ST/ESA/STAT/SER.G/51

DEPARTMENT OF ECONOMIC AND SOCIAL AFFAIRS
STATISTICS DIVISION

DÉPARTEMENT DES AFFAIRES ÉCONOMIQUES ET SOCIALES
DIVISION DE STATISTIQUE

2002
INTERNATIONAL TRADE STATISTICS YEARBOOK
ANNUAIRE STATISTIQUE DU COMMERCE INTERNATIONAL

VOLUME II

TRADE BY COMMODITY

COMMERCE PAR PRODUIT

UNITED NATIONS/NATIONS UNIES
New York, 2004

NOTE

Symbols of United Nations documents are composed of capital letters combined with figures.

General disclaimer

The designations employed and the presentation of material in this publication do not imply the expression of any opinion whatsoever on the part of the Secretariat of the United Nations concerning the legal status of any country, territory, city or area, or of its authorities, or concerning the delimitation of its frontiers or boundaries.

Where the designation "country or area" appears in this publication, it covers countries, territories, cities or areas. In previous issues of this publication, where the designation "country" appears in the headings of tables, it should be interpreted to cover countries, territories, cities or areas.

In some tables, the designation "developed" or "developing" economies is intended for statistical convenience and does not necessarily express a judgement about the stage reached by a particular country or area in the development process.

NOTE

Les cotes des documents de l'Organisation des Nations Unies se composent de lettres majuscules et de chiffres.

Déni de responsabilité

Les appellations employées dans cette publication et la présentation des données qui y figurent n'impliquent, de la part du Secrétariat de l'Organisation des Nations Unies, aucune prise de position quant au statut juridique des pays, territoires, villes ou zones, ou de leurs autorités, ni quant au tracé de leurs frontières ou limites.

L'appellation "pays ou zone", figurant dans cette publication, désigne des pays, des territoires, des villes ou des zones. L'appellation "pays", figurant dans certaines rubriques des tableaux de numéros antérieurs de cette publication, doit être interprétée comme désignant des pays, des territoires, des villes ou des zones.

L'appellation économie "développée" ou économie "en voie de développement" qui figure dans certains tableaux est utilisée pour plus de commodité dans la présentation des statistiques et n'implique pas nécessairement un jugement quant au stade de développement auquel est parvenu un pays ou une zone donnée.

ST/ESA/STAT/SER.G/51

UNITED NATIONS PUBLICATION
Sales No. E/F.04.XVII.3, vol. II

PUBLICATION DES NATIONS UNIES
Numéro de vente : E/F.04.XVII.3, vol. II

ISBN 92-1-061205-1

Enquiries should be directed to:
MEETINGS AND
PUBLISHING DIVISION
UNITED NATIONS
NEW YORK, NY 10017

Adresser toutes demandes de renseignements à la :
DIVISION DES SÉANCES
ET DES SERVICES DE PUBLICATION
NATIONS UNIES
NEW YORK, NY 10017

Printed by the United Nations Publishing Section, New York
Imprimé par la Section de la publication des Nations Unies, New York

The Department of Economic and Social Affairs (DESA) of the United Nations Secretariat is a vital interface between global policies in the economic, social and environmental spheres and national action. The Department works in three main interlinked areas: (i) it compiles, generates and analyses a wide range of economic, social and environmental data and information on which United Nations Member States draw to review common problems and take stock of policy options; (ii) it facilitates the negotiations of Member States in many intergovernmental bodies on joint courses of action to address ongoing or emerging global challenges; and (iii) it advises interested Governments on the ways and means of translating policy frameworks developed in United Nations conferences and summits into programmes at the country level and, through technical assistance, helps build national capacities.

Le Département des affaires économiques et sociales du Secrétariat de l'Organisation des Nations Unies sert de relais entre les orientations arrêtées au niveau international dans les domaines économiques, sociaux et environnementaux et les politiques exécutées à l'échelon national. Il intervient dans trois grands domaines liés les uns aux autres : i) il compile, produit et analyse une vaste gamme de données et d'éléments d'information sur des questions écono-miques, sociales et environnementales dont les Etats Membres de l'Organisation se servent pour examiner des problèmes communs et évaluer les options qui s'offrent à eux; ii) il facilite les négociations entre les Etats Membres dans de nombreux organes intergouvernementaux sur les orientations à suivre de façon collective afin de faire face aux problèmes mondiaux existants ou en voie d'apparition; iii) il conseille les gouvernements intéressés sur la façon de transposer les orientations politiques arrêtées à l'occasion des conférences et sommets des Nations Unies en programmes exécutables au niveau national et aide à renforcer les capacités nationales au moyen de programmes d'assistance technique.

TABLE OF CONTENTS

Volume II

SPECIAL TABLES

TABLES DES MATIERES

Volume II

TABLEAUX SPECIAUX

ABBREVIATIONS AND COUNTRY NOMENCLATURE

Names of some countries (or areas) or groups of countries (or areas) and of some commodities or groups of commodities have been abbreviated. Exact titles and the composition of groups of countries or commodities will be found in various editions of the following publications referred to in the Introduction (see para 3(a), 3(b) and 3(c)):

(i) Standard Country or Area Codes for Statistical Use

(ii) Standard International Trade Classification (SITC)

(iii) Classification by Broad Economic Categories (BEC)

(iv) Classification of Commodities by Industrial Origin

(v) International Standard Industrial Classification of all Economic Activities (ISIC)

1. Data relating to the People's Republic of China generally include those for Taiwan Province in the field of statistics relating to population, area, natural resources, natural conditions such as climate, etc. In other fields of statistics, they do not include Taiwan Province unless otherwise stated. Therefore, in this publication the data published under the heading China exclude those for Taiwan Province. Figures representing the trade with Taiwan Province, which may have been reported by any reporting country or area, are included in the grouping Asia. Pursuant to a Joint Declaration signed on 19 December 1984, the United Kingdom restored Hong Kong to the People's Republic of China with effect from 1 July 1997; the People's Republic of China resumed the exercise of sovereignty over the territory with effect from that date. For statistical purposes, the data for China do not include those for Hong Kong Special Administrative Region. Pursuant to a Joint Declaration signed on 13 April 1987, Portugal restored Macao to the People's Republic of China with effect from 20 December 1999; the People's Republic of China resumed the exercise of sovereignty over the territory with effect from that date. For statistical purposes, the data for China do not include those for Macao Special Administrative Region.

2. On 22 May 1990 Democratic Yemen and Yemen merged to form a single State. Since that date they have been represented as one Member with the name "Yemen". All data shown in this publication relating to the period prior to 1990 refer to the former Democratic Yemen and the former Yemen.

3. Through accession of the German Democratic Republic to the Federal Republic of Germany with effect from 3 October 1990, the two German States have united to form one sovereign State. As from the date of unification, the Federal Republic of Germany acts in the United Nations under the designation of "Germany". All data shown which pertain to Germany prior to 3 October 1990 are indicated separately for the Federal Republic of Germany and the former German Democratic Republic based on their respective territories at the time indicated.

Where data for united Germany (subsequent to 3 October 1990) are not available, they are shown separately and pertain to the territorial boundaries prior to 3 October 1990.

4. In 1991, the Union of Soviet Socialist Republics formally dissolved into fifteen independent countries (Armenia, Azerbaijan, Belarus, Estonia, Georgia, Kazakhstan, Kyrgyzstan, Latvia, Lithuania, Republic of Moldova, Russian Federation, Tajikistan, Turkmenistan, Ukraine and Uzbekistan). From 1992 onwards data are shown for the individual countries. Prior to 1992 data are shown for the former USSR.

5. On 4 February 2003, the official name of the Federal Republic of Yugoslavia has been changed to Serbia and Montenegro. Data provided for Yugoslavia prior to 1 January 1992 refer to the Socialist Federal Republic of Yugoslavia which was composed of six republics; data referring to the years 1992 and later are attributed to Bosnia and Herzegovina, Croatia, Serbia and Montenegro, Slovenia and the former Yugoslav republic of Macedonia.

6. Data for the Czech Republic and Slovakia, where available, are shown separately under the appropriate country name. For periods prior to 1 January 1993, where no separate data are available for the Czech Republic and Slovakia, unless otherwise indicated, data for the former Czechoslovakia are shown under the country name "former Czechoslovakia".

7. Beginning 1 January 1997, the overseas departments of France were included in the statistical territory of France for the purposes of international trade statistics. Values on this basis have been provided by France for 1996 also, and values are published on that basis in this publication.

8. Beginning 1 January 1999, Belgium and Luxembourg provide their international trade statistics separately. For periods prior to 1 January 1999, unless otherwise indicated, data are shown for the Economic Union of Belgium and Luxembourg under the name "Belgium-Luxembourg".

9. Beginning 1 January 2000, Botswana, Lesotho, Namibia, South Africa and Swaziland provide their international trade statistics separately. For periods prior to 1 January 2000, unless otherwise indicated, data are shown for the Southern African Customs Union.

ABREVIATIONS ET CODES DES PAYS

Les noms de certains pays (ou zones) ou groupes de pays (ou zones) et de certains produits ou groupes de produits ont dû être abrégés. On trouvera les intitulés exacts de ces noms dans des différentes éditions des publications suivantes qui figurent dans l'Introduction (voir aussi para 3(a), 3(b) et 3(c)):

(i) Codes standard des pays et des zones à usage statistique

(ii) Classification type pour le commerce international (CTCI)

(iii) Classification par grandes catégories économiques (CGCE)

(iv) Classification des marchandises par origine industrielle

(v) Classification internationale type, par industrie, de toutes les branches d'activité économique (CITI)

1. Les données relatives à la République populaire de Chine comprennent en général les données relatives à la province de Taïwan lorsqu'il s'agit de statistiques concernant la population, la superficie, les ressources naturelles, les conditions naturelles tel que le climat, etc. Dans les statistiques relevant d'autres domaines, la province de Taïwan n'est pas comprise, sauf indication contraire. C'est le cas dans cet Annuaire où les données pour la Chine ne comprennent pas celles de la province de Taïwan. Lorsque des pays partenaires ont déclaré des échanges avec Taïwan ceux-ci sont inclus dans Asie. Conformément à une Déclaration commune signée le 19 décembre 1984, le Royaume-Uni a rétrocédé Hong-kong à la République populaire de Chine, avec effet au ler juillet 1997; la souveraineté de la République populaire de Chine s'exerce à nouveau sur le territoire à compter de cette date. Pour les statistiques, les données de la Chine ne comprennent pas celles de la région administrative spéciale de Hong Kong. Conformément à une Déclaration commune signée le 13 décembre 1987, le Portugal a rétrocédé Macao à la République populaire de Chine, avec effet au 20ième décembre 1999; la souveraineté de la République populaire de Chine s'exerce à nouveau sur le territoire à compter de cette date. Pour les statistiques, les données de la Chine ne comprennent pas celles de la région administrative spéciale de Macao.

2. Le Yémen et le Yémen démocratique ont fusionné le 22 mai 1990 pour ne plus former qu'un seul Etat, qui est depuis lors représenté comme tel à l'Organisation, sous le nom 'Yémen'. Toutes les données présentées dans cet Annuaire qui se rapportent à la période antérieure à l'année 1990 se réfèrent aux anciens Yémen démocratique et Yémen.

3. En vertu de l'adhésion de la République démocratique allemande à la République fédérale d'Allemagne, prenant effet le 3 octobre 1990, les deux Etats allemands se sont unis pour former un seul Etat souverain. A compter de la date de l'unification, la République fédérale

d'Allemagne est désignée à l'ONU sous le nom 'Allemagne'. Toutes les données se rapportant à l'Allemagne avant le 3 octobre 1990 figurent dans deux rubriques séparées, basées sur les territoires respectifs de la République fédérale d'Allemagne et l'ancienne République démocratique allemande selon la période indiquée. En l'absence de données pour l'Allemagne unifiée (à compter du 3 octobre 1990), les données sont fournies séparément sous les rubriques Allemagne (République fédérale d') et Allemagne (ancienne République démocratique) et se rapportent aux limites territoriales antérieures au 3 octobre 1990 lorsqu'elles sont disponibles.

4. En 1991, l'ex Union Soviétique a été scindée officiellement en quinze républiques indépendantes (Arménie, Azerbaïdjan, Bélarus, Estonie, Fédération de Russie, Géorgie, Kazakstan, Kirghizistan, Lettonie, Lituanie, Ouzbékistan, République de Moldova, Tadjikistan, Turkménistan et Ukraine). A partir de 1992 les données sont indiquées pour chaque république individuellement. Avant 1992, les données sont indiquées pour l'ancienne URSS.

5. Le 4 février 2003 la République fédérative de Yougoslavie a changé officiellement son nom en Serbie et Monténégro. Les données fournies pour la Yougoslavie avant le 1er janvier 1992 se rapportent à la République fédérative socialiste de Yougoslavie, qui était composée de six républiques; les données relatives à l'année 1992 et après sont attribuées à la Bosnie-Herzégovine, la Croatie, la Serbie et Monténégro, la Slovénie et l'ex-République yougoslave de Macédoine.

6. Les données relatives à la République tchèque, et à la Slovaquie, lorsqu'elles sont disponibles, sont présentées séparément sous le nom de chacun des pays. En ce qui concerne la période antérieure au 1er janvier 1993, pour laquelle on ne possède pas de données séparées pour les deux Républiques, les données relatives à l'ancienne Tchécoslovaquie sont, sauf indication contraire, présentées sous le titre 'ancienne Tchécoslovaquie'.

7. A partir du ler janvier 1997, pour les statistiques du commerce international, le territoire statistique de la France comprend les départements d'outre-mer. Les valeurs ont été fournies aussi sur cette base par la France pour 1996, et sont publiées dans cet annuaire.

8. A partir du ler janvier 1999, la Belgique et Luxembourg présentent leurs statistiques du commerce international séparément. En ce qui concerne la période antérieure au 1er janvier 1999, sauf indication contraire, les données relatives à l'Union économique de la Belgique et Luxembourg sont présentées sous le titre 'Belgique-Luxembourg'.

9. A partir du ler janvier 2000, Botswana, Lesotho, la Namibie, Swaziland et l'Afrique du Sud présentent leurs statistiques du commerce international séparément. En ce qui concerne la période antérieure au 1er janvier 2000, sauf indication contraire, les données sont présentées pour l'Union douanière d'Afrique australe.

EXPLANATION OF SYMBOLS
EXPLICATION DES SIGNES

Category not applicable .... Ne s'applique pas	–
Not available.......... Aucune donnée disponible	blank
Magnitude of less than half the unit used.......... Grandeur inférieure à la moitié de l'unité utilisée	0 or 0.0
Provisional or estimated figures.......... Donnée provisoire ou estimation	e
Area (1,000 square metres).......... Superficie (1,000 mètres carrés)	A
1,000 kilowatt-hours.......... 1,000 kilowatts-heures	H
Weight (kilograms).......... Poids (kilogrammes)	K
Length (1,000 metres).......... Longueur (1,000 mètres)	L
1,000 times unit shown.......... 1,000 fois l'unité indiquée	M
Number.......... Nombre	N
Other.......... Autres	O
Number of pairs.......... Paires	P
Volume (cubic metres).......... Volume (mètre cube)	V
Weight (metric tons).......... Poids (tonnes métriques)	W
1,000,000 times unit shown.......... 1 million de fois l'unité indiquée	Y
Decimal figures are always preceded by a period except for the Country Notes in French where they are preceded by a comma.......... Les décimales sont toujours précédées d'un point, à l'exception des notes de pays en français où elles sont précédées par une virgule.	(.)

TRADE DATA IN ELECTRONIC FORM

External trade data, for the majority of countries from 1962 to the latest year, are available in electronic form and can be transmitted on diskettes and on CD-ROM or by electronic mail. Detailed information on coverage and prices is available, on request, from the United Nations Statistics Division, New York, N.Y. 10017, USA; tel. (+1) (212) 963-6170; fax (+1) (212) 963-9851 and e-mail tradestat@un.org. Since June 2003 the trade data are also accessible via the internet at http://unstats.un.org/unsd/comtrade. Data can be browsed freely by any internet user or can be downloaded by registered subscribers. See the website for prices on subscriptions.

DONNEES DU COMMERCE EXTÉRIEUR SOUS FORME ÉLECTRONIQUE

Les données du commerce extérieur pour la majorité des pays de 1962 à la dernière année écoulée sont disponibles sous forme électronique et peuvent être envoyées sur disquette, sur CD-ROM, ou par message électronique. Les informations détaillées sur le champ d'application et les prix peuvent être obtenues auprès de la Division de Statistique des Nations Unies, New York, N.Y. 10017, Etats-Unis; Tél. (+1) (212) 963-6170; fax (+1) (212) 963-9851 et e-mail tradestat@un.org. Depuis juin 2003 ces données du commerce extérieur sont accessibles sur l'Internet à l'adresse http://unstats.un.org/unsd/comtrade. Elles peuvent être inspectées gratuitement par tous les utilisateurs, ou peuvent être téléchargées par abonnement. Voir le site Internet pour les coûts des abonnements.

INTRODUCTION

1. The fifty-first edition of the International Trade Statistics Yearbook (the Yearbook) provides the basic information for individual countries' external trade performances in terms of value, as well as in volume and price, the importance of trading partners and the significance of individual commodities imported and exported. This edition shows annual statistics for 183 countries or areas. It is published in two volumes.

2. A difference between the fiftieth and this fifty-first edition is that the Special Table L Export price index numbers of primary commodities and non-ferrous base metals has been discontinued. For information on prices of primary commodities and non-ferrous metals see, for example, the UNCTAD Commodity Yearbook 2003.

VOLUME I

3. Volume I contains detailed data for individual countries or areas. For each country or area the following tables usually appear:

(a) Tables 1 and 2, showing up to the most recent five years available, the value in United States dollars of import and export trade analyzed by the principal countries or areas and regions of origin and destination. The analysis is made according to the United Nations Standard Country or Area Codes for Statistical Use[1/]. In some instances, owing to the nature of the national country classification, the conversion to the United Nations country classification could not be done precisely. A maximum of 30 trading partners are shown, in order of magnitude, based on the sum of the values over the years included in the table, with imports and exports ranked separately. Below the value table is a listing showing the percentage breakdown of trade by regions for the latest available ten years. The line for the European Union (EU) is calculated for all years on the basis of the current membership (fifteen countries). The lines for the Asian part of the former USSR (Armenia, Azerbaijan, Georgia, Kazakhstan, Kyrgyzstan, Tajikistan, Turkmenistan, and Uzbekistan) and the European part of the former USSR (Belarus, Estonia, Latvia, Lithuania, Republic of Moldova, Russian Federation and Ukraine) are calculated as the sum of the appropriate independent countries from 1992 to date. For years prior to 1992 this was not possible and the line for the European part of the former USSR includes the entire former USSR for those years. Eastern Europe comprises Albania, Bulgaria, Czech Republic, Hungary, Poland, Romania and Slovakia. Regional totals are calculated only if the available partner detail exceeds 80% of the reported total imports or exports. Furthermore, if the available partner detail is less than 50% for all years, the table will not be shown.

(b) Tables 3 and 4, showing up to the most recent four years available, the quantity and the value in United States dollars of imports and exports analyzed by principal commodities. The commodities are shown in terms of the Standard International Trade Classification [2/] (SITC), Revision 2, codes and headings (abbreviated). Data for a commodity will appear if the value in any year is greater than or equal to 0.5 per cent of the total trade for that year. Lines for 2-, 3- or 4-digit commodity codes are omitted in cases where the line of the more detailed commodity code (for instance at 5-digit level) contains exactly the same information in terms of value and quantity for all four years shown.

(c) Tables 5 and 6, showing up to the most recent seven years available, percentage breakdowns of imports by broad economic categories and of exports by industrial origin. The analysis for imports is based on the Classification by Broad Economic Categories[3/] and for exports on the Classification of Commodities by Industrial Origin [4/]. Reclassification of foreign trade according to broad economic categories or industrial origin requires statistical information at the five-digit level of the Standard International Trade Classification, Revised[2/]. (For history and background of the SITC, see pages xxii-xxiii). When such details are not available, approximate allocations are made, using the three-digit level of the SITC Revised. In comparing statistics of international trade with statistics of production, problems of limitation exist in addition to those of classification. Exports of products which are obviously not produced in the reporting countries (e.g., exports of tea and cocoa from the Netherlands or the United Kingdom) have been allocated to the industrial origin in which they would have been classified in the producing countries; in the case of tea and cocoa: Agriculture. The industrial origin in the reporting country of these exports is, in fact, the wholesale trade. In the Classification of Commodities by Industrial Origin, SITC, Revised headings are subdivided to correspond, roughly, to groups of the International Standard Industrial Classification of All Economic Activities, (Revision 1)[5/]. The breakdown of exports by industrial origin is derived as much as possible from national or special exports.

4. In some instances the figures shown in United States dollars in the tables indicated under 3(a) and 3(b) above may not correspond to those in United States dollars in the Special Table A or to those in national currency in Special Table B after the application of the currency conversion factors in Special Table C. These discrepancies arise in part from revisions to the more recent data at the total level and these revisions were not broken down for the more detailed data by commodity and partner. In some cases the differences may be due to differences in coverage/definitions of the data. It was felt, however, that a partial revision of the tables referred to under 3(a) and 3(b) above to make the totals consistent with those in the Special Tables should not be made. More information on the Special Tables is given in para 11 and 12.

5. For all countries, the data in Tables 3 and 4 are presented according to SITC Revision 2. Most countries report data according to the Harmonized Commodity Description and Coding System (HS). The data so reported for these countries, were converted to SITC Revision 2. This is a difficult conversion and results in data for some SITC Revision 2 codes, which are not comparable with data reported in terms of SITC, Revision 2 to a very significant extent. Trade data according to HS and SITC, Revision 3, can be found on the web site of the United Nations Statistics Division at http://unstats.un.org/unsd/comtrade.

6. Detailed descriptions of the concepts and definitions applied by countries are available in the United Nations mimeograph "National Reporting Practices in International Merchandise Trade Statistics" (ST/ESA/STAT/112), issued February 1996 and available from the United Nations Statistics Division. A computerized and updated version of the national reporting practices are available on the internet at http://unstats.un.org/unsd/tradereport/default.asp.

VOLUME II

7. Volume II contains commodity tables showing the total trade of certain commodities analyzed by regions and countries. The regional structure is identical to that which is used in Volume I.

8. Commodity tables. These tables show imports and exports of commodities at the group (3-digit) level of the SITC, Revision 2. All groups are covered except for 264, Jute, raw or semi-processed; 286, Ores and concentrates of uranium and thorium; 351, Electric current; 675, Hoops and strip, of iron or steel, hot-rolled or cold-rolled; 688, Uranium depleted in U235 and thorium (including waste), and their alloys, unwrought or wrought, and articles thereof; 911, Postal packages not classified according to kind; 961, Coin (other than gold coin), not being legal tender and 971, Gold, non-monetary (excluding gold ores and concentrates) (for an explanation, see paragraph 9 below). The years covered are the five years 1998 to 2002. The values are in U.S. dollars and both imports and exports are analyzed by regions and principal trading countries. A maximum of 30 countries are shown in order of magnitude, based on the sum of the values over the years 1998 to 2002, with imports and exports ranked separately. No quantity data are shown.

9. In preparing these tables, in many cases estimates were made for countries whose data were not yet available and these are shown with an 'e'. In some cases, estimates were made for particular countries, and they were considered adequate to include in regional and world totals but not sufficiently explained to be published separately for the country; consequently, they have been suppressed and only an 'e' appears in the table. The commodity groups mentioned in paragraph 8 above, (264, 286, 351, 675, 688, 911, 961 and 971) are suppressed from publication because they were poorly reported and contain many estimates which are not sufficiently explainable. Strictly speaking, a regional or world total that contains estimates should be shown with an 'e'. However, virtually all the regional and world totals include estimates and the 'e' has been omitted for cosmetic purposes.

10. The procedure for estimating trade data for a given year and a given country takes some reported ('true') data as a starting point. The minimum required reported input data are the import and export totals of a country. Sometimes other aggregated commodity information is also available and is taken into account; this may include some 3-digit or other commodity totals reported by the country. The estimation procedure then takes the available reported data and initial estimates (which may be either (1) the 3-digit commodity totals of the country for an adjacent (reported) year or (2) the 3-digit commodity totals for the country as reported by all its trading partners combined, for the given year) and scales them in such a way that at every level of the commodity classification the total of the commodity estimates and any reported data add up to the reported ('true') totals at the higher level and ultimately to the totals of the imports and exports.

11. Volume II also contains special tables showing, inter alia, (a) the contribution of the trade of each country to the trade of its region and of the world, (b) the flow of trade between countries and regions and (c) the fluctuations of the prices at which goods are traded internationally. The special tables are:

A. Total imports and exports by regions and countries and areas (in US dollars);
B. Total imports and exports by countries and areas (in national currency);
C. Trade Conversion Factors;
D. World exports by commodity classes and by regions;
E. Growth of world exports by commodity classes and by regions;
F. Structure of world exports by commodity classes and by regions;
G. Total imports and exports: index numbers by countries or areas, terms of trade, and purchasing power of exports;
H. Total exports and imports: index numbers of quantum, unit value and terms of trade by regions;
I. Manufactured goods exports;
J. Fuel imports: developed economies;
K. Some indicators on fuel imports: developed economies;

SPECIAL TABLES

12. The economic and geographic groupings in all the special tables are in accordance with those of Special Table A in this issue, although Special Table A sometimes includes more detailed geographic sub-groups. (See Special Table A for the details)

(A) Total imports and exports by regions and countries and areas (in US dollars). The regional, economic and world totals have been adjusted: (a) to include estimates for countries or areas for which full data are not available; (b) to include estimates of insurance and freight for imports valued FOB; (c) to include countries or areas not listed separately; (d) to approximate special trade for regional groups; (e) to approximate calendar years; and (f) where possible, to eliminate incomparability owing to geographical changes, by adjusting the figures for periods before the change to be comparable to those for periods after the change, for example, the European Union and the European Free Trade Association. The figures shown for individual countries correspond to the figures, which appear and are described in Special Table B. For footnotes see the end of the table.

Monthly and quarterly data appear in the Monthly Bulletin of Statistics.

(B) Total imports and exports by countries and areas (in national currency). The table contains totals of trade by countries reported in terms of national currency. For totals in terms of U.S. dollars for all countries and areas see Special Table A. For general note and footnotes, see the end of the table.

Monthly and quarterly data appear in the Monthly Bulletin of Statistics.

(C) Trade Conversion Factors. The conversion factors shown in the table were used to convert trade data expressed in terms of national currency to U.S. dollars. For general note and footnotes, see the end of the table.

Quarterly data appear in the Monthly Bulletin of Statistics.

(D) World exports by commodity classes and by regions. For the general note and footnotes, see the end of the table.

(E) Growth of world exports by commodity classes and by regions. The annual average rates of change in percentage terms given in this table have been uniformly calculated by the use of the compound interest formula:

$$r = \left(\sqrt[t]{\frac{Vn}{Vo}} - 1 \right) * 100$$

r = Annual average rate of change in percentage terms.
Vn = Value of exports during the last year of the period.
Vo = Value of exports during the first year of the period.
t = Number of years in period.

For the general note and footnotes, see the end of Special Table F.

(F) Structure of world exports by commodity classes and by regions. The figures shown under the heading 'Origin of Exports' refer to the exports of the region or country appearing in the 'Area' column; those shown under the heading 'Destination of Exports' refer to the exports of the world to the region or country appearing in the 'Area' column. For the general note and footnotes, see the end of the table.

(G) Total imports and exports: index numbers by countries or areas, terms of trade, and purchasing power of exports. The unit value indices are in terms of US dollars. For the general note and footnotes, see the end of the table.

(H) Total exports and imports: index numbers of quantum, unit value and terms of trade by regions. For the footnotes, see the end of the table.

Quarterly data appear in the Monthly Bulletin of Statistics.

(I) Manufactured goods exports. For the general note and footnotes, see the end of Table K.

Quarterly data appear in the Monthly Bulletin of Statistics.

(J) Fuel imports: developed economies. For the general note and footnotes, see the end of Table K.

Quarterly data appear in the Monthly Bulletin of Statistics.

(K) Some indicators on fuel imports: developed economies. This table shows the share of fuel imports in the total value of imports and in the total value of exports, and the ratio of unit value indices of manufactured goods exports to those of fuel imports. For the general note and footnotes, see the end of the table.

Quarterly data appear in the Monthly Bulletin of Statistics.

13. The compositions of the economic groups which are used in Special Tables A to K are as follows:

ANCOM-Andean Common Market
Bolivia, Colombia, Ecuador, Peru and Venezuela

APEC-Asian-Pacific Economic Co-operation
Australia, Brunei Darussalam, Canada, Chile, China, Hong Kong Special Administrative Region of China, Indonesia, Japan, Malaysia, Mexico, New Zealand, Papua New Guinea, Peru, Philippines, Republic of Korea, Russian Federation, Singapore, Taiwan Province of China, Thailand, United States of America and Viet Nam

ASEAN-Association of South-East Asian Nations
Brunei Darussalam, Cambodia, Indonesia, Lao People's Democratic Republic, Malaysia, Myanmar, Philippines, Singapore Thailand and Viet Nam

CACM-Central American Common Market
Costa Rica, El Salvador, Guatemala, Honduras and Nicaragua

CARICOM-Caribbean Community and Common Market
Antigua and Barbuda, Bahamas (member of the Community only), Barbados, Belize, Dominica, Grenada, Guyana, Haiti, Jamaica, Montserrat, Saint Kitts and Nevis, Saint Lucia Saint Vincent and the Grenadines, Suriname, Trinidad and Tobago

CIS-Commonwealth of Independent States
Armenia, Azerbaijan, Belarus, Georgia, Kazakhstan, Kyrgyzstan, Republic of Moldova, Russian Federation, Tajikistan, Turkmenistan, Ukraine and Uzbekistan

COMESA-Common Market for Eastern and Southern Africa
Angola, Burundi, Comoros, Democratic Republic of the Congo, Djibouti, Egypt, Eritrea, Ethiopia, Kenya, Madagascar, Malawi, Mauritius, Namibia, Rwanda, Seychelles, Sudan, Swaziland, Uganda, Zambia and Zimbabwe

EMCCA - Economic and Monetary Community of Central Africa
Cameroon, Central African Republic, Chad, Congo, Equatorial Guinea and Gabon

EU-European Union
Austria, Belgium, Denmark, Finland, France, Germany, Greece, Ireland, Italy, Luxembourg, Netherlands, Portugal, Spain, Sweden and United Kingdom

ECOWAS-Economic Community of West African States
Benin, Burkina Faso, Cape Verde, Cote d'Ivoire, Gambia, Ghana, Guinea, Guinea-Bissau, Liberia, Mali, Niger, Nigeria, Senegal, Sierra Leone and Togo

EFTA-European Free Trade Association
Iceland, Liechtenstein, Norway and Switzerland

LAIA-Latin American Integration Association (formerly Latin American Free Trade Association)
Argentina, Bolivia, Brazil, Chile, Colombia, Ecuador, Mexico, Paraguay, Peru, Uruguay and Venezuela

LDCs-Least developed countries
Afghanistan, Angola, Bangladesh, Benin, Bhutan, Burkina Faso, Burundi, Cambodia, Cape Verde, Central African Republic, Chad, Comoros, Democratic Republic of the Congo, Djibouti, Equatorial

Guinea, Eritrea, Ethiopia, Gambia, Guinea, Guinea-Bissau, Haiti, Kiribati, Lao People's Democratic Republic, Lesotho, Liberia, Madagascar, Malawi, Maldives, Mali, Mauritania, Mozambique, Myanmar, Nepal, Niger, Rwanda, Samoa, Sao Tome and Principe, Senegal, Sierra Leone, Solomon Islands, Somalia, Sudan, Togo, Tuvalu, Uganda, United Republic of Tanzania, Vanuatu, Yemen and Zambia

MERCOSUR-Mercado Comun Sud-Americano
Argentina, Brazil, Paraguay and Uruguay

NAFTA-Northern American Free Trade Area
Canada, Mexico and United States of America

OECD-Organization for Economic Cooperation and Development
Australia, Austria, Belgium, Canada, Czech Republic, Denmark, Finland, France, Germany, Greece, Hungary, Iceland, Ireland, Italy, Japan, Luxembourg, Mexico, Netherlands, New Zealand, Norway, Poland, Portugal, Republic of Korea, Slovakia, Spain, Sweden, Switzerland, Turkey, United Kingdom and United States of America

OPEC-Organization of Petroleum Exporting Countries
Algeria, Indonesia, Iran (Islamic. Republic of), Iraq, Kuwait, Libyan Arab Jamahiriya, Nigeria, Qatar, Saudi Arabia, United Arab Emirates and Venezuela.

SOURCES AND PRESENTATION

14. The figures for Volumes I and II are obtained from national published sources, from data supplied by the Governments for use in this publication, from data supplied by the International Monetary Fund, the Inter-American Development Bank, the Organization for Economic Co-operation and Development, the Economic Commission for Latin America and the Caribbean, the Economic Community of West African States, The Common Market of Eastern and Southern Africa, the Food and Agriculture Organization of the United Nations; and from the United Nations publications: Monthly Bulletin of Statistics, and Statistical Yearbook. Estimates for some missing data are made by the United Nations Statistics Division.

15. The country and regional names used by various countries are not uniform for their trade statistics. Also, where former geographical entities commonly referred to in national statistics have changed, countries may introduce the corresponding changes in their statistics at different times. Wherever possible, however, parts of the world have been designated by the names they currently bear. To satisfy the needs of some users for analytical data over time, the ability to reconstruct some former geographic/political entities has been maintained e.g. data relating to the former USSR.

16. The regional aggregates shown throughout this publication are based on those set forth in the United Nations Standard Country or Area Codes for Statistical Use[1/], except where indicated.

17. Generally, data refer to calendar years; however, for those countries which report according to some other reference year, the data are presented in the year which covers the majority of the reference year used by the country. The countries concerned are Bangladesh (reference year July-June), India (April-March), Nepal (July-June) and Myanmar (April-March).

NATIONAL INDEX NUMBERS

18. National index numbers of unit value and of volume, which were previously shown in Table 1 of Volume I in national currency, are now shown in Special Table G of Volume II converted to US dollars. They are the official indices which show the changes in the volume, and the average price (unit value index) of the aggregate merchandise imports or exports. Each index number represents a change between the period to which the number refers, called the current period, and a reference period, in which the index is represented by the percentage 100. In order to facilitate comparison, the indices shown have been rebased to 1990, where necessary. When changes are made in the coverage, formula or base period of an index, the two series are linked together if they have an overlapping period and are sufficiently comparable.

19. Annual, quarterly and monthly figures for these index series in national currency appear in the United Nations Monthly Bulletin of Statistics and a more detailed description of their compilation is given in the 1977 Supplement to the Statistical Yearbook and the Monthly Bulletin of Statistics[7/].

TRANSITION COUNTRIES

20. For the period covered by this Yearbook, countries formerly classified for statistical purposes as centrally planned economies had systems of official rates between their currencies and other currencies, all consistent with rates of 0.90 new roubles to the United States dollar prior to 24 December 1971 and 0.829 new roubles to the United States dollar until February 1973; since then these rates have been fluctuating. They generally used these rates when it was necessary to convert foreign into domestic currencies for the purpose of compiling external trade statistics. The resulting data are for comparison with the external transactions of the rest of the world rather than with domestic monetary transactions.

21. The trade statistics of these countries had definitions somewhat different from those which exist in other countries. Differences in definition contribute to the discrepancies which can be observed between statistical records referring to the same flow of goods but kept by two trading partners having different economic systems. The trade among these countries was carried out on a basis not comparable to that governing trade with other countries. The concept of transaction value, for instance, as applied outside those countries is based on the existence of a market between exporters and importers in which the interaction of supply and demand has more effect than it can be assumed to have had in those countries; in the absence of data on the unit values of specific commodities entering the trade of those countries with one another, it is difficult to assess the possible effects on the trade statistics of this kind of incomparability. Increasingly since 1992, the transition countries have adopted similar concepts and definitions for international trade statistics as are in effect in other countries.

GENERAL STATEMENTS

22. The statistics in this Yearbook have been compiled by national statistical authorities largely consistent with the United Nations recommended International Trade Statistics Concepts and Definitions, Revision 1.[8/] In 1998 the United Nations issued a further revision of this publication;[8/] countries have been requested to commence introduction of the new concepts and definitions with data for 1999. The main elements of the concepts and definitions (Revision 1) are:

1. Territory. The statistics reported by a country generally refer to the customs area of the country. In most cases this coincides with the geographical area of the country. Unless otherwise stated, the combination of two territories, formerly separate, results in the elimination from the statistics of their trade with each other. The separation of two territories, formerly together, results in the appearance of their trade with each other in the statistics for each territory.

2. System of trade. Two systems of recording trade are in common use, differing mainly in the way warehoused and re-exported goods are recorded:

(a) Special trade: special imports are the combined total of imports declared directly from abroad for home use or inward processing and withdrawals from bonded warehouses or free zones for home use. Special exports comprise exports of goods of national origin, namely, goods wholly or partly produced or manufactured in the country, including goods exported after inward processing, and re-exports of imported goods that have been in free circulation.

(b) General trade: general imports are the combined total of imports declared directly from abroad for home use or inward processing, and imports into bonded warehouses or free zones. General exports comprise exports of goods of national origin, including goods exported after inward processing, re-exports of imported goods that have been in free circulation and re-exports of goods from bonded warehouses or free zones.

Direct transit trade, i.e., goods merely being trans-shipped or moving through the country for purposes of transport only, is excluded from the statistics of both special and general trade.

Tables 1 to 4 of Volume I indicate in their headings the system of trade to which the figures relate.

3. Valuation. At its fifteenth session, in 1953, the Economic and Social Council, taking the view that trade statistics must reflect economic realities, recommended that the Governments of Member States of the United Nations, wherever possible, use transaction values in the compilation of their national statistics of external trade or, when national practices are based on other values, endeavor to provide supplementary statistical data based on transaction values (Economic and Social Council resolution 469 B (XV)). In the case of imports, the transaction value is the value at which the goods were purchased by the importer plus the cost of transportation and insurance to the frontier of the importing country (a CIF-type valuation). In

the case of exports, the transaction value is the value at which the goods were sold by the exporter, including the cost of transportation and insurance, to bring the goods onto the transporting vehicle at the frontier of the exporting country (a FOB-type valuation).

4. Currency conversion. For data in this publication, conversion of values from national currencies into United States dollars is done by means of currency conversion factors based on official exchange rates. Values in currencies subject to fluctuation (such currencies increased in number beginning December 1971) are converted into United States dollars using weighted average exchange rates specially calculated for this purpose. The weighted average exchange rate for a given currency for a given year is the component monthly factors, mostly furnished by the International Monetary Fund, weighted by the value of the relevant trade in each month; a monthly factor is the exchange rate (or the simple average rate) in effect during that month. These factors are applicable to total imports and exports respectively, but not necessarily to trade in individual commodities or with individual countries.

5. Merchandise. In order that external trade statistics shall be suited to the measurement of the influence of national economies upon one another, merchandise trade is defined to include, as far as possible, all goods which add to or subtract from the material resources of a country as a result of their movements into or out of the country. Unless, therefore, statements to the contrary are made in footnotes to the country tables, the treatment of the classes of goods listed below is as indicated:

(a) Gold. Gold traded internationally is usually defined as encompassing the three following types:

i) Gold coins (issued and unissued) and bullion, including banking and monetary gold;
ii) Unrefined gold, including gold ores and concentrates;
iii) Partly-worked gold in which the value of the gold is 80 per cent or more of the total value, including scrap, jewelers' sweepings, dust, primary shapes (such as rods, wire and gold leaf) and gold alloys (crude or in primary shapes).

Of the types of gold listed above, those belonging to the category of monetary gold are excluded from merchandise trade, and those classified as non-monetary gold are included, except as indicated below. Any gold shipment received by the central monetary authority of a country is treated as monetary gold. All other gold shipments (whether to commercial banks or to individuals), on the other hand, are considered non-monetary.

(b) Silver ore, concentrates, bullion, unissued coin (as noted below), scrap and partly-worked and manufactured silver are all included in merchandise trade statistics.

(c) Currency and titles of ownership which have been issued into circulation, e.g., issued silver and base metal coins, bank notes, other paper currency and securities, are excluded from merchandise trade statistics. Unissued currency and titles of ownership are included at their intrinsic value as stamped metal or printed paper rather than at face value.

(d) Trade on government account is included as merchandise trade. Movements under government foreign aid programmes (civil and military), war reparations and restitutions and military goods[9/] moving internationally are therefore included. When goods are destined for use of national agencies (including embassies and military forces) stationed abroad they are, however, not considered to have moved in external trade and are excluded.

(e) Temporary imports and exports. Goods for exhibitions or study, animals admitted to a country temporarily, merely for racing or breeding, returnable containers, etc., the movements of all of which are expected to be reversed within a limited time, are excluded.

(f) Improvement and repair trade. Countries sending goods abroad for improvement or repair and later returned are said to be engaging in the passive improvement and repair trade; countries receiving goods from other countries for improvement or repair and eventual return engage in the active improvement and repair trade. Inward and outward movement in this trade are generally excluded from imports and exports.

(g) Postal trade is included in merchandise trade.

(h) Trade in fish, etc. Fish and salvage sold abroad or to foreign vessels off national vessels, and fish and salvage landed from foreign vessels in national ports are excluded from merchandise trade statistics.

(i) Trade in ships and aircraft. Ships and aircraft bought and sold should be included.

(j) Bunkers and stores for ships and aircraft. In general, bunkers and stores should be included in aggregate merchandise exports.

6. Partner country. The following terms describe methods that may be used by reporting countries in determining, for each shipment of goods, the partner country under whose name it should be recorded: (a) for imports: country of origin or production, country of consignment, country of purchase or country of provenance; (b) for exports: country of consumption or consignment, or country of sale.

7. Trade analyzed by commodity. Analysis is according to the Standard International Trade Classification.

THE STANDARD INTERNATIONAL TRADE CLASSIFICATION (SITC) AND THE HARMONIZED COMMODITY DESCRIPTION AND CODING SYSTEM (HS)

23. In July 1950, the United Nations Economic and Social Council, on the advice of its Statistical Commission, recommended that Governments compile trade by commodity statistics according to the original SITC[2/] in order to have available data in internationally comparable categories suitable for the economic analysis of trade. The original SITC had been prepared by the United Nations Secretariat with the assistance of expert consultants and in co-operation with Member Governments and interested international organizations.

24. In May 1960, the Statistical Commission approved a revision, similarly prepared, of the original SITC, known as the SITC, Revised, designed to take account of the changes in the pattern of trade since 1950 and to simplify the relation between the SITC and internationally agreed customs tariff nomenclatures. The SITC, Revised, is a rearrangement into statistical order of the items of the 1955 Tariff Nomenclature (CCCN) of the Customs Co-operation Council.

25. The SITC, Revised, is based on 625 subgroups (identified by code numbers of four digits), most of which correspond to items of the original SITC. A number of subgroups are further subdivided either to distinguish commodities of statistical importance or to permit exact correspondence with the CCCN; this results in a basic (5-digit code) level for the SITC, Revised, consisting of 1,312 items. The subgroups are combined, progressively, into 177 groups, 56 divisions and 10 sections.

26. The headings of the SITC, Revised, are fully determined by their code numbers. The precise composition of each number is defined in the SITC, Revised, itself. In comparing data according to the SITC, Revised, with data according to a national commodity classification it must be remembered that the same brief description may refer to aggregates differing somewhat in composition.

27. Although the SITC, Revised, of 1960 represented a great improvement on the original SITC, basically the same reasons which led to the creation of the SITC and its first revision were found, in the late nineteen-sixties, to be once more valid. Since 1960 the volume of trade had increased rapidly and its geographic and commodity patterns had changed fundamentally. Consequently, a second revision of the SITC was undertaken. In October 1974 the Statistical Commission approved of this revision, known as SITC, Revision 2[2/], and in May 1975 the Economic and Social Council recommended that Member States of the United Nations should report data on external trade according to the SITC, Revision 2, as far and as soon as possible. Starting with data for 1976, some countries began reporting trade statistics based on the SITC, Revision 2.

28. The basic headings of the SITC, Revision 2 had a one-to-one correspondence with the subdivisions of the Customs Co-operation Council Nomenclature (CCCN). However, there were a number of users who found the subdivisions of CCCN (and thus SITC, Revision 2) insufficient for their needs[10/]. There was also an expressed need for the harmonization of economic classifications[11/]. Partly to satisfy these needs, the Customs Co-operation Council in May 1973

undertook responsibility for the development and completion of the Harmonized Commodity Description and Coding System (HS)[12/].

29. At its twenty-first session, in January 1981, the Statistical Commission had taken note of the fact that a third revision of SITC would have to be made available when both the revised CCCN and HS came into force[13/]. Accordingly, later that year, the United Nations Secretariat commenced work on the revision of SITC, Revision 2, based on the principle that every effort should be made to maintain its general character and structure but taking into account the need for its harmonization with the revised CCCN, the International Standard Industrial Classification (ISIC) Revision 3[14/] and a Central Product Classification[15/] which was developed jointly by the United Nations Statistics Division and the Statistical Office of the European Communities.

30. The final draft was revised and approved by the Statistical Commission at its twenty-third session, in February 1985,[16/] and a resolution was adopted by the Economic and Social Council on 28 May 1985 which, inter alia, recommended that Member States should report internationally external trade statistics according to the Standard International Trade Classification, Revision 3 (resolution 1985/7).

31. The Harmonized System was adopted by the Customs Cooperation Council in June 1983, and the International Convention on the Harmonized System (HS Convention) entered into force 1 January 1988 (HS88). As of 30 June 2003 there were 112 Contracting Parties, and another 65 countries or territories which were not contracting parties but were using the HS for customs/statistical purposes.

32. The United Nations Statistical Commission, at its twenty-seventh session, held from 22 February to 3 March 1993, recommended that countries "adopt the HS for compilation and dissemination of their international trade statistics"[17/].

33. In accordance with the preamble of the HS Convention, which recognized the importance of ensuring that the HS be kept up-to-date in the light of changes in technology or in patterns of international trade, the HS is regularly reviewed and revised. The United Nations Statistical Commission at its twenty-seventh session "recommended that the Customs Cooperation Council take fully into account the statistical implications of any changes proposed for HS and the statistical needs and capacities of developing countries"[18/]. Some minor revisions to the HS88, which also resulted in the deletion of one six-digit code, were made in 1992 (HS92). A more comprehensive set of amendments was adopted in 1993 and these amendments entered into force 1 January 1996 (HS96). In 1999 yet another set of amendments was adopted and these entered into force 1 January 2002 (HS02).

34. The Statistical Commission, at its twenty-eighth session, 27 February - 3 March 1995 considered changes that would be required to the SITC, Rev. 3 to bring it into correlation with HS96; the Commission decided that the changes required in SITC, Rev. 3 to make it fully correlated with HS96 were minor in scale. The Commission therefore decided that it would not be necessary to issue a fourth revision of the SITC[19/].

1/ United Nations Standard Country Codes, Statistical Papers, Series M No. 49, (United Nations publication, Sales No. E.70.XVII.13).

United Nations Standard Country or Area Codes for Statistical Use, Statistical Papers, Series M No. 49, Rev. 1, (United Nations publication, Sales No. E.75.XVII.8).

Standard Country or Area Codes for Statistical Use, Statistical Papers, Series M No. 49, Rev.2, (United Nations publication, Sales No. E.82.XVII.8).

Standard Country or Area Codes for Statistical Use, Series M No. 49, Rev. 3, (non-sales publication).

Standard Country or Area Codes for Statistical Use, Series M No. 49, Rev.4, (United Nations publication, Sales No. M.98.XVII.9).

2/ Standard International Trade Classification, Original , Statistical Papers, Series M No.10, Second Edition, 1951 (United Nations publication, Sales No. E.51.XVII.1).

Standard International Trade Classification, Revised, Statistical Papers, Series M No.34, 1961 (United Nations publication, Sales No. E.61.XVII.6).

Standard International Trade Classification, Revision 2, Statistical Papers, Series M No.34/Rev.2, (United Nations publication, Sales No. E.75.XVII.6).

Standard International Trade Classification, Revision 3, Statistical Papers, Series M No.34/Rev.3, (United Nations publication, Sales No. E.86.XVII.12).

3/ Classification by Broad Economic Categories (in terms of the SITC Revised), Statistical Papers, Series M No.53, (United Nations publication, Sales No. 71.XVII.12).

4/ Classification of Commodities by Industrial Origin (Relationship of the Standard International Trade Classification Revised to the International Standard Industrial Classification of All Economic Activities, Revision 1), Statistical Papers, Series M No.43, (United Nations publication, Sales No. 66.XVII.7).

5/ International Standard Industrial Classification of All Economic Activities (Revision 1), Statistical Papers, Series M No. 4, Rev. 1, (United Nations publication, Sales No. 58.XVII.7).

6/ SITC, Revision 1, is used interchangeably with SITC, Revised, and refers therefore to the Standard International Trade Classification, Revised, Statistical Papers, Series M No.34, 1961 (United Nations publication, Sales No. E.61.XVII.6).

7/ 1977 Supplement to the Statistical Yearbook and Monthly Bulletin of Statistics, ST/ESA/STAT/SER.S/SUPPL.2, ST/ESA/STAT/SER.Q/SUPPL.2, (United Nations publication, Sales No. E.78.XVII.10).

8/ Statistical Papers, Series M No. 52, Rev.1, (United Nations publication, Sales No. E.82.XVII.14).

Statistical Papers, Series M No. 52, Rev.2, (United Nations publication, Sales No. E.98.XVII.16).

9/ Countries excluding military goods from imports or exports use varying definitions of this category of merchandise, but for most countries concerned, weapons and their ammunition constitute a major part of the military goods excluded.

10/ United Nations Statistics Division and Statistical Office of the European Communities Joint Working Group on World Level Classifications, "A Harmonized Commodity Description and Coding System for Use in International Trade" (UNSO/SOEC/1/2).

11/ United Nations Secretariat, "The Harmonization of Statistical Classifications: report of an expert group meeting". (ST/ESA/STAT/78).

12/ Customs Co-operation Council, "The Harmonized Commodity Description and Coding System", Brussels, 1985.

13/ Official Records of the Economic and Social Council, 1981, Supplement No. 2, (E/1981/12), para. 41.

14/ International Standard Industrial Classification of All Economic Activities, Statistical Papers, Series M No.4, Rev.3, (United Nations publication, Sales No.E.90.XVII.11).

15/ Provisional Central Product Classification, Statistical Papers, Series M No.77, (United Nations publication, Sales No.E.91.XVII.7).

16/ Official Records of the Economic and Social Council, 1985, Supplement No. 6, (E/1985/26), para. 57 (d).

17/ Official Records of the Economic and Social Council, 1993, Supplement No. 6, (E/1993/26), para. 162 (d).

18/ Official Records of the Economic and Social Council, 1993, Supplement No. 6, (E/1993/26), para. 162 (e).

19/ Official Records of the Economic and Social Council, 1995, Supplement No. 8, (E/CN.3/1995/28), para. 19 (e).

INTRODUCTION

1. La cinquante-et-unième édition de l'annuaire statistique du commerce international (l'Annuaire) présente les informations nécessaires à l'étude des échanges de chaque pays, en termes de valeur et de prix ainsi que l'importance des différents pays partenaires et des principaux produits importés et exportés. Cette édition présente des données annuelles pour 183 pays ou zones. L'annuaire est publié en deux volumes.

2. La différence entre la cinquantième édition et cette édition est que le Tableau Spécial L Indices des prix des exportations des matières premières et des métaux non-ferreux a été discontinué. Pour plus d'information sur les prix des matières premières et des métaux non-ferreux veuillez voir, par exemple, l'Annuaire de Produits de Base 2003 de la CNUCED.

VOLUME I

3. Le Volume I fournit des renseignements détaillés sur chaque pays ou zone au sujet duquel on trouvera généralement les tableaux suivants:

(a) Tableau 1 et 2, présentant jusqu'aux cinq années les plus récentes la valeur en dollars des États-unis des importations et des exportations selon les principaux pays ou zones et régions d'origine et de destination. La distribution géographique est faite selon le Codes standard des pays et des zones à usage statistique[1/] des Nations Unies. Parfois, étant donné la nature des codes géographiques nationaux, la conversion des données selon le code des Nations Unies n'a pu être effectuée que moyennant quelques imprécisions. Dans ces tableaux figurent les 30 pays partenaires les plus importants classés par ordre d'importance selon la somme des valeurs sur les années comprises dans le tableau. Une classification est effectuée séparément pour les importations et les exportations. La ventilation en pourcentage est également indiquée pour les zones d'origine et de destination pour les dix plus récentes années. Les totaux pour l'union européenne (UE) sont calculés pour toutes les années sur la base des pays membres actuels. Les totaux pour la partie asiatique de l'ancienne URSS (Arménie, Azerbaïdjan, Géorgie, Kazakhstan, Kirghizistan, Tadjikistan, Turkménistan, et Ouzbékistan) et pour la partie européenne de l'ancienne URSS (Bélarus, Estonie, Lettonie, Lituanie, République de Moldova, Fédération de Russie et Ukraine) sont calculés sur la base des pays indiqués à partir de l'année 1992. Pour les années avant 1992 cette division n'était pas possible et, par conséquent, les totaux pour la partie européenne de l'ancienne URSS incluent la totalité de l'ancienne URSS pour ces années. L'Europe de l'Est comprend l'Albanie, la Bulgarie, la République tchèque, l'Hongrie, la Pologne, la Roumanie et la Slovaquie. Les totaux régionaux sont calculés seulement si la ventilation des partenaires disponibles dépasse 80% du total rapporté pour les importations et également pour les exportations. En outre, si la ventilation des partenaires disponibles ne dépasse pas 50% du total rapporté pour toutes les années le tableau ne sera pas publié.

(b) Tableaux 3 et 4, présentant les quantités et les valeurs en dollars des États-unis des importations et des exportations par marchandises principales jusqu'aux quatre plus récentes années. Les chiffres sont publiés pour une marchandise donnée si sa valeur pour une année donnée est égale ou supérieure à 0,5 pour cent de la valeur totale pour ladite année. Les marchandises sont présentées selon les titres de la Classification type du commerce international[2/] (CTCI), révision 2; les lignes pour les 2-, 3- ou 4-chiffre des codes produits, qui contiennent exactement la même information pour tous les 4 années (en terme des valeurs et des quantités) que la ligne du code produit plus détaillé (par exemple le code à 5-chiffre), sont supprimées.

(c) Tableau 5 et 6, présentant jusqu'aux sept années les plus récentes disponible, les pourcentages par rapport au commerce total des importations par grandes catégories économiques et les exportations par branches d'origine. Les pourcentages pour des années moins récentes ont été publiés dans les éditions précédentes de cet Annuaire. L'analyse pour les importations est basée sur la Classification par grandes catégories économiques;[3/] pour les exportations sur la Classification des marchandises par origine industrielle[4/]. Toute re-classification du commerce extérieur par grandes catégories économiques ou par origine industrielle nécessite le détail au niveau des 5 chiffres de la CTCI, révisée. (Se référer aux pages xxxvii à xxxix pour l'histoire et le fond de la CTCI). Lorsque les statistiques n'étaient pas disponibles à ce niveau on a utilisé les données au niveau des trois chiffres de la CTCI, révisée. En comparant des statistiques du commerce extérieur avec des statistiques de production on se heurte à certaines incohérences qui s'ajoutent aux problèmes de classification. Les exportations de marchandises qui de toute évidence n'ont pas été produites dans les pays exportateurs (exportation de thé et de cacao des Pays-Bas ou du Royaume-uni) ont été classées dans la branche où elles auraient été classées dans le pays d'origine; dans le cas du thé et du cacao: l'agriculture. La branche dans le pays déclarant est en fait dans ce cas le commerce de gros. Pour obtenir la Classification des marchandises par origine industrielle, les postes de la CTCI, révisée sont regroupés afin de correspondre approximativement aux groupes de la Classification international type, par industrie, de toutes les branches d'activité économique (révisée) (CITI, Révision 1)[5/]. Dans toute la mesure du possible les exportations nationales ou spéciales ont été utilisées.

4. Parfois les données en dollars des tableaux décrits en 3(a) et 3(b) ci-dessus peuvent ne pas correspondre à celles en dollars des Etats Unis du tableau décrit en Tableau Spécial A ou à celles en monnaies nationales du Tableau Spécial B après l'application des facteurs de conversion du Tableau Spécial C. Les différences sont dues pour la plupart à des révisions au niveau du total du commerce qui parfois ne sont pas disponibles à un plus grand niveau de détail par produit et partenaire et qui n'ont donc pas été apportées aux tableaux décrits en 3(a) et 3(b). Plus d'information concernant les Tableaux Spéciaux est donnée dans les paragraphes 11 et 12.

5. Pour tous les pays, les données présentées aux tableaux 3 et 4 sont fondées sur la CTCI, Révision 2. Presque tous les pays déclarent leurs données fondées sur le Système Harmonisé de désignation et de codification des marchandises (SH). Les données ainsi déclarées ont été converties en CTCI, Révision 2. C'est une conversion difficile qui, pour certains codes de la CTCI, Révision 2 produit des données qui ne sont pas comparables avec celles déclarées en termes de CTCI, Révision 2, de façon très substantielle. Des données en SH et CTCI, Révision 3, sont disponibles sur l'Internet à l'adresse http://unstats.un.org/unsd/comtrade.

6. Des descriptions détaillées des concepts et définitions actuels appliqués par les pays sont disponibles dans le document des Nations Unies « Pratiques nationales du rapportage en matière de statistiques du commerce international des marchandises » (ST/ESA/STAT/112), publié en février 1996 et disponible auprès de la Division de statistique des Nations Unies. Une version électronique et mise à jour de ces pratiques nationales du rapportage est disponible sur le site Internet de la division (voir http://unstats.un.org/unsd/tradereport/default.asp).

VOLUME II

7. Le volume II contient des tableaux présentant le commerce total de certains produits de base, analysé par régions et pays. Les régions aux noms identiques ont la même composition que celles du Volume I.

8. Tableaux par produits. Ces tableaux comprennent les importations et les exportations au niveau du groupe à 3 chiffres de la CTCI, Révision 2. Tous les groupes sont y compris à l'exception de 264, Jute et autres fibres textiles libériennes, bruts; 286, Minerais et concentrés d'uranium et de thorium; 351, Energie électrique; 675, Feuillards en fer ou en acier; 688, Uranium et thorium et leurs alliages; 911, Colis postaux, non classés par catégorie; 961, Monnaies (autres que les pièces d'or) n'ayant pas cours légal et 971, Or, non monétaire (à l'exclusion des minerais et concentrés d'or). Les années couvertes sont les cinq années de 1998 à 2002. Les valeurs sont exprimées en dollars des Etats-Unis et les échanges sont analysés par pays et régions. Dans ces tableaux figurent les 30 pays les plus importants classés selon la somme des valeurs sur les années 1998 jusqu'à 2002. Les quantités ne figurent pas dans ces tableaux.

9. Lors de la préparation de ces tableaux, on a eu recours à des estimations pour les pays dont les données n'étaient pas encore disponibles et ces estimations sont signalées par un 'e'. Dans quelques cas, des estimations ont été faites pour certains pays qui ont été jugées adéquates pour être incluses dans les totaux régionaux et du monde mais non suffisamment élaborées pour être publiées séparément pour ces pays. Elles ont de ce fait été éliminées et remplacées par un 'e'. Les groupes des produits mentionnés dans paragraphe 8 au-dessus, (264, 286, 351, 675, 688, 911, 961 et 971) sont supprimés de la publication parce que ils étaient rapportés insuffisamment et portaient beaucoup d'estimations qui n'étaient pas assez expliquées. A vrai dire, les totaux régionaux et du monde, qui comprennent des estimations, devraient avoir un 'e'. Cependant, et en général, pratiquement tous les totaux régionaux et du monde comprennent des estimations et les 'e' ont été omis dans ces cas pour des raisons d'esthétique.

10. La procédure pour estimer les données du commerce extérieur pour une certaine année et un certain pays attend au départ quelques données déclarées ('vraies'). Au moins il faut les totaux pour les importations et les exportations. Parfois des autres informations sur la ventilation des produits sont disponibles et sont utilisées; ça pourrait être des valeurs au niveau de 1-, 2- ou 3- chiffre de la classification des produits, qui sont déclarés par le pays. Ensuite la procédure d'estimation prend les données déclarées disponibles et les estimations initiales, qui comprennent soit (1) les valeurs des produits au niveau 3-chiffre qui étaient déclarées par le pays pour une année adjointe, soit (2) les totaux des valeurs au niveau 3- chiffre sur la base des données déclarées par les partenaires du pays concerné. Ensuite ces estimations initiales sont

recalculées dans la façon que sur tous les niveaux de la classification des produits le total des valeurs estimés plus les valeurs déclarés est égale au valeur déclaré au niveau au-dessus et finalement est égale au valeur total pour les importations et les exportations.

11. Le Volume II aussi fournit des tableaux spéciaux où sont indiqués, entre autres, (a) la contribution des échanges de chaque pays par rapport à sa région et par rapport au monde; (b) le flux du commerce entre pays et régions et (c) les fluctuations des prix sur la base desquels les produits étaient échangés au niveau international. Les titres des tableaux spéciaux sont:

A. Importations et exportations totales par régions et pays ou zones (en dollars E-U);
B. Importations et exportation totales par pays ou zone (en monnaie nationale);
C. Facteurs de conversion pour le commerce extérieur;
D. Exportations mondiales par classes de marchandises et par régions;
E. Croissance des exportations mondiales par catégories de marchandises et par régions;
F. Structure des exportations mondiales par catégories de marchandises et par régions;
G. Importations et exportations totales: indices par pays ou zones;
H. Exportations et importations totales: indices du quantum, de la valeur unitaire et des termes de l'échange par régions;
I. Exportations des produits manufacturés;
J. Importations des produits énergétiques: pays à économies développées;
K. Quelques indicateurs sur les importations des produits énergétiques: pays à économies développées;

TABLEAUX SPECIAUX

12. Les groupes économiques et géographiques dans tous les tableaux spéciaux sont conformes aux groupes de pays ou zones sont présentés dans le Tableau Spécial A de cet annuaire, bien que le Tableau Spécial A comprend quelquefois plus de détails en ce qui concerne les sous-groupes géographiques. (Voir le Tableau Spécial A pour les détails).

(A) Importations et exportations totales par régions et pays ou zones (en dollars E-U). Les totaux régionaux, économiques et mondiaux, ont été ajustés: a) pour y inclure des estimations pour les données non disponibles; b) pour transformer le cas échéant les importations FOB en importations CIF; c) pour y inclure les pays ou zones pour lesquels il n'existe pas de liste séparée; d) pour ramener les données au commerce spécial pour les groupes régionaux; e) pour ramener les données à l'année civile; et f) autant que possible, éliminer les incompatibilités dues à des modifications géographiques pour obtenir des séries comparables par exemple, l'union européenne et l'Association européenne de libre-échange. Les données ci-dessus pour chaque pays correspondent aux données qui apparaissent et qui sont décrites au Tableau Spécial B. Voir la fin du tableau pour les notes.

Le Bulletin Mensuel de Statistique présente des données mensuelles et trimestrielles.

(B) Importations et exportation totales par pays ou zone (en monnaie nationale). Ce tableau montre les totaux du commerce par pays déclarés en monnaie nationale. Pour les totaux en dollars E-U de tous les pays ou zones veuillez voir Tableau Spécial A. Voir la fin du tableau pour les notes.

Le Bulletin Mensuel de Statistique présente des données mensuelles et trimestrielles

(C) Facteurs de conversion pour le commerce extérieur. Les facteurs de conversion montrés dans ce tableau étaient utilisés pour convertir les données du commerce exprimées en monnaie nationale à celles exprimées en dollars E-U. Voir la fin du tableau pour les notes.

Le Bulletin Mensuel de Statistique présente des données trimestrielles

(D) Exportations mondiales par classes de marchandises et par régions. Voir la fin du tableau pour la remarque générale et les notes.

(E) Croissance des exportations mondiales par catégories de marchandises et par régions. Les taux annuels de croissance ont tous été calculés à l'aide de la formule des intérêts composés:

$$r = \left(\sqrt[t]{\frac{Vn}{Vo}} - 1 \right) * 100$$

r = Le taux annuel de croissance en pourcentage.
Vn = La valeur des exportations durant la dernière année de la période.
Vo = La valeur des exportations durant la première année de la période.
t = Le nombre d'années.

Voir la fin du Tableau Spécial F pour la remarque générale et les notes.

(F) Structure des exportations mondiales par catégories de marchandises et par régions. Les chiffres publiés sous le titre 'Origine des exportations' se réfèrent aux exportations de la région ou du pays indiqués dans la colonne zone. Il en est de même pour les 'Destinations des exportations'. Voir la fin du tableau pour la remarque générale et les notes.

(G) Importations et exportations totales: indices par pays ou zones. Les indices de la valeur unitaire sont exprimés en dollars E-U . Voir la fin du tableau pour la remarque générale et les notes.

(H) Exportations et importations totales: indices du quantum, de la valeur unitaire et des termes de l'échange par régions. Voir la fin du tableau pour les notes.

Le Bulletin Mensuel de Statistique présente des données trimestrielles.

(I) Exportations des produits manufacturés. Voir la fin du tableau K pour la remarque générale et les notes.

Le Bulletin Mensuel de Statistique présente des données trimestrielles.

(J) Importations des produits énergétiques: pays à économies développées. Voir la fin du tableau K pour la remarque générale et les notes.

Le Bulletin Mensuel de Statistique présente des données trimestrielles.

(K) Quelques indicateurs sur les importations des produits énergétiques: pays à économies développées. Ce tableau indique la part des importations de combustibles dans la valeur totale des importations et des exportations ainsi que le rapport de l'indice de la valeur unitaire des produits manufacturés qu'ils exportent et de l'indice de la valeur unitaire des combustibles qu'ils importent. Voir la fin du tableau pour la remarque générale et les notes.

Le Bulletin Mensuel de Statistique présente des données trimestrielles.

13. Les compositions des groupes économiques qui étaient utilisés dans les Tableaux Spéciaux A jusqu'à L sont les suivantes:

AELE-Association européenne de libre-échange
Islande, Liechtenstein, Norvège et Suisse

ALAI-Association Latino-américaine pour l'integration (antérieurement Association Latino-américaine de libre-échange)
Argentine, Bolivie, Brésil, Chili, Colombie, Equateur, Mexique, Paraguay, Pérou, Uruguay et Venezuela

ALENA---Accord de libre-échange nord-américain
Canada, Etats-Unis d'Amérique et Mexique

ANASE-Association des nations de l'Asie du Sud-Est
Brunei Darussalam, Cambodge, Indonésie, Malaisie, Myanmar, Philippines, République démocratique populaire lao, Singapour, Thaïlande et Vietnam

ANCOM-Marché commun andin
Bolivie, Colombie, Equateur, Pérou et Venezuela

CARICOM-Communauté des caraïbes et marché commun des caraïbes
Antigua-et-Barbuda, Bahamas (membre de la communauté seulement), Barbade, Belize, Dominique, Grenade, Guyane, Haïti, Jamaïque, Montserrat, Sainte-Lucie, Saint-Kitts-et-Nevis, Saint-Vincent-et-les Grenadines, Suriname, Trinité-et-Tobago.

CEAP-Coopération économique d'Asie-Pacifique
Australie, Brunei Darussalam, Canada, Chili, Chine, Etats-Unis d'Amérique, Fédération de Russie, Hong Kong (région administrative spéciale de Chine), Indonésie, Japon, Malaisie, Mexique, Nouvelle-Zélande, Papouasie Nouvelle-Guinée, Pérou, Philippines, Province chinoise de Taiwan, République de Corée, Singapour, Thaïlande et Vietnam

CEDEAO-Communauté économique des états de l'Afrique de l'Ouest
Bénin, Burkina Faso, Cap-Vert, Cote d'Ivoire, Gambie, Ghana, Guinée, Guinée-Bissau, Liberia, Mali, Niger, Nigeria, Sénégal, Sierra Leone et Togo

CEI-Communauté d'Etats indépendants
Arménie, Azerbaïdjan, Belarus, Fédération de Russie, Georgie, Kazakhstan, Kirghizistan, Ouzbékistan, République de Moldova, Tadjikistan, Turkménistan et Ukraine

CEMAC-Communauté économique et monétaire de I'Afrique centrale
Cameroun, Congo, Gabon, Guinée équatoriale, République Centrafricaine et Tchad

COMESA-Marché commun de l'Afrique de l'Est et de 1'Afrique australe
Angola, Burundi, Comores, Djibouti, Egypte, Erythrée, Ethiopie, Kenya, Madagascar, Malawi, Maurice, Namibie, Ouganda, République démocratique du Congo, Rwanda, Seychelles, Soudan, Swaziland, Zambie et Zimbabwe

MCC-Marché commun centraméricain
Costa Rica, El Salvador, Guatemala, Honduras et Nicaragua

Mercosur-Marché commun sud-américain
Argentine, Brésil, Paraguay et Uruguay

OCDE-Organisation de coopération et de développement économique
Allemagne, Australie, Autriche, Belgique, Canada, Danemark, Espagne, Etats-Unis d'Amérique, Finlande, France, Grèce, Hongrie, Irlande, Islande, Italie, Japon, Luxembourg, Mexique, Norv6ge, Nouvelle-Zélande, Pays-Bas, Pologne, Portugal, République de Corée, République tchèque, Royaume-Uni, Slovaquie, Suède, Suisse et Turquie

OPEP-Organisation des pays exportateurs de pétrole
Algérie, Arabie Saoudite, Emirats arabes unis, Indonésie, Iran (République islamique d') Iraq, Jamahiriya arabe libyenne, Koweït, Nigeria, Qatar et Venezuela

PMA-Pays les moins avancés
Afghanistan, Angola, Bangladesh, Bénin, Bhoutan, Burkina Faso, Burundi, Cambodge, Cap-Vert, Comores, Djibouti, Erythrée, Ethiopie, Gambie, Guinée, Guinée Bissau, Guinée équatoriale, Haïti, Iles Salomon, Kiribati, Lesotho, Liberia, Madagascar, Malawi, Maldives, Mali, Mauritanie, Mozambique, Myanmar, Népal, Niger, Ouganda, République centrafricaine, République démocratique du Congo, République démocratique populaire Lao, République-Unie de Tanzanie, Rwanda, Samoa, Sao Tome-et-Principe, Sénégal, Sierra Leone, Somalie, Soudan, Tchad, Togo, Tuvalu, Vanuatu, Yémen et Zambie

UE-Union européenne
Allemagne, Autriche, Belgique, Danemark, Espagne, Finlande, France, Grèce, Irlande, Italie, Luxembourg, Pays-Bas, Portugal, Royaume-Uni et Suède

SOURCE ET PRESENTATION

14. Les données pour les Volumes I et II sont obtenues à partir de publications nationales, d'états soumis par les gouvernements pour cet ouvrage, par le Fonds monétaire international, par la Banque de développement interaméricaine, par l'Organisation de coopération de développement économiques, par la Commission économique d'Amérique latin et le Caraïbe, par la Communauté économique des états africains occidentaux et par l'Organisation des Nations Unies pour l'alimentation et l'agriculture; et à partir d'autres publications des Nations Unies telles que: Bulletin Mensuel de Statistique, et Annuaire Statistique. Des estimations pour quelques données faisant défaut sont préparées par la Division de Statistique des Nations Unies.

15. Les noms de pays et régions utilisés par divers pays pour leurs statistiques du commerce extérieur ne sont pas uniformes. Aussi, lorsque d'anciennes entités géographiques généralement indiquées dans les statistiques nationales ont changé, les pays peuvent avoir introduit les changements correspondants dans leurs statistiques à différentes époques. Dans la mesure du

possible toutefois, les pays ou zones ont été désignés par leur nom actuel. Pour satisfaire les demandes des certains utilisateurs d'avoir des données d'un série des années consécutives la possibilité de reconstruire des anciennes entités géographiques ou politiques était gardée pour, par exemple, les données relatives à l'ancienne URSS.

16. Sauf indication contraire, les groupements de pays sont conformes à ceux des Codes standard des pays et des zones à usage statistique[1/] des Nations Unies.

17. En général, les données se réfèrent aux années selon le calendrier; cependant, pour les pays, qui déclarent leurs données selon l'année fiscale, les données sont présentées dans l'année qui couvre la plupart de l'année en référence. Les pays concernés sont Bangladesh (la période juillet - juin), l'Inde (avril – mars), Népal (juillet – juin) et Myanmar (avril – mars).

INDICES NATIONAUX

18. Les indices nationaux de la valeur unitaire et du volume antérieurement présentés dans le tableau 1 du Volume I en monnaie nationale sont maintenant présentés dans Tableau Spécial G du Volume II en dollars E-U. Ils indiquent les modifications dans le volume et dans les prix (valeur unitaire) des agrégats des importations et des exportations. Chaque indice représente une modification entre la période à laquelle l'indice se réfère, la période courante, et une période de référence pour laquelle l'indice est représenté par 100. Pour faciliter les comparaisons, chaque fois qu'il était nécessaire de le faire, les indices ont été ramenés à la base de l'année 1990. Lorsque des modifications sont faites dans la couverture, la formule ou la période de base d'un indice, si cela est techniquement possible les deux séries s'enchaînent.

19. Les indices mensuels, trimestriels et annuels en monnaie nationale sont publiés dans le Bulletin Mensuel de Statistique des Nations Unies. On trouvera également dans le Supplément de 1977 à l'Annuaire Statistique et au Bulletin Mensuel de Statistique[7/] des notes plus détaillées sur les méthodes de calcul des indices nationaux.

PAYS EN TRANSITION

20. Pour la période couverte par l'Annuaire les pays classifiés antérieurement pour des raisons statistiques à économies planifiées centralement avaient un système de taux de change officiel entre leurs monnaies et celles des pays extérieurs consistant avec le taux de 0,90 nouveau roubles pour 1 dollar des Etats-Unis avant le 24 décembre 1971 et 0,829 jusqu'à février 1973; depuis cette date le taux a fluctué. Les pays d'Europe orientale utilisaient généralement ces taux lorsqu'il était nécessaire de convertir des devises en monnaie nationale pour préparer les statistiques du commerce extérieur. Les données qui en résultent permettent davantage une comparaison avec les transactions des autres pays qu'une comparaison avec les transactions monétaires intérieures.

21. Les statistiques du commerce extérieur de ces pays ont des définitions différentes de celles qui peuvent exister dans les autres pays. Les différentes définitions peuvent être la source des divergences observées pour le même flux de marchandise enregistré par deux pays

partenaires ayant un système économique différent. Les échanges entre ces pays peuvent être conduits sur une base différente de celle qui régit les échanges entre autres pays. Le concept de la valeur de transaction, par exemple, est basé sur l'existence d'un prix de marché entre l'importateur et l'exportateur sur lequel les variations de l'offre et de la demande ont plus d'influence qu'ils ne peuvent en avoir dans les échanges de ces pays. Faute de données précises sur les valeurs unitaires des produits de base échangés entre ces pays, il est difficile de connaître les effets possibles de ces différences sur les statistiques du commerce extérieur. De plus en plus, depuis 1992, les pays en transition ont adopté les concepts et définitions pour la statistique du commerce international comparables à celles qui sont en vigueur dans les autres pays.

NOTE GENERALE

22. Les statistiques dans cet Annuaire ont été compilées par les autorités nationales des statistiques principalement conforme aux recommandations des Nations Unies publiées dans les Statistiques du Commerce international concepts et définitions, révision 1.[8/] En 1998 les Nations Unies ont fait paraître une révision de suite de cette publication; les pays étaient demandées d'introduire ces nouveaux concepts et définitions à partir des données pour l'année 1999. Les éléments principaux de ces concepts et définitions (Révision 1) sont:

1. Territoire. Les statistiques rapportées par un pays s'appliquent en général au territoire douanier de cet état. Généralement territoire douanier et territoire géographique coïncident, le cas contraire étant indiqué dans les notes par pays. Les modifications dans le territoire douanier sont également indiquées dans les notes par pays. Sauf information contraire, l'unification de deux territoires séparés auparavant donne lieu à l'élimination des échanges entre ces deux territoires. Dans le cas d'une séparation d'un territoire en deux, les échanges entre ces deux territoires viennent à apparaître.

2. Système du commerce. Deux systèmes sont généralement utilisés ne différant que par la façon dont le commerce d'entrepôt et les réexportations sont enregistrés.

a) Commerce spécial. Les importations spéciales comprennent les marchandises entrées directement pour la consommation (y compris les transformations et réparations) et les marchandises sorties des entrepôts douaniers ou des zones franches pour être mises à la consommation. Les exportations spéciales comprennent les exportations de produits nationaux, c'est-à-dire les marchandises entièrement ou partiellement produites ou fabriquées dans le pays, ainsi que les exportations nationalisées (ces dernières sont des biens qui ayant été inclus dans les importations spéciales sont réexportés en l'état.)

b) Commerce général. Les importations générales comprennent les importations pour la consommation et les importations en entrepôt douanier ou en zone franche. Les exportations générales comprennent les exportations de produits nationaux et les réexportations. Ces dernières, dans le système du commerce général, comprennent les exportations nationalisées et les marchandises exportées des entrepôts douaniers et des zones franches sans avoir été transformées depuis leur importation.

Le transit direct, c'est-à-dire les marchandises uniquement transbordées ou traversant le pays pour des raisons de transport, est exclu du commerce général aussi bien que du commerce spécial.

Les titres des tableaux 1 à 4 du Volume I indiquent le système du commerce auquel se réfèrent les données.

3. Evaluation. Lors de sa quinzième session en 1953, le Conseil Economique et Social, tenant compte du fait que les statistiques du commerce extérieur doivent refléter la réalité économique, a recommandé que les gouvernements des pays membres des Nations Unies utilisent, dans la mesure du possible, les valeurs de transaction en préparant leurs statistiques du commerce international ou qu'ils fournissent des informations supplémentaires basées sur les valeurs de transaction quand les politiques nationales font état d'autres valeurs (Résolution 469 B (XV) du Conseil Economique et Social). La valeur de transaction à l'importation est la valeur à laquelle les marchandises ont été achetées par l'importateur plus le coût de l'assurance et du fret jusqu'à la frontière des pays importateurs (valeur type CIF). A l'exportation, la valeur de transaction représente la valeur à laquelle les marchandises ont été vendues par l'exportateur y compris le coût de l'assurance du transport pour amener les marchandises à la frontière des pays exportateurs (valeur type FOB).

4. Conversion des monnaies. Pour les données dans cet Annuaire la conversion des valeurs nationales en dollars des Etats-Unis est effectuée au moyen de taux de conversion basés sur les taux de change officiels. Pour les monnaies sujettes à de larges marges de fluctuations par rapport au dollar, dont le nombre s'est accru considérablement depuis 1971, on utilise des moyennes pondérées des taux de change calculées spécialement dans ce but. La moyenne pondérée est le résultat des taux de change mensuels, généralement fournis par le Fonds Monétaire International, pondérés par les valeurs des importations et des exportations correspondantes. Les facteurs de conversion s'appliquent aux totaux des échanges mais pas nécessairement aux importations ou à l'exportation d'une marchandise donnée.

5. Marchandise. Dans la définition du commerce extérieur on entend par marchandises tous les biens dont l'importation ou l'exportation contribue à l'accroissement ou à la diminution du stock des ressources matérielles dans un pays. Sauf information contraire dans les notes par pays, le traitement des catégories de marchandises suit les règles énoncées ci-dessous:

a) Or. L'or dans le commerce international se présente sous trois formes:
   i) Pièces d'or et lingots y compris l'or monétaire;
   ii) Or non raffiné y compris les minerais et les concentrés;
   iii) Or semi-ouvré dont la valeur de l'or représente au moins 80% de la valeur totale, y compris la limaille et les poussières et les formes primaires telles que feuilles et barres et les alliages d'or.

De ces différents types d'or, l'or monétaire est exclu du commerce des marchandises tandis que les autres types sont inclus, à l'exception de ceux indiqués ci-dessous. Tout transfert d'or entre les autorités monétaires doit être traité comme échange d'or monétaire, les autres échanges portant sur l'or sont classés comme or non-monétaire.

b) Minerai d'argent. Concentrés, lingots, pièces non émises, limailles et argent ouvré ou semi-ouvré sont tous inclus dans les échanges de marchandises.

c) Monnaie et titres de propriété. Pièces de monnaie d'argent et de métal, billets de banque et titres en circulation sont exclus du commerce. Les pièces, billets et titres non en circulation sont inclus à la valeur intrinsèque du papier ou du métal frappé.

d) Le commerce pour le compte de l'Etat. Il est inclus dans le commerce des marchandises. Les échanges au titre des programmes d'aide civile et militaire, les réparations de guerre et les équipements militaires[9/] sont donc inclus. Quand les marchandises sont destinées à des institutions nationales (ambassades ou forces armées) stationnées à l'étranger, elles ne sont pas comprises dans les statistiques.

e) Importations et exportations temporaires. Les effets des touristes et des voyageurs (y compris les véhicules) qui n'ont pas été acquis à l'étranger, les objets pour expositions ou études, les animaux pour la course ou la reproduction, les échantillons et les emballages en retour qui sont considérés comme devant être retournés dans un intervalle de temps assez court sont exclus.

f) Trafic de perfectionnement et de réparation. Les pays qui envoient à l'étranger temporairement des marchandises pour réparation ou complément d'ouvraison effectuent un trafic passif de réparation. Les pays recevant des marchandises dans les mêmes conditions effectuent un trafic actif de réparation. Les mouvements d'entrée et de sortie sont généralement exclus des importations et des exportations.

g) Commerce par poste. Il est inclus dans le commerce des marchandises.

h) Poisson. Le poisson et les épaves débarqués dans des ports étrangers par des navires nationaux et ceux débarqués dans des ports du pays par des navires étrangers sont exclus des statistiques.

i) Vente et achat de navires et d'aéronefs. La vente et l'achat de navires et d'aéronefs neufs sont inclus. Les navires et les aéronefs d'occasion inscrits sur le registre d'immatriculation du pays ou radiés de ce registre sont exclus du commerce quand ces mouvements sont dûs à un transfert de propriété.

j) Avitaillement des navires et des avions. Ils doivent être généralement inclus dans les exportations de marchandises.

6. Pays Partenaire. Les pays partenaires peuvent être distingués: a) à l'importation, suivant: l'origine ou la production, la consignation ou la provenance ou l'achat; b) à l'exportation, suivant: la consommation, la dernière destination connue ou la vente.

7. Echanges par produits. L'analyse est selon la Classification Type pour le Commerce International.

CLASSIFICATION TYPE POUR LE COMMERCE INTERNATIONAL (CTCI) ET UN SYSTEME HARMONISE DE DESIGNATION ET DE CODIFICATION DES MARCHANDISES (SH)

23. En juillet 1950, le Conseil Economique et Social des Nations Unies, sur avis de la Commission de Statistique, a recommandé aux pays de rassembler leurs statistiques des échanges par produits selon la CTCI originale[2/] afin de disposer au niveau mondial de données comparables pour l'analyse du commerce extérieur. La CTCI originale a été préparée par le Secrétariat des Nations Unies avec l'aide d'experts et en coopération avec les gouvernements et les organisations internationales concernées.

24. En mai 1960 la Commission de Statistique a approuvé une révision de la CTCI appelée la CTCI, révisée, qui tenait compte des modifications dans les courants commerciaux intervenus depuis 1950 et qui permettait un passage plus facile entre la CTCI et les nomenclatures internationales. La CTCI, révisée présentait selon une classification statistique les positions de la nomenclature tarifaire NCCD du Conseil de Coopération Douanière.

25. La CTCI, révisée comprend 625 sous-groupes (identifiés par un code à quatre chiffres) qui correspondent pour l'essentiel aux postes de la CTCI originale. Un certain nombre de sous-groupes ont été subdivisés soit pour obtenir des détails supplémentaires soit pour assurer une concordance exacte avec la NCCD. La CTCI, révisée comporte donc 1312 rubriques de base (niveau des 5 chiffres de la CTCI). Les sous-groupes sont rassemblés en 177 groupes, 56 divisions et 10 sections.

26. Les positions de la CTCI sont individualisées par leur numéro de code. Le contenu précis de chaque code est défini dans la CTCI, révisée. Si l'on compare les données selon la CTCI, révisée avec des données classées selon une nomenclature nationale, il faut tenir compte de ce que la même description, généralement abrégée, peut s'appliquer à des groupes de marchandises légèrement différents.

27. La révision de 1960 représentait par rapport à la CTCI initiale une amélioration considérable. Néanmoins vers la fin des années 1960 on a constaté que, pour l'essentiel, les raisons qui avaient conduit à l'établissement de la CTCI puis à sa première révision, se retrouvaient à nouveau valables. Depuis 1960 le volume des échanges commerciaux s'est accru rapidement tandis que leur répartition géographique et leur composition par produits se modifiaient radicalement. Une nouvelle révision de la CTCI fut donc entreprise. En octobre 1974, la Commission Statistique a approuvé cette révision, la désignation de la nouvelle révision est CTCI, Révision 2[2/]. En mai 1975 le Conseil Economique et Social a recommandé aux Etats membres des Nations Unies de communiquer les données sur les statistiques du commerce extérieur en se conformant autant que possible et le plus tôt possible à la CTCI, Révision 2. A partir des données pour 1976, certains pays ont commencé à communiquer leurs données selon la CTCI, Révision 2.

28. Il y avait entre les titres de base de la Classification type pour le commerce international, Révision 2 et les subdivisions de la Nomenclature du Conseil de Coopération Douanière une correspondance biunivoque. Toutefois, un certain nombre d'utilisateurs ont estimé que les subdivisions des positions de la NCCD (et par conséquent celles de la CTCI, Révision 2) ne suffisaient pas à leurs besoins[10/]. La nécessité d'une harmonisation des classifications économiques a également été signalée[11/]. En partie pour répondre à ces besoins, le Conseil de coopération douanière a assumé en mai 1973 la responsabilité d'élaborer et de mettre au point un système harmonisé de désignation et de codification des marchandises (SH)[12/].

29. A sa vingt et unième session, en janvier 1981, la Commission de statistique a pris note du fait qu'une troisième révision de la CTCI devait être disponible lorsque la NCCD révisée et le SH entreraient tous deux en vigueur[13/]. En conséquence, dans le courant de la même année, le Secrétariat de l'ONU a commencé à travailler à la révision de la CTCI, Révision 2 en partant du principe que le maximum devait être fait pour en conserver le caractère général et la structure, tout en tenant compte de la nécessité de son harmonisation avec la NCCD révisée, avec la Classification internationale type, par industrie, de toutes les branches d'activité économique (CITI), Révision 3[14/] et avec une Classification des produits centrale (CPC)[15/] dont l'élaboration était menée conjointement par la Division de statistique des Nations Unies et l'Office statistique des Communautés européennes.

30. Le projet final a été révisé et approuvé par la Commission de statistique à sa vingt-troisième session, en février 1985[16/], et une résolution a été adoptée par le Conseil économique et social le 28 mai 1985 (résolution 1985/7) qui, inter-alia, a recommandé aux Etats Membres de communiquer des données sur les statistiques du commerce extérieur aux institutions internationales en se conformant autant que possible et le plus rapidement possible à la Classification type pour le commerce international (troisième version révisée).

31. Le système harmonisé de désignation et de codification des marchandises (appelé système harmonisé) (SH) a été adopté par le Conseil de coopération douanière en juin 1983, tandis que la Convention internationale sur le système harmonisé de désignation et de codification des marchandises (Convention SH) est entré en vigueur le ler janvier 1988 (SH88). Dès le 30 juin 2003, les parties contractantes étaient au nombre de 112 et 65 autres pays ou territoires ne figuraient pas parmi les parties contractantes, mais utilisaient le système harmonisé à des fins douanières/statistiques.

32. Lors de la vingt-septième session, qui s'est tenue à New York du 22 février au 3 mars 1993, la Commission de statistique des Nations Unies a recommandé "que les pays adoptent le SH pour l'établissement et la diffusion de leurs statistiques du commerce international"[17/].

33. Conformément au préambule à la Convention SH, qui reconnaissait l'importance d'une actualisation effective du système harmonisé compte tenu de l'évolution de la technologie ou des courants commerciaux internationaux, le système harmonisé est régulièrement passé en revue et corrigé. Lors de sa vingt-septième session, la Commission de statistique des Nations Unies a "recommandé que le Conseil de coopération douanière tienne pleinement compte des effets que les modifications proposées pourraient avoir sur le plan statistique et de prendre dûment en

considération les besoins et les capacités des pays en développement"[18/]. Quelques corrections mineures du système harmonisé de 1988, résultant par ailleurs de la suppression d'un code à 6 chiffres, ont été introduites en 1992 (SH92). Une série plus complète de modifications a été adoptée en 1993 et celles-ci sont entrées en vigueur le ler janvier 1996 (SH96). En 1999 encore une autre série de modifications a été adoptée et celles-ci sont entrées en vigueur le ler janvier 2002 (SH02).

35. A sa vingt-huitième session (27 février - 3 mars 1995), la Commission de statistique a examiné les changements qu'il faudrait apporter à la troisième version révisée de la CTCI pour l'adapter au SH96. La Commission a décidé que les changements à apporter à la troisième version révisée de la CTCI pour préserver une parfaite correspondance avec le système harmonisé étaient simplement des modifications mineures. La Commission a donc décidé qu'il serait inutile de publier une quatrième version révisée de la CTCI[19/].

1/ United Nations Standard Country Code, Statistical Papers, Series M N° 49, (United Nations publication, Sales No. E.70.XVII.13).

United Nations Standard Country or Area Code for Statistical Use, Statistical Papers, Series M N° 49, Rev. 1, (United Nations publication, Sales No. E.75.XVII.8).

Standard Country or Area Codes for Statistical Use, Statistical Papers Series M N° 49, Rev.2, (United Nations publication, Sales No. E.82.XVII.8).

Codes standard des pays et des zones à usage statistique, Documents statistiques, Series M N° 49, Rev. 3 (publication interne)

Codes standard des pays et des zones à usage statistique, Documents statistiques, Series M N° 49, Rev. 4, (United Nations publication, Sales No. M.98.XVII.9).

2/ Classification type pour le commerce international, original, Etudes statistiques, Série M No.10, Deuxième èdition, 1951 (publication des Nations Unies, numéro de vente F.51.XVII.1).

Classification type pour le commerce international, (révisée), Etudes statistiques, Série M N° 34, (publication des Nations Unies, numéro de vente F.61.XVII.6).

Classification type pour le commerce international, (deuxième version révisée), Etudes statistiques, Série M N° 34/rév. 2, (publication des Nations Unies, numéro de vente F.75.XVII.6).

Classification type pour le commerce international (troisième version révisée), Etudes statistiques, Série M N° 34/rév. 3, (publication des Nations Unies, numéro de vente F.86.XVII.12).

3/ Classification par grandes catégories économiques, (selon les définitions de la CTCI, révisée), Etudes statistiques, Série M N° 53, (publication des Nations Unies, numéro de vente 71.XVII.12).

4/ Classification des marchandises par origine industrielle (Relation entre la Classification type pour le commerce international et la Classification internationale type, par industrie, de toutes les branches d'activité économique), Etudes statistiques, Série M N° 43, (publication des Nations Unies, numéro de vente 66.XVII.7).

5/ Classification internationale type, par industrie, de toutes les branches d'activité économique (révisée), Etudes statistiques, Série M N° 4, rév. 1. (publication des Nations Unies, numéro de vente 58.XVII.7).

6/ Classification type pour le commerce international, (révisée), Etudes statistiques, Série M N° 34, (publication des Nations Unies, numéro de vente F.61.XVII.6).

7/ Supplément de 1977 à l'Annuaire Statistique et au Bulletin mensuel de statistique, ST/ESA/STAT/SER.S/SUPPL.2, ST/ESA/STAT/SER.Q/SUPPL.2, (publication des Nations Unies, numéro de vente F.78.XVII.10).

8/ Statistiques du commerce international concepts et définitions, Etudes statistiques, Série M N° 52 Révision 1, (publication des Nations Unies, numéro de vente F.82.XVII.14).

Statistiques du commerce international concepts et définitions, Etudes statistiques, Série M N° 52 Révision 2, (publication des Nations Unies, numéro de vente F.98.XVII.16).

9/ Les pays qui excluent l'équipement militaire utilisent des définitions différentes pour cette catégorie de marchandise, pour la majorité des pays cependant, armes et munitions constituent la plupart de l'équipement militaire exclu des statistiques.

10/ Groupe de travail commun Division de statistique de l'ONU - Office statistique des communautés européennes sur les nomenclatures au niveau mondial, "Système harmonisé de désignation et de codification des marchandises pour les besoins du commerce international" (UNSO/SOEC/1/2).

11/ Secrétariat de l'ONU, "L'harmonisation des classifications statistiques: compte rendu d'une réunion d'un groupe d'experts" (ST/ESA/STAT/78).

12/ Conseil de coopération douanière, "Système harmonisé de désignation et de codification des marchandises", 1985.

13/ Documents officiels du Conseil économique et social, 1981, Supplément N° 2. (E/1981/12).

14/ Classification International Type, par industrie, de toutes les branches d'activité économique, Etudes statistiques, Série M N° 4, Révision 3 (publication des Nations Unies, numéro de vente F.90.XVII.11)

15/ Classification centrale de produits (CPC) provisoire, Etudes statistiques, Série M N° 77 (publication des Nations Unies, numéro de vente F.91.XVII.7).

16/ Documents officiels du Conseil économique et social, 1985, Supplément N° 6 (E/1985/26), para. 57 (d).

17/ Documents officiels du Conseil économique et social, 1993, Supplément N° 6 (E/1993/26), para. 162 (d).

18/ Documents officiels du Conseil économique et social, 1993, Supplément N° 6 (E/1993/26), para. 162 (e).

19/ Documents officiels du Conseil économique et social, 1995, Supplément N° 8 (E/CN.3/1995/28), para. 19 (e).

TOTAL TRADE
COMMODITY TABLES

GROUP (3-DIGIT) LEVEL OF THE SITC, REVISION 2

Excluding*/ 264, Jute, raw or semi-processed;
286, Ores and concentrates of uranium and thorium;
351, Electric current; 675, Hoops and strip, of iron or steel, hot-rolled or cold-rolled;
688, Uranium depleted in U235 and thorium (including waste) and their alloys and articles thereof;
911, Postal packages not classified according to kind;
961, Coins (other than gold coin), not being legal tender; and
971, Gold, non-monetary (excluding gold ores and concentrates).

NOTES ON ESTIMATES

In preparing these tables, estimates are made for countries whose data are not yet available. At the country level these estimates are shown with a sign 'e'. They are included in the regional and world totals. Some estimates have been suppressed (see Introduction paragraph 9) and appear only as an "e".

COMMERCE TOTAL
TABLEAUX PAR PRODUITS

NIVEAU DES GROUPES (3-CHIFFRES) DE LA CTCI REVISION 2

A l'exclusion**/ des groupes 264, Jute et autres fibres textiles libériennes, bruts;
286, Minerais et concentrés d'uranium et de thorium;
351, Energie électrique; 675, Feuillards en fer ou en acier;
688, Uranium appauvri en U235, et thorium et leurs alliages;
911, Colis postaux, non classés par catégorie;
961, Monnaies (autres que les pièces d'or) n'ayant pas cours légal ; et
971, Or, non monétaire (à l'exclusion des minerais et concentrés d'or).

NOTES SUR LES ESTIMATIONS

Pour la préparation de ces tableaux, des estimations ont été effectuées pour les pays dont les données n'étaient pas disponibles. Ces estimations au niveau des pays apparaissent avec le signe 'e'. Elles sont comprises dans les totaux régionaux et le total du monde. Certaines estimations sont supprimées (voir L'introduction, paragraphe 9) et apparaissent seulement avec le signe "e".

---

*/ These codes are suppressed from publication because they were poorly reported and contain many estimates which are not sufficiently explainable.

**/ Ces groupes sont supprimés de la publication parce que ils étaient rapports insuffisamment et portaient beaucoup d'estimations qui n'étaient par assez expliquées.

001 Live animals chiefly for food

TRADE BY COMMODITY (Value in million US dollars)
Imports by principal countries or areas

COMMERCE PAR PRODUIT (Valeur en millions de dollars EU)
Importations selon les principaux pays ou zones

Country or area	1998	1999	2000	2001	2002	Pays ou zone
World	9004.9	8917.3	9057.2	8354.3	8462.2	Monde
Africa	382.1	383.0	394.9	233.5	181.7	Afrique
Americas	2254.1	2106.6	2517.7	2777.5	2537.0	Amériques
- Northern America	1821.5	1783.2	2150.3	2427.5	2192.8	- Amérique du Nord
- LAIA	392.6	277.0	318.1	288.4	292.9	- ALAI
- CACM	23.8	33.4	38.0	50.4	39.0	- MCC
- Caribbean	10.8	8.3	6.8	7.2	7.3	- Caraïbes
- Rest of America	5.3	4.7	4.6	4.1	5.1	- Autre d'Amérique
Asia excluding former USSR	1997.9	1967.7	1843.7	1599.1	1611.7	Asie ancienne URSS exclus
- Middle East	998.5	1012.3	847.2	689.3	693.7	- Moyen-Orient
Asia former USSR	4.2	4.3	3.2	4.6	6.1	Asie ancienne URSS
Europe excluding former USSR	4237.2	4326.7	4186.4	3639.4	3996.5	Europe ancienne URSS exclus
- European Union	4000.3	4107.2	3946.0	3410.6	3694.5	- Union Européenne
- Eastern Europe	107.2	76.9	104.7	130.9	131.1	- Europe de l'Est
- Rest of Europe	129.7	142.6	135.7	97.9	170.9	- Autre de l'Europe
Europe former USSR	31.7	19.9	20.4	35.5	53.5	Europe ancienne URSS
Oceania	97.7	109.0	90.8	64.6	75.7	Océanie
United States	1694.7	1611.8	1904.9	2207.0	2079.0	Etats-Unis d'Amérique
Italy-San Marino-Holy See	1561.5	1595.7	1396.6	1129.9	1255.0	Italie-Saint-Marin-Saint-Siège
United Kingdom	377.7	360.4	503.8	461.4	508.2	Royaume-Uni
Germany	389.0	389.0	336.5	470.4	382.1	Allemagne
Spain	429.2	413.4	351.0	245.2	363.8	Espagne
China, Hong Kong SAR	376.0	352.2	354.5	338.7	327.3	Chine - RAS de Hong-Kong
Netherlands	329.4	369.5	336.3	206.7	273.1	Pays-Bas
France-Monaco	260.5	327.3	319.2	201.0	184.8	France-Monaco
Saudi Arabia	238.8	270.2	239.6	158.5	e164.0	Arabie saoudite
Mexico	199.2	190.9	232.4	217.0	221.0	Mexique
Belgium	–	208.6	209.3	238.4	e261.5	Belgique
United Arab Emirates	296.6	310.8	164.0	68.0	e69.8	Emirates arabes unis
Canada	126.7	171.2	245.4	220.4	113.7	Canada
Ireland	130.9	158.7	208.6	181.3	157.5	Irlande
Japan	145.9	155.7	198.4	170.8	163.9	Japon
Lebanon	141.4	128.7	125.1	153.5	e140.0	Liban
Singapore	207.8	123.9	101.3	101.6	101.7	Singapour
Egypt	66.5	144.0	e161.7	147.2	89.4	Egypte
Portugal	61.8	94.1	114.5	112.9	116.3	Portugal
Kuwait	102.9	84.5	e79.4	e87.3	e126.2	Koweït
Libyan Arab Jamahiriya	194.5	e142.1	e127.5	e	e	Jamahiriya arabe libyenne
Greece	71.8	90.6	68.4	68.2	e75.4	Grèce
Austria	57.6	63.2	67.9	59.9	81.9	Autriche
Indonesia	41.3	50.1	104.0	73.8	59.5	Indonésie
Philippines	76.1	93.0	67.2	35.1	41.7	Philippines
Belgium-Luxembourg	309.6	–	–	–	–	Belgique-Luxembourg
Australia	75.5	79.5	60.0	33.9	46.2	Australie
Oman	49.5	49.4	44.5	52.1	44.5	Oman
Malaysia	31.1	42.2	41.8	54.2	e59.2	Malaisie
Croatia	40.0	29.2	45.8	31.6	64.0	Croatie

(Value as percentages of World total) **(Valeur en pourcentage du total mondial)**

Regions of the world	1993	1994	1995	1996	1997	1998	1999	2000	2001	2002	Régions du monde
World	100.0	100.0	100.0	100.0	100.0	100.0	100.0	100.0	100.0	100.0	Monde
Africa	2.6	3.4	3.8	3.3	3.2	4.2	4.3	4.4	2.8	2.1	Afrique
Americas	22.7	22.7	21.3	19.5	23.6	25.0	23.6	27.8	33.2	30.0	Amériques
- Northern America	19.5	17.4	18.0	16.6	19.0	20.2	20.0	23.7	29.1	25.9	- Amérique du Nord
- LAIA	2.8	4.9	3.0	2.6	4.2	4.4	3.1	3.5	3.5	3.5	- ALAI
- CACM	0.3	0.3	0.1	0.2	0.2	0.3	0.4	0.4	0.6	0.5	- MCC
- Caribbean	0.1	0.1	0.1	0.1	0.1	0.1	0.1	0.1	0.1	0.1	- Caraïbes
- Rest of America	0.0	0.0	0.0	0.0	0.0	0.1	0.1	0.1	0.0	0.1	- Autre d'Amérique
Asia excluding former USSR	25.4	21.1	26.6	28.1	26.5	22.2	22.1	20.4	19.1	19.0	Asie ancienne URSS exclus
- Middle East	13.5	9.1	14.0	14.3	12.0	11.1	11.4	9.4	8.3	8.2	- Moyen-Orient
Asia former USSR	0.0	0.0	0.0	0.0	0.0	0.0	0.0	0.0	0.1	0.1	Asie ancienne URSS
Europe excluding former USSR	48.4	51.5	47.2	47.9	45.2	47.1	48.5	46.2	43.6	47.2	Europe ancienne URSS exclus
- European Union	46.8	49.3	45.0	45.8	42.7	44.4	46.1	43.6	40.8	43.7	- Union Européenne
- Eastern Europe	0.7	1.2	1.1	0.9	0.9	1.2	0.9	1.2	1.6	1.5	- Europe de l'Est
- Rest of Europe	0.9	1.0	1.2	1.2	1.5	1.4	1.6	1.5	1.2	2.0	- Autre de l'Europe
Europe former USSR	0.3	0.4	0.3	0.3	0.4	0.4	0.2	0.2	0.4	0.6	Europe ancienne URSS
Oceania	0.7	0.9	0.8	0.8	1.1	1.1	1.2	1.0	0.8	0.9	Océanie

Animaux vivants destinés principalement à l'alimentation humaine 001

TRADE BY COMMODITY (Value in million US dollars) — COMMERCE PAR PRODUIT (Valeur en millions de dollars EU)

Exports by principal countries or areas — **Exportations selon les principaux pays ou zones**

Country or area	1998	1999	2000	2001	2002	Pays ou zone
World	8712.4	8426.1	8781.9	8537.0	9160.6	Monde
Africa	302.9	285.6	356.7	225.5	315.7	Afrique
Americas	2370.9	2042.7	2500.6	2931.0	2552.5	Amériques
- Northern America	1957.1	1638.2	1958.8	2366.4	2159.8	- Amérique du Nord
- LAIA	392.8	368.9	494.6	494.0	350.9	- ALAI
- CACM	17.3	24.1	29.6	32.0	27.4	- MCC
- Caribbean	1.1	0.9	0.9	1.2	1.1	- Caraïbes
- Rest of America	2.6	10.7	16.8	37.4	13.4	- Autre d'Amérique
Asia excluding former USSR	846.1	722.5	685.1	732.4	945.1	Asie ancienne URSS exclus
- Middle East	194.4	152.0	140.4	204.4	407.0	- Moyen-Orient
Asia former USSR	0.6	0.3	0.1	0.1	0.4	Asie ancienne URSS
Europe excluding former USSR	4749.5	4839.5	4680.6	4025.3	4605.3	Europe ancienne URSS exclus
- European Union	4310.3	4449.1	4261.8	3586.1	4141.6	- Union Européenne
- Eastern Europe	416.8	372.5	395.6	417.4	439.2	- Europe de l'Est
- Rest of Europe	22.3	17.9	23.3	21.9	24.4	- Autre de l'Europe
Europe former USSR	10.4	13.7	25.1	27.8	37.3	Europe ancienne URSS
Oceania	432.0	521.8	533.7	594.9	704.4	Océanie
France-Monaco	1719.9	1600.3	1429.2	1076.0	1507.9	France-Monaco
Canada	1306.5	1016.3	1132.8	1510.4	1560.5	Canada
United States	650.3	621.8	825.9	856.0	599.2	Etats-Unis d'Amérique
Germany	725.6	604.2	503.8	509.8	529.8	Allemagne
Netherlands	343.2	483.3	506.5	585.6	602.2	Pays-Bas
Australia	350.0	446.3	456.2	531.0	633.2	Australie
United Kingdom	424.8	478.3	478.2	518.3	514.3	Royaume-Uni
China	428.0	374.3	374.5	333.1	330.3	Chine
Mexico	212.0	292.4	422.2	430.1	309.2	Mexique
Belgium	–	388.7	359.5	238.3	e267.4	Belgique
Spain	208.0	241.3	287.1	248.9	248.3	Espagne
Ireland	185.7	317.1	359.8	137.6	193.0	Irlande
Denmark	170.9	149.5	185.9	161.2	156.7	Danemark
Poland	183.5	155.4	131.0	115.6	133.7	Pologne
Syrian Arab Republic	49.5	54.4	99.8	e113.1	330.4	République arabe syrienne
Malaysia	172.9	116.0	93.3	102.0	e108.1	Malaisie
Hungary	104.6	89.0	118.6	146.9	127.1	Hongrie
Somalia	e119.4	e138.3	e150.7	e	e60.3	Somalie
Romania	52.2	80.7	96.9	98.8	107.2	Roumanie
Austria	100.2	90.8	76.0	51.8	59.3	Autriche
New Zealand	81.8	75.4	77.4	63.8	70.6	Nouvelle-Zélande
Belgium-Luxembourg	363.3	–	–	–	–	Belgique-Luxembourg
Sudan	68.3	e24.9	60.5	0.0	122.8	Soudan
Mali	50.0	53.3	51.0	67.6	e0.1	Mali
Niger	26.2	29.8	45.5	41.0	e74.3	Niger
Czech Republic	57.1	30.4	23.7	32.1	39.1	République tchèque
Italy-San Marino-Holy See	48.5	50.0	33.7	16.2	18.6	Italie-Saint-Marin-Saint-Siège
Indonesia	20.0	28.6	36.1	38.2	29.6	Indonésie
Turkey	46.7	9.8	0.7	42.0	29.4	Turquie
Oman	25.5	24.0	21.2	28.8	21.4	Oman

(Value as percentages of World total) — **(Valeur en pourcentage du total mondial)**

Regions of the world	1993	1994	1995	1996	1997	1998	1999	2000	2001	2002	Régions du monde
World	100.0	100.0	100.0	100.0	100.0	100.0	100.0	100.0	100.0	100.0	Monde
Africa	1.8	1.3	2.8	2.9	2.6	3.5	3.4	4.1	2.6	3.4	Afrique
Americas	24.8	22.8	23.3	21.8	26.2	27.2	24.2	28.5	34.3	27.9	Amériques
- Northern America	18.6	16.8	15.6	19.3	22.3	22.5	19.4	22.3	27.7	23.6	- Amérique du Nord
- LAIA	6.0	5.7	7.6	2.4	3.6	4.5	4.4	5.6	5.8	3.8	- ALAI
- CACM	0.2	0.2	0.1	0.1	0.1	0.2	0.3	0.3	0.4	0.3	- MCC
- Caribbean	0.0	0.0	0.0	0.0	0.0	0.0	0.0	0.0	0.0	0.0	- Caraïbes
- Rest of America	0.0	0.0	0.0	0.0	0.1	0.0	0.1	0.2	0.4	0.1	- Autre d'Amérique
Asia excluding former USSR	13.1	11.8	10.0	10.3	11.1	9.7	8.6	7.8	8.6	10.3	Asie ancienne URSS exclus
- Middle East	5.1	4.0	2.7	2.5	3.1	2.2	1.8	1.6	2.4	4.4	- Moyen-Orient
Asia former USSR	0.0	0.0	0.1	0.0	0.0	0.0	0.0	0.0	0.0	0.0	Asie ancienne URSS
Europe excluding former USSR	56.3	59.6	57.9	58.1	53.0	54.5	57.4	53.3	47.2	50.3	Europe ancienne URSS exclus
- European Union	50.3	53.5	52.9	53.2	47.9	49.5	52.8	48.5	42.0	45.2	- Union Européenne
- Eastern Europe	5.2	5.7	4.7	4.6	4.9	4.8	4.4	4.5	4.9	4.8	- Europe de l'Est
- Rest of Europe	0.8	0.4	0.4	0.3	0.2	0.3	0.2	0.3	0.3	0.3	- Autre de l'Europe
Europe former USSR	0.4	0.5	1.1	0.6	0.2	0.1	0.2	0.3	0.3	0.4	Europe ancienne URSS
Oceania	3.5	4.0	4.9	6.1	6.9	5.0	6.2	6.1	7.0	7.7	Océanie

011 Meat and edible meat offal, fresh, chilled or frozen

TRADE BY COMMODITY (Value in million US dollars)
Imports by principal countries or areas

COMMERCE PAR PRODUIT (Valeur en millions de dollars EU)
Importations selon les principaux pays ou zones

Country or area	1998	1999	2000	2001	2002	Pays ou zone
World	36407.1	37089.3	38031.4	38666.2	39552.9	Monde
Africa	613.1	650.6	700.3	634.9	740.8	Afrique
Americas	5303.5	5589.8	6632.0	7404.5	7308.5	Amériques
- Northern America	3188.3	3598.5	4193.3	4696.6	4688.2	- Amérique du Nord
- LAIA	1658.1	1559.7	2036.8	2235.5	2203.2	- ALAI
- CACM	66.9	66.8	83.3	88.1	94.7	- MCC
- Caribbean	365.8	337.2	289.9	359.0	299.0	- Caraïbes
- Rest of America	24.4	27.7	28.7	25.3	23.5	- Autre d'Amérique
Asia excluding former USSR	10591.4	12409.7	13430.1	12592.2	12185.0	Asie ancienne URSS exclus
- Middle East	1622.3	1511.3	1301.8	1270.8	1180.1	- Moyen-Orient
Asia former USSR	118.3	117.2	99.7	88.9	86.1	Asie ancienne URSS
Europe excluding former USSR	17568.3	16727.7	15774.5	15817.4	16508.8	Europe ancienne URSS exclus
- European Union	16490.7	15899.2	14875.6	14802.0	15333.7	- Union Européenne
- Eastern Europe	485.1	286.3	324.3	431.4	548.0	- Europe de l'Est
- Rest of Europe	592.5	542.2	574.6	584.0	627.1	- Autre de l'Europe
Europe former USSR	2027.8	1392.9	1128.3	1853.1	2406.0	Europe ancienne URSS
Oceania	184.7	201.3	266.4	275.1	317.7	Océanie
Japan	6109.5	7058.2	7652.0	7397.3	6690.3	Japon
United States	2481.1	2872.4	3438.6	3841.6	3819.9	Etats-Unis d'Amérique
Germany	3880.8	3420.5	2819.7	3036.7	2814.4	Allemagne
Italy-San Marino-Holy See	3365.0	3061.7	2947.7	2846.9	2860.3	Italie-Saint-Marin-Saint-Siège
France-Monaco	2680.1	2584.1	2473.1	2193.9	2242.3	France-Monaco
United Kingdom	1948.9	2029.5	2057.5	2191.0	2359.2	Royaume-Uni
Russian Federation	1758.8	1168.6	985.0	1690.4	2229.2	Fédération de Russie
Mexico	985.3	1088.6	1537.5	1815.4	1832.3	Mexique
China, Hong Kong SAR	1434.9	1451.1	1512.8	1419.5	1287.9	Chine - RAS de Hong-Kong
Netherlands	818.7	936.3	868.2	903.6	1092.1	Pays-Bas
Korea, Republic of	443.3	790.0	1128.3	834.4	1261.9	République de Corée
Canada	676.4	692.6	741.3	837.0	844.5	Canada
Greece	817.3	729.6	650.7	586.6	e648.6	Grèce
Spain	712.0	716.7	651.1	598.9	684.1	Espagne
Belgium	–	731.2	650.4	743.7	e815.6	Belgique
Saudi Arabia	581.3	577.3	582.3	538.7	e557.5	Arabie saoudite
China	146.2	506.4	643.2	616.2	642.4	Chine
Portugal	357.4	415.9	437.8	418.0	429.5	Portugal
Denmark	385.4	390.4	400.7	331.2	394.8	Danemark
United Arab Emirates	448.5	470.0	285.9	283.2	e290.6	Emirates arabes unis
Switzerland-Liechtenstein	318.7	308.1	325.6	304.0	326.5	Suisse-Liechtenstein
Sweden	246.8	282.7	314.6	313.1	363.6	Suède
Austria	278.2	301.0	289.6	296.9	290.6	Autriche
Singapore	165.6	238.8	271.3	264.4	276.6	Singapour
Egypt	221.1	271.7	e177.1	161.2	226.7	Egypte
Malaysia	131.7	162.7	195.7	211.8	e231.4	Malaisie
Ireland	132.0	143.0	170.6	213.7	206.3	Irlande
Chile	175.2	166.4	177.5	167.0	175.9	Chili
Belgium-Luxembourg	786.7	–	–	–	–	Belgique-Luxembourg
Israel	147.2	129.7	149.4	127.2	125.0	Israël

(Value as percentages of World total) **(Valeur en pourcentage du total mondial)**

Regions of the world	1993	1994	1995	1996	1997	1998	1999	2000	2001	2002	Régions du monde
World	100.0	100.0	100.0	100.0	100.0	100.0	100.0	100.0	100.0	100.0	Monde
Africa	1.6	1.7	1.8	1.4	1.6	1.7	1.8	1.8	1.6	1.9	Afrique
Americas	13.7	12.8	9.9	10.2	12.7	14.6	15.1	17.4	19.1	18.5	Amériques
- Northern America	9.7	8.4	6.6	6.5	7.9	8.8	9.7	11.0	12.1	11.9	- Amérique du Nord
- LAIA	2.9	3.5	2.3	2.9	3.9	4.6	4.2	5.4	5.8	5.6	- ALAI
- CACM	0.1	0.1	0.1	0.1	0.1	0.2	0.2	0.2	0.2	0.2	- MCC
- Caribbean	1.0	0.8	0.8	0.6	0.7	1.0	0.9	0.8	0.9	0.8	- Caraïbes
- Rest of America	0.1	0.1	0.1	0.0	0.0	0.1	0.1	0.1	0.1	0.1	- Autre d'Amérique
Asia excluding former USSR	29.8	30.0	33.3	33.4	31.0	29.1	33.5	35.3	32.6	30.8	Asie ancienne URSS exclus
- Middle East	3.9	2.7	3.4	3.7	4.1	4.5	4.1	3.4	3.3	3.0	- Moyen-Orient
Asia former USSR	0.2	0.4	0.3	0.4	0.4	0.3	0.3	0.3	0.2	0.2	Asie ancienne URSS
Europe excluding former USSR	52.2	50.7	49.9	49.2	47.2	48.3	45.1	41.5	40.9	41.7	Europe ancienne URSS exclus
- European Union	49.7	47.9	47.4	46.7	44.7	45.3	42.9	39.1	38.3	38.8	- Union Européenne
- Eastern Europe	0.9	1.2	0.9	0.8	0.9	1.3	0.8	0.9	1.1	1.4	- Europe de l'Est
- Rest of Europe	1.5	1.6	1.6	1.7	1.6	1.6	1.5	1.5	1.5	1.6	- Autre de l'Europe
Europe former USSR	2.0	3.9	4.3	4.8	6.6	5.6	3.8	3.0	4.8	6.1	Europe ancienne URSS
Oceania	0.5	0.5	0.5	0.7	0.5	0.5	0.5	0.7	0.7	0.8	Océanie

TRADE BY COMMODITY (Value in million US dollars)
Exports by principal countries or areas

COMMERCE PAR PRODUIT (Valeur en millions de dollars EU)
Exportations selon les principaux pays ou zones

Country or area	1998	1999	2000	2001	2002	Pays ou zone
World	35888.9	36353.3	37445.5	38812.1	38589.0	Monde
Africa	112.4	81.3	180.9	206.1	220.1	Afrique
Americas	10037.4	10666.4	12419.3	13043.5	12169.3	Amériques
- Northern America	7369.7	7758.9	9297.1	9453.8	8465.7	- Amérique du Nord
- LAIA	2568.0	2803.9	3000.2	3464.8	3562.3	- ALAI
- CACM	79.2	84.5	105.9	106.6	118.5	- MCC
- Caribbean	9.4	5.7	4.3	3.8	2.5	- Caraïbes
- Rest of America	11.1	13.4	11.9	14.6	20.3	- Autre d'Amérique
Asia excluding former USSR	2712.8	2602.4	2580.7	2699.0	2506.5	Asie ancienne URSS exclus
- Middle East	126.3	108.4	74.1	79.3	78.8	- Moyen-Orient
Asia former USSR	18.3	13.1	1.8	5.5	6.0	Asie ancienne URSS
Europe excluding former USSR	18707.6	18496.6	17412.6	17486.9	18193.7	Europe ancienne URSS exclus
- European Union	17734.7	17655.5	16589.0	16490.2	17166.8	- Union Européenne
- Eastern Europe	901.2	772.3	764.6	922.2	958.8	- Europe de l'Est
- Rest of Europe	71.6	68.8	58.9	74.5	68.1	- Autre de l'Europe
Europe former USSR	324.4	265.9	297.7	317.0	320.6	Europe ancienne URSS
Oceania	3976.0	4227.6	4552.5	5054.2	5172.7	Océanie
United States	5797.5	5841.9	6946.9	6679.9	5770.4	Etats-Unis d'Amérique
Netherlands	3657.8	3795.7	3583.6	3201.0	3358.2	Pays-Bas
Australia	2418.4	2644.8	2870.4	3236.5	3184.5	Australie
France-Monaco	3256.3	3029.9	2825.0	2351.2	2448.0	France-Monaco
Denmark	2595.9	2545.7	2584.2	2904.0	2735.0	Danemark
Canada	1570.8	1916.2	2349.9	2773.7	2695.1	Canada
Germany	1832.9	2062.9	1686.7	2224.2	2260.3	Allemagne
Brazil	1237.4	1520.4	1596.1	2542.4	e2635.8	Brésil
New Zealand	1552.2	1578.6	1677.8	1813.2	1983.0	Nouvelle-Zélande
Belgium	–	1639.2	1790.8	2057.0	e2308.0	Belgique
Ireland	1374.2	1632.4	1361.8	1116.5	1236.6	Irlande
Spain	917.0	996.1	1018.0	1142.9	1118.0	Espagne
China	828.9	688.2	748.2	852.9	677.5	Chine
United Kingdom	1036.7	879.9	786.8	457.5	570.8	Royaume-Uni
China, Hong Kong SAR	720.0	739.6	809.2	744.2	685.0	Chine - RAS de Hong-Kong
Hungary	524.1	484.2	482.8	561.8	539.8	Hongrie
Italy-San Marino-Holy See	535.9	531.3	469.2	483.5	523.0	Italie-Saint-Marin-Saint-Siège
Thailand	425.9	435.9	427.7	596.2	e629.7	Thaïlande
Argentina	600.7	653.1	619.9	221.6	e214.1	Argentine
Belgium-Luxembourg	2008.2	–	–	–	–	Belgique-Luxembourg
Austria	349.5	366.3	333.6	391.0	432.2	Autriche
Uruguay	443.6	375.4	424.3	257.8	283.9	Uruguay
India	183.3	184.4	323.5	250.1	278.2	Inde
Poland	255.5	206.5	200.3	239.9	289.9	Pologne
Ukraine	159.7	167.7	194.6	190.1	209.6	Ukraine
Mexico	138.8	148.7	191.3	206.5	201.5	Mexique
Korea, Republic of	315.6	340.2	76.5	46.3	20.2	République de Corée
Chile	62.4	60.5	85.2	133.0	e130.1	Chili
Sweden	91.7	83.7	54.8	63.2	67.6	Suède
Paraguay	68.3	35.1	72.7	78.5	e85.7	Paraguay

(Value as percentages of World total) **(Valeur en pourcentage du total mondial)**

Regions of the world	1993	1994	1995	1996	1997	1998	1999	2000	2001	2002	Régions du monde
World	100.0	100.0	100.0	100.0	100.0	100.0	100.0	100.0	100.0	100.0	Monde
Africa	0.4	0.2	0.2	0.3	0.2	0.3	0.2	0.5	0.5	0.6	Afrique
Americas	21.0	22.6	23.6	25.8	27.6	28.0	29.3	33.2	33.6	31.5	Amériques
- Northern America	15.0	16.4	17.8	19.3	20.4	20.5	21.3	24.8	24.4	21.9	- Amérique du Nord
- LAIA	5.3	5.7	5.5	6.3	7.0	7.2	7.7	8.0	8.9	9.2	- ALAI
- CACM	0.6	0.5	0.3	0.3	0.2	0.2	0.2	0.3	0.3	0.3	- MCC
- Caribbean	0.0	0.0	0.0	0.0	0.0	0.0	0.0	0.0	0.0	0.0	- Caraïbes
- Rest of America	0.1	0.0	0.0	0.0	0.0	0.0	0.0	0.0	0.0	0.1	- Autre d'Amérique
Asia excluding former USSR	10.6	8.6	9.9	10.8	7.7	7.6	7.2	6.9	7.0	6.5	Asie ancienne URSS exclus
- Middle East	0.4	0.4	0.4	0.3	0.3	0.4	0.3	0.2	0.2	0.2	- Moyen-Orient
Asia former USSR	0.0	0.0	0.1	0.1	0.2	0.1	0.0	0.0	0.0	0.0	Asie ancienne URSS
Europe excluding former USSR	54.8	55.1	54.3	51.8	51.8	52.1	50.9	46.5	45.1	47.1	Europe ancienne URSS exclus
- European Union	52.2	52.8	52.0	49.2	49.1	49.4	48.6	44.3	42.5	44.5	- Union Européenne
- Eastern Europe	2.2	2.1	2.1	2.4	2.6	2.5	2.1	2.0	2.4	2.5	- Europe de l'Est
- Rest of Europe	0.3	0.3	0.2	0.2	0.2	0.2	0.2	0.2	0.2	0.2	- Autre de l'Europe
Europe former USSR	0.3	0.9	1.0	1.1	1.2	0.9	0.7	0.8	0.8	0.8	Europe ancienne URSS
Oceania	13.0	12.5	10.8	10.1	11.2	11.1	11.6	12.2	13.0	13.4	Océanie

012 Meat and edible meat offal, in brine, dried, salted or smoked

TRADE BY COMMODITY (Value in million US dollars) COMMERCE PAR PRODUIT (Valeur en millions de dollars EU)
Imports by principal countries or areas **Importations selon les principaux pays ou zones**

Country or area	1998	1999	2000	2001	2002	Pays ou zone
World	1507.4	1425.5	1454.9	1647.1	1730.9	Monde
Africa	7.1	11.5	11.4	8.6	6.4	Afrique
Americas	139.7	155.0	200.1	202.1	202.4	Amériques
- Northern America	71.4	95.1	134.6	135.9	149.6	- Amérique du Nord
- LAIA	43.9	40.0	43.5	44.9	34.8	- ALAI
- CACM	1.3	1.4	1.3	1.3	1.1	- MCC
- Caribbean	19.5	14.6	17.0	16.5	14.0	- Caraïbes
- Rest of America	3.5	3.8	3.7	3.4	3.0	- Autre d'Amérique
Asia excluding former USSR	65.1	65.8	48.1	44.6	46.3	Asie ancienne URSS exclus
- Middle East	25.9	26.9	5.3	5.3	5.6	- Moyen-Orient
Asia former USSR	0.6	0.4	0.5	0.4	0.3	Asie ancienne URSS
Europe excluding former USSR	1209.0	1187.8	1189.2	1386.4	1469.7	Europe ancienne URSS exclus
- European Union	1167.2	1149.7	1153.3	1347.3	1428.3	- Union Européenne
- Eastern Europe	2.0	1.9	1.8	1.8	2.6	- Europe de l'Est
- Rest of Europe	39.9	36.2	34.0	37.3	38.8	- Autre de l'Europe
Europe former USSR	83.7	2.4	2.6	2.6	2.3	Europe ancienne URSS
Oceania	2.3	2.8	3.0	2.5	3.4	Océanie
United Kingdom	622.0	642.3	684.6	816.7	852.7	Royaume-Uni
France-Monaco	199.6	177.5	177.1	187.1	201.2	France-Monaco
Germany	143.3	117.7	91.8	125.4	113.1	Allemagne
United States	61.3	78.9	110.5	105.7	118.8	Etats-Unis d'Amérique
Belgium	–	57.0	54.1	54.9	e60.2	Belgique
Italy-San Marino-Holy See	35.8	33.2	29.4	39.6	44.4	Italie-Saint-Marin-Saint-Siège
Netherlands	26.9	28.0	28.0	33.8	33.8	Pays-Bas
Canada	9.7	15.8	23.6	29.6	30.0	Canada
Switzerland-Liechtenstein	22.1	20.8	21.0	19.1	19.8	Suisse-Liechtenstein
Ireland	20.6	20.8	18.4	17.3	23.3	Irlande
Portugal	15.8	16.6	16.4	20.5	28.8	Portugal
Mexico	10.2	11.8	20.4	28.7	26.2	Mexique
Argentina	29.5	25.1	20.2	13.5	e6.0	Argentine
Russian Federation	81.8	0.7	1.0	1.1	1.4	Fédération de Russie
Japan	15.0	15.2	18.4	16.5	18.5	Japon
China, Hong Kong SAR	17.5	16.4	17.1	15.9	15.8	Chine - RAS de Hong-Kong
Denmark	15.2	16.2	17.1	11.6	17.3	Danemark
Austria	13.3	10.9	10.0	12.1	14.6	Autriche
United Arab Emirates	23.6	24.8	2.9	3.3	e3.4	Emirates arabes unis
Belgium-Luxembourg	52.4	–	–	–	–	Belgique-Luxembourg
Spain	8.7	8.8	7.1	6.7	11.7	Espagne
Sweden	8.4	6.4	5.9	6.8	10.9	Suède
Luxembourg	–	9.4	8.9	9.2	e9.7	Luxembourg
Bahamas	5.1	5.0	7.2	6.4	e5.4	Bahamas
Angola	e3.8	e7.1	e8.1	e5.6	e2.8	Angola
Croatia	6.5	3.8	3.2	5.2	5.5	Croatie
Bosnia and Herzegovina	e3.4	e4.8	e3.0	e5.3	e3.7	Bosnie-Herzégovine
Singapore	3.7	3.9	4.5	4.2	3.8	Singapour
Andorra	4.0	3.8	3.5	3.8	4.3	Andorre
Greece	2.6	2.7	2.4	2.8	e3.1	Grèce

(Value as percentages of World total) **(Valeur en pourcentage du total mondial)**

Regions of the world	1993	1994	1995	1996	1997	1998	1999	2000	2001	2002	Régions du monde
World	100.0	100.0	100.0	100.0	100.0	100.0	100.0	100.0	100.0	100.0	Monde
Africa	0.8	0.4	0.4	0.4	0.4	0.5	0.8	0.8	0.5	0.4	Afrique
Americas	9.7	10.1	8.3	7.5	8.6	9.3	10.9	13.8	12.3	11.7	Amériques
- Northern America	4.8	5.2	4.4	4.1	4.6	4.7	6.7	9.3	8.3	8.6	- Amérique du Nord
- LAIA	2.5	3.2	2.2	2.1	2.6	2.9	2.8	3.0	2.7	2.0	- ALAI
- CACM	0.0	0.0	0.0	0.0	0.1	0.1	0.1	0.1	0.1	0.1	- MCC
- Caribbean	2.0	1.4	1.4	1.1	1.1	1.3	1.0	1.2	1.0	0.8	- Caraïbes
- Rest of America	0.4	0.4	0.3	0.1	0.2	0.2	0.3	0.3	0.2	0.2	- Autre d'Amérique
Asia excluding former USSR	2.2	2.5	2.4	2.1	2.6	4.3	4.6	3.3	2.7	2.7	Asie ancienne URSS exclus
- Middle East	0.1	0.1	0.1	0.1	0.2	1.7	1.9	0.4	0.3	0.3	- Moyen-Orient
Asia former USSR	0.0	0.0	0.0	0.0	0.0	0.0	0.0	0.0	0.0	0.0	Asie ancienne URSS
Europe excluding former USSR	86.4	84.9	87.0	88.3	82.5	80.2	83.3	81.7	84.2	84.9	Europe ancienne URSS exclus
- European Union	84.8	83.3	85.0	86.4	80.2	77.4	80.6	79.3	81.8	82.5	- Union Européenne
- Eastern Europe	0.1	0.0	0.1	0.1	0.1	0.1	0.1	0.1	0.1	0.2	- Europe de l'Est
- Rest of Europe	1.5	1.6	1.9	1.8	2.2	2.6	2.5	2.3	2.3	2.2	- Autre de l'Europe
Europe former USSR	0.6	1.9	1.8	1.6	5.7	5.6	0.2	0.2	0.2	0.1	Europe ancienne URSS
Oceania	0.2	0.1	0.1	0.1	0.1	0.2	0.2	0.2	0.2	0.2	Océanie

Viandes et abats comestibles, salés ou en saumure, séchés ou fumés 012

TRADE BY COMMODITY (Value in million US dollars)
Exports by principal countries or areas

COMMERCE PAR PRODUIT (Valeur en millions de dollars EU)
Exportations selon les principaux pays ou zones

Country or area	1998	1999	2000	2001	2002	Pays ou zone
World	1543.7	1552.1	1604.0	1698.8	1785.3	Monde
Africa	0.7	0.8	0.6	0.9	1.2	Afrique
Americas	124.1	132.9	187.2	186.1	209.8	Amériques
- Northern America	116.0	120.1	175.0	176.8	201.5	- Amérique du Nord
- LAIA	8.1	12.5	12.1	9.1	8.0	- ALAI
- CACM	0.0	0.2	0.0	0.2	0.2	- MCC
- Caribbean	0.1	0.0	0.1	0.0	0.0	- Caraïbes
- Rest of America	0.0	0.0	0.0	0.0	0.0	- Autre d'Amérique
Asia excluding former USSR	8.9	5.6	6.7	5.5	6.8	Asie ancienne URSS exclus
- Middle East	0.2	0.3	0.3	0.2	0.3	- Moyen-Orient
Asia former USSR	0.0	0.0	0.0	0.0	0.0	Asie ancienne URSS
Europe excluding former USSR	1406.6	1408.5	1404.8	1502.0	1562.1	Europe ancienne URSS exclus
- European Union	1365.2	1383.6	1381.6	1479.4	1539.0	- Union Européenne
- Eastern Europe	18.0	3.9	4.0	5.3	4.1	- Europe de l'Est
- Rest of Europe	23.4	21.0	19.2	17.3	19.0	- Autre de l'Europe
Europe former USSR	0.9	0.4	0.1	0.2	0.2	Europe ancienne URSS
Oceania	2.6	3.9	4.5	4.1	5.3	Océanie
Denmark	345.0	324.1	330.9	394.3	387.2	Danemark
Netherlands	284.9	356.2	361.6	321.3	331.0	Pays-Bas
Italy-San Marino-Holy See	322.0	318.9	303.4	345.3	344.9	Italie-Saint-Marin-Saint-Siège
Spain	95.0	94.5	94.6	91.0	112.8	Espagne
France-Monaco	88.3	88.8	85.8	115.1	100.6	France-Monaco
United States	71.7	62.4	85.0	92.4	116.8	Etats-Unis d'Amérique
Belgium	–	86.5	84.1	96.7	e108.5	Belgique
Canada	44.2	57.7	90.1	84.4	84.7	Canada
Germany	57.5	50.4	51.0	49.3	60.5	Allemagne
United Kingdom	31.5	23.8	33.0	31.6	46.4	Royaume-Uni
Belgium-Luxembourg	103.1	–	–	–	–	Belgique-Luxembourg
Ireland	15.7	17.8	15.1	12.1	19.2	Irlande
Austria	16.1	14.4	12.4	13.1	16.8	Autriche
Switzerland-Liechtenstein	13.5	13.8	13.1	10.7	13.2	Suisse-Liechtenstein
Brazil	3.6	5.1	5.4	5.1	e5.3	Brésil
Poland	13.9	2.0	2.4	2.9	1.6	Pologne
Slovenia	4.7	3.7	4.1	4.6	4.2	Slovénie
Luxembourg	–	3.1	5.9	5.9	e6.0	Luxembourg
Mexico	2.7	6.4	5.5	2.7	1.3	Mexique
China	5.9	2.6	3.4	2.6	2.6	Chine
Australia	2.4	3.7	4.4	3.7	2.5	Australie
Portugal	3.4	3.9	2.3	2.8	3.9	Portugal
Hungary	3.4	1.5	1.5	2.3	2.4	Hongrie
Sweden	2.4	1.0	0.6	0.8	1.0	Suède
Uruguay	1.4	0.9	1.1	1.0	1.2	Uruguay
Bosnia and Herzegovina	e2.1	e1.6	e0.7	e0.9	e0.4	Bosnie-Herzégovine
Malaysia	1.3	1.3	1.3	0.3	e0.3	Malaisie
New Zealand	0.3	0.2	0.1	0.4	2.8	Nouvelle-Zélande
Croatia	1.9	0.5	0.5	0.2	0.6	Croatie
Serbia and Montenegro	0.4	0.8	0.5	e0.6	e0.4	Serbie-et-Monténégro

(Value as percentages of World total) **(Valeur en pourcentage du total mondial)**

Regions of the world	1993	1994	1995	1996	1997	1998	1999	2000	2001	2002	Régions du monde
World	100.0	100.0	100.0	100.0	100.0	100.0	100.0	100.0	100.0	100.0	Monde
Africa	0.1	0.1	0.0	0.0	0.0	0.0	0.1	0.0	0.1	0.1	Afrique
Americas	7.2	8.8	8.8	7.3	7.2	8.0	8.6	11.7	11.0	11.7	Amériques
- Northern America	6.7	7.9	8.1	6.7	6.8	7.5	7.7	10.9	10.4	11.3	- Amérique du Nord
- LAIA	0.6	0.8	0.7	0.6	0.3	0.5	0.8	0.8	0.5	0.4	- ALAI
- CACM	0.0	0.0	0.0	0.0	0.0	0.0	0.0	0.0	0.0	0.0	- MCC
- Caribbean	0.0	0.0	0.0	0.0	0.0	0.0	0.0	0.0	0.0	0.0	- Caraïbes
- Rest of America	0.0	0.0	0.0	0.0	0.0	0.0	0.0	0.0	0.0	0.0	- Autre d'Amérique
Asia excluding former USSR	0.8	1.1	1.1	0.9	0.9	0.6	0.4	0.4	0.3	0.4	Asie ancienne URSS exclus
- Middle East	0.0	0.0	0.0	0.1	0.2	0.0	0.0	0.0	0.0	0.0	- Moyen-Orient
Asia former USSR	0.0	0.0	0.1	0.0	0.0	0.0	0.0	0.0	0.0	0.0	Asie ancienne URSS
Europe excluding former USSR	91.4	89.7	89.6	91.5	91.4	91.1	90.7	87.6	88.4	87.5	Europe ancienne URSS exclus
- European Union	89.7	87.5	88.0	89.5	89.2	88.4	89.1	86.1	87.1	86.2	- Union Européenne
- Eastern Europe	0.2	0.4	0.1	0.8	1.0	1.2	0.3	0.2	0.3	0.2	- Europe de l'Est
- Rest of Europe	1.5	1.8	1.6	1.2	1.2	1.5	1.4	1.2	1.0	1.1	- Autre de l'Europe
Europe former USSR	0.0	0.0	0.0	0.0	0.2	0.1	0.0	0.0	0.0	0.0	Europe ancienne URSS
Oceania	0.4	0.3	0.3	0.2	0.2	0.2	0.3	0.3	0.2	0.3	Océanie

014 Meat and edible meat offal, prepared, preserved, nes; fish extracts

TRADE BY COMMODITY (Value in million US dollars)
Imports by principal countries or areas

COMMERCE PAR PRODUIT (Valeur en millions de dollars EU)
Importations selon les principaux pays ou zones

Country or area	1998	1999	2000	2001	2002	Pays ou zone
World	5643.2	5679.6	5835.1	6606.9	6692.6	Monde
Africa	64.2	63.9	75.0	71.8	84.9	Afrique
Americas	982.8	1059.5	1048.5	1105.6	1104.4	Amériques
- Northern America	691.2	695.9	706.0	732.6	773.1	- Amérique du Nord
- LAIA	159.6	219.5	191.5	219.5	186.0	- ALAI
- CACM	26.9	31.2	32.5	34.1	32.4	- MCC
- Caribbean	88.4	93.4	97.7	102.1	94.6	- Caraïbes
- Rest of America	16.8	19.6	20.8	17.3	18.3	- Autre d'Amérique
Asia excluding former USSR	1040.5	1174.3	1315.6	1436.0	1520.7	Asie ancienne URSS exclus
- Middle East	120.4	125.7	131.5	123.1	121.2	- Moyen-Orient
Asia former USSR	44.8	23.8	35.6	30.9	32.6	Asie ancienne URSS
Europe excluding former USSR	3200.9	3208.3	3208.6	3799.5	3786.7	Europe ancienne URSS exclus
- European Union	2903.9	2941.4	2987.4	3580.3	3550.8	- Union Européenne
- Eastern Europe	93.5	60.8	57.5	55.9	58.4	- Europe de l'Est
- Rest of Europe	203.5	206.2	163.7	163.3	177.5	- Autre de l'Europe
Europe former USSR	251.4	88.1	83.3	92.0	95.8	Europe ancienne URSS
Oceania	58.7	61.7	68.5	71.1	67.5	Océanie
United Kingdom	783.8	802.3	848.9	983.2	1061.1	Royaume-Uni
Japan	634.0	739.8	880.2	995.3	1067.1	Japon
Germany	754.4	715.5	677.5	896.8	662.4	Allemagne
United States	473.8	476.2	465.6	471.6	500.7	Etats-Unis d'Amérique
Netherlands	249.1	266.0	338.4	412.9	417.0	Pays-Bas
France-Monaco	267.5	236.3	244.2	270.6	273.2	France-Monaco
Canada	209.0	210.7	236.1	255.4	263.7	Canada
Belgium	–	245.1	238.1	279.2	e306.2	Belgique
China, Hong Kong SAR	175.3	158.5	162.3	165.4	161.3	Chine - RAS de Hong-Kong
Mexico	88.9	91.0	124.3	162.9	147.1	Mexique
Italy-San Marino-Holy See	119.4	122.0	115.1	126.5	127.9	Italie-Saint-Marin-Saint-Siège
Spain	111.7	111.8	92.2	115.3	118.3	Espagne
Ireland	97.1	95.8	83.5	115.8	128.6	Irlande
Russian Federation	221.3	74.6	64.3	64.4	62.5	Fédération de Russie
Sweden	84.5	87.2	84.2	91.5	109.9	Suède
Denmark	61.2	65.3	74.6	79.9	106.7	Danemark
Austria	58.7	70.0	76.3	80.5	94.7	Autriche
Switzerland-Liechtenstein	73.3	69.4	64.5	67.2	72.1	Suisse-Liechtenstein
Singapore	50.1	70.1	64.0	63.5	66.8	Singapour
Belgium-Luxembourg	227.8	–	–	–	–	Belgique-Luxembourg
Portugal	36.4	42.9	39.3	44.9	51.1	Portugal
Bosnia and Herzegovina	e40.2	e63.5	e33.0	e30.9	e33.9	Bosnie-Herzégovine
Greece	36.8	33.0	32.0	34.4	e38.0	Grèce
Korea, Republic of	21.2	28.6	34.7	41.4	42.8	République de Corée
Cuba	e29.4	30.8	30.8	32.8	e28.2	Cuba
Lebanon	37.9	33.0	28.8	25.6	e23.3	Liban
Angola	e23.1	e22.9	e27.2	e30.1	e37.2	Angola
United Arab Emirates	22.4	23.5	32.6	28.4	e29.1	Emirates arabes unis
Luxembourg	–	30.6	29.7	32.1	e34.1	Luxembourg
Argentina	25.2	31.8	31.4	23.3	e10.3	Argentine

(Value as percentages of World total) **(Valeur en pourcentage du total mondial)**

Regions of the world	1993	1994	1995	1996	1997	1998	1999	2000	2001	2002	Régions du monde
World	100.0	100.0	100.0	100.0	100.0	100.0	100.0	100.0	100.0	100.0	Monde
Africa	1.5	2.6	2.2	1.1	1.1	1.1	1.1	1.3	1.1	1.3	Afrique
Americas	19.4	19.2	15.3	14.5	16.3	17.4	18.7	18.0	16.7	16.5	Amériques
- Northern America	14.0	13.6	11.3	11.1	11.8	12.2	12.3	12.1	11.1	11.6	- Amérique du Nord
- LAIA	2.9	3.5	1.8	2.0	2.5	2.8	3.9	3.3	3.3	2.8	- ALAI
- CACM	0.1	0.1	0.1	0.2	0.3	0.5	0.5	0.6	0.5	0.5	- MCC
- Caribbean	1.9	1.5	1.7	1.0	1.4	1.6	1.6	1.7	1.5	1.4	- Caraïbes
- Rest of America	0.4	0.4	0.3	0.2	0.3	0.3	0.3	0.4	0.3	0.3	- Autre d'Amérique
Asia excluding former USSR	12.9	14.8	16.3	19.4	19.2	18.4	20.7	22.5	21.7	22.7	Asie ancienne URSS exclus
- Middle East	1.2	1.6	1.7	1.5	1.8	2.1	2.2	2.3	1.9	1.8	- Moyen-Orient
Asia former USSR	0.2	0.3	0.4	0.7	0.7	0.8	0.4	0.6	0.5	0.5	Asie ancienne URSS
Europe excluding former USSR	51.3	55.4	57.4	55.5	54.7	56.7	56.5	55.0	57.5	56.6	Europe ancienne URSS exclus
- European Union	47.9	51.6	52.2	51.0	50.0	51.5	51.8	51.2	54.2	53.1	- Union Européenne
- Eastern Europe	0.8	0.7	1.1	0.9	1.3	1.7	1.1	1.0	0.8	0.9	- Europe de l'Est
- Rest of Europe	2.7	3.1	4.1	3.7	3.5	3.6	3.6	2.8	2.5	2.7	- Autre de l'Europe
Europe former USSR	13.8	6.8	7.4	7.7	7.1	4.5	1.6	1.4	1.4	1.4	Europe ancienne URSS
Oceania	0.8	0.8	0.9	1.0	0.9	1.0	1.1	1.2	1.1	1.0	Océanie

TRADE BY COMMODITY (Value in million US dollars)
Exports by principal countries or areas

COMMERCE PAR PRODUIT (Valeur en millions de dollars EU)
Exportations selon les principaux pays ou zones

Country or area	1998	1999	2000	2001	2002	Pays ou zone
World	6134.1	5565.9	5640.2	6275.9	6581.9	Monde
Africa	19.3	21.2	17.9	11.4	11.9	Afrique
Americas	1350.7	1278.6	1286.7	1378.4	1359.5	Amériques
- Northern America	695.4	620.7	694.3	789.5	781.4	- Amérique du Nord
- LAIA	638.4	638.4	572.5	567.6	559.1	- ALAI
- CACM	9.2	9.9	12.0	14.5	12.3	- MCC
- Caribbean	6.1	6.7	6.7	5.8	5.4	- Caraïbes
- Rest of America	1.7	2.9	1.2	0.9	1.2	- Autre d'Amérique
Asia excluding former USSR	630.8	754.4	963.1	1141.0	1246.3	Asie ancienne URSS exclus
- Middle East	23.8	25.0	28.1	30.7	27.6	- Moyen-Orient
Asia former USSR	1.0	0.5	0.7	0.4	0.5	Asie ancienne URSS
Europe excluding former USSR	3982.2	3397.3	3245.8	3610.4	3815.2	Europe ancienne URSS exclus
- European Union	3393.3	3052.7	2931.6	3317.2	3516.9	- Union Européenne
- Eastern Europe	487.3	251.8	243.9	221.1	218.3	- Europe de l'Est
- Rest of Europe	101.7	92.8	70.3	72.0	79.9	- Autre de l'Europe
Europe former USSR	91.1	47.1	54.7	55.1	63.3	Europe ancienne URSS
Oceania	59.0	66.9	71.3	79.1	85.3	Océanie
United States	563.4	471.8	520.5	609.5	592.0	Etats-Unis d'Amérique
France-Monaco	526.8	545.7	510.9	461.1	478.3	France-Monaco
China	313.5	374.6	502.2	625.9	704.9	Chine
Denmark	633.8	475.6	420.2	443.1	457.1	Danemark
Germany	380.3	373.0	362.7	597.8	541.5	Allemagne
Netherlands	347.1	367.4	348.5	411.0	427.2	Pays-Bas
Belgium	–	439.9	418.1	454.8	e510.3	Belgique
Brazil	350.9	403.6	325.7	335.5	e347.8	Brésil
Thailand	224.8	277.7	349.3	395.9	e418.1	Thaïlande
Ireland	220.9	235.0	249.2	299.3	383.8	Irlande
Italy-San Marino-Holy See	224.9	222.5	221.9	241.4	265.4	Italie-Saint-Marin-Saint-Siège
Argentina	229.1	175.5	169.9	142.3	e137.5	Argentine
Canada	132.0	148.9	173.8	180.0	189.4	Canada
Spain	161.4	146.7	176.4	165.0	174.3	Espagne
Poland	297.1	119.3	113.7	81.4	86.8	Pologne
Belgium-Luxembourg	623.9	–	–	–	–	Belgique-Luxembourg
United Kingdom	128.1	115.7	108.5	116.9	126.2	Royaume-Uni
Hungary	143.8	100.8	95.3	100.0	100.9	Hongrie
Austria	51.9	55.3	48.1	54.7	67.2	Autriche
Australia	36.2	37.5	38.1	40.8	44.8	Australie
Slovenia	40.1	36.4	34.1	36.1	41.0	Slovénie
Sweden	35.4	32.5	28.0	27.9	40.1	Suède
Mexico	17.8	24.8	42.8	46.4	29.9	Mexique
New Zealand	20.7	27.2	31.1	35.0	36.7	Nouvelle-Zélande
Croatia	38.2	28.6	19.2	16.1	19.8	Croatie
Israel	15.6	16.3	30.9	31.2	23.1	Israël
Czech Republic	35.9	22.6	21.4	21.5	15.3	République tchèque
Uruguay	26.9	21.6	17.9	18.0	18.9	Uruguay
Portugal	24.1	16.2	14.6	22.4	24.3	Portugal
China, Hong Kong SAR	19.7	20.4	14.8	16.4	20.5	Chine - RAS de Hong-Kong

(Value as percentages of World total) **(Valeur en pourcentage du total mondial)**

Regions of the world	1993	1994	1995	1996	1997	1998	1999	2000	2001	2002	Régions du monde
World	100.0	100.0	100.0	100.0	100.0	100.0	100.0	100.0	100.0	100.0	Monde
Africa	0.6	0.6	0.6	0.4	0.4	0.3	0.4	0.3	0.2	0.2	Afrique
Americas	22.2	20.9	21.2	20.0	20.3	22.0	23.0	22.8	22.0	20.7	Amériques
- Northern America	8.4	8.4	8.5	10.2	11.3	11.3	11.2	12.3	12.6	11.9	- Amérique du Nord
- LAIA	13.5	12.4	12.4	9.6	8.7	10.4	11.5	10.1	9.0	8.5	- ALAI
- CACM	0.2	0.1	0.1	0.1	0.1	0.1	0.2	0.2	0.2	0.2	- MCC
- Caribbean	0.1	0.1	0.1	0.1	0.1	0.1	0.1	0.1	0.1	0.1	- Caraïbes
- Rest of America	0.0	0.0	0.0	0.0	0.0	0.0	0.1	0.0	0.0	0.0	- Autre d'Amérique
Asia excluding former USSR	10.4	9.3	10.1	10.9	11.0	10.3	13.6	17.1	18.2	18.9	Asie ancienne URSS exclus
- Middle East	0.3	0.4	0.4	1.3	1.7	0.4	0.4	0.5	0.5	0.4	- Moyen-Orient
Asia former USSR	0.0	0.1	0.5	0.2	0.1	0.0	0.0	0.0	0.0	0.0	Asie ancienne URSS
Europe excluding former USSR	65.4	66.6	64.9	65.1	64.0	64.9	61.0	57.5	57.5	58.0	Europe ancienne URSS exclus
- European Union	59.2	59.5	57.8	56.9	53.8	55.3	54.8	52.0	52.9	53.4	- Union Européenne
- Eastern Europe	4.9	5.0	5.3	6.7	8.9	7.9	4.5	4.3	3.5	3.3	- Europe de l'Est
- Rest of Europe	1.2	2.1	1.8	1.5	1.4	1.7	1.7	1.2	1.1	1.2	- Autre de l'Europe
Europe former USSR	0.4	1.4	1.6	2.2	3.2	1.5	0.8	1.0	0.9	1.0	Europe ancienne URSS
Oceania	0.9	1.2	1.3	1.3	1.0	1.0	1.2	1.3	1.3	1.3	Océanie

022 Milk and cream

TRADE BY COMMODITY (Value in million US dollars)
Imports by principal countries or areas

COMMERCE PAR PRODUIT (Valeur en millions de dollars EU)
Importations selon les principaux pays ou zones

Country or area	1998	1999	2000	2001	2002	Pays ou zone
World	13124.3	13173.9	13530.0	13898.7	13581.2	Monde
Africa	1087.9	1151.2	1075.9	1279.7	1310.5	Afrique
Americas	1905.1	1676.6	1790.0	1839.7	1573.5	Amériques
- Northern America	228.1	262.6	319.5	286.4	287.1	- Amérique du Nord
- LAIA	1173.4	956.8	1025.3	1046.6	846.5	- ALAI
- CACM	146.5	152.6	159.3	170.4	140.1	- MCC
- Caribbean	306.4	254.4	255.4	300.0	269.3	- Caraïbes
- Rest of America	50.7	50.3	30.4	36.4	30.5	- Autre d'Amérique
Asia excluding former USSR	2947.7	3234.0	3818.7	3993.5	3889.5	Asie ancienne URSS exclus
- Middle East	791.6	1001.5	1145.2	999.4	1066.3	- Moyen-Orient
Asia former USSR	42.3	41.1	42.3	43.1	48.7	Asie ancienne URSS
Europe excluding former USSR	6824.3	6805.9	6538.1	6480.0	6544.5	Europe ancienne URSS exclus
- European Union	6564.9	6533.5	6280.8	6241.8	6293.7	- Union Européenne
- Eastern Europe	127.9	149.7	137.0	120.0	132.8	- Europe de l'Est
- Rest of Europe	131.5	122.7	120.3	118.2	118.1	- Autre de l'Europe
Europe former USSR	244.9	186.4	184.1	180.8	136.2	Europe ancienne URSS
Oceania	72.1	78.5	80.9	81.8	78.3	Océanie
Netherlands	1319.6	1384.5	1344.3	1075.7	1166.9	Pays-Bas
Italy-San Marino-Holy See	1389.1	1329.6	1217.4	1185.6	1067.5	Italie-Saint-Marin-Saint-Siège
France-Monaco	853.5	853.3	840.2	842.3	733.2	France-Monaco
Belgium	–	869.6	863.1	849.3	e931.4	Belgique
Germany	610.5	602.1	559.6	672.7	729.0	Allemagne
Spain	486.9	477.1	486.9	567.4	554.4	Espagne
Algeria	411.1	365.9	373.9	e452.3	e515.2	Algérie
Mexico	333.1	310.8	409.1	560.1	377.4	Mexique
Philippines	262.0	280.6	352.0	398.3	305.6	Philippines
United Kingdom	338.6	299.0	303.8	312.7	324.5	Royaume-Uni
Brazil	432.5	384.9	326.4	157.1	223.3	Brésil
Malaysia	226.3	234.7	268.8	335.9	e367.1	Malaisie
China, Hong Kong SAR	319.7	270.7	276.9	297.6	249.2	Chine - RAS de Hong-Kong
Saudi Arabia	212.1	240.2	317.3	309.1	e319.9	Arabie saoudite
Thailand	254.5	222.0	223.9	262.8	e273.9	Thaïlande
Greece	240.8	234.2	214.5	200.7	e221.9	Grèce
United States	167.3	197.2	226.9	181.6	188.6	Etats-Unis d'Amérique
Indonesia	90.4	108.8	225.7	296.4	210.2	Indonésie
Belgium-Luxembourg	921.3	–	–	–	–	Belgique-Luxembourg
China	82.6	150.2	206.0	210.1	256.1	Chine
Singapore	156.2	166.9	177.7	214.1	188.6	Singapour
Viet Nam	64.9	86.2	227.5	236.1	287.2	Viet Nam
Nigeria	109.1	232.4	130.4	e178.7	e169.5	Nigéria
Japan	159.2	153.9	148.7	184.0	146.4	Japon
Ireland	165.3	187.5	146.1	122.1	123.9	Irlande
United Arab Emirates	92.7	97.1	170.7	187.1	e191.9	Emirates arabes unis
Venezuela	177.7	123.5	142.2	152.8	e128.5	Venezuela
Portugal	89.9	104.6	125.9	195.8	173.3	Portugal
Russian Federation	196.8	157.0	102.9	99.3	48.1	Fédération de Russie
Sri Lanka	e113.0	102.0	e137.7	109.4	105.1	Sri Lanka

(Value as percentages of World total) **(Valeur en pourcentage du total mondial)**

Regions of the world	1993	1994	1995	1996	1997	1998	1999	2000	2001	2002	Régions du monde
World	100.0	100.0	100.0	100.0	100.0	100.0	100.0	100.0	100.0	100.0	Monde
Africa	11.2	8.8	7.7	7.1	7.8	8.3	8.7	8.0	9.2	9.6	Afrique
Americas	12.3	11.8	11.5	12.7	13.2	14.5	12.7	13.2	13.2	11.6	Amériques
- Northern America	0.7	0.9	0.6	1.1	1.3	1.7	2.0	2.4	2.1	2.1	- Amérique du Nord
- LAIA	8.0	7.6	7.7	8.3	8.2	8.9	7.3	7.6	7.5	6.2	- ALAI
- CACM	0.9	0.8	0.7	0.8	1.0	1.1	1.2	1.2	1.2	1.0	- MCC
- Caribbean	2.5	2.2	2.2	2.2	2.3	2.3	1.9	1.9	2.2	2.0	- Caraïbes
- Rest of America	0.2	0.3	0.3	0.3	0.4	0.4	0.4	0.2	0.3	0.2	- Autre d'Amérique
Asia excluding former USSR	24.4	23.1	23.2	25.8	27.2	22.5	24.5	28.2	28.7	28.6	Asie ancienne URSS exclus
- Middle East	5.1	4.3	4.5	5.9	6.9	6.0	7.6	8.5	7.2	7.9	- Moyen-Orient
Asia former USSR	0.2	0.3	0.3	0.5	0.3	0.3	0.3	0.3	0.3	0.4	Asie ancienne URSS
Europe excluding former USSR	49.9	54.0	55.1	51.5	48.9	52.0	51.7	48.3	46.6	48.2	Europe ancienne URSS exclus
- European Union	48.5	52.8	53.8	50.0	47.2	50.0	49.6	46.4	44.9	46.3	- Union Européenne
- Eastern Europe	0.7	0.5	0.4	0.6	0.6	1.0	1.1	1.0	0.9	1.0	- Europe de l'Est
- Rest of Europe	0.7	0.7	0.9	1.0	1.0	1.0	0.9	0.9	0.9	0.9	- Autre de l'Europe
Europe former USSR	1.4	1.3	1.6	1.9	2.1	1.9	1.4	1.4	1.3	1.0	Europe ancienne URSS
Oceania	0.6	0.7	0.6	0.6	0.6	0.5	0.6	0.6	0.6	0.6	Océanie

TRADE BY COMMODITY (Value in million US dollars)
Exports by principal countries or areas

COMMERCE PAR PRODUIT (Valeur en millions de dollars EU)
Exportations selon les principaux pays ou zones

Country or area	1998	1999	2000	2001	2002	Pays ou zone
World	12866.4	12472.4	12785.0	13652.5	12613.2	Monde
Africa	72.9	84.6	74.3	59.2	78.6	Afrique
Americas	970.2	993.8	983.1	1126.9	991.7	Amériques
- Northern America	502.1	466.4	510.4	613.3	480.3	- Amérique du Nord
- LAIA	426.9	488.3	428.7	471.7	454.7	- ALAI
- CACM	21.7	21.1	24.9	24.9	41.3	- MCC
- Caribbean	8.9	9.2	9.0	7.5	6.3	- Caraïbes
- Rest of America	10.5	8.8	10.0	9.5	9.0	- Autre d'Amérique
Asia excluding former USSR	492.1	535.3	621.8	774.6	831.2	Asie ancienne URSS exclus
- Middle East	126.8	181.9	182.9	213.4	245.3	- Moyen-Orient
Asia former USSR	0.8	0.7	0.7	1.3	1.3	Asie ancienne URSS
Europe excluding former USSR	9367.5	8990.5	8832.9	8872.9	8147.5	Europe ancienne URSS exclus
- European Union	9010.2	8664.5	8425.3	8338.9	7720.3	- Union Européenne
- Eastern Europe	287.6	245.9	329.4	467.3	336.4	- Europe de l'Est
- Rest of Europe	69.7	80.1	78.3	66.7	90.7	- Autre de l'Europe
Europe former USSR	226.1	153.6	308.9	299.6	282.8	Europe ancienne URSS
Oceania	1736.8	1713.8	1963.2	2518.1	2280.2	Océanie
Germany	2883.7	2646.6	2390.3	2511.9	1872.2	Allemagne
France-Monaco	1694.9	1616.0	1587.3	1550.1	1534.7	France-Monaco
Netherlands	1273.0	1244.7	1238.1	1216.4	1183.9	Pays-Bas
New Zealand	1018.9	968.9	1105.2	1621.0	1367.6	Nouvelle-Zélande
Belgium	–	1003.1	1016.0	1018.4	e1142.6	Belgique
Australia	717.3	744.3	856.8	896.0	911.3	Australie
United Kingdom	675.7	581.3	543.3	456.4	461.9	Royaume-Uni
United States	368.1	349.5	414.2	447.7	354.5	Etats-Unis d'Amérique
Ireland	335.8	383.7	443.5	306.8	245.2	Irlande
Denmark	345.6	319.7	311.6	290.8	301.9	Danemark
Spain	223.1	263.3	269.8	370.3	324.7	Espagne
Austria	214.4	264.0	263.3	281.6	314.9	Autriche
Argentina	241.7	300.3	247.0	226.0	e218.3	Argentine
Belgium-Luxembourg	1083.6	–	–	–	–	Belgique-Luxembourg
Poland	161.1	120.9	170.8	258.0	170.5	Pologne
Canada	134.0	116.9	95.6	165.2	125.3	Canada
China, Hong Kong SAR	163.4	125.9	122.2	124.9	94.7	Chine - RAS de Hong-Kong
Saudi Arabia	103.7	116.8	113.8	115.7	e104.3	Arabie saoudite
Portugal	110.7	105.2	113.3	83.5	103.8	Portugal
Czech Republic	86.9	80.2	100.7	127.5	92.5	République tchèque
Singapore	62.7	66.4	62.3	81.2	147.2	Singapour
Uruguay	108.7	88.0	72.8	66.0	77.6	Uruguay
Finland	69.3	63.2	68.2	69.3	68.5	Finlande
Lithuania	71.3	42.1	59.9	60.7	e73.5	Lituanie
Luxembourg	–	74.4	66.8	72.7	e74.3	Luxembourg
Thailand	33.4	32.3	35.8	89.6	e94.6	Thaïlande
Ukraine	38.8	40.4	75.2	53.5	59.0	Ukraine
Malaysia	49.0	45.5	51.3	55.0	e58.2	Malaisie
Indonesia	7.7	16.8	74.5	92.5	54.6	Indonésie
Russian Federation	32.3	17.2	78.0	62.2	48.8	Fédération de Russie

(Value as percentages of World total) **(Valeur en pourcentage du total mondial)**

Regions of the world	1993	1994	1995	1996	1997	1998	1999	2000	2001	2002	Régions du monde
World	100.0	100.0	100.0	100.0	100.0	100.0	100.0	100.0	100.0	100.0	Monde
Africa	0.4	0.4	0.4	0.5	0.5	0.6	0.7	0.6	0.4	0.6	Afrique
Americas	5.4	5.1	5.8	5.8	6.8	7.5	8.0	7.7	8.3	7.9	Amériques
- Northern America	3.8	3.2	3.5	2.9	3.9	3.9	3.7	4.0	4.5	3.8	- Amérique du Nord
- LAIA	1.3	1.6	2.1	2.6	2.6	3.3	3.9	3.4	3.5	3.6	- ALAI
- CACM	0.1	0.1	0.1	0.1	0.1	0.2	0.2	0.2	0.2	0.3	- MCC
- Caribbean	0.1	0.1	0.1	0.1	0.1	0.1	0.1	0.1	0.1	0.1	- Caraïbes
- Rest of America	0.1	0.1	0.0	0.1	0.1	0.1	0.1	0.1	0.1	0.1	- Autre d'Amérique
Asia excluding former USSR	3.4	4.2	3.6	4.2	4.5	3.8	4.3	4.9	5.7	6.6	Asie ancienne URSS exclus
- Middle East	0.8	0.8	0.7	1.0	1.1	1.0	1.5	1.4	1.6	1.9	- Moyen-Orient
Asia former USSR	0.0	0.0	0.0	0.0	0.0	0.0	0.0	0.0	0.0	0.0	Asie ancienne URSS
Europe excluding former USSR	78.1	75.4	77.2	71.6	70.6	72.8	72.1	69.1	65.0	64.6	Europe ancienne URSS exclus
- European Union	74.5	72.3	74.1	68.9	67.8	70.0	69.5	65.9	61.1	61.2	- Union Européenne
- Eastern Europe	3.2	2.7	2.6	2.2	2.4	2.2	2.0	2.6	3.4	2.7	- Europe de l'Est
- Rest of Europe	0.5	0.4	0.5	0.5	0.5	0.5	0.6	0.6	0.5	0.7	- Autre de l'Europe
Europe former USSR	1.3	1.8	2.4	3.3	2.7	1.8	1.2	2.4	2.2	2.2	Europe ancienne URSS
Oceania	11.3	13.0	10.6	14.6	14.8	13.5	13.7	15.4	18.4	18.1	Océanie

023 Butter

TRADE BY COMMODITY (Value in million US dollars)
Imports by principal countries or areas

COMMERCE PAR PRODUIT (Valeur en millions de dollars EU)
Importations selon les principaux pays ou zones

Country or area	1998	1999	2000	2001	2002	Pays ou zone
World	3391.8	3004.0	2785.2	2883.8	2789.4	Monde
Africa	155.9	160.9	167.6	162.8	164.6	Afrique
Americas	230.3	200.8	187.3	260.2	210.5	Amériques
- Northern America	92.6	66.2	59.7	145.6	93.1	- Amérique du Nord
- LAIA	103.5	105.5	96.7	85.7	90.5	- ALAI
- CACM	10.3	7.8	9.3	9.3	6.5	- MCC
- Caribbean	22.3	19.2	18.6	17.2	17.7	- Caraïbes
- Rest of America	1.6	2.2	3.0	2.4	2.7	- Autre d'Amérique
Asia excluding former USSR	373.7	346.5	354.1	323.3	353.8	Asie ancienne URSS exclus
- Middle East	200.2	153.1	168.6	156.0	170.8	- Moyen-Orient
Asia former USSR	57.1	39.1	58.3	50.5	55.3	Asie ancienne URSS
Europe excluding former USSR	2370.7	2153.0	1906.6	1928.5	1835.4	Europe ancienne URSS exclus
- European Union	2337.5	2110.5	1853.6	1888.8	1792.8	- Union Européenne
- Eastern Europe	8.9	17.6	25.2	15.3	23.5	- Europe de l'Est
- Rest of Europe	24.3	24.9	27.7	24.3	19.0	- Autre de l'Europe
Europe former USSR	180.2	77.3	81.4	131.9	144.7	Europe ancienne URSS
Oceania	23.9	26.4	30.0	26.6	25.1	Océanie
Germany	552.1	493.6	374.7	378.2	415.1	Allemagne
France-Monaco	482.0	395.1	398.5	362.4	341.9	France-Monaco
United Kingdom	350.7	367.3	354.9	354.1	198.2	Royaume-Uni
Belgium	–	317.1	302.6	282.4	e309.7	Belgique
Netherlands	243.9	235.6	167.0	219.8	217.9	Pays-Bas
Italy-San Marino-Holy See	178.0	147.9	114.6	131.3	134.2	Italie-Saint-Marin-Saint-Siège
Russian Federation	146.7	61.7	74.9	123.7	132.3	Fédération de Russie
Belgium-Luxembourg	366.9	–	–	–	–	Belgique-Luxembourg
United States	85.9	55.4	37.3	103.1	64.4	Etats-Unis d'Amérique
Egypt	60.2	76.0	e73.5	66.9	66.1	Egypte
Mexico	52.6	68.3	62.3	68.3	69.6	Mexique
Denmark	56.0	46.4	47.2	46.8	50.3	Danemark
Morocco	43.7	33.9	43.3	45.4	e47.9	Maroc
Saudi Arabia	46.7	35.9	41.5	39.9	e41.2	Arabie saoudite
Spain	35.8	34.7	32.0	43.5	39.8	Espagne
Iran (Islamic Republic of)	59.0	22.4	36.1	25.3	38.8	Iran (République islamique d')
Singapore	32.3	36.1	32.6	32.8	30.6	Singapour
China, Hong Kong SAR	23.7	23.4	24.5	25.9	24.0	Chine - RAS de Hong-Kong
Greece	32.4	26.9	17.4	18.1	e20.0	Grèce
United Arab Emirates	21.5	22.5	21.0	21.7	e22.3	Emirates arabes unis
Canada	6.1	10.3	21.9	41.7	27.5	Canada
Thailand	22.3	22.0	20.3	20.3	e21.1	Thaïlande
Austria	12.7	16.1	15.8	21.6	26.1	Autriche
Malaysia	14.8	19.0	19.0	17.7	e19.4	Malaisie
Algeria	18.1	22.3	13.4	e16.3	e18.5	Algérie
Brazil	27.0	23.3	20.7	4.4	11.4	Brésil
Uzbekistan	e32.9	e14.0	e8.4	e9.5	e14.2	Ouzbékistan
Lebanon	18.5	15.4	14.0	15.5	e14.1	Liban
Philippines	18.9	17.7	17.8	12.1	10.8	Philippines
Portugal	11.1	10.1	12.1	13.9	21.1	Portugal

(Value as percentages of World total) **(Valeur en pourcentage du total mondial)**

Regions of the world	1993	1994	1995	1996	1997	1998	1999	2000	2001	2002	Régions du monde
World	100.0	100.0	100.0	100.0	100.0	100.0	100.0	100.0	100.0	100.0	Monde
Africa	7.3	6.7	5.4	6.5	4.4	4.6	5.4	6.0	5.6	5.9	Afrique
Americas	4.2	4.4	3.5	4.0	4.1	6.8	6.7	6.7	9.0	7.5	Amériques
- Northern America	0.2	0.2	0.1	0.5	0.9	2.7	2.2	2.1	5.1	3.3	- Amérique du Nord
- LAIA	2.9	3.3	2.5	2.6	2.3	3.1	3.5	3.5	3.0	3.2	- ALAI
- CACM	0.1	0.2	0.1	0.2	0.2	0.3	0.3	0.3	0.3	0.2	- MCC
- Caribbean	1.0	0.7	0.6	0.6	0.6	0.7	0.6	0.7	0.6	0.6	- Caraïbes
- Rest of America	0.1	0.1	0.1	0.1	0.1	0.0	0.1	0.1	0.1	0.1	- Autre d'Amérique
Asia excluding former USSR	12.1	10.4	10.4	12.0	10.3	11.0	11.5	12.7	11.2	12.7	Asie ancienne URSS exclus
- Middle East	6.1	3.8	3.9	4.5	4.4	5.9	5.1	6.1	5.4	6.1	- Moyen-Orient
Asia former USSR	1.1	1.5	0.6	1.1	0.8	1.7	1.3	2.1	1.8	2.0	Asie ancienne URSS
Europe excluding former USSR	65.2	70.3	73.4	68.9	70.3	69.9	71.7	68.5	66.9	65.8	Europe ancienne URSS exclus
- European Union	63.6	69.4	72.5	68.0	69.2	68.9	70.3	66.6	65.5	64.3	- Union Européenne
- Eastern Europe	1.2	0.6	0.3	0.3	0.4	0.3	0.6	0.9	0.5	0.8	- Europe de l'Est
- Rest of Europe	0.4	0.3	0.6	0.6	0.7	0.7	0.8	1.0	0.8	0.7	- Autre de l'Europe
Europe former USSR	9.7	6.0	6.0	6.6	9.2	5.3	2.6	2.9	4.6	5.2	Europe ancienne URSS
Oceania	0.5	0.6	0.8	0.8	0.8	0.7	0.9	1.1	0.9	0.9	Océanie

TRADE BY COMMODITY (Value in million US dollars)
Exports by principal countries or areas

COMMERCE PAR PRODUIT (Valeur en millions de dollars EU)
Exportations selon les principaux pays ou zones

Country or area	1998	1999	2000	2001	2002	Pays ou zone
World	3507.1	3001.3	2712.7	2693.2	2684.0	Monde
Africa	10.0	9.5	4.6	4.2	4.2	Afrique
Americas	74.2	64.4	43.8	68.8	62.2	Amériques
- Northern America	40.2	25.5	19.5	38.0	31.3	- Amérique du Nord
- LAIA	33.2	37.5	21.9	27.4	27.6	- ALAI
- CACM	0.8	1.3	2.1	3.1	3.0	- MCC
- Caribbean	0.1	0.1	0.3	0.3	0.3	- Caraïbes
- Rest of America	0.0	0.0	0.0	0.0	0.0	- Autre d'Amérique
Asia excluding former USSR	35.9	39.2	72.2	68.6	57.8	Asie ancienne URSS exclus
- Middle East	12.4	12.7	9.3	6.5	5.8	- Moyen-Orient
Asia former USSR	2.4	0.3	0.3	0.4	0.4	Asie ancienne URSS
Europe excluding former USSR	2488.5	2106.8	1813.1	1883.0	1838.3	Europe ancienne URSS exclus
- European Union	2421.0	2048.9	1765.0	1816.6	1781.8	- Union Européenne
- Eastern Europe	58.2	45.9	39.3	58.3	47.5	- Europe de l'Est
- Rest of Europe	9.3	12.1	8.8	8.1	9.1	- Autre de l'Europe
Europe former USSR	149.3	81.8	102.9	83.3	91.5	Europe ancienne URSS
Oceania	746.9	699.3	675.8	584.9	629.6	Océanie
New Zealand	576.2	514.5	507.9	437.0	487.3	Nouvelle-Zélande
Netherlands	539.7	468.4	333.3	414.0	392.0	Pays-Bas
Ireland	481.8	384.6	321.2	294.6	300.6	Irlande
Belgium	–	328.6	313.9	300.5	e337.1	Belgique
France-Monaco	205.5	190.4	180.2	176.9	179.5	France-Monaco
Australia	170.5	184.7	167.8	147.8	142.1	Australie
United Kingdom	201.0	168.1	125.3	114.9	106.1	Royaume-Uni
Germany	141.1	150.7	134.4	143.4	115.9	Allemagne
Denmark	149.6	138.7	126.3	123.2	143.3	Danemark
Belgium-Luxembourg	412.4	–	–	–	–	Belgique-Luxembourg
Finland	68.8	65.2	69.9	71.2	70.9	Finlande
Spain	49.1	27.0	47.3	62.1	43.4	Espagne
Sweden	55.8	46.1	42.6	46.1	37.0	Suède
Italy-San Marino-Holy See	81.8	42.1	33.4	28.7	25.1	Italie-Saint-Marin-Saint-Siège
Belarus	40.1	26.2	23.5	36.3	40.1	Bélarus
Czech Republic	40.9	31.9	29.1	28.8	25.1	République tchèque
Canada	25.8	20.4	10.9	32.5	24.2	Canada
Ukraine	19.7	13.9	43.4	17.2	19.0	Ukraine
Lithuania	49.6	19.5	15.1	12.2	e14.8	Lituanie
Nepal	0.3	0.6	38.3	e39.9	e30.7	Népal
Portugal	23.7	20.7	20.6	24.7	13.3	Portugal
Uruguay	23.3	20.1	8.3	14.9	15.4	Uruguay
Estonia	25.1	14.6	9.7	8.9	11.9	Estonie
Poland	9.3	4.8	6.1	25.0	17.1	Pologne
Austria	10.2	11.3	10.4	9.3	10.5	Autriche
Argentina	8.5	16.0	12.7	7.1	e6.9	Argentine
Singapore	9.3	10.0	8.3	6.1	8.1	Singapour
United States	14.4	5.1	8.6	5.5	7.1	Etats-Unis d'Amérique
China, Hong Kong SAR	9.2	8.5	6.8	6.8	3.9	Chine - RAS de Hong-Kong
Luxembourg	–	6.7	6.2	6.8	e6.9	Luxembourg

(Value as percentages of World total) **(Valeur en pourcentage du total mondial)**

Regions of the world	1993	1994	1995	1996	1997	1998	1999	2000	2001	2002	Régions du monde
World	100.0	100.0	100.0	100.0	100.0	100.0	100.0	100.0	100.0	100.0	Monde
Africa	0.2	0.1	0.1	0.3	0.2	0.3	0.3	0.2	0.2	0.2	Afrique
Americas	5.4	4.1	2.5	2.9	2.5	2.1	2.1	1.6	2.6	2.3	Amériques
- Northern America	5.1	3.5	1.8	1.8	1.4	1.1	0.9	0.7	1.4	1.2	- Amérique du Nord
- LAIA	0.2	0.6	0.7	1.1	1.1	0.9	1.2	0.8	1.0	1.0	- ALAI
- CACM	0.0	0.0	0.0	0.0	0.0	0.0	0.0	0.1	0.1	0.1	- MCC
- Caribbean	0.0	0.0	0.0	0.0	0.0	0.0	0.0	0.0	0.0	0.0	- Caraïbes
- Rest of America	0.0	0.0	0.0	0.0	0.0	0.0	0.0	0.0	0.0	0.0	- Autre d'Amérique
Asia excluding former USSR	2.4	1.1	1.0	1.1	0.9	1.0	1.3	2.7	2.5	2.2	Asie ancienne URSS exclus
- Middle East	1.7	0.2	0.3	0.1	0.2	0.4	0.4	0.3	0.2	0.2	- Moyen-Orient
Asia former USSR	0.0	0.1	0.3	0.1	0.0	0.1	0.0	0.0	0.0	0.0	Asie ancienne URSS
Europe excluding former USSR	74.3	72.1	75.7	70.5	69.7	71.0	70.2	66.8	69.9	68.5	Europe ancienne URSS exclus
- European Union	71.9	70.7	73.5	68.2	68.2	69.0	68.3	65.1	67.5	66.4	- Union Européenne
- Eastern Europe	2.1	1.3	2.0	2.0	1.3	1.7	1.5	1.4	2.2	1.8	- Europe de l'Est
- Rest of Europe	0.3	0.2	0.3	0.2	0.2	0.3	0.4	0.3	0.3	0.3	- Autre de l'Europe
Europe former USSR	1.2	3.5	4.8	3.8	3.9	4.3	2.7	3.8	3.1	3.4	Europe ancienne URSS
Oceania	16.5	18.9	15.6	21.4	22.8	21.3	23.3	24.9	21.7	23.5	Océanie

024 Cheese and curd

TRADE BY COMMODITY (Value in million US dollars)
Imports by principal countries or areas

COMMERCE PAR PRODUIT (Valeur en millions de dollars EU)
Importations selon les principaux pays ou zones

Country or area	1998	1999	2000	2001	2002	Pays ou zone
World	10391.5	10501.6	9600.7	10467.1	10911.2	Monde
Africa	176.5	162.1	152.5	156.0	166.6	Afrique
Americas	1152.1	1239.1	1277.8	1363.8	1389.9	Amériques
- Northern America	795.1	881.2	864.9	917.3	977.4	- Amérique du Nord
- LAIA	238.3	225.9	265.7	292.7	260.1	- ALAI
- CACM	27.3	32.4	43.4	45.6	46.4	- MCC
- Caribbean	80.8	85.2	85.5	88.0	87.7	- Caraïbes
- Rest of America	10.7	14.3	18.2	20.3	18.4	- Autre d'Amérique
Asia excluding former USSR	1194.3	1213.1	1279.3	1292.7	1340.1	Asie ancienne URSS exclus
- Middle East	460.2	473.8	505.8	478.7	507.4	- Moyen-Orient
Asia former USSR	7.0	5.5	5.6	4.0	4.7	Asie ancienne URSS
Europe excluding former USSR	7628.4	7704.0	6682.2	7324.9	7610.3	Europe ancienne URSS exclus
- European Union	7245.4	7342.5	6330.8	6956.5	7204.0	- Union Européenne
- Eastern Europe	88.4	74.2	91.6	98.1	114.6	- Europe de l'Est
- Rest of Europe	294.6	287.3	259.8	270.3	291.7	- Autre de l'Europe
Europe former USSR	117.4	46.7	76.2	192.8	261.0	Europe ancienne URSS
Oceania	115.8	131.2	127.1	132.7	138.6	Océanie
Germany	2065.4	2154.9	1529.1	1795.3	1718.2	Allemagne
Italy-San Marino-Holy See	1148.7	1128.7	1029.7	1080.2	1063.9	Italie-Saint-Marin-Saint-Siège
United Kingdom	977.6	987.0	905.0	936.2	958.9	Royaume-Uni
United States	675.2	754.7	730.0	785.4	835.1	Etats-Unis d'Amérique
France-Monaco	682.7	680.7	654.1	653.7	678.2	France-Monaco
Belgium	–	735.3	677.4	730.5	e801.1	Belgique
Japan	558.9	542.7	548.2	555.4	575.0	Japon
Spain	394.0	407.1	372.2	418.6	456.5	Espagne
Netherlands	315.1	286.4	273.1	349.7	348.3	Pays-Bas
Greece	273.1	237.4	211.9	220.5	e243.8	Grèce
Saudi Arabia	193.4	185.4	220.8	197.3	e204.1	Arabie saoudite
Austria	173.5	200.8	178.1	188.3	214.8	Autriche
Switzerland-Liechtenstein	188.0	179.8	159.4	165.3	170.5	Suisse-Liechtenstein
Belgium-Luxembourg	774.8	–	–	–	–	Belgique-Luxembourg
Sweden	150.3	151.9	136.9	145.9	167.1	Suède
Mexico	82.7	103.9	142.6	191.0	179.3	Mexique
Denmark	98.7	109.9	112.3	121.5	213.5	Danemark
Canada	117.1	123.7	132.0	128.4	137.0	Canada
Russian Federation	97.8	36.5	63.8	165.6	235.0	Fédération de Russie
Australia	91.0	107.7	103.7	110.5	114.1	Australie
Lebanon	88.5	87.1	79.8	75.4	e68.8	Liban
Finland	77.7	78.5	73.4	78.1	81.6	Finlande
Ireland	61.6	77.2	74.2	78.9	85.7	Irlande
Korea, Republic of	35.9	55.2	70.6	88.1	85.1	République de Corée
Portugal	52.4	63.1	63.2	66.9	74.6	Portugal
Luxembourg	–	43.6	40.1	92.5	e98.1	Luxembourg
United Arab Emirates	40.4	42.3	54.4	63.0	e64.7	Emirates arabes unis
Kuwait	49.6	47.4	e44.5	e49.0	e68.3	Koweït
Algeria	42.2	38.1	36.8	e44.5	e50.6	Algérie
Brazil	73.7	46.9	40.2	23.8	22.3	Brésil

(Value as percentages of World total) **(Valeur en pourcentage du total mondial)**

Regions of the world	1993	1994	1995	1996	1997	1998	1999	2000	2001	2002	Régions du monde
World	100.0	100.0	100.0	100.0	100.0	100.0	100.0	100.0	100.0	100.0	Monde
Africa	1.4	1.4	1.5	1.2	1.4	1.7	1.5	1.6	1.5	1.5	Afrique
Americas	9.9	10.3	10.0	9.7	10.2	11.1	11.8	13.3	13.0	12.7	Amériques
- Northern America	7.0	6.8	6.5	6.8	6.9	7.7	8.4	9.0	8.8	9.0	- Amérique du Nord
- LAIA	1.7	2.5	2.5	2.0	2.2	2.3	2.2	2.8	2.8	2.4	- ALAI
- CACM	0.1	0.1	0.1	0.2	0.3	0.3	0.3	0.5	0.4	0.4	- MCC
- Caribbean	1.0	0.7	0.8	0.6	0.7	0.8	0.8	0.9	0.8	0.8	- Caraïbes
- Rest of America	0.2	0.2	0.1	0.1	0.1	0.1	0.1	0.2	0.2	0.2	- Autre d'Amérique
Asia excluding former USSR	9.6	8.4	9.1	9.7	11.3	11.5	11.6	13.3	12.4	12.3	Asie ancienne URSS exclus
- Middle East	4.3	3.0	3.3	3.2	4.0	4.4	4.5	5.3	4.6	4.7	- Moyen-Orient
Asia former USSR	0.1	0.1	0.1	0.1	0.0	0.1	0.1	0.1	0.0	0.0	Asie ancienne URSS
Europe excluding former USSR	76.9	77.2	76.7	76.5	74.1	73.4	73.4	69.6	70.0	69.7	Europe ancienne URSS exclus
- European Union	73.1	73.7	72.8	72.6	70.3	69.7	69.9	65.9	66.5	66.0	- Union Européenne
- Eastern Europe	1.0	0.7	0.8	0.8	0.8	0.9	0.7	1.0	0.9	1.0	- Europe de l'Est
- Rest of Europe	2.8	2.8	3.1	3.1	3.0	2.8	2.7	2.7	2.6	2.7	- Autre de l'Europe
Europe former USSR	1.1	1.5	1.5	1.5	1.7	1.1	0.4	0.8	1.8	2.4	Europe ancienne URSS
Oceania	1.1	1.1	1.1	1.2	1.2	1.1	1.2	1.3	1.3	1.3	Océanie

TRADE BY COMMODITY (Value in million US dollars)
Exports by principal countries or areas

COMMERCE PAR PRODUIT (Valeur en millions de dollars EU)
Exportations selon les principaux pays ou zones

Country or area	1998	1999	2000	2001	2002	Pays ou zone
World	10945.2	10431.0	9924.1	10967.6	11054.0	Monde
Africa	25.4	33.9	26.0	30.8	47.9	Afrique
Americas	376.5	375.5	369.8	387.5	367.3	Amériques
- Northern America	231.3	236.5	217.8	239.4	230.6	- Amérique du Nord
- LAIA	120.2	111.7	119.5	120.2	102.2	- ALAI
- CACM	17.6	17.2	21.3	15.8	24.4	- MCC
- Caribbean	4.6	7.8	8.7	10.6	7.7	- Caraïbes
- Rest of America	2.7	2.3	2.6	1.5	2.3	- Autre d'Amérique
Asia excluding former USSR	53.3	57.2	66.3	68.0	85.1	Asie ancienne URSS exclus
- Middle East	39.2	45.6	52.2	54.1	70.1	- Moyen-Orient
Asia former USSR	1.7	1.2	1.0	2.6	2.6	Asie ancienne URSS
Europe excluding former USSR	9386.1	8890.4	8297.6	9144.7	9275.7	Europe ancienne URSS exclus
- European Union	8751.7	8293.4	7750.9	8543.1	8657.4	- Union Européenne
- Eastern Europe	187.9	163.3	173.5	220.7	222.7	- Europe de l'Est
- Rest of Europe	446.5	433.7	373.2	380.8	395.6	- Autre de l'Europe
Europe former USSR	153.6	99.8	141.2	220.9	243.6	Europe ancienne URSS
Oceania	948.5	972.9	1022.0	1113.1	1031.7	Océanie
France-Monaco	2015.0	1952.2	1822.8	1773.6	1866.9	France-Monaco
Netherlands	1892.6	1662.2	1509.7	1700.3	1703.5	Pays-Bas
Germany	1668.1	1505.1	1395.1	1672.8	1491.3	Allemagne
Denmark	949.0	916.1	858.1	872.6	916.2	Danemark
Italy-San Marino-Holy See	791.5	821.0	801.4	882.4	927.4	Italie-Saint-Marin-Saint-Siège
New Zealand	520.1	509.8	496.3	606.2	545.4	Nouvelle-Zélande
Australia	428.3	463.0	525.6	506.8	486.2	Australie
Belgium	–	418.8	385.0	424.7	e476.5	Belgique
Switzerland-Liechtenstein	345.5	340.1	287.1	296.7	305.5	Suisse-Liechtenstein
Ireland	309.4	290.9	265.4	345.8	336.0	Irlande
United Kingdom	207.0	217.1	192.9	210.7	227.2	Royaume-Uni
Austria	133.2	153.0	157.4	206.2	232.4	Autriche
United States	130.6	147.8	148.3	168.9	167.3	Etats-Unis d'Amérique
Spain	94.9	111.5	101.0	126.4	147.1	Espagne
Finland	101.2	79.1	100.1	113.6	120.1	Finlande
Greece	96.4	89.7	82.9	93.3	e93.4	Grèce
Belgium-Luxembourg	419.2	–	–	–	–	Belgique-Luxembourg
Canada	100.7	88.7	69.5	70.5	63.3	Canada
Lithuania	70.4	50.0	72.4	86.4	e104.7	Lituanie
Norway	78.8	74.8	69.7	65.1	71.5	Norvège
Poland	69.0	52.4	54.7	86.2	88.1	Pologne
Sweden	60.8	57.2	60.2	50.1	48.3	Suède
Argentina	60.9	57.0	59.4	49.4	e47.7	Argentine
Uruguay	48.0	46.2	44.3	48.0	33.0	Uruguay
Czech Republic	46.6	41.1	37.0	40.6	39.0	République tchèque
Hungary	33.2	30.3	40.2	45.9	41.3	Hongrie
Belarus	49.0	25.4	31.0	42.1	43.2	Bélarus
Ukraine	6.7	7.6	18.6	56.7	62.5	Ukraine
Luxembourg	–	9.2	8.6	60.4	e61.7	Luxembourg
Slovakia	23.7	21.5	21.2	26.6	29.0	Slovaquie

(Value as percentages of World total) **(Valeur en pourcentage du total mondial)**

Regions of the world	1993	1994	1995	1996	1997	1998	1999	2000	2001	2002	Régions du monde
World	100.0	100.0	100.0	100.0	100.0	100.0	100.0	100.0	100.0	100.0	Monde
Africa	0.1	0.1	0.1	0.2	0.3	0.2	0.3	0.3	0.3	0.4	Afrique
Americas	1.8	2.1	2.4	2.6	3.4	3.4	3.6	3.7	3.5	3.3	Amériques
- Northern America	1.1	1.2	1.4	1.6	2.1	2.1	2.3	2.2	2.2	2.1	- Amérique du Nord
- LAIA	0.6	0.8	0.9	0.9	1.1	1.1	1.1	1.2	1.1	0.9	- ALAI
- CACM	0.0	0.0	0.1	0.1	0.1	0.2	0.2	0.2	0.1	0.2	- MCC
- Caribbean	0.1	0.0	0.0	0.0	0.0	0.0	0.1	0.1	0.1	0.1	- Caraïbes
- Rest of America	0.1	0.0	0.0	0.0	0.0	0.0	0.0	0.0	0.0	0.0	- Autre d'Amérique
Asia excluding former USSR	0.4	0.4	0.4	0.4	0.5	0.5	0.5	0.7	0.6	0.8	Asie ancienne URSS exclus
- Middle East	0.3	0.3	0.3	0.3	0.4	0.4	0.4	0.5	0.5	0.6	- Moyen-Orient
Asia former USSR	0.0	0.0	0.0	0.0	0.0	0.0	0.0	0.0	0.0	0.0	Asie ancienne URSS
Europe excluding former USSR	91.8	90.5	89.6	88.4	85.8	85.8	85.2	83.6	83.4	83.9	Europe ancienne URSS exclus
- European Union	85.1	84.4	83.6	82.9	79.9	80.0	79.5	78.1	77.9	78.3	- Union Européenne
- Eastern Europe	1.5	1.1	1.0	1.3	1.7	1.7	1.6	1.7	2.0	2.0	- Europe de l'Est
- Rest of Europe	5.1	4.9	4.9	4.2	4.2	4.1	4.2	3.8	3.5	3.6	- Autre de l'Europe
Europe former USSR	0.3	0.5	1.0	0.9	1.1	1.4	1.0	1.4	2.0	2.2	Europe ancienne URSS
Oceania	5.6	6.5	6.5	7.5	8.9	8.7	9.3	10.3	10.1	9.3	Océanie

025 Eggs, birds', and egg yolks, fresh, dried or preserved

TRADE BY COMMODITY (Value in million US dollars)
Imports by principal countries or areas

COMMERCE PAR PRODUIT (Valeur en millions de dollars EU)
Importations selon les principaux pays ou zones

Country or area	1998	1999	2000	2001	2002	Pays ou zone
World	1438.2	1270.1	1279.5	1351.3	1427.1	Monde
Africa	37.8	33.9	39.1	52.6	63.8	Afrique
Americas	209.2	149.7	161.1	189.4	186.5	Amériques
- Northern America	72.5	65.6	56.9	66.2	68.7	- Amérique du Nord
- LAIA	76.7	38.8	56.0	71.6	69.2	- ALAI
- CACM	26.0	18.5	19.5	21.0	16.7	- MCC
- Caribbean	28.1	22.5	23.6	24.5	24.4	- Caraïbes
- Rest of America	5.9	4.4	5.1	6.1	7.5	- Autre d'Amérique
Asia excluding former USSR	280.8	289.0	289.3	272.3	287.4	Asie ancienne URSS exclus
- Middle East	77.4	76.8	92.0	83.8	87.2	- Moyen-Orient
Asia former USSR	19.3	17.2	13.8	8.7	8.9	Asie ancienne URSS
Europe excluding former USSR	864.7	764.7	762.5	797.6	848.4	Europe ancienne URSS exclus
- European Union	760.7	684.6	686.9	711.8	759.4	- Union Européenne
- Eastern Europe	40.5	21.4	22.6	29.9	26.5	- Europe de l'Est
- Rest of Europe	63.5	58.7	53.0	55.9	62.5	- Autre de l'Europe
Europe former USSR	22.5	9.8	7.9	21.2	26.0	Europe ancienne URSS
Oceania	3.9	5.7	5.8	9.5	6.1	Océanie
Germany	357.5	304.0	253.9	312.6	291.6	Allemagne
China, Hong Kong SAR	90.0	78.2	74.5	75.0	72.2	Chine - RAS de Hong-Kong
France-Monaco	74.4	65.3	77.7	76.5	88.9	France-Monaco
Netherlands	72.5	77.4	63.8	55.8	82.9	Pays-Bas
United Kingdom	34.6	37.2	53.1	59.7	77.0	Royaume-Uni
Japan	43.5	43.6	46.3	48.3	56.7	Japon
Canada	58.5	44.3	38.6	45.2	41.4	Canada
Singapore	44.0	52.3	49.1	39.8	42.5	Singapour
Switzerland-Liechtenstein	49.1	46.9	40.8	42.1	45.9	Suisse-Liechtenstein
Italy-San Marino-Holy See	35.3	35.7	80.9	29.7	31.9	Italie-Saint-Marin-Saint-Siège
Belgium	–	55.4	51.0	48.4	e53.0	Belgique
Austria	31.9	29.7	26.5	32.8	32.0	Autriche
Mexico	38.1	19.8	23.2	22.3	27.7	Mexique
Denmark	28.6	23.6	22.1	23.8	24.5	Danemark
United Arab Emirates	19.0	19.9	27.0	26.0	e26.7	Emirates arabes unis
Spain	24.6	16.3	20.4	27.5	28.3	Espagne
United States	13.1	20.3	17.3	19.6	25.4	Etats-Unis d'Amérique
Belgium-Luxembourg	63.0	–	–	–	–	Belgique-Luxembourg
Jamaica	11.2	10.0	12.9	e13.6	e14.3	Jamaïque
Oman	11.6	10.6	11.8	11.9	11.9	Oman
Kuwait	12.5	10.5	e9.9	e10.9	e9.1	Koweït
Venezuela	7.5	3.4	9.7	16.7	e14.0	Venezuela
Portugal	9.1	8.1	9.4	11.7	11.8	Portugal
Sweden	10.1	8.1	10.1	10.1	11.5	Suède
Greece	12.3	11.4	5.9	8.2	e9.1	Grèce
Iraq	e12.5	e11.6	e13.9	e6.8	e1.9	Iraq
Angola	e8.7	e5.7	e10.0	e9.2	e12.7	Angola
Algeria	10.4	11.6	5.5	e6.6	e7.5	Algérie
Saudi Arabia	5.3	7.0	8.1	9.5	e9.9	Arabie saoudite
Hungary	7.8	2.9	4.3	10.4	11.4	Hongrie

(Value as percentages of World total) **(Valeur en pourcentage du total mondial)**

Regions of the world	1993	1994	1995	1996	1997	1998	1999	2000	2001	2002	Régions du monde
World	100.0	100.0	100.0	100.0	100.0	100.0	100.0	100.0	100.0	100.0	Monde
Africa	1.6	2.1	1.5	1.5	2.3	2.6	2.7	3.1	3.9	4.5	Afrique
Americas	11.2	11.3	11.0	8.9	11.0	14.5	11.8	12.6	14.0	13.1	Amériques
- Northern America	5.9	5.7	4.2	4.2	4.5	5.0	5.2	4.4	4.9	4.8	- Amérique du Nord
- LAIA	3.0	3.4	4.3	2.6	3.7	5.3	3.1	4.4	5.3	4.9	- ALAI
- CACM	0.6	0.6	0.6	0.7	1.1	1.8	1.5	1.5	1.6	1.2	- MCC
- Caribbean	1.4	1.4	1.6	1.2	1.4	2.0	1.8	1.8	1.8	1.7	- Caraïbes
- Rest of America	0.2	0.2	0.2	0.2	0.3	0.4	0.3	0.4	0.5	0.5	- Autre d'Amérique
Asia excluding former USSR	25.7	21.6	22.5	20.8	20.4	19.5	22.8	22.6	20.2	20.1	Asie ancienne URSS exclus
- Middle East	8.0	5.3	5.9	4.0	4.6	5.4	6.1	7.2	6.2	6.1	- Moyen-Orient
Asia former USSR	0.1	0.3	0.8	1.1	1.3	1.3	1.4	1.1	0.6	0.6	Asie ancienne URSS
Europe excluding former USSR	61.0	63.6	63.0	66.6	63.0	60.1	60.2	59.6	59.0	59.5	Europe ancienne URSS exclus
- European Union	53.7	56.4	55.7	59.7	56.5	52.9	53.9	53.7	52.7	53.2	- Union Européenne
- Eastern Europe	3.0	2.7	1.8	1.9	2.1	2.8	1.7	1.8	2.2	1.9	- Europe de l'Est
- Rest of Europe	4.3	4.6	5.5	5.0	4.4	4.4	4.6	4.1	4.1	4.4	- Autre de l'Europe
Europe former USSR	0.2	0.7	0.9	0.6	1.5	1.6	0.8	0.6	1.6	1.8	Europe ancienne URSS
Oceania	0.2	0.5	0.4	0.4	0.5	0.3	0.5	0.5	0.7	0.4	Océanie

TRADE BY COMMODITY (Value in million US dollars)
Exports by principal countries or areas

COMMERCE PAR PRODUIT (Valeur en millions de dollars EU)
Exportations selon les principaux pays ou zones

Country or area	1998	1999	2000	2001	2002	Pays ou zone
World	1426.3	1283.5	1304.1	1310.8	1396.7	Monde
Africa	9.7	8.9	9.0	9.4	30.3	Afrique
Americas	265.6	201.4	215.5	231.8	231.4	Amériques
- Northern America	213.9	172.5	178.1	180.6	187.6	- Amérique du Nord
- LAIA	36.2	18.8	25.2	40.5	34.6	- ALAI
- CACM	12.0	9.0	11.1	7.6	5.5	- MCC
- Caribbean	0.0	0.0	0.0	0.2	0.2	- Caraïbes
- Rest of America	3.4	1.0	1.1	3.0	3.5	- Autre d'Amérique
Asia excluding former USSR	186.0	161.7	173.8	200.7	160.5	Asie ancienne URSS exclus
- Middle East	72.3	50.2	49.3	59.0	28.4	- Moyen-Orient
Asia former USSR	0.9	0.3	0.4	0.6	0.5	Asie ancienne URSS
Europe excluding former USSR	904.8	852.1	857.3	825.7	939.4	Europe ancienne URSS exclus
- European Union	863.1	822.2	830.8	795.2	903.5	- Union Européenne
- Eastern Europe	35.0	24.1	20.3	23.6	31.0	- Europe de l'Est
- Rest of Europe	6.7	5.7	6.2	7.0	4.9	- Autre de l'Europe
Europe former USSR	54.1	53.2	44.0	38.7	30.2	Europe ancienne URSS
Oceania	5.2	5.9	3.9	3.9	4.4	Océanie
Netherlands	376.1	379.4	393.0	345.1	381.5	Pays-Bas
United States	187.5	143.7	148.8	151.6	149.1	Etats-Unis d'Amérique
France-Monaco	122.1	130.2	125.3	113.5	137.0	France-Monaco
Germany	99.6	91.6	88.4	102.1	105.9	Allemagne
Belgium	–	91.1	96.0	95.5	e107.2	Belgique
Spain	24.2	35.7	41.9	47.4	61.1	Espagne
Malaysia	35.4	49.6	48.2	36.3	e38.5	Malaisie
United Kingdom	49.4	33.7	30.4	33.1	46.0	Royaume-Uni
China	36.6	27.3	33.2	36.2	40.5	Chine
Belarus	39.4	42.8	32.3	28.7	21.9	Bélarus
Canada	26.4	28.8	29.4	29.0	38.6	Canada
Belgium-Luxembourg	120.7	–	–	–	–	Belgique-Luxembourg
India	16.3	13.6	21.8	30.6	36.3	Inde
Denmark	22.2	22.4	24.4	16.5	13.8	Danemark
Turkey	34.0	16.3	3.7	18.4	3.8	Turquie
Italy-San Marino-Holy See	17.9	16.0	7.3	15.7	18.2	Italie-Saint-Marin-Saint-Siège
Iran (Islamic Republic of)	1.6	14.4	23.1	17.4	9.4	Iran (République islamique d')
Brazil	17.3	7.4	11.0	14.8	e15.4	Brésil
Hungary	18.4	11.9	9.9	11.8	13.3	Hongrie
Saudi Arabia	16.8	12.8	8.4	7.1	e6.4	Arabie saoudite
Thailand	9.6	7.1	8.9	6.1	e6.4	Thaïlande
Czech Republic	7.8	6.9	6.1	5.8	8.2	République tchèque
El Salvador	8.3	6.9	9.7	6.1	3.8	El Salvador
Jordan	13.5	1.6	5.8	8.5	4.6	Jordanie
Portugal	5.3	5.4	5.7	7.0	9.8	Portugal
Sweden	6.1	5.1	6.7	4.1	8.2	Suède
Finland	9.0	5.3	5.4	5.8	4.0	Finlande
Austria	8.1	4.0	3.8	6.1	5.5	Autriche
Colombia	3.7	2.6	6.6	10.3	4.1	Colombie
Zimbabwe	e3.3	3.1	3.4	0.4	16.7	Zimbabwe

(Value as percentages of World total) **(Valeur en pourcentage du total mondial)**

Regions of the world	1993	1994	1995	1996	1997	1998	1999	2000	2001	2002	Régions du monde
World	100.0	100.0	100.0	100.0	100.0	100.0	100.0	100.0	100.0	100.0	Monde
Africa	1.1	1.0	0.7	0.6	0.5	0.7	0.7	0.7	0.7	2.2	Afrique
Americas	13.9	16.1	16.6	15.1	17.2	18.6	15.7	16.5	17.7	16.6	Amériques
- Northern America	12.6	14.4	13.4	13.6	14.6	15.0	13.4	13.7	13.8	13.4	- Amérique du Nord
- LAIA	1.0	1.2	2.6	0.9	1.8	2.5	1.5	1.9	3.1	2.5	- ALAI
- CACM	0.2	0.4	0.5	0.4	0.5	0.8	0.7	0.9	0.6	0.4	- MCC
- Caribbean	0.0	0.0	0.0	0.0	0.2	0.0	0.0	0.0	0.0	0.0	- Caraïbes
- Rest of America	0.0	0.1	0.1	0.1	0.1	0.2	0.1	0.1	0.2	0.3	- Autre d'Amérique
Asia excluding former USSR	11.2	10.7	9.6	12.6	14.4	13.0	12.6	13.3	15.3	11.5	Asie ancienne URSS exclus
- Middle East	2.8	2.1	2.1	2.9	4.3	5.1	3.9	3.8	4.5	2.0	- Moyen-Orient
Asia former USSR	0.0	0.0	0.3	0.1	0.1	0.1	0.0	0.0	0.0	0.0	Asie ancienne URSS
Europe excluding former USSR	71.0	71.0	68.2	68.6	63.9	63.4	66.4	65.7	63.0	67.3	Europe ancienne URSS exclus
- European Union	67.9	68.3	65.3	65.7	60.9	60.5	64.1	63.7	60.7	64.7	- Union Européenne
- Eastern Europe	2.6	1.7	2.1	2.4	2.4	2.5	1.9	1.6	1.8	2.2	- Europe de l'Est
- Rest of Europe	0.6	1.0	0.8	0.5	0.6	0.5	0.4	0.5	0.5	0.4	- Autre de l'Europe
Europe former USSR	2.6	0.9	4.2	2.5	3.4	3.8	4.1	3.4	3.0	2.2	Europe ancienne URSS
Oceania	0.2	0.2	0.4	0.5	0.4	0.4	0.5	0.3	0.3	0.3	Océanie

034 Fish, fresh, chilled or frozen

TRADE BY COMMODITY (Value in million US dollars)
Imports by principal countries or areas

COMMERCE PAR PRODUIT (Valeur en millions de dollars EU)
Importations selon les principaux pays ou zones

Country or area	1998	1999	2000	2001	2002	Pays ou zone
World	23464.1	25106.4	25164.4	26187.3	27015.0	Monde
Africa	806.1	723.5	723.6	821.0	892.9	Afrique
Americas	3763.2	4020.3	4227.3	4162.2	4374.5	Amériques
- Northern America	3354.2	3717.0	3912.9	3787.0	4023.6	- Amérique du Nord
- LAIA	319.8	229.6	252.5	262.1	273.1	- ALAI
- CACM	29.2	17.8	15.6	16.3	25.5	- MCC
- Caribbean	59.0	55.2	45.5	95.9	51.2	- Caraïbes
- Rest of America	1.0	0.7	0.9	0.9	1.1	- Autre d'Amérique
Asia excluding former USSR	8194.8	10111.5	10380.1	10295.3	10517.9	Asie ancienne URSS exclus
- Middle East	174.0	183.0	200.2	194.4	209.3	- Moyen-Orient
Asia former USSR	9.4	10.8	15.7	12.6	13.4	Asie ancienne URSS
Europe excluding former USSR	10071.7	9765.3	9320.5	10252.9	10429.9	Europe ancienne URSS exclus
- European Union	9036.8	8888.1	8428.8	9208.0	9445.7	- Union Européenne
- Eastern Europe	400.0	291.4	331.0	405.0	379.4	- Europe de l'Est
- Rest of Europe	634.9	585.8	560.7	639.9	604.9	- Autre de l'Europe
Europe former USSR	460.6	292.7	321.0	445.7	569.9	Europe ancienne URSS
Oceania	158.4	182.2	176.1	197.5	216.5	Océanie
Japan	5446.6	6833.0	6838.8	6277.4	6209.3	Japon
United States	2948.6	3268.2	3460.6	3335.2	3563.5	Etats-Unis d'Amérique
Spain	1595.1	1483.6	1426.7	1752.6	1825.8	Espagne
France-Monaco	1484.4	1488.7	1339.2	1330.2	1372.6	France-Monaco
Germany	1528.9	1348.9	1213.5	1420.7	1389.1	Allemagne
Italy-San Marino-Holy See	1012.5	1008.6	934.2	985.3	1000.0	Italie-Saint-Marin-Saint-Siège
United Kingdom	926.9	956.6	951.5	957.9	1004.5	Royaume-Uni
Korea, Republic of	392.2	841.8	945.5	1118.4	1214.6	République de Corée
China	485.0	624.4	773.0	917.0	1065.6	Chine
Denmark	692.7	648.5	650.1	726.3	704.7	Danemark
Thailand	619.7	558.1	457.6	672.2	e700.4	Thaïlande
Netherlands	448.8	505.0	505.7	523.5	488.9	Pays-Bas
Canada	403.7	446.6	441.4	436.8	457.4	Canada
China, Hong Kong SAR	425.4	365.6	411.5	423.1	414.8	Chine - RAS de Hong-Kong
Portugal	335.0	405.5	359.1	409.0	430.8	Portugal
Sweden	335.2	378.5	396.0	383.8	439.9	Suède
Norway	351.2	326.0	322.6	372.3	330.0	Norvège
Belgium	–	357.6	391.9	429.9	e471.5	Belgique
Poland	278.2	203.2	247.0	301.9	267.4	Pologne
Nigeria	213.1	171.9	241.6	e331.2	e314.1	Nigéria
Singapore	169.4	186.2	222.9	203.1	180.7	Singapour
Malaysia	145.1	169.5	187.2	204.0	e223.0	Malaisie
Switzerland-Liechtenstein	175.4	174.1	168.1	171.9	166.4	Suisse-Liechtenstein
Russian Federation	160.7	108.4	120.4	187.1	275.1	Fédération de Russie
Côte d'Ivoire	188.7	169.7	128.2	e136.1	e175.7	Côte d'Ivoire
Brazil	223.7	140.4	157.2	135.0	118.3	Brésil
Australia	133.0	150.4	147.2	140.0	155.6	Australie
Greece	121.6	128.4	107.5	109.7	e121.3	Grèce
Egypt	90.4	97.3	e99.8	90.8	64.4	Egypte
Israel	98.1	81.4	82.5	91.3	83.9	Israël

(Value as percentages of World total) **(Valeur en pourcentage du total mondial)**

Regions of the world	1993	1994	1995	1996	1997	1998	1999	2000	2001	2002	Régions du monde
World	100.0	100.0	100.0	100.0	100.0	100.0	100.0	100.0	100.0	100.0	Monde
Africa	2.2	1.7	2.7	3.1	2.9	3.4	2.9	2.9	3.1	3.3	Afrique
Americas	14.2	13.7	13.9	13.7	14.8	16.0	16.0	16.8	15.9	16.2	Amériques
- Northern America	13.0	12.4	12.2	12.0	13.2	14.3	14.8	15.5	14.5	14.9	- Amérique du Nord
- LAIA	0.7	0.9	1.3	1.3	1.2	1.4	0.9	1.0	1.0	1.0	- ALAI
- CACM	0.2	0.1	0.1	0.1	0.2	0.1	0.1	0.1	0.1	0.1	- MCC
- Caribbean	0.3	0.3	0.3	0.3	0.3	0.3	0.2	0.2	0.4	0.2	- Caraïbes
- Rest of America	0.0	0.0	0.0	0.0	0.0	0.0	0.0	0.0	0.0	0.0	- Autre d'Amérique
Asia excluding former USSR	45.3	45.5	43.8	42.2	42.1	34.9	40.3	41.2	39.3	38.9	Asie ancienne URSS exclus
- Middle East	0.8	0.8	0.9	0.7	0.9	0.7	0.7	0.8	0.7	0.8	- Moyen-Orient
Asia former USSR	0.0	0.0	0.0	0.0	0.0	0.0	0.0	0.1	0.0	0.0	Asie ancienne URSS
Europe excluding former USSR	37.1	37.2	37.3	37.9	37.1	42.9	38.9	37.0	39.2	38.6	Europe ancienne URSS exclus
- European Union	34.4	34.2	34.1	34.5	33.8	38.5	35.4	33.5	35.2	35.0	- Union Européenne
- Eastern Europe	0.8	1.0	1.0	1.3	1.3	1.7	1.2	1.3	1.5	1.4	- Europe de l'Est
- Rest of Europe	1.9	1.9	2.2	2.1	2.1	2.7	2.3	2.2	2.4	2.2	- Autre de l'Europe
Europe former USSR	0.5	1.2	1.5	2.0	2.2	2.0	1.2	1.3	1.7	2.1	Europe ancienne URSS
Oceania	0.7	0.7	0.8	1.0	0.7	0.7	0.7	0.7	0.8	0.8	Océanie

TRADE BY COMMODITY (Value in million US dollars)
Exports by principal countries or areas

COMMERCE PAR PRODUIT (Valeur en millions de dollars EU)
Exportations selon les principaux pays ou zones

Country or area	1998	1999	2000	2001	2002	Pays ou zone
World	19458.6	20794.6	21330.5	22442.2	22946.3	Monde
Africa	720.9	667.5	1026.7	1165.3	928.0	Afrique
Americas	4359.1	4752.8	5021.3	5528.7	5525.3	Amériques
- Northern America	2279.6	2696.7	2760.7	3089.5	3087.9	- Amérique du Nord
- LAIA	1848.7	1843.6	1969.9	2094.3	2054.7	- ALAI
- CACM	121.9	83.9	109.6	117.1	131.3	- MCC
- Caribbean	34.2	24.9	20.3	20.4	17.4	- Caraïbes
- Rest of America	74.7	103.7	160.7	207.4	234.1	- Autre d'Amérique
Asia excluding former USSR	4525.9	4910.6	5373.8	5471.4	5759.8	Asie ancienne URSS exclus
- Middle East	98.4	117.3	129.1	103.8	157.2	- Moyen-Orient
Asia former USSR	7.3	5.8	5.4	10.4	11.4	Asie ancienne URSS
Europe excluding former USSR	8739.3	9269.9	8742.5	8985.6	9462.8	Europe ancienne URSS exclus
- European Union	5125.2	5367.3	5012.9	5364.0	5647.4	- Union Européenne
- Eastern Europe	138.5	139.6	131.0	135.1	132.5	- Europe de l'Est
- Rest of Europe	3475.6	3762.9	3598.7	3486.5	3682.8	- Autre de l'Europe
Europe former USSR	400.8	314.1	357.3	451.0	443.0	Europe ancienne URSS
Oceania	705.4	874.0	803.5	829.9	816.0	Océanie
Norway	2485.2	2694.7	2609.3	2449.2	2629.6	Norvège
United States	1354.9	1706.4	1800.5	2102.7	2041.0	Etats-Unis d'Amérique
China	993.2	1142.7	1309.6	1622.0	1736.6	Chine
Chile	920.7	1060.4	1190.1	1259.3	e1232.1	Chili
Denmark	1005.4	1017.4	909.9	978.6	1022.3	Danemark
Canada	871.7	919.6	899.3	937.3	990.6	Canada
Spain	692.0	833.2	831.5	913.4	949.0	Espagne
Netherlands	686.7	805.4	714.0	777.5	833.7	Pays-Bas
Iceland	695.2	728.8	641.7	636.7	718.9	Islande
Korea, Republic of	598.7	724.7	671.8	547.6	544.5	République de Corée
France-Monaco	608.2	542.8	512.0	535.8	590.8	France-Monaco
United Kingdom	547.5	551.4	469.2	497.9	519.7	Royaume-Uni
Germany	484.3	453.5	427.6	412.8	396.6	Allemagne
New Zealand	417.4	462.0	397.6	386.4	422.2	Nouvelle-Zélande
Thailand	372.3	410.2	379.5	383.3	e404.8	Thaïlande
Argentina	474.4	411.2	343.4	335.5	e324.1	Argentine
Indonesia	394.8	420.6	341.2	336.3	370.3	Indonésie
Japan	343.1	344.9	385.7	385.0	379.6	Japon
Faeroe Islands	267.8	315.0	e311.9	e342.7	e262.2	Iles Féroé
Russian Federation	262.6	206.3	263.6	341.8	314.1	Fédération de Russie
Sweden	222.5	267.8	289.4	272.4	316.1	Suède
India	158.3	215.9	316.0	270.7	295.7	Inde
Singapore	244.7	236.5	280.4	240.6	178.3	Singapour
Australia	154.6	236.0	246.0	254.0	275.7	Australie
Ireland	197.1	173.5	178.0	238.3	238.1	Irlande
Greece	200.1	242.2	194.9	177.4	e177.6	Grèce
Belgium	–	185.3	190.3	281.1	e315.4	Belgique
Viet Nam	71.8	116.0	228.7	237.8	264.3	Viet Nam
Italy-San Marino-Holy See	169.2	170.4	169.4	150.9	150.4	Italie-Saint-Marin-Saint-Siège
Mauritania	e180.9	e137.5	e129.3	e131.4	e112.6	Mauritanie

(Value as percentages of World total) **(Valeur en pourcentage du total mondial)**

Regions of the world	1993	1994	1995	1996	1997	1998	1999	2000	2001	2002	Régions du monde
World	100.0	100.0	100.0	100.0	100.0	100.0	100.0	100.0	100.0	100.0	Monde
Africa	2.8	2.9	2.8	2.9	3.0	3.7	3.2	4.8	5.2	4.0	Afrique
Americas	23.5	25.0	25.0	24.0	23.2	22.4	22.9	23.5	24.6	24.1	Amériques
- Northern America	16.2	16.2	15.2	14.0	13.1	11.7	13.0	12.9	13.8	13.5	- Amérique du Nord
- LAIA	6.7	7.6	8.7	8.6	9.3	9.5	8.9	9.2	9.3	9.0	- ALAI
- CACM	0.3	0.3	0.3	0.4	0.5	0.6	0.4	0.5	0.5	0.6	- MCC
- Caribbean	0.1	0.7	0.7	0.7	0.1	0.2	0.1	0.1	0.1	0.1	- Caraïbes
- Rest of America	0.2	0.2	0.2	0.2	0.2	0.4	0.5	0.8	0.9	1.0	- Autre d'Amérique
Asia excluding former USSR	26.3	26.3	26.6	24.5	25.6	23.3	23.6	25.2	24.4	25.1	Asie ancienne URSS exclus
- Middle East	0.6	0.6	0.6	0.6	0.7	0.5	0.6	0.6	0.5	0.7	- Moyen-Orient
Asia former USSR	0.0	0.1	0.1	0.1	0.1	0.0	0.0	0.0	0.0	0.0	Asie ancienne URSS
Europe excluding former USSR	36.6	41.6	40.6	42.6	42.7	44.9	44.6	41.0	40.0	41.2	Europe ancienne URSS exclus
- European Union	22.3	25.0	24.4	25.0	25.2	26.3	25.8	23.5	23.9	24.6	- Union Européenne
- Eastern Europe	0.3	0.4	0.5	0.7	0.7	0.7	0.7	0.6	0.6	0.6	- Europe de l'Est
- Rest of Europe	14.0	16.1	15.7	16.9	16.8	17.9	18.1	16.9	15.5	16.0	- Autre de l'Europe
Europe former USSR	7.4	1.0	1.2	1.4	1.8	2.1	1.5	1.7	2.0	1.9	Europe ancienne URSS
Oceania	3.3	3.3	3.6	4.5	3.6	3.6	4.2	3.8	3.7	3.6	Océanie

035 Fish, dried, salted or in brine; smoked fish

TRADE BY COMMODITY (Value in million US dollars)
Imports by principal countries or areas

COMMERCE PAR PRODUIT (Valeur en millions de dollars EU)
Importations selon les principaux pays ou zones

Country or area	1998	1999	2000	2001	2002	Pays ou zone
World	2717.9	2755.6	2813.9	2824.2	2628.8	Monde
Africa	25.6	27.2	32.2	29.4	28.8	Afrique
Americas	497.1	418.4	419.7	413.7	400.0	Amériques
- Northern America	192.6	195.0	203.6	200.7	208.0	- Amérique du Nord
- LAIA	216.2	153.4	154.9	147.0	119.9	- ALAI
- CACM	2.5	1.2	1.0	1.2	1.1	- MCC
- Caribbean	83.5	66.6	58.0	62.9	68.6	- Caraïbes
- Rest of America	2.3	2.3	2.3	1.9	2.4	- Autre d'Amérique
Asia excluding former USSR	660.4	712.3	943.8	791.2	808.4	Asie ancienne URSS exclus
- Middle East	9.8	8.5	9.0	10.2	11.3	- Moyen-Orient
Asia former USSR	1.2	0.9	1.2	1.0	1.0	Asie ancienne URSS
Europe excluding former USSR	1500.6	1561.3	1388.9	1558.5	1352.9	Europe ancienne URSS exclus
- European Union	1439.2	1501.9	1339.7	1509.0	1300.2	- Union Européenne
- Eastern Europe	9.6	11.0	12.3	9.7	12.7	- Europe de l'Est
- Rest of Europe	51.7	48.4	37.0	39.9	40.0	- Autre de l'Europe
Europe former USSR	15.8	11.6	12.0	16.6	20.2	Europe ancienne URSS
Oceania	17.1	23.8	16.1	13.7	17.4	Océanie
China, Hong Kong SAR	298.4	315.2	485.2	378.2	370.6	Chine - RAS de Hong-Kong
Portugal	366.8	394.8	305.5	314.1	287.0	Portugal
Italy-San Marino-Holy See	255.7	273.3	235.0	262.9	231.2	Italie-Saint-Marin-Saint-Siège
Japan	226.9	256.7	266.9	249.9	256.7	Japon
Spain	195.9	207.3	177.6	190.6	205.9	Espagne
Germany	211.5	189.4	166.6	192.1	132.9	Allemagne
United States	140.0	148.3	151.2	153.6	162.4	Etats-Unis d'Amérique
Brazil	201.1	134.8	135.4	122.2	97.3	Brésil
Sweden	79.6	97.0	100.9	141.7	139.5	Suède
France-Monaco	124.8	111.2	105.7	114.7	101.6	France-Monaco
Netherlands	46.9	57.3	95.6	129.8	23.7	Pays-Bas
Canada	52.5	46.6	52.1	46.4	44.7	Canada
Denmark	32.6	39.8	40.5	46.6	56.3	Danemark
Sri Lanka	e39.1	35.3	e47.7	49.7	41.3	Sri Lanka
Belgium	–	52.3	46.1	46.3	e50.8	Belgique
China	32.0	32.2	41.5	27.8	34.9	Chine
Singapore	27.9	32.0	38.7	29.3	35.8	Singapour
Greece	37.3	40.0	29.6	25.4	e28.1	Grèce
Dominican Republic	e41.0	e23.9	e22.1	e24.8	e30.8	République dominicaine
Jamaica	23.1	25.6	19.3	e20.3	e21.3	Jamaïque
Switzerland-Liechtenstein	20.7	21.5	20.1	21.5	23.1	Suisse-Liechtenstein
Australia	15.7	22.1	14.3	12.0	15.2	Australie
Norway	24.8	20.3	11.2	12.9	8.9	Norvège
Korea, Republic of	6.2	7.2	24.1	16.2	22.8	République de Corée
Austria	15.0	12.6	12.9	17.3	14.3	Autriche
United Kingdom	13.1	12.9	12.2	15.2	14.4	Royaume-Uni
Mexico	7.4	10.2	12.0	17.9	17.5	Mexique
Malaysia	7.1	11.7	13.3	14.1	e15.4	Malaisie
Belgium-Luxembourg	52.8	–	–	–	–	Belgique-Luxembourg
Nigeria	2.0	3.1	5.7	e7.8	e7.4	Nigéria

(Value as percentages of World total) **(Valeur en pourcentage du total mondial)**

Regions of the world	1993	1994	1995	1996	1997	1998	1999	2000	2001	2002	Régions du monde
World	100.0	100.0	100.0	100.0	100.0	100.0	100.0	100.0	100.0	100.0	Monde
Africa	1.1	2.0	1.2	1.1	1.2	0.9	1.0	1.1	1.0	1.1	Afrique
Americas	14.0	14.1	16.0	15.8	17.4	18.3	15.2	14.9	14.6	15.2	Amériques
- Northern America	6.4	6.3	6.4	6.0	6.6	7.1	7.1	7.2	7.1	7.9	- Amérique du Nord
- LAIA	4.9	5.8	7.3	7.4	7.8	8.0	5.6	5.5	5.2	4.6	- ALAI
- CACM	0.0	0.0	0.0	0.0	0.1	0.1	0.0	0.0	0.0	0.0	- MCC
- Caribbean	2.6	2.0	2.3	2.3	2.8	3.1	2.4	2.1	2.2	2.6	- Caraïbes
- Rest of America	0.1	0.1	0.1	0.1	0.1	0.1	0.1	0.1	0.1	0.1	- Autre d'Amérique
Asia excluding former USSR	34.7	32.5	32.1	31.8	30.5	24.3	25.9	33.5	28.0	30.8	Asie ancienne URSS exclus
- Middle East	0.3	0.3	0.3	0.3	0.3	0.4	0.3	0.3	0.4	0.4	- Moyen-Orient
Asia former USSR	0.0	0.1	0.1	0.1	0.1	0.0	0.0	0.0	0.0	0.0	Asie ancienne URSS
Europe excluding former USSR	48.9	49.4	48.5	49.5	49.4	55.2	56.7	49.4	55.2	51.5	Europe ancienne URSS exclus
- European Union	47.4	48.0	46.7	47.5	47.3	53.0	54.5	47.6	53.4	49.5	- Union Européenne
- Eastern Europe	0.2	0.2	0.3	0.3	0.3	0.4	0.4	0.4	0.3	0.5	- Europe de l'Est
- Rest of Europe	1.3	1.2	1.5	1.7	1.8	1.9	1.8	1.3	1.4	1.5	- Autre de l'Europe
Europe former USSR	0.7	1.3	1.5	1.1	0.8	0.6	0.4	0.4	0.6	0.8	Europe ancienne URSS
Oceania	0.6	0.6	0.6	0.6	0.7	0.6	0.9	0.6	0.5	0.7	Océanie

TRADE BY COMMODITY (Value in million US dollars)
Exports by principal countries or areas

COMMERCE PAR PRODUIT (Valeur en millions de dollars EU)
Exportations selon les principaux pays ou zones

Country or area	1998	1999	2000	2001	2002	Pays ou zone
World	2786.5	2661.4	2733.9	2781.5	2717.1	Monde
Africa	21.2	19.5	37.3	47.6	45.2	Afrique
Americas	432.3	374.8	406.7	405.5	348.6	Amériques
- Northern America	265.2	283.8	290.6	285.3	238.7	- Amérique du Nord
- LAIA	68.0	64.7	77.5	84.5	82.7	- ALAI
- CACM	63.1	8.8	10.9	10.6	9.5	- MCC
- Caribbean	0.2	0.3	0.4	0.4	0.2	- Caraïbes
- Rest of America	35.8	17.2	27.2	24.7	17.5	- Autre d'Amérique
Asia excluding former USSR	443.6	442.4	614.0	530.6	614.3	Asie ancienne URSS exclus
- Middle East	16.2	16.8	19.1	9.7	20.1	- Moyen-Orient
Asia former USSR	1.8	1.8	1.2	0.8	1.0	Asie ancienne URSS
Europe excluding former USSR	1850.0	1783.4	1620.9	1743.6	1663.5	Europe ancienne URSS exclus
- European Union	719.3	695.1	676.9	726.4	687.9	- Union Européenne
- Eastern Europe	21.1	25.7	26.7	27.6	25.4	- Europe de l'Est
- Rest of Europe	1109.6	1062.6	917.3	989.6	950.2	- Autre de l'Europe
Europe former USSR	16.0	14.7	18.3	26.0	17.1	Europe ancienne URSS
Oceania	21.6	24.9	35.5	27.4	27.4	Océanie
Norway	770.9	689.1	568.4	615.4	598.7	Norvège
Iceland	277.5	300.9	275.8	294.5	286.8	Islande
Denmark	258.6	248.4	226.1	262.3	253.1	Danemark
Canada	197.3	196.9	205.4	182.5	169.7	Canada
China, Hong Kong SAR	114.3	129.6	194.1	139.3	153.6	Chine - RAS de Hong-Kong
China	84.2	84.1	110.2	101.1	131.6	Chine
Sweden	57.8	74.9	77.5	107.6	103.3	Suède
Germany	119.7	66.9	77.3	64.7	57.4	Allemagne
United States	60.8	78.8	78.2	95.2	59.7	Etats-Unis d'Amérique
Faeroe Islands	60.2	71.3	e70.6	e77.5	e60.1	Iles Féroé
Viet Nam	47.0	27.2	75.4	78.5	87.2	Viet Nam
Netherlands	58.7	72.1	68.5	62.7	37.9	Pays-Bas
United Kingdom	70.3	57.0	62.9	55.2	52.1	Royaume-Uni
Indonesia	59.8	52.9	54.1	55.1	73.2	Indonésie
Spain	57.8	55.9	47.5	47.9	59.4	Espagne
France-Monaco	41.2	43.5	52.8	53.3	48.3	France-Monaco
Chile	31.4	35.2	42.7	46.4	e45.4	Chili
Thailand	21.1	21.1	33.3	35.6	e37.6	Thaïlande
Singapore	23.5	29.8	30.7	20.8	27.1	Singapour
Portugal	12.1	21.6	22.1	32.5	36.4	Portugal
Poland	19.8	25.2	26.5	27.0	25.0	Pologne
Costa Rica	61.2	7.4	8.6	7.2	5.8	Costa Rica
Panama	6.6	14.4	25.0	22.1	15.0	Panama
Japan	14.1	12.7	23.4	16.1	11.9	Japon
Argentina	21.5	13.5	12.2	15.1	e14.6	Argentine
Korea, Republic of	9.5	13.8	14.1	16.5	17.5	République de Corée
Ireland	14.9	19.0	12.4	11.5	11.8	Irlande
Maldives	12.2	11.0	13.1	12.9	10.7	Maldives
Pakistan	12.7	12.6	11.6	11.0	10.5	Pakistan
Papua New Guinea	8.4	e11.8	14.8	e11.1	e9.5	Papouasie-Nouvelle-Guinée

(Value as percentages of World total) **(Valeur en pourcentage du total mondial)**

Regions of the world	1993	1994	1995	1996	1997	1998	1999	2000	2001	2002	Régions du monde
World	100.0	100.0	100.0	100.0	100.0	100.0	100.0	100.0	100.0	100.0	Monde
Africa	1.5	1.2	1.0	0.9	1.1	0.8	0.7	1.4	1.7	1.7	Afrique
Americas	21.3	15.7	16.4	19.5	18.5	15.5	14.1	14.9	14.6	12.8	Amériques
- Northern America	17.7	12.4	12.9	14.6	10.4	9.5	10.7	10.6	10.3	8.8	- Amérique du Nord
- LAIA	2.5	2.5	2.4	2.8	3.6	2.4	2.4	2.8	3.0	3.0	- ALAI
- CACM	0.9	0.6	1.0	1.9	2.7	2.3	0.3	0.4	0.4	0.3	- MCC
- Caribbean	0.0	0.0	0.0	0.0	0.1	0.0	0.0	0.0	0.0	0.0	- Caraïbes
- Rest of America	0.2	0.2	0.2	0.2	1.8	1.3	0.6	1.0	0.9	0.6	- Autre d'Amérique
Asia excluding former USSR	17.7	20.2	19.9	16.2	17.4	15.9	16.6	22.5	19.1	22.6	Asie ancienne URSS exclus
- Middle East	1.4	1.6	1.2	0.2	0.3	0.6	0.6	0.7	0.3	0.7	- Moyen-Orient
Asia former USSR	0.0	0.0	0.1	0.1	0.1	0.1	0.1	0.0	0.0	0.0	Asie ancienne URSS
Europe excluding former USSR	57.9	61.7	60.6	61.0	60.7	66.4	67.0	59.3	62.7	61.2	Europe ancienne URSS exclus
- European Union	24.3	26.0	23.9	24.1	24.8	25.8	26.1	24.8	26.1	25.3	- Union Européenne
- Eastern Europe	0.3	0.5	0.7	0.7	0.6	0.8	1.0	1.0	1.0	0.9	- Europe de l'Est
- Rest of Europe	33.3	35.2	35.9	36.3	35.3	39.8	39.9	33.6	35.6	35.0	- Autre de l'Europe
Europe former USSR	1.0	0.5	0.7	0.8	0.7	0.6	0.6	0.7	0.9	0.6	Europe ancienne URSS
Oceania	0.6	0.6	1.3	1.6	1.5	0.8	0.9	1.3	1.0	1.0	Océanie

036 Crustaceans and molluscs, fresh, chilled, frozen, salted, etc

TRADE BY COMMODITY (Value in million US dollars)
Imports by principal countries or areas

COMMERCE PAR PRODUIT (Valeur en millions de dollars EU)
Importations selon les principaux pays ou zones

Country or area	1998	1999	2000	2001	2002	Pays ou zone
World	16789.8	17556.1	19229.2	18217.8	18226.5	Monde
Africa	27.6	33.3	41.4	43.8	35.3	Afrique
Americas	4544.6	4907.6	5684.9	5530.1	5315.7	Amériques
- Northern America	4451.4	4823.6	5583.5	5422.1	5219.5	- Amérique du Nord
- LAIA	60.3	48.8	54.5	63.2	54.8	- ALAI
- CACM	16.0	17.0	20.9	17.0	14.1	- MCC
- Caribbean	14.0	14.4	18.9	22.8	21.8	- Caraïbes
- Rest of America	2.9	3.9	7.2	5.0	5.4	- Autre d'Amérique
Asia excluding former USSR	6622.4	7136.3	8014.4	6883.2	6975.3	Asie ancienne URSS exclus
- Middle East	54.1	51.4	63.8	77.6	79.9	- Moyen-Orient
Asia former USSR	0.5	0.4	0.4	0.5	0.5	Asie ancienne URSS
Europe excluding former USSR	5411.8	5289.1	5293.6	5566.9	5682.9	Europe ancienne URSS exclus
- European Union	5220.9	5089.1	5093.6	5381.2	5499.3	- Union Européenne
- Eastern Europe	26.2	24.0	17.3	16.9	17.7	- Europe de l'Est
- Rest of Europe	164.7	176.0	182.7	168.8	165.9	- Autre de l'Europe
Europe former USSR	18.2	12.9	14.7	25.5	42.2	Europe ancienne URSS
Oceania	164.7	176.5	179.8	167.8	174.5	Océanie
Japan	4997.7	5283.9	5698.3	4628.3	4506.2	Japon
United States	4003.3	4266.6	4980.7	4839.8	4688.8	Etats-Unis d'Amérique
Spain	1537.7	1447.4	1571.1	1719.1	1729.1	Espagne
France-Monaco	1014.2	984.9	925.7	933.9	952.3	France-Monaco
Italy-San Marino-Holy See	937.1	935.7	887.0	971.9	1031.1	Italie-Saint-Marin-Saint-Siège
China, Hong Kong SAR	742.1	761.6	894.1	817.3	814.7	Chine - RAS de Hong-Kong
Canada	438.5	545.8	601.1	578.9	527.5	Canada
United Kingdom	310.9	303.5	341.9	330.7	340.9	Royaume-Uni
China	145.6	217.6	391.0	367.8	448.1	Chine
Belgium	–	358.5	346.6	361.7	e396.7	Belgique
Korea, Republic of	100.3	195.2	260.3	330.4	426.5	République de Corée
Denmark	256.8	263.8	237.9	219.8	241.7	Danemark
Thailand	183.3	206.6	230.1	258.6	e269.4	Thaïlande
Germany	238.3	207.8	206.1	239.1	186.5	Allemagne
Netherlands	203.0	173.4	206.9	214.1	217.2	Pays-Bas
Portugal	186.9	190.9	175.0	190.0	198.3	Portugal
Singapore	147.9	145.4	173.6	134.7	146.2	Singapour
Australia	143.9	153.7	154.5	145.3	148.7	Australie
Greece	92.1	83.9	77.9	86.5	e95.6	Grèce
Malaysia	52.1	50.2	64.9	78.5	e85.8	Malaisie
Belgium-Luxembourg	328.0	–	–	–	–	Belgique-Luxembourg
Sweden	65.0	72.3	58.8	56.7	56.8	Suède
Switzerland-Liechtenstein	59.8	51.3	56.1	60.4	46.9	Suisse-Liechtenstein
Norway	54.0	53.1	52.8	38.4	40.7	Norvège
Iceland	22.4	43.7	45.7	39.9	48.3	Islande
United Arab Emirates	26.1	27.3	36.8	45.1	e46.3	Emirates arabes unis
Mexico	27.6	21.0	24.2	33.2	34.5	Mexique
Ireland	26.0	29.1	24.4	22.5	19.1	Irlande
Austria	20.8	20.6	16.2	17.5	15.9	Autriche
Indonesia	8.9	15.2	17.2	17.0	14.6	Indonésie

(Value as percentages of World total) **(Valeur en pourcentage du total mondial)**

Regions of the world	1993	1994	1995	1996	1997	1998	1999	2000	2001	2002	Régions du monde
World	100.0	100.0	100.0	100.0	100.0	100.0	100.0	100.0	100.0	100.0	Monde
Africa	0.2	0.2	0.2	0.2	0.2	0.2	0.2	0.2	0.2	0.2	Afrique
Americas	23.4	23.6	21.5	21.9	25.7	27.1	28.0	29.6	30.4	29.2	Amériques
- Northern America	22.9	23.2	21.1	21.5	25.3	26.5	27.5	29.0	29.8	28.6	- Amérique du Nord
- LAIA	0.3	0.3	0.2	0.3	0.3	0.4	0.3	0.3	0.3	0.3	- ALAI
- CACM	0.0	0.0	0.0	0.0	0.0	0.1	0.1	0.1	0.1	0.1	- MCC
- Caribbean	0.2	0.1	0.2	0.1	0.1	0.1	0.1	0.1	0.1	0.1	- Caraïbes
- Rest of America	0.0	0.0	0.0	0.0	0.0	0.0	0.0	0.0	0.0	0.0	- Autre d'Amérique
Asia excluding former USSR	50.6	50.8	50.8	49.5	45.2	39.4	40.6	41.7	37.8	38.3	Asie ancienne URSS exclus
- Middle East	0.3	0.4	0.3	0.3	0.4	0.3	0.3	0.3	0.4	0.4	- Moyen-Orient
Asia former USSR	0.0	0.0	0.0	0.0	0.0	0.0	0.0	0.0	0.0	0.0	Asie ancienne URSS
Europe excluding former USSR	24.9	24.4	26.3	27.3	27.8	32.2	30.1	27.5	30.6	31.2	Europe ancienne URSS exclus
- European Union	23.9	23.6	25.4	26.3	26.9	31.1	29.0	26.5	29.5	30.2	- Union Européenne
- Eastern Europe	0.1	0.1	0.1	0.1	0.1	0.2	0.1	0.1	0.1	0.1	- Europe de l'Est
- Rest of Europe	0.8	0.7	0.8	0.8	0.7	1.0	1.0	1.0	0.9	0.9	- Autre de l'Europe
Europe former USSR	0.2	0.1	0.2	0.1	0.1	0.1	0.1	0.1	0.1	0.2	Europe ancienne URSS
Oceania	0.7	0.9	0.9	1.0	1.0	1.0	1.0	0.9	0.9	1.0	Océanie

Crustacés et mollusques, y compris les coquillages 036

TRADE BY COMMODITY (Value in million US dollars)
Exports by principal countries or areas

COMMERCE PAR PRODUIT (Valeur en millions de dollars EU)
Exportations selon les principaux pays ou zones

Country or area	1998	1999	2000	2001	2002	Pays ou zone
World	15243.0	15540.6	17453.8	16630.9	17219.4	Monde
Africa	913.8	843.3	1151.8	988.7	997.6	Afrique
Americas	4581.3	4744.6	4830.5	4672.1	4657.4	Amériques
- Northern America	1581.3	2029.4	2200.2	2076.5	2361.3	- Amérique du Nord
- LAIA	2233.6	1971.9	1896.5	1950.0	1809.3	- ALAI
- CACM	387.2	356.7	360.0	292.2	127.6	- MCC
- Caribbean	176.3	209.4	188.0	163.4	197.7	- Caraïbes
- Rest of America	202.9	177.2	185.9	190.1	161.6	- Autre d'Amérique
Asia excluding former USSR	6682.1	6703.9	8214.8	7735.5	8121.1	Asie ancienne URSS exclus
- Middle East	53.6	60.7	68.2	57.6	78.0	- Moyen-Orient
Asia former USSR	3.2	2.8	1.0	0.6	2.2	Asie ancienne URSS
Europe excluding former USSR	2246.9	2410.8	2348.8	2427.1	2578.8	Europe ancienne URSS exclus
- European Union	2109.5	2265.6	2211.1	2309.2	2452.9	- Union Européenne
- Eastern Europe	15.5	19.0	10.0	10.0	9.7	- Europe de l'Est
- Rest of Europe	121.9	126.3	127.8	108.0	116.2	- Autre de l'Europe
Europe former USSR	89.2	48.8	63.4	42.3	65.2	Europe ancienne URSS
Oceania	726.6	786.4	843.3	764.6	797.1	Océanie
Thailand	1754.8	1648.3	1865.0	1603.9	e1693.9	Thaïlande
Canada	883.6	1147.7	1291.1	1292.5	1554.1	Canada
Viet Nam	619.2	811.8	1364.9	1419.2	1577.5	Viet Nam
Indonesia	1038.0	953.0	1080.4	1033.9	944.5	Indonésie
India	865.4	940.7	1074.5	952.7	1088.5	Inde
China	650.7	709.3	840.8	845.6	983.7	Chine
United States	585.3	749.3	784.1	656.9	672.6	Etats-Unis d'Amérique
Australia	510.0	574.6	626.2	557.6	554.9	Australie
Mexico	550.4	493.7	565.0	507.8	399.2	Mexique
Morocco	451.2	447.7	633.6	456.2	e496.3	Maroc
Argentina	363.1	355.9	466.9	584.1	e564.4	Argentine
Spain	411.7	461.3	420.5	487.3	530.1	Espagne
Ecuador	873.2	608.5	274.3	282.7	254.7	Equateur
United Kingdom	394.2	408.8	397.0	406.0	431.8	Royaume-Uni
Denmark	376.4	363.5	342.3	329.5	374.7	Danemark
Korea, Republic of	332.3	326.1	370.4	314.0	229.9	République de Corée
Bangladesh	260.7	e202.0	e281.4	334.0	e268.4	Bangladesh
France-Monaco	254.4	254.1	246.7	254.1	251.7	France-Monaco
Netherlands	160.7	220.8	273.4	285.9	264.0	Pays-Bas
Philippines	198.1	194.7	212.7	195.2	210.0	Philippines
Malaysia	171.2	170.0	219.8	211.8	e224.5	Malaisie
New Zealand	175.8	173.5	178.6	173.7	210.4	Nouvelle-Zélande
Honduras	191.6	191.1	183.0	209.7	57.7	Honduras
Belgium	–	177.3	165.9	169.3	e189.9	Belgique
Brazil	68.5	82.1	157.1	190.0	e196.9	Brésil
Japan	123.2	103.8	125.5	132.1	152.7	Japon
Greenland	110.2	132.1	124.8	126.8	e134.5	Groenland
Myanmar	e135.2	e94.4	e126.6	e109.4	e157.3	Myanmar
Italy-San Marino-Holy See	114.7	115.7	120.9	131.1	135.7	Italie-Saint-Marin-Saint-Siège
China, Hong Kong SAR	97.8	104.6	183.1	127.5	104.3	Chine - RAS de Hong-Kong

(Value as percentages of World total) **(Valeur en pourcentage du total mondial)**

Regions of the world	1993	1994	1995	1996	1997	1998	1999	2000	2001	2002	Régions du monde
World	100.0	100.0	100.0	100.0	100.0	100.0	100.0	100.0	100.0	100.0	Monde
Africa	5.9	6.3	6.3	6.2	5.7	6.0	5.4	6.6	5.9	5.8	Afrique
Americas	27.0	26.1	27.6	27.4	29.4	30.1	30.5	27.7	28.1	27.0	Amériques
- Northern America	12.3	12.3	12.4	11.6	11.1	10.4	13.1	12.6	12.5	13.7	- Amérique du Nord
- LAIA	10.9	10.8	12.2	12.6	14.3	14.7	12.7	10.9	11.7	10.5	- ALAI
- CACM	1.3	1.3	1.2	1.6	1.7	2.5	2.3	2.1	1.8	0.7	- MCC
- Caribbean	0.9	0.5	0.7	0.5	1.3	1.2	1.3	1.1	1.0	1.1	- Caraïbes
- Rest of America	1.6	1.2	1.2	1.0	1.0	1.3	1.1	1.1	1.1	0.9	- Autre d'Amérique
Asia excluding former USSR	47.0	49.8	47.5	45.8	44.5	43.8	43.1	47.1	46.5	47.2	Asie ancienne URSS exclus
- Middle East	0.4	0.5	0.4	0.3	0.4	0.4	0.4	0.4	0.3	0.5	- Moyen-Orient
Asia former USSR	0.0	0.0	0.0	0.0	0.0	0.0	0.0	0.0	0.0	0.0	Asie ancienne URSS
Europe excluding former USSR	12.0	12.1	12.5	14.4	14.3	14.7	15.5	13.5	14.6	15.0	Europe ancienne URSS exclus
- European Union	10.8	11.0	11.5	13.2	13.3	13.8	14.6	12.7	13.9	14.2	- Union Européenne
- Eastern Europe	0.1	0.0	0.0	0.1	0.1	0.1	0.1	0.1	0.1	0.1	- Europe de l'Est
- Rest of Europe	1.1	1.0	1.0	1.1	0.9	0.8	0.8	0.7	0.6	0.7	- Autre de l'Europe
Europe former USSR	3.0	0.3	0.3	0.4	0.5	0.6	0.3	0.4	0.3	0.4	Europe ancienne URSS
Oceania	5.2	5.5	5.8	5.8	5.5	4.8	5.1	4.8	4.6	4.6	Océanie

037 Fish, crustaceans and molluscs, prepared or preserved, nes

TRADE BY COMMODITY (Value in million US dollars)
Imports by principal countries or areas

COMMERCE PAR PRODUIT (Valeur en millions de dollars EU)
Importations selon les principaux pays ou zones

Country or area	1998	1999	2000	2001	2002	Pays ou zone
World	9481.5	9575.2	9815.2	9867.6	10550.1	Monde
Africa	186.3	152.2	171.8	153.2	145.9	Afrique
Americas	2043.2	2256.4	2379.8	2518.8	2699.0	Amériques
- Northern America	1670.5	1943.0	2059.2	2194.6	2416.3	- Amérique du Nord
- LAIA	263.3	217.4	219.1	226.3	186.2	- ALAI
- CACM	26.9	20.4	18.5	22.1	22.0	- MCC
- Caribbean	69.4	62.0	68.3	62.4	59.8	- Caraïbes
- Rest of America	13.2	13.6	14.8	13.4	14.8	- Autre d'Amérique
Asia excluding former USSR	2445.9	2733.9	3174.9	2921.2	3034.5	Asie ancienne URSS exclus
- Middle East	158.9	152.0	123.8	155.3	133.6	- Moyen-Orient
Asia former USSR	8.3	8.1	9.1	8.8	8.6	Asie ancienne URSS
Europe excluding former USSR	4461.6	4136.3	3785.8	3928.3	4308.2	Europe ancienne URSS exclus
- European Union	4143.2	3841.4	3506.5	3629.8	3982.3	- Union Européenne
- Eastern Europe	98.6	82.6	81.7	91.3	106.8	- Europe de l'Est
- Rest of Europe	219.8	212.3	197.6	207.2	219.1	- Autre de l'Europe
Europe former USSR	124.7	74.1	78.6	121.6	129.7	Europe ancienne URSS
Oceania	211.4	214.2	215.2	215.6	224.0	Océanie
Japan	1904.0	2105.2	2499.0	2238.7	2283.7	Japon
United States	1431.0	1689.8	1820.5	1950.6	2157.0	Etats-Unis d'Amérique
United Kingdom	898.3	803.7	713.9	780.3	792.1	Royaume-Uni
France-Monaco	793.2	613.9	608.5	613.3	716.0	France-Monaco
Germany	574.2	547.6	485.2	531.9	563.3	Allemagne
Italy-San Marino-Holy See	531.4	510.8	458.2	495.2	583.5	Italie-Saint-Marin-Saint-Siège
Canada	238.2	252.0	237.8	242.7	257.3	Canada
Denmark	229.5	231.9	231.2	224.5	216.9	Danemark
Spain	237.2	234.5	206.7	204.0	225.4	Espagne
Netherlands	225.9	216.6	203.6	156.0	205.9	Pays-Bas
Belgium	-	254.6	215.0	211.3	e231.7	Belgique
Australia	165.2	173.1	172.4	170.8	178.9	Australie
Sweden	155.9	160.6	147.4	152.2	161.9	Suède
China, Hong Kong SAR	140.2	146.0	152.6	146.3	168.8	Chine - RAS de Hong-Kong
Switzerland-Liechtenstein	123.1	120.7	108.0	106.8	109.3	Suisse-Liechtenstein
Singapore	70.5	110.0	117.3	106.0	133.7	Singapour
Korea, Republic of	40.1	70.8	107.7	120.2	142.7	République de Corée
Austria	85.2	79.8	60.9	70.6	82.8	Autriche
Russian Federation	75.9	38.9	29.7	72.7	69.8	Fédération de Russie
Argentina	62.4	65.6	54.3	54.6	e24.2	Argentine
Finland	56.9	49.2	46.5	51.9	52.2	Finlande
Norway	53.2	46.7	47.0	51.1	55.4	Norvège
Belgium-Luxembourg	250.0	-	-	-	-	Belgique-Luxembourg
Colombia	60.7	40.0	44.8	43.0	48.0	Colombie
Portugal	32.0	41.6	39.0	43.6	48.6	Portugal
Saudi Arabia	40.8	36.3	29.8	44.3	e45.8	Arabie saoudite
Egypt	49.4	27.7	e46.2	42.0	28.9	Egypte
Ireland	37.2	35.5	34.1	41.5	43.7	Irlande
Mexico	24.9	28.5	38.5	50.6	48.5	Mexique
Greece	36.3	42.6	36.9	35.4	e39.2	Grèce

(Value as percentages of World total) **(Valeur en pourcentage du total mondial)**

Regions of the world	1993	1994	1995	1996	1997	1998	1999	2000	2001	2002	Régions du monde
World	100.0	100.0	100.0	100.0	100.0	100.0	100.0	100.0	100.0	100.0	Monde
Africa	2.1	1.4	1.6	1.2	1.4	2.0	1.6	1.8	1.6	1.4	Afrique
Americas	17.5	17.8	16.4	16.8	18.8	21.5	23.6	24.2	25.5	25.6	Amériques
- Northern America	14.9	14.9	13.5	13.8	15.5	17.6	20.3	21.0	22.2	22.9	- Amérique du Nord
- LAIA	1.7	2.2	2.2	2.3	2.4	2.8	2.3	2.2	2.3	1.8	- ALAI
- CACM	0.1	0.1	0.1	0.1	0.2	0.3	0.2	0.2	0.2	0.2	- MCC
- Caribbean	0.5	0.4	0.5	0.4	0.5	0.7	0.6	0.7	0.6	0.6	- Caraïbes
- Rest of America	0.2	0.2	0.1	0.2	0.1	0.1	0.1	0.2	0.1	0.1	- Autre d'Amérique
Asia excluding former USSR	29.7	31.9	32.8	32.8	33.0	25.8	28.6	32.3	29.6	28.8	Asie ancienne URSS exclus
- Middle East	0.8	1.6	1.6	1.1	1.3	1.7	1.6	1.3	1.6	1.3	- Moyen-Orient
Asia former USSR	0.0	0.1	0.1	0.2	0.1	0.1	0.1	0.1	0.1	0.1	Asie ancienne URSS
Europe excluding former USSR	45.6	44.3	44.9	45.3	43.4	47.1	43.2	38.6	39.8	40.8	Europe ancienne URSS exclus
- European Union	42.4	41.2	41.7	42.3	40.3	43.7	40.1	35.7	36.8	37.7	- Union Européenne
- Eastern Europe	0.7	0.8	0.8	0.8	0.9	1.0	0.9	0.8	0.9	1.0	- Europe de l'Est
- Rest of Europe	2.5	2.3	2.4	2.2	2.1	2.3	2.2	2.0	2.1	2.1	- Autre de l'Europe
Europe former USSR	1.9	1.4	1.7	1.3	1.2	1.3	0.8	0.8	1.2	1.2	Europe ancienne URSS
Oceania	3.3	3.1	2.5	2.4	2.2	2.2	2.2	2.2	2.2	2.1	Océanie

TRADE BY COMMODITY (Value in million US dollars)
Exports by principal countries or areas

COMMERCE PAR PRODUIT (Valeur en millions de dollars EU)
Exportations selon les principaux pays ou zones

Country or area	1998	1999	2000	2001	2002	Pays ou zone
World	9117.4	9025.5	9356.5	9428.8	10037.8	Monde
Africa	586.4	550.2	502.4	552.1	576.8	Afrique
Americas	1374.2	1426.0	1396.3	1483.5	1557.7	Amériques
- Northern America	645.3	750.1	770.6	792.9	781.4	- Amérique du Nord
- LAIA	691.3	652.7	605.8	652.8	724.6	- ALAI
- CACM	36.4	20.2	15.5	21.3	29.1	- MCC
- Caribbean	1.1	1.3	0.9	0.9	0.8	- Caraïbes
- Rest of America	0.1	1.9	3.5	15.6	21.8	- Autre d'Amérique
Asia excluding former USSR	4041.9	4042.0	4643.4	4484.6	4839.2	Asie ancienne URSS exclus
- Middle East	101.8	71.0	92.2	72.2	56.1	- Moyen-Orient
Asia former USSR	6.5	6.9	7.4	9.0	10.3	Asie ancienne URSS
Europe excluding former USSR	2852.6	2728.4	2527.3	2575.5	2742.2	Europe ancienne URSS exclus
- European Union	2325.4	2248.5	2094.0	2134.7	2293.7	- Union Européenne
- Eastern Europe	86.2	76.1	73.7	89.7	104.6	- Europe de l'Est
- Rest of Europe	441.0	403.8	359.5	351.0	343.9	- Autre de l'Europe
Europe former USSR	131.9	123.9	114.5	205.4	206.6	Europe ancienne URSS
Oceania	123.9	148.1	165.2	118.7	105.0	Océanie
Thailand	1875.8	2016.0	2057.9	2011.9	e2124.8	Thaïlande
China	923.4	1021.8	1391.2	1427.8	1628.2	Chine
Denmark	462.6	436.1	396.7	445.5	453.9	Danemark
Spain	365.5	328.2	340.6	407.8	397.7	Espagne
Canada	301.3	356.8	409.0	377.1	352.3	Canada
Germany	364.3	362.9	295.4	363.8	391.6	Allemagne
United States	271.0	323.1	293.2	351.9	361.2	Etats-Unis d'Amérique
Netherlands	315.5	329.4	287.8	281.5	313.4	Pays-Bas
Korea, Republic of	287.0	311.4	312.1	261.6	230.9	République de Corée
Ecuador	253.9	262.9	220.1	268.0	342.0	Equateur
Japan	229.1	239.1	251.3	222.2	230.5	Japon
Morocco	190.5	200.2	201.9	229.1	e249.2	Maroc
Chile	189.0	200.9	209.5	220.1	e215.3	Chili
Norway	217.2	205.1	188.7	174.0	162.3	Norvège
France-Monaco	169.1	209.8	263.2	134.2	159.8	France-Monaco
Iceland	180.4	159.8	134.4	136.1	140.6	Islande
Côte d'Ivoire	206.6	141.4	120.3	e131.2	135.9	Côte d'Ivoire
United Kingdom	219.7	159.4	117.2	105.5	105.4	Royaume-Uni
Indonesia	121.9	99.7	107.6	106.8	99.1	Indonésie
Philippines	139.0	84.8	72.6	85.7	116.1	Philippines
Italy-San Marino-Holy See	76.1	74.9	83.3	97.0	129.4	Italie-Saint-Marin-Saint-Siège
Portugal	102.8	92.2	79.7	64.5	78.6	Portugal
Belgium	–	107.9	88.3	97.0	e108.9	Belgique
Malaysia	83.9	74.9	74.5	78.7	e83.4	Malaisie
Poland	81.1	65.2	64.8	79.8	100.0	Pologne
Sweden	83.3	76.3	74.4	70.5	82.7	Suède
Australia	71.3	80.0	94.1	63.4	44.4	Australie
Greenland	73.0	70.1	68.4	63.9	e67.7	Groenland
Viet Nam	118.6	13.3	65.6	68.2	75.8	Viet Nam
Mexico	56.5	62.1	65.7	61.5	76.5	Mexique

(Value as percentages of World total) **(Valeur en pourcentage du total mondial)**

Regions of the world	1993	1994	1995	1996	1997	1998	1999	2000	2001	2002	Régions du monde
World	100.0	100.0	100.0	100.0	100.0	100.0	100.0	100.0	100.0	100.0	Monde
Africa	5.0	4.6	5.8	5.8	5.8	6.4	6.1	5.4	5.9	5.7	Afrique
Americas	14.8	14.6	14.6	14.0	14.5	15.1	15.8	14.9	15.7	15.5	Amériques
- Northern America	8.6	8.3	7.6	7.3	6.6	7.1	8.3	8.2	8.4	7.8	- Amérique du Nord
- LAIA	5.5	6.0	6.4	6.3	7.5	7.6	7.2	6.5	6.9	7.2	- ALAI
- CACM	0.4	0.3	0.6	0.5	0.3	0.4	0.2	0.2	0.2	0.3	- MCC
- Caribbean	0.3	0.0	0.0	0.0	0.0	0.0	0.0	0.0	0.0	0.0	- Caraïbes
- Rest of America	0.0	0.0	0.0	0.0	0.0	0.0	0.0	0.0	0.2	0.2	- Autre d'Amérique
Asia excluding former USSR	47.8	46.5	44.7	46.3	47.8	44.3	44.8	49.6	47.6	48.2	Asie ancienne URSS exclus
- Middle East	1.0	1.0	0.9	1.0	1.0	1.1	0.8	1.0	0.8	0.6	- Moyen-Orient
Asia former USSR	0.1	0.1	0.1	0.1	0.1	0.1	0.1	0.1	0.1	0.1	Asie ancienne URSS
Europe excluding former USSR	27.2	29.8	30.2	29.3	27.9	31.3	30.2	27.0	27.3	27.3	Europe ancienne URSS exclus
- European Union	21.8	23.5	24.0	23.6	22.5	25.5	24.9	22.4	22.6	22.9	- Union Européenne
- Eastern Europe	0.8	0.9	0.9	0.8	0.8	0.9	0.8	0.8	1.0	1.0	- Europe de l'Est
- Rest of Europe	4.6	5.4	5.3	5.0	4.6	4.8	4.5	3.8	3.7	3.4	- Autre de l'Europe
Europe former USSR	2.7	2.1	2.6	2.5	1.8	1.4	1.4	1.2	2.2	2.1	Europe ancienne URSS
Oceania	2.3	2.3	2.0	1.9	2.1	1.4	1.6	1.8	1.3	1.0	Océanie

041 Wheat and meslin, unmilled

TRADE BY COMMODITY (Value in million US dollars)
Imports by principal countries or areas

COMMERCE PAR PRODUIT (Valeur en millions de dollars EU)
Importations selon les principaux pays ou zones

Country or area	1998	1999	2000	2001	2002	Pays ou zone
World	16634.1	15684.1	15565.4	15804.8	16526.4	Monde
Africa	3314.3	3036.6	3282.5	3591.2	4078.0	Afrique
Americas	2757.2	2757.8	2664.3	2957.4	2945.2	Amériques
- Northern America	308.7	293.3	248.3	313.5	300.7	- Amérique du Nord
- LAIA	2037.0	2029.8	2010.4	2176.6	2185.9	- ALAI
- CACM	137.2	188.3	165.8	195.1	208.9	- MCC
- Caribbean	242.9	220.9	210.2	239.5	223.5	- Caraïbes
- Rest of America	31.3	25.5	29.6	32.7	26.2	- Autre d'Amérique
Asia excluding former USSR	6016.6	5611.4	5412.7	5122.0	5179.2	Asie ancienne URSS exclus
- Middle East	1379.0	1469.3	1517.7	1338.9	963.1	- Moyen-Orient
Asia former USSR	319.5	186.3	318.9	252.2	264.9	Asie ancienne URSS
Europe excluding former USSR	3963.9	3582.6	3300.8	3653.0	3884.5	Europe ancienne URSS exclus
- European Union	3697.5	3401.2	3015.2	3350.6	3642.3	- Union Européenne
- Eastern Europe	107.2	45.2	129.9	128.2	69.2	- Europe de l'Est
- Rest of Europe	159.2	136.2	155.7	174.2	173.1	- Autre de l'Europe
Europe former USSR	201.2	436.5	520.8	153.2	82.8	Europe ancienne URSS
Oceania	61.5	72.9	65.5	75.8	91.7	Océanie
Japan	1096.1	1074.7	1030.4	1037.8	1124.5	Japon
Italy-San Marino-Holy See	1212.9	968.8	961.1	1087.3	1055.0	Italie-Saint-Marin-Saint-Siège
Brazil	943.3	938.2	981.2	977.3	966.4	Brésil
Algeria	691.2	660.8	803.9	e972.4	e1107.7	Algérie
Egypt	813.9	602.8	e734.2	668.5	819.2	Egypte
Iran (Islamic Republic of)	530.0	801.3	860.0	876.8	499.3	Iran (République islamique d')
Korea, Republic of	662.7	533.2	470.4	529.7	542.7	République de Corée
Spain	552.5	514.8	333.5	513.8	743.0	Espagne
Indonesia	630.4	404.4	502.4	399.5	614.4	Indonésie
Morocco	388.8	388.7	516.3	547.8	e578.0	Maroc
Netherlands	443.0	428.8	433.1	466.5	483.1	Pays-Bas
Philippines	286.9	402.8	391.0	485.1	486.7	Philippines
Mexico	339.4	360.0	353.6	444.8	467.5	Mexique
Belgium	–	474.8	438.8	379.0	e415.6	Belgique
Nigeria	297.0	434.1	251.3	e344.5	e326.7	Nigéria
United States	297.9	290.4	244.8	300.1	282.5	Etats-Unis d'Amérique
United Kingdom	235.6	207.7	194.6	209.9	209.3	Royaume-Uni
Portugal	242.0	222.5	171.9	208.4	210.8	Portugal
Malaysia	187.6	215.4	187.1	206.2	e225.3	Malaisie
Pakistan	357.5	389.1	144.5	26.7	58.0	Pakistan
Bangladesh	150.3	e164.6	e221.5	214.6	e209.7	Bangladesh
Peru	197.3	179.6	170.7	206.9	199.2	Pérou
Israel	187.5	184.6	191.1	170.6	191.4	Israël
Germany	178.5	204.3	166.8	181.0	187.6	Allemagne
Tunisia	217.4	131.5	160.5	198.6	e198.6	Tunisie
Venezuela	177.7	174.8	170.7	193.6	e162.8	Venezuela
Colombia	178.0	151.1	152.2	181.3	199.7	Colombie
Russian Federation	123.4	320.5	277.7	102.3	24.2	Fédération de Russie
Sudan	87.0	e148.7	174.2	156.2	203.3	Soudan
Turkey	232.1	185.9	126.1	49.6	148.0	Turquie

(Value as percentages of World total) **(Valeur en pourcentage du total mondial)**

Regions of the world	1993	1994	1995	1996	1997	1998	1999	2000	2001	2002	Régions du monde
World	100.0	100.0	100.0	100.0	100.0	100.0	100.0	100.0	100.0	100.0	Monde
Africa	11.8	15.5	19.0	16.4	16.8	19.9	19.4	21.1	22.7	24.7	Afrique
Americas	10.3	11.5	9.1	14.0	14.9	16.6	17.6	17.1	18.7	17.8	Amériques
- Northern America	1.6	2.1	1.4	1.2	2.1	1.9	1.9	1.6	2.0	1.8	- Amérique du Nord
- LAIA	6.0	6.3	5.6	10.3	10.1	12.2	12.9	12.9	13.8	13.2	- ALAI
- CACM	0.9	1.3	0.8	1.1	1.0	0.8	1.2	1.1	1.2	1.3	- MCC
- Caribbean	1.6	1.5	1.2	1.2	1.6	1.5	1.4	1.4	1.5	1.4	- Caraïbes
- Rest of America	0.1	0.3	0.2	0.2	0.2	0.2	0.2	0.2	0.2	0.2	- Autre d'Amérique
Asia excluding former USSR	36.9	42.8	44.1	42.7	41.5	36.2	35.8	34.8	32.4	31.3	Asie ancienne URSS exclus
- Middle East	4.5	4.4	8.5	9.2	10.8	8.3	9.4	9.8	8.5	5.8	- Moyen-Orient
Asia former USSR	3.9	3.1	1.9	2.6	1.4	1.9	1.2	2.0	1.6	1.6	Asie ancienne URSS
Europe excluding former USSR	27.8	24.2	23.1	21.7	22.8	23.8	22.8	21.2	23.1	23.5	Europe ancienne URSS exclus
- European Union	24.3	22.5	21.4	18.4	20.3	22.2	21.7	19.4	21.2	22.0	- Union Européenne
- Eastern Europe	2.8	0.7	0.9	2.6	1.4	0.6	0.3	0.8	0.8	0.4	- Europe de l'Est
- Rest of Europe	0.8	1.0	0.8	0.7	1.1	1.0	0.9	1.0	1.1	1.0	- Autre de l'Europe
Europe former USSR	9.0	2.6	2.4	2.2	2.3	1.2	2.8	3.3	1.0	0.5	Europe ancienne URSS
Oceania	0.4	0.4	0.3	0.4	0.3	0.4	0.5	0.4	0.5	0.6	Océanie

TRADE BY COMMODITY (Value in million US dollars)
Exports by principal countries or areas

COMMERCE PAR PRODUIT (Valeur en millions de dollars EU)
Exportations selon les principaux pays ou zones

Country or area	1998	1999	2000	2001	2002	Pays ou zone
World	15442.5	14337.7	14189.4	15045.7	15379.1	Monde
Africa	17.1	31.5	25.1	54.1	33.1	Afrique
Americas	7885.2	6945.2	7193.4	7324.3	6908.8	Amériques
- Northern America	6503.0	5868.6	5868.0	5931.5	5570.7	- Amérique du Nord
- LAIA	1368.2	1062.1	1303.8	1386.3	1330.9	- ALAI
- CACM	0.2	0.0	3.0	4.8	6.6	- MCC
- Caribbean	13.8	14.5	18.6	1.7	0.6	- Caraïbes
- Rest of America	0.0	0.0	0.0	0.0	0.0	- Autre d'Amérique
Asia excluding former USSR	255.9	212.5	300.8	517.2	701.3	Asie ancienne URSS exclus
- Middle East	249.9	210.0	203.1	145.9	127.5	- Moyen-Orient
Asia former USSR	261.5	271.8	456.0	320.7	360.4	Asie ancienne URSS
Europe excluding former USSR	4450.6	4275.5	3936.2	3771.7	3572.6	Europe ancienne URSS exclus
- European Union	4125.5	3975.4	3665.3	3460.0	3252.1	- Union Européenne
- Eastern Europe	306.0	280.0	224.9	265.1	288.1	- Europe de l'Est
- Rest of Europe	19.1	20.0	45.9	46.7	32.4	- Autre de l'Europe
Europe former USSR	364.9	463.9	73.5	819.9	1547.9	Europe ancienne URSS
Oceania	2207.3	2137.3	2204.4	2237.9	2254.9	Océanie
United States	3714.0	3581.0	3387.5	3381.7	3631.9	Etats-Unis d'Amérique
Canada	2789.0	2287.0	2480.2	2549.9	1938.8	Canada
Australia	2207.3	2137.1	2203.9	2237.7	2254.7	Australie
France-Monaco	1975.0	2256.3	2101.7	1791.3	1646.0	France-Monaco
Argentina	1307.6	999.2	1218.1	1301.5	e1257.5	Argentine
Germany	974.9	760.0	615.7	863.9	758.0	Allemagne
Ukraine	212.4	379.5	19.0	619.3	682.6	Ukraine
United Kingdom	580.3	377.2	420.0	193.5	178.1	Royaume-Uni
Kazakhstan	259.0	270.1	453.7	319.2	e359.5	Kazakhstan
Russian Federation	127.5	48.3	41.9	143.8	773.1	Fédération de Russie
India	e	e	92.3	282.0	361.9	Inde
Turkey	163.4	190.5	196.1	136.2	9.8	Turquie
Hungary	160.7	55.9	67.9	150.7	119.1	Hongrie
Denmark	132.5	103.9	102.1	84.1	91.2	Danemark
Spain	49.2	39.6	67.9	145.1	200.6	Espagne
Belgium	–	195.1	141.6	61.3	e68.7	Belgique
Austria	88.9	73.9	74.1	79.3	102.5	Autriche
Sweden	75.2	38.7	44.1	102.1	48.3	Suède
Bulgaria	75.2	62.3	51.8	e54.9	e61.8	Bulgarie
Mexico	27.2	45.4	76.4	77.8	65.8	Mexique
Syrian Arab Republic	78.1	14.0	e	e	111.6	République arabe syrienne
Greece	30.7	40.3	19.4	56.1	e56.2	Grèce
Romania	42.6	71.9	11.8	40.2	24.6	Roumanie
Czech Republic	16.2	50.2	90.6	18.0	14.4	République tchèque
Pakistan	1.6	0.0	4.3	39.8	134.2	Pakistan
Netherlands	47.2	37.2	26.4	27.9	34.8	Pays-Bas
Italy-San Marino-Holy See	16.2	33.3	38.4	35.2	37.0	Italie-Saint-Marin-Saint-Siège
Lithuania	20.0	24.0	11.0	43.5	e52.7	Lituanie
Belgium-Luxembourg	137.5	–	–	–	–	Belgique-Luxembourg
China	1.4	0.2	0.2	46.9	70.1	Chine

(Value as percentages of World total) **(Valeur en pourcentage du total mondial)**

Regions of the world	1993	1994	1995	1996	1997	1998	1999	2000	2001	2002	Régions du monde
World	100.0	100.0	100.0	100.0	100.0	100.0	100.0	100.0	100.0	100.0	Monde
Africa	0.0	0.0	0.1	0.0	0.1	0.1	0.2	0.2	0.4	0.2	Afrique
Americas	52.2	53.8	55.2	53.1	52.2	51.1	48.4	50.7	48.7	44.9	Amériques
- Northern America	47.1	48.7	48.9	47.7	44.1	42.1	40.9	41.4	39.4	36.2	- Amérique du Nord
- LAIA	5.0	5.1	6.4	5.4	8.1	8.9	7.4	9.2	9.2	8.7	- ALAI
- CACM	0.0	0.0	0.0	0.0	0.0	0.0	0.0	0.0	0.0	0.0	- MCC
- Caribbean	0.0	0.0	0.0	0.0	0.0	0.1	0.1	0.1	0.0	0.0	- Caraïbes
- Rest of America	0.0	0.0	0.0	0.0	0.0	0.0	0.0	0.0	0.0	0.0	- Autre d'Amérique
Asia excluding former USSR	1.9	1.8	1.5	1.3	0.7	1.7	1.5	2.1	3.4	4.6	Asie ancienne URSS exclus
- Middle East	1.8	1.6	0.8	0.3	0.7	1.6	1.5	1.4	1.0	0.8	- Moyen-Orient
Asia former USSR	0.1	0.5	1.3	1.6	2.4	1.7	1.9	3.2	2.1	2.3	Asie ancienne URSS
Europe excluding former USSR	35.5	31.0	33.5	27.5	25.8	28.8	29.8	27.7	25.1	23.2	Europe ancienne URSS exclus
- European Union	35.1	29.7	29.1	25.8	24.7	26.7	27.7	25.8	23.0	21.1	- Union Européenne
- Eastern Europe	0.3	0.6	3.8	1.5	1.1	2.0	2.0	1.6	1.8	1.9	- Europe de l'Est
- Rest of Europe	0.1	0.7	0.7	0.1	0.0	0.1	0.1	0.3	0.3	0.2	- Autre de l'Europe
Europe former USSR	0.1	0.6	0.7	1.1	0.9	2.4	3.2	0.5	5.4	10.1	Europe ancienne URSS
Oceania	10.3	12.2	7.6	15.3	17.9	14.3	14.9	15.5	14.9	14.7	Océanie

042 Rice

TRADE BY COMMODITY (Value in million US dollars)
Imports by principal countries or areas

COMMERCE PAR PRODUIT (Valeur en millions de dollars EU)
Importations selon les principaux pays ou zones

Country or area	1998	1999	2000	2001	2002	Pays ou zone
World	9066.9	8596.1	6665.2	6188.9	6206.8	Monde
Africa	1335.1	1093.1	1067.4	1135.9	1233.7	Afrique
Americas	1798.8	1281.9	970.0	961.1	854.4	Amériques
- Northern America	322.4	331.8	322.6	301.3	289.4	- Amérique du Nord
- LAIA	1042.9	527.3	315.3	334.3	260.0	- ALAI
- CACM	99.5	93.3	77.3	79.0	63.1	- MCC
- Caribbean	312.1	327.3	251.7	244.0	237.1	- Caraïbes
- Rest of America	21.9	2.2	3.1	2.6	4.8	- Autre d'Amérique
Asia excluding former USSR	4314.7	4600.5	3261.2	2739.6	2716.2	Asie ancienne URSS exclus
- Middle East	1401.1	1599.6	1572.8	1139.2	1181.4	- Moyen-Orient
Asia former USSR	14.9	14.5	14.8	25.4	34.8	Asie ancienne URSS
Europe excluding former USSR	1345.3	1298.6	1130.1	1121.0	1142.1	Europe ancienne URSS exclus
- European Union	1182.0	1124.5	984.4	987.8	998.2	- Union Européenne
- Eastern Europe	104.8	115.6	90.2	80.7	88.7	- Europe de l'Est
- Rest of Europe	58.5	58.6	55.5	52.5	55.2	- Autre de l'Europe
Europe former USSR	109.4	191.6	96.8	81.4	101.2	Europe ancienne URSS
Oceania	148.7	115.9	124.9	124.6	124.4	Océanie
Indonesia	861.1	1327.5	319.1	134.9	342.5	Indonésie
Saudi Arabia	502.7	485.2	494.7	366.6	e379.4	Arabie saoudite
Philippines	646.6	239.9	135.6	153.1	211.8	Philippines
Iran (Islamic Republic of)	205.6	325.9	337.1	209.6	237.1	Iran (République islamique d')
Brazil	621.7	290.5	140.7	142.6	118.8	Brésil
United Kingdom	283.7	288.7	227.9	247.2	226.8	Royaume-Uni
Japan	273.2	314.8	264.3	195.9	221.8	Japon
France-Monaco	239.8	230.5	220.3	207.8	213.4	France-Monaco
United States	203.0	217.0	209.9	198.6	189.9	Etats-Unis d'Amérique
United Arab Emirates	197.8	207.3	163.0	176.3	e180.8	Emirates arabes unis
Malaysia	232.6	189.2	181.8	140.5	e153.6	Malaisie
Bangladesh	246.2	e269.6	e99.3	96.2	e94.0	Bangladesh
China, Hong Kong SAR	186.7	164.3	156.6	135.9	129.2	Chine - RAS de Hong-Kong
Germany	165.6	157.9	144.2	141.8	140.8	Allemagne
Nigeria	186.5	107.4	119.7	e164.1	e155.6	Nigéria
Senegal	146.4	158.9	109.4	142.6	171.8	Sénégal
Singapore	121.4	147.3	131.7	118.2	119.3	Singapour
Cuba	e145.9	152.6	106.4	99.0	e85.1	Cuba
Côte d'Ivoire	141.8	111.6	97.5	e103.6	e134.3	Côte d'Ivoire
Canada	119.1	114.4	112.5	102.4	99.1	Canada
Mexico	111.5	125.1	102.6	106.4	86.6	Mexique
Korea, Democratic People's Republic of	e53.2	e24.0	e45.4	e374.6	e13.0	République démocratique populaire de Corée
China	120.0	78.2	112.7	98.9	79.7	Chine
Iraq	e82.5	e134.6	e156.7	e62.1	e32.1	Iraq
Netherlands	118.8	101.3	86.3	75.4	86.1	Pays-Bas
Turkey	96.5	97.6	107.8	57.7	86.4	Turquie
Russian Federation	80.1	160.4	69.4	54.1	69.4	Fédération de Russie
Kuwait	82.5	85.7	e80.5	e88.6	e63.6	Koweït
Belgium	-	104.0	90.0	96.2	e105.5	Belgique
Haiti	e54.6	e80.5	e80.7	e73.5	e89.0	Haïti

(Value as percentages of World total)
(Valeur en pourcentage du total mondial)

Regions of the world	1993	1994	1995	1996	1997	1998	1999	2000	2001	2002	Régions du monde
World	100.0	100.0	100.0	100.0	100.0	100.0	100.0	100.0	100.0	100.0	Monde
Africa	15.0	10.2	20.4	15.3	18.3	14.7	12.7	16.0	18.4	19.9	Afrique
Americas	18.1	17.3	15.4	16.4	18.2	19.8	14.9	14.6	15.5	13.8	Amériques
- Northern America	4.2	3.6	3.2	3.4	4.8	3.6	3.9	4.8	4.9	4.7	- Amérique du Nord
- LAIA	8.7	9.3	7.1	8.0	8.7	11.5	6.1	4.7	5.4	4.2	- ALAI
- CACM	0.8	1.0	0.9	1.2	1.4	1.1	1.1	1.2	1.3	1.0	- MCC
- Caribbean	4.3	3.3	4.1	3.8	3.2	3.4	3.8	3.8	3.9	3.8	- Caraïbes
- Rest of America	0.0	0.0	0.1	0.0	0.0	0.2	0.0	0.0	0.0	0.1	- Autre d'Amérique
Asia excluding former USSR	39.4	48.1	41.5	44.3	39.5	47.6	53.5	48.9	44.3	43.8	Asie ancienne URSS exclus
- Middle East	25.2	12.2	14.9	12.9	16.6	15.5	18.6	23.6	18.4	19.0	- Moyen-Orient
Asia former USSR	0.3	0.1	0.2	0.4	0.2	0.2	0.2	0.2	0.4	0.6	Asie ancienne URSS
Europe excluding former USSR	24.8	21.7	19.4	19.5	19.2	14.8	15.1	17.0	18.1	18.4	Europe ancienne URSS exclus
- European Union	22.1	19.9	17.4	17.5	17.0	13.0	13.1	14.8	16.0	16.1	- Union Européenne
- Eastern Europe	1.9	1.0	1.2	1.4	1.5	1.2	1.3	1.4	1.3	1.4	- Europe de l'Est
- Rest of Europe	0.8	0.8	0.7	0.6	0.7	0.6	0.7	0.8	0.8	0.9	- Autre de l'Europe
Europe former USSR	1.4	1.8	2.2	2.1	2.2	1.2	2.2	1.5	1.3	1.6	Europe ancienne URSS
Oceania	1.1	0.8	1.0	2.0	2.4	1.6	1.3	1.9	2.0	2.0	Océanie

TRADE BY COMMODITY (Value in million US dollars)
Exports by principal countries or areas

COMMERCE PAR PRODUIT (Valeur en millions de dollars EU)
Exportations selon les principaux pays ou zones

Country or area	1998	1999	2000	2001	2002	Pays ou zone
World	9571.2	7885.5	6410.9	6911.8	6705.7	Monde
Africa	149.3	102.1	116.3	156.4	124.1	Afrique
Americas	1896.1	1448.5	1199.3	1082.6	1083.4	Amériques
- Northern America	1212.7	947.2	837.6	718.7	777.2	- Amérique du Nord
- LAIA	583.2	407.5	300.6	293.9	244.3	- ALAI
- CACM	4.2	3.2	1.5	3.3	3.0	- MCC
- Caribbean	7.9	5.9	7.1	11.8	7.0	- Caraïbes
- Rest of America	88.1	84.8	52.4	54.9	51.9	- Autre d'Amérique
Asia excluding former USSR	6363.6	5141.6	4124.9	4806.0	4629.1	Asie ancienne URSS exclus
- Middle East	80.1	96.8	86.3	77.2	75.8	- Moyen-Orient
Asia former USSR	8.7	8.9	1.6	0.9	1.0	Asie ancienne URSS
Europe excluding former USSR	922.8	913.7	734.9	677.9	777.8	Europe ancienne URSS exclus
- European Union	904.4	899.2	727.4	673.3	771.9	- Union Européenne
- Eastern Europe	12.2	9.9	4.6	1.9	3.1	- Europe de l'Est
- Rest of Europe	6.1	4.6	3.0	2.8	2.8	- Autre de l'Europe
Europe former USSR	5.1	2.6	5.8	3.0	3.6	Europe ancienne URSS
Oceania	225.7	268.2	228.0	184.9	86.7	Océanie
Thailand	2102.4	1946.7	1628.5	1578.2	e1666.8	Thaïlande
India	1492.4	720.9	654.3	672.8	1212.5	Inde
United States	1208.4	945.5	836.0	717.5	775.3	Etats-Unis d'Amérique
Viet Nam	1019.7	1025.1	599.6	623.5	693.1	Viet Nam
China	924.0	651.9	561.1	329.0	380.4	Chine
Pakistan	573.3	584.3	534.1	521.0	463.1	Pakistan
Italy-San Marino-Holy See	351.9	364.9	294.4	258.6	282.2	Italie-Saint-Marin-Saint-Siège
Japan	143.8	66.7	13.7	935.3	5.9	Japon
Australia	225.5	268.1	227.8	184.7	86.5	Australie
Uruguay	273.4	195.8	165.4	167.9	140.2	Uruguay
Spain	156.5	157.2	121.8	114.3	145.1	Espagne
Argentina	236.5	173.2	103.6	76.6	e74.0	Argentine
Egypt	135.2	87.6	104.6	143.0	106.0	Egypte
Belgium	–	123.0	102.8	100.9	e113.2	Belgique
Netherlands	105.2	87.3	60.2	54.2	75.6	Pays-Bas
United Arab Emirates	71.5	73.8	61.1	68.2	e71.1	Emirates arabes unis
Guyana	68.1	73.3	40.9	43.5	41.3	Guyana
France-Monaco	47.1	57.3	44.2	55.4	55.9	France-Monaco
Germany	35.6	46.4	42.8	38.9	41.0	Allemagne
United Kingdom	42.7	36.4	36.7	34.2	39.4	Royaume-Uni
Myanmar	e	e11.4	e22.7	e41.9	e101.2	Myanmar
Belgium-Luxembourg	128.1	–	–	–	–	Belgique-Luxembourg
Venezuela	42.6	11.2	18.7	13.5	e14.4	Venezuela
Greece	29.6	19.7	16.4	11.4	e11.4	Grèce
Ecuador	21.9	10.6	3.4	27.7	7.2	Equateur
Suriname	18.2	e11.3	11.2	e11.3	e10.6	Suriname
Brazil	3.9	13.7	6.5	5.5	e5.7	Brésil
Saint Vincent and the Grenadines	6.4	5.0	4.6	e8.6	4.2	Saint-Vincent-et-les Grenadies
Iraq	e	e11.4	e15.9	e	e	Iraq
Kazakhstan	8.1	8.7	1.5	0.9	e1.0	Kazakhstan

(Value as percentages of World total)

(Valeur en pourcentage du total mondial)

Regions of the world	1993	1994	1995	1996	1997	1998	1999	2000	2001	2002	Régions du monde
World	100.0	100.0	100.0	100.0	100.0	100.0	100.0	100.0	100.0	100.0	Monde
Africa	0.9	1.4	1.0	1.9	1.2	1.6	1.3	1.8	2.3	1.9	Afrique
Americas	24.7	23.2	21.4	22.3	22.2	19.8	18.4	18.7	15.7	16.2	Amériques
- Northern America	15.3	16.0	13.6	13.9	12.5	12.7	12.0	13.1	10.4	11.6	- Amérique du Nord
- LAIA	5.0	4.4	4.7	5.5	6.9	6.1	5.2	4.7	4.3	3.6	- ALAI
- CACM	0.1	0.0	0.0	0.1	0.1	0.0	0.0	0.0	0.0	0.0	- MCC
- Caribbean	2.0	1.3	1.5	1.1	1.2	0.1	0.1	0.1	0.2	0.1	- Caraïbes
- Rest of America	2.2	1.4	1.6	1.7	1.5	0.9	1.1	0.8	0.8	0.8	- Autre d'Amérique
Asia excluding former USSR	54.2	56.2	60.4	57.3	59.8	66.5	65.2	64.3	69.5	69.0	Asie ancienne URSS exclus
- Middle East	0.9	0.6	0.5	0.7	0.7	0.8	1.2	1.3	1.1	1.1	- Moyen-Orient
Asia former USSR	0.0	0.0	0.2	0.1	0.1	0.1	0.1	0.0	0.0	0.0	Asie ancienne URSS
Europe excluding former USSR	16.9	14.8	14.1	14.8	12.9	9.6	11.6	11.5	9.8	11.6	Europe ancienne URSS exclus
- European Union	16.8	14.7	13.9	14.5	12.7	9.4	11.4	11.3	9.7	11.5	- Union Européenne
- Eastern Europe	0.1	0.1	0.1	0.3	0.2	0.1	0.1	0.1	0.0	0.0	- Europe de l'Est
- Rest of Europe	0.0	0.1	0.0	0.1	0.1	0.1	0.1	0.0	0.0	0.0	- Autre de l'Europe
Europe former USSR	0.1	0.2	0.2	0.2	0.1	0.1	0.0	0.1	0.0	0.1	Europe ancienne URSS
Oceania	3.3	4.2	2.8	3.3	3.7	2.4	3.4	3.6	2.7	1.3	Océanie

043 Barley, unmilled

TRADE BY COMMODITY (Value in million US dollars)
Imports by principal countries or areas

COMMERCE PAR PRODUIT (Valeur en millions de dollars EU)
Importations selon les principaux pays ou zones

Country or area	1998	1999	2000	2001	2002	Pays ou zone
World	2307.8	2570.4	3013.6	2858.9	2672.2	Monde
Africa	199.8	202.5	270.0	298.1	319.6	Afrique
Americas	223.2	184.4	214.2	208.7	196.1	Amériques
- Northern America	106.5	88.1	86.7	100.0	90.7	- Amérique du Nord
- LAIA	116.2	95.8	118.3	102.4	97.6	- ALAI
- CACM	0.1	0.1	0.0	0.0	0.0	- MCC
- Caribbean	0.4	0.2	9.2	6.2	7.7	- Caraïbes
- Rest of America	0.0	0.0	0.0	0.0	0.0	- Autre d'Amérique
Asia excluding former USSR	1112.5	1411.4	1730.4	1476.8	1171.0	Asie ancienne URSS exclus
- Middle East	563.5	797.3	1097.0	783.9	581.2	- Moyen-Orient
Asia former USSR	4.4	2.8	2.0	2.3	2.7	Asie ancienne URSS
Europe excluding former USSR	734.2	710.1	689.5	809.4	936.1	Europe ancienne URSS exclus
- European Union	668.6	647.8	575.3	711.3	875.7	- Union Européenne
- Eastern Europe	36.0	43.0	90.3	70.6	29.9	- Europe de l'Est
- Rest of Europe	29.5	19.3	23.9	27.4	30.5	- Autre de l'Europe
Europe former USSR	32.3	50.2	106.6	58.9	46.4	Europe ancienne URSS
Oceania	1.5	9.0	0.8	4.7	0.3	Océanie
Saudi Arabia	354.1	496.9	669.1	414.0	e428.4	Arabie saoudite
China	241.0	293.6	313.3	381.9	291.0	Chine
Japan	216.7	218.9	243.6	214.7	200.8	Japon
Belgium	–	178.9	157.8	163.5	e179.3	Belgique
Netherlands	94.0	126.2	86.3	95.4	116.2	Pays-Bas
Germany	78.3	83.5	90.4	108.9	113.2	Allemagne
Italy-San Marino-Holy See	87.8	91.6	90.7	91.5	109.4	Italie-Saint-Marin-Saint-Siège
Morocco	61.8	73.7	104.8	98.6	e104.0	Maroc
United States	101.3	84.4	83.0	90.5	70.5	Etats-Unis d'Amérique
Iran (Islamic Republic of)	30.4	53.6	158.4	134.0	24.1	Iran (République islamique d')
Algeria	59.3	67.5	68.6	e83.0	e94.6	Algérie
Spain	32.8	30.2	10.8	93.3	177.8	Espagne
Jordan	66.8	79.3	54.3	44.4	31.5	Jordanie
Israel	43.3	57.0	40.0	41.6	46.6	Israël
Belgium-Luxembourg	224.1	–	–	–	–	Belgique-Luxembourg
Tunisia	12.1	17.3	43.9	67.9	e67.9	Tunisie
Syrian Arab Republic	e	54.4	56.9	e70.9	16.3	République arabe syrienne
Portugal	36.2	29.8	26.7	38.1	46.7	Portugal
Cyprus	34.2	24.9	39.5	39.3	30.7	Chypre
Russian Federation	22.1	30.8	48.8	34.1	23.8	Fédération de Russie
Mexico	40.6	47.8	42.5	14.3	8.9	Mexique
Libyan Arab Jamahiriya	42.2	e30.8	e27.7	e22.3	e20.4	Jamahiriya arabe libyenne
Denmark	12.2	17.6	25.2	40.1	47.6	Danemark
Poland	24.2	30.2	38.7	25.9	22.5	Pologne
Colombia	30.5	19.0	24.5	36.6	27.5	Colombie
Greece	27.2	24.5	24.8	23.5	e26.0	Grèce
Kuwait	12.4	32.6	e30.6	e33.7	e16.6	Koweït
United Arab Emirates	25.0	26.2	23.7	16.4	e16.9	Emirates arabes unis
Belarus	7.0	17.3	42.1	19.5	16.3	Bélarus
United Kingdom	34.3	24.5	10.8	15.8	15.5	Royaume-Uni

(Value as percentages of World total)

(Valeur en pourcentage du total mondial)

Regions of the world	1993	1994	1995	1996	1997	1998	1999	2000	2001	2002	Régions du monde
World	100.0	100.0	100.0	100.0	100.0	100.0	100.0	100.0	100.0	100.0	Monde
Africa	9.0	8.6	7.9	2.8	6.4	8.7	7.9	9.0	10.4	12.0	Afrique
Americas	5.6	10.6	7.2	9.5	8.9	9.7	7.2	7.1	7.3	7.3	Amériques
- Northern America	2.3	7.5	4.0	3.5	4.0	4.6	3.4	2.9	3.5	3.4	- Amérique du Nord
- LAIA	3.2	3.0	3.2	5.7	4.8	5.0	3.7	3.9	3.6	3.7	- ALAI
- CACM	0.0	0.0	0.0	0.0	0.0	0.0	0.0	0.0	0.0	0.0	- MCC
- Caribbean	0.0	0.0	0.1	0.2	0.0	0.0	0.0	0.3	0.2	0.3	- Caraïbes
- Rest of America	0.0	0.0	0.0	0.0	0.0	0.0	0.0	0.0	0.0	0.0	- Autre d'Amérique
Asia excluding former USSR	35.3	45.3	42.1	46.6	54.3	48.2	54.9	57.4	51.7	43.8	Asie ancienne URSS exclus
- Middle East	15.8	24.6	23.2	26.6	31.9	24.4	31.0	36.4	27.4	21.7	- Moyen-Orient
Asia former USSR	0.5	0.1	0.0	0.0	0.1	0.2	0.1	0.1	0.1	0.1	Asie ancienne URSS
Europe excluding former USSR	42.6	32.6	39.1	38.0	28.1	31.8	27.6	22.9	28.3	35.0	Europe ancienne URSS exclus
- European Union	33.0	28.4	35.9	32.3	24.9	29.0	25.2	19.1	24.9	32.8	- Union Européenne
- Eastern Europe	8.5	2.7	1.7	3.9	2.4	1.6	1.7	3.0	2.5	1.1	- Europe de l'Est
- Rest of Europe	1.1	1.5	1.4	1.7	0.8	1.3	0.8	0.8	1.0	1.1	- Autre de l'Europe
Europe former USSR	6.9	2.7	3.0	3.1	2.3	1.4	2.0	3.5	2.1	1.7	Europe ancienne URSS
Oceania	0.1	0.1	0.7	0.1	0.0	0.1	0.3	0.0	0.2	0.0	Océanie

TRADE BY COMMODITY (Value in million US dollars)
Exports by principal countries or areas

COMMERCE PAR PRODUIT (Valeur en millions de dollars EU)
Exportations selon les principaux pays ou zones

Country or area	1998	1999	2000	2001	2002	Pays ou zone
World	2107.8	2364.5	2833.4	2389.5	2367.2	Monde
Africa	0.1	0.0	0.1	5.4	5.7	Afrique
Americas	298.3	279.6	369.3	405.4	230.3	Amériques
- Northern America	276.1	257.6	364.2	369.3	196.2	- Amérique du Nord
- LAIA	22.2	22.0	5.1	36.0	34.1	- ALAI
- CACM	0.0	0.0	0.0	0.0	0.0	- MCC
- Caribbean	0.0	0.0	0.0	0.0	0.0	- Caraïbes
Asia excluding former USSR	122.2	25.4	21.8	45.3	106.7	Asie ancienne URSS exclus
- Middle East	119.7	24.1	20.9	44.5	106.2	- Moyen-Orient
Asia former USSR	24.8	32.4	40.5	19.2	21.7	Asie ancienne URSS
Europe excluding former USSR	1198.2	1513.4	1883.4	1288.6	1163.0	Europe ancienne URSS exclus
- European Union	1172.3	1468.7	1835.1	1234.6	1097.1	- Union Européenne
- Eastern Europe	25.4	43.3	47.5	53.3	65.2	- Europe de l'Est
- Rest of Europe	0.6	1.4	0.8	0.6	0.7	- Autre de l'Europe
Europe former USSR	66.5	90.5	129.0	343.6	458.5	Europe ancienne URSS
Oceania	397.7	423.1	389.1	282.0	381.5	Océanie
France-Monaco	584.9	698.5	587.2	489.1	521.3	France-Monaco
Australia	393.4	423.1	387.2	282.0	381.5	Australie
Germany	141.1	291.7	696.8	363.0	249.5	Allemagne
Canada	199.2	172.9	241.5	253.8	123.2	Canada
United Kingdom	177.8	158.7	204.4	87.2	106.6	Royaume-Uni
Ukraine	39.7	80.2	82.5	211.8	233.5	Ukraine
Denmark	120.3	97.1	128.6	123.3	128.2	Danemark
United States	77.0	84.7	122.5	115.5	73.0	Etats-Unis d'Amérique
Russian Federation	24.5	6.7	44.6	121.4	214.3	Fédération de Russie
Turkey	117.2	21.2	20.1	16.2	58.9	Turquie
Sweden	35.1	47.3	78.8	37.5	13.3	Suède
Netherlands	22.5	23.4	26.2	42.1	25.9	Pays-Bas
Kazakhstan	24.8	32.4	40.5	19.2	e21.7	Kazakhstan
Spain	17.4	55.7	25.1	26.2	6.0	Espagne
Austria	11.7	44.7	28.1	12.4	10.0	Autriche
Argentina	21.7	16.3	5.0	27.3	e26.4	Argentine
Belgium	–	38.4	37.1	9.9	e11.1	Belgique
Romania	2.9	5.5	8.3	22.0	30.2	Roumanie
Iraq	e	e	e	e26.8	e39.0	Iraq
Ireland	18.9	2.5	14.9	19.9	6.0	Irlande
Hungary	14.2	10.1	9.6	13.2	13.6	Hongrie
Finland	15.0	8.1	4.2	19.9	10.4	Finlande
Bulgaria	0.9	2.1	15.7	e16.7	e18.7	Bulgarie
Czech Republic	2.5	13.1	11.6	0.9	1.9	République tchèque
Belgium-Luxembourg	27.0	–	–	–	–	Belgique-Luxembourg
Slovakia	4.4	12.3	2.2	0.6	0.7	Slovaquie
Republic of Moldova	0.8	2.9	0.9	6.4	6.6	République de Moldova
Brazil	0.0			7.3	e7.6	Brésil
Tunisia		0.0		5.1	e5.3	Tunisie
Lithuania	0.2	0.7	0.8	3.3	e4.0	Lituanie

(Value as percentages of World total) **(Valeur en pourcentage du total mondial)**

Regions of the world	1993	1994	1995	1996	1997	1998	1999	2000	2001	2002	Régions du monde
World	100.0	100.0	100.0	100.0	100.0	100.0	100.0	100.0	100.0	100.0	Monde
Africa	0.0	0.4	0.4	0.3	0.5	0.0	0.0	0.0	0.2	0.2	Afrique
Americas	21.8	22.3	17.8	21.0	23.1	14.2	11.8	13.0	17.0	9.7	Amériques
- Northern America	20.1	21.7	17.6	20.4	21.3	13.1	10.9	12.9	15.5	8.3	- Amérique du Nord
- LAIA	1.7	0.6	0.1	0.5	1.8	1.1	0.9	0.2	1.5	1.4	- ALAI
- CACM	0.0	0.0	0.0	0.0	0.0	0.0	0.0	0.0	0.0	0.0	- MCC
- Caribbean	0.0	0.0	0.0	0.0	0.0	0.0	0.0	0.0	0.0	0.0	- Caraïbes
Asia excluding former USSR	1.3	4.2	3.8	2.9	2.3	5.8	1.1	0.8	1.9	4.5	Asie ancienne URSS exclus
- Middle East	1.3	4.2	3.7	2.9	2.3	5.7	1.0	0.7	1.9	4.5	- Moyen-Orient
Asia former USSR	0.1	0.9	2.1	2.4	2.3	1.2	1.4	1.4	0.8	0.9	Asie ancienne URSS
Europe excluding former USSR	66.4	59.8	64.5	51.9	48.4	56.8	64.0	66.5	53.9	49.1	Europe ancienne URSS exclus
- European Union	65.6	59.2	63.2	51.0	46.9	55.6	62.1	64.8	51.7	46.3	- Union Européenne
- Eastern Europe	0.7	0.5	1.2	0.9	1.5	1.2	1.8	1.7	2.2	2.8	- Europe de l'Est
- Rest of Europe	0.1	0.1	0.1	0.0	0.0	0.0	0.1	0.0	0.0	0.0	- Autre de l'Europe
Europe former USSR	0.6	1.8	3.7	4.1	5.8	3.2	3.8	4.6	14.4	19.4	Europe ancienne URSS
Oceania	9.9	10.6	7.8	17.4	17.6	18.9	17.9	13.7	11.8	16.1	Océanie
Oceania	9.9	10.6	17.4	17.6	18.8	18.8	17.9	13.9			Océanie

044 Maize, unmilled

TRADE BY COMMODITY (Value in million US dollars)
Imports by principal countries or areas

COMMERCE PAR PRODUIT (Valeur en millions de dollars EU)
Importations selon les principaux pays ou zones

Country or area	1998	1999	2000	2001	2002	Pays ou zone
World	10398.7	9866.9	10259.5	10110.0	10736.1	Monde
Africa	1134.3	1173.3	1253.6	1137.6	1406.5	Afrique
Americas	2242.5	1994.7	2154.7	2195.2	2313.8	Amériques
- Northern America	325.0	292.7	344.6	465.2	576.1	- Amérique du Nord
- LAIA	1600.7	1390.4	1480.4	1356.7	1331.1	- ALAI
- CACM	152.7	170.2	177.1	204.2	220.2	- MCC
- Caribbean	130.8	107.2	116.3	133.7	143.9	- Caraïbes
- Rest of America	33.2	34.2	36.3	35.4	42.4	- Autre d'Amérique
Asia excluding former USSR	4784.0	4454.3	4789.3	4777.7	4841.8	Asie ancienne URSS exclus
- Middle East	586.0	594.6	711.6	717.3	654.9	- Moyen-Orient
Asia former USSR	2.0	3.0	6.0	3.4	4.4	Asie ancienne URSS
Europe excluding former USSR	2173.1	2110.8	1871.7	1929.5	2076.9	Europe ancienne URSS exclus
- European Union	2013.8	1964.1	1692.0	1650.6	1907.7	- Union Européenne
- Eastern Europe	93.3	69.2	106.7	168.0	88.4	- Europe de l'Est
- Rest of Europe	66.0	77.5	73.0	110.9	80.9	- Autre de l'Europe
Europe former USSR	58.1	124.3	180.3	61.8	86.3	Europe ancienne URSS
Oceania	4.8	6.4	3.9	4.8	6.4	Océanie
Japan	2118.6	1886.7	1885.8	1951.9	1995.1	Japon
Korea, Republic of	910.8	883.7	933.2	925.5	973.4	République de Corée
Mexico	624.1	648.6	608.1	703.2	644.3	Mexique
Egypt	388.1	652.5	e609.1	554.6	594.2	Egypte
Spain	422.6	423.4	469.8	366.7	477.7	Espagne
Netherlands	337.2	298.5	250.5	280.2	312.2	Pays-Bas
Malaysia	226.5	259.9	255.1	218.4	e238.7	Malaisie
Canada	157.5	117.9	170.2	319.4	428.8	Canada
Colombia	267.9	210.5	217.8	200.6	250.2	Colombie
United Kingdom	228.7	219.1	214.0	219.0	206.7	Royaume-Uni
Germany	266.6	245.4	176.7	181.8	183.9	Allemagne
Algeria	132.2	140.0	175.2	e212.0	e241.5	Algérie
Portugal	195.7	178.2	146.3	155.1	162.0	Portugal
Italy-San Marino-Holy See	166.3	252.2	131.9	104.9	157.7	Italie-Saint-Marin-Saint-Siège
United States	167.6	174.8	174.3	145.7	147.3	Etats-Unis d'Amérique
Saudi Arabia	168.3	142.4	170.8	146.7	e151.9	Arabie saoudite
Iran (Islamic Republic of)	112.2	138.0	146.6	224.7	138.6	Iran (République islamique d')
Chile	113.7	146.0	136.4	139.7	135.9	Chili
Brazil	231.2	98.4	202.0	67.6	36.0	Brésil
Venezuela	140.0	114.1	151.1	110.4	e92.8	Venezuela
Peru	144.4	118.4	96.9	97.8	109.8	Pérou
Indonesia	47.8	80.3	157.9	125.5	138.0	Indonésie
Turkey	97.5	98.2	146.9	65.6	133.8	Turquie
Morocco	94.7	88.7	108.1	116.8	e123.2	Maroc
France-Monaco	104.1	83.1	82.5	96.3	127.7	France-Monaco
Syrian Arab Republic	57.6	71.5	105.0	e130.9	93.9	République arabe syrienne
Israel	71.7	77.0	90.9	108.1	101.8	Israël
Greece	83.1	93.4	70.0	85.4	e94.4	Grèce
Tunisia	58.1	73.2	75.1	90.8	e90.8	Tunisie
Belgium	–	99.4	87.4	87.3	e95.8	Belgique

(Value as percentages of World total) **(Valeur en pourcentage du total mondial)**

Regions of the world	1993	1994	1995	1996	1997	1998	1999	2000	2001	2002	Régions du monde
World	100.0	100.0	100.0	100.0	100.0	100.0	100.0	100.0	100.0	100.0	Monde
Africa	7.7	8.5	7.6	7.0	9.4	10.9	11.9	12.2	11.3	13.1	Afrique
Americas	9.1	15.2	13.4	18.0	15.1	21.6	20.2	21.0	21.7	21.6	Amériques
- Northern America	1.5	1.9	1.6	2.0	2.3	3.1	3.0	3.4	4.6	5.4	- Amérique du Nord
- LAIA	5.7	11.0	9.3	12.7	9.5	15.4	14.1	14.4	13.4	12.4	- ALAI
- CACM	0.8	1.1	1.0	1.3	1.6	1.5	1.7	1.7	2.0	2.1	- MCC
- Caribbean	1.0	0.9	1.3	1.6	1.5	1.3	1.1	1.1	1.3	1.3	- Caraïbes
- Rest of America	0.2	0.2	0.2	0.3	0.2	0.3	0.3	0.4	0.4	0.4	- Autre d'Amérique
Asia excluding former USSR	49.8	49.2	55.3	54.1	54.0	46.0	45.1	46.7	47.3	45.1	Asie ancienne URSS exclus
- Middle East	5.9	4.0	5.4	5.9	6.5	5.6	6.0	6.9	7.1	6.1	- Moyen-Orient
Asia former USSR	0.3	0.1	0.0	0.1	0.0	0.0	0.0	0.1	0.0	0.0	Asie ancienne URSS
Europe excluding former USSR	23.7	26.2	22.8	20.2	20.4	20.9	21.4	18.2	19.1	19.3	Europe ancienne URSS exclus
- European Union	21.3	24.9	21.6	18.2	18.6	19.4	19.9	16.5	16.3	17.8	- Union Européenne
- Eastern Europe	1.9	0.5	0.6	1.3	1.1	0.9	0.7	1.0	1.7	0.8	- Europe de l'Est
- Rest of Europe	0.5	0.8	0.6	0.7	0.8	0.6	0.8	0.7	1.1	0.8	- Autre de l'Europe
Europe former USSR	9.3	0.8	0.7	0.7	1.0	0.6	1.3	1.8	0.6	0.8	Europe ancienne URSS
Oceania	0.1	0.1	0.1	0.0	0.0	0.0	0.1	0.0	0.0	0.1	Océanie

TRADE BY COMMODITY (Value in million US dollars)
Exports by principal countries or areas

COMMERCE PAR PRODUIT (Valeur en millions de dollars EU)
Exportations selon les principaux pays ou zones

Country or area	1998	1999	2000	2001	2002	Pays ou zone
World	9136.0	8746.6	8800.7	8908.6	10173.4	Monde
Africa	179.8	122.8	105.9	129.4	187.5	Afrique
Americas	6192.7	6184.2	5894.2	6412.4	6797.2	Amériques
- Northern America	4662.5	5223.9	4752.9	4790.4	5168.5	- Amérique du Nord
- LAIA	1519.9	944.3	1134.9	1616.3	1623.8	- ALAI
- CACM	9.6	15.9	6.2	5.0	4.4	- MCC
- Caribbean	0.5	0.1	0.1	0.4	0.4	- Caraïbes
- Rest of America	0.1	0.0	0.0	0.4	0.1	- Autre d'Amérique
Asia excluding former USSR	641.1	492.3	1098.4	743.0	1277.1	Asie ancienne URSS exclus
- Middle East	7.0	6.7	7.0	9.9	12.1	- Moyen-Orient
Asia former USSR	0.9	0.6	2.6	1.6	1.8	Asie ancienne URSS
Europe excluding former USSR	2041.7	1902.2	1660.9	1564.6	1839.7	Europe ancienne URSS exclus
- European Union	1677.5	1625.8	1454.6	1347.6	1539.9	- Union Européenne
- Eastern Europe	293.7	239.2	180.4	188.9	260.7	- Europe de l'Est
- Rest of Europe	70.5	37.2	25.9	28.2	39.1	- Autre de l'Europe
Europe former USSR	75.9	37.3	29.9	49.9	61.6	Europe ancienne URSS
Oceania	3.9	7.1	8.7	7.7	8.5	Océanie
United States	4619.0	5127.0	4713.9	4765.0	5127.6	Etats-Unis d'Amérique
France-Monaco	1408.0	1395.2	1224.8	1046.9	1260.7	France-Monaco
Argentina	1346.3	817.1	1015.6	988.9	e955.4	Argentine
China	531.7	450.0	1051.7	625.6	1167.3	Chine
Brazil	11.8	7.2	9.4	497.3	e515.6	Brésil
Hungary	204.1	176.8	138.0	163.9	210.4	Hongrie
Germany	95.3	93.0	86.6	109.6	108.8	Allemagne
Chile	84.3	61.9	66.6	65.3	e63.9	Chili
South Africa	–	–	72.3	81.3	135.2	Afrique du Sud
Canada	43.3	95.9	38.2	25.4	40.8	Canada
Southern African Customs Union	125.8	80.5	–	–	–	Union douanière d'Afrique australe
Austria	49.7	32.0	25.5	41.8	35.0	Autriche
Italy-San Marino-Holy See	33.3	21.4	38.8	51.1	39.1	Italie-Saint-Marin-Saint-Siège
Ukraine	52.3	23.8	17.1	41.4	45.6	Ukraine
Netherlands	27.5	34.3	32.4	38.7	31.9	Pays-Bas
Thailand	19.2	12.2	8.4	55.5	e58.6	Thaïlande
Serbia and Montenegro	49.3	28.3	21.1	e24.5	e18.3	Serbie-et-Monténégro
Paraguay	17.4	14.8	22.1	41.3	e45.1	Paraguay
Spain	33.3	19.7	18.1	32.8	32.5	Espagne
Romania	40.1	16.3	13.3	5.0	21.1	Roumanie
Indonesia	65.5	11.0	5.0	10.5	3.3	Indonésie
Slovakia	34.7	17.2	15.2	5.8	10.2	Slovaquie
Mexico	35.2	7.9	3.9	3.8	25.7	Mexique
Bulgaria	10.7	26.1	11.2	e11.9	e13.4	Bulgarie
Republic of Moldova	18.5	13.3	12.6	8.0	15.4	République de Moldova
Belgium	–	19.2	12.6	16.4	e18.4	Belgique
Zimbabwe	e22.9	21.5	8.6	0.6	8.1	Zimbabwe
Croatia	19.6	8.0	3.6	2.7	19.9	Croatie
Ecuador	4.8	12.3	10.9	12.4	8.8	Equateur
Myanmar	e6.1	e5.1	e11.5	e11.1	e12.1	Myanmar

(Value as percentages of World total) **(Valeur en pourcentage du total mondial)**

Regions of the world	1993	1994	1995	1996	1997	1998	1999	2000	2001	2002	Régions du monde
World	100.0	100.0	100.0	100.0	100.0	100.0	100.0	100.0	100.0	100.0	Monde
Africa	1.3	7.5	2.5	3.7	3.4	2.0	1.4	1.2	1.5	1.8	Afrique
Americas	58.8	55.6	76.8	79.0	69.0	67.8	70.7	67.0	72.0	66.8	Amériques
- Northern America	52.3	49.1	69.6	68.0	53.7	51.0	59.7	54.0	53.8	50.8	- Amérique du Nord
- LAIA	6.5	6.4	7.1	10.9	15.0	16.6	10.8	12.9	18.1	16.0	- ALAI
- CACM	0.0	0.0	0.1	0.1	0.3	0.1	0.2	0.1	0.1	0.0	- MCC
- Caribbean	0.0	0.0	0.0	0.0	0.0	0.0	0.0	0.0	0.0	0.0	- Caraïbes
- Rest of America	0.0	0.0	0.0	0.0	0.0	0.0	0.0	0.0	0.0	0.0	- Autre d'Amérique
Asia excluding former USSR	14.2	11.7	0.7	1.1	9.0	7.0	5.6	12.5	8.3	12.6	Asie ancienne URSS exclus
- Middle East	0.2	0.2	0.0	0.1	0.1	0.1	0.1	0.1	0.1	0.1	- Moyen-Orient
Asia former USSR	0.0	0.0	0.0	0.1	0.1	0.0	0.0	0.0	0.0	0.0	Asie ancienne URSS
Europe excluding former USSR	25.3	24.7	19.8	15.8	18.2	22.3	21.7	18.9	17.6	18.1	Europe ancienne URSS exclus
- European Union	23.2	22.8	17.7	15.1	16.4	18.4	18.6	16.5	15.1	15.1	- Union Européenne
- Eastern Europe	1.2	1.2	1.5	0.6	1.8	3.2	2.7	2.1	2.1	2.6	- Europe de l'Est
- Rest of Europe	0.9	0.8	0.6	0.2	0.0	0.8	0.4	0.3	0.3	0.4	- Autre de l'Europe
Europe former USSR	0.3	0.5	0.2	0.4	0.4	0.8	0.4	0.3	0.6	0.6	Europe ancienne URSS
Oceania	0.1	0.0	0.0	0.1	0.0	0.0	0.1	0.1	0.1	0.1	Océanie

045 Cereals, unmilled

TRADE BY COMMODITY (Value in million US dollars)
Imports by principal countries or areas

COMMERCE PAR PRODUIT (Valeur en millions de dollars EU)
Importations selon les principaux pays ou zones

Country or area	1998	1999	2000	2001	2002	Pays ou zone
World	1619.5	1637.3	1670.6	1680.2	1698.6	Monde
Africa	20.8	32.2	44.0	56.5	57.6	Afrique
Americas	670.3	738.0	813.3	893.4	873.3	Amériques
- Northern America	221.7	195.4	190.1	254.0	254.5	- Amérique du Nord
- LAIA	438.0	537.3	617.5	633.0	612.0	- ALAI
- CACM	3.1	2.4	2.8	2.9	2.4	- MCC
- Caribbean	6.7	2.4	2.1	2.9	3.7	- Caraïbes
- Rest of America	0.7	0.5	0.7	0.6	0.6	- Autre d'Amérique
Asia excluding former USSR	588.7	537.7	423.7	408.1	415.3	Asie ancienne URSS exclus
- Middle East	107.1	104.7	12.5	65.5	71.6	- Moyen-Orient
Asia former USSR	4.2	3.4	5.1	2.7	2.3	Asie ancienne URSS
Europe excluding former USSR	315.2	280.3	276.9	291.4	333.1	Europe ancienne URSS exclus
- European Union	281.6	253.4	226.4	229.5	295.0	- Union Européenne
- Eastern Europe	5.9	5.5	25.9	38.4	9.6	- Europe de l'Est
- Rest of Europe	27.8	21.4	24.6	23.4	28.5	- Autre de l'Europe
Europe former USSR	17.4	44.0	102.1	18.5	6.3	Europe ancienne URSS
Oceania	2.9	1.7	5.5	9.6	10.7	Océanie
Mexico	374.5	478.5	532.4	581.9	552.4	Mexique
Japan	416.1	335.3	315.3	298.8	287.7	Japon
United States	216.1	189.3	184.5	245.6	245.2	Etats-Unis d'Amérique
Spain	69.4	52.4	47.5	31.7	83.5	Espagne
United Arab Emirates	81.3	85.2	2.4	56.4	e57.8	Emirates arabes unis
Netherlands	54.2	41.0	27.4	43.9	60.4	Pays-Bas
Germany	31.4	31.4	33.0	37.4	30.1	Allemagne
Brazil	23.1	17.5	51.0	20.8	20.8	Brésil
Italy-San Marino-Holy See	24.8	29.6	30.5	23.1	22.9	Italie-Saint-Marin-Saint-Siège
Belgium	–	26.7	28.2	32.4	e35.5	Belgique
Korea, Republic of	8.6	25.8	43.6	9.6	19.9	République de Corée
Belarus	6.4	19.6	62.7	2.4	0.5	Bélarus
Israel	11.8	22.2	28.9	14.9	9.5	Israël
France-Monaco	14.9	13.3	12.9	17.0	13.0	France-Monaco
Poland	3.8	4.2	22.7	31.6	2.6	Pologne
Russian Federation	5.2	19.2	30.6	8.5	0.6	Fédération de Russie
China	24.6	31.4	0.3	0.5	6.8	Chine
Denmark	9.9	18.5	13.8	7.3	9.2	Danemark
Colombia	16.8	11.6	7.6	9.7	11.8	Colombie
Switzerland-Liechtenstein	11.4	8.5	11.5	10.4	14.1	Suisse-Liechtenstein
United Kingdom	11.4	10.5	10.6	10.7	12.2	Royaume-Uni
Turkey	21.6	14.5	3.8	0.3	2.6	Turquie
Portugal	10.7	8.5	5.5	7.1	8.1	Portugal
Chile	3.6	10.6	7.2	7.3	10.6	Chili
Austria	7.0	8.2	7.6	8.7	6.2	Autriche
Norway	9.8	7.2	6.4	6.2	7.3	Norvège
Finland	11.1	9.0	5.6	4.5	6.4	Finlande
Canada	5.2	5.6	5.5	8.3	9.2	Canada
Belgium-Luxembourg	31.5	–	–	–	–	Belgique-Luxembourg
Venezuela	5.1	6.6	7.6	6.6	e5.6	Venezuela

(Value as percentages of World total)

(Valeur en pourcentage du total mondial)

Regions of the world	1993	1994	1995	1996	1997	1998	1999	2000	2001	2002	Régions du monde
World	100.0	100.0	100.0	100.0	100.0	100.0	100.0	100.0	100.0	100.0	Monde
Africa	2.9	4.2	2.7	3.4	1.9	1.3	2.0	2.6	3.4	3.4	Afrique
Americas	38.5	41.3	29.3	28.0	39.0	41.4	45.1	48.7	53.2	51.4	Amériques
- Northern America	10.3	12.6	10.7	9.4	17.4	13.7	11.9	11.4	15.1	15.0	- Amérique du Nord
- LAIA	26.3	27.4	17.8	18.0	20.5	27.0	32.8	37.0	37.7	36.0	- ALAI
- CACM	0.2	0.4	0.2	0.3	0.8	0.2	0.1	0.2	0.2	0.1	- MCC
- Caribbean	0.4	0.3	0.3	0.3	0.3	0.4	0.1	0.1	0.2	0.2	- Caraïbes
- Rest of America	1.1	0.6	0.4	0.1	0.1	0.0	0.0	0.0	0.0	0.0	- Autre d'Amérique
Asia excluding former USSR	34.2	31.6	37.2	37.3	37.1	36.4	32.8	25.4	24.3	24.5	Asie ancienne URSS exclus
- Middle East	3.1	0.2	0.7	0.4	1.7	6.6	6.4	0.7	3.9	4.2	- Moyen-Orient
Asia former USSR	0.0	0.5	0.0	0.0	0.1	0.3	0.2	0.3	0.2	0.1	Asie ancienne URSS
Europe excluding former USSR	20.8	19.0	25.1	27.5	20.4	19.5	17.1	16.6	17.3	19.6	Europe ancienne URSS exclus
- European Union	16.5	17.1	23.1	23.1	17.6	17.4	15.5	13.5	13.7	17.4	- Union Européenne
- Eastern Europe	3.1	0.4	0.2	2.3	1.0	0.4	0.3	1.6	2.3	0.6	- Europe de l'Est
- Rest of Europe	1.2	1.5	1.9	2.1	1.8	1.7	1.3	1.5	1.4	1.7	- Autre de l'Europe
Europe former USSR	3.4	3.0	3.8	3.4	1.2	1.1	2.7	6.1	1.1	0.4	Europe ancienne URSS
Oceania	0.2	0.5	1.8	0.2	0.3	0.2	0.1	0.3	0.6	0.6	Océanie

Céréales non moulues, autres que le froment, le riz, l'orge et le maïs 045

TRADE BY COMMODITY (Value in million US dollars) | COMMERCE PAR PRODUIT (Valeur en millions de dollars EU)

Exports by principal countries or areas | **Exportations selon les principaux pays ou zones**

Country or area	1998	1999	2000	2001	2002	Pays ou zone
World	1407.9	1340.3	1407.1	1458.6	1452.2	Monde
Africa	16.1	12.2	22.5	26.9	28.2	Afrique
Americas	917.2	832.9	948.8	954.7	908.3	Amériques
- Northern America	776.5	767.3	872.0	896.5	854.6	- Amérique du Nord
- LAIA	140.2	65.3	76.4	57.7	53.1	- ALAI
- CACM	0.4	0.3	0.4	0.5	0.6	- MCC
- Caribbean	0.1	0.0	0.0	0.0	0.0	- Caraïbes
- Rest of America	0.0	0.0	0.0	0.0	0.0	- Autre d'Amérique
Asia excluding former USSR	48.3	49.3	43.5	48.9	48.2	Asie ancienne URSS exclus
- Middle East	4.2	10.7	2.8	1.5	1.0	- Moyen-Orient
Asia former USSR	3.0	1.7	3.5	1.1	1.2	Asie ancienne URSS
Europe excluding former USSR	352.1	376.3	352.3	361.6	377.1	Europe ancienne URSS exclus
- European Union	330.4	357.6	339.0	350.0	358.5	- Union Européenne
- Eastern Europe	21.0	18.1	12.8	10.7	18.0	- Europe de l'Est
- Rest of Europe	0.7	0.6	0.6	0.8	0.6	- Autre de l'Europe
Europe former USSR	18.8	32.5	12.5	40.9	51.1	Europe ancienne URSS
Oceania	52.4	35.4	24.1	24.6	38.2	Océanie
United States	594.8	600.3	673.5	673.6	637.1	Etats-Unis d'Amérique
Canada	181.7	167.0	198.1	222.9	217.4	Canada
Germany	105.7	142.1	153.1	135.4	114.7	Allemagne
Argentina	130.1	57.2	71.9	47.8	e46.2	Argentine
France-Monaco	65.5	57.3	46.3	42.8	46.9	France-Monaco
Sweden	64.9	46.8	44.4	36.8	54.5	Suède
Finland	31.3	24.4	27.6	63.4	63.1	Finlande
Australia	52.3	35.2	23.8	24.4	38.1	Australie
China	35.0	31.4	30.3	32.8	32.5	Chine
Ukraine	9.3	23.3	4.2	32.6	36.0	Ukraine
Denmark	10.3	33.1	15.8	17.3	18.8	Danemark
Netherlands	16.3	16.6	13.2	13.7	14.4	Pays-Bas
United Kingdom	9.7	5.4	13.1	13.4	16.1	Royaume-Uni
Hungary	16.7	12.5	5.2	6.6	10.8	Hongrie
Belgium	–	12.0	9.4	11.4	e12.8	Belgique
Ethiopia	2.0	2.0	3.4	18.1	12.0	Ethiopie
Spain	6.1	6.3	7.6	8.7	7.5	Espagne
Thailand	6.4	4.3	6.2	7.6	e8.0	Thaïlande
Sudan	4.3	e5.7	14.0	0.3	3.1	Soudan
Austria	3.8	8.3	3.7	3.5	4.5	Autriche
Russian Federation	6.7	3.2	5.2	3.5	4.1	Fédération de Russie
Mali	e5.1	e1.6	e0.8	e1.3	e7.2	Mali
India	1.6	1.1	2.6	5.3	4.8	Inde
Belgium-Luxembourg	13.5	–	–	–	–	Belgique-Luxembourg
Italy-San Marino-Holy See	1.4	2.9	2.2	2.3	3.1	Italie-Saint-Marin-Saint-Siège
Bolivia	1.9	2.7	1.8	2.5	e2.4	Bolivie
Kazakhstan	2.7	1.7	3.5	1.1	e1.2	Kazakhstan
Poland	1.7	3.2	1.8	1.6	1.7	Pologne
Lithuania	1.8	4.7	1.6	0.7	e0.9	Lituanie
Turkey	0.3	6.5	1.8	0.3	0.1	Turquie

(Value as percentages of World total) | **(Valeur en pourcentage du total mondial)**

Regions of the world	1993	1994	1995	1996	1997	1998	1999	2000	2001	2002	Régions du monde
World	100.0	100.0	100.0	100.0	100.0	100.0	100.0	100.0	100.0	100.0	Monde
Africa	3.2	1.2	2.4	1.1	0.3	1.1	0.9	1.6	1.8	1.9	Afrique
Americas	62.4	65.4	58.9	55.1	65.2	65.1	62.1	67.4	65.5	62.5	Amériques
- Northern America	55.1	59.2	56.0	49.6	59.7	55.2	57.2	62.0	61.5	58.8	- Amérique du Nord
- LAIA	7.2	5.9	2.7	5.4	5.4	10.0	4.9	5.4	4.0	3.7	- ALAI
- CACM	0.0	0.3	0.1	0.0	0.1	0.0	0.0	0.0	0.0	0.0	- MCC
- Caribbean	0.0	0.0	0.0	0.0	0.0	0.0	0.0	0.0	0.0	0.0	- Caraïbes
- Rest of America	0.0	0.0	0.0	0.0	0.0	0.0	0.0	0.0	0.0	0.0	- Autre d'Amérique
Asia excluding former USSR	5.0	5.4	3.2	3.1	7.3	3.4	3.7	3.1	3.3	3.3	Asie ancienne URSS exclus
- Middle East	0.1	0.1	0.1	0.1	2.9	0.3	0.8	0.2	0.1	0.1	- Moyen-Orient
Asia former USSR	0.1	0.2	0.5	0.5	0.1	0.2	0.1	0.2	0.1	0.1	Asie ancienne URSS
Europe excluding former USSR	26.2	22.0	31.4	30.7	22.9	25.0	28.1	25.0	24.8	26.0	Europe ancienne URSS exclus
- European Union	25.0	21.2	30.4	29.5	21.9	23.5	26.7	24.1	24.0	24.7	- Union Européenne
- Eastern Europe	1.1	0.7	0.9	1.2	1.0	1.5	1.3	0.9	0.7	1.2	- Europe de l'Est
- Rest of Europe	0.1	0.1	0.0	0.0	0.0	0.1	0.0	0.0	0.1	0.0	- Autre de l'Europe
Europe former USSR	0.5	1.8	1.8	1.8	0.9	1.3	2.4	0.9	2.8	3.5	Europe ancienne URSS
Oceania	2.7	4.0	1.8	7.6	3.2	3.7	2.6	1.7	1.7	2.6	Océanie

046 Meal and flour of wheat and flour of meslin

TRADE BY COMMODITY (Value in million US dollars)
Imports by principal countries or areas

COMMERCE PAR PRODUIT (Valeur en millions de dollars EU)
Importations selon les principaux pays ou zones

Country or area	1998	1999	2000	2001	2002	Pays ou zone
World	1976.1	1669.2	1674.3	1588.5	1650.1	Monde
Africa	645.3	470.9	463.9	572.4	577.3	Afrique
Americas	278.6	227.9	250.1	269.2	267.7	Amériques
- Northern America	53.3	56.2	60.3	65.0	83.5	- Amérique du Nord
- LAIA	121.0	79.6	96.0	94.0	75.6	- ALAI
- CACM	4.7	3.9	6.3	9.7	22.4	- MCC
- Caribbean	95.3	84.6	86.1	98.9	83.1	- Caraïbes
- Rest of America	4.3	3.6	1.4	1.6	3.1	- Autre d'Amérique
Asia excluding former USSR	369.8	392.7	413.6	283.9	286.7	Asie ancienne URSS exclus
- Middle East	106.8	97.7	134.8	53.2	41.0	- Moyen-Orient
Asia former USSR	145.4	91.1	75.3	53.6	56.8	Asie ancienne URSS
Europe excluding former USSR	420.1	411.9	366.7	353.2	408.8	Europe ancienne URSS exclus
- European Union	319.6	324.1	286.5	280.8	341.5	- Union Européenne
- Eastern Europe	66.4	55.6	58.9	52.7	46.8	- Europe de l'Est
- Rest of Europe	34.0	32.2	21.4	19.6	20.6	- Autre de l'Europe
Europe former USSR	94.4	56.3	86.0	36.9	31.1	Europe ancienne URSS
Oceania	22.5	18.5	18.7	19.3	21.7	Océanie
Libyan Arab Jamahiriya	175.3	e128.0	e114.9	e239.4	e240.1	Jamahiriya arabe libyenne
Netherlands	71.0	67.6	63.9	57.3	75.3	Pays-Bas
France-Monaco	71.8	60.1	59.1	62.1	63.1	France-Monaco
China, Hong Kong SAR	63.5	63.4	58.9	57.1	57.2	Chine - RAS de Hong-Kong
Indonesia	4.9	67.7	81.4	48.5	69.3	Indonésie
United States	44.8	44.5	49.8	56.5	73.7	Etats-Unis d'Amérique
Angola	e39.7	e52.3	e74.1	e39.3	e58.2	Angola
Yemen	81.2	e75.0	e87.0	e	e	Yémen
Brazil	79.8	46.5	46.2	40.1	22.1	Brésil
Cuba	e26.7	27.9	44.3	51.0	e43.9	Cuba
Sudan	42.3	e26.6	31.2	40.1	22.5	Soudan
Denmark	32.0	39.9	28.1	28.2	32.8	Danemark
Belgium	–	42.9	37.4	35.4	e38.8	Belgique
Russian Federation	59.9	24.7	25.6	18.7	13.4	Fédération de Russie
Singapore	26.5	39.0	28.4	22.8	22.5	Singapour
Albania	39.4	39.5	21.1	19.1	19.9	Albanie
Ireland	25.5	28.4	23.2	22.9	33.3	Irlande
Viet Nam	62.0	31.6	11.7	12.1	14.7	Viet Nam
United Kingdom	23.7	27.5	29.8	20.9	28.9	Royaume-Uni
Bolivia	14.9	12.0	28.5	36.1	e37.4	Bolivie
Algeria	112.5	8.4	1.6	e2.0	e2.2	Algérie
Haiti	e36.8	e23.9	e17.8	e18.4	e16.6	Haïti
Uzbekistan	e22.8	e29.3	e28.1	e15.4	e16.1	Ouzbékistan
Germany	28.5	23.2	14.0	18.0	22.6	Allemagne
Georgia	e32.6	14.9	20.4	14.8	e18.6	Géorgie
Chad	e17.1	e24.6	e17.5	e13.9	e22.0	Tchad
Democratic Republic of the Congo	e11.5	e25.4	e18.8	e19.0	e16.9	République démocratique du Congo
Mauritania	e24.4	e15.4	e18.7	e14.8	e11.4	Mauritanie
Belarus	21.9	20.8	27.2	6.7	6.1	Bélarus
Somalia	e9.9	e11.0	e19.0	e16.6	e25.9	Somalie

(Value as percentages of World total) **(Valeur en pourcentage du total mondial)**

Regions of the world	1993	1994	1995	1996	1997	1998	1999	2000	2001	2002	Régions du monde
World	100.0	100.0	100.0	100.0	100.0	100.0	100.0	100.0	100.0	100.0	Monde
Africa	41.2	39.0	35.9	32.6	35.9	32.7	28.2	27.7	36.0	35.0	Afrique
Americas	9.9	10.3	8.3	11.1	13.6	14.1	13.7	14.9	16.9	16.2	Amériques
- Northern America	1.6	2.8	2.2	2.1	2.1	2.7	3.4	3.6	4.1	5.1	- Amérique du Nord
- LAIA	2.7	3.2	2.1	4.3	6.8	6.1	4.8	5.7	5.9	4.6	- ALAI
- CACM	0.1	0.2	0.1	0.1	0.1	0.2	0.2	0.4	0.6	1.4	- MCC
- Caribbean	5.2	3.9	3.7	4.6	4.4	4.8	5.1	5.1	6.2	5.0	- Caraïbes
- Rest of America	0.3	0.3	0.2	0.1	0.2	0.2	0.2	0.1	0.1	0.2	- Autre d'Amérique
Asia excluding former USSR	23.0	16.2	19.8	18.9	15.9	18.7	23.5	24.7	17.9	17.4	Asie ancienne URSS exclus
- Middle East	11.2	5.5	6.2	5.0	2.7	5.4	5.9	8.1	3.3	2.5	- Moyen-Orient
Asia former USSR	5.1	6.1	8.0	10.6	9.5	7.4	5.5	4.5	3.4	3.4	Asie ancienne URSS
Europe excluding former USSR	18.1	18.4	17.4	16.7	17.6	21.3	24.7	21.9	22.2	24.8	Europe ancienne URSS exclus
- European Union	13.6	14.2	11.9	11.9	12.9	16.2	19.4	17.1	17.7	20.7	- Union Européenne
- Eastern Europe	3.1	3.3	3.6	3.2	2.8	3.4	3.3	3.5	3.3	2.8	- Europe de l'Est
- Rest of Europe	1.4	0.9	1.9	1.6	1.8	1.7	1.9	1.3	1.2	1.2	- Autre de l'Europe
Europe former USSR	1.9	9.3	9.6	9.2	6.3	4.8	3.4	5.1	2.3	1.9	Europe ancienne URSS
Oceania	0.8	0.7	0.9	0.9	1.1	1.1	1.1	1.1	1.2	1.3	Océanie

TRADE BY COMMODITY (Value in million US dollars)
Exports by principal countries or areas

COMMERCE PAR PRODUIT (Valeur en millions de dollars EU)
Exportations selon les principaux pays ou zones

Country or area	1998	1999	2000	2001	2002	Pays ou zone
World	2195.2	1850.0	1784.2	1773.4	1890.9	Monde
Africa	111.3	79.7	85.6	97.2	98.5	Afrique
Americas	338.4	319.6	289.8	293.4	342.3	Amériques
- Northern America	181.8	219.1	194.1	181.0	229.7	- Amérique du Nord
- LAIA	122.9	83.6	77.3	84.1	80.8	- ALAI
- CACM	2.7	2.9	4.6	8.4	19.0	- MCC
- Caribbean	30.9	14.1	13.8	19.9	12.8	- Caraïbes
- Rest of America	0.0	0.0	0.0	0.0	0.0	- Autre d'Amérique
Asia excluding former USSR	380.5	316.7	376.2	403.4	455.7	Asie ancienne URSS exclus
- Middle East	175.1	122.5	148.7	116.4	126.7	- Moyen-Orient
Asia former USSR	63.2	47.8	49.6	29.4	32.7	Asie ancienne URSS
Europe excluding former USSR	1205.7	1000.1	897.7	862.1	889.4	Europe ancienne URSS exclus
- European Union	1154.8	963.5	854.6	829.4	865.3	- Union Européenne
- Eastern Europe	28.5	28.4	40.5	30.4	22.1	- Europe de l'Est
- Rest of Europe	22.4	8.2	2.7	2.3	2.0	- Autre de l'Europe
Europe former USSR	44.1	33.3	39.2	36.7	21.0	Europe ancienne URSS
Oceania	52.1	52.7	46.1	51.3	51.3	Océanie
France-Monaco	303.9	230.4	221.4	168.3	207.7	France-Monaco
Germany	159.9	152.5	134.6	146.3	135.0	Allemagne
Italy-San Marino-Holy See	209.0	147.3	118.4	122.8	124.9	Italie-Saint-Marin-Saint-Siège
United States	129.4	166.0	137.9	121.7	150.5	Etats-Unis d'Amérique
Belgium	–	194.5	160.1	158.6	e177.9	Belgique
Netherlands	96.2	81.7	91.2	87.0	79.1	Pays-Bas
Japan	76.3	85.6	82.6	85.3	84.5	Japon
Argentina	101.1	73.5	66.5	68.7	e66.3	Argentine
Spain	92.6	63.6	49.6	69.4	59.9	Espagne
Turkey	99.1	48.1	69.2	34.1	51.8	Turquie
Canada	52.4	53.1	56.3	59.3	79.1	Canada
China	73.9	45.6	45.3	58.5	61.8	Chine
Australia	49.5	49.8	43.8	48.9	48.6	Australie
United Arab Emirates	52.7	54.4	40.0	42.9	e44.7	Emirates arabes unis
Kazakhstan	56.4	41.9	42.1	26.6	e30.0	Kazakhstan
Belgium-Luxembourg	186.4	–	–	–	–	Belgique-Luxembourg
United Kingdom	34.0	31.6	25.9	30.5	36.6	Royaume-Uni
India	1.3	0.3	33.7	40.8	63.4	Inde
Malaysia	20.6	24.3	26.3	26.4	e28.0	Malaisie
Oman	18.6	12.9	29.5	29.8	29.6	Oman
Russian Federation	14.7	19.0	31.2	31.5	16.9	Fédération de Russie
Tunisia	20.3	16.9	27.4	20.0	e20.9	Tunisie
Pakistan	0.0	0.0	5.4	41.6	57.4	Pakistan
Hungary	22.0	18.8	26.4	19.5	12.9	Hongrie
Morocco	17.3	9.5	13.4	28.1	e30.6	Maroc
Greece	19.9	15.0	14.1	14.0	e14.0	Grèce
South Africa	–	–	17.6	15.9	19.3	Afrique du Sud
Denmark	14.3	14.3	12.4	5.3	3.5	Danemark
Singapore	13.8	8.6	7.8	9.0	10.4	Singapour
China, Hong Kong SAR	8.7	9.2	10.2	10.0	9.0	Chine - RAS de Hong-Kong

(Value as percentages of World total) **(Valeur en pourcentage du total mondial)**

Regions of the world	1993	1994	1995	1996	1997	1998	1999	2000	2001	2002	Régions du monde
World	100.0	100.0	100.0	100.0	100.0	100.0	100.0	100.0	100.0	100.0	Monde
Africa	3.0	1.9	3.4	3.1	4.2	5.1	4.3	4.8	5.5	5.2	Afrique
Americas	15.7	17.0	13.8	10.6	12.4	15.4	17.3	16.2	16.5	18.1	Amériques
- Northern America	12.5	12.9	10.7	6.4	6.6	8.3	11.8	10.9	10.2	12.1	- Amérique du Nord
- LAIA	2.1	3.1	2.4	3.8	5.2	5.6	4.5	4.3	4.7	4.3	- ALAI
- CACM	0.0	0.0	0.0	0.0	0.0	0.1	0.2	0.3	0.5	1.0	- MCC
- Caribbean	1.0	0.9	0.7	0.3	0.5	1.4	0.8	0.8	1.1	0.7	- Caraïbes
- Rest of America	0.0	0.0	0.0	0.0	0.0	0.0	0.0	0.0	0.0	0.0	- Autre d'Amérique
Asia excluding former USSR	13.3	13.1	16.7	21.7	22.0	17.3	17.1	21.1	22.7	24.1	Asie ancienne URSS exclus
- Middle East	5.1	5.4	6.0	7.7	11.9	8.0	6.6	8.3	6.6	6.7	- Moyen-Orient
Asia former USSR	0.0	0.3	1.3	2.2	2.6	2.9	2.6	2.8	1.7	1.7	Asie ancienne URSS
Europe excluding former USSR	66.7	61.2	54.9	53.1	53.3	54.9	54.1	50.3	48.6	47.0	Europe ancienne URSS exclus
- European Union	65.4	58.5	49.9	51.1	51.1	52.6	52.1	47.9	46.8	45.8	- Union Européenne
- Eastern Europe	0.8	0.7	4.0	1.8	2.0	1.3	1.5	2.3	1.7	1.2	- Europe de l'Est
- Rest of Europe	0.6	1.9	0.9	0.3	0.2	1.0	0.4	0.1	0.1	0.1	- Autre de l'Europe
Europe former USSR	0.3	5.6	9.2	8.1	3.9	2.0	1.8	2.2	2.1	1.1	Europe ancienne URSS
Oceania	1.0	0.9	0.7	1.2	1.5	2.4	2.8	2.6	2.9	2.7	Océanie

047 Other cereal meals and flour

TRADE BY COMMODITY (Value in million US dollars)
Imports by principal countries or areas

COMMERCE PAR PRODUIT (Valeur en millions de dollars EU)
Importations selon les principaux pays ou zones

Country or area	1998	1999	2000	2001	2002	Pays ou zone
World	468.5	474.9	466.1	517.3	530.4	Monde
Africa	77.9	78.3	98.2	116.9	146.8	Afrique
Americas	126.0	120.6	125.4	125.9	137.2	Amériques
- Northern America	57.2	55.2	51.2	62.8	75.3	- Amérique du Nord
- LAIA	33.2	28.0	26.2	20.8	21.6	- ALAI
- CACM	17.0	20.0	27.4	27.4	26.3	- MCC
- Caribbean	17.3	15.9	19.3	13.5	12.7	- Caraïbes
- Rest of America	1.3	1.5	1.2	1.3	1.3	- Autre d'Amérique
Asia excluding former USSR	89.7	103.8	105.6	114.9	104.1	Asie ancienne URSS exclus
- Middle East	13.4	12.8	19.5	24.9	26.4	- Moyen-Orient
Asia former USSR	6.5	3.9	6.8	7.3	6.9	Asie ancienne URSS
Europe excluding former USSR	130.8	129.9	106.7	108.2	116.4	Europe ancienne URSS exclus
- European Union	112.1	109.9	88.9	87.0	94.4	- Union Européenne
- Eastern Europe	8.7	8.2	9.4	11.9	12.7	- Europe de l'Est
- Rest of Europe	10.0	11.8	8.4	9.3	9.3	- Autre de l'Europe
Europe former USSR	32.0	32.4	16.2	37.4	11.0	Europe ancienne URSS
Oceania	5.5	6.0	7.2	6.8	8.1	Océanie
United States	24.1	24.5	23.2	35.3	50.9	Etats-Unis d'Amérique
Canada	32.9	30.5	27.6	27.2	24.0	Canada
Angola	e11.7	e25.0	e31.0	e24.4	e31.4	Angola
Israel	18.1	18.2	20.7	23.2	23.6	Israël
Mexico	17.3	18.0	16.6	13.4	16.8	Mexique
France-Monaco	21.3	15.9	14.5	12.0	11.8	France-Monaco
Netherlands	15.0	21.8	14.6	11.5	12.5	Pays-Bas
United Kingdom	13.5	19.0	15.5	13.1	13.2	Royaume-Uni
Malaysia	12.0	11.5	13.9	14.3	e15.7	Malaisie
China, Hong Kong SAR	13.0	11.2	12.2	13.6	13.4	Chine - RAS de Hong-Kong
Russian Federation	19.9	23.2	6.1	7.4	5.5	Fédération de Russie
Belarus	8.4	6.8	7.4	28.5	3.3	Bélarus
Germany	13.7	9.4	8.8	10.5	11.6	Allemagne
United Arab Emirates	3.4	3.6	7.0	16.4	e16.8	Emirates arabes unis
Spain	7.4	8.8	8.1	10.1	12.6	Espagne
Honduras	5.0	8.5	11.3	10.4	8.9	Honduras
India	11.3	16.5	9.0	5.2	0.1	Inde
Denmark	12.2	7.3	4.7	7.2	6.6	Danemark
United Republic of Tanzania	9.4	8.2	2.7	8.9	e8.6	République-Unie de Tanzanie
Lesotho	–	–	e13.0	10.7	e13.9	Lesotho
Belgium	–	8.7	7.3	7.3	e8.0	Belgique
China	4.6	10.0	4.7	9.7	1.7	Chine
Nicaragua	6.0	5.6	7.3	6.6	4.8	Nicaragua
Singapore	7.0	6.5	6.3	5.2	4.9	Singapour
Poland	4.8	4.9	4.4	7.1	8.5	Pologne
Zimbabwe	e0.0	0.0	e0.0	0.0	25.6	Zimbabwe
Democratic Republic of the Congo	e4.2	e5.9	e3.7	e5.9	e5.0	République démocratique du Congo
Egypt	4.2	3.3	e5.9	5.4	3.9	Egypte
Indonesia	2.4	5.3	5.9	4.1	4.0	Indonésie
Saudi Arabia	2.9	3.9	5.1	3.8	e3.9	Arabie saoudite

(Value as percentages of World total) **(Valeur en pourcentage du total mondial)**

Regions of the world	1993	1994	1995	1996	1997	1998	1999	2000	2001	2002	Régions du monde
World	100.0	100.0	100.0	100.0	100.0	100.0	100.0	100.0	100.0	100.0	Monde
Africa	19.3	22.5	17.8	16.3	17.8	16.6	16.5	21.1	22.6	27.7	Afrique
Americas	24.5	25.7	20.3	23.5	25.9	26.9	25.4	26.9	24.3	25.9	Amériques
- Northern America	10.9	10.2	9.4	11.3	12.1	12.2	11.6	11.0	12.1	14.2	- Amérique du Nord
- LAIA	8.8	8.5	5.9	7.1	6.8	7.1	5.9	5.6	4.0	4.1	- ALAI
- CACM	1.7	4.3	2.6	3.2	3.2	3.6	4.2	5.9	5.3	5.0	- MCC
- Caribbean	2.8	2.5	1.9	1.9	3.6	3.7	3.3	4.1	2.6	2.4	- Caraïbes
- Rest of America	0.2	0.2	0.4	0.2	0.3	0.3	0.3	0.3	0.3	0.2	- Autre d'Amérique
Asia excluding former USSR	19.8	15.1	19.7	19.2	20.3	19.2	21.8	22.6	22.2	19.6	Asie ancienne URSS exclus
- Middle East	4.6	2.4	3.2	1.8	1.9	2.9	2.7	4.2	4.8	5.0	- Moyen-Orient
Asia former USSR	0.0	0.7	0.8	1.8	1.1	1.4	0.8	1.5	1.4	1.3	Asie ancienne URSS
Europe excluding former USSR	29.2	26.6	28.1	28.5	26.8	27.9	27.4	22.9	20.9	22.0	Europe ancienne URSS exclus
- European Union	25.7	23.0	24.6	24.4	23.5	23.9	23.1	19.1	16.8	17.8	- Union Européenne
- Eastern Europe	1.2	1.3	1.4	1.8	1.5	1.9	1.7	2.0	2.3	2.4	- Europe de l'Est
- Rest of Europe	2.2	2.3	2.1	2.4	1.9	2.1	2.5	1.8	1.8	1.8	- Autre de l'Europe
Europe former USSR	6.1	8.1	10.8	9.4	6.7	6.8	6.8	3.5	7.2	2.1	Europe ancienne URSS
Oceania	1.0	1.3	2.5	1.2	1.5	1.2	1.3	1.5	1.3	1.5	Océanie

TRADE BY COMMODITY (Value in million US dollars)
Exports by principal countries or areas

COMMERCE PAR PRODUIT (Valeur en millions de dollars EU)
Exportations selon les principaux pays ou zones

Country or area	1998	1999	2000	2001	2002	Pays ou zone
World	480.2	450.1	426.8	468.0	527.0	Monde
Africa	49.4	47.1	24.4	29.8	44.5	Afrique
Americas	172.8	176.9	177.9	182.1	217.2	Amériques
- Northern America	136.2	142.9	135.9	139.0	176.3	- Amérique du Nord
- LAIA	24.5	20.5	22.0	18.6	21.5	- ALAI
- CACM	11.6	12.8	19.0	23.4	18.4	- MCC
- Caribbean	0.5	0.7	1.0	0.9	1.0	- Caraïbes
- Rest of America	0.0	0.1	0.0	0.0	0.0	- Autre d'Amérique
Asia excluding former USSR	64.4	65.2	74.8	76.2	74.7	Asie ancienne URSS exclus
- Middle East	1.6	1.6	3.2	4.0	4.4	- Moyen-Orient
Asia former USSR	0.0	0.0	1.1	1.0	1.2	Asie ancienne URSS
Europe excluding former USSR	146.4	135.9	129.7	156.5	171.7	Europe ancienne URSS exclus
- European Union	137.1	125.4	118.3	144.9	160.6	- Union Européenne
- Eastern Europe	7.0	7.5	8.1	8.1	8.3	- Europe de l'Est
- Rest of Europe	2.2	3.0	3.3	3.5	2.8	- Autre de l'Europe
Europe former USSR	37.2	13.4	10.6	12.5	9.1	Europe ancienne URSS
Oceania	9.9	11.6	8.2	9.8	8.6	Océanie
United States	113.9	117.9	115.4	109.1	132.0	Etats-Unis d'Amérique
France-Monaco	48.7	44.0	40.9	47.0	54.7	France-Monaco
Thailand	41.7	41.9	46.0	42.4	e44.7	Thaïlande
Italy-San Marino-Holy See	31.0	34.4	36.9	48.2	48.0	Italie-Saint-Marin-Saint-Siège
Canada	22.3	25.0	19.6	30.0	44.3	Canada
Germany	17.4	15.8	13.8	16.2	17.0	Allemagne
Southern African Customs Union	34.4	30.7	–	–	–	Union douanière d'Afrique australe
South Africa	–	–	10.6	10.5	27.5	Afrique du Sud
Ukraine	25.3	9.9	3.4	4.6	5.1	Ukraine
Venezuela	15.4	8.7	8.2	6.9	e7.4	Venezuela
United Kingdom	8.7	7.8	6.9	6.6	10.4	Royaume-Uni
Belgium	–	8.4	8.7	9.7	e10.9	Belgique
Australia	7.8	9.1	6.3	7.4	6.8	Australie
Netherlands	12.3	5.6	2.9	7.2	8.8	Pays-Bas
El Salvador	3.6	5.7	9.3	9.1	7.0	El Salvador
Hungary	5.5	5.5	6.5	7.1	7.5	Hongrie
China	4.4	6.3	5.6	5.3	5.8	Chine
Guatemala	4.0	2.9	4.3	9.4	6.2	Guatemala
Tunisia	10.3	6.7	3.8	1.6	e1.7	Tunisie
Spain	5.0	4.0	3.3	4.5	5.4	Espagne
Argentina	2.9	4.0	4.9	4.5	e4.4	Argentine
Singapore	5.2	4.7	5.2	3.9	1.1	Singapour
Costa Rica	3.5	3.4	4.4	4.3	4.2	Costa Rica
Russian Federation	2.1	1.7	6.2	5.8	3.5	Fédération de Russie
China, Hong Kong SAR	2.8	2.5	2.8	7.0	4.1	Chine - RAS de Hong-Kong
Mexico	1.5	2.7	2.8	2.8	4.0	Mexique
Uganda	2.1	0.9	1.2	5.0	4.6	Ouganda
Lesotho	–	–	e3.5	4.4	e5.8	Lesotho
Indonesia	2.5	1.8	2.7	3.0	3.2	Indonésie
Belarus	8.7	0.9	0.5	1.4	0.1	Bélarus

(Value as percentages of World total) **(Valeur en pourcentage du total mondial)**

Regions of the world	1993	1994	1995	1996	1997	1998	1999	2000	2001	2002	Régions du monde
World	100.0	100.0	100.0	100.0	100.0	100.0	100.0	100.0	100.0	100.0	Monde
Africa	1.5	7.1	8.7	9.4	7.9	10.3	10.5	5.7	6.4	8.5	Afrique
Americas	36.8	36.9	30.3	28.3	32.6	36.0	39.3	41.7	38.9	41.2	Amériques
- Northern America	25.4	25.3	23.8	23.7	28.4	28.4	31.7	31.8	29.7	33.5	- Amérique du Nord
- LAIA	10.5	10.4	4.8	1.8	1.5	5.1	4.6	5.2	4.0	4.1	- ALAI
- CACM	0.6	0.7	1.3	2.5	2.3	2.4	2.8	4.5	5.0	3.5	- MCC
- Caribbean	0.2	0.6	0.4	0.3	0.3	0.1	0.1	0.2	0.2	0.2	- Caraïbes
- Rest of America	0.0	0.0	0.0	0.0	0.0	0.0	0.0	0.0	0.0	0.0	- Autre d'Amérique
Asia excluding former USSR	18.9	17.8	14.1	18.0	18.1	13.4	14.5	17.5	16.3	14.2	Asie ancienne URSS exclus
- Middle East	0.2	0.2	0.3	0.6	0.5	0.3	0.4	0.7	0.9	0.8	- Moyen-Orient
Asia former USSR	0.1	0.4	0.1	0.1	0.0	0.0	0.0	0.3	0.2	0.2	Asie ancienne URSS
Europe excluding former USSR	40.8	32.2	36.2	34.4	34.0	30.5	30.2	30.4	33.4	32.6	Europe ancienne URSS exclus
- European Union	40.0	31.2	34.2	32.4	32.4	28.6	27.9	27.7	31.0	30.5	- Union Européenne
- Eastern Europe	0.4	0.4	1.3	1.6	1.3	1.5	1.7	1.9	1.7	1.6	- Europe de l'Est
- Rest of Europe	0.4	0.6	0.7	0.3	0.3	0.5	0.7	0.8	0.8	0.5	- Autre de l'Europe
Europe former USSR	0.9	4.3	8.4	7.5	5.3	7.8	3.0	2.5	2.7	1.7	Europe ancienne URSS
Oceania	0.9	1.3	2.2	2.2	2.1	2.1	2.6	1.9	2.1	1.6	Océanie

048 Cereal, flour or starch preparations of fruits or vegetables

TRADE BY COMMODITY (Value in million US dollars)
Imports by principal countries or areas

COMMERCE PAR PRODUIT (Valeur en millions de dollars EU)
Importations selon les principaux pays ou zones

Country or area	1998	1999	2000	2001	2002	Pays ou zone
World	17513.3	17965.7	17636.2	19289.4	21168.1	Monde
Africa	477.2	492.3	506.2	578.7	624.1	Afrique
Americas	3928.3	4118.0	4357.7	4889.8	5372.4	Amériques
- Northern America	2414.3	2668.8	2868.6	3099.5	3500.6	- Amérique du Nord
- LAIA	1031.2	972.5	988.4	1228.7	1299.9	- ALAI
- CACM	201.5	210.0	230.9	257.0	276.1	- MCC
- Caribbean	225.8	207.5	201.9	241.1	225.8	- Caraïbes
- Rest of America	55.4	59.2	68.0	63.5	70.0	- Autre d'Amérique
Asia excluding former USSR	2948.2	3040.5	3268.4	3507.1	3740.1	Asie ancienne URSS exclus
- Middle East	539.0	589.3	650.9	677.1	711.2	- Moyen-Orient
Asia former USSR	61.4	66.4	69.0	65.6	69.5	Asie ancienne URSS
Europe excluding former USSR	9311.4	9668.2	8775.3	9474.3	10554.4	Europe ancienne URSS exclus
- European Union	8296.0	8568.5	7778.1	8397.6	9314.0	- Union Européenne
- Eastern Europe	399.1	449.0	393.2	439.7	501.6	- Europe de l'Est
- Rest of Europe	616.4	650.7	604.0	637.0	738.8	- Autre de l'Europe
Europe former USSR	480.7	259.1	303.4	437.1	445.3	Europe ancienne URSS
Oceania	306.1	321.4	356.1	336.7	362.5	Océanie
United States	1617.9	1813.2	1958.5	2117.9	2445.4	Etats-Unis d'Amérique
France-Monaco	1530.3	1542.0	1452.2	1436.1	1626.6	France-Monaco
Germany	1648.2	1570.2	1244.0	1515.8	1579.2	Allemagne
United Kingdom	1274.7	1275.0	1226.8	1309.8	1446.9	Royaume-Uni
Japan	937.7	906.3	918.6	980.4	1009.9	Japon
Canada	778.5	835.4	902.6	973.3	1044.3	Canada
Belgium	–	794.5	707.3	831.4	e911.8	Belgique
Netherlands	464.4	605.8	556.5	534.8	672.5	Pays-Bas
Italy-San Marino-Holy See	469.2	527.6	478.2	486.3	567.0	Italie-Saint-Marin-Saint-Siège
Spain	405.0	436.2	411.8	493.1	554.1	Espagne
Mexico	275.5	329.4	407.1	546.3	685.4	Mexique
Austria	356.8	359.3	333.9	373.0	406.8	Autriche
Ireland	331.9	346.2	350.5	377.8	385.1	Irlande
China, Hong Kong SAR	262.5	271.7	273.0	275.9	308.0	Chine - RAS de Hong-Kong
Sweden	252.8	254.8	227.6	254.4	287.3	Suède
Russian Federation	363.9	162.3	197.2	255.8	284.2	Fédération de Russie
Brazil	330.6	211.3	221.4	242.8	235.6	Brésil
Switzerland-Liechtenstein	231.0	238.3	225.5	236.1	271.2	Suisse-Liechtenstein
Saudi Arabia	178.4	194.1	230.8	267.6	e276.9	Arabie saoudite
Denmark	235.8	229.0	209.4	212.3	249.8	Danemark
Portugal	178.7	215.7	219.3	215.9	244.7	Portugal
Malaysia	163.6	182.4	192.1	249.7	e272.9	Malaisie
Norway	170.1	176.6	164.1	175.2	210.4	Norvège
Australia	149.1	160.6	191.8	175.4	187.0	Australie
Singapore	146.4	166.9	175.8	174.1	174.7	Singapour
Greece	183.3	190.9	151.4	145.6	e161.0	Grèce
Belgium-Luxembourg	811.6	–	–	–	–	Belgique-Luxembourg
Finland	153.3	157.3	149.1	150.5	156.6	Finlande
Thailand	132.3	127.8	145.1	168.4	e175.4	Thaïlande
Venezuela	109.1	179.7	114.1	153.1	e128.8	Venezuela

(Value as percentages of World total) **(Valeur en pourcentage du total mondial)**

Regions of the world	1993	1994	1995	1996	1997	1998	1999	2000	2001	2002	Régions du monde
World	100.0	100.0	100.0	100.0	100.0	100.0	100.0	100.0	100.0	100.0	Monde
Africa	2.8	2.8	2.7	2.6	2.6	2.7	2.7	2.9	3.0	2.9	Afrique
Americas	23.8	24.1	23.5	20.6	20.9	22.4	22.9	24.7	25.3	25.4	Amériques
- Northern America	10.8	11.4	10.6	11.2	12.8	13.8	14.9	16.3	16.1	16.5	- Amérique du Nord
- LAIA	10.8	10.6	10.7	7.3	5.6	5.9	5.4	5.6	6.4	6.1	- ALAI
- CACM	0.6	0.7	0.8	0.8	1.0	1.2	1.2	1.3	1.3	1.3	- MCC
- Caribbean	1.2	1.1	1.2	1.0	1.2	1.3	1.2	1.1	1.3	1.1	- Caraïbes
- Rest of America	0.3	0.3	0.3	0.3	0.3	0.3	0.3	0.4	0.3	0.3	- Autre d'Amérique
Asia excluding former USSR	18.3	17.6	17.8	19.3	19.4	16.8	16.9	18.5	18.2	17.7	Asie ancienne URSS exclus
- Middle East	2.7	2.1	2.3	2.1	2.6	3.1	3.3	3.7	3.5	3.4	- Moyen-Orient
Asia former USSR	0.3	0.3	1.0	0.8	0.4	0.4	0.4	0.4	0.3	0.3	Asie ancienne URSS
Europe excluding former USSR	50.6	50.5	50.2	51.4	51.0	53.2	53.8	49.8	49.1	49.9	Europe ancienne URSS exclus
- European Union	46.2	45.9	45.2	46.3	45.8	47.4	47.7	44.1	43.5	44.0	- Union Européenne
- Eastern Europe	1.2	1.4	1.6	1.8	1.9	2.3	2.5	2.2	2.3	2.4	- Europe de l'Est
- Rest of Europe	3.2	3.3	3.4	3.4	3.4	3.5	3.6	3.4	3.3	3.5	- Autre de l'Europe
Europe former USSR	2.7	3.2	3.5	3.6	3.9	2.7	1.4	1.7	2.3	2.1	Europe ancienne URSS
Oceania	1.5	1.5	1.4	1.6	1.8	1.7	1.8	2.0	1.7	1.7	Océanie

Préparations à base de céréales et de farines et de fécules de fruits ou de légumes 048

TRADE BY COMMODITY (Value in million US dollars)
Exports by principal countries or areas

COMMERCE PAR PRODUIT (Valeur en millions de dollars EU)
Exportations selon les principaux pays ou zones

Country or area	1998	1999	2000	2001	2002	Pays ou zone
World	17922.6	17913.4	17722.2	19133.9	21032.4	Monde
Africa	97.8	89.6	92.7	96.1	130.6	Afrique
Americas	3099.0	3174.5	3404.1	3755.4	4031.3	Amériques
- Northern America	2292.9	2407.8	2594.4	2854.5	3093.1	- Amérique du Nord
- LAIA	639.2	587.8	634.3	707.3	730.9	- ALAI
- CACM	114.3	126.9	123.2	138.2	160.4	- MCC
- Caribbean	51.9	51.1	51.1	54.1	44.9	- Caraïbes
- Rest of America	0.6	0.8	1.1	1.3	1.9	- Autre d'Amérique
Asia excluding former USSR	1692.8	1753.1	1947.7	2070.5	2224.7	Asie ancienne URSS exclus
- Middle East	350.8	276.2	265.5	280.7	304.2	- Moyen-Orient
Asia former USSR	4.6	4.7	5.6	6.2	6.9	Asie ancienne URSS
Europe excluding former USSR	12620.9	12477.3	11839.9	12753.0	14127.4	Europe ancienne URSS exclus
- European Union	11918.1	11861.9	11194.5	12057.9	13335.7	- Union Européenne
- Eastern Europe	367.6	281.4	315.6	354.8	431.5	- Europe de l'Est
- Rest of Europe	335.1	334.0	329.7	340.3	360.3	- Autre de l'Europe
Europe former USSR	86.2	85.0	99.1	128.8	137.0	Europe ancienne URSS
Oceania	321.4	329.2	333.0	324.1	374.5	Océanie
Germany	1912.1	1922.6	1888.3	2009.6	2256.4	Allemagne
Italy-San Marino-Holy See	1940.7	1866.1	1761.3	1898.5	2079.0	Italie-Saint-Marin-Saint-Siège
France-Monaco	1798.1	1743.3	1622.6	1687.8	1878.4	France-Monaco
United States	1422.0	1417.2	1498.2	1644.9	1720.5	Etats-Unis d'Amérique
United Kingdom	1486.4	1461.9	1323.4	1344.9	1436.7	Royaume-Uni
Belgium	–	1453.6	1352.9	1578.8	e1771.3	Belgique
Canada	871.0	990.5	1096.2	1209.6	1372.7	Canada
Netherlands	1063.7	1137.4	1049.9	1035.5	1183.2	Pays-Bas
Ireland	676.4	750.7	762.0	841.7	785.3	Irlande
Denmark	553.4	469.8	430.1	495.3	601.9	Danemark
Spain	383.9	373.9	359.8	466.8	519.4	Espagne
China	260.2	287.7	358.5	410.4	453.1	Chine
Belgium-Luxembourg	1460.7	–	–	–	–	Belgique-Luxembourg
Australia	254.1	259.0	267.5	259.4	289.8	Australie
Mexico	205.0	228.8	249.1	272.8	297.3	Mexique
Switzerland-Liechtenstein	239.0	240.0	245.3	247.0	261.0	Suisse-Liechtenstein
Korea, Republic of	214.5	198.9	229.8	265.0	296.9	République de Corée
Austria	198.9	240.0	218.7	239.5	295.0	Autriche
Sweden	213.1	221.5	210.2	228.1	271.5	Suède
Malaysia	141.9	172.4	202.9	197.2	e209.0	Malaisie
Thailand	136.1	156.0	166.7	178.1	e188.1	Thaïlande
Japan	144.2	167.1	174.2	158.6	158.5	Japon
Turkey	197.5	109.3	113.9	133.7	167.3	Turquie
Singapore	139.3	137.9	131.7	134.9	147.7	Singapour
Argentina	150.7	117.6	139.3	127.1	e122.8	Argentine
Poland	131.3	86.8	106.7	122.9	160.3	Pologne
China, Hong Kong SAR	119.9	105.7	113.0	101.6	102.5	Chine - RAS de Hong-Kong
Czech Republic	113.9	86.7	94.4	97.0	116.1	République tchèque
Finland	95.7	69.1	71.8	77.8	84.2	Finlande
Greece	82.5	75.0	67.7	67.4	e67.5	Grèce

(Value as percentages of World total) **(Valeur en pourcentage du total mondial)**

Regions of the world	1993	1994	1995	1996	1997	1998	1999	2000	2001	2002	Régions du monde
World	100.0	100.0	100.0	100.0	100.0	100.0	100.0	100.0	100.0	100.0	Monde
Africa	0.4	0.4	0.5	0.6	0.6	0.5	0.5	0.5	0.5	0.6	Afrique
Americas	14.6	14.7	13.5	14.4	16.2	17.3	17.7	19.2	19.6	19.2	Amériques
- Northern America	11.9	11.7	10.0	10.7	12.0	12.8	13.4	14.6	14.9	14.7	- Amérique du Nord
- LAIA	2.1	2.3	2.8	3.0	3.4	3.6	3.3	3.6	3.7	3.5	- ALAI
- CACM	0.4	0.4	0.5	0.4	0.5	0.6	0.7	0.7	0.7	0.8	- MCC
- Caribbean	0.2	0.2	0.2	0.3	0.3	0.3	0.3	0.3	0.3	0.2	- Caraïbes
- Rest of America	0.0	0.0	0.0	0.0	0.0	0.0	0.0	0.0	0.0	0.0	- Autre d'Amérique
Asia excluding former USSR	11.2	11.3	11.8	12.2	12.0	9.4	9.8	11.0	10.8	10.6	Asie ancienne URSS exclus
- Middle East	1.6	1.5	2.6	3.0	2.9	2.0	1.5	1.5	1.5	1.4	- Moyen-Orient
Asia former USSR	0.0	0.0	0.1	0.1	0.0	0.0	0.0	0.0	0.0	0.0	Asie ancienne URSS
Europe excluding former USSR	72.0	71.3	71.7	70.1	68.6	70.4	69.7	66.8	66.7	67.2	Europe ancienne URSS exclus
- European Union	68.8	68.0	68.1	66.4	64.8	66.5	66.2	63.2	63.0	63.4	- Union Européenne
- Eastern Europe	1.2	1.3	1.8	1.9	2.0	2.1	1.6	1.8	1.9	2.1	- Europe de l'Est
- Rest of Europe	2.0	1.9	1.9	1.8	1.7	1.9	1.9	1.9	1.8	1.7	- Autre de l'Europe
Europe former USSR	0.1	0.3	0.4	0.5	0.5	0.5	0.5	0.6	0.7	0.7	Europe ancienne URSS
Oceania	1.7	2.0	2.0	2.1	2.1	1.8	1.8	1.9	1.7	1.8	Océanie

054 Vegetables, fresh or simply preserved; roots and tubers, nes

TRADE BY COMMODITY (Value in million US dollars)
Imports by principal countries or areas

COMMERCE PAR PRODUIT (Valeur en millions de dollars EU)
Importations selon les principaux pays ou zones

Country or area	1998	1999	2000	2001	2002	Pays ou zone
World	26543.4	26190.1	24814.0	26800.4	27721.5	Monde
Africa	628.6	722.2	739.8	749.6	918.0	Afrique
Americas	5763.1	5495.0	5644.1	6082.8	6308.3	Amériques
- Northern America	4206.0	4215.6	4422.5	4813.8	5143.2	- Amérique du Nord
- LAIA	1172.8	889.5	859.9	872.1	785.3	- ALAI
- CACM	90.4	121.9	118.6	124.0	132.5	- MCC
- Caribbean	258.3	232.9	211.0	243.5	216.1	- Caraïbes
- Rest of America	35.5	35.0	32.0	29.3	31.2	- Autre d'Amérique
Asia excluding former USSR	5099.0	5034.7	5042.1	5776.9	5313.3	Asie ancienne URSS exclus
- Middle East	1216.7	1085.3	989.5	995.6	917.0	- Moyen-Orient
Asia former USSR	25.7	29.5	28.3	31.5	30.3	Asie ancienne URSS
Europe excluding former USSR	14387.1	14241.1	12729.5	13644.3	14541.6	Europe ancienne URSS exclus
- European Union	13345.3	13263.4	11778.1	12594.6	13360.2	- Union Européenne
- Eastern Europe	399.2	330.4	357.3	411.0	486.0	- Europe de l'Est
- Rest of Europe	642.5	647.2	594.0	638.7	695.5	- Autre de l'Europe
Europe former USSR	486.5	508.7	461.9	357.0	433.5	Europe ancienne URSS
Oceania	153.5	158.9	168.3	158.4	176.5	Océanie
Germany	3814.9	3686.3	3018.0	3500.4	3319.5	Allemagne
United States	3179.7	3176.6	3294.9	3646.5	3830.4	Etats-Unis d'Amérique
United Kingdom	2451.3	2423.3	2274.5	2433.6	2642.5	Royaume-Uni
Japan	2169.3	2272.4	2231.3	2197.4	1905.6	Japon
France-Monaco	1741.2	1751.5	1656.3	1671.7	1907.4	France-Monaco
Canada	1015.7	1028.8	1121.9	1159.4	1302.2	Canada
Netherlands	1187.6	1164.2	1102.0	999.4	1174.4	Pays-Bas
Italy-San Marino-Holy See	882.3	917.1	818.7	857.9	1021.8	Italie-Saint-Marin-Saint-Siège
Belgium	-	908.1	791.1	857.3	e940.2	Belgique
Spain	674.5	716.0	649.6	682.3	640.7	Espagne
Switzerland-Liechtenstein	359.9	371.9	341.5	353.7	388.8	Suisse-Liechtenstein
Sweden	342.5	371.1	333.9	348.3	396.5	Suède
India	196.1	96.5	117.2	727.1	629.4	Inde
Russian Federation	379.7	414.9	366.9	258.0	314.4	Fédération de Russie
United Arab Emirates	388.9	407.6	266.2	283.9	e291.3	Emirates arabes unis
Brazil	555.2	310.9	251.7	272.0	219.9	Brésil
Austria	296.3	289.0	253.5	285.3	295.2	Autriche
Mexico	262.4	227.4	250.0	284.6	297.5	Mexique
Malaysia	225.7	251.9	237.7	264.4	e289.0	Malaisie
Denmark	271.1	259.2	219.6	242.9	256.9	Danemark
China, Hong Kong SAR	249.0	261.4	253.7	233.2	214.0	Chine - RAS de Hong-Kong
Portugal	234.8	222.6	195.8	223.6	227.1	Portugal
Ireland	221.4	220.4	186.5	205.9	222.9	Irlande
Saudi Arabia	222.2	234.7	175.2	181.8	e188.2	Arabie saoudite
Singapore	197.7	185.7	182.3	196.3	208.0	Singapour
Belgium-Luxembourg	949.4	-	-	-	-	Belgique-Luxembourg
Algeria	137.3	180.2	144.9	e175.3	e199.6	Algérie
Egypt	107.1	181.4	e177.6	161.7	204.2	Egypte
Korea, Republic of	137.5	145.2	152.8	174.2	149.2	République de Corée
Czech Republic	151.3	133.5	130.0	143.2	181.6	République tchèque

(Value as percentages of World total) **(Valeur en pourcentage du total mondial)**

Regions of the world	1993	1994	1995	1996	1997	1998	1999	2000	2001	2002	Régions du monde
World	100.0	100.0	100.0	100.0	100.0	100.0	100.0	100.0	100.0	100.0	Monde
Africa	2.1	2.6	3.0	2.8	2.4	2.4	2.8	3.0	2.8	3.3	Afrique
Americas	17.1	16.7	16.2	17.1	19.6	21.7	21.0	22.7	22.7	22.8	Amériques
- Northern America	13.2	12.2	12.0	13.1	14.6	15.8	16.1	17.8	18.0	18.6	- Amérique du Nord
- LAIA	2.7	3.4	3.1	3.0	3.7	4.4	3.4	3.5	3.3	2.8	- ALAI
- CACM	0.1	0.2	0.2	0.2	0.3	0.3	0.5	0.5	0.5	0.5	- MCC
- Caribbean	1.0	0.8	0.8	0.7	1.0	1.0	0.9	0.9	0.9	0.8	- Caraïbes
- Rest of America	0.1	0.1	0.1	0.1	0.1	0.1	0.1	0.1	0.1	0.1	- Autre d'Amérique
Asia excluding former USSR	18.8	19.1	18.1	19.1	20.8	19.2	19.2	20.3	21.6	19.2	Asie ancienne URSS exclus
- Middle East	3.4	2.9	2.8	3.2	4.5	4.6	4.1	4.0	3.7	3.3	- Moyen-Orient
Asia former USSR	0.2	0.2	0.1	0.2	0.1	0.1	0.1	0.1	0.1	0.1	Asie ancienne URSS
Europe excluding former USSR	60.4	59.2	60.3	58.4	54.3	54.2	54.4	51.3	50.9	52.5	Europe ancienne URSS exclus
- European Union	56.6	55.3	56.0	54.5	50.4	50.3	50.6	47.5	47.0	48.2	- Union Européenne
- Eastern Europe	1.1	1.0	1.3	1.2	1.4	1.5	1.3	1.4	1.5	1.8	- Europe de l'Est
- Rest of Europe	2.7	2.9	3.0	2.7	2.4	2.4	2.5	2.4	2.4	2.5	- Autre de l'Europe
Europe former USSR	0.7	1.6	1.7	1.7	2.1	1.8	1.9	1.9	1.3	1.6	Europe ancienne URSS
Oceania	0.7	0.6	0.6	0.7	0.7	0.6	0.6	0.7	0.6	0.6	Océanie

Légumes frais, congelés ou conservés; autres produits végétaux comestibles, n.d.a. 054

TRADE BY COMMODITY (Value in million US dollars)
Exports by principal countries or areas

COMMERCE PAR PRODUIT (Valeur en millions de dollars EU)
Exportations selon les principaux pays ou zones

Country or area	1998	1999	2000	2001	2002	Pays ou zone
World	24261.7	24641.7	23128.1	25373.1	26957.7	Monde
Africa	550.8	612.9	576.5	551.2	625.9	Afrique
Americas	6502.4	6471.5	6768.8	7245.7	6965.5	Amériques
- Northern America	3380.0	3479.8	3779.6	3905.0	3850.8	- Amérique du Nord
- LAIA	2872.0	2747.0	2756.9	3130.3	2900.1	- ALAI
- CACM	183.7	199.9	185.6	161.7	167.6	- MCC
- Caribbean	53.9	33.7	35.3	33.1	28.4	- Caraïbes
- Rest of America	12.9	11.2	11.4	15.6	18.6	- Autre d'Amérique
Asia excluding former USSR	3711.2	3821.1	3547.9	4285.6	4465.7	Asie ancienne URSS exclus
- Middle East	1008.2	927.9	792.9	995.2	891.2	- Moyen-Orient
Asia former USSR	107.7	113.8	86.6	93.4	97.9	Asie ancienne URSS
Europe excluding former USSR	12790.1	12992.9	11471.5	12480.4	14076.8	Europe ancienne URSS exclus
- European Union	12281.1	12487.8	11023.6	11938.6	13507.8	- Union Européenne
- Eastern Europe	430.7	438.3	388.7	482.2	515.4	- Europe de l'Est
- Rest of Europe	78.3	66.8	59.2	59.6	53.6	- Autre de l'Europe
Europe former USSR	93.6	89.6	99.3	98.9	108.8	Europe ancienne URSS
Oceania	505.8	539.8	577.4	617.9	617.3	Océanie
Netherlands	3501.0	3563.7	3285.0	3336.9	3834.5	Pays-Bas
Spain	2795.4	2775.0	2542.8	2852.4	3218.2	Espagne
United States	2206.0	2122.5	2271.6	2257.1	2302.6	Etats-Unis d'Amérique
Mexico	2051.9	2038.7	2175.8	2476.7	2246.0	Mexique
Italy-San Marino-Holy See	1585.6	1641.2	1391.0	1562.9	1715.4	Italie-Saint-Marin-Saint-Siège
China	1315.4	1353.1	1374.6	1660.4	1881.7	Chine
Canada	1173.8	1357.3	1508.0	1647.9	1548.2	Canada
France-Monaco	1384.4	1410.0	1166.3	1207.7	1456.8	France-Monaco
Belgium	–	1548.3	1355.3	1495.1	e1677.4	Belgique
Germany	491.9	554.5	463.0	594.6	590.2	Allemagne
Turkey	530.4	403.2	359.1	453.3	398.8	Turquie
Thailand	391.0	460.8	317.8	389.7	e411.6	Thaïlande
Australia	300.2	325.1	396.5	413.9	396.1	Australie
Argentina	497.8	317.9	258.0	281.2	e271.7	Argentine
Belgium-Luxembourg	1484.7	–	–	–	–	Belgique-Luxembourg
United Kingdom	315.3	327.5	273.9	255.4	309.8	Royaume-Uni
Poland	188.1	196.0	193.6	250.2	285.2	Pologne
India	144.7	198.6	245.6	224.8	238.4	Inde
Morocco	219.3	255.0	176.4	180.5	e196.4	Maroc
Greece	278.9	213.8	160.5	186.9	e187.1	Grèce
Myanmar	e165.0	e71.8	e93.5	e276.6	e341.2	Myanmar
New Zealand	187.1	193.5	164.2	187.5	198.8	Nouvelle-Zélande
Israel	160.2	169.3	154.7	172.5	162.4	Israël
Syrian Arab Republic	231.9	198.5	133.7	e151.6	95.6	République arabe syrienne
Chile	166.8	176.9	120.0	145.0	e141.8	Chili
Portugal	137.9	150.5	139.9	140.0	178.9	Portugal
Hungary	123.3	121.1	105.7	122.1	117.2	Hongrie
Peru	79.0	101.5	100.2	119.8	149.2	Pérou
Ireland	113.0	105.2	92.4	120.7	118.3	Irlande
Egypt	92.5	82.2	118.3	91.3	114.2	Egypte

(Value as percentages of World total) **(Valeur en pourcentage du total mondial)**

Regions of the world	1993	1994	1995	1996	1997	1998	1999	2000	2001	2002	Régions du monde
World	100.0	100.0	100.0	100.0	100.0	100.0	100.0	100.0	100.0	100.0	Monde
Africa	2.3	1.8	2.4	2.6	2.2	2.3	2.5	2.5	2.2	2.3	Afrique
Americas	20.7	21.4	21.9	22.1	24.9	26.8	26.3	29.3	28.6	25.8	Amériques
- Northern America	11.1	11.8	11.4	11.8	13.5	13.9	14.1	16.3	15.4	14.3	- Amérique du Nord
- LAIA	8.8	8.9	9.7	9.5	10.5	11.8	11.1	11.9	12.3	10.8	- ALAI
- CACM	0.5	0.6	0.5	0.6	0.7	0.8	0.8	0.8	0.6	0.6	- MCC
- Caribbean	0.2	0.2	0.2	0.2	0.2	0.2	0.1	0.2	0.1	0.1	- Caraïbes
- Rest of America	0.0	0.0	0.0	0.0	0.0	0.1	0.0	0.0	0.1	0.1	- Autre d'Amérique
Asia excluding former USSR	20.7	18.5	17.1	17.6	17.6	15.3	15.5	15.3	16.9	16.6	Asie ancienne URSS exclus
- Middle East	5.2	4.3	4.1	4.7	5.0	4.2	3.8	3.4	3.9	3.3	- Moyen-Orient
Asia former USSR	0.0	0.9	0.2	0.8	0.3	0.4	0.5	0.4	0.4	0.4	Asie ancienne URSS
Europe excluding former USSR	53.7	54.6	55.6	54.0	52.0	52.7	52.7	49.6	49.2	52.2	Europe ancienne URSS exclus
- European Union	51.1	51.9	53.3	51.6	50.0	50.6	50.7	47.7	47.1	50.1	- Union Européenne
- Eastern Europe	2.2	2.2	1.8	2.1	1.8	1.8	1.8	1.7	1.9	1.9	- Europe de l'Est
- Rest of Europe	0.3	0.5	0.5	0.3	0.2	0.3	0.3	0.3	0.2	0.2	- Autre de l'Europe
Europe former USSR	0.5	0.4	0.8	0.4	0.4	0.4	0.4	0.4	0.4	0.4	Europe ancienne URSS
Oceania	2.1	2.4	2.0	2.4	2.5	2.1	2.2	2.5	2.4	2.3	Océanie

056 Vegetables, roots and tubers, prepared or preserved, nes

TRADE BY COMMODITY (Value in million US dollars)
Imports by principal countries or areas

COMMERCE PAR PRODUIT (Valeur en millions de dollars EU)
Importations selon les principaux pays ou zones

Country or area	1998	1999	2000	2001	2002	Pays ou zone
World	6227.1	6517.9	6082.0	6135.9	6596.0	Monde
Africa	137.5	116.6	157.0	121.8	130.5	Afrique
Americas	1336.5	1419.1	1415.6	1462.8	1505.1	Amériques
- Northern America	1016.7	1121.9	1148.4	1201.5	1281.7	- Amérique du Nord
- LAIA	232.5	208.2	189.7	171.4	148.6	- ALAI
- CACM	23.1	26.3	25.9	28.2	26.6	- MCC
- Caribbean	51.6	49.2	38.5	47.1	32.6	- Caraïbes
- Rest of America	12.6	13.5	13.1	14.7	15.6	- Autre d'Amérique
Asia excluding former USSR	1251.7	1428.2	1416.6	1325.0	1324.8	Asie ancienne URSS exclus
- Middle East	173.1	175.8	183.2	173.1	197.1	- Moyen-Orient
Asia former USSR	5.6	7.3	7.2	8.3	9.1	Asie ancienne URSS
Europe excluding former USSR	3198.9	3327.9	2841.8	2953.9	3311.5	Europe ancienne URSS exclus
- European Union	2917.7	3048.1	2570.5	2689.7	3016.8	- Union Européenne
- Eastern Europe	100.3	93.9	100.2	98.1	114.6	- Europe de l'Est
- Rest of Europe	180.8	185.9	171.1	166.1	180.1	- Autre de l'Europe
Europe former USSR	193.4	110.1	133.4	159.7	197.9	Europe ancienne URSS
Oceania	103.6	108.7	110.4	104.5	117.1	Océanie
United States	796.1	898.0	917.9	954.3	1009.5	Etats-Unis d'Amérique
Germany	820.2	822.5	659.3	746.7	807.3	Allemagne
Japan	668.2	783.8	791.5	759.2	719.3	Japon
France-Monaco	472.9	479.8	421.8	435.5	502.0	France-Monaco
United Kingdom	440.4	429.6	344.5	325.3	381.4	Royaume-Uni
Italy-San Marino-Holy See	292.2	285.4	247.6	262.3	265.4	Italie-Saint-Marin-Saint-Siège
Canada	218.6	222.1	228.6	244.8	267.9	Canada
Netherlands	217.6	271.4	219.0	200.5	242.5	Pays-Bas
Spain	148.9	183.6	174.8	188.8	221.1	Espagne
Belgium	–	232.6	202.9	207.4	e227.5	Belgique
China, Hong Kong SAR	149.2	147.5	125.2	99.1	101.4	Chine - RAS de Hong-Kong
Russian Federation	152.9	75.1	103.1	119.5	146.2	Fédération de Russie
Switzerland-Liechtenstein	86.7	87.7	84.4	78.0	83.3	Suisse-Liechtenstein
Sweden	85.2	86.0	74.1	75.5	85.0	Suède
Australia	72.9	77.2	78.0	72.3	84.4	Australie
Mexico	70.5	68.8	70.5	71.2	78.8	Mexique
Korea, Republic of	50.1	74.8	77.7	68.0	78.2	République de Corée
Denmark	75.3	68.8	57.5	60.5	67.6	Danemark
Austria	54.4	55.9	46.7	54.1	60.2	Autriche
Saudi Arabia	42.7	45.6	60.8	59.0	e61.0	Arabie saoudite
Singapore	49.7	57.3	50.5	47.6	49.6	Singapour
Brazil	88.9	51.4	46.5	37.4	26.5	Brésil
Ireland	32.6	39.4	40.1	49.6	63.7	Irlande
United Arab Emirates	38.4	40.3	39.0	45.4	e46.6	Emirates arabes unis
Belgium-Luxembourg	200.5	–	–	–	–	Belgique-Luxembourg
Libyan Arab Jamahiriya	71.2	e52.0	e46.7	e	e	Jamahiriya arabe libyenne
Israel	37.4	32.9	33.5	31.4	36.1	Israël
Portugal	28.4	33.4	30.8	29.9	34.1	Portugal
Algeria	5.1	3.1	40.6	e49.1	e56.0	Algérie
Poland	33.8	29.4	30.0	25.8	30.3	Pologne

(Value as percentages of World total) **(Valeur en pourcentage du total mondial)**

Regions of the world	1993	1994	1995	1996	1997	1998	1999	2000	2001	2002	Régions du monde
World	100.0	100.0	100.0	100.0	100.0	100.0	100.0	100.0	100.0	100.0	Monde
Africa	2.0	1.0	1.5	1.5	1.6	2.2	1.8	2.6	2.0	2.0	Afrique
Americas	17.7	19.0	17.6	17.4	19.6	21.5	21.8	23.3	23.8	22.8	Amériques
- Northern America	14.7	15.2	14.3	14.1	15.3	16.3	17.2	18.9	19.6	19.4	- Amérique du Nord
- LAIA	1.8	2.5	2.2	2.3	3.0	3.7	3.2	3.1	2.8	2.3	- ALAI
- CACM	0.2	0.2	0.2	0.2	0.3	0.4	0.4	0.4	0.5	0.4	- MCC
- Caribbean	0.7	0.9	0.8	0.6	0.8	0.8	0.8	0.6	0.8	0.5	- Caraïbes
- Rest of America	0.2	0.2	0.2	0.1	0.2	0.2	0.2	0.2	0.2	0.2	- Autre d'Amérique
Asia excluding former USSR	25.0	24.3	23.2	22.7	23.0	20.1	21.9	23.3	21.6	20.1	Asie ancienne URSS exclus
- Middle East	2.2	2.0	2.2	1.8	2.2	2.8	2.7	3.0	2.8	3.0	- Moyen-Orient
Asia former USSR	0.1	0.1	0.1	0.1	0.1	0.1	0.1	0.1	0.1	0.1	Asie ancienne URSS
Europe excluding former USSR	51.7	51.5	53.2	53.9	50.1	51.4	51.1	46.7	48.1	50.2	Europe ancienne URSS exclus
- European Union	47.8	47.6	48.9	49.8	46.0	46.9	46.8	42.3	43.8	45.7	- Union Européenne
- Eastern Europe	1.1	0.9	1.0	1.2	1.3	1.6	1.4	1.6	1.6	1.7	- Europe de l'Est
- Rest of Europe	2.9	3.0	3.2	2.9	2.8	2.9	2.9	2.8	2.7	2.7	- Autre de l'Europe
Europe former USSR	1.8	2.5	2.6	2.8	3.9	3.1	1.7	2.2	2.6	3.0	Europe ancienne URSS
Oceania	1.8	1.7	1.7	1.6	1.6	1.7	1.7	1.8	1.7	1.8	Océanie

TRADE BY COMMODITY (Value in million US dollars)
Exports by principal countries or areas

COMMERCE PAR PRODUIT (Valeur en millions de dollars EU)
Exportations selon les principaux pays ou zones

Country or area	1998	1999	2000	2001	2002	Pays ou zone
World	6006.2	6236.7	5773.8	5895.8	6354.3	Monde
Africa	150.8	178.6	127.5	144.0	177.0	Afrique
Americas	1033.4	1095.1	1016.6	968.8	978.4	Amériques
- Northern America	675.9	713.1	660.0	623.1	610.8	- Amérique du Nord
- LAIA	334.7	366.6	339.0	331.4	354.1	- ALAI
- CACM	9.6	11.2	14.0	10.7	10.2	- MCC
- Caribbean	13.2	3.9	3.6	3.3	3.1	- Caraïbes
- Rest of America	0.0	0.2	0.2	0.2	0.1	- Autre d'Amérique
Asia excluding former USSR	1598.9	1625.1	1676.6	1645.4	1792.7	Asie ancienne URSS exclus
- Middle East	222.4	197.9	181.7	220.8	221.3	- Moyen-Orient
Asia former USSR	5.7	7.1	7.2	8.9	6.2	Asie ancienne URSS
Europe excluding former USSR	3148.2	3272.6	2882.4	3065.1	3321.9	Europe ancienne URSS exclus
- European Union	2837.9	2998.4	2630.5	2760.3	3020.8	- Union Européenne
- Eastern Europe	250.4	224.7	211.5	260.7	254.1	- Europe de l'Est
- Rest of Europe	60.0	49.5	40.5	44.1	47.0	- Autre de l'Europe
Europe former USSR	41.0	32.7	32.9	35.3	42.6	Europe ancienne URSS
Oceania	28.3	25.4	30.4	28.3	35.6	Océanie
China	823.3	839.2	906.1	913.5	1036.8	Chine
Spain	572.9	630.0	591.4	618.5	689.4	Espagne
Netherlands	563.5	713.1	589.1	554.5	612.8	Pays-Bas
United States	621.4	638.0	565.8	517.2	496.7	Etats-Unis d'Amérique
France-Monaco	460.7	405.3	363.3	387.5	380.8	France-Monaco
Germany	317.7	282.9	262.8	305.3	345.4	Allemagne
Belgium	–	334.7	266.4	298.8	e335.2	Belgique
Italy-San Marino-Holy See	213.7	219.7	204.3	224.1	271.4	Italie-Saint-Marin-Saint-Siège
Turkey	178.6	155.5	144.2	182.5	182.9	Turquie
Thailand	163.0	151.2	158.2	150.1	e158.5	Thaïlande
Greece	173.7	157.8	128.5	123.7	e123.9	Grèce
Mexico	114.2	151.0	138.4	135.2	143.2	Mexique
United Kingdom	102.9	118.5	107.9	111.4	117.9	Royaume-Uni
Hungary	109.9	106.0	96.0	121.4	106.3	Hongrie
Peru	93.5	110.5	97.9	106.3	122.8	Pérou
Poland	100.8	82.0	91.4	106.1	111.8	Pologne
Morocco	91.3	114.9	84.4	95.5	e103.9	Maroc
Canada	54.5	75.1	94.2	105.9	114.1	Canada
Korea, Republic of	62.0	95.4	94.3	84.1	94.6	République de Corée
China, Hong Kong SAR	83.5	72.8	65.8	44.4	36.4	Chine - RAS de Hong-Kong
Belgium-Luxembourg	297.4	–	–	–	–	Belgique-Luxembourg
Argentina	79.5	61.9	59.5	46.9	e45.3	Argentine
India	38.9	48.3	64.3	50.6	60.6	Inde
Denmark	44.8	46.4	41.6	42.7	46.8	Danemark
Portugal	34.4	37.1	28.6	35.0	38.5	Portugal
Indonesia	28.3	44.5	41.2	31.7	26.4	Indonésie
Israel	34.9	27.4	26.1	25.7	26.5	Israël
Japan	31.8	32.9	26.9	24.2	23.0	Japon
Ireland	19.0	25.7	20.9	26.5	25.3	Irlande
New Zealand	16.3	14.5	18.6	21.7	27.1	Nouvelle-Zélande

(Value as percentages of World total) **(Valeur en pourcentage du total mondial)**

Regions of the world	1993	1994	1995	1996	1997	1998	1999	2000	2001	2002	Régions du monde
World	100.0	100.0	100.0	100.0	100.0	100.0	100.0	100.0	100.0	100.0	Monde
Africa	2.5	2.5	2.9	3.0	2.9	2.5	2.9	2.2	2.4	2.8	Afrique
Americas	13.1	13.4	12.6	13.8	15.7	17.2	17.6	17.6	16.4	15.4	Amériques
- Northern America	8.1	8.8	7.9	8.5	10.1	11.3	11.4	11.4	10.6	9.6	- Amérique du Nord
- LAIA	4.5	4.3	4.4	5.0	5.4	5.6	5.9	5.9	5.6	5.6	- ALAI
- CACM	0.3	0.2	0.1	0.1	0.1	0.2	0.2	0.2	0.2	0.2	- MCC
- Caribbean	0.1	0.2	0.2	0.1	0.1	0.2	0.1	0.1	0.1	0.0	- Caraïbes
- Rest of America	0.0	0.0	0.0	0.0	0.0	0.0	0.0	0.0	0.0	0.0	- Autre d'Amérique
Asia excluding former USSR	32.3	32.4	32.5	30.0	28.8	26.6	26.1	29.0	27.9	28.2	Asie ancienne URSS exclus
- Middle East	3.6	4.2	3.7	3.6	4.0	3.7	3.2	3.1	3.7	3.5	- Moyen-Orient
Asia former USSR	0.0	0.1	0.1	0.1	0.0	0.1	0.1	0.1	0.2	0.1	Asie ancienne URSS
Europe excluding former USSR	51.5	50.8	51.1	52.1	51.7	52.4	52.5	49.9	52.0	52.3	Europe ancienne URSS exclus
- European Union	47.8	46.1	46.1	47.5	46.3	47.2	48.1	45.6	46.8	47.5	- Union Européenne
- Eastern Europe	2.8	3.4	3.8	4.0	4.8	4.2	3.6	3.7	4.4	4.0	- Europe de l'Est
- Rest of Europe	0.9	1.3	1.2	0.6	0.6	1.0	0.8	0.7	0.7	0.7	- Autre de l'Europe
Europe former USSR	0.3	0.4	0.5	0.6	0.5	0.7	0.5	0.6	0.6	0.7	Europe ancienne URSS
Oceania	0.4	0.4	0.4	0.4	0.4	0.5	0.4	0.5	0.5	0.6	Océanie

057 Fruit and nuts, fresh, dried

TRADE BY COMMODITY (Value in million US dollars) — COMMERCE PAR PRODUIT (Valeur en millions de dollars EU)

Imports by principal countries or areas — **Importations selon les principaux pays ou zones**

Country or area	1998	1999	2000	2001	2002	Pays ou zone
World	32840.0	33160.8	31349.5	31963.1	33902.0	Monde
Africa	209.8	199.1	223.8	209.2	232.0	Afrique
Americas	6425.1	7128.8	7244.4	7313.0	7560.5	Amériques
- Northern America	5263.1	5961.2	5949.7	5937.0	6408.9	- Amérique du Nord
- LAIA	1019.6	1011.4	1113.8	1182.7	948.2	- ALAI
- CACM	64.4	76.4	97.1	99.0	113.8	- MCC
- Caribbean	62.8	62.0	64.8	77.3	72.4	- Caraïbes
- Rest of America	15.2	17.9	18.9	17.0	17.3	- Autre d'Amérique
Asia excluding former USSR	5606.7	6021.8	6250.9	5840.5	6199.6	Asie ancienne URSS exclus
- Middle East	1103.8	1188.9	1209.0	1226.4	1228.3	- Moyen-Orient
Asia former USSR	19.9	20.7	21.8	19.7	18.5	Asie ancienne URSS
Europe excluding former USSR	19405.8	18861.6	16477.3	17435.3	18553.0	Europe ancienne URSS exclus
- European Union	17429.8	16980.5	14776.9	15572.8	16498.7	- Union Européenne
- Eastern Europe	874.3	879.0	812.8	914.1	1022.8	- Europe de l'Est
- Rest of Europe	1101.7	1002.2	887.6	948.5	1031.5	- Autre de l'Europe
Europe former USSR	917.4	654.1	873.2	910.2	1070.2	Europe ancienne URSS
Oceania	255.3	274.7	258.1	235.3	268.1	Océanie
United States	3971.0	4604.6	4570.1	4525.9	4870.7	Etats-Unis d'Amérique
Germany	4727.2	4524.5	3658.9	4007.0	3918.5	Allemagne
United Kingdom	2911.0	2707.0	2463.3	2494.7	2778.4	Royaume-Uni
France-Monaco	2393.0	2220.2	2039.9	2096.0	2247.5	France-Monaco
Japan	1680.8	1918.0	1968.8	1754.3	1840.9	Japon
Netherlands	1503.6	1662.8	1443.1	1404.4	1518.4	Pays-Bas
Canada	1283.0	1347.0	1375.5	1407.7	1534.5	Canada
Belgium	-	1660.8	1525.6	1532.5	e1680.8	Belgique
Italy-San Marino-Holy See	1291.1	1291.1	1141.5	1203.3	1330.1	Italie-Saint-Marin-Saint-Siège
China, Hong Kong SAR	1030.8	942.8	906.7	905.6	1008.4	Chine - RAS de Hong-Kong
Spain	666.7	811.6	670.7	813.5	854.3	Espagne
Russian Federation	711.6	434.7	640.4	673.3	805.0	Fédération de Russie
Switzerland-Liechtenstein	569.0	530.9	485.8	507.7	522.1	Suisse-Liechtenstein
Sweden	507.4	476.7	428.0	424.8	488.1	Suède
Poland	442.2	444.9	417.1	484.0	487.6	Pologne
Mexico	248.3	386.8	508.5	572.6	490.3	Mexique
Austria	454.0	421.7	361.5	383.3	391.1	Autriche
United Arab Emirates	329.2	344.9	421.7	418.1	e428.9	Emirates arabes unis
Belgium-Luxembourg	1844.8	-	-	-	-	Belgique-Luxembourg
India	390.0	412.8	392.5	252.0	387.3	Inde
Saudi Arabia	324.5	377.6	324.2	309.9	e320.7	Arabie saoudite
China	241.1	257.6	367.0	365.2	371.9	Chine
Portugal	314.9	305.6	273.8	350.4	338.1	Portugal
Denmark	279.2	295.7	247.3	270.0	298.9	Danemark
Singapore	283.0	297.2	286.1	260.6	261.5	Singapour
Norway	231.4	230.0	209.7	225.2	264.9	Norvège
Brazil	342.5	231.7	205.0	187.5	142.1	Brésil
Finland	220.0	210.7	175.4	199.0	213.0	Finlande
Czech Republic	204.2	199.0	172.0	192.3	235.9	République tchèque
Korea, Republic of	105.9	161.4	207.9	222.6	174.0	République de Corée

(Value as percentages of World total) — **(Valeur en pourcentage du total mondial)**

Regions of the world	1993	1994	1995	1996	1997	1998	1999	2000	2001	2002	Régions du monde
World	100.0	100.0	100.0	100.0	100.0	100.0	100.0	100.0	100.0	100.0	Monde
Africa	0.5	0.5	0.6	0.5	0.5	0.6	0.6	0.7	0.7	0.7	Afrique
Americas	19.3	18.1	17.4	17.7	18.4	19.6	21.5	23.1	22.9	22.3	Amériques
- Northern America	16.5	14.8	14.2	14.5	15.1	16.0	18.0	19.0	18.6	18.9	- Amérique du Nord
- LAIA	2.4	3.0	2.9	2.8	2.9	3.1	3.0	3.6	3.7	2.8	- ALAI
- CACM	0.1	0.1	0.1	0.1	0.2	0.2	0.2	0.3	0.3	0.3	- MCC
- Caribbean	0.2	0.2	0.2	0.2	0.2	0.2	0.2	0.2	0.2	0.2	- Caraïbes
- Rest of America	0.1	0.1	0.1	0.0	0.1	0.0	0.1	0.1	0.1	0.1	- Autre d'Amérique
Asia excluding former USSR	19.8	18.4	18.0	17.7	18.7	17.1	18.2	19.9	18.3	18.3	Asie ancienne URSS exclus
- Middle East	3.5	3.2	3.1	3.0	3.4	3.4	3.6	3.9	3.8	3.6	- Moyen-Orient
Asia former USSR	0.0	0.0	0.1	0.1	0.0	0.1	0.1	0.1	0.1	0.1	Asie ancienne URSS
Europe excluding former USSR	57.4	59.2	59.7	59.9	58.1	59.1	56.9	52.6	54.5	54.7	Europe ancienne URSS exclus
- European Union	51.9	53.5	53.9	54.3	52.7	53.1	51.2	47.1	48.7	48.7	- Union Européenne
- Eastern Europe	1.9	1.9	2.1	2.4	2.4	2.7	2.7	2.6	2.9	3.0	- Europe de l'Est
- Rest of Europe	3.6	3.8	3.7	3.3	3.0	3.4	3.0	2.8	3.0	3.0	- Autre de l'Europe
Europe former USSR	2.2	3.0	3.4	3.3	3.5	2.8	2.0	2.8	2.8	3.2	Europe ancienne URSS
Oceania	0.8	0.8	0.8	0.8	0.8	0.8	0.8	0.8	0.7	0.8	Océanie

TRADE BY COMMODITY (Value in million US dollars)
Exports by principal countries or areas

COMMERCE PAR PRODUIT (Valeur en millions de dollars EU)
Exportations selon les principaux pays ou zones

Country or area	1998	1999	2000	2001	2002	Pays ou zone
World	28956.2	28554.6	27161.6	27748.0	29773.4	Monde
Africa	1562.0	1729.1	1408.7	1335.5	1445.2	Afrique
Americas	9990.2	9593.8	9702.6	9905.3	10109.3	Amériques
- Northern America	3792.4	3642.9	3967.5	4056.0	4260.0	- Amérique du Nord
- LAIA	4345.0	4372.2	4212.0	4303.8	4407.3	- ALAI
- CACM	1438.2	1179.7	1188.7	1228.1	1128.9	- MCC
- Caribbean	221.0	165.8	131.8	144.1	133.4	- Caraïbes
- Rest of America	193.7	233.3	202.7	173.2	179.7	- Autre d'Amérique
Asia excluding former USSR	4786.6	5054.2	5010.7	4950.9	5351.6	Asie ancienne URSS exclus
- Middle East	2170.8	2112.8	1839.6	2049.7	2124.3	- Moyen-Orient
Asia former USSR	133.8	92.6	189.4	161.1	126.8	Asie ancienne URSS
Europe excluding former USSR	11653.2	11143.0	9960.0	10571.8	11762.8	Europe ancienne URSS exclus
- European Union	11368.7	10918.7	9725.9	10350.3	11520.9	- Union Européenne
- Eastern Europe	256.3	188.5	208.0	193.0	219.0	- Europe de l'Est
- Rest of Europe	28.1	35.9	26.1	28.5	22.9	- Autre de l'Europe
Europe former USSR	89.3	65.8	79.5	96.8	100.4	Europe ancienne URSS
Oceania	741.2	876.0	810.8	726.6	877.2	Océanie
United States	3692.8	3548.6	3870.6	3953.7	4142.0	Etats-Unis d'Amérique
Spain	3820.2	3532.7	3199.0	3352.9	4001.1	Espagne
Italy-San Marino-Holy See	2026.6	1991.5	1801.4	1936.1	1946.6	Italie-Saint-Marin-Saint-Siège
France-Monaco	1391.2	1273.6	1211.2	1255.9	1479.2	France-Monaco
Belgium	–	1722.6	1454.4	1490.7	e1672.5	Belgique
Turkey	1250.7	1212.4	1003.1	1178.3	1145.0	Turquie
Chile	1065.9	1109.8	1191.7	1221.0	e1194.6	Chili
Netherlands	1117.1	1198.1	1049.2	1073.2	1132.4	Pays-Bas
Ecuador	1081.1	967.1	835.1	866.8	998.0	Equateur
Costa Rica	875.6	853.2	753.5	722.9	708.3	Costa Rica
Mexico	748.7	747.2	742.0	762.7	730.7	Mexique
India	455.3	669.2	545.9	470.8	518.6	Inde
Iran (Islamic Republic of)	548.2	482.2	461.7	512.5	627.5	Iran (République islamique d')
Argentina	521.9	492.9	449.1	534.2	e516.1	Argentine
New Zealand	457.0	573.2	493.0	415.4	507.3	Nouvelle-Zélande
Colombia	488.8	572.3	494.1	424.6	454.7	Colombie
Greece	492.8	477.9	417.5	476.4	e477.0	Grèce
Philippines	360.7	392.6	434.1	430.8	472.0	Philippines
Germany	464.5	427.5	311.6	429.7	452.6	Allemagne
China	369.8	342.1	348.4	353.1	463.8	Chine
Belgium-Luxembourg	1772.7	–	–	–	–	Belgique-Luxembourg
South Africa	–	–	569.6	539.0	581.9	Afrique du Sud
Brazil	284.0	317.5	364.8	339.9	e352.3	Brésil
Australia	283.0	301.7	316.5	309.9	368.6	Australie
China, Hong Kong SAR	296.8	259.9	319.3	327.2	340.9	Chine - RAS de Hong-Kong
Viet Nam	137.6	150.6	366.3	380.9	423.4	Viet Nam
Southern African Customs Union	645.4	714.7	–	–	–	Union douanière d'Afrique australe
Morocco	302.3	296.4	232.0	222.1	e241.6	Maroc
Guatemala	237.4	192.9	243.3	223.3	253.2	Guatemala
Israel	263.2	244.6	206.0	179.0	163.7	Israël

(Value as percentages of World total) **(Valeur en pourcentage du total mondial)**

Regions of the world	1993	1994	1995	1996	1997	1998	1999	2000	2001	2002	Régions du monde
World	100.0	100.0	100.0	100.0	100.0	100.0	100.0	100.0	100.0	100.0	Monde
Africa	6.3	5.3	5.4	5.2	4.7	5.4	6.1	5.2	4.8	4.9	Afrique
Americas	34.8	33.7	35.1	35.2	34.8	34.5	33.6	35.7	35.7	34.0	Amériques
- Northern America	14.7	14.8	14.9	14.9	14.0	13.1	12.8	14.6	14.6	14.3	- Amérique du Nord
- LAIA	12.6	12.9	13.6	14.6	15.2	15.0	15.3	15.5	15.5	14.8	- ALAI
- CACM	4.8	3.8	4.3	4.2	4.0	5.0	4.1	4.4	4.4	3.8	- MCC
- Caribbean	1.6	1.2	1.4	0.8	0.7	0.8	0.6	0.5	0.5	0.4	- Caraïbes
- Rest of America	1.2	1.0	0.9	0.8	0.8	0.7	0.8	0.7	0.6	0.6	- Autre d'Amérique
Asia excluding former USSR	20.5	18.8	17.3	17.0	16.8	16.5	17.7	18.4	17.8	18.0	Asie ancienne URSS exclus
- Middle East	10.0	8.5	7.0	6.6	6.8	7.5	7.4	6.8	7.4	7.1	- Moyen-Orient
Asia former USSR	0.0	0.8	0.2	0.6	0.5	0.5	0.3	0.7	0.6	0.4	Asie ancienne URSS
Europe excluding former USSR	34.9	38.1	38.3	38.4	40.0	40.2	39.0	36.7	38.1	39.5	Europe ancienne URSS exclus
- European Union	33.9	37.0	37.2	37.4	39.0	39.3	38.2	35.8	37.3	38.7	- Union Européenne
- Eastern Europe	1.0	0.9	0.9	0.8	0.9	0.9	0.7	0.8	0.7	0.7	- Europe de l'Est
- Rest of Europe	0.1	0.2	0.2	0.2	0.1	0.1	0.1	0.1	0.1	0.1	- Autre de l'Europe
Europe former USSR	0.4	0.4	0.4	0.3	0.3	0.3	0.2	0.3	0.3	0.3	Europe ancienne URSS
Oceania	3.1	2.8	3.3	3.3	2.9	2.6	3.1	3.0	2.6	2.9	Océanie

058 Fruit, preserved, and fruits preparations

TRADE BY COMMODITY (Value in million US dollars)
Imports by principal countries or areas

COMMERCE PAR PRODUIT (Valeur en millions de dollars EU)
Importations selon les principaux pays ou zones

Country or area	1998	1999	2000	2001	2002	Pays ou zone
World	13176.2	13952.8	13276.4	12704.8	13787.9	Monde
Africa	109.0	105.9	140.6	125.7	141.1	Afrique
Americas	2736.6	3046.3	3066.3	2960.9	3127.0	Amériques
- Northern America	2219.6	2524.8	2489.7	2351.8	2564.8	- Amérique du Nord
- LAIA	344.1	327.7	373.9	390.6	342.7	- ALAI
- CACM	60.4	70.9	77.2	86.2	89.7	- MCC
- Caribbean	93.1	103.6	105.5	113.0	107.2	- Caraïbes
- Rest of America	19.3	19.3	20.1	19.3	22.6	- Autre d'Amérique
Asia excluding former USSR	1878.6	2166.3	2212.5	2193.1	2258.5	Asie ancienne URSS exclus
- Middle East	253.0	250.9	283.0	310.0	345.4	- Moyen-Orient
Asia former USSR	14.2	13.2	10.6	11.9	13.9	Asie ancienne URSS
Europe excluding former USSR	7969.6	8222.9	7465.1	6985.9	7688.9	Europe ancienne URSS exclus
- European Union	7321.4	7579.1	6846.3	6414.1	7033.9	- Union Européenne
- Eastern Europe	305.4	295.8	289.6	261.4	302.6	- Europe de l'Est
- Rest of Europe	342.8	348.0	329.2	310.4	352.3	- Autre de l'Europe
Europe former USSR	284.5	170.9	174.0	237.7	345.1	Europe ancienne URSS
Oceania	183.9	227.3	207.2	189.6	213.5	Océanie
United States	1625.0	1889.8	1878.0	1754.9	1921.3	Etats-Unis d'Amérique
Germany	1925.8	1889.6	1685.1	1715.6	1793.1	Allemagne
Japan	1037.7	1238.5	1242.0	1207.7	1132.7	Japon
France-Monaco	1220.2	1240.4	1201.0	1020.9	1163.9	France-Monaco
Netherlands	926.0	1064.4	927.2	786.6	869.0	Pays-Bas
United Kingdom	974.9	924.7	826.4	781.0	852.0	Royaume-Uni
Canada	583.5	622.4	609.0	589.7	638.8	Canada
Belgium	–	769.3	729.1	646.7	e709.3	Belgique
Italy-San Marino-Holy See	361.8	371.8	350.7	347.8	368.5	Italie-Saint-Marin-Saint-Siège
Austria	256.8	279.6	240.0	250.4	256.5	Autriche
Spain	221.3	256.7	203.8	213.2	247.9	Espagne
Sweden	200.4	218.6	180.2	173.4	199.4	Suède
Korea, Republic of	116.4	163.9	182.5	173.8	203.1	République de Corée
Switzerland-Liechtenstein	157.8	164.8	156.5	144.5	168.2	Suisse-Liechtenstein
Russian Federation	198.1	99.1	101.0	150.5	228.7	Fédération de Russie
Belgium-Luxembourg	742.6	–	–	–	–	Belgique-Luxembourg
Mexico	63.1	107.5	174.2	195.9	184.1	Mexique
Denmark	129.4	137.3	126.6	123.7	178.1	Danemark
Australia	115.3	149.0	137.7	118.4	131.1	Australie
Saudi Arabia	116.0	111.1	129.2	129.6	e134.1	Arabie saoudite
China, Hong Kong SAR	141.4	121.5	116.4	111.3	109.6	Chine - RAS de Hong-Kong
Poland	117.2	126.4	118.9	109.2	117.4	Pologne
Finland	104.7	112.8	94.8	89.0	92.1	Finlande
Portugal	103.5	122.0	96.0	76.5	87.7	Portugal
Ireland	80.4	91.4	93.5	95.6	114.0	Irlande
Singapore	83.2	98.8	91.2	88.9	92.9	Singapour
Norway	85.9	90.7	78.4	72.9	84.5	Norvège
Greece	73.6	75.2	64.9	67.0	e74.1	Grèce
Czech Republic	82.4	74.3	60.8	59.3	72.4	République tchèque
Israel	66.5	64.6	70.5	64.8	82.3	Israël

(Value as percentages of World total) **(Valeur en pourcentage du total mondial)**

Regions of the world	1993	1994	1995	1996	1997	1998	1999	2000	2001	2002	Régions du monde
World	100.0	100.0	100.0	100.0	100.0	100.0	100.0	100.0	100.0	100.0	Monde
Africa	0.6	0.6	0.8	0.8	0.8	0.8	0.8	1.1	1.0	1.0	Afrique
Americas	21.1	20.0	18.1	20.4	22.2	20.8	21.8	23.1	23.3	22.7	Amériques
- Northern America	18.0	16.6	14.6	17.3	18.8	16.8	18.1	18.8	18.5	18.6	- Amérique du Nord
- LAIA	1.9	2.4	2.3	2.0	2.2	2.6	2.3	2.8	3.1	2.5	- ALAI
- CACM	0.2	0.3	0.3	0.3	0.4	0.5	0.5	0.6	0.7	0.7	- MCC
- Caribbean	0.8	0.6	0.6	0.5	0.6	0.7	0.7	0.8	0.9	0.8	- Caraïbes
- Rest of America	0.2	0.2	0.2	0.2	0.2	0.1	0.1	0.2	0.2	0.2	- Autre d'Amérique
Asia excluding former USSR	18.0	18.8	18.8	16.9	16.5	14.3	15.5	16.7	17.3	16.4	Asie ancienne URSS exclus
- Middle East	1.6	1.4	1.5	1.5	1.7	1.9	1.8	2.1	2.4	2.5	- Moyen-Orient
Asia former USSR	0.1	0.0	0.1	0.1	0.1	0.1	0.1	0.1	0.1	0.1	Asie ancienne URSS
Europe excluding former USSR	56.4	56.6	58.1	57.6	56.5	60.5	58.9	56.2	55.0	55.8	Europe ancienne URSS exclus
- European Union	52.6	52.2	53.3	52.9	52.0	55.6	54.3	51.6	50.5	51.0	- Union Européenne
- Eastern Europe	1.2	1.5	1.8	2.1	2.1	2.3	2.1	2.2	2.1	2.2	- Europe de l'Est
- Rest of Europe	2.6	2.9	3.0	2.6	2.4	2.6	2.5	2.5	2.4	2.6	- Autre de l'Europe
Europe former USSR	2.7	2.5	2.7	2.6	2.5	2.2	1.2	1.3	1.9	2.5	Europe ancienne URSS
Oceania	1.3	1.4	1.5	1.6	1.4	1.4	1.6	1.6	1.5	1.5	Océanie

TRADE BY COMMODITY (Value in million US dollars)
Exports by principal countries or areas

COMMERCE PAR PRODUIT (Valeur en millions de dollars EU)
Exportations selon les principaux pays ou zones

Country or area	1998	1999	2000	2001	2002	Pays ou zone
World	12746.6	13036.4	12435.5	12265.3	12865.4	Monde
Africa	354.0	348.5	397.0	397.1	417.8	Afrique
Americas	3837.9	3975.9	3786.3	3411.1	3500.9	Amériques
- Northern America	1387.3	1479.1	1489.8	1439.3	1485.8	- Amérique du Nord
- LAIA	2150.1	2196.5	1935.4	1708.7	1761.6	- ALAI
- CACM	167.0	169.9	193.2	180.1	179.7	- MCC
- Caribbean	97.9	88.4	103.7	77.3	66.8	- Caraïbes
- Rest of America	35.8	42.0	64.2	5.7	7.0	- Autre d'Amérique
Asia excluding former USSR	2091.8	2453.6	2409.2	2592.1	2718.5	Asie ancienne URSS exclus
- Middle East	494.0	465.8	413.1	450.1	432.2	- Moyen-Orient
Asia former USSR	14.0	27.1	21.8	24.1	22.3	Asie ancienne URSS
Europe excluding former USSR	6149.4	5960.8	5549.7	5549.6	5898.2	Europe ancienne URSS exclus
- European Union	5336.7	5209.7	4800.1	4802.2	5059.0	- Union Européenne
- Eastern Europe	626.2	544.5	562.7	545.3	650.5	- Europe de l'Est
- Rest of Europe	186.5	206.6	186.9	202.1	188.7	- Autre de l'Europe
Europe former USSR	134.3	90.7	99.2	124.0	136.8	Europe ancienne URSS
Oceania	165.2	179.9	172.4	167.3	170.9	Océanie
United States	1236.5	1293.2	1286.9	1228.4	1266.5	Etats-Unis d'Amérique
Brazil	1347.5	1329.3	1122.6	912.7	e946.2	Brésil
Germany	971.9	942.7	856.9	961.8	894.4	Allemagne
China	533.3	615.2	729.7	849.7	935.6	Chine
Netherlands	683.4	786.8	718.3	696.4	736.7	Pays-Bas
Italy-San Marino-Holy See	719.3	708.6	665.4	649.0	676.7	Italie-Saint-Marin-Saint-Siège
Spain	617.5	614.8	537.2	539.9	642.2	Espagne
Belgium	–	801.6	678.6	688.4	e772.4	Belgique
Thailand	428.3	645.9	504.7	521.9	e551.2	Thaïlande
France-Monaco	449.0	476.1	444.1	363.4	401.5	France-Monaco
Poland	388.0	351.3	379.1	364.8	458.3	Pologne
Turkey	387.9	362.2	298.8	328.5	304.4	Turquie
Greece	349.8	268.1	292.7	283.0	e283.3	Grèce
Mexico	299.2	276.3	265.3	208.9	231.4	Mexique
Austria	228.2	241.9	249.2	239.3	256.5	Autriche
Argentina	204.6	230.9	201.7	232.3	e224.4	Argentine
Chile	174.7	228.0	208.4	230.5	e225.5	Chili
Canada	150.7	185.8	202.8	210.9	219.2	Canada
Philippines	184.5	174.9	190.7	213.3	205.5	Philippines
Belgium-Luxembourg	749.1	–	–	–	–	Belgique-Luxembourg
United Kingdom	147.3	133.8	123.1	125.6	125.6	Royaume-Uni
Costa Rica	120.7	120.1	137.1	131.3	127.4	Costa Rica
South Africa	–	–	214.0	192.6	222.7	Afrique du Sud
Australia	122.6	135.9	123.5	114.9	124.5	Australie
Hungary	141.6	114.6	115.6	108.0	112.9	Hongrie
Denmark	115.2	116.1	103.5	114.7	113.7	Danemark
Israel	121.0	106.0	109.8	96.7	96.2	Israël
Serbia and Montenegro	106.8	94.6	89.0	e103.3	e77.1	Serbie-et-Monténégro
Indonesia	36.7	117.8	89.1	101.4	119.2	Indonésie
Southern African Customs Union	214.0	218.8	–	–	–	Union douanière d'Afrique australe

(Value as percentages of World total) **(Valeur en pourcentage du total mondial)**

Regions of the world	1993	1994	1995	1996	1997	1998	1999	2000	2001	2002	Régions du monde
World	100.0	100.0	100.0	100.0	100.0	100.0	100.0	100.0	100.0	100.0	Monde
Africa	3.5	3.2	3.2	3.0	3.3	2.8	2.7	3.2	3.2	3.2	Afrique
Americas	28.5	28.2	28.1	30.5	30.0	30.1	30.5	30.4	27.8	27.2	Amériques
- Northern America	13.1	12.5	10.6	10.8	12.1	10.9	11.3	12.0	11.7	11.5	- Amérique du Nord
- LAIA	14.2	14.5	16.1	18.1	15.9	16.9	16.8	15.6	13.9	13.7	- ALAI
- CACM	0.5	0.6	0.7	0.9	1.1	1.3	1.3	1.6	1.5	1.4	- MCC
- Caribbean	0.4	0.4	0.4	0.4	0.6	0.8	0.7	0.8	0.6	0.5	- Caraïbes
- Rest of America	0.2	0.2	0.3	0.3	0.3	0.3	0.3	0.5	0.0	0.1	- Autre d'Amérique
Asia excluding former USSR	20.6	19.5	18.4	18.5	18.9	16.4	18.8	19.4	21.1	21.1	Asie ancienne URSS exclus
- Middle East	2.9	3.5	3.3	3.3	4.1	3.9	3.6	3.3	3.7	3.4	- Moyen-Orient
Asia former USSR	0.1	0.2	0.1	0.2	0.2	0.1	0.2	0.2	0.2	0.2	Asie ancienne URSS
Europe excluding former USSR	44.9	46.4	47.2	44.8	44.7	48.2	45.7	44.6	45.2	45.8	Europe ancienne URSS exclus
- European Union	38.3	38.7	40.4	39.1	39.0	41.9	40.0	38.6	39.2	39.3	- Union Européenne
- Eastern Europe	5.0	5.4	4.7	5.0	5.1	4.9	4.2	4.5	4.4	5.1	- Europe de l'Est
- Rest of Europe	1.7	2.3	2.0	0.7	0.6	1.5	1.6	1.5	1.6	1.5	- Autre de l'Europe
Europe former USSR	0.8	0.8	1.3	1.4	1.3	1.1	0.7	0.8	1.0	1.1	Europe ancienne URSS
Oceania	1.5	1.8	1.7	1.6	1.6	1.3	1.4	1.4	1.4	1.3	Océanie

061 Sugar and honey

TRADE BY COMMODITY (Value in million US dollars)
Imports by principal countries or areas

COMMERCE PAR PRODUIT (Valeur en millions de dollars EU)
Importations selon les principaux pays ou zones

Country or area	1998	1999	2000	2001	2002	Pays ou zone
World	14418.7	13187.9	11522.9	13630.1	13356.0	Monde
Africa	1648.3	1344.3	1256.9	1484.0	1463.2	Afrique
Americas	2253.9	1803.6	1652.9	1877.1	1899.9	Amériques
- Northern America	1504.2	1252.6	1185.5	1284.6	1386.6	- Amérique du Nord
- LAIA	575.7	385.6	333.6	416.4	330.6	- ALAI
- CACM	12.7	22.8	12.6	13.1	14.1	- MCC
- Caribbean	146.9	129.3	110.2	152.2	158.1	- Caraïbes
- Rest of America	14.3	13.3	11.0	10.9	10.5	- Autre d'Amérique
Asia excluding former USSR	3837.7	3714.4	3349.3	3667.8	3180.9	Asie ancienne URSS exclus
- Middle East	905.6	947.0	829.0	731.2	740.6	- Moyen-Orient
Asia former USSR	274.7	275.2	316.2	335.6	293.9	Asie ancienne URSS
Europe excluding former USSR	4822.0	4577.0	3850.7	4636.0	5213.4	Europe ancienne URSS exclus
- European Union	4343.2	4138.8	3378.9	4057.4	4619.7	- Union Européenne
- Eastern Europe	244.7	200.2	250.6	309.3	277.3	- Europe de l'Est
- Rest of Europe	234.1	238.1	221.2	269.3	316.5	- Autre de l'Europe
Europe former USSR	1494.9	1386.1	1004.1	1526.2	1202.6	Europe ancienne URSS
Oceania	87.2	87.3	92.9	103.4	102.1	Océanie
Russian Federation	1247.0	1194.3	790.2	1266.2	936.6	Fédération de Russie
United States	1136.8	959.5	876.5	921.2	1058.5	Etats-Unis d'Amérique
United Kingdom	1066.1	964.6	831.5	874.9	890.3	Royaume-Uni
Germany	571.3	527.2	463.7	542.2	646.5	Allemagne
Belgium	–	651.8	374.1	769.2	e843.6	Belgique
Japan	552.7	407.0	432.6	497.8	414.7	Japon
France-Monaco	391.6	428.8	391.5	376.9	463.8	France-Monaco
Korea, Republic of	448.5	334.3	356.0	432.0	358.4	République de Corée
Spain	425.4	365.1	282.8	356.6	410.6	Espagne
Italy-San Marino-Holy See	369.0	326.7	306.7	365.9	445.3	Italie-Saint-Marin-Saint-Siège
Indonesia	371.6	552.8	306.8	268.3	228.2	Indonésie
Canada	364.6	290.1	307.4	361.4	325.5	Canada
Malaysia	282.8	270.5	269.0	304.7	e333.0	Malaisie
Algeria	278.7	223.0	222.2	e268.7	e306.1	Algérie
Netherlands	223.3	256.6	213.8	207.3	236.9	Pays-Bas
Iran (Islamic Republic of)	230.2	280.8	239.2	187.0	189.6	Iran (République islamique d')
China	157.4	156.7	147.3	349.7	256.7	Chine
Nigeria	203.6	116.0	146.7	e201.1	e190.7	Nigéria
Saudi Arabia	181.6	115.1	124.3	191.6	e198.3	Arabie saoudite
Portugal	163.5	162.8	141.4	143.5	161.0	Portugal
Egypt	203.0	195.4	e125.6	114.3	115.0	Egypte
Belgium-Luxembourg	735.0	–	–	–	–	Belgique-Luxembourg
Morocco	157.1	136.6	139.2	137.8	e145.4	Maroc
Israel	150.8	132.5	116.7	136.0	122.5	Israël
Belarus	150.7	107.9	117.8	141.2	127.4	Bélarus
Sri Lanka	e120.4	108.6	e146.7	128.2	138.2	Sri Lanka
Denmark	114.8	142.2	85.4	95.4	150.6	Danemark
India	271.7	264.1	14.2	18.3	19.6	Inde
Kazakhstan	107.4	89.0	93.8	125.0	e127.7	Kazakhstan
Romania	100.9	74.2	109.6	146.2	97.0	Roumanie

(Value as percentages of World total) **(Valeur en pourcentage du total mondial)**

Regions of the world	1993	1994	1995	1996	1997	1998	1999	2000	2001	2002	Régions du monde
World	100.0	100.0	100.0	100.0	100.0	100.0	100.0	100.0	100.0	100.0	Monde
Africa	10.0	9.6	10.5	9.0	10.1	11.4	10.2	10.9	10.9	11.0	Afrique
Americas	16.1	15.2	13.0	14.2	14.8	15.6	13.7	14.3	13.8	14.2	Amériques
- Northern America	12.3	10.5	8.7	10.7	11.2	10.4	9.5	10.3	9.4	10.4	- Amérique du Nord
- LAIA	2.6	3.8	3.4	2.5	2.7	4.0	2.9	2.9	3.1	2.5	- ALAI
- CACM	0.2	0.1	0.1	0.0	0.1	0.1	0.2	0.1	0.1	0.1	- MCC
- Caribbean	0.8	0.7	0.8	0.9	0.8	1.0	1.0	1.0	1.1	1.2	- Caraïbes
- Rest of America	0.2	0.1	0.1	0.1	0.1	0.1	0.1	0.1	0.1	0.1	- Autre d'Amérique
Asia excluding former USSR	26.8	32.8	32.3	33.1	33.7	26.6	28.2	29.1	26.9	23.8	Asie ancienne URSS exclus
- Middle East	7.0	7.0	7.7	11.8	12.8	6.3	7.2	7.2	5.4	5.5	- Moyen-Orient
Asia former USSR	1.2	1.0	1.8	2.2	1.7	1.9	2.1	2.7	2.5	2.2	Asie ancienne URSS
Europe excluding former USSR	35.6	31.9	33.0	30.6	30.3	33.4	34.7	33.4	34.0	39.0	Europe ancienne URSS exclus
- European Union	31.7	28.2	28.7	26.8	26.8	30.1	31.4	29.3	29.8	34.6	- Union Européenne
- Eastern Europe	1.9	1.1	1.9	2.2	1.6	1.7	1.5	2.2	2.3	2.1	- Europe de l'Est
- Rest of Europe	2.0	2.6	2.4	1.6	1.9	1.6	1.8	1.9	2.0	2.4	- Autre de l'Europe
Europe former USSR	9.5	8.7	8.8	10.2	8.7	10.4	10.5	8.7	11.2	9.0	Europe ancienne URSS
Oceania	0.8	0.8	0.7	0.7	0.6	0.6	0.7	0.8	0.8	0.8	Océanie

TRADE BY COMMODITY (Value in million US dollars)
Exports by principal countries or areas

COMMERCE PAR PRODUIT (Valeur en millions de dollars EU)
Exportations selon les principaux pays ou zones

Country or area	1998	1999	2000	2001	2002	Pays ou zone
World	12486.8	10361.8	9716.9	11938.2	12100.8	Monde
Africa	973.2	827.8	922.1	1058.5	991.1	Afrique
Americas	4833.6	4147.6	3379.0	4680.3	4725.4	Amériques
- Northern America	537.8	510.3	514.3	566.9	576.9	- Amérique du Nord
- LAIA	2833.7	2477.1	1722.7	2845.5	3004.4	- ALAI
- CACM	516.6	332.1	325.5	431.1	382.4	- MCC
- Caribbean	753.0	642.1	635.8	702.1	620.7	- Caraïbes
- Rest of America	192.4	186.0	180.6	134.7	140.9	- Autre d'Amérique
Asia excluding former USSR	1718.5	1407.6	1546.6	2000.2	1923.5	Asie ancienne URSS exclus
- Middle East	157.0	197.2	200.9	286.9	120.9	- Moyen-Orient
Asia former USSR	14.1	8.5	12.3	11.2	9.8	Asie ancienne URSS
Europe excluding former USSR	4512.5	3584.3	3496.3	3746.4	3931.3	Europe ancienne URSS exclus
- European Union	4208.3	3378.0	3285.8	3480.3	3634.9	- Union Européenne
- Eastern Europe	293.8	196.2	198.8	226.2	239.3	- Europe de l'Est
- Rest of Europe	10.4	10.1	11.7	39.9	57.1	- Autre de l'Europe
Europe former USSR	229.8	168.6	162.9	238.0	307.9	Europe ancienne URSS
Oceania	205.1	217.6	197.8	203.6	211.8	Océanie
Brazil	1953.3	1925.1	1203.9	2289.2	e2373.3	Brésil
France-Monaco	1469.9	1303.5	1271.8	1119.9	1247.1	France-Monaco
Thailand	689.5	582.0	689.9	765.2	e808.1	Thaïlande
Germany	781.3	720.8	616.8	720.0	617.5	Allemagne
Cuba	e475.7	470.6	459.1	551.1	e476.1	Cuba
Belgium	–	385.6	488.3	454.1	e509.5	Belgique
United States	351.7	326.2	336.7	373.9	357.4	Etats-Unis d'Amérique
Mauritius	372.4	318.3	211.8	283.3	287.5	Maurice
United Kingdom	394.2	254.0	229.8	257.0	225.2	Royaume-Uni
Netherlands	365.1	109.2	128.9	351.1	348.1	Pays-Bas
Guatemala	332.3	201.0	197.6	224.1	244.9	Guatemala
Colombia	305.9	192.0	205.0	225.7	226.1	Colombie
Canada	186.1	184.1	177.6	193.0	219.5	Canada
Italy-San Marino-Holy See	181.5	206.9	187.3	172.0	193.5	Italie-Saint-Marin-Saint-Siège
India	11.4	13.2	118.0	385.8	391.7	Inde
Mexico	324.1	153.4	108.3	119.8	211.0	Mexique
China	216.2	161.1	176.6	166.9	179.0	Chine
South Africa	–	–	267.7	321.8	222.6	Afrique du Sud
Argentina	152.9	141.2	151.6	128.8	e124.5	Argentine
Turkey	94.7	125.1	145.0	237.7	68.3	Turquie
Denmark	105.8	118.6	112.5	117.8	151.5	Danemark
Pakistan	269.5	157.1	49.4	61.6	62.9	Pakistan
Southern African Customs Union	330.6	235.4	–	–	–	Union douanière d'Afrique australe
Fiji	e105.8	e126.4	97.3	118.8	113.9	Fidji
Guyana	121.2	130.3	123.4	90.3	93.5	Guyana
Belgium-Luxembourg	550.7	–	–	–	–	Belgique-Luxembourg
Poland	140.3	111.9	109.7	106.1	76.1	Pologne
Korea, Republic of	120.8	86.5	83.1	96.9	93.0	République de Corée
Belarus	94.9	73.5	80.4	88.4	123.6	Bélarus
Spain	113.4	79.7	79.7	79.6	69.5	Espagne

(Value as percentages of World total) **(Valeur en pourcentage du total mondial)**

Regions of the world	1993	1994	1995	1996	1997	1998	1999	2000	2001	2002	Régions du monde
World	100.0	100.0	100.0	100.0	100.0	100.0	100.0	100.0	100.0	100.0	Monde
Africa	6.3	6.7	5.8	6.7	5.8	7.8	8.0	9.5	8.9	8.2	Afrique
Americas	29.5	27.8	30.7	30.0	34.9	38.7	40.0	34.8	39.2	39.1	Amériques
- Northern America	3.5	3.6	3.2	3.3	3.5	4.3	4.9	5.3	4.7	4.8	- Amérique du Nord
- LAIA	10.9	11.8	17.0	15.6	17.4	22.7	23.9	17.7	23.8	24.8	- ALAI
- CACM	2.4	2.1	2.4	2.3	3.1	4.1	3.2	3.4	3.6	3.2	- MCC
- Caribbean	11.0	8.7	6.8	8.4	9.4	6.0	6.2	6.5	5.9	5.1	- Caraïbes
- Rest of America	1.8	1.5	1.3	0.5	1.5	1.5	1.8	1.9	1.1	1.2	- Autre d'Amérique
Asia excluding former USSR	18.1	15.4	15.4	17.1	14.1	13.8	13.6	15.9	16.8	15.9	Asie ancienne URSS exclus
- Middle East	1.8	1.7	0.5	1.0	1.6	1.3	1.9	2.1	2.4	1.0	- Moyen-Orient
Asia former USSR	0.1	0.2	0.2	0.5	0.5	0.1	0.1	0.1	0.1	0.1	Asie ancienne URSS
Europe excluding former USSR	36.7	33.4	32.0	29.8	31.3	36.1	34.6	36.0	31.4	32.5	Europe ancienne URSS exclus
- European Union	34.8	32.0	31.0	28.1	28.8	33.7	32.6	33.8	29.2	30.0	- Union Européenne
- Eastern Europe	1.7	1.3	0.9	1.6	2.4	2.4	1.9	2.0	1.9	2.0	- Europe de l'Est
- Rest of Europe	0.2	0.1	0.1	0.1	0.1	0.1	0.1	0.1	0.3	0.5	- Autre de l'Europe
Europe former USSR	0.6	5.1	5.5	6.1	3.6	1.8	1.6	1.7	2.0	2.5	Europe ancienne URSS
Oceania	8.7	11.5	10.4	9.8	9.7	1.6	2.1	2.0	1.7	1.8	Océanie

062 Sugar confectionery and preparations, non-chocolate

TRADE BY COMMODITY (Value in million US dollars)
Imports by principal countries or areas

COMMERCE PAR PRODUIT (Valeur en millions de dollars EU)
Importations selon les principaux pays ou zones

Country or area	1998	1999	2000	2001	2002	Pays ou zone
World	3699.8	3880.6	3962.2	4014.5	4302.8	Monde
Africa	63.9	54.9	90.4	91.5	83.6	Afrique
Americas	1165.1	1261.0	1339.1	1382.1	1488.8	Amériques
- Northern America	816.2	922.8	994.9	994.7	1140.9	- Amérique du Nord
- LAIA	253.3	236.2	235.4	270.3	228.9	- ALAI
- CACM	41.7	46.2	51.7	60.0	65.1	- MCC
- Caribbean	45.2	45.9	46.3	46.5	43.3	- Caraïbes
- Rest of America	8.7	9.9	10.8	10.6	10.6	- Autre d'Amérique
Asia excluding former USSR	496.9	519.8	568.3	570.9	588.6	Asie ancienne URSS exclus
- Middle East	129.1	117.1	132.3	138.8	130.6	- Moyen-Orient
Asia former USSR	30.2	29.5	36.2	32.6	37.4	Asie ancienne URSS
Europe excluding former USSR	1731.9	1834.4	1703.1	1720.5	1902.8	Europe ancienne URSS exclus
- European Union	1467.9	1574.3	1465.6	1465.4	1632.4	- Union Européenne
- Eastern Europe	110.6	105.5	101.5	112.1	116.5	- Europe de l'Est
- Rest of Europe	153.3	154.6	136.0	143.0	153.9	- Autre de l'Europe
Europe former USSR	128.8	97.0	139.0	132.8	102.9	Europe ancienne URSS
Oceania	83.0	83.9	86.1	84.1	98.7	Océanie
United States	641.1	747.3	812.2	802.1	940.5	Etats-Unis d'Amérique
Germany	301.4	332.1	290.5	293.9	288.1	Allemagne
United Kingdom	184.5	194.9	206.0	225.7	257.9	Royaume-Uni
Canada	170.2	170.2	181.2	190.9	198.0	Canada
France-Monaco	190.9	173.7	162.9	146.5	172.3	France-Monaco
China, Hong Kong SAR	150.5	148.0	141.5	130.6	129.8	Chine - RAS de Hong-Kong
Netherlands	115.2	126.9	118.4	109.8	139.1	Pays-Bas
Sweden	101.2	107.0	98.7	111.8	136.0	Suède
Italy-San Marino-Holy See	109.4	111.4	100.0	97.9	100.7	Italie-Saint-Marin-Saint-Siège
Belgium	–	117.9	115.3	118.4	e129.9	Belgique
Russian Federation	88.5	65.7	105.1	96.1	58.7	Fédération de Russie
Spain	67.2	70.3	70.0	69.7	81.9	Espagne
Ireland	57.2	71.5	69.4	68.2	75.3	Irlande
Denmark	74.8	79.1	60.2	57.8	67.4	Danemark
Austria	61.3	72.9	62.7	59.0	65.0	Autriche
Mexico	29.7	44.9	59.4	80.6	73.1	Mexique
Japan	42.6	48.2	65.5	58.9	69.5	Japon
Norway	58.2	58.5	50.8	51.2	55.1	Norvège
Australia	51.2	53.2	56.9	49.4	58.4	Australie
Switzerland-Liechtenstein	41.6	45.3	41.6	45.9	48.2	Suisse-Liechtenstein
Finland	43.5	43.8	44.4	41.6	44.1	Finlande
Poland	49.2	45.5	37.7	37.7	45.8	Pologne
Brazil	70.6	49.5	36.7	25.0	14.8	Brésil
Saudi Arabia	39.8	29.5	34.2	38.8	e40.1	Arabie saoudite
Venezuela	30.3	31.1	38.3	43.6	e36.7	Venezuela
Portugal	34.5	34.4	33.7	30.9	37.3	Portugal
Korea, Republic of	22.9	24.2	33.3	41.2	46.3	République de Corée
United Arab Emirates	25.3	26.5	34.3	38.8	e39.8	Emirates arabes unis
Israel	29.5	26.5	24.6	33.5	34.0	Israël
Singapore	24.5	28.4	29.7	28.8	34.7	Singapour

(Value as percentages of World total) **(Valeur en pourcentage du total mondial)**

Regions of the world	1993	1994	1995	1996	1997	1998	1999	2000	2001	2002	Régions du monde
World	100.0	100.0	100.0	100.0	100.0	100.0	100.0	100.0	100.0	100.0	Monde
Africa	1.7	1.3	1.2	1.3	1.5	1.7	1.4	2.3	2.3	1.9	Afrique
Americas	21.3	20.7	20.6	24.2	27.0	31.5	32.5	33.8	34.4	34.6	Amériques
- Northern America	15.3	14.3	14.4	17.1	19.2	22.1	23.8	25.1	24.8	26.5	- Amérique du Nord
- LAIA	4.2	4.8	4.5	5.2	5.7	6.8	6.1	5.9	6.7	5.3	- ALAI
- CACM	0.7	0.7	0.7	0.8	0.9	1.1	1.2	1.3	1.5	1.5	- MCC
- Caribbean	0.8	0.6	0.7	0.9	1.0	1.2	1.2	1.2	1.2	1.0	- Caraïbes
- Rest of America	0.2	0.2	0.2	0.2	0.2	0.2	0.3	0.3	0.3	0.2	- Autre d'Amérique
Asia excluding former USSR	19.7	25.5	26.3	16.9	16.1	13.4	13.4	14.3	14.2	13.7	Asie ancienne URSS exclus
- Middle East	3.1	2.7	2.4	2.6	2.8	3.5	3.0	3.3	3.5	3.0	- Moyen-Orient
Asia former USSR	0.4	0.7	2.0	2.0	1.2	0.8	0.8	0.9	0.8	0.9	Asie ancienne URSS
Europe excluding former USSR	46.8	45.4	42.5	48.7	47.1	46.8	47.3	43.0	42.9	44.2	Europe ancienne URSS exclus
- European Union	39.6	38.4	35.8	41.5	40.4	39.7	40.6	37.0	36.5	37.9	- Union Européenne
- Eastern Europe	3.0	2.7	2.7	3.0	2.9	3.0	2.7	2.6	2.8	2.7	- Europe de l'Est
- Rest of Europe	4.1	4.2	4.0	4.2	3.9	4.1	4.0	3.4	3.6	3.6	- Autre de l'Europe
Europe former USSR	8.0	4.5	5.5	4.5	4.8	3.5	2.5	3.5	3.3	2.4	Europe ancienne URSS
Oceania	2.1	2.0	1.9	2.3	2.3	2.2	2.2	2.2	2.1	2.3	Océanie

TRADE BY COMMODITY (Value in million US dollars)
Exports by principal countries or areas

COMMERCE PAR PRODUIT (Valeur en millions de dollars EU)
Exportations selon les principaux pays ou zones

Country or area	1998	1999	2000	2001	2002	Pays ou zone
World	4102.9	3984.2	4149.1	4117.9	4388.7	Monde
Africa	62.7	62.6	84.1	76.3	91.2	Afrique
Americas	956.3	965.9	1105.8	1172.2	1143.1	Amériques
- Northern America	446.6	436.1	540.6	590.2	547.2	- Amérique du Nord
- LAIA	477.5	494.8	510.9	528.8	553.0	- ALAI
- CACM	24.3	26.7	46.6	45.9	37.2	- MCC
- Caribbean	7.4	7.8	7.2	6.8	5.2	- Caraïbes
- Rest of America	0.5	0.6	0.6	0.5	0.5	- Autre d'Amérique
Asia excluding former USSR	585.0	589.0	655.9	648.4	678.9	Asie ancienne URSS exclus
- Middle East	179.1	137.8	140.5	151.9	148.1	- Moyen-Orient
Asia former USSR	7.5	8.6	4.8	2.9	1.1	Asie ancienne URSS
Europe excluding former USSR	2329.7	2204.8	2091.9	2074.5	2323.2	Europe ancienne URSS exclus
- European Union	2085.4	2011.1	1905.6	1858.6	2067.3	- Union Européenne
- Eastern Europe	134.5	85.0	91.7	118.1	153.2	- Europe de l'Est
- Rest of Europe	109.8	108.6	94.7	97.8	102.7	- Autre de l'Europe
Europe former USSR	117.7	102.6	150.0	80.8	82.7	Europe ancienne URSS
Oceania	44.1	50.6	56.6	62.8	68.6	Océanie
Germany	384.0	358.1	315.8	358.0	405.2	Allemagne
Spain	322.9	353.0	396.2	360.9	338.0	Espagne
United Kingdom	378.7	347.9	326.4	251.3	262.0	Royaume-Uni
United States	268.7	264.4	322.0	319.2	256.9	Etats-Unis d'Amérique
Canada	177.9	171.7	218.6	271.0	290.3	Canada
Belgium	–	247.2	234.7	252.1	e282.9	Belgique
Mexico	198.9	202.6	206.1	182.5	205.0	Mexique
Netherlands	182.5	154.9	134.6	140.9	209.7	Pays-Bas
France-Monaco	164.9	148.9	132.0	137.6	160.6	France-Monaco
Denmark	126.8	116.1	107.4	116.9	133.9	Danemark
Colombia	89.7	103.7	95.1	117.3	114.6	Colombie
Turkey	135.1	91.4	91.7	99.8	98.8	Turquie
China, Hong Kong SAR	116.0	91.5	107.5	101.3	92.1	Chine - RAS de Hong-Kong
Brazil	73.8	85.0	91.2	114.7	e118.9	Brésil
China	49.9	53.1	80.0	83.9	120.4	Chine
Korea, Republic of	61.0	71.5	82.5	73.6	63.3	République de Corée
Italy-San Marino-Holy See	73.3	70.7	69.5	65.9	71.1	Italie-Saint-Marin-Saint-Siège
Switzerland-Liechtenstein	76.0	74.2	65.1	64.6	66.1	Suisse-Liechtenstein
Argentina	72.4	60.4	71.9	62.1	e60.0	Argentine
Poland	81.6	41.3	43.0	45.2	61.0	Pologne
Ireland	50.6	50.7	48.4	52.7	68.1	Irlande
Austria	63.3	64.3	51.0	40.3	50.7	Autriche
Ukraine	49.6	56.8	89.4	22.6	24.9	Ukraine
Australia	36.5	42.2	49.0	54.3	57.1	Australie
Indonesia	18.4	53.3	51.2	54.0	60.2	Indonésie
Belgium-Luxembourg	236.7	–	–	–	–	Belgique-Luxembourg
Japan	42.2	49.3	45.8	37.4	39.1	Japon
Czech Republic	28.8	27.7	34.5	53.5	66.8	République tchèque
Sweden	48.7	50.5	44.3	33.0	33.1	Suède
Thailand	22.6	30.4	40.7	37.3	e39.3	Thaïlande

(Value as percentages of World total)

(Valeur en pourcentage du total mondial)

Regions of the world	1993	1994	1995	1996	1997	1998	1999	2000	2001	2002	Régions du monde
World	100.0	100.0	100.0	100.0	100.0	100.0	100.0	100.0	100.0	100.0	Monde
Africa	1.3	1.3	1.2	1.3	1.5	1.5	1.6	2.0	1.9	2.1	Afrique
Americas	17.6	16.9	16.7	17.3	20.9	23.3	24.2	26.7	28.5	26.0	Amériques
- Northern America	9.9	9.0	7.9	8.2	10.2	10.9	10.9	13.0	14.3	12.5	- Amérique du Nord
- LAIA	6.8	7.0	8.0	8.4	10.1	11.6	12.4	12.3	12.8	12.6	- ALAI
- CACM	0.8	0.8	0.6	0.6	0.5	0.6	0.7	1.1	1.1	0.8	- MCC
- Caribbean	0.2	0.1	0.2	0.2	0.2	0.2	0.2	0.2	0.2	0.1	- Caraïbes
- Rest of America	0.0	0.0	0.0	0.0	0.0	0.0	0.0	0.0	0.0	0.0	- Autre d'Amérique
Asia excluding former USSR	15.5	16.4	18.8	18.4	17.5	14.3	14.8	15.8	15.7	15.5	Asie ancienne URSS exclus
- Middle East	3.2	4.9	5.8	6.4	5.6	4.4	3.5	3.4	3.7	3.4	- Moyen-Orient
Asia former USSR	0.0	0.1	0.1	0.1	0.1	0.2	0.2	0.1	0.1	0.0	Asie ancienne URSS
Europe excluding former USSR	63.8	62.5	59.8	59.4	56.6	56.8	55.3	50.4	50.4	52.9	Europe ancienne URSS exclus
- European Union	57.5	56.2	53.8	52.6	49.8	50.8	50.5	45.9	45.1	47.1	- Union Européenne
- Eastern Europe	2.3	2.5	2.8	3.8	4.3	3.3	2.1	2.2	2.9	3.5	- Europe de l'Est
- Rest of Europe	4.0	3.8	3.2	2.9	2.6	2.7	2.7	2.3	2.4	2.3	- Autre de l'Europe
Europe former USSR	0.7	1.8	2.1	2.1	2.2	2.9	2.6	3.6	2.0	1.9	Europe ancienne URSS
Oceania	1.0	1.0	1.2	1.4	1.2	1.1	1.3	1.4	1.5	1.6	Océanie

071 Coffee and coffee substitutes

TRADE BY COMMODITY (Value in million US dollars)
Imports by principal countries or areas

COMMERCE PAR PRODUIT (Valeur en millions de dollars EU
Importations selon les principaux pays ou zone

Country or area	1998	1999	2000	2001	2002	Pays ou zone
World	16653.7	13584.6	12360.4	9717.1	9380.8	Monde
Africa	361.5	340.3	391.1	428.7	448.8	Afrique
Americas	4374.3	3691.7	3441.6	2352.3	2308.4	Amériques
- Northern America	4156.9	3517.8	3278.3	2189.6	2183.3	- Amérique du Nord
- LAIA	185.8	135.7	128.9	124.8	88.2	- ALAI
- CACM	7.1	10.0	13.1	13.6	14.4	- MCC
- Caribbean	21.1	24.5	17.1	20.6	19.0	- Caraïbes
- Rest of America	3.4	3.6	4.3	3.6	3.5	- Autre d'Amérique
Asia excluding former USSR	1948.2	1639.1	1555.3	1261.1	1245.3	Asie ancienne URSS exclus
- Middle East	279.6	237.5	231.0	209.6	209.3	- Moyen-Orient
Asia former USSR	17.8	25.8	23.1	21.1	16.7	Asie ancienne URSS
Europe excluding former USSR	9389.8	7406.0	6471.5	5126.9	4803.5	Europe ancienne URSS exclus
- European Union	8166.9	6365.6	5532.2	4321.3	4056.9	- Union Européenne
- Eastern Europe	639.8	575.7	506.5	431.2	401.0	- Europe de l'Est
- Rest of Europe	583.1	464.7	432.8	374.3	345.7	- Autre de l'Europe
Europe former USSR	345.2	285.8	301.6	377.6	397.3	Europe ancienne URSS
Oceania	216.9	195.8	176.3	149.5	160.8	Océanie
United States	3533.5	3001.2	2814.5	1789.1	1799.2	Etats-Unis d'Amérique
Germany	2469.1	1893.1	1637.1	1248.6	1141.5	Allemagne
Japan	1176.4	974.1	916.7	687.7	668.1	Japon
France-Monaco	1148.9	887.6	763.8	592.5	586.7	France-Monaco
Italy-San Marino-Holy See	936.2	736.9	659.8	514.4	428.8	Italie-Saint-Marin-Saint-Siège
Canada	620.8	514.1	462.7	398.8	382.5	Canada
United Kingdom	636.8	472.6	423.0	324.9	309.8	Royaume-Uni
Spain	549.2	452.7	354.3	273.7	248.7	Espagne
Netherlands	423.3	381.0	396.5	297.8	281.8	Pays-Bas
Belgium	-	435.5	392.6	322.9	e354.2	Belgique
Sweden	342.3	250.8	205.9	160.0	162.7	Suède
Poland	297.5	259.9	214.2	164.4	163.8	Pologne
Russian Federation	204.9	131.9	172.7	248.9	228.7	Fédération de Russie
Austria	268.0	222.3	152.8	148.6	131.7	Autriche
Switzerland-Liechtenstein	233.0	180.0	170.9	150.1	125.8	Suisse-Liechtenstein
Algeria	160.7	150.4	123.7	e149.6	e170.4	Algérie
Finland	238.6	173.4	144.5	108.7	86.7	Finlande
Australia	170.6	156.0	137.2	112.3	123.4	Australie
Belgium-Luxembourg	671.0	-	-	-	-	Belgique-Luxembourg
Denmark	190.6	134.7	116.9	87.4	88.1	Danemark
Korea, Republic of	165.3	134.4	124.0	85.1	83.8	République de Corée
Portugal	134.4	119.5	108.2	85.9	68.9	Portugal
Greece	125.0	110.6	97.7	83.1	e91.9	Grèce
Czech Republic	146.4	91.9	88.6	85.6	79.4	République tchèque
Norway	142.5	115.9	89.1	69.1	65.9	Norvège
Nigeria	1.4	1.9	105.3	e144.4	e136.9	Nigéria
Hungary	87.9	91.2	73.7	59.0	52.7	Hongrie
Serbia and Montenegro	72.9	54.3	75.8	e71.8	e72.7	Serbie-et-Monténégro
Romania	50.0	77.6	75.0	69.4	54.0	Roumanie
Saudi Arabia	71.5	64.3	67.0	56.4	e58.4	Arabie saoudite

(Value as percentages of World total) **(Valeur en pourcentage du total mondial)**

Regions of the world	1993	1994	1995	1996	1997	1998	1999	2000	2001	2002	Régions du monde
World	100.0	100.0	100.0	100.0	100.0	100.0	100.0	100.0	100.0	100.0	Monde
Africa	2.4	3.5	2.3	2.2	1.8	2.2	2.5	3.2	4.4	4.8	Afrique
Americas	22.7	23.4	23.2	24.4	27.0	26.3	27.2	27.8	24.2	24.6	Amériques
- Northern America	21.6	22.0	21.9	23.0	25.6	25.0	25.9	26.5	22.5	23.3	- Amérique du Nord
- LAIA	0.9	1.2	1.2	1.2	1.2	1.1	1.0	1.0	1.3	0.9	- ALAI
- CACM	0.0	0.0	0.0	0.0	0.0	0.0	0.1	0.1	0.1	0.2	- MCC
- Caribbean	0.2	0.1	0.1	0.1	0.1	0.1	0.2	0.1	0.2	0.2	- Caraïbes
- Rest of America	0.0	0.0	0.0	0.0	0.0	0.0	0.0	0.0	0.0	0.0	- Autre d'Amérique
Asia excluding former USSR	12.2	13.2	12.4	12.3	11.5	11.7	12.1	12.6	13.0	13.3	Asie ancienne URSS exclus
- Middle East	1.3	1.2	1.5	1.7	1.3	1.7	1.7	1.9	2.2	2.2	- Moyen-Orient
Asia former USSR	0.0	0.0	0.1	0.1	0.2	0.1	0.2	0.2	0.2	0.2	Asie ancienne URSS
Europe excluding former USSR	58.3	57.7	59.3	58.2	56.1	56.4	54.5	52.4	52.8	51.2	Europe ancienne URSS exclus
- European Union	51.6	51.0	52.6	51.5	50.0	49.0	46.9	44.8	44.5	43.2	- Union Européenne
- Eastern Europe	3.6	3.5	3.6	3.6	3.3	3.8	4.2	4.1	4.4	4.3	- Europe de l'Est
- Rest of Europe	3.2	3.2	3.1	3.1	2.8	3.5	3.4	3.5	3.9	3.7	- Autre de l'Europe
Europe former USSR	3.0	1.0	1.3	1.5	2.2	2.1	2.1	2.4	3.9	4.2	Europe ancienne URSS
Oceania	1.3	1.3	1.4	1.4	1.3	1.3	1.4	1.4	1.5	1.7	Océanie

TRADE BY COMMODITY (Value in million US dollars)
Exports by principal countries or areas

COMMERCE PAR PRODUIT (Valeur en millions de dollars EU)
Exportations selon les principaux pays ou zones

Country or area	1998	1999	2000	2001	2002	Pays ou zone
World	15790.9	13092.2	11558.6	8891.1	8764.3	Monde
Africa	1732.3	1357.0	1180.1	872.3	630.5	Afrique
Americas	8575.7	7196.1	6294.4	4302.0	4193.9	Amériques
- Northern America	667.1	583.8	530.0	513.1	512.5	- Amérique du Nord
- LAIA	5852.1	5016.8	3996.3	2860.9	2823.5	- ALAI
- CACM	1920.0	1517.1	1684.8	864.7	800.4	- MCC
- Caribbean	111.8	58.2	67.1	52.0	48.0	- Caraïbes
- Rest of America	24.7	20.2	16.2	11.3	9.6	- Autre d'Amérique
Asia excluding former USSR	1995.4	1705.2	1329.6	1142.8	1218.4	Asie ancienne URSS exclus
- Middle East	28.6	43.0	64.9	10.7	9.3	- Moyen-Orient
Asia former USSR	0.5	0.5	0.3	0.3	0.9	Asie ancienne URSS
Europe excluding former USSR	3075.3	2663.9	2556.2	2412.7	2564.8	Europe ancienne URSS exclus
- European Union	2792.0	2398.9	2285.8	2153.3	2296.4	- Union Européenne
- Eastern Europe	171.9	164.3	180.6	162.5	150.3	- Europe de l'Est
- Rest of Europe	111.4	100.7	89.8	96.9	118.1	- Autre de l'Europe
Europe former USSR	46.0	29.0	25.2	28.5	39.5	Europe ancienne URSS
Oceania	365.7	140.6	172.7	132.5	116.4	Océanie
Brazil	2604.7	2463.9	1784.6	1417.1	e1469.1	Brésil
Colombia	2038.8	1454.8	1185.5	859.0	864.8	Colombie
Germany	1067.9	844.5	875.8	795.0	839.9	Allemagne
Mexico	761.8	677.7	727.9	337.2	237.6	Mexique
Viet Nam	593.8	586.9	379.4	394.5	438.5	Viet Nam
Guatemala	586.8	561.9	575.4	306.9	262.0	Guatemala
United States	481.7	408.8	367.0	366.0	365.2	Etats-Unis d'Amérique
Indonesia	615.8	488.8	339.9	203.5	239.6	Indonésie
Italy-San Marino-Holy See	286.6	284.9	281.6	298.4	335.0	Italie-Saint-Marin-Saint-Siège
India	410.7	331.1	264.2	232.5	204.7	Inde
Honduras	429.8	256.1	340.6	163.6	182.5	Honduras
Côte d'Ivoire	398.7	209.5	303.0	e330.4	119.4	Côte d'Ivoire
Costa Rica	411.8	310.9	289.1	168.9	170.3	Costa Rica
Belgium	-	353.0	322.3	264.3	e296.6	Belgique
Ethiopia	381.9	269.1	255.4	145.1	159.9	Ethiopie
Peru	288.7	268.3	224.3	180.7	188.1	Pérou
France-Monaco	298.4	239.8	197.2	191.4	192.3	France-Monaco
El Salvador	324.5	247.0	301.5	118.7	109.2	El Salvador
Uganda	287.1	288.0	125.3	97.7	96.6	Ouganda
Canada	185.1	174.9	163.0	147.1	147.2	Canada
Papua New Guinea	347.0	e117.2	146.5	e110.3	e94.2	Papouasie-Nouvelle-Guinée
United Kingdom	158.0	139.9	129.9	128.5	131.3	Royaume-Uni
Nicaragua	167.0	141.2	178.2	106.6	76.5	Nicaragua
Spain	128.5	124.3	105.8	138.2	129.7	Espagne
Kenya	213.1	171.7	153.9	e49.1	35.4	Kenya
Netherlands	119.7	121.9	119.8	100.7	122.9	Pays-Bas
Singapore	105.7	89.0	97.3	98.8	110.8	Singapour
Switzerland-Liechtenstein	99.8	93.1	82.2	91.0	111.3	Suisse-Liechtenstein
Belgium-Luxembourg	470.5	-	-	-	-	Belgique-Luxembourg
Poland	94.2	95.3	109.7	86.9	77.5	Pologne

(Value as percentages of World total) **(Valeur en pourcentage du total mondial)**

Regions of the world	1993	1994	1995	1996	1997	1998	1999	2000	2001	2002	Régions du monde
World	100.0	100.0	100.0	100.0	100.0	100.0	100.0	100.0	100.0	100.0	Monde
Africa	14.3	11.6	12.7	12.7	10.1	11.0	10.4	10.2	9.8	7.2	Afrique
Americas	51.0	53.8	51.2	51.6	57.7	54.3	55.0	54.5	48.4	47.9	Amériques
- Northern America	3.4	3.4	3.1	3.3	3.4	4.2	4.5	4.6	5.8	5.8	- Amérique du Nord
- LAIA	36.4	41.2	35.9	36.2	41.8	37.1	38.3	34.6	32.2	32.2	- ALAI
- CACM	10.3	8.3	11.0	11.1	11.6	12.2	11.6	14.6	9.7	9.1	- MCC
- Caribbean	0.8	0.7	1.0	0.9	0.8	0.7	0.4	0.6	0.6	0.5	- Caraïbes
- Rest of America	0.1	0.1	0.2	0.1	0.1	0.2	0.2	0.1	0.1	0.1	- Autre d'Amérique
Asia excluding former USSR	11.8	15.0	16.2	13.0	11.6	12.6	13.0	11.5	12.9	13.9	Asie ancienne URSS exclus
- Middle East	0.4	0.1	0.2	0.1	0.1	0.2	0.3	0.6	0.1	0.1	- Moyen-Orient
Asia former USSR	0.0	0.0	0.0	0.0	0.0	0.0	0.0	0.0	0.0	0.0	Asie ancienne URSS
Europe excluding former USSR	19.1	17.1	17.5	19.8	18.4	19.5	20.3	22.1	27.1	29.3	Europe ancienne URSS exclus
- European Union	18.0	16.2	16.3	18.5	16.9	17.7	18.3	19.8	24.2	26.2	- Union Européenne
- Eastern Europe	0.4	0.3	0.5	0.6	0.8	1.1	1.3	1.6	1.8	1.7	- Europe de l'Est
- Rest of Europe	0.7	0.6	0.6	0.7	0.7	0.7	0.8	0.8	1.1	1.3	- Autre de l'Europe
Europe former USSR	0.0	0.2	0.2	0.4	0.5	0.3	0.2	0.2	0.3	0.5	Europe ancienne URSS
Oceania	3.7	2.4	2.2	2.5	1.7	2.3	1.1	1.5	1.5	1.3	Océanie

TRADE BY COMMODITY (Value in million US dollars)
Imports by principal countries or areas

COMMERCE PAR PRODUIT (Valeur en millions de dollars EU)
Importations selon les principaux pays ou zones

Country or area	1998	1999	2000	2001	2002	Pays ou zone
World	6447.8	6007.0	4630.0	4888.9	6516.2	Monde
Africa	47.6	54.6	39.4	42.1	47.6	Afrique
Americas	1529.0	1377.2	1140.0	1133.5	1409.5	Amériques
- Northern America	1365.7	1164.9	972.8	996.9	1172.7	- Amérique du Nord
- LAIA	149.6	201.6	159.3	125.8	218.5	- ALAI
- CACM	7.9	5.2	4.5	6.7	14.0	- MCC
- Caribbean	3.7	3.6	2.7	3.4	3.4	- Caraïbes
- Rest of America	2.0	1.8	0.7	0.8	0.9	- Autre d'Amérique
Asia excluding former USSR	533.9	476.6	461.5	511.1	651.4	Asie ancienne URSS exclus
- Middle East	67.7	70.6	65.5	80.4	109.3	- Moyen-Orient
Asia former USSR	2.5	3.3	4.4	5.5	6.3	Asie ancienne URSS
Europe excluding former USSR	3881.7	3720.9	2642.4	2828.0	3828.4	Europe ancienne URSS exclus
- European Union	3505.3	3377.7	2383.0	2549.7	3452.0	- Union Européenne
- Eastern Europe	197.8	170.0	138.2	155.7	217.4	- Europe de l'Est
- Rest of Europe	178.6	173.3	121.2	122.6	159.1	- Autre de l'Europe
Europe former USSR	344.1	261.2	257.2	289.2	457.9	Europe ancienne URSS
Oceania	109.0	113.2	85.1	79.4	115.0	Océanie
United States	1161.2	997.3	820.1	830.2	961.3	Etats-Unis d'Amérique
Netherlands	687.0	853.8	572.4	699.0	845.7	Pays-Bas
Germany	852.8	727.2	505.6	477.0	667.2	Allemagne
France-Monaco	539.4	551.6	396.3	407.9	636.7	France-Monaco
United Kingdom	486.6	475.0	231.5	290.2	412.0	Royaume-Uni
Belgium	–	296.5	300.7	277.6	e304.4	Belgique
Canada	204.6	167.6	152.7	166.6	211.4	Canada
Italy-San Marino-Holy See	190.3	167.2	140.8	142.4	195.2	Italie-Saint-Marin-Saint-Siège
Japan	170.3	162.0	134.7	133.0	175.8	Japon
Russian Federation	137.0	114.4	108.8	125.2	243.8	Fédération de Russie
Spain	126.1	114.9	85.4	95.7	182.9	Espagne
Poland	123.2	105.0	86.1	93.9	133.6	Pologne
Switzerland-Liechtenstein	128.1	128.6	86.8	85.5	112.2	Suisse-Liechtenstein
Estonia	124.8	77.4	70.3	81.2	117.5	Estonie
Malaysia	88.8	63.6	82.6	97.8	e106.9	Malaisie
Australia	87.8	93.0	67.8	62.3	92.7	Australie
Belgium-Luxembourg	377.0	–	–	–	–	Belgique-Luxembourg
Brazil	22.7	94.3	69.2	37.6	111.9	Brésil
Ukraine	57.7	46.6	55.5	63.6	68.6	Ukraine
Turkey	51.3	54.6	43.7	54.9	83.0	Turquie
Austria	68.0	56.5	36.2	42.1	66.0	Autriche
Singapore	57.1	45.3	39.3	42.7	61.7	Singapour
Argentina	75.2	52.9	38.8	42.0	e18.6	Argentine
China	49.3	35.3	36.1	37.3	32.3	Chine
Sweden	49.5	40.3	27.8	26.8	35.5	Suède
Ireland	35.9	23.2	25.1	33.7	41.6	Irlande
Mexico	24.4	23.1	30.1	24.4	40.0	Mexique
Indonesia	10.1	13.1	16.6	32.0	45.4	Indonésie
Czech Republic	23.2	23.4	20.7	22.8	25.3	République tchèque
Greece	29.0	24.6	19.7	19.6	e21.7	Grèce

(Value as percentages of World total)

(Valeur en pourcentage du total mondial)

Regions of the world	1993	1994	1995	1996	1997	1998	1999	2000	2001	2002	Régions du monde
World	100.0	100.0	100.0	100.0	100.0	100.0	100.0	100.0	100.0	100.0	Monde
Africa	1.4	0.8	0.8	0.8	0.8	0.7	0.9	0.9	0.9	0.7	Afrique
Americas	24.7	20.1	18.4	20.8	23.0	23.7	22.9	24.6	23.2	21.6	Amériques
- Northern America	23.1	18.0	16.3	19.1	20.5	21.2	19.4	21.0	20.4	18.0	- Amérique du Nord
- LAIA	1.4	1.8	1.9	1.5	2.3	2.3	3.4	3.4	2.6	3.4	- ALAI
- CACM	0.1	0.1	0.1	0.1	0.1	0.1	0.1	0.1	0.1	0.2	- MCC
- Caribbean	0.1	0.1	0.1	0.0	0.0	0.1	0.1	0.1	0.1	0.1	- Caraïbes
- Rest of America	0.0	0.0	0.0	0.0	0.0	0.0	0.0	0.0	0.0	0.0	- Autre d'Amérique
Asia excluding former USSR	8.5	8.2	8.7	7.9	8.6	8.3	7.9	10.0	10.5	10.0	Asie ancienne URSS exclus
- Middle East	0.8	0.9	1.1	0.9	1.1	1.0	1.2	1.4	1.6	1.7	- Moyen-Orient
Asia former USSR	0.0	0.0	0.0	0.0	0.0	0.0	0.1	0.1	0.1	0.1	Asie ancienne URSS
Europe excluding former USSR	62.4	66.6	67.7	65.9	60.3	60.2	61.9	57.1	57.8	58.8	Europe ancienne URSS exclus
- European Union	56.3	60.5	61.6	60.0	54.2	54.4	56.2	51.5	52.2	53.0	- Union Européenne
- Eastern Europe	3.0	3.0	2.9	3.4	3.5	3.1	2.8	3.0	3.2	3.3	- Europe de l'Est
- Rest of Europe	3.1	3.1	3.2	2.5	2.6	2.8	2.9	2.6	2.5	2.4	- Autre de l'Europe
Europe former USSR	1.5	2.7	2.8	3.1	5.5	5.3	4.3	5.6	5.9	7.0	Europe ancienne URSS
Oceania	1.5	1.6	1.5	1.5	1.7	1.7	1.9	1.8	1.6	1.8	Océanie

TRADE BY COMMODITY (Value in million US dollars)
Exports by principal countries or areas

COMMERCE PAR PRODUIT (Valeur en millions de dollars EU)
Exportations selon les principaux pays ou zones

Country or area	1998	1999	2000	2001	2002	Pays ou zone
World	5571.8	5013.5	3796.5	4160.4	6238.0	Monde
Africa	2297.3	2157.0	1448.8	1674.7	2869.7	Afrique
Americas	528.5	451.5	354.7	368.2	487.6	Amériques
- Northern America	160.7	165.0	131.9	149.5	198.5	- Amérique du Nord
- LAIA	257.2	260.5	196.3	196.4	257.4	- ALAI
- CACM	13.8	6.1	6.0	3.7	6.7	- MCC
- Caribbean	95.9	19.4	19.9	18.3	24.5	- Caraïbes
- Rest of America	0.9	0.5	0.6	0.3	0.5	- Autre d'Amérique
Asia excluding former USSR	908.7	766.9	614.0	651.0	1012.4	Asie ancienne URSS exclus
- Middle East	3.4	13.6	17.3	23.6	25.6	- Moyen-Orient
Asia former USSR	0.0	0.0	0.0	0.0	0.0	Asie ancienne URSS
Europe excluding former USSR	1682.1	1538.3	1290.5	1370.4	1705.1	Europe ancienne URSS exclus
- European Union	1671.6	1527.3	1269.9	1337.2	1664.0	- Union Européenne
- Eastern Europe	8.3	9.3	18.3	28.9	34.8	- Europe de l'Est
- Rest of Europe	2.2	1.7	2.2	4.3	6.3	- Autre de l'Europe
Europe former USSR	122.6	83.8	71.4	81.4	144.0	Europe ancienne URSS
Oceania	32.7	16.1	17.0	14.6	19.2	Océanie
Côte d'Ivoire	1630.9	1567.1	1017.9	e1110.1	2203.0	Côte d'Ivoire
Netherlands	967.4	936.3	753.8	830.4	979.8	Pays-Bas
Indonesia	489.2	386.7	308.4	359.3	666.3	Indonésie
Ghana	512.5	450.5	305.4	e399.7	e403.5	Ghana
France-Monaco	287.7	283.3	245.1	237.1	320.8	France-Monaco
Malaysia	183.3	174.7	133.6	146.6	e155.4	Malaisie
United States	140.4	145.3	112.0	128.6	176.8	Etats-Unis d'Amérique
Cameroon	e94.7	e90.2	103.6	143.9	235.2	Cameroun
Singapore	151.2	119.7	102.9	76.6	114.7	Singapour
Brazil	152.2	107.4	101.1	94.2	e97.6	Brésil
Estonia	119.7	82.5	70.4	80.8	142.5	Estonie
Germany	147.1	96.9	62.0	62.8	62.8	Allemagne
Ecuador	43.5	102.7	71.1	79.1	119.6	Equateur
United Kingdom	72.9	63.0	52.7	48.1	83.9	Royaume-Uni
Spain	58.8	63.0	48.3	55.5	91.9	Espagne
Belgium	–	57.6	80.0	79.8	e89.6	Belgique
China	35.4	31.1	18.1	16.9	16.6	Chine
Belgium-Luxembourg	115.6	–	–	–	–	Belgique-Luxembourg
Dominican Republic	e81.0	e5.0	e5.5	e8.8	e13.6	République dominicaine
Canada	20.3	19.7	20.0	20.9	21.7	Canada
Italy-San Marino-Holy See	19.2	17.3	15.4	12.8	23.8	Italie-Saint-Marin-Saint-Siège
Turkey	2.8	12.6	16.8	22.2	24.0	Turquie
Thailand	17.3	17.4	13.3	13.3	e14.1	Thaïlande
Papua New Guinea	25.2	e9.9	12.4	e9.3	e8.0	Papouasie-Nouvelle-Guinée
Peru	17.1	15.0	9.8	7.3	14.2	Pérou
Mexico	17.9	14.5	4.8	5.2	11.9	Mexique
Philippines	18.5	10.6	7.1	8.0	9.2	Philippines
Nigeria	19.3	22.5	2.1	e1.4	e1.2	Nigéria
Poland	7.1	6.5	7.2	13.2	10.7	Pologne
Colombia	10.9	10.9	2.6	6.8	8.4	Colombie

(Value as percentages of World total) **(Valeur en pourcentage du total mondial)**

Regions of the world	1993	1994	1995	1996	1997	1998	1999	2000	2001	2002	Régions du monde
World	100.0	100.0	100.0	100.0	100.0	100.0	100.0	100.0	100.0	100.0	Monde
Africa	40.9	36.3	40.4	47.7	40.3	41.2	43.0	38.2	40.3	46.0	Afrique
Americas	14.0	14.5	11.1	10.1	9.8	9.5	9.0	9.3	8.8	7.8	Amériques
- Northern America	2.1	2.4	1.9	2.0	2.5	2.9	3.3	3.5	3.6	3.2	- Amérique du Nord
- LAIA	10.4	10.4	6.9	6.7	5.8	4.6	5.2	5.2	4.7	4.1	- ALAI
- CACM	0.2	0.2	0.7	0.2	0.2	0.2	0.1	0.2	0.1	0.1	- MCC
- Caribbean	1.2	1.5	1.6	1.2	1.3	1.7	0.4	0.5	0.4	0.4	- Caraïbes
- Rest of America	0.0	0.0	0.0	0.0	0.0	0.0	0.0	0.0	0.0	0.0	- Autre d'Amérique
Asia excluding former USSR	17.2	17.5	15.8	14.3	16.3	16.3	15.3	16.2	15.6	16.2	Asie ancienne URSS exclus
- Middle East	0.0	0.0	0.1	0.0	0.1	0.1	0.3	0.5	0.6	0.4	- Moyen-Orient
Asia former USSR	0.0	0.0	0.0	0.0	0.0	0.0	0.0	0.0	0.0	0.0	Asie ancienne URSS
Europe excluding former USSR	26.8	30.5	31.6	26.4	30.0	30.2	30.7	34.0	32.9	27.3	Europe ancienne URSS exclus
- European Union	26.6	30.3	31.4	26.0	29.7	30.0	30.5	33.5	32.1	26.7	- Union Européenne
- Eastern Europe	0.1	0.1	0.1	0.2	0.2	0.1	0.2	0.5	0.7	0.6	- Europe de l'Est
- Rest of Europe	0.1	0.2	0.2	0.1	0.1	0.0	0.0	0.1	0.1	0.1	- Autre de l'Europe
Europe former USSR	0.1	0.1	0.1	0.3	2.4	2.2	1.7	1.9	2.0	2.3	Europe ancienne URSS
Oceania	1.1	1.0	0.9	1.3	1.1	0.6	0.3	0.4	0.4	0.3	Océanie

073 Chocolate and other preparations containing cocoa, nes

TRADE BY COMMODITY (Value in million US dollars)
Imports by principal countries or areas

COMMERCE PAR PRODUIT (Valeur en millions de dollars EU
Importations selon les principaux pays ou zones

Country or area	1998	1999	2000	2001	2002	Pays ou zone
World	6979.1	6927.3	6766.8	7266.3	7864.4	Monde
Africa	45.6	37.0	49.9	62.0	62.6	Afrique
Americas	1187.3	1196.6	1292.3	1501.7	1559.5	Amériques
- Northern America	870.0	890.4	962.1	1106.2	1213.8	- Amérique du Nord
- LAIA	261.7	246.8	263.3	322.7	273.6	- ALAI
- CACM	17.2	20.7	24.7	28.2	28.8	- MCC
- Caribbean	29.3	27.1	30.4	33.5	31.0	- Caraïbes
- Rest of America	9.1	11.7	11.8	11.2	12.4	- Autre d'Amérique
Asia excluding former USSR	850.6	903.8	1012.5	1033.0	1043.2	Asie ancienne URSS exclus
- Middle East	235.2	242.4	276.0	299.4	280.1	- Moyen-Orient
Asia former USSR	35.8	37.6	59.2	60.7	70.3	Asie ancienne URSS
Europe excluding former USSR	4528.6	4518.8	4084.2	4286.0	4755.8	Europe ancienne URSS exclus
- European Union	4053.6	4050.6	3646.0	3778.6	4181.3	- Union Européenne
- Eastern Europe	193.9	186.0	185.0	232.0	266.7	- Europe de l'Est
- Rest of Europe	281.1	282.2	253.2	275.4	307.8	- Autre de l'Europe
Europe former USSR	195.9	107.9	148.1	210.0	249.9	Europe ancienne URSS
Oceania	135.4	125.5	120.5	112.7	122.9	Océanie
France-Monaco	926.2	865.9	808.0	764.2	862.1	France-Monaco
Germany	930.3	832.0	645.8	801.2	811.2	Allemagne
United States	593.2	612.7	675.7	795.3	877.7	Etats-Unis d'Amérique
United Kingdom	541.8	605.9	584.3	566.7	644.1	Royaume-Uni
Japan	286.7	298.9	317.4	303.1	298.9	Japon
Canada	274.7	275.8	284.4	309.0	333.5	Canada
Netherlands	257.1	287.8	280.6	250.9	317.3	Pays-Bas
Italy-San Marino-Holy See	184.5	209.3	187.2	191.2	220.1	Italie-Saint-Marin-Saint-Siège
Belgium	-	242.3	217.5	247.8	e271.7	Belgique
Austria	186.9	189.6	158.9	177.8	186.8	Autriche
Spain	166.9	173.1	153.2	169.9	188.6	Espagne
Denmark	142.5	136.9	141.1	134.9	141.7	Danemark
Ireland	141.2	138.9	126.4	123.7	133.3	Irlande
Sweden	111.7	115.1	113.5	125.7	154.1	Suède
Mexico	75.1	96.6	123.1	154.9	147.3	Mexique
Russian Federation	109.6	52.8	88.6	136.0	159.4	Fédération de Russie
Portugal	94.4	112.2	95.0	96.6	110.1	Portugal
Australia	91.8	84.4	83.3	72.1	71.4	Australie
China, Hong Kong SAR	73.5	69.9	75.8	75.0	80.3	Chine - RAS de Hong-Kong
Norway	76.2	73.7	66.6	70.1	82.1	Norvège
Czech Republic	57.7	64.6	62.7	73.4	85.2	République tchèque
Korea, Republic of	46.0	54.9	71.9	76.1	91.7	République de Corée
Switzerland-Liechtenstein	66.8	70.1	61.4	68.4	73.4	Suisse-Liechtenstein
Greece	63.1	72.5	66.9	56.2	e62.2	Grèce
Saudi Arabia	51.9	56.2	66.8	65.9	e68.2	Arabie saoudite
United Arab Emirates	45.6	47.8	56.3	62.2	e63.8	Emirates arabes unis
Poland	44.7	41.3	44.6	64.1	71.1	Pologne
Singapore	39.2	47.3	56.0	55.6	64.6	Singapour
Belgium-Luxembourg	261.1	-	-	-	-	Belgique-Luxembourg
Finland	45.9	42.9	41.6	45.3	49.8	Finlande

(Value as percentages of World total) **(Valeur en pourcentage du total mondial)**

Regions of the world	1993	1994	1995	1996	1997	1998	1999	2000	2001	2002	Régions du monde
World	100.0	100.0	100.0	100.0	100.0	100.0	100.0	100.0	100.0	100.0	Monde
Africa	0.7	0.7	0.7	0.7	0.6	0.7	0.5	0.7	0.9	0.8	Afrique
Americas	13.2	13.7	14.0	14.4	15.9	17.0	17.3	19.1	20.7	19.8	Amériques
- Northern America	9.8	9.3	9.0	10.0	11.8	12.5	12.9	14.2	15.2	15.4	- Amérique du Nord
- LAIA	2.6	3.5	4.0	3.8	3.4	3.8	3.6	3.9	4.4	3.5	- ALAI
- CACM	0.1	0.2	0.2	0.2	0.2	0.2	0.3	0.4	0.4	0.4	- MCC
- Caribbean	0.5	0.5	0.4	0.3	0.4	0.4	0.4	0.4	0.5	0.4	- Caraïbes
- Rest of America	0.2	0.2	0.4	0.1	0.1	0.1	0.2	0.2	0.2	0.2	- Autre d'Amérique
Asia excluding former USSR	12.3	12.9	12.8	13.9	14.4	12.2	13.0	15.0	14.2	13.3	Asie ancienne URSS exclus
- Middle East	2.3	2.3	2.6	2.6	3.1	3.4	3.5	4.1	4.1	3.6	- Moyen-Orient
Asia former USSR	0.2	0.5	1.1	1.1	0.5	0.5	0.5	0.9	0.8	0.9	Asie ancienne URSS
Europe excluding former USSR	59.6	67.0	64.3	64.0	62.8	64.9	65.2	60.4	59.0	60.5	Europe ancienne URSS exclus
- European Union	53.4	60.3	57.3	57.2	56.3	58.1	58.5	53.9	52.0	53.2	- Union Européenne
- Eastern Europe	2.9	2.8	2.9	3.1	2.9	2.8	2.7	2.7	3.2	3.4	- Europe de l'Est
- Rest of Europe	3.3	3.9	4.1	3.6	3.7	4.0	4.1	3.7	3.8	3.9	- Autre de l'Europe
Europe former USSR	12.6	3.7	5.6	4.1	3.8	2.8	1.6	2.2	2.9	3.2	Europe ancienne URSS
Oceania	1.5	1.5	1.5	1.8	2.0	1.9	1.8	1.8	1.6	1.6	Océanie

TRADE BY COMMODITY (Value in million US dollars)
Exports by principal countries or areas

COMMERCE PAR PRODUIT (Valeur en millions de dollars EU)
Exportations selon les principaux pays ou zones

Country or area	1998	1999	2000	2001	2002	Pays ou zone
World	7370.3	7063.4	6969.0	7576.4	8135.4	Monde
Africa	37.1	35.4	36.4	39.5	61.6	Afrique
Americas	919.9	936.9	1122.4	1369.5	1324.3	Amériques
- Northern America	670.9	694.6	862.0	1064.4	1008.8	- Amérique du Nord
- LAIA	232.6	218.0	239.2	283.1	296.7	- ALAI
- CACM	10.4	13.8	12.2	12.4	10.9	- MCC
- Caribbean	5.9	10.4	9.0	9.5	7.6	- Caraïbes
- Rest of America	0.1	0.1	0.1	0.1	0.3	- Autre d'Amérique
Asia excluding former USSR	279.6	309.7	329.0	341.3	366.0	Asie ancienne URSS exclus
- Middle East	97.3	82.3	86.8	102.8	108.8	- Moyen-Orient
Asia former USSR	0.9	1.0	1.2	1.0	0.9	Asie ancienne URSS
Europe excluding former USSR	5921.6	5561.7	5191.6	5474.5	5982.6	Europe ancienne URSS exclus
- European Union	5277.5	5017.4	4648.2	4840.9	5339.5	- Union Européenne
- Eastern Europe	255.5	177.2	223.1	253.4	283.2	- Europe de l'Est
- Rest of Europe	388.6	367.1	320.4	380.2	359.9	- Autre de l'Europe
Europe former USSR	105.0	79.6	145.1	209.5	242.7	Europe ancienne URSS
Oceania	106.3	139.0	143.4	141.0	157.4	Océanie
Germany	1290.1	1079.2	932.9	1130.3	1254.8	Allemagne
Belgium	–	1030.0	1006.4	999.8	e1121.7	Belgique
France-Monaco	782.1	735.7	632.4	622.1	706.8	France-Monaco
Netherlands	510.8	596.4	591.4	606.7	657.7	Pays-Bas
United Kingdom	579.2	500.1	482.4	435.9	451.8	Royaume-Uni
United States	325.3	349.0	471.3	602.9	477.7	Etats-Unis d'Amérique
Canada	345.6	345.6	390.6	461.5	531.2	Canada
Italy-San Marino-Holy See	351.1	323.9	300.5	311.1	355.4	Italie-Saint-Marin-Saint-Siège
Switzerland-Liechtenstein	315.6	291.6	254.8	308.2	287.8	Suisse-Liechtenstein
Ireland	196.0	200.4	201.1	197.1	222.9	Irlande
Belgium-Luxembourg	959.5	–	–	–	–	Belgique-Luxembourg
Austria	210.4	183.9	153.6	173.5	177.0	Autriche
Poland	146.3	99.0	138.7	147.5	151.7	Pologne
Sweden	122.4	133.6	123.9	131.6	140.3	Suède
Australia	76.7	102.3	110.5	103.4	117.7	Australie
Spain	125.9	88.9	90.5	94.8	101.3	Espagne
Argentina	109.5	79.0	79.4	84.0	e81.2	Argentine
Denmark	66.4	76.2	68.4	77.4	82.3	Danemark
Singapore	53.9	67.6	78.5	81.1	78.4	Singapour
Turkey	71.3	59.2	62.1	68.8	79.1	Turquie
Ukraine	22.5	21.9	62.0	108.9	120.1	Ukraine
Brazil	53.6	50.5	62.4	79.9	e82.9	Brésil
Finland	68.6	54.5	51.4	43.5	49.1	Finlande
Russian Federation	35.7	30.6	50.4	60.4	74.4	Fédération de Russie
Mexico	23.6	37.2	47.4	45.9	60.4	Mexique
Czech Republic	41.9	29.0	33.3	38.5	50.7	République tchèque
China, Hong Kong SAR	37.0	38.5	45.3	33.5	37.0	Chine - RAS de Hong-Kong
New Zealand	29.2	36.3	32.5	37.2	39.4	Nouvelle-Zélande
Norway	35.0	41.5	30.1	29.0	27.8	Norvège
Hungary	34.8	25.8	27.0	31.9	38.8	Hongrie

(Value as percentages of World total) **(Valeur en pourcentage du total mondial)**

Regions of the world	1993	1994	1995	1996	1997	1998	1999	2000	2001	2002	Régions du monde
World	100.0	100.0	100.0	100.0	100.0	100.0	100.0	100.0	100.0	100.0	Monde
Africa	0.5	0.6	0.4	0.5	0.6	0.5	0.5	0.5	0.5	0.8	Afrique
Americas	11.4	9.7	8.6	9.3	11.8	12.5	13.3	16.1	18.1	16.3	Amériques
- Northern America	9.7	8.0	6.8	7.2	9.0	9.1	9.8	12.4	14.0	12.4	- Amérique du Nord
- LAIA	1.5	1.5	1.7	1.9	2.7	3.2	3.1	3.4	3.7	3.6	- ALAI
- CACM	0.1	0.1	0.1	0.1	0.1	0.1	0.2	0.2	0.2	0.1	- MCC
- Caribbean	0.1	0.0	0.0	0.1	0.1	0.1	0.1	0.1	0.1	0.1	- Caraïbes
- Rest of America	0.0	0.0	0.0	0.0	0.0	0.0	0.0	0.0	0.0	0.0	- Autre d'Amérique
Asia excluding former USSR	4.5	4.3	4.3	4.2	4.4	3.8	4.4	4.7	4.5	4.5	Asie ancienne URSS exclus
- Middle East	1.1	1.2	1.6	1.4	1.6	1.3	1.2	1.2	1.4	1.3	- Moyen-Orient
Asia former USSR	0.0	0.0	0.0	0.0	0.0	0.0	0.0	0.0	0.0	0.0	Asie ancienne URSS
Europe excluding former USSR	81.5	82.3	83.7	82.6	79.6	80.3	78.7	74.5	72.3	73.5	Europe ancienne URSS exclus
- European Union	74.0	74.7	76.0	74.9	70.9	71.6	71.0	66.7	63.9	65.6	- Union Européenne
- Eastern Europe	2.1	2.2	2.6	3.2	4.4	3.5	2.5	3.2	3.3	3.5	- Europe de l'Est
- Rest of Europe	5.4	5.4	5.1	4.5	4.3	5.3	5.2	4.6	5.0	4.4	- Autre de l'Europe
Europe former USSR	0.2	1.3	1.4	1.6	1.8	1.4	1.1	2.1	2.8	3.0	Europe ancienne URSS
Oceania	1.8	1.9	1.5	1.8	1.7	1.4	2.0	2.1	1.9	1.9	Océanie

074 Tea and mate

TRADE BY COMMODITY (Value in million US dollars)
Imports by principal countries or areas

COMMERCE PAR PRODUIT (Valeur en millions de dollars EU)
Importations selon les principaux pays ou zones

Country or area	1998	1999	2000	2001	2002	Pays ou zone
World	3230.5	2997.8	3015.0	2979.8	2957.5	Monde
Africa	412.2	344.2	374.8	372.9	376.3	Afrique
Americas	343.2	319.6	314.5	329.1	315.1	Amériques
- Northern America	252.7	239.0	237.0	249.3	249.4	- Amérique du Nord
- LAIA	78.8	67.9	64.4	67.7	53.3	- ALAI
- CACM	3.6	3.4	2.5	2.1	2.5	- MCC
- Caribbean	6.1	6.3	7.5	7.4	7.2	- Caraïbes
- Rest of America	2.1	3.0	3.1	2.6	2.7	- Autre d'Amérique
Asia excluding former USSR	1045.8	1019.2	1133.9	1105.2	1054.9	Asie ancienne URSS exclus
- Middle East	475.7	510.0	535.4	493.8	456.5	- Moyen-Orient
Asia former USSR	61.4	76.8	63.7	79.4	70.3	Asie ancienne URSS
Europe excluding former USSR	936.7	842.6	787.7	776.4	790.1	Europe ancienne URSS exclus
- European Union	791.9	732.2	690.4	676.1	692.9	- Union Européenne
- Eastern Europe	105.8	74.0	66.1	69.2	62.9	- Europe de l'Est
- Rest of Europe	39.0	36.4	31.2	31.1	34.2	- Autre de l'Europe
Europe former USSR	361.1	330.3	271.0	257.0	285.0	Europe ancienne URSS
Oceania	70.0	65.1	69.4	59.7	65.8	Océanie
United Kingdom	364.8	323.3	313.1	290.6	282.0	Royaume-Uni
Russian Federation	311.7	283.8	225.9	205.0	228.8	Fédération de Russie
Pakistan	246.6	208.0	222.6	178.9	154.2	Pakistan
Japan	181.2	178.8	207.9	209.5	179.7	Japon
United States	182.7	165.9	163.0	174.2	175.3	Etats-Unis d'Amérique
United Arab Emirates	143.4	150.3	148.2	151.8	e155.8	Emirates arabes unis
Germany	132.8	127.4	98.9	101.0	98.4	Allemagne
Egypt	99.6	98.4	e109.9	100.1	141.8	Egypte
Saudi Arabia	61.0	86.6	129.1	114.6	e118.6	Arabie saoudite
France-Monaco	76.3	82.7	73.1	74.6	84.3	France-Monaco
Canada	69.6	72.7	73.8	74.8	73.8	Canada
Morocco	78.1	72.4	69.6	59.4	e62.7	Maroc
Iraq	e90.9	e70.3	e70.1	e37.9	e45.9	Iraq
Poland	86.9	59.9	51.3	53.1	47.9	Pologne
Afghanistan	e18.2	e	45.2	91.0	131.2	Afghanistan
Australia	53.3	49.8	55.2	46.3	52.2	Australie
Netherlands	55.9	42.0	46.4	51.8	57.5	Pays-Bas
Syrian Arab Republic	48.3	58.7	35.4	e44.2	66.6	République arabe syrienne
China, Hong Kong SAR	48.6	45.5	44.1	41.9	32.3	Chine - RAS de Hong-Kong
Libyan Arab Jamahiriya	62.8	e45.9	e41.2	e44.4	e	Jamahiriya arabe libyenne
Iran (Islamic Republic of)	29.4	49.2	53.9	50.1	0.4	Iran (République islamique d')
Italy-San Marino-Holy See	33.4	34.2	32.2	31.1	36.9	Italie-Saint-Marin-Saint-Siège
Sudan	34.4	e24.0	28.1	44.0	30.5	Soudan
Uruguay	32.9	29.5	27.5	27.5	20.6	Uruguay
Kuwait	30.6	31.9	e29.9	e32.9	e10.8	Koweït
Ireland	27.5	25.8	26.0	24.2	27.7	Irlande
Ukraine	18.4	22.1	23.1	32.5	35.1	Ukraine
Kazakhstan	27.6	27.8	21.2	25.1	e25.6	Kazakhstan
Chile	29.2	25.3	23.7	25.4	22.8	Chili
Sweden	26.0	25.2	27.2	23.1	24.1	Suède

(Value as percentages of World total)

(Valeur en pourcentage du total mondial)

Regions of the world	1993	1994	1995	1996	1997	1998	1999	2000	2001	2002	Régions du monde
World	100.0	100.0	100.0	100.0	100.0	100.0	100.0	100.0	100.0	100.0	Monde
Africa	11.5	12.0	13.1	12.5	12.4	12.8	11.5	12.4	12.5	12.7	Afrique
Americas	9.8	11.7	10.8	11.6	10.8	10.6	10.7	10.4	11.0	10.7	Amériques
- Northern America	7.3	8.6	7.4	8.0	7.7	7.8	8.0	7.9	8.4	8.4	- Amérique du Nord
- LAIA	2.2	2.7	3.1	3.2	2.8	2.4	2.3	2.1	2.3	1.8	- ALAI
- CACM	0.1	0.1	0.1	0.1	0.1	0.1	0.1	0.1	0.1	0.1	- MCC
- Caribbean	0.2	0.2	0.2	0.2	0.2	0.2	0.2	0.2	0.2	0.2	- Caraïbes
- Rest of America	0.1	0.1	0.1	0.1	0.1	0.1	0.1	0.1	0.1	0.1	- Autre d'Amérique
Asia excluding former USSR	31.4	33.3	32.4	30.0	31.3	32.4	34.0	37.6	37.1	35.7	Asie ancienne URSS exclus
- Middle East	11.5	11.7	11.8	11.3	13.5	14.7	17.0	17.8	16.6	15.4	- Moyen-Orient
Asia former USSR	2.1	1.4	1.9	2.2	1.1	1.9	2.6	2.1	2.7	2.4	Asie ancienne URSS
Europe excluding former USSR	30.2	31.7	31.0	32.6	30.9	29.0	28.1	26.1	26.1	26.7	Europe ancienne URSS exclus
- European Union	26.4	27.6	26.7	28.2	26.6	24.5	24.4	22.9	22.7	23.4	- Union Européenne
- Eastern Europe	2.8	2.9	3.1	3.3	3.2	3.3	2.5	2.2	2.3	2.1	- Europe de l'Est
- Rest of Europe	1.0	1.2	1.3	1.2	1.1	1.2	1.2	1.0	1.0	1.2	- Autre de l'Europe
Europe former USSR	13.0	7.5	8.6	8.6	11.2	11.2	11.0	9.0	8.6	9.6	Europe ancienne URSS
Oceania	2.0	2.3	2.1	2.5	2.2	2.2	2.2	2.3	2.0	2.2	Océanie

TRADE BY COMMODITY (Value in million US dollars)
Exports by principal countries or areas

COMMERCE PAR PRODUIT (Valeur en millions de dollars EU)
Exportations selon les principaux pays ou zones

Country or area	1998	1999	2000	2001	2002	Pays ou zone
World	3324.8	2917.3	3087.1	2630.6	2597.7	Monde
Africa	716.2	623.0	633.2	345.0	316.7	Afrique
Americas	153.1	133.1	136.0	139.3	140.6	Amériques
- Northern America	21.6	25.9	30.7	30.8	33.8	- Amérique du Nord
- LAIA	127.5	102.2	101.4	105.8	104.4	- ALAI
- CACM	2.0	2.0	0.9	1.0	1.3	- MCC
- Caribbean	0.8	0.9	1.1	1.3	1.1	- Caraïbes
- Rest of America	1.1	2.2	1.9	0.3	0.0	- Autre d'Amérique
Asia excluding former USSR	1931.9	1715.0	1908.9	1715.0	1664.6	Asie ancienne URSS exclus
- Middle East	110.8	107.6	103.5	73.3	78.1	- Moyen-Orient
Asia former USSR	15.3	17.6	9.4	11.2	10.4	Asie ancienne URSS
Europe excluding former USSR	478.9	405.9	382.5	407.7	451.4	Europe ancienne URSS exclus
- European Union	451.7	384.8	354.5	381.5	418.5	- Union Européenne
- Eastern Europe	21.8	15.5	23.3	21.3	27.0	- Europe de l'Est
- Rest of Europe	5.4	5.7	4.7	4.9	5.9	- Autre de l'Europe
Europe former USSR	16.3	12.4	6.6	5.8	8.2	Europe ancienne URSS
Oceania	13.2	10.3	10.5	6.7	5.8	Océanie
Sri Lanka	e648.5	612.0	e744.3	680.0	650.4	Sri Lanka
India	513.1	403.3	430.8	349.7	326.7	Inde
Kenya	546.2	469.3	463.6	e195.5	140.9	Kenya
China	370.5	338.4	347.4	342.1	331.8	Chine
United Kingdom	246.0	195.2	160.4	170.2	191.5	Royaume-Uni
Indonesia	113.2	97.5	112.2	101.5	107.2	Indonésie
Germany	79.9	70.5	71.4	79.1	88.2	Allemagne
United Arab Emirates	81.9	84.5	77.3	55.9	e58.3	Emirates arabes unis
Argentina	82.9	63.0	63.3	65.3	e63.1	Argentine
Viet Nam	50.5	45.1	75.1	78.1	86.9	Viet Nam
Malawi	e54.7	e44.4	36.1	35.1	e32.1	Malawi
Belgium	–	42.2	44.2	47.9	e53.8	Belgique
Brazil	40.6	35.5	34.7	34.2	e35.4	Brésil
France-Monaco	32.5	31.8	30.3	34.3	34.9	France-Monaco
Uganda	28.2	21.4	37.1	30.3	31.3	Ouganda
United Republic of Tanzania	24.6	30.2	32.3	28.2	e32.3	République-Unie de Tanzanie
Bangladesh	47.4	e36.7	e18.6	22.1	e17.8	Bangladesh
China, Hong Kong SAR	28.3	25.8	26.4	20.8	13.5	Chine - RAS de Hong-Kong
Netherlands	24.3	17.9	22.2	22.9	27.1	Pays-Bas
United States	16.8	21.6	25.0	23.8	26.5	Etats-Unis d'Amérique
Zimbabwe	e21.3	20.0	18.9	6.6	30.2	Zimbabwe
Singapore	21.8	15.8	17.4	15.5	15.8	Singapour
Rwanda	23.1	14.6	e15.6	16.6	11.8	Rwanda
Poland	15.4	10.5	13.5	9.9	13.9	Pologne
Japan	9.5	11.9	11.2	10.0	11.8	Japon
South Africa	–	–	20.2	14.6	18.1	Afrique du Sud
Sweden	8.6	8.9	11.9	11.8	8.7	Suède
Belgium-Luxembourg	44.0	–	–	–	–	Belgique-Luxembourg
Iran (Islamic Republic of)	6.2	11.3	12.2	6.3	6.2	Iran (République islamique d')
Georgia	e10.0	11.4	6.1	5.8	e3.1	Géorgie

(Value as percentages of World total) **(Valeur en pourcentage du total mondial)**

Regions of the world	1993	1994	1995	1996	1997	1998	1999	2000	2001	2002	Régions du monde
World	100.0	100.0	100.0	100.0	100.0	100.0	100.0	100.0	100.0	100.0	Monde
Africa	18.4	20.4	18.4	18.9	18.2	21.5	21.4	20.5	13.1	12.2	Afrique
Americas	5.6	5.6	5.9	5.6	5.1	4.6	4.6	4.4	5.3	5.4	Amériques
- Northern America	0.8	0.9	0.9	1.0	0.8	0.6	0.9	1.0	1.2	1.3	- Amérique du Nord
- LAIA	4.5	4.7	4.9	4.6	4.2	3.8	3.5	3.3	4.0	4.0	- ALAI
- CACM	0.2	0.0	0.0	0.0	0.0	0.1	0.1	0.0	0.0	0.0	- MCC
- Caribbean	0.0	0.0	0.0	0.0	0.0	0.0	0.0	0.0	0.0	0.0	- Caraïbes
- Rest of America	0.0	0.0	0.0	0.0	0.0	0.0	0.1	0.1	0.0	0.0	- Autre d'Amérique
Asia excluding former USSR	60.2	55.7	56.2	55.4	59.1	58.1	58.8	61.8	65.2	64.1	Asie ancienne URSS exclus
- Middle East	2.5	1.0	0.9	0.8	1.1	3.3	3.7	3.4	2.8	3.0	- Moyen-Orient
Asia former USSR	0.1	0.2	0.4	0.9	0.6	0.5	0.6	0.3	0.4	0.4	Asie ancienne URSS
Europe excluding former USSR	15.0	16.7	17.5	17.5	15.7	14.4	13.9	12.4	15.5	17.4	Europe ancienne URSS exclus
- European Union	14.3	15.7	16.6	16.7	15.0	13.6	13.2	11.5	14.5	16.1	- Union Européenne
- Eastern Europe	0.4	0.7	0.5	0.6	0.6	0.7	0.5	0.8	0.8	1.0	- Europe de l'Est
- Rest of Europe	0.3	0.4	0.3	0.2	0.2	0.2	0.2	0.2	0.2	0.2	- Autre de l'Europe
Europe former USSR	0.0	0.6	0.7	0.8	0.7	0.5	0.4	0.2	0.2	0.3	Europe ancienne URSS
Oceania	0.7	0.8	0.9	0.9	0.7	0.4	0.4	0.3	0.3	0.2	Océanie

075 Spices

TRADE BY COMMODITY (Value in million US dollars)
Imports by principal countries or areas

COMMERCE PAR PRODUIT (Valeur en millions de dollars EU)
Importations selon les principaux pays ou zones

Country or area	1998	1999	2000	2001	2002	Pays ou zone
World	2623.0	2796.7	2867.6	2713.0	2650.9	Monde
Africa	81.8	67.5	83.8	80.7	86.8	Afrique
Americas	698.9	721.3	760.1	731.7	739.7	Amériques
- Northern America	535.3	588.4	609.3	570.2	596.1	- Amérique du Nord
- LAIA	128.3	107.4	122.7	135.6	118.2	- ALAI
- CACM	8.6	7.7	9.2	9.1	9.1	- MCC
- Caribbean	23.1	14.4	15.2	14.1	13.5	- Caraïbes
- Rest of America	3.5	3.4	3.7	2.7	2.8	- Autre d'Amérique
Asia excluding former USSR	852.2	1007.1	1044.8	1012.0	910.4	Asie ancienne URSS exclus
- Middle East	233.2	246.1	280.0	266.2	272.6	- Moyen-Orient
Asia former USSR	1.3	1.2	1.6	1.7	1.6	Asie ancienne URSS
Europe excluding former USSR	913.7	925.6	895.2	821.8	840.5	Europe ancienne URSS exclus
- European Union	794.8	814.8	789.3	728.0	740.3	- Union Européenne
- Eastern Europe	70.3	62.6	60.9	49.7	52.7	- Europe de l'Est
- Rest of Europe	48.6	48.2	45.0	44.2	47.5	- Autre de l'Europe
Europe former USSR	45.5	44.6	49.5	38.6	41.6	Europe ancienne URSS
Oceania	29.6	29.4	32.6	26.5	30.2	Océanie
United States	478.5	522.7	548.1	514.6	541.4	Etats-Unis d'Amérique
Japan	185.7	198.3	200.1	198.3	163.8	Japon
Germany	191.3	202.7	180.3	162.2	165.3	Allemagne
Singapore	148.2	201.2	185.2	194.1	128.9	Singapour
Netherlands	131.2	157.6	145.7	113.6	105.9	Pays-Bas
United Arab Emirates	116.8	122.4	123.8	117.7	e120.7	Emirates arabes unis
France-Monaco	97.6	98.9	102.6	99.7	120.9	France-Monaco
United Kingdom	96.2	88.3	95.6	95.1	90.6	Royaume-Uni
Spain	96.5	83.0	80.9	91.2	79.8	Espagne
Saudi Arabia	64.2	72.2	98.8	93.0	e96.2	Arabie saoudite
India	58.0	45.2	44.5	80.8	92.7	Inde
Mexico	60.0	51.8	62.0	73.6	67.5	Mexique
Canada	56.8	65.6	61.2	55.5	54.5	Canada
Malaysia	41.2	59.1	64.2	60.9	e66.6	Malaisie
Italy-San Marino-Holy See	40.1	40.5	39.1	31.4	33.1	Italie-Saint-Marin-Saint-Siège
Indonesia	5.9	55.8	62.9	32.0	14.8	Indonésie
Belgium	–	42.9	40.3	40.9	e44.9	Belgique
Korea, Republic of	30.7	33.7	34.8	35.5	30.4	République de Corée
China, Hong Kong SAR	27.9	31.0	38.0	29.3	25.4	Chine - RAS de Hong-Kong
Sri Lanka	e30.6	27.6	e37.2	26.6	28.3	Sri Lanka
Austria	25.9	25.2	25.4	22.1	23.8	Autriche
Pakistan	22.4	31.2	22.2	18.8	19.5	Pakistan
Sweden	22.0	23.3	24.8	20.6	21.3	Suède
Australia	21.0	21.7	24.3	18.5	21.7	Australie
Poland	25.4	22.2	23.4	16.8	18.6	Pologne
Switzerland-Liechtenstein	20.3	20.6	20.0	20.2	23.3	Suisse-Liechtenstein
Denmark	19.5	19.1	17.9	16.3	17.9	Danemark
Egypt	22.2	13.4	e19.2	17.5	16.2	Egypte
Brazil	19.8	14.8	15.4	19.2	18.6	Brésil
Russian Federation	15.3	16.5	17.4	14.6	16.1	Fédération de Russie

(Value as percentages of World total) **(Valeur en pourcentage du total mondial)**

Regions of the world	1993	1994	1995	1996	1997	1998	1999	2000	2001	2002	Régions du monde
World	100.0	100.0	100.0	100.0	100.0	100.0	100.0	100.0	100.0	100.0	Monde
Africa	3.6	3.5	3.1	2.8	2.7	3.1	2.4	2.9	3.0	3.3	Afrique
Americas	26.5	27.5	24.1	22.6	22.7	26.6	25.8	26.5	27.0	27.9	Amériques
- Northern America	20.6	21.8	19.3	18.2	18.0	20.4	21.0	21.2	21.0	22.5	- Amérique du Nord
- LAIA	4.7	4.6	3.7	3.5	3.8	4.9	3.8	4.3	5.0	4.5	- ALAI
- CACM	0.3	0.3	0.3	0.2	0.3	0.3	0.3	0.3	0.3	0.3	- MCC
- Caribbean	0.7	0.7	0.6	0.5	0.5	0.9	0.5	0.5	0.5	0.5	- Caraïbes
- Rest of America	0.2	0.2	0.1	0.1	0.1	0.1	0.1	0.1	0.1	0.1	- Autre d'Amérique
Asia excluding former USSR	36.7	34.2	36.0	41.0	39.4	32.5	36.0	36.4	37.3	34.3	Asie ancienne URSS exclus
- Middle East	7.4	7.9	8.7	13.0	13.2	8.9	8.8	9.8	9.8	10.3	- Moyen-Orient
Asia former USSR	0.1	0.0	0.1	0.1	0.0	0.0	0.0	0.1	0.1	0.1	Asie ancienne URSS
Europe excluding former USSR	30.6	32.3	33.8	29.6	31.6	34.8	33.1	31.2	30.3	31.7	Europe ancienne URSS exclus
- European Union	26.6	27.9	29.3	25.7	27.7	30.3	29.1	27.5	26.8	27.9	- Union Européenne
- Eastern Europe	2.1	2.4	2.6	2.2	2.4	2.7	2.2	2.1	1.8	2.0	- Europe de l'Est
- Rest of Europe	1.9	2.0	2.0	1.6	1.5	1.9	1.7	1.6	1.6	1.8	- Autre de l'Europe
Europe former USSR	1.5	1.3	1.8	2.9	2.7	1.7	1.6	1.7	1.4	1.6	Europe ancienne URSS
Oceania	1.1	1.2	1.1	1.0	1.0	1.1	1.1	1.1	1.0	1.1	Océanie

TRADE BY COMMODITY (Value in million US dollars)
Exports by principal countries or areas

COMMERCE PAR PRODUIT (Valeur en millions de dollars EU)
Exportations selon les principaux pays ou zones

Country or area	1998	1999	2000	2001	2002	Pays ou zone
World	2459.5	2625.8	2541.4	2239.6	2494.4	Monde
Africa	110.4	99.6	96.4	107.8	168.3	Afrique
Americas	342.4	346.2	352.2	382.5	388.9	Amériques
- Northern America	79.1	83.0	90.9	79.1	80.2	- Amérique du Nord
- LAIA	138.1	160.6	149.1	172.2	183.3	- ALAI
- CACM	105.7	74.7	88.2	105.8	102.9	- MCC
- Caribbean	18.3	26.4	22.5	23.9	21.4	- Caraïbes
- Rest of America	1.2	1.6	1.5	1.6	1.2	- Autre d'Amérique
Asia excluding former USSR	1522.4	1682.1	1630.0	1268.3	1406.6	Asie ancienne URSS exclus
- Middle East	173.2	182.8	186.6	193.3	266.7	- Moyen-Orient
Asia former USSR	1.4	1.6	2.1	2.8	3.5	Asie ancienne URSS
Europe excluding former USSR	463.9	461.9	438.1	458.8	509.9	Europe ancienne URSS exclus
- European Union	415.7	417.8	399.2	422.5	471.5	- Union Européenne
- Eastern Europe	35.5	30.8	27.6	25.9	28.2	- Europe de l'Est
- Rest of Europe	12.6	13.3	11.2	10.4	10.2	- Autre de l'Europe
Europe former USSR	9.1	23.5	11.2	9.4	5.2	Europe ancienne URSS
Oceania	10.0	10.9	11.5	10.1	12.0	Océanie
India	279.0	315.3	261.4	206.2	212.0	Inde
Singapore	308.7	317.0	290.1	175.4	160.3	Singapour
Indonesia	284.5	279.2	317.4	176.1	190.2	Indonésie
China	142.3	142.6	152.4	190.0	209.2	Chine
Viet Nam	65.9	145.6	108.7	113.1	125.7	Viet Nam
Netherlands	113.5	129.2	115.8	99.4	89.3	Pays-Bas
Brazil	86.1	103.4	84.1	93.2	e96.6	Brésil
Malaysia	97.4	115.4	103.6	57.4	e60.9	Malaisie
Sri Lanka	e85.0	80.2	e97.6	66.3	95.6	Sri Lanka
Spain	82.0	76.5	77.5	83.3	86.7	Espagne
Germany	85.9	81.3	70.6	79.5	87.1	Allemagne
Guatemala	37.0	57.8	80.7	97.1	94.2	Guatemala
United States	65.1	65.5	71.8	65.0	63.4	Etats-Unis d'Amérique
Turkey	68.2	52.3	52.5	53.3	61.3	Turquie
Iran (Islamic Republic of)	49.1	47.8	53.8	61.5	67.2	Iran (République islamique d')
France-Monaco	40.6	41.9	42.7	54.9	80.0	France-Monaco
United Arab Emirates	41.4	42.7	43.3	34.2	e35.6	Emirates arabes unis
Syrian Arab Republic	7.8	30.9	29.8	e33.8	94.0	République arabe syrienne
Madagascar	17.9	33.0	e33.5	e36.7	e74.6	Madagascar
United Kingdom	30.9	25.8	29.7	43.4	37.6	Royaume-Uni
Mexico	23.1	31.6	34.5	33.1	36.9	Mexique
China, Hong Kong SAR	17.2	24.2	30.9	20.3	17.9	Chine - RAS de Hong-Kong
Chile	22.8	16.9	18.7	21.9	e21.4	Chili
Austria	14.5	15.1	14.9	17.1	34.3	Autriche
Thailand	15.6	19.2	23.7	15.2	e16.0	Thaïlande
Costa Rica	66.4	12.5	3.4	3.5	3.6	Costa Rica
Canada	14.0	17.5	19.1	14.1	16.8	Canada
Belgium	–	21.6	18.6	17.6	e19.7	Belgique
Grenada	10.1	17.4	13.4	14.9	13.7	Grenade
Pakistan	12.7	14.0	15.5	11.2	13.9	Pakistan

(Value as percentages of World total) **(Valeur en pourcentage du total mondial)**

Regions of the world	1993	1994	1995	1996	1997	1998	1999	2000	2001	2002	Régions du monde
World	100.0	100.0	100.0	100.0	100.0	100.0	100.0	100.0	100.0	100.0	Monde
Africa	7.6	8.2	6.2	4.3	4.0	4.5	3.8	3.8	4.8	6.7	Afrique
Americas	11.2	12.0	11.5	12.4	11.4	13.9	13.2	13.9	17.1	15.6	Amériques
- Northern America	3.9	3.7	3.1	3.1	2.7	3.2	3.2	3.6	3.5	3.2	- Amérique du Nord
- LAIA	3.5	4.1	4.8	5.1	4.6	5.6	6.1	5.9	7.7	7.3	- ALAI
- CACM	3.1	3.4	3.0	3.6	3.4	4.3	2.8	3.5	4.7	4.1	- MCC
- Caribbean	0.6	0.8	0.6	0.6	0.6	0.7	1.0	0.9	1.1	0.9	- Caraïbes
- Rest of America	0.0	0.0	0.0	0.0	0.0	0.0	0.1	0.1	0.1	0.0	- Autre d'Amérique
Asia excluding former USSR	61.0	60.0	62.6	64.3	66.7	61.9	64.1	64.1	56.6	56.4	Asie ancienne URSS exclus
- Middle East	13.5	7.9	6.0	9.2	9.1	7.0	7.0	7.3	8.6	10.7	- Moyen-Orient
Asia former USSR	0.0	0.1	0.1	0.1	0.1	0.1	0.1	0.1	0.1	0.1	Asie ancienne URSS
Europe excluding former USSR	19.2	18.9	18.8	18.0	16.9	18.9	17.6	17.2	20.5	20.4	Europe ancienne URSS exclus
- European Union	15.4	16.4	16.6	16.0	15.1	16.9	15.9	15.7	18.9	18.9	- Union Européenne
- Eastern Europe	2.6	1.6	1.5	1.7	1.5	1.4	1.2	1.1	1.2	1.1	- Europe de l'Est
- Rest of Europe	1.2	0.8	0.7	0.3	0.3	0.5	0.5	0.4	0.5	0.4	- Autre de l'Europe
Europe former USSR	0.3	0.2	0.2	0.5	0.6	0.4	0.9	0.4	0.4	0.2	Europe ancienne URSS
Oceania	0.7	0.7	0.7	0.5	0.4	0.4	0.4	0.5	0.5	0.5	Océanie

081 Feeding stuff for animals (not including unmilled cereals)

TRADE BY COMMODITY (Value in million US dollars)
Imports by principal countries or areas

COMMERCE PAR PRODUIT (Valeur en millions de dollars EU)
Importations selon les principaux pays ou zones

Country or area	1998	1999	2000	2001	2002	Pays ou zone
World	23192.2	20757.5	22423.3	23828.0	24782.1	Monde
Africa	767.9	721.0	963.6	922.5	922.7	Afrique
Americas	2750.4	2575.1	2836.0	3063.0	3169.6	Amériques
- Northern America	1315.0	1213.2	1316.9	1354.0	1419.9	- Amérique du Nord
- LAIA	1045.7	996.4	1145.2	1306.2	1336.3	- ALAI
- CACM	121.1	128.4	134.8	170.2	189.4	- MCC
- Caribbean	208.7	187.4	183.8	181.4	169.9	- Caraïbes
- Rest of America	59.8	49.5	55.3	51.2	54.2	- Autre d'Amérique
Asia excluding former USSR	6684.2	5766.6	6818.8	6926.6	7115.8	Asie ancienne URSS exclus
- Middle East	843.1	772.5	888.2	837.5	811.4	- Moyen-Orient
Asia former USSR	6.6	8.3	11.1	15.7	20.2	Asie ancienne URSS
Europe excluding former USSR	12462.8	11164.6	11312.7	12253.4	12779.7	Europe ancienne URSS exclus
- European Union	10675.7	9719.4	9798.2	10557.6	10919.3	- Union Européenne
- Eastern Europe	1062.2	781.3	873.3	1024.9	1116.3	- Europe de l'Est
- Rest of Europe	724.9	663.9	641.1	670.9	744.2	- Autre de l'Europe
Europe former USSR	336.5	344.3	300.5	434.0	509.6	Europe ancienne URSS
Oceania	183.8	177.7	180.8	212.8	264.5	Océanie
Japan	2045.7	1943.5	2035.6	2114.0	2155.3	Japon
Germany	1831.6	1422.3	1479.5	1679.4	1664.7	Allemagne
France-Monaco	1526.5	1268.5	1463.7	1486.2	1526.2	France-Monaco
Netherlands	912.1	1130.4	1029.2	1192.5	1286.3	Pays-Bas
United Kingdom	1164.8	1049.9	1048.3	1128.2	1114.7	Royaume-Uni
Italy-San Marino-Holy See	1129.7	989.9	1005.6	1179.2	1158.6	Italie-Saint-Marin-Saint-Siège
Spain	886.3	917.0	885.8	873.6	1004.5	Espagne
China	1405.6	619.8	908.6	641.8	777.7	Chine
Belgium	–	912.8	897.9	940.2	e1031.1	Belgique
United States	696.2	635.3	684.2	665.7	707.7	Etats-Unis d'Amérique
Denmark	717.7	595.6	641.4	648.3	661.5	Danemark
Canada	614.5	573.1	631.2	685.8	708.0	Canada
Korea, Republic of	504.0	480.4	577.1	692.1	688.1	République de Corée
Thailand	369.3	436.1	486.8	571.0	e595.0	Thaïlande
Indonesia	282.5	274.3	487.4	585.7	508.7	Indonésie
Poland	444.0	311.3	348.7	416.6	427.9	Pologne
Mexico	277.9	319.3	337.3	425.6	463.8	Mexique
Ireland	348.3	360.9	328.3	341.8	365.3	Irlande
Egypt	264.9	251.1	e408.6	372.0	352.3	Egypte
Philippines	323.2	225.8	305.2	339.1	355.3	Philippines
Portugal	307.2	300.6	274.4	267.2	250.8	Portugal
Malaysia	235.7	231.4	246.6	264.7	e289.3	Malaisie
Austria	235.3	211.5	220.7	256.2	279.6	Autriche
Hungary	248.4	193.3	219.7	256.4	273.4	Hongrie
Switzerland-Liechtenstein	235.7	214.3	213.5	225.6	247.2	Suisse-Liechtenstein
Sweden	234.7	217.0	216.1	214.3	199.1	Suède
Greece	230.5	220.6	179.9	197.5	e218.4	Grèce
Belgium-Luxembourg	1039.5	–	–	–	–	Belgique-Luxembourg
Norway	205.3	204.9	199.4	189.2	232.9	Norvège
Russian Federation	179.4	207.6	145.9	209.3	263.7	Fédération de Russie

(Value as percentages of World total)

(Valeur en pourcentage du total mondial)

Regions of the world	1993	1994	1995	1996	1997	1998	1999	2000	2001	2002	Régions du monde
World	100.0	100.0	100.0	100.0	100.0	100.0	100.0	100.0	100.0	100.0	Monde
Africa	3.0	3.0	3.1	2.9	3.3	3.3	3.5	4.3	3.9	3.7	Afrique
Americas	9.3	9.8	9.2	9.5	10.7	11.9	12.4	12.6	12.9	12.8	Amériques
- Northern America	5.0	5.2	4.9	5.0	5.4	5.7	5.8	5.9	5.7	5.7	- Amérique du Nord
- LAIA	3.1	3.3	3.0	3.0	3.5	4.5	4.8	5.1	5.5	5.4	- ALAI
- CACM	0.3	0.4	0.4	0.4	0.6	0.5	0.6	0.6	0.7	0.8	- MCC
- Caribbean	0.7	0.7	0.8	0.9	1.0	0.9	0.9	0.8	0.8	0.7	- Caraïbes
- Rest of America	0.2	0.2	0.2	0.2	0.2	0.3	0.2	0.2	0.2	0.2	- Autre d'Amérique
Asia excluding former USSR	27.5	25.3	27.6	30.1	32.8	28.8	27.8	30.4	29.1	28.7	Asie ancienne URSS exclus
- Middle East	3.3	2.6	3.1	2.9	3.2	3.6	3.7	4.0	3.5	3.3	- Moyen-Orient
Asia former USSR	0.1	0.0	0.0	0.0	0.0	0.0	0.0	0.0	0.1	0.1	Asie ancienne URSS
Europe excluding former USSR	58.0	60.4	58.3	55.7	51.2	53.7	53.8	50.5	51.4	51.6	Europe ancienne URSS exclus
- European Union	52.3	54.2	51.5	49.2	44.9	46.0	46.8	43.7	44.3	44.1	- Union Européenne
- Eastern Europe	3.2	3.4	3.9	4.2	4.0	4.6	3.8	3.9	4.3	4.5	- Europe de l'Est
- Rest of Europe	2.5	2.8	2.9	2.3	2.4	3.1	3.2	2.9	2.8	3.0	- Autre de l'Europe
Europe former USSR	1.5	0.9	1.1	1.1	1.3	1.5	1.7	1.3	1.8	2.1	Europe ancienne URSS
Oceania	0.6	0.7	0.6	0.6	0.7	0.8	0.9	0.8	0.9	1.1	Océanie

Nourriture destinée aux animaux (à l'exclusions des céréales non moulues) 081

TRADE BY COMMODITY (Value in million US dollars)
Exports by principal countries or areas

COMMERCE PAR PRODUIT (Valeur en millions de dollars EU)
Exportations selon les principaux pays ou zones

Country or area	1998	1999	2000	2001	2002	Pays ou zone
World	20646.7	18949.9	20294.5	21926.9	22438.6	Monde
Africa	132.7	105.0	143.6	169.3	231.4	Afrique
Americas	9886.8	9005.7	10370.4	11481.6	11066.2	Amériques
- Northern America	4999.9	4239.8	4711.4	5123.4	4750.3	- Amérique du Nord
- LAIA	4835.2	4734.3	5617.1	6300.9	6260.8	- ALAI
- CACM	18.3	16.8	17.6	23.7	31.0	- MCC
- Caribbean	23.3	9.4	14.7	21.3	16.8	- Caraïbes
- Rest of America	10.0	5.4	9.6	12.3	7.3	- Autre d'Amérique
Asia excluding former USSR	1529.1	1462.1	1627.4	1686.2	1626.2	Asie ancienne URSS exclus
- Middle East	66.3	84.8	80.1	76.4	61.8	- Moyen-Orient
Asia former USSR	13.8	18.0	16.6	20.6	16.3	Asie ancienne URSS
Europe excluding former USSR	8597.3	7835.7	7357.5	7785.7	8668.6	Europe ancienne URSS exclus
- European Union	7803.3	7141.9	6680.3	7003.4	7756.8	- Union Européenne
- Eastern Europe	234.0	237.3	270.3	355.3	387.8	- Europe de l'Est
- Rest of Europe	560.0	456.5	406.9	427.0	524.1	- Autre de l'Europe
Europe former USSR	106.1	80.4	134.2	208.2	233.3	Europe ancienne URSS
Oceania	381.0	442.9	644.8	575.3	596.5	Océanie
United States	4305.2	3635.8	4088.7	4478.1	4114.7	Etats-Unis d'Amérique
Argentina	2006.3	2049.4	2433.2	2626.7	e2537.8	Argentine
Brazil	1800.7	1587.1	1716.0	2166.8	e2246.4	Brésil
Netherlands	1805.8	1673.1	1673.2	1619.5	1888.8	Pays-Bas
Germany	1597.9	1294.1	1210.3	1444.7	1467.5	Allemagne
France-Monaco	1354.2	1301.1	1189.2	1170.4	1273.2	France-Monaco
Belgium	–	943.5	863.3	974.3	e1093.1	Belgique
Peru	413.2	564.9	902.0	858.9	848.0	Pérou
Canada	693.5	601.7	622.4	645.0	634.8	Canada
Denmark	672.3	594.3	500.0	497.7	571.6	Danemark
United Kingdom	609.6	541.3	486.6	421.5	465.6	Royaume-Uni
Australia	331.8	404.2	564.7	483.3	501.2	Australie
India	477.9	388.8	469.2	509.4	316.3	Inde
Chile	371.8	303.6	255.0	328.3	e321.2	Chili
China	218.6	239.2	303.1	337.5	431.2	Chine
Thailand	252.5	258.5	292.6	272.1	e287.4	Thaïlande
Spain	260.7	224.3	214.9	283.0	306.2	Espagne
Italy-San Marino-Holy See	232.7	225.9	222.6	218.3	245.7	Italie-Saint-Marin-Saint-Siège
Belgium-Luxembourg	932.5	–	–	–	–	Belgique-Luxembourg
Norway	206.8	167.4	130.2	133.5	162.9	Norvège
Bolivia	105.9	114.5	147.8	194.4	e186.9	Bolivie
Iceland	169.0	121.6	119.9	134.8	198.0	Islande
Austria	125.1	120.4	112.3	130.0	179.2	Autriche
Ireland	115.9	121.1	111.6	119.8	133.1	Irlande
Hungary	64.2	78.0	104.0	134.5	165.0	Hongrie
Malaysia	99.1	103.0	95.5	106.4	e112.8	Malaisie
Switzerland-Liechtenstein	103.4	105.2	96.6	93.8	96.7	Suisse-Liechtenstein
Indonesia	112.1	88.4	95.6	85.9	107.1	Indonésie
Japan	68.2	79.6	82.3	77.1	80.4	Japon
Poland	60.2	58.4	49.1	93.4	101.7	Pologne

(Value as percentages of World total) **(Valeur en pourcentage du total mondial)**

Regions of the world	1993	1994	1995	1996	1997	1998	1999	2000	2001	2002	Régions du monde
World	100.0	100.0	100.0	100.0	100.0	100.0	100.0	100.0	100.0	100.0	Monde
Africa	0.8	0.7	0.8	0.5	0.5	0.6	0.6	0.7	0.8	1.0	Afrique
Americas	47.7	47.3	45.7	50.7	52.6	47.9	47.5	51.1	52.4	49.3	Amériques
- Northern America	22.4	21.2	21.3	21.2	23.1	24.2	22.4	23.2	23.4	21.2	- Amérique du Nord
- LAIA	25.2	25.9	24.1	29.2	29.3	23.4	25.0	27.7	28.7	27.9	- ALAI
- CACM	0.1	0.1	0.1	0.1	0.1	0.1	0.1	0.1	0.1	0.1	- MCC
- Caribbean	0.1	0.1	0.1	0.2	0.1	0.1	0.0	0.1	0.1	0.1	- Caraïbes
- Rest of America	0.0	0.0	0.0	0.0	0.0	0.0	0.0	0.0	0.1	0.0	- Autre d'Amérique
Asia excluding former USSR	12.1	10.8	10.2	10.4	9.0	7.4	7.7	8.0	7.7	7.2	Asie ancienne URSS exclus
- Middle East	0.3	0.3	0.3	0.3	0.3	0.3	0.4	0.4	0.3	0.3	- Moyen-Orient
Asia former USSR	0.0	0.1	0.1	0.1	0.0	0.1	0.1	0.1	0.1	0.1	Asie ancienne URSS
Europe excluding former USSR	37.3	39.0	41.2	36.0	35.6	41.6	41.3	36.3	35.5	38.6	Europe ancienne URSS exclus
- European Union	35.0	36.4	38.3	33.1	32.8	37.8	37.7	32.9	31.9	34.6	- Union Européenne
- Eastern Europe	0.7	0.8	1.0	1.0	0.9	1.1	1.3	1.3	1.6	1.7	- Europe de l'Est
- Rest of Europe	1.5	1.8	1.9	2.0	1.9	2.7	2.4	2.0	1.9	2.3	- Autre de l'Europe
Europe former USSR	0.3	0.4	0.3	0.5	0.4	0.5	0.4	0.7	0.9	1.0	Europe ancienne URSS
Oceania	1.8	1.8	1.7	1.9	1.9	1.8	2.3	3.2	2.6	2.7	Océanie

091 Margarine and shortening

TRADE BY COMMODITY (Value in million US dollars)
Imports by principal countries or areas

COMMERCE PAR PRODUIT (Valeur en millions de dollars EU)
Importations selon les principaux pays ou zones

Country or area	1998	1999	2000	2001	2002	Pays ou zone
World	1633.8	1654.6	1641.1	1615.9	1670.4	Monde
Africa	133.7	119.9	116.4	123.1	141.5	Afrique
Americas	197.5	225.3	272.5	308.3	338.4	Amériques
- Northern America	40.1	47.2	43.8	60.3	69.5	- Amérique du Nord
- LAIA	104.3	117.3	170.8	188.6	215.3	- ALAI
- CACM	13.2	15.2	18.0	18.6	15.2	- MCC
- Caribbean	33.7	39.0	32.5	34.4	32.7	- Caraïbes
- Rest of America	6.2	6.7	7.4	6.3	5.8	- Autre d'Amérique
Asia excluding former USSR	255.9	358.8	458.6	390.0	262.8	Asie ancienne URSS exclus
- Middle East	94.6	136.8	171.5	151.6	76.6	- Moyen-Orient
Asia former USSR	22.4	19.6	26.8	21.6	21.5	Asie ancienne URSS
Europe excluding former USSR	782.2	756.4	652.6	653.4	768.9	Europe ancienne URSS exclus
- European Union	680.3	644.9	561.9	559.1	664.6	- Union Européenne
- Eastern Europe	59.5	66.0	56.9	57.7	58.5	- Europe de l'Est
- Rest of Europe	42.4	45.5	33.7	36.6	45.7	- Autre de l'Europe
Europe former USSR	218.3	147.8	92.5	98.0	109.3	Europe ancienne URSS
Oceania	23.9	26.9	21.8	21.6	28.1	Océanie
France-Monaco	141.0	126.4	104.0	112.1	170.4	France-Monaco
United Kingdom	83.3	108.6	98.4	72.6	58.8	Royaume-Uni
Russian Federation	122.4	82.6	42.3	41.1	46.5	Fédération de Russie
China, Hong Kong SAR	75.5	83.9	64.4	54.0	52.4	Chine - RAS de Hong-Kong
Chile	17.4	19.0	63.7	76.8	117.8	Chili
Iraq	e51.2	e95.6	e78.6	e42.6	e23.6	Iraq
China	12.5	47.7	123.1	75.2	26.4	Chine
Germany	65.8	60.9	48.6	51.7	55.9	Allemagne
Netherlands	66.6	50.9	51.5	43.6	65.9	Pays-Bas
Algeria	60.1	49.3	39.3	e47.5	e54.1	Algérie
Belgium	–	63.9	56.0	58.6	e64.3	Belgique
Denmark	41.7	46.5	42.1	39.3	36.0	Danemark
Mexico	39.8	35.8	39.0	41.3	40.4	Mexique
Italy-San Marino-Holy See	41.5	42.5	35.5	34.5	38.1	Italie-Saint-Marin-Saint-Siège
Spain	30.3	32.2	27.7	34.0	49.0	Espagne
Syrian Arab Republic	e	e	61.1	e76.2	20.7	République arabe syrienne
Canada	27.3	29.5	26.3	38.1	36.7	Canada
Finland	33.0	29.8	22.7	26.0	26.1	Finlande
Ireland	23.6	24.0	23.4	29.6	32.2	Irlande
Ukraine	34.3	17.3	18.1	25.3	27.3	Ukraine
Belgium-Luxembourg	98.2	–	–	–	–	Belgique-Luxembourg
United States	11.1	15.9	16.8	21.3	31.6	Etats-Unis d'Amérique
Colombia	17.3	37.0	14.9	17.8	8.4	Colombie
Venezuela	5.1	8.8	30.2	22.6	e19.0	Venezuela
Japan	14.4	14.6	14.7	17.2	18.7	Japon
Lithuania	29.2	21.2	8.9	7.4	e9.1	Lituanie
Korea, Republic of	7.5	10.7	13.9	20.8	22.1	République de Corée
Portugal	9.7	15.6	14.2	15.7	18.7	Portugal
Austria	14.7	13.3	12.2	13.8	17.6	Autriche
Greece	18.9	16.2	12.4	11.3	e12.5	Grèce

(Value as percentages of World total) **(Valeur en pourcentage du total mondial)**

Regions of the world	1993	1994	1995	1996	1997	1998	1999	2000	2001	2002	Régions du monde
World	100.0	100.0	100.0	100.0	100.0	100.0	100.0	100.0	100.0	100.0	Monde
Africa	6.7	7.1	6.0	7.5	6.9	8.2	7.2	7.1	7.6	8.5	Afrique
Americas	8.6	8.5	9.4	9.8	11.4	12.1	13.6	16.6	19.1	20.3	Amériques
- Northern America	2.0	1.8	1.7	2.2	2.4	2.5	2.9	2.7	3.7	4.2	- Amérique du Nord
- LAIA	3.3	4.0	4.3	4.6	6.2	6.4	7.1	10.4	11.7	12.9	- ALAI
- CACM	0.5	0.4	1.0	0.5	0.6	0.8	0.9	1.1	1.2	0.9	- MCC
- Caribbean	2.4	1.9	2.1	2.2	1.9	2.1	2.4	2.0	2.1	2.0	- Caraïbes
- Rest of America	0.4	0.4	0.3	0.4	0.3	0.4	0.4	0.4	0.4	0.3	- Autre d'Amérique
Asia excluding former USSR	19.7	20.5	21.2	16.8	18.7	15.7	21.7	27.9	24.1	15.7	Asie ancienne URSS exclus
- Middle East	8.6	10.2	7.4	6.4	9.1	5.8	8.3	10.5	9.4	4.6	- Moyen-Orient
Asia former USSR	3.1	3.3	3.2	1.6	1.2	1.4	1.2	1.6	1.3	1.3	Asie ancienne URSS
Europe excluding former USSR	51.4	51.1	48.3	52.4	45.6	47.9	45.7	39.8	40.4	46.0	Europe ancienne URSS exclus
- European Union	43.3	45.5	43.0	47.0	40.9	41.6	39.0	34.2	34.6	39.8	- Union Européenne
- Eastern Europe	6.0	3.7	3.0	3.2	2.7	3.6	4.0	3.5	3.6	3.5	- Europe de l'Est
- Rest of Europe	2.1	1.9	2.2	2.2	2.0	2.6	2.7	2.1	2.3	2.7	- Autre de l'Europe
Europe former USSR	8.8	8.1	10.6	10.1	14.1	13.4	8.9	5.6	6.1	6.5	Europe ancienne URSS
Oceania	1.6	1.4	1.2	1.8	2.1	1.5	1.6	1.3	1.3	1.7	Océanie

TRADE BY COMMODITY (Value in million US dollars)
Exports by principal countries or areas

COMMERCE PAR PRODUIT (Valeur en millions de dollars EU)
Exportations selon les principaux pays ou zones

Country or area	1998	1999	2000	2001	2002	Pays ou zone
World	2125.6	1846.9	1576.2	1526.7	1686.7	Monde
Africa	43.9	39.6	21.5	17.1	18.3	Afrique
Americas	262.2	299.7	305.3	284.3	280.1	Amériques
- Northern America	171.5	178.3	164.9	170.3	194.5	- Amérique du Nord
- LAIA	70.3	94.9	116.8	91.7	64.7	- ALAI
- CACM	11.1	17.3	14.3	13.0	12.5	- MCC
- Caribbean	9.3	9.1	9.1	9.1	8.3	- Caraïbes
- Rest of America	0.0	0.2	0.1	0.2	0.2	- Autre d'Amérique
Asia excluding former USSR	441.3	446.6	402.1	354.6	362.6	Asie ancienne URSS exclus
- Middle East	137.6	104.2	71.4	59.2	65.8	- Moyen-Orient
Asia former USSR	0.1	0.6	0.5	0.7	1.1	Asie ancienne URSS
Europe excluding former USSR	1303.5	996.9	781.9	808.3	960.1	Europe ancienne URSS exclus
- European Union	1201.6	888.9	708.7	745.3	901.0	- Union Européenne
- Eastern Europe	89.2	96.3	63.9	52.4	46.9	- Europe de l'Est
- Rest of Europe	12.7	11.6	9.3	10.6	12.1	- Autre de l'Europe
Europe former USSR	19.1	11.5	17.9	14.8	15.1	Europe ancienne URSS
Oceania	55.6	52.1	47.1	46.8	49.4	Océanie
Netherlands	240.0	219.2	158.9	160.3	205.7	Pays-Bas
Germany	343.1	154.1	98.3	127.2	128.2	Allemagne
United States	158.2	160.3	144.2	144.8	162.2	Etats-Unis d'Amérique
Belgium	–	195.5	160.8	162.9	e182.8	Belgique
Malaysia	106.8	99.8	110.6	112.0	e118.7	Malaisie
Indonesia	70.2	121.8	89.0	82.0	94.6	Indonésie
Turkey	114.3	80.6	57.9	54.3	60.2	Turquie
Denmark	72.6	50.0	56.5	63.2	94.6	Danemark
United Kingdom	54.2	46.2	43.0	60.8	90.4	Royaume-Uni
Sweden	65.3	53.5	47.6	40.7	40.9	Suède
Belgium-Luxembourg	237.2	–	–	–	–	Belgique-Luxembourg
Australia	53.5	49.5	44.1	43.6	42.2	Australie
France-Monaco	57.1	49.7	40.3	37.8	45.5	France-Monaco
China, Hong Kong SAR	47.3	47.0	61.0	47.6	26.4	Chine - RAS de Hong-Kong
Argentina	42.8	43.9	45.1	34.4	e33.3	Argentine
Italy-San Marino-Holy See	33.9	42.4	34.4	29.3	33.5	Italie-Saint-Marin-Saint-Siège
Singapore	31.0	35.0	31.4	28.0	28.3	Singapour
Poland	35.7	41.0	24.1	17.2	14.6	Pologne
Ireland	22.7	29.1	29.3	23.7	25.2	Irlande
Finland	46.8	27.1	19.0	10.1	10.3	Finlande
Canada	13.3	18.0	20.7	25.5	32.2	Canada
Czech Republic	27.5	26.6	13.6	15.1	14.2	République tchèque
Colombia	3.0	14.8	34.5	29.3	4.3	Colombie
Bolivia	9.0	22.5	24.2	14.7	e14.1	Bolivie
Spain	12.7	11.6	10.6	16.2	30.1	Espagne
United Arab Emirates	22.0	22.7	12.3	4.0	e4.2	Emirates arabes unis
China	22.5	11.0	13.5	6.6	9.9	Chine
Slovakia	14.3	14.7	13.5	10.1	8.3	Slovaquie
Hungary	9.8	12.7	10.6	8.2	7.3	Hongrie
Kenya	23.3	19.2	3.2	e0.6	0.5	Kenya

(Value as percentages of World total) **(Valeur en pourcentage du total mondial)**

Regions of the world	1993	1994	1995	1996	1997	1998	1999	2000	2001	2002	Régions du monde
World	100.0	100.0	100.0	100.0	100.0	100.0	100.0	100.0	100.0	100.0	Monde
Africa	2.3	1.5	1.1	2.6	1.9	2.1	2.1	1.4	1.1	1.1	Afrique
Americas	13.1	14.0	12.0	11.1	9.9	12.3	16.2	19.4	18.6	16.6	Amériques
- Northern America	10.5	11.8	9.6	8.6	7.1	8.1	9.7	10.5	11.2	11.5	- Amérique du Nord
- LAIA	1.6	1.5	1.6	1.7	2.0	3.3	5.1	7.4	6.0	3.8	- ALAI
- CACM	0.4	0.3	0.3	0.3	0.4	0.5	0.9	0.9	0.9	0.7	- MCC
- Caribbean	0.5	0.4	0.4	0.5	0.4	0.4	0.5	0.6	0.6	0.5	- Caraïbes
- Rest of America	0.0	0.0	0.0	0.0	0.0	0.0	0.0	0.0	0.0	0.0	- Autre d'Amérique
Asia excluding former USSR	19.2	19.0	19.6	16.5	20.8	20.8	24.2	25.5	23.2	21.5	Asie ancienne URSS exclus
- Middle East	7.2	7.6	7.5	6.7	6.1	6.5	5.6	4.5	3.9	3.9	- Moyen-Orient
Asia former USSR	0.0	0.0	0.0	0.0	0.0	0.0	0.0	0.0	0.0	0.1	Asie ancienne URSS
Europe excluding former USSR	62.2	61.3	63.1	65.1	63.2	61.3	54.0	49.6	52.9	56.9	Europe ancienne URSS exclus
- European Union	57.6	58.9	59.8	61.4	58.8	56.5	48.1	45.0	48.8	53.4	- Union Européenne
- Eastern Europe	3.5	1.6	2.8	3.3	4.0	4.2	5.2	4.1	3.4	2.8	- Europe de l'Est
- Rest of Europe	1.1	0.8	0.5	0.4	0.4	0.6	0.6	0.6	0.7	0.7	- Autre de l'Europe
Europe former USSR	0.4	1.1	1.6	1.7	1.1	0.9	0.6	1.1	1.0	0.9	Europe ancienne URSS
Oceania	2.8	3.0	2.6	2.9	3.0	2.6	2.8	3.0	3.1	2.9	Océanie

098 Edible products and preparations, nes

TRADE BY COMMODITY (Value in million US dollars)
Imports by principal countries or areas

COMMERCE PAR PRODUIT (Valeur en millions de dollars EU)
Importations selon les principaux pays ou zones

Country or area	1998	1999	2000	2001	2002	Pays ou zone
World	16612.5	17105.4	16470.0	17658.2	19348.5	Monde
Africa	518.1	513.8	610.8	642.3	666.4	Afrique
Americas	3225.1	3456.8	3645.9	4091.1	4303.9	Amériques
- Northern America	1592.3	1819.9	1865.8	2077.3	2395.0	- Amérique du Nord
- LAIA	1014.6	1009.8	1133.5	1287.1	1225.1	- ALAI
- CACM	300.6	309.3	324.3	388.4	358.9	- MCC
- Caribbean	253.8	245.2	246.9	263.2	241.5	- Caraïbes
- Rest of America	63.8	72.6	75.4	75.2	83.3	- Autre d'Amérique
Asia excluding former USSR	3428.7	3752.5	3961.4	4173.9	4406.3	Asie ancienne URSS exclus
- Middle East	648.3	676.1	737.5	732.0	836.4	- Moyen-Orient
Asia former USSR	67.0	45.2	54.5	49.6	53.0	Asie ancienne URSS
Europe excluding former USSR	8267.1	8401.9	7224.3	7669.5	8719.8	Europe ancienne URSS exclus
- European Union	7092.7	7219.4	6130.2	6477.2	7317.4	- Union Européenne
- Eastern Europe	532.1	511.5	465.9	550.8	644.7	- Europe de l'Est
- Rest of Europe	642.2	671.1	628.2	641.5	757.7	- Autre de l'Europe
Europe former USSR	510.9	301.7	283.5	390.8	494.6	Europe ancienne URSS
Oceania	595.6	633.6	689.6	640.9	704.5	Océanie
Germany	1570.1	1507.6	1139.0	1339.3	1335.7	Allemagne
United States	952.7	1158.1	1203.0	1411.3	1646.1	Etats-Unis d'Amérique
United Kingdom	1404.3	1413.1	1112.0	1131.9	1280.7	Royaume-Uni
Japan	877.9	943.5	958.5	996.9	1023.8	Japon
France-Monaco	839.5	844.9	751.0	741.3	892.2	France-Monaco
Canada	618.1	638.4	649.1	653.8	730.7	Canada
Spain	620.4	684.6	610.0	628.9	745.2	Espagne
China, Hong Kong SAR	573.0	588.6	493.6	477.6	504.9	Chine - RAS de Hong-Kong
Mexico	332.1	428.8	516.4	591.0	639.6	Mexique
Netherlands	394.9	502.7	452.0	435.0	564.4	Pays-Bas
Australia	418.7	441.8	487.4	435.3	477.8	Australie
Italy-San Marino-Holy See	353.6	388.3	362.5	375.4	437.1	Italie-Saint-Marin-Saint-Siège
Belgium	–	468.8	435.5	459.2	e503.6	Belgique
Korea, Republic of	158.1	240.5	323.3	401.0	436.4	République de Corée
Sweden	278.2	300.4	281.9	302.4	332.4	Suède
Switzerland-Liechtenstein	264.2	285.2	263.7	267.3	325.0	Suisse-Liechtenstein
Austria	308.9	283.4	225.1	255.0	314.5	Autriche
Russian Federation	350.0	163.3	137.0	207.2	271.0	Fédération de Russie
Denmark	230.7	220.8	202.5	214.3	247.4	Danemark
Saudi Arabia	199.0	208.2	222.2	215.0	e222.5	Arabie saoudite
Singapore	179.0	197.0	206.6	212.2	231.9	Singapour
Poland	208.3	177.5	142.7	202.1	223.3	Pologne
Ireland	170.0	165.5	147.5	166.8	181.1	Irlande
Israel	158.6	162.9	160.1	162.9	167.5	Israël
China	90.1	132.1	157.7	190.6	189.2	Chine
Malaysia	134.4	139.1	147.4	157.0	e171.6	Malaisie
Philippines	92.0	134.8	155.7	175.6	174.2	Philippines
Czech Republic	141.9	145.8	138.6	140.9	162.5	République tchèque
Portugal	120.1	144.4	135.9	156.6	167.7	Portugal
Finland	145.3	136.4	138.2	132.3	163.5	Finlande

(Value as percentages of World total) **(Valeur en pourcentage du total mondial)**

Regions of the world	1993	1994	1995	1996	1997	1998	1999	2000	2001	2002	Régions du monde
World	100.0	100.0	100.0	100.0	100.0	100.0	100.0	100.0	100.0	100.0	Monde
Africa	3.3	2.6	2.7	2.6	2.8	3.1	3.0	3.7	3.6	3.4	Afrique
Americas	14.7	16.1	14.2	14.8	17.0	19.4	20.2	22.1	23.2	22.2	Amériques
- Northern America	8.2	9.0	7.6	8.0	8.8	9.6	10.6	11.3	11.8	12.4	- Amérique du Nord
- LAIA	3.7	4.3	3.9	4.1	4.8	6.1	5.9	6.9	7.3	6.3	- ALAI
- CACM	1.3	1.3	1.2	1.3	1.6	1.8	1.8	2.0	2.2	1.9	- MCC
- Caribbean	1.2	1.3	1.1	1.1	1.4	1.5	1.4	1.5	1.5	1.2	- Caraïbes
- Rest of America	0.4	0.3	0.3	0.3	0.3	0.4	0.4	0.5	0.4	0.4	- Autre d'Amérique
Asia excluding former USSR	20.3	20.3	21.0	23.0	24.3	20.6	21.9	24.1	23.6	22.8	Asie ancienne URSS exclus
- Middle East	3.0	2.7	3.2	3.3	3.8	3.9	4.0	4.5	4.1	4.3	- Moyen-Orient
Asia former USSR	0.1	0.1	0.3	0.4	0.2	0.4	0.3	0.3	0.3	0.3	Asie ancienne URSS
Europe excluding former USSR	55.3	54.1	54.7	51.6	48.1	49.8	49.1	43.9	43.4	45.1	Europe ancienne URSS exclus
- European Union	48.4	47.0	47.1	44.5	41.3	42.7	42.2	37.2	36.7	37.8	- Union Européenne
- Eastern Europe	3.1	3.3	3.4	3.3	3.2	3.2	3.0	2.8	3.1	3.3	- Europe de l'Est
- Rest of Europe	3.9	3.8	4.2	3.8	3.6	3.9	3.9	3.8	3.6	3.9	- Autre de l'Europe
Europe former USSR	2.8	3.3	3.6	3.9	3.9	3.1	1.8	1.7	2.2	2.6	Europe ancienne URSS
Oceania	3.4	3.5	3.5	3.7	3.7	3.6	3.7	4.2	3.6	3.6	Océanie

TRADE BY COMMODITY (Value in million US dollars)
Exports by principal countries or areas

COMMERCE PAR PRODUIT (Valeur en millions de dollars EU)
Exportations selon les principaux pays ou zones

Country or area	1998	1999	2000	2001	2002	Pays ou zone
World	15446.6	15371.7	15403.2	16514.0	18197.4	Monde
Africa	117.1	112.6	208.4	249.2	332.7	Afrique
Americas	3801.9	4100.7	4367.8	4703.7	4784.5	Amériques
- Northern America	2936.9	3203.2	3278.9	3552.8	3619.5	- Amérique du Nord
- LAIA	603.3	648.0	835.4	891.2	877.6	- ALAI
- CACM	197.9	195.0	195.3	197.0	230.0	- MCC
- Caribbean	51.7	41.8	46.8	51.2	43.6	- Caraïbes
- Rest of America	12.0	12.8	11.4	11.5	13.9	- Autre d'Amérique
Asia excluding former USSR	2177.6	2265.2	2395.2	2457.0	2651.6	Asie ancienne URSS exclus
- Middle East	216.9	194.4	170.0	180.4	210.4	- Moyen-Orient
Asia former USSR	2.3	1.6	2.2	4.1	4.0	Asie ancienne URSS
Europe excluding former USSR	9038.8	8556.9	8045.6	8619.0	9887.2	Europe ancienne URSS exclus
- European Union	8142.4	7713.9	7212.2	7744.6	8811.8	- Union Européenne
- Eastern Europe	349.2	295.2	329.0	352.1	497.7	- Europe de l'Est
- Rest of Europe	547.2	547.9	504.4	522.3	577.7	- Autre de l'Europe
Europe former USSR	85.2	60.7	87.0	113.8	125.3	Europe ancienne URSS
Oceania	223.9	274.0	297.0	367.1	412.1	Océanie
United States	2491.7	2696.4	2769.4	2930.1	2944.4	Etats-Unis d'Amérique
France-Monaco	1760.8	1244.5	1132.3	1145.3	1296.7	France-Monaco
Germany	1248.9	1259.6	1128.9	1299.1	1383.1	Allemagne
Netherlands	900.9	970.8	998.7	1092.4	1303.5	Pays-Bas
Ireland	863.1	839.5	727.0	717.9	777.8	Irlande
United Kingdom	766.0	799.0	757.7	759.1	800.7	Royaume-Uni
Italy-San Marino-Holy See	658.2	666.5	645.3	728.5	846.9	Italie-Saint-Marin-Saint-Siège
Canada	445.2	506.8	509.5	622.7	675.1	Canada
Belgium	–	638.7	613.1	661.5	e742.1	Belgique
Denmark	492.0	494.0	440.7	472.7	611.6	Danemark
Spain	387.4	394.9	386.8	428.8	438.5	Espagne
China	328.1	341.9	377.6	415.9	478.3	Chine
Switzerland-Liechtenstein	366.9	377.5	355.1	366.3	397.5	Suisse-Liechtenstein
Japan	279.0	333.9	391.5	362.6	386.0	Japon
Thailand	252.9	307.1	324.2	337.6	e356.5	Thaïlande
China, Hong Kong SAR	331.5	300.5	233.2	197.0	201.9	Chine - RAS de Hong-Kong
Brazil	121.0	172.4	354.1	283.6	e294.0	Brésil
Mexico	167.6	200.8	227.0	306.9	271.2	Mexique
Sweden	160.3	156.0	144.4	159.6	277.1	Suède
Singapore	154.2	157.3	184.1	193.2	186.9	Singapour
Australia	134.5	165.4	175.8	174.7	192.9	Australie
Hungary	152.1	139.8	132.8	142.9	185.8	Hongrie
New Zealand	87.4	106.7	119.1	190.1	217.1	Nouvelle-Zélande
Israel	146.0	140.7	146.2	135.0	148.0	Israël
Chile	137.4	123.9	118.5	166.4	e162.8	Chili
Austria	112.9	121.0	115.6	154.0	191.0	Autriche
Belgium-Luxembourg	658.2	–	–	–	–	Belgique-Luxembourg
Korea, Republic of	125.5	102.3	113.9	130.7	151.2	République de Corée
Poland	105.5	84.5	106.9	106.7	173.9	Pologne
Turkey	104.9	85.5	92.1	101.5	128.5	Turquie

(Value as percentages of World total) **(Valeur en pourcentage du total mondial)**

Regions of the world	1993	1994	1995	1996	1997	1998	1999	2000	2001	2002	Régions du monde
World	100.0	100.0	100.0	100.0	100.0	100.0	100.0	100.0	100.0	100.0	Monde
Africa	0.6	0.5	0.7	0.7	0.7	0.8	0.7	1.4	1.5	1.8	Afrique
Americas	20.1	21.0	18.4	20.7	23.2	24.6	26.7	28.4	28.5	26.3	Amériques
- Northern America	17.3	17.9	14.8	16.7	18.9	19.0	20.8	21.3	21.5	19.9	- Amérique du Nord
- LAIA	1.8	2.1	2.7	2.9	3.0	3.9	4.2	5.4	5.4	4.8	- ALAI
- CACM	0.6	0.6	0.5	0.7	0.9	1.3	1.3	1.3	1.2	1.3	- MCC
- Caribbean	0.3	0.2	0.3	0.4	0.3	0.3	0.3	0.3	0.3	0.2	- Caraïbes
- Rest of America	0.1	0.1	0.1	0.1	0.1	0.1	0.1	0.1	0.1	0.1	- Autre d'Amérique
Asia excluding former USSR	12.7	12.6	12.5	14.3	15.4	14.1	14.7	15.6	14.9	14.6	Asie ancienne URSS exclus
- Middle East	0.9	0.7	0.7	1.0	1.3	1.4	1.3	1.1	1.1	1.2	- Moyen-Orient
Asia former USSR	0.0	0.0	0.0	0.1	0.0	0.0	0.0	0.0	0.0	0.0	Asie ancienne URSS
Europe excluding former USSR	65.2	64.0	66.6	62.3	58.3	58.5	55.7	52.2	52.2	54.3	Europe ancienne URSS exclus
- European Union	59.7	58.4	61.4	56.5	52.6	52.7	50.2	46.8	46.9	48.4	- Union Européenne
- Eastern Europe	1.6	1.5	1.5	2.0	2.4	2.3	1.9	2.1	2.1	2.7	- Europe de l'Est
- Rest of Europe	3.9	4.1	3.7	3.7	3.4	3.5	3.6	3.3	3.2	3.2	- Autre de l'Europe
Europe former USSR	0.3	0.3	0.3	0.5	0.6	0.6	0.4	0.6	0.7	0.7	Europe ancienne URSS
Oceania	1.1	1.5	1.5	1.6	1.6	1.4	1.8	1.9	2.2	2.3	Océanie

111 Non-alcoholic beverages, nes

TRADE BY COMMODITY (Value in million US dollars)
Imports by principal countries or areas

COMMERCE PAR PRODUIT (Valeur en millions de dollars EU)
Importations selon les principaux pays ou zones

Country or area	1998	1999	2000	2001	2002	Pays ou zone
World	4458.0	5050.7	5173.1	5762.9	6372.4	Monde
Africa	72.7	92.6	163.4	157.8	193.7	Afrique
Americas	1048.1	1099.7	1172.0	1313.8	1387.8	Amériques
- Northern America	808.1	877.5	945.5	1017.2	1106.2	- Amérique du Nord
- LAIA	83.5	77.8	96.0	120.5	118.3	- ALAI
- CACM	30.0	31.4	33.0	45.7	57.7	- MCC
- Caribbean	114.2	102.3	86.9	114.1	89.6	- Caraïbes
- Rest of America	12.3	10.7	10.7	16.3	16.0	- Autre d'Amérique
Asia excluding former USSR	897.8	1027.0	1119.9	1185.3	1179.0	Asie ancienne URSS exclus
- Middle East	139.1	169.3	231.1	232.6	228.2	- Moyen-Orient
Asia former USSR	20.0	15.2	11.1	11.0	12.2	Asie ancienne URSS
Europe excluding former USSR	2223.7	2692.7	2555.5	2930.1	3408.6	Europe ancienne URSS exclus
- European Union	1951.0	2388.6	2251.5	2593.8	3004.0	- Union Européenne
- Eastern Europe	59.0	61.7	72.1	86.3	111.6	- Europe de l'Est
- Rest of Europe	213.7	242.5	231.9	250.1	293.0	- Autre de l'Europe
Europe former USSR	140.2	58.1	60.5	73.2	97.2	Europe ancienne URSS
Oceania	55.4	65.4	90.7	91.6	94.0	Océanie
United States	622.4	670.9	746.7	817.1	902.3	Etats-Unis d'Amérique
Germany	334.8	463.0	433.6	563.3	680.7	Allemagne
United Kingdom	307.2	427.9	431.7	483.4	461.2	Royaume-Uni
China, Hong Kong SAR	398.6	424.4	398.7	439.2	433.0	Chine - RAS de Hong-Kong
France-Monaco	306.9	308.4	301.7	334.8	395.8	France-Monaco
Belgium	–	420.3	347.6	370.3	e406.1	Belgique
Netherlands	212.0	189.2	212.9	229.2	332.3	Pays-Bas
Japan	154.1	198.5	241.4	248.7	257.3	Japon
Canada	178.5	198.5	194.9	196.6	199.7	Canada
Ireland	127.1	168.5	137.3	142.4	162.9	Irlande
Switzerland-Liechtenstein	97.4	107.0	109.3	114.7	128.8	Suisse-Liechtenstein
Italy-San Marino-Holy See	65.8	95.3	96.9	101.8	124.9	Italie-Saint-Marin-Saint-Siège
Spain	58.5	67.2	65.8	82.5	108.8	Espagne
Belgium-Luxembourg	372.6	–	–	–	–	Belgique-Luxembourg
Singapore	56.5	60.5	76.0	87.6	85.5	Singapour
Saudi Arabia	7.4	27.3	75.0	85.5	e88.4	Arabie saoudite
Portugal	35.0	57.1	55.0	58.8	70.2	Portugal
Mexico	34.9	46.5	51.7	64.9	68.6	Mexique
Bosnia and Herzegovina	e33.3	e52.4	e48.2	e52.1	e60.9	Bosnie-Herzégovine
Sweden	39.6	39.4	27.2	62.7	75.4	Suède
Luxembourg	–	58.0	54.8	62.4	e66.3	Luxembourg
Angola	e27.9	e37.2	e58.2	e41.7	e61.4	Angola
Austria	40.1	42.3	35.3	42.8	50.7	Autriche
Russian Federation	90.4	15.2	22.4	27.2	36.1	Fédération de Russie
Oman	44.0	38.3	34.9	26.0	31.3	Oman
Australia	12.6	19.3	42.9	43.3	46.0	Australie
Kuwait	31.1	36.2	e34.0	e37.4	e18.1	Koweït
Greece	26.9	28.6	21.4	26.2	e28.9	Grèce
Czech Republic	15.3	18.8	25.6	26.6	32.6	République tchèque
Croatia	17.2	18.9	20.6	26.6	32.9	Croatie

(Value as percentages of World total) **(Valeur en pourcentage du total mondial)**

Regions of the world	1993	1994	1995	1996	1997	1998	1999	2000	2001	2002	Régions du monde
World	100.0	100.0	100.0	100.0	100.0	100.0	100.0	100.0	100.0	100.0	Monde
Africa	2.6	2.2	2.2	2.1	1.7	1.6	1.8	3.2	2.7	3.0	Afrique
Americas	19.4	20.9	19.8	18.7	23.2	23.5	21.8	22.7	22.8	21.8	Amériques
- Northern America	12.7	13.1	12.0	14.1	17.4	18.1	17.4	18.3	17.7	17.4	- Amérique du Nord
- LAIA	3.7	4.8	4.0	2.0	2.3	1.9	1.5	1.9	2.1	1.9	- ALAI
- CACM	0.3	0.3	0.3	0.3	0.5	0.7	0.6	0.6	0.8	0.9	- MCC
- Caribbean	2.4	2.3	3.0	2.1	2.7	2.6	2.0	1.7	2.0	1.4	- Caraïbes
- Rest of America	0.4	0.4	0.4	0.2	0.2	0.3	0.2	0.2	0.3	0.3	- Autre d'Amérique
Asia excluding former USSR	21.8	22.8	23.4	24.0	23.2	20.1	20.3	21.6	20.6	18.5	Asie ancienne URSS exclus
- Middle East	3.6	3.2	2.7	2.9	3.0	3.1	3.4	4.5	4.0	3.6	- Moyen-Orient
Asia former USSR	0.2	1.0	0.6	0.7	0.6	0.4	0.3	0.2	0.2	0.2	Asie ancienne URSS
Europe excluding former USSR	48.3	47.9	48.0	48.7	46.2	49.9	53.3	49.4	50.8	53.5	Europe ancienne URSS exclus
- European Union	42.9	43.1	42.2	42.5	40.8	43.8	47.3	43.5	45.0	47.1	- Union Européenne
- Eastern Europe	2.3	1.2	1.3	1.6	1.4	1.3	1.2	1.4	1.5	1.8	- Europe de l'Est
- Rest of Europe	3.1	3.6	4.5	4.5	4.0	4.8	4.8	4.5	4.3	4.6	- Autre de l'Europe
Europe former USSR	6.6	4.2	4.9	4.8	3.9	3.1	1.1	1.2	1.3	1.5	Europe ancienne URSS
Oceania	1.2	1.0	1.1	1.1	1.2	1.2	1.3	1.8	1.6	1.5	Océanie

TRADE BY COMMODITY (Value in million US dollars)
Exports by principal countries or areas

COMMERCE PAR PRODUIT (Valeur en millions de dollars EU)
Exportations selon les principaux pays ou zones

Country or area	1998	1999	2000	2001	2002	Pays ou zone
World	4439.7	5113.7	5231.7	5762.8	6407.7	Monde
Africa	37.3	41.2	93.6	97.3	108.0	Afrique
Americas	816.5	869.5	841.1	861.1	1012.9	Amériques
- Northern America	607.8	643.8	580.3	571.5	632.7	- Amérique du Nord
- LAIA	129.4	152.3	183.2	193.0	284.2	- ALAI
- CACM	22.5	23.7	25.2	34.9	49.1	- MCC
- Caribbean	54.6	48.0	51.3	60.7	46.1	- Caraïbes
- Rest of America	2.2	1.6	1.1	1.0	0.8	- Autre d'Amérique
Asia excluding former USSR	653.4	701.5	750.2	790.4	826.7	Asie ancienne URSS exclus
- Middle East	91.0	81.6	118.0	92.0	104.4	- Moyen-Orient
Asia former USSR	10.4	4.3	14.9	16.9	10.5	Asie ancienne URSS
Europe excluding former USSR	2847.7	3426.5	3442.0	3908.1	4342.4	Europe ancienne URSS exclus
- European Union	2587.7	3202.6	3171.2	3632.7	4012.3	- Union Européenne
- Eastern Europe	107.7	77.8	122.5	132.6	163.4	- Europe de l'Est
- Rest of Europe	152.2	146.1	148.3	142.8	166.7	- Autre de l'Europe
Europe former USSR	48.5	34.5	30.6	37.4	45.8	Europe ancienne URSS
Oceania	25.8	36.2	59.2	51.6	61.4	Océanie
France-Monaco	822.5	844.3	858.1	835.4	968.8	France-Monaco
Austria	287.9	505.3	544.7	683.3	655.4	Autriche
Netherlands	289.2	347.7	351.0	428.8	440.1	Pays-Bas
Germany	283.1	345.8	292.4	397.9	468.3	Allemagne
Belgium	–	406.8	403.6	455.9	e511.5	Belgique
China	294.1	333.3	319.5	350.9	354.7	Chine
United States	305.6	328.6	314.3	313.8	336.6	Etats-Unis d'Amérique
Canada	302.3	315.3	266.0	257.7	296.1	Canada
Italy-San Marino-Holy See	157.9	194.2	217.3	269.9	352.3	Italie-Saint-Marin-Saint-Siège
United Kingdom	218.1	277.2	206.5	215.2	159.7	Royaume-Uni
Spain	82.9	96.0	113.7	149.9	211.3	Espagne
Mexico	67.5	93.8	117.8	128.4	216.4	Mexique
Thailand	46.8	72.2	72.4	74.3	e78.4	Thaïlande
Ireland	60.8	67.2	52.8	55.7	81.4	Irlande
Belgium-Luxembourg	300.4	–	–	–	–	Belgique-Luxembourg
Switzerland-Liechtenstein	56.6	70.9	65.9	51.4	52.8	Suisse-Liechtenstein
Malaysia	32.3	39.8	47.2	60.7	e64.3	Malaisie
Czech Republic	21.5	27.5	48.9	54.5	71.6	République tchèque
Slovenia	36.8	34.1	42.3	49.1	59.4	Slovénie
Trinidad and Tobago	46.8	40.4	42.4	50.5	e38.3	Trinité-et-Tobago
Denmark	35.1	40.9	46.1	42.2	53.4	Danemark
China, Hong Kong SAR	51.9	41.2	43.1	42.7	32.4	Chine - RAS de Hong-Kong
Hungary	63.5	22.7	30.7	30.8	29.7	Hongrie
Singapore	42.5	34.1	33.6	32.5	29.8	Singapour
Korea, Republic of	34.9	20.2	24.7	33.6	38.5	République de Corée
Japan	17.5	24.2	25.3	27.7	37.6	Japon
Saudi Arabia	29.6	31.3	29.7	19.4	e17.4	Arabie saoudite
South Africa	–	–	37.9	37.7	49.3	Afrique du Sud
United Arab Emirates	11.4	11.8	43.0	27.1	e28.2	Emirates arabes unis
Brazil	21.5	20.5	27.9	22.1	e23.0	Brésil

(Value as percentages of World total) **(Valeur en pourcentage du total mondial)**

Regions of the world	1993	1994	1995	1996	1997	1998	1999	2000	2001	2002	Régions du monde
World	100.0	100.0	100.0	100.0	100.0	100.0	100.0	100.0	100.0	100.0	Monde
Africa	1.5	1.0	0.8	1.2	0.9	0.8	0.8	1.8	1.7	1.7	Afrique
Americas	13.1	15.2	15.5	13.5	16.8	18.4	17.0	16.1	14.9	15.8	Amériques
- Northern America	10.2	12.4	11.2	10.3	12.9	13.7	12.6	11.1	9.9	9.9	- Amérique du Nord
- LAIA	1.7	1.7	2.9	2.1	2.5	2.9	3.0	3.5	3.3	4.4	- ALAI
- CACM	0.2	0.2	0.2	0.3	0.4	0.5	0.5	0.5	0.6	0.8	- MCC
- Caribbean	1.0	0.9	1.2	0.9	1.0	1.2	0.9	1.0	1.1	0.7	- Caraïbes
- Rest of America	0.0	0.0	0.0	0.0	0.0	0.0	0.0	0.0	0.0	0.0	- Autre d'Amérique
Asia excluding former USSR	21.0	19.2	17.4	17.6	16.5	14.7	13.7	14.3	13.7	12.9	Asie ancienne URSS exclus
- Middle East	3.9	3.3	3.0	2.3	1.8	2.1	1.6	2.3	1.6	1.6	- Moyen-Orient
Asia former USSR	0.0	0.1	0.1	0.2	0.1	0.2	0.1	0.3	0.3	0.2	Asie ancienne URSS
Europe excluding former USSR	63.6	63.1	64.5	65.2	64.0	64.1	67.0	65.8	67.8	67.8	Europe ancienne URSS exclus
- European Union	59.0	56.7	60.2	59.2	57.6	58.3	62.6	60.6	63.0	62.6	- Union Européenne
- Eastern Europe	2.4	3.8	1.9	3.3	2.9	2.4	1.5	2.3	2.3	2.5	- Europe de l'Est
- Rest of Europe	2.3	2.6	2.4	2.7	3.4	3.4	2.9	2.8	2.5	2.6	- Autre de l'Europe
Europe former USSR	0.3	0.9	0.9	1.4	1.2	1.1	0.7	0.6	0.6	0.7	Europe ancienne URSS
Oceania	0.4	0.5	0.7	0.8	0.5	0.6	0.7	1.1	0.9	1.0	Océanie

112 Alcoholic beverages

TRADE BY COMMODITY (Value in million US dollars)
Imports by principal countries or areas

COMMERCE PAR PRODUIT (Valeur en millions de dollars EU)
Importations selon les principaux pays ou zones

Country or area	1998	1999	2000	2001	2002	Pays ou zone
World	29476.5	30402.2	29523.8	30755.9	33078.0	Monde
Africa	387.0	381.2	422.9	412.4	481.0	Afrique
Americas	8116.4	9024.2	9786.1	10323.0	11231.2	Amériques
- Northern America	7106.9	8112.2	8830.5	9225.8	10196.7	- Amérique du Nord
- LAIA	763.2	664.1	695.9	817.4	699.9	- ALAI
- CACM	49.0	52.6	56.9	59.1	71.3	- MCC
- Caribbean	172.5	164.1	174.2	185.3	234.0	- Caraïbes
- Rest of America	24.9	31.2	28.6	35.4	29.2	- Autre d'Amérique
Asia excluding former USSR	4093.8	3797.5	3856.8	3728.2	3781.3	Asie ancienne URSS exclus
- Middle East	153.5	151.1	159.5	159.1	199.7	- Moyen-Orient
Asia former USSR	49.4	27.8	34.1	32.6	36.2	Asie ancienne URSS
Europe excluding former USSR	15463.3	16221.5	14343.8	15030.6	16176.9	Europe ancienne URSS exclus
- European Union	14103.2	14736.4	13008.8	13634.8	14649.1	- Union Européenne
- Eastern Europe	239.7	259.8	247.3	269.2	314.4	- Europe de l'Est
- Rest of Europe	1120.4	1225.3	1087.7	1126.5	1213.4	- Autre de l'Europe
Europe former USSR	937.8	459.1	557.9	715.8	848.3	Europe ancienne URSS
Oceania	428.6	491.0	522.4	513.3	523.0	Océanie
United States	6274.0	7145.3	7819.9	8146.9	9056.6	Etats-Unis d'Amérique
United Kingdom	4017.2	4049.9	3644.4	3728.0	4142.1	Royaume-Uni
Germany	2971.7	3126.0	2521.2	2769.4	2661.8	Allemagne
Japan	2265.9	1870.6	1753.8	1686.3	1636.2	Japon
France-Monaco	1421.1	1384.0	1206.4	1193.0	1329.5	France-Monaco
Spain	1029.1	1069.3	998.8	1146.1	1134.9	Espagne
Canada	803.2	930.7	992.7	1053.9	1101.8	Canada
Netherlands	751.1	881.6	842.8	837.1	924.3	Pays-Bas
Belgium	–	1120.4	1000.7	950.9	e1042.9	Belgique
Switzerland-Liechtenstein	764.5	838.0	733.7	758.0	789.3	Suisse-Liechtenstein
Italy-San Marino-Holy See	751.6	788.1	733.3	729.2	819.7	Italie-Saint-Marin-Saint-Siège
Russian Federation	690.7	297.1	383.0	514.1	588.3	Fédération de Russie
Denmark	498.4	513.7	460.1	462.5	524.1	Danemark
China, Hong Kong SAR	473.0	440.7	418.4	400.7	355.2	Chine - RAS de Hong-Kong
Sweden	426.7	388.0	343.6	400.9	458.3	Suède
Singapore	366.7	401.7	424.6	379.3	397.4	Singapour
Ireland	258.1	285.4	263.9	389.8	483.5	Irlande
Australia	259.5	300.0	333.6	327.8	322.6	Australie
Portugal	257.1	333.6	278.3	245.1	267.7	Portugal
Greece	274.8	274.5	238.1	262.4	e290.2	Grèce
Austria	232.9	226.9	203.8	228.3	257.0	Autriche
Korea, Republic of	122.6	144.1	225.5	261.3	321.3	République de Corée
Belgium-Luxembourg	1047.0	–	–	–	–	Belgique-Luxembourg
Norway	157.8	181.2	177.6	182.0	217.7	Norvège
Mexico	135.5	134.9	152.9	229.7	231.3	Mexique
Finland	166.4	171.9	157.9	177.8	191.8	Finlande
Venezuela	142.0	119.8	167.8	206.2	e173.5	Venezuela
Brazil	153.2	145.8	134.8	139.5	117.6	Brésil
New Zealand	111.1	127.4	125.9	122.4	139.3	Nouvelle-Zélande
China	70.6	116.5	155.2	139.6	139.3	Chine

(Value as percentages of World total) **(Valeur en pourcentage du total mondial)**

Regions of the world	1993	1994	1995	1996	1997	1998	1999	2000	2001	2002	Régions du monde
World	100.0	100.0	100.0	100.0	100.0	100.0	100.0	100.0	100.0	100.0	Monde
Africa	1.5	1.5	1.5	1.4	1.4	1.3	1.3	1.4	1.3	1.5	Afrique
Americas	24.1	24.0	23.3	24.3	26.3	27.5	29.7	33.1	33.6	34.0	Amériques
- Northern America	20.2	20.2	19.4	21.3	23.0	24.1	26.7	29.9	30.0	30.8	- Amérique du Nord
- LAIA	2.8	2.8	2.8	2.3	2.5	2.6	2.2	2.4	2.7	2.1	- ALAI
- CACM	0.1	0.1	0.1	0.1	0.2	0.2	0.2	0.2	0.2	0.2	- MCC
- Caribbean	0.9	0.7	0.7	0.5	0.6	0.6	0.5	0.6	0.6	0.7	- Caraïbes
- Rest of America	0.2	0.2	0.2	0.1	0.1	0.1	0.1	0.1	0.1	0.1	- Autre d'Amérique
Asia excluding former USSR	17.5	17.8	17.8	16.4	15.8	13.9	12.5	13.1	12.1	11.4	Asie ancienne URSS exclus
- Middle East	0.8	0.9	1.0	0.7	0.7	0.5	0.5	0.5	0.5	0.6	- Moyen-Orient
Asia former USSR	0.3	1.6	0.3	0.5	0.4	0.2	0.1	0.1	0.1	0.1	Asie ancienne URSS
Europe excluding former USSR	50.1	49.9	50.9	52.2	50.9	52.5	53.4	48.6	48.9	48.9	Europe ancienne URSS exclus
- European Union	46.0	45.9	46.1	47.4	46.4	47.8	48.5	44.1	44.3	44.3	- Union Européenne
- Eastern Europe	0.8	0.7	0.7	0.9	0.8	0.8	0.9	0.8	0.9	1.0	- Europe de l'Est
- Rest of Europe	3.2	3.4	4.0	3.9	3.6	3.8	4.0	3.7	3.7	3.7	- Autre de l'Europe
Europe former USSR	5.0	3.5	4.7	3.5	3.7	3.2	1.5	1.9	2.3	2.6	Europe ancienne URSS
Oceania	1.5	1.6	1.5	1.6	1.6	1.5	1.6	1.8	1.7	1.6	Océanie

TRADE BY COMMODITY (Value in million US dollars)
Exports by principal countries or areas

COMMERCE PAR PRODUIT (Valeur en millions de dollars EU)
Exportations selon les principaux pays ou zones

Country or area	1998	1999	2000	2001	2002	Pays ou zone
World	29130.5	29976.8	28865.6	29653.5	32748.4	Monde
Africa	293.3	303.2	377.7	403.2	460.2	Afrique
Americas	3668.1	3889.1	4375.1	4654.8	4724.4	Amériques
- Northern America	1805.6	1898.9	1931.5	2005.7	1896.6	- Amérique du Nord
- LAIA	1698.9	1822.1	2260.9	2448.9	2603.5	- ALAI
- CACM	10.7	11.6	15.5	16.0	16.1	- MCC
- Caribbean	144.7	147.9	155.5	170.1	185.8	- Caraïbes
- Rest of America	8.2	8.5	11.6	14.1	22.3	- Autre d'Amérique
Asia excluding former USSR	1219.7	1218.4	1266.3	1202.2	1304.4	Asie ancienne URSS exclus
- Middle East	66.9	64.1	60.5	52.5	61.2	- Moyen-Orient
Asia former USSR	62.2	38.2	68.3	87.2	74.8	Asie ancienne URSS
Europe excluding former USSR	22766.1	23345.5	21422.7	21735.9	24218.9	Europe ancienne URSS exclus
- European Union	22090.8	22822.2	20972.2	21264.2	23674.8	- Union Européenne
- Eastern Europe	449.1	328.2	289.9	301.1	345.2	- Europe de l'Est
- Rest of Europe	226.2	195.1	160.5	170.6	198.8	- Autre de l'Europe
Europe former USSR	363.0	217.1	251.0	352.9	451.3	Europe ancienne URSS
Oceania	758.1	965.4	1104.6	1217.2	1514.3	Océanie
France-Monaco	8011.1	8169.5	7245.5	6764.5	7593.6	France-Monaco
United Kingdom	4567.7	4434.5	4411.6	4445.8	4814.3	Royaume-Uni
Italy-San Marino-Holy See	2864.2	3054.7	2819.9	2878.1	3276.1	Italie-Saint-Marin-Saint-Siège
Spain	1645.2	1704.8	1392.4	1596.9	1656.7	Espagne
Germany	1420.8	1482.8	1219.8	1454.7	1536.1	Allemagne
Netherlands	921.8	1381.1	1317.7	1405.2	1749.8	Pays-Bas
Mexico	862.3	1017.7	1406.8	1525.3	1699.7	Mexique
United States	1218.1	1237.5	1237.2	1290.9	1301.5	Etats-Unis d'Amérique
Australia	668.9	855.1	977.0	1077.3	1354.0	Australie
Ireland	694.2	723.8	717.2	700.2	762.3	Irlande
Canada	585.6	655.7	690.7	712.9	592.2	Canada
Chile	548.8	553.6	591.1	656.2	e642.0	Chili
Portugal	576.7	589.9	525.4	500.0	572.5	Portugal
Belgium	-	612.6	602.0	573.1	e643.0	Belgique
Singapore	337.3	356.4	362.0	327.9	359.5	Singapour
China, Hong Kong SAR	351.0	304.4	293.7	280.9	256.4	Chine - RAS de Hong-Kong
Denmark	267.4	256.2	351.3	277.6	307.5	Danemark
Sweden	252.6	87.4	98.2	393.5	464.9	Suède
South Africa	-	-	284.6	298.4	345.6	Afrique du Sud
Argentina	184.0	163.9	170.8	168.6	e162.9	Argentine
Republic of Moldova	208.0	109.2	127.6	174.2	195.7	République de Moldova
China	103.2	101.7	123.4	136.3	196.3	Chine
Japan	150.0	133.2	131.6	105.0	106.3	Japon
Korea, Republic of	85.3	106.6	134.7	138.1	150.3	République de Corée
New Zealand	87.5	103.4	119.4	133.0	154.1	Nouvelle-Zélande
Greece	137.3	125.4	103.0	96.8	e96.9	Grèce
Belgium-Luxembourg	532.2	-	-	-	-	Belgique-Luxembourg
Southern African Customs Union	229.3	251.5	-	-	-	Union douanière d'Afrique australe
Czech Republic	103.0	87.9	84.0	89.7	102.7	République tchèque
Austria	112.6	87.0	73.9	86.6	102.1	Autriche

(Value as percentages of World total) **(Valeur en pourcentage du total mondial)**

Regions of the world	1993	1994	1995	1996	1997	1998	1999	2000	2001	2002	Régions du monde
World	100.0	100.0	100.0	100.0	100.0	100.0	100.0	100.0	100.0	100.0	Monde
Africa	0.7	0.9	1.3	1.1	1.0	1.0	1.0	1.3	1.4	1.4	Afrique
Americas	9.7	9.8	9.8	10.2	11.3	12.6	13.0	15.2	15.7	14.4	Amériques
- Northern America	6.5	6.3	5.9	5.9	6.0	6.2	6.3	6.7	6.8	5.8	- Amérique du Nord
- LAIA	2.6	3.0	3.4	3.8	4.7	5.8	6.1	7.8	8.3	8.0	- ALAI
- CACM	0.0	0.0	0.0	0.0	0.0	0.0	0.0	0.1	0.1	0.0	- MCC
- Caribbean	0.6	0.5	0.5	0.4	0.5	0.5	0.5	0.5	0.6	0.6	- Caraïbes
- Rest of America	0.1	0.1	0.0	0.1	0.1	0.0	0.0	0.0	0.0	0.1	- Autre d'Amérique
Asia excluding former USSR	5.6	5.9	5.8	5.3	5.3	4.2	4.1	4.4	4.1	4.0	Asie ancienne URSS exclus
- Middle East	0.3	0.3	0.4	0.4	0.3	0.2	0.2	0.2	0.2	0.2	- Moyen-Orient
Asia former USSR	0.0	0.3	0.2	0.3	0.3	0.2	0.1	0.2	0.3	0.2	Asie ancienne URSS
Europe excluding former USSR	81.1	79.6	79.5	78.3	77.8	78.2	77.9	74.2	73.3	74.0	Europe ancienne URSS exclus
- European Union	78.1	77.3	76.5	75.6	75.5	75.8	76.1	72.7	71.7	72.3	- Union Européenne
- Eastern Europe	2.2	1.6	2.3	2.0	1.6	1.5	1.1	1.0	1.0	1.1	- Europe de l'Est
- Rest of Europe	0.8	0.7	0.7	0.7	0.7	0.8	0.7	0.6	0.6	0.6	- Autre de l'Europe
Europe former USSR	1.3	1.8	1.8	2.9	1.9	1.2	0.7	0.9	1.2	1.4	Europe ancienne URSS
Oceania	1.6	1.7	1.6	2.0	2.4	2.6	3.2	3.8	4.1	4.6	Océanie

121 Tobacco unmanufactured; tobacco refuse

TRADE BY COMMODITY (Value in million US dollars)
Imports by principal countries or areas

COMMERCE PAR PRODUIT (Valeur en millions de dollars EU)
Importations selon les principaux pays ou zones

Country or area	1998	1999	2000	2001	2002	Pays ou zone
World	7693.1	7696.7	7021.0	7087.1	7259.5	Monde
Africa	436.1	473.8	441.5	436.9	461.4	Afrique
Americas	1286.1	1079.3	900.0	1016.2	1012.4	Amériques
- Northern America	849.1	793.3	613.8	759.1	755.4	- Amérique du Nord
- LAIA	193.9	128.1	142.0	142.0	131.8	- ALAI
- CACM	62.2	28.3	33.7	20.6	32.3	- MCC
- Caribbean	178.7	129.2	109.8	94.1	92.5	- Caraïbes
- Rest of America	2.3	0.5	0.6	0.4	0.4	- Autre d'Amérique
Asia excluding former USSR	1618.1	1614.4	1725.2	1686.5	1605.5	Asie ancienne URSS exclus
- Middle East	308.0	292.3	371.5	263.2	185.2	- Moyen-Orient
Asia former USSR	32.2	31.4	43.1	54.4	49.3	Asie ancienne URSS
Europe excluding former USSR	3670.1	3758.1	3187.7	3100.4	3274.3	Europe ancienne URSS exclus
- European Union	2913.1	2982.4	2607.1	2574.7	2647.0	- Union Européenne
- Eastern Europe	485.7	501.9	287.4	303.2	367.4	- Europe de l'Est
- Rest of Europe	271.3	273.8	293.3	222.4	259.8	- Autre de l'Europe
Europe former USSR	575.3	664.3	662.3	737.9	762.7	Europe ancienne URSS
Oceania	75.3	75.4	61.1	54.9	94.0	Océanie
Germany	739.9	837.7	705.5	788.2	778.9	Allemagne
United States	810.5	781.7	595.5	746.2	738.0	Etats-Unis d'Amérique
Japan	567.0	550.3	519.2	518.8	518.7	Japon
Russian Federation	416.1	509.8	517.1	576.2	588.2	Fédération de Russie
Netherlands	505.1	554.0	508.3	461.9	438.7	Pays-Bas
United Kingdom	545.4	460.9	345.6	282.4	327.0	Royaume-Uni
Spain	330.8	302.3	298.4	228.0	190.9	Espagne
Turkey	255.5	247.6	308.2	243.4	162.1	Turquie
Egypt	149.0	161.4	e183.7	167.2	170.1	Egypte
Switzerland-Liechtenstein	162.8	157.6	191.6	137.2	164.3	Suisse-Liechtenstein
Poland	183.5	227.0	81.0	110.9	189.8	Pologne
Italy-San Marino-Holy See	170.3	169.1	124.4	96.1	146.7	Italie-Saint-Marin-Saint-Siège
China	35.1	51.8	164.0	233.2	215.6	Chine
Belgium	–	164.4	133.2	184.0	e201.7	Belgique
Ukraine	125.8	110.9	107.8	122.0	131.5	Ukraine
France-Monaco	101.6	107.4	107.2	134.5	131.8	France-Monaco
Indonesia	76.0	128.0	114.8	139.6	104.0	Indonésie
Malaysia	73.8	89.7	96.1	133.8	e146.2	Malaisie
Dominican Republic	e157.0	e111.7	e91.4	e79.9	e79.7	République dominicaine
Greece	89.7	107.5	96.5	93.3	e103.1	Grèce
Philippines	86.1	113.4	109.8	69.2	70.9	Philippines
Denmark	96.3	95.6	84.3	89.2	82.7	Danemark
Korea, Republic of	85.8	87.1	73.9	66.9	81.8	République de Corée
Czech Republic	121.5	77.7	66.2	52.7	45.4	République tchèque
Romania	63.8	83.9	69.0	66.7	62.7	Roumanie
Thailand	72.7	73.1	57.3	42.1	e43.9	Thaïlande
Australia	51.4	59.0	45.9	44.0	80.1	Australie
Austria	33.9	34.3	56.4	65.7	80.8	Autriche
Sri Lanka	e50.8	45.9	e61.9	49.1	35.8	Sri Lanka
Hungary	67.7	63.4	30.0	32.5	26.1	Hongrie

(Value as percentages of World total) **(Valeur en pourcentage du total mondial)**

Regions of the world	1993	1994	1995	1996	1997	1998	1999	2000	2001	2002	Régions du monde
World	100.0	100.0	100.0	100.0	100.0	100.0	100.0	100.0	100.0	100.0	Monde
Africa	5.2	6.3	5.9	5.6	4.6	5.7	6.2	6.3	6.2	6.4	Afrique
Americas	19.3	14.9	13.0	19.4	20.1	16.7	14.0	12.8	14.3	13.9	Amériques
- Northern America	16.7	12.7	9.9	15.7	15.1	11.0	10.3	8.7	10.7	10.4	- Amérique du Nord
- LAIA	1.8	1.4	1.9	1.8	2.2	2.5	1.7	2.0	2.0	1.8	- ALAI
- CACM	0.1	0.2	0.2	0.5	0.8	0.8	0.4	0.5	0.3	0.4	- MCC
- Caribbean	0.6	0.6	0.9	1.3	2.0	2.3	1.7	1.6	1.3	1.3	- Caraïbes
- Rest of America	0.1	0.0	0.1	0.1	0.1	0.0	0.0	0.0	0.0	0.0	- Autre d'Amérique
Asia excluding former USSR	23.6	24.2	24.1	21.2	23.9	21.0	21.0	24.6	23.8	22.1	Asie ancienne URSS exclus
- Middle East	2.4	2.2	3.0	3.7	4.5	4.0	3.8	5.3	3.7	2.6	- Moyen-Orient
Asia former USSR	0.0	0.1	0.3	0.5	0.3	0.4	0.4	0.6	0.8	0.7	Asie ancienne URSS
Europe excluding former USSR	47.5	49.9	51.5	49.1	45.8	47.7	48.8	45.4	43.7	45.1	Europe ancienne URSS exclus
- European Union	40.9	41.8	43.6	40.6	36.6	37.9	38.7	37.1	36.3	36.5	- Union Européenne
- Eastern Europe	3.2	4.2	4.3	5.1	5.7	6.3	6.5	4.1	4.3	5.1	- Europe de l'Est
- Rest of Europe	3.3	3.9	3.7	3.5	3.5	3.5	3.6	4.2	3.1	3.6	- Autre de l'Europe
Europe former USSR	3.0	2.9	3.6	2.8	4.3	7.5	8.6	9.4	10.4	10.5	Europe ancienne URSS
Oceania	1.3	1.6	1.6	1.4	1.1	1.0	1.0	0.9	0.8	1.3	Océanie

TRADE BY COMMODITY (Value in million US dollars)
Exports by principal countries or areas

COMMERCE PAR PRODUIT (Valeur en millions de dollars EU)
Exportations selon les principaux pays ou zones

Country or area	1998	1999	2000	2001	2002	Pays ou zone
World	6604.7	6298.3	5524.8	5916.3	5253.4	Monde
Africa	1140.8	1042.3	928.1	1033.1	583.5	Afrique
Americas	2884.2	2598.3	2382.4	2668.3	2464.8	Amériques
- Northern America	1572.0	1377.0	1296.8	1365.6	1132.6	- Amérique du Nord
- LAIA	1164.1	1140.9	1001.9	1220.8	1268.0	- ALAI
- CACM	52.1	42.0	53.3	51.9	38.9	- MCC
- Caribbean	95.3	37.7	29.9	29.7	25.1	- Caraïbes
- Rest of America	0.7	0.7	0.6	0.3	0.2	- Autre d'Amérique
Asia excluding former USSR	1226.0	1167.9	924.6	947.8	910.2	Asie ancienne URSS exclus
- Middle East	552.6	514.5	397.6	400.0	323.5	- Moyen-Orient
Asia former USSR	79.4	116.6	101.8	64.9	59.0	Asie ancienne URSS
Europe excluding former USSR	1243.1	1331.7	1151.4	1172.2	1214.2	Europe ancienne URSS exclus
- European Union	1042.0	1093.5	979.6	985.3	1033.5	- Union Européenne
- Eastern Europe	73.8	86.6	67.6	81.5	83.7	- Europe de l'Est
- Rest of Europe	127.3	151.6	104.1	105.5	96.9	- Autre de l'Europe
Europe former USSR	29.2	35.7	35.6	28.2	18.3	Europe ancienne URSS
Oceania	2.0	5.8	0.9	1.7	3.4	Océanie
United States	1467.4	1301.3	1234.6	1289.9	1072.8	Etats-Unis d'Amérique
Brazil	939.8	892.7	812.9	921.1	e955.0	Brésil
Zimbabwe	e671.8	630.1	579.2	584.7	173.6	Zimbabwe
Turkey	520.5	478.6	368.4	354.3	285.4	Turquie
Greece	333.6	360.1	264.0	224.7	e225.0	Grèce
Malawi	e344.1	e279.3	227.4	258.8	e236.4	Malawi
Italy-San Marino-Holy See	203.1	186.3	176.7	190.3	228.9	Italie-Saint-Marin-Saint-Siège
China	181.7	208.3	151.3	189.4	205.3	Chine
Germany	145.0	157.4	171.5	187.9	191.7	Allemagne
India	136.0	187.3	147.0	123.4	151.9	Inde
Argentina	130.3	165.8	120.1	162.1	e156.6	Argentine
Netherlands	95.6	107.2	136.0	103.2	62.9	Pays-Bas
Indonesia	147.6	91.8	71.3	91.4	76.7	Indonésie
France-Monaco	86.9	99.2	56.5	62.7	76.0	France-Monaco
Canada	104.6	75.6	62.2	75.8	59.8	Canada
Belgium	–	59.0	74.5	100.7	e113.0	Belgique
Spain	65.4	67.6	56.5	69.3	66.7	Espagne
Thailand	72.5	47.6	58.4	57.1	e60.3	Thaïlande
The former Yugoslav Republic of Macedonia	49.6	77.9	47.7	48.6	e46.8	Ex-République yougoslave de Macédoine
Bulgaria	50.7	63.1	45.9	e48.6	e54.7	Bulgarie
United Republic of Tanzania	43.1	55.1	38.1	35.4	e40.6	République-Unie de Tanzanie
Switzerland-Liechtenstein	45.9	41.6	33.3	39.5	37.2	Suisse-Liechtenstein
Paraguay	8.2	6.2	3.7	85.2	e93.0	Paraguay
Sri Lanka	e39.1	36.9	e44.9	35.9	37.7	Sri Lanka
Kyrgyzstan	49.2	42.1	e47.4	e20.6	19.8	Kirghizistan
Mexico	41.6	35.8	34.7	26.5	33.6	Mexique
Guatemala	36.7	29.2	42.8	33.2	16.0	Guatemala
United Kingdom	38.1	26.8	24.9	24.9	41.7	Royaume-Uni
Uganda	22.4	14.7	26.3	31.8	44.1	Ouganda
Lebanon	21.3	24.8	20.2	37.6	e32.8	Liban

(Value as percentages of World total) **(Valeur en pourcentage du total mondial)**

Regions of the world	1993	1994	1995	1996	1997	1998	1999	2000	2001	2002	Régions du monde
World	100.0	100.0	100.0	100.0	100.0	100.0	100.0	100.0	100.0	100.0	Monde
Africa	12.5	18.3	16.2	17.6	15.3	17.3	16.5	16.8	17.5	11.1	Afrique
Americas	46.8	46.0	48.7	43.8	45.8	43.7	41.3	43.1	45.1	46.9	Amériques
- Northern America	27.2	27.4	28.6	22.9	24.4	23.8	21.9	23.5	23.1	21.6	- Amérique du Nord
- LAIA	17.3	17.1	18.3	19.5	19.7	17.6	18.1	18.1	20.6	24.1	- ALAI
- CACM	1.0	0.6	0.4	0.5	0.7	0.8	0.7	1.0	0.9	0.7	- MCC
- Caribbean	1.2	0.9	1.4	0.9	1.0	1.4	0.6	0.5	0.5	0.5	- Caraïbes
- Rest of America	0.1	0.0	0.0	0.0	0.0	0.0	0.0	0.0	0.0	0.0	- Autre d'Amérique
Asia excluding former USSR	18.3	16.1	14.1	18.8	20.0	18.6	18.5	16.7	16.0	17.3	Asie ancienne URSS exclus
- Middle East	8.0	8.2	5.6	9.0	8.6	8.4	8.2	7.2	6.8	6.2	- Moyen-Orient
Asia former USSR	0.1	1.3	0.9	0.6	0.7	1.2	1.9	1.8	1.1	1.1	Asie ancienne URSS
Europe excluding former USSR	21.8	17.8	19.6	18.8	17.8	18.8	21.1	20.8	19.8	23.1	Europe ancienne URSS exclus
- European Union	15.2	15.6	16.6	15.9	14.9	15.8	17.4	17.7	16.7	19.7	- Union Européenne
- Eastern Europe	4.3	0.1	0.8	1.1	0.9	1.1	1.4	1.2	1.4	1.6	- Europe de l'Est
- Rest of Europe	2.3	2.0	2.2	1.8	2.0	1.9	2.4	1.9	1.8	1.8	- Autre de l'Europe
Europe former USSR	0.3	0.4	0.4	0.4	0.4	0.4	0.6	0.6	0.5	0.3	Europe ancienne URSS
Oceania	0.2	0.1	0.1	0.1	0.0	0.0	0.1	0.0	0.0	0.1	Océanie

122 Tobacco, manufactured

TRADE BY COMMODITY (Value in million US dollars)
Imports by principal countries or areas

COMMERCE PAR PRODUIT (Valeur en millions de dollars EU)
Importations selon les principaux pays ou zones

Country or area	1998	1999	2000	2001	2002	Pays ou zone
World	14179.8	13860.2	13764.5	14371.4	14938.9	Monde
Africa	446.4	419.7	511.4	425.8	456.4	Afrique
Americas	1017.9	807.0	870.7	823.1	893.9	Amériques
- Northern America	548.1	519.7	616.7	591.2	695.7	- Amérique du Nord
- LAIA	410.7	232.3	187.9	153.6	121.5	- ALAI
- CACM	14.5	15.3	23.8	34.6	32.8	- MCC
- Caribbean	33.5	26.6	28.3	29.7	28.3	- Caraïbes
- Rest of America	11.0	13.1	14.0	14.0	15.6	- Autre d'Amérique
Asia excluding former USSR	5734.5	5714.1	6213.5	6060.0	5849.1	Asie ancienne URSS exclus
- Middle East	1308.2	1267.0	1438.6	1525.3	1385.1	- Moyen-Orient
Asia former USSR	111.0	185.0	100.8	98.5	94.5	Asie ancienne URSS
Europe excluding former USSR	5720.4	6123.0	5544.4	6455.1	7133.7	Europe ancienne URSS exclus
- European Union	5369.7	5704.6	5146.4	5961.8	6608.6	- Union Européenne
- Eastern Europe	166.7	210.1	187.2	220.6	223.7	- Europe de l'Est
- Rest of Europe	184.0	208.3	210.8	272.7	301.5	- Autre de l'Europe
Europe former USSR	1070.6	523.4	430.9	408.1	401.7	Europe ancienne URSS
Oceania	79.1	88.0	93.0	100.8	109.6	Océanie
Japan	1871.1	2145.2	2381.5	2025.1	2046.4	Japon
France-Monaco	1612.6	1633.1	1352.1	1632.4	1816.7	France-Monaco
Italy-San Marino-Holy See	1144.1	1258.7	1156.0	1269.5	1304.2	Italie-Saint-Marin-Saint-Siège
Germany	713.0	672.4	647.3	670.7	674.7	Allemagne
Spain	378.4	529.8	547.9	830.4	956.6	Espagne
Singapore	902.6	666.7	603.6	587.8	445.8	Singapour
United States	493.6	468.9	574.4	542.5	635.8	Etats-Unis d'Amérique
China, Hong Kong SAR	608.8	525.3	526.5	468.4	441.8	Chine - RAS de Hong-Kong
Netherlands	438.0	392.7	361.7	454.9	421.5	Pays-Bas
Oman	233.4	317.3	385.9	478.0	411.8	Oman
Russian Federation	770.3	286.5	206.8	155.7	168.0	Fédération de Russie
Belgium	-	411.2	371.5	334.0	e366.3	Belgique
Cyprus	362.8	341.1	335.5	269.6	118.0	Chypre
United Kingdom	248.3	204.0	151.9	215.9	348.2	Royaume-Uni
Saudi Arabia	176.8	168.7	312.2	247.7	e256.4	Arabie saoudite
Korea, Republic of	80.5	129.5	208.7	215.2	261.6	République de Corée
Lebanon	246.2	133.4	107.1	150.7	e137.5	Liban
Greece	168.2	166.9	133.1	125.5	e138.8	Grèce
Paraguay	323.6	144.5	111.5	70.2	46.2	Paraguay
Luxembourg	-	198.8	190.8	139.3	e147.9	Luxembourg
United Arab Emirates	115.2	120.8	109.3	156.7	e160.8	Emirates arabes unis
Cambodia	e134.5	e114.8	e87.8	e94.3	e71.7	Cambodge
Israel	78.8	94.8	97.5	110.9	110.2	Israël
Belarus	110.8	81.5	59.8	84.0	84.2	Bélarus
Belgium-Luxembourg	391.9	-	-	-	-	Belgique-Luxembourg
Sweden	73.0	27.1	29.2	78.2	179.2	Suède
Egypt	71.5	74.7	e77.4	70.4	49.7	Egypte
Philippines	33.7	26.4	41.1	94.1	114.4	Philippines
Australia	46.0	53.8	64.2	68.0	74.6	Australie
Kuwait	55.5	63.4	e59.5	e65.5	e49.0	Koweït

(Value as percentages of World total) **(Valeur en pourcentage du total mondial)**

Regions of the world	1993	1994	1995	1996	1997	1998	1999	2000	2001	2002	Régions du monde
World	100.0	100.0	100.0	100.0	100.0	100.0	100.0	100.0	100.0	100.0	Monde
Africa	2.3	2.3	2.1	2.2	2.4	3.1	3.0	3.7	3.0	3.1	Afrique
Americas	6.3	2.8	3.4	4.5	6.6	7.2	5.8	6.3	5.7	6.0	Amériques
- Northern America	5.5	1.6	1.5	2.2	3.7	3.9	3.7	4.5	4.1	4.7	- Amérique du Nord
- LAIA	0.5	0.8	1.5	2.1	2.6	2.9	1.7	1.4	1.1	0.8	- ALAI
- CACM	0.0	0.0	0.1	0.1	0.1	0.1	0.1	0.2	0.2	0.2	- MCC
- Caribbean	0.2	0.2	0.3	0.1	0.2	0.2	0.2	0.2	0.2	0.2	- Caraïbes
- Rest of America	0.1	0.1	0.1	0.0	0.1	0.1	0.1	0.1	0.1	0.1	- Autre d'Amérique
Asia excluding former USSR	52.3	51.9	50.6	51.0	45.3	40.4	41.2	45.1	42.2	39.2	Asie ancienne URSS exclus
- Middle East	11.2	10.3	10.6	10.8	9.3	9.2	9.1	10.5	10.6	9.3	- Moyen-Orient
Asia former USSR	0.1	0.8	0.5	0.8	1.3	0.8	1.3	0.7	0.7	0.6	Asie ancienne URSS
Europe excluding former USSR	34.0	38.0	38.2	36.2	36.1	40.3	44.2	40.3	44.9	47.8	Europe ancienne URSS exclus
- European Union	30.4	35.4	35.2	33.2	33.2	37.9	41.2	37.4	41.5	44.2	- Union Européenne
- Eastern Europe	2.1	1.4	1.3	1.5	1.3	1.2	1.5	1.4	1.5	1.5	- Europe de l'Est
- Rest of Europe	1.5	1.2	1.7	1.5	1.6	1.3	1.5	1.5	1.9	2.0	- Autre de l'Europe
Europe former USSR	4.6	3.6	4.7	4.8	7.9	7.6	3.8	3.1	2.8	2.7	Europe ancienne URSS
Oceania	0.5	0.5	0.5	0.6	0.4	0.6	0.6	0.7	0.7	0.7	Océanie

TRADE BY COMMODITY (Value in million US dollars)
Exports by principal countries or areas

COMMERCE PAR PRODUIT (Valeur en millions de dollars EU)
Exportations selon les principaux pays ou zones

Country or area	1998	1999	2000	2001	2002	Pays ou zone
World	18290.2	16156.1	16103.2	15262.2	15666.2	Monde
Africa	217.3	160.3	212.8	189.6	244.9	Afrique
Americas	6296.8	4538.2	4617.9	3406.0	2558.6	Amériques
- Northern America	4888.6	3937.1	4069.2	2791.0	2014.5	- Amérique du Nord
- LAIA	926.7	319.4	267.3	227.6	232.4	- ALAI
- CACM	39.3	32.1	28.5	54.6	37.4	- MCC
- Caribbean	438.0	239.1	212.1	304.6	271.3	- Caraïbes
- Rest of America	4.3	10.5	40.7	28.2	2.9	- Autre d'Amérique
Asia excluding former USSR	3828.2	3014.3	3112.1	3540.9	3440.7	Asie ancienne URSS exclus
- Middle East	818.8	793.8	964.5	1263.5	1150.1	- Moyen-Orient
Asia former USSR	28.9	32.0	30.0	33.7	35.2	Asie ancienne URSS
Europe excluding former USSR	7806.5	8262.1	7953.8	7897.4	9129.6	Europe ancienne URSS exclus
- European Union	7127.6	7646.0	7263.8	7243.8	8452.9	- Union Européenne
- Eastern Europe	320.4	257.0	198.9	209.7	195.1	- Europe de l'Est
- Rest of Europe	358.5	359.1	491.1	443.8	481.6	- Autre de l'Europe
Europe former USSR	65.6	108.1	138.9	152.7	200.9	Europe ancienne URSS
Oceania	46.9	41.2	37.8	41.9	56.4	Océanie
United States	4842.0	3897.0	4034.7	2750.1	1959.9	Etats-Unis d'Amérique
Netherlands	2681.5	2787.2	2604.5	2539.7	3354.2	Pays-Bas
Germany	1498.2	1700.9	1638.9	1875.3	1886.6	Allemagne
United Kingdom	1729.1	1635.1	1515.2	1317.7	1434.7	Royaume-Uni
Singapore	1218.3	750.5	706.4	663.3	606.1	Singapour
China, Hong Kong SAR	813.8	654.6	575.7	528.8	530.2	Chine - RAS de Hong-Kong
United Arab Emirates	248.3	256.2	396.5	505.7	e526.8	Emirates arabes unis
Belgium	-	490.5	393.9	375.6	e421.4	Belgique
France-Monaco	285.5	286.3	319.1	332.2	420.9	France-Monaco
Switzerland-Liechtenstein	232.6	228.1	334.2	294.9	321.1	Suisse-Liechtenstein
Cyprus	380.4	335.9	292.1	263.0	107.7	Chypre
Oman	112.8	103.0	133.1	385.0	373.0	Oman
China	396.3	128.0	150.6	196.8	227.3	Chine
Japan	190.5	253.4	167.2	239.9	227.4	Japon
Malaysia	155.7	172.2	200.9	213.6	e226.4	Malaisie
Cuba	e180.2	178.2	146.4	241.1	e208.3	Cuba
Denmark	162.9	156.2	136.3	144.1	196.9	Danemark
Brazil	619.1	68.6	28.6	23.2	e24.0	Brésil
Indonesia	106.8	120.2	149.7	183.5	171.2	Indonésie
Luxembourg	-	157.5	181.7	153.4	e156.8	Luxembourg
Greece	113.6	142.5	129.6	122.8	e123.0	Grèce
Czech Republic	164.7	110.9	84.6	84.6	86.3	République tchèque
Austria	77.4	83.1	83.4	99.9	151.6	Autriche
Turkey	66.7	83.3	123.0	81.1	99.6	Turquie
Ireland	56.4	63.1	95.1	102.3	101.2	Irlande
Korea, Republic of	36.2	42.1	70.9	116.0	147.4	République de Corée
Belgium-Luxembourg	398.1	-	-	-	-	Belgique-Luxembourg
Dominican Republic	e219.0	e35.9	e42.0	e36.9	e39.9	République dominicaine
Venezuela	156.0	77.6	41.4	47.8	e50.8	Venezuela
Spain	58.0	71.0	77.5	71.2	82.6	Espagne

(Value as percentages of World total) **(Valeur en pourcentage du total mondial)**

Regions of the world	1993	1994	1995	1996	1997	1998	1999	2000	2001	2002	Régions du monde
World	100.0	100.0	100.0	100.0	100.0	100.0	100.0	100.0	100.0	100.0	Monde
Africa	0.4	0.6	0.9	1.0	1.3	1.2	1.0	1.3	1.2	1.6	Afrique
Americas	35.2	35.4	32.0	29.9	31.4	34.4	28.1	28.7	22.3	16.3	Amériques
- Northern America	32.3	32.2	28.3	26.2	26.2	26.7	24.4	25.3	18.3	12.9	- Amérique du Nord
- LAIA	2.2	2.6	2.9	2.9	3.6	5.1	2.0	1.7	1.5	1.5	- ALAI
- CACM	0.1	0.1	0.1	0.2	0.5	0.2	0.2	0.2	0.4	0.2	- MCC
- Caribbean	0.6	0.5	0.8	0.6	1.0	2.4	1.5	1.3	2.0	1.7	- Caraïbes
- Rest of America	0.0	0.0	0.0	0.0	0.0	0.0	0.1	0.3	0.2	0.0	- Autre d'Amérique
Asia excluding former USSR	27.1	25.2	25.5	26.1	23.9	20.9	18.7	19.3	23.2	22.0	Asie ancienne URSS exclus
- Middle East	4.1	3.8	4.3	4.6	5.5	4.5	4.9	6.0	8.3	7.3	- Moyen-Orient
Asia former USSR	0.0	0.0	0.0	0.2	0.3	0.2	0.2	0.2	0.2	0.2	Asie ancienne URSS
Europe excluding former USSR	36.9	38.1	41.0	42.0	42.5	42.7	51.1	49.4	51.7	58.3	Europe ancienne URSS exclus
- European Union	33.8	34.3	36.9	37.5	38.2	39.0	47.3	45.1	47.5	54.0	- Union Européenne
- Eastern Europe	0.9	0.9	1.4	2.1	2.1	1.8	1.6	1.2	1.4	1.2	- Europe de l'Est
- Rest of Europe	2.2	2.8	2.7	2.4	2.2	2.0	2.2	3.0	2.9	3.1	- Autre de l'Europe
Europe former USSR	0.2	0.6	0.4	0.5	0.4	0.4	0.7	0.9	1.0	1.3	Europe ancienne URSS
Oceania	0.1	0.2	0.2	0.2	0.2	0.3	0.3	0.2	0.3	0.4	Océanie

211 Hides and skins, excluding furs, raw

TRADE BY COMMODITY (Value in million US dollars)
Imports by principal countries or areas

COMMERCE PAR PRODUIT (Valeur en millions de dollars EU)
Importations selon les principaux pays ou zones

Country or area	1998	1999	2000	2001	2002	Pays ou zone
World	4867.7	4123.2	5186.7	5791.2	5457.8	Monde
Africa	40.0	37.4	37.9	36.9	26.4	Afrique
Americas	404.3	364.3	365.8	354.5	337.3	Amériques
- Northern America	170.5	150.2	168.2	147.2	128.8	- Amérique du Nord
- LAIA	224.9	207.1	191.3	201.3	201.6	- ALAI
- CACM	2.5	1.3	1.3	2.6	3.7	- MCC
- Caribbean	6.4	5.7	4.9	3.4	3.0	- Caraïbes
- Rest of America	0.0	0.0	0.0	0.0	0.1	- Autre d'Amérique
Asia excluding former USSR	2207.5	1889.9	2487.4	2960.8	2863.0	Asie ancienne URSS exclus
- Middle East	378.3	107.5	222.3	281.8	459.3	- Moyen-Orient
Asia former USSR	0.4	0.9	1.0	2.9	3.4	Asie ancienne URSS
Europe excluding former USSR	2178.3	1785.5	2246.6	2367.6	2122.9	Europe ancienne URSS exclus
- European Union	2008.0	1690.2	2095.6	2213.6	1964.2	- Union Européenne
- Eastern Europe	111.0	61.0	96.9	99.3	102.5	- Europe de l'Est
- Rest of Europe	59.3	34.2	54.1	54.7	56.2	- Autre de l'Europe
Europe former USSR	32.3	33.5	34.0	45.1	83.1	Europe ancienne URSS
Oceania	4.8	11.6	14.0	23.4	21.8	Océanie
Italy-San Marino-Holy See	1055.2	896.4	1260.2	1259.9	1090.5	Italie-Saint-Marin-Saint-Siège
Korea, Republic of	544.3	535.3	677.9	706.9	566.7	République de Corée
China	351.0	362.4	573.9	786.1	713.2	Chine
Turkey	369.8	100.8	216.5	274.6	451.1	Turquie
China, Hong Kong SAR	130.8	142.4	234.8	359.2	355.7	Chine - RAS de Hong-Kong
Japan	229.5	221.2	222.0	225.9	157.4	Japon
Mexico	197.4	191.2	177.5	176.6	170.0	Mexique
Thailand	123.9	121.6	145.1	192.1	e200.2	Thaïlande
Spain	191.4	120.3	140.7	178.7	151.5	Espagne
Germany	155.9	135.3	132.9	175.2	171.1	Allemagne
Austria	99.2	125.5	104.6	144.6	124.1	Autriche
Netherlands	94.6	97.0	110.2	116.3	108.3	Pays-Bas
United States	112.7	102.8	111.3	102.4	87.1	Etats-Unis d'Amérique
United Kingdom	131.9	106.3	97.0	98.8	79.0	Royaume-Uni
France-Monaco	120.0	80.0	103.8	100.3	97.5	France-Monaco
India	54.4	48.1	57.9	67.3	57.6	Inde
Canada	57.7	47.3	56.9	44.8	41.7	Canada
Belgium	-	46.7	63.6	53.5	e58.7	Belgique
Poland	37.4	21.7	47.5	45.3	49.2	Pologne
Portugal	50.2	36.0	35.1	35.4	29.1	Portugal
Slovakia	31.1	23.7	29.8	34.3	32.7	Slovaquie
Slovenia	30.1	17.5	28.4	27.3	21.8	Slovénie
Singapore	15.6	17.5	23.2	26.2	24.3	Singapour
Sweden	21.4	17.6	19.3	22.8	24.7	Suède
Lithuania	11.3	18.5	15.3	17.9	e22.1	Lituanie
South Africa	-	-	27.8	27.1	16.9	Afrique du Sud
New Zealand	4.1	10.7	13.1	22.1	20.7	Nouvelle-Zélande
Pakistan	11.0	9.8	11.3	18.2	18.4	Pakistan
Belarus	4.6	2.8	4.3	15.0	38.3	Bélarus
Czech Republic	17.4	9.7	11.2	11.2	8.9	République tchèque

(Value as percentages of World total) **(Valeur en pourcentage du total mondial)**

Regions of the world	1993	1994	1995	1996	1997	1998	1999	2000	2001	2002	Régions du monde
World	100.0	100.0	100.0	100.0	100.0	100.0	100.0	100.0	100.0	100.0	Monde
Africa	0.3	0.4	0.5	0.4	0.6	0.8	0.9	0.7	0.6	0.5	Afrique
Americas	6.8	6.0	4.8	6.2	7.3	8.3	8.8	7.1	6.1	6.2	Amériques
- Northern America	3.6	3.4	3.2	3.2	3.4	3.5	3.6	3.2	2.5	2.4	- Amérique du Nord
- LAIA	3.0	2.5	1.6	3.0	3.7	4.6	5.0	3.7	3.5	3.7	- ALAI
- CACM	0.1	0.0	0.0	0.0	0.0	0.1	0.0	0.0	0.0	0.1	- MCC
- Caribbean	0.0	0.0	0.0	0.0	0.1	0.1	0.1	0.1	0.1	0.1	- Caraïbes
- Rest of America	0.0	0.0	0.0	0.0	0.0	0.0	0.0	0.0	0.0	0.0	- Autre d'Amérique
Asia excluding former USSR	53.2	46.5	49.6	49.3	50.5	45.4	45.8	48.0	51.1	52.5	Asie ancienne URSS exclus
- Middle East	4.6	5.1	7.2	10.8	9.7	7.8	2.6	4.3	4.9	8.4	- Moyen-Orient
Asia former USSR	0.0	0.1	0.0	0.0	0.0	0.0	0.0	0.0	0.0	0.1	Asie ancienne URSS
Europe excluding former USSR	39.1	46.4	43.9	43.2	41.0	44.8	43.3	43.3	40.9	38.9	Europe ancienne URSS exclus
- European Union	36.2	43.1	40.6	39.6	37.2	41.3	41.0	40.4	38.2	36.0	- Union Européenne
- Eastern Europe	1.8	2.1	2.2	2.7	2.7	2.3	1.5	1.9	1.7	1.9	- Europe de l'Est
- Rest of Europe	1.1	1.1	1.1	1.0	1.1	1.2	0.8	1.0	0.9	1.0	- Autre de l'Europe
Europe former USSR	0.2	0.3	0.7	0.4	0.4	0.7	0.8	0.7	0.8	1.5	Europe ancienne URSS
Oceania	0.4	0.4	0.4	0.4	0.2	0.1	0.3	0.3	0.4	0.4	Océanie

TRADE BY COMMODITY (Value in million US dollars)
Exports by principal countries or areas

COMMERCE PAR PRODUIT (Valeur en millions de dollars EU)
Exportations selon les principaux pays ou zones

Country or area	1998	1999	2000	2001	2002	Pays ou zone
World	4591.3	3883.6	5076.6	5704.4	5447.1	Monde
Africa	119.3	82.3	144.8	203.5	198.6	Afrique
Americas	1444.3	1327.8	1858.1	2211.6	1991.8	Amériques
- Northern America	1304.7	1190.7	1689.7	2018.9	1792.0	- Amérique du Nord
- LAIA	125.2	114.8	150.4	178.0	190.2	- ALAI
- CACM	12.1	20.8	15.2	11.6	6.5	- MCC
- Caribbean	2.2	0.8	1.5	1.7	1.6	- Caraïbes
- Rest of America	0.2	0.6	1.3	1.5	1.5	- Autre d'Amérique
Asia excluding former USSR	370.9	352.3	486.8	559.9	545.0	Asie ancienne URSS exclus
- Middle East	92.4	86.2	113.6	93.5	81.8	- Moyen-Orient
Asia former USSR	44.6	36.4	34.9	45.1	44.6	Asie ancienne URSS
Europe excluding former USSR	1784.3	1546.3	1871.2	1898.4	1984.9	Europe ancienne URSS exclus
- European Union	1574.6	1324.0	1596.0	1608.0	1715.3	- Union Européenne
- Eastern Europe	92.7	98.8	121.5	136.7	112.7	- Europe de l'Est
- Rest of Europe	117.0	123.5	153.7	153.7	156.9	- Autre de l'Europe
Europe former USSR	338.4	183.4	179.0	167.8	169.3	Europe ancienne URSS
Oceania	489.5	355.2	501.8	618.1	512.9	Océanie
United States	1130.5	1029.0	1522.6	1834.3	1600.6	Etats-Unis d'Amérique
France-Monaco	352.3	280.2	340.8	358.2	350.2	France-Monaco
Australia	320.1	222.3	343.6	427.4	358.1	Australie
Germany	244.0	221.7	212.6	236.5	240.3	Allemagne
United Kingdom	252.0	163.7	220.1	179.2	215.2	Royaume-Uni
Netherlands	194.1	192.9	217.1	192.8	180.2	Pays-Bas
China, Hong Kong SAR	89.9	110.2	187.3	291.5	284.2	Chine - RAS de Hong-Kong
Canada	174.0	160.9	166.8	184.6	191.4	Canada
New Zealand	167.8	131.8	157.1	189.8	153.9	Nouvelle-Zélande
Russian Federation	287.1	125.6	118.8	85.8	44.9	Fédération de Russie
Spain	120.6	83.7	129.0	149.8	177.7	Espagne
Italy-San Marino-Holy See	69.3	76.4	117.4	117.0	151.7	Italie-Saint-Marin-Saint-Siège
Mexico	84.5	78.5	102.5	115.0	123.5	Mexique
Ireland	82.2	78.4	87.2	87.7	96.2	Irlande
Belgium	–	74.6	99.3	89.8	e100.8	Belgique
Japan	77.7	48.0	33.8	56.7	63.0	Japon
Austria	47.9	50.4	53.8	62.4	50.0	Autriche
Denmark	53.1	48.1	47.2	48.3	52.7	Danemark
Switzerland-Liechtenstein	43.1	41.9	41.1	42.9	44.9	Suisse-Liechtenstein
South Africa	–	–	55.3	66.1	80.6	Afrique du Sud
Iran (Islamic Republic of)	44.7	46.2	40.3	41.8	26.5	Iran (République islamique d')
Poland	31.2	41.0	37.8	48.2	28.0	Pologne
Ukraine	23.9	22.5	26.3	47.9	52.8	Ukraine
Sweden	29.5	24.7	32.3	33.5	33.6	Suède
Czech Republic	30.5	28.6	30.0	31.3	30.0	République tchèque
Norway	27.2	24.9	27.8	29.0	29.3	Norvège
Turkey	21.3	9.5	25.1	30.5	34.3	Turquie
Singapore	12.5	19.5	36.6	26.0	24.6	Singapour
Kazakhstan	29.9	28.2	22.5	16.2	e18.2	Kazakhstan
Slovenia	21.8	21.3	24.5	24.3	21.0	Slovénie

(Value as percentages of World total)

(Valeur en pourcentage du total mondial)

Regions of the world	1993	1994	1995	1996	1997	1998	1999	2000	2001	2002	Régions du monde
World	100.0	100.0	100.0	100.0	100.0	100.0	100.0	100.0	100.0	100.0	Monde
Africa	4.5	4.1	3.1	3.1	3.0	2.6	2.1	2.9	3.6	3.6	Afrique
Americas	32.7	31.2	32.6	32.1	32.6	31.5	34.2	36.6	38.8	36.6	Amériques
- Northern America	31.4	29.7	30.9	30.2	30.7	28.4	30.7	33.3	35.4	32.9	- Amérique du Nord
- LAIA	1.1	1.4	1.6	1.7	1.7	2.7	3.0	3.0	3.1	3.5	- ALAI
- CACM	0.3	0.1	0.1	0.1	0.1	0.3	0.5	0.3	0.2	0.1	- MCC
- Caribbean	0.0	0.0	0.0	0.0	0.1	0.0	0.0	0.0	0.0	0.0	- Caraïbes
- Rest of America	0.0	0.0	0.0	0.0	0.0	0.0	0.0	0.0	0.0	0.0	- Autre d'Amérique
Asia excluding former USSR	9.5	9.9	9.4	8.2	7.5	8.1	9.1	9.6	9.8	10.0	Asie ancienne URSS exclus
- Middle East	3.8	3.7	2.9	2.5	1.8	2.0	2.2	2.2	1.6	1.5	- Moyen-Orient
Asia former USSR	0.8	0.7	0.9	1.6	1.7	1.0	0.9	0.7	0.8	0.8	Asie ancienne URSS
Europe excluding former USSR	37.4	38.4	36.9	38.0	37.4	38.9	39.8	36.9	33.3	36.4	Europe ancienne URSS exclus
- European Union	33.7	34.5	33.5	34.6	33.3	34.3	34.1	31.4	28.2	31.5	- Union Européenne
- Eastern Europe	1.6	1.6	1.1	1.2	1.8	2.0	2.5	2.4	2.4	2.1	- Europe de l'Est
- Rest of Europe	2.1	2.2	2.4	2.3	2.4	2.5	3.2	3.0	2.7	2.9	- Autre de l'Europe
Europe former USSR	4.6	4.6	6.1	4.7	5.9	7.4	4.7	3.5	2.9	3.1	Europe ancienne URSS
Oceania	10.4	11.1	11.0	12.1	11.9	10.7	9.1	9.9	10.8	9.4	Océanie

212 Furskins, raw

TRADE BY COMMODITY (Value in million US dollars)
Imports by principal countries or areas

COMMERCE PAR PRODUIT (Valeur en millions de dollars EU)
Importations selon les principaux pays ou zones

Country or area	1998	1999	2000	2001	2002	Pays ou zone
World	1179.7	913.0	1042.8	1114.4	1183.1	Monde
Africa	2.9	0.8	1.0	0.2	0.2	Afrique
Americas	132.7	112.2	107.3	118.7	121.1	Amériques
- Northern America	127.0	111.2	106.2	117.8	120.6	- Amérique du Nord
- LAIA	5.2	0.9	0.5	0.5	0.2	- ALAI
- CACM	0.0	0.0	0.3	0.0	0.1	- MCC
- Caribbean	0.5	0.1	0.3	0.4	0.2	- Caraïbes
- Rest of America	0.0	0.0	0.0	0.0	0.0	- Autre d'Amérique
Asia excluding former USSR	427.5	417.3	542.9	550.0	571.5	Asie ancienne URSS exclus
- Middle East	3.9	2.0	1.9	0.7	0.7	- Moyen-Orient
Asia former USSR	0.1	2.0	0.1	0.1	0.1	Asie ancienne URSS
Europe excluding former USSR	590.0	358.7	354.6	403.1	442.4	Europe ancienne URSS exclus
- European Union	554.4	336.0	318.8	356.9	386.3	- Union Européenne
- Eastern Europe	27.9	18.5	31.5	41.0	48.2	- Europe de l'Est
- Rest of Europe	7.8	4.2	4.3	5.2	7.9	- Autre de l'Europe
Europe former USSR	26.3	21.3	36.1	42.2	47.3	Europe ancienne URSS
Oceania	0.1	0.6	0.7	0.1	0.6	Océanie
China, Hong Kong SAR	321.0	283.4	371.7	394.6	405.4	Chine - RAS de Hong-Kong
Denmark	146.1	75.2	79.9	105.2	100.3	Danemark
Italy-San Marino-Holy See	106.3	76.4	75.2	65.8	72.2	Italie-Saint-Marin-Saint-Siège
Finland	89.0	71.0	60.7	66.9	85.9	Finlande
Korea, Republic of	41.0	71.9	90.1	67.7	89.9	République de Corée
Canada	64.9	62.4	47.1	55.3	61.8	Canada
United States	62.1	48.8	59.0	62.4	58.7	Etats-Unis d'Amérique
China	49.4	45.5	63.8	67.7	62.2	Chine
Greece	74.4	32.8	30.9	49.9	e55.2	Grèce
Germany	64.0	36.9	34.3	28.5	24.3	Allemagne
Poland	24.4	16.9	28.9	39.0	45.7	Pologne
France-Monaco	23.2	16.5	13.8	14.5	19.0	France-Monaco
Estonia	10.8	11.9	16.8	21.9	23.4	Estonie
Japan	9.5	12.7	12.9	16.8	12.9	Japon
United Kingdom	19.6	10.3	10.5	10.1	9.4	Royaume-Uni
Spain	15.7	8.9	7.9	7.8	7.3	Espagne
Ukraine	6.2	3.7	5.5	7.8	8.4	Ukraine
Lithuania	2.4	2.9	7.1	7.3	e8.9	Lituanie
Norway	7.0	3.5	3.9	4.8	7.5	Norvège
Netherlands	2.4	1.4	1.7	4.5	8.9	Pays-Bas
Belarus	2.0	1.1	4.4	3.4	5.5	Bélarus
Belgium	–	5.5	2.5	2.3	e2.5	Belgique
Belgium-Luxembourg	12.6	–	–	–	–	Belgique-Luxembourg
Russian Federation	4.9	1.6	2.3	1.8	1.1	Fédération de Russie
Czech Republic	2.8	0.9	1.3	1.4	1.3	République tchèque
China, Macao SAR	2.3	1.2	2.1	2.1		Chine - RAS de Macao
Argentina	5.0	0.7	0.4	0.4	e0.2	Argentine
Turkey	3.3	1.5	1.1	0.2	0.2	Turquie
Tunisia	2.8	0.8	0.5	0.1	e0.1	Tunisie
Portugal	0.6	0.6	0.7	1.1	0.8	Portugal

(Value as percentages of World total) **(Valeur en pourcentage du total mondial)**

Regions of the world	1993	1994	1995	1996	1997	1998	1999	2000	2001	2002	Régions du monde
World	100.0	100.0	100.0	100.0	100.0	100.0	100.0	100.0	100.0	100.0	Monde
Africa	0.0	0.1	0.1	0.1	0.2	0.2	0.1	0.1	0.0	0.0	Afrique
Americas	11.6	11.9	9.4	8.8	11.4	11.2	12.3	10.3	10.7	10.2	Amériques
- Northern America	11.4	11.7	9.2	8.6	11.0	10.8	12.2	10.2	10.6	10.2	- Amérique du Nord
- LAIA	0.2	0.3	0.1	0.1	0.1	0.4	0.1	0.1	0.0	0.0	- ALAI
- CACM	0.0	0.0	0.0	0.0	0.0	0.0	0.0	0.0	0.0	0.0	- MCC
- Caribbean	0.0	0.0	0.0	0.1	0.2	0.0	0.0	0.0	0.0	0.0	- Caraïbes
- Rest of America	0.0	0.0	0.0	0.0	0.0	0.0	0.0	0.0	0.0	0.0	- Autre d'Amérique
Asia excluding former USSR	49.8	49.1	48.9	50.7	40.7	36.2	45.7	52.1	49.4	48.3	Asie ancienne URSS exclus
- Middle East	0.1	0.1	0.1	0.2	0.3	0.3	0.2	0.2	0.1	0.1	- Moyen-Orient
Asia former USSR	0.0	0.1	0.0	0.0	0.0	0.0	0.2	0.0	0.0	0.0	Asie ancienne URSS
Europe excluding former USSR	38.0	37.7	39.8	38.9	46.2	50.0	39.3	34.0	36.2	37.4	Europe ancienne URSS exclus
- European Union	36.0	34.9	36.7	36.2	43.7	47.0	36.8	30.6	32.0	32.7	- Union Européenne
- Eastern Europe	1.0	1.6	2.0	1.8	1.8	2.4	2.0	3.0	3.7	4.1	- Europe de l'Est
- Rest of Europe	1.0	1.2	1.0	0.9	0.7	0.7	0.5	0.4	0.5	0.7	- Autre de l'Europe
Europe former USSR	0.5	1.0	1.8	1.5	1.5	2.2	2.3	3.5	3.8	4.0	Europe ancienne URSS
Oceania	0.0	0.1	0.0	0.0	0.0	0.0	0.1	0.1	0.0	0.0	Océanie

TRADE BY COMMODITY (Value in million US dollars)
Exports by principal countries or areas

COMMERCE PAR PRODUIT (Valeur en millions de dollars EU)
Exportations selon les principaux pays ou zones

Country or area	1998	1999	2000	2001	2002	Pays ou zone
World	1368.8	1144.1	1405.4	1494.0	1584.2	Monde
Africa	0.6	0.5	0.5	0.8	0.9	Afrique
Americas	251.0	219.8	265.5	292.1	286.7	Amériques
- Northern America	248.5	217.4	263.9	290.1	285.1	- Amérique du Nord
- LAIA	2.4	2.3	1.6	2.0	1.6	- ALAI
- CACM	0.2	0.1	0.0	0.0	0.0	- MCC
- Caribbean	0.0	0.0	0.0	0.0	0.0	- Caraïbes
- Rest of America	0.0	0.0	0.0	0.0	0.0	- Autre d'Amérique
Asia excluding former USSR	226.6	246.5	319.1	297.3	315.3	Asie ancienne URSS exclus
- Middle East	0.2	0.2	0.0	0.1	0.0	- Moyen-Orient
Asia former USSR	0.6	0.2	0.5	0.5	1.6	Asie ancienne URSS
Europe excluding former USSR	849.4	646.1	774.7	859.5	926.1	Europe ancienne URSS exclus
- European Union	752.8	595.2	724.6	801.0	850.8	- Union Européenne
- Eastern Europe	14.1	9.3	11.0	17.5	25.1	- Europe de l'Est
- Rest of Europe	82.5	41.5	39.0	41.0	50.2	- Autre de l'Europe
Europe former USSR	40.3	30.9	44.5	43.4	51.2	Europe ancienne URSS
Oceania	0.3	0.2	0.5	0.4	2.5	Océanie
Denmark	355.8	320.6	368.6	396.6	433.7	Danemark
China, Hong Kong SAR	204.8	233.3	304.7	286.6	301.5	Chine - RAS de Hong-Kong
Finland	293.9	178.5	244.0	279.7	283.6	Finlande
United States	148.8	127.0	144.8	163.5	157.7	Etats-Unis d'Amérique
Canada	98.8	89.6	118.3	125.4	126.1	Canada
Norway	78.1	36.6	34.9	37.1	44.0	Norvège
Germany	44.3	30.0	32.1	40.0	36.1	Allemagne
Netherlands	14.4	29.3	41.5	41.0	50.9	Pays-Bas
Russian Federation	24.0	17.5	24.7	27.7	35.8	Fédération de Russie
Sweden	22.5	17.4	16.8	17.4	23.1	Suède
Poland	10.9	7.0	8.7	14.8	22.2	Pologne
Belarus	6.8	8.8	12.6	9.9	7.2	Bélarus
United Kingdom	5.2	4.3	5.1	10.4	5.5	Royaume-Uni
China	9.4	3.4	5.1	4.2	4.9	Chine
Afghanistan	e7.5	e2.3	e1.8	e5.5	e8.2	Afghanistan
Belgium	–	3.6	5.1	6.7	e7.5	Belgique
Iceland	4.2	4.8	3.9	3.7	5.1	Islande
France-Monaco	2.4	4.7	3.7	2.6	3.2	France-Monaco
Italy-San Marino-Holy See	2.6	3.3	3.4	2.6	3.0	Italie-Saint-Marin-Saint-Siège
Estonia	2.0	1.8	3.0	3.2	4.0	Estonie
Mongolia	2.8	5.7	3.6	0.0	0.0	Mongolie
Lithuania	3.0	1.4	3.2	1.6	e2.0	Lituanie
Ireland	3.9	1.5	1.6	1.5	1.1	Irlande
Czech Republic	1.8	1.5	1.7	1.5	1.2	République tchèque
Spain	1.1	1.0	1.2	1.9	2.3	Espagne
Latvia	2.4	1.0	0.6	0.6	1.8	Lettonie
Argentina	1.4	1.6	1.0	1.1	e1.1	Argentine
China, Macao SAR	1.0	1.1	2.3	0.7		Chine - RAS de Macao
Greenland	0.9	0.9	0.8	1.2	e1.3	Groenland
Belgium-Luxembourg	4.6	–	–	–	–	Belgique-Luxembourg

(Value as percentages of World total) **(Valeur en pourcentage du total mondial)**

Regions of the world	1993	1994	1995	1996	1997	1998	1999	2000	2001	2002	Régions du monde
World	100.0	100.0	100.0	100.0	100.0	100.0	100.0	100.0	100.0	100.0	Monde
Africa	0.0	0.0	0.0	0.0	0.0	0.0	0.0	0.0	0.1	0.1	Afrique
Americas	19.6	17.8	16.2	17.1	19.2	18.3	19.2	18.9	19.6	18.1	Amériques
- Northern America	19.2	17.5	16.1	16.9	18.9	18.2	19.0	18.8	19.4	18.0	- Amérique du Nord
- LAIA	0.3	0.3	0.1	0.2	0.2	0.2	0.2	0.1	0.1	0.1	- ALAI
- CACM	0.0	0.0	0.0	0.0	0.0	0.0	0.0	0.0	0.0	0.0	- MCC
- Caribbean	0.1	0.0	0.0	0.0	0.0	0.0	0.0	0.0	0.0	0.0	- Caraïbes
- Rest of America	0.0	0.0	0.0	0.0	0.0	0.0	0.0	0.0	0.0	0.0	- Autre d'Amérique
Asia excluding former USSR	12.2	10.8	13.0	9.9	13.5	16.6	21.5	22.7	19.9	19.9	Asie ancienne URSS exclus
- Middle East	0.1	0.0	0.0	0.0	0.1	0.0	0.0	0.0	0.0	0.0	- Moyen-Orient
Asia former USSR	0.1	0.2	0.1	0.2	0.0	0.0	0.0	0.0	0.0	0.1	Asie ancienne URSS
Europe excluding former USSR	64.2	65.6	64.1	67.7	63.6	62.1	56.5	55.1	57.5	58.5	Europe ancienne URSS exclus
- European Union	59.0	60.6	57.4	62.0	56.7	55.0	52.0	51.6	53.6	53.7	- Union Européenne
- Eastern Europe	1.4	0.9	1.2	1.0	0.9	1.0	0.8	0.8	1.2	1.6	- Europe de l'Est
- Rest of Europe	3.9	4.1	5.5	4.6	6.0	6.0	3.6	2.8	2.7	3.2	- Autre de l'Europe
Europe former USSR	3.6	5.2	6.5	4.9	3.6	2.9	2.7	3.2	2.9	3.2	Europe ancienne URSS
Oceania	0.3	0.3	0.1	0.2	0.1	0.0	0.0	0.0	0.0	0.2	Océanie

222 Seeds and oleaginous fruit, whole or broken, for 'soft' fixed oil

TRADE BY COMMODITY (Value in million US dollars) | COMMERCE PAR PRODUIT (Valeur en millions de dollars EU)

Imports by principal countries or areas | **Importations selon les principaux pays ou zones**

Country or area	1998	1999	2000	2001	2002	Pays ou zone
World	15195.6	14175.7	15473.3	16486.0	16353.0	Monde
Africa	241.7	205.4	326.0	248.7	241.7	Afrique
Americas	2155.8	1949.8	2186.9	2327.3	2317.8	Amériques
- Northern America	452.7	452.3	500.2	519.7	484.6	- Amérique du Nord
- LAIA	1586.0	1412.0	1592.1	1653.6	1727.0	- ALAI
- CACM	63.5	58.4	58.4	57.3	65.8	- MCC
- Caribbean	52.3	25.6	34.2	95.1	38.9	- Caraïbes
- Rest of America	1.4	1.4	2.0	1.7	1.6	- Autre d'Amérique
Asia excluding former USSR	5844.3	6164.4	7608.9	7620.5	7398.4	Asie ancienne URSS exclus
- Middle East	471.5	443.0	546.1	419.9	437.0	- Moyen-Orient
Asia former USSR	30.2	19.7	15.1	30.1	23.2	Asie ancienne URSS
Europe excluding former USSR	6805.5	5700.2	5242.4	6160.8	6244.8	Europe ancienne URSS exclus
- European Union	6448.9	5428.4	4981.5	5886.6	5919.0	- Union Européenne
- Eastern Europe	169.0	105.0	107.5	127.5	151.2	- Europe de l'Est
- Rest of Europe	187.5	166.8	153.4	146.7	174.6	- Autre de l'Europe
Europe former USSR	93.3	113.4	74.8	83.0	101.5	Europe ancienne URSS
Oceania	24.9	22.9	19.2	15.6	25.5	Océanie
China	1221.2	1527.1	2942.3	3193.7	2636.5	Chine
Japan	2321.0	2012.8	1942.2	1877.2	1963.6	Japon
Germany	1607.1	1442.9	1253.2	1392.1	1357.7	Allemagne
Netherlands	1374.6	1217.1	1317.9	1532.6	1373.8	Pays-Bas
Mexico	1190.2	1145.6	1182.5	1228.9	1237.8	Mexique
Spain	1043.6	854.5	730.1	823.5	911.3	Espagne
Korea, Republic of	435.7	377.8	399.6	358.9	377.5	République de Corée
Belgium	–	518.3	440.8	465.7	e510.8	Belgique
United Kingdom	489.9	310.9	327.7	413.4	389.8	Royaume-Uni
Italy-San Marino-Holy See	358.8	280.0	242.3	348.5	375.8	Italie-Saint-Marin-Saint-Siège
Indonesia	121.3	341.8	322.7	278.6	344.8	Indonésie
France-Monaco	328.1	269.2	167.6	270.9	279.9	France-Monaco
United States	294.2	249.5	296.5	252.6	204.3	Etats-Unis d'Amérique
Thailand	175.2	213.7	297.3	295.2	e307.5	Thaïlande
Portugal	228.3	183.4	195.0	244.0	294.1	Portugal
Canada	158.5	202.8	203.2	267.1	280.3	Canada
Turkey	303.8	217.8	230.7	133.1	222.4	Turquie
Malaysia	156.3	175.9	164.0	177.4	e193.9	Malaisie
Israel	167.8	170.5	156.7	161.6	187.1	Israël
Brazil	101.1	94.2	145.4	143.8	182.0	Brésil
Greece	149.2	115.3	98.4	127.0	e140.4	Grèce
Belgium-Luxembourg	601.7	–	–	–	–	Belgique-Luxembourg
Egypt	66.5	60.2	e152.6	138.9	113.1	Egypte
Iran (Islamic Republic of)	53.6	98.2	156.9	120.6	88.8	Iran (République islamique d')
Pakistan	3.0	71.8	116.4	121.3	185.9	Pakistan
Philippines	82.0	137.2	77.5	97.1	103.4	Philippines
Norway	88.0	90.8	94.1	89.7	98.6	Norvège
Denmark	88.3	80.7	67.1	93.9	119.4	Danemark
Colombia	47.3	59.9	75.1	90.6	132.6	Colombie
Morocco	80.1	78.4	81.9	55.3	e58.3	Maroc

(Value as percentages of World total) | **(Valeur en pourcentage du total mondial)**

Regions of the world	1993	1994	1995	1996	1997	1998	1999	2000	2001	2002	Régions du monde
World	100.0	100.0	100.0	100.0	100.0	100.0	100.0	100.0	100.0	100.0	Monde
Africa	1.4	1.5	2.2	1.6	1.4	1.6	1.4	2.1	1.5	1.5	Afrique
Americas	10.8	12.4	11.3	13.7	16.6	14.2	13.8	14.1	14.1	14.2	Amériques
- Northern America	2.4	2.7	2.4	2.6	3.1	3.0	3.2	3.2	3.2	3.0	- Amérique du Nord
- LAIA	7.4	8.9	8.2	10.2	12.7	10.4	10.0	10.3	10.0	10.6	- ALAI
- CACM	0.4	0.3	0.4	0.5	0.4	0.4	0.4	0.4	0.3	0.4	- MCC
- Caribbean	0.5	0.5	0.3	0.3	0.4	0.3	0.2	0.2	0.6	0.2	- Caraïbes
- Rest of America	0.0	0.0	0.0	0.0	0.0	0.0	0.0	0.0	0.0	0.0	- Autre d'Amérique
Asia excluding former USSR	41.6	34.4	35.0	36.4	39.6	38.5	43.5	49.2	46.2	45.2	Asie ancienne URSS exclus
- Middle East	1.8	1.0	2.2	2.1	2.2	3.1	3.1	3.5	2.5	2.7	- Moyen-Orient
Asia former USSR	0.1	0.0	0.0	0.0	0.0	0.2	0.1	0.1	0.2	0.1	Asie ancienne URSS
Europe excluding former USSR	45.5	51.0	50.6	47.4	41.6	44.8	40.2	33.9	37.4	38.2	Europe ancienne URSS exclus
- European Union	44.1	48.8	48.4	44.7	39.4	42.4	38.3	32.2	35.7	36.2	- Union Européenne
- Eastern Europe	0.9	1.0	0.8	1.5	1.0	1.1	0.7	0.7	0.8	0.9	- Europe de l'Est
- Rest of Europe	0.6	1.2	1.4	1.1	1.2	1.2	1.2	1.0	0.9	1.1	- Autre de l'Europe
Europe former USSR	0.4	0.4	0.5	0.7	0.5	0.6	0.8	0.5	0.5	0.6	Europe ancienne URSS
Oceania	0.3	0.3	0.4	0.3	0.2	0.2	0.2	0.1	0.1	0.2	Océanie

Graines de fruits oléagineux servant à l'extraction d'huiles végétales fixes douces 222

TRADE BY COMMODITY (Value in million US dollars) | COMMERCE PAR PRODUIT (Valeur en millions de dollars EU)

Exports by principal countries or areas | **Exportations selon les principaux pays ou zones**

Country or area	1998	1999	2000	2001	2002	Pays ou zone
World	14086.8	12354.7	13565.9	14339.0	14555.2	Monde
Africa	257.2	173.2	269.8	217.9	218.6	Afrique
Americas	10555.7	8989.6	10401.9	11409.5	11581.0	Amériques
- Northern America	6722.8	6031.0	6736.4	6798.6	6856.0	- Amérique du Nord
- LAIA	3782.6	2911.8	3608.5	4552.7	4672.8	- ALAI
- CACM	50.2	46.5	56.9	57.7	52.0	- MCC
- Caribbean	0.1	0.2	0.1	0.5	0.1	- Caraïbes
- Rest of America	0.0	0.1	0.0	0.0	0.1	- Autre d'Amérique
Asia excluding former USSR	562.0	678.6	740.8	735.0	680.2	Asie ancienne URSS exclus
- Middle East	28.7	19.9	21.1	19.8	22.9	- Moyen-Orient
Asia former USSR	4.4	5.8	17.2	17.3	5.5	Asie ancienne URSS
Europe excluding former USSR	1953.5	1814.8	1366.8	1476.3	1579.8	Europe ancienne URSS exclus
- European Union	1768.1	1403.2	1115.6	1159.2	1292.2	- Union Européenne
- Eastern Europe	178.2	405.8	243.3	312.0	279.0	- Europe de l'Est
- Rest of Europe	7.2	5.7	7.9	5.1	8.6	- Autre de l'Europe
Europe former USSR	495.4	208.4	366.0	113.9	90.5	Europe ancienne URSS
Oceania	258.6	484.4	403.4	369.1	399.6	Océanie
United States	5315.3	4921.4	5710.0	5807.9	6042.2	Etats-Unis d'Amérique
Brazil	2176.7	1594.3	2189.4	2730.6	e2830.9	Brésil
Argentina	1038.0	859.3	1002.0	1388.5	e1341.5	Argentine
Canada	1407.1	1106.7	1026.4	990.7	813.8	Canada
France-Monaco	946.2	641.0	557.5	432.2	522.1	France-Monaco
Australia	258.1	482.5	403.0	368.6	399.3	Australie
China	272.5	354.5	394.3	411.8	424.6	Chine
Paraguay	442.5	312.5	289.2	364.0	e397.4	Paraguay
Netherlands	414.0	289.5	276.9	341.1	345.6	Pays-Bas
Germany	179.3	253.9	140.0	230.8	204.1	Allemagne
India	102.8	165.1	202.7	175.3	115.7	Inde
Russian Federation	241.4	65.8	183.0	44.2	20.3	Fédération de Russie
Ukraine	208.1	106.3	148.3	20.8	22.9	Ukraine
Sudan	109.5	e56.3	137.0	102.4	72.2	Soudan
Hungary	57.7	67.6	94.0	78.4	125.8	Hongrie
Czech Republic	21.5	83.8	80.1	76.7	65.1	République tchèque
Romania	38.0	98.7	35.8	43.7	32.4	Roumanie
United Kingdom	78.1	70.8	14.3	6.8	51.9	Royaume-Uni
Viet Nam	46.0	36.6	42.8	44.5	49.5	Viet Nam
Belgium	–	43.6	39.5	47.9	e53.8	Belgique
Poland	23.6	63.6	5.3	65.6	8.7	Pologne
Bolivia	49.6	42.1	46.9	3.1	e2.9	Bolivie
Nicaragua	24.6	23.0	32.8	32.8	27.3	Nicaragua
Slovakia	22.8	30.2	16.5	35.3	33.1	Slovaquie
Greece	17.4	32.5	26.7	29.9	e30.0	Grèce
Israel	28.1	30.5	24.9	25.5	25.6	Israël
Ethiopia	31.3	23.0	22.2	24.9	32.1	Ethiopie
Venezuela	22.8	33.2	30.6	21.3	e22.6	Venezuela
Mexico	31.3	25.0	27.3	24.3	13.6	Mexique
Bulgaria	14.5	61.9	11.6	e12.3	e13.9	Bulgarie

(Value as percentages of World total) | **(Valeur en pourcentage du total mondial)**

Regions of the world	1993	1994	1995	1996	1997	1998	1999	2000	2001	2002	Régions du monde
World	100.0	100.0	100.0	100.0	100.0	100.0	100.0	100.0	100.0	100.0	Monde
Africa	2.1	1.9	1.4	1.2	1.5	1.8	1.4	2.0	1.5	1.5	Afrique
Americas	77.9	74.1	75.8	76.8	78.6	74.9	72.8	76.7	79.6	79.6	Amériques
- Northern America	57.6	51.1	59.3	59.8	56.8	47.7	48.8	49.7	47.4	47.1	- Amérique du Nord
- LAIA	19.9	22.6	16.0	16.6	21.4	26.9	23.6	26.6	31.8	32.1	- ALAI
- CACM	0.4	0.4	0.5	0.5	0.4	0.4	0.4	0.4	0.4	0.4	- MCC
- Caribbean	0.0	0.0	0.0	0.0	0.0	0.0	0.0	0.0	0.0	0.0	- Caraïbes
- Rest of America	0.0	0.0	0.0	0.0	0.0	0.0	0.0	0.0	0.0	0.0	- Autre d'Amérique
Asia excluding former USSR	7.0	8.0	6.8	5.8	4.3	4.0	5.5	5.5	5.1	4.7	Asie ancienne URSS exclus
- Middle East	0.2	0.1	0.1	0.2	0.2	0.2	0.2	0.2	0.1	0.2	- Moyen-Orient
Asia former USSR	0.0	0.0	0.0	0.0	0.0	0.0	0.0	0.1	0.1	0.0	Asie ancienne URSS
Europe excluding former USSR	11.2	11.3	11.6	10.4	11.0	13.9	14.7	10.1	10.3	10.9	Europe ancienne URSS exclus
- European Union	9.7	10.2	9.5	9.0	10.1	12.6	11.4	8.2	8.1	8.9	- Union Européenne
- Eastern Europe	1.4	1.1	1.9	1.3	0.9	1.3	3.3	1.8	2.2	1.9	- Europe de l'Est
- Rest of Europe	0.0	0.1	0.2	0.1	0.0	0.1	0.0	0.1	0.0	0.1	- Autre de l'Europe
Europe former USSR	1.4	4.0	3.7	4.7	3.4	3.5	1.7	2.7	0.8	0.6	Europe ancienne URSS
Oceania	0.5	0.6	0.6	1.1	1.1	1.8	3.9	3.0	2.6	2.7	Océanie

223 Seeds and oleaginous fruit, whole or broken, for other fixed oils

TRADE BY COMMODITY (Value in million US dollars)
Imports by principal countries or areas

COMMERCE PAR PRODUIT (Valeur en millions de dollars EU)
Importations selon les principaux pays ou zones

Country or area	1998	1999	2000	2001	2002	Pays ou zone
World	1100.4	945.6	828.2	831.7	900.8	Monde
Africa	12.9	13.8	13.5	16.7	42.7	Afrique
Americas	210.9	186.3	173.4	168.2	173.9	Amériques
- Northern America	126.1	117.4	99.5	84.0	99.9	- Amérique du Nord
- LAIA	61.7	46.6	51.8	61.3	51.0	- ALAI
- CACM	14.9	13.5	12.1	9.9	10.8	- MCC
- Caribbean	7.6	7.4	7.9	9.7	7.0	- Caraïbes
- Rest of America	0.6	1.3	2.1	3.3	5.2	- Autre d'Amérique
Asia excluding former USSR	211.2	227.6	172.9	153.7	154.6	Asie ancienne URSS exclus
- Middle East	20.2	15.8	18.0	12.6	13.3	- Moyen-Orient
Asia former USSR	0.1	1.4	0.9	2.3	1.5	Asie ancienne URSS
Europe excluding former USSR	577.3	455.7	395.2	456.1	495.9	Europe ancienne URSS exclus
- European Union	528.0	418.5	365.3	417.8	450.1	- Union Européenne
- Eastern Europe	30.1	21.7	18.4	23.9	29.1	- Europe de l'Est
- Rest of Europe	19.2	15.5	11.6	14.3	16.7	- Autre de l'Europe
Europe former USSR	58.5	26.6	16.5	14.7	19.6	Europe ancienne URSS
Oceania	29.5	34.1	55.9	20.1	12.7	Océanie
Germany	161.1	131.0	118.3	108.6	109.8	Allemagne
Belgium	–	108.2	95.5	102.9	e112.8	Belgique
United States	103.0	98.6	81.2	58.2	69.2	Etats-Unis d'Amérique
Netherlands	80.9	55.9	44.9	48.4	47.5	Pays-Bas
Japan	64.5	58.4	49.2	35.6	24.8	Japon
Bangladesh	48.5	e53.1	e28.8	27.9	e27.2	Bangladesh
France-Monaco	35.1	33.4	35.9	34.7	37.8	France-Monaco
United Kingdom	45.8	15.6	12.9	28.4	41.4	Royaume-Uni
Spain	18.9	24.0	15.6	37.4	31.5	Espagne
Belgium-Luxembourg	120.5	–	–	–	–	Belgique-Luxembourg
Canada	23.1	18.7	18.3	25.8	30.7	Canada
Australia	23.7	28.2	45.2	11.0	3.2	Australie
Mexico	14.6	16.2	19.8	25.9	20.3	Mexique
Malaysia	22.8	27.9	23.5	9.4	e10.2	Malaisie
Austria	16.2	16.5	12.5	18.0	26.8	Autriche
Korea, Republic of	8.9	11.6	10.1	9.6	24.6	République de Corée
Colombia	24.5	8.9	17.4	7.7	4.4	Colombie
Poland	15.0	10.5	8.8	11.6	12.6	Pologne
Peru	15.5	7.4	7.1	12.6	15.1	Pérou
Sweden	9.1	7.7	9.6	13.4	11.1	Suède
Pakistan	9.8	10.8	9.3	8.2	12.5	Pakistan
Russian Federation	16.3	8.9	4.8	7.8	11.6	Fédération de Russie
United Arab Emirates	9.5	10.0	10.1	6.9	e7.1	Emirates arabes unis
Denmark	10.1	7.0	5.7	6.3	8.9	Danemark
China	5.4	4.2	1.3	22.4	4.8	Chine
Italy-San Marino-Holy See	8.8	9.0	6.8	5.8	7.3	Italie-Saint-Marin-Saint-Siège
Guatemala	8.7	7.5	6.9	6.5	7.9	Guatemala
Lithuania	15.8	3.9	3.9	4.4	e5.4	Lituanie
Cuba	e5.1	5.3	6.8	7.2	e6.2	Cuba
New Zealand	4.0	3.4	7.6	6.5	7.8	Nouvelle-Zélande

(Value as percentages of World total) **(Valeur en pourcentage du total mondial)**

Regions of the world	1993	1994	1995	1996	1997	1998	1999	2000	2001	2002	Régions du monde
World	100.0	100.0	100.0	100.0	100.0	100.0	100.0	100.0	100.0	100.0	Monde
Africa	1.6	1.5	1.3	0.8	2.5	1.2	1.5	1.6	2.0	4.7	Afrique
Americas	18.7	16.9	16.0	20.0	20.4	19.2	19.7	20.9	20.2	19.3	Amériques
- Northern America	10.5	9.9	10.0	13.1	13.4	11.5	12.4	12.0	10.1	11.1	- Amérique du Nord
- LAIA	6.6	4.9	3.9	5.2	5.4	5.6	4.9	6.2	7.4	5.7	- ALAI
- CACM	1.0	1.9	1.7	1.2	0.9	1.4	1.4	1.5	1.2	1.2	- MCC
- Caribbean	0.6	0.2	0.3	0.5	0.6	0.7	0.8	1.0	1.2	0.8	- Caraïbes
- Rest of America	0.1	0.1	0.1	0.1	0.1	0.1	0.1	0.3	0.4	0.6	- Autre d'Amérique
Asia excluding former USSR	28.1	24.3	25.9	20.5	18.5	19.2	24.1	20.9	18.5	17.2	Asie ancienne URSS exclus
- Middle East	2.3	1.3	1.5	1.5	1.3	1.8	1.7	2.2	1.5	1.5	- Moyen-Orient
Asia former USSR	0.0	0.1	0.2	0.1	0.1	0.0	0.2	0.1	0.3	0.2	Asie ancienne URSS
Europe excluding former USSR	44.1	45.3	45.2	47.5	48.4	52.5	48.2	47.7	54.8	55.0	Europe ancienne URSS exclus
- European Union	40.9	42.1	43.1	44.7	45.5	48.0	44.3	44.1	50.2	50.0	- Union Européenne
- Eastern Europe	1.4	1.8	1.1	1.6	1.8	2.7	2.3	2.2	2.9	3.2	- Europe de l'Est
- Rest of Europe	1.7	1.4	1.1	1.3	1.0	1.7	1.6	1.4	1.7	1.9	- Autre de l'Europe
Europe former USSR	3.0	5.4	4.0	5.2	5.5	5.3	2.8	2.0	1.8	2.2	Europe ancienne URSS
Oceania	4.5	6.4	7.5	5.9	4.5	2.7	3.6	6.7	2.4	1.4	Océanie

TRADE BY COMMODITY (Value in million US dollars)
Exports by principal countries or areas

COMMERCE PAR PRODUIT (Valeur en millions de dollars EU)
Exportations selon les principaux pays ou zones

Country or area	1998	1999	2000	2001	2002	Pays ou zone
World	966.0	804.0	821.6	827.4	930.5	Monde
Africa	32.1	28.5	57.5	66.5	67.6	Afrique
Americas	472.4	349.3	324.2	363.0	438.1	Amériques
- Northern America	407.0	301.4	249.1	315.8	397.2	- Amérique du Nord
- LAIA	49.3	31.5	65.6	38.2	36.7	- ALAI
- CACM	13.9	13.9	7.7	8.8	4.0	- MCC
- Caribbean	0.2	0.1	0.1	0.1	0.1	- Caraïbes
- Rest of America	2.1	2.4	1.6	0.1	0.1	- Autre d'Amérique
Asia excluding former USSR	128.7	123.0	136.0	146.9	132.7	Asie ancienne URSS exclus
- Middle East	26.3	29.3	17.4	21.3	18.2	- Moyen-Orient
Asia former USSR	2.1	4.8	4.1	1.6	1.7	Asie ancienne URSS
Europe excluding former USSR	246.0	226.6	218.7	204.1	248.7	Europe ancienne URSS exclus
- European Union	195.5	175.6	171.1	155.3	181.6	- Union Européenne
- Eastern Europe	47.8	48.6	43.7	44.5	63.5	- Europe de l'Est
- Rest of Europe	2.7	2.4	3.9	4.3	3.6	- Autre de l'Europe
Europe former USSR	26.9	28.1	45.5	12.8	12.0	Europe ancienne URSS
Oceania	58.0	43.7	35.5	32.5	29.8	Océanie
Canada	281.4	185.4	140.7	193.5	242.6	Canada
United States	125.6	116.0	108.5	122.4	154.6	Etats-Unis d'Amérique
Belgium	–	41.8	57.7	44.1	e49.5	Belgique
Netherlands	38.7	28.9	28.2	34.5	46.3	Pays-Bas
India	19.5	24.5	40.9	25.4	31.4	Inde
China	14.4	18.1	22.4	48.7	37.0	Chine
Germany	25.6	30.8	19.1	17.5	26.9	Allemagne
Czech Republic	18.3	20.8	19.8	17.6	24.2	République tchèque
Hungary	20.8	20.5	14.3	15.7	27.3	Hongrie
Bolivia	15.0	14.0	40.4	13.7	e13.1	Bolivie
Turkey	19.5	22.6	12.2	19.1	15.7	Turquie
Ukraine	21.2	22.1	35.6	3.3	3.6	Ukraine
Australia	25.4	19.1	14.5	10.5	12.4	Australie
United Kingdom	19.0	27.6	15.4	10.9	6.7	Royaume-Uni
Venezuela	21.6	7.0	14.6	16.2	e17.3	Venezuela
France-Monaco	18.4	14.3	13.5	9.1	13.6	France-Monaco
Austria	11.6	12.0	12.7	15.1	17.0	Autriche
Indonesia	16.1	15.5	13.7	6.7	14.1	Indonésie
Belgium-Luxembourg	64.3	–	–	–	–	Belgique-Luxembourg
Sudan	8.0	e4.9	12.0	15.5	10.2	Soudan
Vanuatu	e11.6	e8.9	8.0	e9.0	e11.5	Vanuatu
Sri Lanka	e9.5	9.0	e10.9	6.9	9.9	Sri Lanka
Singapore	7.6	10.0	8.3	7.0	8.0	Singapour
Nigeria	0.4	0.4	17.8	e11.7	e10.0	Nigéria
Ethiopia	2.5	8.7	6.5	12.9	7.9	Ethiopie
Ghana	4.2	2.3	8.2	e10.7	e10.8	Ghana
Costa Rica	8.2	7.7	3.7	7.1	3.4	Costa Rica
Spain	5.9	5.3	7.2	4.9	5.5	Espagne
Myanmar	e8.1	e6.4	e9.1	e4.6	e	Myanmar
Bulgaria	3.0	3.9	6.4	e6.8	e7.7	Bulgarie

(Value as percentages of World total) **(Valeur en pourcentage du total mondial)**

Regions of the world	1993	1994	1995	1996	1997	1998	1999	2000	2001	2002	Régions du monde
World	100.0	100.0	100.0	100.0	100.0	100.0	100.0	100.0	100.0	100.0	Monde
Africa	3.0	4.0	4.4	7.0	3.5	3.3	3.5	7.0	8.0	7.3	Afrique
Americas	38.0	40.9	48.2	45.2	48.7	48.9	43.4	39.5	43.9	47.1	Amériques
- Northern America	31.9	37.3	40.9	40.7	44.2	42.1	37.5	30.3	38.2	42.7	- Amérique du Nord
- LAIA	4.6	2.2	5.8	3.0	2.3	5.1	3.9	8.0	4.6	3.9	- ALAI
- CACM	1.4	1.3	1.1	1.4	2.0	1.4	1.7	0.9	1.1	0.4	- MCC
- Caribbean	0.2	0.1	0.0	0.0	0.0	0.0	0.0	0.0	0.0	0.0	- Caraïbes
- Rest of America	0.0	0.0	0.4	0.1	0.2	0.2	0.3	0.2	0.0	0.0	- Autre d'Amérique
Asia excluding former USSR	22.4	19.9	16.1	12.6	12.1	13.3	15.3	16.6	17.8	14.3	Asie ancienne URSS exclus
- Middle East	4.7	2.1	1.8	1.8	2.7	2.7	3.6	2.1	2.6	2.0	- Moyen-Orient
Asia former USSR	0.4	0.7	0.4	0.6	0.6	0.2	0.6	0.5	0.2	0.2	Asie ancienne URSS
Europe excluding former USSR	25.5	24.3	22.1	23.7	25.4	25.5	28.2	26.6	24.7	26.7	Europe ancienne URSS exclus
- European Union	20.6	19.9	17.8	18.6	21.0	20.2	21.8	20.8	18.8	19.5	- Union Européenne
- Eastern Europe	4.5	4.0	4.0	4.9	4.2	4.9	6.0	5.3	5.4	6.8	- Europe de l'Est
- Rest of Europe	0.4	0.4	0.3	0.2	0.2	0.3	0.3	0.5	0.5	0.4	- Autre de l'Europe
Europe former USSR	2.6	1.8	2.0	2.8	2.3	2.8	3.5	5.5	1.6	1.3	Europe ancienne URSS
Oceania	8.1	8.4	7.0	8.1	7.4	6.0	5.4	4.3	3.9	3.2	Océanie

232 Natural rubber latex; rubber and gums

TRADE BY COMMODITY (Value in million US dollars)
Imports by principal countries or areas

COMMERCE PAR PRODUIT (Valeur en millions de dollars EU)
Importations selon les principaux pays ou zones

Country or area	1998	1999	2000	2001	2002	Pays ou zone
World	4867.8	3933.1	4825.2	4131.4	4632.5	Monde
Africa	97.9	65.2	72.9	61.3	80.4	Afrique
Americas	1533.5	1138.5	1356.6	1037.5	1209.9	Amériques
- Northern America	1216.3	911.4	1069.8	799.9	970.5	- Amérique du Nord
- LAIA	301.5	212.8	277.8	223.1	232.6	- ALAI
- CACM	3.7	3.8	4.4	4.1	3.4	- MCC
- Caribbean	11.2	10.1	4.0	9.8	3.0	- Caraïbes
- Rest of America	0.7	0.4	0.6	0.7	0.3	- Autre d'Amérique
Asia excluding former USSR	1951.7	1716.0	2179.3	1947.5	2215.7	Asie ancienne URSS exclus
- Middle East	122.5	87.8	111.9	111.2	127.9	- Moyen-Orient
Asia former USSR	1.9	0.1	0.1	0.2	0.1	Asie ancienne URSS
Europe excluding former USSR	1200.7	948.8	1130.6	1026.8	1070.5	Europe ancienne URSS exclus
- European Union	1050.1	826.7	980.0	881.9	905.6	- Union Européenne
- Eastern Europe	115.8	93.7	122.6	119.0	138.5	- Europe de l'Est
- Rest of Europe	34.8	28.4	27.9	25.9	26.3	- Autre de l'Europe
Europe former USSR	45.8	31.3	51.2	35.2	29.2	Europe ancienne URSS
Oceania	36.4	33.3	34.6	22.8	26.8	Océanie
United States	1067.7	798.3	952.4	706.2	844.2	Etats-Unis d'Amérique
Japan	591.8	517.7	578.7	501.0	560.6	Japon
China	322.1	285.6	588.6	595.0	695.9	Chine
Malaysia	302.6	242.2	332.2	280.7	e306.8	Malaisie
Korea, Republic of	228.6	214.6	240.4	206.8	234.3	République de Corée
France-Monaco	198.8	187.8	247.7	202.9	200.1	France-Monaco
Germany	246.2	179.4	209.2	181.3	200.8	Allemagne
Spain	148.0	129.8	134.6	136.9	144.6	Espagne
Singapore	175.2	153.7	143.1	88.9	117.4	Singapour
Italy-San Marino-Holy See	145.0	106.8	121.4	115.7	125.1	Italie-Saint-Marin-Saint-Siège
Canada	148.7	113.1	117.3	93.7	126.3	Canada
United Kingdom	132.9	103.7	116.6	91.4	84.6	Royaume-Uni
Brazil	102.0	72.1	111.7	92.8	114.2	Brésil
Mexico	91.7	79.4	87.3	62.9	62.9	Mexique
Turkey	75.8	50.0	68.0	56.0	76.7	Turquie
China, Hong Kong SAR	59.3	79.4	49.8	26.3	33.3	Chine - RAS de Hong-Kong
Poland	37.1	31.3	42.9	40.0	50.9	Pologne
Iran (Islamic Republic of)	37.1	31.6	37.5	49.0	44.3	Iran (République islamique d')
Czech Republic	26.6	24.4	33.1	31.5	35.2	République tchèque
Austria	33.0	28.3	29.8	27.7	21.4	Autriche
Australia	34.4	28.4	28.4	17.7	19.1	Australie
South Africa	-	-	41.9	30.7	48.2	Afrique du Sud
Pakistan	26.3	21.3	22.4	23.0	24.9	Pakistan
Slovakia	21.5	16.8	19.7	22.3	30.7	Slovaquie
Belgium	-	25.3	24.6	26.3	e28.8	Belgique
Argentina	38.6	17.2	20.2	16.5	e7.3	Argentine
Luxembourg	-	11.8	27.7	28.4	e30.1	Luxembourg
India	22.0	13.3	7.1	31.0	20.6	Inde
Colombia	19.8	15.2	20.2	15.7	15.3	Colombie
Finland	14.4	14.1	16.2	16.7	21.0	Finlande

(Value as percentages of World total)

(Valeur en pourcentage du total mondial)

Regions of the world	1993	1994	1995	1996	1997	1998	1999	2000	2001	2002	Régions du monde
World	100.0	100.0	100.0	100.0	100.0	100.0	100.0	100.0	100.0	100.0	Monde
Africa	2.1	2.2	2.2	2.0	2.0	2.0	1.7	1.5	1.5	1.7	Afrique
Americas	30.8	29.7	30.8	28.7	29.7	31.5	28.9	28.1	25.1	26.1	Amériques
- Northern America	24.4	23.4	24.5	23.3	23.7	25.0	23.2	22.2	19.4	21.0	- Amérique du Nord
- LAIA	6.2	6.0	6.0	5.2	5.7	6.2	5.4	5.8	5.4	5.0	- ALAI
- CACM	0.1	0.1	0.1	0.1	0.1	0.1	0.1	0.1	0.1	0.1	- MCC
- Caribbean	0.1	0.1	0.1	0.2	0.2	0.2	0.3	0.1	0.2	0.1	- Caraïbes
- Rest of America	0.0	0.0	0.0	0.0	0.0	0.0	0.0	0.0	0.0	0.0	- Autre d'Amérique
Asia excluding former USSR	43.1	43.6	42.1	46.1	44.7	40.1	43.6	45.2	47.1	47.8	Asie ancienne URSS exclus
- Middle East	2.8	2.6	2.6	2.7	2.7	2.5	2.2	2.3	2.7	2.8	- Moyen-Orient
Asia former USSR	0.0	0.0	0.0	0.0	0.0	0.0	0.0	0.0	0.0	0.0	Asie ancienne URSS
Europe excluding former USSR	21.8	23.2	23.5	21.8	22.3	24.7	24.1	23.4	24.9	23.1	Europe ancienne URSS exclus
- European Union	19.6	20.9	20.9	19.1	19.8	21.6	21.0	20.3	21.3	19.5	- Union Européenne
- Eastern Europe	1.7	1.7	2.1	2.2	2.1	2.4	2.4	2.5	2.9	3.0	- Europe de l'Est
- Rest of Europe	0.5	0.6	0.5	0.4	0.4	0.7	0.7	0.6	0.6	0.6	- Autre de l'Europe
Europe former USSR	1.2	0.2	0.3	0.3	0.4	0.9	0.8	1.1	0.9	0.6	Europe ancienne URSS
Oceania	1.1	1.2	1.1	1.0	0.9	0.7	0.8	0.7	0.6	0.6	Océanie

TRADE BY COMMODITY (Value in million US dollars)
Exports by principal countries or areas

COMMERCE PAR PRODUIT (Valeur en millions de dollars EU)
Exportations selon les principaux pays ou zones

Country or area	1998	1999	2000	2001	2002	Pays ou zone
World	3981.1	3308.5	3909.9	3329.2	3783.0	Monde
Africa	115.1	107.0	119.8	120.4	124.6	Afrique
Americas	99.3	91.2	102.9	96.1	102.2	Amériques
- Northern America	67.4	61.6	71.7	69.0	70.9	- Amérique du Nord
- LAIA	4.2	3.7	2.6	1.5	1.9	- ALAI
- CACM	27.5	25.9	28.6	25.5	29.2	- MCC
- Caribbean	0.1	0.0	0.0	0.0	0.0	- Caraïbes
- Rest of America	0.1	0.0	0.0	0.0	0.1	- Autre d'Amérique
Asia excluding former USSR	3629.6	2996.6	3586.3	3020.7	3452.1	Asie ancienne URSS exclus
- Middle East	1.8	2.4	0.9	0.4	1.1	- Moyen-Orient
Asia former USSR	0.0	0.0	0.0	0.0	0.0	Asie ancienne URSS
Europe excluding former USSR	132.2	108.9	95.1	86.5	98.7	Europe ancienne URSS exclus
- European Union	128.5	106.0	91.3	83.6	94.6	- Union Européenne
- Eastern Europe	2.9	2.4	2.5	1.8	3.3	- Europe de l'Est
- Rest of Europe	0.8	0.5	1.2	1.1	0.8	- Autre de l'Europe
Europe former USSR	0.9	1.4	1.1	0.6	1.0	Europe ancienne URSS
Oceania	4.0	3.4	4.7	4.9	4.5	Océanie
Thailand	1343.8	1160.8	1510.6	1321.2	e1395.4	Thaïlande
Indonesia	1106.3	850.0	889.3	786.6	1038.4	Indonésie
Malaysia	724.1	618.2	677.6	497.7	e527.4	Malaisie
Singapore	242.9	219.1	208.9	147.5	160.5	Singapour
Viet Nam	e	e	159.6	166.0	184.5	Viet Nam
Côte d'Ivoire	75.3	67.8	78.0	e85.1	86.2	Côte d'Ivoire
United States	50.0	54.1	61.1	60.2	66.2	Etats-Unis d'Amérique
China, Hong Kong SAR	64.6	43.9	31.9	19.9	25.5	Chine - RAS de Hong-Kong
Sri Lanka	e34.6	32.6	e39.7	23.7	26.4	Sri Lanka
Cambodia	e56.9	e34.2	e25.1	e21.7	e14.5	Cambodge
Guatemala	27.4	25.9	28.6	25.5	29.1	Guatemala
Germany	30.6	25.9	23.5	18.2	21.9	Allemagne
France-Monaco	20.4	24.1	15.5	19.7	24.4	France-Monaco
Cameroon	e18.4	e17.5	20.1	19.9	23.0	Cameroun
Myanmar	e19.3	e12.6	e14.2	e10.6	e16.5	Myanmar
Philippines	14.3	11.8	14.3	13.2	18.2	Philippines
Italy-San Marino-Holy See	11.3	14.1	15.2	15.9	13.9	Italie-Saint-Marin-Saint-Siège
United Kingdom	23.5	13.3	11.0	8.5	6.9	Royaume-Uni
Canada	17.4	7.5	10.5	8.8	4.8	Canada
India	1.3	1.4	3.9	4.4	30.7	Inde
Belgium	–	5.4	6.3	8.3	e9.3	Belgique
Ghana	4.6	6.8	4.9	e6.4	e6.5	Ghana
Netherlands	11.8	5.6	4.0	2.7	4.3	Pays-Bas
Liberia	e1.8	e7.1	e	e2.8	e2.6	Libéria
Spain	6.4	4.5	4.3	4.0	4.9	Espagne
China	14.0	2.7	0.6	0.5	1.0	Chine
Belgium-Luxembourg	17.9	–	–	–	–	Belgique-Luxembourg
Sweden	2.9	2.5	1.8	2.5	5.9	Suède
Ireland	0.3	6.9	6.3	0.9	0.2	Irlande
Gabon	e5.5	3.1	1.3	e1.3	e1.3	Gabon

(Value as percentages of World total) **(Valeur en pourcentage du total mondial)**

Regions of the world	1993	1994	1995	1996	1997	1998	1999	2000	2001	2002	Régions du monde
World	100.0	100.0	100.0	100.0	100.0	100.0	100.0	100.0	100.0	100.0	Monde
Africa	4.6	3.8	2.6	5.1	3.1	2.9	3.2	3.1	3.6	3.3	Afrique
Americas	1.6	1.6	1.4	1.6	1.9	2.5	2.8	2.6	2.9	2.7	Amériques
- Northern America	1.1	1.0	0.9	0.8	1.1	1.7	1.9	1.8	2.1	1.9	- Amérique du Nord
- LAIA	0.1	0.1	0.1	0.1	0.1	0.1	0.1	0.1	0.0	0.1	- ALAI
- CACM	0.5	0.5	0.5	0.7	0.7	0.7	0.8	0.7	0.8	0.8	- MCC
- Caribbean	0.0	0.0	0.0	0.0	0.0	0.0	0.0	0.0	0.0	0.0	- Caraïbes
- Rest of America	0.0	0.0	0.0	0.0	0.0	0.0	0.0	0.0	0.0	0.0	- Autre d'Amérique
Asia excluding former USSR	91.9	92.6	94.2	91.5	92.2	91.2	90.6	91.7	90.7	91.3	Asie ancienne URSS exclus
- Middle East	0.0	0.0	0.0	0.0	0.0	0.0	0.1	0.0	0.0	0.0	- Moyen-Orient
Asia former USSR	0.0	0.0	0.0	0.0	0.0	0.0	0.0	0.0	0.0	0.0	Asie ancienne URSS
Europe excluding former USSR	1.6	1.8	1.7	1.7	2.5	3.3	3.3	2.4	2.6	2.6	Europe ancienne URSS exclus
- European Union	1.6	1.4	1.6	1.6	2.4	3.2	3.2	2.3	2.5	2.5	- Union Européenne
- Eastern Europe	0.1	0.3	0.1	0.0	0.1	0.1	0.1	0.1	0.1	0.1	- Europe de l'Est
- Rest of Europe	0.0	0.0	0.0	0.0	0.0	0.0	0.0	0.0	0.0	0.0	- Autre de l'Europe
Europe former USSR	0.0	0.0	0.0	0.0	0.2	0.0	0.0	0.0	0.0	0.0	Europe ancienne URSS
Oceania	0.2	0.1	0.1	0.1	0.2	0.1	0.1	0.1	0.1	0.1	Océanie

233 Synthetic rubber, latex, etc; waste, scrap of unhardened rubber

TRADE BY COMMODITY (Value in million US dollars)
Imports by principal countries or areas

COMMERCE PAR PRODUIT (Valeur en millions de dollars EU)
Importations selon les principaux pays ou zones

Country or area	1998	1999	2000	2001	2002	Pays ou zone
World	7017.5	7047.2	7764.9	7455.7	7738.4	Monde
Africa	85.6	75.0	70.2	75.6	82.4	Afrique
Americas	1557.9	1593.3	1852.7	1764.4	1689.5	Amériques
- Northern America	1087.3	1151.3	1326.9	1276.3	1245.1	- Amérique du Nord
- LAIA	445.9	423.3	503.4	465.0	421.8	- ALAI
- CACM	17.4	11.3	14.1	15.1	15.0	- MCC
- Caribbean	6.8	7.1	8.1	7.9	7.5	- Caraïbes
- Rest of America	0.5	0.3	0.1	0.2	0.1	- Autre d'Amérique
Asia excluding former USSR	1771.1	2031.5	2429.0	2364.4	2644.3	Asie ancienne URSS exclus
- Middle East	120.1	125.4	138.3	129.9	167.0	- Moyen-Orient
Asia former USSR	9.6	2.0	3.4	4.7	3.9	Asie ancienne URSS
Europe excluding former USSR	3342.9	3150.2	3209.6	3060.3	3142.9	Europe ancienne URSS exclus
- European Union	3000.8	2851.5	2861.2	2689.8	2757.1	- Union Européenne
- Eastern Europe	238.9	204.6	244.7	267.5	280.1	- Europe de l'Est
- Rest of Europe	103.2	94.1	103.6	103.0	105.6	- Autre de l'Europe
Europe former USSR	206.9	141.1	139.7	119.5	110.8	Europe ancienne URSS
Oceania	43.5	54.1	60.3	66.8	64.6	Océanie
United States	738.3	786.5	893.2	856.0	840.9	Etats-Unis d'Amérique
China	468.1	613.2	731.9	797.7	960.6	Chine
Germany	596.6	543.5	529.2	571.1	551.8	Allemagne
France-Monaco	472.1	439.7	447.7	402.1	407.0	France-Monaco
Belgium	–	530.2	532.8	467.9	e513.2	Belgique
Italy-San Marino-Holy See	416.3	379.3	397.1	401.0	390.7	Italie-Saint-Marin-Saint-Siège
Canada	349.0	364.7	433.6	420.3	404.1	Canada
United Kingdom	291.3	271.5	240.5	217.1	236.7	Royaume-Uni
Spain	273.6	256.3	229.3	180.0	175.9	Espagne
Netherlands	211.0	207.9	240.1	224.1	232.0	Pays-Bas
Korea, Republic of	177.4	204.6	237.7	220.1	226.9	République de Corée
Japan	158.5	195.1	248.6	223.1	222.8	Japon
China, Hong Kong SAR	161.3	164.9	207.3	185.4	209.9	Chine - RAS de Hong-Kong
Brazil	144.6	136.3	177.9	164.8	155.3	Brésil
India	123.7	130.4	148.0	145.9	160.2	Inde
Thailand	98.6	124.0	138.7	146.6	e152.7	Thaïlande
Mexico	122.9	123.4	143.5	124.9	127.0	Mexique
Indonesia	100.2	82.6	134.2	114.9	116.5	Indonésie
Malaysia	89.8	106.3	116.9	111.8	e122.1	Malaisie
Belgium-Luxembourg	532.0	–	–	–	–	Belgique-Luxembourg
Turkey	91.4	85.4	90.2	74.3	105.7	Turquie
Poland	78.9	68.8	83.7	93.1	100.6	Pologne
Czech Republic	67.5	62.3	73.6	82.6	85.4	République tchèque
Sweden	63.2	58.8	81.3	71.2	66.0	Suède
Ukraine	106.7	71.1	59.4	38.3	41.2	Ukraine
Portugal	51.4	57.7	55.6	50.4	56.7	Portugal
Singapore	39.7	43.1	49.6	42.2	51.5	Singapour
Australia	38.7	39.7	44.2	50.5	48.2	Australie
Colombia	41.6	35.5	44.2	38.6	35.3	Colombie
Belarus	62.2	33.6	33.0	36.8	27.3	Bélarus

(Value as percentages of World total) **(Valeur en pourcentage du total mondial)**

Regions of the world	1993	1994	1995	1996	1997	1998	1999	2000	2001	2002	Régions du monde
World	100.0	100.0	100.0	100.0	100.0	100.0	100.0	100.0	100.0	100.0	Monde
Africa	1.3	1.4	1.4	1.3	1.4	1.2	1.1	0.9	1.0	1.1	Afrique
Americas	22.0	21.8	19.4	19.8	21.5	22.2	22.6	23.9	23.7	21.8	Amériques
- Northern America	14.7	14.7	12.8	13.1	14.7	15.5	16.3	17.1	17.1	16.1	- Amérique du Nord
- LAIA	6.8	6.7	6.2	6.3	6.4	6.4	6.0	6.5	6.2	5.5	- ALAI
- CACM	0.3	0.3	0.3	0.3	0.2	0.2	0.2	0.2	0.2	0.2	- MCC
- Caribbean	0.1	0.1	0.1	0.1	0.1	0.1	0.1	0.1	0.1	0.1	- Caraïbes
- Rest of America	0.0	0.0	0.0	0.0	0.0	0.0	0.0	0.0	0.0	0.0	- Autre d'Amérique
Asia excluding former USSR	31.3	28.0	28.0	29.3	29.6	25.2	28.8	31.3	31.7	34.2	Asie ancienne URSS exclus
- Middle East	2.3	1.7	1.9	2.1	1.9	1.7	1.8	1.8	1.7	2.2	- Moyen-Orient
Asia former USSR	0.0	0.2	0.1	0.2	0.0	0.1	0.0	0.0	0.1	0.1	Asie ancienne URSS
Europe excluding former USSR	43.9	45.8	47.3	47.2	44.9	47.6	44.7	41.3	41.0	40.6	Europe ancienne URSS exclus
- European Union	39.5	41.2	42.1	42.1	40.5	42.8	40.5	36.8	36.1	35.6	- Union Européenne
- Eastern Europe	2.7	2.9	3.5	3.8	3.3	3.4	2.9	3.2	3.6	3.6	- Europe de l'Est
- Rest of Europe	1.7	1.7	1.7	1.3	1.2	1.5	1.3	1.3	1.4	1.4	- Autre de l'Europe
Europe former USSR	0.5	1.8	3.0	1.3	1.7	2.9	2.0	1.8	1.6	1.4	Europe ancienne URSS
Oceania	1.0	1.0	0.9	0.9	0.8	0.6	0.8	0.8	0.9	0.8	Océanie

TRADE BY COMMODITY (Value in million US dollars)
Exports by principal countries or areas

COMMERCE PAR PRODUIT (Valeur en millions de dollars EU)
Exportations selon les principaux pays ou zones

Country or area	1998	1999	2000	2001	2002	Pays ou zone
World	5621.7	5444.7	6198.8	6148.4	6605.6	Monde
Africa	16.3	16.8	20.0	20.1	24.7	Afrique
Americas	1641.3	1679.3	2041.2	1991.4	1993.3	Amériques
- Northern America	1421.5	1454.1	1749.8	1697.4	1694.0	- Amérique du Nord
- LAIA	219.6	225.0	291.2	293.5	299.1	- ALAI
- CACM	0.1	0.2	0.2	0.4	0.2	- MCC
- Caribbean	0.1	0.0	0.0	0.0	0.0	- Caraïbes
- Rest of America	0.0	0.0	0.0	0.0	0.0	- Autre d'Amérique
Asia excluding former USSR	1521.1	1683.2	1944.4	1833.6	1998.6	Asie ancienne URSS exclus
- Middle East	28.0	26.2	25.0	21.4	21.4	- Moyen-Orient
Asia former USSR	8.6	7.6	8.4	12.6	5.7	Asie ancienne URSS
Europe excluding former USSR	2127.1	1773.6	1862.7	1968.7	2197.6	Europe ancienne URSS exclus
- European Union	1987.5	1658.9	1728.2	1828.5	2060.5	- Union Européenne
- Eastern Europe	111.6	90.5	115.3	123.5	122.2	- Europe de l'Est
- Rest of Europe	28.1	24.3	19.2	16.7	14.9	- Autre de l'Europe
Europe former USSR	302.3	277.7	318.2	316.6	377.3	Europe ancienne URSS
Oceania	4.9	6.5	4.0	5.4	8.4	Océanie
United States	1123.0	1132.0	1393.2	1376.1	1357.0	Etats-Unis d'Amérique
Japan	754.4	841.5	875.8	808.2	886.9	Japon
Germany	364.5	381.2	423.0	424.8	612.3	Allemagne
France-Monaco	363.0	328.1	361.8	375.5	361.1	France-Monaco
Belgium	–	487.5	463.1	388.8	e436.2	Belgique
Canada	298.6	322.1	356.6	321.3	337.0	Canada
Korea, Republic of	271.0	284.6	366.9	348.2	361.3	République de Corée
Russian Federation	287.8	267.8	301.5	307.1	368.5	Fédération de Russie
United Kingdom	415.0	258.0	260.7	256.4	255.0	Royaume-Uni
Netherlands	357.7	100.0	86.3	265.9	271.1	Pays-Bas
China, Hong Kong SAR	120.0	134.9	158.6	133.9	156.7	Chine - RAS de Hong-Kong
Mexico	102.2	95.2	140.5	150.4	152.4	Mexique
Brazil	93.6	100.1	115.4	109.1	e113.1	Brésil
Italy-San Marino-Holy See	75.7	72.8	77.8	76.3	78.3	Italie-Saint-Marin-Saint-Siège
Belgium-Luxembourg	377.9	–	–	–	–	Belgique-Luxembourg
China	27.4	35.2	53.2	66.6	80.6	Chine
Czech Republic	42.8	34.9	45.5	50.8	44.8	République tchèque
Thailand	15.6	36.1	57.0	52.5	e55.5	Thaïlande
Poland	40.2	35.1	44.6	44.7	46.3	Pologne
Argentina	18.1	23.0	28.1	27.1	e26.2	Argentine
Singapore	23.0	21.6	21.2	20.4	22.7	Singapour
Bulgaria	23.0	18.2	18.9	e20.0	e22.5	Bulgarie
Indonesia	3.7	11.6	22.9	21.6	20.8	Indonésie
Spain	15.5	14.5	20.5	13.9	16.3	Espagne
Iran (Islamic Republic of)	18.1	15.8	11.7	11.7	13.0	Iran (République islamique d')
Switzerland-Liechtenstein	14.2	18.5	14.8	11.2	9.8	Suisse-Liechtenstein
South Africa	–	–	19.2	19.3	24.0	Afrique du Sud
Finland	2.1	1.4	17.0	13.5	16.7	Finlande
Malaysia	8.8	9.5	7.5	9.3	e9.8	Malaisie
Estonia	8.9	7.8	8.8	8.0	7.3	Estonie

(Value as percentages of World total) **(Valeur en pourcentage du total mondial)**

Regions of the world	1993	1994	1995	1996	1997	1998	1999	2000	2001	2002	Régions du monde
World	100.0	100.0	100.0	100.0	100.0	100.0	100.0	100.0	100.0	100.0	Monde
Africa	0.5	0.1	0.3	0.4	0.4	0.3	0.3	0.3	0.3	0.4	Afrique
Americas	27.5	26.5	27.5	28.7	30.1	29.2	30.8	32.9	32.4	30.2	Amériques
- Northern America	25.2	23.9	23.6	24.9	26.2	25.3	26.7	28.2	27.6	25.6	- Amérique du Nord
- LAIA	2.2	2.6	3.9	3.8	3.9	3.9	4.1	4.7	4.8	4.5	- ALAI
- CACM	0.0	0.0	0.0	0.0	0.0	0.0	0.0	0.0	0.0	0.0	- MCC
- Caribbean	0.0	0.0	0.0	0.0	0.0	0.0	0.0	0.0	0.0	0.0	- Caraïbes
- Rest of America	0.0	0.0	0.0	0.0	0.0	0.0	0.0	0.0	0.0	0.0	- Autre d'Amérique
Asia excluding former USSR	23.3	21.4	25.4	24.3	26.5	27.1	30.9	31.4	29.8	30.3	Asie ancienne URSS exclus
- Middle East	0.1	0.3	0.6	0.6	0.4	0.5	0.5	0.4	0.3	0.3	- Moyen-Orient
Asia former USSR	0.0	0.1	0.2	0.2	0.1	0.2	0.1	0.1	0.2	0.1	Asie ancienne URSS
Europe excluding former USSR	45.0	45.0	39.4	38.7	36.2	37.8	32.6	30.0	32.0	33.3	Europe ancienne URSS exclus
- European Union	43.5	43.2	36.3	36.0	34.0	35.4	30.5	27.9	29.7	31.2	- Union Européenne
- Eastern Europe	1.3	1.5	2.8	2.6	2.0	2.0	1.7	1.9	2.0	1.9	- Europe de l'Est
- Rest of Europe	0.2	0.3	0.3	0.2	0.2	0.5	0.4	0.3	0.3	0.2	- Autre de l'Europe
Europe former USSR	3.6	6.7	7.1	7.6	6.5	5.4	5.1	5.1	5.1	5.7	Europe ancienne URSS
Oceania	0.1	0.1	0.1	0.1	0.1	0.1	0.1	0.1	0.1	0.1	Océanie

244 Cork, natural, raw and waste

TRADE BY COMMODITY (Value in million US dollars)
Imports by principal countries or areas

COMMERCE PAR PRODUIT (Valeur en millions de dollars EU)
Importations selon les principaux pays ou zones

Country or area	1998	1999	2000	2001	2002	Pays ou zone
World	170.0	198.5	257.0	216.7	200.1	Monde
Africa	1.7	1.1	1.5	0.7	0.4	Afrique
Americas	15.1	11.1	13.2	9.5	5.7	Amériques
- Northern America	6.6	5.5	5.2	3.7	2.4	- Amérique du Nord
- LAIA	7.4	5.5	7.8	5.4	3.1	- ALAI
- CACM	0.9	0.0	0.1	0.2	0.0	- MCC
- Caribbean	0.1	0.1	0.1	0.2	0.1	- Caraïbes
- Rest of America	0.0	0.0	0.0	0.0	0.0	- Autre d'Amérique
Asia excluding former USSR	13.0	17.3	18.0	15.1	13.5	Asie ancienne URSS exclus
- Middle East	0.9	0.8	1.3	1.2	1.4	- Moyen-Orient
Asia former USSR	0.0	0.0	0.0	0.0	0.0	Asie ancienne URSS
Europe excluding former USSR	139.2	167.3	223.1	190.8	179.7	Europe ancienne URSS exclus
- European Union	137.6	165.2	221.6	189.6	178.4	- Union Européenne
- Eastern Europe	1.2	1.1	0.9	0.6	0.8	- Europe de l'Est
- Rest of Europe	0.5	1.0	0.7	0.6	0.5	- Autre de l'Europe
Europe former USSR	0.6	1.4	1.0	0.6	0.8	Europe ancienne URSS
Oceania	0.4	0.3	0.2	0.1	0.1	Océanie
Portugal	66.4	72.9	112.4	95.3	98.8	Portugal
Spain	22.7	36.8	50.4	40.4	37.5	Espagne
Italy-San Marino-Holy See	26.4	24.9	24.2	24.9	20.0	Italie-Saint-Marin-Saint-Siège
France-Monaco	14.9	21.5	24.1	19.5	13.1	France-Monaco
China	3.8	6.8	6.5	5.0	5.5	Chine
United States	4.9	3.2	3.8	3.1	1.8	Etats-Unis d'Amérique
Japan	3.2	3.7	3.9	3.6	2.2	Japon
Germany	2.9	3.1	2.8	3.2	1.7	Allemagne
Netherlands	1.1	2.7	3.1	1.5	2.5	Pays-Bas
Brazil	2.4	2.1	2.9	1.8	1.0	Brésil
Argentina	3.2	1.5	2.4	1.5	e0.7	Argentine
United Kingdom	1.6	1.2	2.0	1.8	1.3	Royaume-Uni
India	1.5	1.6	1.4	1.1	1.3	Inde
Korea, Republic of	1.0	1.9	1.6	1.1	1.1	République de Corée
Canada	1.6	2.3	1.3	0.6	0.6	Canada
China, Hong Kong SAR	0.5	0.7	1.6	1.9	0.4	Chine - RAS de Hong-Kong
Belgium	–	0.3	1.1	1.7	e1.8	Belgique
Mexico	0.8	0.8	1.4	1.0	0.7	Mexique
Russian Federation	0.6	1.3	0.9	0.5	0.7	Fédération de Russie
Austria	0.7	0.7	0.3	0.3	0.3	Autriche
Saudi Arabia	0.4	0.5	0.5	0.5	e0.5	Arabie saoudite
Greece	0.1	0.4	0.5	0.6	e0.6	Grèce
Venezuela	0.3	0.6	0.3	0.5	e0.4	Venezuela
Czech Republic	0.6	0.5	0.4	0.3	0.3	République tchèque
Turkey	0.4	0.2	0.4	0.3	0.4	Turquie
Chile	0.4	0.2	0.6	0.3	0.1	Chili
Eritrea	e0.7	e0.5	0.5			Erythrée
Ireland	0.1	0.4	0.5	0.2	0.4	Irlande
Switzerland-Liechtenstein	0.3	0.4	0.2	0.4	0.3	Suisse-Liechtenstein
Indonesia	0.2	0.2	0.3	0.2	0.2	Indonésie

(Value as percentages of World total) **(Valeur en pourcentage du total mondial)**

Regions of the world	1993	1994	1995	1996	1997	1998	1999	2000	2001	2002	Régions du monde
World	100.0	100.0	100.0	100.0	100.0	100.0	100.0	100.0	100.0	100.0	Monde
Africa	1.0	0.3	0.6	0.8	0.6	1.0	0.5	0.6	0.3	0.2	Afrique
Americas	13.6	12.9	10.1	9.5	8.9	8.9	5.6	5.1	4.4	2.9	Amériques
- Northern America	4.6	3.7	3.7	3.8	3.6	3.9	2.8	2.0	1.7	1.2	- Amérique du Nord
- LAIA	8.7	9.2	6.2	5.6	5.2	4.3	2.8	3.0	2.5	1.6	- ALAI
- CACM	0.0	0.0	0.0	0.0	0.0	0.5	0.0	0.0	0.1	0.0	- MCC
- Caribbean	0.3	0.0	0.1	0.1	0.1	0.1	0.1	0.0	0.1	0.1	- Caraïbes
- Rest of America	0.0	0.0	0.0	0.0	0.0	0.0	0.0	0.0	0.0	0.0	- Autre d'Amérique
Asia excluding former USSR	12.5	11.0	11.2	10.0	8.7	7.6	8.7	7.0	7.0	6.7	Asie ancienne URSS exclus
- Middle East	1.2	0.9	1.5	1.0	0.9	0.5	0.4	0.5	0.6	0.7	- Moyen-Orient
Asia former USSR	0.0	0.0	0.0	0.0	0.0	0.0	0.0	0.0	0.0	0.0	Asie ancienne URSS
Europe excluding former USSR	72.3	75.0	77.3	78.7	81.0	81.9	84.3	86.8	88.0	89.8	Europe ancienne URSS exclus
- European Union	70.2	73.1	75.8	77.7	79.6	80.9	83.2	86.2	87.5	89.1	- Union Européenne
- Eastern Europe	1.6	1.3	1.0	0.9	1.0	0.7	0.5	0.3	0.3	0.4	- Europe de l'Est
- Rest of Europe	0.4	0.6	0.5	0.2	0.4	0.3	0.5	0.3	0.3	0.3	- Autre de l'Europe
Europe former USSR	0.4	0.4	0.4	0.5	0.6	0.4	0.7	0.4	0.3	0.4	Europe ancienne URSS
Oceania	0.3	0.3	0.3	0.4	0.2	0.2	0.1	0.1	0.0	0.0	Océanie

TRADE BY COMMODITY (Value in million US dollars)
Exports by principal countries or areas

COMMERCE PAR PRODUIT (Valeur en millions de dollars EU)
Exportations selon les principaux pays ou zones

Country or area	1998	1999	2000	2001	2002	Pays ou zone
World	161.8	178.5	245.9	202.1	197.1	Monde
Africa	19.0	20.4	35.5	18.2	19.1	Afrique
Americas	4.3	7.4	3.1	2.5	1.8	Amériques
- Northern America	4.3	7.4	2.9	2.2	1.7	- Amérique du Nord
- LAIA	0.0	0.0	0.2	0.2	0.1	- ALAI
- CACM	0.0	0.0	0.0	0.0	0.0	- MCC
- Caribbean	0.0	0.0	0.0	0.0	0.0	- Caraïbes
Asia excluding former USSR	1.1	1.6	6.2	7.3	5.5	Asie ancienne URSS exclus
- Middle East	0.0	0.1	0.1	1.5	2.0	- Moyen-Orient
Asia former USSR	0.0	0.0	0.0	0.0	0.0	Asie ancienne URSS
Europe excluding former USSR	137.4	149.1	201.1	174.0	170.4	Europe ancienne URSS exclus
- European Union	137.2	149.0	200.9	173.8	170.1	- Union Européenne
- Eastern Europe	0.1	0.0	0.1	0.1	0.2	- Europe de l'Est
- Rest of Europe	0.0	0.0	0.1	0.1	0.1	- Autre de l'Europe
Europe former USSR	0.0	0.0	0.0	0.0	0.0	Europe ancienne URSS
Oceania	0.0	0.1	0.0	0.1	0.3	Océanie
Spain	80.3	81.5	107.4	104.6	111.1	Espagne
Portugal	50.1	58.9	78.4	57.7	50.8	Portugal
Morocco	10.8	12.9	22.2	9.9	e10.8	Maroc
Algeria	6.6	3.9	9.0	e6.2	e6.0	Algérie
Italy-San Marino-Holy See	2.3	4.1	9.0	6.9	3.2	Italie-Saint-Marin-Saint-Siège
France-Monaco	3.4	3.1	4.0	2.8	3.5	France-Monaco
United States	3.7	6.8	2.4	1.7	1.3	Etats-Unis d'Amérique
Tunisia	1.5	3.6	4.2	2.1	e2.2	Tunisie
China	0.1	0.3	3.1	2.6	1.9	Chine
China, Hong Kong SAR	0.1	0.4	1.8	2.2	0.3	Chine - RAS de Hong-Kong
United Kingdom	0.3	0.3	1.2	1.0	0.6	Royaume-Uni
Saudi Arabia	0.0	0.0	0.1	1.4	e1.3	Arabie saoudite
Germany	0.4	0.8	0.4	0.3	0.4	Allemagne
Canada	0.6	0.5	0.4	0.5	0.4	Canada
Indonesia	0.3	0.1	0.4	0.6	0.5	Indonésie
Japan	0.3	0.5	0.3	0.2	0.2	Japon
Netherlands	0.1	0.1	0.2	0.2	0.4	Pays-Bas
Austria	0.2	0.1	0.1	0.1	0.1	Autriche
Singapore	0.0	0.1	0.0	0.0	0.4	Singapour
Syrian Arab Republic	0.0	0.0	0.0	0.0	0.6	République arabe syrienne
Australia	0.0	0.1	0.0	0.1	0.3	Australie
India	0.0	0.0	0.2	0.1	0.1	Inde
Mexico	0.0	0.0	0.2	0.2	0.0	Mexique
Poland			0.1	0.1	0.1	Pologne
Czech Republic	0.1	0.0	0.0	0.0	0.0	République tchèque
United Arab Emirates	0.0	0.0	0.0	0.1	e0.1	Emirates arabes unis
South Africa	–	–	0.1	0.0	0.1	Afrique du Sud
Belgium	–	0.0	0.0	0.0	e0.1	Belgique
Sweden	0.0	0.0	0.1	0.0	0.0	Suède
Finland	0.0	0.1	0.0		0.0	Finlande

(Value as percentages of World total) **(Valeur en pourcentage du total mondial)**

Regions of the world	1993	1994	1995	1996	1997	1998	1999	2000	2001	2002	Régions du monde
World	100.0	100.0	100.0	100.0	100.0	100.0	100.0	100.0	100.0	100.0	Monde
Africa	7.8	8.1	6.7	5.8	7.5	11.7	11.4	14.4	9.0	9.7	Afrique
Americas	4.4	1.9	1.7	2.1	1.9	2.7	4.1	1.3	1.2	0.9	Amériques
- Northern America	4.3	1.8	1.6	2.1	1.9	2.7	4.1	1.2	1.1	0.9	- Amérique du Nord
- LAIA	0.1	0.1	0.1	0.0	0.0	0.0	0.0	0.1	0.1	0.0	- ALAI
- CACM	0.0	0.0	0.0	0.0	0.0	0.0	0.0	0.0	0.0	0.0	- MCC
- Caribbean	0.0	0.0	0.0	0.0	0.0	0.0	0.0	0.0	0.0	0.0	- Caraïbes
Asia excluding former USSR	1.2	1.2	1.6	0.7	0.8	0.7	0.9	2.5	3.6	2.8	Asie ancienne URSS exclus
- Middle East	0.0	0.0	0.0	0.0	0.0	0.0	0.1	0.0	0.8	1.0	- Moyen-Orient
Asia former USSR	0.0	0.0	0.0	0.0	0.0	0.0	0.0	0.0	0.0	0.0	Asie ancienne URSS
Europe excluding former USSR	86.2	88.7	89.9	91.2	89.7	84.9	83.5	81.8	86.1	86.4	Europe ancienne URSS exclus
- European Union	86.1	88.6	89.9	91.2	89.5	84.8	83.5	81.7	86.0	86.3	- Union Européenne
- Eastern Europe	0.0	0.0	0.0	0.0	0.1	0.1	0.0	0.1	0.1	0.1	- Europe de l'Est
- Rest of Europe	0.0	0.0	0.0	0.0	0.1	0.0	0.0	0.0	0.0	0.0	- Autre de l'Europe
Europe former USSR	0.1	0.0	0.0	0.0	0.0	0.0	0.0	0.0	0.0	0.0	Europe ancienne URSS
Oceania	0.4	0.1	0.1	0.2	0.1	0.0	0.0	0.0	0.1	0.2	Océanie
Oceania	0.4	0.1	0.2	0.1	0.0	0.0	0.0	0.0			Océanie

245 Fuel wood and wood charcoal

TRADE BY COMMODITY (Value in million US dollars)
Imports by principal countries or areas

COMMERCE PAR PRODUIT (Valeur en millions de dollars EU)
Importations selon les principaux pays ou zones

Country or area	1998	1999	2000	2001	2002	Pays ou zone
World	319.0	324.0	348.7	376.4	397.8	Monde
Africa	1.1	3.0	3.7	4.3	4.2	Afrique
Americas	29.6	27.7	17.7	31.8	23.9	Amériques
- Northern America	15.5	14.9	14.6	17.0	21.5	- Amérique du Nord
- LAIA	1.3	0.9	1.3	2.0	1.9	- ALAI
- CACM	0.1	0.1	1.3	0.1	0.1	- MCC
- Caribbean	12.7	11.7	0.5	12.7	0.2	- Caraïbes
- Rest of America	0.1	0.1	0.1	0.1	0.2	- Autre d'Amérique
Asia excluding former USSR	115.8	122.2	153.0	152.5	156.0	Asie ancienne URSS exclus
- Middle East	30.2	21.4	27.5	23.7	26.9	- Moyen-Orient
Asia former USSR	0.9	0.7	0.7	0.8	0.8	Asie ancienne URSS
Europe excluding former USSR	170.1	169.0	172.4	185.7	211.8	Europe ancienne URSS exclus
- European Union	144.1	147.8	153.9	157.4	185.1	- Union Européenne
- Eastern Europe	0.6	0.8	1.3	1.9	2.5	- Europe de l'Est
- Rest of Europe	25.4	20.4	17.3	26.4	24.2	- Autre de l'Europe
Europe former USSR	1.1	0.7	0.4	0.5	0.3	Europe ancienne URSS
Oceania	0.3	0.6	0.8	0.8	0.9	Océanie
Japan	53.4	62.0	73.6	76.0	76.4	Japon
Germany	37.0	37.8	35.1	34.8	39.2	Allemagne
Italy-San Marino-Holy See	19.8	24.8	30.8	29.5	35.8	Italie-Saint-Marin-Saint-Siège
Korea, Republic of	15.2	21.6	30.3	30.5	32.3	République de Corée
United Kingdom	17.5	15.5	18.1	17.1	17.4	Royaume-Uni
Norway	18.5	12.8	10.5	20.3	16.8	Norvège
France-Monaco	12.8	12.1	12.0	11.5	11.1	France-Monaco
United States	10.2	10.3	10.4	12.9	15.3	Etats-Unis d'Amérique
Greece	8.3	8.0	9.2	12.0	e13.3	Grèce
Sweden	7.9	6.7	7.8	8.3	16.4	Suède
Denmark	7.1	7.5	8.1	8.9	12.2	Danemark
Austria	8.0	7.3	7.7	8.9	9.2	Autriche
Turkey	11.1	6.6	11.6	3.7	7.6	Turquie
Aruba	12.0	11.3		12.1	e0.0	Aruba
Netherlands	8.3	7.9	6.4	5.3	6.6	Pays-Bas
Belgium	–	8.8	8.4	7.4	e8.2	Belgique
Saudi Arabia	7.9	4.7	5.4	6.4	e6.7	Arabie saoudite
Spain	3.6	4.9	4.5	5.6	6.7	Espagne
Switzerland-Liechtenstein	5.5	4.8	4.5	4.5	5.2	Suisse-Liechtenstein
Canada	5.3	4.7	4.2	4.0	6.2	Canada
Kuwait	5.4	4.4	e4.2	e4.6	e1.8	Koweït
Portugal	1.3	2.2	2.4	4.6	4.4	Portugal
United Arab Emirates	1.5	1.6	2.0	3.5	e3.6	Emirates arabes unis
China, Hong Kong SAR	2.5	2.5	2.3	2.0	2.3	Chine - RAS de Hong-Kong
Israel	1.7	1.4	2.0	3.0	1.8	Israël
Finland	2.3	2.3	1.3	1.6	2.3	Finlande
Belgium-Luxembourg	9.6	–	–	–	–	Belgique-Luxembourg
China	0.9	1.1	1.7	3.0	1.5	Chine
Lebanon	1.2	1.1	1.3	2.2	e2.0	Liban
Bhutan	2.1	1.9	e1.3	e1.4	e0.0	Bhoutan

(Value as percentages of World total) **(Valeur en pourcentage du total mondial)**

Regions of the world	1993	1994	1995	1996	1997	1998	1999	2000	2001	2002	Régions du monde
World	100.0	100.0	100.0	100.0	100.0	100.0	100.0	100.0	100.0	100.0	Monde
Africa	1.9	1.3	1.4	0.9	0.5	0.3	0.9	1.1	1.1	1.1	Afrique
Americas	9.8	16.3	12.0	10.7	9.2	9.3	8.6	5.1	8.5	6.0	Amériques
- Northern America	9.2	11.3	7.4	6.6	5.3	4.9	4.6	4.2	4.5	5.4	- Amérique du Nord
- LAIA	0.2	0.5	0.3	0.3	0.4	0.4	0.3	0.4	0.5	0.5	- ALAI
- CACM	0.0	0.0	0.0	0.1	0.0	0.0	0.0	0.4	0.0	0.0	- MCC
- Caribbean	0.2	4.4	4.2	3.7	3.5	4.0	3.6	0.1	3.4	0.1	- Caraïbes
- Rest of America	0.1	0.1	0.0	0.0	0.0	0.0	0.0	0.0	0.0	0.0	- Autre d'Amérique
Asia excluding former USSR	34.9	32.2	34.5	35.8	38.4	36.3	37.7	43.9	40.5	39.2	Asie ancienne URSS exclus
- Middle East	8.2	4.8	4.9	6.9	7.0	9.5	6.6	7.9	6.3	6.8	- Moyen-Orient
Asia former USSR	0.0	0.4	0.4	0.2	0.1	0.3	0.2	0.2	0.2	0.2	Asie ancienne URSS
Europe excluding former USSR	52.9	49.5	51.3	52.2	51.5	53.3	52.2	49.4	49.3	53.2	Europe ancienne URSS exclus
- European Union	46.7	41.3	42.7	45.8	44.6	45.2	45.6	44.1	41.8	46.5	- Union Européenne
- Eastern Europe	0.5	0.3	0.4	0.4	0.2	0.2	0.2	0.4	0.5	0.6	- Europe de l'Est
- Rest of Europe	5.7	7.9	8.3	6.0	6.6	8.0	6.3	5.0	7.0	6.1	- Autre de l'Europe
Europe former USSR	0.4	0.2	0.2	0.1	0.2	0.4	0.2	0.1	0.1	0.1	Europe ancienne URSS
Oceania	0.1	0.1	0.2	0.1	0.1	0.1	0.2	0.2	0.2	0.2	Océanie

TRADE BY COMMODITY (Value in million US dollars)
Exports by principal countries or areas

COMMERCE PAR PRODUIT (Valeur en millions de dollars EU)
Exportations selon les principaux pays ou zones

Country or area	1998	1999	2000	2001	2002	Pays ou zone
World	310.6	275.9	296.5	337.4	333.7	Monde
Africa	30.3	27.3	40.3	72.7	49.0	Afrique
Americas	41.0	31.5	32.1	36.1	37.8	Amériques
- Northern America	17.1	14.2	14.3	13.2	15.0	- Amérique du Nord
- LAIA	19.0	15.9	17.8	22.7	22.7	- ALAI
- CACM	0.9	0.3	0.0	0.1	0.0	- MCC
- Caribbean	0.2	0.1	0.1	0.1	0.0	- Caraïbes
- Rest of America	3.7	1.0	0.0	0.0	0.1	- Autre d'Amérique
Asia excluding former USSR	91.6	89.4	112.7	109.2	107.9	Asie ancienne URSS exclus
- Middle East	0.9	0.5	1.0	2.0	2.0	- Moyen-Orient
Asia former USSR	0.0	0.2	0.0	0.0	0.0	Asie ancienne URSS
Europe excluding former USSR	95.4	96.7	95.8	103.8	115.3	Europe ancienne URSS exclus
- European Union	45.1	44.1	37.9	39.2	42.5	- Union Européenne
- Eastern Europe	42.2	44.3	49.3	54.2	60.4	- Europe de l'Est
- Rest of Europe	8.1	8.4	8.6	10.4	12.5	- Autre de l'Europe
Europe former USSR	51.7	30.1	13.9	14.8	22.2	Europe ancienne URSS
Oceania	0.7	0.6	1.7	0.8	1.4	Océanie
China	29.6	30.9	43.5	55.6	56.7	Chine
Indonesia	29.7	27.1	31.4	21.0	16.6	Indonésie
Somalia	e17.0	e10.9	e	e56.7	e30.9	Somalie
Latvia	46.6	22.7	6.3	5.2	8.3	Lettonie
Poland	15.3	15.2	15.4	18.0	18.5	Pologne
Hungary	12.0	12.8	15.7	15.2	18.0	Hongrie
France-Monaco	18.1	15.7	12.1	11.5	12.6	France-Monaco
Malaysia	8.3	10.4	13.7	10.4	e11.0	Malaisie
Argentina	12.2	8.2	9.4	12.1	e11.6	Argentine
United States	12.8	10.0	9.5	7.8	9.6	Etats-Unis d'Amérique
South Africa	–	–	21.3	9.1	12.1	Afrique du Sud
Spain	8.2	8.3	8.2	8.3	8.3	Espagne
Philippines	10.1	7.5	7.5	5.3	5.1	Philippines
Czech Republic	6.3	6.1	6.6	7.5	7.6	République tchèque
Singapore	7.3	6.8	6.2	5.3	6.3	Singapour
Mexico	4.1	4.4	4.8	6.2	6.3	Mexique
United Kingdom	6.5	4.1	4.3	4.5	5.1	Royaume-Uni
Canada	4.3	4.1	4.8	5.4	5.3	Canada
Southern African Customs Union	9.7	13.0	–	–	–	Union douanière d'Afrique australe
Bulgaria	2.9	4.3	4.1	e4.4	e4.9	Bulgarie
Slovakia	2.1	2.8	3.5	4.4	5.4	Slovaquie
Estonia	0.9	2.5	3.2	3.7	6.8	Estonie
Romania	2.8	2.5	3.5	3.8	4.6	Roumanie
Germany	2.9	4.9	3.1	3.5	2.6	Allemagne
Croatia	3.1	2.8	2.7	4.0	4.4	Croatie
Netherlands	2.5	3.0	2.7	3.1	4.6	Pays-Bas
Belgium	–	4.6	3.5	3.7	e4.2	Belgique
Bosnia and Herzegovina	e0.9	e2.1	e2.5	e3.1	e5.1	Bosnie-Herzégovine
Russian Federation	2.7	2.8	2.3	1.8	2.8	Fédération de Russie
Slovenia	2.8	2.4	1.8	1.6	1.8	Slovénie

(Value as percentages of World total) **(Valeur en pourcentage du total mondial)**

Regions of the world	1993	1994	1995	1996	1997	1998	1999	2000	2001	2002	Régions du monde
World	100.0	100.0	100.0	100.0	100.0	100.0	100.0	100.0	100.0	100.0	Monde
Africa	8.5	7.5	9.4	7.6	7.1	9.8	9.9	13.6	21.5	14.7	Afrique
Americas	17.0	20.7	14.0	15.2	13.9	13.2	11.4	10.8	10.7	11.3	Amériques
- Northern America	11.9	14.6	8.7	8.6	6.0	5.5	5.1	4.8	3.9	4.5	- Amérique du Nord
- LAIA	5.0	6.0	4.8	6.4	6.5	6.1	5.8	6.0	6.7	6.8	- ALAI
- CACM	0.0	0.1	0.0	0.1	0.3	0.3	0.1	0.0	0.0	0.0	- MCC
- Caribbean	0.0	0.1	0.1	0.0	0.0	0.1	0.0	0.0	0.0	0.0	- Caraïbes
- Rest of America	0.0	0.0	0.4	0.0	1.1	1.2	0.4	0.0	0.0	0.0	- Autre d'Amérique
Asia excluding former USSR	32.0	34.3	33.6	36.8	34.2	29.5	32.4	38.0	32.4	32.3	Asie ancienne URSS exclus
- Middle East	0.5	0.3	0.4	0.1	0.1	0.3	0.2	0.3	0.6	0.6	- Moyen-Orient
Asia former USSR	0.0	0.0	0.0	0.0	0.0	0.0	0.1	0.0	0.0	0.0	Asie ancienne URSS
Europe excluding former USSR	38.1	35.1	37.6	34.0	32.8	30.7	35.1	32.3	30.8	34.6	Europe ancienne URSS exclus
- European Union	13.7	17.3	19.2	14.3	15.4	14.5	16.0	12.8	11.6	12.7	- Union Européenne
- Eastern Europe	21.0	14.5	16.1	16.8	15.0	13.6	16.1	16.6	16.1	18.1	- Europe de l'Est
- Rest of Europe	3.5	3.3	2.3	2.8	2.4	2.6	3.0	2.9	3.1	3.7	- Autre de l'Europe
Europe former USSR	4.4	2.1	5.1	6.1	11.7	16.6	10.9	4.7	4.4	6.7	Europe ancienne URSS
Oceania	0.1	0.3	0.3	0.3	0.2	0.2	0.2	0.6	0.2	0.4	Océanie

246 Pulpwood (including chips and wood waste)

TRADE BY COMMODITY (Value in million US dollars)
Imports by principal countries or areas

COMMERCE PAR PRODUIT (Valeur en millions de dollars EU)
Importations selon les principaux pays ou zones

Country or area	1998	1999	2000	2001	2002	Pays ou zone
World	2652.0	2625.0	2603.3	2452.3	2407.9	Monde
Africa	0.3	0.9	1.1	1.2	1.5	Afrique
Americas	130.1	135.1	165.2	160.3	152.3	Amériques
- Northern America	126.8	132.5	159.0	155.0	147.0	- Amérique du Nord
- LAIA	1.8	1.7	4.5	3.6	3.1	- ALAI
- CACM	0.7	0.3	0.5	0.6	0.8	- MCC
- Caribbean	0.4	0.6	0.9	0.7	1.4	- Caraïbes
- Rest of America	0.3	0.0	0.3	0.3	0.1	- Autre d'Amérique
Asia excluding former USSR	2159.8	2097.9	2093.5	1920.7	1821.8	Asie ancienne URSS exclus
- Middle East	18.0	11.5	6.8	5.9	7.5	- Moyen-Orient
Asia former USSR	0.0	0.0	0.0	0.1	0.1	Asie ancienne URSS
Europe excluding former USSR	359.7	388.9	341.7	368.3	429.8	Europe ancienne URSS exclus
- European Union	308.4	341.3	302.0	324.0	380.5	- Union Européenne
- Eastern Europe	3.4	4.2	3.7	2.8	5.6	- Europe de l'Est
- Rest of Europe	47.9	43.4	36.0	41.5	43.7	- Autre de l'Europe
Europe former USSR	1.2	1.2	0.7	0.8	1.2	Europe ancienne URSS
Oceania	1.0	1.1	1.1	1.0	1.1	Océanie
Japan	2017.7	1905.0	1915.0	1761.4	1672.1	Japon
United States	77.6	67.8	79.8	90.2	84.2	Etats-Unis d'Amérique
Korea, Republic of	51.0	91.4	83.5	80.9	64.6	République de Corée
Canada	49.2	64.8	79.2	64.8	62.8	Canada
Sweden	44.3	45.7	66.3	65.7	80.9	Suède
Italy-San Marino-Holy See	39.2	37.9	37.7	35.3	41.0	Italie-Saint-Marin-Saint-Siège
Finland	28.2	31.7	32.9	44.6	47.0	Finlande
France-Monaco	48.3	42.6	25.2	22.4	26.3	France-Monaco
Denmark	17.7	38.3	15.1	27.3	42.7	Danemark
Belgium	–	40.4	30.4	32.0	e35.1	Belgique
Germany	27.0	28.8	26.2	28.5	25.4	Allemagne
Norway	29.6	23.8	20.8	26.8	25.2	Norvège
Austria	25.7	30.3	20.0	22.4	26.6	Autriche
Netherlands	12.0	16.7	13.2	16.2	27.4	Pays-Bas
Switzerland-Liechtenstein	14.8	15.4	11.3	11.0	13.7	Suisse-Liechtenstein
United Kingdom	8.1	7.2	12.8	11.8	14.4	Royaume-Uni
Belgium-Luxembourg	38.8	–	–	–	–	Belgique-Luxembourg
Spain	10.2	8.2	9.1	6.8	3.6	Espagne
China	5.9	8.9	5.0	4.6	7.4	Chine
Saudi Arabia	15.3	9.0	1.2	0.4	e0.5	Arabie saoudite
Portugal	7.3	6.4	4.9	4.1	3.3	Portugal
Slovenia	2.8	3.6	3.3	3.1	4.0	Slovénie
Luxembourg	–	5.6	4.4	2.7	e2.9	Luxembourg
United Arab Emirates	1.5	1.5	2.8	4.2	e4.3	Emirates arabes unis
Ireland	1.1	1.4	3.4	3.8	3.5	Irlande
Czech Republic	1.4	1.2	1.4	0.9	2.7	République tchèque
Philippines	0.3	1.5	2.1	1.3	0.1	Philippines
Mexico	0.3	0.2	2.4	1.0	1.3	Mexique
Australia	0.9	1.0	1.1	0.9	0.7	Australie
Argentina	0.6	0.7	1.0	1.4	e0.6	Argentine

(Value as percentages of World total) **(Valeur en pourcentage du total mondial)**

Regions of the world	1993	1994	1995	1996	1997	1998	1999	2000	2001	2002	Régions du monde
World	100.0	100.0	100.0	100.0	100.0	100.0	100.0	100.0	100.0	100.0	Monde
Africa	0.0	0.0	0.0	0.1	0.0	0.0	0.0	0.0	0.1	0.1	Afrique
Americas	3.9	3.4	4.9	4.5	5.3	4.9	5.1	6.3	6.5	6.3	Amériques
- Northern America	3.8	3.4	4.9	4.4	5.2	4.8	5.0	6.1	6.3	6.1	- Amérique du Nord
- LAIA	0.0	0.0	0.0	0.0	0.0	0.1	0.1	0.2	0.1	0.1	- ALAI
- CACM	0.0	0.0	0.0	0.0	0.0	0.0	0.0	0.0	0.0	0.0	- MCC
- Caribbean	0.0	0.0	0.0	0.0	0.0	0.0	0.0	0.0	0.0	0.1	- Caraïbes
- Rest of America	0.0	0.0	0.0	0.0	0.0	0.0	0.0	0.0	0.0	0.0	- Autre d'Amérique
Asia excluding former USSR	85.9	77.5	82.8	83.7	82.1	81.4	79.9	80.4	78.3	75.7	Asie ancienne URSS exclus
- Middle East	1.2	0.3	0.4	0.3	0.4	0.7	0.4	0.3	0.2	0.3	- Moyen-Orient
Asia former USSR	0.0	0.0	0.0	0.0	0.0	0.0	0.0	0.0	0.0	0.0	Asie ancienne URSS
Europe excluding former USSR	10.1	19.0	12.2	11.7	12.5	13.6	14.8	13.1	15.0	17.8	Europe ancienne URSS exclus
- European Union	8.6	17.5	10.7	9.9	11.0	11.6	13.0	11.6	13.2	15.8	- Union Européenne
- Eastern Europe	0.1	0.1	0.1	0.1	0.1	0.1	0.2	0.1	0.1	0.2	- Europe de l'Est
- Rest of Europe	1.3	1.5	1.5	1.7	1.4	1.8	1.7	1.4	1.7	1.8	- Autre de l'Europe
Europe former USSR	0.0	0.0	0.0	0.0	0.0	0.0	0.0	0.0	0.0	0.0	Europe ancienne URSS
Oceania	0.0	0.0	0.0	0.0	0.0	0.0	0.0	0.0	0.0	0.0	Océanie

Bois de trituration (y compris les plaquettes et des déchets du bois) 246

TRADE BY COMMODITY (Value in million US dollars)
Exports by principal countries or areas

COMMERCE PAR PRODUIT (Valeur en millions de dollars EU)
Exportations selon les principaux pays ou zones

Country or area	1998	1999	2000	2001	2002	Pays ou zone
World	1827.5	1793.3	1856.3	1767.1	1792.6	Monde
Africa	141.8	140.0	152.0	172.5	186.9	Afrique
Americas	776.3	741.9	742.5	666.1	555.7	Amériques
- Northern America	585.6	554.0	539.5	442.8	337.4	- Amérique du Nord
- LAIA	188.9	184.9	200.9	221.6	216.4	- ALAI
- CACM	1.8	2.9	2.1	1.7	1.7	- MCC
- Caribbean	0.0	0.0	0.0	0.0	0.0	- Caraïbes
- Rest of America	0.0	0.0	0.0	0.0	0.1	- Autre d'Amérique
Asia excluding former USSR	154.2	165.1	205.3	207.0	206.3	Asie ancienne URSS exclus
- Middle East	0.5	0.5	0.2	1.8	1.9	- Moyen-Orient
Asia former USSR	0.0	0.0	0.0	0.0	0.0	Asie ancienne URSS
Europe excluding former USSR	267.4	280.2	239.9	236.8	276.5	Europe ancienne URSS exclus
- European Union	240.3	250.1	212.8	207.3	239.5	- Union Européenne
- Eastern Europe	13.6	17.3	15.8	17.9	21.4	- Europe de l'Est
- Rest of Europe	13.5	12.7	11.4	11.6	15.6	- Autre de l'Europe
Europe former USSR	45.9	46.8	53.6	69.8	94.4	Europe ancienne URSS
Oceania	441.9	419.3	463.0	414.9	472.8	Océanie
Australia	394.3	378.6	420.1	366.9	428.6	Australie
United States	491.8	465.6	418.6	305.7	208.7	Etats-Unis d'Amérique
Chile	130.5	133.0	133.7	166.0	e162.4	Chili
Canada	93.8	88.5	120.9	137.1	128.8	Canada
China	121.3	113.2	120.9	105.9	91.3	Chine
South Africa	–	–	151.2	172.0	186.4	Afrique du Sud
Germany	97.6	89.8	71.2	62.1	60.4	Allemagne
Southern African Customs Union	141.1	139.4	–	–	–	Union douanière d'Afrique australe
Brazil	38.5	36.6	52.5	48.6	e50.4	Brésil
France-Monaco	41.7	45.5	45.1	37.9	43.6	France-Monaco
Thailand	19.2	25.3	29.7	39.6	e41.8	Thaïlande
New Zealand	30.7	22.2	26.9	34.3	30.1	Nouvelle-Zélande
Estonia	17.9	18.4	20.5	25.5	36.0	Estonie
Austria	19.3	23.3	23.2	23.2	28.8	Autriche
Belgium	–	25.4	20.2	26.8	e30.0	Belgique
Latvia	6.9	9.6	15.4	23.6	38.0	Lettonie
Russian Federation	20.8	18.4	16.2	18.1	17.3	Fédération de Russie
Viet Nam	e	e	26.4	27.5	30.5	Viet Nam
Netherlands	13.8	16.8	13.9	13.2	21.4	Pays-Bas
Sweden	12.9	13.5	12.7	14.4	16.3	Suède
Indonesia	2.4	8.9	9.1	17.3	23.6	Indonésie
Fiji	e12.5	e14.9	11.5	10.3	11.3	Fidji
Malaysia	6.9	11.4	14.5	10.8	e11.5	Malaisie
Finland	9.3	7.5	8.3	11.6	16.5	Finlande
Czech Republic	6.9	9.2	8.1	8.3	8.7	République tchèque
Denmark	15.2	14.2	3.3	3.3	2.1	Danemark
Switzerland-Liechtenstein	8.1	7.6	6.4	5.8	6.8	Suisse-Liechtenstein
Mexico	4.4	7.5	6.1	6.2	3.4	Mexique
Poland	4.0	5.2	4.9	5.8	7.4	Pologne
Argentina	8.1	7.7	8.2	0.0	e0.0	Argentine

(Value as percentages of World total) **(Valeur en pourcentage du total mondial)**

Regions of the world	1993	1994	1995	1996	1997	1998	1999	2000	2001	2002	Régions du monde
World	100.0	100.0	100.0	100.0	100.0	100.0	100.0	100.0	100.0	100.0	Monde
Africa	1.5	4.8	5.3	5.1	6.6	7.8	7.8	8.2	9.8	10.4	Afrique
Americas	50.0	46.7	43.8	44.1	42.9	42.5	41.4	40.0	37.7	31.0	Amériques
- Northern America	38.3	35.3	31.9	33.3	33.0	32.0	30.9	29.1	25.1	18.8	- Amérique du Nord
- LAIA	11.8	11.4	11.9	10.8	9.9	10.3	10.3	10.8	12.5	12.1	- ALAI
- CACM	0.0	0.0	0.0	0.0	0.0	0.1	0.2	0.1	0.1	0.1	- MCC
- Caribbean	0.0	0.0	0.0	0.0	0.0	0.0	0.0	0.0	0.0	0.0	- Caraïbes
- Rest of America	0.0	0.0	0.0	0.0	0.0	0.0	0.0	0.0	0.0	0.0	- Autre d'Amérique
Asia excluding former USSR	7.3	7.6	11.2	11.6	11.6	8.4	9.2	11.1	11.7	11.5	Asie ancienne URSS exclus
- Middle East	0.0	0.0	0.0	0.0	0.0	0.0	0.0	0.0	0.1	0.1	- Moyen-Orient
Asia former USSR	0.0	0.0	0.0	0.0	0.0	0.0	0.0	0.0	0.0	0.0	Asie ancienne URSS
Europe excluding former USSR	13.9	14.8	15.3	14.3	12.8	14.6	15.6	12.9	13.4	15.4	Europe ancienne URSS exclus
- European Union	12.6	13.4	13.9	12.8	11.2	13.1	13.9	11.5	11.7	13.4	- Union Européenne
- Eastern Europe	0.7	0.7	0.7	0.9	0.9	0.7	1.0	0.9	1.0	1.2	- Europe de l'Est
- Rest of Europe	0.5	0.6	0.7	0.7	0.7	0.7	0.7	0.6	0.7	0.9	- Autre de l'Europe
Europe former USSR	2.2	1.2	1.0	1.4	1.7	2.5	2.6	2.9	4.0	5.3	Europe ancienne URSS
Oceania	25.1	24.9	23.2	23.5	24.4	24.2	23.4	24.9	23.5	26.4	Océanie

247 Other wood in the rough or roughly squared

TRADE BY COMMODITY (Value in million US dollars)
Imports by principal countries or areas

COMMERCE PAR PRODUIT (Valeur en millions de dollars EU)
Importations selon les principaux pays ou zones

Country or area	1998	1999	2000	2001	2002	Pays ou zone
World	8568.6	9451.1	9891.3	9380.4	9407.0	Monde
Africa	129.1	131.1	126.9	104.9	106.8	Afrique
Americas	581.1	601.3	721.0	678.6	673.8	Amériques
- Northern America	514.1	558.0	660.1	630.9	639.9	- Amérique du Nord
- LAIA	32.3	24.0	41.2	27.9	16.6	- ALAI
- CACM	4.6	2.8	5.3	2.0	1.8	- MCC
- Caribbean	28.7	15.0	13.0	14.2	14.1	- Caraïbes
- Rest of America	1.4	1.6	1.4	3.6	1.4	- Autre d'Amérique
Asia excluding former USSR	4209.4	5418.7	5938.4	5335.7	5395.1	Asie ancienne URSS exclus
- Middle East	172.3	145.3	188.9	138.0	155.5	- Moyen-Orient
Asia former USSR	7.7	3.9	5.3	7.0	7.4	Asie ancienne URSS
Europe excluding former USSR	3599.7	3252.3	3050.6	3196.2	3153.7	Europe ancienne URSS exclus
- European Union	3268.4	2936.0	2731.3	2912.0	2865.6	- Union Européenne
- Eastern Europe	81.5	93.8	105.0	102.2	103.3	- Europe de l'Est
- Rest of Europe	249.8	222.5	214.2	182.0	184.7	- Autre de l'Europe
Europe former USSR	37.5	39.9	40.8	50.5	65.4	Europe ancienne URSS
Oceania	4.0	3.9	8.3	7.4	4.8	Océanie
Japan	2117.3	2333.3	2330.7	1875.3	1599.7	Japon
China	599.1	1248.6	1655.6	1694.0	2138.3	Chine
Korea, Republic of	349.7	520.7	560.4	536.3	597.0	République de Corée
Italy-San Marino-Holy See	568.0	530.6	508.6	439.1	415.7	Italie-Saint-Marin-Saint-Siège
India	339.7	429.0	465.7	515.2	371.3	Inde
Finland	399.6	391.9	350.6	429.5	469.5	Finlande
Austria	343.4	465.7	432.4	372.6	399.6	Autriche
Canada	366.5	359.3	390.8	392.8	377.2	Canada
Germany	286.1	318.1	297.4	288.3	223.2	Allemagne
France-Monaco	292.5	286.7	279.3	248.5	228.7	France-Monaco
Sweden	435.2	54.0	45.9	365.6	395.3	Suède
Spain	232.1	244.8	258.3	271.3	226.0	Espagne
United States	141.2	192.0	268.6	237.2	262.2	Etats-Unis d'Amérique
China, Hong Kong SAR	241.1	215.7	193.7	133.4	88.0	Chine - RAS de Hong-Kong
Portugal	256.2	179.8	160.4	127.4	120.9	Portugal
Norway	187.2	153.7	147.3	126.3	121.7	Norvège
Belgium	–	167.9	152.9	127.7	e140.1	Belgique
Turkey	122.9	104.1	121.6	66.5	78.4	Turquie
Thailand	50.7	96.0	125.8	98.0	e102.2	Thaïlande
United Kingdom	117.4	86.2	75.9	82.7	90.1	Royaume-Uni
Denmark	82.0	70.0	52.2	44.5	36.5	Danemark
Malaysia	21.0	51.7	63.5	69.0	e75.4	Malaisie
Philippines	54.9	69.5	54.3	44.7	34.5	Philippines
Morocco	34.7	50.1	48.2	35.0	e36.9	Maroc
Indonesia	33.4	42.1	46.6	34.7	36.0	Indonésie
Czech Republic	36.1	36.1	40.8	34.2	42.4	République tchèque
Netherlands	40.7	38.6	34.3	36.5	36.6	Pays-Bas
Ireland	32.6	33.6	33.7	34.3	35.9	Irlande
Greece	39.7	35.1	28.8	27.2	e30.1	Grèce
Poland	21.0	30.3	36.1	39.9	30.5	Pologne

(Value as percentages of World total) **(Valeur en pourcentage du total mondial)**

Regions of the world	1993	1994	1995	1996	1997	1998	1999	2000	2001	2002	Régions du monde
World	100.0	100.0	100.0	100.0	100.0	100.0	100.0	100.0	100.0	100.0	Monde
Africa	0.9	1.2	1.3	1.4	1.4	1.5	1.4	1.3	1.1	1.1	Afrique
Americas	2.8	3.7	4.1	4.0	4.7	6.8	6.4	7.3	7.2	7.2	Amériques
- Northern America	2.5	3.3	3.9	3.7	4.3	6.0	5.9	6.7	6.7	6.8	- Amérique du Nord
- LAIA	0.2	0.3	0.1	0.1	0.2	0.4	0.3	0.4	0.3	0.2	- ALAI
- CACM	0.0	0.0	0.0	0.0	0.0	0.1	0.0	0.1	0.0	0.0	- MCC
- Caribbean	0.1	0.1	0.1	0.1	0.2	0.3	0.2	0.1	0.2	0.1	- Caraïbes
- Rest of America	0.0	0.0	0.0	0.0	0.0	0.0	0.0	0.0	0.0	0.0	- Autre d'Amérique
Asia excluding former USSR	76.9	68.9	61.0	65.8	63.6	49.1	57.3	60.0	56.9	57.4	Asie ancienne URSS exclus
- Middle East	3.0	1.9	1.4	1.7	1.6	2.0	1.5	1.9	1.5	1.7	- Moyen-Orient
Asia former USSR	0.0	0.1	0.1	0.2	0.1	0.1	0.0	0.1	0.1	0.1	Asie ancienne URSS
Europe excluding former USSR	19.3	25.8	33.2	28.5	30.0	42.0	34.4	30.8	34.1	33.5	Europe ancienne URSS exclus
- European Union	17.9	23.6	29.9	25.9	27.3	38.1	31.1	27.6	31.0	30.5	- Union Européenne
- Eastern Europe	0.6	0.4	0.7	0.6	0.6	1.0	1.0	1.1	1.1	1.1	- Europe de l'Est
- Rest of Europe	0.9	1.8	2.6	2.0	2.0	2.9	2.4	2.2	1.9	2.0	- Autre de l'Europe
Europe former USSR	0.1	0.2	0.2	0.2	0.2	0.4	0.4	0.4	0.5	0.7	Europe ancienne URSS
Oceania	0.0	0.0	0.0	0.0	0.0	0.0	0.0	0.1	0.1	0.1	Océanie

TRADE BY COMMODITY (Value in million US dollars)
Exports by principal countries or areas

COMMERCE PAR PRODUIT (Valeur en millions de dollars EU)
Exportations selon les principaux pays ou zones

Country or area	1998	1999	2000	2001	2002	Pays ou zone
World	6693.6	7366.3	7814.4	6909.2	7210.4	Monde
Africa	748.9	580.8	654.7	578.4	600.9	Afrique
Americas	1750.2	1816.5	2001.5	1760.2	1824.5	Amériques
- Northern America	1602.2	1674.9	1860.2	1635.9	1696.1	- Amérique du Nord
- LAIA	138.0	137.9	136.0	118.9	119.2	- ALAI
- CACM	9.0	2.0	1.4	1.8	4.1	- MCC
- Caribbean	0.2	0.1	0.2	0.0	0.0	- Caraïbes
- Rest of America	0.7	1.6	3.7	3.6	5.1	- Autre d'Amérique
Asia excluding former USSR	976.2	1273.7	1239.9	920.6	885.8	Asie ancienne URSS exclus
- Middle East	10.2	7.9	7.1	7.9	10.7	- Moyen-Orient
Asia former USSR	0.5	4.3	7.1	3.4	3.1	Asie ancienne URSS
Europe excluding former USSR	1607.9	1706.3	1695.0	1486.8	1379.2	Europe ancienne URSS exclus
- European Union	1170.4	1194.9	1181.9	1035.3	940.3	- Union Européenne
- Eastern Europe	272.6	335.6	277.1	246.5	255.2	- Europe de l'Est
- Rest of Europe	164.9	175.8	236.0	205.0	183.7	- Autre de l'Europe
Europe former USSR	1271.6	1563.1	1723.3	1723.6	2010.1	Europe ancienne URSS
Oceania	338.4	421.6	492.9	436.3	506.7	Océanie
United States	1399.6	1388.2	1498.6	1289.0	1250.9	Etats-Unis d'Amérique
Russian Federation	937.1	1203.6	1338.3	1388.2	1647.8	Fédération de Russie
Malaysia	481.7	709.5	664.5	412.1	e436.7	Malaisie
Germany	355.1	390.8	363.4	347.0	290.4	Allemagne
Canada	202.6	286.6	361.4	346.9	445.2	Canada
Gabon	e453.8	259.3	291.8	e296.9	e305.5	Gabon
New Zealand	219.5	289.1	329.3	297.5	359.2	Nouvelle-Zélande
France-Monaco	295.1	282.8	384.4	263.8	210.4	France-Monaco
Myanmar	e170.4	e249.8	e274.8	e244.0	e288.8	Myanmar
China, Hong Kong SAR	220.3	203.5	185.8	139.4	86.9	Chine - RAS de Hong-Kong
Estonia	151.9	145.0	135.5	107.4	100.6	Estonie
Switzerland-Liechtenstein	93.5	97.5	162.5	129.0	98.8	Suisse-Liechtenstein
Czech Republic	134.7	146.2	91.1	98.0	108.7	République tchèque
Latvia	89.6	89.9	117.8	104.0	117.9	Lettonie
Congo	e114.1	e98.5	e99.1	e83.1	e112.8	Congo
Belgium	–	128.0	96.4	72.1	e80.9	Belgique
Equatorial Guinea	e65.3	e101.9	e88.1	e65.7	e48.9	Guinée équatoriale
Austria	72.8	83.4	63.6	67.9	67.8	Autriche
Finland	76.8	80.4	65.3	51.0	56.6	Finlande
Ukraine	42.2	72.3	70.2	59.5	65.6	Ukraine
Solomon Islands	e31.8	e60.6	e76.3	e69.2	e60.6	Iles Salomon
Sweden	83.1	30.9	23.5	65.0	94.0	Suède
Hungary	54.7	54.8	50.1	47.3	45.1	Hongrie
Chile	34.2	60.0	54.7	48.2	e47.2	Chili
Slovakia	31.5	51.2	54.9	57.1	47.2	Slovaquie
Denmark	36.8	56.5	69.6	40.4	21.4	Danemark
Cameroon	e55.7	e53.0	60.9	25.2	26.8	Cameroun
Portugal	41.8	41.1	35.3	48.1	48.8	Portugal
Papua New Guinea	67.8	e34.9	43.7	e32.9	e28.1	Papouasie-Nouvelle-Guinée
Lithuania	28.4	32.7	40.3	41.8	e50.6	Lituanie

(Value as percentages of World total) **(Valeur en pourcentage du total mondial)**

Regions of the world	1993	1994	1995	1996	1997	1998	1999	2000	2001	2002	Régions du monde
World	100.0	100.0	100.0	100.0	100.0	100.0	100.0	100.0	100.0	100.0	Monde
Africa	6.1	8.8	9.6	10.2	11.3	11.2	7.9	8.4	8.4	8.3	Afrique
Americas	37.6	35.5	32.6	32.6	28.3	26.1	24.7	25.6	25.5	25.3	Amériques
- Northern America	35.3	32.9	29.0	29.8	24.8	23.9	22.7	23.8	23.7	23.5	- Amérique du Nord
- LAIA	2.2	2.5	3.4	2.6	3.0	2.1	1.9	1.7	1.7	1.7	- ALAI
- CACM	0.2	0.2	0.1	0.2	0.2	0.1	0.0	0.0	0.0	0.1	- MCC
- Caribbean	0.0	0.0	0.0	0.0	0.0	0.0	0.0	0.0	0.0	0.0	- Caraïbes
- Rest of America	0.0	0.1	0.0	0.1	0.3	0.0	0.0	0.0	0.1	0.1	- Autre d'Amérique
Asia excluding former USSR	18.2	17.2	17.2	16.3	16.8	14.6	17.3	15.9	13.3	12.3	Asie ancienne URSS exclus
- Middle East	0.1	0.1	0.0	0.1	0.1	0.2	0.1	0.1	0.1	0.1	- Moyen-Orient
Asia former USSR	0.1	0.0	0.0	0.0	0.0	0.0	0.1	0.1	0.0	0.0	Asie ancienne URSS
Europe excluding former USSR	16.1	19.2	20.4	17.9	19.1	24.0	23.2	21.7	21.5	19.1	Europe ancienne URSS exclus
- European Union	11.1	13.6	15.0	12.7	13.3	17.5	16.2	15.1	15.0	13.0	- Union Européenne
- Eastern Europe	3.2	3.7	3.4	3.3	3.6	4.1	4.6	3.5	3.6	3.5	- Europe de l'Est
- Rest of Europe	1.8	1.9	2.0	1.9	2.2	2.5	2.4	3.0	3.0	2.5	- Autre de l'Europe
Europe former USSR	14.1	11.1	13.1	13.6	15.7	19.0	21.2	22.1	24.9	27.9	Europe ancienne URSS
Oceania	7.9	8.1	7.0	9.4	8.8	5.1	5.7	6.3	6.3	7.0	Océanie

248 Wood, simply worked, and railway sleepers of wood

TRADE BY COMMODITY (Value in million US dollars)
Imports by principal countries or areas

COMMERCE PAR PRODUIT (Valeur en millions de dollars EU)
Importations selon les principaux pays ou zones

Country or area	1998	1999	2000	2001	2002	Pays ou zone
World	26669.5	29220.0	29172.1	26726.7	27351.3	Monde
Africa	1090.2	1001.1	1003.3	993.4	1029.8	Afrique
Americas	9087.2	10423.9	9800.8	9485.2	9497.7	Amériques
- Northern America	8435.4	9797.1	9116.2	8789.0	8830.4	- Amérique du Nord
- LAIA	379.7	376.5	437.0	450.5	458.8	- ALAI
- CACM	19.3	19.3	21.7	35.0	18.7	- MCC
- Caribbean	251.5	228.3	222.1	207.7	186.7	- Caraïbes
- Rest of America	1.2	2.8	3.8	3.1	3.2	- Autre d'Amérique
Asia excluding former USSR	5206.7	6419.1	7042.9	6224.0	6208.5	Asie ancienne URSS exclus
- Middle East	508.1	494.7	518.8	537.6	540.5	- Moyen-Orient
Asia former USSR	74.6	45.9	67.0	68.7	74.3	Asie ancienne URSS
Europe excluding former USSR	10784.5	10884.4	10668.0	9566.1	10038.4	Europe ancienne URSS exclus
- European Union	9810.3	9963.4	9711.1	8641.4	9017.2	- Union Européenne
- Eastern Europe	244.1	259.9	301.2	308.3	374.5	- Europe de l'Est
- Rest of Europe	730.0	661.1	655.8	616.4	646.7	- Autre de l'Europe
Europe former USSR	88.2	75.5	88.4	109.1	136.5	Europe ancienne URSS
Oceania	338.1	370.1	501.6	280.2	366.2	Océanie
United States	7812.8	9093.4	8336.3	8126.6	8096.0	Etats-Unis d'Amérique
Japan	2588.7	3260.2	3542.1	2971.5	2701.4	Japon
Italy-San Marino-Holy See	1866.9	1920.0	1825.1	1624.5	1694.0	Italie-Saint-Marin-Saint-Siège
United Kingdom	1808.7	1763.3	1825.8	1675.4	1844.6	Royaume-Uni
Germany	1561.2	1515.1	1219.0	1009.5	993.2	Allemagne
China	365.7	673.9	989.8	997.8	1183.5	Chine
France-Monaco	790.3	817.9	873.0	806.7	829.8	France-Monaco
Netherlands	794.8	902.9	908.9	748.1	759.2	Pays-Bas
Spain	751.4	831.4	801.6	792.3	803.9	Espagne
Canada	618.8	698.5	776.9	658.9	728.8	Canada
Denmark	576.1	541.7	526.3	458.2	474.9	Danemark
China, Hong Kong SAR	466.9	566.7	545.9	466.1	488.5	Chine - RAS de Hong-Kong
Belgium	–	616.6	688.1	555.7	e609.4	Belgique
Egypt	553.3	473.2	e464.3	422.8	408.7	Egypte
Mexico	236.7	264.4	339.6	352.7	388.3	Mexique
Australia	299.4	311.1	432.8	224.3	304.3	Australie
Austria	283.3	307.9	295.5	274.4	291.4	Autriche
Norway	299.5	261.9	275.0	262.3	277.5	Norvège
Korea, Republic of	201.9	289.3	278.4	257.6	263.1	République de Corée
Thailand	165.3	201.6	234.7	245.7	e255.9	Thaïlande
Ireland	209.6	209.6	228.7	207.1	204.2	Irlande
Switzerland-Liechtenstein	211.5	202.4	188.1	173.5	167.1	Suisse-Liechtenstein
Algeria	155.8	153.9	163.7	e198.0	e225.5	Algérie
Greece	191.2	163.8	148.7	142.2	e157.3	Grèce
Portugal	130.2	154.8	141.8	128.1	131.4	Portugal
Morocco	136.0	138.6	122.0	124.1	e130.9	Maroc
Belgium-Luxembourg	649.4	–	–	–	–	Belgique-Luxembourg
Saudi Arabia	104.7	101.3	136.5	149.9	e155.1	Arabie saoudite
Hungary	102.4	111.8	128.2	129.2	161.5	Hongrie
Sweden	124.4	121.4	127.7	121.2	132.8	Suède

(Value as percentages of World total) **(Valeur en pourcentage du total mondial)**

Regions of the world	1993	1994	1995	1996	1997	1998	1999	2000	2001	2002	Régions du monde
World	100.0	100.0	100.0	100.0	100.0	100.0	100.0	100.0	100.0	100.0	Monde
Africa	2.4	3.3	4.2	3.4	3.6	4.1	3.4	3.4	3.7	3.8	Afrique
Americas	27.7	28.1	25.1	30.2	31.6	34.1	35.7	33.6	35.5	34.7	Amériques
- Northern America	25.5	26.2	23.5	28.6	29.6	31.6	33.5	31.2	32.9	32.3	- Amérique du Nord
- LAIA	1.6	1.4	0.9	0.9	1.0	1.4	1.3	1.5	1.7	1.7	- ALAI
- CACM	0.0	0.0	0.0	0.1	0.2	0.1	0.1	0.1	0.1	0.1	- MCC
- Caribbean	0.6	0.5	0.7	0.7	0.8	0.9	0.8	0.8	0.8	0.7	- Caraïbes
- Rest of America	0.0	0.0	0.0	0.0	0.0	0.0	0.0	0.0	0.0	0.0	- Autre d'Amérique
Asia excluding former USSR	32.4	27.6	29.8	29.1	27.3	19.5	22.0	24.1	23.3	22.7	Asie ancienne URSS exclus
- Middle East	2.0	1.8	1.9	1.5	1.3	1.9	1.7	1.8	2.0	2.0	- Moyen-Orient
Asia former USSR	0.0	0.4	0.3	0.4	0.2	0.3	0.2	0.2	0.3	0.3	Asie ancienne URSS
Europe excluding former USSR	35.4	38.6	38.9	35.4	35.8	40.4	37.2	36.6	35.8	36.7	Europe ancienne URSS exclus
- European Union	33.1	35.9	35.6	32.4	32.9	36.8	34.1	33.3	32.3	33.0	- Union Européenne
- Eastern Europe	0.5	0.5	0.7	0.7	0.7	0.9	0.9	1.0	1.2	1.4	- Europe de l'Est
- Rest of Europe	1.7	2.3	2.6	2.3	2.2	2.7	2.3	2.2	2.3	2.4	- Autre de l'Europe
Europe former USSR	0.1	0.2	0.2	0.1	0.2	0.3	0.3	0.3	0.4	0.5	Europe ancienne URSS
Oceania	2.0	1.7	1.5	1.3	1.3	1.3	1.3	1.7	1.0	1.3	Océanie

TRADE BY COMMODITY (Value in million US dollars)
Exports by principal countries or areas

COMMERCE PAR PRODUIT (Valeur en millions de dollars EU)
Exportations selon les principaux pays ou zones

Country or area	1998	1999	2000	2001	2002	Pays ou zone
World	24517.4	25385.1	24953.9	24464.9	25319.0	Monde
Africa	630.3	613.7	660.4	685.6	593.7	Afrique
Americas	11610.0	13089.4	12453.7	11348.2	10888.7	Amériques
- Northern America	10393.3	11673.1	11018.1	9789.1	9288.1	- Amérique du Nord
- LAIA	1170.6	1355.0	1378.7	1475.9	1518.7	- ALAI
- CACM	29.3	42.6	38.8	61.8	60.2	- MCC
- Caribbean	1.5	1.2	1.2	1.1	0.9	- Caraïbes
- Rest of America	15.4	17.6	16.9	20.2	20.9	- Autre d'Amérique
Asia excluding former USSR	2008.6	2359.4	2594.0	2274.4	2481.3	Asie ancienne URSS exclus
- Middle East	32.9	31.8	23.9	52.8	47.4	- Moyen-Orient
Asia former USSR	3.7	8.0	10.7	9.9	9.2	Asie ancienne URSS
Europe excluding former USSR	8687.6	7445.0	7151.4	8146.9	8934.7	Europe ancienne URSS exclus
- European Union	7196.6	5812.9	5494.2	6667.6	7362.2	- Union Européenne
- Eastern Europe	962.4	1060.8	1096.0	971.9	1057.9	- Europe de l'Est
- Rest of Europe	528.6	571.2	561.2	507.4	514.6	- Autre de l'Europe
Europe former USSR	1225.2	1441.8	1628.6	1571.8	1876.2	Europe ancienne URSS
Oceania	351.9	427.8	455.2	428.1	535.2	Océanie
Canada	8168.2	9244.9	8532.3	7765.4	7318.5	Canada
United States	2224.9	2428.0	2485.6	2023.7	1969.5	Etats-Unis d'Amérique
Finland	1597.2	1551.1	1469.3	1356.8	1422.8	Finlande
Sweden	2258.4	557.1	420.2	1901.1	2175.2	Suède
Austria	1043.2	1206.4	1103.3	1031.1	1134.7	Autriche
Malaysia	860.7	979.4	1067.5	806.0	e854.2	Malaisie
Germany	716.7	777.7	777.1	822.8	924.9	Allemagne
Russian Federation	575.5	644.0	756.2	712.4	886.9	Fédération de Russie
Brazil	456.2	568.6	621.1	621.2	e644.0	Brésil
Chile	360.8	456.3	455.0	566.1	e553.8	Chili
China, Hong Kong SAR	390.3	473.9	476.2	380.2	406.0	Chine - RAS de Hong-Kong
France-Monaco	419.6	406.8	409.5	366.6	388.1	France-Monaco
New Zealand	312.0	377.9	401.2	374.0	481.1	Nouvelle-Zélande
Latvia	334.9	385.7	406.8	368.3	396.1	Lettonie
Romania	266.3	325.9	377.8	334.2	381.5	Roumanie
Italy-San Marino-Holy See	309.3	351.6	346.8	306.5	309.5	Italie-Saint-Marin-Saint-Siège
Belgium	–	347.5	402.3	343.4	e385.3	Belgique
Indonesia	153.2	241.3	292.4	317.3	375.4	Indonésie
China	156.8	221.6	278.9	291.2	315.3	Chine
Czech Republic	214.5	252.0	235.2	218.3	211.1	République tchèque
Côte d'Ivoire	229.4	195.4	239.8	e261.5	160.9	Côte d'Ivoire
Cameroon	e213.9	e203.7	234.1	226.9	203.6	Cameroun
Poland	227.5	226.6	233.2	175.3	197.4	Pologne
Estonia	126.7	173.3	161.7	161.1	206.3	Estonie
Netherlands	166.2	180.8	173.7	149.6	154.4	Pays-Bas
Slovakia	135.8	128.3	127.4	123.4	136.5	Slovaquie
Mexico	168.3	159.3	126.9	101.2	91.7	Mexique
Croatia	129.5	136.6	132.7	116.9	129.3	Croatie
Bosnia and Herzegovina	e77.8	e126.4	e152.0	e140.9	e126.4	Bosnie-Herzégovine
Norway	137.3	147.3	113.6	94.5	106.1	Norvège

(Value as percentages of World total) **(Valeur en pourcentage du total mondial)**

Regions of the world	1993	1994	1995	1996	1997	1998	1999	2000	2001	2002	Régions du monde
World	100.0	100.0	100.0	100.0	100.0	100.0	100.0	100.0	100.0	100.0	Monde
Africa	2.3	2.0	2.6	2.3	1.9	2.6	2.4	2.6	2.8	2.3	Afrique
Americas	49.6	48.8	45.3	49.9	50.2	47.4	51.6	49.9	46.4	43.0	Amériques
- Northern America	46.1	45.0	41.2	45.5	45.2	42.4	46.0	44.2	40.0	36.7	- Amérique du Nord
- LAIA	3.4	3.6	4.0	4.2	4.8	4.8	5.3	5.5	6.0	6.0	- ALAI
- CACM	0.1	0.1	0.1	0.1	0.1	0.1	0.2	0.2	0.3	0.2	- MCC
- Caribbean	0.0	0.0	0.0	0.0	0.0	0.0	0.0	0.0	0.0	0.0	- Caraïbes
- Rest of America	0.0	0.0	0.0	0.0	0.1	0.1	0.1	0.1	0.1	0.1	- Autre d'Amérique
Asia excluding former USSR	15.2	12.5	12.5	11.0	9.7	8.2	9.3	10.4	9.3	9.8	Asie ancienne URSS exclus
- Middle East	0.2	0.2	0.1	0.1	0.1	0.1	0.1	0.1	0.2	0.2	- Moyen-Orient
Asia former USSR	0.0	0.0	0.0	0.0	0.0	0.0	0.0	0.0	0.0	0.0	Asie ancienne URSS
Europe excluding former USSR	28.2	32.6	34.8	31.6	32.2	35.4	29.3	28.7	33.3	35.3	Europe ancienne URSS exclus
- European Union	23.5	27.5	29.4	26.5	27.0	29.4	22.9	22.0	27.3	29.1	- Union Européenne
- Eastern Europe	2.7	3.2	3.4	3.4	3.4	3.9	4.2	4.4	4.0	4.2	- Europe de l'Est
- Rest of Europe	2.0	2.0	2.1	1.7	1.9	2.2	2.3	2.2	2.1	2.0	- Autre de l'Europe
Europe former USSR	3.3	2.7	3.4	4.0	4.5	5.0	5.7	6.5	6.4	7.4	Europe ancienne URSS
Oceania	1.4	1.4	1.4	1.3	1.4	1.4	1.7	1.8	1.7	2.1	Océanie

251 Pulp and waste paper

TRADE BY COMMODITY (Value in million US dollars)
Imports by principal countries or areas

COMMERCE PAR PRODUIT (Valeur en millions de dollars EU)
Importations selon les principaux pays ou zones

Country or area	1998	1999	2000	2001	2002	Pays ou zone
World	18628.0	19776.3	27155.7	21743.8	21372.6	Monde
Africa	150.3	141.6	156.7	132.5	143.9	Afrique
Americas	3826.2	4098.5	5237.3	4159.3	3888.8	Amériques
- Northern America	2916.7	3097.2	4001.7	3099.9	2862.3	- Amérique du Nord
- LAIA	874.0	964.6	1189.2	1009.6	973.3	- ALAI
- CACM	20.8	21.3	26.4	34.0	38.6	- MCC
- Caribbean	12.3	12.8	16.4	12.9	10.9	- Caraïbes
- Rest of America	2.4	2.7	3.6	2.8	3.7	- Autre d'Amérique
Asia excluding former USSR	5856.7	6799.5	9695.1	7794.8	7800.4	Asie ancienne URSS exclus
- Middle East	241.6	254.0	373.6	290.4	309.7	- Moyen-Orient
Asia former USSR	2.3	2.2	1.4	2.1	3.2	Asie ancienne URSS
Europe excluding former USSR	8585.1	8484.4	11725.6	9420.3	9291.4	Europe ancienne URSS exclus
- European Union	7884.8	7721.8	10676.5	8654.5	8464.6	- Union Européenne
- Eastern Europe	315.4	340.4	460.9	349.6	414.5	- Europe de l'Est
- Rest of Europe	384.9	422.2	588.2	416.2	412.2	- Autre de l'Europe
Europe former USSR	96.4	111.2	123.2	98.4	104.9	Europe ancienne URSS
Oceania	111.1	138.9	216.3	136.5	140.1	Océanie
United States	2579.1	2732.2	3513.6	2749.6	2481.8	Etats-Unis d'Amérique
Germany	2195.8	2007.1	2717.7	2415.2	2293.8	Allemagne
China	1094.5	1659.7	2677.9	2734.5	2899.9	Chine
Italy-San Marino-Holy See	1536.4	1574.0	2072.7	1609.0	1557.4	Italie-Saint-Marin-Saint-Siège
Japan	1618.9	1526.6	1985.4	1359.6	1140.1	Japon
Korea, Republic of	973.7	1228.9	1686.3	1195.0	1217.9	République de Corée
France-Monaco	1086.4	1138.2	1725.9	1162.4	1115.8	France-Monaco
United Kingdom	885.1	912.8	1249.8	963.2	822.4	Royaume-Uni
Indonesia	612.8	647.4	1064.8	713.7	629.3	Indonésie
Netherlands	717.6	682.7	771.8	601.0	642.6	Pays-Bas
Mexico	424.1	491.9	597.3	532.0	557.7	Mexique
Belgium	–	391.9	752.0	620.1	e680.1	Belgique
Spain	350.0	339.5	492.5	422.3	441.8	Espagne
Austria	348.3	341.8	480.1	354.3	408.6	Autriche
Canada	337.3	364.7	488.0	350.2	380.4	Canada
Thailand	252.9	307.1	425.7	300.2	e312.8	Thaïlande
India	236.0	255.0	287.0	297.8	341.8	Inde
Switzerland-Liechtenstein	224.5	242.9	326.9	241.4	228.3	Suisse-Liechtenstein
Brazil	191.4	203.1	249.8	196.7	185.1	Brésil
Turkey	153.3	164.2	236.6	149.0	191.1	Turquie
Sweden	189.9	80.3	96.6	200.2	238.0	Suède
Australia	107.9	130.8	213.4	127.8	136.8	Australie
Poland	87.8	121.6	175.8	142.5	170.4	Pologne
Slovenia	82.7	85.8	130.3	95.7	102.2	Slovénie
Philippines	86.9	106.3	128.4	80.9	61.9	Philippines
Venezuela	87.0	99.0	121.3	81.8	e68.8	Venezuela
Finland	67.7	75.6	95.2	111.9	81.3	Finlande
Hungary	82.3	82.3	111.4	61.5	80.1	Hongrie
Czech Republic	83.1	81.1	89.4	76.2	85.4	République tchèque
Colombia	57.7	58.1	89.2	75.0	73.3	Colombie

(Value as percentages of World total) **(Valeur en pourcentage du total mondial)**

Regions of the world	1993	1994	1995	1996	1997	1998	1999	2000	2001	2002	Régions du monde
World	100.0	100.0	100.0	100.0	100.0	100.0	100.0	100.0	100.0	100.0	Monde
Africa	0.9	0.9	0.9	1.0	0.7	0.8	0.7	0.6	0.6	0.7	Afrique
Americas	20.8	20.0	20.1	18.8	20.5	20.5	20.7	19.3	19.1	18.2	Amériques
- Northern America	15.9	15.3	15.5	15.0	15.9	15.7	15.7	14.7	14.3	13.4	- Amérique du Nord
- LAIA	4.7	4.5	4.5	3.6	4.4	4.7	4.9	4.4	4.6	4.6	- ALAI
- CACM	0.1	0.1	0.1	0.1	0.1	0.1	0.1	0.1	0.2	0.2	- MCC
- Caribbean	0.0	0.0	0.1	0.0	0.0	0.1	0.1	0.1	0.1	0.1	- Caraïbes
- Rest of America	0.0	0.0	0.0	0.0	0.0	0.0	0.0	0.0	0.0	0.0	- Autre d'Amérique
Asia excluding former USSR	34.5	31.5	31.2	34.3	32.4	31.4	34.4	35.7	35.8	36.5	Asie ancienne URSS exclus
- Middle East	1.1	0.9	1.1	1.0	1.2	1.3	1.3	1.4	1.3	1.4	- Moyen-Orient
Asia former USSR	0.0	0.0	0.0	0.0	0.0	0.0	0.0	0.0	0.0	0.0	Asie ancienne URSS
Europe excluding former USSR	43.1	46.7	47.0	44.8	45.3	46.1	42.9	43.2	43.3	43.5	Europe ancienne URSS exclus
- European Union	39.8	43.1	43.3	41.1	41.6	42.3	39.0	39.3	39.8	39.6	- Union Européenne
- Eastern Europe	1.2	1.2	1.4	1.7	1.7	1.7	1.7	1.7	1.6	1.9	- Europe de l'Est
- Rest of Europe	2.1	2.3	2.3	2.0	2.1	2.1	2.1	2.2	1.9	1.9	- Autre de l'Europe
Europe former USSR	0.1	0.2	0.2	0.5	0.6	0.5	0.6	0.5	0.5	0.5	Europe ancienne URSS
Oceania	0.7	0.6	0.6	0.6	0.5	0.6	0.7	0.8	0.6	0.7	Océanie

TRADE BY COMMODITY (Value in million US dollars)
Exports by principal countries or areas

COMMERCE PAR PRODUIT (Valeur en millions de dollars EU)
Exportations selon les principaux pays ou zones

Country or area	1998	1999	2000	2001	2002	Pays ou zone
World	16794.3	16829.0	22606.7	18877.5	19286.9	Monde
Africa	381.1	418.5	625.3	421.5	489.6	Afrique
Americas	9968.3	10873.3	14404.0	10944.3	10916.9	Amériques
- Northern America	8080.8	8719.0	11470.8	8481.3	8436.9	- Amérique du Nord
- LAIA	1874.2	2148.3	2921.3	2452.8	2469.2	- ALAI
- CACM	4.1	4.1	9.7	7.8	8.8	- MCC
- Caribbean	9.1	1.9	1.8	1.8	1.1	- Caraïbes
- Rest of America	0.1	0.0	0.4	0.6	0.9	- Autre d'Amérique
Asia excluding former USSR	1089.6	858.1	1271.6	1061.9	1243.6	Asie ancienne URSS exclus
- Middle East	15.8	19.9	24.7	27.7	28.4	- Moyen-Orient
Asia former USSR	0.3	0.7	0.5	0.6	1.0	Asie ancienne URSS
Europe excluding former USSR	4759.9	4070.1	5377.3	5643.4	5805.6	Europe ancienne URSS exclus
- European Union	4285.8	3589.7	4754.5	5115.5	5268.4	- Union Européenne
- Eastern Europe	197.5	191.5	279.9	214.9	229.8	- Europe de l'Est
- Rest of Europe	276.6	288.9	342.9	312.9	307.5	- Autre de l'Europe
Europe former USSR	367.0	379.7	599.1	531.3	564.8	Europe ancienne URSS
Oceania	228.1	228.5	328.8	274.5	265.4	Océanie
Canada	4596.0	5102.8	6756.8	4712.1	4496.8	Canada
United States	3484.8	3616.2	4714.0	3769.0	3939.8	Etats-Unis d'Amérique
Brazil	1049.4	1243.6	1602.4	1247.6	e1293.4	Brésil
Sweden	1322.8	179.2	196.0	1527.9	1485.0	Suède
Chile	693.7	768.3	1113.8	1068.2	e1045.1	Chili
Finland	716.5	819.9	983.6	810.3	874.2	Finlande
Indonesia	690.0	476.1	714.0	566.7	709.3	Indonésie
Germany	417.5	443.1	668.7	522.9	553.5	Allemagne
Russian Federation	356.8	372.0	587.1	519.9	556.8	Fédération de Russie
Portugal	451.8	503.8	555.9	424.6	403.5	Portugal
Spain	309.1	372.0	510.1	375.4	348.5	Espagne
Belgium	–	314.8	585.3	468.3	e525.4	Belgique
France-Monaco	321.7	305.1	389.0	303.7	337.2	France-Monaco
Netherlands	264.4	321.1	423.3	297.7	290.9	Pays-Bas
New Zealand	213.2	208.6	297.6	247.1	237.5	Nouvelle-Zélande
South Africa	–	–	493.2	307.1	276.1	Afrique du Sud
Austria	145.1	184.6	215.2	189.4	171.3	Autriche
Norway	171.7	175.5	174.8	179.9	176.2	Norvège
Southern African Customs Union	340.8	358.3	–	–	–	Union douanière d'Afrique australe
Czech Republic	106.7	109.8	172.6	129.1	135.7	République tchèque
Thailand	74.2	109.9	170.3	128.3	e135.5	Thaïlande
Japan	50.9	60.4	127.7	139.5	206.5	Japon
Argentina	99.4	95.6	155.5	103.2	e99.8	Argentine
United Kingdom	78.5	86.1	114.7	114.7	156.7	Royaume-Uni
Switzerland-Liechtenstein	69.2	80.1	114.1	84.2	88.6	Suisse-Liechtenstein
Singapore	155.7	80.8	66.1	64.6	27.5	Singapour
China, Hong Kong SAR	37.1	47.6	84.9	66.8	57.0	Chine - RAS de Hong-Kong
Belgium-Luxembourg	209.0	–	–	–	–	Belgique-Luxembourg
Swaziland	–	–	60.5	60.7	e84.1	Swaziland
Slovakia	38.8	37.1	42.0	32.7	37.0	Slovaquie

(Value as percentages of World total) **(Valeur en pourcentage du total mondial)**

Regions of the world	1993	1994	1995	1996	1997	1998	1999	2000	2001	2002	Régions du monde
World	100.0	100.0	100.0	100.0	100.0	100.0	100.0	100.0	100.0	100.0	Monde
Africa	2.7	2.7	2.5	2.2	2.5	2.3	2.5	2.8	2.2	2.5	Afrique
Americas	64.7	63.2	62.8	62.0	61.1	59.4	64.6	63.7	58.0	56.6	Amériques
- Northern America	54.4	53.1	52.2	51.4	50.6	48.1	51.8	50.7	44.9	43.7	- Amérique du Nord
- LAIA	10.3	10.0	10.6	10.5	10.4	11.2	12.8	12.9	13.0	12.8	- ALAI
- CACM	0.0	0.0	0.0	0.0	0.0	0.0	0.0	0.0	0.0	0.0	- MCC
- Caribbean	0.0	0.0	0.0	0.0	0.0	0.1	0.0	0.0	0.0	0.0	- Caraïbes
- Rest of America	0.0	0.0	0.0	0.0	0.0	0.0	0.0	0.0	0.0	0.0	- Autre d'Amérique
Asia excluding former USSR	1.8	2.3	3.5	3.9	4.3	6.5	5.1	5.6	5.6	6.4	Asie ancienne URSS exclus
- Middle East	0.2	0.2	0.1	0.1	0.1	0.1	0.1	0.1	0.1	0.1	- Moyen-Orient
Asia former USSR	0.0	0.0	0.0	0.0	0.0	0.0	0.0	0.0	0.0	0.0	Asie ancienne URSS
Europe excluding former USSR	26.4	28.2	28.2	27.7	28.7	28.3	24.2	23.8	29.9	30.1	Europe ancienne URSS exclus
- European Union	24.6	25.4	25.4	24.9	26.1	25.5	21.3	21.0	27.1	27.3	- Union Européenne
- Eastern Europe	1.1	1.1	1.1	1.1	1.0	1.2	1.1	1.2	1.1	1.2	- Europe de l'Est
- Rest of Europe	0.6	1.6	1.7	1.7	1.5	1.6	1.7	1.5	1.7	1.6	- Autre de l'Europe
Europe former USSR	2.7	2.1	1.6	2.6	2.2	2.2	2.3	2.7	2.8	2.9	Europe ancienne URSS
Oceania	1.6	1.6	1.4	1.6	1.3	1.4	1.4	1.5	1.5	1.4	Océanie

261 Silk

TRADE BY COMMODITY (Value in million US dollars)
Imports by principal countries or areas

COMMERCE PAR PRODUIT (Valeur en millions de dollars EU)
Importations selon les principaux pays ou zones

Country or area	1998	1999	2000	2001	2002	Pays ou zone
World	502.0	507.7	481.4	434.4	380.4	Monde
Africa	1.5	2.4	1.9	1.9	2.8	Afrique
Americas	1.9	2.8	2.7	3.1	3.7	Amériques
- Northern America	1.0	1.0	0.9	0.9	0.8	- Amérique du Nord
- LAIA	0.7	1.7	1.7	2.1	2.9	- ALAI
- CACM	0.0	0.0	0.0	0.0	0.0	- MCC
- Caribbean	0.1	0.0	0.0	0.0	0.0	- Caraïbes
- Rest of America	0.0	0.0	0.0	0.0	0.0	- Autre d'Amérique
Asia excluding former USSR	336.3	360.3	312.4	291.7	270.7	Asie ancienne URSS exclus
- Middle East	3.5	3.3	6.3	6.2	5.5	- Moyen-Orient
Asia former USSR	1.4	0.2	0.0	0.0	0.0	Asie ancienne URSS
Europe excluding former USSR	160.9	141.8	164.1	137.5	103.1	Europe ancienne URSS exclus
- European Union	155.6	137.5	157.5	131.5	91.4	- Union Européenne
- Eastern Europe	0.1	0.1	1.1	2.5	8.9	- Europe de l'Est
- Rest of Europe	5.3	4.2	5.5	3.5	2.7	- Autre de l'Europe
Europe former USSR	0.1	0.1	0.1	0.0	0.0	Europe ancienne URSS
Oceania	0.0	0.0	0.1	0.2	0.1	Océanie
India	63.1	96.4	106.0	134.2	135.2	Inde
Italy-San Marino-Holy See	101.5	94.7	108.5	92.9	63.1	Italie-Saint-Marin-Saint-Siège
Japan	73.2	77.3	87.1	60.6	48.9	Japon
Korea, Republic of	36.3	47.4	43.7	35.8	34.9	République de Corée
Bangladesh	65.1	e71.3	e14.8	14.4	e14.0	Bangladesh
Germany	33.9	29.5	33.8	21.8	14.7	Allemagne
China, Hong Kong SAR	37.3	21.3	14.6	4.2	1.0	Chine - RAS de Hong-Kong
Nepal	19.7	13.1	10.2	e9.7	e9.3	Népal
China	12.0	12.3	14.3	10.2	7.1	Chine
Thailand	12.8	11.0	9.0	11.1	e11.5	Thaïlande
France-Monaco	13.9	8.0	9.4	11.3	8.3	France-Monaco
Switzerland-Liechtenstein	5.0	4.2	5.4	3.5	2.7	Suisse-Liechtenstein
Singapore	10.6	2.8	1.9	2.5	0.8	Singapour
United Kingdom	3.4	2.4	3.8	3.4	2.9	Royaume-Uni
Turkey	2.5	2.2	2.8	3.8	2.9	Turquie
Romania	0.0	0.0	1.1	2.5	8.9	Roumanie
United Arab Emirates	0.9	0.9	3.3	2.4	e2.5	Emirates arabes unis
Tunisia	0.8	1.0	1.6	1.5	e1.5	Tunisie
Spain	1.7	1.4	1.1	1.2	0.8	Espagne
Myanmar	e0.7	e0.8	e1.0	e1.1	e0.9	Myanmar
United States	0.8	0.9	0.6	0.8	0.7	Etats-Unis d'Amérique
Egypt	0.5	1.2	e0.3	0.3	1.1	Egypte
Brazil	0.1	1.1	1.1	0.3	0.4	Brésil
Indonesia	0.3	0.8	1.0	0.4	0.4	Indonésie
Paraguay	0.5	0.2	0.2	0.9	0.6	Paraguay
Uruguay	0.0	0.0	0.1	0.4	1.5	Uruguay
Pakistan	0.4	0.4	0.5	0.3	0.4	Pakistan
Greece	0.3	0.4	0.3	0.4	e0.4	Grèce
Ireland	0.0	0.4	0.2	0.2	0.8	Irlande
Peru	0.0	0.4	0.3	0.3	0.3	Pérou

(Value as percentages of World total) **(Valeur en pourcentage du total mondial)**

Regions of the world	1993	1994	1995	1996	1997	1998	1999	2000	2001	2002	Régions du monde
World	100.0	100.0	100.0	100.0	100.0	100.0	100.0	100.0	100.0	100.0	Monde
Africa	0.4	0.2	0.5	0.7	0.3	0.3	0.5	0.4	0.4	0.7	Afrique
Americas	1.1	1.0	0.9	1.0	0.6	0.4	0.6	0.6	0.7	1.0	Amériques
- Northern America	1.0	0.9	0.7	0.9	0.5	0.2	0.2	0.2	0.2	0.2	- Amérique du Nord
- LAIA	0.0	0.1	0.1	0.0	0.2	0.1	0.3	0.4	0.5	0.8	- ALAI
- CACM	0.0	0.0	0.0	0.0	0.0	0.0	0.0	0.0	0.0	0.0	- MCC
- Caribbean	0.0	0.0	0.0	0.0	0.0	0.0	0.0	0.0	0.0	0.0	- Caraïbes
- Rest of America	0.0	0.0	0.0	0.0	0.0	0.0	0.0	0.0	0.0	0.0	- Autre d'Amérique
Asia excluding former USSR	73.1	67.8	68.1	70.7	68.1	67.0	71.0	64.9	67.1	71.2	Asie ancienne URSS exclus
- Middle East	0.7	0.4	0.5	0.8	1.0	0.7	0.6	1.3	1.4	1.4	- Moyen-Orient
Asia former USSR	0.0	0.1	0.4	0.4	0.3	0.3	0.0	0.0	0.0	0.0	Asie ancienne URSS
Europe excluding former USSR	25.3	30.8	30.0	27.3	30.7	32.1	27.9	34.1	31.7	27.1	Europe ancienne URSS exclus
- European Union	24.4	30.0	29.3	26.9	30.1	31.0	27.1	32.7	30.3	24.0	- Union Européenne
- Eastern Europe	0.1	0.0	0.0	0.0	0.0	0.0	0.0	0.2	0.6	2.4	- Europe de l'Est
- Rest of Europe	0.7	0.8	0.6	0.4	0.6	1.0	0.8	1.1	0.8	0.7	- Autre de l'Europe
Europe former USSR	0.1	0.0	0.1	0.1	0.0	0.0	0.0	0.0	0.0	0.0	Europe ancienne URSS
Oceania	0.0	0.0	0.0	0.0	0.0	0.0	0.0	0.0	0.0	0.0	Océanie

TRADE BY COMMODITY (Value in million US dollars)
Exports by principal countries or areas

COMMERCE PAR PRODUIT (Valeur en millions de dollars EU)
Exportations selon les principaux pays ou zones

Country or area	1998	1999	2000	2001	2002	Pays ou zone
World	393.0	376.0	425.3	352.1	322.5	Monde
Africa	0.1	0.4	0.0	0.0	0.0	Afrique
Americas	9.1	3.7	4.3	4.6	4.7	Amériques
- Northern America	1.3	1.4	2.2	2.4	2.3	- Amérique du Nord
- LAIA	7.9	2.3	2.0	2.2	2.3	- ALAI
- CACM	0.0	0.0	0.1	0.1	0.0	- MCC
- Caribbean	0.0	0.0	0.0	0.0	0.0	- Caraïbes
Asia excluding former USSR	330.6	327.6	376.7	309.7	284.6	Asie ancienne URSS exclus
- Middle East	3.3	3.6	4.0	2.1	1.8	- Moyen-Orient
Asia former USSR	11.4	10.3	6.9	8.2	6.8	Asie ancienne URSS
Europe excluding former USSR	41.1	30.2	33.9	29.1	25.3	Europe ancienne URSS exclus
- European Union	39.8	29.0	31.5	27.4	24.3	- Union Européenne
- Eastern Europe	0.0	0.0	0.0	0.0	0.2	- Europe de l'Est
- Rest of Europe	1.3	1.1	2.4	1.6	0.9	- Autre de l'Europe
Europe former USSR	0.4	0.0	0.0	0.0	0.0	Europe ancienne URSS
Oceania	0.1	3.8	3.5	0.5	1.1	Océanie
China	250.3	281.6	331.0	281.2	267.6	Chine
Germany	30.4	25.0	25.2	21.7	12.6	Allemagne
China, Hong Kong SAR	43.4	21.3	17.2	4.7	2.0	Chine - RAS de Hong-Kong
India	11.8	8.6	11.3	11.3	4.1	Inde
Uzbekistan	e2.6	e6.6	e2.6	e5.1	e3.8	Ouzbékistan
Italy-San Marino-Holy See	1.6	1.3	3.2	3.8	9.3	Italie-Saint-Marin-Saint-Siège
Thailand	3.6	4.6	4.2	3.3	e3.5	Thaïlande
Singapore	10.7	3.5	1.7	2.0	0.6	Singapour
Turkmenistan	5.7	3.1	3.5	e2.6	e2.5	Turkménistan
Brazil	7.3	2.1	1.3	2.1	e2.2	Brésil
United Arab Emirates	3.2	3.3	3.4	1.4	e1.5	Emirates arabes unis
United Kingdom	4.7	1.0	2.3	1.5	1.4	Royaume-Uni
United States	1.3	1.4	2.2	2.4	2.3	Etats-Unis d'Amérique
Australia	0.1	3.8	3.5	0.5	1.1	Australie
Korea, Democratic People's Republic of	e2.8	e1.9	e1.5	e1.1	e1.0	République démocratique populaire de Corée
Japan	2.8	1.5	2.2	1.1	0.6	Japon
Switzerland-Liechtenstein	1.3	1.1	2.4	1.6	0.8	Suisse-Liechtenstein
Viet Nam	0.0	0.0	1.2	1.3	1.4	Viet Nam
Spain	2.2	1.2	0.4	0.1	0.0	Espagne
Kyrgyzstan	1.7	0.5	e0.6	e0.4	0.3	Kirghizistan
Malaysia	0.2	0.2	0.9	0.3	e0.3	Malaisie
Azerbaijan	1.4	0.1	0.1	0.1	0.0	Azerbaïdjan
Korea, Republic of	0.9	0.3	0.3	0.1	0.0	République de Corée
Iran (Islamic Republic of)	0.1	0.1	0.2	0.7	0.2	Iran (République islamique d')
Pakistan	0.4	0.2	0.4	0.1	0.1	Pakistan
Paraguay	0.4	0.1	0.6	0.1	e0.1	Paraguay
Netherlands	0.4	0.2	0.1		0.5	Pays-Bas
France-Monaco	0.1	0.1	0.1	0.2	0.2	France-Monaco
Indonesia	0.1	0.2	0.1	0.1	0.2	Indonésie
Turkey	0.0	0.1	0.3	0.0	0.0	Turquie

(Value as percentages of World total) **(Valeur en pourcentage du total mondial)**

Regions of the world	1993	1994	1995	1996	1997	1998	1999	2000	2001	2002	Régions du monde
World	100.0	100.0	100.0	100.0	100.0	100.0	100.0	100.0	100.0	100.0	Monde
Africa	0.0	0.0	0.1	0.0	0.0	0.0	0.1	0.0	0.0	0.0	Afrique
Americas	3.1	2.0	1.5	1.4	2.5	2.3	1.0	1.0	1.3	1.4	Amériques
- Northern America	0.2	0.3	0.1	0.1	0.1	0.3	0.4	0.5	0.7	0.7	- Amérique du Nord
- LAIA	2.8	1.8	1.4	1.2	1.4	2.0	0.6	0.5	0.6	0.7	- ALAI
- CACM	0.0	0.0	0.0	0.0	0.9	0.0	0.0	0.0	0.0	0.0	- MCC
- Caribbean	0.0	0.0	0.0	0.0	0.0	0.0	0.0	0.0	0.0	0.0	- Caraïbes
Asia excluding former USSR	86.9	89.5	88.2	86.4	86.9	84.1	87.1	88.6	88.0	88.2	Asie ancienne URSS exclus
- Middle East	0.0	0.2	0.2	0.4	0.6	0.8	0.9	0.9	0.6	0.5	- Moyen-Orient
Asia former USSR	1.1	1.9	2.2	2.6	1.9	2.9	2.8	1.6	2.3	2.1	Asie ancienne URSS
Europe excluding former USSR	6.4	6.3	7.5	9.2	8.7	10.5	8.0	8.0	8.3	7.9	Europe ancienne URSS exclus
- European Union	6.0	6.1	7.3	9.0	8.5	10.1	7.7	7.4	7.8	7.5	- Union Européenne
- Eastern Europe	0.0	0.0	0.0	0.0	0.0	0.0	0.0	0.0	0.0	0.1	- Europe de l'Est
- Rest of Europe	0.4	0.2	0.2	0.2	0.2	0.3	0.3	0.6	0.5	0.3	- Autre de l'Europe
Europe former USSR	2.5	0.3	0.5	0.3	0.1	0.1	0.0	0.0	0.0	0.0	Europe ancienne URSS
Oceania	0.0	0.0	0.0	0.0	0.0	0.0	1.0	0.8	0.1	0.3	Océanie
Oceania	0.0	0.0	0.0	0.0	0.0	0.0	1.0	0.8			Océanie

TRADE BY COMMODITY (Value in million US dollars)
Imports by principal countries or areas

COMMERCE PAR PRODUIT (Valeur en millions de dollars EU)
Importations selon les principaux pays ou zones

Country or area	1998	1999	2000	2001	2002	Pays ou zone
World	9539.0	7769.9	8169.1	8121.6	7069.4	Monde
Africa	263.5	161.6	216.3	244.6	239.8	Afrique
Americas	1682.9	1282.4	1344.3	1039.5	877.3	Amériques
- Northern America	177.4	261.1	154.8	142.8	118.1	- Amérique du Nord
- LAIA	1409.4	962.1	1112.8	828.7	698.7	- ALAI
- CACM	86.0	48.0	60.8	48.0	50.0	- MCC
- Caribbean	9.1	9.9	14.7	19.1	9.5	- Caraïbes
- Rest of America	1.1	1.2	1.1	0.8	0.9	- Autre d'Amérique
Asia excluding former USSR	4816.9	4167.1	4369.4	4748.8	4207.1	Asie ancienne URSS exclus
- Middle East	632.5	378.8	703.8	531.0	528.4	- Moyen-Orient
Asia former USSR	1.1	2.1	1.4	1.2	0.5	Asie ancienne URSS
Europe excluding former USSR	2451.6	1742.8	1730.1	1654.0	1420.5	Europe ancienne URSS exclus
- European Union	1936.8	1411.1	1386.3	1299.9	1114.3	- Union Européenne
- Eastern Europe	388.1	247.1	254.8	262.1	231.3	- Europe de l'Est
- Rest of Europe	126.7	84.5	89.1	92.1	74.9	- Autre de l'Europe
Europe former USSR	320.8	411.8	506.0	432.6	323.6	Europe ancienne URSS
Oceania	2.2	2.1	1.6	1.0	0.7	Océanie
Indonesia	763.7	672.6	729.9	1066.3	707.6	Indonésie
Turkey	607.9	354.2	681.1	500.5	496.5	Turquie
Mexico	627.4	396.4	556.8	525.6	450.9	Mexique
Italy-San Marino-Holy See	661.9	476.9	494.7	474.3	403.9	Italie-Saint-Marin-Saint-Siège
Thailand	449.7	396.7	472.6	492.8	e513.5	Thaïlande
Korea, Republic of	524.7	487.4	408.3	451.5	375.8	République de Corée
Japan	553.5	426.1	373.8	343.3	266.0	Japon
Bangladesh	237.4	e260.0	e410.5	397.7	e388.7	Bangladesh
Russian Federation	184.2	315.9	384.7	339.9	236.4	Fédération de Russie
Brazil	525.6	379.1	348.9	102.8	69.0	Brésil
India	91.2	289.4	263.7	435.1	254.6	Inde
Germany	311.2	211.5	230.7	238.7	179.3	Allemagne
Portugal	303.8	209.3	194.9	169.2	146.2	Portugal
China	381.3	104.8	137.2	116.6	199.5	Chine
Pakistan	117.4	322.7	81.6	166.9	225.6	Pakistan
France-Monaco	215.3	164.5	152.7	126.4	110.1	France-Monaco
China, Hong Kong SAR	205.2	140.3	129.1	126.4	88.1	Chine - RAS de Hong-Kong
Malaysia	137.1	116.2	110.6	89.4	e97.7	Malaisie
Canada	148.6	92.2	115.4	108.2	84.7	Canada
Viet Nam	91.3	83.3	111.3	115.5	140.5	Viet Nam
Czech Republic	127.6	76.3	82.8	93.6	82.2	République tchèque
Spain	135.0	97.9	80.9	68.2	61.0	Espagne
Poland	122.2	79.6	78.5	67.7	59.5	Pologne
Belgium	-	76.6	85.9	78.4	e86.0	Belgique
Colombia	70.1	48.4	76.1	66.3	63.2	Colombie
United States	28.8	168.9	39.4	34.5	33.4	Etats-Unis d'Amérique
United Kingdom	83.4	63.3	48.2	55.1	47.5	Royaume-Uni
Philippines	66.8	72.8	56.6	58.0	41.9	Philippines
Peru	84.4	67.9	41.0	52.0	50.4	Pérou
Switzerland-Liechtenstein	73.2	48.8	55.0	51.7	41.5	Suisse-Liechtenstein

(Value as percentages of World total) **(Valeur en pourcentage du total mondial)**

Regions of the world	1993	1994	1995	1996	1997	1998	1999	2000	2001	2002	Régions du monde
World	100.0	100.0	100.0	100.0	100.0	100.0	100.0	100.0	100.0	100.0	Monde
Africa	3.5	2.8	3.2	3.4	2.9	2.8	2.1	2.6	3.0	3.4	Afrique
Americas	16.4	12.2	10.7	16.1	15.5	17.6	16.5	16.5	12.8	12.4	Amériques
- Northern America	1.2	1.1	1.2	3.7	1.2	1.9	3.4	1.9	1.8	1.7	- Amérique du Nord
- LAIA	14.8	10.6	9.1	11.8	13.4	14.8	12.4	13.6	10.2	9.9	- ALAI
- CACM	0.3	0.4	0.3	0.5	0.7	0.9	0.6	0.7	0.6	0.7	- MCC
- Caribbean	0.1	0.1	0.1	0.1	0.1	0.1	0.1	0.2	0.2	0.1	- Caraïbes
- Rest of America	0.0	0.0	0.0	0.0	0.0	0.0	0.0	0.0	0.0	0.0	- Autre d'Amérique
Asia excluding former USSR	52.0	54.8	56.6	52.5	52.9	50.5	53.6	53.5	58.5	59.5	Asie ancienne URSS exclus
- Middle East	3.6	2.7	3.3	3.5	6.8	6.6	4.9	8.6	6.5	7.5	- Moyen-Orient
Asia former USSR	0.0	0.0	0.1	0.0	0.0	0.0	0.0	0.0	0.0	0.0	Asie ancienne URSS
Europe excluding former USSR	27.4	27.5	26.6	24.3	24.0	25.7	22.4	21.2	20.4	20.1	Europe ancienne URSS exclus
- European Union	21.2	21.7	20.7	19.7	19.3	20.3	18.2	17.0	16.0	15.8	- Union Européenne
- Eastern Europe	4.1	4.1	4.7	3.6	3.7	4.1	3.2	3.1	3.2	3.3	- Europe de l'Est
- Rest of Europe	2.1	1.7	1.2	1.0	1.0	1.3	1.1	1.1	1.1	1.1	- Autre de l'Europe
Europe former USSR	0.7	2.7	2.7	3.7	4.7	3.4	5.3	6.2	5.3	4.6	Europe ancienne URSS
Oceania	0.0	0.0	0.0	0.0	0.0	0.0	0.0	0.0	0.0	0.0	Océanie

TRADE BY COMMODITY (Value in million US dollars)
Exports by principal countries or areas

COMMERCE PAR PRODUIT (Valeur en millions de dollars EU)
Exportations selon les principaux pays ou zones

Country or area	1998	1999	2000	2001	2002	Pays ou zone
World	9062.7	7223.1	7600.5	7731.3	7590.0	Monde
Africa	1686.3	1579.6	1242.5	1403.0	2100.5	Afrique
Americas	3037.5	1402.3	2220.8	2594.9	2478.7	Amériques
- Northern America	2621.3	1047.5	1982.4	2221.2	2108.4	- Amérique du Nord
- LAIA	412.9	352.0	236.4	371.7	368.1	- ALAI
- CACM	2.5	2.2	1.5	1.6	1.4	- MCC
- Caribbean	0.6	0.5	0.3	0.3	0.8	- Caraïbes
- Rest of America	0.0	0.1	0.2	0.1	0.1	- Autre d'Amérique
Asia excluding former USSR	775.8	794.9	1014.9	641.9	651.7	Asie ancienne URSS exclus
- Middle East	395.4	285.2	293.6	316.7	277.3	- Moyen-Orient
Asia former USSR	1990.9	1889.4	1667.4	1535.3	1174.5	Asie ancienne URSS
Europe excluding former USSR	573.1	604.9	543.4	506.2	494.3	Europe ancienne URSS exclus
- European Union	548.3	592.2	526.2	493.4	478.0	- Union Européenne
- Eastern Europe	14.7	5.1	10.0	6.6	11.2	- Europe de l'Est
- Rest of Europe	10.1	7.5	7.2	6.2	5.1	- Autre de l'Europe
Europe former USSR	12.9	10.3	23.9	18.8	6.8	Europe ancienne URSS
Oceania	986.2	941.8	887.6	1031.1	683.6	Océanie
United States	2619.1	1042.5	1980.5	2220.5	2108.0	Etats-Unis d'Amérique
Uzbekistan	e1661.2	e1499.0	e1208.7	e1133.5	e748.7	Ouzbékistan
Australia	986.0	941.0	887.5	1031.1	683.5	Australie
Mali	284.1	217.6	208.4	276.2	e667.7	Mali
Greece	253.1	350.8	305.0	271.0	e271.3	Grèce
Syrian Arab Republic	274.2	139.4	200.4	e227.2	193.0	République arabe syrienne
Egypt	158.3	239.5	26.8	187.2	331.1	Egypte
Turkmenistan	136.5	215.3	233.4	e172.4	e171.7	Turkménistan
China	59.3	285.8	307.3	82.0	172.4	Chine
Benin	156.1	169.4	128.4	118.6	e246.1	Bénin
Chad	e218.9	e159.2	e141.6	e148.5	e144.9	Tchad
Côte d'Ivoire	168.1	151.1	148.2	e161.6	134.1	Côte d'Ivoire
Burkina Faso	162.5	156.1	106.3	104.2	e131.3	Burkina Faso
Zimbabwe	e117.0	109.7	178.0	113.2	117.1	Zimbabwe
Argentina	230.3	180.4	55.0	75.5	e73.0	Argentine
Pakistan	85.1	40.5	205.9	102.1	81.9	Pakistan
Turkey	101.3	124.2	71.9	80.4	75.4	Turquie
Tajikistan	e72.2	e82.6	83.1	e80.7	e88.6	Tadjikistan
Paraguay	76.2	62.0	79.4	84.9	e92.7	Paraguay
Cameroon	e62.6	e59.6	68.5	98.1	93.9	Cameroun
Brazil	5.4	6.5	36.0	164.2	e170.2	Brésil
Kazakhstan	52.2	49.6	81.5	86.5	e97.4	Kazakhstan
Germany	76.8	61.9	59.8	66.9	56.6	Allemagne
Togo	96.4	87.2	42.1	22.3	39.9	Togo
Mexico	78.9	80.5	50.5	38.6	26.7	Mexique
Sudan	92.9	e24.4	59.3	41.2	55.2	Soudan
Spain	76.1	57.7	39.2	44.5	27.8	Espagne
Israel	67.9	50.1	54.9	25.8	28.0	Israël
Italy-San Marino-Holy See	39.7	40.2	37.1	42.2	45.1	Italie-Saint-Marin-Saint-Siège
United Republic of Tanzania	30.1	47.7	36.1	35.1	e40.3	République-Unie de Tanzanie

(Value as percentages of World total) **(Valeur en pourcentage du total mondial)**

Regions of the world	1993	1994	1995	1996	1997	1998	1999	2000	2001	2002	Régions du monde
World	100.0	100.0	100.0	100.0	100.0	100.0	100.0	100.0	100.0	100.0	Monde
Africa	20.4	15.3	13.6	13.6	18.3	18.6	21.9	16.3	18.1	27.7	Afrique
Americas	23.6	31.2	42.6	32.2	41.8	33.5	19.4	29.2	33.6	32.7	Amériques
- Northern America	20.6	27.0	33.2	24.0	34.1	28.9	14.5	26.1	28.7	27.8	- Amérique du Nord
- LAIA	2.9	4.1	9.3	8.0	7.6	4.6	4.9	3.1	4.8	4.8	- ALAI
- CACM	0.1	0.1	0.1	0.1	0.1	0.0	0.0	0.0	0.0	0.0	- MCC
- Caribbean	0.0	0.0	0.0	0.0	0.0	0.0	0.0	0.0	0.0	0.0	- Caraïbes
- Rest of America	0.0	0.0	0.0	0.0	0.0	0.0	0.0	0.0	0.0	0.0	- Autre d'Amérique
Asia excluding former USSR	14.9	7.9	7.9	13.2	12.7	8.6	11.0	13.4	8.3	8.6	Asie ancienne URSS exclus
- Middle East	4.6	2.5	2.6	3.4	5.0	4.4	3.9	3.9	4.1	3.7	- Moyen-Orient
Asia former USSR	21.7	34.1	23.7	27.9	7.1	22.0	26.2	21.9	19.9	15.5	Asie ancienne URSS
Europe excluding former USSR	5.9	6.1	6.7	7.0	8.2	6.3	8.4	7.1	6.5	6.5	Europe ancienne URSS exclus
- European Union	5.2	5.0	6.0	6.7	7.9	6.0	8.2	6.9	6.4	6.3	- Union Européenne
- Eastern Europe	0.6	0.9	0.5	0.2	0.2	0.2	0.1	0.1	0.1	0.1	- Europe de l'Est
- Rest of Europe	0.1	0.1	0.1	0.1	0.1	0.1	0.1	0.1	0.1	0.1	- Autre de l'Europe
Europe former USSR	7.5	0.6	0.4	0.2	0.2	0.1	0.1	0.3	0.2	0.1	Europe ancienne URSS
Oceania	6.0	4.9	5.0	5.9	11.8	10.9	13.0	11.7	13.3	9.0	Océanie

265 Vegetable textile fibres, excluding cotton, jute, and waste

TRADE BY COMMODITY (Value in million US dollars)
Imports by principal countries or areas

COMMERCE PAR PRODUIT (Valeur en millions de dollars EU)
Importations selon les principaux pays ou zones

Country or area	1998	1999	2000	2001	2002	Pays ou zone
World	451.8	510.1	618.7	552.9	557.5	Monde
Africa	11.4	12.3	9.9	11.1	12.2	Afrique
Americas	58.7	59.4	50.8	44.6	35.6	Amériques
- Northern America	42.0	40.6	38.2	32.5	23.7	- Amérique du Nord
- LAIA	14.0	16.6	10.5	9.9	10.0	- ALAI
- CACM	0.4	0.1	0.2	0.4	0.2	- MCC
- Caribbean	1.9	1.6	1.7	1.5	1.3	- Caraïbes
- Rest of America	0.4	0.5	0.2	0.3	0.3	- Autre d'Amérique
Asia excluding former USSR	94.3	116.6	170.2	160.3	167.5	Asie ancienne URSS exclus
- Middle East	5.6	5.7	6.5	5.9	7.3	- Moyen-Orient
Asia former USSR	0.0	0.1	0.1	0.1	0.1	Asie ancienne URSS
Europe excluding former USSR	264.4	281.6	337.7	300.9	305.2	Europe ancienne URSS exclus
- European Union	241.2	255.4	301.8	268.4	263.4	- Union Européenne
- Eastern Europe	19.9	23.1	32.4	29.4	38.5	- Europe de l'Est
- Rest of Europe	3.3	3.1	3.5	3.1	3.2	- Autre de l'Europe
Europe former USSR	21.4	38.0	46.0	34.9	35.6	Europe ancienne URSS
Oceania	1.7	2.1	1.9	1.1	1.3	Océanie
China	41.9	65.8	114.9	115.0	120.2	Chine
Belgium	–	75.0	97.4	89.6	e98.3	Belgique
Italy-San Marino-Holy See	38.5	42.5	52.9	46.6	38.2	Italie-Saint-Marin-Saint-Siège
United Kingdom	36.6	38.1	45.4	29.9	25.7	Royaume-Uni
United States	40.7	38.7	36.7	30.2	21.1	Etats-Unis d'Amérique
France-Monaco	24.1	24.9	34.0	29.8	29.3	France-Monaco
Japan	28.1	26.6	26.1	21.0	22.5	Japon
Spain	17.1	17.5	17.2	20.1	23.6	Espagne
Germany	17.4	16.5	15.4	16.3	17.6	Allemagne
Belgium-Luxembourg	65.1	–	–	–	–	Belgique-Luxembourg
Portugal	17.7	15.2	8.4	10.3	6.8	Portugal
Austria	10.4	7.5	12.3	11.6	11.0	Autriche
Poland	7.2	7.3	11.8	11.9	13.4	Pologne
Lithuania	6.1	9.0	11.7	11.1	e13.6	Lituanie
Russian Federation	4.0	14.4	19.3	7.0	5.7	Fédération de Russie
Netherlands	7.1	11.0	10.4	6.9	9.3	Pays-Bas
Czech Republic	5.7	8.0	9.8	9.6	9.7	République tchèque
Estonia	3.0	4.2	8.0	10.5	9.1	Estonie
Hungary	3.7	5.3	8.0	5.9	12.0	Hongrie
Belarus	6.1	7.5	5.9	5.1	5.6	Bélarus
Brazil	7.8	10.5	3.5	1.8	2.6	Brésil
India	3.8	4.5	6.3	4.7	6.9	Inde
Tunisia	3.8	4.4	3.9	5.7	e5.7	Tunisie
Mexico	4.0	3.5	4.3	6.2	4.9	Mexique
Korea, Republic of	4.1	3.6	4.6	4.4	3.4	République de Corée
Turkey	3.5	3.0	3.3	3.1	4.3	Turquie
Ireland	4.2	3.2	3.7	2.0	0.3	Irlande
Morocco	2.2	1.7	2.4	1.7	e1.8	Maroc
Canada	1.2	1.9	1.5	2.3	2.6	Canada
Latvia	2.0	2.4	2.1	1.1	1.4	Lettonie

(Value as percentages of World total) **(Valeur en pourcentage du total mondial)**

Regions of the world	1993	1994	1995	1996	1997	1998	1999	2000	2001	2002	Régions du monde
World	100.0	100.0	100.0	100.0	100.0	100.0	100.0	100.0	100.0	100.0	Monde
Africa	2.1	2.1	1.9	2.7	2.9	2.5	2.4	1.6	2.0	2.2	Afrique
Americas	14.4	13.6	14.3	15.7	14.4	13.0	11.6	8.2	8.1	6.4	Amériques
- Northern America	7.8	7.4	7.3	11.2	9.7	9.3	8.0	6.2	5.9	4.3	- Amérique du Nord
- LAIA	6.4	6.1	6.8	4.3	4.3	3.1	3.3	1.7	1.8	1.8	- ALAI
- CACM	0.2	0.1	0.1	0.0	0.2	0.1	0.0	0.0	0.1	0.0	- MCC
- Caribbean	0.0	0.0	0.1	0.2	0.2	0.4	0.3	0.3	0.3	0.2	- Caraïbes
- Rest of America	0.0	0.0	0.0	0.1	0.1	0.1	0.1	0.0	0.0	0.1	- Autre d'Amérique
Asia excluding former USSR	25.8	22.0	21.3	21.8	21.4	20.9	22.9	27.5	29.0	30.0	Asie ancienne URSS exclus
- Middle East	1.3	1.7	1.5	1.4	1.2	1.2	1.1	1.1	1.1	1.3	- Moyen-Orient
Asia former USSR	0.0	0.0	0.2	0.2	0.2	0.0	0.0	0.0	0.0	0.0	Asie ancienne URSS
Europe excluding former USSR	55.9	60.5	58.5	55.8	57.5	58.5	55.2	54.6	54.4	54.7	Europe ancienne URSS exclus
- European Union	50.2	54.1	53.2	51.2	52.2	53.4	50.1	48.8	48.5	47.3	- Union Européenne
- Eastern Europe	4.8	5.5	4.4	3.7	4.4	4.4	4.5	5.2	5.3	6.9	- Europe de l'Est
- Rest of Europe	0.9	0.9	0.9	1.0	0.8	0.7	0.6	0.6	0.6	0.6	- Autre de l'Europe
Europe former USSR	1.3	1.4	3.4	3.1	3.2	4.7	7.5	7.8	6.3	6.4	Europe ancienne URSS
Oceania	0.5	0.4	0.4	0.7	0.5	0.4	0.4	0.3	0.2	0.2	Océanie

TRADE BY COMMODITY (Value in million US dollars)
Exports by principal countries or areas

COMMERCE PAR PRODUIT (Valeur en millions de dollars EU)
Exportations selon les principaux pays ou zones

Country or area	1998	1999	2000	2001	2002	Pays ou zone
World	429.7	497.8	596.7	511.7	540.9	Monde
Africa	25.9	25.7	18.8	28.5	30.6	Afrique
Americas	51.5	41.8	37.6	37.5	33.2	Amériques
- Northern America	22.6	20.8	19.9	21.0	15.4	- Amérique du Nord
- LAIA	28.7	20.9	17.5	16.3	17.7	- ALAI
- CACM	0.1	0.0	0.1	0.1	0.0	- MCC
- Caribbean	0.0	0.0	0.0	0.1	0.0	- Caraïbes
- Rest of America	0.0	0.0	0.0	0.0	0.0	- Autre d'Amérique
Asia excluding former USSR	76.6	75.2	84.1	59.1	61.6	Asie ancienne URSS exclus
- Middle East	0.6	0.7	0.6	0.5	1.0	- Moyen-Orient
Asia former USSR	0.9	0.3	0.3	0.1	0.1	Asie ancienne URSS
Europe excluding former USSR	259.0	337.2	439.4	364.0	385.9	Europe ancienne URSS exclus
- European Union	253.7	332.8	432.2	358.1	378.9	- Union Européenne
- Eastern Europe	4.8	3.9	6.2	5.3	6.6	- Europe de l'Est
- Rest of Europe	0.5	0.5	0.9	0.5	0.4	- Autre de l'Europe
Europe former USSR	15.7	17.4	16.6	22.3	29.5	Europe ancienne URSS
Oceania	0.1	0.1	0.0	0.3	0.1	Océanie
France-Monaco	116.4	151.3	198.8	171.3	168.3	France-Monaco
Belgium	–	144.9	196.3	154.0	e172.8	Belgique
Sri Lanka	e35.3	33.3	e40.5	28.9	30.4	Sri Lanka
Belgium-Luxembourg	110.6	–	–	–	–	Belgique-Luxembourg
Canada	21.0	19.6	17.3	18.3	11.8	Canada
Philippines	18.5	21.0	20.3	10.4	10.7	Philippines
Netherlands	9.0	12.1	16.7	14.3	19.2	Pays-Bas
Brazil	15.2	9.7	8.5	8.8	e9.1	Brésil
China	11.8	10.7	12.2	7.3	9.3	Chine
Lithuania	8.3	10.5	10.4	9.6	e11.6	Lituanie
Ecuador	12.6	10.4	8.3	6.7	8.0	Equateur
Italy-San Marino-Holy See	6.7	7.4	7.7	8.2	9.8	Italie-Saint-Marin-Saint-Siège
Kenya	11.4	9.1	7.5	e6.6	4.8	Kenya
Egypt	4.8	5.5	2.2	10.3	14.2	Egypte
United Republic of Tanzania	7.3	7.1	5.6	6.7	e7.7	République-Unie de Tanzanie
Ukraine	3.4	3.4	2.4	6.0	6.6	Ukraine
Belarus	2.3	2.8	2.7	5.6	7.4	Bélarus
United Kingdom	4.1	5.7	5.0	2.5	1.0	Royaume-Uni
India	1.8	2.4	2.9	3.4	4.9	Inde
Poland	0.8	2.1	4.3	3.3	4.4	Pologne
Austria	1.6	3.5	3.0	2.1	2.4	Autriche
China, Hong Kong SAR	3.7	1.1	2.8	4.2	0.5	Chine - RAS de Hong-Kong
Germany	2.2	2.0	1.6	2.9	3.5	Allemagne
United States	1.6	1.3	2.6	2.7	3.6	Etats-Unis d'Amérique
Madagascar	1.4	2.2	e2.2	e2.4	e1.6	Madagascar
Denmark	1.1	2.4	1.5	1.0	0.5	Danemark
Thailand	0.8	1.1	1.2	1.6	e1.7	Thaïlande
Russian Federation	1.2	0.2	0.6	0.6	3.0	Fédération de Russie
Czech Republic	0.8	0.9	1.1	1.0	0.7	République tchèque
Hungary	2.6	0.5	0.3	0.4	0.8	Hongrie

(Value as percentages of World total) **(Valeur en pourcentage du total mondial)**

Regions of the world	1993	1994	1995	1996	1997	1998	1999	2000	2001	2002	Régions du monde
World	100.0	100.0	100.0	100.0	100.0	100.0	100.0	100.0	100.0	100.0	Monde
Africa	5.4	4.9	5.7	8.8	6.8	6.0	5.2	3.1	5.6	5.7	Afrique
Americas	8.1	6.9	9.6	14.4	12.7	12.0	8.4	6.3	7.3	6.1	Amériques
- Northern America	2.9	2.2	3.3	5.9	5.0	5.3	4.2	3.3	4.1	2.8	- Amérique du Nord
- LAIA	5.2	4.7	6.3	8.5	7.6	6.7	4.2	2.9	3.2	3.3	- ALAI
- CACM	0.0	0.0	0.0	0.0	0.0	0.0	0.0	0.0	0.0	0.0	- MCC
- Caribbean	0.0	0.0	0.0	0.0	0.0	0.0	0.0	0.0	0.0	0.0	- Caraïbes
- Rest of America	0.0	0.0	0.0	0.0	0.0	0.0	0.0	0.0	0.0	0.0	- Autre d'Amérique
Asia excluding former USSR	18.6	13.6	14.3	19.7	20.9	17.8	15.1	14.1	11.5	11.4	Asie ancienne URSS exclus
- Middle East	0.1	0.1	0.1	0.1	0.1	0.1	0.1	0.1	0.1	0.2	- Moyen-Orient
Asia former USSR	0.0	0.0	0.0	0.0	0.0	0.2	0.1	0.0	0.0	0.0	Asie ancienne URSS
Europe excluding former USSR	62.2	70.1	65.0	53.8	56.3	60.3	67.7	73.6	71.1	71.3	Europe ancienne URSS exclus
- European Union	60.7	67.9	63.2	52.2	54.4	59.0	66.9	72.4	70.0	70.0	- Union Européenne
- Eastern Europe	1.3	1.9	1.6	1.3	1.7	1.1	0.8	1.0	1.0	1.2	- Europe de l'Est
- Rest of Europe	0.2	0.3	0.2	0.3	0.2	0.1	0.1	0.2	0.1	0.1	- Autre de l'Europe
Europe former USSR	5.7	4.5	5.3	3.2	3.2	3.6	3.5	2.8	4.4	5.4	Europe ancienne URSS
Oceania	0.0	0.0	0.0	0.1	0.0	0.0	0.0	0.0	0.1	0.0	Océanie

266 Synthetic fibres suitable for spinning

TRADE BY COMMODITY (Value in million US dollars)
Imports by principal countries or areas

COMMERCE PAR PRODUIT (Valeur en millions de dollars EU)
Importations selon les principaux pays ou zones

Country or area	1998	1999	2000	2001	2002	Pays ou zone
World	5677.2	4983.8	5814.1	5290.8	5509.0	Monde
Africa	244.9	211.3	202.6	197.4	218.1	Afrique
Americas	954.9	865.3	1013.0	966.4	969.5	Amériques
- Northern America	627.6	574.6	623.4	606.7	633.0	- Amérique du Nord
- LAIA	301.7	271.1	364.8	338.9	296.1	- ALAI
- CACM	20.9	15.1	19.2	14.8	18.4	- MCC
- Caribbean	4.4	4.3	5.6	5.9	21.9	- Caraïbes
- Rest of America	0.2	0.1	0.1	0.1	0.1	- Autre d'Amérique
Asia excluding former USSR	2456.6	1994.3	2636.2	2308.6	2442.6	Asie ancienne URSS exclus
- Middle East	380.3	313.5	410.5	363.1	444.5	- Moyen-Orient
Asia former USSR	2.0	1.4	1.8	1.2	2.0	Asie ancienne URSS
Europe excluding former USSR	1932.0	1838.1	1869.8	1730.1	1772.7	Europe ancienne URSS exclus
- European Union	1759.9	1698.6	1697.6	1542.2	1579.4	- Union Européenne
- Eastern Europe	113.0	87.6	118.0	134.9	139.7	- Europe de l'Est
- Rest of Europe	59.0	51.9	54.2	53.0	53.6	- Autre de l'Europe
Europe former USSR	41.7	30.1	44.0	46.2	58.7	Europe ancienne URSS
Oceania	45.3	43.4	46.7	40.9	45.2	Océanie
China	1020.0	770.9	1097.3	962.8	1062.9	Chine
United States	469.3	429.3	448.1	441.3	477.2	Etats-Unis d'Amérique
Italy-San Marino-Holy See	394.9	364.9	398.4	343.1	370.5	Italie-Saint-Marin-Saint-Siège
Germany	344.8	350.0	347.9	362.0	334.5	Allemagne
United Kingdom	260.4	243.8	227.8	219.0	220.6	Royaume-Uni
China, Hong Kong SAR	319.6	252.1	251.5	170.7	161.0	Chine - RAS de Hong-Kong
Indonesia	183.6	136.2	237.6	232.3	169.4	Indonésie
France-Monaco	195.4	189.7	181.0	160.9	159.0	France-Monaco
Canada	158.3	145.3	175.3	165.4	155.8	Canada
Turkey	129.0	108.2	171.5	135.9	229.7	Turquie
Iran (Islamic Republic of)	153.6	156.6	154.4	144.8	140.1	Iran (République islamique d')
Belgium	–	193.8	183.3	173.9	e190.8	Belgique
Spain	153.2	145.8	158.6	98.4	108.8	Espagne
Mexico	93.8	96.4	128.5	131.9	132.6	Mexique
Thailand	60.9	63.0	68.9	61.3	e63.9	Thaïlande
Brazil	55.2	51.7	72.2	69.3	50.9	Brésil
Korea, Republic of	55.0	56.6	55.5	67.2	50.9	République de Corée
Netherlands	55.5	65.4	55.0	54.2	47.9	Pays-Bas
Viet Nam	e	e	84.2	87.4	106.3	Viet Nam
Egypt	77.9	71.7	e44.0	40.1	43.2	Egypte
Malaysia	44.9	57.6	60.5	53.3	e58.3	Malaisie
Morocco	55.1	48.0	48.2	52.2	e55.1	Maroc
Japan	53.4	54.5	50.6	47.4	44.0	Japon
Philippines	46.2	47.4	58.0	52.0	45.1	Philippines
India	58.2	33.2	47.7	43.8	60.0	Inde
Austria	46.7	43.9	43.5	39.2	42.4	Autriche
Poland	48.8	32.5	39.5	42.5	41.4	Pologne
Pakistan	65.5	43.3	35.4	25.7	31.8	Pakistan
Saudi Arabia	71.7	24.6	40.1	29.7	e30.8	Arabie saoudite
Belgium-Luxembourg	192.5	–	–	–	–	Belgique-Luxembourg

(Value as percentages of World total) **(Valeur en pourcentage du total mondial)**

Regions of the world	1993	1994	1995	1996	1997	1998	1999	2000	2001	2002	Régions du monde
World	100.0	100.0	100.0	100.0	100.0	100.0	100.0	100.0	100.0	100.0	Monde
Africa	5.3	4.8	4.4	3.8	4.4	4.3	4.2	3.5	3.7	4.0	Afrique
Americas	16.1	15.6	14.8	14.3	15.0	16.8	17.4	17.4	18.3	17.6	Amériques
- Northern America	10.2	10.5	9.6	9.1	9.5	11.1	11.5	10.7	11.5	11.5	- Amérique du Nord
- LAIA	5.4	4.8	4.9	4.8	5.0	5.3	5.4	6.3	6.4	5.4	- ALAI
- CACM	0.4	0.3	0.3	0.3	0.3	0.4	0.3	0.3	0.3	0.3	- MCC
- Caribbean	0.0	0.1	0.0	0.1	0.1	0.1	0.1	0.1	0.1	0.4	- Caraïbes
- Rest of America	0.0	0.0	0.0	0.0	0.0	0.0	0.0	0.0	0.0	0.0	- Autre d'Amérique
Asia excluding former USSR	44.5	43.9	46.3	47.9	47.8	43.3	40.0	45.3	43.6	44.3	Asie ancienne URSS exclus
- Middle East	8.0	5.6	5.5	6.1	6.4	6.7	6.3	7.1	6.9	8.1	- Moyen-Orient
Asia former USSR	0.0	0.1	0.1	0.1	0.1	0.0	0.0	0.0	0.0	0.0	Asie ancienne URSS
Europe excluding former USSR	32.6	34.2	33.0	32.0	31.0	34.0	36.9	32.2	32.7	32.2	Europe ancienne URSS exclus
- European Union	29.6	31.3	30.4	29.1	28.2	31.0	34.1	29.2	29.1	28.7	- Union Européenne
- Eastern Europe	1.7	1.7	1.4	2.0	1.9	2.0	1.8	2.0	2.5	2.5	- Europe de l'Est
- Rest of Europe	1.2	1.3	1.2	0.9	0.8	1.0	1.0	0.9	1.0	1.0	- Autre de l'Europe
Europe former USSR	0.3	0.4	0.4	1.0	0.9	0.7	0.6	0.8	0.9	1.1	Europe ancienne URSS
Oceania	1.1	1.1	1.0	0.9	0.8	0.8	0.9	0.8	0.8	0.8	Océanie

Fibres synthétiques de longueur suffisante pour pouvoir être filées 266

TRADE BY COMMODITY (Value in million US dollars)
Exports by principal countries or areas

COMMERCE PAR PRODUIT (Valeur en millions de dollars EU)
Exportations selon les principaux pays ou zones

Country or area	1998	1999	2000	2001	2002	Pays ou zone
World	4812.1	4231.6	4707.5	4140.3	4732.1	Monde
Africa	33.8	35.1	30.2	32.3	23.1	Afrique
Americas	709.4	606.0	692.5	580.0	675.4	Amériques
- Northern America	467.6	424.6	457.5	373.1	445.8	- Amérique du Nord
- LAIA	241.4	181.1	234.6	206.6	229.4	- ALAI
- CACM	0.4	0.3	0.3	0.3	0.2	- MCC
- Caribbean	0.0	0.0	0.0	0.0	0.0	- Caraïbes
- Rest of America	0.0	0.0	0.0	0.0	0.0	- Autre d'Amérique
Asia excluding former USSR	2790.5	2515.1	2878.6	2484.5	2591.7	Asie ancienne URSS exclus
- Middle East	104.9	99.5	115.6	129.3	47.3	- Moyen-Orient
Asia former USSR	9.8	11.2	12.7	9.4	9.1	Asie ancienne URSS
Europe excluding former USSR	1146.5	957.0	940.8	891.9	1302.6	Europe ancienne URSS exclus
- European Union	1027.0	865.0	842.4	796.8	1203.3	- Union Européenne
- Eastern Europe	73.9	53.4	69.2	72.8	74.8	- Europe de l'Est
- Rest of Europe	45.6	38.6	29.2	22.4	24.5	- Autre de l'Europe
Europe former USSR	111.3	94.2	146.3	141.1	129.0	Europe ancienne URSS
Oceania	10.9	13.1	6.5	1.1	1.3	Océanie
Korea, Republic of	753.3	722.5	840.8	659.8	647.8	République de Corée
Japan	749.8	655.5	724.7	655.2	656.2	Japon
United States	412.8	386.4	445.9	368.9	441.0	Etats-Unis d'Amérique
Germany	121.0	138.6	123.3	110.2	536.3	Allemagne
China, Hong Kong SAR	311.6	175.2	113.1	94.6	134.3	Chine - RAS de Hong-Kong
Mexico	184.3	132.5	169.1	159.8	177.4	Mexique
Thailand	126.7	151.5	187.7	170.2	e179.7	Thaïlande
Belgium	–	171.3	178.2	183.2	e205.5	Belgique
Belarus	107.4	91.9	138.6	135.7	122.2	Bélarus
Spain	99.7	105.2	120.4	121.4	125.6	Espagne
France-Monaco	126.3	120.3	116.5	106.1	75.1	France-Monaco
United Kingdom	218.9	73.8	69.0	77.0	76.5	Royaume-Uni
Ireland	117.1	111.4	89.1	88.0	94.4	Irlande
Italy-San Marino-Holy See	93.8	88.2	85.7	81.6	67.4	Italie-Saint-Marin-Saint-Siège
Turkey	85.6	81.2	92.0	107.8	26.6	Turquie
China	50.7	37.4	37.8	51.8	99.4	Chine
Indonesia	40.9	29.1	37.2	45.2	74.4	Indonésie
Malaysia	42.4	45.2	49.0	40.1	e42.5	Malaisie
Belgium-Luxembourg	182.1	–	–	–	–	Belgique-Luxembourg
Portugal	45.8	44.3	44.5	8.4	7.2	Portugal
India	18.2	41.3	32.9	19.1	35.9	Inde
Switzerland-Liechtenstein	35.1	31.3	23.6	20.7	23.2	Suisse-Liechtenstein
Peru	22.9	18.3	28.0	20.2	24.7	Pérou
Canada	54.8	38.1	11.6	4.1	4.9	Canada
Poland	22.6	14.9	23.9	18.1	20.2	Pologne
Czech Republic	15.9	12.4	19.1	22.8	26.1	République tchèque
Saudi Arabia	18.2	17.0	21.8	19.3	e17.4	Arabie saoudite
South Africa	–	–	27.8	29.5	20.4	Afrique du Sud
Netherlands	20.3	10.3	8.8	17.6	11.4	Pays-Bas
Southern African Customs Union	31.1	30.5	–	–	–	Union douanière d'Afrique australe

(Value as percentages of World total) **(Valeur en pourcentage du total mondial)**

Regions of the world	1993	1994	1995	1996	1997	1998	1999	2000	2001	2002	Régions du monde
World	100.0	100.0	100.0	100.0	100.0	100.0	100.0	100.0	100.0	100.0	Monde
Africa	0.3	0.5	0.6	0.6	0.9	0.7	0.8	0.6	0.8	0.5	Afrique
Americas	11.8	14.4	14.8	14.8	13.8	14.7	14.3	14.7	14.0	14.3	Amériques
- Northern America	7.9	8.8	8.7	9.3	8.4	9.7	10.0	9.7	9.0	9.4	- Amérique du Nord
- LAIA	3.9	5.6	6.1	5.5	5.4	5.0	4.3	5.0	5.0	4.8	- ALAI
- CACM	0.0	0.0	0.0	0.0	0.0	0.0	0.0	0.0	0.0	0.0	- MCC
- Caribbean	0.0	0.0	0.0	0.0	0.0	0.0	0.0	0.0	0.0	0.0	- Caraïbes
- Rest of America	0.0	0.0	0.0	0.0	0.0	0.0	0.0	0.0	0.0	0.0	- Autre d'Amérique
Asia excluding former USSR	50.7	47.6	51.2	51.0	53.4	58.0	59.4	61.1	60.0	54.8	Asie ancienne URSS exclus
- Middle East	0.7	1.6	1.7	2.0	1.8	2.2	2.4	2.5	3.1	1.0	- Moyen-Orient
Asia former USSR	0.0	0.0	0.0	0.1	0.0	0.2	0.3	0.3	0.2	0.2	Asie ancienne URSS
Europe excluding former USSR	34.4	36.2	31.4	32.0	29.7	23.8	22.6	20.0	21.5	27.5	Europe ancienne URSS exclus
- European Union	31.4	32.9	28.1	29.3	26.9	21.3	20.4	17.9	19.2	25.4	- Union Européenne
- Eastern Europe	1.3	1.5	1.7	1.3	1.8	1.5	1.3	1.5	1.8	1.6	- Europe de l'Est
- Rest of Europe	1.7	1.8	1.7	1.3	1.0	0.9	0.9	0.6	0.5	0.5	- Autre de l'Europe
Europe former USSR	2.7	1.2	2.0	1.6	1.9	2.3	2.2	3.1	3.4	2.7	Europe ancienne URSS
Oceania	0.0	0.0	0.0	0.1	0.3	0.2	0.3	0.1	0.0	0.0	Océanie

267 Other man-made fibres suitable for spinning, and waste

TRADE BY COMMODITY (Value in million US dollars)
Imports by principal countries or areas

COMMERCE PAR PRODUIT (Valeur en millions de dollars EU)
Importations selon les principaux pays ou zones

Country or area	1998	1999	2000	2001	2002	Pays ou zone
World	2240.0	2136.5	2214.9	2146.2	2308.5	Monde
Africa	67.5	68.6	62.6	62.6	63.1	Afrique
Americas	215.0	208.4	191.5	168.6	175.3	Amériques
- Northern America	77.0	84.4	70.8	61.7	82.4	- Amérique du Nord
- LAIA	128.9	114.5	112.7	99.0	83.4	- ALAI
- CACM	4.1	4.6	4.4	4.9	6.1	- MCC
- Caribbean	5.0	4.8	3.7	2.9	3.3	- Caraïbes
- Rest of America	0.1	0.0	0.0	0.0	0.0	- Autre d'Amérique
Asia excluding former USSR	951.5	905.5	1016.0	962.7	1059.2	Asie ancienne URSS exclus
- Middle East	184.0	186.2	204.1	190.9	239.1	- Moyen-Orient
Asia former USSR	9.6	10.3	9.9	12.7	15.5	Asie ancienne URSS
Europe excluding former USSR	939.0	864.2	837.5	833.2	866.3	Europe ancienne URSS exclus
- European Union	774.4	714.9	685.3	669.4	704.4	- Union Européenne
- Eastern Europe	114.2	95.6	100.0	108.7	104.9	- Europe de l'Est
- Rest of Europe	50.4	53.7	52.2	55.1	57.1	- Autre de l'Europe
Europe former USSR	41.8	61.9	79.4	89.9	111.6	Europe ancienne URSS
Oceania	15.5	17.7	17.8	16.6	17.5	Océanie
China	307.8	293.4	349.8	388.1	399.0	Chine
Turkey	149.1	144.1	156.5	140.6	186.5	Turquie
Italy-San Marino-Holy See	157.6	139.8	150.3	145.5	140.0	Italie-Saint-Marin-Saint-Siège
Germany	128.1	116.4	109.0	125.7	134.1	Allemagne
Korea, Republic of	71.4	91.6	105.9	95.7	98.1	République de Corée
France-Monaco	89.0	76.5	78.7	70.4	81.2	France-Monaco
Netherlands	84.1	77.3	68.7	69.7	67.7	Pays-Bas
Spain	81.6	72.8	65.6	60.3	60.2	Espagne
United Kingdom	83.1	67.1	53.3	43.3	46.7	Royaume-Uni
Belgium	–	66.4	71.8	72.1	e79.1	Belgique
China, Hong Kong SAR	110.7	48.0	37.9	23.9	32.7	Chine - RAS de Hong-Kong
Pakistan	53.8	43.3	40.8	48.8	50.9	Pakistan
United States	51.4	53.6	37.3	34.2	57.2	Etats-Unis d'Amérique
Russian Federation	25.3	33.0	45.8	48.6	64.5	Fédération de Russie
Poland	49.3	43.1	40.6	42.0	38.5	Pologne
Philippines	40.1	43.7	39.8	22.1	23.3	Philippines
Japan	22.9	30.6	40.8	31.6	33.7	Japon
Canada	25.6	30.8	33.5	27.4	25.3	Canada
Brazil	46.2	26.3	34.7	15.1	12.2	Brésil
Mexico	22.6	30.5	26.9	28.1	23.1	Mexique
Indonesia	22.6	15.2	31.5	26.7	32.6	Indonésie
Switzerland-Liechtenstein	25.5	22.1	25.8	25.8	26.1	Suisse-Liechtenstein
Czech Republic	25.5	19.5	25.2	24.8	25.0	République tchèque
Iran (Islamic Republic of)	19.3	32.3	24.4	20.9	19.0	Iran (République islamique d')
Israel	16.9	17.0	21.8	26.7	31.8	Israël
Argentina	25.4	24.6	18.6	17.8	e7.9	Argentine
Portugal	17.6	20.3	19.4	16.3	18.1	Portugal
Ukraine	6.3	13.4	17.9	25.4	27.4	Ukraine
India	15.1	15.0	18.4	17.7	23.8	Inde
Finland	22.9	24.5	18.0	12.6	11.9	Finlande

(Value as percentages of World total) **(Valeur en pourcentage du total mondial)**

Regions of the world	1993	1994	1995	1996	1997	1998	1999	2000	2001	2002	Régions du monde
World	100.0	100.0	100.0	100.0	100.0	100.0	100.0	100.0	100.0	100.0	Monde
Africa	4.5	3.6	3.1	3.5	3.3	3.0	3.2	2.8	2.9	2.7	Afrique
Americas	13.9	9.3	7.9	7.8	8.4	9.6	9.8	8.6	7.9	7.6	Amériques
- Northern America	7.7	4.8	3.3	3.0	3.3	3.4	4.0	3.2	2.9	3.6	- Amérique du Nord
- LAIA	5.7	4.2	4.3	4.5	4.6	5.8	5.4	5.1	4.6	3.6	- ALAI
- CACM	0.4	0.3	0.2	0.1	0.2	0.2	0.2	0.2	0.2	0.3	- MCC
- Caribbean	0.1	0.1	0.1	0.2	0.3	0.2	0.2	0.2	0.1	0.1	- Caraïbes
- Rest of America	0.0	0.0	0.0	0.0	0.0	0.0	0.0	0.0	0.0	0.0	- Autre d'Amérique
Asia excluding former USSR	35.7	41.3	42.1	42.9	42.2	42.5	42.4	45.9	44.9	45.9	Asie ancienne URSS exclus
- Middle East	6.3	5.4	8.0	8.6	8.7	8.2	8.7	9.2	8.9	10.4	- Moyen-Orient
Asia former USSR	0.0	0.1	0.2	0.4	0.4	0.4	0.5	0.4	0.6	0.7	Asie ancienne URSS
Europe excluding former USSR	44.0	43.8	44.9	43.2	42.9	41.9	40.5	37.8	38.8	37.5	Europe ancienne URSS exclus
- European Union	36.6	37.3	37.2	36.2	36.0	34.6	33.5	30.9	31.2	30.5	- Union Européenne
- Eastern Europe	3.7	3.3	4.8	4.7	4.7	5.1	4.5	4.5	5.1	4.5	- Europe de l'Est
- Rest of Europe	3.7	3.2	2.9	2.2	2.2	2.3	2.5	2.4	2.6	2.5	- Autre de l'Europe
Europe former USSR	0.5	0.7	0.8	1.3	2.1	1.9	2.9	3.6	4.2	4.8	Europe ancienne URSS
Oceania	1.3	1.1	0.9	1.0	0.7	0.7	0.8	0.8	0.8	0.8	Océanie

TRADE BY COMMODITY (Value in million US dollars) — COMMERCE PAR PRODUIT (Valeur en millions de dollars EU)

Exports by principal countries or areas — **Exportations selon les principaux pays ou zones**

Country or area	1998	1999	2000	2001	2002	Pays ou zone
World	2566.3	2124.4	2264.7	2240.3	1924.9	Monde
Africa	4.3	4.6	23.5	14.5	17.6	Afrique
Americas	713.4	634.8	668.7	670.6	657.0	Amériques
- Northern America	619.0	546.7	570.9	564.5	546.5	- Amérique du Nord
- LAIA	94.3	88.0	97.7	106.0	110.4	- ALAI
- CACM	0.0	0.1	0.1	0.0	0.0	- MCC
- Caribbean	0.0	0.0	0.1	0.1	0.0	- Caraïbes
Asia excluding former USSR	505.3	460.6	518.0	473.5	519.1	Asie ancienne URSS exclus
- Middle East	3.5	2.0	5.0	6.0	4.8	- Moyen-Orient
Asia former USSR	0.0	0.2	0.6	0.7	0.4	Asie ancienne URSS
Europe excluding former USSR	1310.3	1000.7	1023.2	1058.8	699.1	Europe ancienne URSS exclus
- European Union	1265.7	980.5	1007.6	1042.4	684.5	- Union Européenne
- Eastern Europe	31.1	14.5	3.7	4.2	4.0	- Europe de l'Est
- Rest of Europe	13.5	5.7	11.9	12.2	10.7	- Autre de l'Europe
Europe former USSR	32.2	23.1	30.5	21.9	31.4	Europe ancienne URSS
Oceania	0.7	0.3	0.2	0.2	0.3	Océanie
Germany	818.4	767.1	798.8	818.7	438.2	Allemagne
United States	528.5	460.6	472.0	468.2	453.2	Etats-Unis d'Amérique
Japan	205.4	206.2	223.0	226.2	219.5	Japon
Canada	90.5	86.1	98.9	96.3	93.3	Canada
Indonesia	87.0	50.0	71.9	55.8	83.4	Indonésie
Finland	76.9	66.6	62.9	67.1	73.2	Finlande
United Kingdom	202.0	11.3	10.8	22.7	19.4	Royaume-Uni
Mexico	48.4	44.5	45.9	55.2	56.5	Mexique
Thailand	39.4	42.4	53.6	50.1	e53.0	Thaïlande
China, Hong Kong SAR	63.0	53.8	25.1	17.1	22.8	Chine - RAS de Hong-Kong
Sweden	44.2	33.7	32.2	30.2	31.6	Suède
Spain	30.1	24.9	29.0	31.2	37.8	Espagne
Venezuela	25.2	20.8	28.9	32.5	e34.5	Venezuela
Russian Federation	28.9	21.2	27.8	19.3	29.0	Fédération de Russie
Belgium	–	28.6	25.5	21.6	e24.2	Belgique
Brazil	19.3	21.8	21.8	17.5	e18.2	Brésil
Netherlands	22.0	17.2	11.8	17.5	27.1	Pays-Bas
Korea, Republic of	4.6	10.8	17.9	30.2	26.3	République de Corée
France-Monaco	17.2	17.6	18.3	17.9	16.7	France-Monaco
Italy-San Marino-Holy See	8.0	11.3	14.0	10.7	10.3	Italie-Saint-Marin-Saint-Siège
Singapore	14.1	16.3	6.6	4.8	7.5	Singapour
Belgium-Luxembourg	44.2	–	–	–	–	Belgique-Luxembourg
Swaziland	–	–	17.4	8.2	e11.4	Swaziland
Czech Republic	19.2	11.4	0.6	1.1	1.0	République tchèque
India	2.8	3.6	6.7	5.9	13.4	Inde
China	5.8	3.1	5.5	3.9	8.8	Chine
Serbia and Montenegro	6.9	0.1	6.6	e7.6	e5.7	Serbie-et-Monténégro
Switzerland-Liechtenstein	3.4	2.6	2.5	2.6	3.1	Suisse-Liechtenstein
Turkey	1.6	1.0	3.8	4.1	3.7	Turquie
Romania	8.0	0.4	0.6	1.1	1.1	Roumanie

(Value as percentages of World total) — **(Valeur en pourcentage du total mondial)**

Regions of the world	1993	1994	1995	1996	1997	1998	1999	2000	2001	2002	Régions du monde
World	100.0	100.0	100.0	100.0	100.0	100.0	100.0	100.0	100.0	100.0	Monde
Africa	0.2	0.1	0.2	0.2	0.2	0.2	0.2	1.0	0.6	0.9	Afrique
Americas	28.5	27.4	34.0	30.6	35.2	27.8	29.9	29.5	29.9	34.1	Amériques
- Northern America	26.1	25.8	30.3	27.7	32.1	24.1	25.7	25.2	25.2	28.4	- Amérique du Nord
- LAIA	2.4	1.6	3.6	2.8	3.2	3.7	4.1	4.3	4.7	5.7	- ALAI
- CACM	0.0	0.0	0.0	0.0	0.0	0.0	0.0	0.0	0.0	0.0	- MCC
- Caribbean	0.0	0.0	0.0	0.0	0.0	0.0	0.0	0.0	0.0	0.0	- Caraïbes
Asia excluding former USSR	23.6	23.9	23.1	24.1	25.9	19.7	21.7	22.9	21.1	27.0	Asie ancienne URSS exclus
- Middle East	0.0	0.1	0.1	0.1	0.1	0.1	0.1	0.2	0.3	0.3	- Moyen-Orient
Asia former USSR	0.0	0.0	0.0	0.1	0.0	0.0	0.0	0.0	0.0	0.0	Asie ancienne URSS
Europe excluding former USSR	45.0	47.0	41.2	43.8	36.5	51.1	47.1	45.2	47.3	36.3	Europe ancienne URSS exclus
- European Union	41.4	43.4	37.8	41.7	34.9	49.3	46.2	44.5	46.5	35.6	- Union Européenne
- Eastern Europe	3.1	3.1	2.7	1.8	1.3	1.2	0.7	0.2	0.2	0.2	- Europe de l'Est
- Rest of Europe	0.5	0.5	0.7	0.3	0.3	0.5	0.3	0.5	0.5	0.6	- Autre de l'Europe
Europe former USSR	2.8	1.5	1.5	1.3	2.1	1.3	1.1	1.3	1.0	1.6	Europe ancienne URSS
Oceania	0.0	0.0	0.0	0.0	0.0	0.0	0.0	0.0	0.0	0.0	Océanie
Oceania	0.0	0.0	0.0	0.1	0.0	0.0	0.0	0.0			Océanie

268 Wool and other animal hair (excluding tops)

TRADE BY COMMODITY (Value in million US dollars)
Imports by principal countries or areas

COMMERCE PAR PRODUIT (Valeur en millions de dollars EU)
Importations selon les principaux pays ou zones

Country or area	1998	1999	2000	2001	2002	Pays ou zone
World	3635.1	3164.3	3759.3	3383.4	3316.3	Monde
Africa	45.0	36.4	31.1	24.1	30.3	Afrique
Americas	224.8	123.4	143.5	128.0	106.3	Amériques
- Northern America	172.9	94.3	101.7	82.1	57.5	- Amérique du Nord
- LAIA	50.2	28.7	41.5	43.9	40.3	- ALAI
- CACM	0.0	0.0	0.1	0.0	0.0	- MCC
- Caribbean	1.5	0.2	0.2	2.1	8.5	- Caraïbes
- Rest of America	0.2	0.1	0.0	0.0	0.0	- Autre d'Amérique
Asia excluding former USSR	1281.0	1328.2	1656.8	1588.2	1624.6	Asie ancienne URSS exclus
- Middle East	135.0	99.0	109.8	89.3	94.9	- Moyen-Orient
Asia former USSR	1.3	0.5	1.0	1.1	1.3	Asie ancienne URSS
Europe excluding former USSR	1995.8	1587.7	1840.9	1575.2	1475.3	Europe ancienne URSS exclus
- European Union	1864.7	1495.6	1739.4	1462.4	1346.3	- Union Européenne
- Eastern Europe	111.1	69.4	82.2	96.5	113.5	- Europe de l'Est
- Rest of Europe	20.1	22.6	19.2	16.3	15.5	- Autre de l'Europe
Europe former USSR	55.4	50.2	52.6	40.8	42.4	Europe ancienne URSS
Oceania	31.7	37.9	33.4	26.1	36.0	Océanie
Italy-San Marino-Holy See	766.4	699.5	871.0	734.0	590.4	Italie-Saint-Marin-Saint-Siège
China	440.8	490.1	836.6	849.3	843.1	Chine
United Kingdom	268.5	254.2	264.4	220.3	199.5	Royaume-Uni
Germany	327.0	181.9	212.6	166.2	207.0	Allemagne
Japan	209.1	241.5	216.9	151.8	145.8	Japon
France-Monaco	263.9	166.2	171.4	166.7	169.1	France-Monaco
India	122.7	117.9	106.7	137.9	170.6	Inde
Korea, Republic of	81.7	117.0	126.8	129.4	134.3	République de Corée
United States	161.6	84.2	89.6	72.3	49.3	Etats-Unis d'Amérique
Belgium	-	87.1	107.7	76.9	e84.3	Belgique
Turkey	99.2	63.6	71.1	56.4	65.2	Turquie
Czech Republic	60.9	42.6	48.2	60.0	73.3	République tchèque
Thailand	41.2	40.4	45.9	45.0	e46.8	Thaïlande
Spain	47.0	43.1	48.1	39.9	39.3	Espagne
China, Hong Kong SAR	90.5	33.4	38.7	28.6	17.3	Chine - RAS de Hong-Kong
Australia	30.0	33.4	30.3	24.4	34.4	Australie
Iran (Islamic Republic of)	25.4	28.6	33.6	29.1	25.6	Iran (République islamique d')
Belgium-Luxembourg	110.9	-	-	-	-	Belgique-Luxembourg
Nepal	22.6	30.2	19.4	e18.4	e17.7	Népal
Belarus	21.8	27.7	26.8	12.1	16.8	Bélarus
Malaysia	11.9	17.2	20.9	22.5	e24.6	Malaisie
Mexico	16.7	12.0	21.6	20.3	13.7	Mexique
Uruguay	24.1	9.5	11.1	16.6	21.0	Uruguay
China, Macao SAR	10.8	13.0	18.1	14.2	24.0	Chine - RAS de Macao
Portugal	17.7	16.4	14.6	13.8	13.5	Portugal
Poland	22.4	11.2	12.3	10.5	8.2	Pologne
Denmark	12.6	9.4	11.4	11.5	14.1	Danemark
Switzerland-Liechtenstein	10.4	15.1	12.3	7.9	7.6	Suisse-Liechtenstein
Netherlands	20.1	9.5	11.3	7.3	4.7	Pays-Bas
Canada	11.4	10.1	12.1	9.7	8.2	Canada

(Value as percentages of World total) **(Valeur en pourcentage du total mondial)**

Regions of the world	1993	1994	1995	1996	1997	1998	1999	2000	2001	2002	Régions du monde
World	100.0	100.0	100.0	100.0	100.0	100.0	100.0	100.0	100.0	100.0	Monde
Africa	0.9	0.9	1.0	1.0	1.0	1.2	1.2	0.8	0.7	0.9	Afrique
Americas	6.3	5.2	5.8	5.3	5.7	6.2	3.9	3.8	3.8	3.2	Amériques
- Northern America	5.2	4.1	4.3	4.1	4.6	4.8	3.0	2.7	2.4	1.7	- Amérique du Nord
- LAIA	1.2	1.1	1.5	1.2	1.0	1.4	0.9	1.1	1.3	1.2	- ALAI
- CACM	0.0	0.0	0.0	0.0	0.0	0.0	0.0	0.0	0.0	0.0	- MCC
- Caribbean	0.0	0.0	0.0	0.0	0.0	0.0	0.0	0.0	0.1	0.3	- Caraïbes
- Rest of America	0.0	0.0	0.0	0.0	0.0	0.0	0.0	0.0	0.0	0.0	- Autre d'Amérique
Asia excluding former USSR	49.3	43.5	43.2	44.9	40.1	35.2	42.0	44.1	46.9	49.0	Asie ancienne URSS exclus
- Middle East	3.1	1.8	2.9	2.6	2.7	3.7	3.1	2.9	2.6	2.9	- Moyen-Orient
Asia former USSR	0.0	0.1	0.2	0.1	0.0	0.0	0.0	0.0	0.0	0.0	Asie ancienne URSS
Europe excluding former USSR	41.8	48.8	47.8	46.4	50.9	54.9	50.2	49.0	46.6	44.5	Europe ancienne URSS exclus
- European Union	39.1	46.1	45.2	43.6	47.9	51.3	47.3	46.3	43.2	40.6	- Union Européenne
- Eastern Europe	1.9	1.9	2.0	2.2	2.5	3.1	2.2	2.2	2.9	3.4	- Europe de l'Est
- Rest of Europe	0.8	0.8	0.6	0.5	0.5	0.6	0.7	0.5	0.5	0.5	- Autre de l'Europe
Europe former USSR	0.8	0.5	1.0	1.2	1.3	1.5	1.6	1.4	1.2	1.3	Europe ancienne URSS
Oceania	0.8	1.0	1.0	1.0	0.9	0.9	1.2	0.9	0.8	1.1	Océanie

TRADE BY COMMODITY (Value in million US dollars)
Exports by principal countries or areas

COMMERCE PAR PRODUIT (Valeur en millions de dollars EU)
Exportations selon les principaux pays ou zones

Country or area	1998	1999	2000	2001	2002	Pays ou zone
World	3224.0	3029.6	3447.0	3049.2	3354.5	Monde
Africa	116.3	119.6	109.4	92.2	122.6	Afrique
Americas	156.1	168.6	185.2	137.1	145.3	Amériques
- Northern America	29.9	37.5	33.0	19.7	36.0	- Amérique du Nord
- LAIA	125.4	130.9	152.0	116.9	108.6	- ALAI
- CACM	0.5	0.0	0.1	0.1	0.1	- MCC
- Caribbean	0.1	0.0	0.0	0.2	0.0	- Caraïbes
- Rest of America	0.3	0.2	0.1	0.3	0.6	- Autre d'Amérique
Asia excluding former USSR	428.9	534.0	586.5	457.0	474.6	Asie ancienne URSS exclus
- Middle East	32.5	34.0	42.9	39.4	33.3	- Moyen-Orient
Asia former USSR	14.7	17.2	15.3	13.2	14.3	Asie ancienne URSS
Europe excluding former USSR	508.0	467.2	525.7	440.6	466.0	Europe ancienne URSS exclus
- European Union	465.6	430.7	485.3	401.4	427.2	- Union Européenne
- Eastern Europe	22.9	16.9	17.4	23.4	25.1	- Europe de l'Est
- Rest of Europe	19.5	19.7	23.0	15.8	13.7	- Autre de l'Europe
Europe former USSR	20.4	9.0	7.6	5.3	15.7	Europe ancienne URSS
Oceania	1979.5	1713.9	2017.2	1903.8	2116.0	Océanie
Australia	1508.8	1324.3	1611.7	1545.5	1724.4	Australie
New Zealand	470.7	389.6	405.6	358.3	391.5	Nouvelle-Zélande
China	192.1	331.5	353.9	273.8	315.7	Chine
United Kingdom	177.1	178.4	203.2	144.5	144.7	Royaume-Uni
France-Monaco	86.1	69.7	68.4	57.0	57.6	France-Monaco
Mongolia	42.3	73.2	84.6	68.6	42.1	Mongolie
Argentina	61.6	59.8	70.2	52.6	e50.8	Argentine
South Africa	–	–	100.7	81.0	106.9	Afrique du Sud
Germany	60.9	54.7	58.6	52.5	51.5	Allemagne
Southern African Customs Union	113.7	118.1	–	–	–	Union douanière d'Afrique australe
China, Hong Kong SAR	93.0	40.1	45.6	30.9	19.5	Chine - RAS de Hong-Kong
Italy-San Marino-Holy See	31.0	30.5	40.2	54.6	64.5	Italie-Saint-Marin-Saint-Siège
Belgium	–	44.8	64.2	49.4	e55.5	Belgique
United States	27.2	35.8	30.7	17.6	33.9	Etats-Unis d'Amérique
Peru	17.8	33.3	45.6	25.8	19.7	Pérou
Spain	32.7	22.6	21.1	21.0	23.7	Espagne
Uruguay	24.2	22.6	22.9	24.4	25.1	Uruguay
China, Macao SAR	9.0	9.1	11.5	9.9	24.3	Chine - RAS de Macao
Switzerland-Liechtenstein	12.9	14.4	17.8	10.5	6.9	Suisse-Liechtenstein
Ireland	15.4	10.0	9.3	7.3	12.0	Irlande
Turkey	10.4	9.7	8.3	10.3	15.1	Turquie
Netherlands	15.0	12.4	13.0	6.2	7.1	Pays-Bas
Iran (Islamic Republic of)	3.0	6.6	15.5	15.3	8.1	Iran (République islamique d')
Belgium-Luxembourg	38.8	–	–	–	–	Belgique-Luxembourg
Czech Republic	5.6	6.9	4.8	8.8	8.7	République tchèque
Romania	5.5	5.0	6.6	5.1	7.3	Roumanie
Brazil	10.5	4.7	2.9	5.6	e5.8	Brésil
Russian Federation	12.4	2.3	2.2	1.8	9.2	Fédération de Russie
Kazakhstan	5.3	7.6	4.5	4.6	e5.1	Kazakhstan
Chile	6.7	4.8	3.9	4.7	e4.6	Chili

(Value as percentages of World total) **(Valeur en pourcentage du total mondial)**

Regions of the world	1993	1994	1995	1996	1997	1998	1999	2000	2001	2002	Régions du monde
World	100.0	100.0	100.0	100.0	100.0	100.0	100.0	100.0	100.0	100.0	Monde
Africa	3.1	3.0	3.0	3.1	2.7	3.6	3.9	3.2	3.0	3.7	Afrique
Americas	5.5	5.5	5.6	5.4	4.9	4.8	5.6	5.4	4.5	4.3	Amériques
- Northern America	0.7	1.1	1.1	1.0	0.8	0.9	1.2	1.0	0.6	1.1	- Amérique du Nord
- LAIA	4.7	4.4	4.5	4.4	4.0	3.9	4.3	4.4	3.8	3.2	- ALAI
- CACM	0.0	0.0	0.0	0.0	0.0	0.0	0.0	0.0	0.0	0.0	- MCC
- Caribbean	0.0	0.0	0.0	0.0	0.0	0.0	0.0	0.0	0.0	0.0	- Caraïbes
- Rest of America	0.0	0.0	0.0	0.0	0.0	0.0	0.0	0.0	0.0	0.0	- Autre d'Amérique
Asia excluding former USSR	18.7	17.9	14.9	14.7	12.1	13.3	17.6	17.0	15.0	14.1	Asie ancienne URSS exclus
- Middle East	0.5	1.1	0.6	0.8	0.9	1.0	1.1	1.2	1.3	1.0	- Moyen-Orient
Asia former USSR	0.7	0.9	1.6	0.6	0.8	0.5	0.6	0.4	0.4	0.4	Asie ancienne URSS
Europe excluding former USSR	14.0	14.6	16.2	14.9	14.1	15.8	15.4	15.3	14.4	13.9	Europe ancienne URSS exclus
- European Union	12.5	13.3	14.4	13.7	12.9	14.4	14.2	14.1	13.2	12.7	- Union Européenne
- Eastern Europe	1.0	0.7	1.2	0.6	0.7	0.7	0.6	0.5	0.8	0.7	- Europe de l'Est
- Rest of Europe	0.5	0.6	0.6	0.6	0.5	0.6	0.6	0.7	0.5	0.4	- Autre de l'Europe
Europe former USSR	0.5	0.5	0.9	0.8	1.0	0.6	0.3	0.2	0.2	0.5	Europe ancienne URSS
Oceania	57.5	57.5	57.9	60.5	64.4	61.4	56.6	58.5	62.4	63.1	Océanie

269 Old clothing and other old textile articles; rags

TRADE BY COMMODITY (Value in million US dollars) COMMERCE PAR PRODUIT (Valeur en millions de dollars EU)
Imports by principal countries or areas **Importations selon les principaux pays ou zones**

Country or area	1998	1999	2000	2001	2002	Pays ou zone
World	1412.4	1412.0	1367.9	1366.6	1468.3	Monde
Africa	439.5	434.8	389.3	391.2	428.6	Afrique
Americas	160.6	152.1	179.6	183.5	220.0	Amériques
- Northern America	54.9	52.3	62.1	63.0	89.6	- Amérique du Nord
- LAIA	45.4	35.8	46.8	44.5	46.7	- ALAI
- CACM	35.6	40.2	40.2	44.0	49.7	- MCC
- Caribbean	22.4	21.6	28.0	29.2	29.6	- Caraïbes
- Rest of America	2.4	2.2	2.4	2.9	4.4	- Autre d'Amérique
Asia excluding former USSR	286.7	358.6	406.7	349.5	344.5	Asie ancienne URSS exclus
- Middle East	41.6	35.5	38.4	43.1	40.9	- Moyen-Orient
Asia former USSR	6.2	10.0	10.5	15.2	19.4	Asie ancienne URSS
Europe excluding former USSR	459.5	402.3	321.1	345.5	368.4	Europe ancienne URSS exclus
- European Union	333.6	248.7	207.9	227.4	242.5	- Union Européenne
- Eastern Europe	114.8	145.7	103.6	107.3	116.1	- Europe de l'Est
- Rest of Europe	11.1	7.8	9.5	10.8	9.8	- Autre de l'Europe
Europe former USSR	46.6	43.8	48.7	70.2	75.1	Europe ancienne URSS
Oceania	13.3	10.4	12.0	11.5	12.2	Océanie
Ghana	78.5	74.3	64.2	e68.3	e69.9	Ghana
Malaysia	35.5	72.6	77.5	68.0	e74.3	Malaisie
Japan	53.2	55.4	65.9	61.9	64.0	Japon
Italy-San Marino-Holy See	80.1	56.3	47.2	49.9	47.0	Italie-Saint-Marin-Saint-Siège
Tunisia	41.9	50.5	43.3	44.2	e44.2	Tunisie
Spain	53.7	41.9	37.9	39.0	40.8	Espagne
Singapore	25.7	55.6	60.7	37.4	31.7	Singapour
India	28.7	31.8	39.0	37.5	41.3	Inde
Benin	39.7	44.3	28.6	30.0	e33.1	Bénin
Canada	32.6	26.3	35.6	34.0	45.6	Canada
Poland	42.6	36.4	29.1	30.0	30.6	Pologne
Netherlands	52.7	33.3	24.3	25.8	30.9	Pays-Bas
United Republic of Tanzania	30.5	26.8	35.0	32.9	e32.1	République-Unie de Tanzanie
Kenya	34.1	32.0	31.0	e30.3	29.2	Kenya
Pakistan	31.9	32.7	25.6	27.5	36.5	Pakistan
United States	22.3	26.0	26.5	28.9	44.0	Etats-Unis d'Amérique
France-Monaco	40.4	29.8	25.3	23.4	21.2	France-Monaco
Germany	22.5	23.2	18.4	26.5	35.8	Allemagne
Romania	14.8	28.8	32.4	24.4	23.5	Roumanie
Belgium	-	30.6	26.3	29.7	e32.5	Belgique
Uganda	21.1	20.9	18.3	22.1	24.9	Ouganda
Cambodia	e14.8	e25.3	e30.5	e18.7	e17.2	Cambodge
China, Hong Kong SAR	29.8	20.7	24.9	19.3	6.5	Chine - RAS de Hong-Kong
Guatemala	15.4	16.1	18.0	21.5	24.8	Guatemala
Cameroon	23.0	21.1	17.5	15.5	14.1	Cameroun
United Kingdom	21.1	17.2	14.1	19.0	16.7	Royaume-Uni
Lebanon	15.0	14.1	11.1	21.3	e19.4	Liban
Congo	e12.1	e15.7	e12.8	e19.5	e20.9	Congo
Mexico	11.1	11.6	12.5	19.5	25.5	Mexique
Zambia	18.7	20.3	15.4	13.7	11.7	Zambie

(Value as percentages of World total) **(Valeur en pourcentage du total mondial)**

Regions of the world	1993	1994	1995	1996	1997	1998	1999	2000	2001	2002	Régions du monde
World	100.0	100.0	100.0	100.0	100.0	100.0	100.0	100.0	100.0	100.0	Monde
Africa	22.6	21.0	21.3	22.0	22.9	31.1	30.8	28.5	28.6	29.2	Afrique
Americas	11.5	11.2	9.5	9.6	10.4	11.4	10.8	13.1	13.4	15.0	Amériques
- Northern America	2.5	2.3	2.8	3.1	3.8	3.9	3.7	4.5	4.6	6.1	- Amérique du Nord
- LAIA	7.1	7.1	4.1	3.8	3.0	3.2	2.5	3.4	3.3	3.2	- ALAI
- CACM	1.3	1.2	1.7	1.8	2.4	2.5	2.8	2.9	3.2	3.4	- MCC
- Caribbean	0.4	0.5	0.7	0.8	1.1	1.6	1.5	2.0	2.1	2.0	- Caraïbes
- Rest of America	0.1	0.1	0.1	0.1	0.1	0.2	0.2	0.2	0.2	0.3	- Autre d'Amérique
Asia excluding former USSR	29.5	30.5	33.8	32.0	27.7	20.3	25.4	29.7	25.6	23.5	Asie ancienne URSS exclus
- Middle East	2.8	2.5	2.2	2.4	2.6	2.9	2.5	2.8	3.2	2.8	- Moyen-Orient
Asia former USSR	0.2	0.2	0.1	0.2	0.3	0.4	0.7	0.8	1.1	1.3	Asie ancienne URSS
Europe excluding former USSR	32.3	34.2	32.6	31.1	31.8	32.5	28.5	23.5	25.3	25.1	Europe ancienne URSS exclus
- European Union	27.1	28.1	26.4	24.2	24.1	23.6	17.6	15.2	16.6	16.5	- Union Européenne
- Eastern Europe	4.6	5.7	5.8	6.5	7.3	8.1	10.3	7.6	7.8	7.9	- Europe de l'Est
- Rest of Europe	0.5	0.4	0.4	0.4	0.4	0.8	0.6	0.7	0.8	0.7	- Autre de l'Europe
Europe former USSR	2.5	1.4	1.7	3.9	5.7	3.3	3.1	3.6	5.1	5.1	Europe ancienne URSS
Oceania	1.4	1.4	1.0	1.2	1.2	0.9	0.7	0.9	0.8	0.8	Océanie

TRADE BY COMMODITY (Value in million US dollars)
Exports by principal countries or areas

COMMERCE PAR PRODUIT (Valeur en millions de dollars EU)
Exportations selon les principaux pays ou zones

Country or area	1998	1999	2000	2001	2002	Pays ou zone
World	1643.9	1537.3	1493.4	1538.8	1629.8	Monde
Africa	46.8	81.9	36.8	37.0	52.1	Afrique
Americas	458.4	402.6	413.7	369.6	402.9	Amériques
- Northern America	386.5	349.7	348.0	328.5	337.1	- Amérique du Nord
- LAIA	60.9	43.0	54.2	34.3	57.9	- ALAI
- CACM	1.0	0.5	0.5	2.3	1.6	- MCC
- Caribbean	9.8	9.1	10.6	4.2	6.1	- Caraïbes
- Rest of America	0.3	0.3	0.3	0.3	0.2	- Autre d'Amérique
Asia excluding former USSR	240.0	282.7	334.0	363.2	346.8	Asie ancienne URSS exclus
- Middle East	58.5	45.4	34.7	99.8	93.1	- Moyen-Orient
Asia former USSR	1.8	1.8	1.6	2.0	2.6	Asie ancienne URSS
Europe excluding former USSR	866.2	737.8	676.8	737.1	789.0	Europe ancienne URSS exclus
- European Union	795.9	670.8	610.3	648.7	685.5	- Union Européenne
- Eastern Europe	39.4	38.0	40.9	57.9	67.0	- Europe de l'Est
- Rest of Europe	30.9	29.0	25.5	30.5	36.5	- Autre de l'Europe
Europe former USSR	6.9	7.8	9.2	11.9	17.8	Europe ancienne URSS
Oceania	23.7	22.7	21.3	18.1	18.6	Océanie
United States	328.8	288.4	297.9	268.0	275.7	Etats-Unis d'Amérique
Germany	248.3	202.6	172.6	204.2	187.9	Allemagne
United Kingdom	126.0	107.2	113.1	107.3	136.1	Royaume-Uni
Netherlands	118.2	99.6	89.2	95.7	101.0	Pays-Bas
Korea, Republic of	52.0	76.6	98.4	95.2	99.4	République de Corée
Belgium	–	97.3	84.8	80.2	e90.0	Belgique
Italy-San Marino-Holy See	82.7	67.3	58.1	64.4	69.2	Italie-Saint-Marin-Saint-Siège
Canada	57.7	61.3	50.1	60.6	61.4	Canada
France-Monaco	59.1	50.6	51.4	50.8	48.4	France-Monaco
Mexico	60.3	42.5	53.9	34.0	57.5	Mexique
Japan	35.5	47.9	50.2	46.2	41.8	Japon
Singapore	25.6	42.2	46.7	30.6	26.4	Singapour
Saudi Arabia	36.5	23.8	10.4	46.8	e42.2	Arabie saoudite
Poland	22.1	20.0	22.1	28.1	28.9	Pologne
Belgium-Luxembourg	113.2	–	–	–	–	Belgique-Luxembourg
Switzerland-Liechtenstein	22.0	20.0	17.4	21.4	29.4	Suisse-Liechtenstein
Australia	21.9	21.1	19.2	16.8	16.0	Australie
Malaysia	11.0	17.0	20.7	22.5	e23.8	Malaisie
Turkey	17.4	15.8	16.1	14.8	16.9	Turquie
China, Hong Kong SAR	19.4	16.1	22.3	15.7	7.2	Chine - RAS de Hong-Kong
Lebanon	3.3	3.6	4.4	35.4	e30.8	Liban
Tunisia	13.4	14.2	16.0	14.7	e15.3	Tunisie
Austria	12.1	10.5	7.6	11.0	12.8	Autriche
Sweden	8.6	10.6	10.5	8.7	9.7	Suède
Zambia	7.2	32.5	1.9	1.2	1.0	Zambie
Czech Republic	5.9	5.0	7.7	10.3	12.7	République tchèque
Slovakia	5.1	5.9	4.8	10.7	15.1	Slovaquie
Zimbabwe	e5.7	5.3	4.5	0.2	22.2	Zimbabwe
China	7.3	6.9	10.1	7.7	5.5	Chine
Ireland	5.3	6.6	5.8	6.8	9.6	Irlande

(Value as percentages of World total) **(Valeur en pourcentage du total mondial)**

Regions of the world	1993	1994	1995	1996	1997	1998	1999	2000	2001	2002	Régions du monde
World	100.0	100.0	100.0	100.0	100.0	100.0	100.0	100.0	100.0	100.0	Monde
Africa	0.9	1.2	1.8	2.9	2.5	2.8	5.3	2.5	2.4	3.2	Afrique
Americas	35.1	32.9	30.1	30.7	32.2	27.9	26.2	27.7	24.0	24.7	Amériques
- Northern America	28.5	26.9	25.9	25.3	26.0	23.5	22.7	23.3	21.4	20.7	- Amérique du Nord
- LAIA	6.5	6.0	3.9	5.1	5.9	3.7	2.8	3.6	2.2	3.6	- ALAI
- CACM	0.0	0.0	0.0	0.1	0.0	0.1	0.0	0.0	0.1	0.1	- MCC
- Caribbean	0.2	0.0	0.3	0.3	0.3	0.6	0.6	0.7	0.3	0.4	- Caraïbes
- Rest of America	0.0	0.0	0.0	0.0	0.0	0.0	0.0	0.0	0.0	0.0	- Autre d'Amérique
Asia excluding former USSR	14.0	16.0	17.8	18.2	17.9	14.6	18.4	22.4	23.6	21.3	Asie ancienne URSS exclus
- Middle East	0.9	1.9	3.3	3.2	3.9	3.6	3.0	2.3	6.5	5.7	- Moyen-Orient
Asia former USSR	0.0	0.0	0.0	0.1	0.1	0.1	0.1	0.1	0.1	0.2	Asie ancienne URSS
Europe excluding former USSR	48.2	48.0	48.5	46.1	45.3	52.7	48.0	45.3	47.9	48.4	Europe ancienne URSS exclus
- European Union	46.0	45.5	45.7	43.2	42.3	48.4	43.6	40.9	42.2	42.1	- Union Européenne
- Eastern Europe	0.9	1.1	1.3	1.5	1.7	2.4	2.5	2.7	3.8	4.1	- Europe de l'Est
- Rest of Europe	1.2	1.4	1.5	1.4	1.3	1.9	1.9	1.7	2.0	2.2	- Autre de l'Europe
Europe former USSR	0.1	0.2	0.1	0.2	0.3	0.4	0.5	0.6	0.8	1.1	Europe ancienne URSS
Oceania	1.6	1.7	1.6	1.8	1.7	1.4	1.5	1.4	1.2	1.1	Océanie

271 Fertilizers, crude

TRADE BY COMMODITY (Value in million US dollars)
Imports by principal countries or areas

COMMERCE PAR PRODUIT (Valeur en millions de dollars EU)
Importations selon les principaux pays ou zones

Country or area	1998	1999	2000	2001	2002	Pays ou zone
World	2006.6	1904.5	1727.6	1596.7	1576.3	Monde
Africa	37.2	19.0	25.1	15.6	20.0	Afrique
Americas	303.8	264.7	242.1	233.3	212.6	Amériques
- Northern America	124.5	106.5	77.6	78.6	86.1	- Amérique du Nord
- LAIA	171.3	154.7	161.0	151.6	124.5	- ALAI
- CACM	4.3	2.2	2.3	1.9	0.8	- MCC
- Caribbean	3.3	0.5	0.7	0.8	0.9	- Caraïbes
- Rest of America	0.3	0.8	0.6	0.4	0.2	- Autre d'Amérique
Asia excluding former USSR	663.6	644.5	647.9	578.0	566.6	Asie ancienne URSS exclus
- Middle East	95.7	87.6	106.1	71.4	81.4	- Moyen-Orient
Asia former USSR	23.5	35.8	20.6	22.2	21.8	Asie ancienne URSS
Europe excluding former USSR	745.9	711.4	594.1	580.0	597.8	Europe ancienne URSS exclus
- European Union	544.0	528.7	411.5	408.0	424.0	- Union Européenne
- Eastern Europe	127.9	110.7	111.4	103.7	102.5	- Europe de l'Est
- Rest of Europe	74.0	72.0	71.2	68.3	71.3	- Autre de l'Europe
Europe former USSR	125.4	138.9	89.0	54.2	60.4	Europe ancienne URSS
Oceania	107.2	90.3	108.7	113.3	97.1	Océanie
India	198.5	204.1	226.9	168.6	184.0	Inde
Spain	117.3	127.6	103.9	102.5	91.5	Espagne
Japan	106.3	100.0	98.9	83.9	87.1	Japon
Belgium	–	119.6	88.2	96.3	e105.6	Belgique
Korea, Republic of	86.6	85.4	81.1	66.9	63.5	République de Corée
Netherlands	112.4	100.0	65.9	44.4	53.5	Pays-Bas
Mexico	89.8	88.8	79.0	71.5	46.0	Mexique
United States	69.4	72.6	62.4	68.5	78.3	Etats-Unis d'Amérique
Poland	87.1	75.5	67.8	60.7	59.9	Pologne
France-Monaco	85.7	80.7	63.4	57.8	56.2	France-Monaco
New Zealand	54.6	56.4	62.4	75.1	59.5	Nouvelle-Zélande
Brazil	54.2	44.2	62.8	60.7	61.1	Brésil
Norway	43.0	47.3	43.3	45.7	48.1	Norvège
Lithuania	44.0	57.8	54.0	28.4	e35.0	Lituanie
Australia	52.0	33.6	45.9	37.8	37.1	Australie
Indonesia	41.0	42.7	23.7	50.8	42.1	Indonésie
Turkey	46.4	40.2	30.6	23.5	31.7	Turquie
Malaysia	40.4	38.0	31.6	21.2	e23.2	Malaisie
Philippines	32.7	23.0	12.3	42.7	13.7	Philippines
Ukraine	48.8	50.4	11.7	5.9	6.3	Ukraine
Canada	55.1	33.8	15.2	10.1	7.8	Canada
Belgium-Luxembourg	120.4	–	–	–	–	Belgique-Luxembourg
Italy-San Marino-Holy See	17.2	19.3	18.0	29.5	30.8	Italie-Saint-Marin-Saint-Siège
Belarus	28.9	26.4	20.0	18.5	17.3	Bélarus
Greece	27.4	23.6	17.8	18.7	e20.7	Grèce
Iran (Islamic Republic of)	29.1	26.7	22.8	12.9	14.1	Iran (République islamique d')
Germany	25.2	18.9	16.8	20.8	23.4	Allemagne
Bulgaria	18.8	10.7	18.8	e20.9	e23.0	Bulgarie
Romania	15.2	19.4	20.0	16.8	14.7	Roumanie
Thailand	16.5	12.2	14.3	18.9	e19.7	Thaïlande

(Value as percentages of World total) **(Valeur en pourcentage du total mondial)**

Regions of the world	1993	1994	1995	1996	1997	1998	1999	2000	2001	2002	Régions du monde
World	100.0	100.0	100.0	100.0	100.0	100.0	100.0	100.0	100.0	100.0	Monde
Africa	0.9	1.4	1.3	1.3	1.9	1.9	1.0	1.5	1.0	1.3	Afrique
Americas	11.5	12.6	12.0	12.3	14.4	15.1	13.9	14.0	14.6	13.5	Amériques
- Northern America	7.3	6.0	5.7	5.3	6.0	6.2	5.6	4.5	4.9	5.5	- Amérique du Nord
- LAIA	3.8	6.3	5.9	6.8	8.2	8.5	8.1	9.3	9.5	7.9	- ALAI
- CACM	0.2	0.1	0.2	0.1	0.1	0.2	0.1	0.1	0.1	0.1	- MCC
- Caribbean	0.1	0.1	0.1	0.0	0.0	0.2	0.0	0.0	0.1	0.1	- Caraïbes
- Rest of America	0.1	0.1	0.1	0.1	0.1	0.0	0.0	0.0	0.0	0.0	- Autre d'Amérique
Asia excluding former USSR	40.4	36.7	35.6	35.2	32.5	33.1	33.8	37.5	36.2	35.9	Asie ancienne URSS exclus
- Middle East	5.6	3.3	4.1	4.4	5.0	4.8	4.6	6.1	4.5	5.2	- Moyen-Orient
Asia former USSR	0.0	0.4	0.2	0.3	0.5	1.2	1.9	1.2	1.4	1.4	Asie ancienne URSS
Europe excluding former USSR	40.3	38.3	38.5	38.9	38.4	37.2	37.4	34.4	36.3	37.9	Europe ancienne URSS exclus
- European Union	28.1	27.7	26.8	27.7	27.3	27.1	27.8	23.8	25.6	26.9	- Union Européenne
- Eastern Europe	7.3	6.3	7.7	7.7	7.5	6.4	5.8	6.4	6.5	6.5	- Europe de l'Est
- Rest of Europe	4.9	4.2	3.9	3.6	3.6	3.7	3.8	4.1	4.3	4.5	- Autre de l'Europe
Europe former USSR	0.8	4.6	7.1	7.1	7.0	6.3	7.3	5.2	3.4	3.8	Europe ancienne URSS
Oceania	6.1	6.1	5.4	4.8	5.3	5.3	4.7	6.3	7.1	6.2	Océanie

TRADE BY COMMODITY (Value in million US dollars)
Exports by principal countries or areas

COMMERCE PAR PRODUIT (Valeur en millions de dollars EU)
Exportations selon les principaux pays ou zones

Country or area	1998	1999	2000	2001	2002	Pays ou zone
World	1817.5	1678.8	1274.6	1381.4	1380.0	Monde
Africa	667.9	615.9	510.5	483.8	523.8	Afrique
Americas	50.0	58.9	43.6	41.7	43.0	Amériques
- Northern America	2.6	4.7	3.9	4.6	5.1	- Amérique du Nord
- LAIA	46.5	53.0	39.3	36.0	36.4	- ALAI
- CACM	0.8	1.2	0.3	0.2	0.2	- MCC
- Caribbean	0.0	0.0	0.1	0.8	1.3	- Caraïbes
- Rest of America	0.0	0.0	0.0	0.0	0.0	- Autre d'Amérique
Asia excluding former USSR	595.5	569.1	345.6	589.9	554.1	Asie ancienne URSS exclus
- Middle East	407.5	380.1	141.8	361.8	372.8	- Moyen-Orient
Asia former USSR	16.9	20.5	10.1	9.1	10.2	Asie ancienne URSS
Europe excluding former USSR	127.8	119.1	110.6	104.0	119.5	Europe ancienne URSS exclus
- European Union	113.4	112.2	104.0	97.6	112.5	- Union Européenne
- Eastern Europe	4.0	3.8	3.5	2.7	3.1	- Europe de l'Est
- Rest of Europe	10.3	3.1	3.1	3.6	3.9	- Autre de l'Europe
Europe former USSR	203.0	174.5	143.6	118.1	116.6	Europe ancienne URSS
Oceania	156.6	120.8	110.6	34.8	12.7	Océanie
Morocco	460.2	454.8	389.3	373.3	e406.1	Maroc
Jordan	354.5	340.2	106.1	322.9	328.9	Jordanie
Russian Federation	200.8	172.8	141.7	116.7	115.1	Fédération de Russie
China	100.8	112.0	135.1	168.8	130.1	Chine
Nauru	e150.3	e116.2	e106.2	e32.9	e11.5	Nauru
Togo	115.7	65.0	48.2	43.7	41.4	Togo
Israel	80.1	67.3	58.5	45.5	38.8	Israël
Chile	42.0	48.4	34.1	32.1	e31.4	Chili
Tunisia	33.7	33.1	34.1	33.7	e35.1	Tunisie
Syrian Arab Republic	41.8	29.5	27.8	e31.6	35.4	République arabe syrienne
Netherlands	24.6	24.3	23.7	18.4	27.6	Pays-Bas
Senegal	30.5	35.1	16.5	16.4	19.1	Sénégal
Belgium	–	31.8	26.5	25.5	e28.6	Belgique
Algeria	26.4	26.9	20.6	e14.0	e13.7	Algérie
Italy-San Marino-Holy See	13.7	14.7	14.0	13.1	13.6	Italie-Saint-Marin-Saint-Siège
Kazakhstan	16.7	20.5	9.8	8.8	e9.9	Kazakhstan
Germany	12.0	10.5	10.3	11.7	11.3	Allemagne
France-Monaco	8.7	9.5	9.1	7.4	9.1	France-Monaco
Saudi Arabia	10.5	9.9	6.5	5.9	e5.4	Arabie saoudite
Belgium-Luxembourg	34.5	–	–	–	–	Belgique-Luxembourg
Spain	7.9	6.4	5.5	5.6	6.6	Espagne
United Kingdom	6.2	7.1	6.0	5.6	5.9	Royaume-Uni
Austria	2.7	3.0	4.6	5.3	5.6	Autriche
Canada	2.6	4.7	3.9	4.6	5.1	Canada
Australia	5.7	4.3	4.0	1.5	0.9	Australie
Ireland	2.5	3.2	3.1	4.2	3.5	Irlande
Indonesia	0.9	2.0	2.4	4.2	5.8	Indonésie
Norway	2.0	2.7	2.9	3.2	3.6	Norvège
Peru	2.7	2.1	2.0	1.6	1.5	Pérou
Malaysia	1.8	2.8	2.2	1.1	e1.1	Malaisie

(Value as percentages of World total) **(Valeur en pourcentage du total mondial)**

Regions of the world	1993	1994	1995	1996	1997	1998	1999	2000	2001	2002	Régions du monde
World	100.0	100.0	100.0	100.0	100.0	100.0	100.0	100.0	100.0	100.0	Monde
Africa	35.4	33.1	31.8	34.0	36.7	36.7	36.7	40.1	35.0	38.0	Afrique
Americas	4.7	2.8	3.6	3.2	3.3	2.7	3.5	3.4	3.0	3.1	Amériques
- Northern America	0.1	0.1	0.1	0.2	0.2	0.1	0.3	0.3	0.3	0.4	- Amérique du Nord
- LAIA	4.4	2.6	3.5	2.9	3.0	2.6	3.2	3.1	2.6	2.6	- ALAI
- CACM	0.0	0.0	0.0	0.0	0.0	0.0	0.1	0.0	0.0	0.0	- MCC
- Caribbean	0.2	0.1	0.1	0.1	0.1	0.0	0.0	0.0	0.1	0.1	- Caraïbes
- Rest of America	0.0	0.0	0.0	0.0	0.0	0.0	0.0	0.0	0.0	0.0	- Autre d'Amérique
Asia excluding former USSR	35.2	33.8	34.9	34.6	32.1	32.8	33.9	27.1	42.7	40.2	Asie ancienne URSS exclus
- Middle East	25.1	24.7	26.1	23.7	22.4	22.4	22.6	11.1	26.2	27.0	- Moyen-Orient
Asia former USSR	0.0	0.0	0.0	0.0	0.1	0.9	1.2	0.8	0.7	0.7	Asie ancienne URSS
Europe excluding former USSR	7.3	8.0	9.0	8.0	6.7	7.0	7.1	8.7	7.5	8.7	Europe ancienne URSS exclus
- European Union	6.8	7.6	8.4	7.4	6.3	6.2	6.7	8.2	7.1	8.2	- Union Européenne
- Eastern Europe	0.3	0.2	0.4	0.5	0.3	0.2	0.2	0.3	0.2	0.2	- Europe de l'Est
- Rest of Europe	0.2	0.2	0.2	0.2	0.1	0.6	0.2	0.2	0.3	0.3	- Autre de l'Europe
Europe former USSR	8.0	11.5	11.8	11.4	12.0	11.2	10.4	11.3	8.6	8.5	Europe ancienne URSS
Oceania	9.5	10.7	8.8	8.9	9.0	8.6	7.2	8.7	2.5	0.9	Océanie

273 Stone, sand and gravel

TRADE BY COMMODITY (Value in million US dollars) COMMERCE PAR PRODUIT (Valeur en millions de dollars EU

Imports by principal countries or areas **Importations selon les principaux pays ou zone**

Country or area	1998	1999	2000	2001	2002	Pays ou zone
World	4668.5	4798.9	5202.5	4753.2	4890.4	Monde
Africa	80.1	79.7	74.1	87.5	90.7	Afrique
Americas	544.1	581.4	618.8	585.1	591.6	Amériques
- Northern America	411.5	448.7	490.6	456.3	485.8	- Amérique du Nord
- LAIA	97.0	96.8	96.4	91.3	76.8	- ALAI
- CACM	7.2	7.2	8.3	9.5	9.0	- MCC
- Caribbean	24.0	25.1	18.6	24.3	17.4	- Caraïbes
- Rest of America	4.3	3.7	4.9	3.6	2.7	- Autre d'Amérique
Asia excluding former USSR	1251.5	1353.4	1777.1	1481.1	1404.0	Asie ancienne URSS exclus
- Middle East	200.3	179.9	256.9	220.5	197.4	- Moyen-Orient
Asia former USSR	15.7	11.9	14.5	15.1	16.8	Asie ancienne URSS
Europe excluding former USSR	2638.7	2676.6	2613.9	2471.6	2639.7	Europe ancienne URSS exclus
- European Union	2306.6	2360.3	2306.5	2158.7	2288.2	- Union Européenne
- Eastern Europe	121.6	119.9	120.6	124.4	144.6	- Europe de l'Est
- Rest of Europe	210.5	196.4	186.7	188.5	206.9	- Autre de l'Europe
Europe former USSR	102.9	63.5	71.9	88.2	119.5	Europe ancienne URSS
Oceania	35.5	32.4	32.2	24.6	28.1	Océanie
Italy-San Marino-Holy See	546.9	535.6	572.5	532.9	530.4	Italie-Saint-Marin-Saint-Siège
Germany	457.0	481.0	463.9	396.5	370.5	Allemagne
United States	307.5	342.7	381.5	337.1	360.9	Etats-Unis d'Amérique
China	100.5	216.0	375.8	430.6	436.9	Chine
Netherlands	359.7	319.0	283.3	240.5	308.5	Pays-Bas
Japan	268.2	239.1	297.3	232.1	195.0	Japon
France-Monaco	187.0	202.8	193.1	187.3	193.0	France-Monaco
Belgium	–	235.5	203.9	206.3	e226.3	Belgique
Spain	145.0	152.9	158.5	175.5	185.0	Espagne
United Kingdom	126.5	128.8	150.6	127.1	151.5	Royaume-Uni
Singapore	97.7	127.0	270.4	100.7	74.6	Singapour
Switzerland-Liechtenstein	116.0	112.7	107.9	109.7	118.9	Suisse-Liechtenstein
Canada	103.9	105.7	108.8	118.4	124.2	Canada
China, Hong Kong SAR	88.7	108.5	111.4	94.7	83.3	Chine - RAS de Hong-Kong
Poland	71.3	72.9	73.9	74.5	82.5	Pologne
Kuwait	77.7	62.2	e58.4	e64.2	e20.3	Koweït
Denmark	67.2	64.3	49.3	47.1	52.1	Danemark
Korea, Republic of	43.6	47.3	59.2	58.5	54.9	République de Corée
Portugal	34.8	44.7	45.3	54.9	57.3	Portugal
Belgium-Luxembourg	230.8	–	–	–	–	Belgique-Luxembourg
Mexico	39.5	46.9	54.0	46.0	41.7	Mexique
Russian Federation	59.4	22.6	35.8	43.3	63.7	Fédération de Russie
India	32.9	43.7	46.9	35.1	45.3	Inde
Austria	39.9	41.0	36.5	35.9	37.9	Autriche
Ireland	29.0	33.6	33.5	37.5	46.5	Irlande
Sweden	35.0	39.2	32.6	31.5	39.2	Suède
Indonesia	38.3	20.6	27.7	42.0	37.4	Indonésie
Finland	30.0	30.4	31.2	33.9	34.3	Finlande
United Arab Emirates	11.6	12.2	42.5	41.2	e42.2	Emirates arabes unis
Malaysia	36.7	26.3	26.1	28.4	e31.0	Malaisie

(Value as percentages of World total) **(Valeur en pourcentage du total mondial)**

Regions of the world	1993	1994	1995	1996	1997	1998	1999	2000	2001	2002	Régions du monde
World	100.0	100.0	100.0	100.0	100.0	100.0	100.0	100.0	100.0	100.0	Monde
Africa	1.2	1.1	1.2	1.4	1.4	1.7	1.7	1.4	1.8	1.9	Afrique
Americas	9.2	9.4	9.0	8.6	10.1	11.7	12.1	11.9	12.3	12.1	Amériques
- Northern America	7.4	7.2	6.9	6.7	7.7	8.8	9.3	9.4	9.6	9.9	- Amérique du Nord
- LAIA	1.4	1.7	1.6	1.3	1.7	2.1	2.0	1.9	1.9	1.6	- ALAI
- CACM	0.1	0.1	0.1	0.1	0.1	0.2	0.1	0.2	0.2	0.2	- MCC
- Caribbean	0.2	0.3	0.4	0.3	0.6	0.5	0.5	0.4	0.5	0.4	- Caraïbes
- Rest of America	0.1	0.1	0.1	0.1	0.1	0.1	0.1	0.1	0.1	0.1	- Autre d'Amérique
Asia excluding former USSR	34.7	31.7	29.5	30.6	34.3	26.8	28.2	34.2	31.2	28.7	Asie ancienne URSS exclus
- Middle East	2.7	2.7	2.5	2.5	3.2	4.3	3.7	4.9	4.6	4.0	- Moyen-Orient
Asia former USSR	0.0	0.3	0.2	2.2	0.3	0.3	0.2	0.3	0.3	0.3	Asie ancienne URSS
Europe excluding former USSR	53.9	55.2	57.5	54.6	51.0	56.5	55.8	50.2	52.0	54.0	Europe ancienne URSS exclus
- European Union	48.1	49.1	51.1	48.3	45.3	49.4	49.2	44.3	45.4	46.8	- Union Européenne
- Eastern Europe	1.5	1.5	1.6	1.9	2.0	2.6	2.5	2.3	2.6	3.0	- Europe de l'Est
- Rest of Europe	4.2	4.6	4.8	4.4	3.8	4.5	4.1	3.6	4.0	4.2	- Autre de l'Europe
Europe former USSR	0.2	1.6	1.9	2.0	2.2	2.2	1.3	1.4	1.9	2.4	Europe ancienne URSS
Oceania	0.7	0.8	0.6	0.6	0.5	0.8	0.7	0.6	0.5	0.6	Océanie

TRADE BY COMMODITY (Value in million US dollars)
Exports by principal countries or areas

COMMERCE PAR PRODUIT (Valeur en millions de dollars EU)
Exportations selon les principaux pays ou zones

Country or area	1998	1999	2000	2001	2002	Pays ou zone
World	3602.4	3702.1	3844.7	3759.8	4013.9	Monde
Africa	102.8	99.5	199.0	104.1	167.2	Afrique
Americas	553.6	541.2	632.8	585.6	575.2	Amériques
- Northern America	446.4	434.2	501.3	453.0	443.3	- Amérique du Nord
- LAIA	85.5	93.1	111.1	111.3	110.7	- ALAI
- CACM	4.4	4.3	5.0	3.0	2.8	- MCC
- Caribbean	17.1	9.3	12.4	14.9	16.5	- Caraïbes
- Rest of America	0.3	0.3	3.0	3.3	1.9	- Autre d'Amérique
Asia excluding former USSR	646.0	793.8	858.2	893.0	934.3	Asie ancienne URSS exclus
- Middle East	168.2	168.0	133.1	180.4	211.9	- Moyen-Orient
Asia former USSR	10.4	4.0	5.2	5.7	6.0	Asie ancienne URSS
Europe excluding former USSR	2166.1	2166.9	2048.8	2051.8	2204.4	Europe ancienne URSS exclus
- European Union	1887.2	1895.5	1780.0	1784.3	1903.0	- Union Européenne
- Eastern Europe	66.1	58.1	58.7	55.9	58.2	- Europe de l'Est
- Rest of Europe	212.8	213.3	210.0	211.6	243.2	- Autre de l'Europe
Europe former USSR	62.7	34.0	37.4	57.9	70.5	Europe ancienne URSS
Oceania	60.8	62.7	63.3	61.6	56.3	Océanie
United States	322.7	287.3	331.4	323.9	313.0	Etats-Unis d'Amérique
Germany	319.8	319.4	283.8	313.9	301.1	Allemagne
Spain	266.6	276.5	296.7	295.1	321.3	Espagne
Italy-San Marino-Holy See	283.0	270.4	279.4	252.9	269.0	Italie-Saint-Marin-Saint-Siège
India	131.7	241.5	265.2	281.6	320.0	Inde
France-Monaco	261.9	256.1	233.8	213.5	227.5	France-Monaco
Belgium	–	234.5	210.8	226.6	e254.3	Belgique
Norway	174.6	167.4	164.5	161.6	193.3	Norvège
Canada	123.7	146.6	169.7	129.0	130.3	Canada
China	102.0	99.7	128.7	131.6	158.0	Chine
Austria	113.0	112.8	99.4	104.2	115.2	Autriche
United Kingdom	97.8	114.7	93.6	97.9	105.0	Royaume-Uni
Netherlands	76.9	78.2	56.9	67.6	82.0	Pays-Bas
Thailand	66.9	57.9	85.6	64.6	e68.3	Thaïlande
Sweden	65.9	68.3	61.2	51.4	56.9	Suède
Indonesia	21.4	51.8	66.2	98.4	56.6	Indonésie
Australia	59.6	60.8	59.6	59.8	52.6	Australie
Mexico	69.9	61.0	52.3	49.9	55.2	Mexique
United Arab Emirates	87.1	89.8	31.7	38.4	e40.0	Emirates arabes unis
Turkey	29.8	40.4	45.6	73.1	88.3	Turquie
Egypt	30.1	25.1	118.5	34.2	57.1	Egypte
Portugal	62.9	45.0	41.3	45.7	57.0	Portugal
Belgium-Luxembourg	230.6	–	–	–	–	Belgique-Luxembourg
Finland	42.0	42.6	37.0	38.0	41.4	Finlande
China, Hong Kong SAR	29.2	52.2	51.4	38.8	23.5	Chine - RAS de Hong-Kong
Japan	33.5	31.4	33.9	33.1	33.5	Japon
Brazil	2.7	21.5	46.3	41.9	e43.4	Brésil
Greece	25.9	25.6	36.8	31.7	e31.7	Grèce
Denmark	26.3	30.6	31.3	28.0	24.0	Danemark
Poland	31.3	27.8	27.1	22.4	20.7	Pologne

(Value as percentages of World total) **(Valeur en pourcentage du total mondial)**

Regions of the world	1993	1994	1995	1996	1997	1998	1999	2000	2001	2002	Régions du monde
World	100.0	100.0	100.0	100.0	100.0	100.0	100.0	100.0	100.0	100.0	Monde
Africa	2.6	2.7	2.6	2.6	2.7	2.9	2.7	5.2	2.8	4.2	Afrique
Americas	12.7	12.1	11.7	11.4	13.5	15.4	14.6	16.5	15.6	14.3	Amériques
- Northern America	10.3	9.7	9.4	9.2	10.6	12.4	11.7	13.0	12.0	11.0	- Amérique du Nord
- LAIA	2.0	2.0	1.9	1.8	2.3	2.4	2.5	2.9	3.0	2.8	- ALAI
- CACM	0.1	0.1	0.1	0.1	0.1	0.1	0.1	0.1	0.1	0.1	- MCC
- Caribbean	0.3	0.4	0.3	0.3	0.5	0.5	0.3	0.3	0.4	0.4	- Caraïbes
- Rest of America	0.0	0.0	0.0	0.0	0.0	0.0	0.0	0.1	0.1	0.0	- Autre d'Amérique
Asia excluding former USSR	22.5	23.2	22.3	22.3	21.9	17.9	21.4	22.3	23.8	23.3	Asie ancienne URSS exclus
- Middle East	3.0	3.1	2.8	2.6	3.2	4.7	4.5	3.5	4.8	5.3	- Moyen-Orient
Asia former USSR	0.0	0.2	0.3	1.3	0.3	0.3	0.1	0.1	0.2	0.2	Asie ancienne URSS
Europe excluding former USSR	60.3	59.6	60.0	59.6	58.7	60.1	58.5	53.3	54.6	54.9	Europe ancienne URSS exclus
- European Union	50.6	51.4	51.7	50.8	51.0	52.4	51.2	46.3	47.5	47.4	- Union Européenne
- Eastern Europe	4.3	2.7	2.7	3.6	2.0	1.8	1.6	1.5	1.5	1.4	- Europe de l'Est
- Rest of Europe	5.4	5.5	5.6	5.3	5.7	5.9	5.8	5.5	5.6	6.1	- Autre de l'Europe
Europe former USSR	0.5	0.9	1.2	1.3	1.2	1.7	0.9	1.0	1.5	1.8	Europe ancienne URSS
Oceania	1.4	1.3	2.0	1.5	1.6	1.7	1.7	1.6	1.6	1.4	Océanie

274 Sulphur and unroasted iron pyrites

TRADE BY COMMODITY (Value in million US dollars)
Imports by principal countries or areas

COMMERCE PAR PRODUIT (Valeur en millions de dollars EU)
Importations selon les principaux pays ou zones

Country or area	1998	1999	2000	2001	2002	Pays ou zone
World	858.6	918.6	1034.1	787.4	920.1	Monde
Africa	236.9	220.3	257.0	202.4	223.0	Afrique
Americas	179.5	188.4	204.7	127.8	135.6	Amériques
- Northern America	78.5	72.3	60.0	36.2	45.2	- Amérique du Nord
- LAIA	90.5	104.7	132.4	82.1	82.0	- ALAI
- CACM	0.9	0.7	1.1	1.1	1.2	- MCC
- Caribbean	9.4	10.6	11.1	8.4	7.3	- Caraïbes
- Rest of America	0.1	0.0	0.0	0.0	0.0	- Autre d'Amérique
Asia excluding former USSR	252.6	362.0	394.1	316.9	407.4	Asie ancienne URSS exclus
- Middle East	37.3	44.6	44.6	38.9	55.5	- Moyen-Orient
Asia former USSR	0.7	1.7	1.5	0.7	0.7	Asie ancienne URSS
Europe excluding former USSR	135.3	95.9	113.8	101.2	104.2	Europe ancienne URSS exclus
- European Union	102.7	69.2	84.0	72.4	74.6	- Union Européenne
- Eastern Europe	11.8	9.2	11.7	12.2	12.8	- Europe de l'Est
- Rest of Europe	20.8	17.5	18.1	16.6	16.7	- Autre de l'Europe
Europe former USSR	34.8	30.3	27.9	12.8	15.1	Europe ancienne URSS
Oceania	18.9	19.9	35.0	25.6	34.1	Océanie
China	45.3	94.8	150.6	134.8	187.1	Chine
Morocco	111.3	108.6	134.1	100.6	e106.2	Maroc
India	66.7	115.8	90.8	58.0	83.0	Inde
Brazil	58.0	66.6	91.6	58.8	63.7	Brésil
Tunisia	63.2	56.0	69.2	54.5	e54.5	Tunisie
United States	72.7	67.0	54.6	30.4	39.8	Etats-Unis d'Amérique
Israel	27.5	28.2	33.1	29.1	25.4	Israël
Philippines	29.1	36.9	28.0	18.4	25.1	Philippines
Jordan	18.1	28.1	25.6	23.3	41.7	Jordanie
Mexico	20.9	27.1	29.4	13.6	9.5	Mexique
Australia	9.6	10.5	20.8	16.4	25.0	Australie
Indonesia	18.3	15.7	16.7	17.4	12.2	Indonésie
Belgium	–	20.8	22.8	15.7	e17.2	Belgique
Senegal	16.2	9.9	4.0	15.2	19.2	Sénégal
South Africa	–	–	29.1	12.8	18.7	Afrique du Sud
Italy-San Marino-Holy See	15.9	4.9	13.2	10.0	11.3	Italie-Saint-Marin-Saint-Siège
Spain	5.2	4.3	13.1	14.9	15.8	Espagne
New Zealand	8.3	8.5	13.8	9.0	9.0	Nouvelle-Zélande
Ukraine	15.9	12.5	9.5	3.8	4.1	Ukraine
Cuba	e9.3	9.7	11.1	8.4	e7.2	Cuba
France-Monaco	11.0	9.7	10.2	7.8	6.5	France-Monaco
Southern African Customs Union	17.4	23.4	–	–	–	Union douanière d'Afrique australe
Turkey	10.6	7.7	7.7	5.3	6.4	Turquie
Korea, Republic of	9.0	8.3	9.4	5.9	5.0	République de Corée
Belarus	8.6	7.7	7.6	5.7	5.2	Bélarus
Norway	7.9	6.8	6.1	5.2	6.8	Norvège
Germany	11.5	6.2	4.6	5.2	4.6	Allemagne
Lebanon	6.4	4.9	7.9	6.1	e5.6	Liban
Greece	7.5	7.8	6.6	3.9	e4.4	Grèce
Canada	5.9	5.3	5.4	5.8	5.4	Canada

(Value as percentages of World total) **(Valeur en pourcentage du total mondial)**

Regions of the world	1993	1994	1995	1996	1997	1998	1999	2000	2001	2002	Régions du monde
World	100.0	100.0	100.0	100.0	100.0	100.0	100.0	100.0	100.0	100.0	Monde
Africa	32.5	28.0	28.3	28.5	30.2	27.6	24.0	24.9	25.7	24.2	Afrique
Americas	21.9	22.0	23.7	21.4	23.3	20.9	20.5	19.8	16.2	14.7	Amériques
- Northern America	10.7	9.6	10.6	8.5	8.1	9.1	7.9	5.8	4.6	4.9	- Amérique du Nord
- LAIA	10.5	11.2	12.1	11.8	13.3	10.5	11.4	12.8	10.4	8.9	- ALAI
- CACM	0.2	0.2	0.1	0.2	0.1	0.1	0.1	0.1	0.1	0.1	- MCC
- Caribbean	0.6	1.1	0.9	0.9	1.8	1.1	1.2	1.1	1.1	0.8	- Caraïbes
- Rest of America	0.0	0.0	0.0	0.0	0.0	0.0	0.0	0.0	0.0	0.0	- Autre d'Amérique
Asia excluding former USSR	25.8	29.9	26.1	28.2	25.2	29.4	39.4	38.1	40.2	44.3	Asie ancienne URSS exclus
- Middle East	3.2	3.5	3.3	4.4	4.0	4.3	4.9	4.3	4.9	6.0	- Moyen-Orient
Asia former USSR	0.0	0.1	0.1	0.2	0.1	0.1	0.2	0.1	0.1	0.1	Asie ancienne URSS
Europe excluding former USSR	17.2	15.5	16.8	15.6	15.3	15.8	10.4	11.0	12.8	11.3	Europe ancienne URSS exclus
- European Union	13.2	12.0	13.3	12.2	12.0	12.0	7.5	8.1	9.2	8.1	- Union Européenne
- Eastern Europe	2.1	1.2	1.5	1.2	1.2	1.4	1.0	1.1	1.5	1.4	- Europe de l'Est
- Rest of Europe	2.0	2.3	2.0	2.2	2.1	2.4	1.9	1.8	2.1	1.8	- Autre de l'Europe
Europe former USSR	0.4	2.6	2.4	4.1	3.8	4.1	3.3	2.7	1.6	1.6	Europe ancienne URSS
Oceania	2.1	1.9	2.5	2.1	2.0	2.2	2.2	3.4	3.3	3.7	Océanie

TRADE BY COMMODITY (Value in million US dollars)
Exports by principal countries or areas

COMMERCE PAR PRODUIT (Valeur en millions de dollars EU)
Exportations selon les principaux pays ou zones

Country or area	1998	1999	2000	2001	2002	Pays ou zone
World	469.6	482.3	580.9	392.7	452.3	Monde
Africa	4.7	9.1	7.5	2.6	4.6	Afrique
Americas	237.9	247.8	276.6	175.2	168.4	Amériques
- Northern America	209.1	220.1	255.5	166.1	155.1	- Amérique du Nord
- LAIA	28.6	27.4	20.6	8.5	12.9	- ALAI
- CACM	0.1	0.1	0.1	0.4	0.1	- MCC
- Caribbean	0.0	0.1	0.4	0.3	0.3	- Caraïbes
- Rest of America	0.0	0.0	0.0	0.0	0.0	- Autre d'Amérique
Asia excluding former USSR	50.8	54.7	66.1	55.7	84.2	Asie ancienne URSS exclus
- Middle East	14.8	19.1	21.2	17.3	46.1	- Moyen-Orient
Asia former USSR	2.4	2.4	0.7	0.5	0.5	Asie ancienne URSS
Europe excluding former USSR	149.0	137.6	162.4	132.7	131.3	Europe ancienne URSS exclus
- European Union	114.5	105.5	116.0	103.7	106.5	- Union Européenne
- Eastern Europe	33.9	31.7	45.5	28.5	23.9	- Europe de l'Est
- Rest of Europe	0.6	0.4	0.9	0.6	0.9	- Autre de l'Europe
Europe former USSR	23.9	30.1	66.8	25.6	62.6	Europe ancienne URSS
Oceania	1.0	0.5	0.7	0.3	0.6	Océanie
Canada	173.3	178.7	194.7	116.9	114.8	Canada
Germany	45.8	49.0	60.7	56.1	53.1	Allemagne
United States	35.9	41.4	60.8	49.2	40.3	Etats-Unis d'Amérique
Russian Federation	21.1	28.3	64.2	24.3	61.0	Fédération de Russie
Poland	33.3	30.8	44.6	27.8	21.8	Pologne
Japan	21.2	21.3	25.5	26.9	26.1	Japon
France-Monaco	24.0	16.9	18.4	14.6	22.1	France-Monaco
Mexico	27.4	26.6	19.7	7.6	11.9	Mexique
Netherlands	17.6	13.8	11.1	12.6	9.3	Pays-Bas
Korea, Republic of	7.8	8.9	12.0	5.6	4.7	République de Corée
Finland	8.9	9.3	7.6	5.5	6.7	Finlande
Italy-San Marino-Holy See	5.3	6.2	8.7	8.1	8.3	Italie-Saint-Marin-Saint-Siège
Jordan		7.6	1.8	4.9	14.9	Jordanie
Saudi Arabia	9.5	4.3	5.8	3.6	e3.2	Arabie saoudite
Qatar	3.4	3.3	6.3	2.7	4.3	Qatar
Spain	4.6	3.8	4.2	3.8	3.4	Espagne
Kuwait	0.0	0.0	0.0	0.0	e	Koweït
Iran (Islamic Republic of)	1.5	3.1	5.4	4.4	3.8	Iran (République islamique d')
Singapore	3.5	2.7	3.9	2.3	2.5	Singapour
Southern African Customs Union	4.4	8.8	-	-	-	Union douanière d'Afrique australe
South Africa	-	-	6.9	2.2	3.5	Afrique du Sud
United Kingdom	4.5	3.4	2.1	1.0	1.4	Royaume-Uni
Ukraine	2.3	1.8	2.6	1.2	1.3	Ukraine
China	2.1	1.2	1.6	2.1	1.7	Chine
Belgium	-	2.2	2.5	1.2	e1.3	Belgique
Bahrain	e0.4	e0.5	0.8	1.1	e1.0	Bahreïn
Kazakhstan	2.1	0.9		0.0	e0.0	Kazakhstan
Peru	0.4	0.5	0.6	0.5	0.5	Pérou
Uzbekistan	e0.0	e1.3	e0.5	e0.3	e0.3	Ouzbékistan
Belgium-Luxembourg	2.2	-	-	-	-	Belgique-Luxembourg

(Value as percentages of World total)

(Valeur en pourcentage du total mondial)

Regions of the world	1993	1994	1995	1996	1997	1998	1999	2000	2001	2002	Régions du monde
World	100.0	100.0	100.0	100.0	100.0	100.0	100.0	100.0	100.0	100.0	Monde
Africa	0.3	0.3	0.4	0.6	0.7	1.0	1.9	1.3	0.7	1.0	Afrique
Americas	35.9	39.9	49.8	52.4	48.4	50.7	51.4	47.6	44.6	37.2	Amériques
- Northern America	30.4	36.0	45.6	48.6	44.8	44.5	45.6	44.0	42.3	34.3	- Amérique du Nord
- LAIA	5.4	3.8	4.2	3.8	3.5	6.1	5.7	3.6	2.2	2.8	- ALAI
- CACM	0.0	0.0	0.0	0.0	0.0	0.0	0.0	0.0	0.1	0.0	- MCC
- Caribbean	0.0	0.1	0.0	0.0	0.0	0.0	0.0	0.1	0.1	0.1	- Caraïbes
- Rest of America	0.0	0.0	0.0	0.0	0.0	0.0	0.0	0.0	0.0	0.0	- Autre d'Amérique
Asia excluding former USSR	30.9	26.4	14.4	11.9	15.6	10.8	11.3	11.4	14.2	18.6	Asie ancienne URSS exclus
- Middle East	26.9	22.5	10.1	6.9	10.3	3.2	4.0	3.7	4.4	10.2	- Moyen-Orient
Asia former USSR	0.7	1.3	0.5	0.6	0.4	0.5	0.5	0.1	0.1	0.1	Asie ancienne URSS
Europe excluding former USSR	31.6	27.3	29.9	28.3	25.0	31.7	28.5	28.0	33.8	29.0	Europe ancienne URSS exclus
- European Union	16.7	15.9	18.4	19.5	17.8	24.4	21.9	20.0	26.4	23.6	- Union Européenne
- Eastern Europe	14.8	11.2	11.4	8.7	7.1	7.2	6.6	7.8	7.2	5.3	- Europe de l'Est
- Rest of Europe	0.1	0.1	0.0	0.1	0.1	0.1	0.1	0.1	0.2	0.2	- Autre de l'Europe
Europe former USSR	0.4	4.7	4.8	6.0	9.8	5.1	6.3	11.5	6.5	13.8	Europe ancienne URSS
Oceania	0.1	0.2	0.1	0.1	0.1	0.2	0.1	0.1	0.1	0.1	Océanie

277 Natural abrasives, nes

TRADE BY COMMODITY (Value in million US dollars)
Imports by principal countries or areas

COMMERCE PAR PRODUIT (Valeur en millions de dollars EU
Importations selon les principaux pays ou zone

Country or area	1998	1999	2000	2001	2002	Pays ou zone
World	1186.4	1706.2	1176.0	1034.7	1001.2	Monde
Africa	24.9	22.6	31.4	35.1	38.4	Afrique
Americas	183.6	175.6	208.4	174.6	160.3	Amériques
- Northern America	164.6	154.5	179.4	151.9	142.5	- Amérique du Nord
- LAIA	16.6	19.0	25.8	20.4	15.0	- ALAI
- CACM	1.0	0.9	0.7	0.8	0.8	- MCC
- Caribbean	1.4	1.0	2.4	1.4	1.9	- Caraïbes
- Rest of America	0.0	0.2	0.1	0.0	0.1	- Autre d'Amérique
Asia excluding former USSR	257.5	343.1	369.5	309.6	298.2	Asie ancienne URSS exclus
- Middle East	12.7	9.7	11.3	18.3	17.8	- Moyen-Orient
Asia former USSR	0.1	0.2	1.2	1.0	2.2	Asie ancienne URSS
Europe excluding former USSR	711.6	1156.0	557.8	507.8	495.1	Europe ancienne URSS exclus
- European Union	610.0	1051.4	446.6	405.7	399.4	- Union Européenne
- Eastern Europe	6.7	5.4	6.0	6.3	7.2	- Europe de l'Est
- Rest of Europe	94.9	99.2	105.2	95.9	88.6	- Autre de l'Europe
Europe former USSR	1.0	0.8	1.0	0.8	1.0	Europe ancienne URSS
Oceania	7.7	8.0	6.7	5.9	6.0	Océanie
United Kingdom	163.1	642.9	54.8	43.8	38.0	Royaume-Uni
United States	150.0	141.2	165.6	138.8	129.7	Etats-Unis d'Amérique
Switzerland-Liechtenstein	92.1	97.0	102.1	93.5	86.2	Suisse-Liechtenstein
Italy-San Marino-Holy See	89.6	88.6	92.9	85.5	78.1	Italie-Saint-Marin-Saint-Siège
Belgium	–	118.0	97.9	84.1	e92.2	Belgique
Japan	77.0	77.9	79.1	70.5	70.9	Japon
Germany	77.8	71.4	71.0	66.5	53.4	Allemagne
Israel	33.6	51.6	104.6	60.4	43.4	Israël
Korea, Republic of	29.2	48.4	57.8	48.1	49.9	République de Corée
Ireland	43.9	36.7	36.3	33.9	59.1	Irlande
China, Hong Kong SAR	28.0	69.5	19.0	21.0	18.4	Chine - RAS de Hong-Kong
Belgium-Luxembourg	140.7	–	–	–	–	Belgique-Luxembourg
Spain	18.6	22.9	21.7	26.5	21.9	Espagne
Singapore	16.2	22.0	21.0	24.1	21.0	Singapour
France-Monaco	17.9	18.9	20.9	21.0	18.4	France-Monaco
Canada	14.6	13.3	13.8	13.0	12.7	Canada
Thailand	8.8	13.2	14.6	14.4	e15.0	Thaïlande
Austria	16.3	13.9	12.0	10.9	7.6	Autriche
China	10.9	9.3	10.1	9.7	18.8	Chine
Greece	14.4	13.5	12.8	8.2	e9.0	Grèce
Mauritius	12.1	12.0	8.1	8.1	9.2	Maurice
India	5.5	8.3	13.2	11.9	9.8	Inde
Botswana	–	–	12.6	16.7	e19.1	Botswana
Brazil	7.2	8.9	10.7	8.3	7.3	Brésil
Mexico	6.6	7.5	12.2	9.9	5.9	Mexique
Malaysia	4.8	6.2	11.4	9.2	e10.1	Malaisie
Sweden	8.2	8.3	9.1	9.5	5.5	Suède
Netherlands	9.7	7.5	5.6	4.3	5.5	Pays-Bas
Australia	6.6	6.9	5.4	4.6	4.7	Australie
Portugal	6.7	5.4	5.0	5.0	4.8	Portugal

(Value as percentages of World total) **(Valeur en pourcentage du total mondia**

Regions of the world	1993	1994	1995	1996	1997	1998	1999	2000	2001	2002	Régions du monde
World	100.0	100.0	100.0	100.0	100.0	100.0	100.0	100.0	100.0	100.0	Monde
Africa	1.3	1.9	1.5	2.3	2.2	2.1	1.3	2.7	3.4	3.8	Afrique
Americas	10.8	12.8	14.2	17.1	17.0	15.5	10.3	17.7	16.9	16.0	Amériques
- Northern America	9.5	11.0	12.6	15.4	15.5	13.9	9.1	15.3	14.7	14.2	- Amérique du Nord
- LAIA	1.2	1.6	1.2	1.3	1.3	1.4	1.1	2.2	2.0	1.5	- ALAI
- CACM	0.0	0.0	0.1	0.1	0.1	0.1	0.1	0.1	0.1	0.1	- MCC
- Caribbean	0.0	0.1	0.2	0.3	0.1	0.1	0.1	0.2	0.1	0.2	- Caraïbes
- Rest of America	0.0	0.0	0.0	0.0	0.0	0.0	0.0	0.0	0.0	0.0	- Autre d'Amérique
Asia excluding former USSR	32.0	31.4	35.0	30.8	30.7	21.7	20.1	31.4	29.9	29.8	Asie ancienne URSS exclus
- Middle East	0.7	1.0	1.0	1.2	2.0	1.1	0.6	1.0	1.8	1.8	- Moyen-Orient
Asia former USSR	0.0	0.0	0.0	0.1	0.1	0.0	0.0	0.1	0.1	0.2	Asie ancienne URSS
Europe excluding former USSR	55.4	53.2	48.3	48.7	49.0	60.0	67.8	47.4	49.1	49.5	Europe ancienne URSS exclus
- European Union	49.8	46.5	41.2	40.8	40.5	51.4	61.6	38.0	39.2	39.9	- Union Européenne
- Eastern Europe	0.4	0.6	0.6	0.6	0.7	0.6	0.3	0.5	0.6	0.7	- Europe de l'Est
- Rest of Europe	5.1	6.2	6.6	7.3	7.8	8.0	5.8	8.9	9.3	8.8	- Autre de l'Europe
Europe former USSR	0.0	0.1	0.2	0.2	0.2	0.1	0.0	0.1	0.1	0.1	Europe ancienne URSS
Oceania	0.5	0.6	0.7	0.8	0.7	0.6	0.5	0.6	0.6	0.6	Océanie

TRADE BY COMMODITY (Value in million US dollars)
Exports by principal countries or areas

COMMERCE PAR PRODUIT (Valeur en millions de dollars EU)
Exportations selon les principaux pays ou zones

Country or area	1998	1999	2000	2001	2002	Pays ou zone
World	1006.4	960.1	1038.3	946.4	903.5	Monde
Africa	121.5	48.1	91.6	84.9	85.8	Afrique
Americas	169.7	150.0	155.2	133.1	117.2	Amériques
- Northern America	167.8	147.6	151.9	131.1	116.1	- Amérique du Nord
- LAIA	1.8	2.3	3.3	1.8	1.0	- ALAI
- CACM	0.0	0.1	0.1	0.1	0.2	- MCC
- Caribbean	0.1	0.0	0.0	0.0	0.0	- Caraïbes
- Rest of America	0.0	0.0	0.0	0.0	0.0	- Autre d'Amérique
Asia excluding former USSR	245.3	430.4	471.5	441.6	450.0	Asie ancienne URSS exclus
- Middle East	9.9	8.1	8.6	10.4	10.5	- Moyen-Orient
Asia former USSR	0.1	0.1	0.1	0.0	0.1	Asie ancienne URSS
Europe excluding former USSR	353.2	323.0	312.1	278.2	241.0	Europe ancienne URSS exclus
- European Union	278.7	249.9	237.0	210.5	192.5	- Union Européenne
- Eastern Europe	0.2	0.1	0.3	0.2	0.6	- Europe de l'Est
- Rest of Europe	74.3	72.9	74.8	67.5	47.8	- Autre de l'Europe
Europe former USSR	106.9	0.5	0.8	0.2	0.0	Europe ancienne URSS
Oceania	9.7	8.1	7.1	8.4	9.5	Océanie
Thailand	93.5	167.1	194.9	158.8	e167.7	Thaïlande
United States	166.1	145.8	150.3	129.2	114.0	Etats-Unis d'Amérique
Israel	11.6	52.1	99.1	119.2	121.4	Israël
Belgium	–	79.3	86.9	81.5	e91.4	Belgique
Switzerland-Liechtenstein	70.5	70.5	71.4	65.3	46.4	Suisse-Liechtenstein
United Kingdom	75.0	57.6	69.0	49.5	48.1	Royaume-Uni
Korea, Republic of	43.5	45.4	46.3	33.0	29.9	République de Corée
Germany	49.2	38.0	37.6	33.5	15.9	Allemagne
China, Hong Kong SAR	27.5	81.0	15.1	14.6	9.8	Chine - RAS de Hong-Kong
India	12.3	15.7	40.4	32.8	27.6	Inde
Russian Federation	106.7	0.4	0.0	0.0	0.0	Fédération de Russie
Belgium-Luxembourg	103.9	–	–	–	–	Belgique-Luxembourg
Japan	18.9	22.3	24.8	20.8	15.8	Japon
Sierra Leone	20.8	1.2	10.1	26.3	40.5	Sierra Leone
China	16.6	15.6	18.8	22.3	23.6	Chine
Singapore	7.8	17.8	16.2	22.0	25.8	Singapour
Ireland	17.9	47.0	9.9	8.8	5.7	Irlande
Botswana	–	–	23.6	27.4	e27.1	Botswana
Ghana	9.8	6.7	11.2	e14.7	e14.8	Ghana
South Africa	–	–	42.3	13.6	0.3	Afrique du Sud
Southern African Customs Union	25.8	26.2	–	–	–	Union douanière d'Afrique australe
Italy-San Marino-Holy See	8.0	9.1	9.0	9.9	9.9	Italie-Saint-Marin-Saint-Siège
Australia	9.4	7.8	6.7	8.0	9.2	Australie
Turkey	9.6	7.8	7.6	6.5	9.2	Turquie
Netherlands	8.6	4.7	7.2	7.4	3.5	Pays-Bas
Greece	7.0	6.4	6.5	5.6	e5.6	Grèce
Central African Republic	e28.0	e0.0	e0.0	e0.0	e0.0	République centrafricaine
France-Monaco	2.1	3.0	6.6	8.2	7.4	France-Monaco
Indonesia	0.7	2.9	3.4	4.8	14.8	Indonésie
Guinea	24.4	0.0	0.0	0.0	e0.0	Guinée

(Value as percentages of World total)

(Valeur en pourcentage du total mondial)

Regions of the world	1993	1994	1995	1996	1997	1998	1999	2000	2001	2002	Régions du monde
World	100.0	100.0	100.0	100.0	100.0	100.0	100.0	100.0	100.0	100.0	Monde
Africa	26.1	9.7	11.6	9.5	8.6	12.1	5.0	8.8	9.0	9.5	Afrique
Americas	21.2	26.5	17.4	19.1	21.6	16.9	15.6	15.0	14.1	13.0	Amériques
- Northern America	21.0	26.3	16.8	18.9	21.4	16.7	15.4	14.6	13.9	12.8	- Amérique du Nord
- LAIA	0.2	0.2	0.3	0.1	0.2	0.2	0.2	0.3	0.2	0.1	- ALAI
- CACM	0.0	0.0	0.0	0.0	0.0	0.0	0.0	0.0	0.0	0.0	- MCC
- Caribbean	0.0	0.0	0.3	0.0	0.0	0.0	0.0	0.0	0.0	0.0	- Caraïbes
- Rest of America	0.0	0.0	0.0	0.1	0.0	0.0	0.0	0.0	0.0	0.0	- Autre d'Amérique
Asia excluding former USSR	18.1	23.4	28.9	23.5	23.1	24.4	44.8	45.4	46.7	49.8	Asie ancienne URSS exclus
- Middle East	1.1	1.2	1.3	1.6	1.3	1.0	0.8	0.8	1.1	1.2	- Moyen-Orient
Asia former USSR	0.0	0.0	0.2	0.3	0.2	0.0	0.0	0.0	0.0	0.0	Asie ancienne URSS
Europe excluding former USSR	29.8	39.3	40.8	46.5	45.4	35.1	33.6	30.1	29.4	26.7	Europe ancienne URSS exclus
- European Union	22.4	30.5	32.4	38.0	35.5	27.7	26.0	22.8	22.2	21.3	- Union Européenne
- Eastern Europe	0.3	0.4	0.0	0.1	0.5	0.0	0.0	0.0	0.0	0.1	- Europe de l'Est
- Rest of Europe	7.1	8.4	8.4	8.4	9.4	7.4	7.6	7.2	7.1	5.3	- Autre de l'Europe
Europe former USSR	3.6	0.1	0.2	0.2	0.2	10.6	0.0	0.1	0.0	0.0	Europe ancienne URSS
Oceania	1.2	0.9	0.9	1.0	0.8	1.0	0.8	0.7	0.9	1.0	Océanie

278 Other crude minerals

TRADE BY COMMODITY (Value in million US dollars)
Imports by principal countries or areas

COMMERCE PAR PRODUIT (Valeur en millions de dollars EU)
Importations selon les principaux pays ou zones

Country or area	1998	1999	2000	2001	2002	Pays ou zone
World	9333.4	9000.3	9332.5	9310.3	9270.1	Monde
Africa	336.4	286.1	242.9	256.6	280.7	Afrique
Americas	1816.6	1679.6	1890.3	1930.8	1770.0	Amériques
- Northern America	1308.8	1242.0	1392.1	1407.8	1300.1	- Amérique du Nord
- LAIA	429.7	360.2	420.1	447.0	399.5	- ALAI
- CACM	29.8	36.2	38.1	34.1	35.7	- MCC
- Caribbean	40.9	33.6	34.6	36.0	29.6	- Caraïbes
- Rest of America	7.4	7.6	5.5	5.9	5.1	- Autre d'Amérique
Asia excluding former USSR	2558.0	2593.3	2795.3	2753.3	2685.5	Asie ancienne URSS exclus
- Middle East	215.3	205.4	248.6	235.6	262.8	- Moyen-Orient
Asia former USSR	46.2	31.9	36.5	41.0	39.4	Asie ancienne URSS
Europe excluding former USSR	4263.6	4121.7	4062.1	4030.9	4173.9	Europe ancienne URSS exclus
- European Union	3723.2	3607.7	3559.1	3521.7	3631.5	- Union Européenne
- Eastern Europe	253.3	243.7	249.5	256.2	283.1	- Europe de l'Est
- Rest of Europe	287.1	270.3	253.5	253.0	259.4	- Autre de l'Europe
Europe former USSR	258.5	231.2	240.2	238.8	256.6	Europe ancienne URSS
Oceania	54.2	56.5	65.2	59.0	64.0	Océanie
Japan	1136.4	1094.0	1145.6	1126.6	987.2	Japon
United States	1006.7	931.9	1062.1	1072.8	962.1	Etats-Unis d'Amérique
Germany	718.5	639.9	613.2	625.5	639.4	Allemagne
Italy-San Marino-Holy See	534.9	595.0	626.3	641.8	631.8	Italie-Saint-Marin-Saint-Siège
France-Monaco	425.1	387.7	369.9	390.2	407.4	France-Monaco
United Kingdom	361.8	319.8	338.8	316.9	342.6	Royaume-Uni
Canada	300.3	307.8	328.8	333.6	335.8	Canada
Netherlands	286.4	306.0	313.9	293.9	308.2	Pays-Bas
Korea, Republic of	225.2	256.2	263.6	275.6	258.3	République de Corée
Belgium	–	319.3	280.9	296.0	e324.6	Belgique
Finland	235.8	216.5	237.1	222.1	211.8	Finlande
Spain	219.5	212.0	209.0	203.6	217.8	Espagne
Sweden	213.6	226.1	202.9	186.1	203.0	Suède
Mexico	171.0	162.8	205.9	240.6	208.2	Mexique
China	111.6	136.1	186.0	203.1	218.2	Chine
Indonesia	127.6	140.6	168.9	151.7	148.4	Indonésie
Austria	158.3	136.3	128.9	97.2	98.7	Autriche
Norway	127.6	120.6	110.4	112.1	116.9	Norvège
Russian Federation	121.1	91.3	101.7	115.3	118.6	Fédération de Russie
Denmark	109.7	97.0	90.2	101.9	85.7	Danemark
India	96.1	95.7	85.1	103.6	102.7	Inde
Malaysia	78.5	93.8	94.4	97.8	e106.9	Malaisie
Thailand	66.1	88.5	100.4	99.1	e103.2	Thaïlande
Ukraine	78.9	91.6	92.9	78.5	84.6	Ukraine
Poland	85.5	74.4	79.3	79.1	93.9	Pologne
Brazil	87.2	62.8	76.3	71.2	68.8	Brésil
Turkey	83.4	60.4	84.3	55.4	74.0	Turquie
Belgium-Luxembourg	338.1	–	–	–	–	Belgique-Luxembourg
Viet Nam	37.8	52.1	71.2	73.9	89.9	Viet Nam
Czech Republic	60.3	61.6	58.2	60.5	62.7	République tchèque

(Value as percentages of World total) **(Valeur en pourcentage du total mondial)**

Regions of the world	1993	1994	1995	1996	1997	1998	1999	2000	2001	2002	Régions du monde
World	100.0	100.0	100.0	100.0	100.0	100.0	100.0	100.0	100.0	100.0	Monde
Africa	3.5	2.7	2.7	3.1	3.9	3.6	3.2	2.6	2.8	3.0	Afrique
Americas	16.8	17.4	16.8	17.5	19.1	19.5	18.7	20.3	20.7	19.1	Amériques
- Northern America	11.8	12.7	12.2	12.3	13.9	14.0	13.8	14.9	15.1	14.0	- Amérique du Nord
- LAIA	4.3	4.1	4.1	4.6	4.5	4.6	4.0	4.5	4.8	4.3	- ALAI
- CACM	0.2	0.2	0.2	0.2	0.3	0.3	0.4	0.4	0.4	0.4	- MCC
- Caribbean	0.2	0.2	0.2	0.3	0.4	0.4	0.4	0.4	0.4	0.3	- Caraïbes
- Rest of America	0.2	0.2	0.1	0.1	0.1	0.1	0.1	0.1	0.1	0.1	- Autre d'Amérique
Asia excluding former USSR	33.0	29.5	29.9	29.1	30.1	27.4	28.8	30.0	29.6	29.0	Asie ancienne URSS exclus
- Middle East	1.8	1.6	2.2	2.2	2.5	2.3	2.3	2.7	2.5	2.8	- Moyen-Orient
Asia former USSR	0.0	0.3	0.8	2.3	0.3	0.5	0.4	0.4	0.4	0.4	Asie ancienne URSS
Europe excluding former USSR	44.7	47.3	46.9	44.9	42.7	45.7	45.8	43.5	43.3	45.0	Europe ancienne URSS exclus
- European Union	39.1	41.5	41.1	39.3	37.4	39.9	40.1	38.1	37.8	39.2	- Union Européenne
- Eastern Europe	2.6	2.5	2.6	2.8	2.6	2.7	2.7	2.7	2.8	3.1	- Europe de l'Est
- Rest of Europe	3.1	3.3	3.2	2.8	2.6	3.1	3.0	2.7	2.7	2.8	- Autre de l'Europe
Europe former USSR	1.3	1.9	2.2	2.5	3.3	2.8	2.6	2.6	2.6	2.8	Europe ancienne URSS
Oceania	0.7	0.8	0.7	0.6	0.7	0.6	0.6	0.7	0.6	0.7	Océanie

TRADE BY COMMODITY (Value in million US dollars)
Exports by principal countries or areas

COMMERCE PAR PRODUIT (Valeur en millions de dollars EU)
Exportations selon les principaux pays ou zones

Country or area	1998	1999	2000	2001	2002	Pays ou zone
World	7047.5	6866.5	6952.2	6941.3	7091.8	Monde
Africa	305.8	275.5	432.5	336.1	359.5	Afrique
Americas	1972.0	1940.0	2116.8	2066.6	1929.7	Amériques
- Northern America	1540.8	1491.1	1612.5	1575.0	1436.5	- Amérique du Nord
- LAIA	402.0	418.2	473.5	461.7	454.2	- ALAI
- CACM	3.9	4.0	4.3	4.4	4.5	- MCC
- Caribbean	24.9	26.0	26.4	25.3	34.5	- Caraïbes
- Rest of America	0.5	0.6	0.1	0.2	0.1	- Autre d'Amérique
Asia excluding former USSR	1270.3	1334.7	1344.6	1386.4	1338.9	Asie ancienne URSS exclus
- Middle East	134.2	262.7	140.5	148.1	169.4	- Moyen-Orient
Asia former USSR	47.0	33.6	33.7	42.5	45.8	Asie ancienne URSS
Europe excluding former USSR	2998.0	2886.7	2632.4	2682.3	2963.7	Europe ancienne URSS exclus
- European Union	2715.0	2617.4	2367.9	2414.3	2651.3	- Union Européenne
- Eastern Europe	172.8	168.4	176.3	172.8	210.4	- Europe de l'Est
- Rest of Europe	110.2	100.9	88.3	95.2	102.1	- Autre de l'Europe
Europe former USSR	219.1	181.4	194.9	216.5	234.7	Europe ancienne URSS
Oceania	235.4	214.6	197.4	211.0	219.5	Océanie
United States	1151.3	1139.5	1247.2	1215.9	1103.7	Etats-Unis d'Amérique
China	762.5	711.6	818.9	856.5	786.0	Chine
United Kingdom	613.4	541.8	525.7	496.9	496.2	Royaume-Uni
Germany	563.3	546.3	443.8	508.0	533.5	Allemagne
Netherlands	359.9	379.4	352.5	367.2	420.8	Pays-Bas
Canada	389.5	351.2	365.3	359.0	332.8	Canada
France-Monaco	298.0	282.1	252.1	228.1	259.1	France-Monaco
Spain	210.4	216.3	200.0	202.2	255.9	Espagne
Brazil	178.9	193.4	233.8	222.3	e230.5	Brésil
Australia	206.9	193.7	191.2	205.7	213.7	Australie
Belgium	-	244.9	228.3	246.5	e276.6	Belgique
Mexico	136.4	139.1	155.4	142.0	128.1	Mexique
Italy-San Marino-Holy See	146.3	134.4	130.0	132.8	145.1	Italie-Saint-Marin-Saint-Siège
Turkey	91.1	222.5	107.4	98.2	117.7	Turquie
Ukraine	81.1	79.9	92.3	111.0	122.4	Ukraine
Japan	93.5	97.3	97.7	88.5	101.5	Japon
Russian Federation	106.8	86.0	88.9	92.2	95.4	Fédération de Russie
South Africa	-	-	121.2	142.1	141.4	Afrique du Sud
Norway	79.9	70.4	62.3	72.4	77.1	Norvège
Zimbabwe	e66.9	62.7	68.3	50.6	68.5	Zimbabwe
Greece	81.8	68.9	54.1	53.2	e53.3	Grèce
Austria	65.5	59.5	53.1	58.6	62.0	Autriche
Slovakia	56.4	56.3	57.3	59.1	59.5	Slovaquie
India	42.4	40.5	64.0	71.6	63.5	Inde
Czech Republic	55.0	51.3	50.4	52.9	54.0	République tchèque
Belgium-Luxembourg	239.9	-	-	-	-	Belgique-Luxembourg
Denmark	50.2	48.9	45.3	43.8	49.9	Danemark
Southern African Customs Union	118.1	108.8	-	-	-	Union douanière d'Afrique australe
Finland	44.2	46.6	41.0	35.4	38.9	Finlande
Chile	28.8	35.4	32.5	49.8	e48.7	Chili

(Value as percentages of World total) **(Valeur en pourcentage du total mondial)**

Regions of the world	1993	1994	1995	1996	1997	1998	1999	2000	2001	2002	Régions du monde
World	100.0	100.0	100.0	100.0	100.0	100.0	100.0	100.0	100.0	100.0	Monde
Africa	6.5	4.5	4.7	4.3	4.5	4.3	4.0	6.2	4.8	5.1	Afrique
Americas	28.3	29.4	26.5	27.1	28.1	28.0	28.3	30.4	29.8	27.2	Amériques
- Northern America	22.6	23.6	20.9	21.5	22.2	21.9	21.7	23.2	22.7	20.3	- Amérique du Nord
- LAIA	5.0	5.3	5.2	5.1	5.5	5.7	6.1	6.8	6.7	6.4	- ALAI
- CACM	0.0	0.0	0.1	0.1	0.0	0.1	0.1	0.1	0.1	0.1	- MCC
- Caribbean	0.5	0.4	0.3	0.3	0.3	0.4	0.4	0.4	0.4	0.5	- Caraïbes
- Rest of America	0.1	0.1	0.0	0.0	0.0	0.0	0.0	0.0	0.0	0.0	- Autre d'Amérique
Asia excluding former USSR	18.5	19.1	21.1	17.8	19.3	18.0	19.4	19.3	20.0	18.9	Asie ancienne URSS exclus
- Middle East	3.6	3.6	3.3	1.5	1.8	1.9	3.8	2.0	2.1	2.4	- Moyen-Orient
Asia former USSR	0.2	0.3	1.0	2.4	0.8	0.7	0.5	0.5	0.6	0.6	Asie ancienne URSS
Europe excluding former USSR	40.9	41.4	41.4	42.9	41.2	42.5	42.0	37.9	38.6	41.8	Europe ancienne URSS exclus
- European Union	36.4	37.9	37.9	38.5	37.4	38.5	38.1	34.1	34.8	37.4	- Union Européenne
- Eastern Europe	2.6	2.1	2.2	3.1	2.5	2.5	2.5	2.5	2.5	3.0	- Europe de l'Est
- Rest of Europe	1.9	1.3	1.3	1.3	1.3	1.6	1.5	1.3	1.4	1.4	- Autre de l'Europe
Europe former USSR	2.1	1.8	2.0	2.3	3.0	3.1	2.6	2.8	3.1	3.3	Europe ancienne URSS
Oceania	3.5	3.5	3.3	3.3	3.1	3.3	3.1	2.8	3.0	3.1	Océanie

281 Iron ore and concentrates

TRADE BY COMMODITY (Value in million US dollars)
Imports by principal countries or areas

COMMERCE PAR PRODUIT (Valeur en millions de dollars EU)
Importations selon les principaux pays ou zones

Country or area	1998	1999	2000	2001	2002	Pays ou zone
World	12900.6	11217.6	13060.1	12769.9	13054.8	Monde
Africa	124.7	106.1	11.7	83.1	38.9	Afrique
Americas	1222.5	944.4	993.8	785.2	737.2	Amériques
- Northern America	870.1	716.2	722.9	559.4	604.9	- Amérique du Nord
- LAIA	292.5	223.8	241.0	222.5	129.2	- ALAI
- CACM	0.4	0.0	0.6	0.1	0.4	- MCC
- Caribbean	59.5	4.5	29.4	3.3	2.7	- Caraïbes
- Rest of America	0.0	0.0	0.0	0.0	0.0	- Autre d'Amérique
Asia excluding former USSR	6487.2	6180.6	7335.4	7851.0	7999.6	Asie ancienne URSS exclus
- Middle East	446.8	427.1	493.5	443.9	550.9	- Moyen-Orient
Asia former USSR	9.2	0.0	0.1	0.5	0.6	Asie ancienne URSS
Europe excluding former USSR	4679.7	3773.2	4190.3	3689.7	3884.0	Europe ancienne URSS exclus
- European Union	3802.0	3181.7	3389.8	2985.4	3127.5	- Union Européenne
- Eastern Europe	859.4	539.6	784.5	686.7	740.9	- Europe de l'Est
- Rest of Europe	18.3	52.0	16.0	17.6	15.6	- Autre de l'Europe
Europe former USSR	307.1	155.1	433.9	304.1	331.7	Europe ancienne URSS
Oceania	70.1	58.2	95.0	56.3	62.8	Océanie
Japan	3050.0	2847.7	3225.5	3072.0	3046.9	Japon
China	1467.8	1379.0	1857.7	2502.8	2769.1	Chine
Germany	1398.9	1128.3	1299.0	1144.5	1271.8	Allemagne
Korea, Republic of	830.3	808.5	939.5	1090.9	998.0	République de Corée
Italy-San Marino-Holy See	465.3	413.9	503.9	460.0	423.9	Italie-Saint-Marin-Saint-Siège
United States	610.4	463.6	480.7	343.2	364.8	Etats-Unis d'Amérique
France-Monaco	479.5	445.7	464.7	314.5	433.2	France-Monaco
United Kingdom	524.9	451.1	393.3	357.9	277.7	Royaume-Uni
Canada	259.7	252.5	242.2	216.2	240.1	Canada
Belgium	–	286.0	291.4	269.6	e295.6	Belgique
Poland	282.2	178.4	258.6	198.3	182.1	Pologne
Russian Federation	205.2	60.2	243.6	227.3	248.7	Fédération de Russie
Czech Republic	220.3	137.9	173.6	179.6	217.8	République tchèque
Spain	221.7	164.7	160.5	172.7	160.8	Espagne
Saudi Arabia	132.2	164.9	140.0	177.6	e183.8	Arabie saoudite
Netherlands	181.9	164.2	140.7	132.1	143.1	Pays-Bas
Romania	165.5	96.4	142.3	115.6	145.6	Roumanie
Argentina	190.0	123.1	133.9	145.6	e64.4	Argentine
Turkey	142.0	89.5	115.5	82.1	164.0	Turquie
Finland	124.3	104.6	109.8	117.6	107.7	Finlande
Slovakia	116.2	94.1	108.9	121.1	120.1	Slovaquie
Ukraine	101.8	94.8	190.0	76.5	82.4	Ukraine
Philippines	89.2	84.8	151.5	102.1	4.7	Philippines
Mexico	98.5	98.0	101.9	70.4	57.7	Mexique
Belgium-Luxembourg	379.1	–	–	–	–	Belgique-Luxembourg
Indonesia	66.4	97.9	84.0	59.2	53.6	Indonésie
Australia	69.1	58.1	94.9	56.3	62.6	Australie
Iran (Islamic Republic of)	62.9	62.9	87.5	53.0	69.7	Iran (République islamique d')
Malaysia	44.9	55.3	67.5	68.7	e75.1	Malaisie
Bahrain	e53.8	e60.0	75.2	55.3	e64.7	Bahreïn

(Value as percentages of World total) **(Valeur en pourcentage du total mondial)**

Regions of the world	1993	1994	1995	1996	1997	1998	1999	2000	2001	2002	Régions du monde
World	100.0	100.0	100.0	100.0	100.0	100.0	100.0	100.0	100.0	100.0	Monde
Africa	0.7	0.9	0.3	0.4	0.4	1.0	0.9	0.1	0.7	0.3	Afrique
Americas	7.2	8.5	8.2	9.4	9.3	9.5	8.4	7.6	6.1	5.6	Amériques
- Northern America	6.0	6.8	6.1	7.0	6.8	6.7	6.4	5.5	4.4	4.6	- Amérique du Nord
- LAIA	1.1	1.1	1.5	1.9	2.2	2.3	2.0	1.8	1.7	1.0	- ALAI
- CACM	0.0	0.0	0.0	0.0	0.0	0.0	0.0	0.0	0.0	0.0	- MCC
- Caribbean	0.1	0.5	0.5	0.5	0.4	0.5	0.0	0.2	0.0	0.0	- Caraïbes
- Rest of America	0.0	0.0	0.0	0.0	0.0	0.0	0.0	0.0	0.0	0.0	- Autre d'Amérique
Asia excluding former USSR	56.2	50.3	50.3	52.0	53.8	50.3	55.1	56.2	61.5	61.3	Asie ancienne URSS exclus
- Middle East	3.8	2.6	3.1	3.4	3.1	3.5	3.8	3.8	3.5	4.2	- Moyen-Orient
Asia former USSR	0.0	0.0	0.0	0.0	0.0	0.1	0.0	0.0	0.0	0.0	Asie ancienne URSS
Europe excluding former USSR	35.5	38.4	39.2	35.8	33.6	36.3	33.6	32.1	28.9	29.8	Europe ancienne URSS exclus
- European Union	30.0	32.4	32.2	29.2	26.7	29.5	28.4	26.0	23.4	24.0	- Union Européenne
- Eastern Europe	5.2	5.7	6.8	6.5	6.7	6.7	4.8	6.0	5.4	5.7	- Europe de l'Est
- Rest of Europe	0.3	0.3	0.3	0.1	0.1	0.1	0.5	0.1	0.1	0.1	- Autre de l'Europe
Europe former USSR	0.0	1.4	1.5	1.8	2.2	2.4	1.4	3.3	2.4	2.5	Europe ancienne URSS
Oceania	0.4	0.5	0.5	0.5	0.7	0.5	0.5	0.7	0.4	0.5	Océanie

TRADE BY COMMODITY (Value in million US dollars)
Exports by principal countries or areas

COMMERCE PAR PRODUIT (Valeur en millions de dollars EU)
Exportations selon les principaux pays ou zones

Country or area	1998	1999	2000	2001	2002	Pays ou zone
World	9984.3	8192.8	9228.8	9110.6	9972.2	Monde
Africa	631.7	516.9	516.7	594.0	623.0	Afrique
Americas	4834.6	3991.8	4319.7	4105.1	4325.6	Amériques
- Northern America	1120.2	957.7	957.9	846.6	953.9	- Amérique du Nord
- LAIA	3714.4	3034.2	3361.5	3258.6	3370.6	- ALAI
- CACM	0.0	0.0	0.0	0.0	1.1	- MCC
- Caribbean	0.0	0.0	0.3	0.0	0.0	- Caraïbes
- Rest of America	0.0	0.0	0.0	0.0	0.0	- Autre d'Amérique
Asia excluding former USSR	551.1	492.7	649.7	745.7	1109.7	Asie ancienne URSS exclus
- Middle East	102.5	144.9	207.2	250.9	241.2	- Moyen-Orient
Asia former USSR	178.3	38.2	51.3	84.8	95.5	Asie ancienne URSS
Europe excluding former USSR	556.3	382.2	415.4	339.9	413.8	Europe ancienne URSS exclus
- European Union	550.2	371.9	409.2	333.0	396.2	- Union Européenne
- Eastern Europe	2.7	9.2	3.7	4.1	3.9	- Europe de l'Est
- Rest of Europe	3.3	1.0	2.4	2.9	13.6	- Autre de l'Europe
Europe former USSR	717.7	451.3	706.9	527.5	549.9	Europe ancienne URSS
Oceania	2514.7	2319.7	2569.1	2713.6	2854.7	Océanie
Brazil	3251.1	2746.0	3048.2	2931.5	e3039.3	Brésil
Australia	2504.6	2303.5	2560.4	2703.9	2844.6	Australie
Canada	875.2	714.4	711.7	617.3	704.9	Canada
India	383.9	271.1	363.2	431.1	863.9	Inde
Sweden	536.1	355.6	390.6	321.1	386.4	Suède
Ukraine	417.5	286.4	403.7	320.4	353.2	Ukraine
United States	245.0	243.3	246.2	229.3	249.0	Etats-Unis d'Amérique
Russian Federation	300.3	164.9	303.2	207.1	196.7	Fédération de Russie
South Africa	–	–	324.7	407.3	418.2	Afrique du Sud
Mauritania	e253.6	e170.4	e190.9	e186.2	e199.7	Mauritanie
Bahrain	e102.0	e139.0	197.4	240.3	e232.7	Bahreïn
Southern African Customs Union	377.4	345.9	–	–	–	Union douanière d'Afrique australe
Chile	163.6	125.7	141.7	134.9	e132.0	Chili
Venezuela	197.0	97.1	101.6	102.1	e108.4	Venezuela
Kazakhstan	177.7	38.2	51.3	84.8	e95.5	Kazakhstan
Peru	96.0	65.3	67.7	77.9	82.6	Pérou
Philippines	60.5	73.4	76.6	61.2	e60.0	Philippines
New Zealand	10.0	16.2	8.7	9.7	10.0	Nouvelle-Zélande
Mexico	6.6		2.2	12.2	8.4	Mexique
Iran (Islamic Republic of)		5.0	5.9	8.6	6.8	Iran (République islamique d')
Netherlands	5.2	6.2	7.7	3.6	3.3	Pays-Bas
Norway	3.1	0.6	0.8	1.1	11.7	Norvège
Slovakia	2.5	3.0	3.3	3.5	3.3	Slovaquie
Belgium	–	4.8	2.3	2.2	e2.5	Belgique
France-Monaco	2.7	1.9	1.7	2.5	1.5	France-Monaco
Malaysia	2.5	2.2	2.2	1.2	e1.3	Malaisie
Albania	0.0	6.0	0.0	0.0	0.0	Albanie
Italy-San Marino-Holy See	0.9	1.3	1.7	1.2	1.0	Italie-Saint-Marin-Saint-Siège
Spain	2.3	1.1	1.0	0.6	0.7	Espagne
Libyan Arab Jamahiriya					e4.8	Jamahiriya arabe libyenne

(Value as percentages of World total) **(Valeur en pourcentage du total mondial)**

Regions of the world	1993	1994	1995	1996	1997	1998	1999	2000	2001	2002	Régions du monde
World	100.0	100.0	100.0	100.0	100.0	100.0	100.0	100.0	100.0	100.0	Monde
Africa	6.3	6.7	8.0	7.3	7.5	6.3	6.3	5.6	6.5	6.2	Afrique
Americas	42.0	47.1	44.8	45.6	44.7	48.4	48.7	46.8	45.1	43.4	Amériques
- Northern America	10.2	11.4	10.5	11.7	12.2	11.2	11.7	10.4	9.3	9.6	- Amérique du Nord
- LAIA	31.7	35.7	34.2	34.0	32.5	37.2	37.0	36.4	35.8	33.8	- ALAI
- CACM	0.0	0.0	0.0	0.0	0.0	0.0	0.0	0.0	0.0	0.0	- MCC
- Caribbean	0.0	0.0	0.0	0.0	0.0	0.0	0.0	0.0	0.0	0.0	- Caraïbes
- Rest of America	0.0	0.0	0.0	0.0	0.0	0.0	0.0	0.0	0.0	0.0	- Autre d'Amérique
Asia excluding former USSR	5.9	5.6	6.9	6.5	6.1	5.5	6.0	7.0	8.2	11.1	Asie ancienne URSS exclus
- Middle East	0.0	0.0	0.1	0.0	0.0	1.0	1.8	2.2	2.8	2.4	- Moyen-Orient
Asia former USSR	0.1	0.3	0.6	1.0	2.0	1.8	0.5	0.6	0.9	1.0	Asie ancienne URSS
Europe excluding former USSR	8.3	6.7	6.9	6.7	6.3	5.6	4.7	4.5	3.7	4.1	Europe ancienne URSS exclus
- European Union	7.3	5.9	6.4	6.3	6.2	5.5	4.5	4.4	3.7	4.0	- Union Européenne
- Eastern Europe	0.1	0.1	0.1	0.1	0.0	0.0	0.1	0.0	0.0	0.0	- Europe de l'Est
- Rest of Europe	0.9	0.7	0.4	0.3	0.1	0.0	0.0	0.0	0.0	0.1	- Autre de l'Europe
Europe former USSR	11.8	7.9	7.4	6.3	5.4	7.2	5.5	7.7	5.8	5.5	Europe ancienne URSS
Oceania	25.6	25.6	25.4	26.6	28.0	25.2	28.3	27.8	29.8	28.6	Océanie

282 Waste and scrap metal of iron or steel

TRADE BY COMMODITY (Value in million US dollars)
Imports by principal countries or areas

COMMERCE PAR PRODUIT (Valeur en millions de dollars EU)
Importations selon les principaux pays ou zones

Country or area	1998	1999	2000	2001	2002	Pays ou zone
World	7533.9	6809.9	8927.1	8272.3	9283.3	Monde
Africa	35.3	54.6	58.4	54.2	84.0	Afrique
Americas	787.7	745.3	818.9	590.5	778.0	Amériques
- Northern America	587.9	582.8	567.0	415.5	557.2	- Amérique du Nord
- LAIA	195.2	160.0	240.1	160.3	203.9	- ALAI
- CACM	4.1	2.1	10.8	13.3	15.3	- MCC
- Caribbean	0.4	0.3	0.9	1.4	1.6	- Caraïbes
- Rest of America	0.1	0.1	0.0	0.0	0.0	- Autre d'Amérique
Asia excluding former USSR	2751.0	2822.2	3836.4	4025.6	4438.2	Asie ancienne URSS exclus
- Middle East	824.3	672.9	718.1	495.6	1043.7	- Moyen-Orient
Asia former USSR	0.2	0.2	0.3	0.4	0.4	Asie ancienne URSS
Europe excluding former USSR	3829.1	3083.3	4055.7	3523.7	3893.2	Europe ancienne URSS exclus
- European Union	3670.0	2966.6	3899.6	3346.6	3651.3	- Union Européenne
- Eastern Europe	46.2	27.8	52.2	80.7	107.7	- Europe de l'Est
- Rest of Europe	112.9	88.8	103.8	96.5	134.2	- Autre de l'Europe
Europe former USSR	129.9	103.5	154.6	76.0	87.0	Europe ancienne URSS
Oceania	0.7	0.8	2.8	1.9	2.4	Océanie
Korea, Republic of	762.8	792.4	1100.4	935.3	974.0	République de Corée
Spain	882.7	719.7	830.9	731.2	734.0	Espagne
Turkey	808.9	660.3	694.1	477.8	1019.0	Turquie
China	211.4	303.5	481.6	1017.7	886.6	Chine
Italy-San Marino-Holy See	701.3	425.8	509.0	517.6	518.9	Italie-Saint-Marin-Saint-Siège
Germany	394.6	332.2	525.2	423.9	477.0	Allemagne
United States	426.8	418.1	407.9	293.8	405.0	Etats-Unis d'Amérique
Belgium	–	378.5	522.9	386.0	e423.4	Belgique
India	263.3	332.2	302.8	423.6	346.4	Inde
France-Monaco	292.6	274.4	358.0	296.3	332.9	France-Monaco
Netherlands	219.8	193.0	297.2	222.7	285.1	Pays-Bas
Luxembourg	–	203.4	217.3	250.3	e265.7	Luxembourg
Sweden	189.6	150.8	224.4	164.1	184.5	Suède
Mexico	159.8	146.0	226.3	150.6	195.2	Mexique
Malaysia	50.5	96.0	183.7	256.9	e280.8	Malaisie
Canada	161.1	164.7	159.2	121.5	152.1	Canada
Japan	100.9	135.0	220.5	105.5	115.0	Japon
Belgium-Luxembourg	605.2	–	–	–	–	Belgique-Luxembourg
Finland	105.5	78.4	135.3	87.7	137.5	Finlande
Indonesia	58.1	71.0	136.8	139.3	131.8	Indonésie
Thailand	46.2	94.4	115.0	105.2	e109.6	Thaïlande
Austria	87.2	57.4	73.8	83.0	92.8	Autriche
United Kingdom	69.5	65.2	108.1	70.2	70.3	Royaume-Uni
Belarus	60.9	45.9	81.2	52.3	62.2	Bélarus
Egypt	31.0	50.1	e52.7	48.0	78.6	Egypte
China, Hong Kong SAR	58.0	45.6	57.7	43.7	41.3	Chine - RAS de Hong-Kong
Slovenia	45.9	38.3	47.8	44.3	61.8	Slovénie
Greece	50.1	23.2	28.2	61.3	e67.7	Grèce
Pakistan	18.3	20.2	31.3	53.1	46.1	Pakistan
Norway	39.6	28.2	34.1	28.6	34.2	Norvège

(Value as percentages of World total) **(Valeur en pourcentage du total mondial)**

Regions of the world	1993	1994	1995	1996	1997	1998	1999	2000	2001	2002	Régions du monde
World	100.0	100.0	100.0	100.0	100.0	100.0	100.0	100.0	100.0	100.0	Monde
Africa	0.3	0.4	0.3	0.3	0.2	0.5	0.8	0.7	0.7	0.9	Afrique
Americas	6.7	7.9	7.0	8.6	10.0	10.5	10.9	9.2	7.1	8.4	Amériques
- Northern America	4.4	5.4	5.1	6.2	6.7	7.8	8.6	6.4	5.0	6.0	- Amérique du Nord
- LAIA	2.2	2.5	1.8	2.3	3.2	2.6	2.3	2.7	1.9	2.2	- ALAI
- CACM	0.1	0.0	0.1	0.1	0.0	0.1	0.0	0.1	0.2	0.2	- MCC
- Caribbean	0.0	0.0	0.0	0.0	0.0	0.0	0.0	0.0	0.0	0.0	- Caraïbes
- Rest of America	0.0	0.0	0.0	0.0	0.0	0.0	0.0	0.0	0.0	0.0	- Autre d'Amérique
Asia excluding former USSR	55.8	45.5	41.7	43.9	42.7	36.5	41.4	43.0	48.7	47.8	Asie ancienne URSS exclus
- Middle East	11.8	11.1	11.4	12.3	11.3	10.9	9.9	8.0	6.0	11.2	- Moyen-Orient
Asia former USSR	0.0	0.0	0.0	0.0	0.0	0.0	0.0	0.0	0.0	0.0	Asie ancienne URSS
Europe excluding former USSR	36.9	46.0	50.0	46.0	45.7	50.8	45.3	45.4	42.6	41.9	Europe ancienne URSS exclus
- European Union	35.2	44.5	48.5	44.9	44.5	48.7	43.6	43.7	40.5	39.3	- Union Européenne
- Eastern Europe	0.4	0.3	0.4	0.3	0.2	0.6	0.4	0.6	1.0	1.2	- Europe de l'Est
- Rest of Europe	1.4	1.3	1.2	0.9	1.0	1.5	1.3	1.2	1.2	1.4	- Autre de l'Europe
Europe former USSR	0.1	0.2	1.0	1.0	1.4	1.7	1.5	1.7	0.9	0.9	Europe ancienne URSS
Oceania	0.2	0.1	0.0	0.1	0.0	0.0	0.0	0.0	0.0	0.0	Océanie

Ferrailles, déchets et débris d'ouvrages de fonte, de fer ou d'acier 282

TRADE BY COMMODITY (Value in million US dollars)
Exports by principal countries or areas

COMMERCE PAR PRODUIT (Valeur en millions de dollars EU)
Exportations selon les principaux pays ou zones

Country or area	1998	1999	2000	2001	2002	Pays ou zone
World	6663.6	5967.8	7533.3	7281.6	8540.2	Monde
Africa	95.2	67.9	68.0	70.6	94.2	Afrique
Americas	1257.7	1145.8	1429.6	1500.4	1700.6	Amériques
- Northern America	1098.5	952.7	1240.7	1342.2	1561.0	- Amérique du Nord
- LAIA	139.9	178.7	148.6	139.7	129.0	- ALAI
- CACM	2.4	2.1	30.9	12.7	5.1	- MCC
- Caribbean	14.8	11.2	8.0	5.3	4.8	- Caraïbes
- Rest of America	2.1	1.0	1.5	0.5	0.6	- Autre d'Amérique
Asia excluding former USSR	888.6	829.3	943.4	1176.6	1331.7	Asie ancienne URSS exclus
- Middle East	93.9	103.2	120.9	106.3	109.5	- Moyen-Orient
Asia former USSR	46.6	78.3	139.6	130.9	125.6	Asie ancienne URSS
Europe excluding former USSR	2991.3	2736.6	3758.0	3472.1	4276.3	Europe ancienne URSS exclus
- European Union	2597.4	2357.7	3152.2	2930.4	3555.9	- Union Européenne
- Eastern Europe	297.3	294.7	500.0	435.2	591.1	- Europe de l'Est
- Rest of Europe	96.6	84.2	105.8	106.6	129.3	- Autre de l'Europe
Europe former USSR	1293.9	1017.8	1072.4	803.5	898.1	Europe ancienne URSS
Oceania	90.3	92.2	122.3	127.5	113.7	Océanie
United States	804.9	738.9	1004.2	1132.3	1297.7	Etats-Unis d'Amérique
Germany	936.8	824.6	1012.2	915.9	970.7	Allemagne
Russian Federation	846.3	620.4	507.5	424.3	493.3	Fédération de Russie
Japan	463.0	476.0	427.6	685.6	727.7	Japon
United Kingdom	394.5	335.9	483.8	530.1	700.9	Royaume-Uni
Netherlands	400.5	359.9	477.2	483.3	609.5	Pays-Bas
France-Monaco	427.6	369.9	494.7	413.5	540.8	France-Monaco
Ukraine	328.7	308.9	437.8	288.7	318.2	Ukraine
Canada	293.6	213.9	236.5	209.9	263.4	Canada
Belgium	–	181.4	220.9	182.1	e204.3	Belgique
Romania	74.0	100.9	207.2	132.5	189.6	Roumanie
Mexico	110.8	162.7	127.3	121.8	110.1	Mexique
China, Hong Kong SAR	122.6	88.5	117.1	116.8	131.7	Chine - RAS de Hong-Kong
Poland	56.1	71.3	107.9	114.9	163.8	Pologne
Australia	78.2	82.0	106.0	110.1	93.8	Australie
Czech Republic	86.1	60.4	80.7	82.2	104.4	République tchèque
Denmark	62.9	49.7	79.9	81.5	132.2	Danemark
Singapore	73.4	52.0	95.9	86.8	87.5	Singapour
Austria	73.2	57.5	78.0	76.3	95.7	Autriche
Kazakhstan	29.0	49.4	91.9	89.1	e100.3	Kazakhstan
Italy-San Marino-Holy See	20.2	63.0	108.1	73.8	73.4	Italie-Saint-Marin-Saint-Siège
Finland	43.4	40.7	93.9	53.1	60.6	Finlande
Estonia	72.8	60.8	75.0	44.6	37.5	Estonie
Switzerland-Liechtenstein	55.3	46.9	60.1	55.9	60.4	Suisse-Liechtenstein
Sweden	37.0	35.8	43.6	48.3	72.6	Suède
Hungary	52.6	33.3	50.1	42.0	55.2	Hongrie
United Arab Emirates	44.0	45.3	43.2	39.7	e41.3	Emirates arabes unis
Korea, Republic of	17.0	13.0	20.4	32.5	109.9	République de Corée
Belgium-Luxembourg	164.5	–	–	–	–	Belgique-Luxembourg
Thailand	45.7	21.9	34.3	25.1	e26.5	Thaïlande

(Value as percentages of World total) (Valeur en pourcentage du total mondial)

Regions of the world	1993	1994	1995	1996	1997	1998	1999	2000	2001	2002	Régions du monde
World	100.0	100.0	100.0	100.0	100.0	100.0	100.0	100.0	100.0	100.0	Monde
Africa	1.0	1.0	1.4	1.6	1.7	1.4	1.1	0.9	1.0	1.1	Afrique
Americas	25.4	24.8	26.7	26.0	23.8	18.9	19.2	19.0	20.6	19.9	Amériques
- Northern America	24.2	23.5	25.4	24.3	22.2	16.5	16.0	16.5	18.4	18.3	- Amérique du Nord
- LAIA	1.0	1.1	1.1	1.3	1.5	2.1	3.0	2.0	1.9	1.5	- ALAI
- CACM	0.0	0.0	0.0	0.0	0.0	0.0	0.0	0.4	0.2	0.1	- MCC
- Caribbean	0.1	0.2	0.2	0.2	0.1	0.2	0.2	0.1	0.1	0.1	- Caraïbes
- Rest of America	0.0	0.0	0.0	0.0	0.0	0.0	0.0	0.0	0.0	0.0	- Autre d'Amérique
Asia excluding former USSR	10.2	9.7	9.5	10.8	10.7	13.3	13.9	12.5	16.2	15.6	Asie ancienne URSS exclus
- Middle East	2.3	2.7	1.6	1.3	0.8	1.4	1.7	1.6	1.5	1.3	- Moyen-Orient
Asia former USSR	0.2	0.2	0.5	0.6	0.9	0.7	1.3	1.9	1.8	1.5	Asie ancienne URSS
Europe excluding former USSR	55.1	57.5	54.4	52.0	50.9	44.9	45.9	49.9	47.7	50.1	Europe ancienne URSS exclus
- European Union	49.3	52.1	49.6	47.0	45.3	39.0	39.5	41.8	40.2	41.6	- Union Européenne
- Eastern Europe	5.1	4.2	3.4	3.6	4.0	4.5	4.9	6.6	6.0	6.9	- Europe de l'Est
- Rest of Europe	0.7	1.1	1.4	1.4	1.6	1.5	1.4	1.4	1.5	1.5	- Autre de l'Europe
Europe former USSR	6.5	5.6	5.9	7.3	10.4	19.4	17.1	14.2	11.0	10.5	Europe ancienne URSS
Oceania	1.6	1.2	1.5	1.8	1.7	1.4	1.5	1.6	1.8	1.3	Océanie

287 Ores and concentrates of base metals, nes

TRADE BY COMMODITY (Value in million US dollars)
Imports by principal countries or areas

COMMERCE PAR PRODUIT (Valeur en millions de dollars EU)
Importations selon les principaux pays ou zones

Country or area	1998	1999	2000	2001	2002	Pays ou zone
World	19283.2	18811.4	22922.1	21992.3	20767.0	Monde
Africa	455.0	433.9	672.7	614.0	660.7	Afrique
Americas	3957.5	3516.6	3916.7	3549.7	3243.9	Amériques
- Northern America	3330.0	2855.0	3098.0	2876.2	2667.3	- Amérique du Nord
- LAIA	611.9	653.7	815.8	669.6	573.2	- ALAI
- CACM	1.1	0.5	0.3	1.9	1.8	- MCC
- Caribbean	14.5	7.3	2.6	1.9	1.5	- Caraïbes
- Rest of America	0.0	0.0	0.0	0.1	0.0	- Autre d'Amérique
Asia excluding former USSR	6520.7	7166.1	9039.4	8860.7	8708.9	Asie ancienne URSS exclus
- Middle East	315.8	341.5	443.5	381.7	411.6	- Moyen-Orient
Asia former USSR	75.7	64.1	162.1	132.4	134.5	Asie ancienne URSS
Europe excluding former USSR	6935.1	6315.5	7423.6	7249.0	6648.4	Europe ancienne URSS exclus
- European Union	5254.4	4785.5	5509.0	5400.9	4910.6	- Union Européenne
- Eastern Europe	421.4	388.0	529.6	498.2	468.1	- Europe de l'Est
- Rest of Europe	1259.3	1142.0	1385.0	1349.9	1269.7	- Autre de l'Europe
Europe former USSR	1191.7	1150.8	1520.0	1416.4	1195.5	Europe ancienne URSS
Oceania	147.5	164.3	187.6	170.0	175.1	Océanie
Japan	3119.4	3371.9	4097.2	3453.2	3352.7	Japon
China	1159.8	1152.4	1922.4	2302.1	2275.6	Chine
United States	2061.6	1739.0	1732.2	1483.7	1395.2	Etats-Unis d'Amérique
Canada	1268.4	1116.1	1365.5	1392.5	1272.1	Canada
Korea, Republic of	987.3	1193.5	1417.8	1273.3	1342.6	République de Corée
Russian Federation	1063.4	1016.9	1269.4	1213.1	969.2	Fédération de Russie
Norway	1022.1	985.0	1186.1	1145.0	1059.7	Norvège
Germany	1012.4	1002.9	1010.8	1251.5	1069.3	Allemagne
Spain	666.1	652.0	758.1	703.4	751.6	Espagne
Finland	549.4	663.9	819.9	693.0	610.0	Finlande
France-Monaco	662.8	578.3	661.9	647.6	545.2	France-Monaco
United Kingdom	590.3	488.3	573.8	580.4	381.7	Royaume-Uni
Netherlands	511.3	350.5	440.5	358.7	326.0	Pays-Bas
Italy-San Marino-Holy See	447.5	326.2	388.7	349.4	363.7	Italie-Saint-Marin-Saint-Siège
Belgium	–	471.5	489.4	379.3	e415.9	Belgique
Brazil	284.4	345.8	395.9	353.3	314.8	Brésil
India	203.1	256.3	271.1	425.7	410.5	Inde
Philippines	231.0	321.8	240.4	297.5	227.9	Philippines
Sweden	122.4	109.4	207.8	271.6	290.8	Suède
Bahrain	e140.4	e156.6	196.2	213.9	e250.1	Bahreïn
South Africa	–	–	332.6	271.8	327.3	Afrique du Sud
Mexico	155.3	169.0	253.3	152.4	140.2	Mexique
Thailand	121.1	136.4	161.4	219.9	e229.1	Thaïlande
Ukraine	123.3	127.6	224.1	185.0	199.3	Ukraine
Bulgaria	126.6	130.6	170.6	e190.5	e209.5	Bulgarie
Egypt	100.0	108.1	e177.4	161.6	175.2	Egypte
New Zealand	126.2	126.7	132.8	125.6	127.1	Nouvelle-Zélande
Malaysia	119.0	111.5	113.6	134.9	e147.5	Malaisie
Ireland	112.3	103.8	109.6	118.0	110.1	Irlande
Belgium-Luxembourg	543.6	–	–	–	–	Belgique-Luxembourg

(Value as percentages of World total) **(Valeur en pourcentage du total mondial)**

Regions of the world	1993	1994	1995	1996	1997	1998	1999	2000	2001	2002	Régions du monde
World	100.0	100.0	100.0	100.0	100.0	100.0	100.0	100.0	100.0	100.0	Monde
Africa	2.1	1.2	1.8	2.3	2.3	2.4	2.3	2.9	2.8	3.2	Afrique
Americas	24.3	20.6	19.9	20.0	19.4	20.5	18.7	17.1	16.1	15.6	Amériques
- Northern America	19.5	16.3	15.5	16.6	15.6	17.3	15.2	13.5	13.1	12.8	- Amérique du Nord
- LAIA	4.7	4.2	4.5	3.4	3.8	3.2	3.5	3.6	3.0	2.8	- ALAI
- CACM	0.0	0.0	0.0	0.0	0.0	0.0	0.0	0.0	0.0	0.0	- MCC
- Caribbean	0.1	0.0	0.0	0.0	0.0	0.1	0.0	0.0	0.0	0.0	- Caraïbes
- Rest of America	0.0	0.0	0.0	0.0	0.0	0.0	0.0	0.0	0.0	0.0	- Autre d'Amérique
Asia excluding former USSR	36.3	34.8	37.1	34.6	35.7	33.8	38.1	39.4	40.3	41.9	Asie ancienne URSS exclus
- Middle East	2.3	1.7	1.6	2.1	2.0	1.6	1.8	1.9	1.7	2.0	- Moyen-Orient
Asia former USSR	0.0	1.0	1.1	0.3	0.1	0.4	0.3	0.7	0.6	0.6	Asie ancienne URSS
Europe excluding former USSR	34.6	34.7	33.1	35.3	35.9	36.0	33.6	32.4	33.0	32.0	Europe ancienne URSS exclus
- European Union	26.1	26.4	25.7	27.0	28.5	27.2	25.4	24.0	24.6	23.6	- Union Européenne
- Eastern Europe	1.4	1.2	1.3	2.0	1.8	2.2	2.1	2.3	2.3	2.3	- Europe de l'Est
- Rest of Europe	7.1	7.2	6.2	6.3	5.6	6.5	6.1	6.0	6.1	6.1	- Autre de l'Europe
Europe former USSR	1.6	6.8	6.2	6.6	5.7	6.2	6.1	6.6	6.4	5.8	Europe ancienne URSS
Oceania	1.0	1.1	0.8	1.0	0.8	0.8	0.9	0.8	0.8	0.8	Océanie

TRADE BY COMMODITY (Value in million US dollars)
Exports by principal countries or areas

COMMERCE PAR PRODUIT (Valeur en millions de dollars EU)
Exportations selon les principaux pays ou zones

Country or area	1998	1999	2000	2001	2002	Pays ou zone
World	17211.2	16847.9	20834.3	19383.1	19117.4	Monde
Africa	1178.2	1260.9	1363.4	1280.5	1474.5	Afrique
Americas	7402.6	7423.9	8914.3	8354.9	8248.7	Amériques
- Northern America	2498.8	2192.0	2505.9	2471.1	2389.7	- Amérique du Nord
- LAIA	3422.0	3729.8	4630.8	4294.6	4485.6	- ALAI
- CACM	17.2	6.3	47.9	35.5	12.9	- MCC
- Caribbean	1092.4	1090.3	1334.8	1151.7	1028.5	- Caraïbes
- Rest of America	372.2	405.5	395.0	402.1	331.9	- Autre d'Amérique
Asia excluding former USSR	2162.3	2193.9	3004.4	3013.1	3150.2	Asie ancienne URSS exclus
- Middle East	139.3	160.8	177.1	163.8	141.4	- Moyen-Orient
Asia former USSR	69.2	97.6	375.3	363.6	414.3	Asie ancienne URSS
Europe excluding former USSR	2003.5	1858.2	2137.0	1860.3	1663.6	Europe ancienne URSS exclus
- European Union	1850.3	1689.1	1878.7	1639.4	1479.6	- Union Européenne
- Eastern Europe	116.3	131.9	173.2	165.9	144.1	- Europe de l'Est
- Rest of Europe	36.9	37.2	85.1	54.9	39.9	- Autre de l'Europe
Europe former USSR	436.0	321.0	454.3	276.1	311.3	Europe ancienne URSS
Oceania	3959.5	3692.5	4585.6	4234.5	3854.9	Océanie
Australia	3657.2	3403.2	4154.0	3914.3	3535.3	Australie
Chile	1598.2	1897.5	2578.3	2358.0	e2307.0	Chili
Indonesia	1453.3	1451.6	1943.2	1987.2	1889.3	Indonésie
Canada	1292.8	1096.7	1300.9	1323.1	1342.0	Canada
United States	1206.0	1095.1	1203.5	1147.6	1047.1	Etats-Unis d'Amérique
Peru	604.9	612.4	669.0	725.1	959.1	Pérou
Jamaica	681.7	684.0	737.2	e688.0	e627.8	Jamaïque
Cuba	e410.7	406.2	597.4	463.7	e400.6	Cuba
Argentina	446.0	465.5	403.6	401.0	e387.4	Argentine
Brazil	359.4	365.3	446.1	418.0	e433.3	Brésil
Ireland	352.7	364.3	431.8	404.0	313.3	Irlande
South Africa	-	-	617.2	565.8	582.1	Afrique du Sud
Guinea	341.9	291.9	269.9	309.8	e400.2	Guinée
Suriname	295.2	e322.8	319.1	e323.5	e302.8	Suriname
Ukraine	245.1	225.0	373.6	219.7	242.2	Ukraine
Southern African Customs Union	583.6	637.2	-	-	-	Union douanière d'Afrique australe
Belgium	-	336.7	349.4	216.5	e242.9	Belgique
Kazakhstan	54.4	75.3	305.4	319.1	e359.5	Kazakhstan
Germany	182.2	174.2	199.1	183.2	200.1	Allemagne
Mexico	177.4	164.0	248.2	152.8	157.6	Mexique
Papua New Guinea	189.1	e171.6	214.4	e161.5	e137.9	Papouasie-Nouvelle-Guinée
India	108.5	92.5	147.1	155.9	360.6	Inde
Japan	79.9	95.8	256.6	193.1	203.9	Japon
Bolivia	178.7	166.7	188.5	136.0	e130.7	Bolivie
New Caledonia	e113.1	117.7	217.1	e158.7	e181.4	Nouvelle-Calédonie
Mongolia	136.9	128.3	166.6	153.1	150.4	Mongolie
Netherlands	256.7	115.5	142.3	121.5	98.7	Pays-Bas
Italy-San Marino-Holy See	114.5	116.3	124.1	148.8	155.8	Italie-Saint-Marin-Saint-Siège
Sweden	126.4	147.0	165.2	96.9	83.1	Suède
Turkey	116.4	118.1	134.5	89.7	103.6	Turquie

(Value as percentages of World total) **(Valeur en pourcentage du total mondial)**

Regions of the world	1993	1994	1995	1996	1997	1998	1999	2000	2001	2002	Régions du monde
World	100.0	100.0	100.0	100.0	100.0	100.0	100.0	100.0	100.0	100.0	Monde
Africa	8.8	8.2	7.8	8.4	6.3	6.8	7.5	6.5	6.6	7.7	Afrique
Americas	43.8	41.5	44.9	42.1	45.7	43.0	44.1	42.8	43.1	43.1	Amériques
- Northern America	17.7	16.2	18.6	16.8	17.2	14.5	13.0	12.0	12.7	12.5	- Amérique du Nord
- LAIA	14.2	16.6	19.2	17.8	19.9	19.9	22.1	22.2	22.2	23.5	- ALAI
- CACM	0.1	0.0	0.0	0.1	0.1	0.1	0.0	0.2	0.2	0.1	- MCC
- Caribbean	4.4	5.6	5.2	5.7	6.4	6.3	6.5	6.4	5.9	5.4	- Caraïbes
- Rest of America	7.5	3.2	2.0	1.7	2.1	2.2	2.4	1.9	2.1	1.7	- Autre d'Amérique
Asia excluding former USSR	12.4	15.1	15.6	16.1	13.3	12.6	13.0	14.4	15.5	16.5	Asie ancienne URSS exclus
- Middle East	0.9	1.1	1.1	0.9	1.1	0.8	1.0	0.8	0.8	0.7	- Moyen-Orient
Asia former USSR	0.4	0.8	0.5	0.3	0.3	0.4	0.6	1.8	1.9	2.2	Asie ancienne URSS
Europe excluding former USSR	11.3	10.7	10.7	11.1	12.4	11.6	11.0	10.3	9.6	8.7	Europe ancienne URSS exclus
- European Union	9.8	9.9	10.0	10.0	11.5	10.8	10.0	9.0	8.5	7.7	- Union Européenne
- Eastern Europe	1.0	0.5	0.4	0.7	0.7	0.7	0.8	0.8	0.9	0.8	- Europe de l'Est
- Rest of Europe	0.5	0.4	0.4	0.4	0.2	0.2	0.2	0.4	0.3	0.2	- Autre de l'Europe
Europe former USSR	1.0	2.3	2.0	1.5	1.4	2.5	1.9	2.2	1.4	1.6	Europe ancienne URSS
Oceania	22.3	21.4	18.4	20.4	20.6	23.0	21.9	22.0	21.8	20.2	Océanie

288 Non-ferrous base metal waste and scrap, nes

TRADE BY COMMODITY (Value in million US dollars)
Imports by principal countries or areas

COMMERCE PAR PRODUIT (Valeur en millions de dollars EU)
Importations selon les principaux pays ou zones

Country or area	1998	1999	2000	2001	2002	Pays ou zone
World	9213.0	9096.7	10944.7	10389.7	9648.0	Monde
Africa	20.5	16.7	28.6	29.4	32.9	Afrique
Americas	1699.3	1771.9	2003.9	1726.1	1457.5	Amériques
- Northern America	1599.7	1646.1	1854.9	1599.9	1325.4	- Amérique du Nord
- LAIA	91.3	119.6	145.6	124.7	121.9	- ALAI
- CACM	1.0	0.7	0.3	0.5	0.4	- MCC
- Caribbean	5.8	4.9	3.0	1.0	9.7	- Caraïbes
- Rest of America	1.6	0.7	0.1	0.0	0.0	- Autre d'Amérique
Asia excluding former USSR	2245.9	2751.3	3730.9	3558.1	3426.0	Asie ancienne URSS exclus
- Middle East	91.5	94.5	152.0	121.5	88.4	- Moyen-Orient
Asia former USSR	19.6	13.1	18.7	26.1	26.2	Asie ancienne URSS
Europe excluding former USSR	5162.4	4487.4	5088.9	4980.1	4615.7	Europe ancienne URSS exclus
- European Union	4871.6	4234.2	4794.7	4696.7	4329.6	- Union Européenne
- Eastern Europe	92.0	77.6	93.3	77.1	91.9	- Europe de l'Est
- Rest of Europe	198.8	175.6	200.9	206.3	194.2	- Autre de l'Europe
Europe former USSR	38.8	35.7	55.3	50.4	68.3	Europe ancienne URSS
Oceania	26.5	20.4	18.4	19.5	21.4	Océanie
Germany	1532.4	1286.5	1277.7	1150.8	1194.4	Allemagne
China	447.7	763.4	1538.0	1501.8	1330.1	Chine
United States	1143.4	1112.5	1198.2	1031.5	889.4	Etats-Unis d'Amérique
Italy-San Marino-Holy See	789.8	639.4	729.3	825.0	600.0	Italie-Saint-Marin-Saint-Siège
Japan	579.1	689.7	777.7	748.7	745.4	Japon
United Kingdom	572.5	579.9	745.1	808.0	597.2	Royaume-Uni
Canada	456.3	533.5	656.6	568.4	435.9	Canada
Belgium	–	510.2	632.2	600.2	e658.2	Belgique
Korea, Republic of	202.8	378.8	450.1	411.6	486.5	République de Corée
Netherlands	380.1	329.9	408.1	346.0	285.6	Pays-Bas
France-Monaco	381.9	299.0	305.1	288.8	282.6	France-Monaco
India	252.2	260.8	212.4	288.5	254.9	Inde
Spain	142.2	138.2	170.8	180.3	190.0	Espagne
Sweden	154.2	127.6	169.2	146.2	161.8	Suède
China, Hong Kong SAR	271.5	152.9	141.5	90.7	68.2	Chine - RAS de Hong-Kong
Norway	132.8	123.1	136.6	149.6	148.8	Norvège
Belgium-Luxembourg	637.1	–	–	–	–	Belgique-Luxembourg
Austria	133.0	111.9	106.6	83.4	109.6	Autriche
Mexico	83.0	112.0	131.8	103.4	103.2	Mexique
Luxembourg	–	82.3	100.3	149.1	e158.3	Luxembourg
Finland	95.1	77.3	70.7	48.6	21.0	Finlande
Malaysia	43.2	64.8	61.0	46.6	e50.9	Malaisie
Switzerland-Liechtenstein	54.3	41.4	44.1	33.6	23.9	Suisse-Liechtenstein
Singapore	41.2	31.5	40.5	34.8	44.6	Singapour
Czech Republic	39.1	35.2	38.9	27.7	26.1	République tchèque
Turkey	28.9	34.5	48.5	16.9	17.4	Turquie
Denmark	33.1	25.3	29.0	28.4	25.9	Danemark
United Arab Emirates	15.3	16.0	43.6	32.7	e33.6	Emirates arabes unis
Iran (Islamic Republic of)	24.1	23.5	31.4	35.5	25.8	Iran (République islamique d')
Pakistan	23.1	26.4	26.5	28.7	31.9	Pakistan

(Value as percentages of World total)

(Valeur en pourcentage du total mondial)

Regions of the world	1993	1994	1995	1996	1997	1998	1999	2000	2001	2002	Régions du monde
World	100.0	100.0	100.0	100.0	100.0	100.0	100.0	100.0	100.0	100.0	Monde
Africa	5.4	0.1	0.1	0.1	0.2	0.2	0.2	0.3	0.3	0.3	Afrique
Americas	16.0	17.7	16.4	17.4	17.9	18.4	19.5	18.3	16.6	15.1	Amériques
- Northern America	15.2	16.9	15.4	16.7	16.8	17.4	18.1	16.9	15.4	13.7	- Amérique du Nord
- LAIA	0.7	0.8	0.9	0.7	1.0	1.0	1.3	1.3	1.2	1.3	- ALAI
- CACM	0.0	0.0	0.0	0.0	0.0	0.0	0.0	0.0	0.0	0.0	- MCC
- Caribbean	0.0	0.0	0.0	0.0	0.1	0.1	0.1	0.0	0.0	0.1	- Caraïbes
- Rest of America	0.0	0.0	0.0	0.0	0.0	0.0	0.0	0.0	0.0	0.0	- Autre d'Amérique
Asia excluding former USSR	29.8	27.3	31.5	29.7	29.0	24.4	30.2	34.1	34.2	35.5	Asie ancienne URSS exclus
- Middle East	0.5	0.5	0.6	0.8	1.0	1.0	1.0	1.4	1.2	0.9	- Moyen-Orient
Asia former USSR	0.0	0.2	0.2	0.1	0.0	0.2	0.1	0.2	0.3	0.3	Asie ancienne URSS
Europe excluding former USSR	48.3	54.1	50.8	51.7	52.3	56.0	49.3	46.5	47.9	47.8	Europe ancienne URSS exclus
- European Union	46.6	51.6	48.5	49.2	49.6	52.9	46.5	43.8	45.2	44.9	- Union Européenne
- Eastern Europe	0.4	0.3	0.5	0.4	0.8	1.0	0.9	0.9	0.7	1.0	- Europe de l'Est
- Rest of Europe	1.4	2.2	1.7	2.0	1.9	2.2	1.9	1.8	2.0	2.0	- Autre de l'Europe
Europe former USSR	0.2	0.2	0.8	0.7	0.4	0.4	0.4	0.5	0.5	0.7	Europe ancienne URSS
Oceania	0.3	0.3	0.4	0.3	0.2	0.3	0.2	0.2	0.2	0.2	Océanie

TRADE BY COMMODITY (Value in million US dollars)
Exports by principal countries or areas

COMMERCE PAR PRODUIT (Valeur en millions de dollars EU)
Exportations selon les principaux pays ou zones

Country or area	1998	1999	2000	2001	2002	Pays ou zone
World	7809.5	7274.8	8370.7	7717.3	7836.1	Monde
Africa	105.2	111.8	162.2	154.8	177.0	Afrique
Americas	1912.6	1890.3	2293.2	2194.4	2145.3	Amériques
- Northern America	1496.9	1400.9	1777.6	1716.3	1706.2	- Amérique du Nord
- LAIA	382.9	438.1	474.8	448.0	409.7	- ALAI
- CACM	11.8	35.6	19.3	12.4	13.7	- MCC
- Caribbean	13.4	9.0	13.0	9.7	9.0	- Caraïbes
- Rest of America	7.5	6.7	8.6	8.0	6.8	- Autre d'Amérique
Asia excluding former USSR	961.0	872.0	1068.0	898.8	925.6	Asie ancienne URSS exclus
- Middle East	136.4	155.1	204.8	192.3	182.8	- Moyen-Orient
Asia former USSR	75.9	82.0	132.2	69.0	45.8	Asie ancienne URSS
Europe excluding former USSR	3435.3	3480.3	4251.5	4087.3	4182.4	Europe ancienne URSS exclus
- European Union	3053.8	3053.3	3616.2	3485.6	3575.0	- Union Européenne
- Eastern Europe	177.0	219.4	361.3	314.2	334.2	- Europe de l'Est
- Rest of Europe	204.6	207.6	274.1	287.5	273.3	- Autre de l'Europe
Europe former USSR	1179.2	696.9	300.4	126.1	131.8	Europe ancienne URSS
Oceania	140.3	141.4	163.2	187.0	228.3	Océanie
United States	945.4	872.7	1211.6	1169.0	1205.8	Etats-Unis d'Amérique
Germany	1097.0	961.3	1016.0	1026.2	920.7	Allemagne
Canada	551.0	527.3	565.4	547.3	500.4	Canada
France-Monaco	395.0	461.2	573.6	514.2	540.0	France-Monaco
United Kingdom	392.3	378.3	518.3	539.6	578.0	Royaume-Uni
Spain	204.4	311.4	319.3	371.9	407.2	Espagne
Russian Federation	958.3	502.8	95.9	28.1	19.2	Fédération de Russie
Netherlands	282.9	296.2	347.8	278.8	312.6	Pays-Bas
Mexico	205.5	232.1	252.9	240.5	202.3	Mexique
Belgium	–	227.5	297.0	275.6	e309.2	Belgique
China, Hong Kong SAR	283.2	198.0	185.8	117.9	75.7	Chine - RAS de Hong-Kong
Australia	124.8	125.8	144.6	167.7	205.1	Australie
Switzerland-Liechtenstein	132.6	140.3	168.8	157.4	153.2	Suisse-Liechtenstein
Singapore	152.2	132.1	156.4	138.6	147.9	Singapour
Italy-San Marino-Holy See	96.8	100.5	146.5	111.1	107.2	Italie-Saint-Marin-Saint-Siège
Japan	68.9	70.0	106.6	124.7	150.1	Japon
Sweden	88.7	78.3	115.2	98.1	106.7	Suède
Chile	76.5	79.8	97.1	93.6	e91.6	Chili
Denmark	72.5	65.3	79.2	85.9	79.1	Danemark
Ukraine	154.8	113.0	90.6	8.8	9.7	Ukraine
Poland	31.0	40.0	87.7	98.2	105.2	Pologne
Austria	80.2	61.6	69.4	65.6	79.5	Autriche
Czech Republic	55.0	55.6	68.5	79.3	82.1	République tchèque
Thailand	54.3	34.4	111.5	43.9	e46.3	Thaïlande
Philippines	55.7	50.7	65.2	55.7	59.5	Philippines
South Africa	–	–	86.3	83.5	89.8	Afrique du Sud
Belgium-Luxembourg	246.0	–	–	–	–	Belgique-Luxembourg
Hungary	39.5	34.8	55.8	61.7	52.1	Hongrie
Romania	31.9	60.7	93.6	20.6	31.7	Roumanie
Malaysia	45.6	45.7	44.3	48.2	e51.0	Malaisie

(Value as percentages of World total) **(Valeur en pourcentage du total mondial)**

Regions of the world	1993	1994	1995	1996	1997	1998	1999	2000	2001	2002	Régions du monde
World	100.0	100.0	100.0	100.0	100.0	100.0	100.0	100.0	100.0	100.0	Monde
Africa	1.5	1.3	1.6	1.8	1.5	1.3	1.5	1.9	2.0	2.3	Afrique
Americas	23.8	27.5	29.5	27.8	24.9	24.5	26.0	27.4	28.4	27.4	Amériques
- Northern America	20.8	23.2	24.2	22.6	20.7	19.2	19.3	21.2	22.2	21.8	- Amérique du Nord
- LAIA	2.8	4.0	4.9	4.8	3.9	4.9	6.0	5.7	5.8	5.2	- ALAI
- CACM	0.0	0.1	0.1	0.1	0.1	0.2	0.5	0.2	0.2	0.2	- MCC
- Caribbean	0.1	0.1	0.2	0.2	0.1	0.2	0.1	0.2	0.1	0.1	- Caraïbes
- Rest of America	0.1	0.0	0.1	0.1	0.1	0.1	0.1	0.1	0.1	0.1	- Autre d'Amérique
Asia excluding former USSR	12.7	12.9	15.0	14.0	13.6	12.3	12.0	12.8	11.6	11.8	Asie ancienne URSS exclus
- Middle East	3.0	3.5	3.1	1.7	1.4	1.7	2.1	2.4	2.5	2.3	- Moyen-Orient
Asia former USSR	1.7	0.6	0.9	0.9	1.0	1.0	1.1	1.6	0.9	0.6	Asie ancienne URSS
Europe excluding former USSR	48.1	50.0	45.2	46.4	46.8	44.0	47.8	50.8	53.0	53.4	Europe ancienne URSS exclus
- European Union	42.8	44.9	40.8	42.0	42.7	39.1	42.0	43.2	45.2	45.6	- Union Européenne
- Eastern Europe	2.5	2.2	1.8	1.5	1.5	2.3	3.0	4.3	4.1	4.3	- Europe de l'Est
- Rest of Europe	2.8	3.0	2.7	2.8	2.6	2.6	2.9	3.3	3.7	3.5	- Autre de l'Europe
Europe former USSR	10.2	5.3	5.5	6.5	10.4	15.1	9.6	3.6	1.6	1.7	Europe ancienne URSS
Oceania	2.1	2.4	2.3	2.7	1.7	1.8	1.9	1.9	2.4	2.9	Océanie

289 Ores and concentrates of precious metals, waste, scrap

TRADE BY COMMODITY (Value in million US dollars)
Imports by principal countries or areas

COMMERCE PAR PRODUIT (Valeur en millions de dollars EU)
Importations selon les principaux pays ou zones

Country or area	1998	1999	2000	2001	2002	Pays ou zone
World	2899.3	2928.4	3911.2	3973.9	3598.7	Monde
Africa	22.8	4.4	6.6	2.6	26.6	Afrique
Americas	311.3	368.9	439.2	580.5	631.8	Amériques
- Northern America	299.2	328.7	359.2	439.6	402.0	- Amérique du Nord
- LAIA	11.9	40.0	79.9	140.7	226.8	- ALAI
- CACM	0.0	0.0	0.0	0.0	0.0	- MCC
- Caribbean	0.1	0.2	0.0	0.2	2.9	- Caraïbes
- Rest of America	0.1	0.0	0.0	0.0	0.0	- Autre d'Amérique
Asia excluding former USSR	385.7	361.5	395.6	393.3	375.6	Asie ancienne URSS exclus
- Middle East	0.6	0.1	0.4	0.4	0.4	- Moyen-Orient
Asia former USSR	0.3	1.6	0.5	1.7	0.7	Asie ancienne URSS
Europe excluding former USSR	2141.1	2144.1	3049.4	2974.8	2551.0	Europe ancienne URSS exclus
- European Union	2061.3	2052.5	2946.3	2869.5	2261.3	- Union Européenne
- Eastern Europe	1.5	1.7	2.8	5.2	5.1	- Europe de l'Est
- Rest of Europe	78.4	89.9	100.3	100.0	284.6	- Autre de l'Europe
Europe former USSR	15.5	35.5	10.7	0.3	6.0	Europe ancienne URSS
Oceania	22.7	12.5	9.2	20.8	7.0	Océanie
Germany	816.3	794.4	1192.0	1052.7	800.2	Allemagne
United Kingdom	584.4	655.8	1090.6	1243.7	894.2	Royaume-Uni
Japan	366.3	334.2	355.6	366.0	349.0	Japon
Belgium	–	309.3	382.9	190.2	e208.6	Belgique
Spain	187.0	217.3	163.9	262.1	258.0	Espagne
United States	191.9	172.6	231.0	264.4	209.4	Etats-Unis d'Amérique
Canada	107.3	156.1	128.2	175.2	192.6	Canada
Switzerland-Liechtenstein	60.7	72.9	81.2	82.9	269.1	Suisse-Liechtenstein
Mexico	3.0	36.7	74.3	134.6	222.7	Mexique
Belgium-Luxembourg	349.2	–	–	–	–	Belgique-Luxembourg
Italy-San Marino-Holy See	69.8	20.7	40.1	40.5	42.4	Italie-Saint-Marin-Saint-Siège
France-Monaco	28.5	12.7	32.0	55.5	23.6	France-Monaco
Sweden	21.5	36.4	38.2	16.5	29.7	Suède
Norway	17.5	17.0	19.0	17.1	15.4	Norvège
China, Hong Kong SAR	10.7	14.7	22.7	15.0	17.6	Chine - RAS de Hong-Kong
Australia	22.4	12.3	9.1	20.6	6.8	Australie
Russian Federation	12.8	35.3	10.3	0.1	4.1	Fédération de Russie
South Africa	–	–	5.2	1.1	25.4	Afrique du Sud
Southern African Customs Union	22.4	4.1	–	–	–	Union douanière d'Afrique australe
Netherlands	2.7	4.7	4.6	6.3	2.5	Pays-Bas
Brazil	0.9	2.3	4.2	6.0	3.4	Brésil
Korea, Republic of	0.5	0.4	8.7	4.8	0.9	République de Corée
Peru	7.1	1.0	1.2	0.1	0.5	Pérou
Singapore	1.5	2.0	1.5	2.7	1.7	Singapour
Malaysia	1.0	1.3	2.6	2.1	e2.3	Malaisie
China	3.2	1.1	0.6	0.9	2.8	Chine
Czech Republic	1.2	1.2	1.1	2.0	2.0	République tchèque
Estonia	2.6	0.1	0.4	0.0	1.8	Estonie
Austria	1.0	0.6	1.3	0.8	0.8	Autriche
Democratic Republic of the Congo		e0.3	e1.3	e1.4	e1.1	République démocratique du Congo

(Value as percentages of World total) **(Valeur en pourcentage du total mondial)**

Regions of the world	1993	1994	1995	1996	1997	1998	1999	2000	2001	2002	Régions du monde
World	100.0	100.0	100.0	100.0	100.0	100.0	100.0	100.0	100.0	100.0	Monde
Africa	0.2	0.1	0.1	0.6	0.5	0.8	0.1	0.2	0.1	0.7	Afrique
Americas	13.1	13.6	18.0	12.3	10.4	10.7	12.6	11.2	14.6	17.6	Amériques
- Northern America	13.1	13.6	17.5	11.9	10.3	10.3	11.2	9.2	11.1	11.2	- Amérique du Nord
- LAIA	0.0	0.0	0.5	0.4	0.1	0.4	1.4	2.0	3.5	6.3	- ALAI
- CACM	0.0	0.0	0.0	0.0	0.0	0.0	0.0	0.0	0.0	0.0	- MCC
- Caribbean	0.0	0.0	0.0	0.0	0.0	0.0	0.0	0.0	0.0	0.1	- Caraïbes
- Rest of America	0.0	0.0	0.0	0.0	0.0	0.0	0.0	0.0	0.0	0.0	- Autre d'Amérique
Asia excluding former USSR	7.0	4.8	3.7	12.2	16.4	13.3	12.3	10.1	9.9	10.4	Asie ancienne URSS exclus
- Middle East	0.2	0.0	0.0	0.0	0.0	0.0	0.0	0.0	0.0	0.0	- Moyen-Orient
Asia former USSR	0.0	0.0	0.0	0.0	0.0	0.0	0.1	0.0	0.0	0.0	Asie ancienne URSS
Europe excluding former USSR	79.5	80.2	76.9	73.5	71.6	73.8	73.2	78.0	74.9	70.9	Europe ancienne URSS exclus
- European Union	76.7	77.2	73.6	71.4	68.6	71.1	70.1	75.3	72.2	62.8	- Union Européenne
- Eastern Europe	0.1	0.0	0.5	0.0	0.0	0.1	0.1	0.1	0.1	0.1	- Europe de l'Est
- Rest of Europe	2.6	2.9	2.8	2.1	2.9	2.7	3.1	2.6	2.5	7.9	- Autre de l'Europe
Europe former USSR	0.1	1.2	1.2	1.0	0.9	0.5	1.2	0.3	0.0	0.2	Europe ancienne URSS
Oceania	0.0	0.0	0.1	0.4	0.2	0.8	0.4	0.2	0.5	0.2	Océanie

TRADE BY COMMODITY (Value in million US dollars)
Exports by principal countries or areas

COMMERCE PAR PRODUIT (Valeur en millions de dollars EU)
Exportations selon les principaux pays ou zones

Country or area	1998	1999	2000	2001	2002	Pays ou zone
World	2508.3	2815.1	3547.8	3446.2	3035.4	Monde
Africa	209.0	261.5	406.8	303.7	217.4	Afrique
Americas	695.3	917.3	1138.2	1319.8	1313.9	Amériques
- Northern America	576.7	764.7	947.0	1138.1	1107.4	- Amérique du Nord
- LAIA	102.0	140.8	175.3	158.1	160.1	- ALAI
- CACM	8.2	3.4	8.4	13.3	37.7	- MCC
- Caribbean	8.3	8.4	7.5	10.3	8.7	- Caraïbes
- Rest of America	0.0	0.0	0.0	0.0	0.0	- Autre d'Amérique
Asia excluding former USSR	234.2	242.7	238.4	218.3	146.7	Asie ancienne URSS exclus
- Middle East	3.5	1.2	3.5	0.8	4.6	- Moyen-Orient
Asia former USSR	6.1	41.5	29.3	46.2	26.2	Asie ancienne URSS
Europe excluding former USSR	432.4	508.1	693.8	760.8	645.1	Europe ancienne URSS exclus
- European Union	345.8	389.4	552.6	581.3	513.5	- Union Européenne
- Eastern Europe	19.1	22.2	25.2	35.3	17.4	- Europe de l'Est
- Rest of Europe	67.5	96.5	116.0	144.2	114.1	- Autre de l'Europe
Europe former USSR	23.0	25.3	18.5	13.2	18.0	Europe ancienne URSS
Oceania	908.3	818.7	1022.8	784.1	668.1	Océanie
Papua New Guinea	900.6	e816.0	1019.6	e767.8	e655.8	Papouasie-Nouvelle-Guinée
United States	423.6	607.6	689.6	857.8	878.9	Etats-Unis d'Amérique
Canada	153.1	157.1	257.4	280.3	228.5	Canada
South Africa	–	–	324.2	257.6	164.1	Afrique du Sud
France-Monaco	72.5	117.2	139.7	158.6	80.1	France-Monaco
Germany	45.4	53.2	101.9	168.2	184.2	Allemagne
Switzerland-Liechtenstein	57.5	88.3	108.7	138.7	107.8	Suisse-Liechtenstein
Southern African Customs Union	177.9	237.8	–	–	–	Union douanière d'Afrique australe
United Kingdom	63.0	65.9	93.0	75.9	69.5	Royaume-Uni
China, Hong Kong SAR	112.6	117.0	61.2	39.0	29.7	Chine - RAS de Hong-Kong
Japan	58.1	50.6	72.9	77.8	32.3	Japon
Bolivia	58.8	55.9	65.3	48.9	e47.0	Bolivie
Sweden	50.3	46.6	59.9	56.0	43.3	Suède
Belgium	–	41.6	63.4	51.4	e57.6	Belgique
Chile	18.8	60.7	58.3	34.1	e33.4	Chili
Philippines	37.2	49.1	46.8	35.1	21.3	Philippines
Peru	11.9	2.7	34.1	52.4	45.1	Pérou
Netherlands	22.1	24.8	42.1	28.6	23.2	Pays-Bas
United Republic of Tanzania		0.0	0.1	45.5	e52.2	République-Unie de Tanzanie
Uzbekistan	e5.9	e26.0	e8.8	e33.4	e17.7	Ouzbékistan
Spain	7.4	11.1	19.5	24.2	19.0	Espagne
Namibia	–	–	79.6	0.0	e	Namibie
Finland	20.4	13.1	11.5	10.5	11.1	Finlande
Honduras	5.2	1.8	7.1	13.3	36.5	Honduras
Mexico	8.8	17.2	12.2	6.1	16.2	Mexique
Austria	27.4	3.2	9.7	0.9	16.3	Autriche
Korea, Republic of	6.0	4.4	9.6	19.7	10.8	République de Corée
Zimbabwe	e22.3	20.9	1.9	0.0	0.7	Zimbabwe
Georgia	e0.2	12.7	17.4	9.2	e5.0	Géorgie
Cuba	e7.9	7.8	7.0	9.6	e8.3	Cuba

(Value as percentages of World total) **(Valeur en pourcentage du total mondial)**

Regions of the world	1993	1994	1995	1996	1997	1998	1999	2000	2001	2002	Régions du monde
World	100.0	100.0	100.0	100.0	100.0	100.0	100.0	100.0	100.0	100.0	Monde
Africa	3.6	3.0	3.6	7.2	8.7	8.3	9.3	11.5	8.8	7.2	Afrique
Americas	26.6	28.0	32.6	30.5	30.1	27.7	32.6	32.1	38.3	43.3	Amériques
- Northern America	20.6	20.3	24.8	21.8	23.0	23.0	27.2	26.7	33.0	36.5	- Amérique du Nord
- LAIA	6.0	6.9	7.5	8.2	6.3	4.1	5.0	4.9	4.6	5.3	- ALAI
- CACM	0.1	0.3	0.2	0.3	0.8	0.3	0.1	0.2	0.4	1.2	- MCC
- Caribbean	0.0	0.5	0.1	0.2	0.0	0.3	0.3	0.2	0.3	0.3	- Caraïbes
- Rest of America	0.0	0.0	0.0	0.0	0.0	0.0	0.0	0.0	0.0	0.0	- Autre d'Amérique
Asia excluding former USSR	6.9	7.4	5.3	5.4	6.7	9.3	8.6	6.7	6.3	4.8	Asie ancienne URSS exclus
- Middle East	0.6	0.1	0.9	0.8	0.9	0.1	0.0	0.1	0.0	0.2	- Moyen-Orient
Asia former USSR	0.5	0.1	0.0	0.1	0.6	0.2	1.5	0.8	1.3	0.9	Asie ancienne URSS
Europe excluding former USSR	17.4	16.4	15.4	15.9	17.8	17.2	18.0	19.6	22.1	21.3	Europe ancienne URSS exclus
- European Union	13.5	13.9	12.6	13.3	13.8	13.8	13.8	15.6	16.9	16.9	- Union Européenne
- Eastern Europe	1.8	0.6	0.6	0.4	0.7	0.8	0.8	0.7	1.0	0.6	- Europe de l'Est
- Rest of Europe	2.1	1.8	2.3	2.3	3.3	2.7	3.4	3.3	4.2	3.8	- Autre de l'Europe
Europe former USSR	1.3	1.4	2.2	1.4	1.4	0.9	0.9	0.5	0.4	0.6	Europe ancienne URSS
Oceania	43.7	43.8	40.9	39.5	34.7	36.2	29.1	28.8	22.8	22.0	Océanie

291 Crude animal materials, nes

TRADE BY COMMODITY (Value in million US dollars)
Imports by principal countries or areas

COMMERCE PAR PRODUIT (Valeur en millions de dollars EU)
Importations selon les principaux pays ou zones

Country or area	1998	1999	2000	2001	2002	Pays ou zone
World	4283.3	4001.6	4133.3	3812.4	3853.2	Monde
Africa	107.5	64.9	45.8	53.8	48.3	Afrique
Americas	753.3	754.5	868.1	851.1	873.5	Amériques
- Northern America	542.3	553.8	643.1	627.1	671.9	- Amérique du Nord
- LAIA	202.6	195.7	217.9	216.4	194.2	- ALAI
- CACM	4.0	2.4	2.8	2.8	2.7	- MCC
- Caribbean	3.7	2.1	3.7	4.5	4.3	- Caraïbes
- Rest of America	0.6	0.5	0.5	0.4	0.4	- Autre d'Amérique
Asia excluding former USSR	1098.0	1179.7	1309.4	1124.6	1085.3	Asie ancienne URSS exclus
- Middle East	77.7	81.3	35.0	32.1	40.3	- Moyen-Orient
Asia former USSR	0.8	0.9	2.3	1.4	1.5	Asie ancienne URSS
Europe excluding former USSR	2223.5	1881.8	1784.2	1677.1	1728.6	Europe ancienne URSS exclus
- European Union	1923.0	1622.9	1531.3	1446.1	1460.5	- Union Européenne
- Eastern Europe	182.9	163.8	152.7	140.3	161.3	- Europe de l'Est
- Rest of Europe	117.5	95.1	100.1	90.7	106.9	- Autre de l'Europe
Europe former USSR	36.5	45.4	45.8	38.9	44.9	Europe ancienne URSS
Oceania	63.7	74.5	77.8	65.4	71.2	Océanie
Japan	608.3	646.6	696.2	561.8	451.5	Japon
United States	476.4	488.5	571.5	546.1	585.8	Etats-Unis d'Amérique
Germany	640.4	534.8	510.7	444.9	422.5	Allemagne
France-Monaco	307.4	255.2	228.7	240.1	234.3	France-Monaco
Italy-San Marino-Holy See	184.5	158.0	150.1	136.2	142.6	Italie-Saint-Marin-Saint-Siège
China	101.3	111.8	157.7	172.3	190.9	Chine
United Kingdom	145.6	125.8	113.6	100.7	99.2	Royaume-Uni
Netherlands	141.9	120.6	122.2	91.3	105.5	Pays-Bas
Denmark	128.0	105.9	95.6	111.6	128.5	Danemark
Mexico	79.3	85.3	114.4	115.5	104.2	Mexique
Poland	113.5	98.9	91.8	79.5	91.0	Pologne
Korea, Republic of	64.3	94.0	111.3	83.3	102.9	République de Corée
Spain	91.1	89.9	86.4	70.2	80.3	Espagne
Canada	65.8	65.1	70.8	79.0	83.7	Canada
China, Hong Kong SAR	60.2	61.1	75.2	63.8	80.6	Chine - RAS de Hong-Kong
Belgium	-	70.8	72.0	78.8	e86.4	Belgique
Australia	45.7	58.1	57.9	41.5	45.8	Australie
Austria	54.9	50.8	43.1	48.1	49.9	Autriche
Brazil	60.6	49.3	47.5	44.2	41.0	Brésil
Switzerland-Liechtenstein	54.0	53.3	47.1	37.5	38.3	Suisse-Liechtenstein
Sweden	48.0	36.2	35.8	52.5	37.5	Suède
Thailand	27.8	22.3	35.9	46.6	e48.6	Thaïlande
Portugal	35.6	35.2	32.7	32.1	30.8	Portugal
Czech Republic	28.6	25.6	23.4	25.9	31.4	République tchèque
Norway	17.0	16.1	24.0	22.6	36.2	Norvège
United Arab Emirates	51.2	53.6	1.5	2.6	e2.7	Emirates arabes unis
Russian Federation	16.8	26.9	20.3	18.4	21.1	Fédération de Russie
Belgium-Luxembourg	102.8	-	-	-	-	Belgique-Luxembourg
Turkey	18.0	17.1	23.2	15.9	26.3	Turquie
Hungary	22.4	20.8	18.9	16.8	17.0	Hongrie

(Value as percentages of World total) **(Valeur en pourcentage du total mondial)**

Regions of the world	1993	1994	1995	1996	1997	1998	1999	2000	2001	2002	Régions du monde
World	100.0	100.0	100.0	100.0	100.0	100.0	100.0	100.0	100.0	100.0	Monde
Africa	1.7	1.3	1.0	1.5	2.1	2.5	1.6	1.1	1.4	1.3	Afrique
Americas	11.1	12.3	13.3	14.3	16.3	17.6	18.9	21.0	22.3	22.7	Amériques
- Northern America	7.7	8.7	9.8	10.5	11.9	12.7	13.8	15.6	16.4	17.4	- Amérique du Nord
- LAIA	3.1	3.4	3.0	3.6	4.2	4.7	4.9	5.3	5.7	5.0	- ALAI
- CACM	0.2	0.1	0.1	0.1	0.1	0.1	0.1	0.1	0.1	0.1	- MCC
- Caribbean	0.1	0.1	0.3	0.2	0.1	0.1	0.1	0.1	0.1	0.1	- Caraïbes
- Rest of America	0.0	0.0	0.0	0.0	0.0	0.0	0.0	0.0	0.0	0.0	- Autre d'Amérique
Asia excluding former USSR	36.4	33.0	32.7	32.2	30.1	25.6	29.5	31.7	29.5	28.2	Asie ancienne URSS exclus
- Middle East	0.6	0.4	0.5	1.3	1.6	1.8	2.0	0.8	0.8	1.0	- Moyen-Orient
Asia former USSR	0.0	0.1	0.0	0.0	0.0	0.0	0.0	0.1	0.0	0.0	Asie ancienne URSS
Europe excluding former USSR	48.9	51.1	50.6	49.4	48.9	51.9	47.0	43.2	44.0	44.9	Europe ancienne URSS exclus
- European Union	44.0	45.9	45.0	43.4	42.5	44.9	40.6	37.0	37.9	37.9	- Union Européenne
- Eastern Europe	2.5	2.7	3.1	3.8	4.0	4.3	4.1	3.7	3.7	4.2	- Europe de l'Est
- Rest of Europe	2.4	2.5	2.4	2.3	2.4	2.7	2.4	2.4	2.4	2.8	- Autre de l'Europe
Europe former USSR	0.4	0.7	0.8	0.9	0.8	0.9	1.1	1.1	1.0	1.2	Europe ancienne URSS
Oceania	1.5	1.6	1.6	1.6	1.9	1.5	1.9	1.9	1.7	1.8	Océanie

TRADE BY COMMODITY (Value in million US dollars)
Exports by principal countries or areas

COMMERCE PAR PRODUIT (Valeur en millions de dollars EU)
Exportations selon les principaux pays ou zones

Country or area	1998	1999	2000	2001	2002	Pays ou zone
World	3588.8	3291.2	3456.6	3321.3	3502.3	Monde
Africa	46.4	86.7	47.1	48.9	53.9	Afrique
Americas	718.2	630.8	726.1	868.2	874.8	Amériques
- Northern America	487.7	476.6	553.4	712.7	714.1	- Amérique du Nord
- LAIA	149.0	142.4	158.2	147.2	149.8	- ALAI
- CACM	76.5	2.9	2.4	3.4	5.2	- MCC
- Caribbean	4.3	5.6	4.0	3.3	4.4	- Caraïbes
- Rest of America	0.7	3.3	8.1	1.6	1.4	- Autre d'Amérique
Asia excluding former USSR	1122.2	1065.3	1240.7	1067.2	1100.9	Asie ancienne URSS exclus
- Middle East	106.4	103.3	90.4	70.2	75.6	- Moyen-Orient
Asia former USSR	5.5	5.2	8.2	13.3	9.6	Asie ancienne URSS
Europe excluding former USSR	1458.1	1266.7	1214.9	1108.7	1239.6	Europe ancienne URSS exclus
- European Union	1256.2	1084.4	1015.1	922.0	1010.8	- Union Européenne
- Eastern Europe	137.0	136.8	148.3	130.1	161.2	- Europe de l'Est
- Rest of Europe	64.9	45.5	51.4	56.5	67.6	- Autre de l'Europe
Europe former USSR	11.3	14.5	19.5	24.0	19.6	Europe ancienne URSS
Oceania	227.2	222.0	200.2	191.2	203.8	Océanie
China	643.0	614.5	750.4	642.7	647.7	Chine
United States	383.7	361.7	434.7	584.4	590.0	Etats-Unis d'Amérique
Germany	383.0	321.2	302.5	292.8	309.3	Allemagne
Netherlands	185.1	172.7	161.8	126.1	156.4	Pays-Bas
France-Monaco	165.2	143.4	135.6	113.1	139.5	France-Monaco
New Zealand	154.7	149.9	127.0	120.8	128.4	Nouvelle-Zélande
Canada	103.9	114.8	118.4	128.3	123.8	Canada
Denmark	115.3	99.4	92.6	83.2	94.0	Danemark
Brazil	69.2	73.9	76.4	82.6	e85.6	Brésil
Hungary	72.0	71.2	75.3	65.2	74.8	Hongrie
Australia	66.4	64.7	67.6	63.5	70.1	Australie
United Kingdom	91.2	67.3	66.9	49.8	55.2	Royaume-Uni
Spain	69.9	65.1	49.4	68.6	63.7	Espagne
Belgium	–	71.3	69.8	62.8	e70.5	Belgique
Poland	50.4	49.3	54.8	47.3	59.9	Pologne
Italy-San Marino-Holy See	52.6	48.0	53.3	50.5	48.6	Italie-Saint-Marin-Saint-Siège
China, Hong Kong SAR	44.0	43.7	51.1	44.1	54.3	Chine - RAS de Hong-Kong
India	38.4	38.5	43.5	42.3	41.7	Inde
Turkey	44.9	42.8	38.2	28.1	37.6	Turquie
Iran (Islamic Republic of)	34.3	32.6	31.1	28.3	25.8	Iran (République islamique d')
Thailand	23.9	29.0	31.5	29.3	e31.0	Thaïlande
Sweden	34.5	28.2	23.4	18.9	18.8	Suède
Korea, Republic of	23.7	21.2	26.6	22.2	20.6	République de Corée
Norway	21.8	15.5	17.2	22.2	32.1	Norvège
Portugal	23.4	22.0	21.2	18.8	18.7	Portugal
Viet Nam	12.0	11.9	22.4	23.3	25.9	Viet Nam
Uruguay	18.4	18.1	22.6	15.3	18.8	Uruguay
Austria	20.2	18.8	16.4	17.3	16.8	Autriche
Belgium-Luxembourg	88.1	–	–	–	–	Belgique-Luxembourg
Ireland	20.5	19.2	16.4	14.3	13.2	Irlande

(Value as percentages of World total) **(Valeur en pourcentage du total mondial)**

Regions of the world	1993	1994	1995	1996	1997	1998	1999	2000	2001	2002	Régions du monde
World	100.0	100.0	100.0	100.0	100.0	100.0	100.0	100.0	100.0	100.0	Monde
Africa	0.8	0.9	0.8	0.9	1.0	1.3	2.6	1.4	1.5	1.5	Afrique
Americas	17.3	17.5	17.5	19.0	18.9	20.0	19.2	21.0	26.1	25.0	Amériques
- Northern America	12.9	12.4	13.2	13.7	13.0	13.6	14.5	16.0	21.5	20.4	- Amérique du Nord
- LAIA	4.1	4.6	4.0	4.3	4.4	4.2	4.3	4.6	4.4	4.3	- ALAI
- CACM	0.1	0.3	0.2	0.9	1.3	2.1	0.1	0.1	0.1	0.1	- MCC
- Caribbean	0.1	0.1	0.1	0.1	0.1	0.1	0.2	0.1	0.1	0.1	- Caraïbes
- Rest of America	0.0	0.0	0.0	0.0	0.0	0.0	0.1	0.2	0.0	0.0	- Autre d'Amérique
Asia excluding former USSR	37.8	36.0	37.5	34.7	33.4	31.3	32.4	35.9	32.1	31.4	Asie ancienne URSS exclus
- Middle East	4.0	3.4	3.0	3.2	2.8	3.0	3.1	2.6	2.1	2.2	- Moyen-Orient
Asia former USSR	0.1	0.1	0.1	0.2	0.1	0.2	0.2	0.2	0.4	0.3	Asie ancienne URSS
Europe excluding former USSR	34.0	37.3	36.6	37.5	39.0	40.6	38.5	35.1	33.4	35.4	Europe ancienne URSS exclus
- European Union	28.7	31.3	31.5	32.4	33.3	35.0	32.9	29.4	27.8	28.9	- Union Européenne
- Eastern Europe	4.0	4.7	3.6	3.7	3.9	3.8	4.2	4.3	3.9	4.6	- Europe de l'Est
- Rest of Europe	1.3	1.3	1.5	1.5	1.7	1.8	1.4	1.5	1.7	1.9	- Autre de l'Europe
Europe former USSR	2.2	0.4	0.4	0.3	0.3	0.3	0.4	0.6	0.7	0.6	Europe ancienne URSS
Oceania	7.8	7.8	7.1	7.3	7.4	6.3	6.7	5.8	5.8	5.8	Océanie

292 Crude vegetable materials, nes

TRADE BY COMMODITY (Value in million US dollars)
Imports by principal countries or areas

COMMERCE PAR PRODUIT (Valeur en millions de dollars EU
Importations selon les principaux pays ou zones

Country or area	1998	1999	2000	2001	2002	Pays ou zone
World	17221.7	17091.4	15717.7	15736.2	16523.3	Monde
Africa	251.7	266.5	268.0	239.3	234.2	Afrique
Americas	3560.6	3481.5	3518.9	3486.0	3338.1	Amériques
- Northern America	2825.6	2751.9	2794.9	2748.7	2672.3	- Amérique du Nord
- LAIA	650.6	640.4	632.3	648.9	570.6	- ALAI
- CACM	36.0	41.1	39.4	40.4	51.4	- MCC
- Caribbean	40.8	39.0	42.4	39.9	34.9	- Caraïbes
- Rest of America	7.7	9.1	10.0	8.1	8.9	- Autre d'Amérique
Asia excluding former USSR	2948.0	3149.3	2740.3	2559.5	2631.4	Asie ancienne URSS exclus
- Middle East	696.3	723.1	286.0	280.2	296.7	- Moyen-Orient
Asia former USSR	13.2	15.3	18.2	20.3	17.4	Asie ancienne URSS
Europe excluding former USSR	10122.2	9886.3	8845.7	9080.1	9903.1	Europe ancienne URSS exclus
- European Union	9128.8	8913.2	7912.1	8113.9	8824.8	- Union Européenne
- Eastern Europe	309.0	309.3	303.9	334.4	396.4	- Europe de l'Est
- Rest of Europe	684.5	663.8	629.8	631.8	681.8	- Autre de l'Europe
Europe former USSR	177.6	136.3	177.5	221.8	256.6	Europe ancienne URSS
Oceania	148.4	156.1	149.1	129.3	142.6	Océanie
United States	2461.1	2370.8	2397.6	2343.6	2261.1	Etats-Unis d'Amérique
Germany	2838.4	2558.0	1907.2	2127.7	1985.1	Allemagne
France-Monaco	1338.8	1334.5	1254.7	1158.3	1297.2	France-Monaco
United Kingdom	1151.8	1163.5	1122.3	1211.5	1554.4	Royaume-Uni
Netherlands	1078.0	1114.1	1122.3	1076.1	1202.5	Pays-Bas
Japan	1000.5	1094.0	1047.8	1017.8	1017.6	Japon
Italy-San Marino-Holy See	729.9	783.5	706.7	656.0	687.2	Italie-Saint-Marin-Saint-Siège
Switzerland-Liechtenstein	459.8	443.1	418.4	407.1	451.9	Suisse-Liechtenstein
Spain	459.9	410.6	350.6	363.6	424.6	Espagne
Canada	362.2	378.6	396.7	404.3	410.2	Canada
Belgium	–	417.4	393.9	411.1	e450.8	Belgique
China, Hong Kong SAR	339.2	327.1	355.3	282.7	288.9	Chine - RAS de Hong-Kong
Mexico	276.4	294.3	287.8	319.9	300.7	Mexique
Denmark	265.6	289.1	281.9	303.1	330.8	Danemark
Austria	289.5	301.0	258.4	280.3	306.7	Autriche
United Arab Emirates	446.6	468.0	51.6	55.2	e56.6	Emirates arabes unis
Korea, Republic of	157.4	214.5	254.4	228.5	218.8	République de Corée
Sweden	205.6	184.6	176.9	200.6	230.6	Suède
China	161.5	171.2	202.3	197.9	232.3	Chine
Poland	129.6	130.5	126.9	145.6	165.1	Pologne
Norway	127.7	124.4	121.9	129.0	126.5	Norvège
Australia	116.7	123.6	117.6	98.3	108.3	Australie
Russian Federation	97.9	64.1	97.5	133.9	164.2	Fédération de Russie
Singapore	109.4	110.8	109.7	101.7	106.2	Singapour
Brazil	96.6	87.8	92.2	89.2	90.2	Brésil
Argentina	117.5	114.7	92.7	84.4	e37.3	Argentine
Portugal	86.1	87.9	86.7	82.9	94.0	Portugal
Belgium-Luxembourg	434.7	–	–	–	–	Belgique-Luxembourg
Ireland	77.1	81.0	84.7	85.4	95.1	Irlande
Finland	89.0	81.0	78.8	83.3	85.2	Finlande

(Value as percentages of World total) **(Valeur en pourcentage du total mondial**

Regions of the world	1993	1994	1995	1996	1997	1998	1999	2000	2001	2002	Régions du monde
World	100.0	100.0	100.0	100.0	100.0	100.0	100.0	100.0	100.0	100.0	Monde
Africa	1.6	1.4	1.4	1.3	1.4	1.5	1.6	1.7	1.5	1.4	Afrique
Americas	17.0	17.2	17.4	17.7	19.4	20.7	20.4	22.4	22.2	20.2	Amériques
- Northern America	13.6	13.4	13.8	14.1	15.5	16.4	16.1	17.8	17.5	16.2	- Amérique du Nord
- LAIA	3.0	3.1	3.0	3.2	3.5	3.8	3.7	4.0	4.1	3.5	- ALAI
- CACM	0.2	0.2	0.1	0.1	0.2	0.2	0.2	0.3	0.3	0.3	- MCC
- Caribbean	0.2	0.5	0.4	0.4	0.2	0.2	0.2	0.3	0.3	0.2	- Caraïbes
- Rest of America	0.0	0.0	0.0	0.0	0.0	0.0	0.1	0.1	0.1	0.1	- Autre d'Amérique
Asia excluding former USSR	22.1	20.3	19.5	20.5	20.2	17.1	18.4	17.4	16.3	15.9	Asie ancienne URSS exclus
- Middle East	1.5	1.5	1.5	3.0	3.8	4.0	4.2	1.8	1.8	1.8	- Moyen-Orient
Asia former USSR	0.0	0.1	0.1	0.0	0.0	0.1	0.1	0.1	0.1	0.1	Asie ancienne URSS
Europe excluding former USSR	57.9	59.3	59.7	58.6	57.0	58.8	57.8	56.3	57.7	59.9	Europe ancienne URSS exclus
- European Union	52.3	53.5	53.6	52.8	51.2	53.0	52.2	50.3	51.6	53.4	- Union Européenne
- Eastern Europe	1.3	1.4	1.5	1.6	1.6	1.8	1.8	1.9	2.1	2.4	- Europe de l'Est
- Rest of Europe	4.3	4.4	4.6	4.2	4.1	4.0	3.9	4.0	4.0	4.1	- Autre de l'Europe
Europe former USSR	0.6	0.8	1.0	1.0	1.1	1.0	0.8	1.1	1.4	1.6	Europe ancienne URSS
Oceania	0.8	0.9	0.8	0.9	0.9	0.9	0.9	0.9	0.8	0.9	Océanie

TRADE BY COMMODITY (Value in million US dollars)
Exports by principal countries or areas

COMMERCE PAR PRODUIT (Valeur en millions de dollars EU)
Exportations selon les principaux pays ou zones

Country or area	1998	1999	2000	2001	2002	Pays ou zone
World	14688.2	15157.2	14492.1	14512.8	15886.4	Monde
Africa	470.6	466.5	469.2	518.2	541.9	Afrique
Americas	2912.7	2917.4	2998.0	3107.9	3328.0	Amériques
- Northern America	1516.0	1516.1	1563.0	1579.8	1667.0	- Amérique du Nord
- LAIA	1170.4	1184.2	1203.1	1306.9	1434.2	- ALAI
- CACM	208.3	205.2	221.9	209.8	210.8	- MCC
- Caribbean	16.1	10.2	8.3	9.1	13.8	- Caraïbes
- Rest of America	1.9	1.7	1.7	2.4	2.3	- Autre d'Amérique
Asia excluding former USSR	2432.2	2521.6	2488.1	2294.9	2386.5	Asie ancienne URSS exclus
- Middle East	86.9	103.0	68.6	74.5	94.7	- Moyen-Orient
Asia former USSR	13.2	13.8	21.1	23.2	15.8	Asie ancienne URSS
Europe excluding former USSR	8654.1	9026.3	8314.9	8366.7	9422.6	Europe ancienne URSS exclus
- European Union	8340.5	8768.1	8053.5	8093.5	9122.1	- Union Européenne
- Eastern Europe	204.9	156.1	160.0	157.7	186.3	- Europe de l'Est
- Rest of Europe	108.8	102.1	101.4	115.5	114.3	- Autre de l'Europe
Europe former USSR	31.7	26.9	36.4	38.6	34.1	Europe ancienne URSS
Oceania	173.5	184.7	164.5	163.3	157.5	Océanie
Netherlands	4408.9	4865.6	4557.8	4415.9	5053.9	Pays-Bas
United States	1120.7	1117.6	1133.7	1107.8	1192.2	Etats-Unis d'Amérique
Germany	790.5	758.0	648.1	715.7	780.7	Allemagne
Italy-San Marino-Holy See	708.9	747.0	658.1	637.4	697.6	Italie-Saint-Marin-Saint-Siège
Denmark	635.8	602.1	520.4	622.2	703.8	Danemark
France-Monaco	612.0	641.5	600.5	545.9	598.6	France-Monaco
Colombia	562.0	555.7	585.1	614.8	675.5	Colombie
China	484.2	453.7	459.4	462.9	503.4	Chine
Canada	395.3	398.5	429.2	471.9	474.8	Canada
Belgium	-	470.0	442.7	485.1	e544.3	Belgique
India	408.5	393.9	378.2	353.0	377.8	Inde
Spain	363.7	350.2	315.3	352.8	381.1	Espagne
Israel	319.8	325.8	280.6	240.6	255.5	Israël
China, Hong Kong SAR	247.0	244.4	270.6	192.1	189.5	Chine - RAS de Hong-Kong
Korea, Republic of	217.7	237.6	230.7	224.7	196.8	République de Corée
Ecuador	164.6	183.8	158.7	233.1	294.9	Equateur
Chile	194.6	184.5	197.2	196.6	e192.4	Chili
United Kingdom	164.2	152.5	141.7	143.7	180.8	Royaume-Uni
Costa Rica	151.7	148.9	158.2	152.7	160.2	Costa Rica
Mexico	130.1	148.6	158.0	150.4	154.2	Mexique
Japan	127.1	145.1	147.3	129.6	139.7	Japon
Kenya	107.4	109.9	117.6	e182.7	131.7	Kenya
Singapore	131.5	120.0	118.4	106.0	102.4	Singapour
Australia	90.1	100.6	90.3	91.4	93.2	Australie
Thailand	83.4	87.5	97.9	95.1	e100.4	Thaïlande
Belgium-Luxembourg	453.9	-	-	-	-	Belgique-Luxembourg
Philippines	68.8	90.7	89.7	81.8	78.1	Philippines
Ireland	97.9	80.2	72.4	70.3	66.6	Irlande
Indonesia	40.2	72.5	88.0	90.1	87.2	Indonésie
New Zealand	77.9	78.4	69.0	65.3	62.7	Nouvelle-Zélande

(Value as percentages of World total) **(Valeur en pourcentage du total mondial)**

Regions of the world	1993	1994	1995	1996	1997	1998	1999	2000	2001	2002	Régions du monde
World	100.0	100.0	100.0	100.0	100.0	100.0	100.0	100.0	100.0	100.0	Monde
Africa	2.8	3.2	4.2	3.1	3.2	3.2	3.1	3.2	3.6	3.4	Afrique
Americas	15.7	15.4	15.0	16.3	18.6	19.8	19.2	20.7	21.4	20.9	Amériques
- Northern America	8.9	8.2	7.8	8.3	9.7	10.3	10.0	10.8	10.9	10.5	- Amérique du Nord
- LAIA	5.8	6.0	6.1	6.6	7.6	8.0	7.8	8.3	9.0	9.0	- ALAI
- CACM	0.9	1.0	1.1	1.3	1.3	1.4	1.4	1.5	1.4	1.3	- MCC
- Caribbean	0.1	0.1	0.1	0.1	0.1	0.1	0.1	0.1	0.1	0.1	- Caraïbes
- Rest of America	0.0	0.0	0.0	0.0	0.0	0.0	0.0	0.0	0.0	0.0	- Autre d'Amérique
Asia excluding former USSR	20.2	19.2	18.6	18.2	18.5	16.6	16.6	17.2	15.8	15.0	Asie ancienne URSS exclus
- Middle East	0.6	0.6	0.6	0.5	0.6	0.6	0.7	0.5	0.5	0.6	- Moyen-Orient
Asia former USSR	0.1	0.1	0.2	0.1	0.1	0.1	0.1	0.1	0.2	0.1	Asie ancienne URSS
Europe excluding former USSR	59.7	60.7	60.7	61.0	58.2	58.9	59.6	57.4	57.7	59.3	Europe ancienne URSS exclus
- European Union	58.2	59.1	59.0	59.2	56.4	56.8	57.8	55.6	55.8	57.4	- Union Européenne
- Eastern Europe	0.8	0.8	0.9	1.1	1.1	1.4	1.0	1.1	1.1	1.2	- Europe de l'Est
- Rest of Europe	0.7	0.8	0.8	0.7	0.7	0.7	0.7	0.7	0.8	0.7	- Autre de l'Europe
Europe former USSR	0.2	0.1	0.2	0.2	0.1	0.2	0.2	0.3	0.3	0.2	Europe ancienne URSS
Oceania	1.2	1.2	1.2	1.2	1.3	1.2	1.2	1.1	1.1	1.0	Océanie

322 Coal, lignite and peat

TRADE BY COMMODITY (Value in million US dollars)
Imports by principal countries or areas

COMMERCE PAR PRODUIT (Valeur en millions de dollars EU)
Importations selon les principaux pays ou zones

Country or area	1998	1999	2000	2001	2002	Pays ou zone
World	23395.7	20564.1	21824.5	25685.6	25897.4	Monde
Africa	337.7	279.5	222.0	391.7	377.4	Afrique
Americas	2174.4	2087.0	2230.2	2686.2	2725.1	Amériques
- Northern America	1120.7	1119.3	1248.1	1614.5	1540.5	- Amérique du Nord
- LAIA	1039.1	957.7	964.5	1031.1	1150.1	- ALAI
- CACM	0.7	3.0	9.4	21.5	19.0	- MCC
- Caribbean	11.4	4.2	6.0	17.8	15.3	- Caraïbes
- Rest of America	2.5	2.8	2.2	1.2	0.2	- Autre d'Amérique
Asia excluding former USSR	12252.4	10959.7	11607.8	12740.5	13677.7	Asie ancienne URSS exclus
- Middle East	503.9	396.7	672.1	342.5	716.4	- Moyen-Orient
Asia former USSR	48.9	40.7	31.3	16.5	22.1	Asie ancienne URSS
Europe excluding former USSR	7931.4	6833.9	7299.5	9434.4	8687.6	Europe ancienne URSS exclus
- European Union	6901.1	6137.8	6550.9	8553.5	7777.4	- Union Européenne
- Eastern Europe	878.8	545.0	581.7	711.3	744.5	- Europe de l'Est
- Rest of Europe	151.5	151.2	166.9	169.6	165.7	- Autre de l'Europe
Europe former USSR	629.5	344.4	416.1	398.1	386.5	Europe ancienne URSS
Oceania	21.5	18.7	17.7	18.2	20.8	Océanie
Japan	6169.1	5487.6	5446.5	6232.5	6315.8	Japon
Korea, Republic of	2206.1	1943.6	2159.5	2322.2	2331.7	République de Corée
United Kingdom	1097.5	968.6	1048.5	1735.6	1319.6	Royaume-Uni
Germany	982.6	857.6	895.1	1312.6	1159.2	Allemagne
India	846.1	818.4	902.1	961.1	1027.2	Inde
Italy-San Marino-Holy See	824.4	779.6	886.0	1041.4	981.0	Italie-Saint-Marin-Saint-Siège
Netherlands	920.2	713.4	753.6	1265.4	838.4	Pays-Bas
Spain	613.5	708.8	797.3	803.9	972.0	Espagne
France-Monaco	773.8	764.8	807.8	714.1	832.5	France-Monaco
United States	492.7	498.0	610.7	948.0	842.7	Etats-Unis d'Amérique
Brazil	684.4	595.1	614.5	678.0	727.3	Brésil
Canada	627.9	621.3	637.3	664.7	697.8	Canada
Turkey	463.8	310.6	611.6	299.7	681.9	Turquie
Belgium	-	521.9	489.5	577.3	e633.2	Belgique
Israel	372.3	323.6	339.0	450.8	468.2	Israël
Ukraine	372.8	209.5	262.4	192.4	207.3	Ukraine
Slovakia	243.4	202.5	206.2	234.5	216.9	Slovaquie
Finland	206.1	140.0	191.4	292.1	242.5	Finlande
Austria	220.8	174.3	165.8	225.9	246.3	Autriche
China, Hong Kong SAR	220.4	179.3	153.0	201.4	243.7	Chine - RAS de Hong-Kong
Portugal	208.2	192.4	201.0	187.2	208.3	Portugal
Romania	222.5	120.5	126.8	180.8	181.3	Roumanie
Sweden	175.8	144.7	159.2	175.4	159.4	Suède
Mexico	111.6	125.3	131.1	175.6	247.6	Mexique
Russian Federation	185.6	90.4	112.3	179.1	152.4	Fédération de Russie
Chile	162.6	173.5	144.8	104.8	114.6	Chili
Bulgaria	163.6	85.8	129.5	e144.6	e159.0	Bulgarie
Philippines	174.4	131.6	129.7	140.1	103.0	Philippines
Belgium-Luxembourg	660.4	-	-	-	-	Belgique-Luxembourg
China	68.5	61.0	69.0	89.6	338.6	Chine

(Value as percentages of World total) **(Valeur en pourcentage du total mondial)**

Regions of the world	1993	1994	1995	1996	1997	1998	1999	2000	2001	2002	Régions du monde
World	100.0	100.0	100.0	100.0	100.0	100.0	100.0	100.0	100.0	100.0	Monde
Africa	1.2	1.1	1.3	1.3	1.2	1.4	1.4	1.0	1.5	1.5	Afrique
Americas	7.3	7.7	7.6	7.7	8.3	9.3	10.1	10.2	10.5	10.5	Amériques
- Northern America	3.4	3.6	3.3	3.4	3.8	4.8	5.4	5.7	6.3	5.9	- Amérique du Nord
- LAIA	3.8	4.0	4.2	4.3	4.5	4.4	4.7	4.4	4.0	4.4	- ALAI
- CACM	0.0	0.0	0.0	0.0	0.0	0.0	0.0	0.0	0.1	0.1	- MCC
- Caribbean	0.0	0.0	0.0	0.0	0.0	0.0	0.0	0.0	0.1	0.1	- Caraïbes
- Rest of America	0.1	0.1	0.0	0.0	0.0	0.0	0.0	0.0	0.0	0.0	- Autre d'Amérique
Asia excluding former USSR	55.2	51.7	50.8	52.5	53.9	52.4	53.3	53.2	49.6	52.8	Asie ancienne URSS exclus
- Middle East	1.8	2.1	1.4	2.5	2.4	2.2	1.9	3.1	1.3	2.8	- Moyen-Orient
Asia former USSR	0.0	0.3	0.4	0.3	0.2	0.2	0.2	0.1	0.1	0.1	Asie ancienne URSS
Europe excluding former USSR	35.0	36.1	35.8	34.3	33.7	33.9	33.2	33.4	36.7	33.5	Europe ancienne URSS exclus
- European Union	30.1	32.0	30.8	29.2	28.6	29.5	29.8	30.0	33.3	30.0	- Union Européenne
- Eastern Europe	4.2	3.4	4.3	4.5	4.5	3.8	2.7	2.7	2.8	2.9	- Europe de l'Est
- Rest of Europe	0.8	0.7	0.7	0.6	0.6	0.6	0.7	0.8	0.7	0.6	- Autre de l'Europe
Europe former USSR	1.1	3.0	4.0	3.8	2.6	2.7	1.7	1.9	1.5	1.5	Europe ancienne URSS
Oceania	0.1	0.1	0.0	0.1	0.1	0.1	0.1	0.1	0.1	0.1	Océanie

TRADE BY COMMODITY (Value in million US dollars)
Exports by principal countries or areas

COMMERCE PAR PRODUIT (Valeur en millions de dollars EU)
Exportations selon les principaux pays ou zones

Country or area	1998	1999	2000	2001	2002	Pays ou zone
World	19163.8	16438.5	17281.4	20908.5	21027.4	Monde
Africa	1407.4	1384.9	1337.8	1453.3	1852.0	Afrique
Americas	5852.3	4553.4	4350.8	4618.0	4101.0	Amériques
- Northern America	4789.2	3595.5	3352.5	3204.1	2857.5	- Amérique du Nord
- LAIA	1063.1	957.8	997.2	1412.9	1242.6	- ALAI
- CACM	0.0	0.0	0.0	0.0	0.0	- MCC
- Caribbean	0.1	0.1	1.1	0.9	0.8	- Caraïbes
- Rest of America	0.0	0.0	0.0	0.0	0.0	- Autre d'Amérique
Asia excluding former USSR	2462.1	2432.3	2907.9	4495.9	4519.9	Asie ancienne URSS exclus
- Middle East	0.4	3.1	5.0	6.0	5.1	- Moyen-Orient
Asia former USSR	324.9	153.4	169.3	224.8	253.1	Asie ancienne URSS
Europe excluding former USSR	2155.6	1910.6	1855.2	2315.7	1975.2	Europe ancienne URSS exclus
- European Union	782.4	810.2	819.2	1063.5	845.6	- Union Européenne
- Eastern Europe	1365.8	1091.0	1028.7	1245.1	1124.9	- Europe de l'Est
- Rest of Europe	7.4	9.5	7.3	7.2	4.8	- Autre de l'Europe
Europe former USSR	737.8	547.3	1260.3	1348.3	1322.7	Europe ancienne URSS
Oceania	6223.7	5456.6	5400.0	6452.6	7003.5	Océanie
Australia	6172.7	5417.6	5399.7	6452.2	7003.1	Australie
United States	3039.6	2140.1	2045.1	1834.6	1607.5	Etats-Unis d'Amérique
China	1068.3	1084.1	1460.5	2667.4	2535.0	Chine
Indonesia	1346.6	1303.9	1276.1	1617.7	1762.4	Indonésie
Canada	1749.5	1455.4	1307.4	1369.5	1250.0	Canada
Colombia	922.2	844.8	842.1	1159.2	972.1	Colombie
South Africa	–	–	1326.3	1440.6	1839.0	Afrique du Sud
Russian Federation	630.1	442.2	1144.2	1206.3	1154.5	Fédération de Russie
Poland	959.9	767.7	741.6	917.8	817.8	Pologne
Southern African Customs Union	1403.5	1381.3	–	–	–	Union douanière d'Afrique australe
Netherlands	242.9	303.5	369.1	618.6	374.7	Pays-Bas
Czech Republic	404.5	322.3	286.0	325.7	305.5	République tchèque
Kazakhstan	324.3	153.0	168.9	224.0	e252.3	Kazakhstan
Germany	228.6	204.5	174.1	162.8	158.3	Allemagne
Venezuela	140.6	111.0	154.5	253.0	e268.8	Venezuela
Belgium	–	131.5	133.2	138.8	e155.8	Belgique
Ukraine	66.2	67.9	66.4	88.9	98.0	Ukraine
Viet Nam	e	e	109.0	113.3	126.0	Viet Nam
United Kingdom	79.0	69.5	66.2	53.6	51.1	Royaume-Uni
Ireland	42.3	50.5	35.6	46.3	58.5	Irlande
India	33.6	27.3	37.3	61.5	53.2	Inde
Belgium-Luxembourg	136.5	–	–	–	–	Belgique-Luxembourg
Estonia	19.3	14.9	24.1	23.1	29.2	Estonie
New Zealand	50.9	39.0	0.3	0.3	0.5	Nouvelle-Zélande
Latvia	8.2	10.3	14.1	17.0	23.5	Lettonie
Lithuania	12.6	10.1	10.7	12.2	e14.8	Lituanie
Finland	11.8	13.8	9.4	10.0	11.6	Finlande
Denmark	11.8	13.9	9.4	10.7	9.9	Danemark
Myanmar	e0.0	e1.6	e9.0	e14.4	e20.5	Myanmar
Korea, Democratic People's Republic of	e9.6	e6.9	e7.0	e10.2	e11.7	République démocratique populaire de Corée

(Value as percentages of World total) **(Valeur en pourcentage du total mondial)**

Regions of the world	1993	1994	1995	1996	1997	1998	1999	2000	2001	2002	Régions du monde
World	100.0	100.0	100.0	100.0	100.0	100.0	100.0	100.0	100.0	100.0	Monde
Africa	9.4	7.7	8.3	7.4	7.5	7.3	8.4	7.7	7.0	8.8	Afrique
Americas	31.4	30.8	31.1	31.5	30.1	30.5	27.7	25.2	22.1	19.5	Amériques
- Northern America	27.4	26.9	27.5	27.4	25.9	25.0	21.9	19.4	15.3	13.6	- Amérique du Nord
- LAIA	4.0	3.9	3.6	4.0	4.2	5.5	5.8	5.8	6.8	5.9	- ALAI
- CACM	0.0	0.0	0.0	0.0	0.0	0.0	0.0	0.0	0.0	0.0	- MCC
- Caribbean	0.0	0.0	0.0	0.0	0.0	0.0	0.0	0.0	0.0	0.0	- Caraïbes
- Rest of America	0.0	0.0	0.0	0.0	0.0	0.0	0.0	0.0	0.0	0.0	- Autre d'Amérique
Asia excluding former USSR	8.7	10.1	11.1	11.7	13.5	12.8	14.8	16.8	21.5	21.5	Asie ancienne URSS exclus
- Middle East	0.0	0.0	0.0	0.0	0.0	0.0	0.0	0.0	0.0	0.0	- Moyen-Orient
Asia former USSR	0.2	1.8	1.9	1.9	1.8	1.7	0.9	1.0	1.1	1.2	Asie ancienne URSS
Europe excluding former USSR	12.8	14.4	13.9	12.2	11.2	11.2	11.6	10.7	11.1	9.4	Europe ancienne URSS exclus
- European Union	4.6	5.5	4.9	4.3	3.7	4.1	4.9	4.7	5.1	4.0	- Union Européenne
- Eastern Europe	8.2	8.8	8.9	7.8	7.4	7.1	6.6	6.0	6.0	5.3	- Europe de l'Est
- Rest of Europe	0.0	0.0	0.0	0.0	0.0	0.0	0.1	0.0	0.0	0.0	- Autre de l'Europe
Europe former USSR	6.5	5.7	5.5	5.7	4.6	3.8	3.3	7.3	6.4	6.3	Europe ancienne URSS
Oceania	30.9	29.5	28.4	29.7	31.4	32.5	33.2	31.2	30.9	33.3	Océanie

323 Briquettes; coke and semi-coke; lignite or peat; retort carbon

TRADE BY COMMODITY (Value in million US dollars)
Imports by principal countries or areas

COMMERCE PAR PRODUIT (Valeur en millions de dollars EU)
Importations selon les principaux pays ou zones

Country or area	1998	1999	2000	2001	2002	Pays ou zone
World	2557.8	2157.8	2713.6	2771.6	2983.2	Monde
Africa	67.4	81.5	60.3	67.9	67.3	Afrique
Americas	707.9	516.6	679.2	560.2	612.7	Amériques
- Northern America	433.2	347.7	410.9	310.1	350.8	- Amérique du Nord
- LAIA	258.7	151.0	240.8	239.4	254.1	- ALAI
- CACM	4.0	5.1	6.9	4.9	2.3	- MCC
- Caribbean	9.6	7.4	19.5	5.7	5.4	- Caraïbes
- Rest of America	2.3	5.5	1.0	0.2	0.1	- Autre d'Amérique
Asia excluding former USSR	390.1	448.2	640.7	540.5	564.7	Asie ancienne URSS exclus
- Middle East	82.5	70.4	101.0	96.1	88.1	- Moyen-Orient
Asia former USSR	46.2	42.5	48.6	57.2	58.4	Asie ancienne URSS
Europe excluding former USSR	1301.0	1020.4	1244.9	1452.3	1585.5	Europe ancienne URSS exclus
- European Union	1116.6	801.3	1028.3	1197.8	1332.0	- Union Européenne
- Eastern Europe	73.8	71.8	114.3	158.7	162.4	- Europe de l'Est
- Rest of Europe	110.6	147.3	102.4	95.9	91.1	- Autre de l'Europe
Europe former USSR	39.1	39.0	33.6	91.1	88.1	Europe ancienne URSS
Oceania	6.1	9.6	6.3	2.3	6.5	Océanie
Germany	415.9	323.8	430.2	572.5	594.2	Allemagne
United States	341.6	271.8	321.8	221.3	285.2	Etats-Unis d'Amérique
India	134.5	189.2	222.4	194.3	206.8	Inde
France-Monaco	208.9	115.4	145.9	145.4	142.2	France-Monaco
Japan	89.3	95.9	209.2	160.6	176.2	Japon
Brazil	153.0	77.8	134.4	163.6	184.6	Brésil
Belgium	–	81.7	115.1	119.9	e131.5	Belgique
Austria	77.5	51.2	87.5	108.0	118.2	Autriche
Canada	91.6	75.9	89.1	88.8	65.6	Canada
Italy-San Marino-Holy See	66.4	39.3	52.3	57.4	115.7	Italie-Saint-Marin-Saint-Siège
Mexico	80.2	53.4	78.4	50.9	44.8	Mexique
Turkey	57.4	34.3	61.1	48.4	60.0	Turquie
Norway	65.2	51.5	52.4	50.0	38.4	Norvège
Finland	51.6	49.0	49.6	54.7	48.6	Finlande
Kazakhstan	43.3	39.3	44.6	51.7	e52.8	Kazakhstan
Netherlands	39.5	45.2	45.0	42.4	48.5	Pays-Bas
United Kingdom	79.4	34.6	42.2	24.1	35.5	Royaume-Uni
Sweden	43.3	35.2	33.9	42.4	56.3	Suède
Romania	12.5	22.8	43.1	57.8	43.9	Roumanie
Ukraine	13.1	11.5	4.3	72.6	78.2	Ukraine
Czech Republic	16.9	19.0	41.3	40.0	38.6	République tchèque
Korea, Republic of	22.7	22.2	26.4	24.8	28.5	République de Corée
Serbia and Montenegro	6.8	60.2	19.1	e18.1	e18.3	Serbie-et-Monténégro
Iran (Islamic Republic of)	9.6	22.1	28.5	35.7	16.3	Iran (République islamique d')
Belgium-Luxembourg	106.7	–	–	–	–	Belgique-Luxembourg
South Africa	–	–	35.9	36.2	33.2	Afrique du Sud
Southern African Customs Union	53.0	46.9	–	–	–	Union douanière d'Afrique australe
Bulgaria	22.2	14.7	14.8	e16.5	e18.2	Bulgarie
Peru	16.3	17.1	15.8	16.9	20.0	Pérou
Slovakia	16.5	11.0	9.1	18.2	15.4	Slovaquie

(Value as percentages of World total) **(Valeur en pourcentage du total mondial)**

Regions of the world	1993	1994	1995	1996	1997	1998	1999	2000	2001	2002	Régions du monde
World	100.0	100.0	100.0	100.0	100.0	100.0	100.0	100.0	100.0	100.0	Monde
Africa	1.4	1.0	0.8	2.4	2.7	2.6	3.8	2.2	2.5	2.3	Afrique
Americas	23.6	26.9	27.5	24.7	26.2	27.7	23.9	25.0	20.2	20.5	Amériques
- Northern America	13.3	16.4	16.7	14.5	14.6	16.9	16.1	15.1	11.2	11.8	- Amérique du Nord
- LAIA	10.1	10.0	10.4	9.8	10.9	10.1	7.0	8.9	8.6	8.5	- ALAI
- CACM	0.0	0.1	0.0	0.1	0.2	0.2	0.2	0.3	0.2	0.1	- MCC
- Caribbean	0.2	0.4	0.4	0.3	0.4	0.4	0.3	0.7	0.2	0.2	- Caraïbes
- Rest of America	0.0	0.0	0.0	0.0	0.1	0.1	0.3	0.0	0.0	0.0	- Autre d'Amérique
Asia excluding former USSR	12.4	10.5	12.6	14.5	20.7	15.3	20.8	23.6	19.5	18.9	Asie ancienne URSS exclus
- Middle East	2.1	1.4	1.6	2.4	3.7	3.2	3.3	3.7	3.5	3.0	- Moyen-Orient
Asia former USSR	0.0	3.1	3.3	3.1	2.1	1.8	2.0	1.8	2.1	2.0	Asie ancienne URSS
Europe excluding former USSR	61.0	56.8	53.9	52.8	46.5	50.9	47.3	45.9	52.4	53.1	Europe ancienne URSS exclus
- European Union	48.3	44.6	42.9	42.4	37.7	43.7	37.1	37.9	43.2	44.6	- Union Européenne
- Eastern Europe	7.2	6.3	6.2	6.3	5.1	2.9	3.3	4.2	5.7	5.4	- Europe de l'Est
- Rest of Europe	5.5	5.8	4.8	4.1	3.7	4.3	6.8	3.8	3.5	3.1	- Autre de l'Europe
Europe former USSR	1.1	1.4	1.5	2.3	1.6	1.5	1.8	1.2	3.3	3.0	Europe ancienne URSS
Oceania	0.4	0.4	0.3	0.1	0.2	0.2	0.4	0.2	0.1	0.2	Océanie

TRADE BY COMMODITY (Value in million US dollars)
Exports by principal countries or areas

COMMERCE PAR PRODUIT (Valeur en millions de dollars EU)
Exportations selon les principaux pays ou zones

Country or area	1998	1999	2000	2001	2002	Pays ou zone
World	2214.9	1792.6	2383.2	2355.5	2460.1	Monde
Africa	60.2	56.1	170.8	69.2	61.4	Afrique
Americas	186.3	157.8	177.5	147.3	113.0	Amériques
- Northern America	172.9	142.6	154.0	124.1	88.8	- Amérique du Nord
- LAIA	13.4	15.2	23.5	23.2	21.9	- ALAI
- CACM	0.0	0.0	0.0	0.0	2.3	- MCC
- Caribbean	0.0	0.0	0.0	0.0	0.0	- Caraïbes
Asia excluding former USSR	1073.6	775.4	1141.6	1130.4	1187.6	Asie ancienne URSS exclus
- Middle East	2.2	1.4	0.4	1.2	1.2	- Moyen-Orient
Asia former USSR	1.4	0.2	0.4	0.1	0.2	Asie ancienne URSS
Europe excluding former USSR	777.6	653.1	759.7	828.9	850.3	Europe ancienne URSS exclus
- European Union	376.6	328.3	386.3	386.5	367.5	- Union Européenne
- Eastern Europe	399.2	320.6	372.4	441.6	480.1	- Europe de l'Est
- Rest of Europe	1.7	4.3	1.1	0.8	2.6	- Autre de l'Europe
Europe former USSR	100.7	141.1	126.7	168.8	235.1	Europe ancienne URSS
Oceania	15.3	8.9	6.5	10.7	12.5	Océanie
China	800.4	554.2	918.4	928.3	960.6	Chine
Poland	271.8	213.5	263.6	321.5	352.0	Pologne
Japan	266.8	217.4	198.3	190.4	214.7	Japon
United States	152.4	120.8	129.4	112.7	68.3	Etats-Unis d'Amérique
Russian Federation	74.6	117.2	72.4	108.1	168.2	Fédération de Russie
Czech Republic	95.3	84.4	70.7	83.8	97.0	République tchèque
Netherlands	83.5	64.9	43.7	84.2	72.1	Pays-Bas
Egypt	31.8	30.8	159.8	60.6	44.3	Egypte
France-Monaco	61.0	57.5	84.2	75.5	47.1	France-Monaco
Spain	47.9	39.2	80.2	67.3	75.2	Espagne
Belgium	–	62.9	60.8	62.9	e70.5	Belgique
Ukraine	21.9	20.7	54.1	60.6	66.8	Ukraine
United Kingdom	40.0	34.0	47.1	40.0	47.3	Royaume-Uni
Germany	50.5	38.1	39.4	37.2	31.2	Allemagne
Canada	20.5	21.8	24.7	11.4	20.6	Canada
Italy-San Marino-Holy See	13.6	15.7	17.7	13.5	19.4	Italie-Saint-Marin-Saint-Siège
Colombia	11.3	11.8	19.1	19.5	18.0	Colombie
Zimbabwe	e24.7	23.2	10.6	5.2	15.9	Zimbabwe
Belgium-Luxembourg	64.3	–	–	–	–	Belgique-Luxembourg
Australia	15.3	8.9	6.5	10.7	12.5	Australie
Bulgaria	1.4	1.7	15.6	e16.5	e18.6	Bulgarie
Hungary	17.8	14.1	18.9	0.0	0.0	Hongrie
Indonesia	3.0	1.6	20.3	7.5	8.3	Indonésie
Slovakia	3.7	2.4	3.2	19.4	11.9	Slovaquie
Portugal	7.4	8.6	8.0	1.1	0.1	Portugal
Sweden	5.4	3.3	2.7	2.6	1.5	Suède
Romania	9.2	4.5	0.4	0.1	0.1	Roumanie
Ireland	2.0	2.7	2.0	2.0	2.7	Irlande
Estonia	4.2	3.0	0.1	0.1	0.1	Estonie
Argentina	0.9	2.0	1.6	1.3	e1.3	Argentine

(Value as percentages of World total) **(Valeur en pourcentage du total mondial)**

Regions of the world	1993	1994	1995	1996	1997	1998	1999	2000	2001	2002	Régions du monde
World	100.0	100.0	100.0	100.0	100.0	100.0	100.0	100.0	100.0	100.0	Monde
Africa	2.0	2.6	2.5	2.6	2.8	2.7	3.1	7.2	2.9	2.5	Afrique
Americas	8.6	7.0	7.0	8.6	8.6	8.4	8.8	7.4	6.3	4.6	Amériques
- Northern America	8.0	6.4	6.5	8.1	8.2	7.8	8.0	6.5	5.3	3.6	- Amérique du Nord
- LAIA	0.6	0.6	0.5	0.5	0.4	0.6	0.8	1.0	1.0	0.9	- ALAI
- CACM	0.0	0.0	0.0	0.0	0.0	0.0	0.0	0.0	0.0	0.1	- MCC
- Caribbean	0.0	0.0	0.0	0.0	0.0	0.0	0.0	0.0	0.0	0.0	- Caraïbes
Asia excluding former USSR	28.3	32.6	42.1	41.1	47.6	48.5	43.3	47.9	48.0	48.3	Asie ancienne URSS exclus
- Middle East	0.0	0.1	0.0	0.0	0.1	0.1	0.1	0.0	0.1	0.0	- Moyen-Orient
Asia former USSR	0.0	0.1	0.0	0.0	0.1	0.1	0.0	0.0	0.0	0.0	Asie ancienne URSS
Europe excluding former USSR	54.1	50.5	42.0	39.2	34.3	35.1	36.4	31.9	35.2	34.6	Europe ancienne URSS exclus
- European Union	32.3	26.4	20.0	19.1	16.3	17.0	18.3	16.2	16.4	14.9	- Union Européenne
- Eastern Europe	19.4	22.7	21.9	20.0	17.9	18.0	17.9	15.6	18.7	19.5	- Europe de l'Est
- Rest of Europe	2.4	1.3	0.1	0.0	0.0	0.1	0.2	0.0	0.0	0.1	- Autre de l'Europe
Europe former USSR	3.3	5.0	4.9	6.5	5.3	4.5	7.9	5.3	7.2	9.6	Europe ancienne URSS
Oceania	3.7	2.2	1.5	1.9	1.3	0.7	0.5	0.3	0.5	0.5	Océanie
Oceania	3.7	2.2	1.5	1.3	0.7	0.5	0.5	0.3	0.5		Océanie

333 Crude petroleum and oils obtained from bituminous minerals

TRADE BY COMMODITY (Value in million US dollars)
Imports by principal countries or areas

COMMERCE PAR PRODUIT (Valeur en millions de dollars EU)
Importations selon les principaux pays ou zones

Country or area	1998	1999	2000	2001	2002	Pays ou zone
World	178959.7	226621.0	391437.1	343087.8	344343.5	Monde
Africa	4192.6	4904.1	7158.1	6424.9	5751.0	Afrique
Americas	51079.8	65160.0	114739.7	98189.1	99851.8	Amériques
- Northern America	45038.3	58081.8	103141.4	87455.3	90242.1	- Amérique du Nord
- LAIA	3749.3	4213.8	6757.4	6493.7	6104.3	- ALAI
- CACM	303.1	316.7	591.1	554.0	517.9	- MCC
- Caribbean	1804.5	2245.8	3802.8	3260.2	2765.8	- Caraïbes
- Rest of America	184.6	302.0	447.0	426.0	221.7	- Autre d'Amérique
Asia excluding former USSR	60508.5	80307.9	139645.5	122040.6	122036.6	Asie ancienne URSS exclus
- Middle East	3916.1	4855.2	6496.4	6125.4	6624.2	- Moyen-Orient
Asia former USSR	195.2	27.6	85.4	233.2	238.3	Asie ancienne URSS
Europe excluding former USSR	57612.6	70299.1	120064.2	106286.9	106097.6	Europe ancienne URSS exclus
- European Union	52216.9	63757.6	110449.8	97426.3	96244.5	- Union Européenne
- Eastern Europe	4019.3	4857.1	7295.1	6765.1	7830.5	- Europe de l'Est
- Rest of Europe	1376.5	1684.3	2319.2	2095.5	2022.7	- Autre de l'Europe
Europe former USSR	2806.0	2342.2	4246.7	5092.1	5621.5	Europe ancienne URSS
Oceania	2565.1	3580.0	5497.5	4820.9	4746.6	Océanie
United States	40734.1	53425.2	93939.3	79288.9	82588.5	Etats-Unis d'Amérique
Japan	22146.7	26534.0	44553.8	38761.1	36487.1	Japon
Korea, Republic of	11240.6	14782.7	25215.6	21367.8	18812.4	République de Corée
Germany	10477.5	13400.7	21969.7	19153.0	18733.9	Allemagne
France-Monaco	8694.6	10382.6	17997.3	15435.5	14731.4	France-Monaco
Italy-San Marino-Holy See	7905.8	9725.0	17071.2	14790.6	14356.6	Italie-Saint-Marin-Saint-Siège
India	3694.2	9409.0	14711.3	13026.4	15986.7	Inde
China	3274.5	4641.2	14860.7	11661.3	12757.3	Chine
Netherlands	5722.4	7598.4	12191.3	10805.0	10106.0	Pays-Bas
Spain	5251.2	6509.4	11585.2	9943.2	10154.8	Espagne
Singapore	5090.5	5330.0	8737.6	7589.9	7381.0	Singapour
Canada	4304.2	4656.6	9202.1	8166.4	7653.7	Canada
United Kingdom	3602.4	3677.7	7705.8	7135.9	7484.5	Royaume-Uni
Thailand	2905.4	3897.1	6108.5	5773.7	e6015.6	Thaïlande
Belgium	–	3979.3	6452.5	6477.8	e7104.3	Belgique
Australia	2082.5	3021.5	4492.8	3976.8	3746.7	Australie
Turkey	2083.9	2754.9	4208.3	3878.0	4087.8	Turquie
Sweden	1894.9	2471.0	4285.7	3527.0	3447.3	Suède
Brazil	2141.7	2277.9	3304.9	3320.9	3412.1	Brésil
Greece	1705.3	1006.2	3015.0	3323.4	e3674.8	Grèce
Poland	1376.3	1823.3	3464.2	2888.9	2922.1	Pologne
Philippines	1524.5	2066.8	3170.8	2822.9	2262.8	Philippines
Indonesia	1058.3	1587.7	2524.9	2887.5	3216.9	Indonésie
Portugal	1218.4	1640.7	2436.5	2216.1	2079.7	Portugal
South Africa	–	–	3486.8	3112.9	2796.4	Afrique du Sud
Finland	1087.9	1464.4	2422.3	2005.2	2173.1	Finlande
Bahrain	e1467.9	e1636.7	2050.7	1504.9	e1760.0	Bahreïn
Ukraine	1054.6	884.4	1090.7	2256.0	2430.8	Ukraine
Israel	1103.7	1183.8	2094.0	1671.0	1649.0	Israël
Netherlands Antilles	1103.5	1379.6	1950.5	1746.2	1354.4	Antilles néerlandaises

(Value as percentages of World total) **(Valeur en pourcentage du total mondial)**

Regions of the world	1993	1994	1995	1996	1997	1998	1999	2000	2001	2002	Régions du monde
World	100.0	100.0	100.0	100.0	100.0	100.0	100.0	100.0	100.0	100.0	Monde
Africa	0.9	1.0	2.1	1.8	2.2	2.3	2.2	1.8	1.9	1.7	Afrique
Americas	27.0	28.0	27.7	26.9	28.0	28.5	28.8	29.3	28.6	29.0	Amériques
- Northern America	23.7	24.9	24.5	23.5	24.8	25.2	25.6	26.3	25.5	26.2	- Amérique du Nord
- LAIA	1.8	2.0	2.1	2.3	2.1	2.1	1.9	1.7	1.9	1.8	- ALAI
- CACM	0.2	0.2	0.2	0.2	0.2	0.2	0.1	0.2	0.2	0.2	- MCC
- Caribbean	1.1	0.9	0.7	0.9	0.8	1.0	1.0	1.0	1.0	0.8	- Caraïbes
- Rest of America	0.1	0.1	0.1	0.1	0.1	0.1	0.1	0.1	0.1	0.1	- Autre d'Amérique
Asia excluding former USSR	35.4	33.3	34.1	33.8	35.3	33.8	35.4	35.7	35.6	35.4	Asie ancienne URSS exclus
- Middle East	2.3	1.6	1.7	1.6	1.5	2.2	2.1	1.7	1.8	1.9	- Moyen-Orient
Asia former USSR	0.0	0.3	0.1	0.0	0.1	0.1	0.0	0.0	0.1	0.1	Asie ancienne URSS
Europe excluding former USSR	35.6	35.8	34.1	34.9	32.0	32.2	31.0	30.7	31.0	30.8	Europe ancienne URSS exclus
- European Union	32.2	32.7	30.8	31.5	29.0	29.2	28.1	28.2	28.4	28.0	- Union Européenne
- Eastern Europe	2.5	2.3	2.3	2.6	2.3	2.2	2.1	1.9	2.0	2.3	- Europe de l'Est
- Rest of Europe	0.8	0.8	0.9	0.8	0.7	0.8	0.7	0.6	0.6	0.6	- Autre de l'Europe
Europe former USSR	0.0	0.6	0.8	1.1	1.1	1.6	1.0	1.1	1.5	1.6	Europe ancienne URSS
Oceania	1.1	1.1	1.2	1.3	1.3	1.4	1.6	1.4	1.4	1.4	Océanie

TRADE BY COMMODITY (Value in million US dollars)
Exports by principal countries or areas

COMMERCE PAR PRODUIT (Valeur en millions de dollars EU)
Exportations selon les principaux pays ou zones

Country or area	1998	1999	2000	2001	2002	Pays ou zone
World	162411.8	225418.5	368353.5	311898.1	313136.5	Monde
Africa	23579.1	35582.3	55461.5	42054.0	40918.3	Afrique
Americas	25610.6	34142.9	56748.3	45190.7	48583.3	Amériques
- Northern America	6586.7	7600.0	13533.0	10639.9	11573.8	- Amérique du Nord
- LAIA	18675.7	26048.9	42441.4	33948.2	36471.4	- ALAI
- CACM	58.3	80.9	159.3	100.8	149.4	- MCC
- Caribbean	272.3	390.5	592.4	479.3	367.6	- Caraïbes
- Rest of America	17.6	22.6	22.3	22.6	21.2	- Autre d'Amérique
Asia excluding former USSR	80018.7	108939.2	173716.2	145174.6	142130.5	Asie ancienne URSS exclus
- Middle East	70931.8	97830.2	157241.2	130508.7	127110.8	- Moyen-Orient
Asia former USSR	1843.3	2584.8	5744.5	6181.7	6466.9	Asie ancienne URSS
Europe excluding former USSR	20176.2	28297.5	47580.2	44390.7	43349.1	Europe ancienne URSS exclus
- European Union	8078.1	11155.6	18202.0	17530.8	17432.7	- Union Européenne
- Eastern Europe	15.5	23.1	37.7	87.9	110.5	- Europe de l'Est
- Rest of Europe	12082.7	17118.9	29340.5	26772.1	25805.9	- Autre de l'Europe
Europe former USSR	9516.9	13659.8	23805.3	24751.4	27690.3	Europe ancienne URSS
Oceania	1667.0	2211.9	5297.4	4155.0	3997.9	Océanie
Saudi Arabia	27354.1	34556.2	61397.7	55110.8	e49665.7	Arabie saoudite
Norway	12079.5	17117.4	29339.3	26765.1	25802.7	Norvège
Russian Federation	9456.4	13466.8	23644.3	24562.6	27445.4	Fédération de Russie
Iran (Islamic Republic of)	10227.8	16648.7	24226.0	18997.2	23919.6	Iran (République islamique d')
United Arab Emirates	13612.7	14044.3	22010.9	16607.2	17298.0	Emirates arabes unis
Nigeria	6658.7	15952.4	26956.1	e17731.4	e15051.8	Nigéria
Venezuela	7788.1	10775.3	18238.0	14755.9	e15675.3	Venezuela
Iraq	e5315.1	e12560.6	e20349.0	e15652.2	e13042.3	Iraq
United Kingdom	7167.0	9699.9	15488.1	15116.1	14615.6	Royaume-Uni
Mexico	6398.8	8858.8	14878.5	11597.9	13110.2	Mexique
Canada	5911.0	6814.5	13051.2	10391.5	11482.2	Canada
Kuwait	4501.7	5441.7	e8712.2	e7262.9	e8722.6	Koweït
Libyan Arab Jamahiriya	4524.8	e5854.3	e7523.6	e7232.3	e8372.5	Jamahiriya arabe libyenne
Oman	3586.0	5376.5	8727.2	7632.8	7533.4	Oman
Algeria	4084.2	4975.1	9254.4	e6301.9	e6155.9	Algérie
Indonesia	3348.6	4517.3	6090.1	5714.7	5227.6	Indonésie
Angola	e2990.3	e3991.0	e4640.1	e4709.3	e4844.0	Angola
Qatar	2984.8	4013.0	3840.6	5610.5	2881.4	Qatar
Kazakhstan	1650.5	2040.2	4502.4	4268.1	e4807.5	Kazakhstan
Malaysia	2078.5	2668.9	3904.7	2999.1	e3178.3	Malaisie
Colombia	2070.7	3337.0	4014.8	2590.5	2577.7	Colombie
Syrian Arab Republic	1378.5	2180.0	3203.7	e3632.2	4044.6	République arabe syrienne
Australia	1097.8	1489.0	4367.6	3366.6	3330.3	Australie
Viet Nam	1232.2	2091.6	3006.0	3125.6	3474.3	Viet Nam
Gabon	e2774.0	1585.2	2117.1	e2154.5	e2217.1	Gabon
Argentina	1462.7	1599.4	2844.0	2394.1	e2313.1	Argentine
Denmark	756.1	1186.1	2363.6	2045.6	2364.0	Danemark
Ecuador	789.0	1312.3	2144.0	1722.3	1838.5	Equateur
China	1523.0	765.3	2132.0	1383.3	1296.2	Chine
Yemen	1227.0	e1993.2	e3334.1			Yémen

(Value as percentages of World total) **(Valeur en pourcentage du total mondial)**

Regions of the world	1993	1994	1995	1996	1997	1998	1999	2000	2001	2002	Régions du monde
World	100.0	100.0	100.0	100.0	100.0	100.0	100.0	100.0	100.0	100.0	Monde
Africa	17.6	15.5	16.1	15.5	15.5	14.5	15.8	15.1	13.5	13.1	Afrique
Americas	12.7	13.4	14.6	12.0	12.3	15.8	15.1	15.4	14.5	15.5	Amériques
- Northern America	3.0	3.1	3.6	3.9	4.3	4.1	3.4	3.7	3.4	3.7	- Amérique du Nord
- LAIA	9.4	10.1	10.8	7.9	7.8	11.5	11.6	11.5	10.9	11.6	- ALAI
- CACM	0.0	0.0	0.0	0.0	0.0	0.0	0.0	0.0	0.0	0.0	- MCC
- Caribbean	0.2	0.2	0.2	0.2	0.2	0.2	0.2	0.2	0.2	0.1	- Caraïbes
- Rest of America	0.0	0.0	0.0	0.0	0.0	0.0	0.0	0.0	0.0	0.0	- Autre d'Amérique
Asia excluding former USSR	50.8	50.4	47.2	48.8	48.9	49.3	48.3	47.2	46.5	45.4	Asie ancienne URSS exclus
- Middle East	43.8	43.9	41.0	42.4	42.4	43.7	43.4	42.7	41.8	40.6	- Moyen-Orient
Asia former USSR	0.1	0.4	0.5	0.7	0.9	1.1	1.1	1.6	2.0	2.1	Asie ancienne URSS
Europe excluding former USSR	11.9	13.0	13.5	15.4	14.5	12.4	12.6	12.9	14.2	13.8	Europe ancienne URSS exclus
- European Union	4.6	5.6	5.7	5.8	5.4	5.0	4.9	4.9	5.6	5.6	- Union Européenne
- Eastern Europe	0.0	0.0	0.0	0.0	0.0	0.0	0.0	0.0	0.0	0.0	- Europe de l'Est
- Rest of Europe	7.3	7.4	7.8	9.6	9.1	7.4	7.6	8.0	8.6	8.2	- Autre de l'Europe
Europe former USSR	5.8	6.4	7.0	6.9	7.0	5.9	6.1	6.5	7.9	8.8	Europe ancienne URSS
Oceania	1.0	1.0	1.0	0.7	0.8	1.0	1.0	1.4	1.3	1.3	Océanie

334 Petroleum products, refined

TRADE BY COMMODITY (Value in million US dollars)
Imports by principal countries or areas

COMMERCE PAR PRODUIT (Valeur en millions de dollars EU)
Importations selon les principaux pays ou zones

Country or area	1998	1999	2000	2001	2002	Pays ou zone
World	84996.0	99928.2	156273.3	144173.3	140813.3	Monde
Africa	3929.7	3620.1	5299.9	6094.1	5156.0	Afrique
Americas	22158.0	25991.8	43532.4	41226.9	34455.1	Amériques
- Northern America	13570.6	16928.6	29632.2	28098.3	23453.5	- Amérique du Nord
- LAIA	5683.6	5946.6	9395.8	8501.1	6382.7	- ALAI
- CACM	959.2	1058.6	1523.8	1641.3	1630.3	- MCC
- Caribbean	1636.5	1816.8	2615.6	2578.1	2517.5	- Caraïbes
- Rest of America	308.1	241.1	365.0	408.0	471.0	- Autre d'Amérique
Asia excluding former USSR	27011.4	34346.7	49559.1	44034.7	47095.1	Asie ancienne URSS exclus
- Middle East	1752.3	2090.0	3496.2	3378.3	3705.0	- Moyen-Orient
Asia former USSR	665.0	396.7	567.4	643.7	681.6	Asie ancienne URSS
Europe excluding former USSR	28057.6	32552.6	52670.3	48704.4	49653.4	Europe ancienne URSS exclus
- European Union	23515.7	27591.6	45262.4	41160.0	42221.2	- Union Européenne
- Eastern Europe	1732.6	1807.3	2276.9	2518.6	2551.5	- Europe de l'Est
- Rest of Europe	2809.3	3153.6	5131.1	5025.8	4880.7	- Autre de l'Europe
Europe former USSR	2120.7	1620.9	2301.1	1267.6	1388.9	Europe ancienne URSS
Oceania	1053.6	1399.6	2343.1	2202.0	2383.3	Océanie
United States	12290.7	15557.9	27845.1	26210.7	21918.0	Etats-Unis d'Amérique
Germany	6151.8	5744.8	10020.2	8779.4	7171.8	Allemagne
Japan	4164.1	5781.1	8731.8	7272.2	6438.8	Japon
Singapore	3090.7	4748.1	7499.6	7011.8	7826.1	Singapour
France-Monaco	2966.1	3748.6	6172.2	5163.7	5711.4	France-Monaco
Korea, Republic of	2410.1	2861.4	5000.2	4775.0	4922.3	République de Corée
United Kingdom	2158.6	2977.3	4858.1	4977.4	4543.4	Royaume-Uni
Netherlands	2208.0	2638.3	4319.7	3688.5	4756.4	Pays-Bas
Belgium	–	2956.9	4814.6	4677.3	e5129.6	Belgique
China	2466.7	2780.8	3776.8	3898.2	4003.7	Chine
Italy-San Marino-Holy See	2397.5	2823.6	4134.8	3421.4	3947.3	Italie-Saint-Marin-Saint-Siège
China, Hong Kong SAR	2202.1	2620.2	3444.0	2836.2	2892.0	Chine - RAS de Hong-Kong
Brazil	2098.6	2245.7	3671.3	3202.1	2243.9	Brésil
Indonesia	1611.6	2098.5	3562.5	2652.9	3409.3	Indonésie
Mexico	1838.5	2048.0	3532.4	3419.3	2442.3	Mexique
Spain	998.4	1577.0	2940.7	3035.5	3107.3	Espagne
India	2735.6	3228.8	1231.8	1155.9	1612.3	Inde
Switzerland-Liechtenstein	1419.2	1394.8	2366.1	2333.7	2024.5	Suisse-Liechtenstein
Malaysia	1333.5	1281.8	2252.1	1870.6	e2044.4	Malaisie
Pakistan	931.6	1441.3	2324.1	1600.1	1666.0	Pakistan
Viet Nam	845.4	1076.0	1822.1	1890.9	2300.7	Viet Nam
Canada	1198.1	1282.5	1686.2	1811.9	1431.5	Canada
Austria	816.9	1049.6	1464.4	1408.0	1509.2	Autriche
Sweden	911.3	837.4	1188.4	1327.9	1485.9	Suède
Denmark	670.4	623.0	1236.5	1081.3	1071.6	Danemark
Turkey	474.9	721.1	1393.3	770.5	1202.2	Turquie
Australia	454.2	633.3	1147.2	993.2	1112.1	Australie
Ireland	460.4	733.6	1124.7	938.9	1020.0	Irlande
Lebanon	410.8	490.4	940.5	1213.0	e1106.6	Liban
Thailand	468.2	802.6	1152.7	830.9	e865.7	Thaïlande

(Value as percentages of World total) **(Valeur en pourcentage du total mondial)**

Regions of the world	1993	1994	1995	1996	1997	1998	1999	2000	2001	2002	Régions du monde
World	100.0	100.0	100.0	100.0	100.0	100.0	100.0	100.0	100.0	100.0	Monde
Africa	2.6	2.9	2.9	3.6	3.8	4.6	3.6	3.4	4.2	3.7	Afrique
Americas	22.2	22.7	21.0	22.4	24.0	26.1	26.0	27.9	28.6	24.5	Amériques
- Northern America	14.9	14.8	12.3	14.8	15.4	16.0	16.9	19.0	19.5	16.7	- Amérique du Nord
- LAIA	5.2	5.0	5.6	4.8	6.2	6.7	6.0	6.0	5.9	4.5	- ALAI
- CACM	0.7	0.7	0.9	0.9	0.9	1.1	1.1	1.0	1.1	1.2	- MCC
- Caribbean	1.0	1.7	1.8	1.7	1.2	1.9	1.8	1.7	1.8	1.8	- Caraïbes
- Rest of America	0.3	0.4	0.4	0.3	0.3	0.4	0.2	0.2	0.3	0.3	- Autre d'Amérique
Asia excluding former USSR	33.8	33.6	37.1	36.3	35.5	31.8	34.4	31.7	30.5	33.4	Asie ancienne URSS exclus
- Middle East	2.3	1.6	2.1	1.9	1.8	2.1	2.1	2.2	2.3	2.6	- Moyen-Orient
Asia former USSR	0.1	0.6	0.8	0.8	0.5	0.8	0.4	0.4	0.4	0.5	Asie ancienne URSS
Europe excluding former USSR	37.5	36.5	34.5	33.2	32.4	33.0	32.6	33.7	33.8	35.3	Europe ancienne URSS exclus
- European Union	32.1	31.7	29.6	28.9	27.6	27.7	27.6	29.0	28.5	30.0	- Union Européenne
- Eastern Europe	2.5	1.5	1.7	1.7	1.3	2.0	1.8	1.5	1.7	1.8	- Europe de l'Est
- Rest of Europe	2.8	3.3	3.2	2.7	3.6	3.3	3.2	3.3	3.5	3.5	- Autre de l'Europe
Europe former USSR	2.2	2.2	2.0	1.9	2.4	2.5	1.6	1.5	0.9	1.0	Europe ancienne URSS
Oceania	1.6	1.5	1.7	1.8	1.4	1.2	1.4	1.5	1.5	1.7	Océanie

TRADE BY COMMODITY (Value in million US dollars)
Exports by principal countries or areas

COMMERCE PAR PRODUIT (Valeur en millions de dollars EU)
Exportations selon les principaux pays ou zones

Country or area	1998	1999	2000	2001	2002	Pays ou zone
World	88413.2	107302.3	172309.5	153120.9	154777.4	Monde
Africa	4349.7	6774.3	11548.5	8832.0	8508.5	Afrique
Americas	14156.2	18055.8	27865.5	26417.7	25997.5	Amériques
- Northern America	6244.4	7300.8	11431.1	11341.2	11271.6	- Amérique du Nord
- LAIA	6080.1	8140.5	12417.3	10853.8	11530.0	- ALAI
- CACM	75.2	83.5	104.3	116.8	122.0	- MCC
- Caribbean	1726.5	2454.2	3845.2	4037.3	3016.8	- Caraïbes
- Rest of America	30.1	76.7	67.7	68.6	57.1	- Autre d'Amérique
Asia excluding former USSR	32255.3	38711.1	60082.2	52420.5	52170.1	Asie ancienne URSS exclus
- Middle East	13664.1	17300.4	24733.6	23366.7	23120.1	- Moyen-Orient
Asia former USSR	598.6	691.2	1194.9	1006.9	1088.9	Asie ancienne URSS
Europe excluding former USSR	30578.7	35273.7	56682.0	50398.1	50575.4	Europe ancienne URSS exclus
- European Union	27256.3	31272.1	50078.0	44731.1	44645.4	- Union Européenne
- Eastern Europe	1423.7	1618.4	2908.2	3059.5	3543.7	- Europe de l'Est
- Rest of Europe	1898.8	2383.1	3695.8	2607.5	2386.3	- Autre de l'Europe
Europe former USSR	5468.2	6584.2	13236.4	12637.5	14976.7	Europe ancienne URSS
Oceania	1006.5	1212.1	1700.0	1408.3	1460.4	Océanie
Netherlands	6717.3	7855.5	12414.2	11658.1	10800.3	Pays-Bas
Singapore	7864.0	8715.2	12905.5	8682.6	9114.6	Singapour
Saudi Arabia	6185.8	8088.5	9690.5	9884.6	e8908.0	Arabie saoudite
Russian Federation	4174.4	5364.5	10717.5	9412.5	11144.3	Fédération de Russie
Korea, Republic of	4354.4	5472.8	9039.4	7764.7	6215.9	République de Corée
United States	4335.4	4973.1	7579.8	6843.1	6626.2	Etats-Unis d'Amérique
Venezuela	4111.8	5451.2	8237.1	5980.3	e6353.0	Venezuela
Belgium	–	4179.8	6852.2	6545.8	e7344.2	Belgique
United Kingdom	3055.6	3528.6	5778.4	4645.0	4998.8	Royaume-Uni
Germany	2960.1	3537.2	5045.3	4555.8	4871.8	Allemagne
Kuwait	2521.3	3461.5	e5541.9	e4620.0	e4712.9	Koweït
France-Monaco	2837.4	2958.5	4788.5	4071.9	3859.9	France-Monaco
Italy-San Marino-Holy See	2582.0	2676.9	4602.6	4380.4	4005.5	Italie-Saint-Marin-Saint-Siège
United Arab Emirates	2436.2	2513.5	4833.0	3786.0	3943.5	Emirates arabes unis
Canada	1901.4	2319.6	3849.9	4497.9	4644.8	Canada
Bahrain	e1578.2	e2150.9	3054.2	3651.1	e3535.3	Bahreïn
Spain	1977.0	2126.2	3617.4	2830.3	2460.6	Espagne
Algeria	1340.4	1882.6	3146.1	e2142.4	e2092.8	Algérie
Norway	1376.2	1783.0	2782.0	1796.3	1601.7	Norvège
China	740.9	1099.0	2134.9	2130.9	2398.7	Chine
Sweden	1124.8	1309.4	2057.1	2067.6	1936.9	Suède
Netherlands Antilles	991.8	1466.5	1855.1	2262.9	1609.0	Antilles néerlandaises
Malaysia	679.0	1062.0	1907.8	2004.5	e2124.2	Malaisie
Libyan Arab Jamahiriya	1062.7	e1374.9	e1767.0	e1040.8	e1477.9	Jamahiriya arabe libyenne
India	92.1	44.4	1905.4	2127.9	2517.3	Inde
Australia	992.6	1195.2	1677.8	1394.1	1349.6	Australie
Egypt	733.5	960.3	2138.1	1255.7	1181.0	Egypte
Finland	784.6	999.4	1545.8	1354.3	1450.5	Finlande
Japan	1045.9	1130.9	1377.0	1323.1	1247.0	Japon
Trinidad and Tobago	688.8	913.0	1661.5	1504.4	e1141.7	Trinité-et-Tobago

(Value as percentages of World total) **(Valeur en pourcentage du total mondial)**

Regions of the world	1993	1994	1995	1996	1997	1998	1999	2000	2001	2002	Régions du monde
World	100.0	100.0	100.0	100.0	100.0	100.0	100.0	100.0	100.0	100.0	Monde
Africa	4.7	5.2	6.1	5.8	5.6	4.9	6.3	6.7	5.8	5.5	Afrique
Americas	18.4	17.1	16.9	12.2	11.5	16.0	16.8	16.2	17.3	16.8	Amériques
- Northern America	8.2	7.1	6.7	8.1	7.6	7.1	6.8	6.6	7.4	7.3	- Amérique du Nord
- LAIA	8.1	7.9	8.1	2.3	2.2	6.9	7.6	7.2	7.1	7.4	- ALAI
- CACM	0.0	0.0	0.0	0.1	0.1	0.1	0.1	0.1	0.1	0.1	- MCC
- Caribbean	2.1	1.9	2.0	1.7	1.7	2.0	2.3	2.2	2.6	1.9	- Caraïbes
- Rest of America	0.0	0.0	0.0	0.0	0.0	0.0	0.1	0.0	0.0	0.0	- Autre d'Amérique
Asia excluding former USSR	29.4	31.5	34.0	32.4	36.3	36.5	36.1	34.9	34.2	33.7	Asie ancienne URSS exclus
- Middle East	8.9	11.1	14.5	9.9	14.0	15.5	16.1	14.4	15.3	14.9	- Moyen-Orient
Asia former USSR	0.6	0.5	0.6	1.0	0.6	0.7	0.6	0.7	0.7	0.7	Asie ancienne URSS
Europe excluding former USSR	38.3	37.2	33.5	38.6	36.1	34.6	32.9	32.9	32.9	32.7	Europe ancienne URSS exclus
- European Union	34.5	33.3	29.9	34.3	32.0	30.8	29.1	29.1	29.2	28.8	- Union Européenne
- Eastern Europe	1.7	1.7	1.6	1.9	1.6	1.6	1.5	1.7	2.0	2.3	- Europe de l'Est
- Rest of Europe	2.1	2.3	2.0	2.4	2.5	2.1	2.2	2.1	1.7	1.5	- Autre de l'Europe
Europe former USSR	7.4	7.4	7.8	8.4	8.5	6.2	6.1	7.7	8.3	9.7	Europe ancienne URSS
Oceania	1.2	1.2	1.1	1.6	1.4	1.1	1.1	1.0	0.9	0.9	Océanie

335 Residual petroleum products, nes and related materials

TRADE BY COMMODITY (Value in million US dollars)
Imports by principal countries or areas

COMMERCE PAR PRODUIT (Valeur en millions de dollars EU)
Importations selon les principaux pays ou zones

Country or area	1998	1999	2000	2001	2002	Pays ou zone
World	7272.7	7737.0	9838.6	9910.9	10476.0	Monde
Africa	326.9	330.4	314.6	362.0	375.0	Afrique
Americas	1446.5	1598.6	1983.6	2029.1	2192.9	Amériques
- Northern America	904.4	1013.3	1346.7	1219.1	1464.2	- Amérique du Nord
- LAIA	487.2	511.4	556.3	758.2	671.6	- ALAI
- CACM	19.7	22.6	25.8	33.0	36.8	- MCC
- Caribbean	19.2	13.2	13.5	13.5	16.2	- Caraïbes
- Rest of America	15.9	38.1	41.3	5.2	4.1	- Autre d'Amérique
Asia excluding former USSR	1876.0	2373.3	3058.3	2911.7	3188.1	Asie ancienne URSS exclus
- Middle East	238.8	197.3	253.7	279.4	296.6	- Moyen-Orient
Asia former USSR	68.1	85.2	58.0	75.5	86.7	Asie ancienne URSS
Europe excluding former USSR	3105.1	2962.9	4012.0	4090.2	4212.0	Europe ancienne URSS exclus
- European Union	2686.0	2544.4	3486.3	3501.5	3554.4	- Union Européenne
- Eastern Europe	145.8	146.9	225.0	282.5	294.7	- Europe de l'Est
- Rest of Europe	273.3	271.6	300.7	306.2	363.0	- Autre de l'Europe
Europe former USSR	244.5	217.4	195.2	230.4	188.4	Europe ancienne URSS
Oceania	205.7	169.3	216.9	212.1	232.8	Océanie
United States	671.7	796.7	1124.6	979.3	1207.1	Etats-Unis d'Amérique
Germany	583.9	557.9	790.2	739.6	600.8	Allemagne
Netherlands	504.1	546.4	759.0	628.6	766.7	Pays-Bas
Japan	495.1	492.4	603.9	490.4	556.3	Japon
India	360.4	333.7	591.7	465.8	491.1	Inde
China	200.2	291.7	411.9	490.2	669.1	Chine
Korea, Republic of	175.6	390.5	456.6	467.5	476.4	République de Corée
France-Monaco	337.1	324.8	377.8	406.6	419.3	France-Monaco
Italy-San Marino-Holy See	418.7	271.1	383.9	362.7	357.6	Italie-Saint-Marin-Saint-Siège
Belgium	–	165.1	324.5	448.1	e491.4	Belgique
Spain	211.8	181.8	243.8	273.9	268.2	Espagne
Canada	232.1	216.0	221.7	239.1	256.0	Canada
Mexico	148.7	185.9	217.4	228.2	227.3	Mexique
United Kingdom	152.1	144.0	192.4	198.9	180.1	Royaume-Uni
Norway	142.7	143.1	149.3	158.8	171.7	Norvège
Australia	156.0	124.4	162.4	145.4	161.2	Australie
Russian Federation	184.4	162.1	110.9	154.7	112.4	Fédération de Russie
Malaysia	60.4	105.4	163.8	187.1	e204.5	Malaisie
Brazil	112.4	111.3	144.9	191.3	153.3	Brésil
Venezuela	57.9	85.2	80.9	174.2	e146.5	Venezuela
Poland	55.8	54.9	103.5	122.1	130.9	Pologne
Thailand	55.3	75.7	110.6	102.7	e107.0	Thaïlande
Israel	25.7	51.8	114.6	101.8	91.0	Israël
Portugal	50.5	49.8	74.3	94.0	99.8	Portugal
Austria	69.8	71.3	78.3	71.9	76.7	Autriche
Indonesia	54.4	87.5	75.3	83.3	52.4	Indonésie
Sweden	58.7	57.4	68.9	83.5	69.7	Suède
United Arab Emirates	52.4	55.0	77.1	73.9	e75.8	Emirates arabes unis
Denmark	57.8	63.4	64.4	53.5	61.6	Danemark
Turkey	59.0	43.9	66.9	62.1	66.0	Turquie

(Value as percentages of World total) **(Valeur en pourcentage du total mondial)**

Regions of the world	1993	1994	1995	1996	1997	1998	1999	2000	2001	2002	Régions du monde
World	100.0	100.0	100.0	100.0	100.0	100.0	100.0	100.0	100.0	100.0	Monde
Africa	4.4	2.8	3.2	4.3	3.7	4.5	4.3	3.2	3.7	3.6	Afrique
Americas	14.6	16.8	16.8	16.9	18.5	19.9	20.7	20.2	20.5	20.9	Amériques
- Northern America	7.8	10.4	10.2	11.6	12.5	12.4	13.1	13.7	12.3	14.0	- Amérique du Nord
- LAIA	5.8	5.4	5.7	4.5	5.2	6.7	6.6	5.7	7.7	6.4	- ALAI
- CACM	0.4	0.3	0.3	0.2	0.2	0.3	0.3	0.3	0.3	0.4	- MCC
- Caribbean	0.3	0.5	0.4	0.5	0.3	0.3	0.2	0.1	0.1	0.2	- Caraïbes
- Rest of America	0.3	0.2	0.2	0.1	0.3	0.2	0.5	0.4	0.1	0.0	- Autre d'Amérique
Asia excluding former USSR	28.1	27.8	28.5	28.3	31.8	25.8	30.7	31.1	29.4	30.4	Asie ancienne URSS exclus
- Middle East	4.0	3.2	3.0	3.3	2.8	3.3	2.5	2.6	2.8	2.8	- Moyen-Orient
Asia former USSR	0.0	0.3	0.8	0.5	0.3	0.9	1.1	0.6	0.8	0.8	Asie ancienne URSS
Europe excluding former USSR	48.2	47.0	45.9	44.3	40.0	42.7	38.3	40.8	41.3	40.2	Europe ancienne URSS exclus
- European Union	42.8	41.5	40.1	38.8	35.1	36.9	32.9	35.4	35.3	33.9	- Union Européenne
- Eastern Europe	1.5	1.6	1.7	1.7	1.7	2.0	1.9	2.3	2.8	2.8	- Europe de l'Est
- Rest of Europe	4.0	4.0	4.0	3.8	3.2	3.8	3.5	3.1	3.1	3.5	- Autre de l'Europe
Europe former USSR	1.9	2.6	2.7	2.8	3.3	3.4	2.8	2.0	2.3	1.8	Europe ancienne URSS
Oceania	2.8	2.7	2.1	2.9	2.4	2.8	2.2	2.2	2.1	2.2	Océanie

TRADE BY COMMODITY (Value in million US dollars)
Exports by principal countries or areas

COMMERCE PAR PRODUIT (Valeur en millions de dollars EU)
Exportations selon les principaux pays ou zones

Country or area	1998	1999	2000	2001	2002	Pays ou zone
World	7085.2	7699.0	11201.1	10647.7	8953.4	Monde
Africa	219.3	235.5	364.7	334.3	298.1	Afrique
Americas	1870.1	1898.0	2663.8	2591.7	2500.1	Amériques
- Northern America	1671.7	1618.6	2185.3	2172.5	2118.9	- Amérique du Nord
- LAIA	192.5	269.5	465.3	238.9	242.3	- ALAI
- CACM	2.6	5.3	3.9	9.6	5.3	- MCC
- Caribbean	3.3	3.6	8.7	169.7	132.5	- Caraïbes
- Rest of America	0.0	1.0	0.6	1.0	1.1	- Autre d'Amérique
Asia excluding former USSR	2341.7	2811.8	4167.9	3746.4	2172.8	Asie ancienne URSS exclus
- Middle East	1111.6	1634.3	2666.8	2165.2	320.5	- Moyen-Orient
Asia former USSR	30.3	27.1	25.6	23.5	30.5	Asie ancienne URSS
Europe excluding former USSR	2454.0	2533.2	3670.2	3723.2	3722.3	Europe ancienne URSS exclus
- European Union	2233.1	2333.1	3424.9	3445.1	3415.6	- Union Européenne
- Eastern Europe	158.2	150.1	181.5	214.6	233.4	- Europe de l'Est
- Rest of Europe	62.7	50.1	63.9	63.5	73.3	- Autre de l'Europe
Europe former USSR	132.2	137.4	215.4	207.9	211.9	Europe ancienne URSS
Oceania	37.6	55.9	93.4	20.7	17.7	Océanie
United States	1470.7	1398.0	1877.3	1885.1	1770.3	Etats-Unis d'Amérique
Kuwait	985.3	1486.8	e2380.3	e1984.4	e124.2	Koweït
Germany	489.4	491.1	689.3	639.0	650.6	Allemagne
Netherlands	343.1	378.6	590.3	743.2	701.6	Pays-Bas
United Kingdom	317.1	332.2	498.4	451.3	438.6	Royaume-Uni
China	397.4	380.3	405.9	426.0	373.8	Chine
Belgium	–	367.2	431.6	449.4	e504.2	Belgique
France-Monaco	203.3	241.2	352.1	337.6	345.0	France-Monaco
Spain	205.6	222.3	355.5	368.1	293.3	Espagne
Singapore	195.4	229.1	265.6	297.6	407.3	Singapour
Canada	201.0	220.7	308.0	287.4	348.6	Canada
Japan	157.5	158.0	243.4	243.2	246.3	Japon
Sweden	94.9	112.1	219.1	209.3	217.8	Suède
Thailand	59.8	74.3	206.2	229.0	e241.9	Thaïlande
Korea, Republic of	107.2	117.8	161.0	156.5	266.1	République de Corée
Algeria	77.6	82.3	190.5	e129.8	e126.8	Algérie
Iran (Islamic Republic of)	52.6	40.8	100.4	156.2	183.7	Iran (République islamique d')
Italy-San Marino-Holy See	66.2	70.8	121.2	104.4	102.4	Italie-Saint-Marin-Saint-Siège
Russian Federation	51.7	74.4	138.6	96.7	98.8	Fédération de Russie
Indonesia	221.1	111.3	35.2	38.1	48.2	Indonésie
Belgium-Luxembourg	404.3	–	–	–	–	Belgique-Luxembourg
Argentina	61.4	74.9	68.5	92.9	e89.8	Argentine
South Africa	–	–	127.5	125.2	120.8	Afrique du Sud
Czech Republic	52.4	53.0	81.5	73.7	83.8	République tchèque
Colombia	34.9	91.9	206.6	2.0	1.1	Colombie
Portugal	43.7	49.3	82.1	56.6	70.6	Portugal
Yemen	56.1	e91.1	e152.4	e	e	Yémen
Trinidad and Tobago	3.2	3.4	2.0	156.3	e118.6	Trinité-et-Tobago
Ukraine	53.4	44.0	49.9	62.7	69.1	Ukraine
Poland	43.1	35.6	50.9	67.2	70.4	Pologne

(Value as percentages of World total) **(Valeur en pourcentage du total mondial)**

Regions of the world	1993	1994	1995	1996	1997	1998	1999	2000	2001	2002	Régions du monde
World	100.0	100.0	100.0	100.0	100.0	100.0	100.0	100.0	100.0	100.0	Monde
Africa	3.1	3.4	2.7	3.4	3.8	3.1	3.1	3.3	3.1	3.3	Afrique
Americas	31.2	33.0	27.6	36.9	30.0	26.4	24.7	23.8	24.3	27.9	Amériques
- Northern America	28.5	30.0	25.3	33.2	27.4	23.6	21.0	19.5	20.4	23.7	- Amérique du Nord
- LAIA	1.9	2.1	1.7	3.0	2.0	2.7	3.5	4.2	2.2	2.7	- ALAI
- CACM	0.0	0.0	0.0	0.0	0.0	0.0	0.1	0.0	0.1	0.1	- MCC
- Caribbean	0.9	0.9	0.7	0.7	0.6	0.0	0.0	0.1	1.6	1.5	- Caraïbes
- Rest of America	0.0	0.0	0.0	0.0	0.0	0.0	0.0	0.0	0.0	0.0	- Autre d'Amérique
Asia excluding former USSR	19.1	16.7	32.7	16.6	32.1	33.1	36.5	37.2	35.2	24.3	Asie ancienne URSS exclus
- Middle East	3.3	2.3	20.5	1.5	18.7	15.7	21.2	23.8	20.3	3.6	- Moyen-Orient
Asia former USSR	0.1	1.8	0.9	0.8	0.5	0.4	0.4	0.2	0.2	0.3	Asie ancienne URSS
Europe excluding former USSR	43.9	42.9	34.1	40.1	31.6	34.6	32.9	32.8	35.0	41.6	Europe ancienne URSS exclus
- European Union	39.9	39.1	30.9	36.4	29.2	31.5	30.3	30.6	32.4	38.1	- Union Européenne
- Eastern Europe	2.7	2.8	2.3	2.6	1.7	2.2	1.9	1.6	2.0	2.6	- Europe de l'Est
- Rest of Europe	1.3	1.0	0.9	1.1	0.7	0.9	0.7	0.6	0.6	0.8	- Autre de l'Europe
Europe former USSR	2.2	1.8	1.5	1.7	1.5	1.9	1.8	1.9	2.0	2.4	Europe ancienne URSS
Oceania	0.4	0.3	0.4	0.5	0.5	0.5	0.7	0.8	0.2	0.2	Océanie

341 Gas, natural and manufactured

TRADE BY COMMODITY (Value in million US dollars)
Imports by principal countries or areas

COMMERCE PAR PRODUIT (Valeur en millions de dollars EU)
Importations selon les principaux pays ou zones

Country or area	1998	1999	2000	2001	2002	Pays ou zone
World	50296.3	52737.3	81858.6	92290.2	86434.9	Monde
Africa	376.3	534.6	796.2	743.7	792.5	Afrique
Americas	8415.9	9640.1	17164.9	22769.7	18016.1	Amériques
- Northern America	6813.3	7622.1	13482.9	19110.4	14542.9	- Amérique du Nord
- LAIA	1414.1	1797.2	3374.0	3338.2	3149.8	- ALAI
- CACM	88.3	113.5	164.0	165.8	147.2	- MCC
- Caribbean	79.2	79.9	120.4	134.7	127.6	- Caraïbes
- Rest of America	21.0	27.5	23.5	20.6	48.7	- Autre d'Amérique
Asia excluding former USSR	15667.2	19388.5	28838.9	28385.9	27231.0	Asie ancienne URSS exclus
- Middle East	533.4	1600.8	1256.9	1125.6	1125.7	- Moyen-Orient
Asia former USSR	383.5	317.1	332.2	527.1	572.6	Asie ancienne URSS
Europe excluding former USSR	20499.4	18531.2	29698.1	35420.3	35009.6	Europe ancienne URSS exclus
- European Union	16207.6	15059.9	23982.0	28664.7	28677.1	- Union Européenne
- Eastern Europe	3305.3	2809.7	4852.7	5711.0	5354.9	- Europe de l'Est
- Rest of Europe	986.4	661.7	863.4	1044.7	977.6	- Autre de l'Europe
Europe former USSR	4891.0	4252.5	4890.4	4356.0	4729.2	Europe ancienne URSS
Oceania	63.1	73.4	137.9	87.5	83.9	Océanie
Japan	10272.0	11557.8	17942.9	17507.0	15719.4	Japon
United States	6654.3	7464.7	13153.7	18757.8	14021.8	Etats-Unis d'Amérique
Germany	6987.1	5870.7	8992.0	11387.6	10962.4	Allemagne
France-Monaco	3480.0	3341.3	5127.2	5968.0	5791.7	France-Monaco
Korea, Republic of	2243.9	3003.2	5355.2	5236.6	5399.5	République de Corée
Ukraine	3544.1	3264.6	3332.9	3268.3	3521.6	Ukraine
Spain	1380.1	1475.3	2913.1	3139.1	3273.6	Espagne
Belgium	–	1537.2	2585.8	2927.8	e3211.0	Belgique
Netherlands	914.2	980.7	1628.9	2269.9	2491.1	Pays-Bas
China	824.0	1198.6	1540.9	1384.0	1597.0	Chine
Mexico	521.6	739.5	1638.6	1686.2	1578.8	Mexique
Turkey	418.4	1466.8	1082.4	955.4	990.3	Turquie
Hungary	750.0	615.6	1040.0	1274.1	1227.3	Hongrie
Poland	755.2	632.3	1016.3	1319.9	1167.5	Pologne
Czech Republic	692.5	573.6	1051.4	1223.2	1075.4	République tchèque
Brazil	470.6	579.6	1042.4	898.1	872.0	Brésil
Slovakia	491.0	436.1	893.5	953.5	822.9	Slovaquie
Belarus	821.8	523.0	565.3	576.4	567.9	Bélarus
Italy-San Marino-Holy See	515.6	655.8	628.7	515.0	518.1	Italie-Saint-Marin-Saint-Siège
Bulgaria	262.8	340.8	510.7	e570.2	e627.1	Bulgarie
Portugal	189.7	331.7	577.6	584.6	577.5	Portugal
Switzerland-Liechtenstein	378.9	310.0	393.0	532.7	516.3	Suisse-Liechtenstein
Finland	401.7	291.8	456.9	519.2	460.5	Finlande
Chile	201.3	299.5	418.3	486.1	439.5	Chili
Belgium-Luxembourg	1757.8	–	–	–	–	Belgique-Luxembourg
China, Hong Kong SAR	309.8	312.9	341.8	358.5	384.1	Chine - RAS de Hong-Kong
Romania	351.7	207.6	333.8	360.2	423.0	Roumanie
United Kingdom	154.4	124.7	393.3	438.1	551.7	Royaume-Uni
Canada	157.8	156.2	328.9	351.8	520.3	Canada
Thailand	0.5	0.5	109.1	650.9	e678.1	Thaïlande

(Value as percentages of World total) **(Valeur en pourcentage du total mondial)**

Regions of the world	1993	1994	1995	1996	1997	1998	1999	2000	2001	2002	Régions du monde
World	100.0	100.0	100.0	100.0	100.0	100.0	100.0	100.0	100.0	100.0	Monde
Africa	0.7	0.8	0.9	0.7	0.7	0.7	1.0	1.0	0.8	0.9	Afrique
Americas	16.3	16.8	13.8	14.1	15.3	16.7	18.3	21.0	24.7	20.8	Amériques
- Northern America	13.8	14.4	11.0	11.5	12.4	13.5	14.5	16.5	20.7	16.8	- Amérique du Nord
- LAIA	2.2	2.0	2.2	2.2	2.5	2.8	3.4	4.1	3.6	3.6	- ALAI
- CACM	0.1	0.2	0.1	0.2	0.2	0.2	0.2	0.2	0.2	0.2	- MCC
- Caribbean	0.1	0.1	0.3	0.2	0.1	0.2	0.2	0.1	0.1	0.1	- Caraïbes
- Rest of America	0.1	0.1	0.1	0.1	0.0	0.0	0.1	0.0	0.0	0.1	- Autre d'Amérique
Asia excluding former USSR	36.5	32.4	32.7	32.9	33.7	31.1	36.8	35.2	30.8	31.5	Asie ancienne URSS exclus
- Middle East	1.7	1.7	2.3	2.4	1.3	1.1	3.0	1.5	1.2	1.3	- Moyen-Orient
Asia former USSR	0.0	0.4	1.2	0.8	0.6	0.8	0.6	0.4	0.6	0.7	Asie ancienne URSS
Europe excluding former USSR	45.2	39.5	38.9	38.9	38.2	40.8	35.1	36.3	38.4	40.5	Europe ancienne URSS exclus
- European Union	37.5	33.0	32.0	31.8	30.7	32.2	28.6	29.3	31.1	33.2	- Union Européenne
- Eastern Europe	5.7	5.1	5.6	5.9	6.3	6.6	5.3	5.9	6.2	6.2	- Europe de l'Est
- Rest of Europe	2.0	1.4	1.3	1.2	1.1	2.0	1.3	1.1	1.1	1.1	- Autre de l'Europe
Europe former USSR	1.2	10.1	12.6	12.4	11.4	9.7	8.1	6.0	4.7	5.5	Europe ancienne URSS
Oceania	0.1	0.1	0.1	0.2	0.1	0.1	0.1	0.2	0.1	0.1	Océanie

TRADE BY COMMODITY (Value in million US dollars)
Exports by principal countries or areas

COMMERCE PAR PRODUIT (Valeur en millions de dollars EU)
Exportations selon les principaux pays ou zones

Country or area	1998	1999	2000	2001	2002	Pays ou zone
World	48536.1	51881.9	83321.6	82584.5	76277.7	Monde
Africa	4235.5	5473.6	9373.8	6542.7	6362.6	Afrique
Americas	7721.0	9533.2	17643.5	20733.5	15980.0	Amériques
- Northern America	7385.8	8850.3	16390.9	19188.5	14698.4	- Amérique du Nord
- LAIA	271.3	442.8	694.1	1027.0	889.5	- ALAI
- CACM	0.4	3.9	3.8	2.4	0.8	- MCC
- Caribbean	63.2	236.0	554.7	515.6	391.2	- Caraïbes
- Rest of America	0.3	0.1	0.1	0.0	0.1	- Autre d'Amérique
Asia excluding former USSR	11076.3	13520.7	19806.5	20101.4	20068.0	Asie ancienne URSS exclus
- Middle East	3607.9	4919.6	7017.5	8320.4	7848.5	- Moyen-Orient
Asia former USSR	355.1	711.9	1662.4	1332.6	1348.9	Asie ancienne URSS
Europe excluding former USSR	10494.5	9802.6	15745.6	13851.1	15041.4	Europe ancienne URSS exclus
- European Union	6478.7	6022.4	9657.0	6067.7	6485.1	- Union Européenne
- Eastern Europe	29.0	45.9	75.2	64.6	71.2	- Europe de l'Est
- Rest of Europe	3986.8	3734.3	6013.5	7718.7	8485.0	- Autre de l'Europe
Europe former USSR	13478.6	11614.0	17206.8	18088.4	15710.0	Europe ancienne URSS
Oceania	1175.1	1226.0	1883.0	1934.9	1766.8	Océanie
Russian Federation	13406.7	11531.8	16990.7	17881.6	15472.8	Fédération de Russie
Canada	6829.5	8151.3	15089.0	18068.6	13002.6	Canada
Algeria	4041.8	5227.2	9016.9	e6140.2	e5998.0	Algérie
Norway	3941.3	3675.1	5900.2	7581.3	8340.5	Norvège
Indonesia	3815.5	4357.1	6624.9	5732.2	5577.6	Indonésie
Qatar	1105.0	2197.2	3863.0	4098.8	3736.7	Qatar
Malaysia	1754.7	2012.1	3615.5	3513.1	e3723.0	Malaisie
Netherlands	3446.0	2911.4	4491.9	283.4	277.0	Pays-Bas
Germany	1708.8	1257.4	1799.5	2562.6	2493.9	Allemagne
United Arab Emirates	1859.3	1918.2	1912.4	1755.6	e1828.6	Emirates arabes unis
United Kingdom	659.1	1171.3	2073.2	2154.0	2198.1	Royaume-Uni
Australia	1165.5	1213.4	1865.8	1919.3	1754.1	Australie
Brunei Darussalam	1212.4	e1374.7	e1359.1	e1037.8	e1183.1	Brunéi Darussalam
United States	555.2	699.0	1301.9	1115.5	1691.7	Etats-Unis d'Amérique
Kuwait	427.4	613.4	e982.1	e818.7	e777.6	Koweït
Turkmenistan	69.9	390.0	1248.9	e922.1	e918.4	Turkménistan
Oman	0.1	0.7	3.2	1176.3	1138.6	Oman
Argentina	162.1	278.5	446.6	621.7	e600.7	Argentine
France-Monaco	323.9	273.8	510.0	426.2	477.7	France-Monaco
Trinidad and Tobago	63.2	235.9	554.7	515.4	e391.2	Trinité-et-Tobago
Uzbekistan	e262.2	e294.9	e372.7	e292.8	e298.5	Ouzbékistan
Myanmar	e	e	e91.6	e548.6	e780.1	Myanmar
Iran (Islamic Republic of)	189.5	150.7	193.5	425.5	306.4	Iran (République islamique d')
China	202.4	228.6	221.5	223.7	266.7	Chine
Singapore	172.2	179.0	260.0	262.8	243.7	Singapour
Belgium	–	175.3	325.7	252.3	e283.1	Belgique
Thailand	117.2	146.0	273.6	188.8	e199.4	Thaïlande
Korea, Republic of	151.6	240.8	202.3	116.1	65.2	République de Corée
Libyan Arab Jamahiriya	90.9	e117.6	e151.2	e184.8	e180.4	Jamahiriya arabe libyenne
Bolivia	56.2	38.5	127.2	241.9	e232.5	Bolivie

(Value as percentages of World total) **(Valeur en pourcentage du total mondial)**

Regions of the world	1993	1994	1995	1996	1997	1998	1999	2000	2001	2002	Régions du monde
World	100.0	100.0	100.0	100.0	100.0	100.0	100.0	100.0	100.0	100.0	Monde
Africa	10.5	8.1	7.1	7.4	9.8	8.7	10.6	11.3	7.9	8.3	Afrique
Americas	19.1	19.1	15.5	16.5	15.3	15.9	18.4	21.2	25.1	20.9	Amériques
- Northern America	18.2	18.1	14.6	15.6	14.7	15.2	17.1	19.7	23.2	19.3	- Amérique du Nord
- LAIA	0.8	0.8	0.8	0.8	0.5	0.6	0.9	0.8	1.2	1.2	- ALAI
- CACM	0.0	0.0	0.0	0.0	0.0	0.0	0.0	0.0	0.0	0.0	- MCC
- Caribbean	0.1	0.1	0.2	0.1	0.1	0.1	0.5	0.7	0.6	0.5	- Caraïbes
- Rest of America	0.0	0.0	0.0	0.0	0.0	0.0	0.0	0.0	0.0	0.0	- Autre d'Amérique
Asia excluding former USSR	28.7	19.8	21.5	19.3	22.6	22.8	26.1	23.8	24.3	26.3	Asie ancienne URSS exclus
- Middle East	8.9	2.7	5.4	2.5	6.3	7.4	9.5	8.4	10.1	10.3	- Moyen-Orient
Asia former USSR	0.2	1.2	2.5	2.9	0.5	0.7	1.4	2.0	1.6	1.8	Asie ancienne URSS
Europe excluding former USSR	22.2	20.0	20.8	23.4	21.9	21.6	18.9	18.9	16.8	19.7	Europe ancienne URSS exclus
- European Union	15.2	12.9	14.2	15.9	13.9	13.3	11.6	11.6	7.3	8.5	- Union Européenne
- Eastern Europe	0.1	0.1	0.1	0.1	0.1	0.1	0.1	0.1	0.1	0.1	- Europe de l'Est
- Rest of Europe	6.9	7.0	6.5	7.3	7.9	8.2	7.2	7.2	9.3	11.1	- Autre de l'Europe
Europe former USSR	16.9	29.5	30.0	27.9	27.2	27.8	22.4	20.7	21.9	20.6	Europe ancienne URSS
Oceania	2.5	2.4	2.6	2.6	2.6	2.4	2.4	2.3	2.3	2.3	Océanie

411 Animal oils and fats

TRADE BY COMMODITY (Value in million US dollars)
Imports by principal countries or areas

COMMERCE PAR PRODUIT (Valeur en millions de dollars EU)
Importations selon les principaux pays ou zones

Country or area	1998	1999	2000	2001	2002	Pays ou zone
World	2040.9	1768.7	1479.3	1489.0	1609.7	Monde
Africa	191.9	130.1	84.5	78.4	96.7	Afrique
Americas	511.5	444.3	357.3	357.8	365.7	Amériques
- Northern America	90.2	82.8	78.1	90.2	94.6	- Amérique du Nord
- LAIA	305.5	257.5	200.6	191.9	185.0	- ALAI
- CACM	75.4	71.2	53.1	44.3	60.0	- MCC
- Caribbean	36.6	30.1	23.0	28.7	23.6	- Caraïbes
- Rest of America	3.7	2.7	2.6	2.6	2.5	- Autre d'Amérique
Asia excluding former USSR	488.4	529.9	449.6	378.9	417.3	Asie ancienne URSS exclus
- Middle East	161.3	130.8	73.0	46.1	60.5	- Moyen-Orient
Asia former USSR	4.6	2.8	3.6	5.6	5.7	Asie ancienne URSS
Europe excluding former USSR	753.9	586.6	514.1	575.0	600.5	Europe ancienne URSS exclus
- European Union	606.6	482.3	412.9	433.4	444.4	- Union Européenne
- Eastern Europe	18.5	10.2	20.7	28.9	35.1	- Europe de l'Est
- Rest of Europe	128.9	94.1	80.5	112.7	120.9	- Autre de l'Europe
Europe former USSR	78.8	65.0	57.9	81.4	108.3	Europe ancienne URSS
Oceania	11.7	9.9	12.3	11.8	15.4	Océanie
Mexico	167.9	151.8	128.6	116.4	124.4	Mexique
China	81.4	112.5	129.9	91.3	117.4	Chine
Norway	115.9	83.5	66.5	99.3	106.0	Norvège
Japan	81.8	73.2	81.9	113.5	89.2	Japon
United Kingdom	98.8	81.0	76.0	89.6	73.5	Royaume-Uni
Netherlands	91.1	80.0	60.8	52.3	56.6	Pays-Bas
Russian Federation	60.8	53.2	45.2	66.8	92.4	Fédération de Russie
Germany	74.0	57.4	54.4	51.8	54.9	Allemagne
Belgium	-	76.3	61.9	60.5	e66.4	Belgique
United States	47.9	48.7	52.5	55.5	59.4	Etats-Unis d'Amérique
Spain	65.6	51.1	42.9	43.4	55.9	Espagne
Turkey	73.1	52.0	51.2	33.4	48.8	Turquie
France-Monaco	68.5	44.9	41.5	47.5	43.1	France-Monaco
Italy-San Marino-Holy See	59.0	43.3	29.4	37.8	44.5	Italie-Saint-Marin-Saint-Siège
Korea, Republic of	25.9	46.8	35.8	33.1	42.3	République de Corée
Canada	42.4	34.0	25.5	34.8	35.1	Canada
Pakistan	38.2	47.7	33.9	19.9	32.1	Pakistan
Guatemala	37.1	33.8	21.2	18.4	19.2	Guatemala
Chile	11.5	27.4	23.6	32.4	19.6	Chili
Sudan	26.8	e16.4	19.2	25.2	25.4	Soudan
Colombia	31.6	27.3	12.0	13.3	14.8	Colombie
Belgium-Luxembourg	95.2	-	-	-	-	Belgique-Luxembourg
Denmark	21.3	16.5	19.2	18.6	17.8	Danemark
El Salvador	19.5	21.8	18.0	14.8	18.9	El Salvador
Nigeria	10.9	18.7	16.0	e21.9	e20.8	Nigéria
Syrian Arab Republic	46.9	40.5	0.1	e0.1	0.0	République arabe syrienne
Philippines	17.2	21.4	13.7	13.3	8.6	Philippines
Brazil	20.7	13.3	20.5	7.9	6.9	Brésil
Venezuela	28.4	24.7	2.5	4.8	e4.1	Venezuela
Iran (Islamic Republic of)	21.0	16.2	11.3	7.1	5.8	Iran (République islamique d')

(Value as percentages of World total) **(Valeur en pourcentage du total mondial)**

Regions of the world	1993	1994	1995	1996	1997	1998	1999	2000	2001	2002	Régions du monde
World	100.0	100.0	100.0	100.0	100.0	100.0	100.0	100.0	100.0	100.0	Monde
Africa	11.5	9.3	10.2	8.1	6.4	9.4	7.4	5.7	5.3	6.0	Afrique
Americas	19.9	21.1	18.9	19.7	21.5	25.1	25.1	24.2	24.0	22.7	Amériques
- Northern America	3.8	3.9	3.2	4.3	5.0	4.4	4.7	5.3	6.1	5.9	- Amérique du Nord
- LAIA	12.4	13.1	11.6	10.9	12.0	15.0	14.6	13.6	12.9	11.5	- ALAI
- CACM	2.6	2.8	2.5	2.8	2.8	3.7	4.0	3.6	3.0	3.7	- MCC
- Caribbean	1.0	1.1	1.5	1.8	1.6	1.8	1.7	1.6	1.9	1.5	- Caraïbes
- Rest of America	0.1	0.1	0.1	0.1	0.1	0.2	0.2	0.2	0.2	0.2	- Autre d'Amérique
Asia excluding former USSR	25.5	22.9	26.4	27.2	24.0	23.9	30.0	30.4	25.4	25.9	Asie ancienne URSS exclus
- Middle East	5.0	3.2	4.3	4.9	4.8	7.9	7.4	4.9	3.1	3.8	- Moyen-Orient
Asia former USSR	0.2	0.3	0.3	0.4	0.1	0.2	0.2	0.2	0.4	0.4	Asie ancienne URSS
Europe excluding former USSR	41.7	44.7	42.5	42.3	44.3	36.9	33.2	34.8	38.6	37.3	Europe ancienne URSS exclus
- European Union	37.2	39.7	37.4	36.8	37.3	29.7	27.3	27.9	29.1	27.6	- Union Européenne
- Eastern Europe	0.8	1.1	0.9	0.9	0.9	0.9	0.6	1.4	1.9	2.2	- Europe de l'Est
- Rest of Europe	3.6	4.0	4.2	4.6	6.2	6.3	5.3	5.4	7.6	7.5	- Autre de l'Europe
Europe former USSR	0.8	1.1	1.1	1.7	3.0	3.9	3.7	3.9	5.5	6.7	Europe ancienne URSS
Oceania	0.5	0.6	0.5	0.6	0.6	0.6	0.6	0.8	0.8	1.0	Océanie

TRADE BY COMMODITY (Value in million US dollars)
Exports by principal countries or areas

COMMERCE PAR PRODUIT (Valeur en millions de dollars EU)
Exportations selon les principaux pays ou zones

Country or area	1998	1999	2000	2001	2002	Pays ou zone
World	1732.2	1423.8	1270.9	1287.0	1512.4	Monde
Africa	6.4	4.8	10.1	14.5	20.6	Afrique
Americas	782.1	653.3	525.3	525.4	648.8	Amériques
- Northern America	723.9	541.4	400.7	396.6	536.6	- Amérique du Nord
- LAIA	51.8	110.3	121.1	122.9	107.5	- ALAI
- CACM	0.5	0.5	1.6	0.7	1.3	- MCC
- Caribbean	0.1	0.3	0.1	0.0	0.0	- Caraïbes
- Rest of America	5.7	0.8	1.8	5.2	3.4	- Autre d'Amérique
Asia excluding former USSR	43.8	44.9	61.8	53.9	60.6	Asie ancienne URSS exclus
- Middle East	5.8	5.0	7.5	6.5	8.0	- Moyen-Orient
Asia former USSR	0.0	0.1	0.0	0.0	0.0	Asie ancienne URSS
Europe excluding former USSR	675.3	529.9	511.3	546.1	626.2	Europe ancienne URSS exclus
- European Union	547.3	439.0	430.2	456.2	530.5	- Union Européenne
- Eastern Europe	18.6	19.1	17.2	14.6	14.8	- Europe de l'Est
- Rest of Europe	109.5	71.7	63.9	75.3	80.9	- Autre de l'Europe
Europe former USSR	3.3	1.8	2.0	2.6	3.2	Europe ancienne URSS
Oceania	221.3	189.2	160.3	144.5	152.9	Océanie
United States	614.9	447.7	324.3	312.2	450.6	Etats-Unis d'Amérique
Australia	165.7	144.8	123.7	111.7	113.0	Australie
Canada	109.0	93.7	76.5	84.4	86.1	Canada
Germany	88.4	79.8	66.4	80.8	82.7	Allemagne
France-Monaco	97.7	72.6	74.1	63.5	82.9	France-Monaco
Denmark	75.4	58.6	55.3	72.0	80.1	Danemark
Peru	18.3	68.3	80.6	91.0	69.7	Pérou
Netherlands	59.7	43.4	47.8	43.6	57.4	Pays-Bas
United Kingdom	48.0	46.6	47.4	43.5	53.5	Royaume-Uni
New Zealand	55.6	44.3	36.6	32.8	39.9	Nouvelle-Zélande
Iceland	65.5	33.9	24.1	41.3	41.1	Islande
Norway	41.6	35.0	37.2	31.4	37.5	Norvège
Italy-San Marino-Holy See	38.2	30.2	38.5	39.6	34.5	Italie-Saint-Marin-Saint-Siège
Belgium	–	31.9	31.0	40.2	e45.1	Belgique
Spain	16.9	16.5	19.2	28.5	40.2	Espagne
Ireland	28.6	22.7	20.1	15.6	20.7	Irlande
Sweden	21.6	20.5	16.6	15.2	16.7	Suède
Japan	13.3	18.0	19.6	18.5	17.0	Japon
Uruguay	11.9	10.8	13.9	6.5	12.1	Uruguay
Belgium-Luxembourg	52.9	–	–	–	–	Belgique-Luxembourg
Poland	13.4	13.7	10.6	8.1	6.8	Pologne
Austria	12.1	7.4	7.0	5.7	7.9	Autriche
Brazil	6.7	4.2	4.5	10.7	e11.0	Brésil
Singapore	3.1	5.6	9.1	9.3	8.3	Singapour
Chile	5.2	14.9	4.4	4.7	e4.6	Chili
Argentina	5.6	8.1	10.8	3.7	e3.6	Argentine
Morocco	2.0	1.3	2.5	10.5	e11.4	Maroc
China	2.8	2.1	8.7	5.2	7.1	Chine
China, Hong Kong SAR	7.8	3.5	4.9	1.8	6.6	Chine - RAS de Hong-Kong
Mexico	2.6	3.5	6.3	4.4	6.0	Mexique

(Value as percentages of World total) **(Valeur en pourcentage du total mondial)**

Regions of the world	1993	1994	1995	1996	1997	1998	1999	2000	2001	2002	Régions du monde
World	100.0	100.0	100.0	100.0	100.0	100.0	100.0	100.0	100.0	100.0	Monde
Africa	0.6	0.4	0.8	0.5	0.6	0.4	0.3	0.8	1.1	1.4	Afrique
Americas	46.2	49.3	50.4	44.8	43.7	45.1	45.9	41.3	40.8	42.9	Amériques
- Northern America	40.4	40.0	42.2	36.2	35.1	41.8	38.0	31.5	30.8	35.5	- Amérique du Nord
- LAIA	5.6	9.1	8.1	8.5	8.3	3.0	7.7	9.5	9.5	7.1	- ALAI
- CACM	0.0	0.0	0.0	0.0	0.0	0.0	0.0	0.1	0.1	0.1	- MCC
- Caribbean	0.0	0.0	0.0	0.0	0.0	0.0	0.0	0.0	0.0	0.0	- Caraïbes
- Rest of America	0.2	0.2	0.1	0.0	0.2	0.3	0.1	0.1	0.4	0.2	- Autre d'Amérique
Asia excluding former USSR	3.6	2.8	2.7	3.5	2.3	2.5	3.2	4.9	4.2	4.0	Asie ancienne URSS exclus
- Middle East	0.4	0.4	0.7	0.9	0.4	0.3	0.4	0.6	0.5	0.5	- Moyen-Orient
Asia former USSR	0.0	0.0	0.0	0.0	0.0	0.0	0.0	0.0	0.0	0.0	Asie ancienne URSS
Europe excluding former USSR	36.2	34.5	34.2	38.9	41.2	39.0	37.2	40.2	42.4	41.4	Europe ancienne URSS exclus
- European Union	28.5	28.5	28.9	31.2	33.0	31.6	30.8	33.9	35.4	35.1	- Union Européenne
- Eastern Europe	1.5	1.2	0.8	1.4	1.6	1.1	1.3	1.4	1.1	1.0	- Europe de l'Est
- Rest of Europe	6.3	4.9	4.5	6.2	6.6	6.3	5.0	5.0	5.9	5.4	- Autre de l'Europe
Europe former USSR	0.7	0.5	0.3	0.2	0.3	0.2	0.1	0.2	0.2	0.2	Europe ancienne URSS
Oceania	12.6	12.5	11.6	12.0	11.9	12.8	13.3	12.6	11.2	10.1	Océanie

423 Fixed vegetable oils, soft, crude refined or purified

TRADE BY COMMODITY (Value in million US dollars)
Imports by principal countries or areas

COMMERCE PAR PRODUIT (Valeur en millions de dollars EU)
Importations selon les principaux pays ou zones

Country or area	1998	1999	2000	2001	2002	Pays ou zone
World	12504.7	10628.0	8391.8	8421.2	9911.8	Monde
Africa	1322.9	1132.8	875.7	746.8	782.4	Afrique
Americas	2363.7	1925.7	1762.1	1545.7	1750.4	Amériques
- Northern America	871.4	819.8	886.0	800.1	922.1	- Amérique du Nord
- LAIA	1188.6	838.1	677.4	552.5	644.7	- ALAI
- CACM	85.4	84.2	65.1	68.1	77.3	- MCC
- Caribbean	195.3	157.7	115.5	107.7	88.7	- Caraïbes
- Rest of America	23.1	25.8	18.0	17.3	17.7	- Autre d'Amérique
Asia excluding former USSR	4229.6	3081.8	2382.4	2281.3	2629.0	Asie ancienne URSS exclus
- Middle East	961.1	800.4	612.1	635.7	606.6	- Moyen-Orient
Asia former USSR	81.4	62.9	66.8	69.3	77.2	Asie ancienne URSS
Europe excluding former USSR	4032.7	3862.7	2883.7	3293.2	4064.7	Europe ancienne URSS exclus
- European Union	3506.3	3526.0	2578.1	2939.4	3631.7	- Union Européenne
- Eastern Europe	305.5	148.3	150.8	180.6	208.9	- Europe de l'Est
- Rest of Europe	220.9	188.5	154.8	173.2	224.1	- Autre de l'Europe
Europe former USSR	362.2	444.5	296.4	369.1	457.6	Europe ancienne URSS
Oceania	112.4	117.6	124.8	115.8	150.5	Océanie
Italy-San Marino-Holy See	982.2	1073.4	854.8	990.5	1224.8	Italie-Saint-Marin-Saint-Siège
United States	755.5	706.7	736.9	676.0	756.9	Etats-Unis d'Amérique
India	727.3	647.9	442.2	555.1	564.4	Inde
France-Monaco	528.6	473.9	405.4	407.7	498.0	France-Monaco
Iran (Islamic Republic of)	598.1	486.4	328.0	357.3	332.9	Iran (République islamique d')
China	707.8	474.7	167.1	51.0	456.3	Chine
China, Hong Kong SAR	917.2	210.9	286.7	246.8	176.6	Chine - RAS de Hong-Kong
Netherlands	415.5	339.4	208.3	240.7	449.8	Pays-Bas
United Kingdom	365.0	335.8	270.7	278.5	299.7	Royaume-Uni
Germany	311.4	277.8	237.3	301.1	375.2	Allemagne
Russian Federation	233.7	346.9	203.1	257.1	332.8	Fédération de Russie
Bangladesh	125.8	e137.7	e324.1	314.0	e306.9	Bangladesh
Belgium	–	310.8	241.9	294.3	e322.8	Belgique
Brazil	312.3	205.1	150.7	112.7	142.0	Brésil
Mexico	264.1	206.5	168.0	111.3	168.9	Mexique
Algeria	251.2	179.6	128.2	e155.1	e176.6	Algérie
Japan	212.8	169.7	157.2	148.8	170.0	Japon
Egypt	240.2	226.4	e112.7	102.6	96.6	Egypte
Turkey	219.4	172.2	125.9	124.3	134.3	Turquie
Morocco	153.9	137.0	128.5	135.8	e143.3	Maroc
Spain	106.2	314.7	71.8	102.7	97.9	Espagne
Canada	115.7	112.9	149.1	123.9	165.0	Canada
Portugal	148.4	137.3	88.9	105.7	119.2	Portugal
Venezuela	139.9	135.0	102.2	85.0	e71.5	Venezuela
Peru	134.0	80.6	66.0	97.3	117.2	Pérou
Colombia	125.9	90.3	92.4	83.3	89.4	Colombie
Pakistan	176.8	169.0	87.7	26.2	13.5	Pakistan
Poland	141.5	76.0	61.0	68.4	81.0	Pologne
Malaysia	107.7	103.7	44.0	65.6	e71.6	Malaisie
Korea, Republic of	55.8	88.0	68.0	78.8	98.5	République de Corée

(Value as percentages of World total) **(Valeur en pourcentage du total mondial)**

Regions of the world	1993	1994	1995	1996	1997	1998	1999	2000	2001	2002	Régions du monde
World	100.0	100.0	100.0	100.0	100.0	100.0	100.0	100.0	100.0	100.0	Monde
Africa	11.9	8.9	11.7	10.4	9.1	10.6	10.7	10.4	8.9	7.9	Afrique
Americas	21.3	19.2	17.6	18.3	17.4	18.9	18.1	21.0	18.4	17.7	Amériques
- Northern America	9.5	8.1	7.1	9.4	8.2	7.0	7.7	10.6	9.5	9.3	- Amérique du Nord
- LAIA	9.5	9.2	8.4	7.0	7.1	9.5	7.9	8.1	6.6	6.5	- ALAI
- CACM	1.0	0.7	0.8	0.7	0.7	0.7	0.8	0.8	0.8	0.8	- MCC
- Caribbean	1.0	0.9	1.1	1.0	1.3	1.6	1.5	1.4	1.3	0.9	- Caraïbes
- Rest of America	0.3	0.3	0.2	0.2	0.1	0.2	0.2	0.2	0.2	0.2	- Autre d'Amérique
Asia excluding former USSR	23.1	31.3	32.8	28.7	32.6	33.8	29.0	28.4	27.1	26.5	Asie ancienne URSS exclus
- Middle East	11.2	9.4	8.1	7.2	6.9	7.7	7.5	7.3	7.5	6.1	- Moyen-Orient
Asia former USSR	0.2	0.7	0.5	0.5	0.4	0.7	0.6	0.8	0.8	0.8	Asie ancienne URSS
Europe excluding former USSR	39.7	36.4	33.9	37.8	35.7	32.2	36.3	34.4	39.1	41.0	Europe ancienne URSS exclus
- European Union	36.1	33.6	31.0	34.6	32.5	28.0	33.2	30.7	34.9	36.6	- Union Européenne
- Eastern Europe	1.9	1.6	1.5	1.6	1.8	2.4	1.4	1.8	2.1	2.1	- Europe de l'Est
- Rest of Europe	1.6	1.1	1.4	1.6	1.4	1.8	1.8	1.8	2.1	2.3	- Autre de l'Europe
Europe former USSR	2.1	2.1	2.3	2.9	3.6	2.9	4.2	3.5	4.4	4.6	Europe ancienne URSS
Oceania	1.7	1.4	1.3	1.4	1.2	0.9	1.1	1.5	1.4	1.5	Océanie

TRADE BY COMMODITY (Value in million US dollars)
Exports by principal countries or areas

COMMERCE PAR PRODUIT (Valeur en millions de dollars EU)
Exportations selon les principaux pays ou zones

Country or area	1998	1999	2000	2001	2002	Pays ou zone
World	12562.5	10399.7	7821.5	8181.3	9431.3	Monde
Africa	310.9	402.0	313.3	252.3	248.1	Afrique
Americas	5589.9	4300.7	2877.0	2964.5	3109.8	Amériques
- Northern America	1864.5	1155.2	746.5	715.2	895.5	- Amérique du Nord
- LAIA	3690.0	3123.3	2111.0	2228.2	2195.6	- ALAI
- CACM	26.2	15.9	15.1	15.7	14.0	- MCC
- Caribbean	9.1	5.2	3.4	4.3	3.7	- Caraïbes
- Rest of America	0.1	1.1	1.0	1.0	1.0	- Autre d'Amérique
Asia excluding former USSR	940.0	630.0	408.3	507.5	446.6	Asie ancienne URSS exclus
- Middle East	161.5	224.6	97.0	209.9	135.9	- Moyen-Orient
Asia former USSR	13.8	13.7	11.9	13.5	21.3	Asie ancienne URSS
Europe excluding former USSR	5497.3	4886.6	3869.9	4039.0	5152.1	Europe ancienne URSS exclus
- European Union	5204.4	4672.6	3730.3	3899.4	5029.8	- Union Européenne
- Eastern Europe	244.0	185.9	99.0	102.5	78.9	- Europe de l'Est
- Rest of Europe	48.8	28.1	40.5	37.1	43.4	- Autre de l'Europe
Europe former USSR	170.2	136.0	319.4	384.0	425.8	Europe ancienne URSS
Oceania	40.4	30.7	21.8	20.5	27.6	Océanie
Argentina	2656.0	2255.2	1579.4	1526.2	e1474.5	Argentine
Spain	1238.8	892.7	947.7	1008.5	1481.3	Espagne
Italy-San Marino-Holy See	683.5	782.5	790.4	727.6	852.2	Italie-Saint-Marin-Saint-Siège
United States	1347.9	783.8	485.6	481.0	661.2	Etats-Unis d'Amérique
Germany	898.6	739.6	491.3	595.5	724.2	Allemagne
Brazil	841.9	701.7	368.9	523.5	e542.7	Brésil
Netherlands	751.5	641.4	416.8	477.3	632.0	Pays-Bas
France-Monaco	452.1	320.2	272.9	262.9	344.4	France-Monaco
Greece	352.2	555.8	241.8	237.8	e238.1	Grèce
Canada	516.6	371.4	260.9	234.3	234.4	Canada
Belgium	–	433.0	322.8	342.7	e384.5	Belgique
Ukraine	123.7	108.2	234.6	306.2	337.5	Ukraine
Tunisia	188.8	321.0	196.5	140.4	e146.1	Tunisie
Turkey	143.4	199.9	54.6	151.7	61.6	Turquie
China, Hong Kong SAR	340.5	106.6	62.1	45.7	52.2	Chine - RAS de Hong-Kong
United Kingdom	172.1	116.1	67.5	65.0	152.4	Royaume-Uni
Malaysia	148.3	135.5	98.4	92.0	e97.5	Malaisie
Portugal	122.8	86.8	95.1	96.3	106.0	Portugal
China	202.9	75.2	65.0	68.6	51.4	Chine
Belgium-Luxembourg	428.8	–	–	–	–	Belgique-Luxembourg
Bolivia	72.5	60.9	76.3	94.2	e90.6	Bolivie
Hungary	116.8	76.0	41.3	30.1	30.8	Hongrie
Senegal	43.2	22.2	67.8	71.4	53.2	Sénégal
Paraguay	65.4	45.8	38.9	44.1	e48.1	Paraguay
Denmark	52.8	42.5	31.4	31.9	50.2	Danemark
Russian Federation	24.3	16.2	73.3	47.9	42.4	Fédération de Russie
Singapore	40.6	43.0	36.1	30.8	33.9	Singapour
Mexico	47.6	48.4	34.5	23.5	22.2	Mexique
Romania	68.2	51.9	18.4	22.8	7.1	Roumanie
Australia	40.2	30.2	21.6	19.9	27.1	Australie

(Value as percentages of World total) **(Valeur en pourcentage du total mondial)**

Regions of the world	1993	1994	1995	1996	1997	1998	1999	2000	2001	2002	Régions du monde
World	100.0	100.0	100.0	100.0	100.0	100.0	100.0	100.0	100.0	100.0	Monde
Africa	4.2	4.9	3.8	2.2	3.3	2.5	3.9	4.0	3.1	2.6	Afrique
Americas	36.6	40.5	41.5	36.2	37.1	44.5	41.4	36.8	36.2	33.0	Amériques
- Northern America	13.2	12.7	13.2	10.6	12.6	14.8	11.1	9.5	8.7	9.5	- Amérique du Nord
- LAIA	23.2	27.6	28.0	25.4	24.4	29.4	30.0	27.0	27.2	23.3	- ALAI
- CACM	0.1	0.1	0.2	0.1	0.1	0.2	0.2	0.2	0.2	0.1	- MCC
- Caribbean	0.1	0.1	0.1	0.1	0.1	0.1	0.1	0.0	0.1	0.0	- Caraïbes
- Rest of America	0.0	0.0	0.0	0.0	0.0	0.0	0.0	0.0	0.0	0.0	- Autre d'Amérique
Asia excluding former USSR	5.2	6.9	7.3	6.6	10.3	7.5	6.1	5.2	6.2	4.7	Asie ancienne URSS exclus
- Middle East	0.9	1.1	1.9	1.4	1.8	1.3	2.2	1.2	2.6	1.4	- Moyen-Orient
Asia former USSR	0.0	0.1	0.1	0.1	0.0	0.1	0.1	0.2	0.2	0.2	Asie ancienne URSS
Europe excluding former USSR	52.7	45.6	45.9	52.5	47.7	43.8	47.0	49.5	49.4	54.6	Europe ancienne URSS exclus
- European Union	49.7	43.8	44.4	50.9	44.7	41.4	44.9	47.7	47.7	53.3	- Union Européenne
- Eastern Europe	2.8	1.6	1.3	1.5	2.8	1.9	1.8	1.3	1.3	0.8	- Europe de l'Est
- Rest of Europe	0.2	0.2	0.2	0.2	0.2	0.4	0.3	0.5	0.5	0.5	- Autre de l'Europe
Europe former USSR	1.2	1.9	1.4	2.3	1.4	1.4	1.3	4.1	4.7	4.5	Europe ancienne URSS
Oceania	0.0	0.0	0.0	0.1	0.2	0.3	0.3	0.3	0.3	0.3	Océanie

424 Other fixed vegetable oils, fluid or solid, crude, refined

TRADE BY COMMODITY (Value in million US dollars)
Imports by principal countries or areas

COMMERCE PAR PRODUIT (Valeur en millions de dollars EU)
Importations selon les principaux pays ou zones

Country or area	1998	1999	2000	2001	2002	Pays ou zone
World	9912.0	8987.5	7529.1	7086.5	8996.6	Monde
Africa	696.8	639.0	477.7	664.2	671.9	Afrique
Americas	1018.1	888.9	832.3	690.7	769.2	Amériques
- Northern America	693.0	631.6	578.4	440.3	486.8	- Amérique du Nord
- LAIA	228.3	165.6	181.0	155.1	196.0	- ALAI
- CACM	59.5	57.1	49.7	63.5	64.3	- MCC
- Caribbean	26.2	24.7	17.2	27.0	18.1	- Caraïbes
- Rest of America	11.1	9.9	5.9	4.7	4.0	- Autre d'Amérique
Asia excluding former USSR	4679.6	4401.4	3678.1	3301.2	4553.4	Asie ancienne URSS exclus
- Middle East	735.1	701.6	671.8	490.6	538.0	- Moyen-Orient
Asia former USSR	12.3	17.5	10.4	15.8	18.8	Asie ancienne URSS
Europe excluding former USSR	3244.9	2813.3	2330.2	2171.2	2658.1	Europe ancienne URSS exclus
- European Union	3054.9	2666.6	2198.4	2044.4	2494.7	- Union Européenne
- Eastern Europe	134.1	95.7	87.4	85.3	115.1	- Europe de l'Est
- Rest of Europe	56.0	51.0	44.4	41.5	48.4	- Autre de l'Europe
Europe former USSR	154.7	125.1	114.0	174.7	236.9	Europe ancienne URSS
Oceania	105.5	102.2	86.4	68.6	88.3	Océanie
India	1116.8	1233.5	928.3	823.1	1244.4	Inde
China	676.7	706.6	587.7	540.2	954.8	Chine
Germany	683.4	589.7	528.4	460.2	571.7	Allemagne
Netherlands	725.8	626.5	392.7	436.3	580.7	Pays-Bas
United States	642.9	580.0	532.0	394.5	446.9	Etats-Unis d'Amérique
Pakistan	737.9	443.0	326.7	342.8	488.1	Pakistan
United Kingdom	351.0	337.3	301.8	252.7	321.5	Royaume-Uni
Japan	349.9	310.3	249.6	204.2	263.7	Japon
Italy-San Marino-Holy See	324.0	284.9	259.0	213.0	249.7	Italie-Saint-Marin-Saint-Siège
France-Monaco	264.6	239.8	218.7	237.6	266.6	France-Monaco
Turkey	197.8	180.6	165.6	144.6	202.2	Turquie
Singapore	205.0	200.6	140.5	114.1	154.5	Singapour
Saudi Arabia	183.9	191.0	149.9	101.9	e105.4	Arabie saoudite
Belgium	–	203.7	194.8	157.1	e172.3	Belgique
Spain	196.8	148.3	123.1	112.7	129.8	Espagne
Korea, Republic of	160.2	153.9	117.6	101.2	125.7	République de Corée
Kenya	128.4	111.8	88.7	e156.5	150.9	Kenya
Bangladesh	96.8	e106.0	e147.1	142.5	e139.3	Bangladesh
China, Hong Kong SAR	92.8	65.6	77.7	160.0	214.6	Chine - RAS de Hong-Kong
Mexico	101.9	111.3	110.6	110.0	145.0	Mexique
Egypt	226.8	143.0	e66.6	60.6	75.3	Egypte
Malaysia	110.5	126.8	89.2	116.5	e127.3	Malaisie
Russian Federation	112.4	79.0	84.0	114.4	170.4	Fédération de Russie
Myanmar	e156.1	e82.1	e54.2	e65.0	e42.1	Myanmar
Denmark	126.8	72.1	58.1	59.4	74.9	Danemark
Australia	83.2	85.8	67.5	52.7	64.1	Australie
Sri Lanka	e60.3	54.4	e73.4	19.0	59.5	Sri Lanka
United Arab Emirates	51.2	53.6	67.1	33.6	e34.5	Emirates arabes unis
Yemen	79.7	e73.6	e85.3	e	e	Yémen
Jordan	56.0	42.5	40.6	34.6	62.9	Jordanie

(Value as percentages of World total) **(Valeur en pourcentage du total mondial)**

Regions of the world	1993	1994	1995	1996	1997	1998	1999	2000	2001	2002	Régions du monde
World	100.0	100.0	100.0	100.0	100.0	100.0	100.0	100.0	100.0	100.0	Monde
Africa	7.2	6.6	6.8	7.7	7.3	7.0	7.1	6.3	9.4	7.5	Afrique
Americas	12.4	11.2	9.4	10.4	11.6	10.3	9.9	11.1	9.7	8.6	Amériques
- Northern America	8.3	7.5	6.6	7.1	8.2	7.0	7.0	7.7	6.2	5.4	- Amérique du Nord
- LAIA	3.1	2.9	2.2	2.4	2.5	2.3	1.8	2.4	2.2	2.2	- ALAI
- CACM	0.3	0.4	0.3	0.4	0.5	0.6	0.6	0.7	0.9	0.7	- MCC
- Caribbean	0.6	0.4	0.2	0.4	0.4	0.3	0.3	0.2	0.4	0.2	- Caraïbes
- Rest of America	0.0	0.0	0.0	0.1	0.1	0.1	0.1	0.1	0.1	0.0	- Autre d'Amérique
Asia excluding former USSR	46.5	48.6	51.8	45.9	47.2	47.2	49.0	48.9	46.6	50.6	Asie ancienne URSS exclus
- Middle East	10.1	8.6	8.9	8.0	8.4	7.4	7.8	8.9	6.9	6.0	- Moyen-Orient
Asia former USSR	0.0	0.0	0.1	0.1	0.1	0.1	0.2	0.1	0.2	0.2	Asie ancienne URSS
Europe excluding former USSR	31.8	31.0	29.4	33.0	30.4	32.7	31.3	30.9	30.6	29.5	Europe ancienne URSS exclus
- European Union	30.4	29.5	28.0	31.4	28.4	30.8	29.7	29.2	28.8	27.7	- Union Européenne
- Eastern Europe	0.9	0.8	0.8	1.1	1.4	1.4	1.1	1.2	1.2	1.3	- Europe de l'Est
- Rest of Europe	0.6	0.6	0.5	0.6	0.5	0.6	0.6	0.6	0.6	0.5	- Autre de l'Europe
Europe former USSR	0.8	1.5	1.4	1.6	2.3	1.6	1.4	1.5	2.5	2.6	Europe ancienne URSS
Oceania	1.3	1.2	1.1	1.3	1.3	1.1	1.1	1.1	1.0	1.0	Océanie

TRADE BY COMMODITY (Value in million US dollars)
Exports by principal countries or areas

COMMERCE PAR PRODUIT (Valeur en millions de dollars EU)
Exportations selon les principaux pays ou zones

Country or area	1998	1999	2000	2001	2002	Pays ou zone
World	9320.0	8481.0	6861.6	6263.6	7723.6	Monde
Africa	181.8	167.1	103.1	109.9	99.1	Afrique
Americas	725.0	648.0	546.2	496.7	635.8	Amériques
- Northern America	502.8	425.9	359.5	345.6	442.6	- Amérique du Nord
- LAIA	131.6	134.6	105.5	79.6	96.2	- ALAI
- CACM	86.3	84.4	78.9	68.5	93.3	- MCC
- Caribbean	2.0	1.5	1.2	1.0	0.9	- Caraïbes
- Rest of America	2.4	1.6	1.2	1.9	2.9	- Autre d'Amérique
Asia excluding former USSR	6913.0	6463.2	5248.1	4742.8	6007.7	Asie ancienne URSS exclus
- Middle East	108.0	118.1	115.5	83.4	83.3	- Moyen-Orient
Asia former USSR	2.1	0.8	1.6	1.0	0.9	Asie ancienne URSS
Europe excluding former USSR	1109.6	1058.7	800.2	789.2	870.4	Europe ancienne URSS exclus
- European Union	1087.0	1043.7	791.6	777.1	857.7	- Union Européenne
- Eastern Europe	16.5	8.8	2.7	5.3	5.4	- Europe de l'Est
- Rest of Europe	6.1	6.2	6.0	6.8	7.3	- Autre de l'Europe
Europe former USSR	1.8	2.5	2.2	2.6	3.7	Europe ancienne URSS
Oceania	386.6	140.7	160.2	121.5	105.9	Océanie
Malaysia	4426.5	3789.9	2574.2	2504.3	e2653.9	Malaisie
Indonesia	1152.1	1674.4	1648.9	1341.1	2511.3	Indonésie
Philippines	706.8	342.7	464.2	417.7	352.7	Philippines
United States	481.8	400.4	340.2	319.9	415.5	Etats-Unis d'Amérique
Netherlands	442.6	429.2	282.6	272.5	346.8	Pays-Bas
Papua New Guinea	364.9	e118.5	148.0	e111.5	e95.2	Papouasie-Nouvelle-Guinée
India	145.5	224.5	196.9	144.8	109.0	Inde
Singapore	166.1	155.6	105.3	89.0	114.2	Singapour
Germany	113.4	122.6	93.7	101.8	118.5	Allemagne
Belgium	–	164.0	113.3	116.6	e130.8	Belgique
Italy-San Marino-Holy See	82.4	99.2	120.3	116.7	73.6	Italie-Saint-Marin-Saint-Siège
Spain	127.8	67.1	56.7	37.2	34.0	Espagne
Côte d'Ivoire	90.1	93.2	47.5	e51.8	36.8	Côte d'Ivoire
United Kingdom	74.7	65.9	43.2	36.4	48.4	Royaume-Uni
Thailand	36.5	32.8	31.9	66.5	e70.2	Thaïlande
France-Monaco	49.1	45.9	36.9	44.7	49.0	France-Monaco
China, Hong Kong SAR	66.9	55.6	37.3	28.7	33.6	Chine - RAS de Hong-Kong
Colombia	44.1	50.3	41.1	32.7	37.7	Colombie
China	72.6	36.0	30.7	28.3	29.0	Chine
Costa Rica	33.8	43.1	36.7	24.8	38.3	Costa Rica
United Arab Emirates	35.3	36.4	37.8	28.4	e29.6	Emirates arabes unis
Honduras	41.2	27.8	25.6	25.4	32.4	Honduras
Belgium-Luxembourg	148.9	–	–	–	–	Belgique-Luxembourg
Canada	21.0	25.5	19.3	25.7	27.1	Canada
Brazil	33.8	15.5	23.6	19.5	e20.2	Brésil
Viet Nam	13.6	13.0	25.5	26.5	29.5	Viet Nam
Sweden	24.4	19.1	18.3	18.7	21.6	Suède
Oman	23.3	18.7	21.1	17.5	19.6	Oman
Denmark	14.6	22.9	17.7	19.8	23.2	Danemark
Kenya	30.3	20.6	12.2	e17.9	12.9	Kenya

(Value as percentages of World total) **(Valeur en pourcentage du total mondial)**

Regions of the world	1993	1994	1995	1996	1997	1998	1999	2000	2001	2002	Régions du monde
World	100.0	100.0	100.0	100.0	100.0	100.0	100.0	100.0	100.0	100.0	Monde
Africa	2.7	2.0	2.1	2.2	1.5	2.0	2.0	1.5	1.8	1.3	Afrique
Americas	6.4	5.4	5.3	5.6	6.1	7.8	7.6	8.0	7.9	8.2	Amériques
- Northern America	4.9	4.1	3.7	4.1	4.3	5.4	5.0	5.2	5.5	5.7	- Amérique du Nord
- LAIA	1.1	1.0	1.2	1.1	1.3	1.4	1.6	1.5	1.3	1.2	- ALAI
- CACM	0.5	0.3	0.3	0.4	0.5	0.9	1.0	1.1	1.1	1.2	- MCC
- Caribbean	0.0	0.0	0.0	0.0	0.0	0.0	0.0	0.0	0.0	0.0	- Caraïbes
- Rest of America	0.0	0.0	0.0	0.0	0.0	0.0	0.0	0.0	0.0	0.0	- Autre d'Amérique
Asia excluding former USSR	75.8	80.2	79.2	74.4	76.5	74.2	76.2	76.5	75.7	77.8	Asie ancienne URSS exclus
- Middle East	3.2	2.7	2.2	2.1	1.9	1.2	1.4	1.7	1.3	1.1	- Moyen-Orient
Asia former USSR	0.0	0.0	0.0	0.0	0.0	0.0	0.0	0.0	0.0	0.0	Asie ancienne URSS
Europe excluding former USSR	10.0	8.9	10.2	10.1	9.8	11.9	12.5	11.7	12.6	11.3	Europe ancienne URSS exclus
- European Union	9.7	8.8	10.0	10.0	9.7	11.7	12.3	11.5	12.4	11.1	- Union Européenne
- Eastern Europe	0.1	0.0	0.1	0.1	0.1	0.2	0.1	0.0	0.1	0.1	- Europe de l'Est
- Rest of Europe	0.2	0.1	0.1	0.1	0.1	0.1	0.1	0.1	0.1	0.1	- Autre de l'Europe
Europe former USSR	0.0	0.0	0.0	0.0	0.0	0.0	0.0	0.0	0.0	0.0	Europe ancienne URSS
Oceania	5.0	3.5	3.3	7.7	6.0	4.1	1.7	2.3	1.9	1.4	Océanie

431 Animal and vegetable oils and fats, processed, and waxes

TRADE BY COMMODITY (Value in million US dollars)
Imports by principal countries or areas

COMMERCE PAR PRODUIT (Valeur en millions de dollars EU)
Importations selon les principaux pays ou zones

Country or area	1998	1999	2000	2001	2002	Pays ou zone
World	3367.3	3472.3	3081.1	3045.9	3332.9	Monde
Africa	190.4	212.0	182.9	171.2	198.3	Afrique
Americas	432.4	426.1	465.3	422.0	452.5	Amériques
- Northern America	220.4	209.6	230.5	205.1	222.7	- Amérique du Nord
- LAIA	145.5	154.4	176.5	160.7	170.2	- ALAI
- CACM	29.5	28.4	20.2	24.1	26.0	- MCC
- Caribbean	34.3	31.1	35.2	28.4	28.4	- Caraïbes
- Rest of America	2.6	2.5	3.0	3.8	5.2	- Autre d'Amérique
Asia excluding former USSR	899.1	1108.2	881.9	877.7	918.6	Asie ancienne URSS exclus
- Middle East	260.3	308.3	205.5	203.5	214.1	- Moyen-Orient
Asia former USSR	14.1	13.5	16.5	19.5	20.6	Asie ancienne URSS
Europe excluding former USSR	1739.9	1596.4	1413.5	1438.7	1612.7	Europe ancienne URSS exclus
- European Union	1541.5	1421.6	1252.7	1268.1	1414.4	- Union Européenne
- Eastern Europe	146.7	131.6	120.0	124.4	144.1	- Europe de l'Est
- Rest of Europe	51.8	43.2	40.7	46.2	54.3	- Autre de l'Europe
Europe former USSR	63.1	82.5	89.2	90.3	99.2	Europe ancienne URSS
Oceania	28.3	33.5	31.8	26.5	31.0	Océanie
Germany	325.5	295.1	252.8	256.7	277.7	Allemagne
Netherlands	247.5	251.1	191.7	199.6	215.9	Pays-Bas
France-Monaco	218.0	168.5	163.0	166.4	179.9	France-Monaco
India	157.1	180.0	128.4	193.8	138.9	Inde
United States	145.4	149.2	170.2	150.0	163.1	Etats-Unis d'Amérique
United Kingdom	144.3	135.4	142.1	172.1	168.2	Royaume-Uni
Belgium	–	142.6	137.5	114.0	e125.0	Belgique
Spain	109.4	98.7	83.5	90.7	120.1	Espagne
Japan	71.3	117.4	104.8	84.5	84.6	Japon
Iraq	e94.9	e131.0	e55.6	e57.9	e61.4	Iraq
Italy-San Marino-Holy See	85.4	79.8	75.7	63.5	90.2	Italie-Saint-Marin-Saint-Siège
Mexico	56.1	64.6	65.6	69.6	82.8	Mexique
Poland	76.6	65.6	58.1	62.3	75.8	Pologne
Korea, Republic of	62.6	70.1	64.3	56.2	69.6	République de Corée
China	19.4	58.2	77.7	73.0	93.6	Chine
Canada	74.3	59.7	60.3	55.0	59.6	Canada
Denmark	58.9	62.9	53.5	60.7	52.5	Danemark
Ireland	47.1	61.7	46.2	38.6	40.4	Irlande
Russian Federation	31.1	42.9	48.1	42.8	44.2	Fédération de Russie
Austria	48.2	41.2	36.2	37.6	43.6	Autriche
United Arab Emirates	66.5	69.7	9.5	26.4	e27.1	Emirates arabes unis
Israel	45.0	46.1	41.0	25.4	39.8	Israël
Sweden	41.9	34.2	32.5	30.7	52.2	Suède
Thailand	21.5	33.8	35.6	39.0	e40.6	Thaïlande
Belgium-Luxembourg	167.9	–	–	–	–	Belgique-Luxembourg
Pakistan	32.2	33.5	27.1	34.4	39.0	Pakistan
Malaysia	45.2	45.8	22.4	22.9	e25.0	Malaisie
Algeria	26.3	30.8	28.6	e34.6	e39.4	Algérie
Singapore	40.9	34.1	27.6	23.9	29.0	Singapour
Turkey	30.9	31.6	31.9	18.8	28.5	Turquie

(Value as percentages of World total)

(Valeur en pourcentage du total mondial)

Regions of the world	1993	1994	1995	1996	1997	1998	1999	2000	2001	2002	Régions du monde
World	100.0	100.0	100.0	100.0	100.0	100.0	100.0	100.0	100.0	100.0	Monde
Africa	5.2	5.6	5.0	6.8	5.6	5.7	6.1	5.9	5.6	5.9	Afrique
Americas	10.9	10.3	10.2	11.0	11.9	12.8	12.3	15.1	13.9	13.6	Amériques
- Northern America	5.9	5.7	5.6	5.0	6.2	6.5	6.0	7.5	6.7	6.7	- Amérique du Nord
- LAIA	4.0	3.6	3.9	4.8	3.9	4.3	4.4	5.7	5.3	5.1	- ALAI
- CACM	0.4	0.4	0.3	0.6	0.7	0.9	0.8	0.7	0.8	0.8	- MCC
- Caribbean	0.5	0.5	0.3	0.6	1.1	1.0	0.9	1.1	0.9	0.9	- Caraïbes
- Rest of America	0.1	0.1	0.1	0.1	0.1	0.1	0.1	0.1	0.1	0.2	- Autre d'Amérique
Asia excluding former USSR	32.2	28.3	31.0	26.9	27.9	26.7	31.9	28.6	28.8	27.6	Asie ancienne URSS exclus
- Middle East	3.7	6.1	8.8	8.4	8.3	7.7	8.9	6.7	6.7	6.4	- Moyen-Orient
Asia former USSR	0.2	1.1	0.6	0.6	0.7	0.4	0.4	0.5	0.6	0.6	Asie ancienne URSS
Europe excluding former USSR	47.4	52.4	51.0	52.2	51.3	51.7	46.0	45.9	47.2	48.4	Europe ancienne URSS exclus
- European Union	43.4	48.8	47.1	47.0	45.4	45.8	40.9	40.7	41.6	42.4	- Union Européenne
- Eastern Europe	2.3	2.1	2.7	3.8	4.3	4.4	3.8	3.9	4.1	4.3	- Europe de l'Est
- Rest of Europe	1.6	1.5	1.3	1.4	1.6	1.5	1.2	1.3	1.5	1.6	- Autre de l'Europe
Europe former USSR	3.1	1.2	1.1	1.3	1.5	1.9	2.4	2.9	3.0	3.0	Europe ancienne URSS
Oceania	1.0	1.1	1.1	1.2	1.0	0.8	1.0	1.0	0.9	0.9	Océanie

Huiles et graisses animals et végétales, préparées, et cires d'origine animale et végétale 431

TRADE BY COMMODITY (Value in million US dollars)
Exports by principal countries or areas

COMMERCE PAR PRODUIT (Valeur en millions de dollars EU)
Exportations selon les principaux pays ou zones

Country or area	1998	1999	2000	2001	2002	Pays ou zone
World	3847.5	3503.1	3023.7	2906.4	3938.8	Monde
Africa	34.5	52.9	30.1	29.3	27.9	Afrique
Americas	478.7	453.0	451.2	467.1	569.4	Amériques
- Northern America	322.3	315.1	298.1	278.5	382.8	- Amérique du Nord
- LAIA	134.1	120.8	140.2	173.8	170.1	- ALAI
- CACM	21.5	16.8	11.9	13.9	15.6	- MCC
- Caribbean	0.7	0.3	1.0	0.9	0.8	- Caraïbes
- Rest of America	0.0	0.0	0.0	0.0	0.1	- Autre d'Amérique
Asia excluding former USSR	1678.6	1491.2	1195.2	1064.9	1729.0	Asie ancienne URSS exclus
- Middle East	193.1	132.7	87.3	98.0	146.2	- Moyen-Orient
Asia former USSR	1.3	1.8	1.5	1.6	2.1	Asie ancienne URSS
Europe excluding former USSR	1577.5	1419.4	1269.4	1271.5	1541.6	Europe ancienne URSS exclus
- European Union	1511.5	1369.8	1226.7	1237.1	1501.9	- Union Européenne
- Eastern Europe	41.1	29.1	25.3	20.3	21.7	- Europe de l'Est
- Rest of Europe	24.8	20.4	17.3	14.1	17.9	- Autre de l'Europe
Europe former USSR	11.1	13.0	10.9	10.2	9.4	Europe ancienne URSS
Oceania	65.9	71.7	65.3	61.7	59.4	Océanie
Malaysia	892.0	885.6	731.7	646.0	e684.6	Malaisie
Germany	424.5	399.0	328.6	336.3	412.7	Allemagne
Netherlands	420.7	385.7	318.0	316.8	389.8	Pays-Bas
United States	222.0	234.4	228.7	213.1	314.5	Etats-Unis d'Amérique
Indonesia	364.7	148.8	120.0	100.1	129.7	Indonésie
Belgium	–	127.7	187.0	210.1	e235.7	Belgique
Israel	0.5	0.2	0.0	0.0	508.4	Israël
United Kingdom	94.5	85.5	69.5	69.3	76.7	Royaume-Uni
Brazil	97.4	75.2	78.7	69.8	e72.4	Brésil
Canada	100.3	80.7	69.4	65.4	68.3	Canada
Denmark	106.4	95.1	66.0	56.8	55.4	Danemark
Sweden	68.7	60.4	61.8	65.7	115.5	Suède
Singapore	83.8	80.7	67.9	61.2	67.1	Singapour
Italy-San Marino-Holy See	72.8	64.3	62.6	59.8	68.1	Italie-Saint-Marin-Saint-Siège
Jordan	82.8	55.6	11.1	58.0	92.5	Jordanie
France-Monaco	60.2	52.5	52.4	41.1	50.7	France-Monaco
Spain	49.0	47.7	44.1	43.2	57.1	Espagne
Argentina	19.5	20.0	35.7	64.5	e62.3	Argentine
Turkey	81.4	40.8	26.1	14.7	18.1	Turquie
India	25.7	36.0	34.1	31.6	50.1	Inde
New Zealand	34.4	34.5	30.7	31.4	24.8	Nouvelle-Zélande
Japan	24.7	32.1	32.7	31.6	29.1	Japon
Australia	31.5	32.1	28.1	25.4	30.4	Australie
Belgium-Luxembourg	136.0	–	–	–	–	Belgique-Luxembourg
Thailand	11.2	35.8	32.1	25.5	e26.9	Thaïlande
Finland	33.5	29.7	18.5	19.8	19.6	Finlande
Pakistan	8.7	19.6	22.8	12.9	17.2	Pakistan
China	28.6	18.3	11.7	8.9	10.0	Chine
Philippines	14.0	11.6	11.0	13.6	22.2	Philippines
Czech Republic	16.8	12.3	11.6	12.4	13.0	République tchèque

(Value as percentages of World total) **(Valeur en pourcentage du total mondial)**

Regions of the world	1993	1994	1995	1996	1997	1998	1999	2000	2001	2002	Régions du monde
World	100.0	100.0	100.0	100.0	100.0	100.0	100.0	100.0	100.0	100.0	Monde
Africa	0.5	0.6	0.6	1.1	1.5	0.9	1.5	1.0	1.0	0.7	Afrique
Americas	10.2	9.0	10.1	11.4	13.1	12.4	12.9	14.9	16.1	14.5	Amériques
- Northern America	6.6	5.9	5.8	6.7	8.1	8.4	9.0	9.9	9.6	9.7	- Amérique du Nord
- LAIA	3.4	2.9	4.1	4.5	4.6	3.5	3.4	4.6	6.0	4.3	- ALAI
- CACM	0.1	0.2	0.2	0.3	0.4	0.6	0.5	0.4	0.5	0.4	- MCC
- Caribbean	0.0	0.0	0.0	0.0	0.0	0.0	0.0	0.0	0.0	0.0	- Caraïbes
- Rest of America	0.0	0.0	0.0	0.0	0.0	0.0	0.0	0.0	0.0	0.0	- Autre d'Amérique
Asia excluding former USSR	43.7	48.2	50.6	46.8	41.6	43.6	42.6	39.5	36.6	43.9	Asie ancienne URSS exclus
- Middle East	3.7	5.4	7.6	8.4	6.6	5.0	3.8	2.9	3.4	3.7	- Moyen-Orient
Asia former USSR	0.0	0.1	0.1	0.2	0.0	0.0	0.1	0.1	0.1	0.1	Asie ancienne URSS
Europe excluding former USSR	43.5	40.1	36.8	38.5	41.4	41.0	40.5	42.0	43.7	39.1	Europe ancienne URSS exclus
- European Union	40.4	38.5	35.7	37.2	39.8	39.3	39.1	40.6	42.6	38.1	- Union Européenne
- Eastern Europe	1.3	1.1	0.8	0.9	1.0	1.1	0.8	0.8	0.7	0.6	- Europe de l'Est
- Rest of Europe	1.9	0.4	0.4	0.5	0.6	0.6	0.6	0.6	0.5	0.5	- Autre de l'Europe
Europe former USSR	0.1	0.3	0.3	0.2	0.2	0.3	0.4	0.4	0.3	0.2	Europe ancienne URSS
Oceania	2.0	1.7	1.6	1.8	2.1	1.7	2.0	2.2	2.1	1.5	Océanie

511 Hydrocarbons, nes, and derivatives

TRADE BY COMMODITY (Value in million US dollars)
Imports by principal countries or areas

COMMERCE PAR PRODUIT (Valeur en millions de dollars EU)
Importations selon les principaux pays ou zones

Country or area	1998	1999	2000	2001	2002	Pays ou zone
World	16709.5	18228.6	26464.9	21923.1	23050.0	Monde
Africa	222.6	200.7	262.1	258.5	259.0	Afrique
Americas	2773.1	3085.9	4650.8	3973.3	3826.2	Amériques
- Northern America	1479.5	1650.3	2501.0	2212.2	2086.6	- Amérique du Nord
- LAIA	1219.0	1366.8	2084.8	1688.2	1667.0	- ALAI
- CACM	36.1	29.7	28.9	34.8	36.5	- MCC
- Caribbean	34.1	33.2	31.3	32.1	30.9	- Caraïbes
- Rest of America	4.4	5.9	4.7	6.1	5.2	- Autre d'Amérique
Asia excluding former USSR	5719.6	7130.7	10237.8	8379.0	8951.6	Asie ancienne URSS exclus
- Middle East	282.2	290.7	452.4	427.2	354.1	- Moyen-Orient
Asia former USSR	18.4	5.7	7.8	4.7	5.3	Asie ancienne URSS
Europe excluding former USSR	7776.3	7569.3	11044.8	9108.9	9812.7	Europe ancienne URSS exclus
- European Union	7193.1	6981.5	10239.1	8438.4	9138.1	- Union Européenne
- Eastern Europe	355.4	361.5	503.6	392.1	397.7	- Europe de l'Est
- Rest of Europe	227.8	226.3	302.1	278.4	277.0	- Autre de l'Europe
Europe former USSR	138.6	154.9	179.0	142.1	128.2	Europe ancienne URSS
Oceania	61.0	81.3	82.7	56.6	67.0	Océanie
Belgium	–	1852.0	2597.4	2311.0	e2534.5	Belgique
China	687.3	1215.3	2022.6	1968.3	2387.6	Chine
United States	1134.5	1289.8	2060.0	1811.9	1733.3	Etats-Unis d'Amérique
Germany	1302.5	1128.3	1813.5	1519.4	1515.9	Allemagne
Netherlands	1050.7	946.0	1661.0	1116.7	1481.4	Pays-Bas
Korea, Republic of	820.8	918.6	1282.3	1076.4	1106.7	République de Corée
Mexico	591.1	760.6	1234.9	971.7	956.2	Mexique
France-Monaco	770.9	728.5	1088.3	929.0	933.8	France-Monaco
Indonesia	443.0	827.8	1113.9	978.6	897.0	Indonésie
United Kingdom	633.1	604.9	785.2	672.2	694.4	Royaume-Uni
Spain	441.5	472.4	767.4	638.0	705.7	Espagne
Italy-San Marino-Holy See	539.7	477.4	548.0	472.8	474.1	Italie-Saint-Marin-Saint-Siège
India	440.8	539.1	520.7	477.4	486.9	Inde
Japan	418.3	444.6	587.9	491.8	521.3	Japon
Malaysia	290.8	320.9	502.4	425.1	e464.6	Malaisie
Canada	344.8	360.2	440.9	400.0	352.9	Canada
Belgium-Luxembourg	1878.3	–	–	–	–	Belgique-Luxembourg
Thailand	256.2	283.9	430.6	262.2	e273.2	Thaïlande
Sweden	158.2	321.6	350.6	210.8	200.7	Suède
China, Hong Kong SAR	212.9	222.2	317.0	222.7	260.7	Chine - RAS de Hong-Kong
Brazil	214.1	212.7	270.5	252.1	267.3	Brésil
Colombia	188.3	197.6	309.4	236.9	281.3	Colombie
Finland	131.2	155.4	272.0	238.0	238.7	Finlande
Turkey	149.9	169.7	266.0	227.8	156.9	Turquie
Singapore	134.7	123.5	203.2	207.9	243.0	Singapour
Poland	135.3	143.9	199.9	173.4	167.0	Pologne
Philippines	98.8	147.7	185.5	159.3	162.5	Philippines
Pakistan	55.2	109.6	175.2	180.1	176.6	Pakistan
Hungary	99.7	107.1	156.3	94.5	103.4	Hongrie
Portugal	89.6	87.9	112.6	109.4	117.6	Portugal

(Value as percentages of World total) **(Valeur en pourcentage du total mondial)**

Regions of the world	1993	1994	1995	1996	1997	1998	1999	2000	2001	2002	Régions du monde
World	100.0	100.0	100.0	100.0	100.0	100.0	100.0	100.0	100.0	100.0	Monde
Africa	1.2	1.1	0.9	1.1	1.1	1.3	1.1	1.0	1.2	1.1	Afrique
Americas	14.1	14.8	14.2	15.3	15.2	16.6	16.9	17.6	18.1	16.6	Amériques
- Northern America	8.9	9.0	7.9	8.8	8.1	8.9	9.1	9.5	10.1	9.1	- Amérique du Nord
- LAIA	4.9	5.6	6.0	6.1	6.7	7.3	7.5	7.9	7.7	7.2	- ALAI
- CACM	0.2	0.1	0.1	0.2	0.2	0.2	0.2	0.1	0.2	0.2	- MCC
- Caribbean	0.1	0.1	0.1	0.1	0.2	0.2	0.2	0.1	0.1	0.1	- Caraïbes
- Rest of America	0.0	0.0	0.0	0.0	0.0	0.0	0.0	0.0	0.0	0.0	- Autre d'Amérique
Asia excluding former USSR	43.4	37.8	42.1	41.0	38.7	34.2	39.1	38.7	38.2	38.8	Asie ancienne URSS exclus
- Middle East	1.8	1.6	1.7	1.7	1.7	1.7	1.6	1.7	1.9	1.5	- Moyen-Orient
Asia former USSR	0.0	0.1	0.2	0.1	0.0	0.1	0.0	0.0	0.0	0.0	Asie ancienne URSS
Europe excluding former USSR	40.4	44.8	41.6	40.9	43.6	46.5	41.5	41.7	41.5	42.6	Europe ancienne URSS exclus
- European Union	36.9	40.9	37.4	37.6	40.1	43.0	38.3	38.7	38.5	39.6	- Union Européenne
- Eastern Europe	1.9	2.4	2.9	2.1	2.4	2.1	2.0	1.9	1.8	1.7	- Europe de l'Est
- Rest of Europe	1.7	1.4	1.4	1.3	1.2	1.4	1.2	1.1	1.3	1.2	- Autre de l'Europe
Europe former USSR	0.1	0.4	0.4	0.8	0.7	0.8	0.8	0.7	0.6	0.6	Europe ancienne URSS
Oceania	0.8	1.0	0.7	0.7	0.7	0.4	0.4	0.3	0.3	0.3	Océanie

TRADE BY COMMODITY (Value in million US dollars)
Exports by principal countries or areas

COMMERCE PAR PRODUIT (Valeur en millions de dollars EU)
Exportations selon les principaux pays ou zones

Country or area	1998	1999	2000	2001	2002	Pays ou zone
World	14943.5	16739.8	23312.2	19767.8	21475.6	Monde
Africa	190.0	279.2	392.4	257.2	208.0	Afrique
Americas	3419.1	4110.8	5791.8	4208.1	4599.6	Amériques
- Northern America	3014.3	3669.2	5119.7	3781.4	4185.0	- Amérique du Nord
- LAIA	387.8	434.0	663.7	420.3	408.1	- ALAI
- CACM	2.1	1.6	2.0	1.9	1.9	- MCC
- Caribbean	14.8	6.0	6.5	4.5	4.5	- Caraïbes
- Rest of America	0.0	0.0	0.0	0.0	0.0	- Autre d'Amérique
Asia excluding former USSR	4646.2	5697.2	8235.6	6952.1	7708.3	Asie ancienne URSS exclus
- Middle East	656.9	614.2	863.5	988.2	912.4	- Moyen-Orient
Asia former USSR	22.0	6.0	13.3	2.2	4.0	Asie ancienne URSS
Europe excluding former USSR	6366.3	6346.0	8397.7	7906.8	8500.1	Europe ancienne URSS exclus
- European Union	6003.8	5979.4	7975.2	7499.2	8127.1	- Union Européenne
- Eastern Europe	282.0	298.4	329.8	313.9	296.9	- Europe de l'Est
- Rest of Europe	80.5	68.1	92.7	93.7	76.0	- Autre de l'Europe
Europe former USSR	281.8	281.1	473.1	439.4	452.4	Europe ancienne URSS
Oceania	18.1	19.5	8.1	1.9	3.2	Océanie
United States	2387.9	2959.1	4002.6	2808.8	3183.7	Etats-Unis d'Amérique
Japan	1614.1	2044.8	2697.3	2401.5	2565.5	Japon
Netherlands	1626.2	1672.5	2263.6	2323.9	2859.1	Pays-Bas
Korea, Republic of	1301.5	1572.3	2424.5	1741.5	1988.0	République de Corée
Germany	1089.4	1149.6	1494.9	1357.1	1314.6	Allemagne
United Kingdom	1138.6	1028.2	1334.3	1363.7	1208.8	Royaume-Uni
Canada	626.3	710.1	1117.1	971.9	1001.2	Canada
Belgium	-	810.0	946.0	911.4	e1022.6	Belgique
Saudi Arabia	529.6	511.3	725.7	822.2	e741.0	Arabie saoudite
France-Monaco	604.0	533.1	763.8	561.1	610.3	France-Monaco
Italy-San Marino-Holy See	329.0	295.0	535.3	437.8	477.0	Italie-Saint-Marin-Saint-Siège
Singapore	341.0	356.6	399.6	337.0	486.0	Singapour
Thailand	95.3	240.5	498.1	302.2	e319.2	Thaïlande
Russian Federation	196.2	223.8	391.2	313.4	315.2	Fédération de Russie
Spain	179.4	197.7	288.6	286.8	297.8	Espagne
Brazil	223.6	261.5	375.2	188.7	e195.6	Brésil
China	143.8	188.4	235.8	276.0	355.5	Chine
Israel	181.6	207.8	269.8	196.6	211.0	Israël
Portugal	136.7	161.1	222.9	153.8	207.3	Portugal
Czech Republic	176.6	181.1	183.0	188.7	143.2	République tchèque
Indonesia	104.6	128.6	275.1	138.8	181.7	Indonésie
Belgium-Luxembourg	774.1	-	-	-	-	Belgique-Luxembourg
Malaysia	41.1	61.4	179.7	226.4	e239.9	Malaisie
India	76.2	161.8	158.8	117.5	210.9	Inde
Libyan Arab Jamahiriya	113.7	e147.1	e189.0	e95.0	e53.4	Jamahiriya arabe libyenne
Iran (Islamic Republic of)	89.6	62.9	89.3	122.0	108.0	Iran (République islamique d')
Ukraine	75.7	48.9	71.0	121.5	134.0	Ukraine
Mexico	49.4	71.7	141.4	87.1	73.2	Mexique
South Africa	-	-	149.4	125.8	117.3	Afrique du Sud
Argentina	53.2	68.3	83.9	90.6	e87.5	Argentine

(Value as percentages of World total) **(Valeur en pourcentage du total mondial)**

Regions of the world	1993	1994	1995	1996	1997	1998	1999	2000	2001	2002	Régions du monde
World	100.0	100.0	100.0	100.0	100.0	100.0	100.0	100.0	100.0	100.0	Monde
Africa	1.9	0.7	1.1	1.0	1.3	1.3	1.7	1.7	1.3	1.0	Afrique
Americas	27.1	23.1	24.8	21.1	24.3	22.9	24.6	24.8	21.3	21.4	Amériques
- Northern America	23.1	20.3	22.2	18.9	21.6	20.2	21.9	22.0	19.1	19.5	- Amérique du Nord
- LAIA	4.0	2.8	2.5	2.0	2.5	2.6	2.6	2.8	2.1	1.9	- ALAI
- CACM	0.0	0.0	0.0	0.0	0.0	0.0	0.0	0.0	0.0	0.0	- MCC
- Caribbean	0.0	0.0	0.1	0.1	0.1	0.1	0.0	0.0	0.0	0.0	- Caraïbes
- Rest of America	0.0	0.0	0.0	0.0	0.0	0.0	0.0	0.0	0.0	0.0	- Autre d'Amérique
Asia excluding former USSR	20.7	21.8	28.2	24.3	30.7	31.1	34.0	35.3	35.2	35.9	Asie ancienne URSS exclus
- Middle East	3.6	3.1	3.4	3.5	3.6	4.4	3.7	3.7	5.0	4.2	- Moyen-Orient
Asia former USSR	0.0	0.0	0.0	0.0	0.0	0.1	0.0	0.1	0.0	0.0	Asie ancienne URSS
Europe excluding former USSR	48.2	52.4	43.7	51.5	41.5	42.6	37.9	36.0	40.0	39.6	Europe ancienne URSS exclus
- European Union	44.9	50.4	41.7	49.7	39.5	40.2	35.7	34.2	37.9	37.8	- Union Européenne
- Eastern Europe	1.9	1.6	1.7	1.6	1.7	1.9	1.8	1.4	1.6	1.4	- Europe de l'Est
- Rest of Europe	1.5	0.3	0.3	0.2	0.3	0.5	0.4	0.4	0.5	0.4	- Autre de l'Europe
Europe former USSR	2.0	2.0	2.1	2.0	2.1	1.9	1.7	2.0	2.2	2.1	Europe ancienne URSS
Oceania	0.1	0.1	0.1	0.1	0.2	0.1	0.1	0.0	0.0	0.0	Océanie

512 Alcohols, phenols etc, and their derivatives

TRADE BY COMMODITY (Value in million US dollars)
Imports by principal countries or areas

COMMERCE PAR PRODUIT (Valeur en millions de dollars EU)
Importations selon les principaux pays ou zones

Country or area	1998	1999	2000	2001	2002	Pays ou zone
World	14194.7	13654.3	16560.6	16881.0	16905.6	Monde
Africa	199.7	175.4	178.8	196.9	222.8	Afrique
Americas	2629.4	2499.9	3191.3	3500.1	3103.6	Amériques
- Northern America	1775.4	1682.3	2146.0	2467.1	2200.7	- Amérique du Nord
- LAIA	781.7	745.8	968.6	968.6	836.7	- ALAI
- CACM	34.7	35.7	30.4	26.3	28.7	- MCC
- Caribbean	35.6	34.0	44.3	36.1	35.6	- Caraïbes
- Rest of America	2.1	2.1	2.1	2.1	1.8	- Autre d'Amérique
Asia excluding former USSR	5097.6	5433.6	6974.8	7096.9	7529.4	Asie ancienne URSS exclus
- Middle East	202.8	220.3	270.4	255.7	273.2	- Moyen-Orient
Asia former USSR	26.7	17.8	19.5	19.5	19.8	Asie ancienne URSS
Europe excluding former USSR	6045.3	5358.6	5996.5	5868.9	5821.9	Europe ancienne URSS exclus
- European Union	5453.1	4873.7	5451.4	5329.9	5257.7	- Union Européenne
- Eastern Europe	254.1	186.9	260.5	257.5	265.4	- Europe de l'Est
- Rest of Europe	338.1	297.9	284.6	281.6	298.7	- Autre de l'Europe
Europe former USSR	118.1	82.6	104.5	105.5	108.0	Europe ancienne URSS
Oceania	77.8	86.4	95.2	93.2	100.2	Océanie
United States	1477.0	1407.2	1840.4	2129.5	1872.8	Etats-Unis d'Amérique
China	648.8	1029.8	1603.6	1928.2	2304.5	Chine
Japan	1016.4	904.7	1060.4	1092.3	982.4	Japon
Korea, Republic of	724.1	796.4	1038.4	1032.9	1049.4	République de Corée
Germany	870.4	775.4	949.2	981.6	963.1	Allemagne
Netherlands	799.0	733.9	871.8	749.7	674.3	Pays-Bas
Italy-San Marino-Holy See	719.2	641.8	752.3	746.0	723.2	Italie-Saint-Marin-Saint-Siège
France-Monaco	692.4	609.9	686.0	658.4	628.4	France-Monaco
United Kingdom	767.9	576.2	540.2	572.4	573.3	Royaume-Uni
Belgium	–	681.7	752.7	734.7	e805.7	Belgique
Spain	386.7	358.0	368.9	397.1	393.3	Espagne
Thailand	220.5	285.6	424.7	425.4	e443.3	Thaïlande
Singapore	288.6	262.5	323.2	426.5	424.2	Singapour
Indonesia	273.4	278.6	402.9	352.8	299.5	Indonésie
Mexico	267.6	274.3	359.2	338.2	330.4	Mexique
Canada	298.4	275.1	305.5	337.4	326.3	Canada
Brazil	250.1	231.6	323.1	340.5	286.7	Brésil
Malaysia	195.9	188.3	286.2	276.6	e302.3	Malaisie
Switzerland-Liechtenstein	251.1	226.1	209.6	213.0	221.1	Suisse-Liechtenstein
India	158.6	194.1	156.1	215.7	259.5	Inde
Turkey	134.4	127.0	172.9	140.5	151.7	Turquie
Belgium-Luxembourg	686.2	–	–	–	–	Belgique-Luxembourg
China, Hong Kong SAR	121.1	113.5	138.0	128.7	136.2	Chine - RAS de Hong-Kong
Sweden	138.7	106.4	119.0	100.0	93.3	Suède
Pakistan	102.7	94.3	119.8	92.7	116.0	Pakistan
Poland	100.4	77.7	109.5	112.4	121.5	Pologne
Argentina	98.0	93.7	109.6	111.9	e49.5	Argentine
Finland	81.7	87.9	84.4	77.9	88.7	Finlande
Israel	89.2	82.8	97.3	75.6	72.7	Israël
Austria	76.3	62.1	78.8	81.0	79.1	Autriche

(Value as percentages of World total)

(Valeur en pourcentage du total mondial)

Regions of the world	1993	1994	1995	1996	1997	1998	1999	2000	2001	2002	Régions du monde
World	100.0	100.0	100.0	100.0	100.0	100.0	100.0	100.0	100.0	100.0	Monde
Africa	1.5	1.2	1.3	1.3	1.4	1.4	1.3	1.1	1.2	1.3	Afrique
Americas	16.5	20.4	18.4	18.7	18.3	18.5	18.3	19.3	20.7	18.4	Amériques
- Northern America	10.1	12.0	10.3	11.3	11.3	12.5	12.3	13.0	14.6	13.0	- Amérique du Nord
- LAIA	6.0	8.1	7.7	6.9	6.6	5.5	5.5	5.8	5.7	4.9	- ALAI
- CACM	0.2	0.2	0.2	0.2	0.2	0.2	0.3	0.2	0.2	0.2	- MCC
- Caribbean	0.1	0.1	0.2	0.2	0.2	0.3	0.2	0.3	0.2	0.2	- Caraïbes
- Rest of America	0.0	0.0	0.0	0.0	0.0	0.0	0.0	0.0	0.0	0.0	- Autre d'Amérique
Asia excluding former USSR	38.2	32.4	36.9	35.4	37.6	35.9	39.8	42.1	42.0	44.5	Asie ancienne URSS exclus
- Middle East	1.5	1.3	1.6	1.7	1.5	1.4	1.6	1.6	1.5	1.6	- Moyen-Orient
Asia former USSR	0.2	0.4	0.3	0.5	0.5	0.2	0.1	0.1	0.1	0.1	Asie ancienne URSS
Europe excluding former USSR	41.0	43.8	41.1	41.9	40.6	42.6	39.2	36.2	34.8	34.4	Europe ancienne URSS exclus
- European Union	36.8	39.6	37.0	37.9	36.9	38.4	35.7	32.9	31.6	31.1	- Union Européenne
- Eastern Europe	2.0	1.9	1.8	1.8	1.7	1.8	1.4	1.6	1.5	1.6	- Europe de l'Est
- Rest of Europe	2.2	2.4	2.3	2.2	2.1	2.4	2.2	1.7	1.7	1.8	- Autre de l'Europe
Europe former USSR	1.8	1.1	1.4	1.6	1.0	0.8	0.6	0.6	0.6	0.6	Europe ancienne URSS
Oceania	0.7	0.7	0.7	0.6	0.6	0.5	0.6	0.6	0.6	0.6	Océanie

TRADE BY COMMODITY (Value in million US dollars)
Exports by principal countries or areas

COMMERCE PAR PRODUIT (Valeur en millions de dollars EU)
Exportations selon les principaux pays ou zones

Country or area	1998	1999	2000	2001	2002	Pays ou zone
World	12327.9	11591.0	13759.2	14206.1	14684.6	Monde
Africa	112.2	111.9	141.3	263.3	307.9	Afrique
Americas	2962.8	2781.7	3544.5	3591.4	3558.3	Amériques
- Northern America	2137.4	2060.0	2465.1	2420.5	2453.3	- Amérique du Nord
- LAIA	621.0	512.4	730.0	834.7	837.6	- ALAI
- CACM	33.8	35.2	29.4	28.8	24.0	- MCC
- Caribbean	167.8	171.1	316.9	304.4	240.3	- Caraïbes
- Rest of America	2.8	3.0	3.1	2.9	3.1	- Autre d'Amérique
Asia excluding former USSR	3386.1	3378.4	4360.9	4544.0	4815.2	Asie ancienne URSS exclus
- Middle East	772.8	670.6	1168.8	1256.7	1320.0	- Moyen-Orient
Asia former USSR	7.9	9.1	6.7	9.2	11.1	Asie ancienne URSS
Europe excluding former USSR	5489.5	4982.1	5303.0	5342.4	5540.0	Europe ancienne URSS exclus
- European Union	5095.4	4627.5	4871.0	4964.1	5102.9	- Union Européenne
- Eastern Europe	210.9	168.3	258.1	211.6	252.5	- Europe de l'Est
- Rest of Europe	183.2	186.4	173.9	166.7	184.5	- Autre de l'Europe
Europe former USSR	199.2	213.1	340.6	341.7	382.4	Europe ancienne URSS
Oceania	170.2	114.6	62.3	114.1	69.7	Océanie
United States	1724.9	1667.9	1982.3	1884.6	1929.5	Etats-Unis d'Amérique
Germany	1794.4	1665.2	1683.5	1731.4	1712.6	Allemagne
Saudi Arabia	725.9	620.1	1097.2	1149.3	e1035.7	Arabie saoudite
Japan	894.0	941.0	916.5	787.0	878.7	Japon
Netherlands	849.5	605.0	728.7	872.2	914.1	Pays-Bas
Belgium	–	848.9	952.5	836.9	e939.0	Belgique
Canada	412.5	392.1	482.8	532.8	522.7	Canada
France-Monaco	490.6	442.7	480.2	438.0	456.5	France-Monaco
United Kingdom	541.4	460.8	420.2	409.1	415.7	Royaume-Uni
Malaysia	379.5	366.8	447.5	441.1	e467.4	Malaisie
Singapore	218.5	240.3	286.4	392.2	466.6	Singapour
Chile	141.9	148.4	305.7	369.8	e361.8	Chili
Russian Federation	160.2	191.1	311.2	301.0	341.5	Fédération de Russie
China	204.7	208.4	260.3	307.0	297.7	Chine
Korea, Republic of	194.0	168.0	273.6	268.6	287.1	République de Corée
Indonesia	182.4	212.9	253.7	258.9	251.9	Indonésie
Spain	173.1	214.2	242.1	224.3	251.5	Espagne
Trinidad and Tobago	147.7	143.4	267.2	257.1	e195.1	Trinité-et-Tobago
Italy-San Marino-Holy See	201.8	183.1	151.1	146.5	183.5	Italie-Saint-Marin-Saint-Siège
Israel	182.0	190.1	190.4	133.3	154.3	Israël
Brazil	148.1	154.2	152.3	188.4	e195.3	Brésil
Switzerland-Liechtenstein	157.2	168.3	152.8	144.1	163.9	Suisse-Liechtenstein
Belgium-Luxembourg	759.2	–	–	–	–	Belgique-Luxembourg
India	86.6	111.4	162.0	139.3	126.1	Inde
China, Hong Kong SAR	111.2	102.5	147.2	142.6	120.3	Chine - RAS de Hong-Kong
Venezuela	131.2	75.1	105.6	145.9	e155.0	Venezuela
Finland	109.0	112.0	116.5	102.6	115.9	Finlande
Poland	83.0	80.1	115.8	76.3	96.1	Pologne
New Zealand	148.4	97.5	43.3	96.9	47.3	Nouvelle-Zélande
Mexico	129.4	68.7	90.5	57.9	54.5	Mexique

(Value as percentages of World total)

(Valeur en pourcentage du total mondial)

Regions of the world	1993	1994	1995	1996	1997	1998	1999	2000	2001	2002	Régions du monde
World	100.0	100.0	100.0	100.0	100.0	100.0	100.0	100.0	100.0	100.0	Monde
Africa	1.9	3.6	1.3	1.6	1.2	0.9	1.0	1.0	1.9	2.1	Afrique
Americas	22.3	23.3	26.1	24.4	25.1	24.0	24.0	25.8	25.3	24.2	Amériques
- Northern America	17.1	17.6	20.3	18.8	18.9	17.3	17.8	17.9	17.0	16.7	- Amérique du Nord
- LAIA	4.3	5.4	5.4	4.0	4.4	5.0	4.4	5.3	5.9	5.7	- ALAI
- CACM	0.3	0.2	0.2	0.3	0.2	0.3	0.3	0.2	0.2	0.2	- MCC
- Caribbean	0.6	0.0	0.1	1.1	1.5	1.4	1.5	2.3	2.1	1.6	- Caraïbes
- Rest of America	0.1	0.1	0.0	0.1	0.0	0.0	0.0	0.0	0.0	0.0	- Autre d'Amérique
Asia excluding former USSR	24.6	24.6	24.3	25.5	25.9	27.5	29.1	31.7	32.0	32.8	Asie ancienne URSS exclus
- Middle East	7.5	8.4	7.7	7.2	6.8	6.3	5.8	8.5	8.8	9.0	- Moyen-Orient
Asia former USSR	0.1	0.4	0.3	0.4	0.4	0.1	0.1	0.0	0.1	0.1	Asie ancienne URSS
Europe excluding former USSR	46.2	41.7	42.3	42.7	42.4	44.5	43.0	38.5	37.6	37.7	Europe ancienne URSS exclus
- European Union	41.7	37.9	38.4	39.0	39.1	41.3	39.9	35.4	34.9	34.8	- Union Européenne
- Eastern Europe	2.8	2.3	2.4	2.2	2.1	1.7	1.5	1.9	1.5	1.7	- Europe de l'Est
- Rest of Europe	1.6	1.5	1.4	1.5	1.3	1.5	1.6	1.3	1.2	1.3	- Autre de l'Europe
Europe former USSR	3.7	4.1	3.7	3.7	2.8	1.6	1.8	2.5	2.4	2.6	Europe ancienne URSS
Oceania	1.2	2.3	2.1	1.9	2.2	1.4	1.0	0.5	0.8	0.5	Océanie

513 Carboxylic acids, and their derivatives

TRADE BY COMMODITY (Value in million US dollars)
Imports by principal countries or areas

COMMERCE PAR PRODUIT (Valeur en millions de dollars EU)
Importations selon les principaux pays ou zones

Country or area	1998	1999	2000	2001	2002	Pays ou zone
World	17668.7	17619.4	20136.8	20534.6	21863.4	Monde
Africa	327.5	286.7	296.8	317.2	345.0	Afrique
Americas	3647.2	3711.2	4281.4	4587.0	4375.1	Amériques
- Northern America	2335.9	2431.3	2855.9	3104.8	3111.4	- Amérique du Nord
- LAIA	1240.8	1216.9	1360.2	1415.5	1193.4	- ALAI
- CACM	43.2	37.9	39.4	42.6	45.4	- MCC
- Caribbean	22.9	21.6	22.1	20.8	21.6	- Caraïbes
- Rest of America	4.4	3.5	3.8	3.4	3.3	- Autre d'Amérique
Asia excluding former USSR	4609.8	5061.8	6440.1	6295.2	7371.8	Asie ancienne URSS exclus
- Middle East	428.5	438.2	520.8	458.6	551.9	- Moyen-Orient
Asia former USSR	9.3	12.5	12.7	12.2	13.8	Asie ancienne URSS
Europe excluding former USSR	8716.7	8191.9	8721.4	8983.9	9424.2	Europe ancienne URSS exclus
- European Union	7813.3	7500.8	7971.6	8170.2	8571.5	- Union Européenne
- Eastern Europe	280.7	250.6	262.5	277.5	289.6	- Europe de l'Est
- Rest of Europe	622.7	440.5	487.3	536.2	563.1	- Autre de l'Europe
Europe former USSR	100.6	80.0	104.0	89.8	95.4	Europe ancienne URSS
Oceania	257.6	275.3	280.6	249.3	238.2	Océanie
United States	1855.6	1945.7	2362.2	2607.7	2601.9	Etats-Unis d'Amérique
China	829.7	1402.5	2233.6	2471.4	3472.8	Chine
Germany	1273.2	1185.0	1312.4	1435.5	1474.9	Allemagne
Italy-San Marino-Holy See	1091.2	1062.9	1152.4	1145.7	1120.9	Italie-Saint-Marin-Saint-Siège
Belgium	–	1046.8	1124.6	1473.1	e1615.6	Belgique
France-Monaco	1015.3	1011.2	1035.2	952.9	1101.3	France-Monaco
United Kingdom	1087.9	944.6	929.7	791.0	766.2	Royaume-Uni
Netherlands	847.2	792.3	881.8	847.9	785.2	Pays-Bas
Japan	558.1	604.2	710.8	648.8	625.7	Japon
Spain	615.5	613.2	579.1	585.6	665.6	Espagne
Canada	480.3	485.5	492.5	496.9	509.4	Canada
Mexico	357.5	404.0	452.7	481.6	461.8	Mexique
Korea, Republic of	318.8	399.4	485.1	423.1	435.0	République de Corée
Switzerland-Liechtenstein	503.8	335.4	372.5	413.2	431.6	Suisse-Liechtenstein
Brazil	391.7	358.6	387.0	378.6	332.4	Brésil
Turkey	282.8	277.5	367.5	299.4	389.7	Turquie
Ireland	308.1	284.1	347.1	270.6	333.6	Irlande
Thailand	323.1	238.6	262.7	284.2	e296.1	Thaïlande
China, Hong Kong SAR	287.0	300.0	319.2	242.3	181.9	Chine - RAS de Hong-Kong
Singapore	275.0	296.7	266.9	257.2	222.4	Singapour
Indonesia	252.2	209.6	283.3	229.5	226.8	Indonésie
Australia	227.1	246.9	248.6	219.3	208.0	Australie
Malaysia	179.2	153.2	264.7	246.2	e269.1	Malaisie
Belgium-Luxembourg	1006.9	–	–	–	–	Belgique-Luxembourg
Argentina	186.7	194.0	204.6	233.8	e103.4	Argentine
India	180.5	159.9	127.7	180.4	213.4	Inde
Pakistan	194.4	133.2	130.5	158.1	150.5	Pakistan
Sweden	132.8	120.6	140.2	148.5	137.8	Suède
Colombia	122.6	107.9	132.7	139.0	122.7	Colombie
Austria	125.1	107.8	106.1	111.4	115.8	Autriche

(Value as percentages of World total)

(Valeur en pourcentage du total mondial)

Regions of the world	1993	1994	1995	1996	1997	1998	1999	2000	2001	2002	Régions du monde
World	100.0	100.0	100.0	100.0	100.0	100.0	100.0	100.0	100.0	100.0	Monde
Africa	2.0	2.0	2.1	2.0	1.8	1.9	1.6	1.5	1.5	1.6	Afrique
Americas	18.9	17.8	16.2	18.4	20.1	20.6	21.1	21.3	22.3	20.0	Amériques
- Northern America	12.8	11.5	10.2	12.2	12.9	13.2	13.8	14.2	15.1	14.2	- Amérique du Nord
- LAIA	5.8	5.8	5.7	5.8	6.7	7.0	6.9	6.8	6.9	5.5	- ALAI
- CACM	0.2	0.2	0.2	0.2	0.2	0.2	0.2	0.2	0.2	0.2	- MCC
- Caribbean	0.1	0.1	0.1	0.2	0.2	0.1	0.1	0.1	0.1	0.1	- Caraïbes
- Rest of America	0.0	0.0	0.0	0.0	0.0	0.0	0.0	0.0	0.0	0.0	- Autre d'Amérique
Asia excluding former USSR	33.4	30.1	32.8	30.8	29.4	26.1	28.7	32.0	30.7	33.7	Asie ancienne URSS exclus
- Middle East	2.0	1.9	2.4	2.6	2.7	2.4	2.5	2.6	2.2	2.5	- Moyen-Orient
Asia former USSR	0.0	0.0	0.0	0.1	0.1	0.1	0.1	0.1	0.1	0.1	Asie ancienne URSS
Europe excluding former USSR	44.1	48.2	47.1	46.6	46.5	49.3	46.5	43.3	43.8	43.1	Europe ancienne URSS exclus
- European Union	39.8	43.5	42.7	41.8	42.4	44.2	42.6	39.6	39.8	39.2	- Union Européenne
- Eastern Europe	1.5	1.4	1.4	1.5	1.6	1.6	1.4	1.3	1.4	1.3	- Europe de l'Est
- Rest of Europe	2.7	3.2	3.0	3.3	2.6	3.5	2.5	2.4	2.6	2.6	- Autre de l'Europe
Europe former USSR	0.3	0.5	0.5	0.6	0.6	0.6	0.5	0.5	0.4	0.4	Europe ancienne URSS
Oceania	1.3	1.4	1.3	1.5	1.6	1.5	1.6	1.4	1.2	1.1	Océanie

Acides carboxyliques, leurs anhydrides, halogénures, peroxides et peracides; leurs dérivés 513

TRADE BY COMMODITY (Value in million US dollars)
Exports by principal countries or areas

COMMERCE PAR PRODUIT (Valeur en millions de dollars EU)
Exportations selon les principaux pays ou zones

Country or area	1998	1999	2000	2001	2002	Pays ou zone
World	15138.5	14570.3	16627.1	16506.3	17388.9	Monde
Africa	14.8	25.1	17.1	23.6	28.0	Afrique
Americas	3040.2	3017.1	3478.7	3172.5	3396.4	Amériques
- Northern America	2461.2	2427.4	2767.3	2522.2	2727.3	- Amérique du Nord
- LAIA	577.0	587.2	709.4	647.3	666.5	- ALAI
- CACM	1.2	1.8	1.5	2.7	2.2	- MCC
- Caribbean	0.8	0.6	0.3	0.3	0.3	- Caraïbes
- Rest of America	0.0	0.0	0.0	0.1	0.1	- Autre d'Amérique
Asia excluding former USSR	4571.9	4832.2	6038.8	6150.5	6749.9	Asie ancienne URSS exclus
- Middle East	13.8	12.4	27.0	49.4	48.2	- Moyen-Orient
Asia former USSR	3.0	3.0	3.7	0.9	0.9	Asie ancienne URSS
Europe excluding former USSR	7374.3	6532.2	6885.2	6957.0	7010.3	Europe ancienne URSS exclus
- European Union	6699.3	5889.4	6252.3	6332.5	6364.7	- Union Européenne
- Eastern Europe	209.7	187.1	209.1	222.1	225.9	- Europe de l'Est
- Rest of Europe	465.2	455.7	423.8	402.4	419.7	- Autre de l'Europe
Europe former USSR	118.3	119.2	185.3	172.5	178.1	Europe ancienne URSS
Oceania	16.2	41.5	18.5	29.3	25.3	Océanie
United States	2296.8	2267.0	2589.1	2354.7	2594.0	Etats-Unis d'Amérique
Japan	2031.5	1794.6	1941.7	1762.7	1958.5	Japon
Germany	1572.2	1512.7	1722.8	1656.5	1727.1	Allemagne
Korea, Republic of	697.6	811.1	1140.7	1148.8	1274.6	République de Corée
Netherlands	1064.8	805.8	870.8	1133.5	1071.8	Pays-Bas
Belgium	–	1087.0	1341.4	1112.9	e1248.7	Belgique
United Kingdom	1259.7	791.3	671.4	804.0	741.8	Royaume-Uni
France-Monaco	678.7	673.3	629.6	628.8	603.4	France-Monaco
China	491.2	549.2	650.0	670.5	747.2	Chine
Italy-San Marino-Holy See	467.6	457.2	449.0	447.6	410.1	Italie-Saint-Marin-Saint-Siège
Singapore	255.0	330.1	423.0	511.1	537.6	Singapour
Mexico	364.8	376.8	461.6	417.4	435.7	Mexique
Switzerland-Liechtenstein	399.4	407.9	366.5	358.3	378.2	Suisse-Liechtenstein
Malaysia	158.0	169.2	278.6	455.9	e483.2	Malaisie
Indonesia	201.6	259.1	297.3	290.4	347.2	Indonésie
Spain	244.0	274.2	302.5	282.2	281.5	Espagne
China, Hong Kong SAR	255.6	288.7	308.5	230.6	166.4	Chine - RAS de Hong-Kong
Belgium-Luxembourg	1002.6	–	–	–	–	Belgique-Luxembourg
India	72.7	106.4	225.7	171.0	260.1	Inde
Canada	164.3	160.5	177.6	167.5	133.3	Canada
Thailand	79.9	127.5	164.9	137.0	e144.7	Thaïlande
Ireland	160.3	99.0	95.7	108.4	135.1	Irlande
Brazil	98.9	95.3	122.8	117.2	e121.6	Brésil
Czech Republic	120.6	100.9	107.5	96.7	92.0	République tchèque
Israel	73.2	81.4	74.6	81.0	97.1	Israël
Sweden	127.1	79.2	61.6	51.5	46.8	Suède
Ukraine	57.0	56.8	81.2	66.5	73.3	Ukraine
Russian Federation	24.1	37.1	82.0	88.5	86.4	Fédération de Russie
Argentina	61.2	55.3	55.2	48.6	e47.0	Argentine
Poland	25.9	24.1	42.1	55.1	55.1	Pologne

(Value as percentages of World total) **(Valeur en pourcentage du total mondial)**

Regions of the world	1993	1994	1995	1996	1997	1998	1999	2000	2001	2002	Régions du monde
World	100.0	100.0	100.0	100.0	100.0	100.0	100.0	100.0	100.0	100.0	Monde
Africa	0.1	0.1	0.1	0.1	0.1	0.1	0.2	0.1	0.1	0.2	Afrique
Americas	21.0	20.8	22.0	18.4	20.6	20.1	20.7	20.9	19.2	19.5	Amériques
- Northern America	16.4	16.3	16.3	14.1	16.4	16.3	16.7	16.6	15.3	15.7	- Amérique du Nord
- LAIA	4.5	4.5	5.8	4.3	4.2	3.8	4.0	4.3	3.9	3.8	- ALAI
- CACM	0.0	0.0	0.0	0.0	0.0	0.0	0.0	0.0	0.0	0.0	- MCC
- Caribbean	0.0	0.1	0.0	0.0	0.0	0.0	0.0	0.0	0.0	0.0	- Caraïbes
- Rest of America	0.0	0.0	0.0	0.0	0.0	0.0	0.0	0.0	0.0	0.0	- Autre d'Amérique
Asia excluding former USSR	24.8	25.5	31.3	31.4	30.7	30.2	33.2	36.3	37.3	38.8	Asie ancienne URSS exclus
- Middle East	0.2	0.1	0.2	0.1	0.1	0.1	0.1	0.2	0.3	0.3	- Moyen-Orient
Asia former USSR	0.0	0.1	0.1	0.1	0.0	0.0	0.0	0.0	0.0	0.0	Asie ancienne URSS
Europe excluding former USSR	52.9	52.7	45.8	49.2	47.7	48.7	44.8	41.4	42.1	40.3	Europe ancienne URSS exclus
- European Union	49.1	48.3	41.5	44.8	43.7	44.3	40.4	37.6	38.4	36.6	- Union Européenne
- Eastern Europe	1.0	1.2	1.6	1.4	1.4	1.4	1.3	1.3	1.3	1.3	- Europe de l'Est
- Rest of Europe	2.9	3.2	2.7	3.0	2.5	3.1	3.1	2.5	2.4	2.4	- Autre de l'Europe
Europe former USSR	1.2	0.7	0.7	0.8	1.0	0.8	0.8	1.1	1.0	1.0	Europe ancienne URSS
Oceania	0.0	0.0	0.0	0.1	0.0	0.1	0.3	0.1	0.2	0.1	Océanie

514 Nitrogen-function compounds

TRADE BY COMMODITY (Value in million US dollars) COMMERCE PAR PRODUIT (Valeur en millions de dollars EU)

Imports by principal countries or areas **Importations selon les principaux pays ou zones**

Country or area	1998	1999	2000	2001	2002	Pays ou zone
World	37608.5	39775.8	41719.6	45918.6	40080.7	Monde
Africa	484.1	446.6	469.2	505.0	506.7	Afrique
Americas	8821.9	9851.8	13484.0	13304.8	11450.9	Amériques
- Northern America	6430.7	7671.4	11267.0	11001.1	9433.4	- Amérique du Nord
- LAIA	2311.6	2109.6	2144.1	2221.6	1936.5	- ALAI
- CACM	50.6	40.9	46.9	52.6	55.0	- MCC
- Caribbean	20.8	22.3	18.7	22.4	19.1	- Caraïbes
- Rest of America	8.2	7.5	7.4	7.2	7.0	- Autre d'Amérique
Asia excluding former USSR	6022.1	6753.7	7885.9	7392.5	7938.3	Asie ancienne URSS exclus
- Middle East	590.6	587.0	688.9	544.1	641.5	- Moyen-Orient
Asia former USSR	10.0	14.2	17.0	13.9	11.9	Asie ancienne URSS
Europe excluding former USSR	21603.6	22016.1	19267.2	24107.8	19577.3	Europe ancienne URSS exclus
- European Union	19642.9	20445.2	17343.1	21012.1	16333.8	- Union Européenne
- Eastern Europe	432.4	373.5	419.0	458.5	500.8	- Europe de l'Est
- Rest of Europe	1528.4	1197.4	1505.1	2637.2	2742.7	- Autre de l'Europe
Europe former USSR	158.6	147.5	157.8	172.5	176.7	Europe ancienne URSS
Oceania	508.2	545.9	438.5	422.0	418.8	Océanie
United States	5636.7	6841.3	10396.8	9970.3	8379.3	Etats-Unis d'Amérique
Germany	5832.4	8794.1	5666.7	9027.5	3096.1	Allemagne
France-Monaco	2470.3	2043.6	2267.4	2473.3	2874.5	France-Monaco
United Kingdom	2333.2	2366.9	2035.1	2091.6	2027.8	Royaume-Uni
Japan	1739.9	1997.9	2360.6	2262.6	2408.4	Japon
Belgium	–	1843.4	2264.3	2462.3	e2700.4	Belgique
Italy-San Marino-Holy See	2033.1	1964.3	1735.3	1705.2	1824.4	Italie-Saint-Marin-Saint-Siège
Switzerland-Liechtenstein	1269.3	979.9	1283.8	2397.4	2491.3	Suisse-Liechtenstein
Spain	1041.2	1108.2	1098.5	1153.0	1520.3	Espagne
China	571.7	900.9	1186.4	1170.3	1391.3	Chine
Brazil	993.6	929.5	914.1	953.2	820.0	Brésil
Canada	793.9	829.6	868.7	1026.7	1049.9	Canada
Netherlands	1073.9	915.1	909.4	835.0	803.5	Pays-Bas
Korea, Republic of	549.0	641.5	736.6	714.2	761.4	République de Corée
Mexico	558.3	562.3	599.4	628.9	646.5	Mexique
Belgium-Luxembourg	2981.4	–	–	–	–	Belgique-Luxembourg
Ireland	444.9	567.1	630.1	491.8	647.3	Irlande
Australia	469.8	508.4	400.2	382.2	378.3	Australie
China, Hong Kong SAR	440.1	406.0	480.8	420.5	340.1	Chine - RAS de Hong-Kong
Turkey	431.1	404.2	506.0	332.5	401.6	Turquie
Sweden	794.9	295.3	212.7	235.9	246.2	Suède
Thailand	217.3	254.8	315.2	300.7	e313.3	Thaïlande
India	241.1	267.6	233.1	300.2	348.4	Inde
Argentina	344.6	273.4	254.7	244.7	e108.2	Argentine
Singapore	220.1	272.0	242.1	231.8	237.5	Singapour
Israel	211.4	194.9	219.5	241.2	264.3	Israël
Indonesia	184.9	189.4	230.9	219.9	212.1	Indonésie
Poland	145.4	142.0	173.4	192.1	215.2	Pologne
Malaysia	142.3	153.2	201.1	166.8	e182.3	Malaisie
Colombia	177.9	133.7	141.8	145.7	143.3	Colombie

(Value as percentages of World total) **(Valeur en pourcentage du total mondial)**

Regions of the world	1993	1994	1995	1996	1997	1998	1999	2000	2001	2002	Régions du monde
World	100.0	100.0	100.0	100.0	100.0	100.0	100.0	100.0	100.0	100.0	Monde
Africa	1.5	1.8	1.6	1.7	1.5	1.3	1.1	1.1	1.1	1.3	Afrique
Americas	22.9	22.2	20.8	22.6	24.1	23.5	24.8	32.3	29.0	28.6	Amériques
- Northern America	16.0	15.5	14.5	16.1	16.9	17.1	19.3	27.0	24.0	23.5	- Amérique du Nord
- LAIA	6.7	6.5	6.1	6.2	6.9	6.1	5.3	5.1	4.8	4.8	- ALAI
- CACM	0.1	0.1	0.1	0.1	0.2	0.1	0.1	0.1	0.1	0.1	- MCC
- Caribbean	0.1	0.1	0.1	0.1	0.1	0.1	0.1	0.0	0.0	0.0	- Caraïbes
- Rest of America	0.0	0.0	0.0	0.0	0.0	0.0	0.0	0.0	0.0	0.0	- Autre d'Amérique
Asia excluding former USSR	24.0	22.1	24.2	22.2	21.1	16.0	17.0	18.9	16.1	19.8	Asie ancienne URSS exclus
- Middle East	1.9	1.6	1.9	1.7	2.0	1.6	1.5	1.7	1.2	1.6	- Moyen-Orient
Asia former USSR	0.0	0.0	0.0	0.0	0.0	0.0	0.0	0.0	0.0	0.0	Asie ancienne URSS
Europe excluding former USSR	49.3	51.9	51.5	51.3	51.1	57.4	55.4	46.2	52.5	48.8	Europe ancienne URSS exclus
- European Union	43.9	46.7	46.6	45.7	45.0	52.2	51.4	41.6	45.8	40.8	- Union Européenne
- Eastern Europe	1.2	1.1	1.2	1.3	1.4	1.1	0.9	1.0	1.0	1.2	- Europe de l'Est
- Rest of Europe	4.2	4.0	3.7	4.2	4.8	4.1	3.0	3.6	5.7	6.8	- Autre de l'Europe
Europe former USSR	0.5	0.4	0.4	0.5	0.5	0.4	0.4	0.4	0.4	0.4	Europe ancienne URSS
Oceania	1.6	1.6	1.4	1.7	1.6	1.4	1.4	1.1	0.9	1.0	Océanie

TRADE BY COMMODITY (Value in million US dollars)
Exports by principal countries or areas

COMMERCE PAR PRODUIT (Valeur en millions de dollars EU)
Exportations selon les principaux pays ou zones

Country or area	1998	1999	2000	2001	2002	Pays ou zone
World	31895.3	31812.7	35095.0	34345.3	35244.2	Monde
Africa	78.6	51.2	47.4	47.5	41.3	Afrique
Americas	4476.7	4271.0	4840.1	4575.2	4322.0	Amériques
- Northern America	3950.5	3817.6	4375.1	4179.8	3921.1	- Amérique du Nord
- LAIA	518.4	439.2	459.9	391.8	398.5	- ALAI
- CACM	6.8	14.0	4.5	3.1	1.9	- MCC
- Caribbean	1.1	0.2	0.5	0.4	0.3	- Caraïbes
- Rest of America	0.0	0.1	0.1	0.1	0.1	- Autre d'Amérique
Asia excluding former USSR	5491.9	5857.8	6112.7	5930.7	6433.0	Asie ancienne URSS exclus
- Middle East	38.6	36.8	43.1	50.3	46.7	- Moyen-Orient
Asia former USSR	0.3	0.2	0.2	0.2	0.2	Asie ancienne URSS
Europe excluding former USSR	21781.6	21566.7	23902.0	23703.2	24340.4	Europe ancienne URSS exclus
- European Union	18630.7	18776.5	20879.2	20256.6	20010.8	- Union Européenne
- Eastern Europe	447.3	395.6	461.8	452.3	555.7	- Europe de l'Est
- Rest of Europe	2703.5	2394.5	2561.1	2994.3	3773.9	- Autre de l'Europe
Europe former USSR	47.5	51.0	181.7	76.7	94.5	Europe ancienne URSS
Oceania	18.6	14.7	10.7	11.8	12.9	Océanie
Ireland	5813.7	6263.4	8320.3	7657.5	6429.4	Irlande
United States	3789.9	3653.5	4211.4	3988.8	3708.6	Etats-Unis d'Amérique
Germany	3143.8	3065.5	2849.2	2847.3	3504.5	Allemagne
Switzerland-Liechtenstein	2459.8	2102.0	2234.3	2644.2	3364.6	Suisse-Liechtenstein
United Kingdom	2344.6	2706.1	2221.6	2353.1	2186.3	Royaume-Uni
Japan	2213.2	2424.4	2507.8	2217.2	2392.3	Japon
Belgium	-	2228.1	2816.4	2771.6	e3109.7	Belgique
France-Monaco	1493.4	1586.5	1744.3	1662.4	1508.9	France-Monaco
Italy-San Marino-Holy See	1090.0	1133.2	1144.0	1090.2	1101.4	Italie-Saint-Marin-Saint-Siège
Netherlands	1616.4	912.9	907.2	970.3	1133.6	Pays-Bas
China	682.4	702.7	855.3	977.7	1239.5	Chine
Singapore	616.4	940.7	692.4	706.4	748.4	Singapour
Korea, Republic of	634.4	536.9	672.3	613.4	534.6	République de Corée
Spain	436.3	477.0	462.9	492.1	575.1	Espagne
Belgium-Luxembourg	2276.3	-	-	-	-	Belgique-Luxembourg
Norway	230.4	286.3	317.4	340.5	401.1	Norvège
Indonesia	255.8	227.0	291.0	347.9	305.8	Indonésie
China, Hong Kong SAR	343.9	298.0	282.8	251.4	246.8	Chine - RAS de Hong-Kong
Brazil	329.5	250.0	239.3	206.9	e214.5	Brésil
India	194.3	204.3	241.7	232.3	280.6	Inde
Israel	160.4	158.0	181.3	180.3	259.0	Israël
Sweden	194.1	190.9	181.2	176.5	179.9	Suède
Canada	145.0	148.8	150.7	182.6	203.9	Canada
Hungary	100.4	124.4	127.4	143.1	218.0	Hongrie
Thailand	105.3	112.1	106.8	119.9	e126.7	Thaïlande
Mexico	101.9	104.4	134.5	113.7	112.5	Mexique
Czech Republic	125.3	101.3	121.6	105.4	109.5	République tchèque
Austria	89.1	70.4	76.2	86.1	122.3	Autriche
Finland	65.1	68.6	70.3	71.0	82.7	Finlande
Slovakia	70.8	58.1	59.8	66.9	71.3	Slovaquie

(Value as percentages of World total) **(Valeur en pourcentage du total mondial)**

Regions of the world	1993	1994	1995	1996	1997	1998	1999	2000	2001	2002	Régions du monde
World	100.0	100.0	100.0	100.0	100.0	100.0	100.0	100.0	100.0	100.0	Monde
Africa	0.3	0.1	0.1	0.2	0.2	0.2	0.2	0.1	0.1	0.1	Afrique
Americas	16.6	16.8	16.2	15.1	15.6	14.0	13.4	13.8	13.3	12.3	Amériques
- Northern America	15.1	15.3	14.7	13.3	13.9	12.4	12.0	12.5	12.2	11.1	- Amérique du Nord
- LAIA	1.5	1.5	1.5	1.7	1.7	1.6	1.4	1.3	1.1	1.1	- ALAI
- CACM	0.0	0.0	0.0	0.0	0.0	0.0	0.0	0.0	0.0	0.0	- MCC
- Caribbean	0.0	0.0	0.0	0.0	0.0	0.0	0.0	0.0	0.0	0.0	- Caraïbes
- Rest of America	0.0	0.0	0.0	0.0	0.0	0.0	0.0	0.0	0.0	0.0	- Autre d'Amérique
Asia excluding former USSR	16.6	17.5	19.0	19.4	19.7	17.2	18.4	17.4	17.3	18.3	Asie ancienne URSS exclus
- Middle East	0.2	0.2	0.1	0.1	0.1	0.1	0.1	0.1	0.1	0.1	- Moyen-Orient
Asia former USSR	0.0	0.0	0.0	0.0	0.0	0.0	0.0	0.0	0.0	0.0	Asie ancienne URSS
Europe excluding former USSR	66.1	65.4	64.3	65.1	64.1	68.3	67.8	68.1	69.0	69.1	Europe ancienne URSS exclus
- European Union	54.2	53.2	51.3	52.2	51.6	58.4	59.0	59.5	59.0	56.8	- Union Européenne
- Eastern Europe	1.0	1.0	1.2	1.1	1.5	1.4	1.2	1.3	1.3	1.6	- Europe de l'Est
- Rest of Europe	11.0	11.1	11.8	11.7	11.0	8.5	7.5	7.3	8.7	10.7	- Autre de l'Europe
Europe former USSR	0.3	0.2	0.3	0.2	0.3	0.1	0.2	0.5	0.2	0.3	Europe ancienne URSS
Oceania	0.0	0.0	0.0	0.0	0.1	0.1	0.0	0.0	0.0	0.0	Océanie

515 Organo-inorganic and heterocyclic compounds

TRADE BY COMMODITY (Value in million US dollars)
Imports by principal countries or areas

COMMERCE PAR PRODUIT (Valeur en millions de dollars EU)
Importations selon les principaux pays ou zones

Country or area	1998	1999	2000	2001	2002	Pays ou zone
World	29259.9	33549.2	34182.9	36809.4	41848.5	Monde
Africa	240.7	233.1	196.7	206.9	225.8	Afrique
Americas	9707.5	11712.3	12642.6	14323.2	16517.8	Amériques
- Northern America	7146.4	9303.7	10246.0	11727.9	14400.1	- Amérique du Nord
- LAIA	2506.9	2358.9	2350.7	2548.4	2068.6	- ALAI
- CACM	34.2	31.9	31.1	33.2	34.5	- MCC
- Caribbean	14.4	11.8	12.6	11.4	12.3	- Caraïbes
- Rest of America	5.6	6.1	2.2	2.4	2.1	- Autre d'Amérique
Asia excluding former USSR	5121.1	5805.5	6355.6	6369.8	6435.6	Asie ancienne URSS exclus
- Middle East	444.5	460.9	494.0	452.8	486.5	- Moyen-Orient
Asia former USSR	8.8	11.2	13.7	13.1	10.8	Asie ancienne URSS
Europe excluding former USSR	13559.5	15105.2	14129.9	15315.0	18139.9	Europe ancienne URSS exclus
- European Union	12260.2	13567.4	12702.8	14087.0	16689.0	- Union Européenne
- Eastern Europe	236.9	213.7	255.9	255.7	296.7	- Europe de l'Est
- Rest of Europe	1062.4	1324.1	1171.2	972.3	1154.2	- Autre de l'Europe
Europe former USSR	86.9	74.5	75.7	78.9	78.0	Europe ancienne URSS
Oceania	535.4	607.4	768.9	502.5	440.8	Océanie
United States	6525.3	8525.1	9587.3	11023.2	13748.8	Etats-Unis d'Amérique
France-Monaco	2456.1	3005.6	3429.3	2837.0	2776.2	France-Monaco
United Kingdom	2304.6	1898.4	2063.9	2499.6	3807.2	Royaume-Uni
Japan	1800.5	2303.3	2345.0	2626.0	2527.5	Japon
Italy-San Marino-Holy See	1734.4	1896.1	2159.4	1930.6	2246.6	Italie-Saint-Marin-Saint-Siège
Germany	1816.4	1770.7	1669.8	2036.5	2508.7	Allemagne
Belgium	–	1985.2	1001.1	1848.3	e2027.0	Belgique
Brazil	1170.9	1080.1	1018.3	1093.7	836.5	Brésil
Switzerland-Liechtenstein	927.9	1209.8	1042.1	847.4	1019.1	Suisse-Liechtenstein
Spain	800.4	813.2	701.8	787.4	961.2	Espagne
Korea, Republic of	659.6	763.4	897.8	734.4	778.8	République de Corée
Canada	621.0	778.6	658.7	704.7	651.3	Canada
China	423.1	521.5	732.7	783.0	805.1	Chine
Netherlands	600.3	565.6	494.1	755.7	712.2	Pays-Bas
Mexico	437.2	504.2	534.4	672.2	733.6	Mexique
Ireland	456.0	513.9	375.3	448.6	820.6	Irlande
Australia	477.6	555.1	714.5	455.2	402.6	Australie
Sweden	42.6	669.8	438.8	536.7	367.7	Suède
Argentina	492.2	423.9	427.1	433.3	e191.7	Argentine
Belgium-Luxembourg	1610.6	–	–	–	–	Belgique-Luxembourg
Turkey	281.4	301.2	349.2	320.5	345.7	Turquie
Indonesia	259.1	265.0	296.2	296.0	267.3	Indonésie
Singapore	200.2	177.5	151.2	174.8	203.0	Singapour
Thailand	163.9	175.4	176.7	181.0	e188.5	Thaïlande
Colombia	213.5	152.4	166.3	158.6	136.5	Colombie
Malaysia	144.3	144.2	154.0	162.5	e177.6	Malaisie
China, Hong Kong SAR	202.8	181.1	150.0	124.9	94.5	Chine - RAS de Hong-Kong
Austria	115.9	125.7	111.5	123.1	132.7	Autriche
India	103.9	105.3	101.8	115.3	137.1	Inde
Greece	114.1	104.9	97.7	93.8	e103.7	Grèce

(Value as percentages of World total) **(Valeur en pourcentage du total mondial)**

Regions of the world	1993	1994	1995	1996	1997	1998	1999	2000	2001	2002	Régions du monde
World	100.0	100.0	100.0	100.0	100.0	100.0	100.0	100.0	100.0	100.0	Monde
Africa	1.4	1.5	1.3	1.2	1.1	0.8	0.7	0.6	0.6	0.5	Afrique
Americas	23.9	25.5	25.6	26.6	31.4	33.2	34.9	37.0	38.9	39.5	Amériques
- Northern America	15.8	16.7	17.3	18.8	22.8	24.4	27.7	30.0	31.9	34.4	- Amérique du Nord
- LAIA	7.6	8.5	8.0	7.7	8.4	8.6	7.0	6.9	6.9	4.9	- ALAI
- CACM	0.2	0.2	0.1	0.1	0.1	0.1	0.1	0.1	0.1	0.1	- MCC
- Caribbean	0.2	0.1	0.1	0.0	0.1	0.0	0.0	0.0	0.0	0.0	- Caraïbes
- Rest of America	0.0	0.0	0.0	0.0	0.0	0.0	0.0	0.0	0.0	0.0	- Autre d'Amérique
Asia excluding former USSR	25.6	24.1	24.8	23.0	20.7	17.5	17.3	18.6	17.3	15.4	Asie ancienne URSS exclus
- Middle East	1.8	1.8	1.8	1.6	1.6	1.5	1.4	1.4	1.2	1.2	- Moyen-Orient
Asia former USSR	0.0	0.0	0.0	0.0	0.0	0.0	0.0	0.0	0.0	0.0	Asie ancienne URSS
Europe excluding former USSR	46.5	46.3	46.0	46.6	44.6	46.3	45.0	41.3	41.6	43.3	Europe ancienne URSS exclus
- European Union	42.3	41.8	41.8	42.4	40.5	41.9	40.4	37.2	38.3	39.9	- Union Européenne
- Eastern Europe	0.9	0.9	1.0	0.9	0.9	0.8	0.6	0.7	0.7	0.7	- Europe de l'Est
- Rest of Europe	3.3	3.6	3.3	3.3	3.3	3.6	3.9	3.4	2.6	2.8	- Autre de l'Europe
Europe former USSR	0.6	0.3	0.4	0.4	0.4	0.3	0.2	0.2	0.2	0.2	Europe ancienne URSS
Oceania	1.9	2.3	1.9	2.1	1.8	1.8	1.8	2.2	1.4	1.1	Océanie

TRADE BY COMMODITY (Value in million US dollars)
Exports by principal countries or areas

COMMERCE PAR PRODUIT (Valeur en millions de dollars EU)
Exportations selon les principaux pays ou zones

Country or area	1998	1999	2000	2001	2002	Pays ou zone
World	26797.4	29356.7	31343.5	32754.9	35799.4	Monde
Africa	30.4	20.5	21.7	21.6	17.1	Afrique
Americas	3575.2	3653.6	4091.0	3979.2	3423.9	Amériques
- Northern America	3251.4	3346.2	3838.5	3712.1	3136.8	- Amérique du Nord
- LAIA	305.2	283.4	221.2	253.0	266.7	- ALAI
- CACM	1.1	0.8	1.0	1.3	1.7	- MCC
- Caribbean	17.5	23.3	30.2	12.8	18.7	- Caraïbes
- Rest of America	0.0	0.0	0.0	0.0	0.0	- Autre d'Amérique
Asia excluding former USSR	4255.8	4701.6	4662.8	5271.8	6204.1	Asie ancienne URSS exclus
- Middle East	7.0	14.0	10.8	7.1	8.1	- Moyen-Orient
Asia former USSR	3.3	1.9	0.7	0.9	0.3	Asie ancienne URSS
Europe excluding former USSR	18671.8	20700.7	22295.8	23182.4	25841.0	Europe ancienne URSS exclus
- European Union	16517.1	18728.5	20190.2	20980.5	23036.9	- Union Européenne
- Eastern Europe	290.1	236.4	320.8	319.1	387.1	- Europe de l'Est
- Rest of Europe	1864.6	1735.9	1784.8	1882.8	2417.0	- Autre de l'Europe
Europe former USSR	251.9	263.6	254.5	288.6	301.2	Europe ancienne URSS
Oceania	8.9	14.7	17.0	10.5	11.8	Océanie
Ireland	5165.4	5472.1	6737.3	7297.0	9931.0	Irlande
Germany	3213.8	3281.4	3588.9	3924.1	2932.9	Allemagne
United States	3178.8	3280.8	3769.6	3628.7	3065.8	Etats-Unis d'Amérique
France-Monaco	1986.4	2564.2	2956.1	2488.7	2551.3	France-Monaco
United Kingdom	2162.4	2619.9	2604.0	2483.7	2447.6	Royaume-Uni
Japan	2075.0	2038.7	2191.9	2169.6	2097.8	Japon
Switzerland-Liechtenstein	1834.8	1706.4	1753.4	1850.4	2378.8	Suisse-Liechtenstein
Belgium	–	2204.8	1769.7	2032.3	e2280.2	Belgique
Singapore	748.0	1267.3	952.6	1426.8	2326.0	Singapour
Italy-San Marino-Holy See	813.2	847.6	784.5	801.1	868.9	Italie-Saint-Marin-Saint-Siège
Netherlands	587.8	697.5	718.8	935.2	838.0	Pays-Bas
China	605.7	602.7	677.0	781.6	871.1	Chine
Spain	414.6	410.3	421.1	444.6	439.5	Espagne
Belgium-Luxembourg	1737.9	–	–	–	–	Belgique-Luxembourg
Austria	257.8	409.5	298.6	290.5	304.2	Autriche
Israel	185.9	216.3	237.0	319.3	324.8	Israël
Denmark	87.5	135.3	225.1	226.1	354.0	Danemark
Russian Federation	169.3	183.5	239.2	203.1	206.2	Fédération de Russie
Korea, Republic of	242.5	186.5	181.4	159.0	173.8	République de Corée
India	97.8	114.6	172.9	173.7	180.1	Inde
China, Hong Kong SAR	184.1	160.9	124.7	94.4	74.7	Chine - RAS de Hong-Kong
Mexico	69.3	123.4	112.7	128.4	135.8	Mexique
Poland	114.3	102.9	125.4	103.9	105.2	Pologne
Brazil	118.6	98.3	68.2	89.5	e92.8	Brésil
Hungary	57.6	42.4	67.2	90.0	131.1	Hongrie
Canada	72.6	65.4	69.0	83.3	69.4	Canada
Czech Republic	60.9	52.5	63.6	60.5	82.2	République tchèque
Belarus	61.9	67.4	3.9	63.7	71.2	Bélarus
Slovakia	40.4	37.1	56.5	55.6	61.1	Slovaquie
Sweden	52.1	48.8	50.3	40.3	55.1	Suède

(Value as percentages of World total) **(Valeur en pourcentage du total mondial)**

Regions of the world	1993	1994	1995	1996	1997	1998	1999	2000	2001	2002	Régions du monde
World	100.0	100.0	100.0	100.0	100.0	100.0	100.0	100.0	100.0	100.0	Monde
Africa	0.2	0.1	0.2	0.2	0.1	0.1	0.1	0.1	0.1	0.0	Afrique
Americas	13.1	12.4	13.6	13.9	15.5	13.3	12.4	13.1	12.1	9.6	Amériques
- Northern America	12.0	11.4	12.4	12.6	14.2	12.1	11.4	12.2	11.3	8.8	- Amérique du Nord
- LAIA	1.0	0.9	1.2	1.2	1.2	1.1	1.0	0.7	0.8	0.7	- ALAI
- CACM	0.0	0.0	0.0	0.0	0.0	0.0	0.0	0.0	0.0	0.0	- MCC
- Caribbean	0.1	0.1	0.1	0.1	0.1	0.1	0.1	0.1	0.0	0.1	- Caraïbes
- Rest of America	0.0	0.0	0.0	0.0	0.0	0.0	0.0	0.0	0.0	0.0	- Autre d'Amérique
Asia excluding former USSR	20.9	18.3	19.6	18.6	17.8	15.9	16.0	14.9	16.1	17.3	Asie ancienne URSS exclus
- Middle East	0.0	0.1	0.1	0.1	0.1	0.0	0.0	0.0	0.0	0.0	- Moyen-Orient
Asia former USSR	0.0	0.0	0.0	0.0	0.0	0.0	0.0	0.0	0.0	0.0	Asie ancienne URSS
Europe excluding former USSR	64.7	67.9	65.0	65.9	64.9	69.7	70.5	71.1	70.8	72.2	Europe ancienne URSS exclus
- European Union	54.8	58.2	54.4	55.7	55.9	61.6	63.8	64.4	64.1	64.4	- Union Européenne
- Eastern Europe	1.2	1.0	1.3	1.4	1.3	1.1	0.8	1.0	1.0	1.1	- Europe de l'Est
- Rest of Europe	8.6	8.7	9.3	8.9	7.7	7.0	5.9	5.7	5.7	6.8	- Autre de l'Europe
Europe former USSR	0.9	1.1	1.4	1.3	1.5	0.9	0.9	0.8	0.9	0.8	Europe ancienne URSS
Oceania	0.1	0.1	0.1	0.1	0.1	0.0	0.1	0.1	0.0	0.0	Océanie

516 Other organic chemicals

TRADE BY COMMODITY (Value in million US dollars)
Imports by principal countries or areas

COMMERCE PAR PRODUIT (Valeur en millions de dollars EU)
Importations selon les principaux pays ou zones

Country or area	1998	1999	2000	2001	2002	Pays ou zone
World	12487.6	12933.2	14483.8	14140.9	14261.5	Monde
Africa	164.8	159.8	147.9	154.3	166.3	Afrique
Americas	3574.4	3721.2	4356.1	4273.2	3937.1	Amériques
- Northern America	2576.4	2727.3	3297.5	3253.5	3035.4	- Amérique du Nord
- LAIA	939.6	933.3	992.9	961.6	840.6	- ALAI
- CACM	31.8	30.3	33.1	34.7	36.0	- MCC
- Caribbean	24.3	27.9	29.9	20.9	22.7	- Caraïbes
- Rest of America	2.3	2.4	2.6	2.5	2.5	- Autre d'Amérique
Asia excluding former USSR	2654.5	2831.7	3450.1	3224.1	3524.5	Asie ancienne URSS exclus
- Middle East	250.3	234.9	263.7	268.6	331.7	- Moyen-Orient
Asia former USSR	14.8	14.6	15.1	13.5	12.5	Asie ancienne URSS
Europe excluding former USSR	5862.4	5981.6	6305.8	6264.4	6405.9	Europe ancienne URSS exclus
- European Union	5061.3	5197.0	5475.9	5414.0	5486.6	- Union Européenne
- Eastern Europe	222.1	204.2	232.9	238.5	310.0	- Europe de l'Est
- Rest of Europe	579.0	580.4	597.1	612.0	609.3	- Autre de l'Europe
Europe former USSR	102.5	93.8	91.5	110.1	112.2	Europe ancienne URSS
Oceania	114.2	130.6	117.2	101.2	103.0	Océanie
United States	2239.5	2385.6	2933.7	2773.0	2534.7	Etats-Unis d'Amérique
Germany	853.4	895.0	1019.0	1001.7	1003.4	Allemagne
Netherlands	668.1	732.6	810.3	836.9	819.5	Pays-Bas
France-Monaco	691.1	691.2	725.3	701.6	670.2	France-Monaco
United Kingdom	661.7	665.3	630.9	617.3	637.0	Royaume-Uni
Italy-San Marino-Holy See	529.6	568.8	664.8	616.1	592.3	Italie-Saint-Marin-Saint-Siège
Belgium	–	690.8	692.2	687.9	e754.5	Belgique
Japan	430.9	506.1	519.8	472.7	505.0	Japon
China	351.8	348.3	522.5	546.6	617.7	Chine
Switzerland-Liechtenstein	478.4	473.6	470.8	452.6	489.1	Suisse-Liechtenstein
Canada	336.5	341.3	363.8	480.4	500.5	Canada
Spain	373.5	402.5	387.5	397.2	429.2	Espagne
Mexico	378.2	415.2	449.1	382.5	333.7	Mexique
Korea, Republic of	229.2	308.7	382.7	350.4	375.9	République de Corée
India	281.7	271.3	277.3	336.3	431.2	Inde
Singapore	224.4	215.9	326.1	277.4	250.3	Singapour
Brazil	229.8	229.1	246.8	251.7	245.3	Brésil
Thailand	128.1	152.9	167.5	172.1	e179.3	Thaïlande
Belgium-Luxembourg	731.3	–	–	–	–	Belgique-Luxembourg
Indonesia	78.8	110.4	149.1	112.0	102.8	Indonésie
Ireland	103.9	120.1	91.9	104.7	107.7	Irlande
Finland	96.0	92.2	114.1	112.2	104.5	Finlande
China, Hong Kong SAR	116.6	92.5	112.7	88.3	95.2	Chine - RAS de Hong-Kong
Argentina	119.9	107.6	102.5	104.2	e46.1	Argentine
Australia	98.4	113.9	98.3	80.5	83.2	Australie
Venezuela	100.4	87.7	78.6	103.7	e87.2	Venezuela
Denmark	97.8	85.8	76.7	91.4	100.2	Danemark
Turkey	84.5	81.8	83.9	77.2	100.9	Turquie
Sweden	93.9	86.3	79.3	76.6	87.7	Suède
Malaysia	56.6	71.5	100.7	92.0	e100.5	Malaisie

(Value as percentages of World total) **(Valeur en pourcentage du total mondial)**

Regions of the world	1993	1994	1995	1996	1997	1998	1999	2000	2001	2002	Régions du monde
World	100.0	100.0	100.0	100.0	100.0	100.0	100.0	100.0	100.0	100.0	Monde
Africa	1.6	1.5	1.3	1.3	1.5	1.3	1.2	1.0	1.1	1.2	Afrique
Americas	22.1	24.3	25.4	26.0	27.6	28.6	28.8	30.1	30.2	27.6	Amériques
- Northern America	15.8	17.7	18.2	19.3	20.6	20.6	21.1	22.8	23.0	21.3	- Amérique du Nord
- LAIA	5.9	6.3	6.8	6.2	6.5	7.5	7.2	6.9	6.8	5.9	- ALAI
- CACM	0.3	0.2	0.2	0.2	0.3	0.3	0.2	0.2	0.2	0.3	- MCC
- Caribbean	0.2	0.1	0.2	0.2	0.2	0.2	0.2	0.2	0.1	0.2	- Caraïbes
- Rest of America	0.0	0.0	0.0	0.0	0.0	0.0	0.0	0.0	0.0	0.0	- Autre d'Amérique
Asia excluding former USSR	24.5	22.7	23.8	23.8	23.3	21.3	21.9	23.8	22.8	24.7	Asie ancienne URSS exclus
- Middle East	1.4	1.6	1.9	2.1	2.4	2.0	1.8	1.8	1.9	2.3	- Moyen-Orient
Asia former USSR	0.0	0.1	0.1	0.1	0.1	0.1	0.1	0.1	0.1	0.1	Asie ancienne URSS
Europe excluding former USSR	50.4	49.5	47.7	46.9	45.8	46.9	46.2	43.5	44.3	44.9	Europe ancienne URSS exclus
- European Union	43.8	42.9	41.2	40.2	39.6	40.5	40.2	37.8	38.3	38.5	- Union Européenne
- Eastern Europe	1.5	1.6	1.7	1.7	1.7	1.8	1.6	1.6	1.7	2.2	- Europe de l'Est
- Rest of Europe	5.1	5.1	4.9	5.0	4.5	4.6	4.5	4.1	4.3	4.3	- Autre de l'Europe
Europe former USSR	0.4	0.7	0.6	0.8	0.9	0.8	0.7	0.6	0.8	0.8	Europe ancienne URSS
Oceania	1.0	1.2	1.0	1.1	0.9	0.9	1.0	0.8	0.7	0.7	Océanie

TRADE BY COMMODITY (Value in million US dollars)
Exports by principal countries or areas

COMMERCE PAR PRODUIT (Valeur en millions de dollars EU)
Exportations selon les principaux pays ou zones

Country or area	1998	1999	2000	2001	2002	Pays ou zone
World	12189.1	12257.8	13871.7	13584.0	14410.3	Monde
Africa	100.4	99.4	88.9	97.4	107.3	Afrique
Americas	2538.2	2590.9	3289.2	3254.5	3188.0	Amériques
- Northern America	2163.5	2261.0	2801.0	2772.5	2690.1	- Amérique du Nord
- LAIA	355.2	326.3	482.9	477.0	492.1	- ALAI
- CACM	2.5	3.0	3.6	3.6	3.6	- MCC
- Caribbean	17.0	0.7	1.8	1.4	2.2	- Caraïbes
- Rest of America	0.0	0.0	0.0	0.0	0.1	- Autre d'Amérique
Asia excluding former USSR	2892.7	3033.4	3641.1	3540.3	3862.2	Asie ancienne URSS exclus
- Middle East	530.8	611.4	779.0	726.4	679.7	- Moyen-Orient
Asia former USSR	0.8	1.0	3.3	2.2	2.9	Asie ancienne URSS
Europe excluding former USSR	6542.0	6433.5	6688.9	6521.8	7102.5	Europe ancienne URSS exclus
- European Union	6024.9	5922.6	6176.4	6047.1	6613.3	- Union Européenne
- Eastern Europe	140.9	112.3	145.8	120.5	122.4	- Europe de l'Est
- Rest of Europe	376.3	398.6	366.8	354.2	366.8	- Autre de l'Europe
Europe former USSR	95.4	84.5	145.9	151.8	132.2	Europe ancienne URSS
Oceania	19.7	15.1	14.3	16.0	15.2	Océanie
United States	1881.4	1966.5	2408.2	2318.0	2385.7	Etats-Unis d'Amérique
Germany	1549.5	1597.6	1659.7	1566.1	1725.0	Allemagne
Netherlands	1168.5	869.5	1066.6	1297.2	1368.8	Pays-Bas
Japan	766.3	899.5	947.5	849.7	898.6	Japon
France-Monaco	683.0	722.6	715.2	629.5	779.1	France-Monaco
United Kingdom	721.1	697.4	607.8	598.9	655.8	Royaume-Uni
Saudi Arabia	505.8	578.1	738.6	678.3	e611.3	Arabie saoudite
Belgium	–	653.0	734.9	642.0	e720.3	Belgique
India	419.8	464.9	529.4	538.5	698.1	Inde
China	477.6	345.6	435.4	454.7	597.0	Chine
Denmark	424.7	432.7	414.9	470.3	482.7	Danemark
Switzerland-Liechtenstein	370.8	392.5	359.3	345.3	358.1	Suisse-Liechtenstein
Canada	282.1	294.5	392.7	454.5	304.4	Canada
Singapore	218.5	218.6	293.0	301.6	294.8	Singapour
Italy-San Marino-Holy See	189.0	216.6	220.3	214.0	259.8	Italie-Saint-Marin-Saint-Siège
Spain	152.4	171.1	179.6	190.5	216.2	Espagne
Brazil	136.0	156.8	221.2	185.9	e192.7	Brésil
Finland	163.1	170.1	171.2	175.9	195.9	Finlande
Ireland	169.5	266.2	254.4	121.5	56.8	Irlande
Venezuela	108.7	54.0	144.0	182.3	e193.7	Venezuela
Belgium-Luxembourg	668.5	–	–	–	–	Belgique-Luxembourg
Korea, Republic of	110.3	115.1	142.3	130.7	122.1	République de Corée
Russian Federation	78.4	73.1	134.1	142.3	120.3	Fédération de Russie
Malaysia	45.8	61.4	165.5	112.5	e119.2	Malaisie
China, Hong Kong SAR	89.1	86.4	97.3	90.9	85.7	Chine - RAS de Hong-Kong
Israel	80.3	72.3	66.0	105.5	116.2	Israël
Austria	79.5	75.7	75.1	84.3	98.7	Autriche
Mexico	71.4	66.5	68.4	67.7	68.0	Mexique
South Africa	–	–	86.5	91.9	104.3	Afrique du Sud
Slovakia	52.7	44.2	62.1	43.7	39.1	Slovaquie

(Value as percentages of World total) **(Valeur en pourcentage du total mondial)**

Regions of the world	1993	1994	1995	1996	1997	1998	1999	2000	2001	2002	Régions du monde
World	100.0	100.0	100.0	100.0	100.0	100.0	100.0	100.0	100.0	100.0	Monde
Africa	0.5	0.6	0.6	0.8	0.7	0.8	0.8	0.6	0.7	0.7	Afrique
Americas	22.5	21.4	20.8	20.6	20.2	20.8	21.1	23.7	24.0	22.1	Amériques
- Northern America	19.4	18.5	18.0	18.7	18.4	17.7	18.4	20.2	20.4	18.7	- Amérique du Nord
- LAIA	3.1	2.9	2.7	1.8	1.7	2.9	2.7	3.5	3.5	3.4	- ALAI
- CACM	0.0	0.0	0.0	0.0	0.0	0.0	0.0	0.0	0.0	0.0	- MCC
- Caribbean	0.0	0.1	0.1	0.1	0.1	0.1	0.0	0.0	0.0	0.0	- Caraïbes
- Rest of America	0.0	0.0	0.0	0.0	0.0	0.0	0.0	0.0	0.0	0.0	- Autre d'Amérique
Asia excluding former USSR	17.4	19.6	22.4	22.5	23.0	23.7	24.7	26.2	26.1	26.8	Asie ancienne URSS exclus
- Middle East	0.9	2.5	5.0	4.5	4.3	4.4	5.0	5.6	5.3	4.7	- Moyen-Orient
Asia former USSR	0.0	0.1	0.0	0.0	0.0	0.0	0.0	0.0	0.0	0.0	Asie ancienne URSS
Europe excluding former USSR	58.8	57.7	55.5	55.4	55.3	53.7	52.5	48.2	48.0	49.3	Europe ancienne URSS exclus
- European Union	53.9	53.0	50.9	50.9	50.9	49.4	48.3	44.5	44.5	45.9	- Union Européenne
- Eastern Europe	1.2	1.1	1.3	1.3	1.3	1.2	0.9	1.1	0.9	0.8	- Europe de l'Est
- Rest of Europe	3.7	3.6	3.3	3.2	3.1	3.1	3.3	2.6	2.6	2.5	- Autre de l'Europe
Europe former USSR	0.6	0.5	0.5	0.5	0.6	0.8	0.7	1.1	1.1	0.9	Europe ancienne URSS
Oceania	0.1	0.2	0.1	0.2	0.2	0.2	0.1	0.1	0.1	0.1	Océanie

522 Inorganic chemical elements, oxides and halogen salts

TRADE BY COMMODITY (Value in million US dollars)
Imports by principal countries or areas

COMMERCE PAR PRODUIT (Valeur en millions de dollars EU)
Importations selon les principaux pays ou zones

Country or area	1998	1999	2000	2001	2002	Pays ou zone
World	18827.3	17495.4	18725.1	19329.5	18559.6	Monde
Africa	626.8	555.5	521.4	569.3	584.5	Afrique
Americas	4221.7	3905.3	4492.3	4818.5	4382.8	Amériques
- Northern America	3066.0	2896.4	3352.9	3499.4	3245.3	- Amérique du Nord
- LAIA	885.9	798.4	959.9	1107.0	951.6	- ALAI
- CACM	74.9	71.1	73.5	82.5	79.7	- MCC
- Caribbean	141.1	116.4	98.2	121.3	97.3	- Caraïbes
- Rest of America	53.7	22.9	7.9	8.3	8.9	- Autre d'Amérique
Asia excluding former USSR	5596.1	5726.7	6137.9	5973.5	6002.3	Asie ancienne URSS exclus
- Middle East	683.9	695.4	683.2	708.4	759.6	- Moyen-Orient
Asia former USSR	286.6	245.3	249.2	260.5	273.1	Asie ancienne URSS
Europe excluding former USSR	7481.0	6508.1	6673.8	7001.9	6775.7	Europe ancienne URSS exclus
- European Union	6660.2	5741.4	5901.3	6191.5	5930.6	- Union Européenne
- Eastern Europe	387.4	369.4	397.4	431.5	459.3	- Europe de l'Est
- Rest of Europe	433.4	397.2	375.0	378.9	385.7	- Autre de l'Europe
Europe former USSR	236.2	229.9	261.5	237.4	251.3	Europe ancienne URSS
Oceania	379.0	324.6	389.0	468.5	289.9	Océanie
United States	2484.7	2369.3	2809.0	2977.3	2760.0	Etats-Unis d'Amérique
Japan	1238.0	1152.3	1335.1	1174.5	1138.5	Japon
Germany	1247.8	1065.3	1080.5	1227.8	1138.1	Allemagne
India	1186.7	1238.7	1004.8	1078.3	1013.7	Inde
France-Monaco	1033.7	874.7	912.4	837.7	853.1	France-Monaco
United Kingdom	853.0	733.5	714.7	744.7	655.1	Royaume-Uni
Korea, Republic of	506.7	587.8	710.9	685.3	642.3	République de Corée
Italy-San Marino-Holy See	651.5	584.8	608.3	635.5	598.3	Italie-Saint-Marin-Saint-Siège
Netherlands	683.0	572.8	565.9	547.7	620.4	Pays-Bas
Canada	580.9	525.3	543.3	521.3	484.6	Canada
Belgium	–	607.5	628.6	616.4	e676.0	Belgique
Spain	492.9	444.6	487.1	483.0	480.5	Espagne
China	318.9	356.4	471.6	516.0	615.6	Chine
Brazil	301.6	248.2	316.5	391.6	367.7	Brésil
Australia	320.6	266.2	340.2	414.3	237.2	Australie
Mexico	240.0	269.4	333.7	345.5	298.9	Mexique
Turkey	272.2	221.1	273.2	205.0	250.6	Turquie
Tajikistan	e238.1	e205.0	198.8	e214.1	e228.5	Tadjikistan
United Arab Emirates	181.7	190.4	180.5	250.0	e256.5	Emirates arabes unis
Singapore	171.3	194.8	223.8	224.4	234.5	Singapour
Austria	227.4	185.7	183.1	235.1	183.6	Autriche
China, Hong Kong SAR	218.7	186.5	207.3	166.5	176.8	Chine - RAS de Hong-Kong
Malaysia	206.5	198.0	205.0	163.1	e178.2	Malaisie
Sweden	237.2	138.3	160.6	217.0	168.5	Suède
Indonesia	169.8	187.0	193.6	190.0	174.1	Indonésie
Finland	204.6	154.6	164.2	226.5	155.4	Finlande
Thailand	131.4	153.5	191.8	207.0	e215.7	Thaïlande
Norway	168.9	152.1	128.0	136.1	132.2	Norvège
Denmark	140.6	130.3	134.6	161.4	138.3	Danemark
Switzerland-Liechtenstein	153.7	136.0	133.2	129.3	135.1	Suisse-Liechtenstein

(Value as percentages of World total) **(Valeur en pourcentage du total mondial)**

Regions of the world	1993	1994	1995	1996	1997	1998	1999	2000	2001	2002	Régions du monde
World	100.0	100.0	100.0	100.0	100.0	100.0	100.0	100.0	100.0	100.0	Monde
Africa	4.2	3.1	2.9	3.0	3.2	3.3	3.2	2.8	2.9	3.1	Afrique
Americas	21.4	23.3	22.6	22.1	22.9	22.4	22.3	24.0	24.9	23.6	Amériques
- Northern America	15.3	17.5	16.7	16.5	17.5	16.3	16.6	17.9	18.1	17.5	- Amérique du Nord
- LAIA	4.6	4.7	4.6	4.5	4.4	4.7	4.6	5.1	5.7	5.1	- ALAI
- CACM	0.4	0.4	0.4	0.3	0.4	0.4	0.4	0.4	0.4	0.4	- MCC
- Caribbean	0.5	0.4	0.6	0.7	0.6	0.7	0.7	0.5	0.6	0.5	- Caraïbes
- Rest of America	0.6	0.3	0.4	0.1	0.1	0.3	0.1	0.0	0.0	0.0	- Autre d'Amérique
Asia excluding former USSR	31.5	29.7	29.4	30.2	31.6	29.7	32.7	32.8	30.9	32.3	Asie ancienne URSS exclus
- Middle East	3.8	3.0	3.1	3.1	2.9	3.6	4.0	3.6	3.7	4.1	- Moyen-Orient
Asia former USSR	0.0	0.3	0.5	0.4	0.2	1.5	1.4	1.3	1.3	1.5	Asie ancienne URSS
Europe excluding former USSR	40.5	41.0	40.9	40.1	38.8	39.7	37.2	35.6	36.2	36.5	Europe ancienne URSS exclus
- European Union	35.9	37.0	36.8	36.0	34.6	35.4	32.8	31.5	32.0	32.0	- Union Européenne
- Eastern Europe	2.3	1.9	1.8	2.0	2.0	2.1	2.1	2.1	2.2	2.5	- Europe de l'Est
- Rest of Europe	2.3	2.2	2.3	2.1	2.2	2.3	2.3	2.0	2.0	2.1	- Autre de l'Europe
Europe former USSR	0.4	1.1	1.2	1.5	1.5	1.3	1.3	1.4	1.2	1.4	Europe ancienne URSS
Oceania	2.1	1.5	2.5	2.6	1.8	2.0	1.9	2.1	2.4	1.6	Océanie

TRADE BY COMMODITY (Value in million US dollars)
Exports by principal countries or areas

COMMERCE PAR PRODUIT (Valeur en millions de dollars EU)
Exportations selon les principaux pays ou zones

Country or area	1998	1999	2000	2001	2002	Pays ou zone
World	15996.4	15196.3	16368.8	16646.1	16411.0	Monde
Africa	1367.5	1502.2	1418.6	1385.9	1601.0	Afrique
Americas	3741.1	3629.6	4228.4	4186.9	3910.3	Amériques
- Northern America	2592.5	2548.5	2935.1	2883.2	2710.8	- Amérique du Nord
- LAIA	878.1	755.2	896.0	827.6	825.8	- ALAI
- CACM	12.8	16.7	15.5	20.0	24.8	- MCC
- Caribbean	256.7	305.1	377.7	452.1	345.6	- Caraïbes
- Rest of America	1.0	4.0	4.1	4.1	3.3	- Autre d'Amérique
Asia excluding former USSR	3888.4	3883.8	4319.5	4468.8	4504.1	Asie ancienne URSS exclus
- Middle East	568.0	554.4	371.4	639.3	601.5	- Moyen-Orient
Asia former USSR	220.1	196.1	63.1	58.9	59.8	Asie ancienne URSS
Europe excluding former USSR	5837.4	5126.6	5216.9	5573.4	5437.9	Europe ancienne URSS exclus
- European Union	5110.7	4497.3	4511.8	4799.8	4714.9	- Union Européenne
- Eastern Europe	390.4	303.3	342.3	382.1	345.5	- Europe de l'Est
- Rest of Europe	336.3	326.0	362.8	391.5	377.5	- Autre de l'Europe
Europe former USSR	793.6	693.3	920.9	774.0	706.5	Europe ancienne URSS
Oceania	148.4	164.5	201.4	198.1	191.5	Océanie
United States	1808.1	1855.4	2166.5	2185.5	1997.5	Etats-Unis d'Amérique
Germany	1920.6	1760.9	1773.6	1851.2	1846.2	Allemagne
China	1164.3	1057.4	1315.6	1323.1	1397.8	Chine
Japan	1054.7	1178.4	1323.5	1183.0	1248.6	Japon
Canada	784.4	693.2	768.5	697.4	713.0	Canada
Netherlands	727.7	547.8	503.3	521.8	504.2	Pays-Bas
Morocco	499.2	588.9	507.5	453.0	e492.8	Maroc
Belgium	-	576.4	551.4	635.5	e713.1	Belgique
Russian Federation	477.8	414.8	579.2	533.2	449.0	Fédération de Russie
United Kingdom	609.5	374.1	397.5	565.9	480.7	Royaume-Uni
France-Monaco	499.3	467.7	505.2	484.5	440.0	France-Monaco
Trinidad and Tobago	249.1	294.8	361.3	439.5	e333.6	Trinité-et-Tobago
South Africa	-	-	438.8	423.2	452.3	Afrique du Sud
Saudi Arabia	347.8	238.1	125.3	307.7	e277.3	Arabie saoudite
Norway	212.0	229.1	263.0	282.2	279.2	Norvège
Italy-San Marino-Holy See	269.3	252.1	254.4	233.0	239.2	Italie-Saint-Marin-Saint-Siège
Brazil	237.1	231.5	268.5	224.2	e232.5	Brésil
Israel	253.6	266.7	244.4	228.1	185.5	Israël
Korea, Republic of	199.6	205.3	266.1	273.0	230.5	République de Corée
Ukraine	265.4	216.5	264.1	196.8	216.9	Ukraine
Mexico	231.9	194.8	240.5	200.9	203.3	Mexique
Tunisia	246.6	230.7	178.6	166.1	e172.7	Tunisie
Chile	225.4	178.9	190.0	189.4	e185.3	Chili
Australia	146.7	163.2	200.4	196.7	190.5	Australie
Spain	153.5	174.4	169.1	181.7	155.9	Espagne
Finland	183.1	153.2	163.8	142.1	137.8	Finlande
China, Hong Kong SAR	144.2	132.3	149.3	139.6	156.6	Chine - RAS de Hong-Kong
Indonesia	94.6	78.0	172.3	188.2	153.3	Indonésie
Southern African Customs Union	312.6	370.0	-	-	-	Union douanière d'Afrique australe
Belgium-Luxembourg	561.2	-	-	-	-	Belgique-Luxembourg

(Value as percentages of World total) **(Valeur en pourcentage du total mondial)**

Regions of the world	1993	1994	1995	1996	1997	1998	1999	2000	2001	2002	Régions du monde
World	100.0	100.0	100.0	100.0	100.0	100.0	100.0	100.0	100.0	100.0	Monde
Africa	7.7	8.6	10.1	9.7	9.4	8.5	9.9	8.7	8.3	9.8	Afrique
Americas	20.9	20.0	21.2	21.8	22.7	23.4	23.9	25.8	25.2	23.8	Amériques
- Northern America	15.5	14.3	15.1	15.3	15.7	16.2	16.8	17.9	17.3	16.5	- Amérique du Nord
- LAIA	4.1	3.9	4.4	4.6	5.2	5.5	5.0	5.5	5.0	5.0	- ALAI
- CACM	0.0	0.0	0.0	0.0	0.0	0.1	0.1	0.1	0.1	0.2	- MCC
- Caribbean	1.3	1.7	1.6	1.9	1.7	1.6	2.0	2.3	2.7	2.1	- Caraïbes
- Rest of America	0.0	0.0	0.0	0.0	0.0	0.0	0.0	0.0	0.0	0.0	- Autre d'Amérique
Asia excluding former USSR	21.4	20.8	23.0	22.9	23.8	24.3	25.6	26.4	26.8	27.4	Asie ancienne URSS exclus
- Middle East	3.8	3.6	4.1	3.7	3.8	3.6	3.6	2.3	3.8	3.7	- Moyen-Orient
Asia former USSR	0.5	0.9	1.7	1.7	1.4	1.4	1.3	0.4	0.4	0.4	Asie ancienne URSS
Europe excluding former USSR	40.2	42.0	36.0	34.9	34.4	36.5	33.7	31.9	33.5	33.1	Europe ancienne URSS exclus
- European Union	35.8	38.2	32.1	30.8	30.3	31.9	29.6	27.6	28.8	28.7	- Union Européenne
- Eastern Europe	1.9	2.2	2.2	2.2	2.1	2.4	2.0	2.1	2.3	2.1	- Europe de l'Est
- Rest of Europe	2.5	1.6	1.7	1.8	2.0	2.1	2.1	2.2	2.4	2.3	- Autre de l'Europe
Europe former USSR	8.2	6.7	7.0	8.0	7.2	5.0	4.6	5.6	4.6	4.3	Europe ancienne URSS
Oceania	1.1	1.0	1.1	1.0	1.0	0.9	1.1	1.2	1.2	1.2	Océanie

523 Other inorganic chemicals; compounds of precious metals

TRADE BY COMMODITY (Value in million US dollars)
Imports by principal countries or areas

COMMERCE PAR PRODUIT (Valeur en millions de dollars EU)
Importations selon les principaux pays ou zones

Country or area	1998	1999	2000	2001	2002	Pays ou zone
World	13471.1	13280.1	14740.2	14524.8	13983.2	Monde
Africa	609.0	537.1	517.9	526.5	558.6	Afrique
Americas	3197.5	3123.5	3483.5	3447.2	3201.4	Amériques
- Northern America	1828.2	1753.0	2024.5	1940.4	1876.5	- Amérique du Nord
- LAIA	1193.5	1205.2	1299.9	1323.8	1139.3	- ALAI
- CACM	87.7	83.2	83.0	96.5	100.3	- MCC
- Caribbean	71.4	68.9	65.2	74.9	72.0	- Caraïbes
- Rest of America	16.8	13.3	11.0	11.6	13.4	- Autre d'Amérique
Asia excluding former USSR	3465.9	3654.9	4214.2	4088.7	4069.7	Asie ancienne URSS exclus
- Middle East	650.3	590.8	628.1	609.4	587.8	- Moyen-Orient
Asia former USSR	82.7	78.0	107.3	93.9	102.6	Asie ancienne URSS
Europe excluding former USSR	5683.6	5506.2	6031.8	5982.3	5649.1	Europe ancienne URSS exclus
- European Union	4978.2	4818.4	5336.8	5283.1	4939.0	- Union Européenne
- Eastern Europe	391.7	351.9	349.4	363.8	401.4	- Europe de l'Est
- Rest of Europe	313.7	335.9	345.7	335.4	308.8	- Autre de l'Europe
Europe former USSR	198.2	152.9	155.5	175.9	200.2	Europe ancienne URSS
Oceania	234.1	227.4	230.0	210.2	201.5	Océanie
United States	1429.4	1332.1	1508.1	1439.5	1393.4	Etats-Unis d'Amérique
Germany	947.5	1062.2	1380.3	1423.6	993.9	Allemagne
France-Monaco	767.9	728.0	778.5	780.2	748.5	France-Monaco
Japan	573.6	626.3	751.6	765.9	661.7	Japon
Belgium	-	582.8	797.1	712.1	e781.0	Belgique
United Kingdom	516.4	468.2	487.3	532.1	519.8	Royaume-Uni
Italy-San Marino-Holy See	548.4	517.4	482.9	436.4	438.0	Italie-Saint-Marin-Saint-Siège
Canada	398.3	420.3	516.3	500.6	482.9	Canada
Mexico	359.6	407.2	481.8	496.3	408.1	Mexique
Netherlands	481.2	342.7	316.5	357.1	402.9	Pays-Bas
Korea, Republic of	276.2	346.2	383.4	384.6	410.1	République de Corée
China	241.0	272.0	382.0	375.2	454.7	Chine
Spain	331.2	335.5	290.1	256.1	278.6	Espagne
Brazil	280.4	274.1	284.4	292.6	294.9	Brésil
China, Hong Kong SAR	308.3	278.8	298.7	273.2	238.6	Chine - RAS de Hong-Kong
Malaysia	219.0	248.6	259.5	229.4	e250.7	Malaisie
Indonesia	214.3	183.6	238.6	244.8	232.4	Indonésie
Thailand	143.6	176.7	222.3	259.6	e270.4	Thaïlande
Singapore	167.2	175.8	213.4	159.4	180.8	Singapour
Switzerland-Liechtenstein	142.5	168.3	197.4	187.8	149.5	Suisse-Liechtenstein
Turkey	192.9	172.1	165.5	141.9	171.7	Turquie
Finland	154.2	153.2	155.1	143.2	156.8	Finlande
Australia	158.8	150.2	164.0	142.8	140.5	Australie
Sweden	158.0	138.9	142.7	161.2	148.2	Suède
Saudi Arabia	153.9	133.1	150.5	117.3	e121.4	Arabie saoudite
Czech Republic	139.1	132.6	118.7	128.3	139.9	République tchèque
Belgium-Luxembourg	599.6	-	-	-	-	Belgique-Luxembourg
Argentina	130.4	134.1	133.1	128.6	e56.9	Argentine
Austria	118.9	111.0	103.3	120.2	124.7	Autriche
Denmark	108.5	96.5	110.6	101.8	118.5	Danemark

(Value as percentages of World total) **(Valeur en pourcentage du total mondial)**

Regions of the world	1993	1994	1995	1996	1997	1998	1999	2000	2001	2002	Régions du monde
World	100.0	100.0	100.0	100.0	100.0	100.0	100.0	100.0	100.0	100.0	Monde
Africa	4.7	3.9	3.8	4.4	4.3	4.5	4.0	3.5	3.6	4.0	Afrique
Americas	21.1	20.9	20.6	20.6	22.6	23.7	23.5	23.6	23.7	22.9	Amériques
- Northern America	12.1	12.5	11.8	12.0	13.3	13.6	13.2	13.7	13.4	13.4	- Amérique du Nord
- LAIA	7.7	7.2	7.8	7.4	8.0	8.9	9.1	8.8	9.1	8.1	- ALAI
- CACM	0.6	0.6	0.5	0.6	0.6	0.7	0.6	0.6	0.7	0.7	- MCC
- Caribbean	0.6	0.4	0.4	0.5	0.6	0.5	0.5	0.4	0.5	0.5	- Caraïbes
- Rest of America	0.2	0.2	0.1	0.1	0.1	0.1	0.1	0.1	0.1	0.1	- Autre d'Amérique
Asia excluding former USSR	30.6	28.4	29.0	29.1	29.1	25.7	27.5	28.6	28.1	29.1	Asie ancienne URSS exclus
- Middle East	4.9	4.0	4.4	4.7	4.7	4.8	4.4	4.3	4.2	4.2	- Moyen-Orient
Asia former USSR	0.0	0.5	0.6	0.7	0.6	0.6	0.6	0.7	0.6	0.7	Asie ancienne URSS
Europe excluding former USSR	41.0	42.9	42.3	41.1	39.7	42.2	41.5	40.9	41.2	40.4	Europe ancienne URSS exclus
- European Union	35.2	37.6	37.0	35.5	34.7	37.0	36.3	36.2	36.4	35.3	- Union Européenne
- Eastern Europe	2.8	2.2	2.5	2.8	2.6	2.9	2.6	2.4	2.5	2.9	- Europe de l'Est
- Rest of Europe	3.0	3.1	2.9	2.7	2.4	2.3	2.5	2.3	2.3	2.2	- Autre de l'Europe
Europe former USSR	0.4	1.4	1.7	2.0	1.8	1.5	1.2	1.1	1.2	1.4	Europe ancienne URSS
Oceania	2.2	2.0	2.1	2.2	2.0	1.7	1.7	1.6	1.4	1.4	Océanie

TRADE BY COMMODITY (Value in million US dollars)
Exports by principal countries or areas

COMMERCE PAR PRODUIT (Valeur en millions de dollars EU)
Exportations selon les principaux pays ou zones

Country or area	1998	1999	2000	2001	2002	Pays ou zone
World	11058.5	10812.3	12233.7	12555.1	11825.2	Monde
Africa	325.2	283.3	298.8	290.1	270.0	Afrique
Americas	2922.3	2841.1	3198.6	3360.9	3175.1	Amériques
- Northern America	2341.4	2270.0	2562.7	2698.7	2509.4	- Amérique du Nord
- LAIA	570.1	560.9	625.4	652.1	656.4	- ALAI
- CACM	4.3	6.2	6.9	6.8	6.4	- MCC
- Caribbean	5.7	3.4	3.0	2.8	2.6	- Caraïbes
- Rest of America	0.8	0.5	0.5	0.5	0.3	- Autre d'Amérique
Asia excluding former USSR	2240.1	2559.3	2751.4	2864.7	2922.0	Asie ancienne URSS exclus
- Middle East	59.7	212.3	65.6	116.8	89.1	- Moyen-Orient
Asia former USSR	40.5	50.6	59.4	65.9	71.1	Asie ancienne URSS
Europe excluding former USSR	5258.2	4780.2	5604.2	5565.7	4993.7	Europe ancienne URSS exclus
- European Union	4634.8	4245.9	5021.9	4875.4	4320.1	- Union Européenne
- Eastern Europe	356.8	232.9	239.5	246.4	256.4	- Europe de l'Est
- Rest of Europe	266.6	301.4	342.8	443.9	417.2	- Autre de l'Europe
Europe former USSR	215.3	210.6	235.8	309.8	284.8	Europe ancienne URSS
Oceania	56.8	87.2	85.5	98.0	108.6	Océanie
United States	1899.1	1853.2	2127.7	2261.2	2056.5	Etats-Unis d'Amérique
Germany	1550.0	1503.4	1548.9	1608.9	1446.8	Allemagne
China	908.1	977.3	1108.6	1299.2	1369.8	Chine
United Kingdom	805.8	683.3	953.7	931.2	691.5	Royaume-Uni
Japan	447.0	522.4	656.6	527.0	560.5	Japon
Canada	442.3	416.8	434.5	436.6	452.8	Canada
Italy-San Marino-Holy See	261.4	293.5	610.7	579.8	387.5	Italie-Saint-Marin-Saint-Siège
France-Monaco	394.5	364.5	424.5	342.1	340.0	France-Monaco
Netherlands	566.6	284.9	262.7	347.5	400.9	Pays-Bas
Belgium	–	348.6	376.0	338.0	e379.2	Belgique
Switzerland-Liechtenstein	171.9	212.3	288.9	251.2	194.2	Suisse-Liechtenstein
Israel	246.5	240.5	212.0	226.8	188.6	Israël
Mexico	220.7	198.2	199.4	184.5	193.8	Mexique
Russian Federation	141.6	140.7	171.5	251.0	219.3	Fédération de Russie
Ireland	159.7	181.0	285.7	174.2	94.6	Irlande
Finland	176.7	174.0	161.1	175.4	181.2	Finlande
Sweden	196.3	188.2	174.8	149.6	152.7	Suède
Chile	143.9	158.7	168.5	192.7	e188.5	Chili
Korea, Republic of	139.5	152.9	180.1	177.0	178.0	République de Corée
Spain	174.5	152.5	148.8	156.8	169.5	Espagne
China, Hong Kong SAR	123.2	112.9	144.5	128.6	118.2	Chine - RAS de Hong-Kong
Poland	120.7	98.4	108.1	111.3	124.2	Pologne
Tunisia	85.0	82.0	88.9	102.0	e106.1	Tunisie
India	54.7	72.3	94.7	128.5	105.7	Inde
South Africa	–	–	172.8	144.3	124.3	Afrique du Sud
Brazil	53.6	57.4	98.1	105.8	e109.7	Brésil
Argentina	71.8	75.9	89.9	89.6	e86.6	Argentine
Australia	50.9	80.5	80.3	92.3	105.1	Australie
Norway	26.6	21.0	16.6	152.5	188.3	Norvège
Southern African Customs Union	214.1	183.0	–	–	–	Union douanière d'Afrique australe

(Value as percentages of World total) **(Valeur en pourcentage du total mondial)**

Regions of the world	1993	1994	1995	1996	1997	1998	1999	2000	2001	2002	Régions du monde
World	100.0	100.0	100.0	100.0	100.0	100.0	100.0	100.0	100.0	100.0	Monde
Africa	3.0	3.7	2.5	3.1	3.3	2.9	2.6	2.4	2.3	2.3	Afrique
Americas	21.9	25.2	25.6	25.9	27.1	26.4	26.3	26.1	26.8	26.8	Amériques
- Northern America	17.9	20.4	20.7	20.9	21.7	21.2	21.0	20.9	21.5	21.2	- Amérique du Nord
- LAIA	3.9	4.7	4.8	5.0	5.3	5.2	5.2	5.1	5.2	5.6	- ALAI
- CACM	0.0	0.0	0.0	0.0	0.0	0.0	0.1	0.1	0.1	0.1	- MCC
- Caribbean	0.1	0.0	0.0	0.0	0.0	0.1	0.0	0.0	0.0	0.0	- Caraïbes
- Rest of America	0.0	0.0	0.0	0.0	0.0	0.0	0.0	0.0	0.0	0.0	- Autre d'Amérique
Asia excluding former USSR	16.1	18.9	22.1	20.2	20.8	20.3	23.7	22.5	22.8	24.7	Asie ancienne URSS exclus
- Middle East	1.1	1.5	1.4	0.5	0.7	0.5	2.0	0.5	0.9	0.8	- Moyen-Orient
Asia former USSR	0.2	0.8	0.9	0.8	0.5	0.4	0.5	0.5	0.5	0.6	Asie ancienne URSS
Europe excluding former USSR	56.8	48.6	46.0	46.6	45.4	47.5	44.2	45.8	44.3	42.2	Europe ancienne URSS exclus
- European Union	51.2	43.7	39.8	40.6	39.9	41.9	39.3	41.0	38.8	36.5	- Union Européenne
- Eastern Europe	2.3	2.3	3.7	3.6	3.2	3.2	2.2	2.0	2.0	2.2	- Europe de l'Est
- Rest of Europe	3.3	2.6	2.5	2.5	2.3	2.4	2.8	2.8	3.5	3.5	- Autre de l'Europe
Europe former USSR	1.7	2.1	2.1	2.4	2.1	1.9	1.9	1.9	2.5	2.4	Europe ancienne URSS
Oceania	0.3	0.7	1.0	1.0	0.7	0.5	0.8	0.7	0.8	0.9	Océanie

524 Radioactive and associated material

TRADE BY COMMODITY (Value in million US dollars)
Imports by principal countries or areas

COMMERCE PAR PRODUIT (Valeur en millions de dollars EU)
Importations selon les principaux pays ou zones

Country or area	1998	1999	2000	2001	2002	Pays ou zone
World	6109.5	6210.8	6891.0	6994.3	7319.6	Monde
Africa	21.4	19.6	17.5	13.7	15.6	Afrique
Americas	1720.7	2024.0	2343.6	2395.2	2460.5	Amériques
- Northern America	1669.6	1972.8	2293.5	2333.6	2394.4	- Amérique du Nord
- LAIA	48.6	48.9	48.1	59.5	64.2	- ALAI
- CACM	0.7	0.6	0.4	0.4	0.4	- MCC
- Caribbean	1.7	1.7	1.5	1.7	1.4	- Caraïbes
- Rest of America	0.1	0.1	0.0	0.0	0.0	- Autre d'Amérique
Asia excluding former USSR	1587.1	1494.7	1855.3	1559.9	1730.8	Asie ancienne URSS exclus
- Middle East	15.2	19.7	19.2	33.4	14.4	- Moyen-Orient
Asia former USSR	52.8	24.0	108.0	137.6	140.4	Asie ancienne URSS
Europe excluding former USSR	2701.2	2606.1	2408.3	2565.0	2675.3	Europe ancienne URSS exclus
- European Union	2550.5	2568.9	2372.4	2528.2	2635.5	- Union Européenne
- Eastern Europe	124.8	13.6	15.0	15.1	18.1	- Europe de l'Est
- Rest of Europe	25.9	23.7	20.9	21.7	21.7	- Autre de l'Europe
Europe former USSR	16.8	32.9	147.0	314.7	286.9	Europe ancienne URSS
Oceania	9.5	9.4	11.5	8.1	10.1	Océanie
United States	1513.1	1769.7	2117.9	2170.7	2236.1	Etats-Unis d'Amérique
Japan	1139.5	1041.1	1413.4	971.8	1111.4	Japon
France-Monaco	669.0	620.9	701.0	660.9	701.8	France-Monaco
Belgium	–	681.5	559.1	596.9	e654.6	Belgique
United Kingdom	385.1	484.8	392.1	483.4	448.3	Royaume-Uni
Germany	465.4	403.6	277.5	320.4	334.9	Allemagne
Korea, Republic of	296.7	327.0	274.9	288.4	332.6	République de Corée
Canada	156.5	203.1	175.6	162.8	158.3	Canada
Russian Federation	13.2	29.6	145.4	312.6	282.6	Fédération de Russie
Netherlands	95.1	85.8	153.7	166.7	246.5	Pays-Bas
Spain	180.5	124.8	130.2	165.5	122.1	Espagne
Belgium-Luxembourg	557.1	–	–	–	–	Belgique-Luxembourg
Kazakhstan	41.4	23.7	107.7	137.2	e140.1	Kazakhstan
Sweden	107.3	76.9	73.9	51.8	48.6	Suède
China	28.0	31.3	37.7	128.0	124.2	Chine
Italy-San Marino-Holy See	44.0	44.9	38.8	35.5	37.6	Italie-Saint-Marin-Saint-Siège
Brazil	20.0	23.6	22.2	34.3	41.1	Brésil
Austria	21.9	19.2	24.0	26.5	20.8	Autriche
Singapore	10.6	16.2	30.6	25.1	29.2	Singapour
Bulgaria	107.7	0.5	0.4	e0.4	e0.5	Bulgarie
Switzerland-Liechtenstein	17.3	15.0	14.6	14.8	14.3	Suisse-Liechtenstein
Malaysia	9.5	14.5	8.7	20.7	e22.6	Malaisie
Mexico	11.0	10.5	11.4	12.1	14.3	Mexique
Argentina	11.8	9.4	10.4	8.5	e3.7	Argentine
Denmark	7.8	9.4	8.8	8.2	7.2	Danemark
Australia	8.4	8.1	10.1	6.4	8.2	Australie
Israel	6.1	7.1	7.0	6.7	6.6	Israël
Turkey	6.5	9.6	5.9	5.2	5.2	Turquie
Czech Republic	6.5	6.5	5.7	6.3	7.1	République tchèque
Greece	7.8	7.6	5.7	5.1	e5.7	Grèce

(Value as percentages of World total) **(Valeur en pourcentage du total mondial)**

Regions of the world	1993	1994	1995	1996	1997	1998	1999	2000	2001	2002	Régions du monde
World	100.0	100.0	100.0	100.0	100.0	100.0	100.0	100.0	100.0	100.0	Monde
Africa	0.3	0.3	0.3	0.3	0.3	0.3	0.3	0.3	0.2	0.2	Afrique
Americas	21.4	23.6	24.5	28.7	25.7	28.2	32.6	34.0	34.2	33.6	Amériques
- Northern America	20.3	23.1	23.8	28.1	25.0	27.3	31.8	33.3	33.4	32.7	- Amérique du Nord
- LAIA	1.0	0.5	0.6	0.6	0.6	0.8	0.8	0.7	0.9	0.9	- ALAI
- CACM	0.0	0.0	0.0	0.0	0.0	0.0	0.0	0.0	0.0	0.0	- MCC
- Caribbean	0.1	0.0	0.1	0.0	0.0	0.0	0.0	0.0	0.0	0.0	- Caraïbes
- Rest of America	0.0	0.0	0.0	0.0	0.0	0.0	0.0	0.0	0.0	0.0	- Autre d'Amérique
Asia excluding former USSR	35.5	33.1	33.1	27.7	28.6	26.0	24.1	26.9	22.3	23.6	Asie ancienne URSS exclus
- Middle East	0.4	0.5	0.4	0.3	0.3	0.2	0.3	0.3	0.5	0.2	- Moyen-Orient
Asia former USSR	0.0	0.0	0.0	0.5	0.5	0.9	0.4	1.6	2.0	1.9	Asie ancienne URSS
Europe excluding former USSR	41.8	42.4	41.7	42.4	44.6	44.2	42.0	34.9	36.7	36.5	Europe ancienne URSS exclus
- European Union	40.9	41.7	39.7	40.8	42.5	41.7	41.4	34.4	36.1	36.0	- Union Européenne
- Eastern Europe	0.3	0.2	1.5	1.0	1.7	2.0	0.2	0.2	0.2	0.2	- Europe de l'Est
- Rest of Europe	0.6	0.5	0.6	0.6	0.4	0.4	0.4	0.3	0.3	0.3	- Autre de l'Europe
Europe former USSR	0.7	0.4	0.2	0.2	0.1	0.3	0.5	2.1	4.5	3.9	Europe ancienne URSS
Oceania	0.2	0.2	0.2	0.2	0.2	0.2	0.2	0.2	0.1	0.1	Océanie

TRADE BY COMMODITY (Value in million US dollars)
Exports by principal countries or areas

COMMERCE PAR PRODUIT (Valeur en millions de dollars EU)
Exportations selon les principaux pays ou zones

Country or area	1998	1999	2000	2001	2002	Pays ou zone
World	4367.5	4270.5	4514.8	5085.5	5658.5	Monde
Africa	68.5	42.9	31.7	32.8	32.9	Afrique
Americas	1753.5	1528.5	1663.9	1893.9	2162.5	Amériques
- Northern America	1666.8	1469.7	1647.4	1888.7	2157.4	- Amérique du Nord
- LAIA	86.6	58.7	16.3	4.9	4.9	- ALAI
- CACM	0.0	0.0	0.0	0.0	0.0	- MCC
- Caribbean	0.0	0.1	0.2	0.2	0.2	- Caraïbes
- Rest of America	0.0	0.0	0.0	0.0	0.0	- Autre d'Amérique
Asia excluding former USSR	292.2	308.4	279.8	317.7	351.8	Asie ancienne URSS exclus
- Middle East	0.7	0.9	0.8	2.7	2.6	- Moyen-Orient
Asia former USSR	140.2	133.7	156.7	215.5	141.4	Asie ancienne URSS
Europe excluding former USSR	1942.7	2093.5	2207.6	2470.0	2845.6	Europe ancienne URSS exclus
- European Union	1894.2	2043.8	2162.8	2438.7	2797.6	- Union Européenne
- Eastern Europe	40.2	39.4	34.2	22.4	38.5	- Europe de l'Est
- Rest of Europe	8.3	10.2	10.6	9.0	9.5	- Autre de l'Europe
Europe former USSR	168.8	161.3	173.0	153.7	122.0	Europe ancienne URSS
Oceania	1.6	2.1	2.1	1.9	2.4	Océanie
United States	1127.0	990.1	1212.6	1282.3	1555.9	Etats-Unis d'Amérique
France-Monaco	891.0	1032.8	970.2	1033.3	1232.3	France-Monaco
United Kingdom	510.2	515.8	680.5	752.0	761.1	Royaume-Uni
Canada	539.8	479.6	434.8	606.4	601.5	Canada
Netherlands	268.5	215.7	268.2	322.9	334.2	Pays-Bas
China	254.4	237.9	195.1	231.2	254.0	Chine
Germany	127.7	147.3	116.2	191.3	332.0	Allemagne
Russian Federation	164.1	156.3	172.2	152.1	116.0	Fédération de Russie
Kazakhstan	80.8	111.4	127.8	110.5	e124.5	Kazakhstan
Belgium	–	78.9	59.9	98.1	e110.1	Belgique
Japan	22.6	49.1	53.0	46.0	53.7	Japon
Uzbekistan	e50.3	e19.6	e26.5	e103.2	e15.6	Ouzbékistan
Argentina	86.3	57.9	15.2	4.4	e4.3	Argentine
Czech Republic	36.7	36.4	32.8	18.3	35.0	République tchèque
Sweden	22.6	32.2	32.6	10.3	9.5	Suède
South Africa	–	–	31.7	32.6	32.6	Afrique du Sud
Southern African Customs Union	57.3	36.7	–	–	–	Union douanière d'Afrique australe
Singapore	3.7	5.5	17.7	17.5	18.0	Singapour
Belgium-Luxembourg	53.7	–	–	–	–	Belgique-Luxembourg
Italy-San Marino-Holy See	11.6	10.7	12.0	9.0	8.8	Italie-Saint-Marin-Saint-Siège
Spain	3.6	0.5	17.3	15.8	3.4	Espagne
Switzerland-Liechtenstein	7.3	6.4	7.1	7.8	8.0	Suisse-Liechtenstein
Israel	1.6	2.8	4.3	9.5	13.9	Israël
China, Hong Kong SAR	5.8	6.0	1.1	2.8	2.3	Chine - RAS de Hong-Kong
Gabon	e10.7	6.1	0.0	e0.0	e0.0	Gabon
Estonia	4.6	4.9	0.4	1.1	5.5	Estonie
Finland	3.5	3.1	3.0	2.9	2.9	Finlande
Korea, Republic of	1.4	2.8	1.3	3.4	3.1	République de Corée
Ireland	1.1	4.1	1.6	2.0	1.6	Irlande
India	0.6	0.1	4.5	2.4	2.1	Inde

(Value as percentages of World total) **(Valeur en pourcentage du total mondial)**

Regions of the world	1993	1994	1995	1996	1997	1998	1999	2000	2001	2002	Régions du monde
World	100.0	100.0	100.0	100.0	100.0	100.0	100.0	100.0	100.0	100.0	Monde
Africa	1.7	4.9	1.3	1.4	1.9	1.6	1.0	0.7	0.6	0.6	Afrique
Americas	32.0	38.2	34.1	37.8	45.8	40.1	35.8	36.9	37.2	38.2	Amériques
- Northern America	31.9	38.2	33.9	37.8	45.8	38.2	34.4	36.5	37.1	38.1	- Amérique du Nord
- LAIA	0.1	0.0	0.1	0.0	0.1	2.0	1.4	0.4	0.1	0.1	- ALAI
- CACM	0.0	0.0	0.0	0.0	0.0	0.0	0.0	0.0	0.0	0.0	- MCC
- Caribbean	0.0	0.0	0.0	0.0	0.0	0.0	0.0	0.0	0.0	0.0	- Caraïbes
- Rest of America	0.0	0.0	0.0	0.0	0.0	0.0	0.0	0.0	0.0	0.0	- Autre d'Amérique
Asia excluding former USSR	4.9	3.2	6.4	6.0	5.9	6.7	7.2	6.2	6.2	6.2	Asie ancienne URSS exclus
- Middle East	0.0	0.0	0.0	0.0	0.0	0.0	0.0	0.0	0.1	0.0	- Moyen-Orient
Asia former USSR	0.8	2.5	1.7	2.6	2.1	3.2	3.1	3.5	4.2	2.5	Asie ancienne URSS
Europe excluding former USSR	49.1	45.9	50.2	45.7	43.7	44.5	49.0	48.9	48.6	50.3	Europe ancienne URSS exclus
- European Union	48.7	45.6	49.8	45.3	42.1	43.4	47.9	47.9	48.0	49.4	- Union Européenne
- Eastern Europe	0.1	0.0	0.1	0.2	1.3	0.9	0.9	0.8	0.4	0.7	- Europe de l'Est
- Rest of Europe	0.2	0.2	0.3	0.2	0.2	0.2	0.2	0.2	0.2	0.2	- Autre de l'Europe
Europe former USSR	11.6	5.2	6.3	6.5	0.5	3.9	3.8	3.8	3.0	2.2	Europe ancienne URSS
Oceania	0.0	0.0	0.0	0.0	0.0	0.0	0.1	0.0	0.0	0.0	Océanie

531 Synthetic dye, natural indigo, lakes

TRADE BY COMMODITY (Value in million US dollars)
Imports by principal countries or areas

COMMERCE PAR PRODUIT (Valeur en millions de dollars EU)
Importations selon les principaux pays ou zones

Country or area	1998	1999	2000	2001	2002	Pays ou zone
World	10442.3	9741.1	9582.4	8687.3	9032.0	Monde
Africa	302.4	251.3	232.4	239.2	251.2	Afrique
Americas	1910.6	1852.0	1822.2	1597.6	1587.3	Amériques
- Northern America	1196.1	1178.6	1087.9	893.1	931.1	- Amérique du Nord
- LAIA	662.3	628.9	689.3	659.8	607.2	- ALAI
- CACM	36.8	32.0	35.0	34.8	38.4	- MCC
- Caribbean	10.4	8.4	8.1	7.6	8.5	- Caraïbes
- Rest of America	5.0	4.1	1.9	2.3	2.2	- Autre d'Amérique
Asia excluding former USSR	2723.3	2768.1	2900.4	2653.0	2918.7	Asie ancienne URSS exclus
- Middle East	431.9	363.7	343.1	320.8	382.8	- Moyen-Orient
Asia former USSR	6.2	5.5	9.3	10.3	8.2	Asie ancienne URSS
Europe excluding former USSR	5319.9	4685.7	4446.8	4025.6	4087.1	Europe ancienne URSS exclus
- European Union	4394.3	3879.9	3665.2	3365.1	3397.0	- Union Européenne
- Eastern Europe	168.9	153.4	150.2	148.9	168.5	- Europe de l'Est
- Rest of Europe	756.6	652.4	631.4	511.6	521.7	- Autre de l'Europe
Europe former USSR	70.5	65.5	72.4	73.7	85.7	Europe ancienne URSS
Oceania	109.4	113.2	98.9	87.9	93.8	Océanie
United States	987.8	955.1	860.6	699.2	736.2	Etats-Unis d'Amérique
Germany	910.0	766.8	752.9	710.4	702.9	Allemagne
Italy-San Marino-Holy See	668.1	591.3	559.6	512.5	475.8	Italie-Saint-Marin-Saint-Siège
France-Monaco	679.2	581.5	536.9	480.6	494.2	France-Monaco
Switzerland-Liechtenstein	620.0	519.7	499.6	379.2	379.8	Suisse-Liechtenstein
United Kingdom	512.6	454.1	449.9	376.7	355.8	Royaume-Uni
China, Hong Kong SAR	386.5	357.7	372.8	329.7	380.2	Chine - RAS de Hong-Kong
China	253.2	291.4	328.6	352.3	428.1	Chine
Japan	335.1	322.6	333.1	293.8	294.5	Japon
Korea, Republic of	261.5	312.2	311.0	282.5	297.8	République de Corée
Belgium	–	349.6	335.2	306.7	e336.4	Belgique
Turkey	319.8	262.1	251.3	209.8	284.5	Turquie
Netherlands	296.3	287.1	266.2	236.2	236.0	Pays-Bas
Mexico	233.7	246.0	257.7	234.3	227.9	Mexique
Spain	246.6	235.3	203.3	203.7	223.1	Espagne
Canada	208.4	223.4	227.2	193.8	194.8	Canada
Indonesia	210.5	175.2	232.4	184.7	190.5	Indonésie
Singapore	96.5	134.1	186.6	159.0	180.0	Singapour
Brazil	156.9	141.6	160.9	143.9	140.4	Brésil
Denmark	171.5	136.5	133.5	131.5	160.0	Danemark
Thailand	110.4	137.6	138.6	137.1	e142.8	Thaïlande
Austria	139.2	110.3	108.0	107.3	101.8	Autriche
Sweden	114.2	118.6	97.3	92.8	94.3	Suède
Norway	87.4	89.9	91.3	91.0	95.7	Norvège
Portugal	109.0	96.0	83.0	74.8	77.0	Portugal
Chile	68.8	76.1	92.7	97.9	88.3	Chili
Australia	82.7	86.5	80.3	68.6	73.9	Australie
Belgium-Luxembourg	386.6	–	–	–	–	Belgique-Luxembourg
Pakistan	83.4	76.7	71.3	67.7	77.3	Pakistan
Finland	88.3	72.7	74.9	67.4	69.4	Finlande

(Value as percentages of World total) **(Valeur en pourcentage du total mondial)**

Regions of the world	1993	1994	1995	1996	1997	1998	1999	2000	2001	2002	Régions du monde
World	100.0	100.0	100.0	100.0	100.0	100.0	100.0	100.0	100.0	100.0	Monde
Africa	3.5	3.4	2.5	2.9	2.7	2.9	2.6	2.4	2.8	2.8	Afrique
Americas	17.6	17.6	16.2	16.9	18.4	18.3	19.0	19.0	18.4	17.6	Amériques
- Northern America	11.8	11.8	10.7	10.8	11.5	11.5	12.1	11.4	10.3	10.3	- Amérique du Nord
- LAIA	5.4	5.4	5.2	5.8	6.3	6.3	6.5	7.2	7.6	6.7	- ALAI
- CACM	0.3	0.3	0.3	0.3	0.5	0.4	0.3	0.4	0.4	0.4	- MCC
- Caribbean	0.1	0.1	0.1	0.1	0.1	0.1	0.1	0.1	0.1	0.1	- Caraïbes
- Rest of America	0.0	0.0	0.0	0.0	0.0	0.0	0.0	0.0	0.0	0.0	- Autre d'Amérique
Asia excluding former USSR	34.9	30.6	29.7	29.4	29.0	26.1	28.4	30.3	30.5	32.3	Asie ancienne URSS exclus
- Middle East	3.9	3.5	4.1	4.5	4.6	4.1	3.7	3.6	3.7	4.2	- Moyen-Orient
Asia former USSR	0.0	0.1	0.1	0.1	0.0	0.1	0.1	0.1	0.1	0.1	Asie ancienne URSS
Europe excluding former USSR	42.2	46.4	49.8	48.8	48.0	50.9	48.1	46.4	46.3	45.3	Europe ancienne URSS exclus
- European Union	33.8	37.5	40.2	39.9	38.8	42.1	39.8	38.2	38.7	37.6	- Union Européenne
- Eastern Europe	1.4	1.4	1.4	1.7	1.6	1.6	1.6	1.6	1.7	1.9	- Europe de l'Est
- Rest of Europe	7.0	7.6	8.2	7.3	7.6	7.2	6.7	6.6	5.9	5.8	- Autre de l'Europe
Europe former USSR	0.3	0.3	0.4	0.5	0.7	0.7	0.7	0.8	0.8	0.9	Europe ancienne URSS
Oceania	1.4	1.5	1.3	1.3	1.1	1.0	1.2	1.0	1.0	1.0	Océanie

TRADE BY COMMODITY (Value in million US dollars)
Exports by principal countries or areas

COMMERCE PAR PRODUIT (Valeur en millions de dollars EU)
Exportations selon les principaux pays ou zones

Country or area	1998	1999	2000	2001	2002	Pays ou zone
World	10016.0	9215.4	9001.7	8482.2	9146.5	Monde
Africa	13.4	14.6	12.0	13.3	12.6	Afrique
Americas	947.9	900.8	953.2	848.1	819.4	Amériques
- Northern America	729.3	709.3	752.1	652.6	610.2	- Amérique du Nord
- LAIA	214.0	187.1	195.2	191.9	205.9	- ALAI
- CACM	2.5	3.0	4.3	2.0	2.0	- MCC
- Caribbean	0.1	0.1	0.1	0.1	0.1	- Caraïbes
- Rest of America	1.9	1.2	1.4	1.4	1.1	- Autre d'Amérique
Asia excluding former USSR	2629.8	2649.2	2867.5	2666.3	2938.9	Asie ancienne URSS exclus
- Middle East	16.9	14.2	13.8	16.1	20.4	- Moyen-Orient
Asia former USSR	1.6	0.2	0.4	0.1	0.1	Asie ancienne URSS
Europe excluding former USSR	6386.4	5557.3	5098.7	4895.7	5343.4	Europe ancienne URSS exclus
- European Union	4876.7	4245.0	3885.2	3746.4	4119.0	- Union Européenne
- Eastern Europe	78.4	65.5	65.5	57.2	59.5	- Europe de l'Est
- Rest of Europe	1431.3	1246.8	1148.0	1092.0	1165.0	- Autre de l'Europe
Europe former USSR	23.3	82.5	62.3	50.0	17.8	Europe ancienne URSS
Oceania	13.6	10.8	7.6	8.7	14.3	Océanie
Germany	2167.7	2025.0	1834.5	1534.1	1778.2	Allemagne
Switzerland-Liechtenstein	1425.6	1241.1	1142.7	1087.4	1157.0	Suisse-Liechtenstein
China	654.8	667.2	764.9	781.2	891.4	Chine
United States	699.3	682.5	726.6	632.5	586.0	Etats-Unis d'Amérique
United Kingdom	753.8	416.6	309.5	492.8	510.9	Royaume-Uni
Japan	549.1	528.4	482.8	333.7	311.4	Japon
India	354.8	409.8	470.4	431.0	497.2	Inde
France-Monaco	486.8	459.7	397.9	371.8	379.9	France-Monaco
China, Hong Kong SAR	336.5	316.0	329.8	316.5	325.9	Chine - RAS de Hong-Kong
Netherlands	366.6	278.1	317.9	318.0	290.3	Pays-Bas
Belgium	–	383.5	345.6	328.3	e368.4	Belgique
Korea, Republic of	245.5	239.8	256.3	236.9	260.0	République de Corée
Denmark	168.9	162.2	201.0	216.2	250.9	Danemark
Italy-San Marino-Holy See	220.0	202.9	176.2	171.6	184.2	Italie-Saint-Marin-Saint-Siège
Singapore	105.5	125.3	170.3	185.2	226.1	Singapour
Spain	158.3	156.2	143.4	151.8	187.9	Espagne
Brazil	92.8	76.5	88.1	75.7	e78.5	Brésil
Belgium-Luxembourg	382.2	–	–	–	–	Belgique-Luxembourg
Indonesia	68.9	56.6	75.8	68.5	86.3	Indonésie
Mexico	60.9	65.2	67.8	67.2	80.1	Mexique
Austria	63.5	56.4	59.5	59.7	55.5	Autriche
Czech Republic	59.8	51.0	48.1	39.0	37.7	République tchèque
Russian Federation	18.5	78.1	58.1	47.2	14.6	Fédération de Russie
Thailand	42.8	42.2	43.2	42.2	e44.5	Thaïlande
Sweden	36.9	31.0	28.3	31.5	38.0	Suède
Argentina	42.1	27.7	24.2	31.4	e30.3	Argentine
Greece	31.7	29.5	26.1	22.7	e22.8	Grèce
Finland	24.8	26.7	26.3	26.2	27.7	Finlande
Canada	29.9	26.8	25.6	20.1	24.0	Canada
Portugal	11.9	11.9	11.1	13.5	16.2	Portugal

(Value as percentages of World total)

(Valeur en pourcentage du total mondial)

Regions of the world	1993	1994	1995	1996	1997	1998	1999	2000	2001	2002	Régions du monde
World	100.0	100.0	100.0	100.0	100.0	100.0	100.0	100.0	100.0	100.0	Monde
Africa	0.1	0.1	0.1	0.1	0.1	0.1	0.2	0.1	0.2	0.1	Afrique
Americas	6.2	6.7	6.8	7.5	8.9	9.5	9.8	10.6	10.0	9.0	Amériques
- Northern America	5.1	5.5	5.3	5.8	6.8	7.3	7.7	8.4	7.7	6.7	- Amérique du Nord
- LAIA	1.1	1.1	1.4	1.7	2.0	2.1	2.0	2.2	2.3	2.3	- ALAI
- CACM	0.0	0.0	0.0	0.0	0.0	0.0	0.0	0.0	0.0	0.0	- MCC
- Caribbean	0.0	0.0	0.0	0.0	0.0	0.0	0.0	0.0	0.0	0.0	- Caraïbes
- Rest of America	0.0	0.0	0.0	0.0	0.0	0.0	0.0	0.0	0.0	0.0	- Autre d'Amérique
Asia excluding former USSR	27.0	25.2	24.3	24.6	27.0	26.3	28.7	31.9	31.4	32.1	Asie ancienne URSS exclus
- Middle East	0.1	0.2	0.3	0.2	0.3	0.2	0.2	0.2	0.2	0.2	- Moyen-Orient
Asia former USSR	0.0	0.0	0.0	0.0	0.0	0.0	0.0	0.0	0.0	0.0	Asie ancienne URSS
Europe excluding former USSR	66.4	67.7	68.5	67.3	63.6	63.8	60.3	56.6	57.7	58.4	Europe ancienne URSS exclus
- European Union	48.1	49.7	50.5	51.3	48.5	48.7	46.1	43.2	44.2	45.0	- Union Européenne
- Eastern Europe	0.8	0.8	0.8	0.7	0.8	0.8	0.7	0.7	0.7	0.7	- Europe de l'Est
- Rest of Europe	17.4	17.3	17.3	15.2	14.3	14.3	13.5	12.8	12.9	12.7	- Autre de l'Europe
Europe former USSR	0.2	0.2	0.2	0.2	0.2	0.2	0.9	0.7	0.6	0.2	Europe ancienne URSS
Oceania	0.1	0.1	0.1	0.2	0.2	0.1	0.1	0.1	0.1	0.2	Océanie

532 Dyeing and tanning extracts, and synthetic tanning materials

TRADE BY COMMODITY (Value in million US dollars)
Imports by principal countries or areas

COMMERCE PAR PRODUIT (Valeur en millions de dollars EU)
Importations selon les principaux pays ou zones

Country or area	1998	1999	2000	2001	2002	Pays ou zone
World	1023.9	998.8	1046.4	1059.3	1104.9	Monde
Africa	33.7	30.9	35.4	41.8	39.1	Afrique
Americas	198.9	206.3	200.5	191.5	170.4	Amériques
- Northern America	82.0	88.3	89.2	78.4	67.8	- Amérique du Nord
- LAIA	103.5	105.5	97.9	100.9	88.7	- ALAI
- CACM	8.0	8.4	8.6	7.7	8.9	- MCÇC
- Caribbean	4.3	3.0	3.5	3.6	4.1	- Caraïbes
- Rest of America	1.1	1.2	1.3	1.0	0.9	- Autre d'Amérique
Asia excluding former USSR	367.1	375.5	419.5	437.9	480.2	Asie ancienne URSS exclus
- Middle East	30.1	24.2	28.0	25.5	32.2	- Moyen-Orient
Asia former USSR	0.9	0.7	0.7	0.7	0.7	Asie ancienne URSS
Europe excluding former USSR	384.8	347.6	354.8	355.7	377.3	Europe ancienne URSS exclus
- European Union	344.2	304.0	304.5	305.6	316.1	- Union Européenne
- Eastern Europe	25.8	25.8	26.0	25.1	27.7	- Europe de l'Est
- Rest of Europe	14.8	17.7	24.4	25.0	33.5	- Autre de l'Europe
Europe former USSR	15.2	14.2	13.5	14.2	17.3	Europe ancienne URSS
Oceania	23.4	23.6	22.1	17.4	19.8	Océanie
Italy-San Marino-Holy See	86.8	78.2	83.4	82.2	86.3	Italie-Saint-Marin-Saint-Siège
United States	74.0	79.7	82.8	72.7	62.3	Etats-Unis d'Amérique
China	38.0	44.4	65.6	78.6	100.5	Chine
China, Hong Kong SAR	52.6	51.9	55.7	64.3	79.6	Chine - RAS de Hong-Kong
Japan	55.5	57.1	61.4	65.8	62.6	Japon
Korea, Republic of	41.7	49.3	52.1	49.1	50.5	République de Corée
Germany	52.6	42.4	42.5	43.8	46.9	Allemagne
Spain	38.2	35.1	41.9	43.5	35.2	Espagne
India	38.6	33.7	37.0	42.0	38.6	Inde
Mexico	36.4	39.9	34.0	32.8	35.2	Mexique
France-Monaco	37.3	35.2	34.9	29.5	31.4	France-Monaco
United Kingdom	34.1	29.8	26.0	24.3	25.8	Royaume-Uni
Brazil	21.8	21.6	21.3	21.8	19.3	Brésil
Pakistan	18.5	16.6	18.2	18.3	17.2	Pakistan
Argentina	18.6	20.9	18.9	18.1	e8.0	Argentine
Netherlands	17.8	16.9	13.9	14.7	20.7	Pays-Bas
Australia	19.0	18.2	16.9	12.5	14.0	Australie
Turkey	15.8	11.3	14.4	14.0	21.2	Turquie
Switzerland-Liechtenstein	6.1	9.0	15.8	17.7	25.8	Suisse-Liechtenstein
Bangladesh	9.7	e10.6	e18.2	17.6	e17.2	Bangladesh
Denmark	11.5	9.9	13.4	17.7	16.4	Danemark
Ireland	22.2	12.7	12.1	8.0	9.6	Irlande
Poland	13.0	13.0	13.2	11.6	12.5	Pologne
Portugal	11.8	12.2	10.1	9.4	9.6	Portugal
Austria	10.4	10.5	8.2	11.1	11.1	Autriche
Thailand	8.5	9.7	9.7	10.2	e10.7	Thaïlande
Indonesia	10.3	7.8	9.0	8.6	8.7	Indonésie
Singapore	4.4	7.4	9.4	10.3	11.7	Singapour
Nigeria	3.8	2.5	8.9	e12.2	e11.6	Nigéria
Belgium	–	8.7	8.2	10.2	e11.2	Belgique

(Value as percentages of World total) **(Valeur en pourcentage du total mondial)**

Regions of the world	1993	1994	1995	1996	1997	1998	1999	2000	2001	2002	Régions du monde
World	100.0	100.0	100.0	100.0	100.0	100.0	100.0	100.0	100.0	100.0	Monde
Africa	5.9	4.1	2.9	2.9	3.1	3.3	3.1	3.4	3.9	3.5	Afrique
Americas	18.1	17.1	16.0	16.2	17.4	19.4	20.7	19.2	18.1	15.4	Amériques
- Northern America	9.6	8.6	7.2	7.2	7.5	8.0	8.8	8.5	7.4	6.1	- Amérique du Nord
- LAIA	7.0	7.2	7.7	7.9	8.8	10.1	10.6	9.4	9.5	8.0	- ALAI
- CACM	1.2	1.0	0.9	0.7	0.7	0.8	0.8	0.8	0.7	0.8	- MCC
- Caribbean	0.3	0.2	0.2	0.3	0.3	0.4	0.3	0.3	0.3	0.4	- Caraïbes
- Rest of America	0.1	0.1	0.1	0.1	0.1	0.1	0.1	0.1	0.1	0.1	- Autre d'Amérique
Asia excluding former USSR	42.6	39.2	41.0	40.7	39.3	35.8	37.6	40.1	41.3	43.5	Asie ancienne URSS exclus
- Middle East	2.4	2.1	2.9	3.6	3.6	2.9	2.4	2.7	2.4	2.9	- Moyen-Orient
Asia former USSR	0.0	0.1	0.1	0.1	0.1	0.1	0.1	0.1	0.1	0.1	Asie ancienne URSS
Europe excluding former USSR	30.0	35.7	36.5	36.6	36.5	37.6	34.8	33.9	33.6	34.2	Europe ancienne URSS exclus
- European Union	27.1	32.2	32.8	32.9	32.7	33.6	30.4	29.1	28.9	28.6	- Union Européenne
- Eastern Europe	1.6	1.7	2.0	2.3	2.4	2.5	2.6	2.5	2.4	2.5	- Europe de l'Est
- Rest of Europe	1.4	1.7	1.6	1.4	1.3	1.4	1.8	2.3	2.4	3.0	- Autre de l'Europe
Europe former USSR	0.7	1.0	0.9	0.8	0.9	1.5	1.4	1.3	1.3	1.6	Europe ancienne URSS
Oceania	2.6	2.9	2.6	2.7	2.8	2.3	2.4	2.1	1.6	1.8	Océanie

Extraits utilisés pour la teinture et le tannage et produits tannants synthétiques 532

TRADE BY COMMODITY (Value in million US dollars)
Exports by principal countries or areas

COMMERCE PAR PRODUIT (Valeur en millions de dollars EU)
Exportations selon les principaux pays ou zones

Country or area	1998	1999	2000	2001	2002	Pays ou zone
World	921.2	899.5	919.4	907.2	976.2	Monde
Africa	46.3	55.5	52.4	46.6	51.3	Afrique
Americas	201.5	181.6	187.7	188.3	183.9	Amériques
- Northern America	41.6	35.4	41.9	46.1	51.1	- Amérique du Nord
- LAIA	154.3	145.8	145.2	141.4	132.0	- ALAI
- CACM	5.1	0.3	0.5	0.5	0.6	- MCC
- Caribbean	0.5	0.1	0.1	0.2	0.1	- Caraïbes
- Rest of America	0.0	0.0	0.0	0.0	0.1	- Autre d'Amérique
Asia excluding former USSR	121.6	141.7	152.7	159.7	187.4	Asie ancienne URSS exclus
- Middle East	15.0	17.4	17.8	16.7	18.1	- Moyen-Orient
Asia former USSR	1.2	0.3	0.2	0.1	0.1	Asie ancienne URSS
Europe excluding former USSR	532.4	513.2	518.1	504.8	546.5	Europe ancienne URSS exclus
- European Union	521.2	503.0	506.3	491.6	531.0	- Union Européenne
- Eastern Europe	1.6	1.0	1.5	1.8	1.9	- Europe de l'Est
- Rest of Europe	9.6	9.2	10.2	11.4	13.6	- Autre de l'Europe
Europe former USSR	2.0	1.9	1.5	4.6	4.8	Europe ancienne URSS
Oceania	16.1	5.4	6.8	3.3	2.4	Océanie
Italy-San Marino-Holy See	122.0	123.3	120.1	117.3	123.0	Italie-Saint-Marin-Saint-Siège
Germany	133.9	116.1	111.8	111.4	116.1	Allemagne
France-Monaco	76.2	84.2	82.2	70.8	75.0	France-Monaco
Spain	63.9	63.5	71.7	70.7	74.6	Espagne
China, Hong Kong SAR	43.8	48.4	53.9	51.5	64.6	Chine - RAS de Hong-Kong
Argentina	56.0	48.9	49.5	49.6	e48.0	Argentine
United Kingdom	53.5	48.9	50.1	46.5	47.5	Royaume-Uni
United States	40.8	34.5	40.0	44.1	47.9	Etats-Unis d'Amérique
Mexico	40.5	40.0	40.7	33.4	21.5	Mexique
Netherlands	29.6	25.1	32.0	34.3	43.9	Pays-Bas
Brazil	33.2	32.0	29.3	28.1	e29.1	Brésil
South Africa	–	–	40.8	37.9	44.6	Afrique du Sud
China	10.1	19.2	17.6	25.7	30.8	Chine
Denmark	17.8	13.7	14.3	26.2	28.0	Danemark
Peru	15.0	16.2	18.5	21.5	26.4	Pérou
Southern African Customs Union	33.7	44.6	–	–	–	Union douanière d'Afrique australe
Turkey	13.4	15.5	15.8	15.4	16.7	Turquie
Japan	12.4	14.0	14.5	15.3	17.8	Japon
Ireland	16.7	20.1	15.4	6.0	13.5	Irlande
India	9.8	10.1	10.8	11.1	14.4	Inde
Indonesia	8.6	9.1	6.8	7.5	7.7	Indonésie
Singapore	4.7	4.8	8.8	10.1	10.5	Singapour
Slovenia	6.4	6.8	6.3	6.5	7.2	Slovénie
Australia	15.6	4.9	6.6	3.2	2.3	Australie
Korea, Republic of	4.2	3.7	6.2	7.0	7.8	République de Corée
Thailand	5.3	4.6	4.2	3.5	e3.7	Thaïlande
Uruguay	3.6	4.4	3.6	4.3	3.8	Uruguay
Switzerland-Liechtenstein	2.9	2.1	3.0	3.7	6.1	Suisse-Liechtenstein
Belgium	–	3.3	4.1	4.1	e4.6	Belgique
Zimbabwe	e3.3	3.1	2.9	2.7	1.1	Zimbabwe

(Value as percentages of World total) **(Valeur en pourcentage du total mondial)**

Regions of the world	1993	1994	1995	1996	1997	1998	1999	2000	2001	2002	Régions du monde
World	100.0	100.0	100.0	100.0	100.0	100.0	100.0	100.0	100.0	100.0	Monde
Africa	6.4	7.3	6.1	5.8	5.6	5.0	6.2	5.7	5.1	5.3	Afrique
Americas	22.9	22.9	21.8	20.0	21.5	21.9	20.2	20.4	20.7	18.8	Amériques
- Northern America	4.0	4.1	3.9	4.0	4.0	4.5	3.9	4.6	5.1	5.2	- Amérique du Nord
- LAIA	18.5	18.3	17.3	15.4	16.8	16.7	16.2	15.8	15.6	13.5	- ALAI
- CACM	0.4	0.5	0.7	0.7	0.6	0.6	0.0	0.1	0.1	0.1	- MCC
- Caribbean	0.0	0.0	0.0	0.0	0.0	0.1	0.0	0.0	0.0	0.0	- Caraïbes
- Rest of America	0.0	0.0	0.0	0.0	0.0	0.0	0.0	0.0	0.0	0.0	- Autre d'Amérique
Asia excluding former USSR	17.1	13.5	13.1	13.5	14.2	13.2	15.8	16.6	17.6	19.2	Asie ancienne URSS exclus
- Middle East	1.1	1.0	1.7	1.5	1.6	1.6	1.9	1.9	1.8	1.9	- Moyen-Orient
Asia former USSR	0.2	0.2	0.0	0.0	0.0	0.1	0.0	0.0	0.0	0.0	Asie ancienne URSS
Europe excluding former USSR	51.8	54.9	57.5	59.4	57.2	57.8	57.1	56.4	55.6	56.0	Europe ancienne URSS exclus
- European Union	50.1	53.6	56.2	58.3	56.0	56.6	55.9	55.1	54.2	54.4	- Union Européenne
- Eastern Europe	0.3	0.2	0.1	0.1	0.1	0.2	0.1	0.2	0.2	0.2	- Europe de l'Est
- Rest of Europe	1.3	1.0	1.2	1.0	1.0	1.0	1.0	1.1	1.3	1.4	- Autre de l'Europe
Europe former USSR	0.5	0.1	0.1	0.1	0.2	0.2	0.2	0.2	0.5	0.5	Europe ancienne URSS
Oceania	1.2	1.1	1.3	1.1	1.3	1.7	0.6	0.7	0.4	0.2	Océanie

533 Pigments, paints, varnishes and related materials

TRADE BY COMMODITY (Value in million US dollars)
Imports by principal countries or areas

COMMERCE PAR PRODUIT (Valeur en millions de dollars EU)
Importations selon les principaux pays ou zones

Country or area	1998	1999	2000	2001	2002	Pays ou zone
World	21446.6	22418.5	24035.7	23626.4	24748.9	Monde
Africa	598.3	603.5	567.0	603.6	644.1	Afrique
Americas	4101.4	4520.8	4881.7	4760.7	4521.1	Amériques
- Northern America	2441.6	2749.0	2946.5	2885.2	2798.2	- Amérique du Nord
- LAIA	1388.3	1506.9	1638.1	1573.3	1419.1	- ALAI
- CACM	105.1	101.6	113.9	114.7	126.9	- MCC
- Caribbean	138.7	132.3	147.6	156.9	141.2	- Caraïbes
- Rest of America	27.6	31.0	35.6	30.5	35.6	- Autre d'Amérique
Asia excluding former USSR	4934.0	5545.7	6780.7	6333.9	6863.3	Asie ancienne URSS exclus
- Middle East	780.5	731.0	815.4	819.6	934.6	- Moyen-Orient
Asia former USSR	69.3	83.2	95.3	89.6	93.3	Asie ancienne URSS
Europe excluding former USSR	10752.1	10777.6	10752.0	10826.9	11491.8	Europe ancienne URSS exclus
- European Union	8787.4	8772.3	8751.7	8692.8	9017.1	- Union Européenne
- Eastern Europe	1190.5	1204.0	1239.6	1277.8	1448.6	- Europe de l'Est
- Rest of Europe	774.2	801.2	760.8	856.2	1026.1	- Autre de l'Europe
Europe former USSR	696.8	546.2	595.1	673.3	788.1	Europe ancienne URSS
Oceania	294.8	341.5	363.9	338.5	347.2	Océanie
United States	1465.6	1661.3	1801.9	1773.2	1627.8	Etats-Unis d'Amérique
Germany	1415.6	1365.8	1311.8	1426.6	1330.7	Allemagne
France-Monaco	1236.5	1323.7	1345.2	1263.8	1337.7	France-Monaco
China	768.9	944.9	1233.9	1322.4	1507.3	Chine
Canada	969.5	1080.7	1141.8	1107.5	1164.7	Canada
United Kingdom	1128.2	1035.6	1072.4	1032.8	1071.8	Royaume-Uni
Italy-San Marino-Holy See	979.5	977.4	1000.2	975.0	1011.6	Italie-Saint-Marin-Saint-Siège
Belgium	–	938.1	955.7	951.2	e1043.2	Belgique
China, Hong Kong SAR	660.8	667.3	760.9	674.5	719.4	Chine - RAS de Hong-Kong
Spain	616.9	628.4	686.0	696.6	791.9	Espagne
Mexico	469.7	657.2	749.8	686.6	671.5	Mexique
Netherlands	631.0	638.1	592.3	554.2	597.5	Pays-Bas
Korea, Republic of	375.7	502.8	611.3	621.2	670.5	République de Corée
Poland	514.5	539.0	548.6	542.0	605.6	Pologne
Japan	417.7	439.4	484.3	455.2	434.7	Japon
Thailand	231.2	340.8	499.8	518.9	e540.6	Thaïlande
Switzerland-Liechtenstein	351.1	370.5	345.9	427.7	548.3	Suisse-Liechtenstein
Austria	400.1	404.7	403.4	411.3	388.4	Autriche
Singapore	307.7	390.1	570.5	343.8	378.7	Singapour
Russian Federation	364.5	261.8	305.1	364.1	425.7	Fédération de Russie
Brazil	360.1	349.2	342.8	352.9	304.0	Brésil
Sweden	333.0	350.6	320.5	322.5	334.1	Suède
Turkey	326.9	301.7	329.4	258.0	364.1	Turquie
Czech Republic	283.2	277.3	276.6	290.7	329.3	République tchèque
Portugal	277.2	272.7	269.7	269.0	288.4	Portugal
Denmark	261.4	261.8	246.0	256.2	264.3	Danemark
Malaysia	167.4	207.6	253.6	211.5	e231.1	Malaisie
Australia	189.1	213.4	231.8	205.8	203.2	Australie
Belgium-Luxembourg	976.7	–	–	–	–	Belgique-Luxembourg
Indonesia	163.4	144.8	223.6	210.8	205.9	Indonésie

(Value as percentages of World total) **(Valeur en pourcentage du total mondial)**

Regions of the world	1993	1994	1995	1996	1997	1998	1999	2000	2001	2002	Régions du monde
World	100.0	100.0	100.0	100.0	100.0	100.0	100.0	100.0	100.0	100.0	Monde
Africa	3.6	3.0	2.6	2.7	2.6	2.8	2.7	2.4	2.6	2.6	Afrique
Americas	15.5	16.2	15.8	16.4	18.4	19.1	20.2	20.3	20.1	18.3	Amériques
- Northern America	9.7	10.1	9.7	10.0	11.2	11.4	12.3	12.3	12.2	11.3	- Amérique du Nord
- LAIA	4.7	5.2	5.1	5.3	6.0	6.5	6.7	6.8	6.7	5.7	- ALAI
- CACM	0.4	0.4	0.4	0.4	0.4	0.5	0.5	0.5	0.5	0.5	- MCC
- Caribbean	0.6	0.5	0.5	0.6	0.6	0.6	0.6	0.6	0.7	0.6	- Caraïbes
- Rest of America	0.2	0.2	0.1	0.1	0.1	0.1	0.1	0.1	0.1	0.1	- Autre d'Amérique
Asia excluding former USSR	27.9	26.2	26.3	26.3	26.5	23.0	24.7	28.2	26.8	27.7	Asie ancienne URSS exclus
- Middle East	3.7	3.1	3.6	3.5	3.5	3.6	3.3	3.4	3.5	3.8	- Moyen-Orient
Asia former USSR	0.0	0.3	0.3	0.5	0.2	0.3	0.4	0.4	0.4	0.4	Asie ancienne URSS
Europe excluding former USSR	49.7	50.4	51.0	49.7	47.4	50.1	48.1	44.7	45.8	46.4	Europe ancienne URSS exclus
- European Union	41.8	42.3	42.4	41.0	38.9	41.0	39.1	36.4	36.8	36.4	- Union Européenne
- Eastern Europe	3.5	3.7	4.3	4.8	5.0	5.6	5.4	5.2	5.4	5.9	- Europe de l'Est
- Rest of Europe	4.4	4.4	4.3	3.9	3.5	3.6	3.6	3.2	3.6	4.1	- Autre de l'Europe
Europe former USSR	1.9	2.5	2.8	3.0	3.5	3.2	2.4	2.5	2.8	3.2	Europe ancienne URSS
Oceania	1.3	1.4	1.3	1.4	1.4	1.4	1.5	1.5	1.4	1.4	Océanie

TRADE BY COMMODITY (Value in million US dollars)
Exports by principal countries or areas

COMMERCE PAR PRODUIT (Valeur en millions de dollars EU)
Exportations selon les principaux pays ou zones

Country or area	1998	1999	2000	2001	2002	Pays ou zone
World	22075.3	22729.1	24183.8	23643.5	25327.9	Monde
Africa	83.0	82.6	87.2	94.0	101.8	Afrique
Americas	3922.3	4229.9	4876.0	4659.1	4675.7	Amériques
- Northern America	3236.2	3474.1	3933.1	3707.3	3848.8	- Amérique du Nord
- LAIA	629.6	700.4	883.3	890.8	761.3	- ALAI
- CACM	35.2	37.6	39.6	42.5	51.5	- MCC
- Caribbean	18.8	16.7	18.5	17.2	12.9	- Caraïbes
- Rest of America	2.5	1.2	1.5	1.4	1.3	- Autre d'Amérique
Asia excluding former USSR	3650.2	4166.0	4902.0	4464.3	4830.0	Asie ancienne URSS exclus
- Middle East	201.4	175.3	170.6	183.5	198.4	- Moyen-Orient
Asia former USSR	8.9	3.7	4.3	4.6	2.9	Asie ancienne URSS
Europe excluding former USSR	13840.6	13697.9	13705.8	13817.4	15099.5	Europe ancienne URSS exclus
- European Union	12776.0	12595.9	12557.2	12659.3	13850.9	- Union Européenne
- Eastern Europe	242.1	231.3	254.3	264.7	316.6	- Europe de l'Est
- Rest of Europe	822.5	870.8	894.2	893.4	932.0	- Autre de l'Europe
Europe former USSR	256.7	212.2	252.2	272.5	252.8	Europe ancienne URSS
Oceania	313.6	336.7	356.3	331.7	365.2	Océanie
Germany	4119.4	4161.3	4016.0	4089.2	4404.4	Allemagne
United States	2718.7	2900.3	3345.9	3138.9	3266.9	Etats-Unis d'Amérique
Japan	1418.8	1736.9	1938.7	1543.6	1635.6	Japon
United Kingdom	1654.1	1520.6	1535.5	1488.8	1647.6	Royaume-Uni
France-Monaco	1235.0	1294.9	1326.7	1232.9	1337.4	France-Monaco
Belgium	–	1473.4	1498.2	1540.5	e1728.5	Belgique
Netherlands	1255.4	992.4	1014.4	988.8	1098.0	Pays-Bas
Italy-San Marino-Holy See	965.8	995.3	1009.4	1032.7	1133.5	Italie-Saint-Marin-Saint-Siège
Spain	691.1	756.2	774.2	844.5	950.9	Espagne
Switzerland-Liechtenstein	578.8	634.7	645.0	646.7	671.5	Suisse-Liechtenstein
Canada	517.4	573.7	587.2	568.4	581.9	Canada
Singapore	312.3	416.0	588.0	547.1	573.3	Singapour
China, Hong Kong SAR	451.4	446.7	531.5	485.0	498.0	Chine - RAS de Hong-Kong
Sweden	356.3	395.0	397.8	404.9	470.2	Suède
Finland	360.4	354.0	364.4	399.3	403.2	Finlande
China	302.1	272.3	348.6	397.7	454.6	Chine
Australia	300.2	319.6	340.0	315.9	346.9	Australie
Korea, Republic of	225.4	267.7	337.5	361.8	413.0	République de Corée
Mexico	138.5	230.3	370.9	422.1	356.0	Mexique
Belgium-Luxembourg	1480.1	–	–	–	–	Belgique-Luxembourg
Colombia	178.3	315.9	348.8	295.0	231.4	Colombie
Austria	267.1	259.8	251.4	262.6	283.9	Autriche
Denmark	268.2	256.7	224.9	216.3	210.7	Danemark
Malaysia	154.5	170.6	191.9	189.2	e200.5	Malaisie
Slovenia	140.6	144.4	160.1	154.6	173.0	Slovénie
Czech Republic	99.5	103.3	112.2	102.7	111.3	République tchèque
Poland	80.3	75.2	90.6	111.1	151.4	Pologne
Brazil	116.0	91.3	92.1	93.6	e97.0	Brésil
Ukraine	65.9	74.3	101.0	72.3	79.7	Ukraine
Turkey	76.5	61.1	63.3	68.9	82.4	Turquie

(Value as percentages of World total) **(Valeur en pourcentage du total mondial)**

Regions of the world	1993	1994	1995	1996	1997	1998	1999	2000	2001	2002	Régions du monde
World	100.0	100.0	100.0	100.0	100.0	100.0	100.0	100.0	100.0	100.0	Monde
Africa	0.3	0.4	0.4	0.3	0.3	0.4	0.4	0.4	0.4	0.4	Afrique
Americas	14.1	14.2	13.8	14.3	16.1	17.8	18.6	20.2	19.7	18.5	Amériques
- Northern America	12.5	12.6	12.0	12.5	14.2	14.7	15.3	16.3	15.7	15.2	- Amérique du Nord
- LAIA	1.4	1.5	1.6	1.6	1.6	2.9	3.1	3.7	3.8	3.0	- ALAI
- CACM	0.1	0.1	0.1	0.1	0.1	0.2	0.2	0.2	0.2	0.2	- MCC
- Caribbean	0.1	0.1	0.1	0.1	0.1	0.1	0.1	0.1	0.1	0.1	- Caraïbes
- Rest of America	0.0	0.0	0.0	0.0	0.0	0.0	0.0	0.0	0.0	0.0	- Autre d'Amérique
Asia excluding former USSR	18.2	18.0	19.0	17.7	18.7	16.5	18.3	20.3	18.9	19.1	Asie ancienne URSS exclus
- Middle East	0.9	0.8	0.7	0.9	1.0	0.9	0.8	0.7	0.8	0.8	- Moyen-Orient
Asia former USSR	0.0	0.0	0.0	0.0	0.0	0.0	0.0	0.0	0.0	0.0	Asie ancienne URSS
Europe excluding former USSR	65.3	65.0	64.3	64.7	62.2	62.7	60.3	56.7	58.4	59.6	Europe ancienne URSS exclus
- European Union	60.0	59.9	59.1	59.7	57.5	57.9	55.4	51.9	53.5	54.7	- Union Européenne
- Eastern Europe	0.8	0.9	1.1	1.0	1.0	1.1	1.0	1.1	1.1	1.2	- Europe de l'Est
- Rest of Europe	4.5	4.2	4.1	4.0	3.6	3.7	3.8	3.7	3.8	3.7	- Autre de l'Europe
Europe former USSR	0.4	0.8	0.9	1.3	1.2	1.2	0.9	1.0	1.2	1.0	Europe ancienne URSS
Oceania	1.7	1.6	1.6	1.6	1.5	1.4	1.5	1.5	1.4	1.4	Océanie

541 Medicinal and pharmaceutical products

TRADE BY COMMODITY (Value in million US dollars)
Imports by principal countries or areas

COMMERCE PAR PRODUIT (Valeur en millions de dollars EU)
Importations selon les principaux pays ou zones

Country or area	1998	1999	2000	2001	2002	Pays ou zone
World	96726.7	108247.1	113209.5	134665.5	162451.2	Monde
Africa	3177.4	3126.5	3243.6	3550.3	3760.6	Afrique
Americas	19955.3	23678.7	25863.6	31173.0	37564.4	Amériques
- Northern America	13708.2	16921.7	18705.1	23213.6	29921.5	- Amérique du Nord
- LAIA	5171.2	5612.9	5831.3	6458.9	6138.2	- ALAI
- CACM	592.1	676.0	807.8	926.7	961.7	- MCC
- Caribbean	356.8	326.3	364.6	421.3	401.4	- Caraïbes
- Rest of America	127.0	141.8	154.7	152.3	141.6	- Autre d'Amérique
Asia excluding former USSR	13656.0	15721.1	16498.1	17647.8	19211.6	Asie ancienne URSS exclus
- Middle East	3468.4	3724.0	4039.2	4185.6	4601.2	- Moyen-Orient
Asia former USSR	253.9	254.9	310.4	316.1	331.3	Asie ancienne URSS
Europe excluding former USSR	55077.8	61120.9	62186.0	76164.1	95374.9	Europe ancienne URSS exclus
- European Union	45943.1	50932.6	51631.1	63316.0	80022.6	- Union Européenne
- Eastern Europe	3579.5	3660.1	3746.9	4418.9	5181.3	- Europe de l'Est
- Rest of Europe	5555.3	6528.3	6808.0	8429.2	10171.0	- Autre de l'Europe
Europe former USSR	2340.0	1776.8	2286.1	2975.6	2893.9	Europe ancienne URSS
Oceania	2266.3	2568.2	2821.8	2838.6	3314.6	Océanie
United States	10982.2	13649.3	14855.2	18753.1	24873.7	Etats-Unis d'Amérique
Germany	8373.1	8669.6	8812.4	10680.9	17388.9	Allemagne
France-Monaco	7166.0	7748.7	7972.3	9272.6	10781.1	France-Monaco
United Kingdom	5631.6	6805.7	7348.2	9178.4	11085.6	Royaume-Uni
Italy-San Marino-Holy See	5435.5	6195.8	6000.9	7059.2	8705.8	Italie-Saint-Marin-Saint-Siège
Switzerland-Liechtenstein	4108.2	5050.5	5274.9	6856.4	8265.6	Suisse-Liechtenstein
Belgium	–	5023.6	5550.8	8353.9	e9161.8	Belgique
Japan	3751.2	4593.4	4775.0	5051.5	5426.2	Japon
Netherlands	3426.9	4174.6	3993.1	4880.0	6080.4	Pays-Bas
Spain	3214.9	3509.1	3613.3	4407.0	5724.4	Espagne
Canada	2693.8	3237.6	3802.5	4321.7	4870.0	Canada
Australia	1785.5	2068.7	2358.2	2385.3	2829.8	Australie
Austria	2223.7	2177.9	1791.6	2027.3	2448.7	Autriche
Brazil	1606.3	1950.5	1804.3	1910.2	1930.9	Brésil
Poland	1527.5	1504.1	1597.7	1891.9	2099.2	Pologne
Mexico	1089.3	1253.9	1445.4	1651.4	1859.9	Mexique
Ireland	1012.2	1197.5	1417.2	1723.0	1948.8	Irlande
Sweden	1322.7	1443.9	1340.6	1448.9	1647.9	Suède
Russian Federation	1383.6	917.5	1325.4	1867.0	1627.1	Fédération de Russie
Turkey	1017.9	1159.3	1344.3	1345.3	1717.2	Turquie
Greece	1080.3	1193.3	1133.2	1160.6	e1283.3	Grèce
Denmark	920.1	921.9	902.1	1097.0	1329.0	Danemark
Portugal	783.8	1002.4	923.0	1079.3	1303.3	Portugal
China	533.5	820.8	952.9	1217.5	1434.1	Chine
Belgium-Luxembourg	4695.4	–	–	–	–	Belgique-Luxembourg
China, Hong Kong SAR	1055.8	980.1	934.3	882.5	825.7	Chine - RAS de Hong-Kong
Saudi Arabia	902.6	908.9	883.1	967.2	e1000.9	Arabie saoudite
Korea, Republic of	561.0	726.2	825.4	1002.4	1174.1	République de Corée
Czech Republic	738.4	776.0	754.4	891.2	1064.2	République tchèque
Norway	696.6	722.9	742.2	747.9	939.9	Norvège

(Value as percentages of World total) **(Valeur en pourcentage du total mondial)**

Regions of the world	1993	1994	1995	1996	1997	1998	1999	2000	2001	2002	Régions du monde
World	100.0	100.0	100.0	100.0	100.0	100.0	100.0	100.0	100.0	100.0	Monde
Africa	4.2	4.2	3.8	3.2	3.2	3.3	2.9	2.9	2.6	2.3	Afrique
Americas	15.9	16.3	15.5	17.2	18.9	20.6	21.9	22.8	23.1	23.1	Amériques
- Northern America	10.6	10.4	9.9	11.5	12.9	14.2	15.6	16.5	17.2	18.4	- Amérique du Nord
- LAIA	3.9	4.5	4.3	4.7	4.9	5.3	5.2	5.2	4.8	3.8	- ALAI
- CACM	0.7	0.6	0.6	0.6	0.6	0.6	0.6	0.7	0.7	0.6	- MCC
- Caribbean	0.6	0.5	0.5	0.4	0.4	0.4	0.3	0.3	0.3	0.2	- Caraïbes
- Rest of America	0.2	0.2	0.2	0.1	0.1	0.1	0.1	0.1	0.1	0.1	- Autre d'Amérique
Asia excluding former USSR	20.9	19.1	18.8	17.7	16.4	14.1	14.5	14.6	13.1	11.8	Asie ancienne URSS exclus
- Middle East	4.1	3.3	3.5	3.5	3.4	3.6	3.4	3.6	3.1	2.8	- Moyen-Orient
Asia former USSR	0.2	0.2	0.2	0.3	0.3	0.3	0.2	0.3	0.2	0.2	Asie ancienne URSS
Europe excluding former USSR	53.7	55.5	57.1	56.7	55.5	56.9	56.5	54.9	56.6	58.7	Europe ancienne URSS exclus
- European Union	45.4	47.0	48.5	48.1	46.4	47.5	47.1	45.6	47.0	49.3	- Union Européenne
- Eastern Europe	3.0	3.1	3.2	3.6	3.6	3.7	3.4	3.3	3.3	3.2	- Europe de l'Est
- Rest of Europe	5.4	5.4	5.4	5.0	5.4	5.7	6.0	6.0	6.3	6.3	- Autre de l'Europe
Europe former USSR	2.6	2.2	2.3	2.4	3.2	2.4	1.6	2.0	2.2	1.8	Europe ancienne URSS
Oceania	2.4	2.5	2.3	2.6	2.5	2.3	2.4	2.5	2.1	2.0	Océanie

TRADE BY COMMODITY (Value in million US dollars)
Exports by principal countries or areas

COMMERCE PAR PRODUIT (Valeur en millions de dollars EU)
Exportations selon les principaux pays ou zones

Country or area	1998	1999	2000	2001	2002	Pays ou zone
World	94572.1	104870.4	107481.7	132797.0	151861.6	Monde
Africa	232.7	189.3	191.7	186.2	237.1	Afrique
Americas	12660.3	14408.6	16555.6	19429.3	20310.3	Amériques
- Northern America	10711.4	12379.2	14351.8	16873.2	17697.9	- Amérique du Nord
- LAIA	1637.8	1721.3	1835.4	2165.6	2225.0	- ALAI
- CACM	233.5	234.1	287.3	297.7	304.0	- MCC
- Caribbean	59.1	54.8	62.8	70.9	60.3	- Caraïbes
- Rest of America	18.5	19.1	18.4	22.0	23.1	- Autre d'Amérique
Asia excluding former USSR	7421.4	8644.9	9095.0	9831.6	10760.4	Asie ancienne URSS exclus
- Middle East	351.8	395.1	384.7	490.4	545.4	- Moyen-Orient
Asia former USSR	17.3	9.0	12.2	10.4	11.1	Asie ancienne URSS
Europe excluding former USSR	73012.7	80273.3	80065.2	101665.6	119023.0	Europe ancienne URSS exclus
- European Union	61303.5	67122.5	67565.0	86095.1	100754.0	- Union Européenne
- Eastern Europe	957.2	835.7	906.9	1082.2	1138.9	- Europe de l'Est
- Rest of Europe	10752.0	12315.1	11593.3	14488.3	17130.1	- Autre de l'Europe
Europe former USSR	395.9	318.9	322.0	326.2	375.2	Europe ancienne URSS
Oceania	831.8	1026.5	1239.9	1347.7	1144.5	Océanie
Germany	14220.2	14977.9	12944.6	18054.5	15048.9	Allemagne
United States	9660.8	11247.5	13122.0	15421.4	16144.4	Etats-Unis d'Amérique
Switzerland-Liechtenstein	9854.4	11451.6	10654.9	13459.5	15870.7	Suisse-Liechtenstein
United Kingdom	9666.6	10053.7	10782.6	13009.2	14918.8	Royaume-Uni
France-Monaco	9314.5	10043.3	10321.2	12635.7	14941.4	France-Monaco
Ireland	4745.9	5122.2	4908.4	8007.9	14781.3	Irlande
Italy-San Marino-Holy See	4698.3	5607.4	6380.0	7339.0	8933.0	Italie-Saint-Marin-Saint-Siège
Belgium	-	6437.7	6834.2	9359.6	e10501.3	Belgique
Netherlands	3519.6	3851.6	4214.5	4927.4	6381.7	Pays-Bas
Sweden	3567.0	4010.9	3912.7	4169.0	4447.2	Suède
Denmark	2213.3	2813.0	2810.1	3376.3	3818.4	Danemark
Japan	1915.1	2407.4	2731.5	2731.1	2811.9	Japon
Spain	1761.4	1960.1	2056.6	2435.3	3672.5	Espagne
China	1692.3	1678.7	1788.5	1978.5	2323.6	Chine
Austria	1343.1	1559.3	1593.9	1830.4	2228.8	Autriche
Canada	1049.2	1130.8	1227.5	1450.3	1550.2	Canada
India	933.7	1068.2	1255.2	1348.2	1760.0	Inde
Belgium-Luxembourg	5481.8	-	-	-	-	Belgique-Luxembourg
Australia	768.6	956.4	1166.0	1258.6	1058.1	Australie
Singapore	592.0	1177.7	1011.0	1125.5	924.4	Singapour
Mexico	715.9	782.2	880.4	1086.0	1171.6	Mexique
China, Hong Kong SAR	882.4	818.1	724.7	735.2	639.7	Chine - RAS de Hong-Kong
Israel	396.6	399.9	428.8	638.4	927.4	Israël
Slovenia	387.8	379.0	396.4	468.3	602.9	Slovénie
Hungary	311.6	290.0	342.4	418.2	416.8	Hongrie
Korea, Republic of	292.3	299.4	337.0	324.0	353.9	République de Corée
Argentina	303.0	324.4	308.7	337.2	e325.8	Argentine
Finland	231.4	237.1	261.8	305.8	417.3	Finlande
Portugal	205.9	242.8	281.6	308.2	326.0	Portugal
Brazil	248.1	277.8	266.3	277.2	e287.4	Brésil

(Value as percentages of World total) **(Valeur en pourcentage du total mondial)**

Regions of the world	1993	1994	1995	1996	1997	1998	1999	2000	2001	2002	Régions du monde
World	100.0	100.0	100.0	100.0	100.0	100.0	100.0	100.0	100.0	100.0	Monde
Africa	0.3	0.3	0.2	0.2	0.2	0.2	0.2	0.2	0.1	0.2	Afrique
Americas	13.5	12.8	11.6	12.1	13.1	13.4	13.7	15.4	14.6	13.4	Amériques
- Northern America	12.0	11.2	9.9	10.3	11.0	11.3	11.8	13.4	12.7	11.7	- Amérique du Nord
- LAIA	1.0	1.1	1.3	1.5	1.7	1.7	1.6	1.7	1.6	1.5	- ALAI
- CACM	0.3	0.3	0.2	0.2	0.2	0.2	0.2	0.3	0.2	0.2	- MCC
- Caribbean	0.2	0.2	0.1	0.1	0.1	0.1	0.1	0.1	0.1	0.0	- Caraïbes
- Rest of America	0.0	0.0	0.0	0.0	0.0	0.0	0.0	0.0	0.0	0.0	- Autre d'Amérique
Asia excluding former USSR	9.6	9.7	9.6	9.3	8.8	7.8	8.2	8.5	7.4	7.1	Asie ancienne URSS exclus
- Middle East	0.6	0.5	0.4	0.4	0.3	0.4	0.4	0.4	0.4	0.4	- Moyen-Orient
Asia former USSR	0.0	0.0	0.0	0.0	0.0	0.0	0.0	0.0	0.0	0.0	Asie ancienne URSS
Europe excluding former USSR	75.3	75.9	77.1	76.8	76.4	77.2	76.5	74.5	76.6	78.4	Europe ancienne URSS exclus
- European Union	61.7	62.8	64.3	63.7	64.1	64.8	64.0	62.9	64.8	66.3	- Union Européenne
- Eastern Europe	1.6	1.3	1.2	1.3	1.4	1.0	0.8	0.8	0.8	0.7	- Europe de l'Est
- Rest of Europe	12.0	11.8	11.6	11.8	10.8	11.4	11.7	10.8	10.9	11.3	- Autre de l'Europe
Europe former USSR	0.3	0.4	0.4	0.5	0.5	0.4	0.3	0.3	0.2	0.2	Europe ancienne URSS
Oceania	0.9	1.0	1.0	1.0	1.0	0.9	1.0	1.2	1.0	0.8	Océanie

551 Essential oils, perfume and flavour materials

TRADE BY COMMODITY (Value in million US dollars)
Imports by principal countries or areas

COMMERCE PAR PRODUIT (Valeur en millions de dollars EU)
Importations selon les principaux pays ou zones

Country or area	1998	1999	2000	2001	2002	Pays ou zone
World	6928.6	7153.1	7733.6	8135.7	9009.5	Monde
Africa	315.3	293.7	318.6	372.7	406.9	Afrique
Americas	1190.3	1199.6	1257.4	1398.7	1595.1	Amériques
- Northern America	659.5	648.6	665.2	652.5	792.6	- Amérique du Nord
- LAIA	410.2	430.3	483.6	595.8	610.6	- ALAI
- CACM	60.3	66.3	70.5	88.5	148.5	- MCC
- Caribbean	53.9	49.7	33.9	56.3	36.3	- Caraïbes
- Rest of America	6.5	4.6	4.2	5.5	7.1	- Autre d'Amérique
Asia excluding former USSR	1560.5	1680.1	1677.4	1753.8	1822.0	Asie ancienne URSS exclus
- Middle East	277.6	260.9	261.1	252.9	277.4	- Moyen-Orient
Asia former USSR	10.4	13.1	18.1	12.7	12.9	Asie ancienne URSS
Europe excluding former USSR	3648.7	3775.3	4249.2	4360.9	4899.3	Europe ancienne URSS exclus
- European Union	2997.4	3164.6	3662.6	3761.2	4201.6	- Union Européenne
- Eastern Europe	340.8	324.8	312.1	300.6	372.4	- Europe de l'Est
- Rest of Europe	310.5	286.0	274.6	299.1	325.4	- Autre de l'Europe
Europe former USSR	124.6	110.7	129.6	156.2	186.9	Europe ancienne URSS
Oceania	78.9	80.6	83.2	80.6	86.4	Océanie
France-Monaco	713.4	811.0	1032.8	1011.1	1157.5	France-Monaco
United Kingdom	470.9	554.9	688.1	637.0	735.4	Royaume-Uni
United States	473.8	440.2	442.1	415.5	467.4	Etats-Unis d'Amérique
Germany	332.4	318.8	412.4	453.7	487.6	Allemagne
Italy-San Marino-Holy See	395.6	398.1	368.8	383.0	434.8	Italie-Saint-Marin-Saint-Siège
Spain	320.8	317.3	311.9	369.4	432.9	Espagne
Japan	288.7	348.0	297.5	351.4	355.7	Japon
Netherlands	255.7	172.7	264.4	256.4	244.3	Pays-Bas
Canada	179.2	201.1	222.9	236.8	324.7	Canada
Mexico	113.3	134.1	155.1	249.9	299.7	Mexique
China, Hong Kong SAR	211.7	188.7	161.0	166.4	135.3	Chine - RAS de Hong-Kong
Switzerland-Liechtenstein	151.6	135.3	134.1	150.6	166.5	Suisse-Liechtenstein
Belgium	–	163.2	140.0	199.4	e218.7	Belgique
Ireland	128.1	123.2	166.9	145.4	143.9	Irlande
Indonesia	120.4	117.2	144.1	136.7	141.5	Indonésie
Poland	128.7	136.2	120.1	101.7	132.7	Pologne
Turkey	143.4	118.4	111.6	99.6	125.2	Turquie
Korea, Republic of	88.9	111.8	123.6	125.6	135.8	République de Corée
Thailand	80.7	95.6	118.1	127.0	e132.3	Thaïlande
Russian Federation	82.4	73.2	91.8	110.7	136.8	Fédération de Russie
Singapore	83.2	101.3	96.6	93.6	102.0	Singapour
China	49.0	78.8	86.9	100.5	127.3	Chine
Philippines	99.7	85.7	90.1	81.8	70.3	Philippines
Austria	52.0	82.4	88.4	92.8	104.2	Autriche
Norway	94.7	83.1	72.4	79.4	85.5	Norvège
Brazil	73.0	81.0	83.1	84.3	85.5	Brésil
Czech Republic	76.4	65.2	70.0	68.6	85.5	République tchèque
Greece	84.8	72.7	61.1	65.8	e72.8	Grèce
Malaysia	49.9	64.6	63.5	75.1	e82.0	Malaisie
Colombia	59.0	56.0	57.9	68.1	64.2	Colombie

(Value as percentages of World total) **(Valeur en pourcentage du total mondial)**

Regions of the world	1993	1994	1995	1996	1997	1998	1999	2000	2001	2002	Régions du monde
World	100.0	100.0	100.0	100.0	100.0	100.0	100.0	100.0	100.0	100.0	Monde
Africa	5.2	6.9	5.7	4.1	3.8	4.6	4.1	4.1	4.6	4.5	Afrique
Americas	17.7	16.4	17.3	16.5	16.6	17.2	16.8	16.3	17.2	17.7	Amériques
- Northern America	10.3	9.6	10.4	9.9	9.4	9.5	9.1	8.6	8.0	8.8	- Amérique du Nord
- LAIA	5.9	5.4	5.6	5.1	5.5	5.9	6.0	6.3	7.3	6.8	- ALAI
- CACM	0.8	0.8	0.8	0.7	0.8	0.9	0.9	0.9	1.1	1.6	- MCC
- Caribbean	0.4	0.6	0.6	0.7	0.8	0.8	0.7	0.4	0.7	0.4	- Caraïbes
- Rest of America	0.2	0.1	0.1	0.1	0.1	0.1	0.1	0.1	0.1	0.1	- Autre d'Amérique
Asia excluding former USSR	27.9	26.4	26.1	26.9	25.6	22.5	23.5	21.7	21.6	20.2	Asie ancienne URSS exclus
- Middle East	3.2	3.0	3.4	4.1	4.0	4.0	3.6	3.4	3.1	3.1	- Moyen-Orient
Asia former USSR	0.0	0.0	0.0	0.1	0.1	0.1	0.2	0.2	0.2	0.1	Asie ancienne URSS
Europe excluding former USSR	47.1	47.8	48.4	49.8	51.1	52.7	52.8	54.9	53.6	54.4	Europe ancienne URSS exclus
- European Union	41.5	41.3	41.4	41.7	42.8	43.3	44.2	47.4	46.2	46.6	- Union Européenne
- Eastern Europe	2.2	2.2	2.9	4.1	4.2	4.9	4.5	4.0	3.7	4.1	- Europe de l'Est
- Rest of Europe	3.4	4.2	4.0	4.0	4.1	4.5	4.0	3.6	3.7	3.6	- Autre de l'Europe
Europe former USSR	0.8	1.2	1.4	1.4	1.8	1.8	1.5	1.7	1.9	2.1	Europe ancienne URSS
Oceania	1.3	1.3	1.2	1.2	1.1	1.1	1.1	1.1	1.0	1.0	Océanie

TRADE BY COMMODITY (Value in million US dollars)
Exports by principal countries or areas

COMMERCE PAR PRODUIT (Valeur en millions de dollars EU)
Exportations selon les principaux pays ou zones

Country or area	1998	1999	2000	2001	2002	Pays ou zone
World	7442.2	8024.2	7824.6	8566.5	9643.0	Monde
Africa	55.1	56.5	220.6	194.5	264.7	Afrique
Americas	1062.5	1092.9	1251.4	1329.4	1452.8	Amériques
- Northern America	829.5	839.4	956.1	1018.5	1112.3	- Amérique du Nord
- LAIA	212.7	234.1	277.6	293.7	318.6	- ALAI
- CACM	4.3	4.2	6.2	6.5	7.3	- MCC
- Caribbean	15.5	14.4	11.2	10.4	13.5	- Caraïbes
- Rest of America	0.5	0.9	0.3	0.2	1.0	- Autre d'Amérique
Asia excluding former USSR	793.3	858.0	882.1	896.2	976.0	Asie ancienne URSS exclus
- Middle East	20.3	29.6	33.3	61.9	63.0	- Moyen-Orient
Asia former USSR	0.4	0.2	0.1	0.2	0.5	Asie ancienne URSS
Europe excluding former USSR	5486.5	5964.3	5411.4	6100.2	6876.0	Europe ancienne URSS exclus
- European Union	4755.1	5190.7	4616.5	5246.4	5825.1	- Union Européenne
- Eastern Europe	30.3	26.4	23.7	24.5	36.2	- Europe de l'Est
- Rest of Europe	701.1	747.2	771.1	829.3	1014.6	- Autre de l'Europe
Europe former USSR	10.2	12.1	21.7	13.1	21.6	Europe ancienne URSS
Oceania	34.2	40.2	37.3	33.0	51.4	Océanie
Ireland	1693.7	1952.6	1598.6	2212.6	2399.9	Irlande
France-Monaco	976.7	1150.5	1138.2	1007.3	1163.7	France-Monaco
United States	802.6	813.0	924.7	990.4	1087.1	Etats-Unis d'Amérique
Switzerland-Liechtenstein	682.4	725.0	750.6	809.4	991.5	Suisse-Liechtenstein
Germany	668.9	636.9	559.3	661.2	734.1	Allemagne
United Kingdom	603.6	599.5	573.3	584.3	621.3	Royaume-Uni
Netherlands	391.7	415.8	353.5	338.2	406.8	Pays-Bas
Singapore	157.9	172.1	166.4	171.0	219.9	Singapour
Spain	128.0	129.8	122.7	172.1	201.9	Espagne
Japan	117.2	144.2	152.7	154.3	168.7	Japon
China, Hong Kong SAR	137.0	139.9	129.7	114.4	84.8	Chine - RAS de Hong-Kong
Swaziland	–	–	169.6	132.7	e183.8	Swaziland
China	106.5	95.7	84.0	90.3	103.4	Chine
Italy-San Marino-Holy See	95.0	98.2	90.9	84.4	85.7	Italie-Saint-Marin-Saint-Siège
Argentina	58.5	69.9	84.5	88.1	e85.2	Argentine
Mexico	61.2	67.9	74.0	77.9	98.9	Mexique
Belgium	–	97.2	78.6	84.4	e94.7	Belgique
Brazil	58.9	55.0	71.7	77.2	e80.0	Brésil
India	62.3	63.0	76.1	61.3	77.6	Inde
Israel	45.0	58.1	81.9	70.2	78.5	Israël
Indonesia	75.1	56.0	56.0	72.6	71.0	Indonésie
Austria	50.3	51.1	48.5	54.8	64.6	Autriche
Thailand	28.5	49.2	53.6	56.9	e60.1	Thaïlande
Australia	31.5	36.0	33.2	27.2	45.4	Australie
Canada	27.0	26.3	31.0	28.1	25.2	Canada
Denmark	25.9	28.3	26.0	22.6	20.7	Danemark
Sweden	20.6	23.6	19.8	17.0	23.1	Suède
Colombia	16.9	20.4	20.6	19.9	19.8	Colombie
Belgium-Luxembourg	94.3	–	–	–	–	Belgique-Luxembourg
Slovenia	14.5	14.9	15.9	15.1	18.5	Slovénie

(Value as percentages of World total) **(Valeur en pourcentage du total mondial)**

Regions of the world	1993	1994	1995	1996	1997	1998	1999	2000	2001	2002	Régions du monde
World	100.0	100.0	100.0	100.0	100.0	100.0	100.0	100.0	100.0	100.0	Monde
Africa	1.2	1.0	1.3	4.1	0.9	0.7	0.7	2.8	2.3	2.7	Afrique
Americas	19.8	20.0	19.1	17.4	16.2	14.3	13.6	16.0	15.5	15.1	Amériques
- Northern America	15.9	16.4	14.8	13.6	12.6	11.1	10.5	12.2	11.9	11.5	- Amérique du Nord
- LAIA	3.4	3.4	4.0	3.6	3.3	2.9	2.9	3.5	3.4	3.3	- ALAI
- CACM	0.1	0.1	0.1	0.0	0.0	0.1	0.1	0.1	0.1	0.1	- MCC
- Caribbean	0.3	0.2	0.2	0.2	0.2	0.2	0.2	0.1	0.1	0.1	- Caraïbes
- Rest of America	0.0	0.0	0.0	0.0	0.0	0.0	0.0	0.0	0.0	0.0	- Autre d'Amérique
Asia excluding former USSR	13.5	13.9	13.5	12.9	11.9	10.7	10.7	11.3	10.5	10.1	Asie ancienne URSS exclus
- Middle East	0.4	0.3	0.4	0.4	0.3	0.3	0.4	0.4	0.7	0.7	- Moyen-Orient
Asia former USSR	0.0	0.0	0.0	0.0	0.0	0.0	0.0	0.0	0.0	0.0	Asie ancienne URSS
Europe excluding former USSR	64.6	64.2	65.4	64.6	70.0	73.7	74.3	69.2	71.2	71.3	Europe ancienne URSS exclus
- European Union	51.2	50.8	52.2	53.6	60.4	63.9	64.7	59.0	61.2	60.4	- Union Européenne
- Eastern Europe	1.1	0.2	0.4	0.4	0.4	0.4	0.3	0.3	0.3	0.4	- Europe de l'Est
- Rest of Europe	12.2	13.2	12.8	10.6	9.2	9.4	9.3	9.9	9.7	10.5	- Autre de l'Europe
Europe former USSR	0.3	0.2	0.2	0.3	0.4	0.1	0.2	0.3	0.2	0.2	Europe ancienne URSS
Oceania	0.6	0.7	0.6	0.7	0.6	0.5	0.5	0.5	0.4	0.5	Océanie

553 Perfumery, cosmetics, toilet preparations, etc

TRADE BY COMMODITY (Value in million US dollars) COMMERCE PAR PRODUIT (Valeur en millions de dollars EU)
Imports by principal countries or areas **Importations selon les principaux pays ou zones**

Country or area	1998	1999	2000	2001	2002	Pays ou zone
World	20518.0	21446.2	22542.3	24529.3	26636.8	Monde
Africa	247.4	266.3	341.0	395.7	403.9	Afrique
Americas	3999.7	4291.8	4875.9	5421.0	5661.8	Amériques
- Northern America	2650.6	2945.9	3326.0	3610.8	3970.1	- Amérique du Nord
- LAIA	984.3	995.9	1172.0	1392.8	1248.3	- ALAI
- CACM	147.1	147.8	161.7	190.8	214.8	- MCC
- Caribbean	169.6	149.5	166.9	175.1	174.5	- Caraïbes
- Rest of America	48.0	52.7	49.4	51.4	54.1	- Autre d'Amérique
Asia excluding former USSR	4088.0	4548.8	5159.9	5331.8	5654.8	Asie ancienne URSS exclus
- Middle East	1066.1	1106.9	1230.0	1256.0	1299.3	- Moyen-Orient
Asia former USSR	63.5	59.6	80.1	82.2	87.6	Asie ancienne URSS
Europe excluding former USSR	11011.2	11398.2	11106.5	12047.9	13307.5	Europe ancienne URSS exclus
- European Union	9293.7	9674.0	9446.9	10277.1	11293.6	- Union Européenne
- Eastern Europe	721.6	729.6	727.3	799.7	948.9	- Europe de l'Est
- Rest of Europe	996.0	994.6	932.3	971.1	1064.9	- Autre de l'Europe
Europe former USSR	629.5	365.7	449.7	697.0	898.7	Europe ancienne URSS
Oceania	478.7	515.7	529.3	553.7	622.4	Océanie
United States	1825.0	2061.3	2374.6	2581.0	2850.1	Etats-Unis d'Amérique
Germany	1856.2	1814.9	1702.9	2048.4	1997.6	Allemagne
United Kingdom	1448.2	1506.7	1642.0	1877.6	2146.4	Royaume-Uni
France-Monaco	1147.0	1167.3	1122.6	1045.2	1205.6	France-Monaco
Italy-San Marino-Holy See	1002.3	1067.5	1050.1	1055.9	1139.6	Italie-Saint-Marin-Saint-Siège
Japan	852.2	1001.7	1102.8	1075.8	1157.9	Japon
Canada	820.5	879.0	948.0	1025.8	1114.0	Canada
Spain	730.2	784.9	773.4	923.8	1007.6	Espagne
Netherlands	577.7	687.6	664.8	668.4	780.1	Pays-Bas
China, Hong Kong SAR	616.4	596.9	660.9	691.1	711.0	Chine - RAS de Hong-Kong
Belgium	–	663.6	616.3	651.9	e714.9	Belgique
Singapore	436.2	502.3	554.4	557.0	580.9	Singapour
Switzerland-Liechtenstein	507.6	485.2	431.6	455.0	483.8	Suisse-Liechtenstein
Mexico	312.0	334.4	441.1	551.4	532.5	Mexique
Australia	314.2	353.0	373.0	393.0	444.2	Australie
United Arab Emirates	317.0	332.2	379.3	418.7	e429.6	Emirates arabes unis
Austria	371.4	349.8	342.7	345.1	425.3	Autriche
Ireland	277.6	310.7	320.5	436.2	476.3	Irlande
Korea, Republic of	145.4	230.5	357.3	475.0	592.9	République de Corée
Russian Federation	376.4	163.2	249.8	406.1	552.3	Fédération de Russie
Denmark	314.1	303.4	302.7	296.4	346.8	Danemark
Poland	283.4	293.6	276.4	294.2	335.5	Pologne
Saudi Arabia	248.7	259.9	321.1	291.2	e301.4	Arabie saoudite
Sweden	267.0	285.9	237.0	247.7	290.8	Suède
Greece	264.3	258.6	256.3	248.8	e275.1	Grèce
Portugal	241.4	260.1	237.6	248.5	289.8	Portugal
Norway	202.3	197.9	201.1	199.7	216.3	Norvège
Malaysia	148.4	177.0	184.1	203.4	e222.3	Malaisie
Czech Republic	158.9	155.9	154.0	156.8	190.3	République tchèque
Turkey	126.5	140.2	158.7	137.9	164.1	Turquie

(Value as percentages of World total) **(Valeur en pourcentage du total mondial)**

Regions of the world	1993	1994	1995	1996	1997	1998	1999	2000	2001	2002	Régions du monde
World	100.0	100.0	100.0	100.0	100.0	100.0	100.0	100.0	100.0	100.0	Monde
Africa	1.1	1.4	1.2	1.0	1.1	1.2	1.2	1.5	1.6	1.5	Afrique
Americas	17.6	17.0	16.2	16.4	18.2	19.5	20.0	21.6	22.1	21.3	Amériques
- Northern America	12.5	11.6	11.3	11.7	12.2	12.9	13.7	14.8	14.7	14.9	- Amérique du Nord
- LAIA	3.2	3.7	3.2	3.4	4.2	4.8	4.6	5.2	5.7	4.7	- ALAI
- CACM	0.4	0.5	0.5	0.5	0.7	0.7	0.7	0.7	0.8	0.8	- MCC
- Caribbean	1.2	0.8	0.9	0.7	1.0	0.8	0.7	0.7	0.7	0.7	- Caraïbes
- Rest of America	0.3	0.3	0.2	0.2	0.2	0.2	0.2	0.2	0.2	0.2	- Autre d'Amérique
Asia excluding former USSR	22.6	21.7	22.6	23.0	23.8	19.9	21.2	22.9	21.7	21.2	Asie ancienne URSS exclus
- Middle East	5.5	4.9	4.9	4.4	5.1	5.2	5.2	5.5	5.1	4.9	- Moyen-Orient
Asia former USSR	0.1	0.2	0.2	0.3	0.2	0.3	0.3	0.4	0.3	0.3	Asie ancienne URSS
Europe excluding former USSR	53.5	54.2	54.0	53.1	50.1	53.7	53.1	49.3	49.1	50.0	Europe ancienne URSS exclus
- European Union	46.1	46.5	45.8	44.7	42.3	45.3	45.1	41.9	41.9	42.4	- Union Européenne
- Eastern Europe	2.6	2.5	2.5	3.1	3.2	3.5	3.4	3.2	3.3	3.6	- Europe de l'Est
- Rest of Europe	4.8	5.2	5.7	5.3	4.7	4.9	4.6	4.1	4.0	4.0	- Autre de l'Europe
Europe former USSR	2.7	3.2	3.6	3.7	4.2	3.1	1.7	2.0	2.8	3.4	Europe ancienne URSS
Oceania	2.3	2.4	2.2	2.5	2.4	2.3	2.4	2.3	2.3	2.3	Océanie

TRADE BY COMMODITY (Value in million US dollars)
Exports by principal countries or areas

COMMERCE PAR PRODUIT (Valeur en millions de dollars EU)
Exportations selon les principaux pays ou zones

Country or area	1998	1999	2000	2001	2002	Pays ou zone
World	21905.7	22415.6	23404.5	25567.6	28202.8	Monde
Africa	186.1	193.7	181.5	208.5	272.4	Afrique
Americas	3649.7	3768.1	4287.0	4859.8	5030.1	Amériques
- Northern America	3109.4	3172.7	3591.2	3984.8	4013.1	- Amérique du Nord
- LAIA	434.8	477.6	596.2	767.2	913.7	- ALAI
- CACM	70.2	64.1	63.0	76.0	68.9	- MCC
- Caribbean	30.5	36.9	27.4	28.0	31.6	- Caraïbes
- Rest of America	4.7	16.8	9.1	3.8	2.8	- Autre d'Amérique
Asia excluding former USSR	2177.2	2342.6	2802.8	3123.7	3338.3	Asie ancienne URSS exclus
- Middle East	293.5	301.0	365.3	514.5	532.9	- Moyen-Orient
Asia former USSR	5.1	1.7	3.3	4.2	3.1	Asie ancienne URSS
Europe excluding former USSR	15669.6	15882.0	15872.8	17109.3	19234.0	Europe ancienne URSS exclus
- European Union	14687.4	14907.6	14871.9	16043.3	17932.1	- Union Européenne
- Eastern Europe	392.7	372.3	435.5	487.5	687.0	- Europe de l'Est
- Rest of Europe	589.5	602.1	565.4	578.5	614.8	- Autre de l'Europe
Europe former USSR	95.9	79.0	107.9	114.3	138.4	Europe ancienne URSS
Oceania	122.1	148.6	149.2	147.9	186.5	Océanie
France-Monaco	5847.9	5898.4	5749.7	6006.1	6709.1	France-Monaco
United States	2678.6	2712.4	3038.5	3350.7	3322.5	Etats-Unis d'Amérique
Germany	2370.3	2274.1	2335.2	2741.1	3188.1	Allemagne
United Kingdom	2500.3	2438.6	2375.5	2412.2	2606.1	Royaume-Uni
Italy-San Marino-Holy See	1171.5	1190.2	1296.9	1493.4	1633.8	Italie-Saint-Marin-Saint-Siège
Spain	648.2	733.7	758.3	875.1	1005.4	Espagne
Belgium	–	743.9	740.2	797.8	e895.1	Belgique
Canada	430.5	460.1	552.3	633.9	689.9	Canada
Ireland	520.6	590.5	505.2	529.4	470.8	Irlande
Japan	396.7	472.6	544.7	515.5	543.8	Japon
Netherlands	352.1	406.3	504.0	524.1	672.1	Pays-Bas
Switzerland-Liechtenstein	478.2	473.6	443.6	457.6	474.9	Suisse-Liechtenstein
Singapore	389.1	423.6	463.0	461.4	441.4	Singapour
Mexico	189.6	232.9	302.0	397.6	533.6	Mexique
China	193.4	195.5	266.1	318.1	413.9	Chine
China, Hong Kong SAR	275.7	214.4	255.1	283.0	296.5	Chine - RAS de Hong-Kong
Poland	191.4	183.5	228.5	263.0	388.4	Pologne
United Arab Emirates	142.5	147.0	185.8	326.5	e340.1	Emirates arabes unis
Thailand	113.0	149.2	196.0	271.9	e287.2	Thaïlande
Sweden	144.4	161.1	146.5	155.3	170.5	Suède
Denmark	112.9	118.9	113.4	169.5	188.1	Danemark
Austria	129.7	129.1	133.3	145.4	163.4	Autriche
Belgium-Luxembourg	693.1	–	–	–	–	Belgique-Luxembourg
India	96.1	107.2	140.3	162.3	154.2	Inde
Australia	95.6	117.2	126.2	120.3	155.6	Australie
Korea, Republic of	68.8	77.9	115.4	132.6	158.6	République de Corée
Argentina	77.9	89.4	101.1	114.6	e110.8	Argentine
Greece	80.1	83.3	97.0	98.5	e98.7	Grèce
Bulgaria	72.6	70.1	76.3	e80.9	e90.9	Bulgarie
Brazil	57.8	60.4	72.7	90.5	e93.9	Brésil

(Value as percentages of World total) **(Valeur en pourcentage du total mondial)**

Regions of the world	1993	1994	1995	1996	1997	1998	1999	2000	2001	2002	Régions du monde
World	100.0	100.0	100.0	100.0	100.0	100.0	100.0	100.0	100.0	100.0	Monde
Africa	0.5	0.5	0.7	0.7	0.7	0.8	0.9	0.8	0.8	1.0	Afrique
Americas	14.2	14.6	14.2	14.8	16.8	16.7	16.8	18.3	19.0	17.8	Amériques
- Northern America	12.6	12.9	12.2	13.0	14.7	14.2	14.2	15.3	15.6	14.2	- Amérique du Nord
- LAIA	1.3	1.4	1.6	1.4	1.7	2.0	2.1	2.5	3.0	3.2	- ALAI
- CACM	0.2	0.2	0.3	0.3	0.3	0.3	0.3	0.3	0.3	0.2	- MCC
- Caribbean	0.1	0.1	0.1	0.1	0.1	0.1	0.2	0.1	0.1	0.1	- Caraïbes
- Rest of America	0.0	0.0	0.0	0.0	0.0	0.0	0.1	0.0	0.0	0.0	- Autre d'Amérique
Asia excluding former USSR	11.3	10.1	9.7	9.6	10.1	9.9	10.5	12.0	12.2	11.8	Asie ancienne URSS exclus
- Middle East	1.1	1.1	1.0	1.0	1.2	1.3	1.3	1.6	2.0	1.9	- Moyen-Orient
Asia former USSR	0.0	0.0	0.0	0.0	0.0	0.0	0.0	0.0	0.0	0.0	Asie ancienne URSS
Europe excluding former USSR	72.7	73.6	74.2	73.7	71.2	71.5	70.9	67.8	66.9	68.2	Europe ancienne URSS exclus
- European Union	67.9	68.8	68.9	68.5	66.6	67.0	66.5	63.5	62.7	63.6	- Union Européenne
- Eastern Europe	0.6	0.5	1.2	1.6	1.9	1.8	1.7	1.9	1.9	2.4	- Europe de l'Est
- Rest of Europe	4.2	4.3	4.1	3.5	2.7	2.7	2.7	2.4	2.3	2.2	- Autre de l'Europe
Europe former USSR	0.3	0.3	0.3	0.4	0.5	0.4	0.4	0.5	0.4	0.5	Europe ancienne URSS
Oceania	0.9	1.0	0.9	0.9	0.8	0.6	0.7	0.6	0.6	0.7	Océanie

554 Soap, cleansing and polishing preparations

TRADE BY COMMODITY (Value in million US dollars)
Imports by principal countries or areas

COMMERCE PAR PRODUIT (Valeur en millions de dollars EU)
Importations selon les principaux pays ou zones

Country or area	1998	1999	2000	2001	2002	Pays ou zone
World	11933.2	12679.3	12818.6	13404.1	14700.3	Monde
Africa	386.4	398.6	432.5	436.1	482.5	Afrique
Americas	2233.0	2405.7	2571.2	2736.3	2792.0	Amériques
- Northern America	1180.4	1288.2	1435.2	1511.8	1705.1	- Amérique du Nord
- LAIA	703.5	763.0	764.4	821.2	703.5	- ALAI
- CACM	166.2	170.4	191.4	218.9	204.3	- MCC
- Caribbean	150.7	146.1	137.9	140.8	132.0	- Caraïbes
- Rest of America	32.2	38.0	42.3	43.7	47.0	- Autre d'Amérique
Asia excluding former USSR	2157.0	2449.0	2638.6	2599.2	2713.9	Asie ancienne URSS exclus
- Middle East	508.4	544.0	564.1	588.0	616.4	- Moyen-Orient
Asia former USSR	73.0	83.5	99.7	100.1	97.1	Asie ancienne URSS
Europe excluding former USSR	6545.7	6891.5	6614.9	7015.9	8020.4	Europe ancienne URSS exclus
- European Union	5425.1	5726.1	5491.3	5840.2	6660.1	- Union Européenne
- Eastern Europe	590.9	609.3	607.1	642.0	754.9	- Europe de l'Est
- Rest of Europe	529.6	556.0	516.5	533.6	605.4	- Autre de l'Europe
Europe former USSR	311.4	207.3	216.6	274.8	340.7	Europe ancienne URSS
Oceania	226.7	243.7	245.2	241.8	253.7	Océanie
France-Monaco	872.7	1020.5	1019.0	1033.8	1233.4	France-Monaco
Germany	795.3	860.0	827.1	979.6	1099.1	Allemagne
United Kingdom	809.9	783.3	737.0	820.0	911.1	Royaume-Uni
United States	667.6	728.6	823.6	840.5	972.1	Etats-Unis d'Amérique
Canada	503.5	549.5	608.1	666.4	726.7	Canada
Belgium	–	735.1	655.9	672.4	e737.5	Belgique
Italy-San Marino-Holy See	404.4	456.7	444.3	453.6	501.1	Italie-Saint-Marin-Saint-Siège
Netherlands	395.4	415.4	405.7	353.9	458.9	Pays-Bas
Japan	310.4	375.3	398.6	341.2	364.0	Japon
Spain	281.6	266.2	265.2	325.4	393.3	Espagne
China	183.0	205.7	240.9	257.3	307.9	Chine
Poland	227.4	233.8	224.1	227.5	272.4	Pologne
Mexico	189.8	197.4	254.2	268.1	250.7	Mexique
Austria	245.8	214.0	210.5	207.1	223.4	Autriche
Sweden	233.9	224.4	198.0	210.0	224.1	Suède
China, Hong Kong SAR	224.8	233.6	229.7	194.0	195.5	Chine - RAS de Hong-Kong
Switzerland-Liechtenstein	203.1	214.2	193.7	196.6	222.9	Suisse-Liechtenstein
Portugal	192.2	169.3	155.3	171.5	198.0	Portugal
Ireland	182.6	171.8	160.9	169.3	186.7	Irlande
Greece	149.9	138.6	161.3	163.5	e180.8	Grèce
Korea, Republic of	113.4	160.4	175.5	180.7	157.1	République de Corée
Australia	144.8	160.3	157.7	154.0	161.5	Australie
Thailand	103.7	128.0	154.6	171.5	e178.7	Thaïlande
Singapore	113.9	132.7	146.0	151.6	146.0	Singapour
Denmark	142.4	134.8	124.8	135.4	147.4	Danemark
Russian Federation	161.1	74.0	93.4	132.1	176.2	Fédération de Russie
Norway	131.7	130.8	121.2	117.9	127.7	Norvège
Belgium-Luxembourg	619.4	–	–	–	–	Belgique-Luxembourg
Czech Republic	123.5	124.1	111.3	120.4	134.9	République tchèque
Argentina	133.4	172.9	117.6	121.5	e53.7	Argentine

(Value as percentages of World total) **(Valeur en pourcentage du total mondial)**

Regions of the world	1993	1994	1995	1996	1997	1998	1999	2000	2001	2002	Régions du monde
World	100.0	100.0	100.0	100.0	100.0	100.0	100.0	100.0	100.0	100.0	Monde
Africa	3.0	3.1	3.0	2.8	2.9	3.2	3.1	3.4	3.3	3.3	Afrique
Americas	14.6	15.1	14.6	15.2	17.7	18.7	19.0	20.1	20.4	19.0	Amériques
- Northern America	8.4	8.6	8.1	8.8	9.9	9.9	10.2	11.2	11.3	11.6	- Amérique du Nord
- LAIA	3.8	4.4	4.4	4.4	5.1	5.9	6.0	6.0	6.1	4.8	- ALAI
- CACM	0.8	0.8	0.8	0.9	1.2	1.4	1.3	1.5	1.6	1.4	- MCC
- Caribbean	1.4	1.0	1.0	0.9	1.3	1.3	1.2	1.1	1.1	0.9	- Caraïbes
- Rest of America	0.3	0.3	0.2	0.2	0.2	0.3	0.3	0.3	0.3	0.3	- Autre d'Amérique
Asia excluding former USSR	22.2	20.5	20.3	20.2	20.8	18.1	19.3	20.6	19.4	18.5	Asie ancienne URSS exclus
- Middle East	5.0	4.2	3.6	3.6	4.0	4.3	4.3	4.4	4.4	4.2	- Moyen-Orient
Asia former USSR	0.1	0.3	0.6	0.7	0.6	0.6	0.7	0.8	0.7	0.7	Asie ancienne URSS
Europe excluding former USSR	56.3	57.0	57.1	56.6	53.2	54.9	54.4	51.6	52.3	54.6	Europe ancienne URSS exclus
- European Union	47.9	48.8	48.2	47.2	44.4	45.5	45.2	42.8	43.6	45.3	- Union Européenne
- Eastern Europe	3.9	3.7	4.2	4.9	4.6	5.0	4.8	4.7	4.8	5.1	- Europe de l'Est
- Rest of Europe	4.5	4.5	4.7	4.5	4.2	4.4	4.4	4.0	4.0	4.1	- Autre de l'Europe
Europe former USSR	1.8	1.9	2.6	2.4	2.8	2.6	1.6	1.7	2.0	2.3	Europe ancienne URSS
Oceania	1.9	2.0	2.0	2.1	2.0	1.9	1.9	1.9	1.8	1.7	Océanie

TRADE BY COMMODITY (Value in million US dollars)
Exports by principal countries or areas

COMMERCE PAR PRODUIT (Valeur en millions de dollars EU)
Exportations selon les principaux pays ou zones

Country or area	1998	1999	2000	2001	2002	Pays ou zone
World	12441.1	13025.5	13050.1	13585.7	15271.2	Monde
Africa	184.4	174.4	196.2	179.5	236.8	Afrique
Americas	2345.2	2465.9	2689.0	2821.4	2909.0	Amériques
- Northern America	1652.5	1758.2	1833.6	1955.8	2024.4	- Amérique du Nord
- LAIA	463.9	487.9	642.9	631.4	672.8	- ALAI
- CACM	166.5	168.5	165.0	191.2	175.7	- MCC
- Caribbean	61.9	50.4	46.9	42.3	34.9	- Caraïbes
- Rest of America	0.4	0.9	0.7	0.8	1.2	- Autre d'Amérique
Asia excluding former USSR	1851.2	2011.1	2185.9	2128.5	2364.7	Asie ancienne URSS exclus
- Middle East	525.3	502.9	463.4	502.3	560.0	- Moyen-Orient
Asia former USSR	2.1	1.6	2.7	6.3	6.8	Asie ancienne URSS
Europe excluding former USSR	7896.0	8191.3	7777.6	8238.1	9524.5	Europe ancienne URSS exclus
- European Union	7165.5	7490.0	7063.4	7440.8	8529.8	- Union Européenne
- Eastern Europe	470.2	430.6	446.9	523.1	679.9	- Europe de l'Est
- Rest of Europe	260.3	270.6	267.3	274.2	314.7	- Autre de l'Europe
Europe former USSR	65.8	67.9	100.9	110.8	119.3	Europe ancienne URSS
Oceania	96.4	113.4	97.8	101.1	110.1	Océanie
Germany	1884.4	1825.3	1778.3	1823.0	2098.7	Allemagne
United States	1395.6	1481.2	1574.3	1671.7	1692.0	Etats-Unis d'Amérique
France-Monaco	993.0	1011.5	862.9	888.9	1037.8	France-Monaco
United Kingdom	924.9	929.8	890.2	903.6	964.9	Royaume-Uni
Belgium	–	1131.2	1034.7	1000.8	e1122.9	Belgique
Italy-San Marino-Holy See	740.3	811.2	780.3	839.1	967.7	Italie-Saint-Marin-Saint-Siège
Spain	511.7	556.9	570.7	715.7	818.1	Espagne
Netherlands	488.1	587.1	528.3	567.6	741.2	Pays-Bas
Japan	324.0	395.3	501.4	415.2	454.8	Japon
Mexico	243.8	256.7	425.5	411.8	454.2	Mexique
Canada	256.8	277.0	259.3	284.0	332.4	Canada
Turkey	285.3	237.1	225.6	228.5	255.9	Turquie
Czech Republic	218.6	211.5	178.0	200.2	297.6	République tchèque
Belgium-Luxembourg	1048.6	–	–	–	–	Belgique-Luxembourg
Malaysia	166.3	185.7	190.9	173.3	e183.6	Malaisie
Indonesia	101.8	183.5	197.2	186.7	223.3	Indonésie
Denmark	174.7	167.5	165.4	178.4	206.0	Danemark
Switzerland-Liechtenstein	168.1	176.9	168.5	166.8	190.3	Suisse-Liechtenstein
Poland	162.7	125.8	145.6	164.5	179.0	Pologne
Sweden	136.3	153.8	152.2	159.2	171.5	Suède
China, Hong Kong SAR	157.6	145.0	161.5	121.4	134.5	Chine - RAS de Hong-Kong
Singapore	124.3	123.6	137.3	135.0	137.4	Singapour
Korea, Republic of	103.1	113.2	129.0	139.1	146.7	République de Corée
China	121.1	91.5	112.3	124.1	159.6	Chine
Austria	97.9	85.3	76.6	111.2	133.6	Autriche
Saudi Arabia	87.8	98.3	105.0	110.5	e99.5	Arabie saoudite
Brazil	79.5	83.7	85.2	70.4	e72.9	Brésil
Hungary	35.1	39.3	60.3	95.9	118.7	Hongrie
Guatemala	54.9	65.0	64.1	73.7	65.1	Guatemala
Russian Federation	27.0	40.4	73.7	82.2	94.6	Fédération de Russie

(Value as percentages of World total) **(Valeur en pourcentage du total mondial)**

Regions of the world	1993	1994	1995	1996	1997	1998	1999	2000	2001	2002	Régions du monde
World	100.0	100.0	100.0	100.0	100.0	100.0	100.0	100.0	100.0	100.0	Monde
Africa	0.8	2.1	1.2	1.4	1.6	1.5	1.3	1.5	1.3	1.6	Afrique
Americas	16.6	16.4	15.9	16.8	18.4	18.9	18.9	20.6	20.8	19.0	Amériques
- Northern America	13.3	13.0	12.2	13.1	13.9	13.3	13.5	14.1	14.4	13.3	- Amérique du Nord
- LAIA	2.2	2.4	2.7	2.5	3.2	3.7	3.7	4.9	4.6	4.4	- ALAI
- CACM	0.6	0.6	0.6	0.8	0.9	1.3	1.3	1.3	1.4	1.2	- MCC
- Caribbean	0.5	0.4	0.4	0.4	0.5	0.5	0.4	0.4	0.3	0.2	- Caraïbes
- Rest of America	0.0	0.0	0.0	0.0	0.0	0.0	0.0	0.0	0.0	0.0	- Autre d'Amérique
Asia excluding former USSR	15.3	15.1	15.7	15.7	16.2	14.9	15.4	16.7	15.7	15.5	Asie ancienne URSS exclus
- Middle East	3.1	3.0	3.7	4.2	4.7	4.2	3.9	3.6	3.7	3.7	- Moyen-Orient
Asia former USSR	0.0	0.0	0.0	0.0	0.0	0.0	0.0	0.0	0.0	0.0	Asie ancienne URSS
Europe excluding former USSR	66.1	65.0	65.6	64.2	62.2	63.5	62.9	59.6	60.6	62.4	Europe ancienne URSS exclus
- European Union	61.6	60.6	60.9	58.6	56.5	57.6	57.5	54.1	54.8	55.9	- Union Européenne
- Eastern Europe	1.4	1.8	2.1	3.2	3.5	3.8	3.3	3.4	3.9	4.5	- Europe de l'Est
- Rest of Europe	3.2	2.6	2.5	2.5	2.1	2.1	2.1	2.0	2.0	2.1	- Autre de l'Europe
Europe former USSR	0.4	0.5	0.5	0.7	0.7	0.5	0.5	0.8	0.8	0.8	Europe ancienne URSS
Oceania	0.8	0.9	1.1	1.1	0.9	0.8	0.9	0.7	0.7	0.7	Océanie

562 Fertilizers, manufactured

TRADE BY COMMODITY (Value in million US dollars)
Imports by principal countries or areas

COMMERCE PAR PRODUIT (Valeur en millions de dollars EU)
Importations selon les principaux pays ou zones

Country or area	1998	1999	2000	2001	2002	Pays ou zone
World	18352.7	17385.9	17463.1	17378.7	17742.7	Monde
Africa	817.9	716.4	878.4	972.4	1099.5	Afrique
Americas	4664.3	4388.2	5197.1	5407.3	4868.2	Amériques
- Northern America	2000.0	1908.5	2232.8	2441.3	2053.8	- Amérique du Nord
- LAIA	2274.9	2137.2	2656.4	2634.8	2508.9	- ALAI
- CACM	228.0	202.0	189.9	196.1	183.0	- MCC
- Caribbean	123.1	106.0	89.2	105.1	83.9	- Caraïbes
- Rest of America	38.3	34.5	28.8	30.0	38.5	- Autre d'Amérique
Asia excluding former USSR	6645.4	6764.8	5725.9	5345.8	6292.5	Asie ancienne URSS exclus
- Middle East	588.0	537.2	680.5	575.6	547.3	- Moyen-Orient
Asia former USSR	62.0	61.0	52.1	51.8	56.3	Asie ancienne URSS
Europe excluding former USSR	5403.2	4720.1	4839.7	4806.6	4635.8	Europe ancienne URSS exclus
- European Union	4820.9	4173.2	4271.4	4158.9	3941.3	- Union Européenne
- Eastern Europe	304.7	278.4	290.6	369.1	405.3	- Europe de l'Est
- Rest of Europe	277.6	268.5	277.8	278.6	289.2	- Autre de l'Europe
Europe former USSR	139.1	120.9	128.3	183.6	187.8	Europe ancienne URSS
Oceania	620.8	614.5	641.7	611.2	602.6	Océanie
China	2503.5	2242.3	1725.1	1552.3	2350.0	Chine
United States	1728.2	1652.2	1863.5	2115.2	1785.3	Etats-Unis d'Amérique
Brazil	1062.6	940.0	1381.0	1321.7	1338.6	Brésil
France-Monaco	1145.1	936.3	1003.2	927.1	826.8	France-Monaco
Germany	856.6	696.2	683.9	658.0	539.1	Allemagne
India	812.2	1078.5	448.5	459.5	356.0	Inde
Italy-San Marino-Holy See	598.7	531.8	490.5	455.8	508.2	Italie-Saint-Marin-Saint-Siège
Japan	471.8	469.5	508.8	463.7	514.9	Japon
Australia	486.4	482.5	493.0	430.1	430.7	Australie
Thailand	426.3	452.2	450.9	484.7	e505.0	Thaïlande
Viet Nam	474.0	442.7	402.7	417.9	508.4	Viet Nam
United Kingdom	396.2	389.1	457.6	436.5	388.4	Royaume-Uni
Mexico	308.1	331.5	423.6	443.8	431.5	Mexique
Spain	430.0	350.4	386.1	381.6	376.0	Espagne
Belgium	–	411.8	414.3	403.9	e443.0	Belgique
Malaysia	311.3	343.4	348.0	268.2	e293.1	Malaisie
Turkey	364.1	271.5	374.9	265.5	265.0	Turquie
Canada	270.8	255.1	368.9	325.6	267.9	Canada
Netherlands	251.7	220.2	207.6	212.1	251.4	Pays-Bas
Pakistan	262.4	255.4	202.3	186.1	218.1	Pakistan
Argentina	235.3	261.8	208.1	186.7	e82.6	Argentine
Philippines	201.7	180.6	192.1	211.1	162.0	Philippines
Indonesia	101.4	225.2	180.6	195.0	241.1	Indonésie
Ireland	164.4	187.8	202.9	196.2	175.2	Irlande
Colombia	176.7	162.3	190.0	187.2	189.2	Colombie
Nigeria	56.3	5.8	203.0	e278.3	e263.9	Nigéria
Chile	185.4	157.8	154.4	141.8	132.7	Chili
Korea, Republic of	119.8	132.6	164.9	157.0	185.6	République de Corée
Poland	117.0	136.9	125.6	152.3	171.2	Pologne
Iran (Islamic Republic of)	95.2	137.1	154.0	164.1	125.4	Iran (République islamique d')

(Value as percentages of World total) **(Valeur en pourcentage du total mondial)**

Regions of the world	1993	1994	1995	1996	1997	1998	1999	2000	2001	2002	Régions du monde
World	100.0	100.0	100.0	100.0	100.0	100.0	100.0	100.0	100.0	100.0	Monde
Africa	4.5	4.2	3.1	3.7	3.7	4.5	4.1	5.0	5.6	6.2	Afrique
Americas	22.1	22.8	18.6	21.7	23.7	25.4	25.2	29.8	31.1	27.4	Amériques
- Northern America	11.4	10.9	8.7	8.7	9.5	10.9	11.0	12.8	14.0	11.6	- Amérique du Nord
- LAIA	8.8	9.8	7.8	10.8	11.8	12.4	12.3	15.2	15.2	14.1	- ALAI
- CACM	1.0	1.2	1.0	1.1	1.6	1.2	1.2	1.1	1.1	1.0	- MCC
- Caribbean	0.5	0.6	0.8	0.8	0.7	0.7	0.6	0.5	0.6	0.5	- Caraïbes
- Rest of America	0.3	0.3	0.2	0.2	0.2	0.2	0.2	0.2	0.2	0.2	- Autre d'Amérique
Asia excluding former USSR	40.0	37.8	44.0	39.3	40.1	36.2	38.9	32.8	30.8	35.5	Asie ancienne URSS exclus
- Middle East	4.7	3.0	3.2	3.1	3.2	3.2	3.1	3.9	3.3	3.1	- Moyen-Orient
Asia former USSR	0.0	0.1	0.4	0.5	0.4	0.3	0.4	0.3	0.3	0.3	Asie ancienne URSS
Europe excluding former USSR	30.5	31.8	30.5	30.5	27.9	29.4	27.1	27.7	27.7	26.1	Europe ancienne URSS exclus
- European Union	27.6	28.8	27.9	27.8	25.0	26.3	24.0	24.5	23.9	22.2	- Union Européenne
- Eastern Europe	1.0	1.3	1.2	1.5	1.6	1.7	1.6	1.7	2.1	2.3	- Europe de l'Est
- Rest of Europe	1.8	1.6	1.4	1.2	1.3	1.5	1.5	1.6	1.6	1.6	- Autre de l'Europe
Europe former USSR	0.2	0.4	0.4	0.7	0.8	0.8	0.7	0.7	1.1	1.1	Europe ancienne URSS
Oceania	2.7	3.0	3.0	3.6	3.5	3.4	3.5	3.7	3.5	3.4	Océanie

TRADE BY COMMODITY (Value in million US dollars)
Exports by principal countries or areas

COMMERCE PAR PRODUIT (Valeur en millions de dollars EU)
Exportations selon les principaux pays ou zones

Country or area	1998	1999	2000	2001	2002	Pays ou zone
World	15537.1	14797.4	15019.4	14457.4	12388.3	Monde
Africa	1076.4	1035.8	1129.0	943.2	1056.1	Afrique
Americas	5571.3	5496.7	5016.1	4560.7	2376.4	Amériques
- Northern America	5076.6	5058.6	4626.4	4118.6	2015.5	- Amérique du Nord
- LAIA	400.8	352.3	306.9	357.5	292.2	- ALAI
- CACM	33.4	36.6	20.1	16.9	16.7	- MCC
- Caribbean	60.5	49.3	62.6	67.6	51.7	- Caraïbes
- Rest of America	0.0	0.0	0.1	0.2	0.2	- Autre d'Amérique
Asia excluding former USSR	2010.4	1906.9	2113.4	2174.5	2128.1	Asie ancienne URSS exclus
- Middle East	750.8	612.0	654.5	754.8	714.0	- Moyen-Orient
Asia former USSR	80.2	70.1	64.8	61.5	49.4	Asie ancienne URSS
Europe excluding former USSR	4204.2	3779.1	3920.6	3832.4	3861.0	Europe ancienne URSS exclus
- European Union	3583.0	3283.6	3185.1	3146.8	3218.7	- Union Européenne
- Eastern Europe	516.6	407.9	626.8	594.4	551.5	- Europe de l'Est
- Rest of Europe	104.6	87.6	108.7	91.2	90.9	- Autre de l'Europe
Europe former USSR	2572.2	2463.3	2728.8	2802.8	2849.0	Europe ancienne URSS
Oceania	22.3	45.4	46.7	82.2	68.3	Océanie
United States	3282.1	3117.4	2485.4	2246.7		Etats-Unis d'Amérique
Canada	1794.5	1941.2	2140.1	1871.8	2015.5	Canada
Russian Federation	1494.0	1439.9	1579.7	1665.2	1644.0	Fédération de Russie
Germany	1041.3	980.8	876.4	912.8	941.9	Allemagne
Netherlands	767.4	718.6	683.7	687.7	654.0	Pays-Bas
Belgium	–	663.2	821.0	758.4	e850.9	Belgique
Belarus	505.0	510.5	487.0	538.2	540.5	Bélarus
Israel	429.0	430.8	418.5	410.9	414.3	Israël
Ukraine	326.7	289.5	413.7	363.3	400.5	Ukraine
Morocco	343.1	316.7	323.3	349.3	e380.0	Maroc
Tunisia	303.7	288.6	266.5	288.8	e300.4	Tunisie
China	151.0	219.9	313.4	377.7	337.6	Chine
Saudi Arabia	270.7	229.6	245.3	321.6	e289.8	Arabie saoudite
Poland	235.5	185.7	249.5	189.8	171.9	Pologne
Lithuania	182.7	177.6	192.6	171.9	e208.3	Lituanie
France-Monaco	212.3	187.7	190.4	152.5	111.6	France-Monaco
Spain	188.3	217.3	141.3	144.5	152.8	Espagne
Qatar	140.0	135.1	188.9	173.1	187.0	Qatar
Indonesia	168.1	185.3	209.4	126.8	129.2	Indonésie
Belgium-Luxembourg	720.5	–	–	–	–	Belgique-Luxembourg
Korea, Republic of	176.4	142.6	125.7	127.4	126.7	République de Corée
United Kingdom	203.7	112.7	102.9	100.3	105.4	Royaume-Uni
Romania	48.2	83.7	146.7	168.0	144.4	Roumanie
Mexico	197.9	154.6	95.2	103.1	33.2	Mexique
Malaysia	66.7	88.5	134.9	141.8	e150.3	Malaisie
Libyan Arab Jamahiriya	95.8	e123.9	e159.3	e	e71.5	Jamahiriya arabe libyenne
Finland	94.0	113.3	89.4	92.1	102.5	Finlande
Jordan	145.8	110.5	38.3	86.3	90.4	Jordanie
Japan	84.0	91.0	91.5	79.4	83.0	Japon
Bulgaria	79.9	35.2	95.1	e100.9	e113.4	Bulgarie

(Value as percentages of World total) **(Valeur en pourcentage du total mondial)**

Regions of the world	1993	1994	1995	1996	1997	1998	1999	2000	2001	2002	Régions du monde
World	100.0	100.0	100.0	100.0	100.0	100.0	100.0	100.0	100.0	100.0	Monde
Africa	6.0	5.7	6.5	6.6	6.4	6.9	7.0	7.5	6.5	8.5	Afrique
Americas	27.8	33.2	30.6	29.0	32.9	35.9	37.1	33.4	31.5	19.2	Amériques
- Northern America	25.7	31.1	27.4	25.9	30.1	32.7	34.2	30.8	28.5	16.3	- Amérique du Nord
- LAIA	1.4	1.5	2.5	2.2	2.0	2.6	2.4	2.0	2.5	2.4	- ALAI
- CACM	0.2	0.2	0.1	0.2	0.3	0.2	0.2	0.1	0.1	0.1	- MCC
- Caribbean	0.5	0.5	0.6	0.7	0.5	0.4	0.3	0.4	0.5	0.4	- Caraïbes
- Rest of America	0.0	0.0	0.0	0.0	0.0	0.0	0.0	0.0	0.0	0.0	- Autre d'Amérique
Asia excluding former USSR	12.8	13.8	14.0	14.0	14.4	12.9	12.9	14.1	15.0	17.2	Asie ancienne URSS exclus
- Middle East	4.3	5.4	5.4	5.0	4.8	4.8	4.1	4.4	5.2	5.8	- Moyen-Orient
Asia former USSR	0.6	0.3	0.6	1.1	0.4	0.5	0.5	0.4	0.4	0.4	Asie ancienne URSS
Europe excluding former USSR	32.2	31.0	30.1	31.8	28.7	27.1	25.5	26.1	26.5	31.2	Europe ancienne URSS exclus
- European Union	24.7	25.5	23.5	24.5	23.2	23.1	22.2	21.2	21.8	26.0	- Union Européenne
- Eastern Europe	4.2	4.7	5.8	6.5	4.9	3.3	2.8	4.2	4.1	4.5	- Europe de l'Est
- Rest of Europe	3.3	0.8	0.7	0.7	0.6	0.7	0.6	0.7	0.6	0.7	- Autre de l'Europe
Europe former USSR	20.5	15.9	18.0	17.3	17.1	16.6	16.6	18.2	19.4	23.0	Europe ancienne URSS
Oceania	0.1	0.2	0.1	0.3	0.1	0.1	0.3	0.3	0.6	0.6	Océanie

572 Explosives and pyrotechnic products

TRADE BY COMMODITY (Value in million US dollars)
Imports by principal countries or areas

COMMERCE PAR PRODUIT (Valeur en millions de dollars EU)
Importations selon les principaux pays ou zones

Country or area	1998	1999	2000	2001	2002	Pays ou zone
World	1344.8	1400.4	1409.8	1341.8	1476.5	Monde
Africa	75.0	78.0	66.0	77.9	80.7	Afrique
Americas	452.1	479.8	529.9	521.5	583.4	Amériques
- Northern America	344.2	363.6	380.4	380.5	387.8	- Amérique du Nord
- LAIA	88.4	97.5	133.3	122.2	177.5	- ALAI
- CACM	7.1	5.7	5.4	7.1	8.0	- MCC
- Caribbean	8.3	9.0	7.6	7.1	6.2	- Caraïbes
- Rest of America	4.2	4.1	3.2	4.6	3.9	- Autre d'Amérique
Asia excluding former USSR	182.2	180.6	185.3	214.9	208.3	Asie ancienne URSS exclus
- Middle East	38.9	34.2	31.6	31.6	37.0	- Moyen-Orient
Asia former USSR	57.4	52.5	60.4	64.3	65.9	Asie ancienne URSS
Europe excluding former USSR	520.7	562.3	517.8	411.7	471.0	Europe ancienne URSS exclus
- European Union	432.9	476.2	432.8	329.7	384.8	- Union Européenne
- Eastern Europe	17.2	22.4	22.8	20.4	24.8	- Europe de l'Est
- Rest of Europe	70.6	63.7	62.1	61.6	61.4	- Autre de l'Europe
Europe former USSR	18.3	9.1	10.4	9.6	12.8	Europe ancienne URSS
Oceania	39.1	38.0	39.9	41.8	54.5	Océanie
United States	253.7	279.9	276.1	295.2	316.8	Etats-Unis d'Amérique
Germany	139.6	152.5	142.8	94.8	119.1	Allemagne
Canada	89.2	82.7	103.3	84.5	69.6	Canada
Mexico	21.7	43.3	75.0	68.9	131.5	Mexique
Italy-San Marino-Holy See	68.0	77.9	69.7	54.2	54.7	Italie-Saint-Marin-Saint-Siège
Japan	54.5	48.4	56.3	77.1	64.9	Japon
France-Monaco	35.2	42.4	38.4	30.5	42.7	France-Monaco
United Kingdom	55.6	33.6	33.3	28.9	28.5	Royaume-Uni
Kazakhstan	36.8	27.4	36.6	32.9	e33.6	Kazakhstan
Australia	26.4	26.2	28.3	30.9	41.1	Australie
Switzerland-Liechtenstein	30.3	25.8	30.3	27.4	20.0	Suisse-Liechtenstein
Norway	25.3	26.0	22.3	24.1	27.6	Norvège
Netherlands	21.4	27.0	27.5	17.9	22.2	Pays-Bas
Singapore	17.6	18.0	21.1	31.0	22.4	Singapour
Indonesia	17.5	20.7	24.3	22.9	24.5	Indonésie
Austria	17.3	21.3	19.5	16.0	19.9	Autriche
Uzbekistan	e11.9	e17.3	e14.4	e23.6	e22.8	Ouzbékistan
Sweden	24.8	22.4	15.5	11.1	14.1	Suède
Greece	12.3	14.2	16.6	17.1	e18.9	Grèce
China, Hong Kong SAR	20.0	21.8	15.1	8.6	11.6	Chine - RAS de Hong-Kong
Belgium	–	23.6	16.3	16.2	e17.7	Belgique
Denmark	11.9	21.7	15.6	11.0	13.5	Danemark
Venezuela	11.3	9.2	14.8	13.1	e11.0	Venezuela
Argentina	13.8	15.5	15.1	9.9	e4.4	Argentine
Spain	13.0	12.6	13.6	8.9	9.5	Espagne
Portugal	10.2	10.0	10.7	9.2	11.2	Portugal
Finland	8.1	12.0	8.8	9.0	9.5	Finlande
Zimbabwe	e12.5	8.4	e7.4	5.4	12.1	Zimbabwe
South Africa	–	–	14.5	14.6	13.0	Afrique du Sud
Colombia	8.9	7.9	7.6	7.6	9.0	Colombie

(Value as percentages of World total)

(Valeur en pourcentage du total mondial)

Regions of the world	1993	1994	1995	1996	1997	1998	1999	2000	2001	2002	Régions du monde
World	100.0	100.0	100.0	100.0	100.0	100.0	100.0	100.0	100.0	100.0	Monde
Africa	7.6	7.1	6.1	6.5	5.7	5.6	5.6	4.7	5.8	5.5	Afrique
Americas	29.2	30.5	26.8	28.3	30.3	33.6	34.3	37.6	38.9	39.5	Amériques
- Northern America	24.1	25.0	21.6	22.7	24.3	25.6	26.0	27.0	28.4	26.3	- Amérique du Nord
- LAIA	3.7	4.0	4.0	3.8	4.7	6.6	7.0	9.5	9.1	12.0	- ALAI
- CACM	0.3	0.3	0.3	0.4	0.4	0.5	0.4	0.4	0.5	0.5	- MCC
- Caribbean	0.4	0.4	0.5	1.0	0.6	0.6	0.6	0.5	0.5	0.4	- Caraïbes
- Rest of America	0.7	0.8	0.4	0.4	0.3	0.3	0.3	0.2	0.3	0.3	- Autre d'Amérique
Asia excluding former USSR	23.3	21.9	19.0	16.5	15.5	13.5	12.9	13.1	16.0	14.1	Asie ancienne URSS exclus
- Middle East	4.4	3.5	2.2	2.2	2.6	2.9	2.4	2.2	2.4	2.5	- Moyen-Orient
Asia former USSR	0.0	3.2	5.4	5.0	6.2	4.3	3.8	4.3	4.8	4.5	Asie ancienne URSS
Europe excluding former USSR	37.0	32.7	37.8	37.9	36.7	38.7	40.2	36.7	30.7	31.9	Europe ancienne URSS exclus
- European Union	29.9	27.1	30.9	31.0	30.4	32.2	34.0	30.7	24.6	26.1	- Union Européenne
- Eastern Europe	1.1	1.3	1.5	1.7	1.3	1.3	1.6	1.6	1.5	1.7	- Europe de l'Est
- Rest of Europe	6.0	4.3	5.4	5.2	5.0	5.3	4.5	4.4	4.6	4.2	- Autre de l'Europe
Europe former USSR	0.7	1.7	2.2	2.8	2.9	1.4	0.6	0.7	0.7	0.9	Europe ancienne URSS
Oceania	2.1	3.0	2.8	3.1	2.6	2.9	2.7	2.8	3.1	3.7	Océanie

TRADE BY COMMODITY (Value in million US dollars)
Exports by principal countries or areas

COMMERCE PAR PRODUIT (Valeur en millions de dollars EU)
Exportations selon les principaux pays ou zones

Country or area	1998	1999	2000	2001	2002	Pays ou zone
World	1210.7	1162.3	1202.0	1130.0	1225.9	Monde
Africa	45.0	29.8	67.5	30.6	34.2	Afrique
Americas	407.6	371.5	443.1	388.7	405.8	Amériques
- Northern America	352.3	326.5	393.7	331.7	350.1	- Amérique du Nord
- LAIA	50.9	41.1	44.9	52.5	52.0	- ALAI
- CACM	3.7	3.3	3.9	4.0	3.3	- MCC
- Caribbean	0.7	0.6	0.6	0.4	0.4	- Caraïbes
- Rest of America	0.0	0.0	0.0	0.1	0.0	- Autre d'Amérique
Asia excluding former USSR	305.4	381.7	322.9	315.4	362.3	Asie ancienne URSS exclus
- Middle East	3.4	2.4	3.4	3.8	5.4	- Moyen-Orient
Asia former USSR	7.2	8.3	8.4	14.3	15.6	Asie ancienne URSS
Europe excluding former USSR	381.9	298.7	289.2	308.6	343.4	Europe ancienne URSS exclus
- European Union	313.9	227.7	211.7	219.0	234.4	- Union Européenne
- Eastern Europe	32.1	33.7	36.1	39.2	47.8	- Europe de l'Est
- Rest of Europe	35.9	37.4	41.4	50.4	61.2	- Autre de l'Europe
Europe former USSR	46.5	52.5	51.9	54.7	47.3	Europe ancienne URSS
Oceania	17.0	19.8	19.0	17.8	17.3	Océanie
China	250.6	324.5	269.4	273.1	307.9	Chine
United States	284.4	255.8	316.4	257.9	280.7	Etats-Unis d'Amérique
Germany	92.3	81.0	78.7	79.0	76.8	Allemagne
Canada	67.9	70.7	77.3	73.8	69.4	Canada
France-Monaco	59.9	55.9	46.2	52.7	62.0	France-Monaco
Russian Federation	44.1	51.4	46.2	45.9	37.0	Fédération de Russie
Switzerland-Liechtenstein	29.1	31.1	36.7	45.7	54.2	Suisse-Liechtenstein
South Africa	–	–	63.7	27.6	30.1	Afrique du Sud
Czech Republic	20.5	19.7	22.1	25.1	29.2	République tchèque
United Kingdom	90.4	2.2	1.6	1.5	1.1	Royaume-Uni
Belgium	–	29.6	22.6	19.8	e22.2	Belgique
China, Hong Kong SAR	23.8	24.4	16.6	10.6	17.3	Chine - RAS de Hong-Kong
Italy-San Marino-Holy See	15.6	18.0	17.7	16.0	14.2	Italie-Saint-Marin-Saint-Siège
Australia	14.4	17.8	17.2	16.2	15.7	Australie
Mexico	11.8	10.6	14.3	20.8	22.2	Mexique
Spain	13.9	16.4	15.0	15.9	14.3	Espagne
Netherlands	8.0	8.3	15.6	13.4	18.8	Pays-Bas
Southern African Customs Union	39.0	24.3	–	–	–	Union douanière d'Afrique australe
Chile	15.5	12.0	11.7	11.8	e11.5	Chili
Tajikistan	e7.1	e8.2	8.2	e8.0	e8.8	Tadjikistan
Brazil	7.9	6.9	7.8	7.9	e8.2	Brésil
Poland	6.9	8.3	6.4	6.1	7.8	Pologne
India	5.0	5.9	9.2	7.4	6.9	Inde
Peru	8.6	7.2	6.1	6.5	4.8	Pérou
Finland	6.5	5.1	5.1	7.3	8.7	Finlande
Singapore	2.2	4.2	4.5	8.2	10.8	Singapour
Ukraine	2.3	1.0	5.5	8.5	9.3	Ukraine
Argentina	6.2	4.2	4.8	5.2	e5.0	Argentine
Philippines	6.3	6.2	6.6	3.1	1.8	Philippines
Slovakia	2.6	2.9	4.5	4.9	4.4	Slovaquie

(Value as percentages of World total) **(Valeur en pourcentage du total mondial)**

Regions of the world	1993	1994	1995	1996	1997	1998	1999	2000	2001	2002	Régions du monde
World	100.0	100.0	100.0	100.0	100.0	100.0	100.0	100.0	100.0	100.0	Monde
Africa	2.1	2.5	3.3	2.3	2.8	3.7	2.6	5.6	2.7	2.8	Afrique
Americas	30.5	28.6	27.5	30.6	31.2	33.7	32.0	36.9	34.4	33.1	Amériques
- Northern America	28.4	26.4	24.7	27.4	27.3	29.1	28.1	32.8	29.4	28.6	- Amérique du Nord
- LAIA	1.9	2.1	2.6	3.0	3.6	4.2	3.5	3.7	4.6	4.2	- ALAI
- CACM	0.1	0.1	0.1	0.2	0.3	0.3	0.3	0.3	0.4	0.3	- MCC
- Caribbean	0.0	0.0	0.0	0.0	0.0	0.1	0.1	0.0	0.0	0.0	- Caraïbes
- Rest of America	0.0	0.0	0.0	0.0	0.0	0.0	0.0	0.0	0.0	0.0	- Autre d'Amérique
Asia excluding former USSR	28.6	28.9	28.2	25.8	24.5	25.2	32.8	26.9	27.9	29.6	Asie ancienne URSS exclus
- Middle East	0.6	0.3	0.2	0.3	0.4	0.3	0.2	0.3	0.3	0.4	- Moyen-Orient
Asia former USSR	0.0	0.0	0.0	0.1	1.0	0.6	0.7	0.7	1.3	1.3	Asie ancienne URSS
Europe excluding former USSR	35.3	32.4	31.9	32.8	30.0	31.5	25.7	24.1	27.3	28.0	Europe ancienne URSS exclus
- European Union	31.3	29.2	27.2	27.6	24.7	25.9	19.6	17.6	19.4	19.1	- Union Européenne
- Eastern Europe	1.0	1.3	1.9	2.7	2.9	2.7	2.9	3.0	3.5	3.9	- Europe de l'Est
- Rest of Europe	2.9	1.9	2.8	2.5	2.4	3.0	3.2	3.4	4.5	5.0	- Autre de l'Europe
Europe former USSR	2.2	5.8	6.9	6.8	8.6	3.8	4.5	4.3	4.8	3.9	Europe ancienne URSS
Oceania	1.2	1.8	2.1	1.7	1.9	1.4	1.7	1.6	1.6	1.4	Océanie

582 Condensation, polycondensation and polyaddition products

TRADE BY COMMODITY (Value in million US dollars)
Imports by principal countries or areas

COMMERCE PAR PRODUIT (Valeur en millions de dollars EU)
Importations selon les principaux pays ou zones

Country or area	1998	1999	2000	2001	2002	Pays ou zone
World	31341.2	32235.4	35564.7	34004.0	35908.6	Monde
Africa	613.7	590.7	599.1	600.8	640.4	Afrique
Americas	5438.3	5647.5	6271.8	6079.7	6129.6	Amériques
- Northern America	3338.6	3569.6	3933.7	3516.7	3768.1	- Amérique du Nord
- LAIA	1942.4	1926.5	2190.5	2384.3	2184.5	- ALAI
- CACM	70.7	77.4	86.5	96.3	108.7	- MCC
- Caribbean	73.4	61.1	51.8	69.0	57.5	- Caraïbes
- Rest of America	13.2	12.8	9.3	13.4	10.7	- Autre d'Amérique
Asia excluding former USSR	8416.5	9795.7	12181.4	10898.5	12298.3	Asie ancienne URSS exclus
- Middle East	760.4	753.5	805.8	804.9	949.5	- Moyen-Orient
Asia former USSR	16.7	18.0	30.1	35.1	33.0	Asie ancienne URSS
Europe excluding former USSR	16272.6	15558.2	15778.4	15610.4	15860.8	Europe ancienne URSS exclus
- European Union	14588.9	13931.2	13917.8	13692.4	13786.2	- Union Européenne
- Eastern Europe	781.4	782.9	965.9	1026.6	1160.1	- Europe de l'Est
- Rest of Europe	902.4	844.1	894.7	891.4	914.5	- Autre de l'Europe
Europe former USSR	237.0	219.0	304.7	408.5	540.8	Europe ancienne URSS
Oceania	346.3	406.3	399.3	371.0	405.7	Océanie
Germany	3201.6	2888.1	2833.5	3007.2	2753.1	Allemagne
China	1583.9	2001.2	2651.0	2578.4	3395.0	Chine
United States	2069.4	2205.1	2464.6	2230.1	2427.9	Etats-Unis d'Amérique
France-Monaco	2033.9	1957.3	2123.4	2087.7	1966.5	France-Monaco
Italy-San Marino-Holy See	1992.4	1963.6	2052.8	1983.3	2062.0	Italie-Saint-Marin-Saint-Siège
United Kingdom	1643.5	1555.1	1489.8	1388.3	1378.7	Royaume-Uni
China, Hong Kong SAR	1267.8	1398.1	1667.9	1348.7	1511.7	Chine - RAS de Hong-Kong
Canada	1268.9	1364.3	1469.1	1286.4	1340.1	Canada
Belgium	-	1725.4	1654.7	1554.9	e1705.2	Belgique
Japan	901.6	1076.5	1347.9	1254.3	1291.0	Japon
Mexico	765.2	914.8	1015.2	1128.2	1131.5	Mexique
Spain	915.5	1012.6	885.7	912.3	1030.7	Espagne
Netherlands	1048.0	941.0	968.8	869.1	827.3	Pays-Bas
Korea, Republic of	654.2	823.3	952.3	828.4	875.8	République de Corée
Singapore	551.9	683.3	887.4	608.8	618.2	Singapour
Malaysia	404.6	535.1	663.0	617.0	e674.3	Malaisie
Switzerland-Liechtenstein	568.3	536.2	557.8	549.0	554.7	Suisse-Liechtenstein
Brazil	519.4	489.7	564.4	600.4	540.7	Brésil
Austria	541.6	504.6	510.4	514.0	551.3	Autriche
Thailand	336.4	411.3	539.6	482.6	e502.9	Thaïlande
Sweden	403.8	383.6	390.7	347.9	365.4	Suède
Turkey	375.7	335.9	392.9	322.4	449.6	Turquie
Belgium-Luxembourg	1811.1	-	-	-	-	Belgique-Luxembourg
Poland	296.0	287.5	334.2	334.5	375.7	Pologne
Australia	313.6	319.7	314.3	283.5	311.7	Australie
Denmark	310.1	282.4	270.0	272.4	326.1	Danemark
Indonesia	248.5	195.1	349.7	310.2	309.5	Indonésie
Czech Republic	213.0	222.2	276.0	306.5	349.2	République tchèque
Viet Nam	161.6	194.2	267.9	278.0	338.2	Viet Nam
Argentina	302.4	210.4	213.1	221.8	e98.1	Argentine

(Value as percentages of World total) **(Valeur en pourcentage du total mondial)**

Regions of the world	1993	1994	1995	1996	1997	1998	1999	2000	2001	2002	Régions du monde
World	100.0	100.0	100.0	100.0	100.0	100.0	100.0	100.0	100.0	100.0	Monde
Africa	2.5	2.1	2.0	2.1	2.0	2.0	1.8	1.7	1.8	1.8	Afrique
Americas	14.3	15.2	14.2	15.5	16.7	17.4	17.5	17.6	17.9	17.1	Amériques
- Northern America	9.3	9.9	8.8	9.7	10.3	10.7	11.1	11.1	10.3	10.5	- Amérique du Nord
- LAIA	4.5	4.9	5.0	5.4	5.9	6.2	6.0	6.2	7.0	6.1	- ALAI
- CACM	0.3	0.2	0.2	0.2	0.3	0.2	0.2	0.2	0.3	0.3	- MCC
- Caribbean	0.1	0.1	0.1	0.2	0.2	0.2	0.2	0.1	0.2	0.2	- Caraïbes
- Rest of America	0.0	0.0	0.0	0.0	0.0	0.0	0.0	0.0	0.0	0.0	- Autre d'Amérique
Asia excluding former USSR	29.9	27.5	27.7	27.8	29.5	26.9	30.4	34.3	32.1	34.2	Asie ancienne URSS exclus
- Middle East	2.2	1.7	1.9	2.0	2.4	2.4	2.3	2.3	2.4	2.6	- Moyen-Orient
Asia former USSR	0.0	0.0	0.1	0.0	0.0	0.1	0.1	0.1	0.1	0.1	Asie ancienne URSS
Europe excluding former USSR	50.9	53.1	54.0	52.4	49.6	51.9	48.3	44.4	45.9	44.2	Europe ancienne URSS exclus
- European Union	46.1	48.2	48.8	47.3	44.7	46.5	43.2	39.1	40.3	38.4	- Union Européenne
- Eastern Europe	1.5	1.5	1.9	2.1	2.2	2.5	2.4	2.7	3.0	3.2	- Europe de l'Est
- Rest of Europe	3.3	3.4	3.3	3.0	2.8	2.9	2.6	2.5	2.6	2.5	- Autre de l'Europe
Europe former USSR	0.7	0.5	0.5	0.7	0.8	0.8	0.7	0.9	1.2	1.5	Europe ancienne URSS
Oceania	1.7	1.6	1.6	1.5	1.4	1.1	1.3	1.1	1.1	1.1	Océanie

TRADE BY COMMODITY (Value in million US dollars)
Exports by principal countries or areas

COMMERCE PAR PRODUIT (Valeur en millions de dollars EU)
Exportations selon les principaux pays ou zones

Country or area	1998	1999	2000	2001	2002	Pays ou zone
World	27712.9	28113.9	31751.9	30326.4	34766.5	Monde
Africa	73.5	90.3	114.5	65.7	59.0	Afrique
Americas	5920.4	6032.5	7086.2	6533.3	6694.1	Amériques
- Northern America	5376.3	5531.2	6501.2	5977.5	6174.2	- Amérique du Nord
- LAIA	530.5	492.6	574.8	545.5	507.7	- ALAI
- CACM	9.7	7.4	7.6	8.6	8.8	- MCC
- Caribbean	3.9	1.4	2.6	1.6	3.3	- Caraïbes
- Rest of America	0.0	0.0	0.0	0.1	0.1	- Autre d'Amérique
Asia excluding former USSR	7132.3	8009.3	10029.1	9167.1	10185.8	Asie ancienne URSS exclus
- Middle East	118.8	105.5	100.5	133.5	134.9	- Moyen-Orient
Asia former USSR	2.6	1.5	1.8	1.2	1.6	Asie ancienne URSS
Europe excluding former USSR	14451.4	13855.0	14385.9	14418.4	17660.8	Europe ancienne URSS exclus
- European Union	13294.9	12750.9	13294.3	13339.2	16500.2	- Union Européenne
- Eastern Europe	196.0	187.4	251.2	270.0	286.5	- Europe de l'Est
- Rest of Europe	960.6	916.7	840.4	809.1	874.1	- Autre de l'Europe
Europe former USSR	81.5	67.8	82.8	80.4	94.6	Europe ancienne URSS
Oceania	51.2	57.4	51.8	60.3	70.7	Océanie
United States	4770.7	4853.6	5700.3	5237.8	5434.5	Etats-Unis d'Amérique
Germany	3094.1	3040.4	3230.1	3191.3	5424.1	Allemagne
Japan	2365.6	2712.1	3100.3	2554.2	2866.1	Japon
Netherlands	2995.4	2345.9	2426.3	2624.7	2780.5	Pays-Bas
Belgium	-	2290.6	2149.4	2115.2	e2373.2	Belgique
Italy-San Marino-Holy See	1590.2	1627.2	1764.8	1802.3	1944.3	Italie-Saint-Marin-Saint-Siège
Korea, Republic of	1207.9	1271.3	1523.9	1447.3	1720.4	République de Corée
United Kingdom	1141.8	1123.8	1154.2	1140.7	1249.3	Royaume-Uni
China, Hong Kong SAR	864.0	911.5	1126.1	1006.5	1121.7	Chine - RAS de Hong-Kong
Spain	677.6	781.2	960.6	941.2	1130.8	Espagne
Singapore	535.1	654.3	906.1	908.1	881.4	Singapour
Switzerland-Liechtenstein	844.9	797.7	717.7	685.9	735.2	Suisse-Liechtenstein
France-Monaco	731.8	785.2	796.8	677.6	726.2	France-Monaco
Canada	605.4	677.6	800.9	734.7	738.8	Canada
Belgium-Luxembourg	2458.1	-	-	-	-	Belgique-Luxembourg
Thailand	199.4	304.9	435.0	475.0	e501.6	Thaïlande
Indonesia	275.7	275.3	409.7	355.3	364.4	Indonésie
China	244.0	243.8	333.3	357.8	490.3	Chine
Malaysia	201.4	252.4	381.8	376.0	e398.5	Malaisie
Austria	232.3	237.9	243.0	242.5	236.2	Autriche
Mexico	269.7	229.3	217.3	224.9	197.1	Mexique
Sweden	171.2	163.8	176.2	174.6	178.4	Suède
India	99.8	105.8	164.6	174.2	212.3	Inde
Luxembourg	-	148.2	171.4	163.3	e166.9	Luxembourg
Brazil	119.7	105.8	158.5	113.3	e117.4	Brésil
Israel	107.4	125.3	128.7	98.8	91.9	Israël
Poland	68.1	73.9	121.2	137.5	145.1	Pologne
Argentina	55.6	81.3	115.7	124.5	e120.3	Argentine
Slovenia	68.6	75.4	86.0	85.6	103.1	Slovénie
Portugal	45.6	42.2	57.3	79.1	103.5	Portugal

(Value as percentages of World total) **(Valeur en pourcentage du total mondial)**

Regions of the world	1993	1994	1995	1996	1997	1998	1999	2000	2001	2002	Régions du monde
World	100.0	100.0	100.0	100.0	100.0	100.0	100.0	100.0	100.0	100.0	Monde
Africa	0.2	0.1	0.3	0.2	0.2	0.3	0.3	0.4	0.2	0.2	Afrique
Americas	18.3	19.2	17.1	18.3	19.7	21.4	21.5	22.3	21.5	19.3	Amériques
- Northern America	17.1	17.7	15.4	16.7	18.0	19.4	19.7	20.5	19.7	17.8	- Amérique du Nord
- LAIA	1.2	1.5	1.6	1.5	1.6	1.9	1.8	1.8	1.8	1.5	- ALAI
- CACM	0.0	0.0	0.0	0.0	0.0	0.0	0.0	0.0	0.0	0.0	- MCC
- Caribbean	0.0	0.0	0.0	0.0	0.0	0.0	0.0	0.0	0.0	0.0	- Caraïbes
- Rest of America	0.0	0.0	0.0	0.0	0.0	0.0	0.0	0.0	0.0	0.0	- Autre d'Amérique
Asia excluding former USSR	23.7	23.6	26.9	24.9	25.0	25.7	28.5	31.6	30.2	29.3	Asie ancienne URSS exclus
- Middle East	0.3	1.1	1.1	1.1	0.5	0.4	0.4	0.3	0.4	0.4	- Moyen-Orient
Asia former USSR	0.0	0.0	0.0	0.0	0.0	0.0	0.0	0.0	0.0	0.0	Asie ancienne URSS
Europe excluding former USSR	57.2	56.5	55.2	55.9	54.6	52.1	49.3	45.3	47.5	50.8	Europe ancienne URSS exclus
- European Union	53.1	52.7	51.3	52.0	50.7	48.0	45.4	41.9	44.0	47.5	- Union Européenne
- Eastern Europe	0.4	0.4	0.7	0.6	0.6	0.7	0.7	0.8	0.9	0.8	- Europe de l'Est
- Rest of Europe	3.8	3.4	3.2	3.4	3.3	3.5	3.3	2.6	2.7	2.5	- Autre de l'Europe
Europe former USSR	0.2	0.2	0.3	0.3	0.3	0.3	0.2	0.3	0.3	0.3	Europe ancienne URSS
Oceania	0.3	0.3	0.3	0.4	0.3	0.2	0.2	0.2	0.2	0.2	Océanie

583 Polymerization and copolymerization products

TRADE BY COMMODITY (Value in million US dollars)
Imports by principal countries or areas

COMMERCE PAR PRODUIT (Valeur en millions de dollars EU)
Importations selon les principaux pays ou zones

Country or area	1998	1999	2000	2001	2002	Pays ou zone
World	77548.6	77970.0	88331.3	85312.8	89517.1	Monde
Africa	1961.7	1812.3	2019.1	2142.2	2151.4	Afrique
Americas	14121.2	14919.1	17633.0	17225.0	17251.7	Amériques
- Northern America	8392.0	9150.9	10528.5	10315.2	10648.6	- Amérique du Nord
- LAIA	5034.4	5111.0	6345.0	6098.6	5753.4	- ALAI
- CACM	405.5	401.2	461.0	489.4	493.0	- MCC
- Caribbean	245.4	217.3	235.0	262.6	298.3	- Caraïbes
- Rest of America	43.9	38.7	63.5	59.1	58.4	- Autre d'Amérique
Asia excluding former USSR	21473.5	22624.4	27509.7	26254.1	28476.9	Asie ancienne URSS exclus
- Middle East	2234.2	2118.9	2709.1	2518.8	3017.5	- Moyen-Orient
Asia former USSR	116.6	75.7	107.7	111.9	126.9	Asie ancienne URSS
Europe excluding former USSR	38287.5	36789.1	39076.4	37488.2	39096.4	Europe ancienne URSS exclus
- European Union	33625.5	32123.1	33963.2	32306.9	33316.5	- Union Européenne
- Eastern Europe	2561.8	2639.7	2970.3	3147.3	3639.8	- Europe de l'Est
- Rest of Europe	2100.2	2026.3	2142.9	2034.1	2140.1	- Autre de l'Europe
Europe former USSR	832.5	737.8	897.7	1133.4	1356.2	Europe ancienne URSS
Oceania	755.7	1011.6	1087.7	958.1	1057.6	Océanie
China	7798.8	8315.9	10273.4	11142.7	12138.8	Chine
United States	5596.3	6056.0	7099.4	7016.2	7143.3	Etats-Unis d'Amérique
Germany	6613.5	6073.6	6079.1	6157.8	5698.4	Allemagne
Italy-San Marino-Holy See	4570.9	4693.0	5184.5	4726.9	4636.0	Italie-Saint-Marin-Saint-Siège
France-Monaco	4739.8	4483.1	4846.6	4281.4	4356.0	France-Monaco
China, Hong Kong SAR	4118.5	4017.7	5079.0	4155.5	4549.3	Chine - RAS de Hong-Kong
United Kingdom	4136.6	3877.5	4130.8	3935.4	4033.8	Royaume-Uni
Canada	2794.9	3094.4	3428.1	3298.1	3504.0	Canada
Belgium	–	3649.2	4051.1	3977.6	e4362.2	Belgique
Mexico	2372.0	2780.9	3440.3	3358.2	3363.5	Mexique
Spain	2079.7	2203.0	2201.4	2240.3	2647.4	Espagne
Netherlands	2226.9	2069.3	2107.4	1959.5	2170.4	Pays-Bas
Poland	1206.7	1289.8	1430.9	1456.2	1655.8	Pologne
Japan	1066.3	1194.9	1336.3	1228.1	1151.9	Japon
Turkey	1110.8	1065.2	1313.8	1011.8	1415.4	Turquie
Switzerland-Liechtenstein	1135.6	1117.1	1169.0	1089.8	1114.7	Suisse-Liechtenstein
Austria	1033.5	988.9	1049.1	1000.0	1055.3	Autriche
Sweden	1055.3	1012.0	1077.0	957.6	1010.5	Suède
Denmark	952.3	850.2	910.2	847.4	956.2	Danemark
Brazil	871.4	733.6	1017.7	913.8	866.4	Brésil
Korea, Republic of	566.9	822.1	993.9	930.5	1065.1	République de Corée
Malaysia	629.7	807.4	997.6	831.8	e909.1	Malaisie
Thailand	691.1	794.4	944.4	837.7	e872.8	Thaïlande
Belgium-Luxembourg	4052.9	–	–	–	–	Belgique-Luxembourg
Singapore	703.6	754.7	858.5	714.5	762.0	Singapour
Czech Republic	624.1	601.1	681.1	739.9	870.0	République tchèque
Australia	643.6	704.2	757.6	635.4	726.5	Australie
Indonesia	432.9	455.2	665.9	623.5	599.3	Indonésie
Finland	592.4	532.5	565.7	505.8	571.8	Finlande
Portugal	500.3	516.9	565.6	535.2	573.1	Portugal

(Value as percentages of World total) **(Valeur en pourcentage du total mondial)**

Regions of the world	1993	1994	1995	1996	1997	1998	1999	2000	2001	2002	Régions du monde
World	100.0	100.0	100.0	100.0	100.0	100.0	100.0	100.0	100.0	100.0	Monde
Africa	2.7	2.4	2.2	2.3	2.5	2.5	2.3	2.3	2.5	2.4	Afrique
Americas	15.2	15.1	14.5	15.6	17.2	18.2	19.1	20.0	20.2	19.3	Amériques
- Northern America	9.6	9.7	8.9	9.7	10.4	10.8	11.7	11.9	12.1	11.9	- Amérique du Nord
- LAIA	4.8	4.7	4.8	5.2	6.0	6.5	6.6	7.2	7.1	6.4	- ALAI
- CACM	0.5	0.4	0.5	0.4	0.5	0.5	0.5	0.5	0.6	0.6	- MCC
- Caribbean	0.2	0.2	0.2	0.2	0.3	0.3	0.3	0.3	0.3	0.3	- Caraïbes
- Rest of America	0.1	0.1	0.1	0.1	0.1	0.1	0.0	0.1	0.1	0.1	- Autre d'Amérique
Asia excluding former USSR	31.4	29.9	29.9	30.6	30.5	27.7	29.0	31.1	30.8	31.8	Asie ancienne URSS exclus
- Middle East	3.1	2.5	2.7	2.9	2.9	2.9	2.7	3.1	3.0	3.4	- Moyen-Orient
Asia former USSR	0.0	0.1	0.1	0.1	0.1	0.2	0.1	0.1	0.1	0.1	Asie ancienne URSS
Europe excluding former USSR	48.7	50.3	51.3	48.9	47.2	49.4	47.2	44.2	43.9	43.7	Europe ancienne URSS exclus
- European Union	44.0	45.6	46.2	43.7	41.9	43.4	41.2	38.4	37.9	37.2	- Union Européenne
- Eastern Europe	1.7	1.7	2.2	2.7	2.9	3.3	3.4	3.4	3.7	4.1	- Europe de l'Est
- Rest of Europe	3.0	3.0	2.9	2.6	2.5	2.7	2.6	2.4	2.4	2.4	- Autre de l'Europe
Europe former USSR	0.7	0.7	0.8	1.1	1.3	1.1	0.9	1.0	1.3	1.5	Europe ancienne URSS
Oceania	1.4	1.4	1.3	1.3	1.3	1.0	1.3	1.2	1.1	1.2	Océanie

TRADE BY COMMODITY (Value in million US dollars)
Exports by principal countries or areas

COMMERCE PAR PRODUIT (Valeur en millions de dollars EU)
Exportations selon les principaux pays ou zones

Country or area	1998	1999	2000	2001	2002	Pays ou zone
World	76891.8	77650.5	88575.1	84964.1	87601.4	Monde
Africa	164.3	245.7	201.3	285.9	292.3	Afrique
Americas	14079.7	14581.3	17533.1	17361.6	17686.0	Amériques
- Northern America	12286.1	12719.3	15078.6	14936.7	15111.5	- Amérique du Nord
- LAIA	1700.1	1763.8	2329.7	2269.1	2376.5	- ALAI
- CACM	55.4	54.4	62.4	75.5	71.5	- MCC
- Caribbean	37.4	43.3	61.6	79.3	125.5	- Caraïbes
- Rest of America	0.6	0.6	0.7	0.9	1.0	- Autre d'Amérique
Asia excluding former USSR	19873.7	20935.1	26209.0	23657.0	25447.8	Asie ancienne URSS exclus
- Middle East	1911.0	1862.5	2350.2	2884.6	2367.8	- Moyen-Orient
Asia former USSR	11.1	16.2	22.4	16.4	24.6	Asie ancienne URSS
Europe excluding former USSR	42003.7	41058.1	43624.1	42711.7	43267.8	Europe ancienne URSS exclus
- European Union	39468.8	38717.1	40828.8	40017.3	40337.5	- Union Européenne
- Eastern Europe	1398.3	1288.5	1770.8	1667.7	1837.1	- Europe de l'Est
- Rest of Europe	1136.6	1052.5	1024.6	1026.6	1093.2	- Autre de l'Europe
Europe former USSR	548.4	595.5	783.3	739.9	687.1	Europe ancienne URSS
Oceania	211.0	218.6	201.8	191.6	195.8	Océanie
Germany	12834.0	12813.6	13114.1	13107.1	11308.7	Allemagne
United States	9488.3	9623.1	11415.1	11208.3	11396.0	Etats-Unis d'Amérique
Belgium	–	7284.0	8079.8	7781.1	e8730.2	Belgique
Japan	4260.2	4792.0	5474.8	4606.0	5200.2	Japon
France-Monaco	4937.2	4745.7	5294.4	4531.0	4714.3	France-Monaco
Netherlands	4353.8	4030.7	3958.9	4184.3	4483.0	Pays-Bas
Korea, Republic of	3686.2	3787.5	4684.5	4207.2	4339.0	République de Corée
China, Hong Kong SAR	3915.9	3932.0	4538.8	3875.8	4259.1	Chine - RAS de Hong-Kong
Canada	2797.8	3096.1	3663.3	3728.3	3715.2	Canada
Italy-San Marino-Holy See	3314.6	3293.5	3493.6	3380.2	3477.6	Italie-Saint-Marin-Saint-Siège
United Kingdom	2228.4	1873.9	1917.8	1952.2	2384.6	Royaume-Uni
Spain	1428.9	1469.5	1572.5	1712.3	1639.8	Espagne
Belgium-Luxembourg	7104.9	–	–	–	–	Belgique-Luxembourg
Singapore	1102.7	1187.9	1452.3	1214.3	1757.6	Singapour
Thailand	991.3	1119.8	1653.6	1412.2	e1491.4	Thaïlande
Saudi Arabia	976.7	826.9	913.7	1536.8	e1385.0	Arabie saoudite
Sweden	1076.4	1038.9	1108.8	1009.2	1118.4	Suède
Mexico	606.2	687.8	873.1	833.8	872.5	Mexique
Switzerland-Liechtenstein	692.4	684.5	678.7	693.7	756.2	Suisse-Liechtenstein
Malaysia	499.1	501.8	802.5	735.3	e779.3	Malaisie
Austria	645.7	632.0	629.0	651.9	723.0	Autriche
Kuwait	471.0	584.7	e936.0	e780.3	e320.0	Koweït
Finland	564.1	548.7	600.3	611.3	631.4	Finlande
Hungary	472.4	423.4	625.4	585.3	623.2	Hongrie
China	549.0	398.3	526.0	508.1	623.0	Chine
Brazil	440.0	420.3	587.8	488.2	e506.2	Brésil
Russian Federation	353.7	429.7	557.8	477.8	410.3	Fédération de Russie
Indonesia	291.3	349.6	464.3	365.8	356.5	Indonésie
Czech Republic	325.7	313.3	382.9	365.2	369.9	République tchèque
Denmark	378.4	326.3	319.6	347.3	371.6	Danemark

(Value as percentages of World total) **(Valeur en pourcentage du total mondial)**

Regions of the world	1993	1994	1995	1996	1997	1998	1999	2000	2001	2002	Régions du monde
World	100.0	100.0	100.0	100.0	100.0	100.0	100.0	100.0	100.0	100.0	Monde
Africa	0.3	0.3	0.2	0.2	0.2	0.2	0.3	0.2	0.3	0.3	Afrique
Americas	16.9	16.9	17.0	17.4	19.2	18.3	18.8	19.8	20.4	20.2	Amériques
- Northern America	14.7	14.7	14.7	15.4	17.0	16.0	16.4	17.0	17.6	17.3	- Amérique du Nord
- LAIA	2.1	2.1	2.3	1.9	2.1	2.2	2.3	2.6	2.7	2.7	- ALAI
- CACM	0.1	0.1	0.0	0.1	0.1	0.1	0.1	0.1	0.1	0.1	- MCC
- Caribbean	0.0	0.0	0.0	0.0	0.0	0.0	0.1	0.1	0.1	0.1	- Caraïbes
- Rest of America	0.0	0.0	0.0	0.0	0.0	0.0	0.0	0.0	0.0	0.0	- Autre d'Amérique
Asia excluding former USSR	26.2	24.5	26.3	25.5	26.9	25.8	27.0	29.6	27.8	29.0	Asie ancienne URSS exclus
- Middle East	1.9	1.9	2.3	1.9	1.9	2.5	2.4	2.7	3.4	2.7	- Moyen-Orient
Asia former USSR	0.0	0.1	0.1	0.1	0.0	0.0	0.0	0.0	0.0	0.0	Asie ancienne URSS
Europe excluding former USSR	55.8	57.3	55.4	55.7	52.5	54.6	52.9	49.3	50.3	49.4	Europe ancienne URSS exclus
- European Union	51.7	53.7	51.5	52.3	49.3	51.3	49.9	46.1	47.1	46.0	- Union Européenne
- Eastern Europe	1.8	1.7	1.9	1.9	1.9	1.8	1.7	2.0	2.0	2.1	- Europe de l'Est
- Rest of Europe	2.3	1.9	2.0	1.5	1.3	1.5	1.4	1.2	1.2	1.2	- Autre de l'Europe
Europe former USSR	0.4	0.6	0.7	0.8	0.8	0.7	0.8	0.9	0.9	0.8	Europe ancienne URSS
Oceania	0.3	0.3	0.3	0.3	0.4	0.3	0.3	0.2	0.2	0.2	Océanie

584 Regenerated cellulose; derivatives of cellulose; vulcanized fibre

TRADE BY COMMODITY (Value in million US dollars)
Imports by principal countries or areas

COMMERCE PAR PRODUIT (Valeur en millions de dollars EU)
Importations selon les principaux pays ou zones

Country or area	1998	1999	2000	2001	2002	Pays ou zone
World	2936.6	2765.0	2724.0	2825.4	2989.3	Monde
Africa	105.9	115.5	89.4	100.0	96.5	Afrique
Americas	602.1	578.1	641.2	643.2	684.6	Amériques
- Northern America	336.2	340.0	354.1	331.7	352.0	- Amérique du Nord
- LAIA	242.4	218.9	262.4	287.1	304.0	- ALAI
- CACM	15.7	11.2	11.6	12.2	13.7	- MCC
- Caribbean	5.7	6.3	10.1	9.4	12.9	- Caraïbes
- Rest of America	2.2	1.8	3.1	2.8	2.0	- Autre d'Amérique
Asia excluding former USSR	672.9	692.6	740.6	746.6	799.8	Asie ancienne URSS exclus
- Middle East	158.1	134.7	119.1	110.2	104.0	- Moyen-Orient
Asia former USSR	3.1	4.9	5.6	6.9	5.7	Asie ancienne URSS
Europe excluding former USSR	1459.5	1296.0	1165.0	1237.5	1301.4	Europe ancienne URSS exclus
- European Union	1308.7	1151.1	1022.0	1095.8	1143.7	- Union Européenne
- Eastern Europe	88.0	80.8	80.6	81.7	92.5	- Europe de l'Est
- Rest of Europe	62.8	64.1	62.5	60.0	65.2	- Autre de l'Europe
Europe former USSR	56.9	39.2	44.4	59.6	68.7	Europe ancienne URSS
Oceania	36.2	38.7	37.8	31.6	32.6	Océanie
United States	243.2	250.6	271.3	254.6	270.3	Etats-Unis d'Amérique
Germany	252.4	233.3	211.3	196.2	183.8	Allemagne
France-Monaco	152.5	149.2	147.5	136.4	162.5	France-Monaco
Belgium	–	131.4	125.7	206.4	e226.3	Belgique
Italy-San Marino-Holy See	191.4	177.3	101.1	96.6	103.5	Italie-Saint-Marin-Saint-Siège
United Kingdom	140.6	132.3	136.9	124.6	123.4	Royaume-Uni
China	116.7	121.5	82.3	92.6	105.6	Chine
Spain	99.1	101.8	90.9	103.5	117.8	Espagne
Mexico	56.4	62.3	102.5	125.9	139.2	Mexique
Netherlands	178.0	71.3	64.7	85.5	77.6	Pays-Bas
Korea, Republic of	62.8	75.4	89.4	109.3	138.1	République de Corée
Japan	62.7	84.9	99.3	105.2	94.3	Japon
Canada	92.9	89.4	82.7	77.2	81.6	Canada
China, Hong Kong SAR	59.4	61.3	74.0	63.6	70.7	Chine - RAS de Hong-Kong
Brazil	62.3	56.2	54.2	56.1	81.0	Brésil
Turkey	42.0	43.2	44.9	36.1	49.0	Turquie
Poland	41.5	38.6	39.8	38.8	44.1	Pologne
Indonesia	36.0	35.4	47.5	38.7	44.3	Indonésie
Austria	45.5	36.7	31.5	28.0	25.8	Autriche
Venezuela	31.5	29.9	35.1	37.2	e31.3	Venezuela
Switzerland-Liechtenstein	34.3	33.5	31.0	27.6	29.7	Suisse-Liechtenstein
Australia	34.1	32.5	32.5	26.9	27.5	Australie
Russian Federation	22.5	18.6	23.1	39.0	44.0	Fédération de Russie
Viet Nam	e	e	44.5	46.1	56.1	Viet Nam
Argentina	42.0	33.2	27.7	26.0	e11.5	Argentine
Singapore	33.5	26.8	30.6	25.4	23.1	Singapour
Belgium-Luxembourg	135.8	–	–	–	–	Belgique-Luxembourg
Thailand	20.5	25.0	25.7	31.2	e32.5	Thaïlande
Denmark	29.0	25.7	23.9	24.0	24.9	Danemark
Ireland	17.5	25.9	25.3	29.0	28.6	Irlande

(Value as percentages of World total) **(Valeur en pourcentage du total mondial)**

Regions of the world	1993	1994	1995	1996	1997	1998	1999	2000	2001	2002	Régions du monde
World	100.0	100.0	100.0	100.0	100.0	100.0	100.0	100.0	100.0	100.0	Monde
Africa	3.6	2.9	3.1	3.2	3.3	3.6	4.2	3.3	3.5	3.2	Afrique
Americas	20.6	19.4	17.4	17.5	18.7	20.5	20.9	23.5	22.8	22.9	Amériques
- Northern America	11.1	10.3	9.4	10.3	11.0	11.4	12.3	13.0	11.7	11.8	- Amérique du Nord
- LAIA	8.3	8.2	7.2	6.4	6.9	8.3	7.9	9.6	10.2	10.2	- ALAI
- CACM	0.8	0.6	0.6	0.6	0.6	0.5	0.4	0.4	0.4	0.5	- MCC
- Caribbean	0.2	0.1	0.1	0.1	0.2	0.2	0.2	0.4	0.3	0.4	- Caraïbes
- Rest of America	0.2	0.2	0.1	0.1	0.1	0.1	0.1	0.1	0.1	0.1	- Autre d'Amérique
Asia excluding former USSR	27.5	23.8	23.0	23.6	24.3	22.9	25.1	27.2	26.4	26.8	Asie ancienne URSS exclus
- Middle East	4.0	3.5	4.1	4.7	4.1	5.4	4.9	4.4	3.9	3.5	- Moyen-Orient
Asia former USSR	0.0	0.1	0.1	0.1	0.1	0.1	0.2	0.2	0.2	0.2	Asie ancienne URSS
Europe excluding former USSR	45.4	50.2	52.8	51.4	49.8	49.7	46.9	42.8	43.8	43.5	Europe ancienne URSS exclus
- European Union	41.1	45.2	47.8	46.6	44.6	44.6	41.6	37.5	38.8	38.3	- Union Européenne
- Eastern Europe	1.7	2.1	2.3	2.6	2.6	3.0	2.9	3.0	2.9	3.1	- Europe de l'Est
- Rest of Europe	2.6	2.9	2.7	2.2	2.6	2.1	2.3	2.3	2.1	2.2	- Autre de l'Europe
Europe former USSR	0.7	1.4	1.8	2.5	2.4	1.9	1.4	1.6	2.1	2.3	Europe ancienne URSS
Oceania	2.3	2.3	1.9	1.7	1.5	1.2	1.4	1.4	1.1	1.1	Océanie

TRADE BY COMMODITY (Value in million US dollars)
Exports by principal countries or areas

COMMERCE PAR PRODUIT (Valeur en millions de dollars EU)
Exportations selon les principaux pays ou zones

Country or area	1998	1999	2000	2001	2002	Pays ou zone
World	2542.8	2300.7	2352.4	2619.6	2782.2	Monde
Africa	3.6	3.6	3.4	2.7	2.3	Afrique
Americas	776.7	755.8	744.6	770.2	801.2	Amériques
- Northern America	692.5	661.4	671.9	715.8	746.7	- Amérique du Nord
- LAIA	83.1	93.8	71.7	52.7	52.7	- ALAI
- CACM	0.7	0.3	0.7	1.5	1.7	- MCC
- Caribbean	0.1	0.1	0.1	0.1	0.1	- Caraïbes
- Rest of America	0.4	0.2	0.2	0.1	0.1	- Autre d'Amérique
Asia excluding former USSR	321.0	377.6	440.9	443.5	510.7	Asie ancienne URSS exclus
- Middle East	17.1	20.5	23.5	20.5	12.0	- Moyen-Orient
Asia former USSR	0.5	0.3	0.2	0.2	0.4	Asie ancienne URSS
Europe excluding former USSR	1437.0	1158.3	1159.8	1397.6	1461.6	Europe ancienne URSS exclus
- European Union	1382.8	1106.3	1110.7	1355.4	1416.3	- Union Européenne
- Eastern Europe	35.2	26.7	28.6	25.7	26.6	- Europe de l'Est
- Rest of Europe	19.0	25.3	20.5	16.6	18.8	- Autre de l'Europe
Europe former USSR	2.7	4.4	2.8	3.0	3.2	Europe ancienne URSS
Oceania	1.4	0.7	0.7	2.4	2.7	Océanie
United States	683.3	657.9	668.9	711.5	742.0	Etats-Unis d'Amérique
Germany	389.8	374.8	394.2	417.1	431.1	Allemagne
Japan	175.9	199.6	229.9	234.6	279.8	Japon
Belgium	-	153.0	141.1	249.8	e280.2	Belgique
Netherlands	267.4	65.8	53.6	184.3	195.2	Pays-Bas
United Kingdom	158.5	116.1	129.1	144.8	150.3	Royaume-Uni
Sweden	95.0	105.9	104.7	101.3	111.0	Suède
Finland	82.7	84.1	97.6	99.8	97.5	Finlande
Ireland	77.7	83.9	74.7	73.4	69.0	Irlande
Italy-San Marino-Holy See	95.4	56.4	60.9	48.4	48.0	Italie-Saint-Marin-Saint-Siège
China, Hong Kong SAR	36.9	40.4	52.1	43.4	48.4	Chine - RAS de Hong-Kong
Belgium-Luxembourg	149.2	-	-	-	-	Belgique-Luxembourg
Spain	47.2	40.6	31.0	16.6	9.1	Espagne
Mexico	38.2	52.5	25.7	10.1	9.7	Mexique
Brazil	24.6	23.9	29.5	28.4	e29.5	Brésil
Korea, Republic of	10.2	18.2	25.1	32.6	44.9	République de Corée
China	12.9	22.7	23.9	25.4	34.4	Chine
Switzerland-Liechtenstein	16.9	23.8	19.8	15.9	16.6	Suisse-Liechtenstein
Singapore	16.9	16.7	17.8	16.3	15.3	Singapour
France-Monaco	9.4	12.8	13.9	13.7	18.2	France-Monaco
Czech Republic	12.9	11.8	11.8	11.6	11.9	République tchèque
Hungary	10.7	9.1	10.5	7.8	7.7	Hongrie
Argentina	11.4	10.2	8.4	6.4	e6.2	Argentine
Kuwait	7.6	8.3	e13.2	e11.0	e1.5	Koweït
Turkey	7.7	9.4	7.7	6.0	7.0	Turquie
Colombia	8.4	6.7	7.9	7.5	7.1	Colombie
India	3.6	6.5	7.5	8.1	9.5	Inde
Canada	9.2	3.5	3.0	4.3	4.7	Canada
Slovakia	8.7	3.7	4.1	3.3	2.6	Slovaquie
Malaysia	3.5	3.7	3.9	5.2	e5.5	Malaisie

(Value as percentages of World total) **(Valeur en pourcentage du total mondial)**

Regions of the world	1993	1994	1995	1996	1997	1998	1999	2000	2001	2002	Régions du monde
World	100.0	100.0	100.0	100.0	100.0	100.0	100.0	100.0	100.0	100.0	Monde
Africa	0.1	0.1	0.2	0.2	0.1	0.1	0.2	0.1	0.1	0.1	Afrique
Americas	35.7	38.6	37.0	36.4	33.3	30.5	32.9	31.7	29.4	28.8	Amériques
- Northern America	31.7	34.9	33.2	32.3	29.7	27.2	28.7	28.6	27.3	26.8	- Amérique du Nord
- LAIA	3.9	3.7	3.7	4.1	3.6	3.3	4.1	3.0	2.0	1.9	- ALAI
- CACM	0.1	0.1	0.1	0.1	0.0	0.0	0.0	0.0	0.1	0.1	- MCC
- Caribbean	0.0	0.0	0.0	0.0	0.0	0.0	0.0	0.0	0.0	0.0	- Caraïbes
- Rest of America	0.0	0.0	0.0	0.0	0.0	0.0	0.0	0.0	0.0	0.0	- Autre d'Amérique
Asia excluding former USSR	12.8	11.9	12.6	13.4	12.2	12.6	16.4	18.7	16.9	18.4	Asie ancienne URSS exclus
- Middle East	0.7	0.7	0.8	0.8	0.7	0.7	0.9	1.0	0.8	0.4	- Moyen-Orient
Asia former USSR	0.0	0.2	0.1	0.1	0.0	0.0	0.0	0.0	0.0	0.0	Asie ancienne URSS
Europe excluding former USSR	51.2	49.0	48.8	49.6	54.2	56.5	50.3	49.3	53.4	52.5	Europe ancienne URSS exclus
- European Union	49.6	46.8	46.4	47.0	52.2	54.4	48.1	47.2	51.7	50.9	- Union Européenne
- Eastern Europe	1.0	1.4	1.6	1.8	1.4	1.4	1.2	1.2	1.0	1.0	- Europe de l'Est
- Rest of Europe	0.6	0.7	0.8	0.7	0.6	0.7	1.1	0.9	0.6	0.7	- Autre de l'Europe
Europe former USSR	0.1	0.1	0.1	0.2	0.1	0.1	0.2	0.1	0.1	0.1	Europe ancienne URSS
Oceania	0.0	0.1	1.1	0.1	0.1	0.1	0.0	0.0	0.1	0.1	Océanie

585 Other artificial resins and plastic materials

TRADE BY COMMODITY (Value in million US dollars)
Imports by principal countries or areas

COMMERCE PAR PRODUIT (Valeur en millions de dollars EU)
Importations selon les principaux pays ou zones

Country or area	1998	1999	2000	2001	2002	Pays ou zone
World	708.3	736.2	728.6	862.8	911.7	Monde
Africa	12.4	12.3	11.0	18.3	18.0	Afrique
Americas	265.9	277.9	255.0	335.8	360.9	Amériques
- Northern America	140.4	148.8	138.0	224.3	248.8	- Amérique du Nord
- LAIA	122.4	126.1	113.7	107.9	109.1	- ALAI
- CACM	1.2	1.5	1.3	1.4	0.9	- MCC
- Caribbean	1.5	1.3	1.6	2.0	1.9	- Caraïbes
- Rest of America	0.3	0.3	0.4	0.2	0.2	- Autre d'Amérique
Asia excluding former USSR	144.2	161.2	170.7	172.7	179.9	Asie ancienne URSS exclus
- Middle East	17.8	13.2	17.0	17.6	16.6	- Moyen-Orient
Asia former USSR	0.4	0.3	1.3	1.3	0.6	Asie ancienne URSS
Europe excluding former USSR	268.8	269.0	271.8	317.8	331.5	Europe ancienne URSS exclus
- European Union	231.6	229.9	230.5	272.3	277.5	- Union Européenne
- Eastern Europe	9.0	7.7	9.4	10.5	11.6	- Europe de l'Est
- Rest of Europe	28.3	31.4	31.9	35.0	42.4	- Autre de l'Europe
Europe former USSR	2.9	3.9	7.7	7.5	9.2	Europe ancienne URSS
Oceania	13.6	11.5	11.1	9.5	11.4	Océanie
United States	122.0	131.4	117.4	201.7	220.2	Etats-Unis d'Amérique
Mexico	84.2	90.9	73.0	64.3	73.7	Mexique
Japan	46.8	64.7	73.2	66.7	71.7	Japon
Germany	60.7	64.2	58.4	50.9	46.2	Allemagne
United Kingdom	37.0	36.0	35.5	41.4	43.6	Royaume-Uni
France-Monaco	28.2	31.6	29.5	49.3	40.6	France-Monaco
Belgium	–	18.7	22.1	37.7	e41.3	Belgique
Switzerland-Liechtenstein	20.0	22.4	21.7	23.1	31.8	Suisse-Liechtenstein
Korea, Republic of	21.5	24.0	23.3	23.2	25.0	République de Corée
Italy-San Marino-Holy See	26.6	21.6	19.8	21.5	23.1	Italie-Saint-Marin-Saint-Siège
Canada	18.5	17.4	20.7	22.6	28.6	Canada
Brazil	15.7	15.5	19.9	22.7	21.3	Brésil
Netherlands	15.2	13.8	15.2	15.7	18.8	Pays-Bas
Spain	13.6	12.9	15.2	14.1	20.4	Espagne
Denmark	13.8	13.0	13.3	14.2	15.4	Danemark
Indonesia	13.5	10.8	11.4	12.0	8.4	Indonésie
Australia	13.2	9.6	9.4	7.9	9.9	Australie
Argentina	8.9	10.3	7.7	8.6	e3.8	Argentine
Norway	6.1	6.5	7.9	10.1	8.5	Norvège
Turkey	10.7	7.1	7.3	6.0	7.2	Turquie
Sweden	7.7	5.3	5.9	9.1	10.1	Suède
Singapore	6.9	7.8	6.8	6.9	7.1	Singapour
China	4.8	3.7	5.3	9.0	11.2	Chine
Thailand	5.1	6.8	5.5	6.6	e6.9	Thaïlande
Philippines	3.7	7.0	4.4	6.8	8.5	Philippines
Ireland	5.6	6.1	5.2	7.6	3.3	Irlande
Austria	2.6	2.8	5.6	5.8	9.1	Autriche
Nigeria	4.9	4.6	3.6	e4.9	e4.7	Nigéria
Colombia	4.7	3.8	4.8	4.3	3.5	Colombie
Russian Federation	1.3	2.5	5.5	4.9	6.3	Fédération de Russie

(Value as percentages of World total) **(Valeur en pourcentage du total mondial)**

Regions of the world	1993	1994	1995	1996	1997	1998	1999	2000	2001	2002	Régions du monde
World	100.0	100.0	100.0	100.0	100.0	100.0	100.0	100.0	100.0	100.0	Monde
Africa	5.2	2.0	3.1	2.1	2.8	1.8	1.7	1.5	2.1	2.0	Afrique
Americas	33.4	34.2	34.5	36.1	38.3	37.5	37.8	35.0	38.9	39.6	Amériques
- Northern America	19.2	20.4	19.8	22.5	23.4	19.8	20.2	18.9	26.0	27.3	- Amérique du Nord
- LAIA	13.0	13.2	14.4	13.2	14.5	17.3	17.1	15.6	12.5	12.0	- ALAI
- CACM	0.9	0.2	0.1	0.2	0.2	0.2	0.2	0.2	0.2	0.1	- MCC
- Caribbean	0.1	0.1	0.1	0.2	0.2	0.2	0.2	0.2	0.2	0.2	- Caraïbes
- Rest of America	0.1	0.2	0.1	0.1	0.0	0.0	0.0	0.1	0.0	0.0	- Autre d'Amérique
Asia excluding former USSR	29.3	26.3	26.3	24.3	22.8	20.4	21.9	23.4	20.0	19.7	Asie ancienne URSS exclus
- Middle East	3.8	4.3	3.3	3.0	3.8	2.5	1.8	2.3	2.0	1.8	- Moyen-Orient
Asia former USSR	0.0	0.0	0.0	0.0	0.1	0.1	0.0	0.2	0.1	0.1	Asie ancienne URSS
Europe excluding former USSR	29.5	34.4	33.3	34.8	33.3	38.0	36.5	37.3	36.8	36.4	Europe ancienne URSS exclus
- European Union	26.6	30.4	28.9	30.4	29.2	32.7	31.2	31.6	31.6	30.4	- Union Européenne
- Eastern Europe	0.9	0.9	1.0	0.9	1.0	1.3	1.0	1.3	1.2	1.3	- Europe de l'Est
- Rest of Europe	1.9	3.0	3.4	3.4	3.1	4.0	4.3	4.4	4.1	4.7	- Autre de l'Europe
Europe former USSR	0.2	0.3	0.3	0.4	0.3	0.4	0.5	1.1	0.9	1.0	Europe ancienne URSS
Oceania	2.5	2.9	2.4	2.3	2.3	1.9	1.6	1.5	1.1	1.3	Océanie

TRADE BY COMMODITY (Value in million US dollars)
Exports by principal countries or areas

COMMERCE PAR PRODUIT (Valeur en millions de dollars EU)
Exportations selon les principaux pays ou zones

Country or area	1998	1999	2000	2001	2002	Pays ou zone
World	553.3	592.1	673.2	734.7	808.4	Monde
Africa	0.9	0.8	0.7	0.6	0.5	Afrique
Americas	195.8	216.4	248.7	240.3	257.8	Amériques
- Northern America	174.6	187.9	209.1	219.5	234.7	- Amérique du Nord
- LAIA	21.1	28.4	39.5	20.7	23.1	- ALAI
- CACM	0.0	0.0	0.0	0.1	0.1	- MCC
- Caribbean	0.0	0.0	0.0	0.0	0.0	- Caraïbes
- Rest of America	0.0	0.0	0.0	0.0	0.0	- Autre d'Amérique
Asia excluding former USSR	89.9	88.4	109.7	181.1	193.1	Asie ancienne URSS exclus
- Middle East	0.3	0.9	1.0	1.5	0.7	- Moyen-Orient
Asia former USSR	0.0	0.1	0.0	0.0	0.0	Asie ancienne URSS
Europe excluding former USSR	265.6	285.8	312.9	312.0	355.6	Europe ancienne URSS exclus
- European Union	257.6	279.1	303.2	300.4	337.7	- Union Européenne
- Eastern Europe	1.2	0.5	0.6	0.5	0.4	- Europe de l'Est
- Rest of Europe	6.8	6.2	9.0	11.1	17.5	- Autre de l'Europe
Europe former USSR	0.0	0.1	0.4	0.1	0.1	Europe ancienne URSS
Oceania	1.1	0.5	0.9	0.6	1.2	Océanie
United States	171.0	183.5	204.0	215.3	230.1	Etats-Unis d'Amérique
Sweden	67.5	71.4	93.8	104.0	123.8	Suède
China	42.7	38.7	53.8	71.5	98.5	Chine
France-Monaco	55.9	59.1	61.7	59.8	61.6	France-Monaco
Germany	48.9	42.7	55.2	43.2	40.7	Allemagne
Japan	29.0	33.2	34.1	46.1	35.6	Japon
Spain	24.2	28.8	32.9	30.1	38.2	Espagne
United Kingdom	15.6	29.1	18.4	27.1	34.0	Royaume-Uni
Singapore	3.9	2.6	7.9	50.8	47.2	Singapour
Italy-San Marino-Holy See	18.8	16.1	17.3	16.3	20.0	Italie-Saint-Marin-Saint-Siège
Argentina	9.9	13.2	12.9	11.4	e11.0	Argentine
Belgium	–	21.5	12.8	7.6	e8.5	Belgique
Netherlands	7.0	8.1	9.2	10.6	9.2	Pays-Bas
Mexico	6.0	9.0	21.0	0.8	2.3	Mexique
Switzerland-Liechtenstein	5.1	3.9	4.4	5.7	13.3	Suisse-Liechtenstein
Canada	3.6	4.4	5.1	4.2	4.6	Canada
Chile	4.0	4.3	3.9	3.9	e3.8	Chili
Belgium-Luxembourg	17.6	–	–	–	–	Belgique-Luxembourg
China, Hong Kong SAR	5.7	3.2	3.1	2.3	1.0	Chine - RAS de Hong-Kong
Korea, Republic of	3.5	3.3	2.4	2.2	2.6	République de Corée
Norway	1.7	2.2	3.8	3.7	1.0	Norvège
Malaysia	0.9	2.3	2.7	1.6	e1.7	Malaisie
Uruguay	0.8	1.7	1.6	1.6	2.9	Uruguay
India	1.7	1.0	1.6	1.4	1.9	Inde
Brazil	0.1	0.2	0.1	2.9	e3.0	Brésil
Iceland			0.8	1.7	3.1	Islande
Bangladesh	1.1	e0.8	e1.0	1.2	e0.9	Bangladesh
Ireland	1.0	1.5	0.5	0.9	1.0	Irlande
Australia	1.0	0.5	0.7	0.6	1.2	Australie
Thailand	0.2	0.3	0.7	0.7	e0.8	Thaïlande

(Value as percentages of World total) **(Valeur en pourcentage du total mondial)**

Regions of the world	1993	1994	1995	1996	1997	1998	1999	2000	2001	2002	Régions du monde
World	100.0	100.0	100.0	100.0	100.0	100.0	100.0	100.0	100.0	100.0	Monde
Africa	0.5	0.3	0.1	0.2	0.2	0.2	0.1	0.1	0.1	0.1	Afrique
Americas	31.5	29.8	30.9	29.3	32.7	35.4	36.5	36.9	32.7	31.9	Amériques
- Northern America	23.7	24.6	26.9	25.4	27.9	31.6	31.7	31.1	29.9	29.0	- Amérique du Nord
- LAIA	6.4	3.7	2.7	3.9	4.8	3.8	4.8	5.9	2.8	2.9	- ALAI
- CACM	0.2	0.0	0.0	0.0	0.0	0.0	0.0	0.0	0.0	0.0	- MCC
- Caribbean	1.2	1.5	1.3	0.0	0.0	0.0	0.0	0.0	0.0	0.0	- Caraïbes
- Rest of America	0.0	0.0	0.0	0.0	0.0	0.0	0.0	0.0	0.0	0.0	- Autre d'Amérique
Asia excluding former USSR	18.1	19.0	19.9	19.6	18.9	16.2	14.9	16.3	24.6	23.9	Asie ancienne URSS exclus
- Middle East	0.6	0.8	0.4	0.4	0.1	0.1	0.2	0.1	0.2	0.1	- Moyen-Orient
Asia former USSR	0.0	0.0	0.0	0.0	0.0	0.0	0.0	0.0	0.0	0.0	Asie ancienne URSS
Europe excluding former USSR	48.6	49.5	48.0	50.2	47.7	48.0	48.3	46.5	42.5	44.0	Europe ancienne URSS exclus
- European Union	47.1	47.8	46.3	48.6	46.1	46.6	47.1	45.0	40.9	41.8	- Union Européenne
- Eastern Europe	0.2	0.2	0.0	0.1	0.2	0.2	0.1	0.1	0.1	0.0	- Europe de l'Est
- Rest of Europe	1.4	1.5	1.6	1.5	1.5	1.2	1.0	1.3	1.5	2.2	- Autre de l'Europe
Europe former USSR	0.1	0.1	0.2	0.0	0.0	0.0	0.0	0.1	0.0	0.0	Europe ancienne URSS
Oceania	1.2	1.3	0.9	0.7	0.5	0.2	0.1	0.1	0.1	0.1	Océanie

591 Pesticides, disinfectants

TRADE BY COMMODITY (Value in million US dollars)
Imports by principal countries or areas

COMMERCE PAR PRODUIT (Valeur en millions de dollars EU)
Importations selon les principaux pays ou zones

Country or area	1998	1999	2000	2001	2002	Pays ou zone
World	11699.1	11476.3	10778.4	10946.4	11557.8	Monde
Africa	637.8	574.9	555.8	587.7	620.1	Afrique
Americas	2992.0	2740.0	2566.7	2809.1	2706.1	Amériques
- Northern America	1189.4	1087.2	989.4	1123.8	1122.0	- Amérique du Nord
- LAIA	1365.3	1227.8	1189.1	1288.0	1189.7	- ALAI
- CACM	240.3	225.9	215.1	224.2	237.2	- MCC
- Caribbean	147.4	145.9	120.0	120.7	113.9	- Caraïbes
- Rest of America	49.8	53.1	53.0	52.4	43.4	- Autre d'Amérique
Asia excluding former USSR	1893.6	2112.6	2069.4	2013.3	1983.9	Asie ancienne URSS exclus
- Middle East	423.2	431.7	433.7	392.5	403.1	- Moyen-Orient
Asia former USSR	43.8	39.1	63.6	66.4	65.2	Asie ancienne URSS
Europe excluding former USSR	5524.2	5533.7	5003.5	4870.8	5550.5	Europe ancienne URSS exclus
- European Union	4648.0	4663.9	4208.9	3971.6	4517.4	- Union Européenne
- Eastern Europe	573.5	607.0	561.1	639.2	744.1	- Europe de l'Est
- Rest of Europe	302.7	262.8	233.5	260.0	289.0	- Autre de l'Europe
Europe former USSR	415.8	203.3	246.8	344.5	364.5	Europe ancienne URSS
Oceania	191.8	272.8	272.6	254.6	267.4	Océanie
France-Monaco	1426.7	1467.3	1362.7	1176.1	1303.4	France-Monaco
Germany	645.8	660.4	594.0	547.1	610.5	Allemagne
Canada	695.1	592.0	518.0	587.9	610.0	Canada
United States	493.1	493.9	471.2	535.2	511.1	Etats-Unis d'Amérique
United Kingdom	525.3	499.8	429.4	459.9	490.8	Royaume-Uni
Italy-San Marino-Holy See	430.0	419.6	339.0	337.0	408.6	Italie-Saint-Marin-Saint-Siège
Spain	362.6	354.7	323.1	315.0	401.8	Espagne
Brazil	291.6	300.6	265.8	309.3	311.0	Brésil
Netherlands	280.1	273.7	262.4	200.1	281.5	Pays-Bas
Japan	254.4	235.2	269.7	264.0	249.0	Japon
Mexico	245.4	253.9	235.9	262.2	271.8	Mexique
Belgium	–	284.3	270.8	336.8	e369.4	Belgique
Poland	216.1	218.2	208.2	228.9	270.0	Pologne
China	186.0	242.6	192.2	165.0	136.1	Chine
Argentina	289.1	205.8	170.0	163.5	e72.3	Argentine
Australia	158.3	185.6	197.1	178.9	178.6	Australie
Thailand	130.2	169.3	192.8	193.0	e201.1	Thaïlande
Viet Nam	184.0	165.9	144.7	150.1	182.7	Viet Nam
Switzerland-Liechtenstein	184.9	154.4	127.3	150.2	162.5	Suisse-Liechtenstein
Hungary	124.4	130.3	128.5	141.6	173.5	Hongrie
Russian Federation	174.5	76.7	102.3	147.2	148.7	Fédération de Russie
Greece	131.9	118.5	106.3	101.8	e112.6	Grèce
Iran (Islamic Republic of)	82.6	119.1	120.0	118.4	121.8	Iran (République islamique d')
Czech Republic	104.9	99.9	90.4	115.5	133.8	République tchèque
Ecuador	112.6	91.6	104.9	106.6	110.8	Equateur
Denmark	112.2	133.1	93.4	78.5	97.7	Danemark
Chile	105.2	98.3	104.4	104.3	96.8	Chili
Colombia	94.0	84.9	91.6	99.3	106.6	Colombie
Turkey	114.4	101.5	96.3	77.4	85.6	Turquie
Costa Rica	98.4	91.9	84.3	84.3	90.8	Costa Rica

(Value as percentages of World total) **(Valeur en pourcentage du total mondial)**

Regions of the world	1993	1994	1995	1996	1997	1998	1999	2000	2001	2002	Régions du monde
World	100.0	100.0	100.0	100.0	100.0	100.0	100.0	100.0	100.0	100.0	Monde
Africa	6.2	5.8	5.5	5.5	5.7	5.5	5.0	5.2	5.4	5.4	Afrique
Americas	18.6	20.7	20.3	20.7	24.9	25.6	23.9	23.8	25.7	23.4	Amériques
- Northern America	7.9	8.3	8.2	8.6	9.8	10.2	9.5	9.2	10.3	9.7	- Amérique du Nord
- LAIA	6.6	8.4	8.0	8.6	11.4	11.7	10.7	11.0	11.8	10.3	- ALAI
- CACM	2.2	2.1	2.0	1.9	2.0	2.1	2.0	2.0	2.0	2.1	- MCC
- Caribbean	1.4	1.4	1.5	1.3	1.2	1.3	1.3	1.1	1.1	1.0	- Caraïbes
- Rest of America	0.6	0.6	0.5	0.5	0.5	0.4	0.5	0.5	0.5	0.4	- Autre d'Amérique
Asia excluding former USSR	20.7	18.2	17.6	17.4	17.1	16.2	18.4	19.2	18.4	17.2	Asie ancienne URSS exclus
- Middle East	5.5	4.4	3.6	3.5	3.5	3.6	3.8	4.0	3.6	3.5	- Moyen-Orient
Asia former USSR	0.8	1.1	0.5	0.8	0.3	0.4	0.3	0.6	0.6	0.6	Asie ancienne URSS
Europe excluding former USSR	47.1	49.7	50.9	50.7	46.9	47.2	48.2	46.4	44.5	48.0	Europe ancienne URSS exclus
- European Union	40.7	43.3	44.5	43.4	39.3	39.7	40.6	39.0	36.3	39.1	- Union Européenne
- Eastern Europe	4.3	4.2	4.4	5.4	5.5	4.9	5.3	5.2	5.8	6.4	- Europe de l'Est
- Rest of Europe	2.1	2.2	2.1	2.0	2.1	2.6	2.3	2.2	2.4	2.5	- Autre de l'Europe
Europe former USSR	5.1	2.8	3.4	2.7	2.8	3.6	1.8	2.3	3.1	3.2	Europe ancienne URSS
Oceania	1.5	1.7	1.7	2.1	2.4	1.6	2.4	2.5	2.3	2.3	Océanie

TRADE BY COMMODITY (Value in million US dollars)
Exports by principal countries or areas

COMMERCE PAR PRODUIT (Valeur en millions de dollars EU)
Exportations selon les principaux pays ou zones

Country or area	1998	1999	2000	2001	2002	Pays ou zone
World	11516.1	11267.1	10743.0	10680.9	10945.7	Monde
Africa	147.1	141.9	143.3	147.8	150.4	Afrique
Americas	2576.8	2347.2	2278.3	2383.3	2336.5	Amériques
- Northern America	1858.1	1676.0	1620.9	1686.8	1657.2	- Amérique du Nord
- LAIA	626.5	568.0	554.8	585.6	579.4	- ALAI
- CACM	72.5	85.0	83.5	92.3	82.8	- MCC
- Caribbean	18.6	17.2	17.7	17.5	15.7	- Caraïbes
- Rest of America	1.1	1.1	1.3	1.1	1.4	- Autre d'Amérique
Asia excluding former USSR	1328.6	1607.3	1719.2	1774.2	1818.0	Asie ancienne URSS exclus
- Middle East	41.3	43.9	47.3	64.7	60.5	- Moyen-Orient
Asia former USSR	1.7	1.8	3.2	1.3	1.3	Asie ancienne URSS
Europe excluding former USSR	7318.0	7025.3	6474.0	6252.7	6509.0	Europe ancienne URSS exclus
- European Union	6431.3	6226.1	5771.1	5502.8	5874.6	- Union Européenne
- Eastern Europe	115.5	91.6	110.1	119.1	138.3	- Europe de l'Est
- Rest of Europe	771.1	707.6	592.8	630.9	496.1	- Autre de l'Europe
Europe former USSR	21.0	19.1	16.0	15.8	21.7	Europe ancienne URSS
Oceania	122.9	124.6	109.0	105.6	108.9	Océanie
Germany	1780.0	1851.5	1741.2	1509.8	1539.1	Allemagne
France-Monaco	2051.5	1716.7	1528.8	1476.7	1572.8	France-Monaco
United States	1746.1	1577.9	1492.4	1547.5	1547.2	Etats-Unis d'Amérique
United Kingdom	1264.4	1209.3	1058.1	980.6	1023.4	Royaume-Uni
Switzerland-Liechtenstein	742.5	679.8	562.5	597.7	460.1	Suisse-Liechtenstein
China	325.0	439.6	463.0	549.2	592.0	Chine
Netherlands	336.4	305.1	311.8	325.0	373.8	Pays-Bas
Belgium	–	357.2	350.9	427.3	e479.4	Belgique
Italy-San Marino-Holy See	298.8	312.6	308.5	305.6	334.6	Italie-Saint-Marin-Saint-Siège
India	209.6	231.6	270.1	287.5	305.9	Inde
Japan	249.5	256.9	274.8	253.7	240.0	Japon
Spain	134.6	163.3	249.1	247.5	317.9	Espagne
Colombia	194.1	182.0	184.4	191.7	190.5	Colombie
Brazil	197.4	153.6	146.3	143.9	e149.2	Brésil
Israel	105.2	117.2	143.0	177.9	203.4	Israël
Argentina	108.1	123.1	109.3	131.3	e126.8	Argentine
Canada	112.0	98.1	128.5	139.3	110.0	Canada
Singapore	81.7	134.6	148.9	111.2	94.8	Singapour
China, Hong Kong SAR	94.5	103.9	80.3	51.2	25.8	Chine - RAS de Hong-Kong
Belgium-Luxembourg	350.7	–	–	–	–	Belgique-Luxembourg
Mexico	73.5	66.0	72.8	69.4	62.2	Mexique
Austria	55.3	85.7	64.0	75.1	61.1	Autriche
South Africa	–	–	108.8	123.1	106.0	Afrique du Sud
Australia	64.5	62.9	52.3	52.2	70.5	Australie
Malaysia	60.8	67.4	60.2	50.6	e53.7	Malaisie
Indonesia	41.8	58.1	70.4	57.6	59.3	Indonésie
Denmark	54.8	55.0	53.8	51.9	64.1	Danemark
Hungary	47.6	44.1	51.4	63.4	66.9	Hongrie
New Zealand	58.4	61.6	56.6	53.2	38.3	Nouvelle-Zélande
Thailand	37.6	47.1	48.9	54.0	e57.1	Thaïlande

(Value as percentages of World total) **(Valeur en pourcentage du total mondial)**

Regions of the world	1993	1994	1995	1996	1997	1998	1999	2000	2001	2002	Régions du monde
World	100.0	100.0	100.0	100.0	100.0	100.0	100.0	100.0	100.0	100.0	Monde
Africa	1.4	1.2	1.6	1.8	1.9	1.3	1.3	1.3	1.4	1.4	Afrique
Americas	19.9	17.5	17.5	17.5	21.8	22.4	20.8	21.2	22.3	21.3	Amériques
- Northern America	15.7	13.7	13.2	12.9	15.4	16.1	14.9	15.1	15.8	15.1	- Amérique du Nord
- LAIA	3.6	3.3	3.7	3.9	5.5	5.4	5.0	5.2	5.5	5.3	- ALAI
- CACM	0.4	0.4	0.5	0.5	0.7	0.6	0.8	0.8	0.9	0.8	- MCC
- Caribbean	0.1	0.1	0.1	0.1	0.1	0.2	0.2	0.2	0.2	0.1	- Caraïbes
- Rest of America	0.0	0.0	0.0	0.0	0.0	0.0	0.0	0.0	0.0	0.0	- Autre d'Amérique
Asia excluding former USSR	10.9	10.5	11.5	11.0	11.8	11.5	14.3	16.0	16.6	16.6	Asie ancienne URSS exclus
- Middle East	0.5	0.8	0.5	0.4	0.4	0.4	0.4	0.4	0.6	0.6	- Moyen-Orient
Asia former USSR	0.0	0.0	0.0	0.1	0.0	0.0	0.0	0.0	0.0	0.0	Asie ancienne URSS
Europe excluding former USSR	66.8	69.5	68.2	68.4	63.1	63.5	62.4	60.3	58.5	59.5	Europe ancienne URSS exclus
- European Union	58.0	61.9	60.1	60.4	55.3	55.8	55.3	53.7	51.5	53.7	- Union Européenne
- Eastern Europe	1.5	1.1	1.0	1.0	1.1	1.0	0.8	1.0	1.1	1.3	- Europe de l'Est
- Rest of Europe	7.2	6.6	7.1	7.0	6.7	6.7	6.3	5.5	5.9	4.5	- Autre de l'Europe
Europe former USSR	0.2	0.2	0.3	0.2	0.1	0.2	0.2	0.1	0.1	0.2	Europe ancienne URSS
Oceania	0.9	1.0	0.9	1.0	1.3	1.1	1.1	1.0	1.0	1.0	Océanie

592 Starches, insulin and wheat gluten; albuminoidal substances; glues

TRADE BY COMMODITY (Value in million US dollars)
Imports by principal countries or areas

COMMERCE PAR PRODUIT (Valeur en millions de dollars EU)
Importations selon les principaux pays ou zones

Country or area	1998	1999	2000	2001	2002	Pays ou zone
World	9225.6	9177.7	9557.4	9923.2	10131.3	Monde
Africa	186.4	165.1	174.9	178.5	188.8	Afrique
Americas	2102.6	2060.6	2324.9	2349.2	2263.8	Amériques
- Northern America	1434.0	1394.4	1579.1	1550.0	1539.7	- Amérique du Nord
- LAIA	581.5	580.2	658.9	699.9	626.9	- ALAI
- CACM	39.5	41.5	44.0	48.7	51.1	- MCC
- Caribbean	36.8	33.8	31.9	41.1	36.1	- Caraïbes
- Rest of America	10.8	10.7	11.0	9.4	10.1	- Autre d'Amérique
Asia excluding former USSR	2123.9	2283.6	2516.8	2503.2	2661.1	Asie ancienne URSS exclus
- Middle East	181.8	176.2	196.4	191.7	214.0	- Moyen-Orient
Asia former USSR	15.9	12.8	17.8	19.4	19.2	Asie ancienne URSS
Europe excluding former USSR	4473.2	4329.5	4196.8	4544.0	4640.6	Europe ancienne URSS exclus
- European Union	3891.6	3755.6	3627.2	3902.7	3948.4	- Union Européenne
- Eastern Europe	337.4	344.9	348.4	414.3	440.1	- Europe de l'Est
- Rest of Europe	244.2	228.9	221.3	227.0	252.1	- Autre de l'Europe
Europe former USSR	210.1	194.2	196.4	205.0	219.8	Europe ancienne URSS
Oceania	113.5	132.0	129.9	123.9	137.9	Océanie
United States	1097.7	1020.4	1181.9	1136.0	1085.3	Etats-Unis d'Amérique
Germany	860.9	778.7	773.0	888.5	840.9	Allemagne
Japan	560.4	595.8	615.7	646.2	624.6	Japon
United Kingdom	525.5	502.8	464.8	485.7	470.1	Royaume-Uni
France-Monaco	472.3	468.1	459.2	451.6	503.1	France-Monaco
China	309.0	380.2	447.3	445.5	530.6	Chine
Canada	335.6	373.3	396.9	413.7	454.1	Canada
Italy-San Marino-Holy See	361.8	369.0	353.5	394.0	374.4	Italie-Saint-Marin-Saint-Siège
Mexico	277.4	299.1	367.3	396.5	356.1	Mexique
Netherlands	301.1	321.1	299.5	331.1	346.1	Pays-Bas
Spain	265.0	252.9	241.4	287.2	275.1	Espagne
Belgium	-	309.1	305.7	314.4	e344.8	Belgique
Korea, Republic of	169.3	205.0	219.1	226.5	251.4	République de Corée
China, Hong Kong SAR	207.8	207.3	230.0	202.0	214.8	Chine - RAS de Hong-Kong
Poland	170.4	178.8	174.0	209.8	212.6	Pologne
Sweden	151.8	146.1	136.1	149.8	164.7	Suède
Finland	141.2	134.3	136.0	137.1	127.6	Finlande
Austria	145.1	122.0	127.8	132.0	135.3	Autriche
Indonesia	120.4	100.4	158.9	144.0	129.0	Indonésie
Switzerland-Liechtenstein	129.5	119.6	115.0	115.1	131.1	Suisse-Liechtenstein
Russian Federation	125.8	121.5	117.9	104.5	120.9	Fédération de Russie
Denmark	120.9	114.9	99.1	101.1	107.8	Danemark
Ireland	108.3	109.4	110.6	93.4	112.8	Irlande
Brazil	116.9	107.8	104.9	96.5	101.2	Brésil
Singapore	81.3	84.4	97.2	86.0	106.0	Singapour
Australia	78.4	90.9	95.0	89.4	97.7	Australie
Malaysia	77.6	89.8	85.5	82.6	e90.2	Malaisie
Thailand	67.1	73.8	80.2	96.6	e100.6	Thaïlande
Turkey	70.4	67.8	75.0	65.1	90.3	Turquie
Philippines	60.0	70.4	77.3	83.2	75.2	Philippines

(Value as percentages of World total) **(Valeur en pourcentage du total mondial)**

Regions of the world	1993	1994	1995	1996	1997	1998	1999	2000	2001	2002	Régions du monde
World	100.0	100.0	100.0	100.0	100.0	100.0	100.0	100.0	100.0	100.0	Monde
Africa	2.3	1.8	1.7	1.7	1.8	2.0	1.8	1.8	1.8	1.9	Afrique
Americas	19.1	19.5	18.3	19.3	20.7	22.8	22.5	24.3	23.7	22.3	Amériques
- Northern America	14.1	14.4	13.3	14.3	14.4	15.5	15.2	16.5	15.6	15.2	- Amérique du Nord
- LAIA	4.2	4.4	4.3	4.3	5.4	6.3	6.3	6.9	7.1	6.2	- ALAI
- CACM	0.3	0.3	0.3	0.3	0.4	0.4	0.5	0.5	0.5	0.5	- MCC
- Caribbean	0.3	0.3	0.3	0.3	0.4	0.4	0.4	0.3	0.4	0.4	- Caraïbes
- Rest of America	0.2	0.2	0.1	0.1	0.1	0.1	0.1	0.1	0.1	0.1	- Autre d'Amérique
Asia excluding former USSR	27.0	25.2	26.3	25.4	26.2	23.0	24.9	26.3	25.2	26.3	Asie ancienne URSS exclus
- Middle East	2.2	1.6	1.7	1.7	1.9	2.0	1.9	2.1	1.9	2.1	- Moyen-Orient
Asia former USSR	0.0	0.1	0.2	0.2	0.2	0.2	0.1	0.2	0.2	0.2	Asie ancienne URSS
Europe excluding former USSR	49.8	50.7	50.5	50.3	47.5	48.5	47.2	43.9	45.8	45.8	Europe ancienne URSS exclus
- European Union	45.2	45.7	44.7	44.5	41.9	42.2	40.9	38.0	39.3	39.0	- Union Européenne
- Eastern Europe	1.9	2.3	2.9	3.1	3.1	3.7	3.8	3.6	4.2	4.3	- Europe de l'Est
- Rest of Europe	2.6	2.7	2.9	2.7	2.6	2.6	2.5	2.3	2.3	2.5	- Autre de l'Europe
Europe former USSR	0.5	1.3	1.7	1.8	2.3	2.3	2.1	2.1	2.1	2.2	Europe ancienne URSS
Oceania	1.2	1.3	1.4	1.3	1.3	1.2	1.4	1.4	1.2	1.4	Océanie

TRADE BY COMMODITY (Value in million US dollars)
Exports by principal countries or areas

COMMERCE PAR PRODUIT (Valeur en millions de dollars EU)
Exportations selon les principaux pays ou zones

Country or area	1998	1999	2000	2001	2002	Pays ou zone
World	8524.0	8500.6	9063.5	9471.0	9730.0	Monde
Africa	25.4	23.9	22.5	26.0	26.7	Afrique
Americas	1477.0	1715.6	1860.1	2058.4	1988.5	Amériques
- Northern America	1200.1	1445.2	1571.7	1766.7	1689.1	- Amérique du Nord
- LAIA	263.2	255.5	272.3	275.8	284.2	- ALAI
- CACM	11.0	11.6	12.1	12.9	12.9	- MCC
- Caribbean	2.5	2.9	3.7	2.8	2.2	- Caraïbes
- Rest of America	0.2	0.2	0.3	0.2	0.1	- Autre d'Amérique
Asia excluding former USSR	1193.5	1323.5	1559.1	1519.9	1727.5	Asie ancienne URSS exclus
- Middle East	32.8	27.9	46.1	37.4	51.0	- Moyen-Orient
Asia former USSR	1.6	0.8	1.0	1.0	0.8	Asie ancienne URSS
Europe excluding former USSR	4838.9	4664.9	4685.4	4892.8	5100.0	Europe ancienne URSS exclus
- European Union	4574.9	4388.2	4409.2	4556.4	4752.5	- Union Européenne
- Eastern Europe	99.7	116.7	128.9	171.8	165.7	- Europe de l'Est
- Rest of Europe	164.3	160.0	147.3	164.6	181.7	- Autre de l'Europe
Europe former USSR	384.8	158.4	225.0	180.6	169.0	Europe ancienne URSS
Oceania	602.7	613.4	710.4	792.4	717.5	Océanie
United States	1073.8	1299.4	1409.5	1619.0	1524.7	Etats-Unis d'Amérique
Germany	1143.6	1094.3	1070.1	1208.3	1337.5	Allemagne
France-Monaco	800.7	856.9	897.0	892.2	869.3	France-Monaco
Netherlands	932.9	733.3	725.3	673.4	715.9	Pays-Bas
New Zealand	478.1	452.4	553.8	647.1	557.9	Nouvelle-Zélande
United Kingdom	304.9	324.2	336.7	330.0	330.9	Royaume-Uni
Italy-San Marino-Holy See	290.7	293.7	279.6	311.4	360.0	Italie-Saint-Marin-Saint-Siège
Thailand	243.7	272.6	305.5	309.0	e326.3	Thaïlande
Belgium	–	358.0	330.6	347.8	e390.2	Belgique
Ireland	261.4	262.3	296.2	286.0	256.6	Irlande
Japan	216.6	251.1	291.8	250.8	302.6	Japon
China, Hong Kong SAR	145.3	150.2	160.2	150.2	179.2	Chine - RAS de Hong-Kong
Canada	126.3	145.8	162.1	147.6	164.3	Canada
Australia	123.9	160.8	156.0	145.2	159.6	Australie
China	96.2	101.0	139.3	172.6	218.3	Chine
Sweden	129.4	122.5	129.3	162.5	181.9	Suède
Switzerland-Liechtenstein	143.5	138.9	126.3	140.1	159.6	Suisse-Liechtenstein
Korea, Republic of	110.9	132.2	144.7	154.5	156.0	République de Corée
Denmark	141.8	153.0	137.3	143.6	110.9	Danemark
Brazil	102.4	96.2	109.4	119.7	e124.1	Brésil
Russian Federation	240.2	48.1	74.4	53.9	44.1	Fédération de Russie
Spain	71.6	82.7	91.7	80.0	83.0	Espagne
Poland	44.5	53.6	72.4	112.7	91.7	Pologne
Belgium-Luxembourg	364.9	–	–	–	–	Belgique-Luxembourg
Ukraine	69.1	57.2	94.5	61.5	67.8	Ukraine
Argentina	63.1	65.9	73.7	65.5	e63.3	Argentine
Austria	80.5	58.7	54.3	56.3	57.4	Autriche
Singapore	49.6	52.6	58.6	53.5	71.6	Singapour
Mexico	44.3	46.4	42.6	42.3	45.8	Mexique
Finland	39.1	35.3	46.3	48.9	39.4	Finlande

(Value as percentages of World total) **(Valeur en pourcentage du total mondial)**

Regions of the world	1993	1994	1995	1996	1997	1998	1999	2000	2001	2002	Régions du monde
World	100.0	100.0	100.0	100.0	100.0	100.0	100.0	100.0	100.0	100.0	Monde
Africa	0.3	0.2	0.3	0.3	0.3	0.3	0.3	0.2	0.3	0.3	Afrique
Americas	13.3	14.2	14.3	15.4	20.0	17.3	20.2	20.5	21.7	20.4	Amériques
- Northern America	10.8	11.6	11.8	12.7	17.1	14.1	17.0	17.3	18.7	17.4	- Amérique du Nord
- LAIA	2.4	2.4	2.4	2.6	2.8	3.1	3.0	3.0	2.9	2.9	- ALAI
- CACM	0.1	0.1	0.1	0.1	0.1	0.1	0.1	0.1	0.1	0.1	- MCC
- Caribbean	0.0	0.0	0.0	0.0	0.0	0.0	0.0	0.0	0.0	0.0	- Caraïbes
- Rest of America	0.0	0.0	0.0	0.0	0.0	0.0	0.0	0.0	0.0	0.0	- Autre d'Amérique
Asia excluding former USSR	15.3	14.9	16.0	15.6	15.9	14.0	15.6	17.2	16.0	17.8	Asie ancienne URSS exclus
- Middle East	0.2	0.2	0.2	0.3	0.3	0.4	0.3	0.5	0.4	0.5	- Moyen-Orient
Asia former USSR	0.0	0.1	0.1	0.1	0.0	0.0	0.0	0.0	0.0	0.0	Asie ancienne URSS
Europe excluding former USSR	61.5	60.5	59.7	59.0	54.4	56.8	54.9	51.7	51.7	52.4	Europe ancienne URSS exclus
- European Union	58.4	57.3	56.6	55.6	51.4	53.7	51.6	48.6	48.1	48.8	- Union Européenne
- Eastern Europe	1.5	1.2	1.1	1.3	1.2	1.2	1.4	1.4	1.8	1.7	- Europe de l'Est
- Rest of Europe	1.7	1.9	2.0	2.2	1.9	1.9	1.9	1.6	1.7	1.9	- Autre de l'Europe
Europe former USSR	2.8	2.4	2.9	2.6	2.4	4.5	1.9	2.5	1.9	1.7	Europe ancienne URSS
Oceania	6.8	7.8	6.7	7.0	7.0	7.1	7.2	7.8	8.4	7.4	Océanie

598 Miscellaneous chemical products, nes

TRADE BY COMMODITY (Value in million US dollars)
Imports by principal countries or areas

COMMERCE PAR PRODUIT (Valeur en millions de dollars EU)
Importations selon les principaux pays ou zones

Country or area	1998	1999	2000	2001	2002	Pays ou zone
World	39896.3	41403.0	46175.3	46186.9	49096.9	Monde
Africa	1115.9	993.9	1005.1	1063.4	1180.6	Afrique
Americas	7363.9	7754.8	8859.2	9086.0	9152.9	Amériques
- Northern America	4529.8	4937.4	5656.4	5753.1	6068.7	- Amérique du Nord
- LAIA	2524.6	2529.9	2899.9	3001.0	2739.3	- ALAI
- CACM	107.0	107.1	115.7	127.3	146.9	- MCC
- Caribbean	171.7	144.0	159.2	176.7	166.0	- Caraïbes
- Rest of America	30.9	36.5	27.9	27.8	31.8	- Autre d'Amérique
Asia excluding former USSR	11986.9	12925.1	16223.2	15215.5	16998.5	Asie ancienne URSS exclus
- Middle East	1416.2	1358.7	1464.2	1550.1	1644.9	- Moyen-Orient
Asia former USSR	76.8	75.5	116.1	118.6	132.1	Asie ancienne URSS
Europe excluding former USSR	18281.4	18515.8	18873.5	19523.8	20335.4	Europe ancienne URSS exclus
- European Union	15958.9	16249.9	16614.8	17203.5	17844.2	- Union Européenne
- Eastern Europe	1124.1	1083.7	1115.2	1161.7	1277.3	- Europe de l'Est
- Rest of Europe	1198.5	1182.1	1143.6	1158.7	1214.0	- Autre de l'Europe
Europe former USSR	541.3	510.3	507.0	629.0	686.9	Europe ancienne URSS
Oceania	530.0	627.5	591.3	550.6	610.4	Océanie
United States	3105.5	3417.0	3960.5	4125.4	4428.2	Etats-Unis d'Amérique
Germany	3095.5	3043.0	3210.6	3574.9	3613.6	Allemagne
France-Monaco	2527.9	2471.7	2456.8	2488.7	2531.9	France-Monaco
Japan	2000.1	2078.1	2903.0	2714.3	2571.4	Japon
China	1440.1	1871.4	2216.0	2325.2	3549.6	Chine
Italy-San Marino-Holy See	2180.6	2231.4	2202.0	2152.5	2274.5	Italie-Saint-Marin-Saint-Siège
United Kingdom	1847.5	1925.3	2184.2	2302.2	2320.3	Royaume-Uni
Korea, Republic of	1424.2	1605.9	1930.1	1833.2	1966.1	République de Corée
Canada	1421.6	1517.0	1694.5	1625.5	1636.8	Canada
Netherlands	1298.0	1333.5	1278.2	1333.6	1333.0	Pays-Bas
Belgium	–	1541.5	1670.8	1585.1	e1738.3	Belgique
Mexico	943.2	1062.0	1365.9	1418.0	1382.0	Mexique
Spain	1070.4	1137.7	1091.2	1211.2	1301.1	Espagne
Singapore	1222.9	978.7	1188.4	975.3	1200.7	Singapour
China, Hong Kong SAR	727.3	743.6	847.8	849.7	876.3	Chine - RAS de Hong-Kong
Switzerland-Liechtenstein	660.9	670.3	652.2	657.3	668.8	Suisse-Liechtenstein
Sweden	519.6	571.6	564.1	591.7	610.0	Suède
Austria	543.8	559.9	554.2	545.3	602.7	Autriche
Thailand	471.9	526.0	602.9	584.8	e609.3	Thaïlande
Brazil	540.7	488.2	499.8	493.8	469.4	Brésil
Poland	464.8	458.2	460.0	464.1	514.5	Pologne
Malaysia	293.9	413.0	471.2	546.4	e597.1	Malaisie
Australia	454.1	472.6	463.7	413.3	470.2	Australie
Turkey	421.8	390.6	396.0	399.4	474.8	Turquie
Indonesia	405.8	386.9	422.2	379.4	432.5	Indonésie
Russian Federation	349.5	325.6	315.2	350.0	383.5	Fédération de Russie
Israel	233.7	273.6	445.6	412.8	354.8	Israël
India	339.3	294.1	277.7	356.5	369.0	Inde
Saudi Arabia	271.5	317.1	314.8	341.8	e353.7	Arabie saoudite
Belgium-Luxembourg	1550.7	–	–	–	–	Belgique-Luxembourg

(Value as percentages of World total) **(Valeur en pourcentage du total mondial)**

Regions of the world	1993	1994	1995	1996	1997	1998	1999	2000	2001	2002	Régions du monde
World	100.0	100.0	100.0	100.0	100.0	100.0	100.0	100.0	100.0	100.0	Monde
Africa	3.8	3.1	2.7	2.7	3.5	2.8	2.4	2.2	2.3	2.4	Afrique
Americas	15.5	15.9	15.7	16.4	17.5	18.5	18.7	19.2	19.7	18.6	Amériques
- Northern America	9.6	10.0	10.1	10.6	11.2	11.4	11.9	12.2	12.5	12.4	- Amérique du Nord
- LAIA	5.0	5.3	5.0	5.0	5.6	6.3	6.1	6.3	6.5	5.6	- ALAI
- CACM	0.3	0.2	0.2	0.2	0.2	0.3	0.3	0.3	0.3	0.3	- MCC
- Caribbean	0.4	0.3	0.3	0.4	0.4	0.4	0.3	0.3	0.4	0.3	- Caraïbes
- Rest of America	0.2	0.1	0.1	0.1	0.1	0.1	0.1	0.1	0.1	0.1	- Autre d'Amérique
Asia excluding former USSR	34.3	32.2	31.9	32.5	31.8	30.0	31.2	35.1	32.9	34.6	Asie ancienne URSS exclus
- Middle East	3.9	3.5	3.2	3.4	3.5	3.5	3.3	3.2	3.4	3.4	- Moyen-Orient
Asia former USSR	0.0	0.2	0.2	0.2	0.1	0.2	0.2	0.3	0.3	0.3	Asie ancienne URSS
Europe excluding former USSR	43.4	45.7	46.7	45.1	43.7	45.8	44.7	40.9	42.3	41.4	Europe ancienne URSS exclus
- European Union	38.6	40.7	41.3	39.7	38.5	40.0	39.2	36.0	37.2	36.3	- Union Européenne
- Eastern Europe	1.8	1.8	2.1	2.4	2.5	2.8	2.6	2.4	2.5	2.6	- Europe de l'Est
- Rest of Europe	3.1	3.2	3.4	3.0	2.7	3.0	2.9	2.5	2.5	2.5	- Autre de l'Europe
Europe former USSR	1.0	1.1	1.2	1.7	1.9	1.4	1.2	1.1	1.4	1.4	Europe ancienne URSS
Oceania	1.8	1.8	1.6	1.5	1.4	1.3	1.5	1.3	1.2	1.2	Océanie

TRADE BY COMMODITY (Value in million US dollars)
Exports by principal countries or areas

COMMERCE PAR PRODUIT (Valeur en millions de dollars EU)
Exportations selon les principaux pays ou zones

Country or area	1998	1999	2000	2001	2002	Pays ou zone
World	38895.6	40321.4	43604.1	43293.8	45908.3	Monde
Africa	148.8	164.4	161.5	184.3	216.8	Afrique
Americas	8873.3	9076.8	10390.2	10377.6	10414.3	Amériques
- Northern America	8180.1	8419.1	9719.6	9715.0	9748.4	- Amérique du Nord
- LAIA	670.1	628.1	638.5	627.1	635.1	- ALAI
- CACM	14.2	18.2	21.9	26.2	23.2	- MCC
- Caribbean	8.4	11.2	10.1	9.0	7.2	- Caraïbes
- Rest of America	0.4	0.2	0.1	0.3	0.4	- Autre d'Amérique
Asia excluding former USSR	7352.6	8301.2	10602.4	9472.4	9948.9	Asie ancienne URSS exclus
- Middle East	142.1	166.9	221.8	217.8	245.7	- Moyen-Orient
Asia former USSR	4.2	3.6	5.3	8.1	7.6	Asie ancienne URSS
Europe excluding former USSR	22224.9	22467.0	22078.2	22887.0	24920.6	Europe ancienne URSS exclus
- European Union	20787.1	21005.2	20770.4	21612.3	23492.0	- Union Européenne
- Eastern Europe	231.3	228.0	238.3	310.4	328.5	- Europe de l'Est
- Rest of Europe	1206.5	1233.7	1069.5	964.3	1100.2	- Autre de l'Europe
Europe former USSR	190.2	195.0	236.8	240.6	270.5	Europe ancienne URSS
Oceania	101.6	113.4	129.6	123.8	129.6	Océanie
United States	7654.8	7885.3	9087.1	9002.2	8989.9	Etats-Unis d'Amérique
Germany	6459.5	6397.0	6506.4	6670.2	6932.4	Allemagne
Japan	3137.3	3736.0	4802.4	3983.8	4479.1	Japon
France-Monaco	2802.9	2896.6	2872.7	2927.2	3197.3	France-Monaco
United Kingdom	3021.2	2723.9	2696.8	2636.2	3017.9	Royaume-Uni
Netherlands	1667.4	1644.8	1737.2	1874.3	2071.3	Pays-Bas
Italy-San Marino-Holy See	1653.1	1667.3	1671.4	1686.3	1792.1	Italie-Saint-Marin-Saint-Siège
Ireland	1253.6	1674.2	1432.5	1754.7	1854.4	Irlande
Belgium	–	1933.3	1813.6	1862.8	e2090.1	Belgique
Singapore	922.0	910.1	1065.7	925.4	1078.0	Singapour
Switzerland-Liechtenstein	850.0	844.9	693.4	692.7	784.9	Suisse-Liechtenstein
China, Hong Kong SAR	696.5	717.0	813.4	783.3	835.1	Chine - RAS de Hong-Kong
China	521.7	551.8	680.3	774.1	853.0	Chine
Canada	525.2	533.8	632.5	712.9	758.4	Canada
Spain	481.2	508.1	496.9	569.8	714.7	Espagne
Korea, Republic of	420.9	453.5	574.8	586.7	681.6	République de Corée
Sweden	436.9	461.2	491.6	601.2	722.8	Suède
Malaysia	451.4	453.0	544.0	485.0	e514.0	Malaisie
Belgium-Luxembourg	1904.9	–	–	–	–	Belgique-Luxembourg
Israel	268.7	321.6	650.1	592.5	35.8	Israël
Austria	354.8	309.9	299.6	309.3	359.4	Autriche
Norway	308.8	347.2	329.6	223.6	262.2	Norvège
Mexico	293.5	266.4	280.6	267.0	274.2	Mexique
Denmark	297.1	313.6	258.0	233.2	222.1	Danemark
Finland	224.1	230.0	238.1	251.9	286.0	Finlande
Brazil	170.4	153.3	159.0	168.1	e174.3	Brésil
Russian Federation	109.9	134.5	165.1	149.2	169.0	Fédération de Russie
India	101.6	144.4	167.3	126.6	141.9	Inde
Portugal	165.2	131.9	116.6	128.4	123.8	Portugal
Australia	87.1	100.1	117.4	109.2	115.9	Australie

(Value as percentages of World total) **(Valeur en pourcentage du total mondial)**

Regions of the world	1993	1994	1995	1996	1997	1998	1999	2000	2001	2002	Régions du monde
World	100.0	100.0	100.0	100.0	100.0	100.0	100.0	100.0	100.0	100.0	Monde
Africa	0.3	0.3	0.4	0.3	0.3	0.4	0.4	0.4	0.4	0.5	Afrique
Americas	22.2	21.1	21.5	21.5	22.7	22.8	22.5	23.8	24.0	22.7	Amériques
- Northern America	20.8	19.8	20.1	20.2	21.2	21.0	20.9	22.3	22.4	21.2	- Amérique du Nord
- LAIA	1.3	1.2	1.3	1.3	1.4	1.7	1.6	1.5	1.4	1.4	- ALAI
- CACM	0.0	0.0	0.0	0.0	0.0	0.0	0.0	0.1	0.1	0.1	- MCC
- Caribbean	0.0	0.0	0.0	0.0	0.0	0.0	0.0	0.0	0.0	0.0	- Caraïbes
- Rest of America	0.0	0.0	0.0	0.0	0.0	0.0	0.0	0.0	0.0	0.0	- Autre d'Amérique
Asia excluding former USSR	18.9	19.0	19.6	20.2	21.0	18.9	20.6	24.3	21.9	21.7	Asie ancienne URSS exclus
- Middle East	0.4	0.4	0.5	0.5	0.5	0.4	0.4	0.5	0.5	0.5	- Moyen-Orient
Asia former USSR	0.0	0.1	0.0	0.0	0.0	0.0	0.0	0.0	0.0	0.0	Asie ancienne URSS
Europe excluding former USSR	58.0	58.6	57.7	57.0	55.1	57.1	55.7	50.6	52.9	54.3	Europe ancienne URSS exclus
- European Union	54.5	55.0	53.9	53.4	51.7	53.4	52.1	47.6	49.9	51.2	- Union Européenne
- Eastern Europe	0.5	0.5	0.7	0.6	0.5	0.6	0.6	0.5	0.7	0.7	- Europe de l'Est
- Rest of Europe	3.0	3.1	3.0	3.0	2.8	3.1	3.1	2.5	2.2	2.4	- Autre de l'Europe
Europe former USSR	0.2	0.5	0.5	0.5	0.6	0.5	0.5	0.5	0.6	0.6	Europe ancienne URSS
Oceania	0.4	0.4	0.3	0.3	0.3	0.3	0.3	0.3	0.3	0.3	Océanie

611 Leather

TRADE BY COMMODITY (Value in million US dollars)
Imports by principal countries or areas

COMMERCE PAR PRODUIT (Valeur en millions de dollars EU)
Importations selon les principaux pays ou zones

Country or area	1998	1999	2000	2001	2002	Pays ou zone
World	13928.8	13239.8	15308.0	16467.8	16353.2	Monde
Africa	279.6	262.6	272.6	289.5	285.6	Afrique
Americas	2117.2	2076.9	2392.4	2246.1	2092.4	Amériques
- Northern America	1271.9	1189.8	1359.1	1198.3	1103.5	- Amérique du Nord
- LAIA	747.2	820.0	966.1	969.9	920.3	- ALAI
- CACM	30.6	28.5	34.0	27.4	29.3	- MCC
- Caribbean	66.5	37.6	32.9	50.0	38.7	- Caraïbes
- Rest of America	1.0	1.0	0.3	0.4	0.6	- Autre d'Amérique
Asia excluding former USSR	5453.0	5615.6	6659.9	6904.1	7020.8	Asie ancienne URSS exclus
- Middle East	165.9	111.9	178.0	172.6	190.3	- Moyen-Orient
Asia former USSR	7.9	3.2	3.1	6.3	2.7	Asie ancienne URSS
Europe excluding former USSR	5889.9	5100.3	5767.9	6804.3	6715.8	Europe ancienne URSS exclus
- European Union	4694.6	3902.0	4453.8	5146.0	4850.2	- Union Européenne
- Eastern Europe	1002.7	1026.4	1102.1	1377.6	1563.4	- Europe de l'Est
- Rest of Europe	192.6	171.9	212.0	280.8	302.3	- Autre de l'Europe
Europe former USSR	101.3	82.7	110.1	120.8	136.5	Europe ancienne URSS
Oceania	79.9	98.6	102.0	96.7	99.4	Océanie
China	1902.2	1965.4	2380.7	2382.4	2547.7	Chine
China, Hong Kong SAR	1851.8	1825.7	2100.3	2282.5	2249.2	Chine - RAS de Hong-Kong
Italy-San Marino-Holy See	1714.0	1349.3	1967.1	2311.4	2135.0	Italie-Saint-Marin-Saint-Siège
United States	1050.3	985.4	1098.0	964.9	882.7	Etats-Unis d'Amérique
Germany	728.0	637.4	543.8	616.9	578.7	Allemagne
Mexico	476.9	562.3	649.3	641.0	700.0	Mexique
Spain	544.5	474.5	515.9	641.6	591.5	Espagne
Korea, Republic of	284.3	358.3	490.6	545.1	551.2	République de Corée
France-Monaco	474.3	419.5	426.2	459.4	404.0	France-Monaco
Romania	278.4	286.1	341.9	479.6	572.2	Roumanie
Portugal	403.5	364.4	327.3	397.0	362.6	Portugal
Poland	227.3	226.0	245.4	312.3	362.3	Pologne
Hungary	245.1	259.0	250.2	282.3	279.8	Hongrie
Thailand	204.9	260.6	246.2	261.8	e272.8	Thaïlande
Canada	221.6	204.3	261.0	233.4	220.6	Canada
United Kingdom	256.2	192.9	228.4	239.4	218.4	Royaume-Uni
Viet Nam	88.7	161.4	216.7	224.9	273.7	Viet Nam
Indonesia	221.3	174.0	188.3	158.0	127.2	Indonésie
Japan	150.7	163.1	184.1	189.5	139.8	Japon
Brazil	141.1	139.3	185.0	184.7	117.4	Brésil
Austria	158.5	126.8	115.0	139.4	187.4	Autriche
Turkey	143.5	94.6	156.9	152.7	167.9	Turquie
Tunisia	123.0	117.9	115.4	145.5	e145.5	Tunisie
India	94.9	103.8	136.4	151.6	142.6	Inde
Czech Republic	118.0	114.9	107.9	119.5	133.2	République tchèque
Netherlands	115.1	100.2	104.2	114.5	124.9	Pays-Bas
Slovakia	70.9	79.8	85.3	98.5	117.0	Slovaquie
Belgium	–	103.7	107.7	97.8	e107.3	Belgique
Australia	70.3	81.3	86.6	84.9	88.1	Australie
Singapore	48.4	73.1	85.4	71.9	84.4	Singapour

(Value as percentages of World total) **(Valeur en pourcentage du total mondial)**

Regions of the world	1993	1994	1995	1996	1997	1998	1999	2000	2001	2002	Régions du monde
World	100.0	100.0	100.0	100.0	100.0	100.0	100.0	100.0	100.0	100.0	Monde
Africa	1.4	1.6	1.7	1.6	1.6	2.0	2.0	1.8	1.8	1.7	Afrique
Americas	13.4	12.2	11.8	11.8	13.3	15.2	15.7	15.6	13.6	12.8	Amériques
- Northern America	8.8	8.4	8.1	7.7	8.5	9.1	9.0	8.9	7.3	6.7	- Amérique du Nord
- LAIA	4.1	3.3	3.2	3.5	4.2	5.4	6.2	6.3	5.9	5.6	- ALAI
- CACM	0.1	0.1	0.1	0.1	0.2	0.2	0.2	0.2	0.2	0.2	- MCC
- Caribbean	0.4	0.3	0.4	0.5	0.4	0.5	0.3	0.2	0.3	0.2	- Caraïbes
- Rest of America	0.0	0.0	0.0	0.0	0.0	0.0	0.0	0.0	0.0	0.0	- Autre d'Amérique
Asia excluding former USSR	47.8	44.4	44.6	45.0	43.8	39.1	42.4	43.5	41.9	42.9	Asie ancienne URSS exclus
- Middle East	1.7	1.4	1.6	1.7	1.5	1.2	0.8	1.2	1.0	1.2	- Moyen-Orient
Asia former USSR	0.0	0.0	0.1	0.1	0.0	0.1	0.0	0.0	0.0	0.0	Asie ancienne URSS
Europe excluding former USSR	36.1	40.6	40.6	40.0	39.7	42.3	38.5	37.7	41.3	41.1	Europe ancienne URSS exclus
- European Union	31.5	35.8	34.6	33.3	32.7	33.7	29.5	29.1	31.2	29.7	- Union Européenne
- Eastern Europe	2.9	3.3	4.6	5.4	5.9	7.2	7.8	7.2	8.4	9.6	- Europe de l'Est
- Rest of Europe	1.6	1.4	1.3	1.2	1.2	1.4	1.3	1.4	1.7	1.8	- Autre de l'Europe
Europe former USSR	0.6	0.4	0.5	0.7	0.7	0.7	0.6	0.7	0.7	0.8	Europe ancienne URSS
Oceania	0.8	0.9	0.8	0.8	0.8	0.6	0.7	0.7	0.6	0.6	Océanie

TRADE BY COMMODITY (Value in million US dollars)
Exports by principal countries or areas

COMMERCE PAR PRODUIT (Valeur en millions de dollars EU)
Exportations selon les principaux pays ou zones

Country or area	1998	1999	2000	2001	2002	Pays ou zone
World	14791.3	14082.5	16550.9	17348.7	17095.3	Monde
Africa	239.1	261.0	484.2	348.1	341.5	Afrique
Americas	2817.2	2757.0	3149.2	3216.6	3097.0	Amériques
- Northern America	908.5	939.1	965.4	932.3	879.7	- Amérique du Nord
- LAIA	1869.1	1784.9	2147.2	2243.6	2182.9	- ALAI
- CACM	25.9	20.8	22.6	27.0	21.3	- MCC
- Caribbean	5.8	4.7	6.1	6.5	5.9	- Caraïbes
- Rest of America	8.0	7.4	7.8	7.2	7.2	- Autre d'Amérique
Asia excluding former USSR	5205.2	4974.9	6042.3	6528.7	6423.3	Asie ancienne URSS exclus
- Middle East	86.0	73.5	123.5	144.5	150.8	- Moyen-Orient
Asia former USSR	2.2	0.7	1.7	13.4	12.0	Asie ancienne URSS
Europe excluding former USSR	5926.5	5584.7	6260.1	6633.1	6470.1	Europe ancienne URSS exclus
- European Union	5599.7	5285.8	5910.4	6235.5	6044.5	- Union Européenne
- Eastern Europe	207.2	196.6	224.4	268.9	283.2	- Europe de l'Est
- Rest of Europe	119.6	102.2	125.3	128.6	142.4	- Autre de l'Europe
Europe former USSR	161.9	109.2	190.5	176.8	249.7	Europe ancienne URSS
Oceania	439.1	395.1	422.9	432.2	501.7	Océanie
Italy-San Marino-Holy See	3068.3	2977.0	3568.7	3753.2	3502.3	Italie-Saint-Marin-Saint-Siège
China, Hong Kong SAR	1518.2	1528.9	1768.0	1866.3	1824.9	Chine - RAS de Hong-Kong
Korea, Republic of	1166.4	1167.0	1353.3	1240.7	1090.7	République de Corée
United States	862.3	890.9	919.7	884.1	843.9	Etats-Unis d'Amérique
Argentina	780.5	748.5	804.8	785.8	e759.2	Argentine
Brazil	657.2	594.8	756.8	872.4	e904.4	Brésil
Germany	779.9	704.1	681.9	757.4	810.3	Allemagne
China	349.9	350.4	538.0	896.4	956.7	Chine
India	268.3	239.6	387.8	464.2	506.5	Inde
Spain	329.8	334.3	374.0	415.7	386.5	Espagne
United Kingdom	365.6	357.8	339.9	293.0	346.8	Royaume-Uni
France-Monaco	318.9	298.3	326.7	328.8	285.1	France-Monaco
Australia	285.8	263.4	277.3	266.5	330.7	Australie
Thailand	222.7	185.1	208.5	255.0	e269.3	Thaïlande
Austria	268.2	191.6	192.9	212.7	234.1	Autriche
Pakistan	195.0	174.2	204.4	245.8	240.5	Pakistan
Uruguay	178.5	171.8	215.7	229.8	208.5	Uruguay
Bangladesh	106.0	e82.2	e209.8	249.1	e200.1	Bangladesh
New Zealand	152.0	130.9	145.0	165.3	170.1	Nouvelle-Zélande
Mexico	143.3	158.1	176.4	140.2	96.7	Mexique
Netherlands	146.7	123.5	120.4	137.8	144.4	Pays-Bas
Japan	118.1	117.8	143.8	124.5	109.0	Japon
Singapore	63.7	80.3	99.4	101.6	101.6	Singapour
Poland	76.9	61.4	77.6	90.4	112.9	Pologne
Indonesia	76.1	63.6	94.7	85.0	68.5	Indonésie
South Africa	–	–	167.4	119.0	93.4	Afrique du Sud
Ukraine	62.4	56.6	77.1	76.7	84.5	Ukraine
Sweden	49.5	62.5	59.3	70.5	80.7	Suède
Colombia	37.5	39.4	72.6	82.7	77.0	Colombie
Belgium	–	64.2	71.3	80.6	e90.4	Belgique

(Value as percentages of World total) **(Valeur en pourcentage du total mondial)**

Regions of the world	1993	1994	1995	1996	1997	1998	1999	2000	2001	2002	Régions du monde
World	100.0	100.0	100.0	100.0	100.0	100.0	100.0	100.0	100.0	100.0	Monde
Africa	1.7	2.9	2.3	2.0	1.9	1.6	1.9	2.9	2.0	2.0	Afrique
Americas	18.6	17.0	17.3	16.9	18.7	19.0	19.6	19.0	18.5	18.1	Amériques
- Northern America	7.3	5.6	4.8	4.9	5.6	6.1	6.7	5.8	5.4	5.1	- Amérique du Nord
- LAIA	11.2	11.2	12.3	11.8	12.9	12.6	12.7	13.0	12.9	12.8	- ALAI
- CACM	0.1	0.2	0.2	0.2	0.2	0.2	0.1	0.1	0.2	0.1	- MCC
- Caribbean	0.0	0.0	0.1	0.0	0.0	0.0	0.0	0.0	0.0	0.0	- Caraïbes
- Rest of America	0.1	0.1	0.1	0.1	0.1	0.1	0.1	0.0	0.0	0.0	- Autre d'Amérique
Asia excluding former USSR	36.2	36.5	37.0	36.7	37.2	35.2	35.3	36.5	37.6	37.6	Asie ancienne URSS exclus
- Middle East	0.6	0.6	0.8	0.9	1.0	0.6	0.5	0.7	0.8	0.9	- Moyen-Orient
Asia former USSR	0.0	0.1	0.0	0.0	0.0	0.0	0.0	0.0	0.1	0.1	Asie ancienne URSS
Europe excluding former USSR	39.4	39.7	39.1	40.0	37.9	40.1	39.7	37.8	38.2	37.8	Europe ancienne URSS exclus
- European Union	36.8	37.0	36.3	38.0	35.8	37.9	37.5	35.7	35.9	35.4	- Union Européenne
- Eastern Europe	1.4	1.4	1.8	1.3	1.4	1.4	1.4	1.4	1.6	1.7	- Europe de l'Est
- Rest of Europe	1.3	1.3	1.0	0.8	0.8	0.8	0.7	0.8	0.7	0.8	- Autre de l'Europe
Europe former USSR	1.3	0.7	0.8	1.1	1.2	1.1	0.8	1.2	1.0	1.5	Europe ancienne URSS
Oceania	2.8	3.1	3.4	3.2	3.2	3.0	2.8	2.6	2.5	2.9	Océanie

612 Manufactures of leather or of composition leather, nes; etc

TRADE BY COMMODITY (Value in million US dollars)
Imports by principal countries or areas

COMMERCE PAR PRODUIT (Valeur en millions de dollars EU)
Importations selon les principaux pays ou zones

Country or area	1998	1999	2000	2001	2002	Pays ou zone
World	6130.2	5887.9	5929.8	6120.1	6086.5	Monde
Africa	163.6	142.2	159.0	145.9	154.1	Afrique
Americas	1283.3	1111.8	1139.7	1100.7	1034.5	Amériques
- Northern America	818.6	744.3	690.8	703.8	697.3	- Amérique du Nord
- LAIA	351.5	300.5	384.7	338.1	294.7	- ALAI
- CACM	10.5	8.1	10.5	9.1	9.8	- MCC
- Caribbean	98.9	54.8	52.0	48.4	31.2	- Caraïbes
- Rest of America	3.7	4.1	1.6	1.2	1.5	- Autre d'Amérique
Asia excluding former USSR	1357.2	1353.0	1453.9	1402.9	1281.7	Asie ancienne URSS exclus
- Middle East	47.4	33.4	41.2	40.8	46.4	- Moyen-Orient
Asia former USSR	4.9	4.3	4.1	3.3	4.0	Asie ancienne URSS
Europe excluding former USSR	3179.3	3152.1	3052.8	3353.1	3473.0	Europe ancienne URSS exclus
- European Union	2469.1	2425.4	2331.5	2506.9	2535.8	- Union Européenne
- Eastern Europe	486.3	498.7	509.4	595.5	670.2	- Europe de l'Est
- Rest of Europe	223.9	227.9	211.9	250.7	267.0	- Autre de l'Europe
Europe former USSR	73.7	53.1	54.8	60.3	82.1	Europe ancienne URSS
Oceania	68.3	71.4	65.6	53.9	57.1	Océanie
Italy-San Marino-Holy See	777.4	754.4	766.8	897.4	963.6	Italie-Saint-Marin-Saint-Siège
United States	752.6	677.8	626.9	639.8	626.4	Etats-Unis d'Amérique
Germany	503.7	495.0	455.0	474.2	421.9	Allemagne
China, Hong Kong SAR	377.8	370.3	373.8	327.1	285.4	Chine - RAS de Hong-Kong
China	275.9	296.3	304.8	323.7	285.2	Chine
France-Monaco	300.7	296.4	279.9	293.2	304.6	France-Monaco
Mexico	281.4	224.5	320.5	273.0	243.8	Mexique
Japan	221.3	231.7	250.7	281.2	271.0	Japon
United Kingdom	258.6	263.3	243.2	242.4	238.1	Royaume-Uni
Romania	145.3	155.3	180.9	218.8	245.8	Roumanie
Portugal	148.9	161.9	152.1	151.3	152.4	Portugal
Austria	140.0	129.2	130.3	138.0	131.3	Autriche
Korea, Republic of	94.4	100.6	117.5	116.6	108.9	République de Corée
Hungary	101.0	112.1	91.4	97.0	123.6	Hongrie
Spain	67.7	75.3	75.4	75.0	89.2	Espagne
Slovenia	51.0	68.3	61.2	86.1	94.1	Slovénie
Czech Republic	57.2	61.0	67.8	82.5	90.6	République tchèque
Indonesia	79.7	65.8	89.4	66.8	57.1	Indonésie
Netherlands	71.9	69.2	60.9	63.9	65.0	Pays-Bas
Canada	64.4	64.6	63.9	64.0	70.5	Canada
Poland	61.2	57.0	58.3	66.9	63.1	Pologne
Switzerland-Liechtenstein	69.5	55.0	48.6	50.8	50.2	Suisse-Liechtenstein
Slovakia	46.7	48.8	48.8	55.3	61.8	Slovaquie
Tunisia	48.5	44.7	46.9	60.6	e60.6	Tunisie
Denmark	68.6	54.9	51.0	49.7	34.2	Danemark
Australia	57.0	54.1	52.6	41.6	43.3	Australie
Croatia	55.0	42.2	39.9	41.2	34.8	Croatie
Dominican Republic	e84.9	e41.3	e38.1	e31.0	e16.0	République dominicaine
Bulgaria	38.1	35.1	33.2	e37.1	e40.8	Bulgarie
Albania	36.7	29.4	28.9	37.9	44.6	Albanie

(Value as percentages of World total) **(Valeur en pourcentage du total mondial)**

Regions of the world	1993	1994	1995	1996	1997	1998	1999	2000	2001	2002	Régions du monde
World	100.0	100.0	100.0	100.0	100.0	100.0	100.0	100.0	100.0	100.0	Monde
Africa	2.0	1.8	2.0	1.9	2.0	2.7	2.4	2.7	2.4	2.5	Afrique
Americas	19.1	20.1	18.0	18.5	20.1	20.9	18.9	19.2	18.0	17.0	Amériques
- Northern America	15.9	16.5	14.1	13.2	13.2	13.4	12.6	11.7	11.5	11.5	- Amérique du Nord
- LAIA	2.6	3.0	3.1	3.8	5.0	5.7	5.1	6.5	5.5	4.8	- ALAI
- CACM	0.1	0.1	0.1	0.1	0.2	0.2	0.1	0.2	0.1	0.2	- MCC
- Caribbean	0.4	0.4	0.6	1.2	1.6	1.6	0.9	0.9	0.8	0.5	- Caraïbes
- Rest of America	0.2	0.1	0.1	0.1	0.1	0.1	0.1	0.0	0.0	0.0	- Autre d'Amérique
Asia excluding former USSR	33.7	30.1	30.0	29.9	28.0	22.1	23.0	24.5	22.9	21.1	Asie ancienne URSS exclus
- Middle East	0.9	0.7	0.8	0.8	0.8	0.8	0.6	0.7	0.7	0.8	- Moyen-Orient
Asia former USSR	0.0	0.0	0.1	0.1	0.1	0.1	0.1	0.1	0.1	0.1	Asie ancienne URSS
Europe excluding former USSR	43.3	46.1	47.8	47.2	47.1	51.9	53.5	51.5	54.8	57.1	Europe ancienne URSS exclus
- European Union	35.0	37.9	38.2	37.4	36.9	40.3	41.2	39.3	41.0	41.7	- Union Européenne
- Eastern Europe	3.1	4.1	5.8	6.5	6.7	7.9	8.5	8.6	9.7	11.0	- Europe de l'Est
- Rest of Europe	5.3	4.1	3.8	3.3	3.5	3.7	3.9	3.6	4.1	4.4	- Autre de l'Europe
Europe former USSR	1.1	1.0	1.2	1.3	1.5	1.2	0.9	0.9	1.0	1.3	Europe ancienne URSS
Oceania	0.8	0.9	1.0	1.1	1.1	1.1	1.2	1.1	0.9	0.9	Océanie

Ouvrages en cuir, n.d.a.; articles de bourrellerie ou de sellerie; parties de chaussures, n.d.a. 612

TRADE BY COMMODITY (Value in million US dollars)
Exports by principal countries or areas

COMMERCE PAR PRODUIT (Valeur en millions de dollars EU)
Exportations selon les principaux pays ou zones

Country or area	1998	1999	2000	2001	2002	Pays ou zone
World	6572.3	6530.5	6830.9	6789.2	6985.6	Monde
Africa	221.4	209.7	194.5	224.2	239.9	Afrique
Americas	967.1	850.5	935.5	779.7	677.1	Amériques
- Northern America	452.3	471.4	524.3	421.8	328.9	- Amérique du Nord
- LAIA	313.9	335.3	378.3	331.0	328.7	- ALAI
- CACM	15.3	13.1	9.2	7.1	6.6	- MCC
- Caribbean	185.6	30.8	23.5	19.8	12.8	- Caraïbes
- Rest of America	0.1	0.0	0.0	0.0	0.0	- Autre d'Amérique
Asia excluding former USSR	2349.7	2371.9	2592.0	2477.9	2542.7	Asie ancienne URSS exclus
- Middle East	16.4	21.2	24.1	27.6	26.3	- Moyen-Orient
Asia former USSR	0.1	0.3	0.4	0.1	0.2	Asie ancienne URSS
Europe excluding former USSR	2970.0	3040.0	3053.2	3251.2	3466.4	Europe ancienne URSS exclus
- European Union	2074.5	2094.4	2113.3	2213.5	2294.6	- Union Européenne
- Eastern Europe	697.8	771.6	759.6	850.7	982.0	- Europe de l'Est
- Rest of Europe	197.8	173.9	180.3	187.0	189.7	- Autre de l'Europe
Europe former USSR	44.5	34.9	34.8	41.9	46.8	Europe ancienne URSS
Oceania	19.5	23.1	20.6	14.2	12.5	Océanie
Italy-San Marino-Holy See	983.5	981.0	1015.6	1117.6	1144.8	Italie-Saint-Marin-Saint-Siège
China	445.0	442.5	555.2	681.9	766.4	Chine
United States	413.2	440.6	493.8	389.2	295.5	Etats-Unis d'Amérique
India	381.0	345.0	420.5	399.7	348.9	Inde
China, Hong Kong SAR	400.3	375.4	391.1	369.4	330.3	Chine - RAS de Hong-Kong
Korea, Republic of	337.1	348.2	368.8	355.7	331.8	République de Corée
Romania	233.7	251.4	280.6	337.3	408.6	Roumanie
Germany	286.4	277.1	259.5	269.2	267.9	Allemagne
France-Monaco	216.1	249.0	283.9	284.3	304.9	France-Monaco
Thailand	196.7	242.8	235.0	168.8	e178.3	Thaïlande
Austria	150.3	152.8	165.7	141.2	151.4	Autriche
Mexico	142.0	155.5	198.4	128.6	130.0	Mexique
Tunisia	141.8	143.1	135.5	159.6	e166.0	Tunisie
Poland	138.0	130.8	120.3	126.8	139.4	Pologne
Hungary	128.8	123.5	101.2	98.8	136.0	Hongrie
Brazil	93.8	106.1	108.6	121.5	e126.0	Brésil
Portugal	121.5	109.4	88.2	92.5	87.1	Portugal
United Kingdom	105.8	94.3	96.9	97.6	100.7	Royaume-Uni
Spain	93.3	97.3	91.6	100.7	111.5	Espagne
Czech Republic	74.3	80.9	78.5	85.1	73.5	République tchèque
Albania	36.3	85.7	66.3	78.2	88.1	Albanie
Slovakia	39.5	52.2	56.4	64.9	69.3	Slovaquie
Croatia	73.5	59.1	47.7	53.5	45.7	Croatie
Bulgaria	47.0	47.1	56.3	e59.7	e67.1	Bulgarie
Dominican Republic	e	e30.6	e23.4	e19.7	e12.7	République dominicaine
Morocco	47.4	51.8	45.1	50.3	e54.8	Maroc
Indonesia	49.5	61.9	68.3	33.1	34.2	Indonésie
Argentina	42.3	42.8	41.9	43.3	e41.8	Argentine
Canada	39.1	30.7	30.6	32.6	33.4	Canada
Netherlands	28.1	32.2	29.3	28.3	35.0	Pays-Bas

(Value as percentages of World total) **(Valeur en pourcentage du total mondial)**

Regions of the world	1993	1994	1995	1996	1997	1998	1999	2000	2001	2002	Régions du monde
World	100.0	100.0	100.0	100.0	100.0	100.0	100.0	100.0	100.0	100.0	Monde
Africa	1.2	1.8	1.9	2.1	2.3	3.4	3.2	2.8	3.3	3.4	Afrique
Americas	9.6	13.4	13.0	11.3	13.0	14.7	13.0	13.7	11.5	9.7	Amériques
- Northern America	3.7	5.1	5.3	6.3	7.3	6.9	7.2	7.7	6.2	4.7	- Amérique du Nord
- LAIA	4.5	6.3	5.0	4.8	5.1	4.8	5.1	5.5	4.9	4.7	- ALAI
- CACM	0.1	0.1	0.1	0.1	0.1	0.2	0.2	0.1	0.1	0.1	- MCC
- Caribbean	1.3	1.9	2.6	0.1	0.6	2.8	0.5	0.3	0.3	0.2	- Caraïbes
- Rest of America	0.0	0.0	0.0	0.0	0.0	0.0	0.0	0.0	0.0	0.0	- Autre d'Amérique
Asia excluding former USSR	63.6	45.4	41.6	42.1	40.9	35.8	36.3	37.9	36.5	36.4	Asie ancienne URSS exclus
- Middle East	0.2	0.1	0.2	0.2	0.4	0.2	0.3	0.4	0.4	0.4	- Moyen-Orient
Asia former USSR	0.0	0.0	0.0	0.0	0.0	0.0	0.0	0.0	0.0	0.0	Asie ancienne URSS
Europe excluding former USSR	25.0	38.6	42.6	43.4	42.5	45.2	46.6	44.7	47.9	49.6	Europe ancienne URSS exclus
- European Union	18.7	28.3	29.9	30.5	30.3	31.6	32.1	30.9	32.6	32.8	- Union Européenne
- Eastern Europe	4.2	6.8	9.5	10.0	9.5	10.6	11.8	11.1	12.5	14.1	- Europe de l'Est
- Rest of Europe	2.1	3.4	3.2	2.9	2.7	3.0	2.7	2.6	2.8	2.7	- Autre de l'Europe
Europe former USSR	0.2	0.4	0.5	0.7	0.8	0.7	0.5	0.5	0.6	0.7	Europe ancienne URSS
Oceania	0.2	0.4	0.4	0.4	0.4	0.3	0.4	0.3	0.2	0.2	Océanie

613 Furskins, tanned or dressed; pieces of furskin, tanned or dressed

TRADE BY COMMODITY (Value in million US dollars)
Imports by principal countries or areas

COMMERCE PAR PRODUIT (Valeur en millions de dollars E
Importations selon les principaux pays ou zone

Country or area	1998	1999	2000	2001	2002	Pays ou zone
World	1125.9	890.2	1064.4	1099.7	1184.4	Monde
Africa	1.5	1.1	1.2	0.6	2.1	Afrique
Americas	39.9	46.6	49.8	53.6	47.7	Amériques
- Northern America	35.4	36.0	42.7	46.8	43.1	- Amérique du Nord
- LAIA	4.3	10.5	6.9	6.7	3.6	- ALAI
- CACM	0.1	0.0	0.0	0.0	0.0	- MCC
- Caribbean	0.1	0.1	0.1	0.0	1.1	- Caraïbes
- Rest of America	0.0	0.0	0.0	0.0	0.0	- Autre d'Amérique
Asia excluding former USSR	406.4	442.0	568.3	561.0	596.8	Asie ancienne URSS exclus
- Middle East	54.9	30.8	68.9	92.6	119.0	- Moyen-Orient
Asia former USSR	0.2	1.5	2.0	0.3	0.3	Asie ancienne URSS
Europe excluding former USSR	651.3	375.2	423.0	464.1	506.3	Europe ancienne URSS exclus
- European Union	606.0	349.3	392.0	427.6	466.2	- Union Européenne
- Eastern Europe	38.8	21.3	25.2	28.8	30.9	- Europe de l'Est
- Rest of Europe	6.4	4.6	5.8	7.7	9.2	- Autre de l'Europe
Europe former USSR	21.8	16.5	14.3	15.3	18.3	Europe ancienne URSS
Oceania	4.8	7.4	5.8	4.8	12.9	Océanie
China, Hong Kong SAR	189.7	220.8	306.9	283.2	295.8	Chine - RAS de Hong-Kong
Greece	255.1	103.1	85.2	103.8	e114.8	Grèce
Italy-San Marino-Holy See	115.6	81.2	118.8	110.9	130.9	Italie-Saint-Marin-Saint-Siège
China	87.0	91.0	101.3	103.9	100.3	Chine
Germany	96.5	70.2	72.6	81.1	69.7	Allemagne
Turkey	53.2	29.0	68.3	91.8	118.1	Turquie
Korea, Republic of	50.6	72.1	62.5	52.7	54.1	République de Corée
United Kingdom	43.8	23.0	29.4	31.1	36.6	Royaume-Uni
United States	26.4	26.0	30.5	34.9	30.0	Etats-Unis d'Amérique
France-Monaco	23.4	19.1	20.7	25.7	34.6	France-Monaco
Netherlands	10.3	6.6	25.2	27.9	27.4	Pays-Bas
Japan	10.3	15.6	18.5	16.9	15.5	Japon
Spain	16.8	14.2	10.4	13.0	16.5	Espagne
Canada	8.9	9.9	12.1	11.8	12.9	Canada
Poland	10.1	7.0	9.6	12.1	12.6	Pologne
Denmark	7.3	5.0	8.8	10.4	8.3	Danemark
Czech Republic	12.0	5.9	6.7	6.4	6.5	République tchèque
Finland	9.0	9.0	4.7	6.2	6.9	Finlande
Hungary	8.0	5.2	6.3	6.4	7.7	Hongrie
Austria	11.8	5.4	5.3	3.8	4.7	Autriche
Thailand	7.9	7.1	4.9	4.3	e4.4	Thaïlande
Russian Federation	8.5	4.2	4.5	4.5	4.5	Fédération de Russie
Belgium	–	5.8	5.1	6.2	e6.8	Belgique
Sweden	4.4	4.1	3.7	4.2	5.7	Suède
Lithuania	8.1	7.1	2.6	1.9	e2.3	Lituanie
Belarus	2.5	3.6	3.9	4.7	6.9	Bélarus
Australia	3.7	4.1	4.3	2.5	6.7	Australie
Portugal	4.9	2.6	2.0	3.1	3.3	Portugal
Argentina	0.6	6.6	3.2	3.6	e1.6	Argentine
New Zealand	1.1	3.2	1.6	2.3	6.2	Nouvelle-Zélande

(Value as percentages of World total) **(Valeur en pourcentage du total mondia**

Regions of the world	1993	1994	1995	1996	1997	1998	1999	2000	2001	2002	Régions du monde
World	100.0	100.0	100.0	100.0	100.0	100.0	100.0	100.0	100.0	100.0	Monde
Africa	0.2	0.1	0.0	0.0	0.0	0.1	0.1	0.1	0.1	0.2	Afrique
Americas	3.8	4.5	4.2	3.5	3.9	3.5	5.2	4.7	4.9	4.0	Amériques
- Northern America	3.4	3.9	3.1	2.9	3.5	3.1	4.0	4.0	4.3	3.6	- Amérique du Nord
- LAIA	0.3	0.6	1.1	0.7	0.4	0.4	1.2	0.7	0.6	0.3	- ALAI
- CACM	0.0	0.0	0.0	0.0	0.0	0.0	0.0	0.0	0.0	0.0	- MCC
- Caribbean	0.0	0.0	0.0	0.0	0.0	0.0	0.0	0.0	0.0	0.1	- Caraïbes
- Rest of America	0.0	0.0	0.0	0.0	0.0	0.0	0.0	0.0	0.0	0.0	- Autre d'Amérique
Asia excluding former USSR	52.7	52.8	52.3	50.8	45.9	36.1	49.6	53.4	51.0	50.4	Asie ancienne URSS exclus
- Middle East	1.5	1.5	2.1	2.8	5.6	4.9	3.5	6.5	8.4	10.0	- Moyen-Orient
Asia former USSR	0.1	0.0	0.1	0.0	0.0	0.0	0.2	0.2	0.0	0.0	Asie ancienne URSS
Europe excluding former USSR	41.4	40.7	41.0	43.2	47.3	57.8	42.1	39.7	42.2	42.7	Europe ancienne URSS exclus
- European Union	38.1	37.2	36.8	39.2	44.3	53.8	39.2	36.8	38.9	39.4	- Union Européenne
- Eastern Europe	1.9	2.3	3.3	3.4	2.4	3.4	2.4	2.4	2.6	2.6	- Europe de l'Est
- Rest of Europe	1.3	1.2	0.8	0.6	0.6	0.6	0.5	0.5	0.7	0.8	- Autre de l'Europe
Europe former USSR	1.2	1.1	1.9	1.8	2.3	1.9	1.9	1.3	1.4	1.5	Europe ancienne URSS
Oceania	0.6	0.7	0.6	0.6	0.6	0.4	0.8	0.5	0.4	1.1	Océanie

Pelleteries tannées ou apprêtées, même assemblées en nappes, sacs; déchets et chutes 613

TRADE BY COMMODITY (Value in million US dollars)
Exports by principal countries or areas

COMMERCE PAR PRODUIT (Valeur en millions de dollars EU)
Exportations selon les principaux pays ou zones

Country or area	1998	1999	2000	2001	2002	Pays ou zone
World	1265.4	964.4	1057.9	1138.7	1187.7	Monde
Africa	6.5	6.6	8.2	2.2	6.6	Afrique
Americas	130.5	71.0	69.2	62.7	67.2	Amériques
- Northern America	73.3	30.7	28.7	29.2	33.5	- Amérique du Nord
- LAIA	57.2	40.0	40.4	33.5	33.7	- ALAI
- CACM	0.0	0.2	0.0	0.0	0.0	- MCC
- Caribbean	0.0	0.0	0.0	0.0	0.0	- Caraïbes
- Rest of America	0.0	0.0	0.0	0.0	0.0	- Autre d'Amérique
Asia excluding former USSR	294.5	281.2	354.2	380.3	370.7	Asie ancienne URSS exclus
- Middle East	11.7	8.9	7.1	6.1	7.5	- Moyen-Orient
Asia former USSR	0.3	0.6	0.6	0.2	0.1	Asie ancienne URSS
Europe excluding former USSR	758.0	545.2	565.5	612.5	656.2	Europe ancienne URSS exclus
- European Union	683.7	494.6	495.9	523.8	568.9	- Union Européenne
- Eastern Europe	54.7	34.0	49.9	64.0	61.0	- Europe de l'Est
- Rest of Europe	19.6	16.6	19.7	24.7	26.3	- Autre de l'Europe
Europe former USSR	32.7	29.4	34.5	45.4	55.0	Europe ancienne URSS
Oceania	42.8	30.5	25.7	35.4	31.9	Océanie
China, Hong Kong SAR	172.8	168.0	206.3	204.2	212.1	Chine - RAS de Hong-Kong
Spain	157.8	120.6	141.2	159.3	193.6	Espagne
China	91.5	93.2	127.7	153.9	138.0	Chine
Italy-San Marino-Holy See	110.6	80.3	78.6	87.4	110.0	Italie-Saint-Marin-Saint-Siège
Germany	122.4	91.4	88.8	87.7	71.3	Allemagne
United Kingdom	64.5	43.4	48.1	46.3	38.7	Royaume-Uni
Poland	36.2	24.1	34.6	51.6	48.3	Pologne
France-Monaco	47.5	32.6	30.4	32.5	38.3	France-Monaco
Finland	50.1	32.7	28.0	32.2	32.4	Finlande
Greece	41.7	30.4	23.9	23.3	e23.3	Grèce
United States	50.3	16.2	15.2	15.0	17.1	Etats-Unis d'Amérique
New Zealand	22.1	21.2	17.6	27.0	24.2	Nouvelle-Zélande
Argentina	25.8	25.0	20.4	15.4	e14.9	Argentine
Estonia	12.2	12.5	17.1	24.6	26.5	Estonie
Canada	23.0	14.4	13.5	14.2	16.4	Canada
Netherlands	15.5	12.2	15.5	15.8	18.9	Pays-Bas
Denmark	16.0	11.0	14.2	13.2	11.1	Danemark
Portugal	10.3	8.6	10.4	13.2	16.5	Portugal
Uruguay	18.8	7.7	10.0	10.5	11.2	Uruguay
Belgium	–	26.3	11.2	8.8	e9.8	Belgique
Australia	20.6	9.3	8.2	8.4	7.7	Australie
Korea, Republic of	14.2	6.9	8.1	7.3	6.3	République de Corée
Lithuania	6.4	8.1	7.6	8.4	e10.2	Lituanie
Turkey	11.4	8.7	7.1	6.0	7.4	Turquie
Iceland	8.8	5.4	7.2	7.3	9.3	Islande
Czech Republic	11.7	5.1	7.1	7.2	6.4	République tchèque
Belgium-Luxembourg	35.0	–	–	–	–	Belgique-Luxembourg
Brazil	8.0	5.2	8.3	6.1	e6.3	Brésil
Norway	2.9	3.8	5.5	8.9	9.1	Norvège
Zimbabwe	e5.8	5.4	7.5	0.1	4.8	Zimbabwe

(Value as percentages of World total) **(Valeur en pourcentage du total mondial)**

Regions of the world	1993	1994	1995	1996	1997	1998	1999	2000	2001	2002	Régions du monde
World	100.0	100.0	100.0	100.0	100.0	100.0	100.0	100.0	100.0	100.0	Monde
Africa	0.2	0.2	0.2	0.2	0.1	0.5	0.7	0.8	0.2	0.6	Afrique
Americas	6.7	8.1	9.4	9.7	9.8	10.3	7.4	6.5	5.5	5.7	Amériques
- Northern America	4.5	4.6	4.0	3.9	4.4	5.8	3.2	2.7	2.6	2.8	- Amérique du Nord
- LAIA	2.2	3.5	5.3	5.7	5.5	4.5	4.2	3.8	2.9	2.8	- ALAI
- CACM	0.0	0.0	0.0	0.0	0.0	0.0	0.0	0.0	0.0	0.0	- MCC
- Caribbean	0.0	0.0	0.0	0.0	0.0	0.0	0.0	0.0	0.0	0.0	- Caraïbes
- Rest of America	0.0	0.0	0.0	0.0	0.0	0.0	0.0	0.0	0.0	0.0	- Autre d'Amérique
Asia excluding former USSR	27.2	24.6	20.7	18.6	18.5	23.3	29.2	33.5	33.4	31.2	Asie ancienne URSS exclus
- Middle East	0.4	0.2	0.5	0.7	0.8	0.9	0.9	0.7	0.5	0.6	- Moyen-Orient
Asia former USSR	0.1	0.1	0.0	0.0	0.0	0.0	0.1	0.1	0.0	0.0	Asie ancienne URSS
Europe excluding former USSR	59.5	62.6	63.8	65.0	65.6	59.9	56.5	53.5	53.8	55.3	Europe ancienne URSS exclus
- European Union	55.2	57.9	57.6	60.0	60.4	54.0	51.3	46.9	46.0	47.9	- Union Européenne
- Eastern Europe	2.7	2.6	4.0	3.0	3.2	4.3	3.5	4.7	5.6	5.1	- Europe de l'Est
- Rest of Europe	1.6	2.2	2.1	2.0	2.0	1.5	1.7	1.9	2.2	2.2	- Autre de l'Europe
Europe former USSR	2.7	1.4	1.9	2.4	2.3	2.6	3.0	3.3	4.0	4.6	Europe ancienne URSS
Oceania	3.6	3.0	4.0	4.0	3.6	3.4	3.2	2.4	3.1	2.7	Océanie

621 Materials of rubber

TRADE BY COMMODITY (Value in million US dollars)
Imports by principal countries or areas

COMMERCE PAR PRODUIT (Valeur en millions de dollars EU)
Importations selon les principaux pays ou zones

Country or area	1998	1999	2000	2001	2002	Pays ou zone
World	7575.7	7483.2	7945.2	7862.7	8366.3	Monde
Africa	280.2	231.7	216.7	143.3	153.3	Afrique
Americas	1989.7	2010.5	2434.6	2334.1	2220.0	Amériques
- Northern America	1320.2	1344.2	1511.3	1442.1	1452.4	- Amérique du Nord
- LAIA	603.6	614.6	872.9	841.2	715.8	- ALAI
- CACM	26.7	21.3	21.5	21.5	25.0	- MCC
- Caribbean	30.9	22.5	23.2	24.1	21.8	- Caraïbes
- Rest of America	8.4	7.8	5.6	5.3	5.0	- Autre d'Amérique
Asia excluding former USSR	904.2	977.0	1150.8	1199.3	1383.0	Asie ancienne URSS exclus
- Middle East	166.4	136.0	162.3	171.5	195.8	- Moyen-Orient
Asia former USSR	23.2	14.1	17.0	20.3	21.0	Asie ancienne URSS
Europe excluding former USSR	4155.8	4050.8	3906.1	3945.1	4339.1	Europe ancienne URSS exclus
- European Union	3626.0	3517.2	3352.8	3337.1	3617.9	- Union Européenne
- Eastern Europe	339.3	349.3	383.5	438.8	540.6	- Europe de l'Est
- Rest of Europe	190.5	184.3	169.8	169.2	180.6	- Autre de l'Europe
Europe former USSR	112.4	78.3	101.9	101.7	113.9	Europe ancienne URSS
Oceania	110.3	120.7	118.1	119.0	136.2	Océanie
United States	757.1	769.3	885.8	848.3	863.8	Etats-Unis d'Amérique
Germany	854.7	820.9	770.4	791.0	830.9	Allemagne
Canada	562.9	574.2	625.4	593.4	588.1	Canada
France-Monaco	516.0	448.8	436.9	434.6	494.5	France-Monaco
Mexico	311.0	382.6	613.0	568.2	423.6	Mexique
United Kingdom	420.8	423.4	417.8	390.4	451.2	Royaume-Uni
Spain	349.7	356.6	355.5	356.4	429.7	Espagne
Italy-San Marino-Holy See	275.6	328.0	312.0	279.7	286.9	Italie-Saint-Marin-Saint-Siège
Belgium	–	324.3	304.8	339.8	e372.6	Belgique
China	135.8	187.4	246.2	304.2	369.0	Chine
Netherlands	237.3	219.2	190.4	176.7	163.1	Pays-Bas
Austria	141.0	145.8	140.9	147.5	149.3	Autriche
Brazil	130.1	114.0	133.8	148.7	193.8	Brésil
Japan	125.4	131.8	145.2	147.4	153.7	Japon
Czech Republic	115.0	113.7	123.0	146.6	161.7	République tchèque
China, Hong Kong SAR	109.1	109.9	130.0	127.0	149.6	Chine - RAS de Hong-Kong
Sweden	126.8	111.5	118.6	110.6	120.3	Suède
Poland	89.7	87.0	95.0	99.5	126.4	Pologne
Portugal	109.1	102.9	88.9	81.6	103.1	Portugal
Australia	93.7	89.5	90.0	90.5	106.8	Australie
Hungary	65.8	82.1	86.4	94.0	103.1	Hongrie
Switzerland-Liechtenstein	88.3	85.7	81.2	78.8	76.9	Suisse-Liechtenstein
Belgium-Luxembourg	377.3	–	–	–	–	Belgique-Luxembourg
Denmark	77.5	77.9	72.8	72.2	65.1	Danemark
Korea, Republic of	41.6	53.4	73.7	71.3	109.9	République de Corée
Turkey	60.7	52.2	66.6	56.7	76.8	Turquie
Libyan Arab Jamahiriya	125.1	e91.4	e82.0	e	e	Jamahiriya arabe libyenne
Singapore	53.6	68.4	57.3	51.4	60.6	Singapour
Finland	55.3	54.3	55.3	54.0	52.9	Finlande
Thailand	35.2	43.1	57.1	64.9	e67.6	Thaïlande

(Value as percentages of World total) **(Valeur en pourcentage du total mondial)**

Regions of the world	1993	1994	1995	1996	1997	1998	1999	2000	2001	2002	Régions du monde
World	100.0	100.0	100.0	100.0	100.0	100.0	100.0	100.0	100.0	100.0	Monde
Africa	3.3	2.7	2.4	2.3	2.4	3.7	3.1	2.7	1.8	1.8	Afrique
Americas	22.5	23.9	23.2	24.1	26.1	26.3	26.9	30.6	29.7	26.5	Amériques
- Northern America	16.3	17.5	16.6	16.5	17.4	17.4	18.0	19.0	18.3	17.4	- Amérique du Nord
- LAIA	5.3	5.8	5.9	6.9	7.9	8.0	8.2	11.0	10.7	8.6	- ALAI
- CACM	0.3	0.3	0.3	0.3	0.4	0.4	0.3	0.3	0.3	0.3	- MCC
- Caribbean	0.4	0.3	0.3	0.3	0.3	0.4	0.3	0.3	0.3	0.3	- Caraïbes
- Rest of America	0.1	0.1	0.1	0.1	0.1	0.1	0.1	0.1	0.1	0.1	- Autre d'Amérique
Asia excluding former USSR	19.4	16.2	16.0	15.5	15.3	11.9	13.1	14.5	15.3	16.5	Asie ancienne URSS exclus
- Middle East	2.8	1.9	2.2	2.2	2.3	2.2	1.8	2.0	2.2	2.3	- Moyen-Orient
Asia former USSR	0.0	0.2	0.2	0.3	0.2	0.3	0.2	0.2	0.3	0.3	Asie ancienne URSS
Europe excluding former USSR	51.5	53.7	55.1	53.7	52.1	54.9	54.1	49.2	50.2	51.9	Europe ancienne URSS exclus
- European Union	46.1	48.3	48.9	47.5	46.0	47.9	47.0	42.2	42.4	43.2	- Union Européenne
- Eastern Europe	2.2	2.1	2.7	3.2	3.6	4.5	4.7	4.8	5.6	6.5	- Europe de l'Est
- Rest of Europe	3.3	3.4	3.5	2.9	2.5	2.5	2.5	2.1	2.2	2.2	- Autre de l'Europe
Europe former USSR	1.1	0.9	1.1	2.1	2.0	1.5	1.0	1.3	1.3	1.4	Europe ancienne URSS
Oceania	2.1	2.3	2.0	2.0	1.9	1.5	1.6	1.5	1.5	1.6	Océanie

TRADE BY COMMODITY (Value in million US dollars)
Exports by principal countries or areas

COMMERCE PAR PRODUIT (Valeur en millions de dollars EU)
Exportations selon les principaux pays ou zones

Country or area	1998	1999	2000	2001	2002	Pays ou zone
World	7456.1	7243.0	7554.5	7543.2	7814.2	Monde
Africa	175.3	14.7	15.3	18.1	21.1	Afrique
Americas	1450.1	1480.0	1731.7	1623.3	1658.1	Amériques
- Northern America	1256.6	1265.3	1450.2	1371.8	1369.5	- Amérique du Nord
- LAIA	187.9	209.5	277.1	246.1	282.2	- ALAI
- CACM	4.4	4.3	3.6	4.1	5.1	- MCC
- Caribbean	0.3	0.3	0.3	0.7	0.8	- Caraïbes
- Rest of America	0.9	0.6	0.4	0.6	0.4	- Autre d'Amérique
Asia excluding former USSR	1057.4	1199.8	1314.6	1252.5	1409.1	Asie ancienne URSS exclus
- Middle East	42.5	49.9	61.0	82.6	73.5	- Moyen-Orient
Asia former USSR	0.7	0.3	0.7	0.5	0.6	Asie ancienne URSS
Europe excluding former USSR	4704.6	4495.3	4426.8	4583.2	4655.5	Europe ancienne URSS exclus
- European Union	4303.5	4095.0	4011.0	4141.8	4182.7	- Union Européenne
- Eastern Europe	292.6	297.0	310.9	335.8	368.6	- Europe de l'Est
- Rest of Europe	108.5	103.3	105.0	105.7	104.2	- Autre de l'Europe
Europe former USSR	49.9	36.1	46.5	45.8	47.7	Europe ancienne URSS
Oceania	18.1	16.9	18.9	19.8	22.1	Océanie
Germany	1320.3	1265.1	1252.0	1340.6	1196.1	Allemagne
United States	980.7	999.0	1126.1	1055.7	1077.0	Etats-Unis d'Amérique
Italy-San Marino-Holy See	721.7	665.7	659.8	650.3	694.8	Italie-Saint-Marin-Saint-Siège
France-Monaco	618.5	592.5	611.2	584.8	650.8	France-Monaco
Japan	426.6	446.5	511.5	436.3	492.3	Japon
United Kingdom	469.6	411.4	383.8	378.3	400.2	Royaume-Uni
Canada	275.9	266.3	324.1	316.2	292.5	Canada
Belgium	–	328.4	314.7	340.6	e382.1	Belgique
Spain	240.8	236.5	263.2	288.8	310.9	Espagne
Malaysia	177.9	177.0	190.5	175.9	e186.4	Malaisie
Netherlands	189.3	219.1	176.4	169.3	127.9	Pays-Bas
Czech Republic	142.3	125.3	133.8	158.2	175.5	République tchèque
Mexico	91.1	121.3	173.2	140.2	179.3	Mexique
Sweden	125.1	121.0	121.0	114.4	111.8	Suède
Austria	136.1	113.1	80.1	110.7	137.0	Autriche
Thailand	72.3	96.1	116.5	117.3	e123.9	Thaïlande
China	62.1	69.5	81.7	92.1	146.9	Chine
China, Hong Kong SAR	70.7	71.4	97.8	97.2	106.5	Chine - RAS de Hong-Kong
Korea, Republic of	71.7	99.8	82.0	72.8	75.2	République de Corée
Belgium-Luxembourg	341.4	–	–	–	–	Belgique-Luxembourg
Hungary	49.7	64.1	69.2	59.3	63.0	Hongrie
Poland	44.4	55.2	61.5	64.4	70.1	Pologne
Denmark	60.1	53.3	51.2	48.1	50.3	Danemark
Turkey	36.4	44.3	51.6	57.1	62.0	Turquie
Brazil	48.8	38.1	48.0	54.4	e56.4	Brésil
Singapore	33.4	61.7	47.7	48.3	54.1	Singapour
Switzerland-Liechtenstein	46.8	51.0	48.3	46.3	47.7	Suisse-Liechtenstein
Ireland	47.8	33.0	36.8	43.6	38.9	Irlande
Slovakia	42.8	39.1	36.2	39.6	39.6	Slovaquie
Southern African Customs Union	171.7	11.4	–	–	–	Union douanière d'Afrique australe

(Value as percentages of World total) **(Valeur en pourcentage du total mondial)**

Regions of the world	1993	1994	1995	1996	1997	1998	1999	2000	2001	2002	Régions du monde
World	100.0	100.0	100.0	100.0	100.0	100.0	100.0	100.0	100.0	100.0	Monde
Africa	0.2	0.2	0.2	0.2	0.3	2.4	0.2	0.2	0.2	0.3	Afrique
Americas	17.0	17.4	16.9	18.5	20.7	19.4	20.4	22.9	21.5	21.2	Amériques
- Northern America	15.1	15.4	15.0	16.3	18.0	16.9	17.5	19.2	18.2	17.5	- Amérique du Nord
- LAIA	1.8	1.9	1.9	2.1	2.6	2.5	2.9	3.7	3.3	3.6	- ALAI
- CACM	0.1	0.1	0.1	0.1	0.0	0.1	0.1	0.0	0.1	0.1	- MCC
- Caribbean	0.0	0.0	0.0	0.0	0.0	0.0	0.0	0.0	0.0	0.0	- Caraïbes
- Rest of America	0.0	0.0	0.0	0.0	0.0	0.0	0.0	0.0	0.0	0.0	- Autre d'Amérique
Asia excluding former USSR	21.4	21.0	20.2	18.6	17.9	14.2	16.6	17.4	16.6	18.0	Asie ancienne URSS exclus
- Middle East	0.4	0.4	0.5	0.4	0.5	0.6	0.7	0.8	1.1	0.9	- Moyen-Orient
Asia former USSR	0.0	0.1	0.0	0.0	0.0	0.0	0.0	0.0	0.0	0.0	Asie ancienne URSS
Europe excluding former USSR	60.9	60.5	61.7	61.3	59.8	63.1	62.1	58.6	60.8	59.6	Europe ancienne URSS exclus
- European Union	58.2	57.7	58.3	57.9	56.1	57.7	56.5	53.1	54.9	53.5	- Union Européenne
- Eastern Europe	1.3	1.2	1.8	2.1	2.5	3.9	4.1	4.1	4.5	4.7	- Europe de l'Est
- Rest of Europe	1.4	1.6	1.6	1.3	1.2	1.5	1.4	1.4	1.4	1.3	- Autre de l'Europe
Europe former USSR	0.3	0.6	0.6	0.9	1.0	0.7	0.5	0.6	0.6	0.6	Europe ancienne URSS
Oceania	0.2	0.3	0.3	0.4	0.3	0.2	0.2	0.2	0.3	0.3	Océanie

625 Rubber tires, tire cases, inner and flaps, for wheels of all kinds

TRADE BY COMMODITY (Value in million US dollars)
Imports by principal countries or areas

COMMERCE PAR PRODUIT (Valeur en millions de dollars EU)
Importations selon les principaux pays ou zones

Country or area	1998	1999	2000	2001	2002	Pays ou zone
World	25330.9	25598.7	25661.3	24786.1	26709.5	Monde
Africa	887.2	818.2	852.5	885.1	945.3	Afrique
Americas	7817.5	8448.9	9112.7	8427.8	8850.7	Amériques
- Northern America	5512.2	6289.1	6572.4	5854.3	6523.4	- Amérique du Nord
- LAIA	1899.9	1782.5	2171.0	2202.0	1956.1	- ALAI
- CACM	170.3	166.0	163.4	174.5	183.0	- MCC
- Caribbean	175.6	161.7	161.3	155.6	145.3	- Caraïbes
- Rest of America	59.5	49.5	44.6	41.4	42.8	- Autre d'Amérique
Asia excluding former USSR	2898.0	2813.7	3230.0	2998.5	3254.4	Asie ancienne URSS exclus
- Middle East	1139.0	1022.7	1411.1	1252.4	1315.4	- Moyen-Orient
Asia former USSR	144.7	99.8	158.6	167.6	171.6	Asie ancienne URSS
Europe excluding former USSR	12538.2	12498.2	11308.4	11310.1	12356.4	Europe ancienne URSS exclus
- European Union	11359.7	11328.7	10177.1	10143.0	10946.7	- Union Européenne
- Eastern Europe	500.6	503.7	510.7	556.0	718.3	- Europe de l'Est
- Rest of Europe	677.9	665.8	620.7	611.2	691.5	- Autre de l'Europe
Europe former USSR	435.3	285.1	333.8	360.3	377.0	Europe ancienne URSS
Oceania	610.0	634.9	665.2	636.7	754.2	Océanie
United States	4310.3	4922.5	5106.2	4484.4	5052.4	Etats-Unis d'Amérique
Germany	2526.3	2451.6	2260.6	2259.3	2310.5	Allemagne
United Kingdom	1442.2	1422.0	1348.0	1264.4	1459.0	Royaume-Uni
Canada	1199.5	1364.0	1464.5	1368.4	1468.3	Canada
France-Monaco	1444.4	1427.1	1314.5	1264.9	1320.7	France-Monaco
Italy-San Marino-Holy See	1318.2	1290.9	1156.1	1130.0	1187.2	Italie-Saint-Marin-Saint-Siège
Netherlands	943.4	1005.9	852.1	886.2	1032.7	Pays-Bas
Spain	974.8	996.7	819.4	810.7	877.7	Espagne
Mexico	635.7	732.0	946.2	1004.5	989.8	Mexique
Belgium	–	936.2	828.9	915.3	e1003.8	Belgique
Australia	537.9	515.1	538.8	509.9	614.7	Australie
Japan	510.4	478.8	467.3	451.8	447.1	Japon
Sweden	446.0	424.0	366.8	390.8	473.3	Suède
Austria	460.6	418.9	369.5	377.4	383.6	Autriche
Saudi Arabia	323.6	270.4	395.6	376.1	e389.3	Arabie saoudite
United Arab Emirates	234.0	245.2	312.4	354.8	e364.0	Emirates arabes unis
Switzerland-Liechtenstein	319.5	316.5	294.1	274.6	298.5	Suisse-Liechtenstein
Brazil	339.2	241.6	295.3	274.8	201.3	Brésil
Portugal	256.9	239.5	209.8	242.4	246.0	Portugal
China, Hong Kong SAR	302.6	202.2	193.2	188.8	267.1	Chine - RAS de Hong-Kong
Denmark	225.8	217.1	196.3	176.9	197.3	Danemark
Singapore	174.9	219.9	204.1	186.3	203.4	Singapour
Argentina	242.7	221.6	230.4	185.3	e82.0	Argentine
Russian Federation	196.8	142.7	167.0	185.0	179.3	Fédération de Russie
Belgium-Luxembourg	856.9	–	–	–	–	Belgique-Luxembourg
Norway	185.6	166.4	154.0	153.6	180.3	Norvège
Poland	147.2	165.7	161.6	153.2	204.9	Pologne
Chile	187.6	143.6	161.8	174.5	162.9	Chili
Greece	184.4	182.2	156.8	143.5	e158.7	Grèce
Colombia	148.3	142.5	164.3	162.0	158.5	Colombie

(Value as percentages of World total) **(Valeur en pourcentage du total mondial)**

Regions of the world	1993	1994	1995	1996	1997	1998	1999	2000	2001	2002	Régions du monde
World	100.0	100.0	100.0	100.0	100.0	100.0	100.0	100.0	100.0	100.0	Monde
Africa	4.1	3.4	3.6	3.7	3.6	3.5	3.2	3.3	3.6	3.5	Afrique
Americas	26.7	27.2	25.2	24.3	28.1	30.9	33.0	35.5	34.0	33.1	Amériques
- Northern America	21.2	21.1	18.8	17.6	19.6	21.8	24.6	25.6	23.6	24.4	- Amérique du Nord
- LAIA	4.1	4.8	4.9	5.4	7.0	7.5	7.0	8.5	8.9	7.3	- ALAI
- CACM	0.5	0.5	0.5	0.5	0.6	0.7	0.6	0.6	0.7	0.7	- MCC
- Caribbean	0.6	0.5	0.7	0.6	0.7	0.7	0.6	0.6	0.6	0.5	- Caraïbes
- Rest of America	0.3	0.2	0.2	0.2	0.2	0.2	0.2	0.2	0.2	0.2	- Autre d'Amérique
Asia excluding former USSR	16.5	13.9	14.2	13.7	14.3	11.4	11.0	12.6	12.1	12.2	Asie ancienne URSS exclus
- Middle East	6.0	4.6	4.6	4.8	4.9	4.5	4.0	5.5	5.1	4.9	- Moyen-Orient
Asia former USSR	0.1	0.6	0.6	1.1	0.5	0.6	0.4	0.6	0.7	0.6	Asie ancienne URSS
Europe excluding former USSR	49.1	50.3	51.8	51.6	48.6	49.5	48.8	44.1	45.6	46.3	Europe ancienne URSS exclus
- European Union	44.8	46.2	47.4	47.1	44.3	44.8	44.3	39.7	40.9	41.0	- Union Européenne
- Eastern Europe	1.3	1.1	1.3	1.6	1.7	2.0	2.0	2.0	2.2	2.7	- Europe de l'Est
- Rest of Europe	3.0	3.0	3.1	2.9	2.7	2.7	2.6	2.4	2.5	2.6	- Autre de l'Europe
Europe former USSR	0.8	1.6	1.8	2.6	2.2	1.7	1.1	1.3	1.5	1.4	Europe ancienne URSS
Oceania	2.7	2.9	2.9	3.0	2.8	2.4	2.5	2.6	2.6	2.8	Océanie

TRADE BY COMMODITY (Value in million US dollars)
Exports by principal countries or areas

COMMERCE PAR PRODUIT (Valeur en millions de dollars EU)
Exportations selon les principaux pays ou zones

Country or area	1998	1999	2000	2001	2002	Pays ou zone
World	25836.8	25704.7	25159.6	24219.5	25977.7	Monde
Africa	176.8	208.4	197.4	204.6	228.3	Afrique
Americas	4930.0	4871.2	5050.9	4741.4	4701.7	Amériques
- Northern America	3822.2	3722.1	3870.5	3712.4	3674.3	- Amérique du Nord
- LAIA	1052.7	1097.1	1128.9	960.4	958.8	- ALAI
- CACM	54.4	51.3	49.1	49.2	53.4	- MCC
- Caribbean	0.7	0.5	2.2	19.0	14.8	- Caraïbes
- Rest of America	0.1	0.2	0.3	0.4	0.4	- Autre d'Amérique
Asia excluding former USSR	7853.1	7939.0	8112.0	7865.1	8778.0	Asie ancienne URSS exclus
- Middle East	450.0	460.3	496.5	591.3	615.1	- Moyen-Orient
Asia former USSR	5.0	4.4	1.0	0.9	1.1	Asie ancienne URSS
Europe excluding former USSR	12174.1	12202.9	11266.6	10932.0	11806.9	Europe ancienne URSS exclus
- European Union	11156.5	11135.0	10130.3	9620.9	9969.5	- Union Européenne
- Eastern Europe	753.9	824.0	906.4	1061.2	1562.0	- Europe de l'Est
- Rest of Europe	263.7	243.8	229.9	249.9	275.4	- Autre de l'Europe
Europe former USSR	594.0	369.4	442.9	400.6	397.7	Europe ancienne URSS
Oceania	103.8	109.5	88.9	74.9	64.0	Océanie
Japan	3460.3	3528.9	3323.5	2988.9	3349.3	Japon
United States	2609.4	2488.8	2531.2	2401.8	2357.7	Etats-Unis d'Amérique
France-Monaco	2788.6	2611.6	2342.8	2059.6	2070.3	France-Monaco
Germany	2125.3	2218.8	2015.4	2119.7	2348.4	Allemagne
Korea, Republic of	1543.0	1485.8	1421.4	1425.7	1484.4	République de Corée
Spain	1400.9	1447.5	1304.1	1298.7	1254.2	Espagne
Canada	1212.7	1233.3	1339.3	1310.6	1316.4	Canada
Italy-San Marino-Holy See	1144.7	1166.8	1021.4	1033.1	1044.9	Italie-Saint-Marin-Saint-Siège
United Kingdom	1345.9	1143.6	1082.2	861.5	789.3	Royaume-Uni
China	642.0	788.4	1088.1	1090.6	1322.1	Chine
Netherlands	588.1	674.4	630.8	583.8	766.5	Pays-Bas
Brazil	525.0	522.9	536.0	475.9	e493.4	Brésil
Belgium	-	575.3	573.6	501.8	e563.0	Belgique
Czech Republic	256.3	318.1	348.4	361.8	614.1	République tchèque
Thailand	324.4	315.7	344.5	380.5	e401.8	Thaïlande
Poland	225.8	233.8	274.1	359.4	437.9	Pologne
Turkey	238.2	241.6	265.0	338.2	359.6	Turquie
Indonesia	213.8	254.1	293.0	273.7	349.3	Indonésie
Austria	316.6	305.6	270.5	245.3	171.3	Autriche
India	201.2	194.6	235.0	258.9	324.0	Inde
Sweden	287.4	260.5	213.7	209.2	175.9	Suède
Portugal	193.6	215.0	222.4	222.6	278.0	Portugal
Luxembourg	-	290.6	214.6	221.0	e225.9	Luxembourg
United Arab Emirates	160.9	166.0	167.7	201.4	e209.7	Emirates arabes unis
Russian Federation	159.4	113.6	175.0	203.4	219.7	Fédération de Russie
Mexico	178.2	228.2	206.9	127.1	126.9	Mexique
Slovenia	156.4	155.3	151.5	169.6	205.0	Slovénie
Finland	149.1	150.7	157.1	169.0	199.9	Finlande
Slovakia	133.0	127.5	137.2	163.2	249.4	Slovaquie
Belgium-Luxembourg	737.6	-	-	-	-	Belgique-Luxembourg

(Value as percentages of World total) **(Valeur en pourcentage du total mondial)**

Regions of the world	1993	1994	1995	1996	1997	1998	1999	2000	2001	2002	Régions du monde
World	100.0	100.0	100.0	100.0	100.0	100.0	100.0	100.0	100.0	100.0	Monde
Africa	0.4	0.6	0.7	0.7	0.6	0.7	0.8	0.8	0.8	0.9	Afrique
Americas	16.9	16.9	16.2	16.0	18.7	19.1	19.0	20.1	19.6	18.1	Amériques
- Northern America	13.3	13.1	12.3	12.3	14.7	14.8	14.5	15.4	15.3	14.1	- Amérique du Nord
- LAIA	3.4	3.6	3.8	3.5	3.8	4.1	4.3	4.5	4.0	3.7	- ALAI
- CACM	0.1	0.2	0.2	0.2	0.2	0.2	0.2	0.2	0.2	0.2	- MCC
- Caribbean	0.0	0.0	0.0	0.0	0.0	0.0	0.0	0.0	0.1	0.1	- Caraïbes
- Rest of America	0.0	0.0	0.0	0.0	0.0	0.0	0.0	0.0	0.0	0.0	- Autre d'Amérique
Asia excluding former USSR	31.2	28.8	30.0	30.5	30.6	30.4	30.9	32.2	32.5	33.8	Asie ancienne URSS exclus
- Middle East	1.4	1.4	1.5	1.5	1.7	1.7	1.8	2.0	2.4	2.4	- Moyen-Orient
Asia former USSR	0.0	0.0	0.0	0.0	0.0	0.0	0.0	0.0	0.0	0.0	Asie ancienne URSS
Europe excluding former USSR	50.6	51.4	49.7	49.5	46.9	47.1	47.5	44.8	45.1	45.5	Europe ancienne URSS exclus
- European Union	47.7	48.1	45.8	46.0	43.4	43.2	43.3	40.3	39.7	38.4	- Union Européenne
- Eastern Europe	1.9	2.2	2.8	2.7	2.6	2.9	3.2	3.6	4.4	6.0	- Europe de l'Est
- Rest of Europe	1.0	1.1	1.1	0.8	0.8	1.0	0.9	0.9	1.0	1.1	- Autre de l'Europe
Europe former USSR	0.5	1.8	2.9	2.8	2.8	2.3	1.4	1.8	1.7	1.5	Europe ancienne URSS
Oceania	0.4	0.5	0.5	0.4	0.4	0.4	0.4	0.4	0.3	0.2	Océanie

628 Articles of rubber, nes

TRADE BY COMMODITY (Value in million US dollars)
Imports by principal countries or areas

COMMERCE PAR PRODUIT (Valeur en millions de dollars EU)
Importations selon les principaux pays ou zones

Country or area	1998	1999	2000	2001	2002	Pays ou zone
World	11501.3	11934.5	12805.7	12755.1	13235.5	Monde
Africa	315.3	287.2	293.8	313.0	342.5	Afrique
Americas	3729.8	3991.7	4751.2	4581.4	4437.5	Amériques
- Northern America	2444.9	2694.6	2890.3	2835.8	3035.4	- Amérique du Nord
- LAIA	1184.2	1193.3	1754.2	1628.1	1288.4	- ALAI
- CACM	35.8	39.4	44.6	54.3	50.7	- MCC
- Caribbean	54.2	53.0	51.9	53.2	52.7	- Caraïbes
- Rest of America	10.6	11.4	10.2	10.0	10.3	- Autre d'Amérique
Asia excluding former USSR	1664.4	1943.2	2180.8	2082.3	2220.0	Asie ancienne URSS exclus
- Middle East	212.8	191.8	225.8	218.6	255.4	- Moyen-Orient
Asia former USSR	32.8	28.0	39.2	43.7	46.0	Asie ancienne URSS
Europe excluding former USSR	5289.6	5270.1	5110.9	5297.9	5721.2	Europe ancienne URSS exclus
- European Union	4509.7	4490.4	4287.9	4422.6	4690.9	- Union Européenne
- Eastern Europe	491.7	505.7	568.2	627.8	758.1	- Europe de l'Est
- Rest of Europe	288.2	273.9	254.8	247.5	272.1	- Autre de l'Europe
Europe former USSR	243.8	163.2	183.7	191.9	200.2	Europe ancienne URSS
Oceania	225.6	251.2	246.2	244.9	268.1	Océanie
United States	1704.7	1864.2	2046.6	2058.4	2231.5	Etats-Unis d'Amérique
Germany	1274.8	1304.7	1182.1	1316.8	1340.6	Allemagne
Mexico	665.4	784.7	1311.9	1162.5	879.2	Mexique
Canada	739.4	829.5	843.2	776.9	803.4	Canada
France-Monaco	577.7	580.5	568.4	575.3	641.5	France-Monaco
United Kingdom	562.4	513.5	513.4	484.2	528.5	Royaume-Uni
Italy-San Marino-Holy See	345.1	368.6	354.3	358.4	381.9	Italie-Saint-Marin-Saint-Siège
Spain	327.5	317.2	316.3	331.6	335.6	Espagne
Belgium	–	382.1	375.3	404.7	e443.8	Belgique
Japan	283.9	289.2	332.3	331.2	356.4	Japon
China	162.7	346.9	296.8	335.7	385.6	Chine
Netherlands	266.1	261.7	241.9	225.9	208.8	Pays-Bas
Sweden	232.2	221.2	211.9	205.6	232.2	Suède
Thailand	158.3	194.3	248.2	229.8	e239.5	Thaïlande
Austria	235.0	211.5	194.8	197.9	215.0	Autriche
Brazil	219.4	175.9	202.0	210.4	206.8	Brésil
Australia	198.3	190.2	196.1	191.6	211.5	Australie
Poland	156.5	165.2	195.4	206.1	245.3	Pologne
Czech Republic	164.5	145.8	165.3	182.4	221.2	République tchèque
Singapore	158.1	161.2	201.8	179.2	161.7	Singapour
China, Hong Kong SAR	131.7	142.0	163.2	129.8	129.9	Chine - RAS de Hong-Kong
Switzerland-Liechtenstein	135.9	134.7	127.6	123.4	128.4	Suisse-Liechtenstein
Hungary	102.8	122.2	130.0	131.7	155.8	Hongrie
Korea, Republic of	80.0	101.1	137.4	114.2	131.7	République de Corée
Malaysia	80.9	103.4	113.6	106.2	e116.1	Malaisie
Portugal	86.8	86.1	103.1	105.0	127.0	Portugal
India	88.4	79.1	91.6	97.7	106.8	Inde
Denmark	90.5	99.9	90.3	83.5	90.6	Danemark
Turkey	101.6	84.6	92.3	69.5	95.5	Turquie
Russian Federation	76.3	60.6	70.0	89.6	84.0	Fédération de Russie

(Value as percentages of World total) **(Valeur en pourcentage du total mondial)**

Regions of the world	1993	1994	1995	1996	1997	1998	1999	2000	2001	2002	Régions du monde
World	100.0	100.0	100.0	100.0	100.0	100.0	100.0	100.0	100.0	100.0	Monde
Africa	3.8	3.4	3.1	3.1	3.1	2.7	2.4	2.3	2.5	2.6	Afrique
Americas	28.6	30.3	30.9	29.2	31.9	32.4	33.4	37.1	35.9	33.5	Amériques
- Northern America	20.8	22.3	20.1	19.9	21.2	21.3	22.6	22.6	22.2	22.9	- Amérique du Nord
- LAIA	6.7	7.2	10.0	8.6	9.9	10.3	10.0	13.7	12.8	9.7	- ALAI
- CACM	0.3	0.3	0.3	0.2	0.3	0.3	0.3	0.3	0.4	0.4	- MCC
- Caribbean	0.6	0.4	0.4	0.5	0.5	0.5	0.4	0.4	0.4	0.4	- Caraïbes
- Rest of America	0.2	0.1	0.1	0.1	0.1	0.1	0.1	0.1	0.1	0.1	- Autre d'Amérique
Asia excluding former USSR	19.9	17.7	17.4	18.0	17.8	14.5	16.3	17.0	16.3	16.8	Asie ancienne URSS exclus
- Middle East	2.6	2.1	1.8	1.9	1.9	1.9	1.6	1.8	1.7	1.9	- Moyen-Orient
Asia former USSR	0.1	0.3	0.3	0.5	0.3	0.3	0.2	0.3	0.3	0.3	Asie ancienne URSS
Europe excluding former USSR	43.4	44.1	44.3	43.4	41.7	46.0	44.2	39.9	41.5	43.2	Europe ancienne URSS exclus
- European Union	38.0	38.8	38.7	37.6	35.9	39.2	37.6	33.5	34.7	35.4	- Union Européenne
- Eastern Europe	2.6	2.6	2.8	3.1	3.4	4.3	4.2	4.4	4.9	5.7	- Europe de l'Est
- Rest of Europe	2.8	2.7	2.8	2.6	2.4	2.5	2.3	2.0	1.9	2.1	- Autre de l'Europe
Europe former USSR	1.4	1.5	1.7	3.1	2.6	2.1	1.4	1.4	1.5	1.5	Europe ancienne URSS
Oceania	2.7	2.8	2.4	2.6	2.4	2.0	2.1	1.9	1.9	2.0	Océanie

TRADE BY COMMODITY (Value in million US dollars)
Exports by principal countries or areas

COMMERCE PAR PRODUIT (Valeur en millions de dollars EU)
Exportations selon les principaux pays ou zones

Country or area	1998	1999	2000	2001	2002	Pays ou zone
World	10543.1	10726.6	11350.0	11271.4	12107.5	Monde
Africa	28.8	31.9	32.3	26.1	36.3	Afrique
Americas	2081.7	2280.0	2683.9	2606.4	2542.4	Amériques
- Northern America	1835.3	1996.1	2331.1	2290.7	2191.6	- Amérique du Nord
- LAIA	208.0	241.7	309.0	269.3	301.8	- ALAI
- CACM	37.6	41.5	42.8	45.4	47.7	- MCC
- Caribbean	0.9	0.6	0.9	0.8	1.1	- Caraïbes
- Rest of America	0.0	0.0	0.0	0.3	0.3	- Autre d'Amérique
Asia excluding former USSR	2476.3	2680.8	3059.4	2813.0	3031.9	Asie ancienne URSS exclus
- Middle East	64.5	67.0	71.3	77.9	113.6	- Moyen-Orient
Asia former USSR	3.7	1.1	1.0	2.6	2.6	Asie ancienne URSS
Europe excluding former USSR	5806.2	5630.2	5466.7	5703.1	6368.5	Europe ancienne URSS exclus
- European Union	5272.7	5102.1	4874.0	5011.1	5521.6	- Union Européenne
- Eastern Europe	314.9	322.5	382.7	485.0	624.4	- Europe de l'Est
- Rest of Europe	218.6	205.7	210.1	207.0	222.5	- Autre de l'Europe
Europe former USSR	108.1	61.5	69.8	83.7	82.8	Europe ancienne URSS
Oceania	38.5	41.1	37.0	36.4	42.9	Océanie
Germany	1710.1	1608.8	1517.1	1635.9	1832.0	Allemagne
United States	1337.2	1435.4	1758.8	1669.4	1542.5	Etats-Unis d'Amérique
Japan	1117.0	1233.0	1405.8	1216.7	1250.7	Japon
France-Monaco	836.2	811.4	818.2	800.0	867.6	France-Monaco
Italy-San Marino-Holy See	672.3	648.5	612.4	619.0	622.5	Italie-Saint-Marin-Saint-Siège
Canada	498.1	560.6	572.3	621.2	649.0	Canada
United Kingdom	606.7	537.2	511.8	481.9	525.9	Royaume-Uni
Spain	336.4	365.3	339.8	377.3	434.2	Espagne
China	229.0	252.9	291.9	316.8	370.8	Chine
Belgium	–	348.2	321.1	350.7	e393.5	Belgique
Sweden	244.7	243.7	222.1	217.0	255.9	Suède
Netherlands	207.9	228.0	227.0	215.5	241.1	Pays-Bas
Thailand	153.1	170.8	222.0	241.7	e255.3	Thaïlande
Mexico	110.5	152.4	209.9	161.3	193.9	Mexique
Singapore	147.7	163.4	176.5	152.8	162.5	Singapour
Czech Republic	125.1	117.8	132.1	149.5	175.5	République tchèque
Korea, Republic of	121.3	127.2	137.4	131.3	146.9	République de Corée
Austria	135.3	129.2	119.0	126.1	146.9	Autriche
Poland	60.0	68.7	105.3	148.9	232.3	Pologne
China, Hong Kong SAR	101.4	126.4	146.8	119.6	99.7	Chine - RAS de Hong-Kong
Malaysia	143.7	113.2	101.9	102.1	e108.2	Malaisie
Switzerland-Liechtenstein	108.1	101.4	106.2	102.6	109.0	Suisse-Liechtenstein
Hungary	67.5	73.7	84.7	99.1	109.9	Hongrie
India	64.8	67.4	93.3	80.2	107.7	Inde
Brazil	79.5	68.7	76.3	79.1	e82.0	Brésil
Belgium-Luxembourg	347.2	–	–	–	–	Belgique-Luxembourg
Turkey	52.5	53.5	55.7	59.1	88.9	Turquie
Slovakia	43.4	36.3	43.0	66.6	81.9	Slovaquie
Russian Federation	64.1	39.7	44.6	52.1	45.6	Fédération de Russie
Indonesia	16.7	28.9	57.1	59.9	79.6	Indonésie

(Value as percentages of World total) **(Valeur en pourcentage du total mondial)**

Regions of the world	1993	1994	1995	1996	1997	1998	1999	2000	2001	2002	Régions du monde
World	100.0	100.0	100.0	100.0	100.0	100.0	100.0	100.0	100.0	100.0	Monde
Africa	0.2	0.2	0.2	0.3	0.3	0.3	0.3	0.3	0.2	0.3	Afrique
Americas	17.2	17.2	16.1	16.8	19.5	19.7	21.3	23.6	23.1	21.0	Amériques
- Northern America	15.3	15.5	14.4	15.0	17.3	17.4	18.6	20.5	20.3	18.1	- Amérique du Nord
- LAIA	1.5	1.4	1.3	1.5	1.8	2.0	2.3	2.7	2.4	2.5	- ALAI
- CACM	0.5	0.4	0.3	0.3	0.3	0.4	0.4	0.4	0.4	0.4	- MCC
- Caribbean	0.0	0.0	0.0	0.0	0.0	0.0	0.0	0.0	0.0	0.0	- Caraïbes
- Rest of America	0.0	0.0	0.0	0.0	0.0	0.0	0.0	0.0	0.0	0.0	- Autre d'Amérique
Asia excluding former USSR	31.8	29.0	28.0	26.7	25.9	23.5	25.0	27.0	25.0	25.0	Asie ancienne URSS exclus
- Middle East	0.2	0.2	0.3	0.3	0.4	0.6	0.6	0.6	0.7	0.9	- Moyen-Orient
Asia former USSR	0.0	0.1	0.1	0.1	0.1	0.0	0.0	0.0	0.0	0.0	Asie ancienne URSS
Europe excluding former USSR	50.0	52.1	54.2	54.5	52.6	55.1	52.5	48.2	50.6	52.6	Europe ancienne URSS exclus
- European Union	45.2	47.5	49.1	50.2	48.3	50.0	47.6	42.9	44.5	45.6	- Union Européenne
- Eastern Europe	2.0	1.9	2.4	2.1	2.4	3.0	3.0	3.4	4.3	5.2	- Europe de l'Est
- Rest of Europe	2.8	2.7	2.6	2.3	2.0	2.1	1.9	1.9	1.8	1.8	- Autre de l'Europe
Europe former USSR	0.2	1.0	1.0	1.2	1.1	1.0	0.6	0.6	0.7	0.7	Europe ancienne URSS
Oceania	0.5	0.5	0.4	0.4	0.5	0.4	0.4	0.3	0.3	0.4	Océanie

633 Cork manufactures

TRADE BY COMMODITY (Value in million US dollars)
Imports by principal countries or areas

COMMERCE PAR PRODUIT (Valeur en millions de dollars EU)
Importations selon les principaux pays ou zones

Country or area	1998	1999	2000	2001	2002	Pays ou zone
World	1247.5	1158.2	1189.9	1154.6	1174.7	Monde
Africa	21.8	25.3	27.8	22.6	29.1	Afrique
Americas	266.5	262.2	285.7	288.9	271.8	Amériques
- Northern America	185.6	181.1	196.7	208.1	214.1	- Amérique du Nord
- LAIA	66.5	67.8	75.3	75.7	54.0	- ALAI
- CACM	0.6	0.3	0.4	0.3	0.4	- MCC
- Caribbean	13.7	12.6	13.2	4.8	3.3	- Caraïbes
- Rest of America	0.1	0.3	0.1	0.1	0.1	- Autre d'Amérique
Asia excluding former USSR	59.1	55.8	62.5	56.9	61.7	Asie ancienne URSS exclus
- Middle East	7.3	7.5	7.7	7.9	8.4	- Moyen-Orient
Asia former USSR	1.8	1.1	2.0	3.0	3.7	Asie ancienne URSS
Europe excluding former USSR	833.4	732.2	724.4	699.8	699.3	Europe ancienne URSS exclus
- European Union	764.7	665.4	658.8	632.9	632.2	- Union Européenne
- Eastern Europe	32.1	29.5	29.2	30.3	33.4	- Europe de l'Est
- Rest of Europe	36.6	37.3	36.4	36.6	33.7	- Autre de l'Europe
Europe former USSR	12.7	8.2	12.4	15.8	12.9	Europe ancienne URSS
Oceania	52.1	73.3	75.1	67.6	96.1	Océanie
France-Monaco	222.4	254.0	255.6	243.0	243.8	France-Monaco
United States	169.9	165.1	177.2	190.5	196.0	Etats-Unis d'Amérique
Germany	161.2	136.5	125.5	123.5	112.4	Allemagne
Italy-San Marino-Holy See	70.9	73.0	78.3	75.5	79.7	Italie-Saint-Marin-Saint-Siège
Spain	57.9	72.1	82.2	78.0	81.7	Espagne
Australia	49.1	63.6	66.3	59.2	86.0	Australie
United Kingdom	155.6	29.3	22.9	22.4	17.4	Royaume-Uni
Austria	30.5	33.7	27.6	27.1	25.6	Autriche
Chile	27.0	28.7	28.7	30.9	27.6	Chili
Portugal	24.3	25.6	30.6	29.9	32.3	Portugal
Switzerland-Liechtenstein	27.1	28.4	27.8	28.4	24.8	Suisse-Liechtenstein
Japan	23.7	22.6	25.1	22.6	23.5	Japon
Argentina	23.2	22.9	23.4	23.4	e10.3	Argentine
Canada	15.7	16.0	18.8	16.6	17.7	Canada
South Africa	–	–	23.2	19.4	23.3	Afrique du Sud
Mexico	8.1	9.9	16.5	13.4	9.4	Mexique
China	9.0	7.1	10.4	10.8	12.3	Chine
Netherlands	13.6	12.2	7.7	6.2	9.2	Pays-Bas
Southern African Customs Union	19.4	22.6	–	–	–	Union douanière d'Afrique australe
New Zealand	2.9	9.6	8.7	8.2	9.9	Nouvelle-Zélande
Belgium	–	10.2	10.0	9.1	e10.0	Belgique
Hungary	6.3	8.1	8.1	8.0	7.8	Hongrie
Bulgaria	9.6	6.9	6.2	e7.0	e7.7	Bulgarie
Denmark	4.8	6.1	7.1	8.1	8.7	Danemark
China, Hong Kong SAR	6.2	6.5	6.0	4.7	7.2	Chine - RAS de Hong-Kong
Czech Republic	6.4	6.2	5.4	5.2	6.1	République tchèque
Cayman Islands	e7.1	e9.0	e9.7	e2.9	e0.0	Iles Caïmans
Greece	6.1	6.4	4.8	5.0	e5.5	Grèce
Poland	5.1	4.6	5.4	5.2	6.4	Pologne
Russian Federation	4.3	3.5	5.2	7.3	3.7	Fédération de Russie

(Value as percentages of World total)

(Valeur en pourcentage du total mondial)

Regions of the world	1993	1994	1995	1996	1997	1998	1999	2000	2001	2002	Régions du monde
World	100.0	100.0	100.0	100.0	100.0	100.0	100.0	100.0	100.0	100.0	Monde
Africa	1.6	2.1	2.0	2.1	2.1	1.8	2.2	2.3	2.0	2.5	Afrique
Americas	17.6	16.9	18.0	19.4	21.2	21.4	22.6	24.0	25.0	23.1	Amériques
- Northern America	14.4	13.4	14.5	15.0	15.1	14.9	15.6	16.5	18.0	18.2	- Amérique du Nord
- LAIA	3.0	3.2	3.4	4.0	5.0	5.3	5.9	6.3	6.6	4.6	- ALAI
- CACM	0.0	0.0	0.0	0.0	0.1	0.1	0.0	0.0	0.0	0.0	- MCC
- Caribbean	0.1	0.1	0.2	0.3	0.9	1.1	1.1	1.1	0.4	0.3	- Caraïbes
- Rest of America	0.0	0.0	0.0	0.0	0.1	0.0	0.0	0.0	0.0	0.0	- Autre d'Amérique
Asia excluding former USSR	6.6	6.4	6.1	5.6	5.6	4.7	4.8	5.3	4.9	5.3	Asie ancienne URSS exclus
- Middle East	0.6	0.5	0.7	0.8	0.7	0.6	0.7	0.6	0.7	0.7	- Moyen-Orient
Asia former USSR	0.0	0.0	0.0	0.0	0.1	0.1	0.1	0.2	0.3	0.3	Asie ancienne URSS
Europe excluding former USSR	68.8	68.7	68.0	66.5	64.4	66.8	63.2	60.9	60.6	59.5	Europe ancienne URSS exclus
- European Union	62.9	62.2	60.3	60.0	58.5	61.3	57.5	55.4	54.8	53.8	- Union Européenne
- Eastern Europe	1.5	1.9	3.4	3.0	2.9	2.6	2.5	2.5	2.6	2.8	- Europe de l'Est
- Rest of Europe	4.4	4.5	4.3	3.5	3.0	2.9	3.2	3.1	3.2	2.9	- Autre de l'Europe
Europe former USSR	0.5	0.7	0.8	1.0	1.3	1.0	0.7	1.0	1.4	1.1	Europe ancienne URSS
Oceania	4.9	5.3	4.9	5.4	5.3	4.2	6.3	6.3	5.9	8.2	Océanie

TRADE BY COMMODITY (Value in million US dollars)
Exports by principal countries or areas

COMMERCE PAR PRODUIT (Valeur en millions de dollars EU)
Exportations selon les principaux pays ou zones

Country or area	1998	1999	2000	2001	2002	Pays ou zone
World	1327.8	1204.7	1236.6	1180.5	1244.7	Monde
Africa	18.4	25.0	26.5	23.2	24.8	Afrique
Americas	71.2	76.4	76.2	51.4	55.9	Amériques
- Northern America	66.8	68.2	68.5	42.7	48.9	- Amérique du Nord
- LAIA	4.3	8.1	7.7	8.6	6.8	- ALAI
- CACM	0.0	0.0	0.0	0.0	0.0	- MCC
- Caribbean	0.0	0.0	0.0	0.0	0.0	- Caraïbes
- Rest of America	0.0	0.0	0.0	0.0	0.0	- Autre d'Amérique
Asia excluding former USSR	12.8	16.5	17.4	18.4	21.6	Asie ancienne URSS exclus
- Middle East	1.1	1.6	0.5	0.7	0.6	- Moyen-Orient
Asia former USSR	0.0	0.1	0.0	0.0	0.0	Asie ancienne URSS
Europe excluding former USSR	1219.5	1081.2	1111.3	1083.2	1134.3	Europe ancienne URSS exclus
- European Union	1201.9	1062.0	1091.5	1061.4	1117.5	- Union Européenne
- Eastern Europe	5.1	2.8	4.8	4.2	4.4	- Europe de l'Est
- Rest of Europe	12.5	16.3	15.0	17.6	12.4	- Autre de l'Europe
Europe former USSR	0.4	0.5	0.5	1.0	0.7	Europe ancienne URSS
Oceania	5.5	5.0	4.7	3.4	7.4	Océanie
Portugal	735.7	746.4	766.7	742.1	800.6	Portugal
Spain	129.0	142.1	152.9	146.5	154.9	Espagne
United States	65.5	66.9	66.2	40.1	44.2	Etats-Unis d'Amérique
France-Monaco	37.3	54.4	60.3	61.9	55.0	France-Monaco
Italy-San Marino-Holy See	49.9	50.1	51.0	51.8	50.2	Italie-Saint-Marin-Saint-Siège
Germany	55.7	40.3	34.2	34.9	33.0	Allemagne
United Kingdom	169.9	4.4	4.2	5.5	3.4	Royaume-Uni
Switzerland-Liechtenstein	12.1	16.1	14.8	17.5	12.3	Suisse-Liechtenstein
Austria	13.2	13.1	11.5	11.0	12.4	Autriche
Morocco	8.4	10.8	10.7	10.5	e11.5	Maroc
China, Hong Kong SAR	4.3	5.8	5.9	5.9	7.9	Chine - RAS de Hong-Kong
Tunisia	5.2	4.4	6.6	6.0	e6.2	Tunisie
Algeria	3.4	7.3	7.3	e5.0	e4.9	Algérie
Netherlands	4.9	5.4	5.1	3.7	3.8	Pays-Bas
Mexico	2.2	6.1	5.3	5.1	3.5	Mexique
China	2.1	2.9	4.4	5.3	7.0	Chine
New Zealand	3.9	3.0	2.0	1.6	3.0	Nouvelle-Zélande
Australia	1.6	2.0	2.6	1.8	4.4	Australie
Canada	1.3	1.3	2.3	2.5	4.7	Canada
Belgium	–	3.4	3.3	2.5	e2.9	Belgique
Bulgaria	3.3	1.6	2.1	e2.2	e2.4	Bulgarie
Sweden	1.3	1.6	1.6	1.0	0.7	Suède
South Africa	–	–	1.6	1.5	1.9	Afrique du Sud
Belgium-Luxembourg	4.6	–	–	–	–	Belgique-Luxembourg
Argentina	0.4	0.5	0.6	1.5	e1.4	Argentine
India	0.2	1.9	1.3	0.3	0.3	Inde
Indonesia	0.0	0.5	0.9	1.8	0.8	Indonésie
Brazil	0.9	0.7	0.9	0.7	e0.7	Brésil
Singapore	1.8	0.4	0.5	0.4	0.9	Singapour
Southern African Customs Union	1.1	2.4	–	–	–	Union douanière d'Afrique australe

(Value as percentages of World total) **(Valeur en pourcentage du total mondial)**

Regions of the world	1993	1994	1995	1996	1997	1998	1999	2000	2001	2002	Régions du monde
World	100.0	100.0	100.0	100.0	100.0	100.0	100.0	100.0	100.0	100.0	Monde
Africa	2.0	1.5	1.4	1.1	1.1	1.4	2.1	2.1	2.0	2.0	Afrique
Americas	4.1	4.4	5.5	6.0	5.2	5.4	6.3	6.2	4.4	4.5	Amériques
- Northern America	3.9	4.1	5.2	5.6	4.8	5.0	5.7	5.5	3.6	3.9	- Amérique du Nord
- LAIA	0.2	0.3	0.3	0.4	0.4	0.3	0.7	0.6	0.7	0.5	- ALAI
- CACM	0.0	0.0	0.0	0.0	0.0	0.0	0.0	0.0	0.0	0.0	- MCC
- Caribbean	0.0	0.0	0.0	0.0	0.0	0.0	0.0	0.0	0.0	0.0	- Caraïbes
- Rest of America	0.0	0.0	0.0	0.0	0.0	0.0	0.0	0.0	0.0	0.0	- Autre d'Amérique
Asia excluding former USSR	1.5	1.4	1.2	1.0	1.0	1.0	1.4	1.4	1.6	1.7	Asie ancienne URSS exclus
- Middle East	0.0	0.0	0.0	0.0	0.0	0.1	0.1	0.0	0.1	0.0	- Moyen-Orient
Asia former USSR	0.0	0.0	0.0	0.0	0.0	0.0	0.0	0.0	0.0	0.0	Asie ancienne URSS
Europe excluding former USSR	91.8	92.0	91.1	91.3	92.1	91.8	89.7	89.9	91.8	91.1	Europe ancienne URSS exclus
- European Union	90.2	90.5	89.4	90.1	90.9	90.5	88.2	88.3	89.9	89.8	- Union Européenne
- Eastern Europe	0.2	0.1	0.5	0.3	0.5	0.4	0.2	0.4	0.4	0.4	- Europe de l'Est
- Rest of Europe	1.5	1.4	1.3	0.9	0.8	0.9	1.4	1.2	1.5	1.0	- Autre de l'Europe
Europe former USSR	0.0	0.0	0.0	0.0	0.0	0.0	0.0	0.0	0.1	0.1	Europe ancienne URSS
Oceania	0.6	0.7	0.7	0.7	0.6	0.4	0.4	0.4	0.3	0.6	Océanie

634 Veneers, plywood, "improved" wood and other wood, worked, nes

TRADE BY COMMODITY (Value in million US dollars)
Imports by principal countries or areas

COMMERCE PAR PRODUIT (Valeur en millions de dollars EU)
Importations selon les principaux pays ou zones

Country or area	1998	1999	2000	2001	2002	Pays ou zone
World	13893.0	14998.5	14810.7	13831.6	14511.2	Monde
Africa	243.5	204.8	278.5	271.5	297.5	Afrique
Americas	3336.8	4147.1	4095.8	3767.3	4172.2	Amériques
- Northern America	2916.9	3710.6	3542.5	3201.9	3652.0	- Amérique du Nord
- LAIA	280.3	301.3	423.6	435.2	400.2	- ALAI
- CACM	24.1	20.6	21.2	26.1	26.6	- MCC
- Caribbean	107.1	103.8	100.3	96.1	85.8	- Caraïbes
- Rest of America	8.3	10.8	8.1	8.0	7.6	- Autre d'Amérique
Asia excluding former USSR	4011.4	4566.2	4717.1	4040.7	4234.4	Asie ancienne URSS exclus
- Middle East	468.7	411.3	486.1	438.0	466.3	- Moyen-Orient
Asia former USSR	38.5	22.7	31.4	38.6	44.9	Asie ancienne URSS
Europe excluding former USSR	6015.7	5844.6	5458.4	5473.0	5460.1	Europe ancienne URSS exclus
- European Union	5200.8	5072.8	4688.5	4675.7	4575.5	- Union Européenne
- Eastern Europe	360.5	329.3	356.8	406.8	483.1	- Europe de l'Est
- Rest of Europe	454.4	442.5	413.0	390.6	401.4	- Autre de l'Europe
Europe former USSR	167.7	115.5	131.5	164.3	198.5	Europe ancienne URSS
Oceania	79.5	97.7	98.0	76.2	103.5	Océanie
United States	2625.2	3359.8	3157.3	2862.4	3244.5	Etats-Unis d'Amérique
Japan	1461.7	2152.6	2123.4	1913.4	1931.6	Japon
Germany	1389.4	1204.5	1051.7	1008.6	857.7	Allemagne
United Kingdom	777.2	784.2	684.6	794.0	789.2	Royaume-Uni
China	776.4	715.4	736.0	463.1	484.5	Chine
Italy-San Marino-Holy See	572.8	553.1	551.4	523.3	572.9	Italie-Saint-Marin-Saint-Siège
France-Monaco	492.1	476.6	472.1	456.9	454.1	France-Monaco
Netherlands	440.5	475.9	451.6	420.2	390.5	Pays-Bas
Korea, Republic of	224.0	371.2	457.3	486.7	598.2	République de Corée
Canada	287.0	347.5	383.1	336.9	403.5	Canada
Spain	261.5	315.9	297.4	338.2	338.1	Espagne
Belgium	–	364.8	329.2	305.0	e334.5	Belgique
Mexico	142.2	194.7	301.0	326.9	302.6	Mexique
China, Hong Kong SAR	401.8	262.4	214.6	185.1	181.7	Chine - RAS de Hong-Kong
Denmark	246.4	229.3	228.3	218.5	222.5	Danemark
Switzerland-Liechtenstein	238.7	236.9	213.0	189.9	181.0	Suisse-Liechtenstein
Sweden	216.9	200.6	189.8	189.5	184.3	Suède
Austria	199.3	202.0	179.9	172.5	167.4	Autriche
Saudi Arabia	181.1	150.0	165.1	130.8	e135.3	Arabie saoudite
Poland	131.5	96.7	107.2	120.0	139.2	Pologne
Egypt	104.9	78.4	e112.9	102.8	105.0	Egypte
United Arab Emirates	83.0	86.9	100.0	108.8	e111.6	Emirates arabes unis
Czech Republic	87.8	81.5	83.0	83.7	91.1	République tchèque
Israel	88.5	83.6	91.0	78.4	80.9	Israël
Norway	96.5	85.0	78.2	77.1	82.4	Norvège
Singapore	81.9	90.2	87.5	64.4	67.4	Singapour
Belgium-Luxembourg	371.6	–	–	–	–	Belgique-Luxembourg
Ireland	72.8	67.8	75.2	74.4	77.1	Irlande
Hungary	53.5	56.3	62.5	68.4	94.4	Hongrie
Portugal	53.2	65.5	78.0	67.0	66.9	Portugal

(Value as percentages of World total)

(Valeur en pourcentage du total mondial)

Regions of the world	1993	1994	1995	1996	1997	1998	1999	2000	2001	2002	Régions du monde
World	100.0	100.0	100.0	100.0	100.0	100.0	100.0	100.0	100.0	100.0	Monde
Africa	2.6	1.9	1.5	1.5	1.4	1.8	1.4	1.9	2.0	2.1	Afrique
Americas	16.3	17.5	16.7	17.8	18.2	24.0	27.7	27.7	27.2	28.8	Amériques
- Northern America	13.7	15.0	14.7	15.6	15.8	21.0	24.7	23.9	23.1	25.2	- Amérique du Nord
- LAIA	1.9	1.9	1.3	1.6	1.6	2.0	2.0	2.9	3.1	2.8	- ALAI
- CACM	0.1	0.1	0.1	0.1	0.1	0.2	0.1	0.1	0.2	0.2	- MCC
- Caribbean	0.5	0.4	0.5	0.5	0.6	0.8	0.7	0.7	0.7	0.6	- Caraïbes
- Rest of America	0.1	0.1	0.0	0.0	0.0	0.1	0.1	0.1	0.1	0.1	- Autre d'Amérique
Asia excluding former USSR	46.0	42.4	40.4	42.1	41.5	28.9	30.4	31.8	29.2	29.2	Asie ancienne URSS exclus
- Middle East	4.4	4.0	3.7	3.5	3.3	3.4	2.7	3.3	3.2	3.2	- Moyen-Orient
Asia former USSR	0.0	0.2	0.2	0.3	0.1	0.3	0.2	0.2	0.3	0.3	Asie ancienne URSS
Europe excluding former USSR	34.3	37.1	40.1	36.9	37.0	43.3	39.0	36.9	39.6	37.6	Europe ancienne URSS exclus
- European Union	31.1	33.3	35.4	32.5	32.2	37.4	33.8	31.7	33.8	31.5	- Union Européenne
- Eastern Europe	0.8	1.0	1.5	1.6	2.1	2.6	2.2	2.4	2.9	3.3	- Europe de l'Est
- Rest of Europe	2.4	2.8	3.1	2.8	2.7	3.3	3.0	2.8	2.8	2.8	- Autre de l'Europe
Europe former USSR	0.2	0.5	0.6	0.9	1.2	1.2	0.8	0.9	1.2	1.4	Europe ancienne URSS
Oceania	0.5	0.6	0.6	0.5	0.5	0.6	0.7	0.7	0.6	0.7	Océanie

TRADE BY COMMODITY (Value in million US dollars)
Exports by principal countries or areas

COMMERCE PAR PRODUIT (Valeur en millions de dollars EU)
Exportations selon les principaux pays ou zones

Country or area	1998	1999	2000	2001	2002	Pays ou zone
World	13608.8	14645.3	13957.9	13161.1	13883.0	Monde
Africa	369.2	299.9	255.9	282.6	293.3	Afrique
Americas	3201.3	3978.4	3893.4	3487.3	3627.4	Amériques
- Northern America	2673.4	3305.2	3190.9	2821.4	2964.0	- Amérique du Nord
- LAIA	473.4	622.5	650.4	622.2	618.2	- ALAI
- CACM	31.1	27.2	27.0	24.1	27.0	- MCC
- Caribbean	0.5	0.4	0.7	0.6	0.4	- Caraïbes
- Rest of America	22.9	23.1	24.4	19.0	17.9	- Autre d'Amérique
Asia excluding former USSR	4152.8	4691.7	4422.2	4000.3	4256.7	Asie ancienne URSS exclus
- Middle East	33.8	36.6	36.2	55.0	63.0	- Moyen-Orient
Asia former USSR	3.5	0.4	0.4	0.4	0.7	Asie ancienne URSS
Europe excluding former USSR	5294.4	5088.0	4816.6	4761.1	4999.3	Europe ancienne URSS exclus
- European Union	4547.4	4338.8	4057.1	3980.0	4151.4	- Union Européenne
- Eastern Europe	452.4	460.5	487.7	536.6	594.8	- Europe de l'Est
- Rest of Europe	294.6	288.7	271.8	244.5	253.1	- Autre de l'Europe
Europe former USSR	481.7	465.4	458.7	519.0	577.1	Europe ancienne URSS
Oceania	105.9	121.6	110.6	110.4	128.5	Océanie
Indonesia	2207.2	2515.8	2286.6	2073.4	2023.4	Indonésie
Canada	1862.4	2469.3	2293.9	2025.8	2088.2	Canada
Malaysia	1130.1	1388.5	1301.4	1114.4	e1181.0	Malaisie
Germany	993.1	930.2	871.3	921.3	917.0	Allemagne
United States	811.0	835.9	897.0	795.5	875.8	Etats-Unis d'Amérique
Finland	630.2	606.0	576.6	579.7	600.7	Finlande
France-Monaco	620.5	594.7	541.5	472.0	465.4	France-Monaco
Austria	477.0	452.5	466.7	487.2	530.1	Autriche
Belgium	–	597.4	547.5	521.7	e585.4	Belgique
Brazil	312.7	425.4	434.4	411.5	e426.6	Brésil
Italy-San Marino-Holy See	326.2	324.5	323.9	328.7	330.9	Italie-Saint-Marin-Saint-Siège
China	118.7	187.4	268.9	340.3	564.3	Chine
Russian Federation	259.0	259.8	250.9	264.2	304.4	Fédération de Russie
Poland	184.6	217.9	234.7	240.2	255.5	Pologne
Sweden	288.2	234.6	183.8	150.1	154.5	Suède
Spain	177.3	175.0	174.3	187.0	207.9	Espagne
China, Hong Kong SAR	258.1	163.6	133.4	105.1	107.4	Chine - RAS de Hong-Kong
Belgium-Luxembourg	638.7	–	–	–	–	Belgique-Luxembourg
Switzerland-Liechtenstein	153.9	143.2	118.5	96.1	99.0	Suisse-Liechtenstein
Czech Republic	120.3	97.8	98.8	113.4	118.4	République tchèque
United Kingdom	106.7	109.6	91.5	90.7	97.5	Royaume-Uni
New Zealand	79.6	94.4	92.7	95.6	115.9	Nouvelle-Zélande
Latvia	99.8	85.7	78.6	91.2	93.3	Lettonie
Portugal	87.4	80.0	73.6	59.8	68.1	Portugal
Netherlands	84.6	82.0	70.6	65.9	65.0	Pays-Bas
Chile	36.0	62.7	64.9	98.8	e96.7	Chili
Ghana	101.2	57.5	51.3	e67.2	e67.8	Ghana
Singapore	78.2	73.9	75.9	54.6	57.1	Singapour
Hungary	60.5	57.4	61.5	72.0	82.2	Hongrie
Thailand	39.9	62.3	74.0	73.9	e78.0	Thaïlande

(Value as percentages of World total) **(Valeur en pourcentage du total mondial)**

Regions of the world	1993	1994	1995	1996	1997	1998	1999	2000	2001	2002	Régions du monde
World	100.0	100.0	100.0	100.0	100.0	100.0	100.0	100.0	100.0	100.0	Monde
Africa	1.9	1.2	1.7	2.4	1.7	2.7	2.0	1.8	2.1	2.1	Afrique
Americas	16.3	17.8	18.4	18.8	19.9	23.5	27.2	27.9	26.5	26.1	Amériques
- Northern America	12.7	13.9	14.7	14.3	15.7	19.6	22.6	22.9	21.4	21.3	- Amérique du Nord
- LAIA	3.3	3.7	3.5	3.8	3.9	3.5	4.3	4.7	4.7	4.5	- ALAI
- CACM	0.1	0.1	0.1	0.1	0.1	0.2	0.2	0.2	0.2	0.2	- MCC
- Caribbean	0.0	0.0	0.0	0.0	0.0	0.0	0.0	0.0	0.0	0.0	- Caraïbes
- Rest of America	0.1	0.1	0.1	0.6	0.2	0.2	0.2	0.2	0.1	0.1	- Autre d'Amérique
Asia excluding former USSR	53.2	48.6	43.5	44.5	42.9	30.5	32.0	31.7	30.4	30.7	Asie ancienne URSS exclus
- Middle East	0.3	0.3	0.3	0.2	0.2	0.2	0.2	0.3	0.4	0.5	- Moyen-Orient
Asia former USSR	0.0	0.0	0.0	0.0	0.0	0.0	0.0	0.0	0.0	0.0	Asie ancienne URSS
Europe excluding former USSR	25.9	29.6	33.0	30.4	31.5	38.9	34.7	34.5	36.2	36.0	Europe ancienne URSS exclus
- European Union	22.9	25.9	28.9	26.6	27.3	33.4	29.6	29.1	30.2	29.9	- Union Européenne
- Eastern Europe	1.3	1.8	2.2	2.0	2.4	3.3	3.1	3.5	4.1	4.3	- Europe de l'Est
- Rest of Europe	1.6	1.8	2.0	1.7	1.7	2.2	2.0	1.9	1.9	1.8	- Autre de l'Europe
Europe former USSR	2.1	1.9	2.3	2.7	3.1	3.5	3.2	3.3	3.9	4.2	Europe ancienne URSS
Oceania	0.6	0.9	1.1	1.1	1.0	0.8	0.8	0.8	0.8	0.9	Océanie

635 Wood manufactures, nes

TRADE BY COMMODITY (Value in million US dollars)
Imports by principal countries or areas

COMMERCE PAR PRODUIT (Valeur en millions de dollars E
Importations selon les principaux pays ou zone

Country or area	1998	1999	2000	2001	2002	Pays ou zone
World	14712.7	15922.0	16286.3	16223.8	17116.4	Monde
Africa	224.2	172.0	204.8	279.7	274.7	Afrique
Americas	4051.8	4851.0	5263.4	5227.7	5589.7	Amériques
- Northern America	3544.5	4328.8	4713.1	4689.0	5117.9	- Amérique du Nord
- LAIA	350.2	360.1	352.2	383.5	316.0	- ALAI
- CACM	25.8	24.1	23.9	25.1	23.3	- MCC
- Caribbean	117.7	126.6	161.2	118.1	114.8	- Caraïbes
- Rest of America	13.5	11.4	13.1	12.0	17.6	- Autre d'Amérique
Asia excluding former USSR	1988.3	2156.5	2473.9	2292.3	2307.7	Asie ancienne URSS exclus
- Middle East	159.4	149.2	204.1	176.9	218.0	- Moyen-Orient
Asia former USSR	97.0	67.7	63.4	61.2	65.1	Asie ancienne URSS
Europe excluding former USSR	7889.2	8210.7	7901.8	7951.2	8406.6	Europe ancienne URSS exclus
- European Union	6722.2	7077.1	6750.2	6771.2	7034.8	- Union Européenne
- Eastern Europe	372.7	337.2	359.0	360.8	411.8	- Europe de l'Est
- Rest of Europe	794.2	796.4	792.7	819.3	960.1	- Autre de l'Europe
Europe former USSR	270.2	222.5	149.0	218.3	244.7	Europe ancienne URSS
Oceania	192.1	241.5	230.0	193.4	228.0	Océanie
United States	3143.5	3913.7	4265.7	4255.1	4660.2	Etats-Unis d'Amérique
Germany	2507.1	2384.4	2039.3	1908.8	1858.2	Allemagne
Japan	998.6	1159.9	1360.7	1298.5	1291.4	Japon
United Kingdom	827.6	913.9	924.6	978.6	1103.2	Royaume-Uni
France-Monaco	686.7	781.4	844.8	849.2	813.8	France-Monaco
Italy-San Marino-Holy See	382.2	469.6	509.2	510.2	570.7	Italie-Saint-Marin-Saint-Siège
Canada	390.7	403.6	438.0	426.4	448.3	Canada
Switzerland-Liechtenstein	407.5	410.6	403.1	403.2	454.5	Suisse-Liechtenstein
Netherlands	410.3	451.2	413.1	390.5	375.8	Pays-Bas
Austria	420.7	433.6	403.0	383.5	356.3	Autriche
China, Hong Kong SAR	345.8	379.7	426.7	381.0	337.1	Chine - RAS de Hong-Kong
Belgium	–	474.3	444.0	449.6	e493.1	Belgique
Spain	262.8	308.1	303.6	338.3	417.9	Espagne
Norway	252.8	247.0	251.1	280.8	351.3	Norvège
Denmark	239.6	265.0	264.8	270.0	317.0	Danemark
Mexico	133.6	183.7	216.1	235.2	202.7	Mexique
Sweden	144.1	157.5	175.7	223.8	219.6	Suède
Australia	129.2	163.0	178.6	146.0	177.7	Australie
Poland	148.5	141.2	142.8	130.9	122.4	Pologne
Portugal	109.9	130.6	131.7	150.5	152.0	Portugal
Russian Federation	182.6	152.2	75.5	121.4	128.6	Fédération de Russie
Ireland	97.4	119.2	131.9	144.1	160.0	Irlande
Belgium-Luxembourg	527.9	–	–	–	–	Belgique-Luxembourg
Korea, Republic of	71.9	77.5	92.7	97.1	125.7	République de Corée
Czech Republic	94.4	80.1	81.0	81.3	98.2	République tchèque
Singapore	87.1	88.0	90.6	79.9	74.4	Singapour
Finland	58.5	62.4	67.6	76.5	91.8	Finlande
Hungary	57.4	46.5	57.4	59.7	85.5	Hongrie
China	97.4	75.5	51.3	31.4	34.4	Chine
Greece	47.4	63.6	43.7	41.5	e45.8	Grèce

(Value as percentages of World total) **(Valeur en pourcentage du total mondial)**

Regions of the world	1993	1994	1995	1996	1997	1998	1999	2000	2001	2002	Régions du monde
World	100.0	100.0	100.0	100.0	100.0	100.0	100.0	100.0	100.0	100.0	Monde
Africa	1.2	1.9	1.2	1.8	2.1	1.5	1.1	1.3	1.7	1.6	Afrique
Americas	21.4	21.7	20.6	20.1	24.0	27.5	30.5	32.3	32.2	32.7	Amériques
- Northern America	18.6	17.9	17.8	17.3	21.0	24.1	27.2	28.9	28.9	29.9	- Amérique du Nord
- LAIA	1.8	2.8	2.0	2.1	2.0	2.4	2.3	2.2	2.4	1.8	- ALAI
- CACM	0.1	0.1	0.1	0.1	0.3	0.2	0.2	0.1	0.2	0.1	- MCC
- Caribbean	0.8	0.7	0.6	0.5	0.6	0.8	0.8	1.0	0.7	0.7	- Caraïbes
- Rest of America	0.2	0.1	0.1	0.1	0.1	0.1	0.1	0.1	0.1	0.1	- Autre d'Amérique
Asia excluding former USSR	18.1	16.8	18.6	20.2	18.5	13.5	13.5	15.2	14.1	13.5	Asie ancienne URSS exclus
- Middle East	1.8	1.3	1.2	1.4	1.2	1.1	0.9	1.3	1.1	1.3	- Moyen-Orient
Asia former USSR	0.2	0.4	0.3	0.3	0.5	0.7	0.4	0.4	0.4	0.4	Asie ancienne URSS
Europe excluding former USSR	53.9	56.2	56.1	54.1	51.7	53.6	51.6	48.5	49.0	49.1	Europe ancienne URSS exclus
- European Union	48.2	50.3	49.3	47.1	44.0	45.7	44.4	41.4	41.7	41.1	- Union Européenne
- Eastern Europe	1.0	1.0	1.2	1.5	1.9	2.5	2.1	2.2	2.2	2.4	- Europe de l'Est
- Rest of Europe	4.7	5.0	5.6	5.5	5.8	5.4	5.0	4.9	5.0	5.6	- Autre de l'Europe
Europe former USSR	4.1	1.8	2.0	2.3	2.1	1.8	1.4	0.9	1.3	1.4	Europe ancienne URSS
Oceania	1.1	1.2	1.2	1.3	1.2	1.3	1.5	1.4	1.2	1.3	Océanie

TRADE BY COMMODITY (Value in million US dollars)
Exports by principal countries or areas

COMMERCE PAR PRODUIT (Valeur en millions de dollars EU)
Exportations selon les principaux pays ou zones

Country or area	1998	1999	2000	2001	2002	Pays ou zone
World	15293.6	16871.4	17045.3	16774.9	17760.9	Monde
Africa	107.0	160.7	132.8	126.1	138.1	Afrique
Americas	3528.0	4122.0	4223.7	3922.4	3898.8	Amériques
- Northern America	2793.7	3257.5	3320.9	3082.5	3078.2	- Amérique du Nord
- LAIA	649.5	765.0	827.2	790.1	776.9	- ALAI
- CACM	61.2	75.4	50.1	25.1	24.6	- MCC
- Caribbean	20.7	19.4	18.7	16.3	12.9	- Caraïbes
- Rest of America	2.8	4.7	6.8	8.4	6.2	- Autre d'Amérique
Asia excluding former USSR	3084.7	3618.8	4165.7	3932.9	4262.3	Asie ancienne URSS exclus
- Middle East	111.3	74.7	71.3	77.7	117.5	- Moyen-Orient
Asia former USSR	3.6	1.9	4.0	4.6	6.3	Asie ancienne URSS
Europe excluding former USSR	8279.3	8658.6	8140.6	8320.5	8891.4	Europe ancienne URSS exclus
- European Union	6525.1	6791.9	6290.8	6484.2	6883.5	- Union Européenne
- Eastern Europe	1198.6	1269.6	1292.0	1320.7	1498.9	- Europe de l'Est
- Rest of Europe	555.6	597.2	557.9	515.6	509.0	- Autre de l'Europe
Europe former USSR	222.0	243.1	310.6	394.2	470.9	Europe ancienne URSS
Oceania	69.0	66.2	68.0	74.2	93.2	Océanie
Canada	1642.2	2139.1	2134.9	2085.3	2175.3	Canada
China	926.3	1150.6	1385.5	1511.9	1805.0	Chine
United States	1151.6	1118.4	1185.9	997.2	902.8	Etats-Unis d'Amérique
Germany	880.5	896.6	783.9	959.2	997.5	Allemagne
Indonesia	507.1	790.3	939.1	816.7	786.8	Indonésie
France-Monaco	767.6	823.0	741.2	755.3	748.9	France-Monaco
Sweden	760.4	709.7	652.8	684.0	805.3	Suède
Italy-San Marino-Holy See	615.9	651.4	614.3	655.8	649.8	Italie-Saint-Marin-Saint-Siège
Denmark	629.5	647.3	594.8	547.4	583.5	Danemark
Poland	536.7	552.6	555.2	561.8	641.1	Pologne
Belgium	–	645.4	676.2	676.9	e759.4	Belgique
Austria	473.0	539.3	531.9	514.8	572.5	Autriche
United Kingdom	443.0	455.0	383.6	370.3	383.0	Royaume-Uni
Finland	415.9	396.7	380.3	395.6	407.7	Finlande
Netherlands	424.9	441.3	376.9	319.7	341.8	Pays-Bas
Spain	346.0	371.8	353.7	386.1	401.3	Espagne
China, Hong Kong SAR	351.7	352.6	406.1	388.5	359.7	Chine - RAS de Hong-Kong
Czech Republic	331.0	348.1	354.0	361.4	387.7	République tchèque
Mexico	297.9	327.7	371.2	249.9	236.1	Mexique
Brazil	209.8	273.8	287.5	337.6	e350.0	Brésil
Thailand	256.5	266.3	301.1	288.8	e305.0	Thaïlande
Malaysia	247.0	276.3	289.4	263.5	e279.2	Malaisie
Slovenia	244.2	236.3	216.8	191.6	199.6	Slovénie
Hungary	161.9	184.0	182.8	171.5	202.6	Hongrie
Norway	153.9	183.0	170.4	154.9	155.9	Norvège
Philippines	118.9	131.7	214.5	120.6	112.8	Philippines
Belgium-Luxembourg	636.1	–	–	–	–	Belgique-Luxembourg
Switzerland-Liechtenstein	119.6	126.1	120.3	123.5	110.0	Suisse-Liechtenstein
Romania	91.6	100.5	113.0	131.5	154.7	Roumanie
Portugal	109.0	103.4	107.0	128.2	131.8	Portugal

(Value as percentages of World total) **(Valeur en pourcentage du total mondial)**

Regions of the world	1993	1994	1995	1996	1997	1998	1999	2000	2001	2002	Régions du monde
World	100.0	100.0	100.0	100.0	100.0	100.0	100.0	100.0	100.0	100.0	Monde
Africa	0.8	1.0	0.8	0.7	0.7	0.7	1.0	0.8	0.8	0.8	Afrique
Americas	17.5	18.5	17.0	19.2	22.0	23.1	24.4	24.8	23.4	22.0	Amériques
- Northern America	13.6	14.2	13.5	15.2	17.6	18.3	19.3	19.5	18.4	17.3	- Amérique du Nord
- LAIA	3.5	3.9	3.2	3.7	3.9	4.2	4.5	4.9	4.7	4.4	- ALAI
- CACM	0.3	0.3	0.3	0.3	0.3	0.4	0.4	0.3	0.1	0.1	- MCC
- Caribbean	0.1	0.1	0.1	0.1	0.1	0.1	0.1	0.1	0.1	0.1	- Caraïbes
- Rest of America	0.0	0.0	0.0	0.0	0.0	0.0	0.0	0.0	0.1	0.0	- Autre d'Amérique
Asia excluding former USSR	30.3	25.9	24.7	23.7	22.2	20.2	21.4	24.4	23.4	24.0	Asie ancienne URSS exclus
- Middle East	0.5	0.6	0.5	0.6	0.6	0.7	0.4	0.4	0.5	0.7	- Moyen-Orient
Asia former USSR	0.0	0.0	0.0	0.1	0.0	0.0	0.0	0.0	0.0	0.0	Asie ancienne URSS
Europe excluding former USSR	50.1	53.5	56.2	54.6	53.0	54.1	51.3	47.8	49.6	50.1	Europe ancienne URSS exclus
- European Union	39.7	42.6	44.5	43.3	42.2	42.7	40.3	36.9	38.7	38.8	- Union Européenne
- Eastern Europe	5.3	6.1	7.0	7.1	7.0	7.8	7.5	7.6	7.9	8.4	- Europe de l'Est
- Rest of Europe	5.1	4.9	4.7	4.2	3.8	3.6	3.5	3.3	3.1	2.9	- Autre de l'Europe
Europe former USSR	0.8	0.7	0.8	1.2	1.5	1.5	1.4	1.8	2.3	2.7	Europe ancienne URSS
Oceania	0.4	0.4	0.5	0.5	0.5	0.5	0.4	0.4	0.4	0.5	Océanie

641 Paper and paperboard

TRADE BY COMMODITY (Value in million US dollars)
Imports by principal countries or areas

COMMERCE PAR PRODUIT (Valeur en millions de dollars EU)
Importations selon les principaux pays ou zones

Country or area	1998	1999	2000	2001	2002	Pays ou zone
World	74942.1	74928.3	79014.4	76947.5	77766.9	Monde
Africa	1780.8	1642.5	1744.9	1845.7	1831.6	Afrique
Americas	18643.0	18942.1	21262.8	20630.0	19199.3	Amériques
- Northern America	13688.0	14401.7	16109.7	15575.6	14845.7	- Amérique du Nord
- LAIA	4022.7	3657.0	4219.4	4093.7	3401.7	- ALAI
- CACM	505.8	515.1	559.7	572.3	577.3	- MCC
- Caribbean	353.7	300.7	298.6	323.8	309.6	- Caraïbes
- Rest of America	72.8	67.7	75.5	64.6	65.0	- Autre d'Amérique
Asia excluding former USSR	12964.4	13859.4	15829.8	14001.1	14699.0	Asie ancienne URSS exclus
- Middle East	1974.1	1957.8	2500.8	2121.8	2317.7	- Moyen-Orient
Asia former USSR	97.0	83.9	131.5	141.3	148.6	Asie ancienne URSS
Europe excluding former USSR	39344.5	38112.4	37424.2	37691.2	38954.8	Europe ancienne URSS exclus
- European Union	35034.2	33908.8	33011.5	33099.4	33909.9	- Union Européenne
- Eastern Europe	2198.7	2158.9	2382.7	2601.7	2966.7	- Europe de l'Est
- Rest of Europe	2111.6	2044.7	2030.0	1990.2	2078.2	- Autre de l'Europe
Europe former USSR	870.1	746.6	918.1	1294.3	1531.0	Europe ancienne URSS
Oceania	1242.3	1541.5	1703.1	1343.8	1402.7	Océanie
United States	11509.2	12013.7	13464.7	12978.4	12206.2	Etats-Unis d'Amérique
Germany	7207.7	7083.8	6631.8	7265.7	7264.1	Allemagne
United Kingdom	6495.6	5952.3	5530.0	5981.4	5812.2	Royaume-Uni
France-Monaco	5162.3	5010.3	5078.0	4734.1	4895.2	France-Monaco
China	3176.4	3583.7	3593.1	3349.7	3841.8	Chine
Italy-San Marino-Holy See	3122.7	3123.1	3398.2	3238.0	3271.1	Italie-Saint-Marin-Saint-Siège
Netherlands	2908.2	2805.7	2489.9	2401.3	2515.0	Pays-Bas
Spain	2653.2	2612.3	2601.5	2427.5	2657.8	Espagne
Canada	2174.4	2383.2	2641.9	2592.4	2633.3	Canada
Belgium	–	2719.4	2702.0	2630.0	e2884.3	Belgique
China, Hong Kong SAR	2105.4	2004.3	2127.8	1582.2	1477.4	Chine - RAS de Hong-Kong
Japan	1448.7	1488.9	1876.7	1782.4	1628.2	Japon
Mexico	1216.4	1373.4	1647.9	1735.8	1629.6	Mexique
Australia	1101.8	1192.5	1360.7	1006.8	1086.0	Australie
Poland	1002.5	1003.4	1070.9	1119.1	1280.3	Pologne
Austria	1034.2	1051.2	1018.1	1057.8	1037.8	Autriche
Switzerland-Liechtenstein	1069.2	1046.4	1029.4	1005.0	1025.6	Suisse-Liechtenstein
Denmark	996.4	942.2	901.6	872.5	934.2	Danemark
Malaysia	580.9	739.0	950.0	800.4	e874.8	Malaisie
Turkey	627.8	642.6	829.2	537.7	740.1	Turquie
Brazil	829.9	617.7	726.8	573.8	404.3	Brésil
Belgium-Luxembourg	2921.8	–	–	–	–	Belgique-Luxembourg
Greece	618.6	585.3	584.5	512.0	e566.2	Grèce
Sweden	576.9	578.5	627.0	515.6	568.2	Suède
Korea, Republic of	308.5	488.2	661.5	598.8	790.1	République de Corée
Argentina	764.0	642.0	609.7	548.0	e242.4	Argentine
Portugal	521.0	532.4	556.3	556.6	569.3	Portugal
Singapore	456.4	505.7	593.2	479.8	462.3	Singapour
Czech Republic	443.4	432.1	478.7	519.4	597.3	République tchèque
Norway	503.0	492.3	470.3	434.6	449.5	Norvège

(Value as percentages of World total) **(Valeur en pourcentage du total mondial)**

Regions of the world	1993	1994	1995	1996	1997	1998	1999	2000	2001	2002	Régions du monde
World	100.0	100.0	100.0	100.0	100.0	100.0	100.0	100.0	100.0	100.0	Monde
Africa	2.6	2.4	2.3	2.4	2.3	2.4	2.2	2.2	2.4	2.4	Afrique
Americas	23.4	22.2	22.4	22.2	23.6	24.9	25.3	26.9	26.8	24.7	Amériques
- Northern America	18.3	16.8	16.9	16.8	17.4	18.3	19.2	20.4	20.2	19.1	- Amérique du Nord
- LAIA	4.0	4.3	4.3	4.3	5.1	5.4	4.9	5.3	5.3	4.4	- ALAI
- CACM	0.6	0.6	0.7	0.6	0.6	0.7	0.7	0.7	0.7	0.7	- MCC
- Caribbean	0.4	0.3	0.3	0.4	0.4	0.5	0.4	0.4	0.4	0.4	- Caraïbes
- Rest of America	0.2	0.2	0.1	0.1	0.1	0.1	0.1	0.1	0.1	0.1	- Autre d'Amérique
Asia excluding former USSR	20.2	19.5	19.3	20.0	20.5	17.3	18.5	20.0	18.2	18.9	Asie ancienne URSS exclus
- Middle East	2.9	2.5	2.9	2.7	2.8	2.6	2.6	3.2	2.8	3.0	- Moyen-Orient
Asia former USSR	0.0	0.1	0.1	0.2	0.1	0.1	0.1	0.2	0.2	0.2	Asie ancienne URSS
Europe excluding former USSR	51.2	52.8	52.9	52.1	50.1	52.5	50.9	47.4	49.0	50.1	Europe ancienne URSS exclus
- European Union	46.8	48.1	48.0	46.8	44.9	46.7	45.3	41.8	43.0	43.6	- Union Européenne
- Eastern Europe	1.6	1.7	1.9	2.5	2.6	2.9	2.9	3.0	3.4	3.8	- Europe de l'Est
- Rest of Europe	2.9	3.0	2.9	2.8	2.6	2.8	2.7	2.6	2.6	2.7	- Autre de l'Europe
Europe former USSR	0.5	0.8	0.9	1.1	1.4	1.2	1.0	1.2	1.7	2.0	Europe ancienne URSS
Oceania	2.1	2.2	2.1	2.0	2.1	1.7	2.1	2.2	1.7	1.8	Océanie

TRADE BY COMMODITY (Value in million US dollars)
Exports by principal countries or areas

COMMERCE PAR PRODUIT (Valeur en millions de dollars EU)
Exportations selon les principaux pays ou zones

Country or area	1998	1999	2000	2001	2002	Pays ou zone
World	72953.5	72674.1	77610.4	74538.8	76720.9	Monde
Africa	364.6	374.1	411.4	467.0	376.4	Afrique
Americas	18017.9	17983.6	19976.2	18913.7	17842.9	Amériques
- Northern America	16459.1	16451.4	18355.6	17189.9	16071.6	- Amérique du Nord
- LAIA	1511.4	1485.9	1577.9	1677.5	1712.6	- ALAI
- CACM	34.9	35.5	30.0	32.9	47.0	- MCC
- Caribbean	6.1	5.3	7.2	8.3	7.2	- Caraïbes
- Rest of America	6.4	5.4	5.5	5.2	4.6	- Autre d'Amérique
Asia excluding former USSR	7568.9	8296.7	9493.1	8279.0	8615.0	Asie ancienne URSS exclus
- Middle East	152.0	154.9	175.8	230.2	233.8	- Moyen-Orient
Asia former USSR	4.9	2.1	1.9	3.3	2.3	Asie ancienne URSS
Europe excluding former USSR	45474.4	44445.9	45891.8	44935.6	47830.3	Europe ancienne URSS exclus
- European Union	41953.8	40923.8	41978.9	40888.1	43412.2	- Union Européenne
- Eastern Europe	1310.6	1266.1	1592.0	1786.4	2031.1	- Europe de l'Est
- Rest of Europe	2210.0	2256.0	2320.9	2261.2	2387.0	- Autre de l'Europe
Europe former USSR	1004.2	1001.5	1258.7	1317.8	1353.4	Europe ancienne URSS
Oceania	518.6	570.2	577.4	622.5	700.7	Océanie
Canada	9390.0	9554.7	10601.5	10221.3	9405.1	Canada
Germany	8582.7	8513.7	8977.9	9061.3	10238.1	Allemagne
Finland	8659.9	8228.0	8246.0	7974.2	7797.3	Finlande
United States	7069.0	6896.7	7754.0	6968.5	6666.4	Etats-Unis d'Amérique
Sweden	6311.4	6041.2	6126.4	5813.7	6059.3	Suède
France-Monaco	4165.6	4170.7	4389.2	4063.3	4209.2	France-Monaco
Austria	2521.1	2473.6	2434.7	2518.2	2812.7	Autriche
Netherlands	2459.1	2486.2	2394.8	2190.7	2390.0	Pays-Bas
Italy-San Marino-Holy See	2266.8	2228.7	2441.0	2296.7	2419.3	Italie-Saint-Marin-Saint-Siège
United Kingdom	2480.0	2209.6	2169.4	2003.4	1952.0	Royaume-Uni
Belgium	–	2191.3	2142.1	2171.6	e2436.5	Belgique
Indonesia	1353.8	1789.3	2042.1	1767.6	1851.6	Indonésie
Japan	1518.1	1825.4	1978.2	1574.7	1787.5	Japon
Korea, Republic of	1440.1	1461.5	1570.5	1344.6	1323.2	République de Corée
Spain	1167.4	1148.8	1330.3	1435.3	1617.0	Espagne
Switzerland-Liechtenstein	1166.6	1238.7	1212.4	1180.4	1307.5	Suisse-Liechtenstein
China, Hong Kong SAR	1447.3	1262.8	1342.1	1031.7	972.4	Chine - RAS de Hong-Kong
Russian Federation	735.0	727.0	916.2	911.9	881.6	Fédération de Russie
Brazil	851.5	813.0	807.4	813.7	e843.6	Brésil
Norway	732.4	720.8	737.1	719.1	684.0	Norvège
Portugal	647.8	591.7	704.8	700.1	788.6	Portugal
Poland	521.4	508.9	662.3	731.0	894.1	Pologne
Belgium-Luxembourg	2293.9	–	–	–	–	Belgique-Luxembourg
Thailand	412.1	448.9	472.9	441.6	e466.4	Thaïlande
China	224.5	189.2	528.4	549.0	588.9	Chine
Slovakia	279.7	268.0	320.3	344.1	369.2	Slovaquie
Czech Republic	292.6	270.7	315.3	336.8	357.4	République tchèque
Malaysia	216.0	276.3	349.3	342.5	e363.0	Malaisie
Chile	185.3	260.7	304.6	380.8	e372.6	Chili
New Zealand	314.5	321.9	277.6	289.6	293.4	Nouvelle-Zélande

(Value as percentages of World total) **(Valeur en pourcentage du total mondial)**

Regions of the world	1993	1994	1995	1996	1997	1998	1999	2000	2001	2002	Régions du monde
World	100.0	100.0	100.0	100.0	100.0	100.0	100.0	100.0	100.0	100.0	Monde
Africa	0.6	0.5	0.5	0.5	0.4	0.5	0.5	0.5	0.6	0.5	Afrique
Americas	27.4	25.9	25.9	26.1	26.0	24.7	24.7	25.7	25.4	23.3	Amériques
- Northern America	25.1	23.4	23.2	24.0	23.9	22.6	22.6	23.7	23.1	20.9	- Amérique du Nord
- LAIA	2.3	2.4	2.6	2.0	2.1	2.1	2.0	2.0	2.3	2.2	- ALAI
- CACM	0.0	0.0	0.0	0.0	0.0	0.0	0.0	0.0	0.0	0.1	- MCC
- Caribbean	0.0	0.0	0.0	0.0	0.0	0.0	0.0	0.0	0.0	0.0	- Caraïbes
- Rest of America	0.0	0.0	0.0	0.0	0.0	0.0	0.0	0.0	0.0	0.0	- Autre d'Amérique
Asia excluding former USSR	9.1	8.9	8.7	8.7	9.9	10.4	11.4	12.2	11.1	11.2	Asie ancienne URSS exclus
- Middle East	0.2	0.3	0.3	0.2	0.2	0.2	0.2	0.2	0.3	0.3	- Moyen-Orient
Asia former USSR	0.0	0.0	0.0	0.0	0.0	0.0	0.0	0.0	0.0	0.0	Asie ancienne URSS
Europe excluding former USSR	61.1	62.7	63.2	62.6	61.5	62.3	61.2	59.1	60.3	62.3	Europe ancienne URSS exclus
- European Union	56.6	58.7	58.6	58.0	56.9	57.5	56.3	54.1	54.9	56.6	- Union Européenne
- Eastern Europe	1.0	1.0	1.4	1.5	1.6	1.8	1.7	2.1	2.4	2.6	- Europe de l'Est
- Rest of Europe	3.5	3.1	3.2	3.1	3.0	3.0	3.1	3.0	3.0	3.1	- Autre de l'Europe
Europe former USSR	0.9	1.2	1.0	1.3	1.3	1.4	1.4	1.6	1.8	1.8	Europe ancienne URSS
Oceania	0.9	0.9	0.7	0.8	0.8	0.7	0.8	0.7	0.8	0.9	Océanie

642 Paper and paperboard, precut, and articles of paper or paperboard

TRADE BY COMMODITY (Value in million US dollars)
Imports by principal countries or areas

COMMERCE PAR PRODUIT (Valeur en millions de dollars EU)
Importations selon les principaux pays ou zones

Country or area	1998	1999	2000	2001	2002	Pays ou zone
World	23948.4	24910.1	26003.1	26796.1	28868.1	Monde
Africa	502.8	461.9	506.2	519.8	580.2	Afrique
Americas	6155.3	6664.1	7609.7	7811.1	8164.0	Amériques
- Northern America	3538.4	3909.2	4520.6	4709.1	5444.4	- Amérique du Nord
- LAIA	2072.7	2220.9	2503.9	2460.6	2092.7	- ALAI
- CACM	225.9	222.2	259.3	295.4	287.3	- MCC
- Caribbean	251.5	236.9	248.2	274.1	265.0	- Caraïbes
- Rest of America	66.9	74.8	77.7	71.9	74.6	- Autre d'Amérique
Asia excluding former USSR	3341.1	3543.0	3887.7	3764.8	3905.6	Asie ancienne URSS exclus
- Middle East	633.3	620.3	728.7	772.8	795.2	- Moyen-Orient
Asia former USSR	90.0	78.7	111.7	107.5	114.2	Asie ancienne URSS
Europe excluding former USSR	12742.5	13153.4	12790.9	13366.9	14695.7	Europe ancienne URSS exclus
- European Union	10374.1	10786.4	10443.9	10926.9	11939.0	- Union Européenne
- Eastern Europe	1090.4	1062.6	1089.5	1179.9	1350.5	- Europe de l'Est
- Rest of Europe	1278.0	1304.4	1257.5	1260.1	1406.2	- Autre de l'Europe
Europe former USSR	789.0	593.8	671.9	854.5	971.0	Europe ancienne URSS
Oceania	327.6	415.3	425.0	371.4	437.4	Océanie
United States	2261.2	2513.8	3023.2	3180.8	3838.3	Etats-Unis d'Amérique
Germany	1892.2	1968.0	1853.1	2198.9	2143.3	Allemagne
France-Monaco	1932.9	1905.3	1917.2	1871.5	2080.3	France-Monaco
Mexico	1351.6	1559.7	1840.0	1748.1	1489.0	Mexique
United Kingdom	1418.3	1464.0	1519.3	1545.1	1712.4	Royaume-Uni
Canada	1259.3	1375.5	1488.8	1517.9	1591.7	Canada
Netherlands	939.7	1144.6	1030.0	961.1	1125.0	Pays-Bas
China, Hong Kong SAR	834.3	828.6	859.9	790.5	778.1	Chine - RAS de Hong-Kong
Belgium	–	965.4	947.7	982.5	e1077.6	Belgique
Switzerland-Liechtenstein	597.4	608.6	584.3	587.0	659.4	Suisse-Liechtenstein
Spain	465.7	491.8	481.5	527.4	655.6	Espagne
Italy-San Marino-Holy See	499.9	500.1	498.8	518.5	565.6	Italie-Saint-Marin-Saint-Siège
Russian Federation	474.8	338.1	406.3	554.9	606.1	Fédération de Russie
Austria	457.8	486.7	449.7	447.6	498.5	Autriche
Denmark	469.4	439.3	392.1	433.8	468.7	Danemark
China	357.9	403.7	435.4	387.4	400.5	Chine
Poland	395.6	385.6	374.1	378.5	425.4	Pologne
Sweden	374.8	371.7	365.1	369.6	429.6	Suède
Japan	271.2	329.5	416.8	403.5	453.4	Japon
Ireland	386.6	373.2	317.3	342.6	381.5	Irlande
Norway	366.5	363.0	350.9	335.1	373.6	Norvège
Singapore	254.4	271.7	264.6	243.6	262.2	Singapour
Czech Republic	225.9	224.4	242.9	277.2	318.8	République tchèque
Hungary	247.5	243.6	254.6	255.4	287.6	Hongrie
Portugal	217.8	249.6	239.5	255.7	293.8	Portugal
Australia	240.9	260.6	266.0	218.5	269.9	Australie
Greece	198.4	212.6	229.0	243.9	e269.7	Grèce
Belgium-Luxembourg	971.3	–	–	–	–	Belgique-Luxembourg
Malaysia	128.8	165.8	168.6	145.4	e158.9	Malaisie
Finland	149.2	143.1	140.0	147.0	150.5	Finlande

(Value as percentages of World total) **(Valeur en pourcentage du total mondial)**

Regions of the world	1993	1994	1995	1996	1997	1998	1999	2000	2001	2002	Régions du monde
World	100.0	100.0	100.0	100.0	100.0	100.0	100.0	100.0	100.0	100.0	Monde
Africa	2.8	2.0	2.3	2.2	2.1	2.1	1.9	1.9	1.9	2.0	Afrique
Americas	20.0	21.6	21.0	22.2	24.1	25.7	26.8	29.3	29.2	28.3	Amériques
- Northern America	11.0	11.6	11.9	12.9	13.7	14.8	15.7	17.4	17.6	18.9	- Amérique du Nord
- LAIA	7.0	8.1	7.3	7.5	8.3	8.7	8.9	9.6	9.2	7.2	- ALAI
- CACM	0.6	0.7	0.7	0.7	0.9	0.9	0.9	1.0	1.1	1.0	- MCC
- Caribbean	1.0	0.9	1.0	0.9	1.0	1.1	1.0	1.0	1.0	0.9	- Caraïbes
- Rest of America	0.4	0.3	0.2	0.2	0.3	0.3	0.3	0.3	0.3	0.3	- Autre d'Amérique
Asia excluding former USSR	18.1	16.4	15.9	15.8	16.0	14.0	14.2	15.0	14.0	13.5	Asie ancienne URSS exclus
- Middle East	3.0	2.7	2.7	2.5	2.7	2.6	2.5	2.8	2.9	2.8	- Moyen-Orient
Asia former USSR	0.0	0.1	0.2	0.4	0.3	0.4	0.3	0.4	0.4	0.4	Asie ancienne URSS
Europe excluding former USSR	56.5	55.7	56.2	54.7	52.0	53.2	52.8	49.2	49.9	50.9	Europe ancienne URSS exclus
- European Union	47.9	46.8	46.7	44.9	42.4	43.3	43.3	40.2	40.8	41.4	- Union Européenne
- Eastern Europe	2.7	3.0	3.6	4.0	4.3	4.6	4.3	4.2	4.4	4.7	- Europe de l'Est
- Rest of Europe	5.9	5.8	5.9	5.8	5.3	5.3	5.2	4.8	4.7	4.9	- Autre de l'Europe
Europe former USSR	0.7	2.3	2.6	2.9	3.8	3.3	2.4	2.6	3.2	3.4	Europe ancienne URSS
Oceania	1.8	1.9	1.7	1.8	1.7	1.4	1.7	1.6	1.4	1.5	Océanie

TRADE BY COMMODITY (Value in million US dollars)
Exports by principal countries or areas

COMMERCE PAR PRODUIT (Valeur en millions de dollars EU)
Exportations selon les principaux pays ou zones

Country or area	1998	1999	2000	2001	2002	Pays ou zone
World	23498.9	24443.6	25224.3	26176.1	27442.1	Monde
Africa	159.8	180.2	192.3	202.0	255.5	Afrique
Americas	5553.8	6005.2	6462.2	6716.4	6694.2	Amériques
- Northern America	4218.3	4516.6	4906.0	5131.9	5136.0	- Amérique du Nord
- LAIA	1092.2	1264.6	1294.8	1300.4	1285.4	- ALAI
- CACM	162.6	146.5	181.0	200.2	201.7	- MCC
- Caribbean	71.3	70.1	68.7	75.9	61.3	- Caraïbes
- Rest of America	9.3	7.4	11.7	8.0	9.8	- Autre d'Amérique
Asia excluding former USSR	3539.7	3845.8	4369.8	4173.5	4499.2	Asie ancienne URSS exclus
- Middle East	325.2	334.1	365.3	443.7	466.0	- Moyen-Orient
Asia former USSR	2.0	1.8	3.1	7.3	8.1	Asie ancienne URSS
Europe excluding former USSR	13987.8	14154.4	13913.9	14794.2	15651.6	Europe ancienne URSS exclus
- European Union	12698.0	12802.0	12427.4	13067.9	13669.7	- Union Européenne
- Eastern Europe	685.4	724.7	855.8	1102.2	1334.9	- Europe de l'Est
- Rest of Europe	604.3	627.6	630.7	624.2	647.0	- Autre de l'Europe
Europe former USSR	138.8	109.7	143.3	149.2	161.7	Europe ancienne URSS
Oceania	117.1	146.5	139.6	133.6	171.7	Océanie
Germany	3563.9	3560.0	3297.8	3730.4	3584.7	Allemagne
United States	3174.1	3375.6	3551.7	3618.2	3390.5	Etats-Unis d'Amérique
France-Monaco	1668.8	1668.7	1647.3	1591.8	1688.0	France-Monaco
Italy-San Marino-Holy See	1548.2	1589.6	1599.2	1701.3	1815.2	Italie-Saint-Marin-Saint-Siège
Canada	1044.1	1141.0	1354.3	1513.7	1745.2	Canada
United Kingdom	1139.9	1074.5	1011.5	1017.2	1106.9	Royaume-Uni
Netherlands	991.9	1079.9	1019.0	1042.4	1144.7	Pays-Bas
Belgium	–	1157.1	1150.6	1171.2	e1314.1	Belgique
China	736.2	702.5	836.7	892.5	1077.3	Chine
China, Hong Kong SAR	786.5	812.5	886.6	770.3	768.4	Chine - RAS de Hong-Kong
Mexico	635.9	816.3	778.8	754.8	720.9	Mexique
Sweden	642.6	685.9	687.6	667.3	763.6	Suède
Spain	522.6	543.2	593.4	656.3	728.9	Espagne
Austria	522.1	516.6	486.3	488.8	581.5	Autriche
Japan	413.7	457.5	537.4	380.8	414.0	Japon
Switzerland-Liechtenstein	361.9	380.0	380.0	382.8	404.8	Suisse-Liechtenstein
Poland	209.3	232.2	348.1	503.3	598.6	Pologne
Denmark	357.7	341.9	369.8	393.7	348.1	Danemark
Finland	418.7	353.0	327.4	348.2	325.4	Finlande
Korea, Republic of	249.7	311.5	343.7	302.1	300.1	République de Corée
Czech Republic	170.5	181.2	204.4	255.4	330.9	République tchèque
Belgium-Luxembourg	1095.7	–	–	–	–	Belgique-Luxembourg
Indonesia	86.1	186.0	258.4	280.8	266.7	Indonésie
Malaysia	167.0	182.6	200.9	197.3	e209.1	Malaisie
Thailand	120.7	159.2	190.5	224.2	e236.8	Thaïlande
Singapore	169.9	180.2	182.1	158.2	179.7	Singapour
Brazil	145.0	154.6	191.5	183.1	e189.8	Brésil
Hungary	180.6	179.5	140.2	156.1	191.8	Hongrie
Slovakia	107.1	117.3	144.7	163.3	183.0	Slovaquie
Saudi Arabia	123.6	131.5	130.0	146.2	e131.8	Arabie saoudite

(Value as percentages of World total)

(Valeur en pourcentage du total mondial)

Regions of the world	1993	1994	1995	1996	1997	1998	1999	2000	2001	2002	Régions du monde
World	100.0	100.0	100.0	100.0	100.0	100.0	100.0	100.0	100.0	100.0	Monde
Africa	0.6	0.8	0.8	1.0	0.8	0.7	0.7	0.8	0.8	0.9	Afrique
Americas	19.2	19.2	19.1	20.8	23.4	23.6	24.6	25.6	25.7	24.4	Amériques
- Northern America	14.5	15.6	15.3	16.6	18.1	18.0	18.5	19.4	19.6	18.7	- Amérique du Nord
- LAIA	3.8	2.8	3.0	3.4	4.3	4.6	5.2	5.1	5.0	4.7	- ALAI
- CACM	0.5	0.5	0.5	0.5	0.6	0.7	0.6	0.7	0.8	0.7	- MCC
- Caribbean	0.3	0.3	0.3	0.3	0.3	0.3	0.3	0.3	0.3	0.2	- Caraïbes
- Rest of America	0.0	0.1	0.1	0.1	0.1	0.0	0.0	0.0	0.0	0.0	- Autre d'Amérique
Asia excluding former USSR	18.3	17.2	16.5	15.6	16.8	15.1	15.7	17.3	15.9	16.4	Asie ancienne URSS exclus
- Middle East	1.5	1.4	1.4	1.2	1.4	1.4	1.4	1.4	1.7	1.7	- Moyen-Orient
Asia former USSR	0.0	0.0	0.0	0.0	0.0	0.0	0.0	0.0	0.0	0.0	Asie ancienne URSS
Europe excluding former USSR	61.2	61.7	62.5	61.3	57.8	59.5	57.9	55.2	56.5	57.0	Europe ancienne URSS exclus
- European Union	57.4	57.7	57.9	56.4	52.5	54.0	52.4	49.3	49.9	49.8	- Union Européenne
- Eastern Europe	1.1	1.3	2.0	2.4	2.7	2.9	3.0	3.4	4.2	4.9	- Europe de l'Est
- Rest of Europe	2.7	2.7	2.7	2.5	2.5	2.6	2.6	2.5	2.4	2.4	- Autre de l'Europe
Europe former USSR	0.2	0.4	0.5	0.7	0.7	0.6	0.4	0.6	0.6	0.6	Europe ancienne URSS
Oceania	0.5	0.6	0.6	0.6	0.6	0.5	0.6	0.6	0.5	0.6	Océanie

651 Textile yarn

TRADE BY COMMODITY (Value in million US dollars)
Imports by principal countries or areas

COMMERCE PAR PRODUIT (Valeur en millions de dollars EU)
Importations selon les principaux pays ou zones

Country or area	1998	1999	2000	2001	2002	Pays ou zone
World	35676.6	33336.4	35695.0	34018.4	34173.9	Monde
Africa	1009.3	910.1	811.5	801.1	859.8	Afrique
Americas	4325.5	4487.6	5112.4	4548.7	4395.0	Amériques
- Northern America	2731.1	2889.6	3139.4	2800.0	2848.3	- Amérique du Nord
- LAIA	1398.8	1459.0	1808.1	1573.9	1366.5	- ALAI
- CACM	88.0	65.4	96.5	102.7	95.3	- MCC
- Caribbean	97.8	65.3	63.8	67.9	80.9	- Caraïbes
- Rest of America	9.8	8.2	4.6	4.3	4.0	- Autre d'Amérique
Asia excluding former USSR	12880.3	12691.8	14622.1	14268.5	14775.9	Asie ancienne URSS exclus
- Middle East	1368.3	1166.7	1418.7	1444.3	1533.4	- Moyen-Orient
Asia former USSR	19.8	17.0	18.8	15.6	16.6	Asie ancienne URSS
Europe excluding former USSR	16792.1	14564.0	14412.8	13722.2	13427.7	Europe ancienne URSS exclus
- European Union	15118.1	13046.7	12776.9	12004.8	11645.8	- Union Européenne
- Eastern Europe	1079.8	1021.0	1158.1	1248.0	1342.2	- Europe de l'Est
- Rest of Europe	594.2	496.3	477.8	469.4	439.7	- Autre de l'Europe
Europe former USSR	232.8	230.7	301.6	325.4	310.1	Europe ancienne URSS
Oceania	416.7	435.2	415.7	336.9	388.8	Océanie
China, Hong Kong SAR	3460.1	3115.7	3672.6	3572.1	3446.9	Chine - RAS de Hong-Kong
China	2738.5	2402.8	3131.5	3295.6	3688.8	Chine
Italy-San Marino-Holy See	2971.0	2552.6	2764.4	2672.1	2640.0	Italie-Saint-Marin-Saint-Siège
Germany	2575.9	2189.1	2014.0	2120.6	1925.1	Allemagne
United States	1963.4	2098.9	2327.4	2106.3	2154.4	Etats-Unis d'Amérique
France-Monaco	2025.7	1744.4	1703.4	1533.6	1456.5	France-Monaco
Korea, Republic of	1066.6	1562.7	1648.0	1542.1	1594.9	République de Corée
United Kingdom	1744.1	1456.4	1369.6	1240.2	1147.5	Royaume-Uni
Japan	1178.0	1123.6	1121.0	1077.3	1059.1	Japon
Belgium	–	1264.6	1198.0	1128.9	e1238.1	Belgique
Spain	1064.7	962.9	971.6	921.1	896.4	Espagne
Turkey	800.8	657.5	804.4	682.8	1002.5	Turquie
Canada	767.0	790.0	811.8	693.5	693.7	Canada
Portugal	766.2	661.1	650.4	648.2	608.0	Portugal
Netherlands	850.0	782.7	768.3	441.2	439.0	Pays-Bas
Mexico	444.8	586.5	735.2	672.6	621.5	Mexique
Brazil	424.8	396.5	518.0	415.5	353.4	Brésil
Austria	468.4	393.8	365.4	350.8	359.9	Autriche
Poland	385.0	330.3	360.3	395.0	418.4	Pologne
Bangladesh	411.3	e450.4	e306.4	296.8	e290.1	Bangladesh
Czech Republic	302.1	296.7	369.0	371.4	391.2	République tchèque
Australia	357.2	359.4	341.8	273.1	322.2	Australie
Belgium-Luxembourg	1608.7	–	–	–	–	Belgique-Luxembourg
Thailand	227.3	269.4	369.8	354.7	e369.6	Thaïlande
Switzerland-Liechtenstein	315.3	273.5	252.8	223.2	191.0	Suisse-Liechtenstein
Syrian Arab Republic	218.0	223.1	286.0	e356.6	165.8	République arabe syrienne
Denmark	275.2	255.4	250.3	242.3	220.0	Danemark
Indonesia	240.5	205.3	289.6	271.7	233.5	Indonésie
Malaysia	187.6	247.9	276.2	236.7	e258.7	Malaisie
Greece	266.4	237.2	216.8	196.7	e217.5	Grèce

(Value as percentages of World total) **(Valeur en pourcentage du total mondial)**

Regions of the world	1993	1994	1995	1996	1997	1998	1999	2000	2001	2002	Régions du monde
World	100.0	100.0	100.0	100.0	100.0	100.0	100.0	100.0	100.0	100.0	Monde
Africa	2.8	2.6	2.3	2.4	2.3	2.8	2.7	2.3	2.4	2.5	Afrique
Americas	9.5	9.0	9.1	10.0	11.3	12.1	13.5	14.3	13.4	12.9	Amériques
- Northern America	6.5	6.3	5.9	6.3	7.0	7.7	8.7	8.8	8.2	8.3	- Amérique du Nord
- LAIA	2.7	2.4	3.0	3.4	3.9	3.9	4.4	5.1	4.6	4.0	- ALAI
- CACM	0.2	0.1	0.1	0.1	0.2	0.2	0.2	0.3	0.3	0.3	- MCC
- Caribbean	0.1	0.1	0.1	0.1	0.2	0.3	0.2	0.2	0.2	0.2	- Caraïbes
- Rest of America	0.0	0.0	0.0	0.0	0.0	0.0	0.0	0.0	0.0	0.0	- Autre d'Amérique
Asia excluding former USSR	40.8	40.4	40.7	41.4	41.6	36.1	38.1	41.0	41.9	43.2	Asie ancienne URSS exclus
- Middle East	4.4	3.4	3.9	3.9	4.0	3.8	3.5	4.0	4.2	4.5	- Moyen-Orient
Asia former USSR	0.0	0.1	0.0	0.1	0.0	0.1	0.1	0.1	0.0	0.0	Asie ancienne URSS
Europe excluding former USSR	44.6	45.8	45.9	44.2	43.0	47.1	43.7	40.4	40.3	39.3	Europe ancienne URSS exclus
- European Union	41.0	42.2	41.9	40.2	39.1	42.4	39.1	35.8	35.3	34.1	- Union Européenne
- Eastern Europe	1.6	1.6	2.0	2.3	2.4	3.0	3.1	3.2	3.7	3.9	- Europe de l'Est
- Rest of Europe	2.1	2.0	2.0	1.7	1.5	1.7	1.5	1.3	1.4	1.3	- Autre de l'Europe
Europe former USSR	0.5	0.5	0.5	0.6	0.6	0.7	0.7	0.8	1.0	0.9	Europe ancienne URSS
Oceania	1.8	1.8	1.4	1.3	1.2	1.2	1.3	1.2	1.0	1.1	Océanie

TRADE BY COMMODITY (Value in million US dollars)
Exports by principal countries or areas

COMMERCE PAR PRODUIT (Valeur en millions de dollars EU)
Exportations selon les principaux pays ou zones

Country or area	1998	1999	2000	2001	2002	Pays ou zone
World	35310.6	32254.8	34938.8	32920.9	33491.7	Monde
Africa	504.1	395.3	316.3	419.6	400.7	Afrique
Americas	3600.4	3515.7	3929.1	3411.1	3407.5	Amériques
- Northern America	2506.4	2473.8	2743.9	2305.4	2311.1	- Amérique du Nord
- LAIA	1043.4	996.1	1150.6	1069.3	1065.0	- ALAI
- CACM	49.8	45.4	33.5	33.7	28.3	- MCC
- Caribbean	0.7	0.3	1.0	2.7	3.1	- Caraïbes
- Rest of America	0.1	0.1	0.1	0.0	0.0	- Autre d'Amérique
Asia excluding former USSR	15150.6	15239.6	17636.7	16532.9	17161.7	Asie ancienne URSS exclus
- Middle East	781.0	827.1	930.0	999.3	823.4	- Moyen-Orient
Asia former USSR	180.7	216.3	192.3	237.2	234.5	Asie ancienne URSS
Europe excluding former USSR	15022.2	12120.8	12058.0	11579.0	11566.7	Europe ancienne URSS exclus
- European Union	13594.0	10861.8	10645.5	10098.4	10027.8	- Union Européenne
- Eastern Europe	723.6	661.1	833.6	900.2	993.6	- Europe de l'Est
- Rest of Europe	704.7	598.0	578.9	580.4	545.3	- Autre de l'Europe
Europe former USSR	433.4	371.4	404.0	379.0	397.3	Europe ancienne URSS
Oceania	419.1	395.7	402.5	362.0	323.3	Océanie
China, Hong Kong SAR	2916.8	2614.6	3042.2	3114.9	3176.4	Chine - RAS de Hong-Kong
Germany	3416.1	2991.2	2825.7	2727.0	2639.2	Allemagne
China	2078.0	2180.4	2711.0	2765.0	3097.1	Chine
Italy-San Marino-Holy See	2590.6	2479.4	2651.7	2533.3	2481.3	Italie-Saint-Marin-Saint-Siège
United States	1928.2	1887.5	2141.9	1743.0	1733.3	Etats-Unis d'Amérique
India	1448.9	1629.0	2002.9	1606.6	1834.0	Inde
Korea, Republic of	1555.3	1446.0	1585.0	1305.1	1423.9	République de Corée
France-Monaco	1599.8	1443.9	1380.0	1193.9	1248.4	France-Monaco
Indonesia	889.8	1178.3	1327.8	1245.2	1230.8	Indonésie
Pakistan	1118.7	1097.8	1188.5	1097.4	973.1	Pakistan
Japan	1003.4	1092.3	1143.6	1017.0	996.8	Japon
United Kingdom	1533.9	852.0	812.6	772.8	670.8	Royaume-Uni
Belgium	–	984.0	900.7	884.5	e992.3	Belgique
Spain	835.1	745.1	747.9	713.8	717.4	Espagne
Turkey	704.5	733.7	751.1	811.3	665.4	Turquie
Canada	578.2	586.2	602.0	562.4	577.8	Canada
Malaysia	507.4	513.3	572.1	447.3	e474.0	Malaisie
Thailand	461.9	468.1	518.9	504.5	e532.9	Thaïlande
Netherlands	1212.9	281.6	269.9	309.1	308.9	Pays-Bas
Mexico	333.3	350.4	440.2	423.1	423.9	Mexique
Switzerland-Liechtenstein	487.3	408.3	382.9	351.7	313.4	Suisse-Liechtenstein
Australia	368.1	341.8	354.6	326.0	272.8	Australie
Austria	286.3	278.1	264.1	252.7	262.1	Autriche
Czech Republic	176.9	191.3	278.8	296.9	312.0	République tchèque
Belgium-Luxembourg	1196.9	–	–	–	–	Belgique-Luxembourg
Ireland	267.5	225.2	253.8	234.0	210.1	Irlande
Singapore	173.9	211.4	245.5	194.9	241.8	Singapour
Brazil	217.1	215.5	232.8	187.6	e194.5	Brésil
Slovakia	212.3	176.1	196.9	204.6	233.5	Slovaquie
Argentina	170.2	173.4	207.1	192.0	e185.5	Argentine

(Value as percentages of World total) **(Valeur en pourcentage du total mondial)**

Regions of the world	1993	1994	1995	1996	1997	1998	1999	2000	2001	2002	Régions du monde
World	100.0	100.0	100.0	100.0	100.0	100.0	100.0	100.0	100.0	100.0	Monde
Africa	1.8	2.3	1.9	1.4	1.6	1.4	1.2	0.9	1.3	1.2	Afrique
Americas	8.6	8.7	9.2	9.7	10.0	10.2	10.9	11.2	10.4	10.2	Amériques
- Northern America	5.2	5.3	5.5	6.2	6.6	7.1	7.7	7.9	7.0	6.9	- Amérique du Nord
- LAIA	3.2	3.3	3.6	3.4	3.3	3.0	3.1	3.3	3.2	3.2	- ALAI
- CACM	0.1	0.1	0.1	0.1	0.1	0.1	0.1	0.1	0.1	0.1	- MCC
- Caribbean	0.0	0.0	0.0	0.0	0.0	0.0	0.0	0.0	0.0	0.0	- Caraïbes
- Rest of America	0.0	0.0	0.0	0.0	0.0	0.0	0.0	0.0	0.0	0.0	- Autre d'Amérique
Asia excluding former USSR	46.3	44.7	44.8	46.0	45.8	42.9	47.2	50.5	50.2	51.2	Asie ancienne URSS exclus
- Middle East	1.4	2.1	1.5	1.6	1.9	2.2	2.6	2.7	3.0	2.5	- Moyen-Orient
Asia former USSR	0.0	0.3	0.1	0.3	0.2	0.5	0.7	0.6	0.7	0.7	Asie ancienne URSS
Europe excluding former USSR	41.7	42.2	41.6	40.0	39.7	42.5	37.6	34.5	35.2	34.5	Europe ancienne URSS exclus
- European Union	37.3	37.8	37.2	36.2	36.0	38.5	33.7	30.5	30.7	29.9	- Union Européenne
- Eastern Europe	1.5	1.5	1.9	1.7	1.8	2.0	2.0	2.4	2.7	3.0	- Europe de l'Est
- Rest of Europe	2.9	2.8	2.6	2.2	1.9	2.0	1.9	1.7	1.8	1.6	- Autre de l'Europe
Europe former USSR	0.7	0.8	1.1	1.2	1.2	1.2	1.2	1.2	1.2	1.2	Europe ancienne URSS
Oceania	0.9	1.0	1.3	1.3	1.4	1.2	1.2	1.2	1.1	1.0	Océanie

652 Cotton fabrics, woven (not including narrow or special fabrics)

TRADE BY COMMODITY (Value in million US dollars)
Imports by principal countries or areas

COMMERCE PAR PRODUIT (Valeur en millions de dollars EU)
Importations selon les principaux pays ou zones

Country or area	1998	1999	2000	2001	2002	Pays ou zone
World	20917.0	19855.6	20192.8	19979.4	21437.5	Monde
Africa	1643.7	1520.3	1438.4	1613.3	1678.0	Afrique
Americas	3304.6	3485.7	3926.6	3543.5	3868.8	Amériques
- Northern America	2161.5	2032.9	2165.4	1893.3	2056.6	- Amérique du Nord
- LAIA	916.9	1281.1	1570.0	1370.9	1457.6	- ALAI
- CACM	54.9	45.7	42.7	47.6	52.0	- MCC
- Caribbean	161.1	118.3	140.0	224.2	297.2	- Caraïbes
- Rest of America	10.1	7.6	8.5	7.4	5.5	- Autre d'Amérique
Asia excluding former USSR	7696.3	7855.8	8339.5	7758.1	8602.2	Asie ancienne URSS exclus
- Middle East	726.8	671.1	746.9	811.9	1214.5	- Moyen-Orient
Asia former USSR	19.9	10.7	14.1	13.2	12.4	Asie ancienne URSS
Europe excluding former USSR	7784.4	6504.0	5991.0	6539.4	6739.0	Europe ancienne URSS exclus
- European Union	5931.9	5010.1	4545.4	4897.8	4854.1	- Union Européenne
- Eastern Europe	1107.8	1076.2	1171.7	1347.9	1589.6	- Europe de l'Est
- Rest of Europe	744.8	417.7	273.9	293.7	295.3	- Autre de l'Europe
Europe former USSR	226.8	205.7	242.4	312.7	319.1	Europe ancienne URSS
Oceania	241.3	273.5	240.9	199.1	218.0	Océanie
China, Hong Kong SAR	2434.8	2363.7	2374.6	2081.7	2322.5	Chine - RAS de Hong-Kong
United States	1778.5	1696.2	1810.8	1591.1	1760.5	Etats-Unis d'Amérique
China	1526.9	1600.5	1796.6	1788.8	1887.2	Chine
Mexico	524.6	980.3	1210.0	994.0	1127.5	Mexique
Germany	1100.2	907.1	802.1	872.6	813.4	Allemagne
Italy-San Marino-Holy See	906.2	774.5	764.3	942.1	918.9	Italie-Saint-Marin-Saint-Siège
United Kingdom	992.9	804.8	676.6	636.1	587.8	Royaume-Uni
France-Monaco	860.0	703.1	677.5	724.5	674.3	France-Monaco
Tunisia	666.5	605.8	558.9	698.4	e698.3	Tunisie
Bangladesh	489.0	e535.4	e469.9	455.2	e444.9	Bangladesh
Turkey	359.4	295.6	352.1	436.4	796.4	Turquie
Morocco	430.4	397.6	397.5	468.2	e494.1	Maroc
Poland	425.1	404.0	409.6	422.0	471.9	Pologne
Belgium	–	504.6	462.5	470.8	e516.4	Belgique
Japan	407.4	421.9	411.1	367.9	321.6	Japon
Romania	247.2	263.2	344.5	444.2	582.4	Roumanie
Sri Lanka	e377.9	340.9	e460.4	336.5	332.4	Sri Lanka
Spain	318.1	313.4	306.6	398.3	462.9	Espagne
Canada	382.9	336.7	354.1	301.7	295.7	Canada
Korea, Republic of	169.3	283.4	317.8	306.9	377.7	République de Corée
Portugal	289.3	255.2	235.2	243.4	254.8	Portugal
Philippines	232.4	247.5	243.1	215.2	199.5	Philippines
Netherlands	239.3	228.1	196.7	177.4	172.0	Pays-Bas
China, Macao SAR	194.2	185.0	195.5	200.7	199.0	Chine - RAS de Macao
Thailand	160.5	199.8	220.6	191.7	e199.7	Thaïlande
Australia	194.6	195.6	171.8	136.5	152.7	Australie
Indonesia	139.2	119.2	184.2	164.9	151.9	Indonésie
Malaysia	161.7	158.4	156.4	129.1	e141.1	Malaisie
Dominican Republic	e114.2	e76.5	e94.5	e175.3	e244.4	République dominicaine
Hungary	140.2	129.4	121.6	140.1	167.6	Hongrie

(Value as percentages of World total) **(Valeur en pourcentage du total mondial)**

Regions of the world	1993	1994	1995	1996	1997	1998	1999	2000	2001	2002	Régions du monde
World	100.0	100.0	100.0	100.0	100.0	100.0	100.0	100.0	100.0	100.0	Monde
Africa	7.9	6.4	6.0	6.0	6.0	7.9	7.7	7.1	8.1	7.8	Afrique
Americas	15.7	13.5	13.5	13.3	14.9	15.8	17.6	19.4	17.7	18.0	Amériques
- Northern America	11.9	10.1	9.9	9.3	10.5	10.3	10.2	10.7	9.5	9.6	- Amérique du Nord
- LAIA	3.0	2.7	2.9	3.1	3.5	4.4	6.5	7.8	6.9	6.8	- ALAI
- CACM	0.3	0.2	0.2	0.2	0.3	0.3	0.2	0.2	0.2	0.2	- MCC
- Caribbean	0.4	0.3	0.4	0.5	0.7	0.8	0.6	0.7	1.1	1.4	- Caraïbes
- Rest of America	0.1	0.1	0.1	0.1	0.0	0.0	0.0	0.0	0.0	0.0	- Autre d'Amérique
Asia excluding former USSR	39.0	40.4	41.9	41.8	40.7	36.8	39.6	41.3	38.8	40.1	Asie ancienne URSS exclus
- Middle East	3.4	3.5	3.7	3.2	3.8	3.5	3.4	3.7	4.1	5.7	- Moyen-Orient
Asia former USSR	0.1	0.1	0.1	0.2	0.1	0.1	0.1	0.1	0.1	0.1	Asie ancienne URSS
Europe excluding former USSR	34.3	36.8	35.4	35.8	35.6	37.2	32.8	29.7	32.7	31.4	Europe ancienne URSS exclus
- European Union	29.0	29.0	28.9	29.0	28.7	28.4	25.2	22.5	24.5	22.6	- Union Européenne
- Eastern Europe	3.0	3.1	4.0	4.5	4.8	5.3	5.4	5.8	6.7	7.4	- Europe de l'Est
- Rest of Europe	2.3	4.7	2.4	2.3	2.1	3.6	2.1	1.4	1.5	1.4	- Autre de l'Europe
Europe former USSR	1.0	1.0	1.2	1.1	1.1	1.1	1.0	1.2	1.6	1.5	Europe ancienne URSS
Oceania	2.1	1.7	1.8	1.7	1.5	1.2	1.4	1.2	1.0	1.0	Océanie

TRADE BY COMMODITY (Value in million US dollars)
Exports by principal countries or areas

COMMERCE PAR PRODUIT (Valeur en millions de dollars EU)
Exportations selon les principaux pays ou zones

Country or area	1998	1999	2000	2001	2002	Pays ou zone
World	22226.9	21386.6	22386.7	22317.9	24520.7	Monde
Africa	304.8	253.2	254.8	309.1	272.3	Afrique
Americas	1944.2	1969.6	2410.7	2271.0	2351.8	Amériques
- Northern America	1135.3	1348.4	1710.9	1681.0	1777.1	- Amérique du Nord
- LAIA	758.6	588.7	670.6	576.6	562.2	- ALAI
- CACM	46.3	30.0	27.4	11.6	11.1	- MCC
- Caribbean	3.9	2.5	1.7	1.7	1.2	- Caraïbes
- Rest of America	0.0	0.0	0.0	0.1	0.2	- Autre d'Amérique
Asia excluding former USSR	11266.1	11609.8	12484.5	11966.1	13658.1	Asie ancienne URSS exclus
- Middle East	548.7	475.1	546.8	632.8	704.7	- Moyen-Orient
Asia former USSR	79.5	99.7	106.8	114.7	118.2	Asie ancienne URSS
Europe excluding former USSR	8333.1	7231.7	6863.6	7407.9	7863.2	Europe ancienne URSS exclus
- European Union	7554.1	6662.2	6335.1	6817.5	7239.3	- Union Européenne
- Eastern Europe	379.1	292.4	282.7	329.5	346.2	- Europe de l'Est
- Rest of Europe	399.9	277.2	245.8	260.8	277.7	- Autre de l'Europe
Europe former USSR	247.0	173.1	221.4	213.6	220.9	Europe ancienne URSS
Oceania	52.4	49.6	45.0	35.6	36.2	Océanie
China	2698.7	2720.4	3122.9	3233.0	4293.2	Chine
China, Hong Kong SAR	3135.8	3090.5	3140.1	2828.7	3045.3	Chine - RAS de Hong-Kong
Italy-San Marino-Holy See	1808.2	1704.8	1769.6	2085.0	2355.6	Italie-Saint-Marin-Saint-Siège
United States	1020.8	1254.0	1619.2	1605.7	1711.9	Etats-Unis d'Amérique
Germany	1574.9	1291.5	1157.0	1226.0	1226.5	Allemagne
Pakistan	1188.8	1171.4	1073.0	1044.3	1241.9	Pakistan
France-Monaco	1167.8	1001.8	986.1	1034.6	1015.1	France-Monaco
India	946.7	990.8	1102.6	974.6	1009.3	Inde
Japan	742.5	884.3	990.5	934.5	989.7	Japon
Belgium	–	881.9	777.6	789.9	e886.3	Belgique
Korea, Republic of	417.1	604.4	703.1	647.0	661.5	République de Corée
Spain	466.2	464.9	485.3	563.9	599.0	Espagne
Turkey	445.8	368.6	413.2	524.2	586.9	Turquie
Indonesia	293.0	374.2	452.1	430.6	373.3	Indonésie
United Kingdom	448.9	381.6	321.5	287.8	303.7	Royaume-Uni
Netherlands	376.9	328.0	304.1	279.3	300.6	Pays-Bas
Thailand	303.4	287.4	319.1	279.9	e295.6	Thaïlande
Mexico	357.1	303.3	355.0	220.5	216.4	Mexique
Austria	277.7	218.8	187.2	198.7	194.7	Autriche
Czech Republic	251.3	191.4	185.5	213.0	220.0	République tchèque
Brazil	208.6	165.2	189.4	225.8	e234.0	Brésil
Belgium-Luxembourg	967.1	–	–	–	–	Belgique-Luxembourg
Switzerland-Liechtenstein	222.0	193.5	179.7	180.8	181.5	Suisse-Liechtenstein
Portugal	202.9	170.3	160.7	168.8	180.0	Portugal
Malaysia	115.9	113.4	116.6	112.9	e119.7	Malaisie
Russian Federation	100.9	82.4	119.8	114.5	115.8	Fédération de Russie
Canada	114.5	94.4	91.7	75.3	65.2	Canada
Singapore	81.3	85.8	79.0	65.4	65.3	Singapour
Uzbekistan	e44.6	e64.0	e63.5	e80.6	e83.1	Ouzbékistan
Denmark	67.0	64.2	60.7	67.2	62.7	Danemark

(Value as percentages of World total) **(Valeur en pourcentage du total mondial)**

Regions of the world	1993	1994	1995	1996	1997	1998	1999	2000	2001	2002	Régions du monde
World	100.0	100.0	100.0	100.0	100.0	100.0	100.0	100.0	100.0	100.0	Monde
Africa	1.9	1.8	1.8	1.6	1.6	1.4	1.2	1.1	1.4	1.1	Afrique
Americas	6.4	6.8	7.5	7.9	8.4	8.7	9.2	10.8	10.2	9.6	Amériques
- Northern America	4.1	4.3	4.3	4.5	4.7	5.1	6.3	7.6	7.5	7.2	- Amérique du Nord
- LAIA	2.3	2.3	3.1	3.3	3.6	3.4	2.8	3.0	2.6	2.3	- ALAI
- CACM	0.1	0.1	0.1	0.1	0.1	0.2	0.1	0.1	0.1	0.0	- MCC
- Caribbean	0.0	0.0	0.0	0.0	0.0	0.0	0.0	0.0	0.0	0.0	- Caraïbes
- Rest of America	0.0	0.0	0.0	0.0	0.0	0.0	0.0	0.0	0.0	0.0	- Autre d'Amérique
Asia excluding former USSR	55.3	54.3	53.4	53.0	53.8	50.7	54.3	55.8	53.6	55.7	Asie ancienne URSS exclus
- Middle East	1.6	2.8	2.2	2.8	3.3	2.5	2.2	2.4	2.8	2.9	- Moyen-Orient
Asia former USSR	0.1	0.6	0.1	0.4	0.3	0.4	0.5	0.5	0.5	0.5	Asie ancienne URSS
Europe excluding former USSR	35.2	35.4	36.0	35.5	34.3	37.5	33.8	30.7	33.2	32.1	Europe ancienne URSS exclus
- European Union	31.8	32.1	32.3	32.5	31.4	34.0	31.2	28.3	30.5	29.5	- Union Européenne
- Eastern Europe	1.3	1.2	1.7	1.4	1.5	1.7	1.4	1.3	1.5	1.4	- Europe de l'Est
- Rest of Europe	2.1	2.0	1.9	1.5	1.4	1.8	1.3	1.1	1.2	1.1	- Autre de l'Europe
Europe former USSR	0.9	0.9	1.0	1.1	1.3	1.1	0.8	1.0	1.0	0.9	Europe ancienne URSS
Oceania	0.2	0.2	0.3	0.4	0.3	0.2	0.2	0.2	0.2	0.1	Océanie

653 Fabrics, woven, of man-made fibres (not narrow or special fabrics)

TRADE BY COMMODITY (Value in million US dollars)
Imports by principal countries or areas

COMMERCE PAR PRODUIT (Valeur en millions de dollars EU)
Importations selon les principaux pays ou zones

Country or area	1998	1999	2000	2001	2002	Pays ou zone
World	30302.3	28476.0	29134.3	26634.7	25976.6	Monde
Africa	1475.8	1346.7	1253.1	1236.3	1293.7	Afrique
Americas	3971.3	3898.6	4397.1	3987.8	4003.9	Amériques
- Northern America	2098.1	1923.1	2029.6	1682.9	1769.3	- Amérique du Nord
- LAIA	1609.4	1767.5	2145.5	2049.7	1956.4	- ALAI
- CACM	74.8	58.2	66.3	62.8	85.1	- MCC
- Caribbean	154.0	120.3	124.6	159.5	167.3	- Caraïbes
- Rest of America	34.9	29.6	31.1	32.9	25.8	- Autre d'Amérique
Asia excluding former USSR	13175.5	12761.3	13871.1	12173.7	11591.1	Asie ancienne URSS exclus
- Middle East	2863.7	2700.2	2671.1	2500.0	2622.3	- Moyen-Orient
Asia former USSR	35.8	45.2	52.0	39.7	40.2	Asie ancienne URSS
Europe excluding former USSR	10637.0	9460.1	8568.9	8234.1	8121.0	Europe ancienne URSS exclus
- European Union	8159.4	7126.1	6283.3	5926.8	5690.3	- Union Européenne
- Eastern Europe	2128.5	2001.4	1966.9	1982.0	2097.8	- Europe de l'Est
- Rest of Europe	349.0	332.6	318.7	325.4	332.9	- Autre de l'Europe
Europe former USSR	565.0	524.5	561.7	609.2	615.7	Europe ancienne URSS
Oceania	442.0	439.6	430.4	353.8	311.0	Océanie
China	3398.0	3485.0	3840.4	3436.9	3180.5	Chine
China, Hong Kong SAR	3021.5	2627.8	2695.8	2144.7	1751.2	Chine - RAS de Hong-Kong
United States	1503.7	1366.2	1445.1	1188.1	1270.5	Etats-Unis d'Amérique
Germany	1688.0	1470.9	1255.1	1212.9	1035.2	Allemagne
Mexico	909.5	1210.6	1481.5	1396.9	1382.5	Mexique
United Kingdom	1591.2	1364.5	1174.6	1095.3	1075.8	Royaume-Uni
United Arab Emirates	1186.5	1243.3	1227.0	1180.1	e1210.7	Emirates arabes unis
France-Monaco	1057.1	924.9	871.9	786.5	787.2	France-Monaco
Italy-San Marino-Holy See	882.3	786.2	737.7	694.4	641.4	Italie-Saint-Marin-Saint-Siège
Romania	582.0	619.2	644.2	698.4	785.0	Roumanie
Poland	810.0	674.3	615.4	592.1	613.3	Pologne
Spain	760.5	675.1	620.0	612.7	590.9	Espagne
Canada	594.3	556.8	584.3	494.6	498.7	Canada
Bangladesh	445.8	e488.2	e577.2	559.1	e546.5	Bangladesh
Korea, Republic of	491.2	553.8	599.7	461.2	417.8	République de Corée
Viet Nam	379.7	422.9	489.2	507.7	617.8	Viet Nam
Saudi Arabia	477.7	507.1	502.8	432.5	e447.6	Arabie saoudite
Turkey	599.1	480.3	451.9	352.5	475.9	Turquie
Morocco	454.6	422.7	400.0	377.3	e398.1	Maroc
Tunisia	410.4	379.0	326.4	359.6	e359.5	Tunisie
Thailand	293.0	330.4	418.4	380.3	e396.2	Thaïlande
Sri Lanka	e371.9	335.5	e453.1	323.7	302.7	Sri Lanka
Belgium	–	421.5	402.3	393.1	e431.1	Belgique
Netherlands	368.6	352.1	291.5	245.9	251.6	Pays-Bas
Portugal	382.0	330.4	278.5	263.9	246.8	Portugal
Singapore	240.8	267.7	295.5	207.9	229.8	Singapour
Philippines	286.4	261.3	285.3	233.3	174.4	Philippines
Japan	272.0	249.4	261.5	234.8	200.2	Japon
Hungary	283.7	259.7	235.7	205.5	194.1	Hongrie
Australia	274.8	247.3	224.7	168.3	171.5	Australie

(Value as percentages of World total) **(Valeur en pourcentage du total mondial)**

Regions of the world	1993	1994	1995	1996	1997	1998	1999	2000	2001	2002	Régions du monde
World	100.0	100.0	100.0	100.0	100.0	100.0	100.0	100.0	100.0	100.0	Monde
Africa	3.0	3.0	3.1	3.0	3.1	4.9	4.7	4.3	4.6	5.0	Afrique
Americas	12.2	11.9	10.6	10.6	12.3	13.1	13.7	15.1	15.0	15.4	Amériques
- Northern America	6.8	6.3	5.6	5.9	6.8	6.9	6.8	7.0	6.3	6.8	- Amérique du Nord
- LAIA	4.7	5.0	4.4	4.0	4.7	5.3	6.2	7.4	7.7	7.5	- ALAI
- CACM	0.2	0.2	0.2	0.2	0.3	0.2	0.2	0.2	0.2	0.3	- MCC
- Caribbean	0.3	0.2	0.3	0.4	0.4	0.5	0.4	0.4	0.6	0.6	- Caraïbes
- Rest of America	0.1	0.1	0.1	0.1	0.1	0.1	0.1	0.1	0.1	0.1	- Autre d'Amérique
Asia excluding former USSR	50.5	51.6	50.8	50.8	48.8	43.5	44.8	47.6	45.7	44.6	Asie ancienne URSS exclus
- Middle East	8.9	8.8	8.3	7.5	8.2	9.5	9.5	9.2	9.4	10.1	- Moyen-Orient
Asia former USSR	0.1	0.1	0.1	0.1	0.1	0.1	0.2	0.2	0.1	0.2	Asie ancienne URSS
Europe excluding former USSR	30.9	30.8	32.5	32.5	32.8	35.1	33.2	29.4	30.9	31.3	Europe ancienne URSS exclus
- European Union	25.7	25.7	26.6	26.1	25.9	26.9	25.0	21.6	22.3	21.9	- Union Européenne
- Eastern Europe	3.9	3.9	4.7	5.3	5.9	7.0	7.0	6.8	7.4	8.1	- Europe de l'Est
- Rest of Europe	1.3	1.3	1.2	1.1	1.1	1.2	1.2	1.1	1.2	1.3	- Autre de l'Europe
Europe former USSR	1.4	0.9	1.3	1.4	1.5	1.9	1.8	1.9	2.3	2.4	Europe ancienne URSS
Oceania	1.9	1.6	1.8	1.5	1.5	1.5	1.5	1.5	1.3	1.2	Océanie

TRADE BY COMMODITY (Value in million US dollars)
Exports by principal countries or areas

COMMERCE PAR PRODUIT (Valeur en millions de dollars EU)
Exportations selon les principaux pays ou zones

Country or area	1998	1999	2000	2001	2002	Pays ou zone
World	32478.2	30617.3	32151.8	28576.6	28388.4	Monde
Africa	93.0	85.4	83.7	91.7	108.8	Afrique
Americas	1726.5	1928.4	2453.4	2113.0	1998.7	Amériques
- Northern America	1425.1	1562.7	1937.7	1774.1	1715.3	- Amérique du Nord
- LAIA	244.8	310.3	466.7	301.8	250.6	- ALAI
- CACM	49.2	48.8	42.7	29.4	27.3	- MCC
- Caribbean	7.4	6.6	6.2	6.8	5.2	- Caraïbes
- Rest of America	0.1	0.0	0.2	1.0	0.3	- Autre d'Amérique
Asia excluding former USSR	19205.8	18575.2	20555.9	17778.2	17672.5	Asie ancienne URSS exclus
- Middle East	1487.4	1456.5	1795.5	1420.8	1577.6	- Moyen-Orient
Asia former USSR	2.5	1.2	1.1	4.9	6.9	Asie ancienne URSS
Europe excluding former USSR	11248.7	9879.3	8911.6	8441.0	8464.9	Europe ancienne URSS exclus
- European Union	10624.2	9303.4	8341.4	7899.0	7919.1	- Union Européenne
- Eastern Europe	339.5	333.6	342.1	344.8	364.6	- Europe de l'Est
- Rest of Europe	285.0	242.3	228.0	197.2	181.2	- Autre de l'Europe
Europe former USSR	131.4	93.6	95.2	101.6	95.4	Europe ancienne URSS
Oceania	70.1	54.1	50.8	46.1	41.3	Océanie
Korea, Republic of	4623.7	4245.8	4308.7	3390.2	2895.7	République de Corée
China	2477.6	2352.4	3124.7	3294.7	3822.7	Chine
Japan	2103.9	2232.9	2280.5	1984.4	1768.6	Japon
China, Hong Kong SAR	2427.7	2178.6	2203.0	1815.8	1578.1	Chine - RAS de Hong-Kong
Italy-San Marino-Holy See	2445.7	2100.4	1936.1	1904.9	1814.9	Italie-Saint-Marin-Saint-Siège
Germany	2626.5	2157.5	1798.2	1711.1	1546.1	Allemagne
United States	1207.6	1343.8	1710.0	1560.7	1494.4	Etats-Unis d'Amérique
France-Monaco	1698.9	1504.5	1390.8	1225.3	1248.7	France-Monaco
Indonesia	905.5	1014.0	1119.4	996.4	836.8	Indonésie
United Arab Emirates	779.8	804.6	1122.0	710.9	e740.4	Emirates arabes unis
Belgium	–	1067.5	981.1	937.4	e1051.7	Belgique
United Kingdom	713.9	659.7	618.5	609.6	674.1	Royaume-Uni
Spain	682.1	652.3	598.4	630.2	681.1	Espagne
Turkey	616.1	576.7	577.9	583.2	668.2	Turquie
India	364.4	394.1	506.0	623.2	759.8	Inde
Thailand	529.0	525.4	522.3	454.5	e480.0	Thaïlande
Pakistan	557.6	414.3	509.3	488.8	447.4	Pakistan
Netherlands	455.9	415.3	370.0	295.3	311.2	Pays-Bas
Malaysia	300.0	304.2	355.5	282.2	e299.0	Malaisie
Belgium-Luxembourg	1159.0	–	–	–	–	Belgique-Luxembourg
Mexico	130.7	224.0	365.4	216.7	166.6	Mexique
Canada	217.5	218.9	227.6	213.4	220.9	Canada
Singapore	278.8	245.5	241.4	168.8	146.3	Singapour
Portugal	217.9	215.7	193.2	186.5	192.9	Portugal
Austria	289.8	199.6	141.4	126.9	123.4	Autriche
Czech Republic	144.1	141.3	151.2	157.0	152.3	République tchèque
Switzerland-Liechtenstein	191.2	164.1	146.3	122.1	110.4	Suisse-Liechtenstein
Denmark	126.5	128.8	126.0	105.8	96.5	Danemark
Sweden	103.4	96.5	91.4	81.5	94.2	Suède
Poland	65.1	63.3	61.9	55.5	64.8	Pologne

(Value as percentages of World total) **(Valeur en pourcentage du total mondial)**

Regions of the world	1993	1994	1995	1996	1997	1998	1999	2000	2001	2002	Régions du monde
World	100.0	100.0	100.0	100.0	100.0	100.0	100.0	100.0	100.0	100.0	Monde
Africa	0.3	0.3	0.3	0.4	0.3	0.3	0.3	0.3	0.3	0.4	Afrique
Americas	4.2	4.3	4.0	4.5	4.8	5.3	6.3	7.6	7.4	7.0	Amériques
- Northern America	3.4	3.4	3.2	3.6	4.0	4.4	5.1	6.0	6.2	6.0	- Amérique du Nord
- LAIA	0.7	0.8	0.7	0.7	0.7	0.8	1.0	1.5	1.1	0.9	- ALAI
- CACM	0.1	0.1	0.1	0.1	0.1	0.2	0.2	0.1	0.1	0.1	- MCC
- Caribbean	0.0	0.0	0.0	0.0	0.0	0.0	0.0	0.0	0.0	0.0	- Caraïbes
- Rest of America	0.0	0.0	0.0	0.0	0.0	0.0	0.0	0.0	0.0	0.0	- Autre d'Amérique
Asia excluding former USSR	64.7	64.0	62.7	62.3	63.2	59.1	60.7	63.9	62.2	62.3	Asie ancienne URSS exclus
- Middle East	1.5	1.6	2.2	2.4	2.8	4.6	4.8	5.6	5.0	5.6	- Moyen-Orient
Asia former USSR	0.0	0.0	0.0	0.0	0.0	0.0	0.0	0.0	0.0	0.0	Asie ancienne URSS
Europe excluding former USSR	30.5	31.0	32.6	32.2	31.1	34.6	32.3	27.7	29.5	29.8	Europe ancienne URSS exclus
- European Union	28.8	29.5	30.8	30.5	29.4	32.7	30.4	25.9	27.6	27.9	- Union Européenne
- Eastern Europe	0.6	0.6	0.9	0.8	0.8	1.0	1.1	1.1	1.2	1.3	- Europe de l'Est
- Rest of Europe	1.0	1.0	0.9	0.9	0.8	0.9	0.8	0.7	0.7	0.6	- Autre de l'Europe
Europe former USSR	0.2	0.2	0.2	0.4	0.4	0.4	0.3	0.3	0.4	0.3	Europe ancienne URSS
Oceania	0.1	0.2	0.2	0.2	0.2	0.2	0.2	0.2	0.2	0.1	Océanie

654 Textile fabrics, woven, other than cotton or man-made fibres

TRADE BY COMMODITY (Value in million US dollars)
Imports by principal countries or areas

COMMERCE PAR PRODUIT (Valeur en millions de dollars EU)
Importations selon les principaux pays ou zones

Country or area	1998	1999	2000	2001	2002	Pays ou zone
World	8754.5	8171.5	8470.1	8072.3	7789.4	Monde
Africa	193.9	201.6	183.2	184.7	206.3	Afrique
Americas	1311.6	1219.6	1294.3	1170.9	1070.9	Amériques
- Northern America	1022.5	972.5	1011.6	873.3	836.9	- Amérique du Nord
- LAIA	225.9	206.6	232.3	244.7	182.3	- ALAI
- CACM	11.8	7.4	10.9	8.0	6.4	- MCC
- Caribbean	50.0	31.8	38.3	44.1	44.2	- Caraïbes
- Rest of America	1.4	1.3	1.2	0.9	1.1	- Autre d'Amérique
Asia excluding former USSR	2755.5	2591.3	3060.3	2846.3	2851.9	Asie ancienne URSS exclus
- Middle East	284.5	253.9	264.1	252.4	291.6	- Moyen-Orient
Asia former USSR	11.7	13.6	11.9	8.9	11.2	Asie ancienne URSS
Europe excluding former USSR	4122.6	3799.5	3574.3	3504.4	3289.2	Europe ancienne URSS exclus
- European Union	3051.8	2853.6	2654.1	2515.4	2313.8	- Union Européenne
- Eastern Europe	850.6	750.8	716.5	758.6	760.1	- Europe de l'Est
- Rest of Europe	220.2	195.1	203.7	230.4	215.3	- Autre de l'Europe
Europe former USSR	242.3	218.4	232.2	244.2	259.4	Europe ancienne URSS
Oceania	116.9	127.5	114.0	112.8	100.5	Océanie
China	727.9	724.7	878.0	897.6	921.6	Chine
United States	803.4	781.0	820.2	691.2	661.3	Etats-Unis d'Amérique
Germany	945.9	829.9	740.5	700.0	538.9	Allemagne
China, Hong Kong SAR	707.5	608.3	686.2	567.4	557.5	Chine - RAS de Hong-Kong
France-Monaco	428.9	402.9	393.9	361.3	338.4	France-Monaco
Japan	389.0	363.7	412.9	396.3	337.0	Japon
Italy-San Marino-Holy See	353.1	330.1	365.1	356.4	341.9	Italie-Saint-Marin-Saint-Siège
United Kingdom	400.2	357.3	306.5	305.4	277.8	Royaume-Uni
Korea, Republic of	241.5	264.6	362.3	323.1	319.9	République de Corée
Romania	217.0	227.4	204.3	231.0	243.3	Roumanie
Poland	246.6	217.9	213.7	211.9	191.0	Pologne
Spain	185.8	233.6	210.3	200.0	207.5	Espagne
Canada	218.4	190.6	191.4	181.9	175.5	Canada
Turkey	145.3	132.1	140.2	125.9	160.3	Turquie
Portugal	143.9	137.5	122.9	113.2	100.4	Portugal
Mexico	101.8	107.2	128.2	142.3	112.1	Mexique
Hungary	133.0	119.4	101.6	105.5	103.6	Hongrie
Netherlands	115.2	116.6	108.9	88.2	98.1	Pays-Bas
Switzerland-Liechtenstein	115.4	106.0	98.9	102.2	93.6	Suisse-Liechtenstein
Belgium	–	126.4	122.3	115.6	e126.7	Belgique
Morocco	89.3	108.9	94.0	91.7	e96.8	Maroc
Austria	111.1	86.4	78.3	83.6	77.1	Autriche
Czech Republic	130.9	72.4	67.6	71.5	71.4	République tchèque
Australia	94.4	94.2	77.5	60.1	60.6	Australie
Denmark	64.5	80.5	69.6	70.2	82.6	Danemark
Bulgaria	54.6	54.7	70.0	e78.2	e86.0	Bulgarie
Ukraine	69.0	50.9	65.5	72.0	77.6	Ukraine
Thailand	58.3	58.2	70.0	66.3	e69.1	Thaïlande
Slovakia	67.2	57.7	57.9	59.3	63.6	Slovaquie
Russian Federation	59.5	57.0	51.3	59.5	54.3	Fédération de Russie

(Value as percentages of World total) **(Valeur en pourcentage du total mondial)**

Regions of the world	1993	1994	1995	1996	1997	1998	1999	2000	2001	2002	Régions du monde
World	100.0	100.0	100.0	100.0	100.0	100.0	100.0	100.0	100.0	100.0	Monde
Africa	1.6	1.8	1.8	1.7	1.5	2.2	2.5	2.2	2.3	2.6	Afrique
Americas	13.4	12.2	11.7	12.4	14.2	15.0	14.9	15.3	14.5	13.7	Amériques
- Northern America	10.8	9.9	9.5	10.1	10.8	11.7	11.9	11.9	10.8	10.7	- Amérique du Nord
- LAIA	2.2	1.9	1.8	1.8	2.8	2.6	2.5	2.7	3.0	2.3	- ALAI
- CACM	0.1	0.0	0.1	0.1	0.2	0.1	0.1	0.1	0.1	0.1	- MCC
- Caribbean	0.3	0.2	0.2	0.4	0.4	0.6	0.4	0.5	0.5	0.6	- Caraïbes
- Rest of America	0.1	0.1	0.0	0.0	0.0	0.0	0.0	0.0	0.0	0.0	- Autre d'Amérique
Asia excluding former USSR	39.3	39.8	38.7	38.9	37.8	31.5	31.7	36.1	35.3	36.6	Asie ancienne URSS exclus
- Middle East	2.8	2.6	2.4	2.8	3.4	3.2	3.1	3.1	3.1	3.7	- Moyen-Orient
Asia former USSR	0.1	0.2	0.1	0.2	0.1	0.1	0.2	0.1	0.1	0.1	Asie ancienne URSS
Europe excluding former USSR	42.5	43.1	44.5	43.4	42.8	47.1	46.5	42.2	43.4	42.2	Europe ancienne URSS exclus
- European Union	35.6	36.1	35.8	34.1	32.7	34.9	34.9	31.3	31.2	29.7	- Union Européenne
- Eastern Europe	4.4	4.6	6.1	7.0	7.9	9.7	9.2	8.5	9.4	9.8	- Europe de l'Est
- Rest of Europe	2.6	2.4	2.6	2.3	2.2	2.5	2.4	2.4	2.9	2.8	- Autre de l'Europe
Europe former USSR	1.7	1.5	1.7	1.7	2.1	2.8	2.7	2.7	3.0	3.3	Europe ancienne URSS
Oceania	1.4	1.4	1.6	1.7	1.6	1.3	1.6	1.3	1.4	1.3	Océanie

TRADE BY COMMODITY (Value in million US dollars)
Exports by principal countries or areas

COMMERCE PAR PRODUIT (Valeur en millions de dollars EU)
Exportations selon les principaux pays ou zones

Country or area	1998	1999	2000	2001	2002	Pays ou zone
World	9656.6	9003.6	9432.3	8857.4	8499.9	Monde
Africa	9.2	20.4	20.6	20.3	8.8	Afrique
Americas	477.8	430.1	486.9	450.4	423.5	Amériques
- Northern America	315.7	291.9	323.8	295.2	288.4	- Amérique du Nord
- LAIA	160.5	137.0	162.0	153.7	133.4	- ALAI
- CACM	1.1	0.9	0.7	0.4	0.3	- MCC
- Caribbean	0.6	0.3	0.5	1.1	1.4	- Caraïbes
- Rest of America	0.0	0.0	0.0	0.0	0.0	- Autre d'Amérique
Asia excluding former USSR	2944.5	2882.4	3475.0	3061.7	3130.1	Asie ancienne URSS exclus
- Middle East	88.9	103.5	118.2	101.9	106.0	- Moyen-Orient
Asia former USSR	3.1	2.1	4.5	1.6	1.0	Asie ancienne URSS
Europe excluding former USSR	6002.8	5415.5	5197.0	5095.7	4676.7	Europe ancienne URSS exclus
- European Union	5675.6	5134.5	4895.3	4780.7	4355.9	- Union Européenne
- Eastern Europe	213.8	186.0	200.4	221.1	230.3	- Europe de l'Est
- Rest of Europe	113.3	95.0	101.4	93.9	90.4	- Autre de l'Europe
Europe former USSR	205.2	233.4	235.2	216.8	246.7	Europe ancienne URSS
Oceania	14.1	19.7	13.0	10.9	13.1	Océanie
Italy-San Marino-Holy See	2682.9	2354.4	2354.8	2394.4	2109.2	Italie-Saint-Marin-Saint-Siège
China	842.1	784.8	1026.0	978.2	1055.0	Chine
Germany	1052.6	923.2	779.4	754.5	630.1	Allemagne
China, Hong Kong SAR	687.9	547.2	625.5	501.3	494.1	Chine - RAS de Hong-Kong
Japan	458.2	547.0	628.7	582.0	534.5	Japon
France-Monaco	566.0	555.6	533.1	471.6	416.6	France-Monaco
United Kingdom	539.8	506.6	489.4	440.3	435.8	Royaume-Uni
India	235.7	264.9	370.4	291.5	346.3	Inde
Korea, Republic of	331.2	310.4	304.7	251.8	245.8	République de Corée
United States	240.3	212.2	237.3	206.4	209.0	Etats-Unis d'Amérique
Spain	141.3	151.5	147.6	157.9	165.4	Espagne
Belgium	–	178.6	181.7	170.8	e191.6	Belgique
Czech Republic	118.8	106.3	119.5	133.2	140.8	République tchèque
Netherlands	142.4	137.5	109.8	107.0	117.4	Pays-Bas
Turkey	81.6	96.4	108.1	88.6	92.0	Turquie
Canada	75.4	79.7	86.4	88.8	79.4	Canada
Russian Federation	60.1	88.5	82.8	68.8	80.3	Fédération de Russie
Bangladesh	72.5	e56.1	e78.5	93.2	e74.9	Bangladesh
Austria	126.3	79.4	65.4	51.3	47.1	Autriche
Portugal	60.3	63.1	59.3	70.1	70.8	Portugal
Switzerland-Liechtenstein	74.5	65.7	65.4	61.4	55.7	Suisse-Liechtenstein
Belarus	67.0	65.0	66.4	58.8	62.4	Bélarus
Mexico	43.3	52.6	73.3	72.5	63.6	Mexique
Sweden	71.0	66.3	49.4	41.9	51.5	Suède
Ireland	50.3	54.3	56.4	56.8	53.7	Irlande
Lithuania	50.2	43.8	43.6	40.4	e48.9	Lituanie
Uruguay	53.4	38.8	41.1	40.9	33.9	Uruguay
Denmark	27.9	36.2	46.1	42.5	47.8	Danemark
Belgium-Luxembourg	191.2	–	–	–	–	Belgique-Luxembourg
Poland	45.1	28.9	32.0	29.1	27.1	Pologne

(Value as percentages of World total) **(Valeur en pourcentage du total mondial)**

Regions of the world	1993	1994	1995	1996	1997	1998	1999	2000	2001	2002	Régions du monde
World	100.0	100.0	100.0	100.0	100.0	100.0	100.0	100.0	100.0	100.0	Monde
Africa	0.1	0.1	0.1	0.1	0.3	0.1	0.2	0.2	0.2	0.1	Afrique
Americas	4.3	4.2	4.3	4.8	5.2	4.9	4.8	5.2	5.1	5.0	Amériques
- Northern America	2.9	2.9	2.9	3.4	3.3	3.3	3.2	3.4	3.3	3.4	- Amérique du Nord
- LAIA	1.4	1.3	1.4	1.4	1.8	1.7	1.5	1.7	1.7	1.6	- ALAI
- CACM	0.0	0.0	0.0	0.0	0.0	0.0	0.0	0.0	0.0	0.0	- MCC
- Caribbean	0.0	0.0	0.0	0.0	0.0	0.0	0.0	0.0	0.0	0.0	- Caraïbes
- Rest of America	0.0	0.0	0.0	0.0	0.0	0.0	0.0	0.0	0.0	0.0	- Autre d'Amérique
Asia excluding former USSR	34.2	35.0	32.3	31.1	32.9	30.5	32.0	36.8	34.6	36.8	Asie ancienne URSS exclus
- Middle East	0.4	0.5	0.8	1.1	1.2	0.9	1.1	1.3	1.2	1.2	- Moyen-Orient
Asia former USSR	0.0	0.1	0.1	0.1	0.1	0.0	0.0	0.0	0.0	0.0	Asie ancienne URSS
Europe excluding former USSR	60.5	59.7	61.6	62.4	59.8	62.2	60.1	55.1	57.5	55.0	Europe ancienne URSS exclus
- European Union	56.7	55.9	57.5	59.2	56.8	58.8	57.0	51.9	54.0	51.2	- Union Européenne
- Eastern Europe	2.1	2.2	2.6	1.8	1.9	2.2	2.1	2.1	2.5	2.7	- Europe de l'Est
- Rest of Europe	1.7	1.6	1.5	1.4	1.1	1.2	1.1	1.1	1.1	1.1	- Autre de l'Europe
Europe former USSR	0.7	0.8	1.4	1.3	1.6	2.1	2.6	2.5	2.4	2.9	Europe ancienne URSS
Oceania	0.1	0.1	0.1	0.2	0.2	0.1	0.2	0.1	0.1	0.2	Océanie

655 Knitted or crocheted fabrics (including tubular, etc, fabrics)

TRADE BY COMMODITY (Value in million US dollars) — COMMERCE PAR PRODUIT (Valeur en millions de dollars EU)

Imports by principal countries or areas — **Importations selon les principaux pays ou zones**

Country or area	1998	1999	2000	2001	2002	Pays ou zone
World	11880.1	12024.9	13213.7	12753.9	12939.4	Monde
Africa	359.2	351.1	381.6	346.8	373.2	Afrique
Americas	1675.8	2031.4	2319.8	2294.5	2198.0	Amériques
- Northern America	1170.2	1326.9	1408.7	1387.2	1421.0	- Amérique du Nord
- LAIA	403.1	629.1	837.5	818.6	662.8	- ALAI
- CACM	14.9	11.2	9.2	14.6	10.4	- MCC
- Caribbean	79.1	58.0	57.9	69.1	97.8	- Caraïbes
- Rest of America	8.6	6.3	6.4	5.0	6.0	- Autre d'Amérique
Asia excluding former USSR	5678.7	5680.2	6650.8	6361.7	6583.6	Asie ancienne URSS exclus
- Middle East	341.5	270.0	456.9	504.1	548.7	- Moyen-Orient
Asia former USSR	5.5	7.3	19.9	15.6	13.4	Asie ancienne URSS
Europe excluding former USSR	3721.1	3465.0	3288.2	3100.3	3055.8	Europe ancienne URSS exclus
- European Union	2992.5	2715.3	2480.6	2248.4	2154.7	- Union Européenne
- Eastern Europe	593.7	617.5	657.5	699.5	739.9	- Europe de l'Est
- Rest of Europe	134.9	132.2	150.1	152.4	161.2	- Autre de l'Europe
Europe former USSR	181.8	181.8	227.2	222.6	252.8	Europe ancienne URSS
Oceania	258.1	308.0	326.3	412.4	462.6	Océanie
China, Hong Kong SAR	1877.3	1927.8	2287.1	2088.0	2285.1	Chine - RAS de Hong-Kong
China	1161.9	1182.8	1339.0	1336.5	1432.0	Chine
United States	835.0	978.2	1058.5	1070.6	1147.0	Etats-Unis d'Amérique
Mexico	235.9	480.1	637.4	636.0	537.3	Mexique
France-Monaco	562.5	528.7	492.8	436.3	404.4	France-Monaco
Germany	542.4	481.2	430.2	404.3	378.1	Allemagne
Italy-San Marino-Holy See	353.9	320.7	351.4	318.6	319.8	Italie-Saint-Marin-Saint-Siège
China, Macao SAR	354.3	321.7	345.0	299.8	302.7	Chine - RAS de Macao
Canada	335.2	348.7	350.0	316.0	273.7	Canada
Sri Lanka	e305.8	275.9	e372.6	299.7	307.4	Sri Lanka
United Kingdom	425.3	362.0	280.5	248.4	226.4	Royaume-Uni
Philippines	261.2	293.3	262.9	268.8	156.2	Philippines
Singapore	223.5	217.9	268.0	226.0	210.6	Singapour
Poland	222.3	213.6	215.2	225.8	250.5	Pologne
Malaysia	223.4	217.4	242.0	194.8	e212.9	Malaisie
Thailand	179.9	196.3	224.9	226.4	e235.9	Thaïlande
Northern Mariana Islands	e88.8	e137.3	e171.1	e294.2	e348.9	Iles Mariannes septentrionales
Spain	155.2	191.8	189.6	173.0	179.0	Espagne
United Arab Emirates	121.3	127.1	230.9	172.3	e176.7	Emirates arabes unis
Morocco	155.3	156.0	179.0	158.3	e167.1	Maroc
Portugal	181.4	165.3	154.2	134.6	114.0	Portugal
Japan	202.3	170.4	129.1	93.6	85.4	Japon
Hungary	132.1	137.8	129.5	127.0	118.5	Hongrie
Belgium	–	184.5	145.5	139.3	e152.8	Belgique
Indonesia	139.4	104.1	145.7	120.2	76.7	Indonésie
Romania	76.5	94.9	103.4	128.3	144.1	Roumanie
Greece	121.1	110.4	90.6	77.8	e86.0	Grèce
Israel	98.0	110.6	102.7	89.8	78.7	Israël
Austria	122.5	93.7	92.4	88.4	75.8	Autriche
Czech Republic	84.5	92.1	99.3	92.0	91.2	République tchèque

(Value as percentages of World total) — **(Valeur en pourcentage du total mondial)**

Regions of the world	1993	1994	1995	1996	1997	1998	1999	2000	2001	2002	Régions du monde
World	100.0	100.0	100.0	100.0	100.0	100.0	100.0	100.0	100.0	100.0	Monde
Africa	2.3	2.0	2.2	2.0	1.8	3.0	2.9	2.9	2.7	2.9	Afrique
Americas	8.2	8.0	8.3	10.4	13.8	14.1	16.9	17.6	18.0	17.0	Amériques
- Northern America	6.2	6.2	5.8	7.4	9.9	9.8	11.0	10.7	10.9	11.0	- Amérique du Nord
- LAIA	1.1	1.2	1.5	1.8	2.9	3.4	5.2	6.3	6.4	5.1	- ALAI
- CACM	0.2	0.1	0.1	0.1	0.1	0.1	0.1	0.1	0.1	0.1	- MCC
- Caribbean	0.6	0.4	0.8	1.1	0.8	0.7	0.5	0.4	0.5	0.8	- Caraïbes
- Rest of America	0.1	0.1	0.1	0.1	0.1	0.1	0.1	0.0	0.0	0.0	- Autre d'Amérique
Asia excluding former USSR	57.8	59.1	56.9	54.7	51.5	47.8	47.2	50.3	49.9	50.9	Asie ancienne URSS exclus
- Middle East	3.1	3.5	2.7	2.5	2.9	2.9	2.2	3.5	4.0	4.2	- Moyen-Orient
Asia former USSR	0.0	0.1	0.1	0.0	0.0	0.0	0.1	0.2	0.1	0.1	Asie ancienne URSS
Europe excluding former USSR	28.9	28.6	29.4	28.7	29.0	31.3	28.8	24.9	24.3	23.6	Europe ancienne URSS exclus
- European Union	24.6	24.2	24.3	23.2	23.7	25.2	22.6	18.8	17.6	16.7	- Union Européenne
- Eastern Europe	2.6	2.8	3.6	4.0	4.2	5.0	5.1	5.0	5.5	5.7	- Europe de l'Est
- Rest of Europe	1.7	1.6	1.5	1.5	1.1	1.1	1.1	1.1	1.2	1.2	- Autre de l'Europe
Europe former USSR	1.2	0.7	1.0	1.2	1.3	1.5	1.5	1.7	1.7	2.0	Europe ancienne URSS
Oceania	1.6	1.5	2.2	3.1	2.5	2.2	2.6	2.5	3.2	3.6	Océanie

Etoffes de bonneterie, y compris les étoffes façon velours, peluches et la bonneterie à jours 655

TRADE BY COMMODITY (Value in million US dollars)
Exports by principal countries or areas

COMMERCE PAR PRODUIT (Valeur en millions de dollars EU)
Exportations selon les principaux pays ou zones

Country or area	1998	1999	2000	2001	2002	Pays ou zone
World	14423.7	14477.4	15730.9	14817.1	16182.9	Monde
Africa	41.6	46.0	44.0	57.4	37.7	Afrique
Americas	972.8	1053.6	1322.2	1480.5	1563.5	Amériques
- Northern America	823.4	903.3	1125.1	1275.5	1376.9	- Amérique du Nord
- LAIA	136.8	141.9	185.2	191.4	175.3	- ALAI
- CACM	11.4	7.9	11.7	13.2	11.0	- MCC
- Caribbean	1.2	0.4	0.3	0.3	0.2	- Caraïbes
- Rest of America	0.0	0.0	0.0	0.0	0.0	- Autre d'Amérique
Asia excluding former USSR	8839.2	9086.1	10336.3	9528.8	10816.3	Asie ancienne URSS exclus
- Middle East	227.1	254.6	275.5	329.5	356.9	- Moyen-Orient
Asia former USSR	10.4	15.5	15.2	12.1	13.1	Asie ancienne URSS
Europe excluding former USSR	4467.7	4201.7	3933.2	3660.9	3667.1	Europe ancienne URSS exclus
- European Union	4214.7	3960.0	3714.9	3469.1	3483.4	- Union Européenne
- Eastern Europe	126.8	105.2	94.6	86.8	88.5	- Europe de l'Est
- Rest of Europe	126.3	136.5	123.6	105.1	95.2	- Autre de l'Europe
Europe former USSR	47.9	26.2	31.5	34.9	40.2	Europe ancienne URSS
Oceania	44.1	48.3	48.4	42.5	45.1	Océanie
Korea, Republic of	1919.2	2169.9	2522.1	2478.1	2687.0	République de Corée
China, Hong Kong SAR	1965.6	1947.4	2371.8	2160.2	2379.6	Chine - RAS de Hong-Kong
China	917.2	977.4	1287.8	1361.0	2006.4	Chine
Germany	1072.3	1043.0	947.4	899.5	888.3	Allemagne
Italy-San Marino-Holy See	980.0	971.6	926.6	838.1	866.6	Italie-Saint-Marin-Saint-Siège
United States	608.6	629.3	806.8	949.4	1100.8	Etats-Unis d'Amérique
France-Monaco	670.8	639.3	611.4	572.3	523.4	France-Monaco
Japan	383.7	428.4	436.4	372.8	410.0	Japon
Spain	298.7	302.3	276.5	259.6	282.1	Espagne
Canada	214.8	274.0	318.3	326.1	276.1	Canada
United Kingdom	308.7	252.4	232.3	205.2	201.1	Royaume-Uni
Turkey	191.3	223.1	210.9	238.9	263.6	Turquie
Austria	272.7	214.9	201.0	179.7	168.3	Autriche
Singapore	145.4	128.7	163.0	149.3	124.8	Singapour
Denmark	138.9	121.5	113.9	119.6	133.6	Danemark
Malaysia	119.7	111.8	130.5	126.0	e133.5	Malaisie
Belgium	–	155.0	145.0	144.8	e162.5	Belgique
Netherlands	135.6	109.3	110.1	98.5	106.2	Pays-Bas
Mexico	66.3	79.5	100.7	102.9	93.9	Mexique
Switzerland-Liechtenstein	93.4	97.8	88.7	67.2	55.5	Suisse-Liechtenstein
Pakistan	85.9	69.5	70.5	73.8	65.7	Pakistan
Thailand	44.3	56.0	66.5	76.3	e80.5	Thaïlande
China, Macao SAR	45.8	67.7	65.6	60.7	74.6	Chine - RAS de Macao
Sweden	60.1	57.1	60.2	49.5	46.4	Suède
Indonesia	19.9	42.8	75.9	51.5	42.3	Indonésie
Greece	41.2	39.9	41.6	53.7	e53.7	Grèce
Poland	67.7	47.8	34.7	26.4	28.6	Pologne
Czech Republic	45.1	40.1	39.2	39.3	32.7	République tchèque
Belgium-Luxembourg	183.4	–	–	–	–	Belgique-Luxembourg
United Arab Emirates	4.2	4.3	37.1	57.4	e59.8	Emirates arabes unis

(Value as percentages of World total) **(Valeur en pourcentage du total mondial)**

Regions of the world	1993	1994	1995	1996	1997	1998	1999	2000	2001	2002	Régions du monde
World	100.0	100.0	100.0	100.0	100.0	100.0	100.0	100.0	100.0	100.0	Monde
Africa	0.2	0.2	0.3	0.3	0.3	0.3	0.3	0.3	0.4	0.2	Afrique
Americas	4.0	4.4	5.2	5.7	6.5	6.7	7.3	8.4	10.0	9.7	Amériques
- Northern America	3.5	3.9	4.4	4.8	5.5	5.7	6.2	7.2	8.6	8.5	- Amérique du Nord
- LAIA	0.4	0.4	0.7	0.8	0.9	0.9	1.0	1.2	1.3	1.1	- ALAI
- CACM	0.0	0.0	0.0	0.0	0.0	0.1	0.1	0.1	0.1	0.1	- MCC
- Caribbean	0.0	0.0	0.0	0.0	0.0	0.0	0.0	0.0	0.0	0.0	- Caraïbes
- Rest of America	0.0	0.0	0.0	0.0	0.0	0.0	0.0	0.0	0.0	0.0	- Autre d'Amérique
Asia excluding former USSR	69.4	65.3	63.5	63.4	64.4	61.3	62.8	65.7	64.3	66.8	Asie ancienne URSS exclus
- Middle East	1.1	1.6	1.0	1.3	1.6	1.6	1.8	1.8	2.2	2.2	- Moyen-Orient
Asia former USSR	0.0	0.0	0.0	0.0	0.0	0.1	0.1	0.1	0.1	0.1	Asie ancienne URSS
Europe excluding former USSR	26.0	29.6	30.6	30.0	28.1	31.0	29.0	25.0	24.7	22.7	Europe ancienne URSS exclus
- European Union	24.0	27.5	28.4	28.0	26.6	29.2	27.4	23.6	23.4	21.5	- Union Européenne
- Eastern Europe	0.8	0.8	1.1	0.9	0.8	0.9	0.7	0.6	0.6	0.5	- Europe de l'Est
- Rest of Europe	1.2	1.4	1.2	1.1	0.8	0.9	0.9	0.8	0.7	0.6	- Autre de l'Europe
Europe former USSR	0.1	0.1	0.2	0.3	0.4	0.3	0.2	0.2	0.2	0.2	Europe ancienne URSS
Oceania	0.2	0.3	0.3	0.3	0.3	0.3	0.3	0.3	0.3	0.3	Océanie

656 Tulle, lace, embroidery, ribbons, trimmings and other small wares

TRADE BY COMMODITY (Value in million US dollars) / COMMERCE PAR PRODUIT (Valeur en millions de dollars EU)

Imports by principal countries or areas / **Importations selon les principaux pays ou zones**

Country or area	1998	1999	2000	2001	2002	Pays ou zone
World	4655.1	4755.8	5237.3	4950.8	5160.8	Monde
Africa	169.2	171.3	173.6	203.7	222.1	Afrique
Americas	1109.5	1118.9	1294.8	1226.6	1202.2	Amériques
- Northern America	537.7	555.4	614.4	589.9	628.5	- Amérique du Nord
- LAIA	443.7	478.3	567.3	525.5	441.9	- ALAI
- CACM	42.9	25.0	35.3	31.0	37.9	- MCC
- Caribbean	79.1	55.1	74.0	77.1	89.9	- Caraïbes
- Rest of America	6.2	5.2	3.8	3.2	4.0	- Autre d'Amérique
Asia excluding former USSR	1523.9	1667.6	1930.0	1750.3	1848.3	Asie ancienne URSS exclus
- Middle East	160.7	154.9	176.8	183.5	203.1	- Moyen-Orient
Asia former USSR	3.5	3.6	7.0	9.7	9.3	Asie ancienne URSS
Europe excluding former USSR	1730.6	1671.9	1697.5	1635.8	1722.3	Europe ancienne URSS exclus
- European Union	1364.3	1294.1	1299.5	1211.1	1217.2	- Union Européenne
- Eastern Europe	263.5	279.1	304.3	332.1	404.8	- Europe de l'Est
- Rest of Europe	102.7	98.7	93.7	92.6	100.3	- Autre de l'Europe
Europe former USSR	54.0	53.1	62.7	75.8	88.6	Europe ancienne URSS
Oceania	64.4	69.5	71.7	49.0	68.0	Océanie
United States	459.7	469.8	523.9	498.3	537.1	Etats-Unis d'Amérique
China	349.9	423.7	502.2	456.4	462.5	Chine
Mexico	349.8	405.0	488.2	458.1	383.7	Mexique
China, Hong Kong SAR	399.4	382.4	433.2	372.4	409.7	Chine - RAS de Hong-Kong
Italy-San Marino-Holy See	218.0	215.9	240.9	206.2	204.2	Italie-Saint-Marin-Saint-Siège
Germany	239.9	223.1	196.8	185.1	159.7	Allemagne
France-Monaco	187.5	192.4	202.4	186.0	182.4	France-Monaco
United Kingdom	204.9	189.4	183.7	177.1	187.0	Royaume-Uni
Spain	101.0	94.3	107.9	101.7	116.2	Espagne
Sri Lanka	e92.8	83.7	e113.0	90.7	94.1	Sri Lanka
Japan	77.4	81.9	93.2	93.5	90.3	Japon
Canada	77.4	84.9	90.4	91.4	91.1	Canada
Romania	50.4	60.1	74.0	93.0	129.2	Roumanie
Hungary	78.1	81.0	74.8	75.8	81.7	Hongrie
Belgium	–	89.9	90.2	99.1	e108.7	Belgique
Viet Nam	26.5	68.6	82.2	85.3	103.8	Viet Nam
Thailand	58.4	74.2	79.8	75.0	e78.2	Thaïlande
Poland	65.0	61.1	66.6	75.9	96.8	Pologne
United Arab Emirates	70.4	73.8	75.0	66.7	e68.4	Emirates arabes unis
Morocco	51.6	62.4	69.1	83.0	e87.6	Maroc
Austria	80.0	72.8	65.2	64.0	62.6	Autriche
Dominican Republic	e62.4	e41.1	e61.4	e62.7	e74.8	République dominicaine
Tunisia	59.2	54.6	50.3	62.8	e62.7	Tunisie
Switzerland-Liechtenstein	64.1	61.2	55.8	51.7	52.4	Suisse-Liechtenstein
Philippines	66.7	57.3	57.8	56.1	38.0	Philippines
Portugal	64.5	56.5	54.9	47.4	45.7	Portugal
Czech Republic	45.4	48.4	52.1	46.5	49.7	République tchèque
Indonesia	46.7	47.1	59.9	48.3	34.1	Indonésie
Singapore	35.5	46.7	54.4	42.5	53.4	Singapour
Netherlands	50.0	43.8	44.2	42.7	42.9	Pays-Bas

(Value as percentages of World total) / **(Valeur en pourcentage du total mondial)**

Regions of the world	1993	1994	1995	1996	1997	1998	1999	2000	2001	2002	Régions du monde
World	100.0	100.0	100.0	100.0	100.0	100.0	100.0	100.0	100.0	100.0	Monde
Africa	3.2	4.2	3.3	2.7	2.6	3.6	3.6	3.3	4.1	4.3	Afrique
Americas	16.8	17.2	16.6	18.4	21.7	23.8	23.5	24.7	24.8	23.3	Amériques
- Northern America	9.7	9.7	9.1	9.6	10.8	11.6	11.7	11.7	11.9	12.2	- Amérique du Nord
- LAIA	5.9	6.5	6.3	7.3	7.9	9.5	10.1	10.8	10.6	8.6	- ALAI
- CACM	0.2	0.2	0.2	0.3	1.4	0.9	0.5	0.7	0.6	0.7	- MCC
- Caribbean	0.8	0.7	0.8	1.1	1.5	1.7	1.2	1.4	1.6	1.7	- Caraïbes
- Rest of America	0.2	0.1	0.1	0.1	0.1	0.1	0.1	0.1	0.1	0.1	- Autre d'Amérique
Asia excluding former USSR	40.3	40.2	40.1	39.2	38.0	32.7	35.1	36.9	35.4	35.8	Asie ancienne URSS exclus
- Middle East	5.2	4.7	3.8	2.9	3.1	3.5	3.3	3.4	3.7	3.9	- Moyen-Orient
Asia former USSR	0.1	0.1	0.1	0.1	0.0	0.1	0.1	0.1	0.2	0.2	Asie ancienne URSS
Europe excluding former USSR	36.6	36.1	37.6	37.1	35.0	37.2	35.2	32.4	33.0	33.4	Europe ancienne URSS exclus
- European Union	31.2	30.6	31.0	30.7	28.5	29.3	27.2	24.8	24.5	23.6	- Union Européenne
- Eastern Europe	2.8	3.0	4.1	4.3	4.6	5.7	5.9	5.8	6.7	7.8	- Europe de l'Est
- Rest of Europe	2.6	2.5	2.5	2.2	2.0	2.2	2.1	1.8	1.9	1.9	- Autre de l'Europe
Europe former USSR	1.1	0.5	0.7	0.8	1.1	1.2	1.1	1.2	1.5	1.7	Europe ancienne URSS
Oceania	1.8	1.6	1.6	1.6	1.6	1.4	1.5	1.4	1.0	1.3	Océanie

Tulles, dentelles, broderies, rubans, passementeries et autres articles de mercerie 656

TRADE BY COMMODITY (Value in million US dollars)
Exports by principal countries or areas

COMMERCE PAR PRODUIT (Valeur en millions de dollars EU)
Exportations selon les principaux pays ou zones

Country or area	1998	1999	2000	2001	2002	Pays ou zone
World	5023.9	5192.3	5709.9	5530.3	6007.9	Monde
Africa	31.9	32.0	31.4	29.7	35.2	Afrique
Americas	699.1	783.9	808.4	877.5	912.9	Amériques
- Northern America	552.3	625.1	650.3	726.1	724.4	- Amérique du Nord
- LAIA	136.0	146.0	145.6	141.8	178.1	- ALAI
- CACM	9.0	10.8	11.0	8.1	9.0	- MCC
- Caribbean	1.8	1.9	1.6	1.4	1.3	- Caraïbes
- Rest of America	0.1	0.0	0.0	0.0	0.0	- Autre d'Amérique
Asia excluding former USSR	2176.0	2423.4	2918.8	2711.6	2966.2	Asie ancienne URSS exclus
- Middle East	124.1	166.5	205.8	275.8	314.3	- Moyen-Orient
Asia former USSR	0.2	0.2	0.5	0.4	0.4	Asie ancienne URSS
Europe excluding former USSR	2094.7	1932.5	1928.2	1889.0	2070.3	Europe ancienne URSS exclus
- European Union	1819.0	1681.5	1685.5	1644.4	1804.5	- Union Européenne
- Eastern Europe	54.9	51.5	58.4	63.5	72.1	- Europe de l'Est
- Rest of Europe	220.8	199.5	184.3	181.1	193.7	- Autre de l'Europe
Europe former USSR	12.9	9.5	12.5	15.2	15.9	Europe ancienne URSS
Oceania	9.0	10.9	10.1	6.9	7.0	Océanie
Korea, Republic of	473.5	554.1	729.2	644.4	652.9	République de Corée
United States	506.2	575.7	591.1	670.2	670.6	Etats-Unis d'Amérique
China, Hong Kong SAR	458.1	466.1	556.2	490.9	535.8	Chine - RAS de Hong-Kong
France-Monaco	445.3	419.6	410.6	383.1	430.9	France-Monaco
Germany	402.5	360.2	332.5	324.6	345.0	Allemagne
Italy-San Marino-Holy See	289.4	271.5	303.1	310.5	349.0	Italie-Saint-Marin-Saint-Siège
China	236.8	226.4	274.7	279.7	392.5	Chine
Japan	192.6	225.6	248.2	198.9	202.9	Japon
Switzerland-Liechtenstein	212.0	191.8	176.5	171.5	183.7	Suisse-Liechtenstein
Austria	202.6	175.6	176.7	184.9	192.2	Autriche
Turkey	104.1	141.6	171.8	227.2	254.9	Turquie
United Kingdom	141.6	135.6	146.0	141.3	152.0	Royaume-Uni
Thailand	81.0	83.7	94.6	104.6	e110.4	Thaïlande
Mexico	76.0	84.5	92.9	90.8	127.2	Mexique
Spain	75.8	85.1	92.4	84.9	95.0	Espagne
India	53.0	83.9	80.6	81.6	88.9	Inde
Netherlands	85.6	79.0	73.1	62.7	72.0	Pays-Bas
Indonesia	37.0	56.2	99.1	67.4	48.9	Indonésie
Belgium	–	77.3	68.8	71.2	e79.9	Belgique
Canada	46.1	49.5	59.2	56.0	53.7	Canada
Czech Republic	33.9	29.4	31.9	32.6	30.9	République tchèque
Colombia	29.7	33.2	29.6	29.5	30.0	Colombie
Singapore	24.0	25.7	23.0	21.7	24.1	Singapour
Philippines	18.7	19.1	22.6	25.6	26.9	Philippines
Sweden	19.7	19.3	18.3	17.9	21.6	Suède
Belgium-Luxembourg	90.4	–	–	–	–	Belgique-Luxembourg
Denmark	15.7	17.5	18.8	16.2	19.4	Danemark
Portugal	15.8	14.8	16.7	18.5	17.9	Portugal
Iran (Islamic Republic of)	5.7	8.4	14.6	24.4	24.5	Iran (République islamique d')
United Arab Emirates	9.3	9.6	12.6	15.8	e16.5	Emirates arabes unis

(Value as percentages of World total) **(Valeur en pourcentage du total mondial)**

Regions of the world	1993	1994	1995	1996	1997	1998	1999	2000	2001	2002	Régions du monde
World	100.0	100.0	100.0	100.0	100.0	100.0	100.0	100.0	100.0	100.0	Monde
Africa	0.6	0.5	0.6	0.6	0.6	0.6	0.6	0.6	0.5	0.6	Afrique
Americas	8.5	10.2	9.8	10.3	12.3	13.9	15.1	14.2	15.9	15.2	Amériques
- Northern America	6.8	8.2	7.8	7.9	9.4	11.0	12.0	11.4	13.1	12.1	- Amérique du Nord
- LAIA	1.5	1.8	1.9	2.2	2.6	2.7	2.8	2.5	2.6	3.0	- ALAI
- CACM	0.1	0.1	0.0	0.0	0.2	0.2	0.2	0.2	0.1	0.1	- MCC
- Caribbean	0.2	0.1	0.1	0.0	0.1	0.0	0.0	0.0	0.0	0.0	- Caraïbes
- Rest of America	0.0	0.0	0.0	0.0	0.0	0.0	0.0	0.0	0.0	0.0	- Autre d'Amérique
Asia excluding former USSR	52.8	46.1	45.8	46.9	48.2	43.3	46.7	51.1	49.0	49.4	Asie ancienne URSS exclus
- Middle East	1.0	1.6	2.0	2.0	2.3	2.5	3.2	3.6	5.0	5.2	- Moyen-Orient
Asia former USSR	0.0	0.0	0.0	0.0	0.0	0.0	0.0	0.0	0.0	0.0	Asie ancienne URSS
Europe excluding former USSR	37.7	42.9	43.4	41.8	38.5	41.7	37.2	33.8	34.2	34.5	Europe ancienne URSS exclus
- European Union	32.5	37.0	37.0	36.3	33.7	36.2	32.4	29.5	29.7	30.0	- Union Européenne
- Eastern Europe	0.5	0.5	1.1	0.9	0.9	1.1	1.0	1.0	1.1	1.2	- Europe de l'Est
- Rest of Europe	4.8	5.4	5.2	4.6	3.8	4.4	3.8	3.2	3.3	3.2	- Autre de l'Europe
Europe former USSR	0.2	0.2	0.2	0.3	0.3	0.3	0.2	0.2	0.3	0.3	Europe ancienne URSS
Oceania	0.2	0.2	0.2	0.2	0.2	0.2	0.2	0.2	0.1	0.1	Océanie

657 Special textile fabrics and related products

TRADE BY COMMODITY (Value in million US dollars)
Imports by principal countries or areas

COMMERCE PAR PRODUIT (Valeur en millions de dollars EU)
Importations selon les principaux pays ou zones

Country or area	1998	1999	2000	2001	2002	Pays ou zone
World	18043.5	18129.0	18911.4	18712.2	19439.1	Monde
Africa	505.8	438.3	437.0	441.3	464.3	Afrique
Americas	3458.4	3585.3	4139.0	4225.2	4254.6	Amériques
- Northern America	2060.3	2103.6	2347.8	2326.2	2571.3	- Amérique du Nord
- LAIA	1254.9	1350.7	1656.5	1765.6	1538.5	- ALAI
- CACM	60.9	52.3	50.1	52.3	61.7	- MCC
- Caribbean	70.6	67.7	74.8	72.0	73.1	- Caraïbes
- Rest of America	11.8	10.9	9.8	9.1	9.9	- Autre d'Amérique
Asia excluding former USSR	5112.4	5315.8	5881.2	5551.7	5672.8	Asie ancienne URSS exclus
- Middle East	506.3	462.5	497.1	494.0	529.1	- Moyen-Orient
Asia former USSR	26.5	20.3	27.1	25.8	25.6	Asie ancienne URSS
Europe excluding former USSR	8276.1	8169.6	7765.4	7849.3	8375.4	Europe ancienne URSS exclus
- European Union	6574.0	6529.2	6065.0	5987.1	6278.6	- Union Européenne
- Eastern Europe	1124.1	1078.6	1146.4	1288.4	1477.6	- Europe de l'Est
- Rest of Europe	577.9	561.7	553.9	573.8	619.1	- Autre de l'Europe
Europe former USSR	377.9	304.2	364.1	363.8	377.0	Europe ancienne URSS
Oceania	286.5	295.7	297.6	255.0	269.3	Océanie
United States	1349.6	1401.7	1634.7	1640.3	1866.1	Etats-Unis d'Amérique
China	1288.5	1385.9	1561.0	1538.6	1615.4	Chine
Germany	1422.5	1389.4	1228.6	1349.7	1326.2	Allemagne
France-Monaco	1021.6	978.1	965.0	912.1	955.8	France-Monaco
Mexico	626.6	816.1	1054.1	1211.6	1067.1	Mexique
China, Hong Kong SAR	1038.4	987.2	1002.8	840.1	825.3	Chine - RAS de Hong-Kong
United Kingdom	908.8	828.6	773.0	674.0	708.8	Royaume-Uni
Canada	708.0	699.7	711.3	682.7	699.9	Canada
Italy-San Marino-Holy See	653.2	685.1	622.4	623.8	640.2	Italie-Saint-Marin-Saint-Siège
Spain	518.1	536.7	505.1	534.0	593.7	Espagne
Japan	456.3	547.0	573.7	538.5	536.0	Japon
Poland	419.0	394.8	387.3	418.5	463.0	Pologne
Belgium	–	502.5	479.4	426.1	e467.3	Belgique
Netherlands	349.5	384.3	325.9	334.8	378.0	Pays-Bas
Korea, Republic of	192.4	253.9	297.6	298.3	327.0	République de Corée
Czech Republic	237.6	211.7	243.6	284.5	369.2	République tchèque
Viet Nam	165.4	210.0	278.4	288.9	351.5	Viet Nam
Portugal	230.1	261.8	271.5	217.5	230.1	Portugal
Indonesia	241.1	202.5	262.5	216.4	193.3	Indonésie
Austria	217.8	223.4	202.2	214.5	229.0	Autriche
Switzerland-Liechtenstein	215.5	215.4	209.8	198.5	214.4	Suisse-Liechtenstein
Sweden	217.6	203.1	201.0	189.9	208.9	Suède
Australia	204.1	210.8	218.5	187.1	197.2	Australie
Thailand	159.6	186.9	215.8	209.4	e218.2	Thaïlande
Turkey	217.7	193.0	182.4	159.5	207.6	Turquie
Brazil	206.1	174.5	194.7	180.2	164.2	Brésil
Romania	156.8	162.6	169.7	207.5	219.1	Roumanie
Denmark	181.5	179.3	165.8	168.6	181.7	Danemark
Hungary	146.7	171.3	178.2	171.2	195.5	Hongrie
Russian Federation	167.7	154.4	174.2	169.5	165.4	Fédération de Russie

(Value as percentages of World total) **(Valeur en pourcentage du total mondial)**

Regions of the world	1993	1994	1995	1996	1997	1998	1999	2000	2001	2002	Régions du monde
World	100.0	100.0	100.0	100.0	100.0	100.0	100.0	100.0	100.0	100.0	Monde
Africa	3.3	2.9	2.5	2.5	2.4	2.8	2.4	2.3	2.4	2.4	Afrique
Americas	16.7	17.0	16.2	16.0	18.0	19.2	19.8	21.9	22.6	21.9	Amériques
- Northern America	10.8	10.8	10.0	10.1	11.0	11.4	11.6	12.4	12.4	13.2	- Amérique du Nord
- LAIA	5.1	5.6	5.5	5.2	6.3	7.0	7.5	8.8	9.4	7.9	- ALAI
- CACM	0.3	0.3	0.3	0.2	0.3	0.3	0.3	0.3	0.3	0.3	- MCC
- Caribbean	0.3	0.3	0.3	0.3	0.4	0.4	0.4	0.4	0.4	0.4	- Caraïbes
- Rest of America	0.1	0.1	0.1	0.1	0.1	0.1	0.1	0.1	0.0	0.1	- Autre d'Amérique
Asia excluding former USSR	34.8	33.5	32.8	33.6	33.1	28.3	29.3	31.1	29.7	29.2	Asie ancienne URSS exclus
- Middle East	3.0	2.6	2.6	2.7	2.9	2.8	2.6	2.6	2.6	2.7	- Moyen-Orient
Asia former USSR	0.0	0.1	0.1	0.2	0.1	0.1	0.1	0.1	0.1	0.1	Asie ancienne URSS
Europe excluding former USSR	42.0	43.1	44.8	44.1	42.6	45.9	45.1	41.1	41.9	43.1	Europe ancienne URSS exclus
- European Union	36.4	36.9	37.3	36.3	34.4	36.4	36.0	32.1	32.0	32.3	- Union Européenne
- Eastern Europe	2.7	3.2	4.3	4.9	5.4	6.2	5.9	6.1	6.9	7.6	- Europe de l'Est
- Rest of Europe	2.9	3.0	3.2	2.9	2.7	3.2	3.1	2.9	3.1	3.2	- Autre de l'Europe
Europe former USSR	1.3	1.6	1.9	2.0	2.2	2.1	1.7	1.9	1.9	1.9	Europe ancienne URSS
Oceania	1.8	1.8	1.7	1.7	1.6	1.6	1.6	1.6	1.4	1.4	Océanie

Tissus spéciaux et produits connexes en matières textiles 657

TRADE BY COMMODITY (Value in million US dollars)
Exports by principal countries or areas

COMMERCE PAR PRODUIT (Valeur en millions de dollars EU)
Exportations selon les principaux pays ou zones

Country or area	1998	1999	2000	2001	2002	Pays ou zone
World	20219.1	20365.9	21077.2	20477.3	21792.5	Monde
Africa	56.7	62.4	57.0	64.2	76.6	Afrique
Americas	3010.5	2955.9	3184.3	3218.9	3351.9	Amériques
- Northern America	2495.7	2455.4	2655.9	2735.2	2869.8	- Amérique du Nord
- LAIA	471.6	473.8	499.4	454.5	454.2	- ALAI
- CACM	22.7	20.2	22.0	21.8	19.9	- MCC
- Caribbean	20.4	6.4	6.8	7.1	7.8	- Caraïbes
- Rest of America	0.0	0.1	0.1	0.2	0.1	- Autre d'Amérique
Asia excluding former USSR	7038.9	7446.8	8226.1	7362.3	7689.7	Asie ancienne URSS exclus
- Middle East	190.9	177.0	183.0	212.4	250.6	- Moyen-Orient
Asia former USSR	38.9	38.2	44.9	48.7	28.4	Asie ancienne URSS
Europe excluding former USSR	9809.2	9652.5	9309.7	9525.2	10371.7	Europe ancienne URSS exclus
- European Union	9035.5	8888.5	8507.5	8661.5	9390.7	- Union Européenne
- Eastern Europe	307.7	305.7	339.2	385.5	454.4	- Europe de l'Est
- Rest of Europe	465.9	458.2	463.1	478.3	526.5	- Autre de l'Europe
Europe former USSR	189.4	129.1	169.6	176.2	198.5	Europe ancienne URSS
Oceania	75.5	81.0	85.6	81.7	75.7	Océanie
Germany	2561.1	2492.4	2306.3	2449.5	2716.4	Allemagne
United States	2096.7	2068.6	2226.6	2288.7	2371.2	Etats-Unis d'Amérique
Korea, Republic of	1618.7	1875.9	2119.2	1821.6	1710.0	République de Corée
Italy-San Marino-Holy See	1616.8	1552.7	1573.8	1529.3	1536.9	Italie-Saint-Marin-Saint-Siège
Japan	1002.9	1091.9	1189.2	1018.9	1034.7	Japon
France-Monaco	927.0	884.7	890.2	871.7	973.7	France-Monaco
China, Hong Kong SAR	912.0	864.6	900.9	763.6	743.3	Chine - RAS de Hong-Kong
United Kingdom	847.9	851.4	795.4	789.4	811.3	Royaume-Uni
China	482.1	498.2	679.2	752.0	957.1	Chine
Belgium	–	757.9	715.3	682.6	e765.9	Belgique
Netherlands	615.4	599.3	559.6	456.9	543.8	Pays-Bas
Canada	399.0	386.8	429.3	446.6	498.6	Canada
Spain	391.5	363.1	336.7	371.2	389.6	Espagne
Switzerland-Liechtenstein	329.6	326.5	320.9	327.0	362.9	Suisse-Liechtenstein
Portugal	224.6	262.3	265.3	364.3	415.8	Portugal
Sweden	266.5	262.2	268.3	267.5	300.8	Suède
Luxembourg	–	303.3	273.6	321.8	e328.9	Luxembourg
Mexico	176.7	204.3	208.4	204.4	229.6	Mexique
Belgium-Luxembourg	1016.8	–	–	–	–	Belgique-Luxembourg
Thailand	152.2	177.7	192.6	220.7	e233.1	Thaïlande
Finland	202.7	203.5	180.1	180.6	194.5	Finlande
Czech Republic	175.1	168.1	182.9	207.7	219.3	République tchèque
Austria	185.7	155.6	151.4	159.7	173.2	Autriche
Turkey	155.8	142.1	152.8	168.5	200.6	Turquie
Denmark	137.4	155.3	143.6	160.3	179.2	Danemark
Indonesia	92.6	140.9	173.1	145.7	135.3	Indonésie
Israel	110.4	108.7	129.8	132.1	155.6	Israël
Brazil	142.4	133.9	131.5	101.6	e105.4	Brésil
Poland	61.2	68.9	91.3	103.2	120.8	Pologne
India	79.7	94.1	91.9	81.0	96.3	Inde

(Value as percentages of World total) **(Valeur en pourcentage du total mondial)**

Regions of the world	1993	1994	1995	1996	1997	1998	1999	2000	2001	2002	Régions du monde
World	100.0	100.0	100.0	100.0	100.0	100.0	100.0	100.0	100.0	100.0	Monde
Africa	0.3	0.3	0.3	0.4	0.3	0.3	0.3	0.3	0.3	0.4	Afrique
Americas	12.1	13.1	12.2	12.6	14.6	14.9	14.5	15.1	15.7	15.4	Amériques
- Northern America	10.3	11.0	10.1	10.4	12.1	12.3	12.1	12.6	13.4	13.2	- Amérique du Nord
- LAIA	1.7	1.9	1.9	2.1	2.5	2.3	2.3	2.4	2.2	2.1	- ALAI
- CACM	0.1	0.1	0.1	0.1	0.1	0.1	0.1	0.1	0.1	0.1	- MCC
- Caribbean	0.1	0.2	0.2	0.0	0.0	0.1	0.0	0.0	0.0	0.0	- Caraïbes
- Rest of America	0.0	0.0	0.0	0.0	0.0	0.0	0.0	0.0	0.0	0.0	- Autre d'Amérique
Asia excluding former USSR	43.7	38.4	37.7	38.2	38.8	34.8	36.6	39.0	36.0	35.3	Asie ancienne URSS exclus
- Middle East	0.6	0.6	0.7	1.0	1.3	0.9	0.9	0.9	1.0	1.2	- Moyen-Orient
Asia former USSR	0.0	0.2	0.1	0.2	0.1	0.2	0.2	0.2	0.2	0.1	Asie ancienne URSS
Europe excluding former USSR	43.1	46.8	48.6	47.2	44.9	48.5	47.4	44.2	46.5	47.6	Europe ancienne URSS exclus
- European Union	39.9	43.3	44.5	43.5	41.5	44.7	43.6	40.4	42.3	43.1	- Union Européenne
- Eastern Europe	0.9	0.9	1.5	1.3	1.3	1.5	1.5	1.6	1.9	2.1	- Europe de l'Est
- Rest of Europe	2.4	2.6	2.5	2.4	2.1	2.3	2.2	2.2	2.3	2.4	- Autre de l'Europe
Europe former USSR	0.3	0.6	0.7	1.0	0.9	0.9	0.6	0.8	0.9	0.9	Europe ancienne URSS
Oceania	0.4	0.4	0.5	0.5	0.4	0.4	0.4	0.4	0.4	0.3	Océanie

658 Made-up articles, wholly or chiefly of textile materials, nes

TRADE BY COMMODITY (Value in million US dollars)
Imports by principal countries or areas

COMMERCE PAR PRODUIT (Valeur en millions de dollars EU
Importations selon les principaux pays ou zone

Country or area	1998	1999	2000	2001	2002	Pays ou zone
World	14970.9	16028.3	17149.2	17545.1	19036.2	Monde
Africa	347.4	306.6	304.9	287.6	322.6	Afrique
Americas	4645.5	5252.8	6062.4	6387.9	7128.8	Amériques
- Northern America	4049.7	4658.9	5348.4	5696.4	6558.6	- Amérique du Nord
- LAIA	445.2	443.4	561.2	540.9	423.9	- ALAI
- CACM	34.5	39.8	43.6	43.7	47.6	- MCC
- Caribbean	94.3	91.6	92.3	90.4	81.2	- Caraïbes
- Rest of America	21.9	19.0	17.0	16.5	17.6	- Autre d'Amérique
Asia excluding former USSR	2478.8	2666.8	3055.5	3026.4	3029.1	Asie ancienne URSS exclus
- Middle East	453.8	416.9	453.5	451.7	483.3	- Moyen-Orient
Asia former USSR	22.9	25.2	25.4	30.0	33.2	Asie ancienne URSS
Europe excluding former USSR	6984.4	7266.7	7132.6	7277.5	7848.5	Europe ancienne URSS exclus
- European Union	6169.4	6406.7	6315.1	6405.0	6868.3	- Union Européenne
- Eastern Europe	283.4	330.8	312.1	362.8	418.4	- Europe de l'Est
- Rest of Europe	531.5	529.1	505.4	509.7	561.9	- Autre de l'Europe
Europe former USSR	146.4	127.6	134.3	155.5	220.0	Europe ancienne URSS
Oceania	345.4	382.6	433.9	380.2	453.8	Océanie
United States	3590.4	4178.8	4826.7	5141.4	5976.9	Etats-Unis d'Amérique
Germany	1676.6	1702.7	1609.7	1627.4	1641.1	Allemagne
Japan	1166.3	1336.0	1617.7	1670.5	1630.7	Japon
United Kingdom	922.6	959.4	1032.7	1102.5	1247.3	Royaume-Uni
France-Monaco	931.2	1014.0	1042.6	996.9	1090.9	France-Monaco
Canada	452.0	472.2	519.0	551.9	577.2	Canada
China, Hong Kong SAR	488.5	478.8	483.8	434.5	402.8	Chine - RAS de Hong-Kong
Netherlands	443.2	466.9	424.9	421.1	485.6	Pays-Bas
Italy-San Marino-Holy See	376.1	403.1	412.5	396.6	425.4	Italie-Saint-Marin-Saint-Siège
Belgium	–	437.9	424.8	440.2	e482.7	Belgique
Spain	311.1	334.1	311.4	317.6	368.4	Espagne
Australia	252.8	283.7	334.5	282.2	342.0	Australie
Switzerland-Liechtenstein	299.4	300.5	284.5	286.1	302.0	Suisse-Liechtenstein
Sweden	245.0	246.8	256.3	268.5	274.2	Suède
Austria	244.0	265.6	243.7	250.8	249.5	Autriche
Mexico	142.1	178.9	264.5	243.4	196.8	Mexique
Denmark	192.9	189.8	178.7	190.8	187.4	Danemark
Norway	155.8	151.4	150.9	150.3	171.5	Norvège
Saudi Arabia	172.2	151.7	150.6	146.1	e151.1	Arabie saoudite
Poland	118.6	132.1	148.0	164.2	181.8	Pologne
United Arab Emirates	119.5	125.3	140.6	144.4	e148.2	Emirates arabes unis
Ireland	108.9	111.0	109.2	113.8	116.6	Irlande
Singapore	80.5	111.4	107.1	95.2	95.7	Singapour
Belgium-Luxembourg	480.1	–	–	–	–	Belgique-Luxembourg
Greece	93.1	102.6	89.2	91.5	e101.2	Grèce
Russian Federation	79.3	71.4	86.6	93.8	140.8	Fédération de Russie
Finland	90.0	86.1	88.1	93.3	92.5	Finlande
Argentina	100.2	98.5	105.9	86.0	e38.1	Argentine
New Zealand	69.7	77.1	75.7	75.1	88.0	Nouvelle-Zélande
Czech Republic	74.9	73.5	58.5	72.3	98.6	République tchèque

(Value as percentages of World total)

(Valeur en pourcentage du total mondia

Regions of the world	1993	1994	1995	1996	1997	1998	1999	2000	2001	2002	Régions du monde
World	100.0	100.0	100.0	100.0	100.0	100.0	100.0	100.0	100.0	100.0	Monde
Africa	2.7	2.2	2.1	2.2	2.3	2.3	1.9	1.8	1.6	1.7	Afrique
Americas	24.0	24.8	24.8	24.2	27.6	31.0	32.8	35.4	36.4	37.4	Amériques
- Northern America	20.2	21.4	21.7	21.0	24.1	27.1	29.1	31.2	32.5	34.5	- Amérique du Nord
- LAIA	2.8	2.5	2.2	2.4	2.6	3.0	2.8	3.3	3.1	2.2	- ALAI
- CACM	0.2	0.2	0.2	0.2	0.3	0.2	0.2	0.3	0.2	0.2	- MCC
- Caribbean	0.7	0.5	0.5	0.5	0.6	0.6	0.6	0.5	0.5	0.4	- Caraïbes
- Rest of America	0.2	0.1	0.1	0.1	0.1	0.1	0.1	0.1	0.1	0.1	- Autre d'Amérique
Asia excluding former USSR	21.7	22.7	22.8	22.1	21.1	16.6	16.6	17.8	17.2	15.9	Asie ancienne URSS exclus
- Middle East	5.6	4.1	3.5	3.2	3.4	3.0	2.6	2.6	2.6	2.5	- Moyen-Orient
Asia former USSR	0.1	0.2	0.2	0.3	0.1	0.2	0.2	0.1	0.2	0.2	Asie ancienne URSS
Europe excluding former USSR	46.3	46.4	46.5	47.4	45.0	46.7	45.3	41.6	41.5	41.2	Europe ancienne URSS exclus
- European Union	41.8	41.7	41.2	42.0	40.0	41.2	40.0	36.8	36.5	36.1	- Union Européenne
- Eastern Europe	0.9	1.1	1.5	1.6	1.6	1.9	2.1	1.8	2.1	2.2	- Europe de l'Est
- Rest of Europe	3.6	3.7	3.9	3.7	3.5	3.6	3.3	2.9	2.9	3.0	- Autre de l'Europe
Europe former USSR	2.5	1.2	1.4	1.3	1.2	1.0	0.8	0.8	0.9	1.2	Europe ancienne URSS
Oceania	2.5	2.5	2.3	2.6	2.7	2.3	2.4	2.5	2.2	2.4	Océanie

Articles façonnés entièrement ou principalement en matières textiles, n.d.a. 658

TRADE BY COMMODITY (Value in million US dollars)
Exports by principal countries or areas

COMMERCE PAR PRODUIT (Valeur en millions de dollars EU)
Exportations selon les principaux pays ou zones

Country or area	1998	1999	2000	2001	2002	Pays ou zone
World	15199.0	16135.9	17098.3	17426.3	19042.7	Monde
Africa	222.8	247.0	142.8	271.2	273.2	Afrique
Americas	1963.0	2136.9	2236.2	2015.1	2119.9	Amériques
- Northern America	847.8	868.8	959.9	896.1	877.6	- Amérique du Nord
- LAIA	1055.3	1219.9	1224.3	1067.3	1191.8	- ALAI
- CACM	33.7	33.8	38.2	35.2	33.8	- MCC
- Caribbean	26.1	14.4	13.6	16.3	16.2	- Caraïbes
- Rest of America	0.0	0.1	0.1	0.2	0.5	- Autre d'Amérique
Asia excluding former USSR	7469.7	8220.4	9444.2	9744.3	10941.1	Asie ancienne URSS exclus
- Middle East	980.7	1008.3	1086.5	1145.3	1345.4	- Moyen-Orient
Asia former USSR	14.8	18.3	24.2	27.2	16.9	Asie ancienne URSS
Europe excluding former USSR	5301.0	5269.1	4996.3	5092.6	5411.8	Europe ancienne URSS exclus
- European Union	4388.8	4350.1	4046.7	4116.2	4360.9	- Union Européenne
- Eastern Europe	724.4	738.2	785.2	824.6	903.8	- Europe de l'Est
- Rest of Europe	187.8	180.8	164.3	151.8	147.1	- Autre de l'Europe
Europe former USSR	161.5	167.6	186.9	213.0	227.2	Europe ancienne URSS
Oceania	66.2	76.6	67.7	63.1	52.6	Océanie
China	2646.9	2874.2	3435.4	3684.7	4377.3	Chine
Pakistan	1087.0	1204.7	1354.1	1497.4	1761.6	Pakistan
India	778.1	906.3	1161.5	1104.6	1255.3	Inde
Turkey	908.5	925.6	992.6	1037.8	1226.4	Turquie
Mexico	745.0	903.7	862.3	702.4	826.2	Mexique
Portugal	823.8	823.6	790.5	779.6	773.3	Portugal
United States	737.0	716.9	792.5	705.2	669.4	Etats-Unis d'Amérique
Germany	672.4	691.0	618.5	661.0	730.3	Allemagne
China, Hong Kong SAR	516.7	526.8	566.5	499.8	432.4	Chine - RAS de Hong-Kong
Italy-San Marino-Holy See	460.3	452.0	460.7	468.0	467.5	Italie-Saint-Marin-Saint-Siège
France-Monaco	417.8	405.7	409.4	391.3	435.3	France-Monaco
Belgium	–	459.9	467.5	459.0	e514.9	Belgique
Korea, Republic of	306.5	367.7	386.3	363.4	406.7	République de Corée
United Kingdom	443.4	378.1	328.8	328.4	303.5	Royaume-Uni
Poland	295.8	298.5	335.3	341.2	369.8	Pologne
Spain	313.4	267.4	255.8	270.5	279.7	Espagne
Netherlands	259.4	319.6	222.0	229.1	270.3	Pays-Bas
Brazil	232.6	231.1	260.0	262.3	e271.9	Brésil
Czech Republic	212.2	230.1	236.5	258.3	272.4	République tchèque
Indonesia	96.8	172.8	225.0	235.5	200.4	Indonésie
Thailand	161.9	171.0	185.4	192.0	e202.7	Thaïlande
Canada	110.7	151.9	167.4	190.8	208.0	Canada
Bangladesh	149.7	e116.0	e154.3	183.2	e147.2	Bangladesh
Denmark	127.1	132.6	126.1	135.0	152.0	Danemark
Sweden	125.3	127.8	118.5	124.4	145.3	Suède
Austria	123.1	133.0	115.4	124.0	136.3	Autriche
Israel	107.8	111.3	113.5	136.2	131.0	Israël
Viet Nam	55.1	139.4	102.3	106.4	118.3	Viet Nam
Belgium-Luxembourg	466.4	–	–	–	–	Belgique-Luxembourg
Egypt	87.2	108.4	5.9	117.7	98.9	Egypte

(Value as percentages of World total) **(Valeur en pourcentage du total mondial)**

Regions of the world	1993	1994	1995	1996	1997	1998	1999	2000	2001	2002	Régions du monde
World	100.0	100.0	100.0	100.0	100.0	100.0	100.0	100.0	100.0	100.0	Monde
Africa	1.3	1.4	1.6	1.8	1.6	1.5	1.5	0.8	1.6	1.4	Afrique
Americas	12.0	11.1	9.6	10.4	11.8	12.9	13.2	13.1	11.6	11.1	Amériques
- Northern America	4.9	4.9	4.5	5.0	5.5	5.6	5.4	5.6	5.1	4.6	- Amérique du Nord
- LAIA	6.7	5.8	4.8	5.1	6.0	6.9	7.6	7.2	6.1	6.3	- ALAI
- CACM	0.2	0.2	0.2	0.2	0.2	0.2	0.2	0.2	0.2	0.2	- MCC
- Caribbean	0.2	0.2	0.2	0.0	0.1	0.2	0.1	0.1	0.1	0.1	- Caraïbes
- Rest of America	0.0	0.0	0.0	0.0	0.0	0.0	0.0	0.0	0.0	0.0	- Autre d'Amérique
Asia excluding former USSR	52.4	52.0	51.7	50.9	51.7	49.1	50.9	55.2	55.9	57.5	Asie ancienne URSS exclus
- Middle East	3.8	4.1	4.5	4.9	6.0	6.5	6.2	6.4	6.6	7.1	- Moyen-Orient
Asia former USSR	0.0	0.2	0.0	0.2	0.1	0.1	0.1	0.1	0.2	0.1	Asie ancienne URSS
Europe excluding former USSR	33.2	34.2	35.6	35.1	33.2	34.9	32.7	29.2	29.2	28.4	Europe ancienne URSS exclus
- European Union	28.6	29.0	30.1	29.5	27.8	28.9	27.0	23.7	23.6	22.9	- Union Européenne
- Eastern Europe	2.8	3.3	3.8	4.1	4.1	4.8	4.6	4.6	4.7	4.7	- Europe de l'Est
- Rest of Europe	1.7	1.9	1.7	1.5	1.2	1.2	1.1	1.0	0.9	0.8	- Autre de l'Europe
Europe former USSR	0.5	0.7	0.8	1.0	1.0	1.1	1.0	1.1	1.2	1.2	Europe ancienne URSS
Oceania	0.6	0.6	0.6	0.6	0.6	0.4	0.5	0.4	0.4	0.3	Océanie

659 Floor coverings, etc

TRADE BY COMMODITY (Value in million US dollars) COMMERCE PAR PRODUIT (Valeur en millions de dollars EU)

Imports by principal countries or areas **Importations selon les principaux pays ou zones**

Country or area	1998	1999	2000	2001	2002	Pays ou zone
World	8822.5	8640.0	8671.3	8547.6	8585.3	Monde
Africa	72.3	68.3	78.5	84.2	79.8	Afrique
Americas	2013.9	2188.3	2531.1	2478.1	2474.6	Amériques
- Northern America	1703.8	1879.5	2120.6	2050.0	2191.5	- Amérique du Nord
- LAIA	273.5	273.7	369.3	393.2	251.1	- ALAI
- CACM	6.4	6.1	12.2	7.0	7.5	- MCC
- Caribbean	24.6	24.3	24.8	24.6	20.5	- Caraïbes
- Rest of America	5.5	4.7	4.1	3.2	3.9	- Autre d'Amérique
Asia excluding former USSR	1181.2	1189.6	1328.5	1325.3	1354.7	Asie ancienne URSS exclus
- Middle East	386.6	356.6	378.6	385.8	405.7	- Moyen-Orient
Asia former USSR	42.9	34.1	62.8	60.9	63.0	Asie ancienne URSS
Europe excluding former USSR	5276.8	4940.6	4451.4	4390.4	4366.5	Europe ancienne URSS exclus
- European Union	4674.5	4367.6	3918.5	3856.0	3788.2	- Union Européenne
- Eastern Europe	243.3	235.7	236.1	253.7	293.3	- Europe de l'Est
- Rest of Europe	359.0	337.3	296.7	280.7	285.0	- Autre de l'Europe
Europe former USSR	85.7	50.3	51.6	71.2	82.2	Europe ancienne URSS
Oceania	149.6	168.9	167.4	137.5	164.5	Océanie
United States	1197.3	1351.4	1592.3	1541.0	1674.2	Etats-Unis d'Amérique
Germany	1625.3	1421.0	1139.0	1174.4	1002.0	Allemagne
United Kingdom	975.8	910.5	933.4	962.5	1044.9	Royaume-Uni
Japan	480.2	505.9	566.1	574.9	562.1	Japon
Canada	501.4	522.6	526.9	506.9	515.4	Canada
France-Monaco	437.3	440.4	416.0	369.1	370.4	France-Monaco
Netherlands	379.3	328.4	284.8	258.3	242.7	Pays-Bas
Italy-San Marino-Holy See	232.9	231.4	217.4	192.3	198.2	Italie-Saint-Marin-Saint-Siège
Mexico	127.4	163.9	253.5	290.2	174.1	Mexique
Switzerland-Liechtenstein	223.5	206.3	181.4	172.5	163.8	Suisse-Liechtenstein
Belgium	–	253.3	222.8	214.0	e234.6	Belgique
Austria	151.6	164.7	145.0	134.0	117.2	Autriche
Spain	130.2	132.2	127.1	126.0	141.6	Espagne
Australia	115.0	128.9	134.5	106.5	126.7	Australie
Sweden	120.5	110.0	117.8	126.7	121.3	Suède
Saudi Arabia	130.1	117.7	101.3	116.4	e120.5	Arabie saoudite
Poland	98.2	97.1	99.9	98.3	100.6	Pologne
China, Hong Kong SAR	100.9	85.3	89.9	82.6	71.2	Chine - RAS de Hong-Kong
Denmark	95.5	86.0	73.9	71.6	86.2	Danemark
Ireland	86.9	77.8	74.5	80.7	70.7	Irlande
Czech Republic	71.6	68.4	65.0	75.8	95.1	République tchèque
Norway	81.1	72.1	64.8	59.9	65.9	Norvège
Greece	85.6	85.7	56.9	45.3	e50.1	Grèce
United Arab Emirates	50.3	52.7	70.5	73.3	e75.2	Emirates arabes unis
Singapore	54.3	54.3	70.6	58.8	44.4	Singapour
Turkey	55.8	46.3	64.4	52.5	59.4	Turquie
Portugal	53.2	63.7	55.7	42.7	47.8	Portugal
Kuwait	54.5	51.0	e47.9	e52.7	e51.1	Koweït
Belgium-Luxembourg	256.7	–	–	–	–	Belgique-Luxembourg
Korea, Republic of	21.5	37.8	55.3	56.9	58.3	République de Corée

(Value as percentages of World total) **(Valeur en pourcentage du total mondial)**

Regions of the world	1993	1994	1995	1996	1997	1998	1999	2000	2001	2002	Régions du monde
World	100.0	100.0	100.0	100.0	100.0	100.0	100.0	100.0	100.0	100.0	Monde
Africa	0.7	0.9	0.8	0.7	0.7	0.8	0.8	0.9	1.0	0.9	Afrique
Americas	15.4	16.3	16.3	16.6	18.3	22.8	25.3	29.2	29.0	28.8	Amériques
- Northern America	13.0	13.7	14.0	14.0	15.4	19.3	21.8	24.5	24.0	25.5	- Amérique du Nord
- LAIA	2.0	2.2	2.0	2.3	2.6	3.1	3.2	4.3	4.6	2.9	- ALAI
- CACM	0.1	0.1	0.1	0.1	0.1	0.1	0.1	0.1	0.1	0.1	- MCC
- Caribbean	0.2	0.2	0.2	0.2	0.2	0.3	0.3	0.3	0.3	0.2	- Caraïbes
- Rest of America	0.1	0.1	0.1	0.0	0.1	0.1	0.1	0.0	0.0	0.0	- Autre d'Amérique
Asia excluding former USSR	18.4	18.2	17.5	17.9	16.0	13.4	13.8	15.3	15.5	15.8	Asie ancienne URSS exclus
- Middle East	6.3	4.7	4.0	4.0	4.2	4.4	4.1	4.4	4.5	4.7	- Moyen-Orient
Asia former USSR	0.1	0.2	0.3	0.6	0.2	0.5	0.4	0.7	0.7	0.7	Asie ancienne URSS
Europe excluding former USSR	60.9	61.4	61.8	60.9	61.3	59.8	57.2	51.3	51.4	50.9	Europe ancienne URSS exclus
- European Union	54.7	55.1	55.2	54.3	55.3	53.0	50.6	45.2	45.1	44.1	- Union Européenne
- Eastern Europe	1.5	1.5	1.8	2.1	2.4	2.8	2.7	2.7	3.0	3.4	- Europe de l'Est
- Rest of Europe	4.7	4.8	4.8	4.5	3.7	4.1	3.9	3.4	3.3	3.3	- Autre de l'Europe
Europe former USSR	3.1	1.3	1.5	1.4	1.7	1.0	0.6	0.6	0.8	1.0	Europe ancienne URSS
Oceania	1.4	1.7	1.8	1.9	1.8	1.7	2.0	1.9	1.6	1.9	Océanie

TRADE BY COMMODITY (Value in million US dollars)
Exports by principal countries or areas

COMMERCE PAR PRODUIT (Valeur en millions de dollars EU)
Exportations selon les principaux pays ou zones

Country or area	1998	1999	2000	2001	2002	Pays ou zone
World	9369.2	9336.1	9003.1	8574.7	8970.1	Monde
Africa	115.4	120.9	62.0	63.6	69.9	Afrique
Americas	1171.4	1135.7	1149.8	1036.1	1032.1	Amériques
- Northern America	1038.6	1012.6	1048.9	947.5	937.5	- Amérique du Nord
- LAIA	132.0	122.2	98.7	87.0	93.2	- ALAI
- CACM	0.5	0.4	1.4	0.7	0.4	- MCC
- Caribbean	0.3	0.4	0.7	0.8	0.9	- Caraïbes
- Rest of America	0.0	0.0	0.0	0.1	0.1	- Autre d'Amérique
Asia excluding former USSR	2880.8	3078.3	3154.4	2947.6	3041.8	Asie ancienne URSS exclus
- Middle East	1049.5	1101.2	1096.1	960.8	998.6	- Moyen-Orient
Asia former USSR	10.6	6.1	4.4	3.9	4.1	Asie ancienne URSS
Europe excluding former USSR	5047.8	4857.8	4486.6	4386.5	4663.3	Europe ancienne URSS exclus
- European Union	4828.5	4627.5	4244.7	4136.4	4412.2	- Union Européenne
- Eastern Europe	89.4	97.0	116.7	125.6	134.8	- Europe de l'Est
- Rest of Europe	130.0	133.4	125.2	124.4	116.3	- Autre de l'Europe
Europe former USSR	52.4	40.7	60.4	57.3	57.1	Europe ancienne URSS
Oceania	90.6	96.5	85.4	79.8	101.8	Océanie
Belgium	-	2137.9	2020.4	1946.1	e2183.5	Belgique
United States	875.5	822.5	825.8	743.7	734.6	Etats-Unis d'Amérique
Iran (Islamic Republic of)	605.2	733.3	708.2	603.6	627.1	Iran (République islamique d')
China	588.2	578.9	654.8	683.3	768.5	Chine
Netherlands	763.6	665.4	570.3	574.3	627.8	Pays-Bas
India	616.7	696.2	650.1	585.3	619.5	Inde
Germany	506.6	481.2	411.4	443.0	431.5	Allemagne
Belgium-Luxembourg	2207.7	-	-	-	-	Belgique-Luxembourg
United Kingdom	405.9	385.3	376.1	354.1	329.8	Royaume-Uni
France-Monaco	356.9	370.7	325.1	256.5	264.1	France-Monaco
Turkey	343.9	270.2	293.7	263.4	286.8	Turquie
Pakistan	209.2	243.8	282.1	265.2	243.7	Pakistan
Canada	163.1	190.1	223.1	203.8	202.9	Canada
Nepal	128.9	146.3	146.4	e152.3	e117.2	Népal
Denmark	144.0	130.7	119.4	122.5	127.5	Danemark
Italy-San Marino-Holy See	138.1	129.7	123.8	126.7	124.4	Italie-Saint-Marin-Saint-Siège
Switzerland-Liechtenstein	113.9	115.7	101.7	98.9	96.7	Suisse-Liechtenstein
Mexico	101.4	98.9	72.9	58.2	64.4	Mexique
Austria	59.4	71.7	68.5	70.8	68.8	Autriche
Saudi Arabia	70.0	65.7	55.3	59.0	e53.2	Arabie saoudite
Spain	61.3	64.9	59.1	49.4	55.1	Espagne
China, Hong Kong SAR	65.3	51.8	49.1	48.7	46.4	Chine - RAS de Hong-Kong
Thailand	36.4	47.8	59.2	52.3	e55.2	Thaïlande
Portugal	51.4	50.7	44.7	45.8	57.9	Portugal
New Zealand	50.6	52.2	45.7	43.3	57.6	Nouvelle-Zélande
Sweden	43.8	46.9	48.7	44.7	47.0	Suède
Ireland	52.7	48.1	44.1	42.6	33.3	Irlande
Korea, Republic of	36.4	47.2	52.9	41.0	32.2	République de Corée
Australia	39.7	44.2	39.5	36.5	44.2	Australie
Poland	24.6	33.6	43.3	47.8	52.3	Pologne

(Value as percentages of World total) **(Valeur en pourcentage du total mondial)**

Regions of the world	1993	1994	1995	1996	1997	1998	1999	2000	2001	2002	Régions du monde
World	100.0	100.0	100.0	100.0	100.0	100.0	100.0	100.0	100.0	100.0	Monde
Africa	1.0	1.1	1.0	0.9	0.8	1.2	1.3	0.7	0.7	0.8	Afrique
Americas	10.6	10.3	9.9	10.9	10.9	12.5	12.2	12.8	12.1	11.5	Amériques
- Northern America	9.6	9.4	9.0	9.7	9.6	11.1	10.8	11.7	11.0	10.5	- Amérique du Nord
- LAIA	1.0	0.9	0.9	1.2	1.3	1.4	1.3	1.1	1.0	1.0	- ALAI
- CACM	0.0	0.0	0.0	0.0	0.0	0.0	0.0	0.0	0.0	0.0	- MCC
- Caribbean	0.0	0.0	0.0	0.0	0.0	0.0	0.0	0.0	0.0	0.0	- Caraïbes
- Rest of America	0.0	0.0	0.0	0.0	0.0	0.0	0.0	0.0	0.0	0.0	- Autre d'Amérique
Asia excluding former USSR	37.3	36.1	31.3	32.9	28.4	30.7	33.0	35.0	34.4	33.9	Asie ancienne URSS exclus
- Middle East	14.6	13.6	10.4	12.4	10.5	11.2	11.8	12.2	11.2	11.1	- Moyen-Orient
Asia former USSR	0.4	0.5	0.2	0.2	0.1	0.1	0.1	0.0	0.0	0.0	Asie ancienne URSS
Europe excluding former USSR	49.7	50.7	56.3	53.5	58.4	53.9	52.0	49.8	51.2	52.0	Europe ancienne URSS exclus
- European Union	47.6	48.8	54.3	51.5	56.6	51.5	49.6	47.1	48.2	49.2	- Union Européenne
- Eastern Europe	0.8	0.7	0.7	0.9	0.8	1.0	1.0	1.3	1.5	1.5	- Europe de l'Est
- Rest of Europe	1.3	1.2	1.3	1.2	1.0	1.4	1.4	1.4	1.5	1.3	- Autre de l'Europe
Europe former USSR	0.3	0.3	0.3	0.5	0.5	0.6	0.4	0.7	0.7	0.6	Europe ancienne URSS
Oceania	0.7	0.9	0.9	1.0	0.9	1.0	1.0	0.9	0.9	1.1	Océanie

661 Lime, cement, and fabricated construction materials

TRADE BY COMMODITY (Value in million US dollars)
Imports by principal countries or areas

COMMERCE PAR PRODUIT (Valeur en millions de dollars EU)
Importations selon les principaux pays ou zones

Country or area	1998	1999	2000	2001	2002	Pays ou zone
World	11608.7	11960.9	12104.8	12403.9	12770.1	Monde
Africa	865.8	1043.2	894.7	1034.0	1149.3	Afrique
Americas	2960.9	3353.5	3677.4	3693.0	3713.2	Amériques
- Northern America	2391.8	2854.2	3127.6	3157.6	3245.9	- Amérique du Nord
- LAIA	301.1	228.2	239.4	240.5	213.1	- ALAI
- CACM	46.9	58.9	62.0	63.0	53.9	- MCC
- Caribbean	168.1	157.0	200.8	194.8	158.0	- Caraïbes
- Rest of America	53.0	55.3	47.6	37.1	42.4	- Autre d'Amérique
Asia excluding former USSR	3312.5	2977.6	3092.7	3147.4	3114.1	Asie ancienne URSS exclus
- Middle East	638.4	572.0	636.1	650.8	654.1	- Moyen-Orient
Asia former USSR	80.3	65.6	70.6	60.5	60.9	Asie ancienne URSS
Europe excluding former USSR	4115.3	4265.0	4094.9	4216.1	4410.3	Europe ancienne URSS exclus
- European Union	3405.3	3552.2	3373.8	3483.3	3568.9	- Union Européenne
- Eastern Europe	347.2	349.3	356.2	344.3	428.3	- Europe de l'Est
- Rest of Europe	362.7	363.5	364.9	388.5	413.1	- Autre de l'Europe
Europe former USSR	151.4	106.5	120.3	141.7	174.5	Europe ancienne URSS
Oceania	122.5	149.4	154.1	111.2	147.8	Océanie
United States	2250.9	2685.4	2944.4	2959.0	3036.1	Etats-Unis d'Amérique
Germany	1083.2	982.4	799.7	778.2	648.8	Allemagne
Japan	724.6	776.1	847.1	871.4	870.6	Japon
France-Monaco	468.9	537.7	572.3	539.4	569.2	France-Monaco
Netherlands	385.2	411.3	351.3	340.6	380.8	Pays-Bas
China, Hong Kong SAR	540.7	376.4	305.1	270.1	233.5	Chine - RAS de Hong-Kong
United Kingdom	309.9	320.7	324.6	324.1	398.0	Royaume-Uni
Spain	229.6	278.7	298.1	393.0	406.4	Espagne
Italy-San Marino-Holy See	150.2	180.2	210.5	245.1	275.5	Italie-Saint-Marin-Saint-Siège
Bangladesh	242.1	e265.1	e188.1	182.2	e178.1	Bangladesh
Nigeria	124.3	270.7	165.6	e226.9	e215.2	Nigéria
Singapore	271.4	181.2	186.0	166.8	140.6	Singapour
Korea, Republic of	57.9	90.6	161.0	238.0	368.3	République de Corée
Belgium	–	221.5	215.9	223.6	e245.3	Belgique
Canada	135.7	163.3	180.3	195.0	206.0	Canada
Switzerland-Liechtenstein	181.2	171.8	165.2	170.1	178.8	Suisse-Liechtenstein
Austria	175.7	177.9	150.9	150.3	155.2	Autriche
Kuwait	163.1	135.3	e127.1	e139.8	e131.4	Koweït
Saudi Arabia	94.4	87.0	136.5	149.3	e154.5	Arabie saoudite
Poland	128.3	135.3	126.6	102.5	123.4	Pologne
United Arab Emirates	120.3	126.1	101.0	115.2	e118.1	Emirates arabes unis
Portugal	88.2	90.3	117.1	145.3	128.7	Portugal
China	152.5	110.3	86.6	113.9	92.2	Chine
Israel	124.3	105.6	106.9	106.7	104.2	Israël
Denmark	86.9	89.3	99.4	102.6	104.7	Danemark
Egypt	147.2	218.7	e46.5	42.3	21.9	Egypte
Ireland	85.3	101.0	84.9	80.7	85.2	Irlande
Australia	73.1	86.3	106.0	66.5	96.6	Australie
Czech Republic	69.0	72.8	70.8	74.5	97.8	République tchèque
Sri Lanka	e79.9	72.1	e97.4	67.4	67.9	Sri Lanka

(Value as percentages of World total) **(Valeur en pourcentage du total mondial)**

Regions of the world	1993	1994	1995	1996	1997	1998	1999	2000	2001	2002	Régions du monde
World	100.0	100.0	100.0	100.0	100.0	100.0	100.0	100.0	100.0	100.0	Monde
Africa	7.3	5.7	7.0	6.7	5.8	7.5	8.7	7.4	8.3	9.0	Afrique
Americas	14.8	16.8	16.4	16.7	20.4	25.5	28.0	30.4	29.8	29.1	Amériques
- Northern America	11.6	13.2	12.7	13.1	16.0	20.6	23.9	25.8	25.5	25.4	- Amérique du Nord
- LAIA	1.7	1.9	2.0	2.0	2.5	2.6	1.9	2.0	1.9	1.7	- ALAI
- CACM	0.2	0.3	0.3	0.3	0.4	0.4	0.5	0.5	0.5	0.4	- MCC
- Caribbean	1.0	1.0	1.1	1.1	1.1	1.4	1.3	1.7	1.6	1.2	- Caraïbes
- Rest of America	0.4	0.4	0.3	0.2	0.3	0.5	0.5	0.4	0.3	0.3	- Autre d'Amérique
Asia excluding former USSR	39.6	37.5	37.1	39.5	38.2	28.5	24.9	25.5	25.4	24.4	Asie ancienne URSS exclus
- Middle East	8.7	8.5	6.7	6.4	5.6	5.5	4.8	5.3	5.2	5.1	- Moyen-Orient
Asia former USSR	0.1	0.2	0.9	0.7	0.6	0.7	0.5	0.6	0.5	0.5	Asie ancienne URSS
Europe excluding former USSR	36.8	37.4	36.3	34.0	32.6	35.4	35.7	33.8	34.0	34.5	Europe ancienne URSS exclus
- European Union	32.8	33.1	31.5	29.1	27.5	29.3	29.7	27.9	28.1	27.9	- Union Européenne
- Eastern Europe	1.4	1.5	1.8	2.1	2.4	3.0	2.9	2.9	2.8	3.4	- Europe de l'Est
- Rest of Europe	2.6	2.8	3.1	2.8	2.7	3.1	3.0	3.0	3.1	3.2	- Autre de l'Europe
Europe former USSR	0.4	1.2	1.3	1.3	1.4	1.3	0.9	1.0	1.1	1.4	Europe ancienne URSS
Oceania	0.9	1.1	1.0	1.0	1.0	1.1	1.2	1.3	0.9	1.2	Océanie

TRADE BY COMMODITY (Value in million US dollars)
Exports by principal countries or areas

COMMERCE PAR PRODUIT (Valeur en millions de dollars EU)
Exportations selon les principaux pays ou zones

Country or area	1998	1999	2000	2001	2002	Pays ou zone
World	10836.6	10876.7	10836.6	11064.7	11683.3	Monde
Africa	309.5	295.3	291.7	328.7	566.2	Afrique
Americas	1420.8	1500.2	1552.1	1592.1	1599.5	Amériques
- Northern America	615.6	673.9	704.4	736.3	768.2	- Amérique du Nord
- LAIA	721.1	740.6	768.8	759.8	745.7	- ALAI
- CACM	18.3	19.8	27.9	32.4	29.7	- MCC
- Caribbean	65.0	65.0	49.9	60.5	55.2	- Caraïbes
- Rest of America	0.8	0.9	1.1	3.2	0.8	- Autre d'Amérique
Asia excluding former USSR	2817.7	3023.6	3274.6	3487.9	3727.8	Asie ancienne URSS exclus
- Middle East	535.4	603.9	741.1	857.1	934.9	- Moyen-Orient
Asia former USSR	44.9	18.9	22.9	24.3	29.3	Asie ancienne URSS
Europe excluding former USSR	6023.3	5864.2	5529.6	5455.9	5568.0	Europe ancienne URSS exclus
- European Union	5416.3	5273.2	4983.6	4907.0	5011.2	- Union Européenne
- Eastern Europe	481.2	447.3	388.6	378.0	379.5	- Europe de l'Est
- Rest of Europe	125.8	143.8	157.4	170.9	177.3	- Autre de l'Europe
Europe former USSR	179.4	138.2	138.2	143.7	160.1	Europe ancienne URSS
Oceania	41.0	36.4	27.5	32.1	32.3	Océanie
Italy-San Marino-Holy See	2215.3	2121.6	2059.3	1953.0	1907.5	Italie-Saint-Marin-Saint-Siège
China	923.5	866.3	955.1	1097.0	1249.3	Chine
Spain	727.7	737.2	703.6	714.6	764.0	Espagne
Canada	411.3	441.4	443.7	481.6	497.8	Canada
Germany	454.0	453.3	412.3	439.2	465.6	Allemagne
Turkey	271.4	286.7	370.2	437.1	551.9	Turquie
France-Monaco	398.2	371.5	345.8	338.5	354.9	France-Monaco
Belgium	–	474.2	424.1	420.3	e471.5	Belgique
India	218.9	276.7	402.2	342.2	427.1	Inde
Thailand	226.0	348.3	316.9	360.4	e380.6	Thaïlande
Greece	303.8	259.9	246.3	253.8	e254.1	Grèce
United States	203.4	232.2	260.7	254.7	270.4	Etats-Unis d'Amérique
Brazil	231.3	224.5	238.8	246.6	e255.6	Brésil
Mexico	238.0	252.9	255.0	239.2	205.8	Mexique
United Kingdom	248.9	218.6	181.4	171.4	155.5	Royaume-Uni
Japan	208.0	164.7	162.6	148.6	154.5	Japon
Portugal	156.7	175.7	176.2	165.9	159.7	Portugal
Indonesia	94.2	165.8	171.5	187.7	138.3	Indonésie
Korea, Republic of	118.5	166.6	148.0	127.9	101.5	République de Corée
Saudi Arabia	124.1	121.5	133.3	132.7	e119.6	Arabie saoudite
Venezuela	107.1	122.1	128.1	116.5	e123.8	Venezuela
Czech Republic	114.5	122.6	119.9	99.3	87.2	République tchèque
Netherlands	127.2	123.7	102.5	95.4	74.7	Pays-Bas
Denmark	105.0	102.5	99.6	104.4	108.5	Danemark
Slovakia	98.3	105.9	86.2	92.9	102.7	Slovaquie
Belgium-Luxembourg	477.2	–	–	–	–	Belgique-Luxembourg
Colombia	85.3	87.5	94.4	99.9	101.4	Colombie
Poland	121.9	94.3	64.3	67.8	61.7	Pologne
China, Hong Kong SAR	178.7	106.9	59.4	37.0	24.3	Chine - RAS de Hong-Kong
Croatia	47.8	62.4	73.4	87.3	85.6	Croatie

(Value as percentages of World total) **(Valeur en pourcentage du total mondial)**

Regions of the world	1993	1994	1995	1996	1997	1998	1999	2000	2001	2002	Régions du monde
World	100.0	100.0	100.0	100.0	100.0	100.0	100.0	100.0	100.0	100.0	Monde
Africa	2.0	2.0	2.8	2.4	2.1	2.9	2.7	2.7	3.0	4.8	Afrique
Americas	9.7	9.2	9.9	10.2	11.5	13.1	13.8	14.3	14.4	13.7	Amériques
- Northern America	5.2	4.9	4.7	5.2	5.8	5.7	6.2	6.5	6.7	6.6	- Amérique du Nord
- LAIA	4.1	3.8	4.8	4.6	5.3	6.7	6.8	7.1	6.9	6.4	- ALAI
- CACM	0.1	0.1	0.1	0.1	0.1	0.2	0.2	0.3	0.3	0.3	- MCC
- Caribbean	0.3	0.4	0.4	0.4	0.3	0.6	0.6	0.5	0.5	0.5	- Caraïbes
- Rest of America	0.0	0.0	0.0	0.0	0.0	0.0	0.0	0.0	0.0	0.0	- Autre d'Amérique
Asia excluding former USSR	28.3	28.6	28.1	28.9	31.2	26.0	27.8	30.2	31.5	31.9	Asie ancienne URSS exclus
- Middle East	4.8	5.6	4.6	4.3	5.1	4.9	5.6	6.8	7.7	8.0	- Moyen-Orient
Asia former USSR	0.1	0.2	0.3	0.5	0.2	0.4	0.2	0.2	0.2	0.3	Asie ancienne URSS
Europe excluding former USSR	58.3	58.6	57.3	56.2	53.2	55.6	53.9	51.0	49.3	47.7	Europe ancienne URSS exclus
- European Union	51.8	52.0	51.1	49.9	47.6	50.0	48.5	46.0	44.3	42.9	- Union Européenne
- Eastern Europe	5.2	5.3	5.1	5.4	4.5	4.4	4.1	3.6	3.4	3.2	- Europe de l'Est
- Rest of Europe	1.3	1.2	1.1	0.9	1.2	1.2	1.3	1.5	1.5	1.5	- Autre de l'Europe
Europe former USSR	1.2	1.1	1.2	1.3	1.4	1.7	1.3	1.3	1.3	1.4	Europe ancienne URSS
Oceania	0.5	0.4	0.4	0.5	0.4	0.4	0.3	0.3	0.3	0.3	Océanie

662 Clay and refractory construction materials

TRADE BY COMMODITY (Value in million US dollars)
Imports by principal countries or areas

COMMERCE PAR PRODUIT (Valeur en millions de dollars EU)
Importations selon les principaux pays ou zones

Country or area	1998	1999	2000	2001	2002	Pays ou zone
World	10705.7	10508.5	10454.6	10432.9	11077.9	Monde
Africa	451.9	389.4	466.5	518.9	552.9	Afrique
Americas	2276.9	2511.8	2756.6	2549.9	2751.4	Amériques
- Northern America	1528.0	1822.2	2060.6	1845.7	2075.0	- Amérique du Nord
- LAIA	530.9	462.5	470.5	467.9	442.0	- ALAI
- CACM	61.5	57.8	65.4	73.2	81.5	- MCC
- Caribbean	134.3	138.3	132.1	140.4	127.1	- Caraïbes
- Rest of America	22.2	31.0	28.1	22.7	25.8	- Autre d'Amérique
Asia excluding former USSR	1728.5	1572.4	1787.9	1903.4	2010.3	Asie ancienne URSS exclus
- Middle East	491.9	457.9	546.7	606.2	672.6	- Moyen-Orient
Asia former USSR	72.5	65.6	88.1	76.0	82.6	Asie ancienne URSS
Europe excluding former USSR	5643.5	5481.4	4817.3	4879.4	5077.1	Europe ancienne URSS exclus
- European Union	4527.0	4366.8	3745.5	3772.7	3875.3	- Union Européenne
- Eastern Europe	682.3	639.2	622.6	632.2	666.1	- Europe de l'Est
- Rest of Europe	434.3	475.5	449.3	474.6	535.7	- Autre de l'Europe
Europe former USSR	275.7	218.3	253.9	297.0	342.5	Europe ancienne URSS
Oceania	256.7	269.5	284.2	208.4	261.1	Océanie
United States	1240.8	1522.4	1756.7	1582.5	1784.7	Etats-Unis d'Amérique
Germany	1540.1	1341.3	916.6	938.3	803.2	Allemagne
France-Monaco	796.5	823.5	777.2	807.4	877.7	France-Monaco
United Kingdom	506.9	453.8	485.4	461.0	544.0	Royaume-Uni
Poland	351.3	336.1	309.8	255.7	225.7	Pologne
Canada	286.7	299.3	302.9	261.4	287.9	Canada
Belgium	–	306.4	301.0	286.2	e313.9	Belgique
Austria	236.4	246.6	220.0	239.4	219.8	Autriche
Australia	212.3	219.0	240.3	166.5	209.9	Australie
Italy-San Marino-Holy See	191.1	212.2	198.8	187.9	199.1	Italie-Saint-Marin-Saint-Siège
Netherlands	191.0	214.4	180.4	168.1	181.1	Pays-Bas
Mexico	150.6	170.6	182.8	189.7	201.3	Mexique
Japan	143.8	153.3	177.6	199.0	208.9	Japon
China, Hong Kong SAR	216.1	177.4	180.6	164.6	129.9	Chine - RAS de Hong-Kong
Switzerland-Liechtenstein	176.9	180.2	158.3	154.9	163.7	Suisse-Liechtenstein
Greece	195.8	187.5	143.1	125.2	e138.5	Grèce
Saudi Arabia	92.1	100.0	171.9	203.3	e210.4	Arabie saoudite
Singapore	189.1	152.1	130.2	109.9	93.6	Singapour
Russian Federation	141.0	91.4	113.3	135.2	168.0	Fédération de Russie
Portugal	124.4	135.5	120.5	117.7	122.5	Portugal
Korea, Republic of	58.2	65.6	106.9	156.9	222.3	République de Corée
Spain	120.6	121.0	91.6	118.6	138.2	Espagne
Israel	117.1	110.6	104.3	117.7	115.1	Israël
Hungary	90.8	85.8	94.4	111.4	126.8	Hongrie
Sweden	91.3	95.3	90.4	98.2	104.9	Suède
Czech Republic	98.4	94.6	83.7	92.3	106.9	République tchèque
China	85.0	67.4	86.3	104.8	88.9	Chine
Norway	92.4	77.5	78.5	79.1	98.6	Norvège
Algeria	36.2	36.9	88.8	e107.4	e122.4	Algérie
Bosnia and Herzegovina	e19.2	e75.2	e82.0	e94.6	e105.9	Bosnie-Herzégovine

(Value as percentages of World total) **(Valeur en pourcentage du total mondial)**

Regions of the world	1993	1994	1995	1996	1997	1998	1999	2000	2001	2002	Régions du monde
World	100.0	100.0	100.0	100.0	100.0	100.0	100.0	100.0	100.0	100.0	Monde
Africa	4.2	4.0	4.1	3.9	3.6	4.2	3.7	4.5	5.0	5.0	Afrique
Americas	17.4	17.4	16.0	16.9	19.2	21.3	23.9	26.4	24.4	24.8	Amériques
- Northern America	12.0	11.4	10.6	11.3	13.0	14.3	17.3	19.7	17.7	18.7	- Amérique du Nord
- LAIA	3.8	4.4	3.7	3.8	4.4	5.0	4.4	4.5	4.5	4.0	- ALAI
- CACM	0.4	0.4	0.4	0.4	0.5	0.6	0.5	0.6	0.7	0.7	- MCC
- Caribbean	1.0	1.0	1.2	1.1	1.2	1.3	1.3	1.3	1.3	1.1	- Caraïbes
- Rest of America	0.2	0.2	0.2	0.2	0.2	0.2	0.3	0.3	0.2	0.2	- Autre d'Amérique
Asia excluding former USSR	20.2	18.4	19.4	20.7	19.8	16.1	15.0	17.1	18.2	18.1	Asie ancienne URSS exclus
- Middle East	5.8	4.5	4.6	5.0	4.6	4.6	4.4	5.2	5.8	6.1	- Moyen-Orient
Asia former USSR	0.0	0.3	0.4	0.7	0.6	0.7	0.6	0.8	0.7	0.7	Asie ancienne URSS
Europe excluding former USSR	54.3	55.1	55.0	53.0	51.5	52.7	52.2	46.1	46.8	45.8	Europe ancienne URSS exclus
- European Union	45.6	47.4	46.4	43.5	41.8	42.3	41.6	35.8	36.2	35.0	- Union Européenne
- Eastern Europe	5.2	4.0	4.6	5.6	5.9	6.4	6.1	6.0	6.1	6.0	- Europe de l'Est
- Rest of Europe	3.5	3.7	4.0	3.9	3.8	4.1	4.5	4.3	4.5	4.8	- Autre de l'Europe
Europe former USSR	1.4	2.1	2.4	2.5	2.9	2.6	2.1	2.4	2.8	3.1	Europe ancienne URSS
Oceania	2.5	2.7	2.6	2.4	2.3	2.4	2.6	2.7	2.0	2.4	Océanie

TRADE BY COMMODITY (Value in million US dollars)
Exports by principal countries or areas

COMMERCE PAR PRODUIT (Valeur en millions de dollars EU)
Exportations selon les principaux pays ou zones

Country or area	1998	1999	2000	2001	2002	Pays ou zone
World	10366.8	10361.5	10127.3	10252.4	11136.2	Monde
Africa	47.4	73.2	50.2	76.3	74.5	Afrique
Americas	939.6	981.5	991.1	960.1	949.7	Amériques
- Northern America	448.3	454.7	452.0	421.2	390.3	- Amérique du Nord
- LAIA	482.4	519.1	529.8	524.2	543.8	- ALAI
- CACM	5.3	5.9	7.4	13.2	14.0	- MCC
- Caribbean	3.3	1.5	1.6	1.4	1.3	- Caraïbes
- Rest of America	0.2	0.3	0.3	0.2	0.2	- Autre d'Amérique
Asia excluding former USSR	944.4	995.6	1126.1	1216.8	1529.4	Asie ancienne URSS exclus
- Middle East	262.5	288.8	308.9	328.3	396.1	- Moyen-Orient
Asia former USSR	1.8	0.3	0.5	0.7	0.9	Asie ancienne URSS
Europe excluding former USSR	8277.0	8163.8	7769.4	7803.0	8379.8	Europe ancienne URSS exclus
- European Union	7892.2	7774.0	7371.5	7383.3	7943.9	- Union Européenne
- Eastern Europe	299.2	280.5	283.5	298.7	324.2	- Europe de l'Est
- Rest of Europe	85.7	109.3	114.4	121.0	111.8	- Autre de l'Europe
Europe former USSR	111.5	98.7	142.6	148.0	154.8	Europe ancienne URSS
Oceania	45.2	48.3	47.4	47.5	47.1	Océanie
Italy-San Marino-Holy See	3556.7	3497.5	3326.6	3277.9	3495.9	Italie-Saint-Marin-Saint-Siège
Spain	1743.2	1786.3	1828.9	1897.9	2074.1	Espagne
Germany	1002.2	1011.3	918.6	955.8	1044.4	Allemagne
France-Monaco	594.9	520.1	458.4	449.5	490.1	France-Monaco
United States	366.7	365.7	367.9	351.9	314.2	Etats-Unis d'Amérique
China	206.8	192.3	251.6	376.8	620.2	Chine
United Kingdom	297.1	254.2	238.4	219.6	207.0	Royaume-Uni
Turkey	190.8	212.6	215.3	221.6	274.2	Turquie
Mexico	189.0	225.4	212.8	212.1	215.3	Mexique
Brazil	193.1	196.6	213.7	205.5	e213.1	Brésil
Japan	177.4	177.7	172.9	145.2	120.9	Japon
Netherlands	193.2	204.0	141.1	115.7	137.5	Pays-Bas
Belgium	–	196.6	181.8	186.4	e209.1	Belgique
Czech Republic	127.2	129.6	128.7	126.1	125.2	République tchèque
Portugal	119.7	115.4	103.5	104.4	120.5	Portugal
Canada	81.7	89.0	84.1	69.2	76.1	Canada
Malaysia	66.7	76.2	86.9	81.3	e86.1	Malaisie
Indonesia	22.0	65.6	73.3	79.8	89.2	Indonésie
Slovakia	58.5	55.9	65.6	65.8	66.7	Slovaquie
Thailand	45.7	59.8	64.4	65.6	e69.3	Thaïlande
Belarus	37.6	36.8	55.8	68.0	72.6	Bélarus
United Arab Emirates	40.7	42.0	50.8	64.7	e67.4	Emirates arabes unis
Poland	46.3	35.4	35.4	46.3	69.9	Pologne
Australia	43.7	47.1	45.9	46.2	45.3	Australie
Hungary	46.2	42.7	40.6	46.5	47.2	Hongrie
Denmark	52.6	48.5	39.0	41.5	29.4	Danemark
Sweden	45.7	41.4	43.6	39.0	41.5	Suède
Russian Federation	34.8	34.4	43.5	44.0	41.5	Fédération de Russie
Belgium-Luxembourg	191.2	–	–	–	–	Belgique-Luxembourg
India	19.7	21.5	42.4	47.2	55.3	Inde

(Value as percentages of World total) **(Valeur en pourcentage du total mondial)**

Regions of the world	1993	1994	1995	1996	1997	1998	1999	2000	2001	2002	Régions du monde
World	100.0	100.0	100.0	100.0	100.0	100.0	100.0	100.0	100.0	100.0	Monde
Africa	0.4	0.4	0.4	0.4	1.1	0.5	0.7	0.5	0.7	0.7	Afrique
Americas	8.8	8.0	8.0	8.3	9.1	9.1	9.5	9.8	9.4	8.5	Amériques
- Northern America	4.5	4.1	4.2	4.5	4.6	4.3	4.4	4.5	4.1	3.5	- Amérique du Nord
- LAIA	4.2	3.8	3.7	3.8	4.4	4.7	5.0	5.2	5.1	4.9	- ALAI
- CACM	0.1	0.0	0.0	0.0	0.0	0.1	0.1	0.1	0.1	0.1	- MCC
- Caribbean	0.0	0.0	0.0	0.0	0.0	0.0	0.0	0.0	0.0	0.0	- Caraïbes
- Rest of America	0.0	0.0	0.0	0.0	0.0	0.0	0.0	0.0	0.0	0.0	- Autre d'Amérique
Asia excluding former USSR	9.0	8.5	8.9	9.1	9.7	9.1	9.6	11.1	11.9	13.7	Asie ancienne URSS exclus
- Middle East	1.8	1.8	1.9	2.1	2.4	2.5	2.8	3.1	3.2	3.6	- Moyen-Orient
Asia former USSR	0.0	0.0	0.1	0.1	0.0	0.0	0.0	0.0	0.0	0.0	Asie ancienne URSS
Europe excluding former USSR	81.1	81.7	81.2	80.4	78.3	79.8	78.8	76.7	76.1	75.2	Europe ancienne URSS exclus
- European Union	77.2	77.7	77.6	76.9	74.7	76.1	75.0	72.8	72.0	71.3	- Union Européenne
- Eastern Europe	2.8	2.6	2.5	2.7	2.9	2.9	2.7	2.8	2.9	2.9	- Europe de l'Est
- Rest of Europe	1.2	1.4	1.1	0.8	0.7	0.8	1.1	1.1	1.2	1.0	- Autre de l'Europe
Europe former USSR	0.2	0.9	0.9	1.2	1.2	1.1	1.0	1.4	1.4	1.4	Europe ancienne URSS
Oceania	0.3	0.5	0.5	0.6	0.5	0.4	0.5	0.5	0.5	0.4	Océanie

663 Mineral manufactures, nes

TRADE BY COMMODITY (Value in million US dollars)
Imports by principal countries or areas

COMMERCE PAR PRODUIT (Valeur en millions de dollars EU)
Importations selon les principaux pays ou zones

Country or area	1998	1999	2000	2001	2002	Pays ou zone
World	12653.9	13148.4	13615.0	13384.4	13847.4	Monde
Africa	249.9	254.8	296.1	293.7	311.2	Afrique
Americas	3390.5	3783.7	4208.0	3969.1	3930.1	Amériques
- Northern America	2573.6	3005.9	3258.9	3119.5	3154.4	- Amérique du Nord
- LAIA	677.2	670.5	810.8	734.0	664.3	- ALAI
- CACM	42.1	43.8	44.8	46.0	50.7	- MCC
- Caribbean	88.1	53.7	76.6	61.0	51.7	- Caraïbes
- Rest of America	9.5	9.8	16.9	8.6	9.0	- Autre d'Amérique
Asia excluding former USSR	2046.2	2121.4	2459.1	2395.9	2592.0	Asie ancienne URSS exclus
- Middle East	302.5	272.8	300.4	305.1	348.0	- Moyen-Orient
Asia former USSR	41.5	28.7	40.4	42.0	47.8	Asie ancienne URSS
Europe excluding former USSR	6455.5	6525.0	6170.2	6220.1	6447.0	Europe ancienne URSS exclus
- European Union	5396.6	5490.1	5152.0	5151.6	5257.2	- Union Européenne
- Eastern Europe	503.8	484.6	500.7	535.1	614.8	- Europe de l'Est
- Rest of Europe	555.1	550.3	517.5	533.4	575.0	- Autre de l'Europe
Europe former USSR	267.2	225.2	234.6	271.5	315.1	Europe ancienne URSS
Oceania	203.2	209.7	206.5	192.0	204.3	Océanie
United States	2080.7	2491.7	2745.4	2645.3	2641.2	Etats-Unis d'Amérique
Germany	1467.6	1454.9	1274.1	1330.0	1256.5	Allemagne
France-Monaco	815.8	799.5	806.7	755.5	783.3	France-Monaco
United Kingdom	502.5	565.5	567.4	541.5	591.9	Royaume-Uni
Italy-San Marino-Holy See	527.7	533.8	527.3	533.0	534.7	Italie-Saint-Marin-Saint-Siège
Canada	461.1	485.4	509.1	470.0	507.0	Canada
Mexico	316.0	369.4	482.0	405.8	376.2	Mexique
Netherlands	375.2	426.4	346.6	334.0	378.5	Pays-Bas
Japan	322.7	326.9	380.0	380.1	405.0	Japon
Spain	291.3	304.4	286.8	330.0	342.7	Espagne
Belgium	–	409.8	377.9	341.7	e374.7	Belgique
Switzerland-Liechtenstein	303.1	295.5	288.3	286.1	288.7	Suisse-Liechtenstein
Korea, Republic of	160.5	230.2	288.0	281.6	319.2	République de Corée
Austria	259.5	257.1	240.1	237.0	246.1	Autriche
China, Hong Kong SAR	246.2	202.9	230.7	247.8	267.4	Chine - RAS de Hong-Kong
China	140.0	163.3	234.7	253.8	290.5	Chine
Sweden	187.2	170.1	168.2	185.3	183.4	Suède
Poland	184.6	168.9	165.1	155.0	177.9	Pologne
Thailand	115.9	137.4	179.0	188.8	e196.7	Thaïlande
Singapore	151.3	172.6	174.4	146.1	138.7	Singapour
Australia	158.6	159.2	158.6	146.0	151.4	Australie
Denmark	147.4	146.7	134.0	142.6	135.8	Danemark
Brazil	146.1	125.3	131.5	138.1	132.7	Brésil
Czech Republic	131.7	118.3	127.9	138.6	151.0	République tchèque
Russian Federation	129.0	108.2	115.1	128.4	150.5	Fédération de Russie
Ireland	113.7	127.1	134.0	127.6	126.2	Irlande
Norway	134.5	122.5	109.7	120.0	139.0	Norvège
Malaysia	106.6	122.8	126.2	120.0	e131.1	Malaisie
Hungary	88.8	101.1	102.8	112.2	135.8	Hongrie
Turkey	105.0	96.3	98.5	79.6	105.2	Turquie

(Value as percentages of World total)

(Valeur en pourcentage du total mondial)

Regions of the world	1993	1994	1995	1996	1997	1998	1999	2000	2001	2002	Régions du monde
World	100.0	100.0	100.0	100.0	100.0	100.0	100.0	100.0	100.0	100.0	Monde
Africa	2.2	2.0	1.7	1.8	1.8	2.0	1.9	2.2	2.2	2.2	Afrique
Americas	19.5	20.9	20.0	21.4	24.6	26.8	28.8	30.9	29.7	28.4	Amériques
- Northern America	15.0	16.1	15.4	16.3	18.6	20.3	22.9	23.9	23.3	22.8	- Amérique du Nord
- LAIA	3.8	4.1	3.9	4.4	5.2	5.4	5.1	6.0	5.5	4.8	- ALAI
- CACM	0.3	0.2	0.2	0.2	0.3	0.3	0.3	0.3	0.3	0.4	- MCC
- Caribbean	0.4	0.3	0.3	0.4	0.4	0.7	0.4	0.6	0.5	0.4	- Caraïbes
- Rest of America	0.1	0.1	0.1	0.1	0.1	0.1	0.1	0.1	0.1	0.1	- Autre d'Amérique
Asia excluding former USSR	23.0	20.4	20.4	20.2	20.2	16.2	16.1	18.1	17.9	18.7	Asie ancienne URSS exclus
- Middle East	3.2	2.8	2.4	2.4	2.3	2.4	2.1	2.2	2.3	2.5	- Moyen-Orient
Asia former USSR	0.1	0.3	0.3	0.4	0.3	0.3	0.2	0.3	0.3	0.3	Asie ancienne URSS
Europe excluding former USSR	52.2	52.9	54.1	52.4	49.3	51.0	49.6	45.3	46.5	46.6	Europe ancienne URSS exclus
- European Union	45.1	46.3	46.7	44.5	41.5	42.6	41.8	37.8	38.5	38.0	- Union Européenne
- Eastern Europe	2.8	2.4	2.9	3.5	3.5	4.0	3.7	3.7	4.0	4.4	- Europe de l'Est
- Rest of Europe	4.2	4.2	4.5	4.4	4.2	4.4	4.2	3.8	4.0	4.2	- Autre de l'Europe
Europe former USSR	1.3	1.7	1.8	2.0	2.1	2.1	1.7	1.7	2.0	2.3	Europe ancienne URSS
Oceania	1.9	1.9	1.7	1.7	1.7	1.6	1.6	1.5	1.4	1.5	Océanie

TRADE BY COMMODITY (Value in million US dollars)
Exports by principal countries or areas

COMMERCE PAR PRODUIT (Valeur en millions de dollars EU)
Exportations selon les principaux pays ou zones

Country or area	1998	1999	2000	2001	2002	Pays ou zone
World	13291.5	13605.4	13828.6	13346.2	13483.7	Monde
Africa	42.3	42.3	39.2	43.5	52.4	Afrique
Americas	2487.8	2645.6	2813.9	2764.3	2630.6	Amériques
- Northern America	2127.9	2239.8	2368.5	2258.8	2201.7	- Amérique du Nord
- LAIA	347.9	389.0	434.0	495.2	418.6	- ALAI
- CACM	7.6	12.2	7.5	6.8	7.6	- MCC
- Caribbean	4.3	4.5	3.9	3.4	2.5	- Caraïbes
- Rest of America	0.1	0.0	0.0	0.1	0.1	- Autre d'Amérique
Asia excluding former USSR	2799.2	2931.3	3432.0	3104.2	3042.4	Asie ancienne URSS exclus
- Middle East	75.4	73.8	82.6	77.2	84.0	- Moyen-Orient
Asia former USSR	4.7	2.1	2.4	2.6	4.4	Asie ancienne URSS
Europe excluding former USSR	7795.8	7833.5	7343.2	7260.3	7560.4	Europe ancienne URSS exclus
- European Union	7052.1	7051.5	6540.7	6411.0	6603.1	- Union Européenne
- Eastern Europe	340.0	372.6	386.5	432.2	507.1	- Europe de l'Est
- Rest of Europe	403.7	409.3	416.1	417.1	450.3	- Autre de l'Europe
Europe former USSR	120.1	106.3	160.6	133.1	150.9	Europe ancienne URSS
Oceania	41.5	44.4	37.3	38.3	42.5	Océanie
Germany	2175.0	2122.1	1954.3	2002.4	2087.0	Allemagne
Japan	1722.0	1693.4	1991.9	1682.6	1501.3	Japon
United States	1528.6	1508.4	1723.6	1656.3	1576.9	Etats-Unis d'Amérique
United Kingdom	835.7	917.1	862.1	814.3	760.4	Royaume-Uni
Italy-San Marino-Holy See	771.2	752.7	770.7	798.8	811.3	Italie-Saint-Marin-Saint-Siège
France-Monaco	805.0	822.2	754.3	720.5	708.1	France-Monaco
Canada	599.2	731.4	645.0	602.4	624.8	Canada
Belgium	–	585.9	561.5	543.5	e609.8	Belgique
Netherlands	403.9	403.4	364.9	308.2	300.4	Pays-Bas
Austria	360.6	349.5	326.2	341.4	367.1	Autriche
Spain	414.1	359.0	265.5	289.7	331.0	Espagne
China	256.9	268.3	274.1	298.0	343.9	Chine
Switzerland-Liechtenstein	253.9	257.3	270.4	260.4	272.8	Suisse-Liechtenstein
Mexico	196.0	243.4	256.3	334.8	256.0	Mexique
Denmark	212.3	221.5	193.2	146.4	157.6	Danemark
Sweden	190.3	189.3	185.1	172.5	181.9	Suède
Korea, Republic of	133.1	157.1	184.2	188.1	193.8	République de Corée
Czech Republic	137.0	149.0	158.1	181.4	207.8	République tchèque
Thailand	71.3	110.1	194.3	191.7	e202.5	Thaïlande
Poland	89.8	119.1	124.6	135.4	166.0	Pologne
Belgium-Luxembourg	613.6	–	–	–	–	Belgique-Luxembourg
Malaysia	102.4	124.9	133.9	102.2	e108.3	Malaisie
Finland	116.8	110.7	107.4	103.3	116.5	Finlande
Brazil	99.3	91.4	124.1	107.9	e111.8	Brésil
Viet Nam	54.9	87.2	117.6	122.3	135.9	Viet Nam
China, Hong Kong SAR	108.6	90.7	101.7	99.4	94.4	Chine - RAS de Hong-Kong
Slovenia	88.8	87.1	84.6	94.1	113.7	Slovénie
Indonesia	29.1	77.5	86.9	96.7	98.0	Indonésie
Hungary	69.0	67.7	60.8	68.4	73.0	Hongrie
Russian Federation	55.1	56.0	98.5	62.7	61.0	Fédération de Russie

(Value as percentages of World total) **(Valeur en pourcentage du total mondial)**

Regions of the world	1993	1994	1995	1996	1997	1998	1999	2000	2001	2002	Régions du monde
World	100.0	100.0	100.0	100.0	100.0	100.0	100.0	100.0	100.0	100.0	Monde
Africa	0.4	0.4	0.3	0.4	0.3	0.3	0.3	0.3	0.3	0.4	Afrique
Americas	14.9	15.6	15.0	15.6	18.4	18.7	19.4	20.3	20.7	19.5	Amériques
- Northern America	12.5	13.2	12.7	13.4	15.8	16.0	16.5	17.1	16.9	16.3	- Amérique du Nord
- LAIA	2.3	2.4	2.3	2.1	2.5	2.6	2.9	3.1	3.7	3.1	- ALAI
- CACM	0.0	0.0	0.0	0.0	0.1	0.1	0.1	0.1	0.1	0.1	- MCC
- Caribbean	0.0	0.0	0.0	0.0	0.0	0.0	0.0	0.0	0.0	0.0	- Caraïbes
- Rest of America	0.0	0.0	0.0	0.0	0.0	0.0	0.0	0.0	0.0	0.0	- Autre d'Amérique
Asia excluding former USSR	26.8	23.7	23.6	23.0	22.7	21.1	21.5	24.8	23.3	22.6	Asie ancienne URSS exclus
- Middle East	0.5	0.6	0.6	0.5	0.5	0.6	0.5	0.6	0.6	0.6	- Moyen-Orient
Asia former USSR	0.0	0.2	0.1	0.1	0.2	0.0	0.0	0.0	0.0	0.0	Asie ancienne URSS
Europe excluding former USSR	57.2	58.4	59.3	58.9	56.6	58.7	57.6	53.1	54.4	56.1	Europe ancienne URSS exclus
- European Union	52.3	53.5	54.2	53.4	51.4	53.1	51.8	47.3	48.0	49.0	- Union Européenne
- Eastern Europe	1.7	1.8	2.0	2.5	2.3	2.6	2.7	2.8	3.2	3.8	- Europe de l'Est
- Rest of Europe	3.3	3.1	3.1	3.1	2.9	3.0	3.0	3.0	3.1	3.3	- Autre de l'Europe
Europe former USSR	0.3	1.3	1.2	1.4	1.4	0.9	0.8	1.2	1.0	1.1	Europe ancienne URSS
Oceania	0.4	0.5	0.5	0.6	0.5	0.3	0.3	0.3	0.3	0.3	Océanie

664 Glass

TRADE BY COMMODITY (Value in million US dollars)
Imports by principal countries or areas

COMMERCE PAR PRODUIT (Valeur en millions de dollars EU)
Importations selon les principaux pays ou zones

Country or area	1998	1999	2000	2001	2002	Pays ou zone
World	16850.3	17764.4	20293.5	21160.6	20178.1	Monde
Africa	350.6	324.5	305.1	314.4	322.6	Afrique
Americas	4313.1	4796.8	5880.4	6174.5	5116.7	Amériques
- Northern America	2983.4	3532.4	4211.6	4449.0	3655.5	- Amérique du Nord
- LAIA	1201.1	1139.2	1532.5	1554.3	1315.5	- ALAI
- CACM	51.3	56.3	56.6	75.0	65.5	- MCC
- Caribbean	60.3	53.1	60.5	77.3	65.9	- Caraïbes
- Rest of America	17.1	15.8	19.1	18.9	14.3	- Autre d'Amérique
Asia excluding former USSR	3995.4	4203.6	5344.6	5267.8	5407.9	Asie ancienne URSS exclus
- Middle East	411.6	383.3	446.2	476.8	528.2	- Moyen-Orient
Asia former USSR	36.3	19.8	35.5	40.9	41.0	Asie ancienne URSS
Europe excluding former USSR	7742.7	8050.1	8320.1	8922.6	8796.3	Europe ancienne URSS exclus
- European Union	6606.2	6921.3	7136.6	7525.2	7298.6	- Union Européenne
- Eastern Europe	647.7	633.5	680.6	842.0	977.8	- Europe de l'Est
- Rest of Europe	488.8	495.2	503.0	555.5	519.9	- Autre de l'Europe
Europe former USSR	226.9	156.6	180.0	231.4	273.2	Europe ancienne URSS
Oceania	185.3	213.0	227.8	209.1	220.4	Océanie
United States	1959.9	2293.8	2784.5	2987.3	2444.4	Etats-Unis d'Amérique
Germany	1432.6	1446.4	1549.1	1679.6	1504.8	Allemagne
Canada	1019.7	1234.0	1391.0	1316.6	1206.8	Canada
France-Monaco	1133.0	1212.7	1218.6	1218.7	1206.6	France-Monaco
China	600.2	728.1	1053.3	1165.7	1267.5	Chine
Japan	785.5	800.3	1095.5	919.1	901.5	Japon
Mexico	628.4	733.7	1047.5	966.7	954.0	Mexique
United Kingdom	733.2	779.1	881.0	907.6	978.6	Royaume-Uni
Italy-San Marino-Holy See	691.7	707.5	683.6	770.4	735.5	Italie-Saint-Marin-Saint-Siège
Belgium	–	619.9	644.7	709.9	e778.5	Belgique
Korea, Republic of	288.2	447.1	529.5	527.8	735.8	République de Corée
Netherlands	448.0	520.6	516.9	495.8	389.6	Pays-Bas
China, Hong Kong SAR	501.6	419.9	518.7	464.5	373.0	Chine - RAS de Hong-Kong
Spain	444.3	480.6	419.4	448.3	471.9	Espagne
Singapore	411.3	312.7	362.0	289.4	252.9	Singapour
Austria	286.9	307.1	289.3	325.9	309.2	Autriche
Poland	247.6	254.4	267.4	283.0	329.5	Pologne
Switzerland-Liechtenstein	234.6	243.7	259.8	290.7	247.6	Suisse-Liechtenstein
Sweden	216.1	240.9	254.6	294.8	259.1	Suède
Thailand	165.2	181.7	218.2	270.0	e281.3	Thaïlande
Czech Republic	177.9	146.2	169.0	247.7	311.3	République tchèque
Denmark	189.5	194.8	217.4	226.3	220.6	Danemark
Malaysia	135.7	172.4	235.8	219.7	e240.1	Malaisie
Brazil	204.8	141.3	187.4	248.3	125.7	Brésil
Australia	128.0	151.2	167.1	144.8	151.7	Australie
Belgium-Luxembourg	624.6	–	–	–	–	Belgique-Luxembourg
Hungary	100.5	118.6	118.9	140.5	137.3	Hongrie
Norway	117.0	117.0	110.7	116.2	106.4	Norvège
India	74.6	77.3	84.8	207.9	118.5	Inde
Portugal	112.7	113.8	109.2	111.7	111.7	Portugal

(Value as percentages of World total)

(Valeur en pourcentage du total mondial)

Regions of the world	1993	1994	1995	1996	1997	1998	1999	2000	2001	2002	Régions du monde
World	100.0	100.0	100.0	100.0	100.0	100.0	100.0	100.0	100.0	100.0	Monde
Africa	2.0	1.8	1.6	1.7	1.8	2.1	1.8	1.5	1.5	1.6	Afrique
Americas	22.7	24.1	21.2	23.7	25.1	25.6	27.0	29.0	29.2	25.4	Amériques
- Northern America	17.1	18.5	15.9	16.8	17.5	17.7	19.9	20.8	21.0	18.1	- Amérique du Nord
- LAIA	5.0	4.9	4.6	6.3	6.8	7.1	6.4	7.6	7.3	6.5	- ALAI
- CACM	0.3	0.3	0.3	0.2	0.3	0.3	0.3	0.3	0.4	0.3	- MCC
- Caribbean	0.3	0.3	0.3	0.3	0.4	0.4	0.3	0.3	0.4	0.3	- Caraïbes
- Rest of America	0.1	0.1	0.1	0.1	0.1	0.1	0.1	0.1	0.1	0.1	- Autre d'Amérique
Asia excluding former USSR	26.4	26.1	28.0	27.6	27.7	23.7	23.7	26.3	24.9	26.8	Asie ancienne URSS exclus
- Middle East	3.3	2.4	2.8	2.5	2.6	2.4	2.2	2.2	2.3	2.6	- Moyen-Orient
Asia former USSR	0.1	0.2	0.1	0.3	0.1	0.2	0.1	0.2	0.2	0.2	Asie ancienne URSS
Europe excluding former USSR	47.0	45.6	46.7	44.4	42.9	45.9	45.3	41.0	42.2	43.6	Europe ancienne URSS exclus
- European Union	41.5	40.2	40.7	38.2	36.6	39.2	39.0	35.2	35.6	36.2	- Union Européenne
- Eastern Europe	2.2	2.2	2.7	3.2	3.5	3.8	3.6	3.4	4.0	4.8	- Europe de l'Est
- Rest of Europe	3.2	3.1	3.2	3.0	2.8	2.9	2.8	2.5	2.6	2.6	- Autre de l'Europe
Europe former USSR	0.5	0.9	1.0	1.0	1.3	1.3	0.9	0.9	1.1	1.4	Europe ancienne URSS
Oceania	1.4	1.4	1.3	1.4	1.2	1.1	1.2	1.1	1.0	1.1	Océanie

TRADE BY COMMODITY (Value in million US dollars)
Exports by principal countries or areas

COMMERCE PAR PRODUIT (Valeur en millions de dollars EU)
Exportations selon les principaux pays ou zones

Country or area	1998	1999	2000	2001	2002	Pays ou zone
World	16644.9	17814.9	20586.5	21493.6	19778.1	Monde
Africa	68.8	113.2	131.5	120.7	115.4	Afrique
Americas	3608.1	3902.1	4777.9	4953.9	4296.4	Amériques
- Northern America	2804.5	3027.7	3751.3	3971.9	3321.2	- Amérique du Nord
- LAIA	794.5	866.5	1015.6	970.5	963.5	- ALAI
- CACM	2.8	4.3	9.5	10.5	11.1	- MCC
- Caribbean	6.3	3.4	1.4	0.9	0.6	- Caraïbes
- Rest of America	0.0	0.2	0.1	0.2	0.1	- Autre d'Amérique
Asia excluding former USSR	3901.9	4558.9	6208.9	6418.2	5388.1	Asie ancienne URSS exclus
- Middle East	191.6	195.3	260.1	311.9	291.5	- Moyen-Orient
Asia former USSR	5.6	1.7	1.8	4.3	3.9	Asie ancienne URSS
Europe excluding former USSR	8814.2	9017.5	9171.0	9660.5	9689.7	Europe ancienne URSS exclus
- European Union	8061.3	8268.1	8340.7	8716.5	8643.6	- Union Européenne
- Eastern Europe	510.6	521.4	616.3	706.9	819.9	- Europe de l'Est
- Rest of Europe	242.3	228.1	214.0	237.0	226.3	- Autre de l'Europe
Europe former USSR	108.8	108.2	143.6	198.2	176.6	Europe ancienne URSS
Oceania	137.6	113.3	151.7	137.6	108.0	Océanie
United States	2325.9	2469.3	3146.7	3303.2	2765.3	Etats-Unis d'Amérique
Japan	1799.5	2224.6	3088.4	3071.2	2065.7	Japon
Germany	2133.2	2150.1	2199.2	2465.7	2314.3	Allemagne
France-Monaco	1139.9	1210.8	1156.2	1146.4	1180.9	France-Monaco
Belgium	–	1334.9	1309.8	1373.6	e1541.2	Belgique
Italy-San Marino-Holy See	891.1	889.5	823.3	820.8	837.1	Italie-Saint-Marin-Saint-Siège
Mexico	600.8	663.1	771.2	703.2	691.2	Mexique
United Kingdom	656.2	632.8	716.9	730.1	586.4	Royaume-Uni
China	344.8	410.8	613.0	671.5	939.6	Chine
Canada	478.5	558.3	604.6	668.6	555.6	Canada
Korea, Republic of	299.2	338.7	543.4	737.4	471.7	République de Corée
Spain	416.9	441.4	450.3	527.9	540.4	Espagne
Netherlands	433.6	474.2	538.1	440.6	375.3	Pays-Bas
China, Hong Kong SAR	347.4	316.9	392.4	352.9	282.2	Chine - RAS de Hong-Kong
Czech Republic	249.9	264.3	301.5	338.9	382.8	République tchèque
Belgium-Luxembourg	1472.5	–	–	–	–	Belgique-Luxembourg
Finland	271.0	269.4	241.8	274.8	292.2	Finlande
Sweden	245.1	203.0	202.1	239.2	209.4	Suède
Malaysia	187.0	181.6	198.2	245.9	e260.6	Malaisie
Singapore	197.8	201.6	212.2	181.3	228.5	Singapour
Denmark	115.5	183.6	212.6	190.4	234.6	Danemark
Thailand	134.4	157.2	219.0	190.2	e200.9	Thaïlande
Indonesia	66.3	164.0	226.9	211.9	216.7	Indonésie
Luxembourg	–	201.8	210.8	228.2	e233.3	Luxembourg
Poland	106.0	107.4	151.8	189.4	234.4	Pologne
Turkey	102.0	106.6	141.1	192.6	176.3	Turquie
Austria	141.6	140.2	133.2	144.9	157.4	Autriche
Brazil	93.4	119.4	157.7	152.6	e158.2	Brésil
Switzerland-Liechtenstein	143.9	123.6	127.0	127.0	120.8	Suisse-Liechtenstein
Australia	127.6	97.5	138.1	117.3	89.1	Australie

(Value as percentages of World total) **(Valeur en pourcentage du total mondial)**

Regions of the world	1993	1994	1995	1996	1997	1998	1999	2000	2001	2002	Régions du monde
World	100.0	100.0	100.0	100.0	100.0	100.0	100.0	100.0	100.0	100.0	Monde
Africa	0.5	0.4	0.3	0.3	0.4	0.4	0.6	0.6	0.6	0.6	Afrique
Americas	20.8	20.1	18.3	20.4	22.6	21.7	21.9	23.2	23.0	21.7	Amériques
- Northern America	17.4	16.7	15.1	17.1	18.8	16.8	17.0	18.2	18.5	16.8	- Amérique du Nord
- LAIA	3.4	3.4	3.2	3.3	3.8	4.8	4.9	4.9	4.5	4.9	- ALAI
- CACM	0.0	0.0	0.0	0.0	0.0	0.0	0.0	0.0	0.0	0.1	- MCC
- Caribbean	0.0	0.0	0.0	0.0	0.0	0.0	0.0	0.0	0.0	0.0	- Caraïbes
- Rest of America	0.0	0.0	0.0	0.0	0.0	0.0	0.0	0.0	0.0	0.0	- Autre d'Amérique
Asia excluding former USSR	23.2	25.1	27.6	25.9	25.0	23.4	25.6	30.2	29.9	27.2	Asie ancienne URSS exclus
- Middle East	1.0	1.1	1.0	1.0	1.0	1.2	1.1	1.3	1.5	1.5	- Moyen-Orient
Asia former USSR	0.0	0.0	0.0	0.1	0.1	0.0	0.0	0.0	0.0	0.0	Asie ancienne URSS
Europe excluding former USSR	54.2	52.9	52.4	51.8	50.5	53.0	50.6	44.5	44.9	49.0	Europe ancienne URSS exclus
- European Union	50.3	49.3	48.5	47.8	46.7	48.4	46.4	40.5	40.6	43.7	- Union Européenne
- Eastern Europe	2.6	2.2	2.5	2.6	2.6	3.1	2.9	3.0	3.3	4.1	- Europe de l'Est
- Rest of Europe	1.3	1.4	1.4	1.4	1.2	1.5	1.3	1.0	1.1	1.1	- Autre de l'Europe
Europe former USSR	0.5	0.5	0.6	0.8	0.7	0.7	0.6	0.7	0.9	0.9	Europe ancienne URSS
Oceania	0.8	0.9	0.7	0.8	0.9	0.8	0.6	0.7	0.6	0.5	Océanie

665 Glassware

TRADE BY COMMODITY (Value in million US dollars)
Imports by principal countries or areas

COMMERCE PAR PRODUIT (Valeur en millions de dollars EU
Importations selon les principaux pays ou zone

Country or area	1998	1999	2000	2001	2002	Pays ou zone
World	9723.9	9929.5	10271.2	10221.7	10845.3	Monde
Africa	288.2	251.6	243.3	248.3	269.3	Afrique
Americas	2613.9	2778.3	3014.1	2838.7	2893.7	Amériques
- Northern America	2016.2	2274.5	2449.4	2271.3	2366.1	- Amérique du Nord
- LAIA	374.8	312.3	360.1	348.1	319.0	- ALAI
- CACM	92.1	72.3	73.3	82.5	75.5	- MCC
- Caribbean	110.5	103.5	112.1	115.0	114.3	- Caraïbes
- Rest of America	20.3	15.6	19.2	21.7	18.8	- Autre d'Amérique
Asia excluding former USSR	1660.7	1826.9	2169.1	2162.0	2408.8	Asie ancienne URSS exclus
- Middle East	382.3	350.6	367.9	401.3	425.5	- Moyen-Orient
Asia former USSR	39.7	29.1	38.9	35.8	40.7	Asie ancienne URSS
Europe excluding former USSR	4716.2	4705.6	4411.3	4500.1	4769.5	Europe ancienne URSS exclus
- European Union	3995.0	4016.4	3727.2	3783.3	3933.7	- Union Européenne
- Eastern Europe	262.8	243.8	259.6	283.9	360.7	- Europe de l'Est
- Rest of Europe	458.4	445.4	424.5	433.0	475.1	- Autre de l'Europe
Europe former USSR	214.9	136.1	171.7	219.5	245.3	Europe ancienne URSS
Oceania	190.3	202.0	222.8	217.2	218.0	Océanie
United States	1671.5	1908.4	2026.4	1843.0	1963.7	Etats-Unis d'Amérique
France-Monaco	810.9	751.6	715.1	705.0	753.2	France-Monaco
Germany	719.7	700.8	613.5	613.4	580.3	Allemagne
United Kingdom	470.3	491.5	507.9	512.3	522.2	Royaume-Uni
Italy-San Marino-Holy See	441.2	449.7	438.6	464.4	496.2	Italie-Saint-Marin-Saint-Siège
Canada	341.1	362.4	421.6	427.4	401.0	Canada
China, Hong Kong SAR	271.8	288.7	347.8	379.1	445.4	Chine - RAS de Hong-Kong
Spain	347.0	365.3	301.3	308.2	356.8	Espagne
Japan	281.6	278.3	307.9	308.5	344.5	Japon
Switzerland-Liechtenstein	307.4	288.4	261.8	261.5	277.4	Suisse-Liechtenstein
Belgium	-	320.4	307.5	317.8	e348.6	Belgique
Netherlands	204.2	260.9	238.5	232.4	220.6	Pays-Bas
Korea, Republic of	112.5	184.0	244.6	243.8	267.1	République de Corée
China	112.2	149.3	211.0	218.2	276.8	Chine
Australia	140.7	155.1	168.2	169.2	163.2	Australie
United Arab Emirates	123.1	129.0	139.9	183.9	e188.7	Emirates arabes unis
Austria	158.5	154.8	135.6	136.6	142.8	Autriche
Mexico	95.4	102.5	135.7	131.9	132.9	Mexique
Malaysia	99.7	114.1	128.4	112.3	e122.7	Malaisie
Singapore	82.2	97.9	113.6	110.0	130.2	Singapour
Russian Federation	100.3	67.5	92.8	124.1	139.9	Fédération de Russie
Denmark	86.3	100.1	109.1	120.1	109.0	Danemark
Sweden	113.6	103.2	94.4	101.0	111.1	Suède
Poland	101.6	83.1	90.0	92.4	122.8	Pologne
Greece	108.8	98.8	77.6	78.8	e87.2	Grèce
Portugal	80.6	89.6	73.0	73.3	89.0	Portugal
Israel	71.5	69.9	72.3	72.7	66.1	Israël
Belgium-Luxembourg	339.7	-	-	-	-	Belgique-Luxembourg
Norway	64.4	67.0	66.6	65.3	74.7	Norvège
Ireland	68.0	75.6	67.1	63.2	58.6	Irlande

(Value as percentages of World total) **(Valeur en pourcentage du total mondial)**

Regions of the world	1993	1994	1995	1996	1997	1998	1999	2000	2001	2002	Régions du monde
World	100.0	100.0	100.0	100.0	100.0	100.0	100.0	100.0	100.0	100.0	Monde
Africa	3.0	2.5	2.5	2.6	2.7	3.0	2.5	2.4	2.4	2.5	Afrique
Americas	22.9	23.2	22.4	22.6	25.3	26.9	28.0	29.3	27.8	26.7	Amériques
- Northern America	17.5	17.7	17.3	17.8	19.6	20.7	22.9	23.8	22.2	21.8	- Amérique du Nord
- LAIA	3.4	3.8	3.4	3.2	3.7	3.9	3.1	3.5	3.4	2.9	- ALAI
- CACM	0.8	0.7	0.7	0.6	0.7	0.9	0.7	0.7	0.8	0.7	- MCC
- Caribbean	1.0	0.8	0.9	0.8	1.1	1.1	1.0	1.1	1.1	1.1	- Caraïbes
- Rest of America	0.2	0.2	0.1	0.1	0.2	0.2	0.2	0.2	0.2	0.2	- Autre d'Amérique
Asia excluding former USSR	22.4	20.7	20.9	21.3	20.2	17.1	18.4	21.1	21.2	22.2	Asie ancienne URSS exclus
- Middle East	4.5	3.7	3.6	3.6	3.6	3.9	3.5	3.6	3.9	3.9	- Moyen-Orient
Asia former USSR	0.1	0.2	0.2	0.3	0.3	0.4	0.3	0.4	0.3	0.4	Asie ancienne URSS
Europe excluding former USSR	49.0	49.9	50.1	49.1	46.8	48.5	47.4	42.9	44.0	44.0	Europe ancienne URSS exclus
- European Union	42.7	43.9	43.7	42.6	40.3	41.1	40.4	36.3	37.0	36.3	- Union Européenne
- Eastern Europe	1.8	1.5	1.8	2.0	2.3	2.7	2.5	2.5	2.8	3.3	- Europe de l'Est
- Rest of Europe	4.4	4.5	4.6	4.6	4.3	4.7	4.5	4.1	4.2	4.4	- Autre de l'Europe
Europe former USSR	0.9	1.6	2.1	2.2	2.7	2.2	1.4	1.7	2.1	2.3	Europe ancienne URSS
Oceania	1.8	1.9	1.8	2.0	2.0	2.0	2.0	2.2	2.1	2.0	Océanie

TRADE BY COMMODITY (Value in million US dollars)
Exports by principal countries or areas

COMMERCE PAR PRODUIT (Valeur en millions de dollars EU)
Exportations selon les principaux pays ou zones

Country or area	1998	1999	2000	2001	2002	Pays ou zone
World	9979.7	9902.3	10321.0	10460.1	11115.4	Monde
Africa	65.6	42.2	37.7	60.3	75.6	Afrique
Americas	1309.0	1336.0	1496.2	1455.9	1330.7	Amériques
- Northern America	823.1	854.8	959.4	938.9	777.2	- Amérique du Nord
- LAIA	398.9	409.1	456.5	420.7	461.4	- ALAI
- CACM	62.1	54.9	62.0	73.7	72.9	- MCC
- Caribbean	22.8	14.1	14.8	21.6	17.3	- Caraïbes
- Rest of America	2.0	3.1	3.4	1.0	1.9	- Autre d'Amérique
Asia excluding former USSR	1554.7	1766.9	2129.7	2138.8	2389.5	Asie ancienne URSS exclus
- Middle East	336.8	325.6	376.8	450.0	466.2	- Moyen-Orient
Asia former USSR	3.4	3.8	4.4	5.0	5.7	Asie ancienne URSS
Europe excluding former USSR	6927.0	6608.1	6495.5	6651.9	7182.8	Europe ancienne URSS exclus
- European Union	5680.7	5393.8	5213.0	5360.6	5753.7	- Union Européenne
- Eastern Europe	870.7	858.4	911.1	965.2	1087.4	- Europe de l'Est
- Rest of Europe	375.6	355.9	371.4	326.2	341.7	- Autre de l'Europe
Europe former USSR	96.6	120.7	136.9	126.9	109.6	Europe ancienne URSS
Oceania	23.3	24.7	20.6	21.3	21.5	Océanie
France-Monaco	1650.4	1597.6	1546.3	1456.6	1524.1	France-Monaco
Germany	1145.9	1069.6	978.4	1070.4	1210.8	Allemagne
Italy-San Marino-Holy See	846.1	843.1	824.9	850.6	873.6	Italie-Saint-Marin-Saint-Siège
United States	673.3	698.3	806.0	783.5	626.2	Etats-Unis d'Amérique
China	362.3	405.6	492.2	552.3	728.8	Chine
Austria	439.1	453.8	495.5	529.9	575.2	Autriche
Czech Republic	430.2	450.0	462.5	512.9	577.9	République tchèque
Mexico	264.9	281.4	340.2	311.6	327.4	Mexique
United Kingdom	320.3	278.1	280.8	255.6	270.6	Royaume-Uni
Japan	186.1	252.3	301.3	254.0	288.7	Japon
Spain	252.5	236.7	213.2	244.4	279.4	Espagne
Switzerland-Liechtenstein	256.2	247.7	258.6	219.8	224.9	Suisse-Liechtenstein
Poland	224.1	213.5	240.0	243.3	271.6	Pologne
Turkey	229.7	209.4	239.7	242.7	263.2	Turquie
Belgium	–	285.3	263.2	257.9	e289.4	Belgique
Portugal	141.0	189.3	180.4	195.0	226.9	Portugal
Netherlands	215.1	125.1	125.0	194.3	184.8	Pays-Bas
China, Hong Kong SAR	135.0	142.6	177.1	168.5	158.5	Chine - RAS de Hong-Kong
Canada	149.8	156.5	153.4	155.3	151.1	Canada
Ireland	119.6	135.1	111.3	113.3	111.2	Irlande
Indonesia	43.6	110.9	132.1	117.0	110.6	Indonésie
Sweden	105.6	95.8	96.1	89.4	103.7	Suède
United Arab Emirates	68.7	70.9	80.0	131.7	e137.2	Emirates arabes unis
Malaysia	46.8	67.1	116.9	109.0	e115.5	Malaisie
Korea, Republic of	75.6	86.2	101.9	97.6	88.1	République de Corée
Slovakia	71.1	66.3	68.9	70.1	83.2	Slovaquie
Belgium-Luxembourg	355.3	–	–	–	–	Belgique-Luxembourg
Romania	68.1	62.6	61.7	59.7	67.2	Roumanie
Denmark	53.8	56.0	71.8	66.3	68.9	Danemark
Thailand	46.9	50.9	72.9	69.1	e73.0	Thaïlande

(Value as percentages of World total) **(Valeur en pourcentage du total mondial)**

Regions of the world	1993	1994	1995	1996	1997	1998	1999	2000	2001	2002	Régions du monde
World	100.0	100.0	100.0	100.0	100.0	100.0	100.0	100.0	100.0	100.0	Monde
Africa	0.7	0.6	0.6	0.7	0.7	0.7	0.4	0.4	0.6	0.7	Afrique
Americas	11.5	12.0	11.6	11.8	13.5	13.1	13.5	14.5	13.9	12.0	Amériques
- Northern America	6.9	7.5	7.5	7.9	9.0	8.2	8.6	9.3	9.0	7.0	- Amérique du Nord
- LAIA	4.0	3.8	3.5	3.3	3.7	4.0	4.1	4.4	4.0	4.2	- ALAI
- CACM	0.5	0.5	0.5	0.5	0.5	0.6	0.6	0.6	0.7	0.7	- MCC
- Caribbean	0.2	0.2	0.2	0.1	0.1	0.2	0.1	0.1	0.2	0.2	- Caraïbes
- Rest of America	0.0	0.0	0.0	0.0	0.0	0.0	0.0	0.0	0.0	0.0	- Autre d'Amérique
Asia excluding former USSR	20.4	16.8	16.6	16.5	16.9	15.6	17.8	20.6	20.4	21.5	Asie ancienne URSS exclus
- Middle East	1.9	2.0	2.1	2.4	2.9	3.4	3.3	3.7	4.3	4.2	- Moyen-Orient
Asia former USSR	0.0	0.0	0.0	0.0	0.0	0.0	0.0	0.0	0.0	0.1	Asie ancienne URSS
Europe excluding former USSR	66.8	69.7	69.9	69.5	67.7	69.4	66.7	62.9	63.6	64.6	Europe ancienne URSS exclus
- European Union	56.7	59.1	58.4	57.8	56.1	56.9	54.5	50.5	51.2	51.8	- Union Européenne
- Eastern Europe	6.8	7.0	7.5	8.0	8.0	8.7	8.7	8.8	9.2	9.8	- Europe de l'Est
- Rest of Europe	3.2	3.7	4.0	3.8	3.6	3.8	3.6	3.6	3.1	3.1	- Autre de l'Europe
Europe former USSR	0.4	0.7	0.9	1.1	0.9	1.0	1.2	1.3	1.2	1.0	Europe ancienne URSS
Oceania	0.2	0.3	0.3	0.3	0.2	0.2	0.2	0.2	0.2	0.2	Océanie

666 Pottery

TRADE BY COMMODITY (Value in million US dollars)
Imports by principal countries or areas

COMMERCE PAR PRODUIT (Valeur en millions de dollars EU)
Importations selon les principaux pays ou zones

Country or area	1998	1999	2000	2001	2002	Pays ou zone
World	5943.4	5908.0	6116.0	5710.5	5711.1	Monde
Africa	77.0	87.7	86.8	83.0	85.6	Afrique
Americas	2240.6	2213.9	2407.3	2223.4	2278.7	Amériques
- Northern America	2057.8	2053.8	2217.8	2022.4	2092.3	- Amérique du Nord
- LAIA	130.1	110.8	135.4	148.0	135.2	- ALAI
- CACM	13.1	12.6	14.8	17.3	18.1	- MCC
- Caribbean	33.6	30.4	34.5	31.5	28.1	- Caraïbes
- Rest of America	6.0	6.2	4.8	4.3	4.9	- Autre d'Amérique
Asia excluding former USSR	909.6	917.2	1023.9	926.9	899.8	Asie ancienne URSS exclus
- Middle East	156.1	147.5	168.1	170.1	174.5	- Moyen-Orient
Asia former USSR	9.1	8.1	8.6	8.4	11.2	Asie ancienne URSS
Europe excluding former USSR	2546.4	2527.0	2409.8	2309.5	2249.8	Europe ancienne URSS exclus
- European Union	2244.1	2236.1	2121.6	2036.1	1945.4	- Union Européenne
- Eastern Europe	97.4	95.0	101.3	99.2	120.2	- Europe de l'Est
- Rest of Europe	204.9	195.8	186.9	174.2	184.2	- Autre de l'Europe
Europe former USSR	36.5	24.4	38.1	54.4	66.9	Europe ancienne URSS
Oceania	124.3	129.8	141.4	104.9	119.1	Océanie
United States	1868.6	1870.6	2022.9	1831.3	1886.9	Etats-Unis d'Amérique
Germany	502.0	468.1	419.2	425.7	361.0	Allemagne
United Kingdom	343.6	324.7	339.9	339.1	326.9	Royaume-Uni
China, Hong Kong SAR	357.6	331.4	351.9	294.1	250.3	Chine - RAS de Hong-Kong
France-Monaco	307.3	294.2	283.6	264.0	270.2	France-Monaco
Japan	251.9	267.6	300.3	282.2	271.6	Japon
Italy-San Marino-Holy See	269.5	290.2	274.7	247.6	234.8	Italie-Saint-Marin-Saint-Siège
Canada	184.4	177.7	193.4	188.6	203.4	Canada
Spain	153.1	166.1	155.2	149.2	150.1	Espagne
Netherlands	149.8	161.1	170.8	154.1	126.1	Pays-Bas
Australia	100.7	103.5	119.2	82.5	93.0	Australie
Belgium	–	125.5	127.9	115.0	e126.2	Belgique
Switzerland-Liechtenstein	100.1	101.2	97.4	88.9	92.0	Suisse-Liechtenstein
Austria	95.4	93.1	79.7	75.2	78.3	Autriche
Sweden	71.9	68.6	63.7	55.4	59.6	Suède
Denmark	66.6	59.3	60.6	65.3	62.0	Danemark
Norway	70.4	62.8	58.8	51.7	54.7	Norvège
Czech Republic	55.3	50.5	49.8	48.5	55.1	République tchèque
United Arab Emirates	40.2	42.1	54.1	60.3	e61.8	Emirates arabes unis
Mexico	28.1	28.5	45.4	55.0	60.1	Mexique
Ireland	40.2	51.3	38.1	39.2	39.8	Irlande
Greece	49.6	42.7	34.8	34.8	e38.4	Grèce
Portugal	41.3	50.2	37.1	33.1	31.9	Portugal
Israel	39.2	33.8	36.0	29.1	23.4	Israël
Korea, Republic of	11.6	27.5	36.3	36.2	46.2	République de Corée
Singapore	28.0	30.3	39.6	29.5	27.0	Singapour
Russian Federation	23.4	12.5	25.3	40.7	51.0	Fédération de Russie
Poland	19.2	24.9	31.2	29.3	39.2	Pologne
Saudi Arabia	25.3	26.4	30.2	29.2	e30.2	Arabie saoudite
Belgium-Luxembourg	132.4	–	–	–	–	Belgique-Luxembourg

(Value as percentages of World total) **(Valeur en pourcentage du total mondial)**

Regions of the world	1993	1994	1995	1996	1997	1998	1999	2000	2001	2002	Régions du monde
World	100.0	100.0	100.0	100.0	100.0	100.0	100.0	100.0	100.0	100.0	Monde
Africa	1.1	1.1	1.2	1.3	1.3	1.3	1.5	1.4	1.5	1.5	Afrique
Americas	36.2	36.4	35.3	33.7	35.7	37.7	37.5	39.4	38.9	39.9	Amériques
- Northern America	33.4	33.5	32.8	31.3	33.0	34.6	34.8	36.3	35.4	36.6	- Amérique du Nord
- LAIA	2.1	2.2	1.8	1.8	2.0	2.2	1.9	2.2	2.6	2.4	- ALAI
- CACM	0.1	0.1	0.2	0.2	0.2	0.2	0.2	0.2	0.3	0.3	- MCC
- Caribbean	0.5	0.4	0.4	0.4	0.4	0.6	0.5	0.6	0.6	0.5	- Caraïbes
- Rest of America	0.1	0.1	0.1	0.1	0.1	0.1	0.1	0.1	0.1	0.1	- Autre d'Amérique
Asia excluding former USSR	19.2	19.1	19.5	20.2	18.7	15.3	15.5	16.7	16.2	15.8	Asie ancienne URSS exclus
- Middle East	2.5	2.1	2.0	2.3	2.4	2.6	2.5	2.7	3.0	3.1	- Moyen-Orient
Asia former USSR	0.0	0.1	0.1	0.2	0.1	0.2	0.1	0.1	0.1	0.2	Asie ancienne URSS
Europe excluding former USSR	40.6	40.5	41.0	41.8	41.2	42.8	42.8	39.4	40.4	39.4	Europe ancienne URSS exclus
- European Union	37.0	37.0	36.7	37.1	36.7	37.8	37.8	34.7	35.7	34.1	- Union Européenne
- Eastern Europe	0.4	0.4	0.9	1.3	1.3	1.6	1.6	1.7	1.7	2.1	- Europe de l'Est
- Rest of Europe	3.2	3.1	3.5	3.4	3.2	3.4	3.3	3.1	3.0	3.2	- Autre de l'Europe
Europe former USSR	0.8	0.5	0.5	0.6	0.7	0.6	0.4	0.6	1.0	1.2	Europe ancienne URSS
Oceania	2.2	2.2	2.3	2.3	2.3	2.1	2.2	2.3	1.8	2.1	Océanie

TRADE BY COMMODITY (Value in million US dollars)
Exports by principal countries or areas

COMMERCE PAR PRODUIT (Valeur en millions de dollars EU)
Exportations selon les principaux pays ou zones

Country or area	1998	1999	2000	2001	2002	Pays ou zone
World	5577.0	5413.4	5504.1	4901.5	5034.4	Monde
Africa	29.4	26.5	22.7	30.8	23.8	Afrique
Americas	270.9	301.8	308.3	258.3	241.1	Amériques
- Northern America	145.7	157.3	159.0	140.6	128.0	- Amérique du Nord
- LAIA	119.5	139.4	144.6	115.3	109.8	- ALAI
- CACM	3.2	3.4	2.5	1.2	2.1	- MCC
- Caribbean	2.5	1.7	2.1	1.0	1.1	- Caraïbes
- Rest of America	0.0	0.0	0.1	0.1	0.0	- Autre d'Amérique
Asia excluding former USSR	2446.1	2449.8	2676.7	2188.9	2375.6	Asie ancienne URSS exclus
- Middle East	60.4	63.2	67.7	68.8	67.2	- Moyen-Orient
Asia former USSR	0.3	0.1	0.1	0.3	0.3	Asie ancienne URSS
Europe excluding former USSR	2800.3	2591.3	2462.0	2387.8	2356.9	Europe ancienne URSS exclus
- European Union	2460.5	2273.9	2131.7	2050.1	2032.6	- Union Européenne
- Eastern Europe	304.2	284.6	298.6	308.0	295.5	- Europe de l'Est
- Rest of Europe	35.5	32.9	31.7	29.7	28.9	- Autre de l'Europe
Europe former USSR	23.2	36.2	26.7	29.6	31.5	Europe ancienne URSS
Oceania	6.8	7.7	7.5	5.7	5.2	Océanie
China	1329.7	1394.2	1549.2	1238.7	1476.9	Chine
Germany	473.8	472.7	415.2	405.5	434.4	Allemagne
United Kingdom	540.3	461.0	436.9	397.1	356.6	Royaume-Uni
China, Hong Kong SAR	423.6	377.2	399.3	334.2	285.3	Chine - RAS de Hong-Kong
Italy-San Marino-Holy See	407.0	353.8	332.7	310.9	286.3	Italie-Saint-Marin-Saint-Siège
Portugal	308.1	266.7	231.2	229.1	230.5	Portugal
France-Monaco	222.4	227.1	217.3	215.0	211.9	France-Monaco
Thailand	170.8	176.7	200.5	181.5	e191.7	Thaïlande
Spain	143.3	158.0	152.3	150.2	155.2	Espagne
Japan	177.0	164.4	167.0	119.4	110.5	Japon
United States	129.2	141.9	141.3	124.1	110.0	Etats-Unis d'Amérique
Czech Republic	123.2	108.1	111.0	115.7	111.8	République tchèque
Netherlands	116.0	106.6	105.4	93.1	83.7	Pays-Bas
Poland	95.4	91.8	98.2	105.0	95.2	Pologne
Denmark	73.7	78.0	85.4	80.5	98.8	Danemark
Mexico	69.4	91.1	93.2	68.6	60.7	Mexique
Indonesia	53.6	67.4	79.5	70.6	67.0	Indonésie
Belgium	–	73.5	78.4	77.6	e87.1	Belgique
Romania	40.0	43.4	44.9	45.6	46.4	Roumanie
Philippines	59.7	51.5	42.5	34.0	30.2	Philippines
Malaysia	47.1	39.0	40.2	40.2	e42.6	Malaisie
Sri Lanka	e42.0	39.6	e48.2	35.4	34.0	Sri Lanka
Hungary	37.8	35.9	38.1	34.7	34.3	Hongrie
United Arab Emirates	33.5	34.6	41.5	33.4	e34.8	Emirates arabes unis
Sweden	26.8	27.5	31.4	45.8	41.8	Suède
Brazil	28.8	27.1	27.0	23.7	e24.5	Brésil
Turkey	21.8	22.4	19.3	28.5	27.4	Turquie
Korea, Republic of	22.8	21.9	22.9	18.0	18.1	République de Corée
Belgium-Luxembourg	103.4	–	–	–	–	Belgique-Luxembourg
Austria	21.4	22.5	21.9	18.7	18.8	Autriche

(Value as percentages of World total) **(Valeur en pourcentage du total mondial)**

Regions of the world	1993	1994	1995	1996	1997	1998	1999	2000	2001	2002	Régions du monde
World	100.0	100.0	100.0	100.0	100.0	100.0	100.0	100.0	100.0	100.0	Monde
Africa	0.3	0.4	0.4	0.4	0.5	0.5	0.5	0.4	0.6	0.5	Afrique
Americas	4.9	4.4	4.2	4.5	4.6	4.9	5.6	5.6	5.3	4.8	Amériques
- Northern America	2.8	2.5	2.3	2.4	2.4	2.6	2.9	2.9	2.9	2.5	- Amérique du Nord
- LAIA	2.0	1.8	1.8	2.1	2.2	2.1	2.6	2.6	2.4	2.2	- ALAI
- CACM	0.0	0.0	0.0	0.0	0.1	0.1	0.1	0.0	0.0	0.0	- MCC
- Caribbean	0.0	0.0	0.0	0.0	0.0	0.0	0.0	0.0	0.0	0.0	- Caraïbes
- Rest of America	0.0	0.0	0.0	0.0	0.0	0.0	0.0	0.0	0.0	0.0	- Autre d'Amérique
Asia excluding former USSR	46.5	46.5	43.8	42.0	44.8	43.9	45.3	48.6	44.7	47.2	Asie ancienne URSS exclus
- Middle East	0.4	0.4	0.6	0.6	0.7	1.1	1.2	1.2	1.4	1.3	- Moyen-Orient
Asia former USSR	0.0	0.0	0.0	0.0	0.0	0.0	0.0	0.0	0.0	0.0	Asie ancienne URSS
Europe excluding former USSR	48.0	48.2	51.1	52.5	49.5	50.2	47.9	44.7	48.7	46.8	Europe ancienne URSS exclus
- European Union	44.2	44.4	46.4	46.7	44.3	44.1	42.0	38.7	41.8	40.4	- Union Européenne
- Eastern Europe	3.1	3.1	4.0	4.9	4.7	5.5	5.3	5.4	6.3	5.9	- Europe de l'Est
- Rest of Europe	0.7	0.6	0.7	0.8	0.5	0.6	0.6	0.6	0.6	0.6	- Autre de l'Europe
Europe former USSR	0.2	0.4	0.4	0.4	0.4	0.4	0.7	0.5	0.6	0.6	Europe ancienne URSS
Oceania	0.1	0.1	0.1	0.1	0.1	0.1	0.1	0.1	0.1	0.1	Océanie

667 Pearl, precious and semi-precious stones, unworked or worked

TRADE BY COMMODITY (Value in million US dollars)
Imports by principal countries or areas

COMMERCE PAR PRODUIT (Valeur en millions de dollars EU)
Importations selon les principaux pays ou zones

Country or area	1998	1999	2000	2001	2002	Pays ou zone
World	43214.8	52572.5	59992.4	53378.8	58495.4	Monde
Africa	319.0	456.6	541.8	149.8	533.1	Afrique
Americas	9777.3	11408.2	13639.4	11984.0	13496.1	Amériques
- Northern America	9677.9	11297.4	13531.1	11822.5	13350.4	- Amérique du Nord
- LAIA	59.4	78.0	95.1	114.3	111.3	- ALAI
- CACM	3.5	1.4	6.3	4.7	8.5	- MCC
- Caribbean	36.0	30.6	6.4	42.3	25.7	- Caraïbes
- Rest of America	0.5	0.7	0.4	0.3	0.2	- Autre d'Amérique
Asia excluding former USSR	13798.3	18961.0	20996.4	18832.9	23031.8	Asie ancienne URSS exclus
- Middle East	362.4	398.3	522.3	597.1	601.6	- Moyen-Orient
Asia former USSR	45.9	82.0	101.2	86.6	185.5	Asie ancienne URSS
Europe excluding former USSR	19069.4	21498.3	24499.8	22149.0	21035.0	Europe ancienne URSS exclus
- European Union	16555.7	19509.4	22126.6	20088.1	19787.0	- Union Européenne
- Eastern Europe	15.7	10.2	13.6	10.6	12.9	- Europe de l'Est
- Rest of Europe	2497.9	1978.7	2359.6	2050.3	1235.1	- Autre de l'Europe
Europe former USSR	4.8	0.2	23.1	8.6	0.3	Europe ancienne URSS
Oceania	200.1	166.2	190.7	167.9	213.5	Océanie
United States	9468.5	11045.4	13256.5	11596.8	13087.9	Etats-Unis d'Amérique
Belgium	–	11166.5	12539.7	11304.4	e12397.7	Belgique
United Kingdom	5329.5	6742.4	7791.9	7145.0	6095.6	Royaume-Uni
Israel	4210.5	5820.5	6784.4	5618.6	7222.2	Israël
India	3763.6	5433.5	4919.4	4671.2	6034.4	Inde
China, Hong Kong SAR	2491.3	3456.6	4393.1	4075.5	4875.6	Chine - RAS de Hong-Kong
Switzerland-Liechtenstein	2484.9	1967.7	2350.5	2042.0	1225.8	Suisse-Liechtenstein
Belgium-Luxembourg	9618.0	–	–	–	–	Belgique-Luxembourg
Japan	1505.9	1866.8	1795.8	1450.9	1404.6	Japon
Thailand	529.3	728.6	909.4	857.8	e893.7	Thaïlande
China	358.2	522.5	779.3	760.4	1090.7	Chine
France-Monaco	405.9	357.3	565.2	566.8	390.1	France-Monaco
Italy-San Marino-Holy See	433.2	480.6	494.4	440.6	353.5	Italie-Saint-Marin-Saint-Siège
United Arab Emirates	327.9	343.6	463.2	515.2	e528.6	Emirates arabes unis
Germany	517.0	481.1	456.4	388.1	312.2	Allemagne
Singapore	243.5	365.3	404.1	384.6	433.3	Singapour
Canada	195.3	236.3	274.4	225.3	261.5	Canada
South Africa	–	–	467.3	92.7	469.5	Afrique du Sud
Sri Lanka	e165.4	149.2	e201.6	151.5	185.5	Sri Lanka
Australia	180.6	142.7	167.8	147.2	186.4	Australie
Southern African Customs Union	264.4	411.4	–	–	–	Union douanière d'Afrique australe
Armenia	43.9	80.9	101.0	86.3	185.3	Arménie
Mexico	56.3	74.9	86.5	105.6	106.8	Mexique
Spain	74.2	87.6	83.5	75.5	76.4	Espagne
Korea, Republic of	38.7	66.6	81.4	75.9	80.2	République de Corée
Portugal	55.6	55.4	59.7	46.3	48.2	Portugal
Malaysia	46.1	58.4	64.8	40.9	e44.7	Malaisie
Netherlands	42.6	52.2	58.8	39.5	40.1	Pays-Bas
Austria	41.1	41.9	35.4	38.0	30.5	Autriche
Lebanon	15.2	20.6	22.2	56.3	e51.4	Liban

(Value as percentages of World total) **(Valeur en pourcentage du total mondial)**

Regions of the world	1993	1994	1995	1996	1997	1998	1999	2000	2001	2002	Régions du monde
World	100.0	100.0	100.0	100.0	100.0	100.0	100.0	100.0	100.0	100.0	Monde
Africa	1.2	1.2	0.8	0.8	0.9	0.7	0.9	0.9	0.3	0.9	Afrique
Americas	16.2	17.4	16.5	16.7	19.2	22.6	21.7	22.7	22.5	23.1	Amériques
- Northern America	16.2	17.2	16.4	16.6	19.0	22.4	21.5	22.6	22.1	22.8	- Amérique du Nord
- LAIA	0.0	0.1	0.0	0.1	0.1	0.1	0.1	0.2	0.2	0.2	- ALAI
- CACM	0.0	0.0	0.0	0.0	0.0	0.0	0.0	0.0	0.0	0.0	- MCC
- Caribbean	0.0	0.1	0.1	0.1	0.1	0.1	0.1	0.0	0.1	0.0	- Caraïbes
- Rest of America	0.0	0.0	0.0	0.0	0.0	0.0	0.0	0.0	0.0	0.0	- Autre d'Amérique
Asia excluding former USSR	36.8	37.0	38.9	37.2	34.7	31.9	36.1	35.0	35.3	39.4	Asie ancienne URSS exclus
- Middle East	0.3	0.3	0.4	0.3	0.4	0.8	0.8	0.9	1.1	1.0	- Moyen-Orient
Asia former USSR	0.1	0.0	0.1	0.1	0.1	0.1	0.2	0.2	0.2	0.3	Asie ancienne URSS
Europe excluding former USSR	45.2	44.0	43.2	44.8	44.6	44.1	40.9	40.8	41.5	36.0	Europe ancienne URSS exclus
- European Union	37.5	37.3	38.8	39.4	39.0	38.3	37.1	36.9	37.6	33.8	- Union Européenne
- Eastern Europe	0.1	0.0	0.0	0.0	0.0	0.0	0.0	0.0	0.0	0.0	- Europe de l'Est
- Rest of Europe	7.7	6.6	4.4	5.4	5.5	5.8	3.8	3.9	3.8	2.1	- Autre de l'Europe
Europe former USSR	0.1	0.1	0.2	0.1	0.1	0.0	0.0	0.0	0.0	0.0	Europe ancienne URSS
Oceania	0.3	0.3	0.3	0.4	0.5	0.5	0.3	0.3	0.3	0.4	Océanie

TRADE BY COMMODITY (Value in million US dollars)
Exports by principal countries or areas

COMMERCE PAR PRODUIT (Valeur en millions de dollars EU)
Exportations selon les principaux pays ou zones

Country or area	1998	1999	2000	2001	2002	Pays ou zone
World	38396.4	45753.1	54104.6	54045.5	56026.9	Monde
Africa	2117.8	2795.5	5621.9	8801.9	4853.3	Afrique
Americas	3186.7	4237.6	5154.1	5233.0	5731.1	Amériques
- Northern America	3011.4	4017.4	4928.2	5010.2	5511.7	- Amérique du Nord
- LAIA	164.3	205.8	209.0	203.2	197.1	- ALAI
- CACM	0.3	0.0	0.0	0.4	0.2	- MCC
- Caribbean	8.5	12.2	12.6	5.5	3.0	- Caraïbes
- Rest of America	2.1	2.3	4.3	13.7	19.1	- Autre d'Amérique
Asia excluding former USSR	14715.4	18361.3	21089.0	19778.1	23664.6	Asie ancienne URSS exclus
- Middle East	135.2	136.4	228.7	371.2	385.3	- Moyen-Orient
Asia former USSR	47.1	84.6	99.9	86.6	198.8	Asie ancienne URSS
Europe excluding former USSR	16437.0	19778.0	21580.5	19724.8	21153.8	Europe ancienne URSS exclus
- European Union	15245.5	18484.4	20241.4	18672.2	20384.3	- Union Européenne
- Eastern Europe	12.9	6.7	2.2	4.7	7.7	- Europe de l'Est
- Rest of Europe	1178.6	1286.9	1336.9	1047.9	761.8	- Autre de l'Europe
Europe former USSR	1512.7	0.2	20.7	13.1	0.2	Europe ancienne URSS
Oceania	379.6	495.9	538.4	408.0	425.1	Océanie
Belgium	–	12074.0	12996.1	11496.8	e12899.2	Belgique
Israel	6365.9	7779.8	9635.8	8767.9	10323.8	Israël
India	4992.3	6642.6	6477.2	6188.2	7592.2	Inde
United Kingdom	4342.3	5673.1	6605.4	6516.0	6857.5	Royaume-Uni
United States	2970.0	3595.2	4520.8	4475.1	4899.7	Etats-Unis d'Amérique
China, Hong Kong SAR	1422.2	1829.4	2492.7	2348.0	2964.2	Chine - RAS de Hong-Kong
Belgium-Luxembourg	10207.1	–	–	–	–	Belgique-Luxembourg
South Africa	–	–	1756.9	e5204.9	1550.9	Afrique du Sud
Botswana	–	–	2262.2	2122.1	e2102.0	Botswana
Switzerland-Liechtenstein	1172.3	1278.0	1317.0	1043.9	740.5	Suisse-Liechtenstein
China	364.0	435.6	613.7	649.1	810.6	Chine
Southern African Customs Union	1225.0	1576.3	–	–	–	Union douanière d'Afrique australe
Thailand	464.9	518.4	580.0	559.4	e590.9	Thaïlande
Japan	482.5	577.3	551.4	390.2	343.2	Japon
Angola	e355.7	e585.0	e421.5	e475.0	e456.9	Angola
Canada	41.4	418.0	406.6	533.8	605.3	Canada
Democratic Republic of the Congo	e300.9	e384.1	e343.9	e348.0	e374.4	République démocratique du Congo
Russian Federation	1512.6	e	e	e	e	Fédération de Russie
Australia	233.0	334.3	353.4	282.9	303.5	Australie
Germany	303.6	344.5	284.8	280.7	232.1	Allemagne
United Arab Emirates	128.5	132.6	223.6	357.7	e372.5	Emirates arabes unis
Namibia	–	–	515.7	448.1	e	Namibie
France-Monaco	164.6	136.8	183.4	216.6	217.7	France-Monaco
Sri Lanka	e136.9	129.2	e157.1	153.3	300.5	Sri Lanka
Singapore	132.4	133.6	194.6	203.9	200.1	Singapour
French Polynesia	139.5	155.1	175.9	117.1	117.4	Polynésie française
Armenia	47.0	84.3	99.2	86.0	198.4	Arménie
Colombia	83.4	107.8	97.1	89.9	92.4	Colombie
Brazil	66.7	81.5	103.0	91.8	e95.2	Brésil
Congo	e87.5	e76.3	e130.2	e39.2	e42.4	Congo

(Value as percentages of World total) **(Valeur en pourcentage du total mondial)**

Regions of the world	1993	1994	1995	1996	1997	1998	1999	2000	2001	2002	Régions du monde
World	100.0	100.0	100.0	100.0	100.0	100.0	100.0	100.0	100.0	100.0	Monde
Africa	10.3	9.8	8.6	8.7	9.9	5.5	6.1	10.4	16.3	8.7	Afrique
Americas	7.7	7.7	7.9	7.3	7.4	8.3	9.3	9.5	9.7	10.2	Amériques
- Northern America	6.0	6.1	6.3	6.5	6.7	7.8	8.8	9.1	9.3	9.8	- Amérique du Nord
- LAIA	1.7	1.5	1.5	0.7	0.6	0.4	0.4	0.4	0.4	0.4	- ALAI
- CACM	0.0	0.0	0.0	0.0	0.0	0.0	0.0	0.0	0.0	0.0	- MCC
- Caribbean	0.0	0.1	0.1	0.1	0.1	0.0	0.0	0.0	0.0	0.0	- Caraïbes
- Rest of America	0.0	0.0	0.0	0.0	0.0	0.0	0.0	0.0	0.0	0.0	- Autre d'Amérique
Asia excluding former USSR	34.4	34.6	36.7	35.7	36.3	38.3	40.1	39.0	36.6	42.2	Asie ancienne URSS exclus
- Middle East	0.2	0.2	0.1	0.1	0.1	0.4	0.3	0.4	0.7	0.7	- Moyen-Orient
Asia former USSR	0.2	0.3	0.1	0.1	0.1	0.1	0.2	0.2	0.2	0.4	Asie ancienne URSS
Europe excluding former USSR	43.8	46.1	45.4	46.9	45.1	42.8	43.2	39.9	36.5	37.8	Europe ancienne URSS exclus
- European Union	34.7	39.4	40.5	41.9	41.4	39.7	40.4	37.4	34.5	36.4	- Union Européenne
- Eastern Europe	0.1	0.1	0.0	0.0	0.0	0.0	0.0	0.0	0.0	0.0	- Europe de l'Est
- Rest of Europe	9.0	6.6	4.9	4.9	3.7	3.1	2.8	2.5	1.9	1.4	- Autre de l'Europe
Europe former USSR	2.6	0.1	0.1	0.1	0.1	3.9	0.0	0.0	0.0	0.0	Europe ancienne URSS
Oceania	1.0	1.3	1.1	1.2	1.1	1.0	1.1	1.0	0.8	0.8	Océanie

671 Pig and sponge iron, spiegeleisen, etc, and ferro-alloys

TRADE BY COMMODITY (Value in million US dollars)
Imports by principal countries or areas

COMMERCE PAR PRODUIT (Valeur en millions de dollars EU)
Importations selon les principaux pays ou zones

Country or area	1998	1999	2000	2001	2002	Pays ou zone
World	11433.9	9883.0	11623.6	10031.3	10504.9	Monde
Africa	99.5	93.3	104.8	81.4	95.1	Afrique
Americas	2834.3	2439.0	2854.1	2175.1	2282.8	Amériques
- Northern America	2419.1	2112.7	2386.4	1748.6	1919.8	- Amérique du Nord
- LAIA	351.2	273.2	449.6	365.3	346.4	- ALAI
- CACM	2.8	1.4	2.5	2.8	3.6	- MCC
- Caribbean	61.1	51.7	15.5	58.4	12.8	- Caraïbes
- Rest of America	0.1	0.1	0.0	0.0	0.1	- Autre d'Amérique
Asia excluding former USSR	3126.0	3155.6	3838.5	3108.9	3380.9	Asie ancienne URSS exclus
- Middle East	201.7	203.7	217.8	187.9	279.9	- Moyen-Orient
Asia former USSR	19.7	20.2	28.8	26.3	32.1	Asie ancienne URSS
Europe excluding former USSR	4979.8	3888.1	4458.0	4299.6	4381.4	Europe ancienne URSS exclus
- European Union	4612.0	3606.8	4117.6	3925.8	3983.9	- Union Européenne
- Eastern Europe	257.6	187.0	247.4	264.5	289.5	- Europe de l'Est
- Rest of Europe	110.2	94.3	93.0	109.3	108.0	- Autre de l'Europe
Europe former USSR	303.0	228.4	290.4	295.1	286.6	Europe ancienne URSS
Oceania	71.6	58.4	48.8	44.8	46.0	Océanie
United States	2186.3	1905.8	2169.7	1517.6	1673.6	Etats-Unis d'Amérique
Japan	1116.4	970.6	1251.7	1022.7	1017.1	Japon
Germany	1053.8	760.4	829.5	887.0	876.2	Allemagne
Korea, Republic of	901.7	893.3	1028.9	780.0	796.9	République de Corée
Italy-San Marino-Holy See	849.0	639.3	671.4	685.5	747.9	Italie-Saint-Marin-Saint-Siège
France-Monaco	560.0	397.5	502.6	416.4	468.1	France-Monaco
Spain	415.5	398.8	471.8	460.6	444.5	Espagne
Netherlands	411.1	368.6	435.5	386.7	279.5	Pays-Bas
United Kingdom	362.4	268.9	248.8	223.0	235.8	Royaume-Uni
Belgium	–	292.1	370.8	317.2	e347.9	Belgique
Mexico	213.9	168.8	311.7	214.0	229.0	Mexique
Canada	232.8	206.9	216.7	230.9	245.9	Canada
Sweden	232.1	166.3	205.4	175.3	178.6	Suède
Finland	167.8	155.8	203.1	187.2	211.6	Finlande
Russian Federation	182.3	141.5	185.6	162.7	149.5	Fédération de Russie
China	35.0	63.5	88.7	224.4	338.1	Chine
Malaysia	51.4	159.7	213.0	144.0	e157.4	Malaisie
Turkey	138.3	116.2	149.5	116.2	193.2	Turquie
Austria	109.4	75.7	80.8	85.4	94.1	Autriche
Czech Republic	85.2	60.4	72.6	80.7	89.5	République tchèque
Poland	60.1	57.9	88.5	88.1	93.6	Pologne
Belgium-Luxembourg	368.6	–	–	–	–	Belgique-Luxembourg
India	42.9	68.8	73.9	46.1	61.6	Inde
Thailand	55.2	55.9	79.2	49.9	e52.0	Thaïlande
Indonesia	42.8	47.3	79.5	58.4	53.4	Indonésie
Ukraine	43.2	20.3	41.9	75.9	81.8	Ukraine
Australia	66.3	52.7	42.9	39.3	40.9	Australie
Brazil	51.6	36.5	44.8	49.7	43.5	Brésil
Belarus	53.4	38.8	48.5	42.6	30.5	Bélarus
Romania	56.3	32.5	38.4	39.3	39.6	Roumanie

(Value as percentages of World total) **(Valeur en pourcentage du total mondial)**

Regions of the world	1993	1994	1995	1996	1997	1998	1999	2000	2001	2002	Régions du monde
World	100.0	100.0	100.0	100.0	100.0	100.0	100.0	100.0	100.0	100.0	Monde
Africa	2.2	1.1	1.3	1.5	1.1	0.9	0.9	0.9	0.8	0.9	Afrique
Americas	18.4	19.2	19.2	21.0	20.8	24.8	24.7	24.6	21.7	21.7	Amériques
- Northern America	16.6	16.7	16.5	17.9	17.5	21.2	21.4	20.5	17.4	18.3	- Amérique du Nord
- LAIA	1.8	2.2	2.5	2.8	3.0	3.1	2.8	3.9	3.6	3.3	- ALAI
- CACM	0.0	0.0	0.0	0.0	0.0	0.0	0.0	0.0	0.0	0.0	- MCC
- Caribbean	0.0	0.2	0.2	0.3	0.3	0.5	0.5	0.1	0.6	0.1	- Caraïbes
- Rest of America	0.0	0.0	0.0	0.0	0.0	0.0	0.0	0.0	0.0	0.0	- Autre d'Amérique
Asia excluding former USSR	41.6	33.1	33.3	33.3	35.5	27.3	31.9	33.0	31.0	32.2	Asie ancienne URSS exclus
- Middle East	3.7	3.5	2.4	2.5	2.3	1.8	2.1	1.9	1.9	2.7	- Moyen-Orient
Asia former USSR	0.0	0.1	0.1	0.2	0.1	0.2	0.2	0.2	0.3	0.3	Asie ancienne URSS
Europe excluding former USSR	36.6	41.7	41.9	38.9	39.1	43.6	39.3	38.4	42.9	41.7	Europe ancienne URSS exclus
- European Union	33.9	39.0	39.1	36.3	36.4	40.3	36.5	35.4	39.1	37.9	- Union Européenne
- Eastern Europe	1.9	1.8	1.9	1.9	2.0	2.3	1.9	2.1	2.6	2.8	- Europe de l'Est
- Rest of Europe	0.8	0.9	0.9	0.7	0.8	1.0	1.0	0.8	1.1	1.0	- Autre de l'Europe
Europe former USSR	0.4	4.3	3.6	4.5	2.7	2.7	2.3	2.5	2.9	2.7	Europe ancienne URSS
Oceania	0.7	0.6	0.6	0.6	0.6	0.6	0.6	0.4	0.4	0.4	Océanie

TRADE BY COMMODITY (Value in million US dollars)
Exports by principal countries or areas

COMMERCE PAR PRODUIT (Valeur en millions de dollars EU)
Exportations selon les principaux pays ou zones

Country or area	1998	1999	2000	2001	2002	Pays ou zone
World	7844.8	7660.3	9088.9	7955.8	8462.7	Monde
Africa	278.2	1323.5	1465.7	1090.9	1343.6	Afrique
Americas	1988.8	1674.1	2063.2	1930.0	1947.9	Amériques
- Northern America	456.8	404.2	432.8	322.0	300.7	- Amérique du Nord
- LAIA	1357.9	1205.1	1506.0	1471.0	1540.7	- ALAI
- CACM	0.3	0.0	0.0	0.3	0.2	- MCC
- Caribbean	173.8	64.7	124.4	136.7	106.3	- Caraïbes
- Rest of America	0.0	0.0	0.0	0.0	0.0	- Autre d'Amérique
Asia excluding former USSR	1817.2	1523.0	1946.2	1395.4	1527.2	Asie ancienne URSS exclus
- Middle East	67.4	80.3	54.4	63.2	73.6	- Moyen-Orient
Asia former USSR	242.3	236.9	315.5	340.5	375.2	Asie ancienne URSS
Europe excluding former USSR	2104.6	1729.0	1790.8	1720.7	1586.2	Europe ancienne URSS exclus
- European Union	1216.4	1007.7	1053.1	1055.1	971.5	- Union Européenne
- Eastern Europe	253.9	157.9	211.9	181.8	175.2	- Europe de l'Est
- Rest of Europe	634.3	563.4	525.8	483.8	439.5	- Autre de l'Europe
Europe former USSR	1144.8	898.8	1113.0	1093.8	1268.0	Europe ancienne URSS
Oceania	268.9	274.9	394.5	384.5	414.7	Océanie
China	1038.9	814.2	1188.7	793.1	838.9	Chine
Brazil	890.3	733.0	905.1	847.1	e878.3	Brésil
South Africa	–	–	1304.3	922.7	1109.8	Afrique du Sud
Russian Federation	550.6	442.8	569.2	569.6	682.5	Fédération de Russie
Ukraine	573.6	432.1	533.3	514.7	567.3	Ukraine
Norway	472.5	445.6	401.0	356.6	317.5	Norvège
Japan	418.0	383.6	350.2	278.5	301.8	Japon
Venezuela	219.8	239.5	314.4	324.9	e345.2	Venezuela
Kazakhstan	224.2	213.0	293.8	316.1	e356.0	Kazakhstan
New Caledonia	e210.5	219.0	367.5	e268.6	e307.1	Nouvelle-Calédonie
Southern African Customs Union	99.9	1166.9	–	–	–	Union douanière d'Afrique australe
Germany	279.4	241.1	225.5	238.5	235.3	Allemagne
United States	258.4	238.7	267.3	182.7	148.0	Etats-Unis d'Amérique
Netherlands	191.9	198.7	283.3	246.1	95.0	Pays-Bas
Colombia	119.7	154.1	211.6	235.5	272.9	Colombie
Canada	198.4	165.5	165.5	139.3	152.7	Canada
United Kingdom	199.8	138.0	139.7	143.1	179.7	Royaume-Uni
France-Monaco	194.8	137.5	126.7	140.0	141.4	France-Monaco
Zimbabwe	e136.7	128.2	133.9	114.7	171.8	Zimbabwe
India	117.8	80.7	140.0	89.7	118.2	Inde
Belgium	–	114.7	114.3	117.0	e131.3	Belgique
Slovakia	93.6	77.0	92.0	82.1	87.8	Slovaquie
Australia	58.4	55.6	26.2	115.6	107.6	Australie
Trinidad and Tobago	27.2	41.5	73.3	109.0	e82.7	Trinité-et-Tobago
Spain	82.2	59.2	50.8	64.0	74.2	Espagne
Indonesia	41.3	52.6	97.6	48.5	34.6	Indonésie
Dominican Republic	e	e22.3	e51.1	e27.7	e23.6	République dominicaine
Iceland	45.4	43.4	49.7	51.9	53.8	Islande
Malaysia	57.4	43.8	35.0	45.3	e48.1	Malaisie
Italy-San Marino-Holy See	50.0	41.1	49.5	40.0	39.2	Italie-Saint-Marin-Saint-Siège

(Value as percentages of World total) **(Valeur en pourcentage du total mondial)**

Regions of the world	1993	1994	1995	1996	1997	1998	1999	2000	2001	2002	Régions du monde
World	100.0	100.0	100.0	100.0	100.0	100.0	100.0	100.0	100.0	100.0	Monde
Africa	11.2	11.9	13.9	13.4	3.7	3.5	17.3	16.1	13.7	15.9	Afrique
Americas	18.7	19.3	18.6	19.1	22.4	25.4	21.9	22.7	24.3	23.0	Amériques
- Northern America	3.8	3.7	3.6	4.3	5.7	5.8	5.3	4.8	4.0	3.6	- Amérique du Nord
- LAIA	12.9	13.1	12.1	12.3	13.7	17.3	15.7	16.6	18.5	18.2	- ALAI
- CACM	0.0	0.0	0.0	0.0	0.0	0.0	0.0	0.0	0.0	0.0	- MCC
- Caribbean	2.1	2.6	2.8	2.6	3.1	2.2	0.8	1.4	1.7	1.3	- Caraïbes
- Rest of America	0.0	0.0	0.0	0.0	0.0	0.0	0.0	0.0	0.0	0.0	- Autre d'Amérique
Asia excluding former USSR	16.2	20.2	26.0	23.0	29.1	23.2	19.9	21.4	17.5	18.0	Asie ancienne URSS exclus
- Middle East	2.3	2.4	2.2	2.4	2.6	0.9	1.0	0.6	0.8	0.9	- Moyen-Orient
Asia former USSR	2.1	4.5	5.1	3.0	2.7	3.1	3.1	3.5	4.3	4.4	Asie ancienne URSS
Europe excluding former USSR	26.6	28.0	22.4	26.2	24.9	26.8	22.6	19.7	21.6	18.7	Europe ancienne URSS exclus
- European Union	17.3	18.3	12.6	15.4	14.0	15.5	13.2	11.6	13.3	11.5	- Union Européenne
- Eastern Europe	2.2	2.5	2.7	3.0	3.3	3.2	2.1	2.3	2.3	2.1	- Europe de l'Est
- Rest of Europe	7.1	7.2	7.1	7.9	7.6	8.1	7.4	5.8	6.1	5.2	- Autre de l'Europe
Europe former USSR	21.3	12.7	10.8	11.3	13.4	14.6	11.7	12.2	13.7	15.0	Europe ancienne URSS
Oceania	3.8	3.4	3.1	3.9	3.8	3.4	3.6	4.3	4.8	4.9	Océanie

672 Ingots and other primary forms, of iron or steel

TRADE BY COMMODITY (Value in million US dollars)
Imports by principal countries or areas

COMMERCE PAR PRODUIT (Valeur en millions de dollars EU)
Importations selon les principaux pays ou zones

Country or area	1998	1999	2000	2001	2002	Pays ou zone
World	28278.0	25000.6	31700.4	26180.4	29305.7	Monde
Africa	879.1	620.3	760.5	760.7	761.1	Afrique
Americas	7348.2	4812.4	6509.9	3749.8	4971.9	Amériques
- Northern America	5922.7	3979.1	5286.5	2633.8	3962.0	- Amérique du Nord
- LAIA	1180.8	665.4	1039.6	939.3	802.1	- ALAI
- CACM	147.8	105.2	106.0	117.3	140.9	- MCC
- Caribbean	84.3	50.8	74.1	55.8	65.3	- Caraïbes
- Rest of America	12.5	11.8	3.7	3.6	1.5	- Autre d'Amérique
Asia excluding former USSR	8198.2	9940.8	13121.7	11328.8	12431.1	Asie ancienne URSS exclus
- Middle East	1425.5	1041.0	1549.2	1325.8	1546.8	- Moyen-Orient
Asia former USSR	26.0	17.3	9.9	10.5	12.4	Asie ancienne URSS
Europe excluding former USSR	11638.8	9471.3	11134.8	10126.2	10934.9	Europe ancienne URSS exclus
- European Union	10846.6	8862.1	10369.7	9412.0	10174.3	- Union Européenne
- Eastern Europe	447.3	327.4	464.3	467.8	513.9	- Europe de l'Est
- Rest of Europe	344.9	281.7	300.9	246.4	246.6	- Autre de l'Europe
Europe former USSR	127.0	72.9	102.4	142.6	124.3	Europe ancienne URSS
Oceania	60.7	65.6	61.2	61.7	70.2	Océanie
United States	5171.2	3540.2	4515.6	2290.1	3426.6	Etats-Unis d'Amérique
China	904.3	1407.9	2394.1	3061.1	3175.0	Chine
Italy-San Marino-Holy See	2538.1	1925.6	2262.8	1964.4	2053.9	Italie-Saint-Marin-Saint-Siège
France-Monaco	1762.8	1504.8	1938.4	1759.8	1817.9	France-Monaco
Korea, Republic of	570.9	1471.8	2228.3	1743.8	2320.9	République de Corée
Germany	1587.6	1199.2	1337.3	1104.3	1063.7	Allemagne
Belgium	–	1243.3	1563.4	1284.9	e1409.2	Belgique
Thailand	630.8	1157.6	1272.5	1164.8	e1213.7	Thaïlande
Spain	967.9	904.3	897.6	984.2	1080.6	Espagne
Viet Nam	356.8	472.3	768.1	797.1	969.9	Viet Nam
Turkey	722.3	539.0	879.9	495.7	643.9	Turquie
Canada	751.4	438.5	770.3	343.7	529.7	Canada
United Kingdom	704.4	421.8	448.7	435.8	775.0	Royaume-Uni
Mexico	549.1	396.3	676.3	536.8	501.1	Mexique
Japan	674.1	554.7	607.6	406.3	351.2	Japon
Sweden	455.1	500.0	491.0	458.0	521.0	Suède
Philippines	302.6	452.1	381.3	345.8	227.8	Philippines
Indonesia	290.5	168.3	480.3	335.6	391.8	Indonésie
Belgium-Luxembourg	1644.9	–	–	–	–	Belgique-Luxembourg
Malaysia	397.3	431.5	310.7	150.6	e164.6	Malaisie
Egypt	414.1	257.4	e274.3	249.7	225.3	Egypte
Luxembourg	–	294.6	340.0	320.3	e340.1	Luxembourg
Greece	260.1	181.7	312.2	256.3	e283.4	Grèce
Saudi Arabia	399.3	156.3	220.0	247.7	e256.3	Arabie saoudite
Netherlands	291.6	237.6	254.8	170.0	251.0	Pays-Bas
Iran (Islamic Republic of)	107.6	165.9	264.0	298.0	318.0	Iran (République islamique d')
Portugal	210.1	159.8	174.7	318.9	197.3	Portugal
China, Hong Kong SAR	163.3	148.4	212.8	208.5	212.0	Chine - RAS de Hong-Kong
Romania	169.5	108.5	191.6	190.7	227.1	Roumanie
Morocco	175.4	119.8	176.0	179.3	e189.2	Maroc

(Value as percentages of World total) **(Valeur en pourcentage du total mondial**

Regions of the world	1993	1994	1995	1996	1997	1998	1999	2000	2001	2002	Régions du monde
World	100.0	100.0	100.0	100.0	100.0	100.0	100.0	100.0	100.0	100.0	Monde
Africa	1.9	1.9	1.8	2.3	2.6	3.1	2.5	2.4	2.9	2.6	Afrique
Americas	12.6	22.1	15.4	18.5	19.7	26.0	19.2	20.5	14.3	17.0	Amériques
- Northern America	9.9	18.3	12.7	15.5	15.8	20.9	15.9	16.7	10.1	13.5	- Amérique du Nord
- LAIA	2.2	3.3	2.4	2.5	3.2	4.2	2.7	3.3	3.6	2.7	- ALAI
- CACM	0.3	0.4	0.2	0.3	0.3	0.5	0.4	0.3	0.4	0.5	- MCC
- Caribbean	0.1	0.1	0.1	0.2	0.2	0.3	0.2	0.2	0.2	0.2	- Caraïbes
- Rest of America	0.1	0.1	0.1	0.0	0.0	0.0	0.0	0.0	0.0	0.0	- Autre d'Amérique
Asia excluding former USSR	61.2	42.7	43.1	42.6	40.4	29.0	39.8	41.4	43.3	42.4	Asie ancienne URSS exclus
- Middle East	6.3	3.4	3.7	3.6	4.1	5.0	4.2	4.9	5.1	5.3	- Moyen-Orient
Asia former USSR	0.0	0.1	0.1	0.1	0.1	0.1	0.1	0.0	0.0	0.0	Asie ancienne URSS
Europe excluding former USSR	23.7	32.2	38.3	35.3	36.4	41.2	37.9	35.1	38.7	37.3	Europe ancienne URSS exclus
- European Union	21.9	29.9	35.6	33.0	33.9	38.4	35.4	32.7	36.0	34.7	- Union Européenne
- Eastern Europe	0.7	1.1	1.5	1.3	1.5	1.6	1.3	1.5	1.8	1.8	- Europe de l'Est
- Rest of Europe	1.1	1.2	1.3	1.0	1.1	1.2	1.1	0.9	0.9	0.8	- Autre de l'Europe
Europe former USSR	0.2	0.6	0.7	0.8	0.5	0.4	0.3	0.3	0.5	0.4	Europe ancienne URSS
Oceania	0.4	0.4	0.5	0.3	0.3	0.2	0.3	0.2	0.2	0.2	Océanie

Lingots et formes primaires équivalents en fer ou en acier 672

TRADE BY COMMODITY (Value in million US dollars)
Exports by principal countries or areas

COMMERCE PAR PRODUIT (Valeur en millions de dollars EU)
Exportations selon les principaux pays ou zones

Country or area	1998	1999	2000	2001	2002	Pays ou zone
World	24955.7	22797.5	28081.5	23529.8	27779.4	Monde
Africa	484.5	451.6	794.4	664.2	788.5	Afrique
Americas	3219.7	2730.8	3313.3	2473.2	2941.3	Amériques
- Northern America	746.8	651.7	774.6	673.8	862.5	- Amérique du Nord
- LAIA	2437.2	2045.7	2486.8	1760.2	2046.5	- ALAI
- CACM	3.9	2.9	1.9	3.1	2.3	- MCC
- Caribbean	31.7	30.4	50.0	36.1	30.0	- Caraïbes
- Rest of America	0.0	0.1	0.0	0.0	0.0	- Autre d'Amérique
Asia excluding former USSR	5647.5	5393.0	7738.6	6142.3	7435.4	Asie ancienne URSS exclus
- Middle East	314.6	356.3	486.7	715.0	887.1	- Moyen-Orient
Asia former USSR	248.4	220.0	198.1	135.3	157.6	Asie ancienne URSS
Europe excluding former USSR	10610.0	9484.5	10474.3	9401.3	10942.5	Europe ancienne URSS exclus
- European Union	9587.0	8652.8	9357.7	8394.6	9708.4	- Union Européenne
- Eastern Europe	861.1	748.3	960.1	908.2	1134.4	- Europe de l'Est
- Rest of Europe	162.0	83.4	156.5	98.5	99.7	- Autre de l'Europe
Europe former USSR	4203.7	4138.4	5276.8	4656.3	5358.1	Europe ancienne URSS
Oceania	541.9	379.2	286.1	57.1	156.0	Océanie
Russian Federation	2643.5	2409.5	3099.0	2577.2	3071.2	Fédération de Russie
Japan	2027.2	2165.2	3100.6	2684.8	3453.9	Japon
France-Monaco	1550.9	1860.9	1912.9	1844.7	2258.8	France-Monaco
Ukraine	1440.9	1619.9	2039.8	1997.7	2201.9	Ukraine
Germany	2127.5	1667.0	1893.8	1569.8	1644.5	Allemagne
Belgium	–	2090.4	2260.3	2040.2	e2289.1	Belgique
Brazil	1549.0	1295.0	1635.0	1221.9	e1266.8	Brésil
Korea, Republic of	1463.3	1065.6	1239.8	1073.1	1078.0	République de Corée
China	706.6	689.6	1437.8	625.6	485.1	Chine
Sweden	698.4	668.9	697.4	688.8	805.1	Suède
Italy-San Marino-Holy See	669.6	496.9	714.5	632.9	790.7	Italie-Saint-Marin-Saint-Siège
Netherlands	563.7	617.3	577.1	471.8	649.7	Pays-Bas
Mexico	739.5	576.6	620.5	302.8	537.6	Mexique
Belgium-Luxembourg	2378.8	–	–	–	–	Belgique-Luxembourg
United Kingdom	620.3	402.9	451.8	375.3	502.3	Royaume-Uni
United States	429.4	338.8	486.4	461.0	450.3	Etats-Unis d'Amérique
Turkey	208.2	186.6	277.7	537.5	682.2	Turquie
South Africa	–	–	659.0	523.0	576.7	Afrique du Sud
Canada	317.4	312.9	288.2	212.7	412.3	Canada
Spain	327.3	309.6	323.4	275.4	235.1	Espagne
Australia	492.7	335.1	240.9	21.6	113.8	Australie
Slovakia	219.9	143.3	190.4	252.8	311.4	Slovaquie
Finland	314.4	191.5	190.4	178.2	218.8	Finlande
Romania	154.1	219.4	246.5	184.6	269.5	Roumanie
India	91.4	134.6	180.3	149.2	506.2	Inde
Kazakhstan	242.9	217.1	196.7	135.0	e152.1	Kazakhstan
Southern African Customs Union	454.3	415.0	–	–	–	Union douanière d'Afrique australe
Poland	170.7	137.0	210.5	160.7	183.8	Pologne
Austria	246.4	135.4	154.1	141.0	176.2	Autriche
Iran (Islamic Republic of)	99.0	161.4	195.0	144.1	188.6	Iran (République islamique d')

(Value as percentages of World total) **(Valeur en pourcentage du total mondial)**

Regions of the world	1993	1994	1995	1996	1997	1998	1999	2000	2001	2002	Régions du monde
World	100.0	100.0	100.0	100.0	100.0	100.0	100.0	100.0	100.0	100.0	Monde
Africa	2.2	2.7	1.8	2.1	2.1	1.9	2.0	2.8	2.8	2.8	Afrique
Americas	14.2	12.8	15.6	13.7	12.9	12.9	12.0	11.8	10.5	10.6	Amériques
- Northern America	3.7	3.1	5.8	3.9	3.5	3.0	2.9	2.8	2.9	3.1	- Amérique du Nord
- LAIA	10.5	9.6	9.7	9.7	9.2	9.8	9.0	8.9	7.5	7.4	- ALAI
- CACM	0.0	0.0	0.0	0.0	0.0	0.0	0.0	0.0	0.0	0.0	- MCC
- Caribbean	0.0	0.1	0.1	0.1	0.1	0.1	0.1	0.2	0.2	0.1	- Caraïbes
- Rest of America	0.0	0.0	0.0	0.0	0.0	0.0	0.0	0.0	0.0	0.0	- Autre d'Amérique
Asia excluding former USSR	22.3	19.3	22.2	18.9	22.2	22.6	23.7	27.6	26.1	26.8	Asie ancienne URSS exclus
- Middle East	3.5	3.7	2.1	2.1	2.2	1.3	1.6	1.7	3.0	3.2	- Moyen-Orient
Asia former USSR	0.4	0.4	0.6	0.8	1.2	1.0	1.0	0.7	0.6	0.6	Asie ancienne URSS
Europe excluding former USSR	44.8	47.8	43.9	46.0	42.7	42.5	41.6	37.3	40.0	39.4	Europe ancienne URSS exclus
- European Union	40.5	43.5	40.0	43.0	38.6	38.4	38.0	33.3	35.7	34.9	- Union Européenne
- Eastern Europe	4.0	3.9	3.6	2.8	3.9	3.5	3.3	3.4	3.9	4.1	- Europe de l'Est
- Rest of Europe	0.3	0.3	0.3	0.2	0.2	0.6	0.4	0.6	0.4	0.4	- Autre de l'Europe
Europe former USSR	13.7	14.4	13.5	16.2	16.9	16.8	18.2	18.8	19.8	19.3	Europe ancienne URSS
Oceania	2.4	2.7	2.3	2.2	1.9	2.2	1.7	1.0	0.2	0.6	Océanie

673 Iron and steel bars, rods, shapes and sections

TRADE BY COMMODITY (Value in million US dollars)
Imports by principal countries or areas

COMMERCE PAR PRODUIT (Valeur en millions de dollars EU)
Importations selon les principaux pays ou zones

Country or area	1998	1999	2000	2001	2002	Pays ou zone
World	25975.2	22561.7	24395.5	23427.3	23830.7	Monde
Africa	1130.5	926.1	788.2	931.1	1029.9	Afrique
Americas	6290.8	5363.4	6262.6	5242.4	5029.9	Amériques
- Northern America	4741.4	3954.4	4869.8	3904.5	3781.1	- Amérique du Nord
- LAIA	1209.3	1105.9	1092.8	1009.4	927.2	- ALAI
- CACM	165.5	133.6	135.5	167.8	163.4	- MCC
- Caribbean	146.8	135.2	139.2	129.3	116.9	- Caraïbes
- Rest of America	27.8	34.3	25.3	31.4	41.3	- Autre d'Amérique
Asia excluding former USSR	5498.1	4799.0	5319.9	5199.8	5670.5	Asie ancienne URSS exclus
- Middle East	1373.2	1258.7	1602.6	1766.5	1764.0	- Moyen-Orient
Asia former USSR	113.0	70.1	134.1	138.0	143.4	Asie ancienne URSS
Europe excluding former USSR	12203.1	10903.5	11211.0	11267.5	11316.9	Europe ancienne URSS exclus
- European Union	10497.1	9453.3	9593.8	9483.3	9422.1	- Union Européenne
- Eastern Europe	814.1	701.7	795.0	948.2	1040.8	- Europe de l'Est
- Rest of Europe	891.9	748.5	822.2	836.0	854.0	- Autre de l'Europe
Europe former USSR	529.3	289.8	461.1	456.3	401.9	Europe ancienne URSS
Oceania	210.6	209.7	218.7	192.2	238.3	Océanie
United States	3911.5	3156.6	3817.7	3118.4	2979.3	Etats-Unis d'Amérique
Germany	2739.5	2287.2	2258.6	2319.1	2038.5	Allemagne
France-Monaco	1595.0	1413.8	1491.8	1362.1	1356.8	France-Monaco
Italy-San Marino-Holy See	1114.5	962.9	1061.5	1033.7	1054.5	Italie-Saint-Marin-Saint-Siège
Canada	829.4	797.0	1050.8	784.2	798.8	Canada
United Kingdom	860.7	749.5	756.5	771.9	796.6	Royaume-Uni
Netherlands	821.6	748.1	731.0	735.5	729.0	Pays-Bas
Spain	592.9	664.8	668.6	675.2	714.1	Espagne
China	973.6	628.4	487.8	516.9	632.6	Chine
Belgium	–	726.8	712.9	666.7	e731.2	Belgique
Mexico	534.3	540.0	635.4	555.1	495.4	Mexique
China, Hong Kong SAR	663.0	520.3	510.5	505.2	458.7	Chine - RAS de Hong-Kong
Korea, Republic of	255.9	449.5	591.5	512.7	778.9	République de Corée
Switzerland-Liechtenstein	455.3	396.7	441.9	428.3	385.1	Suisse-Liechtenstein
Sweden	451.1	367.0	396.9	352.8	376.9	Suède
Singapore	549.1	359.2	357.8	313.1	347.3	Singapour
Portugal	291.0	397.6	368.9	405.6	409.1	Portugal
Austria	371.2	304.9	313.5	328.4	320.8	Autriche
Iran (Islamic Republic of)	161.9	234.0	359.0	521.9	330.1	Iran (République islamique d')
United Arab Emirates	187.8	196.7	358.1	392.9	e403.1	Emirates arabes unis
Thailand	228.4	280.3	331.9	312.4	e325.5	Thaïlande
Algeria	275.8	236.5	245.4	e296.8	e338.1	Algérie
Czech Republic	242.3	196.7	217.1	250.6	268.1	République tchèque
Saudi Arabia	266.2	191.8	191.3	246.7	e255.4	Arabie saoudite
Malaysia	161.5	221.8	264.4	237.7	e259.8	Malaisie
Poland	177.9	183.4	210.3	255.0	280.9	Pologne
Greece	264.8	220.4	190.3	192.3	e212.7	Grèce
Denmark	238.1	199.1	204.4	195.6	235.4	Danemark
Russian Federation	254.6	125.7	237.2	208.8	136.6	Fédération de Russie
Finland	199.1	160.0	175.3	172.1	156.8	Finlande

(Value as percentages of World total) **(Valeur en pourcentage du total mondial)**

Regions of the world	1993	1994	1995	1996	1997	1998	1999	2000	2001	2002	Régions du monde
World	100.0	100.0	100.0	100.0	100.0	100.0	100.0	100.0	100.0	100.0	Monde
Africa	4.4	4.2	3.9	3.9	3.5	4.4	4.1	3.2	4.0	4.3	Afrique
Americas	12.4	14.3	14.4	16.2	19.7	24.2	23.8	25.7	22.4	21.1	Amériques
- Northern America	9.0	10.7	11.0	12.5	14.8	18.3	17.5	20.0	16.7	15.9	- Amérique du Nord
- LAIA	2.6	2.9	2.5	2.9	3.9	4.7	4.9	4.5	4.3	3.9	- ALAI
- CACM	0.3	0.4	0.4	0.4	0.5	0.6	0.6	0.6	0.7	0.7	- MCC
- Caribbean	0.4	0.3	0.4	0.4	0.5	0.6	0.6	0.6	0.6	0.5	- Caraïbes
- Rest of America	0.1	0.1	0.1	0.1	0.1	0.1	0.2	0.1	0.1	0.2	- Autre d'Amérique
Asia excluding former USSR	49.4	40.6	31.5	34.2	30.6	21.2	21.3	21.8	22.2	23.8	Asie ancienne URSS exclus
- Middle East	5.4	6.2	5.7	6.3	6.0	5.3	5.6	6.6	7.5	7.4	- Moyen-Orient
Asia former USSR	0.0	0.2	0.2	0.4	0.3	0.4	0.3	0.5	0.6	0.6	Asie ancienne URSS
Europe excluding former USSR	33.0	38.4	47.6	41.9	42.8	47.0	48.3	46.0	48.1	47.5	Europe ancienne URSS exclus
- European Union	29.5	34.8	42.6	37.0	37.5	40.4	41.9	39.3	40.5	39.5	- Union Européenne
- Eastern Europe	1.0	1.0	1.7	1.9	2.4	3.1	3.1	3.3	4.0	4.4	- Europe de l'Est
- Rest of Europe	2.4	2.7	3.3	3.0	3.0	3.4	3.3	3.4	3.6	3.6	- Autre de l'Europe
Europe former USSR	0.3	1.6	1.6	2.3	2.0	2.0	1.3	1.9	1.9	1.7	Europe ancienne URSS
Oceania	0.6	0.7	0.8	1.0	1.0	0.8	0.9	0.9	0.8	1.0	Océanie

TRADE BY COMMODITY (Value in million US dollars)
Exports by principal countries or areas

COMMERCE PAR PRODUIT (Valeur en millions de dollars EU)
Exportations selon les principaux pays ou zones

Country or area	1998	1999	2000	2001	2002	Pays ou zone
World	24835.5	21370.5	23176.3	22550.0	23192.8	Monde
Africa	430.0	395.0	435.1	335.4	386.9	Afrique
Americas	2545.7	2412.5	2691.1	2530.4	2475.3	Amériques
- Northern America	1733.9	1589.8	1832.5	1659.8	1646.0	- Amérique du Nord
- LAIA	559.4	608.4	638.2	636.5	635.6	- ALAI
- CACM	35.8	35.9	40.3	54.0	52.5	- MCC
- Caribbean	216.5	178.3	180.0	179.7	140.4	- Caraïbes
- Rest of America	0.3	0.1	0.2	0.4	0.8	- Autre d'Amérique
Asia excluding former USSR	5599.3	4901.3	5119.2	4995.3	5456.1	Asie ancienne URSS exclus
- Middle East	1486.0	1520.2	1361.0	1605.9	1656.4	- Moyen-Orient
Asia former USSR	15.6	23.3	31.8	37.2	33.1	Asie ancienne URSS
Europe excluding former USSR	14121.5	11951.6	12777.5	12521.4	12631.6	Europe ancienne URSS exclus
- European Union	12305.4	10518.3	11264.6	10917.8	10975.6	- Union Européenne
- Eastern Europe	1278.2	972.5	1016.3	1076.1	1135.3	- Europe de l'Est
- Rest of Europe	537.8	460.8	496.6	527.5	520.7	- Autre de l'Europe
Europe former USSR	1982.9	1588.9	2049.4	2056.3	2149.3	Europe ancienne URSS
Oceania	140.6	97.8	72.2	74.0	60.6	Océanie
Germany	2745.9	2297.9	2534.1	2406.6	2468.9	Allemagne
Italy-San Marino-Holy See	1810.2	1562.3	1752.1	1774.0	1679.6	Italie-Saint-Marin-Saint-Siège
Japan	1853.5	1492.6	1577.2	1391.7	1607.8	Japon
France-Monaco	1714.8	1335.5	1446.2	1368.4	1277.4	France-Monaco
Turkey	1114.3	1136.8	1021.9	1233.4	1221.3	Turquie
United Kingdom	1375.7	1015.6	971.2	1079.5	1048.4	Royaume-Uni
Ukraine	971.2	876.4	1188.0	1091.2	1202.8	Ukraine
Spain	1088.9	943.5	1123.7	994.1	1139.5	Espagne
Canada	884.1	813.6	929.0	789.4	827.0	Canada
United States	849.7	776.2	903.4	870.4	819.0	Etats-Unis d'Amérique
Luxembourg	-	963.2	980.3	1010.4	e1033.0	Luxembourg
Korea, Republic of	1022.7	762.7	736.5	615.7	567.3	République de Corée
Sweden	792.8	647.8	685.9	596.2	593.6	Suède
Russian Federation	754.2	523.6	660.8	700.0	659.3	Fédération de Russie
Czech Republic	510.5	452.9	433.0	514.6	569.8	République tchèque
Belgium	-	564.7	557.9	529.2	e593.7	Belgique
Poland	487.4	342.8	452.9	412.8	414.0	Pologne
Austria	514.8	390.4	384.7	390.0	387.4	Autriche
China	190.3	169.2	328.5	325.6	465.9	Chine
Belgium-Luxembourg	1423.9	-	-	-	-	Belgique-Luxembourg
Netherlands	298.5	264.7	266.2	258.9	270.9	Pays-Bas
Switzerland-Liechtenstein	273.5	245.0	286.3	272.0	271.9	Suisse-Liechtenstein
Brazil	229.2	270.6	278.8	272.1	e282.1	Brésil
Finland	230.9	210.3	208.7	206.8	190.4	Finlande
India	117.1	127.8	175.8	183.7	235.7	Inde
Trinidad and Tobago	202.8	165.2	168.2	169.8	e128.9	Trinité-et-Tobago
Qatar	155.2	150.3	119.2	170.1	229.4	Qatar
Mexico	155.8	152.8	139.1	165.4	157.1	Mexique
Saudi Arabia	192.1	198.2	149.5	99.4	e89.6	Arabie saoudite
South Africa	-	-	276.8	219.1	221.1	Afrique du Sud

(Value as percentages of World total) **(Valeur en pourcentage du total mondial)**

Regions of the world	1993	1994	1995	1996	1997	1998	1999	2000	2001	2002	Régions du monde
World	100.0	100.0	100.0	100.0	100.0	100.0	100.0	100.0	100.0	100.0	Monde
Africa	2.3	1.6	1.5	1.4	1.6	1.7	1.8	1.9	1.5	1.7	Afrique
Americas	10.1	9.4	9.8	10.5	10.6	10.3	11.3	11.6	11.2	10.7	Amériques
- Northern America	5.4	5.6	5.8	6.8	7.1	7.0	7.4	7.9	7.4	7.1	- Amérique du Nord
- LAIA	4.1	3.7	3.9	2.9	2.6	2.3	2.8	2.8	2.8	2.7	- ALAI
- CACM	0.1	0.1	0.1	0.1	0.1	0.1	0.2	0.2	0.2	0.2	- MCC
- Caribbean	0.5	0.0	0.0	0.7	0.8	0.9	0.8	0.8	0.8	0.6	- Caraïbes
- Rest of America	0.0	0.0	0.0	0.0	0.0	0.0	0.0	0.0	0.0	0.0	- Autre d'Amérique
Asia excluding former USSR	25.6	23.2	19.9	21.6	21.7	22.5	22.9	22.1	22.2	23.5	Asie ancienne URSS exclus
- Middle East	7.2	6.9	5.6	6.5	6.3	6.0	7.1	5.9	7.1	7.1	- Moyen-Orient
Asia former USSR	0.6	0.2	0.2	0.2	0.0	0.1	0.1	0.1	0.2	0.1	Asie ancienne URSS
Europe excluding former USSR	52.2	56.0	59.9	55.9	55.8	56.9	55.9	55.1	55.5	54.5	Europe ancienne URSS exclus
- European Union	43.3	48.4	52.1	48.7	48.6	49.5	49.2	48.6	48.4	47.3	- Union Européenne
- Eastern Europe	6.9	5.7	6.0	5.4	5.4	5.1	4.6	4.4	4.8	4.9	- Europe de l'Est
- Rest of Europe	2.0	1.9	1.8	1.8	1.8	2.2	2.2	2.1	2.3	2.2	- Autre de l'Europe
Europe former USSR	8.7	9.1	8.0	9.7	9.5	8.0	7.4	8.8	9.1	9.3	Europe ancienne URSS
Oceania	0.5	0.5	0.5	0.7	0.7	0.6	0.5	0.3	0.3	0.3	Océanie

674 Universals, plates, and sheets, of iron or steel

TRADE BY COMMODITY (Value in million US dollars)
Imports by principal countries or areas

COMMERCE PAR PRODUIT (Valeur en millions de dollars EU)
Importations selon les principaux pays ou zones

Country or area	1998	1999	2000	2001	2002	Pays ou zone
World	54017.9	48171.2	55001.1	49946.5	52787.5	Monde
Africa	1447.1	1150.7	1123.2	1242.4	1252.5	Afrique
Americas	10103.3	8502.1	9524.3	8249.6	8052.0	Amériques
- Northern America	6833.2	5942.6	6086.4	4968.7	4994.3	- Amérique du Nord
- LAIA	2716.4	2114.1	2946.8	2801.6	2638.6	- ALAI
- CACM	295.0	257.9	278.7	307.2	258.6	- MCC
- Caribbean	198.4	137.2	154.4	123.4	112.2	- Caraïbes
- Rest of America	60.3	50.3	58.0	48.8	48.3	- Autre d'Amérique
Asia excluding former USSR	14880.1	15353.8	17827.3	15839.9	18386.4	Asie ancienne URSS exclus
- Middle East	2191.7	1690.0	2170.4	2013.5	2137.8	- Moyen-Orient
Asia former USSR	75.3	54.5	93.9	94.9	110.9	Asie ancienne URSS
Europe excluding former USSR	26068.9	21934.2	24901.5	23064.8	23467.2	Europe ancienne URSS exclus
- European Union	22774.2	19175.9	21557.1	19626.9	19909.5	- Union Européenne
- Eastern Europe	1837.7	1585.0	1979.7	2146.0	2251.3	- Europe de l'Est
- Rest of Europe	1457.0	1173.3	1364.7	1291.8	1306.4	- Autre de l'Europe
Europe former USSR	918.8	628.3	942.4	987.9	947.8	Europe ancienne URSS
Oceania	524.4	547.6	588.6	467.0	570.7	Océanie
China	3548.7	4578.7	5871.4	5887.3	7908.3	Chine
Germany	4887.7	4195.3	4365.0	4326.6	3978.4	Allemagne
United States	5381.5	4399.0	4377.5	3642.5	3397.6	Etats-Unis d'Amérique
Italy-San Marino-Holy See	3517.6	2889.8	3450.5	3276.5	3160.5	Italie-Saint-Marin-Saint-Siège
France-Monaco	3271.7	2761.2	3320.2	2760.6	2830.5	France-Monaco
China, Hong Kong SAR	2407.1	2036.6	2159.5	1552.6	1512.6	Chine - RAS de Hong-Kong
United Kingdom	2120.2	1669.2	1797.2	1777.7	1732.3	Royaume-Uni
Spain	1850.0	1667.3	1708.8	1604.4	1781.8	Espagne
Mexico	1298.6	1250.5	1810.7	1648.3	1667.3	Mexique
Canada	1451.3	1543.0	1708.3	1325.7	1596.0	Canada
Netherlands	1649.3	1269.7	1426.1	1223.2	1277.8	Pays-Bas
Belgium	–	1445.1	1747.4	1382.7	e1516.4	Belgique
Korea, Republic of	761.9	806.2	995.3	926.6	1097.4	République de Corée
Malaysia	700.7	915.8	1025.2	823.5	e900.0	Malaisie
Thailand	758.9	949.1	858.4	809.3	e843.2	Thaïlande
Sweden	902.5	790.4	910.5	741.7	822.3	Suède
Japan	839.3	875.6	1086.6	703.3	503.0	Japon
Poland	633.4	627.3	775.5	858.3	888.3	Pologne
Turkey	889.9	573.0	848.2	564.1	831.2	Turquie
Czech Republic	736.1	557.7	701.2	705.2	731.9	République tchèque
Denmark	710.8	594.8	666.0	649.2	646.9	Danemark
Switzerland-Liechtenstein	731.9	578.8	705.9	595.8	571.5	Suisse-Liechtenstein
Austria	628.2	542.3	626.7	603.4	666.2	Autriche
Singapore	605.7	618.7	661.8	528.4	604.6	Singapour
Iran (Islamic Republic of)	588.6	442.9	577.5	641.5	552.9	Iran (République islamique d')
India	451.1	449.3	372.8	470.3	495.3	Inde
Portugal	502.0	436.8	485.9	297.8	475.1	Portugal
Indonesia	425.0	249.4	512.4	384.7	456.6	Indonésie
Philippines	305.9	391.4	380.0	384.2	538.5	Philippines
Belgium-Luxembourg	1933.2	–	–	–	–	Belgique-Luxembourg

(Value as percentages of World total) **(Valeur en pourcentage du total mondial)**

Regions of the world	1993	1994	1995	1996	1997	1998	1999	2000	2001	2002	Régions du monde
World	100.0	100.0	100.0	100.0	100.0	100.0	100.0	100.0	100.0	100.0	Monde
Africa	2.8	2.5	2.2	2.4	2.3	2.7	2.4	2.0	2.5	2.4	Afrique
Americas	15.8	18.6	14.0	15.1	16.9	18.7	17.6	17.3	16.5	15.3	Amériques
- Northern America	11.0	14.0	9.7	10.5	11.7	12.6	12.3	11.1	9.9	9.5	- Amérique du Nord
- LAIA	4.0	3.9	3.6	3.9	4.4	5.0	4.4	5.4	5.6	5.0	- ALAI
- CACM	0.3	0.4	0.4	0.4	0.4	0.5	0.5	0.5	0.6	0.5	- MCC
- Caribbean	0.3	0.2	0.3	0.3	0.3	0.4	0.3	0.3	0.2	0.2	- Caraïbes
- Rest of America	0.1	0.1	0.1	0.1	0.1	0.1	0.1	0.1	0.1	0.1	- Autre d'Amérique
Asia excluding former USSR	41.2	32.5	35.1	36.3	35.4	27.5	31.9	32.4	31.7	34.8	Asie ancienne URSS exclus
- Middle East	4.9	2.9	4.3	4.3	4.4	4.1	3.5	3.9	4.0	4.0	- Moyen-Orient
Asia former USSR	0.0	0.1	0.1	0.2	0.1	0.1	0.1	0.2	0.2	0.2	Asie ancienne URSS
Europe excluding former USSR	38.4	44.1	46.7	43.4	42.7	48.3	45.5	45.3	46.2	44.5	Europe ancienne URSS exclus
- European Union	34.0	39.5	41.3	38.4	37.4	42.2	39.8	39.2	39.3	37.7	- Union Européenne
- Eastern Europe	1.6	1.7	2.3	2.4	2.6	3.4	3.3	3.6	4.3	4.3	- Europe de l'Est
- Rest of Europe	2.7	2.9	3.1	2.6	2.7	2.7	2.4	2.5	2.6	2.5	- Autre de l'Europe
Europe former USSR	0.8	1.0	1.0	1.5	1.6	1.7	1.3	1.7	2.0	1.8	Europe ancienne URSS
Oceania	1.1	1.1	1.0	1.0	1.1	1.0	1.1	1.1	0.9	1.1	Océanie

TRADE BY COMMODITY (Value in million US dollars)
Exports by principal countries or areas

COMMERCE PAR PRODUIT (Valeur en millions de dollars EU)
Exportations selon les principaux pays ou zones

Country or area	1998	1999	2000	2001	2002	Pays ou zone
World	52749.7	46710.4	53786.8	47331.1	51047.9	Monde
Africa	533.1	478.4	474.9	464.0	438.3	Afrique
Americas	4377.7	4321.8	4907.5	4275.7	4637.6	Amériques
- Northern America	2543.0	2623.9	3140.4	2833.5	3072.2	- Amérique du Nord
- LAIA	1750.9	1611.0	1669.1	1310.3	1460.1	- ALAI
- CACM	75.6	81.5	90.2	123.3	101.9	- MCC
- Caribbean	8.1	5.3	7.6	8.4	3.4	- Caraïbes
- Rest of America	0.1	0.1	0.2	0.2	0.1	- Autre d'Amérique
Asia excluding former USSR	15909.3	14977.3	17383.0	14299.6	16001.8	Asie ancienne URSS exclus
- Middle East	213.2	150.7	297.8	345.4	342.4	- Moyen-Orient
Asia former USSR	204.7	266.9	597.9	468.1	526.9	Asie ancienne URSS
Europe excluding former USSR	29106.0	24538.4	27865.8	25523.8	26773.3	Europe ancienne URSS exclus
- European Union	26498.8	22775.1	25487.0	23197.8	24320.5	- Union Européenne
- Eastern Europe	1981.7	1314.5	1773.8	1784.5	1905.7	- Europe de l'Est
- Rest of Europe	625.4	448.8	605.1	541.5	547.2	- Autre de l'Europe
Europe former USSR	2171.6	1753.6	2234.8	2157.1	2540.7	Europe ancienne URSS
Oceania	447.4	374.0	322.8	142.9	129.3	Océanie
Japan	6906.8	6574.2	7200.0	5909.8	6840.0	Japon
Germany	6328.9	5398.0	5574.1	5595.3	5723.2	Allemagne
France-Monaco	3892.5	3494.7	4029.9	3427.8	3488.8	France-Monaco
Belgium	–	4026.3	4547.7	3873.1	e4345.5	Belgique
Korea, Republic of	3630.0	3122.0	3620.4	3084.0	2958.2	République de Corée
United States	1783.6	1921.5	2369.7	2145.5	2073.9	Etats-Unis d'Amérique
Netherlands	1681.2	1476.7	1722.4	1514.8	1788.0	Pays-Bas
United Kingdom	1892.3	1521.5	1733.9	1359.0	1307.4	Royaume-Uni
Sweden	1500.1	1387.9	1562.8	1452.3	1590.9	Suède
Italy-San Marino-Holy See	1569.5	1263.9	1662.3	1477.8	1388.2	Italie-Saint-Marin-Saint-Siège
China, Hong Kong SAR	1821.6	1483.4	1513.1	1156.8	1339.9	Chine - RAS de Hong-Kong
Austria	1808.6	1234.1	1218.0	1257.2	1332.9	Autriche
Russian Federation	1209.1	1069.2	1388.7	1174.7	1454.5	Fédération de Russie
Spain	1107.7	1049.5	1280.8	1233.9	1243.5	Espagne
Finland	1075.9	1003.4	1193.1	1110.3	1175.2	Finlande
Belgium-Luxembourg	5111.2	–	–	–	–	Belgique-Luxembourg
Ukraine	860.3	626.2	799.2	924.6	1019.2	Ukraine
Canada	759.4	702.3	770.7	688.0	998.3	Canada
Slovakia	755.5	545.0	677.3	638.1	613.5	Slovaquie
Brazil	701.7	597.8	590.8	477.1	e494.7	Brésil
India	300.9	514.8	596.6	467.8	956.2	Inde
Mexico	622.6	530.8	514.8	342.7	474.2	Mexique
Kazakhstan	203.7	265.7	595.3	467.5	e526.6	Kazakhstan
China	462.3	266.7	531.5	383.7	386.9	Chine
Luxembourg	–	435.0	489.6	455.6	e465.8	Luxembourg
Romania	400.7	219.2	302.9	307.3	402.4	Roumanie
Thailand	207.2	259.2	374.3	282.0	e297.8	Thaïlande
Czech Republic	314.1	199.2	259.4	286.7	287.7	République tchèque
Argentina	176.3	253.7	280.4	250.1	e241.7	Argentine
Denmark	231.8	241.5	216.9	213.6	226.5	Danemark

(Value as percentages of World total) **(Valeur en pourcentage du total mondial)**

Regions of the world	1993	1994	1995	1996	1997	1998	1999	2000	2001	2002	Régions du monde
World	100.0	100.0	100.0	100.0	100.0	100.0	100.0	100.0	100.0	100.0	Monde
Africa	1.4	1.4	1.3	1.1	1.2	1.0	1.0	0.9	1.0	0.9	Afrique
Americas	8.7	8.0	7.8	8.1	8.0	8.3	9.3	9.1	9.0	9.1	Amériques
- Northern America	5.0	4.6	4.1	4.5	4.7	4.8	5.6	5.8	6.0	6.0	- Amérique du Nord
- LAIA	3.6	3.4	3.6	3.5	3.1	3.3	3.4	3.1	2.8	2.9	- ALAI
- CACM	0.0	0.1	0.1	0.1	0.1	0.1	0.2	0.2	0.3	0.2	- MCC
- Caribbean	0.0	0.0	0.0	0.0	0.0	0.0	0.0	0.0	0.0	0.0	- Caraïbes
- Rest of America	0.0	0.0	0.0	0.0	0.0	0.0	0.0	0.0	0.0	0.0	- Autre d'Amérique
Asia excluding former USSR	32.6	28.8	29.7	31.1	32.0	30.2	32.1	32.3	30.2	31.3	Asie ancienne URSS exclus
- Middle East	0.1	0.2	0.2	0.3	0.4	0.4	0.3	0.6	0.7	0.7	- Moyen-Orient
Asia former USSR	0.5	0.4	0.4	0.5	0.6	0.4	0.6	1.1	1.0	1.0	Asie ancienne URSS
Europe excluding former USSR	53.2	56.5	56.0	53.3	52.0	55.2	52.5	51.8	53.9	52.4	Europe ancienne URSS exclus
- European Union	48.9	52.1	51.4	49.9	47.0	50.2	48.8	47.4	49.0	47.6	- Union Européenne
- Eastern Europe	3.4	3.5	3.8	2.6	4.1	3.8	2.8	3.3	3.8	3.7	- Europe de l'Est
- Rest of Europe	0.9	0.9	0.8	0.8	0.9	1.2	1.0	1.1	1.1	1.1	- Autre de l'Europe
Europe former USSR	2.7	4.1	4.1	4.9	5.2	4.1	3.8	4.2	4.6	5.0	Europe ancienne URSS
Oceania	0.9	0.8	0.8	0.9	1.0	0.8	0.8	0.6	0.3	0.3	Océanie

676 Rails and railway track construction materials, of iron or steel

TRADE BY COMMODITY (Value in million US dollars)
Imports by principal countries or areas

COMMERCE PAR PRODUIT (Valeur en millions de dollars EU)
Importations selon les principaux pays ou zones

Country or area	1998	1999	2000	2001	2002	Pays ou zone
World	1816.0	1445.7	1153.0	1301.0	1394.9	Monde
Africa	63.0	40.8	54.7	57.2	65.2	Afrique
Americas	537.6	389.1	379.1	372.9	351.5	Amériques
- Northern America	364.2	283.1	258.5	227.5	249.5	- Amérique du Nord
- LAIA	168.8	101.7	108.6	139.1	97.1	- ALAI
- CACM	0.9	0.6	0.8	0.3	0.3	- MCC
- Caribbean	3.6	3.6	2.4	4.9	4.5	- Caraïbes
- Rest of America	0.2	0.1	8.8	1.1	0.1	- Autre d'Amérique
Asia excluding former USSR	500.5	445.0	235.4	260.3	258.8	Asie ancienne URSS exclus
- Middle East	319.9	225.3	79.2	58.1	50.4	- Moyen-Orient
Asia former USSR	105.0	41.7	43.2	47.1	58.1	Asie ancienne URSS
Europe excluding former USSR	508.3	481.9	397.6	510.2	597.4	Europe ancienne URSS exclus
- European Union	390.0	374.7	311.9	417.0	470.6	- Union Européenne
- Eastern Europe	52.8	48.6	26.8	35.6	50.5	- Europe de l'Est
- Rest of Europe	65.5	58.6	58.8	57.6	76.4	- Autre de l'Europe
Europe former USSR	88.6	38.3	33.7	42.8	53.7	Europe ancienne URSS
Oceania	13.0	8.8	9.3	10.4	10.0	Océanie
United States	282.3	233.0	210.2	170.0	182.7	Etats-Unis d'Amérique
Germany	119.1	128.8	70.1	112.0	114.1	Allemagne
Canada	81.8	50.0	48.2	57.5	66.7	Canada
Iran (Islamic Republic of)	139.5	73.6	34.7	39.4	13.6	Iran (République islamique d')
Syrian Arab Republic	134.4	110.9	e	e	10.5	République arabe syrienne
Brazil	78.4	21.7	42.6	76.9	33.7	Brésil
United Kingdom	25.0	26.6	32.0	75.3	88.0	Royaume-Uni
Mexico	66.7	56.7	41.5	30.3	30.6	Mexique
Switzerland-Liechtenstein	41.7	41.0	38.4	44.0	52.7	Suisse-Liechtenstein
Belgium	–	49.2	48.4	42.5	e46.6	Belgique
Kazakhstan	78.7	21.4	9.5	22.8	e23.3	Kazakhstan
France-Monaco	21.0	33.1	25.2	23.7	32.1	France-Monaco
Italy-San Marino-Holy See	14.9	16.1	26.9	37.2	25.7	Italie-Saint-Marin-Saint-Siège
Thailand	22.9	22.7	28.6	20.9	e21.7	Thaïlande
Turkey	40.1	33.5	31.2	4.9	5.8	Turquie
Malaysia	9.4	7.0	11.0	37.1	e40.5	Malaisie
Finland	29.5	24.9	14.8	18.5	15.2	Finlande
Sweden	28.7	16.4	14.2	17.5	23.5	Suède
Spain	15.2	10.3	18.4	18.2	35.5	Espagne
Netherlands	25.2	16.5	17.3	16.0	20.9	Pays-Bas
India	15.4	49.3	5.9	7.0	6.4	Inde
China	2.6	3.2	2.5	35.4	37.3	Chine
Portugal	29.2	10.7	7.4	12.7	18.7	Portugal
Romania	25.3	27.3	4.5	8.7	12.5	Roumanie
Bangladesh	9.6	e10.5	e17.9	17.3	e16.9	Bangladesh
Indonesia	10.8	40.0	6.8	4.2	8.8	Indonésie
Belarus	20.6	6.6	4.0	10.6	27.1	Bélarus
Russian Federation	34.5	11.7	12.1	3.6	2.1	Fédération de Russie
Austria	11.6	13.6	9.3	12.8	14.4	Autriche
Uzbekistan	e7.6	e10.1	e16.1	e7.9	e14.7	Ouzbékistan

(Value as percentages of World total) **(Valeur en pourcentage du total mondial)**

Regions of the world	1993	1994	1995	1996	1997	1998	1999	2000	2001	2002	Régions du monde
World	100.0	100.0	100.0	100.0	100.0	100.0	100.0	100.0	100.0	100.0	Monde
Africa	5.0	3.7	4.8	4.2	2.8	3.5	2.8	4.7	4.4	4.7	Afrique
Americas	19.9	23.3	21.4	24.9	31.1	29.6	26.9	32.9	28.7	25.2	Amériques
- Northern America	13.7	18.0	15.7	19.1	22.2	20.1	19.6	22.4	17.5	17.9	- Amérique du Nord
- LAIA	6.1	5.1	5.6	5.6	8.8	9.3	7.0	9.4	10.7	7.0	- ALAI
- CACM	0.1	0.1	0.0	0.0	0.0	0.0	0.0	0.1	0.0	0.0	- MCC
- Caribbean	0.1	0.1	0.1	0.1	0.1	0.2	0.3	0.2	0.4	0.3	- Caraïbes
- Rest of America	0.0	0.0	0.0	0.0	0.0	0.0	0.0	0.8	0.1	0.0	- Autre d'Amérique
Asia excluding former USSR	39.1	29.9	26.8	19.6	18.9	27.6	30.8	20.4	20.0	18.6	Asie ancienne URSS exclus
- Middle East	14.4	4.2	4.0	3.6	5.2	17.6	15.6	6.9	4.5	3.6	- Moyen-Orient
Asia former USSR	0.0	1.3	3.7	4.9	5.0	5.8	2.9	3.7	3.6	4.2	Asie ancienne URSS
Europe excluding former USSR	34.5	35.3	35.2	37.0	34.8	28.0	33.3	34.5	39.2	42.8	Europe ancienne URSS exclus
- European Union	24.7	26.3	24.1	25.5	24.4	21.5	25.9	27.1	32.1	33.7	- Union Européenne
- Eastern Europe	3.4	2.9	5.3	3.9	5.4	2.9	3.4	2.3	2.7	3.6	- Europe de l'Est
- Rest of Europe	6.4	6.2	5.9	7.6	4.9	3.6	4.1	5.1	4.4	5.5	- Autre de l'Europe
Europe former USSR	1.0	5.9	7.4	8.3	6.2	4.9	2.6	2.9	3.3	3.9	Europe ancienne URSS
Oceania	0.4	0.5	0.7	1.1	1.2	0.7	0.6	0.8	0.8	0.7	Océanie

TRADE BY COMMODITY (Value in million US dollars)
Exports by principal countries or areas

COMMERCE PAR PRODUIT (Valeur en millions de dollars EU)
Exportations selon les principaux pays ou zones

Country or area	1998	1999	2000	2001	2002	Pays ou zone
World	1407.2	1199.7	1015.6	1238.7	1308.3	Monde
Africa	6.1	6.5	6.2	6.7	5.6	Afrique
Americas	167.5	108.1	124.0	117.8	121.4	Amériques
- Northern America	162.0	103.0	118.7	110.6	113.9	- Amérique du Nord
- LAIA	5.5	4.7	5.0	7.1	7.4	- ALAI
- CACM	0.0	0.5	0.2	0.0	0.1	- MCC
- Caribbean	0.0	0.0	0.1	0.0	0.1	- Caraïbes
- Rest of America	0.0	0.0	0.0	0.0	0.0	- Autre d'Amérique
Asia excluding former USSR	233.0	189.3	215.2	176.3	179.2	Asie ancienne URSS exclus
- Middle East	0.8	3.2	3.6	3.5	3.3	- Moyen-Orient
Asia former USSR	2.8	4.7	4.4	4.8	5.5	Asie ancienne URSS
Europe excluding former USSR	760.2	744.4	552.9	809.2	866.8	Europe ancienne URSS exclus
- European Union	606.3	592.0	450.4	667.2	723.7	- Union Européenne
- Eastern Europe	139.6	139.0	90.0	126.4	121.4	- Europe de l'Est
- Rest of Europe	14.3	13.4	12.5	15.6	21.7	- Autre de l'Europe
Europe former USSR	229.7	134.0	98.1	104.6	109.5	Europe ancienne URSS
Oceania	7.9	12.8	14.8	19.4	20.3	Océanie
Austria	182.5	175.0	130.1	213.0	186.3	Autriche
Japan	169.7	139.2	152.3	112.7	126.6	Japon
Germany	117.9	130.8	108.3	149.5	180.4	Allemagne
Russian Federation	141.4	104.2	68.4	80.1	82.1	Fédération de Russie
United States	99.5	62.7	80.6	80.5	74.5	Etats-Unis d'Amérique
Poland	87.8	105.4	55.0	73.5	47.6	Pologne
United Kingdom	110.9	105.8	47.6	44.8	49.2	Royaume-Uni
France-Monaco	40.7	47.3	47.1	86.6	129.5	France-Monaco
Czech Republic	44.2	27.8	30.8	50.9	71.8	République tchèque
Canada	62.4	40.2	38.1	30.2	39.4	Canada
Spain	54.1	37.8	26.8	40.0	42.3	Espagne
Ukraine	78.2	23.7	27.5	22.0	24.2	Ukraine
Italy-San Marino-Holy See	8.1	18.2	26.4	46.0	61.4	Italie-Saint-Marin-Saint-Siège
Luxembourg	–	39.3	34.5	40.2	e41.1	Luxembourg
China	36.8	28.9	37.1	19.3	27.2	Chine
Sweden	27.3	21.4	12.1	21.8	5.8	Suède
Australia	7.9	12.7	14.8	19.3	20.3	Australie
Korea, Republic of	12.8	10.2	11.7	30.9	7.8	République de Corée
Switzerland-Liechtenstein	11.1	11.1	11.3	14.5	19.0	Suisse-Liechtenstein
Belgium	–	12.3	12.1	15.1	e16.9	Belgique
Belgium-Luxembourg	51.9	–	–	–	–	Belgique-Luxembourg
Netherlands	10.6	2.3	3.9	7.9	6.6	Pays-Bas
Brazil	3.5	3.1	4.0	5.5	e5.7	Brésil
Kazakhstan	2.4	4.5	4.2	4.4	e5.0	Kazakhstan
Romania	6.7	4.7	3.8	1.6	1.4	Roumanie
Singapore	2.3	1.8	2.0	2.3	6.0	Singapour
South Africa	–	–	4.6	5.1	4.1	Afrique du Sud
Belarus	7.5	3.6	0.0	0.2	0.4	Bélarus
India	3.9	0.7	1.5	2.5	2.9	Inde
Southern African Customs Union	5.5	5.9	–	–	–	Union douanière d'Afrique australe

(Value as percentages of World total) **(Valeur en pourcentage du total mondial)**

Regions of the world	1993	1994	1995	1996	1997	1998	1999	2000	2001	2002	Régions du monde
World	100.0	100.0	100.0	100.0	100.0	100.0	100.0	100.0	100.0	100.0	Monde
Africa	0.5	0.5	0.4	0.2	0.4	0.4	0.5	0.6	0.5	0.4	Afrique
Americas	14.0	10.7	10.7	11.3	13.8	11.9	9.0	12.2	9.5	9.3	Amériques
- Northern America	13.5	10.0	9.9	10.7	13.4	11.5	8.6	11.7	8.9	8.7	- Amérique du Nord
- LAIA	0.5	0.6	0.8	0.6	0.4	0.4	0.4	0.5	0.6	0.6	- ALAI
- CACM	0.0	0.1	0.0	0.0	0.0	0.0	0.0	0.0	0.0	0.0	- MCC
- Caribbean	0.0	0.0	0.0	0.0	0.0	0.0	0.0	0.0	0.0	0.0	- Caraïbes
- Rest of America	0.0	0.0	0.0	0.0	0.0	0.0	0.0	0.0	0.0	0.0	- Autre d'Amérique
Asia excluding former USSR	20.3	16.0	16.4	14.6	16.8	16.6	15.8	21.2	14.2	13.7	Asie ancienne URSS exclus
- Middle East	1.1	0.1	0.1	0.1	0.1	0.1	0.3	0.4	0.3	0.3	- Moyen-Orient
Asia former USSR	0.2	0.1	0.2	0.2	0.2	0.2	0.4	0.4	0.4	0.4	Asie ancienne URSS
Europe excluding former USSR	59.1	58.2	57.7	58.8	53.8	54.0	62.0	54.4	65.3	66.3	Europe ancienne URSS exclus
- European Union	53.5	49.8	47.2	48.8	45.1	43.1	49.3	44.3	53.9	55.3	- Union Européenne
- Eastern Europe	4.9	7.9	9.7	9.0	8.0	9.9	11.6	8.9	10.2	9.3	- Europe de l'Est
- Rest of Europe	0.7	0.5	0.8	1.0	0.7	1.0	1.1	1.2	1.3	1.7	- Autre de l'Europe
Europe former USSR	5.1	14.0	14.1	13.6	14.2	16.3	11.2	9.7	8.4	8.4	Europe ancienne URSS
Oceania	0.8	0.6	0.6	1.3	0.8	0.6	1.1	1.5	1.6	1.5	Océanie

677 Iron or steel wire (excluding wire rod), not insulated

TRADE BY COMMODITY (Value in million US dollars)
Imports by principal countries or areas

COMMERCE PAR PRODUIT (Valeur en millions de dollars EU)
Importations selon les principaux pays ou zones

Country or area	1998	1999	2000	2001	2002	Pays ou zone
World	4136.5	3917.6	4312.2	4102.6	4154.6	Monde
Africa	92.0	101.8	87.5	104.7	120.7	Afrique
Americas	1009.0	983.1	1075.4	1007.3	985.4	Amériques
- Northern America	776.5	767.4	821.0	740.8	753.1	- Amérique du Nord
- LAIA	192.4	177.6	221.7	223.0	194.7	- ALAI
- CACM	16.9	17.4	17.3	25.6	21.0	- MCC
- Caribbean	17.5	16.2	10.8	13.2	11.9	- Caraïbes
- Rest of America	5.6	4.5	4.5	4.7	4.8	- Autre d'Amérique
Asia excluding former USSR	852.4	892.3	1144.6	1066.8	1059.3	Asie ancienne URSS exclus
- Middle East	165.9	124.9	240.9	259.1	207.9	- Moyen-Orient
Asia former USSR	20.1	17.1	36.0	21.3	25.9	Asie ancienne URSS
Europe excluding former USSR	2044.9	1823.6	1849.6	1800.8	1844.3	Europe ancienne URSS exclus
- European Union	1726.0	1552.8	1548.1	1483.9	1507.9	- Union Européenne
- Eastern Europe	152.5	126.1	147.2	165.0	185.2	- Europe de l'Est
- Rest of Europe	166.4	144.7	154.2	151.9	151.2	- Autre de l'Europe
Europe former USSR	49.6	30.7	46.0	41.7	45.5	Europe ancienne URSS
Oceania	68.6	68.9	73.1	60.0	73.4	Océanie
United States	657.1	637.8	660.5	596.7	612.8	Etats-Unis d'Amérique
Germany	478.6	423.0	390.2	410.4	404.6	Allemagne
France-Monaco	333.9	307.5	323.6	281.7	285.4	France-Monaco
China	177.3	194.6	254.2	268.4	309.7	Chine
Italy-San Marino-Holy See	184.9	170.4	179.8	159.6	163.3	Italie-Saint-Marin-Saint-Siège
Japan	132.4	152.6	180.1	153.2	137.9	Japon
Canada	119.4	129.4	160.5	143.9	140.2	Canada
United Kingdom	150.0	116.5	123.1	118.7	115.3	Royaume-Uni
Mexico	97.6	104.3	130.0	132.6	117.3	Mexique
Spain	92.8	99.8	99.2	113.5	116.3	Espagne
Switzerland-Liechtenstein	95.3	83.7	91.2	90.0	84.4	Suisse-Liechtenstein
Netherlands	111.3	85.3	82.6	70.9	75.7	Pays-Bas
China, Hong Kong SAR	81.5	81.3	90.3	70.1	77.3	Chine - RAS de Hong-Kong
Syrian Arab Republic	e	e	115.6	e144.2	88.0	République arabe syrienne
Austria	68.2	66.6	59.8	61.3	55.5	Autriche
Sweden	60.6	56.2	58.0	48.6	51.7	Suède
Poland	52.9	44.8	52.5	56.1	63.1	Pologne
Belgium	–	63.1	68.0	65.5	e71.8	Belgique
Singapore	44.7	51.5	55.4	44.7	40.9	Singapour
Thailand	38.3	45.0	48.1	44.4	e46.2	Thaïlande
Australia	43.9	43.5	46.7	36.8	47.1	Australie
Malaysia	31.5	41.6	47.2	40.3	e44.1	Malaisie
Czech Republic	44.0	31.8	35.5	43.7	47.8	République tchèque
Denmark	40.7	38.1	42.6	36.9	42.1	Danemark
Korea, Republic of	26.7	45.2	47.4	38.7	32.5	République de Corée
Portugal	41.6	35.4	34.6	35.3	41.1	Portugal
Indonesia	34.1	34.8	42.5	32.1	38.8	Indonésie
Brazil	33.6	22.5	36.0	38.1	35.7	Brésil
Ireland	32.3	32.6	33.7	33.1	30.9	Irlande
Iran (Islamic Republic of)	49.3	25.2	26.1	29.7	32.3	Iran (République islamique d')

(Value as percentages of World total) **(Valeur en pourcentage du total mondial)**

Regions of the world	1993	1994	1995	1996	1997	1998	1999	2000	2001	2002	Régions du monde
World	100.0	100.0	100.0	100.0	100.0	100.0	100.0	100.0	100.0	100.0	Monde
Africa	4.8	8.0	2.3	2.6	2.3	2.2	2.6	2.0	2.6	2.9	Afrique
Americas	22.7	20.8	19.9	20.9	23.7	24.4	25.1	24.9	24.6	23.7	Amériques
- Northern America	18.1	16.9	16.1	16.4	18.4	18.8	19.6	19.0	18.1	18.1	- Amérique du Nord
- LAIA	3.6	3.2	3.0	3.7	4.5	4.7	4.5	5.1	5.4	4.7	- ALAI
- CACM	0.3	0.3	0.3	0.3	0.3	0.4	0.4	0.4	0.6	0.5	- MCC
- Caribbean	0.5	0.2	0.4	0.4	0.4	0.4	0.4	0.3	0.3	0.3	- Caraïbes
- Rest of America	0.2	0.2	0.1	0.2	0.2	0.1	0.1	0.1	0.1	0.1	- Autre d'Amérique
Asia excluding former USSR	27.9	24.9	24.2	23.7	24.3	20.6	22.8	26.5	26.0	25.5	Asie ancienne URSS exclus
- Middle East	3.5	3.4	3.8	4.1	4.4	4.0	3.2	5.6	6.3	5.0	- Moyen-Orient
Asia former USSR	0.0	0.3	0.4	0.5	0.3	0.5	0.4	0.8	0.5	0.6	Asie ancienne URSS
Europe excluding former USSR	42.6	43.4	50.5	49.1	46.5	49.4	46.5	42.9	43.9	44.4	Europe ancienne URSS exclus
- European Union	36.3	37.7	44.2	42.3	39.9	41.7	39.6	35.9	36.2	36.3	- Union Européenne
- Eastern Europe	2.6	2.2	2.4	3.0	3.0	3.7	3.2	3.4	4.0	4.5	- Europe de l'Est
- Rest of Europe	3.7	3.5	3.9	3.8	3.5	4.0	3.7	3.6	3.7	3.6	- Autre de l'Europe
Europe former USSR	0.2	0.9	1.0	1.4	1.3	1.2	0.8	1.1	1.0	1.1	Europe ancienne URSS
Oceania	1.7	1.6	1.7	1.8	1.8	1.7	1.8	1.7	1.5	1.8	Océanie

TRADE BY COMMODITY (Value in million US dollars)
Exports by principal countries or areas

COMMERCE PAR PRODUIT (Valeur en millions de dollars EU)
Exportations selon les principaux pays ou zones

Country or area	1998	1999	2000	2001	2002	Pays ou zone
World	3907.8	3602.1	3790.2	3549.9	3783.5	Monde
Africa	67.4	72.9	65.5	58.1	65.9	Afrique
Americas	583.3	583.6	568.0	544.0	530.3	Amériques
- Northern America	456.2	465.5	448.2	443.7	420.2	- Amérique du Nord
- LAIA	116.4	112.1	113.4	93.6	101.2	- ALAI
- CACM	8.3	4.9	5.5	5.8	7.9	- MCC
- Caribbean	2.4	1.1	1.0	0.9	1.0	- Caraïbes
- Rest of America	0.0	0.0	0.0	0.0	0.0	- Autre d'Amérique
Asia excluding former USSR	924.0	1025.1	1144.1	987.5	1095.6	Asie ancienne URSS exclus
- Middle East	31.7	40.9	42.0	26.2	24.7	- Moyen-Orient
Asia former USSR	0.0	0.1	0.1	0.2	0.2	Asie ancienne URSS
Europe excluding former USSR	2195.2	1802.4	1857.1	1826.5	1935.7	Europe ancienne URSS exclus
- European Union	1917.2	1557.9	1620.4	1601.6	1675.5	- Union Européenne
- Eastern Europe	205.1	181.2	176.6	172.0	209.3	- Europe de l'Est
- Rest of Europe	72.9	63.2	60.0	53.0	50.8	- Autre de l'Europe
Europe former USSR	112.1	90.8	132.7	117.6	137.0	Europe ancienne URSS
Oceania	25.8	27.2	22.7	15.9	18.9	Océanie
Germany	332.7	313.4	316.3	336.5	364.7	Allemagne
Korea, Republic of	282.9	302.4	336.3	314.4	332.3	République de Corée
Japan	284.4	304.8	331.7	245.7	262.5	Japon
Italy-San Marino-Holy See	309.2	272.2	271.7	258.8	271.3	Italie-Saint-Marin-Saint-Siège
France-Monaco	288.2	257.7	265.3	248.2	266.3	France-Monaco
United States	252.7	273.6	261.7	266.7	247.4	Etats-Unis d'Amérique
Sweden	222.1	205.9	211.2	183.7	183.4	Suède
Canada	203.5	191.9	186.5	177.0	172.7	Canada
United Kingdom	201.8	166.0	164.3	154.0	129.8	Royaume-Uni
Czech Republic	131.1	124.4	111.0	110.6	130.1	République tchèque
Spain	118.1	98.2	131.9	116.8	126.2	Espagne
China	79.9	102.8	104.9	117.7	144.4	Chine
Austria	79.4	73.3	80.2	83.5	92.5	Autriche
China, Hong Kong SAR	55.2	58.3	66.4	53.8	61.7	Chine - RAS de Hong-Kong
India	37.8	34.9	60.0	56.6	84.6	Inde
Belgium-Luxembourg	267.7	–	–	–	–	Belgique-Luxembourg
Luxembourg	–	53.5	61.4	71.2	e72.8	Luxembourg
Netherlands	73.0	30.0	31.8	56.7	64.5	Pays-Bas
Belgium	–	63.2	59.7	60.1	e67.4	Belgique
Switzerland-Liechtenstein	51.1	42.5	44.8	40.9	42.0	Suisse-Liechtenstein
Russian Federation	35.8	24.2	51.8	49.2	55.2	Fédération de Russie
Mexico	43.0	49.0	42.3	36.2	43.6	Mexique
Ukraine	37.2	31.8	37.9	33.3	36.7	Ukraine
South Africa	–	–	49.5	46.5	53.6	Afrique du Sud
Brazil	26.2	24.9	31.0	22.3	e23.1	Brésil
Belarus	25.6	19.4	24.3	24.9	32.6	Bélarus
Romania	30.5	20.7	22.9	18.7	22.3	Roumanie
Malaysia	17.4	26.1	28.4	20.7	e22.0	Malaisie
Thailand	18.7	24.7	23.1	20.3	e21.5	Thaïlande
Southern African Customs Union	48.0	53.0	–	–	–	Union douanière d'Afrique australe

(Value as percentages of World total) **(Valeur en pourcentage du total mondial)**

Regions of the world	1993	1994	1995	1996	1997	1998	1999	2000	2001	2002	Régions du monde
World	100.0	100.0	100.0	100.0	100.0	100.0	100.0	100.0	100.0	100.0	Monde
Africa	2.5	2.0	3.7	2.8	2.8	1.7	2.0	1.7	1.6	1.7	Afrique
Americas	11.2	10.8	10.6	12.2	14.8	14.9	16.2	15.0	15.3	14.0	Amériques
- Northern America	9.0	8.9	8.4	9.6	11.8	11.7	12.9	11.8	12.5	11.1	- Amérique du Nord
- LAIA	2.0	1.8	2.1	2.5	2.8	3.0	3.1	3.0	2.6	2.7	- ALAI
- CACM	0.1	0.1	0.0	0.1	0.1	0.2	0.1	0.1	0.2	0.2	- MCC
- Caribbean	0.1	0.0	0.0	0.0	0.0	0.1	0.0	0.0	0.0	0.0	- Caraïbes
- Rest of America	0.0	0.0	0.0	0.0	0.0	0.0	0.0	0.0	0.0	0.0	- Autre d'Amérique
Asia excluding former USSR	27.1	25.3	26.4	25.2	25.1	23.6	28.5	30.2	27.8	29.0	Asie ancienne URSS exclus
- Middle East	0.5	0.4	0.6	0.7	0.6	0.8	1.1	1.1	0.7	0.7	- Moyen-Orient
Asia former USSR	0.1	0.1	0.1	0.0	0.0	0.0	0.0	0.0	0.0	0.0	Asie ancienne URSS
Europe excluding former USSR	56.6	58.0	54.8	55.4	53.4	56.2	50.0	49.0	51.5	51.2	Europe ancienne URSS exclus
- European Union	50.9	52.4	47.3	48.7	46.8	49.1	43.3	42.8	45.1	44.3	- Union Européenne
- Eastern Europe	4.0	3.9	5.6	4.9	5.0	5.2	5.0	4.7	4.8	5.5	- Europe de l'Est
- Rest of Europe	1.6	1.7	1.9	1.8	1.7	1.9	1.8	1.6	1.5	1.3	- Autre de l'Europe
Europe former USSR	1.8	3.0	3.4	3.4	3.0	2.9	2.5	3.5	3.3	3.6	Europe ancienne URSS
Oceania	0.8	0.9	1.0	1.0	0.8	0.7	0.8	0.6	0.4	0.5	Océanie

678 Tube, pipes and fittings, of iron or steel

TRADE BY COMMODITY (Value in million US dollars)
Imports by principal countries or areas

COMMERCE PAR PRODUIT (Valeur en millions de dollars EU)
Importations selon les principaux pays ou zones

Country or area	1998	1999	2000	2001	2002	Pays ou zone
World	27538.2	22051.0	23582.4	25885.8	26421.6	Monde
Africa	1273.3	1054.8	929.7	1147.8	1278.9	Afrique
Americas	6908.9	5275.2	6489.9	6879.6	6356.4	Amériques
- Northern America	4420.4	3573.1	4799.5	4903.7	4427.8	- Amérique du Nord
- LAIA	2170.6	1452.5	1453.4	1696.3	1666.8	- ALAI
- CACM	82.0	82.5	77.7	78.3	75.1	- MCC
- Caribbean	209.1	143.7	135.7	179.9	159.6	- Caraïbes
- Rest of America	26.8	23.3	23.5	21.4	27.1	- Autre d'Amérique
Asia excluding former USSR	6391.3	4976.9	5571.6	6533.5	7072.5	Asie ancienne URSS exclus
- Middle East	1963.6	1290.4	1842.5	2268.1	2251.3	- Moyen-Orient
Asia former USSR	319.6	289.2	477.0	626.9	723.7	Asie ancienne URSS
Europe excluding former USSR	11342.4	9282.5	8947.7	9491.8	9802.7	Europe ancienne URSS exclus
- European Union	8880.8	7566.3	7311.2	7783.3	7869.5	- Union Européenne
- Eastern Europe	1053.0	759.5	801.2	884.4	985.5	- Europe de l'Est
- Rest of Europe	1408.6	956.6	835.3	824.2	947.7	- Autre de l'Europe
Europe former USSR	894.5	834.2	828.5	850.2	766.9	Europe ancienne URSS
Oceania	408.2	338.1	337.9	356.0	420.6	Océanie
United States	3141.6	2489.8	3487.6	3660.1	3293.1	Etats-Unis d'Amérique
Germany	1934.7	1783.8	1628.4	1735.4	1591.9	Allemagne
Canada	1276.9	1081.2	1309.1	1240.7	1131.1	Canada
France-Monaco	1196.2	1044.5	1108.1	1053.0	1157.3	France-Monaco
United Kingdom	1157.7	800.8	791.4	1099.5	940.9	Royaume-Uni
China	849.9	631.5	618.0	799.5	1206.9	Chine
Italy-San Marino-Holy See	886.2	774.3	758.6	755.2	764.7	Italie-Saint-Marin-Saint-Siège
Mexico	605.4	626.0	681.4	697.1	551.1	Mexique
Russian Federation	603.5	536.3	595.5	623.1	505.2	Fédération de Russie
Netherlands	701.4	598.2	483.7	514.4	535.1	Pays-Bas
Malaysia	360.3	364.4	248.1	760.1	e830.7	Malaisie
Spain	492.8	497.4	476.0	531.8	547.4	Espagne
Singapore	630.8	434.5	442.1	510.6	488.6	Singapour
Norway	891.5	448.8	317.1	343.5	439.8	Norvège
Belgium	–	516.5	536.2	546.3	e599.1	Belgique
Saudi Arabia	518.0	391.9	274.0	394.0	e407.7	Arabie saoudite
Sweden	448.3	401.5	387.9	351.8	370.2	Suède
Korea, Republic of	290.6	329.7	417.4	410.1	432.9	République de Corée
Japan	340.6	307.9	418.5	389.4	356.7	Japon
Indonesia	441.3	361.3	371.0	305.0	331.0	Indonésie
Austria	415.9	324.5	337.3	352.4	340.4	Autriche
Denmark	453.0	298.6	283.6	308.9	347.2	Danemark
Switzerland-Liechtenstein	340.3	336.3	344.6	308.3	302.8	Suisse-Liechtenstein
Poland	491.6	248.7	247.2	246.0	293.9	Pologne
Australia	320.7	256.8	256.1	264.9	321.3	Australie
Turkey	227.5	134.6	297.5	477.1	277.4	Turquie
Venezuela	359.0	211.5	259.1	307.4	e258.6	Venezuela
Iran (Islamic Republic of)	206.7	194.9	309.6	324.5	358.5	Iran (République islamique d')
Kazakhstan	111.2	98.4	226.8	424.0	e433.0	Kazakhstan
United Arab Emirates	113.2	118.7	323.5	322.9	e331.3	Emirates arabes unis

(Value as percentages of World total) **(Valeur en pourcentage du total mondial)**

Regions of the world	1993	1994	1995	1996	1997	1998	1999	2000	2001	2002	Régions du monde
World	100.0	100.0	100.0	100.0	100.0	100.0	100.0	100.0	100.0	100.0	Monde
Africa	6.4	6.5	5.4	5.4	4.6	4.6	4.8	3.9	4.4	4.8	Afrique
Americas	18.5	18.5	17.7	17.7	21.8	25.1	23.9	27.5	26.6	24.1	Amériques
- Northern America	12.6	13.4	11.9	12.4	14.8	16.1	16.2	20.4	18.9	16.8	- Amérique du Nord
- LAIA	4.9	4.3	4.9	4.4	6.0	7.9	6.6	6.2	6.6	6.3	- ALAI
- CACM	0.2	0.2	0.2	0.3	0.3	0.3	0.4	0.3	0.3	0.3	- MCC
- Caribbean	0.6	0.3	0.6	0.5	0.7	0.8	0.7	0.6	0.7	0.6	- Caraïbes
- Rest of America	0.2	0.2	0.1	0.1	0.1	0.1	0.1	0.1	0.1	0.1	- Autre d'Amérique
Asia excluding former USSR	32.4	29.2	25.5	27.3	27.0	23.2	22.6	23.6	25.2	26.8	Asie ancienne URSS exclus
- Middle East	9.4	6.8	5.8	6.7	7.4	7.1	5.9	7.8	8.8	8.5	- Moyen-Orient
Asia former USSR	0.4	0.8	0.9	1.5	0.8	1.2	1.3	2.0	2.4	2.7	Asie ancienne URSS
Europe excluding former USSR	36.8	39.5	44.6	41.8	39.7	41.2	42.1	37.9	36.7	37.1	Europe ancienne URSS exclus
- European Union	29.5	32.2	36.7	34.3	31.6	32.2	34.3	31.0	30.1	29.8	- Union Européenne
- Eastern Europe	2.1	2.0	2.8	3.3	3.2	3.8	3.4	3.4	3.4	3.7	- Europe de l'Est
- Rest of Europe	5.2	5.3	5.1	4.2	4.9	5.1	4.3	3.5	3.2	3.6	- Autre de l'Europe
Europe former USSR	4.3	4.1	4.3	4.7	4.6	3.2	3.8	3.5	3.3	2.9	Europe ancienne URSS
Oceania	1.3	1.4	1.6	1.6	1.6	1.5	1.5	1.4	1.4	1.6	Océanie

TRADE BY COMMODITY (Value in million US dollars)
Exports by principal countries or areas

COMMERCE PAR PRODUIT (Valeur en millions de dollars EU)
Exportations selon les principaux pays ou zones

Country or area	1998	1999	2000	2001	2002	Pays ou zone
World	26889.7	21282.3	22542.1	25114.9	26077.9	Monde
Africa	143.8	128.5	131.7	129.9	148.6	Afrique
Americas	4621.8	3407.4	3895.3	4106.1	4097.0	Amériques
- Northern America	3066.2	2501.7	2789.7	2730.9	2694.7	- Amérique du Nord
- LAIA	1526.4	875.5	1074.0	1338.1	1365.6	- ALAI
- CACM	26.4	27.3	29.4	30.6	31.5	- MCC
- Caribbean	2.6	2.8	2.1	6.3	5.1	- Caraïbes
- Rest of America	0.1	0.0	0.0	0.1	0.0	- Autre d'Amérique
Asia excluding former USSR	6452.3	5127.1	5582.3	6888.5	7155.8	Asie ancienne URSS exclus
- Middle East	348.3	331.2	416.4	647.3	787.5	- Moyen-Orient
Asia former USSR	16.0	7.7	8.9	13.2	15.5	Asie ancienne URSS
Europe excluding former USSR	14896.7	12044.8	11985.4	13090.9	13743.4	Europe ancienne URSS exclus
- European Union	13189.1	10715.6	10649.3	11651.0	12319.3	- Union Européenne
- Eastern Europe	912.4	651.1	724.2	862.1	851.3	- Europe de l'Est
- Rest of Europe	795.2	678.1	611.8	577.8	572.8	- Autre de l'Europe
Europe former USSR	657.9	483.9	866.7	803.3	833.2	Europe ancienne URSS
Oceania	101.2	82.9	71.8	83.2	84.5	Océanie
Germany	3873.4	3002.1	2763.0	3292.4	3376.3	Allemagne
Japan	3211.9	2408.9	2135.2	2961.4	2918.3	Japon
Italy-San Marino-Holy See	2860.8	2230.3	2373.7	2524.4	2663.2	Italie-Saint-Marin-Saint-Siège
United States	2354.9	1838.6	1952.0	1967.7	1904.0	Etats-Unis d'Amérique
France-Monaco	1768.2	1489.3	1531.2	1634.2	1678.9	France-Monaco
United Kingdom	1108.4	812.0	793.5	988.0	1153.7	Royaume-Uni
China	773.3	588.0	762.6	887.5	974.3	Chine
Canada	711.3	663.1	837.7	763.2	790.7	Canada
Korea, Republic of	737.5	631.1	704.7	682.0	674.3	République de Corée
Spain	594.7	511.7	617.2	617.7	646.1	Espagne
Austria	612.8	525.9	610.2	626.6	597.9	Autriche
Sweden	648.6	542.1	568.0	507.6	562.3	Suède
Mexico	672.9	347.5	365.7	408.0	455.8	Mexique
Argentina	521.4	273.5	400.5	500.2	e483.2	Argentine
Netherlands	510.2	425.9	386.4	381.2	454.0	Pays-Bas
Switzerland-Liechtenstein	465.1	428.1	442.0	410.8	400.3	Suisse-Liechtenstein
Ukraine	457.9	311.8	531.6	373.4	411.6	Ukraine
Turkey	247.6	208.3	255.9	445.7	576.8	Turquie
Malaysia	324.2	145.4	248.7	450.0	e476.9	Malaisie
Belgium	–	371.3	361.3	388.7	e436.1	Belgique
Czech Republic	351.2	231.6	257.0	307.6	282.1	République tchèque
Denmark	283.5	399.6	235.7	234.6	246.0	Danemark
Finland	294.4	276.0	271.6	252.6	294.9	Finlande
Russian Federation	153.0	145.4	305.3	396.7	373.3	Fédération de Russie
Brazil	266.8	178.6	196.7	298.5	e309.5	Brésil
Singapore	265.6	192.1	223.8	250.6	249.4	Singapour
Thailand	180.8	182.7	214.8	196.5	e207.6	Thaïlande
Romania	235.4	152.8	150.2	211.7	228.9	Roumanie
India	138.4	116.8	155.7	208.9	249.0	Inde
Poland	143.1	105.8	131.4	151.3	133.5	Pologne

(Value as percentages of World total) **(Valeur en pourcentage du total mondial)**

Regions of the world	1993	1994	1995	1996	1997	1998	1999	2000	2001	2002	Régions du monde
World	100.0	100.0	100.0	100.0	100.0	100.0	100.0	100.0	100.0	100.0	Monde
Africa	0.7	0.9	0.6	0.6	0.5	0.5	0.6	0.6	0.5	0.6	Afrique
Americas	13.6	13.8	14.0	15.1	17.1	17.2	16.0	17.3	16.3	15.7	Amériques
- Northern America	9.1	9.5	9.7	9.8	11.1	11.4	11.8	12.4	10.9	10.3	- Amérique du Nord
- LAIA	4.3	4.2	4.3	5.2	5.9	5.7	4.1	4.8	5.3	5.2	- ALAI
- CACM	0.1	0.1	0.1	0.1	0.1	0.1	0.1	0.1	0.1	0.1	- MCC
- Caribbean	0.0	0.0	0.0	0.0	0.0	0.0	0.0	0.0	0.0	0.0	- Caraïbes
- Rest of America	0.0	0.0	0.0	0.0	0.0	0.0	0.0	0.0	0.0	0.0	- Autre d'Amérique
Asia excluding former USSR	30.9	25.9	23.4	23.0	24.1	24.0	24.1	24.8	27.4	27.4	Asie ancienne URSS exclus
- Middle East	1.2	1.3	1.5	1.1	1.4	1.3	1.6	1.8	2.6	3.0	- Moyen-Orient
Asia former USSR	0.1	0.1	0.2	0.1	0.1	0.1	0.0	0.0	0.1	0.1	Asie ancienne URSS
Europe excluding former USSR	53.8	55.3	57.6	57.0	53.8	55.4	56.6	53.2	52.1	52.7	Europe ancienne URSS exclus
- European Union	48.4	50.1	51.6	51.5	47.6	49.0	50.3	47.2	46.4	47.2	- Union Européenne
- Eastern Europe	2.3	2.3	3.2	3.1	2.9	3.4	3.1	3.2	3.4	3.3	- Europe de l'Est
- Rest of Europe	3.0	2.8	2.8	2.4	3.3	3.0	3.2	2.7	2.3	2.2	- Autre de l'Europe
Europe former USSR	0.7	3.5	3.8	3.7	3.9	2.4	2.3	3.8	3.2	3.2	Europe ancienne URSS
Oceania	0.3	0.4	0.4	0.4	0.4	0.4	0.4	0.3	0.3	0.3	Océanie

679 Iron, steel casting, forging and stamping, in the rough state, nes

TRADE BY COMMODITY (Value in million US dollars) COMMERCE PAR PRODUIT (Valeur en millions de dollars E
Imports by principal countries or areas **Importations selon les principaux pays ou zone**

Country or area	1998	1999	2000	2001	2002	Pays ou zone
World	3570.0	3478.8	3614.1	3705.2	3696.1	Monde
Africa	61.2	59.5	62.8	69.1	77.5	Afrique
Americas	882.7	894.1	1050.4	1032.5	971.7	Amériques
- Northern America	586.9	614.2	705.3	665.9	700.4	- Amérique du Nord
- LAIA	281.0	266.0	321.2	343.9	246.8	- ALAI
- CACM	7.3	7.5	8.0	9.8	8.6	- MCC
- Caribbean	6.3	5.8	9.3	7.2	7.2	- Caraïbes
- Rest of America	1.2	0.5	6.6	5.8	8.7	- Autre d'Amérique
Asia excluding former USSR	686.2	645.8	678.9	651.0	615.1	Asie ancienne URSS exclus
- Middle East	189.0	119.6	86.7	97.0	64.6	- Moyen-Orient
Asia former USSR	13.5	8.4	13.1	13.5	13.6	Asie ancienne URSS
Europe excluding former USSR	1846.0	1791.7	1721.4	1868.0	1932.2	Europe ancienne URSS exclus
- European Union	1595.9	1563.8	1479.7	1588.2	1622.4	- Union Européenne
- Eastern Europe	139.2	132.6	153.9	177.6	201.2	- Europe de l'Est
- Rest of Europe	110.8	95.3	87.9	102.3	108.7	- Autre de l'Europe
Europe former USSR	32.7	20.5	18.9	35.5	46.3	Europe ancienne URSS
Oceania	47.8	58.8	68.5	35.6	39.7	Océanie
United States	371.1	402.4	459.5	467.8	512.2	Etats-Unis d'Amérique
Germany	399.7	383.1	338.4	412.5	369.2	Allemagne
France-Monaco	241.4	241.9	234.5	228.5	252.9	France-Monaco
Italy-San Marino-Holy See	245.7	230.5	220.3	233.0	249.8	Italie-Saint-Marin-Saint-Siège
Canada	215.1	211.4	245.5	197.7	187.6	Canada
Mexico	143.8	150.6	202.8	205.2	126.7	Mexique
United Kingdom	170.2	144.7	141.9	152.7	155.5	Royaume-Uni
Japan	92.5	95.7	105.3	101.7	91.0	Japon
Austria	88.9	100.4	94.8	95.3	97.1	Autriche
Spain	74.2	82.4	85.4	99.3	106.4	Espagne
Malaysia	67.2	83.2	101.4	80.0	e87.5	Malaisie
Belgium	–	111.7	97.0	92.7	e101.7	Belgique
China	71.7	79.1	78.6	77.9	72.4	Chine
Korea, Republic of	52.9	45.1	69.5	88.9	86.5	République de Corée
Sweden	73.9	62.6	68.9	72.0	65.0	Suède
Netherlands	69.7	72.0	62.4	57.6	65.4	Pays-Bas
Brazil	62.1	44.9	52.3	69.6	71.0	Brésil
Singapore	59.3	59.8	51.1	59.9	62.6	Singapour
Indonesia	46.6	59.7	66.6	55.9	55.0	Indonésie
Czech Republic	40.4	39.7	48.7	55.2	60.4	République tchèque
Slovakia	41.8	35.9	41.9	45.6	54.6	Slovaquie
Denmark	33.3	32.9	36.0	46.3	59.9	Danemark
Switzerland-Liechtenstein	44.0	37.1	36.9	42.1	44.2	Suisse-Liechtenstein
Poland	33.3	33.7	37.5	43.9	49.5	Pologne
Syrian Arab Republic	101.6	55.7	5.3	e6.7	1.1	République arabe syrienne
Ireland	33.3	34.5	30.2	26.9	25.8	Irlande
Australia	22.6	24.7	49.1	22.3	24.4	Australie
Norway	36.5	26.8	19.8	26.8	31.8	Norvège
Finland	29.5	26.5	24.1	26.0	21.9	Finlande
Thailand	14.9	20.5	27.0	28.5	e29.7	Thaïlande

(Value as percentages of World total) **(Valeur en pourcentage du total mondia**

Regions of the world	1993	1994	1995	1996	1997	1998	1999	2000	2001	2002	Régions du monde
World	100.0	100.0	100.0	100.0	100.0	100.0	100.0	100.0	100.0	100.0	Monde
Africa	2.6	2.1	1.9	1.6	1.8	1.7	1.7	1.7	1.9	2.1	Afrique
Americas	21.5	21.7	19.1	19.5	23.2	24.7	25.7	29.1	27.9	26.3	Amériques
- Northern America	13.6	14.2	12.1	12.3	15.0	16.4	17.7	19.5	18.0	18.9	- Amérique du Nord
- LAIA	7.2	6.7	6.3	6.7	7.6	7.9	7.6	8.9	9.3	6.7	- ALAI
- CACM	0.4	0.2	0.2	0.2	0.3	0.2	0.2	0.2	0.3	0.2	- MCC
- Caribbean	0.2	0.2	0.3	0.2	0.2	0.2	0.2	0.3	0.2	0.2	- Caraïbes
- Rest of America	0.1	0.3	0.1	0.1	0.2	0.0	0.0	0.2	0.2	0.2	- Autre d'Amérique
Asia excluding former USSR	24.4	22.9	22.4	20.8	21.0	19.2	18.6	18.8	17.6	16.6	Asie ancienne URSS exclus
- Middle East	2.7	2.8	1.9	1.7	2.8	5.3	3.4	2.4	2.6	1.7	- Moyen-Orient
Asia former USSR	0.1	1.3	0.3	1.1	0.2	0.4	0.2	0.4	0.4	0.4	Asie ancienne URSS
Europe excluding former USSR	49.4	49.3	53.7	54.3	51.0	51.7	51.5	47.6	50.4	52.3	Europe ancienne URSS exclus
- European Union	43.7	43.5	47.0	47.6	44.5	44.7	45.0	40.9	42.9	43.9	- Union Européenne
- Eastern Europe	2.3	2.3	3.2	3.4	3.6	3.9	3.8	4.3	4.8	5.4	- Europe de l'Est
- Rest of Europe	3.5	3.5	3.5	3.3	2.9	3.1	2.7	2.4	2.8	2.9	- Autre de l'Europe
Europe former USSR	0.6	1.1	0.9	1.2	1.1	0.9	0.6	0.5	1.0	1.3	Europe ancienne URSS
Oceania	1.3	1.7	1.7	1.6	1.7	1.3	1.7	1.9	1.0	1.1	Océanie

TRADE BY COMMODITY (Value in million US dollars)
Exports by principal countries or areas

COMMERCE PAR PRODUIT (Valeur en millions de dollars EU)
Exportations selon les principaux pays ou zones

Country or area	1998	1999	2000	2001	2002	Pays ou zone
World	4680.9	4545.6	4665.6	4767.5	5008.5	Monde
Africa	16.2	13.9	17.5	14.6	13.0	Afrique
Americas	745.7	723.9	882.0	793.8	791.5	Amériques
- Northern America	590.6	577.3	710.6	611.9	570.8	- Amérique du Nord
- LAIA	152.9	145.1	170.3	179.9	219.3	- ALAI
- CACM	1.5	0.8	0.6	1.5	1.0	- MCC
- Caribbean	0.7	0.7	0.4	0.4	0.4	- Caraïbes
- Rest of America	0.0	0.0	0.0	0.0	0.1	- Autre d'Amérique
Asia excluding former USSR	1115.7	1147.7	1266.8	1250.4	1399.7	Asie ancienne URSS exclus
- Middle East	43.3	47.8	48.6	68.6	72.9	- Moyen-Orient
Asia former USSR	0.3	0.3	1.0	1.6	1.5	Asie ancienne URSS
Europe excluding former USSR	2652.7	2519.5	2394.9	2581.0	2669.7	Europe ancienne URSS exclus
- European Union	2106.9	1978.0	1847.4	1969.4	2046.8	- Union Européenne
- Eastern Europe	439.5	434.9	447.1	511.0	518.3	- Europe de l'Est
- Rest of Europe	106.2	106.6	100.3	100.6	104.6	- Autre de l'Europe
Europe former USSR	84.2	67.3	48.6	64.5	64.3	Europe ancienne URSS
Oceania	66.0	72.8	54.8	61.5	68.8	Océanie
China	548.5	539.5	573.1	586.7	674.3	Chine
France-Monaco	565.5	559.5	533.2	515.1	510.7	France-Monaco
United States	519.6	499.7	602.1	504.5	457.7	Etats-Unis d'Amérique
Italy-San Marino-Holy See	389.8	371.1	349.7	373.5	382.2	Italie-Saint-Marin-Saint-Siège
Germany	355.5	328.1	292.1	357.3	343.6	Allemagne
Czech Republic	228.8	231.3	243.9	266.8	267.9	République tchèque
United Kingdom	259.7	241.9	214.5	229.6	238.8	Royaume-Uni
Poland	149.8	147.5	148.6	174.4	174.6	Pologne
India	103.4	129.5	171.1	175.0	203.8	Inde
Spain	124.3	110.9	112.4	125.3	141.9	Espagne
Korea, Republic of	129.4	120.3	132.3	113.9	110.5	République de Corée
Canada	71.0	77.7	108.6	107.4	113.1	Canada
Belgium	–	120.3	107.2	106.4	e119.3	Belgique
Mexico	59.7	59.4	82.8	83.0	124.0	Mexique
Austria	73.2	70.8	72.4	74.9	75.0	Autriche
Denmark	81.5	67.8	64.2	66.4	67.8	Danemark
Japan	48.4	57.4	60.7	47.5	67.0	Japon
Australia	55.9	62.4	43.4	52.5	58.8	Australie
Netherlands	51.0	44.4	40.2	41.9	56.5	Pays-Bas
Turkey	31.8	35.0	37.8	47.2	57.8	Turquie
Norway	40.5	44.9	40.6	37.6	45.4	Norvège
Brazil	31.0	36.1	43.6	46.5	e48.2	Brésil
Russian Federation	45.2	40.0	23.3	34.4	30.7	Fédération de Russie
Israel	43.0	34.9	28.7	35.3	30.1	Israël
Switzerland-Liechtenstein	34.4	35.4	33.4	35.0	33.2	Suisse-Liechtenstein
Finland	27.0	21.8	19.2	29.7	38.6	Finlande
Belgium-Luxembourg	133.3	–	–	–	–	Belgique-Luxembourg
Chile	20.0	21.1	18.8	32.8	e32.1	Chili
Slovakia	22.5	20.6	23.3	26.8	27.8	Slovaquie
Singapore	22.9	25.9	24.5	21.2	25.9	Singapour

(Value as percentages of World total) **(Valeur en pourcentage du total mondial)**

Regions of the world	1993	1994	1995	1996	1997	1998	1999	2000	2001	2002	Régions du monde
World	100.0	100.0	100.0	100.0	100.0	100.0	100.0	100.0	100.0	100.0	Monde
Africa	0.2	0.3	0.2	0.3	0.3	0.3	0.3	0.4	0.3	0.3	Afrique
Americas	14.3	14.0	11.7	13.6	15.5	15.9	15.9	18.9	16.7	15.8	Amériques
- Northern America	12.4	12.0	9.6	11.7	12.6	12.6	12.7	15.2	12.8	11.4	- Amérique du Nord
- LAIA	1.9	2.0	2.1	1.9	2.9	3.3	3.2	3.6	3.8	4.4	- ALAI
- CACM	0.1	0.0	0.0	0.0	0.0	0.0	0.0	0.0	0.0	0.0	- MCC
- Caribbean	0.0	0.0	0.0	0.0	0.0	0.0	0.0	0.0	0.0	0.0	- Caraïbes
- Rest of America	0.0	0.0	0.0	0.0	0.0	0.0	0.0	0.0	0.0	0.0	- Autre d'Amérique
Asia excluding former USSR	25.3	23.2	22.8	23.9	26.7	23.8	25.2	27.2	26.2	27.9	Asie ancienne URSS exclus
- Middle East	0.5	0.5	0.8	0.8	0.8	0.9	1.1	1.0	1.4	1.5	- Moyen-Orient
Asia former USSR	0.0	0.1	0.0	0.0	0.0	0.0	0.0	0.0	0.0	0.0	Asie ancienne URSS
Europe excluding former USSR	58.2	58.7	61.8	58.4	54.1	56.7	55.4	51.3	54.1	53.3	Europe ancienne URSS exclus
- European Union	48.3	47.8	49.5	46.5	43.4	45.0	43.5	39.6	41.3	40.9	- Union Européenne
- Eastern Europe	7.2	8.1	9.6	9.6	8.7	9.4	9.6	9.6	10.7	10.3	- Europe de l'Est
- Rest of Europe	2.7	2.8	2.7	2.3	2.0	2.3	2.3	2.2	2.1	2.1	- Autre de l'Europe
Europe former USSR	0.8	2.1	2.0	2.1	2.1	1.8	1.5	1.0	1.4	1.3	Europe ancienne URSS
Oceania	1.3	1.5	1.5	1.6	1.4	1.4	1.6	1.2	1.3	1.4	Océanie

681 Silver, platinum and other metals of the platinum group

TRADE BY COMMODITY (Value in million US dollars) | COMMERCE PAR PRODUIT (Valeur en millions de dollars EU)

Imports by principal countries or areas | **Importations selon les principaux pays ou zones**

Country or area	1998	1999	2000	2001	2002	Pays ou zone
World	13439.2	13974.4	21677.1	19994.8	14548.7	Monde
Africa	72.8	115.0	10.5	15.5	14.1	Afrique
Americas	3967.8	4385.2	6885.3	6243.6	3894.8	Amériques
- Northern America	3851.8	4233.5	6662.6	5983.8	3696.0	- Amérique du Nord
- LAIA	112.1	148.5	218.9	255.6	195.2	- ALAI
- CACM	2.1	0.4	0.7	0.7	0.6	- MCC
- Caribbean	1.7	2.7	3.0	3.4	3.0	- Caraïbes
- Rest of America	0.1	0.1	0.1	0.1	0.1	- Autre d'Amérique
Asia excluding former USSR	3341.5	4118.8	6029.1	5042.4	4614.7	Asie ancienne URSS exclus
- Middle East	146.8	146.2	76.4	57.4	79.0	- Moyen-Orient
Asia former USSR	11.3	0.6	0.8	0.3	1.2	Asie ancienne URSS
Europe excluding former USSR	5910.4	5231.9	8715.7	8670.9	5964.9	Europe ancienne URSS exclus
- European Union	4374.7	3586.6	5585.9	4958.0	3834.4	- Union Européenne
- Eastern Europe	28.9	33.9	39.8	51.1	38.3	- Europe de l'Est
- Rest of Europe	1506.9	1611.4	3090.1	3661.8	2092.2	- Autre de l'Europe
Europe former USSR	1.6	1.8	2.8	2.3	1.9	Europe ancienne URSS
Oceania	133.8	121.1	32.9	19.9	57.0	Océanie
United States	3726.7	4135.4	6470.2	5765.2	3517.5	Etats-Unis d'Amérique
Switzerland-Liechtenstein	1468.1	1565.7	3053.6	3630.5	2071.1	Suisse-Liechtenstein
Japan	1699.6	2131.9	3357.2	2316.3	1765.5	Japon
United Kingdom	1742.6	928.7	1647.1	1318.9	882.2	Royaume-Uni
Germany	850.1	911.5	1514.8	1508.9	1421.4	Allemagne
Italy-San Marino-Holy See	560.5	693.9	1195.2	999.8	685.2	Italie-Saint-Marin-Saint-Siège
China, Hong Kong SAR	361.5	534.7	786.4	1134.1	1304.7	Chine - RAS de Hong-Kong
France-Monaco	553.0	566.4	767.7	592.7	362.1	France-Monaco
India	637.6	603.3	619.4	457.0	471.0	Inde
Korea, Republic of	106.6	212.1	442.1	478.9	335.7	République de Corée
Canada	125.1	98.1	192.4	218.6	178.4	Canada
Brazil	84.7	119.7	181.3	210.5	141.4	Brésil
China	65.8	121.3	148.7	120.4	143.2	Chine
Belgium	-	163.5	106.4	156.6	e171.8	Belgique
Singapore	79.5	69.5	139.6	111.9	130.1	Singapour
Thailand	85.6	91.5	112.4	116.1	e121.0	Thaïlande
Spain	111.0	101.4	120.9	107.4	74.5	Espagne
Malaysia	55.5	64.3	102.2	95.6	e104.5	Malaisie
United Arab Emirates	122.3	128.2	43.2	35.8	e36.7	Emirates arabes unis
Netherlands	73.5	80.2	63.0	54.3	51.4	Pays-Bas
Ireland	66.5	34.0	35.4	110.0	75.1	Irlande
Australia	120.3	90.7	30.6	18.0	54.7	Australie
Belgium-Luxembourg	292.4	-	-	-	-	Belgique-Luxembourg
Austria	38.3	21.4	57.9	44.7	48.5	Autriche
Southern African Customs Union	60.8	101.1	-	-	-	Union douanière d'Afrique australe
Czech Republic	21.3	24.0	28.1	29.5	29.4	République tchèque
Norway	25.1	32.5	29.9	25.5	15.8	Norvège
Sweden	30.5	26.7	24.0	18.6	21.2	Suède
Israel	20.8	20.3	22.7	18.5	18.7	Israël
Turkey	13.1	9.2	25.4	12.9	29.0	Turquie

(Value as percentages of World total) | **(Valeur en pourcentage du total mondial)**

Regions of the world	1993	1994	1995	1996	1997	1998	1999	2000	2001	2002	Régions du monde
World	100.0	100.0	100.0	100.0	100.0	100.0	100.0	100.0	100.0	100.0	Monde
Africa	0.5	0.2	0.2	0.3	0.4	0.5	0.8	0.0	0.1	0.1	Afrique
Americas	28.1	27.1	25.8	28.0	24.9	29.5	31.4	31.8	31.2	26.8	Amériques
- Northern America	27.3	26.1	25.0	27.1	23.9	28.7	30.3	30.7	29.9	25.4	- Amérique du Nord
- LAIA	0.8	1.0	0.8	0.9	1.0	0.8	1.1	1.0	1.3	1.3	- ALAI
- CACM	0.0	0.0	0.0	0.0	0.0	0.0	0.0	0.0	0.0	0.0	- MCC
- Caribbean	0.0	0.0	0.0	0.0	0.0	0.0	0.0	0.0	0.0	0.0	- Caraïbes
- Rest of America	0.0	0.0	0.0	0.0	0.0	0.0	0.0	0.0	0.0	0.0	- Autre d'Amérique
Asia excluding former USSR	31.8	32.8	30.6	31.2	31.1	24.9	29.5	27.8	25.2	31.7	Asie ancienne URSS exclus
- Middle East	2.5	1.6	1.4	1.6	1.8	1.1	1.0	0.4	0.3	0.5	- Moyen-Orient
Asia former USSR	0.0	0.0	0.0	0.0	0.0	0.1	0.0	0.0	0.0	0.0	Asie ancienne URSS
Europe excluding former USSR	38.6	38.6	42.8	39.9	42.7	44.0	37.4	40.2	43.4	41.0	Europe ancienne URSS exclus
- European Union	29.3	32.0	36.7	33.3	31.4	32.6	25.7	25.8	24.8	26.4	- Union Européenne
- Eastern Europe	0.2	0.2	0.2	0.2	0.2	0.2	0.2	0.2	0.3	0.3	- Europe de l'Est
- Rest of Europe	9.1	6.3	5.9	6.4	11.0	11.2	11.5	14.3	18.3	14.4	- Autre de l'Europe
Europe former USSR	0.3	0.3	0.2	0.1	0.1	0.0	0.0	0.0	0.0	0.0	Europe ancienne URSS
Oceania	0.9	1.0	0.4	0.5	0.7	1.0	0.9	0.2	0.1	0.4	Océanie

TRADE BY COMMODITY (Value in million US dollars)
Exports by principal countries or areas

COMMERCE PAR PRODUIT (Valeur en millions de dollars EU)
Exportations selon les principaux pays ou zones

Country or area	1998	1999	2000	2001	2002	Pays ou zone
World	10531.4	10741.3	12343.6	10926.7	10608.8	Monde
Africa	79.3	2245.3	86.6	52.5	63.5	Afrique
Americas	2760.6	2285.8	2890.3	2795.4	2791.2	Amériques
- Northern America	1904.7	1537.2	2153.3	2136.0	1938.0	- Amérique du Nord
- LAIA	783.9	740.8	730.0	656.0	838.8	- ALAI
- CACM	8.3	6.1	5.1	3.1	12.9	- MCC
- Caribbean	7.7	1.4	1.8	0.3	1.5	- Caraïbes
- Rest of America	55.9	0.2	0.1	0.1	0.0	- Autre d'Amérique
Asia excluding former USSR	747.6	919.5	1093.0	1180.9	1196.8	Asie ancienne URSS exclus
- Middle East	59.3	61.8	17.9	14.7	14.6	- Moyen-Orient
Asia former USSR	133.2	114.4	197.8	149.8	182.1	Asie ancienne URSS
Europe excluding former USSR	4553.4	5088.2	7983.9	6660.5	6282.1	Europe ancienne URSS exclus
- European Union	2904.0	2736.5	4410.3	4326.2	3851.1	- Union Européenne
- Eastern Europe	215.0	220.7	211.0	196.0	223.0	- Europe de l'Est
- Rest of Europe	1434.3	2131.0	3362.6	2138.3	2208.1	- Autre de l'Europe
Europe former USSR	2171.3	0.3	0.2	0.3	0.3	Europe ancienne URSS
Oceania	86.1	87.7	91.8	87.2	92.7	Océanie
Switzerland-Liechtenstein	1337.5	2022.9	3228.3	2000.3	2072.0	Suisse-Liechtenstein
United States	1542.5	1173.1	1769.7	1800.6	1628.2	Etats-Unis d'Amérique
Germany	976.4	1040.0	1501.3	1526.4	1373.5	Allemagne
United Kingdom	869.6	717.4	1682.9	1546.5	1199.5	Royaume-Uni
Southern African Customs Union	28.2	2203.9	–	–	–	Union douanière d'Afrique australe
Belgium	–	439.5	580.8	554.4	e622.0	Belgique
Russian Federation	2171.1	e	e	e	e	Fédération de Russie
Mexico	426.4	399.3	434.3	361.9	533.0	Mexique
Canada	362.3	364.0	383.4	335.4	309.8	Canada
Japan	264.3	265.9	430.6	429.5	327.9	Japon
France-Monaco	322.9	233.4	297.7	345.9	236.9	France-Monaco
China, Hong Kong SAR	86.4	257.0	278.4	231.5	225.1	Chine - RAS de Hong-Kong
Poland	189.8	191.7	170.0	158.3	184.4	Pologne
Peru	197.3	177.1	180.1	161.2	175.2	Pérou
Italy-San Marino-Holy See	118.7	102.8	160.9	191.9	250.0	Italie-Saint-Marin-Saint-Siège
China	39.2	75.2	97.2	223.2	341.2	Chine
Kazakhstan	100.8	104.9	192.1	136.4	e153.6	Kazakhstan
Singapore	147.9	128.9	119.6	146.1	117.0	Singapour
Norway	72.2	93.9	128.9	132.8	131.6	Norvège
Chile	134.1	125.7	91.4	96.1	e94.1	Chili
Korea, Republic of	97.2	77.5	91.2	98.0	137.3	République de Corée
Australia	85.0	86.6	90.9	86.3	92.1	Australie
Belgium-Luxembourg	402.8	–	–	–	–	Belgique-Luxembourg
Spain	55.2	59.4	74.0	48.9	49.9	Espagne
Netherlands	66.8	73.6	54.5	41.1	37.2	Pays-Bas
Sweden	53.0	36.0	34.2	42.3	60.2	Suède
Morocco	50.3	41.0	43.9	37.8	e41.2	Maroc
Czech Republic	24.3	27.4	38.5	35.5	33.9	République tchèque
United Arab Emirates	54.4	56.1	15.3	10.5	e11.0	Emirates arabes unis
Indonesia	33.9	22.3	30.2	19.3	16.1	Indonésie

(Value as percentages of World total) **(Valeur en pourcentage du total mondial)**

Regions of the world	1993	1994	1995	1996	1997	1998	1999	2000	2001	2002	Régions du monde
World	100.0	100.0	100.0	100.0	100.0	100.0	100.0	100.0	100.0	100.0	Monde
Africa	0.6	0.8	0.9	0.7	0.7	0.8	20.9	0.7	0.5	0.6	Afrique
Americas	22.9	26.3	31.7	31.3	30.5	26.2	21.3	23.4	25.6	26.3	Amériques
- Northern America	15.2	16.9	22.3	21.2	22.0	18.1	14.3	17.4	19.5	18.3	- Amérique du Nord
- LAIA	7.4	9.4	9.4	10.1	8.0	7.4	6.9	5.9	6.0	7.9	- ALAI
- CACM	0.2	0.0	0.0	0.0	0.0	0.1	0.1	0.0	0.0	0.1	- MCC
- Caribbean	0.0	0.0	0.0	0.0	0.0	0.1	0.0	0.0	0.0	0.0	- Caraïbes
- Rest of America	0.0	0.0	0.0	0.0	0.5	0.5	0.0	0.0	0.0	0.0	- Autre d'Amérique
Asia excluding former USSR	4.3	8.2	11.1	11.3	13.0	7.1	8.6	8.9	10.8	11.3	Asie ancienne URSS exclus
- Middle East	0.3	2.0	2.3	0.9	1.5	0.6	0.6	0.1	0.1	0.1	- Moyen-Orient
Asia former USSR	2.7	3.0	0.2	0.5	0.6	1.3	1.1	1.6	1.4	1.7	Asie ancienne URSS
Europe excluding former USSR	50.6	60.3	55.2	55.2	54.2	43.2	47.4	64.7	61.0	59.2	Europe ancienne URSS exclus
- European Union	39.3	42.6	40.9	40.9	36.0	27.6	25.5	35.7	39.6	36.3	- Union Européenne
- Eastern Europe	2.0	3.2	2.6	2.6	2.2	2.0	2.1	1.7	1.8	2.1	- Europe de l'Est
- Rest of Europe	9.3	14.5	11.7	11.8	15.9	13.6	19.8	27.2	19.6	20.8	- Autre de l'Europe
Europe former USSR	17.9	0.0	0.0	0.0	0.3	20.6	0.0	0.0	0.0	0.0	Europe ancienne URSS
Oceania	1.0	1.2	0.9	1.0	0.6	0.8	0.8	0.7	0.8	0.9	Océanie

682 Copper

TRADE BY COMMODITY (Value in million US dollars)
Imports by principal countries or areas

COMMERCE PAR PRODUIT (Valeur en millions de dollars EU)
Importations selon les principaux pays ou zones

Country or area	1998	1999	2000	2001	2002	Pays ou zone
World	28634.5	27419.8	33284.2	29666.3	29049.6	Monde
Africa	380.4	313.1	331.4	335.3	350.8	Afrique
Americas	5115.2	5336.9	6815.5	6314.1	5339.2	Amériques
- Northern America	3610.3	4013.6	5074.9	4655.4	4084.6	- Amérique du Nord
- LAIA	1413.2	1239.5	1651.4	1585.3	1187.9	- ALAI
- CACM	44.8	44.7	49.6	34.6	33.6	- MCC
- Caribbean	40.7	34.6	35.4	35.4	30.4	- Caraïbes
- Rest of America	6.2	4.4	4.1	3.4	2.7	- Autre d'Amérique
Asia excluding former USSR	10335.8	10213.5	12458.0	10830.1	12033.9	Asie ancienne URSS exclus
- Middle East	814.0	676.6	986.5	876.1	1034.5	- Moyen-Orient
Asia former USSR	20.9	7.0	13.4	23.1	23.4	Asie ancienne URSS
Europe excluding former USSR	12415.2	11203.6	13270.8	11770.9	10891.7	Europe ancienne URSS exclus
- European Union	11260.2	10163.0	11986.0	10505.5	9670.6	- Union Européenne
- Eastern Europe	523.8	497.4	655.3	697.7	702.1	- Europe de l'Est
- Rest of Europe	631.3	543.2	629.5	567.7	519.1	- Autre de l'Europe
Europe former USSR	206.6	170.7	197.5	184.9	200.2	Europe ancienne URSS
Oceania	160.4	175.0	197.6	207.9	210.4	Océanie
United States	3134.4	3522.5	4499.1	4210.2	3608.9	Etats-Unis d'Amérique
China	1848.5	2478.9	3498.2	3506.7	4436.6	Chine
Germany	2523.9	2128.3	2469.3	2198.3	1779.1	Allemagne
Italy-San Marino-Holy See	2023.2	1917.5	2217.1	2133.2	1978.5	Italie-Saint-Marin-Saint-Siège
France-Monaco	1911.8	1688.2	2090.1	1717.6	1671.7	France-Monaco
Korea, Republic of	1274.3	1280.0	1362.1	1134.7	1230.0	République de Corée
United Kingdom	1345.3	1155.0	1428.6	1222.1	1113.4	Royaume-Uni
China, Hong Kong SAR	1543.0	1036.1	1267.3	992.1	982.6	Chine - RAS de Hong-Kong
Mexico	714.3	744.5	970.7	979.0	747.8	Mexique
Malaysia	615.2	681.3	868.5	697.2	e762.0	Malaisie
Spain	679.2	616.1	712.0	685.7	579.5	Espagne
Japan	730.8	707.5	752.5	538.4	454.6	Japon
Belgium	–	655.6	821.4	646.0	e708.5	Belgique
Singapore	757.0	620.9	598.7	435.3	393.2	Singapour
Thailand	391.7	454.3	582.9	573.5	e597.5	Thaïlande
Netherlands	448.8	511.2	587.8	464.4	491.2	Pays-Bas
Canada	475.7	490.7	575.2	444.9	475.2	Canada
Switzerland-Liechtenstein	397.7	346.7	406.4	358.7	304.4	Suisse-Liechtenstein
Turkey	331.1	303.4	438.0	307.9	421.7	Turquie
Austria	431.0	334.0	375.2	353.3	307.9	Autriche
Brazil	365.4	272.9	401.1	343.4	248.6	Brésil
Sweden	306.8	318.0	349.5	247.3	209.4	Suède
Saudi Arabia	269.3	185.4	318.0	298.2	e308.6	Arabie saoudite
Greece	235.2	222.1	289.5	243.4	e269.2	Grèce
Czech Republic	176.2	172.0	221.5	232.2	239.8	République tchèque
Portugal	200.8	194.8	214.5	198.5	201.0	Portugal
India	213.7	175.7	133.1	146.5	120.3	Inde
Denmark	183.6	157.3	156.3	147.9	138.8	Danemark
Finland	170.4	155.3	171.3	144.8	118.1	Finlande
Philippines	112.3	137.5	171.1	171.2	167.3	Philippines

(Value as percentages of World total)

(Valeur en pourcentage du total mondial)

Regions of the world	1993	1994	1995	1996	1997	1998	1999	2000	2001	2002	Régions du monde
World	100.0	100.0	100.0	100.0	100.0	100.0	100.0	100.0	100.0	100.0	Monde
Africa	1.0	1.2	1.1	1.1	1.0	1.3	1.1	1.0	1.1	1.2	Afrique
Americas	12.9	14.6	13.6	14.8	16.0	17.9	19.5	20.5	21.3	18.4	Amériques
- Northern America	9.3	10.8	10.1	11.0	11.9	12.6	14.6	15.2	15.7	14.1	- Amérique du Nord
- LAIA	3.4	3.5	3.2	3.5	3.8	4.9	4.5	5.0	5.3	4.1	- ALAI
- CACM	0.1	0.1	0.1	0.1	0.1	0.2	0.2	0.1	0.1	0.1	- MCC
- Caribbean	0.1	0.1	0.1	0.1	0.1	0.1	0.1	0.1	0.1	0.1	- Caraïbes
- Rest of America	0.0	0.0	0.0	0.0	0.0	0.0	0.0	0.0	0.0	0.0	- Autre d'Amérique
Asia excluding former USSR	41.6	35.9	38.1	40.1	39.5	36.1	37.2	37.4	36.5	41.4	Asie ancienne URSS exclus
- Middle East	2.4	2.6	2.5	2.9	3.0	2.8	2.5	3.0	3.0	3.6	- Moyen-Orient
Asia former USSR	0.0	0.0	0.1	0.0	0.0	0.1	0.0	0.0	0.1	0.1	Asie ancienne URSS
Europe excluding former USSR	43.5	47.1	45.8	42.7	42.2	43.4	40.9	39.9	39.7	37.5	Europe ancienne URSS exclus
- European Union	40.2	43.5	42.0	38.9	38.6	39.3	37.1	36.0	35.4	33.3	- Union Européenne
- Eastern Europe	1.2	1.2	1.5	1.6	1.6	1.8	1.8	2.0	2.4	2.4	- Europe de l'Est
- Rest of Europe	2.1	2.3	2.3	2.2	2.0	2.2	2.0	1.9	1.9	1.8	- Autre de l'Europe
Europe former USSR	0.3	0.4	0.5	0.6	0.8	0.7	0.6	0.6	0.6	0.7	Europe ancienne URSS
Oceania	0.7	0.8	0.8	0.7	0.6	0.6	0.6	0.6	0.7	0.7	Océanie

TRADE BY COMMODITY (Value in million US dollars)
Exports by principal countries or areas

COMMERCE PAR PRODUIT (Valeur en millions de dollars EU)
Exportations selon les principaux pays ou zones

Country or area	1998	1999	2000	2001	2002	Pays ou zone
World	28843.5	27961.0	32648.2	29892.2	29322.1	Monde
Africa	875.5	656.1	483.9	684.8	617.7	Afrique
Americas	8182.8	7861.4	9392.3	8679.2	8168.1	Amériques
- Northern America	2505.9	2214.9	2663.4	2297.1	2092.9	- Amérique du Nord
- LAIA	5663.4	5635.4	6721.0	6376.8	6069.6	- ALAI
- CACM	1.7	0.8	1.4	1.2	1.4	- MCC
- Caribbean	11.2	9.5	6.5	4.1	4.2	- Caraïbes
- Rest of America	0.7	0.7	0.0	0.0	0.0	- Autre d'Amérique
Asia excluding former USSR	6861.1	7173.4	8469.3	7136.2	7528.8	Asie ancienne URSS exclus
- Middle East	288.7	300.2	329.7	336.3	239.8	- Moyen-Orient
Asia former USSR	667.5	614.3	776.2	816.3	952.9	Asie ancienne URSS
Europe excluding former USSR	10895.7	9912.4	11309.9	10566.5	10180.6	Europe ancienne URSS exclus
- European Union	9425.3	8631.2	9704.8	9046.6	8647.4	- Union Européenne
- Eastern Europe	977.7	908.6	1217.5	1163.7	1208.4	- Europe de l'Est
- Rest of Europe	492.7	372.6	387.5	356.1	324.8	- Autre de l'Europe
Europe former USSR	950.1	1120.4	1365.8	1123.4	1079.4	Europe ancienne URSS
Oceania	410.8	622.9	850.7	885.8	794.6	Océanie
Chile	4162.7	4249.8	5063.8	4816.2	e4712.1	Chili
Germany	3021.5	2894.2	3193.0	2985.6	2710.0	Allemagne
Japan	1986.9	2116.7	2422.2	2096.2	2081.8	Japon
France-Monaco	1336.3	1148.7	1395.0	1209.4	1145.6	France-Monaco
United States	1304.1	1146.4	1478.1	1129.5	1069.8	Etats-Unis d'Amérique
Canada	1201.8	1068.5	1185.2	1167.5	1023.1	Canada
Russian Federation	917.6	1043.8	1212.9	1008.1	938.5	Fédération de Russie
Korea, Republic of	1185.1	963.8	997.6	806.5	852.8	République de Corée
Belgium	–	1028.4	1264.6	1167.4	e1309.8	Belgique
China, Hong Kong SAR	988.8	812.9	1087.4	880.5	885.5	Chine - RAS de Hong-Kong
Italy-San Marino-Holy See	881.2	777.9	891.2	905.5	805.0	Italie-Saint-Marin-Saint-Siège
Peru	751.6	725.8	866.2	800.7	829.3	Pérou
Australia	363.7	571.0	810.0	852.5	764.7	Australie
Poland	616.3	631.4	738.8	631.3	668.4	Pologne
Kazakhstan	560.6	539.8	687.3	703.9	e792.9	Kazakhstan
United Kingdom	758.4	589.3	626.0	559.7	533.6	Royaume-Uni
China	511.6	508.3	723.2	514.6	627.5	Chine
Mexico	640.4	522.2	627.9	615.3	379.0	Mexique
Spain	544.0	514.6	531.0	474.4	413.0	Espagne
Zambia	647.4	444.7	300.5	537.8	483.9	Zambie
Sweden	485.3	445.6	455.9	478.3	500.3	Suède
Finland	442.7	407.2	443.0	434.8	423.9	Finlande
Malaysia	391.0	409.4	482.1	383.0	e405.9	Malaisie
Singapore	353.0	421.5	367.6	240.5	248.5	Singapour
Indonesia	53.6	290.5	386.3	400.0	453.0	Indonésie
Austria	387.2	288.1	334.3	298.2	252.7	Autriche
Bulgaria	206.4	164.6	340.5	e361.3	e406.0	Bulgarie
Philippines	187.5	281.1	273.2	286.4	234.1	Philippines
Netherlands	251.4	249.8	236.6	220.8	235.6	Pays-Bas
Belgium-Luxembourg	1101.1	–	–	–	–	Belgique-Luxembourg

(Value as percentages of World total) **(Valeur en pourcentage du total mondial)**

Regions of the world	1993	1994	1995	1996	1997	1998	1999	2000	2001	2002	Régions du monde
World	100.0	100.0	100.0	100.0	100.0	100.0	100.0	100.0	100.0	100.0	Monde
Africa	4.7	3.7	3.5	1.0	0.8	3.0	2.3	1.5	2.3	2.1	Afrique
Americas	26.9	27.4	29.2	29.7	30.6	28.4	28.1	28.8	29.0	27.9	Amériques
- Northern America	9.5	9.5	9.8	10.0	9.0	8.7	7.9	8.2	7.7	7.1	- Amérique du Nord
- LAIA	17.5	17.9	19.5	19.7	21.7	19.6	20.2	20.6	21.3	20.7	- ALAI
- CACM	0.0	0.0	0.0	0.0	0.0	0.0	0.0	0.0	0.0	0.0	- MCC
- Caribbean	0.0	0.0	0.0	0.0	0.0	0.0	0.0	0.0	0.0	0.0	- Caraïbes
- Rest of America	0.0	0.0	0.0	0.0	0.0	0.0	0.0	0.0	0.0	0.0	- Autre d'Amérique
Asia excluding former USSR	20.3	18.7	20.1	21.4	22.2	23.8	25.7	25.9	23.9	25.7	Asie ancienne URSS exclus
- Middle East	1.2	1.0	1.0	1.1	1.0	1.0	1.1	1.0	1.1	0.8	- Moyen-Orient
Asia former USSR	0.9	1.1	2.1	2.5	2.1	2.3	2.2	2.4	2.7	3.2	Asie ancienne URSS
Europe excluding former USSR	40.0	42.4	39.6	38.8	38.6	37.8	35.5	34.6	35.3	34.7	Europe ancienne URSS exclus
- European Union	34.3	35.5	33.3	33.7	33.4	32.7	30.9	29.7	30.3	29.5	- Union Européenne
- Eastern Europe	4.2	4.5	4.3	4.0	4.1	3.4	3.2	3.7	3.9	4.1	- Europe de l'Est
- Rest of Europe	1.5	2.4	1.9	1.1	1.1	1.7	1.3	1.2	1.2	1.1	- Autre de l'Europe
Europe former USSR	4.7	4.1	3.4	4.3	4.0	3.3	4.0	4.2	3.8	3.7	Europe ancienne URSS
Oceania	2.4	2.6	2.1	2.3	1.6	1.4	2.2	2.6	3.0	2.7	Océanie

683 Nickel

TRADE BY COMMODITY (Value in million US dollars)
Imports by principal countries or areas

COMMERCE PAR PRODUIT (Valeur en millions de dollars EU)
Importations selon les principaux pays ou zones

Country or area	1998	1999	2000	2001	2002	Pays ou zone
World	5008.6	5434.5	8195.0	6176.7	6628.9	Monde
Africa	10.0	43.6	111.1	30.7	87.4	Afrique
Americas	1078.9	1057.6	1746.0	1328.2	1167.4	Amériques
- Northern America	972.5	951.5	1554.3	1187.8	1024.6	- Amérique du Nord
- LAIA	103.3	104.6	190.4	138.8	141.1	- ALAI
- CACM	0.5	0.2	0.6	0.5	0.9	- MCC
- Caribbean	2.5	1.4	0.7	1.0	0.8	- Caraïbes
- Rest of America	0.0	0.0	0.0	0.0	0.0	- Autre d'Amérique
Asia excluding former USSR	1194.3	1506.6	2263.3	1686.1	1864.9	Asie ancienne URSS exclus
- Middle East	63.1	34.2	32.9	38.8	46.9	- Moyen-Orient
Asia former USSR	1.5	0.9	14.4	4.0	4.3	Asie ancienne URSS
Europe excluding former USSR	2672.2	2790.5	3968.3	3043.0	3432.5	Europe ancienne URSS exclus
- European Union	2543.7	2683.8	3811.9	2890.1	3293.5	- Union Européenne
- Eastern Europe	44.3	36.4	66.8	62.3	57.6	- Europe de l'Est
- Rest of Europe	84.2	70.4	89.7	90.6	81.4	- Autre de l'Europe
Europe former USSR	31.7	20.2	75.2	67.5	57.9	Europe ancienne URSS
Oceania	20.0	14.9	16.6	17.2	14.5	Océanie
United States	907.0	877.1	1442.9	1090.3	944.0	Etats-Unis d'Amérique
Germany	573.0	576.3	913.8	740.0	737.3	Allemagne
Japan	395.6	451.1	713.8	337.6	417.4	Japon
France-Monaco	392.3	404.7	582.1	497.9	422.3	France-Monaco
Italy-San Marino-Holy See	321.6	333.5	496.7	407.5	422.0	Italie-Saint-Marin-Saint-Siège
Netherlands	351.9	448.1	547.1	22.2	411.7	Pays-Bas
United Kingdom	284.8	249.2	333.3	387.2	365.2	Royaume-Uni
Korea, Republic of	164.7	286.8	292.0	195.5	239.1	République de Corée
Belgium	–	225.9	310.7	268.7	e294.7	Belgique
Sweden	156.3	167.1	277.0	189.7	211.2	Suède
China	72.4	79.7	170.4	308.9	364.6	Chine
Spain	130.0	169.1	190.8	205.1	235.1	Espagne
China, Hong Kong SAR	99.6	95.5	201.5	169.3	165.0	Chine - RAS de Hong-Kong
India	66.2	78.4	123.4	158.6	183.5	Inde
Singapore	51.4	65.5	140.6	151.3	109.1	Singapour
Canada	65.5	74.4	111.4	97.3	80.6	Canada
Brazil	51.8	62.7	122.2	74.6	87.5	Brésil
Finland	46.9	38.8	53.3	64.7	101.5	Finlande
Austria	52.7	38.0	66.0	66.3	57.2	Autriche
Switzerland-Liechtenstein	46.9	35.6	46.0	48.5	53.1	Suisse-Liechtenstein
South Africa	–	–	105.7	25.3	78.8	Afrique du Sud
Mexico	36.0	31.6	51.6	47.0	43.4	Mexique
Belgium-Luxembourg	198.1	–	–	–	–	Belgique-Luxembourg
Ukraine	20.8	15.7	47.7	36.6	39.4	Ukraine
Slovenia	28.5	27.9	37.2	30.8	18.1	Slovénie
Ireland	24.6	22.8	23.4	23.2	17.5	Irlande
Malaysia	13.9	50.7	16.5	11.2	e12.2	Malaisie
Israel	20.6	15.1	21.6	23.0	17.1	Israël
Turkey	14.9	14.0	19.4	17.2	21.5	Turquie
Poland	14.8	13.1	23.0	19.1	16.3	Pologne

(Value as percentages of World total) **(Valeur en pourcentage du total mondial)**

Regions of the world	1993	1994	1995	1996	1997	1998	1999	2000	2001	2002	Régions du monde
World	100.0	100.0	100.0	100.0	100.0	100.0	100.0	100.0	100.0	100.0	Monde
Africa	0.3	0.5	1.8	0.8	0.8	0.2	0.8	1.4	0.5	1.3	Afrique
Americas	27.0	24.4	23.2	25.8	23.6	21.5	19.5	21.3	21.5	17.6	Amériques
- Northern America	25.0	22.3	21.3	23.5	21.5	19.4	17.5	19.0	19.2	15.5	- Amérique du Nord
- LAIA	2.0	2.1	1.9	2.2	2.1	2.1	1.9	2.3	2.2	2.1	- ALAI
- CACM	0.0	0.0	0.0	0.0	0.0	0.0	0.0	0.0	0.0	0.0	- MCC
- Caribbean	0.0	0.0	0.0	0.0	0.0	0.0	0.0	0.0	0.0	0.0	- Caraïbes
- Rest of America	0.0	0.0	0.0	0.0	0.0	0.0	0.0	0.0	0.0	0.0	- Autre d'Amérique
Asia excluding former USSR	27.6	25.2	26.2	25.4	26.9	23.8	27.7	27.6	27.3	28.1	Asie ancienne URSS exclus
- Middle East	1.4	0.7	0.5	0.7	0.8	1.3	0.6	0.4	0.6	0.7	- Moyen-Orient
Asia former USSR	0.0	0.0	0.0	0.0	0.0	0.0	0.0	0.2	0.1	0.1	Asie ancienne URSS
Europe excluding former USSR	44.6	49.1	48.2	46.1	47.8	53.4	51.3	48.4	49.3	51.8	Europe ancienne URSS exclus
- European Union	42.4	46.7	45.8	43.5	45.5	50.8	49.4	46.5	46.8	49.7	- Union Européenne
- Eastern Europe	0.8	0.8	1.1	1.0	0.8	0.9	0.7	0.8	1.0	0.9	- Europe de l'Est
- Rest of Europe	1.5	1.6	1.2	1.6	1.5	1.7	1.3	1.1	1.5	1.2	- Autre de l'Europe
Europe former USSR	0.1	0.4	0.4	1.5	0.4	0.6	0.4	0.9	1.1	0.9	Europe ancienne URSS
Oceania	0.4	0.4	0.3	0.3	0.4	0.4	0.3	0.2	0.3	0.2	Océanie

TRADE BY COMMODITY (Value in million US dollars)
Exports by principal countries or areas

COMMERCE PAR PRODUIT (Valeur en millions de dollars EU)
Exportations selon les principaux pays ou zones

Country or area	1998	1999	2000	2001	2002	Pays ou zone
World	4846.8	5231.0	7402.4	6222.1	6861.7	Monde
Africa	131.4	172.3	181.2	207.3	244.5	Afrique
Americas	1125.8	998.7	1513.7	1397.4	1280.2	Amériques
- Northern America	1045.2	922.8	1405.0	1337.2	1218.2	- Amérique du Nord
- LAIA	40.6	73.4	108.5	60.2	62.0	- ALAI
- CACM	0.0	0.0	0.0	0.0	0.0	- MCC
- Caribbean	3.6	2.5	0.2	0.0	0.0	- Caraïbes
- Rest of America	36.5	0.0	0.0	0.0	0.0	- Autre d'Amérique
Asia excluding former USSR	302.2	333.7	567.8	448.0	451.9	Asie ancienne URSS exclus
- Middle East	4.3	2.4	1.8	1.1	1.0	- Moyen-Orient
Asia former USSR	0.1	0.1	0.2	0.6	0.7	Asie ancienne URSS
Europe excluding former USSR	1866.6	2033.2	2526.6	2303.7	2289.3	Europe ancienne URSS exclus
- European Union	1474.7	1566.6	1979.6	1858.5	1785.4	- Union Européenne
- Eastern Europe	2.7	7.3	6.0	3.7	4.5	- Europe de l'Est
- Rest of Europe	389.2	459.3	541.0	441.4	499.5	- Autre de l'Europe
Europe former USSR	1134.9	1235.2	1736.0	1121.7	1760.5	Europe ancienne URSS
Oceania	285.8	457.8	877.0	743.4	834.7	Océanie
Russian Federation	1124.9	1233.0	1730.2	1112.4	1753.1	Fédération de Russie
Canada	670.9	589.1	975.9	796.2	773.4	Canada
Australia	285.8	457.2	876.7	743.4	834.4	Australie
United Kingdom	433.6	405.1	494.1	497.1	439.7	Royaume-Uni
Norway	355.0	424.6	506.1	409.9	469.5	Norvège
Germany	393.5	393.8	445.2	483.9	443.7	Allemagne
United States	373.3	332.4	428.6	541.0	444.8	Etats-Unis d'Amérique
Finland	144.8	175.8	250.5	232.6	268.9	Finlande
Netherlands	126.7	172.2	266.1	191.0	181.6	Pays-Bas
Japan	128.8	136.7	218.4	162.5	173.0	Japon
France-Monaco	133.1	139.7	180.2	192.4	163.4	France-Monaco
Zimbabwe	e80.2	75.3	83.9	142.8	177.3	Zimbabwe
Belgium	–	114.0	151.6	132.8	e149.0	Belgique
China, Hong Kong SAR	38.6	44.6	130.4	127.8	110.3	Chine - RAS de Hong-Kong
Singapore	40.0	65.8	124.0	86.0	100.8	Singapour
Brazil	39.2	72.7	108.2	58.9	e61.1	Brésil
Sweden	65.4	65.3	75.6	62.0	55.6	Suède
China	81.7	73.0	75.5	40.8	34.5	Chine
South Africa	–	–	97.3	63.9	67.1	Afrique du Sud
Italy-San Marino-Holy See	33.3	21.3	37.0	31.5	43.8	Italie-Saint-Marin-Saint-Siège
Southern African Customs Union	50.3	97.0	–	–	–	Union douanière d'Afrique australe
Austria	29.7	24.1	36.0	26.1	28.5	Autriche
Spain	13.9	49.2	36.7	3.5	6.5	Espagne
Switzerland-Liechtenstein	17.5	20.4	17.6	18.7	21.1	Suisse-Liechtenstein
Belgium-Luxembourg	93.8	–	–	–	–	Belgique-Luxembourg
Slovenia	16.6	13.9	17.2	12.8	8.8	Slovénie
Suriname	36.5	0.0	0.0	0.0	0.0	Suriname
Ireland	6.2	5.6	6.1	5.1	4.3	Irlande
Ukraine	8.8	1.3	3.2	2.8	3.0	Ukraine
Korea, Republic of	1.4	1.5	2.2	3.3	9.1	République de Corée

(Value as percentages of World total) **(Valeur en pourcentage du total mondial)**

Regions of the world	1993	1994	1995	1996	1997	1998	1999	2000	2001	2002	Régions du monde
World	100.0	100.0	100.0	100.0	100.0	100.0	100.0	100.0	100.0	100.0	Monde
Africa	3.1	3.3	2.7	2.1	1.8	2.7	3.3	2.4	3.3	3.6	Afrique
Americas	33.5	22.4	22.7	23.7	22.8	23.2	19.1	20.4	22.5	18.7	Amériques
- Northern America	27.2	21.5	21.9	22.8	21.1	21.6	17.6	19.0	21.5	17.8	- Amérique du Nord
- LAIA	0.9	0.9	0.8	0.9	0.7	0.8	1.4	1.5	1.0	0.9	- ALAI
- CACM	0.0	0.0	0.0	0.0	0.0	0.0	0.0	0.0	0.0	0.0	- MCC
- Caribbean	5.4	0.0	0.0	0.0	0.1	0.1	0.0	0.0	0.0	0.0	- Caraïbes
- Rest of America	0.0	0.0	0.0	0.0	0.8	0.8	0.0	0.0	0.0	0.0	- Autre d'Amérique
Asia excluding former USSR	4.7	7.5	5.1	4.5	5.5	6.2	6.4	7.7	7.2	6.6	Asie ancienne URSS exclus
- Middle East	0.0	0.0	0.1	0.0	0.0	0.1	0.0	0.0	0.0	0.0	- Moyen-Orient
Asia former USSR	0.3	0.1	2.9	0.1	0.0	0.0	0.0	0.0	0.0	0.0	Asie ancienne URSS
Europe excluding former USSR	37.7	35.5	36.3	38.4	37.6	38.5	38.9	34.1	37.0	33.4	Europe ancienne URSS exclus
- European Union	26.5	24.1	26.8	28.8	28.8	30.4	29.9	26.7	29.9	26.0	- Union Européenne
- Eastern Europe	0.4	0.1	0.3	0.1	0.4	0.1	0.1	0.1	0.1	0.1	- Europe de l'Est
- Rest of Europe	10.8	11.4	9.2	9.5	8.4	8.0	8.8	7.3	7.1	7.3	- Autre de l'Europe
Europe former USSR	16.2	25.1	22.3	23.8	26.3	23.4	23.6	23.5	18.0	25.7	Europe ancienne URSS
Oceania	4.5	6.1	7.9	7.4	5.9	5.9	8.8	11.8	11.9	12.2	Océanie

684 Aluminium

TRADE BY COMMODITY (Value in million US dollars)
Imports by principal countries or areas

COMMERCE PAR PRODUIT (Valeur en millions de dollars EU)
Importations selon les principaux pays ou zones

Country or area	1998	1999	2000	2001	2002	Pays ou zone
World	44498.6	43995.9	50664.1	48109.2	49262.0	Monde
Africa	484.4	419.4	445.0	464.4	503.2	Afrique
Americas	10131.4	10318.4	11365.8	10601.6	10904.4	Amériques
- Northern America	7706.3	8157.4	9040.2	8231.9	8662.1	- Amérique du Nord
- LAIA	2082.8	1932.9	2082.4	2122.4	2005.0	- ALAI
- CACM	112.3	100.9	116.4	137.0	114.4	- MCC
- Caribbean	209.9	92.0	102.7	91.9	97.8	- Caraïbes
- Rest of America	20.0	35.3	24.2	18.4	25.1	- Autre d'Amérique
Asia excluding former USSR	11849.7	12516.6	15392.3	13355.4	13569.4	Asie ancienne URSS exclus
- Middle East	1067.5	1021.4	1215.0	1210.6	1358.3	- Moyen-Orient
Asia former USSR	43.9	28.9	50.8	76.4	86.8	Asie ancienne URSS
Europe excluding former USSR	21327.6	19964.7	22428.4	22806.4	23355.2	Europe ancienne URSS exclus
- European Union	18488.5	17109.2	18981.4	19257.6	19545.7	- Union Européenne
- Eastern Europe	1414.1	1439.1	1752.8	1861.0	2099.8	- Europe de l'Est
- Rest of Europe	1425.0	1416.3	1694.2	1687.9	1709.7	- Autre de l'Europe
Europe former USSR	314.8	398.2	591.2	467.0	464.7	Europe ancienne URSS
Oceania	346.9	349.7	390.5	338.0	378.3	Océanie
United States	6107.3	6443.8	7117.5	6546.2	6938.1	Etats-Unis d'Amérique
Germany	5029.8	4479.6	5135.6	5431.5	5256.9	Allemagne
Japan	4155.0	3993.9	4887.3	4232.6	3874.3	Japon
France-Monaco	2390.5	2244.8	2647.0	2511.2	2426.1	France-Monaco
Italy-San Marino-Holy See	2266.6	2197.2	2545.0	2381.9	2417.9	Italie-Saint-Marin-Saint-Siège
China	1242.3	1737.6	2544.8	1853.7	2054.8	Chine
United Kingdom	2062.3	1800.1	1627.9	1927.2	1995.1	Royaume-Uni
Canada	1598.7	1713.3	1922.0	1684.6	1723.4	Canada
Korea, Republic of	1252.0	1622.6	1919.4	1732.7	1751.7	République de Corée
Netherlands	1488.3	1408.6	1527.4	1352.8	1402.8	Pays-Bas
Belgium	–	1311.8	1436.6	1566.4	e1717.8	Belgique
Mexico	1036.5	1098.4	1264.0	1252.9	1316.6	Mexique
Spain	887.3	886.8	1011.1	1030.4	1070.3	Espagne
Austria	888.3	780.2	793.8	890.7	923.7	Autriche
Switzerland-Liechtenstein	715.6	661.3	752.5	738.9	700.6	Suisse-Liechtenstein
China, Hong Kong SAR	937.8	616.9	651.9	476.6	523.1	Chine - RAS de Hong-Kong
Sweden	660.4	555.9	598.5	577.1	638.2	Suède
Thailand	438.0	480.7	629.7	655.8	e683.3	Thaïlande
Poland	464.6	517.6	573.5	594.3	702.0	Pologne
Malaysia	402.3	518.0	605.6	524.2	e573.0	Malaisie
Singapore	378.3	385.6	439.4	635.0	645.7	Singapour
Norway	374.0	414.0	540.8	491.6	564.4	Norvège
Hungary	375.3	370.1	492.4	500.9	538.6	Hongrie
Czech Republic	370.4	351.6	409.8	464.0	522.4	République tchèque
Turkey	419.8	381.7	464.0	365.3	479.9	Turquie
Portugal	313.2	407.9	497.7	451.2	439.5	Portugal
Brazil	466.1	406.1	335.7	395.3	298.1	Brésil
Denmark	348.6	333.9	335.9	352.0	433.8	Danemark
Saudi Arabia	284.0	289.5	318.0	300.6	e311.1	Arabie saoudite
Belgium-Luxembourg	1496.7	–	–	–	–	Belgique-Luxembourg

(Value as percentages of World total)

(Valeur en pourcentage du total mondial)

Regions of the world	1993	1994	1995	1996	1997	1998	1999	2000	2001	2002	Régions du monde
World	100.0	100.0	100.0	100.0	100.0	100.0	100.0	100.0	100.0	100.0	Monde
Africa	1.5	1.2	0.9	1.0	0.9	1.1	1.0	0.9	1.0	1.0	Afrique
Americas	19.1	21.2	18.7	18.4	20.0	22.8	23.5	22.4	22.0	22.1	Amériques
- Northern America	15.5	17.9	15.5	14.9	15.9	17.3	18.5	17.8	17.1	17.6	- Amérique du Nord
- LAIA	3.2	3.0	2.9	3.1	3.8	4.7	4.4	4.1	4.4	4.1	- ALAI
- CACM	0.2	0.2	0.2	0.2	0.2	0.3	0.2	0.2	0.3	0.2	- MCC
- Caribbean	0.1	0.1	0.1	0.1	0.2	0.5	0.2	0.2	0.2	0.2	- Caraïbes
- Rest of America	0.0	0.0	0.0	0.1	0.0	0.0	0.1	0.0	0.0	0.1	- Autre d'Amérique
Asia excluding former USSR	34.1	29.9	33.2	33.1	32.7	26.6	28.4	30.4	27.8	27.5	Asie ancienne URSS exclus
- Middle East	2.8	2.2	2.4	2.5	2.6	2.4	2.3	2.4	2.5	2.8	- Moyen-Orient
Asia former USSR	0.0	0.0	0.1	0.1	0.1	0.1	0.1	0.1	0.2	0.2	Asie ancienne URSS
Europe excluding former USSR	44.2	46.4	45.9	46.0	44.9	47.9	45.4	44.3	47.4	47.4	Europe ancienne URSS exclus
- European Union	39.6	41.0	40.5	40.3	38.9	41.5	38.9	37.5	40.0	39.7	- Union Européenne
- Eastern Europe	1.8	2.0	2.4	2.6	2.8	3.2	3.3	3.5	3.9	4.3	- Europe de l'Est
- Rest of Europe	2.8	3.4	3.1	3.1	3.1	3.2	3.2	3.3	3.5	3.5	- Autre de l'Europe
Europe former USSR	0.3	0.5	0.5	0.6	0.7	0.7	0.9	1.2	1.0	0.9	Europe ancienne URSS
Oceania	0.8	0.7	0.7	0.8	0.8	0.8	0.8	0.8	0.7	0.8	Océanie

TRADE BY COMMODITY (Value in million US dollars)
Exports by principal countries or areas

COMMERCE PAR PRODUIT (Valeur en millions de dollars EU)
Exportations selon les principaux pays ou zones

Country or area	1998	1999	2000	2001	2002	Pays ou zone
World	43394.2	43319.2	49082.2	47502.7	48094.9	Monde
Africa	335.9	1107.1	1362.6	1654.1	1674.8	Afrique
Americas	9893.3	9901.8	11117.6	10132.4	10049.4	Amériques
- Northern America	7695.2	7606.1	8284.7	7750.3	7594.6	- Amérique du Nord
- LAIA	2092.9	2228.9	2752.0	2313.5	2384.3	- ALAI
- CACM	60.3	60.2	73.1	63.0	65.3	- MCC
- Caribbean	42.3	2.5	2.7	2.0	2.2	- Caraïbes
- Rest of America	2.7	4.0	5.2	3.5	3.0	- Autre d'Amérique
Asia excluding former USSR	5688.7	5684.6	6818.4	6531.9	7528.5	Asie ancienne URSS exclus
- Middle East	1376.7	1522.1	2000.0	1954.8	2001.1	- Moyen-Orient
Asia former USSR	373.4	420.8	456.9	421.0	461.3	Asie ancienne URSS
Europe excluding former USSR	20018.8	19015.3	20917.9	21227.3	21668.1	Europe ancienne URSS exclus
- European Union	15071.1	14276.8	15380.4	15655.4	16032.8	- Union Européenne
- Eastern Europe	1236.7	1198.1	1440.3	1385.0	1510.5	- Europe de l'Est
- Rest of Europe	3711.0	3540.4	4097.2	4186.9	4124.8	- Autre de l'Europe
Europe former USSR	4470.6	4583.1	5366.4	4629.9	3927.4	Europe ancienne URSS
Oceania	2613.5	2606.6	3042.4	2906.2	2785.5	Océanie
Germany	4488.9	4283.5	4574.0	5028.4	5111.7	Allemagne
Canada	4009.1	3975.5	4429.0	4421.7	4535.3	Canada
Russian Federation	4206.9	4156.8	4777.4	4267.0	3495.7	Fédération de Russie
United States	3684.6	3630.6	3855.7	3328.6	3059.3	Etats-Unis d'Amérique
Australia	2133.8	2144.7	2522.5	2430.2	2318.4	Australie
Norway	2301.0	2069.5	2340.6	2382.5	2353.8	Norvège
France-Monaco	1877.7	1705.2	1737.2	1629.4	1684.8	France-Monaco
Netherlands	1566.7	1462.9	1520.9	1410.6	1448.2	Pays-Bas
United Kingdom	1476.2	1273.8	1488.5	1333.5	1271.7	Royaume-Uni
Italy-San Marino-Holy See	1308.1	1311.1	1369.2	1324.1	1368.2	Italie-Saint-Marin-Saint-Siège
Japan	1245.6	1347.6	1390.1	1132.7	1233.0	Japon
Brazil	1083.4	1213.9	1439.9	1101.5	e1141.9	Brésil
Belgium	–	1206.3	1266.1	1377.5	e1545.5	Belgique
China	690.4	491.0	623.7	928.8	1556.1	Chine
United Arab Emirates	660.9	681.8	901.1	802.4	e835.8	Emirates arabes unis
Spain	729.5	700.5	759.7	796.3	838.9	Espagne
Austria	685.9	647.2	772.0	805.6	791.7	Autriche
Venezuela	688.3	653.1	770.4	748.6	e795.2	Venezuela
Switzerland-Liechtenstein	724.3	681.3	708.6	686.0	698.5	Suisse-Liechtenstein
Bahrain	e402.8	e548.9	779.5	825.2	e799.0	Bahreïn
Korea, Republic of	519.8	545.3	571.8	550.5	630.7	République de Corée
Sweden	533.1	536.8	571.2	550.7	556.8	Suède
China, Hong Kong SAR	668.6	540.9	564.0	425.2	472.3	Chine - RAS de Hong-Kong
South Africa	–	–	867.1	821.0	887.8	Afrique du Sud
Greece	457.5	441.1	455.3	537.6	e538.3	Grèce
New Zealand	479.2	461.6	519.8	475.8	467.1	Nouvelle-Zélande
Hungary	358.9	341.4	413.4	405.9	441.3	Hongrie
Tajikistan	e322.8	e369.5	371.5	e360.8	e396.2	Tadjikistan
Iceland	260.4	312.6	352.7	404.5	421.4	Islande
Ukraine	236.6	333.6	438.7	268.4	295.8	Ukraine

(Value as percentages of World total) **(Valeur en pourcentage du total mondial)**

Regions of the world	1993	1994	1995	1996	1997	1998	1999	2000	2001	2002	Régions du monde
World	100.0	100.0	100.0	100.0	100.0	100.0	100.0	100.0	100.0	100.0	Monde
Africa	1.8	1.4	1.9	2.7	1.1	0.8	2.6	2.8	3.5	3.5	Afrique
Americas	25.3	25.1	23.6	21.9	23.1	22.8	22.9	22.7	21.3	20.9	Amériques
- Northern America	18.4	18.6	17.5	17.9	19.0	17.7	17.6	16.9	16.3	15.8	- Amérique du Nord
- LAIA	6.4	6.3	5.9	3.8	3.9	4.8	5.1	5.6	4.9	5.0	- ALAI
- CACM	0.1	0.1	0.1	0.1	0.1	0.1	0.1	0.1	0.1	0.1	- MCC
- Caribbean	0.0	0.0	0.0	0.0	0.0	0.1	0.0	0.0	0.0	0.0	- Caraïbes
- Rest of America	0.4	0.1	0.1	0.1	0.0	0.0	0.0	0.0	0.0	0.0	- Autre d'Amérique
Asia excluding former USSR	12.8	12.8	13.4	13.4	14.4	13.1	13.1	13.9	13.8	15.7	Asie ancienne URSS exclus
- Middle East	4.8	4.4	3.6	3.4	3.6	3.2	3.5	4.1	4.1	4.2	- Moyen-Orient
Asia former USSR	0.6	0.5	0.9	0.7	0.3	0.9	1.0	0.9	0.9	1.0	Asie ancienne URSS
Europe excluding former USSR	44.3	44.5	45.7	45.1	44.8	46.1	43.9	42.6	44.7	45.1	Europe ancienne URSS exclus
- European Union	34.7	34.3	35.6	34.7	34.1	34.7	33.0	31.3	33.0	33.3	- Union Européenne
- Eastern Europe	1.6	1.9	2.2	2.4	2.8	2.8	2.8	2.9	2.9	3.1	- Europe de l'Est
- Rest of Europe	7.9	8.2	7.9	8.0	7.9	8.6	8.2	8.3	8.8	8.6	- Autre de l'Europe
Europe former USSR	8.8	10.0	8.9	10.5	10.1	10.3	10.6	10.9	9.7	8.2	Europe ancienne URSS
Oceania	6.4	5.8	5.7	5.7	6.2	6.0	6.0	6.2	6.1	5.8	Océanie

685 Lead

TRADE BY COMMODITY (Value in million US dollars)
Imports by principal countries or areas

COMMERCE PAR PRODUIT (Valeur en millions de dollars EU)
Importations selon les principaux pays ou zones

Country or area	1998	1999	2000	2001	2002	Pays ou zone
World	1542.6	1558.8	1542.0	1459.1	1494.4	Monde
Africa	33.6	26.2	24.3	25.0	28.3	Afrique
Americas	375.7	401.3	391.0	260.0	227.5	Amériques
- Northern America	232.7	206.4	235.5	158.1	140.6	- Amérique du Nord
- LAIA	124.7	176.4	151.7	96.3	81.9	- ALAI
- CACM	0.9	0.8	0.3	0.7	0.4	- MCC
- Caribbean	17.1	17.4	3.2	4.7	4.2	- Caraïbes
- Rest of America	0.2	0.2	0.3	0.3	0.3	- Autre d'Amérique
Asia excluding former USSR	424.0	463.5	456.0	461.0	496.1	Asie ancienne URSS exclus
- Middle East	51.4	36.6	43.3	36.3	53.2	- Moyen-Orient
Asia former USSR	1.2	0.3	1.1	2.2	1.2	Asie ancienne URSS
Europe excluding former USSR	670.6	632.3	617.8	677.7	706.9	Europe ancienne URSS exclus
- European Union	611.2	569.9	535.1	591.4	612.6	- Union Européenne
- Eastern Europe	38.3	43.7	62.3	66.0	73.0	- Europe de l'Est
- Rest of Europe	21.1	18.7	20.4	20.3	21.4	- Autre de l'Europe
Europe former USSR	20.7	23.6	40.3	27.9	27.1	Europe ancienne URSS
Oceania	16.8	11.6	11.5	5.3	7.3	Océanie
United States	178.9	190.9	201.9	150.1	137.2	Etats-Unis d'Amérique
United Kingdom	180.8	162.3	161.9	168.8	171.8	Royaume-Uni
Germany	95.7	96.1	82.5	106.0	91.5	Allemagne
Mexico	63.0	126.3	96.0	37.6	31.0	Mexique
Korea, Republic of	74.3	65.6	63.0	72.5	72.1	République de Corée
Spain	64.4	62.0	58.6	69.9	76.0	Espagne
France-Monaco	48.5	60.1	65.3	60.4	62.6	France-Monaco
Italy-San Marino-Holy See	57.9	64.5	52.8	54.6	65.8	Italie-Saint-Marin-Saint-Siège
Malaysia	52.5	78.3	57.6	47.8	e52.3	Malaisie
Singapore	23.9	62.5	49.8	54.0	52.8	Singapour
India	39.8	37.4	33.9	43.2	50.7	Inde
Brazil	41.1	36.0	40.5	42.8	38.9	Brésil
Netherlands	34.5	35.1	28.9	26.6	34.1	Pays-Bas
Thailand	19.3	26.2	36.9	33.2	e34.6	Thaïlande
Turkey	30.5	23.6	29.3	23.1	35.0	Turquie
Czech Republic	19.1	20.4	27.6	32.6	33.3	République tchèque
Austria	34.0	21.8	22.8	25.4	24.8	Autriche
Japan	28.8	19.4	25.1	34.5	17.1	Japon
Belgium	–	23.5	22.1	33.0	e36.2	Belgique
Canada	53.9	15.5	33.6	8.0	3.4	Canada
Indonesia	23.5	16.2	25.9	18.9	24.5	Indonésie
Russian Federation	14.5	17.6	30.5	23.2	23.1	Fédération de Russie
China	12.6	10.4	14.1	18.9	32.3	Chine
Ireland	18.5	14.8	13.8	18.4	21.9	Irlande
Poland	6.6	10.5	20.8	20.5	28.3	Pologne
Portugal	18.6	12.8	11.0	12.1	11.1	Portugal
China, Hong Kong SAR	11.4	8.8	7.2	12.8	12.4	Chine - RAS de Hong-Kong
Philippines	4.7	13.3	11.9	6.3	6.3	Philippines
Belgium-Luxembourg	41.3	–	–	–	–	Belgique-Luxembourg
Australia	13.3	8.1	9.8	3.9	5.5	Australie

(Value as percentages of World total) **(Valeur en pourcentage du total mondial)**

Regions of the world	1993	1994	1995	1996	1997	1998	1999	2000	2001	2002	Régions du monde
World	100.0	100.0	100.0	100.0	100.0	100.0	100.0	100.0	100.0	100.0	Monde
Africa	2.2	1.6	1.7	1.8	2.3	2.2	1.7	1.6	1.7	1.9	Afrique
Americas	14.1	16.2	16.5	18.1	21.2	24.4	25.7	25.4	17.8	15.2	Amériques
- Northern America	9.5	12.3	12.4	13.8	14.3	15.1	13.2	15.3	10.8	9.4	- Amérique du Nord
- LAIA	4.1	3.6	3.7	4.1	6.6	8.1	11.3	9.8	6.6	5.5	- ALAI
- CACM	0.2	0.1	0.1	0.0	0.1	0.1	0.1	0.0	0.1	0.0	- MCC
- Caribbean	0.3	0.2	0.3	0.2	0.3	1.1	1.1	0.2	0.3	0.3	- Caraïbes
- Rest of America	0.0	0.0	0.0	0.0	0.0	0.0	0.0	0.0	0.0	0.0	- Autre d'Amérique
Asia excluding former USSR	40.2	34.8	35.6	36.0	30.8	27.5	29.7	29.6	31.6	33.2	Asie ancienne URSS exclus
- Middle East	3.0	2.4	3.1	3.0	2.8	3.3	2.3	2.8	2.5	3.6	- Moyen-Orient
Asia former USSR	0.0	0.0	0.1	0.0	0.0	0.1	0.0	0.1	0.2	0.1	Asie ancienne URSS
Europe excluding former USSR	43.2	44.6	43.1	41.3	43.4	43.5	40.6	40.1	46.4	47.3	Europe ancienne URSS exclus
- European Union	40.1	41.3	39.7	38.3	40.1	39.6	36.6	34.7	40.5	41.0	- Union Européenne
- Eastern Europe	1.9	1.9	2.0	1.7	1.9	2.5	2.8	4.0	4.5	4.9	- Europe de l'Est
- Rest of Europe	1.2	1.4	1.4	1.3	1.4	1.4	1.2	1.3	1.4	1.4	- Autre de l'Europe
Europe former USSR	0.0	2.4	2.3	2.0	1.6	1.3	1.5	2.6	1.9	1.8	Europe ancienne URSS
Oceania	0.3	0.4	0.8	0.7	0.7	1.1	0.7	0.7	0.4	0.5	Océanie

TRADE BY COMMODITY (Value in million US dollars)
Exports by principal countries or areas

COMMERCE PAR PRODUIT (Valeur en millions de dollars EU)
Exportations selon les principaux pays ou zones

Country or area	1998	1999	2000	2001	2002	Pays ou zone
World	1474.3	1511.8	1448.9	1412.4	1478.1	Monde
Africa	35.5	29.9	24.5	32.8	33.5	Afrique
Americas	369.3	347.2	348.5	229.0	223.9	Amériques
- Northern America	250.8	248.8	260.4	136.7	142.6	- Amérique du Nord
- LAIA	115.9	96.0	85.6	88.3	80.3	- ALAI
- CACM	1.4	1.2	1.0	2.7	0.2	- MCC
- Caribbean	0.3	0.3	0.4	0.0	0.1	- Caraïbes
- Rest of America	0.8	0.8	1.2	1.3	0.7	- Autre d'Amérique
Asia excluding former USSR	259.6	345.9	357.9	390.6	395.6	Asie ancienne URSS exclus
- Middle East	9.9	8.2	6.2	8.3	8.8	- Moyen-Orient
Asia former USSR	41.9	49.7	65.8	56.4	63.3	Asie ancienne URSS
Europe excluding former USSR	556.7	478.8	474.9	492.2	535.1	Europe ancienne URSS exclus
- European Union	468.2	397.8	388.0	399.7	443.6	- Union Européenne
- Eastern Europe	60.9	63.8	67.5	71.2	71.8	- Europe de l'Est
- Rest of Europe	27.6	17.2	19.4	21.2	19.8	- Autre de l'Europe
Europe former USSR	7.3	6.5	5.6	10.0	6.3	Europe ancienne URSS
Oceania	203.9	253.9	171.6	201.5	220.5	Océanie
China	146.1	243.9	231.8	245.8	240.2	Chine
Australia	196.5	247.5	167.9	198.2	216.4	Australie
Canada	130.9	133.2	131.8	98.7	99.4	Canada
Germany	101.0	91.4	100.8	127.5	133.5	Allemagne
United Kingdom	128.7	77.7	69.1	84.3	96.7	Royaume-Uni
United States	119.9	115.7	128.6	38.0	43.2	Etats-Unis d'Amérique
Belgium	–	83.8	91.8	78.6	e88.2	Belgique
Peru	66.7	67.1	60.5	58.4	55.5	Pérou
Kazakhstan	41.5	49.1	65.3	55.1	e62.0	Kazakhstan
France-Monaco	62.6	52.0	49.7	43.5	41.2	France-Monaco
Bulgaria	34.1	36.1	36.2	e38.4	e43.1	Bulgarie
Sweden	36.1	34.6	34.8	30.1	33.9	Suède
Singapore	18.8	12.8	37.3	47.1	34.0	Singapour
Morocco	32.2	27.8	22.7	27.2	e29.6	Maroc
Korea, Republic of	27.3	17.6	20.1	22.2	34.8	République de Corée
Malaysia	15.8	28.5	19.4	27.2	e28.8	Malaisie
Poland	18.4	18.2	17.3	19.0	16.2	Pologne
Belgium-Luxembourg	86.6	–	–	–	–	Belgique-Luxembourg
Mexico	39.1	18.0	10.9	10.5	6.0	Mexique
Italy-San Marino-Holy See	14.5	15.8	13.9	6.2	14.1	Italie-Saint-Marin-Saint-Siège
Ireland	17.5	12.6	9.7	11.2	12.9	Irlande
The former Yugoslav Republic of Macedonia	11.0	9.9	10.0	11.5	e11.1	Ex-République yougoslave de Macédoine
China, Hong Kong SAR	7.1	5.6	9.8	10.0	11.2	Chine - RAS de Hong-Kong
Japan	8.0	6.8	7.9	5.8	14.6	Japon
Netherlands	10.2	10.5	8.0	6.0	6.4	Pays-Bas
Venezuela	6.1	5.4	5.5	6.2	e6.6	Venezuela
Romania	3.9	2.9	7.2	7.7	7.9	Roumanie
Saudi Arabia	7.8	4.3	4.8	4.5	e4.0	Arabie saoudite
New Zealand	7.4	6.4	3.7	3.3	4.1	Nouvelle-Zélande
Argentina	0.2	0.5	4.9	9.8	e9.4	Argentine

(Value as percentages of World total) **(Valeur en pourcentage du total mondial)**

Regions of the world	1993	1994	1995	1996	1997	1998	1999	2000	2001	2002	Régions du monde
World	100.0	100.0	100.0	100.0	100.0	100.0	100.0	100.0	100.0	100.0	Monde
Africa	3.1	2.8	2.4	2.5	2.3	2.4	2.0	1.7	2.3	2.3	Afrique
Americas	21.4	18.8	22.4	24.7	26.4	25.0	23.0	24.1	16.2	15.1	Amériques
- Northern America	12.8	12.1	13.2	16.8	18.0	17.0	16.5	18.0	9.7	9.6	- Amérique du Nord
- LAIA	8.6	6.7	9.1	7.8	8.3	7.9	6.3	5.9	6.2	5.4	- ALAI
- CACM	0.0	0.0	0.0	0.0	0.0	0.1	0.1	0.1	0.2	0.0	- MCC
- Caribbean	0.0	0.0	0.0	0.0	0.0	0.0	0.0	0.0	0.0	0.0	- Caraïbes
- Rest of America	0.0	0.0	0.0	0.1	0.0	0.1	0.1	0.1	0.1	0.0	- Autre d'Amérique
Asia excluding former USSR	15.6	17.0	16.8	17.2	14.3	17.6	22.9	24.7	27.7	26.8	Asie ancienne URSS exclus
- Middle East	0.5	0.5	0.5	0.8	0.9	0.7	0.5	0.4	0.6	0.6	- Moyen-Orient
Asia former USSR	0.9	3.5	2.2	2.6	3.0	2.8	3.3	4.5	4.0	4.3	Asie ancienne URSS
Europe excluding former USSR	37.6	39.8	37.4	34.6	35.5	37.8	31.7	32.8	34.8	36.2	Europe ancienne URSS exclus
- European Union	33.5	34.0	30.3	28.9	29.9	31.8	26.3	26.8	28.3	30.0	- Union Européenne
- Eastern Europe	2.8	3.1	4.6	4.4	4.2	4.1	4.2	4.7	5.0	4.9	- Europe de l'Est
- Rest of Europe	1.4	2.7	2.5	1.3	1.4	1.9	1.1	1.3	1.5	1.3	- Autre de l'Europe
Europe former USSR	0.5	0.7	0.7	1.1	1.1	0.5	0.4	0.4	0.7	0.4	Europe ancienne URSS
Oceania	20.9	17.4	18.0	17.4	17.4	13.8	16.8	11.8	14.3	14.9	Océanie

686 Zinc

TRADE BY COMMODITY (Value in million US dollars)
Imports by principal countries or areas

COMMERCE PAR PRODUIT (Valeur en millions de dollars EU)
Importations selon les principaux pays ou zones

Country or area	1998	1999	2000	2001	2002	Pays ou zone
World	5325.5	5344.6	6003.1	5046.2	4683.7	Monde
Africa	97.6	101.6	112.7	112.5	107.0	Afrique
Americas	1283.4	1442.6	1490.6	1190.0	1130.0	Amériques
- Northern America	1096.7	1249.1	1276.5	1029.0	1006.9	- Amérique du Nord
- LAIA	150.6	158.4	177.8	126.2	92.5	- ALAI
- CACM	27.0	28.4	32.7	29.7	27.2	- MCC
- Caribbean	8.9	6.4	3.5	4.7	3.4	- Caraïbes
- Rest of America	0.2	0.4	0.1	0.5	0.1	- Autre d'Amérique
Asia excluding former USSR	1605.8	1622.0	1939.1	1676.9	1602.6	Asie ancienne URSS exclus
- Middle East	149.0	120.4	158.1	130.8	136.9	- Moyen-Orient
Asia former USSR	2.0	1.2	2.9	1.0	1.0	Asie ancienne URSS
Europe excluding former USSR	2244.1	2119.2	2384.2	2011.3	1793.7	Europe ancienne URSS exclus
- European Union	2037.8	1933.9	2161.7	1809.5	1601.6	- Union Européenne
- Eastern Europe	120.4	106.5	136.1	126.1	123.7	- Europe de l'Est
- Rest of Europe	86.0	78.8	86.4	75.7	68.4	- Autre de l'Europe
Europe former USSR	67.5	29.6	44.0	32.4	30.4	Europe ancienne URSS
Oceania	25.0	28.4	29.7	22.0	19.0	Océanie
United States	1060.6	1209.9	1229.4	996.9	981.8	Etats-Unis d'Amérique
Germany	531.7	510.3	519.1	454.8	345.1	Allemagne
Italy-San Marino-Holy See	241.5	301.7	319.2	236.9	217.2	Italie-Saint-Marin-Saint-Siège
Belgium	–	287.0	347.4	299.2	e328.1	Belgique
France-Monaco	241.7	231.3	286.1	224.2	173.8	France-Monaco
China	134.8	159.1	201.7	214.1	284.0	Chine
China, Hong Kong SAR	173.0	164.6	200.5	179.4	167.2	Chine - RAS de Hong-Kong
Singapore	199.0	156.2	197.1	204.2	123.3	Singapour
Netherlands	188.6	154.6	213.9	165.5	136.2	Pays-Bas
United Kingdom	192.5	161.6	176.0	124.5	103.9	Royaume-Uni
Malaysia	82.3	148.2	130.9	99.9	e109.2	Malaisie
Korea, Republic of	82.3	125.5	152.7	98.4	98.1	République de Corée
Austria	112.7	91.8	90.7	96.5	88.1	Autriche
Japan	150.0	78.4	112.5	78.1	29.1	Japon
Indonesia	82.5	67.5	115.3	97.7	81.0	Indonésie
Turkey	66.1	65.5	99.5	72.2	86.8	Turquie
India	72.1	77.0	67.9	80.1	80.6	Inde
Belgium-Luxembourg	337.1	–	–	–	–	Belgique-Luxembourg
Bangladesh	37.8	e41.4	e76.2	73.8	e72.1	Bangladesh
Sweden	62.9	51.2	47.8	48.3	42.5	Suède
Mexico	49.9	72.1	62.3	24.1	22.3	Mexique
Philippines	46.2	64.0	43.0	43.4	32.7	Philippines
Switzerland-Liechtenstein	42.9	40.4	41.4	39.3	35.6	Suisse-Liechtenstein
Czech Republic	36.2	34.5	42.6	36.7	33.5	République tchèque
Canada	36.1	39.2	47.0	32.2	25.0	Canada
Portugal	36.0	32.3	31.6	29.4	30.8	Portugal
Denmark	30.6	29.5	37.0	31.5	28.8	Danemark
Greece	27.0	25.4	30.9	34.8	e38.4	Grèce
Thailand	33.5	25.9	33.4	28.3	e29.5	Thaïlande
Spain	27.6	30.8	29.8	29.4	31.9	Espagne

(Value as percentages of World total)

(Valeur en pourcentage du total mondial)

Regions of the world	1993	1994	1995	1996	1997	1998	1999	2000	2001	2002	Régions du monde
World	100.0	100.0	100.0	100.0	100.0	100.0	100.0	100.0	100.0	100.0	Monde
Africa	2.2	1.4	1.8	1.7	1.8	1.8	1.9	1.9	2.2	2.3	Afrique
Americas	23.3	24.3	24.2	23.2	23.9	24.1	27.0	24.8	23.6	24.1	Amériques
- Northern America	20.4	21.7	20.6	21.2	21.5	20.6	23.4	21.3	20.4	21.5	- Amérique du Nord
- LAIA	2.5	2.2	3.2	1.6	1.8	2.8	3.0	3.0	2.5	2.0	- ALAI
- CACM	0.4	0.4	0.3	0.3	0.4	0.5	0.5	0.5	0.6	0.6	- MCC
- Caribbean	0.1	0.1	0.1	0.2	0.1	0.2	0.1	0.1	0.1	0.1	- Caraïbes
- Rest of America	0.0	0.0	0.0	0.0	0.0	0.0	0.0	0.0	0.0	0.0	- Autre d'Amérique
Asia excluding former USSR	34.1	30.3	30.7	33.2	34.1	30.2	30.3	32.3	33.2	34.2	Asie ancienne URSS exclus
- Middle East	1.8	1.6	2.3	2.7	2.4	2.8	2.3	2.6	2.6	2.9	- Moyen-Orient
Asia former USSR	0.0	0.0	0.0	0.0	0.0	0.0	0.0	0.0	0.0	0.0	Asie ancienne URSS
Europe excluding former USSR	38.5	41.7	41.3	39.8	38.6	42.1	39.7	39.7	39.9	38.3	Europe ancienne URSS exclus
- European Union	35.0	37.6	37.3	36.0	35.1	38.3	36.2	36.0	35.9	34.2	- Union Européenne
- Eastern Europe	1.7	1.9	1.8	1.9	1.8	2.3	2.0	2.3	2.5	2.6	- Europe de l'Est
- Rest of Europe	1.7	2.2	2.2	1.9	1.7	1.6	1.5	1.4	1.5	1.5	- Autre de l'Europe
Europe former USSR	1.1	1.5	1.4	1.5	1.2	1.3	0.6	0.7	0.6	0.6	Europe ancienne URSS
Oceania	0.8	0.8	0.6	0.5	0.4	0.5	0.5	0.5	0.4	0.4	Océanie

TRADE BY COMMODITY (Value in million US dollars)
Exports by principal countries or areas

COMMERCE PAR PRODUIT (Valeur en millions de dollars EU)
Exportations selon les principaux pays ou zones

Country or area	1998	1999	2000	2001	2002	Pays ou zone
World	4778.6	4933.2	5535.0	4614.9	4379.5	Monde
Africa	61.6	64.5	46.0	38.9	31.7	Afrique
Americas	1129.7	1215.4	1294.6	969.6	911.5	Amériques
- Northern America	746.2	796.3	840.1	588.2	599.5	- Amérique du Nord
- LAIA	347.4	389.1	406.6	380.7	311.5	- ALAI
- CACM	36.1	30.0	47.7	0.5	0.4	- MCC
- Caribbean	0.0	0.0	0.1	0.0	0.1	- Caraïbes
- Rest of America	0.0	0.0	0.1	0.2	0.1	- Autre d'Amérique
Asia excluding former USSR	1112.3	1219.0	1412.4	1220.4	1083.4	Asie ancienne URSS exclus
- Middle East	26.9	12.5	14.0	22.9	27.8	- Moyen-Orient
Asia former USSR	237.0	193.0	259.1	211.2	216.7	Asie ancienne URSS
Europe excluding former USSR	1844.0	1831.3	1923.3	1648.4	1609.6	Europe ancienne URSS exclus
- European Union	1440.8	1424.6	1449.0	1226.1	1225.1	- Union Européenne
- Eastern Europe	179.5	187.2	225.5	220.7	193.2	- Europe de l'Est
- Rest of Europe	223.8	219.6	248.7	201.5	191.3	- Autre de l'Europe
Europe former USSR	129.0	125.7	113.2	103.0	94.4	Europe ancienne URSS
Oceania	264.9	284.2	486.5	423.4	432.3	Océanie
Canada	683.1	722.7	765.9	534.5	545.0	Canada
China	419.3	557.0	674.6	558.1	412.4	Chine
Australia	264.0	283.6	485.7	422.8	431.8	Australie
Netherlands	364.5	306.6	301.8	230.4	213.2	Pays-Bas
Germany	223.6	215.1	252.8	221.1	228.6	Allemagne
Korea, Republic of	185.5	183.7	237.3	229.4	248.9	République de Corée
Belgium	–	223.6	266.6	220.1	e246.9	Belgique
Peru	194.9	210.9	223.3	180.6	131.6	Pérou
Finland	170.7	202.6	201.7	178.6	164.4	Finlande
Kazakhstan	181.6	163.0	198.2	157.7	e177.7	Kazakhstan
China, Hong Kong SAR	144.7	144.5	181.6	169.4	175.1	Chine - RAS de Hong-Kong
France-Monaco	172.9	168.1	161.7	142.9	148.6	France-Monaco
Spain	157.3	197.5	153.0	130.6	115.6	Espagne
Mexico	123.1	141.7	145.4	170.3	149.3	Mexique
Norway	138.6	146.4	151.8	122.9	120.0	Norvège
Russian Federation	128.3	124.6	112.0	101.8	93.8	Fédération de Russie
Singapore	152.9	123.6	138.5	80.7	41.9	Singapour
Poland	90.5	106.1	102.6	91.3	71.0	Pologne
Japan	75.6	101.0	82.4	81.7	98.7	Japon
Bulgaria	66.8	68.2	78.8	e83.6	e94.0	Bulgarie
United States	63.1	73.6	74.2	53.7	54.5	Etats-Unis d'Amérique
United Kingdom	65.8	54.4	53.0	52.0	48.0	Royaume-Uni
The former Yugoslav Republic of Macedonia	54.8	48.3	65.8	51.0	e49.1	Ex-République yougoslave de Macédoine
Uzbekistan	e55.2	e29.9	e60.8	e53.5	e39.0	Ouzbékistan
Belgium-Luxembourg	221.8	–	–	–	–	Belgique-Luxembourg
Thailand	62.4	39.8	35.6	29.2	e30.8	Thaïlande
Austria	23.2	27.1	27.7	20.0	33.5	Autriche
Romania	17.9	6.3	37.9	41.6	25.7	Roumanie
Brazil	16.5	28.3	28.4	22.3	e23.1	Brésil
Honduras	35.9	29.8	47.5	0.2	0.0	Honduras

(Value as percentages of World total) **(Valeur en pourcentage du total mondial)**

Regions of the world	1993	1994	1995	1996	1997	1998	1999	2000	2001	2002	Régions du monde
World	100.0	100.0	100.0	100.0	100.0	100.0	100.0	100.0	100.0	100.0	Monde
Africa	0.7	0.6	0.7	1.1	1.1	1.3	1.3	0.8	0.8	0.7	Afrique
Americas	24.6	24.8	24.9	25.3	23.4	23.6	24.6	23.4	21.0	20.8	Amériques
- Northern America	15.6	16.3	16.3	16.6	15.6	15.6	16.1	15.2	12.7	13.7	- Amérique du Nord
- LAIA	9.0	8.4	8.6	8.6	7.8	7.3	7.9	7.3	8.2	7.1	- ALAI
- CACM	0.0	0.0	0.0	0.0	0.0	0.8	0.6	0.9	0.0	0.0	- MCC
- Caribbean	0.0	0.0	0.0	0.0	0.0	0.0	0.0	0.0	0.0	0.0	- Caraïbes
- Rest of America	0.0	0.0	0.0	0.0	0.0	0.0	0.0	0.0	0.0	0.0	- Autre d'Amérique
Asia excluding former USSR	13.0	15.7	17.9	12.6	23.0	23.3	24.7	25.5	26.4	24.7	Asie ancienne URSS exclus
- Middle East	0.1	0.2	0.2	0.4	0.5	0.6	0.3	0.3	0.5	0.6	- Moyen-Orient
Asia former USSR	2.1	3.6	4.2	4.2	4.1	5.0	3.9	4.7	4.6	4.9	Asie ancienne URSS
Europe excluding former USSR	47.6	45.4	43.0	47.4	40.3	38.6	37.1	34.7	35.7	36.8	Europe ancienne URSS exclus
- European Union	38.1	36.7	33.9	39.1	31.6	30.2	28.9	26.2	26.6	28.0	- Union Européenne
- Eastern Europe	4.7	3.5	4.4	3.6	3.8	3.8	3.8	4.1	4.8	4.4	- Europe de l'Est
- Rest of Europe	4.8	5.2	4.7	4.7	4.8	4.7	4.5	4.5	4.4	4.4	- Autre de l'Europe
Europe former USSR	4.2	2.6	2.7	2.8	2.5	2.7	2.5	2.0	2.2	2.2	Europe ancienne URSS
Oceania	7.8	7.4	6.7	6.6	5.6	5.5	5.8	8.8	9.2	9.9	Océanie

687 Tin

TRADE BY COMMODITY (Value in million US dollars)
Imports by principal countries or areas

COMMERCE PAR PRODUIT (Valeur en millions de dollars EU)
Importations selon les principaux pays ou zones

Country or area	1998	1999	2000	2001	2002	Pays ou zone
World	1437.3	1401.3	1542.9	1283.1	1230.6	Monde
Africa	23.8	17.9	23.2	20.2	18.0	Afrique
Americas	347.3	371.0	374.2	296.8	233.8	Amériques
- Northern America	290.7	311.2	305.9	246.5	192.2	- Amérique du Nord
- LAIA	50.1	53.1	63.7	44.3	36.6	- ALAI
- CACM	0.8	0.7	0.7	0.7	0.6	- MCC
- Caribbean	5.5	5.9	3.9	4.8	4.3	- Caraïbes
- Rest of America	0.0	0.1	0.1	0.4	0.1	- Autre d'Amérique
Asia excluding former USSR	540.5	566.2	672.7	527.2	585.8	Asie ancienne URSS exclus
- Middle East	21.9	18.8	31.4	22.6	20.7	- Moyen-Orient
Asia former USSR	7.0	6.8	11.7	10.0	10.3	Asie ancienne URSS
Europe excluding former USSR	496.2	419.1	442.2	412.2	365.3	Europe ancienne URSS exclus
- European Union	458.1	384.1	402.6	374.7	328.1	- Union Européenne
- Eastern Europe	24.5	23.6	27.4	24.6	25.5	- Europe de l'Est
- Rest of Europe	13.6	11.4	12.2	12.9	11.6	- Autre de l'Europe
Europe former USSR	2.5	4.5	7.6	6.2	7.1	Europe ancienne URSS
Oceania	20.0	15.9	11.4	10.6	10.2	Océanie
United States	263.0	282.4	276.6	226.2	174.0	Etats-Unis d'Amérique
Japan	143.7	154.6	172.8	112.4	110.8	Japon
Germany	136.7	111.5	126.5	131.1	93.7	Allemagne
Korea, Republic of	71.6	72.5	92.1	66.3	75.2	République de Corée
China	54.1	62.9	76.1	79.7	96.6	Chine
China, Hong Kong SAR	100.5	70.3	87.2	55.9	51.0	Chine - RAS de Hong-Kong
Singapore	19.4	39.6	56.9	70.1	99.9	Singapour
United Kingdom	60.2	57.9	62.6	52.1	42.7	Royaume-Uni
France-Monaco	58.0	47.7	50.1	44.1	39.1	France-Monaco
Netherlands	79.7	54.8	36.8	27.8	38.6	Pays-Bas
Italy-San Marino-Holy See	45.6	38.9	42.0	37.1	33.4	Italie-Saint-Marin-Saint-Siège
Malaysia	32.2	34.1	37.3	31.0	e33.9	Malaisie
Spain	28.9	25.9	35.3	36.1	33.9	Espagne
Mexico	28.4	33.2	43.2	28.3	25.0	Mexique
Canada	27.7	28.8	29.3	20.3	18.2	Canada
India	17.9	18.8	20.6	18.0	16.1	Inde
Belgium	–	14.0	15.1	15.9	e17.4	Belgique
Australia	14.3	13.5	9.4	9.6	9.1	Australie
Turkey	9.0	8.3	11.4	6.5	8.2	Turquie
Kazakhstan	6.6	6.6	11.3	9.3	e9.5	Kazakhstan
Poland	7.7	6.8	8.5	6.5	7.8	Pologne
Portugal	8.0	7.0	8.8	6.7	6.1	Portugal
Austria	6.3	7.6	8.0	6.9	6.9	Autriche
United Arab Emirates	4.1	4.3	11.7	6.4	e6.5	Emirates arabes unis
South Africa	–	–	10.7	9.7	8.5	Afrique du Sud
Switzerland-Liechtenstein	6.3	5.6	6.0	6.0	4.8	Suisse-Liechtenstein
Sweden	6.2	5.5	7.3	5.0	4.5	Suède
Argentina	7.7	6.8	6.3	4.9	e2.2	Argentine
Hungary	4.4	5.4	6.7	4.9	4.6	Hongrie
Indonesia	0.6	5.1	4.8	1.9	12.0	Indonésie

(Value as percentages of World total)

(Valeur en pourcentage du total mondial)

Regions of the world	1993	1994	1995	1996	1997	1998	1999	2000	2001	2002	Régions du monde
World	100.0	100.0	100.0	100.0	100.0	100.0	100.0	100.0	100.0	100.0	Monde
Africa	1.9	1.6	1.6	1.5	1.5	1.7	1.3	1.5	1.6	1.5	Afrique
Americas	20.4	22.3	22.9	22.4	22.8	24.2	26.5	24.3	23.1	19.0	Amériques
- Northern America	17.9	19.6	20.2	19.8	19.8	20.2	22.2	19.8	19.2	15.6	- Amérique du Nord
- LAIA	1.7	2.2	2.3	2.3	2.6	3.5	3.8	4.1	3.5	3.0	- ALAI
- CACM	0.1	0.1	0.0	0.0	0.1	0.1	0.1	0.0	0.1	0.0	- MCC
- Caribbean	0.6	0.5	0.4	0.3	0.4	0.4	0.4	0.3	0.4	0.3	- Caraïbes
- Rest of America	0.0	0.0	0.0	0.0	0.0	0.0	0.0	0.0	0.0	0.0	- Autre d'Amérique
Asia excluding former USSR	39.9	39.0	39.7	40.1	39.2	37.6	40.4	43.6	41.1	47.6	Asie ancienne URSS exclus
- Middle East	1.2	1.8	1.4	1.8	1.6	1.5	1.3	2.0	1.8	1.7	- Moyen-Orient
Asia former USSR	0.0	0.3	0.6	0.6	0.6	0.5	0.5	0.8	0.8	0.8	Asie ancienne URSS
Europe excluding former USSR	30.8	35.0	33.8	34.1	34.4	34.5	29.9	28.7	32.1	29.7	Europe ancienne URSS exclus
- European Union	28.5	32.5	31.1	31.3	31.5	31.9	27.4	26.1	29.2	26.7	- Union Européenne
- Eastern Europe	1.3	1.5	1.7	1.9	2.0	1.7	1.7	1.8	1.9	2.1	- Europe de l'Est
- Rest of Europe	1.0	1.0	1.0	0.9	0.9	0.9	0.8	0.8	1.0	0.9	- Autre de l'Europe
Europe former USSR	6.3	0.7	0.3	0.3	0.3	0.2	0.3	0.5	0.5	0.6	Europe ancienne URSS
Oceania	0.8	1.1	1.0	1.1	1.3	1.4	1.1	0.7	0.8	0.8	Océanie

TRADE BY COMMODITY (Value in million US dollars)
Exports by principal countries or areas

COMMERCE PAR PRODUIT (Valeur en millions de dollars EU)
Exportations selon les principaux pays ou zones

Country or area	1998	1999	2000	2001	2002	Pays ou zone
World	1602.9	1563.3	1734.7	1310.2	1236.8	Monde
Africa	0.7	0.6	0.6	0.6	0.8	Afrique
Americas	208.6	198.7	306.1	138.9	135.3	Amériques
- Northern America	77.5	85.1	82.9	54.5	46.1	- Amérique du Nord
- LAIA	131.0	113.5	223.1	84.3	89.1	- ALAI
- CACM	0.0	0.0	0.0	0.0	0.0	- MCC
- Caribbean	0.1	0.1	0.1	0.1	0.1	- Caraïbes
- Rest of America	0.0	0.0	0.0	0.0	0.0	- Autre d'Amérique
Asia excluding former USSR	1178.8	1169.5	1250.5	1019.4	928.2	Asie ancienne URSS exclus
- Middle East	2.2	2.1	7.8	4.1	4.3	- Moyen-Orient
Asia former USSR	0.2	0.0	0.0	0.1	0.0	Asie ancienne URSS
Europe excluding former USSR	189.5	167.0	148.6	125.8	148.9	Europe ancienne URSS exclus
- European Union	187.0	164.8	146.5	124.1	146.5	- Union Européenne
- Eastern Europe	1.1	1.2	1.2	1.0	1.9	- Europe de l'Est
- Rest of Europe	1.4	1.0	0.9	0.6	0.5	- Autre de l'Europe
Europe former USSR	13.0	5.1	16.6	16.2	13.5	Europe ancienne URSS
Oceania	12.1	22.3	12.3	9.2	10.1	Océanie
China	301.9	357.7	467.5	295.8	159.3	Chine
Indonesia	280.6	246.2	232.4	190.5	223.0	Indonésie
Singapore	230.3	229.2	193.3	196.4	190.4	Singapour
Malaysia	148.0	150.3	135.9	138.3	e146.6	Malaisie
Thailand	61.4	65.9	69.9	82.4	e87.0	Thaïlande
United States	69.5	78.8	75.8	51.0	42.9	Etats-Unis d'Amérique
Bolivia	58.2	63.4	66.2	51.1	e49.1	Bolivie
China, Hong Kong SAR	75.9	50.6	64.2	50.5	36.9	Chine - RAS de Hong-Kong
Peru	36.2	17.8	119.1	6.8	12.7	Pérou
Belgium	–	41.7	48.2	40.8	e45.8	Belgique
Netherlands	53.4	49.9	28.7	11.5	27.3	Pays-Bas
Brazil	35.9	31.7	37.3	25.9	e26.9	Brésil
Germany	26.2	29.5	26.9	29.4	26.0	Allemagne
Japan	14.3	22.8	28.8	22.3	30.5	Japon
United Kingdom	27.0	16.8	18.2	15.0	12.9	Royaume-Uni
France-Monaco	16.5	14.7	11.3	17.0	16.2	France-Monaco
Australia	12.0	22.3	12.3	9.2	9.8	Australie
Viet Nam	12.4	11.9	9.5	9.9	11.0	Viet Nam
Russian Federation	12.8	5.1	12.2	9.9	9.1	Fédération de Russie
Belgium-Luxembourg	45.2	–	–	–	–	Belgique-Luxembourg
India	4.0	6.7	14.3	4.9	10.5	Inde
Korea, Republic of	23.1	4.2	3.9	3.5	5.4	République de Corée
Canada	8.0	6.3	7.1	3.6	3.2	Canada
Spain	9.2	4.0	4.4	1.7	1.7	Espagne
United Arab Emirates	1.9	2.0	7.6	3.8	e4.0	Emirates arabes unis
Italy-San Marino-Holy See	4.2	1.9	2.8	3.5	4.9	Italie-Saint-Marin-Saint-Siège
Ireland	0.3	1.9	0.6	1.8	7.7	Irlande
Sweden	2.9	2.4	3.0	1.8	1.7	Suède
Philippines	5.1	1.8	1.0	1.3	1.6	Philippines
Latvia		0.0	2.8	4.2	2.0	Lettonie

(Value as percentages of World total) **(Valeur en pourcentage du total mondial)**

Regions of the world	1993	1994	1995	1996	1997	1998	1999	2000	2001	2002	Régions du monde
World	100.0	100.0	100.0	100.0	100.0	100.0	100.0	100.0	100.0	100.0	Monde
Africa	0.3	0.2	0.1	0.1	0.1	0.0	0.0	0.0	0.0	0.1	Afrique
Americas	23.4	21.6	16.5	17.4	17.8	13.0	12.7	17.6	10.6	10.9	Amériques
- Northern America	6.3	5.8	5.7	5.8	4.7	4.8	5.4	4.8	4.2	3.7	- Amérique du Nord
- LAIA	17.1	15.7	10.7	11.6	13.0	8.2	7.3	12.9	6.4	7.2	- ALAI
- CACM	0.0	0.0	0.0	0.0	0.0	0.0	0.0	0.0	0.0	0.0	- MCC
- Caribbean	0.0	0.0	0.0	0.0	0.0	0.0	0.0	0.0	0.0	0.0	- Caraïbes
- Rest of America	0.0	0.0	0.0	0.0	0.0	0.0	0.0	0.0	0.0	0.0	- Autre d'Amérique
Asia excluding former USSR	66.0	66.1	69.0	69.4	69.9	73.5	74.8	72.1	77.8	75.0	Asie ancienne URSS exclus
- Middle East	0.3	0.4	0.5	0.4	0.4	0.1	0.1	0.5	0.3	0.4	- Moyen-Orient
Asia former USSR	0.1	0.0	0.0	0.0	0.0	0.0	0.0	0.0	0.0	0.0	Asie ancienne URSS
Europe excluding former USSR	8.4	8.5	10.7	8.9	8.8	11.8	10.7	8.6	9.6	12.0	Europe ancienne URSS exclus
- European Union	8.2	8.2	9.5	8.5	8.0	11.7	10.5	8.4	9.5	11.8	- Union Européenne
- Eastern Europe	0.1	0.1	1.1	0.3	0.8	0.1	0.1	0.1	0.1	0.2	- Europe de l'Est
- Rest of Europe	0.1	0.2	0.1	0.1	0.1	0.1	0.1	0.1	0.0	0.0	- Autre de l'Europe
Europe former USSR	1.5	3.4	3.2	3.4	2.6	0.8	0.3	1.0	1.2	1.1	Europe ancienne URSS
Oceania	0.2	0.3	0.4	0.7	0.9	0.8	1.4	0.7	0.7	0.8	Océanie

689 Miscellaneous non-ferrous base metals, employed in metallurgy

TRADE BY COMMODITY (Value in million US dollars)
Imports by principal countries or areas

COMMERCE PAR PRODUIT (Valeur en millions de dollars EU)
Importations selon les principaux pays ou zones

Country or area	1998	1999	2000	2001	2002	Pays ou zone
World	4183.2	3665.8	4073.2	4005.9	3210.4	Monde
Africa	9.1	13.0	15.8	16.8	16.4	Afrique
Americas	1329.1	1072.2	1136.7	1130.2	816.1	Amériques
- Northern America	1203.5	1007.9	1059.0	1053.3	743.7	- Amérique du Nord
- LAIA	124.5	63.4	76.8	76.2	71.6	- ALAI
- CACM	0.2	0.2	0.4	0.1	0.2	- MCC
- Caribbean	0.9	0.7	0.5	0.6	0.6	- Caraïbes
- Rest of America	0.0	0.0	0.0	0.0	0.0	- Autre d'Amérique
Asia excluding former USSR	1011.2	980.8	1287.3	1128.8	950.3	Asie ancienne URSS exclus
- Middle East	28.1	30.4	29.1	23.7	27.1	- Moyen-Orient
Asia former USSR	7.3	1.6	2.9	5.8	5.6	Asie ancienne URSS
Europe excluding former USSR	1759.5	1539.9	1580.8	1667.6	1365.6	Europe ancienne URSS exclus
- European Union	1583.3	1374.9	1385.4	1467.7	1140.6	- Union Européenne
- Eastern Europe	78.6	72.1	104.3	114.3	124.2	- Europe de l'Est
- Rest of Europe	97.6	92.9	91.0	85.6	100.8	- Autre de l'Europe
Europe former USSR	32.8	33.0	28.1	34.4	38.9	Europe ancienne URSS
Oceania	34.2	25.2	21.6	22.1	17.4	Océanie
United States	1058.1	868.6	894.7	939.2	647.0	Etats-Unis d'Amérique
Japan	632.1	501.1	640.1	579.3	434.2	Japon
United Kingdom	464.9	398.9	411.6	453.0	293.2	Royaume-Uni
Germany	399.0	367.3	383.1	401.5	319.6	Allemagne
France-Monaco	173.3	134.5	136.8	131.3	103.1	France-Monaco
Canada	145.4	139.3	164.3	114.1	96.6	Canada
Korea, Republic of	81.4	105.1	126.4	115.9	117.0	République de Corée
Netherlands	118.2	143.4	101.0	94.4	77.1	Pays-Bas
Italy-San Marino-Holy See	123.9	117.0	94.8	91.3	96.0	Italie-Saint-Marin-Saint-Siège
China	40.7	65.8	91.8	103.9	110.2	Chine
Czech Republic	60.3	57.5	85.7	92.6	109.3	République tchèque
Israel	42.9	54.9	74.6	94.6	63.0	Israël
China, Hong Kong SAR	47.1	57.2	130.2	40.5	28.4	Chine - RAS de Hong-Kong
Belgium	–	66.6	69.8	75.5	e82.8	Belgique
Sweden	70.1	53.3	53.9	65.6	35.0	Suède
Norway	50.5	50.4	42.8	37.1	54.9	Norvège
Mexico	77.0	25.1	33.5	31.1	34.6	Mexique
Austria	33.3	29.4	37.2	42.6	36.2	Autriche
Brazil	34.0	28.7	32.3	34.1	29.1	Brésil
Spain	36.7	30.1	31.5	31.0	22.8	Espagne
Switzerland-Liechtenstein	33.3	28.4	29.9	31.3	27.1	Suisse-Liechtenstein
Finland	65.3	6.7	11.6	27.6	23.7	Finlande
India	28.5	22.9	24.4	29.1	29.7	Inde
Singapore	11.9	22.3	32.1	26.7	19.7	Singapour
Australia	32.6	23.2	19.9	20.3	15.6	Australie
Russian Federation	23.0	20.3	14.8	21.5	26.3	Fédération de Russie
Malaysia	21.1	27.2	24.8	14.9	e16.3	Malaisie
Portugal	4.5	5.1	26.9	27.5	24.1	Portugal
Belgium-Luxembourg	74.3	–	–	–	–	Belgique-Luxembourg
Thailand	9.4	13.0	18.6	15.3	e15.9	Thaïlande

(Value as percentages of World total) **(Valeur en pourcentage du total mondial)**

Regions of the world	1993	1994	1995	1996	1997	1998	1999	2000	2001	2002	Régions du monde
World	100.0	100.0	100.0	100.0	100.0	100.0	100.0	100.0	100.0	100.0	Monde
Africa	0.4	0.6	0.5	0.4	0.4	0.2	0.4	0.4	0.4	0.5	Afrique
Americas	28.1	27.3	27.0	31.1	32.7	31.8	29.2	27.9	28.2	25.4	Amériques
- Northern America	25.8	25.4	25.2	29.4	30.9	28.8	27.5	26.0	26.3	23.2	- Amérique du Nord
- LAIA	2.2	1.8	1.8	1.7	1.8	3.0	1.7	1.9	1.9	2.2	- ALAI
- CACM	0.0	0.0	0.0	0.0	0.0	0.0	0.0	0.0	0.0	0.0	- MCC
- Caribbean	0.0	0.0	0.0	0.0	0.0	0.0	0.0	0.0	0.0	0.0	- Caraïbes
- Rest of America	0.0	0.0	0.0	0.0	0.0	0.0	0.0	0.0	0.0	0.0	- Autre d'Amérique
Asia excluding former USSR	28.5	29.4	29.5	28.2	26.7	24.2	26.8	31.6	28.2	29.6	Asie ancienne URSS exclus
- Middle East	1.2	0.4	0.5	0.4	0.7	0.7	0.8	0.7	0.6	0.8	- Moyen-Orient
Asia former USSR	0.1	0.0	0.0	0.1	0.1	0.2	0.0	0.1	0.1	0.2	Asie ancienne URSS
Europe excluding former USSR	41.0	41.1	41.3	38.7	38.5	42.1	42.0	38.8	41.6	42.5	Europe ancienne URSS exclus
- European Union	37.7	37.8	36.4	34.0	34.3	37.8	37.5	34.0	36.6	35.5	- Union Européenne
- Eastern Europe	0.8	0.7	2.2	2.1	2.3	1.9	2.0	2.6	2.9	3.9	- Europe de l'Est
- Rest of Europe	2.5	2.7	2.8	2.5	2.0	2.3	2.5	2.2	2.1	3.1	- Autre de l'Europe
Europe former USSR	0.9	0.6	0.7	0.6	0.7	0.8	0.9	0.7	0.9	1.2	Europe ancienne URSS
Oceania	1.1	0.9	1.0	0.9	0.8	0.8	0.7	0.5	0.6	0.5	Océanie

Autres métaux communs non ferreux utilisés en métallurgie, et cermets 689

TRADE BY COMMODITY (Value in million US dollars)
Exports by principal countries or areas

COMMERCE PAR PRODUIT (Valeur en millions de dollars EU)
Exportations selon les principaux pays ou zones

Country or area	1998	1999	2000	2001	2002	Pays ou zone
World	3574.7	3383.7	3824.8	3727.3	3019.7	Monde
Africa	239.0	269.0	208.2	170.7	149.7	Afrique
Americas	919.8	745.7	796.2	738.4	679.3	Amériques
- Northern America	890.1	713.3	755.2	703.0	638.0	- Amérique du Nord
- LAIA	29.5	32.3	40.9	35.3	41.2	- ALAI
- CACM	0.1	0.0	0.0	0.0	0.1	- MCC
- Caribbean	0.1	0.0	0.1	0.0	0.0	- Caraïbes
- Rest of America	0.0	0.0	0.0	0.0	0.0	- Autre d'Amérique
Asia excluding former USSR	762.3	877.0	1111.3	1105.1	816.3	Asie ancienne URSS exclus
- Middle East	2.6	3.5	0.9	1.6	1.2	- Moyen-Orient
Asia former USSR	130.4	84.4	50.6	92.4	99.7	Asie ancienne URSS
Europe excluding former USSR	1105.4	1063.1	1235.2	1232.3	1008.4	Europe ancienne URSS exclus
- European Union	899.0	887.1	1081.6	1083.1	873.3	- Union Européenne
- Eastern Europe	6.6	9.0	19.2	35.8	39.8	- Europe de l'Est
- Rest of Europe	199.8	167.0	134.4	113.5	95.3	- Autre de l'Europe
Europe former USSR	365.2	294.6	347.8	311.2	226.2	Europe ancienne URSS
Oceania	52.5	50.0	75.6	77.1	40.1	Océanie
China	393.9	440.2	469.1	529.5	453.1	Chine
United States	417.8	359.8	461.1	467.7	377.1	Etats-Unis d'Amérique
Canada	472.2	353.4	294.0	235.3	260.8	Canada
Russian Federation	337.4	259.6	295.3	260.9	172.4	Fédération de Russie
Germany	210.4	216.9	292.9	321.4	245.6	Allemagne
United Kingdom	262.7	220.6	257.8	260.3	211.4	Royaume-Uni
Japan	190.6	203.1	273.0	289.1	152.1	Japon
Finland	93.7	115.2	135.7	122.4	102.1	Finlande
Norway	168.3	136.1	101.3	74.3	63.0	Norvège
France-Monaco	123.6	97.9	123.8	119.3	68.7	France-Monaco
Netherlands	93.9	102.5	115.0	96.5	60.4	Pays-Bas
Kazakhstan	108.6	75.4	41.5	82.7	e93.1	Kazakhstan
Zambia	57.3	107.3	45.2	98.5	83.0	Zambie
Israel	59.3	76.9	76.2	71.8	61.3	Israël
China, Hong Kong SAR	53.1	66.2	136.5	42.2	29.5	Chine - RAS de Hong-Kong
Australia	52.3	49.9	74.0	77.0	40.1	Australie
Ukraine	26.0	30.2	47.2	44.7	49.3	Ukraine
Philippines	16.8	28.0	43.1	73.4	30.0	Philippines
Belgium	–	41.6	40.5	50.0	e56.1	Belgique
Southern African Customs Union	90.1	85.9	–	–	–	Union douanière d'Afrique australe
Thailand	9.6	20.3	54.7	35.1	e37.0	Thaïlande
Congo	e24.9	e24.9	e65.9	e22.6	e8.7	Congo
Switzerland-Liechtenstein	21.9	24.6	27.9	32.1	24.4	Suisse-Liechtenstein
Austria	13.7	14.5	28.3	29.0	45.4	Autriche
Democratic Republic of the Congo	e48.0	e26.1	e19.7	e15.1	e11.3	République démocratique du Congo
Morocco	8.9	13.9	35.1	25.9	e28.2	Maroc
Sweden	23.2	23.1	27.7	18.2	13.7	Suède
Luxembourg	–	20.3	25.1	23.1	e23.6	Luxembourg
Italy-San Marino-Holy See	18.3	17.1	12.3	17.8	25.2	Italie-Saint-Marin-Saint-Siège
Czech Republic	3.2	5.5	13.3	30.1	36.2	République tchèque

(Value as percentages of World total) **(Valeur en pourcentage du total mondial)**

Regions of the world	1993	1994	1995	1996	1997	1998	1999	2000	2001	2002	Régions du monde
World	100.0	100.0	100.0	100.0	100.0	100.0	100.0	100.0	100.0	100.0	Monde
Africa	10.9	5.3	4.2	4.0	4.1	6.7	8.0	5.4	4.6	5.0	Afrique
Americas	22.4	22.3	23.6	25.7	25.3	25.7	22.0	20.8	19.8	22.5	Amériques
- Northern America	21.2	21.0	22.6	24.8	24.4	24.9	21.1	19.7	18.9	21.1	- Amérique du Nord
- LAIA	1.1	1.3	1.1	0.9	1.0	0.8	1.0	1.1	0.9	1.4	- ALAI
- CACM	0.0	0.0	0.0	0.0	0.0	0.0	0.0	0.0	0.0	0.0	- MCC
- Caribbean	0.0	0.0	0.0	0.0	0.0	0.0	0.0	0.0	0.0	0.0	- Caraïbes
- Rest of America	0.0	0.0	0.0	0.0	0.0	0.0	0.0	0.0	0.0	0.0	- Autre d'Amérique
Asia excluding former USSR	16.8	20.8	23.0	19.5	22.2	21.3	25.9	29.1	29.6	27.0	Asie ancienne URSS exclus
- Middle East	0.1	0.1	0.1	0.1	0.1	0.1	0.1	0.0	0.0	0.0	- Moyen-Orient
Asia former USSR	1.2	2.0	2.6	3.0	3.3	3.6	2.5	1.3	2.5	3.3	Asie ancienne URSS
Europe excluding former USSR	34.3	37.2	35.1	35.3	30.7	30.9	31.4	32.3	33.1	33.4	Europe ancienne URSS exclus
- European Union	26.2	30.4	26.8	29.5	25.8	25.1	26.2	28.3	29.1	28.9	- Union Européenne
- Eastern Europe	0.2	0.4	2.1	0.2	0.1	0.2	0.3	0.5	1.0	1.3	- Europe de l'Est
- Rest of Europe	7.8	6.4	6.2	5.5	4.8	5.6	4.9	3.5	3.0	3.2	- Autre de l'Europe
Europe former USSR	14.2	12.3	11.2	12.3	13.9	10.2	8.7	9.1	8.3	7.5	Europe ancienne URSS
Oceania	0.2	0.1	0.1	0.3	0.6	1.5	1.5	2.0	2.1	1.3	Océanie

691 Structures and parts, nes, of iron, steel or aluminium

TRADE BY COMMODITY (Value in million US dollars)
Imports by principal countries or areas

COMMERCE PAR PRODUIT (Valeur en millions de dollars EU)
Importations selon les principaux pays ou zones

Country or area	1998	1999	2000	2001	2002	Pays ou zone
World	13261.0	13208.8	12351.1	12812.9	13742.8	Monde
Africa	546.8	726.7	510.9	530.3	577.6	Afrique
Americas	1891.9	2144.9	2473.1	2575.8	2651.1	Amériques
- Northern America	1167.3	1425.6	1769.9	1984.6	2126.2	- Amérique du Nord
- LAIA	477.0	483.7	445.9	336.8	288.7	- ALAI
- CACM	61.1	71.6	75.3	74.9	55.6	- MCC
- Caribbean	158.2	142.4	162.3	161.8	160.3	- Caraïbes
- Rest of America	28.2	21.6	19.8	17.6	20.3	- Autre d'Amérique
Asia excluding former USSR	3222.9	2622.2	2386.8	2516.1	2579.1	Asie ancienne URSS exclus
- Middle East	760.8	561.1	599.6	611.2	593.9	- Moyen-Orient
Asia former USSR	110.1	195.2	87.5	90.4	113.4	Asie ancienne URSS
Europe excluding former USSR	6973.7	7168.5	6558.1	6706.9	7299.5	Europe ancienne URSS exclus
- European Union	5168.2	5562.7	5184.5	5232.8	5613.7	- Union Européenne
- Eastern Europe	621.7	569.3	540.1	562.3	648.9	- Europe de l'Est
- Rest of Europe	1183.8	1036.5	833.5	911.7	1037.0	- Autre de l'Europe
Europe former USSR	346.0	206.3	206.8	284.7	402.4	Europe ancienne URSS
Oceania	169.6	145.0	128.0	108.6	119.8	Océanie
Germany	1609.6	1694.8	1424.6	1447.3	1382.7	Allemagne
United States	926.4	1161.1	1499.9	1717.3	1830.5	Etats-Unis d'Amérique
France-Monaco	635.8	665.6	724.8	689.0	788.9	France-Monaco
United Kingdom	491.5	497.5	504.9	474.6	630.2	Royaume-Uni
Japan	373.8	369.6	436.2	541.9	594.3	Japon
Switzerland-Liechtenstein	430.3	426.0	417.7	439.4	476.1	Suisse-Liechtenstein
Austria	443.0	435.7	394.0	428.5	434.0	Autriche
Netherlands	403.3	407.0	381.3	377.1	413.7	Pays-Bas
Norway	581.8	419.8	239.7	272.8	322.0	Norvège
Belgium	–	430.6	372.4	386.0	e423.3	Belgique
China, Hong Kong SAR	403.4	270.1	284.6	289.9	326.2	Chine - RAS de Hong-Kong
Denmark	235.3	266.5	258.5	271.9	279.6	Danemark
Canada	230.6	252.6	264.2	259.5	284.8	Canada
Italy-San Marino-Holy See	193.9	244.1	243.0	256.8	289.2	Italie-Saint-Marin-Saint-Siège
Spain	203.9	253.7	213.6	257.4	289.3	Espagne
Poland	268.8	253.7	215.0	192.0	208.1	Pologne
Singapore	272.6	253.0	237.9	199.8	157.0	Singapour
China	342.7	168.9	148.7	164.0	181.7	Chine
Korea, Republic of	169.8	309.3	142.7	138.7	172.0	République de Corée
Sweden	191.5	196.2	135.3	131.1	134.9	Suède
Ireland	124.5	147.9	155.1	155.8	181.2	Irlande
Russian Federation	230.7	123.2	77.5	116.0	169.8	Fédération de Russie
United Arab Emirates	100.7	105.5	164.7	160.8	e165.0	Emirates arabes unis
Mexico	106.8	143.0	168.4	147.6	127.7	Mexique
Czech Republic	132.5	115.0	118.4	125.1	143.4	République tchèque
Turkey	89.3	116.0	97.7	163.3	136.2	Turquie
Portugal	102.2	103.2	108.5	125.0	126.7	Portugal
Philippines	136.8	80.7	96.9	134.1	98.4	Philippines
Hungary	95.8	99.1	97.6	104.9	128.9	Hongrie
Saudi Arabia	95.0	125.8	108.6	77.5	e80.2	Arabie saoudite

(Value as percentages of World total) **(Valeur en pourcentage du total mondial)**

Regions of the world	1993	1994	1995	1996	1997	1998	1999	2000	2001	2002	Régions du monde
World	100.0	100.0	100.0	100.0	100.0	100.0	100.0	100.0	100.0	100.0	Monde
Africa	4.9	3.9	4.2	3.6	5.2	4.1	5.5	4.1	4.1	4.2	Afrique
Americas	8.8	9.3	9.1	10.3	11.7	14.3	16.2	20.0	20.1	19.3	Amériques
- Northern America	4.3	4.6	5.2	6.0	7.0	8.8	10.8	14.3	15.5	15.5	- Amérique du Nord
- LAIA	2.8	2.9	2.2	2.5	3.0	3.6	3.7	3.6	2.6	2.1	- ALAI
- CACM	0.2	0.3	0.3	0.2	0.3	0.5	0.5	0.6	0.6	0.4	- MCC
- Caribbean	1.1	1.1	1.2	1.3	1.2	1.2	1.1	1.3	1.3	1.2	- Caraïbes
- Rest of America	0.4	0.4	0.2	0.1	0.1	0.2	0.2	0.2	0.1	0.1	- Autre d'Amérique
Asia excluding former USSR	29.4	28.0	26.1	28.0	30.4	24.3	19.9	19.3	19.6	18.8	Asie ancienne URSS exclus
- Middle East	7.5	5.7	5.1	4.7	4.8	5.7	4.2	4.9	4.8	4.3	- Moyen-Orient
Asia former USSR	0.2	0.6	0.3	0.7	0.5	0.8	1.5	0.7	0.7	0.8	Asie ancienne URSS
Europe excluding former USSR	53.1	55.5	56.9	53.9	48.1	52.6	54.3	53.1	52.3	53.1	Europe ancienne URSS exclus
- European Union	44.3	43.2	44.8	43.3	37.9	39.0	42.1	42.0	40.8	40.8	- Union Européenne
- Eastern Europe	2.4	2.8	3.4	4.1	4.1	4.7	4.3	4.4	4.4	4.7	- Europe de l'Est
- Rest of Europe	6.4	9.5	8.7	6.6	6.1	8.9	7.8	6.7	7.1	7.5	- Autre de l'Europe
Europe former USSR	2.9	2.2	2.6	2.2	2.5	2.6	1.6	1.7	2.2	2.9	Europe ancienne URSS
Oceania	0.7	0.7	0.8	1.4	1.5	1.3	1.1	1.0	0.8	0.9	Océanie

TRADE BY COMMODITY (Value in million US dollars)
Exports by principal countries or areas

COMMERCE PAR PRODUIT (Valeur en millions de dollars EU)
Exportations selon les principaux pays ou zones

Country or area	1998	1999	2000	2001	2002	Pays ou zone
World	13422.7	13730.4	13431.3	13970.7	15190.5	Monde
Africa	122.1	159.7	186.7	139.5	162.1	Afrique
Americas	1803.0	1884.2	2179.0	2146.7	2184.1	Amériques
- Northern America	1476.7	1563.1	1759.4	1762.0	1769.1	- Amérique du Nord
- LAIA	291.2	295.8	374.3	357.0	391.9	- ALAI
- CACM	9.8	10.5	24.3	13.1	10.2	- MCC
- Caribbean	24.4	13.5	20.1	13.7	11.8	- Caraïbes
- Rest of America	1.0	1.3	0.9	0.9	1.1	- Autre d'Amérique
Asia excluding former USSR	2084.4	2233.3	2259.5	2395.0	2770.8	Asie ancienne URSS exclus
- Middle East	278.5	237.0	302.2	349.0	354.3	- Moyen-Orient
Asia former USSR	3.1	1.9	2.0	2.4	2.3	Asie ancienne URSS
Europe excluding former USSR	9201.1	9170.2	8352.3	8894.5	9542.9	Europe ancienne URSS exclus
- European Union	7855.0	7821.4	6933.9	7339.0	7810.9	- Union Européenne
- Eastern Europe	898.3	920.1	970.5	1125.9	1281.2	- Europe de l'Est
- Rest of Europe	447.8	428.7	447.9	429.6	450.8	- Autre de l'Europe
Europe former USSR	132.3	205.9	396.6	346.1	470.3	Europe ancienne URSS
Oceania	76.7	75.3	55.0	46.4	58.1	Océanie
Germany	2210.6	2181.2	2046.5	2246.1	2352.4	Allemagne
Canada	734.8	825.9	1038.8	1090.7	1130.2	Canada
Italy-San Marino-Holy See	932.3	954.7	835.2	861.5	913.7	Italie-Saint-Marin-Saint-Siège
China	550.6	573.0	702.1	899.5	1100.3	Chine
United States	741.9	737.2	720.6	671.3	638.8	Etats-Unis d'Amérique
Netherlands	605.3	771.8	614.6	611.3	693.5	Pays-Bas
United Kingdom	811.9	704.7	525.2	600.8	549.6	Royaume-Uni
France-Monaco	687.8	693.0	591.1	556.8	577.3	France-Monaco
Belgium	–	652.0	599.8	601.5	e674.9	Belgique
Austria	537.2	543.4	416.9	431.4	499.1	Autriche
Poland	385.7	382.8	415.3	514.9	609.2	Pologne
Korea, Republic of	334.1	553.2	442.5	355.9	501.4	République de Corée
Denmark	382.5	364.0	327.6	363.1	435.1	Danemark
Czech Republic	280.6	292.3	329.1	377.9	393.9	République tchèque
Sweden	320.9	302.9	292.8	287.2	335.0	Suède
Spain	281.8	264.1	280.5	299.0	289.6	Espagne
Finland	326.3	211.7	217.7	277.6	231.4	Finlande
Switzerland-Liechtenstein	257.5	226.3	207.3	202.7	224.5	Suisse-Liechtenstein
Mexico	139.9	182.8	247.9	233.2	259.7	Mexique
Japan	272.4	236.9	162.1	154.7	159.9	Japon
Russian Federation	40.1	120.1	275.8	163.7	225.2	Fédération de Russie
Thailand	96.1	116.3	129.5	165.7	e175.0	Thaïlande
Hungary	128.9	139.4	132.1	132.1	148.9	Hongrie
Turkey	128.2	97.6	102.0	137.8	173.0	Turquie
Malaysia	150.4	118.1	121.2	119.1	e126.3	Malaisie
Belgium-Luxembourg	594.1	–	–	–	–	Belgique-Luxembourg
Norway	93.9	105.1	142.1	112.7	95.1	Norvège
Estonia	65.5	58.5	81.2	122.0	168.7	Estonie
Ireland	86.5	73.4	76.6	71.5	117.2	Irlande
India	88.7	93.7	84.7	62.6	76.9	Inde

(Value as percentages of World total) **(Valeur en pourcentage du total mondial)**

Regions of the world	1993	1994	1995	1996	1997	1998	1999	2000	2001	2002	Régions du monde
World	100.0	100.0	100.0	100.0	100.0	100.0	100.0	100.0	100.0	100.0	Monde
Africa	0.6	0.7	0.9	1.0	1.0	0.9	1.2	1.4	1.0	1.1	Afrique
Americas	7.4	9.1	8.1	10.1	11.6	13.4	13.7	16.2	15.4	14.4	Amériques
- Northern America	6.3	7.6	6.8	8.8	10.0	11.0	11.4	13.1	12.6	11.6	- Amérique du Nord
- LAIA	1.0	1.3	1.2	1.2	1.4	2.2	2.2	2.8	2.6	2.6	- ALAI
- CACM	0.1	0.1	0.1	0.0	0.0	0.1	0.1	0.2	0.1	0.1	- MCC
- Caribbean	0.1	0.1	0.1	0.1	0.1	0.2	0.1	0.1	0.1	0.1	- Caraïbes
- Rest of America	0.0	0.0	0.0	0.0	0.0	0.0	0.0	0.0	0.0	0.0	- Autre d'Amérique
Asia excluding former USSR	21.8	18.4	21.4	16.2	17.9	15.5	16.3	16.8	17.1	18.2	Asie ancienne URSS exclus
- Middle East	1.5	2.1	2.2	1.7	1.8	2.1	1.7	2.3	2.5	2.3	- Moyen-Orient
Asia former USSR	0.0	0.0	0.1	0.1	0.0	0.0	0.0	0.0	0.0	0.0	Asie ancienne URSS
Europe excluding former USSR	68.5	69.6	67.7	70.6	67.8	68.5	66.8	62.2	63.7	62.8	Europe ancienne URSS exclus
- European Union	60.4	61.3	59.0	60.7	59.1	58.5	57.0	51.6	52.5	51.4	- Union Européenne
- Eastern Europe	3.9	4.9	5.5	6.5	5.7	6.7	6.7	7.2	8.1	8.4	- Europe de l'Est
- Rest of Europe	4.2	3.4	3.2	3.3	3.0	3.3	3.1	3.3	3.1	3.0	- Autre de l'Europe
Europe former USSR	0.4	0.6	0.6	0.7	0.8	1.0	1.5	3.0	2.5	3.1	Europe ancienne URSS
Oceania	1.3	1.7	1.2	1.4	0.9	0.6	0.5	0.4	0.3	0.4	Océanie

692 Metal containers for storage and transport

TRADE BY COMMODITY (Value in million US dollars)
Imports by principal countries or areas

COMMERCE PAR PRODUIT (Valeur en millions de dollars EU)
Importations selon les principaux pays ou zones

Country or area	1998	1999	2000	2001	2002	Pays ou zone
World	6697.9	6624.3	6454.2	6680.4	6948.9	Monde
Africa	294.0	288.7	275.1	293.4	300.5	Afrique
Americas	1474.1	1523.7	1489.5	1618.9	1495.0	Amériques
- Northern America	850.4	935.6	935.7	923.9	1001.5	- Amérique du Nord
- LAIA	434.7	421.2	383.8	509.8	321.5	- ALAI
- CACM	99.3	90.8	88.4	94.8	96.1	- MCC
- Caribbean	77.8	67.3	69.8	84.7	68.8	- Caraïbes
- Rest of America	11.8	8.9	11.9	5.6	7.1	- Autre d'Amérique
Asia excluding former USSR	1099.7	1039.4	1140.5	1129.2	1162.3	Asie ancienne URSS exclus
- Middle East	307.2	276.0	326.9	288.4	292.5	- Moyen-Orient
Asia former USSR	24.5	33.7	43.2	40.9	37.1	Asie ancienne URSS
Europe excluding former USSR	3521.2	3570.9	3306.0	3382.7	3680.8	Europe ancienne URSS exclus
- European Union	2935.7	3037.6	2801.1	2857.8	3027.3	- Union Européenne
- Eastern Europe	304.8	271.0	266.9	280.6	356.8	- Europe de l'Est
- Rest of Europe	280.7	262.2	238.0	244.3	296.6	- Autre de l'Europe
Europe former USSR	180.9	73.8	83.5	119.0	171.6	Europe ancienne URSS
Oceania	103.5	94.1	116.3	96.3	101.7	Océanie
United States	487.1	578.4	576.9	595.4	647.7	Etats-Unis d'Amérique
Germany	539.2	530.0	483.8	501.6	482.1	Allemagne
France-Monaco	418.3	396.0	400.7	396.4	450.1	France-Monaco
Netherlands	334.3	448.1	353.3	344.6	389.3	Pays-Bas
Canada	362.3	356.1	358.0	327.6	352.7	Canada
United Kingdom	347.7	362.5	310.2	286.8	329.6	Royaume-Uni
Belgium	–	348.5	338.5	379.2	e415.8	Belgique
Austria	207.4	232.2	248.0	257.3	177.8	Autriche
Spain	158.8	165.2	156.4	187.5	210.4	Espagne
Mexico	133.0	154.0	186.3	147.9	145.8	Mexique
Japan	123.4	129.5	160.0	145.6	157.4	Japon
Italy-San Marino-Holy See	119.3	129.7	113.0	113.3	126.4	Italie-Saint-Marin-Saint-Siège
Denmark	128.5	103.3	92.0	95.9	119.2	Danemark
Switzerland-Liechtenstein	106.8	102.9	90.5	96.6	109.1	Suisse-Liechtenstein
Korea, Republic of	89.3	88.9	100.8	100.2	119.1	République de Corée
Poland	97.8	83.7	95.4	83.2	110.0	Pologne
Chile	75.9	61.3	61.0	206.9	62.2	Chili
China, Hong Kong SAR	82.0	86.7	97.9	98.0	100.6	Chine - RAS de Hong-Kong
China	70.9	76.2	72.5	92.0	97.3	Chine
Ireland	83.8	86.5	78.2	71.1	71.2	Irlande
Belgium-Luxembourg	365.8	–	–	–	–	Belgique-Luxembourg
Russian Federation	119.0	38.8	38.4	61.6	105.5	Fédération de Russie
Sweden	68.2	70.2	67.7	70.5	75.0	Suède
Norway	77.0	69.0	57.0	58.4	79.3	Norvège
Portugal	64.4	70.3	63.8	60.9	79.9	Portugal
Hungary	69.5	63.3	54.0	59.6	81.3	Hongrie
Singapore	75.0	53.4	62.6	60.5	60.0	Singapour
Argentina	73.8	112.6	43.3	46.8	e20.7	Argentine
United Arab Emirates	36.3	38.0	97.3	54.9	e56.3	Emirates arabes unis
Malaysia	57.2	45.7	52.7	60.0	e65.6	Malaisie

(Value as percentages of World total) **(Valeur en pourcentage du total mondial)**

Regions of the world	1993	1994	1995	1996	1997	1998	1999	2000	2001	2002	Régions du monde
World	100.0	100.0	100.0	100.0	100.0	100.0	100.0	100.0	100.0	100.0	Monde
Africa	4.6	3.6	3.7	3.7	3.4	4.4	4.4	4.3	4.4	4.3	Afrique
Americas	18.2	18.7	19.4	18.7	21.2	22.0	23.0	23.1	24.2	21.5	Amériques
- Northern America	10.4	10.0	10.2	10.7	12.0	12.7	14.1	14.5	13.8	14.4	- Amérique du Nord
- LAIA	5.6	6.9	7.2	6.1	6.9	6.5	6.4	5.9	7.6	4.6	- ALAI
- CACM	0.8	0.8	0.9	0.8	1.1	1.5	1.4	1.4	1.4	1.4	- MCC
- Caribbean	1.1	0.9	0.9	1.0	1.1	1.2	1.0	1.1	1.3	1.0	- Caraïbes
- Rest of America	0.3	0.2	0.3	0.2	0.2	0.2	0.1	0.2	0.1	0.1	- Autre d'Amérique
Asia excluding former USSR	23.1	20.0	19.0	19.2	19.3	16.4	15.7	17.7	16.9	16.7	Asie ancienne URSS exclus
- Middle East	6.6	4.4	3.5	3.7	3.9	4.6	4.2	5.1	4.3	4.2	- Moyen-Orient
Asia former USSR	0.1	0.2	0.2	0.4	0.1	0.4	0.5	0.7	0.6	0.5	Asie ancienne URSS
Europe excluding former USSR	51.3	53.5	53.5	53.8	51.5	52.6	53.9	51.2	50.6	53.0	Europe ancienne URSS exclus
- European Union	44.3	46.0	45.6	45.6	43.5	43.8	45.9	43.4	42.8	43.6	- Union Européenne
- Eastern Europe	3.2	3.4	3.7	4.4	4.1	4.5	4.1	4.1	4.2	5.1	- Europe de l'Est
- Rest of Europe	3.7	4.2	4.2	3.8	3.9	4.2	4.0	3.7	3.7	4.3	- Autre de l'Europe
Europe former USSR	1.3	2.4	2.8	2.7	2.9	2.7	1.1	1.3	1.8	2.5	Europe ancienne URSS
Oceania	1.5	1.5	1.4	1.5	1.6	1.5	1.4	1.8	1.4	1.5	Océanie

TRADE BY COMMODITY (Value in million US dollars)
Exports by principal countries or areas

COMMERCE PAR PRODUIT (Valeur en millions de dollars EU)
Exportations selon les principaux pays ou zones

Country or area	1998	1999	2000	2001	2002	Pays ou zone
World	7264.5	6959.6	6768.7	6784.9	7136.0	Monde
Africa	80.7	84.0	47.4	52.1	46.4	Afrique
Americas	1424.4	1305.7	1351.0	1324.1	1352.9	Amériques
- Northern America	1092.9	1002.1	1024.9	1003.3	1001.7	- Amérique du Nord
- LAIA	268.7	252.9	269.7	276.7	310.3	- ALAI
- CACM	36.3	33.1	33.9	24.9	21.2	- MCC
- Caribbean	17.0	12.2	17.1	12.4	11.4	- Caraïbes
- Rest of America	9.5	5.3	5.4	6.8	8.3	- Autre d'Amérique
Asia excluding former USSR	955.4	978.3	1082.6	1049.3	1087.8	Asie ancienne URSS exclus
- Middle East	101.3	120.7	109.2	160.6	147.3	- Moyen-Orient
Asia former USSR	6.7	2.4	3.6	7.1	7.4	Asie ancienne URSS
Europe excluding former USSR	4674.3	4476.4	4153.4	4198.0	4473.8	Europe ancienne URSS exclus
- European Union	4092.8	3914.8	3565.1	3571.8	3812.8	- Union Européenne
- Eastern Europe	410.8	390.0	415.7	457.5	488.2	- Europe de l'Est
- Rest of Europe	170.7	171.5	172.6	168.8	172.9	- Autre de l'Europe
Europe former USSR	48.6	46.6	54.0	74.3	86.0	Europe ancienne URSS
Oceania	74.6	66.2	76.6	80.0	81.6	Océanie
Germany	921.6	870.5	740.4	761.5	812.6	Allemagne
United States	836.7	711.7	728.6	703.6	701.5	Etats-Unis d'Amérique
France-Monaco	582.1	582.5	496.4	467.0	558.5	France-Monaco
Italy-San Marino-Holy See	547.2	504.8	452.3	486.4	477.2	Italie-Saint-Marin-Saint-Siège
United Kingdom	523.1	472.2	450.0	410.9	409.1	Royaume-Uni
Netherlands	297.9	272.4	323.8	309.1	311.4	Pays-Bas
Spain	283.9	303.7	287.8	285.7	328.0	Espagne
Canada	256.2	290.4	296.2	299.7	300.2	Canada
Belgium	–	314.2	250.7	255.5	e286.7	Belgique
Korea, Republic of	245.4	209.7	192.0	132.8	136.1	République de Corée
China	133.9	134.1	156.9	177.5	242.1	Chine
Mexico	149.5	147.8	158.6	153.8	189.6	Mexique
Poland	141.8	136.2	147.1	167.0	186.9	Pologne
Czech Republic	154.6	138.7	150.2	159.9	167.9	République tchèque
Sweden	174.7	141.4	135.4	145.8	161.9	Suède
Austria	134.5	129.4	128.2	128.3	127.4	Autriche
Denmark	134.2	129.6	113.9	125.9	139.6	Danemark
China, Hong Kong SAR	117.2	110.2	120.2	122.9	99.6	Chine - RAS de Hong-Kong
Switzerland-Liechtenstein	101.6	106.2	110.6	107.5	112.0	Suisse-Liechtenstein
Portugal	97.8	97.0	104.1	107.6	127.7	Portugal
Japan	84.0	95.0	111.7	83.7	84.4	Japon
Indonesia	41.3	75.7	88.9	109.6	89.7	Indonésie
Thailand	69.2	69.7	113.0	65.4	e69.1	Thaïlande
Hungary	56.2	63.1	65.8	74.3	64.6	Hongrie
Malaysia	49.5	50.2	61.6	64.6	e68.5	Malaisie
Belgium-Luxembourg	288.9	–	–	–	–	Belgique-Luxembourg
Turkey	41.0	35.3	36.2	46.2	55.6	Turquie
Saudi Arabia	36.2	50.4	42.4	44.8	e40.4	Arabie saoudite
Brazil	44.2	42.9	40.2	33.5	e34.7	Brésil
Australia	35.8	30.1	40.9	43.4	40.3	Australie

(Value as percentages of World total) **(Valeur en pourcentage du total mondial)**

Regions of the world	1993	1994	1995	1996	1997	1998	1999	2000	2001	2002	Régions du monde
World	100.0	100.0	100.0	100.0	100.0	100.0	100.0	100.0	100.0	100.0	Monde
Africa	0.9	1.2	1.3	1.7	1.2	1.1	1.2	0.7	0.8	0.7	Afrique
Americas	18.5	17.4	17.8	18.0	20.3	19.6	18.8	20.0	19.5	19.0	Amériques
- Northern America	14.7	14.1	14.5	14.2	16.0	15.0	14.4	15.1	14.8	14.0	- Amérique du Nord
- LAIA	3.0	2.6	2.5	3.1	3.6	3.7	3.6	4.0	4.1	4.3	- ALAI
- CACM	0.3	0.3	0.3	0.3	0.4	0.5	0.5	0.5	0.4	0.3	- MCC
- Caribbean	0.3	0.3	0.3	0.2	0.2	0.2	0.2	0.3	0.2	0.2	- Caraïbes
- Rest of America	0.1	0.1	0.1	0.2	0.2	0.1	0.1	0.1	0.1	0.1	- Autre d'Amérique
Asia excluding former USSR	16.4	14.2	13.6	12.3	14.6	13.2	14.1	16.0	15.5	15.2	Asie ancienne URSS exclus
- Middle East	2.0	1.8	1.6	1.1	1.3	1.4	1.7	1.6	2.4	2.1	- Moyen-Orient
Asia former USSR	0.0	0.1	0.1	0.1	0.1	0.1	0.0	0.1	0.1	0.1	Asie ancienne URSS
Europe excluding former USSR	62.8	65.0	65.1	66.1	62.0	64.3	64.3	61.4	61.9	62.7	Europe ancienne URSS exclus
- European Union	56.6	59.3	58.6	59.0	54.8	56.3	56.3	52.7	52.6	53.4	- Union Européenne
- Eastern Europe	3.7	3.4	4.0	4.8	4.8	5.7	5.6	6.1	6.7	6.8	- Europe de l'Est
- Rest of Europe	2.5	2.2	2.4	2.3	2.5	2.4	2.5	2.6	2.5	2.4	- Autre de l'Europe
Europe former USSR	0.5	1.0	1.0	0.6	0.6	0.7	0.7	0.8	1.1	1.2	Europe ancienne URSS
Oceania	0.9	1.1	1.0	1.2	1.3	1.0	1.0	1.1	1.2	1.1	Océanie

693 Wire products (excluding insulated electrical wire); fencing grills

TRADE BY COMMODITY (Value in million US dollars)
Imports by principal countries or areas

COMMERCE PAR PRODUIT (Valeur en millions de dollars EU)
Importations selon les principaux pays ou zones

Country or area	1998	1999	2000	2001	2002	Pays ou zone
World	4713.8	4608.9	4677.2	4661.7	4764.8	Monde
Africa	187.3	188.3	179.7	183.9	191.3	Afrique
Americas	1357.9	1383.3	1451.2	1432.3	1338.6	Amériques
- Northern America	902.4	970.9	1025.9	1011.4	952.6	- Amérique du Nord
- LAIA	357.4	311.4	327.7	319.0	290.2	- ALAI
- CACM	35.5	43.6	40.9	42.7	39.7	- MCC
- Caribbean	49.4	47.4	46.3	48.4	42.2	- Caraïbes
- Rest of America	13.2	9.9	10.4	10.7	13.9	- Autre d'Amérique
Asia excluding former USSR	688.5	650.6	732.0	802.2	826.2	Asie ancienne URSS exclus
- Middle East	141.3	133.5	169.9	240.6	240.1	- Moyen-Orient
Asia former USSR	33.2	25.7	31.8	31.7	35.4	Asie ancienne URSS
Europe excluding former USSR	2289.4	2211.3	2111.0	2067.4	2224.2	Europe ancienne URSS exclus
- European Union	1941.4	1873.4	1755.8	1707.9	1814.0	- Union Européenne
- Eastern Europe	154.3	151.4	169.3	191.8	228.8	- Europe de l'Est
- Rest of Europe	193.6	186.5	186.0	167.7	181.4	- Autre de l'Europe
Europe former USSR	79.4	68.0	82.7	75.0	72.2	Europe ancienne URSS
Oceania	78.1	81.7	88.9	69.2	76.9	Océanie
United States	726.0	779.2	804.7	792.0	747.5	Etats-Unis d'Amérique
Germany	396.1	345.9	300.1	310.9	302.8	Allemagne
France-Monaco	315.8	345.7	329.8	286.0	307.0	France-Monaco
Canada	175.0	190.7	220.0	218.4	203.2	Canada
United Kingdom	257.0	209.1	176.5	167.0	191.1	Royaume-Uni
Spain	148.9	172.4	166.4	171.0	205.9	Espagne
Italy-San Marino-Holy See	150.7	151.5	143.8	147.6	154.5	Italie-Saint-Marin-Saint-Siège
Mexico	122.2	117.4	160.8	144.1	115.9	Mexique
Belgium	-	163.0	158.7	143.6	e157.5	Belgique
Austria	106.8	93.9	86.3	95.7	98.1	Autriche
Netherlands	102.1	96.9	85.1	83.7	83.4	Pays-Bas
Singapore	96.9	81.5	78.6	83.1	74.0	Singapour
Japan	68.7	73.0	85.3	83.8	87.1	Japon
China	48.7	55.1	73.8	91.4	112.5	Chine
Denmark	64.5	58.6	63.3	62.7	73.5	Danemark
Sweden	59.6	56.1	68.9	59.8	56.4	Suède
Czech Republic	61.6	50.5	55.2	61.3	69.2	République tchèque
Australia	55.7	58.7	67.8	49.5	53.5	Australie
Switzerland-Liechtenstein	53.3	55.7	68.8	48.7	45.9	Suisse-Liechtenstein
Norway	56.1	57.5	53.0	48.9	53.4	Norvège
Brazil	67.0	46.9	45.4	47.7	61.8	Brésil
Portugal	58.9	54.5	44.8	46.2	48.7	Portugal
Korea, Republic of	35.8	45.4	60.3	56.5	47.3	République de Corée
Poland	43.2	40.4	47.0	48.9	62.9	Pologne
Ireland	46.0	41.4	53.4	50.3	50.3	Irlande
United Arab Emirates	21.9	23.0	41.9	67.2	e68.9	Emirates arabes unis
Saudi Arabia	41.1	29.6	25.0	53.6	e55.5	Arabie saoudite
China, Hong Kong SAR	42.9	39.1	40.8	33.6	30.7	Chine - RAS de Hong-Kong
Belgium-Luxembourg	182.2	-	-	-	-	Belgique-Luxembourg
Thailand	44.0	34.7	32.7	33.4	e34.8	Thaïlande

(Value as percentages of World total) **(Valeur en pourcentage du total mondial)**

Regions of the world	1993	1994	1995	1996	1997	1998	1999	2000	2001	2002	Régions du monde
World	100.0	100.0	100.0	100.0	100.0	100.0	100.0	100.0	100.0	100.0	Monde
Africa	5.0	5.0	4.3	4.8	4.9	4.0	4.1	3.8	3.9	4.0	Afrique
Americas	27.2	25.9	24.9	25.2	27.9	28.8	30.0	31.0	30.7	28.1	Amériques
- Northern America	20.9	19.7	18.7	18.2	19.1	19.1	21.1	21.9	21.7	20.0	- Amérique du Nord
- LAIA	4.2	4.5	4.5	5.3	6.8	7.6	6.8	7.0	6.8	6.1	- ALAI
- CACM	0.6	0.5	0.5	0.5	0.5	0.8	0.9	0.9	0.9	0.8	- MCC
- Caribbean	1.1	0.9	1.0	1.1	1.1	1.0	1.0	1.0	1.0	0.9	- Caraïbes
- Rest of America	0.4	0.3	0.2	0.2	0.2	0.3	0.2	0.2	0.2	0.3	- Autre d'Amérique
Asia excluding former USSR	21.8	19.9	18.4	18.4	17.9	14.6	14.1	15.6	17.2	17.3	Asie ancienne URSS exclus
- Middle East	4.1	3.4	3.6	2.8	2.8	3.0	2.9	3.6	5.2	5.0	- Moyen-Orient
Asia former USSR	0.1	0.4	0.6	0.7	0.5	0.7	0.6	0.7	0.7	0.7	Asie ancienne URSS
Europe excluding former USSR	42.6	45.8	48.9	47.8	46.1	48.6	48.0	45.1	44.3	46.7	Europe ancienne URSS exclus
- European Union	37.3	40.0	42.5	41.1	39.6	41.2	40.6	37.5	36.6	38.1	- Union Européenne
- Eastern Europe	2.0	2.0	2.6	2.9	2.6	3.3	3.3	3.6	4.1	4.8	- Europe de l'Est
- Rest of Europe	3.2	3.8	3.7	3.8	3.9	4.1	4.0	4.0	3.6	3.8	- Autre de l'Europe
Europe former USSR	1.7	1.4	1.5	1.4	1.3	1.7	1.5	1.8	1.6	1.5	Europe ancienne URSS
Oceania	1.6	1.5	1.5	1.7	1.5	1.7	1.8	1.9	1.5	1.6	Océanie

TRADE BY COMMODITY (Value in million US dollars)
Exports by principal countries or areas

COMMERCE PAR PRODUIT (Valeur en millions de dollars EU)
Exportations selon les principaux pays ou zones

Country or area	1998	1999	2000	2001	2002	Pays ou zone
World	4677.2	4811.4	4854.7	4754.6	4959.4	Monde
Africa	60.1	62.4	52.7	46.3	61.3	Afrique
Americas	813.9	815.5	1013.2	860.4	867.2	Amériques
- Northern America	519.2	533.4	715.4	589.3	595.8	- Amérique du Nord
- LAIA	278.5	262.3	273.3	251.1	254.0	- ALAI
- CACM	12.2	15.9	21.0	16.3	14.7	- MCC
- Caribbean	3.8	3.8	3.5	3.7	2.6	- Caraïbes
- Rest of America	0.2	0.1	0.0	0.1	0.0	- Autre d'Amérique
Asia excluding former USSR	1164.2	1255.6	1287.2	1339.9	1410.8	Asie ancienne URSS exclus
- Middle East	101.4	143.1	151.5	156.3	175.8	- Moyen-Orient
Asia former USSR	4.7	3.1	4.2	2.1	1.8	Asie ancienne URSS
Europe excluding former USSR	2479.1	2439.9	2322.5	2348.8	2467.2	Europe ancienne URSS exclus
- European Union	2183.1	2158.6	2036.6	2051.0	2131.0	- Union Européenne
- Eastern Europe	191.1	178.6	180.4	192.0	214.9	- Europe de l'Est
- Rest of Europe	104.9	102.7	105.5	105.8	121.3	- Autre de l'Europe
Europe former USSR	139.5	222.1	156.8	136.4	131.5	Europe ancienne URSS
Oceania	15.8	12.8	18.1	20.7	19.6	Océanie
Germany	496.6	484.7	483.1	526.9	527.2	Allemagne
United States	399.4	398.3	569.5	449.1	451.7	Etats-Unis d'Amérique
Italy-San Marino-Holy See	338.8	324.0	309.9	310.1	318.0	Italie-Saint-Marin-Saint-Siège
Korea, Republic of	281.6	277.8	297.4	309.5	320.0	République de Corée
China	243.3	269.2	278.7	323.7	351.8	Chine
France-Monaco	319.3	323.4	276.5	252.8	268.2	France-Monaco
Japan	257.5	254.1	241.5	218.5	211.6	Japon
United Kingdom	232.3	201.7	196.8	235.2	211.1	Royaume-Uni
Spain	204.9	202.2	192.2	178.2	179.8	Espagne
Belgium	–	225.6	221.3	200.5	e224.9	Belgique
Netherlands	175.3	161.5	129.5	111.7	145.8	Pays-Bas
Canada	119.8	135.1	145.8	140.2	144.0	Canada
Mexico	121.0	129.5	131.2	121.8	116.6	Mexique
Turkey	75.8	90.3	108.0	106.9	123.2	Turquie
Belarus	86.5	81.3	82.7	77.1	78.2	Bélarus
Czech Republic	69.0	73.3	70.9	69.8	63.5	République tchèque
Malaysia	51.5	72.7	55.7	69.8	e74.0	Malaisie
Thailand	27.8	46.3	55.5	73.9	e78.1	Thaïlande
Poland	46.0	47.1	54.7	52.2	71.4	Pologne
Russian Federation	31.5	126.9	45.4	37.9	29.3	Fédération de Russie
India	53.2	52.2	54.8	54.0	56.6	Inde
Venezuela	76.7	42.9	64.6	41.7	e44.3	Venezuela
Switzerland-Liechtenstein	51.4	55.9	51.3	56.3	54.1	Suisse-Liechtenstein
Luxembourg	–	71.9	63.3	61.4	e62.7	Luxembourg
Austria	48.3	50.4	46.0	49.8	56.7	Autriche
Brazil	45.8	52.9	44.8	50.7	e52.6	Brésil
Belgium-Luxembourg	234.5	–	–	–	–	Belgique-Luxembourg
Sweden	37.3	33.3	35.3	27.9	37.8	Suède
Singapore	30.7	29.7	32.3	26.1	47.6	Singapour
Saudi Arabia	19.5	44.8	35.3	33.8	e30.5	Arabie saoudite

(Value as percentages of World total) **(Valeur en pourcentage du total mondial)**

Regions of the world	1993	1994	1995	1996	1997	1998	1999	2000	2001	2002	Régions du monde
World	100.0	100.0	100.0	100.0	100.0	100.0	100.0	100.0	100.0	100.0	Monde
Africa	1.7	1.5	1.4	1.4	1.5	1.3	1.3	1.1	1.0	1.2	Afrique
Americas	14.6	13.8	13.5	13.3	15.1	17.4	16.9	20.9	18.1	17.5	Amériques
- Northern America	10.2	9.4	8.7	8.9	10.7	11.1	11.1	14.7	12.4	12.0	- Amérique du Nord
- LAIA	4.2	4.2	4.6	4.3	4.2	6.0	5.5	5.6	5.3	5.1	- ALAI
- CACM	0.2	0.1	0.1	0.1	0.1	0.3	0.3	0.4	0.3	0.3	- MCC
- Caribbean	0.1	0.1	0.1	0.1	0.1	0.1	0.1	0.1	0.1	0.1	- Caraïbes
- Rest of America	0.0	0.0	0.0	0.0	0.0	0.0	0.0	0.0	0.0	0.0	- Autre d'Amérique
Asia excluding former USSR	27.8	25.3	25.0	26.1	28.0	24.9	26.1	26.5	28.2	28.4	Asie ancienne URSS exclus
- Middle East	1.9	1.9	2.6	3.0	3.3	2.2	3.0	3.1	3.3	3.5	- Moyen-Orient
Asia former USSR	0.1	0.3	0.3	0.5	0.3	0.1	0.1	0.1	0.0	0.0	Asie ancienne URSS
Europe excluding former USSR	54.1	57.0	55.8	55.3	52.0	53.0	50.7	47.8	49.4	49.7	Europe ancienne URSS exclus
- European Union	48.8	52.2	50.4	49.8	46.3	46.7	44.9	42.0	43.1	43.0	- Union Européenne
- Eastern Europe	3.3	2.7	3.2	3.2	3.4	4.1	3.7	3.7	4.0	4.3	- Europe de l'Est
- Rest of Europe	1.9	2.1	2.2	2.3	2.3	2.2	2.1	2.2	2.2	2.4	- Autre de l'Europe
Europe former USSR	1.1	1.5	3.4	2.6	2.8	3.0	4.6	3.2	2.9	2.7	Europe ancienne URSS
Oceania	0.5	0.6	0.5	0.9	0.4	0.3	0.3	0.4	0.4	0.4	Océanie

694 Nails, screws, nuts, bolts, rivets, etc, of iron, steel or copper

TRADE BY COMMODITY (Value in million US dollars)
Imports by principal countries or areas

COMMERCE PAR PRODUIT (Valeur en millions de dollars EU)
Importations selon les principaux pays ou zones

Country or area	1998	1999	2000	2001	2002	Pays ou zone
World	12959.2	13265.0	15096.0	14577.7	14229.5	Monde
Africa	240.7	221.2	251.8	252.1	233.7	Afrique
Americas	4837.8	5194.6	6469.7	6062.0	5214.6	Amériques
- Northern America	3442.2	3651.8	4025.1	3507.3	3737.3	- Amérique du Nord
- LAIA	1294.1	1442.7	2349.6	2453.5	1383.4	- ALAI
- CACM	38.3	37.9	39.5	44.0	41.4	- MCC
- Caribbean	51.1	51.0	44.8	46.7	42.5	- Caraïbes
- Rest of America	12.1	11.3	10.7	10.5	9.9	- Autre d'Amérique
Asia excluding former USSR	1750.5	1861.9	2240.0	2222.7	2423.1	Asie ancienne URSS exclus
- Middle East	283.1	232.1	261.6	299.3	301.9	- Moyen-Orient
Asia former USSR	26.7	17.2	22.5	21.8	24.8	Asie ancienne URSS
Europe excluding former USSR	5805.3	5686.2	5816.3	5720.0	5979.6	Europe ancienne URSS exclus
- European Union	4988.4	4867.1	4913.8	4781.0	4908.9	- Union Européenne
- Eastern Europe	425.3	448.5	529.0	580.5	703.1	- Europe de l'Est
- Rest of Europe	391.6	370.5	373.5	358.5	367.6	- Autre de l'Europe
Europe former USSR	87.6	70.2	82.5	96.5	116.3	Europe ancienne URSS
Oceania	210.6	213.7	213.2	202.6	237.4	Océanie
United States	2539.5	2650.9	3001.3	2593.6	2785.8	Etats-Unis d'Amérique
Mexico	867.3	1114.1	1980.7	2076.7	1063.4	Mexique
Germany	1237.3	1162.9	1160.8	1165.1	1129.8	Allemagne
Canada	902.0	1000.1	1023.3	912.8	950.3	Canada
France-Monaco	714.1	716.6	759.1	732.1	769.1	France-Monaco
United Kingdom	666.3	642.4	680.0	622.9	673.1	Royaume-Uni
Spain	377.8	459.9	398.7	363.8	361.9	Espagne
China	225.7	298.7	380.9	439.6	579.4	Chine
Belgium	–	374.0	381.9	407.5	e446.9	Belgique
Japan	264.8	286.8	339.7	346.6	339.3	Japon
Netherlands	341.9	301.2	305.2	302.0	316.5	Pays-Bas
Italy-San Marino-Holy See	296.7	291.6	309.5	296.5	288.9	Italie-Saint-Marin-Saint-Siège
Austria	285.4	266.4	254.8	262.7	279.8	Autriche
Sweden	273.2	252.9	261.3	227.2	233.8	Suède
Thailand	161.6	206.0	224.1	224.8	e234.2	Thaïlande
Switzerland-Liechtenstein	212.7	199.7	213.4	197.5	189.2	Suisse-Liechtenstein
Brazil	188.1	157.8	190.1	204.0	183.5	Brésil
Singapore	179.3	194.6	205.3	159.5	168.1	Singapour
Australia	168.4	167.0	170.5	160.2	191.3	Australie
Czech Republic	124.0	131.1	158.2	194.3	240.2	République tchèque
Malaysia	122.9	145.7	178.0	176.4	e192.8	Malaisie
Hungary	112.1	132.8	147.3	151.3	167.3	Hongrie
Poland	115.7	115.4	141.7	137.9	175.8	Pologne
China, Hong Kong SAR	126.2	127.0	145.8	130.3	146.5	Chine - RAS de Hong-Kong
Denmark	125.0	118.2	117.5	126.9	125.7	Danemark
Korea, Republic of	63.8	80.9	135.2	104.5	105.4	République de Corée
Norway	98.8	86.8	82.1	81.1	89.2	Norvège
Finland	94.0	83.8	88.6	85.6	81.1	Finlande
Indonesia	62.1	42.8	94.2	100.8	108.5	Indonésie
Belgium-Luxembourg	402.8	–	–	–	–	Belgique-Luxembourg

(Value as percentages of World total) **(Valeur en pourcentage du total mondial)**

Regions of the world	1993	1994	1995	1996	1997	1998	1999	2000	2001	2002	Régions du monde
World	100.0	100.0	100.0	100.0	100.0	100.0	100.0	100.0	100.0	100.0	Monde
Africa	2.7	2.1	2.1	2.0	1.9	1.9	1.7	1.7	1.7	1.6	Afrique
Americas	35.6	35.7	32.6	34.1	36.2	37.3	39.2	42.9	41.6	36.6	Amériques
- Northern America	28.4	28.5	25.6	25.3	26.0	26.6	27.5	26.7	24.1	26.3	- Amérique du Nord
- LAIA	6.3	6.5	6.3	8.0	9.5	10.0	10.9	15.6	16.8	9.7	- ALAI
- CACM	0.3	0.3	0.2	0.2	0.3	0.3	0.3	0.3	0.3	0.3	- MCC
- Caribbean	0.4	0.3	0.3	0.4	0.4	0.4	0.4	0.3	0.3	0.3	- Caraïbes
- Rest of America	0.2	0.1	0.1	0.1	0.1	0.1	0.1	0.1	0.1	0.1	- Autre d'Amérique
Asia excluding former USSR	19.1	17.8	16.7	18.0	16.9	13.5	14.0	14.8	15.2	17.0	Asie ancienne URSS exclus
- Middle East	3.1	2.2	2.2	2.4	2.3	2.2	1.7	1.7	2.1	2.1	- Moyen-Orient
Asia former USSR	0.0	0.1	0.1	0.2	0.1	0.2	0.1	0.1	0.1	0.2	Asie ancienne URSS
Europe excluding former USSR	40.2	41.8	46.0	43.4	42.3	44.8	42.9	38.5	39.2	42.0	Europe ancienne URSS exclus
- European Union	35.7	37.2	40.7	38.0	36.7	38.5	36.7	32.5	32.8	34.5	- Union Européenne
- Eastern Europe	1.0	1.1	1.7	2.0	2.6	3.3	3.4	3.5	4.0	4.9	- Europe de l'Est
- Rest of Europe	3.5	3.4	3.7	3.4	3.1	3.0	2.8	2.5	2.5	2.6	- Autre de l'Europe
Europe former USSR	0.4	0.4	0.5	0.5	0.7	0.7	0.5	0.5	0.7	0.8	Europe ancienne URSS
Oceania	2.1	2.1	2.0	1.9	1.9	1.6	1.6	1.4	1.4	1.7	Océanie

Clous, vis, écrous, boulons, rondelles et articles similaires, en fer, en acier ou en cuivre 694

TRADE BY COMMODITY (Value in million US dollars)
Exports by principal countries or areas

COMMERCE PAR PRODUIT (Valeur en millions de dollars EU)
Exportations selon les principaux pays ou zones

Country or area	1998	1999	2000	2001	2002	Pays ou zone
World	11261.9	11259.8	12172.4	11298.9	12048.0	Monde
Africa	43.3	27.7	18.6	20.9	24.5	Afrique
Americas	2015.8	2134.9	2357.7	2081.9	2107.9	Amériques
- Northern America	1835.5	1966.5	2169.0	1882.7	1921.4	- Amérique du Nord
- LAIA	168.3	158.0	177.6	188.6	171.3	- ALAI
- CACM	7.6	6.8	7.0	6.8	11.8	- MCC
- Caribbean	4.3	3.4	3.8	3.4	3.2	- Caraïbes
- Rest of America	0.1	0.1	0.3	0.3	0.2	- Autre d'Amérique
Asia excluding former USSR	3719.0	3878.4	4575.1	4077.5	4519.7	Asie ancienne URSS exclus
- Middle East	48.7	46.5	55.5	57.3	58.1	- Moyen-Orient
Asia former USSR	0.9	0.8	0.4	0.3	0.2	Asie ancienne URSS
Europe excluding former USSR	5380.0	5137.2	5131.8	5023.2	5292.0	Europe ancienne URSS exclus
- European Union	4420.5	4244.6	4201.6	4115.0	4383.6	- Union Européenne
- Eastern Europe	287.0	234.1	247.0	268.2	291.3	- Europe de l'Est
- Rest of Europe	672.6	658.5	683.3	640.1	617.1	- Autre de l'Europe
Europe former USSR	77.4	51.5	63.9	71.2	78.6	Europe ancienne URSS
Oceania	25.6	29.3	25.0	24.0	25.1	Océanie
Germany	1643.2	1579.2	1574.1	1625.7	1716.6	Allemagne
United States	1458.2	1564.8	1745.2	1541.6	1549.1	Etats-Unis d'Amérique
Japan	994.7	1101.6	1312.2	1127.6	1228.8	Japon
Italy-San Marino-Holy See	755.7	705.5	698.1	681.2	695.8	Italie-Saint-Marin-Saint-Siège
Switzerland-Liechtenstein	626.9	614.9	635.6	586.9	562.1	Suisse-Liechtenstein
China	436.7	488.6	632.1	663.0	794.7	Chine
France-Monaco	544.5	534.1	525.4	469.1	541.2	France-Monaco
Canada	377.2	401.7	423.8	341.1	372.3	Canada
United Kingdom	438.2	423.8	375.8	338.1	335.8	Royaume-Uni
Korea, Republic of	287.6	274.0	262.6	220.3	235.2	République de Corée
Spain	213.9	220.1	210.1	212.3	216.6	Espagne
Netherlands	212.2	184.6	189.2	157.2	167.1	Pays-Bas
Belgium	–	189.3	188.7	209.7	e235.3	Belgique
Sweden	159.0	142.3	151.3	141.9	162.6	Suède
Singapore	112.2	128.0	131.8	120.4	145.7	Singapour
Austria	116.8	111.7	129.1	126.9	140.4	Autriche
Malaysia	105.1	98.6	112.2	103.0	e109.2	Malaisie
Czech Republic	87.0	84.7	97.7	104.4	107.3	République tchèque
Mexico	74.5	83.6	101.7	113.6	95.6	Mexique
China, Hong Kong SAR	80.6	82.8	89.2	81.4	114.3	Chine - RAS de Hong-Kong
Denmark	87.2	85.6	94.5	81.6	93.6	Danemark
Poland	79.4	62.3	75.6	84.3	93.5	Pologne
Thailand	56.1	70.2	99.1	81.9	e86.5	Thaïlande
India	50.2	64.0	87.8	79.0	99.2	Inde
Brazil	57.9	47.5	49.1	44.3	e45.9	Brésil
Belgium-Luxembourg	187.5	–	–	–	–	Belgique-Luxembourg
Hungary	60.1	42.3	26.4	26.2	26.8	Hongrie
Indonesia	13.9	25.3	41.2	53.0	42.9	Indonésie
Turkey	31.7	31.2	34.3	36.1	37.6	Turquie
Russian Federation	31.1	30.4	34.7	36.4	37.2	Fédération de Russie

(Value as percentages of World total) **(Valeur en pourcentage du total mondial)**

Regions of the world	1993	1994	1995	1996	1997	1998	1999	2000	2001	2002	Régions du monde
World	100.0	100.0	100.0	100.0	100.0	100.0	100.0	100.0	100.0	100.0	Monde
Africa	0.3	0.2	0.4	0.3	0.3	0.4	0.2	0.2	0.2	0.2	Afrique
Americas	14.9	16.6	14.7	18.0	18.1	17.9	19.0	19.4	18.4	17.5	Amériques
- Northern America	13.4	15.2	13.5	16.7	16.2	16.3	17.5	17.8	16.7	15.9	- Amérique du Nord
- LAIA	1.3	1.2	1.0	1.3	1.8	1.5	1.4	1.5	1.7	1.4	- ALAI
- CACM	0.0	0.0	0.0	0.0	0.0	0.1	0.1	0.1	0.1	0.1	- MCC
- Caribbean	0.2	0.2	0.1	0.0	0.0	0.0	0.0	0.0	0.0	0.0	- Caraïbes
- Rest of America	0.0	0.0	0.0	0.0	0.0	0.0	0.0	0.0	0.0	0.0	- Autre d'Amérique
Asia excluding former USSR	43.5	37.3	37.1	34.6	35.5	33.0	34.4	37.6	36.1	37.5	Asie ancienne URSS exclus
- Middle East	0.4	0.4	0.5	0.4	0.4	0.4	0.4	0.5	0.5	0.5	- Moyen-Orient
Asia former USSR	0.0	0.0	0.0	0.0	0.0	0.0	0.0	0.0	0.0	0.0	Asie ancienne URSS
Europe excluding former USSR	40.4	44.8	46.9	46.1	45.1	47.8	45.6	42.2	44.5	43.9	Europe ancienne URSS exclus
- European Union	33.2	37.1	38.6	38.2	37.5	39.3	37.7	34.5	36.4	36.4	- Union Européenne
- Eastern Europe	1.6	1.5	2.0	1.9	1.9	2.5	2.1	2.0	2.4	2.4	- Europe de l'Est
- Rest of Europe	5.6	6.2	6.2	6.0	5.7	6.0	5.8	5.6	5.7	5.1	- Autre de l'Europe
Europe former USSR	0.5	0.5	0.6	0.6	0.6	0.7	0.5	0.5	0.6	0.7	Europe ancienne URSS
Oceania	0.4	0.5	0.4	0.4	0.3	0.2	0.3	0.2	0.2	0.2	Océanie

695 Tools for use in the hand or in machines

TRADE BY COMMODITY (Value in million US dollars)
Imports by principal countries or areas

COMMERCE PAR PRODUIT (Valeur en millions de dollars EU)
Importations selon les principaux pays ou zones

Country or area	1998	1999	2000	2001	2002	Pays ou zone
World	19363.7	19356.4	20328.3	20227.7	20424.5	Monde
Africa	522.9	454.3	465.3	501.9	549.7	Afrique
Americas	5848.9	5804.5	6362.6	6047.1	6158.0	Amériques
- Northern America	4350.1	4269.6	4784.8	4424.0	4804.7	- Amérique du Nord
- LAIA	1330.2	1370.7	1421.9	1461.5	1191.1	- ALAI
- CACM	72.4	73.9	67.7	71.4	78.0	- MCC
- Caribbean	79.1	73.7	72.8	76.7	70.4	- Caraïbes
- Rest of America	17.2	16.7	15.4	13.5	13.7	- Autre d'Amérique
Asia excluding former USSR	3096.5	3189.4	3717.4	3515.0	3885.6	Asie ancienne URSS exclus
- Middle East	396.7	388.1	459.5	416.9	467.4	- Moyen-Orient
Asia former USSR	39.7	29.9	45.9	94.5	67.5	Asie ancienne URSS
Europe excluding former USSR	9247.2	9328.7	9156.8	9471.2	9102.6	Europe ancienne URSS exclus
- European Union	8001.1	8126.7	7931.0	8223.2	7717.9	- Union Européenne
- Eastern Europe	511.8	508.8	544.6	575.9	678.7	- Europe de l'Est
- Rest of Europe	734.2	693.2	681.3	672.1	706.0	- Autre de l'Europe
Europe former USSR	219.6	186.0	201.6	261.6	282.8	Europe ancienne URSS
Oceania	389.0	363.6	378.7	336.4	378.3	Océanie
United States	3167.5	3226.4	3511.2	3305.1	3615.4	Etats-Unis d'Amérique
Germany	1828.0	1763.5	1618.3	1807.3	1676.0	Allemagne
Canada	1176.3	1035.3	1271.3	1116.7	1186.5	Canada
United Kingdom	1097.0	1096.1	1126.4	1203.0	1093.7	Royaume-Uni
France-Monaco	924.1	927.1	991.8	946.6	981.7	France-Monaco
Italy-San Marino-Holy See	812.6	867.3	882.7	897.3	851.9	Italie-Saint-Marin-Saint-Siège
Netherlands	796.0	854.5	834.8	811.7	413.7	Pays-Bas
Mexico	562.1	793.0	827.2	816.9	666.1	Mexique
Belgium	–	611.2	614.9	652.9	e716.1	Belgique
Japan	472.5	461.1	533.4	542.6	528.6	Japon
Spain	481.8	525.1	457.7	475.5	540.0	Espagne
Switzerland-Liechtenstein	465.7	446.5	441.5	426.4	419.3	Suisse-Liechtenstein
Sweden	415.1	393.8	376.2	399.2	382.2	Suède
Austria	383.2	353.8	333.6	347.0	350.2	Autriche
Singapore	312.8	295.3	352.0	379.0	414.4	Singapour
China	249.3	240.4	313.8	370.6	544.9	Chine
Thailand	259.3	284.9	354.4	391.8	e408.2	Thaïlande
China, Hong Kong SAR	296.8	294.8	340.5	311.5	337.3	Chine - RAS de Hong-Kong
Australia	306.9	283.8	298.0	253.7	292.9	Australie
Korea, Republic of	170.3	285.9	309.6	277.8	305.3	République de Corée
Malaysia	183.7	196.7	298.9	243.2	e265.8	Malaisie
Denmark	251.4	217.5	201.6	199.0	211.0	Danemark
Brazil	236.8	202.1	180.7	231.0	199.8	Brésil
Poland	205.3	188.5	203.0	167.0	195.0	Pologne
Czech Republic	119.0	143.9	147.0	182.4	208.0	République tchèque
Finland	146.7	141.3	138.1	139.9	137.8	Finlande
Norway	153.3	135.2	124.9	126.8	144.1	Norvège
Portugal	121.6	127.9	124.1	120.1	136.6	Portugal
Russian Federation	107.2	83.8	107.2	149.1	156.4	Fédération de Russie
United Arab Emirates	91.7	96.1	132.6	136.1	e139.7	Emirates arabes unis

(Value as percentages of World total) **(Valeur en pourcentage du total mondial)**

Regions of the world	1993	1994	1995	1996	1997	1998	1999	2000	2001	2002	Régions du monde
World	100.0	100.0	100.0	100.0	100.0	100.0	100.0	100.0	100.0	100.0	Monde
Africa	3.1	3.2	3.0	2.7	2.7	2.7	2.3	2.3	2.5	2.7	Afrique
Americas	27.3	26.5	24.8	25.7	29.5	30.2	30.0	31.3	29.9	30.1	Amériques
- Northern America	20.7	20.0	18.9	18.7	22.0	22.5	22.1	23.5	21.9	23.5	- Amérique du Nord
- LAIA	5.7	5.7	5.0	6.1	6.7	6.9	7.1	7.0	7.2	5.8	- ALAI
- CACM	0.4	0.3	0.3	0.3	0.3	0.4	0.4	0.3	0.4	0.4	- MCC
- Caribbean	0.4	0.3	0.4	0.5	0.4	0.4	0.4	0.4	0.4	0.3	- Caraïbes
- Rest of America	0.2	0.2	0.1	0.1	0.1	0.1	0.1	0.1	0.1	0.1	- Autre d'Amérique
Asia excluding former USSR	22.3	20.6	20.3	20.3	19.1	16.0	16.5	18.3	17.4	19.0	Asie ancienne URSS exclus
- Middle East	3.2	2.7	2.3	1.9	2.0	2.0	2.0	2.3	2.1	2.3	- Moyen-Orient
Asia former USSR	0.1	0.2	0.3	0.2	0.1	0.2	0.2	0.2	0.5	0.3	Asie ancienne URSS
Europe excluding former USSR	44.2	46.2	48.4	48.0	45.3	47.8	48.2	45.0	46.8	44.6	Europe ancienne URSS exclus
- European Union	39.1	40.9	42.3	41.7	39.3	41.3	42.0	39.0	40.7	37.8	- Union Européenne
- Eastern Europe	1.3	1.5	1.7	2.1	2.4	2.6	2.6	2.7	2.8	3.3	- Europe de l'Est
- Rest of Europe	3.8	3.9	4.3	4.2	3.6	3.8	3.6	3.4	3.3	3.5	- Autre de l'Europe
Europe former USSR	0.8	0.9	0.9	0.9	1.0	1.1	1.0	1.0	1.3	1.4	Europe ancienne URSS
Oceania	2.3	2.3	2.3	2.2	2.2	2.0	1.9	1.9	1.7	1.9	Océanie

TRADE BY COMMODITY (Value in million US dollars)
Exports by principal countries or areas

COMMERCE PAR PRODUIT (Valeur en millions de dollars EU)
Exportations selon les principaux pays ou zones

Country or area	1998	1999	2000	2001	2002	Pays ou zone
World	18775.7	19656.2	20673.9	20898.3	21092.6	Monde
Africa	88.8	101.3	104.9	91.9	102.7	Afrique
Americas	3097.7	3075.1	3437.6	3654.1	3419.1	Amériques
- Northern America	2701.3	2645.7	3010.8	2810.9	2749.1	- Amérique du Nord
- LAIA	368.9	407.9	404.4	824.0	649.3	- ALAI
- CACM	14.4	12.8	9.7	10.5	10.7	- MCC
- Caribbean	12.4	8.3	11.8	8.3	9.4	- Caraïbes
- Rest of America	0.6	0.5	1.0	0.5	0.6	- Autre d'Amérique
Asia excluding former USSR	5514.2	5668.7	6405.7	6340.6	6748.8	Asie ancienne URSS exclus
- Middle East	145.4	81.0	82.7	91.4	91.6	- Moyen-Orient
Asia former USSR	7.8	3.3	4.4	7.4	7.7	Asie ancienne URSS
Europe excluding former USSR	9776.4	10032.5	9720.8	9787.5	9992.9	Europe ancienne URSS exclus
- European Union	8555.1	8852.2	8523.7	8550.2	8699.9	- Union Européenne
- Eastern Europe	233.3	232.2	232.7	298.1	329.6	- Europe de l'Est
- Rest of Europe	988.0	948.2	964.5	939.2	963.4	- Autre de l'Europe
Europe former USSR	199.7	677.9	903.8	919.0	724.7	Europe ancienne URSS
Oceania	91.2	97.3	96.8	97.8	96.7	Océanie
Germany	2987.8	2920.8	2719.5	2936.6	3207.6	Allemagne
United States	2283.0	2255.8	2586.0	2416.6	2331.4	Etats-Unis d'Amérique
Japan	1768.4	1926.8	2071.2	2016.8	1989.3	Japon
China	933.2	911.2	1109.6	1180.6	1414.8	Chine
United Kingdom	972.9	928.5	940.7	921.4	908.7	Royaume-Uni
Italy-San Marino-Holy See	891.3	927.7	884.8	920.0	908.7	Italie-Saint-Marin-Saint-Siège
Switzerland-Liechtenstein	871.0	832.9	841.2	805.8	819.3	Suisse-Liechtenstein
Sweden	778.9	908.0	774.0	703.7	752.6	Suède
France-Monaco	728.2	698.8	687.7	660.0	722.9	France-Monaco
Netherlands	697.0	767.9	713.4	635.5	257.4	Pays-Bas
Austria	479.0	469.9	473.4	501.3	521.6	Autriche
Belgium	–	502.6	596.1	583.9	e655.2	Belgique
Russian Federation	158.4	644.5	851.2	348.3	93.0	Fédération de Russie
Israel	404.1	374.6	436.4	431.3	423.6	Israël
Canada	418.1	389.9	424.8	394.2	417.7	Canada
Spain	374.3	406.1	415.4	389.6	431.9	Espagne
Mexico	199.9	242.5	233.4	630.4	454.4	Mexique
China, Hong Kong SAR	306.5	298.9	344.4	311.3	358.5	Chine - RAS de Hong-Kong
Korea, Republic of	241.0	281.9	341.2	361.0	364.0	République de Corée
Singapore	245.4	200.7	253.3	297.6	342.5	Singapour
Ukraine	12.6	12.5	30.0	544.0	599.6	Ukraine
India	109.6	144.8	185.6	176.7	191.9	Inde
Czech Republic	105.5	98.9	105.7	148.2	160.6	République tchèque
Brazil	112.4	93.3	105.0	112.8	e116.9	Brésil
Denmark	89.8	88.5	94.4	95.7	106.4	Danemark
Ireland	83.6	77.6	64.5	75.1	81.5	Irlande
Belgium-Luxembourg	354.2	–	–	–	–	Belgique-Luxembourg
Slovenia	58.9	57.7	62.7	68.2	78.4	Slovénie
Poland	51.5	51.8	59.2	62.9	74.6	Pologne
Australia	48.9	55.8	56.7	59.9	57.6	Australie

(Value as percentages of World total)

(Valeur en pourcentage du total mondial)

Regions of the world	1993	1994	1995	1996	1997	1998	1999	2000	2001	2002	Régions du monde
World	100.0	100.0	100.0	100.0	100.0	100.0	100.0	100.0	100.0	100.0	Monde
Africa	0.4	0.5	0.6	0.5	0.6	0.5	0.5	0.5	0.4	0.5	Afrique
Americas	13.8	14.3	13.4	13.9	16.7	16.5	15.6	16.6	17.5	16.2	Amériques
- Northern America	11.9	12.4	11.8	12.3	14.5	14.4	13.5	14.6	13.5	13.0	- Amérique du Nord
- LAIA	1.6	1.6	1.5	1.5	2.1	2.0	2.1	2.0	3.9	3.1	- ALAI
- CACM	0.1	0.1	0.0	0.1	0.1	0.1	0.1	0.0	0.1	0.1	- MCC
- Caribbean	0.0	0.0	0.1	0.0	0.0	0.1	0.0	0.1	0.0	0.0	- Caraïbes
- Rest of America	0.2	0.2	0.1	0.0	0.0	0.0	0.0	0.0	0.0	0.0	- Autre d'Amérique
Asia excluding former USSR	36.3	31.5	31.2	29.9	31.3	29.4	28.8	31.0	30.3	32.0	Asie ancienne URSS exclus
- Middle East	0.2	0.2	0.2	0.1	0.2	0.8	0.4	0.4	0.4	0.4	- Moyen-Orient
Asia former USSR	0.0	0.1	0.1	0.1	0.1	0.0	0.0	0.0	0.0	0.0	Asie ancienne URSS
Europe excluding former USSR	48.8	52.7	53.9	54.7	50.4	52.1	51.0	47.0	46.8	47.4	Europe ancienne URSS exclus
- European Union	42.9	46.5	47.2	48.1	44.6	45.6	45.0	41.2	40.9	41.2	- Union Européenne
- Eastern Europe	0.9	0.8	1.0	1.0	1.0	1.2	1.2	1.1	1.4	1.6	- Europe de l'Est
- Rest of Europe	5.0	5.5	5.8	5.5	4.8	5.3	4.8	4.7	4.5	4.6	- Autre de l'Europe
Europe former USSR	0.2	0.4	0.4	0.4	0.4	1.1	3.4	4.4	4.4	3.4	Europe ancienne URSS
Oceania	0.5	0.5	0.5	0.5	0.5	0.5	0.5	0.5	0.5	0.5	Océanie

696 Cutlery

TRADE BY COMMODITY (Value in million US dollars)
Imports by principal countries or areas

COMMERCE PAR PRODUIT (Valeur en millions de dollars EU)
Importations selon les principaux pays ou zones

Country or area	1998	1999	2000	2001	2002	Pays ou zone
World	4900.1	5264.5	5371.7	5393.2	5657.9	Monde
Africa	91.2	107.6	93.0	93.1	95.7	Afrique
Americas	1381.7	1580.2	1736.3	1719.1	1735.5	Amériques
- Northern America	1061.7	1230.4	1348.9	1311.0	1383.1	- Amérique du Nord
- LAIA	270.3	300.4	336.9	353.2	294.9	- ALAI
- CACM	24.6	27.4	26.4	30.2	32.8	- MCC
- Caribbean	19.6	16.9	17.6	18.8	17.8	- Caraïbes
- Rest of America	5.5	5.1	6.5	6.0	6.9	- Autre d'Amérique
Asia excluding former USSR	845.6	925.0	955.9	872.0	911.3	Asie ancienne URSS exclus
- Middle East	159.0	148.8	162.3	167.2	168.2	- Moyen-Orient
Asia former USSR	6.6	4.5	7.7	10.9	10.4	Asie ancienne URSS
Europe excluding former USSR	2392.3	2460.3	2400.9	2497.5	2675.4	Europe ancienne URSS exclus
- European Union	2128.2	2178.7	2126.1	2183.8	2324.0	- Union Européenne
- Eastern Europe	115.4	130.4	139.0	172.0	197.9	- Europe de l'Est
- Rest of Europe	148.7	151.1	135.8	141.6	153.5	- Autre de l'Europe
Europe former USSR	52.4	47.3	44.6	69.6	88.9	Europe ancienne URSS
Oceania	130.4	139.6	133.2	131.0	140.8	Océanie
United States	880.1	1044.8	1156.5	1108.2	1159.5	Etats-Unis d'Amérique
United Kingdom	459.9	459.1	523.2	570.5	562.6	Royaume-Uni
Germany	413.4	445.3	406.5	440.6	451.0	Allemagne
France-Monaco	315.4	325.1	287.4	265.3	303.6	France-Monaco
China, Hong Kong SAR	275.4	272.7	309.3	260.2	260.1	Chine - RAS de Hong-Kong
Italy-San Marino-Holy See	240.0	233.5	235.9	231.5	253.3	Italie-Saint-Marin-Saint-Siège
Canada	180.6	184.5	192.1	202.3	223.0	Canada
Japan	134.9	167.1	181.0	169.5	191.1	Japon
Spain	168.0	161.7	136.9	159.1	184.4	Espagne
Netherlands	124.7	128.4	116.7	100.5	118.3	Pays-Bas
Australia	104.0	112.2	108.4	105.2	112.7	Australie
Mexico	62.4	86.0	108.5	130.5	118.5	Mexique
Poland	50.9	63.3	71.4	102.9	120.2	Pologne
Denmark	58.4	77.6	75.4	74.9	76.4	Danemark
Belgium	–	87.1	96.7	85.3	e93.6	Belgique
Switzerland-Liechtenstein	73.1	75.7	69.1	71.4	72.0	Suisse-Liechtenstein
China	42.6	47.0	73.3	75.1	86.7	Chine
Argentina	78.6	83.7	76.5	58.0	e25.7	Argentine
Austria	60.4	60.8	54.1	66.0	66.5	Autriche
United Arab Emirates	47.8	50.1	54.9	65.7	e67.5	Emirates arabes unis
Sweden	53.4	62.9	55.0	52.1	57.0	Suède
Singapore	82.8	79.8	52.3	29.5	27.9	Singapour
Greece	52.3	43.8	41.8	43.8	e48.4	Grèce
Norway	40.0	39.8	34.7	36.6	41.3	Norvège
Ireland	35.4	35.4	34.8	37.4	42.9	Irlande
Chile	39.6	36.9	41.3	35.8	29.8	Chili
Korea, Republic of	15.4	31.8	36.7	46.2	52.1	République de Corée
Portugal	37.0	34.5	35.1	32.3	36.3	Portugal
Russian Federation	30.0	23.9	21.8	37.9	53.6	Fédération de Russie
Turkey	38.0	28.3	33.4	28.9	31.0	Turquie

(Value as percentages of World total) **(Valeur en pourcentage du total mondial)**

Regions of the world	1993	1994	1995	1996	1997	1998	1999	2000	2001	2002	Régions du monde
World	100.0	100.0	100.0	100.0	100.0	100.0	100.0	100.0	100.0	100.0	Monde
Africa	2.4	2.1	1.9	1.7	2.3	1.9	2.0	1.7	1.7	1.7	Afrique
Americas	26.8	27.3	26.5	26.6	27.7	28.2	30.0	32.3	31.9	30.7	Amériques
- Northern America	21.2	21.1	20.3	20.2	21.2	21.7	23.4	25.1	24.3	24.4	- Amérique du Nord
- LAIA	4.6	5.4	5.3	5.4	5.7	5.5	5.7	6.3	6.5	5.2	- ALAI
- CACM	0.5	0.5	0.4	0.4	0.4	0.5	0.5	0.5	0.6	0.6	- MCC
- Caribbean	0.4	0.3	0.4	0.4	0.3	0.4	0.3	0.3	0.3	0.3	- Caraïbes
- Rest of America	0.1	0.1	0.1	0.1	0.1	0.1	0.1	0.1	0.1	0.1	- Autre d'Amérique
Asia excluding former USSR	20.5	20.1	21.0	20.9	21.7	17.3	17.6	17.8	16.2	16.1	Asie ancienne URSS exclus
- Middle East	4.2	3.8	3.3	3.2	3.5	3.2	2.8	3.0	3.1	3.0	- Moyen-Orient
Asia former USSR	0.0	0.1	0.1	0.1	0.1	0.1	0.1	0.1	0.2	0.2	Asie ancienne URSS
Europe excluding former USSR	46.7	46.7	46.8	46.9	44.2	48.8	46.7	44.7	46.3	47.3	Europe ancienne URSS exclus
- European Union	42.6	42.3	42.0	41.9	39.4	43.4	41.4	39.6	40.5	41.1	- Union Européenne
- Eastern Europe	1.2	1.4	1.5	1.9	2.0	2.4	2.5	2.6	3.2	3.5	- Europe de l'Est
- Rest of Europe	2.9	3.0	3.3	3.0	2.9	3.0	2.9	2.5	2.6	2.7	- Autre de l'Europe
Europe former USSR	0.8	0.8	0.9	1.0	1.3	1.1	0.9	0.8	1.3	1.6	Europe ancienne URSS
Oceania	2.8	3.0	2.9	2.8	2.8	2.7	2.7	2.5	2.4	2.5	Océanie

TRADE BY COMMODITY (Value in million US dollars)
Exports by principal countries or areas

COMMERCE PAR PRODUIT (Valeur en millions de dollars EU)
Exportations selon les principaux pays ou zones

Country or area	1998	1999	2000	2001	2002	Pays ou zone
World	4441.4	4826.8	4993.2	5194.5	5475.7	Monde
Africa	14.9	15.4	9.9	19.8	14.0	Afrique
Americas	654.6	746.4	685.4	732.6	791.0	Amériques
- Northern America	428.3	530.8	437.1	483.9	491.1	- Amérique du Nord
- LAIA	224.5	213.9	246.2	247.1	298.2	- ALAI
- CACM	1.6	1.4	1.3	1.0	1.3	- MCC
- Caribbean	0.2	0.2	0.6	0.5	0.4	- Caraïbes
- Rest of America	0.0	0.1	0.1	0.1	0.2	- Autre d'Amérique
Asia excluding former USSR	1904.5	1888.8	2214.5	2077.5	2201.9	Asie ancienne URSS exclus
- Middle East	30.5	34.1	30.7	39.6	42.7	- Moyen-Orient
Asia former USSR	0.4	0.1	2.0	0.3	0.2	Asie ancienne URSS
Europe excluding former USSR	1833.6	2126.1	2044.6	2329.3	2425.1	Europe ancienne URSS exclus
- European Union	1636.5	1914.9	1820.8	2063.2	2170.8	- Union Européenne
- Eastern Europe	47.0	64.1	80.4	133.4	131.6	- Europe de l'Est
- Rest of Europe	150.1	147.1	143.4	132.7	122.7	- Autre de l'Europe
Europe former USSR	19.9	35.7	20.5	20.9	25.3	Europe ancienne URSS
Oceania	13.4	14.1	16.4	14.2	18.3	Océanie
China	646.2	705.4	962.8	1012.2	1174.4	Chine
United Kingdom	397.9	636.1	664.0	865.1	892.7	Royaume-Uni
Germany	598.8	639.3	578.4	664.3	705.3	Allemagne
United States	395.1	483.1	407.7	438.9	452.6	Etats-Unis d'Amérique
China, Hong Kong SAR	359.8	336.9	383.7	366.4	390.0	Chine - RAS de Hong-Kong
Korea, Republic of	265.5	266.4	281.2	230.3	183.4	République de Corée
France-Monaco	200.6	222.4	170.2	135.8	149.4	France-Monaco
Japan	178.1	168.2	186.8	146.5	137.5	Japon
Italy-San Marino-Holy See	182.5	134.0	127.3	121.8	113.9	Italie-Saint-Marin-Saint-Siège
Switzerland-Liechtenstein	144.6	139.6	137.1	126.8	116.7	Suisse-Liechtenstein
Mexico	89.2	96.2	136.0	139.1	198.9	Mexique
Brazil	111.2	96.1	85.1	85.2	e88.3	Brésil
Singapore	121.6	82.2	50.5	25.1	17.3	Singapour
Indonesia	65.2	52.5	78.0	48.5	37.2	Indonésie
Poland	18.7	33.0	40.2	87.3	82.5	Pologne
Netherlands	45.2	44.9	43.2	50.8	43.7	Pays-Bas
Spain	41.0	42.7	43.6	40.7	57.7	Espagne
Portugal	40.8	46.9	41.8	35.7	38.7	Portugal
Belgium	–	38.5	50.4	50.8	e56.9	Belgique
Canada	33.3	47.7	29.4	45.0	38.5	Canada
India	36.6	33.2	41.0	39.6	40.5	Inde
Malaysia	30.2	57.4	35.1	27.5	e29.1	Malaisie
Denmark	21.2	38.9	34.0	35.2	45.6	Danemark
Czech Republic	19.7	22.4	31.1	36.7	38.3	République tchèque
United Arab Emirates	22.9	23.6	22.2	30.7	e32.0	Emirates arabes unis
Sweden	24.8	24.5	23.6	21.7	26.3	Suède
Pakistan	18.3	20.7	26.8	25.0	26.5	Pakistan
Thailand	27.2	24.1	25.5	19.1	e20.1	Thaïlande
Russian Federation	15.8	32.3	16.7	16.4	20.7	Fédération de Russie
Finland	20.5	18.4	14.7	12.9	15.5	Finlande

(Value as percentages of World total) **(Valeur en pourcentage du total mondial)**

Regions of the world	1993	1994	1995	1996	1997	1998	1999	2000	2001	2002	Régions du monde
World	100.0	100.0	100.0	100.0	100.0	100.0	100.0	100.0	100.0	100.0	Monde
Africa	0.4	0.5	0.5	0.5	0.6	0.3	0.3	0.2	0.4	0.3	Afrique
Americas	12.7	14.0	13.0	14.6	14.0	14.7	15.5	13.7	14.1	14.4	Amériques
- Northern America	7.7	9.4	8.8	9.9	9.1	9.6	11.0	8.8	9.3	9.0	- Amérique du Nord
- LAIA	4.9	4.5	4.2	4.6	4.8	5.1	4.4	4.9	4.8	5.4	- ALAI
- CACM	0.1	0.1	0.0	0.0	0.0	0.0	0.0	0.0	0.0	0.0	- MCC
- Caribbean	0.0	0.0	0.0	0.0	0.0	0.0	0.0	0.0	0.0	0.0	- Caraïbes
- Rest of America	0.0	0.0	0.0	0.0	0.0	0.0	0.0	0.0	0.0	0.0	- Autre d'Amérique
Asia excluding former USSR	48.2	43.9	44.3	44.0	45.2	42.9	39.1	44.4	40.0	40.2	Asie ancienne URSS exclus
- Middle East	0.5	0.3	0.4	0.4	0.2	0.7	0.7	0.6	0.8	0.8	- Moyen-Orient
Asia former USSR	0.0	0.0	0.0	0.0	0.0	0.0	0.0	0.0	0.0	0.0	Asie ancienne URSS
Europe excluding former USSR	38.3	41.0	41.6	40.2	39.3	41.3	44.0	40.9	44.8	44.3	Europe ancienne URSS exclus
- European Union	33.9	36.2	36.9	35.4	35.1	36.8	39.7	36.5	39.7	39.6	- Union Européenne
- Eastern Europe	0.7	0.7	0.8	1.0	1.0	1.1	1.3	1.6	2.6	2.4	- Europe de l'Est
- Rest of Europe	3.8	4.1	3.9	3.8	3.2	3.4	3.0	2.9	2.6	2.2	- Autre de l'Europe
Europe former USSR	0.1	0.2	0.2	0.3	0.5	0.4	0.7	0.4	0.4	0.5	Europe ancienne URSS
Oceania	0.3	0.3	0.3	0.4	0.4	0.3	0.3	0.3	0.3	0.3	Océanie

697 Household equipment of base metal, nes

TRADE BY COMMODITY (Value in million US dollars)
Imports by principal countries or areas

COMMERCE PAR PRODUIT (Valeur en millions de dollars EU)
Importations selon les principaux pays ou zones

Country or area	1998	1999	2000	2001	2002	Pays ou zone
World	10930.5	11515.1	12476.3	12542.4	13708.8	Monde
Africa	253.4	237.9	279.6	294.0	304.8	Afrique
Americas	3604.8	4088.5	4646.9	4708.9	5254.9	Amériques
- Northern America	3066.0	3570.4	4069.3	4101.5	4700.0	- Amérique du Nord
- LAIA	369.4	354.4	411.3	443.4	389.8	- ALAI
- CACM	53.2	58.8	57.0	60.5	70.1	- MCC
- Caribbean	97.4	86.1	89.4	87.2	75.8	- Caraïbes
- Rest of America	18.7	18.8	19.9	16.4	19.2	- Autre d'Amérique
Asia excluding former USSR	1946.4	1994.6	2386.5	2305.3	2401.0	Asie ancienne URSS exclus
- Middle East	453.7	418.4	472.3	477.0	472.1	- Moyen-Orient
Asia former USSR	27.4	17.2	22.2	24.2	28.3	Asie ancienne URSS
Europe excluding former USSR	4705.3	4833.9	4737.2	4780.4	5187.2	Europe ancienne URSS exclus
- European Union	3941.1	4076.6	3997.9	4000.9	4283.6	- Union Européenne
- Eastern Europe	309.8	298.8	294.7	324.2	390.8	- Europe de l'Est
- Rest of Europe	454.3	458.5	444.6	455.3	512.9	- Autre de l'Europe
Europe former USSR	180.8	107.2	117.3	185.5	227.5	Europe ancienne URSS
Oceania	212.5	235.7	286.6	244.1	305.0	Océanie
United States	2662.8	3152.7	3615.0	3658.8	4203.9	Etats-Unis d'Amérique
Germany	873.0	852.8	835.3	871.0	843.4	Allemagne
China, Hong Kong SAR	664.7	713.5	892.5	825.8	875.9	Chine - RAS de Hong-Kong
United Kingdom	604.2	639.0	687.6	747.1	865.1	Royaume-Uni
France-Monaco	625.1	647.4	646.9	586.9	608.9	France-Monaco
Japan	398.9	421.0	508.0	500.2	510.5	Japon
Canada	400.2	414.5	451.7	438.9	491.9	Canada
Netherlands	263.4	308.7	282.3	280.4	297.9	Pays-Bas
Spain	269.3	285.0	274.9	267.2	303.3	Espagne
Italy-San Marino-Holy See	254.7	276.2	268.1	249.0	271.8	Italie-Saint-Marin-Saint-Siège
Switzerland-Liechtenstein	258.0	250.9	238.4	231.1	249.0	Suisse-Liechtenstein
Belgium	–	280.1	276.6	266.9	e292.7	Belgique
Austria	226.5	222.0	181.2	178.4	184.0	Autriche
Australia	154.8	175.1	225.0	185.2	233.6	Australie
Mexico	97.7	110.8	155.4	176.1	171.2	Mexique
Poland	149.0	140.7	126.6	134.0	156.3	Pologne
Saudi Arabia	125.5	102.5	129.0	129.7	e134.3	Arabie saoudite
Denmark	99.4	119.5	110.0	130.5	145.4	Danemark
United Arab Emirates	90.8	95.2	123.5	126.0	e129.3	Emirates arabes unis
Sweden	99.3	108.2	103.5	106.9	118.4	Suède
Norway	93.3	92.4	96.7	107.0	125.4	Norvège
Singapore	87.3	97.4	106.5	98.8	101.7	Singapour
Portugal	95.9	103.1	95.8	93.0	103.8	Portugal
Greece	101.2	91.5	94.5	76.3	e84.3	Grèce
Russian Federation	85.3	38.1	51.1	107.6	134.5	Fédération de Russie
Korea, Republic of	35.6	56.1	82.7	97.3	121.2	République de Corée
Ireland	75.9	75.2	74.9	75.0	86.2	Irlande
Israel	69.8	59.2	67.0	65.7	64.5	Israël
Czech Republic	54.9	58.3	57.6	64.1	78.7	République tchèque
Argentina	68.1	63.8	67.4	69.5	e30.7	Argentine

(Value as percentages of World total) **(Valeur en pourcentage du total mondial)**

Regions of the world	1993	1994	1995	1996	1997	1998	1999	2000	2001	2002	Régions du monde
World	100.0	100.0	100.0	100.0	100.0	100.0	100.0	100.0	100.0	100.0	Monde
Africa	3.1	2.8	2.6	2.5	2.4	2.3	2.1	2.2	2.3	2.2	Afrique
Americas	28.3	28.6	27.7	27.4	30.6	33.0	35.5	37.2	37.5	38.3	Amériques
- Northern America	23.4	23.8	23.6	23.3	26.1	28.1	31.0	32.6	32.7	34.3	- Amérique du Nord
- LAIA	3.4	3.4	2.7	2.8	3.1	3.4	3.1	3.3	3.5	2.8	- ALAI
- CACM	0.4	0.4	0.4	0.4	0.5	0.5	0.5	0.5	0.5	0.5	- MCC
- Caribbean	0.8	0.7	0.8	0.8	0.8	0.9	0.7	0.7	0.7	0.6	- Caraïbes
- Rest of America	0.3	0.3	0.2	0.2	0.2	0.2	0.2	0.2	0.1	0.1	- Autre d'Amérique
Asia excluding former USSR	21.4	20.7	21.8	21.3	20.3	17.8	17.3	19.1	18.4	17.5	Asie ancienne URSS exclus
- Middle East	5.8	4.7	4.5	4.4	4.3	4.2	3.6	3.8	3.8	3.4	- Moyen-Orient
Asia former USSR	0.1	0.1	0.1	0.2	0.2	0.3	0.1	0.2	0.2	0.2	Asie ancienne URSS
Europe excluding former USSR	44.5	44.1	43.3	44.4	42.4	43.0	42.0	38.0	38.1	37.8	Europe ancienne URSS exclus
- European Union	38.2	37.6	36.3	36.8	35.8	36.1	35.4	32.0	31.9	31.2	- Union Européenne
- Eastern Europe	2.4	2.4	2.6	3.1	2.6	2.8	2.6	2.4	2.6	2.9	- Europe de l'Est
- Rest of Europe	4.0	4.1	4.4	4.5	3.9	4.2	4.0	3.6	3.6	3.7	- Autre de l'Europe
Europe former USSR	0.8	1.7	2.5	2.1	2.1	1.7	0.9	0.9	1.5	1.7	Europe ancienne URSS
Oceania	1.8	1.9	1.9	2.0	2.1	1.9	2.0	2.3	1.9	2.2	Océanie

TRADE BY COMMODITY (Value in million US dollars)
Exports by principal countries or areas

COMMERCE PAR PRODUIT (Valeur en millions de dollars EU)
Exportations selon les principaux pays ou zones

Country or area	1998	1999	2000	2001	2002	Pays ou zone
World	10677.0	10864.8	12057.2	11877.0	12846.6	Monde
Africa	61.0	81.5	62.6	60.7	69.9	Afrique
Americas	1497.8	1266.2	1648.9	1620.9	1592.8	Amériques
- Northern America	844.5	835.5	929.4	924.8	884.5	- Amérique du Nord
- LAIA	631.2	403.8	691.6	671.2	679.1	- ALAI
- CACM	16.7	20.2	19.1	19.5	23.8	- MCC
- Caribbean	3.4	4.0	5.9	3.2	3.4	- Caraïbes
- Rest of America	2.0	2.7	2.8	2.2	2.0	- Autre d'Amérique
Asia excluding former USSR	4122.0	4585.9	5553.7	5262.6	5932.4	Asie ancienne URSS exclus
- Middle East	199.6	211.6	254.8	295.1	338.7	- Moyen-Orient
Asia former USSR	3.2	2.1	1.7	1.3	1.3	Asie ancienne URSS
Europe excluding former USSR	4885.0	4776.3	4649.6	4767.8	5098.4	Europe ancienne URSS exclus
- European Union	4337.1	4238.3	4094.1	4169.8	4433.7	- Union Européenne
- Eastern Europe	248.4	246.4	272.8	325.1	382.2	- Europe de l'Est
- Rest of Europe	299.5	291.6	282.7	272.9	282.5	- Autre de l'Europe
Europe former USSR	63.5	103.9	87.8	120.0	105.9	Europe ancienne URSS
Oceania	44.5	48.9	53.0	43.7	45.9	Océanie
China	1151.2	1330.1	1821.6	1982.2	2538.7	Chine
Italy-San Marino-Holy See	1583.6	1490.6	1438.9	1506.3	1561.7	Italie-Saint-Marin-Saint-Siège
China, Hong Kong SAR	824.3	896.1	1028.3	892.3	916.2	Chine - RAS de Hong-Kong
Germany	636.8	621.8	618.4	685.3	724.5	Allemagne
United States	583.8	536.7	611.3	602.0	552.6	Etats-Unis d'Amérique
France-Monaco	603.4	576.1	565.6	526.2	570.0	France-Monaco
Mexico	453.9	230.7	493.3	457.0	463.5	Mexique
Korea, Republic of	387.5	475.0	488.8	365.7	342.5	République de Corée
Spain	321.0	313.0	296.2	296.5	347.9	Espagne
Canada	260.7	298.8	318.1	322.8	331.8	Canada
India	151.9	230.8	378.3	373.2	395.7	Inde
Thailand	261.6	225.6	258.8	251.7	e265.9	Thaïlande
Belgium	–	312.9	287.3	284.9	e319.6	Belgique
Netherlands	175.8	214.8	217.5	203.5	212.3	Pays-Bas
United Kingdom	213.4	188.5	179.6	170.3	179.4	Royaume-Uni
Japan	200.0	211.9	207.8	149.8	125.7	Japon
Switzerland-Liechtenstein	198.5	171.9	166.8	153.5	156.2	Suisse-Liechtenstein
Turkey	125.4	133.5	151.2	175.8	231.0	Turquie
Indonesia	118.2	142.3	164.3	137.5	115.0	Indonésie
Denmark	116.9	117.5	124.5	155.4	160.0	Danemark
Brazil	102.0	103.6	119.6	123.3	e127.8	Brésil
Austria	97.7	102.1	113.0	107.0	111.5	Autriche
Portugal	119.4	105.4	97.8	83.9	89.3	Portugal
Sweden	92.3	98.0	90.3	80.1	88.8	Suède
Czech Republic	73.8	76.8	76.9	93.6	103.8	République tchèque
Poland	60.6	50.7	64.2	82.7	106.9	Pologne
Hungary	60.2	64.6	67.0	74.0	85.4	Hongrie
Belgium-Luxembourg	285.5	–	–	–	–	Belgique-Luxembourg
Belarus	36.9	44.0	53.0	83.9	64.4	Bélarus
United Arab Emirates	33.9	35.0	53.9	58.0	e60.4	Emirates arabes unis

(Value as percentages of World total) **(Valeur en pourcentage du total mondial)**

Regions of the world	1993	1994	1995	1996	1997	1998	1999	2000	2001	2002	Régions du monde
World	100.0	100.0	100.0	100.0	100.0	100.0	100.0	100.0	100.0	100.0	Monde
Africa	0.7	0.8	0.8	0.6	0.7	0.6	0.8	0.5	0.5	0.5	Afrique
Americas	12.3	13.6	12.8	12.9	13.4	14.0	11.7	13.7	13.6	12.4	Amériques
- Northern America	7.4	8.0	7.3	7.5	7.7	7.9	7.7	7.7	7.8	6.9	- Amérique du Nord
- LAIA	4.7	5.4	5.3	5.2	5.5	5.9	3.7	5.7	5.7	5.3	- ALAI
- CACM	0.1	0.1	0.1	0.1	0.1	0.2	0.2	0.2	0.2	0.2	- MCC
- Caribbean	0.0	0.0	0.0	0.0	0.0	0.0	0.0	0.0	0.0	0.0	- Caraïbes
- Rest of America	0.0	0.0	0.0	0.0	0.0	0.0	0.0	0.0	0.0	0.0	- Autre d'Amérique
Asia excluding former USSR	41.4	37.0	38.0	37.0	38.9	38.6	42.2	46.1	44.3	46.2	Asie ancienne URSS exclus
- Middle East	1.5	1.4	1.9	2.0	2.0	1.9	1.9	2.1	2.5	2.6	- Moyen-Orient
Asia former USSR	0.0	0.0	0.1	0.0	0.0	0.0	0.0	0.0	0.0	0.0	Asie ancienne URSS
Europe excluding former USSR	45.0	47.7	47.5	48.4	45.9	45.8	44.0	38.6	40.1	39.7	Europe ancienne URSS exclus
- European Union	38.7	41.8	41.9	42.9	40.8	40.6	39.0	34.0	35.1	34.5	- Union Européenne
- Eastern Europe	2.3	2.1	2.1	2.3	2.4	2.3	2.3	2.3	2.7	3.0	- Europe de l'Est
- Rest of Europe	4.0	3.8	3.5	3.2	2.8	2.8	2.7	2.3	2.3	2.2	- Autre de l'Europe
Europe former USSR	0.2	0.3	0.4	0.6	0.7	0.6	1.0	0.7	1.0	0.8	Europe ancienne URSS
Oceania	0.4	0.5	0.5	0.5	0.4	0.4	0.5	0.4	0.4	0.4	Océanie

699 Manufactures of base metal, nes

TRADE BY COMMODITY (Value in million US dollars) | COMMERCE PAR PRODUIT (Valeur en millions de dollars EU)

Imports by principal countries or areas | **Importations selon les principaux pays ou zones**

Country or area	1998	1999	2000	2001	2002	Pays ou zone
World	47680.6	49980.3	53464.5	52188.1	53717.3	Monde
Africa	925.0	981.2	946.4	956.7	994.2	Afrique
Americas	15587.4	17507.6	21121.7	19190.5	18171.2	Amériques
- Northern America	9895.4	10968.9	13009.0	11548.3	12311.2	- Amérique du Nord
- LAIA	5237.3	6101.5	7641.2	7123.8	5413.2	- ALAI
- CACM	154.1	151.9	160.5	164.4	185.3	- MCC
- Caribbean	248.7	234.6	265.6	313.3	222.4	- Caraïbes
- Rest of America	51.8	50.7	45.4	40.8	39.1	- Autre d'Amérique
Asia excluding former USSR	8962.4	9274.6	9609.6	9232.2	9896.1	Asie ancienne URSS exclus
- Middle East	1079.3	941.0	1034.0	1038.9	1098.0	- Moyen-Orient
Asia former USSR	128.8	109.3	110.1	103.0	113.6	Asie ancienne URSS
Europe excluding former USSR	20827.6	20978.5	20479.6	21434.1	23070.1	Europe ancienne URSS exclus
- European Union	17531.7	17638.8	16905.8	17612.9	18557.7	- Union Européenne
- Eastern Europe	1900.3	1992.3	2279.0	2533.5	3116.2	- Europe de l'Est
- Rest of Europe	1395.5	1347.4	1294.8	1287.7	1396.2	- Autre de l'Europe
Europe former USSR	497.2	368.9	436.4	585.0	683.5	Europe ancienne URSS
Oceania	752.2	760.2	760.7	686.6	788.6	Océanie
United States	7249.1	7859.6	8790.3	8381.2	9018.5	Etats-Unis d'Amérique
Mexico	4057.1	5124.2	6659.4	6196.1	4607.1	Mexique
Germany	4245.1	4230.7	3853.4	4342.5	4360.3	Allemagne
Canada	2619.7	3081.5	4213.7	3161.3	3285.1	Canada
France-Monaco	2747.2	2753.8	2824.7	2715.8	2922.2	France-Monaco
United Kingdom	2278.2	2197.8	2198.3	2293.7	2577.1	Royaume-Uni
Japan	1227.2	1259.5	1440.7	1521.2	1564.3	Japon
Thailand	1514.0	1784.3	1284.6	1172.4	e1221.6	Thaïlande
Spain	1194.7	1299.0	1269.8	1318.4	1461.2	Espagne
Italy-San Marino-Holy See	1207.0	1249.4	1277.7	1287.2	1293.2	Italie-Saint-Marin-Saint-Siège
Netherlands	1183.7	1291.9	1088.5	1039.3	1129.9	Pays-Bas
Belgium	–	1369.0	1302.3	1382.5	e1516.2	Belgique
China	842.6	923.5	1070.9	1130.4	1328.4	Chine
China, Hong Kong SAR	1050.9	1027.3	1080.7	1019.6	1015.9	Chine - RAS de Hong-Kong
Austria	1026.6	967.0	887.3	1014.2	1006.1	Autriche
Poland	630.6	725.4	795.0	825.8	1002.4	Pologne
Singapore	811.8	835.9	760.6	689.9	767.0	Singapour
Sweden	700.6	685.3	715.0	656.4	724.7	Suède
Czech Republic	593.0	526.4	623.8	736.5	871.7	République tchèque
Switzerland-Liechtenstein	667.3	656.7	638.3	627.6	644.1	Suisse-Liechtenstein
Korea, Republic of	453.7	591.1	663.8	662.0	751.4	République de Corée
Australia	600.1	601.3	614.5	545.9	626.5	Australie
Malaysia	505.9	474.6	593.2	549.2	e600.2	Malaisie
Hungary	372.4	442.9	513.9	527.3	637.5	Hongrie
Denmark	467.4	449.8	431.0	462.9	463.7	Danemark
Norway	400.6	351.7	320.8	306.2	345.7	Norvège
Brazil	424.7	342.9	331.3	315.1	304.9	Brésil
Portugal	310.2	350.1	324.4	340.6	348.8	Portugal
Israel	287.8	268.5	296.8	301.2	320.1	Israël
Belgium-Luxembourg	1468.3	–	–	–	–	Belgique-Luxembourg

(Value as percentages of World total) | **(Valeur en pourcentage du total mondial)**

Regions of the world	1993	1994	1995	1996	1997	1998	1999	2000	2001	2002	Régions du monde
World	100.0	100.0	100.0	100.0	100.0	100.0	100.0	100.0	100.0	100.0	Monde
Africa	2.5	2.3	2.2	2.1	1.9	1.9	2.0	1.8	1.8	1.9	Afrique
Americas	28.8	29.3	27.5	29.4	31.9	32.7	35.0	39.5	36.8	33.8	Amériques
- Northern America	19.6	20.1	18.3	19.1	20.1	20.8	21.9	24.3	22.1	22.9	- Amérique du Nord
- LAIA	8.2	8.4	8.4	9.4	10.8	11.0	12.2	14.3	13.7	10.1	- ALAI
- CACM	0.3	0.3	0.3	0.2	0.3	0.3	0.3	0.3	0.3	0.3	- MCC
- Caribbean	0.5	0.4	0.5	0.5	0.5	0.5	0.5	0.5	0.6	0.4	- Caraïbes
- Rest of America	0.2	0.1	0.1	0.1	0.1	0.1	0.1	0.1	0.1	0.1	- Autre d'Amérique
Asia excluding former USSR	22.6	21.6	21.4	21.0	20.9	18.8	18.6	18.0	17.7	18.4	Asie ancienne URSS exclus
- Middle East	3.2	2.7	2.5	2.3	2.2	2.3	1.9	1.9	2.0	2.0	- Moyen-Orient
Asia former USSR	0.1	0.2	0.2	0.3	0.2	0.3	0.2	0.2	0.2	0.2	Asie ancienne URSS
Europe excluding former USSR	43.3	43.8	45.8	44.4	42.2	43.7	42.0	38.3	41.1	42.9	Europe ancienne URSS exclus
- European Union	38.3	38.6	39.7	38.4	36.1	36.8	35.3	31.6	33.7	34.5	- Union Européenne
- Eastern Europe	1.6	1.7	2.4	2.7	3.1	4.0	4.0	4.3	4.9	5.8	- Europe de l'Est
- Rest of Europe	3.4	3.5	3.7	3.3	3.0	2.9	2.7	2.4	2.5	2.6	- Autre de l'Europe
Europe former USSR	0.6	0.8	0.9	1.0	1.1	1.0	0.7	0.8	1.1	1.3	Europe ancienne URSS
Oceania	2.0	2.1	2.0	1.8	1.8	1.6	1.5	1.4	1.3	1.5	Océanie

TRADE BY COMMODITY (Value in million US dollars)
Exports by principal countries or areas

COMMERCE PAR PRODUIT (Valeur en millions de dollars EU)
Exportations selon les principaux pays ou zones

Country or area	1998	1999	2000	2001	2002	Pays ou zone
World	46145.7	46953.7	50307.6	49143.0	52009.2	Monde
Africa	182.9	215.7	264.2	248.4	240.0	Afrique
Americas	10121.7	10751.8	13408.3	11821.9	12051.3	Amériques
- Northern America	8082.0	8623.9	10685.4	8959.9	9039.6	- Amérique du Nord
- LAIA	1998.3	2099.3	2683.4	2823.8	2971.2	- ALAI
- CACM	17.8	16.3	20.7	23.3	25.4	- MCC
- Caribbean	23.3	11.7	17.8	14.2	14.5	- Caraïbes
- Rest of America	0.3	0.5	1.0	0.6	0.7	- Autre d'Amérique
Asia excluding former USSR	9932.6	10560.9	11722.4	11039.7	12250.3	Asie ancienne URSS exclus
- Middle East	247.3	282.8	272.0	277.6	312.6	- Moyen-Orient
Asia former USSR	23.7	12.4	19.2	28.8	31.4	Asie ancienne URSS
Europe excluding former USSR	25181.8	24682.3	24060.7	25191.0	26622.7	Europe ancienne URSS exclus
- European Union	22285.9	21873.5	21053.5	22055.0	23141.6	- Union Européenne
- Eastern Europe	1748.9	1704.6	1886.5	2038.8	2359.4	- Europe de l'Est
- Rest of Europe	1146.9	1104.2	1120.7	1097.2	1121.6	- Autre de l'Europe
Europe former USSR	476.4	531.7	645.9	637.2	579.7	Europe ancienne URSS
Oceania	226.6	198.9	186.9	176.0	233.7	Océanie
United States	6155.5	6612.5	8512.7	7024.0	7063.6	Etats-Unis d'Amérique
Germany	6728.0	6815.3	6380.3	6998.3	7355.8	Allemagne
Italy-San Marino-Holy See	4293.5	4138.4	4073.8	4254.2	4384.6	Italie-Saint-Marin-Saint-Siège
France-Monaco	2734.0	2733.1	2742.5	2610.8	2700.8	France-Monaco
China	1968.8	2106.4	2542.7	2844.5	3623.8	Chine
Mexico	1663.5	1834.5	2348.9	2449.8	2588.7	Mexique
Japan	1996.5	2094.4	2397.3	2033.3	2186.2	Japon
Canada	1926.4	2011.3	2172.7	1935.9	1975.9	Canada
United Kingdom	2094.7	1922.5	1845.3	1798.5	1817.9	Royaume-Uni
Austria	1460.0	1417.8	1298.5	1392.5	1386.2	Autriche
Spain	1135.1	1149.7	1185.9	1308.8	1406.0	Espagne
China, Hong Kong SAR	1204.2	1222.2	1282.9	1217.6	1193.5	Chine - RAS de Hong-Kong
Netherlands	1002.9	796.7	756.5	921.6	972.9	Pays-Bas
Czech Republic	753.7	704.6	785.6	844.6	954.8	République tchèque
Belgium	-	971.9	934.2	946.3	e1061.7	Belgique
Sweden	699.2	712.3	683.8	651.9	716.5	Suède
Switzerland-Liechtenstein	719.0	698.6	695.1	673.5	670.0	Suisse-Liechtenstein
Korea, Republic of	532.3	606.7	695.2	731.0	766.9	République de Corée
Poland	611.9	569.9	630.0	655.0	782.5	Pologne
Denmark	493.5	487.2	443.5	434.0	470.1	Danemark
Russian Federation	354.4	424.0	520.7	404.1	324.3	Fédération de Russie
Singapore	406.5	409.9	416.4	359.2	378.4	Singapour
Malaysia	285.1	311.0	323.6	340.7	e361.0	Malaisie
India	233.1	281.7	334.4	308.1	332.4	Inde
Portugal	279.1	292.2	274.2	279.2	355.5	Portugal
Thailand	239.8	252.5	320.4	311.2	e328.7	Thaïlande
Hungary	209.1	235.7	253.7	276.2	305.2	Hongrie
Finland	210.5	199.5	216.8	212.4	229.8	Finlande
Brazil	191.8	151.4	195.6	227.7	e236.1	Brésil
Belgium-Luxembourg	936.0	-	-	-	-	Belgique-Luxembourg

(Value as percentages of World total) **(Valeur en pourcentage du total mondial)**

Regions of the world	1993	1994	1995	1996	1997	1998	1999	2000	2001	2002	Régions du monde
World	100.0	100.0	100.0	100.0	100.0	100.0	100.0	100.0	100.0	100.0	Monde
Africa	0.4	0.5	0.5	0.3	0.4	0.4	0.5	0.5	0.5	0.5	Afrique
Americas	17.6	18.6	17.5	19.4	21.1	21.9	22.9	26.7	24.1	23.2	Amériques
- Northern America	14.0	15.3	14.7	15.9	17.0	17.5	18.4	21.2	18.2	17.4	- Amérique du Nord
- LAIA	3.6	3.3	2.7	3.4	4.0	4.3	4.5	5.3	5.7	5.7	- ALAI
- CACM	0.0	0.0	0.0	0.0	0.0	0.0	0.0	0.0	0.0	0.0	- MCC
- Caribbean	0.0	0.0	0.0	0.0	0.0	0.1	0.0	0.0	0.0	0.0	- Caraïbes
- Rest of America	0.0	0.0	0.0	0.0	0.0	0.0	0.0	0.0	0.0	0.0	- Autre d'Amérique
Asia excluding former USSR	31.1	25.8	25.0	23.4	23.8	21.5	22.5	23.3	22.5	23.6	Asie ancienne URSS exclus
- Middle East	0.4	0.4	0.6	0.5	0.6	0.5	0.6	0.5	0.6	0.6	- Moyen-Orient
Asia former USSR	0.0	0.1	0.1	0.1	0.0	0.1	0.0	0.0	0.1	0.1	Asie ancienne URSS
Europe excluding former USSR	49.9	53.6	55.6	55.4	53.1	54.6	52.6	47.8	51.3	51.2	Europe ancienne URSS exclus
- European Union	45.8	49.0	49.9	49.8	47.5	48.3	46.6	41.8	44.9	44.5	- Union Européenne
- Eastern Europe	1.3	1.7	2.6	2.8	3.0	3.8	3.6	3.7	4.1	4.5	- Europe de l'Est
- Rest of Europe	2.7	2.9	3.0	2.8	2.5	2.5	2.4	2.2	2.2	2.2	- Autre de l'Europe
Europe former USSR	0.3	0.8	0.8	0.8	0.9	1.0	1.1	1.3	1.3	1.1	Europe ancienne URSS
Oceania	0.5	0.6	0.5	0.6	0.6	0.5	0.4	0.4	0.4	0.4	Océanie

711 Steam boilers and auxiliary plant; and parts thereof, nes

TRADE BY COMMODITY (Value in million US dollars)
Imports by principal countries or areas

COMMERCE PAR PRODUIT (Valeur en millions de dollars EU)
Importations selon les principaux pays ou zones

Country or area	1998	1999	2000	2001	2002	Pays ou zone
World	3940.7	3081.6	2797.1	3158.4	3248.5	Monde
Africa	256.6	343.6	126.6	104.0	145.5	Afrique
Americas	658.0	527.2	675.9	947.5	1083.3	Amériques
- Northern America	253.8	261.6	490.0	691.0	892.5	- Amérique du Nord
- LAIA	302.0	199.1	130.7	150.7	143.8	- ALAI
- CACM	22.1	20.8	6.4	9.2	13.9	- MCC
- Caribbean	74.6	43.1	46.6	95.3	31.6	- Caraïbes
- Rest of America	5.5	2.6	2.2	1.3	1.5	- Autre d'Amérique
Asia excluding former USSR	2265.8	1430.5	1266.2	1504.8	1370.2	Asie ancienne URSS exclus
- Middle East	382.0	357.0	333.3	574.7	600.5	- Moyen-Orient
Asia former USSR	38.1	39.3	32.9	24.5	33.6	Asie ancienne URSS
Europe excluding former USSR	562.8	601.7	545.0	492.6	514.7	Europe ancienne URSS exclus
- European Union	328.4	396.9	396.6	333.4	339.4	- Union Européenne
- Eastern Europe	199.0	146.0	102.6	120.9	126.2	- Europe de l'Est
- Rest of Europe	35.5	58.7	45.8	38.3	49.2	- Autre de l'Europe
Europe former USSR	134.9	90.6	68.6	63.3	81.0	Europe ancienne URSS
Oceania	24.4	48.7	81.9	21.8	20.2	Océanie
China	999.0	543.2	363.7	369.2	193.5	Chine
United States	154.5	197.7	437.1	606.6	834.5	Etats-Unis d'Amérique
Turkey	144.3	59.8	32.9	171.1	279.4	Turquie
Saudi Arabia	65.2	178.5	160.6	76.2	e78.8	Arabie saoudite
Korea, Republic of	139.2	121.7	76.3	83.7	128.3	République de Corée
Indonesia	227.0	102.1	117.4	25.6	22.6	Indonésie
Morocco	156.9	258.5	26.7	21.2	e22.3	Maroc
Malaysia	10.3	17.7	31.6	198.2	e216.6	Malaisie
United Arab Emirates	26.6	27.9	56.0	145.8	e149.6	Emirates arabes unis
Canada	99.3	63.9	52.6	84.2	57.7	Canada
Poland	100.7	84.7	48.9	45.8	72.1	Pologne
United Kingdom	68.3	96.7	57.7	31.0	38.2	Royaume-Uni
Argentina	148.1	58.6	39.8	12.4	e5.5	Argentine
Germany	56.8	55.2	50.3	56.5	45.2	Allemagne
Singapore	93.3	56.4	63.7	37.7	11.7	Singapour
Iran (Islamic Republic of)	75.6	22.1	20.4	95.8	25.7	Iran (République islamique d')
Mexico	18.9	24.8	29.5	77.4	68.3	Mexique
Japan	60.3	30.3	39.9	52.8	30.2	Japon
Spain	27.9	36.1	20.6	57.7	62.4	Espagne
Russian Federation	78.2	34.6	27.5	30.9	23.0	Fédération de Russie
France-Monaco	28.1	39.0	55.4	37.0	28.8	France-Monaco
Brazil	56.3	44.8	9.4	30.4	42.4	Brésil
Australia	9.5	22.0	77.6	16.1	11.6	Australie
Czech Republic	57.3	30.9	17.2	11.8	15.3	République tchèque
Iraq	e	e36.1	e24.6	e37.4	e31.3	Iraq
Belgium	–	24.4	18.4	42.3	e46.4	Belgique
Ukraine	35.8	33.5	25.1	16.7	18.0	Ukraine
Netherlands Antilles	37.6	7.7	10.9	61.8	9.3	Antilles néerlandaises
Greece	9.0	7.0	78.3	11.4	e12.6	Grèce
Chile	39.4	33.3	14.6	10.3	12.7	Chili

(Value as percentages of World total)

(Valeur en pourcentage du total mondial)

Regions of the world	1993	1994	1995	1996	1997	1998	1999	2000	2001	2002	Régions du monde
World	100.0	100.0	100.0	100.0	100.0	100.0	100.0	100.0	100.0	100.0	Monde
Africa	16.2	5.9	2.4	2.7	2.5	6.5	11.2	4.5	3.3	4.5	Afrique
Americas	18.4	18.6	14.3	18.8	13.5	16.7	17.1	24.2	30.0	33.3	Amériques
- Northern America	6.5	6.2	7.2	9.5	6.4	6.4	8.5	17.5	21.9	27.5	- Amérique du Nord
- LAIA	9.2	11.5	5.2	8.1	5.9	7.7	6.5	4.7	4.8	4.4	- ALAI
- CACM	0.6	0.2	0.4	0.5	0.5	0.6	0.7	0.2	0.3	0.4	- MCC
- Caribbean	1.8	0.6	1.3	0.7	0.7	1.9	1.4	1.7	3.0	1.0	- Caraïbes
- Rest of America	0.2	0.2	0.2	0.1	0.1	0.1	0.1	0.1	0.0	0.0	- Autre d'Amérique
Asia excluding former USSR	45.3	47.7	50.9	50.1	58.5	57.5	46.4	45.3	47.6	42.2	Asie ancienne URSS exclus
- Middle East	9.0	6.7	10.2	7.9	9.0	9.7	11.6	11.9	18.2	18.5	- Moyen-Orient
Asia former USSR	0.1	0.9	0.9	1.0	0.5	1.0	1.3	1.2	0.8	1.0	Asie ancienne URSS
Europe excluding former USSR	16.4	19.0	23.5	19.6	17.6	14.3	19.5	19.5	15.6	15.8	Europe ancienne URSS exclus
- European Union	10.5	13.9	18.4	13.3	10.9	8.3	12.9	14.2	10.6	10.4	- Union Européenne
- Eastern Europe	3.3	3.9	4.1	4.6	5.1	5.0	4.7	3.7	3.8	3.9	- Europe de l'Est
- Rest of Europe	2.6	1.2	1.0	1.8	1.6	0.9	1.9	1.6	1.2	1.5	- Autre de l'Europe
Europe former USSR	3.3	7.6	7.5	6.6	6.4	3.4	2.9	2.5	2.0	2.5	Europe ancienne URSS
Oceania	0.3	0.3	0.5	1.2	0.9	0.6	1.6	2.9	0.7	0.6	Océanie

TRADE BY COMMODITY (Value in million US dollars)
Exports by principal countries or areas

COMMERCE PAR PRODUIT (Valeur en millions de dollars EU)
Exportations selon les principaux pays ou zones

Country or area	1998	1999	2000	2001	2002	Pays ou zone
World	3597.8	2742.8	2510.1	2806.6	2566.3	Monde
Africa	7.8	6.8	12.1	26.5	7.1	Afrique
Americas	779.1	626.0	553.8	539.9	433.5	Amériques
- Northern America	727.8	578.8	502.3	489.2	380.2	- Amérique du Nord
- LAIA	43.9	46.2	50.7	49.0	52.3	- ALAI
- CACM	0.2	0.1	0.1	0.8	0.4	- MCC
- Caribbean	7.2	0.9	0.7	0.9	0.5	- Caraïbes
- Rest of America	0.0	0.0	0.0	0.0	0.0	- Autre d'Amérique
Asia excluding former USSR	1130.9	723.6	794.9	948.7	893.7	Asie ancienne URSS exclus
- Middle East	24.5	17.1	14.2	11.6	19.0	- Moyen-Orient
Asia former USSR	0.3	1.0	0.7	0.2	0.1	Asie ancienne URSS
Europe excluding former USSR	1493.0	1277.5	1055.0	1150.0	1175.5	Europe ancienne URSS exclus
- European Union	1310.5	1133.0	848.4	960.6	948.3	- Union Européenne
- Eastern Europe	150.0	110.9	169.3	154.3	202.7	- Europe de l'Est
- Rest of Europe	32.5	33.6	37.3	35.1	24.5	- Autre de l'Europe
Europe former USSR	179.9	100.3	89.9	137.2	52.5	Europe ancienne URSS
Oceania	6.8	7.7	3.7	4.1	4.0	Océanie
Japan	802.3	385.4	321.6	293.9	230.2	Japon
United States	616.0	475.3	401.9	295.6	231.3	Etats-Unis d'Amérique
Korea, Republic of	122.4	153.5	265.9	404.6	407.8	République de Corée
Germany	204.6	167.2	135.9	195.7	203.5	Allemagne
United Kingdom	197.1	175.2	142.2	147.0	100.9	Royaume-Uni
Italy-San Marino-Holy See	89.8	128.3	156.4	139.8	183.2	Italie-Saint-Marin-Saint-Siège
France-Monaco	160.4	192.3	114.7	154.0	65.4	France-Monaco
Canada	111.9	103.5	100.4	193.7	148.8	Canada
Finland	167.3	80.1	61.8	103.7	88.7	Finlande
Russian Federation	162.7	88.1	77.8	127.4	41.3	Fédération de Russie
China	97.4	70.8	101.1	113.9	113.2	Chine
Spain	182.7	104.9	70.8	55.9	81.7	Espagne
Belgium	–	63.7	41.3	78.3	e87.9	Belgique
Netherlands	74.8	98.9	32.9	24.0	34.3	Pays-Bas
Czech Republic	19.5	23.5	55.2	65.4	80.4	République tchèque
Poland	61.6	40.3	51.6	40.5	45.9	Pologne
Denmark	70.4	68.2	44.0	19.0	18.7	Danemark
Slovakia	24.0	23.5	36.9	23.6	43.0	Slovaquie
Mexico	21.3	35.5	35.0	23.4	25.6	Mexique
Austria	41.8	27.4	17.9	11.5	19.3	Autriche
Sweden	34.9	18.3	14.9	14.7	19.8	Suède
Brazil	17.2	8.0	13.4	23.0	e23.9	Brésil
Hungary	33.6	15.4	12.2	11.6	10.8	Hongrie
Belgium-Luxembourg	78.2	–	–	–	–	Belgique-Luxembourg
Thailand	2.9	4.8	8.0	29.7	e31.4	Thaïlande
Switzerland-Liechtenstein	14.4	17.4	16.8	17.4	10.7	Suisse-Liechtenstein
India	12.5	11.3	11.9	18.1	16.6	Inde
Romania	10.8	7.8	10.9	10.6	19.6	Roumanie
Turkey	22.8	12.0	5.8	7.8	9.1	Turquie
Malaysia	4.3	4.5	13.5	14.7	e15.6	Malaisie

(Value as percentages of World total) **(Valeur en pourcentage du total mondial)**

Regions of the world	1993	1994	1995	1996	1997	1998	1999	2000	2001	2002	Régions du monde
World	100.0	100.0	100.0	100.0	100.0	100.0	100.0	100.0	100.0	100.0	Monde
Africa	0.3	0.1	0.3	0.4	0.2	0.2	0.2	0.5	0.9	0.3	Afrique
Americas	22.7	21.4	23.3	28.0	28.9	21.7	22.8	22.1	19.2	16.9	Amériques
- Northern America	20.8	19.3	22.3	26.2	27.4	20.2	21.1	20.0	17.4	14.8	- Amérique du Nord
- LAIA	1.8	2.0	1.0	1.8	1.5	1.2	1.7	2.0	1.7	2.0	- ALAI
- CACM	0.0	0.0	0.0	0.0	0.0	0.0	0.0	0.0	0.0	0.0	- MCC
- Caribbean	0.0	0.0	0.0	0.0	0.0	0.2	0.0	0.0	0.0	0.0	- Caraïbes
- Rest of America	0.1	0.0	0.0	0.0	0.0	0.0	0.0	0.0	0.0	0.0	- Autre d'Amérique
Asia excluding former USSR	22.6	28.3	26.3	23.2	20.4	31.4	26.4	31.7	33.8	34.8	Asie ancienne URSS exclus
- Middle East	0.4	0.2	0.5	0.7	0.8	0.7	0.6	0.6	0.4	0.7	- Moyen-Orient
Asia former USSR	0.0	0.0	0.0	0.0	0.0	0.0	0.0	0.0	0.0	0.0	Asie ancienne URSS
Europe excluding former USSR	51.4	46.9	46.5	44.8	45.7	41.5	46.6	42.0	41.0	45.8	Europe ancienne URSS exclus
- European Union	45.4	42.5	41.5	39.4	41.0	36.4	41.3	33.8	34.2	37.0	- Union Européenne
- Eastern Europe	4.7	3.6	4.1	4.3	3.9	4.2	4.0	6.7	5.5	7.9	- Europe de l'Est
- Rest of Europe	1.2	0.8	1.0	1.1	0.8	0.9	1.2	1.5	1.3	1.0	- Autre de l'Europe
Europe former USSR	2.0	2.8	2.9	3.0	4.3	5.0	3.7	3.6	4.9	2.0	Europe ancienne URSS
Oceania	1.0	0.5	0.7	0.6	0.4	0.2	0.3	0.1	0.1	0.2	Océanie

712 Steam engines, turbines

TRADE BY COMMODITY (Value in million US dollars)
Imports by principal countries or areas

COMMERCE PAR PRODUIT (Valeur en millions de dollars EU)
Importations selon les principaux pays ou zones

Country or area	1998	1999	2000	2001	2002	Pays ou zone
World	3351.0	2833.3	2982.2	3216.4	3105.6	Monde
Africa	56.3	46.9	40.1	39.3	58.0	Afrique
Americas	497.8	492.0	500.0	755.3	848.2	Amériques
- Northern America	206.4	276.3	378.9	594.0	683.4	- Amérique du Nord
- LAIA	209.7	158.3	97.0	128.8	134.3	- ALAI
- CACM	54.7	39.6	9.7	3.9	6.0	- MCC
- Caribbean	26.0	17.1	14.0	28.4	23.6	- Caraïbes
- Rest of America	1.1	0.8	0.4	0.2	0.8	- Autre d'Amérique
Asia excluding former USSR	1945.2	1540.6	1752.1	1289.1	1350.3	Asie ancienne URSS exclus
- Middle East	543.8	549.3	639.0	413.7	408.2	- Moyen-Orient
Asia former USSR	16.4	13.1	21.6	16.1	8.5	Asie ancienne URSS
Europe excluding former USSR	773.4	682.0	595.7	1037.0	781.0	Europe ancienne URSS exclus
- European Union	597.9	504.0	464.5	874.4	593.9	- Union Européenne
- Eastern Europe	118.9	115.3	76.1	97.4	113.2	- Europe de l'Est
- Rest of Europe	56.6	62.8	55.1	65.2	73.9	- Autre de l'Europe
Europe former USSR	27.5	31.0	31.7	20.3	19.1	Europe ancienne URSS
Oceania	34.4	27.7	41.0	59.3	40.4	Océanie
United States	165.8	237.5	339.4	545.3	633.8	Etats-Unis d'Amérique
China	438.3	458.8	395.1	222.9	256.4	Chine
Iran (Islamic Republic of)	390.2	424.1	328.2	154.6	85.5	Iran (République islamique d')
Spain	33.3	70.3	40.3	435.6	126.4	Espagne
Germany	133.5	87.4	77.7	129.4	164.3	Allemagne
Korea, Republic of	157.2	92.3	84.3	97.1	161.5	République de Corée
Japan	85.6	45.0	90.2	148.6	154.9	Japon
United Kingdom	86.4	131.0	108.0	94.6	96.8	Royaume-Uni
Turkey	101.3	24.8	13.6	166.8	200.7	Turquie
Indonesia	305.7	65.6	38.3	24.6	32.9	Indonésie
Saudi Arabia	16.1	50.6	227.3	42.0	e43.5	Arabie saoudite
Italy-San Marino-Holy See	59.8	68.1	70.4	61.4	76.1	Italie-Saint-Marin-Saint-Siège
Singapore	74.7	64.5	70.6	67.4	31.7	Singapour
Mexico	23.1	30.2	56.6	82.3	94.8	Mexique
Malaysia	36.1	24.6	20.1	90.1	e98.5	Malaisie
France-Monaco	53.7	28.9	39.0	62.1	62.1	France-Monaco
Poland	42.9	53.0	32.0	45.9	64.7	Pologne
India	64.2	38.2	58.0	33.6	40.4	Inde
Switzerland-Liechtenstein	41.8	34.6	41.5	48.7	61.0	Suisse-Liechtenstein
Canada	40.6	38.8	39.5	48.4	49.5	Canada
Brazil	77.4	77.3	13.9	19.4	22.4	Brésil
Australia	7.7	23.1	39.7	57.4	26.2	Australie
Netherlands	56.6	35.3	22.2	21.1	12.9	Pays-Bas
Czech Republic	52.7	20.7	16.0	20.1	20.6	République tchèque
Finland	73.1	4.2	9.1	14.7	8.4	Finlande
Pakistan	39.6	26.5	14.6	8.7	18.9	Pakistan
Chile	62.0	30.0	1.8	2.5	6.0	Chili
United Arab Emirates	18.6	19.5	41.5	9.2	e9.4	Emirates arabes unis
Philippines	30.6	23.5	26.0	10.5	5.7	Philippines
Israel	35.0	26.5	1.7	24.3	5.2	Israël

(Value as percentages of World total) **(Valeur en pourcentage du total mondial)**

Regions of the world	1993	1994	1995	1996	1997	1998	1999	2000	2001	2002	Régions du monde
World	100.0	100.0	100.0	100.0	100.0	100.0	100.0	100.0	100.0	100.0	Monde
Africa	3.6	2.6	1.2	1.8	1.5	1.7	1.7	1.3	1.2	1.9	Afrique
Americas	16.9	26.2	11.1	12.0	15.9	14.9	17.4	16.8	23.5	27.3	Amériques
- Northern America	8.5	6.8	5.6	4.3	6.0	6.2	9.8	12.7	18.5	22.0	- Amérique du Nord
- LAIA	7.0	18.3	4.0	5.9	8.1	6.3	5.6	3.3	4.0	4.3	- ALAI
- CACM	0.1	0.3	0.2	0.4	0.5	1.6	1.4	0.3	0.1	0.2	- MCC
- Caribbean	1.3	0.8	1.3	1.2	1.2	0.8	0.6	0.5	0.9	0.8	- Caraïbes
- Rest of America	0.1	0.0	0.0	0.0	0.0	0.0	0.0	0.0	0.0	0.0	- Autre d'Amérique
Asia excluding former USSR	54.0	49.1	64.6	57.0	57.4	58.0	54.4	58.8	40.1	43.5	Asie ancienne URSS exclus
- Middle East	13.3	3.4	8.8	10.8	10.9	16.2	19.4	21.4	12.9	13.1	- Moyen-Orient
Asia former USSR	0.0	0.2	0.8	0.6	0.2	0.5	0.5	0.7	0.5	0.3	Asie ancienne URSS
Europe excluding former USSR	23.7	19.0	20.0	25.0	22.0	23.1	24.1	20.0	32.2	25.1	Europe ancienne URSS exclus
- European Union	20.1	16.3	15.1	20.9	17.5	17.8	17.8	15.6	27.2	19.1	- Union Européenne
- Eastern Europe	1.3	0.7	2.5	2.1	2.7	3.5	4.1	2.6	3.0	3.6	- Europe de l'Est
- Rest of Europe	2.3	2.0	2.4	2.0	1.8	1.7	2.2	1.8	2.0	2.4	- Autre de l'Europe
Europe former USSR	1.0	0.9	1.3	1.4	1.1	0.8	1.1	1.1	0.6	0.6	Europe ancienne URSS
Oceania	0.8	1.9	1.0	2.3	1.8	1.0	1.0	1.4	1.8	1.3	Océanie

TRADE BY COMMODITY (Value in million US dollars)
Exports by principal countries or areas

COMMERCE PAR PRODUIT (Valeur en millions de dollars EU)
Exportations selon les principaux pays ou zones

Country or area	1998	1999	2000	2001	2002	Pays ou zone
World	3060.0	2394.3	2513.9	3036.3	3075.6	Monde
Africa	4.5	1.2	1.2	7.2	18.8	Afrique
Americas	673.2	554.5	580.9	637.7	480.7	Amériques
- Northern America	651.3	512.1	509.8	523.1	388.8	- Amérique du Nord
- LAIA	21.2	40.6	66.0	105.2	83.7	- ALAI
- CACM	0.0	0.0	0.8	0.8	0.2	- MCC
- Caribbean	0.6	1.8	4.3	8.6	8.0	- Caraïbes
- Rest of America	0.0	0.0	0.0	0.0	0.0	- Autre d'Amérique
Asia excluding former USSR	1070.4	670.7	793.3	1026.1	1038.7	Asie ancienne URSS exclus
- Middle East	2.3	4.0	4.6	4.5	5.0	- Moyen-Orient
Asia former USSR	2.5	1.2	0.2	0.3	0.3	Asie ancienne URSS
Europe excluding former USSR	1223.4	1098.5	1036.7	1297.3	1363.8	Europe ancienne URSS exclus
- European Union	1028.0	905.4	868.1	1087.6	1189.9	- Union Européenne
- Eastern Europe	120.0	128.8	132.3	149.2	129.1	- Europe de l'Est
- Rest of Europe	75.4	64.3	36.2	60.4	44.8	- Autre de l'Europe
Europe former USSR	79.0	62.6	83.5	31.9	147.7	Europe ancienne URSS
Oceania	7.0	5.7	18.1	35.8	25.5	Océanie
Japan	933.5	590.4	700.0	893.2	873.3	Japon
United States	631.0	498.2	490.8	487.9	371.6	Etats-Unis d'Amérique
Germany	436.5	358.8	296.5	413.7	467.5	Allemagne
Italy-San Marino-Holy See	135.2	156.0	199.9	182.7	196.7	Italie-Saint-Marin-Saint-Siège
United Kingdom	146.7	135.4	122.6	222.7	220.7	Royaume-Uni
France-Monaco	175.1	138.1	121.4	133.5	156.6	France-Monaco
Czech Republic	68.3	61.7	81.7	49.2	64.5	République tchèque
Russian Federation	57.9	42.2	65.7	19.2	139.2	Fédération de Russie
Mexico	14.9	26.3	60.6	97.9	76.3	Mexique
Poland	37.1	40.1	36.7	73.1	41.8	Pologne
Sweden	41.8	38.6	62.7	31.1	33.0	Suède
Switzerland-Liechtenstein	68.8	52.9	24.2	33.0	25.2	Suisse-Liechtenstein
Austria	42.0	20.2	21.3	38.3	48.4	Autriche
Korea, Republic of	29.5	14.2	22.1	34.4	46.9	République de Corée
China	30.4	27.9	12.2	31.6	35.7	Chine
Netherlands	32.7	28.6	15.5	20.5	16.4	Pays-Bas
Canada	20.3	13.9	19.1	35.2	17.1	Canada
India	25.6	2.3	1.7	15.6	30.7	Inde
Australia	1.5	2.0	12.9	32.4	20.0	Australie
Ukraine	21.0	18.0	14.4	7.3	8.0	Ukraine
Belgium	–	18.7	19.5	12.7	e14.2	Belgique
Singapore	10.4	11.7	18.2	7.9	11.9	Singapour
Slovenia	2.8	6.5	10.2	23.1	15.7	Slovénie
Malaysia	24.0	6.8	7.2	9.3	e9.8	Malaisie
Spain	5.5	6.3	2.5	16.7	24.3	Espagne
Hungary	11.0	19.2		12.4	11.7	Hongrie
Indonesia	3.9	4.8	11.8	9.5	10.2	Indonésie
Romania	1.7	6.2	11.5	11.5	8.3	Roumanie
Brazil	4.5	6.7	4.1	5.8	e6.0	Brésil
South Africa	–	–	0.7	6.2	17.0	Afrique du Sud

(Value as percentages of World total) **(Valeur en pourcentage du total mondial)**

Regions of the world	1993	1994	1995	1996	1997	1998	1999	2000	2001	2002	Régions du monde
World	100.0	100.0	100.0	100.0	100.0	100.0	100.0	100.0	100.0	100.0	Monde
Africa	0.1	0.5	0.1	0.0	0.1	0.1	0.1	0.0	0.2	0.6	Afrique
Americas	22.3	23.4	28.7	26.0	33.5	22.0	23.2	23.1	21.0	15.6	Amériques
- Northern America	21.7	23.1	28.4	25.6	32.8	21.3	21.4	20.3	17.2	12.6	- Amérique du Nord
- LAIA	0.6	0.2	0.2	0.4	0.7	0.7	1.7	2.6	3.5	2.7	- ALAI
- CACM	0.0	0.0	0.0	0.0	0.0	0.0	0.0	0.0	0.0	0.0	- MCC
- Caribbean	0.0	0.1	0.0	0.0	0.0	0.0	0.1	0.2	0.3	0.3	- Caraïbes
- Rest of America	0.0	0.0	0.0	0.0	0.0	0.0	0.0	0.0	0.0	0.0	- Autre d'Amérique
Asia excluding former USSR	25.7	28.3	23.2	25.9	21.9	35.0	28.0	31.6	33.8	33.8	Asie ancienne URSS exclus
- Middle East	0.1	0.0	0.1	0.2	0.2	0.1	0.2	0.2	0.1	0.2	- Moyen-Orient
Asia former USSR	0.0	0.0	0.0	0.0	0.0	0.1	0.1	0.0	0.0	0.0	Asie ancienne URSS
Europe excluding former USSR	50.5	46.0	45.9	45.8	42.0	40.0	45.9	41.2	42.7	44.3	Europe ancienne URSS exclus
- European Union	41.4	38.2	36.0	37.3	35.6	33.6	37.8	34.5	35.8	38.7	- Union Européenne
- Eastern Europe	2.0	2.0	3.9	3.5	2.8	3.9	5.4	5.3	4.9	4.2	- Europe de l'Est
- Rest of Europe	7.0	5.8	6.0	5.0	3.5	2.5	2.7	1.4	2.0	1.5	- Autre de l'Europe
Europe former USSR	1.3	1.7	1.9	2.3	2.2	2.6	2.6	3.3	1.1	4.8	Europe ancienne URSS
Oceania	0.1	0.2	0.2	0.0	0.3	0.2	0.2	0.7	1.2	0.8	Océanie

713 Internal combustion piston engines, and parts thereof, nes

TRADE BY COMMODITY (Value in million US dollars)
Imports by principal countries or areas

COMMERCE PAR PRODUIT (Valeur en millions de dollars EU)
Importations selon les principaux pays ou zones

Country or area	1998	1999	2000	2001	2002	Pays ou zone
World	63871.9	67686.9	71133.2	67724.6	73590.4	Monde
Africa	886.8	851.9	818.5	880.0	932.4	Afrique
Americas	25567.0	28933.9	30869.9	27018.8	27798.3	Amériques
- Northern America	20387.3	23608.7	24505.1	21265.0	22004.3	- Amérique du Nord
- LAIA	4879.1	5047.2	6026.1	5472.8	5450.2	- ALAI
- CACM	88.8	96.0	82.6	97.9	153.9	- MCC
- Caribbean	184.6	153.3	224.0	153.3	162.5	- Caraïbes
- Rest of America	27.1	28.6	32.2	29.8	27.5	- Autre d'Amérique
Asia excluding former USSR	6497.4	7201.5	8833.2	8305.0	9938.0	Asie ancienne URSS exclus
- Middle East	1305.0	1220.6	1948.3	1695.2	2101.0	- Moyen-Orient
Asia former USSR	139.4	113.6	138.0	135.8	110.4	Asie ancienne URSS
Europe excluding former USSR	29520.6	29416.8	29214.8	30132.0	33408.4	Europe ancienne URSS exclus
- European Union	26050.5	26044.3	25659.9	26374.1	29311.5	- Union Européenne
- Eastern Europe	2772.0	2824.4	3015.5	3167.1	3439.6	- Europe de l'Est
- Rest of Europe	698.1	548.1	539.3	590.8	657.2	- Autre de l'Europe
Europe former USSR	447.9	313.2	352.3	358.2	379.0	Europe ancienne URSS
Oceania	812.8	855.9	906.4	894.7	1023.8	Océanie
United States	13078.4	15057.5	16056.4	14077.4	14944.0	Etats-Unis d'Amérique
Canada	7297.7	8538.5	8438.3	7176.2	7043.6	Canada
Germany	6545.2	6819.4	7137.9	7717.2	8523.6	Allemagne
Mexico	2603.3	3265.6	4267.3	3770.5	3972.5	Mexique
France-Monaco	3147.6	3206.0	3346.3	3227.1	3845.2	France-Monaco
Spain	3576.7	3340.2	2720.5	2685.5	2960.4	Espagne
United Kingdom	2469.1	2682.5	2822.7	2971.8	3527.0	Royaume-Uni
Belgium	-	3201.9	3007.7	3249.5	e3563.8	Belgique
Italy-San Marino-Holy See	1761.7	1888.9	2062.4	1966.2	2033.4	Italie-Saint-Marin-Saint-Siège
Hungary	1376.5	1333.4	1306.0	1418.7	1549.7	Hongrie
Austria	1274.5	1347.5	1305.2	1461.0	1554.2	Autriche
China	636.1	1073.8	1144.9	1371.3	1757.0	Chine
Netherlands	1410.1	1350.4	1063.3	997.2	1027.7	Pays-Bas
Brazil	1126.7	953.9	919.2	872.8	855.2	Brésil
Korea, Republic of	730.9	788.5	989.3	864.3	1154.2	République de Corée
Japan	707.1	814.2	977.2	851.9	1116.9	Japon
Sweden	974.7	799.1	917.0	790.2	921.5	Suède
Poland	766.9	828.2	919.0	936.0	944.1	Pologne
Australia	688.0	708.5	774.6	768.1	885.3	Australie
Belgium-Luxembourg	3431.7	-	-	-	-	Belgique-Luxembourg
Turkey	617.9	515.6	761.7	548.9	754.5	Turquie
Singapore	508.3	568.1	623.5	650.2	729.8	Singapour
Portugal	631.6	618.2	501.4	493.4	531.4	Portugal
Thailand	212.4	408.0	525.7	597.0	e622.1	Thaïlande
Malaysia	342.2	369.5	465.1	494.6	e540.6	Malaisie
China, Hong Kong SAR	715.7	503.8	361.0	290.7	319.6	Chine - RAS de Hong-Kong
Czech Republic	301.5	362.7	416.6	448.8	516.5	République tchèque
Saudi Arabia	228.6	300.4	553.8	445.9	e461.5	Arabie saoudite
Indonesia	237.6	234.4	577.9	440.5	490.2	Indonésie
Argentina	656.3	426.8	390.8	330.5	e146.2	Argentine

(Value as percentages of World total) **(Valeur en pourcentage du total mondial)**

Regions of the world	1993	1994	1995	1996	1997	1998	1999	2000	2001	2002	Régions du monde
World	100.0	100.0	100.0	100.0	100.0	100.0	100.0	100.0	100.0	100.0	Monde
Africa	2.0	1.9	1.7	1.7	1.5	1.4	1.3	1.2	1.3	1.3	Afrique
Americas	39.6	40.2	38.3	39.5	40.0	40.0	42.7	43.4	39.9	37.8	Amériques
- Northern America	34.6	35.5	32.7	31.9	31.3	31.9	34.9	34.4	31.4	29.9	- Amérique du Nord
- LAIA	4.4	4.3	5.1	7.2	8.2	7.6	7.5	8.5	8.1	7.4	- ALAI
- CACM	0.1	0.1	0.1	0.1	0.2	0.1	0.1	0.1	0.1	0.2	- MCC
- Caribbean	0.3	0.2	0.3	0.2	0.3	0.3	0.2	0.3	0.2	0.2	- Caraïbes
- Rest of America	0.1	0.1	0.1	0.1	0.1	0.0	0.0	0.0	0.0	0.0	- Autre d'Amérique
Asia excluding former USSR	18.5	16.7	16.0	15.4	14.6	10.2	10.6	12.4	12.3	13.5	Asie ancienne URSS exclus
- Middle East	3.0	1.7	1.7	1.9	2.2	2.0	1.8	2.7	2.5	2.9	- Moyen-Orient
Asia former USSR	0.0	0.2	0.1	0.2	0.1	0.2	0.2	0.2	0.2	0.2	Asie ancienne URSS
Europe excluding former USSR	37.4	38.6	41.5	40.8	41.5	46.2	43.5	41.1	44.5	45.4	Europe ancienne URSS exclus
- European Union	35.4	36.6	39.4	38.5	37.4	40.8	38.5	36.1	38.9	39.8	- Union Européenne
- Eastern Europe	0.9	0.9	1.0	1.3	3.1	4.3	4.2	4.2	4.7	4.7	- Europe de l'Est
- Rest of Europe	1.1	1.2	1.1	1.0	1.0	1.1	0.8	0.8	0.9	0.9	- Autre de l'Europe
Europe former USSR	0.7	0.5	0.6	0.8	0.8	0.7	0.5	0.5	0.5	0.5	Europe ancienne URSS
Oceania	1.8	1.9	1.6	1.6	1.5	1.3	1.3	1.3	1.3	1.4	Océanie

Moteurs à explosion ou à combustion interne, à pistons, et pièces détachées 713

TRADE BY COMMODITY (Value in million US dollars)
Exports by principal countries or areas

COMMERCE PAR PRODUIT (Valeur en millions de dollars EU)
Exportations selon les principaux pays ou zones

Country or area	1998	1999	2000	2001	2002	Pays ou zone
World	62342.0	66112.6	68567.3	66158.4	70733.1	Monde
Africa	273.2	116.5	127.9	175.9	274.0	Afrique
Americas	18517.1	21044.2	22745.2	20703.2	21202.4	Amériques
- Northern America	14079.9	16364.2	17827.4	16135.3	16484.8	- Amérique du Nord
- LAIA	4421.6	4670.6	4904.0	4551.3	4684.6	- ALAI
- CACM	1.5	2.4	1.9	6.6	22.4	- MCC
- Caribbean	13.7	6.5	11.2	7.4	9.3	- Caraïbes
- Rest of America	0.4	0.4	0.7	2.5	1.3	- Autre d'Amérique
Asia excluding former USSR	11636.3	13317.5	14717.7	12993.1	13993.9	Asie ancienne URSS exclus
- Middle East	258.8	275.5	319.3	455.8	527.7	- Moyen-Orient
Asia former USSR	11.4	8.1	8.7	7.4	5.2	Asie ancienne URSS
Europe excluding former USSR	31242.5	31011.6	30265.1	31757.7	34776.0	Europe ancienne URSS exclus
- European Union	27876.9	27339.8	25698.3	26638.3	28949.6	- Union Européenne
- Eastern Europe	2973.4	3276.3	4162.5	4687.2	5361.6	- Europe de l'Est
- Rest of Europe	392.3	395.5	404.2	432.2	464.8	- Autre de l'Europe
Europe former USSR	326.5	236.1	275.7	261.7	232.3	Europe ancienne URSS
Oceania	334.9	378.6	427.0	259.4	249.3	Océanie
United States	10832.2	12388.0	13699.9	12631.7	12862.0	Etats-Unis d'Amérique
Japan	9284.4	10774.0	11858.7	10205.9	10796.7	Japon
Germany	9155.7	9398.6	8938.9	9390.1	10813.6	Allemagne
United Kingdom	4040.4	3812.2	3933.4	4013.3	4382.1	Royaume-Uni
France-Monaco	4159.2	4313.4	3589.7	3490.9	3436.4	France-Monaco
Canada	3247.6	3976.2	4127.3	3503.5	3622.4	Canada
Mexico	3038.3	3355.4	3568.5	3250.6	3343.3	Mexique
Hungary	2580.3	2690.2	2575.3	2831.6	3093.1	Hongrie
Austria	2462.5	2592.9	2559.2	2651.6	2783.4	Autriche
Italy-San Marino-Holy See	2261.2	2255.9	2015.9	2016.1	2071.3	Italie-Saint-Marin-Saint-Siège
Spain	1733.7	1743.2	1523.1	1354.6	1317.1	Espagne
Sweden	1775.5	881.6	795.0	1334.9	1533.1	Suède
Brazil	1141.8	1063.2	1108.4	1135.2	e1176.9	Brésil
Poland	147.7	276.4	1262.2	1524.7	1814.6	Pologne
Belgium	–	950.9	865.4	805.5	e903.7	Belgique
Netherlands	631.5	599.4	580.3	632.2	665.7	Pays-Bas
China	245.5	371.7	476.0	530.8	730.1	Chine
Korea, Republic of	318.9	339.9	415.0	458.7	447.5	République de Corée
Finland	417.6	320.1	376.1	413.0	417.3	Finlande
Singapore	317.5	316.7	329.5	317.0	410.0	Singapour
Australia	320.7	365.6	412.6	244.3	238.3	Australie
Turkey	185.4	205.6	260.6	392.4	450.6	Turquie
China, Hong Kong SAR	459.4	363.5	252.2	171.7	173.9	Chine - RAS de Hong-Kong
Czech Republic	184.1	202.5	223.8	251.9	371.1	République tchèque
Thailand	119.9	188.5	322.4	285.8	e301.8	Thaïlande
Switzerland-Liechtenstein	177.2	186.1	201.4	210.3	229.8	Suisse-Liechtenstein
Argentina	221.9	232.5	205.2	143.8	e138.9	Argentine
Malaysia	192.3	188.1	231.7	137.4	e145.7	Malaisie
Denmark	159.4	145.7	176.0	187.4	221.5	Danemark
India	119.0	156.8	199.6	141.6	184.2	Inde

(Value as percentages of World total) **(Valeur en pourcentage du total mondial)**

Regions of the world	1993	1994	1995	1996	1997	1998	1999	2000	2001	2002	Régions du monde
World	100.0	100.0	100.0	100.0	100.0	100.0	100.0	100.0	100.0	100.0	Monde
Africa	0.2	0.2	0.2	0.2	0.3	0.4	0.2	0.2	0.3	0.4	Afrique
Americas	29.2	27.8	26.3	27.2	29.5	29.7	31.8	33.2	31.3	30.0	Amériques
- Northern America	22.7	21.1	19.1	20.0	22.3	22.6	24.8	26.0	24.4	23.3	- Amérique du Nord
- LAIA	6.5	6.7	7.1	7.1	7.2	7.1	7.1	7.2	6.9	6.6	- ALAI
- CACM	0.0	0.0	0.0	0.0	0.0	0.0	0.0	0.0	0.0	0.0	- MCC
- Caribbean	0.0	0.0	0.0	0.0	0.0	0.0	0.0	0.0	0.0	0.0	- Caraïbes
- Rest of America	0.0	0.0	0.0	0.0	0.0	0.0	0.0	0.0	0.0	0.0	- Autre d'Amérique
Asia excluding former USSR	27.3	28.3	27.7	24.4	22.0	18.7	20.1	21.5	19.6	19.8	Asie ancienne URSS exclus
- Middle East	0.2	0.3	0.3	0.3	0.3	0.4	0.4	0.5	0.7	0.7	- Moyen-Orient
Asia former USSR	0.0	0.0	0.0	0.0	0.0	0.0	0.0	0.0	0.0	0.0	Asie ancienne URSS
Europe excluding former USSR	42.4	42.5	44.5	46.7	46.6	50.1	46.9	44.1	48.0	49.2	Europe ancienne URSS exclus
- European Union	41.0	41.3	43.3	45.4	43.2	44.7	41.4	37.5	40.3	40.9	- Union Européenne
- Eastern Europe	0.5	0.4	0.5	0.6	2.9	4.8	5.0	6.1	7.1	7.6	- Europe de l'Est
- Rest of Europe	0.9	0.8	0.8	0.6	0.6	0.6	0.6	0.6	0.7	0.7	- Autre de l'Europe
Europe former USSR	0.2	0.5	0.5	0.7	0.6	0.5	0.4	0.4	0.4	0.3	Europe ancienne URSS
Oceania	0.7	0.7	0.8	0.8	0.9	0.5	0.6	0.6	0.4	0.4	Océanie

714 Engines and motors, non-electric; parts, nes; group 714, item 71888

TRADE BY COMMODITY (Value in million US dollars)
Imports by principal countries or areas

COMMERCE PAR PRODUIT (Valeur en millions de dollars EU)
Importations selon les principaux pays ou zones

Country or area	1998	1999	2000	2001	2002	Pays ou zone
World	41796.2	43838.7	46818.2	51375.5	48367.1	Monde
Africa	635.8	467.8	515.5	487.6	589.4	Afrique
Americas	14182.9	14585.3	15260.5	18601.8	15454.6	Amériques
- Northern America	12550.4	13028.7	13673.8	16494.8	13497.9	- Amérique du Nord
- LAIA	1541.6	1451.4	1525.5	2023.9	1873.1	- ALAI
- CACM	6.3	7.0	28.4	17.1	35.4	- MCC
- Caribbean	67.4	96.4	28.9	65.4	47.4	- Caraïbes
- Rest of America	17.2	1.7	4.0	0.6	0.8	- Autre d'Amérique
Asia excluding former USSR	5775.4	6090.0	7038.6	8503.0	8895.8	Asie ancienne URSS exclus
- Middle East	1184.7	947.0	1000.1	1620.4	1438.3	- Moyen-Orient
Asia former USSR	57.3	73.9	117.8	161.6	119.3	Asie ancienne URSS
Europe excluding former USSR	20426.7	21906.5	23293.8	23042.8	22562.1	Europe ancienne URSS exclus
- European Union	19636.3	20939.9	22349.8	21973.4	21574.3	- Union Européenne
- Eastern Europe	137.5	269.7	232.8	342.3	208.9	- Europe de l'Est
- Rest of Europe	652.9	696.9	711.2	727.2	778.9	- Autre de l'Europe
Europe former USSR	335.4	210.3	181.7	226.4	330.7	Europe ancienne URSS
Oceania	382.7	505.0	410.2	352.3	415.2	Océanie
United States	10354.3	10369.8	10996.4	13680.5	10975.0	Etats-Unis d'Amérique
United Kingdom	6026.7	6535.0	5961.0	6245.8	6782.5	Royaume-Uni
Germany	4333.4	5442.8	6662.6	5656.7	5415.1	Allemagne
France-Monaco	4845.9	4849.0	5162.2	5371.8	4696.4	France-Monaco
Canada	2196.0	2658.4	2677.2	2814.1	2520.8	Canada
Japan	2103.0	2078.1	2666.3	2888.2	2955.0	Japon
Netherlands	1143.2	1062.2	1249.6	1093.5	950.3	Pays-Bas
Italy-San Marino-Holy See	933.2	870.1	907.1	1195.0	1206.1	Italie-Saint-Marin-Saint-Siège
China, Hong Kong SAR	404.8	871.4	1084.8	1276.7	1165.4	Chine - RAS de Hong-Kong
Brazil	619.2	661.4	807.9	1093.0	831.5	Brésil
Sweden	693.7	573.9	776.7	697.7	699.5	Suède
Mexico	503.5	404.6	432.6	616.0	774.2	Mexique
Singapore	325.3	407.4	443.2	553.4	645.8	Singapour
Switzerland-Liechtenstein	367.0	438.5	499.1	469.8	497.8	Suisse-Liechtenstein
China	328.8	331.5	296.1	478.9	714.2	Chine
Spain	364.6	402.8	390.2	441.1	527.8	Espagne
Turkey	455.8	161.0	284.1	784.9	389.3	Turquie
Korea, Republic of	403.0	399.4	350.5	339.9	555.1	République de Corée
Belgium	–	493.8	452.3	406.1	e445.4	Belgique
Israel	411.7	384.0	262.3	279.3	312.7	Israël
Australia	253.8	396.4	330.0	301.7	365.2	Australie
Ireland	251.4	238.3	364.4	375.6	303.3	Irlande
Malaysia	115.3	228.8	216.6	317.4	e346.9	Malaisie
Saudi Arabia	272.3	309.6	209.9	195.3	e202.1	Arabie saoudite
Norway	239.3	198.1	169.1	229.4	245.1	Norvège
Russian Federation	285.3	186.6	144.7	179.1	271.8	Fédération de Russie
Thailand	69.1	94.0	200.4	267.2	e278.4	Thaïlande
United Arab Emirates	131.9	138.2	162.9	190.3	e195.3	Emirates arabes unis
Iran (Islamic Republic of)	54.7	101.8	96.1	249.7	309.0	Iran (République islamique d')
Austria	210.6	157.9	119.5	154.0	134.6	Autriche

(Value as percentages of World total) **(Valeur en pourcentage du total mondial)**

Regions of the world	1993	1994	1995	1996	1997	1998	1999	2000	2001	2002	Régions du monde
World	100.0	100.0	100.0	100.0	100.0	100.0	100.0	100.0	100.0	100.0	Monde
Africa	1.7	2.1	1.2	1.1	1.3	1.5	1.1	1.1	0.9	1.2	Afrique
Americas	28.9	28.3	27.2	28.7	31.0	33.9	33.3	32.6	36.2	32.0	Amériques
- Northern America	26.9	26.8	24.9	26.3	28.0	30.0	29.7	29.2	32.1	27.9	- Amérique du Nord
- LAIA	1.7	1.3	1.8	2.0	2.7	3.7	3.3	3.3	3.9	3.9	- ALAI
- CACM	0.0	0.0	0.1	0.1	0.1	0.0	0.0	0.1	0.0	0.1	- MCC
- Caribbean	0.2	0.2	0.3	0.3	0.2	0.2	0.2	0.1	0.1	0.1	- Caraïbes
- Rest of America	0.1	0.0	0.1	0.0	0.0	0.0	0.0	0.0	0.0	0.0	- Autre d'Amérique
Asia excluding former USSR	21.6	18.9	19.9	17.6	16.5	13.8	13.9	15.0	16.6	18.4	Asie ancienne URSS exclus
- Middle East	5.1	2.2	2.7	2.8	3.3	2.8	2.2	2.1	3.2	3.0	- Moyen-Orient
Asia former USSR	0.0	0.2	0.3	0.2	0.1	0.1	0.2	0.3	0.3	0.2	Asie ancienne URSS
Europe excluding former USSR	46.2	48.3	49.1	50.2	49.0	48.9	50.0	49.8	44.9	46.6	Europe ancienne URSS exclus
- European Union	44.6	46.5	47.2	47.8	46.5	47.0	47.8	47.7	42.8	44.6	- Union Européenne
- Eastern Europe	0.4	0.2	0.3	0.3	0.4	0.3	0.6	0.5	0.7	0.4	- Europe de l'Est
- Rest of Europe	1.2	1.6	1.6	2.1	2.1	1.6	1.6	1.5	1.4	1.6	- Autre de l'Europe
Europe former USSR	0.4	1.0	1.1	1.0	1.3	0.8	0.5	0.4	0.4	0.7	Europe ancienne URSS
Oceania	1.2	1.1	1.1	1.2	1.0	0.9	1.2	0.9	0.7	0.9	Océanie

Moteurs non électriques; parties et pièces détachées, n.d.a., du groupe 714 et 718.88 714

TRADE BY COMMODITY (Value in million US dollars)
Exports by principal countries or areas

COMMERCE PAR PRODUIT (Valeur en millions de dollars EU)
Exportations selon les principaux pays ou zones

Country or area	1998	1999	2000	2001	2002	Pays ou zone
World	43228.5	45943.6	48813.0	56481.9	53630.7	Monde
Africa	44.2	40.6	18.5	23.9	24.0	Afrique
Americas	16411.7	17691.7	19132.3	21812.4	20593.5	Amériques
- Northern America	15866.1	17183.9	18435.2	20900.1	19643.4	- Amérique du Nord
- LAIA	543.9	503.0	691.7	876.2	909.7	- ALAI
- CACM	0.1	3.4	4.2	6.5	14.0	- MCC
- Caribbean	1.5	1.3	1.2	29.5	26.3	- Caraïbes
- Rest of America	0.0	0.1	0.0	0.0	0.1	- Autre d'Amérique
Asia excluding former USSR	2291.0	2315.5	2931.1	3949.0	3673.3	Asie ancienne URSS exclus
- Middle East	84.0	88.8	95.9	119.3	180.9	- Moyen-Orient
Asia former USSR	7.6	7.5	10.7	12.0	14.0	Asie ancienne URSS
Europe excluding former USSR	23795.1	25367.2	26156.7	29838.0	28429.3	Europe ancienne URSS exclus
- European Union	22766.1	24243.8	24911.1	28491.4	26437.1	- Union Européenne
- Eastern Europe	153.6	170.9	210.6	255.2	468.9	- Europe de l'Est
- Rest of Europe	875.4	952.5	1035.0	1091.4	1523.3	- Autre de l'Europe
Europe former USSR	614.5	468.8	497.5	785.2	825.9	Europe ancienne URSS
Oceania	64.3	52.3	66.2	61.3	70.7	Océanie
United States	13814.9	15069.5	15736.2	17676.9	16540.8	Etats-Unis d'Amérique
United Kingdom	9742.3	10465.3	9683.7	11643.3	10659.9	Royaume-Uni
Germany	3936.3	4279.5	5461.4	6413.2	5724.2	Allemagne
France-Monaco	4684.1	5090.4	4797.8	5216.7	4819.3	France-Monaco
Canada	2051.2	2114.4	2699.0	3223.2	3102.6	Canada
Japan	1450.6	1181.4	1882.5	2446.4	1738.1	Japon
Italy-San Marino-Holy See	1310.7	1102.1	1427.0	1911.0	1797.4	Italie-Saint-Marin-Saint-Siège
Netherlands	1064.3	1132.9	1220.0	1088.0	1185.4	Pays-Bas
Sweden	907.8	916.8	1126.3	1075.3	1036.2	Suède
Switzerland-Liechtenstein	680.7	743.7	803.4	866.8	1124.9	Suisse-Liechtenstein
Mexico	421.4	420.7	549.9	673.7	716.9	Mexique
Russian Federation	445.9	391.8	346.1	560.7	578.2	Fédération de Russie
Belgium	–	533.6	594.9	534.0	e599.1	Belgique
China, Hong Kong SAR	153.4	299.4	251.6	348.9	646.8	Chine - RAS de Hong-Kong
Korea, Republic of	199.6	190.8	219.4	246.0	241.9	République de Corée
Norway	159.0	167.2	193.3	190.4	369.0	Norvège
Austria	125.9	276.2	155.6	198.1	134.9	Autriche
Ireland	195.1	169.0	158.5	150.8	203.1	Irlande
Ukraine	145.3	67.1	128.1	201.6	222.2	Ukraine
Malaysia	25.6	143.6	88.6	229.5	e243.3	Malaisie
Spain	74.6	125.0	173.2	157.7	168.5	Espagne
China	51.7	94.4	137.9	167.7	192.2	Chine
Israel	147.1	120.0	92.5	126.9	134.2	Israël
Brazil	103.5	66.2	108.1	157.7	e163.5	Brésil
Belgium-Luxembourg	512.1	–	–	–	–	Belgique-Luxembourg
Singapore	65.9	52.2	75.2	122.2	155.5	Singapour
Hungary	24.5	19.0	26.9	62.6	269.3	Hongrie
Turkey	75.1	66.3	72.5	98.2	86.4	Turquie
Poland	47.2	66.9	81.8	86.3	56.7	Pologne
Czech Republic	48.3	45.7	49.2	64.8	90.3	République tchèque

(Value as percentages of World total) **(Valeur en pourcentage du total mondial)**

Regions of the world	1993	1994	1995	1996	1997	1998	1999	2000	2001	2002	Régions du monde
World	100.0	100.0	100.0	100.0	100.0	100.0	100.0	100.0	100.0	100.0	Monde
Africa	0.2	0.2	0.1	0.1	0.1	0.1	0.1	0.0	0.0	0.0	Afrique
Americas	40.8	39.8	38.9	38.3	38.6	38.0	38.5	39.2	38.6	38.4	Amériques
- Northern America	39.6	37.9	37.5	37.1	37.4	36.7	37.4	37.8	37.0	36.6	- Amérique du Nord
- LAIA	1.2	2.0	1.3	1.2	1.2	1.3	1.1	1.4	1.6	1.7	- ALAI
- CACM	0.0	0.0	0.0	0.0	0.0	0.0	0.0	0.0	0.0	0.0	- MCC
- Caribbean	0.0	0.0	0.0	0.0	0.0	0.0	0.0	0.0	0.1	0.0	- Caraïbes
- Rest of America	0.0	0.0	0.0	0.0	0.0	0.0	0.0	0.0	0.0	0.0	- Autre d'Amérique
Asia excluding former USSR	6.7	6.8	6.7	5.0	5.5	5.3	5.0	6.0	7.0	6.8	Asie ancienne URSS exclus
- Middle East	0.6	0.6	0.5	0.6	0.9	0.2	0.2	0.2	0.2	0.3	- Moyen-Orient
Asia former USSR	0.0	0.0	0.0	0.0	0.0	0.0	0.0	0.0	0.0	0.0	Asie ancienne URSS
Europe excluding former USSR	51.8	51.7	52.6	54.5	54.1	55.0	55.2	53.6	52.8	53.0	Europe ancienne URSS exclus
- European Union	49.4	49.4	49.9	51.5	51.6	52.7	52.8	51.0	50.4	49.3	- Union Européenne
- Eastern Europe	0.4	0.2	0.3	0.4	0.3	0.4	0.4	0.4	0.5	0.9	- Europe de l'Est
- Rest of Europe	2.0	2.1	2.4	2.6	2.2	2.0	2.1	2.1	1.9	2.8	- Autre de l'Europe
Europe former USSR	0.3	1.2	1.5	1.6	1.4	1.4	1.0	1.0	1.4	1.5	Europe ancienne URSS
Oceania	0.2	0.3	0.2	0.4	0.3	0.1	0.1	0.1	0.1	0.1	Océanie

716 Rotating electric plant and parts thereof, nes

TRADE BY COMMODITY (Value in million US dollars)
Imports by principal countries or areas

COMMERCE PAR PRODUIT (Valeur en millions de dollars EU)
Importations selon les principaux pays ou zones

Country or area	1998	1999	2000	2001	2002	Pays ou zone
World	30180.0	31234.8	32665.6	34877.4	36266.8	Monde
Africa	993.8	787.5	811.2	848.6	903.0	Afrique
Americas	8493.7	10126.9	10452.5	12372.8	12030.5	Amériques
- Northern America	5393.5	6815.7	6969.4	8535.1	7925.4	- Amérique du Nord
- LAIA	2685.8	2814.2	3022.7	3530.7	3770.2	- ALAI
- CACM	203.5	258.2	243.6	110.3	180.5	- MCC
- Caribbean	183.3	173.4	186.9	172.2	135.0	- Caraïbes
- Rest of America	27.4	65.3	29.9	24.4	19.4	- Autre d'Amérique
Asia excluding former USSR	10586.0	10013.1	11230.8	10674.7	11729.6	Asie ancienne URSS exclus
- Middle East	914.1	934.5	1164.6	1060.4	1161.3	- Moyen-Orient
Asia former USSR	73.5	110.1	74.9	85.9	83.1	Asie ancienne URSS
Europe excluding former USSR	9309.3	9599.6	9468.4	10173.6	10780.7	Europe ancienne URSS exclus
- European Union	7962.0	8250.5	8037.9	8641.4	9084.2	- Union Européenne
- Eastern Europe	679.1	688.4	802.2	909.6	1062.9	- Europe de l'Est
- Rest of Europe	668.2	660.7	628.2	622.5	633.6	- Autre de l'Europe
Europe former USSR	287.2	174.5	205.0	267.9	326.5	Europe ancienne URSS
Oceania	436.7	423.2	422.7	453.9	413.5	Océanie
United States	4271.0	5606.1	5903.1	7121.0	6658.6	Etats-Unis d'Amérique
Germany	2262.6	2413.7	2352.6	2711.1	2785.8	Allemagne
China	1513.8	1619.4	2018.6	2102.1	2542.2	Chine
China, Hong Kong SAR	1563.7	1620.2	1953.9	1699.4	2006.9	Chine - RAS de Hong-Kong
Mexico	1063.3	1612.1	2019.6	1951.9	1931.5	Mexique
Japan	1282.7	1300.9	1468.2	1437.5	1382.0	Japon
Canada	1120.7	1204.8	1063.9	1411.5	1263.3	Canada
Singapore	1337.7	1212.6	1237.8	1095.0	1125.4	Singapour
France-Monaco	1120.9	1183.2	1152.4	1178.6	1260.3	France-Monaco
United Kingdom	1062.0	1036.5	1035.4	1027.0	1009.2	Royaume-Uni
Italy-San Marino-Holy See	818.3	841.4	851.1	852.1	973.4	Italie-Saint-Marin-Saint-Siège
Brazil	557.4	519.8	347.0	1035.9	1420.8	Brésil
Korea, Republic of	600.2	762.1	846.5	745.6	842.8	République de Corée
Spain	701.8	700.4	607.2	695.2	712.1	Espagne
Malaysia	590.6	533.8	663.8	596.1	e651.5	Malaisie
Thailand	1051.6	510.4	476.5	487.5	e507.9	Thaïlande
Denmark	269.0	372.8	343.2	481.1	548.4	Danemark
Switzerland-Liechtenstein	401.4	394.8	419.5	399.7	369.2	Suisse-Liechtenstein
Netherlands	373.3	366.1	372.4	352.2	365.1	Pays-Bas
Australia	330.8	320.3	353.4	386.9	336.1	Australie
Turkey	301.3	356.2	274.1	257.5	373.3	Turquie
Austria	275.9	282.5	275.6	306.7	322.1	Autriche
Sweden	323.7	297.4	282.3	267.5	278.4	Suède
Czech Republic	258.0	216.3	256.2	318.4	329.2	République tchèque
Belgium	-	324.5	309.9	334.7	e367.0	Belgique
Hungary	171.9	218.6	286.9	277.2	311.4	Hongrie
Argentina	513.1	185.5	258.1	171.0	e75.6	Argentine
Philippines	231.8	220.9	204.6	209.9	93.0	Philippines
Saudi Arabia	162.8	163.7	241.0	151.1	e156.4	Arabie saoudite
Poland	136.5	136.5	150.2	174.6	243.2	Pologne

(Value as percentages of World total)

(Valeur en pourcentage du total mondial)

Regions of the world	1993	1994	1995	1996	1997	1998	1999	2000	2001	2002	Régions du monde
World	100.0	100.0	100.0	100.0	100.0	100.0	100.0	100.0	100.0	100.0	Monde
Africa	3.0	2.7	2.0	2.4	2.5	3.3	2.5	2.5	2.4	2.5	Afrique
Americas	23.2	24.0	23.0	23.4	25.0	28.1	32.4	32.0	35.5	33.2	Amériques
- Northern America	15.3	16.5	16.1	15.7	16.2	17.9	21.8	21.3	24.5	21.9	- Amérique du Nord
- LAIA	6.7	6.4	5.4	6.5	8.0	8.9	9.0	9.3	10.1	10.4	- ALAI
- CACM	0.7	0.5	0.7	0.2	0.2	0.7	0.8	0.7	0.3	0.5	- MCC
- Caribbean	0.4	0.5	0.8	0.9	0.5	0.6	0.6	0.6	0.5	0.4	- Caraïbes
- Rest of America	0.2	0.1	0.1	0.1	0.1	0.1	0.2	0.1	0.1	0.1	- Autre d'Amérique
Asia excluding former USSR	44.0	42.9	43.1	40.7	40.8	35.1	32.1	34.4	30.6	32.3	Asie ancienne URSS exclus
- Middle East	4.7	3.1	3.0	2.7	3.1	3.0	3.0	3.6	3.0	3.2	- Moyen-Orient
Asia former USSR	0.0	0.2	0.2	0.3	0.2	0.2	0.4	0.2	0.2	0.2	Asie ancienne URSS
Europe excluding former USSR	27.1	27.8	29.1	30.3	28.8	30.8	30.7	29.0	29.2	29.7	Europe ancienne URSS exclus
- European Union	23.9	24.6	25.6	26.6	25.0	26.4	26.4	24.6	24.8	25.0	- Union Européenne
- Eastern Europe	0.7	0.7	1.1	1.3	1.6	2.3	2.2	2.5	2.6	2.9	- Europe de l'Est
- Rest of Europe	2.5	2.4	2.4	2.3	2.2	2.2	2.1	1.9	1.8	1.7	- Autre de l'Europe
Europe former USSR	0.9	0.9	1.0	1.0	0.9	1.0	0.6	0.6	0.8	0.9	Europe ancienne URSS
Oceania	1.8	1.5	1.6	2.0	1.8	1.4	1.4	1.3	1.3	1.1	Océanie

TRADE BY COMMODITY (Value in million US dollars)
Exports by principal countries or areas

COMMERCE PAR PRODUIT (Valeur en millions de dollars EU)
Exportations selon les principaux pays ou zones

Country or area	1998	1999	2000	2001	2002	Pays ou zone
World	27783.1	28977.7	30891.6	32562.2	32731.1	Monde
Africa	52.4	57.9	39.6	66.4	64.9	Afrique
Americas	5937.7	6032.0	6272.0	7393.2	6768.7	Amériques
- Northern America	4071.4	3887.5	4020.1	5050.0	4274.8	- Amérique du Nord
- LAIA	1807.7	2127.9	2235.0	2333.5	2483.6	- ALAI
- CACM	5.8	2.8	1.8	3.5	4.6	- MCC
- Caribbean	50.5	13.6	14.7	4.0	4.7	- Caraïbes
- Rest of America	2.4	0.4	0.5	2.1	1.1	- Autre d'Amérique
Asia excluding former USSR	8921.6	9880.6	11357.5	10340.5	11121.6	Asie ancienne URSS exclus
- Middle East	95.7	105.4	143.2	174.8	179.6	- Moyen-Orient
Asia former USSR	26.4	18.2	21.9	18.8	19.7	Asie ancienne URSS
Europe excluding former USSR	12511.3	12707.9	12889.3	14365.8	14469.4	Europe ancienne URSS exclus
- European Union	10730.2	10787.3	10743.5	11918.4	12102.7	- Union Européenne
- Eastern Europe	802.3	828.4	955.0	1195.7	1318.7	- Europe de l'Est
- Rest of Europe	978.8	1092.3	1190.7	1251.8	1047.9	- Autre de l'Europe
Europe former USSR	195.0	175.6	220.7	285.3	236.9	Europe ancienne URSS
Oceania	138.7	105.4	90.8	92.0	50.0	Océanie
United States	3537.3	3353.0	3442.2	4375.1	3709.7	Etats-Unis d'Amérique
Germany	3247.1	3249.9	3196.7	3373.8	3555.3	Allemagne
Japan	2726.6	3076.2	3106.2	2839.4	2714.5	Japon
China	1522.7	1670.5	2212.9	2150.4	2588.6	Chine
Mexico	1503.8	1848.6	1936.0	1950.3	2103.0	Mexique
China, Hong Kong SAR	1468.5	1658.0	1935.2	1662.3	1906.1	Chine - RAS de Hong-Kong
France-Monaco	1602.3	1464.1	1503.6	1698.1	1709.0	France-Monaco
United Kingdom	1509.8	1363.9	1407.4	1493.0	1380.7	Royaume-Uni
Italy-San Marino-Holy See	1359.7	1395.1	1385.5	1396.9	1410.5	Italie-Saint-Marin-Saint-Siège
Denmark	556.1	940.6	724.4	1498.4	1457.0	Danemark
Singapore	914.2	856.0	986.0	862.9	838.9	Singapour
Switzerland-Liechtenstein	745.1	865.2	946.5	989.1	776.7	Suisse-Liechtenstein
Thailand	600.7	790.0	880.0	831.2	e877.8	Thaïlande
Finland	693.1	600.3	797.1	585.7	701.9	Finlande
Canada	534.1	534.4	577.9	674.9	565.0	Canada
Korea, Republic of	376.7	490.8	620.9	561.4	634.3	République de Corée
Austria	487.6	491.9	440.6	530.7	528.9	Autriche
Czech Republic	338.0	361.3	415.3	466.8	510.3	République tchèque
Spain	342.9	365.3	372.0	454.1	448.5	Espagne
Malaysia	378.4	410.6	433.1	348.0	e368.8	Malaisie
Sweden	443.2	359.2	260.5	261.4	289.2	Suède
Netherlands	232.3	277.3	353.9	324.8	289.2	Pays-Bas
Brazil	265.3	221.3	259.2	332.3	e344.6	Brésil
Indonesia	261.6	224.5	346.0	231.3	321.5	Indonésie
Hungary	144.8	153.5	186.5	322.5	333.2	Hongrie
Slovenia	153.0	162.0	177.3	188.6	209.0	Slovénie
Belgium	–	178.6	206.5	204.1	e229.0	Belgique
Poland	118.2	111.6	138.6	159.9	193.9	Pologne
Russian Federation	126.0	111.4	136.6	194.6	131.4	Fédération de Russie
Slovakia	111.9	116.0	120.4	138.1	160.9	Slovaquie

(Value as percentages of World total) **(Valeur en pourcentage du total mondial)**

Regions of the world	1993	1994	1995	1996	1997	1998	1999	2000	2001	2002	Régions du monde
World	100.0	100.0	100.0	100.0	100.0	100.0	100.0	100.0	100.0	100.0	Monde
Africa	0.1	0.1	0.1	0.1	0.1	0.2	0.2	0.1	0.2	0.2	Afrique
Americas	19.7	19.1	18.0	18.7	20.9	21.4	20.8	20.3	22.7	20.7	Amériques
- Northern America	15.4	14.6	13.9	13.6	15.3	14.7	13.4	13.0	15.5	13.1	- Amérique du Nord
- LAIA	4.2	4.5	4.0	5.1	5.5	6.5	7.3	7.2	7.2	7.6	- ALAI
- CACM	0.0	0.0	0.0	0.0	0.0	0.0	0.0	0.0	0.0	0.0	- MCC
- Caribbean	0.0	0.0	0.1	0.0	0.0	0.2	0.0	0.0	0.0	0.0	- Caraïbes
- Rest of America	0.0	0.0	0.0	0.0	0.0	0.0	0.0	0.0	0.0	0.0	- Autre d'Amérique
Asia excluding former USSR	36.0	35.3	35.6	34.1	35.2	32.1	34.1	36.8	31.8	34.0	Asie ancienne URSS exclus
- Middle East	0.3	0.2	0.2	0.3	0.4	0.3	0.4	0.5	0.5	0.5	- Moyen-Orient
Asia former USSR	0.0	0.2	0.1	0.1	0.1	0.1	0.1	0.1	0.1	0.1	Asie ancienne URSS
Europe excluding former USSR	43.4	44.3	45.1	45.7	42.3	45.0	43.9	41.7	44.1	44.2	Europe ancienne URSS exclus
- European Union	38.2	39.1	39.2	39.5	36.4	38.6	37.2	34.8	36.6	37.0	- Union Européenne
- Eastern Europe	1.6	1.5	2.1	2.4	2.5	2.9	2.9	3.1	3.7	4.0	- Europe de l'Est
- Rest of Europe	3.6	3.7	3.8	3.8	3.4	3.5	3.8	3.9	3.8	3.2	- Autre de l'Europe
Europe former USSR	0.5	0.8	0.8	0.9	0.8	0.7	0.6	0.7	0.9	0.7	Europe ancienne URSS
Oceania	0.3	0.3	0.3	0.5	0.6	0.5	0.4	0.3	0.3	0.2	Océanie

718 Other power generating machinery and parts thereof, nes

TRADE BY COMMODITY (Value in million US dollars)
Imports by principal countries or areas

COMMERCE PAR PRODUIT (Valeur en millions de dollars EU)
Importations selon les principaux pays ou zones

Country or area	1998	1999	2000	2001	2002	Pays ou zone
World	5145.6	5773.2	6176.1	6130.8	6066.8	Monde
Africa	97.8	91.6	120.6	75.8	108.1	Afrique
Americas	1050.4	1033.6	1132.3	1178.6	1065.9	Amériques
- Northern America	711.6	765.1	873.9	850.1	789.2	- Amérique du Nord
- LAIA	325.0	227.4	227.7	296.1	255.2	- ALAI
- CACM	9.0	31.6	14.7	24.2	12.6	- MCC
- Caribbean	3.5	4.6	10.6	7.1	5.7	- Caraïbes
- Rest of America	1.3	4.9	5.4	1.2	3.1	- Autre d'Amérique
Asia excluding former USSR	1344.0	1805.3	2249.2	1912.6	1917.7	Asie ancienne URSS exclus
- Middle East	520.3	417.0	381.8	442.0	298.0	- Moyen-Orient
Asia former USSR	7.4	19.5	15.7	15.4	21.2	Asie ancienne URSS
Europe excluding former USSR	2400.1	2576.8	2278.0	2556.7	2502.4	Europe ancienne URSS exclus
- European Union	1947.2	1921.5	1628.3	1936.3	1880.3	- Union Européenne
- Eastern Europe	211.9	362.2	367.2	403.1	348.3	- Europe de l'Est
- Rest of Europe	241.1	293.1	282.5	217.3	273.7	- Autre de l'Europe
Europe former USSR	167.3	176.9	312.5	337.4	377.1	Europe ancienne URSS
Oceania	78.6	69.3	67.8	54.2	74.5	Océanie
China	183.5	543.1	1013.9	669.3	779.8	Chine
United States	492.4	553.2	637.0	630.5	560.3	Etats-Unis d'Amérique
France-Monaco	527.8	516.6	330.3	567.9	517.4	France-Monaco
Germany	457.7	484.1	420.7	521.8	426.9	Allemagne
Japan	141.3	322.0	183.3	261.0	236.5	Japon
Canada	219.1	211.8	236.8	219.4	228.6	Canada
Kuwait	331.5	230.6	e216.7	e238.3	e1.3	Koweït
Ukraine	94.3	92.5	234.9	238.8	257.3	Ukraine
Switzerland-Liechtenstein	143.6	187.2	200.2	128.6	146.7	Suisse-Liechtenstein
United Kingdom	170.8	156.4	156.0	145.5	149.1	Royaume-Uni
Sweden	184.2	140.6	140.5	118.5	178.5	Suède
Italy-San Marino-Holy See	125.8	139.4	147.7	143.2	149.4	Italie-Saint-Marin-Saint-Siège
Czech Republic	101.6	161.6	179.4	161.5	98.3	République tchèque
Korea, Republic of	151.6	124.4	125.7	100.4	122.5	République de Corée
Iran (Islamic Republic of)	64.3	60.5	33.8	129.4	198.0	Iran (République islamique d')
Finland	104.6	103.4	92.7	87.3	92.9	Finlande
Austria	105.1	86.7	78.2	81.9	86.5	Autriche
Mexico	98.9	73.3	84.7	100.0	77.9	Mexique
Belgium	–	94.6	73.4	110.5	e121.2	Belgique
Brazil	95.0	77.9	68.4	77.5	77.7	Brésil
Spain	93.6	84.2	67.3	77.8	71.1	Espagne
Bulgaria	1.2	78.1	83.7	e93.5	e102.8	Bulgarie
Slovakia	58.1	70.1	44.4	87.9	78.6	Slovaquie
Australia	68.1	51.8	57.9	43.6	58.3	Australie
Turkey	77.4	82.9	50.1	27.8	33.6	Turquie
Norway	53.6	45.4	33.2	42.7	78.9	Norvège
Netherlands	49.0	50.3	56.3	38.9	47.2	Pays-Bas
Lithuania	36.4	48.3	34.4	34.6	e42.6	Lituanie
Poland	37.5	33.8	40.7	37.7	44.0	Pologne
South Africa	–	–	72.6	42.1	69.0	Afrique du Sud

(Value as percentages of World total) **(Valeur en pourcentage du total mondial)**

Regions of the world	1993	1994	1995	1996	1997	1998	1999	2000	2001	2002	Régions du monde
World	100.0	100.0	100.0	100.0	100.0	100.0	100.0	100.0	100.0	100.0	Monde
Africa	2.7	1.2	2.2	1.3	2.3	1.9	1.6	2.0	1.2	1.8	Afrique
Americas	18.7	21.0	19.2	18.5	18.8	20.4	17.9	18.3	19.2	17.6	Amériques
- Northern America	11.5	13.6	12.8	12.8	13.2	13.8	13.3	14.1	13.9	13.0	- Amérique du Nord
- LAIA	5.6	6.0	4.2	4.3	4.9	6.3	3.9	3.7	4.8	4.2	- ALAI
- CACM	0.6	0.2	0.6	0.2	0.3	0.2	0.5	0.2	0.4	0.2	- MCC
- Caribbean	0.4	0.8	1.6	1.2	0.3	0.1	0.1	0.2	0.1	0.1	- Caraïbes
- Rest of America	0.6	0.3	0.0	0.0	0.0	0.0	0.1	0.1	0.0	0.1	- Autre d'Amérique
Asia excluding former USSR	22.2	23.9	28.5	32.9	30.1	26.1	31.3	36.4	31.2	31.6	Asie ancienne URSS exclus
- Middle East	7.1	8.5	6.9	10.9	9.5	10.1	7.2	6.2	7.2	4.9	- Moyen-Orient
Asia former USSR	0.0	0.1	0.0	0.1	0.1	0.1	0.3	0.3	0.3	0.3	Asie ancienne URSS
Europe excluding former USSR	53.7	49.6	45.9	42.8	43.2	46.6	44.6	36.9	41.7	41.2	Europe ancienne URSS exclus
- European Union	43.8	42.7	37.5	34.6	34.8	37.8	33.3	26.4	31.6	31.0	- Union Européenne
- Eastern Europe	3.6	1.8	2.7	3.3	3.7	4.1	6.3	5.9	6.6	5.7	- Europe de l'Est
- Rest of Europe	6.3	5.1	5.7	4.9	4.7	4.7	5.1	4.6	3.5	4.5	- Autre de l'Europe
Europe former USSR	0.9	2.3	2.5	2.6	3.7	3.3	3.1	5.1	5.5	6.2	Europe ancienne URSS
Oceania	1.7	2.0	1.7	1.8	1.8	1.5	1.2	1.1	0.9	1.2	Océanie

Autres moteurs et machines motrices et leurs parties et pièces détachées, n.d.a 718

TRADE BY COMMODITY (Value in million US dollars)
Exports by principal countries or areas

COMMERCE PAR PRODUIT (Valeur en millions de dollars EU)
Exportations selon les principaux pays ou zones

Country or area	1998	1999	2000	2001	2002	Pays ou zone
World	4006.1	5169.8	5032.9	5103.5	5612.9	Monde
Africa	5.2	6.6	9.7	10.7	11.3	Afrique
Americas	703.7	845.2	875.9	978.5	895.2	Amériques
- Northern America	625.6	763.5	759.8	864.4	811.9	- Amérique du Nord
- LAIA	77.6	80.3	114.3	113.5	82.8	- ALAI
- CACM	0.1	1.0	0.1	0.0	0.2	- MCC
- Caribbean	0.4	0.4	1.8	0.5	0.3	- Caraïbes
- Rest of America	0.0	0.0	0.0	0.1	0.0	- Autre d'Amérique
Asia excluding former USSR	401.2	499.5	582.0	508.0	537.8	Asie ancienne URSS exclus
- Middle East	4.2	4.3	11.3	28.8	29.5	- Moyen-Orient
Asia former USSR	0.2	0.3	0.3	2.1	2.3	Asie ancienne URSS
Europe excluding former USSR	2465.6	3136.5	3011.9	2834.5	3304.5	Europe ancienne URSS exclus
- European Union	2178.2	2934.4	2798.1	2592.7	2980.5	- Union Européenne
- Eastern Europe	124.8	71.6	87.8	87.1	110.0	- Europe de l'Est
- Rest of Europe	162.7	130.5	125.9	154.7	214.0	- Autre de l'Europe
Europe former USSR	417.6	671.2	537.9	755.2	848.5	Europe ancienne URSS
Oceania	12.6	10.6	15.1	14.7	13.1	Océanie
Germany	877.7	933.2	686.7	653.8	834.7	Allemagne
United States	531.1	596.3	574.4	713.4	665.5	Etats-Unis d'Amérique
Russian Federation	390.9	655.8	513.3	590.9	668.9	Fédération de Russie
Belgium	–	699.0	682.5	660.2	e740.7	Belgique
Japan	315.4	371.1	410.8	327.0	342.3	Japon
France-Monaco	321.6	419.7	342.7	316.3	316.6	France-Monaco
Sweden	195.7	189.5	179.3	216.2	311.0	Suède
United Kingdom	224.0	194.2	181.8	171.6	168.3	Royaume-Uni
Italy-San Marino-Holy See	141.0	147.8	172.2	160.6	161.7	Italie-Saint-Marin-Saint-Siège
Canada	94.4	167.2	185.4	150.9	146.4	Canada
Austria	163.1	130.7	94.1	87.3	98.6	Autriche
Spain	79.7	92.5	182.5	79.3	105.4	Espagne
Switzerland-Liechtenstein	96.2	95.4	80.4	104.9	160.7	Suisse-Liechtenstein
Finland	43.5	41.8	185.7	57.8	61.3	Finlande
Ukraine	14.5	5.8	13.0	150.0	165.3	Ukraine
Denmark	25.6	24.2	22.2	109.7	112.7	Danemark
China	22.3	37.7	56.0	66.8	65.8	Chine
Mexico	43.5	45.0	72.4	51.5	21.2	Mexique
Netherlands	28.6	44.2	49.5	54.5	42.0	Pays-Bas
Czech Republic	75.6	28.2	31.4	31.8	44.6	République tchèque
Norway	57.5	27.8	33.7	38.9	31.8	Norvège
Korea, Republic of	12.8	29.0	54.0	33.5	37.2	République de Corée
Brazil	17.9	18.8	21.2	41.5	e43.0	Brésil
Ireland	14.4	14.8	16.8	23.0	25.4	Irlande
Bulgaria	15.6	17.0	17.6	e18.6	e21.0	Bulgarie
Argentina	14.7	12.4	18.9	17.1	e16.5	Argentine
Singapore	12.1	19.2	8.7	12.4	13.8	Singapour
Slovakia	8.3	7.5	16.8	15.5	16.6	Slovaquie
Belgium-Luxembourg	62.7	–	–	–	–	Belgique-Luxembourg
Australia	10.9	8.6	13.7	13.8	12.0	Australie

(Value as percentages of World total) **(Valeur en pourcentage du total mondial)**

Regions of the world	1993	1994	1995	1996	1997	1998	1999	2000	2001	2002	Régions du monde
World	100.0	100.0	100.0	100.0	100.0	100.0	100.0	100.0	100.0	100.0	Monde
Africa	0.1	0.4	0.2	0.1	0.1	0.1	0.1	0.2	0.2	0.2	Afrique
Americas	17.1	16.8	17.5	16.2	17.2	17.6	16.3	17.4	19.2	15.9	Amériques
- Northern America	15.3	15.6	15.8	14.6	14.7	15.6	14.8	15.1	16.9	14.5	- Amérique du Nord
- LAIA	1.7	1.2	1.6	1.5	2.4	1.9	1.6	2.3	2.2	1.5	- ALAI
- CACM	0.0	0.0	0.0	0.0	0.0	0.0	0.0	0.0	0.0	0.0	- MCC
- Caribbean	0.1	0.1	0.1	0.1	0.1	0.0	0.0	0.0	0.0	0.0	- Caraïbes
- Rest of America	0.0	0.0	0.0	0.0	0.0	0.0	0.0	0.0	0.0	0.0	- Autre d'Amérique
Asia excluding former USSR	12.9	14.9	14.8	12.2	13.0	10.0	9.7	11.6	10.0	9.6	Asie ancienne URSS exclus
- Middle East	0.3	0.2	0.1	0.1	0.1	0.1	0.1	0.2	0.6	0.5	- Moyen-Orient
Asia former USSR	0.0	0.0	0.0	0.1	0.0	0.0	0.0	0.0	0.0	0.0	Asie ancienne URSS
Europe excluding former USSR	66.7	59.9	59.7	62.3	59.2	61.5	60.7	59.8	55.5	58.9	Europe ancienne URSS exclus
- European Union	61.1	55.3	54.8	55.7	53.0	54.4	56.8	55.6	50.8	53.1	- Union Européenne
- Eastern Europe	1.7	1.1	1.5	2.3	2.4	3.1	1.4	1.7	1.7	2.0	- Europe de l'Est
- Rest of Europe	3.9	3.4	3.3	4.4	3.7	4.1	2.5	2.5	3.0	3.8	- Autre de l'Europe
Europe former USSR	2.9	7.7	7.5	8.6	10.0	10.4	13.0	10.7	14.8	15.1	Europe ancienne URSS
Oceania	0.3	0.2	0.3	0.4	0.5	0.3	0.2	0.3	0.3	0.2	Océanie

721 Agricultural machinery (excluding tractors) and parts thereof, nes

TRADE BY COMMODITY (Value in million US dollars)
Imports by principal countries or areas

COMMERCE PAR PRODUIT (Valeur en millions de dollars EU)
Importations selon les principaux pays ou zones

Country or area	1998	1999	2000	2001	2002	Pays ou zone
World	12353.2	11507.9	10867.5	11022.8	12107.7	Monde
Africa	364.1	275.1	261.4	268.0	273.5	Afrique
Americas	3304.8	2721.6	2749.5	2911.1	2885.0	Amériques
- Northern America	2249.2	1939.2	2079.0	2090.1	2186.5	- Amérique du Nord
- LAIA	861.5	585.4	552.2	654.1	594.7	- ALAI
- CACM	63.2	61.7	50.9	46.5	51.9	- MCC
- Caribbean	114.9	114.5	50.5	108.4	38.5	- Caraïbes
- Rest of America	16.0	20.7	16.9	11.9	13.4	- Autre d'Amérique
Asia excluding former USSR	843.5	856.9	976.2	983.0	1034.6	Asie ancienne URSS exclus
- Middle East	217.0	225.7	242.4	236.9	244.8	- Moyen-Orient
Asia former USSR	202.7	156.5	189.7	143.9	141.1	Asie ancienne URSS
Europe excluding former USSR	6624.0	6644.9	5872.3	5900.4	6771.7	Europe ancienne URSS exclus
- European Union	5607.5	5832.0	5089.6	5005.2	5631.7	- Union Européenne
- Eastern Europe	603.1	417.9	407.2	535.1	736.6	- Europe de l'Est
- Rest of Europe	413.3	394.9	375.4	360.1	403.3	- Autre de l'Europe
Europe former USSR	598.6	450.4	383.8	493.0	555.6	Europe ancienne URSS
Oceania	415.6	402.5	434.6	323.4	446.4	Océanie
France-Monaco	1411.9	1396.6	1242.6	1124.8	1206.1	France-Monaco
United States	1192.0	1076.9	1141.9	1195.7	1276.2	Etats-Unis d'Amérique
Germany	1024.1	1075.2	1016.4	1003.2	1100.0	Allemagne
Canada	1057.1	862.2	936.8	893.8	909.4	Canada
United Kingdom	609.4	687.2	587.1	585.3	731.4	Royaume-Uni
Australia	359.1	337.5	365.5	248.6	347.7	Australie
Spain	367.4	347.6	285.3	313.5	326.7	Espagne
Italy-San Marino-Holy See	305.6	340.9	286.6	284.4	297.7	Italie-Saint-Marin-Saint-Siège
Denmark	298.9	304.4	273.3	287.0	350.0	Danemark
Netherlands	288.7	286.7	253.3	277.0	331.7	Pays-Bas
Belgium	–	405.2	297.4	298.3	e327.2	Belgique
Russian Federation	268.2	299.8	210.4	238.2	261.0	Fédération de Russie
Mexico	204.3	197.0	247.2	298.7	323.2	Mexique
Sweden	263.6	253.0	225.0	214.7	257.3	Suède
Austria	269.9	238.4	202.1	204.5	230.8	Autriche
Poland	216.4	151.8	154.1	192.0	240.2	Pologne
Japan	163.3	151.8	177.8	196.8	201.9	Japon
Switzerland-Liechtenstein	175.6	162.6	159.4	162.2	169.8	Suisse-Liechtenstein
Ireland	158.5	165.5	150.7	150.2	171.4	Irlande
China	102.6	141.3	137.3	155.5	168.5	Chine
Norway	133.3	143.9	131.4	117.9	136.4	Norvège
Hungary	142.4	99.3	85.6	122.8	197.0	Hongrie
Finland	132.4	132.0	117.7	114.2	140.9	Finlande
Czech Republic	118.0	85.7	94.0	114.0	152.8	République tchèque
Brazil	206.7	136.4	68.4	75.1	65.0	Brésil
Argentina	233.5	109.8	71.2	86.7	e38.4	Argentine
Ukraine	184.8	47.2	43.1	102.8	110.7	Ukraine
Greece	80.2	99.8	67.6	59.2	e65.4	Grèce
Belarus	52.4	47.2	86.1	80.3	85.8	Bélarus
Portugal	68.7	77.8	66.0	64.4	69.1	Portugal

(Value as percentages of World total) **(Valeur en pourcentage du total mondial)**

Regions of the world	1993	1994	1995	1996	1997	1998	1999	2000	2001	2002	Régions du monde
World	100.0	100.0	100.0	100.0	100.0	100.0	100.0	100.0	100.0	100.0	Monde
Africa	3.4	2.7	2.7	3.1	2.7	2.9	2.4	2.4	2.4	2.3	Afrique
Americas	25.4	25.9	22.2	22.0	26.4	26.8	23.6	25.3	26.4	23.8	Amériques
- Northern America	19.8	19.2	16.8	15.8	18.9	18.2	16.9	19.1	19.0	18.1	- Amérique du Nord
- LAIA	4.8	5.4	4.2	4.9	6.1	7.0	5.1	5.1	5.9	4.9	- ALAI
- CACM	0.4	0.4	0.3	0.3	0.4	0.5	0.5	0.5	0.4	0.4	- MCC
- Caribbean	0.3	0.7	0.7	0.7	0.8	0.9	1.0	0.5	1.0	0.3	- Caraïbes
- Rest of America	0.2	0.2	0.2	0.2	0.1	0.1	0.2	0.2	0.1	0.1	- Autre d'Amérique
Asia excluding former USSR	13.7	10.0	10.0	10.1	9.0	6.8	7.4	9.0	8.9	8.5	Asie ancienne URSS exclus
- Middle East	3.7	1.6	1.6	1.5	1.6	1.8	2.0	2.2	2.1	2.0	- Moyen-Orient
Asia former USSR	0.3	1.6	1.4	1.5	1.3	1.6	1.4	1.7	1.3	1.2	Asie ancienne URSS
Europe excluding former USSR	49.2	53.3	57.1	55.0	51.9	53.6	57.7	54.0	53.5	55.9	Europe ancienne URSS exclus
- European Union	42.7	45.2	47.6	45.1	42.9	45.4	50.7	46.8	45.4	46.5	- Union Européenne
- Eastern Europe	3.1	4.4	5.6	6.5	6.0	4.9	3.6	3.7	4.9	6.1	- Europe de l'Est
- Rest of Europe	3.4	3.7	3.9	3.5	3.1	3.3	3.4	3.5	3.3	3.3	- Autre de l'Europe
Europe former USSR	5.2	3.1	3.7	4.2	5.0	4.8	3.9	3.5	4.5	4.6	Europe ancienne URSS
Oceania	2.7	3.3	3.0	4.0	3.7	3.4	3.5	4.0	2.9	3.7	Océanie

TRADE BY COMMODITY (Value in million US dollars)
Exports by principal countries or areas

COMMERCE PAR PRODUIT (Valeur en millions de dollars EU)
Exportations selon les principaux pays ou zones

Country or area	1998	1999	2000	2001	2002	Pays ou zone
World	12279.0	11071.8	10786.3	10990.3	12271.1	Monde
Africa	27.8	36.7	20.8	21.5	25.8	Afrique
Americas	3568.1	2830.7	3012.2	2868.0	3074.5	Amériques
- Northern America	3203.7	2607.6	2785.7	2673.9	2854.6	- Amérique du Nord
- LAIA	354.4	210.8	214.5	185.5	211.5	- ALAI
- CACM	6.2	9.8	7.9	5.1	4.9	- MCC
- Caribbean	3.8	2.6	4.0	3.2	3.1	- Caraïbes
- Rest of America	0.0	0.0	0.1	0.2	0.4	- Autre d'Amérique
Asia excluding former USSR	460.0	523.6	570.4	530.2	627.1	Asie ancienne URSS exclus
- Middle East	16.9	19.9	27.7	35.9	31.2	- Moyen-Orient
Asia former USSR	5.6	12.8	11.5	9.1	9.1	Asie ancienne URSS
Europe excluding former USSR	8008.2	7438.2	6935.7	7280.0	8233.1	Europe ancienne URSS exclus
- European Union	7420.0	6932.9	6427.6	6741.9	7565.5	- Union Européenne
- Eastern Europe	356.6	292.8	323.4	360.5	458.0	- Europe de l'Est
- Rest of Europe	231.5	212.4	184.7	177.6	209.6	- Autre de l'Europe
Europe former USSR	99.4	116.1	128.6	173.6	173.7	Europe ancienne URSS
Oceania	109.9	113.7	107.1	107.9	127.8	Océanie
United States	2613.7	2171.9	2331.7	2184.8	2284.4	Etats-Unis d'Amérique
Germany	2342.6	2009.6	1804.1	2013.9	2263.8	Allemagne
Italy-San Marino-Holy See	1269.9	1258.8	1194.9	1258.3	1382.9	Italie-Saint-Marin-Saint-Siège
France-Monaco	830.2	767.5	763.4	764.7	868.3	France-Monaco
Netherlands	495.7	548.7	503.3	540.2	652.1	Pays-Bas
Canada	590.0	435.7	454.0	489.1	570.2	Canada
Belgium	–	546.5	540.6	565.2	e634.1	Belgique
Denmark	518.7	476.8	434.7	400.8	411.0	Danemark
United Kingdom	478.5	505.1	396.2	352.5	347.6	Royaume-Uni
Sweden	279.5	275.1	252.5	274.7	337.4	Suède
Austria	233.2	212.0	222.7	215.0	264.7	Autriche
Japan	185.6	210.3	195.5	164.6	177.0	Japon
Spain	156.2	161.3	140.6	162.4	186.0	Espagne
Brazil	222.8	109.8	114.7	133.8	e138.7	Brésil
Hungary	124.9	109.9	118.9	147.3	198.5	Hongrie
Belgium-Luxembourg	652.8	–	–	–	–	Belgique-Luxembourg
Norway	149.4	131.9	103.2	99.3	118.4	Norvège
Finland	104.1	103.1	108.9	113.8	120.3	Finlande
China	47.7	66.1	91.4	102.2	175.5	Chine
Poland	88.5	68.5	100.2	98.8	122.6	Pologne
Czech Republic	107.5	90.6	77.3	83.6	99.5	République tchèque
Mexico	105.8	80.2	77.8	33.1	56.2	Mexique
Australia	61.9	68.6	60.1	66.2	67.7	Australie
Ireland	43.9	49.9	48.6	62.3	76.3	Irlande
Switzerland-Liechtenstein	52.6	55.1	56.4	51.2	52.6	Suisse-Liechtenstein
New Zealand	48.0	45.0	46.9	41.6	60.1	Nouvelle-Zélande
Israel	53.3	40.9	55.8	48.5	40.6	Israël
Belarus	37.6	53.1	51.5	50.9	40.8	Bélarus
Russian Federation	15.1	23.0	36.6	75.5	77.1	Fédération de Russie
Korea, Republic of	23.2	28.1	27.1	29.1	31.6	République de Corée

(Value as percentages of World total) **(Valeur en pourcentage du total mondial)**

Regions of the world	1993	1994	1995	1996	1997	1998	1999	2000	2001	2002	Régions du monde
World	100.0	100.0	100.0	100.0	100.0	100.0	100.0	100.0	100.0	100.0	Monde
Africa	0.2	0.3	0.3	0.4	0.3	0.2	0.3	0.2	0.2	0.2	Afrique
Americas	30.9	29.3	27.3	28.9	32.3	29.1	25.6	27.9	26.1	25.1	Amériques
- Northern America	28.7	26.8	24.9	26.2	29.3	26.1	23.6	25.8	24.3	23.3	- Amérique du Nord
- LAIA	2.2	2.4	2.4	2.7	3.0	2.9	1.9	2.0	1.7	1.7	- ALAI
- CACM	0.0	0.0	0.0	0.0	0.1	0.1	0.1	0.1	0.0	0.0	- MCC
- Caribbean	0.0	0.0	0.0	0.0	0.0	0.0	0.0	0.0	0.0	0.0	- Caraïbes
- Rest of America	0.0	0.0	0.0	0.0	0.0	0.0	0.0	0.0	0.0	0.0	- Autre d'Amérique
Asia excluding former USSR	7.0	5.1	4.4	4.2	4.1	3.7	4.7	5.3	4.8	5.1	Asie ancienne URSS exclus
- Middle East	0.1	0.1	0.1	0.2	0.2	0.1	0.2	0.3	0.3	0.3	- Moyen-Orient
Asia former USSR	0.0	0.1	0.1	0.1	0.1	0.0	0.1	0.1	0.1	0.1	Asie ancienne URSS
Europe excluding former USSR	60.1	63.2	65.1	63.8	61.0	65.2	67.2	64.3	66.2	67.1	Europe ancienne URSS exclus
- European Union	56.2	59.2	60.7	59.4	56.5	60.4	62.6	59.6	61.3	61.7	- Union Européenne
- Eastern Europe	1.9	2.0	2.1	2.2	2.6	2.9	2.6	3.0	3.3	3.7	- Europe de l'Est
- Rest of Europe	2.0	2.0	2.3	2.1	1.9	1.9	1.9	1.7	1.6	1.7	- Autre de l'Europe
Europe former USSR	0.5	1.1	1.5	1.4	0.9	0.8	1.0	1.2	1.6	1.4	Europe ancienne URSS
Oceania	1.2	1.1	1.3	1.2	1.2	0.9	1.0	1.0	1.0	1.0	Océanie

722 Tractors (other than those falling in heading 74411 and 7832)

TRADE BY COMMODITY (Value in million US dollars)
Imports by principal countries or areas

COMMERCE PAR PRODUIT (Valeur en millions de dollars EU)
Importations selon les principaux pays ou zones

Country or area	1998	1999	2000	2001	2002	Pays ou zone
World	9399.3	7756.8	7706.8	7357.6	8362.0	Monde
Africa	296.7	220.4	232.1	200.0	288.0	Afrique
Americas	3458.2	2448.2	2674.5	2580.5	2816.3	Amériques
- Northern America	2932.8	2101.5	2406.1	2287.8	2564.3	- Amérique du Nord
- LAIA	410.8	228.8	178.1	210.4	167.3	- ALAI
- CACM	71.3	65.3	56.6	55.2	53.3	- MCC
- Caribbean	28.3	40.6	22.7	18.7	23.8	- Caraïbes
- Rest of America	15.0	12.1	11.0	8.4	7.7	- Autre d'Amérique
Asia excluding former USSR	481.4	558.3	607.7	634.7	621.5	Asie ancienne URSS exclus
- Middle East	138.7	94.5	132.3	159.2	157.7	- Moyen-Orient
Asia former USSR	121.6	65.7	82.0	54.3	69.4	Asie ancienne URSS
Europe excluding former USSR	4304.4	4024.5	3631.1	3444.7	3972.5	Europe ancienne URSS exclus
- European Union	3821.7	3593.1	3218.4	2956.2	3381.2	- Union Européenne
- Eastern Europe	165.0	117.9	132.8	207.9	284.5	- Europe de l'Est
- Rest of Europe	317.7	313.5	279.9	280.7	306.8	- Autre de l'Europe
Europe former USSR	278.7	102.9	112.3	115.0	129.1	Europe ancienne URSS
Oceania	458.3	336.7	367.0	328.4	465.1	Océanie
United States	2247.5	1618.5	1835.4	1654.6	1901.5	Etats-Unis d'Amérique
France-Monaco	954.6	882.2	881.1	749.1	842.7	France-Monaco
Canada	685.0	482.7	570.4	632.6	662.3	Canada
Spain	633.7	520.7	406.4	413.5	391.3	Espagne
Germany	398.6	332.9	287.4	333.4	373.9	Allemagne
United Kingdom	219.5	334.7	267.4	272.9	388.3	Royaume-Uni
Australia	399.1	281.9	277.3	205.9	305.6	Australie
Italy-San Marino-Holy See	302.5	303.4	248.3	231.3	253.2	Italie-Saint-Marin-Saint-Siège
Netherlands	180.2	177.7	163.2	138.2	182.8	Pays-Bas
Denmark	138.8	138.3	147.5	126.3	167.4	Danemark
Portugal	141.2	159.6	131.3	128.0	140.2	Portugal
Belgium	-	204.4	190.8	135.3	e148.4	Belgique
Sweden	120.5	137.2	151.1	129.2	133.4	Suède
Austria	127.8	124.2	123.7	107.8	134.1	Autriche
Switzerland-Liechtenstein	117.0	116.4	120.2	119.8	112.3	Suisse-Liechtenstein
Japan	88.4	89.4	110.7	122.6	125.1	Japon
Norway	101.9	107.2	88.8	97.4	123.0	Norvège
Ireland	92.5	96.8	88.4	84.1	110.0	Irlande
New Zealand	53.4	48.6	82.1	115.0	152.2	Nouvelle-Zélande
Finland	104.1	79.9	78.5	83.3	89.5	Finlande
Hungary	75.9	54.3	48.5	70.2	96.2	Hongrie
Pakistan	48.8	113.3	52.6	46.0	37.7	Pakistan
Belgium-Luxembourg	288.5	-	-	-	-	Belgique-Luxembourg
Thailand	28.3	44.7	71.3	70.4	e73.4	Thaïlande
Greece	119.3	90.1	43.9	16.2	e17.9	Grèce
Korea, Republic of	18.3	33.3	63.0	87.7	79.4	République de Corée
Argentina	140.0	44.0	33.7	40.0	e17.7	Argentine
Mexico	63.2	43.9	44.0	53.1	51.4	Mexique
Poland	34.4	22.8	33.5	59.8	94.7	Pologne
Ukraine	158.1	19.7	20.0	19.9	21.4	Ukraine

(Value as percentages of World total) **(Valeur en pourcentage du total mondial)**

Regions of the world	1993	1994	1995	1996	1997	1998	1999	2000	2001	2002	Régions du monde
World	100.0	100.0	100.0	100.0	100.0	100.0	100.0	100.0	100.0	100.0	Monde
Africa	5.0	4.9	4.4	4.7	4.1	3.2	2.8	3.0	2.7	3.4	Afrique
Americas	36.3	36.8	32.4	28.5	33.8	36.8	31.6	34.7	35.1	33.7	Amériques
- Northern America	31.0	32.1	28.6	24.5	29.1	31.2	27.1	31.2	31.1	30.7	- Amérique du Nord
- LAIA	3.7	3.7	2.8	3.2	3.6	4.4	2.9	2.3	2.9	2.0	- ALAI
- CACM	0.8	0.5	0.3	0.3	0.6	0.8	0.8	0.7	0.8	0.6	- MCC
- Caribbean	0.2	0.2	0.3	0.3	0.2	0.3	0.5	0.3	0.3	0.3	- Caraïbes
- Rest of America	0.5	0.4	0.4	0.2	0.2	0.2	0.2	0.1	0.1	0.1	- Autre d'Amérique
Asia excluding former USSR	15.0	11.9	12.0	10.8	9.4	5.1	7.2	7.9	8.6	7.4	Asie ancienne URSS exclus
- Middle East	2.9	1.3	0.9	1.0	1.1	1.5	1.2	1.7	2.2	1.9	- Moyen-Orient
Asia former USSR	0.1	0.3	0.9	0.9	0.6	1.3	0.8	1.1	0.7	0.8	Asie ancienne URSS
Europe excluding former USSR	37.8	40.6	45.2	48.7	45.4	45.8	51.9	47.1	46.8	47.5	Europe ancienne URSS exclus
- European Union	33.3	35.5	40.1	43.2	40.3	40.7	46.3	41.8	40.2	40.4	- Union Européenne
- Eastern Europe	1.3	1.6	1.2	1.9	2.0	1.8	1.5	1.7	2.8	3.4	- Europe de l'Est
- Rest of Europe	3.2	3.5	3.9	3.5	3.0	3.4	4.0	3.6	3.8	3.7	- Autre de l'Europe
Europe former USSR	2.0	1.2	1.2	1.6	2.1	3.0	1.3	1.5	1.6	1.5	Europe ancienne URSS
Oceania	3.9	4.4	3.9	4.7	4.6	4.9	4.3	4.8	4.5	5.6	Océanie

TRADE BY COMMODITY (Value in million US dollars)
Exports by principal countries or areas

COMMERCE PAR PRODUIT (Valeur en millions de dollars EU)
Exportations selon les principaux pays ou zones

Country or area	1998	1999	2000	2001	2002	Pays ou zone
World	9612.3	8202.9	7812.5	7423.2	8389.7	Monde
Africa	16.9	22.1	16.4	19.3	23.6	Afrique
Americas	2524.7	1627.9	1698.1	1564.6	1705.1	Amériques
- Northern America	2285.5	1485.4	1547.2	1402.6	1549.8	- Amérique du Nord
- LAIA	233.5	129.8	142.8	160.1	152.2	- ALAI
- CACM	1.4	1.8	1.0	1.0	2.2	- MCC
- Caribbean	4.2	10.8	7.0	0.6	0.7	- Caraïbes
- Rest of America	0.1	0.1	0.1	0.3	0.1	- Autre d'Amérique
Asia excluding former USSR	1062.3	1113.1	1240.0	1070.6	1244.7	Asie ancienne URSS exclus
- Middle East	28.1	40.5	49.1	37.6	45.2	- Moyen-Orient
Asia former USSR	12.1	12.2	10.7	6.6	9.6	Asie ancienne URSS
Europe excluding former USSR	5744.5	5115.3	4562.2	4459.9	5130.9	Europe ancienne URSS exclus
- European Union	5451.3	4960.1	4455.2	4334.3	4985.5	- Union Européenne
- Eastern Europe	254.3	114.8	72.2	86.8	108.1	- Europe de l'Est
- Rest of Europe	38.9	40.5	34.9	38.8	37.3	- Autre de l'Europe
Europe former USSR	247.8	307.8	278.8	296.4	270.0	Europe ancienne URSS
Oceania	4.0	4.5	6.3	5.9	5.8	Océanie
United States	1860.2	1261.1	1292.9	1251.3	1397.8	Etats-Unis d'Amérique
United Kingdom	1872.9	1535.3	1218.3	1062.2	1111.0	Royaume-Uni
Germany	1342.3	1265.3	1231.0	1235.2	1514.6	Allemagne
Italy-San Marino-Holy See	1128.5	1091.2	1032.0	1013.4	1097.7	Italie-Saint-Marin-Saint-Siège
Japan	869.9	933.8	1011.2	844.6	966.2	Japon
France-Monaco	388.7	326.6	287.5	298.2	385.7	France-Monaco
Finland	302.7	357.8	297.8	302.7	343.9	Finlande
Canada	425.4	224.2	254.2	151.3	152.0	Canada
Belarus	193.6	244.4	200.7	207.2	207.8	Bélarus
Austria	152.2	115.5	153.4	223.9	277.9	Autriche
Brazil	148.4	53.7	70.9	95.9	e99.4	Brésil
Mexico	80.1	67.2	68.2	59.3	50.6	Mexique
China	45.8	58.9	63.6	61.4	68.5	Chine
Belgium	–	107.2	80.9	48.1	e54.0	Belgique
Czech Republic	125.0	41.4	15.6	45.0	56.8	République tchèque
Korea, Republic of	36.0	31.2	57.2	73.6	77.7	République de Corée
Netherlands	33.3	35.2	42.6	52.7	75.9	Pays-Bas
Sweden	31.2	56.1	64.0	30.2	49.6	Suède
Poland	65.8	41.7	34.4	27.5	34.1	Pologne
Russian Federation	30.0	41.0	46.9	57.0	27.7	Fédération de Russie
Turkey	22.1	28.9	45.3	30.6	38.8	Turquie
Spain	25.0	34.8	24.2	34.8	39.4	Espagne
Belgium-Luxembourg	149.9	–	–	–	–	Belgique-Luxembourg
India	17.4	14.1	23.3	29.1	64.6	Inde
Denmark	18.5	20.6	18.1	22.4	24.9	Danemark
Switzerland-Liechtenstein	19.7	21.3	19.3	21.7	21.8	Suisse-Liechtenstein
Romania	44.3	20.3	14.2	7.0	8.8	Roumanie
Ukraine	9.1	13.1	22.9	19.8	21.8	Ukraine
Thailand	36.7	15.4	14.4	9.6	e10.2	Thaïlande
Slovakia	15.7	9.2	5.4	5.0	4.9	Slovaquie

(Value as percentages of World total) **(Valeur en pourcentage du total mondial)**

Regions of the world	1993	1994	1995	1996	1997	1998	1999	2000	2001	2002	Régions du monde
World	100.0	100.0	100.0	100.0	100.0	100.0	100.0	100.0	100.0	100.0	Monde
Africa	0.1	0.2	0.1	0.1	0.1	0.2	0.3	0.2	0.3	0.3	Afrique
Americas	23.6	23.5	22.9	23.0	26.1	26.3	19.8	21.7	21.1	20.3	Amériques
- Northern America	22.3	21.8	20.9	20.8	23.4	23.8	18.1	19.8	18.9	18.5	- Amérique du Nord
- LAIA	1.3	1.6	2.0	2.2	2.7	2.4	1.6	1.8	2.2	1.8	- ALAI
- CACM	0.0	0.0	0.0	0.0	0.0	0.0	0.0	0.0	0.0	0.0	- MCC
- Caribbean	0.0	0.0	0.0	0.0	0.0	0.0	0.1	0.1	0.0	0.0	- Caraïbes
- Rest of America	0.0	0.0	0.0	0.0	0.0	0.0	0.0	0.0	0.0	0.0	- Autre d'Amérique
Asia excluding former USSR	13.8	14.9	11.8	10.1	9.9	11.1	13.6	15.9	14.4	14.8	Asie ancienne URSS exclus
- Middle East	0.1	0.1	0.1	0.2	0.1	0.3	0.5	0.6	0.5	0.5	- Moyen-Orient
Asia former USSR	0.2	0.3	0.2	0.4	0.4	0.1	0.1	0.1	0.1	0.1	Asie ancienne URSS
Europe excluding former USSR	58.5	59.4	61.6	63.9	61.0	59.8	62.4	58.4	60.1	61.2	Europe ancienne URSS exclus
- European Union	55.3	57.0	58.5	61.0	58.2	56.7	60.5	57.0	58.4	59.4	- Union Européenne
- Eastern Europe	2.8	2.1	2.8	2.6	2.6	2.6	1.4	0.9	1.2	1.3	- Europe de l'Est
- Rest of Europe	0.4	0.4	0.4	0.3	0.3	0.4	0.5	0.4	0.5	0.4	- Autre de l'Europe
Europe former USSR	3.7	1.6	3.3	2.4	2.4	2.6	3.8	3.6	4.0	3.2	Europe ancienne URSS
Oceania	0.1	0.1	0.0	0.1	0.0	0.0	0.1	0.1	0.1	0.1	Océanie

723 Civil engineering, contractors' plant and equipment and parts, nes

TRADE BY COMMODITY (Value in million US dollars)
Imports by principal countries or areas

COMMERCE PAR PRODUIT (Valeur en millions de dollars EU)
Importations selon les principaux pays ou zones

Country or area	1998	1999	2000	2001	2002	Pays ou zone
World	24358.8	22354.1	22805.5	23339.1	25036.8	Monde
Africa	1641.5	1239.8	1335.3	1659.7	1851.2	Afrique
Americas	8388.9	7147.2	6995.9	6308.1	6229.1	Amériques
- Northern America	6014.2	5475.9	5216.3	4579.8	4516.0	- Amérique du Nord
- LAIA	2025.3	1377.1	1520.2	1507.2	1353.5	- ALAI
- CACM	165.9	142.6	100.0	77.6	98.5	- MCC
- Caribbean	112.2	103.6	122.6	115.4	235.9	- Caraïbes
- Rest of America	71.2	48.0	36.9	28.1	25.1	- Autre d'Amérique
Asia excluding former USSR	5207.4	4327.0	4993.5	5604.8	6433.3	Asie ancienne URSS exclus
- Middle East	1752.8	1338.0	1787.7	2041.3	2270.3	- Moyen-Orient
Asia former USSR	171.1	183.8	330.3	409.6	441.0	Asie ancienne URSS
Europe excluding former USSR	7582.9	8380.2	8005.5	8149.9	8606.9	Europe ancienne URSS exclus
- European Union	6393.1	7262.9	6847.2	7097.3	7377.5	- Union Européenne
- Eastern Europe	445.0	398.1	387.0	400.8	488.6	- Europe de l'Est
- Rest of Europe	744.8	719.2	771.3	651.8	740.8	- Autre de l'Europe
Europe former USSR	546.2	297.6	484.8	592.3	600.7	Europe ancienne URSS
Oceania	820.7	778.4	660.3	614.8	874.6	Océanie
United States	4385.8	4036.9	3674.4	3299.8	3235.2	Etats-Unis d'Amérique
Canada	1623.6	1433.8	1536.9	1273.8	1271.5	Canada
Singapore	1198.2	1001.7	822.3	1068.8	1298.9	Singapour
United Kingdom	1069.5	1091.0	929.3	1109.4	1187.2	Royaume-Uni
France-Monaco	853.0	954.6	1042.9	999.4	964.4	France-Monaco
Italy-San Marino-Holy See	673.6	839.4	798.6	828.6	1028.6	Italie-Saint-Marin-Saint-Siège
Germany	725.5	853.3	665.0	886.6	665.3	Allemagne
Spain	612.8	773.2	664.9	688.1	739.4	Espagne
Netherlands	535.5	630.0	638.6	540.4	689.8	Pays-Bas
United Arab Emirates	463.6	485.8	569.8	736.7	e755.8	Emirates arabes unis
Australia	660.2	586.8	498.5	447.7	656.4	Australie
Mexico	451.5	474.0	655.1	545.6	589.3	Mexique
Belgium	–	527.9	574.1	593.0	e650.3	Belgique
China	362.2	445.1	416.3	448.1	665.2	Chine
Russian Federation	385.7	191.7	363.9	469.5	449.2	Fédération de Russie
China, Hong Kong SAR	340.4	239.1	307.3	369.5	472.7	Chine - RAS de Hong-Kong
Indonesia	378.4	303.2	345.5	327.3	264.4	Indonésie
Denmark	294.9	291.9	325.6	340.1	350.8	Danemark
Norway	356.7	287.3	283.1	250.8	277.7	Norvège
Austria	283.8	296.0	277.9	259.0	274.3	Autriche
Turkey	419.3	210.8	371.3	179.3	186.7	Turquie
Switzerland-Liechtenstein	217.7	243.3	304.2	256.2	260.3	Suisse-Liechtenstein
Portugal	259.0	262.4	279.7	276.9	201.5	Portugal
Oman	209.5	154.3	213.0	278.7	248.4	Oman
Saudi Arabia	181.8	117.5	187.7	298.1	e308.6	Arabie saoudite
Angola	e143.5	e170.0	e149.0	e183.9	e357.2	Angola
Sweden	180.9	216.1	197.1	179.4	178.3	Suède
Chile	293.3	112.2	212.2	167.3	147.2	Chili
Ireland	151.6	195.9	184.0	167.4	186.0	Irlande
South Africa	–	–	253.6	282.4	328.8	Afrique du Sud

(Value as percentages of World total)

(Valeur en pourcentage du total mondial)

Regions of the world	1993	1994	1995	1996	1997	1998	1999	2000	2001	2002	Régions du monde
World	100.0	100.0	100.0	100.0	100.0	100.0	100.0	100.0	100.0	100.0	Monde
Africa	6.3	6.5	5.7	7.6	7.3	6.7	5.5	5.9	7.1	7.4	Afrique
Americas	22.1	29.1	25.0	23.5	29.9	34.4	32.0	30.7	27.0	24.9	Amériques
- Northern America	14.5	20.6	18.3	17.0	21.6	24.7	24.5	22.9	19.6	18.0	- Amérique du Nord
- LAIA	6.6	7.7	5.9	5.7	7.1	8.3	6.2	6.7	6.5	5.4	- ALAI
- CACM	0.3	0.4	0.3	0.3	0.5	0.7	0.6	0.4	0.3	0.4	- MCC
- Caribbean	0.3	0.2	0.3	0.4	0.5	0.5	0.5	0.5	0.5	0.9	- Caraïbes
- Rest of America	0.3	0.2	0.2	0.2	0.2	0.3	0.2	0.2	0.1	0.1	- Autre d'Amérique
Asia excluding former USSR	36.8	28.7	29.4	30.8	27.9	21.4	19.4	21.9	24.0	25.7	Asie ancienne URSS exclus
- Middle East	10.1	6.2	4.6	5.1	6.2	7.2	6.0	7.8	8.7	9.1	- Moyen-Orient
Asia former USSR	0.5	0.6	0.5	0.8	0.5	0.7	0.8	1.4	1.8	1.8	Asie ancienne URSS
Europe excluding former USSR	26.5	28.0	32.3	30.4	27.7	31.1	37.5	35.1	34.9	34.4	Europe ancienne URSS exclus
- European Union	21.9	23.5	26.6	24.4	22.9	26.2	32.5	30.0	30.4	29.5	- Union Européenne
- Eastern Europe	1.9	1.5	1.8	2.0	1.8	1.8	1.8	1.7	1.7	2.0	- Europe de l'Est
- Rest of Europe	2.7	3.0	3.9	4.0	3.0	3.1	3.2	3.4	2.8	3.0	- Autre de l'Europe
Europe former USSR	4.1	2.4	2.6	2.6	3.1	2.2	1.3	2.1	2.5	2.4	Europe ancienne URSS
Oceania	3.7	4.6	4.3	4.3	3.6	3.4	3.5	2.9	2.6	3.5	Océanie

TRADE BY COMMODITY (Value in million US dollars)
Exports by principal countries or areas

COMMERCE PAR PRODUIT (Valeur en millions de dollars EU)
Exportations selon les principaux pays ou zones

Country or area	1998	1999	2000	2001	2002	Pays ou zone
World	28367.6	24777.7	25791.0	27488.0	28700.1	Monde
Africa	114.2	110.7	120.2	147.0	170.8	Afrique
Americas	10112.2	7914.3	8417.0	9325.5	8957.2	Amériques
- Northern America	9411.9	7286.5	7735.1	8596.8	8271.0	- Amérique du Nord
- LAIA	680.4	612.4	652.7	697.8	653.8	- ALAI
- CACM	8.0	3.5	7.3	5.8	11.1	- MCC
- Caribbean	10.8	9.7	20.1	20.9	18.9	- Caraïbes
- Rest of America	1.1	2.1	1.7	4.1	2.4	- Autre d'Amérique
Asia excluding former USSR	6110.4	5444.2	5835.8	5957.1	7154.0	Asie ancienne URSS exclus
- Middle East	230.8	258.1	346.0	485.2	484.4	- Moyen-Orient
Asia former USSR	17.3	18.3	30.1	46.4	47.2	Asie ancienne URSS
Europe excluding former USSR	11676.4	10957.0	11053.6	11567.2	12008.6	Europe ancienne URSS exclus
- European Union	10995.2	10348.3	10523.7	11025.7	11379.4	- Union Européenne
- Eastern Europe	259.9	221.5	241.6	251.0	285.1	- Europe de l'Est
- Rest of Europe	421.2	387.2	288.3	290.5	344.1	- Autre de l'Europe
Europe former USSR	165.5	185.1	176.7	283.0	196.6	Europe ancienne URSS
Oceania	171.5	148.3	157.5	162.0	165.5	Océanie
United States	8820.1	6778.5	7210.0	7940.2	7589.8	Etats-Unis d'Amérique
Japan	3330.1	3345.1	3350.5	3144.2	3821.2	Japon
Germany	2341.7	2203.4	2339.0	2658.4	2817.3	Allemagne
United Kingdom	2408.4	2083.6	1933.9	2032.3	2148.5	Royaume-Uni
France-Monaco	1802.4	1609.0	1671.7	1529.4	1531.0	France-Monaco
Italy-San Marino-Holy See	1128.9	1138.7	1170.2	1185.1	1029.5	Italie-Saint-Marin-Saint-Siège
Belgium	–	1335.7	1333.1	1404.7	e1576.0	Belgique
Singapore	972.2	716.9	814.3	891.4	1036.4	Singapour
Korea, Republic of	650.6	636.7	718.7	680.5	994.6	République de Corée
Canada	591.1	508.0	525.0	656.6	681.0	Canada
Netherlands	496.8	587.5	538.7	628.6	630.0	Pays-Bas
Austria	445.4	416.2	455.8	469.1	518.9	Autriche
Sweden	464.7	446.1	463.3	420.9	443.1	Suède
Brazil	411.6	326.6	314.5	351.2	e364.1	Brésil
Finland	320.2	284.3	333.4	343.9	356.7	Finlande
Belgium-Luxembourg	1369.3	–	–	–	–	Belgique-Luxembourg
China	136.5	111.8	216.9	384.3	421.2	Chine
Norway	318.9	276.9	187.2	180.7	231.0	Norvège
United Arab Emirates	95.7	98.8	198.6	326.0	e339.6	Emirates arabes unis
Mexico	204.1	167.5	275.0	200.7	171.4	Mexique
Denmark	85.4	115.6	159.0	212.0	190.4	Danemark
Australia	138.1	126.4	137.0	147.9	154.4	Australie
China, Hong Kong SAR	198.8	81.5	105.1	95.5	127.5	Chine - RAS de Hong-Kong
Russian Federation	69.3	119.0	112.4	199.3	101.2	Fédération de Russie
Poland	128.4	109.3	108.1	67.5	69.0	Pologne
Thailand	174.9	69.8	68.3	70.0	e73.9	Thaïlande
Malaysia	212.1	73.6	61.4	49.0	e52.0	Malaisie
Switzerland-Liechtenstein	87.1	84.1	82.5	88.5	81.3	Suisse-Liechtenstein
Spain	86.2	82.1	70.6	73.3	59.8	Espagne
Indonesia	94.5	62.8	78.9	43.2	56.4	Indonésie

(Value as percentages of World total) **(Valeur en pourcentage du total mondial)**

Regions of the world	1993	1994	1995	1996	1997	1998	1999	2000	2001	2002	Régions du monde
World	100.0	100.0	100.0	100.0	100.0	100.0	100.0	100.0	100.0	100.0	Monde
Africa	0.4	0.3	0.3	1.0	0.4	0.4	0.4	0.5	0.5	0.6	Afrique
Americas	32.6	32.5	30.6	33.1	36.0	35.6	31.9	32.6	33.9	31.2	Amériques
- Northern America	30.7	29.9	28.3	31.1	33.3	33.2	29.4	30.0	31.3	28.8	- Amérique du Nord
- LAIA	1.9	2.5	2.2	2.0	2.6	2.4	2.5	2.5	2.5	2.3	- ALAI
- CACM	0.0	0.0	0.0	0.0	0.0	0.0	0.0	0.0	0.0	0.0	- MCC
- Caribbean	0.0	0.0	0.0	0.0	0.0	0.0	0.0	0.1	0.1	0.1	- Caraïbes
- Rest of America	0.0	0.0	0.0	0.0	0.0	0.0	0.0	0.0	0.0	0.0	- Autre d'Amérique
Asia excluding former USSR	25.5	24.3	25.1	24.4	23.7	21.5	22.0	22.6	21.7	24.9	Asie ancienne URSS exclus
- Middle East	1.6	1.2	0.8	0.7	0.9	0.8	1.0	1.3	1.8	1.7	- Moyen-Orient
Asia former USSR	0.2	0.1	0.1	0.2	0.1	0.1	0.1	0.1	0.2	0.2	Asie ancienne URSS
Europe excluding former USSR	39.3	41.9	42.4	39.9	38.4	41.2	44.2	42.9	42.1	41.8	Europe ancienne URSS exclus
- European Union	37.4	40.0	40.5	37.7	36.3	38.8	41.8	40.8	40.1	39.6	- Union Européenne
- Eastern Europe	1.0	1.1	1.1	1.2	1.1	0.9	0.9	0.9	0.9	1.0	- Europe de l'Est
- Rest of Europe	0.9	0.8	0.9	1.0	1.0	1.5	1.6	1.1	1.1	1.2	- Autre de l'Europe
Europe former USSR	1.4	0.5	0.6	0.7	0.7	0.6	0.7	0.7	1.0	0.7	Europe ancienne URSS
Oceania	0.7	0.5	0.9	0.7	0.7	0.6	0.6	0.6	0.6	0.6	Océanie

724 Textile and leather machinery, and parts thereof, nes

TRADE BY COMMODITY (Value in million US dollars) COMMERCE PAR PRODUIT (Valeur en millions de dollars EU)
Imports by principal countries or areas **Importations selon les principaux pays ou zones**

Country or area	1998	1999	2000	2001	2002	Pays ou zone
World	21906.5	18086.8	20491.5	19119.2	21017.8	Monde
Africa	894.0	759.5	824.0	787.8	797.6	Afrique
Americas	5399.9	4480.3	4576.6	3640.9	3307.0	Amériques
- Northern America	3178.6	2627.8	2443.1	1917.8	1934.4	- Amérique du Nord
- LAIA	2045.9	1709.4	1958.0	1549.5	1201.3	- ALAI
- CACM	95.8	82.2	106.7	119.7	115.1	- MCC
- Caribbean	73.6	55.2	62.6	49.8	53.3	- Caraïbes
- Rest of America	6.0	5.7	6.1	4.1	2.8	- Autre d'Amérique
Asia excluding former USSR	8550.9	6841.1	9215.0	8929.0	11345.5	Asie ancienne URSS exclus
- Middle East	1967.9	901.5	1423.6	1183.7	2217.7	- Moyen-Orient
Asia former USSR	104.5	86.6	163.2	188.7	156.8	Asie ancienne URSS
Europe excluding former USSR	6578.6	5572.7	5390.7	5187.3	5042.5	Europe ancienne URSS exclus
- European Union	5421.5	4609.0	4407.6	4150.3	3945.2	- Union Européenne
- Eastern Europe	714.4	576.3	598.4	667.3	721.9	- Europe de l'Est
- Rest of Europe	442.7	387.4	384.7	369.8	375.5	- Autre de l'Europe
Europe former USSR	208.4	166.2	175.7	266.8	238.3	Europe ancienne URSS
Oceania	170.2	180.4	146.4	118.7	130.0	Océanie
China	1436.5	1569.0	2368.5	2939.1	4017.1	Chine
United States	2803.3	2282.4	2091.9	1621.2	1637.8	Etats-Unis d'Amérique
Italy-San Marino-Holy See	1181.0	997.4	1046.2	1017.7	1022.3	Italie-Saint-Marin-Saint-Siège
Turkey	1387.6	522.6	932.3	660.0	1700.5	Turquie
China, Hong Kong SAR	749.0	763.4	990.4	924.8	1120.5	Chine - RAS de Hong-Kong
Germany	954.5	856.3	904.7	933.0	888.3	Allemagne
Mexico	1072.5	1017.2	1111.6	734.4	561.0	Mexique
France-Monaco	685.6	552.4	519.6	453.3	395.1	France-Monaco
Japan	463.9	404.8	453.5	430.4	411.1	Japon
Brazil	500.0	403.1	477.6	435.2	317.1	Brésil
Korea, Republic of	275.6	447.0	615.7	378.5	405.7	République de Corée
Spain	511.7	470.8	400.5	401.1	328.0	Espagne
Indonesia	731.5	226.9	414.5	373.8	293.3	Indonésie
India	430.9	341.0	360.5	358.6	495.6	Inde
United Kingdom	557.6	408.6	354.6	316.2	301.6	Royaume-Uni
Thailand	213.5	264.8	432.5	459.8	e479.1	Thaïlande
Canada	374.8	345.0	350.9	296.1	295.6	Canada
Pakistan	235.4	180.4	333.9	465.0	445.9	Pakistan
Belgium	-	366.9	373.7	320.8	e351.8	Belgique
Viet Nam	147.8	199.5	266.6	276.7	336.6	Viet Nam
Switzerland-Liechtenstein	269.8	239.9	249.6	232.2	232.2	Suisse-Liechtenstein
Portugal	325.4	281.8	246.6	216.6	149.4	Portugal
Singapore	185.6	224.8	286.1	258.9	234.8	Singapour
Iran (Islamic Republic of)	333.5	190.2	180.9	208.3	265.6	Iran (République islamique d')
Czech Republic	213.4	181.8	178.9	172.9	205.9	République tchèque
Bangladesh	152.9	e167.5	e193.7	187.6	e183.3	Bangladesh
Poland	228.5	153.1	145.1	167.8	177.7	Pologne
Malaysia	171.5	151.0	185.3	156.8	e171.3	Malaisie
Greece	183.6	215.4	130.9	107.7	e119.1	Grèce
Tunisia	134.9	126.3	125.7	140.0	e139.9	Tunisie

(Value as percentages of World total) **(Valeur en pourcentage du total mondial)**

Regions of the world	1993	1994	1995	1996	1997	1998	1999	2000	2001	2002	Régions du monde
World	100.0	100.0	100.0	100.0	100.0	100.0	100.0	100.0	100.0	100.0	Monde
Africa	3.5	3.5	3.5	3.7	3.6	4.1	4.2	4.0	4.1	3.8	Afrique
Americas	18.0	20.6	18.9	17.2	21.6	24.6	24.8	22.3	19.0	15.7	Amériques
- Northern America	11.9	13.3	11.8	10.5	12.1	14.5	14.5	11.9	10.0	9.2	- Amérique du Nord
- LAIA	5.6	6.8	6.6	6.2	8.7	9.3	9.5	9.6	8.1	5.7	- ALAI
- CACM	0.4	0.3	0.3	0.2	0.4	0.4	0.5	0.5	0.6	0.5	- MCC
- Caribbean	0.1	0.2	0.2	0.3	0.3	0.3	0.3	0.3	0.3	0.3	- Caraïbes
- Rest of America	0.1	0.0	0.0	0.0	0.0	0.0	0.0	0.0	0.0	0.0	- Autre d'Amérique
Asia excluding former USSR	55.5	49.3	50.0	51.5	46.9	39.0	37.8	45.0	46.7	54.0	Asie ancienne URSS exclus
- Middle East	7.2	5.1	8.2	12.0	10.5	9.0	5.0	6.9	6.2	10.6	- Moyen-Orient
Asia former USSR	0.3	0.7	0.6	0.8	0.1	0.5	0.5	0.8	1.0	0.7	Asie ancienne URSS
Europe excluding former USSR	19.0	23.7	25.2	25.0	26.0	30.0	30.8	26.3	27.1	24.0	Europe ancienne URSS exclus
- European Union	15.7	19.8	20.8	20.3	21.3	24.7	25.5	21.5	21.7	18.8	- Union Européenne
- Eastern Europe	1.9	2.2	2.5	2.9	2.9	3.3	3.2	2.9	3.5	3.4	- Europe de l'Est
- Rest of Europe	1.5	1.6	1.9	1.8	1.8	2.0	2.1	1.9	1.9	1.8	- Autre de l'Europe
Europe former USSR	2.7	1.0	0.7	0.8	1.0	1.0	0.9	0.9	1.4	1.1	Europe ancienne URSS
Oceania	0.9	1.2	1.1	0.9	0.8	0.8	1.0	0.7	0.6	0.6	Océanie

Machines pour l'industrie textile et pour le travail des cuirs et peaux, et pièces détachées 724

TRADE BY COMMODITY (Value in million US dollars) — COMMERCE PAR PRODUIT (Valeur en millions de dollars EU)

Exports by principal countries or areas — **Exportations selon les principaux pays ou zones**

Country or area	1998	1999	2000	2001	2002	Pays ou zone
World	20961.3	18159.6	20216.7	18890.5	20094.3	Monde
Africa	33.9	36.5	43.2	37.7	33.6	Afrique
Americas	1571.3	1432.3	1497.5	1346.6	1319.6	Amériques
- Northern America	1448.8	1331.5	1367.2	1231.2	1201.9	- Amérique du Nord
- LAIA	113.1	95.4	122.3	106.0	111.6	- ALAI
- CACM	7.9	4.1	6.4	7.1	5.2	- MCC
- Caribbean	1.3	1.0	1.5	2.2	0.8	- Caraïbes
- Rest of America	0.1	0.3	0.1	0.1	0.1	- Autre d'Amérique
Asia excluding former USSR	6089.5	5791.4	7278.6	6478.3	7207.3	Asie ancienne URSS exclus
- Middle East	63.8	62.1	83.1	97.2	104.4	- Moyen-Orient
Asia former USSR	5.0	7.4	6.7	6.0	4.9	Asie ancienne URSS
Europe excluding former USSR	13187.2	10806.3	11293.2	10935.6	11437.1	Europe ancienne URSS exclus
- European Union	11143.2	9115.1	9365.6	9094.5	9423.3	- Union Européenne
- Eastern Europe	317.4	302.7	400.3	411.9	479.9	- Europe de l'Est
- Rest of Europe	1726.6	1388.5	1527.3	1429.2	1533.9	- Autre de l'Europe
Europe former USSR	42.9	51.1	59.3	47.2	49.5	Europe ancienne URSS
Oceania	31.5	34.5	38.2	39.1	42.3	Océanie
Germany	5504.7	4173.1	4190.4	4040.8	4297.0	Allemagne
Japan	2944.8	2636.0	3098.1	2650.7	2774.2	Japon
Italy-San Marino-Holy See	2729.6	2380.5	2603.2	2690.9	2706.8	Italie-Saint-Marin-Saint-Siège
Switzerland-Liechtenstein	1688.4	1356.1	1491.8	1391.3	1486.9	Suisse-Liechtenstein
United States	1389.2	1266.3	1299.6	1178.3	1135.0	Etats-Unis d'Amérique
France-Monaco	1040.5	820.5	920.5	822.8	807.6	France-Monaco
China, Hong Kong SAR	613.5	598.4	766.4	704.6	862.9	Chine - RAS de Hong-Kong
China	479.6	499.6	766.0	742.7	922.8	Chine
Korea, Republic of	501.4	474.9	684.6	655.7	816.5	République de Corée
United Kingdom	569.2	492.6	428.3	360.0	320.1	Royaume-Uni
Czech Republic	233.3	231.5	298.2	300.7	340.3	République tchèque
Spain	292.8	269.1	252.9	254.9	252.0	Espagne
Singapore	214.8	239.3	293.0	257.1	260.0	Singapour
Belgium	–	294.8	302.5	276.5	e310.2	Belgique
Sweden	202.9	219.3	197.9	182.2	232.1	Suède
Austria	176.0	134.1	152.3	153.4	165.4	Autriche
Netherlands	118.4	124.7	110.5	103.7	106.0	Pays-Bas
Denmark	94.5	99.2	92.0	91.3	100.4	Danemark
India	66.0	63.6	111.7	100.3	93.9	Inde
Brazil	81.4	61.5	73.5	62.9	e65.3	Brésil
Canada	59.5	65.2	66.9	52.8	66.8	Canada
Portugal	60.0	62.6	61.7	58.3	61.3	Portugal
Belgium-Luxembourg	303.3	–	–	–	–	Belgique-Luxembourg
Thailand	47.6	46.0	49.3	53.1	e56.0	Thaïlande
Turkey	40.3	34.6	45.9	60.3	64.3	Turquie
Poland	29.7	23.4	44.4	50.8	53.1	Pologne
Malaysia	28.9	37.0	30.9	42.8	e45.3	Malaisie
Russian Federation	26.9	39.8	41.9	31.3	29.6	Fédération de Russie
Viet Nam	26.6	24.2	35.5	37.0	41.1	Viet Nam
Mexico	20.2	25.8	39.9	32.2	37.0	Mexique

(Value as percentages of World total) — **(Valeur en pourcentage du total mondial)**

Regions of the world	1993	1994	1995	1996	1997	1998	1999	2000	2001	2002	Régions du monde
World	100.0	100.0	100.0	100.0	100.0	100.0	100.0	100.0	100.0	100.0	Monde
Africa	0.1	0.1	0.1	0.1	0.1	0.2	0.2	0.2	0.2	0.2	Afrique
Americas	5.4	6.2	6.0	6.0	7.1	7.5	7.9	7.4	7.1	6.6	Amériques
- Northern America	4.7	5.5	5.3	5.4	6.4	6.9	7.3	6.8	6.5	6.0	- Amérique du Nord
- LAIA	0.7	0.7	0.7	0.6	0.6	0.5	0.5	0.6	0.6	0.6	- ALAI
- CACM	0.0	0.0	0.0	0.0	0.1	0.0	0.0	0.0	0.0	0.0	- MCC
- Caribbean	0.0	0.0	0.0	0.0	0.0	0.0	0.0	0.0	0.0	0.0	- Caraïbes
- Rest of America	0.0	0.0	0.0	0.0	0.0	0.0	0.0	0.0	0.0	0.0	- Autre d'Amérique
Asia excluding former USSR	41.1	35.8	33.6	32.6	33.0	29.1	31.9	36.0	34.3	35.9	Asie ancienne URSS exclus
- Middle East	0.2	0.2	0.2	0.2	0.3	0.3	0.3	0.4	0.5	0.5	- Moyen-Orient
Asia former USSR	0.0	0.0	0.0	0.0	0.0	0.0	0.0	0.0	0.0	0.0	Asie ancienne URSS
Europe excluding former USSR	53.2	57.6	60.0	60.8	59.4	62.9	59.5	55.9	57.9	56.9	Europe ancienne URSS exclus
- European Union	45.2	48.6	49.6	51.2	50.0	53.2	50.2	46.3	48.1	46.9	- Union Européenne
- Eastern Europe	0.8	0.9	1.1	1.2	1.3	1.5	1.7	2.0	2.2	2.4	- Europe de l'Est
- Rest of Europe	7.1	8.1	9.2	8.4	8.1	8.2	7.6	7.6	7.6	7.6	- Autre de l'Europe
Europe former USSR	0.1	0.2	0.2	0.3	0.2	0.2	0.3	0.3	0.2	0.2	Europe ancienne URSS
Oceania	0.1	0.1	0.1	0.1	0.1	0.2	0.2	0.2	0.2	0.2	Océanie

725 Paper and paper manufacture machinery, and parts thereof, nes

TRADE BY COMMODITY (Value in million US dollars)
Imports by principal countries or areas

COMMERCE PAR PRODUIT (Valeur en millions de dollars EU)
Importations selon les principaux pays ou zones

Country or area	1998	1999	2000	2001	2002	Pays ou zone
World	7757.7	6605.5	6505.2	6584.1	6004.3	Monde
Africa	148.6	176.0	124.9	136.6	156.0	Afrique
Americas	1913.6	1817.4	1932.5	2014.6	1360.0	Amériques
- Northern America	1359.7	1329.0	1497.7	1374.6	950.8	- Amérique du Nord
- LAIA	505.7	449.5	390.4	590.6	357.6	- ALAI
- CACM	25.7	27.8	31.6	36.3	37.9	- MCC
- Caribbean	15.3	7.5	9.7	9.0	10.7	- Caraïbes
- Rest of America	7.1	3.6	3.1	4.1	2.9	- Autre d'Amérique
Asia excluding former USSR	2491.1	1390.7	1414.5	1369.2	1567.5	Asie ancienne URSS exclus
- Middle East	158.7	221.5	198.5	174.1	170.0	- Moyen-Orient
Asia former USSR	8.4	5.1	23.3	12.1	17.0	Asie ancienne URSS
Europe excluding former USSR	3003.3	3002.6	2723.9	2835.5	2682.1	Europe ancienne URSS exclus
- European Union	2414.5	2532.4	2261.4	2403.2	2268.7	- Union Européenne
- Eastern Europe	327.7	256.3	216.3	248.1	248.7	- Europe de l'Est
- Rest of Europe	261.2	213.9	246.3	184.2	164.8	- Autre de l'Europe
Europe former USSR	99.0	100.9	126.9	135.7	130.3	Europe ancienne URSS
Oceania	93.7	112.7	159.1	80.4	91.3	Océanie
United States	971.0	936.5	1052.4	1007.5	656.1	Etats-Unis d'Amérique
China	1011.7	400.7	448.0	431.2	691.9	Chine
Germany	479.7	615.9	464.3	583.2	548.7	Allemagne
Canada	388.7	392.5	445.3	367.1	294.6	Canada
France-Monaco	363.2	361.1	352.7	337.0	337.3	France-Monaco
Italy-San Marino-Holy See	303.7	302.5	269.1	385.3	289.8	Italie-Saint-Marin-Saint-Siège
United Kingdom	285.8	291.2	262.4	238.2	233.5	Royaume-Uni
Indonesia	494.3	243.1	130.0	107.0	89.2	Indonésie
Spain	191.2	227.2	199.6	198.3	205.2	Espagne
Mexico	191.9	227.8	202.5	238.7	150.7	Mexique
Sweden	161.8	193.2	161.2	168.6	148.4	Suède
Japan	175.4	130.2	132.8	207.0	123.4	Japon
Poland	172.9	104.2	106.3	122.1	81.2	Pologne
Switzerland-Liechtenstein	127.0	81.0	166.8	104.9	88.7	Suisse-Liechtenstein
Finland	132.2	101.6	104.6	111.3	115.9	Finlande
Netherlands	128.5	105.1	98.4	83.9	94.5	Pays-Bas
Malaysia	178.7	45.9	106.4	78.6	e85.9	Malaisie
Austria	132.3	87.8	75.2	100.2	86.2	Autriche
Belgium	–	115.9	115.8	102.0	e111.8	Belgique
Brazil	80.7	70.9	71.5	131.7	88.7	Brésil
Korea, Republic of	114.9	83.1	86.3	80.5	71.0	République de Corée
Russian Federation	64.8	79.4	102.3	93.5	86.6	Fédération de Russie
Australia	66.2	83.9	132.3	57.6	68.1	Australie
Turkey	79.0	110.9	77.5	57.2	58.0	Turquie
Norway	83.3	92.6	52.8	41.6	36.9	Norvège
Thailand	56.5	33.2	55.2	70.7	e73.7	Thaïlande
China, Hong Kong SAR	62.0	45.9	57.5	61.3	51.5	Chine - RAS de Hong-Kong
Chile	67.9	33.6	44.8	82.6	44.7	Chili
Czech Republic	59.6	46.6	47.0	50.1	65.8	République tchèque
Singapore	69.8	50.3	51.8	36.5	30.6	Singapour

(Value as percentages of World total) **(Valeur en pourcentage du total mondial)**

Regions of the world	1993	1994	1995	1996	1997	1998	1999	2000	2001	2002	Régions du monde
World	100.0	100.0	100.0	100.0	100.0	100.0	100.0	100.0	100.0	100.0	Monde
Africa	2.0	3.0	2.8	2.5	1.9	1.9	2.7	1.9	2.1	2.6	Afrique
Americas	21.2	23.1	22.4	21.4	26.0	24.7	27.5	29.7	30.6	22.7	Amériques
- Northern America	14.7	17.1	16.0	16.2	18.9	17.5	20.1	23.0	20.9	15.8	- Amérique du Nord
- LAIA	5.8	5.7	6.1	4.8	6.6	6.5	6.8	6.0	9.0	6.0	- ALAI
- CACM	0.3	0.2	0.1	0.2	0.2	0.3	0.4	0.5	0.6	0.6	- MCC
- Caribbean	0.2	0.1	0.1	0.2	0.2	0.2	0.1	0.1	0.1	0.2	- Caraïbes
- Rest of America	0.2	0.0	0.0	0.0	0.0	0.1	0.1	0.0	0.1	0.0	- Autre d'Amérique
Asia excluding former USSR	37.1	32.6	33.6	35.5	31.4	32.1	21.1	21.7	20.8	26.1	Asie ancienne URSS exclus
- Middle East	1.5	5.5	2.0	2.0	2.2	2.0	3.4	3.1	2.6	2.8	- Moyen-Orient
Asia former USSR	0.1	0.5	0.0	0.1	0.0	0.1	0.1	0.4	0.2	0.3	Asie ancienne URSS
Europe excluding former USSR	36.0	36.6	37.0	36.7	36.7	38.7	45.5	41.9	43.1	44.7	Europe ancienne URSS exclus
- European Union	30.8	30.8	30.4	31.3	30.5	31.1	38.3	34.8	36.5	37.8	- Union Européenne
- Eastern Europe	2.2	2.7	3.1	3.0	3.4	4.2	3.9	3.3	3.8	4.1	- Europe de l'Est
- Rest of Europe	2.9	3.1	3.5	2.4	2.8	3.4	3.2	3.8	2.8	2.7	- Autre de l'Europe
Europe former USSR	1.3	2.0	1.9	1.7	1.7	1.3	1.5	2.0	2.1	2.2	Europe ancienne URSS
Oceania	2.3	2.3	2.2	2.1	2.3	1.2	1.7	2.4	1.2	1.5	Océanie

TRADE BY COMMODITY (Value in million US dollars)
Exports by principal countries or areas

COMMERCE PAR PRODUIT (Valeur en millions de dollars EU)
Exportations selon les principaux pays ou zones

Country or area	1998	1999	2000	2001	2002	Pays ou zone
World	7636.3	6571.2	6883.9	6659.0	6435.7	Monde
Africa	8.7	3.5	6.4	7.9	8.0	Afrique
Americas	1102.3	1037.3	1060.1	934.0	797.4	Amériques
- Northern America	995.4	926.5	924.5	819.3	683.3	- Amérique du Nord
- LAIA	105.7	109.6	133.2	113.7	113.0	- ALAI
- CACM	0.9	1.0	2.2	0.8	0.9	- MCC
- Caribbean	0.2	0.1	0.2	0.1	0.1	- Caraïbes
- Rest of America	0.0	0.1	0.1	0.2	0.1	- Autre d'Amérique
Asia excluding former USSR	625.7	504.1	613.5	539.6	542.5	Asie ancienne URSS exclus
- Middle East	8.4	10.4	8.9	9.9	7.9	- Moyen-Orient
Asia former USSR	0.1	1.4	1.0	2.4	3.3	Asie ancienne URSS
Europe excluding former USSR	5871.4	4999.9	5171.5	5145.1	5054.3	Europe ancienne URSS exclus
- European Union	5161.2	4296.1	4499.3	4516.8	4419.9	- Union Européenne
- Eastern Europe	93.3	97.0	85.3	82.0	96.2	- Europe de l'Est
- Rest of Europe	616.9	606.8	586.9	546.4	538.2	- Autre de l'Europe
Europe former USSR	12.9	12.9	19.9	18.9	16.2	Europe ancienne URSS
Oceania	15.1	11.9	11.6	11.1	14.1	Océanie
Germany	1891.2	1531.0	1423.0	1546.3	1509.1	Allemagne
United States	780.7	717.2	747.4	655.9	538.1	Etats-Unis d'Amérique
Finland	714.7	482.9	686.6	780.7	642.1	Finlande
Italy-San Marino-Holy See	706.2	664.0	646.3	593.7	642.9	Italie-Saint-Marin-Saint-Siège
Switzerland-Liechtenstein	559.6	537.2	541.9	489.5	497.5	Suisse-Liechtenstein
Sweden	474.9	380.7	486.1	436.0	322.8	Suède
France-Monaco	397.3	399.0	385.3	382.7	444.2	France-Monaco
United Kingdom	353.4	256.9	270.6	233.0	232.7	Royaume-Uni
Austria	263.0	249.8	248.0	193.9	268.7	Autriche
Japan	325.6	211.7	264.1	172.3	180.0	Japon
Canada	214.7	209.4	177.1	163.4	145.2	Canada
Spain	162.3	158.5	171.8	189.3	179.8	Espagne
Brazil	92.1	93.1	103.3	93.0	e96.4	Brésil
Netherlands	98.8	84.7	82.8	83.3	89.4	Pays-Bas
China, Hong Kong SAR	57.6	51.0	54.6	70.0	58.0	Chine - RAS de Hong-Kong
Korea, Republic of	49.3	47.1	66.5	55.2	47.2	République de Corée
Denmark	46.5	49.2	62.0	33.9	39.6	Danemark
Norway	45.4	58.4	34.6	43.9	29.5	Norvège
Czech Republic	39.9	33.9	33.9	44.2	44.1	République tchèque
China	22.5	24.0	36.5	47.7	65.3	Chine
Poland	34.4	44.6	27.7	18.2	29.3	Pologne
Belgium	–	27.4	23.6	30.4	e34.1	Belgique
Singapore	19.3	17.0	12.3	13.6	11.2	Singapour
Mexico	6.6	8.3	23.1	13.6	10.7	Mexique
Malaysia	16.5	10.6	11.6	9.9	e10.5	Malaisie
Hungary	10.9	9.3	13.3	9.4	9.2	Hongrie
India	7.8	6.2	11.9	10.6	8.1	Inde
Australia	9.1	5.6	7.9	7.7	11.8	Australie
Slovenia	9.5	6.9	6.7	11.0	8.0	Slovénie
Slovakia	5.7	7.9	7.5	7.9	10.9	Slovaquie

(Value as percentages of World total) **(Valeur en pourcentage du total mondial)**

Regions of the world	1993	1994	1995	1996	1997	1998	1999	2000	2001	2002	Régions du monde
World	100.0	100.0	100.0	100.0	100.0	100.0	100.0	100.0	100.0	100.0	Monde
Africa	0.1	0.1	0.1	0.1	0.1	0.1	0.1	0.1	0.1	0.1	Afrique
Americas	16.2	15.3	14.2	13.4	15.6	14.4	15.8	15.4	14.0	12.4	Amériques
- Northern America	14.3	14.1	12.9	12.5	14.4	13.0	14.1	13.4	12.3	10.6	- Amérique du Nord
- LAIA	1.8	1.2	1.2	0.9	1.2	1.4	1.7	1.9	1.7	1.8	- ALAI
- CACM	0.0	0.0	0.0	0.0	0.0	0.0	0.0	0.0	0.0	0.0	- MCC
- Caribbean	0.0	0.0	0.0	0.0	0.0	0.0	0.0	0.0	0.0	0.0	- Caraïbes
- Rest of America	0.0	0.0	0.0	0.0	0.0	0.0	0.0	0.0	0.0	0.0	- Autre d'Amérique
Asia excluding former USSR	16.0	12.6	11.9	12.7	11.0	8.2	7.7	8.9	8.1	8.4	Asie ancienne URSS exclus
- Middle East	0.0	0.1	0.1	0.1	0.1	0.1	0.2	0.1	0.1	0.1	- Moyen-Orient
Asia former USSR	0.0	0.0	0.0	0.0	0.0	0.0	0.0	0.0	0.0	0.1	Asie ancienne URSS
Europe excluding former USSR	67.3	71.5	73.4	73.4	72.9	76.9	76.1	75.1	77.3	78.5	Europe ancienne URSS exclus
- European Union	59.0	62.4	64.2	65.2	64.5	67.6	65.4	65.4	67.8	68.7	- Union Européenne
- Eastern Europe	0.4	0.3	0.7	0.8	1.1	1.2	1.5	1.2	1.2	1.5	- Europe de l'Est
- Rest of Europe	8.0	8.7	8.5	7.4	7.4	8.1	9.2	8.5	8.2	8.4	- Autre de l'Europe
Europe former USSR	0.2	0.3	0.2	0.3	0.2	0.2	0.2	0.3	0.3	0.3	Europe ancienne URSS
Oceania	0.2	0.2	0.2	0.2	0.2	0.2	0.2	0.2	0.2	0.2	Océanie

726 Printing, bookbinding machinery, and parts thereof, nes

TRADE BY COMMODITY (Value in million US dollars)
Imports by principal countries or areas

COMMERCE PAR PRODUIT (Valeur en millions de dollars EU)
Importations selon les principaux pays ou zones

Country or area	1998	1999	2000	2001	2002	Pays ou zone
World	13897.0	13780.7	13759.6	13799.9	12895.8	Monde
Africa	384.1	493.3	380.6	408.7	444.4	Afrique
Americas	3761.2	3697.1	3465.5	3207.7	2717.8	Amériques
- Northern America	2724.5	2767.1	2596.2	2292.8	1917.4	- Amérique du Nord
- LAIA	938.2	831.2	775.6	831.7	714.6	- ALAI
- CACM	45.7	57.5	52.8	40.8	49.7	- MCC
- Caribbean	40.9	30.5	27.6	33.4	30.7	- Caraïbes
- Rest of America	12.0	10.8	13.4	9.1	5.3	- Autre d'Amérique
Asia excluding former USSR	2601.5	2644.8	3570.5	3780.2	3839.5	Asie ancienne URSS exclus
- Middle East	377.0	285.5	355.9	410.8	448.1	- Moyen-Orient
Asia former USSR	17.4	16.1	23.7	23.7	27.2	Asie ancienne URSS
Europe excluding former USSR	6552.7	6457.5	5829.4	5821.7	5311.8	Europe ancienne URSS exclus
- European Union	5473.2	5586.6	4958.1	4977.9	4551.1	- Union Européenne
- Eastern Europe	476.0	420.1	473.9	420.1	367.7	- Europe de l'Est
- Rest of Europe	603.6	450.7	397.4	423.8	393.0	- Autre de l'Europe
Europe former USSR	239.2	132.6	178.5	259.5	304.1	Europe ancienne URSS
Oceania	340.9	339.5	311.4	298.3	251.0	Océanie
United States	2266.7	2341.6	2164.7	1929.9	1586.8	Etats-Unis d'Amérique
United Kingdom	1066.6	929.6	883.2	826.5	694.4	Royaume-Uni
China	424.1	712.4	873.1	1282.2	1107.1	Chine
Germany	720.9	842.8	845.6	916.8	774.6	Allemagne
France-Monaco	883.1	841.4	691.6	681.2	602.9	France-Monaco
Italy-San Marino-Holy See	606.7	700.4	687.0	703.8	734.8	Italie-Saint-Marin-Saint-Siège
Spain	536.8	511.7	373.6	421.3	321.2	Espagne
Canada	456.7	424.3	431.1	362.5	330.3	Canada
China, Hong Kong SAR	368.0	354.4	386.6	405.1	403.7	Chine - RAS de Hong-Kong
Belgium	–	534.2	470.4	427.7	e469.1	Belgique
Japan	378.3	317.3	352.5	406.1	359.5	Japon
Mexico	278.1	260.9	310.5	338.0	348.4	Mexique
Netherlands	385.5	331.8	244.3	254.9	312.8	Pays-Bas
Brazil	325.5	292.8	300.0	301.6	204.3	Brésil
Switzerland-Liechtenstein	249.5	248.9	266.3	297.0	241.1	Suisse-Liechtenstein
Australia	281.6	292.1	269.6	254.6	203.5	Australie
Korea, Republic of	87.5	179.2	334.6	270.4	403.3	République de Corée
Malaysia	164.5	142.8	330.1	257.9	e281.9	Malaisie
Poland	280.6	234.7	240.0	186.6	130.6	Pologne
Austria	200.9	160.3	175.3	210.9	162.0	Autriche
Singapore	103.0	125.9	178.4	129.7	197.2	Singapour
Denmark	132.2	189.6	159.4	134.4	117.6	Danemark
Sweden	173.6	171.7	145.6	116.6	101.5	Suède
South Africa	–	–	230.0	227.2	242.2	Afrique du Sud
Turkey	172.1	95.2	124.4	97.9	123.0	Turquie
Russian Federation	126.6	57.9	95.9	119.9	159.6	Fédération de Russie
Norway	254.4	122.1	66.8	52.4	47.5	Norvège
Southern African Customs Union	196.6	302.8	–	–	–	Union douanière d'Afrique australe
Portugal	77.1	120.8	110.3	97.8	78.7	Portugal
Indonesia	154.4	30.8	83.4	98.2	85.7	Indonésie

(Value as percentages of World total) **(Valeur en pourcentage du total mondial)**

Regions of the world	1993	1994	1995	1996	1997	1998	1999	2000	2001	2002	Régions du monde
World	100.0	100.0	100.0	100.0	100.0	100.0	100.0	100.0	100.0	100.0	Monde
Africa	3.4	3.5	3.2	3.4	3.0	2.8	3.6	2.8	3.0	3.4	Afrique
Americas	23.2	24.7	25.1	21.6	26.6	27.1	26.8	25.2	23.2	21.1	Amériques
- Northern America	15.8	16.7	17.4	15.5	17.7	19.6	20.1	18.9	16.6	14.9	- Amérique du Nord
- LAIA	6.6	7.4	7.2	5.6	8.2	6.8	6.0	5.6	6.0	5.5	- ALAI
- CACM	0.7	0.3	0.3	0.2	0.3	0.3	0.4	0.4	0.3	0.4	- MCC
- Caribbean	0.2	0.2	0.2	0.2	0.3	0.3	0.2	0.2	0.2	0.2	- Caraïbes
- Rest of America	0.1	0.1	0.1	0.1	0.1	0.1	0.1	0.1	0.1	0.0	- Autre d'Amérique
Asia excluding former USSR	29.5	27.7	25.8	28.9	25.6	18.7	19.2	25.9	27.4	29.8	Asie ancienne URSS exclus
- Middle East	3.9	2.2	2.1	2.9	2.6	2.7	2.1	2.6	3.0	3.5	- Moyen-Orient
Asia former USSR	0.1	0.1	0.3	0.1	0.1	0.1	0.1	0.2	0.2	0.2	Asie ancienne URSS
Europe excluding former USSR	39.4	39.5	40.8	42.6	41.2	47.2	46.9	42.4	42.2	41.2	Europe ancienne URSS exclus
- European Union	34.4	33.6	34.8	36.2	34.4	39.4	40.5	36.0	36.1	35.3	- Union Européenne
- Eastern Europe	2.2	2.6	2.6	2.8	3.3	3.4	3.0	3.4	3.0	2.9	- Europe de l'Est
- Rest of Europe	2.9	3.4	3.4	3.6	3.4	4.3	3.3	2.9	3.1	3.0	- Autre de l'Europe
Europe former USSR	2.0	1.0	0.9	0.9	1.5	1.7	1.0	1.3	1.9	2.4	Europe ancienne URSS
Oceania	2.3	3.5	4.0	2.5	2.0	2.5	2.5	2.3	2.2	1.9	Océanie

TRADE BY COMMODITY (Value in million US dollars)
Exports by principal countries or areas

COMMERCE PAR PRODUIT (Valeur en millions de dollars EU)
Exportations selon les principaux pays ou zones

Country or area	1998	1999	2000	2001	2002	Pays ou zone
World	14628.1	14290.3	14244.7	14239.5	13218.1	Monde
Africa	15.7	14.0	16.3	19.4	19.1	Afrique
Americas	1779.3	1727.9	1992.9	1571.4	1320.7	Amériques
- Northern America	1726.1	1682.9	1952.2	1532.1	1281.1	- Amérique du Nord
- LAIA	51.2	42.1	39.2	34.5	36.9	- ALAI
- CACM	1.0	1.5	1.1	1.4	1.7	- MCC
- Caribbean	1.0	1.4	0.4	2.7	0.9	- Caraïbes
- Rest of America	0.0	0.0	0.0	0.7	0.1	- Autre d'Amérique
Asia excluding former USSR	2537.3	2682.4	2919.7	2796.9	2627.6	Asie ancienne URSS exclus
- Middle East	12.9	14.6	14.6	26.2	22.1	- Moyen-Orient
Asia former USSR	1.0	0.6	1.3	0.6	0.7	Asie ancienne URSS
Europe excluding former USSR	10212.5	9788.6	9227.0	9766.8	9167.4	Europe ancienne URSS exclus
- European Union	9062.1	8588.7	8056.7	8540.2	8095.5	- Union Européenne
- Eastern Europe	109.4	104.0	107.2	108.3	102.5	- Europe de l'Est
- Rest of Europe	1040.9	1095.9	1063.1	1118.3	969.4	- Autre de l'Europe
Europe former USSR	12.1	10.6	17.9	26.3	30.5	Europe ancienne URSS
Oceania	70.3	66.1	69.6	58.2	52.0	Océanie
Germany	5113.5	4689.1	4381.5	5029.9	4664.4	Allemagne
Japan	1604.9	1693.4	1770.4	1422.6	1297.5	Japon
United States	1506.6	1372.3	1624.0	1275.9	1074.6	Etats-Unis d'Amérique
Switzerland-Liechtenstein	1015.2	1064.1	1023.4	1088.8	938.5	Suisse-Liechtenstein
United Kingdom	942.5	903.9	931.0	796.5	725.4	Royaume-Uni
Italy-San Marino-Holy See	713.4	662.8	602.9	634.5	608.2	Italie-Saint-Marin-Saint-Siège
France-Monaco	696.7	662.7	579.5	637.7	544.1	France-Monaco
Israel	357.4	372.5	405.0	417.2	357.0	Israël
Netherlands	411.1	356.3	352.5	316.0	378.3	Pays-Bas
Belgium	–	533.5	463.1	374.2	e419.9	Belgique
Canada	219.4	310.6	328.2	256.3	206.5	Canada
China, Hong Kong SAR	207.9	240.0	243.3	277.8	301.1	Chine - RAS de Hong-Kong
Denmark	218.2	208.8	222.3	208.7	219.6	Danemark
Austria	214.1	214.2	189.9	225.1	217.2	Autriche
Sweden	137.3	134.5	123.5	116.3	119.0	Suède
Spain	104.1	125.1	122.8	116.7	129.0	Espagne
Singapore	60.3	85.7	77.8	159.9	84.1	Singapour
Malaysia	28.7	33.3	83.3	131.3	e139.1	Malaisie
Belgium-Luxembourg	411.8	–	–	–	–	Belgique-Luxembourg
Czech Republic	84.8	75.4	68.9	69.8	60.7	République tchèque
Australia	57.2	59.2	62.3	53.0	47.5	Australie
Korea, Republic of	72.0	47.4	49.3	41.6	53.3	République de Corée
Portugal	50.5	53.5	57.3	45.4	43.5	Portugal
China	27.7	32.3	44.9	52.1	91.0	Chine
Thailand	22.9	8.7	18.9	44.7	e47.2	Thaïlande
India	22.0	25.0	29.1	27.9	33.9	Inde
Norway	15.2	24.8	31.9	18.5	14.4	Norvège
Brazil	13.9	24.3	17.1	13.7	e14.2	Brésil
Indonesia	20.5	4.0	19.7	18.3	18.1	Indonésie
Poland	8.0	12.0	17.8	18.9	22.7	Pologne

(Value as percentages of World total) **(Valeur en pourcentage du total mondial)**

Regions of the world	1993	1994	1995	1996	1997	1998	1999	2000	2001	2002	Régions du monde
World	100.0	100.0	100.0	100.0	100.0	100.0	100.0	100.0	100.0	100.0	Monde
Africa	0.1	0.1	0.1	0.1	0.1	0.1	0.1	0.1	0.1	0.1	Afrique
Americas	12.8	11.9	11.7	11.8	12.8	12.2	12.1	14.0	11.0	10.0	Amériques
- Northern America	12.4	11.6	11.3	11.5	12.5	11.8	11.8	13.7	10.8	9.7	- Amérique du Nord
- LAIA	0.4	0.3	0.3	0.3	0.3	0.3	0.3	0.3	0.2	0.3	- ALAI
- CACM	0.0	0.0	0.0	0.0	0.0	0.0	0.0	0.0	0.0	0.0	- MCC
- Caribbean	0.0	0.0	0.0	0.0	0.0	0.0	0.0	0.0	0.0	0.0	- Caraïbes
- Rest of America	0.0	0.0	0.0	0.0	0.0	0.0	0.0	0.0	0.0	0.0	- Autre d'Amérique
Asia excluding former USSR	20.3	20.0	19.6	18.8	18.8	17.3	18.8	20.5	19.6	19.9	Asie ancienne URSS exclus
- Middle East	0.1	0.1	0.1	0.1	0.1	0.1	0.1	0.1	0.2	0.2	- Moyen-Orient
Asia former USSR	0.0	0.0	0.0	0.0	0.0	0.0	0.0	0.0	0.0	0.0	Asie ancienne URSS
Europe excluding former USSR	66.4	67.5	68.2	68.7	67.7	69.8	68.5	64.8	68.6	69.4	Europe ancienne URSS exclus
- European Union	57.6	57.9	59.0	60.6	59.7	61.9	60.1	56.6	60.0	61.2	- Union Européenne
- Eastern Europe	0.4	0.5	0.6	0.7	0.7	0.7	0.7	0.8	0.8	0.8	- Europe de l'Est
- Rest of Europe	8.3	9.0	8.6	7.5	7.3	7.1	7.7	7.5	7.9	7.3	- Autre de l'Europe
Europe former USSR	0.0	0.0	0.0	0.1	0.1	0.1	0.1	0.1	0.2	0.2	Europe ancienne URSS
Oceania	0.5	0.4	0.5	0.5	0.5	0.5	0.5	0.5	0.4	0.4	Océanie

727 Food-processing machines (non-domestic) and parts thereof, nes

TRADE BY COMMODITY (Value in million US dollars)
Imports by principal countries or areas

COMMERCE PAR PRODUIT (Valeur en millions de dollars EU)
Importations selon les principaux pays ou zones

Country or area	1998	1999	2000	2001	2002	Pays ou zone
World	6495.3	5871.9	5496.4	5526.0	5828.2	Monde
Africa	415.3	436.9	450.2	485.9	510.6	Afrique
Americas	1423.6	1385.8	1254.3	1214.3	1285.7	Amériques
- Northern America	788.0	800.6	705.7	691.2	794.3	- Amérique du Nord
- LAIA	498.9	455.0	395.4	387.3	366.7	- ALAI
- CACM	68.8	66.0	65.1	71.8	59.1	- MCC
- Caribbean	55.0	49.2	65.3	52.7	48.2	- Caraïbes
- Rest of America	12.9	15.0	22.9	11.2	17.4	- Autre d'Amérique
Asia excluding former USSR	1261.9	1049.4	1183.8	1193.2	1203.0	Asie ancienne URSS exclus
- Middle East	289.0	291.8	278.8	210.6	268.9	- Moyen-Orient
Asia former USSR	128.9	77.5	72.0	80.8	74.7	Asie ancienne URSS
Europe excluding former USSR	2631.2	2460.6	2096.2	2111.5	2207.8	Europe ancienne URSS exclus
- European Union	1923.2	1886.9	1627.8	1628.1	1690.3	- Union Européenne
- Eastern Europe	413.9	300.0	234.5	259.4	276.5	- Europe de l'Est
- Rest of Europe	294.1	273.7	233.9	224.0	241.0	- Autre de l'Europe
Europe former USSR	521.7	343.0	316.3	327.4	420.2	Europe ancienne URSS
Oceania	112.6	118.8	123.6	112.8	126.3	Océanie
United States	593.6	594.2	516.8	508.0	561.1	Etats-Unis d'Amérique
United Kingdom	340.2	342.8	281.7	270.9	277.5	Royaume-Uni
France-Monaco	300.4	265.1	260.6	242.4	282.0	France-Monaco
Russian Federation	376.1	251.9	211.6	203.0	271.2	Fédération de Russie
China	195.5	186.4	249.2	279.7	212.4	Chine
Germany	257.1	239.1	199.1	216.4	180.1	Allemagne
Canada	190.3	200.8	186.7	180.8	229.1	Canada
Spain	163.4	169.7	153.0	174.5	225.9	Espagne
Mexico	151.3	179.0	176.8	154.0	183.4	Mexique
Italy-San Marino-Holy See	173.8	165.6	142.4	149.6	127.0	Italie-Saint-Marin-Saint-Siège
Poland	197.2	150.4	114.0	112.1	113.8	Pologne
Netherlands	115.7	111.5	107.8	107.3	114.4	Pays-Bas
Belgium	–	152.9	131.7	108.2	e118.6	Belgique
Japan	112.7	96.3	99.0	103.1	88.3	Japon
Algeria	33.7	70.7	106.8	e129.2	e147.2	Algérie
Switzerland-Liechtenstein	86.7	95.1	78.4	80.2	85.7	Suisse-Liechtenstein
Norway	103.1	95.7	82.0	70.0	74.5	Norvège
Brazil	127.1	96.7	73.8	71.2	53.8	Brésil
Thailand	21.5	40.2	65.3	135.6	e141.3	Thaïlande
Australia	73.5	78.9	85.8	80.8	84.2	Australie
Indonesia	69.6	46.0	73.2	94.5	96.2	Indonésie
Austria	76.4	76.1	66.5	73.2	86.6	Autriche
Denmark	70.1	81.2	75.4	75.4	71.5	Danemark
Iran (Islamic Republic of)	62.7	65.4	76.1	61.3	81.3	Iran (République islamique d')
Greece	97.2	98.9	58.6	40.3	e44.5	Grèce
Turkey	94.9	60.2	78.6	35.7	65.4	Turquie
Viet Nam	103.5	90.1	41.7	43.2	52.6	Viet Nam
Ukraine	56.0	42.0	39.7	64.9	70.0	Ukraine
Sweden	56.3	59.7	56.1	48.2	52.0	Suède
Korea, Republic of	37.2	42.0	60.0	56.4	69.0	République de Corée

(Value as percentages of World total) **(Valeur en pourcentage du total mondial)**

Regions of the world	1993	1994	1995	1996	1997	1998	1999	2000	2001	2002	Régions du monde
World	100.0	100.0	100.0	100.0	100.0	100.0	100.0	100.0	100.0	100.0	Monde
Africa	5.0	4.9	5.2	5.5	5.8	6.4	7.4	8.2	8.8	8.8	Afrique
Americas	17.6	18.4	18.5	16.7	20.3	21.9	23.6	22.8	22.0	22.1	Amériques
- Northern America	9.4	9.8	10.2	8.8	10.6	12.1	13.6	12.8	12.5	13.6	- Amérique du Nord
- LAIA	6.6	7.2	6.8	6.3	7.7	7.7	7.7	7.2	7.0	6.3	- ALAI
- CACM	1.0	0.6	0.7	0.8	1.0	1.1	1.1	1.2	1.3	1.0	- MCC
- Caribbean	0.5	0.5	0.5	0.5	0.9	0.8	0.8	1.2	1.0	0.8	- Caraïbes
- Rest of America	0.2	0.2	0.3	0.2	0.2	0.2	0.3	0.4	0.2	0.3	- Autre d'Amérique
Asia excluding former USSR	29.8	28.6	29.3	31.9	25.5	19.4	17.9	21.5	21.6	20.6	Asie ancienne URSS exclus
- Middle East	4.2	3.9	4.0	5.1	4.2	4.4	5.0	5.1	3.8	4.6	- Moyen-Orient
Asia former USSR	0.7	1.7	0.7	0.9	0.9	2.0	1.3	1.3	1.5	1.3	Asie ancienne URSS
Europe excluding former USSR	38.6	37.6	36.6	35.8	37.1	40.5	41.9	38.1	38.2	37.9	Europe ancienne URSS exclus
- European Union	28.6	27.2	25.7	24.8	26.7	29.6	32.1	29.6	29.5	29.0	- Union Européenne
- Eastern Europe	7.2	6.7	7.1	7.1	6.3	6.4	5.1	4.3	4.7	4.7	- Europe de l'Est
- Rest of Europe	2.8	3.7	3.8	3.9	4.1	4.5	4.7	4.3	4.1	4.1	- Autre de l'Europe
Europe former USSR	6.6	7.0	7.6	7.4	8.3	8.0	5.8	5.8	5.9	7.2	Europe ancienne URSS
Oceania	1.7	1.7	2.0	1.8	2.0	1.7	2.0	2.2	2.0	2.2	Océanie

TRADE BY COMMODITY (Value in million US dollars)
Exports by principal countries or areas

COMMERCE PAR PRODUIT (Valeur en millions de dollars EU)
Exportations selon les principaux pays ou zones

Country or area	1998	1999	2000	2001	2002	Pays ou zone
World	6520.2	5821.6	5653.9	5628.9	6201.2	Monde
Africa	49.2	39.1	40.4	35.6	34.6	Afrique
Americas	797.6	745.0	767.9	691.6	739.9	Amériques
- Northern America	722.2	672.1	701.4	622.5	660.5	- Amérique du Nord
- LAIA	69.9	68.4	61.4	64.9	63.3	- ALAI
- CACM	3.2	3.3	3.6	2.8	14.3	- MCC
- Caribbean	2.4	1.1	1.5	1.2	1.2	- Caraïbes
- Rest of America	0.0	0.0	0.1	0.2	0.6	- Autre d'Amérique
Asia excluding former USSR	502.9	381.8	511.0	503.9	528.1	Asie ancienne URSS exclus
- Middle East	74.9	49.0	61.8	63.9	65.5	- Moyen-Orient
Asia former USSR	6.8	10.5	9.9	4.5	3.3	Asie ancienne URSS
Europe excluding former USSR	5060.7	4525.8	4212.4	4305.7	4797.1	Europe ancienne URSS exclus
- European Union	4477.3	4033.3	3746.2	3814.3	4243.3	- Union Européenne
- Eastern Europe	146.4	107.2	113.8	120.6	122.9	- Europe de l'Est
- Rest of Europe	437.1	385.4	352.3	370.8	430.9	- Autre de l'Europe
Europe former USSR	44.6	60.6	65.7	38.4	39.4	Europe ancienne URSS
Oceania	58.3	58.8	46.7	49.3	58.8	Océanie
Germany	1243.2	1074.2	1011.5	1051.7	1200.9	Allemagne
Italy-San Marino-Holy See	998.8	916.5	859.2	829.5	853.0	Italie-Saint-Marin-Saint-Siège
United States	669.4	615.4	644.2	563.0	607.9	Etats-Unis d'Amérique
Netherlands	554.8	491.1	454.4	469.6	593.9	Pays-Bas
France-Monaco	350.3	349.4	348.3	364.3	399.1	France-Monaco
Switzerland-Liechtenstein	395.2	336.4	307.7	321.2	386.2	Suisse-Liechtenstein
Denmark	296.6	329.8	305.7	335.2	363.4	Danemark
United Kingdom	391.7	294.8	208.8	188.4	208.8	Royaume-Uni
Austria	208.6	175.2	161.9	175.5	206.7	Autriche
Spain	147.2	170.0	153.9	159.2	164.2	Espagne
Japan	97.3	115.0	143.9	124.6	132.0	Japon
Belgium	-	114.6	130.3	123.3	e138.4	Belgique
China	99.8	46.5	64.3	69.5	85.6	Chine
Sweden	67.4	65.0	70.0	68.6	68.5	Suède
Czech Republic	78.4	55.2	52.2	53.7	54.7	République tchèque
Canada	52.5	56.3	57.0	59.3	52.3	Canada
Turkey	67.7	38.2	53.5	53.0	53.5	Turquie
Malaysia	29.2	19.5	45.1	52.9	e56.0	Malaisie
Australia	41.7	46.0	34.8	34.5	45.4	Australie
Poland	34.0	28.1	35.9	39.5	36.9	Pologne
Belgium-Luxembourg	169.3	-	-	-	-	Belgique-Luxembourg
Korea, Republic of	17.2	24.5	33.2	38.3	32.2	République de Corée
India	40.1	25.0	24.5	21.7	22.1	Inde
Norway	22.8	28.0	23.3	30.0	19.9	Norvège
Brazil	27.9	24.3	22.6	23.0	e23.8	Brésil
Ukraine	22.3	21.3	33.0	15.6	17.2	Ukraine
China, Hong Kong SAR	37.7	15.6	22.8	18.2	14.3	Chine - RAS de Hong-Kong
Singapore	15.2	14.6	25.1	26.0	26.5	Singapour
Mexico	18.1	21.5	21.6	20.1	19.2	Mexique
Thailand	22.4	13.5	24.0	17.8	e18.8	Thaïlande

(Value as percentages of World total) **(Valeur en pourcentage du total mondial)**

Regions of the world	1993	1994	1995	1996	1997	1998	1999	2000	2001	2002	Régions du monde
World	100.0	100.0	100.0	100.0	100.0	100.0	100.0	100.0	100.0	100.0	Monde
Africa	0.3	0.2	0.4	0.4	0.7	0.8	0.7	0.7	0.6	0.6	Afrique
Americas	13.4	13.3	12.5	12.1	12.6	12.2	12.8	13.6	12.3	11.9	Amériques
- Northern America	12.0	11.9	11.4	10.8	11.4	11.1	11.5	12.4	11.1	10.7	- Amérique du Nord
- LAIA	1.3	1.4	1.1	1.2	1.1	1.1	1.2	1.1	1.2	1.0	- ALAI
- CACM	0.0	0.0	0.0	0.1	0.0	0.0	0.1	0.1	0.0	0.2	- MCC
- Caribbean	0.0	0.0	0.0	0.0	0.0	0.0	0.0	0.0	0.0	0.0	- Caraïbes
- Rest of America	0.0	0.0	0.0	0.0	0.0	0.0	0.0	0.0	0.0	0.0	- Autre d'Amérique
Asia excluding former USSR	11.4	9.0	9.2	10.0	8.6	7.7	6.6	9.0	9.0	8.5	Asie ancienne URSS exclus
- Middle East	0.6	0.7	0.6	0.7	1.3	1.1	0.8	1.1	1.1	1.1	- Moyen-Orient
Asia former USSR	0.0	0.0	0.0	0.0	0.1	0.1	0.2	0.2	0.1	0.1	Asie ancienne URSS
Europe excluding former USSR	73.2	75.3	75.9	75.6	76.1	77.6	77.7	74.5	76.5	77.4	Europe ancienne URSS exclus
- European Union	64.6	66.7	67.2	67.0	67.5	68.7	69.3	66.3	67.8	68.4	- Union Européenne
- Eastern Europe	1.5	1.6	1.5	1.8	2.0	2.2	1.8	2.0	2.1	2.0	- Europe de l'Est
- Rest of Europe	7.1	7.0	7.3	6.8	6.6	6.7	6.6	6.2	6.6	6.9	- Autre de l'Europe
Europe former USSR	0.2	0.7	0.8	0.8	0.8	0.7	1.0	1.2	0.7	0.6	Europe ancienne URSS
Oceania	1.4	1.3	1.2	1.0	1.2	0.9	1.0	0.8	0.9	0.9	Océanie

728 Other machinery, equipment, for specialized industries; parts nes

TRADE BY COMMODITY (Value in million US dollars)
Imports by principal countries or areas

COMMERCE PAR PRODUIT (Valeur en millions de dollars EU)
Importations selon les principaux pays ou zones

Country or area	1998	1999	2000	2001	2002	Pays ou zone
World	61314.8	63254.5	74268.7	64921.7	64164.1	Monde
Africa	1940.2	1690.9	1598.3	1768.0	1688.3	Afrique
Americas	15854.4	15515.5	17377.5	14659.5	13167.0	Amériques
- Northern America	10093.4	10530.1	12339.6	9928.5	9063.3	- Amérique du Nord
- LAIA	5303.4	4629.6	4639.7	4380.2	3735.5	- ALAI
- CACM	231.0	171.5	216.1	184.8	195.9	- MCC
- Caribbean	172.8	132.3	149.5	138.5	149.0	- Caraïbes
- Rest of America	53.9	51.9	32.5	27.5	23.3	- Autre d'Amérique
Asia excluding former USSR	21375.3	23883.2	33191.8	26665.0	28640.6	Asie ancienne URSS exclus
- Middle East	2012.8	1610.8	1531.4	1737.7	1857.0	- Moyen-Orient
Asia former USSR	114.9	142.9	206.1	226.2	251.5	Asie ancienne URSS
Europe excluding former USSR	19971.0	20259.7	20256.4	19908.5	18448.2	Europe ancienne URSS exclus
- European Union	16175.7	16446.0	16573.4	15934.4	14502.1	- Union Européenne
- Eastern Europe	2117.4	2210.8	2172.5	2419.2	2393.6	- Europe de l'Est
- Rest of Europe	1677.9	1602.9	1510.5	1554.8	1552.5	- Autre de l'Europe
Europe former USSR	1219.5	939.9	930.2	1027.4	1280.4	Europe ancienne URSS
Oceania	839.5	822.3	708.3	667.0	688.0	Océanie
United States	7971.7	8291.6	9862.0	7882.8	6978.6	Etats-Unis d'Amérique
China	4610.7	4651.3	6046.6	6846.7	8367.6	Chine
Germany	3213.8	3369.6	3258.4	3413.2	2825.6	Allemagne
Korea, Republic of	1429.4	2413.5	4209.8	2762.2	2821.4	République de Corée
Singapore	1800.7	2073.9	3596.1	2397.8	2357.4	Singapour
France-Monaco	2274.3	2368.4	2726.6	2331.9	2143.6	France-Monaco
Mexico	2274.7	2444.8	2639.1	2347.6	2091.8	Mexique
Canada	2120.5	2237.3	2475.1	2042.7	2081.0	Canada
Japan	2158.8	2056.3	2225.7	2150.6	1980.9	Japon
United Kingdom	2213.8	2089.9	2090.7	2031.7	1902.0	Royaume-Uni
Malaysia	1437.3	1381.5	2460.8	1510.3	e1650.6	Malaisie
Italy-San Marino-Holy See	1540.8	1626.4	1861.2	1740.2	1603.3	Italie-Saint-Marin-Saint-Siège
Spain	1369.2	1623.0	1495.2	1590.9	1460.8	Espagne
China, Hong Kong SAR	1083.3	1092.0	1366.9	1221.2	1232.0	Chine - RAS de Hong-Kong
Brazil	1405.0	1228.7	1089.1	1052.0	857.5	Brésil
Thailand	702.5	710.3	1043.4	1018.9	e1061.6	Thaïlande
Poland	972.2	951.2	771.7	748.8	848.2	Pologne
Netherlands	890.0	905.4	837.4	747.0	667.0	Pays-Bas
Switzerland-Liechtenstein	779.2	798.0	787.2	774.9	737.1	Suisse-Liechtenstein
Austria	773.5	786.8	805.6	747.4	704.7	Autriche
Philippines	854.6	771.9	864.9	678.5	640.4	Philippines
Belgium	–	925.6	872.5	904.8	e992.3	Belgique
Turkey	996.1	713.3	620.0	547.4	675.2	Turquie
Russian Federation	785.9	638.6	575.1	620.0	823.6	Fédération de Russie
Sweden	648.4	710.7	721.1	576.2	508.8	Suède
Australia	682.4	665.2	559.4	523.8	548.9	Australie
Indonesia	827.8	381.6	512.6	497.1	458.3	Indonésie
Czech Republic	446.0	457.1	509.3	690.5	555.9	République tchèque
Ireland	889.3	443.0	410.2	393.5	341.0	Irlande
Egypt	677.9	536.2	e444.3	404.5	276.7	Egypte

(Value as percentages of World total) **(Valeur en pourcentage du total mondial)**

Regions of the world	1993	1994	1995	1996	1997	1998	1999	2000	2001	2002	Régions du monde
World	100.0	100.0	100.0	100.0	100.0	100.0	100.0	100.0	100.0	100.0	Monde
Africa	2.7	2.6	2.3	2.3	2.3	3.2	2.7	2.2	2.7	2.6	Afrique
Americas	18.9	20.2	19.7	18.9	23.7	25.9	24.5	23.4	22.6	20.5	Amériques
- Northern America	12.6	13.8	13.6	12.6	15.4	16.5	16.6	16.6	15.3	14.1	- Amérique du Nord
- LAIA	5.8	6.1	5.7	6.0	7.8	8.6	7.3	6.2	6.7	5.8	- ALAI
- CACM	0.2	0.2	0.1	0.1	0.2	0.4	0.3	0.3	0.3	0.3	- MCC
- Caribbean	0.2	0.1	0.2	0.2	0.2	0.3	0.2	0.2	0.2	0.2	- Caraïbes
- Rest of America	0.1	0.1	0.1	0.1	0.1	0.1	0.1	0.0	0.0	0.0	- Autre d'Amérique
Asia excluding former USSR	47.3	47.1	47.3	49.1	43.2	34.9	37.8	44.7	41.1	44.6	Asie ancienne URSS exclus
- Middle East	4.9	3.4	2.3	3.1	3.1	3.3	2.5	2.1	2.7	2.9	- Moyen-Orient
Asia former USSR	0.1	0.3	0.2	0.2	0.1	0.2	0.2	0.3	0.3	0.4	Asie ancienne URSS
Europe excluding former USSR	26.7	26.4	27.1	26.0	27.1	32.6	32.0	27.3	30.7	28.8	Europe ancienne URSS exclus
- European Union	22.2	22.0	22.3	21.3	22.0	26.4	26.0	22.3	24.5	22.6	- Union Européenne
- Eastern Europe	2.2	2.1	2.2	2.5	2.7	3.5	3.5	2.9	3.7	3.7	- Europe de l'Est
- Rest of Europe	2.3	2.3	2.6	2.3	2.3	2.7	2.5	2.0	2.4	2.4	- Autre de l'Europe
Europe former USSR	2.9	2.0	2.0	1.9	2.0	2.0	1.5	1.3	1.6	2.0	Europe ancienne URSS
Oceania	1.4	1.4	1.4	1.6	1.6	1.4	1.3	1.0	1.0	1.1	Océanie

Autres machines spécialisés pour l'industrie particulières, et leurs pièces détachées 728

TRADE BY COMMODITY (Value in million US dollars)
Exports by principal countries or areas

COMMERCE PAR PRODUIT (Valeur en millions de dollars EU)
Exportations selon les principaux pays ou zones

Country or area	1998	1999	2000	2001	2002	Pays ou zone
World	59205.6	63261.2	76192.7	64756.6	62602.1	Monde
Africa	180.6	159.4	190.9	184.5	180.2	Afrique
Americas	12025.5	13291.5	18837.2	13912.6	11552.3	Amériques
- Northern America	11481.6	12679.3	18106.3	13085.1	10857.1	- Amérique du Nord
- LAIA	518.8	577.2	676.1	774.7	669.9	- ALAI
- CACM	15.9	27.2	43.8	44.5	17.4	- MCC
- Caribbean	8.8	7.1	10.2	6.3	6.4	- Caraïbes
- Rest of America	0.4	0.6	0.9	1.9	1.6	- Autre d'Amérique
Asia excluding former USSR	13705.9	16731.8	24248.1	17480.3	17640.9	Asie ancienne URSS exclus
- Middle East	92.7	95.6	97.2	122.4	154.2	- Moyen-Orient
Asia former USSR	8.7	11.8	30.1	18.2	19.8	Asie ancienne URSS
Europe excluding former USSR	32583.6	32515.4	32193.7	32575.4	32619.6	Europe ancienne URSS exclus
- European Union	29126.1	28959.4	28313.9	28724.8	28841.5	- Union Européenne
- Eastern Europe	652.6	700.5	724.1	794.6	964.1	- Europe de l'Est
- Rest of Europe	2804.9	2855.5	3155.7	3056.1	2814.0	- Autre de l'Europe
Europe former USSR	168.6	192.0	328.4	217.4	230.8	Europe ancienne URSS
Oceania	532.6	359.3	364.3	368.2	358.4	Océanie
United States	9964.4	11140.7	16373.9	11563.3	9376.9	Etats-Unis d'Amérique
Japan	8472.1	10714.1	15771.9	10079.5	9741.6	Japon
Germany	10614.0	10541.3	10175.0	10481.0	10471.3	Allemagne
Italy-San Marino-Holy See	7630.2	7353.5	7201.3	7447.3	7482.2	Italie-Saint-Marin-Saint-Siège
Switzerland-Liechtenstein	2498.6	2586.6	2860.3	2718.9	2426.3	Suisse-Liechtenstein
France-Monaco	2484.2	2302.5	2163.2	2143.8	2245.2	France-Monaco
United Kingdom	2313.1	2264.6	2124.8	2205.6	2167.8	Royaume-Uni
Canada	1517.1	1538.6	1732.4	1521.6	1479.7	Canada
Austria	1240.7	1393.1	1311.9	1388.7	1421.2	Autriche
Korea, Republic of	953.0	1013.1	1480.7	1312.9	1497.1	République de Corée
Netherlands	1088.4	1274.6	1364.5	1048.1	985.0	Pays-Bas
Singapore	833.2	1028.0	1782.9	1003.9	1016.8	Singapour
Sweden	993.4	980.2	1055.9	922.7	1052.3	Suède
China, Hong Kong SAR	811.4	796.8	1141.5	1075.2	1090.6	Chine - RAS de Hong-Kong
Finland	670.5	717.2	724.2	784.2	693.6	Finlande
China	351.2	474.7	587.8	789.2	919.9	Chine
Spain	625.2	628.6	618.4	660.2	588.0	Espagne
Belgium	–	651.2	681.8	696.0	e780.9	Belgique
Denmark	509.8	513.1	533.9	580.9	595.9	Danemark
Mexico	307.6	369.8	445.6	515.0	409.0	Mexique
Malaysia	323.9	324.9	423.0	391.8	e415.2	Malaisie
Australia	483.2	315.6	324.7	322.5	317.3	Australie
Czech Republic	278.5	296.2	294.9	325.0	403.4	République tchèque
Norway	215.1	175.1	198.3	226.9	273.3	Norvège
Israel	128.7	172.4	227.2	191.1	172.7	Israël
Poland	175.2	158.4	161.1	164.1	229.8	Pologne
Belgium-Luxembourg	746.8	–	–	–	–	Belgique-Luxembourg
Ireland	122.2	148.0	171.0	155.3	140.3	Irlande
India	98.7	94.1	145.8	170.4	186.5	Inde
Brazil	121.5	125.3	138.5	150.0	e155.5	Brésil

(Value as percentages of World total) **(Valeur en pourcentage du total mondial)**

Regions of the world	1993	1994	1995	1996	1997	1998	1999	2000	2001	2002	Régions du monde
World	100.0	100.0	100.0	100.0	100.0	100.0	100.0	100.0	100.0	100.0	Monde
Africa	0.3	0.3	0.3	0.3	0.4	0.3	0.3	0.3	0.3	0.3	Afrique
Americas	15.6	16.8	18.1	18.6	21.1	20.3	21.0	24.7	21.5	18.5	Amériques
- Northern America	15.0	16.3	17.4	17.9	20.2	19.4	20.0	23.8	20.2	17.3	- Amérique du Nord
- LAIA	0.6	0.5	0.6	0.7	0.8	0.9	0.9	0.9	1.2	1.1	- ALAI
- CACM	0.0	0.0	0.0	0.0	0.0	0.0	0.0	0.1	0.1	0.0	- MCC
- Caribbean	0.0	0.0	0.0	0.0	0.0	0.0	0.0	0.0	0.0	0.0	- Caraïbes
- Rest of America	0.0	0.0	0.0	0.0	0.0	0.0	0.0	0.0	0.0	0.0	- Autre d'Amérique
Asia excluding former USSR	30.6	28.7	28.0	27.3	27.6	23.1	26.4	31.8	27.0	28.2	Asie ancienne URSS exclus
- Middle East	0.1	0.1	0.1	0.1	0.2	0.2	0.2	0.1	0.2	0.2	- Moyen-Orient
Asia former USSR	0.0	0.0	0.0	0.0	0.0	0.0	0.0	0.0	0.0	0.0	Asie ancienne URSS
Europe excluding former USSR	52.6	53.5	52.7	52.8	49.9	55.0	51.4	42.3	50.3	52.1	Europe ancienne URSS exclus
- European Union	48.2	48.8	47.9	48.0	45.2	49.2	45.8	37.2	44.4	46.1	- Union Européenne
- Eastern Europe	0.6	0.6	0.7	0.8	0.8	1.1	1.1	1.0	1.2	1.5	- Europe de l'Est
- Rest of Europe	3.8	4.1	4.1	4.0	3.9	4.7	4.5	4.1	4.7	4.5	- Autre de l'Europe
Europe former USSR	0.4	0.2	0.2	0.3	0.3	0.3	0.3	0.4	0.3	0.4	Europe ancienne URSS
Oceania	0.5	0.6	0.7	0.7	0.7	0.9	0.6	0.5	0.6	0.6	Océanie

736 Metalworking machine-tools, parts and accessories thereof, nes

TRADE BY COMMODITY (Value in million US dollars)
Imports by principal countries or areas

COMMERCE PAR PRODUIT (Valeur en millions de dollars EU)
Importations selon les principaux pays ou zones

Country or area	1998	1999	2000	2001	2002	Pays ou zone
World	30835.2	29224.6	31898.9	30499.8	27500.5	Monde
Africa	355.6	282.5	300.5	331.0	350.6	Afrique
Americas	9762.7	9013.8	9432.0	8533.7	6328.9	Amériques
- Northern America	7679.2	6720.0	7616.9	6415.9	4743.9	- Amérique du Nord
- LAIA	2010.3	2233.3	1761.1	2056.2	1515.8	- ALAI
- CACM	35.9	29.7	26.3	32.5	42.5	- MCC
- Caribbean	26.3	20.4	22.3	22.3	22.3	- Caraïbes
- Rest of America	11.1	10.4	5.3	6.8	4.5	- Autre d'Amérique
Asia excluding former USSR	7534.1	7640.4	10018.9	8993.1	9472.0	Asie ancienne URSS exclus
- Middle East	750.7	722.9	663.2	672.3	750.7	- Moyen-Orient
Asia former USSR	24.9	26.6	22.2	79.3	31.3	Asie ancienne URSS
Europe excluding former USSR	12574.8	11756.9	11697.1	12025.0	10616.7	Europe ancienne URSS exclus
- European Union	10678.2	9985.8	9965.7	10002.4	8521.5	- Union Européenne
- Eastern Europe	963.8	904.2	891.5	1078.0	1272.1	- Europe de l'Est
- Rest of Europe	932.9	866.9	839.9	944.6	823.0	- Autre de l'Europe
Europe former USSR	308.7	275.8	206.1	307.8	415.1	Europe ancienne URSS
Oceania	274.4	228.5	222.1	229.9	285.9	Océanie
United States	6424.9	5528.5	6407.1	5385.4	3870.5	Etats-Unis d'Amérique
Germany	2645.1	2533.8	2457.1	2700.7	2173.6	Allemagne
China	1882.2	1703.3	2081.2	2582.0	3315.9	Chine
France-Monaco	1653.2	1614.1	1725.6	1634.5	1241.0	France-Monaco
Italy-San Marino-Holy See	1513.7	1494.6	1596.2	1501.9	1403.5	Italie-Saint-Marin-Saint-Siège
Mexico	1129.4	1365.2	1225.0	1353.2	1011.6	Mexique
United Kingdom	1513.6	1174.4	1213.9	1146.0	937.8	Royaume-Uni
Canada	1254.1	1191.4	1209.5	1029.9	873.1	Canada
Japan	841.7	855.3	1154.2	846.5	625.5	Japon
Korea, Republic of	509.6	703.9	1270.7	1012.6	814.0	République de Corée
Spain	678.1	713.9	636.4	695.6	642.5	Espagne
Switzerland-Liechtenstein	689.2	655.1	640.5	698.1	588.6	Suisse-Liechtenstein
Belgium	–	626.4	642.4	705.8	e774.0	Belgique
Malaysia	398.0	435.2	645.3	587.1	e641.6	Malaisie
Singapore	392.3	491.6	748.0	496.0	418.4	Singapour
Brazil	557.2	662.7	373.9	488.8	354.9	Brésil
Thailand	396.6	327.8	494.5	555.1	e578.3	Thaïlande
China, Hong Kong SAR	409.8	422.4	520.5	489.5	462.3	Chine - RAS de Hong-Kong
Austria	453.1	423.3	438.2	469.5	363.2	Autriche
Czech Republic	310.0	289.7	331.0	393.4	389.6	République tchèque
Sweden	436.9	339.6	337.5	308.5	282.7	Suède
Turkey	369.5	260.2	274.4	232.3	338.4	Turquie
Poland	294.3	264.5	230.8	259.4	384.2	Pologne
Netherlands	358.6	349.0	220.7	210.1	145.5	Pays-Bas
India	325.7	234.1	205.6	172.0	207.3	Inde
Hungary	208.7	197.9	199.2	212.0	285.5	Hongrie
Iran (Islamic Republic of)	180.0	246.5	225.3	232.4	193.5	Iran (République islamique d')
Indonesia	295.0	71.0	131.6	242.8	321.8	Indonésie
Australia	241.7	193.8	180.3	187.6	237.7	Australie
Russian Federation	218.8	197.2	102.0	174.4	225.9	Fédération de Russie

(Value as percentages of World total) **(Valeur en pourcentage du total mondial)**

Regions of the world	1993	1994	1995	1996	1997	1998	1999	2000	2001	2002	Régions du monde
World	100.0	100.0	100.0	100.0	100.0	100.0	100.0	100.0	100.0	100.0	Monde
Africa	1.8	1.5	1.4	1.4	1.1	1.2	1.0	0.9	1.1	1.3	Afrique
Americas	23.2	26.9	25.7	25.1	29.0	31.7	30.8	29.6	28.0	23.0	Amériques
- Northern America	17.5	21.6	20.8	19.8	23.4	24.9	23.0	23.9	21.0	17.3	- Amérique du Nord
- LAIA	5.5	5.1	4.7	5.2	5.4	6.5	7.6	5.5	6.7	5.5	- ALAI
- CACM	0.1	0.1	0.1	0.1	0.1	0.1	0.1	0.1	0.1	0.2	- MCC
- Caribbean	0.1	0.1	0.1	0.1	0.1	0.1	0.1	0.1	0.1	0.1	- Caraïbes
- Rest of America	0.1	0.0	0.0	0.0	0.0	0.0	0.0	0.0	0.0	0.0	- Autre d'Amérique
Asia excluding former USSR	38.6	35.7	35.1	36.1	32.2	24.4	26.1	31.4	29.5	34.4	Asie ancienne URSS exclus
- Middle East	4.7	2.6	2.1	2.1	2.3	2.4	2.5	2.1	2.2	2.7	- Moyen-Orient
Asia former USSR	0.1	0.4	0.2	0.1	0.0	0.1	0.1	0.1	0.3	0.1	Asie ancienne URSS
Europe excluding former USSR	32.1	32.9	35.3	35.0	35.3	40.8	40.2	36.7	39.4	38.6	Europe ancienne URSS exclus
- European Union	27.8	28.5	30.3	30.2	29.3	34.6	34.2	31.2	32.8	31.0	- Union Européenne
- Eastern Europe	1.8	1.8	1.9	2.1	3.4	3.1	3.1	2.8	3.5	4.6	- Europe de l'Est
- Rest of Europe	2.5	2.5	3.2	2.8	2.5	3.0	3.0	2.6	3.1	3.0	- Autre de l'Europe
Europe former USSR	3.2	1.4	1.0	1.0	1.1	1.0	0.9	0.6	1.0	1.5	Europe ancienne URSS
Oceania	1.0	1.3	1.3	1.3	1.3	0.9	0.8	0.7	0.8	1.0	Océanie

Machines-outils pour le travail des métaux et des carbures métalliques, pièces detachées 736

TRADE BY COMMODITY (Value in million US dollars)
Exports by principal countries or areas

COMMERCE PAR PRODUIT (Valeur en millions de dollars EU)
Exportations selon les principaux pays ou zones

Country or area	1998	1999	2000	2001	2002	Pays ou zone
World	30931.6	29223.1	32068.6	29912.2	27424.8	Monde
Africa	27.6	37.3	19.9	26.5	28.6	Afrique
Americas	4714.0	4696.2	5596.2	4451.1	3932.5	Amériques
- Northern America	4529.0	4516.5	5395.3	4271.2	3740.5	- Amérique du Nord
- LAIA	180.3	173.4	193.5	174.2	185.2	- ALAI
- CACM	3.0	5.2	4.4	3.0	2.8	- MCC
- Caribbean	1.7	1.1	2.9	2.5	4.0	- Caraïbes
- Rest of America	0.0	0.0	0.1	0.2	0.1	- Autre d'Amérique
Asia excluding former USSR	9813.1	9176.1	11558.4	9737.6	8930.5	Asie ancienne URSS exclus
- Middle East	70.1	80.0	93.1	106.7	115.8	- Moyen-Orient
Asia former USSR	10.9	8.4	10.6	14.6	11.7	Asie ancienne URSS
Europe excluding former USSR	16035.6	15006.3	14462.7	15408.2	14286.4	Europe ancienne URSS exclus
- European Union	12907.7	12113.6	11514.9	12446.6	11573.1	- Union Européenne
- Eastern Europe	759.4	676.5	704.5	780.2	749.3	- Europe de l'Est
- Rest of Europe	2368.5	2216.2	2243.2	2181.4	1964.0	- Autre de l'Europe
Europe former USSR	228.8	192.3	283.5	181.6	166.2	Europe ancienne URSS
Oceania	101.6	106.4	137.4	92.6	68.9	Océanie
Japan	6512.1	6135.6	7620.2	6132.1	5162.4	Japon
Germany	5546.6	5076.5	4975.1	5544.0	5181.4	Allemagne
United States	4097.9	4078.4	4915.5	3860.6	3389.0	Etats-Unis d'Amérique
Italy-San Marino-Holy See	2581.0	2504.0	2241.3	2445.8	2229.7	Italie-Saint-Marin-Saint-Siège
Switzerland-Liechtenstein	2263.4	2126.9	2147.2	2084.1	1861.6	Suisse-Liechtenstein
United Kingdom	1305.7	1204.9	1116.4	1152.5	904.6	Royaume-Uni
France-Monaco	909.2	853.7	851.7	849.3	784.9	France-Monaco
Spain	652.9	636.8	551.7	608.4	624.4	Espagne
Belgium	–	540.8	588.6	628.1	e704.8	Belgique
Korea, Republic of	560.5	425.0	487.5	473.8	475.5	République de Corée
Canada	431.1	438.1	479.7	410.6	351.4	Canada
China	313.4	330.9	467.5	464.4	501.6	Chine
China, Hong Kong SAR	353.0	371.4	458.3	430.0	426.6	Chine - RAS de Hong-Kong
Czech Republic	462.6	383.6	366.9	402.4	367.2	République tchèque
Austria	427.2	365.5	351.2	407.7	377.2	Autriche
Sweden	328.7	316.3	331.9	289.4	285.5	Suède
Singapore	250.5	252.2	353.4	304.8	285.9	Singapour
Netherlands	274.4	274.9	172.4	167.3	153.7	Pays-Bas
Finland	157.9	142.8	144.8	163.3	136.3	Finlande
Russian Federation	155.4	140.6	218.6	75.8	57.3	Fédération de Russie
Brazil	113.8	109.6	134.3	116.3	e120.6	Brésil
Belgium-Luxembourg	560.0	–	–	–	–	Belgique-Luxembourg
Poland	87.7	85.3	117.6	129.6	118.3	Pologne
Denmark	100.5	106.7	105.4	111.0	95.3	Danemark
Malaysia	85.7	83.5	90.4	82.7	e87.6	Malaisie
Slovakia	82.8	80.9	82.9	91.5	88.6	Slovaquie
Thailand	76.5	80.5	115.8	72.5	e76.6	Thaïlande
Australia	76.6	87.0	100.6	73.8	53.6	Australie
India	65.2	55.1	83.5	88.3	99.0	Inde
Turkey	57.2	67.0	69.3	78.3	87.4	Turquie

(Value as percentages of World total) **(Valeur en pourcentage du total mondial)**

Regions of the world	1993	1994	1995	1996	1997	1998	1999	2000	2001	2002	Régions du monde
World	100.0	100.0	100.0	100.0	100.0	100.0	100.0	100.0	100.0	100.0	Monde
Africa	0.1	0.1	0.1	0.1	0.1	0.1	0.1	0.1	0.1	0.1	Afrique
Americas	13.7	15.4	14.5	15.1	16.3	15.2	16.1	17.5	14.9	14.3	Amériques
- Northern America	12.9	14.8	13.7	14.4	15.7	14.6	15.5	16.8	14.3	13.6	- Amérique du Nord
- LAIA	0.7	0.5	0.7	0.7	0.6	0.6	0.6	0.6	0.6	0.7	- ALAI
- CACM	0.0	0.0	0.0	0.0	0.0	0.0	0.0	0.0	0.0	0.0	- MCC
- Caribbean	0.0	0.0	0.0	0.0	0.0	0.0	0.0	0.0	0.0	0.0	- Caraïbes
- Rest of America	0.0	0.0	0.0	0.0	0.0	0.0	0.0	0.0	0.0	0.0	- Autre d'Amérique
Asia excluding former USSR	33.6	32.1	34.7	34.4	34.8	31.7	31.4	36.0	32.6	32.6	Asie ancienne URSS exclus
- Middle East	0.1	0.1	0.1	0.1	0.2	0.2	0.3	0.3	0.4	0.4	- Moyen-Orient
Asia former USSR	0.0	0.0	0.0	0.0	0.0	0.0	0.0	0.0	0.0	0.0	Asie ancienne URSS
Europe excluding former USSR	51.7	51.7	49.9	49.5	47.8	51.8	51.4	45.1	51.5	52.1	Europe ancienne URSS exclus
- European Union	42.4	41.5	40.0	40.4	38.9	41.7	41.5	35.9	41.6	42.2	- Union Européenne
- Eastern Europe	1.8	1.5	1.7	1.9	2.0	2.5	2.3	2.2	2.6	2.7	- Europe de l'Est
- Rest of Europe	7.5	8.8	8.3	7.2	6.9	7.7	7.6	7.0	7.3	7.2	- Autre de l'Europe
Europe former USSR	0.6	0.4	0.4	0.5	0.6	0.7	0.7	0.9	0.6	0.6	Europe ancienne URSS
Oceania	0.3	0.3	0.3	0.4	0.4	0.3	0.4	0.4	0.3	0.3	Océanie

737 Metalworking machinery (other than machine-tools), and parts, nes

TRADE BY COMMODITY (Value in million US dollars)
Imports by principal countries or areas

COMMERCE PAR PRODUIT (Valeur en millions de dollars EU)
Importations selon les principaux pays ou zones

Country or area	1998	1999	2000	2001	2002	Pays ou zone
World	10614.7	9790.4	9719.0	8541.8	8930.9	Monde
Africa	402.4	212.3	201.2	184.4	192.8	Afrique
Americas	3056.7	2617.8	2591.1	2228.0	2088.3	Amériques
- Northern America	2151.3	1721.0	1844.0	1523.9	1519.6	- Amérique du Nord
- LAIA	863.7	864.2	710.0	663.0	522.6	- ALAI
- CACM	15.1	12.3	13.2	16.5	22.4	- MCC
- Caribbean	22.3	16.1	18.9	21.4	20.2	- Caraïbes
- Rest of America	4.4	4.1	5.1	3.1	3.5	- Autre d'Amérique
Asia excluding former USSR	3363.3	3463.0	3565.3	2709.4	3327.9	Asie ancienne URSS exclus
- Middle East	529.7	687.7	366.2	342.0	383.5	- Moyen-Orient
Asia former USSR	32.3	32.7	44.7	68.9	70.3	Asie ancienne URSS
Europe excluding former USSR	3482.6	3231.6	3039.7	3065.4	2923.7	Europe ancienne URSS exclus
- European Union	2913.4	2632.0	2471.1	2448.5	2260.7	- Union Européenne
- Eastern Europe	355.6	392.0	334.6	395.8	446.3	- Europe de l'Est
- Rest of Europe	213.6	207.7	234.0	221.1	216.7	- Autre de l'Europe
Europe former USSR	180.4	145.5	183.8	200.9	233.2	Europe ancienne URSS
Oceania	97.0	87.3	93.1	84.9	94.7	Océanie
United States	1544.0	1301.9	1366.7	1200.8	1187.7	Etats-Unis d'Amérique
China	630.8	800.1	739.4	784.5	1270.4	Chine
Germany	572.3	501.1	460.2	550.7	504.5	Allemagne
Canada	606.8	418.9	476.8	322.6	331.2	Canada
Mexico	348.6	488.7	469.6	353.7	326.8	Mexique
United Kingdom	419.1	362.6	333.4	359.8	311.8	Royaume-Uni
France-Monaco	429.4	325.6	341.2	306.5	300.9	France-Monaco
Korea, Republic of	277.0	312.9	406.8	257.1	300.9	République de Corée
Iran (Islamic Republic of)	334.9	508.0	185.9	155.0	210.1	Iran (République islamique d')
Spain	237.8	321.6	317.1	274.2	212.5	Espagne
Italy-San Marino-Holy See	287.7	284.6	251.3	257.2	241.3	Italie-Saint-Marin-Saint-Siège
China, Hong Kong SAR	188.3	218.5	383.2	230.6	178.7	Chine - RAS de Hong-Kong
Brazil	299.9	219.7	133.3	190.0	105.2	Brésil
Thailand	332.8	106.8	177.2	129.5	e134.9	Thaïlande
Malaysia	278.7	135.5	169.1	136.7	e149.4	Malaisie
Japan	175.6	150.1	154.0	152.8	125.9	Japon
Belgium	–	203.2	183.9	166.5	e182.6	Belgique
Indonesia	118.0	197.9	102.4	97.8	186.5	Indonésie
Russian Federation	109.5	121.9	131.5	151.7	168.3	Fédération de Russie
Poland	146.5	131.4	128.8	87.2	132.6	Pologne
Austria	155.5	142.3	110.9	121.2	94.9	Autriche
Singapore	133.2	114.3	154.6	106.9	98.6	Singapour
Netherlands	120.5	146.6	109.2	109.2	110.4	Pays-Bas
Sweden	153.3	99.3	126.6	92.2	83.7	Suède
India	154.6	104.7	108.6	58.7	68.2	Inde
Switzerland-Liechtenstein	96.4	97.8	96.8	92.8	98.2	Suisse-Liechtenstein
Czech Republic	87.2	141.6	74.9	91.1	85.0	République tchèque
Turkey	93.6	85.3	91.1	88.5	81.8	Turquie
Australia	80.2	72.7	73.6	67.1	74.3	Australie
Southern African Customs Union	267.3	91.0	–	–	–	Union douanière d'Afrique australe

(Value as percentages of World total) **(Valeur en pourcentage du total mondial)**

Regions of the world	1993	1994	1995	1996	1997	1998	1999	2000	2001	2002	Régions du monde
World	100.0	100.0	100.0	100.0	100.0	100.0	100.0	100.0	100.0	100.0	Monde
Africa	2.4	4.3	2.0	2.1	2.9	3.8	2.2	2.1	2.2	2.2	Afrique
Americas	20.1	21.7	20.7	23.7	25.5	28.8	26.7	26.7	26.1	23.4	Amériques
- Northern America	13.7	13.2	14.1	17.5	17.0	20.3	17.6	19.0	17.8	17.0	- Amérique du Nord
- LAIA	6.1	8.2	6.2	5.9	8.3	8.1	8.8	7.3	7.8	5.9	- ALAI
- CACM	0.1	0.1	0.1	0.1	0.1	0.1	0.1	0.1	0.2	0.3	- MCC
- Caribbean	0.1	0.1	0.3	0.2	0.1	0.2	0.2	0.2	0.3	0.2	- Caraïbes
- Rest of America	0.1	0.0	0.0	0.0	0.0	0.0	0.0	0.1	0.0	0.0	- Autre d'Amérique
Asia excluding former USSR	46.3	42.6	44.3	42.4	39.6	31.7	35.4	36.7	31.7	37.3	Asie ancienne URSS exclus
- Middle East	3.9	4.5	3.4	2.5	2.6	5.0	7.0	3.8	4.0	4.3	- Moyen-Orient
Asia former USSR	0.1	0.3	0.5	0.4	0.3	0.3	0.3	0.5	0.8	0.8	Asie ancienne URSS
Europe excluding former USSR	26.7	27.6	29.0	28.4	29.2	32.8	33.0	31.3	35.9	32.7	Europe ancienne URSS exclus
- European Union	22.9	23.7	24.0	23.5	24.1	27.4	26.9	25.4	28.7	25.3	- Union Européenne
- Eastern Europe	1.9	2.2	3.0	2.9	3.4	3.3	4.0	3.4	4.6	5.0	- Europe de l'Est
- Rest of Europe	1.9	1.7	2.0	2.1	1.8	2.0	2.1	2.4	2.6	2.4	- Autre de l'Europe
Europe former USSR	3.4	2.1	2.1	1.7	1.5	1.7	1.5	1.9	2.4	2.6	Europe ancienne URSS
Oceania	1.0	1.3	1.3	1.2	0.9	0.9	0.9	1.0	1.0	1.1	Océanie

TRADE BY COMMODITY (Value in million US dollars)
Exports by principal countries or areas

COMMERCE PAR PRODUIT (Valeur en millions de dollars EU)
Exportations selon les principaux pays ou zones

Country or area	1998	1999	2000	2001	2002	Pays ou zone
World	9735.3	9021.0	9344.5	8554.2	8524.0	Monde
Africa	19.6	23.2	28.5	27.2	22.3	Afrique
Americas	1693.0	1656.0	1789.3	1411.3	1303.4	Amériques
- Northern America	1574.0	1569.3	1692.5	1293.0	1187.4	- Amérique du Nord
- LAIA	114.9	83.2	92.7	114.2	112.4	- ALAI
- CACM	2.9	2.4	2.8	2.6	2.0	- MCC
- Caribbean	1.2	1.0	1.1	1.2	1.4	- Caraïbes
- Rest of America	0.0	0.1	0.2	0.2	0.2	- Autre d'Amérique
Asia excluding former USSR	2004.9	1881.9	2506.5	2081.8	2060.4	Asie ancienne URSS exclus
- Middle East	23.9	31.7	28.9	40.3	37.3	- Moyen-Orient
Asia former USSR	3.6	2.2	2.7	2.0	2.2	Asie ancienne URSS
Europe excluding former USSR	5909.4	5325.3	4844.0	4879.5	4948.0	Europe ancienne URSS exclus
- European Union	5151.3	4681.5	4104.7	4212.6	4259.7	- Union Européenne
- Eastern Europe	187.1	132.4	146.3	156.6	177.6	- Europe de l'Est
- Rest of Europe	571.0	511.4	593.0	510.3	510.8	- Autre de l'Europe
Europe former USSR	88.1	103.4	137.8	127.1	174.5	Europe ancienne URSS
Oceania	16.7	28.9	35.6	25.2	13.2	Océanie
Germany	1666.6	1592.8	1349.9	1445.2	1365.8	Allemagne
Japan	1343.5	1200.1	1469.9	1245.2	1134.4	Japon
United States	1236.3	1272.5	1428.3	1071.4	947.3	Etats-Unis d'Amérique
Italy-San Marino-Holy See	1248.7	1090.4	855.5	929.6	976.0	Italie-Saint-Marin-Saint-Siège
Switzerland-Liechtenstein	505.8	458.2	547.1	455.9	458.3	Suisse-Liechtenstein
Sweden	412.5	456.8	458.0	372.9	422.6	Suède
United Kingdom	494.6	393.9	361.6	338.8	307.2	Royaume-Uni
France-Monaco	469.4	343.9	321.6	353.7	349.4	France-Monaco
Canada	337.7	296.7	264.2	221.7	240.2	Canada
Austria	275.8	239.2	232.1	226.8	253.6	Autriche
China, Hong Kong SAR	159.5	197.0	371.6	225.3	227.9	Chine - RAS de Hong-Kong
China	122.1	105.3	215.9	163.2	159.7	Chine
Netherlands	125.3	130.5	156.9	135.0	149.9	Pays-Bas
Spain	127.9	156.1	109.8	139.3	132.4	Espagne
Korea, Republic of	121.2	97.8	139.1	126.6	168.4	République de Corée
Belgium	–	134.6	128.5	144.3	e161.9	Belgique
Ukraine	52.0	53.0	71.8	94.8	104.5	Ukraine
Czech Republic	92.2	57.3	62.2	70.0	73.9	République tchèque
Singapore	59.5	77.0	69.6	60.9	75.6	Singapour
Finland	72.7	53.0	58.4	64.4	69.5	Finlande
Brazil	68.0	34.8	39.7	37.9	e39.3	Brésil
Belgium-Luxembourg	208.3	–	–	–	–	Belgique-Luxembourg
Russian Federation	23.3	44.3	59.6	22.5	51.6	Fédération de Russie
Mexico	22.1	25.3	35.8	59.8	56.8	Mexique
Slovenia	45.4	34.7	33.6	39.4	36.4	Slovénie
India	22.1	19.6	33.0	32.6	60.5	Inde
Malaysia	33.2	26.4	25.1	27.9	e29.6	Malaisie
Denmark	29.0	28.7	29.8	24.5	25.8	Danemark
Slovakia	25.4	23.6	24.7	26.1	29.9	Slovaquie
Turkey	17.4	22.7	19.1	29.9	26.1	Turquie

(Value as percentages of World total) **(Valeur en pourcentage du total mondial)**

Regions of the world	1993	1994	1995	1996	1997	1998	1999	2000	2001	2002	Régions du monde
World	100.0	100.0	100.0	100.0	100.0	100.0	100.0	100.0	100.0	100.0	Monde
Africa	0.1	0.1	0.1	0.2	0.2	0.2	0.3	0.3	0.3	0.3	Afrique
Americas	15.1	15.5	13.0	13.7	16.3	17.4	18.4	19.1	16.5	15.3	Amériques
- Northern America	14.0	14.9	12.0	12.0	15.4	16.2	17.4	18.1	15.1	13.9	- Amérique du Nord
- LAIA	1.1	0.6	1.0	1.6	0.9	1.2	0.9	1.0	1.3	1.3	- ALAI
- CACM	0.0	0.0	0.0	0.0	0.0	0.0	0.0	0.0	0.0	0.0	- MCC
- Caribbean	0.0	0.0	0.0	0.0	0.0	0.0	0.0	0.0	0.0	0.0	- Caraïbes
- Rest of America	0.0	0.0	0.0	0.0	0.0	0.0	0.0	0.0	0.0	0.0	- Autre d'Amérique
Asia excluding former USSR	24.8	26.8	27.2	25.7	24.0	20.6	20.9	26.8	24.3	24.2	Asie ancienne URSS exclus
- Middle East	0.1	0.2	0.2	0.1	0.2	0.2	0.4	0.3	0.5	0.4	- Moyen-Orient
Asia former USSR	0.0	0.1	0.1	0.1	0.0	0.0	0.0	0.0	0.0	0.0	Asie ancienne URSS
Europe excluding former USSR	59.3	56.4	58.4	58.9	58.3	60.7	59.0	51.8	57.0	58.0	Europe ancienne URSS exclus
- European Union	51.8	49.6	50.4	51.8	51.3	52.9	51.9	43.9	49.2	50.0	- Union Européenne
- Eastern Europe	1.7	1.3	1.5	1.3	1.4	1.9	1.5	1.6	1.8	2.1	- Europe de l'Est
- Rest of Europe	5.8	5.6	6.6	5.8	5.6	5.9	5.7	6.3	6.0	6.0	- Autre de l'Europe
Europe former USSR	0.5	0.9	0.9	1.1	1.0	0.9	1.1	1.5	1.5	2.0	Europe ancienne URSS
Oceania	0.2	0.2	0.2	0.2	0.2	0.2	0.3	0.4	0.3	0.2	Océanie

741 Heating and cooling equipment and parts thereof, nes

TRADE BY COMMODITY (Value in million US dollars)
Imports by principal countries or areas

COMMERCE PAR PRODUIT (Valeur en millions de dollars EU)
Importations selon les principaux pays ou zones

Country or area	1998	1999	2000	2001	2002	Pays ou zone
World	42052.8	41695.5	42686.5	42200.9	43399.3	Monde
Africa	1303.4	1191.8	1165.2	1269.2	1312.7	Afrique
Americas	9945.6	10269.3	10669.5	10529.0	10553.3	Amériques
- Northern America	5461.0	6218.8	6957.9	6660.4	7287.9	- Amérique du Nord
- LAIA	3504.0	3530.2	3160.1	3026.9	2504.7	- ALAI
- CACM	156.5	142.0	126.3	131.4	134.9	- MCC
- Caribbean	764.1	324.5	372.1	665.2	582.2	- Caraïbes
- Rest of America	60.2	53.8	53.2	45.2	43.6	- Autre d'Amérique
Asia excluding former USSR	12544.8	11596.1	12810.3	12341.9	12667.0	Asie ancienne URSS exclus
- Middle East	2362.8	2111.5	2432.6	2415.1	2245.7	- Moyen-Orient
Asia former USSR	145.5	163.7	203.0	215.6	228.9	Asie ancienne URSS
Europe excluding former USSR	16145.8	16946.0	16367.7	16113.6	16683.7	Europe ancienne URSS exclus
- European Union	13196.7	14243.1	13920.2	13644.8	13863.1	- Union Européenne
- Eastern Europe	1719.2	1487.3	1380.1	1377.7	1510.5	- Europe de l'Est
- Rest of Europe	1229.9	1215.7	1067.3	1091.1	1310.1	- Autre de l'Europe
Europe former USSR	1128.4	710.7	672.5	972.4	1060.2	Europe ancienne URSS
Oceania	839.2	817.8	798.3	759.1	893.4	Océanie
United States	3357.2	3908.8	4636.3	4531.5	5011.6	Etats-Unis d'Amérique
Germany	2813.5	2831.9	2541.1	2792.9	2641.3	Allemagne
Canada	2084.2	2287.8	2315.5	2120.6	2263.7	Canada
France-Monaco	1737.3	1791.0	1945.4	1758.5	1825.6	France-Monaco
China	1242.6	1391.6	1573.5	2103.9	2532.6	Chine
United Kingdom	1810.0	1693.9	1698.9	1711.0	1621.7	Royaume-Uni
Italy-San Marino-Holy See	1175.7	1597.3	1632.8	1503.4	1516.7	Italie-Saint-Marin-Saint-Siège
Spain	1174.1	1505.9	1446.9	1484.9	1609.0	Espagne
Mexico	1189.0	1399.7	1427.7	1390.7	1243.0	Mexique
Japan	1037.1	1013.2	1138.0	1508.8	1622.3	Japon
China, Hong Kong SAR	1212.2	854.5	943.8	915.2	817.3	Chine - RAS de Hong-Kong
Belgium	–	1176.3	1065.8	1041.8	e1142.5	Belgique
Singapore	847.6	859.8	967.7	759.6	663.3	Singapour
Korea, Republic of	723.9	619.5	916.0	738.8	732.9	République de Corée
Netherlands	711.7	752.5	731.5	706.2	742.8	Pays-Bas
Australia	697.6	669.2	672.8	632.1	764.3	Australie
Malaysia	573.5	866.6	634.3	475.7	e519.9	Malaisie
Russian Federation	785.7	464.1	369.4	607.9	661.1	Fédération de Russie
Poland	835.5	586.5	472.2	421.3	471.7	Pologne
Switzerland-Liechtenstein	517.3	549.3	530.0	529.6	627.3	Suisse-Liechtenstein
Austria	526.1	542.6	513.1	539.1	528.5	Autriche
Turkey	597.4	493.8	554.0	558.5	417.3	Turquie
Brazil	656.8	498.0	448.9	533.8	437.5	Brésil
Sweden	480.8	515.4	506.4	480.8	525.8	Suède
Greece	429.8	540.0	541.4	464.8	e513.9	Grèce
Saudi Arabia	533.5	604.2	474.2	365.8	e378.6	Arabie saoudite
Venezuela	575.8	719.6	488.2	271.7	e228.5	Venezuela
Thailand	489.6	243.0	344.5	443.7	e462.3	Thaïlande
United Arab Emirates	199.9	209.5	454.4	479.4	e491.9	Emirates arabes unis
Argentina	434.0	462.4	340.6	309.9	e137.1	Argentine

(Value as percentages of World total) **(Valeur en pourcentage du total mondial)**

Regions of the world	1993	1994	1995	1996	1997	1998	1999	2000	2001	2002	Régions du monde
World	100.0	100.0	100.0	100.0	100.0	100.0	100.0	100.0	100.0	100.0	Monde
Africa	3.5	3.3	3.2	2.8	3.4	3.1	2.9	2.7	3.0	3.0	Afrique
Americas	18.4	19.8	18.0	18.2	21.6	23.7	24.6	25.0	24.9	24.3	Amériques
- Northern America	11.4	12.6	11.4	11.9	12.2	13.0	14.9	16.3	15.8	16.8	- Amérique du Nord
- LAIA	5.8	6.4	5.3	5.3	6.8	8.3	8.5	7.4	7.2	5.8	- ALAI
- CACM	0.3	0.2	0.2	0.2	0.3	0.4	0.3	0.3	0.3	0.3	- MCC
- Caribbean	0.8	0.5	0.9	0.7	2.3	1.8	0.8	0.9	1.6	1.3	- Caraïbes
- Rest of America	0.1	0.1	0.1	0.1	0.2	0.1	0.1	0.1	0.1	0.1	- Autre d'Amérique
Asia excluding former USSR	41.6	40.6	40.3	39.2	35.5	29.8	27.8	30.0	29.2	29.2	Asie ancienne URSS exclus
- Middle East	8.1	6.3	4.9	4.6	4.5	5.6	5.1	5.7	5.7	5.2	- Moyen-Orient
Asia former USSR	0.2	0.3	0.2	0.3	0.2	0.3	0.4	0.5	0.5	0.5	Asie ancienne URSS
Europe excluding former USSR	32.6	32.4	34.7	36.1	34.1	38.4	40.6	38.3	38.2	38.4	Europe ancienne URSS exclus
- European Union	27.7	27.3	28.9	29.8	28.2	31.4	34.2	32.6	32.3	31.9	- Union Européenne
- Eastern Europe	2.4	2.4	2.9	3.5	3.3	4.1	3.6	3.2	3.3	3.5	- Europe de l'Est
- Rest of Europe	2.5	2.7	2.9	2.7	2.6	2.9	2.9	2.5	2.6	3.0	- Autre de l'Europe
Europe former USSR	2.3	1.9	1.9	1.8	3.3	2.7	1.7	1.6	2.3	2.4	Europe ancienne URSS
Oceania	1.4	1.7	1.6	1.7	1.9	2.0	2.0	1.9	1.8	2.1	Océanie

TRADE BY COMMODITY (Value in million US dollars)
Exports by principal countries or areas

COMMERCE PAR PRODUIT (Valeur en millions de dollars EU)
Exportations selon les principaux pays ou zones

Country or area	1998	1999	2000	2001	2002	Pays ou zone
World	39925.5	39214.5	41304.0	41190.1	42575.9	Monde
Africa	77.0	80.5	120.5	106.2	127.6	Afrique
Americas	8912.3	8734.5	9683.1	9218.2	8956.9	Amériques
- Northern America	7636.3	7276.0	8095.7	7663.3	7185.9	- Amérique du Nord
- LAIA	1235.9	1414.5	1550.0	1503.9	1735.9	- ALAI
- CACM	17.7	16.3	18.4	25.4	14.2	- MCC
- Caribbean	22.3	27.6	18.9	25.1	20.2	- Caraïbes
- Rest of America	0.0	0.2	0.1	0.5	0.7	- Autre d'Amérique
Asia excluding former USSR	9019.0	9369.9	11454.2	10990.7	11603.7	Asie ancienne URSS exclus
- Middle East	314.5	335.6	381.3	405.5	469.5	- Moyen-Orient
Asia former USSR	5.8	3.9	3.2	4.7	4.8	Asie ancienne URSS
Europe excluding former USSR	21568.2	20664.0	19589.3	20317.1	21366.1	Europe ancienne URSS exclus
- European Union	19828.0	19031.5	17893.0	18527.8	19395.3	- Union Européenne
- Eastern Europe	690.7	636.9	734.9	898.8	1048.7	- Europe de l'Est
- Rest of Europe	1049.5	995.6	961.4	890.5	922.1	- Autre de l'Europe
Europe former USSR	136.5	146.1	258.1	358.9	303.7	Europe ancienne URSS
Oceania	206.7	215.6	195.5	194.4	213.0	Océanie
United States	6849.8	6486.6	7218.4	6759.7	6269.9	Etats-Unis d'Amérique
Germany	4741.9	4450.5	3988.1	4482.5	4624.4	Allemagne
Italy-San Marino-Holy See	4485.8	4246.6	4147.8	4112.7	4299.9	Italie-Saint-Marin-Saint-Siège
Japan	3845.7	3726.4	4316.7	3305.0	3120.7	Japon
France-Monaco	2877.6	2755.3	2442.0	2461.4	2489.3	France-Monaco
Korea, Republic of	900.3	1218.3	1771.2	1817.1	1870.8	République de Corée
United Kingdom	1638.4	1557.1	1412.4	1491.3	1399.7	Royaume-Uni
China	522.9	752.8	1226.8	1665.8	2164.6	Chine
Mexico	956.4	1141.7	1260.4	1216.7	1447.6	Mexique
Thailand	877.9	999.9	1150.3	1252.8	e1323.1	Thaïlande
Sweden	968.8	951.3	903.6	902.6	989.4	Suède
Denmark	998.6	889.3	898.7	879.1	962.7	Danemark
Spain	814.3	824.6	900.8	833.8	916.7	Espagne
Canada	786.4	789.3	877.2	903.5	915.9	Canada
Belgium	–	1008.0	1051.9	1023.0	e1147.8	Belgique
Netherlands	852.1	817.1	770.1	828.0	948.9	Pays-Bas
Switzerland-Liechtenstein	791.7	771.9	739.4	674.3	681.5	Suisse-Liechtenstein
Austria	633.6	614.1	542.0	612.9	690.1	Autriche
Malaysia	465.9	573.4	564.7	601.5	e637.4	Malaisie
China, Hong Kong SAR	725.5	460.4	487.4	585.8	553.4	Chine - RAS de Hong-Kong
Singapore	514.3	371.9	429.6	351.0	385.0	Singapour
Czech Republic	343.7	338.8	363.8	448.0	502.7	République tchèque
Ireland	401.8	360.9	308.0	276.2	293.5	Irlande
Finland	277.9	208.0	200.0	244.9	223.5	Finlande
Belgium-Luxembourg	966.1	–	–	–	–	Belgique-Luxembourg
Portugal	114.4	193.5	186.3	193.0	220.4	Portugal
Poland	149.2	119.7	149.4	186.7	225.0	Pologne
Hungary	120.3	121.3	155.6	188.9	218.0	Hongrie
Brazil	125.2	144.3	178.0	164.5	e170.6	Brésil
Israel	192.5	160.1	162.8	143.3	116.6	Israël

(Value as percentages of World total) **(Valeur en pourcentage du total mondial)**

Regions of the world	1993	1994	1995	1996	1997	1998	1999	2000	2001	2002	Régions du monde
World	100.0	100.0	100.0	100.0	100.0	100.0	100.0	100.0	100.0	100.0	Monde
Africa	0.1	0.1	0.2	0.2	0.2	0.2	0.2	0.3	0.3	0.3	Afrique
Americas	19.4	19.5	18.4	18.9	21.9	22.3	22.3	23.4	22.4	21.0	Amériques
- Northern America	17.5	17.4	16.1	16.2	19.1	19.1	18.6	19.6	18.6	16.9	- Amérique du Nord
- LAIA	1.8	2.1	2.3	2.6	2.7	3.1	3.6	3.8	3.7	4.1	- ALAI
- CACM	0.0	0.0	0.0	0.0	0.0	0.0	0.0	0.0	0.1	0.0	- MCC
- Caribbean	0.0	0.0	0.0	0.0	0.1	0.1	0.1	0.0	0.1	0.0	- Caraïbes
- Rest of America	0.0	0.0	0.0	0.0	0.0	0.0	0.0	0.0	0.0	0.0	- Autre d'Amérique
Asia excluding former USSR	31.1	30.4	30.4	28.2	26.1	22.6	23.9	27.7	26.7	27.3	Asie ancienne URSS exclus
- Middle East	0.6	0.7	0.8	0.7	0.8	0.8	0.9	0.9	1.0	1.1	- Moyen-Orient
Asia former USSR	0.0	0.1	0.1	0.0	0.0	0.0	0.0	0.0	0.0	0.0	Asie ancienne URSS
Europe excluding former USSR	48.5	48.7	49.8	51.5	50.7	54.0	52.7	47.4	49.3	50.2	Europe ancienne URSS exclus
- European Union	45.2	45.3	46.2	47.9	46.9	49.7	48.5	43.3	45.0	45.6	- Union Européenne
- Eastern Europe	0.6	0.6	0.9	1.0	1.3	1.7	1.6	1.8	2.2	2.5	- Europe de l'Est
- Rest of Europe	2.7	2.7	2.7	2.5	2.4	2.6	2.5	2.3	2.2	2.2	- Autre de l'Europe
Europe former USSR	0.2	0.3	0.4	0.4	0.4	0.3	0.4	0.6	0.9	0.7	Europe ancienne URSS
Oceania	0.6	0.8	0.7	0.8	0.7	0.5	0.5	0.5	0.5	0.5	Océanie

742 Pumps for liquids; liquid elevators; and parts thereof, nes

TRADE BY COMMODITY (Value in million US dollars)
Imports by principal countries or areas

COMMERCE PAR PRODUIT (Valeur en millions de dollars EU)
Importations selon les principaux pays ou zones

Country or area	1998	1999	2000	2001	2002	Pays ou zone
World	19822.1	19883.0	20401.5	20579.8	21776.1	Monde
Africa	739.2	684.7	667.8	720.4	794.1	Afrique
Americas	5136.4	5262.4	5796.3	5615.6	5742.6	Amériques
- Northern America	3486.6	3707.7	4094.3	3960.1	4100.5	- Amérique du Nord
- LAIA	1441.2	1374.1	1520.0	1463.0	1456.3	- ALAI
- CACM	77.7	70.6	64.6	67.4	71.1	- MCC
- Caribbean	105.2	87.0	98.0	104.9	98.1	- Caraïbes
- Rest of America	25.8	23.0	19.4	20.2	16.7	- Autre d'Amérique
Asia excluding former USSR	3681.5	3861.8	4169.8	4271.0	4721.1	Asie ancienne URSS exclus
- Middle East	863.7	840.7	1010.3	999.1	1017.4	- Moyen-Orient
Asia former USSR	120.2	110.2	135.3	141.3	156.2	Asie ancienne URSS
Europe excluding former USSR	9464.6	9371.1	8987.6	9111.7	9584.6	Europe ancienne URSS exclus
- European Union	8314.6	8252.2	7673.2	7557.1	7911.7	- Union Européenne
- Eastern Europe	668.7	683.8	911.2	1124.6	1225.7	- Europe de l'Est
- Rest of Europe	481.3	435.1	403.2	430.0	447.2	- Autre de l'Europe
Europe former USSR	356.3	280.6	342.3	413.1	446.3	Europe ancienne URSS
Oceania	323.8	312.2	302.3	306.7	331.3	Océanie
United States	2477.4	2547.1	2793.9	2679.4	2882.3	Etats-Unis d'Amérique
Germany	1685.8	1736.0	1581.3	1627.9	1683.3	Allemagne
France-Monaco	1693.6	1625.1	1441.5	1361.3	1583.9	France-Monaco
Canada	1008.0	1159.4	1299.1	1279.0	1216.1	Canada
United Kingdom	1222.7	1140.9	1080.1	1088.0	1081.9	Royaume-Uni
Italy-San Marino-Holy See	920.0	947.9	872.6	771.8	824.6	Italie-Saint-Marin-Saint-Siège
Spain	618.8	684.8	668.0	617.5	544.8	Espagne
Mexico	448.0	504.2	711.6	630.8	634.7	Mexique
Korea, Republic of	408.5	645.1	488.0	558.7	716.7	République de Corée
China	354.4	410.9	465.8	570.5	776.1	Chine
Japan	378.2	393.3	445.6	450.7	448.0	Japon
Netherlands	386.5	408.6	354.8	386.6	410.5	Pays-Bas
Belgium	–	442.7	439.6	472.3	e518.0	Belgique
Sweden	411.8	374.3	358.7	332.2	358.2	Suède
Singapore	333.6	350.8	374.7	347.9	355.8	Singapour
Poland	171.7	210.4	384.1	476.1	495.1	Pologne
Austria	326.3	283.1	261.2	301.3	314.6	Autriche
Indonesia	241.2	196.5	296.0	266.5	281.3	Indonésie
Brazil	280.8	226.7	234.5	246.8	252.9	Brésil
Russian Federation	223.7	181.4	232.8	297.2	304.1	Fédération de Russie
Australia	253.2	241.4	236.3	238.4	259.6	Australie
Czech Republic	191.1	183.8	215.4	267.1	287.3	République tchèque
Hungary	173.9	180.5	200.1	259.6	302.3	Hongrie
Denmark	220.6	227.9	235.6	223.1	200.6	Danemark
Switzerland-Liechtenstein	208.8	194.5	203.5	207.4	199.5	Suisse-Liechtenstein
Turkey	236.0	184.9	206.8	161.7	215.6	Turquie
Saudi Arabia	189.8	198.7	208.6	180.6	e186.9	Arabie saoudite
Venezuela	178.9	217.3	152.9	172.3	e144.9	Venezuela
Thailand	111.0	125.2	188.3	203.1	e211.6	Thaïlande
China, Hong Kong SAR	162.6	140.8	161.9	149.3	148.0	Chine - RAS de Hong-Kong

(Value as percentages of World total) **(Valeur en pourcentage du total mondial)**

Regions of the world	1993	1994	1995	1996	1997	1998	1999	2000	2001	2002	Régions du monde
World	100.0	100.0	100.0	100.0	100.0	100.0	100.0	100.0	100.0	100.0	Monde
Africa	4.6	4.5	3.7	3.9	3.7	3.7	3.4	3.3	3.5	3.6	Afrique
Americas	23.6	23.5	21.8	21.8	24.4	25.9	26.5	28.4	27.3	26.4	Amériques
- Northern America	16.4	17.1	15.7	15.6	17.1	17.6	18.6	20.1	19.2	18.8	- Amérique du Nord
- LAIA	6.1	5.6	5.4	5.4	6.4	7.3	6.9	7.5	7.1	6.7	- ALAI
- CACM	0.3	0.3	0.3	0.3	0.3	0.4	0.4	0.3	0.3	0.3	- MCC
- Caribbean	0.6	0.3	0.3	0.3	0.5	0.5	0.4	0.5	0.5	0.5	- Caraïbes
- Rest of America	0.4	0.2	0.1	0.1	0.1	0.1	0.1	0.1	0.1	0.1	- Autre d'Amérique
Asia excluding former USSR	25.2	23.7	22.9	23.1	22.1	18.6	19.4	20.4	20.8	21.7	Asie ancienne URSS exclus
- Middle East	6.2	4.9	3.9	3.8	4.2	4.4	4.2	5.0	4.9	4.7	- Moyen-Orient
Asia former USSR	0.2	0.4	0.6	0.6	0.4	0.6	0.6	0.7	0.7	0.7	Asie ancienne URSS
Europe excluding former USSR	42.0	44.0	47.1	46.4	45.3	47.7	47.1	44.1	44.3	44.0	Europe ancienne URSS exclus
- European Union	37.5	39.6	42.0	41.4	40.4	41.9	41.5	37.6	36.7	36.3	- Union Européenne
- Eastern Europe	1.8	1.8	2.2	2.6	2.8	3.4	3.4	4.5	5.5	5.6	- Europe de l'Est
- Rest of Europe	2.7	2.6	2.9	2.5	2.1	2.4	2.2	2.0	2.1	2.1	- Autre de l'Europe
Europe former USSR	2.8	2.0	2.1	2.2	2.4	1.8	1.4	1.7	2.0	2.0	Europe ancienne URSS
Oceania	1.6	1.8	1.8	1.9	1.7	1.6	1.6	1.5	1.5	1.5	Océanie

Pompes, moto- et turbo-pompes pour liquides; élévateurs à liquides; pièces détachées 742

TRADE BY COMMODITY (Value in million US dollars)
Exports by principal countries or areas

COMMERCE PAR PRODUIT (Valeur en millions de dollars EU)
Exportations selon les principaux pays ou zones

Country or area	1998	1999	2000	2001	2002	Pays ou zone
World	19116.7	19082.6	19469.2	19719.8	20953.6	Monde
Africa	55.6	113.5	50.7	67.2	59.2	Afrique
Americas	3831.7	3862.0	4336.8	4438.6	4394.1	Amériques
- Northern America	3356.2	3384.3	3778.3	3885.3	3806.2	- Amérique du Nord
- LAIA	470.7	472.4	552.6	545.9	578.1	- ALAI
- CACM	1.0	1.3	1.9	2.3	4.6	- MCC
- Caribbean	3.3	3.7	3.6	4.3	4.6	- Caraïbes
- Rest of America	0.5	0.2	0.4	0.8	0.6	- Autre d'Amérique
Asia excluding former USSR	2378.9	2585.1	3045.5	2968.8	3220.6	Asie ancienne URSS exclus
- Middle East	74.8	86.8	109.1	122.0	138.0	- Moyen-Orient
Asia former USSR	83.6	145.5	7.8	7.5	6.0	Asie ancienne URSS
Europe excluding former USSR	12524.8	12144.3	11720.9	11946.5	12962.1	Europe ancienne URSS exclus
- European Union	11592.7	11289.0	10846.1	10784.2	11612.6	- Union Européenne
- Eastern Europe	420.0	340.1	426.4	632.0	784.6	- Europe de l'Est
- Rest of Europe	512.1	515.1	448.4	530.3	564.9	- Autre de l'Europe
Europe former USSR	162.8	141.3	217.1	200.9	214.8	Europe ancienne URSS
Oceania	79.2	90.9	90.3	90.3	97.0	Océanie
Germany	4811.3	4769.6	4651.9	4500.7	4632.5	Allemagne
United States	2963.6	2948.5	3270.1	3347.3	3248.2	Etats-Unis d'Amérique
Japan	1575.5	1734.4	1906.6	1749.4	1846.0	Japon
Italy-San Marino-Holy See	1595.6	1719.1	1679.6	1783.7	1999.9	Italie-Saint-Marin-Saint-Siège
France-Monaco	1499.0	1416.3	1314.1	1282.9	1446.8	France-Monaco
United Kingdom	1325.0	1032.8	1001.5	955.2	968.8	Royaume-Uni
Canada	392.6	435.7	508.3	538.0	558.0	Canada
Denmark	451.6	444.3	453.7	467.4	525.4	Danemark
Sweden	406.4	405.3	370.7	356.2	398.0	Suède
Spain	387.9	413.5	350.6	339.0	433.1	Espagne
Netherlands	362.4	363.2	336.0	342.3	407.9	Pays-Bas
Czech Republic	278.2	226.4	271.3	426.6	529.4	République tchèque
China	169.8	186.7	279.6	353.4	473.2	Chine
Switzerland-Liechtenstein	295.7	301.8	277.7	290.0	295.6	Suisse-Liechtenstein
Austria	276.7	265.9	234.6	263.6	266.7	Autriche
Mexico	175.3	194.8	250.9	288.5	317.0	Mexique
Brazil	245.5	226.7	239.6	183.8	e190.5	Brésil
Belgium	–	248.9	237.7	262.8	e294.8	Belgique
Singapore	179.4	172.0	194.6	212.4	219.1	Singapour
Norway	178.5	176.2	131.8	198.4	222.5	Norvège
Korea, Republic of	86.1	100.7	147.3	125.3	136.6	République de Corée
Hungary	80.3	55.2	78.6	120.5	156.3	Hongrie
Finland	100.3	95.4	92.8	98.2	100.6	Finlande
Ireland	89.2	88.6	97.8	102.6	107.7	Irlande
Russian Federation	70.4	66.9	104.1	101.7	107.3	Fédération de Russie
China, Hong Kong SAR	89.6	77.9	100.4	86.3	90.3	Chine - RAS de Hong-Kong
Australia	71.9	84.0	81.8	82.1	85.7	Australie
India	65.8	56.4	77.8	96.3	83.9	Inde
Ukraine	48.2	45.7	75.9	56.9	62.7	Ukraine
Belgium-Luxembourg	259.7	–	–	–	–	Belgique-Luxembourg

(Value as percentages of World total) **(Valeur en pourcentage du total mondial)**

Regions of the world	1993	1994	1995	1996	1997	1998	1999	2000	2001	2002	Régions du monde
World	100.0	100.0	100.0	100.0	100.0	100.0	100.0	100.0	100.0	100.0	Monde
Africa	0.3	0.2	0.3	0.3	0.3	0.3	0.6	0.3	0.3	0.3	Afrique
Americas	19.6	18.7	17.2	17.8	20.7	20.0	20.2	22.3	22.5	21.0	Amériques
- Northern America	17.6	16.6	15.0	15.4	18.0	17.6	17.7	19.4	19.7	18.2	- Amérique du Nord
- LAIA	2.0	2.1	2.1	2.3	2.7	2.5	2.5	2.8	2.8	2.8	- ALAI
- CACM	0.0	0.0	0.0	0.0	0.0	0.0	0.0	0.0	0.0	0.0	- MCC
- Caribbean	0.0	0.0	0.0	0.0	0.0	0.0	0.0	0.0	0.0	0.0	- Caraïbes
- Rest of America	0.0	0.0	0.0	0.0	0.0	0.0	0.0	0.0	0.0	0.0	- Autre d'Amérique
Asia excluding former USSR	19.0	18.2	17.5	15.6	14.5	12.4	13.5	15.6	15.1	15.4	Asie ancienne URSS exclus
- Middle East	0.4	0.4	0.3	0.3	0.4	0.4	0.5	0.6	0.6	0.7	- Moyen-Orient
Asia former USSR	0.1	0.1	0.7	0.5	0.4	0.4	0.8	0.0	0.0	0.0	Asie ancienne URSS
Europe excluding former USSR	60.1	61.4	63.0	64.3	62.6	65.5	63.6	60.2	60.6	61.9	Europe ancienne URSS exclus
- European Union	56.5	57.9	58.9	60.3	58.4	60.6	59.2	55.7	54.7	55.4	- Union Européenne
- Eastern Europe	0.9	0.9	1.2	1.2	1.6	2.2	1.8	2.2	3.2	3.7	- Europe de l'Est
- Rest of Europe	2.7	2.6	2.9	2.8	2.5	2.7	2.7	2.3	2.7	2.7	- Autre de l'Europe
Europe former USSR	0.5	0.9	1.0	1.1	1.1	0.9	0.7	1.1	1.0	1.0	Europe ancienne URSS
Oceania	0.5	0.5	0.5	0.5	0.5	0.4	0.5	0.5	0.5	0.5	Océanie

743 Pumps, compressors; centrifuges; filtering apparatus; etc, parts

TRADE BY COMMODITY (Value in million US dollars)
Imports by principal countries or areas

COMMERCE PAR PRODUIT (Valeur en millions de dollars EU)
Importations selon les principaux pays ou zones

Country or area	1998	1999	2000	2001	2002	Pays ou zone
World	36987.9	38149.5	41165.4	43272.0	44797.3	Monde
Africa	1219.5	1084.9	856.8	958.5	1036.1	Afrique
Americas	10159.1	11396.6	12816.8	13103.2	12667.2	Amériques
- Northern America	6839.4	7736.4	8862.9	8618.2	9064.5	- Amérique du Nord
- LAIA	3028.8	3396.2	3685.3	4183.1	3304.0	- ALAI
- CACM	106.5	89.6	90.4	101.0	114.4	- MCC
- Caribbean	157.8	149.1	152.7	178.5	162.2	- Caraïbes
- Rest of America	26.7	25.3	25.5	22.5	22.0	- Autre d'Amérique
Asia excluding former USSR	8225.3	8449.4	9666.0	10092.9	11236.9	Asie ancienne URSS exclus
- Middle East	1399.0	1296.7	1454.5	1410.0	1699.0	- Moyen-Orient
Asia former USSR	149.9	136.3	208.4	180.3	200.1	Asie ancienne URSS
Europe excluding former USSR	15778.1	15875.8	16399.7	17640.3	18019.1	Europe ancienne URSS exclus
- European Union	13472.0	13610.3	14149.6	15114.0	15300.9	- Union Européenne
- Eastern Europe	1261.4	1286.8	1400.1	1669.9	1744.6	- Europe de l'Est
- Rest of Europe	1044.7	978.7	850.1	856.4	973.7	- Autre de l'Europe
Europe former USSR	626.5	462.8	510.3	629.4	821.7	Europe ancienne URSS
Oceania	829.5	743.8	707.3	667.4	816.1	Océanie
United States	4781.9	5393.3	6230.0	6174.0	6739.2	Etats-Unis d'Amérique
Germany	3040.4	3042.9	3109.1	3456.9	3217.3	Allemagne
Canada	2055.9	2340.3	2630.7	2439.6	2320.3	Canada
France-Monaco	1956.9	2030.7	2186.4	2281.7	2383.0	France-Monaco
Mexico	1246.5	1659.8	2170.9	2605.6	1831.1	Mexique
United Kingdom	1951.6	1751.5	1829.3	1959.6	1960.4	Royaume-Uni
China	1026.3	1339.1	1433.1	2031.5	2572.5	Chine
Italy-San Marino-Holy See	1394.6	1596.7	1699.4	1714.5	1748.8	Italie-Saint-Marin-Saint-Siège
Japan	1106.9	1127.8	1213.4	1212.4	1230.0	Japon
Spain	1126.1	1132.4	1108.0	1117.2	1224.7	Espagne
Belgium	-	1085.3	1231.8	1279.3	e1403.0	Belgique
Korea, Republic of	606.3	744.1	1067.2	1027.3	1212.9	République de Corée
Netherlands	655.4	667.8	689.4	861.9	833.9	Pays-Bas
Sweden	585.2	589.2	616.8	637.0	707.9	Suède
Australia	703.0	616.9	590.2	537.2	684.2	Australie
Singapore	540.6	553.1	708.5	609.0	585.9	Singapour
China, Hong Kong SAR	709.8	530.1	577.9	585.4	577.0	Chine - RAS de Hong-Kong
Austria	481.8	533.1	566.4	704.5	669.6	Autriche
Malaysia	378.7	461.6	494.9	688.1	e752.0	Malaisie
Brazil	580.5	447.8	525.1	568.7	603.5	Brésil
Poland	509.3	448.5	473.9	501.0	516.4	Pologne
Thailand	372.1	423.0	490.3	535.1	e557.5	Thaïlande
Switzerland-Liechtenstein	458.2	423.0	444.3	437.6	452.6	Suisse-Liechtenstein
Russian Federation	424.3	291.1	311.9	429.5	587.9	Fédération de Russie
Turkey	385.3	311.0	350.3	295.1	450.5	Turquie
Hungary	218.2	292.2	348.2	423.6	444.0	Hongrie
Denmark	359.4	351.2	327.8	314.0	347.7	Danemark
Saudi Arabia	340.7	419.5	323.1	279.1	e288.9	Arabie saoudite
Czech Republic	284.9	267.9	294.8	391.3	388.7	République tchèque
Indonesia	324.0	233.5	378.4	361.2	315.4	Indonésie

(Value as percentages of World total) **(Valeur en pourcentage du total mondial)**

Regions of the world	1993	1994	1995	1996	1997	1998	1999	2000	2001	2002	Régions du monde
World	100.0	100.0	100.0	100.0	100.0	100.0	100.0	100.0	100.0	100.0	Monde
Africa	3.6	3.3	3.2	3.1	2.9	3.3	2.8	2.1	2.2	2.3	Afrique
Americas	24.4	26.0	24.8	24.0	25.5	27.5	29.9	31.1	30.3	28.3	Amériques
- Northern America	17.0	18.5	17.9	17.0	17.5	18.5	20.3	21.5	19.9	20.2	- Amérique du Nord
- LAIA	6.7	7.0	6.4	6.5	7.4	8.2	8.9	9.0	9.7	7.4	- ALAI
- CACM	0.2	0.2	0.2	0.2	0.2	0.3	0.2	0.2	0.2	0.3	- MCC
- Caribbean	0.3	0.2	0.2	0.2	0.3	0.4	0.4	0.4	0.4	0.4	- Caraïbes
- Rest of America	0.1	0.1	0.1	0.1	0.1	0.1	0.1	0.1	0.1	0.0	- Autre d'Amérique
Asia excluding former USSR	30.1	28.1	28.7	28.9	27.3	22.2	22.1	23.5	23.3	25.1	Asie ancienne URSS exclus
- Middle East	4.9	4.1	3.9	3.7	3.6	3.8	3.4	3.5	3.3	3.8	- Moyen-Orient
Asia former USSR	0.1	0.2	0.3	0.3	0.2	0.4	0.4	0.5	0.4	0.4	Asie ancienne URSS
Europe excluding former USSR	38.1	38.2	39.0	39.5	39.2	42.7	41.6	39.8	40.8	40.2	Europe ancienne URSS exclus
- European Union	32.7	32.8	33.4	33.8	33.6	36.4	35.7	34.4	34.9	34.2	- Union Européenne
- Eastern Europe	2.6	2.5	2.7	3.1	3.1	3.4	3.4	3.4	3.9	3.9	- Europe de l'Est
- Rest of Europe	2.9	2.9	2.9	2.6	2.5	2.8	2.6	2.1	2.0	2.2	- Autre de l'Europe
Europe former USSR	1.6	2.0	1.9	1.9	2.7	1.7	1.2	1.2	1.5	1.8	Europe ancienne URSS
Oceania	2.2	2.3	2.2	2.2	2.2	2.2	1.9	1.7	1.5	1.8	Océanie

Pompes et compresseurs; ventilateurs; centrifigeuses; et leurs pièces détachées 743

TRADE BY COMMODITY (Value in million US dollars)
Exports by principal countries or areas

COMMERCE PAR PRODUIT (Valeur en millions de dollars EU)
Exportations selon les principaux pays ou zones

Country or area	1998	1999	2000	2001	2002	Pays ou zone
World	35364.8	36711.3	39823.7	40783.6	43080.1	Monde
Africa	349.0	559.6	791.0	802.8	1011.6	Afrique
Americas	8397.3	8906.4	10143.4	10523.1	10360.4	Amériques
- Northern America	7222.2	7566.0	8560.5	8893.7	8468.0	- Amérique du Nord
- LAIA	1167.7	1331.4	1575.8	1617.7	1879.1	- ALAI
- CACM	4.1	4.8	3.7	4.1	6.2	- MCC
- Caribbean	3.1	4.1	3.2	6.9	6.8	- Caraïbes
- Rest of America	0.1	0.2	0.2	0.6	0.4	- Autre d'Amérique
Asia excluding former USSR	6757.0	7110.7	8346.7	7868.7	8592.4	Asie ancienne URSS exclus
- Middle East	94.6	99.3	107.1	120.1	139.2	- Moyen-Orient
Asia former USSR	11.3	6.0	10.7	11.3	10.0	Asie ancienne URSS
Europe excluding former USSR	19526.6	19855.4	20119.8	21102.9	22687.9	Europe ancienne URSS exclus
- European Union	18079.6	18498.5	18789.5	19625.6	20954.5	- Union Européenne
- Eastern Europe	322.0	326.7	382.5	505.6	658.9	- Europe de l'Est
- Rest of Europe	1125.1	1030.2	947.8	971.7	1074.5	- Autre de l'Europe
Europe former USSR	176.4	152.0	263.8	338.3	286.9	Europe ancienne URSS
Oceania	147.2	121.2	148.3	136.5	130.9	Océanie
United States	6326.8	6600.2	7490.1	7755.1	7237.5	Etats-Unis d'Amérique
Germany	5672.7	5800.6	5790.0	6464.5	6806.6	Allemagne
Japan	3784.8	4036.0	4650.8	4142.5	4305.2	Japon
Italy-San Marino-Holy See	2931.2	3181.8	3060.3	2937.2	3077.1	Italie-Saint-Marin-Saint-Siège
France-Monaco	2648.3	2647.2	2508.7	2482.5	2781.8	France-Monaco
United Kingdom	2331.1	2199.0	2355.5	2320.1	2296.8	Royaume-Uni
Belgium	–	1514.6	2090.5	2168.2	e2432.6	Belgique
Canada	895.4	965.7	1070.4	1138.5	1230.4	Canada
Mexico	572.5	746.7	915.6	961.5	1207.8	Mexique
Switzerland-Liechtenstein	881.2	809.1	733.5	747.5	804.9	Suisse-Liechtenstein
Netherlands	695.5	671.4	653.7	761.5	819.6	Pays-Bas
Korea, Republic of	667.2	650.0	708.3	717.6	804.3	République de Corée
Sweden	602.0	567.5	554.2	568.3	620.6	Suède
Brazil	529.0	500.9	539.4	517.7	e536.7	Brésil
Austria	522.8	518.4	450.5	519.8	607.6	Autriche
Spain	485.3	489.9	528.9	532.6	576.9	Espagne
China, Hong Kong SAR	528.7	441.6	512.8	486.4	555.9	Chine - RAS de Hong-Kong
South Africa	–	–	769.9	775.2	980.3	Afrique du Sud
Singapore	428.0	425.8	485.4	446.1	530.2	Singapour
China	232.4	275.2	371.6	494.9	655.1	Chine
Denmark	432.4	430.1	360.0	376.0	393.9	Danemark
Belgium-Luxembourg	1392.0	–	–	–	–	Belgique-Luxembourg
Thailand	161.9	231.7	308.5	299.9	e316.7	Thaïlande
Malaysia	188.5	215.6	245.0	227.8	e241.4	Malaisie
Ireland	146.3	187.8	171.2	189.8	212.2	Irlande
Finland	177.8	164.2	154.9	199.4	209.0	Finlande
Southern African Customs Union	329.1	492.3	–	–	–	Union douanière d'Afrique australe
Czech Republic	137.3	128.6	131.5	174.2	234.7	République tchèque
Slovenia	130.3	121.6	125.0	133.8	167.3	Slovénie
Russian Federation	85.9	72.2	155.7	147.2	79.0	Fédération de Russie

(Value as percentages of World total) **(Valeur en pourcentage du total mondial)**

Regions of the world	1993	1994	1995	1996	1997	1998	1999	2000	2001	2002	Régions du monde
World	100.0	100.0	100.0	100.0	100.0	100.0	100.0	100.0	100.0	100.0	Monde
Africa	0.5	0.4	0.5	0.6	0.7	1.0	1.5	2.0	2.0	2.3	Afrique
Americas	22.1	22.5	21.1	22.0	24.9	23.7	24.3	25.5	25.8	24.0	Amériques
- Northern America	19.0	18.9	17.8	19.3	21.8	20.4	20.6	21.5	21.8	19.7	- Amérique du Nord
- LAIA	3.0	3.6	3.3	2.8	3.0	3.3	3.6	4.0	4.0	4.4	- ALAI
- CACM	0.0	0.0	0.0	0.0	0.0	0.0	0.0	0.0	0.0	0.0	- MCC
- Caribbean	0.0	0.0	0.0	0.0	0.0	0.0	0.0	0.0	0.0	0.0	- Caraïbes
- Rest of America	0.0	0.0	0.0	0.0	0.0	0.0	0.0	0.0	0.0	0.0	- Autre d'Amérique
Asia excluding former USSR	26.3	25.3	24.6	22.5	21.0	19.1	19.4	21.0	19.3	19.9	Asie ancienne URSS exclus
- Middle East	0.2	0.2	0.3	0.2	0.2	0.3	0.3	0.3	0.3	0.3	- Moyen-Orient
Asia former USSR	0.0	0.0	0.0	0.0	0.0	0.0	0.0	0.0	0.0	0.0	Asie ancienne URSS
Europe excluding former USSR	50.5	50.9	52.9	53.7	52.2	55.2	54.1	50.5	51.7	52.7	Europe ancienne URSS exclus
- European Union	46.8	47.1	48.9	49.6	48.5	51.1	50.4	47.2	48.1	48.6	- Union Européenne
- Eastern Europe	0.5	0.6	0.7	0.8	0.8	0.9	0.9	1.0	1.2	1.5	- Europe de l'Est
- Rest of Europe	3.2	3.2	3.3	3.4	2.9	3.2	2.8	2.4	2.4	2.5	- Autre de l'Europe
Europe former USSR	0.3	0.4	0.5	0.6	0.7	0.5	0.4	0.7	0.8	0.7	Europe ancienne URSS
Oceania	0.4	0.4	0.4	0.6	0.5	0.4	0.3	0.4	0.3	0.3	Océanie

744 Mechanical handling equipment, and parts thereof, nes

TRADE BY COMMODITY (Value in million US dollars)
Imports by principal countries or areas

COMMERCE PAR PRODUIT (Valeur en millions de dollars EU
Importations selon les principaux pays ou zones

Country or area	1998	1999	2000	2001	2002	Pays ou zone
World	36758.0	35136.5	36066.4	35906.7	36558.6	Monde
Africa	1143.7	936.1	978.7	1036.9	1078.7	Afrique
Americas	10361.7	10259.6	11054.8	10333.5	9846.0	Amériques
- Northern America	7665.2	7973.7	8764.9	7987.9	7951.6	- Amérique du Nord
- LAIA	2324.7	1978.9	1927.7	2012.2	1586.3	- ALAI
- CACM	142.9	91.9	92.0	80.2	86.2	- MCC
- Caribbean	182.2	158.0	198.4	220.1	197.4	- Caraïbes
- Rest of America	46.7	57.1	71.9	33.0	24.4	- Autre d'Amérique
Asia excluding former USSR	7629.6	6364.1	6908.1	6899.9	7552.4	Asie ancienne URSS exclus
- Middle East	1283.2	967.2	1186.4	1124.5	1389.6	- Moyen-Orient
Asia former USSR	173.8	143.8	102.3	145.4	145.4	Asie ancienne URSS
Europe excluding former USSR	15968.9	16243.7	15860.9	16253.2	16498.8	Europe ancienne URSS exclus
- European Union	13804.1	14293.0	13978.9	14264.4	14340.6	- Union Européenne
- Eastern Europe	943.0	807.1	811.9	834.7	938.1	- Europe de l'Est
- Rest of Europe	1221.9	1143.7	1070.1	1154.1	1220.2	- Autre de l'Europe
Europe former USSR	649.4	401.9	401.2	537.7	639.9	Europe ancienne URSS
Oceania	830.9	787.3	760.4	700.1	797.3	Océanie
United States	5988.6	6192.3	6834.5	6290.2	6218.7	Etats-Unis d'Amérique
Germany	2633.4	2581.5	2290.3	2587.8	2343.2	Allemagne
France-Monaco	2205.3	2336.1	2504.0	2567.6	2304.2	France-Monaco
United Kingdom	2342.2	2143.4	2137.7	1998.8	2139.4	Royaume-Uni
Canada	1669.4	1773.0	1925.1	1693.1	1726.8	Canada
China	1323.2	1342.4	1306.9	1504.0	1959.7	Chine
Italy-San Marino-Holy See	1033.7	1161.0	1183.3	1266.4	1312.2	Italie-Saint-Marin-Saint-Siège
Spain	984.3	1137.0	1036.8	1129.9	1313.1	Espagne
Belgium	–	1259.4	1296.0	1250.9	e1371.9	Belgique
Netherlands	947.8	1051.8	989.0	937.6	972.7	Pays-Bas
Singapore	994.4	881.0	925.6	832.5	797.3	Singapour
Mexico	758.2	865.7	926.6	892.0	725.1	Mexique
Austria	689.3	654.6	645.1	669.0	640.5	Autriche
Australia	660.4	642.3	592.4	543.6	593.7	Australie
Switzerland-Liechtenstein	526.1	531.7	538.7	602.7	600.5	Suisse-Liechtenstein
Sweden	502.8	565.7	549.3	515.6	529.5	Suède
Japan	547.0	445.5	494.5	544.5	520.8	Japon
China, Hong Kong SAR	691.5	447.6	454.0	439.5	412.3	Chine - RAS de Hong-Kong
Korea, Republic of	436.4	405.4	518.3	452.6	406.4	République de Corée
Brazil	503.1	354.1	322.3	434.9	350.7	Brésil
Norway	457.1	371.7	301.4	336.5	372.9	Norvège
Denmark	386.3	345.6	333.1	333.4	399.3	Danemark
Indonesia	577.6	260.8	333.8	289.8	303.8	Indonésie
Poland	443.5	334.4	338.3	318.7	320.3	Pologne
Russian Federation	435.1	234.5	242.3	358.0	422.7	Fédération de Russie
Malaysia	264.7	227.8	313.9	353.5	e386.3	Malaisie
Finland	268.3	286.8	297.5	319.1	300.5	Finlande
Portugal	272.5	293.0	322.7	289.4	275.1	Portugal
Saudi Arabia	272.2	236.4	273.7	299.2	e309.6	Arabie saoudite
Turkey	328.9	250.5	264.7	179.0	275.7	Turquie

(Value as percentages of World total) **(Valeur en pourcentage du total mondial)**

Regions of the world	1993	1994	1995	1996	1997	1998	1999	2000	2001	2002	Régions du monde
World	100.0	100.0	100.0	100.0	100.0	100.0	100.0	100.0	100.0	100.0	Monde
Africa	3.5	3.1	2.8	2.8	2.8	3.1	2.7	2.7	2.9	3.0	Afrique
Americas	21.6	23.0	21.9	20.8	24.6	28.2	29.2	30.7	28.8	26.9	Amériques
- Northern America	16.0	17.4	16.3	15.7	18.2	20.9	22.7	24.3	22.2	21.8	- Amérique du Nord
- LAIA	4.8	4.8	4.8	4.5	5.6	6.3	5.6	5.3	5.6	4.3	- ALAI
- CACM	0.2	0.2	0.2	0.2	0.2	0.4	0.3	0.3	0.2	0.2	- MCC
- Caribbean	0.4	0.3	0.4	0.4	0.4	0.5	0.4	0.6	0.6	0.5	- Caraïbes
- Rest of America	0.3	0.2	0.2	0.1	0.1	0.1	0.2	0.2	0.1	0.1	- Autre d'Amérique
Asia excluding former USSR	30.8	30.5	30.4	33.2	30.0	20.8	18.1	19.2	19.2	20.7	Asie ancienne URSS exclus
- Middle East	4.7	3.4	2.8	3.0	3.4	3.5	2.8	3.3	3.1	3.8	- Moyen-Orient
Asia former USSR	0.1	0.5	0.4	0.4	0.3	0.5	0.4	0.3	0.4	0.4	Asie ancienne URSS
Europe excluding former USSR	39.4	38.9	40.5	38.4	37.8	43.4	46.2	44.0	45.3	45.1	Europe ancienne URSS exclus
- European Union	34.6	34.1	35.1	33.2	32.8	37.6	40.7	38.8	39.7	39.2	- Union Européenne
- Eastern Europe	1.7	1.7	1.9	1.9	2.0	2.6	2.3	2.3	2.3	2.6	- Europe de l'Est
- Rest of Europe	3.1	3.1	3.5	3.3	3.0	3.3	3.3	3.0	3.2	3.3	- Autre de l'Europe
Europe former USSR	2.7	1.9	1.7	1.7	1.9	1.8	1.1	1.1	1.5	1.8	Europe ancienne URSS
Oceania	1.8	2.1	2.3	2.6	2.5	2.3	2.2	2.1	1.9	2.2	Océanie

Equipement mécanique de manutention; parties et pièces détachées, n.d.a 744

TRADE BY COMMODITY (Value in million US dollars)
Exports by principal countries or areas

COMMERCE PAR PRODUIT (Valeur en millions de dollars EU)
Exportations selon les principaux pays ou zones

Country or area	1998	1999	2000	2001	2002	Pays ou zone
World	36190.0	35122.4	36390.0	36335.5	37374.8	Monde
Africa	131.0	107.0	105.9	109.0	100.8	Afrique
Americas	7879.7	7564.4	8520.7	7899.4	7530.4	Amériques
- Northern America	7242.2	6951.8	7864.1	7258.2	6870.2	- Amérique du Nord
- LAIA	608.5	574.3	618.4	600.6	616.0	- ALAI
- CACM	4.6	9.0	6.4	3.2	4.2	- MCC
- Caribbean	22.9	25.0	27.7	32.2	35.7	- Caraïbes
- Rest of America	1.5	4.3	4.1	5.2	4.4	- Autre d'Amérique
Asia excluding former USSR	6262.7	5991.7	6640.3	6235.6	6711.9	Asie ancienne URSS exclus
- Middle East	150.7	147.2	217.2	190.9	198.5	- Moyen-Orient
Asia former USSR	20.8	31.3	19.6	15.9	11.8	Asie ancienne URSS
Europe excluding former USSR	21470.1	21063.8	20687.6	21639.7	22515.9	Europe ancienne URSS exclus
- European Union	19759.7	19378.2	19036.8	19878.2	20592.3	- Union Européenne
- Eastern Europe	770.8	778.4	835.9	966.4	1064.4	- Europe de l'Est
- Rest of Europe	939.7	907.2	814.8	795.1	859.2	- Autre de l'Europe
Europe former USSR	223.0	174.9	219.8	231.3	269.7	Europe ancienne URSS
Oceania	202.7	189.2	196.2	204.6	234.3	Océanie
Germany	5915.8	5545.0	5260.4	5808.0	5850.0	Allemagne
United States	5724.3	5246.2	5958.5	5597.0	5246.9	Etats-Unis d'Amérique
Japan	3465.9	3242.9	3576.3	3096.1	3256.0	Japon
Italy-San Marino-Holy See	2465.2	2518.2	2468.8	2576.0	2551.7	Italie-Saint-Marin-Saint-Siège
France-Monaco	2381.3	2313.2	2366.8	2378.8	2550.7	France-Monaco
United Kingdom	2364.5	2079.5	1999.6	2006.5	1942.5	Royaume-Uni
Canada	1517.8	1704.6	1905.5	1661.2	1623.3	Canada
Sweden	1439.0	1412.4	1471.9	1403.9	1496.7	Suède
Netherlands	1070.7	1098.1	1204.6	1195.0	1372.7	Pays-Bas
Austria	952.4	1094.1	1029.4	1055.2	1147.7	Autriche
China	578.6	596.6	846.8	1034.4	1307.3	Chine
Belgium	–	1010.5	1039.9	1073.5	e1204.5	Belgique
Finland	800.2	767.5	759.7	794.9	785.9	Finlande
Korea, Republic of	736.7	776.4	802.3	737.6	729.0	République de Corée
Spain	694.5	716.0	683.1	766.4	771.4	Espagne
Denmark	492.7	510.2	443.4	493.7	546.4	Danemark
Switzerland-Liechtenstein	519.2	491.1	451.5	423.7	412.4	Suisse-Liechtenstein
Singapore	453.9	437.4	452.7	455.2	429.3	Singapour
Mexico	380.3	396.4	440.3	424.3	439.7	Mexique
Czech Republic	274.7	269.5	284.7	323.6	374.8	République tchèque
Norway	275.5	266.4	214.5	202.7	274.1	Norvège
Poland	207.5	203.4	224.0	270.3	286.9	Pologne
China, Hong Kong SAR	261.0	217.1	186.4	193.5	236.0	Chine - RAS de Hong-Kong
Ireland	151.2	190.4	188.1	214.2	242.2	Irlande
Belgium-Luxembourg	951.5	–	–	–	–	Belgique-Luxembourg
Australia	167.9	160.6	165.7	173.4	207.8	Australie
Hungary	110.7	133.3	149.6	174.7	189.8	Hongrie
Slovenia	113.2	116.7	116.4	125.1	127.0	Slovénie
Brazil	118.0	104.2	116.7	101.9	e105.7	Brésil
Turkey	87.3	103.1	100.6	122.2	113.2	Turquie

(Value as percentages of World total) **(Valeur en pourcentage du total mondial)**

Regions of the world	1993	1994	1995	1996	1997	1998	1999	2000	2001	2002	Régions du monde
World	100.0	100.0	100.0	100.0	100.0	100.0	100.0	100.0	100.0	100.0	Monde
Africa	0.3	0.3	0.4	0.3	0.4	0.4	0.3	0.3	0.3	0.3	Afrique
Americas	19.0	18.6	18.0	18.8	21.1	21.8	21.5	23.4	21.7	20.1	Amériques
- Northern America	17.7	17.5	16.7	17.4	19.4	20.0	19.8	21.6	20.0	18.4	- Amérique du Nord
- LAIA	1.2	1.1	1.2	1.3	1.7	1.7	1.6	1.7	1.7	1.6	- ALAI
- CACM	0.0	0.0	0.0	0.0	0.0	0.0	0.0	0.0	0.0	0.0	- MCC
- Caribbean	0.0	0.0	0.0	0.0	0.0	0.1	0.1	0.1	0.1	0.1	- Caraïbes
- Rest of America	0.0	0.0	0.0	0.0	0.0	0.0	0.0	0.0	0.0	0.0	- Autre d'Amérique
Asia excluding former USSR	22.6	23.7	22.9	22.6	22.0	17.3	17.1	18.2	17.2	18.0	Asie ancienne URSS exclus
- Middle East	0.4	0.5	0.4	0.4	0.6	0.4	0.4	0.6	0.5	0.5	- Moyen-Orient
Asia former USSR	0.0	0.1	0.1	0.1	0.1	0.1	0.1	0.1	0.0	0.0	Asie ancienne URSS
Europe excluding former USSR	57.1	56.2	57.5	56.7	55.1	59.3	60.0	56.8	59.6	60.2	Europe ancienne URSS exclus
- European Union	52.6	52.1	53.1	52.2	50.8	54.6	55.2	52.3	54.7	55.1	- Union Européenne
- Eastern Europe	1.5	1.1	1.4	1.7	1.8	2.1	2.2	2.3	2.7	2.8	- Europe de l'Est
- Rest of Europe	3.0	2.9	3.0	2.8	2.5	2.6	2.6	2.2	2.2	2.3	- Autre de l'Europe
Europe former USSR	0.2	0.5	0.5	0.6	0.6	0.6	0.5	0.6	0.6	0.7	Europe ancienne URSS
Oceania	0.7	0.7	0.6	0.8	0.8	0.6	0.5	0.5	0.6	0.6	Océanie

745 Other non-electric machinery, tools and mechanical apparatus, nes

TRADE BY COMMODITY (Value in million US dollars)
Imports by principal countries or areas

COMMERCE PAR PRODUIT (Valeur en millions de dollars EU)
Importations selon les principaux pays ou zones

Country or area	1998	1999	2000	2001	2002	Pays ou zone
World	23505.5	22686.9	22905.2	23197.3	24844.0	Monde
Africa	741.7	755.3	698.7	692.0	761.5	Afrique
Americas	6611.8	6475.1	6837.6	6786.2	6900.7	Amériques
- Northern America	4162.5	4385.6	4674.4	4697.7	5029.9	- Amérique du Nord
- LAIA	2203.8	1862.6	1924.2	1855.2	1619.0	- ALAI
- CACM	121.4	101.3	110.4	107.4	123.9	- MCC
- Caribbean	96.2	92.3	99.2	100.5	104.5	- Caraïbes
- Rest of America	27.9	33.3	29.4	25.5	23.5	- Autre d'Amérique
Asia excluding former USSR	3809.8	3644.9	4271.5	4283.2	4789.9	Asie ancienne URSS exclus
- Middle East	693.1	627.8	683.7	661.5	791.3	- Moyen-Orient
Asia former USSR	61.9	46.1	66.7	67.1	63.6	Asie ancienne URSS
Europe excluding former USSR	11000.8	10765.8	10042.2	10247.6	11081.3	Europe ancienne URSS exclus
- European Union	8990.0	8918.7	8435.5	8647.8	9203.8	- Union Européenne
- Eastern Europe	1077.7	952.3	782.1	817.1	934.9	- Europe de l'Est
- Rest of Europe	933.1	894.7	824.6	782.7	942.7	- Autre de l'Europe
Europe former USSR	732.0	452.7	432.7	600.5	689.7	Europe ancienne URSS
Oceania	547.5	547.0	556.0	520.7	557.1	Océanie
United States	3087.8	3338.9	3606.0	3654.2	3913.8	Etats-Unis d'Amérique
France-Monaco	1553.1	1602.3	1512.4	1465.1	1506.0	France-Monaco
Germany	1510.3	1511.9	1384.4	1514.4	1523.9	Allemagne
United Kingdom	1426.4	1325.0	1286.0	1285.1	1421.3	Royaume-Uni
Canada	1072.6	1043.8	1066.0	1041.1	1112.6	Canada
Mexico	823.5	893.4	1054.3	982.9	922.9	Mexique
Italy-San Marino-Holy See	816.3	825.1	800.0	794.7	837.8	Italie-Saint-Marin-Saint-Siège
China	572.8	601.4	708.0	893.0	1095.1	Chine
Spain	622.4	702.0	645.7	750.5	831.1	Espagne
Japan	561.3	581.7	624.6	597.4	625.3	Japon
Belgium	–	713.4	682.4	735.6	e806.8	Belgique
Netherlands	495.6	529.3	484.1	474.4	524.6	Pays-Bas
Switzerland-Liechtenstein	478.5	480.6	449.5	423.2	513.3	Suisse-Liechtenstein
Australia	439.0	434.6	452.7	407.1	427.4	Australie
Poland	530.2	430.3	343.5	294.0	332.9	Pologne
Austria	440.6	346.0	334.7	364.4	404.1	Autriche
Russian Federation	470.0	319.5	290.2	367.7	421.4	Fédération de Russie
Sweden	368.2	377.0	355.3	365.9	401.5	Suède
Brazil	497.2	359.3	323.4	323.8	276.8	Brésil
China, Hong Kong SAR	353.7	301.7	354.2	322.4	346.9	Chine - RAS de Hong-Kong
Korea, Republic of	224.9	221.0	336.2	312.7	352.8	République de Corée
Denmark	278.2	257.6	308.7	250.7	283.6	Danemark
Turkey	318.4	221.3	217.5	144.3	203.4	Turquie
Singapore	178.9	187.6	215.8	238.3	234.4	Singapour
Thailand	146.5	162.7	209.2	235.3	e245.2	Thaïlande
Malaysia	182.0	177.2	209.0	199.0	e217.5	Malaisie
Norway	222.4	199.2	183.6	170.8	200.1	Norvège
Argentina	293.1	215.5	185.0	159.1	e70.4	Argentine
Finland	197.9	178.4	165.8	174.5	180.5	Finlande
Portugal	176.5	189.4	181.5	174.7	170.2	Portugal

(Value as percentages of World total) **(Valeur en pourcentage du total mondial)**

Regions of the world	1993	1994	1995	1996	1997	1998	1999	2000	2001	2002	Régions du monde
World	100.0	100.0	100.0	100.0	100.0	100.0	100.0	100.0	100.0	100.0	Monde
Africa	3.2	3.1	3.0	3.4	3.2	3.2	3.3	3.1	3.0	3.1	Afrique
Americas	24.1	25.7	24.1	23.5	26.5	28.1	28.5	29.9	29.3	27.8	Amériques
- Northern America	15.6	16.2	15.1	15.2	16.6	17.7	19.3	20.4	20.3	20.2	- Amérique du Nord
- LAIA	7.6	8.9	8.1	7.6	8.9	9.4	8.2	8.4	8.0	6.5	- ALAI
- CACM	0.4	0.3	0.4	0.3	0.5	0.5	0.4	0.5	0.5	0.5	- MCC
- Caribbean	0.4	0.2	0.3	0.3	0.4	0.4	0.4	0.4	0.4	0.4	- Caraïbes
- Rest of America	0.1	0.1	0.2	0.1	0.1	0.1	0.1	0.1	0.1	0.1	- Autre d'Amérique
Asia excluding former USSR	22.4	20.9	22.0	23.6	20.9	16.2	16.1	18.6	18.5	19.3	Asie ancienne URSS exclus
- Middle East	3.5	2.9	2.6	2.6	2.8	2.9	2.8	3.0	2.9	3.2	- Moyen-Orient
Asia former USSR	0.1	0.7	0.2	0.2	0.1	0.3	0.2	0.3	0.3	0.3	Asie ancienne URSS
Europe excluding former USSR	45.6	45.1	45.9	44.5	44.0	46.8	47.5	43.8	44.2	44.6	Europe ancienne URSS exclus
- European Union	38.0	37.8	37.8	36.7	36.0	38.2	39.3	36.8	37.3	37.0	- Union Européenne
- Eastern Europe	3.6	3.4	3.8	4.1	4.2	4.6	4.2	3.4	3.5	3.8	- Europe de l'Est
- Rest of Europe	4.0	3.9	4.3	3.7	3.7	4.0	3.9	3.6	3.4	3.8	- Autre de l'Europe
Europe former USSR	2.0	2.0	2.2	2.2	2.8	3.1	2.0	1.9	2.6	2.8	Europe ancienne URSS
Oceania	2.6	2.6	2.6	2.5	2.6	2.3	2.4	2.4	2.2	2.2	Océanie

Autres machines, appareils et outils, non électriques; et leurs parties et pièces détachées 745

TRADE BY COMMODITY (Value in million US dollars)
Exports by principal countries or areas

COMMERCE PAR PRODUIT (Valeur en millions de dollars EU)
Exportations selon les principaux pays ou zones

Country or area	1998	1999	2000	2001	2002	Pays ou zone
World	23992.3	23028.8	23065.3	23351.9	25392.3	Monde
Africa	69.5	66.7	49.5	60.4	72.4	Afrique
Americas	4300.2	4348.4	4911.2	4737.6	4547.9	Amériques
- Northern America	3896.6	3836.8	4303.7	4161.4	3997.7	- Amérique du Nord
- LAIA	389.4	496.1	585.7	558.2	528.7	- ALAI
- CACM	12.5	12.8	19.6	15.0	17.1	- MCC
- Caribbean	1.5	2.7	2.1	2.6	3.8	- Caraïbes
- Rest of America	0.1	0.0	0.0	0.4	0.7	- Autre d'Amérique
Asia excluding former USSR	2823.4	3005.8	3406.3	3201.9	3694.7	Asie ancienne URSS exclus
- Middle East	44.9	48.1	69.1	105.3	106.4	- Moyen-Orient
Asia former USSR	2.2	2.3	1.7	7.9	6.9	Asie ancienne URSS
Europe excluding former USSR	16634.3	15429.3	14508.3	15161.9	16891.7	Europe ancienne URSS exclus
- European Union	15308.6	14157.6	13256.2	13904.9	15466.6	- Union Européenne
- Eastern Europe	261.2	248.0	297.2	302.8	340.2	- Europe de l'Est
- Rest of Europe	1064.6	1023.7	954.9	954.2	1085.0	- Autre de l'Europe
Europe former USSR	63.1	72.2	86.8	71.7	71.4	Europe ancienne URSS
Oceania	99.6	104.1	101.5	110.5	107.3	Océanie
Germany	5779.3	5393.5	4921.6	5328.2	5940.9	Allemagne
Italy-San Marino-Holy See	3968.7	3733.9	3581.7	3730.8	4090.2	Italie-Saint-Marin-Saint-Siège
United States	3412.5	3334.8	3776.5	3627.5	3450.5	Etats-Unis d'Amérique
Japan	1261.0	1419.3	1477.0	1187.3	1204.0	Japon
United Kingdom	1280.7	1090.4	960.8	997.8	1053.1	Royaume-Uni
Switzerland-Liechtenstein	920.9	871.6	810.2	793.6	900.5	Suisse-Liechtenstein
France-Monaco	920.3	840.8	773.4	717.1	860.4	France-Monaco
Sweden	792.1	718.6	666.6	661.4	807.4	Suède
Netherlands	556.4	590.3	541.3	564.6	616.2	Pays-Bas
Canada	483.9	501.9	527.1	533.9	547.1	Canada
Spain	414.6	445.0	438.2	505.1	534.3	Espagne
Denmark	450.9	415.3	404.5	388.5	462.5	Danemark
Belgium	–	475.4	503.5	491.4	e551.3	Belgique
China	176.7	246.6	353.2	457.1	745.2	Chine
China, Hong Kong SAR	314.5	310.7	384.6	343.1	402.9	Chine - RAS de Hong-Kong
Mexico	180.0	326.3	429.0	376.1	343.2	Mexique
Austria	377.6	223.6	224.3	236.5	295.9	Autriche
Finland	174.9	131.6	150.0	170.9	160.9	Finlande
Singapore	146.3	138.8	145.2	137.6	161.2	Singapour
Czech Republic	115.6	122.7	127.3	130.7	152.0	République tchèque
Korea, Republic of	98.4	99.9	124.7	145.2	159.0	République de Corée
Brazil	136.1	105.2	94.3	118.9	e123.2	Brésil
Belgium-Luxembourg	509.3	–	–	–	–	Belgique-Luxembourg
Norway	90.3	92.2	87.6	89.0	105.7	Norvège
Israel	151.7	80.2	57.3	60.9	70.2	Israël
Australia	66.6	69.0	66.4	75.8	76.6	Australie
Hungary	44.4	48.9	70.1	73.0	69.0	Hongrie
Poland	69.6	47.8	58.5	56.5	69.4	Pologne
Malaysia	37.0	43.1	59.3	55.9	e59.3	Malaisie
Argentina	52.2	44.5	46.5	42.7	e41.3	Argentine

(Value as percentages of World total) **(Valeur en pourcentage du total mondial)**

Regions of the world	1993	1994	1995	1996	1997	1998	1999	2000	2001	2002	Régions du monde
World	100.0	100.0	100.0	100.0	100.0	100.0	100.0	100.0	100.0	100.0	Monde
Africa	0.2	0.2	0.2	0.2	0.3	0.3	0.3	0.2	0.3	0.3	Afrique
Americas	16.7	16.9	15.7	16.1	18.2	17.9	18.9	21.3	20.3	17.9	Amériques
- Northern America	15.1	15.4	14.4	14.7	16.4	16.2	16.7	18.7	17.8	15.7	- Amérique du Nord
- LAIA	1.6	1.5	1.3	1.3	1.7	1.6	2.2	2.5	2.4	2.1	- ALAI
- CACM	0.0	0.0	0.0	0.0	0.0	0.1	0.1	0.1	0.1	0.1	- MCC
- Caribbean	0.0	0.0	0.0	0.0	0.0	0.0	0.0	0.0	0.0	0.0	- Caraïbes
- Rest of America	0.0	0.0	0.0	0.0	0.0	0.0	0.0	0.0	0.0	0.0	- Autre d'Amérique
Asia excluding former USSR	16.6	14.4	14.3	13.9	13.3	11.8	13.1	14.8	13.7	14.6	Asie ancienne URSS exclus
- Middle East	0.1	0.2	0.1	0.2	0.2	0.2	0.2	0.3	0.5	0.4	- Moyen-Orient
Asia former USSR	0.0	0.0	0.0	0.0	0.0	0.0	0.0	0.0	0.0	0.0	Asie ancienne URSS
Europe excluding former USSR	66.0	67.9	69.1	69.0	67.3	69.3	67.0	62.9	64.9	66.5	Europe ancienne URSS exclus
- European Union	60.4	62.0	63.3	63.5	62.0	63.8	61.5	57.5	59.5	60.9	- Union Européenne
- Eastern Europe	0.5	0.4	0.6	0.7	0.9	1.1	1.1	1.3	1.3	1.3	- Europe de l'Est
- Rest of Europe	5.0	5.4	5.1	4.8	4.5	4.4	4.4	4.1	4.1	4.3	- Autre de l'Europe
Europe former USSR	0.1	0.2	0.2	0.3	0.4	0.3	0.3	0.4	0.3	0.3	Europe ancienne URSS
Oceania	0.4	0.4	0.5	0.5	0.6	0.4	0.5	0.4	0.5	0.4	Océanie

749 Non-electric parts and accessories of machinery, nes

TRADE BY COMMODITY (Value in million US dollars)
Imports by principal countries or areas

COMMERCE PAR PRODUIT (Valeur en millions de dollars EU)
Importations selon les principaux pays ou zones

Country or area	1998	1999	2000	2001	2002	Pays ou zone
World	65345.3	65443.7	69181.9	68765.1	72365.0	Monde
Africa	1799.2	1693.5	1618.5	1591.3	1799.8	Afrique
Americas	19862.8	20595.8	22721.2	21459.6	21327.1	Amériques
- Northern America	14019.6	14946.7	15911.2	14631.4	15247.6	- Amérique du Nord
- LAIA	5451.5	5298.5	6435.7	6448.1	5684.5	- ALAI
- CACM	151.3	142.2	148.7	152.2	176.0	- MCC
- Caribbean	207.6	176.7	187.8	190.9	186.2	- Caraïbes
- Rest of America	32.8	31.6	37.8	37.1	32.9	- Autre d'Amérique
Asia excluding former USSR	13393.2	14067.1	16029.7	15962.9	17501.9	Asie ancienne URSS exclus
- Middle East	2328.4	1908.0	2203.6	2322.4	2472.5	- Moyen-Orient
Asia former USSR	105.3	139.0	181.6	197.5	205.4	Asie ancienne URSS
Europe excluding former USSR	28365.0	27350.3	26989.6	27800.0	29580.1	Europe ancienne URSS exclus
- European Union	24121.2	23331.1	22931.3	23466.9	24791.6	- Union Européenne
- Eastern Europe	2282.2	2185.1	2363.4	2621.1	2985.1	- Europe de l'Est
- Rest of Europe	1961.6	1834.1	1694.9	1712.1	1803.4	- Autre de l'Europe
Europe former USSR	647.3	478.2	560.4	733.0	795.0	Europe ancienne URSS
Oceania	1172.6	1120.0	1080.8	1020.9	1155.7	Océanie
United States	10280.3	11080.9	11863.0	10998.9	11675.0	Etats-Unis d'Amérique
Germany	5751.2	5767.2	5611.1	6089.0	6191.9	Allemagne
Canada	3738.1	3862.9	4043.2	3626.6	3566.5	Canada
France-Monaco	3517.4	3319.7	3329.1	3308.8	3500.3	France-Monaco
Mexico	2501.4	2986.9	3990.0	3864.0	3334.5	Mexique
United Kingdom	3040.7	2847.6	2898.0	2933.7	3199.8	Royaume-Uni
Italy-San Marino-Holy See	2867.2	2747.0	2701.0	2672.7	2690.9	Italie-Saint-Marin-Saint-Siège
China	1543.4	2185.9	2507.8	2959.7	3671.2	Chine
Japan	1821.7	1880.2	2049.7	2010.6	2092.0	Japon
Korea, Republic of	1174.5	1371.1	1604.3	1474.7	1609.5	République de Corée
Spain	1363.2	1360.5	1335.2	1372.0	1585.5	Espagne
Singapore	1289.8	1419.8	1499.2	1336.6	1381.4	Singapour
Belgium	–	1716.9	1680.5	1676.6	e1838.8	Belgique
Austria	1347.1	1248.6	1189.3	1221.8	1275.4	Autriche
Netherlands	1238.9	1235.2	1191.4	1224.5	1279.9	Pays-Bas
Brazil	1287.3	1002.8	1090.5	1215.4	1203.1	Brésil
Sweden	1189.8	1148.2	1120.3	1060.2	1163.3	Suède
China, Hong Kong SAR	924.7	900.8	1082.7	1098.5	1229.4	Chine - RAS de Hong-Kong
Thailand	779.0	896.0	1119.9	1097.1	e1143.0	Thaïlande
Switzerland-Liechtenstein	987.2	947.0	960.5	937.9	911.0	Suisse-Liechtenstein
Australia	1003.7	946.6	923.7	867.5	989.3	Australie
Malaysia	623.5	817.9	847.5	906.4	e990.6	Malaisie
Poland	647.4	607.8	700.9	744.8	834.6	Pologne
Czech Republic	593.8	562.2	622.3	746.0	859.7	République tchèque
Hungary	628.0	639.2	640.5	668.3	768.6	Hongrie
Denmark	569.8	613.9	558.4	613.0	714.0	Danemark
India	618.2	554.3	531.0	584.2	640.5	Inde
Turkey	669.5	529.9	596.1	481.7	642.0	Turquie
Saudi Arabia	579.2	587.8	514.5	517.8	e535.8	Arabie saoudite
Norway	646.1	578.6	437.9	459.1	531.9	Norvège

(Value as percentages of World total) **(Valeur en pourcentage du total mondial)**

Regions of the world	1993	1994	1995	1996	1997	1998	1999	2000	2001	2002	Régions du monde
World	100.0	100.0	100.0	100.0	100.0	100.0	100.0	100.0	100.0	100.0	Monde
Africa	4.3	3.4	3.5	3.2	3.0	2.8	2.6	2.3	2.3	2.5	Afrique
Americas	25.4	27.9	26.3	26.0	28.4	30.4	31.5	32.8	31.2	29.5	Amériques
- Northern America	18.6	21.4	20.1	19.3	20.4	21.5	22.8	23.0	21.3	21.1	- Amérique du Nord
- LAIA	6.1	6.1	5.8	6.2	7.5	8.3	8.1	9.3	9.4	7.9	- ALAI
- CACM	0.2	0.2	0.2	0.2	0.2	0.2	0.2	0.2	0.2	0.2	- MCC
- Caribbean	0.4	0.2	0.2	0.3	0.3	0.3	0.3	0.3	0.3	0.3	- Caraïbes
- Rest of America	0.1	0.1	0.1	0.1	0.0	0.1	0.0	0.1	0.1	0.0	- Autre d'Amérique
Asia excluding former USSR	28.5	25.1	24.5	25.6	24.6	20.5	21.5	23.2	23.2	24.2	Asie ancienne URSS exclus
- Middle East	6.2	3.9	3.5	3.5	3.7	3.6	2.9	3.2	3.4	3.4	- Moyen-Orient
Asia former USSR	0.1	0.2	0.2	0.3	0.1	0.2	0.2	0.3	0.3	0.3	Asie ancienne URSS
Europe excluding former USSR	38.5	40.5	42.7	42.0	40.8	43.4	41.8	39.0	40.4	40.9	Europe ancienne URSS exclus
- European Union	33.9	35.9	37.6	36.7	35.1	36.9	35.7	33.1	34.1	34.3	- Union Européenne
- Eastern Europe	1.7	1.7	2.1	2.4	2.9	3.5	3.3	3.4	3.8	4.1	- Europe de l'Est
- Rest of Europe	2.9	2.9	3.1	2.9	2.8	3.0	2.8	2.4	2.5	2.5	- Autre de l'Europe
Europe former USSR	1.2	0.8	0.8	0.9	1.0	1.0	0.7	0.8	1.1	1.1	Europe ancienne URSS
Oceania	2.0	2.1	1.9	2.1	2.0	1.8	1.7	1.6	1.5	1.6	Océanie

TRADE BY COMMODITY (Value in million US dollars)
Exports by principal countries or areas

COMMERCE PAR PRODUIT (Valeur en millions de dollars EU)
Exportations selon les principaux pays ou zones

Country or area	1998	1999	2000	2001	2002	Pays ou zone
World	62765.5	62768.6	65929.0	65737.8	69669.7	Monde
Africa	149.4	142.1	131.7	131.5	136.7	Afrique
Americas	11009.0	11589.9	12849.3	12463.8	12928.6	Amériques
- Northern America	9135.3	9398.3	10356.1	10078.4	10184.0	- Amérique du Nord
- LAIA	1863.8	2182.7	2476.8	2366.5	2723.4	- ALAI
- CACM	5.5	4.6	9.2	9.9	13.3	- MCC
- Caribbean	4.3	4.1	6.9	7.7	7.2	- Caraïbes
- Rest of America	0.1	0.3	0.3	1.3	0.7	- Autre d'Amérique
Asia excluding former USSR	14054.0	15494.9	18430.6	17248.0	18521.6	Asie ancienne URSS exclus
- Middle East	155.9	183.2	212.1	242.0	283.0	- Moyen-Orient
Asia former USSR	28.4	12.2	27.9	29.2	30.4	Asie ancienne URSS
Europe excluding former USSR	36948.0	34979.2	33708.0	34816.6	37339.3	Europe ancienne URSS exclus
- European Union	33917.5	32008.9	30422.8	31313.5	33332.8	- Union Européenne
- Eastern Europe	1374.8	1330.2	1551.3	1844.2	2182.4	- Europe de l'Est
- Rest of Europe	1655.7	1640.1	1733.9	1658.8	1824.0	- Autre de l'Europe
Europe former USSR	390.7	334.9	593.6	857.2	527.0	Europe ancienne URSS
Oceania	185.9	215.4	187.9	191.6	186.2	Océanie
Germany	11814.7	11458.3	10992.7	11634.4	12337.4	Allemagne
Japan	7896.7	8605.4	9866.2	8590.3	8690.4	Japon
United States	6975.6	7078.8	7990.9	7753.8	7684.2	Etats-Unis d'Amérique
Italy-San Marino-Holy See	6428.8	6005.1	5740.9	5914.6	6109.9	Italie-Saint-Marin-Saint-Siège
France-Monaco	4238.3	3976.4	3586.9	3493.2	3827.1	France-Monaco
United Kingdom	3525.2	3028.6	2837.3	2754.7	2801.1	Royaume-Uni
Canada	2159.7	2319.5	2365.1	2324.6	2499.7	Canada
China	1172.7	1488.5	2094.8	2487.2	3143.7	Chine
Mexico	1307.0	1669.4	1875.7	1807.1	2155.2	Mexique
Switzerland-Liechtenstein	1278.0	1234.1	1305.7	1236.8	1270.8	Suisse-Liechtenstein
Singapore	1087.1	1260.4	1372.2	1248.8	1313.9	Singapour
Belgium	–	1597.1	1512.9	1464.2	e1642.8	Belgique
Spain	1225.0	1152.4	1076.7	1199.8	1324.4	Espagne
Austria	1174.1	1031.7	1021.5	1037.4	1117.5	Autriche
Korea, Republic of	782.8	920.1	1146.3	1179.4	1222.5	République de Corée
Sweden	1102.2	1047.6	976.5	919.2	1032.7	Suède
Netherlands	936.0	916.4	965.8	916.7	1056.4	Pays-Bas
China, Hong Kong SAR	604.3	622.5	713.5	733.2	906.8	Chine - RAS de Hong-Kong
Denmark	689.5	647.4	582.9	755.8	765.2	Danemark
Czech Republic	494.0	430.9	467.6	576.7	664.5	République tchèque
Portugal	364.7	395.3	399.6	436.5	462.9	Portugal
Brazil	385.3	360.8	429.9	381.2	e395.2	Brésil
Belgium-Luxembourg	1946.7	–	–	–	–	Belgique-Luxembourg
Poland	300.6	299.8	371.1	412.0	527.6	Pologne
Thailand	309.5	353.6	421.3	399.5	e421.9	Thaïlande
Russian Federation	208.3	205.5	411.8	658.5	322.9	Fédération de Russie
Finland	358.6	344.1	270.7	333.6	395.0	Finlande
Hungary	198.6	206.4	241.7	291.0	353.3	Hongrie
Luxembourg	–	293.7	323.4	332.3	e339.7	Luxembourg
Slovakia	183.2	196.1	244.7	305.3	357.4	Slovaquie

(Value as percentages of World total) **(Valeur en pourcentage du total mondial)**

Regions of the world	1993	1994	1995	1996	1997	1998	1999	2000	2001	2002	Régions du monde
World	100.0	100.0	100.0	100.0	100.0	100.0	100.0	100.0	100.0	100.0	Monde
Africa	0.2	0.2	0.2	0.2	0.2	0.2	0.2	0.2	0.2	0.2	Afrique
Americas	15.4	17.3	14.5	14.9	17.1	17.5	18.5	19.5	19.0	18.6	Amériques
- Northern America	13.1	14.9	12.4	12.8	14.3	14.6	15.0	15.7	15.3	14.6	- Amérique du Nord
- LAIA	2.2	2.3	2.1	2.1	2.7	3.0	3.5	3.8	3.6	3.9	- ALAI
- CACM	0.0	0.0	0.0	0.0	0.0	0.0	0.0	0.0	0.0	0.0	- MCC
- Caribbean	0.0	0.0	0.0	0.0	0.0	0.0	0.0	0.0	0.0	0.0	- Caraïbes
- Rest of America	0.0	0.0	0.0	0.0	0.0	0.0	0.0	0.0	0.0	0.0	- Autre d'Amérique
Asia excluding former USSR	28.2	26.8	27.0	25.9	25.2	22.4	24.7	28.0	26.2	26.6	Asie ancienne URSS exclus
- Middle East	0.2	0.2	0.2	0.2	0.3	0.2	0.3	0.3	0.4	0.4	- Moyen-Orient
Asia former USSR	0.0	0.1	0.1	0.1	0.1	0.0	0.0	0.0	0.0	0.0	Asie ancienne URSS
Europe excluding former USSR	55.6	54.7	57.2	57.8	56.4	58.9	55.7	51.1	53.0	53.6	Europe ancienne URSS exclus
- European Union	51.5	50.6	52.6	53.2	52.1	54.0	51.0	46.1	47.6	47.8	- Union Européenne
- Eastern Europe	1.4	1.4	1.7	1.8	1.8	2.2	2.1	2.4	2.8	3.1	- Europe de l'Est
- Rest of Europe	2.7	2.7	2.9	2.8	2.4	2.6	2.6	2.6	2.5	2.6	- Autre de l'Europe
Europe former USSR	0.2	0.6	0.6	0.7	0.7	0.6	0.5	0.9	1.3	0.8	Europe ancienne URSS
Oceania	0.4	0.4	0.4	0.4	0.4	0.3	0.3	0.3	0.3	0.3	Océanie

751 Office machines

TRADE BY COMMODITY (Value in million US dollars)
Imports by principal countries or areas

COMMERCE PAR PRODUIT (Valeur en millions de dollars EU)
Importations selon les principaux pays ou zones

Country or area	1998	1999	2000	2001	2002	Pays ou zone
World	15560.9	14276.4	13900.2	12951.6	12247.6	Monde
Africa	300.4	311.9	282.5	275.8	288.9	Afrique
Americas	5883.9	4525.1	4062.4	3340.7	3091.6	Amériques
- Northern America	5073.3	3917.5	3485.9	2765.6	2650.9	- Amérique du Nord
- LAIA	710.8	506.5	485.4	487.3	356.9	- ALAI
- CACM	45.1	44.2	42.0	41.8	40.5	- MCC
- Caribbean	42.6	45.6	39.7	39.1	36.5	- Caraïbes
- Rest of America	12.2	11.3	9.5	6.9	6.9	- Autre d'Amérique
Asia excluding former USSR	2792.7	3015.7	3510.0	3258.3	3043.6	Asie ancienne URSS exclus
- Middle East	375.7	335.3	396.8	331.6	352.7	- Moyen-Orient
Asia former USSR	24.4	15.1	22.6	17.0	18.3	Asie ancienne URSS
Europe excluding former USSR	6121.6	5998.7	5600.0	5665.8	5385.7	Europe ancienne URSS exclus
- European Union	5439.8	5365.8	4985.1	5107.3	4839.2	- Union Européenne
- Eastern Europe	316.3	285.0	278.0	249.4	247.2	- Europe de l'Est
- Rest of Europe	365.5	347.9	337.0	309.1	299.3	- Autre de l'Europe
Europe former USSR	114.8	77.9	77.3	101.9	96.5	Europe ancienne URSS
Oceania	323.0	332.1	345.4	292.0	323.0	Océanie
United States	4580.4	3449.4	3006.7	2309.3	2241.7	Etats-Unis d'Amérique
Germany	1199.8	1185.1	1132.8	1103.4	924.9	Allemagne
China, Hong Kong SAR	957.0	907.8	1061.9	1085.8	944.2	Chine - RAS de Hong-Kong
France-Monaco	839.8	788.4	757.9	803.6	848.7	France-Monaco
Netherlands	782.8	815.4	791.4	755.4	670.8	Pays-Bas
United Kingdom	671.6	625.0	619.5	636.1	649.9	Royaume-Uni
Japan	513.2	496.5	539.4	445.2	383.6	Japon
Italy-San Marino-Holy See	490.0	486.0	450.1	447.4	454.5	Italie-Saint-Marin-Saint-Siège
Canada	484.9	459.1	477.6	453.9	406.3	Canada
Singapore	352.0	359.6	449.0	387.2	256.0	Singapour
Spain	370.7	369.6	307.7	387.4	311.3	Espagne
China	119.9	269.2	359.9	307.6	317.8	Chine
Australia	248.1	265.7	289.3	240.9	269.0	Australie
Belgium	-	328.2	245.3	264.5	e290.1	Belgique
Mexico	253.6	189.3	227.1	250.1	161.8	Mexique
Switzerland-Liechtenstein	191.2	201.4	189.4	156.5	154.4	Suisse-Liechtenstein
Korea, Republic of	78.7	183.7	194.5	181.8	250.4	République de Corée
Sweden	162.7	134.5	142.8	117.2	146.3	Suède
Austria	159.1	142.2	124.1	137.4	124.0	Autriche
Turkey	151.2	151.1	174.9	84.4	113.4	Turquie
Denmark	138.6	138.1	120.1	113.6	107.7	Danemark
Poland	154.3	131.6	120.2	99.6	72.3	Pologne
Norway	117.6	99.6	100.1	102.7	89.4	Norvège
Finland	109.5	103.8	75.2	89.2	75.7	Finlande
United Arab Emirates	67.1	70.3	85.0	81.2	e83.3	Emirates arabes unis
Greece	65.2	77.3	67.1	81.8	e90.5	Grèce
Brazil	105.4	63.3	68.5	76.0	66.6	Brésil
Portugal	79.7	86.3	64.7	75.6	69.0	Portugal
Argentina	144.1	108.5	63.2	37.6	e16.6	Argentine
Ireland	68.9	69.4	73.4	82.2	62.4	Irlande

(Value as percentages of World total) **(Valeur en pourcentage du total mondial)**

Regions of the world	1993	1994	1995	1996	1997	1998	1999	2000	2001	2002	Régions du monde
World	100.0	100.0	100.0	100.0	100.0	100.0	100.0	100.0	100.0	100.0	Monde
Africa	1.8	1.8	1.7	1.9	1.9	1.9	2.2	2.0	2.1	2.4	Afrique
Americas	33.4	34.9	33.4	34.4	36.2	37.8	31.7	29.2	25.8	25.2	Amériques
- Northern America	28.3	29.3	28.7	29.9	31.0	32.6	27.4	25.1	21.4	21.6	- Amérique du Nord
- LAIA	4.5	5.1	4.1	4.0	4.6	4.6	3.5	3.5	3.8	2.9	- ALAI
- CACM	0.2	0.2	0.2	0.2	0.3	0.3	0.3	0.3	0.3	0.3	- MCC
- Caribbean	0.3	0.2	0.3	0.2	0.2	0.3	0.3	0.3	0.3	0.3	- Caraïbes
- Rest of America	0.1	0.1	0.1	0.1	0.1	0.1	0.1	0.1	0.1	0.1	- Autre d'Amérique
Asia excluding former USSR	18.2	18.1	19.3	20.9	20.6	17.9	21.1	25.3	25.2	24.9	Asie ancienne URSS exclus
- Middle East	2.1	1.7	1.6	1.8	1.9	2.4	2.3	2.9	2.6	2.9	- Moyen-Orient
Asia former USSR	0.0	0.1	0.2	0.1	0.1	0.2	0.1	0.2	0.1	0.1	Asie ancienne URSS
Europe excluding former USSR	43.0	42.0	42.4	39.8	38.3	39.3	42.0	40.3	43.7	44.0	Europe ancienne URSS exclus
- European Union	38.6	37.8	38.1	35.5	34.3	35.0	37.6	35.9	39.4	39.5	- Union Européenne
- Eastern Europe	1.9	1.7	1.8	1.9	1.8	2.0	2.0	2.0	1.9	2.0	- Europe de l'Est
- Rest of Europe	2.4	2.4	2.5	2.4	2.2	2.3	2.4	2.4	2.4	2.4	- Autre de l'Europe
Europe former USSR	1.4	0.7	0.8	0.8	0.8	0.7	0.5	0.6	0.8	0.8	Europe ancienne URSS
Oceania	2.2	2.4	2.2	2.1	2.1	2.1	2.3	2.5	2.3	2.6	Océanie

TRADE BY COMMODITY (Value in million US dollars)
Exports by principal countries or areas

COMMERCE PAR PRODUIT (Valeur en millions de dollars EU)
Exportations selon les principaux pays ou zones

Country or area	1998	1999	2000	2001	2002	Pays ou zone
World	14838.6	14240.4	14412.0	13598.9	11230.0	Monde
Africa	10.1	8.0	7.2	9.0	9.6	Afrique
Americas	1831.0	1563.8	1709.9	1747.9	1239.5	Amériques
- Northern America	1395.9	1230.1	1391.4	1392.3	999.4	- Amérique du Nord
- LAIA	433.1	329.8	316.0	354.2	238.9	- ALAI
- CACM	1.4	3.3	0.8	0.9	0.6	- MCC
- Caribbean	0.6	0.6	1.7	0.5	0.6	- Caraïbes
- Rest of America	0.0	0.0	0.0	0.1	0.1	- Autre d'Amérique
Asia excluding former USSR	7425.0	7754.8	8167.7	7504.4	5569.2	Asie ancienne URSS exclus
- Middle East	27.6	31.0	40.0	57.4	53.9	- Moyen-Orient
Asia former USSR	0.8	0.5	0.5	0.5	0.7	Asie ancienne URSS
Europe excluding former USSR	5539.5	4875.9	4492.9	4293.9	4365.0	Europe ancienne URSS exclus
- European Union	5279.1	4626.5	4274.7	4057.9	4156.3	- Union Européenne
- Eastern Europe	36.3	27.6	36.4	32.4	38.8	- Europe de l'Est
- Rest of Europe	224.1	221.9	181.8	203.5	169.9	- Autre de l'Europe
Europe former USSR	14.6	12.3	12.9	16.8	20.5	Europe ancienne URSS
Oceania	17.6	25.1	20.9	26.4	25.4	Océanie
Japan	3256.9	3733.0	3553.0	2687.1	624.8	Japon
China	1297.5	1304.0	1550.2	1734.3	2166.6	Chine
China, Hong Kong SAR	1427.8	1346.0	1434.4	1526.8	1316.1	Chine - RAS de Hong-Kong
Netherlands	1218.1	1226.0	989.4	988.1	1055.1	Pays-Bas
United States	1232.0	1078.1	1198.6	1148.5	757.3	Etats-Unis d'Amérique
Germany	1345.8	1022.9	961.0	933.5	1079.2	Allemagne
United Kingdom	1277.7	1115.2	1159.4	946.7	760.9	Royaume-Uni
France-Monaco	534.6	429.0	381.1	360.6	522.9	France-Monaco
Singapore	469.6	371.3	435.8	380.8	278.4	Singapour
Mexico	410.9	303.7	292.4	336.4	221.4	Mexique
Korea, Republic of	206.1	212.4	321.8	299.4	254.3	République de Corée
Thailand	313.6	243.5	269.2	215.5	e227.6	Thaïlande
Malaysia	132.3	178.3	231.4	227.7	e241.3	Malaisie
Italy-San Marino-Holy See	250.0	198.1	214.7	195.1	151.1	Italie-Saint-Marin-Saint-Siège
Canada	163.9	151.9	192.6	243.8	242.1	Canada
Switzerland-Liechtenstein	184.5	176.4	124.9	157.3	111.6	Suisse-Liechtenstein
Belgium	–	201.3	164.3	181.8	e204.0	Belgique
Sweden	144.9	131.8	129.2	146.7	137.3	Suède
Spain	104.4	141.9	87.2	101.4	100.6	Espagne
Ireland	43.4	64.1	50.9	68.0	31.6	Irlande
Belgium-Luxembourg	256.0	–	–	–	–	Belgique-Luxembourg
Philippines	40.5	31.2	47.2	90.8	45.0	Philippines
Norway	37.3	44.1	55.7	44.4	55.0	Norvège
Austria	44.8	41.5	47.4	48.7	47.8	Autriche
Denmark	20.1	26.2	69.4	60.1	44.3	Danemark
Israel	1.7	24.3	37.4	44.2	83.9	Israël
Indonesia	35.5	35.8	25.2	20.3	41.3	Indonésie
United Arab Emirates	18.3	18.9	26.9	43.5	e45.3	Emirates arabes unis
Australia	15.0	22.3	18.7	24.6	22.6	Australie
Finland	33.7	17.6	10.8	15.2	12.9	Finlande

(Value as percentages of World total) **(Valeur en pourcentage du total mondial)**

Regions of the world	1993	1994	1995	1996	1997	1998	1999	2000	2001	2002	Régions du monde
World	100.0	100.0	100.0	100.0	100.0	100.0	100.0	100.0	100.0	100.0	Monde
Africa	0.2	0.1	0.1	0.1	0.1	0.1	0.1	0.0	0.1	0.1	Afrique
Americas	10.9	10.4	10.3	11.4	11.3	12.3	11.0	11.9	12.9	11.0	Amériques
- Northern America	8.2	7.2	7.4	8.5	8.7	9.4	8.6	9.7	10.2	8.9	- Amérique du Nord
- LAIA	2.7	3.1	2.8	2.9	2.6	2.9	2.3	2.2	2.6	2.1	- ALAI
- CACM	0.0	0.0	0.0	0.0	0.0	0.0	0.0	0.0	0.0	0.0	- MCC
- Caribbean	0.0	0.0	0.0	0.0	0.0	0.0	0.0	0.0	0.0	0.0	- Caraïbes
- Rest of America	0.0	0.0	0.0	0.0	0.0	0.0	0.0	0.0	0.0	0.0	- Autre d'Amérique
Asia excluding former USSR	54.0	52.5	50.5	50.7	52.4	50.0	54.5	56.7	55.2	49.6	Asie ancienne URSS exclus
- Middle East	0.2	0.2	0.2	0.2	0.2	0.2	0.2	0.3	0.4	0.5	- Moyen-Orient
Asia former USSR	0.0	0.0	0.0	0.0	0.0	0.0	0.0	0.0	0.0	0.0	Asie ancienne URSS
Europe excluding former USSR	34.8	36.7	38.9	37.5	36.0	37.3	34.2	31.2	31.6	38.9	Europe ancienne URSS exclus
- European Union	33.5	35.5	37.3	35.7	34.5	35.6	32.5	29.7	29.8	37.0	- Union Européenne
- Eastern Europe	0.4	0.2	0.2	0.3	0.2	0.2	0.2	0.3	0.2	0.3	- Europe de l'Est
- Rest of Europe	0.9	0.9	1.3	1.5	1.3	1.5	1.6	1.3	1.5	1.5	- Autre de l'Europe
Europe former USSR	0.0	0.1	0.1	0.1	0.1	0.1	0.1	0.1	0.1	0.2	Europe ancienne URSS
Oceania	0.1	0.1	0.2	0.2	0.2	0.1	0.2	0.1	0.2	0.2	Océanie

752 Automatic data processing machines and units thereof

TRADE BY COMMODITY (Value in million US dollars)
Imports by principal countries or areas

COMMERCE PAR PRODUIT (Valeur en millions de dollars EU)
Importations selon les principaux pays ou zones

Country or area	1998	1999	2000	2001	2002	Pays ou zone
World	179232.2	197921.0	219759.7	199989.1	199257.8	Monde
Africa	1636.4	1571.2	1585.2	1591.2	1621.8	Afrique
Americas	57391.9	63401.9	71956.5	63044.8	64718.1	Amériques
- Northern America	51758.0	57303.9	64739.5	55069.7	57176.1	- Amérique du Nord
- LAIA	5133.3	5562.5	6614.8	7321.6	6859.2	- ALAI
- CACM	217.7	232.9	276.8	272.2	305.4	- MCC
- Caribbean	218.2	219.3	239.7	306.4	295.8	- Caraïbes
- Rest of America	64.7	83.3	85.7	74.8	81.5	- Autre d'Amérique
Asia excluding former USSR	31186.1	39941.8	52064.3	46576.8	47998.1	Asie ancienne URSS exclus
- Middle East	1245.5	1397.4	1801.1	1445.4	1604.8	- Moyen-Orient
Asia former USSR	104.6	93.6	130.9	134.9	144.4	Asie ancienne URSS
Europe excluding former USSR	85179.9	88961.3	89756.4	84959.4	80663.4	Europe ancienne URSS exclus
- European Union	78082.0	81207.8	81974.4	76880.0	71965.9	- Union Européenne
- Eastern Europe	2537.7	2551.7	2724.0	3410.7	4212.4	- Europe de l'Est
- Rest of Europe	4560.2	5201.7	5058.0	4668.8	4485.1	- Autre de l'Europe
Europe former USSR	492.0	475.6	503.2	758.2	902.2	Europe ancienne URSS
Oceania	3241.3	3475.6	3763.3	2923.9	3210.0	Océanie
United States	44825.0	50115.2	57064.7	48492.2	51012.8	Etats-Unis d'Amérique
Germany	16857.3	17430.8	16892.1	16964.9	15588.8	Allemagne
United Kingdom	14996.7	15586.1	16742.5	14597.8	13687.4	Royaume-Uni
Netherlands	14157.8	15635.9	14923.1	14177.3	12713.6	Pays-Bas
Japan	9825.6	12514.6	17459.5	15038.0	14332.6	Japon
France-Monaco	9579.1	8920.1	9393.0	8054.8	7873.2	France-Monaco
Canada	6891.9	7142.4	7662.7	6561.1	6144.8	Canada
China, Hong Kong SAR	5546.3	5613.4	6258.0	6448.6	6846.7	Chine - RAS de Hong-Kong
Singapore	5395.7	5257.4	6363.4	5423.2	4413.3	Singapour
Italy-San Marino-Holy See	4362.3	4965.4	5163.5	4699.0	4544.9	Italie-Saint-Marin-Saint-Siège
Ireland	5023.0	4579.0	4986.6	4535.6	3437.6	Irlande
China	1821.3	3253.3	4516.4	4981.0	6733.3	Chine
Mexico	1794.2	2507.1	3291.5	4224.5	4524.3	Mexique
Switzerland-Liechtenstein	2928.8	3488.9	3503.8	3105.7	2860.0	Suisse-Liechtenstein
Belgium	–	3522.6	3690.6	3840.4	e4211.8	Belgique
Australia	2752.0	2962.6	3255.6	2495.4	2713.4	Australie
Spain	2484.8	2694.3	2905.9	2858.7	2690.5	Espagne
Korea, Republic of	1022.3	2265.6	3814.8	3039.8	3174.9	République de Corée
Sweden	2812.9	2263.7	2087.5	2136.1	2080.4	Suède
Austria	1299.9	1609.2	1383.2	1414.7	1460.1	Autriche
Denmark	1223.4	1496.4	1550.7	1261.0	1471.8	Danemark
Malaysia	914.3	1045.6	920.0	1640.2	e1792.5	Malaisie
Poland	979.4	1102.1	1133.5	1092.7	1035.2	Pologne
Norway	1126.7	1162.6	1034.5	994.7	978.1	Norvège
Finland	1175.2	1117.5	952.9	954.5	904.9	Finlande
Czech Republic	697.6	637.1	726.3	1140.5	1579.6	République tchèque
Brazil	1020.8	856.9	1078.8	1005.6	701.5	Brésil
Israel	617.0	771.5	958.3	764.4	738.4	Israël
Turkey	697.7	782.8	1097.3	539.1	671.2	Turquie
Thailand	281.3	367.0	618.1	1038.7	e1082.2	Thaïlande

(Value as percentages of World total) **(Valeur en pourcentage du total mondial)**

Regions of the world	1993	1994	1995	1996	1997	1998	1999	2000	2001	2002	Régions du monde
World	100.0	100.0	100.0	100.0	100.0	100.0	100.0	100.0	100.0	100.0	Monde
Africa	1.0	1.0	1.0	0.9	0.8	0.9	0.8	0.7	0.8	0.8	Afrique
Americas	34.4	34.6	31.9	32.0	33.6	32.0	32.0	32.7	31.5	32.5	Amériques
- Northern America	31.2	31.2	29.1	29.3	30.6	28.9	29.0	29.5	27.5	28.7	- Amérique du Nord
- LAIA	2.9	3.2	2.6	2.5	2.8	2.9	2.8	3.0	3.7	3.4	- ALAI
- CACM	0.1	0.1	0.1	0.1	0.1	0.1	0.1	0.1	0.1	0.2	- MCC
- Caribbean	0.1	0.1	0.1	0.1	0.1	0.1	0.1	0.1	0.2	0.1	- Caraïbes
- Rest of America	0.0	0.0	0.0	0.0	0.0	0.0	0.0	0.0	0.0	0.0	- Autre d'Amérique
Asia excluding former USSR	15.7	16.7	18.9	21.2	20.4	17.4	20.2	23.7	23.3	24.1	Asie ancienne URSS exclus
- Middle East	0.9	0.6	0.7	0.6	0.7	0.7	0.7	0.8	0.7	0.8	- Moyen-Orient
Asia former USSR	0.0	0.0	0.0	0.1	0.0	0.1	0.0	0.1	0.1	0.1	Asie ancienne URSS
Europe excluding former USSR	46.3	45.1	45.7	43.4	42.8	47.5	44.9	40.8	42.5	40.5	Europe ancienne URSS exclus
- European Union	42.3	41.1	41.5	39.6	39.1	43.6	41.0	37.3	38.4	36.1	- Union Européenne
- Eastern Europe	1.4	1.3	1.3	1.2	1.3	1.4	1.3	1.2	1.7	2.1	- Europe de l'Est
- Rest of Europe	2.7	2.8	2.8	2.5	2.4	2.5	2.6	2.3	2.3	2.3	- Autre de l'Europe
Europe former USSR	0.7	0.3	0.3	0.3	0.3	0.3	0.2	0.2	0.4	0.5	Europe ancienne URSS
Oceania	2.0	2.2	2.2	2.1	2.1	1.8	1.8	1.7	1.5	1.6	Océanie

TRADE BY COMMODITY (Value in million US dollars)
Exports by principal countries or areas

COMMERCE PAR PRODUIT (Valeur en millions de dollars EU)
Exportations selon les principaux pays ou zones

Country or area	1998	1999	2000	2001	2002	Pays ou zone
World	168872.6	180224.4	199047.5	184380.0	181564.4	Monde
Africa	57.4	57.8	63.1	69.0	72.4	Afrique
Americas	32327.9	35211.4	41620.4	38842.3	32603.2	Amériques
- Northern America	27635.2	28451.4	33101.5	28845.7	23028.4	- Amérique du Nord
- LAIA	4679.3	6735.7	8510.4	9981.3	9560.4	- ALAI
- CACM	4.2	9.3	2.9	7.4	7.1	- MCC
- Caribbean	9.1	14.8	5.5	6.4	6.0	- Caraïbes
- Rest of America	0.1	0.2	0.2	1.5	1.2	- Autre d'Amérique
Asia excluding former USSR	73600.2	79613.0	91286.4	82012.2	90993.3	Asie ancienne URSS exclus
- Middle East	96.8	118.9	127.9	109.4	104.7	- Moyen-Orient
Asia former USSR	1.4	2.0	2.2	2.7	2.3	Asie ancienne URSS
Europe excluding former USSR	62520.3	65034.2	65810.7	63163.1	57481.6	Europe ancienne URSS exclus
- European Union	59612.6	61390.6	62038.5	60008.0	53253.2	- Union Européenne
- Eastern Europe	2025.2	2525.9	2728.4	2334.9	3797.5	- Europe de l'Est
- Rest of Europe	882.6	1117.7	1043.8	820.1	430.9	- Autre de l'Europe
Europe former USSR	90.6	94.7	74.1	60.2	116.0	Europe ancienne URSS
Oceania	274.9	211.3	190.6	230.6	295.7	Océanie
United States	25834.6	26714.9	30929.3	27386.3	21812.1	Etats-Unis d'Amérique
Singapore	20364.7	19784.2	19424.0	16532.1	15570.6	Singapour
Netherlands	13993.0	15428.2	15187.0	16081.6	14581.8	Pays-Bas
Japan	15675.5	14472.5	14850.0	12643.6	11140.4	Japon
United Kingdom	13657.0	13920.2	13806.4	12268.7	9379.1	Royaume-Uni
China	7066.6	7922.0	10994.1	13093.8	20132.3	Chine
Ireland	8753.3	9620.8	9751.4	10099.0	8502.6	Irlande
Germany	8741.4	8551.9	9606.8	9137.4	9118.0	Allemagne
Mexico	4428.0	6398.9	8137.8	9692.5	9261.5	Mexique
Korea, Republic of	4536.6	7156.7	9290.5	7484.9	8204.7	République de Corée
Malaysia	5271.0	6416.0	7180.8	7777.2	e8242.0	Malaisie
France-Monaco	7476.2	6627.8	6404.2	5342.3	4398.7	France-Monaco
China, Hong Kong SAR	3618.9	4063.6	4135.8	4615.9	6362.0	Chine - RAS de Hong-Kong
Philippines	2411.1	3610.0	4643.8	4134.4	4495.5	Philippines
Belgium	–	2635.6	3094.6	3029.5	e3399.1	Belgique
Hungary	1735.7	2223.3	2370.9	1595.1	1869.8	Hongrie
Thailand	1810.7	1935.3	1999.2	1785.2	e1885.4	Thaïlande
Canada	1800.3	1735.8	2171.9	1459.0	1216.0	Canada
Italy-San Marino-Holy See	1644.3	1349.6	1100.2	1023.6	1112.7	Italie-Saint-Marin-Saint-Siège
Spain	1193.8	1185.8	1279.5	999.2	509.0	Espagne
Indonesia	80.7	294.1	2017.7	1138.8	1207.4	Indonésie
Czech Republic	191.4	142.6	211.5	625.0	1827.3	République tchèque
Austria	407.1	465.5	521.2	693.6	839.4	Autriche
Switzerland-Liechtenstein	587.0	773.3	758.8	574.5	217.8	Suisse-Liechtenstein
Israel	890.4	1094.7	347.7	218.0	146.3	Israël
Finland	886.1	728.7	309.0	260.1	210.9	Finlande
Sweden	381.5	360.4	370.8	425.8	506.8	Suède
Belgium-Luxembourg	2044.7	–	–	–	–	Belgique-Luxembourg
Denmark	363.9	385.9	446.1	390.3	455.3	Danemark
Brazil	216.9	304.6	329.5	241.0	e249.9	Brésil

(Value as percentages of World total) **(Valeur en pourcentage du total mondial)**

Regions of the world	1993	1994	1995	1996	1997	1998	1999	2000	2001	2002	Régions du monde
World	100.0	100.0	100.0	100.0	100.0	100.0	100.0	100.0	100.0	100.0	Monde
Africa	0.0	0.0	0.0	0.0	0.0	0.0	0.0	0.0	0.0	0.0	Afrique
Americas	21.6	22.8	20.4	19.8	19.8	19.1	19.5	20.9	21.1	18.0	Amériques
- Northern America	20.6	21.4	18.9	17.8	17.4	16.4	15.8	16.6	15.6	12.7	- Amérique du Nord
- LAIA	1.0	1.3	1.4	1.9	2.3	2.8	3.7	4.3	5.4	5.3	- ALAI
- CACM	0.0	0.0	0.0	0.0	0.0	0.0	0.0	0.0	0.0	0.0	- MCC
- Caribbean	0.0	0.0	0.0	0.0	0.0	0.0	0.0	0.0	0.0	0.0	- Caraïbes
- Rest of America	0.0	0.0	0.0	0.0	0.0	0.0	0.0	0.0	0.0	0.0	- Autre d'Amérique
Asia excluding former USSR	48.1	43.8	44.5	46.9	46.8	43.6	44.2	45.9	44.5	50.1	Asie ancienne URSS exclus
- Middle East	0.1	0.1	0.1	0.0	0.1	0.1	0.1	0.1	0.1	0.1	- Moyen-Orient
Asia former USSR	0.0	0.0	0.0	0.0	0.0	0.0	0.0	0.0	0.0	0.0	Asie ancienne URSS
Europe excluding former USSR	30.0	33.0	34.8	33.0	33.2	37.0	36.1	33.1	34.3	31.7	Europe ancienne URSS exclus
- European Union	29.4	32.4	34.1	32.4	31.8	35.3	34.1	31.2	32.5	29.3	- Union Européenne
- Eastern Europe	0.1	0.1	0.1	0.1	0.9	1.2	1.4	1.4	1.3	2.1	- Europe de l'Est
- Rest of Europe	0.6	0.6	0.6	0.5	0.5	0.5	0.6	0.5	0.4	0.2	- Autre de l'Europe
Europe former USSR	0.0	0.1	0.1	0.1	0.1	0.1	0.1	0.0	0.0	0.1	Europe ancienne URSS
Oceania	0.3	0.3	0.2	0.2	0.2	0.2	0.1	0.1	0.1	0.2	Océanie

759 Parts, nes of and accessories for machines of headings 751 or 752

TRADE BY COMMODITY (Value in million US dollars)
Imports by principal countries or areas

COMMERCE PAR PRODUIT (Valeur en millions de dollars EU)
Importations selon les principaux pays ou zones

Country or area	1998	1999	2000	2001	2002	Pays ou zone
World	120472.5	135131.1	154000.6	140403.3	137416.8	Monde
Africa	629.4	724.0	722.1	734.3	731.6	Afrique
Americas	34201.3	38827.8	42321.3	35978.7	34008.3	Amériques
- Northern America	31358.8	35449.0	38034.3	30185.3	28140.8	- Amérique du Nord
- LAIA	2532.4	3061.3	3951.0	5403.0	5445.1	- ALAI
- CACM	142.4	149.9	174.8	219.9	268.6	- MCC
- Caribbean	108.5	118.7	125.1	135.2	125.3	- Caraïbes
- Rest of America	59.3	49.0	36.1	35.3	28.4	- Autre d'Amérique
Asia excluding former USSR	36834.4	41335.5	54289.4	50941.1	54454.9	Asie ancienne URSS exclus
- Middle East	1160.0	1144.6	1312.2	1286.2	1339.1	- Moyen-Orient
Asia former USSR	49.9	48.7	43.6	43.4	42.6	Asie ancienne URSS
Europe excluding former USSR	46820.6	52314.5	54649.0	50944.8	46271.8	Europe ancienne URSS exclus
- European Union	43339.6	48477.4	50165.8	46813.2	42340.2	- Union Européenne
- Eastern Europe	1865.5	2273.4	2761.0	2486.6	2328.4	- Europe de l'Est
- Rest of Europe	1615.4	1563.7	1722.2	1644.9	1603.1	- Autre de l'Europe
Europe former USSR	292.6	230.4	220.4	206.8	279.5	Europe ancienne URSS
Oceania	1644.2	1650.3	1754.8	1554.2	1628.2	Océanie
United States	28665.1	32468.4	34122.1	26558.1	25290.0	Etats-Unis d'Amérique
United Kingdom	9895.3	11099.9	12220.8	8806.1	7863.6	Royaume-Uni
China, Hong Kong SAR	6813.2	7437.5	11021.6	11404.1	12310.0	Chine - RAS de Hong-Kong
Germany	8193.8	9744.0	9614.1	10144.8	9531.5	Allemagne
Singapore	7671.3	8770.1	9869.1	8750.9	9091.1	Singapour
Netherlands	7507.6	8658.7	8239.4	7309.9	7128.0	Pays-Bas
Japan	6551.4	7380.8	9551.8	7996.8	7362.2	Japon
China	3951.4	4212.0	5982.1	7371.2	10042.9	Chine
France-Monaco	5178.2	5325.2	5831.2	5464.0	4489.2	France-Monaco
Ireland	3757.9	4263.7	5350.9	6317.3	4570.1	Irlande
Canada	2686.5	2973.1	3901.8	3615.2	2834.4	Canada
Malaysia	2520.3	2544.4	3475.9	2895.5	e3164.4	Malaisie
Italy-San Marino-Holy See	2793.1	2985.9	2859.5	2638.5	2451.0	Italie-Saint-Marin-Saint-Siège
Philippines	2751.9	2220.3	2202.5	2912.1	3129.8	Philippines
Mexico	1137.9	1661.1	2256.2	3872.7	4258.1	Mexique
Thailand	1846.5	2138.1	3125.3	2789.7	e2906.6	Thaïlande
Korea, Republic of	866.2	1881.2	3701.6	2419.2	2021.8	République de Corée
Spain	1499.2	1566.3	1467.1	1340.7	1286.1	Espagne
Australia	1434.5	1395.6	1498.2	1300.1	1348.0	Australie
Hungary	1056.6	1433.7	1785.3	1333.5	1112.1	Hongrie
Belgium	–	1098.9	1253.6	1438.4	e1577.5	Belgique
Switzerland-Liechtenstein	912.7	899.7	966.6	847.7	740.5	Suisse-Liechtenstein
Austria	739.5	752.5	799.0	822.7	840.1	Autriche
Denmark	768.7	848.5	705.0	771.7	853.7	Danemark
Sweden	927.8	831.4	757.3	700.9	721.0	Suède
Brazil	700.7	694.3	907.6	823.7	689.3	Brésil
Israel	515.7	588.6	697.1	585.5	499.0	Israël
Norway	557.4	504.0	575.8	606.5	636.1	Norvège
India	299.6	451.7	720.6	662.1	673.9	Inde
Finland	576.4	535.1	375.9	368.7	342.5	Finlande

(Value as percentages of World total) **(Valeur en pourcentage du total mondial)**

Regions of the world	1993	1994	1995	1996	1997	1998	1999	2000	2001	2002	Régions du monde
World	100.0	100.0	100.0	100.0	100.0	100.0	100.0	100.0	100.0	100.0	Monde
Africa	0.9	0.9	0.8	0.7	0.6	0.5	0.5	0.5	0.5	0.5	Afrique
Americas	29.7	31.6	29.8	27.9	27.4	28.4	28.7	27.5	25.6	24.7	Amériques
- Northern America	26.9	29.4	27.8	25.8	25.4	26.0	26.2	24.7	21.5	20.5	- Amérique du Nord
- LAIA	2.6	1.9	1.8	1.8	1.9	2.1	2.3	2.6	3.8	4.0	- ALAI
- CACM	0.1	0.1	0.1	0.1	0.1	0.1	0.1	0.1	0.2	0.2	- MCC
- Caribbean	0.1	0.1	0.1	0.1	0.1	0.1	0.1	0.1	0.1	0.1	- Caraïbes
- Rest of America	0.0	0.0	0.0	0.0	0.0	0.0	0.0	0.0	0.0	0.0	- Autre d'Amérique
Asia excluding former USSR	25.1	25.4	29.8	32.2	34.0	30.6	30.6	35.3	36.3	39.6	Asie ancienne URSS exclus
- Middle East	1.0	0.8	0.8	0.7	0.7	1.0	0.8	0.9	0.9	1.0	- Moyen-Orient
Asia former USSR	0.0	0.0	0.1	0.0	0.0	0.0	0.0	0.0	0.0	0.0	Asie ancienne URSS
Europe excluding former USSR	41.5	39.5	37.3	37.1	36.0	38.9	38.7	35.5	36.3	33.7	Europe ancienne URSS exclus
- European Union	38.7	36.8	34.8	34.7	33.3	36.0	35.9	32.6	33.3	30.8	- Union Européenne
- Eastern Europe	0.7	0.6	0.6	0.7	1.3	1.5	1.7	1.8	1.8	1.7	- Europe de l'Est
- Rest of Europe	2.1	2.1	1.9	1.7	1.3	1.3	1.2	1.1	1.2	1.2	- Autre de l'Europe
Europe former USSR	0.5	0.4	0.4	0.4	0.4	0.2	0.2	0.1	0.1	0.2	Europe ancienne URSS
Oceania	2.3	2.3	1.9	1.8	1.6	1.4	1.2	1.1	1.1	1.2	Océanie

Pièces détachées, n.d.a. destinés aux machines et appareils des groupes 751 et 752 759

TRADE BY COMMODITY (Value in million US dollars)
Exports by principal countries or areas

COMMERCE PAR PRODUIT (Valeur en millions de dollars EU)
Exportations selon les principaux pays ou zones

Country or area	1998	1999	2000	2001	2002	Pays ou zone
World	120675.0	136374.3	165520.0	148429.7	150010.2	Monde
Africa	90.4	152.3	90.0	87.9	81.8	Afrique
Americas	27226.3	29424.1	33755.2	27719.9	22641.0	Amériques
- Northern America	23835.9	23714.7	28618.4	23591.8	18859.4	- Amérique du Nord
- LAIA	2834.7	3219.3	3490.5	3323.9	2878.9	- ALAI
- CACM	544.4	2486.6	1629.4	791.7	899.1	- MCC
- Caribbean	11.2	3.3	16.8	11.7	3.3	- Caraïbes
- Rest of America	0.1	0.3	0.1	0.6	0.3	- Autre d'Amérique
Asia excluding former USSR	62703.2	72916.6	92365.0	80904.3	89994.4	Asie ancienne URSS exclus
- Middle East	175.2	189.3	221.0	232.8	238.7	- Moyen-Orient
Asia former USSR	1.1	2.4	1.5	4.6	2.1	Asie ancienne URSS
Europe excluding former USSR	29827.1	33096.3	38589.3	38996.3	36666.0	Europe ancienne URSS exclus
- European Union	28398.8	31076.2	35906.1	36899.6	34957.3	- Union Européenne
- Eastern Europe	922.6	1407.7	1990.5	1489.7	1237.3	- Europe de l'Est
- Rest of Europe	505.7	612.3	692.7	607.0	471.5	- Autre de l'Europe
Europe former USSR	41.5	33.0	35.0	29.5	38.8	Europe ancienne URSS
Oceania	785.4	749.6	683.9	687.2	586.1	Océanie
United States	20692.7	20810.8	25467.2	20868.7	17174.8	Etats-Unis d'Amérique
Japan	14594.9	15003.4	16805.9	13203.3	13924.4	Japon
China, Hong Kong SAR	8099.1	8303.4	10832.2	11603.9	12720.6	Chine - RAS de Hong-Kong
Singapore	9843.1	10131.9	11258.6	10317.4	9858.3	Singapour
Malaysia	6278.7	10561.2	13276.3	8765.2	e9289.0	Malaisie
Ireland	5551.4	6434.3	8119.6	9887.0	7861.3	Irlande
China	3482.2	4142.5	6093.6	8744.3	13928.9	Chine
Netherlands	5570.9	5840.0	6974.9	7602.0	7832.8	Pays-Bas
United Kingdom	5996.0	6366.9	6927.8	6167.9	6733.2	Royaume-Uni
Thailand	5917.8	6033.0	6522.0	6002.8	e6339.8	Thaïlande
Korea, Republic of	676.6	3203.1	10021.1	5714.4	7940.9	République de Corée
Germany	4215.1	4874.0	5745.6	5719.3	5260.8	Allemagne
Mexico	2696.6	3057.7	3326.5	3159.5	2709.4	Mexique
France-Monaco	2820.1	2990.9	3294.4	2629.8	2239.5	France-Monaco
Canada	3142.9	2903.1	3151.0	2723.0	1684.5	Canada
Philippines	2082.3	2344.8	2517.1	2815.5	e2480.0	Philippines
Italy-San Marino-Holy See	1771.0	1907.7	1958.6	1744.9	1232.1	Italie-Saint-Marin-Saint-Siège
Costa Rica	539.8	2484.2	1627.1	789.0	897.8	Costa Rica
Hungary	688.1	1101.5	1510.1	941.8	579.6	Hongrie
Indonesia	683.9	864.2	997.9	903.9	977.6	Indonésie
Belgium	–	725.2	988.0	1101.6	e1236.0	Belgique
Australia	716.8	695.3	629.3	628.6	563.8	Australie
Denmark	520.5	560.9	519.7	488.1	591.1	Danemark
Spain	371.4	478.7	431.3	489.3	602.0	Espagne
Switzerland-Liechtenstein	334.0	442.8	502.6	442.0	304.5	Suisse-Liechtenstein
Austria	279.0	341.4	446.8	394.1	560.3	Autriche
Israel	323.7	310.5	516.5	450.1	408.3	Israël
Sweden	349.0	293.4	259.9	334.7	376.6	Suède
Czech Republic	152.0	136.8	279.9	392.4	531.4	République tchèque
United Arab Emirates	152.9	157.8	182.4	195.7	e203.8	Emirates arabes unis

(Value as percentages of World total) **(Valeur en pourcentage du total mondial)**

Regions of the world	1993	1994	1995	1996	1997	1998	1999	2000	2001	2002	Régions du monde
World	100.0	100.0	100.0	100.0	100.0	100.0	100.0	100.0	100.0	100.0	Monde
Africa	0.1	0.1	0.1	0.1	0.1	0.1	0.1	0.1	0.1	0.1	Afrique
Americas	21.6	22.4	22.5	23.1	23.6	22.6	21.6	20.4	18.7	15.1	Amériques
- Northern America	20.8	21.4	21.6	21.8	21.9	19.8	17.4	17.3	15.9	12.6	- Amérique du Nord
- LAIA	0.8	1.0	0.9	1.2	1.7	2.3	2.4	2.1	2.2	1.9	- ALAI
- CACM	0.0	0.0	0.0	0.0	0.0	0.5	1.8	1.0	0.5	0.6	- MCC
- Caribbean	0.0	0.0	0.0	0.0	0.0	0.0	0.0	0.0	0.0	0.0	- Caraïbes
- Rest of America	0.0	0.0	0.0	0.0	0.0	0.0	0.0	0.0	0.0	0.0	- Autre d'Amérique
Asia excluding former USSR	52.3	51.5	51.1	50.8	51.1	52.0	53.5	55.8	54.5	60.0	Asie ancienne URSS exclus
- Middle East	0.1	0.0	0.1	0.1	0.1	0.1	0.1	0.1	0.2	0.2	- Moyen-Orient
Asia former USSR	0.0	0.0	0.0	0.0	0.0	0.0	0.0	0.0	0.0	0.0	Asie ancienne URSS
Europe excluding former USSR	25.1	24.9	25.2	24.8	24.2	24.7	24.3	23.3	26.3	24.4	Europe ancienne URSS exclus
- European Union	24.6	24.3	24.5	24.2	23.4	23.5	22.8	21.7	24.9	23.3	- Union Européenne
- Eastern Europe	0.1	0.1	0.2	0.2	0.4	0.8	1.0	1.2	1.0	0.8	- Europe de l'Est
- Rest of Europe	0.4	0.5	0.5	0.5	0.4	0.4	0.4	0.4	0.4	0.3	- Autre de l'Europe
Europe former USSR	0.1	0.1	0.1	0.1	0.1	0.0	0.0	0.0	0.0	0.0	Europe ancienne URSS
Oceania	0.8	1.0	1.0	1.1	0.9	0.7	0.5	0.4	0.5	0.4	Océanie

761 Television receivers

TRADE BY COMMODITY (Value in million US dollars)
Imports by principal countries or areas

COMMERCE PAR PRODUIT (Valeur en millions de dollars EU)
Importations selon les principaux pays ou zones

Country or area	1998	1999	2000	2001	2002	Pays ou zone
World	22231.9	22058.3	25918.3	27489.0	30528.5	Monde
Africa	323.8	253.2	318.0	344.5	377.8	Afrique
Americas	8077.7	7976.7	9506.0	10504.2	12573.2	Amériques
- Northern America	6935.4	6953.5	8228.5	9108.5	11276.1	- Amérique du Nord
- LAIA	952.5	847.7	1087.0	1194.7	1084.5	- ALAI
- CACM	76.0	70.7	81.3	96.7	112.5	- MCC
- Caribbean	89.2	78.9	85.6	83.4	76.0	- Caraïbes
- Rest of America	24.6	26.0	23.6	20.8	24.2	- Autre d'Amérique
Asia excluding former USSR	3728.3	3776.6	4930.3	4803.8	4679.2	Asie ancienne URSS exclus
- Middle East	425.0	407.9	606.5	569.3	625.5	- Moyen-Orient
Asia former USSR	49.1	35.5	46.8	39.0	39.2	Asie ancienne URSS
Europe excluding former USSR	9540.7	9423.0	10462.6	11114.1	11939.5	Europe ancienne URSS exclus
- European Union	8555.7	8271.6	9183.2	10011.4	10715.7	- Union Européenne
- Eastern Europe	501.3	706.3	793.7	546.1	604.8	- Europe de l'Est
- Rest of Europe	483.8	445.1	485.6	556.6	618.9	- Autre de l'Europe
Europe former USSR	139.6	133.6	96.5	219.1	241.5	Europe ancienne URSS
Oceania	372.8	459.6	558.2	464.3	678.2	Océanie
United States	6284.9	6274.5	7320.9	8188.5	10194.2	Etats-Unis d'Amérique
Germany	1810.3	1693.3	1691.7	2149.1	2144.0	Allemagne
Japan	1128.4	1410.7	1805.3	1950.2	1549.8	Japon
United Kingdom	1058.8	1339.2	1530.1	1692.9	1964.6	Royaume-Uni
France-Monaco	1313.8	1142.3	1370.5	1213.5	1466.8	France-Monaco
Netherlands	1050.9	1006.5	1257.3	1382.5	1152.6	Pays-Bas
Italy-San Marino-Holy See	878.3	812.6	862.6	1049.4	1157.8	Italie-Saint-Marin-Saint-Siège
China, Hong Kong SAR	1132.0	754.5	864.1	814.8	815.2	Chine - RAS de Hong-Kong
Canada	646.9	675.0	906.3	917.4	1078.9	Canada
Spain	722.7	625.2	635.0	660.9	748.6	Espagne
Mexico	429.7	464.4	594.7	635.7	549.1	Mexique
Singapore	414.2	422.6	617.1	528.2	673.7	Singapour
Australia	299.8	378.0	480.8	389.9	575.1	Australie
Sweden	251.7	283.8	329.3	374.9	469.6	Suède
Belgium	–	305.6	422.8	440.9	e483.6	Belgique
Austria	353.3	297.6	245.5	247.0	273.7	Autriche
Switzerland-Liechtenstein	259.7	241.0	258.9	282.9	301.3	Suisse-Liechtenstein
Poland	205.9	288.0	281.8	208.5	218.6	Pologne
Denmark	228.3	191.7	202.0	221.5	239.1	Danemark
Hungary	149.5	269.1	335.6	112.7	122.9	Hongrie
United Arab Emirates	110.7	116.0	172.4	217.6	e223.3	Emirates arabes unis
Korea, Republic of	40.4	80.6	190.1	221.5	281.7	République de Corée
Portugal	163.2	164.4	145.0	151.6	174.5	Portugal
Greece	162.0	152.7	146.6	151.5	e167.5	Grèce
Norway	134.6	122.5	140.2	182.7	191.8	Norvège
Finland	140.2	145.6	215.2	137.3	114.4	Finlande
Israel	105.9	110.1	192.7	174.5	127.4	Israël
Turkey	93.1	113.1	177.8	97.1	90.8	Turquie
Chile	135.7	111.1	126.9	88.8	99.4	Chili
Czech Republic	89.4	90.8	89.3	106.8	119.4	République tchèque

(Value as percentages of World total) **(Valeur en pourcentage du total mondial)**

Regions of the world	1993	1994	1995	1996	1997	1998	1999	2000	2001	2002	Régions du monde
World	100.0	100.0	100.0	100.0	100.0	100.0	100.0	100.0	100.0	100.0	Monde
Africa	1.1	1.1	1.3	1.4	1.5	1.5	1.1	1.2	1.3	1.2	Afrique
Americas	23.9	26.4	25.1	25.3	30.1	36.3	36.2	36.7	38.2	41.2	Amériques
- Northern America	18.9	21.3	20.6	21.6	25.1	31.2	31.5	31.7	33.1	36.9	- Amérique du Nord
- LAIA	4.6	4.7	3.9	3.1	4.2	4.3	3.8	4.2	4.3	3.6	- ALAI
- CACM	0.2	0.2	0.3	0.2	0.4	0.3	0.3	0.3	0.4	0.4	- MCC
- Caribbean	0.2	0.2	0.3	0.3	0.3	0.4	0.4	0.3	0.3	0.2	- Caraïbes
- Rest of America	0.0	0.0	0.1	0.1	0.1	0.1	0.1	0.1	0.1	0.1	- Autre d'Amérique
Asia excluding former USSR	32.3	34.4	33.1	30.1	25.1	16.8	17.1	19.0	17.5	15.3	Asie ancienne URSS exclus
- Middle East	4.6	4.4	3.2	3.0	3.0	1.9	1.8	2.3	2.1	2.0	- Moyen-Orient
Asia former USSR	0.1	0.4	0.3	0.6	0.4	0.2	0.2	0.2	0.1	0.1	Asie ancienne URSS
Europe excluding former USSR	38.5	34.0	36.0	37.6	39.1	42.9	42.7	40.4	40.4	39.1	Europe ancienne URSS exclus
- European Union	35.7	31.2	33.1	34.4	35.5	38.5	37.5	35.4	36.4	35.1	- Union Européenne
- Eastern Europe	0.8	0.7	0.6	0.9	1.3	2.3	3.2	3.1	2.0	2.0	- Europe de l'Est
- Rest of Europe	2.0	2.1	2.3	2.2	2.3	2.2	2.0	1.9	2.0	2.0	- Autre de l'Europe
Europe former USSR	2.5	1.9	2.2	2.7	1.7	0.6	0.6	0.4	0.8	0.8	Europe ancienne URSS
Oceania	1.7	1.8	1.9	2.3	2.1	1.7	2.1	2.2	1.7	2.2	Océanie

TRADE BY COMMODITY (Value in million US dollars)
Exports by principal countries or areas

COMMERCE PAR PRODUIT (Valeur en millions de dollars EU)
Exportations selon les principaux pays ou zones

Country or area	1998	1999	2000	2001	2002	Pays ou zone
World	23999.7	23436.6	28825.3	28858.4	31881.6	Monde
Africa	17.1	19.6	52.5	65.7	63.1	Afrique
Americas	6337.9	6494.2	7406.6	7953.8	8277.9	Amériques
- Northern America	1390.0	1258.8	1505.4	1530.5	1394.3	- Amérique du Nord
- LAIA	4944.6	5233.1	5899.4	6421.3	6881.7	- ALAI
- CACM	1.6	0.7	0.1	0.2	0.4	- MCC
- Caribbean	1.6	1.3	1.3	1.2	0.9	- Caraïbes
- Rest of America	0.0	0.4	0.4	0.5	0.5	- Autre d'Amérique
Asia excluding former USSR	9515.2	9353.3	12662.9	12159.0	14838.6	Asie ancienne URSS exclus
- Middle East	828.4	785.9	968.1	1019.0	1606.2	- Moyen-Orient
Asia former USSR	22.4	22.2	26.6	16.2	16.1	Asie ancienne URSS
Europe excluding former USSR	8020.6	7471.2	8592.8	8556.2	8589.6	Europe ancienne URSS exclus
- European Union	6920.0	6384.5	7148.0	6323.2	6237.2	- Union Européenne
- Eastern Europe	1038.5	1035.1	1358.5	2087.9	2263.0	- Europe de l'Est
- Rest of Europe	62.0	51.7	86.3	145.2	89.4	- Autre de l'Europe
Europe former USSR	79.0	68.8	71.5	95.8	81.8	Europe ancienne URSS
Oceania	7.6	7.2	12.4	11.7	14.4	Océanie
Mexico	4911.1	5164.8	5736.5	6241.2	6694.3	Mexique
Japan	2436.8	2494.2	3327.0	3242.4	3733.7	Japon
Malaysia	1346.8	1431.3	2009.3	1829.7	e1939.1	Malaisie
Korea, Republic of	1133.0	1293.8	1582.0	1545.9	2084.5	République de Corée
United States	1359.8	1223.0	1474.6	1469.1	1303.5	Etats-Unis d'Amérique
China	686.7	803.1	1297.3	1591.0	2396.3	Chine
France-Monaco	1272.3	1174.7	1420.5	1508.8	1369.9	France-Monaco
United Kingdom	1582.4	1259.1	1340.4	1182.0	918.2	Royaume-Uni
Spain	1046.1	900.3	938.4	1006.1	1240.2	Espagne
Thailand	904.6	728.5	1092.1	915.4	e966.8	Thaïlande
Turkey	733.5	674.9	830.0	865.0	1453.6	Turquie
Germany	721.4	764.2	705.1	822.0	837.0	Allemagne
Poland	510.3	543.3	635.1	905.4	1086.8	Pologne
Belgium	–	635.7	760.9	713.7	e800.8	Belgique
Singapore	645.4	491.7	574.8	566.0	581.2	Singapour
China, Hong Kong SAR	804.5	521.1	477.1	361.9	459.4	Chine - RAS de Hong-Kong
Hungary	330.3	378.1	428.5	536.4	533.9	Hongrie
Netherlands	395.2	559.3	877.9	129.6	137.0	Pays-Bas
Czech Republic	153.3	70.2	227.1	550.6	450.6	République tchèque
Sweden	300.6	211.5	224.5	300.1	252.7	Suède
Denmark	160.8	183.8	200.6	228.8	276.9	Danemark
Indonesia	44.0	38.1	314.5	348.4	298.9	Indonésie
Italy-San Marino-Holy See	273.1	238.1	180.2	148.3	146.0	Italie-Saint-Marin-Saint-Siège
Austria	164.5	180.5	186.7	153.3	99.0	Autriche
Belgium-Luxembourg	779.0	–	–	–	–	Belgique-Luxembourg
Brazil	25.6	62.6	155.9	178.1	e184.7	Brésil
United Arab Emirates	74.3	76.6	118.7	129.7	e135.1	Emirates arabes unis
Finland	176.7	56.3	29.8	61.0	99.4	Finlande
Philippines	120.3	61.4	81.8	64.5	60.0	Philippines
Slovakia	44.0	42.7	67.4	94.5	118.3	Slovaquie

(Value as percentages of World total) **(Valeur en pourcentage du total mondial)**

Regions of the world	1993	1994	1995	1996	1997	1998	1999	2000	2001	2002	Régions du monde
World	100.0	100.0	100.0	100.0	100.0	100.0	100.0	100.0	100.0	100.0	Monde
Africa	0.0	0.1	0.1	0.1	0.1	0.1	0.1	0.2	0.2	0.2	Afrique
Americas	12.4	16.1	16.6	17.2	21.9	26.4	27.7	25.7	27.6	26.0	Amériques
- Northern America	3.8	4.2	4.0	3.9	5.5	5.8	5.4	5.2	5.3	4.4	- Amérique du Nord
- LAIA	8.6	11.9	12.6	13.4	16.4	20.6	22.3	20.5	22.3	21.6	- ALAI
- CACM	0.0	0.0	0.0	0.0	0.0	0.0	0.0	0.0	0.0	0.0	- MCC
- Caribbean	0.0	0.0	0.0	0.0	0.0	0.0	0.0	0.0	0.0	0.0	- Caraïbes
- Rest of America	0.0	0.0	0.0	0.0	0.0	0.0	0.0	0.0	0.0	0.0	- Autre d'Amérique
Asia excluding former USSR	63.9	58.9	57.1	52.5	45.8	39.6	39.9	43.9	42.1	46.5	Asie ancienne URSS exclus
- Middle East	1.0	1.0	1.2	1.1	1.8	3.5	3.4	3.4	3.5	5.0	- Moyen-Orient
Asia former USSR	0.0	0.0	0.0	0.0	0.1	0.1	0.1	0.1	0.1	0.1	Asie ancienne URSS
Europe excluding former USSR	23.3	24.4	25.8	29.5	31.0	33.4	31.9	29.8	29.6	26.9	Europe ancienne URSS exclus
- European Union	22.8	23.7	24.8	28.5	27.9	28.8	27.2	24.8	21.9	19.6	- Union Européenne
- Eastern Europe	0.2	0.4	0.7	0.7	2.7	4.3	4.4	4.7	7.2	7.1	- Europe de l'Est
- Rest of Europe	0.3	0.3	0.3	0.3	0.3	0.3	0.2	0.3	0.5	0.3	- Autre de l'Europe
Europe former USSR	0.3	0.4	0.4	0.6	1.1	0.3	0.3	0.2	0.3	0.3	Europe ancienne URSS
Oceania	0.0	0.0	0.0	0.0	0.0	0.0	0.0	0.0	0.0	0.0	Océanie

762 Radio-broadcast receivers

TRADE BY COMMODITY (Value in million US dollars) COMMERCE PAR PRODUIT (Valeur en millions de dollars EU)
Imports by principal countries or areas **Importations selon les principaux pays ou zones**

Country or area	1998	1999	2000	2001	2002	Pays ou zone
World	20274.2	20167.1	22188.8	20269.8	20724.5	Monde
Africa	236.4	234.0	238.5	238.6	243.7	Afrique
Americas	8326.4	8332.4	9786.6	8930.1	8928.9	Amériques
- Northern America	7105.7	7312.0	8487.3	7478.8	7592.1	- Amérique du Nord
- LAIA	1121.2	931.4	1204.4	1345.6	1226.1	- ALAI
- CACM	57.3	52.3	55.8	66.0	74.4	- MCC
- Caribbean	25.8	24.5	27.2	26.9	25.4	- Caraïbes
- Rest of America	16.4	12.2	11.8	12.8	10.9	- Autre d'Amérique
Asia excluding former USSR	4445.8	4327.0	5287.8	4373.5	4388.9	Asie ancienne URSS exclus
- Middle East	335.3	309.0	382.3	314.8	350.0	- Moyen-Orient
Asia former USSR	10.7	6.7	2.9	4.3	4.5	Asie ancienne URSS
Europe excluding former USSR	6883.2	6908.7	6463.3	6280.4	6609.4	Europe ancienne URSS exclus
- European Union	6256.6	6333.2	5896.6	5758.3	6023.6	- Union Européenne
- Eastern Europe	346.8	317.9	325.6	292.0	357.6	- Europe de l'Est
- Rest of Europe	279.9	257.6	241.2	230.0	228.1	- Autre de l'Europe
Europe former USSR	38.3	29.9	46.3	105.8	170.1	Europe ancienne URSS
Oceania	333.3	328.5	363.5	337.1	378.9	Océanie
United States	6323.4	6474.9	7534.1	6690.6	6752.5	Etats-Unis d'Amérique
China, Hong Kong SAR	2457.1	2009.8	2360.4	1778.0	1882.8	Chine - RAS de Hong-Kong
Germany	1345.1	1429.7	1447.7	1413.5	1349.1	Allemagne
Japan	786.5	983.6	1278.5	1235.1	1066.5	Japon
United Kingdom	921.9	801.7	866.1	848.6	912.1	Royaume-Uni
Canada	781.7	836.5	952.4	787.3	837.8	Canada
Mexico	523.6	558.9	763.1	881.2	810.9	Mexique
France-Monaco	719.0	738.6	693.1	621.3	644.6	France-Monaco
Netherlands	676.8	733.6	630.5	584.2	583.6	Pays-Bas
Belgium	–	759.8	635.8	771.5	e846.1	Belgique
Spain	512.5	542.9	474.6	466.3	558.8	Espagne
Singapore	445.5	526.6	596.1	476.4	478.9	Singapour
Italy-San Marino-Holy See	524.8	525.3	440.4	409.3	449.9	Italie-Saint-Marin-Saint-Siège
Australia	280.4	267.8	312.7	289.9	323.0	Australie
Sweden	232.0	234.1	235.2	217.0	222.0	Suède
Belgium-Luxembourg	757.6	–	–	–	–	Belgique-Luxembourg
Poland	161.6	161.8	160.9	125.1	132.1	Pologne
Korea, Republic of	54.1	101.6	171.4	172.8	210.8	République de Corée
Austria	156.6	161.3	130.6	118.4	117.7	Autriche
United Arab Emirates	122.9	128.8	145.8	130.7	e134.1	Emirates arabes unis
Switzerland-Liechtenstein	142.2	123.4	118.1	109.6	96.8	Suisse-Liechtenstein
Argentina	211.3	127.8	111.2	85.9	e38.0	Argentine
Denmark	117.7	105.2	73.5	70.3	79.5	Danemark
Thailand	40.8	65.1	104.4	103.1	e107.5	Thaïlande
Portugal	93.1	93.4	77.5	63.3	65.9	Portugal
Turkey	103.4	84.9	104.6	40.0	58.6	Turquie
Chile	97.9	64.7	85.5	69.8	62.2	Chili
Czech Republic	75.0	68.8	63.6	69.1	88.1	République tchèque
Greece	78.1	78.7	67.9	59.9	e66.2	Grèce
Finland	80.5	75.3	69.2	60.1	64.1	Finlande

(Value as percentages of World total) **(Valeur en pourcentage du total mondial)**

Regions of the world	1993	1994	1995	1996	1997	1998	1999	2000	2001	2002	Régions du monde
World	100.0	100.0	100.0	100.0	100.0	100.0	100.0	100.0	100.0	100.0	Monde
Africa	1.4	0.7	0.7	0.9	1.1	1.2	1.2	1.1	1.2	1.2	Afrique
Americas	35.7	36.8	35.2	34.6	37.9	41.1	41.3	44.1	44.1	43.1	Amériques
- Northern America	31.2	32.0	30.4	29.7	32.0	35.0	36.3	38.3	36.9	36.6	- Amérique du Nord
- LAIA	4.1	4.4	4.4	4.6	5.5	5.5	4.6	5.4	6.6	5.9	- ALAI
- CACM	0.2	0.2	0.2	0.2	0.2	0.3	0.3	0.3	0.3	0.4	- MCC
- Caribbean	0.1	0.1	0.1	0.1	0.1	0.1	0.1	0.1	0.1	0.1	- Caraïbes
- Rest of America	0.2	0.1	0.1	0.1	0.1	0.1	0.1	0.1	0.1	0.1	- Autre d'Amérique
Asia excluding former USSR	29.6	31.6	31.2	29.6	27.9	21.9	21.5	23.8	21.6	21.2	Asie ancienne URSS exclus
- Middle East	2.6	2.4	2.3	2.1	2.5	1.7	1.5	1.7	1.6	1.7	- Moyen-Orient
Asia former USSR	0.0	0.0	0.0	0.1	0.0	0.1	0.0	0.0	0.0	0.0	Asie ancienne URSS
Europe excluding former USSR	31.2	29.0	31.0	32.6	31.0	34.0	34.3	29.1	31.0	31.9	Europe ancienne URSS exclus
- European Union	29.2	27.0	28.6	29.9	28.3	30.9	31.4	26.6	28.4	29.1	- Union Européenne
- Eastern Europe	0.8	0.6	0.8	1.3	1.4	1.7	1.6	1.5	1.4	1.7	- Europe de l'Est
- Rest of Europe	1.2	1.4	1.6	1.4	1.3	1.4	1.3	1.1	1.1	1.1	- Autre de l'Europe
Europe former USSR	0.4	0.2	0.3	0.3	0.3	0.2	0.1	0.2	0.5	0.8	Europe ancienne URSS
Oceania	1.6	1.8	1.7	1.9	1.8	1.6	1.6	1.6	1.7	1.8	Océanie

TRADE BY COMMODITY (Value in million US dollars)
Exports by principal countries or areas

COMMERCE PAR PRODUIT (Valeur en millions de dollars EU)
Exportations selon les principaux pays ou zones

Country or area	1998	1999	2000	2001	2002	Pays ou zone
World	17719.5	17277.4	19389.3	16905.3	17693.5	Monde
Africa	14.4	24.9	26.7	23.0	29.9	Afrique
Americas	2455.9	2533.2	2809.1	2587.4	2935.0	Amériques
- Northern America	832.8	897.5	1099.4	952.6	950.3	- Amérique du Nord
- LAIA	1623.0	1635.3	1709.3	1634.0	1983.9	- ALAI
- CACM	0.1	0.1	0.1	0.1	0.2	- MCC
- Caribbean	0.1	0.3	0.4	0.6	0.5	- Caraïbes
- Rest of America	0.0	0.0	0.0	0.1	0.1	- Autre d'Amérique
Asia excluding former USSR	11839.7	11007.4	13192.8	11086.4	11269.7	Asie ancienne URSS exclus
- Middle East	71.8	75.1	77.4	76.6	76.3	- Moyen-Orient
Asia former USSR	0.4	0.2	0.0	0.1	0.1	Asie ancienne URSS
Europe excluding former USSR	3392.9	3700.3	3351.1	3191.1	3445.8	Europe ancienne URSS exclus
- European Union	3171.9	3414.9	3044.4	2951.3	3111.5	- Union Européenne
- Eastern Europe	206.0	275.1	297.4	230.8	327.4	- Europe de l'Est
- Rest of Europe	15.1	10.2	9.3	8.9	6.8	- Autre de l'Europe
Europe former USSR	8.3	3.8	4.2	5.0	5.3	Europe ancienne URSS
Oceania	7.8	7.6	5.4	12.3	7.7	Océanie
China, Hong Kong SAR	3390.0	2783.3	3398.4	2626.2	2803.6	Chine - RAS de Hong-Kong
China	2740.6	2432.5	2968.8	2628.9	3046.2	Chine
Malaysia	2031.3	2474.4	2582.0	2041.8	e2163.8	Malaisie
Mexico	1289.3	1368.7	1450.0	1455.2	1799.8	Mexique
Japan	1276.8	1293.1	1129.0	739.7	814.0	Japon
Singapore	1241.8	944.5	1033.4	969.6	569.7	Singapour
United States	804.8	866.2	1062.4	919.9	911.0	Etats-Unis d'Amérique
Portugal	559.8	659.7	642.1	652.3	651.0	Portugal
Germany	510.3	570.8	525.8	619.5	748.8	Allemagne
Belgium	–	681.9	624.1	649.9	e729.2	Belgique
Indonesia	215.6	209.9	610.8	654.6	539.7	Indonésie
France-Monaco	466.8	501.5	393.4	380.3	448.1	France-Monaco
Netherlands	498.6	561.7	431.2	301.4	160.6	Pays-Bas
Korea, Republic of	244.5	255.4	565.4	440.5	342.8	République de Corée
Thailand	292.5	195.3	377.4	364.2	e384.6	Thaïlande
Hungary	199.5	266.4	288.6	218.8	300.3	Hongrie
Brazil	312.9	250.1	248.3	166.7	e172.8	Brésil
Israel	126.3	130.8	221.5	309.5	298.2	Israël
United Kingdom	249.2	138.7	97.7	98.1	78.2	Royaume-Uni
Belgium-Luxembourg	639.5	–	–	–	–	Belgique-Luxembourg
Philippines	87.3	108.0	127.2	129.2	120.2	Philippines
Denmark	96.2	100.3	79.1	72.1	90.2	Danemark
Spain	45.1	95.0	66.2	59.3	87.1	Espagne
United Arab Emirates	63.4	65.4	64.6	65.5	e68.2	Emirates arabes unis
Sweden	49.9	45.3	41.8	43.4	47.7	Suède
Austria	28.4	24.0	98.3	24.1	12.6	Autriche
Canada	27.9	31.3	37.0	32.7	39.3	Canada
Italy-San Marino-Holy See	18.4	17.8	22.0	21.8	29.3	Italie-Saint-Marin-Saint-Siège
Argentina	19.6	15.4	9.8	9.1	e8.8	Argentine
South Africa	–	–	18.4	20.0	24.1	Afrique du Sud

(Value as percentages of World total) **(Valeur en pourcentage du total mondial)**

Regions of the world	1993	1994	1995	1996	1997	1998	1999	2000	2001	2002	Régions du monde
World	100.0	100.0	100.0	100.0	100.0	100.0	100.0	100.0	100.0	100.0	Monde
Africa	0.0	0.0	0.0	0.0	0.1	0.1	0.1	0.1	0.1	0.2	Afrique
Americas	10.1	9.5	9.8	11.6	14.3	13.9	14.7	14.5	15.3	16.6	Amériques
- Northern America	3.1	3.3	3.5	4.1	4.9	4.7	5.2	5.7	5.6	5.4	- Amérique du Nord
- LAIA	6.9	6.3	6.3	7.5	9.4	9.2	9.5	8.8	9.7	11.2	- ALAI
- CACM	0.0	0.0	0.0	0.0	0.0	0.0	0.0	0.0	0.0	0.0	- MCC
- Caribbean	0.0	0.0	0.0	0.0	0.0	0.0	0.0	0.0	0.0	0.0	- Caraïbes
- Rest of America	0.0	0.0	0.0	0.0	0.0	0.0	0.0	0.0	0.0	0.0	- Autre d'Amérique
Asia excluding former USSR	77.6	78.2	75.8	71.2	68.8	66.8	63.7	68.0	65.6	63.7	Asie ancienne URSS exclus
- Middle East	0.2	0.2	0.2	0.2	0.2	0.4	0.4	0.4	0.5	0.4	- Moyen-Orient
Asia former USSR	0.0	0.0	0.0	0.0	0.0	0.0	0.0	0.0	0.0	0.0	Asie ancienne URSS
Europe excluding former USSR	12.3	12.2	14.4	17.1	16.6	19.1	21.4	17.3	18.9	19.5	Europe ancienne URSS exclus
- European Union	12.2	12.0	14.2	16.8	16.1	17.9	19.8	15.7	17.5	17.6	- Union Européenne
- Eastern Europe	0.1	0.2	0.1	0.2	0.4	1.2	1.6	1.5	1.4	1.9	- Europe de l'Est
- Rest of Europe	0.1	0.0	0.1	0.1	0.1	0.1	0.1	0.0	0.1	0.0	- Autre de l'Europe
Europe former USSR	0.0	0.0	0.0	0.1	0.2	0.0	0.0	0.0	0.0	0.0	Europe ancienne URSS
Oceania	0.0	0.1	0.0	0.0	0.1	0.0	0.0	0.0	0.1	0.0	Océanie

763 Gramophones, dictating machines and other sound recorders

TRADE BY COMMODITY (Value in million US dollars)
Imports by principal countries or areas

COMMERCE PAR PRODUIT (Valeur en millions de dollars EU)
Importations selon les principaux pays ou zones

Country or area	1998	1999	2000	2001	2002	Pays ou zone
World	21469.5	24170.0	29350.7	29622.4	34244.6	Monde
Africa	171.0	160.7	173.1	180.4	201.1	Afrique
Americas	9603.1	11074.2	13615.0	12308.4	14483.8	Amériques
- Northern America	8641.9	10245.9	12666.3	11296.3	13196.2	- Amérique du Nord
- LAIA	894.0	763.8	876.6	943.9	1211.8	- ALAI
- CACM	19.8	20.5	20.9	25.6	32.8	- MCC
- Caribbean	32.2	29.0	38.9	31.7	31.5	- Caraïbes
- Rest of America	15.1	14.9	12.3	10.9	11.5	- Autre d'Amérique
Asia excluding former USSR	3920.2	4339.0	5895.8	6879.4	8209.1	Asie ancienne URSS exclus
- Middle East	276.8	279.0	358.2	346.4	419.2	- Moyen-Orient
Asia former USSR	25.7	17.2	23.3	18.2	13.5	Asie ancienne URSS
Europe excluding former USSR	7299.5	8075.8	9028.1	9656.2	10594.7	Europe ancienne URSS exclus
- European Union	6678.2	7383.3	8331.1	8866.5	9628.9	- Union Européenne
- Eastern Europe	258.3	298.4	252.1	326.5	409.9	- Europe de l'Est
- Rest of Europe	363.0	394.1	444.9	463.2	555.8	- Autre de l'Europe
Europe former USSR	53.2	47.4	45.3	76.6	107.0	Europe ancienne URSS
Oceania	396.9	455.7	570.1	503.2	635.5	Océanie
United States	8013.5	9561.9	11851.9	10478.2	12243.3	Etats-Unis d'Amérique
China, Hong Kong SAR	1598.7	1601.0	2244.6	2669.4	3703.5	Chine - RAS de Hong-Kong
United Kingdom	1401.0	1485.6	1665.7	1732.8	2187.5	Royaume-Uni
Germany	1420.6	1648.5	1793.3	1998.0	1373.8	Allemagne
Japan	921.4	1097.8	1506.1	1973.8	1898.2	Japon
France-Monaco	987.0	1029.3	1253.7	1218.1	1457.4	France-Monaco
Netherlands	562.7	780.9	919.6	949.3	975.5	Pays-Bas
Singapore	647.3	705.1	824.1	823.9	891.1	Singapour
Canada	626.2	681.6	813.1	816.2	950.0	Canada
Mexico	593.1	532.4	605.6	686.4	963.9	Mexique
Italy-San Marino-Holy See	518.4	544.9	664.4	711.0	847.4	Italie-Saint-Marin-Saint-Siège
Spain	433.9	497.3	535.7	634.1	806.8	Espagne
Belgium	-	501.8	446.0	609.5	e668.5	Belgique
Australia	337.6	389.9	493.9	441.4	557.4	Australie
Korea, Republic of	112.5	162.9	358.1	407.8	520.7	République de Corée
Sweden	194.8	218.1	283.2	251.7	359.1	Suède
Switzerland-Liechtenstein	202.2	227.7	254.1	261.4	286.2	Suisse-Liechtenstein
Austria	267.8	206.4	206.9	212.6	230.8	Autriche
Denmark	147.9	129.3	129.5	150.6	232.4	Danemark
Norway	92.4	97.9	121.6	123.4	162.2	Norvège
Portugal	112.6	101.9	114.6	97.8	107.6	Portugal
Saudi Arabia	79.3	92.8	117.9	118.3	e122.4	Arabie saoudite
Poland	86.4	87.4	95.2	98.3	126.1	Pologne
China	28.9	64.5	85.1	112.3	189.6	Chine
Finland	76.1	78.0	100.1	93.3	120.0	Finlande
Hungary	70.1	103.9	56.8	108.7	121.5	Hongrie
United Arab Emirates	69.9	73.3	109.0	99.9	e102.5	Emirates arabes unis
Thailand	40.8	69.2	107.3	108.8	e113.4	Thaïlande
Belgium-Luxembourg	431.8	-	-	-	-	Belgique-Luxembourg
Ireland	50.5	57.5	102.2	88.9	132.5	Irlande

(Value as percentages of World total) **(Valeur en pourcentage du total mondial)**

Regions of the world	1993	1994	1995	1996	1997	1998	1999	2000	2001	2002	Régions du monde
World	100.0	100.0	100.0	100.0	100.0	100.0	100.0	100.0	100.0	100.0	Monde
Africa	0.7	0.7	0.6	0.5	0.6	0.8	0.7	0.6	0.6	0.6	Afrique
Americas	37.9	38.4	38.4	37.7	41.9	44.7	45.8	46.4	41.6	42.3	Amériques
- Northern America	33.3	32.9	32.9	33.9	37.9	40.3	42.4	43.2	38.1	38.5	- Amérique du Nord
- LAIA	4.4	5.2	5.1	3.6	3.7	4.2	3.2	3.0	3.2	3.5	- ALAI
- CACM	0.1	0.1	0.1	0.1	0.1	0.1	0.1	0.1	0.1	0.1	- MCC
- Caribbean	0.1	0.1	0.1	0.1	0.1	0.2	0.1	0.1	0.1	0.1	- Caraïbes
- Rest of America	0.1	0.1	0.1	0.1	0.1	0.1	0.1	0.0	0.0	0.0	- Autre d'Amérique
Asia excluding former USSR	27.2	29.5	28.6	25.1	23.6	18.3	18.0	20.1	23.2	24.0	Asie ancienne URSS exclus
- Middle East	2.9	3.2	2.3	1.6	2.1	1.3	1.2	1.2	1.2	1.2	- Moyen-Orient
Asia former USSR	0.0	0.1	0.2	0.2	0.1	0.1	0.1	0.1	0.1	0.0	Asie ancienne URSS
Europe excluding former USSR	31.4	29.1	29.9	33.9	31.3	34.0	33.4	30.8	32.6	30.9	Europe ancienne URSS exclus
- European Union	29.5	27.2	27.8	31.5	28.5	31.1	30.5	28.4	29.9	28.1	- Union Européenne
- Eastern Europe	0.6	0.6	0.7	0.8	1.1	1.2	1.2	0.9	1.1	1.2	- Europe de l'Est
- Rest of Europe	1.3	1.3	1.4	1.5	1.6	1.7	1.6	1.5	1.6	1.6	- Autre de l'Europe
Europe former USSR	1.2	0.6	0.7	0.8	0.5	0.2	0.2	0.2	0.3	0.3	Europe ancienne URSS
Oceania	1.4	1.5	1.7	1.8	2.0	1.8	1.9	1.9	1.7	1.9	Océanie

Appareils d'enregistrement et de reproduction du son et des images, par procédé magnétique 763

TRADE BY COMMODITY (Value in million US dollars) COMMERCE PAR PRODUIT (Valeur en millions de dollars EU)

Exports by principal countries or areas **Exportations selon les principaux pays ou zones**

Country or area	1998	1999	2000	2001	2002	Pays ou zone
World	20343.4	23221.6	27580.7	27064.5	32280.4	Monde
Africa	10.0	8.9	11.0	9.3	9.3	Afrique
Americas	1732.5	2079.0	2096.3	1715.4	1599.9	Amériques
- Northern America	1223.4	1319.1	1370.6	1234.3	1197.1	- Amérique du Nord
- LAIA	508.3	758.5	724.6	479.3	400.8	- ALAI
- CACM	0.1	0.2	0.3	0.2	0.2	- MCC
- Caribbean	0.8	1.0	0.7	1.3	1.8	- Caraïbes
- Rest of America	0.0	0.1	0.0	0.2	0.0	- Autre d'Amérique
Asia excluding former USSR	14679.3	16924.6	21534.4	21129.0	26802.0	Asie ancienne URSS exclus
- Middle East	78.1	67.1	82.8	97.7	97.3	- Moyen-Orient
Asia former USSR	2.6	2.2	1.2	0.7	0.6	Asie ancienne URSS
Europe excluding former USSR	3892.3	4182.1	3907.8	4184.1	3842.9	Europe ancienne URSS exclus
- European Union	3043.4	3248.0	3002.3	3420.4	3093.3	- Union Européenne
- Eastern Europe	790.7	881.8	858.4	725.6	698.3	- Europe de l'Est
- Rest of Europe	58.3	52.3	47.2	38.1	51.3	- Autre de l'Europe
Europe former USSR	14.1	4.9	4.4	6.1	6.0	Europe ancienne URSS
Oceania	12.4	20.0	25.5	19.9	19.7	Océanie
Japan	6712.6	8352.6	9940.2	8157.9	9290.0	Japon
China	1430.7	1865.1	2873.9	4130.2	6469.8	Chine
Malaysia	1901.0	1812.0	2382.0	2336.7	e2476.4	Malaisie
China, Hong Kong SAR	1488.5	1465.6	2084.6	2408.2	3350.7	Chine - RAS de Hong-Kong
Korea, Republic of	1055.3	1430.1	1716.2	1683.9	1872.9	République de Corée
United States	1140.1	1239.2	1279.9	1141.5	1080.0	Etats-Unis d'Amérique
Singapore	844.8	808.6	796.9	776.3	1141.9	Singapour
Germany	783.6	858.9	815.5	1064.1	616.6	Allemagne
Indonesia	486.7	445.0	823.3	829.5	1356.4	Indonésie
Hungary	771.4	867.8	844.4	673.5	622.8	Hongrie
United Kingdom	790.3	751.1	527.4	448.0	481.7	Royaume-Uni
Mexico	505.4	752.4	711.0	466.6	387.6	Mexique
Netherlands	330.2	475.3	540.1	617.8	437.1	Pays-Bas
Belgium	–	459.6	360.0	571.2	e640.8	Belgique
Thailand	461.6	418.1	381.2	316.2	e334.0	Thaïlande
France-Monaco	303.3	301.6	275.0	257.4	263.1	France-Monaco
Spain	121.8	129.6	193.2	145.6	188.3	Espagne
Canada	83.3	80.0	90.7	92.7	116.9	Canada
Belgium-Luxembourg	424.5	–	–	–	–	Belgique-Luxembourg
United Arab Emirates	42.9	44.3	70.6	82.8	e86.2	Emirates arabes unis
Sweden	51.5	46.5	46.8	54.6	118.8	Suède
Denmark	47.5	44.1	37.7	64.9	107.5	Danemark
Austria	60.1	60.1	46.9	41.9	51.4	Autriche
Ireland	16.1	26.2	50.7	67.2	94.3	Irlande
Italy-San Marino-Holy See	43.3	35.2	37.3	38.2	52.0	Italie-Saint-Marin-Saint-Siège
Switzerland-Liechtenstein	47.2	43.7	37.2	29.9	39.4	Suisse-Liechtenstein
Portugal	39.9	27.8	30.1	15.1	12.5	Portugal
Finland	27.6	15.1	23.5	19.4	13.8	Finlande
Slovakia	1.1	0.7	0.9	38.2	49.0	Slovaquie
Australia	10.6	18.5	22.1	17.9	19.2	Australie

(Value as percentages of World total) **(Valeur en pourcentage du total mondial)**

Regions of the world	1993	1994	1995	1996	1997	1998	1999	2000	2001	2002	Régions du monde
World	100.0	100.0	100.0	100.0	100.0	100.0	100.0	100.0	100.0	100.0	Monde
Africa	0.0	0.0	0.1	0.0	0.0	0.0	0.0	0.0	0.0	0.0	Afrique
Americas	5.4	5.6	6.7	6.9	8.7	8.5	9.0	7.6	6.3	5.0	Amériques
- Northern America	4.0	3.9	4.2	5.0	6.4	6.0	5.7	5.0	4.6	3.7	- Amérique du Nord
- LAIA	1.4	1.7	2.5	2.0	2.3	2.5	3.3	2.6	1.8	1.2	- ALAI
- CACM	0.0	0.0	0.0	0.0	0.0	0.0	0.0	0.0	0.0	0.0	- MCC
- Caribbean	0.0	0.0	0.0	0.0	0.0	0.0	0.0	0.0	0.0	0.0	- Caraïbes
- Rest of America	0.0	0.0	0.0	0.0	0.0	0.0	0.0	0.0	0.0	0.0	- Autre d'Amérique
Asia excluding former USSR	77.4	78.2	77.5	73.5	72.5	72.2	72.9	78.1	78.1	83.0	Asie ancienne URSS exclus
- Middle East	0.3	0.2	0.2	0.2	0.3	0.4	0.3	0.3	0.4	0.3	- Moyen-Orient
Asia former USSR	0.0	0.0	0.0	0.0	0.0	0.0	0.0	0.0	0.0	0.0	Asie ancienne URSS
Europe excluding former USSR	17.1	15.9	15.5	19.3	18.3	19.1	18.0	14.2	15.5	11.9	Europe ancienne URSS exclus
- European Union	16.6	15.5	14.8	18.8	15.2	15.0	14.0	10.9	12.6	9.6	- Union Européenne
- Eastern Europe	0.1	0.1	0.4	0.1	2.8	3.9	3.8	3.1	2.7	2.2	- Europe de l'Est
- Rest of Europe	0.4	0.3	0.3	0.3	0.3	0.3	0.2	0.2	0.1	0.2	- Autre de l'Europe
Europe former USSR	0.1	0.1	0.1	0.2	0.4	0.1	0.0	0.0	0.0	0.0	Europe ancienne URSS
Oceania	0.0	0.0	0.1	0.1	0.1	0.1	0.1	0.1	0.1	0.1	Océanie

764 Telecommunication equipment, nes; parts and accessories, nes

TRADE BY COMMODITY (Value in million US dollars) — COMMERCE PAR PRODUIT (Valeur en millions de dollars EU)

Imports by principal countries or areas — **Importations selon les principaux pays ou zones**

Country or area	1998	1999	2000	2001	2002	Pays ou zone
World	146172.9	169101.3	222184.2	205721.4	195069.3	Monde
Africa	3736.8	3251.1	4023.9	3477.3	3436.7	Afrique
Americas	39316.7	47559.4	68838.0	59661.6	54257.4	Amériques
- Northern America	27010.3	34915.8	52656.6	44383.7	43527.3	- Amérique du Nord
- LAIA	11379.0	11549.6	14968.3	14060.6	9521.1	- ALAI
- CACM	324.3	522.0	552.0	464.1	507.7	- MCC
- Caribbean	433.5	439.4	538.8	597.4	558.6	- Caraïbes
- Rest of America	169.5	132.6	122.4	155.7	142.7	- Autre d'Amérique
Asia excluding former USSR	43906.2	48378.5	65389.1	63102.1	65808.3	Asie ancienne URSS exclus
- Middle East	3795.5	4424.8	4948.7	4155.0	4019.9	- Moyen-Orient
Asia former USSR	377.4	296.8	439.7	366.1	365.8	Asie ancienne URSS
Europe excluding former USSR	54746.0	64860.8	77603.1	73835.1	66184.6	Europe ancienne URSS exclus
- European Union	47578.1	57509.9	68750.8	65348.5	57767.8	- Union Européenne
- Eastern Europe	4085.8	4040.3	5150.0	5242.8	5343.9	- Europe de l'Est
- Rest of Europe	3082.1	3310.5	3702.3	3243.8	3072.8	- Autre de l'Europe
Europe former USSR	1938.2	1357.9	1599.5	2226.1	2341.0	Europe ancienne URSS
Oceania	2151.5	3396.8	4291.0	3053.1	2675.5	Océanie
United States	22497.0	29629.8	45062.0	38471.8	38272.9	Etats-Unis d'Amérique
China, Hong Kong SAR	11710.1	11006.4	15273.2	15086.0	16852.8	Chine - RAS de Hong-Kong
United Kingdom	10193.1	11941.4	15176.7	12184.1	10587.8	Royaume-Uni
China	7625.3	9117.0	12230.8	13121.3	13893.3	Chine
Germany	8083.6	9102.9	10669.3	12860.4	12026.4	Allemagne
Japan	6049.0	6701.7	8879.9	8216.2	7437.6	Japon
France-Monaco	5529.3	6098.9	7597.3	7097.2	5803.2	France-Monaco
Mexico	4273.5	5342.8	7808.3	7814.3	5505.5	Mexique
Canada	4474.8	5248.2	7390.4	5861.2	5222.6	Canada
Italy-San Marino-Holy See	4754.4	5355.7	6149.0	5350.3	4980.7	Italie-Saint-Marin-Saint-Siège
Netherlands	3066.4	5106.0	6826.8	6894.2	4323.8	Pays-Bas
Singapore	3830.6	4125.8	4832.4	4602.1	4517.2	Singapour
Spain	3001.6	4801.4	5003.3	4116.3	3794.2	Espagne
Korea, Republic of	1788.6	3160.6	5110.7	4019.4	3850.4	République de Corée
Sweden	3447.1	3032.6	3413.4	2747.3	2191.7	Suède
Malaysia	1923.2	2111.4	3254.9	3072.5	e3357.9	Malaisie
Australia	1684.0	2764.1	3574.1	2520.6	2232.3	Australie
Brazil	2563.9	2526.6	3045.8	3032.0	1484.1	Brésil
Belgium	–	2602.3	2813.7	3343.2	e3666.5	Belgique
Ireland	1102.7	2023.6	2277.0	2619.0	1809.0	Irlande
Denmark	1574.4	1721.5	2013.5	1950.9	2550.4	Danemark
Austria	1644.4	2026.2	2038.7	1582.0	1681.1	Autriche
Thailand	861.4	1094.8	1615.0	2452.0	e2554.7	Thaïlande
Switzerland-Liechtenstein	1527.4	1690.3	1930.6	1617.9	1480.3	Suisse-Liechtenstein
Turkey	1325.7	2120.1	2642.6	1036.3	881.6	Turquie
Hungary	1300.5	1299.8	1627.0	1732.4	2020.2	Hongrie
Finland	1030.3	1194.8	2130.8	1933.1	1624.4	Finlande
Poland	1271.1	1428.3	1639.3	1584.4	1485.4	Pologne
Philippines	1194.2	1106.5	1832.1	1822.0	1204.2	Philippines
Israel	1000.4	1245.1	1356.4	1118.8	1113.4	Israël

(Value as percentages of World total) — **(Valeur en pourcentage du total mondial)**

Regions of the world	1993	1994	1995	1996	1997	1998	1999	2000	2001	2002	Régions du monde
World	100.0	100.0	100.0	100.0	100.0	100.0	100.0	100.0	100.0	100.0	Monde
Africa	1.9	2.1	1.8	1.8	2.0	2.6	1.9	1.8	1.7	1.8	Afrique
Americas	27.3	27.2	24.4	24.0	25.0	26.9	28.1	31.0	29.0	27.8	Amériques
- Northern America	21.0	20.5	18.5	17.5	17.0	18.5	20.6	23.7	21.6	22.3	- Amérique du Nord
- LAIA	5.7	6.2	5.4	6.1	7.5	7.8	6.8	6.7	6.8	4.9	- ALAI
- CACM	0.3	0.2	0.2	0.2	0.2	0.2	0.3	0.2	0.2	0.3	- MCC
- Caribbean	0.2	0.2	0.2	0.2	0.3	0.3	0.3	0.2	0.3	0.3	- Caraïbes
- Rest of America	0.1	0.1	0.1	0.1	0.1	0.1	0.1	0.1	0.1	0.1	- Autre d'Amérique
Asia excluding former USSR	38.0	37.4	38.8	37.2	35.5	30.0	28.6	29.4	30.7	33.7	Asie ancienne URSS exclus
- Middle East	2.7	2.5	2.5	2.2	2.2	2.6	2.6	2.2	2.0	2.1	- Moyen-Orient
Asia former USSR	0.1	0.2	0.2	0.3	0.2	0.3	0.2	0.2	0.2	0.2	Asie ancienne URSS
Europe excluding former USSR	29.8	30.2	31.6	33.5	34.0	37.5	38.4	34.9	35.9	33.9	Europe ancienne URSS exclus
- European Union	26.2	26.7	27.8	29.3	29.5	32.5	34.0	30.9	31.8	29.6	- Union Européenne
- Eastern Europe	1.7	1.6	1.6	2.1	2.5	2.8	2.4	2.3	2.5	2.7	- Europe de l'Est
- Rest of Europe	1.9	2.0	2.2	2.0	2.0	2.1	2.0	1.7	1.6	1.6	- Autre de l'Europe
Europe former USSR	1.3	1.1	1.2	1.3	1.6	1.3	0.8	0.7	1.1	1.2	Europe ancienne URSS
Oceania	1.7	1.7	2.0	1.9	1.7	1.5	2.0	1.9	1.5	1.4	Océanie

Equipement de télécommunication, et pièces détachées; des appareils de la division 76 764

TRADE BY COMMODITY (Value in million US dollars)
Exports by principal countries or areas

COMMERCE PAR PRODUIT (Valeur en millions de dollars EU)
Exportations selon les principaux pays ou zones

Country or area	1998	1999	2000	2001	2002	Pays ou zone
World	151650.8	171831.1	223560.9	208622.7	208392.1	Monde
Africa	283.1	251.9	265.4	270.2	258.6	Afrique
Americas	33224.5	38319.1	53326.4	44508.4	37299.7	Amériques
- Northern America	27426.4	30731.8	40661.7	31955.2	26371.8	- Amérique du Nord
- LAIA	5671.5	7559.8	12637.6	12493.1	10860.0	- ALAI
- CACM	108.5	14.0	15.8	31.5	37.5	- MCC
- Caribbean	18.0	13.0	10.8	27.6	27.1	- Caraïbes
- Rest of America	0.1	0.5	0.5	1.1	3.2	- Autre d'Amérique
Asia excluding former USSR	51691.1	58946.0	79565.9	77930.1	87965.2	Asie ancienne URSS exclus
- Middle East	432.2	415.3	456.7	827.0	836.4	- Moyen-Orient
Asia former USSR	17.2	6.5	6.6	11.1	10.5	Asie ancienne URSS
Europe excluding former USSR	65103.8	72898.9	88292.1	84001.7	81510.5	Europe ancienne URSS exclus
- European Union	62457.2	70362.3	84181.4	78515.3	74598.4	- Union Européenne
- Eastern Europe	1027.8	1049.2	2483.3	3812.0	5495.5	- Europe de l'Est
- Rest of Europe	1618.7	1487.5	1627.4	1674.3	1416.7	- Autre de l'Europe
Europe former USSR	690.2	737.1	1171.7	1128.2	881.9	Europe ancienne URSS
Oceania	640.9	671.5	932.7	773.1	465.5	Océanie
United States	22673.2	24381.1	29163.0	26133.5	21587.2	Etats-Unis d'Amérique
United Kingdom	12862.3	12932.3	16146.1	17111.5	17409.2	Royaume-Uni
Germany	10451.7	12461.4	13945.7	15614.2	15298.0	Allemagne
Japan	12698.8	13296.9	16120.0	12047.0	10781.9	Japon
China, Hong Kong SAR	9893.7	10455.1	13658.0	13300.2	16264.0	Chine - RAS de Hong-Kong
China	6253.0	7960.3	12368.2	15408.7	20104.5	Chine
Korea, Republic of	4556.8	7523.5	10500.4	12273.2	15755.7	République de Corée
France-Monaco	8322.4	8945.4	11828.7	8910.4	8398.0	France-Monaco
Sweden	10357.3	11016.6	11646.8	6613.1	5899.5	Suède
Mexico	5369.6	7093.7	11323.6	10979.2	9283.6	Mexique
Finland	6191.8	7134.9	9677.9	8035.6	8173.4	Finlande
Canada	4750.3	6349.7	11497.6	5820.6	4783.6	Canada
Malaysia	3752.7	4162.8	5991.1	5961.3	e6317.5	Malaisie
Singapore	4688.5	5031.2	5860.7	4948.1	5488.0	Singapour
Netherlands	2335.0	3536.7	5346.0	5314.7	3032.4	Pays-Bas
Italy-San Marino-Holy See	3283.8	3483.2	3845.3	4559.5	3314.4	Italie-Saint-Marin-Saint-Siège
Israel	2413.2	2879.1	4008.9	3260.2	2394.9	Israël
Ireland	1892.9	3679.8	3179.2	3115.9	2341.6	Irlande
Belgium	–	2307.2	3151.6	3508.7	e3936.7	Belgique
Denmark	1660.0	1771.4	1829.6	1806.7	2872.4	Danemark
Thailand	1432.6	1655.2	2163.7	1914.6	e2022.1	Thaïlande
Hungary	429.7	472.3	1436.7	2410.0	3894.7	Hongrie
Spain	1384.1	1622.8	1528.1	1617.6	1444.0	Espagne
Indonesia	614.3	775.1	1751.6	1521.2	1164.4	Indonésie
Austria	928.4	875.9	1091.2	1151.5	1311.9	Autriche
Brazil	255.4	407.0	1233.3	1437.3	e1490.1	Brésil
Philippines	919.1	793.1	1044.2	938.2	857.1	Philippines
Switzerland-Liechtenstein	760.6	747.5	838.8	830.4	660.9	Suisse-Liechtenstein
Estonia	388.4	385.3	934.1	826.9	538.6	Estonie
Norway	666.9	617.5	613.5	599.2	509.1	Norvège

(Value as percentages of World total) **(Valeur en pourcentage du total mondial)**

Regions of the world	1993	1994	1995	1996	1997	1998	1999	2000	2001	2002	Régions du monde
World	100.0	100.0	100.0	100.0	100.0	100.0	100.0	100.0	100.0	100.0	Monde
Africa	0.2	0.1	0.1	0.1	0.1	0.2	0.1	0.1	0.1	0.1	Afrique
Americas	19.4	19.7	19.8	20.4	22.0	21.9	22.3	23.9	21.3	17.9	Amériques
- Northern America	17.2	17.3	17.2	17.7	18.8	18.1	17.9	18.2	15.3	12.7	- Amérique du Nord
- LAIA	2.1	2.4	2.5	2.7	3.2	3.7	4.4	5.7	6.0	5.2	- ALAI
- CACM	0.0	0.0	0.0	0.0	0.1	0.1	0.0	0.0	0.0	0.0	- MCC
- Caribbean	0.0	0.0	0.0	0.0	0.0	0.0	0.0	0.0	0.0	0.0	- Caraïbes
- Rest of America	0.0	0.0	0.0	0.0	0.0	0.0	0.0	0.0	0.0	0.0	- Autre d'Amérique
Asia excluding former USSR	52.2	48.9	44.8	41.0	37.9	34.1	34.3	35.6	37.4	42.2	Asie ancienne URSS exclus
- Middle East	0.2	0.2	0.1	0.2	0.1	0.3	0.2	0.2	0.4	0.4	- Moyen-Orient
Asia former USSR	0.0	0.0	0.0	0.0	0.0	0.0	0.0	0.0	0.0	0.0	Asie ancienne URSS
Europe excluding former USSR	27.7	30.4	34.5	37.6	38.9	42.9	42.4	39.5	40.3	39.1	Europe ancienne URSS exclus
- European Union	26.2	28.8	32.9	35.9	37.2	41.2	40.9	37.7	37.6	35.8	- Union Européenne
- Eastern Europe	0.4	0.5	0.5	0.5	0.6	0.7	0.6	1.1	1.8	2.6	- Europe de l'Est
- Rest of Europe	1.1	1.1	1.2	1.2	1.1	1.1	0.9	0.7	0.8	0.7	- Autre de l'Europe
Europe former USSR	0.1	0.3	0.3	0.4	0.5	0.5	0.4	0.5	0.5	0.4	Europe ancienne URSS
Oceania	0.4	0.6	0.5	0.5	0.6	0.4	0.4	0.4	0.4	0.2	Océanie

771 Electric power machinery, and parts thereof, nes

TRADE BY COMMODITY (Value in million US dollars)
Imports by principal countries or areas

COMMERCE PAR PRODUIT (Valeur en millions de dollars EU)
Importations selon les principaux pays ou zones

Country or area	1998	1999	2000	2001	2002	Pays ou zone
World	31674.8	33683.1	39748.8	36496.0	34413.7	Monde
Africa	460.7	438.4	580.7	608.4	665.3	Afrique
Americas	9937.7	11067.3	13306.7	11908.8	10054.9	Amériques
- Northern America	7284.0	8205.9	9902.0	8127.3	7449.8	- Amérique du Nord
- LAIA	2440.8	2687.1	3204.5	3587.9	2425.0	- ALAI
- CACM	89.1	71.9	87.3	87.1	89.6	- MCC
- Caribbean	104.0	72.6	82.1	80.8	70.1	- Caraïbes
- Rest of America	19.8	29.8	30.8	25.7	20.4	- Autre d'Amérique
Asia excluding former USSR	10478.9	11283.8	14188.6	12962.6	13188.1	Asie ancienne URSS exclus
- Middle East	630.9	611.2	731.3	687.7	864.8	- Moyen-Orient
Asia former USSR	36.4	40.7	77.6	69.6	60.0	Asie ancienne URSS
Europe excluding former USSR	10307.4	10422.3	11108.2	10464.4	9953.5	Europe ancienne URSS exclus
- European Union	8868.4	9044.6	9559.2	8804.2	8282.1	- Union Européenne
- Eastern Europe	796.8	763.6	918.4	999.9	1020.4	- Europe de l'Est
- Rest of Europe	642.2	614.1	630.7	660.2	650.9	- Autre de l'Europe
Europe former USSR	191.1	149.3	200.3	224.2	246.1	Europe ancienne URSS
Oceania	262.7	281.3	286.7	258.0	246.0	Océanie
United States	6463.5	7207.8	8697.1	7122.1	6574.4	Etats-Unis d'Amérique
China, Hong Kong SAR	2644.5	2806.0	3540.5	3196.6	2978.8	Chine - RAS de Hong-Kong
Germany	2239.5	2227.3	2243.6	2264.3	2176.9	Allemagne
Japan	1682.3	1909.4	2421.3	2175.6	2047.6	Japon
Mexico	1445.7	1758.9	2312.0	2734.1	1835.3	Mexique
China	1189.8	1451.9	1903.9	2128.7	2554.9	Chine
United Kingdom	1603.1	1649.8	1614.4	1361.4	1137.2	Royaume-Uni
France-Monaco	1221.2	1232.2	1452.7	1130.6	1069.9	France-Monaco
Singapore	1131.8	1157.0	1422.6	1032.5	872.3	Singapour
Canada	820.1	997.7	1204.3	1004.2	874.1	Canada
Netherlands	622.4	767.0	898.8	900.8	837.7	Pays-Bas
Malaysia	646.1	646.2	1003.6	796.8	e870.8	Malaisie
Korea, Republic of	422.8	659.0	873.7	899.8	911.9	République de Corée
Italy-San Marino-Holy See	749.7	733.7	783.3	752.1	726.2	Italie-Saint-Marin-Saint-Siège
Thailand	496.8	438.6	521.0	466.8	e486.3	Thaïlande
Brazil	419.1	478.8	456.8	505.7	318.0	Brésil
Ireland	437.1	420.6	442.4	391.8	347.8	Irlande
Switzerland-Liechtenstein	406.0	393.4	422.2	412.5	378.2	Suisse-Liechtenstein
Sweden	396.7	379.4	428.2	339.2	315.5	Suède
Spain	311.5	341.9	354.8	377.8	400.9	Espagne
Austria	356.4	335.5	314.7	305.2	312.9	Autriche
Belgium	–	298.1	337.8	326.9	e358.6	Belgique
Finland	252.1	229.4	267.7	271.7	241.2	Finlande
Czech Republic	263.2	205.0	265.1	269.3	256.6	République tchèque
Hungary	172.7	175.1	245.0	290.8	319.2	Hongrie
Poland	224.1	244.4	231.2	232.9	220.2	Pologne
Australia	204.4	217.4	228.3	194.7	181.9	Australie
Philippines	261.6	201.6	203.4	203.8	146.8	Philippines
Denmark	175.3	202.9	216.2	189.8	193.3	Danemark
Turkey	191.8	187.9	195.6	124.7	197.9	Turquie

(Value as percentages of World total) **(Valeur en pourcentage du total mondial)**

Regions of the world	1993	1994	1995	1996	1997	1998	1999	2000	2001	2002	Régions du monde
World	100.0	100.0	100.0	100.0	100.0	100.0	100.0	100.0	100.0	100.0	Monde
Africa	2.5	2.1	1.6	1.4	1.4	1.5	1.3	1.5	1.7	1.9	Afrique
Americas	25.4	24.7	24.5	27.1	29.4	31.4	32.9	33.5	32.6	29.2	Amériques
- Northern America	19.4	18.2	18.2	20.9	22.1	23.0	24.4	24.9	22.3	21.6	- Amérique du Nord
- LAIA	5.5	5.9	5.9	5.7	6.8	7.7	8.0	8.1	9.8	7.0	- ALAI
- CACM	0.1	0.2	0.2	0.2	0.2	0.3	0.2	0.2	0.2	0.3	- MCC
- Caribbean	0.2	0.2	0.2	0.2	0.2	0.3	0.2	0.2	0.2	0.2	- Caraïbes
- Rest of America	0.2	0.1	0.1	0.1	0.1	0.1	0.1	0.1	0.1	0.1	- Autre d'Amérique
Asia excluding former USSR	40.9	40.8	40.3	39.1	36.0	33.1	33.5	35.7	35.5	38.3	Asie ancienne URSS exclus
- Middle East	3.8	2.6	1.9	2.2	1.5	2.0	1.8	1.8	1.9	2.5	- Moyen-Orient
Asia former USSR	0.0	0.1	0.1	0.1	0.1	0.1	0.1	0.2	0.2	0.2	Asie ancienne URSS
Europe excluding former USSR	30.0	30.7	31.8	30.5	31.4	32.5	30.9	27.9	28.7	28.9	Europe ancienne URSS exclus
- European Union	26.5	27.3	27.8	26.6	27.7	28.0	26.9	24.0	24.1	24.1	- Union Européenne
- Eastern Europe	1.0	1.1	1.5	1.7	1.9	2.5	2.3	2.3	2.7	3.0	- Europe de l'Est
- Rest of Europe	2.4	2.2	2.5	2.2	1.9	2.0	1.8	1.6	1.8	1.9	- Autre de l'Europe
Europe former USSR	0.3	0.6	0.6	0.6	0.7	0.6	0.4	0.5	0.6	0.7	Europe ancienne URSS
Oceania	1.0	1.0	1.1	1.2	0.9	0.8	0.8	0.7	0.7	0.7	Océanie

TRADE BY COMMODITY (Value in million US dollars)
Exports by principal countries or areas

COMMERCE PAR PRODUIT (Valeur en millions de dollars EU)
Exportations selon les principaux pays ou zones

Country or area	1998	1999	2000	2001	2002	Pays ou zone
World	29462.1	31291.8	37000.8	33906.5	32216.6	Monde
Africa	90.5	128.1	140.9	133.8	139.3	Afrique
Americas	5826.7	6402.6	7874.1	7341.5	5860.3	Amériques
- Northern America	3709.6	4005.9	4976.1	4539.1	3551.2	- Amérique du Nord
- LAIA	2084.6	2381.0	2869.2	2782.6	2289.3	- ALAI
- CACM	7.4	8.2	7.6	8.4	9.7	- MCC
- Caribbean	25.0	7.5	21.2	11.1	10.0	- Caraïbes
- Rest of America	0.0	0.0	0.0	0.4	0.1	- Autre d'Amérique
Asia excluding former USSR	12450.8	13926.2	17495.3	14942.7	15308.1	Asie ancienne URSS exclus
- Middle East	129.2	111.1	131.9	172.1	199.6	- Moyen-Orient
Asia former USSR	9.8	5.4	11.3	10.0	6.6	Asie ancienne URSS
Europe excluding former USSR	10817.6	10628.0	11250.1	11257.3	10667.5	Europe ancienne URSS exclus
- European Union	9658.9	9502.6	9991.1	9920.8	9241.5	- Union Européenne
- Eastern Europe	491.0	529.0	625.8	666.8	771.9	- Europe de l'Est
- Rest of Europe	667.7	596.5	633.2	669.7	654.0	- Autre de l'Europe
Europe former USSR	159.0	115.3	129.2	132.7	149.6	Europe ancienne URSS
Oceania	107.8	86.2	99.9	88.6	85.1	Océanie
China, Hong Kong SAR	2927.0	3447.2	4629.3	3892.9	3604.5	Chine - RAS de Hong-Kong
United States	3118.6	3336.1	4233.9	3798.0	2857.0	Etats-Unis d'Amérique
China	2399.9	2831.5	3610.2	3626.9	4226.8	Chine
Germany	2652.9	2558.6	2699.5	2811.0	2708.5	Allemagne
Mexico	1971.9	2252.5	2693.8	2599.2	2098.8	Mexique
Japan	2225.7	2327.9	2771.0	1995.6	1817.8	Japon
France-Monaco	1167.3	1145.5	1205.1	1126.0	1079.6	France-Monaco
United Kingdom	1019.2	1078.3	1256.8	1092.7	949.3	Royaume-Uni
Italy-San Marino-Holy See	891.0	868.1	889.7	900.3	872.5	Italie-Saint-Marin-Saint-Siège
Singapore	823.9	806.3	1049.3	845.6	813.4	Singapour
Thailand	630.5	744.6	796.1	795.9	e840.5	Thaïlande
Netherlands	543.7	742.4	871.8	857.8	731.3	Pays-Bas
Korea, Republic of	570.6	703.2	837.0	695.9	705.9	République de Corée
Canada	590.9	669.7	742.1	741.1	694.0	Canada
Finland	674.0	610.1	586.6	654.4	561.4	Finlande
Malaysia	440.2	557.7	818.8	574.5	e608.8	Malaisie
Austria	590.0	453.9	451.2	491.1	552.9	Autriche
Sweden	544.3	491.6	497.2	517.1	460.5	Suède
Switzerland-Liechtenstein	418.4	380.5	420.9	445.8	440.3	Suisse-Liechtenstein
Ireland	427.0	471.9	457.5	443.9	280.0	Irlande
Denmark	288.2	280.1	315.5	264.3	262.2	Danemark
Spain	250.5	260.4	245.5	263.6	285.6	Espagne
Belgium	–	294.5	265.5	313.4	e351.6	Belgique
Portugal	258.5	223.0	223.8	161.0	121.6	Portugal
Poland	150.4	165.8	186.1	213.5	235.6	Pologne
Indonesia	74.8	83.1	228.2	221.8	289.6	Indonésie
Czech Republic	139.8	127.2	161.0	170.0	180.5	République tchèque
Hungary	110.8	114.5	134.1	140.7	167.0	Hongrie
Turkey	107.6	88.2	108.0	145.7	167.8	Turquie
Brazil	68.5	90.1	130.4	127.4	e132.0	Brésil

(Value as percentages of World total) **(Valeur en pourcentage du total mondial)**

Regions of the world	1993	1994	1995	1996	1997	1998	1999	2000	2001	2002	Régions du monde
World	100.0	100.0	100.0	100.0	100.0	100.0	100.0	100.0	100.0	100.0	Monde
Africa	0.3	0.3	0.3	0.3	0.3	0.3	0.4	0.4	0.4	0.4	Afrique
Americas	16.3	17.0	15.4	17.1	18.5	19.8	20.5	21.3	21.7	18.2	Amériques
- Northern America	11.1	11.9	10.7	11.5	12.6	12.6	12.8	13.4	13.4	11.0	- Amérique du Nord
- LAIA	5.2	5.1	4.6	5.5	5.8	7.1	7.6	7.8	8.2	7.1	- ALAI
- CACM	0.0	0.0	0.0	0.1	0.1	0.0	0.0	0.0	0.0	0.0	- MCC
- Caribbean	0.0	0.0	0.0	0.0	0.0	0.1	0.0	0.1	0.0	0.0	- Caraïbes
- Rest of America	0.0	0.0	0.0	0.0	0.0	0.0	0.0	0.0	0.0	0.0	- Autre d'Amérique
Asia excluding former USSR	50.6	47.1	47.5	44.5	43.5	42.3	44.5	47.3	44.1	47.5	Asie ancienne URSS exclus
- Middle East	0.4	0.4	0.5	0.7	0.5	0.4	0.4	0.4	0.5	0.6	- Moyen-Orient
Asia former USSR	0.0	0.1	0.1	0.0	0.0	0.0	0.0	0.0	0.0	0.0	Asie ancienne URSS
Europe excluding former USSR	32.2	34.6	35.7	37.0	36.7	36.7	34.0	30.4	33.2	33.1	Europe ancienne URSS exclus
- European Union	28.8	31.3	32.2	33.4	33.5	32.8	30.4	27.0	29.3	28.7	- Union Européenne
- Eastern Europe	0.6	0.7	0.9	1.2	1.2	1.7	1.7	1.7	2.0	2.4	- Europe de l'Est
- Rest of Europe	2.7	2.7	2.7	2.4	1.9	2.3	1.9	1.7	2.0	2.0	- Autre de l'Europe
Europe former USSR	0.3	0.4	0.5	0.6	0.6	0.5	0.4	0.3	0.4	0.5	Europe ancienne URSS
Oceania	0.4	0.4	0.5	0.4	0.3	0.4	0.3	0.3	0.3	0.3	Océanie

772 Electrical apparatus for making and breaking electrical circuits

TRADE BY COMMODITY (Value in million US dollars)
Imports by principal countries or areas

COMMERCE PAR PRODUIT (Valeur en millions de dollars EU)
Importations selon les principaux pays ou zones

Country or area	1998	1999	2000	2001	2002	Pays ou zone
World	76978.4	80997.1	96487.7	90882.9	88832.9	Monde
Africa	1328.6	1318.2	1368.8	1469.8	1541.8	Afrique
Americas	22390.8	24648.4	30661.5	27953.0	24378.5	Amériques
- Northern America	14300.1	15962.1	19746.9	15954.4	15227.9	- Amérique du Nord
- LAIA	7467.4	8242.6	10347.3	11505.2	8681.2	- ALAI
- CACM	226.1	133.2	231.4	175.1	156.0	- MCC
- Caribbean	360.9	277.0	303.6	285.1	281.3	- Caraïbes
- Rest of America	36.4	33.5	32.3	33.2	32.2	- Autre d'Amérique
Asia excluding former USSR	22564.7	24506.3	30868.4	28714.1	31756.7	Asie ancienne URSS exclus
- Middle East	1920.8	1799.8	1929.0	1953.0	2199.1	- Moyen-Orient
Asia former USSR	116.8	110.8	145.4	125.3	134.6	Asie ancienne URSS
Europe excluding former USSR	29190.3	29137.4	31938.8	31236.6	29411.8	Europe ancienne URSS exclus
- European Union	24266.4	24346.8	26627.9	25622.3	23427.9	- Union Européenne
- Eastern Europe	2909.7	2872.6	3398.4	3710.2	4122.0	- Europe de l'Est
- Rest of Europe	2014.1	1918.0	1912.6	1904.1	1861.9	- Autre de l'Europe
Europe former USSR	616.3	511.5	705.1	690.4	831.2	Europe ancienne URSS
Oceania	771.0	764.5	799.7	693.7	778.2	Océanie
United States	11317.2	12434.7	15552.1	12595.0	12237.4	Etats-Unis d'Amérique
Mexico	5310.4	6472.5	8486.5	9644.6	7230.1	Mexique
Germany	5646.0	5613.6	5893.3	6682.7	5750.8	Allemagne
China	3036.8	3731.9	5419.9	6294.9	7870.0	Chine
China, Hong Kong SAR	2801.6	3095.3	4321.9	4056.2	4620.3	Chine - RAS de Hong-Kong
United Kingdom	3644.1	3645.2	4255.2	3462.9	3118.4	Royaume-Uni
Canada	2976.1	3521.3	4188.5	3351.5	2981.0	Canada
France-Monaco	3036.7	3160.6	3614.0	3015.7	2992.2	France-Monaco
Singapore	3028.3	3310.7	3675.6	2802.3	2777.4	Singapour
Malaysia	2382.2	2687.5	3653.7	3033.5	e3315.3	Malaisie
Japan	2063.3	2386.8	3024.2	2754.2	2814.9	Japon
Italy-San Marino-Holy See	2493.1	2467.6	2692.2	2690.2	2438.9	Italie-Saint-Marin-Saint-Siège
Korea, Republic of	1347.8	1896.8	2334.1	2023.2	2351.8	République de Corée
Thailand	1623.0	1522.9	1835.0	1694.3	e1765.3	Thaïlande
Spain	1403.5	1509.6	1526.5	1682.1	1482.6	Espagne
Netherlands	1412.6	1348.2	1567.0	1633.3	1371.4	Pays-Bas
Sweden	1272.4	1274.9	1488.1	1070.0	994.1	Suède
Hungary	700.5	989.1	1312.9	1398.0	1525.3	Hongrie
Switzerland-Liechtenstein	1182.3	1156.5	1177.7	1131.6	1030.9	Suisse-Liechtenstein
Belgium	-	1295.5	1340.9	1392.5	e1527.2	Belgique
Austria	1110.7	1057.3	1037.9	1035.4	1014.5	Autriche
Czech Republic	1176.5	812.2	942.6	1049.4	1173.1	République tchèque
Ireland	1034.5	983.0	1145.6	1086.0	876.1	Irlande
Brazil	960.9	908.5	1064.4	1099.5	846.9	Brésil
Philippines	1031.2	712.3	702.7	852.9	636.6	Philippines
Poland	673.6	672.6	681.9	700.3	766.7	Pologne
Finland	603.8	629.4	691.9	631.9	599.9	Finlande
Australia	605.1	595.2	638.7	542.1	611.5	Australie
Portugal	527.8	550.0	510.5	453.6	482.7	Portugal
Israel	521.5	539.4	590.9	436.4	363.9	Israël

(Value as percentages of World total) **(Valeur en pourcentage du total mondial)**

Regions of the world	1993	1994	1995	1996	1997	1998	1999	2000	2001	2002	Régions du monde
World	100.0	100.0	100.0	100.0	100.0	100.0	100.0	100.0	100.0	100.0	Monde
Africa	2.4	2.4	2.1	1.9	1.8	1.7	1.6	1.4	1.6	1.7	Afrique
Americas	26.6	27.6	25.8	26.5	28.1	29.1	30.4	31.8	30.8	27.4	Amériques
- Northern America	19.8	20.2	19.0	18.5	19.0	18.6	19.7	20.5	17.6	17.1	- Amérique du Nord
- LAIA	6.3	7.0	6.4	7.5	8.5	9.7	10.2	10.7	12.7	9.8	- ALAI
- CACM	0.1	0.1	0.1	0.1	0.2	0.3	0.2	0.2	0.2	0.2	- MCC
- Caribbean	0.3	0.3	0.3	0.3	0.4	0.5	0.3	0.3	0.3	0.3	- Caraïbes
- Rest of America	0.1	0.1	0.1	0.0	0.0	0.0	0.0	0.0	0.0	0.0	- Autre d'Amérique
Asia excluding former USSR	33.7	32.5	32.9	32.8	32.4	29.3	30.3	32.0	31.6	35.7	Asie ancienne URSS exclus
- Middle East	3.6	2.8	2.8	3.2	2.5	2.5	2.2	2.0	2.1	2.5	- Moyen-Orient
Asia former USSR	0.0	0.1	0.1	0.1	0.1	0.2	0.1	0.2	0.1	0.2	Asie ancienne URSS
Europe excluding former USSR	35.4	35.5	37.4	36.9	35.7	37.9	36.0	33.1	34.4	33.1	Europe ancienne URSS exclus
- European Union	31.6	31.5	32.5	31.7	30.5	31.5	30.1	27.6	28.2	26.4	- Union Européenne
- Eastern Europe	1.2	1.3	2.0	2.5	2.8	3.8	3.5	3.5	4.1	4.6	- Europe de l'Est
- Rest of Europe	2.6	2.6	2.8	2.7	2.4	2.6	2.4	2.0	2.1	2.1	- Autre de l'Europe
Europe former USSR	0.5	0.5	0.5	0.6	0.7	0.8	0.6	0.7	0.8	0.9	Europe ancienne URSS
Oceania	1.3	1.4	1.2	1.2	1.1	1.0	0.9	0.8	0.8	0.9	Océanie

Appareillage pour coupure ou connexion des circuits électriques; et leurs pièces détachées 772

TRADE BY COMMODITY (Value in million US dollars)
Exports by principal countries or areas

COMMERCE PAR PRODUIT (Valeur en millions de dollars EU)
Exportations selon les principaux pays ou zones

Country or area	1998	1999	2000	2001	2002	Pays ou zone
World	77683.1	81868.5	96264.5	86871.5	88346.5	Monde
Africa	225.2	269.1	311.0	333.2	357.9	Afrique
Americas	15776.6	17596.1	22212.5	18883.1	18629.1	Amériques
- Northern America	12100.9	13648.5	16614.0	13870.9	12954.8	- Amérique du Nord
- LAIA	3359.7	3815.3	5406.6	4814.0	5496.9	- ALAI
- CACM	55.8	54.5	98.9	120.9	93.2	- MCC
- Caribbean	260.1	77.9	92.9	77.0	79.6	- Caraïbes
- Rest of America	0.1	0.1	0.1	0.2	4.7	- Autre d'Amérique
Asia excluding former USSR	27135.7	30056.5	38787.0	32274.0	33807.4	Asie ancienne URSS exclus
- Middle East	169.0	169.5	190.7	245.0	275.5	- Moyen-Orient
Asia former USSR	17.0	8.4	15.1	13.6	8.5	Asie ancienne URSS
Europe excluding former USSR	34007.9	33367.4	34343.8	34691.2	34875.2	Europe ancienne URSS exclus
- European Union	29566.4	29202.6	29850.7	30112.5	29867.0	- Union Européenne
- Eastern Europe	1864.5	1680.1	2000.9	2196.2	2572.2	- Europe de l'Est
- Rest of Europe	2576.9	2484.7	2492.3	2382.5	2436.0	- Autre de l'Europe
Europe former USSR	211.7	229.4	229.1	301.7	312.2	Europe ancienne URSS
Oceania	309.2	341.7	366.0	374.7	356.2	Océanie
United States	10875.2	12412.9	15128.7	12498.1	11648.4	Etats-Unis d'Amérique
Germany	11313.8	10975.8	10752.3	11228.2	11423.4	Allemagne
Japan	9838.7	10681.2	13327.0	9901.9	10018.9	Japon
France-Monaco	5162.7	4932.5	5168.0	5023.9	5014.3	France-Monaco
Mexico	3050.6	3590.0	5155.6	4546.6	5221.3	Mexique
China, Hong Kong SAR	2739.9	3126.3	4359.7	4157.5	4621.1	Chine - RAS de Hong-Kong
United Kingdom	3502.0	3463.5	3566.4	3291.4	3099.0	Royaume-Uni
China	2248.6	2634.2	3376.9	3564.4	4243.2	Chine
Singapore	2351.3	2846.9	3261.8	2774.8	2881.1	Singapour
Malaysia	2481.9	2402.0	2562.2	2512.8	e2663.0	Malaisie
Italy-San Marino-Holy See	2134.1	2041.0	2132.6	2305.0	2277.8	Italie-Saint-Marin-Saint-Siège
Switzerland-Liechtenstein	2089.3	1976.1	2006.1	1898.8	1908.3	Suisse-Liechtenstein
Thailand	1210.9	1471.6	1886.7	1484.5	e1567.8	Thaïlande
Netherlands	1218.2	1334.8	1498.7	1439.9	1380.1	Pays-Bas
Canada	1225.6	1235.6	1485.3	1372.8	1306.3	Canada
Korea, Republic of	925.1	1064.8	1422.1	1253.0	1472.4	République de Corée
Austria	1099.9	1070.3	1227.4	1258.7	1334.8	Autriche
Philippines	1105.2	1321.6	1622.4	960.9	315.1	Philippines
Spain	973.9	1054.1	1055.2	1085.2	1019.5	Espagne
Sweden	1017.9	958.0	1071.1	1009.8	956.3	Suède
Ireland	785.6	923.3	1046.6	1100.0	794.9	Irlande
Belgium	–	1061.2	1066.2	1065.3	e1195.2	Belgique
Czech Republic	903.4	671.1	785.0	801.2	985.6	République tchèque
Hungary	558.8	599.3	758.0	841.4	916.4	Hongrie
Israel	408.5	410.1	489.2	400.7	277.4	Israël
Finland	371.8	340.7	364.7	399.7	383.8	Finlande
Denmark	357.7	363.0	348.4	340.4	342.2	Danemark
Indonesia	99.4	117.5	470.6	483.8	575.7	Indonésie
Poland	292.6	289.8	313.1	365.1	470.6	Pologne
Portugal	344.7	371.0	248.0	246.2	320.6	Portugal

(Value as percentages of World total) **(Valeur en pourcentage du total mondial)**

Regions of the world	1993	1994	1995	1996	1997	1998	1999	2000	2001	2002	Régions du monde
World	100.0	100.0	100.0	100.0	100.0	100.0	100.0	100.0	100.0	100.0	Monde
Africa	0.2	0.2	0.3	0.3	0.2	0.3	0.3	0.3	0.4	0.4	Afrique
Americas	18.9	19.7	18.0	18.9	20.0	20.3	21.5	23.1	21.7	21.1	Amériques
- Northern America	14.9	15.4	14.1	14.9	15.8	15.6	16.7	17.3	16.0	14.7	- Amérique du Nord
- LAIA	3.7	4.1	3.5	3.9	4.1	4.3	4.7	5.6	5.5	6.2	- ALAI
- CACM	0.0	0.0	0.0	0.0	0.1	0.1	0.1	0.1	0.1	0.1	- MCC
- Caribbean	0.3	0.3	0.2	0.0	0.1	0.3	0.1	0.1	0.1	0.1	- Caraïbes
- Rest of America	0.0	0.0	0.0	0.0	0.0	0.0	0.0	0.0	0.0	0.0	- Autre d'Amérique
Asia excluding former USSR	36.4	35.8	36.2	34.9	36.0	34.9	36.7	40.3	37.2	38.3	Asie ancienne URSS exclus
- Middle East	0.2	0.2	0.2	0.2	0.2	0.2	0.2	0.2	0.3	0.3	- Moyen-Orient
Asia former USSR	0.0	0.0	0.0	0.0	0.0	0.0	0.0	0.0	0.0	0.0	Asie ancienne URSS
Europe excluding former USSR	43.9	43.5	44.8	45.2	43.0	43.8	40.8	35.7	39.9	39.5	Europe ancienne URSS exclus
- European Union	39.4	38.9	39.5	40.0	38.0	38.1	35.7	31.0	34.7	33.8	- Union Européenne
- Eastern Europe	0.7	0.8	1.4	1.5	1.8	2.4	2.1	2.1	2.5	2.9	- Europe de l'Est
- Rest of Europe	3.8	3.8	3.8	3.7	3.3	3.3	3.0	2.6	2.7	2.8	- Autre de l'Europe
Europe former USSR	0.1	0.2	0.2	0.2	0.3	0.3	0.3	0.2	0.3	0.4	Europe ancienne URSS
Oceania	0.5	0.5	0.5	0.6	0.5	0.4	0.4	0.4	0.4	0.4	Océanie

773 Equipment for distribution of electricity

TRADE BY COMMODITY (Value in million US dollars)
Imports by principal countries or areas

COMMERCE PAR PRODUIT (Valeur en millions de dollars EU)
Importations selon les principaux pays ou zones

Country or area	1998	1999	2000	2001	2002	Pays ou zone
World	36827.0	38378.1	41743.3	40753.0	40984.7	Monde
Africa	793.5	780.7	720.4	778.0	825.5	Afrique
Americas	13401.1	14454.6	16077.9	15342.1	14347.2	Amériques
- Northern America	9125.1	10117.6	10992.7	9896.3	10457.5	- Amérique du Nord
- LAIA	4009.6	4092.5	4801.5	5158.2	3631.7	- ALAI
- CACM	100.5	87.9	113.3	110.8	105.3	- MCC
- Caribbean	131.9	128.2	134.7	142.2	122.1	- Caraïbes
- Rest of America	34.0	28.4	35.7	34.7	30.6	- Autre d'Amérique
Asia excluding former USSR	7831.1	8204.6	9480.0	8944.2	9442.2	Asie ancienne URSS exclus
- Middle East	810.7	686.2	975.1	951.1	1012.7	- Moyen-Orient
Asia former USSR	95.7	85.0	107.3	104.6	111.4	Asie ancienne URSS
Europe excluding former USSR	13948.0	14156.5	14580.1	14818.0	15456.5	Europe ancienne URSS exclus
- European Union	11678.0	11880.4	12115.9	12257.5	12625.0	- Union Européenne
- Eastern Europe	1606.7	1639.0	1828.1	1921.9	2186.5	- Europe de l'Est
- Rest of Europe	663.4	637.1	636.1	638.6	645.0	- Autre de l'Europe
Europe former USSR	384.9	287.8	346.2	397.9	475.2	Europe ancienne URSS
Oceania	372.7	408.9	431.3	368.2	326.8	Océanie
United States	7424.1	8206.2	8996.1	8149.8	8670.8	Etats-Unis d'Amérique
Germany	3665.2	3714.6	3647.3	3841.6	3847.7	Allemagne
Mexico	3098.9	3429.2	3965.7	4066.8	3106.5	Mexique
Japan	1432.7	1678.4	1994.6	1981.5	2128.5	Japon
Canada	1698.8	1909.1	1993.9	1743.4	1783.3	Canada
United Kingdom	1536.2	1593.0	1671.2	1601.8	1580.1	Royaume-Uni
France-Monaco	1496.0	1444.5	1491.1	1441.7	1604.0	France-Monaco
China, Hong Kong SAR	1269.5	1282.8	1476.7	1375.8	1382.3	Chine - RAS de Hong-Kong
China	956.6	1175.9	1414.3	1435.7	1718.7	Chine
Spain	724.8	869.3	878.2	978.8	972.1	Espagne
Austria	652.5	645.1	665.7	714.8	746.9	Autriche
Belgium	–	818.3	736.5	873.7	e958.2	Belgique
Italy-San Marino-Holy See	607.9	621.5	688.9	710.9	740.1	Italie-Saint-Marin-Saint-Siège
Thailand	622.2	620.7	652.9	621.1	e647.1	Thaïlande
Singapore	691.9	632.3	669.6	599.6	490.1	Singapour
Hungary	458.0	532.6	591.3	563.6	613.5	Hongrie
Netherlands	570.1	578.6	567.2	525.9	502.2	Pays-Bas
Sweden	492.4	491.8	564.8	465.2	524.3	Suède
Czech Republic	448.4	377.9	417.7	467.7	519.8	République tchèque
Korea, Republic of	337.7	437.6	544.8	407.0	464.8	République de Corée
Brazil	304.5	249.8	397.1	657.9	196.1	Brésil
Malaysia	308.2	334.9	395.0	326.6	e357.0	Malaisie
Portugal	325.3	310.2	343.9	332.9	398.0	Portugal
Poland	290.5	310.1	319.3	350.4	394.9	Pologne
Australia	293.7	333.7	347.7	300.1	258.4	Australie
Philippines	306.2	302.8	283.3	266.0	226.0	Philippines
Finland	256.6	256.5	267.7	248.9	255.7	Finlande
Switzerland-Liechtenstein	255.8	251.0	261.8	251.6	240.3	Suisse-Liechtenstein
Ireland	221.5	234.1	313.2	244.9	226.7	Irlande
Slovakia	215.2	197.5	243.1	262.8	304.0	Slovaquie

(Value as percentages of World total) **(Valeur en pourcentage du total mondial)**

Regions of the world	1993	1994	1995	1996	1997	1998	1999	2000	2001	2002	Régions du monde
World	100.0	100.0	100.0	100.0	100.0	100.0	100.0	100.0	100.0	100.0	Monde
Africa	3.1	2.6	2.4	2.4	2.4	2.2	2.0	1.7	1.9	2.0	Afrique
Americas	34.0	35.6	33.7	33.3	35.5	36.4	37.7	38.5	37.6	35.0	Amériques
- Northern America	23.3	25.1	23.0	22.8	24.1	24.8	26.4	26.3	24.3	25.5	- Amérique du Nord
- LAIA	9.9	9.9	10.0	9.9	10.6	10.9	10.7	11.5	12.7	8.9	- ALAI
- CACM	0.2	0.2	0.2	0.2	0.3	0.3	0.2	0.3	0.3	0.3	- MCC
- Caribbean	0.4	0.3	0.5	0.3	0.4	0.4	0.3	0.3	0.3	0.3	- Caraïbes
- Rest of America	0.1	0.1	0.1	0.1	0.1	0.1	0.1	0.1	0.1	0.1	- Autre d'Amérique
Asia excluding former USSR	27.1	24.4	23.7	24.7	24.7	21.3	21.4	22.7	21.9	23.0	Asie ancienne URSS exclus
- Middle East	4.9	3.2	2.6	2.7	2.3	2.2	1.8	2.3	2.3	2.5	- Moyen-Orient
Asia former USSR	0.1	0.2	0.5	0.5	0.3	0.3	0.2	0.3	0.3	0.3	Asie ancienne URSS
Europe excluding former USSR	33.0	35.0	37.4	36.8	35.1	37.9	36.9	34.9	36.4	37.7	Europe ancienne URSS exclus
- European Union	29.5	31.1	32.7	31.8	29.8	31.7	31.0	29.0	30.1	30.8	- Union Européenne
- Eastern Europe	1.6	1.9	2.5	3.0	3.5	4.4	4.3	4.4	4.7	5.3	- Europe de l'Est
- Rest of Europe	1.9	2.0	2.1	1.9	1.7	1.8	1.7	1.5	1.6	1.6	- Autre de l'Europe
Europe former USSR	1.4	1.0	1.1	1.1	1.1	1.0	0.7	0.8	1.0	1.2	Europe ancienne URSS
Oceania	1.3	1.3	1.3	1.1	1.0	1.0	1.1	1.0	0.9	0.8	Océanie

TRADE BY COMMODITY (Value in million US dollars)
Exports by principal countries or areas

COMMERCE PAR PRODUIT (Valeur en millions de dollars EU)
Exportations selon les principaux pays ou zones

Country or area	1998	1999	2000	2001	2002	Pays ou zone
World	34379.1	35749.4	39921.0	37229.2	38245.6	Monde
Africa	461.9	520.3	540.0	605.2	644.6	Afrique
Americas	11209.6	11935.2	13913.9	12050.8	11520.6	Amériques
- Northern America	5685.7	5681.9	6832.0	5761.3	5330.0	- Amérique du Nord
- LAIA	5439.1	6190.1	6995.5	6227.3	6146.4	- ALAI
- CACM	73.8	53.7	65.6	47.6	38.0	- MCC
- Caribbean	10.9	9.4	20.9	14.3	6.1	- Caraïbes
- Rest of America	0.1	0.0	0.0	0.3	0.2	- Autre d'Amérique
Asia excluding former USSR	7933.4	8688.0	10262.1	9278.4	9694.4	Asie ancienne URSS exclus
- Middle East	553.1	506.9	587.9	704.5	668.7	- Moyen-Orient
Asia former USSR	16.7	6.3	7.8	7.0	5.5	Asie ancienne URSS
Europe excluding former USSR	14307.2	14217.5	14744.7	14796.8	15825.4	Europe ancienne URSS exclus
- European Union	11522.5	11281.5	11403.5	11095.1	11457.9	- Union Européenne
- Eastern Europe	2094.6	2268.4	2624.0	2962.4	3630.7	- Europe de l'Est
- Rest of Europe	690.2	667.5	717.2	739.3	736.9	- Autre de l'Europe
Europe former USSR	309.9	273.2	336.9	369.4	409.3	Europe ancienne URSS
Oceania	140.3	108.9	115.6	121.7	145.8	Océanie
Mexico	5223.1	6008.2	6719.8	5949.7	5886.8	Mexique
United States	5097.0	5034.0	6060.2	5065.2	4742.0	Etats-Unis d'Amérique
Germany	3105.0	3007.1	2873.1	3110.4	3285.1	Allemagne
Japan	1767.1	1905.2	2157.2	1628.4	1654.9	Japon
China	1082.5	1325.6	1688.1	1764.4	2229.4	Chine
China, Hong Kong SAR	1259.7	1333.2	1648.4	1402.7	1473.6	Chine - RAS de Hong-Kong
France-Monaco	1415.9	1307.7	1321.5	1340.2	1425.2	France-Monaco
Italy-San Marino-Holy See	996.7	990.0	1050.5	1085.3	1053.0	Italie-Saint-Marin-Saint-Siège
United Kingdom	1106.9	983.0	983.4	917.1	835.5	Royaume-Uni
Portugal	927.3	923.1	998.7	747.6	1003.0	Portugal
Spain	865.7	883.9	823.6	866.4	799.9	Espagne
Hungary	667.1	724.4	848.0	830.6	896.9	Hongrie
Canada	588.7	647.9	771.8	696.1	587.9	Canada
Czech Republic	545.4	571.6	619.5	706.6	819.0	République tchèque
Poland	443.0	514.5	632.7	743.6	895.8	Pologne
Austria	620.9	556.7	604.7	632.5	650.3	Autriche
Korea, Republic of	516.0	575.3	634.2	671.4	651.8	République de Corée
Sweden	549.6	717.3	675.4	491.7	478.1	Suède
Philippines	483.9	576.3	652.4	550.4	534.2	Philippines
Belgium	–	632.9	659.3	660.0	e740.5	Belgique
Netherlands	457.7	444.4	519.3	481.3	482.0	Pays-Bas
Thailand	494.3	549.0	484.6	415.6	e439.0	Thaïlande
Turkey	373.6	334.1	379.7	479.3	475.0	Turquie
Singapore	365.7	397.3	475.3	389.9	331.8	Singapour
Switzerland-Liechtenstein	400.5	385.1	374.4	363.5	378.3	Suisse-Liechtenstein
Malaysia	318.0	341.0	423.2	365.0	e386.8	Malaisie
Slovakia	287.4	299.8	323.3	369.7	459.9	Slovaquie
Ireland	370.7	385.5	363.6	263.9	208.5	Irlande
Indonesia	226.4	267.8	337.6	373.3	232.6	Indonésie
Tunisia	257.8	252.0	239.2	279.4	e290.6	Tunisie

(Value as percentages of World total) **(Valeur en pourcentage du total mondial)**

Regions of the world	1993	1994	1995	1996	1997	1998	1999	2000	2001	2002	Régions du monde
World	100.0	100.0	100.0	100.0	100.0	100.0	100.0	100.0	100.0	100.0	Monde
Africa	0.9	1.0	1.0	1.0	1.1	1.3	1.5	1.4	1.6	1.7	Afrique
Americas	31.3	30.9	29.0	30.6	32.6	32.6	33.4	34.9	32.4	30.1	Amériques
- Northern America	17.1	17.4	16.1	15.9	17.1	16.5	15.9	17.1	15.5	13.9	- Amérique du Nord
- LAIA	14.1	13.4	12.7	14.6	15.2	15.8	17.3	17.5	16.7	16.1	- ALAI
- CACM	0.1	0.1	0.1	0.1	0.2	0.2	0.2	0.2	0.1	0.1	- MCC
- Caribbean	0.1	0.1	0.1	0.0	0.0	0.0	0.0	0.1	0.0	0.0	- Caraïbes
- Rest of America	0.0	0.0	0.0	0.0	0.0	0.0	0.0	0.0	0.0	0.0	- Autre d'Amérique
Asia excluding former USSR	28.9	26.9	26.1	25.6	25.4	23.1	24.3	25.7	24.9	25.3	Asie ancienne URSS exclus
- Middle East	1.7	1.6	1.8	2.0	1.7	1.6	1.4	1.5	1.9	1.7	- Moyen-Orient
Asia former USSR	0.0	0.1	0.1	0.1	0.0	0.0	0.0	0.0	0.0	0.0	Asie ancienne URSS
Europe excluding former USSR	38.0	39.9	42.4	41.2	39.5	41.6	39.8	36.9	39.7	41.4	Europe ancienne URSS exclus
- European Union	33.7	35.3	36.6	34.9	32.7	33.5	31.6	28.6	29.8	30.0	- Union Européenne
- Eastern Europe	2.1	2.2	3.4	4.0	4.8	6.1	6.3	6.6	8.0	9.5	- Europe de l'Est
- Rest of Europe	2.2	2.3	2.3	2.3	2.0	2.0	1.9	1.8	2.0	1.9	- Autre de l'Europe
Europe former USSR	0.4	0.7	0.8	0.9	0.9	0.9	0.8	0.8	1.0	1.1	Europe ancienne URSS
Oceania	0.6	0.6	0.7	0.5	0.4	0.4	0.3	0.3	0.3	0.4	Océanie

774 Electro-medical and radiological equipment

TRADE BY COMMODITY (Value in million US dollars)
Imports by principal countries or areas

COMMERCE PAR PRODUIT (Valeur en millions de dollars EU)
Importations selon les principaux pays ou zones

Country or area	1998	1999	2000	2001	2002	Pays ou zone
World	12613.7	13022.5	13847.0	15419.5	16791.7	Monde
Africa	168.2	189.6	196.2	221.0	247.7	Afrique
Americas	3883.5	4068.4	4434.7	4908.3	5687.4	Amériques
- Northern America	2970.2	3301.0	3634.9	4096.1	4996.0	- Amérique du Nord
- LAIA	846.0	688.7	712.0	734.6	609.1	- ALAI
- CACM	27.1	43.7	51.2	37.7	36.0	- MCC
- Caribbean	25.6	26.9	28.0	33.3	41.1	- Caraïbes
- Rest of America	14.6	8.0	8.5	6.7	5.2	- Autre d'Amérique
Asia excluding former USSR	2713.5	2917.1	3608.8	3912.0	3968.3	Asie ancienne URSS exclus
- Middle East	437.4	379.5	444.2	469.7	495.0	- Moyen-Orient
Asia former USSR	55.9	48.6	29.0	42.7	26.5	Asie ancienne URSS
Europe excluding former USSR	4928.6	5099.7	5054.6	5593.5	6130.3	Europe ancienne URSS exclus
- European Union	4287.8	4567.0	4471.2	4967.5	5451.5	- Union Européenne
- Eastern Europe	317.9	220.7	292.4	329.3	322.8	- Europe de l'Est
- Rest of Europe	323.0	311.9	290.9	296.7	356.0	- Autre de l'Europe
Europe former USSR	601.4	403.1	258.9	508.6	439.6	Europe ancienne URSS
Oceania	262.7	296.1	264.8	233.3	291.9	Océanie
United States	2664.9	2929.4	3253.6	3679.9	4539.8	Etats-Unis d'Amérique
Germany	1103.1	1208.2	1066.6	1215.2	1336.8	Allemagne
Japan	815.5	945.6	1052.4	1047.3	1064.8	Japon
France-Monaco	705.0	703.3	805.0	948.7	1060.5	France-Monaco
China	332.7	501.4	683.1	1048.3	942.2	Chine
Netherlands	492.8	640.0	572.0	638.6	690.8	Pays-Bas
United Kingdom	440.7	380.4	436.7	591.1	620.5	Royaume-Uni
Italy-San Marino-Holy See	410.9	442.0	450.4	460.4	555.6	Italie-Saint-Marin-Saint-Siège
Canada	304.9	370.8	381.0	415.4	454.0	Canada
Russian Federation	510.2	338.6	205.0	433.0	360.8	Fédération de Russie
Spain	276.7	330.8	294.3	287.2	321.2	Espagne
Brazil	421.2	271.6	225.6	338.0	249.6	Brésil
Korea, Republic of	145.5	214.0	312.8	296.2	335.5	République de Corée
China, Hong Kong SAR	330.6	232.6	228.7	246.3	223.2	Chine - RAS de Hong-Kong
Australia	229.9	255.6	227.9	201.0	254.3	Australie
Mexico	131.5	213.4	283.0	219.0	221.7	Mexique
India	128.4	133.4	156.1	196.3	241.7	Inde
Sweden	190.1	177.9	159.8	159.5	160.4	Suède
Belgium	–	214.0	216.8	194.2	e213.0	Belgique
Switzerland-Liechtenstein	164.0	171.3	161.7	159.8	178.8	Suisse-Liechtenstein
Austria	174.2	166.3	163.5	146.0	166.1	Autriche
Israel	76.0	96.8	157.4	175.1	184.6	Israël
Turkey	169.3	134.2	129.6	101.1	96.5	Turquie
Singapore	71.9	76.2	119.7	85.0	132.6	Singapour
Iran (Islamic Republic of)	106.6	67.6	77.8	88.0	145.1	Iran (République islamique d')
Poland	150.2	76.4	89.3	81.2	87.4	Pologne
Saudi Arabia	78.2	74.3	81.4	111.7	e115.6	Arabie saoudite
Norway	92.8	79.0	76.2	86.5	119.7	Norvège
Finland	64.3	72.3	66.8	71.1	82.0	Finlande
Denmark	63.3	66.3	72.6	81.4	71.3	Danemark

(Value as percentages of World total) **(Valeur en pourcentage du total mondial)**

Regions of the world	1993	1994	1995	1996	1997	1998	1999	2000	2001	2002	Régions du monde
World	100.0	100.0	100.0	100.0	100.0	100.0	100.0	100.0	100.0	100.0	Monde
Africa	1.8	2.4	2.2	1.9	1.7	1.3	1.5	1.4	1.4	1.5	Afrique
Americas	31.1	28.4	26.0	25.3	28.6	30.8	31.2	32.0	31.8	33.9	Amériques
- Northern America	26.0	22.8	21.2	20.2	22.2	23.5	25.3	26.3	26.6	29.8	- Amérique du Nord
- LAIA	4.8	5.1	4.4	4.7	5.9	6.7	5.3	5.1	4.8	3.6	- ALAI
- CACM	0.2	0.3	0.2	0.2	0.3	0.2	0.3	0.4	0.2	0.2	- MCC
- Caribbean	0.1	0.1	0.1	0.2	0.2	0.2	0.2	0.2	0.2	0.2	- Caraïbes
- Rest of America	0.1	0.1	0.1	0.1	0.1	0.1	0.1	0.1	0.0	0.0	- Autre d'Amérique
Asia excluding former USSR	21.9	22.3	24.0	25.6	24.5	21.5	22.4	26.1	25.4	23.6	Asie ancienne URSS exclus
- Middle East	3.2	2.5	3.6	4.2	3.8	3.5	2.9	3.2	3.0	2.9	- Moyen-Orient
Asia former USSR	0.1	0.2	0.5	0.5	0.4	0.4	0.4	0.2	0.3	0.2	Asie ancienne URSS
Europe excluding former USSR	39.2	39.5	40.0	40.1	38.1	39.1	39.2	36.5	36.3	36.5	Europe ancienne URSS exclus
- European Union	33.6	33.8	34.4	34.7	33.2	34.0	35.1	32.3	32.2	32.5	- Union Européenne
- Eastern Europe	3.2	3.0	2.8	2.5	2.6	2.5	1.7	2.1	2.1	1.9	- Europe de l'Est
- Rest of Europe	2.4	2.7	2.8	2.8	2.4	2.6	2.4	2.1	1.9	2.1	- Autre de l'Europe
Europe former USSR	3.8	4.7	5.0	4.5	4.6	4.8	3.1	1.9	3.3	2.6	Europe ancienne URSS
Oceania	2.1	2.5	2.3	2.2	2.1	2.1	2.3	1.9	1.5	1.7	Océanie

TRADE BY COMMODITY (Value in million US dollars)
Exports by principal countries or areas

COMMERCE PAR PRODUIT (Valeur en millions de dollars EU)
Exportations selon les principaux pays ou zones

Country or area	1998	1999	2000	2001	2002	Pays ou zone
World	13954.7	14123.1	14784.2	15783.9	17045.9	Monde
Africa	25.3	12.1	19.4	17.0	13.7	Afrique
Americas	4412.2	4728.9	5045.7	5438.7	5638.3	Amériques
- Northern America	4176.5	4483.8	4789.7	5271.9	5387.7	- Amérique du Nord
- LAIA	233.3	242.4	251.9	158.4	243.8	- ALAI
- CACM	1.0	1.2	2.6	2.3	1.6	- MCC
- Caribbean	1.4	1.4	1.4	5.8	5.1	- Caraïbes
- Rest of America	0.1	0.0	0.1	0.3	0.1	- Autre d'Amérique
Asia excluding former USSR	2776.8	2833.3	3160.2	3435.9	3374.7	Asie ancienne URSS exclus
- Middle East	8.1	10.0	12.0	11.3	21.8	- Moyen-Orient
Asia former USSR	2.9	1.3	2.5	2.7	2.0	Asie ancienne URSS
Europe excluding former USSR	6693.3	6487.7	6460.1	6786.1	7907.6	Europe ancienne URSS exclus
- European Union	6448.1	6242.2	6187.4	6466.1	7514.8	- Union Européenne
- Eastern Europe	47.9	37.1	41.9	55.1	81.1	- Europe de l'Est
- Rest of Europe	197.4	208.4	230.8	264.9	311.8	- Autre de l'Europe
Europe former USSR	15.8	12.4	45.8	56.4	64.7	Europe ancienne URSS
Oceania	28.4	47.4	50.4	47.1	45.0	Océanie
United States	4062.3	4346.4	4621.1	5088.0	5143.1	Etats-Unis d'Amérique
Germany	2721.0	2401.8	2344.3	2857.0	3468.1	Allemagne
Japan	1849.5	1916.9	1932.7	1934.0	1970.7	Japon
Netherlands	1183.2	1316.9	1253.7	815.2	865.7	Pays-Bas
France-Monaco	683.5	703.4	765.2	898.9	1026.1	France-Monaco
Israel	438.1	361.0	512.5	631.8	472.0	Israël
United Kingdom	448.1	419.1	408.2	449.8	513.4	Royaume-Uni
Finland	297.3	314.4	292.9	338.2	339.4	Finlande
Italy-San Marino-Holy See	261.4	261.1	272.2	275.3	289.4	Italie-Saint-Marin-Saint-Siège
Sweden	273.1	252.6	227.6	212.6	243.4	Suède
Mexico	216.5	229.3	236.9	142.6	228.5	Mexique
Korea, Republic of	121.7	153.6	232.8	236.7	183.5	République de Corée
China, Hong Kong SAR	203.9	169.8	148.5	191.3	178.2	Chine - RAS de Hong-Kong
Canada	114.1	137.4	168.5	183.9	244.5	Canada
Switzerland-Liechtenstein	148.8	139.3	164.7	190.1	203.7	Suisse-Liechtenstein
Denmark	163.6	130.7	157.4	151.7	172.8	Danemark
Austria	104.2	144.7	147.9	142.4	198.5	Autriche
China	50.7	52.6	113.1	175.0	240.2	Chine
Belgium	–	155.9	137.9	124.0	e139.1	Belgique
India	21.5	79.8	92.4	134.6	168.4	Inde
Spain	97.5	82.8	79.3	96.9	94.8	Espagne
Ireland	27.3	51.1	93.6	95.9	155.9	Irlande
Norway	43.7	62.9	54.4	64.0	93.9	Norvège
Singapore	55.4	57.6	61.3	58.6	69.6	Singapour
Australia	24.2	43.1	45.8	42.0	43.7	Australie
Belgium-Luxembourg	176.7	–	–	–	–	Belgique-Luxembourg
Hungary	33.0	23.8	23.8	29.1	54.8	Hongrie
Malaysia	13.1	17.2	21.9	26.6	e28.2	Malaisie
Indonesia	7.4	8.2	18.4	23.5	29.0	Indonésie
Ukraine	0.6	0.3	3.1	38.8	42.8	Ukraine

(Value as percentages of World total) **(Valeur en pourcentage du total mondial)**

Regions of the world	1993	1994	1995	1996	1997	1998	1999	2000	2001	2002	Régions du monde
World	100.0	100.0	100.0	100.0	100.0	100.0	100.0	100.0	100.0	100.0	Monde
Africa	0.1	0.1	0.1	0.1	0.1	0.2	0.1	0.1	0.1	0.1	Afrique
Americas	27.8	28.4	27.9	30.3	31.8	31.6	33.5	34.1	34.5	33.1	Amériques
- Northern America	27.2	27.8	27.5	29.6	30.4	29.9	31.7	32.4	33.4	31.6	- Amérique du Nord
- LAIA	0.6	0.6	0.4	0.7	1.3	1.7	1.7	1.7	1.0	1.4	- ALAI
- CACM	0.0	0.0	0.0	0.0	0.0	0.0	0.0	0.0	0.0	0.0	- MCC
- Caribbean	0.0	0.0	0.0	0.0	0.0	0.0	0.0	0.0	0.0	0.0	- Caraïbes
- Rest of America	0.0	0.0	0.0	0.0	0.0	0.0	0.0	0.0	0.0	0.0	- Autre d'Amérique
Asia excluding former USSR	21.4	19.5	18.9	18.2	19.8	19.9	20.1	21.4	21.8	19.8	Asie ancienne URSS exclus
- Middle East	0.1	0.1	0.2	0.1	0.1	0.1	0.1	0.1	0.1	0.1	- Moyen-Orient
Asia former USSR	0.0	0.0	0.0	0.1	0.0	0.0	0.0	0.0	0.0	0.0	Asie ancienne URSS
Europe excluding former USSR	50.4	51.4	52.4	50.8	47.9	48.0	45.9	43.7	43.0	46.4	Europe ancienne URSS exclus
- European Union	48.4	49.5	50.4	49.0	46.3	46.2	44.2	41.9	41.0	44.1	- Union Européenne
- Eastern Europe	0.3	0.3	0.3	0.2	0.3	0.3	0.3	0.3	0.3	0.5	- Europe de l'Est
- Rest of Europe	1.7	1.7	1.7	1.5	1.3	1.4	1.5	1.6	1.7	1.8	- Autre de l'Europe
Europe former USSR	0.1	0.1	0.1	0.1	0.1	0.1	0.1	0.3	0.4	0.4	Europe ancienne URSS
Oceania	0.4	0.4	0.5	0.4	0.2	0.2	0.3	0.3	0.3	0.3	Océanie

775 Household type equipment, nes

TRADE BY COMMODITY (Value in million US dollars)
Imports by principal countries or areas

COMMERCE PAR PRODUIT (Valeur en millions de dollars EU
Importations selon les principaux pays ou zone

Country or area	1998	1999	2000	2001	2002	Pays ou zone
World	35301.6	36500.7	38675.9	40082.1	43985.9	Monde
Africa	541.2	493.0	600.1	625.7	666.2	Afrique
Americas	9190.9	9864.0	11063.4	11860.0	12667.9	Amériques
- Northern America	7216.3	8035.8	8971.2	9722.1	10759.8	- Amérique du Nord
- LAIA	1501.1	1431.4	1707.1	1729.9	1482.6	- ALAI
- CACM	168.3	149.3	156.1	175.9	199.9	- MCC
- Caribbean	243.9	188.7	178.8	186.3	175.2	- Caraïbes
- Rest of America	61.2	58.8	50.2	45.8	50.4	- Autre d'Amérique
Asia excluding former USSR	6214.4	6652.0	7746.6	7733.3	8137.4	Asie ancienne URSS exclus
- Middle East	1235.2	1075.9	1295.2	1099.2	1135.1	- Moyen-Orient
Asia former USSR	127.1	88.4	69.2	76.3	82.8	Asie ancienne URSS
Europe excluding former USSR	18007.0	18277.6	17933.8	18398.4	20507.9	Europe ancienne URSS exclus
- European Union	15475.9	15798.9	15536.1	15981.2	17683.0	- Union Européenne
- Eastern Europe	1294.6	1224.5	1230.6	1260.6	1501.5	- Europe de l'Est
- Rest of Europe	1236.5	1254.2	1167.1	1156.5	1323.4	- Autre de l'Europe
Europe former USSR	422.6	291.3	360.6	610.6	951.0	Europe ancienne URSS
Oceania	798.3	834.6	902.3	777.8	972.7	Océanie
United States	5930.5	6700.5	7570.8	8302.8	9209.8	Etats-Unis d'Amérique
Germany	3332.6	3235.7	3057.9	3170.1	3321.5	Allemagne
United Kingdom	2069.3	2472.1	2681.7	2811.4	3268.5	Royaume-Uni
China, Hong Kong SAR	2414.9	2499.5	2696.4	2689.9	2524.1	Chine - RAS de Hong-Kong
France-Monaco	2478.4	2503.7	2417.2	2471.7	2707.0	France-Monaco
Japan	1045.3	1305.2	1628.6	1849.7	2119.1	Japon
Canada	1281.7	1330.9	1393.9	1413.7	1542.0	Canada
Netherlands	1325.2	1336.3	1325.5	1327.5	1358.2	Pays-Bas
Spain	1053.5	1095.4	1209.0	1131.2	1314.4	Espagne
Italy-San Marino-Holy See	921.8	1010.5	975.2	1001.1	1209.5	Italie-Saint-Marin-Saint-Siège
Belgium	–	989.1	865.0	907.0	e994.7	Belgique
Australia	634.6	665.6	741.4	624.1	778.7	Australie
Austria	787.7	696.1	610.8	628.7	675.2	Autriche
Mexico	464.8	576.6	766.8	766.4	733.5	Mexique
Sweden	636.4	582.3	599.2	627.1	711.5	Suède
Switzerland-Liechtenstein	578.5	586.5	544.9	512.5	553.9	Suisse-Liechtenstein
Poland	508.0	480.5	483.1	469.3	521.8	Pologne
Denmark	433.0	377.9	380.3	418.6	493.5	Danemark
Greece	436.1	421.2	356.9	408.1	e451.2	Grèce
Portugal	389.2	401.9	387.8	359.8	394.2	Portugal
Finland	380.2	320.4	329.6	349.5	409.7	Finlande
Norway	368.5	362.2	333.9	330.4	383.8	Norvège
Czech Republic	328.9	315.3	298.8	305.7	354.3	République tchèque
Turkey	436.4	359.0	400.7	194.8	180.4	Turquie
Singapore	275.3	327.4	311.7	304.2	314.8	Singapour
Ireland	269.0	299.4	291.0	315.3	316.4	Irlande
China	202.4	225.8	293.1	303.1	456.9	Chine
Russian Federation	181.3	94.3	178.5	344.5	645.2	Fédération de Russie
Korea, Republic of	121.1	188.8	301.5	300.7	380.6	République de Corée
Israel	232.8	224.7	271.8	297.9	258.2	Israël

(Value as percentages of World total) **(Valeur en pourcentage du total mondial**

Regions of the world	1993	1994	1995	1996	1997	1998	1999	2000	2001	2002	Régions du monde
World	100.0	100.0	100.0	100.0	100.0	100.0	100.0	100.0	100.0	100.0	Monde
Africa	1.8	1.6	1.5	1.5	1.5	1.5	1.4	1.6	1.6	1.5	Afrique
Americas	23.8	24.1	21.5	21.6	23.9	26.0	27.0	28.6	29.6	28.8	Amériques
- Northern America	18.5	18.6	16.8	17.0	18.5	20.4	22.0	23.2	24.3	24.5	- Amérique du Nord
- LAIA	4.4	4.4	3.6	3.7	4.3	4.3	3.9	4.4	4.3	3.4	- ALAI
- CACM	0.3	0.4	0.4	0.3	0.4	0.5	0.4	0.4	0.4	0.5	- MCC
- Caribbean	0.5	0.4	0.5	0.5	0.5	0.7	0.5	0.5	0.5	0.4	- Caraïbes
- Rest of America	0.2	0.2	0.1	0.1	0.2	0.2	0.2	0.1	0.1	0.1	- Autre d'Amérique
Asia excluding former USSR	21.6	20.6	22.9	23.1	21.5	17.6	18.2	20.0	19.3	18.5	Asie ancienne URSS exclus
- Middle East	4.4	3.3	4.0	4.0	3.6	3.5	2.9	3.3	2.7	2.6	- Moyen-Orient
Asia former USSR	0.0	0.3	0.3	0.3	0.2	0.4	0.2	0.2	0.2	0.2	Asie ancienne URSS
Europe excluding former USSR	49.4	50.0	50.3	49.7	48.7	51.0	50.1	46.4	45.9	46.6	Europe ancienne URSS exclus
- European Union	44.0	44.6	44.3	43.2	42.2	43.8	43.3	40.2	39.9	40.2	- Union Européenne
- Eastern Europe	2.1	2.0	2.4	3.1	3.2	3.7	3.4	3.2	3.1	3.4	- Europe de l'Est
- Rest of Europe	3.2	3.5	3.6	3.4	3.3	3.5	3.4	3.0	2.9	3.0	- Autre de l'Europe
Europe former USSR	1.4	1.3	1.5	1.7	1.8	1.2	0.8	0.9	1.5	2.2	Europe ancienne URSS
Oceania	1.9	2.2	2.0	2.1	2.3	2.3	2.3	2.3	1.9	2.2	Océanie

TRADE BY COMMODITY (Value in million US dollars)
Exports by principal countries or areas

COMMERCE PAR PRODUIT (Valeur en millions de dollars EU)
Exportations selon les principaux pays ou zones

Country or area	1998	1999	2000	2001	2002	Pays ou zone
World	36022.3	36831.5	38057.5	39219.6	43324.0	Monde
Africa	42.5	33.8	78.8	55.0	69.5	Afrique
Americas	4859.6	5031.9	5289.9	5407.8	5500.5	Amériques
- Northern America	3260.8	3199.2	3255.8	3107.0	3054.6	- Amérique du Nord
- LAIA	1496.1	1721.9	1940.9	2195.7	2330.3	- ALAI
- CACM	97.0	108.3	90.3	102.3	112.5	- MCC
- Caribbean	5.6	2.3	2.7	2.4	2.5	- Caraïbes
- Rest of America	0.1	0.3	0.3	0.5	0.6	- Autre d'Amérique
Asia excluding former USSR	10802.0	11912.6	13605.3	14546.8	16539.1	Asie ancienne URSS exclus
- Middle East	553.4	592.5	574.2	684.8	909.9	- Moyen-Orient
Asia former USSR	6.2	2.4	1.8	1.2	1.3	Asie ancienne URSS
Europe excluding former USSR	19888.8	19394.0	18630.0	18683.4	20605.9	Europe ancienne URSS exclus
- European Union	18244.4	17655.1	16782.8	16686.6	18207.3	- Union Européenne
- Eastern Europe	737.8	858.1	953.8	1051.7	1293.8	- Europe de l'Est
- Rest of Europe	906.6	880.8	893.4	945.1	1104.7	- Autre de l'Europe
Europe former USSR	244.9	251.8	273.4	328.3	389.6	Europe ancienne URSS
Oceania	178.2	205.0	178.2	197.1	218.2	Océanie
Italy-San Marino-Holy See	5323.5	5039.3	4953.8	5036.1	5362.3	Italie-Saint-Marin-Saint-Siège
Germany	4819.7	4965.5	4637.8	4875.3	5619.9	Allemagne
China	2993.7	3498.1	4473.2	5352.5	6787.0	Chine
China, Hong Kong SAR	2996.3	3002.8	3279.8	3379.7	3267.9	Chine - RAS de Hong-Kong
United States	2738.0	2650.1	2654.2	2571.6	2451.0	Etats-Unis d'Amérique
Korea, Republic of	1721.4	2077.3	2268.9	2209.3	2590.4	République de Corée
France-Monaco	2186.5	1954.1	1857.9	1717.2	1696.2	France-Monaco
Mexico	1260.3	1496.5	1649.6	1884.6	2041.4	Mexique
Spain	1149.0	1143.3	1046.9	1127.9	1217.7	Espagne
United Kingdom	1187.7	1087.8	987.2	895.3	939.8	Royaume-Uni
Sweden	889.8	858.7	843.6	860.8	1027.6	Suède
Thailand	586.1	680.1	883.7	917.9	e969.4	Thaïlande
Netherlands	809.0	769.3	708.3	445.0	456.5	Pays-Bas
Japan	647.5	680.9	679.7	534.6	493.2	Japon
Canada	522.7	549.1	601.6	535.4	603.6	Canada
Slovenia	520.5	507.3	498.3	539.5	650.2	Slovénie
Singapore	418.3	485.8	539.2	508.0	488.7	Singapour
Turkey	346.9	376.8	397.7	479.1	706.3	Turquie
Austria	416.6	435.6	408.0	355.0	398.0	Autriche
Hungary	259.5	326.8	343.3	352.7	437.1	Hongrie
Belgium	–	429.6	404.8	409.8	e459.8	Belgique
Denmark	401.3	333.5	322.7	298.4	310.3	Danemark
Poland	184.3	211.8	277.6	340.8	433.0	Pologne
Malaysia	225.8	225.6	245.9	341.7	e362.1	Malaisie
Switzerland-Liechtenstein	250.9	253.7	287.0	287.9	320.6	Suisse-Liechtenstein
Ireland	275.5	208.6	183.2	210.0	175.4	Irlande
Finland	221.1	157.3	147.9	186.9	240.1	Finlande
Portugal	163.9	158.5	162.9	167.9	202.4	Portugal
Brazil	145.7	153.1	190.4	169.9	e176.1	Brésil
Belarus	118.8	138.4	159.7	188.6	218.2	Bélarus

(Value as percentages of World total) **(Valeur en pourcentage du total mondial)**

Regions of the world	1993	1994	1995	1996	1997	1998	1999	2000	2001	2002	Régions du monde
World	100.0	100.0	100.0	100.0	100.0	100.0	100.0	100.0	100.0	100.0	Monde
Africa	0.2	0.2	0.2	0.1	0.1	0.1	0.1	0.2	0.1	0.2	Afrique
Americas	12.3	11.9	11.4	11.8	13.0	13.5	13.7	13.9	13.8	12.7	Amériques
- Northern America	9.2	9.0	8.3	8.4	8.9	9.1	8.7	8.6	7.9	7.1	- Amérique du Nord
- LAIA	3.0	2.8	3.0	3.2	3.8	4.2	4.7	5.1	5.6	5.4	- ALAI
- CACM	0.0	0.1	0.1	0.1	0.2	0.3	0.3	0.2	0.3	0.3	- MCC
- Caribbean	0.0	0.0	0.0	0.0	0.0	0.0	0.0	0.0	0.0	0.0	- Caraïbes
- Rest of America	0.0	0.0	0.0	0.0	0.0	0.0	0.0	0.0	0.0	0.0	- Autre d'Amérique
Asia excluding former USSR	33.6	31.3	31.3	31.9	31.7	30.0	32.3	35.7	37.1	38.2	Asie ancienne URSS exclus
- Middle East	0.7	0.7	0.9	0.9	1.0	1.5	1.6	1.5	1.7	2.1	- Moyen-Orient
Asia former USSR	0.0	0.0	0.0	0.0	0.0	0.0	0.0	0.0	0.0	0.0	Asie ancienne URSS
Europe excluding former USSR	52.8	55.3	55.8	54.7	53.7	55.2	52.7	49.0	47.6	47.6	Europe ancienne URSS exclus
- European Union	49.0	51.5	52.1	51.1	49.6	50.6	47.9	44.1	42.5	42.0	- Union Européenne
- Eastern Europe	1.2	1.2	1.4	1.5	1.8	2.0	2.3	2.5	2.7	3.0	- Europe de l'Est
- Rest of Europe	2.5	2.6	2.4	2.2	2.2	2.5	2.4	2.3	2.4	2.5	- Autre de l'Europe
Europe former USSR	0.7	0.5	0.6	0.8	1.0	0.7	0.7	0.7	0.8	0.9	Europe ancienne URSS
Oceania	0.6	0.7	0.6	0.7	0.6	0.5	0.6	0.5	0.5	0.5	Océanie

776 Thermionic, microcircuits, transistors, valves, etc

TRADE BY COMMODITY (Value in million US dollars)
Imports by principal countries or areas

COMMERCE PAR PRODUIT (Valeur en millions de dollars EU)
Importations selon les principaux pays ou zones

Country or area	1998	1999	2000	2001	2002	Pays ou zone
World	208984.0	242449.6	323598.0	260336.3	266426.5	Monde
Africa	909.5	925.9	814.0	711.9	681.9	Afrique
Americas	51314.9	58253.9	75916.4	54040.0	44832.2	Amériques
- Northern America	40828.4	45734.0	57900.7	36028.1	30080.2	- Amérique du Nord
- LAIA	9838.9	12053.7	17266.9	16966.7	13617.4	- ALAI
- CACM	607.7	428.9	706.8	997.2	1088.7	- MCC
- Caribbean	34.1	30.6	35.6	42.7	41.6	- Caraïbes
- Rest of America	5.7	6.7	6.4	5.3	4.3	- Autre d'Amérique
Asia excluding former USSR	110239.6	134120.4	180320.8	150787.5	169213.4	Asie ancienne URSS exclus
- Middle East	961.4	1004.6	1199.1	1091.0	1513.1	- Moyen-Orient
Asia former USSR	11.5	13.1	34.7	27.8	29.5	Asie ancienne URSS
Europe excluding former USSR	45468.6	48015.4	65250.4	53701.8	50400.5	Europe ancienne URSS exclus
- European Union	41820.3	44051.7	58935.9	47076.0	42909.8	- Union Européenne
- Eastern Europe	1868.6	2043.2	3671.1	4746.8	5782.2	- Europe de l'Est
- Rest of Europe	1779.7	1920.4	2643.4	1879.0	1708.4	- Autre de l'Europe
Europe former USSR	238.1	251.8	309.1	369.9	571.9	Europe ancienne URSS
Oceania	801.8	869.1	952.7	697.4	697.2	Océanie
United States	34718.7	38866.2	49581.3	31646.5	27167.7	Etats-Unis d'Amérique
Singapore	18406.9	22113.5	30556.3	23192.0	24118.8	Singapour
China	8331.6	13391.0	21155.6	23611.9	35167.4	Chine
Malaysia	16247.4	19343.6	24513.0	19773.6	e21610.5	Malaisie
China, Hong Kong SAR	12817.4	14223.9	20286.1	18179.4	21598.4	Chine - RAS de Hong-Kong
Korea, Republic of	12610.2	16892.6	20470.4	15865.2	17080.3	République de Corée
Japan	10773.3	13474.3	19845.6	15725.4	15267.3	Japon
Germany	10356.2	10846.2	14347.9	12898.2	11403.8	Allemagne
Mexico	7891.6	10106.0	14279.5	14467.6	11531.5	Mexique
United Kingdom	7818.0	8367.9	11987.5	9239.2	6568.0	Royaume-Uni
Philippines	7912.4	8926.6	7604.7	6264.3	e8619.5	Philippines
France-Monaco	6809.0	6597.5	9212.8	6074.7	5492.2	France-Monaco
Thailand	4910.4	5928.1	8365.8	6791.5	e7076.1	Thaïlande
Canada	6109.7	6867.6	8313.9	4368.9	2905.4	Canada
Netherlands	3934.6	4527.0	6785.8	2687.0	1058.0	Pays-Bas
Ireland	2192.5	2802.9	3002.6	3986.1	6690.3	Irlande
Italy-San Marino-Holy See	3258.1	3180.0	3970.4	3314.8	2819.1	Italie-Saint-Marin-Saint-Siège
Brazil	1513.6	1634.8	2638.6	2118.9	1835.7	Brésil
Hungary	646.3	826.7	1665.6	2372.0	2548.4	Hongrie
Belgium	–	1452.2	2059.0	2113.2	e2317.5	Belgique
Sweden	1441.8	1455.0	1959.1	1218.4	924.2	Suède
Finland	1325.0	1247.2	1525.0	1266.9	1362.9	Finlande
Spain	1229.6	1213.7	1460.2	1303.8	1204.4	Espagne
Austria	967.6	928.0	1000.9	1274.7	1189.6	Autriche
Malta	791.8	897.4	1309.7	752.6	e783.7	Malte
Turkey	730.9	769.3	936.8	777.3	1172.1	Turquie
Israel	624.8	719.6	1508.4	868.7	636.3	Israël
Czech Republic	383.4	360.2	669.0	1073.6	1561.4	République tchèque
Poland	609.1	576.2	742.6	859.8	1046.4	Pologne
Switzerland-Liechtenstein	681.8	731.1	984.8	770.4	592.4	Suisse-Liechtenstein

(Value as percentages of World total) **(Valeur en pourcentage du total mondial)**

Regions of the world	1993	1994	1995	1996	1997	1998	1999	2000	2001	2002	Régions du monde
World	100.0	100.0	100.0	100.0	100.0	100.0	100.0	100.0	100.0	100.0	Monde
Africa	0.3	0.3	0.2	0.3	0.2	0.4	0.4	0.3	0.3	0.3	Afrique
Americas	25.1	27.0	27.1	25.5	24.6	24.6	24.0	23.5	20.8	16.8	Amériques
- Northern America	22.2	23.8	23.9	21.9	20.6	19.5	18.9	17.9	13.8	11.3	- Amérique du Nord
- LAIA	2.9	3.2	3.1	3.6	4.0	4.7	5.0	5.3	6.5	5.1	- ALAI
- CACM	0.0	0.0	0.0	0.0	0.0	0.3	0.2	0.2	0.4	0.4	- MCC
- Caribbean	0.0	0.0	0.0	0.0	0.0	0.0	0.0	0.0	0.0	0.0	- Caraïbes
- Rest of America	0.0	0.0	0.0	0.0	0.0	0.0	0.0	0.0	0.0	0.0	- Autre d'Amérique
Asia excluding former USSR	52.3	49.8	51.5	52.6	53.8	52.8	55.3	55.7	57.9	63.5	Asie ancienne URSS exclus
- Middle East	0.4	0.3	0.3	0.4	0.4	0.5	0.4	0.4	0.4	0.6	- Moyen-Orient
Asia former USSR	0.0	0.0	0.0	0.0	0.0	0.0	0.0	0.0	0.0	0.0	Asie ancienne URSS
Europe excluding former USSR	21.7	22.3	20.6	21.1	20.8	21.8	19.8	20.2	20.6	18.9	Europe ancienne URSS exclus
- European Union	20.3	20.8	19.3	19.8	19.4	20.0	18.2	18.2	18.1	16.1	- Union Européenne
- Eastern Europe	0.4	0.3	0.4	0.4	0.6	0.9	0.8	1.1	1.8	2.2	- Europe de l'Est
- Rest of Europe	1.1	1.2	1.0	0.8	0.7	0.9	0.8	0.8	0.7	0.6	- Autre de l'Europe
Europe former USSR	0.1	0.1	0.1	0.1	0.1	0.1	0.1	0.1	0.1	0.2	Europe ancienne URSS
Oceania	0.5	0.5	0.5	0.5	0.4	0.4	0.4	0.3	0.3	0.3	Océanie

TRADE BY COMMODITY (Value in million US dollars)
Exports by principal countries or areas

COMMERCE PAR PRODUIT (Valeur en millions de dollars EU)
Exportations selon les principaux pays ou zones

Country or area	1998	1999	2000	2001	2002	Pays ou zone
World	205206.1	242244.7	311198.1	241582.7	243300.0	Monde
Africa	415.9	556.3	531.1	464.8	533.2	Afrique
Americas	45797.0	54679.5	69645.6	52352.4	48292.1	Amériques
- Northern America	43153.6	52103.2	66283.1	50031.9	46123.7	- Amérique du Nord
- LAIA	2193.5	2495.3	3302.8	2260.4	2113.9	- ALAI
- CACM	443.3	75.0	51.3	54.4	51.7	- MCC
- Caribbean	6.6	6.0	8.3	5.8	2.8	- Caraïbes
- Rest of America	0.0	0.0	0.1	0.0	0.0	- Autre d'Amérique
Asia excluding former USSR	119977.5	145466.0	186916.4	143449.4	146922.4	Asie ancienne URSS exclus
- Middle East	15.8	19.5	23.9	29.6	33.2	- Moyen-Orient
Asia former USSR	0.8	1.4	6.1	3.2	3.5	Asie ancienne URSS
Europe excluding former USSR	38685.5	41092.9	53563.1	44851.9	47071.2	Europe ancienne URSS exclus
- European Union	36627.0	38967.7	50517.6	42033.8	44075.2	- Union Européenne
- Eastern Europe	595.4	540.6	799.3	1113.9	1285.8	- Europe de l'Est
- Rest of Europe	1463.1	1584.6	2246.1	1704.2	1710.2	- Autre de l'Europe
Europe former USSR	210.0	306.1	386.4	313.9	322.3	Europe ancienne URSS
Oceania	119.5	142.5	149.3	146.9	155.2	Océanie
United States	40156.0	49350.9	62823.9	47622.0	44518.4	Etats-Unis d'Amérique
Japan	28378.1	32725.9	42454.3	30037.7	30926.9	Japon
Singapore	19449.2	23037.3	34436.3	27275.2	29404.4	Singapour
Korea, Republic of	19415.2	21843.4	24688.1	14741.9	15991.3	République de Corée
Malaysia	13930.2	17232.1	18728.9	15929.1	e16881.0	Malaisie
Philippines	12925.3	17068.1	16662.8	12569.9	e14771.6	Philippines
China, Hong Kong SAR	7910.4	9480.3	14045.6	13715.0	16250.7	Chine - RAS de Hong-Kong
Germany	8882.4	9382.6	12887.5	11415.0	11126.4	Allemagne
United Kingdom	6255.5	6970.7	9224.0	9567.4	10004.8	Royaume-Uni
France-Monaco	7593.3	7405.7	8424.4	6797.6	5959.8	France-Monaco
China	2386.9	3709.8	5351.8	4931.8	7276.9	Chine
Thailand	3169.2	4031.1	5876.3	4699.9	e4963.7	Thaïlande
Ireland	2283.9	2821.2	4167.0	5574.0	7641.2	Irlande
Netherlands	5720.1	6024.1	7625.3	1195.6	1567.5	Pays-Bas
Canada	2997.6	2752.2	3459.2	2409.7	1605.3	Canada
Italy-San Marino-Holy See	2278.4	2230.3	3158.7	2631.2	2811.1	Italie-Saint-Marin-Saint-Siège
Mexico	2071.1	2344.8	3064.4	2045.6	1891.6	Mexique
Malta	956.8	1017.1	1513.7	1003.0	e1091.1	Malte
Belgium	–	1078.0	1349.9	1461.1	e1639.3	Belgique
Israel	395.4	413.8	1781.5	1630.0	1120.7	Israël
Austria	794.1	796.5	1024.4	1225.4	1304.5	Autriche
Spain	478.0	587.2	605.2	610.2	602.9	Espagne
Switzerland-Liechtenstein	465.6	531.7	690.1	553.9	479.2	Suisse-Liechtenstein
Sweden	587.4	518.7	771.9	414.0	342.5	Suède
Indonesia	195.7	314.0	738.9	520.7	558.6	Indonésie
Morocco	393.9	531.5	480.2	386.2	e420.1	Maroc
Portugal	260.0	390.4	389.4	570.1	535.2	Portugal
Finland	299.1	314.9	465.0	263.1	214.2	Finlande
Czech Republic	220.9	145.4	218.0	321.6	489.0	République tchèque
Poland	261.5	245.1	256.0	266.5	330.1	Pologne

(Value as percentages of World total) **(Valeur en pourcentage du total mondial)**

Regions of the world	1993	1994	1995	1996	1997	1998	1999	2000	2001	2002	Régions du monde
World	100.0	100.0	100.0	100.0	100.0	100.0	100.0	100.0	100.0	100.0	Monde
Africa	0.1	0.1	0.0	0.0	0.0	0.2	0.2	0.2	0.2	0.2	Afrique
Americas	22.0	22.0	20.2	21.7	22.1	22.3	22.6	22.4	21.7	19.8	Amériques
- Northern America	21.2	21.3	19.6	20.7	21.2	21.0	21.5	21.3	20.7	19.0	- Amérique du Nord
- LAIA	0.7	0.8	0.6	1.0	0.9	1.1	1.0	1.1	0.9	0.9	- ALAI
- CACM	0.0	0.0	0.0	0.0	0.0	0.2	0.0	0.0	0.0	0.0	- MCC
- Caribbean	0.0	0.0	0.0	0.0	0.0	0.0	0.0	0.0	0.0	0.0	- Caraïbes
- Rest of America	0.0	0.0	0.0	0.0	0.0	0.0	0.0	0.0	0.0	0.0	- Autre d'Amérique
Asia excluding former USSR	59.1	58.9	62.0	59.6	58.9	58.5	60.0	60.1	59.4	60.4	Asie ancienne URSS exclus
- Middle East	0.0	0.0	0.0	0.0	0.0	0.0	0.0	0.0	0.0	0.0	- Moyen-Orient
Asia former USSR	0.0	0.0	0.0	0.0	0.0	0.0	0.0	0.0	0.0	0.0	Asie ancienne URSS
Europe excluding former USSR	18.6	18.8	17.6	18.5	18.8	18.9	17.0	17.2	18.6	19.3	Europe ancienne URSS exclus
- European Union	17.6	17.8	16.6	17.6	18.0	17.8	16.1	16.2	17.4	18.1	- Union Européenne
- Eastern Europe	0.1	0.1	0.2	0.2	0.2	0.3	0.2	0.3	0.5	0.5	- Europe de l'Est
- Rest of Europe	0.9	0.9	0.8	0.7	0.6	0.7	0.7	0.7	0.7	0.7	- Autre de l'Europe
Europe former USSR	0.1	0.1	0.1	0.1	0.1	0.1	0.1	0.1	0.1	0.1	Europe ancienne URSS
Oceania	0.1	0.0	0.0	0.0	0.1	0.1	0.1	0.0	0.1	0.1	Océanie

778 Electrical machinery and apparatus, nes

TRADE BY COMMODITY (Value in million US dollars)
Imports by principal countries or areas

COMMERCE PAR PRODUIT (Valeur en millions de dollars EU)
Importations selon les principaux pays ou zones

Country or area	1998	1999	2000	2001	2002	Pays ou zone
World	82428.8	88267.5	106406.0	95189.0	95552.7	Monde
Africa	1219.9	1102.0	1115.5	1154.6	1170.8	Afrique
Americas	23203.3	25238.9	30565.4	27079.1	25174.8	Amériques
- Northern America	15984.3	18188.0	21322.7	18183.5	18361.5	- Amérique du Nord
- LAIA	6652.7	6550.3	8689.2	8391.5	6295.7	- ALAI
- CACM	199.9	192.5	236.6	220.0	234.1	- MCC
- Caribbean	319.0	260.0	270.1	241.0	242.2	- Caraïbes
- Rest of America	47.4	48.0	46.8	43.1	41.4	- Autre d'Amérique
Asia excluding former USSR	20812.4	24123.1	32950.3	29196.6	32123.7	Asie ancienne URSS exclus
- Middle East	1582.8	1484.7	1718.4	1493.2	1639.5	- Moyen-Orient
Asia former USSR	116.1	97.7	115.4	109.8	112.4	Asie ancienne URSS
Europe excluding former USSR	35099.0	35854.6	39512.1	35785.1	34913.1	Europe ancienne URSS exclus
- European Union	31019.5	31748.0	34810.5	30930.2	30068.5	- Union Européenne
- Eastern Europe	2396.1	2386.6	2979.1	3139.0	3113.9	- Europe de l'Est
- Rest of Europe	1683.4	1720.0	1722.5	1715.9	1730.6	- Autre de l'Europe
Europe former USSR	844.1	679.1	885.9	738.4	854.9	Europe ancienne URSS
Oceania	1134.0	1172.0	1261.5	1125.4	1203.1	Océanie
United States	12821.3	14607.5	17552.6	15068.6	15320.5	Etats-Unis d'Amérique
Germany	7652.3	7753.6	9228.7	8540.6	7936.0	Allemagne
Mexico	4063.1	4445.6	6294.8	6122.0	4629.6	Mexique
United Kingdom	5220.1	5103.0	5679.2	4591.2	4251.8	Royaume-Uni
China	2620.9	3388.1	4771.7	5080.8	6778.7	Chine
France-Monaco	4363.0	4435.8	4928.0	4159.7	4130.6	France-Monaco
China, Hong Kong SAR	3380.9	3661.7	4856.7	4236.0	4774.1	Chine - RAS de Hong-Kong
Japan	3042.9	3538.3	5016.6	4093.0	3747.2	Japon
Canada	3139.2	3554.1	3765.0	3109.5	3033.9	Canada
Singapore	2488.5	2823.0	3748.4	2572.8	2439.6	Singapour
Korea, Republic of	1420.6	2249.0	2997.5	2832.7	3463.8	République de Corée
Italy-San Marino-Holy See	2482.8	2538.3	2614.3	2519.9	2381.8	Italie-Saint-Marin-Saint-Siège
Malaysia	1409.5	1634.3	2584.7	2149.1	e2348.7	Malaisie
Netherlands	2062.8	2097.9	2150.2	1912.0	1881.9	Pays-Bas
Spain	1810.3	1841.7	1822.1	1834.0	2117.2	Espagne
Belgium	–	2162.2	2162.5	2231.0	e2446.7	Belgique
Sweden	1339.2	1499.0	1617.8	1153.6	1077.9	Suède
Thailand	977.2	1093.6	1407.5	1280.5	e1334.1	Thaïlande
Austria	1111.5	1017.8	1091.9	1056.6	988.9	Autriche
Brazil	1116.7	941.4	1152.6	1076.1	807.0	Brésil
Australia	923.8	954.7	1041.9	918.4	988.8	Australie
Finland	818.0	972.2	1063.2	862.2	830.2	Finlande
Czech Republic	817.4	781.2	881.1	1056.6	861.9	République tchèque
Hungary	589.6	680.6	1037.2	997.6	1019.9	Hongrie
Switzerland-Liechtenstein	795.8	872.8	864.4	821.1	736.5	Suisse-Liechtenstein
Israel	402.6	446.6	704.5	1317.3	1153.0	Israël
Ireland	685.4	756.0	999.1	675.4	566.0	Irlande
Denmark	628.2	802.2	729.0	672.8	716.9	Danemark
Poland	657.8	620.1	670.0	670.5	737.5	Pologne
Turkey	592.7	532.3	632.0	424.3	535.6	Turquie

(Value as percentages of World total)
(Valeur en pourcentage du total mondial)

Regions of the world	1993	1994	1995	1996	1997	1998	1999	2000	2001	2002	Régions du monde
World	100.0	100.0	100.0	100.0	100.0	100.0	100.0	100.0	100.0	100.0	Monde
Africa	1.8	1.8	1.6	1.4	1.4	1.5	1.2	1.0	1.2	1.2	Afrique
Americas	26.1	25.5	23.8	24.9	26.4	28.1	28.6	28.7	28.4	26.3	Amériques
- Northern America	19.3	19.4	17.6	17.9	18.4	19.4	20.6	20.0	19.1	19.2	- Amérique du Nord
- LAIA	6.2	5.6	5.8	6.5	7.4	8.1	7.4	8.2	8.8	6.6	- ALAI
- CACM	0.2	0.2	0.2	0.2	0.2	0.2	0.2	0.2	0.2	0.2	- MCC
- Caribbean	0.3	0.2	0.2	0.3	0.3	0.4	0.3	0.3	0.3	0.3	- Caraïbes
- Rest of America	0.1	0.1	0.1	0.0	0.0	0.1	0.1	0.0	0.0	0.0	- Autre d'Amérique
Asia excluding former USSR	28.4	27.7	28.0	28.7	28.5	25.2	27.3	31.0	30.7	33.6	Asie ancienne URSS exclus
- Middle East	2.7	2.0	2.2	2.2	1.9	1.9	1.7	1.6	1.6	1.7	- Moyen-Orient
Asia former USSR	0.1	0.1	0.1	0.2	0.1	0.1	0.1	0.1	0.1	0.1	Asie ancienne URSS
Europe excluding former USSR	40.8	42.3	43.9	42.0	41.1	42.6	40.6	37.1	37.6	36.5	Europe ancienne URSS exclus
- European Union	37.0	38.8	39.9	37.8	36.7	37.6	36.0	32.7	32.5	31.5	- Union Européenne
- Eastern Europe	1.3	1.3	1.7	2.1	2.4	2.9	2.7	2.8	3.3	3.3	- Europe de l'Est
- Rest of Europe	2.4	2.3	2.3	2.1	1.9	2.0	1.9	1.6	1.8	1.8	- Autre de l'Europe
Europe former USSR	1.1	0.8	0.9	1.0	1.0	1.0	0.8	0.8	0.8	0.9	Europe ancienne URSS
Oceania	1.7	1.7	1.7	1.8	1.5	1.4	1.3	1.2	1.2	1.3	Océanie

TRADE BY COMMODITY (Value in million US dollars)
Exports by principal countries or areas

COMMERCE PAR PRODUIT (Valeur en millions de dollars EU)
Exportations selon les principaux pays ou zones

Country or area	1998	1999	2000	2001	2002	Pays ou zone
World	81139.6	87685.6	103349.3	90054.3	92450.5	Monde
Africa	184.8	169.9	180.8	245.2	262.7	Afrique
Americas	16968.7	19055.3	22811.7	18413.8	18322.4	Amériques
- Northern America	11847.3	12645.9	15574.4	12636.6	12447.3	- Amérique du Nord
- LAIA	4959.3	6283.5	7049.0	5625.1	5706.9	- ALAI
- CACM	91.5	102.6	159.0	124.7	142.0	- MCC
- Caribbean	70.3	22.7	28.9	26.4	25.1	- Caraïbes
- Rest of America	0.2	0.6	0.5	1.0	1.1	- Autre d'Amérique
Asia excluding former USSR	28604.7	33133.1	43454.0	36545.2	38755.5	Asie ancienne URSS exclus
- Middle East	208.9	210.1	235.3	265.4	268.2	- Moyen-Orient
Asia former USSR	23.6	26.0	25.2	25.9	25.8	Asie ancienne URSS
Europe excluding former USSR	34773.6	34576.1	36062.1	33989.1	34178.6	Europe ancienne URSS exclus
- European Union	30588.8	30369.8	31334.5	29293.4	29407.8	- Union Européenne
- Eastern Europe	2275.0	2384.8	2905.3	2970.9	2976.8	- Europe de l'Est
- Rest of Europe	1909.8	1821.5	1822.3	1724.8	1794.0	- Autre de l'Europe
Europe former USSR	352.5	439.2	515.8	546.5	598.8	Europe ancienne URSS
Oceania	231.8	286.0	299.6	288.5	306.6	Océanie
Japan	13415.2	15943.4	20231.7	14396.8	14010.7	Japon
United States	10655.8	11306.0	14170.3	11350.0	11105.3	Etats-Unis d'Amérique
Germany	9974.5	9798.4	9824.7	9951.2	9863.6	Allemagne
China	3437.0	4438.1	6042.1	6571.2	7842.1	Chine
Mexico	4432.1	5835.6	6543.8	5117.6	5193.1	Mexique
United Kingdom	5405.5	5291.4	5762.2	4910.9	4522.1	Royaume-Uni
France-Monaco	4004.0	4023.9	3958.4	3686.4	3956.8	France-Monaco
China, Hong Kong SAR	2932.6	3133.5	4246.2	3911.0	4622.3	Chine - RAS de Hong-Kong
Singapore	2408.3	2444.3	3387.5	2863.4	2451.8	Singapour
Italy-San Marino-Holy See	2385.6	2181.4	2162.6	2072.4	2058.2	Italie-Saint-Marin-Saint-Siège
Belgium	–	2278.7	2241.7	2504.3	e2809.8	Belgique
Netherlands	2019.4	1877.6	1968.0	1446.0	1448.0	Pays-Bas
Korea, Republic of	1194.5	1234.2	1651.3	1596.9	1889.4	République de Corée
Spain	1409.5	1534.6	1645.2	1398.9	1528.8	Espagne
Switzerland-Liechtenstein	1553.2	1463.7	1435.0	1331.3	1317.1	Suisse-Liechtenstein
Canada	1191.5	1339.8	1404.0	1286.6	1341.9	Canada
Czech Republic	902.0	992.3	1260.9	1274.4	1135.3	République tchèque
Malaysia	726.7	956.7	1336.1	1186.8	e1257.7	Malaisie
Hungary	788.4	862.6	1027.6	1033.6	1052.1	Hongrie
Sweden	906.2	943.7	1010.6	821.2	888.4	Suède
Thailand	598.9	672.8	952.2	948.1	e1001.3	Thaïlande
Austria	821.3	778.4	815.1	838.5	798.7	Autriche
Ireland	590.9	595.7	699.7	579.9	486.0	Irlande
Indonesia	382.0	510.4	662.2	581.3	631.4	Indonésie
Poland	451.7	405.8	475.1	507.5	597.4	Pologne
Belgium-Luxembourg	2219.9	–	–	–	–	Belgique-Luxembourg
Israel	274.8	253.6	636.4	396.9	654.6	Israël
Denmark	341.2	400.0	409.7	445.6	440.2	Danemark
Brazil	361.9	305.8	364.1	362.6	e375.9	Brésil
Finland	287.3	352.7	341.7	239.3	257.4	Finlande

(Value as percentages of World total) **(Valeur en pourcentage du total mondial)**

Regions of the world	1993	1994	1995	1996	1997	1998	1999	2000	2001	2002	Régions du monde
World	100.0	100.0	100.0	100.0	100.0	100.0	100.0	100.0	100.0	100.0	Monde
Africa	0.2	0.2	0.2	0.2	0.2	0.2	0.2	0.2	0.3	0.3	Afrique
Americas	19.4	18.6	17.3	18.4	21.0	20.9	21.7	22.1	20.4	19.8	Amériques
- Northern America	14.8	14.0	12.6	13.7	14.8	14.6	14.4	15.1	14.0	13.5	- Amérique du Nord
- LAIA	4.4	4.4	4.6	4.6	6.1	6.1	7.2	6.8	6.2	6.2	- ALAI
- CACM	0.0	0.1	0.0	0.0	0.1	0.1	0.1	0.2	0.1	0.2	- MCC
- Caribbean	0.1	0.1	0.1	0.0	0.0	0.1	0.0	0.0	0.0	0.0	- Caraïbes
- Rest of America	0.0	0.0	0.0	0.0	0.0	0.0	0.0	0.0	0.0	0.0	- Autre d'Amérique
Asia excluding former USSR	39.8	39.9	40.6	38.4	36.2	35.3	37.8	42.0	40.6	41.9	Asie ancienne URSS exclus
- Middle East	0.2	0.1	0.2	0.3	0.2	0.3	0.2	0.2	0.3	0.3	- Moyen-Orient
Asia former USSR	0.0	0.0	0.0	0.1	0.0	0.0	0.0	0.0	0.0	0.0	Asie ancienne URSS
Europe excluding former USSR	40.1	40.4	41.0	41.9	41.7	42.9	39.4	34.9	37.7	37.0	Europe ancienne URSS exclus
- European Union	36.0	36.5	36.9	37.7	37.2	37.7	34.6	30.3	32.5	31.8	- Union Européenne
- Eastern Europe	1.4	1.2	1.6	1.8	2.2	2.8	2.7	2.8	3.3	3.2	- Europe de l'Est
- Rest of Europe	2.8	2.7	2.5	2.5	2.3	2.4	2.1	1.8	1.9	1.9	- Autre de l'Europe
Europe former USSR	0.2	0.4	0.4	0.5	0.4	0.4	0.5	0.5	0.6	0.6	Europe ancienne URSS
Oceania	0.3	0.4	0.4	0.4	0.4	0.3	0.3	0.3	0.3	0.3	Océanie

781 Passenger motor vehicles (excluding buses)

TRADE BY COMMODITY (Value in million US dollars)
Imports by principal countries or areas

COMMERCE PAR PRODUIT (Valeur en millions de dollars EU)
Importations selon les principaux pays ou zones

Country or area	1998	1999	2000	2001	2002	Pays ou zone
World	272744.7	294109.2	306038.2	313098.2	340331.1	Monde
Africa	3028.4	3023.1	3315.2	3464.6	4176.1	Afrique
Americas	106499.4	120063.8	136533.3	134679.1	144582.0	Amériques
- Northern America	94521.5	111725.5	125902.4	122735.2	132616.4	- Amérique du Nord
- LAIA	9809.2	6499.4	8841.5	10183.7	10097.6	- ALAI
- CACM	854.2	604.7	609.8	670.0	828.9	- MCC
- Caribbean	934.5	862.3	895.8	872.8	794.4	- Caraïbes
- Rest of America	380.0	371.9	283.9	217.5	244.7	- Autre d'Amérique
Asia excluding former USSR	18550.4	18536.4	24691.8	23411.3	26396.2	Asie ancienne URSS exclus
- Middle East	6513.2	6138.6	9339.9	8858.7	10117.9	- Moyen-Orient
Asia former USSR	116.1	108.6	303.4	306.9	337.6	Asie ancienne URSS
Europe excluding former USSR	137410.5	145498.0	133814.0	143065.5	155131.7	Europe ancienne URSS exclus
- European Union	125543.0	133017.9	121760.7	130181.3	140629.9	- Union Européenne
- Eastern Europe	3441.2	3762.6	3896.7	4709.5	5963.1	- Europe de l'Est
- Rest of Europe	8426.3	8717.5	8156.6	8174.6	8538.7	- Autre de l'Europe
Europe former USSR	1825.8	944.3	1162.8	2319.0	2731.9	Europe ancienne URSS
Oceania	5314.0	5935.0	6217.7	5851.8	6975.5	Océanie
United States	82430.3	98328.7	110919.9	108187.8	115629.9	Etats-Unis d'Amérique
Germany	24864.4	26050.1	21990.8	24314.9	25309.4	Allemagne
United Kingdom	23273.3	24172.4	20995.0	24606.4	27551.3	Royaume-Uni
Italy-San Marino-Holy See	18050.5	19009.0	17370.7	18564.1	20565.9	Italie-Saint-Marin-Saint-Siège
France-Monaco	14835.1	16457.7	16815.5	16121.6	17488.9	France-Monaco
Canada	12072.3	13376.5	14813.2	14528.2	16960.8	Canada
Spain	9797.5	12092.4	11340.2	11712.2	12279.3	Espagne
Belgium	–	10722.2	10573.0	12410.7	e13611.0	Belgique
Netherlands	7225.8	7832.5	7086.6	7222.8	7110.3	Pays-Bas
Japan	5554.4	6214.4	6947.5	6236.5	6259.0	Japon
Switzerland-Liechtenstein	4858.9	5183.5	4849.2	4982.3	4991.5	Suisse-Liechtenstein
Australia	4102.9	4370.5	4874.7	4481.6	5242.5	Australie
Mexico	2113.5	2584.1	4521.2	5170.6	6072.2	Mexique
Austria	4184.1	4082.0	3609.2	3659.3	3801.9	Autriche
Portugal	2824.0	3366.1	2922.4	2600.1	2623.2	Portugal
Saudi Arabia	1626.0	1548.4	2307.7	3362.5	e3479.8	Arabie saoudite
Ireland	2244.5	2300.6	2813.7	2070.2	2267.5	Irlande
Sweden	3343.4	1022.0	1166.8	2342.4	2559.6	Suède
Belgium-Luxembourg	10040.1	–	–	–	–	Belgique-Luxembourg
Poland	1379.5	1585.4	1713.9	1997.2	2532.1	Pologne
Greece	1570.2	2121.4	1886.1	1297.4	e1434.6	Grèce
Norway	1838.3	1562.2	1518.3	1529.5	1756.8	Norvège
Denmark	1943.2	1673.7	1311.7	1418.6	1848.6	Danemark
Brazil	2728.3	1248.3	1248.4	1438.0	749.9	Brésil
China, Hong Kong SAR	2003.6	869.4	1318.0	1557.8	1612.1	Chine - RAS de Hong-Kong
United Arab Emirates	822.8	862.2	1534.7	1851.0	e1899.1	Emirates arabes unis
Turkey	1392.4	1324.7	2595.9	586.8	813.3	Turquie
Israel	1152.9	1183.9	1524.6	1418.1	1172.1	Israël
Finland	1347.0	1344.4	1157.7	997.7	1283.6	Finlande
New Zealand	987.2	1289.1	1079.3	1106.1	1451.2	Nouvelle-Zélande

(Value as percentages of World total) **(Valeur en pourcentage du total mondial)**

Regions of the world	1993	1994	1995	1996	1997	1998	1999	2000	2001	2002	Régions du monde
World	100.0	100.0	100.0	100.0	100.0	100.0	100.0	100.0	100.0	100.0	Monde
Africa	1.6	1.3	1.5	1.2	1.1	1.1	1.0	1.1	1.1	1.2	Afrique
Americas	36.9	39.5	36.7	35.1	38.1	39.0	40.8	44.6	43.0	42.5	Amériques
- Northern America	33.5	35.4	32.8	32.1	34.1	34.7	38.0	41.1	39.2	39.0	- Amérique du Nord
- LAIA	2.7	3.5	3.2	2.4	3.3	3.6	2.2	2.9	3.3	3.0	- ALAI
- CACM	0.3	0.2	0.2	0.2	0.2	0.3	0.2	0.2	0.2	0.2	- MCC
- Caribbean	0.3	0.3	0.4	0.3	0.3	0.3	0.3	0.3	0.3	0.2	- Caraïbes
- Rest of America	0.1	0.1	0.1	0.1	0.1	0.1	0.1	0.1	0.1	0.1	- Autre d'Amérique
Asia excluding former USSR	14.0	12.3	12.2	11.3	10.0	6.8	6.3	8.1	7.5	7.8	Asie ancienne URSS exclus
- Middle East	3.2	2.5	2.0	2.2	2.6	2.4	2.1	3.1	2.8	3.0	- Moyen-Orient
Asia former USSR	0.1	0.1	0.0	0.0	0.0	0.0	0.0	0.1	0.1	0.1	Asie ancienne URSS
Europe excluding former USSR	44.9	44.7	47.3	49.9	47.9	50.4	49.5	43.7	45.7	45.6	Europe ancienne URSS exclus
- European Union	41.5	40.9	43.2	45.5	43.9	46.0	45.2	39.8	41.6	41.3	- Union Européenne
- Eastern Europe	0.8	0.7	0.8	1.3	1.1	1.3	1.3	1.3	1.5	1.8	- Europe de l'Est
- Rest of Europe	2.6	3.0	3.2	3.2	2.9	3.1	3.0	2.7	2.6	2.5	- Autre de l'Europe
Europe former USSR	0.8	0.3	0.4	0.4	0.8	0.7	0.3	0.4	0.7	0.8	Europe ancienne URSS
Oceania	1.7	1.9	1.9	2.1	2.0	1.9	2.0	2.0	1.9	2.0	Océanie

Voitures à tous moteurs, pour le transport des personnes; autre que en commun 781

TRADE BY COMMODITY (Value in million US dollars) | COMMERCE PAR PRODUIT (Valeur en millions de dollars EU)

Exports by principal countries or areas | **Exportations selon les principaux pays ou zones**

Country or area	1998	1999	2000	2001	2002	Pays ou zone
World	277342.7	292742.9	300748.1	307740.4	341766.1	Monde
Africa	353.9	900.6	1092.1	924.7	1675.7	Afrique
Americas	59428.3	65748.9	71042.9	68342.7	69968.3	Amériques
- Northern America	44877.0	51428.9	51859.9	49620.3	52708.9	- Amérique du Nord
- LAIA	14538.2	14297.3	19166.5	18703.2	17241.7	- ALAI
- CACM	1.4	1.4	2.1	4.3	4.2	- MCC
- Caribbean	11.2	19.8	12.6	12.2	11.1	- Caraïbes
- Rest of America	0.5	1.5	1.8	2.7	2.4	- Autre d'Amérique
Asia excluding former USSR	60818.9	66897.1	71307.1	68404.3	80356.4	Asie ancienne URSS exclus
- Middle East	921.6	1371.0	1477.0	1800.5	2284.1	- Moyen-Orient
Asia former USSR	162.5	92.1	91.3	99.2	90.0	Asie ancienne URSS
Europe excluding former USSR	155222.7	157742.4	155337.0	167733.5	187353.2	Europe ancienne URSS exclus
- European Union	148913.0	150776.3	147090.0	159178.8	178066.5	- Union Européenne
- Eastern Europe	5143.7	5980.3	7326.5	7631.0	8178.2	- Europe de l'Est
- Rest of Europe	1166.0	985.9	920.5	923.7	1108.5	- Autre de l'Europe
Europe former USSR	618.7	308.0	532.0	637.4	741.3	Europe ancienne URSS
Oceania	737.7	1053.8	1345.6	1598.6	1581.2	Océanie
Germany	60355.3	62241.7	60560.0	67390.6	75210.4	Allemagne
Japan	50194.8	54684.3	56809.4	52884.8	62582.9	Japon
Canada	28440.3	34634.9	34909.7	31576.5	31908.1	Canada
France-Monaco	19414.4	19309.2	19388.3	21046.3	24862.8	France-Monaco
United States	16436.4	16794.0	16950.2	18043.7	20800.8	Etats-Unis d'Amérique
Spain	16014.6	16492.5	17313.0	16929.9	17657.1	Espagne
Belgium	–	17435.5	16354.5	19745.5	e22154.1	Belgique
United Kingdom	14488.7	15665.1	14042.9	11734.5	15740.5	Royaume-Uni
Mexico	10974.2	12407.5	16296.7	15297.4	13948.1	Mexique
Korea, Republic of	8603.6	9968.0	11894.1	12025.7	13281.1	République de Corée
Italy-San Marino-Holy See	6884.4	6853.4	7252.4	6650.4	6656.4	Italie-Saint-Marin-Saint-Siège
Netherlands	4236.2	4390.6	3861.1	3467.0	3449.1	Pays-Bas
Belgium-Luxembourg	17373.1	–	–	–	–	Belgique-Luxembourg
Sweden	4084.4	1491.4	1861.3	4679.7	4344.3	Suède
Austria	2346.3	2951.0	2694.3	2831.9	3203.8	Autriche
Portugal	2595.3	2515.7	2224.4	2767.8	2811.6	Portugal
Czech Republic	2053.3	2140.5	2459.4	2921.2	3095.8	République tchèque
Slovakia	1507.2	1390.9	1937.5	1763.4	2142.6	Slovaquie
Brazil	1618.7	1138.5	1768.5	1951.4	e2023.1	Brésil
Poland	1008.4	1091.7	1461.0	1411.3	1389.7	Pologne
Hungary	546.9	1342.6	1423.6	1466.6	1481.2	Hongrie
Australia	728.4	1038.9	1310.1	1574.2	1579.2	Australie
Argentina	1630.8	588.4	730.3	947.8	e915.7	Argentine
Slovenia	983.7	794.7	746.4	727.6	848.0	Slovénie
Finland	702.8	740.5	742.5	928.2	920.3	Finlande
Turkey	140.2	688.1	628.5	972.9	1297.3	Turquie
South Africa	–	–	1041.6	871.9	1614.5	Afrique du Sud
China, Hong Kong SAR	522.2	384.2	478.5	677.5	1008.5	Chine - RAS de Hong-Kong
Thailand	70.9	124.6	219.3	674.2	e712.1	Thaïlande
Oman	377.1	282.5	365.0	307.3	412.3	Oman

(Value as percentages of World total) | **(Valeur en pourcentage du total mondial)**

Regions of the world	1993	1994	1995	1996	1997	1998	1999	2000	2001	2002	Régions du monde
World	100.0	100.0	100.0	100.0	100.0	100.0	100.0	100.0	100.0	100.0	Monde
Africa	0.1	0.1	0.1	0.1	0.1	0.1	0.3	0.4	0.3	0.5	Afrique
Americas	21.1	22.4	21.8	21.7	21.9	21.4	22.5	23.6	22.2	20.5	Amériques
- Northern America	18.2	19.4	18.1	17.2	16.9	16.2	17.6	17.2	16.1	15.4	- Amérique du Nord
- LAIA	2.9	3.0	3.7	4.6	5.0	5.2	4.9	6.4	6.1	5.0	- ALAI
- CACM	0.0	0.0	0.0	0.0	0.0	0.0	0.0	0.0	0.0	0.0	- MCC
- Caribbean	0.0	0.0	0.0	0.0	0.0	0.0	0.0	0.0	0.0	0.0	- Caraïbes
- Rest of America	0.0	0.0	0.0	0.0	0.0	0.0	0.0	0.0	0.0	0.0	- Autre d'Amérique
Asia excluding former USSR	29.3	25.1	21.9	20.8	22.9	21.9	22.9	23.7	22.2	23.5	Asie ancienne URSS exclus
- Middle East	0.6	0.5	0.4	0.4	0.4	0.3	0.5	0.5	0.6	0.7	- Moyen-Orient
Asia former USSR	0.0	0.0	0.0	0.0	0.0	0.1	0.0	0.0	0.0	0.0	Asie ancienne URSS
Europe excluding former USSR	48.8	51.9	55.6	56.8	54.5	56.0	53.9	51.7	54.5	54.8	Europe ancienne URSS exclus
- European Union	47.8	50.9	54.5	55.5	53.0	53.7	51.5	48.9	51.7	52.1	- Union Européenne
- Eastern Europe	0.7	0.7	0.7	0.9	1.2	1.9	2.0	2.4	2.5	2.4	- Europe de l'Est
- Rest of Europe	0.3	0.3	0.4	0.4	0.4	0.4	0.3	0.3	0.3	0.3	- Autre de l'Europe
Europe former USSR	0.5	0.3	0.3	0.4	0.3	0.2	0.1	0.2	0.2	0.2	Europe ancienne URSS
Oceania	0.2	0.2	0.2	0.3	0.3	0.3	0.4	0.4	0.5	0.5	Océanie

782 Lorries and special purposes motor vehicles

TRADE BY COMMODITY (Value in million US dollars)
Imports by principal countries or areas

COMMERCE PAR PRODUIT (Valeur en millions de dollars EU)
Importations selon les principaux pays ou zones

Country or area	1998	1999	2000	2001	2002	Pays ou zone
World	55102.8	57529.5	60240.3	59716.6	64062.0	Monde
Africa	1999.3	1814.0	1929.8	2317.5	2660.0	Afrique
Americas	21108.1	23316.5	25227.6	25822.7	27092.8	Amériques
- Northern America	15078.6	19389.8	20508.6	21402.1	22420.7	- Amérique du Nord
- LAIA	4970.7	2893.0	3730.8	3489.2	3666.6	- ALAI
- CACM	594.2	554.7	507.3	496.4	572.1	- MCC
- Caribbean	370.3	369.0	413.9	381.6	373.3	- Caraïbes
- Rest of America	94.2	110.0	66.9	53.4	60.1	- Autre d'Amérique
Asia excluding former USSR	4829.7	4495.7	6052.1	5662.2	5692.7	Asie ancienne URSS exclus
- Middle East	2506.5	2204.2	2939.2	2746.9	2663.6	- Moyen-Orient
Asia former USSR	306.4	396.0	254.5	275.0	289.1	Asie ancienne URSS
Europe excluding former USSR	24450.5	25136.8	24417.4	23395.8	25554.5	Europe ancienne URSS exclus
- European Union	21638.1	22501.9	21589.6	20383.0	22023.4	- Union Européenne
- Eastern Europe	1180.8	1120.5	1172.6	1342.3	1880.2	- Europe de l'Est
- Rest of Europe	1631.5	1514.4	1655.2	1670.4	1650.9	- Autre de l'Europe
Europe former USSR	668.9	371.1	391.4	673.4	715.1	Europe ancienne URSS
Oceania	1740.0	1999.3	1967.5	1570.1	2057.8	Océanie
United States	11084.6	15128.0	15779.6	17002.1	17169.5	Etats-Unis d'Amérique
Canada	3982.2	4247.8	4712.9	4388.8	5234.1	Canada
Germany	4233.6	4363.7	3674.4	3234.8	3419.7	Allemagne
France-Monaco	3336.2	3337.5	3385.3	3594.2	3857.5	France-Monaco
United Kingdom	2982.4	2865.3	3309.4	2962.7	3345.4	Royaume-Uni
Italy-San Marino-Holy See	2065.8	2459.2	2480.1	2278.6	2786.5	Italie-Saint-Marin-Saint-Siège
Spain	1623.6	2022.8	1745.0	1642.2	1783.4	Espagne
Netherlands	1766.0	1684.2	1448.4	1307.4	1257.7	Pays-Bas
Australia	1390.0	1554.8	1549.7	1141.8	1500.2	Australie
Belgium	–	1644.8	1606.6	1739.5	e1907.8	Belgique
Mexico	825.6	807.5	1598.5	1317.0	1928.8	Mexique
Portugal	874.4	918.3	1030.4	922.0	721.4	Portugal
Austria	800.6	709.6	716.0	597.2	617.6	Autriche
Saudi Arabia	444.5	459.1	640.6	896.1	e927.3	Arabie saoudite
Norway	743.7	615.4	588.7	600.9	617.3	Norvège
Denmark	719.3	673.0	528.2	503.8	529.6	Danemark
Switzerland-Liechtenstein	509.5	514.9	654.5	662.0	535.8	Suisse-Liechtenstein
Brazil	903.3	465.0	514.6	516.9	313.5	Brésil
Argentina	1180.2	579.9	399.0	318.5	e140.9	Argentine
Turkey	694.1	471.0	889.4	269.5	251.1	Turquie
Chile	681.4	299.9	548.1	467.2	454.3	Chili
Sweden	461.7	447.7	484.4	489.1	528.3	Suède
Ireland	498.3	501.5	478.9	411.2	490.1	Irlande
Poland	320.7	346.5	372.5	373.1	628.1	Pologne
Finland	450.0	370.6	342.5	371.9	418.9	Finlande
Hungary	362.4	372.2	343.7	369.8	463.1	Hongrie
Israel	322.2	343.5	435.8	391.2	358.0	Israël
China	295.4	273.7	320.9	372.6	473.4	Chine
Singapore	283.7	266.8	497.2	364.3	269.4	Singapour
Greece	320.3	425.9	296.3	246.9	e273.0	Grèce

(Value as percentages of World total) **(Valeur en pourcentage du total mondial)**

Regions of the world	1993	1994	1995	1996	1997	1998	1999	2000	2001	2002	Régions du monde
World	100.0	100.0	100.0	100.0	100.0	100.0	100.0	100.0	100.0	100.0	Monde
Africa	4.9	4.9	4.9	3.8	3.8	3.6	3.2	3.2	3.9	4.2	Afrique
Americas	40.0	38.5	36.7	36.0	40.0	38.3	40.5	41.9	43.2	42.3	Amériques
- Northern America	32.9	30.1	28.4	29.0	30.7	27.4	33.7	34.0	35.8	35.0	- Amérique du Nord
- LAIA	5.4	6.8	6.5	5.7	7.7	9.0	5.0	6.2	5.8	5.7	- ALAI
- CACM	0.8	0.9	0.9	0.8	0.8	1.1	1.0	0.8	0.8	0.9	- MCC
- Caribbean	0.6	0.4	0.6	0.5	0.6	0.7	0.6	0.7	0.6	0.6	- Caraïbes
- Rest of America	0.2	0.2	0.2	0.1	0.1	0.2	0.2	0.1	0.1	0.1	- Autre d'Amérique
Asia excluding former USSR	20.7	16.1	12.6	13.2	11.4	8.8	7.8	10.0	9.5	8.9	Asie ancienne URSS exclus
- Middle East	6.3	5.2	3.9	4.0	4.1	4.5	3.8	4.9	4.6	4.2	- Moyen-Orient
Asia former USSR	0.1	0.3	0.6	0.7	0.5	0.6	0.7	0.4	0.5	0.5	Asie ancienne URSS
Europe excluding former USSR	29.2	35.0	40.1	41.2	39.5	44.4	43.7	40.5	39.2	39.9	Europe ancienne URSS exclus
- European Union	25.3	30.6	35.2	36.4	34.8	39.3	39.1	35.8	34.1	34.4	- Union Européenne
- Eastern Europe	1.7	1.4	1.5	1.8	1.8	2.1	1.9	1.9	2.2	2.9	- Europe de l'Est
- Rest of Europe	2.2	2.9	3.4	3.0	3.0	3.0	2.6	2.7	2.8	2.6	- Autre de l'Europe
Europe former USSR	1.6	1.1	1.2	1.4	1.5	1.2	0.6	0.6	1.1	1.1	Europe ancienne URSS
Oceania	3.4	4.3	4.0	3.8	3.3	3.2	3.5	3.3	2.6	3.2	Océanie

Voitures à tous moteurs, pour le transport des merchandises et à usages spéciaux 782

TRADE BY COMMODITY (Value in million US dollars)
Exports by principal countries or areas

COMMERCE PAR PRODUIT (Valeur en millions de dollars EU)
Exportations selon les principaux pays ou zones

Country or area	1998	1999	2000	2001	2002	Pays ou zone
World	55497.7	54232.6	57665.4	57167.8	60147.2	Monde
Africa	197.3	217.2	242.6	247.4	302.8	Afrique
Americas	19720.6	21197.4	23519.0	23383.9	23915.2	Amériques
- Northern America	13949.8	15801.0	17200.1	15633.8	16267.4	- Amérique du Nord
- LAIA	5758.4	5363.0	6301.0	7736.8	7629.6	- ALAI
- CACM	4.6	3.2	1.8	3.6	7.4	- MCC
- Caribbean	6.7	29.6	15.5	7.4	8.3	- Caraïbes
- Rest of America	0.9	0.6	0.5	2.3	2.5	- Autre d'Amérique
Asia excluding former USSR	10324.6	9024.7	9159.9	8371.1	9680.1	Asie ancienne URSS exclus
- Middle East	221.5	233.8	320.3	663.8	1049.0	- Moyen-Orient
Asia former USSR	13.2	20.2	20.0	19.6	17.5	Asie ancienne URSS
Europe excluding former USSR	24477.4	23156.8	24075.4	24304.5	25268.0	Europe ancienne URSS exclus
- European Union	23466.1	22270.1	23091.9	23429.3	24220.8	- Union Européenne
- Eastern Europe	670.6	581.7	683.3	528.2	675.4	- Europe de l'Est
- Rest of Europe	340.7	305.0	300.2	346.9	371.9	- Autre de l'Europe
Europe former USSR	672.1	525.1	578.2	772.6	914.3	Europe ancienne URSS
Oceania	92.6	91.3	70.3	68.8	49.3	Océanie
Canada	6308.9	9506.2	9712.7	9237.3	9472.9	Canada
Germany	7391.9	7193.6	6990.9	7470.0	6820.8	Allemagne
United States	7640.9	6294.8	7487.5	6396.5	6794.5	Etats-Unis d'Amérique
Japan	8298.3	6610.0	6291.8	5389.2	6270.2	Japon
Mexico	3595.8	4107.6	4826.1	6453.0	6356.3	Mexique
France-Monaco	3074.0	3167.4	3329.5	3162.8	3239.3	France-Monaco
Spain	3409.4	2928.3	2806.4	2745.2	2781.7	Espagne
Italy-San Marino-Holy See	2770.4	2785.2	2759.6	2847.6	2926.5	Italie-Saint-Marin-Saint-Siège
Belgium	–	1938.3	2563.2	2483.8	e2786.8	Belgique
United Kingdom	1546.0	1180.2	1191.6	1359.7	1886.1	Royaume-Uni
Netherlands	1246.5	1279.5	1274.1	1216.6	1369.9	Pays-Bas
Thailand	643.8	1148.9	1406.3	1244.1	e1314.0	Thaïlande
Austria	757.4	646.9	912.0	978.5	991.1	Autriche
Korea, Republic of	794.8	766.6	781.9	694.0	601.8	République de Corée
Brazil	1019.8	628.9	699.1	486.8	e504.7	Brésil
Argentina	806.8	446.4	584.9	531.7	e513.7	Argentine
Portugal	506.7	428.8	364.0	308.3	545.3	Portugal
Belgium-Luxembourg	2133.3	–	–	–	–	Belgique-Luxembourg
Poland	345.0	359.1	458.3	377.3	517.4	Pologne
Belarus	465.0	376.5	382.9	395.4	349.4	Bélarus
Sweden	224.1	316.3	487.9	373.7	358.8	Suède
Turkey	30.1	39.5	89.5	384.7	720.1	Turquie
Russian Federation	145.8	110.1	133.8	289.8	466.6	Fédération de Russie
Finland	187.7	172.2	191.1	206.4	188.3	Finlande
Switzerland-Liechtenstein	197.3	164.1	156.0	192.8	201.9	Suisse-Liechtenstein
Czech Republic	286.5	186.4	191.3	105.3	104.3	République tchèque
Denmark	139.5	122.6	122.4	118.2	157.3	Danemark
South Africa	–	–	200.8	194.3	230.5	Afrique du Sud
Norway	116.8	114.9	118.0	118.8	113.7	Norvège
China	108.6	60.5	120.3	112.1	167.8	Chine

(Value as percentages of World total) **(Valeur en pourcentage du total mondial)**

Regions of the world	1993	1994	1995	1996	1997	1998	1999	2000	2001	2002	Régions du monde
World	100.0	100.0	100.0	100.0	100.0	100.0	100.0	100.0	100.0	100.0	Monde
Africa	0.2	0.3	0.4	0.5	0.4	0.4	0.4	0.4	0.4	0.5	Afrique
Americas	34.7	32.1	32.7	35.5	38.6	35.5	39.1	40.8	40.9	39.8	Amériques
- Northern America	31.0	27.8	26.3	26.8	28.5	25.1	29.1	29.8	27.3	27.0	- Amérique du Nord
- LAIA	3.6	4.3	6.4	8.7	10.2	10.4	9.9	10.9	13.5	12.7	- ALAI
- CACM	0.0	0.0	0.0	0.0	0.0	0.0	0.0	0.0	0.0	0.0	- MCC
- Caribbean	0.0	0.0	0.0	0.0	0.0	0.0	0.1	0.0	0.0	0.0	- Caraïbes
- Rest of America	0.0	0.0	0.0	0.0	0.0	0.0	0.0	0.0	0.0	0.0	- Autre d'Amérique
Asia excluding former USSR	29.2	27.9	23.9	21.4	20.6	18.6	16.6	15.9	14.6	16.1	Asie ancienne URSS exclus
- Middle East	0.6	0.7	0.5	0.5	0.6	0.4	0.4	0.6	1.2	1.7	- Moyen-Orient
Asia former USSR	0.1	0.0	0.1	0.0	0.0	0.0	0.0	0.0	0.0	0.0	Asie ancienne URSS
Europe excluding former USSR	34.3	38.8	40.9	41.0	38.9	44.1	42.7	41.8	42.5	42.0	Europe ancienne URSS exclus
- European Union	32.6	37.2	39.3	39.5	37.3	42.3	41.1	40.0	41.0	40.3	- Union Européenne
- Eastern Europe	1.0	0.9	0.9	0.8	1.1	1.2	1.1	1.2	0.9	1.1	- Europe de l'Est
- Rest of Europe	0.7	0.8	0.7	0.6	0.5	0.6	0.6	0.5	0.6	0.6	- Autre de l'Europe
Europe former USSR	1.5	0.7	1.9	1.5	1.3	1.2	1.0	1.0	1.4	1.5	Europe ancienne URSS
Oceania	0.2	0.2	0.2	0.2	0.2	0.2	0.2	0.1	0.1	0.1	Océanie

783 Road motor vehicles, nes

TRADE BY COMMODITY (Value in million US dollars)
Imports by principal countries or areas

COMMERCE PAR PRODUIT (Valeur en millions de dollars EU)
Importations selon les principaux pays ou zones

Country or area	1998	1999	2000	2001	2002	Pays ou zone
World	16218.3	16572.4	15322.0	13566.9	14951.5	Monde
Africa	714.9	740.3	686.7	839.4	875.6	Afrique
Americas	6532.5	7306.2	5252.8	3734.4	4071.1	Amériques
- Northern America	4654.2	6213.1	3940.1	2694.8	3098.1	- Amérique du Nord
- LAIA	1438.9	722.6	925.8	719.0	602.7	- ALAI
- CACM	190.9	174.9	188.0	186.7	193.8	- MCC
- Caribbean	192.5	137.6	151.9	103.4	136.8	- Caraïbes
- Rest of America	55.9	58.0	47.0	30.5	39.6	- Autre d'Amérique
Asia excluding former USSR	1581.8	1289.2	1969.7	1736.8	2000.3	Asie ancienne URSS exclus
- Middle East	703.5	541.8	858.0	744.7	911.3	- Moyen-Orient
Asia former USSR	95.0	81.0	102.3	107.3	117.7	Asie ancienne URSS
Europe excluding former USSR	6503.3	6625.7	6683.8	6389.3	6971.7	Europe ancienne URSS exclus
- European Union	5485.9	5743.6	5634.8	5129.3	5469.1	- Union Européenne
- Eastern Europe	612.1	504.8	638.8	819.8	1002.2	- Europe de l'Est
- Rest of Europe	405.3	377.3	410.1	440.2	500.3	- Autre de l'Europe
Europe former USSR	563.4	266.9	343.9	578.7	685.8	Europe ancienne URSS
Oceania	227.4	263.0	282.7	180.9	229.5	Océanie
United States	3232.5	4510.5	2737.9	1941.1	2010.1	Etats-Unis d'Amérique
France-Monaco	1510.8	1404.6	1197.3	958.2	1132.3	France-Monaco
Canada	1420.7	1701.3	1201.4	751.1	1085.0	Canada
Italy-San Marino-Holy See	725.2	1010.3	953.6	917.8	898.7	Italie-Saint-Marin-Saint-Siège
Spain	544.5	736.7	744.4	627.3	575.5	Espagne
Germany	529.6	520.0	683.6	663.6	741.9	Allemagne
United Kingdom	540.7	442.1	487.3	437.4	494.4	Royaume-Uni
Belgium	–	510.4	457.8	495.5	e543.4	Belgique
Austria	379.3	338.6	338.3	311.9	354.8	Autriche
Netherlands	340.3	266.7	289.5	254.1	257.5	Pays-Bas
Philippines	88.1	173.4	282.3	301.8	345.9	Philippines
Czech Republic	171.6	166.6	190.9	228.0	250.5	République tchèque
Russian Federation	286.1	114.7	142.4	199.2	263.8	Fédération de Russie
Poland	173.8	127.4	163.2	195.7	326.7	Pologne
Saudi Arabia	152.8	137.0	202.8	240.9	e249.3	Arabie saoudite
Turkey	324.8	129.4	309.7	88.7	127.2	Turquie
China, Hong Kong SAR	373.0	159.0	161.9	123.5	118.0	Chine - RAS de Hong-Kong
Australia	181.7	209.5	232.5	127.3	171.3	Australie
Brazil	294.6	163.9	211.4	143.9	97.6	Brésil
Switzerland-Liechtenstein	154.1	136.2	180.1	205.7	198.4	Suisse-Liechtenstein
Mexico	122.5	143.5	284.8	147.0	99.9	Mexique
Chile	171.6	82.7	130.3	130.9	147.5	Chili
Portugal	106.0	152.6	151.6	143.8	100.8	Portugal
China	127.7	80.2	118.6	115.3	141.1	Chine
Hungary	106.0	112.5	89.2	100.8	138.5	Hongrie
Algeria	84.0	153.9	84.8	e102.6	e116.9	Algérie
Nigeria	68.1	87.0	103.4	e141.7	e134.4	Nigéria
Belgium-Luxembourg	509.8	–	–	–	–	Belgique-Luxembourg
Venezuela	211.8	56.4	58.7	80.9	e68.1	Venezuela
Sweden	76.1	92.3	91.4	78.1	131.9	Suède

(Value as percentages of World total) **(Valeur en pourcentage du total mondial)**

Regions of the world	1993	1994	1995	1996	1997	1998	1999	2000	2001	2002	Régions du monde
World	100.0	100.0	100.0	100.0	100.0	100.0	100.0	100.0	100.0	100.0	Monde
Africa	5.9	5.2	5.2	4.5	4.8	4.4	4.5	4.5	6.2	5.9	Afrique
Americas	30.7	34.5	28.3	27.6	35.8	40.3	44.1	34.3	27.5	27.2	Amériques
- Northern America	18.6	24.1	21.5	22.0	27.3	28.7	37.5	25.7	19.9	20.7	- Amérique du Nord
- LAIA	9.5	8.2	5.4	4.0	6.3	8.9	4.4	6.0	5.3	4.0	- ALAI
- CACM	0.7	1.0	0.8	0.7	1.0	1.2	1.1	1.2	1.4	1.3	- MCC
- Caribbean	0.7	0.4	0.4	0.6	0.8	1.2	0.8	1.0	0.8	0.9	- Caraïbes
- Rest of America	1.1	0.9	0.2	0.2	0.3	0.3	0.4	0.3	0.2	0.3	- Autre d'Amérique
Asia excluding former USSR	21.4	19.5	11.2	13.1	14.4	9.8	7.8	12.9	12.8	13.4	Asie ancienne URSS exclus
- Middle East	6.7	5.2	3.7	4.2	4.8	4.3	3.3	5.6	5.5	6.1	- Moyen-Orient
Asia former USSR	1.0	0.9	0.4	0.7	0.3	0.6	0.5	0.7	0.8	0.8	Asie ancienne URSS
Europe excluding former USSR	33.8	35.4	50.9	49.6	38.1	40.1	40.0	43.6	47.1	46.6	Europe ancienne URSS exclus
- European Union	28.1	30.3	45.6	44.5	33.0	33.8	34.7	36.8	37.8	36.6	- Union Européenne
- Eastern Europe	2.8	2.0	2.1	2.6	2.6	3.8	3.0	4.2	6.0	6.7	- Europe de l'Est
- Rest of Europe	2.9	3.1	3.2	2.4	2.5	2.5	2.3	2.7	3.2	3.3	- Autre de l'Europe
Europe former USSR	5.7	2.6	2.6	3.0	5.2	3.5	1.6	2.2	4.3	4.6	Europe ancienne URSS
Oceania	1.6	1.8	1.3	1.5	1.3	1.4	1.6	1.8	1.3	1.5	Océanie

TRADE BY COMMODITY (Value in million US dollars)
Exports by principal countries or areas

COMMERCE PAR PRODUIT (Valeur en millions de dollars EU)
Exportations selon les principaux pays ou zones

Country or area	1998	1999	2000	2001	2002	Pays ou zone
World	17891.4	17775.1	16188.4	14653.5	16416.5	Monde
Africa	38.8	47.7	60.4	108.9	125.4	Afrique
Americas	5349.2	6591.5	4458.8	2988.9	3593.0	Amériques
- Northern America	4559.0	5089.0	3712.8	2522.8	2566.9	- Amérique du Nord
- LAIA	784.8	1500.1	743.3	463.7	1023.2	- ALAI
- CACM	0.3	1.4	1.6	1.2	1.3	- MCC
- Caribbean	5.0	1.0	0.8	0.8	1.3	- Caraïbes
- Rest of America	0.1	0.0	0.2	0.4	0.2	- Autre d'Amérique
Asia excluding former USSR	2020.3	1788.4	2021.2	2052.3	2347.0	Asie ancienne URSS exclus
- Middle East	284.9	351.6	351.0	423.3	448.4	- Moyen-Orient
Asia former USSR	1.0	6.9	10.0	20.7	16.4	Asie ancienne URSS
Europe excluding former USSR	10325.3	9206.7	9419.3	9241.1	10018.3	Europe ancienne URSS exclus
- European Union	10002.5	8926.6	9079.5	8866.1	9572.7	- Union Européenne
- Eastern Europe	240.7	223.0	308.7	321.3	360.6	- Europe de l'Est
- Rest of Europe	82.1	57.1	31.1	53.8	84.9	- Autre de l'Europe
Europe former USSR	148.8	121.8	207.1	212.4	281.4	Europe ancienne URSS
Oceania	8.1	12.2	11.7	29.1	35.1	Océanie
Germany	3295.1	3093.1	3103.6	3285.5	3461.8	Allemagne
Canada	2805.8	3181.6	2140.5	1534.5	1255.8	Canada
Netherlands	1924.5	1827.4	1821.5	1773.4	1876.7	Pays-Bas
United States	1753.2	1907.5	1572.3	988.4	1311.1	Etats-Unis d'Amérique
France-Monaco	1370.6	1205.5	1290.6	1058.6	1181.6	France-Monaco
Belgium	–	1497.5	1406.8	1332.9	e1495.5	Belgique
Japan	1050.3	897.0	1045.8	961.9	1146.8	Japon
Mexico	331.4	1202.0	421.8	188.7	729.6	Mexique
Korea, Republic of	498.0	370.2	468.2	521.7	596.7	République de Corée
Sweden	504.0	342.5	537.7	466.9	548.8	Suède
Belgium-Luxembourg	1815.7	–	–	–	–	Belgique-Luxembourg
Spain	321.6	341.3	259.7	317.2	356.8	Espagne
Turkey	211.0	268.2	271.7	334.8	366.3	Turquie
United Kingdom	243.1	171.4	270.1	220.0	234.0	Royaume-Uni
Brazil	301.8	206.3	211.1	205.5	e213.1	Brésil
Austria	246.8	135.0	124.4	148.3	153.2	Autriche
Belarus	92.4	66.6	139.0	124.3	160.3	Bélarus
Poland	33.8	60.7	131.3	109.8	158.6	Pologne
Hungary	120.1	80.2	90.8	122.2	78.7	Hongrie
Italy-San Marino-Holy See	124.7	108.3	92.8	78.6	75.2	Italie-Saint-Marin-Saint-Siège
Argentina	118.9	86.5	101.7	63.2	e61.0	Argentine
Czech Republic	79.0	75.8	78.6	81.8	114.5	République tchèque
Finland	74.6	90.1	70.8	76.2	70.1	Finlande
India	53.6	61.0	67.2	31.5	53.7	Inde
Russian Federation	32.7	33.6	37.5	58.4	80.2	Fédération de Russie
Denmark	27.6	48.8	41.7	48.5	71.2	Danemark
China	27.9	26.5	38.1	55.3	50.2	Chine
China, Hong Kong SAR	62.4	31.7	23.8	24.5	21.4	Chine - RAS de Hong-Kong
Portugal	39.2	30.3	32.6	29.8	25.6	Portugal
Switzerland-Liechtenstein	32.6	21.1	10.7	29.4	49.4	Suisse-Liechtenstein

(Value as percentages of World total) **(Valeur en pourcentage du total mondial)**

Regions of the world	1993	1994	1995	1996	1997	1998	1999	2000	2001	2002	Régions du monde
World	100.0	100.0	100.0	100.0	100.0	100.0	100.0	100.0	100.0	100.0	Monde
Africa	0.3	0.2	0.3	0.2	0.4	0.2	0.3	0.4	0.7	0.8	Afrique
Americas	26.2	28.1	22.0	22.4	28.6	29.9	37.1	27.5	20.4	21.9	Amériques
- Northern America	21.7	24.9	20.9	21.0	25.5	25.5	28.6	22.9	17.2	15.6	- Amérique du Nord
- LAIA	4.5	3.2	1.1	1.4	3.1	4.4	8.4	4.6	3.2	6.2	- ALAI
- CACM	0.0	0.0	0.0	0.0	0.0	0.0	0.0	0.0	0.0	0.0	- MCC
- Caribbean	0.0	0.0	0.0	0.0	0.0	0.0	0.0	0.0	0.0	0.0	- Caraïbes
- Rest of America	0.0	0.0	0.0	0.0	0.0	0.0	0.0	0.0	0.0	0.0	- Autre d'Amérique
Asia excluding former USSR	23.4	22.0	11.9	13.8	14.6	11.3	10.1	12.5	14.0	14.3	Asie ancienne URSS exclus
- Middle East	2.2	3.1	2.0	2.7	1.9	1.6	2.0	2.2	2.9	2.7	- Moyen-Orient
Asia former USSR	0.0	0.0	0.0	0.0	0.0	0.0	0.0	0.1	0.1	0.1	Asie ancienne URSS
Europe excluding former USSR	49.1	48.9	64.5	62.6	55.3	57.7	51.8	58.2	63.1	61.0	Europe ancienne URSS exclus
- European Union	44.8	47.0	63.0	61.1	52.8	55.9	50.2	56.1	60.5	58.3	- Union Européenne
- Eastern Europe	3.3	1.3	1.1	1.3	2.2	1.3	1.3	1.9	2.2	2.2	- Europe de l'Est
- Rest of Europe	1.0	0.6	0.4	0.3	0.3	0.5	0.3	0.2	0.4	0.5	- Autre de l'Europe
Europe former USSR	0.9	0.7	1.1	0.9	1.0	0.8	0.7	1.3	1.4	1.7	Europe ancienne URSS
Oceania	0.1	0.1	0.1	0.1	0.1	0.0	0.1	0.1	0.2	0.2	Océanie

784 Motor vehicle parts and accessories, nes

TRADE BY COMMODITY (Value in million US dollars)
Imports by principal countries or areas

COMMERCE PAR PRODUIT (Valeur en millions de dollars EU)
Importations selon les principaux pays ou zones

Country or area	1998	1999	2000	2001	2002	Pays ou zone
World	128880.5	138795.6	146517.0	142193.6	157785.2	Monde
Africa	1498.7	1323.9	1357.6	1368.1	1479.4	Afrique
Americas	51837.8	57900.0	64061.6	59103.6	61195.7	Amériques
- Northern America	40506.9	45927.5	48032.8	44217.7	48379.8	- Amérique du Nord
- LAIA	10923.1	11579.2	15649.8	14515.4	12426.0	- ALAI
- CACM	131.9	123.5	119.9	121.8	140.2	- MCC
- Caribbean	207.8	200.1	197.4	200.3	196.4	- Caraïbes
- Rest of America	68.1	69.8	61.6	48.4	53.3	- Autre d'Amérique
Asia excluding former USSR	11013.7	11203.7	15596.5	15333.8	18759.2	Asie ancienne URSS exclus
- Middle East	3791.4	3095.3	3982.0	3650.8	5625.7	- Moyen-Orient
Asia former USSR	307.3	352.6	296.6	311.5	228.6	Asie ancienne URSS
Europe excluding former USSR	62014.4	66005.5	62989.5	64114.5	74028.3	Europe ancienne URSS exclus
- European Union	55660.3	59542.6	56757.6	57982.0	67272.2	- Union Européenne
- Eastern Europe	4699.7	4904.5	4739.8	4648.4	5121.1	- Europe de l'Est
- Rest of Europe	1654.3	1558.3	1492.1	1484.1	1634.9	- Autre de l'Europe
Europe former USSR	765.9	477.3	505.6	665.9	725.0	Europe ancienne URSS
Oceania	1442.6	1532.7	1709.7	1296.2	1368.9	Océanie
United States	23455.3	26790.6	29219.3	27620.0	30563.2	Etats-Unis d'Amérique
Canada	17043.8	19128.5	18810.1	16593.3	17810.3	Canada
Germany	10379.9	10884.1	9776.8	10748.1	14840.8	Allemagne
United Kingdom	9933.2	10842.9	9535.7	9332.4	10754.9	Royaume-Uni
Mexico	6623.9	8230.1	12054.8	11192.7	9813.1	Mexique
Spain	7723.0	9162.4	10073.4	9401.4	10380.1	Espagne
France-Monaco	6597.1	7055.0	6990.8	7440.0	8206.3	France-Monaco
Belgium	–	6623.3	5981.6	6777.9	e7433.4	Belgique
Italy-San Marino-Holy See	3179.9	3394.5	3461.1	3547.4	3942.1	Italie-Saint-Marin-Saint-Siège
Netherlands	3321.9	3234.7	2677.6	2334.1	2706.7	Pays-Bas
Sweden	2339.5	2389.5	2682.6	2531.9	2910.3	Suède
Austria	1938.8	2482.0	2451.9	2754.9	2743.6	Autriche
Japan	1591.3	1631.2	2041.2	2121.8	2555.6	Japon
China	947.3	1273.0	2127.8	2549.7	3005.0	Chine
Brazil	1682.1	1581.7	1741.2	1644.9	1473.4	Brésil
Poland	2206.0	1992.8	1532.0	1123.7	1109.0	Pologne
Belgium-Luxembourg	7021.4	–	–	–	–	Belgique-Luxembourg
Portugal	1341.7	1380.2	1301.1	1297.8	1385.8	Portugal
Australia	1304.5	1388.3	1565.6	1141.8	1198.0	Australie
Czech Republic	936.0	1000.4	1123.6	1491.9	1670.3	République tchèque
Iran (Islamic Republic of)	1044.1	596.7	696.3	1043.7	2813.5	Iran (République islamique d')
Thailand	290.6	724.4	1442.7	1586.7	e1653.2	Thaïlande
Turkey	1177.6	1009.9	1532.0	815.2	1033.4	Turquie
Korea, Republic of	647.9	950.2	1209.2	1194.9	1515.7	République de Corée
Argentina	1693.3	1065.7	1084.2	800.4	e354.1	Argentine
Hungary	584.4	1057.0	1075.9	968.1	1056.4	Hongrie
Slovakia	820.2	721.2	867.3	901.4	1053.8	Slovaquie
Indonesia	387.9	305.3	1120.9	936.4	829.7	Indonésie
Finland	637.0	678.1	655.4	699.2	750.5	Finlande
Singapore	442.9	566.4	693.7	654.4	753.4	Singapour

(Value as percentages of World total)

(Valeur en pourcentage du total mondial)

Regions of the world	1993	1994	1995	1996	1997	1998	1999	2000	2001	2002	Régions du monde
World	100.0	100.0	100.0	100.0	100.0	100.0	100.0	100.0	100.0	100.0	Monde
Africa	2.1	2.2	1.8	1.2	1.1	1.2	1.0	0.9	1.0	0.9	Afrique
Americas	44.3	39.4	36.1	36.5	39.3	40.2	41.7	43.7	41.6	38.8	Amériques
- Northern America	33.2	34.9	30.6	29.0	30.6	31.4	33.1	32.8	31.1	30.7	- Amérique du Nord
- LAIA	10.8	4.2	5.2	7.2	8.4	8.5	8.3	10.7	10.2	7.9	- ALAI
- CACM	0.1	0.1	0.1	0.1	0.1	0.1	0.1	0.1	0.1	0.1	- MCC
- Caribbean	0.2	0.1	0.1	0.1	0.2	0.2	0.1	0.1	0.1	0.1	- Caraïbes
- Rest of America	0.1	0.1	0.1	0.0	0.1	0.1	0.1	0.0	0.0	0.0	- Autre d'Amérique
Asia excluding former USSR	13.2	12.6	13.7	12.8	11.2	8.5	8.1	10.6	10.8	11.9	Asie ancienne URSS exclus
- Middle East	2.8	2.0	2.5	2.4	2.6	2.9	2.2	2.7	2.6	3.6	- Moyen-Orient
Asia former USSR	0.0	0.1	0.1	0.3	0.1	0.2	0.3	0.2	0.2	0.1	Asie ancienne URSS
Europe excluding former USSR	38.7	43.9	46.8	47.7	46.6	48.1	47.6	43.0	45.1	46.9	Europe ancienne URSS exclus
- European Union	36.8	42.0	44.3	44.6	42.6	43.2	42.9	38.7	40.8	42.6	- Union Européenne
- Eastern Europe	0.8	0.9	1.3	1.9	3.0	3.6	3.5	3.2	3.3	3.2	- Europe de l'Est
- Rest of Europe	1.1	1.1	1.2	1.2	1.1	1.3	1.1	1.0	1.0	1.0	- Autre de l'Europe
Europe former USSR	0.5	0.4	0.4	0.5	0.6	0.6	0.3	0.3	0.5	0.5	Europe ancienne URSS
Oceania	1.2	1.4	1.1	1.1	1.1	1.1	1.1	1.2	0.9	0.9	Océanie

Pièces détachées des voitures routières et des tracteurs des groupes 722, 781, 782 et 783 784

TRADE BY COMMODITY (Value in million US dollars)
Exports by principal countries or areas

COMMERCE PAR PRODUIT (Valeur en millions de dollars EU)
Exportations selon les principaux pays ou zones

Country or area	1998	1999	2000	2001	2002	Pays ou zone
World	127127.5	134081.7	142592.0	137503.2	157626.5	Monde
Africa	462.6	516.0	482.2	457.5	506.3	Afrique
Americas	43719.6	46903.0	50787.0	47123.2	49240.4	Amériques
- Northern America	37007.0	39612.2	42573.0	39227.0	40289.5	- Amérique du Nord
- LAIA	6702.9	7279.2	8196.9	7869.9	8930.6	- ALAI
- CACM	5.0	6.3	3.0	7.6	4.2	- MCC
- Caribbean	4.3	4.7	13.1	9.6	8.8	- Caraïbes
- Rest of America	0.4	0.6	1.0	9.0	7.2	- Autre d'Amérique
Asia excluding former USSR	18557.0	21307.7	25461.7	24141.4	27102.3	Asie ancienne URSS exclus
- Middle East	777.0	864.8	958.2	1162.9	1344.4	- Moyen-Orient
Asia former USSR	12.1	9.4	11.8	11.6	14.9	Asie ancienne URSS
Europe excluding former USSR	63522.6	64502.2	64889.2	64815.4	79653.2	Europe ancienne URSS exclus
- European Union	59732.7	60213.8	60110.2	59030.7	72281.1	- Union Européenne
- Eastern Europe	2697.1	3172.2	3709.2	4634.0	6034.2	- Europe de l'Est
- Rest of Europe	1092.8	1116.2	1069.8	1150.7	1337.9	- Autre de l'Europe
Europe former USSR	466.8	364.8	413.4	413.4	444.4	Europe ancienne URSS
Oceania	386.8	478.6	546.8	540.8	664.9	Océanie
United States	28324.9	29397.9	31641.4	29165.3	29248.8	Etats-Unis d'Amérique
Germany	16191.9	16062.5	15949.3	17294.6	26332.7	Allemagne
Japan	12742.4	14496.9	17444.8	15632.2	17100.6	Japon
France-Monaco	10894.6	11921.7	12479.1	11229.1	12203.5	France-Monaco
Canada	8682.1	10214.3	10931.2	10061.5	11040.0	Canada
Italy-San Marino-Holy See	7504.9	7280.1	7165.9	7066.0	7471.8	Italie-Saint-Marin-Saint-Siège
United Kingdom	7084.8	6598.6	7297.1	6070.3	6146.5	Royaume-Uni
Spain	5461.3	5825.6	5842.0	6051.1	6970.3	Espagne
Mexico	4173.7	5107.9	5812.5	5579.3	6608.5	Mexique
Sweden	4449.2	3891.7	3246.1	3095.8	3618.2	Suède
Belgium	–	3734.0	3545.9	3533.6	e3964.7	Belgique
Austria	1832.0	2030.9	1927.6	1903.7	2086.9	Autriche
Korea, Republic of	1281.0	1708.6	1792.2	1905.5	2247.7	République de Corée
Czech Republic	1242.4	1464.8	1627.7	2028.0	2545.3	République tchèque
Brazil	1788.9	1446.5	1572.9	1584.0	e1642.2	Brésil
Netherlands	1480.1	1507.8	1301.8	1371.7	1838.9	Pays-Bas
China	533.1	782.7	1129.4	1360.2	1859.2	Chine
Poland	414.6	534.9	790.3	1081.4	1451.7	Pologne
Hungary	567.2	624.4	748.0	903.3	1172.5	Hongrie
Belgium-Luxembourg	3515.1	–	–	–	–	Belgique-Luxembourg
Portugal	480.3	540.8	595.4	648.1	798.9	Portugal
Philippines	337.5	442.1	568.6	625.1	741.0	Philippines
Switzerland-Liechtenstein	466.4	503.2	473.9	515.2	579.9	Suisse-Liechtenstein
Turkey	358.4	390.7	456.5	539.1	706.4	Turquie
Denmark	495.1	494.8	439.5	455.8	525.3	Danemark
Slovakia	396.9	427.1	432.9	473.9	617.1	Slovaquie
Argentina	457.0	496.8	520.8	426.6	e412.2	Argentine
Australia	342.7	423.5	475.3	464.9	577.3	Australie
Singapore	363.6	429.5	460.3	435.0	524.5	Singapour
Thailand	234.5	343.7	508.1	500.5	e528.6	Thaïlande

(Value as percentages of World total) **(Valeur en pourcentage du total mondial)**

Regions of the world	1993	1994	1995	1996	1997	1998	1999	2000	2001	2002	Régions du monde
World	100.0	100.0	100.0	100.0	100.0	100.0	100.0	100.0	100.0	100.0	Monde
Africa	0.4	0.3	0.3	0.3	0.3	0.4	0.4	0.3	0.3	0.3	Afrique
Americas	33.1	32.2	29.7	30.2	33.0	34.4	35.0	35.6	34.3	31.2	Amériques
- Northern America	28.9	28.0	25.9	26.1	28.6	29.1	29.5	29.9	28.5	25.6	- Amérique du Nord
- LAIA	4.1	4.1	3.8	4.1	4.5	5.3	5.4	5.7	5.7	5.7	- ALAI
- CACM	0.0	0.0	0.0	0.0	0.0	0.0	0.0	0.0	0.0	0.0	- MCC
- Caribbean	0.0	0.0	0.0	0.0	0.0	0.0	0.0	0.0	0.0	0.0	- Caraïbes
- Rest of America	0.0	0.0	0.0	0.0	0.0	0.0	0.0	0.0	0.0	0.0	- Autre d'Amérique
Asia excluding former USSR	21.4	20.9	19.8	18.3	16.6	14.6	15.9	17.9	17.6	17.2	Asie ancienne URSS exclus
- Middle East	0.4	0.3	0.4	0.4	0.5	0.6	0.6	0.7	0.8	0.9	- Moyen-Orient
Asia former USSR	0.0	0.0	0.0	0.0	0.0	0.0	0.0	0.0	0.0	0.0	Asie ancienne URSS
Europe excluding former USSR	44.6	46.1	49.7	50.5	49.3	50.0	48.1	45.5	47.1	50.5	Europe ancienne URSS exclus
- European Union	43.3	44.8	48.0	48.6	46.9	47.0	44.9	42.2	42.9	45.9	- Union Européenne
- Eastern Europe	0.6	0.6	0.9	1.2	1.6	2.1	2.4	2.6	3.4	3.8	- Europe de l'Est
- Rest of Europe	0.7	0.7	0.8	0.7	0.7	0.9	0.8	0.8	0.8	0.8	- Autre de l'Europe
Europe former USSR	0.2	0.2	0.3	0.4	0.4	0.4	0.3	0.3	0.3	0.3	Europe ancienne URSS
Oceania	0.3	0.3	0.3	0.3	0.4	0.3	0.4	0.4	0.4	0.4	Océanie

785 Cycles, scooters, motorized or not; invalid carriages

TRADE BY COMMODITY (Value in million US dollars)
Imports by principal countries or areas

COMMERCE PAR PRODUIT (Valeur en millions de dollars EU
Importations selon les principaux pays ou zone

Country or area	1998	1999	2000	2001	2002	Pays ou zone
World	18222.0	18992.0	20437.6	19841.3	20506.8	Monde
Africa	371.3	343.2	370.3	385.3	405.8	Afrique
Americas	3914.1	4490.3	5658.8	5691.1	5951.9	Amériques
- Northern America	3058.9	3739.3	4817.1	4841.2	5122.2	- Amérique du Nord
- LAIA	674.2	603.5	677.4	696.8	666.9	- ALAI
- CACM	78.5	67.8	72.0	74.7	79.2	- MCC
- Caribbean	88.6	66.3	79.6	68.0	72.7	- Caraïbes
- Rest of America	13.9	13.5	12.8	10.4	10.9	- Autre d'Amérique
Asia excluding former USSR	3738.8	3608.1	4304.4	4054.8	4403.3	Asie ancienne URSS exclus
- Middle East	237.0	224.5	256.7	272.1	324.1	- Moyen-Orient
Asia former USSR	3.5	3.6	3.8	4.2	4.6	Asie ancienne URSS
Europe excluding former USSR	9763.4	10061.6	9553.5	9211.6	9179.9	Europe ancienne URSS exclus
- European Union	8946.5	9267.3	8739.9	8422.6	8309.8	- Union Européenne
- Eastern Europe	249.5	250.2	260.9	259.3	315.2	- Europe de l'Est
- Rest of Europe	567.4	544.1	552.7	529.8	555.0	- Autre de l'Europe
Europe former USSR	48.5	42.3	46.6	66.5	83.8	Europe ancienne URSS
Oceania	382.4	442.9	500.2	427.8	477.6	Océanie
United States	2665.0	3268.0	4254.9	4284.0	4526.3	Etats-Unis d'Amérique
Germany	2191.8	2026.5	1817.9	1781.3	1635.3	Allemagne
France-Monaco	1323.3	1434.5	1274.9	1225.4	1338.4	France-Monaco
Italy-San Marino-Holy See	1138.9	1304.0	1381.5	1328.3	1128.2	Italie-Saint-Marin-Saint-Siège
United Kingdom	1061.8	1125.2	1148.3	1009.8	1032.8	Royaume-Uni
Netherlands	960.6	1008.2	925.9	893.2	816.9	Pays-Bas
Japan	614.5	774.4	928.5	957.7	1021.9	Japon
Spain	639.6	712.6	564.4	609.2	631.4	Espagne
Viet Nam	387.4	432.7	707.6	734.3	893.4	Viet Nam
China, Hong Kong SAR	892.9	535.4	488.0	341.4	318.3	Chine - RAS de Hong-Kong
Canada	387.9	464.5	559.7	553.5	591.5	Canada
Belgium	–	519.9	495.6	535.0	e586.7	Belgique
Australia	318.7	379.2	431.4	360.9	396.8	Australie
Switzerland-Liechtenstein	328.9	314.0	333.6	316.4	328.2	Suisse-Liechtenstein
Indonesia	205.5	132.6	333.9	433.4	420.9	Indonésie
Austria	304.6	293.3	295.2	259.6	267.4	Autriche
Singapore	245.3	221.5	255.4	195.0	210.6	Singapour
China	171.6	216.1	241.2	187.1	194.0	Chine
Sweden	185.5	190.4	208.9	190.0	223.9	Suède
Mexico	120.4	159.6	196.8	232.6	251.6	Mexique
Greece	167.8	177.7	169.2	175.0	e193.5	Grèce
Denmark	205.9	171.7	160.6	157.8	183.9	Danemark
Philippines	116.3	159.7	185.2	191.4	165.1	Philippines
Norway	170.0	158.5	152.9	148.9	146.5	Norvège
Brazil	164.5	113.9	138.3	142.5	119.7	Brésil
Argentina	171.3	155.7	159.4	119.5	e52.9	Argentine
Portugal	150.5	145.5	128.1	107.3	113.2	Portugal
Poland	118.1	113.9	111.5	96.9	108.8	Pologne
Belgium-Luxembourg	497.6	–	–	–	–	Belgique-Luxembourg
Czech Republic	70.1	75.9	79.7	80.2	95.6	République tchèque

(Value as percentages of World total)

(Valeur en pourcentage du total mondial)

Regions of the world	1993	1994	1995	1996	1997	1998	1999	2000	2001	2002	Régions du monde
World	100.0	100.0	100.0	100.0	100.0	100.0	100.0	100.0	100.0	100.0	Monde
Africa	1.9	1.8	1.7	2.1	1.8	2.0	1.8	1.8	1.9	2.0	Afrique
Americas	19.5	20.3	19.3	17.9	19.6	21.5	23.6	27.7	28.7	29.0	Amériques
- Northern America	13.6	14.1	15.0	14.4	15.0	16.8	19.7	23.6	24.4	25.0	- Amérique du Nord
- LAIA	5.0	5.5	3.7	2.9	3.9	3.7	3.2	3.3	3.5	3.3	- ALAI
- CACM	0.3	0.3	0.3	0.3	0.4	0.4	0.4	0.4	0.4	0.4	- MCC
- Caribbean	0.4	0.2	0.2	0.2	0.3	0.5	0.3	0.4	0.3	0.4	- Caraïbes
- Rest of America	0.1	0.1	0.1	0.1	0.1	0.1	0.1	0.1	0.1	0.1	- Autre d'Amérique
Asia excluding former USSR	32.8	31.8	31.8	29.3	26.7	20.5	19.0	21.1	20.4	21.5	Asie ancienne URSS exclus
- Middle East	1.2	0.9	0.9	1.2	1.3	1.3	1.2	1.3	1.4	1.6	- Moyen-Orient
Asia former USSR	0.0	0.0	0.0	0.0	0.0	0.0	0.0	0.0	0.0	0.0	Asie ancienne URSS
Europe excluding former USSR	44.2	44.1	45.1	48.4	49.5	53.6	53.0	46.7	46.4	44.8	Europe ancienne URSS exclus
- European Union	40.6	40.1	40.9	43.9	45.1	49.1	48.8	42.8	42.4	40.5	- Union Européenne
- Eastern Europe	0.8	1.0	1.2	1.4	1.4	1.4	1.3	1.3	1.3	1.5	- Europe de l'Est
- Rest of Europe	2.8	3.0	3.0	3.1	2.9	3.1	2.9	2.7	2.7	2.7	- Autre de l'Europe
Europe former USSR	0.1	0.1	0.1	0.2	0.3	0.3	0.2	0.2	0.3	0.4	Europe ancienne URSS
Oceania	1.5	1.8	1.9	2.1	2.1	2.1	2.3	2.4	2.2	2.3	Océanie

TRADE BY COMMODITY (Value in million US dollars)
Exports by principal countries or areas

COMMERCE PAR PRODUIT (Valeur en millions de dollars EU)
Exportations selon les principaux pays ou zones

Country or area	1998	1999	2000	2001	2002	Pays ou zone
World	18692.9	19256.7	21371.4	19901.3	20752.8	Monde
Africa	29.6	28.7	25.8	24.5	26.3	Afrique
Americas	1309.1	1294.3	1397.3	1394.9	1401.6	Amériques
- Northern America	1116.4	1068.3	1166.4	1189.3	1243.3	- Amérique du Nord
- LAIA	187.7	222.1	223.7	200.8	155.6	- ALAI
- CACM	4.0	2.9	4.4	2.7	0.6	- MCC
- Caribbean	0.9	0.9	2.6	1.5	1.6	- Caraïbes
- Rest of America	0.2	0.1	0.2	0.6	0.5	- Autre d'Amérique
Asia excluding former USSR	11558.8	12062.5	14229.0	12465.8	12847.6	Asie ancienne URSS exclus
- Middle East	50.3	47.9	47.8	61.4	60.5	- Moyen-Orient
Asia former USSR	0.1	0.0	0.1	0.1	0.1	Asie ancienne URSS
Europe excluding former USSR	5723.1	5786.1	5612.7	5881.4	6320.4	Europe ancienne URSS exclus
- European Union	5433.0	5505.6	5325.1	5591.8	5991.7	- Union Européenne
- Eastern Europe	182.1	157.7	165.3	178.1	202.5	- Europe de l'Est
- Rest of Europe	108.0	122.8	122.3	111.5	126.2	- Autre de l'Europe
Europe former USSR	61.6	68.0	75.2	77.7	86.1	Europe ancienne URSS
Oceania	10.6	17.0	31.3	56.9	70.7	Océanie
Japan	5666.6	5902.7	6660.1	6065.5	5834.4	Japon
China	1175.3	1404.9	2475.5	2552.5	2902.6	Chine
Italy-San Marino-Holy See	1948.0	1896.9	1888.5	1834.5	1868.9	Italie-Saint-Marin-Saint-Siège
United States	1047.3	995.7	1089.8	1108.9	1151.8	Etats-Unis d'Amérique
Germany	698.3	727.9	707.5	696.1	905.5	Allemagne
Netherlands	688.1	669.1	669.2	696.4	606.6	Pays-Bas
France-Monaco	670.0	702.0	617.5	508.1	553.3	France-Monaco
Spain	475.6	485.5	454.9	542.9	625.3	Espagne
China, Hong Kong SAR	547.8	508.3	473.3	327.1	298.1	Chine - RAS de Hong-Kong
Thailand	311.4	337.8	343.8	322.6	e340.7	Thaïlande
Belgium	-	278.7	267.2	485.3	e544.5	Belgique
India	199.8	224.3	302.9	296.4	350.3	Inde
United Kingdom	267.6	292.7	284.2	287.2	241.9	Royaume-Uni
Singapore	312.6	276.4	300.0	210.8	243.4	Singapour
Indonesia	164.5	196.5	227.5	170.2	196.0	Indonésie
Austria	126.6	145.6	149.5	218.0	292.5	Autriche
Korea, Republic of	177.0	214.3	226.3	147.7	133.7	République de Corée
Malaysia	131.5	148.2	164.2	128.0	e135.7	Malaisie
Mexico	125.5	151.0	116.1	102.0	59.5	Mexique
Sweden	86.3	102.9	103.8	116.3	130.8	Suède
Viet Nam	26.5	43.2	131.7	136.9	152.2	Viet Nam
Canada	69.1	72.6	76.6	80.4	91.5	Canada
Czech Republic	88.7	68.2	69.7	70.2	74.0	République tchèque
Denmark	62.0	67.4	59.6	77.5	91.1	Danemark
Portugal	75.1	76.6	66.4	67.4	66.9	Portugal
Poland	65.1	62.9	67.3	71.2	76.9	Pologne
Brazil	40.9	46.6	80.5	76.4	e79.2	Brésil
Switzerland-Liechtenstein	59.1	65.2	63.3	58.8	65.3	Suisse-Liechtenstein
Belgium-Luxembourg	289.2	-	-	-	-	Belgique-Luxembourg
Philippines	30.1	54.3	60.8	52.7	56.1	Philippines

(Value as percentages of World total)

(Valeur en pourcentage du total mondial)

Regions of the world	1993	1994	1995	1996	1997	1998	1999	2000	2001	2002	Régions du monde
World	100.0	100.0	100.0	100.0	100.0	100.0	100.0	100.0	100.0	100.0	Monde
Africa	0.1	0.1	0.1	0.1	0.1	0.2	0.1	0.1	0.1	0.1	Afrique
Americas	5.2	5.8	6.1	6.6	7.0	7.0	6.7	6.5	7.0	6.8	Amériques
- Northern America	4.7	5.2	5.6	5.9	6.2	6.0	5.5	5.5	6.0	6.0	- Amérique du Nord
- LAIA	0.5	0.5	0.5	0.7	0.7	1.0	1.2	1.0	1.0	0.7	- ALAI
- CACM	0.0	0.0	0.0	0.0	0.0	0.0	0.0	0.0	0.0	0.0	- MCC
- Caribbean	0.0	0.0	0.0	0.0	0.0	0.0	0.0	0.0	0.0	0.0	- Caraïbes
- Rest of America	0.0	0.0	0.0	0.0	0.0	0.0	0.0	0.0	0.0	0.0	- Autre d'Amérique
Asia excluding former USSR	76.3	70.7	68.7	64.7	63.9	61.8	62.6	66.6	62.6	61.9	Asie ancienne URSS exclus
- Middle East	0.1	0.1	0.2	0.2	0.2	0.3	0.2	0.2	0.3	0.3	- Moyen-Orient
Asia former USSR	0.0	0.0	0.0	0.0	0.0	0.0	0.0	0.0	0.0	0.0	Asie ancienne URSS
Europe excluding former USSR	18.0	23.2	24.7	28.2	28.6	30.6	30.0	26.3	29.6	30.5	Europe ancienne URSS exclus
- European Union	16.9	21.8	23.2	26.6	27.2	29.1	28.6	24.9	28.1	28.9	- Union Européenne
- Eastern Europe	0.5	0.6	0.8	0.9	0.9	1.0	0.8	0.8	0.9	1.0	- Europe de l'Est
- Rest of Europe	0.6	0.7	0.7	0.7	0.6	0.6	0.6	0.6	0.6	0.6	- Autre de l'Europe
Europe former USSR	0.3	0.2	0.2	0.3	0.4	0.3	0.4	0.4	0.4	0.4	Europe ancienne URSS
Oceania	0.1	0.1	0.1	0.1	0.1	0.1	0.1	0.1	0.3	0.3	Océanie

786 Trailers, and other vehicles, not motorized, nes

TRADE BY COMMODITY (Value in million US dollars)
Imports by principal countries or areas

COMMERCE PAR PRODUIT (Valeur en millions de dollars EU)
Importations selon les principaux pays ou zones

Country or area	1998	1999	2000	2001	2002	Pays ou zone
World	8143.6	8290.7	9284.8	8337.9	8722.8	Monde
Africa	201.4	216.9	182.6	220.8	241.5	Afrique
Americas	2089.3	2286.5	2928.7	1960.4	1991.1	Amériques
- Northern America	1653.7	1867.3	2455.6	1560.0	1648.9	- Amérique du Nord
- LAIA	376.4	352.9	409.4	337.9	277.5	- ALAI
- CACM	25.2	27.4	22.9	27.2	28.5	- MCC
- Caribbean	27.3	29.5	33.4	29.3	29.2	- Caraïbes
- Rest of America	6.7	9.4	7.3	6.0	7.1	- Autre d'Amérique
Asia excluding former USSR	636.2	636.9	801.1	685.7	694.0	Asie ancienne URSS exclus
- Middle East	151.8	136.4	158.7	157.4	212.8	- Moyen-Orient
Asia former USSR	19.4	14.6	32.5	38.8	30.4	Asie ancienne URSS
Europe excluding former USSR	4883.4	4925.5	5085.7	5069.8	5325.3	Europe ancienne URSS exclus
- European Union	4017.6	4128.8	4251.5	4129.5	4249.4	- Union Européenne
- Eastern Europe	451.4	389.2	407.3	492.6	589.9	- Europe de l'Est
- Rest of Europe	414.5	407.6	426.8	447.7	485.9	- Autre de l'Europe
Europe former USSR	225.2	110.1	149.2	255.4	313.6	Europe ancienne URSS
Oceania	88.7	100.2	105.0	107.0	126.8	Océanie
United States	720.2	945.6	1561.8	881.4	871.5	Etats-Unis d'Amérique
Germany	924.4	896.0	1033.4	892.5	813.5	Allemagne
Canada	932.6	920.4	887.7	670.8	761.7	Canada
France-Monaco	519.0	551.5	541.7	565.9	601.7	France-Monaco
United Kingdom	401.6	407.8	431.0	415.5	498.8	Royaume-Uni
Netherlands	409.7	442.2	423.8	397.6	404.2	Pays-Bas
Denmark	365.3	286.5	324.1	336.9	328.6	Danemark
Belgium	–	360.6	329.5	322.7	e353.9	Belgique
Austria	248.9	259.4	231.0	257.7	255.8	Autriche
Italy-San Marino-Holy See	182.5	242.9	272.2	269.4	280.1	Italie-Saint-Marin-Saint-Siège
Spain	218.3	237.2	226.5	232.2	263.3	Espagne
Mexico	187.1	232.4	308.2	249.6	199.0	Mexique
Sweden	157.7	175.4	175.5	188.1	185.4	Suède
Switzerland-Liechtenstein	160.2	165.4	176.7	187.3	185.0	Suisse-Liechtenstein
Norway	172.5	150.6	155.0	163.5	186.9	Norvège
Poland	208.6	160.1	136.5	124.7	183.8	Pologne
China, Hong Kong SAR	128.2	170.7	217.7	113.3	88.6	Chine - RAS de Hong-Kong
Japan	145.7	125.2	149.4	149.2	143.7	Japon
Czech Republic	106.6	100.8	107.9	116.1	149.9	République tchèque
Hungary	75.0	78.8	67.3	98.2	118.9	Hongrie
Australia	64.8	75.1	82.4	82.3	98.4	Australie
Portugal	68.6	81.7	84.2	77.6	66.7	Portugal
Finland	85.8	62.9	60.3	72.4	85.6	Finlande
Belgium-Luxembourg	355.8	–	–	–	–	Belgique-Luxembourg
Russian Federation	70.4	32.7	47.3	81.3	105.7	Fédération de Russie
Ireland	52.7	62.2	63.1	53.0	60.0	Irlande
Israel	40.6	40.0	53.1	82.7	73.7	Israël
Romania	16.8	15.4	52.2	93.0	68.1	Roumanie
Lithuania	44.7	16.6	29.8	56.9	e70.1	Lituanie
Singapore	24.5	30.6	67.0	43.8	26.6	Singapour

(Value as percentages of World total) **(Valeur en pourcentage du total mondial)**

Regions of the world	1993	1994	1995	1996	1997	1998	1999	2000	2001	2002	Régions du monde
World	100.0	100.0	100.0	100.0	100.0	100.0	100.0	100.0	100.0	100.0	Monde
Africa	3.6	2.9	2.9	2.9	2.5	2.5	2.6	2.0	2.6	2.8	Afrique
Americas	21.0	22.6	21.2	19.7	23.2	25.7	27.6	31.5	23.5	22.8	Amériques
- Northern America	16.2	17.7	17.2	16.0	18.2	20.3	22.5	26.4	18.7	18.9	- Amérique du Nord
- LAIA	4.0	4.0	3.2	3.0	4.2	4.6	4.3	4.4	4.1	3.2	- ALAI
- CACM	0.3	0.3	0.2	0.2	0.3	0.3	0.3	0.2	0.3	0.3	- MCC
- Caribbean	0.3	0.3	0.4	0.4	0.4	0.3	0.4	0.4	0.4	0.3	- Caraïbes
- Rest of America	0.2	0.3	0.2	0.1	0.1	0.1	0.1	0.1	0.1	0.1	- Autre d'Amérique
Asia excluding former USSR	15.0	13.0	12.0	11.9	11.5	7.8	7.7	8.6	8.2	8.0	Asie ancienne URSS exclus
- Middle East	3.4	2.8	2.0	1.9	1.8	1.9	1.6	1.7	1.9	2.4	- Moyen-Orient
Asia former USSR	0.5	0.3	0.5	0.2	0.1	0.2	0.2	0.4	0.5	0.3	Asie ancienne URSS
Europe excluding former USSR	55.1	58.1	60.0	62.0	58.4	60.0	59.4	54.8	60.8	61.1	Europe ancienne URSS exclus
- European Union	46.7	49.3	50.6	52.0	48.3	49.3	49.8	45.8	49.5	48.7	- Union Européenne
- Eastern Europe	3.3	3.0	3.5	4.4	4.9	5.5	4.7	4.4	5.9	6.8	- Europe de l'Est
- Rest of Europe	5.1	5.7	5.9	5.6	5.3	5.1	4.9	4.6	5.4	5.6	- Autre de l'Europe
Europe former USSR	3.4	1.7	2.1	2.1	2.9	2.8	1.3	1.6	3.1	3.6	Europe ancienne URSS
Oceania	1.3	1.4	1.2	1.4	1.4	1.1	1.2	1.1	1.3	1.5	Océanie

Remorques et autres véhicules non automobiles et containers pour tous modes de transport 786

TRADE BY COMMODITY (Value in million US dollars)
Exports by principal countries or areas

COMMERCE PAR PRODUIT (Valeur en millions de dollars EU)
Exportations selon les principaux pays ou zones

Country or area	1998	1999	2000	2001	2002	Pays ou zone
World	10873.8	10299.0	11030.3	10402.7	10905.2	Monde
Africa	292.1	222.8	153.3	125.2	144.7	Afrique
Americas	1860.7	1962.5	2006.5	1572.8	1556.8	Amériques
- Northern America	1472.3	1505.2	1518.8	1280.3	1375.4	- Amérique du Nord
- LAIA	383.4	451.8	471.3	285.9	173.9	- ALAI
- CACM	2.5	1.8	6.1	3.6	3.3	- MCC
- Caribbean	2.4	3.5	10.0	2.7	3.8	- Caraïbes
- Rest of America	0.0	0.3	0.3	0.4	0.4	- Autre d'Amérique
Asia excluding former USSR	2590.1	2432.7	3451.8	2953.7	3053.6	Asie ancienne URSS exclus
- Middle East	92.7	67.6	78.4	73.3	84.3	- Moyen-Orient
Asia former USSR	3.2	4.6	5.1	7.3	8.1	Asie ancienne URSS
Europe excluding former USSR	5986.0	5553.3	5278.3	5590.6	5983.8	Europe ancienne URSS exclus
- European Union	5377.3	4917.4	4621.9	4896.0	5241.6	- Union Européenne
- Eastern Europe	481.5	505.6	520.2	558.9	593.9	- Europe de l'Est
- Rest of Europe	127.2	130.3	136.2	135.6	148.3	- Autre de l'Europe
Europe former USSR	122.2	96.5	113.4	125.2	129.9	Europe ancienne URSS
Oceania	19.6	26.6	21.9	27.9	28.3	Océanie
China	1719.9	1655.8	2771.8	2510.9	2583.1	Chine
Germany	2152.9	1906.8	1824.7	2223.8	2266.5	Allemagne
United States	1266.0	1250.5	1251.1	1000.6	1022.4	Etats-Unis d'Amérique
France-Monaco	720.4	671.6	635.0	562.6	602.7	France-Monaco
United Kingdom	564.5	523.6	500.1	397.4	428.0	Royaume-Uni
Belgium	–	396.9	371.3	371.0	e416.2	Belgique
Mexico	309.3	407.5	424.8	254.9	141.4	Mexique
Italy-San Marino-Holy See	336.0	322.9	286.1	287.2	298.1	Italie-Saint-Marin-Saint-Siège
Netherlands	288.1	309.4	287.1	282.2	358.5	Pays-Bas
Canada	206.3	254.6	267.6	279.6	353.0	Canada
Korea, Republic of	398.4	397.0	273.4	68.5	58.6	République de Corée
Austria	237.4	213.8	202.9	212.0	259.5	Autriche
Hungary	152.6	175.2	171.4	190.0	206.9	Hongrie
Denmark	206.4	172.1	145.0	174.9	193.2	Danemark
Poland	142.4	153.6	161.6	171.7	177.4	Pologne
Spain	179.9	128.9	110.7	120.9	137.0	Espagne
Sweden	101.2	111.7	111.2	118.0	131.5	Suède
Czech Republic	110.0	107.5	115.1	114.6	119.8	République tchèque
Finland	107.6	100.4	93.4	97.5	93.6	Finlande
Southern African Customs Union	248.0	205.5	–	–	–	Union douanière d'Afrique australe
Belgium-Luxembourg	424.4	–	–	–	–	Belgique-Luxembourg
South Africa	–	–	138.4	100.1	109.4	Afrique du Sud
Slovenia	59.0	62.8	66.0	67.5	78.2	Slovénie
Belarus	66.5	52.4	56.1	59.3	57.0	Bélarus
Slovakia	50.4	45.3	50.3	59.9	67.0	Slovaquie
Japan	59.3	61.7	42.3	46.0	49.8	Japon
Turkey	64.4	33.4	39.8	41.1	53.0	Turquie
Norway	43.6	42.5	43.9	41.1	42.2	Norvège
Malaysia	70.8	37.3	21.6	36.7	e38.8	Malaisie
Singapore	29.8	30.9	43.8	42.8	36.3	Singapour

(Value as percentages of World total) **(Valeur en pourcentage du total mondial)**

Regions of the world	1993	1994	1995	1996	1997	1998	1999	2000	2001	2002	Régions du monde
World	100.0	100.0	100.0	100.0	100.0	100.0	100.0	100.0	100.0	100.0	Monde
Africa	2.7	2.2	2.2	2.3	3.0	2.7	2.2	1.4	1.2	1.3	Afrique
Americas	13.2	14.3	13.2	13.4	16.2	17.1	19.1	18.2	15.1	14.3	Amériques
- Northern America	10.8	11.2	10.4	10.2	12.3	13.5	14.6	13.8	12.3	12.6	- Amérique du Nord
- LAIA	2.4	3.0	2.8	3.1	3.9	3.5	4.4	4.3	2.7	1.6	- ALAI
- CACM	0.0	0.0	0.0	0.0	0.0	0.0	0.0	0.1	0.0	0.0	- MCC
- Caribbean	0.0	0.0	0.0	0.0	0.0	0.0	0.0	0.1	0.0	0.0	- Caraïbes
- Rest of America	0.0	0.1	0.0	0.0	0.0	0.0	0.0	0.0	0.0	0.0	- Autre d'Amérique
Asia excluding former USSR	32.2	29.4	31.5	28.4	24.0	23.8	23.6	31.3	28.4	28.0	Asie ancienne URSS exclus
- Middle East	1.1	1.6	1.2	1.4	1.3	0.9	0.7	0.7	0.7	0.8	- Moyen-Orient
Asia former USSR	0.0	0.0	0.0	0.0	0.0	0.0	0.0	0.0	0.1	0.1	Asie ancienne URSS
Europe excluding former USSR	49.3	53.3	51.4	54.4	55.1	55.0	53.9	47.9	53.7	54.9	Europe ancienne URSS exclus
- European Union	44.4	48.6	46.5	49.3	49.8	49.5	47.7	41.9	47.1	48.1	- Union Européenne
- Eastern Europe	3.5	3.5	3.7	3.9	4.1	4.4	4.9	4.7	5.4	5.4	- Europe de l'Est
- Rest of Europe	1.5	1.2	1.2	1.2	1.2	1.2	1.3	1.2	1.3	1.4	- Autre de l'Europe
Europe former USSR	2.4	0.5	1.2	1.1	1.3	1.1	0.9	1.0	1.2	1.2	Europe ancienne URSS
Oceania	0.3	0.3	0.4	0.4	0.3	0.2	0.3	0.2	0.3	0.3	Océanie

791 Railway vehicles and associated equipment

TRADE BY COMMODITY (Value in million US dollars)
Imports by principal countries or areas

COMMERCE PAR PRODUIT (Valeur en millions de dollars EU)
Importations selon les principaux pays ou zones

Country or area	1998	1999	2000	2001	2002	Pays ou zone
World	8965.0	8989.9	8116.4	8703.4	8962.6	Monde
Africa	136.1	235.8	142.4	141.3	122.2	Afrique
Americas	3542.8	3716.9	3107.0	2647.2	1935.3	Amériques
- Northern America	2987.1	2878.0	2476.6	2080.2	1448.5	- Amérique du Nord
- LAIA	541.9	825.6	608.5	517.3	455.4	- ALAI
- CACM	0.5	0.9	1.8	1.4	0.5	- MCC
- Caribbean	13.0	12.3	19.2	32.7	30.9	- Caraïbes
- Rest of America	0.3	0.1	0.9	15.7	0.1	- Autre d'Amérique
Asia excluding former USSR	1708.1	1322.6	1112.5	1350.1	1611.9	Asie ancienne URSS exclus
- Middle East	150.5	193.3	211.8	144.6	178.6	- Moyen-Orient
Asia former USSR	175.6	100.8	196.8	105.1	116.0	Asie ancienne URSS
Europe excluding former USSR	2999.9	3348.3	3354.4	4148.8	4542.3	Europe ancienne URSS exclus
- European Union	2314.0	2719.8	2564.0	3414.4	3700.9	- Union Européenne
- Eastern Europe	446.9	347.4	426.8	414.6	421.9	- Europe de l'Est
- Rest of Europe	239.0	281.1	363.5	319.8	419.4	- Autre de l'Europe
Europe former USSR	361.5	210.2	159.6	260.1	493.5	Europe ancienne URSS
Oceania	40.9	55.2	43.7	50.8	141.4	Océanie
United States	2029.9	2200.7	1742.7	1278.7	973.4	Etats-Unis d'Amérique
Canada	957.1	677.2	733.7	801.4	475.0	Canada
Germany	703.3	651.8	575.8	588.8	731.5	Allemagne
United Kingdom	394.6	582.6	606.2	511.5	461.8	Royaume-Uni
Mexico	214.1	456.8	396.4	286.4	203.3	Mexique
Greece	195.7	162.2	15.4	471.2	e521.0	Grèce
China	217.6	204.4	250.3	234.1	379.6	Chine
France-Monaco	157.3	266.1	335.9	234.4	282.0	France-Monaco
Belgium	-	195.4	168.8	396.0	e434.3	Belgique
Austria	166.9	181.9	184.4	230.4	305.1	Autriche
Korea, Republic of	188.0	251.9	305.2	196.5	99.2	République de Corée
Italy-San Marino-Holy See	164.4	144.3	156.4	242.8	204.9	Italie-Saint-Marin-Saint-Siège
China, Hong Kong SAR	289.6	48.3	19.4	137.7	305.7	Chine - RAS de Hong-Kong
Denmark	31.0	60.5	156.7	305.4	220.6	Danemark
Switzerland-Liechtenstein	119.9	142.4	129.6	155.5	220.4	Suisse-Liechtenstein
Brazil	131.8	285.0	125.8	95.5	95.2	Brésil
Russian Federation	146.2	67.1	65.4	124.0	307.9	Fédération de Russie
Sweden	97.7	133.9	86.7	110.5	124.3	Suède
Poland	82.1	97.8	137.5	109.1	116.5	Pologne
Czech Republic	145.1	105.7	89.0	95.4	78.8	République tchèque
Norway	85.3	114.2	127.9	60.3	123.9	Norvège
Slovakia	123.2	63.1	79.8	95.3	91.3	Slovaquie
Spain	80.8	77.2	87.6	89.0	112.8	Espagne
Kazakhstan	130.8	73.1	89.6	64.1	e65.5	Kazakhstan
Japan	75.7	95.5	78.4	87.1	68.6	Japon
Turkey	40.4	74.5	133.5	100.0	32.2	Turquie
Portugal	53.7	165.0	40.6	52.3	54.4	Portugal
Ukraine	110.0	72.1	45.5	60.8	65.5	Ukraine
Malaysia	91.9	19.6	9.7	107.2	e117.2	Malaisie
Iran (Islamic Republic of)	79.3	91.0	54.1	12.4	79.8	Iran (République islamique d')

(Value as percentages of World total) **(Valeur en pourcentage du total mondial)**

Regions of the world	1993	1994	1995	1996	1997	1998	1999	2000	2001	2002	Régions du monde
World	100.0	100.0	100.0	100.0	100.0	100.0	100.0	100.0	100.0	100.0	Monde
Africa	3.3	2.3	2.6	2.5	3.0	1.5	2.6	1.8	1.6	1.4	Afrique
Americas	17.2	21.5	26.9	27.0	30.3	39.5	41.3	38.3	30.4	21.6	Amériques
- Northern America	13.7	17.4	23.5	23.9	27.1	33.3	32.0	30.5	23.9	16.2	- Amérique du Nord
- LAIA	3.4	4.0	3.2	2.9	3.1	6.0	9.2	7.5	5.9	5.1	- ALAI
- CACM	0.0	0.0	0.0	0.0	0.0	0.0	0.0	0.0	0.0	0.0	- MCC
- Caribbean	0.1	0.1	0.1	0.1	0.1	0.1	0.1	0.2	0.4	0.3	- Caraïbes
- Rest of America	0.0	0.0	0.0	0.0	0.0	0.0	0.0	0.0	0.2	0.0	- Autre d'Amérique
Asia excluding former USSR	25.4	11.7	19.2	22.6	21.0	19.1	14.7	13.7	15.5	18.0	Asie ancienne URSS exclus
- Middle East	5.6	2.1	2.5	3.7	2.5	1.7	2.1	2.6	1.7	2.0	- Moyen-Orient
Asia former USSR	0.5	1.6	1.0	1.1	1.5	2.0	1.1	2.4	1.2	1.3	Asie ancienne URSS
Europe excluding former USSR	44.2	55.7	40.5	37.3	36.7	33.5	37.2	41.3	47.7	50.7	Europe ancienne URSS exclus
- European Union	38.1	51.6	31.0	25.6	27.3	25.8	30.3	31.6	39.2	41.3	- Union Européenne
- Eastern Europe	2.8	1.7	5.3	4.0	4.9	5.0	3.9	5.3	4.8	4.7	- Europe de l'Est
- Rest of Europe	3.2	2.3	4.2	7.6	4.4	2.7	3.1	4.5	3.7	4.7	- Autre de l'Europe
Europe former USSR	8.6	6.2	8.6	8.8	6.9	4.0	2.3	2.0	3.0	5.5	Europe ancienne URSS
Oceania	0.7	1.1	1.1	0.8	0.6	0.5	0.6	0.5	0.6	1.6	Océanie

TRADE BY COMMODITY (Value in million US dollars)
Exports by principal countries or areas

COMMERCE PAR PRODUIT (Valeur en millions de dollars EU)
Exportations selon les principaux pays ou zones

Country or area	1998	1999	2000	2001	2002	Pays ou zone
World	9679.6	8932.2	8251.9	8898.1	9116.1	Monde
Africa	43.5	27.2	24.5	23.9	33.1	Afrique
Americas	3428.8	3541.2	2962.3	2760.3	2039.6	Amériques
- Northern America	3143.5	2973.8	2373.4	2196.2	1508.6	- Amérique du Nord
- LAIA	284.5	566.8	588.6	563.7	530.5	- ALAI
- CACM	0.1	0.2	0.1	0.1	0.2	- MCC
- Caribbean	0.7	0.4	0.2	0.1	0.1	- Caraïbes
- Rest of America	0.0	0.0	0.0	0.2	0.2	- Autre d'Amérique
Asia excluding former USSR	581.5	532.7	675.3	727.6	788.0	Asie ancienne URSS exclus
- Middle East	13.6	7.2	4.6	5.5	13.4	- Moyen-Orient
Asia former USSR	18.2	8.9	10.5	13.1	16.1	Asie ancienne URSS
Europe excluding former USSR	5142.0	4528.8	4296.9	4904.7	5702.8	Europe ancienne URSS exclus
- European Union	3992.8	3517.6	3343.2	3815.1	4676.5	- Union Européenne
- Eastern Europe	717.3	700.4	647.2	801.1	736.5	- Europe de l'Est
- Rest of Europe	432.0	310.8	306.4	288.5	289.8	- Autre de l'Europe
Europe former USSR	409.5	267.1	263.6	440.9	514.6	Europe ancienne URSS
Oceania	56.1	26.2	18.8	27.6	21.9	Océanie
United States	1584.5	1459.0	1331.0	1437.4	1033.2	Etats-Unis d'Amérique
Germany	1117.8	980.0	1029.2	1266.6	1537.4	Allemagne
Canada	1559.0	1514.7	1042.3	758.8	475.4	Canada
France-Monaco	698.3	634.0	698.0	560.8	753.1	France-Monaco
Austria	497.2	624.7	478.9	493.6	691.5	Autriche
Mexico	245.1	534.1	545.6	511.7	478.0	Mexique
Italy-San Marino-Holy See	469.4	295.6	354.4	414.9	494.2	Italie-Saint-Marin-Saint-Siège
Japan	207.5	354.9	374.3	521.6	417.2	Japon
Spain	380.9	320.3	278.2	270.8	353.1	Espagne
Switzerland-Liechtenstein	403.4	279.8	253.6	215.4	227.6	Suisse-Liechtenstein
Czech Republic	330.3	307.6	235.7	247.7	244.3	République tchèque
United Kingdom	288.9	259.6	169.5	256.9	210.6	Royaume-Uni
Russian Federation	250.9	164.9	169.3	159.1	200.1	Fédération de Russie
Ukraine	128.7	85.1	85.1	266.8	294.1	Ukraine
China	234.5	130.8	184.6	77.8	179.6	Chine
Belgium	-	136.2	63.0	280.2	e314.4	Belgique
Poland	85.5	117.4	151.4	190.1	199.6	Pologne
Sweden	166.0	150.6	143.3	123.6	145.4	Suède
Slovakia	150.3	138.5	101.9	148.9	103.5	Slovaquie
Hungary	69.6	82.0	82.0	137.5	86.6	Hongrie
Korea, Republic of	95.9	16.6	84.9	81.3	124.0	République de Corée
Romania	77.4	52.0	73.6	74.1	99.4	Roumanie
Netherlands	44.7	57.2	80.3	77.7	60.5	Pays-Bas
Belgium-Luxembourg	223.7	-	-	-	-	Belgique-Luxembourg
Brazil	32.5	26.1	35.7	46.4	e48.1	Brésil
Denmark	27.9	12.1	17.3	35.7	84.5	Danemark
Slovenia	8.7	10.2	30.7	51.8	41.1	Slovénie
Australia	52.2	21.7	18.4	26.1	21.7	Australie
Finland	54.9	22.1	7.4	10.7	14.0	Finlande
Portugal	22.7	23.4	21.5	16.7	10.6	Portugal

(Value as percentages of World total) **(Valeur en pourcentage du total mondial)**

Regions of the world	1993	1994	1995	1996	1997	1998	1999	2000	2001	2002	Régions du monde
World	100.0	100.0	100.0	100.0	100.0	100.0	100.0	100.0	100.0	100.0	Monde
Africa	0.5	0.3	0.3	1.1	2.0	0.4	0.3	0.3	0.3	0.4	Afrique
Americas	20.8	20.3	26.5	26.5	30.0	35.4	39.6	35.9	31.0	22.4	Amériques
- Northern America	19.4	19.7	25.4	25.7	28.9	32.5	33.3	28.8	24.7	16.5	- Amérique du Nord
- LAIA	1.3	0.6	1.1	0.8	1.0	2.9	6.3	7.1	6.3	5.8	- ALAI
- CACM	0.0	0.0	0.0	0.0	0.0	0.0	0.0	0.0	0.0	0.0	- MCC
- Caribbean	0.0	0.0	0.0	0.0	0.0	0.0	0.0	0.0	0.0	0.0	- Caraïbes
- Rest of America	0.0	0.0	0.0	0.0	0.0	0.0	0.0	0.0	0.0	0.0	- Autre d'Amérique
Asia excluding former USSR	4.6	3.4	6.5	8.1	8.1	6.0	6.0	8.2	8.2	8.6	Asie ancienne URSS exclus
- Middle East	0.1	0.0	0.2	0.2	0.1	0.1	0.1	0.1	0.1	0.1	- Moyen-Orient
Asia former USSR	0.0	0.0	0.0	0.1	0.1	0.2	0.1	0.1	0.1	0.2	Asie ancienne URSS
Europe excluding former USSR	71.9	70.2	56.8	56.1	51.4	53.1	50.7	52.1	55.1	62.6	Europe ancienne URSS exclus
- European Union	62.3	63.5	46.7	44.7	41.7	41.2	39.4	40.5	42.9	51.3	- Union Européenne
- Eastern Europe	5.4	3.8	6.5	5.5	6.3	7.4	7.8	7.8	9.0	8.1	- Europe de l'Est
- Rest of Europe	4.2	2.9	3.6	6.0	3.3	4.5	3.5	3.7	3.2	3.2	- Autre de l'Europe
Europe former USSR	1.9	5.5	7.9	7.2	6.6	4.2	3.0	3.2	5.0	5.6	Europe ancienne URSS
Oceania	0.4	0.3	1.9	0.9	1.8	0.6	0.3	0.2	0.3	0.2	Océanie

792 Aircraft and associated equipment, and parts thereof, nes

TRADE BY COMMODITY (Value in million US dollars)
Imports by principal countries or areas

COMMERCE PAR PRODUIT (Valeur en millions de dollars EU)
Importations selon les principaux pays ou zones

Country or area	1998	1999	2000	2001	2002	Pays ou zone
World	88554.1	90983.7	91043.2	98892.1	98651.2	Monde
Africa	1102.0	1564.1	1849.0	1442.3	1873.9	Afrique
Americas	19747.3	22048.5	25336.6	28679.1	24729.6	Amériques
- Northern America	16774.9	19170.6	22651.1	26266.3	22786.0	- Amérique du Nord
- LAIA	2728.8	2528.6	2342.6	2143.7	1796.0	- ALAI
- CACM	25.3	22.0	27.8	19.1	16.1	- MCC
- Caribbean	212.5	315.6	305.4	237.7	118.6	- Caraïbes
- Rest of America	5.8	11.6	9.7	12.3	12.8	- Autre d'Amérique
Asia excluding former USSR	24076.0	21255.4	14878.0	20940.2	21361.7	Asie ancienne URSS exclus
- Middle East	4341.0	2925.5	3843.6	3072.0	3513.3	- Moyen-Orient
Asia former USSR	218.4	290.3	61.4	196.1	68.8	Asie ancienne URSS
Europe excluding former USSR	40316.8	43222.7	46056.1	45757.5	46876.9	Europe ancienne URSS exclus
- European Union	37131.6	39045.1	41471.5	42778.2	44295.1	- Union Européenne
- Eastern Europe	663.7	778.2	1046.8	492.7	623.8	- Europe de l'Est
- Rest of Europe	2521.5	3399.4	3537.8	2486.6	1958.0	- Autre de l'Europe
Europe former USSR	963.4	66.9	89.3	165.1	275.4	Europe ancienne URSS
Oceania	2130.2	2535.6	2772.8	1711.7	3465.0	Océanie
United States	13106.1	15087.9	18265.3	21180.1	18063.4	Etats-Unis d'Amérique
Germany	10486.9	9811.7	11917.2	13979.2	13119.6	Allemagne
United Kingdom	9576.5	8687.5	9068.2	11584.0	12798.8	Royaume-Uni
France-Monaco	6684.6	6704.3	7001.4	6172.4	6711.5	France-Monaco
Canada	3657.9	4075.8	4364.1	5049.6	4564.2	Canada
Japan	5216.6	5683.5	2997.9	1970.3	3723.9	Japon
China	3174.1	3174.4	2170.0	4542.7	4051.1	Chine
Italy-San Marino-Holy See	2790.2	2993.1	3439.6	3404.4	3933.4	Italie-Saint-Marin-Saint-Siège
Singapore	2591.0	2232.8	1152.5	3805.1	3136.3	Singapour
Spain	1269.9	2711.7	2967.9	1805.5	1782.1	Espagne
Australia	1461.4	1883.2	2252.8	1254.1	2851.1	Australie
Switzerland-Liechtenstein	1639.7	2375.4	1870.9	1107.5	1000.6	Suisse-Liechtenstein
Saudi Arabia	2210.6	1239.6	1242.3	1413.0	e1462.3	Arabie saoudite
Thailand	605.9	1809.4	330.5	1371.3	e1428.8	Thaïlande
Ireland	790.7	1435.8	769.0	875.0	1353.8	Irlande
Netherlands	1082.3	761.0	1542.9	957.4	803.1	Pays-Bas
United Arab Emirates	685.0	717.7	1191.1	1044.4	e1071.5	Emirates arabes unis
Norway	514.4	762.9	1383.0	1235.3	782.1	Norvège
China, Hong Kong SAR	1926.1	726.5	364.4	1438.5	160.5	Chine - RAS de Hong-Kong
Malaysia	1804.1	1073.5	486.0	594.2	e649.4	Malaisie
Brazil	957.5	932.9	1091.8	821.5	664.6	Brésil
Korea, Republic of	857.7	825.5	919.6	706.3	721.6	République de Corée
Austria	822.1	785.4	888.7	529.9	615.6	Autriche
Sweden	555.9	806.9	1028.8	693.4	420.2	Suède
Israel	381.8	1068.8	462.2	946.6	592.3	Israël
Denmark	582.7	537.1	331.5	564.4	931.7	Danemark
Colombia	419.3	494.7	359.9	865.2	787.1	Colombie
Turkey	795.9	551.6	935.7	249.8	274.0	Turquie
Belgium	–	823.6	702.4	583.6	e640.0	Belgique
Luxembourg	–	1023.5	515.0	543.5	e577.0	Luxembourg

(Value as percentages of World total) **(Valeur en pourcentage du total mondial)**

Regions of the world	1993	1994	1995	1996	1997	1998	1999	2000	2001	2002	Régions du monde
World	100.0	100.0	100.0	100.0	100.0	100.0	100.0	100.0	100.0	100.0	Monde
Africa	1.6	1.9	1.5	0.8	1.8	1.2	1.7	2.0	1.5	1.9	Afrique
Americas	14.9	16.4	15.7	17.4	20.2	22.3	24.2	27.8	29.0	25.1	Amériques
- Northern America	12.9	13.5	14.0	15.3	17.4	18.9	21.1	24.9	26.6	23.1	- Amérique du Nord
- LAIA	1.8	2.7	1.5	1.8	2.5	3.1	2.8	2.6	2.2	1.8	- ALAI
- CACM	0.0	0.0	0.0	0.0	0.0	0.0	0.0	0.0	0.0	0.0	- MCC
- Caribbean	0.1	0.1	0.1	0.2	0.2	0.2	0.3	0.3	0.2	0.1	- Caraïbes
- Rest of America	0.1	0.1	0.2	0.0	0.0	0.0	0.0	0.0	0.0	0.0	- Autre d'Amérique
Asia excluding former USSR	38.2	34.5	36.0	34.1	30.6	27.2	23.4	16.3	21.2	21.7	Asie ancienne URSS exclus
- Middle East	9.6	5.7	7.7	5.3	5.2	4.9	3.2	4.2	3.1	3.6	- Moyen-Orient
Asia former USSR	0.0	0.2	0.1	0.4	0.1	0.2	0.3	0.1	0.2	0.1	Asie ancienne URSS
Europe excluding former USSR	43.6	44.3	43.6	44.1	45.2	45.5	47.5	50.6	46.3	47.5	Europe ancienne URSS exclus
- European Union	41.5	42.1	40.0	40.0	41.6	41.9	42.9	45.6	43.3	44.9	- Union Européenne
- Eastern Europe	0.3	0.4	0.1	0.4	0.6	0.7	0.9	1.1	0.5	0.6	- Europe de l'Est
- Rest of Europe	1.8	1.7	3.5	3.7	3.0	2.8	3.7	3.9	2.5	2.0	- Autre de l'Europe
Europe former USSR	0.1	0.1	0.2	0.1	0.1	1.1	0.1	0.1	0.2	0.3	Europe ancienne URSS
Oceania	1.6	2.6	2.8	3.1	2.0	2.4	2.8	3.0	1.7	3.5	Océanie

Appareils de navigation aérienne et materiel connexe; leurs parties et pièces détachées 792

TRADE BY COMMODITY (Value in million US dollars)
Exports by principal countries or areas

COMMERCE PAR PRODUIT (Valeur en millions de dollars EU)
Exportations selon les principaux pays ou zones

Country or area	1998	1999	2000	2001	2002	Pays ou zone
World	112375.4	110586.4	109613.8	117219.7	116824.8	Monde
Africa	280.1	302.5	372.0	318.9	195.6	Afrique
Americas	59788.9	57831.0	52133.1	57569.4	55662.4	Amériques
- Northern America	57274.0	55063.9	47692.8	53229.8	51293.6	- Amérique du Nord
- LAIA	2474.4	2698.3	4363.7	4210.8	4332.6	- ALAI
- CACM	6.7	6.8	20.5	23.4	15.7	- MCC
- Caribbean	33.3	61.7	56.0	105.3	20.2	- Caraïbes
- Rest of America	0.5	0.2	0.1	0.2	0.2	- Autre d'Amérique
Asia excluding former USSR	6314.3	5976.9	5911.7	6292.5	5408.7	Asie ancienne URSS exclus
- Middle East	224.2	736.0	927.7	1070.2	618.9	- Moyen-Orient
Asia former USSR	46.9	88.1	79.6	96.6	74.7	Asie ancienne URSS
Europe excluding former USSR	44581.0	45509.2	50248.9	52008.4	53946.3	Europe ancienne URSS exclus
- European Union	43279.2	43872.0	49131.1	50648.5	51845.3	- Union Européenne
- Eastern Europe	490.6	616.1	283.1	368.3	250.4	- Europe de l'Est
- Rest of Europe	811.2	1021.2	834.7	991.6	1850.6	- Autre de l'Europe
Europe former USSR	774.8	246.8	354.0	460.5	541.7	Europe ancienne URSS
Oceania	589.3	631.8	514.6	473.3	995.4	Océanie
United States	52366.7	49610.7	40954.4	44688.6	43876.4	Etats-Unis d'Amérique
France-Monaco	15053.9	15101.6	16605.5	17209.6	17169.7	France-Monaco
Germany	12238.7	13954.2	14855.4	17174.5	17364.2	Allemagne
United Kingdom	8726.7	7822.6	9831.8	9211.2	8741.9	Royaume-Uni
Canada	4907.1	5445.1	6726.4	8530.7	7416.4	Canada
Italy-San Marino-Holy See	2745.8	2804.0	3581.9	2751.1	3856.1	Italie-Saint-Marin-Saint-Siège
Brazil	1317.5	1899.2	3574.5	3553.5	e3684.1	Brésil
Japan	1734.5	1804.4	1492.1	1729.4	1294.6	Japon
Spain	995.4	1357.6	1401.8	1342.6	1846.4	Espagne
Israel	748.2	853.6	933.3	945.1	1073.3	Israël
Switzerland-Liechtenstein	601.3	882.7	714.0	621.7	1065.6	Suisse-Liechtenstein
Singapore	597.5	477.7	669.8	850.4	936.7	Singapour
Sweden	1081.1	481.6	370.7	473.6	592.8	Suède
Belgium	–	712.1	535.2	709.3	e795.8	Belgique
Korea, Republic of	968.1	442.7	631.8	449.4	245.6	République de Corée
Netherlands	521.0	347.1	630.3	599.1	586.5	Pays-Bas
Australia	487.3	436.8	346.4	397.3	966.0	Australie
Malaysia	1162.8	704.2	302.4	224.3	e237.7	Malaisie
Mexico	931.1	382.8	298.4	383.5	400.1	Mexique
China	438.0	566.0	533.2	397.0	436.7	Chine
Turkey	123.4	517.4	670.9	524.7	126.8	Turquie
Denmark	280.7	502.8	328.9	238.1	259.7	Danemark
Russian Federation	603.6	101.4	166.4	319.3	380.7	Fédération de Russie
Austria	486.3	235.6	269.4	266.5	272.2	Autriche
Norway	102.3	58.6	83.6	352.2	768.6	Norvège
Ireland	347.4	301.7	260.8	201.1	105.2	Irlande
Czech Republic	362.2	487.9	43.0	115.6	82.2	République tchèque
Saudi Arabia	19.8	50.3	86.5	353.5	e318.6	Arabie saoudite
Argentina	35.4	82.0	259.8	192.7	e186.2	Argentine
Portugal	67.3	90.9	206.3	221.7	134.1	Portugal

(Value as percentages of World total) **(Valeur en pourcentage du total mondial)**

Regions of the world	1993	1994	1995	1996	1997	1998	1999	2000	2001	2002	Régions du monde
World	100.0	100.0	100.0	100.0	100.0	100.0	100.0	100.0	100.0	100.0	Monde
Africa	0.1	0.3	0.2	0.2	0.3	0.2	0.3	0.3	0.3	0.2	Afrique
Americas	49.0	47.6	41.2	46.9	48.9	53.2	52.3	47.6	49.1	47.6	Amériques
- Northern America	48.1	46.8	40.2	45.8	47.8	51.0	49.8	43.5	45.4	43.9	- Amérique du Nord
- LAIA	0.8	0.7	0.9	1.1	1.1	2.2	2.4	4.0	3.6	3.7	- ALAI
- CACM	0.0	0.0	0.0	0.0	0.0	0.0	0.0	0.0	0.0	0.0	- MCC
- Caribbean	0.1	0.0	0.1	0.0	0.0	0.0	0.1	0.1	0.1	0.0	- Caraïbes
- Rest of America	0.0	0.0	0.0	0.0	0.0	0.0	0.0	0.0	0.0	0.0	- Autre d'Amérique
Asia excluding former USSR	4.5	6.1	5.6	5.5	6.2	5.6	5.4	5.4	5.4	4.6	Asie ancienne URSS exclus
- Middle East	0.4	0.5	0.2	0.2	0.4	0.2	0.7	0.8	0.9	0.5	- Moyen-Orient
Asia former USSR	0.0	0.0	0.0	0.1	0.0	0.0	0.1	0.1	0.1	0.1	Asie ancienne URSS
Europe excluding former USSR	44.7	45.0	51.3	45.9	43.7	39.7	41.2	45.8	44.4	46.2	Europe ancienne URSS exclus
- European Union	44.1	44.4	50.2	44.5	42.4	38.5	39.7	44.8	43.2	44.4	- Union Européenne
- Eastern Europe	0.1	0.1	0.1	0.3	0.4	0.4	0.6	0.3	0.3	0.2	- Europe de l'Est
- Rest of Europe	0.6	0.5	1.0	1.1	0.9	0.7	0.9	0.8	0.8	1.6	- Autre de l'Europe
Europe former USSR	1.0	0.4	0.4	0.4	0.1	0.7	0.2	0.3	0.4	0.5	Europe ancienne URSS
Oceania	0.7	0.7	1.2	0.9	0.8	0.5	0.6	0.5	0.4	0.9	Océanie

793 Ships, boats and floating structures

TRADE BY COMMODITY (Value in million US dollars)
Imports by principal countries or areas

COMMERCE PAR PRODUIT (Valeur en millions de dollars EU)
Importations selon les principaux pays ou zones

Country or area	1998	1999	2000	2001	2002	Pays ou zone
World	17669.8	18606.1	18589.1	19334.5	19044.9	Monde
Africa	513.7	818.9	510.7	1177.4	571.5	Afrique
Americas	2180.2	2042.3	2350.0	2861.5	2851.3	Amériques
- Northern America	1588.7	1471.8	1914.0	1921.6	1734.0	- Amérique du Nord
- LAIA	354.1	341.3	264.6	357.4	366.8	- ALAI
- CACM	23.6	56.8	11.1	9.4	15.1	- MCC
- Caribbean	203.4	154.0	153.4	562.6	725.4	- Caraïbes
- Rest of America	10.4	18.3	7.0	10.5	10.0	- Autre d'Amérique
Asia excluding former USSR	6276.2	5933.4	4420.8	4861.8	4685.6	Asie ancienne URSS exclus
- Middle East	1064.8	999.2	512.0	900.4	808.9	- Moyen-Orient
Asia former USSR	23.1	187.8	41.8	25.9	48.6	Asie ancienne URSS
Europe excluding former USSR	7664.2	7782.8	10661.7	9691.5	9942.5	Europe ancienne URSS exclus
- European Union	4362.6	5331.0	7072.0	6827.4	6639.2	- Union Européenne
- Eastern Europe	76.3	92.1	249.0	755.0	1446.7	- Europe de l'Est
- Rest of Europe	3225.3	2359.7	3340.7	2109.2	1856.6	- Autre de l'Europe
Europe former USSR	686.7	476.8	296.2	350.2	381.9	Europe ancienne URSS
Oceania	325.7	1364.2	308.0	366.2	563.6	Océanie
Norway	2623.7	1757.1	2839.1	1491.3	1308.4	Norvège
United States	1174.2	1161.9	1210.5	1239.2	1362.4	Etats-Unis d'Amérique
Greece	1132.1	1047.3	1568.3	1133.2	e1253.0	Grèce
Germany	367.2	1089.1	1182.8	1699.4	1296.3	Allemagne
Singapore	1819.2	1483.0	694.0	199.7	256.2	Singapour
France-Monaco	453.8	785.1	524.2	1035.9	1369.8	France-Monaco
Spain	591.3	685.8	550.3	684.9	762.6	Espagne
Italy-San Marino-Holy See	273.4	454.8	756.6	852.7	784.6	Italie-Saint-Marin-Saint-Siège
Indonesia	174.1	286.9	867.2	947.9	550.9	Indonésie
Poland	8.0	52.2	173.7	712.9	1400.0	Pologne
Canada	402.0	285.0	634.6	635.0	319.5	Canada
India	219.3	570.8	340.9	577.3	554.3	Inde
Denmark	486.1	212.0	840.6	399.6	303.5	Danemark
United Kingdom	285.7	356.6	1022.7	305.4	245.4	Royaume-Uni
Malaysia	1115.3	626.4	206.1	116.1	e126.8	Malaisie
China	188.3	252.9	336.4	699.2	607.1	Chine
Russian Federation	657.8	446.7	221.2	285.2	299.9	Fédération de Russie
Turkey	229.2	281.1	128.3	608.7	501.4	Turquie
Australia	177.6	764.7	137.5	205.5	387.1	Australie
Korea, Republic of	382.4	243.6	192.5	374.2	425.8	République de Corée
Croatia	413.1	352.1	210.6	243.6	192.2	Croatie
Netherlands	214.4	306.8	249.3	250.5	259.1	Pays-Bas
United Arab Emirates	446.7	468.1	138.1	97.4	e99.9	Emirates arabes unis
Bangladesh	225.4	e246.8	e249.4	241.5	e236.1	Bangladesh
Angola	e14.9	e178.0	e114.7	e771.3	e13.8	Angola
Japan	178.1	209.1	201.5	222.5	267.9	Japon
Trinidad and Tobago	45.4	42.7	31.8	398.6	e	Trinité-et-Tobago
New Zealand	60.0	519.5	91.0	61.4	57.0	Nouvelle-Zélande
Saudi Arabia	310.6	75.7	101.4	69.7	e72.2	Arabie saoudite
Venezuela	96.0	124.5	79.8	139.3	e117.1	Venezuela

(Value as percentages of World total)

(Valeur en pourcentage du total mondial)

Regions of the world	1993	1994	1995	1996	1997	1998	1999	2000	2001	2002	Régions du monde
World	100.0	100.0	100.0	100.0	100.0	100.0	100.0	100.0	100.0	100.0	Monde
Africa	3.0	3.9	3.3	1.5	4.8	2.9	4.4	2.7	6.1	3.0	Afrique
Americas	12.3	12.5	12.1	11.0	8.7	12.3	11.0	12.6	14.8	15.0	Amériques
- Northern America	7.2	7.1	6.9	7.4	6.1	9.0	7.9	10.3	9.9	9.1	- Amérique du Nord
- LAIA	3.8	3.2	3.0	2.3	1.4	2.0	1.8	1.4	1.8	1.9	- ALAI
- CACM	0.1	0.1	0.1	0.1	0.1	0.1	0.3	0.1	0.0	0.1	- MCC
- Caribbean	1.1	2.1	1.9	1.1	1.0	1.2	0.8	0.8	2.9	3.8	- Caraïbes
- Rest of America	0.1	0.0	0.2	0.1	0.2	0.1	0.1	0.0	0.1	0.1	- Autre d'Amérique
Asia excluding former USSR	36.4	52.9	51.2	51.9	41.4	35.5	31.9	23.8	25.1	24.6	Asie ancienne URSS exclus
- Middle East	4.0	4.3	5.9	4.9	5.0	6.0	5.4	2.8	4.7	4.2	- Moyen-Orient
Asia former USSR	0.0	0.0	0.0	0.0	0.0	0.1	1.0	0.2	0.1	0.3	Asie ancienne URSS
Europe excluding former USSR	41.1	27.6	26.9	30.5	35.2	43.4	41.8	57.4	50.1	52.2	Europe ancienne URSS exclus
- European Union	29.0	19.9	20.2	21.9	20.6	24.7	28.7	38.0	35.3	34.9	- Union Européenne
- Eastern Europe	0.1	0.1	0.1	0.1	0.5	0.4	0.5	1.3	3.9	7.6	- Europe de l'Est
- Rest of Europe	12.0	7.7	6.6	8.5	14.1	18.3	12.7	18.0	10.9	9.7	- Autre de l'Europe
Europe former USSR	3.4	1.9	2.4	2.1	4.7	3.9	2.6	1.6	1.8	2.0	Europe ancienne URSS
Oceania	3.9	1.1	4.1	3.0	5.2	1.8	7.3	1.7	1.9	3.0	Océanie

Navires, bateaux et engines flattants, y compris les aéroglisseurs 793

TRADE BY COMMODITY (Value in million US dollars)
Exports by principal countries or areas

COMMERCE PAR PRODUIT (Valeur en millions de dollars EU)
Exportations selon les principaux pays ou zones

Country or area	1998	1999	2000	2001	2002	Pays ou zone
World	42004.1	40194.5	39788.0	43484.7	45109.0	Monde
Africa	305.0	267.4	173.6	99.2	533.6	Afrique
Americas	2498.6	2382.1	1814.8	3265.0	2516.6	Amériques
- Northern America	2204.1	2207.3	1582.6	2451.7	1813.1	- Amérique du Nord
- LAIA	271.5	136.7	174.4	126.4	147.4	- ALAI
- CACM	4.7	5.6	3.2	5.2	4.6	- MCC
- Caribbean	17.1	30.0	44.5	678.8	548.3	- Caraïbes
- Rest of America	1.1	2.5	10.0	2.9	3.2	- Autre d'Amérique
Asia excluding former USSR	22844.8	20943.4	22273.0	21970.0	23465.5	Asie ancienne URSS exclus
- Middle East	204.4	258.5	269.0	500.1	474.2	- Moyen-Orient
Asia former USSR	7.3	9.5	41.5	39.4	44.4	Asie ancienne URSS
Europe excluding former USSR	14497.2	14924.0	13884.8	17193.4	17441.6	Europe ancienne URSS exclus
- European Union	10555.1	10872.5	10674.4	12343.9	12717.3	- Union Européenne
- Eastern Europe	1598.7	1363.5	1339.6	2182.6	2695.8	- Europe de l'Est
- Rest of Europe	2343.4	2688.0	1870.8	2666.9	2028.4	- Autre de l'Europe
Europe former USSR	1241.4	859.6	1103.5	569.5	649.0	Europe ancienne URSS
Oceania	609.8	808.6	496.7	348.3	458.2	Océanie
Japan	10127.6	9945.9	10267.9	8450.6	9214.2	Japon
Korea, Republic of	8014.1	7490.3	8229.4	9699.2	10671.6	République de Corée
Germany	1576.7	2498.3	1555.6	3244.2	3275.3	Allemagne
Italy-San Marino-Holy See	2737.1	2063.4	2234.1	2135.0	2624.0	Italie-Saint-Marin-Saint-Siège
China	1860.6	1618.5	1634.5	1927.7	1924.5	Chine
France-Monaco	1322.4	1038.1	2197.1	2406.2	1866.0	France-Monaco
United States	1773.0	1671.9	1113.6	1899.0	1238.8	Etats-Unis d'Amérique
Norway	1453.2	1857.0	1152.3	1808.9	1333.5	Norvège
Poland	1209.5	1030.8	1031.4	1887.3	2322.3	Pologne
Finland	1045.6	1068.1	1046.8	1623.6	1417.6	Finlande
Spain	1106.6	1430.9	1079.6	692.8	1073.3	Espagne
United Kingdom	846.8	1048.3	904.4	642.9	648.0	Royaume-Uni
Russian Federation	1008.5	724.2	987.2	387.5	442.4	Fédération de Russie
Netherlands	394.7	737.2	723.9	811.0	879.5	Pays-Bas
Croatia	760.6	690.7	617.4	713.7	604.7	Croatie
Singapore	908.2	482.0	716.7	643.2	322.8	Singapour
Canada	420.9	525.2	459.0	535.5	556.6	Canada
Denmark	736.4	653.9	351.1	265.2	485.8	Danemark
Australia	528.7	718.2	379.3	220.6	341.3	Australie
Sweden	352.2	147.9	355.5	332.3	237.4	Suède
Trinidad and Tobago	7.9	19.3	3.1	668.9	e	Trinité-et-Tobago
Romania	163.3	247.6	226.6	224.4	316.9	Roumanie
Turkey	152.4	166.6	118.2	308.6	290.1	Turquie
Malaysia	387.1	173.8	42.9	53.0	e56.1	Malaisie
Indonesia	365.4	98.4	64.7	49.3	74.1	Indonésie
Ukraine	198.9	90.5	41.7	104.1	114.8	Ukraine
Côte d'Ivoire	43.6	93.3	2.4	e2.6	407.6	Côte d'Ivoire
New Zealand	43.0	55.7	84.2	85.0	76.6	Nouvelle-Zélande
India	55.6	79.4	53.1	37.2	112.7	Inde
Portugal	107.6	30.7	61.8	56.4	66.3	Portugal

(Value as percentages of World total) **(Valeur en pourcentage du total mondial)**

Regions of the world	1993	1994	1995	1996	1997	1998	1999	2000	2001	2002	Régions du monde
World	100.0	100.0	100.0	100.0	100.0	100.0	100.0	100.0	100.0	100.0	Monde
Africa	0.5	0.6	1.3	0.4	1.3	0.7	0.7	0.4	0.2	1.2	Afrique
Americas	5.4	6.6	6.1	5.9	6.2	5.9	5.9	4.6	7.5	5.6	Amériques
- Northern America	4.1	4.8	4.8	4.8	5.3	5.2	5.5	4.0	5.6	4.0	- Amérique du Nord
- LAIA	1.2	1.6	1.1	0.9	0.8	0.6	0.3	0.4	0.3	0.3	- ALAI
- CACM	0.0	0.0	0.0	0.0	0.0	0.0	0.0	0.0	0.0	0.0	- MCC
- Caribbean	0.1	0.2	0.2	0.2	0.1	0.0	0.1	0.1	1.6	1.2	- Caraïbes
- Rest of America	0.0	0.0	0.0	0.0	0.0	0.0	0.0	0.0	0.0	0.0	- Autre d'Amérique
Asia excluding former USSR	54.7	57.7	51.3	53.2	54.5	54.4	52.1	56.0	50.5	52.0	Asie ancienne URSS exclus
- Middle East	0.6	0.4	0.5	0.2	0.4	0.5	0.6	0.7	1.2	1.1	- Moyen-Orient
Asia former USSR	0.0	0.0	0.0	0.0	0.0	0.0	0.0	0.1	0.1	0.1	Asie ancienne URSS
Europe excluding former USSR	37.6	31.3	37.3	35.8	35.3	34.5	37.1	34.9	39.5	38.7	Europe ancienne URSS exclus
- European Union	29.1	23.0	28.2	27.7	28.9	25.1	27.0	26.8	28.4	28.2	- Union Européenne
- Eastern Europe	2.6	3.1	3.4	3.8	1.6	3.8	3.4	3.4	5.0	6.0	- Europe de l'Est
- Rest of Europe	5.9	5.1	5.6	4.3	4.8	5.6	6.7	4.7	6.1	4.5	- Autre de l'Europe
Europe former USSR	0.7	3.0	3.0	3.5	0.3	3.0	2.1	2.8	1.3	1.4	Europe ancienne URSS
Oceania	1.2	0.9	1.0	1.3	2.4	1.5	2.0	1.2	0.8	1.0	Océanie

812 Sanitary, plumbing, heating, lighting fixtures and fittings, nes

TRADE BY COMMODITY (Value in million US dollars)
Imports by principal countries or areas

COMMERCE PAR PRODUIT (Valeur en millions de dollars EU)
Importations selon les principaux pays ou zones

Country or area	1998	1999	2000	2001	2002	Pays ou zone
World	17872.6	19588.1	20240.9	19909.8	21540.4	Monde
Africa	281.1	261.7	254.3	279.6	278.1	Afrique
Americas	4655.6	5699.2	6603.6	6279.8	7002.9	Amériques
- Northern America	4097.7	5180.0	6019.1	5688.1	6450.9	- Amérique du Nord
- LAIA	418.4	377.3	427.5	440.6	398.2	- ALAI
- CACM	41.6	45.0	48.4	51.5	57.9	- MCC
- Caribbean	80.0	77.7	90.7	83.1	79.8	- Caraïbes
- Rest of America	17.8	19.2	17.9	16.5	16.1	- Autre d'Amérique
Asia excluding former USSR	2767.3	2927.2	3202.1	2936.8	2998.8	Asie ancienne URSS exclus
- Middle East	708.2	671.8	726.9	668.1	729.8	- Moyen-Orient
Asia former USSR	72.7	49.4	52.7	53.4	54.1	Asie ancienne URSS
Europe excluding former USSR	9551.5	10175.5	9625.7	9801.0	10561.0	Europe ancienne URSS exclus
- European Union	8030.9	8645.9	8179.4	8287.3	8822.7	- Union Européenne
- Eastern Europe	745.4	740.3	715.9	769.4	922.5	- Europe de l'Est
- Rest of Europe	775.2	789.3	730.4	744.3	815.8	- Autre de l'Europe
Europe former USSR	292.2	205.3	213.1	302.9	351.8	Europe ancienne URSS
Oceania	252.2	269.9	289.4	256.4	293.7	Océanie
United States	3420.4	4418.8	5208.8	4914.7	5583.8	Etats-Unis d'Amérique
Germany	2149.6	2127.3	1811.2	1921.0	1766.3	Allemagne
United Kingdom	1037.7	1173.9	1239.1	1352.1	1588.1	Royaume-Uni
China, Hong Kong SAR	1074.2	1167.3	1267.9	1084.4	1034.0	Chine - RAS de Hong-Kong
France-Monaco	1035.0	1133.9	1170.0	1070.5	1170.2	France-Monaco
Canada	669.0	752.5	805.9	768.2	861.0	Canada
Netherlands	611.3	696.7	586.2	599.6	606.7	Pays-Bas
Spain	479.4	580.4	569.5	582.0	712.5	Espagne
Italy-San Marino-Holy See	492.7	550.4	550.6	557.2	602.6	Italie-Saint-Marin-Saint-Siège
Austria	503.6	554.5	492.4	477.8	507.6	Autriche
Belgium	-	639.2	610.1	579.5	e635.5	Belgique
Japan	289.3	337.3	423.4	440.4	437.8	Japon
Switzerland-Liechtenstein	374.5	388.0	369.0	375.4	397.6	Suisse-Liechtenstein
Poland	320.8	329.2	278.2	256.9	280.2	Pologne
Sweden	255.1	275.6	277.8	270.4	299.2	Suède
Denmark	245.4	246.8	238.3	235.3	257.3	Danemark
United Arab Emirates	184.9	193.8	213.1	223.4	e229.2	Emirates arabes unis
Australia	183.7	197.0	220.6	192.2	217.6	Australie
Norway	211.0	200.9	192.3	192.7	200.3	Norvège
Mexico	141.1	149.4	206.9	216.6	222.5	Mexique
Czech Republic	172.6	163.6	159.8	175.4	199.7	République tchèque
Ireland	150.2	176.4	172.9	171.1	170.6	Irlande
Singapore	162.2	181.1	175.4	154.2	151.8	Singapour
Portugal	137.6	166.1	161.3	166.3	178.4	Portugal
Turkey	190.0	179.7	190.2	100.9	123.4	Turquie
Greece	145.4	151.2	130.3	128.3	e141.9	Grèce
Hungary	120.6	130.0	132.2	134.7	168.1	Hongrie
Belgium-Luxembourg	668.4	-	-	-	-	Belgique-Luxembourg
Russian Federation	145.7	85.8	89.3	149.5	169.8	Fédération de Russie
Finland	119.6	120.3	121.5	126.0	132.4	Finlande

(Value as percentages of World total)

(Valeur en pourcentage du total mondial)

Regions of the world	1993	1994	1995	1996	1997	1998	1999	2000	2001	2002	Régions du monde
World	100.0	100.0	100.0	100.0	100.0	100.0	100.0	100.0	100.0	100.0	Monde
Africa	1.6	1.8	1.6	1.4	1.4	1.6	1.3	1.3	1.4	1.3	Afrique
Americas	21.7	22.0	21.0	21.5	24.0	26.0	29.1	32.6	31.5	32.5	Amériques
- Northern America	19.0	19.2	18.4	19.0	20.9	22.9	26.4	29.7	28.6	29.9	- Amérique du Nord
- LAIA	1.8	2.1	1.9	1.9	2.3	2.3	1.9	2.1	2.2	1.8	- ALAI
- CACM	0.2	0.2	0.2	0.2	0.2	0.2	0.2	0.2	0.3	0.3	- MCC
- Caribbean	0.5	0.4	0.5	0.4	0.4	0.4	0.4	0.4	0.4	0.4	- Caraïbes
- Rest of America	0.1	0.1	0.1	0.1	0.1	0.1	0.1	0.1	0.1	0.1	- Autre d'Amérique
Asia excluding former USSR	19.2	18.4	18.9	18.8	18.0	15.5	14.9	15.8	14.8	13.9	Asie ancienne URSS exclus
- Middle East	4.3	3.9	3.7	3.4	3.6	4.0	3.4	3.6	3.4	3.4	- Moyen-Orient
Asia former USSR	0.1	0.2	0.1	0.4	0.3	0.4	0.3	0.3	0.3	0.3	Asie ancienne URSS
Europe excluding former USSR	54.7	54.6	55.1	54.6	52.5	53.4	51.9	47.6	49.2	49.0	Europe ancienne URSS exclus
- European Union	48.2	47.9	47.4	46.5	44.2	44.9	44.1	40.4	41.6	41.0	- Union Européenne
- Eastern Europe	2.4	2.6	3.0	3.6	3.9	4.2	3.8	3.5	3.9	4.3	- Europe de l'Est
- Rest of Europe	4.1	4.2	4.7	4.5	4.4	4.3	4.0	3.6	3.7	3.8	- Autre de l'Europe
Europe former USSR	1.5	1.6	1.8	1.9	2.3	1.6	1.0	1.1	1.5	1.6	Europe ancienne URSS
Oceania	1.4	1.4	1.4	1.4	1.5	1.4	1.4	1.4	1.3	1.4	Océanie

TRADE BY COMMODITY (Value in million US dollars)
Exports by principal countries or areas

COMMERCE PAR PRODUIT (Valeur en millions de dollars EU)
Exportations selon les principaux pays ou zones

Country or area	1998	1999	2000	2001	2002	Pays ou zone
World	17006.2	17786.7	18078.4	18174.1	19609.8	Monde
Africa	84.6	107.1	69.1	89.9	94.9	Afrique
Americas	2203.3	2282.2	2557.4	2697.2	2846.5	Amériques
- Northern America	1347.4	1341.2	1475.3	1451.9	1531.0	- Amérique du Nord
- LAIA	818.5	903.0	1040.2	1203.1	1270.6	- ALAI
- CACM	29.8	32.7	34.3	33.5	39.0	- MCC
- Caribbean	7.6	5.1	7.6	7.4	5.7	- Caraïbes
- Rest of America	0.0	0.2	0.1	1.3	0.3	- Autre d'Amérique
Asia excluding former USSR	3910.7	4526.5	5201.7	5091.4	5758.3	Asie ancienne URSS exclus
- Middle East	208.2	215.5	243.0	281.6	357.5	- Moyen-Orient
Asia former USSR	6.8	1.5	1.9	1.4	1.2	Asie ancienne URSS
Europe excluding former USSR	10660.9	10764.0	10121.3	10142.9	10730.3	Europe ancienne URSS exclus
- European Union	9633.0	9710.3	9039.1	8934.6	9312.7	- Union Européenne
- Eastern Europe	638.2	657.0	704.7	831.4	1029.3	- Europe de l'Est
- Rest of Europe	389.7	396.7	377.5	376.9	388.4	- Autre de l'Europe
Europe former USSR	102.8	64.3	86.1	107.5	129.7	Europe ancienne URSS
Oceania	37.0	41.1	40.8	43.8	48.8	Océanie
Italy-San Marino-Holy See	2372.7	2372.5	2276.7	2194.2	2225.6	Italie-Saint-Marin-Saint-Siège
Germany	2284.4	2294.6	2113.1	2137.2	2319.4	Allemagne
China	1308.1	1655.3	2165.7	2358.9	3020.3	Chine
China, Hong Kong SAR	1364.3	1545.5	1676.3	1469.2	1384.3	Chine - RAS de Hong-Kong
United States	1044.6	1011.6	1103.6	1086.5	1134.8	Etats-Unis d'Amérique
France-Monaco	1144.2	1124.7	1017.4	997.4	973.2	France-Monaco
Mexico	733.6	826.4	950.9	1082.6	1138.0	Mexique
Belgium	-	769.9	715.0	657.4	e737.6	Belgique
Spain	559.1	541.0	509.4	581.2	586.4	Espagne
Netherlands	587.1	632.1	549.6	508.8	452.3	Pays-Bas
United Kingdom	605.5	552.9	464.6	466.6	504.6	Royaume-Uni
Austria	435.3	463.6	469.4	491.7	528.8	Autriche
Canada	302.7	329.5	371.6	365.4	396.2	Canada
Sweden	302.2	294.6	278.3	262.6	297.2	Suède
Denmark	234.3	239.0	250.8	228.4	260.3	Danemark
Czech Republic	217.0	197.3	219.3	264.5	303.4	République tchèque
Switzerland-Liechtenstein	216.5	224.0	209.2	200.8	202.7	Suisse-Liechtenstein
Poland	155.3	167.0	184.6	214.8	293.7	Pologne
Hungary	165.4	175.2	161.9	176.8	204.1	Hongrie
Finland	196.8	173.6	166.6	172.5	161.3	Finlande
Turkey	139.2	143.4	151.1	174.7	249.9	Turquie
Belgium-Luxembourg	690.9	-	-	-	-	Belgique-Luxembourg
Portugal	116.8	146.9	129.0	131.0	151.8	Portugal
Thailand	103.1	131.1	143.8	138.3	e146.0	Thaïlande
Japan	115.0	113.6	103.1	95.7	84.4	Japon
Norway	91.8	96.7	87.6	88.1	87.5	Norvège
Slovakia	59.5	60.8	68.7	95.9	130.7	Slovaquie
Korea, Republic of	79.6	85.8	83.5	73.8	74.3	République de Corée
Singapore	85.8	79.4	75.0	70.5	66.3	Singapour
Malaysia	59.1	67.5	59.4	90.8	e96.3	Malaisie

(Value as percentages of World total) **(Valeur en pourcentage du total mondial)**

Regions of the world	1993	1994	1995	1996	1997	1998	1999	2000	2001	2002	Régions du monde
World	100.0	100.0	100.0	100.0	100.0	100.0	100.0	100.0	100.0	100.0	Monde
Africa	0.4	0.3	0.4	0.4	0.5	0.5	0.6	0.4	0.5	0.5	Afrique
Americas	10.6	10.9	10.2	10.4	12.4	13.0	12.8	14.1	14.8	14.5	Amériques
- Northern America	7.1	7.6	7.3	7.1	8.3	7.9	7.5	8.2	8.0	7.8	- Amérique du Nord
- LAIA	3.4	3.1	2.7	3.1	3.8	4.8	5.1	5.8	6.6	6.5	- ALAI
- CACM	0.1	0.1	0.1	0.2	0.2	0.2	0.2	0.2	0.2	0.2	- MCC
- Caribbean	0.0	0.0	0.0	0.0	0.0	0.0	0.0	0.0	0.0	0.0	- Caraïbes
- Rest of America	0.0	0.0	0.0	0.0	0.0	0.0	0.0	0.0	0.0	0.0	- Autre d'Amérique
Asia excluding former USSR	31.6	25.8	25.3	24.7	24.0	23.0	25.4	28.8	28.0	29.4	Asie ancienne URSS exclus
- Middle East	1.0	1.1	1.1	1.0	1.1	1.2	1.2	1.3	1.5	1.8	- Moyen-Orient
Asia former USSR	0.0	0.0	0.2	0.1	0.1	0.0	0.0	0.0	0.0	0.0	Asie ancienne URSS
Europe excluding former USSR	57.0	62.3	63.3	63.6	62.2	62.7	60.5	56.0	55.8	54.7	Europe ancienne URSS exclus
- European Union	52.4	57.1	58.0	58.3	56.6	56.6	54.6	50.0	49.2	47.5	- Union Européenne
- Eastern Europe	1.9	2.3	2.4	2.7	3.3	3.8	3.7	3.9	4.6	5.2	- Europe de l'Est
- Rest of Europe	2.6	2.9	2.9	2.6	2.3	2.3	2.2	2.1	2.1	2.0	- Autre de l'Europe
Europe former USSR	0.2	0.4	0.4	0.5	0.6	0.6	0.4	0.5	0.6	0.7	Europe ancienne URSS
Oceania	0.2	0.2	0.3	0.3	0.3	0.2	0.2	0.2	0.2	0.2	Océanie

821 Furniture and parts thereof

TRADE BY COMMODITY (Value in million US dollars)
Imports by principal countries or areas

COMMERCE PAR PRODUIT (Valeur en millions de dollars EU)
Importations selon les principaux pays ou zones

Country or area	1998	1999	2000	2001	2002	Pays ou zone
World	54823.4	60923.4	66668.7	67370.5	72261.7	Monde
Africa	446.6	543.9	633.0	662.9	721.6	Afrique
Americas	18910.2	22819.1	27611.0	27495.5	29249.3	Amériques
- Northern America	17006.6	20720.7	24225.7	23704.2	27092.3	- Amérique du Nord
- LAIA	1466.2	1641.4	2877.1	3276.5	1675.3	- ALAI
- CACM	112.0	128.2	136.2	136.8	154.9	- MCC
- Caribbean	276.0	267.4	307.9	328.7	276.8	- Caraïbes
- Rest of America	49.4	61.5	64.1	49.2	50.0	- Autre d'Amérique
Asia excluding former USSR	6493.9	7099.9	8471.9	8339.5	8634.5	Asie ancienne URSS exclus
- Middle East	1138.6	1055.0	1226.1	1213.5	1266.8	- Moyen-Orient
Asia former USSR	161.0	115.1	113.1	119.4	123.0	Asie ancienne URSS
Europe excluding former USSR	27607.6	29248.4	28541.0	29472.5	31927.2	Europe ancienne URSS exclus
- European Union	23503.0	25055.1	24399.1	25259.7	27197.3	- Union Européenne
- Eastern Europe	1163.3	1200.2	1282.4	1370.0	1585.4	- Europe de l'Est
- Rest of Europe	2941.3	2993.0	2859.5	2842.8	3144.5	- Autre de l'Europe
Europe former USSR	542.4	313.2	372.9	497.4	610.8	Europe ancienne URSS
Oceania	661.7	783.8	925.8	783.4	995.3	Océanie
United States	14406.0	17750.4	20952.4	20613.7	23887.8	Etats-Unis d'Amérique
Germany	7318.3	7192.2	6408.3	6788.9	6782.9	Allemagne
France-Monaco	3492.3	3732.3	3841.9	3843.9	4164.2	France-Monaco
United Kingdom	2858.1	3221.8	3560.3	3832.1	4741.8	Royaume-Uni
Japan	2749.6	3108.9	3858.1	3929.6	3918.2	Japon
Canada	2564.3	2930.3	3257.0	3065.7	3174.5	Canada
Netherlands	1750.9	2049.0	1937.7	1919.7	1960.6	Pays-Bas
Switzerland-Liechtenstein	1713.3	1769.2	1666.0	1614.7	1709.6	Suisse-Liechtenstein
Belgium	-	2113.9	1966.5	1994.1	e2186.9	Belgique
Mexico	678.8	895.7	2184.2	2620.1	1167.8	Mexique
Austria	1434.8	1495.8	1496.4	1537.3	1466.0	Autriche
China, Hong Kong SAR	1096.6	1242.7	1377.7	1285.0	1315.5	Chine - RAS de Hong-Kong
Italy-San Marino-Holy See	899.2	1054.4	1087.0	1094.1	1162.7	Italie-Saint-Marin-Saint-Siège
Spain	812.0	984.3	998.4	1119.2	1275.2	Espagne
Sweden	910.1	1005.7	1001.4	972.7	1142.2	Suède
Norway	794.6	769.3	752.8	744.5	862.0	Norvège
Denmark	740.9	775.7	722.1	738.7	762.5	Danemark
Australia	512.0	613.5	757.0	625.8	805.8	Australie
Belgium-Luxembourg	2174.4	-	-	-	-	Belgique-Luxembourg
Singapore	389.3	474.0	475.2	390.8	363.3	Singapour
Poland	366.4	392.4	395.7	423.4	452.1	Pologne
Czech Republic	365.2	346.1	343.6	360.8	418.0	République tchèque
Portugal	315.7	374.2	345.3	355.8	397.9	Portugal
Finland	293.6	323.7	322.5	334.3	343.5	Finlande
Saudi Arabia	285.9	267.8	337.0	323.3	e334.5	Arabie saoudite
Israel	298.9	285.6	319.8	327.5	299.2	Israël
Ireland	265.9	295.1	307.2	307.8	352.6	Irlande
Hungary	208.7	250.0	272.8	270.0	354.1	Hongrie
Korea, Republic of	127.7	186.4	269.9	293.5	466.7	République de Corée
Russian Federation	320.3	140.2	193.6	291.7	371.7	Fédération de Russie

(Value as percentages of World total)

(Valeur en pourcentage du total mondial)

Regions of the world	1993	1994	1995	1996	1997	1998	1999	2000	2001	2002	Régions du monde
World	100.0	100.0	100.0	100.0	100.0	100.0	100.0	100.0	100.0	100.0	Monde
Africa	0.9	1.0	1.0	0.9	0.9	0.8	0.9	0.9	1.0	1.0	Afrique
Americas	28.2	29.2	27.5	27.9	31.6	34.5	37.5	41.4	40.8	40.5	Amériques
- Northern America	25.4	26.1	24.8	25.3	28.3	31.0	34.0	36.3	35.2	37.5	- Amérique du Nord
- LAIA	2.0	2.4	1.9	2.0	2.5	2.7	2.7	4.3	4.9	2.3	- ALAI
- CACM	0.1	0.1	0.1	0.1	0.2	0.2	0.2	0.2	0.2	0.2	- MCC
- Caribbean	0.6	0.5	0.5	0.4	0.4	0.5	0.4	0.5	0.5	0.4	- Caraïbes
- Rest of America	0.1	0.1	0.1	0.1	0.1	0.1	0.1	0.1	0.1	0.1	- Autre d'Amérique
Asia excluding former USSR	14.7	15.1	15.1	15.5	15.3	11.8	11.7	12.7	12.4	11.9	Asie ancienne URSS exclus
- Middle East	2.8	2.1	1.9	2.0	2.3	2.1	1.7	1.8	1.8	1.8	- Moyen-Orient
Asia former USSR	0.1	0.2	0.3	0.3	0.2	0.3	0.2	0.2	0.2	0.2	Asie ancienne URSS
Europe excluding former USSR	52.5	51.8	53.2	52.7	49.1	50.4	48.0	42.8	43.7	44.2	Europe ancienne URSS exclus
- European Union	45.2	44.5	45.3	45.2	42.0	42.9	41.1	36.6	37.5	37.6	- Union Européenne
- Eastern Europe	1.4	1.4	1.6	1.7	1.9	2.1	2.0	1.9	2.0	2.2	- Europe de l'Est
- Rest of Europe	5.9	5.9	6.3	5.8	5.2	5.4	4.9	4.3	4.2	4.4	- Autre de l'Europe
Europe former USSR	2.6	1.6	1.8	1.5	1.7	1.0	0.5	0.6	0.7	0.8	Europe ancienne URSS
Oceania	1.1	1.1	1.1	1.2	1.3	1.2	1.3	1.4	1.2	1.4	Océanie

TRADE BY COMMODITY (Value in million US dollars)
Exports by principal countries or areas

COMMERCE PAR PRODUIT (Valeur en millions de dollars EU)
Exportations selon les principaux pays ou zones

Country or area	1998	1999	2000	2001	2002	Pays ou zone
World	55444.6	59414.5	63838.2	63451.4	67606.0	Monde
Africa	540.9	550.9	527.0	496.8	609.6	Afrique
Americas	12105.1	12975.1	15284.2	14463.8	14249.8	Amériques
- Northern America	9536.8	9896.4	10992.1	10162.1	9844.3	- Amérique du Nord
- LAIA	2433.1	2970.3	4200.1	4213.1	4333.8	- ALAI
- CACM	107.0	81.2	59.4	57.9	44.6	- MCC
- Caribbean	26.5	25.8	29.6	25.6	24.3	- Caraïbes
- Rest of America	1.7	1.5	3.0	5.2	2.9	- Autre d'Amérique
Asia excluding former USSR	8879.9	11251.1	13694.0	13133.2	15387.8	Asie ancienne URSS exclus
- Middle East	285.4	320.5	398.9	438.8	512.5	- Moyen-Orient
Asia former USSR	5.6	3.6	3.2	1.7	1.6	Asie ancienne URSS
Europe excluding former USSR	33253.0	33939.7	33565.2	34470.7	36327.5	Europe ancienne URSS exclus
- European Union	27494.9	28039.4	27291.8	27582.8	28426.2	- Union Européenne
- Eastern Europe	3903.9	3959.4	4362.6	4959.6	5851.2	- Europe de l'Est
- Rest of Europe	1854.3	1940.8	1910.8	1928.3	2050.0	- Autre de l'Europe
Europe former USSR	531.0	527.5	629.7	743.0	866.4	Europe ancienne URSS
Oceania	129.0	166.7	134.8	142.2	163.3	Océanie
Italy-San Marino-Holy See	8791.0	8586.8	8631.2	8673.9	8845.6	Italie-Saint-Marin-Saint-Siège
Germany	5198.2	5569.5	5230.0	5669.8	5762.6	Allemagne
United States	5238.2	5250.1	5765.4	5398.1	5018.7	Etats-Unis d'Amérique
Canada	4298.5	4646.2	5226.6	4763.8	4825.5	Canada
China	2837.8	3466.2	4593.5	5074.2	6700.5	Chine
Mexico	1851.2	2302.1	3331.6	3308.8	3429.3	Mexique
France-Monaco	2494.4	2582.0	2542.1	2357.5	2419.8	France-Monaco
Poland	1917.9	1964.3	2203.7	2505.5	2895.1	Pologne
Denmark	2079.4	1992.8	1951.8	1947.5	2082.9	Danemark
United Kingdom	1676.7	1654.0	1558.7	1494.7	1377.1	Royaume-Uni
Spain	1495.2	1509.8	1519.8	1522.3	1519.1	Espagne
Belgium	–	1866.0	1725.9	1763.5	e1978.6	Belgique
Malaysia	1115.2	1401.6	1598.1	1388.2	e1471.1	Malaisie
Sweden	1404.1	1371.5	1355.0	1219.5	1279.6	Suède
Indonesia	355.3	1241.5	1528.2	1433.5	1519.6	Indonésie
Austria	1092.5	1153.1	1121.5	1271.9	1349.7	Autriche
China, Hong Kong SAR	852.7	995.8	1124.2	1036.8	1144.9	Chine - RAS de Hong-Kong
Czech Republic	872.3	771.1	797.9	930.8	1095.1	République tchèque
Netherlands	780.3	965.8	899.1	839.1	877.1	Pays-Bas
Thailand	630.9	795.7	949.6	865.7	e914.3	Thaïlande
Switzerland-Liechtenstein	777.6	800.3	774.2	722.1	723.8	Suisse-Liechtenstein
Slovenia	568.9	617.1	589.9	642.2	726.8	Slovénie
Hungary	433.0	558.1	568.6	620.8	682.0	Hongrie
Japan	435.4	466.8	615.7	560.3	621.7	Japon
Romania	435.8	427.9	444.7	500.6	615.0	Roumanie
Brazil	361.1	404.1	515.0	504.9	e523.4	Brésil
Portugal	345.2	346.9	347.9	413.4	493.0	Portugal
Norway	341.9	349.3	347.2	329.6	337.7	Norvège
Philippines	324.7	355.4	382.5	298.5	316.3	Philippines
Belgium-Luxembourg	1629.7	–	–	–	–	Belgique-Luxembourg

(Value as percentages of World total) **(Valeur en pourcentage du total mondial)**

Regions of the world	1993	1994	1995	1996	1997	1998	1999	2000	2001	2002	Régions du monde
World	100.0	100.0	100.0	100.0	100.0	100.0	100.0	100.0	100.0	100.0	Monde
Africa	0.4	0.7	1.0	1.0	1.0	1.0	0.9	0.8	0.8	0.9	Afrique
Americas	16.4	17.8	16.6	17.9	20.6	21.8	21.8	23.9	22.8	21.1	Amériques
- Northern America	13.6	14.6	13.6	14.1	16.0	17.2	16.7	17.2	16.0	14.6	- Amérique du Nord
- LAIA	2.7	3.0	2.9	3.7	4.5	4.4	5.0	6.6	6.6	6.4	- ALAI
- CACM	0.1	0.1	0.1	0.1	0.1	0.2	0.1	0.1	0.1	0.1	- MCC
- Caribbean	0.0	0.0	0.0	0.0	0.0	0.0	0.0	0.0	0.0	0.0	- Caraïbes
- Rest of America	0.0	0.0	0.0	0.0	0.0	0.0	0.0	0.0	0.0	0.0	- Autre d'Amérique
Asia excluding former USSR	23.3	19.4	17.9	17.4	18.0	16.0	18.9	21.5	20.7	22.8	Asie ancienne URSS exclus
- Middle East	0.4	0.4	0.4	0.5	0.5	0.5	0.5	0.6	0.7	0.8	- Moyen-Orient
Asia former USSR	0.0	0.0	0.0	0.0	0.0	0.0	0.0	0.0	0.0	0.0	Asie ancienne URSS
Europe excluding former USSR	58.9	61.2	63.7	62.5	59.1	60.0	57.1	52.6	54.3	53.7	Europe ancienne URSS exclus
- European Union	51.4	52.8	54.2	53.0	49.7	49.6	47.2	42.8	43.5	42.0	- Union Européenne
- Eastern Europe	4.0	4.8	5.8	6.1	6.3	7.0	6.7	6.8	7.8	8.7	- Europe de l'Est
- Rest of Europe	3.6	3.7	3.7	3.3	3.1	3.3	3.3	3.0	3.0	3.0	- Autre de l'Europe
Europe former USSR	0.6	0.5	0.6	0.9	1.0	1.0	0.9	1.0	1.2	1.3	Europe ancienne URSS
Oceania	0.3	0.3	0.3	0.3	0.3	0.2	0.3	0.2	0.2	0.2	Océanie

831 Travel goods, handbags etc, of leather, plastics, textile, others

TRADE BY COMMODITY (Value in million US dollars)
Imports by principal countries or areas

COMMERCE PAR PRODUIT (Valeur en millions de dollars EU)
Importations selon les principaux pays ou zones

Country or area	1998	1999	2000	2001	2002	Pays ou zone
World	17253.1	18506.5	19696.5	19646.2	19716.4	Monde
Africa	118.1	134.7	133.5	131.0	138.5	Afrique
Americas	4919.3	5201.1	5587.7	5509.5	5648.8	Amériques
- Northern America	4509.9	4787.1	5135.7	4984.7	5186.8	- Amérique du Nord
- LAIA	328.0	350.8	388.6	446.1	380.2	- ALAI
- CACM	34.3	20.3	22.4	29.4	38.5	- MCC
- Caribbean	36.7	33.0	30.8	39.0	32.0	- Caraïbes
- Rest of America	10.3	10.1	10.2	10.2	11.3	- Autre d'Amérique
Asia excluding former USSR	6422.9	7077.2	7681.6	7512.7	7208.3	Asie ancienne URSS exclus
- Middle East	302.1	303.6	313.3	306.9	322.2	- Moyen-Orient
Asia former USSR	3.7	4.1	3.9	3.6	4.2	Asie ancienne URSS
Europe excluding former USSR	5505.9	5766.3	5916.8	6071.5	6288.4	Europe ancienne URSS exclus
- European Union	4936.5	5221.6	5330.5	5457.2	5658.1	- Union Européenne
- Eastern Europe	140.0	133.5	145.8	156.4	180.9	- Europe de l'Est
- Rest of Europe	429.4	411.3	440.5	457.8	449.3	- Autre de l'Europe
Europe former USSR	38.1	29.5	43.2	124.1	119.2	Europe ancienne URSS
Oceania	245.2	293.5	329.7	293.9	309.1	Océanie
United States	4171.4	4449.0	4777.8	4623.7	4818.8	Etats-Unis d'Amérique
China, Hong Kong SAR	3349.1	3542.0	3694.3	3437.2	3249.4	Chine - RAS de Hong-Kong
Japan	2315.9	2665.4	2996.1	3044.8	2836.2	Japon
Germany	1076.9	1119.4	1073.0	1072.7	967.1	Allemagne
United Kingdom	903.1	934.6	1015.6	1010.2	1020.3	Royaume-Uni
France-Monaco	886.0	893.3	943.0	971.9	1060.7	France-Monaco
Italy-San Marino-Holy See	556.0	587.9	637.2	675.9	751.6	Italie-Saint-Marin-Saint-Siège
Spain	283.1	330.2	348.9	371.4	435.0	Espagne
Canada	338.2	337.7	357.0	359.6	366.5	Canada
Belgium	-	379.0	360.6	424.0	e465.0	Belgique
Netherlands	327.3	346.0	306.6	286.7	286.0	Pays-Bas
Switzerland-Liechtenstein	286.6	279.8	309.7	335.0	315.6	Suisse-Liechtenstein
Australia	226.9	246.4	279.4	246.0	254.2	Australie
Singapore	150.4	183.7	208.2	190.9	179.6	Singapour
Mexico	114.8	158.2	179.3	214.4	187.1	Mexique
Korea, Republic of	58.6	96.0	146.7	182.9	249.0	République de Corée
Austria	142.6	146.4	135.2	140.2	143.2	Autriche
Sweden	108.0	118.4	126.4	105.9	109.6	Suède
United Arab Emirates	95.2	99.7	99.8	108.4	e111.2	Emirates arabes unis
Denmark	105.3	105.6	95.6	94.1	101.2	Danemark
Saudi Arabia	88.4	90.8	92.7	77.2	e79.9	Arabie saoudite
Norway	82.4	81.1	77.8	67.8	72.3	Norvège
Greece	67.4	74.3	74.7	74.8	e82.7	Grèce
Ireland	52.1	55.2	81.9	94.2	90.5	Irlande
Portugal	62.1	70.4	68.8	73.8	79.1	Portugal
Belgium-Luxembourg	323.4	-	-	-	-	Belgique-Luxembourg
Poland	47.0	45.0	53.1	54.1	63.5	Pologne
Brazil	63.3	40.4	47.5	49.2	48.3	Brésil
Russian Federation	19.3	12.5	23.9	99.0	89.1	Fédération de Russie
Finland	43.2	47.6	48.1	47.4	51.1	Finlande

(Value as percentages of World total) **(Valeur en pourcentage du total mondial)**

Regions of the world	1993	1994	1995	1996	1997	1998	1999	2000	2001	2002	Régions du monde
World	100.0	100.0	100.0	100.0	100.0	100.0	100.0	100.0	100.0	100.0	Monde
Africa	0.7	0.8	0.7	0.6	0.6	0.7	0.7	0.7	0.7	0.7	Afrique
Americas	25.2	25.4	24.4	23.9	26.4	28.5	28.1	28.4	28.0	28.7	Amériques
- Northern America	23.8	24.1	22.9	22.5	24.5	26.1	25.9	26.1	25.4	26.3	- Amérique du Nord
- LAIA	1.1	1.1	1.2	1.1	1.5	1.9	1.9	2.0	2.3	1.9	- ALAI
- CACM	0.1	0.1	0.1	0.1	0.1	0.2	0.1	0.1	0.1	0.2	- MCC
- Caribbean	0.2	0.2	0.2	0.1	0.2	0.2	0.2	0.2	0.2	0.2	- Caraïbes
- Rest of America	0.1	0.1	0.1	0.0	0.0	0.1	0.1	0.1	0.1	0.1	- Autre d'Amérique
Asia excluding former USSR	41.7	43.4	43.7	43.4	41.7	37.2	38.2	39.0	38.2	36.6	Asie ancienne URSS exclus
- Middle East	1.8	1.5	1.4	1.3	1.5	1.8	1.6	1.6	1.6	1.6	- Moyen-Orient
Asia former USSR	0.0	0.0	0.0	0.0	0.0	0.0	0.0	0.0	0.0	0.0	Asie ancienne URSS
Europe excluding former USSR	30.1	28.2	29.0	29.2	29.1	31.9	31.2	30.0	30.9	31.9	Europe ancienne URSS exclus
- European Union	26.9	25.1	25.7	26.2	26.2	28.6	28.2	27.1	27.8	28.7	- Union Européenne
- Eastern Europe	0.5	0.5	0.6	0.6	0.7	0.8	0.7	0.7	0.8	0.9	- Europe de l'Est
- Rest of Europe	2.6	2.7	2.7	2.4	2.3	2.5	2.2	2.2	2.3	2.3	- Autre de l'Europe
Europe former USSR	0.6	0.3	0.4	0.4	0.4	0.2	0.2	0.2	0.6	0.6	Europe ancienne URSS
Oceania	1.7	1.8	1.8	2.5	1.7	1.4	1.6	1.7	1.5	1.6	Océanie

TRADE BY COMMODITY (Value in million US dollars)
Exports by principal countries or areas

COMMERCE PAR PRODUIT (Valeur en millions de dollars EU)
Exportations selon les principaux pays ou zones

Country or area	1998	1999	2000	2001	2002	Pays ou zone
World	14724.2	15281.8	16509.6	16299.4	16182.4	Monde
Africa	54.5	51.4	49.4	57.7	63.4	Afrique
Americas	738.9	760.6	813.6	704.2	627.9	Amériques
- Northern America	390.0	439.6	483.7	473.0	445.4	- Amérique du Nord
- LAIA	279.2	270.5	293.5	198.6	151.2	- ALAI
- CACM	38.9	40.0	29.4	27.6	27.3	- MCC
- Caribbean	30.6	10.2	6.9	4.8	3.9	- Caraïbes
- Rest of America	0.2	0.3	0.1	0.2	0.2	- Autre d'Amérique
Asia excluding former USSR	9790.1	10111.3	10973.4	10417.0	10260.9	Asie ancienne URSS exclus
- Middle East	67.1	64.2	86.7	111.9	95.1	- Moyen-Orient
Asia former USSR	0.1	0.1	0.2	0.3	0.3	Asie ancienne URSS
Europe excluding former USSR	4105.1	4326.7	4641.5	5085.3	5195.3	Europe ancienne URSS exclus
- European Union	3811.2	4041.3	4329.0	4724.0	4824.0	- Union Européenne
- Eastern Europe	153.8	149.3	157.0	174.4	206.7	- Europe de l'Est
- Rest of Europe	140.2	136.2	155.5	186.9	164.6	- Autre de l'Europe
Europe former USSR	22.5	17.5	17.0	19.3	20.2	Europe ancienne URSS
Oceania	13.1	14.2	14.5	15.7	14.5	Océanie
China, Hong Kong SAR	4369.8	4542.3	4731.9	4377.7	4092.4	Chine - RAS de Hong-Kong
China	3262.2	3416.7	3881.7	3919.9	4410.7	Chine
Italy-San Marino-Holy See	1306.7	1282.9	1504.9	1598.0	1486.2	Italie-Saint-Marin-Saint-Siège
France-Monaco	1096.2	1252.9	1363.1	1557.9	1661.4	France-Monaco
Thailand	415.8	448.7	477.2	440.6	e465.3	Thaïlande
Belgium	–	474.1	438.0	500.2	e561.2	Belgique
United States	343.4	383.9	421.6	413.6	383.4	Etats-Unis d'Amérique
Germany	337.0	316.0	329.0	362.2	364.8	Allemagne
India	331.2	306.0	349.5	322.3	337.2	Inde
Korea, Republic of	354.6	388.4	332.9	233.1	135.2	République de Corée
United Kingdom	234.3	236.6	229.1	227.9	233.5	Royaume-Uni
Philippines	236.3	232.0	276.4	270.0	83.3	Philippines
Spain	142.5	165.8	171.7	207.3	237.5	Espagne
Mexico	209.2	217.7	228.5	140.6	106.2	Mexique
Netherlands	165.6	201.6	171.5	156.3	158.3	Pays-Bas
Viet Nam	131.3	102.7	176.3	183.3	203.7	Viet Nam
Indonesia	94.8	139.5	163.9	187.1	116.6	Indonésie
Switzerland-Liechtenstein	104.8	112.0	133.0	158.9	135.4	Suisse-Liechtenstein
Sri Lanka	e130.5	123.1	e149.7	108.0	55.4	Sri Lanka
Belgium-Luxembourg	420.7	–	–	–	–	Belgique-Luxembourg
Canada	46.6	55.7	62.1	59.3	62.0	Canada
Colombia	52.3	39.0	49.6	43.5	30.0	Colombie
Czech Republic	47.1	39.9	37.4	40.2	47.4	République tchèque
Hungary	44.4	40.1	39.3	36.8	41.3	Hongrie
Singapore	42.2	38.6	41.7	38.2	32.6	Singapour
Turkey	36.2	30.6	33.7	39.5	42.6	Turquie
Romania	20.0	23.6	28.2	44.8	60.0	Roumanie
Japan	26.9	34.5	39.2	34.2	34.7	Japon
Denmark	29.3	27.5	32.3	27.2	26.6	Danemark
Costa Rica	32.7	34.9	25.6	23.8	22.2	Costa Rica

(Value as percentages of World total) **(Valeur en pourcentage du total mondial)**

Regions of the world	1993	1994	1995	1996	1997	1998	1999	2000	2001	2002	Régions du monde
World	100.0	100.0	100.0	100.0	100.0	100.0	100.0	100.0	100.0	100.0	Monde
Africa	0.4	0.4	0.5	0.4	0.3	0.4	0.3	0.3	0.4	0.4	Afrique
Americas	4.4	4.0	3.6	3.9	4.6	5.0	5.0	4.9	4.3	3.9	Amériques
- Northern America	2.2	2.3	2.1	2.5	2.7	2.6	2.9	2.9	2.9	2.8	- Amérique du Nord
- LAIA	1.9	1.5	1.2	1.4	1.7	1.9	1.8	1.8	1.2	0.9	- ALAI
- CACM	0.1	0.1	0.0	0.0	0.2	0.3	0.3	0.2	0.2	0.2	- MCC
- Caribbean	0.3	0.2	0.2	0.0	0.0	0.2	0.1	0.0	0.0	0.0	- Caraïbes
- Rest of America	0.0	0.0	0.0	0.0	0.0	0.0	0.0	0.0	0.0	0.0	- Autre d'Amérique
Asia excluding former USSR	70.0	67.6	66.4	64.4	67.1	66.5	66.2	66.5	63.9	63.4	Asie ancienne URSS exclus
- Middle East	0.4	0.4	0.4	0.4	0.4	0.5	0.4	0.5	0.7	0.6	- Moyen-Orient
Asia former USSR	0.0	0.0	0.0	0.0	0.0	0.0	0.0	0.0	0.0	0.0	Asie ancienne URSS
Europe excluding former USSR	25.1	27.8	29.4	31.1	27.8	27.9	28.3	28.1	31.2	32.1	Europe ancienne URSS exclus
- European Union	23.2	25.7	27.5	29.2	26.2	25.9	26.4	26.2	29.0	29.8	- Union Européenne
- Eastern Europe	0.9	0.8	0.8	1.0	0.9	1.0	1.0	1.0	1.1	1.3	- Europe de l'Est
- Rest of Europe	1.0	1.2	1.1	0.9	0.8	1.0	0.9	0.9	1.1	1.0	- Autre de l'Europe
Europe former USSR	0.0	0.1	0.1	0.1	0.1	0.2	0.1	0.1	0.1	0.1	Europe ancienne URSS
Oceania	0.1	0.1	0.1	0.1	0.1	0.1	0.1	0.1	0.1	0.1	Océanie

842 Men's and boys' outerwear, textile fabrics not knitted or crocheted

TRADE BY COMMODITY (Value in million US dollars)
Imports by principal countries or areas

COMMERCE PAR PRODUIT (Valeur en millions de dollars EU)
Importations selon les principaux pays ou zones

Country or area	1998	1999	2000	2001	2002	Pays ou zone
World	32894.9	32716.4	34287.5	33599.2	32750.5	Monde
Africa	272.8	257.0	257.5	254.5	282.9	Afrique
Americas	11200.9	10942.0	12444.5	11582.9	10930.5	Amériques
- Northern America	9644.1	9806.0	11224.6	10466.2	10012.9	- Amérique du Nord
- LAIA	930.3	746.4	767.8	763.8	653.3	- ALAI
- CACM	126.7	55.8	92.7	92.2	71.3	- MCC
- Caribbean	461.7	295.7	327.4	240.7	172.4	- Caraïbes
- Rest of America	38.2	38.1	32.1	20.0	20.6	- Autre d'Amérique
Asia excluding former USSR	5494.2	5785.8	6679.0	6391.6	5812.0	Asie ancienne URSS exclus
- Middle East	641.0	583.4	579.7	578.7	580.2	- Moyen-Orient
Asia former USSR	29.1	20.4	20.0	23.3	23.7	Asie ancienne URSS
Europe excluding former USSR	15468.1	15285.2	14436.6	14907.6	15183.4	Europe ancienne URSS exclus
- European Union	14031.4	13908.6	13163.1	13642.9	13751.3	- Union Européenne
- Eastern Europe	327.1	306.8	270.7	285.2	370.8	- Europe de l'Est
- Rest of Europe	1109.5	1069.7	1002.8	979.5	1061.3	- Autre de l'Europe
Europe former USSR	125.7	90.1	97.3	129.1	190.5	Europe ancienne URSS
Oceania	304.1	335.9	352.6	310.2	327.5	Océanie
United States	9078.4	9273.7	10628.9	9870.5	9457.3	Etats-Unis d'Amérique
Germany	3958.9	3707.6	3240.3	3422.0	3145.8	Allemagne
Japan	2509.9	2833.5	3336.8	3250.9	2873.3	Japon
France-Monaco	2111.1	1985.8	1946.5	2006.5	1974.1	France-Monaco
United Kingdom	1818.7	1921.7	1997.3	1964.7	2018.9	Royaume-Uni
China, Hong Kong SAR	1766.6	1695.3	1803.0	1595.3	1335.6	Chine - RAS de Hong-Kong
Italy-San Marino-Holy See	1559.4	1494.6	1488.8	1631.6	1708.5	Italie-Saint-Marin-Saint-Siège
Netherlands	1079.7	1115.7	1001.1	976.9	913.6	Pays-Bas
Belgium	–	1036.8	998.9	1081.4	e1186.0	Belgique
Spain	592.0	699.9	704.1	773.4	933.0	Espagne
Switzerland-Liechtenstein	635.3	603.3	563.4	594.7	656.0	Suisse-Liechtenstein
Canada	563.1	529.7	592.7	592.2	550.9	Canada
Mexico	645.7	513.9	487.7	471.3	423.8	Mexique
Sweden	450.7	456.2	427.0	400.4	385.8	Suède
Austria	457.0	419.2	371.2	374.6	391.6	Autriche
Denmark	342.2	379.3	328.6	343.8	370.2	Danemark
Korea, Republic of	133.7	202.4	389.6	445.0	489.1	République de Corée
Australia	238.2	266.3	283.6	243.3	259.5	Australie
Norway	255.2	256.6	231.0	216.4	225.2	Norvège
Dominican Republic	e364.0	e204.1	e265.6	e153.5	e124.7	République dominicaine
Saudi Arabia	244.6	206.8	205.4	208.2	e215.4	Arabie saoudite
Belgium-Luxembourg	986.6	–	–	–	–	Belgique-Luxembourg
Ireland	174.8	174.7	185.4	184.6	187.3	Irlande
Greece	189.2	179.8	164.8	158.0	e174.7	Grèce
United Arab Emirates	163.1	170.9	169.4	171.3	e175.8	Emirates arabes unis
Singapore	159.4	185.5	184.3	144.3	133.1	Singapour
Finland	163.3	163.0	145.5	155.5	164.7	Finlande
Portugal	147.7	142.2	132.6	138.7	164.5	Portugal
Poland	130.7	111.2	81.2	68.1	111.7	Pologne
Slovenia	106.3	97.8	87.0	81.6	81.5	Slovénie

(Value as percentages of World total) **(Valeur en pourcentage du total mondial)**

Regions of the world	1993	1994	1995	1996	1997	1998	1999	2000	2001	2002	Régions du monde
World	100.0	100.0	100.0	100.0	100.0	100.0	100.0	100.0	100.0	100.0	Monde
Africa	1.2	0.9	1.0	0.9	0.9	0.8	0.8	0.8	0.8	0.9	Afrique
Americas	25.8	27.5	27.4	27.1	31.2	34.1	33.4	36.3	34.5	33.4	Amériques
- Northern America	23.0	24.3	23.9	23.5	26.9	29.3	30.0	32.7	31.2	30.6	- Amérique du Nord
- LAIA	1.9	2.3	2.4	2.3	2.6	2.8	2.3	2.2	2.3	2.0	- ALAI
- CACM	0.1	0.1	0.1	0.1	0.2	0.4	0.2	0.3	0.3	0.2	- MCC
- Caribbean	0.8	0.8	0.9	1.2	1.4	1.4	0.9	1.0	0.7	0.5	- Caraïbes
- Rest of America	0.1	0.1	0.1	0.1	0.1	0.1	0.1	0.1	0.1	0.1	- Autre d'Amérique
Asia excluding former USSR	20.8	21.0	21.9	22.8	20.7	16.7	17.7	19.5	19.0	17.7	Asie ancienne URSS exclus
- Middle East	2.3	2.0	2.2	1.8	1.9	1.9	1.8	1.7	1.7	1.8	- Moyen-Orient
Asia former USSR	0.1	0.1	0.1	0.1	0.1	0.1	0.1	0.1	0.1	0.1	Asie ancienne URSS
Europe excluding former USSR	49.2	49.2	48.3	47.8	45.8	47.0	46.7	42.1	44.4	46.4	Europe ancienne URSS exclus
- European Union	45.0	44.8	43.9	43.3	41.7	42.7	42.5	38.4	40.6	42.0	- Union Européenne
- Eastern Europe	0.5	0.5	0.6	0.8	0.9	1.0	0.9	0.8	0.8	1.1	- Europe de l'Est
- Rest of Europe	3.6	3.9	3.8	3.7	3.3	3.4	3.3	2.9	2.9	3.2	- Autre de l'Europe
Europe former USSR	2.3	0.4	0.5	0.4	0.4	0.4	0.3	0.3	0.4	0.6	Europe ancienne URSS
Oceania	0.7	0.8	0.8	0.9	0.9	0.9	1.0	1.0	0.9	1.0	Océanie

Vêtements de dessus pour hommes et garçonnets, en matières textiles, n.d.a. 842

TRADE BY COMMODITY (Value in million US dollars)
Exports by principal countries or areas

COMMERCE PAR PRODUIT (Valeur en millions de dollars EU)
Exportations selon les principaux pays ou zones

Country or area	1998	1999	2000	2001	2002	Pays ou zone
World	34614.4	33554.7	34862.0	34112.8	33698.9	Monde
Africa	2156.6	1987.8	1836.0	2082.8	2265.2	Afrique
Americas	4391.4	3860.8	4258.6	3615.9	3503.2	Amériques
- Northern America	1785.3	1566.4	1561.5	1199.9	1111.8	- Amérique du Nord
- LAIA	1798.9	2029.2	2403.5	2173.8	2187.3	- ALAI
- CACM	101.6	82.9	83.1	71.1	32.6	- MCC
- Caribbean	683.6	161.4	189.4	168.0	168.8	- Caraïbes
- Rest of America	22.0	20.9	21.1	3.1	2.8	- Autre d'Amérique
Asia excluding former USSR	15709.0	15594.9	17740.8	16902.4	15950.4	Asie ancienne URSS exclus
- Middle East	901.9	949.4	1005.4	1126.2	1311.7	- Moyen-Orient
Asia former USSR	25.2	20.3	26.0	30.1	27.7	Asie ancienne URSS
Europe excluding former USSR	11536.9	11281.2	10217.1	10671.4	11114.7	Europe ancienne URSS exclus
- European Union	8652.1	8383.8	7476.8	7842.5	8127.2	- Union Européenne
- Eastern Europe	2025.0	2072.1	1984.6	2046.7	2151.6	- Europe de l'Est
- Rest of Europe	859.7	825.3	755.7	782.2	835.8	- Autre de l'Europe
Europe former USSR	436.8	436.0	422.5	458.9	496.6	Europe ancienne URSS
Oceania	358.4	373.7	361.1	351.3	341.0	Océanie
China	5639.0	5669.2	6797.1	6735.4	6727.7	Chine
China, Hong Kong SAR	2920.2	2760.8	2986.9	2506.9	2002.3	Chine - RAS de Hong-Kong
Italy-San Marino-Holy See	2538.1	2344.2	2281.7	2421.3	2445.0	Italie-Saint-Marin-Saint-Siège
Mexico	1563.2	1806.1	2149.2	1928.4	1973.2	Mexique
Germany	1504.1	1492.6	1262.3	1387.9	1483.1	Allemagne
Tunisia	1123.7	1021.9	945.6	1142.8	e1188.6	Tunisie
Bangladesh	1193.8	e925.1	e1044.1	1239.3	e995.8	Bangladesh
United States	1403.2	1163.9	1163.3	846.9	738.4	Etats-Unis d'Amérique
Belgium	–	1110.1	950.5	1037.3	e1163.8	Belgique
Indonesia	647.3	761.6	1003.0	917.5	716.8	Indonésie
Viet Nam	537.1	821.4	720.9	749.6	833.2	Viet Nam
Romania	604.5	635.4	660.3	722.3	805.6	Roumanie
Turkey	637.1	643.0	665.3	671.8	789.9	Turquie
Morocco	720.1	673.0	588.6	587.7	e639.3	Maroc
Portugal	748.4	678.2	569.6	527.0	481.0	Portugal
Netherlands	640.3	658.5	528.5	569.7	570.0	Pays-Bas
Poland	608.7	582.0	504.3	486.5	471.4	Pologne
Thailand	560.1	482.3	521.0	498.8	e526.8	Thaïlande
United Kingdom	594.6	559.7	477.5	469.0	417.8	Royaume-Uni
France-Monaco	525.6	479.0	467.0	458.5	504.3	France-Monaco
Korea, Republic of	559.1	532.0	499.0	352.8	329.5	République de Corée
Canada	382.1	402.6	398.2	353.0	373.4	Canada
Sri Lanka	e356.1	336.1	e408.7	392.3	373.9	Sri Lanka
Pakistan	332.3	352.7	416.2	381.2	384.2	Pakistan
Spain	344.6	369.3	321.5	343.4	407.8	Espagne
India	268.0	287.2	442.6	404.5	376.9	Inde
Philippines	358.2	337.7	368.6	332.4	186.4	Philippines
Switzerland-Liechtenstein	251.4	243.3	232.5	272.0	345.7	Suisse-Liechtenstein
Northern Mariana Islands	250.0	260.0	270.0	270.0	270.0	Iles Mariannes septentrionales
Hungary	263.0	279.8	255.5	252.8	259.4	Hongrie

(Value as percentages of World total) **(Valeur en pourcentage du total mondial)**

Regions of the world	1993	1994	1995	1996	1997	1998	1999	2000	2001	2002	Régions du monde
World	100.0	100.0	100.0	100.0	100.0	100.0	100.0	100.0	100.0	100.0	Monde
Africa	5.0	4.8	5.5	5.3	4.6	6.2	5.9	5.3	6.1	6.7	Afrique
Americas	7.8	8.1	9.0	9.1	10.5	12.7	11.5	12.2	10.6	10.4	Amériques
- Northern America	5.0	5.1	5.2	5.5	5.5	5.2	4.7	4.5	3.5	3.3	- Amérique du Nord
- LAIA	1.9	2.2	2.8	3.5	4.5	5.2	6.0	6.9	6.4	6.5	- ALAI
- CACM	0.1	0.1	0.1	0.1	0.3	0.3	0.2	0.2	0.2	0.1	- MCC
- Caribbean	0.7	0.7	0.8	0.1	0.1	2.0	0.5	0.5	0.5	0.5	- Caraïbes
- Rest of America	0.1	0.1	0.1	0.1	0.1	0.1	0.1	0.1	0.0	0.0	- Autre d'Amérique
Asia excluding former USSR	52.9	52.9	48.2	47.2	47.7	45.4	46.5	50.9	49.5	47.3	Asie ancienne URSS exclus
- Middle East	2.4	2.1	2.5	2.2	2.2	2.6	2.8	2.9	3.3	3.9	- Moyen-Orient
Asia former USSR	0.0	0.1	0.1	0.1	0.1	0.1	0.1	0.1	0.1	0.1	Asie ancienne URSS
Europe excluding former USSR	33.4	33.1	36.2	36.2	35.1	33.3	33.6	29.3	31.3	33.0	Europe ancienne URSS exclus
- European Union	26.7	26.0	28.5	28.1	27.4	25.0	25.0	21.4	23.0	24.1	- Union Européenne
- Eastern Europe	3.9	4.5	4.9	5.4	5.5	5.9	6.2	5.7	6.0	6.4	- Europe de l'Est
- Rest of Europe	2.8	2.6	2.8	2.6	2.3	2.5	2.5	2.2	2.3	2.5	- Autre de l'Europe
Europe former USSR	0.7	0.7	0.9	1.1	1.2	1.3	1.3	1.2	1.3	1.5	Europe ancienne URSS
Oceania	0.2	0.3	0.3	1.0	0.9	1.0	1.1	1.0	1.0	1.0	Océanie

843 Womens, girls, infants outerwear, textile, not knitted or crocheted

TRADE BY COMMODITY (Value in million US dollars)
Imports by principal countries or areas

COMMERCE PAR PRODUIT (Valeur en millions de dollars EU)
Importations selon les principaux pays ou zones

Country or area	1998	1999	2000	2001	2002	Pays ou zone
World	47450.0	47480.2	50917.6	52114.0	54635.1	Monde
Africa	249.0	235.0	263.8	274.9	315.2	Afrique
Americas	16632.7	16440.2	19133.4	18883.2	18691.5	Amériques
- Northern America	15058.8	15212.9	17749.2	17685.8	17619.9	- Amérique du Nord
- LAIA	1108.9	950.5	1079.8	942.8	833.0	- ALAI
- CACM	168.8	48.6	64.5	80.0	101.6	- MCC
- Caribbean	257.0	185.3	202.3	141.1	97.2	- Caraïbes
- Rest of America	39.2	43.0	37.6	33.5	39.9	- Autre d'Amérique
Asia excluding former USSR	8489.7	9178.0	10703.4	11028.7	11173.3	Asie ancienne URSS exclus
- Middle East	929.5	849.1	896.3	922.0	934.2	- Moyen-Orient
Asia former USSR	20.1	23.6	15.2	13.6	18.4	Asie ancienne URSS
Europe excluding former USSR	21552.0	21075.1	20226.4	21306.4	23634.5	Europe ancienne URSS exclus
- European Union	19509.0	19136.9	18377.2	19396.6	21462.0	- Union Européenne
- Eastern Europe	330.2	335.8	342.5	399.0	528.1	- Europe de l'Est
- Rest of Europe	1712.8	1602.5	1506.7	1510.8	1644.3	- Autre de l'Europe
Europe former USSR	113.1	76.0	78.1	134.9	247.1	Europe ancienne URSS
Oceania	393.6	452.4	497.2	472.2	555.0	Océanie
United States	14333.3	14480.0	16915.4	16752.0	16641.5	Etats-Unis d'Amérique
Germany	6646.2	6003.0	5327.1	5454.1	5473.5	Allemagne
Japan	3387.7	4038.3	4892.0	4980.6	4780.0	Japon
China, Hong Kong SAR	3208.5	3234.8	3549.5	3690.0	3715.3	Chine - RAS de Hong-Kong
United Kingdom	2945.4	3103.9	3328.7	3550.2	4150.6	Royaume-Uni
France-Monaco	2723.6	2743.2	2759.0	2938.9	3339.2	France-Monaco
Italy-San Marino-Holy See	1100.8	1148.6	1190.6	1336.7	1648.7	Italie-Saint-Marin-Saint-Siège
Netherlands	1326.8	1303.2	1158.1	1171.0	1246.6	Pays-Bas
Belgium	-	1254.8	1181.7	1295.8	e1421.1	Belgique
Switzerland-Liechtenstein	1022.5	966.2	884.4	910.3	988.3	Suisse-Liechtenstein
Canada	722.4	729.8	829.9	926.9	968.8	Canada
Spain	623.6	705.2	733.7	889.3	1147.9	Espagne
Austria	783.5	744.2	647.6	675.3	730.8	Autriche
Mexico	789.8	656.9	761.8	628.7	570.1	Mexique
Denmark	596.4	594.2	582.9	608.5	654.4	Danemark
Sweden	486.9	497.4	473.9	450.4	486.3	Suède
Australia	284.7	328.1	380.2	362.9	432.4	Australie
Norway	355.5	348.0	338.2	333.4	383.2	Norvège
Saudi Arabia	338.2	274.0	312.2	311.7	e322.6	Arabie saoudite
Singapore	249.9	290.1	363.3	304.9	312.2	Singapour
Ireland	270.5	277.4	297.7	309.3	347.1	Irlande
Belgium-Luxembourg	1330.4	-	-	-	-	Belgique-Luxembourg
Korea, Republic of	88.2	143.3	248.3	294.7	513.9	République de Corée
Portugal	213.4	234.1	224.7	240.1	292.4	Portugal
Finland	241.0	232.1	213.1	215.8	238.5	Finlande
China	136.7	161.8	193.7	220.0	266.1	Chine
Greece	220.5	206.9	172.6	171.9	e190.1	Grèce
United Arab Emirates	183.1	191.8	198.5	173.8	e178.3	Emirates arabes unis
Kuwait	176.0	170.5	e160.2	e176.1	e146.1	Koweït
Israel	125.2	113.8	143.0	171.6	173.6	Israël

(Value as percentages of World total) **(Valeur en pourcentage du total mondial)**

Regions of the world	1993	1994	1995	1996	1997	1998	1999	2000	2001	2002	Régions du monde
World	100.0	100.0	100.0	100.0	100.0	100.0	100.0	100.0	100.0	100.0	Monde
Africa	0.6	0.5	0.5	0.5	0.5	0.5	0.5	0.5	0.5	0.6	Afrique
Americas	32.1	31.7	29.5	29.8	32.8	35.1	34.6	37.6	36.2	34.2	Amériques
- Northern America	30.2	29.6	27.4	27.3	30.1	31.7	32.0	34.9	33.9	32.3	- Amérique du Nord
- LAIA	1.5	1.7	1.6	1.8	2.1	2.3	2.0	2.1	1.8	1.5	- ALAI
- CACM	0.0	0.1	0.1	0.1	0.1	0.4	0.1	0.1	0.2	0.2	- MCC
- Caribbean	0.4	0.3	0.4	0.5	0.5	0.5	0.4	0.4	0.3	0.2	- Caraïbes
- Rest of America	0.1	0.1	0.1	0.1	0.1	0.1	0.1	0.1	0.1	0.1	- Autre d'Amérique
Asia excluding former USSR	20.3	21.2	22.2	22.7	21.1	17.9	19.3	21.0	21.2	20.5	Asie ancienne URSS exclus
- Middle East	1.8	1.9	2.0	1.7	1.9	2.0	1.8	1.8	1.8	1.7	- Moyen-Orient
Asia former USSR	0.0	0.1	0.0	0.0	0.0	0.0	0.0	0.0	0.0	0.0	Asie ancienne URSS
Europe excluding former USSR	44.8	45.6	46.6	45.9	44.5	45.4	44.4	39.7	40.9	43.3	Europe ancienne URSS exclus
- European Union	40.3	40.9	41.8	41.3	40.2	41.1	40.3	36.1	37.2	39.3	- Union Européenne
- Eastern Europe	0.5	0.5	0.5	0.6	0.6	0.7	0.7	0.7	0.8	1.0	- Europe de l'Est
- Rest of Europe	3.9	4.1	4.3	4.0	3.7	3.6	3.4	3.0	2.9	3.0	- Autre de l'Europe
Europe former USSR	1.7	0.3	0.3	0.3	0.3	0.2	0.2	0.2	0.3	0.5	Europe ancienne URSS
Oceania	0.6	0.6	0.7	0.9	0.8	0.8	1.0	1.0	0.9	1.0	Océanie

Vêtements de dessus pour femmes, fillettes et jeunes enfants, en matières textiles, n.d.a. 843

TRADE BY COMMODITY (Value in million US dollars)
Exports by principal countries or areas

COMMERCE PAR PRODUIT (Valeur en millions de dollars EU)
Exportations selon les principaux pays ou zones

Country or area	1998	1999	2000	2001	2002	Pays ou zone
World	45961.6	44983.3	48205.7	48444.1	51334.6	Monde
Africa	1695.3	1660.7	1580.5	1723.2	1869.8	Afrique
Americas	4109.4	3745.3	4195.7	3643.2	3479.2	Amériques
- Northern America	1557.7	1360.9	1412.0	1155.5	1071.7	- Amérique du Nord
- LAIA	2037.5	2229.0	2617.8	2353.8	2284.2	- ALAI
- CACM	94.9	64.4	53.6	40.0	46.8	- MCC
- Caribbean	409.9	82.8	100.9	84.3	67.6	- Caraïbes
- Rest of America	9.3	8.1	11.4	9.5	9.0	- Autre d'Amérique
Asia excluding former USSR	22071.3	22429.3	26224.4	25901.6	27488.2	Asie ancienne URSS exclus
- Middle East	1834.8	1866.8	2038.7	2254.0	2658.1	- Moyen-Orient
Asia former USSR	13.2	10.5	9.1	18.5	16.7	Asie ancienne URSS
Europe excluding former USSR	16879.8	15954.5	15016.6	15920.4	17226.2	Europe ancienne URSS exclus
- European Union	13358.5	12772.8	11939.7	12534.5	13701.6	- Union Européenne
- Eastern Europe	2761.3	2584.5	2537.1	2809.9	2967.9	- Europe de l'Est
- Rest of Europe	760.1	597.2	539.8	576.0	556.6	- Autre de l'Europe
Europe former USSR	794.0	752.4	771.2	839.0	895.2	Europe ancienne URSS
Oceania	398.6	430.6	408.1	398.2	359.3	Océanie
China	6318.0	6646.7	8243.8	8558.7	10107.6	Chine
China, Hong Kong SAR	5540.5	5605.0	6015.6	5965.6	6013.1	Chine - RAS de Hong-Kong
Italy-San Marino-Holy See	3748.3	3399.8	3445.4	3793.2	4030.5	Italie-Saint-Marin-Saint-Siège
Germany	2989.1	2802.8	2329.0	2505.9	2651.6	Allemagne
Mexico	1855.3	2083.5	2422.1	2117.0	2036.9	Mexique
France-Monaco	2068.9	1986.0	1901.6	1865.0	2073.5	France-Monaco
India	1886.6	1832.6	2136.8	1812.0	1950.4	Inde
Turkey	1409.3	1412.8	1505.0	1638.7	2023.8	Turquie
Indonesia	700.9	1056.1	1329.3	1239.7	1155.7	Indonésie
Romania	767.9	761.4	879.7	1086.5	1272.3	Roumanie
United States	1200.9	993.8	983.4	759.5	673.3	Etats-Unis d'Amérique
Poland	1135.3	962.7	823.3	841.1	785.1	Pologne
United Kingdom	1090.7	965.8	852.1	796.0	790.9	Royaume-Uni
Morocco	830.1	820.2	813.6	813.1	e884.6	Maroc
Sri Lanka	e844.8	797.2	e969.6	755.6	731.5	Sri Lanka
Korea, Republic of	941.3	876.4	880.4	710.1	645.2	République de Corée
Belgium	–	852.2	909.9	1051.0	e1179.2	Belgique
Philippines	796.5	782.3	940.6	887.6	571.3	Philippines
Bangladesh	659.6	e511.1	e701.3	832.4	e668.9	Bangladesh
Tunisia	653.3	647.3	587.3	696.9	e724.8	Tunisie
Spain	468.5	592.4	610.4	699.2	927.0	Espagne
Thailand	607.4	613.4	669.7	635.6	e671.3	Thaïlande
Netherlands	569.0	633.7	517.7	489.2	589.3	Pays-Bas
Denmark	488.1	495.8	486.8	516.2	585.0	Danemark
Canada	356.7	367.1	428.6	396.0	398.4	Canada
Hungary	407.3	402.1	362.7	385.9	369.4	Hongrie
China, Macao SAR	290.0	305.2	368.4	362.1	387.0	Chine - RAS de Macao
Viet Nam	351.4	230.3	330.5	343.6	382.0	Viet Nam
Portugal	372.9	336.7	293.2	278.4	304.1	Portugal
Northern Mariana Islands	250.0	260.0	270.0	270.0	270.0	Iles Mariannes septentrionales

(Value as percentages of World total) **(Valeur en pourcentage du total mondial)**

Regions of the world	1993	1994	1995	1996	1997	1998	1999	2000	2001	2002	Régions du monde
World	100.0	100.0	100.0	100.0	100.0	100.0	100.0	100.0	100.0	100.0	Monde
Africa	1.7	1.8	2.1	2.0	1.9	3.7	3.7	3.3	3.6	3.6	Afrique
Americas	5.0	5.2	5.7	6.2	7.6	8.9	8.3	8.7	7.5	6.8	Amériques
- Northern America	2.5	2.7	2.8	2.9	3.3	3.4	3.0	2.9	2.4	2.1	- Amérique du Nord
- LAIA	1.9	2.1	2.5	3.1	4.0	4.4	5.0	5.4	4.9	4.4	- ALAI
- CACM	0.1	0.1	0.1	0.0	0.2	0.2	0.1	0.1	0.1	0.1	- MCC
- Caribbean	0.4	0.3	0.3	0.1	0.1	0.9	0.2	0.2	0.2	0.1	- Caraïbes
- Rest of America	0.0	0.0	0.0	0.0	0.0	0.0	0.0	0.0	0.0	0.0	- Autre d'Amérique
Asia excluding former USSR	56.0	55.1	52.2	50.4	50.4	48.0	49.9	54.4	53.5	53.5	Asie ancienne URSS exclus
- Middle East	3.1	3.2	4.0	3.7	3.7	4.0	4.2	4.2	4.7	5.2	- Moyen-Orient
Asia former USSR	0.0	0.0	0.0	0.0	0.0	0.0	0.0	0.0	0.0	0.0	Asie ancienne URSS
Europe excluding former USSR	36.1	36.6	38.6	39.2	37.8	36.7	35.5	31.2	32.9	33.6	Europe ancienne URSS exclus
- European Union	29.8	30.3	31.5	32.0	30.8	29.1	28.4	24.8	25.9	26.7	- Union Européenne
- Eastern Europe	4.2	4.7	5.4	5.8	5.6	6.0	5.7	5.3	5.8	5.8	- Europe de l'Est
- Rest of Europe	2.0	1.7	1.7	1.5	1.4	1.7	1.3	1.1	1.2	1.1	- Autre de l'Europe
Europe former USSR	1.0	0.9	1.2	1.4	1.5	1.7	1.7	1.6	1.7	1.7	Europe ancienne URSS
Oceania	0.2	0.2	0.2	0.7	0.7	0.9	1.0	0.8	0.8	0.7	Océanie

844 Under garments of textile fabrics, not knitted or crocheted

TRADE BY COMMODITY (Value in million US dollars)
Imports by principal countries or areas

COMMERCE PAR PRODUIT (Valeur en millions de dollars EU)
Importations selon les principaux pays ou zones

Country or area	1998	1999	2000	2001	2002	Pays ou zone
World	14400.7	13871.6	14150.6	13570.0	13320.0	Monde
Africa	243.9	244.8	233.4	239.7	257.6	Afrique
Americas	5494.0	5194.7	5535.1	5133.8	4719.2	Amériques
- Northern America	4290.8	4388.7	4814.0	4487.5	4162.8	- Amérique du Nord
- LAIA	631.8	573.9	494.1	466.6	386.9	- ALAI
- CACM	120.9	34.6	41.6	35.2	42.3	- MCC
- Caribbean	438.7	183.3	172.8	133.3	113.6	- Caraïbes
- Rest of America	11.9	14.3	12.6	11.2	13.6	- Autre d'Amérique
Asia excluding former USSR	3460.1	3512.9	3728.6	3559.7	3355.1	Asie ancienne URSS exclus
- Middle East	334.7	318.8	294.9	314.9	293.2	- Moyen-Orient
Asia former USSR	13.5	8.1	3.8	4.7	6.4	Asie ancienne URSS
Europe excluding former USSR	4938.9	4649.6	4390.0	4400.1	4698.4	Europe ancienne URSS exclus
- European Union	4393.7	4178.1	3928.7	3883.6	4112.0	- Union Européenne
- Eastern Europe	275.4	224.1	220.6	260.2	317.6	- Europe de l'Est
- Rest of Europe	269.7	247.4	240.6	256.3	268.8	- Autre de l'Europe
Europe former USSR	98.1	86.3	73.0	79.4	103.1	Europe ancienne URSS
Oceania	152.1	175.1	186.8	152.8	180.2	Océanie
United States	4060.8	4164.9	4578.7	4255.1	3939.6	Etats-Unis d'Amérique
China, Hong Kong SAR	1237.8	1209.4	1138.2	1039.9	1038.0	Chine - RAS de Hong-Kong
Japan	1039.0	1111.2	1222.0	1166.7	1029.8	Japon
Germany	1168.7	1069.7	947.1	921.0	863.3	Allemagne
United Kingdom	841.0	815.9	842.7	806.4	888.6	Royaume-Uni
France-Monaco	643.8	617.3	575.3	574.8	590.5	France-Monaco
China	517.4	474.3	453.1	410.9	368.1	Chine
Italy-San Marino-Holy See	414.2	366.2	346.6	378.9	476.3	Italie-Saint-Marin-Saint-Siège
Mexico	454.1	425.0	361.5	337.3	283.0	Mexique
Spain	218.7	242.1	245.6	262.0	310.8	Espagne
Netherlands	278.4	263.9	237.3	239.8	251.4	Pays-Bas
Canada	229.8	223.5	234.6	230.3	222.0	Canada
Belgium	–	218.9	190.0	203.5	e223.2	Belgique
Tunisia	154.4	152.2	139.9	149.3	e149.3	Tunisie
Switzerland-Liechtenstein	158.4	149.6	139.5	138.5	145.4	Suisse-Liechtenstein
Australia	108.9	129.3	145.3	117.2	138.9	Australie
Bangladesh	55.3	e60.6	e178.7	173.1	e169.2	Bangladesh
Romania	125.5	88.3	100.4	130.0	164.3	Roumanie
Dominican Republic	e	e89.4	e83.0	e46.3	e30.3	République dominicaine
Austria	128.0	110.3	92.1	100.8	103.5	Autriche
Saudi Arabia	104.7	95.9	95.8	105.1	e108.7	Arabie saoudite
Korea, Republic of	34.5	57.2	109.2	131.7	157.7	République de Corée
United Arab Emirates	104.0	109.0	92.4	90.4	e92.7	Emirates arabes unis
Denmark	107.0	106.8	95.5	89.9	88.0	Danemark
Singapore	84.5	97.9	111.7	99.2	89.4	Singapour
Sweden	106.2	100.9	95.0	82.3	76.7	Suède
Ireland	79.9	83.3	79.4	70.9	79.2	Irlande
Greece	65.6	72.8	85.4	51.3	e56.7	Grèce
Jamaica	97.6	48.0	49.4	e52.0	e54.7	Jamaïque
Kuwait	75.9	64.4	e60.5	e66.5	e26.6	Koweït

(Value as percentages of World total) **(Valeur en pourcentage du total mondial)**

Regions of the world	1993	1994	1995	1996	1997	1998	1999	2000	2001	2002	Régions du monde
World	100.0	100.0	100.0	100.0	100.0	100.0	100.0	100.0	100.0	100.0	Monde
Africa	0.9	1.3	1.1	1.2	1.4	1.7	1.8	1.6	1.8	1.9	Afrique
Americas	35.5	34.7	33.8	33.3	35.5	38.2	37.4	39.1	37.8	35.4	Amériques
- Northern America	31.9	30.8	28.9	27.1	28.4	29.8	31.6	34.0	33.1	31.3	- Amérique du Nord
- LAIA	1.9	2.3	2.7	2.9	3.8	4.4	4.1	3.5	3.4	2.9	- ALAI
- CACM	0.2	0.2	0.2	0.3	0.4	0.8	0.2	0.3	0.3	0.3	- MCC
- Caribbean	1.3	1.4	1.8	3.0	2.9	3.0	1.3	1.2	1.0	0.9	- Caraïbes
- Rest of America	0.1	0.1	0.1	0.1	0.1	0.1	0.1	0.1	0.1	0.1	- Autre d'Amérique
Asia excluding former USSR	23.1	24.6	24.9	26.0	26.3	24.0	25.3	26.3	26.2	25.2	Asie ancienne URSS exclus
- Middle East	3.0	3.1	2.7	2.1	2.2	2.3	2.3	2.1	2.3	2.2	- Moyen-Orient
Asia former USSR	0.0	0.1	0.1	0.1	0.0	0.1	0.1	0.0	0.0	0.0	Asie ancienne URSS
Europe excluding former USSR	38.2	37.6	38.1	37.5	34.9	34.3	33.5	31.0	32.4	35.3	Europe ancienne URSS exclus
- European Union	35.1	34.3	34.5	33.5	31.1	30.5	30.1	27.8	28.6	30.9	- Union Européenne
- Eastern Europe	1.0	1.0	1.3	1.7	1.8	1.9	1.6	1.6	1.9	2.4	- Europe de l'Est
- Rest of Europe	2.1	2.3	2.3	2.2	2.0	1.9	1.8	1.7	1.9	2.0	- Autre de l'Europe
Europe former USSR	1.3	0.6	0.9	0.7	0.7	0.7	0.6	0.5	0.6	0.8	Europe ancienne URSS
Oceania	1.0	1.2	1.2	1.3	1.1	1.1	1.3	1.3	1.1	1.4	Océanie

Vêtements de dessus en matières textiles, autres que de bonneterie 844

TRADE BY COMMODITY (Value in million US dollars)
Exports by principal countries or areas

COMMERCE PAR PRODUIT (Valeur en millions de dollars EU)
Exportations selon les principaux pays ou zones

Country or area	1998	1999	2000	2001	2002	Pays ou zone
World	14699.4	13786.6	14218.7	13462.3	13270.1	Monde
Africa	574.6	538.9	432.9	427.4	426.5	Afrique
Americas	2009.7	1368.2	1409.5	1051.1	944.7	Amériques
- Northern America	1519.4	982.1	972.0	660.2	588.0	- Amérique du Nord
- LAIA	324.1	284.9	336.0	287.2	252.1	- ALAI
- CACM	62.4	61.8	61.7	74.4	80.1	- MCC
- Caribbean	91.1	28.7	32.6	24.7	22.0	- Caraïbes
- Rest of America	12.7	10.7	7.3	4.6	2.6	- Autre d'Amérique
Asia excluding former USSR	8384.1	8254.3	8929.5	8460.5	8102.8	Asie ancienne URSS exclus
- Middle East	459.8	413.9	368.2	400.1	561.9	- Moyen-Orient
Asia former USSR	2.9	0.9	0.8	1.0	1.0	Asie ancienne URSS
Europe excluding former USSR	3384.8	3257.7	3081.1	3165.0	3434.2	Europe ancienne URSS exclus
- European Union	2710.2	2625.4	2479.7	2542.1	2757.1	- Union Européenne
- Eastern Europe	476.9	470.7	453.3	478.0	537.2	- Europe de l'Est
- Rest of Europe	197.6	161.5	148.2	144.8	139.8	- Autre de l'Europe
Europe former USSR	61.8	68.5	65.1	57.9	68.1	Europe ancienne URSS
Oceania	281.6	298.3	299.7	299.5	292.9	Océanie
China	2258.1	2271.4	2630.5	2634.6	2589.7	Chine
China, Hong Kong SAR	1454.0	1393.5	1407.7	1310.5	1214.1	Chine - RAS de Hong-Kong
United States	1464.2	927.4	906.2	605.7	535.1	Etats-Unis d'Amérique
India	823.4	844.3	1020.7	780.9	805.2	Inde
Bangladesh	959.4	e743.5	e727.6	863.6	e693.9	Bangladesh
Italy-San Marino-Holy See	752.8	736.9	698.8	756.9	851.0	Italie-Saint-Marin-Saint-Siège
United Kingdom	577.9	546.7	572.8	497.5	511.6	Royaume-Uni
Korea, Republic of	406.4	420.0	505.2	449.8	414.8	République de Corée
Indonesia	359.8	494.4	490.2	430.6	420.3	Indonésie
Germany	371.4	360.9	311.8	334.5	355.1	Allemagne
Turkey	336.9	282.4	253.9	267.9	348.8	Turquie
Northern Mariana Islands	250.0	260.0	270.0	270.0	270.0	Iles Mariannes septentrionales
Sri Lanka	e248.9	234.9	e285.7	257.7	229.6	Sri Lanka
Mexico	264.5	245.8	286.7	233.5	207.9	Mexique
France-Monaco	190.1	188.6	190.3	199.2	233.5	France-Monaco
Portugal	237.1	227.4	180.8	169.9	163.8	Portugal
Philippines	216.2	223.4	237.3	226.9	51.3	Philippines
Romania	141.1	146.0	178.0	206.9	257.5	Roumanie
Thailand	184.6	194.6	200.3	166.2	e175.5	Thaïlande
Pakistan	177.2	158.2	160.9	152.7	168.6	Pakistan
Netherlands	174.4	155.2	136.4	149.4	171.3	Pays-Bas
Morocco	187.4	157.4	127.5	124.7	e135.7	Maroc
Malaysia	145.8	144.7	150.5	130.9	e138.7	Malaisie
Mauritius	137.4	167.0	161.5	120.8	103.3	Maurice
Tunisia	140.3	128.2	105.8	111.8	e116.3	Tunisie
China, Macao SAR	127.5	127.2	132.3	97.8	73.7	Chine - RAS de Macao
Poland	149.2	124.8	102.5	95.1	85.0	Pologne
Belgium	-	136.4	116.7	126.3	e141.7	Belgique
Spain	90.4	90.2	92.6	104.5	134.7	Espagne
Singapore	75.3	89.2	95.9	77.3	73.5	Singapour

(Value as percentages of World total) **(Valeur en pourcentage du total mondial)**

Regions of the world	1993	1994	1995	1996	1997	1998	1999	2000	2001	2002	Régions du monde
World	100.0	100.0	100.0	100.0	100.0	100.0	100.0	100.0	100.0	100.0	Monde
Africa	3.5	3.6	3.5	3.3	2.8	3.9	3.9	3.0	3.2	3.2	Afrique
Americas	7.4	7.9	9.7	10.1	12.5	13.7	9.9	9.9	7.8	7.1	Amériques
- Northern America	4.4	5.0	6.1	8.2	9.5	10.3	7.1	6.8	4.9	4.4	- Amérique du Nord
- LAIA	1.2	1.4	1.6	1.6	2.2	2.2	2.1	2.4	2.1	1.9	- ALAI
- CACM	0.2	0.1	0.1	0.1	0.6	0.4	0.4	0.4	0.6	0.6	- MCC
- Caribbean	1.5	1.3	1.8	0.1	0.1	0.6	0.2	0.2	0.2	0.2	- Caraïbes
- Rest of America	0.1	0.1	0.1	0.1	0.1	0.1	0.1	0.1	0.0	0.0	- Autre d'Amérique
Asia excluding former USSR	69.6	68.6	64.1	61.4	60.3	57.0	59.9	62.8	62.8	61.1	Asie ancienne URSS exclus
- Middle East	3.5	3.8	4.2	3.4	3.3	3.1	3.0	2.6	3.0	4.2	- Moyen-Orient
Asia former USSR	0.0	0.0	0.0	0.0	0.0	0.0	0.0	0.0	0.0	0.0	Asie ancienne URSS
Europe excluding former USSR	19.1	19.4	21.8	23.0	22.2	23.0	23.6	21.7	23.5	25.9	Europe ancienne URSS exclus
- European Union	15.7	16.2	18.0	18.9	18.2	18.4	19.0	17.4	18.9	20.8	- Union Européenne
- Eastern Europe	2.1	2.2	2.8	2.9	2.9	3.2	3.4	3.2	3.6	4.0	- Europe de l'Est
- Rest of Europe	1.3	1.0	1.0	1.2	1.1	1.3	1.2	1.0	1.1	1.1	- Autre de l'Europe
Europe former USSR	0.2	0.2	0.4	0.3	0.3	0.4	0.5	0.5	0.4	0.5	Europe ancienne URSS
Oceania	0.2	0.3	0.5	1.9	1.9	1.9	2.2	2.1	2.2	2.2	Océanie

845 Outerwear knitted or crocheted, not elastic nor rubberized

TRADE BY COMMODITY (Value in million US dollars)
Imports by principal countries or areas

COMMERCE PAR PRODUIT (Valeur en millions de dollars EU)
Importations selon les principaux pays ou zones

Country or area	1998	1999	2000	2001	2002	Pays ou zone
World	47952.6	50544.8	53672.2	55154.5	56736.6	Monde
Africa	220.6	222.6	244.1	275.3	273.5	Afrique
Americas	16264.1	17956.1	20515.9	21367.1	22196.5	Amériques
- Northern America	14958.7	16521.7	18776.0	19581.5	20523.8	- Amérique du Nord
- LAIA	988.6	1179.6	1461.2	1499.6	1324.7	- ALAI
- CACM	64.2	34.1	35.6	47.3	52.6	- MCC
- Caribbean	230.8	198.4	219.4	216.3	271.5	- Caraïbes
- Rest of America	21.8	22.3	23.7	22.5	23.9	- Autre d'Amérique
Asia excluding former USSR	10575.9	11194.1	12800.5	12989.9	12908.3	Asie ancienne URSS exclus
- Middle East	382.2	353.9	429.7	447.5	524.6	- Moyen-Orient
Asia former USSR	14.0	31.4	24.9	26.7	33.1	Asie ancienne URSS
Europe excluding former USSR	20285.0	20557.1	19467.9	19867.3	20628.1	Europe ancienne URSS exclus
- European Union	18369.9	18638.7	17600.5	17973.1	18642.6	- Union Européenne
- Eastern Europe	325.5	366.7	399.1	504.5	612.8	- Europe de l'Est
- Rest of Europe	1589.7	1551.6	1468.3	1389.7	1372.7	- Autre de l'Europe
Europe former USSR	105.2	84.8	93.0	134.9	189.7	Europe ancienne URSS
Oceania	487.8	498.8	525.9	493.3	507.4	Océanie
United States	14171.2	15708.6	17920.0	18626.0	19484.6	Etats-Unis d'Amérique
China, Hong Kong SAR	4431.4	4793.4	5221.3	5615.7	5570.4	Chine - RAS de Hong-Kong
Japan	4604.1	4661.0	5406.9	4958.1	4476.9	Japon
Germany	5316.9	5048.7	4532.4	4336.5	4218.7	Allemagne
United Kingdom	2968.0	2989.0	2983.3	3207.8	3605.0	Royaume-Uni
France-Monaco	2869.9	2878.9	2833.1	2784.7	2859.6	France-Monaco
Italy-San Marino-Holy See	1256.6	1402.4	1412.2	1586.4	1670.4	Italie-Saint-Marin-Saint-Siège
Netherlands	1157.4	1231.0	1072.1	1076.2	1064.1	Pays-Bas
Spain	763.3	914.6	921.5	1035.6	1150.6	Espagne
Mexico	688.9	881.4	1098.2	1095.1	992.6	Mexique
Switzerland-Liechtenstein	996.3	984.8	936.6	867.6	874.7	Suisse-Liechtenstein
Belgium	–	1127.3	1013.2	1067.5	e1170.7	Belgique
Canada	740.6	762.4	851.6	949.2	1033.3	Canada
Austria	682.1	671.7	608.6	619.5	610.6	Autriche
Singapore	463.8	569.7	665.8	633.9	769.9	Singapour
Denmark	634.8	667.1	594.1	625.9	572.6	Danemark
Sweden	488.8	500.7	461.6	421.2	433.8	Suède
Australia	370.0	375.9	401.8	378.6	388.6	Australie
Korea, Republic of	135.8	199.5	311.2	459.4	658.5	République de Corée
Norway	395.1	378.1	321.3	308.6	321.9	Norvège
Ireland	322.3	334.8	328.2	342.6	362.4	Irlande
Greece	270.2	318.5	320.6	342.5	e378.7	Grèce
Portugal	265.6	288.1	273.9	280.7	297.7	Portugal
China	143.6	181.8	260.0	350.2	376.5	Chine
Belgium-Luxembourg	1159.2	–	–	–	–	Belgique-Luxembourg
Finland	214.6	210.1	194.5	189.2	187.4	Finlande
Poland	110.8	113.3	120.7	124.6	184.6	Pologne
United Arab Emirates	74.0	77.6	131.0	138.5	e142.1	Emirates arabes unis
Chile	89.2	89.8	120.1	120.8	119.4	Chili
China, Macao SAR	79.2	99.6	103.0	115.1	125.9	Chine - RAS de Macao

(Value as percentages of World total) **(Valeur en pourcentage du total mondial)**

Regions of the world	1993	1994	1995	1996	1997	1998	1999	2000	2001	2002	Régions du monde
World	100.0	100.0	100.0	100.0	100.0	100.0	100.0	100.0	100.0	100.0	Monde
Africa	0.4	0.5	0.5	0.5	0.4	0.5	0.4	0.5	0.5	0.5	Afrique
Americas	27.3	28.7	28.3	27.6	30.0	33.9	35.5	38.2	38.7	39.1	Amériques
- Northern America	26.1	27.2	26.6	25.9	27.7	31.2	32.7	35.0	35.5	36.2	- Amérique du Nord
- LAIA	0.9	1.2	1.3	1.4	1.8	2.1	2.3	2.7	2.7	2.3	- ALAI
- CACM	0.1	0.1	0.1	0.1	0.1	0.1	0.1	0.1	0.1	0.1	- MCC
- Caribbean	0.2	0.1	0.2	0.3	0.3	0.5	0.4	0.4	0.4	0.5	- Caraïbes
- Rest of America	0.1	0.1	0.1	0.0	0.0	0.0	0.0	0.0	0.0	0.0	- Autre d'Amérique
Asia excluding former USSR	21.7	24.2	25.2	25.0	23.1	22.1	22.1	23.8	23.6	22.8	Asie ancienne URSS exclus
- Middle East	0.9	0.8	0.8	0.7	0.8	0.8	0.7	0.8	0.8	0.9	- Moyen-Orient
Asia former USSR	0.1	0.1	0.1	0.0	0.0	0.0	0.1	0.0	0.0	0.1	Asie ancienne URSS
Europe excluding former USSR	48.0	45.2	44.6	45.6	45.2	42.3	40.7	36.3	36.0	36.4	Europe ancienne URSS exclus
- European Union	43.3	40.8	40.1	41.1	41.4	38.3	36.9	32.8	32.6	32.9	- Union Européenne
- Eastern Europe	0.5	0.5	0.6	0.6	0.6	0.7	0.7	0.7	0.9	1.1	- Europe de l'Est
- Rest of Europe	4.2	3.9	4.0	3.8	3.3	3.3	3.1	2.7	2.5	2.4	- Autre de l'Europe
Europe former USSR	1.5	0.3	0.4	0.3	0.2	0.2	0.2	0.2	0.2	0.3	Europe ancienne URSS
Oceania	0.9	1.0	1.0	1.0	1.0	1.0	1.0	1.0	0.9	0.9	Océanie

Vêtements de dessus de bonneterie non élastique ni caoutchoutée 845

TRADE BY COMMODITY (Value in million US dollars) — COMMERCE PAR PRODUIT (Valeur en millions de dollars EU)

Exports by principal countries or areas — **Exportations selon les principaux pays ou zones**

Country or area	1998	1999	2000	2001	2002	Pays ou zone
World	43431.9	44677.7	47350.5	47558.1	49890.2	Monde
Africa	972.2	956.6	1041.4	1002.2	1097.5	Afrique
Americas	3556.1	3940.7	4238.0	4163.6	3906.0	Amériques
- Northern America	1762.9	1946.9	2107.2	1928.4	1721.7	- Amérique du Nord
- LAIA	1441.8	1834.3	1956.0	2062.5	1969.3	- ALAI
- CACM	52.9	52.3	51.5	51.2	69.4	- MCC
- Caribbean	292.8	101.0	121.2	115.4	137.9	- Caraïbes
- Rest of America	5.7	6.2	2.0	6.1	7.7	- Autre d'Amérique
Asia excluding former USSR	24712.7	25723.5	28854.2	28866.5	30964.0	Asie ancienne URSS exclus
- Middle East	2374.2	2055.6	1935.4	1947.4	2381.9	- Moyen-Orient
Asia former USSR	4.3	7.5	16.6	17.7	26.9	Asie ancienne URSS
Europe excluding former USSR	13822.9	13672.6	12835.2	13095.6	13490.1	Europe ancienne URSS exclus
- European Union	12593.3	12348.1	11458.9	11518.1	11788.4	- Union Européenne
- Eastern Europe	934.6	1012.4	1082.0	1258.6	1377.0	- Europe de l'Est
- Rest of Europe	294.9	312.2	294.3	318.9	324.8	- Autre de l'Europe
Europe former USSR	260.0	258.1	253.7	274.3	298.8	Europe ancienne URSS
Oceania	103.7	118.7	111.5	138.3	107.0	Océanie
China	6968.1	7512.8	8798.5	9013.2	10708.9	Chine
China, Hong Kong SAR	7054.8	7190.9	7710.8	7863.7	7615.2	Chine - RAS de Hong-Kong
Italy-San Marino-Holy See	3837.8	3683.2	3707.9	3552.5	3378.1	Italie-Saint-Marin-Saint-Siège
Turkey	2203.7	1890.9	1702.5	1720.8	2097.7	Turquie
Mexico	1204.4	1584.5	1646.6	1721.6	1627.0	Mexique
United States	1326.9	1425.1	1524.4	1426.1	1216.3	Etats-Unis d'Amérique
Germany	1330.0	1357.3	1318.1	1379.1	1495.3	Allemagne
France-Monaco	1307.6	1315.6	1285.6	1309.8	1395.4	France-Monaco
Korea, Republic of	1280.1	1406.8	1295.1	1204.8	1095.0	République de Corée
Thailand	1011.2	1025.1	1094.2	1073.7	e1133.9	Thaïlande
United Kingdom	1187.7	1022.9	890.8	885.9	907.7	Royaume-Uni
Portugal	1129.5	1055.0	860.4	854.2	827.5	Portugal
Singapore	609.3	707.2	807.1	761.4	873.0	Singapour
China, Macao SAR	730.9	730.9	782.1	709.8	748.5	Chine - RAS de Macao
Indonesia	397.1	695.3	893.0	861.6	744.6	Indonésie
Belgium	–	861.0	767.6	807.5	e906.0	Belgique
Netherlands	721.9	719.4	539.8	589.6	602.7	Pays-Bas
India	419.0	585.0	675.5	594.7	840.6	Inde
Greece	623.7	661.3	564.2	563.6	e564.3	Grèce
Denmark	571.4	638.7	563.6	593.1	577.5	Danemark
Spain	396.2	497.5	512.8	580.1	717.4	Espagne
Canada	436.0	521.5	582.8	502.4	505.3	Canada
Bangladesh	512.9	e397.5	e507.3	602.2	e483.9	Bangladesh
Philippines	466.6	469.6	506.0	489.7	351.5	Philippines
Morocco	449.3	431.6	424.4	364.0	e396.0	Maroc
Malaysia	387.9	409.4	433.1	397.4	e421.2	Malaisie
Viet Nam	21.8	32.1	560.5	582.9	647.9	Viet Nam
Cambodia	e336.8	e346.2	e350.8	e414.3	e366.1	Cambodge
Sri Lanka	e341.7	322.5	e392.2	349.5	360.3	Sri Lanka
Romania	222.3	231.1	292.9	371.6	466.6	Roumanie

(Value as percentages of World total) — **(Valeur en pourcentage du total mondial)**

Regions of the world	1993	1994	1995	1996	1997	1998	1999	2000	2001	2002	Régions du monde
World	100.0	100.0	100.0	100.0	100.0	100.0	100.0	100.0	100.0	100.0	Monde
Africa	2.2	2.0	2.1	2.0	1.7	2.2	2.1	2.2	2.1	2.2	Afrique
Americas	4.3	5.1	5.9	6.3	6.8	8.2	8.8	9.0	8.8	7.8	Amériques
- Northern America	2.8	3.3	3.7	4.0	3.8	4.1	4.4	4.5	4.1	3.5	- Amérique du Nord
- LAIA	1.2	1.5	2.0	2.2	2.9	3.3	4.1	4.1	4.3	3.9	- ALAI
- CACM	0.1	0.1	0.1	0.1	0.1	0.1	0.1	0.1	0.1	0.1	- MCC
- Caribbean	0.2	0.2	0.1	0.1	0.0	0.7	0.2	0.3	0.2	0.3	- Caraïbes
- Rest of America	0.0	0.0	0.0	0.0	0.0	0.0	0.0	0.0	0.0	0.0	- Autre d'Amérique
Asia excluding former USSR	59.6	57.9	55.9	54.4	53.2	56.9	57.6	60.9	60.7	62.1	Asie ancienne URSS exclus
- Middle East	5.6	5.8	6.8	6.1	5.3	5.5	4.6	4.1	4.1	4.8	- Moyen-Orient
Asia former USSR	0.0	0.0	0.0	0.0	0.0	0.0	0.0	0.0	0.0	0.1	Asie ancienne URSS
Europe excluding former USSR	33.4	34.5	35.4	36.3	37.3	31.8	30.6	27.1	27.5	27.0	Europe ancienne URSS exclus
- European Union	31.0	31.9	32.7	33.4	34.9	29.0	27.6	24.2	24.2	23.6	- Union Européenne
- Eastern Europe	1.6	1.6	1.9	2.1	1.8	2.2	2.3	2.3	2.6	2.8	- Europe de l'Est
- Rest of Europe	0.8	0.9	0.8	0.7	0.6	0.7	0.7	0.6	0.7	0.7	- Autre de l'Europe
Europe former USSR	0.3	0.3	0.4	0.5	0.6	0.6	0.6	0.5	0.6	0.6	Europe ancienne URSS
Oceania	0.2	0.3	0.4	0.4	0.4	0.2	0.3	0.2	0.3	0.2	Océanie

846 Under-garments, knitted or crocheted

TRADE BY COMMODITY (Value in million US dollars)
Imports by principal countries or areas

COMMERCE PAR PRODUIT (Valeur en millions de dollars EU)
Importations selon les principaux pays ou zones

Country or area	1998	1999	2000	2001	2002	Pays ou zone
World	31038.7	32509.7	33970.0	33861.0	35289.4	Monde
Africa	342.0	361.9	359.6	368.0	386.8	Afrique
Americas	10829.5	11712.4	12407.7	11887.0	12128.8	Amériques
- Northern America	9115.2	9988.1	10523.4	10181.8	10575.0	- Amérique du Nord
- LAIA	1027.9	1116.6	1188.4	1119.5	930.6	- ALAI
- CACM	213.8	105.0	166.6	147.8	150.5	- MCC
- Caribbean	458.4	487.8	512.5	424.9	459.0	- Caraïbes
- Rest of America	14.2	14.8	16.8	13.0	13.8	- Autre d'Amérique
Asia excluding former USSR	4916.9	5485.0	6398.7	6337.4	6263.4	Asie ancienne URSS exclus
- Middle East	272.7	263.0	291.4	299.9	366.0	- Moyen-Orient
Asia former USSR	10.2	14.4	8.0	10.4	16.5	Asie ancienne URSS
Europe excluding former USSR	14457.6	14417.3	14199.0	14707.3	15862.7	Europe ancienne URSS exclus
- European Union	13249.8	13145.7	12924.9	13423.0	14456.9	- Union Européenne
- Eastern Europe	482.1	546.7	564.9	585.4	624.8	- Europe de l'Est
- Rest of Europe	725.7	724.9	709.1	698.9	781.0	- Autre de l'Europe
Europe former USSR	102.6	87.4	104.7	132.3	174.8	Europe ancienne URSS
Oceania	379.9	431.3	492.3	418.6	456.4	Océanie
United States	8585.3	9429.7	9943.6	9568.4	9959.2	Etats-Unis d'Amérique
Germany	3586.2	3441.1	3342.4	3298.6	3275.2	Allemagne
United Kingdom	2134.2	2326.3	2310.0	2609.1	2926.5	Royaume-Uni
China, Hong Kong SAR	2172.4	2299.7	2513.5	2416.4	2379.5	Chine - RAS de Hong-Kong
Japan	1754.2	2102.8	2592.2	2597.7	2388.4	Japon
France-Monaco	2122.9	2124.7	2100.0	2116.4	2351.8	France-Monaco
Italy-San Marino-Holy See	853.2	905.2	983.2	1031.9	1198.7	Italie-Saint-Marin-Saint-Siège
Netherlands	893.8	895.3	879.5	843.6	807.3	Pays-Bas
Mexico	721.4	824.4	861.3	774.2	641.9	Mexique
Belgium	–	862.7	841.6	827.2	e907.2	Belgique
Spain	557.4	616.7	610.6	743.8	883.2	Espagne
Canada	528.7	557.4	577.2	610.3	612.0	Canada
Austria	556.8	501.9	451.3	463.9	501.5	Autriche
Denmark	410.7	416.7	388.9	387.1	406.4	Danemark
Singapore	324.5	373.4	432.3	389.0	378.5	Singapour
Switzerland-Liechtenstein	356.6	365.7	348.6	358.3	405.5	Suisse-Liechtenstein
Sweden	382.1	305.4	301.1	364.6	406.4	Suède
Australia	285.6	323.3	380.6	312.3	344.7	Australie
Dominican Republic	e268.2	e240.6	e239.3	e201.9	e219.5	République dominicaine
Ireland	198.7	204.3	214.8	228.2	223.6	Irlande
Belgium-Luxembourg	1058.2	–	–	–	–	Belgique-Luxembourg
Norway	202.4	198.4	201.1	189.1	210.2	Norvège
Portugal	169.2	175.4	162.8	172.3	200.4	Portugal
Greece	178.8	184.5	163.1	154.0	e170.3	Grèce
Hungary	145.7	160.2	160.4	159.9	154.2	Hongrie
Finland	147.4	152.0	143.9	147.3	161.1	Finlande
Morocco	120.5	155.4	143.8	154.5	e163.1	Maroc
United Arab Emirates	119.3	125.0	139.4	143.0	e146.7	Emirates arabes unis
Poland	114.5	119.2	124.7	128.1	161.8	Pologne
Costa Rica	181.6	74.7	131.5	110.1	100.7	Costa Rica

(Value as percentages of World total) **(Valeur en pourcentage du total mondial)**

Regions of the world	1993	1994	1995	1996	1997	1998	1999	2000	2001	2002	Régions du monde
World	100.0	100.0	100.0	100.0	100.0	100.0	100.0	100.0	100.0	100.0	Monde
Africa	0.7	0.9	0.8	0.7	0.7	1.1	1.1	1.1	1.1	1.1	Afrique
Americas	22.5	25.2	26.9	27.7	32.5	34.9	36.0	36.5	35.1	34.4	Amériques
- Northern America	19.2	21.7	23.3	23.9	27.4	29.4	30.7	31.0	30.1	30.0	- Amérique du Nord
- LAIA	1.9	2.3	2.4	2.5	3.2	3.3	3.4	3.5	3.3	2.6	- ALAI
- CACM	0.1	0.1	0.1	0.2	0.5	0.7	0.3	0.5	0.4	0.4	- MCC
- Caribbean	1.1	1.0	1.0	1.0	1.3	1.5	1.5	1.5	1.3	1.3	- Caraïbes
- Rest of America	0.1	0.1	0.1	0.0	0.0	0.0	0.0	0.0	0.0	0.0	- Autre d'Amérique
Asia excluding former USSR	22.0	22.4	22.8	21.9	19.5	15.8	16.9	18.8	18.7	17.7	Asie ancienne URSS exclus
- Middle East	1.7	1.4	1.1	0.7	0.9	0.9	0.8	0.9	0.9	1.0	- Moyen-Orient
Asia former USSR	0.0	0.1	0.1	0.1	0.0	0.0	0.0	0.0	0.0	0.0	Asie ancienne URSS
Europe excluding former USSR	52.4	49.6	47.7	48.1	45.6	46.6	44.3	41.8	43.4	45.0	Europe ancienne URSS exclus
- European Union	48.3	45.7	43.7	44.0	41.8	42.7	40.4	38.0	39.6	41.0	- Union Européenne
- Eastern Europe	1.4	1.3	1.4	1.5	1.4	1.6	1.7	1.7	1.7	1.8	- Europe de l'Est
- Rest of Europe	2.8	2.6	2.6	2.6	2.4	2.3	2.2	2.1	2.1	2.2	- Autre de l'Europe
Europe former USSR	1.1	0.4	0.5	0.4	0.4	0.3	0.3	0.3	0.4	0.5	Europe ancienne URSS
Oceania	1.1	1.3	1.1	1.2	1.3	1.2	1.3	1.4	1.2	1.3	Océanie

TRADE BY COMMODITY (Value in million US dollars)
Exports by principal countries or areas

COMMERCE PAR PRODUIT (Valeur en millions de dollars EU)
Exportations selon les principaux pays ou zones

Country or area	1998	1999	2000	2001	2002	Pays ou zone
World	31912.1	32245.3	33518.4	32346.2	33700.3	Monde
Africa	1104.8	1131.9	1217.2	1281.4	1420.3	Afrique
Americas	5497.2	5782.4	6135.2	5410.3	4989.8	Amériques
- Northern America	2647.9	2910.5	3088.0	2499.4	2209.4	- Amérique du Nord
- LAIA	1847.0	2207.2	2386.7	2269.2	2177.5	- ALAI
- CACM	188.5	218.5	232.8	282.0	271.2	- MCC
- Caribbean	812.9	443.8	417.4	352.5	323.9	- Caraïbes
- Rest of America	1.0	2.3	10.3	7.0	7.8	- Autre d'Amérique
Asia excluding former USSR	15526.0	15602.6	17039.1	16275.2	17095.8	Asie ancienne URSS exclus
- Middle East	1961.1	1851.2	1890.9	1774.6	2194.0	- Moyen-Orient
Asia former USSR	4.0	9.5	26.2	24.3	32.7	Asie ancienne URSS
Europe excluding former USSR	9483.9	9377.5	8764.2	9014.9	9790.9	Europe ancienne URSS exclus
- European Union	8246.7	8072.7	7435.3	7589.5	8327.4	- Union Européenne
- Eastern Europe	857.6	935.7	997.8	1109.9	1155.5	- Europe de l'Est
- Rest of Europe	379.5	369.1	331.0	315.5	308.0	- Autre de l'Europe
Europe former USSR	206.7	242.3	251.0	267.4	307.9	Europe ancienne URSS
Oceania	89.5	99.2	85.5	72.7	63.0	Océanie
China	4546.6	4083.3	4295.4	3930.5	4609.5	Chine
China, Hong Kong SAR	3124.7	3309.0	3575.4	3305.1	3300.2	Chine - RAS de Hong-Kong
United States	2429.7	2664.4	2804.2	2205.7	1920.8	Etats-Unis d'Amérique
Turkey	1831.7	1698.4	1769.6	1652.2	2005.4	Turquie
Mexico	1406.9	1700.3	1736.9	1647.0	1565.8	Mexique
Italy-San Marino-Holy See	1633.2	1506.5	1476.3	1552.4	1672.4	Italie-Saint-Marin-Saint-Siège
India	822.6	973.2	1087.7	1261.3	1508.2	Inde
France-Monaco	1086.4	1146.3	1025.2	1027.4	1180.1	France-Monaco
Germany	952.2	939.8	893.2	1006.8	1102.3	Allemagne
Portugal	791.9	785.0	759.0	748.9	852.5	Portugal
Thailand	720.2	711.4	762.8	714.0	e754.1	Thaïlande
Indonesia	383.5	653.7	740.3	796.5	678.8	Indonésie
Korea, Republic of	622.4	677.7	723.4	596.1	519.2	République de Corée
United Kingdom	695.1	616.7	550.5	545.8	539.0	Royaume-Uni
Belgium	-	707.0	679.4	691.4	e775.8	Belgique
Bangladesh	452.9	e350.9	e563.6	668.9	e537.5	Bangladesh
Pakistan	453.7	492.8	527.2	537.8	520.8	Pakistan
Greece	625.4	566.9	439.4	381.0	e381.4	Grèce
Sri Lanka	e444.8	419.8	e510.5	491.0	465.4	Sri Lanka
Netherlands	483.3	496.3	424.4	420.8	466.9	Pays-Bas
Austria	494.3	461.2	412.1	410.0	437.2	Autriche
Morocco	320.6	380.3	407.6	409.6	e445.6	Maroc
Singapore	362.7	392.2	451.4	403.7	353.3	Singapour
Spain	272.5	325.3	304.5	324.7	435.9	Espagne
Mauritius	336.1	315.3	331.2	305.8	369.9	Maurice
Philippines	370.4	329.3	363.8	335.7	142.5	Philippines
Denmark	281.3	319.2	292.9	304.8	291.9	Danemark
Tunisia	283.4	268.6	286.2	313.2	e325.8	Tunisie
Peru	214.6	275.8	334.9	304.2	318.9	Pérou
Hungary	287.0	300.9	288.9	295.9	260.6	Hongrie

(Value as percentages of World total) **(Valeur en pourcentage du total mondial)**

Regions of the world	1993	1994	1995	1996	1997	1998	1999	2000	2001	2002	Régions du monde
World	100.0	100.0	100.0	100.0	100.0	100.0	100.0	100.0	100.0	100.0	Monde
Africa	2.7	3.0	3.0	3.0	2.6	3.5	3.5	3.6	4.0	4.2	Afrique
Americas	10.7	11.5	12.6	13.3	14.5	17.2	17.9	18.3	16.7	14.8	Amériques
- Northern America	6.8	6.9	7.2	7.7	8.1	8.3	9.0	9.2	7.7	6.6	- Amérique du Nord
- LAIA	2.8	3.1	3.9	4.6	5.1	5.8	6.8	7.1	7.0	6.5	- ALAI
- CACM	0.1	0.2	0.1	0.2	0.6	0.6	0.7	0.7	0.9	0.8	- MCC
- Caribbean	1.0	1.2	1.3	0.8	0.7	2.5	1.4	1.2	1.1	1.0	- Caraïbes
- Rest of America	0.0	0.0	0.0	0.0	0.0	0.0	0.0	0.0	0.0	0.0	- Autre d'Amérique
Asia excluding former USSR	53.8	52.7	51.5	50.6	51.1	48.7	48.4	50.8	50.3	50.7	Asie ancienne URSS exclus
- Middle East	6.6	6.1	6.2	5.7	5.8	6.1	5.7	5.6	5.5	6.5	- Moyen-Orient
Asia former USSR	0.0	0.0	0.0	0.0	0.0	0.0	0.0	0.1	0.1	0.1	Asie ancienne URSS
Europe excluding former USSR	32.3	32.3	31.9	32.1	30.8	29.7	29.1	26.1	27.9	29.1	Europe ancienne URSS exclus
- European Union	28.6	28.3	28.1	28.3	27.3	25.8	25.0	22.2	23.5	24.7	- Union Européenne
- Eastern Europe	1.8	2.1	2.2	2.4	2.2	2.7	2.9	3.0	3.4	3.4	- Europe de l'Est
- Rest of Europe	1.9	1.8	1.6	1.4	1.2	1.2	1.1	1.0	1.0	0.9	- Autre de l'Europe
Europe former USSR	0.3	0.3	0.4	0.6	0.6	0.6	0.8	0.7	0.8	0.9	Europe ancienne URSS
Oceania	0.3	0.3	0.6	0.4	0.3	0.3	0.3	0.3	0.2	0.2	Océanie

847 Clothing accessories, of textile fabrics, nes

TRADE BY COMMODITY (Value in million US dollars) COMMERCE PAR PRODUIT (Valeur en millions de dollars EU)

Imports by principal countries or areas **Importations selon les principaux pays ou zones**

Country or area	1998	1999	2000	2001	2002	Pays ou zone
World	8292.8	8476.6	9135.4	9053.0	9601.6	Monde
Africa	58.7	50.4	63.9	72.5	73.9	Afrique
Americas	2019.5	2096.6	2458.4	2452.0	2583.9	Amériques
- Northern America	1540.1	1648.9	1931.0	1921.6	2069.9	- Amérique du Nord
- LAIA	402.3	321.9	369.5	372.8	348.6	- ALAI
- CACM	9.6	21.3	40.7	60.2	65.3	- MCC
- Caribbean	64.2	101.5	114.6	95.2	97.5	- Caraïbes
- Rest of America	3.3	3.0	2.6	2.2	2.6	- Autre d'Amérique
Asia excluding former USSR	2346.4	2468.7	2854.1	2813.6	2870.4	Asie ancienne URSS exclus
- Middle East	124.1	117.9	136.6	148.7	176.2	- Moyen-Orient
Asia former USSR	8.4	7.2	8.4	7.0	5.0	Asie ancienne URSS
Europe excluding former USSR	3705.5	3716.1	3593.4	3560.7	3887.8	Europe ancienne URSS exclus
- European Union	3241.8	3263.8	3133.2	3072.6	3313.9	- Union Européenne
- Eastern Europe	195.9	197.1	202.2	237.5	300.0	- Europe de l'Est
- Rest of Europe	267.8	255.2	258.1	250.7	273.8	- Autre de l'Europe
Europe former USSR	61.5	43.3	51.9	60.5	77.1	Europe ancienne URSS
Oceania	92.8	94.2	105.3	86.7	103.3	Océanie
United States	1380.2	1499.8	1754.8	1748.4	1890.6	Etats-Unis d'Amérique
Japan	803.3	879.5	1161.1	1068.2	1015.3	Japon
Germany	916.1	889.7	774.8	736.8	752.8	Allemagne
China, Hong Kong SAR	580.7	646.0	725.9	748.2	732.3	Chine - RAS de Hong-Kong
France-Monaco	542.0	537.6	552.8	533.3	572.4	France-Monaco
United Kingdom	485.1	512.4	532.7	533.9	606.5	Royaume-Uni
Viet Nam	460.3	442.5	435.3	451.8	549.7	Viet Nam
Mexico	325.1	253.0	294.1	297.5	285.9	Mexique
Netherlands	215.3	225.5	219.2	198.0	221.4	Pays-Bas
Italy-San Marino-Holy See	168.8	186.3	203.9	202.2	241.9	Italie-Saint-Marin-Saint-Siège
Spain	165.2	197.6	190.5	201.4	213.4	Espagne
Canada	159.3	148.5	175.4	172.1	178.1	Canada
Belgium	–	213.7	194.4	197.7	e216.8	Belgique
Switzerland-Liechtenstein	154.3	149.5	150.0	140.7	145.1	Suisse-Liechtenstein
Austria	135.2	134.6	116.5	109.8	113.7	Autriche
China	127.3	120.8	84.6	77.3	77.6	Chine
Sweden	102.0	77.0	73.4	87.4	96.8	Suède
Denmark	93.0	91.7	83.5	84.0	80.6	Danemark
Australia	76.3	77.3	88.2	70.4	78.8	Australie
Dominican Republic	e44.9	e85.4	e96.2	e79.0	e83.6	République dominicaine
Romania	39.8	55.0	63.2	85.7	116.3	Roumanie
Norway	71.2	66.7	63.2	60.1	72.2	Norvège
Korea, Republic of	29.6	49.1	75.3	82.4	92.8	République de Corée
United Arab Emirates	51.4	53.9	69.6	75.1	e77.1	Emirates arabes unis
Singapore	57.8	68.4	59.9	59.9	65.6	Singapour
Portugal	64.7	65.1	58.9	55.1	56.8	Portugal
Ireland	53.3	47.3	48.4	47.3	47.8	Irlande
Czech Republic	56.2	48.8	42.7	46.1	47.8	République tchèque
Finland	50.7	45.2	46.5	47.2	50.8	Finlande
Belgium-Luxembourg	219.2	–	–	–	–	Belgique-Luxembourg

(Value as percentages of World total) **(Valeur en pourcentage du total mondial)**

Regions of the world	1993	1994	1995	1996	1997	1998	1999	2000	2001	2002	Régions du monde
World	100.0	100.0	100.0	100.0	100.0	100.0	100.0	100.0	100.0	100.0	Monde
Africa	1.3	1.5	1.1	0.9	0.7	0.7	0.6	0.7	0.8	0.8	Afrique
Americas	19.1	19.4	19.5	19.7	24.6	24.4	24.7	26.9	27.1	26.9	Amériques
- Northern America	16.7	16.7	16.3	16.2	18.6	18.6	19.5	21.1	21.2	21.6	- Amérique du Nord
- LAIA	1.8	2.1	2.7	2.9	5.2	4.9	3.8	4.0	4.1	3.6	- ALAI
- CACM	0.1	0.2	0.2	0.1	0.1	0.1	0.3	0.4	0.7	0.7	- MCC
- Caribbean	0.4	0.3	0.4	0.5	0.7	0.8	1.2	1.3	1.1	1.0	- Caraïbes
- Rest of America	0.1	0.0	0.0	0.0	0.0	0.0	0.0	0.0	0.0	0.0	- Autre d'Amérique
Asia excluding former USSR	26.9	28.4	28.2	27.6	25.6	28.3	29.1	31.2	31.1	29.9	Asie ancienne URSS exclus
- Middle East	2.8	2.4	2.2	1.6	1.7	1.5	1.4	1.5	1.6	1.8	- Moyen-Orient
Asia former USSR	0.1	0.2	0.1	0.1	0.1	0.1	0.1	0.1	0.1	0.1	Asie ancienne URSS
Europe excluding former USSR	50.4	48.4	48.8	49.2	46.6	44.7	43.8	39.3	39.3	40.5	Europe ancienne URSS exclus
- European Union	45.0	43.4	42.9	43.4	41.2	39.1	38.5	34.3	33.9	34.5	- Union Européenne
- Eastern Europe	1.5	1.4	2.3	2.3	2.2	2.4	2.3	2.2	2.6	3.1	- Europe de l'Est
- Rest of Europe	3.8	3.6	3.7	3.6	3.3	3.2	3.0	2.8	2.8	2.9	- Autre de l'Europe
Europe former USSR	1.0	0.8	0.9	0.9	1.1	0.7	0.5	0.6	0.7	0.8	Europe ancienne URSS
Oceania	1.2	1.3	1.3	1.5	1.3	1.1	1.1	1.2	1.0	1.1	Océanie

TRADE BY COMMODITY (Value in million US dollars)
Exports by principal countries or areas

COMMERCE PAR PRODUIT (Valeur en millions de dollars EU)
Exportations selon les principaux pays ou zones

Country or area	1998	1999	2000	2001	2002	Pays ou zone
World	8338.3	8346.8	9159.5	9083.4	9339.5	Monde
Africa	40.5	37.9	43.0	51.4	63.2	Afrique
Americas	819.9	980.1	1152.2	1040.6	955.8	Amériques
- Northern America	589.0	745.7	861.3	751.8	638.2	- Amérique du Nord
- LAIA	137.4	168.2	218.0	221.8	247.0	- ALAI
- CACM	40.7	42.3	45.9	48.1	50.8	- MCC
- Caribbean	49.9	21.8	25.1	16.3	17.7	- Caraïbes
- Rest of America	2.9	2.2	2.0	2.7	2.2	- Autre d'Amérique
Asia excluding former USSR	4097.6	4149.0	4973.8	4966.2	5205.3	Asie ancienne URSS exclus
- Middle East	295.9	294.5	386.9	501.6	488.9	- Moyen-Orient
Asia former USSR	8.9	4.1	6.6	7.1	2.8	Asie ancienne URSS
Europe excluding former USSR	3309.4	3129.5	2931.8	2963.2	3030.6	Europe ancienne URSS exclus
- European Union	3038.7	2854.2	2657.7	2666.6	2711.1	- Union Européenne
- Eastern Europe	160.8	168.2	175.5	188.3	205.0	- Europe de l'Est
- Rest of Europe	109.9	107.1	98.7	108.3	114.5	- Autre de l'Europe
Europe former USSR	24.8	23.3	31.8	32.0	37.0	Europe ancienne URSS
Oceania	37.2	23.0	20.3	22.9	44.8	Océanie
China	1380.1	1143.4	1524.2	1535.4	1822.8	Chine
Italy-San Marino-Holy See	1378.3	1211.0	1115.6	1092.3	1043.2	Italie-Saint-Marin-Saint-Siège
China, Hong Kong SAR	799.8	876.1	996.2	1026.8	914.4	Chine - RAS de Hong-Kong
United States	495.4	628.6	746.7	642.2	516.7	Etats-Unis d'Amérique
Korea, Republic of	520.6	575.8	648.7	596.2	598.5	République de Corée
Germany	375.9	378.8	335.6	353.3	359.1	Allemagne
Turkey	276.1	273.4	286.5	329.3	394.8	Turquie
United Kingdom	313.2	273.5	284.5	280.9	273.8	Royaume-Uni
France-Monaco	299.9	283.9	261.7	254.5	271.1	France-Monaco
India	144.9	239.9	300.4	209.0	230.2	Inde
Pakistan	116.3	121.7	142.4	183.3	269.2	Pakistan
Mexico	108.0	138.8	182.1	185.5	212.5	Mexique
Portugal	160.3	165.9	147.0	153.7	164.5	Portugal
Belgium	–	188.1	180.8	197.8	e221.9	Belgique
Netherlands	101.1	109.8	111.0	114.1	137.9	Pays-Bas
Canada	93.6	117.1	114.6	109.6	121.5	Canada
Sri Lanka	e91.9	86.8	e105.5	90.1	84.3	Sri Lanka
Malaysia	71.9	82.7	93.7	86.6	e91.8	Malaisie
Thailand	75.2	81.9	85.6	79.3	e83.7	Thaïlande
Viet Nam	57.4	100.6	76.8	79.8	88.7	Viet Nam
Indonesia	29.2	74.1	106.1	98.6	89.3	Indonésie
Switzerland-Liechtenstein	70.9	71.1	63.5	69.8	68.6	Suisse-Liechtenstein
Spain	55.8	56.6	59.5	65.7	80.1	Espagne
Japan	67.9	61.7	63.3	47.1	45.5	Japon
Czech Republic	58.9	58.5	52.6	54.6	49.9	République tchèque
Israel	67.1	63.9	45.4	47.8	46.9	Israël
Austria	56.5	65.0	50.0	46.5	47.6	Autriche
Philippines	56.8	49.5	48.2	58.7	23.8	Philippines
Romania	19.4	28.7	38.9	44.1	55.2	Roumanie
Denmark	34.0	37.9	35.0	35.9	39.7	Danemark

(Value as percentages of World total) **(Valeur en pourcentage du total mondial)**

Regions of the world	1993	1994	1995	1996	1997	1998	1999	2000	2001	2002	Régions du monde
World	100.0	100.0	100.0	100.0	100.0	100.0	100.0	100.0	100.0	100.0	Monde
Africa	0.9	0.6	0.7	0.7	0.6	0.5	0.5	0.5	0.6	0.7	Afrique
Americas	4.7	5.6	7.1	6.8	8.3	9.8	11.7	12.6	11.5	10.2	Amériques
- Northern America	3.8	4.4	5.6	5.6	6.2	7.1	8.9	9.4	8.3	6.8	- Amérique du Nord
- LAIA	0.7	0.9	1.1	1.1	1.7	1.6	2.0	2.4	2.4	2.6	- ALAI
- CACM	0.1	0.1	0.1	0.1	0.4	0.5	0.5	0.5	0.5	0.5	- MCC
- Caribbean	0.1	0.1	0.2	0.1	0.1	0.6	0.3	0.3	0.2	0.2	- Caraïbes
- Rest of America	0.0	0.0	0.0	0.0	0.0	0.0	0.0	0.0	0.0	0.0	- Autre d'Amérique
Asia excluding former USSR	50.4	47.6	46.5	45.8	50.7	49.1	49.7	54.3	54.7	55.7	Asie ancienne URSS exclus
- Middle East	2.7	3.3	3.7	3.5	3.8	3.5	3.5	4.2	5.5	5.2	- Moyen-Orient
Asia former USSR	0.0	0.3	0.1	0.2	0.1	0.1	0.0	0.1	0.1	0.0	Asie ancienne URSS
Europe excluding former USSR	43.6	45.5	45.1	45.9	39.7	39.7	37.5	32.0	32.6	32.4	Europe ancienne URSS exclus
- European Union	40.5	42.6	41.8	43.0	36.9	36.4	34.2	29.0	29.4	29.0	- Union Européenne
- Eastern Europe	1.5	1.3	1.9	1.6	1.6	1.9	2.0	1.9	2.1	2.2	- Europe de l'Est
- Rest of Europe	1.7	1.6	1.4	1.3	1.2	1.3	1.3	1.1	1.2	1.2	- Autre de l'Europe
Europe former USSR	0.3	0.3	0.4	0.4	0.3	0.3	0.3	0.3	0.4	0.4	Europe ancienne URSS
Oceania	0.1	0.2	0.2	0.2	0.3	0.4	0.3	0.2	0.3	0.5	Océanie

848 Articles of apparel, clothing accessories, non-textile, headgear

TRADE BY COMMODITY (Value in million US dollars)
Imports by principal countries or areas

COMMERCE PAR PRODUIT (Valeur en millions de dollars EU)
Importations selon les principaux pays ou zones

Country or area	1998	1999	2000	2001	2002	Pays ou zone
World	13308.9	12925.9	15056.0	15781.4	15541.9	Monde
Africa	106.2	101.2	103.5	102.2	129.1	Afrique
Americas	5023.1	5101.5	6422.0	6728.0	6401.4	Amériques
- Northern America	4654.2	4754.5	6032.6	6236.6	6024.8	- Amérique du Nord
- LAIA	309.6	282.7	327.5	415.8	303.5	- ALAI
- CACM	16.3	17.5	17.7	20.5	24.0	- MCC
- Caribbean	35.1	38.8	37.5	48.6	42.0	- Caraïbes
- Rest of America	7.9	7.9	6.7	6.6	7.1	- Autre d'Amérique
Asia excluding former USSR	2293.1	2197.5	2781.8	2876.0	2731.2	Asie ancienne URSS exclus
- Middle East	191.7	171.1	175.3	206.1	216.3	- Moyen-Orient
Asia former USSR	14.8	18.5	16.2	11.4	8.2	Asie ancienne URSS
Europe excluding former USSR	5590.4	5228.5	5425.3	5724.8	5911.8	Europe ancienne URSS exclus
- European Union	5023.0	4712.5	4880.5	5122.8	5243.7	- Union Européenne
- Eastern Europe	190.8	178.5	200.8	234.0	261.6	- Europe de l'Est
- Rest of Europe	376.6	337.5	344.0	368.1	406.5	- Autre de l'Europe
Europe former USSR	98.0	81.5	87.9	144.7	137.2	Europe ancienne URSS
Oceania	183.2	197.3	219.3	194.3	223.1	Océanie
United States	4311.0	4405.8	5584.5	5772.3	5565.5	Etats-Unis d'Amérique
Germany	1497.3	1287.5	1165.7	1163.3	1134.6	Allemagne
China, Hong Kong SAR	917.7	891.8	1077.0	1015.6	947.3	Chine - RAS de Hong-Kong
Japan	646.9	801.4	1125.3	1198.4	1069.4	Japon
United Kingdom	665.2	647.9	818.7	815.3	836.1	Royaume-Uni
France-Monaco	645.2	681.7	717.9	743.8	768.5	France-Monaco
Italy-San Marino-Holy See	502.1	465.9	508.3	532.4	593.6	Italie-Saint-Marin-Saint-Siège
Canada	341.1	346.5	445.4	462.5	457.2	Canada
Spain	281.0	305.3	362.6	408.0	393.6	Espagne
Netherlands	324.9	289.1	283.6	302.6	282.8	Pays-Bas
Belgium	–	301.3	279.0	345.4	e378.8	Belgique
Switzerland-Liechtenstein	205.7	192.4	202.0	220.2	235.2	Suisse-Liechtenstein
Austria	225.9	210.4	182.4	196.8	218.4	Autriche
Australia	161.1	164.6	184.6	159.0	183.2	Australie
Mexico	125.1	114.0	154.5	232.8	146.2	Mexique
Sweden	156.3	135.7	153.9	152.9	167.7	Suède
Denmark	131.6	124.1	136.6	145.8	147.5	Danemark
Norway	97.9	83.6	82.6	83.1	100.0	Norvège
Greece	99.1	77.7	70.8	84.2	e93.1	Grèce
Korea, Republic of	37.3	52.3	78.3	97.1	133.3	République de Corée
Saudi Arabia	77.1	73.7	67.7	76.5	e79.2	Arabie saoudite
Finland	76.1	66.4	68.6	78.4	79.4	Finlande
Portugal	63.3	62.9	71.6	86.5	80.6	Portugal
Russian Federation	53.2	40.8	51.6	97.1	86.8	Fédération de Russie
Singapore	70.9	65.8	65.2	65.8	60.0	Singapour
Belgium-Luxembourg	308.5	–	–	–	–	Belgique-Luxembourg
Viet Nam	225.7	15.1	19.0	19.7	24.0	Viet Nam
Poland	58.3	49.4	58.3	58.3	67.7	Pologne
Hungary	48.1	49.8	54.3	64.2	64.4	Hongrie
China	41.8	43.8	57.0	60.5	68.2	Chine

(Value as percentages of World total) **(Valeur en pourcentage du total mondial)**

Regions of the world	1993	1994	1995	1996	1997	1998	1999	2000	2001	2002	Régions du monde
World	100.0	100.0	100.0	100.0	100.0	100.0	100.0	100.0	100.0	100.0	Monde
Africa	0.7	0.7	0.7	0.7	0.7	0.8	0.8	0.7	0.6	0.8	Afrique
Americas	35.2	35.7	33.5	33.9	35.5	37.7	39.5	42.7	42.6	41.2	Amériques
- Northern America	33.3	33.7	31.6	31.7	32.9	35.0	36.8	40.1	39.5	38.8	- Amérique du Nord
- LAIA	1.5	1.7	1.5	1.8	2.1	2.3	2.2	2.2	2.6	2.0	- ALAI
- CACM	0.1	0.1	0.1	0.1	0.1	0.1	0.1	0.1	0.1	0.2	- MCC
- Caribbean	0.2	0.2	0.3	0.3	0.3	0.3	0.3	0.2	0.3	0.3	- Caraïbes
- Rest of America	0.0	0.0	0.1	0.1	0.1	0.1	0.1	0.0	0.0	0.0	- Autre d'Amérique
Asia excluding former USSR	20.8	21.5	22.2	21.5	18.6	17.2	17.0	18.5	18.2	17.6	Asie ancienne URSS exclus
- Middle East	1.3	1.1	1.4	1.3	1.6	1.4	1.3	1.2	1.3	1.4	- Moyen-Orient
Asia former USSR	0.1	0.2	0.1	0.2	0.0	0.1	0.1	0.1	0.1	0.1	Asie ancienne URSS
Europe excluding former USSR	37.8	39.9	41.1	41.6	42.6	42.0	40.4	36.0	36.3	38.0	Europe ancienne URSS exclus
- European Union	34.5	36.2	36.9	37.5	38.5	37.7	36.5	32.4	32.5	33.7	- Union Européenne
- Eastern Europe	0.6	0.7	1.0	1.1	1.4	1.4	1.4	1.3	1.5	1.7	- Europe de l'Est
- Rest of Europe	2.7	3.0	3.1	2.9	2.8	2.8	2.6	2.3	2.3	2.6	- Autre de l'Europe
Europe former USSR	4.2	0.6	0.9	0.7	1.0	0.7	0.6	0.6	0.9	0.9	Europe ancienne URSS
Oceania	1.2	1.3	1.5	1.5	1.6	1.4	1.5	1.5	1.2	1.4	Océanie

TRADE BY COMMODITY (Value in million US dollars)
Exports by principal countries or areas

COMMERCE PAR PRODUIT (Valeur en millions de dollars EU)
Exportations selon les principaux pays ou zones

Country or area	1998	1999	2000	2001	2002	Pays ou zone
World	12784.6	12165.4	14064.1	14608.8	14806.2	Monde
Africa	50.1	45.2	52.7	56.2	63.6	Afrique
Americas	1034.3	975.9	1040.2	1078.7	925.6	Amériques
- Northern America	647.9	646.5	712.9	770.1	687.4	- Amérique du Nord
- LAIA	321.5	298.6	293.2	280.8	222.0	- ALAI
- CACM	16.2	17.7	18.3	14.6	4.8	- MCC
- Caribbean	46.3	11.8	14.7	12.1	9.9	- Caraïbes
- Rest of America	2.4	1.4	1.2	1.2	1.5	- Autre d'Amérique
Asia excluding former USSR	8338.6	7954.7	9787.8	9901.5	9999.0	Asie ancienne URSS exclus
- Middle East	377.8	330.6	362.6	403.8	416.7	- Moyen-Orient
Asia former USSR	1.1	0.9	2.7	1.6	0.8	Asie ancienne URSS
Europe excluding former USSR	3283.4	3090.3	3075.9	3461.0	3713.0	Europe ancienne URSS exclus
- European Union	2986.8	2834.7	2796.6	3116.7	3365.8	- Union Européenne
- Eastern Europe	212.7	183.2	198.0	249.9	253.6	- Europe de l'Est
- Rest of Europe	83.9	72.5	81.3	94.5	93.7	- Autre de l'Europe
Europe former USSR	32.2	51.7	54.4	53.2	48.6	Europe ancienne URSS
Oceania	44.7	46.6	50.3	56.5	55.6	Océanie
China	3011.2	2819.7	3857.8	4315.8	4818.7	Chine
China, Hong Kong SAR	1288.6	1256.8	1547.1	1493.7	1394.3	Chine - RAS de Hong-Kong
Malaysia	1094.4	1005.9	924.2	877.0	e929.4	Malaisie
Italy-San Marino-Holy See	862.6	798.4	905.4	1038.8	1074.3	Italie-Saint-Marin-Saint-Siège
United States	480.0	471.0	506.1	531.6	435.4	Etats-Unis d'Amérique
Germany	495.0	439.5	400.9	476.0	500.1	Allemagne
Thailand	417.3	387.2	456.4	450.9	e476.2	Thaïlande
India	432.8	407.6	529.2	433.4	336.3	Inde
Pakistan	432.1	388.3	468.2	465.0	373.4	Pakistan
Korea, Republic of	332.9	393.8	488.0	409.6	318.6	République de Corée
Turkey	363.4	315.3	350.5	380.6	396.3	Turquie
France-Monaco	270.9	287.0	296.7	302.1	364.7	France-Monaco
Belgium	-	276.2	247.8	296.9	e333.1	Belgique
United Kingdom	232.0	256.5	227.1	196.6	223.6	Royaume-Uni
Greece	253.5	199.1	178.2	205.8	e206.0	Grèce
Canada	167.2	174.7	206.3	237.9	251.4	Canada
Indonesia	163.3	179.8	244.8	253.0	195.4	Indonésie
Mexico	201.3	213.9	207.7	179.0	128.5	Mexique
Netherlands	171.2	167.8	170.9	178.5	175.5	Pays-Bas
Spain	102.5	119.0	108.4	135.1	184.7	Espagne
Japan	108.7	125.3	145.1	111.8	96.7	Japon
Sri Lanka	e100.2	94.6	e115.0	106.8	107.2	Sri Lanka
Austria	104.1	96.5	68.9	81.3	87.7	Autriche
Sweden	78.3	79.4	80.1	83.0	95.0	Suède
Philippines	86.4	83.7	111.3	92.0	39.4	Philippines
Hungary	69.1	65.7	72.5	85.2	79.9	Hongrie
Denmark	81.1	62.9	64.9	73.9	69.8	Danemark
Czech Republic	58.6	48.0	50.7	65.3	66.5	République tchèque
Belgium-Luxembourg	255.7	-	-	-	-	Belgique-Luxembourg
Poland	45.0	38.7	40.3	45.1	47.0	Pologne

(Value as percentages of World total) **(Valeur en pourcentage du total mondial)**

Regions of the world	1993	1994	1995	1996	1997	1998	1999	2000	2001	2002	Régions du monde
World	100.0	100.0	100.0	100.0	100.0	100.0	100.0	100.0	100.0	100.0	Monde
Africa	0.4	0.4	0.4	0.4	0.3	0.4	0.4	0.4	0.4	0.4	Afrique
Americas	8.5	8.9	8.5	8.6	8.5	8.1	8.0	7.4	7.4	6.3	Amériques
- Northern America	4.9	5.3	5.2	5.3	5.4	5.1	5.3	5.1	5.3	4.6	- Amérique du Nord
- LAIA	3.0	3.2	3.1	3.1	2.9	2.5	2.5	2.1	1.9	1.5	- ALAI
- CACM	0.0	0.1	0.0	0.1	0.1	0.1	0.1	0.1	0.1	0.0	- MCC
- Caribbean	0.5	0.3	0.1	0.0	0.0	0.4	0.1	0.1	0.1	0.1	- Caraïbes
- Rest of America	0.0	0.0	0.0	0.0	0.0	0.0	0.0	0.0	0.0	0.0	- Autre d'Amérique
Asia excluding former USSR	70.3	67.6	68.1	65.8	65.8	65.2	65.4	69.6	67.8	67.5	Asie ancienne URSS exclus
- Middle East	4.2	4.1	3.8	2.8	3.2	3.0	2.7	2.6	2.8	2.8	- Moyen-Orient
Asia former USSR	0.0	0.0	0.0	0.0	0.0	0.0	0.0	0.0	0.0	0.0	Asie ancienne URSS
Europe excluding former USSR	20.2	22.3	22.2	24.4	24.6	25.7	25.4	21.9	23.7	25.1	Europe ancienne URSS exclus
- European Union	18.5	20.3	20.3	22.4	22.4	23.4	23.3	19.9	21.3	22.7	- Union Européenne
- Eastern Europe	0.9	1.1	1.2	1.3	1.6	1.7	1.5	1.4	1.7	1.7	- Europe de l'Est
- Rest of Europe	0.7	0.9	0.7	0.6	0.6	0.7	0.6	0.6	0.6	0.6	- Autre de l'Europe
Europe former USSR	0.2	0.2	0.2	0.3	0.3	0.3	0.4	0.4	0.4	0.3	Europe ancienne URSS
Oceania	0.5	0.6	0.6	0.5	0.4	0.3	0.4	0.4	0.4	0.4	Océanie

851 Footwear

TRADE BY COMMODITY (Value in million US dollars)
Imports by principal countries or areas

COMMERCE PAR PRODUIT (Valeur en millions de dollars EU)
Importations selon les principaux pays ou zones

Country or area	1998	1999	2000	2001	2002	Pays ou zone
World	44797.5	45292.3	46719.9	48186.0	50033.0	Monde
Africa	447.4	475.0	556.0	552.8	598.0	Afrique
Americas	15900.3	16213.5	17391.0	17976.9	18166.4	Amériques
- Northern America	14803.4	15255.6	16261.3	16625.9	16871.7	- Amérique du Nord
- LAIA	773.9	650.1	804.8	981.3	898.8	- ALAI
- CACM	102.8	95.4	112.7	143.1	168.5	- MCC
- Caribbean	160.1	151.3	152.9	172.6	159.0	- Caraïbes
- Rest of America	60.1	61.0	59.3	54.0	68.3	- Autre d'Amérique
Asia excluding former USSR	9566.4	9376.2	10112.5	9793.2	9789.1	Asie ancienne URSS exclus
- Middle East	771.3	690.9	732.9	787.5	778.7	- Moyen-Orient
Asia former USSR	72.5	66.7	69.5	60.6	60.7	Asie ancienne URSS
Europe excluding former USSR	17990.0	18404.3	17732.9	18847.0	20357.1	Europe ancienne URSS exclus
- European Union	16126.1	16667.9	16100.9	17140.5	18407.4	- Union Européenne
- Eastern Europe	591.6	510.3	509.5	563.1	724.6	- Europe de l'Est
- Rest of Europe	1272.3	1226.2	1122.4	1143.4	1225.1	- Autre de l'Europe
Europe former USSR	258.1	170.0	214.7	371.1	381.5	Europe ancienne URSS
Oceania	562.8	586.7	643.4	584.6	680.2	Océanie
United States	13876.5	14302.5	15290.8	15638.3	15838.7	Etats-Unis d'Amérique
China, Hong Kong SAR	5447.2	4973.5	5318.2	4863.1	4766.8	Chine - RAS de Hong-Kong
Germany	4158.7	4101.6	3636.1	3808.2	3696.7	Allemagne
United Kingdom	2907.7	3112.4	2858.5	3118.7	3410.8	Royaume-Uni
France-Monaco	2574.6	2477.7	2639.0	2712.6	3121.6	France-Monaco
Japan	2265.3	2582.5	2776.1	2819.0	2719.6	Japon
Italy-San Marino-Holy See	1420.5	1561.2	1667.2	1877.7	2123.1	Italie-Saint-Marin-Saint-Siège
Netherlands	1018.9	1182.7	1252.0	1329.2	1268.9	Pays-Bas
Belgium	–	1221.4	1165.0	1347.9	e1478.2	Belgique
Canada	915.8	941.0	966.5	982.6	1026.6	Canada
Spain	596.3	611.9	616.4	663.4	810.6	Espagne
Austria	658.8	663.0	591.3	645.7	671.0	Autriche
Switzerland-Liechtenstein	649.4	637.5	605.9	664.3	668.4	Suisse-Liechtenstein
Australia	446.5	465.1	515.2	457.7	539.9	Australie
Denmark	434.7	439.2	417.0	408.1	457.8	Danemark
Sweden	401.9	381.6	375.2	350.0	398.7	Suède
Viet Nam	371.4	364.4	317.1	329.0	400.4	Viet Nam
Norway	275.5	268.1	241.6	232.0	274.4	Norvège
Greece	263.1	261.0	252.7	236.6	e261.6	Grèce
Ireland	250.9	247.8	253.0	239.1	255.1	Irlande
Belgium-Luxembourg	1091.7	–	–	–	–	Belgique-Luxembourg
Poland	227.9	191.0	180.5	196.9	275.5	Pologne
United Arab Emirates	194.2	203.5	212.4	227.8	e233.7	Emirates arabes unis
Singapore	172.0	201.0	250.4	223.6	221.2	Singapour
Portugal	179.9	199.2	198.0	211.5	243.8	Portugal
Saudi Arabia	214.7	180.4	178.0	189.0	e195.6	Arabie saoudite
Israel	160.6	158.5	182.8	187.4	175.8	Israël
Chile	169.7	142.2	173.1	179.7	182.7	Chili
Korea, Republic of	77.8	102.1	166.3	200.2	300.9	République de Corée
Czech Republic	149.7	138.3	143.2	163.1	195.4	République tchèque

(Value as percentages of World total) **(Valeur en pourcentage du total mondial)**

Regions of the world	1993	1994	1995	1996	1997	1998	1999	2000	2001	2002	Régions du monde
World	100.0	100.0	100.0	100.0	100.0	100.0	100.0	100.0	100.0	100.0	Monde
Africa	0.9	1.0	1.1	1.0	1.0	1.0	1.0	1.2	1.1	1.2	Afrique
Americas	34.3	33.7	32.5	31.6	33.5	35.5	35.8	37.2	37.3	36.3	Amériques
- Northern America	32.2	31.5	30.2	29.7	31.3	33.0	33.7	34.8	34.5	33.7	- Amérique du Nord
- LAIA	1.5	1.7	1.7	1.5	1.6	1.7	1.4	1.7	2.0	1.8	- ALAI
- CACM	0.1	0.1	0.2	0.2	0.2	0.2	0.2	0.2	0.3	0.3	- MCC
- Caribbean	0.3	0.3	0.3	0.2	0.3	0.4	0.3	0.3	0.4	0.3	- Caraïbes
- Rest of America	0.1	0.1	0.1	0.1	0.1	0.1	0.1	0.1	0.1	0.1	- Autre d'Amérique
Asia excluding former USSR	22.0	23.6	25.2	25.6	24.7	21.4	20.7	21.6	20.3	19.6	Asie ancienne URSS exclus
- Middle East	1.7	1.8	1.8	1.4	1.6	1.7	1.5	1.6	1.6	1.6	- Moyen-Orient
Asia former USSR	0.1	0.2	0.2	0.2	0.1	0.2	0.1	0.1	0.1	0.1	Asie ancienne URSS
Europe excluding former USSR	38.1	38.8	38.3	38.8	38.5	40.2	40.6	38.0	39.1	40.7	Europe ancienne URSS exclus
- European Union	34.0	34.8	34.0	34.8	34.6	36.0	36.8	34.5	35.6	36.8	- Union Européenne
- Eastern Europe	0.9	1.0	1.1	1.1	1.2	1.3	1.1	1.1	1.2	1.4	- Europe de l'Est
- Rest of Europe	3.2	3.0	3.2	2.9	2.7	2.8	2.7	2.4	2.4	2.4	- Autre de l'Europe
Europe former USSR	3.5	1.4	1.5	1.4	0.9	0.6	0.4	0.5	0.8	0.8	Europe ancienne URSS
Oceania	1.1	1.2	1.2	1.3	1.2	1.3	1.3	1.4	1.2	1.4	Océanie

TRADE BY COMMODITY (Value in million US dollars)
Exports by principal countries or areas

COMMERCE PAR PRODUIT (Valeur en millions de dollars EU)
Exportations selon les principaux pays ou zones

Country or area	1998	1999	2000	2001	2002	Pays ou zone
World	40968.3	40418.4	41630.0	42201.7	43474.5	Monde
Africa	312.7	317.0	347.9	391.2	424.1	Afrique
Americas	2627.3	2413.5	2724.8	2688.0	2689.0	Amériques
- Northern America	693.2	678.6	716.8	662.1	652.3	- Amérique du Nord
- LAIA	1805.1	1677.7	1951.6	1966.6	1987.3	- ALAI
- CACM	46.9	40.9	38.8	41.0	34.8	- MCC
- Caribbean	81.7	15.9	17.4	18.1	14.3	- Caraïbes
- Rest of America	0.4	0.3	0.2	0.2	0.3	- Autre d'Amérique
Asia excluding former USSR	19505.3	19832.7	21530.4	21002.0	21655.1	Asie ancienne URSS exclus
- Middle East	366.3	263.6	253.5	318.3	324.8	- Moyen-Orient
Asia former USSR	8.1	10.2	4.9	5.3	4.1	Asie ancienne URSS
Europe excluding former USSR	18176.1	17542.7	16743.5	17841.6	18462.7	Europe ancienne URSS exclus
- European Union	16577.9	15942.2	15097.3	15944.7	16437.8	- Union Européenne
- Eastern Europe	1147.0	1205.2	1252.1	1439.2	1604.8	- Europe de l'Est
- Rest of Europe	451.3	395.3	394.2	457.7	420.0	- Autre de l'Europe
Europe former USSR	272.9	229.0	218.1	211.8	182.3	Europe ancienne URSS
Oceania	65.9	73.4	60.3	61.6	57.1	Océanie
China	8054.9	8355.8	9466.6	9676.4	10680.6	Chine
Italy-San Marino-Holy See	6837.1	6372.0	6204.3	6529.6	6415.9	Italie-Saint-Marin-Saint-Siège
China, Hong Kong SAR	6323.8	5819.2	6134.1	5575.0	5466.3	Chine - RAS de Hong-Kong
Spain	2103.7	1918.3	1805.2	1895.5	2024.0	Espagne
Brazil	1330.5	1277.8	1554.8	1615.3	e1674.7	Brésil
Portugal	1605.2	1581.0	1395.1	1431.1	1417.4	Portugal
Viet Nam	1031.0	1387.1	1567.8	1630.2	1812.1	Viet Nam
Indonesia	1156.7	1541.1	1605.1	1474.1	1115.1	Indonésie
Belgium	–	1461.4	1367.1	1643.1	e1843.6	Belgique
Germany	1253.0	1221.4	1112.4	1186.2	1440.6	Allemagne
France-Monaco	929.6	937.2	836.8	828.2	931.9	France-Monaco
Thailand	844.5	771.3	780.2	784.5	e828.6	Thaïlande
United Kingdom	856.8	820.2	735.4	670.1	639.1	Royaume-Uni
Netherlands	601.5	659.1	746.4	875.5	742.6	Pays-Bas
Romania	371.4	429.2	507.2	643.1	754.8	Roumanie
United States	550.6	533.3	558.8	529.0	514.9	Etats-Unis d'Amérique
Austria	504.8	484.1	460.7	514.0	503.1	Autriche
Korea, Republic of	480.1	460.9	437.7	352.1	236.1	République de Corée
India	336.5	386.1	399.1	409.3	431.1	Inde
Mexico	357.2	327.3	329.4	285.1	254.8	Mexique
Belgium-Luxembourg	1428.2	–	–	–	–	Belgique-Luxembourg
Denmark	263.8	300.4	256.4	182.3	278.9	Danemark
Hungary	233.6	235.8	222.9	247.6	251.6	Hongrie
Poland	187.0	183.6	194.7	197.0	212.0	Pologne
Slovakia	146.7	141.1	160.8	175.6	222.5	Slovaquie
Tunisia	109.0	127.8	135.6	176.6	e183.7	Tunisie
Canada	142.5	145.3	157.9	133.0	137.3	Canada
Turkey	180.0	95.6	100.3	112.9	117.6	Turquie
Singapore	99.4	115.0	137.1	112.2	111.5	Singapour
Morocco	115.3	114.4	104.9	114.8	e124.9	Maroc

(Value as percentages of World total) **(Valeur en pourcentage du total mondial)**

Regions of the world	1993	1994	1995	1996	1997	1998	1999	2000	2001	2002	Régions du monde
World	100.0	100.0	100.0	100.0	100.0	100.0	100.0	100.0	100.0	100.0	Monde
Africa	0.6	0.6	0.6	0.6	0.6	0.8	0.8	0.8	0.9	1.0	Afrique
Americas	8.2	6.9	6.2	6.2	6.3	6.4	6.0	6.5	6.4	6.2	Amériques
- Northern America	1.7	1.9	1.7	1.6	1.6	1.7	1.7	1.7	1.6	1.5	- Amérique du Nord
- LAIA	6.3	4.9	4.3	4.5	4.6	4.4	4.2	4.7	4.7	4.6	- ALAI
- CACM	0.1	0.1	0.1	0.1	0.1	0.1	0.1	0.1	0.1	0.1	- MCC
- Caribbean	0.0	0.1	0.1	0.0	0.0	0.2	0.0	0.0	0.0	0.0	- Caraïbes
- Rest of America	0.0	0.0	0.0	0.0	0.0	0.0	0.0	0.0	0.0	0.0	- Autre d'Amérique
Asia excluding former USSR	53.1	51.2	51.3	49.7	50.8	47.6	49.1	51.7	49.8	49.8	Asie ancienne URSS exclus
- Middle East	0.5	0.7	0.7	0.8	0.9	0.9	0.7	0.6	0.8	0.7	- Moyen-Orient
Asia former USSR	0.0	0.0	0.0	0.0	0.0	0.0	0.0	0.0	0.0	0.0	Asie ancienne URSS
Europe excluding former USSR	37.7	40.8	41.4	42.6	41.3	44.4	43.4	40.2	42.3	42.5	Europe ancienne URSS exclus
- European Union	34.2	36.8	37.5	38.8	37.7	40.5	39.4	36.3	37.8	37.8	- Union Européenne
- Eastern Europe	2.0	2.3	2.5	2.6	2.5	2.8	3.0	3.0	3.4	3.7	- Europe de l'Est
- Rest of Europe	1.6	1.7	1.4	1.2	1.1	1.1	1.0	0.9	1.1	1.0	- Autre de l'Europe
Europe former USSR	0.3	0.4	0.4	0.7	0.7	0.7	0.6	0.5	0.5	0.4	Europe ancienne URSS
Oceania	0.1	0.2	0.2	0.2	0.2	0.2	0.2	0.1	0.1	0.1	Océanie

871 Optical instruments and apparatus

TRADE BY COMMODITY (Value in million US dollars)
Imports by principal countries or areas

COMMERCE PAR PRODUIT (Valeur en millions de dollars EU)
Importations selon les principaux pays ou zones

Country or area	1998	1999	2000	2001	2002	Pays ou zone
World	11085.6	14814.9	21110.9	19939.2	19048.4	Monde
Africa	115.9	85.8	98.9	74.1	67.2	Afrique
Americas	2812.9	4116.4	6638.7	4667.8	3116.2	Amériques
- Northern America	2473.6	3506.2	5795.8	3905.2	2347.5	- Amérique du Nord
- LAIA	312.6	583.0	824.2	732.6	747.6	- ALAI
- CACM	7.8	8.6	9.4	8.8	11.2	- MCC
- Caribbean	17.1	16.4	7.3	19.6	8.4	- Caraïbes
- Rest of America	1.8	2.3	1.9	1.7	1.4	- Autre d'Amérique
Asia excluding former USSR	4434.7	6453.1	8971.5	9621.7	11500.6	Asie ancienne URSS exclus
- Middle East	118.0	97.7	131.0	139.3	126.6	- Moyen-Orient
Asia former USSR	1.7	2.4	3.9	8.8	5.1	Asie ancienne URSS
Europe excluding former USSR	3549.2	3981.9	5192.1	5368.7	4170.9	Europe ancienne URSS exclus
- European Union	3142.4	3553.4	4681.3	4822.9	3679.1	- Union Européenne
- Eastern Europe	115.3	136.0	204.6	234.3	163.8	- Europe de l'Est
- Rest of Europe	291.5	292.4	306.3	311.4	328.0	- Autre de l'Europe
Europe former USSR	42.4	42.5	49.6	57.6	59.8	Europe ancienne URSS
Oceania	128.7	132.7	156.3	140.6	128.6	Océanie
United States	2057.4	2883.8	4766.8	3348.0	1976.2	Etats-Unis d'Amérique
China	461.6	712.6	1532.2	2631.5	5278.8	Chine
Japan	865.4	1441.1	2000.0	1666.8	1722.1	Japon
China, Hong Kong SAR	901.2	1184.9	1670.7	2077.5	1049.0	Chine - RAS de Hong-Kong
Korea, Republic of	529.8	1059.3	1482.0	1103.4	1375.2	République de Corée
Germany	843.4	882.2	1044.3	1244.3	994.6	Allemagne
United Kingdom	606.5	740.9	1218.4	998.7	676.7	Royaume-Uni
Canada	409.7	615.8	1012.8	556.9	370.4	Canada
France-Monaco	461.5	518.8	735.6	656.6	526.0	France-Monaco
Singapore	477.3	538.2	466.8	390.8	321.2	Singapour
Mexico	123.0	361.9	530.5	439.6	486.0	Mexique
Italy-San Marino-Holy See	238.5	310.7	449.6	563.8	350.3	Italie-Saint-Marin-Saint-Siège
Netherlands	281.3	311.2	417.0	394.4	320.4	Pays-Bas
Switzerland-Liechtenstein	187.9	206.6	234.1	245.9	249.0	Suisse-Liechtenstein
Spain	139.7	151.1	192.5	246.8	185.2	Espagne
Brazil	106.3	141.0	207.7	190.8	185.1	Brésil
Israel	101.6	120.6	148.2	140.7	134.9	Israël
Belgium	-	138.1	132.2	162.3	e178.0	Belgique
Sweden	113.6	114.7	123.2	156.5	98.9	Suède
Australia	105.7	109.4	132.4	119.6	107.2	Australie
Malaysia	71.4	63.2	126.0	141.5	e154.6	Malaisie
Austria	89.2	110.0	120.4	111.9	111.2	Autriche
Denmark	64.1	66.9	75.8	96.5	74.0	Danemark
Turkey	72.4	55.9	88.9	57.9	48.2	Turquie
Finland	49.3	82.9	48.3	67.6	41.7	Finlande
Norway	75.2	63.1	53.3	44.3	53.7	Norvège
Hungary	26.5	38.3	80.5	90.2	44.1	Hongrie
India	30.9	40.4	46.6	98.5	61.2	Inde
Portugal	34.9	52.1	58.5	63.9	54.7	Portugal
Thailand	29.9	36.6	63.1	63.7	e66.3	Thaïlande

(Value as percentages of World total) **(Valeur en pourcentage du total mondial)**

Regions of the world	1993	1994	1995	1996	1997	1998	1999	2000	2001	2002	Régions du monde
World	100.0	100.0	100.0	100.0	100.0	100.0	100.0	100.0	100.0	100.0	Monde
Africa	0.7	0.7	0.7	0.7	0.5	1.0	0.6	0.5	0.4	0.4	Afrique
Americas	21.1	21.7	21.1	20.8	20.7	25.4	27.8	31.4	23.4	16.4	Amériques
- Northern America	19.1	19.1	18.5	18.0	17.9	22.3	23.7	27.5	19.6	12.3	- Amérique du Nord
- LAIA	1.9	2.3	2.3	2.6	2.6	2.8	3.9	3.9	3.7	3.9	- ALAI
- CACM	0.1	0.0	0.0	0.1	0.0	0.1	0.1	0.0	0.0	0.1	- MCC
- Caribbean	0.1	0.2	0.2	0.1	0.2	0.2	0.1	0.0	0.1	0.0	- Caraïbes
- Rest of America	0.0	0.0	0.0	0.0	0.0	0.0	0.0	0.0	0.0	0.0	- Autre d'Amérique
Asia excluding former USSR	42.8	43.9	44.6	46.8	48.1	40.0	43.6	42.5	48.3	60.4	Asie ancienne URSS exclus
- Middle East	2.1	1.4	0.9	0.9	0.9	1.1	0.7	0.6	0.7	0.7	- Moyen-Orient
Asia former USSR	0.0	0.0	0.0	0.0	0.0	0.0	0.0	0.0	0.0	0.0	Asie ancienne URSS
Europe excluding former USSR	33.5	31.9	32.0	30.2	29.3	32.0	26.9	24.6	26.9	21.9	Europe ancienne URSS exclus
- European Union	29.4	28.3	28.8	26.8	26.1	28.3	24.0	22.2	24.2	19.3	- Union Européenne
- Eastern Europe	0.6	0.6	0.7	0.8	0.9	1.0	0.9	1.0	1.2	0.9	- Europe de l'Est
- Rest of Europe	3.5	3.0	2.5	2.6	2.3	2.6	2.0	1.5	1.6	1.7	- Autre de l'Europe
Europe former USSR	0.5	0.4	0.4	0.4	0.4	0.4	0.3	0.2	0.3	0.3	Europe ancienne URSS
Oceania	1.3	1.4	1.3	1.2	1.1	1.2	0.9	0.7	0.7	0.7	Océanie

TRADE BY COMMODITY (Value in million US dollars)
Exports by principal countries or areas

COMMERCE PAR PRODUIT (Valeur en millions de dollars EU)
Exportations selon les principaux pays ou zones

Country or area	1998	1999	2000	2001	2002	Pays ou zone
World	13543.1	18276.8	23662.0	21277.6	18368.1	Monde
Africa	6.9	6.7	13.1	13.6	8.8	Afrique
Americas	2781.6	3617.9	6518.4	5062.9	3382.2	Amériques
- Northern America	2669.0	3494.1	6326.9	4837.8	3193.6	- Amérique du Nord
- LAIA	111.6	122.6	190.5	224.0	186.8	- ALAI
- CACM	0.6	0.6	0.3	0.4	0.9	- MCC
- Caribbean	0.5	0.6	0.7	0.8	0.9	- Caraïbes
- Rest of America	0.0	0.0	0.0	0.0	0.0	- Autre d'Amérique
Asia excluding former USSR	7214.6	10868.4	12668.5	11418.0	10943.5	Asie ancienne URSS exclus
- Middle East	6.7	5.4	8.0	9.1	11.2	- Moyen-Orient
Asia former USSR	1.5	0.4	0.0	0.1	0.1	Asie ancienne URSS
Europe excluding former USSR	3387.6	3546.8	4134.9	4429.7	3814.9	Europe ancienne URSS exclus
- European Union	3065.3	3243.3	3731.4	3938.1	3386.6	- Union Européenne
- Eastern Europe	78.9	68.7	99.9	118.1	129.8	- Europe de l'Est
- Rest of Europe	243.4	234.7	303.7	373.5	298.5	- Autre de l'Europe
Europe former USSR	79.5	93.7	101.1	133.2	142.3	Europe ancienne URSS
Oceania	71.4	143.0	225.9	220.1	76.2	Océanie
Japan	2719.4	4136.4	5976.1	5182.8	5288.3	Japon
United States	2220.0	2760.9	4605.7	4026.3	2958.5	Etats-Unis d'Amérique
China, Hong Kong SAR	1227.6	1529.7	2184.1	2457.4	1328.1	Chine - RAS de Hong-Kong
Germany	1262.7	1389.6	1577.9	1800.9	1666.9	Allemagne
Korea, Republic of	1496.5	2565.9	471.4	480.2	498.6	République de Corée
China	654.5	938.9	1402.3	1026.7	1400.6	Chine
Canada	449.0	733.2	1721.1	811.5	235.1	Canada
United Kingdom	556.3	591.9	613.9	676.5	557.4	Royaume-Uni
France-Monaco	474.6	469.1	499.1	483.0	397.2	France-Monaco
Switzerland-Liechtenstein	229.9	226.9	285.3	348.3	272.2	Suisse-Liechtenstein
Singapore	245.9	290.5	260.7	229.5	272.8	Singapour
Denmark	102.4	153.7	367.6	257.1	55.0	Danemark
Netherlands	223.0	159.9	167.5	185.2	149.2	Pays-Bas
Thailand	118.8	145.9	167.4	172.6	e182.3	Thaïlande
Australia	68.1	140.0	223.7	218.0	75.9	Australie
Mexico	95.0	92.8	145.3	176.6	138.0	Mexique
Ireland	133.3	136.8	117.2	104.5	113.5	Irlande
Italy-San Marino-Holy See	84.7	84.8	116.5	171.7	146.0	Italie-Saint-Marin-Saint-Siège
Malaysia	35.9	47.7	67.2	185.6	e196.7	Malaisie
Israel	98.3	116.0	111.0	89.6	87.2	Israël
Czech Republic	61.1	45.5	62.3	77.8	81.8	République tchèque
Philippines	48.5	64.6	71.0	73.3	70.4	Philippines
Austria	51.2	60.0	64.7	69.4	82.1	Autriche
Russian Federation	57.7	69.4	66.4	63.7	62.0	Fédération de Russie
Belgium	–	91.0	85.5	64.1	e71.9	Belgique
Sweden	59.1	62.1	66.7	65.8	51.0	Suède
Belarus	15.1	16.1	24.6	47.9	56.4	Bélarus
Brazil	14.8	26.5	39.4	38.5	e39.9	Brésil
Indonesia	4.3	13.4	24.7	46.6	42.3	Indonésie
Spain	13.8	18.1	18.4	17.7	56.1	Espagne

(Value as percentages of World total) **(Valeur en pourcentage du total mondial)**

Regions of the world	1993	1994	1995	1996	1997	1998	1999	2000	2001	2002	Régions du monde
World	100.0	100.0	100.0	100.0	100.0	100.0	100.0	100.0	100.0	100.0	Monde
Africa	0.0	0.0	0.1	0.1	0.3	0.1	0.0	0.1	0.1	0.0	Afrique
Americas	19.9	19.4	17.3	19.2	19.4	20.5	19.8	27.5	23.8	18.4	Amériques
- Northern America	18.7	18.5	16.5	18.5	18.7	19.7	19.1	26.7	22.7	17.4	- Amérique du Nord
- LAIA	1.2	0.9	0.8	0.7	0.7	0.8	0.7	0.8	1.1	1.0	- ALAI
- CACM	0.0	0.0	0.0	0.0	0.0	0.0	0.0	0.0	0.0	0.0	- MCC
- Caribbean	0.0	0.0	0.0	0.0	0.0	0.0	0.0	0.0	0.0	0.0	- Caraïbes
- Rest of America	0.0	0.0	0.0	0.0	0.0	0.0	0.0	0.0	0.0	0.0	- Autre d'Amérique
Asia excluding former USSR	47.0	48.3	50.9	50.2	52.6	53.3	59.5	53.5	53.7	59.6	Asie ancienne URSS exclus
- Middle East	0.0	0.0	0.0	0.1	0.0	0.0	0.0	0.0	0.0	0.1	- Moyen-Orient
Asia former USSR	0.0	0.0	0.0	0.0	0.0	0.0	0.0	0.0	0.0	0.0	Asie ancienne URSS
Europe excluding former USSR	31.3	30.6	30.2	29.0	26.5	25.0	19.4	17.5	20.8	20.8	Europe ancienne URSS exclus
- European Union	27.7	27.5	27.5	26.3	24.3	22.6	17.7	15.8	18.5	18.4	- Union Européenne
- Eastern Europe	0.2	0.2	0.3	0.4	0.3	0.6	0.4	0.4	0.6	0.7	- Europe de l'Est
- Rest of Europe	3.4	2.9	2.4	2.3	1.9	1.8	1.3	1.3	1.8	1.6	- Autre de l'Europe
Europe former USSR	0.5	0.5	0.5	0.6	0.6	0.6	0.5	0.4	0.6	0.8	Europe ancienne URSS
Oceania	1.3	1.1	1.0	0.9	0.5	0.5	0.8	1.0	1.0	0.4	Océanie

872 Medical instruments and appliances, nes

TRADE BY COMMODITY (Value in million US dollars)
Imports by principal countries or areas

COMMERCE PAR PRODUIT (Valeur en millions de dollars EU)
Importations selon les principaux pays ou zones

Country or area	1998	1999	2000	2001	2002	Pays ou zone
World	21757.1	23903.2	25465.4	27968.5	30357.9	Monde
Africa	533.9	508.8	507.7	543.0	592.2	Afrique
Americas	5319.3	6030.7	6769.7	7496.1	8252.5	Amériques
- Northern America	4230.8	4973.6	5536.8	6167.8	6810.0	- Amérique du Nord
- LAIA	814.3	853.5	988.0	1094.4	1136.5	- ALAI
- CACM	66.2	63.7	69.6	74.6	134.6	- MCC
- Caribbean	191.5	119.1	155.2	141.5	156.1	- Caraïbes
- Rest of America	16.6	20.7	20.1	17.9	15.2	- Autre d'Amérique
Asia excluding former USSR	4431.8	4903.5	5591.9	6108.5	6153.8	Asie ancienne URSS exclus
- Middle East	595.7	585.9	659.6	683.1	717.7	- Moyen-Orient
Asia former USSR	22.8	41.2	74.3	53.0	53.0	Asie ancienne URSS
Europe excluding former USSR	10438.8	11576.6	11645.3	12738.9	14271.5	Europe ancienne URSS exclus
- European Union	9299.0	10496.4	10570.7	11546.9	12907.2	- Union Européenne
- Eastern Europe	486.8	429.5	456.6	489.5	584.3	- Europe de l'Est
- Rest of Europe	653.0	650.8	618.0	702.6	780.0	- Autre de l'Europe
Europe former USSR	543.3	338.0	348.4	518.0	461.0	Europe ancienne URSS
Oceania	467.3	504.4	528.0	511.1	574.0	Océanie
United States	3501.7	4119.3	4688.9	5175.0	5833.7	Etats-Unis d'Amérique
Japan	1983.0	2178.8	2434.6	2683.7	2568.2	Japon
Germany	1878.6	2039.0	1886.0	2128.6	2181.7	Allemagne
France-Monaco	1391.7	1383.3	1343.2	1371.8	1554.1	France-Monaco
United Kingdom	1209.7	1175.3	1237.7	1524.1	1642.4	Royaume-Uni
Netherlands	788.5	1150.1	1271.8	1458.8	2061.8	Pays-Bas
Italy-San Marino-Holy See	996.7	1114.2	1118.2	1192.5	1230.6	Italie-Saint-Marin-Saint-Siège
Belgium	–	1271.5	1314.0	1385.4	e1519.4	Belgique
Canada	728.3	853.5	846.2	990.4	972.6	Canada
Spain	607.2	658.1	632.9	624.2	732.4	Espagne
Mexico	284.9	401.1	488.5	580.1	673.8	Mexique
Ireland	341.5	446.9	566.9	520.5	452.9	Irlande
China, Hong Kong SAR	371.7	393.1	450.8	531.7	556.3	Chine - RAS de Hong-Kong
Australia	378.9	404.3	426.9	407.3	460.4	Australie
Switzerland-Liechtenstein	328.2	337.8	332.2	400.7	444.4	Suisse-Liechtenstein
China	155.6	267.8	351.7	470.0	490.3	Chine
Sweden	305.5	303.7	322.5	365.7	405.5	Suède
Austria	282.6	288.3	252.0	276.7	325.2	Autriche
Russian Federation	379.1	189.9	212.4	355.3	287.0	Fédération de Russie
Korea, Republic of	160.8	241.6	288.9	325.0	382.8	République de Corée
Singapore	223.1	247.7	257.0	270.9	266.8	Singapour
Turkey	239.4	227.2	248.8	193.3	213.8	Turquie
Denmark	168.5	177.4	193.5	228.8	283.3	Danemark
India	148.1	167.3	202.4	235.9	218.0	Inde
Greece	203.4	205.2	169.2	179.3	e198.2	Grèce
Belgium-Luxembourg	874.0	–	–	–	–	Belgique-Luxembourg
Brazil	188.4	147.3	174.6	188.3	172.7	Brésil
Norway	171.1	174.8	153.9	161.1	185.6	Norvège
Poland	177.1	140.1	162.9	168.3	183.0	Pologne
Portugal	141.8	159.9	138.2	140.0	159.2	Portugal

(Value as percentages of World total) **(Valeur en pourcentage du total mondial)**

Regions of the world	1993	1994	1995	1996	1997	1998	1999	2000	2001	2002	Régions du monde
World	100.0	100.0	100.0	100.0	100.0	100.0	100.0	100.0	100.0	100.0	Monde
Africa	2.9	2.6	2.6	2.5	2.5	2.5	2.1	2.0	1.9	2.0	Afrique
Americas	23.1	22.7	21.5	21.5	22.5	24.4	25.2	26.6	26.8	27.2	Amériques
- Northern America	18.1	17.7	16.7	16.7	17.7	19.4	20.8	21.7	22.1	22.4	- Amérique du Nord
- LAIA	4.2	4.2	3.7	3.6	3.7	3.7	3.6	3.9	3.9	3.7	- ALAI
- CACM	0.2	0.2	0.2	0.2	0.3	0.3	0.3	0.3	0.3	0.4	- MCC
- Caribbean	0.5	0.5	0.7	0.9	0.8	0.9	0.5	0.6	0.5	0.5	- Caraïbes
- Rest of America	0.1	0.1	0.1	0.1	0.1	0.1	0.1	0.1	0.1	0.1	- Autre d'Amérique
Asia excluding former USSR	22.2	21.3	21.8	21.9	22.4	20.4	20.5	22.0	21.8	20.3	Asie ancienne URSS exclus
- Middle East	3.8	2.7	2.3	2.2	2.4	2.7	2.5	2.6	2.4	2.4	- Moyen-Orient
Asia former USSR	0.1	0.1	0.2	0.1	0.1	0.1	0.2	0.3	0.2	0.2	Asie ancienne URSS
Europe excluding former USSR	47.4	48.3	49.0	49.1	47.9	48.0	48.4	45.7	45.5	47.0	Europe ancienne URSS exclus
- European Union	42.5	42.9	43.4	43.8	42.9	42.7	43.9	41.5	41.3	42.5	- Union Européenne
- Eastern Europe	2.1	2.3	2.4	2.4	2.2	2.2	1.8	1.8	1.8	1.9	- Europe de l'Est
- Rest of Europe	2.7	3.1	3.2	3.0	2.9	3.0	2.7	2.4	2.5	2.6	- Autre de l'Europe
Europe former USSR	2.3	2.6	2.7	2.6	2.3	2.5	1.4	1.4	1.9	1.5	Europe ancienne URSS
Oceania	2.0	2.3	2.1	2.2	2.3	2.1	2.1	2.1	1.8	1.9	Océanie

TRADE BY COMMODITY (Value in million US dollars)
Exports by principal countries or areas

COMMERCE PAR PRODUIT (Valeur en millions de dollars EU)
Exportations selon les principaux pays ou zones

Country or area	1998	1999	2000	2001	2002	Pays ou zone
World	21682.4	23273.5	24233.2	27072.3	29316.7	Monde
Africa	27.8	31.0	31.2	25.3	30.4	Afrique
Americas	7242.2	7489.5	8280.7	9506.1	9755.2	Amériques
- Northern America	5992.7	6308.5	6693.8	7580.4	7497.0	- Amérique du Nord
- LAIA	906.1	1026.3	1332.5	1587.1	1831.7	- ALAI
- CACM	66.5	93.3	183.4	274.9	358.0	- MCC
- Caribbean	276.9	61.4	71.0	63.7	68.3	- Caraïbes
- Rest of America	0.0	0.0	0.1	0.1	0.2	- Autre d'Amérique
Asia excluding former USSR	3415.4	3694.1	3881.1	4056.9	4321.4	Asie ancienne URSS exclus
- Middle East	41.5	42.8	43.9	59.1	62.5	- Moyen-Orient
Asia former USSR	0.8	0.9	0.7	1.6	1.6	Asie ancienne URSS
Europe excluding former USSR	10692.6	11756.7	11714.9	13110.8	14753.6	Europe ancienne URSS exclus
- European Union	9801.2	10859.0	10838.3	12203.7	13700.7	- Union Européenne
- Eastern Europe	153.0	149.6	171.5	198.1	250.9	- Europe de l'Est
- Rest of Europe	738.4	748.1	705.1	709.0	802.0	- Autre de l'Europe
Europe former USSR	66.3	60.7	63.0	75.8	86.4	Europe ancienne URSS
Oceania	237.3	240.5	261.6	295.8	368.1	Océanie
United States	5838.7	6172.1	6551.9	7410.0	7276.8	Etats-Unis d'Amérique
Germany	2527.0	2636.1	2505.1	2928.5	3076.7	Allemagne
Netherlands	969.3	1613.7	1519.9	1683.3	2090.6	Pays-Bas
United Kingdom	1356.2	1295.3	1242.1	1431.8	1501.7	Royaume-Uni
Ireland	1196.8	1217.6	1243.9	1374.4	1604.6	Irlande
Japan	1295.4	1325.8	1339.3	1235.3	1237.8	Japon
Mexico	845.6	971.5	1273.4	1521.9	1765.5	Mexique
France-Monaco	945.8	1067.7	1161.3	1282.9	1412.3	France-Monaco
Belgium	-	1136.4	1148.3	1278.2	e1434.1	Belgique
Italy-San Marino-Holy See	637.6	639.2	664.2	749.3	851.9	Italie-Saint-Marin-Saint-Siège
Switzerland-Liechtenstein	604.3	605.5	574.9	568.8	653.6	Suisse-Liechtenstein
Singapore	568.4	570.0	579.2	596.4	634.9	Singapour
Sweden	591.7	506.0	567.2	547.6	666.2	Suède
China, Hong Kong SAR	381.6	438.4	544.2	679.9	711.8	Chine - RAS de Hong-Kong
China	270.8	316.5	431.9	529.3	631.3	Chine
Denmark	288.4	322.4	359.9	385.5	433.6	Danemark
Spain	225.7	190.9	216.5	242.1	297.0	Espagne
Australia	188.9	184.8	201.2	226.0	291.0	Australie
Israel	232.7	326.3	175.2	129.3	156.8	Israël
Costa Rica	66.1	92.3	181.8	273.8	357.3	Costa Rica
Thailand	171.2	173.3	188.7	187.4	e197.9	Thaïlande
Canada	153.9	136.4	141.8	170.3	219.9	Canada
Malaysia	119.1	149.0	172.7	181.1	e191.9	Malaisie
Belgium-Luxembourg	811.0	-	-	-	-	Belgique-Luxembourg
Pakistan	115.1	114.9	120.6	131.2	141.5	Pakistan
Finland	109.7	103.3	84.9	153.8	169.5	Finlande
Korea, Republic of	85.4	88.2	112.2	124.8	136.3	République de Corée
Dominican Republic	e	e60.3	e69.9	e62.5	e66.5	République dominicaine
Austria	100.1	85.7	79.5	98.4	115.2	Autriche
Norway	74.5	72.1	67.6	72.3	75.7	Norvège

(Value as percentages of World total) **(Valeur en pourcentage du total mondial)**

Regions of the world	1993	1994	1995	1996	1997	1998	1999	2000	2001	2002	Régions du monde
World	100.0	100.0	100.0	100.0	100.0	100.0	100.0	100.0	100.0	100.0	Monde
Africa	0.2	0.2	0.2	0.2	0.1	0.1	0.1	0.1	0.1	0.1	Afrique
Americas	31.4	31.3	30.1	30.2	32.8	33.4	32.2	34.2	35.1	33.3	Amériques
- Northern America	27.4	27.5	25.7	26.7	28.5	27.6	27.1	27.6	28.0	25.6	- Amérique du Nord
- LAIA	2.9	2.8	2.7	3.4	3.9	4.2	4.4	5.5	5.9	6.2	- ALAI
- CACM	0.0	0.0	0.0	0.0	0.4	0.3	0.4	0.8	1.0	1.2	- MCC
- Caribbean	1.1	1.1	1.7	0.0	0.0	1.3	0.3	0.3	0.2	0.2	- Caraïbes
- Rest of America	0.0	0.0	0.0	0.0	0.0	0.0	0.0	0.0	0.0	0.0	- Autre d'Amérique
Asia excluding former USSR	19.8	19.2	18.1	16.7	16.9	15.8	15.9	16.0	15.0	14.7	Asie ancienne URSS exclus
- Middle East	0.2	0.2	0.2	0.1	0.1	0.2	0.2	0.2	0.2	0.2	- Moyen-Orient
Asia former USSR	0.0	0.0	0.0	0.0	0.0	0.0	0.0	0.0	0.0	0.0	Asie ancienne URSS
Europe excluding former USSR	47.7	48.1	50.5	51.6	48.6	49.3	50.5	48.3	48.4	50.3	Europe ancienne URSS exclus
- European Union	43.9	43.6	45.9	47.1	44.6	45.2	46.7	44.7	45.1	46.7	- Union Européenne
- Eastern Europe	0.6	0.9	0.8	0.8	0.8	0.7	0.6	0.7	0.7	0.9	- Europe de l'Est
- Rest of Europe	3.2	3.6	3.8	3.7	3.3	3.4	3.2	2.9	2.6	2.7	- Autre de l'Europe
Europe former USSR	0.1	0.2	0.3	0.3	0.3	0.3	0.3	0.3	0.3	0.3	Europe ancienne URSS
Oceania	0.8	0.9	0.9	1.0	1.2	1.1	1.0	1.1	1.1	1.3	Océanie

873 Meters and counters, nes

TRADE BY COMMODITY (Value in million US dollars)
Imports by principal countries or areas

COMMERCE PAR PRODUIT (Valeur en millions de dollars EU)
Importations selon les principaux pays ou zones

Country or area	1998	1999	2000	2001	2002	Pays ou zone
World	3165.6	3116.1	3207.0	3213.7	3474.9	Monde
Africa	99.8	81.6	76.4	75.8	76.9	Afrique
Americas	1325.7	1381.1	1426.6	1404.7	1375.8	Amériques
- Northern America	983.3	1070.6	1076.5	1105.3	1114.5	- Amérique du Nord
- LAIA	307.2	279.8	309.1	255.9	234.3	- ALAI
- CACM	17.9	14.7	17.0	25.5	12.3	- MCC
- Caribbean	14.9	13.4	17.5	13.3	10.7	- Caraïbes
- Rest of America	2.3	2.7	6.5	4.6	4.0	- Autre d'Amérique
Asia excluding former USSR	376.2	345.7	418.7	392.4	452.1	Asie ancienne URSS exclus
- Middle East	63.5	51.6	75.2	57.7	67.4	- Moyen-Orient
Asia former USSR	19.3	11.2	13.0	13.6	37.2	Asie ancienne URSS
Europe excluding former USSR	1243.9	1212.6	1202.6	1245.2	1435.5	Europe ancienne URSS exclus
- European Union	1058.7	1026.4	1002.6	1052.9	1240.9	- Union Européenne
- Eastern Europe	119.5	124.6	147.0	139.8	138.0	- Europe de l'Est
- Rest of Europe	65.8	61.6	53.0	52.6	56.6	- Autre de l'Europe
Europe former USSR	58.7	45.6	33.5	48.2	57.3	Europe ancienne URSS
Oceania	41.9	38.3	36.1	33.7	40.1	Océanie
United States	770.9	810.6	805.1	850.3	857.6	Etats-Unis d'Amérique
Germany	298.9	279.5	277.0	334.6	324.4	Allemagne
Canada	212.2	259.9	271.3	254.9	256.2	Canada
Mexico	140.1	133.5	180.4	121.9	123.7	Mexique
Italy-San Marino-Holy See	77.4	93.3	83.2	90.9	217.6	Italie-Saint-Marin-Saint-Siège
Belgium	-	123.8	128.3	144.4	e158.4	Belgique
France-Monaco	109.4	92.2	93.5	92.3	85.1	France-Monaco
United Kingdom	98.9	89.1	87.7	91.3	103.4	Royaume-Uni
Sweden	91.8	93.5	78.1	72.0	75.3	Suède
Spain	73.7	82.3	81.1	64.3	89.2	Espagne
Netherlands	54.8	66.2	61.4	51.7	47.7	Pays-Bas
China, Hong Kong SAR	71.9	47.5	49.9	52.1	49.6	Chine - RAS de Hong-Kong
Austria	51.1	46.2	47.3	53.8	63.4	Autriche
Japan	50.6	47.6	45.2	43.2	67.0	Japon
China	21.9	28.4	42.4	51.4	62.7	Chine
Brazil	51.2	33.8	40.9	43.2	32.1	Brésil
Hungary	25.4	31.9	34.6	34.2	44.6	Hongrie
Slovakia	23.7	32.6	36.8	31.4	22.2	Slovaquie
Korea, Republic of	22.9	27.8	28.1	31.4	33.4	République de Corée
Czech Republic	29.9	24.8	27.5	27.7	32.8	République tchèque
Belgium-Luxembourg	134.1	-	-	-	-	Belgique-Luxembourg
Australia	27.9	27.2	25.2	22.9	29.6	Australie
Argentina	32.4	33.7	30.7	24.4	e10.8	Argentine
Poland	25.7	22.9	27.8	25.6	20.7	Pologne
Switzerland-Liechtenstein	26.7	24.5	22.5	20.1	21.4	Suisse-Liechtenstein
Russian Federation	30.0	19.6	12.7	20.9	24.0	Fédération de Russie
Colombia	29.6	27.3	10.5	19.2	15.6	Colombie
Thailand	17.4	14.9	20.5	22.3	e23.2	Thaïlande
Turkey	18.4	15.7	20.6	13.8	26.0	Turquie
Denmark	23.8	21.0	17.4	15.1	16.4	Danemark

(Value as percentages of World total) **(Valeur en pourcentage du total mondial)**

Regions of the world	1993	1994	1995	1996	1997	1998	1999	2000	2001	2002	Régions du monde
World	100.0	100.0	100.0	100.0	100.0	100.0	100.0	100.0	100.0	100.0	Monde
Africa	4.4	3.2	2.8	2.9	2.9	3.2	2.6	2.4	2.4	2.2	Afrique
Americas	32.0	44.5	41.6	39.0	41.6	41.9	44.3	44.5	43.7	39.6	Amériques
- Northern America	24.1	34.2	31.6	29.2	30.7	31.1	34.4	33.6	34.4	32.1	- Amérique du Nord
- LAIA	6.8	9.4	9.2	9.0	10.0	9.7	9.0	9.6	8.0	6.7	- ALAI
- CACM	0.4	0.5	0.4	0.5	0.6	0.6	0.5	0.5	0.8	0.4	- MCC
- Caribbean	0.5	0.3	0.3	0.2	0.2	0.5	0.4	0.5	0.4	0.3	- Caraïbes
- Rest of America	0.2	0.1	0.1	0.1	0.1	0.1	0.1	0.2	0.1	0.1	- Autre d'Amérique
Asia excluding former USSR	18.6	14.0	14.3	15.4	13.6	11.9	11.1	13.1	12.2	13.0	Asie ancienne URSS exclus
- Middle East	3.9	2.5	1.9	1.8	2.1	2.0	1.7	2.3	1.8	1.9	- Moyen-Orient
Asia former USSR	0.0	0.2	0.3	0.4	0.5	0.6	0.4	0.4	0.4	1.1	Asie ancienne URSS
Europe excluding former USSR	41.6	34.3	36.2	38.2	36.9	39.3	38.9	37.5	38.7	41.3	Europe ancienne URSS exclus
- European Union	34.7	28.8	30.7	32.4	31.6	33.4	32.9	31.3	32.8	35.7	- Union Européenne
- Eastern Europe	3.7	3.1	3.0	3.3	3.1	3.8	4.0	4.6	4.4	4.0	- Europe de l'Est
- Rest of Europe	3.1	2.5	2.4	2.5	2.2	2.1	2.0	1.7	1.6	1.6	- Autre de l'Europe
Europe former USSR	1.7	2.3	3.5	2.7	3.0	1.9	1.5	1.0	1.5	1.6	Europe ancienne URSS
Oceania	1.6	1.5	1.4	1.5	1.5	1.3	1.2	1.1	1.0	1.2	Océanie

TRADE BY COMMODITY (Value in million US dollars)
Exports by principal countries or areas

COMMERCE PAR PRODUIT (Valeur en millions de dollars EU)
Exportations selon les principaux pays ou zones

Country or area	1998	1999	2000	2001	2002	Pays ou zone
World	2776.9	2711.7	2739.9	2802.3	3083.7	Monde
Africa	12.5	9.0	12.2	21.6	24.3	Afrique
Americas	720.3	748.6	812.2	847.0	723.4	Amériques
- Northern America	458.4	448.0	531.7	494.9	467.7	- Amérique du Nord
- LAIA	261.7	300.4	280.2	351.7	254.5	- ALAI
- CACM	0.0	0.1	0.2	0.2	1.0	- MCC
- Caribbean	0.1	0.1	0.1	0.1	0.1	- Caraïbes
- Rest of America	0.0	0.0	0.0	0.0	0.0	- Autre d'Amérique
Asia excluding former USSR	457.1	393.0	455.6	445.7	642.6	Asie ancienne URSS exclus
- Middle East	4.2	6.3	3.8	9.0	13.2	- Moyen-Orient
Asia former USSR	1.5	0.7	1.0	1.0	0.7	Asie ancienne URSS
Europe excluding former USSR	1561.6	1534.9	1424.8	1446.3	1647.8	Europe ancienne URSS exclus
- European Union	1342.7	1320.8	1230.8	1252.9	1415.8	- Union Européenne
- Eastern Europe	54.4	51.2	45.9	56.8	83.6	- Europe de l'Est
- Rest of Europe	164.5	163.0	148.1	136.6	148.4	- Autre de l'Europe
Europe former USSR	17.6	19.9	27.7	35.1	37.4	Europe ancienne URSS
Oceania	6.3	5.6	6.4	5.6	7.4	Océanie
Germany	535.0	585.2	559.5	591.2	670.0	Allemagne
United States	413.4	427.7	509.4	470.4	438.9	Etats-Unis d'Amérique
United Kingdom	318.9	249.2	237.7	208.7	201.4	Royaume-Uni
Mexico	211.3	233.5	219.8	283.4	184.2	Mexique
Japan	212.4	191.8	208.1	161.8	156.2	Japon
France-Monaco	164.3	140.7	106.1	125.1	137.2	France-Monaco
China	42.6	38.7	60.7	84.7	288.3	Chine
Slovenia	81.1	85.9	76.0	72.6	79.2	Slovénie
Switzerland-Liechtenstein	78.2	72.9	65.1	58.9	64.4	Suisse-Liechtenstein
China, Hong Kong SAR	67.4	56.6	65.5	72.6	64.5	Chine - RAS de Hong-Kong
Spain	28.3	34.0	58.2	75.3	107.5	Espagne
Italy-San Marino-Holy See	62.7	57.6	49.1	44.2	46.4	Italie-Saint-Marin-Saint-Siège
Netherlands	39.4	50.9	43.0	40.6	52.2	Pays-Bas
Brazil	35.6	50.6	40.4	38.4	e39.8	Brésil
Belgium	–	59.5	49.2	35.6	e40.0	Belgique
Sweden	21.0	30.4	37.0	40.2	36.0	Suède
Austria	44.7	36.1	25.9	21.6	24.1	Autriche
Canada	44.9	20.3	22.3	24.5	28.8	Canada
Finland	29.4	30.7	21.1	23.3	24.8	Finlande
Denmark	17.4	16.7	13.5	18.6	33.4	Danemark
Argentina	11.9	14.3	17.3	25.1	e24.2	Argentine
Slovakia	20.0	14.2	13.3	19.5	24.1	Slovaquie
Greece	22.6	18.6	19.3	13.5	e13.5	Grèce
Indonesia	6.3	10.7	21.5	22.3	13.8	Indonésie
Thailand	41.1	9.1	9.3	6.0	e6.4	Thaïlande
Hungary	11.6	12.6	13.7	13.6	18.1	Hongrie
Singapore	21.7	16.1	9.9	8.6	9.1	Singapour
Israel	13.5	12.1	12.8	13.6	12.6	Israël
Korea, Republic of	6.9	7.0	10.7	14.0	23.7	République de Corée
Poland	14.9	13.3	7.3	10.0	12.3	Pologne

(Value as percentages of World total) **(Valeur en pourcentage du total mondial)**

Regions of the world	1993	1994	1995	1996	1997	1998	1999	2000	2001	2002	Régions du monde
World	100.0	100.0	100.0	100.0	100.0	100.0	100.0	100.0	100.0	100.0	Monde
Africa	0.1	0.1	0.2	0.2	0.3	0.4	0.3	0.4	0.8	0.8	Afrique
Americas	15.0	23.6	18.7	19.0	24.3	25.9	27.6	29.6	30.2	23.5	Amériques
- Northern America	12.8	21.4	16.9	16.0	16.8	16.5	16.5	19.4	17.7	15.2	- Amérique du Nord
- LAIA	2.2	2.2	1.8	3.0	7.5	9.4	11.1	10.2	12.6	8.3	- ALAI
- CACM	0.0	0.0	0.0	0.0	0.0	0.0	0.0	0.0	0.0	0.0	- MCC
- Caribbean	0.0	0.0	0.0	0.0	0.0	0.0	0.0	0.0	0.0	0.0	- Caraïbes
- Rest of America	0.0	0.0	0.0	0.0	0.0	0.0	0.0	0.0	0.0	0.0	- Autre d'Amérique
Asia excluding former USSR	25.8	20.4	20.0	19.3	18.9	16.5	14.5	16.6	15.9	20.8	Asie ancienne URSS exclus
- Middle East	0.1	0.1	0.1	0.1	0.2	0.2	0.2	0.1	0.3	0.4	- Moyen-Orient
Asia former USSR	0.0	0.2	0.1	0.1	0.1	0.1	0.0	0.0	0.0	0.0	Asie ancienne URSS
Europe excluding former USSR	58.5	54.9	60.1	60.4	55.3	56.2	56.6	52.0	51.6	53.4	Europe ancienne URSS exclus
- European Union	48.9	45.4	49.5	50.5	46.8	48.4	48.7	44.9	44.7	45.9	- Union Européenne
- Eastern Europe	2.0	2.0	2.7	2.5	2.8	2.0	1.9	1.7	2.0	2.7	- Europe de l'Est
- Rest of Europe	7.5	7.5	7.9	7.4	5.7	5.9	6.0	5.4	4.9	4.8	- Autre de l'Europe
Europe former USSR	0.4	0.6	0.7	0.8	1.0	0.6	0.7	1.0	1.3	1.2	Europe ancienne URSS
Oceania	0.2	0.3	0.2	0.2	0.2	0.2	0.2	0.2	0.2	0.2	Océanie

874 Measuring, checking, analysis, controlling instruments, nes, parts

TRADE BY COMMODITY (Value in million US dollars)
Imports by principal countries or areas

COMMERCE PAR PRODUIT (Valeur en millions de dollars EU)
Importations selon les principaux pays ou zones

Country or area	1998	1999	2000	2001	2002	Pays ou zone
World	65062.0	67676.3	79024.6	76425.9	76198.7	Monde
Africa	1095.3	1037.0	980.3	1019.5	1094.7	Afrique
Americas	17572.4	18861.4	22453.2	22066.8	20996.1	Amériques
- Northern America	13308.6	14702.3	17646.9	17166.3	16452.9	- Amérique du Nord
- LAIA	3961.2	3915.4	4531.8	4582.5	4214.5	- ALAI
- CACM	128.4	95.3	109.1	116.0	141.1	- MCC
- Caribbean	152.5	125.6	135.1	178.2	167.4	- Caraïbes
- Rest of America	21.7	22.7	30.2	23.9	20.3	- Autre d'Amérique
Asia excluding former USSR	17741.2	19205.5	25374.3	22355.5	23357.2	Asie ancienne URSS exclus
- Middle East	1267.9	1116.7	1349.7	1389.5	1561.4	- Moyen-Orient
Asia former USSR	125.9	121.0	160.3	202.3	194.4	Asie ancienne URSS
Europe excluding former USSR	26581.5	26607.9	28128.7	28876.6	28583.0	Europe ancienne URSS exclus
- European Union	23585.1	23633.7	24993.3	25706.9	25115.1	- Union Européenne
- Eastern Europe	1415.1	1384.5	1540.6	1603.6	1783.3	- Europe de l'Est
- Rest of Europe	1581.3	1589.6	1594.8	1566.1	1684.6	- Autre de l'Europe
Europe former USSR	743.7	624.7	765.8	772.6	805.2	Europe ancienne URSS
Oceania	1202.1	1218.9	1162.1	1132.6	1168.0	Océanie
United States	9824.1	10782.7	13295.8	13002.6	12585.9	Etats-Unis d'Amérique
Germany	5057.6	5090.6	5679.8	6060.3	5778.1	Allemagne
United Kingdom	4847.9	4737.4	5040.6	5484.1	5196.8	Royaume-Uni
Japan	3818.8	3942.9	4756.8	4601.0	4272.7	Japon
Canada	3481.1	3916.6	4346.1	4158.1	3860.2	Canada
France-Monaco	3225.8	3245.0	3422.0	3592.3	3707.1	France-Monaco
China	1898.9	2214.4	3002.3	3881.7	4623.5	Chine
Italy-San Marino-Holy See	2520.0	2556.2	2630.6	2539.1	2420.1	Italie-Saint-Marin-Saint-Siège
Korea, Republic of	1826.4	2135.9	3180.9	2658.8	2779.2	République de Corée
Mexico	1970.5	2244.0	2782.7	2596.3	2546.3	Mexique
Singapore	1620.0	2091.3	2695.7	1719.2	1733.8	Singapour
Netherlands	1843.7	1818.6	1945.0	1897.3	1627.6	Pays-Bas
Spain	1429.3	1578.3	1354.1	1409.1	1617.7	Espagne
China, Hong Kong SAR	1191.7	1219.6	1490.2	1523.2	1419.8	Chine - RAS de Hong-Kong
Malaysia	1042.4	1059.4	1642.6	1478.7	e1616.1	Malaisie
Australia	1031.0	1059.3	1012.2	986.8	994.1	Australie
Sweden	1002.4	979.3	1090.4	1017.5	980.4	Suède
Switzerland-Liechtenstein	969.4	988.1	1021.3	1015.2	1041.3	Suisse-Liechtenstein
Brazil	968.0	856.3	945.7	1106.5	946.5	Brésil
Belgium	-	1106.1	1098.0	1151.8	e1263.2	Belgique
Austria	811.2	798.4	796.8	828.6	818.4	Autriche
Thailand	516.1	616.4	648.8	642.0	e668.9	Thaïlande
India	500.9	480.4	456.4	524.5	666.2	Inde
Russian Federation	483.5	406.5	518.6	506.4	517.5	Fédération de Russie
Israel	403.2	532.2	520.5	498.9	448.7	Israël
Poland	469.2	442.6	457.8	431.7	460.0	Pologne
Denmark	411.5	387.9	414.3	450.1	446.5	Danemark
Turkey	410.6	372.3	480.1	374.8	471.3	Turquie
Czech Republic	394.3	368.3	393.6	443.4	486.1	République tchèque
Finland	375.8	358.3	400.3	405.2	384.1	Finlande

(Value as percentages of World total) **(Valeur en pourcentage du total mondial)**

Regions of the world	1993	1994	1995	1996	1997	1998	1999	2000	2001	2002	Régions du monde
World	100.0	100.0	100.0	100.0	100.0	100.0	100.0	100.0	100.0	100.0	Monde
Africa	2.2	2.1	1.9	1.8	1.8	1.7	1.5	1.2	1.3	1.4	Afrique
Americas	22.0	23.8	22.7	22.8	24.7	27.0	27.9	28.4	28.9	27.6	Amériques
- Northern America	17.1	18.6	17.9	17.5	18.9	20.5	21.7	22.3	22.5	21.6	- Amérique du Nord
- LAIA	4.5	4.9	4.5	5.0	5.4	6.1	5.8	5.7	6.0	5.5	- ALAI
- CACM	0.1	0.1	0.1	0.1	0.1	0.2	0.1	0.1	0.2	0.2	- MCC
- Caribbean	0.2	0.1	0.2	0.2	0.2	0.2	0.2	0.2	0.2	0.2	- Caraïbes
- Rest of America	0.1	0.1	0.1	0.0	0.0	0.0	0.0	0.0	0.0	0.0	- Autre d'Amérique
Asia excluding former USSR	29.8	28.9	30.5	31.9	32.5	27.3	28.4	32.1	29.3	30.7	Asie ancienne URSS exclus
- Middle East	3.0	2.2	2.1	1.9	2.0	1.9	1.7	1.7	1.8	2.0	- Moyen-Orient
Asia former USSR	0.0	0.1	0.1	0.1	0.1	0.2	0.2	0.2	0.3	0.3	Asie ancienne URSS
Europe excluding former USSR	42.6	41.9	41.6	40.2	37.7	40.9	39.3	35.6	37.8	37.5	Europe ancienne URSS exclus
- European Union	37.8	37.3	36.6	35.6	33.6	36.3	34.9	31.6	33.6	33.0	- Union Européenne
- Eastern Europe	1.8	1.7	2.1	2.0	2.0	2.2	2.0	1.9	2.1	2.3	- Europe de l'Est
- Rest of Europe	2.9	2.9	2.8	2.6	2.2	2.4	2.3	2.0	2.0	2.2	- Autre de l'Europe
Europe former USSR	1.1	1.1	1.1	1.1	1.3	1.1	0.9	1.0	1.0	1.1	Europe ancienne URSS
Oceania	2.2	2.3	2.1	2.0	1.9	1.8	1.8	1.5	1.5	1.5	Océanie

Instruments de mesure, d'analyse et de contrôle, pièces détachées des groupes 873 et 874 874

TRADE BY COMMODITY (Value in million US dollars)
Exports by principal countries or areas

COMMERCE PAR PRODUIT (Valeur en millions de dollars EU)
Exportations selon les principaux pays ou zones

Country or area	1998	1999	2000	2001	2002	Pays ou zone
World	61878.4	65033.9	74649.7	74103.5	74026.7	Monde
Africa	159.8	212.3	167.9	147.5	157.3	Afrique
Americas	20114.1	21502.2	26094.8	24771.1	23334.9	Amériques
- Northern America	18698.3	19805.7	24025.6	22320.9	20725.2	- Amérique du Nord
- LAIA	1386.6	1662.0	2041.5	2379.4	2563.4	- ALAI
- CACM	7.9	19.0	10.5	37.7	19.8	- MCC
- Caribbean	20.6	14.4	16.3	31.4	25.5	- Caraïbes
- Rest of America	0.6	1.1	0.9	1.7	1.0	- Autre d'Amérique
Asia excluding former USSR	10644.6	11977.0	16132.6	14696.1	15037.9	Asie ancienne URSS exclus
- Middle East	74.5	89.6	111.3	104.4	111.6	- Moyen-Orient
Asia former USSR	11.4	11.4	31.9	26.3	30.1	Asie ancienne URSS
Europe excluding former USSR	30054.1	30247.3	31097.5	32909.2	34302.8	Europe ancienne URSS exclus
- European Union	27242.3	27497.9	28222.9	29734.4	30760.7	- Union Européenne
- Eastern Europe	377.6	360.7	466.2	619.1	784.2	- Europe de l'Est
- Rest of Europe	2434.2	2388.6	2408.4	2555.7	2757.8	- Autre de l'Europe
Europe former USSR	489.0	588.2	661.3	1107.9	723.5	Europe ancienne URSS
Oceania	405.3	495.7	463.7	445.5	440.3	Océanie
United States	17360.3	18348.2	22344.7	20623.6	18946.2	Etats-Unis d'Amérique
Germany	9658.6	10094.8	9938.8	10634.5	11327.3	Allemagne
Japan	6336.1	7187.9	9839.3	7762.9	7435.8	Japon
United Kingdom	6075.0	6079.1	6277.6	6599.4	6365.8	Royaume-Uni
France-Monaco	3167.1	3054.6	3346.9	3613.6	3846.1	France-Monaco
Netherlands	1968.3	1866.7	2181.2	2028.9	2134.8	Pays-Bas
Switzerland-Liechtenstein	1959.6	1914.0	1950.7	2005.6	2135.3	Suisse-Liechtenstein
Italy-San Marino-Holy See	1849.3	1866.5	1815.2	1917.6	1920.4	Italie-Saint-Marin-Saint-Siège
Mexico	1204.5	1460.3	1787.8	2089.5	2270.3	Mexique
Canada	1337.3	1457.0	1680.5	1696.6	1778.5	Canada
China, Hong Kong SAR	936.4	1063.1	1390.8	1457.2	1567.0	Chine - RAS de Hong-Kong
Singapore	915.0	1052.4	1274.4	1383.3	1757.1	Singapour
Sweden	1059.3	1078.5	1097.2	1180.9	1218.0	Suède
China	643.3	700.4	938.6	1091.6	1259.3	Chine
Denmark	633.1	633.5	669.3	701.2	752.2	Danemark
Spain	599.5	674.1	631.9	678.3	683.0	Espagne
Austria	644.8	561.0	590.2	644.3	645.2	Autriche
Malaysia	315.3	355.0	624.1	818.1	e867.0	Malaisie
Israel	450.1	479.8	666.6	696.8	588.9	Israël
Russian Federation	354.3	466.3	509.6	915.3	509.5	Fédération de Russie
Finland	485.9	521.2	553.3	581.6	589.0	Finlande
Belgium	–	615.6	628.1	647.6	e726.6	Belgique
Norway	371.2	370.6	351.7	421.6	480.8	Norvège
Australia	313.9	403.2	403.0	393.0	398.8	Australie
Korea, Republic of	262.1	271.3	397.1	361.1	380.6	République de Corée
Ireland	356.3	251.4	311.9	303.3	326.4	Irlande
Hungary	94.3	110.7	169.3	258.2	340.0	Hongrie
Czech Republic	164.7	141.5	153.7	204.5	231.7	République tchèque
Brazil	130.1	149.1	171.7	193.2	e200.3	Brésil
Belgium-Luxembourg	578.8	–	–	–	–	Belgique-Luxembourg

(Value as percentages of World total) **(Valeur en pourcentage du total mondial)**

Regions of the world	1993	1994	1995	1996	1997	1998	1999	2000	2001	2002	Régions du monde
World	100.0	100.0	100.0	100.0	100.0	100.0	100.0	100.0	100.0	100.0	Monde
Africa	0.2	0.2	0.2	0.2	0.2	0.3	0.3	0.2	0.2	0.2	Afrique
Americas	30.3	29.6	28.2	29.3	32.0	32.5	33.1	35.0	33.4	31.5	Amériques
- Northern America	29.0	28.3	27.1	27.9	30.2	30.2	30.5	32.2	30.1	28.0	- Amérique du Nord
- LAIA	1.3	1.3	1.1	1.4	1.7	2.2	2.6	2.7	3.2	3.5	- ALAI
- CACM	0.0	0.0	0.0	0.0	0.0	0.0	0.0	0.0	0.1	0.0	- MCC
- Caribbean	0.0	0.0	0.0	0.0	0.0	0.0	0.0	0.0	0.0	0.0	- Caraïbes
- Rest of America	0.0	0.0	0.0	0.0	0.0	0.0	0.0	0.0	0.0	0.0	- Autre d'Amérique
Asia excluding former USSR	19.0	19.6	20.8	19.8	19.6	17.2	18.4	21.6	19.8	20.3	Asie ancienne URSS exclus
- Middle East	0.3	0.3	0.2	0.1	0.1	0.1	0.1	0.1	0.1	0.2	- Moyen-Orient
Asia former USSR	0.0	0.0	0.0	0.0	0.0	0.0	0.0	0.0	0.0	0.0	Asie ancienne URSS
Europe excluding former USSR	49.9	49.6	49.9	49.7	47.1	48.6	46.5	41.7	44.4	46.3	Europe ancienne URSS exclus
- European Union	44.4	44.1	44.4	44.5	42.7	44.0	42.3	37.8	40.1	41.6	- Union Européenne
- Eastern Europe	0.4	0.4	0.6	0.5	0.5	0.6	0.6	0.6	0.8	1.1	- Europe de l'Est
- Rest of Europe	5.1	5.1	5.0	4.6	3.9	3.9	3.7	3.2	3.4	3.7	- Autre de l'Europe
Europe former USSR	0.1	0.4	0.4	0.4	0.5	0.8	0.9	0.9	1.5	1.0	Europe ancienne URSS
Oceania	0.5	0.6	0.5	0.6	0.6	0.7	0.8	0.6	0.6	0.6	Océanie

881 Photographic apparatus and equipment, nes

TRADE BY COMMODITY (Value in million US dollars)
Imports by principal countries or areas

COMMERCE PAR PRODUIT (Valeur en millions de dollars EU)
Importations selon les principaux pays ou zones

Country or area	1998	1999	2000	2001	2002	Pays ou zone
World	13764.8	15080.2	17997.4	15444.7	14585.3	Monde
Africa	103.5	110.9	105.5	87.1	104.2	Afrique
Americas	4085.1	4456.8	5168.7	4291.0	4034.8	Amériques
- Northern America	3647.1	4092.2	4752.1	3817.9	3556.1	- Amérique du Nord
- LAIA	399.4	325.8	373.1	436.7	438.6	- ALAI
- CACM	15.1	15.5	16.7	15.2	17.1	- MCC
- Caribbean	16.1	17.2	17.4	16.9	17.2	- Caraïbes
- Rest of America	7.4	6.0	9.5	4.3	5.8	- Autre d'Amérique
Asia excluding former USSR	5035.8	5772.0	7794.3	6450.5	6385.1	Asie ancienne URSS exclus
- Middle East	229.1	202.0	225.4	211.8	213.9	- Moyen-Orient
Asia former USSR	4.1	4.1	4.5	3.9	4.0	Asie ancienne URSS
Europe excluding former USSR	4284.4	4502.3	4670.7	4374.2	3806.5	Europe ancienne URSS exclus
- European Union	3896.5	4078.8	4276.4	4019.9	3421.0	- Union Européenne
- Eastern Europe	111.0	104.9	118.6	128.0	161.8	- Europe de l'Est
- Rest of Europe	276.9	318.5	275.6	226.3	223.7	- Autre de l'Europe
Europe former USSR	56.2	24.2	30.6	40.1	50.5	Europe ancienne URSS
Oceania	195.7	209.9	223.0	197.9	200.2	Océanie
United States	3363.2	3777.0	4398.3	3467.2	3289.7	Etats-Unis d'Amérique
China, Hong Kong SAR	1591.1	1588.5	1897.9	1870.7	1748.8	Chine - RAS de Hong-Kong
Germany	958.3	943.4	1069.5	1142.3	801.6	Allemagne
Japan	932.6	935.1	1022.5	893.1	786.7	Japon
China	588.0	637.0	813.1	756.3	910.4	Chine
Korea, Republic of	507.3	693.0	960.2	622.6	643.9	République de Corée
United Kingdom	761.6	679.4	695.9	630.6	564.8	Royaume-Uni
France-Monaco	529.9	517.4	582.1	494.9	437.8	France-Monaco
Singapore	278.4	365.6	496.8	519.2	467.1	Singapour
Netherlands	286.7	366.2	466.4	447.5	379.0	Pays-Bas
Italy-San Marino-Holy See	304.5	426.1	396.5	319.6	295.6	Italie-Saint-Marin-Saint-Siège
Canada	281.8	312.9	352.4	349.2	264.4	Canada
Mexico	202.0	192.6	224.8	300.8	321.7	Mexique
Spain	229.8	263.0	245.4	236.3	232.2	Espagne
Belgium	-	370.1	269.8	264.9	e290.5	Belgique
Malaysia	128.6	137.5	201.9	209.4	e228.9	Malaisie
Australia	158.0	167.0	178.0	153.2	151.3	Australie
Switzerland-Liechtenstein	169.5	210.3	178.4	121.8	104.7	Suisse-Liechtenstein
Philippines	197.4	172.0	116.1	83.1	18.7	Philippines
Ireland	103.3	89.0	142.6	98.9	67.0	Irlande
Austria	93.1	102.2	104.5	110.4	81.3	Autriche
Israel	32.0	173.6	155.9	54.0	61.6	Israël
Sweden	97.9	94.2	97.2	77.0	83.2	Suède
Thailand	66.0	60.0	98.4	88.2	e91.9	Thaïlande
United Arab Emirates	50.7	53.1	77.6	76.7	e78.7	Emirates arabes unis
Denmark	67.1	70.7	63.6	65.7	58.4	Danemark
Belgium-Luxembourg	323.2	-	-	-	-	Belgique-Luxembourg
Norway	66.3	66.1	57.0	60.3	65.3	Norvège
Portugal	58.3	59.0	55.5	51.2	47.0	Portugal
Saudi Arabia	66.7	61.0	42.8	40.1	e41.5	Arabie saoudite

(Value as percentages of World total) **(Valeur en pourcentage du total mondial)**

Regions of the world	1993	1994	1995	1996	1997	1998	1999	2000	2001	2002	Régions du monde
World	100.0	100.0	100.0	100.0	100.0	100.0	100.0	100.0	100.0	100.0	Monde
Africa	0.9	0.8	0.7	0.7	0.7	0.8	0.7	0.6	0.6	0.7	Afrique
Americas	26.5	27.4	25.2	25.2	28.0	29.7	29.6	28.7	27.8	27.7	Amériques
- Northern America	23.0	23.8	22.7	22.8	25.2	26.5	27.1	26.4	24.7	24.4	- Amérique du Nord
- LAIA	3.1	3.2	2.2	2.2	2.6	2.9	2.2	2.1	2.8	3.0	- ALAI
- CACM	0.1	0.1	0.1	0.1	0.1	0.1	0.1	0.1	0.1	0.1	- MCC
- Caribbean	0.2	0.2	0.1	0.1	0.1	0.1	0.1	0.1	0.1	0.1	- Caraïbes
- Rest of America	0.1	0.1	0.1	0.0	0.0	0.1	0.0	0.1	0.0	0.0	- Autre d'Amérique
Asia excluding former USSR	36.7	37.0	40.8	41.0	39.6	36.6	38.3	43.3	41.8	43.8	Asie ancienne URSS exclus
- Middle East	2.3	1.7	1.6	1.6	1.7	1.7	1.3	1.3	1.4	1.5	- Moyen-Orient
Asia former USSR	0.0	0.0	0.0	0.0	0.0	0.0	0.0	0.0	0.0	0.0	Asie ancienne URSS
Europe excluding former USSR	33.8	32.4	30.8	30.6	29.5	31.1	29.9	26.0	28.3	26.1	Europe ancienne URSS exclus
- European Union	31.1	29.8	28.1	27.9	26.8	28.3	27.0	23.8	26.0	23.5	- Union Européenne
- Eastern Europe	0.7	0.6	0.7	0.7	0.7	0.8	0.7	0.7	0.8	1.1	- Europe de l'Est
- Rest of Europe	2.0	1.9	2.1	2.1	2.0	2.0	2.1	1.5	1.5	1.5	- Autre de l'Europe
Europe former USSR	0.4	0.8	0.8	0.8	0.7	0.4	0.2	0.2	0.3	0.3	Europe ancienne URSS
Oceania	1.7	1.6	1.5	1.6	1.5	1.4	1.4	1.2	1.3	1.4	Océanie

TRADE BY COMMODITY (Value in million US dollars)
Exports by principal countries or areas

COMMERCE PAR PRODUIT (Valeur en millions de dollars EU)
Exportations selon les principaux pays ou zones

Country or area	1998	1999	2000	2001	2002	Pays ou zone
World	13943.9	15111.7	18935.6	16113.7	15278.0	Monde
Africa	6.0	5.2	7.4	13.6	18.5	Afrique
Americas	1508.7	1715.1	1772.9	1652.0	1639.2	Amériques
- Northern America	1257.2	1414.5	1364.3	1233.0	1249.7	- Amérique du Nord
- LAIA	242.4	291.8	395.3	410.3	382.1	- ALAI
- CACM	5.4	6.9	7.5	5.1	5.7	- MCC
- Caribbean	3.7	1.2	4.3	3.3	1.4	- Caraïbes
- Rest of America	0.0	0.7	1.4	0.3	0.2	- Autre d'Amérique
Asia excluding former USSR	8647.0	9252.2	12078.9	10207.4	8845.7	Asie ancienne URSS exclus
- Middle East	41.5	42.6	45.8	40.7	47.6	- Moyen-Orient
Asia former USSR	0.1	0.1	0.4	0.3	0.3	Asie ancienne URSS
Europe excluding former USSR	3732.0	4087.5	5023.0	4183.1	4719.4	Europe ancienne URSS exclus
- European Union	3394.5	3634.5	4535.4	3842.5	4355.7	- Union Européenne
- Eastern Europe	34.2	27.5	73.3	108.1	134.4	- Europe de l'Est
- Rest of Europe	303.4	425.4	414.3	232.5	229.3	- Autre de l'Europe
Europe former USSR	18.8	11.0	8.5	17.9	18.9	Europe ancienne URSS
Oceania	31.2	40.6	44.5	39.4	36.0	Océanie
Japan	3640.4	4100.9	5766.1	4290.5	3485.4	Japon
China, Hong Kong SAR	1895.5	1959.7	2355.8	2307.3	2181.4	Chine - RAS de Hong-Kong
Netherlands	1013.8	1230.8	2226.1	1548.8	2129.0	Pays-Bas
United States	1186.9	1330.0	1286.8	1186.8	1178.2	Etats-Unis d'Amérique
China	1154.3	1185.0	1447.3	1221.7	1056.3	Chine
Germany	903.9	923.2	880.1	940.3	898.7	Allemagne
Malaysia	445.6	430.9	573.5	590.9	e626.2	Malaisie
Mexico	240.4	289.1	391.1	406.6	378.3	Mexique
Singapore	280.8	283.2	390.3	380.9	340.8	Singapour
United Kingdom	394.0	355.0	344.3	247.6	251.0	Royaume-Uni
Switzerland-Liechtenstein	268.9	397.7	381.2	165.4	181.1	Suisse-Liechtenstein
Italy-San Marino-Holy See	243.9	263.1	277.8	265.5	209.4	Italie-Saint-Marin-Saint-Siège
Belgium	–	322.1	261.2	292.4	e328.1	Belgique
Thailand	189.8	179.2	269.2	255.3	e269.6	Thaïlande
France-Monaco	181.2	187.5	210.4	207.3	213.0	France-Monaco
Korea, Republic of	166.2	178.2	162.1	126.8	106.3	République de Corée
Indonesia	132.5	121.2	141.3	118.9	59.7	Indonésie
Denmark	124.5	135.9	120.0	93.5	81.3	Danemark
Philippines	136.1	64.1	109.2	223.5	10.9	Philippines
Sweden	84.8	76.0	86.5	111.6	91.2	Suède
Israel	48.9	77.3	132.5	85.1	51.4	Israël
Canada	70.2	84.4	77.5	46.2	71.5	Canada
Belgium-Luxembourg	318.1	–	–	–	–	Belgique-Luxembourg
Austria	53.7	57.3	55.0	51.0	55.8	Autriche
Hungary	1.3	8.4	50.1	82.5	96.5	Hongrie
Spain	41.9	48.8	39.6	47.0	52.6	Espagne
Australia	25.9	31.5	37.8	31.7	33.5	Australie
United Arab Emirates	26.0	26.8	28.3	31.9	e33.2	Emirates arabes unis
Norway	12.4	9.3	14.2	46.1	24.2	Norvège
Portugal	25.2	20.5	16.6	19.3	19.2	Portugal

(Value as percentages of World total) **(Valeur en pourcentage du total mondial)**

Regions of the world	1993	1994	1995	1996	1997	1998	1999	2000	2001	2002	Régions du monde
World	100.0	100.0	100.0	100.0	100.0	100.0	100.0	100.0	100.0	100.0	Monde
Africa	0.0	0.1	0.1	0.0	0.0	0.0	0.0	0.0	0.1	0.1	Afrique
Americas	11.8	11.1	9.8	10.1	9.9	10.8	11.3	9.4	10.3	10.7	Amériques
- Northern America	11.0	10.4	9.1	9.2	8.7	9.0	9.4	7.2	7.7	8.2	- Amérique du Nord
- LAIA	0.8	0.7	0.6	0.9	1.1	1.7	1.9	2.1	2.5	2.5	- ALAI
- CACM	0.0	0.0	0.0	0.0	0.0	0.0	0.0	0.0	0.0	0.0	- MCC
- Caribbean	0.0	0.0	0.0	0.0	0.0	0.0	0.0	0.0	0.0	0.0	- Caraïbes
- Rest of America	0.0	0.0	0.0	0.0	0.0	0.0	0.0	0.0	0.0	0.0	- Autre d'Amérique
Asia excluding former USSR	64.5	63.5	65.9	64.3	63.1	62.0	61.2	63.8	63.3	57.9	Asie ancienne URSS exclus
- Middle East	0.2	0.1	0.1	0.1	0.1	0.3	0.3	0.2	0.3	0.3	- Moyen-Orient
Asia former USSR	0.0	0.0	0.0	0.0	0.0	0.0	0.0	0.0	0.0	0.0	Asie ancienne URSS
Europe excluding former USSR	23.2	24.9	23.9	25.1	26.5	26.8	27.0	26.5	26.0	30.9	Europe ancienne URSS exclus
- European Union	21.5	23.2	22.3	23.2	24.4	24.3	24.1	24.0	23.8	28.5	- Union Européenne
- Eastern Europe	0.1	0.1	0.1	0.1	0.1	0.2	0.2	0.4	0.7	0.9	- Europe de l'Est
- Rest of Europe	1.6	1.6	1.6	1.8	2.0	2.2	2.8	2.2	1.4	1.5	- Autre de l'Europe
Europe former USSR	0.2	0.1	0.1	0.2	0.2	0.1	0.1	0.0	0.1	0.1	Europe ancienne URSS
Oceania	0.2	0.3	0.2	0.2	0.2	0.2	0.3	0.2	0.2	0.2	Océanie

882 Photographic and cinematographic supplies

TRADE BY COMMODITY (Value in million US dollars)
Imports by principal countries or areas

COMMERCE PAR PRODUIT (Valeur en millions de dollars EU)
Importations selon les principaux pays ou zones

Country or area	1998	1999	2000	2001	2002	Pays ou zone
World	17291.4	18029.5	18622.4	16550.7	16511.1	Monde
Africa	276.5	256.0	266.2	255.2	276.4	Afrique
Americas	4339.1	4511.3	4786.4	4193.0	4086.4	Amériques
- Northern America	3081.2	3200.0	3329.5	2827.2	2755.9	- Amérique du Nord
- LAIA	1166.1	1215.6	1358.0	1261.6	1236.1	- ALAI
- CACM	44.2	47.3	52.2	54.1	53.2	- MCC
- Caribbean	35.4	36.8	33.3	39.2	32.4	- Caraïbes
- Rest of America	12.3	11.6	13.5	10.9	8.8	- Autre d'Amérique
Asia excluding former USSR	4004.9	4693.1	5324.5	4670.1	4695.3	Asie ancienne URSS exclus
- Middle East	382.7	390.6	384.6	353.7	367.8	- Moyen-Orient
Asia former USSR	6.9	6.4	8.1	8.6	8.0	Asie ancienne URSS
Europe excluding former USSR	8128.6	7964.1	7681.8	6926.1	6905.9	Europe ancienne URSS exclus
- European Union	7458.7	7288.9	7033.6	6298.3	6231.9	- Union Européenne
- Eastern Europe	266.7	264.5	285.3	294.2	331.7	- Europe de l'Est
- Rest of Europe	403.2	410.8	362.8	333.7	342.3	- Autre de l'Europe
Europe former USSR	134.3	127.2	140.7	145.9	156.5	Europe ancienne URSS
Oceania	401.1	471.4	414.7	351.8	382.7	Océanie
United States	2409.1	2462.0	2654.1	2213.0	2132.9	Etats-Unis d'Amérique
Germany	1523.4	1483.6	1314.4	1258.4	1051.2	Allemagne
United Kingdom	1478.2	1366.1	1487.9	1166.3	1077.9	Royaume-Uni
France-Monaco	1185.7	1250.3	1219.6	979.9	1033.4	France-Monaco
China, Hong Kong SAR	797.9	788.7	885.8	859.2	847.0	Chine - RAS de Hong-Kong
Italy-San Marino-Holy See	706.9	704.5	684.4	644.4	680.1	Italie-Saint-Marin-Saint-Siège
Singapore	528.2	695.0	807.5	718.4	667.8	Singapour
Canada	670.2	735.9	674.6	613.3	622.0	Canada
Netherlands	677.2	605.3	548.8	470.4	572.2	Pays-Bas
Mexico	436.6	520.0	628.9	596.5	676.9	Mexique
Korea, Republic of	439.0	549.2	626.1	579.6	590.9	République de Corée
Japan	553.4	627.0	721.5	422.9	358.1	Japon
Spain	431.5	450.7	420.9	412.5	421.5	Espagne
China	221.3	357.3	517.8	458.5	566.6	Chine
Belgium	–	461.5	416.8	469.3	e514.7	Belgique
Australia	366.5	379.7	330.8	270.6	296.7	Australie
Brazil	310.0	283.2	304.2	282.5	254.6	Brésil
Sweden	343.3	230.6	213.9	217.5	217.0	Suède
Austria	233.1	211.8	245.8	216.8	196.1	Autriche
Switzerland-Liechtenstein	241.5	237.1	204.3	178.6	170.1	Suisse-Liechtenstein
India	167.1	168.0	197.2	215.7	207.5	Inde
Turkey	143.2	140.0	137.8	118.6	130.1	Turquie
Denmark	149.2	132.8	131.2	118.4	121.7	Danemark
Argentina	139.0	143.9	141.4	118.9	e52.6	Argentine
Thailand	101.7	130.7	119.1	111.8	e116.4	Thaïlande
Poland	109.9	108.1	112.1	112.4	120.8	Pologne
Malaysia	80.8	110.1	110.5	107.8	e117.9	Malaisie
Portugal	88.2	108.0	102.7	100.7	103.1	Portugal
United Arab Emirates	98.0	102.7	101.3	92.1	e94.4	Emirates arabes unis
Israel	82.9	93.0	109.6	103.8	93.9	Israël

(Value as percentages of World total) **(Valeur en pourcentage du total mondial)**

Regions of the world	1993	1994	1995	1996	1997	1998	1999	2000	2001	2002	Régions du monde
World	100.0	100.0	100.0	100.0	100.0	100.0	100.0	100.0	100.0	100.0	Monde
Africa	1.6	1.7	1.6	1.6	1.6	1.6	1.4	1.4	1.5	1.7	Afrique
Americas	24.3	23.9	22.2	22.3	23.9	25.1	25.0	25.7	25.3	24.7	Amériques
- Northern America	19.1	18.3	16.9	16.7	17.5	17.8	17.7	17.9	17.1	16.7	- Amérique du Nord
- LAIA	4.7	5.0	4.8	5.2	5.9	6.7	6.7	7.3	7.6	7.5	- ALAI
- CACM	0.2	0.2	0.2	0.2	0.2	0.3	0.3	0.3	0.3	0.3	- MCC
- Caribbean	0.2	0.2	0.2	0.2	0.2	0.2	0.2	0.2	0.2	0.2	- Caraïbes
- Rest of America	0.1	0.1	0.1	0.1	0.1	0.1	0.1	0.1	0.1	0.1	- Autre d'Amérique
Asia excluding former USSR	24.3	24.2	24.5	25.4	25.5	23.2	26.0	28.6	28.2	28.4	Asie ancienne URSS exclus
- Middle East	2.2	1.8	1.9	2.0	2.1	2.2	2.2	2.1	2.1	2.2	- Moyen-Orient
Asia former USSR	0.0	0.0	0.0	0.1	0.0	0.0	0.0	0.0	0.1	0.0	Asie ancienne URSS
Europe excluding former USSR	46.9	46.6	48.2	46.6	45.0	47.0	44.2	41.3	41.8	41.8	Europe ancienne URSS exclus
- European Union	43.1	43.0	44.6	43.1	41.6	43.1	40.4	37.8	38.1	37.7	- Union Européenne
- Eastern Europe	1.1	1.1	1.2	1.2	1.3	1.5	1.5	1.5	1.8	2.0	- Europe de l'Est
- Rest of Europe	2.6	2.5	2.4	2.3	2.2	2.3	2.3	1.9	2.0	2.1	- Autre de l'Europe
Europe former USSR	0.5	0.8	1.0	1.1	1.1	0.8	0.7	0.8	0.9	0.9	Europe ancienne URSS
Oceania	2.4	2.8	2.6	2.9	2.9	2.3	2.6	2.2	2.1	2.3	Océanie

TRADE BY COMMODITY (Value in million US dollars)
Exports by principal countries or areas

COMMERCE PAR PRODUIT (Valeur en millions de dollars EU)
Exportations selon les principaux pays ou zones

Country or area	1998	1999	2000	2001	2002	Pays ou zone
World	17354.2	17329.1	18511.9	16266.1	16924.3	Monde
Africa	13.4	12.1	15.0	26.6	24.2	Afrique
Americas	3447.6	3557.7	4347.1	3307.3	3512.5	Amériques
- Northern America	2876.1	2930.0	3656.1	2766.8	2989.6	- Amérique du Nord
- LAIA	569.8	625.7	687.7	537.7	521.2	- ALAI
- CACM	0.8	1.1	2.3	1.8	0.7	- MCC
- Caribbean	1.0	0.8	0.9	0.8	0.8	- Caraïbes
- Rest of America	0.0	0.1	0.1	0.2	0.1	- Autre d'Amérique
Asia excluding former USSR	5177.5	5614.3	6035.6	5588.9	5880.3	Asie ancienne URSS exclus
- Middle East	225.0	232.6	53.4	62.6	60.2	- Moyen-Orient
Asia former USSR	0.2	0.1	0.0	0.0	0.0	Asie ancienne URSS
Europe excluding former USSR	8446.0	7857.4	7844.6	7116.7	7276.8	Europe ancienne URSS exclus
- European Union	8232.6	7659.6	7665.1	6946.1	7095.8	- Union Européenne
- Eastern Europe	46.1	34.2	39.2	41.7	42.5	- Europe de l'Est
- Rest of Europe	167.3	163.6	140.3	128.9	138.5	- Autre de l'Europe
Europe former USSR	11.5	8.5	9.8	7.7	7.3	Europe ancienne URSS
Oceania	257.9	279.1	259.7	218.8	223.1	Océanie
Japan	3465.7	3753.7	3974.0	3597.4	3763.0	Japon
United States	2637.3	2671.3	3416.6	2552.1	2833.4	Etats-Unis d'Amérique
Germany	1974.2	1908.0	1728.3	1619.7	1638.6	Allemagne
United Kingdom	1693.6	1646.7	1719.0	1465.1	1317.2	Royaume-Uni
Belgium	–	1370.9	1434.7	1388.5	e1557.9	Belgique
France-Monaco	1043.0	1114.2	1129.2	967.2	961.5	France-Monaco
Netherlands	1323.7	785.2	819.3	673.2	792.3	Pays-Bas
Singapore	501.5	677.8	794.3	765.9	769.9	Singapour
China, Hong Kong SAR	613.5	463.3	516.1	470.5	471.2	Chine - RAS de Hong-Kong
Mexico	318.5	360.9	427.3	336.2	315.8	Mexique
China	139.6	227.9	426.4	419.2	522.4	Chine
Italy-San Marino-Holy See	388.2	366.5	336.1	300.2	303.9	Italie-Saint-Marin-Saint-Siège
Belgium-Luxembourg	1340.3	–	–	–	–	Belgique-Luxembourg
Australia	253.9	276.1	255.8	215.2	222.4	Australie
Canada	238.7	258.7	239.5	214.8	156.2	Canada
Brazil	210.1	220.5	195.3	155.5	e161.3	Brésil
Spain	155.1	149.9	156.3	185.2	167.6	Espagne
Switzerland-Liechtenstein	152.5	151.7	126.2	113.3	119.4	Suisse-Liechtenstein
Sweden	135.0	124.9	121.1	110.8	120.5	Suède
United Arab Emirates	212.0	218.8	37.4	43.7	e45.5	Emirates arabes unis
Korea, Republic of	77.8	83.1	82.0	107.0	115.5	République de Corée
Austria	80.1	79.0	69.6	79.1	78.8	Autriche
Malaysia	54.2	72.8	74.9	61.4	e65.0	Malaisie
Argentina	37.7	41.9	61.0	43.0	e41.5	Argentine
Denmark	39.7	38.7	47.0	46.7	47.1	Danemark
Greece	9.8	20.2	42.7	40.1	e40.1	Grèce
Finland	25.2	22.1	21.1	20.2	20.9	Finlande
Ireland	18.0	9.7	16.0	23.6	25.6	Irlande
India	18.1	17.7	16.7	8.5	9.1	Inde
Bulgaria	9.8	11.4	14.6	e15.5	e17.4	Bulgarie

(Value as percentages of World total) **(Valeur en pourcentage du total mondial)**

Regions of the world	1993	1994	1995	1996	1997	1998	1999	2000	2001	2002	Régions du monde
World	100.0	100.0	100.0	100.0	100.0	100.0	100.0	100.0	100.0	100.0	Monde
Africa	0.1	0.1	0.1	0.1	0.1	0.1	0.1	0.1	0.2	0.1	Afrique
Americas	19.4	18.2	18.2	19.5	20.0	19.9	20.5	23.5	20.3	20.8	Amériques
- Northern America	16.7	15.3	15.2	16.8	17.1	16.6	16.9	19.7	17.0	17.7	- Amérique du Nord
- LAIA	2.7	2.9	3.0	2.7	3.0	3.3	3.6	3.7	3.3	3.1	- ALAI
- CACM	0.0	0.0	0.0	0.0	0.0	0.0	0.0	0.0	0.0	0.0	- MCC
- Caribbean	0.0	0.0	0.0	0.0	0.0	0.0	0.0	0.0	0.0	0.0	- Caraïbes
- Rest of America	0.0	0.0	0.0	0.0	0.0	0.0	0.0	0.0	0.0	0.0	- Autre d'Amérique
Asia excluding former USSR	30.7	31.0	31.2	30.5	30.1	29.8	32.4	32.6	34.4	34.7	Asie ancienne URSS exclus
- Middle East	0.2	0.2	0.2	0.9	1.1	1.3	1.3	0.3	0.4	0.4	- Moyen-Orient
Asia former USSR	0.0	0.0	0.0	0.0	0.0	0.0	0.0	0.0	0.0	0.0	Asie ancienne URSS
Europe excluding former USSR	48.3	49.1	48.9	48.0	47.8	48.7	45.3	42.4	43.8	43.0	Europe ancienne URSS exclus
- European Union	46.6	47.6	47.3	46.7	46.6	47.4	44.2	41.4	42.7	41.9	- Union Européenne
- Eastern Europe	0.1	0.2	0.2	0.2	0.2	0.3	0.2	0.2	0.3	0.3	- Europe de l'Est
- Rest of Europe	1.6	1.4	1.4	1.2	0.9	1.0	0.9	0.8	0.8	0.8	- Autre de l'Europe
Europe former USSR	0.0	0.1	0.1	0.1	0.1	0.1	0.0	0.1	0.0	0.0	Europe ancienne URSS
Oceania	1.5	1.5	1.5	1.7	1.9	1.5	1.6	1.4	1.3	1.3	Océanie

883 Cinematograph film, exposed and developed

TRADE BY COMMODITY (Value in million US dollars)
Imports by principal countries or areas

COMMERCE PAR PRODUIT (Valeur en millions de dollars EU)
Importations selon les principaux pays ou zones

Country or area	1998	1999	2000	2001	2002	Pays ou zone
World	306.9	344.8	363.1	445.7	421.5	Monde
Africa	6.6	5.0	4.5	4.6	4.2	Afrique
Americas	132.6	164.2	160.5	192.4	209.1	Amériques
- Northern America	120.6	152.0	145.3	177.5	195.0	- Amérique du Nord
- LAIA	9.9	10.8	13.6	13.2	12.3	- ALAI
- CACM	0.6	0.4	0.7	0.6	0.8	- MCC
- Caribbean	0.8	0.5	0.7	0.7	0.6	- Caraïbes
- Rest of America	0.7	0.6	0.3	0.3	0.3	- Autre d'Amérique
Asia excluding former USSR	60.8	69.0	91.3	157.0	98.8	Asie ancienne URSS exclus
- Middle East	7.6	7.4	10.2	7.0	7.2	- Moyen-Orient
Asia former USSR	0.3	0.1	0.1	0.0	0.0	Asie ancienne URSS
Europe excluding former USSR	96.3	96.9	96.0	82.1	95.0	Europe ancienne URSS exclus
- European Union	75.4	76.7	74.6	68.3	83.4	- Union Européenne
- Eastern Europe	4.1	3.2	3.5	4.0	4.2	- Europe de l'Est
- Rest of Europe	16.8	17.1	17.9	9.8	7.3	- Autre de l'Europe
Europe former USSR	0.8	0.7	1.1	1.9	2.1	Europe ancienne URSS
Oceania	9.4	9.0	9.5	7.7	12.4	Océanie
United States	111.3	140.4	135.3	169.4	186.4	Etats-Unis d'Amérique
Korea, Republic of	20.3	23.7	40.7	46.5	51.4	République de Corée
France-Monaco	30.6	30.2	34.2	25.6	30.3	France-Monaco
Japan	9.1	13.0	13.4	80.0	13.7	Japon
Spain	16.3	17.7	12.7	13.1	18.6	Espagne
Switzerland-Liechtenstein	12.7	13.1	14.0	6.1	3.1	Suisse-Liechtenstein
Canada	9.2	11.5	10.0	8.1	8.6	Canada
United Kingdom	8.0	8.9	7.9	8.6	10.9	Royaume-Uni
Australia	8.9	8.1	8.8	6.7	11.1	Australie
Mexico	5.9	5.7	8.1	6.9	6.6	Mexique
Israel	4.6	3.9	5.2	5.4	5.9	Israël
Austria	3.2	4.1	3.3	5.0	6.7	Autriche
Thailand	3.6	4.5	4.6	4.1	e4.3	Thaïlande
Italy-San Marino-Holy See	2.6	2.6	4.1	2.8	2.7	Italie-Saint-Marin-Saint-Siège
Germany	3.7	3.2	3.1	2.3	2.2	Allemagne
Norway	2.2	2.6	2.2	1.9	2.5	Norvège
China, Hong Kong SAR	1.7	2.8	2.5	2.0	2.4	Chine - RAS de Hong-Kong
Portugal	2.6	1.8	2.2	2.2	2.3	Portugal
Belgium	-	1.7	2.2	3.3	e3.6	Belgique
Indonesia	1.9	2.5	2.6	2.1	1.6	Indonésie
Chile	1.2	1.6	2.0	2.6	2.7	Chili
Turkey	1.6	1.6	2.2	1.7	3.0	Turquie
Lebanon	2.1	1.7	1.9	2.0	e1.9	Liban
China	1.7	2.9	2.3	1.1	1.2	Chine
Singapore	1.2	1.2	1.6	1.8	2.5	Singapour
Poland	2.1	1.0	1.6	1.7	1.5	Pologne
South Africa	-	-	2.4	2.8	2.6	Afrique du Sud
Southern African Customs Union	4.2	3.5	-	-	-	Union douanière d'Afrique australe
Venezuela	1.0	0.9	1.7	1.8	e1.5	Venezuela
Greece	1.4	1.2	1.3	1.3	e1.4	Grèce

(Value as percentages of World total) **(Valeur en pourcentage du total mondial)**

Regions of the world	1993	1994	1995	1996	1997	1998	1999	2000	2001	2002	Régions du monde
World	100.0	100.0	100.0	100.0	100.0	100.0	100.0	100.0	100.0	100.0	Monde
Africa	1.8	1.8	1.6	1.5	1.5	2.1	1.4	1.2	1.0	1.0	Afrique
Americas	37.2	28.6	28.8	33.8	35.5	43.2	47.6	44.2	43.2	49.6	Amériques
- Northern America	35.5	26.5	26.6	31.8	32.5	39.3	44.1	40.0	39.8	46.3	- Amérique du Nord
- LAIA	1.1	1.3	1.5	1.5	2.4	3.2	3.1	3.7	3.0	2.9	- ALAI
- CACM	0.0	0.0	0.0	0.1	0.1	0.2	0.1	0.2	0.1	0.2	- MCC
- Caribbean	0.5	0.7	0.6	0.4	0.4	0.3	0.1	0.2	0.2	0.2	- Caraïbes
- Rest of America	0.0	0.0	0.0	0.0	0.2	0.2	0.2	0.1	0.1	0.1	- Autre d'Amérique
Asia excluding former USSR	31.9	35.7	37.2	30.6	30.0	19.8	20.0	25.1	35.2	23.4	Asie ancienne URSS exclus
- Middle East	2.2	3.3	2.7	2.9	3.6	2.5	2.2	2.8	1.6	1.7	- Moyen-Orient
Asia former USSR	0.0	0.0	0.0	0.1	0.1	0.1	0.0	0.0	0.0	0.0	Asie ancienne URSS
Europe excluding former USSR	27.3	31.4	30.4	31.7	30.5	31.4	28.1	26.4	18.4	22.5	Europe ancienne URSS exclus
- European Union	23.0	26.1	21.2	24.0	23.4	24.6	22.2	20.6	15.3	19.8	- Union Européenne
- Eastern Europe	1.0	1.1	0.9	1.7	2.3	1.3	0.9	1.0	0.9	1.0	- Europe de l'Est
- Rest of Europe	3.3	4.3	8.3	6.0	4.7	5.5	5.0	4.9	2.2	1.7	- Autre de l'Europe
Europe former USSR	0.1	0.1	0.1	0.1	0.2	0.3	0.2	0.3	0.4	0.5	Europe ancienne URSS
Oceania	1.7	2.4	1.9	2.1	2.3	3.1	2.6	2.6	1.7	2.9	Océanie

TRADE BY COMMODITY (Value in million US dollars)
Exports by principal countries or areas

COMMERCE PAR PRODUIT (Valeur en millions de dollars EU)
Exportations selon les principaux pays ou zones

Country or area	1998	1999	2000	2001	2002	Pays ou zone
World	391.4	430.9	375.8	386.2	478.3	Monde
Africa	3.8	3.0	1.3	0.4	0.4	Afrique
Americas	109.7	139.1	154.7	173.4	212.1	Amériques
- Northern America	98.0	126.8	134.8	153.2	189.8	- Amérique du Nord
- LAIA	11.5	12.1	19.3	20.0	22.0	- ALAI
- CACM	0.0	0.0	0.0	0.0	0.0	- MCC
- Caribbean	0.2	0.3	0.6	0.2	0.4	- Caraïbes
- Rest of America	0.0	0.0	0.0	0.0	0.0	- Autre d'Amérique
Asia excluding former USSR	131.0	141.1	80.7	52.8	39.9	Asie ancienne URSS exclus
- Middle East	6.1	1.8	2.3	3.0	1.4	- Moyen-Orient
Asia former USSR	0.0	0.1	0.1	0.0	0.0	Asie ancienne URSS
Europe excluding former USSR	140.0	140.6	121.2	149.8	214.6	Europe ancienne URSS exclus
- European Union	136.0	137.6	114.1	129.7	204.7	- Union Européenne
- Eastern Europe	1.6	1.2	5.0	5.7	6.1	- Europe de l'Est
- Rest of Europe	2.4	1.8	2.1	14.4	3.8	- Autre de l'Europe
Europe former USSR	0.9	0.8	0.6	0.4	0.8	Europe ancienne URSS
Oceania	6.1	6.2	17.2	9.3	10.5	Océanie
Canada	65.3	92.9	100.2	121.2	153.8	Canada
Italy-San Marino-Holy See	49.8	60.8	47.4	57.1	105.9	Italie-Saint-Marin-Saint-Siège
United Kingdom	60.3	45.9	37.3	36.1	58.1	Royaume-Uni
Korea, Republic of	80.5	87.4	33.4	10.5	7.4	République de Corée
United States	32.7	33.9	34.6	32.0	36.0	Etats-Unis d'Amérique
India	23.2	27.1	25.1	17.7	15.5	Inde
France-Monaco	16.9	20.0	21.0	22.3	23.5	France-Monaco
Argentina	6.0	8.2	12.1	13.1	e12.7	Argentine
Israel	4.9	12.1	7.5	12.4	7.5	Israël
Australia	4.3	3.7	16.1	7.4	10.1	Australie
Mexico	4.5	3.8	7.1	6.3	8.7	Mexique
Spain	3.2	6.0	2.4	4.1	5.6	Espagne
Japan	2.4	4.5	5.2	3.7	1.5	Japon
China, Hong Kong SAR	3.5	2.8	3.0	2.8	3.8	Chine - RAS de Hong-Kong
Norway	0.3	0.2	0.1	12.4	0.1	Norvège
Bulgaria	0.6	0.3	3.4	e3.6	e4.1	Bulgarie
Belgium	–	1.8	1.7	3.1	e3.4	Belgique
China	4.1	2.9	2.4	0.1	0.2	Chine
Lebanon	5.0	0.9	1.0	1.2	e1.0	Liban
Germany	1.5	1.1	1.3	2.2	2.4	Allemagne
New Zealand	1.7	2.4	1.0	1.8	0.4	Nouvelle-Zélande
Philippines	5.6	1.0	0.1	0.1	0.0	Philippines
Switzerland-Liechtenstein	1.1	1.2	1.5	1.3	1.5	Suisse-Liechtenstein
Southern African Customs Union	3.4	2.7	–	–	–	Union douanière d'Afrique australe
Denmark	0.2	0.1	0.1	2.5	1.8	Danemark
Croatia	0.9	0.1	0.3	0.7	2.2	Croatie
Thailand	0.4	0.5	0.9	0.8	e0.8	Thaïlande
Kuwait	0.8	0.6	e1.0	e0.8	e0.0	Koweït
Czech Republic	0.6	0.7	0.5	0.6	0.7	République tchèque
Russian Federation	0.5	0.7	0.5	0.3	0.7	Fédération de Russie

(Value as percentages of World total) **(Valeur en pourcentage du total mondial)**

Regions of the world	1993	1994	1995	1996	1997	1998	1999	2000	2001	2002	Régions du monde
World	100.0	100.0	100.0	100.0	100.0	100.0	100.0	100.0	100.0	100.0	Monde
Africa	0.1	0.2	0.4	0.3	0.4	1.0	0.7	0.3	0.1	0.1	Afrique
Americas	36.2	26.9	28.9	28.8	25.7	28.0	32.3	41.2	44.9	44.3	Amériques
- Northern America	34.6	25.8	27.2	26.6	23.5	25.0	29.4	35.9	39.7	39.7	- Amérique du Nord
- LAIA	1.5	1.1	1.6	2.1	2.2	2.9	2.8	5.1	5.2	4.6	- ALAI
- CACM	0.0	0.0	0.0	0.0	0.0	0.0	0.0	0.0	0.0	0.0	- MCC
- Caribbean	0.1	0.0	0.1	0.0	0.1	0.0	0.1	0.2	0.1	0.1	- Caraïbes
- Rest of America	0.0	0.0	0.0	0.0	0.0	0.0	0.0	0.0	0.0	0.0	- Autre d'Amérique
Asia excluding former USSR	36.1	39.4	42.5	38.0	40.1	33.5	32.8	21.5	13.7	8.3	Asie ancienne URSS exclus
- Middle East	0.6	0.7	0.7	0.4	0.6	1.6	0.4	0.6	0.8	0.3	- Moyen-Orient
Asia former USSR	0.0	0.0	0.0	0.0	0.0	0.0	0.0	0.0	0.0	0.0	Asie ancienne URSS
Europe excluding former USSR	27.1	32.7	26.8	31.5	32.3	35.8	32.6	32.3	38.8	44.9	Europe ancienne URSS exclus
- European Union	24.9	30.6	25.7	29.3	31.4	34.7	31.9	30.4	33.6	42.8	- Union Européenne
- Eastern Europe	1.8	1.7	0.6	1.9	0.4	0.4	0.3	1.3	1.5	1.3	- Europe de l'Est
- Rest of Europe	0.4	0.4	0.6	0.3	0.5	0.6	0.4	0.6	3.7	0.8	- Autre de l'Europe
Europe former USSR	0.1	0.1	0.2	0.1	0.1	0.2	0.2	0.2	0.1	0.2	Europe ancienne URSS
Oceania	0.4	0.6	1.3	1.3	1.4	1.6	1.4	4.6	2.4	2.2	Océanie

884 Optical goods nes

TRADE BY COMMODITY (Value in million US dollars)
Imports by principal countries or areas

COMMERCE PAR PRODUIT (Valeur en millions de dollars EU)
Importations selon les principaux pays ou zones

Country or area	1998	1999	2000	2001	2002	Pays ou zone
World	8509.5	9308.4	10388.4	10504.1	11028.0	Monde
Africa	90.6	88.0	90.4	91.4	95.5	Afrique
Americas	2724.0	2757.7	3214.9	3154.2	3131.3	Amériques
- Northern America	2399.9	2462.6	2891.2	2778.1	2715.1	- Amérique du Nord
- LAIA	294.1	264.6	292.0	339.9	378.3	- ALAI
- CACM	10.4	10.9	11.0	14.0	14.6	- MCC
- Caribbean	14.4	14.9	16.5	18.2	19.0	- Caraïbes
- Rest of America	5.2	4.7	4.2	4.0	4.2	- Autre d'Amérique
Asia excluding former USSR	1901.8	2218.3	2772.7	2974.1	3355.7	Asie ancienne URSS exclus
- Middle East	158.2	154.9	170.7	161.8	170.5	- Moyen-Orient
Asia former USSR	2.2	3.5	3.4	3.4	3.4	Asie ancienne URSS
Europe excluding former USSR	3573.5	4034.4	4072.7	4054.0	4197.8	Europe ancienne URSS exclus
- European Union	3155.3	3648.1	3688.8	3657.8	3788.8	- Union Européenne
- Eastern Europe	123.6	111.4	113.0	123.4	134.0	- Europe de l'Est
- Rest of Europe	294.5	275.0	270.8	272.8	275.0	- Autre de l'Europe
Europe former USSR	45.4	31.0	29.3	39.2	48.2	Europe ancienne URSS
Oceania	171.9	175.5	204.9	187.8	196.1	Océanie
United States	2101.0	2157.1	2552.4	2439.0	2367.4	Etats-Unis d'Amérique
Japan	631.3	688.0	834.4	961.7	1003.3	Japon
Germany	793.2	825.5	773.0	745.6	627.8	Allemagne
China, Hong Kong SAR	480.1	513.3	577.6	583.3	665.5	Chine - RAS de Hong-Kong
United Kingdom	454.0	515.9	598.0	574.3	667.9	Royaume-Uni
Netherlands	243.0	556.7	554.1	577.5	585.9	Pays-Bas
France-Monaco	401.0	433.6	475.3	470.9	515.3	France-Monaco
Italy-San Marino-Holy See	355.3	394.9	438.9	421.5	458.2	Italie-Saint-Marin-Saint-Siège
Canada	298.5	305.1	338.3	338.4	346.7	Canada
Spain	255.9	239.9	239.6	240.7	266.6	Espagne
China	124.3	158.4	223.8	264.4	450.7	Chine
Singapore	148.6	203.2	242.8	201.8	200.3	Singapour
Korea, Republic of	90.9	152.9	230.6	242.8	276.9	République de Corée
Mexico	133.3	131.7	147.4	193.6	257.3	Mexique
Switzerland-Liechtenstein	157.3	155.7	157.4	153.9	153.3	Suisse-Liechtenstein
Australia	139.9	142.7	170.9	153.2	158.8	Australie
Belgium	–	148.6	138.7	138.5	e151.9	Belgique
Austria	101.3	110.9	112.2	113.3	113.6	Autriche
Sweden	107.5	105.7	107.8	106.6	116.3	Suède
Denmark	79.3	77.2	76.4	84.4	95.0	Danemark
Malaysia	46.1	61.3	81.3	88.5	e96.7	Malaisie
Norway	82.6	71.5	68.2	73.7	72.6	Norvège
Thailand	38.8	54.3	79.6	84.3	e87.9	Thaïlande
Portugal	64.0	60.6	51.4	55.8	61.8	Portugal
Brazil	68.4	52.0	58.9	59.2	52.4	Brésil
Israel	50.2	46.3	54.0	65.0	63.9	Israël
Czech Republic	59.7	51.6	50.7	56.0	58.6	République tchèque
Greece	50.9	56.2	38.7	39.8	e44.0	Grèce
Ireland	75.7	69.4	32.1	28.0	21.1	Irlande
Turkey	50.1	44.2	54.0	36.8	39.3	Turquie

(Value as percentages of World total) **(Valeur en pourcentage du total mondial)**

Regions of the world	1993	1994	1995	1996	1997	1998	1999	2000	2001	2002	Régions du monde
World	100.0	100.0	100.0	100.0	100.0	100.0	100.0	100.0	100.0	100.0	Monde
Africa	1.3	1.1	1.1	1.0	1.0	1.1	0.9	0.9	0.9	0.9	Afrique
Americas	31.4	31.3	30.9	29.8	29.6	32.0	29.6	30.9	30.0	28.4	Amériques
- Northern America	28.3	28.1	27.9	26.7	26.2	28.2	26.5	27.8	26.4	24.6	- Amérique du Nord
- LAIA	2.8	2.8	2.6	2.8	3.0	3.5	2.8	2.8	3.2	3.4	- ALAI
- CACM	0.1	0.1	0.1	0.1	0.1	0.1	0.1	0.1	0.1	0.1	- MCC
- Caribbean	0.2	0.2	0.2	0.1	0.2	0.2	0.2	0.2	0.2	0.2	- Caraïbes
- Rest of America	0.1	0.1	0.1	0.0	0.0	0.1	0.1	0.0	0.0	0.0	- Autre d'Amérique
Asia excluding former USSR	22.6	22.1	22.8	23.8	23.8	22.3	23.8	26.7	28.3	30.4	Asie ancienne URSS exclus
- Middle East	2.2	2.0	1.9	1.9	1.9	1.9	1.7	1.6	1.5	1.5	- Moyen-Orient
Asia former USSR	0.0	0.0	0.0	0.0	0.0	0.0	0.0	0.0	0.0	0.0	Asie ancienne URSS
Europe excluding former USSR	42.2	42.4	42.2	42.5	42.8	42.0	43.3	39.2	38.6	38.1	Europe ancienne URSS exclus
- European Union	37.8	38.1	37.6	37.9	38.5	37.1	39.2	35.5	34.8	34.4	- Union Européenne
- Eastern Europe	0.8	0.8	1.0	1.3	1.2	1.5	1.2	1.1	1.2	1.2	- Europe de l'Est
- Rest of Europe	3.6	3.6	3.6	3.4	3.2	3.5	3.0	2.6	2.6	2.5	- Autre de l'Europe
Europe former USSR	0.5	0.7	0.8	0.8	0.7	0.5	0.3	0.3	0.4	0.4	Europe ancienne URSS
Oceania	2.1	2.2	2.3	2.2	2.1	2.0	1.9	2.0	1.8	1.8	Océanie

TRADE BY COMMODITY (Value in million US dollars)
Exports by principal countries or areas

COMMERCE PAR PRODUIT (Valeur en millions de dollars EU)
Exportations selon les principaux pays ou zones

Country or area	1998	1999	2000	2001	2002	Pays ou zone
World	8857.0	9013.2	10323.4	10576.7	10960.2	Monde
Africa	24.4	18.8	24.6	21.9	20.3	Afrique
Americas	1192.2	1154.9	1336.1	1431.6	1392.1	Amériques
- Northern America	1135.4	1094.4	1287.0	1380.6	1345.3	- Amérique du Nord
- LAIA	56.2	59.2	47.5	47.7	43.9	- ALAI
- CACM	0.1	0.2	0.2	0.1	0.3	- MCC
- Caribbean	0.5	1.1	1.4	3.0	2.5	- Caraïbes
- Rest of America	0.0	0.0	0.0	0.1	0.1	- Autre d'Amérique
Asia excluding former USSR	3592.8	3806.4	4671.5	4593.5	4841.1	Asie ancienne URSS exclus
- Middle East	13.4	13.3	15.0	16.7	16.0	- Moyen-Orient
Asia former USSR	0.2	0.2	0.4	0.7	0.2	Asie ancienne URSS
Europe excluding former USSR	4016.2	3983.4	4202.9	4437.0	4664.3	Europe ancienne URSS exclus
- European Union	3804.8	3788.2	4001.7	4225.8	4451.0	- Union Européenne
- Eastern Europe	94.4	78.4	75.7	86.5	75.6	- Europe de l'Est
- Rest of Europe	117.0	116.8	125.5	124.6	137.7	- Autre de l'Europe
Europe former USSR	12.3	17.9	24.1	13.2	16.3	Europe ancienne URSS
Oceania	19.0	31.7	63.7	78.8	25.9	Océanie
Japan	1403.7	1593.4	1933.7	1696.9	1717.8	Japon
Italy-San Marino-Holy See	1182.8	1113.4	1307.7	1377.7	1481.6	Italie-Saint-Marin-Saint-Siège
United States	1060.3	1041.0	1220.3	1296.4	1241.6	Etats-Unis d'Amérique
Germany	1032.7	1010.0	1068.2	1068.5	1045.5	Allemagne
China, Hong Kong SAR	777.5	775.8	922.5	940.8	1056.4	Chine - RAS de Hong-Kong
China	471.7	493.0	672.7	801.8	872.8	Chine
France-Monaco	438.9	405.9	408.5	369.8	400.2	France-Monaco
United Kingdom	292.3	314.6	353.5	380.9	407.1	Royaume-Uni
Ireland	286.9	303.2	259.8	295.1	366.0	Irlande
Korea, Republic of	237.4	240.1	283.8	265.7	217.4	République de Corée
Singapore	189.1	199.2	263.1	253.5	333.9	Singapour
Netherlands	168.1	231.5	183.2	226.1	255.0	Pays-Bas
Austria	137.9	132.2	156.5	231.0	214.1	Autriche
Thailand	75.4	70.4	88.1	122.3	e129.2	Thaïlande
Canada	75.1	53.4	66.7	84.2	103.7	Canada
Belgium	–	98.8	88.6	82.5	e92.5	Belgique
Switzerland-Liechtenstein	65.2	58.6	67.9	70.2	77.7	Suisse-Liechtenstein
Indonesia	46.0	68.1	77.6	76.7	68.4	Indonésie
Denmark	60.5	63.3	60.7	72.7	62.9	Danemark
Sweden	67.8	56.1	48.8	45.9	48.2	Suède
Czech Republic	65.4	48.2	48.7	53.6	50.5	République tchèque
Malaysia	29.4	33.7	59.3	65.2	e69.1	Malaisie
Spain	37.1	36.1	40.7	48.4	49.9	Espagne
Australia	17.1	29.4	61.7	76.5	25.6	Australie
Israel	16.4	25.7	36.2	60.2	41.6	Israël
Mexico	30.9	37.2	23.0	28.4	24.4	Mexique
Slovenia	20.4	27.0	30.0	29.1	32.7	Slovénie
Hungary	21.3	25.3	21.4	19.9	18.4	Hongrie
Malta	21.6	20.1	18.6	15.0	e16.3	Malte
Belgium-Luxembourg	80.6	–	–	–	–	Belgique-Luxembourg

(Value as percentages of World total)

(Valeur en pourcentage du total mondial)

Regions of the world	1993	1994	1995	1996	1997	1998	1999	2000	2001	2002	Régions du monde
World	100.0	100.0	100.0	100.0	100.0	100.0	100.0	100.0	100.0	100.0	Monde
Africa	0.3	0.4	0.4	0.3	0.3	0.3	0.2	0.2	0.2	0.2	Afrique
Americas	10.3	11.3	10.8	12.0	12.1	13.5	12.8	12.9	13.5	12.7	Amériques
- Northern America	9.7	10.7	10.3	11.6	11.6	12.8	12.1	12.5	13.1	12.3	- Amérique du Nord
- LAIA	0.6	0.5	0.5	0.5	0.5	0.6	0.7	0.5	0.5	0.4	- ALAI
- CACM	0.0	0.0	0.0	0.0	0.0	0.0	0.0	0.0	0.0	0.0	- MCC
- Caribbean	0.0	0.0	0.0	0.0	0.0	0.0	0.0	0.0	0.0	0.0	- Caraïbes
- Rest of America	0.0	0.0	0.0	0.0	0.0	0.0	0.0	0.0	0.0	0.0	- Autre d'Amérique
Asia excluding former USSR	47.4	43.8	43.0	41.1	39.1	40.6	42.2	45.3	43.4	44.2	Asie ancienne URSS exclus
- Middle East	0.2	0.2	0.1	0.1	0.1	0.2	0.1	0.1	0.2	0.1	- Moyen-Orient
Asia former USSR	0.0	0.0	0.0	0.0	0.0	0.0	0.0	0.0	0.0	0.0	Asie ancienne URSS
Europe excluding former USSR	41.6	44.1	45.4	46.1	48.0	45.3	44.2	40.7	42.0	42.6	Europe ancienne URSS exclus
- European Union	39.4	41.6	42.8	43.7	46.1	43.0	42.0	38.8	40.0	40.6	- Union Européenne
- Eastern Europe	0.2	0.3	0.5	0.7	0.7	1.1	0.9	0.7	0.8	0.7	- Europe de l'Est
- Rest of Europe	2.0	2.1	2.1	1.7	1.3	1.3	1.3	1.2	1.2	1.3	- Autre de l'Europe
Europe former USSR	0.1	0.1	0.2	0.1	0.1	0.1	0.2	0.2	0.1	0.1	Europe ancienne URSS
Oceania	0.2	0.3	0.3	0.3	0.3	0.2	0.4	0.6	0.7	0.2	Océanie

885 Watches and clocks

TRADE BY COMMODITY (Value in million US dollars)
Imports by principal countries or areas

COMMERCE PAR PRODUIT (Valeur en millions de dollars EU)
Importations selon les principaux pays ou zones

Country or area	1998	1999	2000	2001	2002	Pays ou zone
World	18889.1	18578.1	18896.4	17997.3	18589.8	Monde
Africa	135.0	131.2	120.8	107.6	110.3	Afrique
Americas	3923.9	3979.4	4262.7	3826.3	3980.7	Amériques
- Northern America	3436.3	3531.8	3776.2	3303.3	3488.3	- Amérique du Nord
- LAIA	391.7	358.2	394.8	414.8	362.5	- ALAI
- CACM	13.0	13.1	15.1	16.1	18.8	- MCC
- Caribbean	73.8	65.9	67.9	85.1	100.6	- Caraïbes
- Rest of America	9.1	10.5	8.7	7.0	10.5	- Autre d'Amérique
Asia excluding former USSR	8588.2	8482.7	8766.7	8384.8	8602.0	Asie ancienne URSS exclus
- Middle East	653.0	645.6	669.6	641.8	700.2	- Moyen-Orient
Asia former USSR	3.0	3.6	12.5	11.2	17.1	Asie ancienne URSS
Europe excluding former USSR	5994.2	5734.0	5472.5	5406.6	5623.6	Europe ancienne URSS exclus
- European Union	5162.7	4982.0	4660.5	4584.6	4735.2	- Union Européenne
- Eastern Europe	124.3	119.5	113.1	106.1	112.7	- Europe de l'Est
- Rest of Europe	707.2	632.5	698.9	715.9	775.6	- Autre de l'Europe
Europe former USSR	40.0	29.0	36.5	52.1	46.1	Europe ancienne URSS
Oceania	204.9	218.1	224.7	208.6	210.0	Océanie
China, Hong Kong SAR	3759.4	3697.7	3802.6	3683.1	3691.6	Chine - RAS de Hong-Kong
United States	3218.5	3292.5	3534.3	3081.3	3238.3	Etats-Unis d'Amérique
Japan	1581.1	1687.5	1718.1	1649.7	1681.8	Japon
Germany	1173.2	1062.6	972.7	935.4	890.4	Allemagne
Italy-San Marino-Holy See	917.7	878.3	833.8	793.0	871.3	Italie-Saint-Marin-Saint-Siège
China	835.8	763.0	785.1	756.5	808.6	Chine
United Kingdom	862.8	780.1	712.9	740.4	767.4	Royaume-Uni
Singapore	832.2	775.5	775.5	668.7	714.2	Singapour
France-Monaco	741.3	719.5	741.3	731.1	781.2	France-Monaco
Switzerland-Liechtenstein	604.5	530.9	604.3	622.2	677.0	Suisse-Liechtenstein
Spain	542.4	564.4	483.3	485.5	504.9	Espagne
United Arab Emirates	232.0	243.1	263.2	272.0	e279.0	Emirates arabes unis
Canada	212.6	233.4	239.0	218.1	244.3	Canada
Malaysia	201.3	208.0	229.9	230.7	e252.1	Malaisie
Netherlands	194.1	218.2	201.7	185.9	170.6	Pays-Bas
Thailand	177.9	158.4	196.9	207.5	e216.2	Thaïlande
Australia	174.2	184.7	193.5	179.0	177.0	Australie
Mexico	141.5	149.5	177.7	210.8	190.3	Mexique
Saudi Arabia	168.9	165.6	157.4	153.4	e158.7	Arabie saoudite
Belgium	–	199.3	188.6	183.0	e200.7	Belgique
Austria	155.9	159.6	141.8	154.2	159.3	Autriche
Korea, Republic of	137.0	137.7	163.1	152.3	173.4	République de Corée
Portugal	94.0	93.5	88.0	94.7	97.2	Portugal
Sweden	87.2	87.1	86.8	78.9	84.4	Suède
Turkey	109.0	87.8	91.6	52.0	74.7	Turquie
Brazil	97.3	77.8	81.1	70.3	66.5	Brésil
Greece	78.9	82.1	74.8	73.5	e81.3	Grèce
Philippines	91.7	76.9	86.6	71.6	21.2	Philippines
Denmark	56.9	55.1	59.9	53.0	52.3	Danemark
Poland	52.6	51.2	48.8	43.0	47.0	Pologne

(Value as percentages of World total) **(Valeur en pourcentage du total mondial)**

Regions of the world	1993	1994	1995	1996	1997	1998	1999	2000	2001	2002	Régions du monde
World	100.0	100.0	100.0	100.0	100.0	100.0	100.0	100.0	100.0	100.0	Monde
Africa	0.7	0.7	0.6	0.6	0.6	0.7	0.7	0.6	0.6	0.6	Afrique
Americas	17.7	17.2	16.3	16.7	17.7	20.8	21.4	22.6	21.3	21.4	Amériques
- Northern America	15.5	15.0	14.2	14.8	15.4	18.2	19.0	20.0	18.4	18.8	- Amérique du Nord
- LAIA	1.8	1.9	1.7	1.6	1.9	2.1	1.9	2.1	2.3	2.0	- ALAI
- CACM	0.1	0.0	0.0	0.0	0.1	0.1	0.1	0.1	0.1	0.1	- MCC
- Caribbean	0.3	0.3	0.3	0.3	0.3	0.4	0.4	0.4	0.5	0.5	- Caraïbes
- Rest of America	0.0	0.0	0.0	0.0	0.0	0.0	0.1	0.0	0.0	0.1	- Autre d'Amérique
Asia excluding former USSR	53.3	53.7	54.2	53.5	52.0	45.5	45.7	46.4	46.6	46.3	Asie ancienne URSS exclus
- Middle East	4.5	4.3	3.8	3.1	3.6	3.5	3.5	3.5	3.6	3.8	- Moyen-Orient
Asia former USSR	0.0	0.0	0.0	0.0	0.0	0.0	0.0	0.1	0.1	0.1	Asie ancienne URSS
Europe excluding former USSR	27.2	27.2	27.8	27.8	28.4	31.7	30.9	29.0	30.0	30.3	Europe ancienne URSS exclus
- European Union	23.5	23.4	23.8	23.7	24.5	27.3	26.8	24.7	25.5	25.5	- Union Européenne
- Eastern Europe	0.3	0.4	0.4	0.5	0.6	0.7	0.6	0.6	0.6	0.6	- Europe de l'Est
- Rest of Europe	3.3	3.5	3.6	3.6	3.4	3.7	3.4	3.7	4.0	4.2	- Autre de l'Europe
Europe former USSR	0.2	0.1	0.1	0.2	0.2	0.2	0.2	0.2	0.3	0.2	Europe ancienne URSS
Oceania	1.0	1.1	1.0	1.2	1.0	1.1	1.2	1.2	1.2	1.1	Océanie

TRADE BY COMMODITY (Value in million US dollars)
Exports by principal countries or areas

COMMERCE PAR PRODUIT (Valeur en millions de dollars EU)
Exportations selon les principaux pays ou zones

Country or area	1998	1999	2000	2001	2002	Pays ou zone
World	19465.3	18759.0	19107.7	18019.0	18476.1	Monde
Africa	35.9	37.2	31.8	25.6	25.4	Afrique
Americas	577.7	615.9	658.0	615.8	572.3	Amériques
- Northern America	456.5	537.5	539.5	471.7	441.9	- Amérique du Nord
- LAIA	115.8	72.9	99.1	138.1	123.8	- ALAI
- CACM	0.8	1.0	0.8	0.5	0.4	- MCC
- Caribbean	4.6	4.0	18.5	5.1	5.7	- Caraïbes
- Rest of America	0.0	0.5	0.1	0.3	0.5	- Autre d'Amérique
Asia excluding former USSR	10813.0	9890.8	10149.3	8961.4	8684.2	Asie ancienne URSS exclus
- Middle East	79.3	82.1	91.5	100.8	105.1	- Moyen-Orient
Asia former USSR	1.2	0.5	0.9	3.8	15.4	Asie ancienne URSS
Europe excluding former USSR	7978.6	8137.2	8195.5	8343.1	9116.8	Europe ancienne URSS exclus
- European Union	2232.5	2235.4	2123.2	2133.4	2349.7	- Union Européenne
- Eastern Europe	34.9	26.7	24.8	23.4	23.9	- Europe de l'Est
- Rest of Europe	5711.3	5875.0	6047.6	6186.3	6743.2	- Autre de l'Europe
Europe former USSR	16.3	21.7	20.7	18.4	19.8	Europe ancienne URSS
Oceania	42.6	55.7	51.6	50.9	42.2	Océanie
Switzerland-Liechtenstein	5693.7	5858.9	6031.1	6171.7	6728.9	Suisse-Liechtenstein
China, Hong Kong SAR	5373.8	5095.0	5260.9	4841.8	4669.0	Chine - RAS de Hong-Kong
China	1849.2	1752.3	1738.9	1528.5	1591.4	Chine
Japan	1577.6	1434.9	1363.2	1026.3	975.5	Japon
Germany	679.6	682.6	644.4	660.5	713.3	Allemagne
Singapore	727.2	604.9	610.3	530.2	532.4	Singapour
France-Monaco	484.6	463.4	466.4	440.0	490.8	France-Monaco
United States	436.9	501.7	508.8	440.9	403.4	Etats-Unis d'Amérique
Italy-San Marino-Holy See	317.9	324.3	340.7	362.9	411.8	Italie-Saint-Marin-Saint-Siège
Thailand	331.8	245.5	282.3	272.3	e287.6	Thaïlande
United Kingdom	335.0	276.5	215.8	235.3	228.8	Royaume-Uni
Korea, Republic of	276.3	189.0	196.9	169.6	154.6	République de Corée
Malaysia	209.6	163.6	201.1	133.6	e141.6	Malaisie
Spain	126.2	131.3	122.5	134.1	155.6	Espagne
Philippines	117.7	92.7	178.7	149.6	2.6	Philippines
Belgium	–	141.1	116.9	107.7	e120.8	Belgique
Mexico	52.5	64.8	88.3	126.3	112.0	Mexique
Netherlands	55.2	87.6	85.9	68.9	67.0	Pays-Bas
United Arab Emirates	54.2	55.9	69.3	77.6	e80.8	Emirates arabes unis
Austria	43.9	42.3	45.1	52.5	71.2	Autriche
Australia	38.8	53.1	49.4	48.5	42.1	Australie
India	26.4	36.2	50.8	47.2	52.6	Inde
Canada	19.2	35.7	30.6	30.8	38.4	Canada
Sweden	21.6	25.0	22.1	22.1	31.0	Suède
Belgium-Luxembourg	121.5	–	–	–	–	Belgique-Luxembourg
Denmark	20.1	17.8	20.5	21.5	27.2	Danemark
Mauritius	21.2	21.4	16.3	11.6	10.0	Maurice
Ireland	8.5	24.1	24.0	7.4	9.2	Irlande
Belarus	9.2	12.7	13.7	10.4	11.4	Bélarus
Peru	55.7	0.2	0.2	0.3	0.2	Pérou

(Value as percentages of World total) **(Valeur en pourcentage du total mondial)**

Regions of the world	1993	1994	1995	1996	1997	1998	1999	2000	2001	2002	Régions du monde
World	100.0	100.0	100.0	100.0	100.0	100.0	100.0	100.0	100.0	100.0	Monde
Africa	0.2	0.2	0.2	0.2	0.1	0.2	0.2	0.2	0.1	0.1	Afrique
Americas	2.4	2.4	2.7	2.2	2.5	3.0	3.3	3.4	3.4	3.1	Amériques
- Northern America	2.1	2.1	1.9	2.0	2.2	2.3	2.9	2.8	2.6	2.4	- Amérique du Nord
- LAIA	0.3	0.3	0.8	0.2	0.2	0.6	0.4	0.5	0.8	0.7	- ALAI
- CACM	0.1	0.0	0.0	0.0	0.0	0.0	0.0	0.0	0.0	0.0	- MCC
- Caribbean	0.0	0.0	0.0	0.0	0.0	0.0	0.0	0.1	0.0	0.0	- Caraïbes
- Rest of America	0.0	0.0	0.0	0.0	0.0	0.0	0.0	0.0	0.0	0.0	- Autre d'Amérique
Asia excluding former USSR	58.5	56.6	56.4	57.4	58.2	55.6	52.7	53.1	49.7	47.0	Asie ancienne URSS exclus
- Middle East	0.4	0.4	0.3	0.3	0.4	0.4	0.4	0.5	0.6	0.6	- Moyen-Orient
Asia former USSR	0.0	0.0	0.0	0.0	0.0	0.0	0.0	0.0	0.0	0.1	Asie ancienne URSS
Europe excluding former USSR	38.4	40.6	40.5	39.9	38.9	41.0	43.4	42.9	46.3	49.3	Europe ancienne URSS exclus
- European Union	10.5	11.0	11.1	11.0	11.3	11.5	11.9	11.1	11.8	12.7	- Union Européenne
- Eastern Europe	0.1	0.1	0.1	0.1	0.2	0.2	0.1	0.1	0.1	0.1	- Europe de l'Est
- Rest of Europe	27.9	29.4	29.3	28.8	27.5	29.3	31.3	31.7	34.3	36.5	- Autre de l'Europe
Europe former USSR	0.2	0.1	0.1	0.1	0.1	0.1	0.1	0.1	0.1	0.1	Europe ancienne URSS
Oceania	0.2	0.2	0.2	0.2	0.2	0.2	0.3	0.3	0.3	0.2	Océanie

892 Printed matter

TRADE BY COMMODITY (Value in million US dollars)
Imports by principal countries or areas

COMMERCE PAR PRODUIT (Valeur en millions de dollars EU)
Importations selon les principaux pays ou zones

Country or area	1998	1999	2000	2001	2002	Pays ou zone
World	27241.4	27412.1	27819.5	28217.8	29019.8	Monde
Africa	711.4	778.0	948.1	1009.4	1013.4	Afrique
Americas	7856.2	8043.3	8776.1	8861.3	8586.6	Amériques
- Northern America	5502.2	5770.8	6192.4	6159.4	6437.9	- Amérique du Nord
- LAIA	1984.8	1914.6	2211.5	2296.2	1714.8	- ALAI
- CACM	129.5	141.3	148.1	157.7	189.6	- MCC
- Caribbean	193.5	171.9	176.6	202.9	198.7	- Caraïbes
- Rest of America	46.1	44.8	47.5	45.0	45.7	- Autre d'Amérique
Asia excluding former USSR	3665.2	3666.2	4141.6	4203.2	4173.5	Asie ancienne URSS exclus
- Middle East	453.1	364.9	412.2	461.0	467.3	- Moyen-Orient
Asia former USSR	76.3	75.5	69.2	87.8	112.6	Asie ancienne URSS
Europe excluding former USSR	13411.3	13550.4	12549.8	12755.4	13768.1	Europe ancienne URSS exclus
- European Union	10661.7	10977.0	10097.2	10265.0	10980.0	- Union Européenne
- Eastern Europe	1012.6	861.1	823.9	906.6	1071.8	- Europe de l'Est
- Rest of Europe	1737.0	1712.4	1628.7	1583.9	1716.4	- Autre de l'Europe
Europe former USSR	748.7	398.2	464.1	537.6	563.5	Europe ancienne URSS
Oceania	772.2	900.5	870.6	763.0	802.0	Océanie
United States	3205.5	3489.0	3870.6	3884.1	4143.2	Etats-Unis d'Amérique
Canada	2278.9	2262.6	2315.3	2268.0	2284.9	Canada
United Kingdom	2034.7	2101.7	2008.3	2094.9	2351.7	Royaume-Uni
Germany	1772.2	1779.0	1599.6	1755.5	1856.1	Allemagne
France-Monaco	1842.9	1802.6	1779.2	1639.2	1630.0	France-Monaco
Switzerland-Liechtenstein	1223.3	1214.9	1123.5	1109.8	1198.8	Suisse-Liechtenstein
Mexico	856.0	993.5	1343.2	1456.6	1077.0	Mexique
Japan	810.9	758.7	781.9	779.6	744.7	Japon
Belgium	-	1010.3	875.2	927.2	e1016.8	Belgique
China, Hong Kong SAR	532.2	612.4	757.7	748.0	768.7	Chine - RAS de Hong-Kong
Austria	699.3	725.0	617.9	645.1	658.5	Autriche
Netherlands	629.7	709.0	636.3	617.5	654.4	Pays-Bas
Italy-San Marino-Holy See	601.7	608.9	596.2	591.6	609.4	Italie-Saint-Marin-Saint-Siège
Australia	640.1	618.0	629.1	535.2	562.2	Australie
China	515.8	489.4	538.1	565.3	534.2	Chine
Spain	445.9	472.8	425.3	433.4	509.6	Espagne
Denmark	370.0	404.7	330.8	354.4	385.3	Danemark
Russian Federation	547.0	230.9	296.8	368.0	372.5	Fédération de Russie
Sweden	389.0	387.2	352.9	320.0	337.6	Suède
Singapore	302.2	334.8	370.0	341.8	335.7	Singapour
Norway	350.1	340.4	332.3	310.2	334.7	Norvège
Ireland	304.0	338.8	290.7	325.5	387.2	Irlande
Czech Republic	307.0	271.5	275.8	327.3	409.9	République tchèque
Poland	359.4	304.5	263.0	267.5	285.9	Pologne
Brazil	411.3	257.4	250.9	215.7	143.4	Brésil
Portugal	217.7	225.8	219.6	214.5	219.7	Portugal
Belgium-Luxembourg	1045.4	-	-	-	-	Belgique-Luxembourg
Argentina	256.8	253.7	222.6	192.0	e84.9	Argentine
India	178.2	153.4	208.1	243.6	223.5	Inde
Korea, Republic of	109.2	148.3	210.7	233.0	238.5	République de Corée

(Value as percentages of World total) **(Valeur en pourcentage du total mondial)**

Regions of the world	1993	1994	1995	1996	1997	1998	1999	2000	2001	2002	Régions du monde
World	100.0	100.0	100.0	100.0	100.0	100.0	100.0	100.0	100.0	100.0	Monde
Africa	3.3	3.1	3.0	3.0	2.7	2.6	2.8	3.4	3.6	3.5	Afrique
Americas	26.1	26.1	25.8	25.3	27.5	28.8	29.3	31.5	31.4	29.6	Amériques
- Northern America	19.3	19.1	19.0	18.5	19.8	20.2	21.1	22.3	21.8	22.2	- Amérique du Nord
- LAIA	5.2	5.7	5.5	5.7	6.6	7.3	7.0	7.9	8.1	5.9	- ALAI
- CACM	0.7	0.3	0.4	0.4	0.4	0.5	0.5	0.5	0.6	0.7	- MCC
- Caribbean	0.8	0.7	0.8	0.6	0.7	0.7	0.6	0.6	0.7	0.7	- Caraïbes
- Rest of America	0.2	0.2	0.2	0.1	0.1	0.2	0.2	0.2	0.2	0.2	- Autre d'Amérique
Asia excluding former USSR	14.1	13.4	14.3	14.9	16.3	13.5	13.4	14.9	14.9	14.4	Asie ancienne URSS exclus
- Middle East	2.2	1.5	1.4	1.4	1.6	1.7	1.3	1.5	1.6	1.6	- Moyen-Orient
Asia former USSR	0.1	0.2	0.2	0.2	0.2	0.3	0.3	0.2	0.3	0.4	Asie ancienne URSS
Europe excluding former USSR	51.1	51.1	50.7	50.8	47.1	49.2	49.4	45.1	45.2	47.4	Europe ancienne URSS exclus
- European Union	42.1	42.0	40.8	40.7	37.8	39.1	40.0	36.3	36.4	37.8	- Union Européenne
- Eastern Europe	2.5	2.4	2.7	3.0	3.0	3.7	3.1	3.0	3.2	3.7	- Europe de l'Est
- Rest of Europe	6.6	6.7	7.2	7.0	6.2	6.4	6.2	5.9	5.6	5.9	- Autre de l'Europe
Europe former USSR	1.4	2.1	2.3	2.2	2.6	2.7	1.5	1.7	1.9	1.9	Europe ancienne URSS
Oceania	3.9	4.1	3.7	3.6	3.6	2.8	3.3	3.1	2.7	2.8	Océanie

TRADE BY COMMODITY (Value in million US dollars)
Exports by principal countries or areas

COMMERCE PAR PRODUIT (Valeur en millions de dollars EU)
Exportations selon les principaux pays ou zones

Country or area	1998	1999	2000	2001	2002	Pays ou zone
World	26851.3	26509.3	26733.0	27378.0	27964.1	Monde
Africa	80.5	92.7	273.3	342.5	229.9	Afrique
Americas	6720.7	6661.5	7156.0	7331.5	6983.0	Amériques
- Northern America	5913.1	5942.4	6352.9	6487.0	6215.1	- Amérique du Nord
- LAIA	749.3	669.8	743.4	727.4	702.1	- ALAI
- CACM	28.3	25.4	27.8	87.9	36.8	- MCC
- Caribbean	29.1	23.2	26.2	27.4	26.7	- Caraïbes
- Rest of America	1.0	0.6	5.7	1.9	2.3	- Autre d'Amérique
Asia excluding former USSR	2955.7	3345.1	3745.9	3821.8	3816.8	Asie ancienne URSS exclus
- Middle East	96.5	95.2	99.3	113.8	110.6	- Moyen-Orient
Asia former USSR	8.7	9.0	2.5	3.8	4.0	Asie ancienne URSS
Europe excluding former USSR	16287.7	15767.8	14915.4	15247.5	16279.6	Europe ancienne URSS exclus
- European Union	15005.5	14489.5	13670.7	13917.9	14832.0	- Union Européenne
- Eastern Europe	526.2	530.7	553.6	659.9	806.6	- Europe de l'Est
- Rest of Europe	756.0	747.6	691.1	669.7	641.1	- Autre de l'Europe
Europe former USSR	575.6	403.2	426.2	425.7	432.6	Europe ancienne URSS
Oceania	222.3	230.1	213.7	205.2	218.2	Océanie
United States	4795.8	4712.5	4996.4	5061.3	4686.5	Etats-Unis d'Amérique
Germany	3730.3	3623.3	3227.0	3521.5	3810.3	Allemagne
United Kingdom	3418.7	3021.2	2949.9	2825.0	3165.6	Royaume-Uni
France-Monaco	1808.0	1756.1	1708.8	1619.3	1600.1	France-Monaco
Italy-San Marino-Holy See	1509.5	1401.8	1383.3	1365.8	1413.6	Italie-Saint-Marin-Saint-Siège
Canada	1117.1	1229.7	1356.2	1425.6	1528.4	Canada
China, Hong Kong SAR	951.2	1107.9	1303.9	1278.6	1351.2	Chine - RAS de Hong-Kong
Spain	1051.1	1059.5	1059.1	1131.3	1136.6	Espagne
Belgium	–	1117.7	1056.1	1073.1	e1204.0	Belgique
Netherlands	768.9	830.0	746.8	748.1	768.3	Pays-Bas
Singapore	487.4	543.3	585.3	694.1	506.6	Singapour
China	380.0	401.7	486.7	539.8	676.9	Chine
Switzerland-Liechtenstein	531.6	500.5	486.1	461.6	420.6	Suisse-Liechtenstein
Japan	416.2	483.1	491.7	410.6	409.1	Japon
Austria	434.3	402.1	356.2	387.8	397.7	Autriche
Denmark	352.7	361.1	340.9	364.1	371.5	Danemark
Russian Federation	474.2	322.5	350.5	317.1	311.3	Fédération de Russie
Mexico	314.3	315.0	356.6	330.8	331.3	Mexique
Finland	385.0	291.5	302.5	332.1	310.3	Finlande
Czech Republic	243.4	288.9	277.0	339.8	426.8	République tchèque
Korea, Republic of	225.2	257.1	281.3	284.1	214.7	République de Corée
Sweden	238.5	241.5	239.6	210.7	245.1	Suède
Ireland	166.1	245.6	191.6	226.5	302.5	Irlande
Belgium-Luxembourg	1073.6	–	–	–	–	Belgique-Luxembourg
Australia	187.2	191.8	179.2	168.6	183.6	Australie
Poland	115.8	110.9	123.2	125.7	174.9	Pologne
Colombia	117.5	104.5	129.2	150.7	127.0	Colombie
Slovakia	109.7	78.3	92.9	118.2	129.8	Slovaquie
Malaysia	72.7	97.0	109.7	114.9	e121.8	Malaisie
Argentina	130.6	96.4	102.1	84.6	e81.7	Argentine

(Value as percentages of World total) **(Valeur en pourcentage du total mondial)**

Regions of the world	1993	1994	1995	1996	1997	1998	1999	2000	2001	2002	Régions du monde
World	100.0	100.0	100.0	100.0	100.0	100.0	100.0	100.0	100.0	100.0	Monde
Africa	0.3	0.5	0.3	0.4	0.3	0.3	0.3	1.0	1.3	0.8	Afrique
Americas	26.0	23.6	22.6	23.0	25.4	25.0	25.1	26.8	26.8	25.0	Amériques
- Northern America	23.3	21.2	20.1	20.0	22.0	22.0	22.4	23.8	23.7	22.2	- Amérique du Nord
- LAIA	2.5	2.2	2.3	2.3	2.6	2.8	2.5	2.8	2.7	2.5	- ALAI
- CACM	0.1	0.1	0.1	0.6	0.6	0.1	0.1	0.1	0.3	0.1	- MCC
- Caribbean	0.1	0.1	0.1	0.1	0.1	0.1	0.1	0.1	0.1	0.1	- Caraïbes
- Rest of America	0.0	0.0	0.0	0.0	0.0	0.0	0.0	0.0	0.0	0.0	- Autre d'Amérique
Asia excluding former USSR	11.7	11.4	11.8	11.3	11.6	11.0	12.6	14.0	14.0	13.6	Asie ancienne URSS exclus
- Middle East	0.4	0.4	0.5	0.6	0.4	0.4	0.4	0.4	0.4	0.4	- Moyen-Orient
Asia former USSR	0.0	0.0	0.0	0.1	0.0	0.0	0.0	0.0	0.0	0.0	Asie ancienne URSS
Europe excluding former USSR	61.0	62.1	62.7	62.5	59.7	60.7	59.5	55.8	55.7	58.2	Europe ancienne URSS exclus
- European Union	56.8	57.8	58.6	58.2	55.6	55.9	54.7	51.1	50.8	53.0	- Union Européenne
- Eastern Europe	0.8	0.9	1.2	1.4	1.6	2.0	2.0	2.1	2.4	2.9	- Europe de l'Est
- Rest of Europe	3.4	3.4	3.0	2.9	2.5	2.8	2.8	2.6	2.4	2.3	- Autre de l'Europe
Europe former USSR	0.1	1.5	1.6	1.8	2.1	2.1	1.5	1.6	1.6	1.5	Europe ancienne URSS
Oceania	0.8	0.9	0.9	1.0	1.0	0.8	0.9	0.8	0.7	0.8	Océanie

893 Articles, nes of plastic materials

TRADE BY COMMODITY (Value in million US dollars) | COMMERCE PAR PRODUIT (Valeur en millions de dollars EU)
Imports by principal countries or areas | **Importations selon les principaux pays ou zones**

Country or area	1998	1999	2000	2001	2002	Pays ou zone
World	59370.2	63308.8	68695.2	68939.0	72147.6	Monde
Africa	951.2	967.1	1043.5	1102.3	1188.1	Afrique
Americas	16770.1	18945.5	22349.3	22645.8	22143.0	Amériques
- Northern America	9731.9	11142.7	12644.0	12853.9	14016.9	- Amérique du Nord
- LAIA	6270.3	7028.2	8766.8	8780.3	7117.6	- ALAI
- CACM	300.5	297.9	392.7	439.2	469.0	- MCC
- Caribbean	376.5	382.3	445.8	482.3	448.2	- Caraïbes
- Rest of America	91.0	94.4	100.0	90.1	91.3	- Autre d'Amérique
Asia excluding former USSR	10539.9	11777.5	13981.2	13150.5	13881.6	Asie ancienne URSS exclus
- Middle East	1210.2	1180.6	1350.1	1366.8	1516.4	- Moyen-Orient
Asia former USSR	124.1	101.4	139.7	141.3	141.9	Asie ancienne URSS
Europe excluding former USSR	29163.6	29725.7	29204.4	29902.2	32529.1	Europe ancienne URSS exclus
- European Union	24422.7	24889.1	24152.4	24569.9	26373.5	- Union Européenne
- Eastern Europe	2597.6	2711.3	2969.5	3197.7	3795.3	- Europe de l'Est
- Rest of Europe	2143.3	2125.2	2082.5	2134.7	2360.3	- Autre de l'Europe
Europe former USSR	883.9	673.8	765.0	910.2	1067.8	Europe ancienne URSS
Oceania	937.4	1117.9	1212.1	1086.6	1196.0	Océanie
United States	7436.2	8590.5	9861.6	10028.5	10989.1	Etats-Unis d'Amérique
Mexico	4582.4	5613.0	7265.2	7265.3	5812.8	Mexique
Germany	5386.8	5392.7	4866.5	5071.6	5116.1	Allemagne
France-Monaco	4081.0	4039.4	4163.6	4044.0	4394.7	France-Monaco
United Kingdom	3326.5	3309.3	3417.5	3434.7	3744.4	Royaume-Uni
China, Hong Kong SAR	2756.9	2817.9	3164.4	2857.5	2742.9	Chine - RAS de Hong-Kong
Canada	2277.7	2534.2	2773.2	2816.0	3014.0	Canada
Japan	1856.7	2185.2	2650.4	2591.4	2688.1	Japon
Netherlands	1828.3	1996.6	1811.6	1903.3	2093.9	Pays-Bas
Belgium	-	2217.9	2120.0	2213.0	e2427.0	Belgique
Italy-San Marino-Holy See	1567.9	1710.2	1721.3	1711.5	1869.8	Italie-Saint-Marin-Saint-Siège
Spain	1381.9	1500.9	1495.2	1530.3	1690.6	Espagne
China	944.8	1153.9	1426.1	1419.5	1714.5	Chine
Austria	1230.3	1234.9	1158.7	1202.5	1242.6	Autriche
Switzerland-Liechtenstein	1142.2	1153.5	1123.2	1134.1	1225.1	Suisse-Liechtenstein
Poland	959.6	957.8	949.0	944.6	1101.3	Pologne
Thailand	769.1	911.6	1120.1	1007.5	e1049.7	Thaïlande
Sweden	857.1	842.6	837.9	810.8	926.0	Suède
Australia	794.1	823.2	917.9	788.1	882.7	Australie
Czech Republic	672.0	730.7	806.8	892.0	1043.5	République tchèque
Singapore	644.9	771.2	875.2	752.1	801.9	Singapour
Denmark	725.7	694.9	663.5	706.6	784.6	Danemark
Ireland	649.7	629.8	638.8	672.5	688.3	Irlande
Hungary	488.4	553.8	670.0	680.6	777.8	Hongrie
Malaysia	440.3	513.6	742.6	625.7	e683.9	Malaisie
Korea, Republic of	353.9	486.4	647.3	643.5	763.1	République de Corée
Norway	557.2	514.5	482.5	488.5	554.9	Norvège
Portugal	456.8	503.6	493.9	477.1	550.4	Portugal
Brazil	522.1	450.1	465.6	448.6	426.2	Brésil
Belgium-Luxembourg	2256.0	-	-	-	-	Belgique-Luxembourg

(Value as percentages of World total) | **(Valeur en pourcentage du total mondial)**

Regions of the world	1993	1994	1995	1996	1997	1998	1999	2000	2001	2002	Régions du monde
World	100.0	100.0	100.0	100.0	100.0	100.0	100.0	100.0	100.0	100.0	Monde
Africa	1.7	1.6	1.9	1.5	1.4	1.6	1.5	1.5	1.6	1.6	Afrique
Americas	25.0	25.2	24.1	25.0	27.3	28.2	29.9	32.5	32.8	30.7	Amériques
- Northern America	16.3	16.2	15.1	15.1	15.7	16.4	17.6	18.4	18.6	19.4	- Amérique du Nord
- LAIA	7.6	8.0	8.0	9.0	10.5	10.6	11.1	12.8	12.7	9.9	- ALAI
- CACM	0.3	0.3	0.3	0.3	0.4	0.5	0.5	0.6	0.6	0.7	- MCC
- Caribbean	0.6	0.5	0.5	0.5	0.6	0.6	0.6	0.6	0.7	0.6	- Caraïbes
- Rest of America	0.2	0.2	0.2	0.1	0.1	0.2	0.1	0.1	0.1	0.1	- Autre d'Amérique
Asia excluding former USSR	20.1	20.0	20.0	20.0	20.4	17.8	18.6	20.4	19.1	19.2	Asie ancienne URSS exclus
- Middle East	2.4	2.1	2.0	1.9	2.0	2.0	1.9	2.0	2.0	2.1	- Moyen-Orient
Asia former USSR	0.0	0.1	0.2	0.2	0.1	0.2	0.2	0.2	0.2	0.2	Asie ancienne URSS
Europe excluding former USSR	49.9	49.9	50.6	50.1	47.3	49.1	47.0	42.5	43.4	45.1	Europe ancienne URSS exclus
- European Union	43.6	43.3	43.5	42.8	39.9	41.1	39.3	35.2	35.6	36.6	- Union Européenne
- Eastern Europe	2.1	2.4	2.9	3.5	3.9	4.4	4.3	4.3	4.6	5.3	- Europe de l'Est
- Rest of Europe	4.2	4.2	4.2	3.9	3.6	3.6	3.4	3.0	3.1	3.3	- Autre de l'Europe
Europe former USSR	1.2	1.1	1.3	1.2	1.4	1.5	1.1	1.1	1.3	1.5	Europe ancienne URSS
Oceania	2.1	2.1	2.0	2.0	1.9	1.6	1.8	1.8	1.6	1.7	Océanie

TRADE BY COMMODITY (Value in million US dollars)
Exports by principal countries or areas

COMMERCE PAR PRODUIT (Valeur en millions de dollars EU)
Exportations selon les principaux pays ou zones

Country or area	1998	1999	2000	2001	2002	Pays ou zone
World	58908.1	61898.1	66957.2	66560.1	70429.3	Monde
Africa	367.0	321.3	579.6	331.4	340.8	Afrique
Americas	11979.7	13456.3	15988.9	15659.8	15354.7	Amériques
- Northern America	10005.4	11315.1	13303.6	12933.6	12659.3	- Amérique du Nord
- LAIA	1790.3	1964.8	2461.8	2470.8	2444.9	- ALAI
- CACM	115.5	132.7	171.4	204.5	205.1	- MCC
- Caribbean	63.2	36.4	41.4	41.4	37.4	- Caraïbes
- Rest of America	5.2	7.4	10.7	9.6	8.1	- Autre d'Amérique
Asia excluding former USSR	15420.6	16837.6	19691.1	18680.3	20030.4	Asie ancienne URSS exclus
- Middle East	500.1	521.9	610.3	726.8	743.7	- Moyen-Orient
Asia former USSR	4.0	7.3	6.7	10.1	10.7	Asie ancienne URSS
Europe excluding former USSR	30713.9	30780.6	30121.6	31273.0	34012.4	Europe ancienne URSS exclus
- European Union	27795.2	27756.7	26927.4	27842.7	30131.4	- Union Européenne
- Eastern Europe	1278.0	1347.8	1524.6	1764.4	2091.0	- Europe de l'Est
- Rest of Europe	1640.7	1676.1	1669.5	1665.9	1790.0	- Autre de l'Europe
Europe former USSR	155.2	193.0	264.8	308.7	350.1	Europe ancienne URSS
Oceania	267.7	302.1	304.4	296.8	330.1	Océanie
United States	7837.5	8775.9	10336.0	9920.7	9458.9	Etats-Unis d'Amérique
Germany	7656.6	7697.0	7418.0	7969.8	8634.9	Allemagne
China	3945.0	4066.5	5078.3	5303.8	6325.3	Chine
Italy-San Marino-Holy See	3932.1	3831.7	3834.8	3870.0	4117.7	Italie-Saint-Marin-Saint-Siège
China, Hong Kong SAR	3480.2	3612.4	4015.5	3609.1	3403.2	Chine - RAS de Hong-Kong
France-Monaco	3762.2	3633.8	3450.3	3400.9	3727.9	France-Monaco
United Kingdom	2944.7	2866.7	2743.8	2656.8	2787.3	Royaume-Uni
Canada	2167.9	2539.1	2967.6	3012.8	3200.2	Canada
Belgium	–	2435.2	2409.1	2484.8	e2787.9	Belgique
Japan	1603.1	1964.9	2360.3	1901.9	2098.0	Japon
Netherlands	1736.7	1754.0	1607.9	1677.2	1885.2	Pays-Bas
Mexico	1325.6	1528.0	1932.0	1860.6	1806.2	Mexique
Spain	1136.5	1172.5	1228.2	1391.7	1467.5	Espagne
Switzerland-Liechtenstein	1225.9	1270.9	1244.9	1213.6	1318.0	Suisse-Liechtenstein
Denmark	1069.5	1089.1	1027.5	1065.2	1190.5	Danemark
Austria	1063.1	1025.0	1022.6	1053.4	1122.1	Autriche
Sweden	986.7	938.7	918.9	877.9	978.0	Suède
Korea, Republic of	728.4	886.7	1033.5	937.2	1052.4	République de Corée
Israel	596.9	711.7	732.9	775.9	736.6	Israël
Singapore	535.7	605.8	762.8	729.6	680.8	Singapour
Malaysia	473.7	566.3	697.8	718.1	e761.0	Malaisie
Czech Republic	485.6	522.5	580.5	663.3	758.4	République tchèque
Thailand	503.0	557.4	635.3	627.5	e662.7	Thaïlande
Poland	428.9	449.9	521.2	611.7	759.8	Pologne
Belgium-Luxembourg	2532.0	–	–	–	–	Belgique-Luxembourg
Ireland	371.4	387.0	378.9	431.1	410.4	Irlande
Hungary	237.6	247.8	285.6	324.5	357.5	Hongrie
Finland	283.4	276.6	277.6	288.5	309.3	Finlande
Turkey	219.4	200.5	242.6	311.2	349.5	Turquie
Luxembourg	–	314.2	278.1	344.6	e352.3	Luxembourg

(Value as percentages of World total) **(Valeur en pourcentage du total mondial)**

Regions of the world	1993	1994	1995	1996	1997	1998	1999	2000	2001	2002	Régions du monde
World	100.0	100.0	100.0	100.0	100.0	100.0	100.0	100.0	100.0	100.0	Monde
Africa	0.3	0.3	0.4	0.7	0.5	0.6	0.5	0.9	0.5	0.5	Afrique
Americas	15.7	17.1	15.5	17.4	18.9	20.3	21.7	23.9	23.5	21.8	Amériques
- Northern America	12.9	14.4	13.0	14.6	15.8	17.0	18.3	19.9	19.4	18.0	- Amérique du Nord
- LAIA	2.6	2.5	2.2	2.5	2.9	3.0	3.2	3.7	3.7	3.5	- ALAI
- CACM	0.1	0.1	0.1	0.1	0.1	0.2	0.2	0.3	0.3	0.3	- MCC
- Caribbean	0.1	0.1	0.1	0.1	0.1	0.1	0.1	0.1	0.1	0.1	- Caraïbes
- Rest of America	0.0	0.0	0.0	0.0	0.0	0.0	0.0	0.0	0.0	0.0	- Autre d'Amérique
Asia excluding former USSR	33.8	28.8	29.4	27.2	28.1	26.2	27.2	29.4	28.1	28.4	Asie ancienne URSS exclus
- Middle East	0.6	0.7	0.9	0.7	0.7	0.8	0.8	0.9	1.1	1.1	- Moyen-Orient
Asia former USSR	0.0	0.0	0.0	0.0	0.0	0.0	0.0	0.0	0.0	0.0	Asie ancienne URSS
Europe excluding former USSR	49.7	53.0	53.9	54.0	51.6	52.1	49.7	45.0	47.0	48.3	Europe ancienne URSS exclus
- European Union	45.9	48.8	49.4	49.3	46.8	47.2	44.8	40.2	41.8	42.8	- Union Européenne
- Eastern Europe	0.9	1.1	1.5	1.8	2.1	2.2	2.2	2.3	2.7	3.0	- Europe de l'Est
- Rest of Europe	2.8	3.1	3.0	2.9	2.7	2.8	2.7	2.5	2.5	2.5	- Autre de l'Europe
Europe former USSR	0.1	0.1	0.2	0.2	0.3	0.3	0.3	0.4	0.5	0.5	Europe ancienne URSS
Oceania	0.5	0.6	0.6	0.6	0.5	0.5	0.5	0.5	0.4	0.5	Océanie

894 Baby carriages, toys, games and sporting goods

TRADE BY COMMODITY (Value in million US dollars)
Imports by principal countries or areas

COMMERCE PAR PRODUIT (Valeur en millions de dollars EU)
Importations selon les principaux pays ou zones

Country or area	1998	1999	2000	2001	2002	Pays ou zone
World	54860.6	56581.7	60683.4	59511.2	62888.2	Monde
Africa	416.7	384.8	393.9	340.4	357.3	Afrique
Americas	23747.5	24401.0	25800.6	26714.5	28114.3	Amériques
- Northern America	21822.6	22733.1	23908.0	24752.3	26209.1	- Amérique du Nord
- LAIA	1681.6	1457.8	1665.4	1702.3	1636.0	- ALAI
- CACM	101.7	89.8	102.5	128.0	134.3	- MCC
- Caribbean	95.7	82.9	85.6	95.4	93.9	- Caraïbes
- Rest of America	45.9	37.3	39.1	36.6	41.1	- Autre d'Amérique
Asia excluding former USSR	12042.7	12847.7	14903.9	13003.6	13283.5	Asie ancienne URSS exclus
- Middle East	693.7	642.2	841.3	728.8	835.1	- Moyen-Orient
Asia former USSR	20.2	21.4	31.4	25.9	24.2	Asie ancienne URSS
Europe excluding former USSR	17494.1	17848.5	18327.1	18159.2	19504.4	Europe ancienne URSS exclus
- European Union	15793.3	16118.4	16593.3	16419.9	17451.6	- Union Européenne
- Eastern Europe	633.2	634.2	656.9	664.7	789.0	- Europe de l'Est
- Rest of Europe	1067.6	1095.9	1076.9	1074.6	1263.7	- Autre de l'Europe
Europe former USSR	232.3	179.4	193.0	345.9	393.9	Europe ancienne URSS
Oceania	907.2	899.0	1033.5	921.7	1210.6	Océanie
United States	19691.2	20458.0	21626.7	22417.6	23631.3	Etats-Unis d'Amérique
China, Hong Kong SAR	6683.1	6949.5	8034.6	6881.2	6789.6	Chine - RAS de Hong-Kong
Japan	3154.9	3387.0	3853.8	3378.3	3301.5	Japon
United Kingdom	3119.2	3236.1	3337.2	3306.9	3907.1	Royaume-Uni
Germany	3297.6	3056.3	2998.0	3248.7	3430.4	Allemagne
France-Monaco	2222.6	2264.4	2570.5	2447.0	2622.4	France-Monaco
Canada	2119.2	2261.6	2274.7	2327.9	2569.5	Canada
Netherlands	1510.5	1666.8	1720.8	1701.3	1127.6	Pays-Bas
Italy-San Marino-Holy See	1302.0	1279.8	1314.6	1274.4	1293.1	Italie-Saint-Marin-Saint-Siège
Spain	1014.1	1157.1	1160.8	1166.8	1288.0	Espagne
Belgium	–	1136.5	1220.0	982.7	e1077.8	Belgique
Australia	709.4	699.6	821.6	726.7	972.8	Australie
Mexico	607.4	620.4	755.8	840.3	918.8	Mexique
Switzerland-Liechtenstein	603.3	610.0	607.6	595.3	674.8	Suisse-Liechtenstein
Austria	556.7	598.7	558.1	539.0	613.8	Autriche
Korea, Republic of	225.1	373.4	530.1	540.5	714.5	République de Corée
Sweden	489.8	441.1	439.8	443.8	536.8	Suède
Denmark	342.2	340.3	331.9	340.4	435.4	Danemark
Singapore	244.4	371.0	450.7	352.2	369.3	Singapour
Norway	292.0	310.1	300.8	297.5	381.6	Norvège
China	278.5	251.5	232.6	275.5	361.0	Chine
Poland	250.7	244.4	262.2	245.1	270.3	Pologne
Portugal	221.8	268.3	242.0	236.7	294.3	Portugal
Ireland	229.6	221.4	238.8	239.0	281.9	Irlande
Greece	238.4	225.8	223.7	211.9	e234.3	Grèce
Belgium-Luxembourg	1071.1	–	–	–	–	Belgique-Luxembourg
United Arab Emirates	171.0	179.2	287.5	210.5	e215.9	Emirates arabes unis
Finland	177.9	168.6	174.3	206.7	229.8	Finlande
Czech Republic	172.3	177.4	169.1	178.4	225.8	République tchèque
Argentina	247.2	220.9	189.2	184.0	e81.4	Argentine

(Value as percentages of World total) **(Valeur en pourcentage du total mondial)**

Regions of the world	1993	1994	1995	1996	1997	1998	1999	2000	2001	2002	Régions du monde
World	100.0	100.0	100.0	100.0	100.0	100.0	100.0	100.0	100.0	100.0	Monde
Africa	0.6	0.6	0.7	0.6	0.7	0.8	0.7	0.6	0.6	0.6	Afrique
Americas	37.9	38.5	37.2	37.5	40.2	43.3	43.1	42.5	44.9	44.7	Amériques
- Northern America	35.1	34.9	33.7	34.4	36.8	39.8	40.2	39.4	41.6	41.7	- Amérique du Nord
- LAIA	2.5	3.2	3.0	2.7	3.1	3.1	2.6	2.7	2.9	2.6	- ALAI
- CACM	0.1	0.2	0.2	0.1	0.2	0.2	0.2	0.2	0.2	0.2	- MCC
- Caribbean	0.2	0.2	0.2	0.2	0.2	0.2	0.1	0.1	0.2	0.1	- Caraïbes
- Rest of America	0.1	0.1	0.1	0.1	0.1	0.1	0.1	0.1	0.1	0.1	- Autre d'Amérique
Asia excluding former USSR	25.1	26.2	28.0	27.5	24.9	22.0	22.7	24.6	21.9	21.1	Asie ancienne URSS exclus
- Middle East	1.1	1.2	1.1	1.1	1.1	1.3	1.1	1.4	1.2	1.3	- Moyen-Orient
Asia former USSR	0.0	0.0	0.0	0.0	0.0	0.0	0.0	0.1	0.0	0.0	Asie ancienne URSS
Europe excluding former USSR	34.3	32.5	31.9	32.0	31.8	31.9	31.5	30.2	30.5	31.0	Europe ancienne URSS exclus
- European Union	31.2	29.4	28.5	28.7	28.8	28.8	28.5	27.3	27.6	27.8	- Union Européenne
- Eastern Europe	0.9	0.9	1.1	1.2	1.1	1.2	1.1	1.1	1.1	1.3	- Europe de l'Est
- Rest of Europe	2.2	2.2	2.4	2.2	2.0	1.9	1.9	1.8	1.8	2.0	- Autre de l'Europe
Europe former USSR	0.3	0.4	0.5	0.5	0.4	0.4	0.3	0.3	0.6	0.6	Europe ancienne URSS
Oceania	1.6	1.7	1.8	1.9	1.9	1.7	1.6	1.7	1.5	1.9	Océanie

Voitures pour le transport des enfants; jouets, articles pour divertissements et pour sports 894

TRADE BY COMMODITY (Value in million US dollars)
Exports by principal countries or areas

COMMERCE PAR PRODUIT (Valeur en millions de dollars EU)
Exportations selon les principaux pays ou zones

Country or area	1998	1999	2000	2001	2002	Pays ou zone
World	45545.5	47083.1	48924.2	46189.6	49848.2	Monde
Africa	43.0	68.5	42.3	44.6	50.8	Afrique
Americas	6274.7	6106.7	6208.6	5949.8	6383.2	Amériques
- Northern America	5027.9	5040.5	5282.3	4977.0	4868.4	- Amérique du Nord
- LAIA	1217.6	1038.6	897.9	944.6	1486.3	- ALAI
- CACM	18.8	21.4	19.8	21.0	23.3	- MCC
- Caribbean	10.3	6.1	8.4	6.2	4.8	- Caraïbes
- Rest of America	0.1	0.1	0.1	1.1	0.5	- Autre d'Amérique
Asia excluding former USSR	28213.5	29764.2	31764.8	27783.7	30503.6	Asie ancienne URSS exclus
- Middle East	148.5	159.5	146.1	182.8	200.7	- Moyen-Orient
Asia former USSR	5.3	0.9	1.7	0.7	0.6	Asie ancienne URSS
Europe excluding former USSR	10765.2	10842.2	10594.9	12121.6	12571.8	Europe ancienne URSS exclus
- European Union	9681.7	9765.1	9498.2	10654.5	10696.0	- Union Européenne
- Eastern Europe	547.0	511.2	564.0	939.5	1351.7	- Europe de l'Est
- Rest of Europe	536.5	565.9	532.7	527.6	524.1	- Autre de l'Europe
Europe former USSR	102.9	150.8	137.8	121.6	130.9	Europe ancienne URSS
Oceania	141.0	149.7	174.0	167.5	207.3	Océanie
China, Hong Kong SAR	12211.9	12086.6	13290.4	11087.2	10984.7	Chine - RAS de Hong-Kong
China	8412.5	8511.0	10112.4	9886.2	12561.2	Chine
United States	4200.2	4131.1	4359.0	4110.8	3875.9	Etats-Unis d'Amérique
Japan	3060.7	4765.7	3261.1	2540.1	2605.6	Japon
Germany	1846.2	1776.1	1767.0	2109.2	2437.9	Allemagne
Italy-San Marino-Holy See	1656.9	1559.5	1478.8	1463.7	1503.8	Italie-Saint-Marin-Saint-Siège
United Kingdom	1338.6	1324.9	1230.8	1166.7	1278.0	Royaume-Uni
Netherlands	1058.1	1127.0	1196.2	1817.7	790.0	Pays-Bas
France-Monaco	1053.5	1112.9	1141.1	1131.3	1285.4	France-Monaco
Mexico	1078.0	902.8	751.8	809.4	1345.7	Mexique
Canada	827.6	909.5	923.2	866.0	992.2	Canada
Spain	668.9	689.6	667.5	738.6	852.1	Espagne
Austria	614.9	667.4	546.7	680.0	787.1	Autriche
Belgium	-	700.0	724.3	738.0	e828.0	Belgique
Korea, Republic of	638.7	606.0	628.6	567.3	463.4	République de Corée
Thailand	462.4	506.4	554.1	540.5	e570.8	Thaïlande
Switzerland-Liechtenstein	379.0	399.7	360.9	348.0	302.6	Suisse-Liechtenstein
Hungary	73.3	97.8	95.6	414.7	731.2	Hongrie
Malaysia	301.7	270.0	262.5	235.1	e249.1	Malaisie
Sweden	248.9	236.1	215.0	230.0	294.5	Suède
Czech Republic	251.4	204.8	218.2	243.1	291.8	République tchèque
Pakistan	257.5	196.2	213.6	208.5	260.1	Pakistan
Indonesia	104.6	221.9	383.6	198.7	169.1	Indonésie
Singapore	165.0	184.1	186.6	170.4	169.5	Singapour
Philippines	190.8	180.0	189.1	154.8	125.1	Philippines
Denmark	145.7	147.3	163.5	158.0	215.4	Danemark
Ireland	198.7	158.6	127.3	133.9	137.2	Irlande
Australia	118.9	126.9	146.8	141.2	186.8	Australie
Poland	137.0	124.8	139.8	141.6	170.6	Pologne
Finland	137.8	136.7	126.8	146.8	147.5	Finlande

(Value as percentages of World total) **(Valeur en pourcentage du total mondial)**

Regions of the world	1993	1994	1995	1996	1997	1998	1999	2000	2001	2002	Régions du monde
World	100.0	100.0	100.0	100.0	100.0	100.0	100.0	100.0	100.0	100.0	Monde
Africa	0.1	0.1	0.1	0.1	0.1	0.1	0.1	0.1	0.1	0.1	Afrique
Americas	12.0	13.6	14.1	14.0	13.9	13.8	13.0	12.7	12.9	12.8	Amériques
- Northern America	10.3	11.6	11.8	11.6	11.4	11.0	10.7	10.8	10.8	9.8	- Amérique du Nord
- LAIA	1.6	2.0	2.3	2.3	2.5	2.7	2.2	1.8	2.0	3.0	- ALAI
- CACM	0.0	0.0	0.0	0.0	0.0	0.0	0.0	0.0	0.0	0.0	- MCC
- Caribbean	0.0	0.0	0.0	0.0	0.0	0.0	0.0	0.0	0.0	0.0	- Caraïbes
- Rest of America	0.0	0.0	0.0	0.0	0.0	0.0	0.0	0.0	0.0	0.0	- Autre d'Amérique
Asia excluding former USSR	65.5	61.4	60.8	61.4	62.7	61.9	63.2	64.9	60.2	61.2	Asie ancienne URSS exclus
- Middle East	0.1	0.1	0.1	0.2	0.3	0.3	0.3	0.3	0.4	0.4	- Moyen-Orient
Asia former USSR	0.0	0.0	0.0	0.0	0.0	0.0	0.0	0.0	0.0	0.0	Asie ancienne URSS
Europe excluding former USSR	22.0	24.4	24.5	23.9	22.8	23.6	23.0	21.7	26.2	25.2	Europe ancienne URSS exclus
- European Union	20.0	22.1	22.3	21.5	20.7	21.3	20.7	19.4	23.1	21.5	- Union Européenne
- Eastern Europe	0.6	0.8	0.9	1.0	1.0	1.2	1.1	1.2	2.0	2.7	- Europe de l'Est
- Rest of Europe	1.4	1.5	1.3	1.3	1.1	1.2	1.2	1.1	1.1	1.1	- Autre de l'Europe
Europe former USSR	0.2	0.1	0.2	0.2	0.2	0.2	0.3	0.3	0.3	0.3	Europe ancienne URSS
Oceania	0.2	0.3	0.4	0.4	0.3	0.3	0.3	0.4	0.4	0.4	Océanie

895 Office and stationary supplies, nes

TRADE BY COMMODITY (Value in million US dollars)
Imports by principal countries or areas

COMMERCE PAR PRODUIT (Valeur en millions de dollars EU)
Importations selon les principaux pays ou zones

Country or area	1998	1999	2000	2001	2002	Pays ou zone
World	8194.4	8543.0	9125.2	8689.5	9019.7	Monde
Africa	177.4	169.7	168.3	173.6	203.2	Afrique
Americas	2413.5	2554.2	2841.3	2554.8	2524.0	Amériques
- Northern America	1674.5	1835.4	2042.9	1833.4	1840.3	- Amérique du Nord
- LAIA	631.4	612.5	673.1	588.4	553.8	- ALAI
- CACM	59.2	60.3	71.5	83.1	82.8	- MCC
- Caribbean	31.8	30.7	38.5	37.2	35.1	- Caraïbes
- Rest of America	16.6	15.3	15.4	12.7	11.9	- Autre d'Amérique
Asia excluding former USSR	1589.0	1783.4	2090.2	1878.2	1882.0	Asie ancienne URSS exclus
- Middle East	252.7	239.2	262.0	243.9	256.1	- Moyen-Orient
Asia former USSR	4.6	4.7	9.8	9.0	8.8	Asie ancienne URSS
Europe excluding former USSR	3786.8	3808.0	3772.6	3851.7	4184.1	Europe ancienne URSS exclus
- European Union	3324.2	3352.4	3291.8	3424.4	3686.5	- Union Européenne
- Eastern Europe	229.9	224.7	258.7	213.5	281.4	- Europe de l'Est
- Rest of Europe	232.7	230.9	222.1	213.8	216.2	- Autre de l'Europe
Europe former USSR	68.6	62.1	82.0	83.2	80.5	Europe ancienne URSS
Oceania	154.5	161.1	160.9	139.0	137.1	Océanie
United States	1417.3	1576.6	1777.4	1579.0	1596.9	Etats-Unis d'Amérique
France-Monaco	631.7	681.4	658.5	681.6	771.8	France-Monaco
United Kingdom	675.7	664.9	593.8	526.8	588.8	Royaume-Uni
Germany	584.0	497.3	507.8	687.9	613.2	Allemagne
China, Hong Kong SAR	426.8	479.4	590.1	512.5	500.6	Chine - RAS de Hong-Kong
Italy-San Marino-Holy See	316.0	352.8	393.7	398.7	431.3	Italie-Saint-Marin-Saint-Siège
Mexico	357.7	377.7	425.8	334.0	357.9	Mexique
Netherlands	244.9	260.6	261.3	247.2	331.2	Pays-Bas
Canada	256.6	258.2	265.0	253.5	242.2	Canada
Spain	231.8	262.2	245.5	245.3	286.8	Espagne
Japan	192.4	219.7	239.0	219.1	202.9	Japon
Singapore	183.2	176.9	214.2	193.1	154.0	Singapour
Malaysia	100.5	150.0	175.4	134.3	e146.7	Malaisie
Switzerland-Liechtenstein	136.5	135.4	134.0	130.3	127.9	Suisse-Liechtenstein
Belgium	–	154.7	151.9	152.9	e167.7	Belgique
Australia	117.3	123.6	124.4	105.8	102.6	Australie
Austria	96.8	106.1	102.1	98.7	110.6	Autriche
Korea, Republic of	70.4	98.4	117.8	110.5	116.1	République de Corée
Sweden	103.1	91.9	86.6	90.2	103.7	Suède
Thailand	57.9	77.3	113.1	110.8	e115.5	Thaïlande
Poland	97.8	94.3	93.3	84.2	94.3	Pologne
China	53.3	71.8	97.8	106.3	130.4	Chine
Ireland	68.2	55.7	80.3	83.8	79.8	Irlande
Denmark	77.8	66.1	67.0	64.6	56.9	Danemark
Turkey	67.6	64.9	79.8	51.5	67.9	Turquie
Saudi Arabia	67.6	60.0	62.6	59.2	e61.2	Arabie saoudite
Hungary	33.1	41.6	78.6	49.9	90.2	Hongrie
Portugal	59.8	66.5	50.4	54.5	52.7	Portugal
Czech Republic	62.4	59.0	56.4	45.4	57.6	République tchèque
Brazil	66.6	49.2	49.5	52.0	44.9	Brésil

(Value as percentages of World total) **(Valeur en pourcentage du total mondial)**

Regions of the world	1993	1994	1995	1996	1997	1998	1999	2000	2001	2002	Régions du monde
World	100.0	100.0	100.0	100.0	100.0	100.0	100.0	100.0	100.0	100.0	Monde
Africa	2.7	2.3	2.4	2.3	2.2	2.2	2.0	1.8	2.0	2.3	Afrique
Americas	28.1	27.9	26.4	26.1	28.0	29.5	29.9	31.1	29.4	28.0	Amériques
- Northern America	21.3	21.3	20.0	19.3	19.1	20.4	21.5	22.4	21.1	20.4	- Amérique du Nord
- LAIA	5.7	5.7	5.3	5.6	7.2	7.7	7.2	7.4	6.8	6.1	- ALAI
- CACM	0.5	0.5	0.5	0.7	1.1	0.7	0.7	0.8	1.0	0.9	- MCC
- Caribbean	0.4	0.3	0.4	0.3	0.3	0.4	0.4	0.4	0.4	0.4	- Caraïbes
- Rest of America	0.2	0.2	0.2	0.2	0.2	0.2	0.2	0.2	0.1	0.1	- Autre d'Amérique
Asia excluding former USSR	24.0	23.8	24.3	24.9	23.8	19.4	20.9	22.9	21.6	20.9	Asie ancienne URSS exclus
- Middle East	4.3	3.7	3.4	3.2	3.2	3.1	2.8	2.9	2.8	2.8	- Moyen-Orient
Asia former USSR	0.0	0.0	0.1	0.1	0.1	0.1	0.1	0.1	0.1	0.1	Asie ancienne URSS
Europe excluding former USSR	42.0	43.0	44.1	43.7	43.1	46.2	44.6	41.3	44.3	46.4	Europe ancienne URSS exclus
- European Union	37.0	37.8	38.5	38.0	37.9	40.6	39.2	36.1	39.4	40.9	- Union Européenne
- Eastern Europe	1.8	1.9	2.2	2.6	2.5	2.8	2.6	2.8	2.5	3.1	- Europe de l'Est
- Rest of Europe	3.2	3.3	3.4	3.1	2.7	2.8	2.7	2.4	2.5	2.4	- Autre de l'Europe
Europe former USSR	0.8	0.6	0.6	0.6	0.8	0.8	0.7	0.9	1.0	0.9	Europe ancienne URSS
Oceania	2.3	2.3	2.2	2.2	2.0	1.9	1.9	1.8	1.6	1.5	Océanie

TRADE BY COMMODITY (Value in million US dollars)
Exports by principal countries or areas

COMMERCE PAR PRODUIT (Valeur en millions de dollars EU)
Exportations selon les principaux pays ou zones

Country or area	1998	1999	2000	2001	2002	Pays ou zone
World	7522.7	7997.8	8331.1	7470.8	7941.9	Monde
Africa	28.4	21.1	27.2	24.1	27.3	Afrique
Americas	1200.6	1207.6	1178.3	1093.0	1123.6	Amériques
- Northern America	855.2	857.2	818.3	722.6	701.4	- Amérique du Nord
- LAIA	328.1	339.1	348.9	352.7	409.7	- ALAI
- CACM	8.6	10.2	10.0	16.4	11.6	- MCC
- Caribbean	8.4	1.0	1.0	1.0	0.8	- Caraïbes
- Rest of America	0.2	0.1	0.0	0.3	0.2	- Autre d'Amérique
Asia excluding former USSR	3061.1	3479.9	4005.3	3286.9	3487.0	Asie ancienne URSS exclus
- Middle East	32.8	32.2	29.6	34.3	36.0	- Moyen-Orient
Asia former USSR	0.2	0.5	0.8	0.7	0.4	Asie ancienne URSS
Europe excluding former USSR	3205.0	3265.8	3096.1	3040.3	3278.1	Europe ancienne URSS exclus
- European Union	2924.2	3005.2	2800.0	2744.7	2945.8	- Union Européenne
- Eastern Europe	113.3	102.0	113.1	112.0	129.8	- Europe de l'Est
- Rest of Europe	167.5	158.5	183.0	183.6	202.5	- Autre de l'Europe
Europe former USSR	4.7	4.4	6.0	7.3	10.5	Europe ancienne URSS
Oceania	22.8	18.5	17.4	18.5	15.0	Océanie
Japan	1249.8	1402.5	1493.3	1195.9	1154.7	Japon
Germany	894.9	845.6	798.0	858.5	849.8	Allemagne
United States	821.8	825.1	779.3	686.2	669.3	Etats-Unis d'Amérique
China	445.6	465.4	552.7	584.2	722.6	Chine
France-Monaco	624.4	573.8	511.1	455.3	508.3	France-Monaco
China, Hong Kong SAR	388.3	456.1	546.5	458.4	486.9	Chine - RAS de Hong-Kong
United Kingdom	423.9	470.8	463.3	420.7	516.8	Royaume-Uni
Netherlands	220.6	369.1	279.5	280.1	311.7	Pays-Bas
Italy-San Marino-Holy See	299.6	287.0	280.2	275.4	267.0	Italie-Saint-Marin-Saint-Siège
Mexico	235.9	276.1	267.2	272.9	329.6	Mexique
Singapore	188.8	283.0	426.5	200.2	258.0	Singapour
Korea, Republic of	149.2	174.3	224.4	221.7	196.2	République de Corée
Switzerland-Liechtenstein	133.2	128.0	152.7	154.1	169.7	Suisse-Liechtenstein
Spain	97.2	107.2	114.6	116.8	146.6	Espagne
Belgium	–	97.6	116.4	112.2	e125.9	Belgique
Malaysia	74.2	86.3	95.4	86.5	e91.6	Malaisie
Czech Republic	71.6	64.3	64.2	64.8	74.8	République tchèque
Austria	48.5	60.6	69.6	73.7	78.4	Autriche
Thailand	57.9	68.6	78.9	60.1	e63.4	Thaïlande
India	43.7	55.4	78.2	74.6	76.5	Inde
Ireland	110.8	77.9	56.5	34.7	25.2	Irlande
Sweden	64.3	61.3	53.1	49.1	54.8	Suède
Brazil	62.8	42.4	51.3	54.2	e56.2	Brésil
Indonesia	36.6	55.0	60.6	52.6	58.1	Indonésie
Canada	33.4	32.1	39.0	36.3	32.1	Canada
Denmark	35.9	30.4	26.8	32.0	26.8	Danemark
Slovenia	26.0	22.4	22.9	22.8	24.8	Slovénie
Hungary	15.6	16.0	20.4	21.3	28.7	Hongrie
Poland	20.0	15.8	21.9	18.9	18.7	Pologne
Belgium-Luxembourg	81.5	–	–	–	–	Belgique-Luxembourg

(Value as percentages of World total) **(Valeur en pourcentage du total mondial)**

Regions of the world	1993	1994	1995	1996	1997	1998	1999	2000	2001	2002	Régions du monde
World	100.0	100.0	100.0	100.0	100.0	100.0	100.0	100.0	100.0	100.0	Monde
Africa	0.3	0.4	0.4	0.5	0.6	0.4	0.3	0.3	0.3	0.3	Afrique
Americas	11.8	13.1	12.8	14.3	15.9	16.0	15.1	14.1	14.6	14.1	Amériques
- Northern America	8.9	9.3	9.1	10.3	11.6	11.4	10.7	9.8	9.7	8.8	- Amérique du Nord
- LAIA	2.8	3.6	3.2	3.1	3.8	4.4	4.2	4.2	4.7	5.2	- ALAI
- CACM	0.1	0.3	0.5	0.8	0.5	0.1	0.1	0.1	0.2	0.1	- MCC
- Caribbean	0.0	0.0	0.0	0.0	0.0	0.1	0.0	0.0	0.0	0.0	- Caraïbes
- Rest of America	0.0	0.0	0.0	0.0	0.0	0.0	0.0	0.0	0.0	0.0	- Autre d'Amérique
Asia excluding former USSR	45.3	42.4	42.6	40.5	40.8	40.7	43.5	48.1	44.0	43.9	Asie ancienne URSS exclus
- Middle East	0.3	0.3	0.4	0.2	0.2	0.4	0.4	0.4	0.5	0.5	- Moyen-Orient
Asia former USSR	0.0	0.0	0.0	0.0	0.0	0.0	0.0	0.0	0.0	0.0	Asie ancienne URSS
Europe excluding former USSR	42.3	43.8	43.8	44.3	42.3	42.6	40.8	37.2	40.7	41.3	Europe ancienne URSS exclus
- European Union	38.8	40.2	39.8	39.9	38.5	38.9	37.6	33.6	36.7	37.1	- Union Européenne
- Eastern Europe	0.7	0.8	0.9	1.3	1.5	1.5	1.3	1.4	1.5	1.6	- Europe de l'Est
- Rest of Europe	2.7	2.8	3.1	3.1	2.3	2.2	2.0	2.2	2.5	2.5	- Autre de l'Europe
Europe former USSR	0.0	0.1	0.1	0.1	0.1	0.1	0.1	0.1	0.1	0.1	Europe ancienne URSS
Oceania	0.2	0.3	0.3	0.4	0.3	0.3	0.2	0.2	0.2	0.2	Océanie

896 Works of art, collectors' pieces and antiques

TRADE BY COMMODITY (Value in million US dollars)
Imports by principal countries or areas

COMMERCE PAR PRODUIT (Valeur en millions de dollars EU)
Importations selon les principaux pays ou zones

Country or area	1998	1999	2000	2001	2002	Pays ou zone
World	9333.5	10024.1	11464.9	11378.7	11307.0	Monde
Africa	20.3	14.3	63.4	50.8	39.5	Afrique
Americas	4156.1	5056.5	6008.6	5624.9	5316.1	Amériques
- Northern America	4095.7	5012.4	5977.6	5580.2	5283.5	- Amérique du Nord
- LAIA	35.2	22.5	20.6	21.7	24.1	- ALAI
- CACM	1.7	1.3	1.5	1.0	1.0	- MCC
- Caribbean	18.5	17.1	7.7	21.0	6.4	- Caraïbes
- Rest of America	5.0	3.2	1.2	1.0	1.1	- Autre d'Amérique
Asia excluding former USSR	570.8	729.8	831.1	531.9	534.6	Asie ancienne URSS exclus
- Middle East	13.0	17.1	126.2	31.4	26.7	- Moyen-Orient
Asia former USSR	0.2	0.3	5.1	1.5	1.2	Asie ancienne URSS
Europe excluding former USSR	4471.1	4105.2	4457.7	5108.2	5349.7	Europe ancienne URSS exclus
- European Union	3558.7	3299.6	3610.7	4129.9	4562.8	- Union Européenne
- Eastern Europe	67.8	131.9	20.0	11.5	52.2	- Europe de l'Est
- Rest of Europe	844.6	673.7	827.0	966.8	734.6	- Autre de l'Europe
Europe former USSR	5.9	2.3	1.5	1.7	2.4	Europe ancienne URSS
Oceania	109.1	115.7	97.5	59.8	63.5	Océanie
United States	4021.8	4933.4	5877.2	5465.3	5177.2	Etats-Unis d'Amérique
United Kingdom	2482.2	2251.6	2479.3	2757.0	3170.1	Royaume-Uni
Switzerland-Liechtenstein	830.0	663.1	812.0	942.7	709.0	Suisse-Liechtenstein
Germany	458.8	303.1	373.4	461.1	325.2	Allemagne
Japan	368.2	455.0	449.8	229.8	220.3	Japon
France-Monaco	194.6	198.0	233.4	187.3	221.2	France-Monaco
Spain	104.0	92.7	147.9	284.3	171.1	Espagne
China, Hong Kong SAR	94.6	117.2	124.7	139.3	155.3	Chine - RAS de Hong-Kong
Netherlands	97.3	77.6	103.9	102.4	92.3	Pays-Bas
Canada	73.2	78.1	99.4	111.8	103.9	Canada
Australia	89.4	104.5	87.3	49.0	52.5	Australie
Sweden	12.9	128.8	41.2	18.4	142.5	Suède
Italy-San Marino-Holy See	43.2	54.3	42.1	42.7	146.3	Italie-Saint-Marin-Saint-Siège
Greece	5.4	9.8	45.4	109.1	e120.6	Grèce
Belgium	-	60.8	53.7	66.4	e72.8	Belgique
Czech Republic	56.2	116.3	2.4	1.5	38.7	République tchèque
Austria	36.3	43.7	37.7	45.3	51.3	Autriche
Korea, Republic of	14.7	16.8	20.0	33.2	63.7	République de Corée
Israel	14.6	34.6	23.5	47.2	22.2	Israël
Singapore	22.9	29.1	44.0	23.0	22.4	Singapour
Turkey	3.2	6.4	111.7	10.7	2.4	Turquie
Ireland	6.2	52.7	20.2	22.8	11.8	Irlande
Denmark	21.4	18.3	19.3	22.3	22.3	Danemark
Belgium-Luxembourg	89.5	-	-	-	-	Belgique-Luxembourg
South Africa	-	-	31.1	12.6	29.6	Afrique du Sud
Mexico	18.5	7.3	10.7	10.0	9.2	Mexique
Egypt	0.0	0.0	e	25.0	0.2	Egypte
Poland	6.2	12.2	15.2	5.4	9.0	Pologne
New Zealand	11.0	8.9	8.2	9.5	9.3	Nouvelle-Zélande
Norway	10.4	6.2	8.0	8.9	8.1	Norvège

(Value as percentages of World total) **(Valeur en pourcentage du total mondial)**

Regions of the world	1993	1994	1995	1996	1997	1998	1999	2000	2001	2002	Régions du monde
World	100.0	100.0	100.0	100.0	100.0	100.0	100.0	100.0	100.0	100.0	Monde
Africa	0.3	0.2	0.3	0.4	0.3	0.2	0.1	0.6	0.4	0.3	Afrique
Americas	38.3	35.1	41.7	43.4	44.1	44.5	50.4	52.4	49.4	47.0	Amériques
- Northern America	37.9	34.3	41.0	42.7	43.6	43.9	50.0	52.1	49.0	46.7	- Amérique du Nord
- LAIA	0.3	0.4	0.5	0.4	0.4	0.4	0.2	0.2	0.2	0.2	- ALAI
- CACM	0.0	0.0	0.0	0.0	0.0	0.0	0.0	0.0	0.0	0.0	- MCC
- Caribbean	0.1	0.4	0.2	0.2	0.1	0.2	0.2	0.1	0.2	0.1	- Caraïbes
- Rest of America	0.0	0.0	0.0	0.0	0.1	0.1	0.0	0.0	0.0	0.0	- Autre d'Amérique
Asia excluding former USSR	10.9	11.2	11.4	12.5	11.6	6.1	7.3	7.2	4.7	4.7	Asie ancienne URSS exclus
- Middle East	0.2	0.3	0.2	0.2	0.2	0.1	0.2	1.1	0.3	0.2	- Moyen-Orient
Asia former USSR	0.0	0.0	0.0	0.0	0.0	0.0	0.0	0.0	0.0	0.0	Asie ancienne URSS
Europe excluding former USSR	49.4	52.4	45.3	42.2	42.6	47.9	41.0	38.9	44.9	47.3	Europe ancienne URSS exclus
- European Union	42.8	44.0	37.5	31.5	30.5	38.1	32.9	31.5	36.3	40.4	- Union Européenne
- Eastern Europe	0.1	0.1	1.1	0.1	2.1	0.7	1.3	0.2	0.1	0.5	- Europe de l'Est
- Rest of Europe	6.6	8.3	6.7	10.6	10.0	9.0	6.7	7.2	8.5	6.5	- Autre de l'Europe
Europe former USSR	0.2	0.1	0.1	0.0	0.0	0.1	0.0	0.0	0.0	0.0	Europe ancienne URSS
Oceania	0.9	1.0	1.4	1.5	1.4	1.2	1.2	0.9	0.5	0.6	Océanie

TRADE BY COMMODITY (Value in million US dollars)
Exports by principal countries or areas

COMMERCE PAR PRODUIT (Valeur en millions de dollars EU)
Exportations selon les principaux pays ou zones

Country or area	1998	1999	2000	2001	2002	Pays ou zone
World	7467.2	7304.3	9806.7	9597.2	9270.7	Monde
Africa	44.4	44.1	45.6	28.5	66.3	Afrique
Americas	2514.8	2073.0	3482.0	3864.4	2632.9	Amériques
- Northern America	2478.6	2044.6	3441.3	3843.2	2610.2	- Amérique du Nord
- LAIA	15.5	19.8	36.7	17.5	13.6	- ALAI
- CACM	0.1	0.0	0.1	0.4	0.5	- MCC
- Caribbean	18.8	8.4	3.4	2.9	8.4	- Caraïbes
- Rest of America	1.8	0.3	0.5	0.4	0.3	- Autre d'Amérique
Asia excluding former USSR	257.8	246.8	292.9	317.4	302.9	Asie ancienne URSS exclus
- Middle East	6.7	3.4	18.3	8.9	6.3	- Moyen-Orient
Asia former USSR	0.8	1.1	2.0	3.1	4.1	Asie ancienne URSS
Europe excluding former USSR	4596.1	4886.1	5916.8	5320.6	6198.4	Europe ancienne URSS exclus
- European Union	3782.5	4089.8	4998.2	4612.3	5273.4	- Union Européenne
- Eastern Europe	123.9	134.6	21.2	15.7	21.6	- Europe de l'Est
- Rest of Europe	689.6	661.7	897.5	692.7	903.4	- Autre de l'Europe
Europe former USSR	1.8	1.9	5.3	3.5	8.6	Europe ancienne URSS
Oceania	51.5	51.2	62.1	59.6	57.5	Océanie
United Kingdom	2380.7	2564.3	3220.5	2998.4	3709.8	Royaume-Uni
United States	2361.2	1908.4	3173.6	3574.6	2444.1	Etats-Unis d'Amérique
Switzerland-Liechtenstein	674.5	633.9	858.6	651.9	859.3	Suisse-Liechtenstein
France-Monaco	525.6	555.7	763.5	620.7	598.5	France-Monaco
Germany	554.3	539.9	526.5	511.7	471.9	Allemagne
Canada	116.4	135.0	264.2	266.3	164.8	Canada
China, Hong Kong SAR	91.0	88.5	110.2	96.8	127.3	Chine - RAS de Hong-Kong
Italy-San Marino-Holy See	50.9	68.2	84.6	82.2	73.4	Italie-Saint-Marin-Saint-Siège
Belgium	–	87.1	92.0	76.3	e85.6	Belgique
Japan	42.1	39.7	70.6	104.4	51.2	Japon
Netherlands	55.6	47.6	67.9	65.6	48.4	Pays-Bas
Spain	25.9	44.3	52.5	57.3	100.9	Espagne
Czech Republic	109.1	117.8	5.8	6.0	6.5	République tchèque
Australia	42.5	41.9	49.8	46.9	50.4	Australie
Austria	36.7	38.5	43.2	59.2	40.0	Autriche
Denmark	40.5	32.3	48.1	43.3	34.7	Danemark
Sweden	25.5	52.5	28.1	19.0	31.7	Suède
Greece	1.9	5.9	35.8	55.1	e55.2	Grèce
China	50.8	38.3	21.3	18.6	20.0	Chine
Norway	11.5	24.5	33.3	28.6	38.4	Norvège
Korea, Republic of	9.9	13.5	18.6	35.6	51.9	République de Corée
Ireland	6.7	46.8	27.3	13.3	11.3	Irlande
Israel	19.2	21.0	24.2	19.3	16.5	Israël
Zimbabwe	e15.9	14.9	16.5	1.6	25.0	Zimbabwe
Singapore	19.3	19.8	11.2	14.0	9.1	Singapour
Belgium-Luxembourg	71.9	–	–	–	–	Belgique-Luxembourg
Mexico	8.5	11.8	25.2	9.0	5.1	Mexique
South Africa	–	–	19.5	15.5	19.6	Afrique du Sud
New Zealand	8.2	8.8	11.6	11.3	6.6	Nouvelle-Zélande
Poland	9.6	11.5	10.8	5.2	6.8	Pologne

(Value as percentages of World total) **(Valeur en pourcentage du total mondial)**

Regions of the world	1993	1994	1995	1996	1997	1998	1999	2000	2001	2002	Régions du monde
World	100.0	100.0	100.0	100.0	100.0	100.0	100.0	100.0	100.0	100.0	Monde
Africa	0.4	0.7	0.6	0.5	0.4	0.6	0.6	0.5	0.3	0.7	Afrique
Americas	32.6	27.5	23.7	23.4	25.0	33.7	28.4	35.5	40.3	28.4	Amériques
- Northern America	30.5	26.8	23.5	23.0	24.7	33.2	28.0	35.1	40.0	28.2	- Amérique du Nord
- LAIA	2.1	0.5	0.1	0.2	0.1	0.2	0.3	0.4	0.2	0.1	- ALAI
- CACM	0.0	0.0	0.0	0.1	0.0	0.0	0.0	0.0	0.0	0.0	- MCC
- Caribbean	0.0	0.2	0.1	0.1	0.1	0.3	0.1	0.0	0.0	0.1	- Caraïbes
- Rest of America	0.0	0.0	0.0	0.0	0.0	0.0	0.0	0.0	0.0	0.0	- Autre d'Amérique
Asia excluding former USSR	4.7	5.4	4.3	3.6	3.7	3.5	3.4	3.0	3.3	3.3	Asie ancienne URSS exclus
- Middle East	0.5	0.5	0.1	0.0	0.0	0.1	0.0	0.2	0.1	0.1	- Moyen-Orient
Asia former USSR	0.1	0.0	0.1	0.0	0.0	0.0	0.0	0.0	0.0	0.0	Asie ancienne URSS
Europe excluding former USSR	60.2	66.0	70.6	72.0	70.4	61.6	66.9	60.3	55.4	66.9	Europe ancienne URSS exclus
- European Union	44.3	49.7	59.8	60.2	57.4	50.7	56.0	51.0	48.1	56.9	- Union Européenne
- Eastern Europe	1.3	3.4	1.6	1.2	4.1	1.7	1.8	0.2	0.2	0.2	- Europe de l'Est
- Rest of Europe	14.6	12.8	9.3	10.6	8.8	9.2	9.1	9.2	7.2	9.7	- Autre de l'Europe
Europe former USSR	1.6	0.0	0.0	0.0	0.0	0.0	0.0	0.1	0.0	0.1	Europe ancienne URSS
Oceania	0.4	0.4	0.6	0.5	0.5	0.7	0.7	0.6	0.6	0.6	Océanie

897 Gold, silver ware, jewelry and articles of precious materials, nes

TRADE BY COMMODITY (Value in million US dollars) | COMMERCE PAR PRODUIT (Valeur en millions de dollars EU)

Imports by principal countries or areas | **Importations selon les principaux pays ou zones**

Country or area	1998	1999	2000	2001	2002	Pays ou zone
World	18354.4	18394.0	20528.2	21155.1	23102.6	Monde
Africa	54.7	57.2	64.5	139.3	134.7	Afrique
Americas	6213.6	6653.5	7501.9	7326.0	8330.0	Amériques
- Northern America	5673.9	6131.1	7032.1	6817.8	7682.2	- Amérique du Nord
- LAIA	386.1	356.4	293.2	301.5	331.5	- ALAI
- CACM	11.0	9.9	11.8	11.5	15.8	- MCC
- Caribbean	132.6	145.6	156.2	189.1	290.7	- Caraïbes
- Rest of America	10.0	10.6	8.6	6.0	9.8	- Autre d'Amérique
Asia excluding former USSR	4428.3	4708.6	5770.0	6089.5	6273.5	Asie ancienne URSS exclus
- Middle East	1150.6	1129.2	1599.6	1819.5	1845.4	- Moyen-Orient
Asia former USSR	7.9	9.2	10.2	22.2	17.6	Asie ancienne URSS
Europe excluding former USSR	7125.0	6712.0	6900.2	7285.4	8006.9	Europe ancienne URSS exclus
- European Union	5240.5	5082.7	5113.5	5522.1	6033.3	- Union Européenne
- Eastern Europe	99.7	116.8	116.3	118.8	140.6	- Europe de l'Est
- Rest of Europe	1784.8	1512.5	1670.4	1644.5	1833.1	- Autre de l'Europe
Europe former USSR	33.4	23.4	26.2	34.4	34.8	Europe ancienne URSS
Oceania	491.4	230.1	255.2	258.3	305.0	Océanie
United States	5415.7	5842.0	6617.3	6417.5	7283.1	Etats-Unis d'Amérique
United Kingdom	2167.4	1730.4	1639.1	2008.9	2356.0	Royaume-Uni
Switzerland-Liechtenstein	1660.6	1392.9	1551.3	1521.6	1694.8	Suisse-Liechtenstein
China, Hong Kong SAR	1093.4	1198.4	1404.6	1362.5	1539.5	Chine - RAS de Hong-Kong
Japan	984.1	1106.4	1234.1	1417.6	1368.9	Japon
United Arab Emirates	697.6	731.0	1196.2	1442.6	e1480.1	Emirates arabes unis
France-Monaco	730.6	766.8	896.8	995.9	992.3	France-Monaco
Germany	864.9	916.1	886.6	821.3	867.5	Allemagne
Singapore	539.6	608.4	583.7	555.7	532.1	Singapour
Italy-San Marino-Holy See	331.0	353.4	413.9	441.0	459.8	Italie-Saint-Marin-Saint-Siège
Canada	257.0	288.7	409.4	392.8	390.5	Canada
Spain	288.7	339.0	268.4	289.8	305.2	Espagne
Mexico	296.9	290.8	228.9	220.1	257.8	Mexique
Australia	443.7	179.5	202.9	207.7	246.1	Australie
Belgium	–	205.1	274.7	294.5	e322.9	Belgique
Austria	185.5	187.3	171.4	169.7	174.1	Autriche
Netherlands	133.9	150.8	152.0	128.8	129.3	Pays-Bas
Kuwait	142.4	153.6	e144.3	e158.7	e91.3	Koweït
Malaysia	155.9	105.9	182.1	112.2	e122.6	Malaisie
China	97.3	106.2	130.1	136.5	123.9	Chine
Israel	100.7	112.3	114.3	126.2	114.5	Israël
Portugal	111.8	122.0	113.0	88.9	96.0	Portugal
Thailand	39.0	52.8	89.3	115.9	e120.7	Thaïlande
Korea, Republic of	39.0	57.5	94.1	97.2	126.4	République de Corée
Sweden	67.7	74.3	79.1	66.6	82.9	Suède
Turkey	62.9	43.4	73.7	66.4	89.0	Turquie
Norway	64.2	63.8	62.5	62.9	75.6	Norvège
Greece	74.5	74.5	65.7	46.7	e51.6	Grèce
Dominican Republic	e34.0	e43.0	e42.4	e75.4	e101.0	République dominicaine
Denmark	53.3	49.8	49.2	60.5	74.6	Danemark

(Value as percentages of World total) | **(Valeur en pourcentage du total mondial)**

Regions of the world	1993	1994	1995	1996	1997	1998	1999	2000	2001	2002	Régions du monde
World	100.0	100.0	100.0	100.0	100.0	100.0	100.0	100.0	100.0	100.0	Monde
Africa	0.4	0.6	0.3	0.3	0.4	0.3	0.3	0.3	0.7	0.6	Afrique
Americas	31.2	31.6	29.0	28.5	28.9	33.9	36.2	36.5	34.6	36.1	Amériques
- Northern America	29.5	29.9	27.5	26.9	27.0	30.9	33.3	34.3	32.2	33.3	- Amérique du Nord
- LAIA	0.9	1.0	0.9	0.9	1.1	2.1	1.9	1.4	1.4	1.4	- ALAI
- CACM	0.1	0.1	0.1	0.1	0.1	0.1	0.1	0.1	0.1	0.1	- MCC
- Caribbean	0.6	0.5	0.5	0.6	0.6	0.7	0.8	0.8	0.9	1.3	- Caraïbes
- Rest of America	0.1	0.1	0.1	0.0	0.0	0.1	0.1	0.0	0.0	0.0	- Autre d'Amérique
Asia excluding former USSR	25.8	26.2	30.4	30.2	28.7	24.1	25.6	28.1	28.8	27.2	Asie ancienne URSS exclus
- Middle East	7.2	6.7	7.3	6.1	5.9	6.3	6.1	7.8	8.6	8.0	- Moyen-Orient
Asia former USSR	0.0	0.0	0.1	0.1	0.0	0.0	0.0	0.0	0.1	0.1	Asie ancienne URSS
Europe excluding former USSR	41.0	40.4	39.0	39.5	40.7	38.8	36.5	33.6	34.4	34.7	Europe ancienne URSS exclus
- European Union	28.9	29.4	28.0	28.7	29.1	28.6	27.6	24.9	26.1	26.1	- Union Européenne
- Eastern Europe	0.4	0.4	0.4	0.4	0.4	0.5	0.6	0.6	0.6	0.6	- Europe de l'Est
- Rest of Europe	11.7	10.5	10.6	10.4	11.2	9.7	8.2	8.1	7.8	7.9	- Autre de l'Europe
Europe former USSR	0.3	0.1	0.1	0.1	0.1	0.2	0.1	0.1	0.2	0.2	Europe ancienne URSS
Oceania	1.3	1.2	1.1	1.4	1.2	2.7	1.3	1.2	1.2	1.3	Océanie

TRADE BY COMMODITY (Value in million US dollars)
Exports by principal countries or areas

COMMERCE PAR PRODUIT (Valeur en millions de dollars EU)
Exportations selon les principaux pays ou zones

Country or area	1998	1999	2000	2001	2002	Pays ou zone
World	23032.6	22086.5	23474.9	24258.8	25967.0	Monde
Africa	77.2	75.1	114.8	103.6	265.5	Afrique
Americas	2495.3	2839.8	3110.6	3458.4	3630.9	Amériques
- Northern America	1654.3	2168.9	2462.3	2836.1	2974.5	- Amérique du Nord
- LAIA	630.2	583.1	574.8	559.5	586.2	- ALAI
- CACM	57.8	52.5	30.8	23.6	28.0	- MCC
- Caribbean	152.2	34.5	42.1	35.5	39.4	- Caraïbes
- Rest of America	0.8	0.8	0.6	3.6	2.7	- Autre d'Amérique
Asia excluding former USSR	9834.3	8665.2	9408.8	9421.6	10336.8	Asie ancienne URSS exclus
- Middle East	429.6	510.1	659.6	813.4	940.9	- Moyen-Orient
Asia former USSR	3.3	4.6	11.6	18.0	18.5	Asie ancienne URSS
Europe excluding former USSR	10504.2	10375.1	10736.2	11147.7	11601.5	Europe ancienne URSS exclus
- European Union	8742.3	8802.4	9075.5	9289.8	9350.2	- Union Européenne
- Eastern Europe	103.1	84.6	91.9	93.1	87.4	- Europe de l'Est
- Rest of Europe	1658.8	1488.1	1568.8	1764.8	2164.0	- Autre de l'Europe
Europe former USSR	31.2	4.9	6.8	13.2	7.9	Europe ancienne URSS
Oceania	87.1	121.8	86.2	96.2	106.0	Océanie
Italy-San Marino-Holy See	4746.2	5086.2	5416.1	4957.0	4876.5	Italie-Saint-Marin-Saint-Siège
China, Hong Kong SAR	1708.6	2036.8	2482.5	2396.8	2717.7	Chine - RAS de Hong-Kong
United States	1477.7	1956.4	2187.9	2604.0	2729.5	Etats-Unis d'Amérique
China	1806.5	2092.2	1883.1	1576.6	1730.3	Chine
Switzerland-Liechtenstein	1592.7	1413.2	1487.5	1684.1	2089.7	Suisse-Liechtenstein
United Kingdom	1723.7	1265.1	1044.8	1482.1	1606.8	Royaume-Uni
India	953.9	865.6	1019.4	1208.8	1444.1	Inde
Thailand	846.2	912.5	901.7	1074.7	e1135.0	Thaïlande
France-Monaco	713.6	772.4	963.1	1122.6	1067.4	France-Monaco
Germany	750.5	802.9	810.1	821.6	825.0	Allemagne
Korea, Republic of	494.3	513.6	645.7	671.3	569.8	République de Corée
Malaysia	403.7	463.5	615.9	506.8	e537.1	Malaisie
Indonesia	1661.7	174.2	111.0	118.1	66.9	Indonésie
Singapore	786.0	296.6	262.8	267.0	307.0	Singapour
Turkey	216.7	295.8	394.5	445.6	561.1	Turquie
Israel	372.2	365.7	355.4	354.2	415.1	Israël
Mexico	342.3	385.1	376.4	350.1	358.2	Mexique
Spain	252.1	282.3	242.2	270.8	255.1	Espagne
Canada	176.5	212.2	274.0	231.6	244.9	Canada
Japan	167.8	217.7	248.8	189.1	199.7	Japon
Austria	197.3	191.9	166.0	173.9	197.5	Autriche
United Arab Emirates	132.3	136.5	145.4	217.3	e226.3	Emirates arabes unis
Belgium	–	158.8	187.7	236.9	e265.8	Belgique
Brazil	64.7	72.3	79.5	81.2	e84.1	Brésil
Peru	144.4	56.5	49.6	47.3	60.5	Pérou
Australia	53.0	86.4	59.6	66.3	74.7	Australie
Lebanon	49.1	53.0	76.5	71.5	e62.3	Liban
Denmark	37.9	43.6	67.1	65.3	94.7	Danemark
Bolivia	61.5	52.0	51.5	50.5	e48.5	Bolivie
Czech Republic	53.6	52.2	55.3	53.5	46.3	République tchèque

(Value as percentages of World total) **(Valeur en pourcentage du total mondial)**

Regions of the world	1993	1994	1995	1996	1997	1998	1999	2000	2001	2002	Régions du monde
World	100.0	100.0	100.0	100.0	100.0	100.0	100.0	100.0	100.0	100.0	Monde
Africa	1.1	0.7	0.5	0.5	0.4	0.3	0.3	0.5	0.4	1.0	Afrique
Americas	8.6	9.5	9.1	9.3	10.6	10.8	12.9	13.3	14.3	14.0	Amériques
- Northern America	6.0	5.5	5.9	7.0	7.5	7.2	9.8	10.5	11.7	11.5	- Amérique du Nord
- LAIA	1.9	3.2	2.5	1.8	2.6	2.7	2.6	2.4	2.3	2.3	- ALAI
- CACM	0.1	0.3	0.3	0.3	0.4	0.3	0.2	0.1	0.1	0.1	- MCC
- Caribbean	0.5	0.5	0.4	0.1	0.1	0.7	0.2	0.2	0.1	0.2	- Caraïbes
- Rest of America	0.0	0.0	0.0	0.0	0.0	0.0	0.0	0.0	0.0	0.0	- Autre d'Amérique
Asia excluding former USSR	35.6	37.4	37.5	36.8	37.9	42.7	39.2	40.1	38.8	39.8	Asie ancienne URSS exclus
- Middle East	2.0	2.0	1.5	1.3	1.5	1.9	2.3	2.8	3.4	3.6	- Moyen-Orient
Asia former USSR	0.0	0.0	0.0	0.0	0.0	0.0	0.0	0.0	0.1	0.1	Asie ancienne URSS
Europe excluding former USSR	54.1	51.9	52.5	53.0	50.6	45.6	47.0	45.7	46.0	44.7	Europe ancienne URSS exclus
- European Union	41.8	41.0	41.7	43.7	41.1	38.0	39.9	38.7	38.3	36.0	- Union Européenne
- Eastern Europe	0.5	0.4	0.4	0.4	0.4	0.4	0.4	0.4	0.4	0.3	- Europe de l'Est
- Rest of Europe	11.9	10.5	10.3	8.8	9.2	7.2	6.7	6.7	7.3	8.3	- Autre de l'Europe
Europe former USSR	0.1	0.1	0.0	0.0	0.0	0.1	0.0	0.0	0.1	0.0	Europe ancienne URSS
Oceania	0.5	0.4	0.4	0.4	0.4	0.4	0.6	0.4	0.4	0.4	Océanie

898 Musical instruments, parts and accessories thereof

TRADE BY COMMODITY (Value in million US dollars)
Imports by principal countries or areas

COMMERCE PAR PRODUIT (Valeur en millions de dollars EU)
Importations selon les principaux pays ou zones

Country or area	1998	1999	2000	2001	2002	Pays ou zone
World	31832.2	33928.0	33983.1	32957.5	33732.1	Monde
Africa	399.8	389.3	381.9	373.1	402.2	Afrique
Americas	7504.3	8019.4	8595.6	8262.4	8477.7	Amériques
- Northern America	6050.2	6495.4	6914.0	6544.7	6980.6	- Amérique du Nord
- LAIA	1307.9	1363.3	1519.7	1541.4	1303.3	- ALAI
- CACM	70.9	76.7	87.6	97.9	114.3	- MCC
- Caribbean	51.7	52.6	51.4	60.4	60.1	- Caraïbes
- Rest of America	23.6	31.3	23.0	18.0	19.5	- Autre d'Amérique
Asia excluding former USSR	7065.8	7607.7	8379.7	8015.0	8400.5	Asie ancienne URSS exclus
- Middle East	386.4	405.7	490.6	544.5	496.6	- Moyen-Orient
Asia former USSR	15.4	27.0	31.6	27.7	28.7	Asie ancienne URSS
Europe excluding former USSR	15811.6	16846.8	15625.7	15434.5	15507.9	Europe ancienne URSS exclus
- European Union	13602.1	14376.0	13292.8	13207.6	13398.5	- Union Européenne
- Eastern Europe	821.2	968.2	701.7	713.0	615.4	- Europe de l'Est
- Rest of Europe	1388.2	1502.6	1631.1	1513.8	1494.0	- Autre de l'Europe
Europe former USSR	162.2	131.4	134.2	177.1	167.3	Europe ancienne URSS
Oceania	873.1	906.4	834.3	667.7	747.8	Océanie
United States	4497.6	4840.4	5333.3	5023.4	5423.3	Etats-Unis d'Amérique
United Kingdom	2704.8	2523.7	2690.0	2629.0	2762.4	Royaume-Uni
Germany	2821.4	3003.5	2489.4	2615.1	2265.0	Allemagne
France-Monaco	1934.2	1867.3	1743.0	1646.3	1900.5	France-Monaco
Japan	1554.6	1668.7	1936.9	1876.3	1661.5	Japon
Canada	1546.3	1647.8	1577.0	1515.2	1548.3	Canada
Singapore	1777.8	1640.9	1288.8	950.5	927.9	Singapour
Italy-San Marino-Holy See	1177.4	1345.6	1259.2	1237.8	1303.1	Italie-Saint-Marin-Saint-Siège
Netherlands	1040.2	1278.8	1275.9	1195.0	1206.7	Pays-Bas
Switzerland-Liechtenstein	892.4	951.8	1147.5	1032.2	963.6	Suisse-Liechtenstein
China	481.9	629.4	887.9	1053.3	1436.4	Chine
Mexico	542.4	668.6	880.4	1003.8	805.8	Mexique
Korea, Republic of	477.1	619.9	859.8	852.0	927.1	République de Corée
China, Hong Kong SAR	670.7	648.9	735.1	850.8	761.1	Chine - RAS de Hong-Kong
Belgium	-	798.2	797.8	885.3	e970.9	Belgique
Spain	713.3	738.2	600.6	603.3	717.0	Espagne
Australia	703.2	743.2	691.8	533.2	595.3	Australie
Austria	520.0	631.0	486.3	480.0	524.1	Autriche
Sweden	428.7	414.8	432.3	478.3	489.2	Suède
Ireland	525.3	542.4	456.5	393.8	304.1	Irlande
India	231.4	320.2	401.8	477.0	756.4	Inde
Hungary	461.5	557.8	320.2	277.5	211.8	Hongrie
Denmark	327.9	424.0	406.5	343.3	239.6	Danemark
Norway	322.0	382.2	334.4	314.2	336.3	Norvège
Thailand	425.0	338.4	280.5	231.4	e241.1	Thaïlande
Malaysia	168.4	256.5	334.5	193.9	e211.9	Malaisie
Finland	204.2	192.0	218.0	213.1	228.6	Finlande
Portugal	194.9	230.2	201.7	215.6	194.5	Portugal
Israel	191.4	214.8	220.7	223.3	162.4	Israël
Argentina	225.6	216.6	204.7	145.2	e64.2	Argentine

(Value as percentages of World total) **(Valeur en pourcentage du total mondial)**

Regions of the world	1993	1994	1995	1996	1997	1998	1999	2000	2001	2002	Régions du monde
World	100.0	100.0	100.0	100.0	100.0	100.0	100.0	100.0	100.0	100.0	Monde
Africa	1.0	1.0	1.0	1.6	1.2	1.3	1.1	1.1	1.1	1.2	Afrique
Americas	23.4	23.7	21.7	21.2	22.7	23.6	23.6	25.3	25.1	25.1	Amériques
- Northern America	19.2	19.1	17.8	17.2	18.2	19.0	19.1	20.3	19.9	20.7	- Amérique du Nord
- LAIA	3.9	4.3	3.6	3.7	4.2	4.1	4.0	4.5	4.7	3.9	- ALAI
- CACM	0.1	0.1	0.1	0.2	0.2	0.2	0.2	0.3	0.3	0.3	- MCC
- Caribbean	0.2	0.2	0.2	0.1	0.1	0.2	0.2	0.2	0.2	0.2	- Caraïbes
- Rest of America	0.0	0.1	0.0	0.0	0.1	0.1	0.1	0.1	0.1	0.1	- Autre d'Amérique
Asia excluding former USSR	22.5	23.4	26.4	27.0	26.4	22.2	22.4	24.7	24.3	24.9	Asie ancienne URSS exclus
- Middle East	1.6	1.3	1.2	0.9	1.0	1.2	1.2	1.4	1.7	1.5	- Moyen-Orient
Asia former USSR	0.0	0.1	0.0	0.1	0.0	0.0	0.1	0.1	0.1	0.1	Asie ancienne URSS
Europe excluding former USSR	49.4	48.2	47.5	47.1	46.4	49.7	49.7	46.0	46.8	46.0	Europe ancienne URSS exclus
- European Union	44.6	43.3	42.3	42.0	40.9	42.7	42.4	39.1	40.1	39.7	- Union Européenne
- Eastern Europe	0.9	0.9	1.0	1.0	1.5	2.6	2.9	2.1	2.2	1.8	- Europe de l'Est
- Rest of Europe	3.9	4.0	4.1	4.1	4.0	4.4	4.4	4.8	4.6	4.4	- Autre de l'Europe
Europe former USSR	0.8	0.4	0.5	0.4	0.5	0.5	0.4	0.4	0.5	0.5	Europe ancienne URSS
Oceania	2.9	3.3	2.9	2.6	2.7	2.7	2.7	2.5	2.0	2.2	Océanie

TRADE BY COMMODITY (Value in million US dollars)
Exports by principal countries or areas

COMMERCE PAR PRODUIT (Valeur en millions de dollars EU)
Exportations selon les principaux pays ou zones

Country or area	1998	1999	2000	2001	2002	Pays ou zone
World	32161.3	34412.3	34285.2	33167.3	33633.5	Monde
Africa	25.0	25.6	21.0	26.1	32.1	Afrique
Americas	7493.9	7312.5	7100.9	6342.2	6030.1	Amériques
- Northern America	6794.3	6572.0	6301.4	5573.3	5323.3	- Amérique du Nord
- LAIA	687.7	728.1	784.9	756.8	693.7	- ALAI
- CACM	9.0	10.0	10.3	8.8	10.8	- MCC
- Caribbean	2.9	2.3	4.3	3.3	2.3	- Caraïbes
- Rest of America	0.0	0.0	0.0	0.1	0.1	- Autre d'Amérique
Asia excluding former USSR	9480.1	10757.1	11951.3	11745.6	12105.4	Asie ancienne URSS exclus
- Middle East	118.8	85.0	64.6	78.9	79.7	- Moyen-Orient
Asia former USSR	5.8	8.3	13.5	9.2	4.8	Asie ancienne URSS
Europe excluding former USSR	14924.7	16049.7	14904.7	14756.2	15228.5	Europe ancienne URSS exclus
- European Union	14260.0	15378.1	14221.9	14150.9	14593.6	- Union Européenne
- Eastern Europe	337.1	262.1	285.5	247.1	266.0	- Europe de l'Est
- Rest of Europe	327.6	409.5	397.3	358.2	368.8	- Autre de l'Europe
Europe former USSR	105.5	138.1	172.3	171.0	99.9	Europe ancienne URSS
Oceania	126.5	121.1	121.5	117.1	132.7	Océanie
United States	6419.5	6130.2	5836.7	5074.4	4852.7	Etats-Unis d'Amérique
Japan	3824.2	3834.0	3654.0	3214.4	3421.6	Japon
Ireland	3663.9	4181.8	4022.7	3113.7	2335.2	Irlande
Germany	2837.2	2891.0	2297.9	2685.0	3223.1	Allemagne
Singapore	1437.9	1964.1	2469.9	2323.6	2019.3	Singapour
United Kingdom	2028.3	1826.1	1674.2	1846.5	2088.4	Royaume-Uni
Netherlands	1713.9	1977.5	1964.5	1810.9	1515.9	Pays-Bas
Austria	1175.8	1256.2	1078.8	1130.5	1325.5	Autriche
France-Monaco	1036.9	1180.9	1076.3	1034.3	1224.9	France-Monaco
Korea, Republic of	968.5	913.7	976.8	979.6	919.7	République de Corée
China, Hong Kong SAR	676.8	737.8	887.3	974.3	995.0	Chine - RAS de Hong-Kong
China	718.3	696.1	720.7	873.4	1156.4	Chine
Mexico	588.4	618.9	688.7	636.4	575.1	Mexique
Belgium	–	488.6	606.7	629.7	e706.5	Belgique
Canada	374.6	441.7	464.7	498.9	470.5	Canada
Sweden	204.6	262.2	275.9	472.0	669.6	Suède
Italy-San Marino-Holy See	345.6	361.7	347.2	336.2	360.8	Italie-Saint-Marin-Saint-Siège
Switzerland-Liechtenstein	268.9	338.8	333.8	289.1	302.5	Suisse-Liechtenstein
Malaysia	238.4	293.5	247.1	310.8	e329.4	Malaisie
Denmark	244.5	261.5	296.8	275.5	269.7	Danemark
Luxembourg	–	345.0	191.5	397.9	e406.8	Luxembourg
India	223.4	213.8	362.7	235.6	258.5	Inde
Spain	193.8	193.9	198.5	269.0	347.2	Espagne
Thailand	232.7	211.4	252.1	238.2	e251.6	Thaïlande
Indonesia	87.1	137.2	280.2	289.3	274.2	Indonésie
Belgium-Luxembourg	695.6	–	–	–	–	Belgique-Luxembourg
Czech Republic	115.6	103.6	113.1	119.7	132.8	République tchèque
Australia	114.2	112.7	112.1	105.0	123.8	Australie
Russian Federation	69.9	113.7	149.5	148.7	74.5	Fédération de Russie
Finland	64.1	77.0	97.5	80.6	65.4	Finlande

(Value as percentages of World total) **(Valeur en pourcentage du total mondial)**

Regions of the world	1993	1994	1995	1996	1997	1998	1999	2000	2001	2002	Régions du monde
World	100.0	100.0	100.0	100.0	100.0	100.0	100.0	100.0	100.0	100.0	Monde
Africa	0.1	0.1	0.1	0.1	0.1	0.1	0.1	0.1	0.1	0.1	Afrique
Americas	26.1	26.7	25.5	24.9	25.0	23.3	21.2	20.7	19.1	17.9	Amériques
- Northern America	23.9	24.3	23.2	22.7	23.0	21.1	19.1	18.4	16.8	15.8	- Amérique du Nord
- LAIA	2.1	2.4	2.3	2.1	1.9	2.1	2.1	2.3	2.3	2.1	- ALAI
- CACM	0.0	0.0	0.1	0.1	0.1	0.0	0.0	0.0	0.0	0.0	- MCC
- Caribbean	0.0	0.0	0.0	0.0	0.0	0.0	0.0	0.0	0.0	0.0	- Caraïbes
- Rest of America	0.0	0.0	0.0	0.0	0.0	0.0	0.0	0.0	0.0	0.0	- Autre d'Amérique
Asia excluding former USSR	33.9	30.7	30.8	29.9	30.3	29.5	31.3	34.9	35.4	36.0	Asie ancienne URSS exclus
- Middle East	0.4	0.4	0.4	0.4	0.3	0.4	0.2	0.2	0.2	0.2	- Moyen-Orient
Asia former USSR	0.0	0.0	0.0	0.0	0.0	0.0	0.0	0.0	0.0	0.0	Asie ancienne URSS
Europe excluding former USSR	39.4	41.9	42.9	44.4	43.7	46.4	46.6	43.5	44.5	45.3	Europe ancienne URSS exclus
- European Union	37.2	39.6	40.8	41.9	42.3	44.3	44.7	41.5	42.7	43.4	- Union Européenne
- Eastern Europe	0.5	0.6	0.7	1.1	0.6	1.0	0.8	0.8	0.7	0.8	- Europe de l'Est
- Rest of Europe	1.7	1.7	1.4	1.4	0.8	1.0	1.2	1.2	1.1	1.1	- Autre de l'Europe
Europe former USSR	0.1	0.3	0.3	0.3	0.6	0.3	0.4	0.5	0.5	0.3	Europe ancienne URSS
Oceania	0.4	0.3	0.4	0.3	0.3	0.4	0.4	0.4	0.4	0.4	Océanie

899 Other miscellaneous manufactured articles, nes

TRADE BY COMMODITY (Value in million US dollars)
Imports by principal countries or areas

COMMERCE PAR PRODUIT (Valeur en millions de dollars EU)
Importations selon les principaux pays ou zones

Country or area	1998	1999	2000	2001	2002	Pays ou zone
World	22360.6	24607.7	25887.6	27398.0	29846.3	Monde
Africa	410.2	413.9	440.8	443.4	458.8	Afrique
Americas	5712.0	6397.7	7114.7	7850.8	8789.3	Amériques
- Northern America	4733.4	5440.1	5934.8	6650.9	7701.0	- Amérique du Nord
- LAIA	822.5	812.1	1011.6	1024.9	906.9	- ALAI
- CACM	61.5	57.3	73.4	74.0	82.9	- MCC
- Caribbean	76.6	70.4	77.7	84.9	79.7	- Caraïbes
- Rest of America	18.0	17.8	17.3	16.1	18.7	- Autre d'Amérique
Asia excluding former USSR	5646.1	6108.1	6677.4	6509.1	6704.0	Asie ancienne URSS exclus
- Middle East	601.8	603.8	619.1	664.1	745.7	- Moyen-Orient
Asia former USSR	20.1	17.8	23.4	30.8	25.0	Asie ancienne URSS
Europe excluding former USSR	9891.7	10975.0	10891.0	11777.7	12971.8	Europe ancienne URSS exclus
- European Union	8506.2	9512.5	9410.9	10198.2	11113.1	- Union Européenne
- Eastern Europe	592.5	582.3	592.2	634.6	763.7	- Europe de l'Est
- Rest of Europe	793.0	880.2	887.9	945.0	1095.0	- Autre de l'Europe
Europe former USSR	204.9	173.5	215.7	288.2	298.3	Europe ancienne URSS
Oceania	475.6	521.6	524.8	497.9	599.1	Océanie
United States	4043.1	4691.4	5152.2	5880.8	6861.0	Etats-Unis d'Amérique
Germany	2044.9	2130.4	1962.8	2079.0	2058.7	Allemagne
China, Hong Kong SAR	1890.8	1970.5	1979.1	1801.6	1688.8	Chine - RAS de Hong-Kong
Japan	1615.6	1736.6	1905.1	1956.1	2019.6	Japon
France-Monaco	1210.4	1273.0	1317.3	1281.2	1407.0	France-Monaco
United Kingdom	1099.9	1147.9	1267.7	1314.1	1423.0	Royaume-Uni
Netherlands	625.0	1026.9	1026.1	1148.6	1352.5	Pays-Bas
Italy-San Marino-Holy See	884.9	999.5	1015.4	1062.8	1135.3	Italie-Saint-Marin-Saint-Siège
Canada	688.3	746.4	780.2	766.9	832.7	Canada
Switzerland-Liechtenstein	506.6	584.2	600.9	646.1	747.9	Suisse-Liechtenstein
Spain	545.2	588.2	582.6	607.0	698.9	Espagne
Ireland	260.2	350.0	286.7	677.4	835.4	Irlande
China	350.7	414.5	541.1	525.6	569.8	Chine
Belgium	–	554.4	549.8	597.2	e655.0	Belgique
Australia	394.6	424.0	426.8	405.8	495.0	Australie
Mexico	308.4	351.6	487.9	483.8	435.9	Mexique
Sweden	329.7	336.7	340.8	350.8	407.5	Suède
Austria	324.1	346.0	312.4	337.3	356.8	Autriche
Korea, Republic of	205.5	287.7	343.7	372.3	421.2	République de Corée
Denmark	290.3	278.1	307.5	281.4	296.4	Danemark
Poland	200.9	182.6	207.3	203.2	240.3	Pologne
Turkey	177.4	187.5	211.6	198.6	233.7	Turquie
United Arab Emirates	174.9	183.3	158.9	207.2	e212.6	Emirates arabes unis
Norway	168.7	177.0	166.9	169.0	199.5	Norvège
Greece	171.7	178.0	159.7	164.9	e182.3	Grèce
Brazil	164.3	139.5	165.5	175.0	173.5	Brésil
Portugal	143.4	166.7	151.5	150.0	153.0	Portugal
Singapore	113.3	135.9	160.6	133.9	157.1	Singapour
Czech Republic	125.0	117.7	117.1	135.6	173.3	République tchèque
Russian Federation	99.9	75.7	109.7	168.9	160.5	Fédération de Russie

(Value as percentages of World total) **(Valeur en pourcentage du total mondial)**

Regions of the world	1993	1994	1995	1996	1997	1998	1999	2000	2001	2002	Régions du monde
World	100.0	100.0	100.0	100.0	100.0	100.0	100.0	100.0	100.0	100.0	Monde
Africa	1.7	1.8	1.7	1.7	1.8	1.8	1.7	1.7	1.6	1.5	Afrique
Americas	22.3	22.3	22.0	21.5	23.6	25.5	26.0	27.5	28.7	29.4	Amériques
- Northern America	18.8	18.6	18.5	17.9	19.4	21.2	22.1	22.9	24.3	25.8	- Amérique du Nord
- LAIA	2.9	3.0	2.9	3.0	3.5	3.7	3.3	3.9	3.7	3.0	- ALAI
- CACM	0.2	0.2	0.2	0.2	0.3	0.3	0.2	0.3	0.3	0.3	- MCC
- Caribbean	0.4	0.3	0.4	0.3	0.3	0.3	0.3	0.3	0.3	0.3	- Caraïbes
- Rest of America	0.1	0.1	0.1	0.1	0.1	0.1	0.1	0.1	0.1	0.1	- Autre d'Amérique
Asia excluding former USSR	31.4	30.9	30.2	29.3	28.2	25.3	24.8	25.8	23.8	22.5	Asie ancienne URSS exclus
- Middle East	2.7	2.5	2.3	1.8	2.0	2.7	2.5	2.4	2.4	2.5	- Moyen-Orient
Asia former USSR	0.0	0.1	0.1	0.1	0.1	0.1	0.1	0.1	0.1	0.1	Asie ancienne URSS
Europe excluding former USSR	41.9	42.5	43.4	44.7	43.4	44.2	44.6	42.1	43.0	43.5	Europe ancienne URSS exclus
- European Union	36.8	37.3	37.8	38.9	37.6	38.0	38.7	36.4	37.2	37.2	- Union Européenne
- Eastern Europe	1.8	2.0	2.3	2.6	2.6	2.6	2.4	2.3	2.3	2.6	- Europe de l'Est
- Rest of Europe	3.3	3.2	3.3	3.2	3.2	3.5	3.6	3.4	3.4	3.7	- Autre de l'Europe
Europe former USSR	0.8	0.6	0.8	0.7	0.9	0.9	0.7	0.8	1.1	1.0	Europe ancienne URSS
Oceania	1.9	1.9	1.9	2.0	2.1	2.1	2.1	2.0	1.8	2.0	Océanie

TRADE BY COMMODITY (Value in million US dollars)
Exports by principal countries or areas

COMMERCE PAR PRODUIT (Valeur en millions de dollars EU)
Exportations selon les principaux pays ou zones

Country or area	1998	1999	2000	2001	2002	Pays ou zone
World	20778.2	22642.4	23992.8	24763.5	26957.5	Monde
Africa	73.4	83.9	100.3	96.6	119.5	Afrique
Americas	3475.1	3864.5	4318.9	4631.0	4910.0	Amériques
- Northern America	2903.9	3234.5	3681.1	4003.8	4245.0	- Amérique du Nord
- LAIA	496.5	534.1	537.3	542.7	591.0	- ALAI
- CACM	40.8	76.4	78.6	61.1	56.1	- MCC
- Caribbean	22.3	8.8	9.6	8.6	8.1	- Caraïbes
- Rest of America	11.5	10.7	12.2	14.7	9.7	- Autre d'Amérique
Asia excluding former USSR	8774.2	9139.9	9688.8	8987.7	9364.6	Asie ancienne URSS exclus
- Middle East	165.6	171.4	131.8	146.6	158.6	- Moyen-Orient
Asia former USSR	1.9	8.1	9.6	4.1	3.7	Asie ancienne URSS
Europe excluding former USSR	8299.1	9409.2	9725.4	10884.7	12355.9	Europe ancienne URSS exclus
- European Union	6905.8	7845.1	7978.4	8873.3	9742.4	- Union Européenne
- Eastern Europe	264.8	274.3	291.8	303.7	363.6	- Europe de l'Est
- Rest of Europe	1128.5	1289.9	1455.2	1707.7	2249.9	- Autre de l'Europe
Europe former USSR	55.0	54.3	61.8	69.0	75.2	Europe ancienne URSS
Oceania	99.5	82.5	88.1	90.4	128.6	Océanie
United States	2661.1	2987.0	3433.5	3765.8	4019.8	Etats-Unis d'Amérique
China	3012.9	3033.5	3351.7	3442.7	3748.5	Chine
China, Hong Kong SAR	2874.0	2944.2	2925.1	2608.1	2465.3	Chine - RAS de Hong-Kong
Germany	1711.5	1711.3	1657.5	1863.4	1966.9	Allemagne
Switzerland-Liechtenstein	1065.3	1223.9	1387.5	1635.3	2169.5	Suisse-Liechtenstein
France-Monaco	1031.0	1033.8	985.8	979.2	1204.8	France-Monaco
Netherlands	488.7	1146.1	1167.2	1080.8	1226.7	Pays-Bas
United Kingdom	995.6	905.7	866.2	943.9	914.7	Royaume-Uni
Ireland	245.0	451.0	760.1	1303.4	1506.4	Irlande
Italy-San Marino-Holy See	790.4	733.3	711.0	719.2	732.0	Italie-Saint-Marin-Saint-Siège
Japan	508.6	579.7	673.2	519.3	487.3	Japon
Korea, Republic of	476.9	557.8	521.9	457.0	450.6	République de Corée
Denmark	409.9	439.9	461.1	467.2	527.2	Danemark
Belgium	-	493.1	510.7	588.0	e659.8	Belgique
Sweden	374.9	398.3	382.3	422.9	452.9	Suède
Mexico	325.1	381.9	374.9	380.7	429.8	Mexique
Spain	231.6	246.8	231.3	275.6	299.8	Espagne
Canada	242.8	247.4	247.6	238.0	225.2	Canada
Singapore	226.2	244.0	243.0	200.4	219.0	Singapour
Thailand	219.7	219.5	231.2	214.8	e226.8	Thaïlande
Indonesia	97.8	186.7	227.6	210.4	238.8	Indonésie
Philippines	162.0	155.6	166.7	156.5	129.5	Philippines
Austria	116.0	150.2	138.6	131.1	148.4	Autriche
Poland	100.7	108.6	124.2	128.8	169.5	Pologne
Israel	50.7	45.4	155.7	105.8	238.9	Israël
Viet Nam	56.4	94.0	125.2	130.2	144.7	Viet Nam
United Arab Emirates	116.0	119.7	74.7	88.1	e91.7	Emirates arabes unis
India	74.6	83.3	103.4	106.0	120.8	Inde
Czech Republic	92.0	89.6	91.7	97.6	107.7	République tchèque
Brazil	89.0	83.7	93.7	92.2	e95.6	Brésil

(Value as percentages of World total) **(Valeur en pourcentage du total mondial)**

Regions of the world	1993	1994	1995	1996	1997	1998	1999	2000	2001	2002	Régions du monde
World	100.0	100.0	100.0	100.0	100.0	100.0	100.0	100.0	100.0	100.0	Monde
Africa	0.3	0.3	0.4	0.4	0.4	0.4	0.4	0.4	0.4	0.4	Afrique
Americas	12.5	13.0	13.0	14.3	15.6	16.7	17.1	18.0	18.7	18.2	Amériques
- Northern America	10.9	11.4	11.1	12.3	13.3	14.0	14.3	15.3	16.2	15.7	- Amérique du Nord
- LAIA	1.4	1.4	1.7	1.8	2.1	2.4	2.4	2.2	2.2	2.2	- ALAI
- CACM	0.1	0.1	0.1	0.1	0.1	0.2	0.3	0.3	0.2	0.2	- MCC
- Caribbean	0.1	0.1	0.1	0.0	0.0	0.1	0.0	0.0	0.0	0.0	- Caraïbes
- Rest of America	0.0	0.1	0.1	0.1	0.1	0.1	0.0	0.1	0.1	0.0	- Autre d'Amérique
Asia excluding former USSR	50.5	48.8	46.8	43.9	44.0	42.2	40.4	40.4	36.3	34.7	Asie ancienne URSS exclus
- Middle East	0.3	0.3	0.3	0.3	0.3	0.8	0.8	0.5	0.6	0.6	- Moyen-Orient
Asia former USSR	0.0	0.0	0.0	0.0	0.0	0.0	0.0	0.0	0.0	0.0	Asie ancienne URSS
Europe excluding former USSR	35.5	37.3	39.2	40.7	39.2	39.9	41.6	40.5	44.0	45.8	Europe ancienne URSS exclus
- European Union	29.8	31.5	33.1	34.7	33.4	33.2	34.6	33.3	35.8	36.1	- Union Européenne
- Eastern Europe	0.9	0.8	1.0	1.1	1.1	1.3	1.2	1.2	1.2	1.3	- Europe de l'Est
- Rest of Europe	4.9	5.0	5.1	4.9	4.7	5.4	5.7	6.1	6.9	8.3	- Autre de l'Europe
Europe former USSR	0.7	0.2	0.2	0.2	0.2	0.3	0.2	0.3	0.3	0.3	Europe ancienne URSS
Oceania	0.4	0.4	0.4	0.5	0.5	0.5	0.4	0.4	0.4	0.5	Océanie

931 Special transactions, commodity not classified according to class

TRADE BY COMMODITY (Value in million US dollars)
Imports by principal countries or areas

COMMERCE PAR PRODUIT (Valeur en millions de dollars EU)
Importations selon les principaux pays ou zones

Country or area	1998	1999	2000	2001	2002	Pays ou zone
World	146933.0	151291.6	194387.7	161309.7	178720.1	Monde
Africa	4864.8	3303.6	3795.8	3787.3	4473.8	Afrique
Americas	44853.8	54490.0	58801.8	55713.8	55519.6	Amériques
- Northern America	39904.8	48643.5	53636.7	53879.8	53499.9	- Amérique du Nord
- LAIA	4571.5	4517.9	4808.9	1263.3	1309.1	- ALAI
- CACM	3.0	965.9	8.2	25.8	49.6	- MCC
- Caribbean	366.1	352.1	341.4	427.1	503.2	- Caraïbes
- Rest of America	8.5	10.7	6.6	117.7	158.0	- Autre d'Amérique
Asia excluding former USSR	22619.8	20299.5	28744.3	29285.7	37070.6	Asie ancienne URSS exclus
- Middle East	4026.7	5642.6	13512.1	13861.9	12087.3	- Moyen-Orient
Asia former USSR	152.6	283.3	151.0	149.9	106.3	Asie ancienne URSS
Europe excluding former USSR	52885.0	57615.0	85224.3	66830.6	78923.7	Europe ancienne URSS exclus
- European Union	50175.3	55157.7	82487.1	63412.6	77073.5	- Union Européenne
- Eastern Europe	1282.2	1474.7	1618.6	2492.1	875.7	- Europe de l'Est
- Rest of Europe	1427.5	982.6	1118.7	926.0	974.5	- Autre de l'Europe
Europe former USSR	20770.4	14302.5	16629.9	4564.0	1197.7	Europe ancienne URSS
Oceania	786.7	997.7	1040.6	978.5	1428.4	Océanie
United States	35420.5	44076.2	48907.2	49053.3	49380.8	Etats-Unis d'Amérique
Germany	30975.8	35500.8	59972.5	21104.3	41187.2	Allemagne
Russian Federation	20309.3	13822.9	15975.4	4165.7	257.9	Fédération de Russie
United Kingdom	2254.8	3690.8	2241.7	21947.1	16222.2	Royaume-Uni
Italy-San Marino-Holy See	5387.6	5397.4	9152.5	10277.8	9619.4	Italie-Saint-Marin-Saint-Siège
Iraq	e2500.0	e5000.0	e8500.0	e8500.0	e6000.0	Iraq
Japan	4241.6	4556.4	5532.6	5807.0	5928.3	Japon
Canada	4378.5	4467.1	4677.0	4786.3	4054.4	Canada
Sweden	4157.8	3785.1	3529.9	2397.2	2297.6	Suède
Ireland	3019.6	2874.8	2888.3	2855.3	3135.8	Irlande
Mexico	3922.8	4179.6	4435.0	870.4	1149.8	Mexique
Viet Nam	2197.7	1725.8	2147.2	2228.3	2711.2	Viet Nam
Philippines	38.5	19.4	9.9	1.6	4529.7	Philippines
Turkey	976.7		2068.3	2425.7	2225.7	Turquie
Occupied Palestinian Territory	-	-	2300.0	2300.0	2900.0	Territoire palestinien occupé
South Africa	-	-	2152.1	2142.9	2351.4	Afrique du Sud
Denmark	1388.5	1211.6	1162.1	1537.2	1063.8	Danemark
Singapore	1243.0	1498.1	1107.9	1166.4	1330.3	Singapour
China	0.0	1370.5	1723.1	1675.7	1563.0	Chine
Malaysia	1035.9	1158.0	1243.7	1352.6	e1478.2	Malaisie
India	2757.5	1069.0	927.3	662.2	707.1	Inde
Southern African Customs Union	3555.8	1949.4	-	-	-	Union douanière d'Afrique australe
Belgium	-	1155.6	1681.2	1259.6	e1381.4	Belgique
Egypt	1080.1	727.2	e956.8	871.2	1237.4	Egypte
Hungary	339.9	332.8	1370.6	1330.8	531.5	Hongrie
Northern Mariana Islands	533.2	750.0	750.0	750.0	800.0	Iles Mariannes septentrionales
Spain	335.8	427.9	603.0	1018.4	1039.2	Espagne
Finland	524.1	650.1	776.2	739.9	662.0	Finlande
Thailand	736.1	784.9	358.9	402.1	e418.9	Thaïlande
Poland	491.2	877.2		904.0	47.5	Pologne

(Value as percentages of World total) **(Valeur en pourcentage du total mondial)**

Regions of the world	1993	1994	1995	1996	1997	1998	1999	2000	2001	2002	Régions du monde
World	100.0	100.0	100.0	100.0	100.0	100.0	100.0	100.0	100.0	100.0	Monde
Africa	2.1	1.5	0.9	2.1	3.9	3.3	2.2	2.0	2.3	2.5	Afrique
Americas	25.6	33.3	28.2	27.0	27.7	30.5	36.0	30.2	34.5	31.1	Amériques
- Northern America	25.0	24.6	22.8	24.3	24.2	27.2	32.2	27.6	33.4	29.9	- Amérique du Nord
- LAIA	0.5	8.1	4.8	2.3	3.1	3.1	3.0	2.5	0.8	0.7	- ALAI
- CACM	0.0	0.0	0.0	0.1	0.0	0.0	0.6	0.0	0.0	0.0	- MCC
- Caribbean	0.2	0.5	0.6	0.3	0.3	0.2	0.2	0.2	0.3	0.3	- Caraïbes
- Rest of America	0.0	0.0	0.0	0.0	0.0	0.0	0.0	0.0	0.1	0.1	- Autre d'Amérique
Asia excluding former USSR	19.2	17.0	13.5	18.4	20.4	15.4	13.4	14.8	18.2	20.7	Asie ancienne URSS exclus
- Middle East	0.8	0.8	0.6	5.0	7.6	2.7	3.7	7.0	8.6	6.8	- Moyen-Orient
Asia former USSR	0.1	0.2	0.0	0.0	0.0	0.1	0.2	0.1	0.1	0.1	Asie ancienne URSS
Europe excluding former USSR	39.8	30.6	41.7	37.5	32.9	36.0	38.1	43.8	41.4	44.2	Europe ancienne URSS exclus
- European Union	37.6	29.3	39.6	35.4	32.0	34.1	36.5	42.4	39.3	43.1	- Union Européenne
- Eastern Europe	1.5	0.7	1.1	1.5	0.4	0.9	1.0	0.8	1.5	0.5	- Europe de l'Est
- Rest of Europe	0.8	0.6	1.0	0.5	0.5	1.0	0.6	0.6	0.6	0.5	- Autre de l'Europe
Europe former USSR	12.8	17.2	15.4	14.6	14.5	14.1	9.5	8.6	2.8	0.7	Europe ancienne URSS
Oceania	0.3	0.3	0.2	0.5	0.5	0.5	0.7	0.5	0.6	0.8	Océanie

TRADE BY COMMODITY (Value in million US dollars)
Exports by principal countries or areas

COMMERCE PAR PRODUIT (Valeur en millions de dollars EU)
Exportations selon les principaux pays ou zones

Country or area	1998	1999	2000	2001	2002	Pays ou zone
World	144993.5	146244.8	163553.8	168936.6	190177.9	Monde
Africa	2747.2	245.8	3409.8	3744.3	521.6	Afrique
Americas	33973.9	37583.5	41330.5	42478.9	43268.3	Amériques
- Northern America	32640.2	35877.8	39361.6	40269.4	41053.1	- Amérique du Nord
- LAIA	1221.3	1670.4	1905.3	2042.3	2075.3	- ALAI
- CACM	9.8	1.2	18.6	12.5	2.1	- MCC
- Caribbean	99.6	29.8	42.9	36.3	38.7	- Caraïbes
- Rest of America	3.0	4.3	2.1	118.4	99.1	- Autre d'Amérique
Asia excluding former USSR	26754.9	21736.7	24904.2	28529.0	45057.6	Asie ancienne URSS exclus
- Middle East	631.6	259.3	1086.4	867.9	1291.0	- Moyen-Orient
Asia former USSR	35.1	264.6	298.2	51.2	53.2	Asie ancienne URSS
Europe excluding former USSR	68490.9	71283.9	78089.1	79832.0	86123.0	Europe ancienne URSS exclus
- European Union	64288.9	67182.6	74547.9	75177.1	82455.9	- Union Européenne
- Eastern Europe	804.0	1335.7	824.1	1913.1	1145.9	- Europe de l'Est
- Rest of Europe	3398.1	2765.6	2717.1	2741.8	2521.2	- Autre de l'Europe
Europe former USSR	9859.0	13032.8	13123.2	11825.0	10035.5	Europe ancienne URSS
Oceania	3132.6	2097.4	2398.8	2476.2	5118.7	Océanie
Germany	24699.8	28642.9	40219.5	22758.7	32814.0	Allemagne
United States	20834.0	21440.2	23502.2	24407.3	24900.9	Etats-Unis d'Amérique
Japan	11708.1	13239.5	16831.9	16099.8	17030.0	Japon
Canada	11799.5	14431.2	15850.9	15837.6	16130.6	Canada
Russian Federation	9389.8	12348.7	12574.2	11553.8	9473.0	Fédération de Russie
United Kingdom	3084.2	5945.8	1601.8	19623.8	15041.2	Royaume-Uni
Belgium	–	7586.8	7632.6	7573.8	e8497.7	Belgique
France-Monaco	7078.0	6169.7	6128.2	5604.5	6221.4	France-Monaco
Sweden	5397.5	4695.8	4360.5	3670.2	4248.7	Suède
Italy-San Marino-Holy See	2826.0	2877.6	2957.1	3990.8	3666.3	Italie-Saint-Marin-Saint-Siège
Austria	3926.3	3043.2	2913.9	2992.0	3318.0	Autriche
Ireland	3157.2	3031.3	3243.6	3308.5	3297.5	Irlande
Philippines	6.5	6.8	9.0	9.9	3736.4	Philippines
Denmark	2841.9	2819.1	2740.0	2765.2	2357.5	Danemark
Norway	2888.3	2653.2	2626.8	2646.8	2425.8	Norvège
Singapore	1489.8	1299.9	1103.1	4665.3	4587.1	Singapour
Australia	2734.9	1581.5	1560.2	1773.5	4330.6	Australie
Thailand	869.7	1671.1	1627.5	2249.7	e2376.0	Thaïlande
Belgium-Luxembourg	8775.3	–	–	–	–	Belgique-Luxembourg
Spain	1622.0	1551.9	1778.3	1872.2	1891.7	Espagne
Indonesia	7548.2	1101.9	7.8	4.3	20.6	Indonésie
Viet Nam	1907.9	1589.9	1243.0	1292.4	1436.6	Viet Nam
South Africa	–	–	3314.0	3364.3	5.7	Afrique du Sud
India	805.0	800.9	994.1	1288.8	1234.3	Inde
Brazil	628.5	823.8	1073.7	1186.1	e1229.6	Brésil
Malaysia	595.7	667.1	730.9	843.5	e894.0	Malaisie
Hungary	407.6	340.3	450.6	780.9	713.6	Hongrie
Southern African Customs Union	2572.6	10.6	–	–	–	Union douanière d'Afrique australe
New Zealand	144.2	243.2	575.9	474.9	542.2	Nouvelle-Zélande
China	0.0	173.9	513.5	573.9	645.6	Chine

(Value as percentages of World total) **(Valeur en pourcentage du total mondial)**

Regions of the world	1993	1994	1995	1996	1997	1998	1999	2000	2001	2002	Régions du monde
World	100.0	100.0	100.0	100.0	100.0	100.0	100.0	100.0	100.0	100.0	Monde
Africa	10.8	9.4	5.7	1.3	1.7	1.9	0.2	2.1	2.2	0.3	Afrique
Americas	25.3	25.3	20.3	23.2	22.3	23.4	25.7	25.3	25.1	22.8	Amériques
- Northern America	24.7	24.1	19.1	20.1	19.0	22.5	24.5	24.1	23.8	21.6	- Amérique du Nord
- LAIA	0.6	0.7	0.7	0.7	0.9	0.8	1.1	1.2	1.2	1.1	- ALAI
- CACM	0.0	0.1	0.1	0.0	0.0	0.0	0.0	0.0	0.0	0.0	- MCC
- Caribbean	0.0	0.4	0.4	2.4	2.4	0.1	0.0	0.0	0.0	0.0	- Caraïbes
- Rest of America	0.0	0.0	0.0	0.0	0.0	0.0	0.0	0.0	0.1	0.1	- Autre d'Amérique
Asia excluding former USSR	16.4	16.2	12.0	21.9	28.7	18.5	14.9	15.2	16.9	23.7	Asie ancienne URSS exclus
- Middle East	0.4	0.2	0.2	10.0	12.3	0.4	0.2	0.7	0.5	0.7	- Moyen-Orient
Asia former USSR	0.0	0.0	0.0	0.7	0.0	0.0	0.2	0.2	0.0	0.0	Asie ancienne URSS
Europe excluding former USSR	38.5	35.0	50.7	41.1	36.2	47.2	48.7	47.7	47.3	45.3	Europe ancienne URSS exclus
- European Union	37.4	31.4	47.7	37.5	34.0	44.3	45.9	45.6	44.5	43.4	- Union Européenne
- Eastern Europe	1.1	1.1	0.8	1.4	0.5	0.6	0.9	0.5	1.1	0.6	- Europe de l'Est
- Rest of Europe	0.0	2.5	2.3	2.2	1.8	2.3	1.9	1.7	1.6	1.3	- Autre de l'Europe
Europe former USSR	8.1	12.5	9.7	10.2	9.7	6.8	8.9	8.0	7.0	5.3	Europe ancienne URSS
Oceania	0.9	1.6	1.6	1.6	1.3	2.2	1.4	1.5	1.5	2.7	Océanie

941 Animals, live, nes, (including zoo animals, pets, insects, etc)

TRADE BY COMMODITY (Value in million US dollars)
Imports by principal countries or areas

COMMERCE PAR PRODUIT (Valeur en millions de dollars EU)
Importations selon les principaux pays ou zones

Country or area	1998	1999	2000	2001	2002	Pays ou zone
World	468.6	537.1	492.6	481.0	484.7	Monde
Africa	9.2	15.8	34.9	30.8	25.8	Afrique
Americas	95.8	97.5	96.2	103.8	110.0	Amériques
- Northern America	88.2	89.7	86.0	92.5	99.2	- Amérique du Nord
- LAIA	6.6	7.0	7.3	8.3	7.5	- ALAI
- CACM	0.3	0.3	0.2	0.3	0.4	- MCC
- Caribbean	0.7	0.4	2.6	2.7	2.8	- Caraïbes
- Rest of America	0.0	0.0	0.1	0.1	0.1	- Autre d'Amérique
Asia excluding former USSR	181.1	231.2	174.4	144.6	125.7	Asie ancienne URSS exclus
- Middle East	16.6	22.9	29.1	31.6	26.3	- Moyen-Orient
Asia former USSR	0.1	0.2	0.7	0.6	0.5	Asie ancienne URSS
Europe excluding former USSR	179.3	189.2	182.5	196.3	218.6	Europe ancienne URSS exclus
- European Union	163.8	174.7	168.0	178.6	199.1	- Union Européenne
- Eastern Europe	4.9	4.2	4.3	5.5	6.6	- Europe de l'Est
- Rest of Europe	10.6	10.3	10.1	12.1	13.0	- Autre de l'Europe
Europe former USSR	2.5	1.6	2.4	3.8	3.0	Europe ancienne URSS
Oceania	0.6	1.7	1.6	1.2	1.1	Océanie
United States	70.5	72.7	71.2	75.6	80.7	Etats-Unis d'Amérique
China, Hong Kong SAR	81.3	108.0	60.8	37.3	20.6	Chine - RAS de Hong-Kong
France-Monaco	46.3	45.5	44.5	44.2	51.2	France-Monaco
Japan	32.8	36.3	33.6	35.1	32.9	Japon
China	30.0	43.8	29.2	14.8	12.4	Chine
Belgium	–	29.1	28.2	34.4	e37.7	Belgique
Italy-San Marino-Holy See	25.6	25.4	22.5	24.2	23.6	Italie-Saint-Marin-Saint-Siège
Egypt	7.1	13.5	e29.7	27.0	20.9	Egypte
Spain	15.2	17.3	16.4	16.6	20.3	Espagne
Canada	17.5	16.8	14.7	16.9	18.5	Canada
Germany	15.7	15.1	14.1	18.1	18.1	Allemagne
Netherlands	14.1	13.8	11.3	7.7	10.6	Pays-Bas
United Kingdom		9.6	12.7	13.3	15.4	Royaume-Uni
Korea, Republic of	6.3	8.5	7.6	8.4	16.4	République de Corée
Saudi Arabia	4.6	9.2	11.2	5.8	e6.0	Arabie saoudite
Portugal	7.6	6.3	5.7	7.4	8.3	Portugal
Switzerland-Liechtenstein	6.4	6.6	6.6	7.2	8.1	Suisse-Liechtenstein
United Arab Emirates	3.9	4.1	7.9	7.7	e7.9	Emirates arabes unis
Belgium-Luxembourg	25.1	–	–	–	–	Belgique-Luxembourg
Mexico	4.4	4.1	4.2	5.1	4.9	Mexique
Oman	3.4	4.1	3.5	4.5	4.0	Oman
Singapore	2.3	2.7	3.2	3.8	5.2	Singapour
Kuwait	2.9	3.2	e3.0	e3.3	e3.2	Koweït
Denmark	4.4	2.3	3.0	2.9	2.1	Danemark
Sweden	3.0	2.5	2.3	2.9	3.9	Suède
Greece	2.6	3.2	2.5	1.9	e2.1	Grèce
Austria	2.4	2.2	2.3	2.3	2.5	Autriche
Norway	2.7	2.3	2.0	2.5	2.1	Norvège
China, Macao SAR	2.0	2.1	2.3	2.1	2.1	Chine - RAS de Macao
Qatar			0.8	7.4	2.3	Qatar

(Value as percentages of World total) **(Valeur en pourcentage du total mondial)**

Regions of the world	1993	1994	1995	1996	1997	1998	1999	2000	2001	2002	Régions du monde
World	100.0	100.0	100.0	100.0	100.0	100.0	100.0	100.0	100.0	100.0	Monde
Africa	0.8	1.1	0.8	1.0	1.0	2.0	2.9	7.1	6.4	5.3	Afrique
Americas	20.5	19.6	16.5	18.5	19.7	20.4	18.1	19.5	21.6	22.7	Amériques
- Northern America	19.2	18.3	15.8	17.4	17.9	18.8	16.7	17.5	19.2	20.5	- Amérique du Nord
- LAIA	0.8	1.0	0.5	0.7	1.7	1.4	1.3	1.5	1.7	1.5	- ALAI
- CACM	0.1	0.1	0.0	0.0	0.0	0.1	0.1	0.0	0.1	0.1	- MCC
- Caribbean	0.4	0.2	0.1	0.3	0.1	0.1	0.1	0.5	0.6	0.6	- Caraïbes
- Rest of America	0.0	0.0	0.0	0.0	0.0	0.0	0.0	0.0	0.0	0.0	- Autre d'Amérique
Asia excluding former USSR	31.0	33.1	36.0	37.8	39.4	38.7	43.0	35.4	30.1	25.9	Asie ancienne URSS exclus
- Middle East	8.9	9.8	8.6	8.9	9.8	3.5	4.3	5.9	6.6	5.4	- Moyen-Orient
Asia former USSR	0.0	0.0	0.0	0.0	0.0	0.0	0.0	0.1	0.1	0.1	Asie ancienne URSS
Europe excluding former USSR	46.7	44.8	40.4	39.9	35.2	38.3	35.2	37.0	40.8	45.1	Europe ancienne URSS exclus
- European Union	43.2	41.0	36.4	36.3	32.2	35.0	32.5	34.1	37.1	41.1	- Union Européenne
- Eastern Europe	1.0	1.1	1.4	1.1	1.0	1.0	0.8	0.9	1.1	1.4	- Europe de l'Est
- Rest of Europe	2.5	2.6	2.5	2.6	2.1	2.3	1.9	2.1	2.5	2.7	- Autre de l'Europe
Europe former USSR	0.1	0.3	0.3	0.3	0.8	0.5	0.3	0.5	0.8	0.6	Europe ancienne URSS
Oceania	0.9	1.2	6.1	2.3	3.9	0.1	0.3	0.3	0.3	0.2	Océanie

TRADE BY COMMODITY (Value in million US dollars)
Exports by principal countries or areas

COMMERCE PAR PRODUIT (Valeur en millions de dollars EU)
Exportations selon les principaux pays ou zones

Country or area	1998	1999	2000	2001	2002	Pays ou zone
World	348.8	372.6	360.5	370.7	410.1	Monde
Africa	49.2	35.5	37.3	37.0	41.6	Afrique
Americas	90.2	95.4	88.8	89.7	88.1	Amériques
- Northern America	71.5	78.4	77.1	78.1	75.5	- Amérique du Nord
- LAIA	11.9	10.6	4.7	4.1	5.4	- ALAI
- CACM	2.7	2.3	2.3	2.5	3.1	- MCC
- Caribbean	2.9	2.7	2.9	1.9	1.6	- Caraïbes
- Rest of America	1.2	1.4	1.8	3.0	2.6	- Autre d'Amérique
Asia excluding former USSR	78.6	85.4	79.3	72.8	79.2	Asie ancienne URSS exclus
- Middle East	14.3	16.6	17.1	18.9	22.7	- Moyen-Orient
Asia former USSR	0.8	0.4	0.8	1.3	1.6	Asie ancienne URSS
Europe excluding former USSR	121.9	148.0	146.0	162.7	189.6	Europe ancienne URSS exclus
- European Union	96.3	123.2	121.3	135.6	159.0	- Union Européenne
- Eastern Europe	22.9	22.3	22.6	25.2	27.6	- Europe de l'Est
- Rest of Europe	2.8	2.4	2.1	2.0	3.0	- Autre de l'Europe
Europe former USSR	0.9	1.3	0.9	1.0	1.0	Europe ancienne URSS
Oceania	7.2	6.7	7.4	6.1	9.1	Océanie
United States	32.8	36.2	38.4	41.5	42.8	Etats-Unis d'Amérique
Canada	37.7	42.1	38.5	36.6	32.7	Canada
Belgium	–	33.1	29.4	38.0	e42.6	Belgique
France-Monaco	21.5	22.0	23.7	22.7	29.7	France-Monaco
Thailand	16.4	33.9	25.0	18.8	e19.8	Thaïlande
Netherlands	15.4	18.8	22.1	25.1	29.8	Pays-Bas
Germany	10.9	13.8	11.9	12.4	14.8	Allemagne
Oman	12.1	13.2	12.8	11.8	12.6	Oman
China	13.0	10.8	10.4	11.4	13.5	Chine
Spain	11.3	11.6	10.4	12.3	11.4	Espagne
United Kingdom		12.6	12.6	10.4	12.8	Royaume-Uni
Mauritius	9.4	8.1	9.6	9.6	10.2	Maurice
Hungary	6.9	6.7	7.5	8.2	8.2	Hongrie
Czech Republic	5.6	6.5	6.8	7.8	8.0	République tchèque
Australia	4.9	4.9	5.6	4.5	7.1	Australie
Slovakia	4.1	4.3	4.9	5.4	7.2	Slovaquie
Sudan	16.5	e1.6	4.0	1.3	1.8	Soudan
Denmark	4.8	4.0	3.9	5.7	6.5	Danemark
Italy-San Marino-Holy See	3.9	4.3	4.0	5.1	7.2	Italie-Saint-Marin-Saint-Siège
Somalia	e6.2	e10.3	e7.3	e	e	Somalie
Belgium-Luxembourg	23.9	–	–	–	–	Belgique-Luxembourg
Egypt	4.1	3.8	0.1	4.5	4.8	Egypte
China, Hong Kong SAR	6.0	2.8	6.6	1.4	0.4	Chine - RAS de Hong-Kong
Chile	6.0	6.3	1.7	1.3	e1.3	Chili
Niger	3.2	2.3	3.0	2.8	e5.1	Niger
South Africa	–	–	5.4	5.8	5.1	Afrique du Sud
Israel	3.1	2.7	2.8	3.0	3.5	Israël
Poland	4.4	2.8	2.2	2.3	2.5	Pologne
Japan	3.2	2.1	2.3	3.6	3.1	Japon
Singapore	4.3	2.7	2.3	2.2	2.7	Singapour

(Value as percentages of World total) **(Valeur en pourcentage du total mondial)**

Regions of the world	1993	1994	1995	1996	1997	1998	1999	2000	2001	2002	Régions du monde
World	100.0	100.0	100.0	100.0	100.0	100.0	100.0	100.0	100.0	100.0	Monde
Africa	6.7	8.4	10.9	12.2	10.8	14.1	9.5	10.3	10.0	10.1	Afrique
Americas	22.6	21.3	19.8	24.0	26.1	25.8	25.6	24.6	24.2	21.5	Amériques
- Northern America	17.4	17.9	16.6	18.5	22.5	20.5	21.0	21.4	21.1	18.4	- Amérique du Nord
- LAIA	1.5	1.3	1.7	2.4	1.6	3.4	2.8	1.3	1.1	1.3	- ALAI
- CACM	0.7	0.7	0.7	0.7	0.7	0.8	0.6	0.6	0.7	0.7	- MCC
- Caribbean	0.4	0.2	0.2	0.3	0.6	0.8	0.7	0.8	0.5	0.4	- Caraïbes
- Rest of America	2.7	1.1	0.6	2.1	0.7	0.3	0.4	0.5	0.8	0.6	- Autre d'Amérique
Asia excluding former USSR	27.6	28.6	29.4	23.8	26.8	22.5	22.9	22.0	19.6	19.3	Asie ancienne URSS exclus
- Middle East	7.8	7.5	6.1	4.6	6.1	4.1	4.5	4.8	5.1	5.5	- Moyen-Orient
Asia former USSR	0.0	0.0	0.0	0.1	0.0	0.2	0.1	0.2	0.4	0.4	Asie ancienne URSS
Europe excluding former USSR	39.4	38.3	36.3	35.3	33.0	35.0	39.7	40.5	43.9	46.2	Europe ancienne URSS exclus
- European Union	32.7	31.8	29.8	29.0	27.4	27.6	33.1	33.6	36.6	38.8	- Union Européenne
- Eastern Europe	6.0	5.6	5.8	5.5	4.8	6.6	6.0	6.3	6.8	6.7	- Europe de l'Est
- Rest of Europe	0.8	0.9	0.7	0.9	0.8	0.8	0.7	0.6	0.5	0.7	- Autre de l'Europe
Europe former USSR	0.7	0.2	0.2	0.2	0.2	0.3	0.3	0.2	0.3	0.2	Europe ancienne URSS
Oceania	2.9	3.1	3.4	4.4	3.1	2.1	1.8	2.1	1.7	2.2	Océanie

951 Armoured fighting vehicles, war firearms, ammunition, parts, nes

TRADE BY COMMODITY (Value in million US dollars)
Imports by principal countries or areas

COMMERCE PAR PRODUIT (Valeur en millions de dollars EU)
Importations selon les principaux pays ou zones

Country or area	1998	1999	2000	2001	2002	Pays ou zone
World	3806.0	3437.6	3031.0	2957.2	4075.1	Monde
Africa	63.3	73.1	48.6	51.3	60.3	Afrique
Americas	871.7	748.3	955.6	865.9	1280.3	Amériques
- Northern America	732.0	627.6	802.7	744.9	1158.1	- Amérique du Nord
- LAIA	127.3	105.7	138.0	98.7	110.0	- ALAI
- CACM	6.6	9.4	10.6	16.0	7.6	- MCC
- Caribbean	5.0	4.4	3.6	5.0	3.9	- Caraïbes
- Rest of America	0.9	1.1	0.8	1.2	0.8	- Autre d'Amérique
Asia excluding former USSR	1611.9	1305.5	998.7	1161.4	1438.2	Asie ancienne URSS exclus
- Middle East	793.7	557.0	504.8	707.6	961.1	- Moyen-Orient
Asia former USSR	3.0	0.5	0.4	0.2	1.3	Asie ancienne URSS
Europe excluding former USSR	1148.3	1211.4	799.2	777.8	1095.8	Europe ancienne URSS exclus
- European Union	778.6	820.1	614.3	593.5	794.8	- Union Européenne
- Eastern Europe	51.8	42.2	41.7	24.5	43.0	- Europe de l'Est
- Rest of Europe	317.9	349.1	143.2	159.8	258.0	- Autre de l'Europe
Europe former USSR	2.5	11.9	80.0	4.0	5.3	Europe ancienne URSS
Oceania	105.3	86.8	148.4	96.6	193.8	Océanie
United States	496.1	474.4	607.7	564.0	785.5	Etats-Unis d'Amérique
United Kingdom	438.3	570.1	338.4	343.1	480.9	Royaume-Uni
Saudi Arabia	482.4	283.4	304.9	430.6	e445.6	Arabie saoudite
Korea, Republic of	444.7	510.9	297.0	163.6	214.4	République de Corée
Canada	235.8	153.2	195.0	180.9	372.5	Canada
Japan	160.8	156.0	147.0	227.4	201.0	Japon
Turkey	205.0	156.6	86.2	118.3	157.4	Turquie
Norway	181.5	207.7	70.4	63.9	126.4	Norvège
Australia	90.4	79.8	138.0	88.4	186.0	Australie
Cyprus	27.7	83.3	50.0	152.1	220.4	Chypre
Switzerland-Liechtenstein	111.2	130.9	69.8	84.5	118.4	Suisse-Liechtenstein
Iran (Islamic Republic of)	77.1	30.4	59.8		92.0	Iran (République islamique d')
Colombia	85.7	37.5	23.5	38.1	59.7	Colombie
Germany	56.4	49.5	49.9	45.2	37.5	Allemagne
Spain	28.1	33.6	57.0	51.8	67.4	Espagne
Indonesia	114.6	34.6	21.1	23.3	19.9	Indonésie
Italy-San Marino-Holy See	27.9	40.0	23.4	25.4	59.0	Italie-Saint-Marin-Saint-Siège
Finland	38.1	20.6	39.2	23.0	46.5	Finlande
Portugal	35.8	30.3	36.5	38.6	23.3	Portugal
Brazil	7.6	25.6	74.1	33.2	8.8	Brésil
Netherlands	85.8	3.7	3.3	3.6	2.9	Pays-Bas
France-Monaco	19.6	23.4	15.0	15.7	24.1	France-Monaco
Mexico	16.9	15.9	20.6	11.3	30.0	Mexique
Poland	15.0	14.3	20.5	9.8	23.0	Pologne
Russian Federation	0.4	4.5	74.6	1.0	1.2	Fédération de Russie
Sweden	21.1	17.7	13.8	7.1	8.3	Suède
Thailand	32.8	10.3	6.2	6.5	e6.8	Thaïlande
Bangladesh	11.1	e12.1	e10.8	10.5	e10.2	Bangladesh
Angola	e0.1	e32.8	e13.4	e0.8	e2.2	Angola
Greece	3.7	10.0	16.0	9.1	e10.1	Grèce

(Value as percentages of World total) **(Valeur en pourcentage du total mondial)**

Regions of the world	1993	1994	1995	1996	1997	1998	1999	2000	2001	2002	Régions du monde
World	100.0	100.0	100.0	100.0	100.0	100.0	100.0	100.0	100.0	100.0	Monde
Africa	0.8	3.0	1.0	0.7	0.8	1.7	2.1	1.6	1.7	1.5	Afrique
Americas	25.5	21.9	22.9	23.4	20.7	22.9	21.8	31.5	29.3	31.4	Amériques
- Northern America	21.0	18.1	20.5	21.3	17.8	19.2	18.3	26.5	25.2	28.4	- Amérique du Nord
- LAIA	4.3	3.6	2.1	1.8	2.5	3.3	3.1	4.6	3.3	2.7	- ALAI
- CACM	0.1	0.1	0.2	0.2	0.2	0.2	0.3	0.3	0.5	0.2	- MCC
- Caribbean	0.1	0.1	0.1	0.1	0.1	0.1	0.1	0.1	0.2	0.1	- Caraïbes
- Rest of America	0.1	0.1	0.1	0.0	0.0	0.0	0.0	0.0	0.0	0.0	- Autre d'Amérique
Asia excluding former USSR	29.9	36.5	36.1	32.9	40.8	42.4	38.0	33.0	39.3	35.3	Asie ancienne URSS exclus
- Middle East	15.0	17.8	17.2	16.5	22.1	20.9	16.2	16.7	23.9	23.6	- Moyen-Orient
Asia former USSR	0.0	0.1	0.0	0.0	0.0	0.1	0.0	0.0	0.0	0.0	Asie ancienne URSS
Europe excluding former USSR	42.5	35.9	35.3	39.5	34.9	30.2	35.2	26.4	26.3	26.9	Europe ancienne URSS exclus
- European Union	33.4	27.5	26.1	29.2	26.9	20.5	23.9	20.3	20.1	19.5	- Union Européenne
- Eastern Europe	0.6	1.1	1.3	4.1	1.3	1.4	1.2	1.4	0.8	1.1	- Europe de l'Est
- Rest of Europe	8.4	7.3	7.9	6.3	6.6	8.4	10.2	4.7	5.4	6.3	- Autre de l'Europe
Europe former USSR	0.1	0.1	0.1	0.1	0.1	0.1	0.3	2.6	0.1	0.1	Europe ancienne URSS
Oceania	1.2	2.6	4.6	3.4	2.7	2.8	2.5	4.9	3.3	4.8	Océanie

TRADE BY COMMODITY (Value in million US dollars)
Exports by principal countries or areas

COMMERCE PAR PRODUIT (Valeur en millions de dollars EU)
Exportations selon les principaux pays ou zones

Country or area	1998	1999	2000	2001	2002	Pays ou zone
World	5718.3	5074.2	5369.0	4204.8	4683.9	Monde
Africa	7.6	125.2	7.9	38.9	16.1	Afrique
Americas	3146.1	2755.6	2689.6	2711.9	2955.4	Amériques
- Northern America	3132.6	2742.1	2674.0	2694.0	2939.3	- Amérique du Nord
- LAIA	13.5	13.0	15.2	16.9	15.9	- ALAI
- CACM	0.0	0.4	0.1	1.0	0.1	- MCC
- Caribbean	0.0	0.1	0.3	0.1	0.1	- Caraïbes
- Rest of America	0.0	0.0	0.0	0.0	0.0	- Autre d'Amérique
Asia excluding former USSR	358.3	225.0	294.2	202.0	275.4	Asie ancienne URSS exclus
- Middle East	15.5	37.4	49.8	37.3	68.7	- Moyen-Orient
Asia former USSR	0.0	3.6	1.9	0.1	0.2	Asie ancienne URSS
Europe excluding former USSR	2196.1	1450.8	1579.3	1240.9	1400.4	Europe ancienne URSS exclus
- European Union	1970.4	1158.8	1338.7	930.5	1047.1	- Union Européenne
- Eastern Europe	69.3	105.9	129.4	120.3	51.6	- Europe de l'Est
- Rest of Europe	156.3	186.0	111.2	190.0	301.6	- Autre de l'Europe
Europe former USSR	3.6	506.1	786.4	4.7	15.4	Europe ancienne URSS
Oceania	6.6	7.9	9.7	6.2	21.1	Océanie
United States	3013.8	2629.6	2539.2	2572.5	2599.2	Etats-Unis d'Amérique
United Kingdom	1301.7	613.7	813.3	474.6	537.3	Royaume-Uni
Russian Federation	3.1	506.0	785.8	4.5	15.2	Fédération de Russie
France-Monaco	168.6	205.3	224.4	204.0	212.7	France-Monaco
Canada	118.8	112.6	134.8	121.3	339.9	Canada
Japan	54.6	108.8	199.8	85.7	120.5	Japon
Norway	71.2	93.9	47.3	98.3	193.8	Norvège
Germany	108.9	109.5	91.9	83.8	98.5	Allemagne
Switzerland-Liechtenstein	79.3	89.8	61.7	87.1	100.7	Suisse-Liechtenstein
Italy-San Marino-Holy See	75.5	79.9	75.4	80.8	76.9	Italie-Saint-Marin-Saint-Siège
China	240.3	3.0	3.7	2.5	2.3	Chine
Korea, Republic of	32.7	61.1	22.9	45.5	50.7	République de Corée
Slovakia	30.8	41.1	59.0	62.2	15.8	Slovaquie
Netherlands	194.9	0.5	0.4	0.3	1.2	Pays-Bas
Czech Republic	22.4	43.9	54.2	27.7	28.9	République tchèque
Finland	18.6	43.1	18.0	7.9	39.9	Finlande
Southern African Customs Union		123.6	–	–	–	Union douanière d'Afrique australe
Sweden	31.4	26.9	30.0	19.7	15.5	Suède
Portugal	20.2	27.2	29.2	20.0	13.6	Portugal
Turkey	12.8	33.1	10.3	10.1	24.7	Turquie
Poland	16.0	20.4	15.2	29.9	6.8	Pologne
Spain	19.7	16.1	18.1	11.2	15.5	Espagne
Belgium	–	20.8	20.7	13.8	e15.5	Belgique
Saudi Arabia	0.5	1.3	16.5	24.9	e22.4	Arabie saoudite
South Africa	–	–	6.1	36.2	7.4	Afrique du Sud
Austria	9.9	8.6	7.2	7.1	11.5	Autriche
Iran (Islamic Republic of)	0.5	0.9	22.8		19.2	Iran (République islamique d')
Australia	3.5	6.1	3.1	4.4	18.0	Australie
Mexico	5.2	5.4	6.8	7.1	6.4	Mexique
Denmark	4.0	3.4	5.4	6.3	8.6	Danemark

(Value as percentages of World total) **(Valeur en pourcentage du total mondial)**

Regions of the world	1993	1994	1995	1996	1997	1998	1999	2000	2001	2002	Régions du monde
World	100.0	100.0	100.0	100.0	100.0	100.0	100.0	100.0	100.0	100.0	Monde
Africa	0.1	0.0	0.1	0.1	0.2	0.1	2.5	0.1	0.9	0.3	Afrique
Americas	60.1	66.4	65.1	65.4	61.4	55.0	54.3	50.1	64.5	63.1	Amériques
- Northern America	59.8	66.0	64.9	65.2	61.2	54.8	54.0	49.8	64.1	62.8	- Amérique du Nord
- LAIA	0.3	0.3	0.2	0.2	0.2	0.2	0.3	0.3	0.4	0.3	- ALAI
- CACM	0.0	0.0	0.0	0.0	0.0	0.0	0.0	0.0	0.0	0.0	- MCC
- Caribbean	0.0	0.0	0.0	0.0	0.0	0.0	0.0	0.0	0.0	0.0	- Caraïbes
- Rest of America	0.0	0.0	0.0	0.0	0.0	0.0	0.0	0.0	0.0	0.0	- Autre d'Amérique
Asia excluding former USSR	2.7	3.4	2.3	1.7	2.4	6.3	4.4	5.5	4.8	5.9	Asie ancienne URSS exclus
- Middle East	0.3	0.3	0.3	0.2	0.4	0.3	0.7	0.9	0.9	1.5	- Moyen-Orient
Asia former USSR	0.0	0.2	0.0	0.0	0.1	0.0	0.1	0.0	0.0	0.0	Asie ancienne URSS
Europe excluding former USSR	35.5	29.8	32.4	32.5	35.8	38.4	28.6	29.4	29.5	29.9	Europe ancienne URSS exclus
- European Union	31.8	25.3	28.1	28.3	31.8	34.5	22.8	24.9	22.1	22.4	- Union Européenne
- Eastern Europe	0.5	1.9	2.6	1.9	1.3	1.2	2.1	2.4	2.9	1.1	- Europe de l'Est
- Rest of Europe	3.2	2.7	1.6	2.3	2.6	2.7	3.7	2.1	4.5	6.4	- Autre de l'Europe
Europe former USSR	1.5	0.1	0.1	0.0	0.0	0.1	10.0	14.6	0.1	0.3	Europe ancienne URSS
Oceania	0.1	0.1	0.1	0.3	0.2	0.1	0.2	0.2	0.1	0.5	Océanie

2002 INTERNATIONAL TRADE STATISTICS YEARBOOK

VOLUME II

SPECIAL TABLES

ANNUAIRE DE STATISTIQUE DU COMMERCE INTERNATIONAL 2002

VOLUME II

TABLEAUX SPECIAUX

Special Table A

Total imports and exports by regions and countries or areas

Imports CIF, exports FOB and balance: million U.S. dollars

Importations et exportations totales par régions et pays ou zones

Importations CIF, exportations FOB et balance: en millions de dollars E.-U.

Country or Area - Pays ou Zone	IMP EXP BAL	G/S	1985	1990	1995	1996	1997	1998	1999	2000	2001	2002
World	IMP		1999357	3490068	4937508	5178436	5351251	5293113	5506955	6234282	5990065	6192522
Monde	EXP		1936290	3375787	4908628	5110378	5298054	5230596	5412607	6062739	5816189	6070693
	BAL		-63067	-114280	-28880	-68059	-53196	-62518	-94347	-171543	-173876	-121829
Developed economies[1,2]	IMP		1380865	2568465	3420423	3543988	3627163	3714991	3894188	4292827	4110645	4206125
Economies développées[1,2]	EXP		1288185	2448513	3452404	3545561	3631086	3653486	3703492	3950715	3823947	3933464
	BAL		-92680	-119952	31982	1573	3922	-61505	-190696	-342112	-286698	-272660
Developing economies[2,3]	IMP		453215	751151	1343844	1439281	1512802	1364123	1421141	1724140	1638323	1718355
Eco. evdd[2,3]	EXP		474480	771370	1274154	1366328	1461478	1376654	1510368	1861690	1728605	1844626
	BAL		21265	20219	-69689	-72954	-51324	12531	89227	137550	90283	126271
Other[4]	IMP		165277	170452	173241	195167	211285	213999	191626	217315	241098	268042
Autres[4]	EXP		173625	155905	182069	198489	205490	200456	198747	250333	263636	292602
	BAL		8347	-14547	8828	3322	-5795	-13543	7121	33019	22539	24560
Devpd. econ.: America	IMP		424448	612670	886786	939950	1037793	1085185	1208522	1414250	1321315	1345511
Eco. dévlpés.: Amérique	EXP		301111	496668	728927	773940	845918	836244	874811	973908	911039	867388
	BAL		-123337	-116003	-157859	-166010	-191875	-248941	-333711	-440342	-410277	-478123
Canada[5]	IMP	G	80642	120242	163954	170694	195980	201061	214791	238812	221757	221961
Canada[5]	EXP	G	90953	127634	192204	201636	214428	214335	238422	276645	259857	252408
	BAL		10311	7392	28250	30942	18448	13274	23631	37833	38100	30447
United States[6]	IMP	G	352463	516987	770852	822025	899019	944353	1059440	1259300	1179180	1202430
Etats-Unis[6]	EXP	G	218815	393592	584743	625073	688696	682138	702098	781125	730803	693860
	BAL		-133648	-123395	-186109	-196952	-210323	-262215	-357342	-478175	-448377	-508570
Devlpg. econ.: America[3]	IMP		84690	128874	246975	274639	320421	335337	323378	373316	366417	343049
Eco. evdd.: Amérique[3]	EXP		106403	144412	225103	252147	279052	276766	294962	353172	338031	343816
	BAL		21713	15539	-21872	-22492	-41368	-58571	-28416	-20144	-28387	767
LAIA	IMP		67013	103761	210438	235615	281439	292164	279504	326208	318368	293537
ALAI	EXP		95479	131589	207459	234240	259458	256389	273344	329605	315975	322369
	BAL		28465	27828	-2979	-1375	-21980	-35775	-6161	3397	-2393	28833
Argentina	IMP	S	3814	4076	20122	23762	30450	31404	25508	25280	20320	8990
Argentine	EXP	S	8396	12353	20967	23811	26370	26441	23333	26341	26543	25709
	BAL		4582	8277	846	49	-4080	-4963	-2175	1061	6223	16720
Bolivia	IMP	G	691	687	1424	1635	1851	1983	1755	1830	1708	1770
Bolivie	EXP	G	623	926	1101	1137	1167	1104	1051	1230	1285	1299
	BAL		-68	239	-323	-498	-684	-879	-704	-600	-423	-471
Brazil	IMP	G	14332	22524	53783	56947	64996	60652	51759	58631	58351	49577
Brésil	EXP	G	25639	31414	46506	47747	52994	51140	48011	55086	58223	60362
	BAL		11307	8890	-7277	-9200	-12001	-9512	-3748	-3545	-128	10785
Chile	IMP	S	3072	7742	15900	19123	20825	19880	15988	18507	17814	17093
Chili	EXP	S	3804	8373	16024	15657	17902	16323	17162	19210	18466	18340
	BAL		733	630	124	-3466	-2923	-3557	1174	703	652	1247
Colombia	IMP	G	4141	5590	13853	13684	15378	14635	10659	11539	12834	12738
Colombie	EXP	G	3552	6766	10056	10587	11522	10852	11576	13040	12257	12001
	BAL		-589	1176	-3797	-3097	-3855	-3782	918	1502	-577	-737
Cuba	IMP	S	9536	6745	2805	3205	...	...	...	...	...	...
Cuba	EXP	S	7086	4910	1625	2015	...	...	...	...	...	...
	BAL		-2450	-1835	-1180	-1190	...	...	...	...	...	...
Ecuador	IMP	G	1767	1865	4153	3935	4955	5576	3017	3721	5363	6431
Equateur	EXP	G	2905	2714	4307	4900	5264	4203	4451	4927	4678	5030
	BAL		1138	849	155	965	310	-1373	1434	1205	-685	-1401

Special Table A

Total imports and exports by regions and countries or areas

Imports CIF, exports FOB and balance: million U.S. dollars *[cont.]*

Importations et exportations totales par régions et pays ou zones

Importations CIF, exportations FOB et balance: en millions de dollars E.-U. *[suite]*

Country or Area - Pays ou Zone	IMP EXP BAL	G/S	1985	1990	1995	1996	1997	1998	1999	2000	2001	2002
Mexico[5,7]	IMP	G	18359	41594	72453	89469	109808	125373	141975	174500	168276	168679
Mexique[5,7]	EXP	G	26757	40711	79542	96000	110431	117460	136391	166367	158547	160682
	BAL		8398	-883	7089	6531	623	-7913	-5584	-8133	-9729	-7997
Paraguay	IMP	S	502	1352	2782	2850	3099	2471	1725	2050	1989	...
Paraguay	EXP	S	304	959	919	1044	1089	1014	741	869	990	...
	BAL		-198	-393	-1863	-1807	-2011	-1457	-984	-1181	-999	...
Peru[5]	IMP	S	1529	2892	7687	7894	8554	8222	6729	7331	7164	7423
Pérou[5]	EXP	S	2979	3231	5575	5897	6841	5757	6113	7028	7100	7669
	BAL		1449	339	-2112	-1997	-1712	-2466	-616	-303	-65	247
Uruguay	IMP	G	708	1343	2867	3323	3727	3811	3357	3466	3061	...
Uruguay	EXP	G	909	1693	2106	2397	2726	2771	2237	2295	2060	...
	BAL		201	350	-761	-926	-1001	-1040	-1120	-1171	-1000	...
Venezuela	IMP	G	8234	7360	12619	9794	14577	15750	13835	16142	18263	...
Venezuela	EXP	G	12538	17549	18740	23053	21073	17175	20880	31737	24345	26881
	BAL		4303	10189	6121	13260	6496	1425	7045	15596	6082	...
CACM	IMP		5087	6473	12817	13110	15355	18029	18380	19618	20734	21947
MCAC	EXP		3794	4354	8284	8568	10005	11455	11861	11907	10600	10599
	BAL		-1293	-2119	-4534	-4543	-5349	-6574	-6519	-7710	-10134	-11349
Costa Rica	IMP	S	1098	1990	4036	4300	4924	6230	6320	6372	6564	7188
Costa Rica	EXP	S	976	1448	3453	3730	4268	5511	6577	5865	5010	5253
	BAL		-122	-542	-583	-569	-656	-719	257	-508	-1555	-1935
El Salvador	IMP	S	961	1263	2853	2671	2981	3121	3140	3795	3866	3907
El Salvador	EXP	S	679	582	998	1024	1371	1256	1177	1332	1214	1234
	BAL		-282	-681	-1855	-1647	-1609	-1865	-1963	-2462	-2653	-2674
Guatemala	IMP	S	1175	1649	3293	3146	3852	4651	4382	4791	5607	6078
Guatemala	EXP	S	1057	1163	2156	2031	2344	2582	2398	2696	2466	2232
	BAL		-118	-486	-1137	-1115	-1508	-2070	-1984	-2095	-3141	-3846
Honduras	IMP	S	888	935	1643	1840	2149	2535	2676	2855	2918	2979
Honduras	EXP	S	780	831	1220	1316	1446	1533	1164	1370	1318	1284
	BAL		-108	-104	-423	-524	-703	-1002	-1512	-1485	-1600	-1694
Nicaragua	IMP	G	964	638	993	1154	1450	1492	1862	1805	1779	1795
Nicaragua	EXP	G	302	331	457	466	577	573	545	645	592	596
	BAL		-663	-307	-536	-687	-873	-918	-1317	-1160	-1187	-1199
Other America	IMP		**12590**	**18640**	**23720**	**25913**	**23627**	**25144**	**25494**	**27490**	**27315**	**27565**
Autres pays d'Amérique	EXP		**7131**	**8469**	**9360**	**9339**	**9589**	**8922**	**9757**	**11659**	**11456**	**10848**
	BAL		**-5459**	**-10171**	**-14359**	**-16574**	**-14039**	**-16222**	**-15737**	**-15831**	**-15860**	**-16717**
Anguilla	IMP	S	...	...	...	...	54	58	...	...	...	..
Anguilla	EXP	S	...	...	...	...	2	5	...	...	...	..
	BAL		...	...	...	...	-53	-53	...	...	...	..
Antigua and Barbuda	IMP	G	112	255	346	365	370	385	414	...	...	..
Antigua-et-Barbuda	EXP	G	13	21	53	38	38	36	38	...	...	..
	BAL		-99	-234	-293	-328	-333	-349	-376	...	...	..
Aruba	IMP	S	.	536	567	578	614	815	782	835	841	841[illegible]
Aruba	EXP	S	.	28	15	12	24	29	29	173	149	128[illegible]
	BAL		.	-508	-552	-566	-590	-786	-753	-662	-693	-71[illegible]
Bahamas[8]	IMP	G	3078	1112	1243	1366	1666	1873	1772	1764	1742	161[illegible]
Bahamas[8]	EXP	G	2728	238	176	180	181	300	532	805	649	61[illegible]
	BAL		-349	-874	-1067	-1186	-1484	-1573	-1240	-959	-1093	-99[illegible]

Special Table A

Total imports and exports by regions and countries or areas

Imports CIF, exports FOB and balance: million U.S. dollars *[cont.]*

Importations et exportations totales par régions et pays ou zones

Importations CIF, exportations FOB et balance: en millions de dollars E.-U. *[suite]*

Country or Area - Pays ou Zone	IMP EXP BAL	G/S	1985	1990	1995	1996	1997	1998	1999	2000	2001	2002
Barbados	IMP	G	611	704	771	834	996	1010	1108	1156	1087	1039
Barbade	EXP	G	357	215	239	281	283	252	264	272	259	206
	BAL		-254	-489	-532	-553	-713	-758	-844	-884	-827	-833
Belize	IMP	G	128	211	257	255	286	295	370	452	500	521
Belize	EXP	G	90	133	162	168	176	172	186	185	174	180
	BAL		-38	-78	-96	-88	-110	-123	-184	-268	-327	-340
Bermuda	IMP	G	402	595	550	569	619	629	712	720	721	...
Bermudes	EXP	G	23	60	56	68	57	45	...	...	...	...
	BAL		-379	-535	-494	-501	-562	-584	...	...	...	...
Cayman Islands	IMP	G	147	288	391	379	...	...	...	...	...	...
Iles Caïmanes	EXP	G	2	4	4	3	...	...	...	...	...	...
	BAL		-145	-284	-387	-377	...	...	...	...	...	...
Dominica	IMP	S	55	118	117	130	125	132	138	148	131	115
Dominique	EXP	S	28	55	45	51	53	62	56	54	43	42
	BAL		-27	-63	-72	-79	-72	-70	-83	-95	-88	-73
Dominican Republic[5,9]	IMP	G	1487	1793	3164	3581	4192	4897	5207	6416	5937	6037
République dominicaine[5,9]	EXP	G	735	735	872	945	1017	880	805	966	805	834
	BAL		-752	-1058	-2292	-2635	-3175	-4016	-4402	-5450	-5132	-5204
French Guiana[10]	IMP	S	257	785	752	...	.	.	.	.	.	.
Guyane française[10]	EXP	S	38	93	131	...	.	.	.	.	.	.
	BAL		-220	-692	-622	...	.	.	.	.	.	.
Greenland	IMP	G	302	446	435	469	397	409	408	351	...	...
Groenland	EXP	G	177	454	373	369	293	254	276	262	...	...
	BAL		-125	8	-63	-100	-104	-155	-132	-88	...	...
Grenada	IMP	S	69	106	124	152	173	200	...	...	...	...
Grenade	EXP	S	22	28	22	20	23	27	...	...	...	...
	BAL		-47	-78	-102	-132	-151	-173	...	...	...	...
Guadeloupe[10]	IMP	S	620	1650	1890	...	.	.	.	.	.	.
Guadeloupe[10]	EXP	S	72	118	159	...	.	.	.	.	.	.
	BAL		-548	-1531	-1731	...	.	.	.	.	.	.
Guyana	IMP	S	226	312	528	598	629	...	...	...	584	563
Guyana	EXP	S	166	256	455	517	643	485	523	498	478	493
	BAL		-59	-56	-73	-81	14	...	...	...	-106	-70
Haiti	IMP	G	442	332	654	666	648	800	1035	1041	1017	1122
Haïti	EXP	G	168	160	112	90	212	320	338	313	275	279
	BAL		-273	-172	-542	-576	-436	-480	-697	-728	-742	-842
Jamaica	IMP	G	1111	1924	2808	2965	3128	3033	2899	3326	3361	3533
Jamaïque	EXP	G	566	1158	1420	1382	1382	1312	1241	1304	1220	1114
	BAL		-545	-765	-1388	-1583	-1746	-1721	-1658	-2022	-2140	-2419
Martinique[10]	IMP	S	683	1779	1963	...	.	.	.	.	.	.
Martinique[10]	EXP	S	162	278	224	...	.	.	.	.	.	.
	BAL		-520	-1500	-1739	...	.	.	.	.	.	.
Montserrat	IMP	S	18	48	...	...	...	...	...	...	...	...
Montserrat	EXP	S	3	1	...	...	...	...	...	...	...	...
	BAL		-15	-47	...	...	...	...	...	...	...	...
Neth. Antilles[11]	IMP	S	1388	2141	1841	2519	2083	...	...	...	...	...
Antilles néer.[11]	EXP	S	1031	1790	1522	1269	1488	...	...	...	...	...
	BAL		-357	-351	-319	-1249	-594	...	...	...	...	...

Special Table A

Total imports and exports by regions and countries or areas

Imports CIF, exports FOB and balance: million U.S. dollars *[cont.]*

Importations et exportations totales par régions et pays ou zones

Importations CIF, exportations FOB et balance: en millions de dollars E.-U. *[suite]*

Country or Area - Pays ou Zone	IMP EXP BAL	G/S	1985	1990	1995	1996	1997	1998	1999	2000	2001	2002
Panama[12]	IMP	S	1392	1539	2511	2780	3002	3398	3516	3379	2964	2982
Panama[12]	EXP	S	336	340	625	723	723	784	822	859	911	846
	BAL		-1056	-1198	-1886	-2057	-2279	-2614	-2694	-2519	-2053	-2136
Saint Kitts-Nevis	IMP	S	51	110	133	149	148	148	...	...	...	...
Saint-Kitts-et-Nevis	EXP	S	20	28	19	22	36	...	...	...	...	...
	BAL		-31	-83	-114	-127	-112	...	...	...	...	...
Saint Lucia	IMP	S	125	271	306	313	332	335	355	355	355	...
Sainte-Lucie	EXP	S	57	127	124	80	61	62	56	43	44	...
	BAL		-68	-144	-182	-234	-271	-273	-299	-312	-311	...
Saint Vincent-Grenadines	IMP	S	79	136	136	132	182	193	201	163	186	174
St.Vincent-Grenadines	EXP	S	63	83	43	46	46	50	49	47	41	38
	BAL		-16	-53	-93	-85	-136	-143	-152	-116	-144	-136
Suriname	IMP	G	299	472	583	501	657	551	...	...	...	...
Suriname	EXP	G	329	472	478	433	700	435	...	...	...	...
	BAL		30	0	-105	-68	43	-116	...	...	...	...
Trinidad and Tobago	IMP	S	1538	1109	1714	2144	2990	2999	2740	3308	3569	3643
Trinité-et-Tobago	EXP	S	2147	1960	2456	2500	2542	2258	2803	4274	4280	3881
	BAL		609	851	742	356	-448	-741	63	965	711	237
Devlpd. econ.: Europe	IMP		**775782**	**1640574**	**2075552**	**2126490**	**2122056**	**2229678**	**2250805**	**2364950**	**2320365**	**2397286**
Eco. dévlpés.: Europe	EXP		**762032**	**1586820**	**2179826**	**2249782**	**2249173**	**2328003**	**2308484**	**2377732**	**2395023**	**2537302**
	BAL		**-13750**	**-53754**	**104274**	**123292**	**127117**	**98325**	**57678**	**12782**	**74658**	**140017**
EU	IMP		726782	1538816	1959683	2010317	2009359	2111690	2134351	2246976	2203519	2276116
UE	EXP		713161	1485823	2055694	2120170	2124285	2207818	2182473	2238027	2253221	2388918
	BAL		-13621	-52992	96011	109854	114925	96129	48122	-8949	49702	112802
Austria	IMP	S	20996	49092	66400	67336	64786	68187	69557	68986	70461	71863
Autriche	EXP	S	17247	41138	57655	57822	58599	62747	64126	64167	66671	72746
	BAL		-3749	-7954	-8745	-9514	-6187	-5441	-5431	-4819	-3789	884
Belgium[13]	IMP	S	56211	120325	159716	163615	157283	162212	164620	177001	178715	195984
Belgique[13]	EXP	S	53762	118328	175884	175367	171906	177666	178965	187885	190352	213525
	BAL		-2449	-1996	16169	11752	14623	15454	14345	10884	11637	17541
Denmark	IMP	S	18252	32230	45082	44434	44044	45427	44067	43713	43430	47707
Danemark	EXP	S	17096	35135	49769	50099	47720	47481	48698	49756	50738	55762
	BAL		-1155	2905	4687	5665	3676	2054	4632	6043	7309	8055
Finland	IMP	G	13234	27003	28114	29265	29786	32301	31617	33900	32114	33642
Finlande	EXP	G	13620	26572	39574	38435	39318	42963	41841	45482	42802	44671
	BAL		386	-430	11460	9171	9533	10662	10224	11582	10688	11029
France[10]	IMP	S	108379	234465	281497	281776	272721	288412	294916	310942	300744	308389
France[10]	EXP	S	101709	216606	284914	287643	290972	305664	302472	300022	296233	309952
	BAL		-6669	-17859	3417	5867	18252	17252	7556	-10920	-4512	156
Germany[14,15]	IMP	S	158548	346179	464366	458808	445683	471448	473551	495480	486053	492112
Allemagne[14,15]	EXP	S	184003	410135	523909	524226	512503	543431	542884	550260	571460	612857
	BAL		25455	63956	59544	65418	66820	71983	69334	54780	85407	120745
Greece	IMP	S	10140	19777	22929	29672	27899	29388	28720	29221	29928	3116
Grèce	EXP	S	4543	8105	10961	11948	11128	10732	10475	10747	9483	1031
	BAL		-5598	-11672	-11968	-17724	-16771	-18656	-18244	-18474	-20444	-2084
Ireland	IMP	G	10019	20682	41987	45577	49814	56684	47195	51444	51304	5150
Irlande	EXP	G	10362	23747	56677	61798	67951	81576	71221	77097	83020	8749
	BAL		343	3066	14689	16221	18137	24893	24026	25653	31715	3598

Special Table A

Total imports and exports by regions and countries or areas

Imports CIF, exports FOB and balance: million U.S. dollars *[cont.]*

Importations et exportations totales par régions et pays ou zones

Importations CIF, exportations FOB et balance: en millions de dollars E.-U. *[suite]*

Country or Area - Pays ou Zone	IMP EXP BAL	G/S	1985	1990	1995	1996	1997	1998	1999	2000	2001	2002
Italy	IMP	S	87720	181983	206059	208097	210297	218459	220327	238071	236128	244292
Italie	EXP	S	76742	170499	234020	252045	240438	245716	235180	239934	244253	253349
	BAL		-10978	-11484	27960	43948	30141	27257	14852	1863	8125	9057
Luxembourg[16]	IMP	S	.	.	.	.	9380	7409	11045	10718	11154	11617
Luxembourg[16]	EXP	S	.	.	.	.	7000	7912	7895	7950	8240	8574
	BAL		.	.	.	.	-2380	503	-3150	-2768	-2914	-3043
Netherlands	IMP	S	73151	126485	176874	180642	178133	187754	187530	198331	194925	193665
Pays-Bas	EXP	S	77894	131787	196276	197420	194909	201382	200290	208889	216117	222410
	BAL		4743	5303	19402	16778	16776	13628	12760	10558	21193	28745
Portugal	IMP	S	7654	25265	33315	35179	35066	38539	39826	38192	39422	38326
Portugal	EXP	S	5686	16422	23212	24606	23974	24816	25228	23279	24449	25536
	BAL		-1968	-8843	-10103	-10572	-11092	-13723	-14599	-14913	-14973	-12791
Spain	IMP	S	29965	87559	113316	121792	122721	133164	144438	152901	153634	163575
Espagne	EXP	S	24249	55524	91041	102003	104368	109240	109966	113348	115175	123563
	BAL		-5716	-32034	-22275	-19788	-18353	-23923	-34473	-39553	-38459	-40012
Sweden	IMP	G	28553	54266	64752	66931	65697	68633	68721	72981	63471	66108
Suède	EXP	G	30467	57542	79813	84904	82956	85003	84772	86963	75791	81141
	BAL		1913	3276	15061	17973	17258	16370	16050	13982	12320	15033
United Kingdom	IMP	G	109593	224551	265322	287472	306592	314036	317963	334371	320956	335458
Royaume-Uni	EXP	G	101414	185326	242036	262130	281083	271851	268203	281525	267357	276315
	BAL		-8179	-39224	-23286	-25342	-25509	-42185	-49760	-52846	-53599	-59143
EFTA	IMP		47177	98590	111734	112118	108781	113852	112114	113024	112293	116293
AELE	EXP		48250	99429	121862	127489	122905	117894	123602	136831	139340	145725
	BAL		1073	839	10128	15371	14124	4042	11488	23807	27048	29432
Iceland	IMP	G	906	1680	1756	2031	1992	2489	2503	2591	2253	2274
Islande	EXP	G	815	1591	1804	1638	1852	2050	2005	1891	2021	2227
	BAL		-90	-89	48	-393	-140	-438	-498	-700	-232	-47
Norway	IMP	G	15560	27219	32972	35616	35713	37478	34172	34351	32954	34890
Norvège	EXP	G	19989	34045	41997	49646	48547	40405	45474	60063	59193	59575
	BAL		4429	6826	9024	14030	12834	2926	11302	25712	26239	24686
Switzerland	IMP	S	30711	69691	77006	74471	71075	73885	75440	76082	77086	79129
Suisse	EXP	S	27446	63793	78061	76205	72506	75439	76124	74876	78126	83922
	BAL		-3266	-5898	1055	1735	1431	1554	684	-1206	1041	4793
Other Developed Europe	IMP		**1824**	**3168**	**4134**	**4056**	**3916**	**4136**	**4340**	**4950**	**4553**	**4877**
Autres pays d'Europe	EXP		**622**	**1567**	**2270**	**2123**	**1983**	**2291**	**2409**	**2874**	**2461**	**2660**
	BAL		**-1202**	**-1601**	**-1865**	**-1933**	**-1933**	**-1846**	**-1931**	**-2076**	**-2092**	**-2217**
Andorra	IMP		...	723	793	816	946	972	...	...	...	...
Andorre	EXP		...	17	37	35	42	52	...	...	...	...
	BAL		...	-707	-756	-781	-904	-920	...	...	...	...
Faeroe Islands	IMP	G	256	338	314	370	358	387	470	532	504	...
Iles Féroé	EXP	G	184	420	362	417	389	435	468	472	520	...
	BAL		-72	82	48	47	31	48	-2	-60	16	...
Gibraltar	IMP		148	...	...	...	...	...	...	...	...	...
Gibraltar	EXP		62	...	...	...	...	...	...	...	...	...
	BAL		-86	...	...	...	...	...	...	...	...	...
Malta	IMP	G	759	1961	2942	2796	2552	2666	2841	3401	2726	2840
Malte	EXP	G	400	1130	1913	1731	1630	1833	1980	2447	1958	2131
	BAL		-359	-831	-1029	-1064	-922	-834	-861	-953	-768	-709

Special Table A

Total imports and exports by regions and countries or areas

Imports CIF, exports FOB and balance: million U.S. dollars *[cont.]*

Importations et exportations totales par régions et pays ou zones

Importations CIF, exportations FOB et balance: en millions de dollars E.-U. *[suite]*

Country or Area - Pays ou Zone	IMP EXP BAL	G/S	1985	1990	1995	1996	1997	1998	1999	2000	2001	2002
Devlpg. econ.: Europe[3]	IMP		12164	18890	**21487**	**23029**	**27989**	27951	**25560**	**26519**	**28655**	**32337**
Eco. evdd.: Europe[3]	EXP		10642	14312	**15770**	**15892**	**16598**	18097	**17029**	**17407**	**17966**	**18368**
	BAL		-1522	-4579	**-5717**	**-7137**	**-11391**	-9854	**-8531**	**-9112**	**-10689**	**-13969**
Bosnia Herzegovina	IMP	S	.	.	...	...	...	2921	3276	3085	3219	4066
Bosnie-Herzégovine	EXP	S	.	.	...	...	...	594	748	1067	1083	1020
	BAL		.	.	...	...	...	-2327	-2528	-2017	-2136	-3047
Croatia	IMP	G	.	.	7510	7788	9104	8383	7799	7887	9147	10714
Croatie	EXP	G	.	.	4633	4512	4171	4541	4303	4432	4666	4899
	BAL		.	.	-2877	-3276	-4933	-3842	-3496	-3455	-4481	-5815
Serbia and Montenegro[17]	IMP	S	12164	18890	2666	4102	4799	4622	...	...	...	...
Serbie-et-Monténégro[17]	EXP	S	10642	14312	1531	1842	2368	2604	...	...	...	...
	BAL		-1522	-4579	-1135	-2260	-2431	-2018	...	...	...	...
Slovenia	IMP	S	.	.	9492	9423	9357	10110	9952	10107	10144	10937
Slovénie	EXP	S	.	.	8316	8312	8372	9048	8604	8733	9251	9471
	BAL		.	.	-1175	-1111	-985	-1062	-1348	-1374	-892	-1466
TFYR Macedonia	IMP	S	.	.	1719	1627	1779	1915	1796	2085	1676	1928
L'ex-Ry de Macédoine	EXP	S	.	.	1204	1148	1237	1311	1192	1319	1154	1112
	BAL		.	.	-515	-479	-542	-604	-604	-766	-522	-816
Eastern Europe	IMP		82138	**49800**	96065	113395	118464	132624	130461	147167	160231	178495
Europe de l'Est	EXP		86344	**51728**	79242	85649	89592	100201	101311	116084	129539	14831[illegible]
	BAL		4206	**1928**	-16823	-27746	-28872	-32422	-29150	-31084	-30692	-3017[illegible]
Albania	IMP	G	64	76	1161	841	649	829	1140	1091	1331	1504
Albanie	EXP	G	53	45	367	208	139	205	264	261	305	33[illegible]
	BAL		-10	-30	-794	-633	-510	-624	-876	-829	-1026	-117[illegible]
Bulgaria	IMP	S	14	396	5651	6861	5223	4954	5454	6505	7263	798[illegible]
Bulgarie	EXP	S	13	400	5353	6602	5322	4197	3964	4809	5115	574[illegible]
	BAL		0	4	-298	-259	99	-757	-1490	-1696	-2148	-223[illegible]
Czech Rep[5]	IMP	S	.	.	25306	27724	27189	28814	28087	32180	36473	4075[illegible]
République. tchèque[5]	EXP	S	.	.	21686	21917	22751	26417	26245	29057	33399	3836[illegible]
	BAL		.	.	-3620	-5807	-4438	-2396	-1842	-3123	-3075	-239[illegible]
Fm Czechoslovakia[5,18]	IMP	G	28001	13106	.	.	.	.	.	.	.	
L'ex-Tchécoslovaquie[5,18]	EXP	G	28881	11882	.	.	.	.	.	.	.	
	BAL		880	-1224	.	.	.	.	.	.	.	
Fm German D.R.[5,14]	IMP	G	23433	...	.	.	.	.	.	.	.	
L'ex-Allemagne rép. dem. du[5,14]	EXP	G	25268	...	.	.	.	.	.	.	.	
	BAL		1835	...	.	.	.	.	.	.	.	
Hungary[19,20]	IMP	S	8224	8670	15379	18058	21116	25679	27923	31955	33725	3778[illegible]
Hongrie[19,20]	EXP	S	8538	9596	12439	15631	18989	22992	24950	28016	30530	3451[illegible]
	BAL		314	926	-2940	-2426	-2126	-2687	-2973	-3939	-3195	-327[illegible]
Poland	IMP	S	11136	9781	29064	37045	42237	46803	45778	48970	50378	5514[illegible]
Pologne	EXP	S	11423	14322	22890	24389	25708	27370	27323	31684	36159	4103[illegible]
	BAL		287	4541	-6173	-12656	-16529	-19433	-18455	-17285	-14219	-1410[illegible]
Romania	IMP	S	11267	9843	10278	11435	11280	11821	10392	13055	15561	1786[illegible]
Roumanie	EXP	S	12167	5775	7910	8085	8431	8300	8505	10367	11391	1387[illegible]
	BAL		900	-4068	-2368	-3351	-2849	-3521	-1887	-2688	-4170	-398[illegible]
Slovakia	IMP	S	.	.	9226	11431	10770	13725	11688	13413	15501	1745[illegible]
Slovaquie	EXP	S	.	.	8596	8818	8251	10721	10062	11889	12641	1445[illegible]
	BAL		.	.	-630	-2613	-2519	-3004	-1625	-1524	-2860	-299[illegible]

Special Table A

Total imports and exports by regions and countries or areas

Imports CIF, exports FOB and balance: million U.S. dollars *[cont.]*

Importations et exportations totales par régions et pays ou zones

Importations CIF, exportations FOB et balance: en millions de dollars E.-U. *[suite]*

Country or Area - Pays ou Zone	IMP EXP BAL	G/S	1985	1990	1995	1996	1997	1998	1999	2000	2001	2002
Former USSR	IMP		83140	120651	.	.	.	.	.	.	.	.
L'-ex URSS	EXP		87281	104177	.	.	.	.	.	.	.	.
	BAL		4141	-16474	.	.	.	.	.	.	.	.
Former USSR-Europe	IMP		.	.	77176	81772	92821	81375	61165	**70148**	**80867**	**89547**
L'ex-URSS -Europe	EXP		.	.	102827	112840	115898	100254	97436	**134250**	**134097**	**144283**
	BAL		.	.	25651	31068	23077	18879	36271	**64102**	**53230**	**54736**
Belarus	IMP	G	.	.	5563	6939	8689	8549	6674	8646	8178	8980
Bélarus	EXP	G	.	.	4707	5652	7301	7070	5909	7326	7448	8098
	BAL		.	.	-856	-1288	-1388	-1480	-765	-1320	-730	-882
Estonia[21]	IMP	G	.	.	2545	3245	4429	4611	4094	4242	4280	4810
Estonie[21]	EXP	G	.	.	1838	2087	2924	3130	2937	3132	3275	3444
	BAL		.	.	-707	-1157	-1506	-1482	-1157	-1109	-1005	-1367
Latvia	IMP	S	.	.	1818	2320	2721	3191	2945	3187	3504	4053
Lettonie	EXP	S	.	.	1305	1443	1672	1811	1723	1867	2001	2284
	BAL		.	.	-513	-876	-1049	-1380	-1222	-1320	-1504	-1769
Lithuania	IMP	G	.	.	3649	4559	5644	5794	4835	5457	6353	7825
Lituanie	EXP	G	.	.	2705	3355	3860	3711	3004	3810	4583	5553
	BAL		.	.	-944	-1204	-1784	-2083	-1831	-1647	-1770	-2271
Moldova, Republic of	IMP	G	.	.	841	1072	1171	1024	586	776	897	...
République de Moldova	EXP	G	.	.	739	795	874	632	463	471	570	...
	BAL		.	.	-102	-277	-297	-392	-123	-305	-327	...
Russian Federation	IMP	G	.	.	46709	46034	53039	43530	30185	33884	41879	46161
Fédération de Russie	EXP	G	.	.	78217	85107	85036	71265	71817	103070	99955	106435
	BAL		.	.	31508	39073	31997	27735	41632	69186	58076	60274
Ukraine	IMP	G	.	.	16052	17603	17128	14676	11846	13956	15775	16977
Ukraine	EXP	G	.	.	13317	14401	14232	12637	11582	14573	16265	17957
	BAL		.	.	-2735	-3203	-2896	-2039	-264	617	490	980
Devlpd. econ.: Afr/S.Afr.[22,23]	IMP		10921	17665	29608	29105	31939	28277	25890	28980	27421	28261
Eco. dévlpés.: Afr/A.S.[22,23]	EXP		15814	22834	26917	28145	29964	25396	25901	29267	28439	28713
	BAL		4893	5169	-2690	-960	-1975	-2881	11	287	1019	452
Devlpg. econ.: Africa[3]	IMP		**60360**	**78925**	**87238**	**88692**	**89167**	**101239**	**99492**	**98306**	**104055**	**108190**
Eco. evdd.: Afrique[3]	EXP		**64007**	**78074**	**77617**	**85557**	**84230**	**75888**	**88870**	**110447**	**98545**	**101123**
	BAL		**3647**	**-851**	**-9621**	**-3135**	**-4937**	**-25351**	**-10622**	**12140**	**-5510**	**-7067**
North Africa	IMP		**32260**	**44780**	**45943**	**45257**	**45367**	**50609**	**48965**	**48351**	**50169**	**54869**
Afrique du Nord	EXP		**32980**	**39171**	**35725**	**38031**	**38097**	**31671**	**37808**	**51325**	**43273**	**44704**
	BAL		**720**	**-5609**	**-10218**	**-7226**	**-7271**	**-18938**	**-11157**	**2974**	**-6896**	**-10165**
Algeria	IMP	S	9841	9780	10250	9112	8691	9404	9190	...	...	...
Algérie	EXP	S	12841	12930	10250	13521	13728	10215	...	...	...	...
	BAL		3000	3150	0	4409	5037	811	...	...	...	...
Egypt[24]	IMP	S	11104	16783	11760	13038	13211	16166	16022	14010	12756	12552
Egypte[24]	EXP	S	3714	4957	3450	3539	3921	3130	3559	4691	4128	4708
	BAL		-7390	-11826	-8310	-9499	-9290	-13036	-12463	-9319	-8628	-7844
Libyan Arab Jamah.	IMP	G	4101	5351	5033	4383	4640	4708	4158	3732	4388	6986
Jamahiriya arabe libyenne	EXP	G	12314	13312	9364	8190	7497	5072	7933	10195	8899	9173
	BAL		8213	7961	4331	3807	2857	364	3775	6463	4510	2188
Morocco	IMP	S	3850	6925	10024	9704	9526	10290	9925	11534	11037	11647
Maroc	EXP	S	2165	4265	6882	6881	7033	7153	7367	6956	7144	7772
	BAL		-1685	-2660	-3142	-2823	-2493	-3137	-2558	-4577	-3893	-3874

Special Table A

Total imports and exports by regions and countries or areas

Imports CIF, exports FOB and balance: million U.S. dollars *[cont.]*

Importations et exportations totales par régions et pays ou zones

Importations CIF, exportations FOB et balance: en millions de dollars E.-U. *[suite]*

Country or Area - Pays ou Zone	IMP EXP BAL	G/S	1985	1990	1995	1996	1997	1998	1999	2000	2001	2002
Sudan[25]	IMP	G	771	619	1219	1548	1580	1915	1415	1553	1586	...
Soudan[25]	EXP	G	374	374	556	620	594	596	780	1807	1699	...
	BAL		-397	-244	-663	-927	-985	-1319	-635	254	113	...
Tunisia	IMP	G	2757	5513	7903	7701	7948	8350	8475	8567	9529	9526
Tunisie	EXP	G	1738	3527	5475	5517	5560	5738	5872	5850	6609	6874
	BAL		-1019	-1985	-2428	-2185	-2388	-2613	-2603	-2717	-2920	-2652
Other Africa	IMP		**28100**	**34145**	**41295**	**43435**	**43799**	**50630**	**50527**	**49956**	**53886**	**53321**
Autres pays d' Afrique	EXP		**31027**	**38903**	**41891**	**47526**	**46133**	**44217**	**51062**	**59122**	**55272**	**56419**
	BAL		**2927**	**4758**	**597**	**4090**	**2334**	**-6413**	**535**	**9166**	**1386**	**3097**
EMCCA	IMP		2920	3455	3345	4498	4192	4108	3850	**3835**	**4748**	**5511**
CEMAC	EXP		3973	5592	6047	6855	7443	5816	6608	**8217**	**7418**	**8135**
	BAL		1053	2137	2703	2357	3251	1709	2758	**4383**	**2670**	**2624**
Cameroon	IMP	S	1151	1413	1201	1226	1359	1503	1314	...	...	...
Cameroun	EXP	S	722	2020	1654	1768	1860	1675	1595	...	...	...
	BAL		-429	606	453	542	501	172	281	...	...	...
Cent. Afr. Rep.	IMP	S	114	155	174	141	141	146	131	118	107	...
Rép. centrafricaine	EXP	S	92	120	171	147	163	151	147	161	143	...
	BAL		-21	-35	-3	5	22	5	15	44	35	...
Chad	IMP	S	168	285	365	332	335	356	317	318	621	995
Tchad	EXP	S	62	188	243	238	238	262	202	184	189	189
	BAL		-105	-97	-122	-94	-97	-94	-115	-135	-432	-806
Congo	IMP	S	604	618	670	1550	925	682	820	464	...	...
Congo	EXP	S	1099	985	1176	1343	1666	1373	1555	2477	...	...
	BAL		494	367	506	-207	741	691	735	2013	...	...
Equatorial Guinea	IMP	G	20	61	50	292	330	317	425	451	...	...
Guinée équatoriale	EXP	G	17	62	86	175	495	438	708	1097	...	...
	BAL		-3	2	36	-117	165	122	284	646	...	...
Gabon	IMP	S	863	923	884	956	1103	1103	844	996	858	...
Gabon	EXP	S	1980	2216	2718	3183	3021	1916	2401	2465	2646	...
	BAL		1117	1294	1834	2227	1918	813	1557	1470	1788	...
ECOWAS	IMP		**14934**	**13520**	**18966**	**17719**	**20354**	**21117**	**21357**	**20335**	**23115**	**21214**
CEDEA	EXP		**18477**	**20589**	**21753**	**26368**	**25114**	**20512**	**24745**	**30515**	**27233**	**26546**
	BAL		**3544**	**7069**	**2787**	**8650**	**4760**	**-605**	**3389**	**10180**	**4117**	**5332**
Benin	IMP	S	332	266	746	654	681	736	749	613	603	664
Bénin	EXP	S	151	122	417	653	417	407	422	392	372	377
	BAL		-181	-143	-329	-1	-264	-328	-327	-221	-231	-286
Burkina Faso	IMP	G	333	540	455	647	588	732	678	611	656	740
Burkina Faso	EXP	G	70	151	276	234	232	319	255	209	234	237
	BAL		-263	-389	-180	-413	-355	-412	-423	-401	-422	-502
Cape Verde	IMP	G	84	136	252	234	237	229	248	237	233	...
Cap-Vert	EXP	G	6	6	9	13	14	10	12	11	10	...
	BAL		-78	-130	-243	-222	-223	-218	-237	-227	-223	...
Cote d'Ivoire	IMP	S	1749	2109	2929	2900	2782	3358	3217	2782	2636	3799
Côte d'Ivoire	EXP	S	2945	3124	3812	4444	4460	4610	4675	3905	3956	5157
	BAL		1196	1015	883	1543	1679	1252	1458	1123	1320	1358
Gambia	IMP	G	93	188	182	258	174	245	192	...	...	...
Gambie	EXP	G	43	31	16	21	15	27	7	...	...	...
	BAL		-50	-157	-166	-237	-159	-218	-185	...	...	...

Special Table A

Total imports and exports by regions and countries or areas

Imports CIF, exports FOB and balance: million U.S. dollars *[cont.]*

Importations et exportations totales par régions et pays ou zones

Importations CIF, exportations FOB et balance: en millions de dollars E.-U. *[suite]*

Country or Area - Pays ou Zone	IMP EXP BAL	G/S	1985	1990	1995	1996	1997	1998	1999	2000	2001	2002
Ghana	IMP	G	866	...	1896	2101	2310	2561	3505	2973	...	...
Ghana	EXP	G	617	...	1754	1670	1636	1792	...	...	...	...
	BAL		-249	...	-142	-431	-674	-769	...	...	...	...
Guinea-Bissau	IMP	G	...	85	134	85	89	63	51	59	74	105
Guinée-Bissau	EXP	G	12	19	45	28	49	26	51	62	62	55
	BAL		...	-66	-89	-57	-40	-37	0	3	-12	-50
Liberia	IMP	S	285	...	...	...	...	...	...	...	...	...
Libéria	EXP	S	436	...	...	...	...	...	...	...	...	...
	BAL		151	...	...	...	...	...	...	...	...	...
Mali	IMP	S	303	609	774	772	738	761	824	807	708	752
Mali	EXP	S	125	361	443	433	561	561	566	547	725	918
	BAL		-178	-248	-331	-340	-177	-199	-258	-261	16	167
Niger	IMP	S	372	389	373	448	374	470	395	395	370	399
Niger	EXP	S	262	282	289	325	272	334	288	285	273	279
	BAL		-110	-107	-85	-123	-102	-136	-107	-111	-97	-120
Nigeria	IMP	G	8877	5627	8222	6438	9501	9211	8588	8721	11586	7547
Nigéria	EXP	G	12537	13596	12342	16154	15207	9855	13856	20975	17261	15107
	BAL		3660	7970	4121	9715	5706	644	5268	12254	5675	7560
Senegal	IMP	G	813	1222	1411	1435	1333	1455	1561	1519	1478	...
Sénégal	EXP	G	555	765	993	987	904	968	1025	920	1005	1106
	BAL		-258	-457	-419	-448	-429	-487	-535	-599	-473	...
Sierra Leone	IMP	S	155	148	134	211	92	95	80	149	182	264
Sierra Leone	EXP	S	127	137	42	47	17	7	6	13	29	49
	BAL		-28	-11	-91	-164	-75	-88	-74	-136	-153	-216
Togo	IMP	S	290	581	594	664	645	589	572	562	553	592
Togo	EXP	S	190	268	378	441	424	969	389	361	357	251
	BAL		-100	-313	-215	-224	-221	381	-183	-201	-196	-341
Rest of Africa	IMP		**10246**	**17170**	**18984**	**21219**	**19253**	**25405**	**25320**	**25786**	**26023**	**26596**
Afrique NDA	EXP		**8577**	**12722**	**14091**	**14302**	**13577**	**17888**	**19708**	**20389**	**20621**	**21738**
	BAL		**-1669**	**-4448**	**-4893**	**-6916**	**-5676**	**-7516**	**-5612**	**-5397**	**-5402**	**-4858**
Angola	IMP	S	671	...	427	...	...	...	...	...	...	...
Angola	EXP	S	2224	3910	3642	...	...	...	...	...	...	...
	BAL		1553	...	3215	...	...	...	...	...	...	...
Botswana	IMP	G	.	.	.	.	.	2320	2197	2469	1816	...
Botswana	EXP	G	.	.	.	.	.	2075	2645	2681	2480	...
	BAL		.	.	.	.	.	-245	447	213	664	...
Burundi	IMP	S	186	231	234	127	121	158	118	148	139	129
Burundi	EXP	S	112	75	106	40	87	65	54	50	39	30
	BAL		-74	-156	-129	-87	-35	-93	-64	-98	-101	-99
Comoros	IMP	S	36	52	63	...	...	...	...	...	...	...
Comores	EXP	S	16	18	11	...	...	...	...	...	...	...
	BAL		-20	-34	-51	...	...	...	...	...	...	...
Dem. Rep. of the Congo	IMP	S	792	888	397	424	...	...	...	...	...	...
Rép. dém. du Congo	EXP	S	950	999	438	592	...	...	...	...	...	...
	BAL		158	111	41	167	...	...	...	...	...	...
Djibouti	IMP	G	201	215	177	179	148	158	153	...	...	...
Djibouti	EXP	G	14	25	14	14	11	12	12	...	...	...
	BAL		-187	-190	-163	-165	-137	-146	-140	...	...	...

Special Table A

Total imports and exports by regions and countries or areas

Imports CIF, exports FOB and balance: million U.S. dollars *[cont.]*

Importations et exportations totales par régions et pays ou zones

Importations CIF, exportations FOB et balance: en millions de dollars E.-U. *[suite]*

Country or Area - Pays ou Zone	IMP EXP BAL	G/S	1985	1990	1995	1996	1997	1998	1999	2000	2001	2002
Eritrea	IMP	G	.	.	...	450	425	356	382	...	...	...
Erythrée	EXP	G	.	.	...	76	52	26	20	...	...	...
	BAL		.	.	...	-374	-373	-330	-362	...	...	...
Ethiopia	IMP	G	993	1081	1142	1401	...	...	1317	...	...	...
Ethiopie	EXP	G	333	298	422	417	587	560	...	...	...	...
	BAL		-660	-784	-720	-984	...	...	...	...	...	...
Kenya	IMP	G	1436	2223	3006	2949	3296	3195	2833	3105	3189	3245
Kenya	EXP	G	958	1032	1890	2068	2054	2007	1747	1734	1943	2116
	BAL		-479	-1191	-1116	-881	-1243	-1188	-1086	-1372	-1246	-1129
Lesotho	IMP	G	.	.	.	.	.	863	781	728	681	776
Lesotho	EXP	G	.	.	.	.	.	194	172	221	280	369
	BAL		.	.	.	.	.	-670	-609	-507	-401	-407
Madagascar	IMP	S	402	652	543	507	467	514	377	...	...	...
Madagascar	EXP	S	274	319	370	299	222	243	221	...	...	...
	BAL		-128	-333	-174	-208	-245	-271	-156	...	...	...
Malawi	IMP	G	295	575	475	623	791	515	673	533	563	669
Malawi	EXP	G	248	417	405	481	537	430	453	379	449	447
	BAL		-47	-159	-69	-143	-255	-85	-221	-153	-113	-222
Mauritania	IMP	S	233	...	...	...	...	...	...	...	...	...
Mauritanie	EXP	S	374	...	...	...	...	...	...	...	...	...
	BAL		140	...	...	...	...	...	...	...	...	...
Mauritius	IMP	G	529	1621	1976	2289	2181	2073	2248	2091	1993	...
Maurice	EXP	G	440	1196	1538	1802	1592	1645	1554	1551	1615	...
	BAL		-88	-425	-438	-487	-588	-428	-694	-540	-377	...
Mozambique	IMP	S	424	878	704	759	739	790	1139	1158	...	...
Mozambique	EXP	S	77	126	168	217	222	230	263	364	...	...
	BAL		-347	-752	-536	-542	-517	-560	-876	-794	...	...
Namibia	IMP	G	.	.	.	.	.	1636	1609	1539	1542	...
Namibie	EXP	G	.	.	.	.	.	1224	1233	1317	1180	...
	BAL		.	.	.	.	.	-412	-376	-222	-362	...
Réunion[10]	IMP	S	841	2165	2625	...	.	.	.	.	.	.
Réunion[10]	EXP	S	97	189	207	...	.	.	.	.	.	.
	BAL		-744	-1976	-2418	...	.	.	.	.	.	.
Rwanda	IMP	G	298	288	241	257	297	284	250	211	250	203
Rwanda	EXP	G	131	110	52	61	87	60	60	52	85	56
	BAL		-167	-178	-189	-197	-210	-224	-190	-159	-165	-148
Sao Tome and Principe	IMP	S	...	21	29	22	16	...	...	...	...	...
Sao Tomé-et-Principe	EXP	S	...	4	5	5	5	...	...	...	...	...
	BAL		...	-17	-24	-18	-11	...	...	...	...	...
Seychelles	IMP	G	99	187	233	379	340	384	434	342	523	...
Seychelles	EXP	G	28	57	53	139	113	122	145	194	216	...
	BAL		-71	-130	-180	-239	-227	-261	-289	-149	-307	...
Somalia	IMP	G	111	81	...	...	...	...	...	...	...	...
Somalie	EXP	G	89	81	...	...	...	...	...	...	...	...
	BAL		-22	0	...	...	...	...	...	...	...	...
Swaziland	IMP	G	.	.	.	.	.	1071	1068	1031	1097	983
Swaziland	EXP	G	.	.	.	.	.	963	937	896	1031	939
	BAL		.	.	.	.	.	-108	-131	-135	-66	-44

Special Table A

Total imports and exports by regions and countries or areas

Imports CIF, exports FOB and balance: million U.S. dollars *[cont.]*

Importations et exportations totales par régions et pays ou zones

Importations CIF, exportations FOB et balance: en millions de dollars E.-U. *[suite]*

Country or Area - Pays ou Zone	IMP EXP BAL	G/ S	1985	1990	1995	1996	1997	1998	1999	2000	2001	2002
Uganda	IMP	G	315	292	1056	1190	1317	1414	1342	1512	1594	1112
Ouganda	EXP	G	472	152	461	587	555	501	517	469	457	442
	BAL		157	-140	-595	-603	-762	-913	-825	-1043	-1137	-670
United Rep. of Tanzania	IMP	G	860	1364	1679	1386	1336	1453	1550	1523	1713	1687
Rép.-Unie de Tanzanie	EXP	G	246	331	685	783	752	589	543	663	777	875
	BAL		-614	-1033	-994	-603	-584	-864	-1007	-860	-935	-812
Zambia	IMP	S	721	1209	702	836	819	...	...	...	...	...
Zambie	EXP	S	482	1312	1046	1049	914	...	...	...	...	...
	BAL		-239	103	344	213	96	...	...	...	...	...
Zimbabwe	IMP	G	896	1839	2661	2817	3058	2700	2178	1863	...	...
Zimbabwe	EXP	G	1110	1722	2114	2419	2456	2044	2140	2109	...	...
	BAL		213	-117	-547	-399	-601	-656	-38	246	...	...
Devlpd. econ.: Asia	IMP		138665	247823	356339	371510	358277	298083	328931	402984	368352	352302
Eco. dévlpés.: Asie	EXP		181737	294829	453076	422252	432218	399238	429180	496439	416378	425652
	BAL		43072	47007	96736	50742	73941	101154	100249	93455	48026	73350
Israel[26]	IMP	S	9875	16794	29579	31620	30782	29342	33166	37686	35449	35517
Israël[26]	EXP	S	6260	11576	19046	20610	22503	22993	25794	31404	29048	29347
	BAL		-3615	-5218	-10533	-11010	-8279	-6349	-7371	-6281	-6401	-6170
Japan	IMP	G	130515	235424	335990	349174	338830	280632	310039	379491	349189	337209
Japon	EXP	G	177202	287648	443259	410926	421050	388135	417659	479227	403616	416730
	BAL		46687	52225	107269	61752	82220	107503	107620	99736	54427	79520
Devlpg. Econ.: Asia[3,27]	IMP		**292538**	**519363**	**981300**	**1045542**	**1067802**	**892374**	**965220**	**1218543**	**1131604**	**1226715**
Eco. evdd.: Asie[3,27]	EXP		**291584**	**531763**	**949865**	**1007080**	**1076361**	**1001233**	**1104339**	**1375305**	**1269272**	**1376723**
	BAL		**-953**	**12400**	**-31436**	**-38462**	**8559**	**108859**	**139119**	**156762**	**137668**	**150007**
Asia Middle East	IMP		86163	105871	**135123**	**151878**	**161667**	**156072**	**151902**	**191201**	**171550**	**189832**
Moyen-Orient d'Asie	EXP		**97696**	**133287**	**151420**	**174238**	**186138**	**157478**	**195905**	**274424**	**243003**	**246395**
	BAL		**11533**	**27415**	**16296**	**22359**	**24471**	**1405**	**44003**	**83223**	**71453**	**56563**
Bahrain	IMP	G	3107	3712	3716	4273	4026	3566	3698	4634	4306	4985
Bahreïn	EXP	G	2897	3761	4113	4702	4384	3270	4363	6195	5577	5369
	BAL		-210	49	397	429	358	-296	665	1561	1271	384
Cyprus	IMP	G	1247	2796	3694	3983	3655	3687	3618	3846	3938	4084
Chypre	EXP	G	476	948	1231	1391	1250	1062	997	954	976	843
	BAL		-771	-1848	-2463	-2591	-2405	-2625	-2621	-2893	-2962	-3240
Fm Yemen A.R.[28]	IMP		1301	.	.	.	.	.	.	.	.	.
Fmr Yémen A.R.[28]	EXP		13	.	.	.	.	.	.	.	.	.
	BAL		-1287	.	.	.	.	.	.	.	.	.
Fm Yemen Dm[28]	IMP	S	698	.	.	.	.	.	.	.	.	.
FMR Yémen Dm[28]	EXP	S	40	.	.	.	.	.	.	.	.	.
	BAL		-658	.	.	.	.	.	.	.	.	.
Iran (Islamic Rep. of)[29,30]	IMP	S	11629	20322	13882	16274	14196	14323	12683	14296	17938	22190
Iran (Rép. islamique d')[29,30]	EXP	S	13448	19305	18360	22391	18381	13118	21030	28345	23716	24440
	BAL		1819	-1017	4478	6117	4185	-1205	8347	14049	5778	2250
Iraq	IMP		7619	4834	...	...	...	...	...	...	...	...
Iraq	EXP		...	...	...	...	...	...	...	...	...	...
	BAL		...	...	...	...	...	...	...	...	...	...
Jordan	IMP	G	2733	2603	3696	4293	4102	3828	3717	4597	4844	...
Jordanie	EXP	G	791	1063	1769	1817	1836	1802	1832	1899	2293	...
	BAL		-1942	-1540	-1928	-2476	-2266	-2026	-1885	-2698	-2551	...

Special Table A

Total imports and exports by regions and countries or areas

Imports CIF, exports FOB and balance: million U.S. dollars *[cont.]*

Importations et exportations totales par régions et pays ou zones

Importations CIF, exportations FOB et balance: en millions de dollars E.-U. *[suite]*

Country or Area - Pays ou Zone	IMP EXP BAL	G/ S	1985	1990	1995	1996	1997	1998	1999	2000	2001	2002
Kuwait	IMP	S	6007	3923	7792	8373	8246	8617	7617	7157	7869	9010
Koweït	EXP	S	10600	6956	12785	14889	14225	9553	12164	19436	16203	15369
	BAL		4593	3033	4992	6515	5979	936	4547	12279	8334	6359
Lebanon	IMP	G	2203	2525	5480	7540	7467	7070	6207	6228	...	...
Liban	EXP	G	482	494	656	736	643	662	677	714	...	...
	BAL		-1721	-2031	-4825	-6804	-6824	-6408	-5530	-5514	...	...
Oman	IMP	G	3153	2681	4248	4578	5026	5682	4674	5040	5798	6005
Oman	EXP	G	3938	5508	6101	7346	7630	5508	7238	11319	11074	11172
	BAL		785	2827	1854	2768	2604	-173	2564	6279	5276	5167
Qatar	IMP	S	1139	1695	3398	2868	3322	3409	2499	...	...	...
Qatar	EXP	S	3542	3529	3481	3752	3791	4880	7059	...	...	...
	BAL		2403	1834	83	884	470	1471	4560	...	...	...
Saudi Arabia	IMP	S	23600	24069	28091	27744	28732	30013	28010	30237	31223	32312
Arabie saoudite	EXP	S	27491	44417	50040	60729	60732	38822	50760	77583	68064	...
	BAL		3891	20347	21949	32985	32000	8809	22750	47345	36841	...
Syrian Arab Rep.	IMP	S	3967	2400	4709	5380	4028	3895	3832	16706	5846	5097
République arab syrienne	EXP	S	1637	4212	3563	3999	3916	2890	3464	19260	6451	6831
	BAL		-2329	1812	-1146	-1381	-111	-1005	-368	2553	605	1734
Turkey	IMP	S	11343	22302	35709	43627	48559	45921	40671	54503	41399	49663
Turquie	EXP	S	7958	12959	21637	23225	26261	26974	26587	27775	31334	34561
	BAL		-3386	-9343	-14072	-20402	-22298	-18947	-14084	-26728	-10065	-15101
United Arab Emirates	IMP	G	6549	11199	20984	22638	29952	24728	33231	38139	...	...
Emirats arabes unis	EXP	G	13124	23544	27753	28085	39613	42666	43307	...	...	...
	BAL		6576	12345	6769	5447	9661	17938	10076	...	...	...
Yemen[28]	IMP	S	.	1571	1817	2442	2017	2172	2006	2326	2309	...
Yémen[28]	EXP	S	.	692	1917	3206	2509	1501	2438	4078	3214	...
	BAL		.	-879	101	763	491	-671	432	1751	905	...
Non Petrol. Export[31]	IMP		...	...	...	...	...	...	...	...	...	...
Pétrole N. Compris[31]	EXP		**18757**	**79352**	**96706**	**111242**	62312	60768	73025	**102397**	**100182**	**92853**
	BAL		...	...	...	...	...	...	...	...	...	...
Other Asia	IMP		**206374**	**413492**	**835673**	**879944**	**892407**	**723341**	**801399**	**1013386**	**943789**	**1020738**
Autres Pays d'Asie	EXP		**193888**	**398476**	**785371**	**817965**	**874701**	**832230**	**895704**	**1082853**	**1007789**	**1110837**
	BAL		**-12486**	**-15015**	**-50302**	**-61979**	**-17707**	**108889**	**94306**	**69467**	**64000**	**90099**
ASEAN	IMP		**66471**	**162236**	**354014**	**374911**	370119	280236	**299142**	**367558**	**337567**	**345796**
ANASE	EXP		**72383**	**144054**	**320313**	**340008**	350776	327666	**357424**	**424563**	**382885**	**403307**
	BAL		**5912**	**-18183**	**-33701**	**-34903**	-19343	47429	**58282**	**57005**	**45318**	**57511**
Brunei Darussalam	IMP	S	615	1001	2078	2494	2203	1552	...	...	...	...
Brunéi Darussalam	EXP	S	2972	2213	2389	2481	2467	2058	...	...	...	...
	BAL		2357	1213	311	-13	264	506	...	...	...	...
Cambodia	IMP	S	...	...	...	...	1116	1129	1243	1424	1456	...
Cambodge	EXP	S	...	...	...	...	626	933	1040	1123	1296	...
	BAL		...	...	...	...	-491	-195	-203	-302	-160	...
Indonesia	IMP	S	10259	21837	40630	42929	41694	27337	24003	33515	31010	25388
Indonésie	EXP	S	18587	25675	45417	49814	53443	48848	48666	62124	56447	58120
	BAL		8328	3838	4787	6885	11749	21511	24662	28609	25437	32732
Lao P.Dem.R.	IMP	S	193	185	589	690	706	553	525	535	528	431
Rép. dém. populaire lao	EXP	S	54	79	311	323	359	370	311	330	331	298
	BAL		-139	-106	-278	-367	-347	-183	-214	-205	-197	-133

Country or Area - Pays ou Zone	IMP EXP BAL	G/S	1985	1990	1995	1996	1997	1998	1999	2000	2001	2002
Malaysia	IMP	G	12253	29259	77545	78408	79030	58278	65385	81963	73867	79868
Malaisie	EXP	G	15316	29453	73779	78318	78742	73255	84617	98230	88006	93264
	BAL		3063	194	-3766	-90	-288	14977	19231	16266	14139	13396
Myanmar	IMP	G	284	270	1335	1371	2056	2695	2323	2401	2877	...
Myanmar	EXP	G	304	325	851	754	874	1077	1136	1647	2382	...
	BAL		20	55	-484	-618	-1182	-1617	-1187	-755	-496	...
Philippines	IMP	G	5456	13042	28328	34127	38604	31542	32569	36887	34944	37202
Philippines	EXP	G	4612	8160	17492	20408	24895	29449	36577	39794	32664	36510
	BAL		-844	-4882	-10836	-13719	-13709	-2093	4008	2907	-2280	-692
Singapore	IMP	G	26288	60774	124502	131340	132443	104728	111062	134546	116004	116448
Singapour	EXP	G	22815	52730	118263	125016	124990	109905	114682	137806	121755	125177
	BAL		-3473	-8044	-6239	-6324	-7453	5177	3620	3259	5752	8730
Thailand	IMP	S	9242	33065	70787	72336	62880	42971	50343	61924	62058	64658
Thaïlande	EXP	S	7121	23084	56440	55721	57402	54458	58440	69057	65114	68768
	BAL		-2121	-9981	-14347	-16616	-5479	11487	8098	7133	3055	4110
Viet Nam	IMP	G	1857	2752	8155	11144	11592	11500	11742	15638	15999	19000
Viet Nam	EXP	G	699	2404	5449	7256	9185	9361	11540	14449	15100	16530
	BAL		-1159	-348	-2707	-3888	-2407	-2139	-202	-1189	-899	-2470
Rest of Asia	IMP		**139903**	**251255**	**481659**	**505032**	**522289**	**443105**	**502256**	**645828**	**606222**	**674942**
Asie NDA	EXP		**121505**	**254423**	**465058**	**477957**	**523925**	**504565**	**538280**	**658291**	**624904**	**707530**
	BAL		**-18398**	**3167**	**-16601**	**-27075**	**1636**	**61460**	**36024**	**12462**	**18682**	**32588**
Afghanistan	IMP	G	1194	936	50	...	...	...	...	...	...	...
Afghanistan	EXP	G	567	235	26	...	...	...	...	...	...	...
	BAL		-627	-701	-24	...	...	...	...	...	...	...
Bangladesh	IMP	G	2505	3618	6501	6621	6896	6978	7685	8358	8349	7913
Bangladesh	EXP	G	986	1671	3173	3297	3778	3831	3919	4787	4826	4566
	BAL		-1519	-1946	-3328	-3324	-3117	-3147	-3766	-3572	-3523	-3348
Bhutan	IMP	G	75	78	113	128	137	135	182	203	...	...
Bhoutan	EXP	G	22	68	103	100	118	108	116	121	...	...
	BAL		-53	-10	-9	-27	-19	-26	-66	-81	...	...
China[32]	IMP	S	42252	53345	129113	138833	142370	140237	165699	225094	243553	295171
Chine[32]	EXP	S	27350	62091	148797	151048	182792	183712	194931	249203	266098	325591
	BAL		-14902	8746	19684	12215	40422	43475	29232	24109	22545	30420
China, Hong Kong SAR[33]	IMP	G	29703	82490	192751	198550	208614	184518	179520	212805	201076	207644
Chine, Hong-Kong RAS[33]	EXP	G	30187	82160	173750	180750	188059	174002	173885	201860	189894	200092
	BAL		484	-330	-19001	-17800	-20555	-10516	-5635	-10945	-11182	-7552
China, Macao SAR[33]	IMP	G	773	1539	2042	2000	2082	1955	2040	2255	2386	2530
Chine, Macao RAS[33]	EXP	G	901	1701	1997	1996	2148	2141	2200	2539	2300	2356
	BAL		129	162	-44	-4	66	186	160	284	-87	-174
India	IMP	G	15935	23583	34710	37944	41430	42999	46971	51563	50390	56496
Inde	EXP	G	9144	17970	30628	33107	35006	33463	35666	42378	43338	49293
	BAL		-6791	-5613	-4082	-4837	-6425	-9536	-11305	-9185	-7052	-7202
Korea, Republic of	IMP	G	31136	69844	135119	150339	144616	93282	119725	160481	141098	152126
Corée, République de	EXP	G	30282	65016	125058	129715	136164	132313	143685	172267	150439	162470
	BAL		-854	-4828	-10061	-20624	-8452	39031	23960	11786	9341	10344
Maldives	IMP	G	53	138	268	302	349	354	402	389	393	392
Maldives	EXP	G	23	52	50	59	73	74	64	76	76	90
	BAL		-30	-86	-218	-243	-276	-280	-338	-313	-317	-301

Special Table A

Total imports and exports by regions and countries or areas

Imports CIF, exports FOB and balance: million U.S. dollars *[cont.]*

Importations et exportations totales par régions et pays ou zones

Importations CIF, exportations FOB et balance: en millions de dollars E.-U. *[suite]*

Country or Area - Pays ou Zone	IMP EXP BAL	G/S	1985	1990	1995	1996	1997	1998	1999	2000	2001	2002
Mongolia	IMP	G	1096	924	415	451	468	503	513	615	630	...
Mongolie	EXP	G	689	661	473	424	452	345	358	466	448	...
	BAL		-406	-263	58	-27	-17	-158	-154	-148	-182	...
Nepal	IMP	G	455	672	1333	1398	1693	1245	1418	1573	1475	1419
Népal	EXP	G	161	204	346	385	406	474	600	804	738	567
	BAL		-295	-468	-988	-1013	-1287	-772	-818	-768	-737	-851
Pakistan	IMP	G	5919	7412	11517	12191	11652	9331	10154	10864	10192	11227
Pakistan	EXP	G	2753	5616	8031	9367	8760	8515	8380	9028	9238	9908
	BAL		-3166	-1796	-3486	-2824	-2893	-816	-1775	-1836	-953	-1319
Sri Lanka	IMP	G	1987	2688	5307	5442	5864	5877	5960	7210	5973	6105
Sri Lanka	EXP	G	1333	1912	3798	4095	4639	4787	4594	5433	4815	4699
	BAL		-654	-776	-1509	-1347	-1225	-1091	-1367	-1776	-1158	-1406
Timor-Leste	IMP	S	...	...	112	132	142	135	82	...	...	...
Timor-Leste	EXP	S	...	...	34	41	48	56	45	...	...	...
	BAL		...	...	-78	-91	-94	-79	-37	...	...	...
Former USSR - Asia	IMP		.	.	10504	**13720**	**13728**	**12961**	**11920**	**13956**	**16265**	**16145**
L'ex-URSS - Asie	EXP		.	.	13074	**14877**	**15523**	**11525**	**12730**	**18028**	**18480**	**19491**
	BAL		.	.	2570	**1157**	**1795**	**-1436**	**810**	**4072**	**2216**	**3346**
Armenia	IMP	S	.	.	674	856	892	902	800	882	874	991
Arménie	EXP	S	.	.	271	290	233	221	232	294	343	507
	BAL		.	.	-403	-566	-660	-682	-568	-588	-532	-484
Azerbaijan	IMP	G	.	.	668	961	794	1077	1036	1172	1431	1666
Azerbaïdjan	EXP	G	.	.	637	631	781	606	929	1745	2314	2164
	BAL		.	.	-30	-329	-13	-471	-107	573	883	499
Georgia	IMP	G	.	.	412	687	944	878	...	...	...	...
Géorgie	EXP	G	.	.	158	199	240	192	...	...	...	...
	BAL		.	.	-255	-489	-704	-686	...	...	...	...
Kazakhstan	IMP	G	.	.	3807	4241	4301	4314	3655	5040	6446	6584
Kazakhstan	EXP	G	.	.	5250	5911	6497	5334	5872	8812	8639	9670
	BAL		.	.	1444	1670	2196	1020	2217	3772	2193	3086
Kyrgyzstan	IMP	S	.	.	522	838	709	842	615	559	472	592
Kirghizistan	EXP	S	.	.	409	505	604	514	463	511	480	488
	BAL		.	.	-113	-332	-105	-328	-152	-48	9	-104
Tajikistan	IMP	G	.	.	810	668	750	711	664	675	688	721
Tadjikistan	EXP	G	.	.	749	770	746	597	689	784	652	737
	BAL		.	.	-61	102	-5	-114	25	109	-36	16
Turkmenistan	IMP	G	.	.	777	...	...	...	...	...	...	...
Turkménistan	EXP	G	.	.	1939	...	...	...	...	...	...	...
	BAL		.	.	1162	...	...	...	...	...	...	...
Uzbekistan	IMP	G	.	.	2893	4721	4523	3289	3111	2947	3137	2712
Ouzbékistan	EXP	G	.	.	3720	4590	4388	3528	3236	3265	3265	2988
	BAL		.	.	827	-131	-136	240	125	317	128	276
Devlpd. econ.: Oceania	IMP		31049	49734	72138	76932	77098	73768	80039	81663	73192	82764
Eco. dévlpés.: Océanie	EXP		27491	47362	63658	71441	73814	64605	65116	73370	73068	74409
	BAL		-3558	-2372	-8480	-5490	-3285	-9163	-14923	-8293	-124	-8355
Australia	IMP	G	25900	42024	61283	65428	65892	64630	69158	71537	63890	72679
Australie	EXP	G	22613	39760	53115	60300	62910	55893	56080	63878	63389	65037
	BAL		-3287	-2265	-8167	-5128	-2982	-8737	-13078	-7659	-501	-7643

Special Table A

Total imports and exports by regions and countries or areas

Imports CIF, exports FOB and balance: million U.S. dollars *[cont.]*

Importations et exportations totales par régions et pays ou zones

Importations CIF, exportations FOB et balance: en millions de dollars E.-U. *[suite]*

Country or Area - Pays ou Zone	IMP EXP BAL	G/ S	1985	1990	1995	1996	1997	1998	1999	2000	2001	2002
New Zealand	IMP	G	5993	9501	13958	14724	14519	12496	14299	13906	13347	15077
Nouvelle-Zélande	EXP	G	5722	9394	13645	14362	14216	12069	12454	13272	13724	14364
	BAL		-271	-107	-312	-362	-303	-427	-1844	-634	377	-713
Devlpg. econ.: Océanie[3]	IMP		**3463**	**5099**	**6844**	**7380**	**7424**	**7222**	**7491**	**7455**	**7590**	**8064**
Eco. evdd.: Océanie[3]	EXP		**1844**	**2809**	**5800**	**5652**	**5237**	**4669**	**5169**	**5359**	**4790**	**4597**
	BAL		**-1619**	**-2290**	**-1044**	**-1727**	**-2186**	**-2553**	**-2322**	**-2097**	**-2800**	**-3467**
American Samoa[3,4]	IMP	S	296	360	...	...	...	...	...	...	...	...
Samoa américaines[3,4]	EXP	S	202	311	...	...	...	...	...	...	...	...
	BAL		-94	-50	...	...	...	...	...	...	...	...
Cook Islands	IMP	G	25	52	49	43	48	38	41	50	47	46
Iles Cook	EXP	G	3	5	5	3	3	3	4	9	7	5
	BAL		-22	-47	-44	-40	-45	-35	-38	-41	-40	-41
Fiji	IMP	G	442	758	892	987	965	721	903	830	794	898
Fidji	EXP	G	236	613	619	749	619	510	609	585	537	550
	BAL		-205	-145	-273	-239	-346	-211	-294	-246	-257	-348
French Polynesia	IMP	S	549	929	1019	1016	936	1096	927	974	1108	...
Polynésie française	EXP	S	41	111	196	251	222	248	253	222	204	...
	BAL		-508	-818	-823	-765	-714	-847	-674	-753	-904	...
Kiribati[5]	IMP	G	15	27	35	38	39	33	41	40	...	...
Kiribati[5]	EXP	G	4	3	7	5	6	6	9	6	...	...
	BAL		-11	-24	-28	-33	-33	-27	-32	-33	...	...
Marshall Is	IMP	G	.	.	75	72	58	67	...	68	...	...
Iles Marshall	EXP	G	.	.	23	18	28	6	8	7	...	...
	BAL		.	.	-52	-54	-30	-62	...	-61	...	...
Micronesia	IMP	S	.	.	100	84	...	49	12	...	...	...
Micronésie	EXP	S	.	.	43	14	...	...	...	...	...	...
	BAL		.	.	-56	-70	...	...	...	...	...	...
N.Mariana Is	IMP	G	.	.	628	...	...	...	...	...	...	...
Iles Mariannes septentrionales	EXP	G	.	.	941	...	...	1000	...	...	...	...
	BAL		.	.	313	...	...	...	...	...	...	...
New Caledonia	IMP	S	348	877	967	1001	928	938	1009	925	977	...
Nouvelle-Calédonie	EXP	S	271	446	570	554	542	382	468	606	465	...
	BAL		-78	-431	-397	-447	-386	-555	-541	-319	-512	...
Niue	IMP	G	2	4	...	...	...	...	...	...	...	...
Nuie	EXP	G	0	0	...	...	...	...	...	...	...	...
	BAL		-2	-4	...	...	...	...	...	...	...	...
Palau	IMP	S	.	.	60	72	69	66	78	123	...	...
Palaos	EXP	S	.	.	14	14	12	11	11	...	...	...
	BAL		.	.	-47	-58	-57	-55	-67	...	...	...
Papua New Guinea	IMP	G	1008	1192	1452	1741	1709	1240	1236	1151	1073	1103
Popouasie-Nouvelle-Guinée	EXP	G	928	1177	2654	2531	2160	1772	1927	2096	1813	1549
	BAL		-80	-15	1202	789	451	532	691	945	740	446
Samoa	IMP	S	51	81	95	100	97	97	115	106	130	113
Samoa	EXP	S	16	9	9	10	15	15	20	14	16	14
	BAL		-35	-72	-86	-90	-82	-82	-95	-92	-115	-99
Solomon Islands	IMP	S	83	91	154	151	183	150	...	...	...	...
Iles Salomon	EXP	S	70	70	168	162	174	126	...	...	...	...
	BAL		-13	-21	14	11	-10	-24	...	...	...	...

Special Table A

Total imports and exports by regions and countries or areas

Imports CIF, exports FOB and balance: million U.S. dollars *[cont.]*

Importations et exportations totales par régions et pays ou zones

Importations CIF, exportations FOB et balance: en millions de dollars E.-U. *[suite]*

Country or Area - Pays ou Zone	IMP EXP BAL	G/S	1985	1990	1995	1996	1997	1998	1999	2000	2001	2002
Tonga	IMP	G	41	62	77	75	73	69	73	69	73	...
Tonga	EXP	G	5	12	15	13	10	8	12	9	7	...
	BAL		-36	-50	-63	-61	-63	-61	-60	-61	-66	...
Tuvalu	IMP	G	2	...	...	...	...	...	...	...	...	...
Tuvalu	EXP	G	0	...	...	...	...	...	...	...	...	...
	BAL		-2	...	...	...	...	...	...	...	...	...
Vanuatu	IMP	G	70	96	95	97	94	88	96	89	...	...
Vanuatu	EXP	G	31	19	28	30	35	34	26	26	...	...
	BAL		-39	-77	-67	-67	-59	-54	-70	-63	...	...
Wallis Fut.I	IMP	S	...	...	14	...	...	...	...	...	...	...
Wallis et Fut.	EXP	S	...	...	0	...	...	...	...	...	...	...
	BAL		...	...	-13	...	...	...	...	...	...	...
Additional Country Groupings												
ANCOM	IMP		16691	18385	39726	36936	45310	46162	35992	40559	45329	42185
ANCO	EXP		22583	31177	39769	45570	45864	39087	44068	57959	49662	52878
	BAL		5892	12793	44	8634	553	-7075	8076	17399	4333	10693
APEC	IMP		782755	1315942	2198779	2329501	2451731	2275662	2500086	3020207	2819943	2912322
CEA	EXP		714497	1247690	2143210	2215152	2368475	2266380	2414351	2824772	2595750	2667605
	BAL		-68259	-68251	-55569	-114348	-83255	-9282	-85735	-195435	-224192	-244716
CARICOM	IMP		5770	6908	9423	10294	12060	12267	12171	13059	13478	13431
CARICOM	EXP		4586	4623	5457	5478	6054	5418	6231	7801	7484	6875
	BAL		-1184	-2285	-3966	-4816	-6006	-6848	-5941	-5258	-5993	-6556
CIS	IMP		...	...	79668	85369	93755	80740	61211	71219	82994	89005
CEI	EXP		...	...	110053	120832	122966	103128	102501	143469	142719	152493
	BAL		...	...	30385	35462	29211	22389	41290	72250	59725	63489
COMESA	IMP		19635	29794	26552	30664	31458	36963	36261	34625	34013	33942
COMESA	EXP		11769	16872	16446	16649	16651	17748	19794	22321	21896	23279
	BAL		-7866	-12922	-10106	-14015	-14807	-19215	-16467	-12303	-12117	-10662
LDCs	IMP		16584	23244	29479	33187	34604	37236	38356	40278	41418	42514
PMA	EXP		11364	15672	20386	21581	21869	22356	25043	30072	30587	31761
	BAL		-5220	-7573	-9094	-11606	-12735	-14880	-13313	-10206	-10831	-10753
MERCOSUR	IMP		19355	29295	79554	86882	102272	98336	82349	89427	83720	62337
MERCOSUR	EXP		35248	46418	70499	74998	83179	81366	74322	84590	87816	88979
	BAL		15893	17123	-9055	-11884	-19093	-16971	-8027	-4836	4096	26642
NAFTA	IMP		442807	654264	959239	1029419	1147601	1210558	1350497	1588750	1489591	1514190
NAFTA	EXP		327868	537378	808469	869940	956349	953704	1011202	1140275	1069586	1028070
	BAL		-114939	-116885	-150770	-159479	-191252	-256854	-339295	-448475	-420006	-486120
OECD	IMP		1438444	2683030	3679358	3856899	3964983	4033014	4246851	4737432	4530283	4659241
OCDE	EXP		1350448	2555140	3696019	3814377	3925354	3967235	4044843	4354445	4217259	4358983
	BAL		-87996	-127890	16661	-42521	-39630	-65779	-202008	-382987	-313024	-300257
OPEC	IMP		97817	115966	151323	151025	164673	149291	145849	167383	175738	173195
OPEP	EXP		148373	187442	209060	241153	251439	207604	254764	352094	306092	306215
	BAL		50556	71475	57737	90128	86767	58312	108915	184711	130355	133021
EU-15[35]	IMP		.	.	.	.	.	.	829780	950433	920531	931745
UE-15[35]	EXP		.	.	.	.	.	.	808092	866124	881834	939448
	BAL		.	.	.	.	.	.	-21688	-84309	-38697	7703

Special Table A

Total imports and exports by regions and countries or areas

Imports CIF, exports FOB and balance: million U.S. dollars *[cont.]*

Importations et exportations totales par régions et pays ou zones

Importations CIF, exportations FOB et balance: en millions de dollars E.-U. *[suite]*

Country or Area - Pays ou Zone	IMP EXP BAL	G/S	1985	1990	1995	1996	1997	1998	1999	2000	2001	2002
Memorandum Items												
World excluding intra-EU trade	IMP		.	.	.	.	.	.	**4202383**	**4937738**	**4707077**	**4848151**
as percent of World total	IMP		.	.	.	.	.	.	**76**	**79**	**79**	**78**
Monde excl. le intra-UE com.	EXP		.	.	.	.	.	.	**4038226**	**4690836**	**4444802**	**4621223**
comme pour cent du Monde	EXP		.	.	.	.	.	.	**75**	**77**	**76**	**76**
	BAL		.	.	.	.	.	.	**-164157**	**-246903**	**-262275**	**-226928**

Special Table A
Total imports and exports by regions and countries or areas
Imports C.I.F., exports F.O.B. and balance: million U.S. dollars *[cont.]*

Importations et exportations totales par régions et pays ou zones
Importations C.I.F., exportations F.O.B., et balance: en millions de dollars E.-U. *[suite]*

General note: System: G=General trade; S=Special trade.

World imports and exports are the sum of imports and exports of Developed economies, Developing economies and Other. The regional totals for exports and imports have been adjusted to exclude the re-exports of countries or areas comprising each region. Estimates for certain countries or areas not shown separately as well as for those shown separately but for which no data are yet available are included in the regional and world totals. Regional totals containing data are printed in bold.
Export and import values in terms of U.S. dollars are derived by the United Nations Statistics Division (UNSD) from data published in national publications, or from data on the Monthly Bulletin of Statistics Questionnaires for the following countries: American Samoa, Angola, Bermuda, Brunei Darussalam, Cayman Is., Cook Is, Cuba, Faeroe Is., French Guiana, French Polynesia, Greenland, Guinea, Iraq, Kiribati, Montserrat, Netherland Antilles, New Caledonia, Russian Federation (beginning 1994), St. Kitts-Nevis, St. Pierre Miquelon, Turkmenistan, Uzbekistan, and Yugoslavia.
Export and import dollar values for all other countries are derived from data published by the International Monetary Fund (IMF) in the International Financial Statistics publication.

1 United States, Canada, Developed Economies of Europe, Israel, Japan, Australia, New Zealand and South Africa.

2 This classification is intended for statistical convenience and does not, necessarily, express a judgement about the stage reached by a particular country in the development process.

3 See footnote in French for "evdd".

4 Comprises Eastern Europe and the European countries of the former USSR.

5 Imports FOB.

6 Including the trade of the U.S. Virgin Islands and Puerto Rico but excluding shipments of merchandise between the United States and its other possessions (Guam, American Samoa, etc.). Data include imports and exports of non-monetary gold.

7 Trade data include maquiladoras and exclude goods from customs-bonded warehouses. Total exports include revaluation and exports of silver.

8 Beginning 1990, trade statistics exclude certain oil and chemical products.

9 Export and import values exclude trade in the processing zone.

10 Beginning 1997, trade data for France include the import and export values of French Guiana, Guadeloupe, Martinique, and Reunion.

11 Prior to 1986, includes Aruba.

12 Exports include re-exports and petroleum products.

13 Economic Union of Belgium and Luxembourg. Intertrade

Note générale: Système: Le commerce de G=General; Le commerce de S=Special.

Les importations et les exportations du monde sont la somme les importations et les exportations des économies développées, d'économies se développantes et d'autre. Les totaux régionaux de pour des exportations et des importations ont été ajustés pour exclure les réexportations les pays ou les secteurs comportant chaque région. Des évaluations pour certains pays ou secteurs non montrés séparément comme pour ceux montrés séparément mais pour ce qui n'est aucune donnée pourtant disponible sont incluses dans les totaux régionaux et du monde. Des totaux régionaux contenant des données sont imprimés dans "bold". Des valeurs d'exportation et d'importation en termes de dollars des E.U.sont dérivées par la Division de statistiques des Nations Unies (DSMU) des données éditées en publications nationales, ou des données sur le bulletin mensuel des questionnaires de statistiques pour les pays suivants: Les Samoa Américaines, Angola, les Bermudes,Brunei Darussalam, Iles Caïmanes, Iles Cook, le Cuba, la Fédération Russe (commençant 1994), Iles Féroé, la Guyane Française, Guinée, le Groenland, l'Irak, le Kiribati, le Montserrat, Netherland Antilles, Nouvelle Calédonie, la Polynésie Française, St. Kitts-Nevis, St. Pierre Miquelon, Turkmenistan, Uzbekistan, et Yougoslavie.
Des valeurs du dollar d'exportation et d'importation pour tous autres pays sont dérivées des données éditées par le Fonds monétaire international (FMI) dans la publication "Statistiques Financière Internationales".

1 Etats-Unis, Canada, pays a économie développés d'Europe, Israël, Japon, Australie, Nouvelle-Zélande et l'Afrique du Sud.

2 Cette classification est utilisée pour plus de commodité dans la présentation des statistiques et n'implique pas nécessairement un jugement quant au stade de développement auquel est parvenu un pays donné.

3 En voie de développement.

4 Compris de l'Europe l'Est et les pays européennes de l'ancienne URSS.

5 Importations FOB.

6 Y compris le commerce des Iles Vierges américaines et de Porto Rico mais non compris les échanges de marchandise, entre les Etats-Unis et leurs autres possessions (Guam, Samoa americaines, etc.). Les données comprennent les importations et exportations d'or non-monétaire.

7 Les statistiques du commerce extérieur comprennent maquiladoras et ne comprennent pas les marchandises provenant des entrepôts en douane. Les exportations comprennent la réevaluation et les données sur les exportations d'argent.

8 A compter de 1990, les statistiques commerciales font exclusion de certains produits pétroliers et chimiques.

9 Les valeurs à l'exportation et à l'importation excluent le commerce de la zone de transformation.

10 A compter de 1997, les valeurs de commerce pour la France comprennent les valeurs des importations et des exportations de la Guyane française, la Guadeloupe, la Martinique, et la Réunion.

11 Avant 1986, comprend Aruba.

12 Exportations comprennent re-exportations et produits pétroliers.

13 L'Union économique belgo-luxembourgeoise. Non compris

between the two countries is excluded. Beginning January 1997, data refer to Belgium only and include trade between Belgium and Luxembourg.

14 Prior to January 1991, excludes trade conducted in accordance with the supplementary protocol to the treaty on the basis of relations between the Federal Republic of Germany and the former German Democratic Republic.

15 Prior to 1991, data refers to the Federal Republic of Germany. See explanatory notes pertaining to Germany on page v.

16 Prior to 1997, included under Belgium. See also footnote for Belgium.

17 See explanatory notes on data pertaining to Yugoslavia on page vi.

18 See explanatory notes pertaining to Czechoslovakia on page vi.

19 Beginning 1989, data exclude re-exports.

20 Prior to 1996 data exclude customs free zones, repairs on goods, and operational leasing.

21 Beginning January 1994, foreign trade statistics exclude re-exports.

22 Exports include gold.

23 Beginning in January 1998, foreign trade data refer to South Africa only, excluding intra-trade of the Southern African Common Customs Area. Prior to January 1998, trade data refer to the Southern African Common Customs Area, which includes Botswana, Lesotho, Namibia, South Africa and Swaziland.

24 Imports exclude petroleum imported without stated value. Exports cover domestic exports.

25 Year ending June 30 through 1994. Year ending December 31 thereafter.

26 Imports and exports net of returned goods. The figures also exclude Judea and Samaria and the Gaza area.

27 Data include Armenia, Azerbaijan, Georgia, Kazakhstan, Kyrgyzstan, Tajikistan, Turkmenistan, and Uzbekistan.

28 See explanatory notes on data pertaining to Yemen on page v.

29 Year ending 20 March of the years stated.

30 Data include oil and gas.. The value of oil exports and total exports are rough estimates based on information published in various petroleum industry journals.

31 Data refer to total exports less petroleum exports of Asia Middle East countries where petroleum, in this case, is the sum of SITC groups 333, 334 and 335.

32 Data for China exclude those for Hong Kong SAR, Macao SAR and Taiwan Province of China.

33 See explanatory notes pertaining to Hong Kong SAR and Macao SAR on page v.

34 Year ending 30 September of the years stated.

35 Excluding intra-EU trade.

le commerce entre ces pays. A partir de janvier 1997, les données se rapportent à Belgique seulement et recouvrent les échanges entre la Belgique et le Luxembourg

14 Avant janvier 1991, non compris le commerce effectué en accord avec le protocole additionnel au traité définissant la base des relations entre la République Fédérale d'Allemagne et l'ancienne République Démocratique Allemande.

15 Avant 1991, les données se rapportent à la République Fédérale d'Allemagne. Voir les notes explicatives concerner l'Allemagne à la page vii.

16 Avant 1997, inclus sous la Belgique. Voir également l'apostille pour la Belgique.

17 Voir les notes explicatives sur les données concernant Yougoslavie à la page viii.

18 Voir les notes explicatives sur les données concernant Tchécoslovaquie à la page viii.

19 A compter 1989, les données non compris les réexportations.

20 Avant de 1996 les données excluent des zones franches, des réparations sur des marchandises, et le crédit-bail opérationnel.

21 A compter de janvier 1994, les statistiques du commerce exterieur non compris les réexportations.

22 Les exportations comprennent l'or.

23 A compter de janvier 1998, les données sur le commerce extérieur ne se rapportent qu'à l'Afrique du Sud. et ne tiennent pas compte des échanges commerciaux entre les pays de l'Union douanière de l'Afrique du Sud. qui incluait l'Afrique du Sud, Botswana, Lesotho, Namibie, et Swaziland.

24 Non compris le petrole brute dont la valeur des importations ne sont pas stipulée. Les exportations sont les exportations d'intérieur.

25 Année finissant juin 30 à 1994. Année finissant décembre 31 ensuite.

26 Importations et exportations nets, ne comprennant pas les marchandises retournées. Sont également exclues les données de la Judée et de Samaria et ainsi que la zone de Gaza.

27 Données compris Arménie, Azerbaïdjan, Géorgie, Kazakhstan, Kirghizistan, Ouzbékistan, Tadjikistan et Turkménistan.

28 Voir les notes explicatives sur les données concernant Yemen à la page vii.

29 Année finissant le 20 mars de l'année indiquée.

30 Les données comprennent le pétrole et le gaz. La valeur des exportations de pétrole et des exportations totales sont des évaluations grossières basées sur l'information pubilée à divers journaux d'industrie de pétrole.

31 Les données se rapportent aux exportations totales moins les exportations pétrolières de moyen-orient d'Asie. Dans ce cas, le pétrole est la somme des groupes CTCI 333, 334 et 335.

32 Non compris les données pour la Hong-Kong RAS, Macao RAS, et province chinoise de Taiwan.

33 Voir les notes explicatives concernant Hong-Kong RAS et Macao RAS à la page v.

34 Année finissant le 30 septembre de l'année indiquée.

35 Non compris le commerce de l'intra-UE.

Special Table B

Total imports and exports by countries and areas

Imports CIF, exports FOB and balance: million of national currency

Importations et exportations totales par pays ou zone

Importations CIF, exportations FOB et balance: en millions de monnaie nationale

Country or Area - Pays ou Zone	IMP EXP BAL	G/S	1985	1990	1995	1996	1997	1998	1999	2000	2001	2002
Albania	IMP	G	3176	3797	66145	87995	95021	124337	157424	157218	190696	210436
Albanie	EXP	G	2665	2273	18712	21603	21044	30656	36369	37547	43771	46193
leks	BAL		-511	-1524	-47433	-66392	-73977	-93681	-121055	-119671	-146925	-164243
Algeria	IMP	S	49491	88895	487586	498325	501598	552359	610673	...	...	...
Algérie	EXP	S	64564	116693	489003	740811	791767	599903	...	...	...	...
dinars	BAL		15073	27797	1417	242486	290169	47544	...	...	...	...
Antigua and Barbuda[1]	IMP	G	302	688	933	...	...	...	...	...	...	...
Antigua-et-Barbuda[1]	EXP	G	36	56	143	...	...	...	...	...	...	...
EC dollars	BAL		-266	-632	-790	...	...	...	...	...	...	...
Australia	IMP	G	37054	53785	82673	83543	88884	102905	107154	123461	123539	133424
Australie	EXP	G	32408	50892	71657	76978	84786	88977	86895	110464	122664	119483
dollars	BAL		-4646	-2893	-11016	-6565	-4098	-13928	-20259	-12997	-875	-13941
Austria[2]	IMP	S	430969	556234	668031	712760	790251	842128	65316	74935	78657	76140
Autriche[2]	EXP	S	353965	466067	580014	612190	715017	774738	60266	69692	74451	77006
euros	BAL		-77004	-90167	-88017	-100570	-75234	-67390	-5050	-5243	-4206	866
Bahamas[3]	IMP	G	3078	1112	1243	1366	1666	1873	1772	1764	1742	1614
Bahamas[3]	EXP	G	2728	238	176	180	181	300	532	805	649	617
dollars	BAL		-349	-874	-1067	-1186	-1484	-1573	-1240	-959	-1093	-997
Bahrain	IMP	G	1168	1396	1397	1607	1514	1341	1390	1742	1619	1875
Bahreïn	EXP	G	1089	1414	1546	1768	1648	1230	1640	2329	2097	2019
dinars	BAL		-79	18	149	161	135	-111	250	587	478	144
Bangladesh	IMP	G	70867	124880	261878	276838	302942	327575	377496	436450	465607	458119
Bangladesh	EXP	G	27997	57885	127782	137944	166087	179614	192571	249860	269150	264295
taka	BAL		-42870	-66995	-134096	-138894	-136855	-147961	-184925	-186590	-196457	-193824
Barbados	IMP	G	1222	1408	1541	1667	1991	2020	2216	2312	2173	2078
Barbade	EXP	G	713	430	478	561	566	503	528	545	519	413
dollars	BAL		-508	-978	-1063	-1106	-1425	-1516	-1689	-1767	-1655	-1666
Belgium[2,4]	IMP	S	3317800	4011600	4701990	5065770	5619160	5879960	154630	192190	199490	207550
Belgique[2,4]	EXP	S	3167700	3944500	5177780	5430210	6142850	6441990	168090	203950	212540	226180
euros	BAL		-150100	-67100	475790	364440	523690	562030	13460	11760	13050	18630
Belize	IMP	G	256	423	514	511	572	590	739	905	1001	1041
Belize	EXP	G	179	266	323	335	353	344	372	370	347	361
dollars	BAL		-77	-157	-191	-176	-219	-246	-367	-535	-654	-681
Benin[5,6]	IMP	S	148777	72193	372200	334700	397900	434000	464580	433300	441300	458900
Bénin[5,6]	EXP	S	67348	33254	209600	334700	243400	240400	259500	279400	273900	261400
CFA francs	BAL		-81429	-38939	-162600	0	-154500	-193600	-205080	-153900	-167400	-197500
Bhutan	IMP	G	927	1368	3642	4525	4978	5516	7835	9049	...	...
Bhoutan	EXP	G	272	1192	3349	3554	4274	4456	4988	5425	...	...
ngultrum	BAL		-655	-176	-293	-971	-704	-1061	-2847	-3624	...	...
Bosnia Herzegovina	IMP	S	.	.	...	...	...	5120	6048	6582	7062	8368
Bosnie-Herzégovine	EXP	S	.	.	...	...	...	1043	1375	2265	2370	2099
marka	BAL		.	.	...	...	...	-4077	-4673	-4317	-4692	-6269
Botswana	IMP	G	.	.	.	.	.	9804	10164	12647	10557	...
Botswana	EXP	G	.	.	.	.	.	8697	12228	13835	14307	...
pula	BAL		.	.	.	.	.	-1107	2063	1188	3750	...
Brunei Darussalam	IMP	S	1348	1813	2960	3516	3258	2598	...	...	...	...
Brunéi Darussalam	EXP	S	6533	4010	3402	3498	3649	3443	...	...	...	...
dollars	BAL		5185	2197	443	-18	391	845	...	...	...	...

Special Table B

Total imports and exports by countries and areas

Imports CIF, exports FOB and balance: million of national currency *[cont.]*

Importations et exportations totales par pays ou zone

Importations CIF, exportations FOB et balance: en millions de monnaie nationale *[suite]*

Country or Area - Pays ou Zone	IMP EXP BAL	G/S	1985	1990	1995	1996	1997	1998	1999	2000	2001	2002
Bulgaria[7]	IMP	S	14	10	380	892	8268	8709	10053	13857	15897	16451
Bulgarie[7]	EXP	S	14	11	360	860	8281	7391	7303	10247	11176	11858
leva	BAL		0	0	-20	-32	13	-1318	-2750	-3610	-4721	-4593
Burkina Faso[5,6]	IMP	G	146243	145833	227000	330963	342353	430334	418500	437300	481200	510400
Burkina Faso[5,6]	EXP	G	31157	41282	138000	119043	133619	190440	156200	146400	168800	164200
CFA francs	BAL		-115086	-104551	-89000	-211920	-208734	-239894	-262300	-290900	-312400	-346200
Burundi	IMP	S	22435	39371	58186	37332	43250	70274	66308	106059	115249	121028
Burundi	EXP	S	13522	12774	25982	11372	30767	28635	30971	35223	31978	28867
francs	BAL		-8913	-26597	-32204	-25960	-12483	-41639	-35337	-70836	-83271	-92161
Cameroon[5,6]	IMP	S	508756	381150	598709	627424	793930	881782	811226	...	...	...
Cameroun[5,6]	EXP	S	321751	545106	824276	904871	1084510	985827	985492	...	...	...
CFA francs	BAL		-187005	163956	225567	277447	290580	104045	174266	...	...	...
Canada[8]	IMP	G	110130	140329	224977	232672	271422	298076	319008	354728	343311	348198
Canada[8]	EXP	G	124249	148912	263697	274884	296928	317903	354108	410994	402172	396020
dollars	BAL		14119	8583	38720	42212	25506	19827	35100	56266	58861	47822
Cape Verde	IMP	G	7663	9495	19394	19355	21936	22395	25484	27517	28694	...
Cap-Vert	EXP	G	524	398	686	1046	1309	1024	1185	1272	1212	...
escudos	BAL		-7139	-9097	-18708	-18309	-20627	-21371	-24299	-26245	-27482	...
Cayman Islands	IMP	G	123	240	333	315	...	...	...	...	...	...
Iles Caïmanes	EXP	G	2	3	3	2	...	...	...	...	...	...
dollars	BAL		-121	-237	-329	-313	...	...	...	...	...	...
Cent. Afr. Rep.[5,6]	IMP	S	50686	42050	86900	72300	82039	86375	80689	83290	78464	...
Rép. centrafricaine[5,6]	EXP	S	41217	32770	85300	75100	94850	89309	90136	114414	104299	...
CFA francs	BAL		-9469	-9280	-1600	2800	12811	2934	9447	31124	25835	...
Chad[5,6]	IMP	S	74708	77742	182400	169733	194732	210207	194523	225700	454600	694700
Tchad[5,6]	EXP	S	27781	51202	121273	121895	138130	154455	124138	130200	138300	132000
CFA francs	BAL		-46927	-26540	-61127	-47838	-56602	-55752	-70385	-95500	-316300	-562700
Comoros	IMP	S	16481	14041	23411	...	...	...	...	...	...	...
Comores	EXP	S	7048	4883	4236	...	...	...	...	...	...	...
francs	BAL		-9433	-9158	-19175	...	...	...	...	...	...	...
Congo	IMP	S	268697	169023	334183	793306	540647	401288	505215	330939	...	...
Congo	EXP	S	488515	267100	585300	688100	973700	806900	960500	1772200	...	...
francs	BAL		219818	98077	251117	-105206	433053	405612	455285	1441261	...	...
Cook Islands	IMP	G	50	86	74	63	72	71	79	112	112	102
Iles Cook	EXP	G	6	8	7	5	4	6	7	20	16	11
NZ dollars	BAL		-43	-78	-67	-58	-68	-65	-72	-92	-95	-91
Cote d'Ivoire[5,6]	IMP	S	772980	571100	1463000	1484500	1623100	1973770	1975000	1982900	1930300	2636600
Côte d'Ivoire[5,6]	EXP	S	1318060	836430	1899700	2274400	2598100	2717600	2870100	2768200	2892700	3601000
CFA francs	BAL		545080	265330	436700	789900	975000	743830	895100	785300	962400	964400
Cuba	IMP	S	8758	6745	2805	3205	...	...	...	...	...	...
Cuba	EXP	S	6531	4910	1625	2015	...	...	...	...	...	...
pesos	BAL		-2227	-1835	-1180	-1190	...	...	...	...	...	...
Cyprus	IMP	G	762	1279	1670	1858	1877	1905	1971	2402	2537	2485
Chypre	EXP	G	291	436	556	649	640	551	543	592	629	515
pounds	BAL		-472	-843	-1115	-1208	-1237	-1354	-1428	-1810	-1908	-1970
Czech Rep[8]	IMP	S	.	.	670445	752343	861770	926559	973169	1241920	1386320	1326340
République. tchèque[8]	EXP	S	.	.	574722	594630	722501	850240	908756	1121100	1269630	1250440
koruny	BAL		.	.	-95723	-157713	-139269	-76319	-64413	-120820	-116690	-75900

Special Table B

Total imports and exports by countries and areas

Imports CIF, exports FOB and balance: million of national currency *[cont.]*

Importations et exportations totales par pays ou zone

Importations CIF, exportations FOB et balance: en millions de monnaie nationale *[suite]*

Country or Area - Pays ou Zone	IMP EXP BAL	G/S	1985	1990	1995	1996	1997	1998	1999	2000	2001	2002
Denmark	IMP	S	191562	198782	252344	257655	290648	303705	307478	353797	361146	375191
Danemark	EXP	S	179578	216444	278515	290543	315001	317423	339896	403044	421830	438368
kroner	BAL		-11984	17662	26171	32888	24353	13718	32418	49247	60684	63177
Djibouti	IMP	G	35670	38174	31395	31805	26322	28120	27131	...	...	...
Djibouti	EXP	G	2488	4420	2414	2439	1917	2195	2168	...	...	...
francs	BAL		-33182	-33754	-28981	-29366	-24405	-25925	-24963	...	...	...
Dominica	IMP	S	149	318	317	351	336	357	373	400	354	311
Dominique	EXP	S	77	149	122	138	143	167	150	145	117	113
EC dollars	BAL		-73	-170	-195	-212	-193	-190	-223	-256	-237	-198
Egypt[9]	IMP	S	7773	24823	39892	44218	44769	54771	54399	48645	50660	56480
Egypte[9]	EXP	S	2600	6954	11704	12004	13286	10606	12086	16274	16343	21184
pounds	BAL		-5173	-17869	-28188	-32214	-31483	-44165	-42313	-32371	-34317	-35297
Equatorial Guinea[5,6]	IMP	G	8947	16586	24897	149384	192800	187167	261784	320800	...	...
Guinée équatoriale[5,6]	EXP	G	7441	16996	42683	89682	289204	258957	436735	780819	...	...
CFA francs	BAL		-1506	410	17786	-59702	96404	71790	174951	460019	...	...
Eritrea	IMP	G	.	.	...	3063	3062	2702	3129	...	...	...
Erythrée	EXP	G	.	.	...	520	375	197	164	...	...	...
nakfa	BAL		.	.	...	-2543	-2687	-2505	-2965	...	...	...
Estonia[10]	IMP	G	.	.	29101	38887	61610	64897	60248	72309	75163	79467
Estonie[10]	EXP	G	.	.	21040	25024	40662	43952	43178	53324	57528	56920
krooni	BAL		.	.	-8061	-13863	-20948	-20945	-17070	-18985	-17635	-22547
Ethiopia	IMP	G	2056	2239	7053	8899	...	...	10515	...	...	...
Ethiopie	EXP	G	689	616	2603	2651	3941	3966	...	...	...	...
birr	BAL		-1367	-1623	-4450	-6249	...	...	...	...	...	...
EU-15[11]	IMP		.	.	.	.	.	.	779825	1032859	1027955	986893
UE-15[11]	EXP		.	.	.	.	.	.	760192	941940	985326	993863
euros	BAL		.	.	.	.	.	.	-19633	-90919	-42629	6969
Faeroe Islands	IMP	G	2631	2084	1759	2147	2363	2592	3281	4306	4147	...
Iles Féroé	EXP	G	1899	2578	2026	2417	2567	2908	3264	3821	4279	...
D kroner	BAL		-732	494	267	270	204	316	-17	-485	132	...
Fiji	IMP	G	508	1119	1254	1384	1393	1434	1779	1756	1808	1953
Fidji	EXP	G	271	901	870	1050	897	1016	1201	1244	1224	1195
dollars	BAL		-237	-218	-384	-335	-496	-418	-578	-513	-584	-758
Finland[2]	IMP	G	81350	103066	122428	134422	154681	172315	29691	36837	35845	35611
Finlande[2]	EXP	G	83976	101380	172380	176592	204202	229233	39306	49485	47768	47245
euros	BAL		2626	-1686	49952	42170	49521	56918	9614	12647	11923	11634
Fm Czechoslovakia[8,12]	IMP	G	191137	238202	.	.	.	.	.	.	.	.
L'ex-Tchécoslovaquie[8,12]	EXP	G	197274	215257	.	.	.	.	.	.	.	.
koruny	BAL		6137	-22945	.	.	.	.	.	.	.	.
Fm German D.R.[8,13]	IMP	G	86701	...	.	.	.	.	.	.	.	.
L'ex-Allemagne rép. dem. du[8,13]	EXP	G	93490	...	.	.	.	.	.	.	.	.
GDR marks	BAL		6789	...	.	.	.	.	.	.	.	.
Fm Yemen A.R.[14]	IMP		9501	.	.	.	.	.	.	.	.	.
Fmr Yémen A.R.[14]	EXP		97	.	.	.	.	.	.	.	.	.
rials	BAL		-9404	.	.	.	.	.	.	.	.	.
Fm Yemen Dm[14]	IMP	S	241	.	.	.	.	.	.	.	.	.
FMR Yémen Dm[14]	EXP	S	14	.	.	.	.	.	.	.	.	.
dinars	BAL		-227	.	.	.	.	.	.	.	.	.

Special Table B

Total imports and exports by countries and areas

Imports CIF, exports FOB and balance: million of national currency *[cont.]*

Importations et exportations totales par pays ou zone

Importations CIF, exportations FOB et balance: en millions de monnaie nationale *[suite]*

Country or Area - Pays ou Zone	IMP EXP BAL	G/ S	1985	1990	1995	1996	1997	1998	1999	2000	2001	2002
France[2,15]	IMP	S	967915	1273620	1403800	1441620	1585340	1698018	277020	337570	335780	326840
France[2,15]	EXP	S	906889	1177160	1420270	1471640	1692650	1801060	284120	325640	330830	328290
euros	BAL		-61026	-96460	16470	30020	107310	103042	7100	-11930	-4950	1450
French Guiana[15]	IMP	S	2287	4278	3750	...	.	.	.	.	.	.
Guyane française[15]	EXP	S	337	506	654	...	.	.	.	.	.	.
francs	BAL		-1950	-3773	-3096	...	.	.	.	.	.	.
French Polynesia[16]	IMP	S	88940	91926	91383	94550	99339	116275	103780	126145	140852	...
Polynésie française[16]	EXP	S	6564	11011	17548	23433	23804	26444	28319	28721	25982	...
CFP francs	BAL		-82376	-80915	-73835	-71117	-75535	-89831	-75460	-97424	-114869	...
Gabon[5,6]	IMP	S	384000	250000	440200	489300	644300	650800	518000	708000	629500	...
Gabon[5,6]	EXP	S	876700	600000	1354400	1628700	1765200	1130200	1473800	1753000	1942000	...
CFA francs	BAL		492700	350000	914200	1139400	1120900	479400	955800	1045000	1312500	...
Gambia	IMP	G	362	1482	1741	2528	1774	2605	2187	...	...	...
Gambie	EXP	G	173	245	155	209	150	286	81	...	...	...
dalasis	BAL		-189	-1237	-1586	-2318	-1624	-2319	-2106	...	...	...
Georgia	IMP	G	.	.	507	868	1225	1230	...	...	...	...
Géorgie	EXP	G	.	.	194	251	312	269	...	...	...	...
lari	BAL		.	.	-313	-617	-914	-961	...	...	...	...
Germany[2,13,17]	IMP	S	463810	556084	664233	690397	772326	828285	444797	538343	542772	520600
Allemagne[2,13,17]	EXP	S	537164	660717	749538	788937	888641	954665	510009	597481	638269	648307
euros	BAL		73354	104633	85305	98540	116315	126380	65212	59138	95497	127707
Ghana	IMP	G	47155	...	2288760	3451760	4769410	5932180	9347000	16171000	...	...
Ghana	EXP	G	33185	...	2069660	2732600	3352870	4150730	...	...	...	...
cedis	BAL		-13970	...	-219100	-719160	-1416540	-1781450	...	...	...	...
Gibraltar	IMP		113	...	...	...	...	...	...	...	...	...
Gibraltar	EXP		48	...	...	...	...	...	...	...	...	...
pounds	BAL		-65	...	...	...	...	...	...	...	...	...
Greenland	IMP	G	3140	2756	2431	2719	2625	2740	2856	2947	...	...
Groenland	EXP	G	1842	2795	2081	2141	1937	1702	1932	2205	...	...
D kroner	BAL		-1298	39	-349	-578	-688	-1038	-924	-742	...	...
Grenada[1]	IMP	S	187	287	334	411	468	540	...	...	...	...
Grenade[1]	EXP	S	60	75	59	54	62	73	...	...	...	...
EC dollars	BAL		-127	-212	-275	-357	-407	-468	...	...	...	...
Guadeloupe[15]	IMP	S	5745	8937	9401	...	.	.	.	.	.	.
Guadeloupe[15]	EXP	S	669	649	788	...	.	.	.	.	.	.
francs	BAL		-5076	-8288	-8613	...	.	.	.	.	.	.
Guinea-Bissau[6,18]	IMP	G	...	2882	36990	35240	51800	37000	31200	42000	54400	72380
Guinée-Bissau[6,18]	EXP	G	...	648	12310	11030	28300	15300	31500	44300	46100	37800
CFA francs	BAL		...	-2235	-24680	-24210	-23500	-21700	300	2300	-8300	-34580
Guyana	IMP	S	960	12290	74912	83895	89747	...	...	...	109362	107274
Guyana	EXP	S	706	10208	64581	72598	91809	73336	93138	90830	89593	93938
dollars	BAL		-254	-2082	-10330	-11297	2062	...	...	...	-19769	-13336
Haiti	IMP	G	2208	1661	9866	10448	10792	13366	17367	21936	24746	33061
Haïti	EXP	G	842	801	1666	1414	3537	5365	5661	6725	6701	8203
gourdes	BAL		-1366	-860	-8200	-9034	-7255	-8001	-11706	-15211	-18045	-24858
Hungary[19,20]	IMP	S	410130	544920	1936380	2763900	3961200	5511500	6645600	9064000	9665100	9704100
Hongrie[19,20]	EXP	S	424610	603600	1576100	2392300	3566800	4934500	5938500	7942800	8748200	8873970
forint	BAL		14480	58680	-360280	-371600	-394400	-577000	-707100	-1121200	-916900	-830130

Special Table B

Total imports and exports by countries and areas

Imports CIF, exports FOB and balance: million of national currency *[cont.]*

Importations et exportations totales par pays ou zone

Importations CIF, exportations FOB et balance: en millions de monnaie nationale *[suite]*

Country or Area - Pays ou Zone	IMP EXP BAL	G/S	1985	1990	1995	1996	1997	1998	1999	2000	2001	2002
Iceland	IMP	G	37600	97559	113388	135165	141355	176521	181321	203847	218296	207632
Islande	EXP	G	33826	92624	116613	108977	131228	145008	145132	148516	196803	204078
kronur	BAL		-3774	-4936	3225	-26188	-10127	-31513	-36189	-55331	-21493	-3554
India	IMP	G	196768	413566	1127480	1344060	1505430	1772310	2024180	2316550	2378110	2746720
Inde	EXP	G	113192	314394	994546	1171910	1270700	1379290	1536150	1906530	2044500	2396860
rupees	BAL		-83576	-99172	-132934	-172150	-234730	-393020	-488030	-410020	-333610	-349860
Iraq	IMP		2368	1503	...	...	...	...	...	...	...	...
Iraq	EXP		...	...	...	...	...	...	...	...	...	...
dinars	BAL		...	...	...	...	...	...	...	...	...	...
Ireland[2]	IMP	G	9428	12469	26181	28479	32863	39715	44327	55909	57230	54805
Irlande[2]	EXP	G	9743	14337	35330	38609	44868	57322	66956	83889	92730	92893
euros	BAL		315	1868	9149	10130	12005	17607	22629	27980	35500	38088
Italy[2]	IMP	S	167095001	217704000	335661000	321286000	357587000	378784000	207016	258507	263756	258528
Italie[2]	EXP	S	145887998	203718000	381175000	388885000	409128000	426182000	221040	260414	272990	267842
euros	BAL		-21207003	-13986000	45514000	67599000	51541000	47398000	14024	1907	9234	9314
Jamaica	IMP	G	6147	13923	99418	109687	110932	110926	113472	141987	154526	171201
Jamaïque	EXP	G	3128	8305	49916	51513	48971	47940	48425	55621	56061	53897
dollars	BAL		-3018	-5618	-49502	-58174	-61961	-62986	-65047	-86366	-98465	-117304
Japan	IMP	G	31076000	33854000	31534000	37992000	40956300	36653000	35270000	40915000	42402000	42177000
Japon	EXP	G	41959000	41457000	41531600	44729000	50938100	50644000	47549000	51649000	49010000	52109000
yen	BAL		10883000	7603000	9997600	6737000	9981800	13991000	12279000	10734000	6608000	9932000
Jordan	IMP	G	1074	1726	2590	3044	2908	2714	2635	3259	3435	...
Jordanie	EXP	G	311	706	1241	1288	1301	1278	1299	1347	1626	..
dinars	BAL		-764	-1020	-1349	-1755	-1607	-1437	-1336	-1913	-1809	..
Kenya	IMP	G	23589	50913	155168	168486	190674	193032	198313	236613	250782	255569
Kenya	EXP	G	15725	23697	97284	118226	119960	121252	122067	132183	152712	166635
shillings	BAL		-7864	-27216	-57884	-50260	-70714	-71780	-76246	-104430	-98070	-88934
Kiribati[8]	IMP	G	22	34	48	49	53	52	64	68	...	..
Kiribati[8]	EXP	G	6	4	10	7	8	9	14	11	...	..
Aust. dollars	BAL		-16	-31	-38	-42	-44	-43	-50	-57	...	..
Kuwait	IMP	S	1806	1146	2323	2507	2502	2626	2318	2195	2413	273[illegible]
Koweït	EXP	S	3185	2031	3815	4458	4314	2912	3703	5963	4970	466[illegible]
dinars	BAL		1379	886	1491	1951	1813	285	1385	3767	2556	193[illegible]
Latvia	IMP	S	.	.	960	1278	1582	1881	1724	1934	2202	249[illegible]
Lettonie	EXP	S	.	.	688	795	972	1069	1008	1131	1256	140[illegible]
lati	BAL		.	.	-271	-483	-611	-812	-716	-803	-945	-108[illegible]
Lesotho	IMP	G	.	.	.	.	.	4699	4773	5048	5824	812[illegible]
Lesotho	EXP	G	.	.	.	.	.	1071	1053	1528	2426	385[illegible]
maloti	BAL		.	.	.	.	.	-3628	-3720	-3520	-3398	-426[illegible]
Liberia	IMP	S	284	...	...	...	...	...	...	...	...	..
Libéria	EXP	S	436	...	...	...	...	...	...	...	...	.
dollars	BAL		151	...	...	...	...	...	...	...	...	.
Libyan Arab Jamah.	IMP	G	1214	1511	1729	1915	2139	2204	1929	1911	2660	886
Jamahiriya arabe libyenne	EXP	G	3646	3745	3222	3579	3456	2374	3682	5222	5394	1164
dinars	BAL		2432	2234	1494	1664	1317	170	1754	3310	2734	277
Lithuania	IMP	G	.	.	14594	18235	22577	23174	19338	21826	25413	2856
Lituanie	EXP	G	.	.	10820	13420	15441	14842	12015	15238	18332	2029
litai	BAL		.	.	-3774	-4815	-7136	-8332	-7323	-6588	-7081	-827

Special Table B

Total imports and exports by countries and areas

Imports CIF, exports FOB and balance: million of national currency *[cont.]*

Importations et exportations totales par pays ou zone

Importations CIF, exportations FOB et balance: en millions de monnaie nationale *[suite]*

Country or Area - Pays ou Zone	IMP EXP BAL	G/ S	1985	1990	1995	1996	1997	1998	1999	2000	2001	2002
Luxembourg[2,21]	IMP	S	.	.	.	.	335700	268200	10379	11647	12470	12294
Luxembourg[2,21]	EXP	S	.	.	.	.	250100	286900	7416	8619	9207	9088
euros	BAL		.	.	.	.	-85600	18700	-2964	-3028	-3263	-3206
Madagascar	IMP	S	265915	969540	2333890	2056110	2392160	2790320	2375270	...	...	...
Madagascar	EXP	S	181630	476682	1569390	1215700	1139070	1310000	1382430	...	...	...
francs	BAL		-84285	-492858	-764500	-840410	-1253090	-1480320	-992840	...	...	...
Malawi	IMP	G	506	1572	7255	9545	12848	16431	29696	32283	39480	51653
Malawi	EXP	G	422	1124	6193	7359	8827	13861	19907	23625	31816	34483
kwacha	BAL		-84	-449	-1062	-2186	-4020	-2570	-9789	-8658	-7664	-17170
Malaysia	IMP	G	30438	79119	194345	197280	220936	228124	248478	311459	280691	303502
Malaisie	EXP	G	38017	79646	184987	197026	220890	286563	321560	373270	334420	354407
ringgit	BAL		7579	527	-9358	-254	-46	58439	73082	61811	53729	50905
Mali[5,6]	IMP	S	134540	164020	385400	395170	431200	448800	507300	573500	519700	522700
Mali[5,6]	EXP	S	55560	97680	220500	221410	327700	331100	348600	388130	531600	638700
CFA francs	BAL		-78980	-66340	-164900	-173760	-103500	-117700	-158700	-185370	11900	116000
Malta	IMP	G	354	621	1038	1008	984	1035	1136	1493	1226	1228
Malte	EXP	G	187	358	675	624	629	712	791	1075	881	920
liri	BAL		-167	-263	-363	-384	-355	-323	-345	-418	-346	-307
Martinique[15]	IMP	S	6050	9681	9769	...	.	.	.	.	.	.
Martinique[15]	EXP	S	1456	1512	1112	...	.	.	.	.	.	.
francs	BAL		-4593	-8168	-8658	...	.	.	.	.	.	.
Mauritania	IMP	S	17806	...	...	...	...	...	...	...	...	...
Mauritanie	EXP	S	28887	...	...	...	...	...	...	...	...	...
ouguiyas	BAL		11081	...	...	...	...	...	...	...	...	...
Mauritius	IMP	G	8119	24019	34363	41082	46093	49811	56629	54928	58115	...
Maurice	EXP	G	6729	17677	26756	32312	33694	39634	39160	40882	47138	...
rupees	BAL		-1390	-6342	-7607	-8770	-12399	-10177	-17469	-14046	-10977	...
Montserrat[1]	IMP	S	50	130	...	...	...	...	...	...	...	...
Montserrat[1]	EXP	S	8	4	...	...	...	...	...	...	...	...
EC dollars	BAL		-42	-126	...	...	...	...	...	...	...	...
Morocco	IMP	S	38675	57021	85493	84612	90712	98676	97454	122527	124718	127855
Maroc	EXP	S	21740	35135	58673	60013	67057	68608	72283	73869	80667	85528
dirhams	BAL		-16935	-21886	-26821	-24600	-23656	-30068	-25171	-48658	-44051	-42327
Myanmar	IMP	G	2402	1709	7564	8032	12736	16921	14464	15426	19248	...
Myanmar	EXP	G	2576	2037	4826	4420	5416	6737	7074	10601	15929	...
kyats	BAL		174	328	-2738	-3613	-7320	-10184	-7390	-4826	-3319	...
Namibia	IMP	G	.	.	.	.	.	9112	9834	10755	13319	...
Namibie	EXP	G	.	.	.	.	.	6812	7539	9164	10148	...
dollars	BAL		.	.	.	.	.	-2300	-2295	-1591	-3171	...
Nepal	IMP	G	8267	19729	69028	79247	97974	81901	97057	111800	110362	110552
Népal	EXP	G	2915	5996	17895	21830	23555	31288	41088	57231	55221	44184
rupees	BAL		-5352	-13733	-51133	-57417	-74419	-50613	-55969	-54569	-55141	-66368
Neth. Antilles[22]	IMP	S	2498	3833	3295	4508	3728	...	...	...	...	...
Antilles néer.[22]	EXP	S	1856	3204	2724	2272	2664	...	...	...	...	...
NA guilders	BAL		-642	-629	-571	-2236	-1064	...	...	...	...	...
Netherlands[2]	IMP	S	241587	229708	283538	304559	347286	371760	176115	215459	217631	205021
Pays-Bas[2]	EXP	S	257267	239181	314693	332920	380018	398686	188046	226903	241300	235383
euros	BAL		15680	9473	31155	28361	32732	26926	11931	11444	23669	30362

Special Table B

Total imports and exports by countries and areas

Imports CIF, exports FOB and balance: million of national currency *[cont.]*

Importations et exportations totales par pays ou zone

Importations CIF, exportations FOB et balance: en millions de monnaie nationale *[suite]*

Country or Area - Pays ou Zone	IMP EXP BAL	G/S	1985	1990	1995	1996	1997	1998	1999	2000	2001	2002
New Caledonia[16]	IMP	S	55931	86930	86894	93087	98561	99531	112888	119766	124171	..
Nouvelle-Calédonie[16]	EXP	S	43864	43931	51180	51471	57612	40621	52387	78454	59053	..
CFP francs	BAL		-12067	-42999	-35714	-41616	-40949	-58910	-60501	-41312	-65118	..
New Zealand	IMP	G	12076	15896	21251	21399	21964	23348	27114	30737	31774	32402
Nouvelle-Zélande	EXP	G	11603	15760	20787	20876	21448	22493	23540	29201	32655	30993
dollars	BAL		-472	-136	-464	-523	-516	-855	-3574	-1536	881	-140[illegible]
Niger[5,6]	IMP	S	165935	105851	186501	229271	218067	277886	242480	279794	271000	278800
Niger[5,6]	EXP	S	116538	76939	143800	166300	158500	197000	176600	201500	199700	195000
CFA francs	BAL		-49397	-28912	-42701	-62971	-59567	-80886	-65880	-78294	-71300	-83800
Niue	IMP	G	4	7	...	...	...	...	...	...	...	..
Nuie	EXP	G	0	0	...	...	...	...	...	...	...	..
NZ dollars	BAL		-4	-7	...	...	...	...	...	...	...	..
Norway	IMP	G	132563	169998	208627	229720	252232	282638	266676	302852	296135	27656[illegible]
Norvège	EXP	G	170733	211579	265883	320130	342421	304653	355171	529814	532041	47326[illegible]
kroner	BAL		38170	41581	57256	90410	90189	22015	88495	226962	235906	19670[illegible]
Oman	IMP	G	1089	1031	1633	1760	1933	2185	1797	1938	2229	230[illegible]
Oman	EXP	G	1360	2118	2346	2825	2934	2118	2783	4352	4258	429[illegible]
rials Omani	BAL		271	1087	713	1064	1001	-67	986	2414	2029	198[illegible]
Pakistan	IMP	G	93793	160134	362686	437769	476346	419311	505451	582681	631005	67057[illegible]
Pakistan	EXP	G	43645	121345	252714	335313	359046	382477	417322	484476	572471	59171[illegible]
rupees	BAL		-50148	-38789	-109972	-102456	-117300	-36834	-88129	-98205	-58534	-7886[illegible]
Panama[23]	IMP	S	1392	1539	2511	2780	3002	3398	3516	3379	2964	298[illegible]
Panama[23]	EXP	S	336	340	625	723	723	784	822	859	911	84[illegible]
balboas	BAL		-1056	-1198	-1886	-2057	-2279	-2614	-2694	-2519	-2053	-213[illegible]
Papua New Guinea	IMP	G	1006	1139	1863	2296	2448	2566	3174	3196	3638	429[illegible]
Popouasie-Nouvelle-Guinée	EXP	G	926	1122	3400	3334	3079	3707	5007	5813	6105	602[illegible]
kina	BAL		-79	-16	1537	1038	631	1141	1833	2617	2467	173[illegible]
Philippines	IMP	G	101518	317977	729960	894665	1139830	1290270	1273000	1636810	1780530	191916[illegible]
Philippines	EXP	G	85811	197962	450487	535054	738415	1206200	1432590	1773140	1665020	188432[illegible]
pesos	BAL		-15707	-120015	-279473	-359611	-401415	-84070	159590	136330	-115510	-3484[illegible]
Poland	IMP	S	165	9292	70502	100231	138898	162458	182362	213072	206253	22481[illegible]
Pologne	EXP	S	169	13606	55515	65819	84480	95015	108705	137909	148114	16733[illegible]
zlotys	BAL		4	4314	-14987	-34412	-54418	-67443	-73657	-75163	-58139	-5747[illegible]
Portugal[2]	IMP	S	1302760	3589730	5028700	5427130	6139710	6914800	37506	41425	44054	4065[illegible]
Portugal[2]	EXP	S	967390	2336460	3501820	3795870	4195050	4461000	23716	25241	27323	2709[illegible]
euros	BAL		-335370	-1253270	-1526880	-1631260	-1944660	-2453800	-13790	-16184	-16731	-1356[illegible]
Qatar	IMP	S	4147	6169	12369	10441	12091	12407	9098	...	...	
Qatar	EXP	S	12894	12847	12671	13659	13801	17763	25703	...	...	
riyals	BAL		8748	6677	302	3218	1710	5355	16605	...	...	
Réunion[15]	IMP	S	7457	11738	13077	...	.	.	.	.	.	
Réunion[15]	EXP	S	868	1016	1027	...	.	.	.	.	.	
francs	BAL		-6589	-10722	-12050	...	.	.	.	.	.	
Rwanda	IMP	G	30244	23059	62193	78837	89694	89218	84508	82586	110488	964[illegible]
Rwanda	EXP	G	13221	9224	14731	18569	26190	18696	20388	20521	37314	263[illegible]
francs	BAL		-17023	-13835	-47463	-60268	-63503	-70523	-64120	-62065	-73174	-701[illegible]
Saint Kitts-Nevis[1]	IMP	S	139	298	359	403	398	400	...	...	...	
Saint-Kitts-et-Nevis[1]	EXP	S	55	75	51	59	97	...	...	...	...	
EC dollars	BAL		-84	-223	-308	-344	-302	...	...	...	...	

Special Table B

Total imports and exports by countries and areas

Imports CIF, exports FOB and balance: million of national currency *[cont.]*

Importations et exportations totales par pays ou zone

Importations CIF, exportations FOB et balance: en millions de monnaie nationale *[suite]*

Country or Area - Pays ou Zone	IMP EXP BAL	G/S	1985	1990	1995	1996	1997	1998	1999	2000	2001	2002
Saint Lucia[1]	IMP	S	338	732	826	846	897	905	957	959	959	...
Sainte-Lucie[1]	EXP	S	153	344	335	215	165	168	150	117	120	...
EC dollars	BAL		-185	-388	-491	-631	-732	-737	-807	-842	-839	...
Saint Vincent-Grenadines[1]	IMP	S	214	367	367	356	491	520	543	440	502	471
St.Vincent-Grenadines[1]	EXP	S	171	223	115	125	125	134	131	128	112	103
EC dollars	BAL		-43	-144	-252	-231	-366	-386	-412	-312	-390	-368
Samoa	IMP	S	115	186	235	247	247	286	347	349	453	381
Samoa	EXP	S	36	20	22	25	39	43	62	47	54	46
talas	BAL		-79	-166	-213	-222	-209	-242	-285	-302	-399	-335
Saudi Arabia	IMP	S	85563	90140	105200	103900	107600	112400	104900	113240	116930	121010
Arabie saoudite	EXP	S	99540	166340	187400	227430	227440	145390	190100	290550	254900	...
riyals	BAL		13977	76200	82200	123530	119840	32990	85200	177310	137970	...
Senegal[5,6]	IMP	G	370970	332120	704900	734600	779000	858500	962700	1081300	1081300	...
Sénégal[5,6]	EXP	G	252490	207380	495800	505400	528000	570900	632400	654900	735300	772700
CFA francs	BAL		-118480	-124740	-209100	-229200	-251000	-287600	-330300	-426400	-346000	...
Seychelles	IMP	G	705	994	1109	1882	1711	2016	2317	1950	3049	...
Seychelles	EXP	G	200	302	254	693	569	644	775	1108	1264	...
rupees	BAL		-505	-692	-856	-1188	-1142	-1372	-1542	-842	-1785	...
Sierra Leone	IMP	S	789	22572	102488	193628	80010	148226	153856	314639	368323	554838
Sierra Leone	EXP	S	649	21023	30148	43004	15412	10482	11347	26771	57897	102010
leones	BAL		-140	-1549	-72340	-150624	-64598	-137744	-142509	-287868	-310426	-452828
Singapore	IMP	G	57819	109806	176317	185183	196606	174867	188143	232176	207694	208324
Singapour	EXP	G	50179	95206	167515	176271	185613	183763	194290	237826	218029	223902
dollars	BAL		-7640	-14600	-8802	-8912	-10993	8896	6147	5650	10335	15578
Slovakia	IMP	S	.	.	273831	350847	361833	483773	492337	619789	749775	785277
Slovaquie	EXP	S	.	.	255096	270643	277434	377807	423648	548527	611325	651256
koruny	BAL		.	.	-18735	-80204	-84399	-105966	-68689	-71262	-138450	-134021
Solomon Islands	IMP	S	123	231	526	537	686	722	...	...	...	...
Iles Salomon	EXP	S	104	178	573	577	649	608	...	...	...	...
dollars	BAL		-19	-53	47	40	-37	-114	...	...	...	...
South Africa[24,25]	IMP	G	25226	47605	110826	129522	151779	161802	163092	206620	241311	307312
Afrique du Sud[24,25]	EXP	G	36312	60929	101051	126101	142937	145518	163182	208476	249348	311679
rands	BAL		11086	13324	-9775	-3421	-8842	-16284	90	1856	8037	4367
Spain[2]	IMP	S	5072998	8898400	14106700	15435700	17965900	19837900	135866	166138	171691	172789
Espagne[2]	EXP	S	4099000	5630600	11339600	12931200	15266900	16290800	103343	123100	128672	130814
euros	BAL		-973998	-3267800	-2767100	-2504500	-2699000	-3547100	-32523	-43038	-43019	-41975
Sri Lanka	IMP	G	54049	107729	272201	301076	346026	380138	421888	554290	532963	584491
Sri Lanka	EXP	G	36207	76624	195117	226801	274193	310398	325171	420114	430372	449850
rupees	BAL		-17843	-31105	-77084	-74275	-71833	-69740	-96717	-134176	-102591	-134641
Suriname	IMP	G	533	843	258917	200951	263902	221388	...	...	...	...
Suriname	EXP	G	587	843	211021	173806	281197	174868	...	...	...	...
guilders	BAL		54	1	-47896	-27145	17295	-46520	...	...	...	...
Swaziland	IMP	G	.	.	.	.	.	5936	6526	7225	9587	10302
Swaziland	EXP	G	.	.	.	.	.	5331	5723	6281	8951	9827
emalangeni	BAL		.	.	.	.	.	-606	-803	-945	-636	-475
Sweden	IMP	G	244609	320380	460500	448700	501100	545300	568100	669200	654000	641800
Suède	EXP	G	260500	340040	567700	569200	632800	675300	700800	796900	781900	788400
kronor	BAL		15891	19660	107200	120500	131700	130000	132700	127700	127900	146600

Special Table B

Total imports and exports by countries and areas

Imports CIF, exports FOB and balance: million of national currency *[cont.]*

Importations et exportations totales par pays ou zone

Importations CIF, exportations FOB et balance: en millions de monnaie nationale *[suite]*

Country or Area - Pays ou Zone	IMP EXP BAL	G/S	1985	1990	1995	1996	1997	1998	1999	2000	2001	2002
Switzerland	IMP	S	74750	96611	90775	91967	103088	106866	113416	128578	130052	12312
Suisse	EXP	S	66624	88257	92012	94174	105133	109113	114446	126565	131717	13038
francs	BAL		-8126	-8354	1237	2207	2045	2247	1030	-2013	1665	725
Syrian Arab Rep.	IMP	S	15570	26940	52860	60390	45210	43720	43010	187530	220000	23572
République arab syrienne	EXP	S	6427	47280	40000	44890	43960	32440	38880	216190	243000	31592
pounds	BAL		-9143	20340	-12860	-15500	-1250	-11280	-4130	28660	23000	8020
Thailand	IMP	S	251169	844448	1763590	1832840	1924280	1774070	1907100	2494160	2756700	277539
Thaïlande	EXP	S	193366	589813	1406310	1412110	1806700	2247450	2213960	2777730	2893180	295207
baht	BAL		-57803	-254635	-357280	-420730	-117580	473380	306860	283570	136480	17668
Togo[5,6]	IMP	S	129406	158287	295700	339900	376400	346700	354500	400000	405300	41000
Togo[5,6]	EXP	S	85380	72942	188400	225400	246600	570900	241000	257400	261900	17362
CFA francs	BAL		-44026	-85345	-107300	-114500	-129800	224200	-113500	-142600	-143400	-23637
Tonga	IMP	G	59	79	98	92	92	102	116	123	155	.
Tonga	EXP	G	8	15	18	16	13	12	20	16	15	.
pa'anga	BAL		-51	-64	-80	-76	-79	-91	-96	-107	-141	.
Trinidad and Tobago	IMP	S	3739	4712	10191	12867	18706	18887	17263	20842	22200	2276
Trinité-et-Tobago	EXP	S	5247	8331	14609	15014	15888	14221	17661	26924	26709	2423
dollars	BAL		1508	3618	4418	2148	-2818	-4666	398	6082	4509	147
Tunisia	IMP	G	2287	4826	7464	7499	8794	9490	10071	11738	13697	1351
Tunisie	EXP	G	1443	3087	5173	5372	6148	6518	6967	8005	9504	974
dinars	BAL		-844	-1739	-2291	-2127	-2645	-2971	-3104	-3733	-4194	-376
Tuvalu	IMP	G	4	...	...	...	...	...	...	...	...	.
Tuvalu	EXP	G	0	...	...	...	...	...	...	...	...	.
Aust. dollars	BAL		-4	...	...	...	...	...	...	...	...	.
Uganda	IMP	G	2003	125059	1024320	1247380	1425900	1753330	1955850	2486270	2798210	199815
Ouganda	EXP	G	3000	64653	446086	613598	594804	624509	748862	759273	802296	79551
shillings	BAL		997	-60406	-578234	-633782	-831096	-1128821	-1206988	-1726997	-1995914	-120263
United Kingdom	IMP	G	85027	126086	168055	184113	187135	189532	196504	221027	222944	22343
Royaume-Uni	EXP	G	78392	103692	153353	167764	171594	164066	165738	186171	185673	18416
pounds	BAL		-6635	-22394	-14702	-16349	-15541	-25466	-30766	-34856	-37271	-3927
United Rep. of Tanzania	IMP	G	14959	265984	968910	804949	818703	967080	1161840	1219380	1502640	163039
Rép.-Unie de Tanzanie	EXP	G	4265	64571	390378	455519	459549	391805	412204	531058	681186	84720
shillings	BAL		-10694	-201413	-578532	-349430	-359154	-575275	-749636	-688322	-821454	-78319
Vanuatu	IMP	G	7378	11211	10659	10888	10888	11257	12337	12317	...	.
Vanuatu	EXP	G	3252	2202	3173	3368	4087	4323	3327	3644	...	.
vatu	BAL		-4126	-9009	-7486	-7520	-6801	-6934	-9010	-8673	...	.
Venezuela	IMP	G	61757	347878	2202000	4179920	7145460	8603970	8380530	10997300	13221100	.
Venezuela	EXP	G	94034	831176	3332640	9803060	10295500	9393450	12751400	21602200	17568900	3252570
bolivares	BAL		32277	483298	1130640	5623140	3150040	789480	4370870	10604900	4347800	.
Yemen[14]	IMP	S	.	18867	64591	191862	260331	294510	312749	375783	389638	.
Yémen[14]	EXP	S	.	8316	79434	251830	323716	203480	380010	659609	542359	.
rials	BAL		.	-10552	14843	59968	63385	-91030	67261	283826	152721	.
Zambia	IMP	S	2133	36554	604791	1004290	1077020	...	...	...	...	.
Zambie	EXP	S	1508	39144	898643	1252670	1203020	...	...	...	...	.
kwacha	BAL		-625	2590	293852	248380	126000	...	...	...	...	.
Zimbabwe	IMP	G	1447	4528	23048	28095	36556	59345	83407	83031	...	.
Zimbabwe	EXP	G	1796	4231	18359	24209	30208	44928	81945	94998	...	.
dollars	BAL		349	-297	-4689	-3886	-6347	-14417	-1463	11968	...	.

Special Table B

Total imports and exports by countries or areas

Imports CIF, exports FOB and balance: millions of national currency *[cont.]*

Importations et exportations totales par pays ou zone

Importations CIF, exportations FOB et balance: en millions de monnaie nationale *[suite]*

General note: System: G=General trade; S=Special trade.

This table contains totals of imports and exports of countries or areas which report data in national currency. Countries that are not included in this table may report their trade in US dollars and are shown in Table A. Export and import values are as compiled by the International Monetary Fund (IMF) except for Brunei Darussalam, Cayman Is., Cook Is, Cuba, Faeroe Is., French Guiana, French Polynesia, Greenland, Guadeloupe, Iraq, Kiribati, Martinique, Montserrat, Netherland Antilles, New Caledonia, Réunion, Russian Federation (beginning 1994), St. Kitts-Nevis, St. Pierre Miquelon, Turkmenistan, Uzbekistan, and Yugoslavia.

1 East Caribbean dollar.

2 Prior to January 1999, trade data are reported as follows: Austria in schillings, Belguim in francs, Finland in markkaa, France in francs, Germany in deutsche marks, Ireland in pounds, Italy in lire, Luxembourg in francs, Netherlands in guilders, Portugal in escudos, and Spain in pesetas.

3 Beginning 1990, trade statistics exclude certain oil and chemical products.

4 Economic Union of Belgium and Luxembourg. Intertrade between the two countries is excluded. Beginning January 1997, data refer to Belgium only and include trade between Belgium and Luxembourg.

5 Prior to 1999, the CFA franc was pegged to the French franc at CFAF 100 per French franc and prior to 1994 CFAF 50 per French franc.. Beginning 1999, the CFAF is pegged to the euro at CFAF 655.957 per euro.

6 Comptoirs Francais du Afrique franc pegged to the euro at CFAF 655.957 per euro.

7 After July 5, 1999 lev is equal to 1,000 of pre-July 5, 1999 leva. All data are expressed in terms of the new leva.

8 Imports FOB.

9 Imports exclude petroleum imported without stated value. Exports cover domestic exports.

Note générale: Système: Le commerce de G=General; Le commerce de S=Special.

Cette table contient des totaux d'd'importations et d'd'exportations les pays ou les secteurs qui rapportent des données dans la monnaie nationale.Les pays qui ne sont pas inclus dans cette table peuvent rapporter leurs échanges des dollars d'USA et sont montrés dans le Tableau A. Export et les valeurs d'importation sont comme compilé par le Fonds monétaire international (FMI) excepté Brunei Darussalam, Iles Caïmanes, Iles Cook, le Cuba, Iles Féroé, la Guyane Française, la Polynésie Française, le Groenland, la Guadeloupe, l'Irak, le Kiribati, la Martinique, le Montserrat, Netherland Antilles, le Nouvelle Calédonie, le Réunion, la Fédération Russe (commençant 1994), St. Kitts-Nevis, St. Pierre Miquelon, Turkmenistan, Uzbekistan, et Yougoslavie.

1 Dollar des caraïbes orientales.

2 Avant janvier 1999, des données commerciales sont rapportées comme suit: Autriche en schillings, Belgique en francs, Finlande en markkaa, France en francs, Allemagne en deutsche marks, Irlande en livres, Italie en lire, Luxembourg, en francs, Pays-Bas en florins, Portugal en escudos, et Espagne en pesetas.

3 A compter de 1990, les statistiques commerciales font exclusion de certains produits pétroliers et chimiques.

4 L'Union économique belgo-luxembourgeoise. Non compris le commerce entre ces pays. A partir de janvier 1997, les données se rapportent à Belgique seulement et recouvrent les échanges entre la Belgique et le Luxembourg

5 Avant 1999, le franc de CFA a été chevillé au franc français à CFAF 100 par franc français et avant 1994, CFAF 50 par franc français. Commençant 1999, le CFAF est chevillé à l'euro à CFAF 655,957 par euro.

6 Comptoirs Francais du Afrique franc est chevillé à l'euro à CFAF 655,957 par euro.

7 Après juillet 5, 1999 le lev est égal à 1,000 pré-Juillet de 5, 1999 leva. Toutes les données sont exprimées en termes de nouveau lev.

8 Importations FOB.

9 Non compris le petrole brute dont la valeur des importations ne sont pas stipulée. Les exportations sont les exportations d'intérieur.

10 Beginning January 1994, foreign trade statistics exclude re-exports.
11 Excluding intra-EU trade.
12 See explanatory notes pertaining to Czechoslovakia on page vi.
13 Prior to January 1991, excludes trade conducted in accordance with the supplementary protocol to the treaty on the basis of relations between the Federal Republic of Germany and the former German Democratic Republic.
14 See explanatory notes on data pertaining to Yemen on page v.
15 Beginning 1997, trade data for France include the import and export values of French Guiana, Guadeloupe, Martinique, and Reunion.
16 Comptoirs Francais du Pacifique franc.
17 Prior to 1991, data refers to the Federal Republic of Germany. See explanatory notes pertaining to Germany on page v.
18 Prior to 1999, the CFA franc was pegged to the French franc at CFAF 100 per French franc. Beginning 1999, the CFAF is pegged to the euro at CFAF 655.957 per euro.
19 Prior to 1996 data exclude customs free zones, repairs on goods, and operational leasing.
20 Beginning 1989, data exclude re-exports.
21 Prior to 1997, included under Belgium. See also footnote for Belgium.
22 Prior to 1986, includes Aruba.
23 Exports include re-exports and petroleum products.
24 Exports include gold.
25 Beginning in January 1998, foreign trade data refer to South Africa only, excluding intra-trade of the Southern African Common Customs Area. Prior to January 1998, trade data refer to the Southern African Common Customs Area, which includes Botswana, Lesotho, Namibia, South Africa and Swaziland.

10 A compter de janvier 1994, les statistiques du commerce exterieur non compris les réexportations.
11 Non compris le commerce de l'intra-UE.
12 Voir les notes explicatives sur les données concernant Tchécoslovaquie à la page viii.
13 Avant janvier 1991, non compris le commerce effectué en accord avec le protocole additionnel au traité définissant la base des relations entre la République Fédérale d'Allemagne et l'ancienne République Démocratique Allemande.
14 Voir les notes explicatives sur les données concernant Yemen à la page vii.
15 A compter de 1997, les valeurs de commerce pour la France comprennent les valeurs des importations et des exportations de la Guyane française, la Guadeloupe, la Martinique, et la Réunion.
16 Comptoirs Francais du Pacifique franc.
17 Avant 1991, les données se rapportent à la République Fédérale d'Allemagne. Voir les notes explicatives concerner l'Allemagne à la page vii.
18 Avant 1999, le franc de CFA a été chevillé au franc français à CFAF 100 par franc français. Commençant 1999, le CFAF est chevillé à l'euro à CFAF 655,957 par euro.
19 Avant de 1996 les données excluent des zones franches, des réparations sur des marchandises, et le crédit-bail opérationnel.
20 A compter 1989, les données non compris les réexportations.
21 Avant 1997, inclus sous la Belgique. Voir également l'apostille pour la Belgique.
22 Avant 1986, comprend Aruba.
23 Exportations comprennent re-exportations et produits pétroliers.
24 Les exportations comprennent l'or.
25 A compter de janvier 1998, les données sur le commerce extérieur ne se rapportent qu'à l'Afrique du Sud. et ne tiennent pas compte des échanges commerciaux entre les pays de l'Union douanière de l'Afrique du Sud. qui incluait l'Afrique du Sud, Botswana, Lesotho, Namibie, et Swaziland.

Special Table C

External trade conversion factors

Imports, exports: US dollars per national currency

Facteurs de conversion pour le commerce extérieur

Importations, exportations: monnaie nationale en dollars É.-U.

Country or Area	Unit	1985	1990	1995	1996	1997	1998	1999	2000	2001	2002
		Imports - Importations									
Albania	lek	...	0.02000	0.01755	0.00956	0.00683	0.00666	0.00724	0.00694	0.00698	0.00715
Algeria	dinar	0.19885	0.11002	0.02102	0.01828	0.01733	0.01702	0.01505	...	...	...
Antigua and Barbuda	EC dollar[1]	0.37037	0.37037	0.37037	...	...	...	...	...	...	...
Australia	dollar	0.69898	0.78134	0.74127	0.78317	0.74133	0.62806	0.64541	0.57943	0.51716	0.54472
Austria	euro[2,3]	0.04872	0.08826	0.09940	0.09447	0.08198	0.08097	1.06493	0.92061	0.89580	0.94383
Bahamas	dollar	1.00000	1.00000	1.00000	1.00000	1.00000	1.00000	1.00000	1.00000	1.00000	1.00000
Bahrain	dinar	2.65960	2.65960	2.65958	2.65958	2.65958	2.65958	2.65958	2.65957	2.65957	2.65957
Bangladesh	taka	0.03535	0.02897	0.02483	0.02392	0.02276	0.02130	0.02036	0.01915	0.01793	0.01727
Barbados	dollar	0.50000	0.50000	0.50000	0.50000	0.50000	0.50000	0.50000	0.50000	0.50000	0.50000
Belgium	euro[2,3]	0.01694	0.02999	0.03397	0.03230	0.02799	0.02759	1.06461	0.92097	0.89586	0.94427
Belize	dollar	0.50000	0.50000	0.50000	0.50000	0.50000	0.50000	0.50000	0.50000	0.50000	0.50000
Benin	CFA franc[4,5,6]	0.00223	0.00368	0.00200	0.00195	0.00171	0.00169	0.00161	0.00142	0.00137	0.00145
Bhutan	ngultrum	0.08087	0.05717	0.03097	0.02826	0.02759	0.02439	0.02326	0.02238	...	...
Bosnia Herzegovina	marka	.	.	...	...	...	0.57051	0.54173	0.46864	0.45585	0.48591
Botswana	pula	0.52895	0.53809	0.36025	0.30005	0.27378	0.23666	0.21618	0.19521	0.17200	...
Brunei Darussalam	dollar	0.45573	0.55193	0.70215	...	...	...	...	...	...	...
Bulgaria	lev[7]	0.97083	38.35230	14.87123	7.69061	0.63173	0.56882	0.54251	0.46942	0.45689	0.48551
Burkina Faso	CFA franc[4,6]	0.00228	0.00370	0.00201	0.00195	0.00172	0.00170	0.00162	0.00140	0.00136	0.00145
Burundi	franc	0.00829	0.00586	0.00403	0.00341	0.00281	0.00225	0.00178	0.00139	0.00121	0.00107
Cameroon	CFA franc[4,6]	0.00226	0.00371	0.00201	0.00195	0.00171	0.00170	0.00162	...	...	...
Canada	dollar	0.73224	0.85686	0.72876	0.73362	0.72205	0.67453	0.67331	0.67323	0.64594	0.63746
Cape Verde	escudo	0.01093	0.01433	0.01302	0.01211	0.01080	0.01021	0.00974	0.00863	0.00812	...
Cayman Islands	dollar	1.20000	1.20000	...	...	...	...	...	...	...	...
Cent. Afr. Rep.	CFA franc[4,5,6]	0.00224	0.00368	0.00200	0.00196	0.00172	0.00170	0.00163	0.00141	0.00137	...
Chad	CFA franc[4,5,6]	0.00224	0.00367	0.00200	0.00196	0.00172	0.00169	0.00163	0.00141	0.00137	0.00143
Comoros	franc	0.00221	0.00371	0.00267	...	...	...	...	...	...	...
Congo	franc[5]	0.00225	0.00365	0.00201	0.00195	0.00171	0.00170	0.00162	0.00140	...	...
Cook Islands	NZ dollar	0.49767	0.59809	0.65694	0.68915	0.65814	0.53433	0.52726	0.44835	0.42000	...
Cote d'Ivoire	CFA franc[4,6]	0.00226	0.00369	0.00200	0.00195	0.00171	0.00170	0.00163	0.00140	0.00137	0.00144
Cuba	peso	1.08888	1.00000	...	1.00000	...	...	...	...	...	...
Cyprus	pound	1.63606	2.18702	2.21154	2.14403	1.94704	1.93563	1.83571	1.60134	1.55231	1.64330
Czech Rep	koruna	.	.	0.03775	0.03685	0.03155	0.03110	0.02886	0.02591	0.02631	0.03073
Denmark	krone	0.09528	0.16214	0.17865	0.17246	0.15154	0.14958	0.14332	0.12355	0.12025	0.12715
Djibouti	franc	0.00563	0.00563	0.00563	0.00563	0.00563	0.00563	0.00563	...	...	...
Dominica	EC dollar[1]	0.37037	0.37037	0.37037	0.37037	0.37037	0.37037	0.37037	0.37037	0.37037	0.37037
Egypt	pound	1.42857	0.67609	0.29479	0.29486	0.29509	0.29516	0.29453	0.28800	0.25179	0.22224
Equatorial Guinea	CFA franc[4,6]	0.00220	0.00367	0.00201	0.00195	0.00171	0.00169	0.00162	0.00140	...	...
Eritrea	nakfa	.	.	...	...	...	...	0.12202	...	...	...
Estonia	kroon	.	.	0.08745	0.08344	0.07189	0.07106	0.06795	0.05866	0.05694	0.06053
Ethiopia	birr	0.48309	0.48309	0.16186	0.15747	...	...	0.12528	...	...	...
EU-15	euro	.	.	.	.	.	.	1.06406	0.92020	0.89550	0.94413
Faeroe Islands	D krone	0.09731	0.16200	0.17871	0.17243	0.15140	0.14934	0.14325	0.12365	...	...
Fiji	dollar	0.86917	0.67753	0.71109	0.71312	0.69316	0.50302	0.50769	0.47282	0.43909	0.45965
Finland	euro[2,3]	0.16268	0.26199	0.22964	0.21771	0.19256	0.18745	1.06487	0.92026	0.89591	0.94471
Fm Czechoslovakia	koruna	0.14650	0.05502	.	.	.	.	.	.	.	.
Fm German D.R.	GDR mark	0.27027	...	.	.	.	.	.	.	.	.
Fm Yemen A.R.	rial[8]	0.13690	.	.	.	.	.	.	.	.	.
Fm Yemen Dm	dinar[8]	2.89520	.	.	.	.	.	.	.	.	.
France	euro[2,3]	0.11197	0.18409	0.20053	0.19546	0.17203	0.16985	1.06460	0.92112	0.89566	0.94355
French Guiana	franc	0.11253	0.18350	0.20065	...	.	.	.	.	.	.

Special Table C
External trade conversion factors
Imports, exports: US dollars per national currency
Facteurs de conversion pour le commerce extérieur
Importations, exportations: monnaie nationale en dollars É.-U.

1985	1990	1995	1996	1997	1998	1999	2000	2001	2002	Unité	Pays ou Zone
				Exports - Exportations							
...	0.02000	0.01962	0.00961	0.00660	0.00668	0.00725	0.00696	0.00697	0.00715	lek	Albanie
0.19889	0.11080	0.02096	0.01825	0.01734	0.01703	...	...	...	...	dinar	Algérie
0.37037	0.37037	0.37037	...	...	...	...	...	...	...	dollar C.O.[1]	Antigua-et-Barbuda
0.69776	0.78126	0.74124	0.78334	0.74199	0.62818	0.64538	0.57827	0.51677	0.54432	dollar	Australie
0.04873	0.08827	0.09940	0.09445	0.08195	0.08099	1.06405	0.92072	0.89550	0.94469	euro[2,3]	Autriche
1.00000	1.00000	1.00000	1.00000	1.00000	1.00000	1.00000	1.00000	1.00000	1.00000	dollar	Bahamas
2.65960	2.65960	2.65958	2.65958	2.65958	2.65958	2.65958	2.65957	2.65957	2.65957	dinar	Bahreïn
0.03522	0.02887	0.02483	0.02390	0.02275	0.02133	0.02035	0.01916	0.01793	0.01727	taka	Bangladesh
0.50000	0.50000	0.50000	0.50000	0.50000	0.50000	0.50000	0.50000	0.50000	0.50000	dollar	Barbade
0.01697	0.03000	0.03397	0.03229	0.02798	0.02758	1.06470	0.92123	0.89561	0.94405	euro[2,3]	Belgique
0.50000	0.50000	0.50000	0.50000	0.50000	0.50000	0.50000	0.50000	0.50000	0.50000	dollar	Belize
0.00224	0.00368	0.00199	0.00195	0.00171	0.00169	0.00163	0.00140	0.00136	0.00144	franc CFA[4,5,6]	Bénin
0.08088	0.05717	0.03088	0.02826	0.02759	0.02434	0.02324	0.02232	...	...	ngultrum	Bhoutan
.	.	...	...	...	0.56912	0.54405	0.47127	0.45686	0.48569	marka	Bosnie-Herzégovine
0.51964	0.53769	0.36056	0.30092	0.27354	0.23858	0.21627	0.19381	0.17336	...	pula	Botswana
0.45489	0.55193	0.70215	...	...	...	...	...	...	...	dollar	Brunéi Darussalam
0.97155	37.88058	14.88441	7.67844	0.64267	0.56786	0.54276	0.46931	0.45769	0.48481	lev[7]	Bulgarie
0.00226	0.00366	0.00200	0.00197	0.00174	0.00168	0.00163	0.00143	0.00138	0.00144	franc CFA[4,6]	Burkina Faso
0.00830	0.00586	0.00407	0.00351	0.00281	0.00225	0.00175	0.00142	0.00120	0.00105	franc	Burundi
0.00224	0.00371	0.00201	0.00195	0.00172	0.00170	0.00162	...	...	...	franc CFA[4,6]	Cameroun
0.73202	0.85711	0.72888	0.73353	0.72215	0.67421	0.67330	0.67311	0.64613	0.63736	dollar	Canada
0.01096	0.01473	0.01302	0.01209	0.01080	0.01024	0.00973	0.00859	0.00813	...	escudo	Cap-Vert
1.20000	1.20000	...	...	...	...	...	...	...	...	dollar	Iles Caïmanes
0.00224	0.00367	0.00200	0.00196	0.00172	0.00170	0.00163	0.00141	0.00137	...	franc CFA[4,5,6]	Rép. centrafricaine
0.00224	0.00367	0.00200	0.00196	0.00172	0.00169	0.00163	0.00141	0.00137	0.00143	franc CFA[4,5,6]	Tchad
0.00232	0.00368	0.00267	...	...	...	...	...	...	...	franc	Comores
0.00225	0.00369	0.00201	0.00195	0.00171	0.00170	0.00162	0.00140	...	...	franc[5]	Congo
0.50826	0.59886	0.65536	0.68639	0.66078	0.53695	0.52820	0.44574	0.42299	...	dollar NZ	Iles Cook
0.00223	0.00373	0.00201	0.00195	0.00172	0.00170	0.00163	0.00141	0.00137	0.00143	franc CFA[4,6]	Côte d'Ivoire
1.08504	1.00000	...	1.00000	...	...	...	...	...	...	peso	Cuba
1.63953	2.17708	2.21501	2.14345	1.95358	1.92718	1.83669	1.61103	1.55189	1.63806	livre	Chypre
.	.	0.03773	0.03686	0.03149	0.03107	0.02888	0.02592	0.02631	0.03068	couronne	République. tchèque
0.09520	0.16233	0.17869	0.17243	0.15149	0.14958	0.14327	0.12345	0.12028	0.12720	couronne	Danemark
0.00563	0.00563	0.00563	0.00563	0.00563	0.00563	0.00563	...	...	...	franc	Djibouti
0.37037	0.37037	0.37037	0.37037	0.37037	0.37037	0.37037	0.37037	0.37037	0.37037	dollar C.O.[1]	Dominique
1.42857	0.71280	0.29476	0.29486	0.29509	0.29516	0.29450	0.28824	0.25257	0.22223	livre	Egypte
0.00223	0.00367	0.00201	0.00195	0.00171	0.00169	0.00162	0.00140	...	...	franc CFA[4,6]	Guinée équatoriale
.	.	...	...	...	...	0.12202	...	...	...	nakfa	Erythrée
.	.	0.08734	0.08341	0.07190	0.07120	0.06803	0.05874	0.05693	0.06050	kroon	Estonie
0.48309	0.48309	0.16214	0.15745	0.14895	0.14127	...	...	...	...	birr	Ethiopie
.	.	.	.	.	.	1.06301	0.91951	0.89497	0.94525	euro	UE-15
0.09711	0.16288	0.17871	0.17252	0.15140	0.14948	0.14326	0.12359	...	...	couronne d	Iles Féroé
0.87058	0.68051	0.71110	0.71323	0.69037	0.50184	0.50761	0.47011	0.43842	0.46027	dollar	Fidji
0.16219	0.26211	0.22957	0.21765	0.19255	0.18742	1.06451	0.91911	0.89603	0.94552	euro[2,3]	Finlande
0.14640	0.05520	.	.	.	.	.	.	.	.	koruna	L'ex-Tchécoslovaquie
0.27027	...	.	.	.	.	.	.	.	.	RDA mark	L'ex-Allemagne rép. dem. du
0.13690	.	.	.	.	.	.	.	.	.	rial[8]	Fmr Yémen A.R.
2.89520	.	.	.	.	.	.	.	.	.	dinar[8]	FMR Yémen Dm
0.11215	0.18401	0.20061	0.19546	0.17190	0.16971	1.06459	0.92133	0.89542	0.94414	euro[2,3]	France
0.11144	0.18317	0.19982	...	.	.	.	.	.	.	franc	Guyane française

Special Table C

External trade conversion factors

Imports, exports: US dollars per national currency *[cont.]*

Facteurs de conversion pour le commerce extérieur

Importations, exportations: monnaie nationale en dollars É.-U. *[suite]*

Country or Area	Unit	1985	1990	1995	1996	1997	1998	1999	2000	2001	2002
						Imports - Importations *[cont.]*					
French Polynesia	CFP franc[9]	0.00617	0.01011	0.01115	0.01075	0.00942	0.00942	0.00893	0.00773	0.00787	...
Gabon	CFA franc[4,5,6]	0.00225	0.00369	0.00201	0.00195	0.00171	0.00170	0.00163	0.00141	0.00136	...
Gambia	dalasi	0.25764	0.12678	0.10470	0.10217	0.09821	0.09401	0.08775	...	...	...
Georgia	lari	.	.	...	0.79175	0.77040	0.71423	...	...	...	...
Germany	euro[2,3]	0.34184	0.62253	0.69910	0.66456	0.57707	0.56919	1.06464	0.92038	0.89550	0.94528
Ghana	cedi	0.01836	...	0.00083	0.00061	0.00048	0.00043	0.00037	0.00018	...	...
Gibraltar	pound	1.30633	...	...	...	...	...	...	...	...	...
Greenland	D krone	0.09623	0.16189	0.17908	0.17240	0.15132	0.14925	0.14280	...	...	...
Grenada	EC dollar[1]	0.37037	0.37037	0.37037	0.37037	0.37037	0.37037	...	...	...	...
Guadeloupe	franc	0.10800	0.18458	0.20103	...	.	.	.	.	.	.
Guinea-Bissau	CFA franc[6,10]	...	0.02955	0.00362	0.00242	0.00171	0.00170	0.00162	0.00140	0.00136	0.00144
Guyana	dollar	0.23526	0.02540	0.00705	0.00712	0.00701	...	...	...	0.00534	0.00525
Haiti	gourde	0.20000	0.20000	0.06625	0.06374	0.06000	0.05988	0.05960	0.04745	0.04108	0.03392
Hungary	forint	0.02005	0.01591	0.00794	0.00653	0.00533	0.00466	0.00420	0.00353	0.00349	0.00389
Iceland	krona	0.02408	0.01722	0.01548	0.01503	0.01409	0.01410	0.01380	0.01271	0.01032	0.01095
India	rupee	0.08098	0.05702	0.03079	0.02823	0.02752	0.02426	0.02321	0.02226	0.02119	0.02057
Iraq	dinar	3.21691	3.21691	...	...	...	...	...	...	...	...
Ireland	euro[2,3]	1.06264	1.65865	1.60373	1.60038	1.51581	1.42726	1.06471	0.92013	0.89646	0.93985
Italy	euro[2,3]	0.00052	0.00084	0.00061	0.00065	0.00059	0.00058	1.06430	0.92095	0.89525	0.94493
Jamaica	dollar	0.18078	0.13817	0.02825	0.02703	0.02820	0.02734	0.02555	0.02343	0.02175	0.02064
Japan	yen	0.00420	0.00695	0.01065	0.00919	0.00827	0.00766	0.00879	0.00928	0.00824	0.00800
Jordan	dinar	2.54392	1.50810	1.42704	1.41044	1.41044	1.41044	1.41044	1.41044	1.41046	...
Kenya	shilling	0.06088	0.04366	0.01937	0.01750	0.01729	0.01655	0.01429	0.01312	0.01272	0.01270
Kiribati	Aust. dollar	0.70080	0.78129	0.74087	0.78388	0.74504	0.62746	0.64557	0.58250	...	...
Kuwait	dinar	3.32611	3.42410	3.35435	3.33975	3.29639	3.28130	3.28546	3.25993	3.26075	3.29358
Latvia	lat	.	.	1.89459	1.81473	1.71957	1.69639	1.70848	1.64778	1.59180	1.62275
Lesotho	loti	0.45194	0.38696	0.27549	0.23221	0.21699	0.18372	0.16368	0.14414	0.11686	0.09558
Liberia	dollar	1.00037	...	...	...	...	...	...	...	...	...
Libyan Arab Jamah.	dinar	3.37780	3.54181	2.91185	2.28908	2.16947	2.13641	2.15599	1.95230	1.64955	0.78773
Lithuania	lita	.	.	0.25000	0.25000	0.25000	0.25000	0.25000	0.25000	0.25000	0.27395
Luxembourg	euro[2,3]	.	.	.	.	0.02794	0.02762	1.06415	0.92029	0.89445	0.94491
Madagascar	franc	0.00151	0.00067	0.00023	0.00025	0.00020	0.00018	0.00016	...	...	...
Malawi	kwacha	0.58313	0.36594	0.06544	0.06532	0.06159	0.03135	0.02267	0.01650	0.01425	0.01296
Malaysia	ringgit	0.40256	0.36981	0.39901	0.39745	0.35771	0.25546	0.26314	0.26316	0.26316	0.26315
Mali	CFA franc[4,5,6]	0.00225	0.00371	0.00201	0.00195	0.00171	0.00169	0.00162	0.00141	0.00136	0.00144
Malta	lira	2.14266	3.16089	2.83531	2.77390	2.59318	2.57647	2.50053	2.27790	2.22245	2.31322
Martinique	franc	0.11282	0.18373	0.20089	...	.	.	.	.	.	.
Mauritania	ouguiya	0.01310	...	...	...	...	...	...	...	...	...
Mauritius	rupee	0.06511	0.06750	0.05752	0.05572	0.04731	0.04161	0.03969	0.03807	0.03429	...
Montserrat	EC dollar[1]	0.37040	0.37040	...	...	...	...	...	...	...	...
Morocco	dirham	0.09955	0.12145	0.11725	0.11469	0.10501	0.10428	0.10185	0.09413	0.08850	0.09109
Myanmar	kyat	0.11825	0.15800	0.17645	0.17073	0.16146	0.15925	0.16062	0.15567	0.14948	...
Namibia	dollar	.	.	.	0.23278	0.21593	0.17952	0.16363	0.14310	0.11577	...
Nepal	rupee	0.05509	0.03407	0.01932	0.01765	0.01728	0.01521	0.01461	0.01407	0.01336	0.01283
Neth. Antilles	NA guilder	0.55550	0.55870	0.55870	0.55870	0.55870	...	...	...	...	...
Netherlands	euro[2,3]	0.30279	0.55063	0.62381	0.59313	0.51293	0.50504	1.06481	0.92050	0.89567	0.94461
New Caledonia	CFP franc[9]	0.00623	0.01009	0.01113	0.01075	0.00941	0.00942	0.00893	0.00773	0.00787	...
New Zealand	dollar	0.49632	0.59772	0.65680	0.68809	0.66102	0.53519	0.52736	0.45242	0.42006	0.46530
Niger	CFA franc[4,6]	0.00224	0.00368	0.00200	0.00196	0.00171	0.00169	0.00163	0.00141	0.00137	0.00143
Niue	NZ dollar	0.49840	0.59626	...	...	...	...	...	...	...	...

Special Table C

External trade conversion factors

Imports, exports: US dollars per national currency *[cont.]*

Facteurs de conversion pour le commerce extérieur

Importations, exportations: monnaie nationale en dollars É.-U. *[suite]*

1985	1990	1995	1996	1997	1998	1999	2000	2001	2002	Unité	Pays ou Zone
				Exports - Exportations *[suite]*							
0.00619	0.01005	0.01119	0.01072	0.00931	0.00939	0.00893	0.00773	0.00787	...	franc CFP[9]	Polynésie française
0.00226	0.00369	0.00201	0.00195	0.00171	0.00170	0.00163	0.00141	0.00136	...	franc CFA[4,5,6]	Gabon
0.24994	0.12577	0.10520	0.10254	0.09902	0.09448	0.08773	...	...	...	dalasi	Gambie
.	.	...	0.79175	0.76984	0.71504	...	...	...	...	lari	Géorgie
0.34254	0.62074	0.69898	0.66447	0.57673	0.56924	1.06446	0.92097	0.89533	0.94532	euro[2,3]	Allemagne
0.01859	...	0.00085	0.00061	0.00049	0.00043	...	...	...	...	cedi	Ghana
1.29633	...	...	...	...	...	...	...	...	...	livre	Gibraltar
0.09618	0.16233	0.17908	0.17242	0.15132	0.14925	0.14267	...	...	...	couronne d	Groenland
0.37037	0.37037	0.37037	0.37037	0.37037	0.37037	...	...	...	...	dollar C.O.[1]	Grenade
0.10763	0.18216	0.20144	...	.	.	.	.	.	.	franc	Guadeloupe
...	0.02955	0.00364	0.00255	0.00172	0.00169	0.00161	0.00140	0.00135	0.00144	franc CFA[6,10]	Guinée-Bissau
0.23595	0.02509	0.00705	0.00712	0.00701	0.00661	0.00562	0.00548	0.00533	0.00524	dollar	Guyana
0.20000	0.20000	0.06698	0.06386	0.05980	0.05973	0.05972	0.04649	0.04101	0.03406	gourde	Haïti
0.02011	0.01590	0.00789	0.00653	0.00532	0.00466	0.00420	0.00353	0.00349	0.00389	forint	Hongrie
0.02410	0.01718	0.01547	0.01503	0.01411	0.01414	0.01381	0.01273	0.01027	0.01091	couronne	Islande
0.08078	0.05716	0.03080	0.02825	0.02755	0.02426	0.02322	0.02223	0.02120	0.02057	roupie	Inde
...	...	...	...	...	...	...	...	...	...	dinar	Iraq
1.06349	1.65637	1.60421	1.60062	1.51447	1.42313	1.06370	0.91904	0.89528	0.94192	euro[2,3]	Irlande
0.00053	0.00084	0.00061	0.00065	0.00059	0.00058	1.06397	0.92136	0.89473	0.94589	euro[2,3]	Italie
0.18092	0.13946	0.02845	0.02683	0.02822	0.02736	0.02562	0.02344	0.02177	0.02066	dollar	Jamaïque
0.00422	0.00694	0.01067	0.00919	0.00827	0.00766	0.00878	0.00928	0.00824	0.00800	yen	Japon
2.54458	1.50548	1.42519	1.41044	1.41044	1.41044	1.41044	1.41044	1.41046	...	dinar	Jordanie
0.06089	0.04355	0.01942	0.01749	0.01712	0.01655	0.01431	0.01312	0.01272	0.01270	shilling	Kenya
0.70080	0.78049	0.74087	0.78377	0.74504	0.62744	0.64556	0.58074	...	...	dollar aust.	Kiribati
3.32810	3.42434	3.35157	3.33979	3.29724	3.28116	3.28505	3.25965	3.26038	3.29362	dinar	Koweït
.	.	1.89569	1.81508	1.72020	1.69447	1.70884	1.65011	1.59240	1.62104	lat	Lettonie
0.44716	0.38624	0.27564	0.23019	0.21691	0.18071	0.16367	0.14443	0.11525	0.09571	loti	Lesotho
1.00037	...	...	...	...	...	...	...	...	...	dollar	Libéria
3.37780	3.55483	2.90622	2.28855	2.16947	2.13641	2.15438	1.95249	1.64973	0.78774	dinar	Jamahiriya arabe libyenne
.	.	0.25000	0.25000	0.25000	0.25000	0.25000	0.25000	0.25000	0.27368	lita	Lituanie
.	.	.	.	0.02799	0.02758	1.06469	0.92240	0.89496	0.94350	euro[2,3]	Luxembourg
0.00151	0.00067	0.00024	0.00025	0.00020	0.00019	0.00016	...	...	...	franc	Madagascar
0.58828	0.37108	0.06545	0.06532	0.06079	0.03102	0.02273	0.01605	0.01413	0.01296	kwacha	Malawi
0.40287	0.36980	0.39883	0.39750	0.35648	0.25563	0.26314	0.26316	0.26316	0.26315	ringgit	Malaisie
0.00225	0.00369	0.00201	0.00195	0.00171	0.00169	0.00162	0.00141	0.00136	0.00144	franc CFA[4,5,6]	Mali
2.13564	3.15816	2.83462	2.77393	2.59200	2.57414	2.50307	2.27740	2.22302	2.31533	lire	Malte
0.11151	0.18411	0.20127	...	.	.	.	.	.	.	franc	Martinique
0.01294	...	...	...	...	...	...	...	...	...	ouguiya	Mauritanie
0.06542	0.06767	0.05749	0.05577	0.04726	0.04151	0.03968	0.03794	0.03427	...	rupee	Maurice
0.37040	0.37040	...	...	...	...	...	...	...	...	dollar C.O.[1]	Montserrat
0.09960	0.12139	0.11729	0.11466	0.10488	0.10426	0.10192	0.09417	0.08856	0.09087	dirham	Maroc
0.11804	0.15954	0.17638	0.17051	0.16146	0.15991	0.16058	0.15536	0.14951	...	kyat	Myanmar
.	.	.	0.23278	0.21593	0.17969	0.16358	0.14372	0.11626	...	dollar	Namibie
0.05512	0.03401	0.01931	0.01764	0.01723	0.01514	0.01459	0.01405	0.01336	0.01284	rupee	Népal
0.55550	0.55870	0.55870	0.55870	0.55870	...	...	...	...	...	guilder NA	Antilles néer.
0.30277	0.55099	0.62371	0.59300	0.51289	0.50511	1.06511	0.92061	0.89564	0.94489	euro[2,3]	Pays-Bas
0.00617	0.01015	0.01114	0.01076	0.00940	0.00941	0.00893	0.00773	0.00787	...	CFP franc[9]	Nouvelle-Calédonie
0.49315	0.59606	0.65643	0.68798	0.66282	0.53656	0.52908	0.45450	0.42026	0.46345	dollar	Nouvelle-Zélande
0.00225	0.00366	0.00201	0.00196	0.00171	0.00170	0.00163	0.00141	0.00137	0.00143	franc CFA[4,6]	Niger
0.48836	0.59255	...	...	...	...	...	...	...	...	dollar NZ	Nuie

Special Table C

External trade conversion factors

Imports, exports: US dollars per national currency *[cont.]*

Facteurs de conversion pour le commerce extérieur

Importations, exportations: monnaie nationale en dollars É.-U. *[suite]*

Country or Area	Unit	1985	1990	1995	1996	1997	1998	1999	2000	2001	2002
		Imports - Importations *[cont.]*									
Norway	krone	0.11738	0.16011	0.15805	0.15504	0.14159	0.13260	0.12814	0.11343	0.11128	0.12615
Oman	rial Omani	2.89519	2.60078	2.60078	2.60078	2.60078	2.60078	2.60071	2.60078	2.60078	2.60077
Pakistan	rupee	0.06311	0.04629	0.03176	0.02785	0.02446	0.02225	0.02009	0.01865	0.01615	0.01674
Panama	balboa	1.00000	1.00000	1.00000	1.00000	1.00000	1.00000	1.00000	1.00000	1.00000	1.00000
Papua New Guinea	kina	1.00185	1.04679	0.77924	0.75844	0.69814	0.48325	0.38939	0.36017	0.29489	0.25646
Philippines	peso	0.05374	0.04102	0.03881	0.03814	0.03387	0.02445	0.02558	0.02254	0.01963	0.01938
Poland	zloty	67.65233	1.05263	0.41224	0.36960	0.30409	0.28809	0.25103	0.22983	0.24425	0.24527
Portugal	euro[2,3]	0.00588	0.00704	0.00662	0.00648	0.00571	0.00557	1.06188	0.92195	0.89485	0.94270
Qatar	riyal	0.27473	0.27473	0.27473	0.27473	0.27473	0.27473	0.27465	...	...	...
Réunion	franc	0.11276	0.18445	0.20073	...	.	.	.	.	.	.
Rwanda	franc	0.00987	0.01250	0.00388	0.00327	0.00332	0.00318	0.00295	0.00255	0.00226	0.00211
Saint Kitts-Nevis	EC dollar[1]	0.37037	0.37037	0.37037	0.37037	0.37037	0.37037	...	...	...	...
Saint Lucia	EC dollar[1]	0.37037	0.37037	0.37037	0.37037	0.37037	0.37037	0.37037	0.37037	0.37037	...
Saint Vincent-Grenadines	EC dollar[1]	0.37037	0.37037	0.37037	0.37037	0.37037	0.37037	0.37037	0.37037	0.37037	0.37037
Samoa	tala	0.44611	0.43355	0.40353	0.40610	0.39104	0.33837	0.33276	0.30374	0.28768	0.29629
Saudi Arabia	riyal	0.27582	0.26702	0.26702	0.26702	0.26702	0.26702	0.26702	0.26702	0.26702	0.26702
Senegal	CFA franc[4,6]	0.00219	0.00368	0.00200	0.00195	0.00171	0.00169	0.00162	0.00140	0.00137	...
Seychelles	rupee	0.14094	0.18807	0.20989	0.20120	0.19889	0.19038	0.18728	0.17549	0.17157	...
Sierra Leone	leone	0.19646	0.00658	0.00130	0.00109	0.00115	0.00064	0.00052	0.00047	0.00049	0.00048
Singapore	dollar	0.45467	0.55347	0.70613	0.70924	0.67364	0.59890	0.59031	0.57950	0.55853	0.55897
Slovakia	koruna	.	.	0.03369	0.03258	0.02977	0.02837	0.02374	0.02164	0.02067	0.02223
Solomon Islands	dollar	0.67254	0.39595	0.29345	0.28057	0.26740	0.20770	...	...	...	...
South Africa	rand	0.45380	0.38651	0.27562	0.23307	0.21744	0.18079	0.16369	0.14374	0.11713	0.09528
Spain	euro[2,3]	0.00591	0.00984	0.00803	0.00789	0.00683	0.00671	1.06309	0.92032	0.89483	0.94667
Sri Lanka	rupee	0.03676	0.02495	0.01950	0.01807	0.01695	0.01546	0.01413	0.01301	0.01121	0.01044
Suriname	guilder	0.56031	0.56029	0.00225	0.00249	0.00249	0.00249	...	...	...	...
Swaziland	lilangeni	0.44749	0.38718	0.27545	0.23300	0.21751	0.18046	0.16366	0.14268	0.11448	0.09539
Sweden	krona	0.11673	0.16938	0.14061	0.14917	0.13111	0.12586	0.12097	0.10906	0.09705	0.10300
Switzerland	franc	0.41085	0.72136	0.84832	0.80975	0.68946	0.69138	0.66516	0.59172	0.59273	0.64268
Syrian Arab Rep.	pound	0.25478	0.08909	0.08909	0.08909	0.08909	0.08909	0.08909	0.08909	0.02657	0.02162
Thailand	baht	0.03680	0.03916	0.04014	0.03947	0.03268	0.02422	0.02640	0.02483	0.02251	0.02330
Togo	CFA franc[4,5,6]	0.00224	0.00367	0.00201	0.00195	0.00171	0.00170	0.00161	0.00141	0.00136	0.00144
Tonga	pa'anga	0.69881	0.78102	0.78714	0.81208	0.78979	0.67195	0.62487	0.56442	0.46889	..
Trinidad and Tobago	dollar	0.41143	0.23529	0.16815	0.16665	0.15984	0.15876	0.15872	0.15873	0.16076	0.16006
Tunisia	dinar	1.20539	1.14217	1.05880	1.02699	0.90381	0.87993	0.84151	0.72984	0.69569	0.70506
Tuvalu	Aust. dollar	0.49840	...	...	...	...	...	...	...	...	...
Uganda	shilling	0.15750	0.00233	0.00103	0.00095	0.00092	0.00081	0.00069	0.00061	0.00057	0.00056
United Kingdom	pound	1.28893	1.78093	1.57878	1.56139	1.63834	1.65690	1.61810	1.51281	1.43963	1.50138
United Rep. of Tanzania	shilling	0.05752	0.00513	0.00173	0.00172	0.00163	0.00150	0.00133	0.00125	0.00114	0.00103
Vanuatu	vatu	0.00953	0.00855	0.00892	0.00895	0.00862	0.00782	0.00775	0.00725	...	..
Venezuela	bolivar	0.13333	0.02116	0.00573	0.00234	0.00204	0.00183	0.00165	0.00147	0.00138	..
Yemen	rial[8]	.	...	0.02813	0.01273	0.00775	0.00738	0.00641	0.00619	0.00593	..
Zambia	kwacha	0.33798	0.03307	0.00116	0.00083	0.00076	...	...	...	...	..
Zimbabwe	dollar	0.61952	0.40619	0.11546	0.10027	0.08365	0.04550	0.02612	0.02244	...	..

Special Table C

External trade conversion factors

Imports, exports: US dollars per national currency *[cont.]*

Facteurs de conversion pour le commerce extérieur

Importations, exportations: monnaie nationale en dollars É.-U. *[suite]*

1985	1990	1995	1996	1997	1998	1999	2000	2001	2002	Unité	Pays ou Zone
				Exports - Exportations *[suite]*							
0.11708	0.16091	0.15795	0.15508	0.14178	0.13263	0.12803	0.11337	0.11126	0.12588	couronne	Norvège
2.89519	2.60078	2.60078	2.60078	2.60078	2.60078	2.60069	2.60078	2.60078	2.60077	rial omani	Oman
0.06308	0.04628	0.03178	0.02794	0.02440	0.02226	0.02008	0.01864	0.01614	0.01674	rupee	Pakistan
1.00000	1.00000	1.00000	1.00000	1.00000	1.00000	1.00000	1.00000	1.00000	1.00000	balboa	Panama
1.00162	1.04859	0.78048	0.75900	0.70163	0.47805	0.38481	0.36050	0.29694	0.25686	kina	Popouasie-Nouvelle-Guinée
0.05374	0.04122	0.03883	0.03814	0.03371	0.02441	0.02553	0.02244	0.01962	0.01938	peso	Philippines
67.55309	1.05263	0.41233	0.37054	0.30431	0.28806	0.25135	0.22975	0.24413	0.24521	zloty	Pologne
0.00588	0.00703	0.00663	0.00648	0.00571	0.00556	1.06376	0.92225	0.89482	0.94263	euro[2,3]	Portugal
0.27473	0.27473	0.27473	0.27473	0.27473	0.27473	0.27465	...	...	...	riyal	Qatar
0.11193	0.18631	0.20123	...	.	.	.	.	.	.	franc	Réunion
0.00994	0.01196	0.00354	0.00326	0.00332	0.00319	0.00295	0.00255	0.00228	0.00212	franc	Rwanda
0.37037	0.37037	0.37037	0.37037	0.37037	...	...	...	...	...	dollar C.O.[1]	Saint-Kitts-et-Nevis
0.37037	0.37037	0.37037	0.37037	0.37037	0.37037	0.37037	0.37037	0.37037	...	dollar C.O.[1]	Sainte-Lucie
0.37037	0.37037	0.37037	0.37037	0.37037	0.37037	0.37037	0.37037	0.37037	0.37037	dollar C.O.[1]	St.Vincent-Grenadines
0.44748	0.43258	0.40322	0.40627	0.39011	0.33822	0.33082	0.30446	0.28776	0.29732	tala	Samoa
0.27618	0.26702	0.26702	0.26702	0.26702	0.26702	0.26702	0.26702	0.26702	...	riyal	Arabie saoudite
0.00220	0.00369	0.00200	0.00195	0.00171	0.00169	0.00162	0.00141	0.00137	0.00143	franc CFA.[4,6]	Sénégal
0.13971	0.18917	0.20959	0.20103	0.19905	0.19010	0.18722	0.17468	0.17112	...	rupee	Seychelles
0.19511	0.00654	0.00140	0.00109	0.00111	0.00063	0.00055	0.00049	0.00050	0.00048	leone	Sierra Leone
0.45468	0.55385	0.70598	0.70923	0.67339	0.59808	0.59026	0.57944	0.55844	0.55907	dollar	Singapour
.	.	0.03370	0.03258	0.02974	0.02838	0.02375	0.02167	0.02068	0.02220	couronne	Slovaquie
0.67227	0.39555	0.29377	0.28037	0.26789	0.20744	...	...	...	...	dollar	Iles Salomon
0.45000	0.38683	0.27566	0.23178	0.21708	0.18122	0.16367	0.14384	0.11744	0.09540	rand	Afrique du Sud
0.00592	0.00986	0.00803	0.00789	0.00684	0.00671	1.06408	0.92078	0.89511	0.94457	euro[2,3]	Espagne
0.03681	0.02496	0.01946	0.01806	0.01692	0.01542	0.01413	0.01293	0.01119	0.01045	rupee	Sri Lanka
0.56031	0.56029	0.00226	0.00249	0.00249	0.00249	...	...	...	...	guilder	Suriname
0.45622	0.38693	0.27525	0.23146	0.21611	0.18062	0.16367	0.14270	0.11524	0.09553	lilangeni	Swaziland
0.11696	0.16922	0.14059	0.14916	0.13109	0.12587	0.12096	0.10913	0.09693	0.10292	couronne	Suède
0.41195	0.72281	0.84838	0.80920	0.68966	0.69139	0.66515	0.59160	0.59314	0.64367	franc	Suisse
0.25478	0.08909	0.08909	0.08909	0.08909	0.08909	0.08909	0.08909	0.02655	0.02162	livre	République arab syrienne
0.03682	0.03914	0.04013	0.03946	0.03177	0.02423	0.02640	0.02486	0.02251	0.02329	baht	Thaïlande
0.00223	0.00368	0.00201	0.00195	0.00172	0.00170	0.00161	0.00140	0.00136	0.00144	franc CFA[4,5,6]	Togo
0.70038	0.77748	0.78835	0.81755	0.77625	0.64723	0.61960	0.55145	0.46059	...	pa'anga	Tonga
0.40920	0.23529	0.16809	0.16651	0.16002	0.15876	0.15872	0.15873	0.16023	0.16014	dollar	Trinité-et-Tobago
1.20445	1.14241	1.05846	1.02693	0.90429	0.88022	0.84282	0.73083	0.69538	0.70516	dinar	Tunisie
0.49840	...	...	...	...	...	...	...	...	...	dollar aust.	Tuvalu
0.15750	0.00235	0.00103	0.00096	0.00093	0.00080	0.00069	0.00062	0.00057	0.00056	shilling	Ouganda
1.29368	1.78728	1.57829	1.56250	1.63807	1.65696	1.61824	1.51219	1.43994	1.50041	livre	Royaume-Uni
0.05779	0.00513	0.00175	0.00172	0.00164	0.00150	0.00132	0.00125	0.00114	0.00103	shilling	Rép.-Unie de Tanzanie
0.00951	0.00854	0.00891	0.00897	0.00863	0.00781	0.00774	0.00725	...	...	vatu	Vanuatu
0.13333	0.02111	0.00562	0.00235	0.00205	0.00183	0.00164	0.00147	0.00139	0.00083	bolívar	Venezuela
.	...	0.02414	0.01273	0.00775	0.00738	0.00641	0.00618	0.00593	...	rial[8]	Yémen
0.31939	0.03351	0.00116	0.00084	0.00076	...	...	...	...	...	kwacha	Zambie
0.61798	0.40696	0.11514	0.09990	0.08132	0.04550	0.02611	0.02220	...	...	dollar	Zimbabwe

Special Table C
External trade conversion factors
Imports, exports: US dollars per national currency *[cont.]*
Facteurs de conversion pour le commerce extérieur
Importations, exportations: monnaie nationale en dollars É.-U. *[suite]*

General note: Trade conversion factors are weighted averages of monthly or quarterly exchange rates, the weights being the corresponding monthly or quarterly values of imports and exports. The exchange rates are as compiled by the IMF or provided by the country concerned. The conversion factors shown in this table are used to obtain trade data in terms of US dollars.

1 East Caribbean dollar.
2 Beginning 1999 U.S. dollars per euro; the conversion factors are calculated for each country of euro zone separately and may vary due to differences in relative weights of monthly or quarterly values of imports and exports.
3 Prior to January 1999 the conversion factors are US dollar per previous national currency: Austria - schillings, Belguim - francs, Finland - markkaa, France - francs, Germany - deutsche marks, Ireland - pounds, Italy -lire, Luxembourg - francs, Netherlands - guilders, Portugal - escudos, and Spain - pesetas.
4 Prior to 1999, the CFA franc was pegged to the French franc at CFAF 100 per French franc and prior to 1994 CFAF 50 per French franc.. Beginning 1999, the CFAF is pegged to the euro at CFAF 655.957 per euro.
5 The conversion factors are not trade weighted.
6 Comptoirs Francais du Afrique franc pegged to the euro at CFAF 655.957 per euro.
7 After July 5, 1999 lev is equal to 1,000 of pre-July 5, 1999 leva. All data are expressed in terms of the new leva.
8 See explanatory notes on data pertaining to Yemen on page v.
9 Comptoirs Francais du Pacifique franc.
10 Prior to 1999, the CFA franc was pegged to the French franc at CFAF 100 per French franc. Beginning 1999, the CFAF is pegged to the euro at CFAF 655.957 per euro.

Note generale: Les facteurs de conversion pour le commerce extérieur sont les moyennes pondérées des taux de change mensuelles ou trimestrielles. Les coefficients de pondération sont les valeurs mensuelles ou trimestrielles correspondantes des importations ou des exportations. Les taux de change sont les taux calculés par le secretariat du FMI ou fournis par le pays. Les facteurs de conversion montrés dans cette table sont employés pour obtenir les données commerciales en termes de dollars de E.U..

1 Dollar des caraïbes orientales.
2 A partir de 1999 dollars des Etats-Unis par euro; les facteurs de conversion sont calculés pour chaque pays d'euro zone séparément et peuvent varier en raison des différences dans les ponderation relatifs de valeurs mensuelles ou trimestrielles des importations et des exportations.
3 Avant janvier 1999 les facteurs de conversion sont dollar des E.U. par monnaie nationale précédente: Autriche - schillings, Belgique - francs, Finlande - markkaa, France - francs, Allemagne - deutsche marks, Irlande - livres, Italie - lire, Luxembourg - francs, Pays-Bas - florins, Portugal - escudos, et Espagne - pesetas.
4 Avant 1999, le franc de CFA a été chevillé au franc français à CFAF 100 par franc français et avant 1994, CFAF 50 par franc français. Commençant 1999, le CFAF est chevillé à l'euro à CFAF 655,957 par euro.
5 Les facteurs de conversion ne sont pas pondérés.
6 Comptoirs Francais du Afrique franc est chevillé à l'euro à CFAF 655,957 par euro.
7 Après juillet 5, 1999 le lev est égal à 1,000 pré-Juillet de 5, 1999 leva. Toutes les données sont exprimées en termes de nouveau lev.
8 Voir les notes explicatives sur les données concernant Yemen à la page vii.
9 Comptoirs Francais du Pacifique franc.
10 Avant 1999, le franc de CFA a été chevillé au franc français à CFAF 100 par franc français. Commençant 1999, le CFAF est chevillé à l'euro à CFAF 655,957 par euro.

SPECIAL TABLE: D

World exports by commodity classes and by regions (continued)

In million U.S. dollars f.o.b.

Exports from ↓ / Exports to →	Year	World Monde 1/	Developed economies: Econ. développées 1/,2/	Developing economies: économies en voie de développement 1/,2/ — Total	Developing economies — OPEC OPEP	Eastern Europe and fmr. USSR-Europe: Europe de l'Est et l'anc. URSS-Europe — Total 1/,5/	Eastern Europe — Former USSR-Eur. 6/	Developed economies: Europe — Total	Europe — EU UE	Europe — EFTA AELE	Developed economies: South Africa — Afrique du Sud
											Total trade (SITC, Rev. 2 and Rev. 3, 0-9) 4/
World 1/	1998	5305813	3594609	1434084	163294	210854	86173	2162318	2030089	126845	24581
	1999	5499822	3780536	1470346	146981	184280	63609	2207136	2079720	121421	21700
	2000	6181017	4150407	1754265	167246	218110	82116	2312109	2181824	123405	23531
	2001	5976350	3977708	1669600	186109	236961	91401	2273138	2145994	120887	23554
	2002	6237861	4151148	1737203	193719	253647	98186	2395810	2261984	127237	24574
Developed economies 1/,2/	1998	3616763	2626442	806025	103032	134653	43047	1758721	1648121	106150	18725
	1999	3683103	2713346	799175	87150	119578	29794	1786414	1677966	103610	15653
	2000	3945295	2844875	920837	93453	131425	34477	1812232	1703565	103074	16748
	2001	3852664	2761298	870983	103969	148855	44202	1794883	1685187	104303	16570
	2002	3960461	2850537	878114	106422	156936	46448	1879733	1764815	109261	17106
Developing economies 1/,2/	1998	1482791	851269	600441	58013	23840	13538	299640	284005	15431	5764
	1999	1614333	945601	643229	57794	20353	10671	311844	299361	12192	5931
	2000	1984564	1157715	792449	70611	25136	14467	367463	353216	13890	6666
	2001	1862280	1067899	759133	78385	28476	16947	342034	329593	12085	6884
	2002	1987273	1135783	815266	83130	30529	18162	364890	351538	12983	7357
OPEC	1998	217196	119643	96652	13147	654	320	39988	39551	428	226
	1999	275291	147015	123404	15512	693	363	49312	48835	460	340
	2000	339151	186591	150952	18155	925	584	62188	61596	579	454
	2001	302141	161562	139465	19420	995	639	52719	52147	508	444
	2002	302263	161627	139521	19428	995	639	52740	52168	508	445
Eastern Europe and the former USSR 1/,5/	1998	206259	116898	27618	2249	52361	29588	103957	97963	5264	92
	1999	202386	121589	27942	2037	44349	23144	108878	102393	5619	116
	2000	251158	147817	40979	3182	61549	33172	132414	125043	6441	117
	2001	261406	148511	39484	3755	59630	30252	136221	131214	4499	100
	2002	290127	164828	43822	4168	66182	33576	151188	145631	4993	111
Former USSR-Europe 6/	1998	103235	43051	19225	1325	32091	22324	34134	29816	3684	37
	1999	100321	44577	19630	1239	27696	18384	36087	31467	3865	62
	2000	135066	61224	31078	2114	42737	27916	51107	45721	4548	43
	2001	132047	51716	28852	2502	37854	23963	44857	42355	2141	19
	2002	142082	55646	31045	2692	40731	25784	48266	45574	2304	20
Developed economies-Europe	1998	2271567	1783031	319309	55325	123898	36808	1497896	1401734	92183	12185
	1999	2270503	1821136	298558	48256	111712	26204	1517222	1423721	89117	10643
	2000	2342743	1856689	322553	50418	122486	30313	1525606	1433399	87137	10846
	2001	2387729	1856032	331556	58929	139563	39585	1530711	1436717	89276	11147
	2002	2529697	1966387	351269	62433	147861	41939	1621723	1522140	94584	11810
European Union	1998	2148086	1678803	303471	53046	120488	35741	1413694	1318836	91025	11735
	1999	2140318	1710412	282329	46219	108486	25443	1430435	1338255	88083	10273
	2000	2196716	1731668	305115	48168	118923	29363	1427814	1336931	86100	10445
	2001	2242327	1733713	312772	56456	135270	38248	1432808	1340210	88192	10799
	2002	2378915	1839320	331824	59895	143510	40578	1520085	1421847	93564	11457
European Free Trade Association	1998	121189	102386	15403	2214	3398	1059	82763	81518	1100	444
	1999	127789	108808	15776	1972	3204	744	85363	84099	977	369
	2000	143334	122908	16892	2196	3533	935	96478	95346	846	399
	2001	143120	120504	18366	2409	4248	1318	96570	95345	913	345
	2002	148500	125034	19056	2500	4408	1368	100200	98929	947	358
Other developed economies	1998	1345196	843411	486716	47707	10755	6239	260825	246387	13967	6540
	1999	1412600	892210	500617	38894	7866	3590	269192	254245	14493	5010
	2000	1602552	988186	598284	43035	8939	4164	286626	270166	15937	5902
	2001	1464935	905266	539427	45040	9292	4617	264172	248470	15027	5423
	2002	1430764	884150	526845	43989	9075	4509	258010	242674	14676	5297

For general note and footnotes see end of table.

Exportations mondiales par classes de marchandises et par régions (suite)

En millions de dollars E.-U. f.o.b.

Economies développées 1/,2/ — Canada	U.S.A. E.-U.	Japan Japon	Australia New Zealand Australie Nouvelle-Zélande	Developing economies / Economies en voie de développement 1/,2/ — Africa Afrique	America Amerique — Total	America Amerique — LAIA ALADI	Asia Asie — Mid. East Moyen Orient	Asia Asie — Other Autres 7/	Oceania Océanie	← Exportations vers / Année	Exportations en provenance de ↓
Commerce total (CTCI, Rev. 2 et Rev. 3, 0-9) 4/											
180387	886738	249441	66909	101096	315673	251590	168450	818748	5499	1998	Monde 1/
192105	988618	272135	71531	96138	298378	229560	151994	894819	5934	1999	
209923	1162542	337034	74731	100895	348229	269336	174140	1099889	6320	2000	
196189	1074657	312645	69648	107556	333035	258203	175076	1020359	6866	2001	
195363	1106334	328036	72119	112664	337377	260711	183316	1068259	7161	2002	
163422	505390	113963	46333	68421	223856	183898	107768	384823	3887	1998	Economies dévelopées 1/,2/
173317	553331	114320	48184	63860	212862	171487	92166	410219	4087	1999	
186332	629723	128368	47921	65468	239123	195875	99357	496583	3813	2000	
174365	589947	118387	45629	70869	227730	187177	97260	453077	4385	2001	
172078	594355	119216	45911	73564	227287	186721	100476	453685	4437	2002	
16449	372586	132809	20417	30271	88615	66262	53990	421445	1574	1998	Economies en voie de développement 1/,2/
18378	426581	155261	23233	29757	81576	56846	54134	471519	1836	1999	
23060	522976	205413	26688	32387	103218	71980	64107	585455	2502	2000	
21308	476600	191689	23891	33724	99735	69569	67110	551060	2429	2001	
22711	502977	205968	26066	35812	103908	72373	70958	596570	2666	2002	
888	27601	44028	1910	5222	4688	3866	17490	66772	83	1998	OPEP
1050	34538	58072	2406	5846	4030	3249	19598	90140	148	1999	
1879	44420	73556	4081	6645	5289	4354	22326	111834	188	2000	
1888	40463	62745	3282	6403	5473	4435	21834	101466	135	2001	
1889	40479	62770	3283	6406	5475	4437	21843	101507	135	2002	
516	8762	2669	159	2404	3202	1430	6692	12480	38	1998	Europe de l'Est et l'ancienne URSS 1/,5/
410	8706	2554	114	2521	3940	1227	5694	13081	11	1999	
531	9843	3253	122	3040	5888	1481	10676	17851	5	2000	
516	8110	2569	128	2963	5570	1457	10706	16222	52	2001	
573	9001	2851	142	3289	6182	1617	11882	18004	58	2002	
185	5778	2382	22	1298	2331	735	4479	10477	6	1998	l'ancienne URSS-Europe 6/
152	5388	2293	18	1426	3151	597	3751	10797	2	1999	
193	5826	2873	21	1994	5010	822	7971	15231	3	2000	
155	4006	2158	29	1795	4547	722	7953	13536	6	2001	
167	4310	2322	31	1931	4893	777	8557	14565	6	2002	
17941	186711	38621	16980	51576	61583	51305	70401	117834	1286	1998	Economies développées-Europe
19735	201124	41094	17353	47828	55072	43750	62352	116550	1459	1999	
21742	221794	44979	16505	48652	56523	44723	69397	130927	1233	2000	
21510	219481	43370	16267	52518	58811	47229	66254	135005	1869	2001	
22789	232531	45949	17234	55641	62308	50037	70193	143032	1980	2002	
15899	174901	34503	16137	50355	58400	48669	67209	110060	1273	1998	Union Européenne
16870	186912	36499	16456	46432	52169	41457	59453	107992	1448	1999	
17542	205566	40337	15683	47408	53532	42390	66188	121406	1216	2000	
18242	204701	39044	15404	50993	55085	44777	63052	125166	1808	2001	
19353	217170	41422	16342	54099	58440	47505	66893	132790	1918	2002	
2035	11469	4071	841	1167	3170	2632	3123	7476	12	1998	Association Européenne de Libre Exchange
2852	13793	4539	894	1337	2893	2289	2866	8207	11	1999	
4172	15558	4545	820	1197	2979	2327	3179	9065	17	2000	
3260	14376	4263	862	1468	3715	2447	3169	9523	61	2001	
3383	14916	4423	894	1523	3855	2539	3288	9881	63	2002	
145481	318679	75342	29353	16845	162273	132593	37367	266989	2601	1998	Autres economies développées
153582	352207	73226	30831	16032	157790	127737	29814	293669	2628	1999	
164590	407929	83389	31416	16816	182600	151152	29960	365656	2580	2000	
152855	370466	75017	29362	18351	168919	139948	31006	318072	2516	2001	
149290	361825	73267	28677	17923	164979	136684	30283	310653	2457	2002	

Voir la fin du tableau pour la remarque générale et les notes

SPECIAL TABLE: D

World exports by commodity classes and by regions (continued)

In million U.S. dollars f.o.b.

Exports to → / ↓ Exports from	Year	World Monde 1/	Developed economies Econ. dévelop-pées 1/,2/	Developing economies economies en voie de développement 1/,2/ Total	OPEC OPEP	Eastern Europe and fmr. USSR-Europe Europe de l'Est et l'anc. URSS-Europe Total 1/,5/	Former USSR-Eur. 6/	Developed economies Europe Total	EU UE	EFTA AELE	South Africa Afrique du Sud
		Total trade (SITC, Rev. 2 and Rev. 3, 0-9) 4/ (continued)									
Canada	1998	214606	200991	13074	2208	540	236	12154	10935	1215	228
	1999	238778	226048	12335	1899	393	153	14217	13369	843	176
	2000	277113	262549	14162	2269	402	177	13600	12722	869	163
	2001	259903	245710	13783	1917	407	217	12676	11796	871	120
	2002	252408	238624	13386	1862	395	211	12310	11456	846	117
United States	1998	634674	363787	263755	25902	6729	4282	148532	140556	7675	3590
	1999	642159	373784	263223	20338	4778	2502	151523	142338	8980	2627
	2000	712212	402507	304277	19291	5111	2731	163567	152802	10411	2830
	2001	666003	377687	282405	20326	5637	3093	158288	147555	10452	2822
	2002	632336	358594	268129	19298	5352	2937	150286	140096	9924	2679
Japan	1998	388136	213633	172258	15359	2241	1101	75389	71687	3562	1794
	1999	417610	227811	187989	13281	1807	574	78451	74580	3652	1640
	2000	479248	246519	230377	15976	2351	719	82090	78414	3551	1863
	2001	403364	207959	193151	16377	2248	830	67546	64489	2711	1495
	2002	416730	214850	199551	16920	2322	858	69784	66626	2801	1545
Australia, New Zealand	1998	64890	36052	27462	3632	422	270	10177	9401	762	707
	1999	65024	30702	24388	2648	182	92	7753	7470	272	338
	2000	76497	40123	34513	4729	341	227	9261	9035	213	778
	2001	78719	41186	35709	5596	337	208	9851	9582	253	736
	2002	79401	41543	36018	5644	340	210	9936	9665	255	742
Developing economies-Africa	1998	65550	47038	15219	2423	871	411	34876	34267	525	707
	1999	83753	59027	21278	2369	842	375	40685	39622	962	1170
	2000	116411	85454	27362	3517	2007	1450	56710	54302	2196	1393
	2001	96632	70387	22666	3439	1474	1003	47274	45960	1177	1954
	2002	101522	74069	23813	3613	1549	1054	49786	48407	1237	2053
Developing economies-America	1998	277390	193286	75501	9067	2914	1873	40459	38768	1678	625
	1999	296386	221087	65444	6775	2468	1550	40709	38625	2067	640
	2000	350790	263949	79820	8168	2260	1196	42922	40215	2694	646
	2001	339986	250187	82427	10651	3070	2105	42371	39912	2444	835
	2002	344520	253545	83530	10793	3111	2133	42957	40465	2477	846
Developing economies-Europe 3/	1998	18221	11179	5159	263	1863	736	10468	9910	486	14
	1999	15979	10132	4428	204	1405	406	9470	8964	405	10
	2000	16673	10477	4605	194	1577	465	9731	9351	325	14
	2001	17532	10862	4826	210	1832	645	10175	9762	349	13
	2002	18500	11471	5092	222	1933	681	10746	10310	368	14
Developing economies-Middle East	1998	147127	76231	66203	15900	3212	1896	38815	38175	606	174
	1999	177020	89318	83808	15354	2217	1116	40983	40286	626	169
	2000	227871	126317	97037	16866	2422	1261	52524	51803	644	257
	2001	226334	120687	100338	21282	3350	1829	51203	50424	639	314
	2002	230452	122883	102164	21669	3411	1863	52135	51342	651	319
Developing economies-Other Asia	1998	969079	520848	437030	30346	14888	8621	174364	162290	12074	4234
	1999	1035670	562859	466301	33071	13407	7222	179215	171199	8016	3935
	2000	1266985	668640	581859	41820	16865	10094	205013	196988	8025	4352
	2001	1176675	613144	547301	42757	18746	11364	190509	183039	7470	3764
	2002	1287195	670734	598706	46773	20507	12431	208403	200231	8172	4118
Former USSR-Asia 7/.	1998	11692	5516	2795	377	3293	2711	5131	4637	495	4
	1999	12622	5511	3970	413	3012	2466	5061	4506	547	3
	2000	18311	7592	5962	605	4645	4059	6962	6134	795	1
	2001	17794	7949	5573	533	4168	3591	7285	6497	776	0
	2002	19598	8828	6138	587	4591	3955	8096	7228	855	0
Developing economies-Oceania	1998	5424	2687	1329	14	92	1	658	595	62	10
	1999	5525	3178	1970	21	14	2	782	665	116	7
	2000	5834	2878	1766	46	5	1	563	557	6	4
	2001	5121	2632	1575	46	4	1	502	496	6	4
	2002	5084	3082	1961	60	19	1	863	783	79	7

For general note and footnotes see end of table.

Exportations mondiales par classes de marchandises et par régions (suite)

En millions de dollars E.-U. f.o.b.

conomies éveloppées 1/,2/				Developing economies Economies en voie de développement 1/,2/						← Exportations vers	
Canada	U.S.A. E.-U.	Japan Japon	Australia New Zealand Australie Nouvelle-Zélande	Africa Afrique	America Amerique Total	America Amerique LAIA ALADI	Asia Asie Mid. East Moyen Orient	Asia Asie Other Autres 7/	Oceania Océanie	Année	Exportations en provenance de ↓
ommerce total (CTCI, Rev. 2 et Rev. 3, 0-9) 4/ (suite)											
.	181854	5806	795	1205	4377	3461	900	6490	22	1998	Canada
.	205020	5651	785	910	3884	2921	992	6451	22	1999	
.	241591	6063	925	887	4261	3427	1167	7752	14	2000	
.	226587	5275	829	876	4537	3659	949	7372	14	2001	
.	220053	5123	805	851	4406	3553	922	7159	14	2002	
137766	.	54845	13370	7356	135515	115244	19470	100672	404	1998	Etats-Unis
145726	.	54309	13262	7015	133652	113671	15988	105809	385	1999	
155587	.	60748	13584	7710	156125	134439	14440	125283	361	2000	
144619	.	53544	12266	9260	145044	124092	14280	113160	318	2001	
137308	.	50837	11646	8792	137712	117819	13558	107440	302	2002	
6348	119845	.	9211	3877	19587	11522	13386	134738	547	1998	Japon
6927	129797	.	9931	3655	17891	9175	10007	155621	658	1999	
7477	143977	.	9835	3044	19477	10902	9914	197365	460	2000	
6565	122549	.	8868	2816	16418	9713	10697	162698	448	2001	
6783	126610	.	9162	2909	16962	10035	11051	168089	463	2002	
963	6308	12450	5359	859	1362	1153	2759	20851	1612	1998	Australie, Nouvelle-Zélande
470	5428	10587	6058	566	1100	869	1717	19442	1558	1999	
1023	8218	14381	6317	906	1252	1035	3265	27339	1739	2000	
1227	8398	14136	6688	1118	1481	1168	3973	27413	1709	2001	
1238	8471	14258	6746	1128	1494	1178	4007	27650	1724	2002	
663	9153	1281	144	6908	1702	1613	2797	3638	5	1998	Economies en voie de développement-Afrique
948	14373	1356	226	7375	3090	2943	2913	7664	22	1999	
1570	23568	1460	329	8289	4334	3659	4035	10392	90	2000	
1090	18054	1444	188	7481	3157	2648	3764	8062	55	2001	
1145	18968	1517	198	7860	3317	2782	3954	8470	58	2002	
4105	140524	6630	572	3032	57440	44740	3872	10970	27	1998	Economies en voie de développement-Amérique
4831	166884	7053	625	2350	48982	35453	2997	10993	30	1999	
5834	205778	7671	778	2413	61121	43526	3388	12788	23	2000	
5646	193728	6595	596	3010	60445	43034	3987	14842	26	2001	
5721	196311	6683	604	3051	61251	43609	4040	15040	26	2002	
48	570	22	27	530	138	84	451	128	0	1998	Economies en voie de développement-Europe 3/
36	536	22	27	341	148	115	411	169	3	1999	
56	583	30	23	385	132	66	420	144	1	2000	
49	504	53	30	288	178	64	372	168	42	2001	
52	532	56	32	304	188	68	393	177	44	2002	
592	12774	22360	1002	5921	786	574	18550	40689	0	1998	Economies en voie de développement-Moyen Orient
643	17222	28398	1234	5949	982	743	20559	56018	0	1999	
1123	26135	43427	2159	6139	1415	1122	22443	66702	7	2000	
1198	25642	39662	1769	6679	1691	1280	25858	65762	20	2001	
1220	26109	40384	1801	6801	1722	1303	26329	66959	20	2002	
11030	209265	101494	18034	13870	28101	18949	28320	365238	1424	1998	Economies en voie de développement-Autres Pays d'Asie
11909	227184	117328	20229	13724	27759	17138	27253	395472	1655	1999	
14447	266578	151556	22747	15149	35715	23138	33816	494361	2292	2000	
13294	238364	142696	20830	16255	33755	22061	33124	461309	2201	2001	
14543	260752	156099	22786	17782	36925	24133	36235	504638	2408	2002	
8	148	216	1	54	169	56	947	1612	0	1998	l'ancienne URSS asiatique 7/
8	190	179	1	49	1289	42	874	1743	0	1999	
9	311	162	1	40	2558	49	1228	2108	1	2000	
9	316	163	1	58	2432	57	1031	2010	2	2001	
10	348	180	1	64	2679	63	1136	2214	2	2002	
11	300	1022	638	10	448	302	0	782	118	1998	Economies en voie de développement-Océanie
11	382	1104	892	18	615	454	1	1203	126	1999	
30	334	1269	652	12	501	469	5	1068	89	2000	
31	308	1239	478	11	509	482	5	917	85	2001	
31	306	1230	645	15	505	479	7	1287	109	2002	

Voir la fin du tableau pour la remarque générale et les notes

SPECIAL TABLE: D

World exports by commodity classes and by regions (continued)

In million U.S. dollars f.o.b.

Exports from ↓ / Exports to →	Year	World Monde 1/	Developed economies — Econ. dévelop-pées 1/,2/	Developing economies — economies en voie de développement 1/,2/: Total	Developing economies: OPEC OPEP	Eastern Europe and fmr. USSR-Europe — Europe de l'Est et l'anc. URSS-Europe: Total 1/,5/	Eastern Europe and fmr. USSR-Europe: Former USSR-Eur. 6/	Developed economies — Europe: Total	Europe: EU UE	Europe: EFTA AELE	South Africa — Afrique du Sud
								Food, beverages and tobacco (SITC, Rev. 2 and Rev. 3, 0 and 1)			
World 1/	1998	405199	274687	103256	20774	21896	14536	185252	178856	5834	1464
	1999	393960	276236	96817	19350	16111	9608	182970	176451	5972	1265
	2000	387901	265012	102879	20527	15717	9265	167710	161676	5520	1165
	2001	407496	274446	109833	23909	18957	11632	176084	169670	5866	1394
	2002	425327	286455	114639	24955	19787	12141	183789	177094	6123	1455
Developed economies 1/,2/	1998	266188	200506	49845	9462	11561	7208	151250	145770	4952	706
	1999	263919	202708	48980	9475	8285	4513	150423	144846	5062	653
	2000	255241	191837	51698	10259	8122	4352	136972	131908	4579	540
	2001	267362	199854	54475	10307	9479	5213	143744	138293	4931	458
	2002	274843	205446	55999	10595	9744	5359	147766	142162	5069	471
Developing economies 1/,2/	1998	127751	69870	51720	11178	5201	3745	30296	29514	754	754
	1999	121065	69512	46352	9750	4371	3028	29007	28196	784	605
	2000	123530	69218	49606	10105	3992	2778	27340	26487	830	617
	2001	129472	69955	53426	13286	5366	3967	28353	27531	802	929
	2002	138162	74650	57012	14177	5726	4233	30256	29378	856	991
OPEC	1998	11846	5084	6444	2419	312	164	1829	1810	18	19
	1999	11371	4592	6508	2234	253	132	1734	1715	16	18
	2000	10566	3978	6275	2302	292	204	1430	1412	18	13
	2001	10520	3993	6229	2595	288	223	1433	1421	10	9
	2002	10524	3995	6232	2596	288	223	1434	1422	10	9
Eastern Europe and the former USSR 1/,5/	1998	11260	4142	1708	134	5134	3583	3536	3402	128	4
	1999	8976	3828	1503	125	3455	2067	3350	3220	126	7
	2000	9130	3821	1593	163	3603	2135	3261	3144	111	8
	2001	10662	4502	1949	316	4112	2452	3851	3710	133	7
	2002	11833	4997	2163	351	4564	2721	4274	4118	148	8
Former USSR-Europe 6/	1998	3418	757	557	16	1909	1779	474	445	28	0
	1999	2460	614	411	3	1252	1145	407	382	24	0
	2000	2590	710	568	24	1296	1210	451	419	30	0
	2001	3327	842	759	91	1636	1553	552	510	39	1
	2002	3580	906	817	98	1760	1671	594	549	42	1
Developed economies-Europe	1998	186234	154630	20729	5206	9560	5587	139562	134594	4465	381
	1999	183689	155900	19781	5428	7048	3536	139865	134777	4597	38[illegible]
	2000	171002	142984	20371	5577	6801	3237	127164	122546	4158	28[illegible]
	2001	179043	149964	20347	5545	7918	3910	133697	128729	4480	27[illegible]
	2002	189688	158880	21557	5875	8389	4142	141646	136383	4746	29[illegible]
European Union	1998	178365	148001	19972	5086	9080	5267	134128	129360	4302	371
	1999	175665	148965	19065	5305	6680	3353	134404	129542	4415	37[illegible]
	2000	163619	136838	19551	5432	6388	2980	122315	117907	3987	27[illegible]
	2001	171704	144030	19509	5391	7357	3540	128951	124191	4316	27[illegible]
	2002	182163	152803	20697	5719	7805	3756	136806	131756	4579	28[illegible]
European Free Trade Association	1998	7430	6219	731	107	479	319	5041	4863	141	1[illegible]
	1999	7529	6475	685	108	368	183	5031	4833	154	1[illegible]
	2000	7016	5816	788	130	413	256	4544	4353	152	1[illegible]
	2001	6921	5556	803	138	561	370	4402	4217	142	[illegible]
	2002	7181	5765	833	143	582	384	4567	4376	147	[illegible]
Other developed economies	1998	79954	45876	29116	4256	2001	1621	11687	11175	486	32[illegible]
	1999	80230	46808	29199	4047	1237	976	10558	10068	465	27[illegible]
	2000	84240	48853	31328	4681	1321	1116	9808	9362	421	25[illegible]
	2001	88318	49889	34128	4761	1561	1302	10047	9564	451	18[illegible]
	2002	86258	48725	33332	4650	1525	1272	9813	9341	440	17[illegible]

For general note and footnotes see end of table.

Exportations mondiales par classes de marchandises et par régions (suite)

En millions de dollars E.-U. f.o.b.

Economies développées 1/,2/				Developing economies Economies en voie de développement 1/,2/						← Exportations vers	
Canada	U.S.A. E.-U.	Japan Japon	Australia New Zealand Australie Nouvelle-Zélande	Africa Afrique	America Amerique Total	America Amerique LAIA ALADI	Asia Asie Mid. East Moyen Orient	Asia Asie Other Autres 7/	Oceania Océanie	Année	Exportations en provenance de ↓
Produits alimentaires, boisson et tabac (CTCI, Rev. 2 et Rev. 3, 0 et 1)											
9541	39866	33991	3185	14758	24764	18256	18668	41657	759	1998	Monde 1/
9773	41778	35563	3541	12974	21229	15065	18529	40851	748	1999	
10514	43391	37138	3662	13891	22136	16193	19488	44227	718	2000	
11117	44771	35905	3661	15137	23858	17427	21054	46344	773	2001	
11604	46730	37476	3821	15799	24902	18190	21975	48372	807	2002	
8127	19214	18213	2039	9632	13339	9329	8034	16904	607	1998	Economies dévelopées 1/,2/
8364	20861	19205	2254	8620	12177	8175	8361	17995	596	1999	
8990	22005	19951	2358	9162	12758	8933	8733	19275	566	2000	
9590	23760	18843	2443	9516	14114	10009	7819	21092	621	2001	
9858	24425	19370	2511	9782	14509	10289	8038	21682	638	2002	
1382	20400	15529	1135	4932	11362	8889	10328	23998	164	1998	Economies en voie de développement 1/,2/
1381	20674	16208	1277	4205	9016	6866	9904	22223	158	1999	
1492	21152	16966	1294	4597	9315	7207	10483	24244	135	2000	
1491	20734	16809	1208	5350	9675	7357	12898	24470	131	2001	
1591	22126	17937	1289	5709	10325	7851	13764	26112	140	2002	
51	1979	1142	62	212	772	580	3507	1934	2	1998	OPEP
43	1727	997	73	196	575	491	3613	2088	13	1999	
44	1373	1041	74	192	515	464	3653	1884	11	2000	
43	1458	972	75	198	573	513	3576	1857	9	2001	
43	1459	972	75	198	573	513	3577	1858	9	2002	
32	252	249	11	194	63	38	306	756	0	1998	Europe de l'Est et l'ancienne URSS 1/,5/
28	243	150	10	149	37	24	264	633	0	1999	
32	234	221	10	133	63	53	273	709	0	2000	
36	277	253	10	272	69	61	337	783	0	2001	
40	307	281	11	302	77	68	374	869	0	2002	
9	86	159	4	10	19	7	67	459	0	1998	l'ancienne URSS-Europe 6/
4	90	95	2	4	12	6	24	369	0	1999	
6	75	145	3	10	6	3	53	495	0	2000	
8	100	143	2	56	10	9	100	584	0	2001	
9	108	154	2	60	11	10	108	628	0	2002	
1284	7939	4193	705	6044	3563	2313	4927	4774	156	1998	Economies développées-Europe
1302	8667	4395	779	5284	2999	1795	5194	4974	156	1999	
1361	8591	4237	832	5666	3143	1990	5070	5227	135	2000	
1436	8928	4269	781	6141	3095	1938	4447	5248	154	2001	
1521	9459	4523	827	6506	3279	2053	4711	5560	163	2002	
1191	7440	3671	673	5943	3284	2080	4787	4568	156	1998	Union Européenne
1207	8090	3674	745	5190	2805	1643	5056	4715	156	1999	
1267	8088	3615	807	5489	2961	1850	4912	4953	135	2000	
1352	8474	3689	756	5947	2913	1797	4299	4976	154	2001	
1434	8990	3914	802	6309	3090	1906	4561	5279	163	2002	
90	488	520	32	95	279	233	122	205	0	1998	Association Européenne de Libre Exchange
89	557	715	34	84	194	152	119	258	0	1999	
90	491	615	24	166	182	139	141	271	0	2000	
79	438	566	25	179	182	141	130	270	0	2001	
82	454	587	26	186	189	146	135	280	0	2002	
6843	11275	14021	1335	3588	9776	7016	3106	12130	451	1998	Autres economies développées
7061	12194	14810	1475	3336	9178	6380	3168	13021	440	1999	
7629	13414	15713	1527	3495	9616	6943	3663	14048	431	2000	
8154	14832	14574	1662	3374	11019	8071	3372	15844	466	2001	
7964	14486	14234	1623	3295	10762	7883	3293	15474	455	2002	

Voir la fin du tableau pour la remarque générale et les notes

SPECIAL TABLE: D

World exports by commodity classes and by regions (continued)

In million U.S. dollars f.o.b.

Exports from ↓ / Exports to →	Year	World Monde 1/	Developed economies Econ. dévelop-pées 1/,2/	Developing economies économies en voie de développement 1/,2/ — Total	OPEC OPEP	Eastern Europe and fmr. USSR-Europe Europe de l'Est et l'anc. URSS-Europe — Total 1/,5/	Former USSR-Eur. 6/	Developed economies — Europe — Total	EU UE	EFTA AELE	South Africa Afrique du Sud
		Food, beverages and tobacco (SITC, Rev. 2 and Rev. 3, 0 and 1) (continued)									
Canada	1998	14400	11219	3079	1087	102	59	951	907	42	[illegible]
	1999	14699	11926	2711	924	62	33	957	899	56	[illegible]
	2000	16031	12859	3120	1102	52	32	846	806	39	[illegible]
	2001	17583	14184	3303	863	96	63	935	872	61	[illegible]
	2002	17076	13775	3208	838	93	61	908	847	59	[illegible]
United States	1998	44727	24729	18358	2024	1522	1258	7022	6680	329	[illegible]
	1999	43630	24236	18279	1996	982	803	5809	5506	289	[illegible]
	2000	45419	24789	19437	2246	1118	981	5293	5026	253	[illegible]
	2001	45343	23967	20031	2280	1248	1076	5399	5123	261	[illegible]
	2002	43051	22755	19018	2165	1185	1022	5126	4864	248	[illegible]
Japan	1998	1984	533	1442	161	9	9	93	89	4	[illegible]
	1999	2085	601	1477	92	8	7	95	91	3	
	2000	2088	618	1461	39	9	9	107	104	3	
	2001	2984	584	2384	38	16	15	105	101	3	
	2002	3083	603	2463	39	17	15	108	104	3	
Australia, New Zealand	1998	15664	7395	5235	844	214	186	2076	2002	64	[illegible]
	1999	16691	8036	5740	886	87	78	2112	2035	68	[illegible]
	2000	17738	8660	6371	1117	68	62	2118	2028	80	[illegible]
	2001	19389	9224	7433	1438	113	103	2209	2116	79	[illegible]
	2002	19557	9304	7497	1450	114	104	2228	2134	80	[illegible]
Developing economies-Africa	1998	11555	7783	2810	901	524	291	6029	5891	132	[illegible]
	1999	10887	7241	2771	751	429	212	5707	5596	100	[illegible]
	2000	10521	7094	3004	935	353	197	5650	5462	178	[illegible]
	2001	11568	7651	3477	1240	366	208	5879	5712	161	[illegible]
	2002	12153	8051	3653	1303	385	219	6191	6016	169	[illegible]
Developing economies-America	1998	52097	33022	16910	2896	1896	1359	15221	14929	284	[illegible]
	1999	47806	32415	13526	2195	1673	1197	14495	14134	357	[illegible]
	2000	47468	31523	14111	2318	1416	960	13472	13103	364	[illegible]
	2001	49760	31215	15927	3382	2353	1808	13781	13410	364	[illegible]
	2002	50424	31634	16140	3427	2384	1832	13972	13596	369	[illegible]
Developing economies-Europe 3/	1998	1525	469	848	21	205	62	412	394	16	
	1999	1368	438	764	19	162	37	376	361	14	
	2000	1281	384	748	19	144	37	327	307	19	
	2001	1393	448	791	27	150	40	363	336	27	
	2002	1470	473	835	28	158	42	383	355	28	
Developing economies-Middle East	1998	10300	2977	6437	3382	654	456	2377	2281	94	
	1999	9766	2781	6376	3140	445	265	2251	2146	102	
	2000	9341	2421	6287	3201	440	280	1941	1854	85	
	2001	11584	2665	8078	4901	538	341	2097	2015	81	
	2002	11795	2713	8225	4990	548	347	2135	2052	82	
Developing economies-Other Asia	1998	51451	24886	24509	3968	1918	1577	5843	5632	199	[illegible]
	1999	50421	25916	22708	3638	1656	1317	5750	5573	169	[illegible]
	2000	54203	27143	25257	3614	1638	1304	5633	5444	183	[illegible]
	2001	54484	27346	24961	3717	1959	1570	5916	5741	168	[illegible]
	2002	59601	29914	27305	4066	2143	1717	6472	6280	184	[illegible]
Former USSR-Asia 7/.	1998	688	46	241	20	400	393	43	38	5	
	1999	665	65	157	9	443	437	56	49	7	
	2000	887	76	326	31	484	478	62	58	4	
	2001	824	54	313	30	456	451	40	37	3	
	2002	908	60	345	33	502	497	44	41	3	
Developing economies-Oceania	1998	822	433	147	7	3	0	205	183	21	
	1999	817	585	207	7	6	0	292	250	42	
	2000	716	428	171	16	1	0	137	136	1	
	2001	683	422	173	17	0	0	136	135	1	
	2002	678	494	215	22	0	0	234	213	13	

For general note and footnotes see end of table.

Exportations mondiales par classes de marchandises et par régions (suite)

En millions de dollars E.-U. f.o.b.

:conomies développées 1/,2/				Developing economies / Economies en voie de développement 1/,2/						← Exportations vers	
Canada	U.S.A. / E.-U.	Japan / Japon	Australia New Zealand / Australie Nouvelle-Zélande	Africa / Afrique	America / Amerique: Total	America / Amerique: LAIA / ALADI	Asia / Asie: Mid. East / Moyen Orient	Asia / Asie: Other / Autres 7/	Oceania / Océanie	Année	Exportations en provenance de ↓
'roduits alimentaires, boisson et tabac (CTCI, Rev. 2 et Rev. 3, 0 et 1) (suite)											
.	9051	1083	69	813	1092	793	227	943	1	1998	Canada
.	9722	1114	85	473	985	667	424	822	2	1999	
.	10603	1278	77	536	1035	796	579	967	1	2000	
.	11780	1346	89	549	1209	942	378	1162	1	2001	
.	11440	1307	86	533	1174	915	367	1128	1	2002	
6541	.	10209	430	1793	8052	5756	2002	6382	86	1998	Etats-Unis
6714	.	10726	432	1887	7732	5397	1844	6713	67	1999	
7228	.	11236	452	2048	8065	5791	2087	7102	76	2000	
7657	.	10022	423	1808	8990	6583	1895	7225	72	2001	
7270	.	9515	402	1717	8536	6250	1799	6860	68	2002	
26	355	.	47	13	24	17	27	1315	62	1998	Japon
31	412	.	56	6	26	19	28	1355	60	1999	
31	399	.	72	12	24	14	27	1343	56	2000	
29	370	.	74	17	24	9	29	2262	52	2001	
30	382	.	76	18	25	9	30	2337	54	2002	
229	1675	2565	754	353	569	419	702	3300	302	1998	Australie, Nouvelle-Zélande
260	1885	2829	862	384	405	278	710	3927	311	1999	
312	2217	3022	885	352	467	325	791	4458	298	2000	
422	2489	2977	1033	435	766	515	945	4946	340	2001	
426	2511	3003	1042	439	773	519	953	4989	343	2002	
71	700	698	49	1323	39	20	808	620	2	1998	Economies en voie de développement-Afrique
56	527	665	52	1156	91	72	742	754	11	1999	
51	462	640	46	1275	74	44	871	764	4	2000	
53	457	681	50	1450	64	44	1179	767	4	2001	
56	480	715	53	1523	67	46	1239	806	4	2002	
667	13990	2647	154	1674	10701	8469	1885	2565	14	1998	Economies en voie de développement-Amérique
644	14264	2513	200	1164	8364	6413	1530	2372	22	1999	
690	14443	2282	290	1262	8642	6749	1696	2426	16	2000	
665	13929	2207	207	1639	9004	6887	2317	2874	17	2001	
674	14115	2236	210	1661	9124	6979	2348	2912	17	2002	
4	34	12	6	17	6	6	57	7	0	1998	Economies en voie de développement-Europe 3/
5	42	8	7	17	6	6	52	4	2	1999	
5	28	17	7	18	6	6	52	7	1	2000	
5	35	38	6	16	5	5	48	9	1	2001	
5	37	40	6	17	5	5	51	9	1	2002	
27	389	94	39	497	64	60	4798	1027	0	1998	Economies en voie de développement-Moyen Orient
26	315	92	40	380	58	52	4870	1013	0	1999	
30	255	101	44	434	53	46	4861	876	0	2000	
30	344	85	43	466	87	77	6516	936	0	2001	
31	350	87	44	474	89	78	6635	953	0	2002	
612	5199	11938	797	1421	511	331	2780	19668	95	1998	Economies en voie de développement-Autres Pays d'Asie
649	5447	12821	875	1488	465	321	2710	17946	83	1999	
713	5889	13720	856	1607	538	362	3004	20012	79	2000	
735	5899	13602	857	1778	512	344	2838	19731	75	2001	
804	6453	14880	937	1945	560	376	3105	21584	82	2002	
0	3	0	0	1	0	0	36	204	0	1998	l'ancienne URSS asiatique 7/
0	7	0	0	1	0	0	16	140	0	1999	
0	10	0	0	1	0	0	42	282	0	2000	
0	11	0	0	1	0	0	44	268	0	2001	
0	12	0	0	1	0	0	48	295	0	2002	
1	63	100	64	0	29	2	0	79	38	1998	Economies en voie de développement-Océanie
1	79	109	103	0	32	2	0	134	40	1999	
3	65	179	44	1	2	0	0	138	30	2000	
3	64	178	41	1	3	0	0	138	31	2001	
3	64	177	55	1	3	0	0	194	40	2002	

Voir la fin du tableau pour la remarque générale et les notes.

SPECIAL TABLE: D

World exports by commodity classes and by regions (continued)

In million U.S. dollars f.o.b.

Cereals (SITC, Rev. 2 and Rev. 3, 041-045

Exports to → / ↓ Exports from	Year	World Monde 1/	Developed economies Econ. dévelop-pées 1/,2/	Developing economies / economies en voie de développement 1/,2/ Total	Developing economies OPEC OPEP	Eastern Europe and fmr. USSR-Europe / Europe de l'Est et l'anc. URSS-Europe Total 1/,5/	Eastern Europe and fmr. USSR-Europe Former USSR-Eur. 6/	Developed economies Europe Total	Developed economies Europe EU UE	Developed economies Europe EFTA AELE	Developed economies South Africa Afrique du Sud
World 1/	1998	36758	12779	20496	5053	694	323	7969	7814	141	38[illegible]
	1999	33718	11855	17895	4780	1207	912	7459	7268	179	28[illegible]
	2000	33662	11026	18900	4931	1192	734	6640	6443	183	25[illegible]
	2001	34506	11655	19375	4563	969	514	7136	6887	234	21[illegible]
	2002	36016	12165	20223	4763	1011	536	7448	7188	244	22[illegible]
Developed economies 1/,2/	1998	24803	11024	10925	2440	117	23	7251	7137	105	11[illegible]
	1999	24414	10314	10798	2771	571	487	6657	6542	104	11[illegible]
	2000	23626	9558	11133	3116	431	241	5855	5741	103	10[illegible]
	2001	24074	9870	11467	2405	273	76	6137	6033	95	4[illegible]
	2002	24748	10146	11788	2472	281	78	6309	6202	98	4[illegible]
Developing economies 1/,2/	1998	11075	1540	9158	2572	329	225	553	523	28	26[illegible]
	1999	8590	1382	6727	1976	455	343	666	599	67	16[illegible]
	2000	9437	1357	7538	1758	503	352	700	623	76	15[illegible]
	2001	9561	1509	7508	2028	499	345	757	635	119	17[illegible]
	2002	10203	1610	8012	2164	532	368	808	678	127	18[illegible]
OPEC	1998	162	2	159	5	0	0	0	0	0	[illegible]
	1999	87	5	81	17	0	0	0	0	0	[illegible]
	2000	66	3	63	22	0	0	0	0	0	[illegible]
	2001	88	2	86	19	0	0	0	0	0	[illegible]
	2002	88	2	86	19	0	0	0	0	0	[illegible]
Eastern Europe and the former USSR 1/,5/	1998	880	215	413	41	248	75	166	155	8	[illegible]
	1999	714	160	370	33	181	83	136	127	7	[illegible]
	2000	598	111	229	56	258	141	85	79	4	[illegible]
	2001	872	275	399	131	197	93	242	218	20	[illegible]
	2002	968	305	443	145	219	103	269	242	22	[illegible]
Former USSR-Europe 6/	1998	221	40	105	13	73	62	20	16	3	[illegible]
	1999	124	20	45	0	55	50	7	6	1	[illegible]
	2000	128	26	66	20	37	36	5	4	0	[illegible]
	2001	352	110	162	78	80	74	84	75	7	[illegible]
	2002	379	118	174	84	86	80	90	81	8	[illegible]
Developed economies-Europe	1998	8211	6538	1583	460	90	17	6387	6316	67	2[illegible]
	1999	8328	6038	1989	951	299	235	5912	5844	64	1[illegible]
	2000	8022	5425	2277	1074	304	124	5262	5185	72	1[illegible]
	2001	7587	5642	1694	671	240	55	5489	5417	69	[illegible]
	2002	8038	5977	1795	711	254	58	5815	5739	73	[illegible]
European Union	1998	8210	6537	1583	460	90	17	6386	6315	67	2[illegible]
	1999	8327	6036	1989	951	299	235	5910	5843	64	1[illegible]
	2000	8021	5424	2277	1074	304	124	5261	5184	72	1[illegible]
	2001	7585	5641	1694	671	240	55	5488	5417	68	[illegible]
	2002	8047	5985	1797	712	255	58	5822	5747	72	[illegible]
European Free Trade Association	1998	1	1	0	0	0	0	1	1	0	[illegible]
	1999	2	2	0	0	0	0	2	1	0	[illegible]
	2000	1	1	0	0	0	0	1	1	0	[illegible]
	2001	2	1	0	0	0	0	1	1	0	[illegible]
	2002	2	1	0	0	0	0	1	1	0	[illegible]
Other developed economies	1998	16591	4486	9343	1979	27	7	863	820	37	9[illegible]
	1999	16086	4276	8809	1821	271	252	745	698	41	10[illegible]
	2000	15604	4134	8856	2042	127	116	593	556	31	9[illegible]
	2001	16487	4228	9773	1733	33	20	647	616	26	3[illegible]
	2002	16102	4129	9545	1693	32	20	632	602	25	3[illegible]

For general note and footnotes see end of table.

Exportations mondiales par classes de marchandises et par régions (suite)

En millions de dollars E.-U. f.o.b.

Economies développées 1/,2/ — Canada	U.S.A. / E.-U.	Japan / Japon	Australia New Zealand / Australie Nouvelle-Zélande	Developing economies / Economies en voie de développement 1/,2/ — Africa / Afrique	America / Amerique — Total	America / Amerique — LAIA / ALADI	Asia / Asie — Mid. East / Moyen Orient	Asia / Asie — Other / Autres 7/	Oceania / Océanie	Année	← Exportations vers / Exportations en provenance de ↓
Céréales (CTCI, Rev. 2 et Rev. 3, 041-045)											
284	919	2982	43	4682	5914	4881	2830	6867	29	1998	Monde 1/
238	877	2721	49	3882	5050	3993	3467	5311	20	1999	
293	841	2655	46	4517	5157	4145	3838	5230	16	2000	
436	862	2694	53	4669	5315	4234	3209	5963	20	2001	
455	900	2812	55	4873	5548	4419	3349	6224	0	2002	
242	652	2611	20	3078	3670	2804	1082	3045	10	1998	Economies dévelopées /1,2
205	612	2531	21	2631	3335	2445	1921	2874	5	1999	
254	571	2521	14	3148	3326	2447	2178	2440	7	2000	
405	653	2445	29	2965	3585	2667	1356	3497	12	2001	
416	671	2513	30	3048	3685	2742	1394	3595	0	2002	
41	265	360	23	1498	2238	2077	1627	3717	19	1998	Economies en voie de développement 1/,2/
33	262	188	29	1182	1713	1547	1452	2340	15	1999	
39	269	133	32	1347	1831	1698	1570	2751	9	2000	
31	206	249	23	1619	1729	1566	1700	2420	9	2001	
33	220	266	25	1728	1845	1671	1814	2582	0	2002	
0	2	0	0	0	86	86	8	65	0	1998	OPEP
0	4	2	0	0	52	52	20	10	0	1999	
0	1	2	0	0	34	34	25	3	0	2000	
0	0	2	0	0	54	54	21	10	0	2001	
0	0	2	0	0	54	54	21	10	0	2002	
0	2	12	0	106	6	0	121	105	0	1998	Europe de l'Est et l'ancienne URSS 1/,5/
1	3	2	0	70	2	0	94	97	0	1999	
0	1	0	0	22	0	0	90	39	0	2000	
0	3	0	0	85	0	0	153	46	0	2001	
0	3	0	0	94	0	0	170	51	0	2002	
0	0	0	0	7	1	0	39	57	0	1998	l'ancienne URSS-Europe 6/
0	2	0	0	1	0	0	10	34	0	1999	
0	0	0	0	4	0	0	31	30	0	2000	
0	3	0	0	42	0	0	81	39	0	2001	
0	3	0	0	45	0	0	87	42	0	2002	
3	86	32	2	913	152	36	283	209	0	1998	Economies développées-Europe
3	71	22	2	757	128	23	876	205	0	1999	
4	62	29	2	1040	138	56	937	139	0	2000	
3	78	31	2	1044	130	45	371	109	0	2001	
3	83	33	2	1106	138	48	393	115	0	2002	
3	86	32	2	913	152	36	283	209	0	1998	Union Européenne
3	71	22	2	757	128	23	876	205	0	1999	
4	62	29	2	1040	138	56	937	139	0	2000	
3	77	31	2	1044	130	45	371	109	0	2001	
3	82	33	2	1108	138	48	394	116	0	2002	
0	0	0	0	0	0	0	0	0	0	1998	Association Européenne de Libre Exchange
0	0	0	0	0	0	0	0	0	0	1999	
0	0	0	0	0	0	0	0	0	0	2000	
0	0	0	0	0	0	0	0	0	0	2001	
0	0	0	0	0	0	0	0	0	0	2002	
240	565	2579	18	2165	3518	2768	800	2836	10	1998	Autres economies développées
202	541	2509	19	1874	3208	2422	1045	2669	5	1999	
250	509	2492	12	2108	3188	2391	1241	2301	7	2000	
402	575	2414	27	1921	3455	2622	984	3388	11	2001	
393	562	2358	26	1876	3374	2561	961	3309	0	2002	

Voir la fin du tableau pour la remarque générale et les notes.

SPECIAL TABLE: D

World exports by commodity classes and by regions (continued)

In million U.S. dollars f.o.b.

Exports to → / ↓ Exports from	Year	World Monde 1/	Developed economies Econ. dévelop-pées 1/,2/	Developing economies economies en voie de développement 1/,2/		Eastern Europe and fmr. USSR-Europe Europe de l'Est et l'anc. URSS-Europe		Developed economies			
								Europe			South Africa
				Total	OPEC OPEP	Total 1/,5/	Former USSR-Eur. 6/	Total	EU UE	EFTA AELE	Afrique du Sud
Cereals (SITC, Rev. 2 and Rev. 3, 041-045) (continued)											
Canada	1998	3215	1114	2092	930	9	0	254	245	7	4[illegible]
	1999	2725	1056	1658	821	10	0	234	218	15	2[illegible]
	2000	2960	966	1989	1002	5	2	174	163	10	2[illegible]
	2001	3053	1074	1972	759	6	0	229	221	8	
	2002	2965	1043	1915	737	6	0	222	215	8	
United States	1998	10207	3261	6811	872	18	7	586	552	30	5[illegible]
	1999	10323	3138	6790	880	261	252	503	472	24	8[illegible]
	2000	9684	2999	6490	953	122	115	414	387	20	5[illegible]
	2001	9632	2987	6524	874	26	20	409	387	17	2[illegible]
	2002	9145	2836	6194	830	25	19	388	367	16	2[illegible]
Japan	1998	144	0	143	127	0	0	0	0	0	
	1999	67	1	66	59	0	0	0	0	0	
	2000	14	1	13	0	0	0	0	0	0	
	2001	935	1	935	0	0	0	0	0	0	
	2002	966	1	966	0	0	0	0	0	0	
Australia, New Zealand	1998	2887	92	177	50	0	0	22	22	0	
	1999	2871	78	196	59	0	0	7	7	0	
	2000	2854	143	298	77	0	0	5	4	0	
	2001	2736	87	292	99	0	0	8	7	0	
	2002	2760	88	295	100	0	0	8	7	0	
Developing economies-Africa	1998	240	22	184	22	34	8	9	9	0	1[illegible]
	1999	153	16	117	9	19	1	8	8	0	
	2000	180	20	134	16	26	1	8	7	1	
	2001	227	28	169	38	29	12	15	15	0	
	2002	238	29	178	40	30	13	16	16	0	
Developing economies-America	1998	3703	650	3028	400	1	1	261	253	8	2[illegible]
	1999	2655	593	2058	224	3	1	376	329	47	2[illegible]
	2000	2956	545	2389	321	17	0	354	302	51	3[illegible]
	2001	3555	747	2765	544	37	0	460	358	99	5[illegible]
	2002	3602	757	2802	551	37	0	466	363	100	5[illegible]
Developing economies-Europe 3/	1998	134	12	70	8	52	17	12	10	1	
	1999	101	13	36	6	52	16	13	12	1	
	2000	115	13	45	5	57	15	13	5	8	
	2001	117	8	51	10	58	15	8	4	4	
	2002	123	8	54	11	61	16	8	4	4	
Developing economies-Middle East	1998	388	39	346	129	0	0	32	32	0	
	1999	268	30	237	34	1	0	24	21	2	
	2000	258	57	173	52	28	13	48	47	1	
	2001	196	40	145	43	11	0	33	32	1	
	2002	200	41	148	44	11	0	34	33	1	
Developing economies-Other Asia	1998	6610	817	5531	2012	241	200	238	218	18	2[illegible]
	1999	5413	730	4279	1702	379	325	246	229	17	1[illegible]
	2000	5921	722	4791	1356	375	323	277	261	15	1[illegible]
	2001	5459	686	4371	1387	364	317	241	225	15	1[illegible]
	2002	5972	750	4782	1517	398	347	264	246	16	1[illegible]
Former USSR-Asia 7/.	1998	300	11	147	19	142	141	11	11	0	
	1999	315	24	78	8	213	213	23	18	5	
	2000	503	24	235	28	244	244	20	17	3	
	2001	476	23	222	26	232	231	19	16	3	
	2002	524	26	245	29	256	254	21	18	3	
Developing economies-Oceania	1998	0	0	0	0	0	0	0	0	0	
	1999	0	0	0	0	0	0	0	0	0	
	2000	7	0	7	7	0	0	0	0	0	
	2001	7	0	7	7	0	0	0	0	0	
	2002	7	0	9	9	0	0	0	0	0	

For general note and footnotes see end of table.

Exportations mondiales par classes de marchandises et par régions (suite)

En millions de dollars E.-U. f.o.b.

Economies développées 1/,2/ — Canada	U.S.A. E.-U.	Japan Japon	Australia New Zealand Australie Nouvelle-Zélande	Developing economies / Economies en voie de développement 1/,2/ — Africa Afrique	America Amerique — Total	America Amerique — LAIA ALADI	Asia Asie — Mid. East Moyen Orient	Asia Asie — Other Autres 7/	Oceania Océanie	Année	← Exportations vers / Exportations en provenance de ↓
Céréales (CTCI, Rev. 2 et Rev. 3, 041-045) (suite)											
.	565	240	12	707	638	567	182	566	0	1998	Canada
.	540	250	11	403	516	431	365	371	1	1999	
.	508	249	5	461	583	495	494	452	0	2000	
.	575	259	7	469	623	542	329	552	0	2001	
.	558	252	7	455	605	526	320	536	0	2002	
240	.	2252	4	1318	2872	2194	551	2050	5	1998	Etats-Unis
202	.	2196	2	1372	2687	1988	596	2127	3	1999	
250	.	2093	2	1589	2600	1890	643	1642	4	2000	
402	.	2023	3	1395	2823	2070	549	1739	4	2001	
382	.	1921	3	1324	2680	1965	521	1651	4	2002	
0	0	.	0	6	1	0	0	135	1	1998	Japon
0	0	.	0	3	0	0	1	63	0	1999	
0	0	.	0	7	0	0	1	5	0	2000	
0	0	.	0	9	0	0	0	925	0	2001	
0	0	.	0	9	0	0	0	956	0	2002	
0	0	68	1	18	7	7	64	84	4	1998	Australie, Nouvelle-Zélande
0	0	63	6	3	3	3	81	108	1	1999	
0	0	125	5	1	6	6	90	197	3	2000	
0	0	54	17	0	9	9	105	170	7	2001	
0	0	54	17	0	9	9	106	171	7	2002	
0	0	0	0	97	0	0	80	5	0	1998	Economies en voie de
0	3	0	0	52	0	0	64	0	0	1999	développement-Afrique
0	2	0	0	49	0	0	82	1	0	2000	
0	0	0	0	91	0	0	76	1	0	2001	
0	0	0	0	96	0	0	80	1	0	2002	
2	121	238	1	394	2048	1977	356	223	0	1998	Economies en voie de
0	102	79	1	171	1560	1463	235	92	0	1999	développement-Amérique
1	101	46	1	335	1667	1595	334	52	0	2000	
2	72	121	1	314	1564	1454	539	342	0	2001	
2	73	123	1	318	1585	1473	546	347	0	2002	
0	0	0	0	5	0	0	14	4	0	1998	Economies en voie de
0	0	0	0	1	0	0	9	0	2	1999	développement-Europe 3/
0	0	0	0	0	0	0	16	0	0	2000	
0	0	0	0	10	0	0	17	1	0	2001	
0	0	0	0	11	0	0	18	1	0	2002	
0	0	0	0	139	0	0	130	77	0	1998	Economies en voie de
0	0	0	0	47	0	0	53	137	0	1999	développement-Moyen Orient
0	0	0	0	93	0	0	59	21	0	2000	
0	0	0	0	91	1	0	45	7	0	2001	
0	0	0	0	93	1	0	46	7	0	2002	
39	144	122	22	863	190	100	1046	3408	19	1998	Economies en voie de
33	157	109	27	910	153	84	1091	2110	12	1999	développement-Autres Pays d'Asie
39	165	87	31	870	164	103	1079	2670	9	2000	
29	134	128	22	1113	164	112	1023	2062	9	2001	
32	147	140	24	1218	179	123	1119	2256	10	2002	
0	0	0	0	0	0	0	29	117	0	1998	l'ancienne URSS asiatique 7/
0	0	0	0	0	0	0	11	67	0	1999	
0	2	0	0	1	0	0	37	197	0	2000	
0	2	0	0	1	0	0	35	185	0	2001	
0	2	0	0	1	0	0	39	204	0	2002	
0	0	0	0	0	0	0	0	0	0	1998	Economies en voie de
0	0	0	0	0	0	0	0	0	0	1999	développement-Océanie
0	0	0	0	0	0	0	0	7	0	2000	
0	0	0	0	0	0	0	0	7	0	2001	
0	0	0	0	0	0	0	0	10	0	2002	

Voir la fin du tableau pour la remarque générale et les notes.

SPECIAL TABLE: D

World exports by commodity classes and by regions (continued)

In million U.S. dollars f.o.b.

Exports from ↓ / Exports to →	Year	World Monde 1/	Developed economies Econ. dévelop-pées 1/,2/	Developing economies économies en voie de développement 1/,2/		Eastern Europe and fmr. USSR-Europe Europe de l'Est et l'anc. URSS-Europe		Developed economies			
								Europe			South Africa
				Total	OPEC OPEP	Total 1/,5/	Former USSR-Eur. 6/	Total	EU UE	EFTA AELE	Afrique du Sud
		Crude materials (excluding fuels), oils, fats (SITC, Rev. 2 and Rev. 3, 2 and 4									
World 1/	1998	211031	130207	66526	6363	7616	3164	82314	78455	3795	852
	1999	200071	123597	64765	6488	6636	2798	74699	71041	3591	771
	2000	213236	128557	72636	6842	6913	3018	76848	72986	3794	818
	2001	205459	120479	72861	6578	7385	3348	73385	69635	3688	822
	2002	214932	125684	76518	6916	7826	3561	76572	72682	3849	858
Developed economies 1/,2/	1998	126008	88621	30586	2886	2883	989	57363	54576	2733	332
	1999	118059	82895	29063	2795	2695	975	50993	48597	2344	275
	2000	126209	85477	33948	3048	2867	950	52440	50069	2321	287
	2001	120997	79868	34126	2782	3229	1144	49882	47457	2374	224
	2002	124383	82103	35081	2860	3319	1176	51278	48785	2440	230
Developing economies 1/,2/	1998	72756	34612	33954	3382	2237	1233	18603	17745	848	520
	1999	70701	34271	33650	3588	1840	1020	17983	16877	1092	493
	2000	76263	36742	36182	3669	2148	1181	18879	17529	1334	531
	2001	74628	34894	36333	3693	2467	1454	18491	17307	1176	59[illegible]
	2002	79637	37236	38772	3941	2633	1552	19732	18469	1255	637
OPEC	1998	7987	3388	4290	259	110	33	1636	1555	80	13
	1999	8270	3659	4502	234	82	36	1745	1689	54	34
	2000	9290	4086	5042	252	141	82	1886	1818	67	58
	2001	9097	3690	5155	314	241	139	1833	1787	44	55
	2002	9101	3691	5157	314	241	139	1834	1788	44	55
Eastern Europe and the former USSR 1/,5/	1998	12267	6974	1985	96	2496	942	6349	6134	214	[illegible]
	1999	11311	6431	2053	105	2100	802	5723	5567	155	[illegible]
	2000	10763	6338	2506	125	1898	886	5529	5388	140	[illegible]
	2001	9833	5717	2402	104	1689	750	5012	4871	138	[illegible]
	2002	10913	6345	2666	115	1875	832	5563	5406	153	[illegible]
Former USSR-Europe 6/	1998	8556	4420	1445	32	1814	779	3870	3692	178	[illegible]
	1999	7357	3665	1398	48	1488	663	3056	2939	117	[illegible]
	2000	6507	3564	1733	72	1209	725	2858	2750	106	[illegible]
	2001	5818	3087	1705	50	1004	610	2485	2381	102	[illegible]
	2002	6260	3322	1835	54	1080	656	2674	2562	110	[illegible]
Developed economies-Europe	1998	57888	46949	7306	1003	2615	899	43439	41214	2177	15[illegible]
	1999	52715	42382	7269	932	2442	862	38701	36821	1832	12[illegible]
	2000	53352	42358	7976	1013	2596	868	38408	36604	1757	13[illegible]
	2001	51967	41104	7425	917	2938	1054	37335	35581	1708	10[illegible]
	2002	55057	43548	7866	972	3113	1117	39555	37697	1810	11[illegible]
European Union	1998	56110	45288	7220	997	2585	894	41853	39696	2109	15[illegible]
	1999	51009	40808	7170	925	2410	856	37203	35370	1788	12[illegible]
	2000	51527	40701	7851	1001	2553	859	36832	35061	1727	13[illegible]
	2001	50190	39487	7303	907	2899	1043	35795	34082	1673	10[illegible]
	2002	53247	41892	7748	962	3076	1107	37975	36158	1775	11[illegible]
European Free Trade Association	1998	1754	1638	86	7	30	5	1563	1505	57	[illegible]
	1999	1692	1562	98	7	32	6	1486	1443	40	[illegible]
	2000	1812	1646	124	12	42	9	1566	1534	28	[illegible]
	2001	1764	1606	120	10	39	10	1529	1491	32	[illegible]
	2002	1830	1666	125	10	40	10	1586	1547	33	[illegible]
Other developed economies	1998	68120	41675	23295	1883	268	91	13926	13363	556	18[illegible]
	1999	65345	40515	21810	1863	253	113	12293	11777	512	15[illegible]
	2000	72857	43094	25991	2035	272	82	14005	13438	564	15[illegible]
	2001	69030	38768	26722	1865	291	90	12549	11878	666	11[illegible]
	2002	67420	37864	26099	1821	284	88	12256	11601	650	11[illegible]

For general note and footnotes see end of table.

Exportations mondiales par classes de marchandises et par régions (suite)

En millions de dollars E.-U. f.o.b.

Economies développées 1/,2/ Canada	U.S.A. E.-U.	Japan Japon	Australia New Zealand Australie Nouvelle-Zélande	Developing economies / Economies en voie de développement 1/,2/ Africa Afrique	America Amerique Total	America Amerique LAIA ALADI	Asia Asie Mid. East Moyen Orient	Asia Asie Other Autres 7/	Oceania Océanie	← Exportations vers / Année	Exportations en provenance de ↓
Matières brutes (sauf combustibles), huiles et graisses (CTCI, Rev. 2 et Rev. 3, 2 et 4)											
5358	21459	18191	1624	5552	11109	9563	6920	41879	116	1998	Monde 1/
5291	22332	18350	1540	5215	9124	7813	5888	43571	107	1999	
5968	22808	19900	1642	4620	10238	8911	6597	50171	104	2000	
5577	21079	17640	1370	4507	9848	8411	6520	50952	115	2001	
5821	22001	18478	1426	4704	10279	8779	6805	53522	120	2002	
4446	14663	10641	790	2703	6671	5774	2674	17962	76	1998	Economies dévelopées 1/,2/
4531	15573	10304	822	2265	5438	4654	2040	18765	68	1999	
5067	15823	10584	880	2049	6091	5333	2430	22800	61	2000	
4698	14520	9423	761	1979	5847	5071	2344	23350	62	2001	
4829	14926	9687	782	2034	6011	5213	2410	24003	64	2002	
884	6666	7110	832	2592	4350	3770	3597	23101	41	1998	Economies en voie de développement 1/,2/
743	6650	7498	716	2712	3632	3128	3259	23789	39	1999	
872	6878	8677	754	2214	4119	3557	3551	26048	43	2000	
854	6443	7678	605	2289	3966	3312	3703	26110	53	2001	
911	6875	8193	639	2443	4232	3534	3952	27862	57	2002	
93	764	842	40	96	281	272	474	3419	2	1998	OPEP
58	737	1030	46	138	251	235	481	3608	4	1999	
70	683	1317	65	137	241	232	527	4106	6	2000	
79	560	1086	61	195	243	232	547	4142	8	2001	
79	560	1086	61	195	243	232	547	4144	8	2002	
27	130	441	2	257	88	19	649	816	0	1998	Europe de l'Est et l'ancienne URSS 1/,5/
17	110	548	2	239	54	31	590	1016	0	1999	
29	107	640	8	356	28	21	615	1323	0	2000	
26	116	539	4	239	34	28	474	1492	0	2001	
29	129	598	4	265	38	31	526	1656	0	2002	
12	111	418	1	121	76	8	452	774	0	1998	l'ancienne URSS-Europe 6/
3	83	516	1	133	27	7	338	890	0	1999	
17	78	597	2	220	14	7	321	1168	0	2000	
14	85	495	1	134	13	7	221	1330	0	2001	
15	91	533	1	144	14	8	238	1431	0	2002	
281	1714	990	172	1933	579	510	1467	2852	16	1998	Economies développées-Europe
262	1775	1129	193	1604	552	465	1161	3462	14	1999	
307	2008	1123	192	1467	625	551	1371	3996	11	2000	
261	1966	1097	171	1346	632	566	1274	3629	11	2001	
277	2083	1162	181	1426	670	600	1350	3845	11	2002	
277	1676	965	168	1924	571	502	1456	2800	16	1998	Union Européenne
258	1739	1100	188	1597	543	457	1151	3399	14	1999	
302	1968	1095	187	1456	616	543	1358	3911	11	2000	
259	1931	1068	163	1340	623	557	1260	3538	11	2001	
275	2049	1133	173	1422	661	591	1337	3754	11	2002	
4	39	25	4	9	8	8	11	52	0	1998	Association Européenne de Libre Exchange
4	36	29	5	7	8	7	9	63	0	1999	
4	39	27	4	10	8	8	13	85	0	2000	
3	35	30	7	6	8	8	13	91	0	2001	
3	36	31	7	6	8	8	13	94	0	2002	
4165	12949	9651	619	770	6092	5265	1207	15112	60	1998	Autres economies développées
4268	13797	9175	630	661	4886	4189	879	15307	53	1999	
4760	13815	9461	688	582	5466	4781	1060	18806	50	2000	
4436	12554	8326	590	633	5216	4505	1070	19724	50	2001	
4333	12261	8132	576	618	5094	4400	1045	19264	51	2002	

Voir la fin du tableau pour la remarque générale et les notes.

SPECIAL TABLE: D

World exports by commodity classes and by regions (continued)

In million U.S. dollars f.o.b.

Exports to → / ↓ Exports from	Year	World Monde 1/	Developed economies Econ. dévelop-pées 1/,2/	Developing economies économies en voie de développement 1/,2/		Eastern Europe and fmr. USSR-Europe Europe de l'Est et l'anc. URSS-Europe		Developed economies: Europe			South Africa
				Total	OPEC OPEP	Total 1/,5/	Former USSR-Eur. 6/	Total	EU UE	EFTA AELE	Afrique du Sud
		Crude materials (excluding fuels), oils, fats (SITC, Rev. 2 and Rev. 3, 2 and 4) (continued)									
Canada	1998	20681	18136	2516	206	29	6	3472	3070	402	29
	1999	21294	18673	2603	282	18	6	3145	2757	388	36
	2000	22565	19570	2972	340	24	6	3814	3381	432	31
	2001	19580	17000	2559	145	21	4	3071	2568	503	18
	2002	19015	16510	2485	141	20	4	2982	2494	488	17
United States	1998	28616	15197	13093	1041	119	63	6687	6615	67	81
	1999	25660	13894	11409	908	118	62	5624	5560	61	72
	2000	29749	15286	14120	1001	110	47	6377	6296	78	75
	2001	28919	13918	14697	1069	138	48	6003	5909	90	56
	2002	27457	13214	13954	1015	131	46	5700	5610	85	53
Japan	1998	2948	709	2230	177	9	4	418	404	14	17
	1999	3002	740	2255	186	8	3	431	421	10	16
	2000	3369	762	2600	197	7	4	433	423	10	17
	2001	3439	684	2748	193	8	4	381	372	9	15
	2002	3553	707	2839	199	8	4	394	384	9	15
Australia, New Zealand	1998	12893	5435	4716	392	69	13	1943	1937	5	51
	1999	12317	5019	4725	421	46	9	1673	1667	6	24
	2000	13867	5105	5413	399	83	14	1806	1798	8	26
	2001	14061	5060	5824	402	99	30	1680	1670	11	20
	2002	14183	5104	5874	405	100	30	1695	1684	11	20
Developing economies-Africa	1998	6569	3353	2558	438	121	30	2659	2574	79	147
	1999	7198	3664	2938	534	134	44	3016	2838	172	146
	2000	7696	4277	3136	531	240	107	3410	3169	230	190
	2001	7738	4369	3121	479	212	84	3379	3168	206	269
	2002	8130	4598	3279	503	223	88	3559	3337	216	283
Developing economies-America	1998	24643	14611	9185	1434	568	386	7768	7315	452	159
	1999	23146	14258	8365	1318	410	291	7220	6661	556	159
	2000	25243	15350	9464	1271	378	176	7714	6926	786	119
	2001	25601	14742	10402	1181	414	233	7336	6618	718	135
	2002	25942	14940	10541	1197	420	236	7437	6710	728	137
Developing economies-Europe 3/	1998	685	411	204	8	70	14	404	398	6	0
	1999	608	382	180	8	46	8	376	370	5	0
	2000	669	422	185	8	62	13	414	406	8	0
	2001	671	417	191	10	63	14	410	400	9	0
	2002	708	440	202	11	66	15	433	422	9	0
Developing economies-Middle East	1998	3971	1123	2621	502	143	67	848	785	62	3
	1999	4144	1263	2724	496	99	54	923	868	53	2
	2000	3788	986	2608	473	125	67	698	658	41	8
	2001	5212	1397	3526	721	214	116	1087	1036	51	5
	2002	5307	1422	3590	734	218	118	1107	1055	52	5
Developing economies-Other Asia	1998	34913	14535	19004	994	1335	736	6736	6519	217	210
	1999	33860	13883	18786	1219	1149	623	6187	5943	242	187
	2000	36885	15101	20402	1376	1342	818	6406	6134	269	213
	2001	33894	13487	18794	1294	1564	1007	6077	5883	191	187
	2002	37078	14754	20559	1416	1711	1102	6648	6436	209	205
Former USSR-Asia 7/	1998	2900	1431	692	78	744	337	1269	1150	119	0
	1999	2718	1374	671	95	643	272	1213	1069	144	0
	2000	3109	1380	789	90	911	548	1226	1056	170	0
	2001	2965	1347	701	82	887	521	1193	1056	137	0
	2002	3266	1496	772	90	977	574	1326	1175	151	0
Developing economies-Oceania	1998	1976	531	382	6	1	0	140	108	32	0
	1999	1745	772	655	13	2	0	213	149	64	0
	2000	1983	557	388	10	0	0	187	187	0	1
	2001	1512	431	298	10	0	0	152	152	0	1
	2002	1501	505	371	13	0	0	261	240	0	2

For general note and footnotes see end of table.

Exportations mondiales par classes de marchandises et par régions (suite)

En millions de dollars E.-U. f.o.b.

...onomies ...veloppées 1/,2/ — ...anada	U.S.A. E.-U.	Japan Japon	Australia New Zealand Australie Nouvelle-Zélande	Developing economies Economies en voie de développement 1/,2/ — Africa Afrique	America Amerique Total	America Amerique LAIA ALADI	Asia Asie Mid. East Moyen Orient	Asia Asie Other Autres 7/	Oceania Océanie	Année	← Exportations vers / Exportations en provenance de ↓
...tières brutes (sauf combustibles), huiles et graisses (CTCI, Rev. 2 et Rev. 3, 2 et 4) (suite)											
.	11999	2487	127	113	396	364	89	1916	0	1998	Canada
.	12847	2491	141	97	293	261	103	2108	1	1999	
.	12780	2763	171	59	372	328	94	2443	3	2000	
.	11582	2214	106	64	384	301	49	2059	3	2001	
.	11248	2150	103	62	373	292	48	2000	3	2002	
4126	.	3991	166	435	5513	4725	771	6314	21	1998	Etats-Unis
4212	.	3651	160	379	4395	3741	561	6040	19	1999	
4687	.	3815	147	336	4921	4291	713	8112	18	2000	
4352	.	3198	132	383	4662	4041	764	8850	17	2001	
4132	.	3036	125	364	4426	3837	725	8403	16	2002	
12	224	.	34	20	36	33	65	2109	1	1998	Japon
13	244	.	33	27	35	33	53	2137	1	1999	
12	268	.	30	27	33	32	39	2498	1	2000	
12	246	.	27	30	35	34	38	2642	1	2001	
12	254	.	28	31	36	35	39	2730	1	2002	
14	366	2778	278	82	78	77	189	4332	32	1998	Australie, Nouvelle-Zélande
33	379	2636	270	40	91	88	88	4473	32	1999	
51	429	2467	325	32	72	68	146	5134	28	2000	
63	484	2505	305	32	51	50	143	5567	30	2001	
64	488	2527	308	32	51	50	144	5615	30	2002	
87	263	154	35	1224	214	200	334	772	1	1998	Economies en voie de développement-Afrique
42	215	187	38	1292	199	187	423	1002	1	1999	
35	265	278	44	983	283	254	509	1337	3	2000	
36	282	279	48	865	306	268	470	1455	2	2001	
38	296	293	50	909	321	282	494	1529	2	2002	
570	3870	2150	58	578	3565	3072	1146	3825	2	1998	Economies en voie de développement-Amérique
528	4024	2262	48	615	2949	2518	925	3868	2	1999	
638	4142	2654	75	496	3339	2861	897	4723	3	2000	
630	4052	2503	58	618	3221	2670	834	5710	3	2001	
638	4106	2536	59	626	3264	2706	845	5786	3	2002	
0	2	1	1	38	1	0	27	2	0	1998	Economies en voie de développement-Europe 3/
0	2	0	1	33	1	0	16	3	0	1999	
0	2	1	1	29	0	0	23	3	0	2000	
0	2	1	1	31	5	0	24	3	0	2001	
0	2	1	1	33	5	0	25	3	0	2002	
5	52	145	33	139	7	5	766	1683	0	1998	Economies en voie de développement-Moyen Orient
5	103	184	8	112	13	11	708	1870	0	1999	
8	48	193	3	102	14	12	768	1705	0	2000	
7	66	199	3	186	7	6	1164	2138	10	2001	
7	67	203	3	189	7	6	1185	2177	10	2002	
222	2451	4473	353	604	554	489	1323	16467	28	1998	Economies en voie de développement-Autres Pays d'Asie
168	2253	4591	343	644	459	408	1187	16436	25	1999	
191	2412	5318	377	599	483	430	1354	17908	28	2000	
180	2033	4497	351	585	427	368	1210	16516	32	2001	
197	2224	4919	384	640	467	403	1324	18067	35	2002	
0	3	159	0	0	30	28	311	339	0	1998	l'ancienne URSS asiatique 7/
0	11	148	0	1	30	26	269	360	0	1999	
0	8	145	0	5	28	25	340	406	0	2000	
0	7	146	0	3	26	26	282	379	0	2001	
0	8	161	0	3	29	29	311	417	0	2002	
0	27	188	176	8	10	3	0	352	9	1998	Economies en voie de développement-Océanie
0	52	274	232	17	11	4	0	610	10	1999	
0	9	232	127	5	0	0	1	372	9	2000	
0	8	199	72	4	0	0	1	287	6	2001	
0	8	198	97	5	0	0	1	403	8	2002	

Voir la fin du tableau pour la remarque générale et les notes.

SPECIAL TABLE: D

World exports by commodity classes and by regions (continued)

In million U.S. dollars f.o.b.

Exports to → / ↓ Exports from	Year	World Monde 1/	Developed economies Econ. dévelop-pées 1/,2/	Developing economies economies en voie de développement 1/,2/ Total	OPEC OPEP	Eastern Europe and fmr. USSR-Europe Europe de l'Est et l'anc. URSS-Europe Total 1/,5/	Former USSR-Eur. 6/	Develop… economi… Europe Total	EU UE	EFTA AELE	South Africa Afriqu… du Su…
		Oil seeds and, oleaginous fruit (SITC, Rev. 2 and Rev. 3, …									
World 1/	1998	15036	9380	5142	426	222	71	6762	6641	119	
	1999	13442	7602	5332	580	208	100	5193	5073	116	
	2000	14436	7299	6731	599	162	71	4891	4753	135	
	2001	15761	7904	7464	711	215	95	5487	5333	152	
	2002	16451	8250	7791	742	224	99	5727	5566	159	
Developed economies 1/,2/	1998	9420	5888	3231	217	95	16	3787	3725	61	
	1999	8468	4567	3585	295	77	38	2611	2584	26	
	2000	8690	4365	4056	223	36	13	2508	2487	19	
	2001	8887	4649	4023	292	48	11	2806	2778	28	
	2002	9136	4779	4136	300	49	11	2885	2856	29	
Developing economies 1/,2/	1998	5020	3130	1783	209	63	29	2626	2594	31	
	1999	4341	2638	1610	285	70	41	2201	2126	72	
	2000	5232	2584	2570	376	68	45	2040	1930	107	
	2001	6415	2931	3366	419	108	59	2362	2255	107	
	2002	6846	3128	3592	447	115	63	2521	2406	114	
OPEC	1998	67	22	44	1	0	0	12	12	0	
	1999	67	17	50	1	0	0	7	7	0	
	2000	106	44	60	2	1	1	5	5	0	
	2001	81	32	48	1	1	1	4	4	0	
	2002	81	32	48	1	1	1	4	4	0	
Eastern Europe and the former USSR 1/,5/	1998	596	362	128	0	64	25	349	322	27	
	1999	633	396	137	0	61	21	381	363	18	
	2000	515	350	106	0	58	14	344	335	8	
	2001	459	325	75	0	59	25	318	300	17	
	2002	509	361	83	0	65	28	353	333	19	
Former USSR-Europe 6/	1998	370	195	102	0	31	21	188	168	20	
	1999	178	78	37	0	25	14	75	65	10	
	2000	228	122	82	0	23	10	117	111	5	
	2001	103	58	15	0	29	22	53	50	2	
	2002	111	62	16	0	31	24	57	54	2	
Developed economies-Europe	1998	1965	1707	183	7	75	14	1659	1640	19	
	1999	1580	1153	385	7	42	13	1129	1111	18	
	2000	1289	1078	182	4	29	11	1061	1046	14	
	2001	1357	1221	102	6	34	8	1201	1186	15	
	2002	1438	1294	108	6	36	8	1272	1257	16	
European Union	1998	1964	1706	183	7	75	14	1658	1639	19	
	1999	1579	1152	384	7	42	13	1128	1110	18	
	2000	1287	1076	182	4	29	11	1059	1044	14	
	2001	1356	1220	102	6	34	8	1200	1185	15	
	2002	1439	1294	108	6	36	8	1273	1257	16	
European Free Trade Association	1998	1	1	0	0	0	0	1	1	0	
	1999	1	1	0	0	0	0	1	1	0	
	2000	2	2	0	0	0	0	2	2	0	
	2001	1	1	0	0	0	0	1	1	0	
	2002	1	1	0	0	0	0	1	1	0	
Other developed economies	1998	7455	4181	3048	211	20	2	2127	2086	42	
	1999	6888	3414	3201	287	35	25	1482	1473	9	
	2000	7401	3287	3874	219	8	2	1447	1442	5	
	2001	7530	3428	3920	286	15	3	1606	1592	14	
	2002	7354	3348	3829	279	15	3	1569	1555	14	

For general note and footnotes see end of table.

Exportations mondiales par classes de marchandises et par régions (suite)

En millions de dollars E.-U. f.o.b.

raines et fruits oléagineaux (CTCI, Rev. 2 et Rev. 3, 22)

conomies éveloppées 1/,2/				Developing economies Economies en voie de développement 1/,2/						← Exportations vers	
Canada	U.S.A. E.-U.	Japan Japon	Australia New Zealand Australie Nouvelle-Zélande	Africa Afrique	America Amerique Total	America Amerique LAIA ALADI	Asia Asie Mid. East Moyen Orient	Asia Asie Other Autres 7/	Oceania Océanie	Année	Exportations en provenance de ↓
194	424	1821	33	173	1664	1538	368	2911	8	1998	Monde 1/
229	333	1654	33	183	1340	1236	361	3428	4	1999	
256	310	1638	26	187	1628	1492	395	4505	5	2000	
301	282	1631	22	232	1718	1539	416	5069	5	2001	
314	294	1702	23	242	1793	1606	434	5291	0	2002	
159	261	1575	21	62	1201	1132	93	1857	6	1998	Economies dévelopées 1/,2/
198	202	1426	18	64	1003	945	138	2371	3	1999	
201	190	1349	15	75	1076	998	122	2774	3	2000	
255	180	1289	15	86	1142	1062	101	2684	4	2001	
262	185	1325	15	88	1174	1092	104	2759	0	2002	
35	157	246	12	110	455	400	181	1035	1	1998	Economies en voie de développement 1/,2/
29	129	228	15	117	321	276	169	999	2	1999	
55	119	288	11	112	547	490	200	1707	2	2000	
46	97	342	7	146	560	461	298	2345	1	2001	
49	104	365	7	156	598	492	318	2502	0	2002	
1	8	0	0	6	25	25	2	12	1	1998	OPEP
1	8	0	0	11	20	20	2	16	0	1999	
1	12	10	0	9	31	30	5	15	0	2000	
0	11	6	0	2	34	34	4	8	0	2001	
0	11	6	0	2	34	34	4	8	0	2002	
0	6	0	0	1	8	6	94	19	0	1998	Europe de l'Est et l'ancienne URSS 1/,5/
2	2	0	0	2	15	15	54	59	0	1999	
0	2	0	0	1	5	5	73	24	0	2000	
0	5	0	0	0	16	16	16	40	0	2001	
0	6	0	0	0	18	18	18	44	0	2002	
0	5	0	0	1	2	0	80	19	0	1998	l'ancienne URSS-Europe 6/
0	2	0	0	0	0	0	31	5	0	1999	
0	1	0	0	1	0	0	64	17	0	2000	
0	5	0	0	0	0	0	6	9	0	2001	
0	5	0	0	0	0	0	6	10	0	2002	
17	10	17	1	11	18	18	13	135	0	1998	Economies développées-Europe
4	9	7	1	9	30	30	15	324	0	1999	
1	11	1	1	14	7	7	17	138	0	2000	
1	7	6	1	9	2	2	11	74	0	2001	
1	7	6	1	10	2	2	12	78	0	2002	
17	10	17	1	11	18	18	13	135	0	1998	Union Européenne
4	9	7	1	9	30	30	15	324	0	1999	
1	11	1	1	14	7	7	17	138	0	2000	
1	7	6	1	9	2	2	11	74	0	2001	
1	7	6	1	10	2	2	12	79	0	2002	
0	0	0	0	0	0	0	0	0	0	1998	Association Européenne de Libre Exchange
0	0	0	0	0	0	0	0	0	0	1999	
0	0	0	0	0	0	0	0	0	0	2000	
0	0	0	0	0	0	0	0	0	0	2001	
0	0	0	0	0	0	0	0	0	0	2002	
142	251	1558	20	51	1182	1114	80	1722	6	1998	Autres economies développées
193	193	1419	17	54	973	915	123	2047	3	1999	
200	179	1348	14	61	1069	991	105	2636	3	2000	
254	173	1283	14	77	1140	1061	90	2610	4	2001	
248	169	1253	14	75	1113	1036	88	2549	0	2002	

Voir la fin du tableau pour la remarque générale et les notes.

SPECIAL TABLE: D

World exports by commodity classes and by regions (continued)

In million U.S. dollars f.o.b.

Exports to → / ↓ Exports from	Year	World Monde 1/	Developed economies Econ. développées 1/,2/	Developing economies economies en voie de développement 1/,2/ Total	OPEC OPEP	Eastern Europe and fmr. USSR-Europe Europe de l'Est et l'anc. URSS-Europe Total 1/,5/	Former USSR-Eur. 6/	Develop[…] economi[…] Europe Total	EU UE	EFTA AELE	South Africa Afrique du Su[…]
Oil seeds and, oleaginous fruit (SITC, Rev. 2 and Rev. 3, 22) (continue[…]											
Canada	1998	1689	1065	614	25	9	0	277	248	29	
	1999	1292	772	520	62	0	0	123	122	1	
	2000	1167	667	499	32	0	0	99	99	0	
	2001	1184	710	474	7	0	0	163	163	0	
	2002	1150	690	460	7	0	0	158	158	0	
United States	1998	5425	2913	2295	186	10	2	1779	1770	9	
	1999	5028	2342	2412	224	35	25	1213	1208	4	
	2000	5763	2424	3100	187	7	2	1308	1306	3	
	2001	5912	2446	3285	275	14	3	1330	1319	11	
	2002	5613	2322	3119	261	13	3	1263	1252	10	
Japan	1998	1	0	0	0	0	0	0	0	0	
	1999	1	0	1	0	0	0	0	0	0	
	2000	1	0	0	0	0	0	0	0	0	
	2001	2	1	0	0	0	0	0	0	0	
	2002	2	1	0	0	0	0	0	0	0	
Australia, New Zealand	1998	284	158	126	0	0	0	36	36	0	
	1999	504	246	258	1	0	0	101	101	0	
	2000	418	155	264	0	0	0	7	6	0	
	2001	380	227	153	3	0	0	75	75	0	
	2002	383	229	154	3	0	0	76	76	0	
Developing economies-	1998	254	116	133	30	5	1	73	69	4	
Africa	1999	273	99	168	37	5	0	54	50	4	
	2000	302	149	146	32	6	1	65	61	3	
	2001	506	192	302	67	11	1	94	88	6	
	2002	532	202	317	70	12	1	99	93	6	
Developing economies-	1998	3901	2676	1173	46	13	2	2399	2372	26	
America	1999	3008	2184	809	42	2	0	1986	1917	67	
	2000	3743	2031	1702	113	1	0	1780	1675	104	
	2001	4660	2340	2297	108	15	0	2069	1967	101	
	2002	4722	2371	2328	109	15	0	2098	1994	102	
Developing economies-	1998	9	1	1	0	7	1	1	1	0	
Europe 3/	1999	8	2	2	0	4	0	2	2	0	
	2000	9	5	2	0	2	0	4	4	0	
	2001	9	5	2	0	2	0	4	4	0	
	2002	9	5	2	0	2	0	4	4	0	
Developing economies-	1998	48	20	19	2	9	4	16	16	0	
Middle East	1999	39	20	9	2	9	5	16	16	0	
	2000	28	14	9	3	5	3	11	11	0	
	2001	38	17	11	2	10	6	14	14	0	
	2002	39	17	11	2	10	6	14	14	0	
Developing economies-	1998	773	303	440	130	29	22	130	130	0	
Other Asia	1999	968	316	603	204	49	36	139	138	0	
	2000	1124	376	695	229	53	40	173	173	0	
	2001	1178	369	739	241	69	52	176	176	0	
	2002	1289	404	808	264	75	57	193	193	0	
Former USSR-Asia 7/.	1998	2	0	0	0	2	2	0	0	0	
	1999	5	0	1	0	4	4	0	0	0	
	2000	6	0	1	0	4	4	0	0	0	
	2001	6	0	1	0	4	4	0	0	0	
	2002	7	0	1	0	4	4	0	0	0	
Developing economies-	1998	35	14	17	0	0	0	6	6	0	
Oceania	1999	45	17	20	0	0	0	5	5	0	
	2000	25	9	16	0	0	0	5	5	0	
	2001	23	8	14	0	0	0	5	5	0	
	2002	23	9	17	0	0	0	9	8	0	

For general note and footnotes see end of table.

Exportations mondiales par classes de marchandises et par régions (suite)

En millions de dollars E.-U. f.o.b.

Economies développées 1/,2/				Developing economies Economies en voie de développement 1/,2/						← Exportations vers	
Canada	U.S.A. E.-U.	Japan Japon	Australia New Zealand Australie Nouvelle-Zélande	Africa Afrique	America Amerique Total	America Amerique LAIA ALADI	Asia Asie Mid. East Moyen Orient	Asia Asie Other Autres 7/	Oceania Océanie	Année	Exportations en provenance de ↓
Graines et fruits oléagineaux (CTCI, Rev. 2 et Rev. 3, 22) (suite)											
.	234	548	0	14	192	191	25	383	0	1998	Canada
.	160	488	0	6	117	116	48	348	0	1999	
.	141	426	0	9	175	169	25	291	0	2000	
.	130	416	0	7	166	165	4	296	0	2001	
.	126	404	0	7	161	160	4	287	0	2002	
140	.	902	16	26	983	916	55	1220	5	1998	Etats-Unis
191	.	818	14	43	813	758	73	1480	2	1999	
198	.	809	10	45	879	808	72	2101	2	2000	
253	.	755	11	66	972	895	81	2163	3	2001	
240	.	717	10	63	923	850	77	2054	3	2002	
0	0	.	0	0	0	0	0	0	0	1998	Japon
0	0	.	0	0	0	0	0	1	0	1999	
0	0	.	0	0	0	0	0	0	0	2000	
0	0	.	0	0	0	0	0	0	0	2001	
0	0	.	0	0	0	0	0	0	0	2002	
2	15	101	3	0	6	6	0	119	1	1998	Australie, Nouvelle-Zélande
2	31	107	2	0	39	39	1	217	1	1999	
2	36	106	3	0	13	13	7	243	1	2000	
1	41	107	3	0	0	0	3	148	1	2001	
1	41	108	3	0	0	0	3	149	1	2002	
1	4	23	0	43	6	0	58	27	0	1998	Economies en voie de
0	11	19	0	53	5	3	70	39	0	1999	développement-Afrique
0	6	26	0	46	3	1	65	33	0	2000	
0	7	42	0	66	6	0	147	83	0	2001	
0	7	44	0	69	6	0	154	87	0	2002	
30	124	84	5	48	445	398	80	601	0	1998	Economies en voie de
24	81	77	3	43	303	270	68	394	0	1999	développement-Amérique
50	70	116	4	31	527	481	83	1061	0	2000	
36	49	163	2	44	532	449	99	1611	0	2001	
36	50	165	2	45	539	455	100	1632	0	2002	
0	0	0	0	0	0	0	0	0	0	1998	Economies en voie de
0	0	0	0	0	0	0	0	0	0	1999	développement-Europe 3/
0	0	0	0	0	0	0	0	0	0	2000	
0	0	0	0	0	0	0	0	0	0	2001	
0	0	0	0	0	0	0	0	0	0	2002	
0	2	1	0	0	0	0	16	2	0	1998	Economies en voie de
0	1	2	0	1	0	0	3	5	0	1999	développement-Moyen Orient
0	0	2	0	0	0	0	6	2	0	2000	
0	0	1	0	1	0	0	9	2	0	2001	
0	0	1	0	1	0	0	9	2	0	2002	
5	27	132	4	19	3	1	28	390	1	1998	Economies en voie de
4	35	123	6	21	11	3	27	543	0	1999	développement-Autres Pays d'Asie
5	42	140	6	34	17	7	46	596	0	2000	
9	40	133	5	36	23	12	43	636	0	2001	
10	44	145	5	39	25	13	47	696	0	2002	
0	0	0	0	0	0	0	0	0	0	1998	l'ancienne URSS asiatique 7/
0	0	0	0	0	0	0	1	0	0	1999	
0	0	0	0	0	0	0	1	0	0	2000	
0	0	0	0	0	0	0	1	0	0	2001	
0	0	0	0	0	0	0	1	0	0	2002	
0	0	5	3	0	2	0	0	15	0	1998	Economies en voie de
0	0	7	5	0	2	0	0	17	2	1999	développement-Océanie
0	0	3	0	0	0	0	0	15	1	2000	
0	0	3	0	0	0	0	0	13	1	2001	
0	0	3	0	0	0	0	0	18	1	2002	

Voir la fin du tableau pour la remarque générale et les notes.

SPECIAL TABLE: D

World exports by commodity classes and by regions (continued)

In million U.S. dollars f.o.b.

Textile fibres (SITC, Rev. 2 and Rev. 3,

Exports to → / ↓ Exports from	Year	World Monde 1/	Developed economies Econ. dévelop-pées 1/,2/	Developing economies economies en voie de développement 1/,2/ Total	OPEC OPEP	Eastern Europe and fmr. USSR-Europe Europe de l'Est et l'anc. URSS-Europe Total 1/,5/	Former USSR-Eur. 6/	Develo[…] econom[…] Europe Total	EU UE	EFTA AELE	Sou[…] Afric[…] Afriq[…] du S[…]
World 1/	1998	24214	10157	12497	1372	1250	312	7502	7245	252	
	1999	20991	8987	10551	1337	1187	359	6667	6401	263	
	2000	22967	9177	12224	1471	1436	524	6886	6587	297	
	2001	23022	9017	12314	1501	1565	540	6835	6557	276	
	2002	24029	9412	12853	1567	1633	564	7134	6844	288	
Developed economies 1/,2/	1998	13842	6355	6849	823	540	110	4710	4610	99	
	1999	11013	5218	5219	668	507	121	3954	3871	81	
	2000	12361	5147	6523	736	623	164	3920	3834	85	
	2001	12376	4759	6829	777	710	178	3642	3558	83	
	2002	12722	4892	7020	799	730	183	3744	3658	85	
Developing economies 1/,2/	1998	9851	3617	5568	545	516	85	2617	2462	152	
	1999	9558	3618	5268	661	528	135	2574	2391	182	
	2000	10182	3863	5635	728	625	217	2804	2593	210	
	2001	10207	4071	5430	716	659	222	3012	2820	192	
	2002	10892	4344	5794	764	703	237	3214	3009	205	
OPEC	1998	228	41	186	7	1	0	29	28	1	
	1999	175	52	118	9	0	0	32	31	1	
	2000	234	55	166	14	10	9	35	34	1	
	2001	227	47	170	17	9	9	27	26	0	
	2002	227	47	170	17	9	9	27	26	0	
Eastern Europe and the former USSR 1/,5/	1998	521	184	81	5	195	118	174	174	1	
	1999	420	150	64	8	152	103	139	139	1	
	2000	424	166	67	7	188	143	162	160	2	
	2001	439	187	56	8	195	141	181	179	2	
	2002	487	208	62	9	216	156	201	199	2	
Former USSR-Europe 6/	1998	304	41	49	3	155	109	33	33	0	
	1999	256	36	39	8	127	97	26	26	0	
	2000	230	42	37	7	151	134	40	39	1	
	2001	215	39	27	7	149	131	34	34	0	
	2002	231	42	29	8	160	141	37	37	0	
Developed economies-Europe	1998	5116	3413	1141	95	465	94	3087	2998	87	
	1999	4463	2865	1082	76	448	105	2584	2513	69	
	2000	4506	2679	1214	84	547	147	2456	2382	74	
	2001	4374	2556	1126	80	617	154	2329	2252	75	
	2002	4634	2708	1193	85	654	163	2467	2386	79	
European Union	1998	5021	3329	1137	95	457	93	3013	2924	87	
	1999	4377	2790	1079	75	440	103	2517	2447	69	
	2000	4427	2614	1209	84	539	143	2398	2323	74	
	2001	4301	2501	1121	80	605	148	2282	2205	75	
	2002	4563	2653	1189	85	642	157	2421	2339	80	
European Free Trade Association	1998	95	83	4	0	8	2	74	74	0	
	1999	86	74	4	0	8	2	66	66	0	
	2000	79	65	5	0	8	4	58	58	0	
	2001	71	54	5	0	12	6	47	46	0	
	2002	74	56	5	0	12	6	49	48	0	
Other developed economies	1998	8726	2942	5709	728	75	16	1624	1611	12	
	1999	6550	2354	4137	593	59	16	1370	1359	11	
	2000	7855	2468	5308	652	76	18	1464	1452	12	
	2001	8002	2203	5703	697	93	24	1314	1306	8	
	2002	7815	2152	5570	681	91	23	1283	1276	8	

For general note and footnotes see end of table.

Exportations mondiales par classes de marchandises et par régions (suite)

En millions de dollars E.-U. f.o.b.

Economies développées 1/,2/ Canada	U.S.A. E.-U.	Japan Japon	Australia New Zealand Australie Nouvelle-Zélande	Developing economies / Economies en voie de développement 1/,2/ Africa Afrique	America Amerique Total	America Amerique LAIA ALADI	Asia Asie Mid. East Moyen Orient	Asia Asie Other Autres 7/	Oceania Océanie	Année	← Exportations vers / Exportations en provenance de ↓
Fibres textiles (CTCI, Rev. 2 et Rev. 3, 26)											
367	817	1185	103	1518	2056	1805	1243	7566	13	1998	Monde 1/
283	787	978	108	1455	1320	1195	976	6697	12	1999	
364	664	991	97	918	1705	1543	1442	8052	12	2000	
342	617	947	102	1018	1494	1330	1427	8243	20	2001	
357	644	988	106	1063	1559	1388	1489	8604	20	2002	
345	407	716	73	671	1401	1183	673	4032	11	1998	Economies dévelopées 1/,2/
265	325	505	78	616	751	657	464	3319	10	1999	
337	248	479	64	574	1112	991	703	4061	10	2000	
312	214	446	64	594	979	855	601	4565	8	2001	
321	220	458	66	611	1006	879	618	4693	8	2002	
21	409	461	29	843	651	618	529	3518	1	1998	Economies en voie de développement 1/,2/
18	460	465	30	837	565	533	473	3366	1	1999	
26	414	511	33	342	592	552	692	3981	2	2000	
30	400	498	38	421	514	475	791	3671	12	2001	
32	427	531	41	449	548	507	844	3917	10	2002	
0	5	5	1	24	28	26	25	109	0	1998	OPEP
0	6	7	4	3	18	15	32	65	0	1999	
0	6	6	7	6	18	17	50	92	0	2000	
0	6	4	9	28	15	14	24	102	0	2001	
0	6	4	9	28	15	14	24	102	0	2002	
0	1	8	0	4	5	5	41	16	0	1998	Europe de l'Est et l'ancienne URSS 1/,5/
0	2	8	0	3	4	4	39	12	0	1999	
0	2	1	0	2	1	1	47	9	0	2000	
0	3	3	0	3	0	0	36	6	0	2001	
0	3	3	0	3	0	0	40	7	0	2002	
0	1	8	0	1	4	4	26	15	0	1998	l'ancienne URSS-Europe 6/
0	1	8	0	0	4	4	23	11	0	1999	
0	1	1	0	0	0	0	27	7	0	2000	
0	2	3	0	1	0	0	20	4	0	2001	
0	2	3	0	1	0	0	22	4	0	2002	
19	170	48	23	447	87	75	310	238	1	1998	Economies développées-Europe
11	151	46	24	411	75	69	284	255	0	1999	
11	99	48	18	398	86	82	341	327	0	2000	
15	103	47	17	396	70	65	292	287	1	2001	
16	109	50	18	420	74	69	309	304	0	2002	
18	162	47	22	445	86	75	310	238	1	1998	Union Européenne
10	144	46	23	409	75	68	284	254	0	1999	
11	93	47	17	395	86	82	341	326	0	2000	
15	97	47	17	392	70	65	291	286	1	2001	
16	103	50	18	416	74	69	309	303	0	2002	
1	8	0	1	2	0	0	0	1	0	1998	Association Européenne de Libre Exchange
1	7	0	1	2	0	0	0	1	0	1999	
1	6	0	0	3	0	0	1	1	0	2000	
0	6	0	0	3	0	0	1	1	0	2001	
0	6	0	0	3	0	0	1	1	0	2002	
327	237	668	50	224	1314	1108	362	3794	11	1998	Autres economies développées
255	174	460	54	205	676	589	180	3064	10	1999	
326	149	431	46	176	1025	909	362	3734	10	2000	
297	111	399	47	198	909	789	309	4278	8	2001	
290	108	390	46	193	888	771	302	4178	8	2002	

Voir la fin du tableu pour la remarque générale et les notes.

SPECIAL TABLE: D

World exports by commodity classes and by regions (continued)

In million U.S. dollars f.o.b.

Exports from ↓ / Exports to →	Year	World Monde 1/	Developed economies Econ. dévelop-pées 1/,2/	Developing economies économies en voie de développement 1/,2/ Total	Developing economies OPEC OPEP	Eastern Europe and fmr. USSR-Europe / Europe de l'Est et l'anc. URSS-Europe Total 1/,5/	Eastern Europe and fmr. USSR-Europe Former USSR-Eur. 6/	Developed economies: Europe Total	Europe EU UE	Europe EFTA AELE	South Africa Afrique du Sud
									Textile fibres (SITC, Rev. 2 and Rev. 3, 26) (continued)		
Canada	1998	229	97	129	4	3	2	5	5	0	0
	1999	212	84	124	3	4	3	5	5	0	0
	2000	183	51	129	2	3	2	5	5	0	0
	2001	183	54	128	3	1	0	10	10	0	0
	2002	178	52	124	3	1	0	10	10	0	0
United States	1998	3913	1064	2839	270	9	3	393	387	7	8
	1999	2208	770	1428	146	10	5	333	324	9	13
	2000	3187	907	2266	242	14	7	367	358	8	12
	2001	3334	777	2540	270	16	8	302	297	5	6
	2002	3165	738	2412	256	15	8	287	282	5	6
Japan	1998	1005	180	821	129	4	1	113	112	1	13
	1999	922	184	733	119	5	0	120	120	1	11
	2000	1008	180	825	117	3	1	116	114	2	12
	2001	934	139	791	111	4	1	87	86	1	10
	2002	965	144	817	115	4	1	90	89	1	10
Australia, New Zealand	1998	3294	1424	1815	318	55	10	953	949	4	3
	1999	2949	1165	1750	317	34	8	777	776	1	2
	2000	3230	1182	1990	284	56	8	849	848	1	5
	2001	3322	1100	2151	306	71	14	793	793	1	5
	2002	3351	1110	2170	309	72	14	800	800	1	5
Developing economies-Africa	1998	1946	492	1359	251	7	0	396	387	7	51
	1999	2079	525	1465	252	7	0	415	384	30	54
	2000	1911	652	1197	228	55	29	538	509	30	50
	2001	2060	673	1317	223	64	38	555	522	32	63
	2002	2164	708	1384	234	67	40	584	550	34	66
Developing economies-America	1998	1200	460	730	42	2	0	229	229	1	2
	1999	1008	439	564	53	4	0	217	214	3	2
	2000	995	447	544	52	1	1	243	235	8	1
	2001	1090	469	615	63	3	1	282	277	5	5
	2002	1105	475	623	64	3	1	286	281	5	5
Developing economies-Europe 3/	1998	27	8	12	0	7	0	8	8	0	0
	1999	17	4	10	0	3	0	4	4	0	0
	2000	22	9	8	0	5	0	9	9	0	0
	2001	18	9	4	0	4	0	9	9	0	0
	2002	19	10	4	0	4	0	10	10	0	0
Developing economies-Middle East	1998	547	264	250	58	15	1	241	222	19	0
	1999	430	215	178	49	9	1	179	174	5	0
	2000	475	214	219	56	24	10	189	183	6	1
	2001	1278	552	667	148	54	14	470	452	18	1
	2002	1301	562	679	151	55	14	479	460	18	1
Developing economies-Other Asia	1998	6125	2393	3211	194	485	83	1742	1616	126	15
	1999	6018	2435	3046	306	504	134	1759	1615	143	9
	2000	6759	2541	3647	387	539	177	1824	1657	167	11
	2001	5742	2367	2807	277	535	169	1696	1559	136	11
	2002	6281	2589	3071	303	585	185	1855	1705	149	12
Former USSR-Asia 7/	1998	2327	1385	435	37	475	78	1225	1111	114	0
	1999	2260	1318	422	71	489	125	1160	1026	135	0
	2000	2276	1296	433	55	518	163	1146	991	155	0
	2001	2214	1274	397	41	513	155	1124	998	126	0
	2002	2438	1415	437	45	565	171	1249	1110	139	0
Developing economies-Oceania	1998	6	0	5	0	0	0	0	0	0	0
	1999	6	1	6	0	0	0	0	0	0	0
	2000	20	0	19	5	0	0	0	0	0	0
	2001	20	0	20	6	0	0	0	0	0	0
	2002	20	0	25	8	0	0	0	0	0	0

For general note and footnotes see end of table.

Exportations mondiales par classes de marchandises et par régions (suite)

En millions de dollars E.-U. f.o.b.

Economies développées 1/,2/ Canada	U.S.A. E.-U.	Japan Japon	Australia New Zealand Australie Nouvelle-Zélande	Developing economies Economies en voie de développement 1/,2/ Africa Afrique	America Amerique Total	America Amerique LAIA ALADI	Asia Asie Mid. East Moyen Orient	Asia Asie Other Autres 7/	Oceania Océanie	Année	← Exportations vers / Exportations en provenance de ↓
Fibres textiles (CTCI, Rev. 2 et Rev. 3, 26) (suite)											
.	87	0	3	35	7	4	2	86	0	1998	Canada
.	73	1	4	37	8	5	1	78	0	1999	
.	44	0	1	25	6	2	1	97	0	2000	
.	41	0	3	32	6	2	2	87	0	2001	
.	40	0	3	31	6	2	2	84	0	2002	
316	.	323	14	130	1249	1047	189	1270	1	1998	Etats-Unis
244	.	153	13	111	633	550	62	623	0	1999	
314	.	187	7	86	975	864	234	970	0	2000	
291	.	162	7	103	864	749	202	1370	0	2001	
276	.	154	7	98	820	711	192	1301	0	2002	
3	45	.	5	16	9	8	56	739	0	1998	Japon
3	42	.	7	25	8	7	40	660	0	1999	
3	40	.	9	25	9	9	26	765	0	2000	
2	30	.	9	28	11	11	25	726	0	2001	
2	31	.	9	29	11	11	26	750	0	2002	
5	100	334	27	24	45	45	82	1652	10	1998	Australie, Nouvelle-Zélande
5	54	296	29	13	22	21	50	1654	10	1999	
5	60	234	28	16	32	30	71	1861	10	2000	
2	36	233	27	13	25	25	52	2052	8	2001	
2	36	235	27	13	25	25	52	2070	8	2002	
0	7	35	3	729	90	89	103	434	0	1998	Economies en voie de développement-Afrique
0	16	38	1	764	86	85	112	499	0	1999	
3	16	43	1	237	155	146	132	666	1	2000	
4	9	41	1	230	169	158	108	804	1	2001	
4	9	43	1	242	178	166	113	845	1	2002	
2	198	28	0	6	478	455	20	227	0	1998	Economies en voie de développement-Amérique
1	202	16	0	5	374	353	18	167	0	1999	
2	176	24	1	2	343	318	35	164	0	2000	
1	161	18	1	5	263	239	20	327	0	2001	
1	163	18	1	5	267	242	20	331	0	2002	
0	0	0	0	0	0	0	2	0	0	1998	Economies en voie de développement-Europe 3/
0	0	0	0	0	0	0	0	0	0	1999	
0	0	0	0	0	0	0	1	0	0	2000	
0	0	0	0	0	0	0	1	0	0	2001	
0	0	0	0	0	0	0	1	0	0	2002	
1	9	9	0	58	3	3	105	83	0	1998	Economies en voie de développement-Moyen Orient
2	22	11	0	30	8	8	55	83	0	1999	
1	8	12	0	38	2	1	118	59	0	2000	
1	21	55	0	123	1	0	332	199	10	2001	
1	21	56	0	125	1	0	338	203	10	2002	
18	195	390	26	50	75	69	300	2773	0	1998	Economies en voie de développement-Autres Pays d'Asie
14	220	399	28	37	91	84	288	2618	1	1999	
20	214	432	32	64	92	86	405	3074	0	2000	
23	210	384	35	63	81	77	330	2322	1	2001	
25	230	420	38	69	89	84	361	2540	1	2002	
0	2	158	0	0	30	28	209	185	0	1998	l'ancienne URSS asiatique 7/
0	10	148	0	1	30	26	202	178	0	1999	
0	6	144	0	4	25	25	226	167	0	2000	
0	4	145	0	3	26	25	193	165	0	2001	
0	4	160	0	3	29	28	213	182	0	2002	
0	0	0	0	0	5	3	0	0	1	1998	Economies en voie de développement-Océanie
0	0	0	0	0	5	3	0	0	1	1999	
0	0	0	0	0	0	0	0	19	0	2000	
0	0	0	0	0	0	0	0	19	0	2001	
0	0	0	0	0	0	0	0	27	0	2002	

Voir la fin du tableau pour la remarque générale et les notes.

SPECIAL TABLE: D

World exports by commodity classes and by regions (continued)

In million U.S. dollars f.o.b.

Exports from ↓ / Exports to →	Year	World / Monde 1/	Developed economies / Econ. dévelop-pées 1/,2/	Developing economies / économies en voie de développement 1/,2/ — Total	Developing economies — OPEC / OPEP	Eastern Europe and fmr. USSR-Europe / Europe de l'Est et l'anc. URSS-Europe — Total 1/,5/	Eastern Europe and fmr. USSR-Europe — Former USSR-Eur. 6/	Developed economies — Europe — Total	Developed economies — Europe — EU / UE	Developed economies — Europe — EFTA / AELE	Developed economies — South Africa / Afrique du Sud
		Crude fertilizers and minerals (SITC, Rev. 2 and Rev. 3, 27)									
World 1/	1998	13723	8918	3659	446	731	330	6027	5638	374	88
	1999	13634	8888	3769	415	650	285	5891	5530	347	82
	2000	13450	8740	3779	442	623	259	5573	5232	328	82
	2001	13449	8544	3863	481	673	278	5586	5235	336	74
	2002	14037	8918	4032	502	702	290	5830	5464	351	77
Developed economies 1/,2/	1998	8535	6234	1708	201	235	47	4727	4419	295	45
	1999	8316	6103	1690	188	226	43	4590	4288	290	41
	2000	8226	5941	1775	202	220	41	4332	4048	274	38
	2001	8065	5821	1645	207	245	51	4305	4013	280	30
	2002	8291	5984	1691	213	252	52	4425	4125	288	31
Developing economies 1/,2/	1998	4377	2374	1805	236	165	79	1003	949	52	43
	1999	4697	2572	1981	215	134	60	1095	1060	33	41
	2000	4609	2590	1852	230	153	73	1045	1011	31	44
	2001	4846	2532	2105	264	195	98	1096	1062	31	43
	2002	5171	2702	2246	282	208	105	1170	1133	33	46
OPEC	1998	200	29	167	58	3	0	18	17	1	0
	1999	212	27	178	24	6	3	15	15	0	0
	2000	239	30	201	31	7	7	19	19	0	0
	2001	287	34	240	46	13	13	20	20	0	0
	2002	287	34	240	46	13	13	20	20	0	0
Eastern Europe and the former USSR 1/,5/	1998	810	310	147	9	330	203	297	270	27	0
	1999	620	213	99	11	290	182	206	181	25	0
	2000	614	209	152	10	250	145	196	172	23	0
	2001	537	191	112	10	233	128	185	160	25	0
	2002	596	212	124	11	259	142	205	178	28	0
Former USSR-Europe 6/	1998	533	178	110	6	225	181	167	143	24	0
	1999	358	96	64	10	180	150	91	68	23	0
	2000	330	94	103	8	132	109	84	61	22	0
	2001	277	89	75	8	113	90	85	61	24	0
	2002	298	96	81	9	122	97	91	66	26	0
Developed economies-Europe	1998	5475	4372	699	103	221	43	4071	3778	281	19
	1999	5327	4291	673	98	218	40	3970	3687	272	14
	2000	4937	3917	676	102	211	39	3590	3332	247	15
	2001	4986	3898	666	119	235	48	3582	3318	253	13
	2002	5282	4130	706	126	249	51	3795	3515	268	14
European Union	1998	5109	4039	672	99	215	42	3758	3476	271	18
	1999	4981	3974	650	96	211	38	3675	3406	258	14
	2000	4605	3624	646	100	202	38	3318	3069	239	15
	2001	4656	3607	636	117	225	47	3313	3054	247	13
	2002	4940	3827	675	124	239	50	3515	3240	262	14
European Free Trade Association	1998	365	332	27	3	6	1	312	301	10	0
	1999	346	316	23	2	7	2	294	280	13	0
	2000	331	293	30	2	9	2	271	263	8	0
	2001	330	290	30	2	10	2	269	263	6	0
	2002	342	301	31	2	10	2	279	273	6	0
Other developed economies	1998	3061	1862	1009	99	14	4	656	642	14	26
	1999	2989	1812	1017	90	8	3	620	602	18	27
	2000	3289	2023	1100	100	9	2	742	716	27	24
	2001	3078	1923	979	88	9	3	722	695	26	17
	2002	3006	1878	956	86	9	3	705	679	25	17

For general note and footnotes see end of table.

Exportations mondiales par classes de marchandises et par régions (suite)

En millions de dollars E.-U. f.o.b.

Economies développées 1/,2/ Canada	U.S.A. E.-U.	Japan Japon	Australia New Zealand Australie Nouvelle-Zélande	Developing economies / Economies en voie de développement 1/,2/ Africa Afrique	America Amerique Total	America Amerique LAIA ALADI	Asia Asie Mid. East Moyen Orient	Asia Asie Other Autres 7/	Oceania Océanie	Année	← Exportations vers / Exportations en provenance de ↓
Engrais et minéraux bruts (CTCI, Rev. 2 et Rev. 3, 27)											
438	1153	831	261	355	705	619	416	2072	15	1998	Monde 1/
408	1204	877	244	306	630	533	364	2350	14	1999	
421	1230	965	232	374	669	562	395	2234	14	2000	
430	1204	835	191	346	611	514	430	2373	12	2001	
449	1257	872	199	361	638	536	449	2477	11	2002	
350	607	382	79	224	450	390	182	794	7	1998	Economies dévelopées 1/,2/
356	600	397	79	196	393	336	150	896	7	1999	
377	660	416	84	178	418	351	153	976	6	2000	
390	625	365	74	203	366	312	153	868	7	2001	
401	642	375	76	209	376	321	157	892	7	2002	
87	539	445	182	97	248	226	223	1200	8	1998	Economies en voie de développement 1/,2/
52	601	477	165	81	231	193	200	1419	7	1999	
38	568	546	148	116	244	206	232	1218	8	2000	
40	577	468	117	105	241	200	265	1458	5	2001	
43	616	499	125	112	257	213	283	1556	5	2002	
0	2	8	1	4	7	6	107	48	0	1998	OPEP
0	3	8	1	2	5	4	84	87	0	1999	
0	2	8	0	4	4	3	82	111	0	2000	
0	3	10	1	6	2	2	84	147	0	2001	
0	3	10	1	6	2	2	84	147	0	2002	
0	7	4	0	34	7	3	11	77	0	1998	Europe de l'Est et l'ancienne URSS 1/,5/
0	3	3	0	30	7	4	14	35	0	1999	
7	2	2	0	80	7	5	11	41	0	2000	
1	1	1	0	38	4	2	12	47	0	2001	
1	1	1	0	42	4	2	13	52	0	2002	
0	6	4	0	19	6	2	8	76	0	1998	l'ancienne URSS-Europe 6/
0	2	3	0	17	2	1	11	33	0	1999	
7	0	2	0	51	3	2	7	39	0	2000	
0	0	1	0	17	3	2	7	45	0	2001	
0	0	1	0	18	3	2	8	48	0	2002	
22	160	60	15	140	77	62	139	293	2	1998	Economies développées-Europe
24	177	68	13	129	73	58	118	306	2	1999	
25	190	65	11	116	77	61	123	315	2	2000	
23	182	64	12	130	68	53	125	296	2	2001	
24	193	68	13	138	72	56	132	314	1	2002	
21	152	49	14	139	74	60	134	274	2	1998	Union Européenne
23	166	59	12	129	71	57	113	290	2	1999	
24	180	55	10	115	75	59	118	293	2	2000	
22	173	54	11	129	65	51	123	272	2	2001	
23	184	57	12	137	69	54	130	289	1	2002	
1	8	11	1	1	3	3	4	19	0	1998	Association Européenne de Libre Exchange
1	11	10	1	0	2	1	4	16	0	1999	
1	10	9	1	1	2	2	5	22	0	2000	
1	9	10	1	1	2	2	2	24	0	2001	
1	9	10	1	1	2	2	2	25	0	2002	
328	447	322	64	84	373	328	43	501	5	1998	Autres economies développées
332	423	329	66	66	320	278	33	590	6	1999	
352	470	351	72	63	341	290	30	661	4	2000	
367	443	301	63	74	298	260	28	572	5	2001	
358	433	294	62	72	291	254	27	559	5	2002	

Voir la fin du tableau pour la remarque générale et les notes.

SPECIAL TABLE: D

World exports by commodity classes and by regions (continued)

In million U.S. dollars f.o.b.

Crude fertilizers and minerals (SITC, Rev. 2 and Rev. 3, 27) (continued)

Exports from ↓ / Exports to →	Year	World Monde 1/	Developed economies Econ. développées 1/,2/	Developing economies économies en voie de développement 1/,2/ Total	Developing economies OPEC OPEP	Eastern Europe and fmr. USSR-Europe Europe de l'Est et l'anc. URSS-Europe Total 1/,5/	Eastern Europe and fmr. USSR-Europe Former USSR-Eur. 6/	Developed economies Europe Total	Developed economies Europe EU UE	Developed economies Europe EFTA AELE	Developed economies South Africa Afrique du Sud
Canada	1998	691	472	218	18	1	0	22	22	0	17
	1999	683	451	231	22	1	0	19	18	1	19
	2000	735	484	250	20	1	0	21	20	1	15
	2001	612	439	172	20	0	0	17	16	1	10
	2002	594	426	167	19	0	0	17	16	1	10
United States	1998	1599	1071	523	61	6	4	444	437	7	8
	1999	1534	1031	498	47	4	2	407	396	10	6
	2000	1717	1145	569	64	3	1	462	448	14	5
	2001	1654	1116	533	51	4	3	464	450	13	5
	2002	1570	1060	506	48	4	3	441	427	12	5
Japan	1998	168	44	122	8	2	0	18	13	5	1
	1999	174	46	127	7	0	0	18	12	6	0
	2000	184	47	136	8	1	1	19	14	5	0
	2001	171	43	128	7	0	0	19	14	5	0
	2002	177	44	132	7	0	0	20	14	5	0
Australia, New Zealand	1998	303	80	47	9	0	0	34	34	0	0
	1999	281	82	46	11	0	0	27	27	0	0
	2000	271	80	33	4	0	0	28	28	0	1
	2001	284	83	34	5	0	0	34	34	0	0
	2002	286	84	34	5	0	0	34	34	0	0
Developing economies-Africa	1998	999	543	398	49	58	0	326	282	43	29
	1999	906	506	345	56	54	2	305	282	20	28
	2000	895	480	351	55	61	5	279	255	22	27
	2001	917	497	356	46	61	5	280	254	23	28
	2002	963	523	374	48	64	5	295	268	24	29
Developing economies-America	1998	642	475	162	24	4	1	135	133	2	2
	1999	717	540	173	23	3	1	159	157	2	1
	2000	752	551	193	27	5	1	188	187	1	2
	2001	715	524	186	28	3	1	170	169	1	1
	2002	725	531	188	28	3	1	172	171	1	1
Developing economies-Europe 3/	1998	36	16	18	1	2	0	15	15	0	0
	1999	41	15	24	1	3	0	15	15	0	0
	2000	41	18	22	1	2	0	17	17	0	0
	2001	43	22	17	1	4	0	22	22	0	0
	2002	45	23	18	1	4	0	23	23	0	0
Developing economies-Middle East	1998	684	225	409	103	18	7	168	167	1	2
	1999	778	308	443	67	19	8	226	225	0	2
	2000	447	161	250	57	27	17	131	130	1	3
	2001	807	201	535	101	61	32	170	169	0	3
	2002	822	205	545	103	62	33	173	172	0	3
Developing economies-Other Asia	1998	1871	1020	768	59	82	72	358	352	7	10
	1999	2102	1102	944	68	55	49	391	380	10	10
	2000	2352	1300	994	90	57	51	429	423	6	11
	2001	2318	1257	994	87	66	60	454	448	6	11
	2002	2536	1375	1087	95	72	66	497	490	7	12
Former USSR-Asia 7/.	1998	77	1	41	4	34	34	1	1	0	0
	1999	59	4	37	3	17	17	4	3	1	0
	2000	49	1	28	2	20	20	1	1	0	0
	2001	46	1	27	1	18	18	0	0	0	0
	2002	51	1	30	1	20	20	0	0	0	0
Developing economies-Oceania	1998	144	95	50	0	0	0	0	0	0	0
	1999	153	100	53	0	0	0	0	0	0	0
	2000	122	79	43	0	0	0	0	0	0	0
	2001	47	30	17	0	0	0	0	0	0	0
	2002	47	35	21	0	0	0	0	0	0	0

For general note and footnotes see end of table.

Exportations mondiales par classes de marchandises et par régions (suite)

En millions de dollars E.-U. f.o.b.

conomies éveloppées 1/,2/ Canada	U.S.A. E.-U.	Japan Japon	Australia New Zealand Australie Nouvelle-Zélande	Developing economies Economies en voie de développement 1/,2/ Africa Afrique	America Amerique Total	America Amerique LAIA ALADI	Asia Asie Mid. East Moyen Orient	Asia Asie Other Autres 7/	Oceania Océanie	← Exportations vers Année	Exportations en provenance de ↓
ngrais et minéraux bruts (CTCI, Rev. 2 et Rev. 3, 27) (suite)											
.	381	31	9	50	86	70	6	76	0	1998	Canada
.	359	33	13	34	79	62	4	114	0	1999	
.	397	27	19	18	96	75	3	133	0	2000	
.	377	23	8	18	58	46	2	94	0	2001	
.	366	22	8	17	56	45	2	91	0	2002	
323	.	261	28	12	258	229	17	235	0	1998	Etats-Unis
329	.	256	28	7	209	184	16	265	1	1999	
348	.	293	32	17	218	188	20	314	0	2000	
362	.	245	35	22	215	188	18	278	1	2001	
344	.	233	33	21	204	178	17	264	1	2002	
0	15	.	10	2	0	0	2	118	0	1998	Japon
0	18	.	9	0	0	0	1	125	0	1999	
0	21	.	6	1	0	0	1	134	0	2000	
0	17	.	5	0	0	0	0	126	0	2001	
0	18	.	5	0	0	0	0	130	0	2002	
1	19	15	12	0	0	0	1	40	5	1998	Australie, Nouvelle-Zélande
0	17	26	12	1	1	1	4	37	4	1999	
1	19	18	12	0	1	1	1	27	4	2000	
2	14	21	11	1	1	1	3	26	5	2001	
2	14	21	11	1	1	1	3	26	5	2002	
56	76	26	29	55	104	104	56	173	0	1998	Economies en voie de développement-Afrique
26	91	21	34	44	90	90	49	146	0	1999	
8	76	17	37	62	98	96	49	129	0	2000	
8	77	17	43	68	97	95	41	138	0	2001	
8	81	18	45	71	102	100	43	145	0	2002	
14	273	47	4	6	123	104	2	31	0	1998	Economies en voie de développement-Amérique
12	278	86	4	8	122	90	3	40	0	1999	
14	258	88	1	7	125	91	3	58	0	2000	
13	275	64	1	7	125	87	2	51	0	2001	
13	279	65	1	7	127	88	2	52	0	2002	
0	0	0	0	0	0	0	1	0	0	1998	Economies en voie de développement-Europe 3/
0	0	0	0	0	0	0	1	0	0	1999	
0	0	0	0	0	0	0	1	0	0	2000	
0	0	0	0	0	0	0	1	0	0	2001	
0	0	0	0	0	0	0	1	0	0	2002	
1	4	13	32	22	2	2	135	249	0	1998	Economies en voie de développement-Moyen Orient
1	42	25	6	19	1	0	120	301	0	1999	
1	6	9	1	17	5	4	124	104	0	2000	
1	7	11	0	16	4	3	179	334	0	2001	
1	7	11	0	16	4	3	182	340	0	2002	
17	187	358	23	14	17	16	29	705	3	1998	Economies en voie de développement-Autres Pays d'Asie
14	190	345	21	10	15	13	28	886	2	1999	
14	227	431	29	30	16	15	55	889	2	2000	
18	218	376	43	13	16	14	41	919	2	2001	
20	238	411	47	14	18	15	45	1005	2	2002	
0	0	0	0	0	0	0	4	38	0	1998	l'ancienne URSS asiatique 7/
0	0	0	0	0	0	0	3	34	0	1999	
0	1	0	0	0	0	0	4	24	0	2000	
0	1	0	0	0	0	0	4	23	0	2001	
0	1	0	0	0	0	0	4	25	0	2002	
0	0	0	94	0	2	1	0	43	5	1998	Economies en voie de développement-Océanie
0	0	0	100	0	2	1	0	45	5	1999	
0	0	0	79	0	0	0	0	38	5	2000	
0	0	0	29	0	0	0	0	14	2	2001	
0	0	0	39	0	0	0	0	20	3	2002	

Voir la fin du tableau pour la remarque générale et les notes.

SPECIAL TABLE: D

World exports by commodity classes and by regions (continued)

In million U.S. dollars f.o.b.

Exports to → / ↓ Exports from	Year	World Monde 1/	Developed economies Econ. dévelop-pées 1/,2/	Developing economies economies en voie de développement 1/,2/ Total	OPEC OPEP	Eastern Europe and fmr. USSR-Europe Europe de l'Est et l'anc. URSS-Europe Total 1/,5/	Former USSR-Eur. 6/	Developed economies Europe Total	EU UE	EFTA AELE	South Africa Afrique du Sud
						Metalliferous ores and metal scraps (SITC, Rev. 2 and Rev. 3, 28					
World 1/	1998	45485	27748	11415	609	2142	1004	17185	15905	1279	73
	1999	42186	25910	11712	679	1647	730	15529	14121	1406	100
	2000	49473	29199	14844	873	1684	933	17562	15934	1622	155
	2001	47475	26897	15619	877	1652	967	16398	14827	1571	114
	2002	49552	28074	16302	915	1724	1009	17116	15476	1640	119
Developed economies 1/,2/	1998	24045	16150	5083	140	296	134	10553	9804	748	44
	1999	22680	15122	5025	170	261	99	9740	9035	705	35
	2000	26926	17173	6637	216	336	100	11424	10660	764	53
	2001	26577	15978	7678	204	331	135	10660	9810	850	32
	2002	27321	16425	7893	210	340	139	10958	10084	874	33
Developing economies 1/,2/	1998	17263	9553	5778	466	931	655	4707	4208	499	29
	1999	16279	9426	6180	502	637	458	4517	3851	664	64
	2000	20235	10834	7606	653	831	539	5022	4184	832	102
	2001	19024	9928	7424	673	957	677	4803	4106	697	82
	2002	20301	10594	7922	718	1021	722	5125	4382	744	88
OPEC	1998	3164	1242	1664	42	60	14	529	463	65	0
	1999	3168	1405	1719	36	37	15	525	481	42	1
	2000	3750	1836	1829	41	79	45	692	635	57	2
	2001	3849	1674	2018	50	157	74	780	748	32	1
	2002	3851	1675	2019	50	157	74	780	748	32	1
Eastern Europe and the former USSR 1/,5/	1998	4177	2045	554	2	915	216	1925	1893	32	0
	1999	3227	1362	506	7	749	173	1273	1235	37	2
	2000	2312	1192	601	4	518	294	1116	1090	26	0
	2001	1874	991	517	0	364	155	935	911	24	0
	2002	2080	1100	574	0	404	172	1038	1011	27	0
Former USSR-Europe 6/	1998	3564	1568	484	1	850	214	1474	1446	28	0
	1999	2550	865	404	4	672	158	805	776	29	0
	2000	1248	510	372	2	365	222	457	439	19	0
	2001	919	382	332	0	204	107	344	322	22	0
	2002	989	411	357	0	220	115	370	346	24	0
Developed economies-Europe	1998	8740	7462	936	102	221	95	6910	6561	349	20
	1999	8214	6952	1051	122	202	69	6326	6006	319	15
	2000	10048	8198	1567	172	263	82	7535	7182	353	29
	2001	9453	7560	1616	125	277	115	7024	6707	317	14
	2002	10015	8009	1712	132	293	122	7442	7106	336	15
European Union	1998	8420	7146	933	102	221	95	6596	6248	347	20
	1999	7870	6617	1042	122	202	69	5992	5674	318	15
	2000	9618	7785	1552	172	263	82	7127	6776	351	29
	2001	8989	7118	1594	125	277	115	6585	6270	315	14
	2002	9537	7552	1691	133	294	122	6986	6652	334	15
European Free Trade Association	1998	315	313	3	0	0	0	311	309	1	0
	1999	341	332	9	0	0	0	331	329	1	0
	2000	425	408	16	0	1	0	404	402	2	0
	2001	460	439	21	0	0	0	435	434	1	0
	2002	477	456	22	0	0	0	451	450	1	0
Other developed economies	1998	15305	8688	4147	39	75	39	3643	3244	399	23
	1999	14466	8170	3974	48	59	30	3415	3029	386	20
	2000	16879	8975	5069	43	72	18	3889	3478	411	24
	2001	17124	8418	6062	78	54	20	3636	3103	533	18
	2002	16725	8222	5921	76	53	20	3551	3031	521	18

For general note and footnotes see end of table.

Exportations mondiales par classes de marchandises et par régions (suite)

En millions de dollars E.-U. f.o.b.

conomies éveloppées 1/,2/				Developing economies Economies en voie de développement 1/,2/						← Exportations vers	
Canada	U.S.A. E.-U.	Japan Japon	Australia New Zealand Australie Nouvelle-Zélande	Africa Afrique	America Amerique Total	America Amerique LAIA ALADI	Asia Asie Mid. East Moyen Orient	Asia Asie Other Autres 7/	Oceania Océanie	Année	Exportations en provenance de ↓
nérais metalliféres et dechets de metaux (CTCI, Rev. 2 et Rev. 3, 28)											
1825	3218	5305	135	437	1334	1195	1066	8432	5	1998	Monde 1/
1783	2965	5373	155	381	1165	1061	891	9153	3	1999	
1964	3198	6148	166	613	1405	1299	1167	11502	2	2000	
1832	2868	5509	167	450	1430	1264	1174	12395	2	2001	
1912	2993	5750	174	470	1493	1319	1225	12937	2	2002	
1276	1757	2466	48	89	391	380	401	4123	3	1998	Economies dévelopées 1/,2/
1305	1646	2324	67	84	331	323	197	4331	1	1999	
1389	1793	2452	58	78	426	417	306	5730	1	2000	
1269	1536	2405	68	79	531	473	370	6596	0	2001	
1305	1579	2472	70	81	546	486	380	6781	0	2002	
524	1399	2805	87	341	882	814	475	4051	2	1998	Economies en voie de développement 1/,2/
467	1281	3010	88	288	815	734	500	4554	2	1999	
566	1379	3657	107	526	973	878	656	5422	2	2000	
554	1309	3080	99	363	892	786	629	5510	2	2001	
591	1397	3287	106	387	952	839	671	5880	2	2002	
27	46	634	6	5	81	81	51	1527	0	1998	OPEP
10	53	811	5	7	63	61	59	1590	0	1999	
19	57	1055	12	14	36	36	65	1711	0	2000	
38	47	792	16	21	32	31	67	1899	0	2001	
38	47	792	16	21	32	31	67	1900	0	2002	
25	61	33	0	7	61	2	190	257	0	1998	Europe de l'Est et l'ancienne URSS 1/,5/
11	38	39	0	9	19	4	193	268	0	1999	
9	27	39	1	8	6	4	205	350	0	2000	
9	22	24	0	8	6	5	175	288	0	2001	
10	24	27	0	9	7	6	194	320	0	2002	
11	56	27	0	6	59	0	163	251	0	1998	l'ancienne URSS-Europe 6/
1	34	26	0	8	16	0	131	248	0	1999	
0	25	28	1	7	4	2	92	268	0	2000	
0	20	18	0	7	3	2	102	220	0	2001	
0	22	19	0	8	3	2	110	237	0	2002	
90	259	176	3	66	34	32	311	455	0	1998	Economies développées-Europe
88	303	215	3	65	26	25	171	709	1	1999	
108	346	177	2	68	60	59	263	1082	0	2000	
62	294	157	6	56	128	127	272	1058	0	2001	
66	311	166	6	59	136	135	288	1121	0	2002	
90	258	176	3	66	34	32	311	453	0	1998	Union Européenne
88	302	215	3	65	26	25	171	704	1	1999	
107	341	177	2	68	60	59	263	1066	0	2000	
62	293	157	4	56	128	127	271	1038	0	2001	
66	311	167	4	59	136	135	288	1101	0	2002	
0	1	0	0	0	0	0	0	2	0	1998	Association Européenne de Libre Exchange
0	1	0	0	0	0	0	0	5	0	1999	
1	4	0	0	0	0	0	0	15	0	2000	
0	1	0	2	0	0	0	0	21	0	2001	
0	1	0	2	0	0	0	0	22	0	2002	
1186	1498	2290	45	23	357	348	89	3668	2	1998	Autres economies développées
1217	1343	2109	64	19	305	298	26	3622	0	1999	
1281	1447	2275	56	10	366	358	43	4648	1	2000	
1206	1243	2248	62	22	403	346	98	5538	0	2001	
1178	1214	2196	61	21	394	338	96	5409	0	2002	

Voir la fin du tableau pour la remarque générale et les notes.

SPECIAL TABLE: D

World exports by commodity classes and by regions (continued)

In million U.S. dollars f.o.b.

Exports to → / ↓ Exports from	Year	World Monde 1/	Developed economies Econ. dévelop-pées 1/,2/	Developing economies economies en voie de développement 1/,2/ Total	Developing economies 1/,2/ OPEC OPEP	Eastern Europe and fmr. USSR-Europe Europe de l'Est et l'anc. URSS-Europe Total 1/,5/	Eastern Europe and fmr. USSR-Europe Former USSR-Eur. 6/	Developed economies Europe Total	Europe EU UE	Europe EFTA AELE	South Africa Afrique du Sud
		Metalliferous ores and metal scraps (SITC, Rev. 2 and Rev. 3, 28) (continued)									
Canada	1998	3168	2905	263	0	0	0	1419	1087	332	[illegible]
	1999	2711	2546	160	1	5	2	1299	959	340	[illegible]
	2000	3072	2811	255	0	7	0	1413	1042	372	[illegible]
	2001	2978	2624	343	0	12	1	1355	883	473	
	2002	2892	2548	333	0	12	1	1316	858	459	
United States	1998	3592	2358	1195	26	40	39	890	885	5	1
	1999	3501	2328	1173	18	1	0	849	846	4	1
	2000	4235	2511	1715	20	9	8	920	907	13	1
	2001	4448	2421	2020	34	7	7	962	951	11	1
	2002	4223	2299	1918	32	7	7	913	903	10	[illegible]
Japan	1998	675	71	604	3	0	0	55	48	7	[illegible]
	1999	702	67	635	8	0	0	54	53	1	
	2000	879	106	773	5	0	0	78	77	1	
	2001	1096	104	992	20	0	0	70	67	3	
	2002	1132	107	1025	21	0	0	72	69	3	
Australia, New Zealand	1998	6576	2325	1849	5	7	0	690	690	0	1
	1999	6182	2190	1721	13	8	0	608	605	4	[illegible]
	2000	7257	2435	2039	13	21	3	768	763	5	[illegible]
	2001	7203	2279	2313	21	22	12	607	598	8	[illegible]
	2002	7265	2299	2333	21	22	12	612	603	8	
Developing economies-Africa	1998	991	812	150	5	18	4	654	649	5	1
	1999	1000	831	134	20	19	4	750	653	97	2
	2000	1387	979	360	23	33	13	793	631	156	3
	2001	1284	1031	207	19	33	16	799	678	121	3
	2002	1349	1085	217	20	35	17	841	714	127	3
Developing economies-America	1998	9280	6206	2470	341	390	234	3102	2727	375	1
	1999	8934	6020	2616	283	284	180	2884	2484	400	2
	2000	10331	6738	3272	394	304	114	3181	2613	568	3
	2001	9828	6196	3367	355	262	104	2926	2404	523	3
	2002	9959	6279	3412	360	265	105	2966	2437	530	3
Developing economies-Europe 3/	1998	100	47	33	3	19	0	47	46	2	[illegible]
	1999	90	39	32	3	19	1	39	39	1	[illegible]
	2000	113	52	39	3	22	0	52	49	3	[illegible]
	2001	121	58	47	3	16	0	58	54	4	[illegible]
	2002	128	61	50	3	17	0	61	57	4	[illegible]
Developing economies-Middle East	1998	1600	290	1257	54	51	21	168	135	33	
	1999	1809	309	1450	126	45	28	167	127	37	[illegible]
	2000	1943	344	1536	160	59	30	168	140	28	
	2001	1964	275	1605	203	83	60	146	122	24	
	2002	2000	280	1634	207	85	61	149	124	24	
Developing economies-Other Asia	1998	4083	1957	1674	63	452	395	643	591	52	[illegible]
	1999	3686	1854	1561	70	270	245	543	479	64	1
	2000	4997	2409	2174	72	414	381	700	624	76	3
	2001	4706	2115	2027	92	564	497	771	746	25	1
	2002	5148	2314	2217	101	617	544	843	816	27	1
Former USSR-Asia 7/.	1998	406	39	153	37	214	208	39	35	4	[illegible]
	1999	313	44	153	21	116	113	43	34	8	
	2000	690	68	270	32	352	349	67	52	15	
	2001	614	58	226	38	330	327	57	46	11	
	2002	676	64	249	42	363	360	63	51	12	[illegible]
Developing economies-Oceania	1998	1209	242	195	0	0	0	92	60	32	[illegible]
	1999	760	372	388	0	0	0	133	69	64	[illegible]
	2000	1463	312	224	1	0	0	128	128	0	[illegible]
	2001	1122	253	171	1	0	0	103	103	0	[illegible]
	2002	1114	296	213	1	0	0	177	163	0	[illegible]

For general note and footnotes see end of table.

Exportations mondiales par classes de marchandises et par régions (suite)

En millions de dollars E.-U. f.o.b.

Economies développées 1/,2/ Canada	U.S.A. E.-U.	Japan Japon	Australia New Zealand Australie Nouvelle-Zélande	Developing economies / Economies en voie de développement 1/,2/ Africa Afrique	America Amerique Total	America Amerique LAIA ALADI	Asia Asie Mid. East Moyen Orient	Asia Asie Other Autres 7/	Oceania Océanie	Année	← Exportations vers / Exportations en provenance de ↓
Minérais metalliféres et dechets de metaux (CTCI, Rev. 2 et Rev. 3, 28) (suite)											
.	1185	278	22	2	17	17	5	239	0	1998	Canada
.	1054	169	24	0	11	11	0	149	0	1999	
.	1141	232	24	0	6	6	8	241	0	2000	
.	986	253	29	4	60	11	9	269	0	2001	
.	958	246	28	4	58	11	9	261	0	2002	
1179	.	271	4	11	326	317	54	804	0	1998	Etats-Unis
1195	.	252	15	8	276	270	8	880	0	1999	
1242	.	315	14	2	344	338	12	1357	0	2000	
1155	.	273	16	10	306	298	51	1653	0	2001	
1097	.	259	15	9	291	283	48	1569	0	2002	
0	14	.	2	0	0	0	0	603	0	1998	Japon
1	10	.	1	0	0	0	1	634	0	1999	
2	24	.	1	0	0	0	1	772	0	2000	
0	32	.	1	0	0	0	1	991	0	2001	
0	33	.	1	0	0	0	1	1024	0	2002	
1	53	1557	15	0	0	0	17	1832	0	1998	Australie, Nouvelle-Zélande
18	53	1492	14	1	7	7	4	1709	0	1999	
35	85	1530	12	2	3	1	15	2019	1	2000	
48	76	1533	9	2	4	4	18	2289	0	2001	
48	77	1546	9	2	4	4	18	2309	0	2002	
27	117	3	0	129	1	0	4	15	0	1998	Economies en voie de développement-Afrique
11	40	6	0	77	3	3	19	34	0	1999	
20	105	24	1	270	2	1	23	64	0	2000	
21	131	43	1	121	2	1	19	62	0	2001	
22	138	45	1	127	2	1	20	65	0	2002	
461	1148	1468	13	186	800	737	296	1181	2	1998	Economies en voie de développement-Amérique
438	1137	1523	9	175	757	679	268	1412	1	1999	
522	1198	1768	35	209	933	842	356	1769	1	2000	
505	1090	1623	21	203	861	762	323	1975	1	2001	
512	1105	1645	21	206	872	772	327	2001	1	2002	
0	0	0	0	16	0	0	4	1	0	1998	Economies en voie de développement-Europe 3/
0	0	0	0	16	0	0	4	0	0	1999	
0	0	0	0	17	0	0	4	0	0	2000	
0	0	0	0	17	5	0	4	1	0	2001	
0	0	0	0	18	5	0	4	1	0	2002	
0	13	106	0	5	0	0	69	1177	0	1998	Economies en voie de développement-Moyen Orient
0	10	132	0	12	2	2	124	1312	0	1999	
3	15	155	0	15	1	1	153	1365	0	2000	
2	11	116	0	15	0	0	175	1415	0	2001	
2	11	118	0	15	0	0	178	1441	0	2002	
36	98	1135	38	3	80	77	102	1489	0	1998	Economies en voie de développement-Autres Pays d'Asie
18	49	1205	29	3	52	51	86	1420	0	1999	
21	57	1563	38	11	36	33	121	2005	0	2000	
25	75	1179	49	4	25	23	107	1891	0	2001	
27	82	1290	54	4	27	25	117	2069	0	2002	
0	1	0	0	0	0	0	78	75	0	1998	l'ancienne URSS asiatique 7/
0	1	0	0	0	0	0	47	106	0	1999	
0	2	0	0	0	2	0	87	181	0	2000	
0	2	0	0	0	0	0	65	160	0	2001	
0	2	0	0	0	0	0	72	176	0	2002	
0	22	92	35	2	1	0	0	188	0	1998	Economies en voie de développement-Océanie
0	45	144	50	5	1	0	0	375	0	1999	
0	3	147	34	5	0	0	0	219	0	2000	
0	2	118	28	4	0	0	0	167	0	2001	
0	2	117	38	5	0	0	0	234	0	2002	

Voir la fin du tableau pour la remarque générale et les notes.

SPECIAL TABLE: D

World exports by commodity classes and by regions (continued)

In million U.S. dollars f.o.b.

Exports to → / ↓ Exports from	Year	World Monde 1/	Developed economies Econ. dévelop-pées 1/,2/	Developing economies economies en voie de développement 1/,2/ Total	Developing economies OPEC OPEP	Eastern Europe and fmr. USSR-Europe Europe de l'Est et l'anc. URSS-Europe Total 1/,5/	Eastern Europe and fmr. USSR-Europe Former USSR-Eur. 6/	Developed economies Europe Total	Developed economies Europe EU UE	Developed economies Europe EFTA AELE	Developed economies South Africa Afrique du Sud
		Animal and vegetable oils, fats and waxes (SITC, Rev. 2 and Rev. 3, 4)									
World 1/	1998	27788	11673	14482	1978	1170	732	8527	8295	219	303
	1999	24489	10926	12118	1712	965	669	8052	7855	186	244
	2000	19101	8794	9323	1316	720	428	6183	6008	165	166
	2001	19038	9082	8808	1252	960	619	6723	6505	208	203
	2002	19871	9479	9193	1307	1002	646	7017	6790	217	212
Developed economies 1/,2/	1998	12538	7476	4248	559	684	389	5925	5724	188	54
	1999	10630	6799	3018	388	645	432	5388	5231	146	29
	2000	8574	5681	2271	335	499	293	4279	4143	127	21
	2001	8692	6041	1953	291	618	367	4714	4544	161	18
	2002	8935	6210	2008	299	635	377	4846	4671	166	19
Developing economies 1/,2/	1998	14799	4142	10105	1399	258	215	2547	2517	30	249
	1999	13504	4071	8980	1319	175	158	2609	2569	40	215
	2000	10280	3085	6934	961	120	103	1878	1839	38	146
	2001	10108	3013	6768	953	221	203	1984	1936	47	184
	2002	10786	3215	7222	1017	236	217	2117	2066	50	196
OPEC	1998	1785	642	1137	114	6	2	545	543	2	3
	1999	2120	826	1288	132	5	4	691	689	2	21
	2000	2065	691	1361	131	13	9	564	562	1	21
	2001	1771	480	1266	152	23	21	427	426	0	31
	2002	1772	480	1267	152	23	21	427	426	0	31
Eastern Europe and the former USSR 1/,5/	1998	451	55	130	20	228	127	55	54	1	0
	1999	355	56	121	5	145	78	55	54	1	0
	2000	247	28	119	20	100	32	27	26	0	0
	2001	238	28	88	8	121	49	25	25	0	0
	2002	264	31	98	9	134	54	28	28	0	0
Former USSR-Europe 6/	1998	125	16	41	1	31	24	16	16	0	0
	1999	104	10	34	0	26	21	10	10	0	0
	2000	96	4	74	20	19	15	3	3	0	0
	2001	90	6	49	8	34	30	4	4	0	0
	2002	97	6	53	9	37	32	4	4	0	0
Developed economies-Europe	1998	8618	6266	1554	335	667	377	5608	5417	178	14
	1999	7725	5788	1151	222	619	407	5162	5015	135	12
	2000	6357	4799	956	217	479	273	4089	3959	121	12
	2001	6570	5162	729	157	599	349	4512	4351	152	13
	2002	6961	5469	772	166	635	370	4780	4610	161	14
European Union	1998	8482	6143	1547	335	662	376	5494	5335	146	14
	1999	7626	5702	1142	222	614	406	5087	4961	115	12
	2000	6259	4716	948	216	473	273	4019	3901	109	11
	2001	6472	5070	725	156	597	348	4431	4291	132	13
	2002	6866	5379	769	166	633	369	4701	4552	140	14
European Free Trade Association	1998	135	122	8	0	5	1	113	81	32	0
	1999	98	84	9	0	5	1	73	54	19	0
	2000	96	82	8	1	6	1	68	57	11	0
	2001	97	90	4	0	2	1	80	60	18	0
	2002	101	93	4	0	2	1	83	62	19	0
Other developed economies	1998	3920	1210	2694	224	17	12	317	307	10	40
	1999	2904	1011	1867	166	26	25	226	216	10	16
	2000	2217	882	1315	118	21	19	190	184	5	9
	2001	2123	880	1224	135	19	18	202	192	10	6
	2002	2073	859	1195	132	19	18	197	188	10	6

For general note and footnotes see end of table.

Exportations mondiales par classes de marchandises et par régions (suite)

En millions de dollars E.-U. f.o.b.

Economies développées 1/,2/				Developing economies / Economies en voie de développement 1/,2/						← Exportations vers	
Canada	U.S.A. / E.-U.	Japan / Japon	Australia New Zealand / Australie Nouvelle-Zélande	Africa / Afrique	America / Amerique: Total	America / Amerique: LAIA / ALADI	Asia / Asie: Mid. East / Moyen Orient	Asia / Asie: Other / Autres 7/	Oceania / Océanie	Année	Exportations en provenance de ↓
Huiles et graisses d'origine animale ou vegetale (CTCI, Rev. 2 et Rev. 3, 4)											
253	1552	710	261	1842	2270	1764	2188	7936	28	1998	Monde 1/
252	1429	622	265	1781	1719	1278	1857	6597	23	1999	
264	1407	526	200	1296	1462	1109	1469	4964	21	2000	
254	1183	502	170	1297	1435	1060	1399	4536	21	2001	
265	1235	524	177	1354	1498	1106	1460	4734	22	2002	
226	837	299	89	920	1054	797	507	1675	14	1998	Economies dévelopées 1/,2/
228	776	248	95	734	833	578	422	959	12	1999	
244	782	227	98	571	677	502	327	639	8	2000	
226	729	242	83	480	637	461	283	489	9	2001	
232	749	249	85	493	655	474	291	503	8	2002	
28	715	411	172	888	1216	966	1649	6229	14	1998	Economies en voie de développement 1/,2/
23	652	374	170	1036	885	700	1399	5612	11	1999	
19	624	299	102	688	785	607	1124	4294	12	2000	
27	453	260	87	803	796	598	1109	4015	12	2001	
29	483	277	93	857	849	638	1183	4284	11	2002	
9	54	21	10	49	31	29	234	807	1	1998	OPEP
5	84	25	1	94	67	63	245	865	1	1999	
1	88	14	2	86	61	59	252	943	3	2000	
1	10	8	3	108	72	68	282	784	4	2001	
1	10	8	3	108	72	68	282	784	4	2002	
0	1	0	0	33	0	0	32	32	0	1998	Europe de l'Est et l'ancienne URSS 1/,5/
1	0	0	0	12	0	0	36	26	0	1999	
1	1	0	0	37	0	0	17	31	0	2000	
1	1	0	0	15	2	0	7	33	0	2001	
1	1	0	0	17	2	0	8	37	0	2002	
0	0	0	0	3	0	0	17	21	0	1998	l'ancienne URSS-Europe 6/
0	0	0	0	3	0	0	16	15	0	1999	
0	1	0	0	36	0	0	8	30	0	2000	
0	1	0	0	14	2	0	1	31	0	2001	
0	1	0	0	15	2	0	1	33	0	2002	
48	382	122	66	636	151	130	226	476	10	1998	Economies développées-Europe
49	363	105	78	510	143	104	191	250	9	1999	
54	439	105	82	420	144	118	169	176	6	2000	
50	395	108	67	326	132	113	102	118	6	2001	
53	418	114	71	345	140	120	108	125	6	2002	
46	376	122	65	634	150	129	226	474	10	1998	Union Européenne
47	355	105	78	508	142	103	191	248	9	1999	
52	429	105	81	419	143	117	168	173	6	2000	
49	387	108	66	326	131	112	102	115	6	2001	
52	411	115	70	346	139	119	108	122	6	2002	
2	6	0	1	1	1	1	0	2	0	1998	Association Européenne de Libre Exchange
2	8	0	1	2	1	1	0	2	0	1999	
2	11	0	1	2	1	1	1	3	0	2000	
1	8	0	1	0	1	1	0	3	0	2001	
1	8	0	1	0	1	1	0	3	0	2002	
178	455	177	23	285	903	667	281	1199	4	1998	Autres economies développées
179	414	143	16	224	690	474	231	709	3	1999	
190	343	122	16	150	533	383	158	463	2	2000	
176	334	133	16	154	505	349	181	371	3	2001	
172	326	130	16	150	493	341	177	362	3	2002	

Voir la fin du tableau pour la remarque générale et les notes.

SPECIAL TABLE: D

World exports by commodity classes and by regions (continued)

In million U.S. dollars f.o.b.

Exports from ↓ / Exports to →	Year	World Monde 1/	Developed economies Econ. dévelop-pées 1/,2/	Developing economies economies en voie de développement 1/,2/ Total	Developing economies OPEC OPEP	Eastern Europe and fmr. USSR-Europe Europe de l'Est et l'anc. URSS-Europe Total 1/,5/	Eastern Europe and fmr. USSR-Europe Former USSR-Eur. 6/	Developed economies Europe Total	Developed economies Europe EU UE	Developed economies Europe EFTA AELE	Developed economies South Africa Afrique du Sud
		Animal and vegetable oils, fats and waxes (SITC, Rev. 2 and Rev. 3, 4) (continued)									
Canada	1998	751	511	237	0	3	3	36	36	0	0
	1999	576	430	146	2	0	0	22	22	1	1
	2000	432	350	81	5	1	1	16	16	0	0
	2001	416	349	66	0	1	1	17	17	0	1
	2002	404	339	64	0	1	1	17	17	0	1
United States	1998	2729	571	2146	215	12	8	255	245	10	16
	1999	1922	459	1436	151	26	25	179	170	9	5
	2000	1421	404	998	104	20	18	142	138	4	2
	2001	1364	402	943	122	18	17	155	146	9	2
	2002	1295	382	895	116	17	16	147	139	9	2
Japan	1998	62	30	32	1	0	0	11	11	0	0
	1999	79	37	42	3	0	0	12	11	0	0
	2000	81	37	44	3	0	0	11	10	1	0
	2001	74	34	40	1	0	0	10	10	0	0
	2002	76	35	41	1	0	0	10	10	0	0
Australia, New Zealand	1998	330	89	239	8	1	1	7	7	0	24
	1999	284	80	203	9	0	0	9	9	0	11
	2000	243	84	159	6	0	0	15	15	0	6
	2001	234	87	147	10	0	0	14	13	0	3
	2002	236	88	148	10	0	0	14	13	0	3
Developing economies-Africa	1998	506	349	137	18	1	0	323	313	10	11
	1999	637	438	186	73	0	0	414	405	9	6
	2000	478	319	150	60	0	0	299	290	8	7
	2001	562	400	153	37	0	0	379	364	14	6
	2002	590	421	161	39	0	0	399	383	15	6
Developing economies-America	1998	4146	603	3413	814	123	118	281	278	3	125
	1999	3608	626	2887	711	94	90	374	355	19	112
	2000	2585	395	2138	461	41	41	205	181	24	55
	2001	2716	405	2210	424	96	96	180	154	26	89
	2002	2752	410	2240	430	97	97	182	156	26	90
Developing economies-Europe 3/	1998	54	7	29	0	19	10	7	6	0	0
	1999	27	5	18	0	4	3	5	5	0	0
	2000	30	6	15	0	9	5	6	5	1	0
	2001	35	6	19	0	11	6	6	5	1	0
	2002	37	6	20	0	12	6	6	5	1	0
Developing economies-Middle East	1998	648	93	499	254	45	32	52	47	4	0
	1999	640	189	437	220	8	6	139	133	6	0
	2000	465	53	400	171	5	3	20	18	2	0
	2001	627	148	471	217	2	1	104	100	4	0
	2002	638	151	480	221	2	1	106	102	4	0
Developing economies-Other Asia	1998	9064	3021	5973	307	70	56	1849	1837	12	113
	1999	8105	2685	5346	304	69	59	1614	1608	6	97
	2000	6552	2256	4227	269	65	53	1301	1297	3	83
	2001	6036	2009	3912	274	111	100	1278	1276	1	89
	2002	6603	2198	4279	300	121	109	1398	1396	1	97
Former USSR-Asia 7/.	1998	7	0	2	0	4	1	0	0	0	0
	1999	8	0	4	0	5	1	0	0	0	0
	2000	11	0	7	0	4	1	0	0	0	0
	2001	10	0	6	0	4	1	0	0	0	0
	2002	11	0	7	0	4	1	0	0	0	0
Developing economies-Oceania	1998	380	69	53	6	0	0	36	36	0	0
	1999	487	127	105	11	0	0	64	64	0	0
	2000	171	57	4	0	0	0	48	48	0	0
	2001	132	46	4	0	0	0	38	38	0	0
	2002	131	54	5	0	0	0	65	60	0	0

For general note and footnotes see end of table.

Exportations mondiales par classes de marchandises et par régions (suite)

En millions de dollars E.-U. f.o.b.

Economies développées 1/,2/ Canada	U.S.A. E.-U.	Japan Japon	Australia New Zealand Australie Nouvelle-Zélande	Developing economies / Economies en voie de développement 1/,2/ Africa Afrique	America Amerique Total	America Amerique LAIA ALADI	Asia Asie Mid. East Moyen Orient	Asia Asie Other Autres 7/	Oceania Océanie	Année	← Exportations vers / Exportations en provenance de ↓
Huiles et graisses d'origine animale ou vegetale (CTCI, Rev. 2 et Rev. 3, 4) (suite)											
.	433	38	3	5	22	15	0	210	0	1998	Canada
.	386	20	0	11	11	6	0	123	0	1999	
.	314	19	1	2	8	3	4	67	0	2000	
.	307	24	1	0	13	3	1	52	0	2001	
.	298	23	1	0	13	3	1	51	0	2002	
176	.	93	11	203	880	651	273	768	0	1998	Etats-Unis
177	.	76	4	168	679	468	222	358	0	1999	
189	.	55	4	115	524	380	149	201	0	2000	
174	.	55	3	123	491	345	176	144	0	2001	
165	.	52	3	117	466	328	167	137	0	2002	
1	17	.	0	0	0	0	0	31	0	1998	Japon
1	23	.	0	0	0	0	0	42	0	1999	
1	24	.	1	0	0	0	0	44	0	2000	
1	22	.	1	0	0	0	0	40	0	2001	
1	23	.	1	0	0	0	0	41	0	2002	
0	4	44	9	50	0	0	6	179	4	1998	Australie, Nouvelle-Zélande
0	3	46	11	17	0	0	8	175	3	1999	
0	5	48	10	7	0	0	5	145	2	2000	
0	4	54	12	10	0	0	5	130	2	2001	
0	4	54	12	10	0	0	5	131	2	2002	
1	12	2	0	111	4	2	13	8	0	1998	Economies en voie de développement-Afrique
1	17	1	0	136	5	2	34	12	0	1999	
1	11	2	0	88	6	3	44	11	0	2000	
1	12	2	0	94	12	4	21	26	0	2001	
1	13	2	0	99	13	4	22	27	0	2002	
6	139	26	24	286	1104	890	680	1280	0	1998	Economies en voie de développement-Amérique
7	94	25	9	347	806	637	519	1211	1	1999	
5	83	32	12	209	702	535	363	863	1	2000	
14	68	38	13	322	715	535	331	843	0	2001	
14	69	39	13	326	725	542	335	854	0	2002	
0	0	0	0	1	0	0	1	0	0	1998	Economies en voie de développement-Europe 3/
0	0	0	0	1	0	0	1	0	0	1999	
0	0	0	0	0	0	0	1	0	0	2000	
0	0	0	0	0	0	0	1	0	0	2001	
0	0	0	0	0	0	0	1	0	0	2002	
3	23	0	1	48	1	0	373	61	0	1998	Economies en voie de développement-Moyen Orient
2	26	0	2	45	1	1	332	42	0	1999	
2	16	0	1	25	5	5	304	50	0	2000	
3	24	1	2	25	2	2	364	63	0	2001	
3	24	1	2	25	2	2	371	64	0	2002	
18	538	383	116	436	107	74	582	4834	14	1998	Economies en voie de développement-Autres Pays d'Asie
13	511	347	100	496	73	61	513	4254	10	1999	
11	510	265	84	365	71	63	411	3368	11	2000	
9	346	218	67	362	67	57	390	3081	11	2001	
10	378	238	73	396	73	62	427	3370	12	2002	
0	0	0	0	0	0	0	0	2	0	1998	l'ancienne URSS asiatique 7/
0	0	0	0	0	0	0	0	3	0	1999	
0	0	0	0	0	0	0	1	6	0	2000	
0	0	0	0	0	0	0	0	6	0	2001	
0	0	0	0	0	0	0	0	7	0	2002	
0	2	0	31	6	0	0	0	47	0	1998	Economies en voie de développement-Océanie
0	5	0	59	11	0	0	0	93	0	1999	
0	4	0	5	0	0	0	1	3	0	2000	
0	3	0	5	0	0	0	1	3	0	2001	
0	3	0	7	0	0	0	1	4	0	2002	

Voir la fin du tableau pour la remarque générale et les notes.

SPECIAL TABLE: D

World exports by commodity classes and by regions (continued)

In million U.S. dollars f.o.b.

Exports to → / ↓ Exports from	Year	World Monde 1/	Developed economies Econ. dévelop-pées 1/,2/	Developing economies économies en voie de développement 1/,2/ Total	Developing economies OPEC OPEP	Eastern Europe and fmr. USSR-Europe Europe de l'Est et l'anc. URSS-Europe Total 1/,5/	Eastern Europe and fmr. USSR-Europe Former USSR-Eur. 6/	Developed economies Europe Total	Developed economies Europe EU UE	Developed economies Europe EFTA AELE	Developed economies South Africa Afrique du Sud
		Mineral fuels and related materials (SITC, Rev. 2 and Rev. 3, 3)									
World 1/	1998	307457	198229	82911	5231	17431	8819	101417	94820	5324	564
	1999	388072	248082	113671	5845	16654	7599	120605	113212	5791	733
	2000	607183	405646	163991	9090	26319	11790	191432	181695	7316	737
	2001	545654	359609	146967	8622	25834	12114	168922	161316	6194	690
	2002	569530	375344	153398	9000	26964	12644	176314	168375	6465	720
Developed economies 1/,2/	1998	106519	84738	13730	992	2011	475	54069	49854	3630	346
	1999	121418	98260	15269	927	1856	356	63955	59852	3368	170
	2000	191758	160628	22128	1366	2264	342	98028	92324	4462	240
	2001	181110	151201	19110	1310	2037	257	90555	85482	4185	262
	2002	186177	155432	19645	1347	2094	264	93089	87874	4302	269
Developing economies 1/,2/	1998	165608	97041	65187	4199	1664	1408	31386	30725	538	210
	1999	228758	130585	93381	4902	1600	1301	37839	36701	984	558
	2000	355025	213866	131687	7639	4009	3576	63125	61813	950	497
	2001	302872	178432	118053	7247	3096	2747	49056	48076	810	428
	2002	323200	190408	125977	7734	3304	2932	52349	51303	864	456
OPEC	1998	126595	77111	49390	2959	94	86	19939	19832	107	51
	1999	172276	96845	75256	6179	175	146	28084	27940	144	109
	2000	231559	134839	96527	7917	194	155	38927	38700	227	194
	2001	197966	111704	86094	7375	168	136	30198	30000	198	146
	2002	198046	111749	86128	7378	168	136	30210	30012	198	146
Eastern Europe and the former USSR 1/,5/	1998	35330	16451	3994	40	13757	6936	15961	14241	1156	8
	1999	37896	18673	5022	16	13198	5942	18247	16094	1439	5
	2000	60400	30146	10177	85	20046	7872	29272	26551	1904	0
	2001	61672	29339	9805	65	20701	9110	28673	27121	1199	0
	2002	68448	32563	10882	72	22975	10111	31823	30101	1331	0
Former USSR-Europe 6/	1998	31596	14344	3529	17	12628	6711	13873	12244	1094	8
	1999	34196	16656	4473	1	12065	5799	16264	14195	1369	5
	2000	55306	27657	9308	20	18339	7639	26826	24235	1825	0
	2001	56037	26295	8888	7	19029	8978	25729	24337	1115	0
	2002	60296	28293	9563	8	20475	9660	27684	26187	1200	0
Developed economies-Europe	1998	66321	56138	3946	513	1800	416	50088	45919	3596	195
	1999	78129	67502	4803	539	1744	325	58140	54120	3291	67
	2000	124216	111511	6718	949	2132	288	94226	88636	4372	87
	2001	114336	100766	5373	876	1943	220	86174	81169	4122	93
	2002	121134	106757	5692	928	2059	233	91298	85995	4367	99
European Union	1998	48655	38986	3592	509	1641	394	35212	31154	3513	191
	1999	55216	45505	4090	534	1542	310	40085	36194	3199	62
	2000	85625	73771	6128	943	1871	278	62725	57279	4309	76
	2001	77743	65463	4475	867	1552	207	56225	51305	4082	80
	2002	82479	69451	4748	920	1647	220	59650	54430	4331	85
European Free Trade Association	1998	17647	17141	349	3	157	21	14864	14754	83	4
	1999	22894	21986	708	4	201	14	18043	17914	91	5
	2000	38573	37728	585	5	260	9	31489	31346	63	12
	2001	36575	35292	893	8	390	11	29937	29852	40	13
	2002	37950	36619	927	8	405	11	31062	30974	42	13
Other developed economies	1998	40199	28600	9784	479	210	58	3981	3935	33	151
	1999	43290	30758	10466	389	112	31	5815	5733	77	103
	2000	67542	49118	15410	417	132	54	3802	3688	90	153
	2001	66774	50435	13736	434	94	37	4381	4312	63	169
	2002	65216	49259	13416	424	92	36	4279	4211	62	165

For general note and footnotes see end of table.

Exportations mondiales par classes de marchandises et par régions (suite)

En millions de dollars E.-U. f.o.b.

Economies développées 1/,2/				Developing economies Economies en voie de développement 1/,2/						← Exportations vers	
Canada	U.S.A. E.-U.	Japan Japon	Australia New Zealand Australie Nouvelle-Zélande	Africa Afrique	America Amerique Total	America Amerique LAIA ALADI	Asia Asie Mid. East Moyen Orient	Asia Asie Other Autres 7/	Oceania Océanie	Année	Exportations en provenance de ↓
Combustibles minéraux et produits assimiles (CTCI, Rev. 2 et Rev. 3, 3)											
5189	53986	33322	3141	4499	16619	9420	5365	54446	425	1998	Monde 1/
6398	74179	41289	4120	6182	21429	10852	7494	76377	452	1999	
9469	132115	64484	6008	9013	35058	17082	13067	103225	581	2000	
9391	115385	58428	5488	7376	29756	14289	11423	94920	495	2001	
9802	120434	60985	5728	7699	31058	14914	11923	99073	491	2002	
3820	20776	4838	626	1483	4748	3685	1153	5589	268	1998	Economies dévelopées 1/,2/
4368	24117	4597	692	1722	4689	3639	1262	6765	299	1999	
6356	49443	5123	904	3031	7392	5762	2041	8459	429	2000	
6767	47431	4842	910	2740	6093	4718	1294	7976	341	2001	
6956	48758	4977	935	2817	6263	4850	1330	8199	350	2002	
1353	33012	28289	2515	2951	10628	5686	3303	47642	278	1998	Economies en voie de développement 1/,2/
2014	49885	36534	3428	4392	14431	7172	5286	68492	362	1999	
3112	82467	59059	5104	5831	24097	11293	7315	92999	816	2000	
2619	67813	53384	4578	4404	20494	9518	6825	85094	709	2001	
2795	72364	56967	4885	4700	21870	10157	7283	90805	710	2002	
403	16750	33860	1108	1541	750	603	4087	40610	50	1998	OPEP
516	22860	46990	1286	2413	991	826	5334	62865	70	1999	
1290	30960	60630	2838	3096	1677	1419	7095	79980	82	2000	
1320	27600	50400	2040	2400	1800	1440	6942	70800	52	2001	
1321	27611	50420	2041	2401	1801	1441	6945	70828	51	2002	
16	198	195	0	65	1243	50	909	1215	5	1998	Europe de l'Est et l'ancienne URSS 1/,5/
16	178	158	0	68	2309	41	946	1120	1	1999	
1	205	302	0	151	3569	28	3711	1767	0	2000	
5	141	202	0	232	3169	54	3304	1850	2	2001	
6	156	224	0	257	3517	60	3667	2053	2	2002	
16	180	195	0	6	1202	15	834	1111	5	1998	l'ancienne URSS-Europe 6/
16	152	158	0	11	2258	0	854	1044	1	1999	
1	192	302	0	46	3541	21	3544	1677	0	2000	
2	106	202	0	155	3114	19	3148	1761	2	2001	
2	114	217	0	167	3351	20	3387	1895	1	2002	
1458	4155	175	22	1253	845	612	770	585	5	1998	Economies développées-Europe
2223	6741	192	21	1250	752	408	962	1305	5	1999	
3711	13053	103	34	2259	820	346	1686	1179	6	2000	
3177	11127	56	19	1902	709	353	1007	1099	5	2001	
3366	11789	59	20	2015	751	374	1067	1164	5	2002	
208	3255	55	21	1248	816	604	729	333	5	1998	Union Européenne
222	4946	51	21	1246	689	391	916	718	5	1999	
498	10072	72	34	2252	712	321	1555	868	6	2000	
889	8081	50	19	1892	503	263	878	549	5	2001	
943	8573	53	20	2007	534	279	931	582	5	2002	
1249	901	120	2	5	29	7	40	249	0	1998	Association Européenne de Libre Exchange
2000	1796	141	0	4	62	16	45	584	0	1999	
3214	2981	31	0	6	108	25	130	307	0	2000	
2288	3046	6	0	9	205	90	128	547	0	2001	
2374	3161	6	0	9	213	93	133	568	0	2002	
2362	16621	4663	603	230	3903	3073	382	5004	263	1998	Autres economies développées
2146	17375	4405	671	471	3937	3232	300	5460	294	1999	
2644	36390	5020	869	772	6572	5415	355	7280	423	2000	
3590	36304	4787	890	838	5384	4364	287	6878	336	2001	
3506	35457	4675	869	818	5258	4262	280	6718	355	2002	

Voir la fin du tableau pour la remarque générale et les notes.

SPECIAL TABLE: D

World exports by commodity classes and by regions (continued)

In million U.S. dollars f.o.b.

Exports to → / ↓ Exports from	Year	World Monde 1/	Developed economies Econ. dévelop-pées 1/,2/	Developing economies economies en voie de développement 1/,2/ Total	Developing economies OPEC OPEP	Eastern Europe and fmr. USSR-Europe Europe de l'Est et l'anc. URSS-Europe Total 1/,5/	Eastern Europe and fmr. USSR-Europe Former USSR-Eur. 6/	Developed economies Europe Total	Europe EU UE	Europe EFTA AELE	South Africa Afrique du Sud
		Mineral fuels and related materials (SITC, Rev. 2 and Rev. 3, 3) (continued)									
Canada	1998	17676	17119	549	3	8	0	290	284	6	0
	1999	20261	19782	471	1	8	0	2459	2451	8	6
	2000	36344	35950	382	3	12	0	225	190	35	9
	2001	36673	36266	403	3	4	0	415	414	1	0
	2002	35615	35220	391	3	4	0	403	402	1	0
United States	1998	9957	5288	4546	302	124	29	1841	1805	22	126
	1999	9794	4841	4908	207	45	8	1604	1543	55	[illegible]
	2000	13134	5540	7518	266	76	11	1775	1715	36	[illegible]
	2001	12550	6286	6222	239	42	15	1850	1787	58	[illegible]
	2002	11916	5968	5907	227	40	14	1756	1697	55	[illegible]
Japan	1998	1237	340	864	24	31	28	52	52	0	[illegible]
	1999	1226	366	842	31	17	14	34	34	0	[illegible]
	2000	1520	517	994	35	8	7	38	37	1	[illegible]
	2001	1509	416	1082	39	11	9	56	56	0	[illegible]
	2002	1559	430	1118	40	11	9	58	58	0	[illegible]
Australia, New Zealand	1998	9711	4775	3410	143	34	0	930	928	2	[illegible]
	1999	9594	4676	3411	118	26	0	864	860	4	[illegible]
	2000	13652	6004	5526	72	0	0	861	859	2	[illegible]
	2001	13504	6219	5100	112	19	0	1108	1106	2	[illegible]
	2002	13621	6273	5144	113	19	0	1118	1116	2	[illegible]
Developing economies-Africa	1998	28884	22735	5071	123	151	54	14649	14483	100	[illegible]
	1999	46974	34527	11085	238	217	85	20053	19509	467	[illegible]
	2000	72967	54345	16319	943	1260	1042	30323	29715	433	[illegible]
	2001	51641	38574	11248	654	757	615	20659	20208	335	[illegible]
	2002	54254	40592	11817	687	795	646	21757	21284	352	[illegible]
Developing economies-America	1998	28482	20093	8168	329	14	6	2283	2278	3	[illegible]
	1999	38908	27813	9727	134	6	4	2455	2346	102	[illegible]
	2000	61653	43785	16298	233	2	1	3919	3877	40	
	2001	52315	35733	15254	287	7	1	3773	3731	37	[illegible]
	2002	53013	36213	15458	291	7	1	3825	3783	37	[illegible]
Developing economies-Europe 3/	1998	445	114	286	1	44	1	113	94	17	
	1999	446	141	260	1	44	7	136	111	25	[illegible]
	2000	615	194	371	4	50	1	181	159	17	
	2001	615	245	322	1	48	2	230	211	12	
	2002	649	259	340	1	51	2	243	223	13	
Developing economies-Middle East	1998	64126	36662	27408	2961	56	51	11904	11840	64	[illegible]
	1999	93326	48111	45104	3608	110	92	12930	12840	90	[illegible]
	2000	140701	83621	56960	4557	120	96	24141	24000	141	[illegible]
	2001	129210	74470	54628	4370	112	90	20132	20000	132	[illegible]
	2002	131561	75825	55622	4450	114	92	20498	20364	134	[illegible]
Developing economies-Other Asia	1998	43221	17148	24044	785	1399	1296	2389	1981	354	[illegible]
	1999	48461	19593	26906	921	1223	1113	2210	1840	300	[illegible]
	2000	78234	31309	41348	1902	2577	2436	4399	3901	319	[illegible]
	2001	68407	28944	36291	1935	2172	2039	4147	3810	294	[illegible]
	2002	74832	31663	39700	2117	2376	2231	4537	4168	322	[illegible]
Former USSR-Asia 7/.	1998	3018	949	846	181	1185	1112	939	712	227	
	1999	4018	1015	1946	160	1022	941	930	721	202	
	2000	8590	2723	3455	245	2378	2260	2564	2336	196	
	2001	8446	3166	3261	190	1983	1875	2971	2742	217	
	2002	9302	3516	3592	209	2184	2065	3302	3051	239	
Developing economies-Oceania	1998	450	240	210	0	0	0	0	0	0	
	1999	643	344	298	0	0	0	0	0	0	
	2000	855	450	390	0	0	0	0	0	0	
	2001	684	350	310	0	0	0	0	0	0	
	2002	679	410	386	0	0	0	0	0	0	

For general note and footnotes see end of table.

Exportations mondiales par classes de marchandises et par régions (suite)

En millions de dollars E.-U. f.o.b.

Economies développées 1/,2/: Canada	Economies développées 1/,2/: U.S.A. E.-U.	Economies développées 1/,2/: Japan Japon	Economies développées 1/,2/: Australia New Zealand Australie Nouvelle-Zélande	Developing economies Economies en voie de développement 1/,2/: Africa Afrique	America Amerique: Total	America Amerique: LAIA ALADI	Asia Asie: Mid. East Moyen Orient	Asia Asie: Other Autres 7/	Oceania Océanie	Année	← Exportations vers / Exportations en provenance de ↓
Combustibles minéraux et produits assimiles (CTCI, Rev. 2 et Rev. 3, 3) (suite)											
.	15997	814	18	10	148	142	26	365	0	1998	Canada
.	16696	621	1	14	134	131	33	291	0	1999	
.	35232	483	1	9	88	84	37	248	0	2000	
.	35432	418	1	12	106	102	37	247	0	2001	
.	34410	406	1	12	103	99	36	240	0	2002	
2353	.	716	164	115	3351	2544	172	902	4	1998	Etats-Unis
2141	.	758	158	100	3469	2777	114	1213	8	1999	
2642	.	806	155	138	6122	4976	171	1082	2	2000	
3573	.	517	172	132	4894	3882	125	1059	1	2001	
3392	.	491	163	125	4647	3686	119	1005	1	2002	
6	263	.	18	0	41	24	11	809	2	1998	Japon
0	307	.	23	0	29	21	9	804	0	1999	
1	394	.	83	0	42	38	4	948	0	2000	
0	282	.	76	0	39	37	5	1038	0	2001	
0	291	.	79	0	40	38	5	1072	0	2002	
0	347	3044	398	38	302	302	122	2691	257	1998	Australie, Nouvelle-Zélande
0	349	2956	466	16	258	258	101	2749	286	1999	
0	735	3695	595	9	274	274	73	4750	420	2000	
16	494	3820	629	24	275	275	99	4367	334	2001	
16	498	3853	634	24	277	277	100	4405	337	2002	
471	7214	202	11	1641	1336	1298	1015	958	0	1998	Economies en voie de développement-Afrique
817	12627	332	101	2511	2390	2328	1158	4860	8	1999	
1429	21588	256	164	3455	3743	3203	1760	7124	78	2000	
957	16254	234	32	2530	2616	2201	1180	4781	45	2001	
1005	17077	246	34	2658	2748	2312	1240	5023	47	2002	
551	16946	155	13	151	7809	3721	15	187	0	1998	Economies en voie de développement-Amérique
830	24097	307	33	52	9316	4133	43	311	0	1999	
797	38555	379	67	77	15354	6889	45	813	0	2000	
743	30726	356	3	97	13743	5860	138	1262	1	2001	
753	31136	361	3	98	13926	5938	140	1279	1	2002	
0	1	0	0	0	1	0	6	0	0	1998	Economies en voie de développement-Europe 3/
0	2	0	0	11	1	0	10	0	0	1999	
0	13	0	0	14	1	0	8	1	0	2000	
0	15	0	0	1	1	0	2	0	0	2001	
0	16	0	0	1	1	0	2	0	0	2002	
288	7360	16400	680	920	448	360	1640	24400	0	1998	Economies en voie de développement-Moyen Orient
312	11280	22640	880	1520	624	520	3360	39600	0	1999	
800	19200	37600	1760	1920	1040	880	4400	49600	0	2000	
880	18400	33600	1360	1600	1200	960	4628	47200	0	2001	
896	18735	34211	1385	1629	1222	977	4712	48059	0	2002	
43	1461	11532	1651	239	1009	305	627	21886	271	1998	Economies en voie de développement-Autres Pays d'Asie
55	1819	13255	2130	298	2072	189	715	23459	346	1999	
86	3021	20780	2823	365	3929	321	1102	35190	732	2000	
39	2348	19149	3018	176	2910	497	877	31611	659	2001	
43	2569	20948	3301	193	3183	544	959	34580	721	2002	
0	11	0	0	1	93	0	357	393	0	1998	l'ancienne URSS asiatique 7/
0	28	0	0	10	1194	8	295	443	0	1999	
0	25	0	0	10	2469	7	419	542	1	2000	
0	31	0	0	31	2346	14	325	533	2	2001	
0	34	0	0	34	2584	15	358	587	2	2002	
0	30	0	160	0	25	2	0	210	7	1998	Economies en voie de développement-Océanie
0	60	0	284	0	28	2	0	262	8	1999	
0	90	44	290	0	30	0	0	270	6	2000	
0	70	45	165	0	24	0	0	240	4	2001	
0	69	45	223	0	24	0	0	337	5	2002	

Voir la fin du tableau pour la remarque générale et les notes.

SPECIAL TABLE: D

World exports by commodity classes and by regions (continued)

In million U.S. dollars f.o.b.

Exports to → / ↓ Exports from	Year	World Monde 1/	Developed economies Econ. dévelop-pées 1/,2/	Developing economies économies en voie de développement 1/,2/ Total	OPEC OPEP	Eastern Europe and fmr. USSR-Europe Europe de l'Est et l'anc. URSS-Europe Total 1/,5/	Former USSR-Eur. 6/	Developed economies Europe Total	EU UE	EFTA AELE	South Africa Afrique du Sud
								Chemicals (SITC, Rev. 2 and Rev. 3, 5)			
World 1/	1998	513058	334959	144356	15447	21617	7813	236194	220937	14905	2860
	1999	527577	347220	151077	15544	20048	6170	238486	222695	15439	2653
	2000	568544	366901	174783	17490	22531	7839	246537	230927	15239	2768
	2001	593345	388837	171890	19393	26203	9790	263925	246845	16652	2920
	2002	619308	405852	179412	20242	27350	10218	275474	257646	17381	3048
Developed economies 1/,2/	1998	414278	302763	85967	9774	15257	4467	219943	205633	13984	2420
	1999	425672	313723	90232	9494	14379	3313	222161	207178	14662	2232
	2000	449889	327976	101904	10242	16159	4442	227933	213174	14417	2270
	2001	475143	349724	100046	11084	19363	6123	245446	229329	15767	2264
	2002	488437	359509	102845	11394	19905	6294	252314	235746	16208	2327
Developing economies 1/,2/	1998	83173	26130	54977	5584	1650	947	10960	10503	440	422
	1999	87607	27993	57444	5953	1535	923	11538	11119	395	408
	2000	104046	32078	69360	7124	1786	1129	12563	12091	445	488
	2001	103407	32911	68154	8135	2001	1281	13111	12563	472	642
	2002	110348	35120	72728	8681	2135	1367	13991	13406	504	68[illegible]
OPEC	1998	11108	2837	8223	2003	24	5	1174	1147	23	43
	1999	10928	2047	8174	1703	22	6	675	643	26	18
	2000	13476	2550	9703	1837	67	43	814	780	28	3[illegible]
	2001	13906	3539	10277	2408	49	29	1490	1403	32	97
	2002	13912	3540	10281	2409	49	29	1491	1404	32	97
Eastern Europe and the former USSR 1/,5/	1998	15608	6056	3422	89	4710	2399	5280	4790	481	1[illegible]
	1999	14300	5494	3412	97	4134	1934	4776	4387	382	1[illegible]
	2000	14611	6420	3529	124	4586	2268	5613	5234	377	1[illegible]
	2001	14797	6203	3702	174	4839	2386	5368	4954	413	1[illegible]
	2002	16423	6885	4109	193	5371	2648	5958	5498	458	1[illegible]
Former USSR-Europe 6/	1998	8208	2514	2567	50	1774	1309	2023	1659	356	1[illegible]
	1999	7738	2346	2563	51	1583	1119	1889	1616	267	[illegible]
	2000	6659	2535	2407	69	1716	1293	2069	1829	239	[illegible]
	2001	6543	2340	2536	108	1631	1202	1879	1623	256	[illegible]
	2002	7040	2518	2729	116	1755	1293	2022	1746	275	[illegible]
Developed economies-Europe	1998	298799	233852	40076	6948	14692	4199	192113	179283	12524	181[illegible]
	1999	303017	241657	40229	6568	13916	3162	193511	180438	12765	167[illegible]
	2000	310310	248207	42897	6850	15495	4086	196343	183596	12444	163[illegible]
	2001	339592	269688	45508	7725	18540	5634	212842	198636	13879	165[illegible]
	2002	359783	285723	48214	8184	19642	5969	225497	210446	14704	175[illegible]
European Union	1998	274965	214690	36268	6391	13827	4013	177219	164486	12438	164[illegible]
	1999	278093	221340	36462	6046	13075	3033	177965	164989	12677	153[illegible]
	2000	286402	229132	38954	6287	14605	3913	182138	169471	12373	149[illegible]
	2001	312275	247665	41306	7125	17449	5364	196252	182169	13768	151[illegible]
	2002	331297	262751	43822	7559	18512	5691	208206	193266	14607	160[illegible]
European Free Trade Association	1998	23795	19129	3802	554	864	186	14862	14765	85	16[illegible]
	1999	24883	20282	3760	520	840	129	15513	15415	87	14[illegible]
	2000	23873	19049	3935	558	889	173	14180	14099	71	13[illegible]
	2001	27274	21989	4195	597	1091	269	16559	16438	111	14[illegible]
	2002	28299	22816	4353	619	1132	279	17181	17056	115	14[illegible]
Other developed economies	1998	115479	68911	45891	2826	564	268	27830	26350	1461	60[illegible]
	1999	122655	72066	50003	2926	464	151	28650	26740	1898	55[illegible]
	2000	139579	79769	59007	3392	665	356	31589	29578	1974	63[illegible]
	2001	135551	80036	54538	3359	823	489	32605	30693	1888	60[illegible]
	2002	132389	78169	53266	3281	804	478	31844	29977	1844	59[illegible]

For general note and footnotes see end of table.

Exportations mondiales par classes de marchandises et par régions (suite)

En millions de dollars E.-U. f.o.b.

Economies développées 1/,2/ — Canada	U.S.A. E.-U.	Japan Japon	Australia New Zealand Australie Nouvelle-Zélande	Developing economies Economies en voie de développement 1/,2/ — Africa Afrique	America Amerique — Total	LAIA ALADI	Asia Asie — Mid. East Moyen Orient	Other Autres 7/	Oceania Océanie	← Exportations vers / Année	Exportations en provenance de ↓
Produits chimiques (CTCI, Rev. 2 et Rev. 3, 5)											
16385	51863	17527	7837	9949	34564	29980	16814	79941	399	1998	Monde 1/
17539	58957	18925	8308	9243	33322	28563	16643	88875	415	1999	
19136	66572	21297	8094	9496	38348	33145	18113	105570	400	2000	
19484	69912	21428	8565	10998	39858	33971	18479	99009	452	2001	
20337	72971	22366	8940	11479	41602	35457	19288	103341	458	2002	
15927	42848	13146	6411	7298	25409	22603	10778	40311	247	1998	Economies dévelopées 1/,2/
17089	49007	14434	6706	6947	24393	21588	10569	46241	263	1999	
18617	54885	15739	6340	6947	27758	24708	11443	53468	246	2000	
18943	58236	15823	6704	8025	28586	25216	11636	49318	298	2001	
19473	59865	16266	6892	8250	29386	25922	11962	50698	299	2002	
416	8432	4304	1409	2503	8691	6955	5345	37804	65	1998	Economies en voie de développement 1/,2/
415	9394	4427	1587	2168	8460	6549	5567	40611	72	1999	
476	11063	5477	1744	2394	10032	7938	6027	50264	71	2000	
501	11038	5529	1848	2842	10697	8274	6280	47665	70	2001	
535	11779	5900	1972	3033	11415	8829	6702	50864	73	2002	
14	930	401	275	605	789	716	3159	3659	3	1998	OPEP
5	838	203	306	337	618	533	3341	3864	7	1999	
11	1103	293	298	377	695	598	3516	5090	16	2000	
33	1068	471	380	619	695	591	3492	5454	10	2001	
33	1068	471	380	619	695	591	3493	5456	11	2002	
42	583	77	17	148	466	424	691	1830	0	1998	Europe de l'Est et l'ancienne URSS 1/,5/
35	556	64	15	128	471	427	507	2027	0	1999	
43	624	81	10	155	559	500	644	1842	2	2000	
40	638	76	13	131	577	483	564	2030	2	2001	
44	708	84	14	145	640	536	626	2253	1	2002	
28	393	43	6	71	371	343	483	1608	0	1998	l'ancienne URSS-Europe 6/
18	391	30	6	67	389	356	293	1779	0	1999	
18	406	29	2	87	468	417	272	1554	1	2000	
18	397	31	4	64	460	377	238	1741	0	2001	
19	427	33	4	69	495	406	256	1873	0	2002	
2444	25582	7050	3195	6129	9354	8255	9356	13218	147	1998	Economies développées-Europe
2483	30659	8148	3495	5789	8926	7836	9045	14553	147	1999	
2724	33904	8747	3160	5627	9370	8224	9730	16087	144	2000	
3454	37542	8919	3501	6461	10397	9055	9925	16445	180	2001	
3659	39774	9449	3709	6845	11015	9593	10515	17423	170	2002	
2176	23346	5889	2885	5842	8134	7142	8481	11916	145	1998	Union Européenne
2201	28017	6911	3179	5528	7816	6846	8179	13151	147	1999	
2357	31219	7490	2876	5354	8222	7222	8838	14589	143	2000	
2968	34519	7631	3186	6154	9200	8019	8980	14827	179	2001	
3149	36622	8096	3380	6529	9760	8507	9527	15730	180	2002	
268	2236	1161	310	285	1219	1112	873	1301	1	1998	Association Européenne de Libre Exchange
282	2642	1238	316	258	1110	989	864	1401	1	1999	
367	2685	1256	284	270	1147	1001	890	1497	1	2000	
485	3021	1288	315	305	1195	1034	943	1616	1	2001	
503	3135	1336	327	316	1240	1073	978	1677	0	2002	
13483	17266	6096	3217	1169	16055	14348	1423	27093	100	1998	Autres economies développées
14606	18348	6286	3211	1158	15467	13752	1524	31688	115	1999	
15893	20980	6992	3180	1320	18388	16484	1712	37381	102	2000	
15490	20694	6904	3203	1565	18189	16161	1710	32873	118	2001	
15129	20211	6743	3128	1528	17765	15784	1670	32106	115	2002	

Voir la fin du tableau pour la remarque générale et les notes.

SPECIAL TABLE: D

World exports by commodity classes and by regions (continued)

In million U.S. dollars f.o.b.

Exports to → / ↓ Exports from	Year	World Monde 1/	Developed economies Econ. dévelop-pées 1/,2/	Developing economies economies en voie de développement 1/,2/		Eastern Europe and fmr. USSR-Europe Europe de l'Est et l'anc. URSS-Europe		Developed economies			
								Europe			South Africa
				Total	OPEC OPEP	Total 1/,5/	Former USSR-Eur. 6/	Total	EU UE	EFTA AELE	Afrique du Sud
											Chemicals (SITC, Rev. 2 and Rev. 3, 5) (continued)
Canada	1998	12180	10884	1271	76	24	12	685	587	97	13
	1999	12861	11508	1319	85	34	10	707	642	65	13
	2000	14796	13107	1661	117	28	7	653	620	33	11
	2001	14995	13477	1498	70	21	6	624	599	24	6
	2002	14563	13088	1455	68	20	6	606	582	23	6
United States	1998	68066	41259	26416	1783	390	198	19761	18702	1049	445
	1999	70483	42949	27264	1746	270	86	20301	18813	1483	395
	2000	79911	47791	31661	2031	458	275	22997	21372	1608	478
	2001	80140	48775	30738	2162	625	407	24424	22914	1505	447
	2002	76089	46309	29184	2053	593	386	23189	21756	1429	424
Japan	1998	27238	11847	15325	788	66	18	5193	4914	275	67
	1999	30722	12466	18189	891	67	18	5351	5043	304	64
	2000	35158	13222	21861	994	74	23	5433	5136	293	75
	2001	30680	12115	18494	833	70	22	5225	4900	321	79
	2002	31697	12516	19107	861	72	23	5398	5062	332	82
Australia, New Zealand	1998	2856	1720	1033	96	5	2	374	364	10	30
	1999	3183	1911	1167	98	5	1	431	416	14	30
	2000	3619	2148	1358	123	5	1	590	582	8	33
	2001	3977	2402	1433	131	18	9	529	514	14	39
	2002	4011	2423	1445	132	18	9	534	518	14	39
Developing economies-Africa	1998	3061	977	1996	288	36	24	892	877	14	20
	1999	3012	1002	1932	307	30	23	911	901	8	17
	2000	3098	1161	1804	323	84	71	970	963	5	59
	2001	3133	1185	1819	309	78	62	911	906	4	155
	2002	3292	1247	1911	325	82	65	959	954	4	163
Developing economies-America	1998	14225	6269	7818	813	29	15	1856	1697	159	50
	1999	14056	6561	7438	749	29	8	1743	1602	141	64
	2000	16471	7685	8672	1012	31	10	2144	1993	150	73
	2001	16801	7502	9170	1189	42	17	2209	2023	186	71
	2002	17025	7603	9293	1205	43	17	2240	2051	188	72
Developing economies-Europe 3/	1998	1870	690	626	27	553	229	628	612	16	0
	1999	1679	614	611	21	451	153	547	541	7	0
	2000	1748	656	615	17	475	191	580	570	10	4
	2001	1808	611	631	21	564	243	518	508	10	3
	2002	1908	645	666	22	595	256	547	537	11	3
Developing economies-Middle East	1998	9325	1971	6765	2255	337	218	852	817	29	43
	1999	9338	1518	6675	1905	247	136	580	537	37	16
	2000	10652	1587	7512	1990	281	151	569	520	42	27
	2001	12010	2746	8742	2746	328	192	1443	1345	40	92
	2002	12229	2796	8901	2796	334	195	1469	1369	41	94
Developing economies-Other Asia	1998	54645	16211	37731	2201	695	461	6726	6493	222	306
	1999	59470	17940	40742	2971	778	603	7404	7187	202	308
	2000	72060	20387	50745	3778	915	706	7703	7447	238	322
	2001	69637	20853	47781	3866	989	767	8020	7772	232	318
	2002	76178	22812	52269	4229	1082	839	8773	8502	254	348
Former USSR-Asia 7/	1998	495	128	103	3	264	249	74	74	0	0
	1999	506	172	100	2	234	220	133	133	0	0
	2000	417	181	109	5	127	114	101	100	0	0
	2001	380	167	93	3	120	108	91	91	0	0
	2002	419	185	102	3	132	119	101	101	0	0
Developing economies-Oceania	1998	47	7	40	0	0	0	2	2	0	3
	1999	52	7	45	0	0	0	2	2	0	3
	2000	17	6	12	4	0	0	2	2	0	3
	2001	18	6	12	4	0	0	2	2	0	3
	2002	18	7	15	5	0	0	3	3	0	5

For general note and footnotes see end of table.

Exportations mondiales par classes de marchandises et par régions (suite)

En millions de dollars E.-U. f.o.b.

Economies développées 1/,2/ Canada	U.S.A. E.-U.	Japan Japon	Australia New Zealand Australie Nouvelle-Zélande	Developing economies Economies en voie de développement 1/,2/ Africa Afrique	America Amerique Total	America Amerique LAIA ALADI	Asia Asie Mid. East Moyen Orient	Asia Asie Other Autres 7/	Oceania Océanie	← Exportations vers Année	Exportations en provenance de ↓
Produits chimiques (CTCI, Rev. 2 et Rev. 3, 5) (suite)											
.	9877	183	116	25	318	265	39	886	1	1998	Canada
.	10485	173	121	32	315	254	45	924	1	1999	
.	12115	211	111	14	435	381	38	1172	1	2000	
.	12556	171	112	19	336	279	32	1109	1	2001	
.	12194	166	109	18	326	271	31	1077	1	2002	
13266	.	5459	1980	416	14722	13152	851	10393	11	1998	Etats-Unis
14364	.	5689	1851	348	14186	12623	926	11773	10	1999	
15624	.	6346	1927	408	16892	15128	990	13328	10	2000	
15218	.	6305	1918	691	16843	14941	1025	12145	13	2001	
14449	.	5986	1821	656	15992	14186	973	11531	12	2002	
120	6022	.	404	75	534	489	248	14453	5	1998	Japon
142	6444	.	423	70	519	470	239	17344	7	1999	
162	7114	.	385	75	542	493	212	21014	6	2000	
145	6250	.	375	51	481	448	206	17741	6	2001	
150	6457	.	387	53	497	463	213	18329	6	2002	
35	415	259	604	15	69	66	49	816	82	1998	Australie, Nouvelle-Zélande
34	494	240	678	24	63	60	37	945	98	1999	
37	592	256	635	29	92	86	50	1101	84	2000	
63	829	264	673	42	126	117	40	1126	98	2001	
64	836	266	679	42	127	118	40	1136	99	2002	
2	15	4	37	826	90	78	307	772	0	1998	Economies en voie de développement-Afrique
1	43	2	23	702	87	75	312	828	0	1999	
4	80	9	30	627	131	107	356	682	2	2000	
4	75	6	27	700	118	98	339	657	1	2001	
4	79	6	28	735	124	103	356	690	1	2002	
168	3790	292	97	85	7260	5697	72	397	0	1998	Economies en voie de développement-Amérique
135	4305	229	67	76	6921	5214	55	384	0	1999	
122	5032	235	61	91	7981	6120	62	534	0	2000	
122	4848	171	70	102	8528	6391	58	479	0	2001	
124	4913	173	71	103	8642	6476	59	485	0	2002	
5	52	1	3	31	9	8	30	32	0	1998	Economies en voie de développement-Europe 3/
6	55	1	4	16	7	7	35	42	0	1999	
5	61	1	3	7	10	10	57	31	0	2000	
4	81	1	3	10	9	9	36	39	0	2001	
4	85	1	3	11	9	9	38	41	0	2002	
12	632	238	173	554	40	35	3538	2621	0	1998	Economies en voie de développement-Moyen Orient
7	647	14	215	322	47	41	3676	2605	0	1999	
6	735	16	206	398	50	45	3808	3237	0	2000	
20	670	225	256	688	45	33	3984	4004	0	2001	
20	682	229	261	701	46	34	4056	4077	0	2002	
229	3943	3769	1098	1007	1260	1119	1398	33982	57	1998	Economies en voie de développement-Autres Pays d'Asie
266	4344	4181	1276	1052	1362	1192	1489	36751	64	1999	
339	5155	5216	1443	1270	1860	1656	1744	45774	64	2000	
351	5364	5126	1491	1341	1996	1743	1862	42481	64	2001	
384	5868	5607	1631	1467	2183	1907	2037	46471	70	2002	
0	52	1	1	1	1	0	14	88	0	1998	l'ancienne URSS asiatique 7/
0	38	1	1	0	0	0	19	81	0	1999	
2	75	1	1	0	0	0	18	90	0	2000	
2	72	1	1	0	0	0	12	81	0	2001	
2	79	1	1	0	0	0	13	89	0	2002	
0	0	0	1	0	32	18	0	0	8	1998	Economies en voie de développement-Océanie
0	0	0	2	0	36	20	0	1	8	1999	
0	0	0	1	1	0	0	0	6	5	2000	
0	0	0	1	1	0	0	0	6	5	2001	
0	0	0	1	1	0	0	0	8	6	2002	

Voir la fin du tableau pour la remarque générale et les notes.

SPECIAL TABLE: D

World exports by commodity classes and by regions (continued)

In million U.S. dollars f.o.b.

Exports from ↓ / Exports to →	Year	World Monde 1/	Developed economies Econ. dévelop-pées 1/,2/	Developing economies économies en voie de développement 1/,2/ Total	Developing economies OPEC OPEP	Eastern Europe and fmr. USSR-Europe Europe de l'Est et l'anc. URSS-Europe Total 1/,5/	Eastern Europe and fmr. USSR-Europe Former USSR-Eur. 6/	Developed economies Europe Total	Developed economies Europe EU UE	Developed economies Europe EFTA AELE	Developed economies South Africa Afrique du Sud
		Machinery and transport equipment (SITC, Rev. 2 and Rev. 3, 7)									
World 1/	1998	2158363	1480692	593595	65792	70107	23658	844412	799609	42299	11955
	1999	2263530	1580638	600417	55186	61780	15818	879519	835651	41056	10015
	2000	2527376	1704263	730780	62586	72606	19442	907906	863833	40872	11229
	2001	2395162	1616328	686454	72810	83218	26066	891883	847429	41212	11155
	2002	2499969	1687055	716492	75996	86860	27206	930910	884511	43015	11643
Developed economies 1/,2/	1998	1643064	1164821	408668	52826	56985	17072	731497	690036	39624	10386
	1999	1687692	1218980	398380	42256	50700	11186	754480	714045	38361	8438
	2000	1809243	1259812	467177	45857	59644	13577	756168	716614	37215	9290
	2001	1718707	1208061	434715	53731	67917	18598	747366	707238	37661	9419
	2002	1766796	1241863	446878	55234	69817	19118	768277	727026	38715	9683
Developing economies 1/,2/	1998	467765	282901	179575	12481	4572	1828	82295	79728	2031	1544
	1999	527476	325679	197149	12458	4075	1051	91248	88714	1922	1551
	2000	660542	397264	257759	16113	4759	1418	107273	103757	2732	1900
	2001	612069	360305	245173	18079	5759	2167	98991	95978	2310	1704
	2002	653150	384488	261629	19293	6146	2312	105635	102420	2465	1818
OPEC	1998	10437	4206	6204	2301	21	6	2377	2368	8	32
	1999	10755	4387	6317	2059	36	7	2495	2467	27	35
	2000	16544	7354	9124	2336	54	16	3527	3489	36	30
	2001	14821	6564	8164	2574	56	8	3218	3195	22	25
	2002	14827	6567	8167	2575	56	8	3219	3196	22	25
Eastern Europe and the former USSR 1/,5/	1998	47536	32995	5544	487	8551	4759	30631	29855	644	25
	1999	48363	36004	5088	474	7006	3581	33801	32902	773	26
	2000	57592	43060	6131	617	8203	4447	40322	39319	925	39
	2001	64388	47996	6795	1001	9543	5301	45544	44230	1241	32
	2002	71462	53269	7542	1111	10592	5883	50548	49090	1377	36
Former USSR-Europe 6/	1998	9812	2411	3103	205	4033	3343	1709	1539	88	7
	1999	8521	2304	2638	239	3337	2677	1949	1849	60	4
	2000	9986	3038	2990	235	3958	3364	2778	2641	87	2
	2001	10581	2665	3479	624	4416	3884	2384	2274	88	2
	2002	11385	2868	3743	671	4752	4179	2565	2447	95	2
Developed economies-Europe	1998	941141	725259	153509	24670	51135	13794	592158	556621	34063	6654
	1999	944106	741191	138142	20733	46466	9479	606602	571766	33129	5657
	2000	978156	744898	157212	22890	54975	11861	599210	565454	31788	6114
	2001	993199	758586	164777	29274	63200	16684	609797	575249	32648	6441
	2002	1052252	803690	174574	31015	66958	17676	646054	609452	34589	6824
European Union	1998	908827	699750	147708	23911	50130	13515	571713	536581	33696	6469
	1999	911725	715595	132314	20071	45509	9250	586704	552312	32846	5519
	2000	945816	719875	150962	22172	53908	11610	580198	546950	31392	5952
	2001	961151	734488	158016	28466	62011	16344	590879	556869	32273	6324
	2002	1019698	779228	167641	30200	65788	17340	626872	590790	34239	6709
European Free Trade Association	1998	31109	24670	5438	727	1001	277	19932	19536	357	180
	1999	31129	24733	5455	636	941	216	19440	19006	273	138
	2000	30609	23776	5787	701	1045	241	18487	18134	240	160
	2001	30789	23209	6426	780	1154	327	18425	18017	245	113
	2002	31946	24081	6668	809	1197	339	19118	18694	254	117
Other developed economies	1998	701923	439562	255160	28156	5850	3277	139339	133416	5562	3732
	1999	743586	477789	260238	21523	4233	1707	147878	142279	5232	2781
	2000	831088	514915	309966	22967	4669	1716	156958	151160	5428	3175
	2001	725508	449475	269938	24457	4718	1915	137569	131989	5013	2978
	2002	708585	438991	263642	23887	4608	1870	134360	128910	4896	2909

For general note and footnotes see end of table.

Exportations mondiales par classes de marchandises et par régions (suite)

En millions de dollars E.-U. f.o.b.

Economies développées 1/,2/				Developing economies Economies en voie de développement 1/,2/						← Exportations vers	
Canada	U.S.A. E.-U.	Japan Japon	Australia New Zealand Australie Nouvelle-Zélande	Africa Afrique	America Amerique Total	America Amerique LAIA ALADI	Asia Asie Mid. East Moyen Orient	Asia Asie Other Autres 7/	Oceania Océanie	Année	Exportations en provenance de ↓
Machines et matériél de transport (CTCI, Rev. 2 et Rev. 3, 7)											
92778	425538	67356	29763	37488	139725	116109	66875	340354	1607	1998	Monde 1/
99634	475272	74030	32043	34633	129162	103689	55876	371571	1900	1999	
105946	541516	93669	32975	36267	146537	120641	63074	475805	1486	2000	
94680	493887	84349	30209	39731	139500	115816	62614	434168	2127	2001	
98823	515499	88039	31530	41470	145604	120884	65353	453167	2170	2002	
88009	266474	37213	23212	29098	113787	95192	55577	202356	1425	1998	Economies dévelopées 1/,2/
93798	291241	37285	24715	27120	107863	87482	45859	209728	1740	1999	
98129	319319	42682	24801	28252	120242	99484	49996	261251	1333	2000	
87806	293348	37865	23430	30977	113141	94955	49082	232970	1931	2001	
90263	301556	38924	24086	31844	116307	97612	50455	239488	1980	2002	
4633	157086	30053	6466	7896	25438	20567	10187	135033	209	1998	Economies en voie de développement 1/,2/
5730	182121	36689	7290	6999	20840	15883	9248	158912	364	1999	
7691	219997	50838	8125	7577	25774	20842	11890	211102	607	2000	
6733	198583	46321	6732	8217	25674	20530	11958	197750	700	2001	
7185	211912	49429	7183	8769	27397	21908	12760	211023	720	2002	
35	946	755	61	1890	628	565	978	2702	6	1998	OPEP
36	978	766	76	1864	297	228	957	3188	7	1999	
54	1875	1697	171	1904	492	389	1232	5474	16	2000	
44	1689	1431	157	1905	541	449	1168	4539	8	2001	
44	1690	1432	157	1906	541	449	1168	4541	8	2002	
136	1978	90	86	497	503	352	1113	2967	30	1998	Europe de l'Est et l'ancienne URSS 1/,5/
106	1912	56	38	518	463	326	770	2934	8	1999	
126	2201	149	50	441	525	317	1189	3455	1	2000	
141	1957	163	47	540	688	332	1575	3451	44	2001	
156	2172	181	52	599	764	368	1748	3830	30	2002	
10	626	42	8	227	152	70	398	2219	0	1998	l'ancienne URSS-Europe 6/
16	310	11	2	145	114	51	375	1942	0	1999	
13	201	35	4	126	122	47	457	2188	0	2000	
18	189	61	6	149	217	35	834	2192	3	2001	
19	203	66	6	160	233	38	897	2359	2	2002	
7692	93511	13737	7678	21364	31587	26719	31884	61992	583	1998	Economies développées-Europe
8013	94792	14310	7581	19771	28282	22392	27733	55928	750	1999	
8242	102091	16737	7436	20893	29600	23202	33347	67024	567	2000	
8453	105420	15991	7604	22518	31073	24889	31646	72040	1136	2001	
8956	111688	16942	8056	23857	32921	26369	33528	76323	1120	2002	
7476	89915	13055	7447	20781	30592	25902	30893	58932	579	1998	Union Européenne
7749	90574	13630	7337	19010	27335	21658	26870	52856	747	1999	
7955	97713	15950	7198	20325	28700	22469	32411	63345	562	2000	
8248	101753	15205	7352	21767	29579	24127	30827	68524	1090	2001	
8750	107951	16131	7800	23093	31381	25597	32705	72698	1099	2002	
214	3317	644	230	553	985	816	949	2780	4	1998	Association Européenne de Libre Exchange
257	3869	632	242	733	942	733	858	2739	3	1999	
264	3768	700	237	551	894	731	933	3244	5	2000	
202	3321	741	252	723	1489	760	815	3219	45	2001	
210	3446	769	261	750	1545	789	846	3340	40	2002	
80317	172963	23476	15534	7733	82200	68472	23693	140364	842	1998	Autres economies développées
85785	196449	22975	17135	7349	79581	65090	18126	153800	990	1999	
89887	217229	25945	17365	7359	90642	76282	16649	194226	766	2000	
79354	187928	21875	15826	8459	82068	70066	17436	160930	795	2001	
77503	183544	21365	15457	8262	80154	68432	17029	157176	798	2002	

Voir la fin du tableau pour la remarque générale et les notes.

SPECIAL TABLE: D

World exports by commodity classes and by regions (continued)

In million U.S. dollars f.o.b.

Exports to → / ↓ Exports from	Year	World Monde 1/	Developed economies Econ. dévelop-pées 1/,2/	Developing economies économies en voie de développement 1/,2/ Total	Developing economies OPEC OPEP	Eastern Europe and fmr. USSR-Europe Europe de l'Est et l'anc. URSS-Europe Total 1/,5/	Eastern Europe and fmr. USSR-Europe Former USSR-Eur. 6/	Developed economies Europe Total	Developed economies Europe EU UE	Developed economies Europe EFTA AELE	Developed economies South Africa Afrique du Sud
		Machinery and transport equipment (SITC, Rev. 2 and Rev. 3, 7) (continued)									
Canada	1998	87393	83888	3288	563	218	86	3424	3190	234	92
	1999	101708	98459	3096	365	152	59	3748	3575	172	56
	2000	111436	107496	3770	489	170	82	4847	4659	183	36
	2001	99287	95269	3846	577	172	103	4423	4268	152	47
	2002	96424	92522	3735	560	167	100	4295	4145	148	46
United States	1998	328822	186637	138622	16356	3485	2232	76592	73392	2966	2078
	1999	335882	195750	137692	11798	2437	1214	81300	78555	2595	1335
	2000	365990	206061	157586	10206	2341	1034	85244	82020	2975	1521
	2001	331933	185448	144015	10985	2466	1106	79441	76114	3101	1623
	2002	315153	176073	136735	10430	2341	1050	75425	72266	2944	1541
Japan	1998	268466	158767	107924	10684	1773	833	54941	52590	2230	1376
	1999	286790	171248	114190	8612	1349	362	57343	54839	2298	1237
	2000	329661	186554	141277	11105	1829	486	60545	58396	2037	1443
	2001	271287	154903	114602	11439	1780	608	48143	46284	1528	1116
	2002	280276	160036	118399	11818	1839	628	49738	47818	1579	1153
Australia, New Zealand	1998	6105	3467	2421	445	8	2	813	794	18	101
	1999	6733	4281	2323	650	9	3	1086	1054	31	74
	2000	8259	4612	3225	1037	19	5	1065	1052	13	80
	2001	8405	4690	3378	1294	14	6	1024	999	24	105
	2002	8478	4731	3407	1305	14	6	1033	1008	24	106
Developing economies- Africa	1998	2108	1592	473	120	6	2	1454	1437	17	58
	1999	2564	1943	584	120	7	2	1720	1699	21	116
	2000	2882	2245	585	176	23	11	1930	1902	26	207
	2001	2861	2247	552	172	22	12	1941	1919	21	220
	2002	3006	2365	580	181	23	13	2044	2021	22	231
Developing economies- America	1998	88811	72791	15523	1551	269	50	4139	4043	96	113
	1999	100615	89350	10964	930	277	25	5870	5731	139	111
	2000	121795	108040	13336	1322	361	18	5969	5609	359	151
	2001	119245	105169	13840	2115	175	9	5594	5169	425	247
	2002	120835	106581	14025	2143	177	9	5671	5241	431	250
Developing economies- Europe 3/	1998	5143	3402	1275	112	463	278	3275	3130	79	9
	1999	4606	3206	1114	76	284	118	3084	2824	161	5
	2000	4691	3294	1054	69	341	122	3189	3091	49	5
	2001	5094	3542	1111	66	440	212	3439	3329	54	6
	2002	5375	3741	1172	70	464	224	3632	3516	57	6
Developing economies- Middle East	1998	10129	4567	4968	2870	285	149	4194	4149	40	24
	1999	11073	5534	4921	2785	239	101	5002	4941	33	17
	2000	12077	5926	5285	2952	397	163	5161	5094	32	26
	2001	13557	6893	5494	3473	605	255	6023	5946	42	31
	2002	13804	7018	5594	3536	616	260	6133	6054	43	32
Developing economies- Other Asia	1998	361301	200384	157236	7828	3547	1348	69143	66879	1799	1340
	1999	408320	225471	179450	8547	3265	803	75518	73467	1568	1302
	2000	518929	277667	237431	11586	3635	1103	90982	88018	2265	1511
	2001	471164	242372	224117	12245	4516	1678	81955	79576	1767	1200
	2002	515419	265137	245167	13396	4940	1835	89653	87050	1933	1312
Former USSR-Asia 7/.	1998	415	50	163	24	202	194	41	39	2	3
	1999	493	69	247	47	177	169	57	49	8	2
	2000	453	121	128	23	204	199	94	80	14	1
	2001	419	123	123	24	173	168	92	82	10	0
	2002	461	137	135	26	191	185	102	91	11	0
Developing economies- Oceania	1998	273	164	100	0	2	1	89	89	0	0
	1999	298	164	116	0	3	2	42	42	0	0
	2000	168	88	68	8	2	1	40	40	1	0
	2001	148	81	59	8	1	1	38	38	1	0
	2002	147	95	73	10	5	1	65	60	13	0

For general note and footnotes see end of table.

Exportations mondiales par classes de marchandises et par régions (suite)

En millions de dollars E.-U. f.o.b.

conomies éveloppées 1/,2/				Developing economies Economies en voie de développement 1/,2/						← Exportations vers	
Canada	U.S.A. E.-U.	Japan Japon	Australia New Zealand Australie Nouvelle-Zélande	Africa Afrique	America Amerique Total	America Amerique LAIA ALADI	Asia Asie Mid. East Moyen Orient	Asia Asie Other Autres 7/	Oceania Océanie	Année	Exportations en provenance de ↓
achines et matériél de transport (CTCI, Rev. 2 et Rev. 3, 7) (suite)											
.	79746	292	284	146	1479	1242	325	1265	18	1998	Canada
.	93934	333	287	184	1352	1079	202	1306	14	1999	
.	101692	385	417	178	1452	1198	258	1825	6	2000	
.	89878	415	390	145	1627	1395	275	1786	5	2001	
.	87286	403	379	141	1580	1355	267	1734	5	2002	
75112	.	22743	6762	3309	63437	57856	12342	59192	185	1998	Etats-Unis
79939	.	22124	7157	3094	62463	56835	9544	62202	189	1999	
83612	.	24882	7503	3639	72094	66347	7863	73664	157	2000	
73808	.	20788	6666	4945	66184	60913	7930	64648	133	2001	
70077	.	19737	6329	4695	62838	57834	7529	61380	126	2002	
5007	89582	.	7089	3085	16577	8826	10438	77375	362	1998	Japon
5679	98495	.	7724	2950	15189	6738	7480	87951	496	1999	
6064	109917	.	7675	2400	16429	8148	7517	114546	303	2000	
5350	92695	.	6919	2189	13610	7179	7933	90510	312	2001	
5527	95767	.	7148	2262	14061	7417	8196	93509	322	2002	
93	1044	238	1168	64	171	152	483	1433	270	1998	Australie, Nouvelle-Zélande
72	1153	263	1627	67	187	123	600	1181	288	1999	
95	1630	287	1443	80	150	134	859	1840	296	2000	
88	1721	206	1536	76	123	106	1109	1727	340	2001	
89	1736	208	1549	77	124	107	1119	1742	343	2002	
2	71	3	1	404	3	2	30	31	0	1998	Economies en voie de développement-Afrique
3	97	5	1	287	174	171	78	44	0	1999	
7	72	7	18	398	12	7	81	91	1	2000	
8	54	7	12	352	12	6	108	78	1	2001	
8	57	7	13	370	13	6	113	82	1	2002	
1220	67052	143	108	248	13747	12498	279	1234	7	1998	Economies en voie de développement-Amérique
1854	81027	340	125	156	9330	8178	150	1322	2	1999	
2654	98568	544	131	180	11787	10240	165	1199	1	2000	
2520	96382	277	127	231	11663	10507	221	1716	1	2001	
2554	97667	281	129	234	11819	10647	224	1739	1	2002	
15	87	1	10	384	70	22	190	57	0	1998	Economies en voie de développement-Europe 3/
4	100	2	7	213	105	80	169	81	0	1999	
6	83	2	6	271	73	31	92	54	0	2000	
7	78	4	6	174	116	37	91	74	41	2001	
7	82	4	6	184	122	39	96	78	43	2002	
11	269	7	16	2314	45	27	1739	835	0	1998	Economies en voie de développement-Moyen Orient
15	417	7	18	2372	72	40	1693	732	0	1999	
13	577	12	61	2299	76	44	1969	841	7	2000	
10	627	10	23	2420	122	74	2133	747	10	2001	
10	638	10	23	2464	124	75	2172	761	10	2002	
3377	89577	29899	6295	4546	11512	7987	7949	132858	182	1998	Economies en voie de développement-Autres Pays d'Asie
3846	100424	36335	7082	3971	11092	7379	7158	156708	338	1999	
5010	120678	50272	7881	4429	13824	10520	9579	208872	584	2000	
4187	101427	46022	6538	5040	13760	9906	9401	195099	634	2001	
4580	110954	50344	7152	5513	15053	10837	10283	213424	693	2002	
0	5	0	0	14	1	0	43	104	0	1998	l'ancienne URSS asiatique 7/
0	5	0	0	22	13	7	64	146	0	1999	
1	23	2	0	4	1	0	28	95	0	2000	
1	27	2	0	3	3	2	28	86	0	2001	
1	30	2	0	3	3	2	31	95	0	2002	
8	30	0	36	0	61	31	0	18	20	1998	Economies en voie de développement-Océanie
8	56	0	57	0	67	35	0	25	24	1999	
1	18	1	28	0	1	0	4	45	14	2000	
1	15	1	26	0	1	0	4	36	13	2001	
1	15	1	35	0	1	0	6	51	17	2002	

Voir la fin du tableau pour la remarque générale et les notes.

World exports by commodity classes and by regions (continued)

In million U.S. dollars f.o.b.

Exports from ↓ / Exports to →	Year	World / Monde 1/	Developed economies / Econ. dévelop-pées 1/,2/	Developing economies / economies en voie de développement 1/,2/: Total	Developing economies: OPEC / OPEP	Eastern Europe and fmr. USSR-Europe / Europe de l'Est et l'anc. URSS-Europe: Total 1/,5/	Eastern Europe and fmr. USSR-Europe: Former USSR-Eur. 6/	Developed economies – Europe: Total	Europe: EU / UE	Europe: EFTA / AELE	South Africa / Afrique du Sud
		Passenger road vehicles and their parts (SITC, Rev. 2, 781.0, 784.1, 785.1, 785.2, 785.3 (SITC, Rev. 3, 781.2, 784.1, 785.1, 785.2, 785.3									
World 1/	1998	290319	251438	31764	7306	6850	2556	143113	135653	7242	9
	1999	305582	275049	25036	5721	5406	1264	150039	143057	6736	7
	2000	314946	275132	33639	7549	6037	1755	137156	130506	6411	10
	2001	320683	278292	34169	10041	8095	3191	145132	138183	6686	11
	2002	334715	290469	35664	10480	8449	3331	151483	144230	6979	12
Developed economies 1/,2/	1998	254604	226257	23266	5732	5063	1928	132376	125255	6912	7
	1999	268025	244791	19113	4418	4105	987	137135	130531	6377	6
	2000	267982	238467	24532	5559	4916	1431	124527	118362	5939	9
	2001	273520	241461	25318	7762	6679	2579	132287	125771	6260	10
	2002	281173	248217	26026	7979	6866	2651	135988	129290	6435	10
Developing economies 1/,2/	1998	29698	20434	8071	1553	975	226	6017	5829	179	1
	1999	31016	24745	5512	1281	709	67	7416	7214	185	1
	2000	38903	29981	8505	1975	353	53	5979	5747	221	1
	2001	38686	30034	8264	2226	325	134	6097	5908	183	1
	2002	41283	32050	8819	2375	347	143	6506	6305	195	1
OPEC	1998	433	44	387	84	1	1	34	34	0	
	1999	174	55	118	29	1	1	43	43	0	
	2000	283	57	225	78	1	1	46	46	0	
	2001	298	57	237	122	0	0	48	48	0	
	2002	298	57	237	122	0	0	48	48	0	
Eastern Europe and the former USSR 1/,5/	1998	6018	4747	427	21	812	403	4720	4568	150	
	1999	6540	5512	410	23	591	211	5487	5312	174	
	2000	8061	6684	601	15	769	271	6650	6398	250	
	2001	8478	6797	588	53	1091	478	6748	6504	243	
	2002	9409	7544	653	59	1211	531	7489	7219	270	
Former USSR-Europe 6/	1998	736	120	213	6	375	321	108	106	2	
	1999	421	77	148	7	169	149	73	72	1	
	2000	597	117	237	1	243	206	116	112	4	
	2001	705	102	246	2	355	346	101	97	3	
	2002	759	110	265	2	382	372	109	104	3	
Developed economies-Europe	1998	154072	139805	9905	1660	4345	1570	115427	109539	5707	4
	1999	155840	144570	7593	1308	3662	852	119267	113778	5292	4
	2000	151798	136269	11013	1833	4451	1251	109524	104387	4928	6
	2001	163507	146527	10689	2698	6231	2312	118816	113175	5404	7
	2002	173229	155239	11325	2858	6601	2449	125880	119904	5725	7
European Union	1998	153841	139651	9865	1653	4309	1560	115284	109402	5701	4
	1999	155582	144396	7543	1295	3628	844	119104	113621	5286	4
	2000	151581	136127	10963	1826	4425	1245	109394	104263	4923	6
	2001	163292	146396	10640	2692	6196	2297	118701	113064	5399	7
	2002	173239	155313	11288	2856	6573	2437	125931	119951	5728	7
European Free Trade Association	1998	220	145	39	7	36	10	134	127	6	
	1999	247	166	49	12	33	8	154	148	5	
	2000	206	133	49	6	25	6	121	115	5	
	2001	204	122	48	6	34	14	106	101	4	
	2002	212	127	50	6	35	15	110	105	4	
Other developed economies	1998	100531	86452	13361	4072	718	357	16949	15716	1205	2
	1999	112185	100221	11520	3110	444	134	17868	16753	1086	2
	2000	116184	102198	13519	3727	465	180	15004	13974	1011	2
	2001	110012	94935	14628	5064	448	267	13471	12596	856	3
	2002	107446	92721	14287	4946	438	261	13157	12302	836	3

For general note and footnotes see end of table.

Exportations mondiales par classes de marchandises et par régions (suite)

En millions de dollars E.-U. f.o.b.

Véhicules routiers et pièces détachées pour transport passagère (CTCI, Rev. 2, 781.0, 784.1, 785.1, 785.2 et 785.31
CTCI, Rev. 3, 781.2, 784.1, 785.1, 785.2 et 785.31)

Economies développées 1/,2/				Developing economies Economies en voie de développement 1/,2/						← Exportations vers	
Canada	U.S.A. E.-U.	Japan Japon	Australia New Zealand Australie Nouvelle-Zélande	Africa Afrique	America Amerique Total	America Amerique LAIA ALADI	Asia Asie Mid. East Moyen Orient	Asia Asie Other Autres 7/	Oceania Océanie	Année	Exportations en provenance de ↓
12078	83004	5791	5340	2879	11863	10041	8834	6565	231	1998	Monde 1/
13472	97590	6073	5850	2798	8095	6337	6936	5738	198	1999	
14885	107617	6602	6063	2637	10892	8739	9910	8813	192	2000	
14388	104142	5918	6066	3156	11916	10406	8967	8653	230	2001	
15018	108699	6177	6331	3294	12437	10861	9359	9032	222	2002	
11496	70364	5500	4685	2218	7271	5845	7510	5034	188	1998	Economies dévelopées 1/,2/
12267	82791	5689	5199	2121	5698	4302	5893	4231	177	1999	
12841	87289	6103	5330	2059	6743	5339	8640	6028	176	2000	
12213	83707	5323	5547	2612	7784	6591	7810	5911	216	2001	
12555	86049	5472	5702	2685	8002	6775	8029	6076	210	2002	
581	12634	291	653	617	4554	4172	1241	1471	28	1998	Economies en voie de développement 1/,2/
1205	14796	382	651	632	2363	2016	975	1396	21	1999	
2044	20325	498	732	522	4112	3381	1140	2603	17	2000	
2175	20431	594	513	487	4060	3782	1082	2525	14	2001	
2321	21802	634	547	520	4333	4036	1155	2694	15	2002	
1	5	0	1	38	276	266	42	32	0	1998	OPEP
2	7	2	1	6	64	57	26	21	1	1999	
3	2	4	1	10	125	113	56	32	1	2000	
1	3	3	2	7	157	154	41	31	1	2001	
1	3	3	2	7	157	154	41	31	0	2002	
2	7	0	1	44	38	24	83	60	15	1998	Europe de l'Est et l'ancienne URSS 1/,5/
1	3	2	0	45	34	19	67	111	0	1999	
0	3	1	1	56	37	18	130	182	0	2000	
0	4	1	6	57	72	33	75	217	0	2001	
0	4	1	7	63	80	37	83	241	0	2002	
2	4	0	0	15	8	7	54	49	0	1998	l'ancienne URSS-Europe 6/
0	1	0	0	2	20	15	42	54	0	1999	
0	1	0	0	2	17	13	45	137	0	2000	
0	1	0	0	6	25	1	28	139	0	2001	
0	1	0	0	6	27	1	30	150	0	2002	
785	16837	4356	1341	1507	2359	2116	3178	1774	93	1998	Economies développées-Europe
681	17582	4755	1246	1513	1304	1061	2428	1358	91	1999	
801	18121	5069	1240	1591	1621	1324	4783	2100	102	2000	
774	19267	4375	1646	2086	2224	1892	2835	2453	139	2001	
820	20413	4635	1744	2210	2356	2004	3004	2599	137	2002	
785	16830	4356	1340	1485	2357	2114	3166	1772	93	1998	Union Européenne
680	17575	4754	1246	1484	1303	1060	2415	1356	91	1999	
801	18115	5067	1239	1562	1620	1324	4770	2098	102	2000	
773	19253	4374	1646	2053	2223	1891	2825	2450	139	2001	
820	20426	4640	1746	2178	2358	2006	2997	2599	140	2002	
0	8	1	0	22	2	1	12	1	0	1998	Association Européenne de Libre Exchange
1	7	1	0	29	1	1	13	2	0	1999	
0	6	2	1	28	1	0	12	2	0	2000	
1	14	1	0	33	1	1	10	2	0	2001	
1	15	1	0	34	1	1	10	2	0	2002	
10710	53526	1143	3345	710	4912	3729	4331	3260	95	1998	Autres economies développées
11586	65209	934	3952	608	4394	3241	3464	2872	87	1999	
12040	69169	1035	4091	469	5122	4015	3857	3927	74	2000	
11439	64440	948	3901	526	5560	4699	4975	3458	77	2001	
11172	62937	926	3810	514	5430	4589	4859	3377	78	2002	

Voir la fin du tableau pour la remarque générale et les notes.

SPECIAL TABLE: D

World exports by commodity classes and by regions (continued)

In million U.S. dollars f.o.b.

Exports to → / ↓ Exports from	Year	World Monde 1/	Developed economies Econ. dévelop-pées 1/,2/	Developing economies economies en voie de développement 1/,2/ Total	OPEC OPEP	Eastern Europe and fmr. USSR-Europe Europe de l'Est et l'anc. URSS-Europe Total 1/,5/	Former USSR-Eur. 6/	Developed economies Europe Total	EU UE	EFTA AELE	South Africa Afrique du Sud
		Passenger road vehicles and their parts (SITC, Rev. 2, 781.0, 784.1, 785.1, 785.2, 785.31 (SITC, Rev. 3, 781.2, 784.1, 785.1, 785.2, 785.31) (continued									
Canada	1998	28484	28396	66	8	21	9	151	140	11	[illegible]
	1999	34676	34572	92	4	12	3	188	176	12	[illegible]
	2000	34956	34810	138	16	8	5	110	96	14	[illegible]
	2001	31621	31484	128	19	8	7	82	67	15	[illegible]
	2002	30709	30576	124	18	8	7	80	65	15	[illegible]
United States	1998	16129	12913	3119	701	96	53	2649	2528	119	54
	1999	16153	13006	3107	340	41	14	2529	2442	85	17
	2000	16655	12926	3686	430	43	16	2172	2079	91	42
	2001	18139	13498	4579	757	63	33	3363	3216	145	13
	2002	17222	12816	4348	719	60	31	3193	3053	138	12
Japan	1998	54896	44627	9668	3074	600	295	13999	12899	1074	20
	1999	59435	51455	7589	2269	391	116	14488	13473	988	17
	2000	62188	53154	8620	2509	413	159	12190	11269	905	21
	2001	57766	48735	8655	3312	376	226	9729	9018	695	15
	2002	59680	50350	8942	3422	388	233	10051	9317	718	16
Australia, New Zealand	1998	727	320	407	289	0	0	7	6	0	[illegible]
	1999	1037	431	606	496	0	0	6	6	0	1
	2000	1333	432	901	771	0	0	11	11	0	
	2001	1604	540	1063	972	0	0	11	11	0	1
	2002	1618	545	1072	980	0	0	11	11	0	1
Developing economies-Africa	1998	42	23	19	4	0	0	20	20	0	
	1999	48	13	34	17	0	0	10	9	0	[illegible]
	2000	174	112	61	30	0	0	72	72	0	2
	2001	117	86	30	3	0	0	50	50	0	2
	2002	123	90	32	3	0	0	53	53	0	2
Developing economies-America	1998	15200	11324	3665	354	36	16	910	900	11	3
	1999	14967	13189	1776	153	0	0	1718	1715	3	3
	2000	19581	16421	3159	313	0	0	734	733	1	4
	2001	19113	15890	3220	694	0	0	675	675	0	4
	2002	19368	16103	3263	703	0	0	684	684	0	4
Developing economies-Europe 3/	1998	1007	973	31	1	3	0	971	970	0	
	1999	818	772	31	1	15	0	769	768	1	
	2000	776	673	47	1	55	0	670	664	7	
	2001	758	666	44	1	47	0	663	657	6	
	2002	800	703	46	1	50	0	700	694	6	
Developing economies-Middle East	1998	623	58	536	269	28	26	54	54	0	
	1999	1026	631	370	232	23	13	628	628	0	
	2000	1089	548	478	303	57	15	545	544	1	
	2001	1375	845	426	283	97	46	834	828	6	
	2002	1400	860	434	288	99	47	849	843	6	
Developing economies-Other Asia	1998	12802	8055	3798	925	908	184	4061	3885	168	12
	1999	14131	10138	3278	878	671	54	4291	4093	181	8
	2000	17281	12227	4758	1327	241	38	3958	3734	213	10
	2001	17321	12545	4543	1245	181	88	3875	3698	171	6
	2002	18948	13723	4970	1362	198	96	4239	4045	187	6
Former USSR-Asia 7/.	1998	7	1	6	1	0	0	1	1	0	
	1999	6	0	5	2	1	1	0	0	0	
	2000	6	0	4	0	1	1	0	0	0	
	2001	5	0	4	0	1	1	0	0	0	
	2002	6	0	4	0	1	1	0	0	0	
Developing economies-Oceania	1998	22	1	21	0	0	0	1	1	0	
	1999	26	2	24	0	0	0	1	1	0	
	2000	1	0	1	0	0	0	0	0	0	
	2001	1	0	1	0	0	0	0	0	0	
	2002	1	0	1	0	0	0	0	0	0	

For general note and footnotes see end of table.

Exportations mondiales par classes de marchandises et par régions (suite)

En millions de dollars E.-U. f.o.b.

Economies développées 1/,2/				Developing economies / Economies en voie de développement 1/,2/						← Exportations vers	
Canada	U.S.A. / E.-U.	Japan / Japon	Australia New Zealand / Australie Nouvelle-Zélande	Africa / Afrique	America / Amerique: Total	America / Amerique: LAIA / ALADI	Asia / Asie: Mid. East / Moyen Orient	Asia / Asie: Other / Autres 7/	Oceania / Océanie	Année	Exportations en provenance de ↓
Véhicules routiers et pièces détachées pour transport passagère (CTCI, Rev. 2, 781.0, 784.1, 785.1, 785.2 et 785.31 (CTCI, Rev. 3, 781.2, 784.1, 785.1, 785.2 et 785.31) (suite)											
.	28191	44	4	5	30	20	10	18	1	1998	Canada
.	34274	105	2	7	69	60	8	6	0	1999	
.	34581	103	2	4	91	87	22	22	0	2000	
.	31315	82	1	3	86	82	21	18	0	2001	
.	30412	80	1	3	84	80	20	17	0	2002	
8845	.	1079	247	80	2029	1677	668	333	3	1998	Etats-Unis
9366	.	795	263	66	2476	2151	323	220	2	1999	
9579	.	773	298	48	2872	2510	426	330	3	2000	
8962	.	645	337	53	3520	3234	702	297	3	2001	
8509	.	612	320	50	3342	3071	667	282	3	2002	
1865	25224	.	2867	563	2797	1992	3304	2874	87	1998	Japon
2220	30766	.	3376	477	1825	1007	2612	2522	78	1999	
2461	34278	.	3482	330	2126	1385	2644	3392	67	2000	
2477	32808	.	3195	388	1951	1381	3259	2958	71	2001	
2559	33895	.	3301	401	2016	1427	3367	3056	73	2002	
0	107	19	180	1	40	40	348	14	4	1998	Australie, Nouvelle-Zélande
0	162	33	219	0	23	22	521	56	6	1999	
0	216	28	176	1	33	33	765	97	3	2000	
0	310	10	194	2	0	0	991	66	3	2001	
0	313	10	196	2	0	0	1000	67	3	2002	
0	0	1	0	16	0	0	0	2	0	1998	Economies en voie de développement-Afrique
0	1	1	0	30	0	0	1	4	0	1999	
0	1	2	9	49	0	0	1	11	0	2000	
0	1	2	5	20	0	0	1	8	0	2001	
0	1	2	5	21	0	0	1	8	0	2002	
313	10060	3	4	31	3502	3340	111	15	6	1998	Economies en voie de développement-Amérique
850	10574	12	3	13	1709	1587	48	7	0	1999	
1454	14174	14	3	21	3104	2583	4	29	0	2000	
1482	13646	38	2	21	3074	2965	26	98	0	2001	
1502	13828	39	2	21	3115	3005	26	99	0	2002	
0	2	1	0	3	1	1	2	0	0	1998	Economies en voie de développement-Europe 3/
0	3	0	0	0	1	1	1	0	0	1999	
0	3	0	0	4	1	1	1	0	0	2000	
0	3	0	0	4	1	1	1	0	0	2001	
0	3	0	0	4	1	1	1	0	0	2002	
0	1	1	0	129	0	0	336	68	0	1998	Economies en voie de développement-Moyen Orient
0	2	1	0	93	0	0	254	20	0	1999	
0	1	1	0	80	0	0	366	29	0	2000	
0	1	1	1	89	1	0	301	31	0	2001	
0	1	1	1	91	1	0	306	32	0	2002	
268	2571	286	648	438	1034	822	793	1383	20	1998	Economies en voie de développement-Autres Pays d'Asie
354	4217	368	647	497	635	419	671	1362	18	1999	
589	6145	481	720	368	1006	796	768	2533	16	2000	
692	6779	553	504	353	984	815	753	2387	13	2001	
757	7416	605	551	386	1076	892	824	2611	14	2002	
0	0	0	0	0	0	0	2	4	0	1998	l'ancienne URSS asiatique 7/
0	0	0	0	0	0	0	2	3	0	1999	
0	0	0	0	0	0	0	1	3	0	2000	
0	0	0	0	0	0	0	0	3	0	2001	
0	0	0	0	0	0	0	0	3	0	2002	
0	0	0	1	0	16	8	0	3	2	1998	Economies en voie de développement-Océanie
0	0	0	1	0	18	9	0	3	3	1999	
0	0	0	0	0	0	0	0	1	0	2000	
0	0	0	0	0	0	0	0	1	0	2001	
0	0	0	0	0	0	0	0	1	0	2002	

Voir la fin du tableau pour la remarque générale et les notes.

SPECIAL TABLE: D

World exports by commodity classes and by regions (continued)

In million U.S. dollars f.o.b.

Exports from ↓ / Exports to →	Year	World Monde 1/	Developed economies Econ. dévelop-pées 1/,2/	Developing economies economies en voie de développement 1/,2/ — Total	Developing economies — OPEC OPEP	Eastern Europe and fmr. USSR-Europe / Europe de l'Est et l'anc. URSS-Europe — Total 1/,5/	Eastern Europe and fmr. USSR-Europe — Former USSR-Eur. 6/	Developed economies — Europe — Total	Developed economies — Europe — EU UE	Developed economies — Europe — EFTA AELE	Developed economies — South Africa Afrique du Sud
Other manufactured goods (SITC, Rev. 2 and Rev. 3, 6 and 8)											
World 1/	1998	1486566	1038414	375181	42188	60707	21539	639612	595877	42558	5695
	1999	1494464	1057090	374484	38166	53948	16431	633038	592434	39388	5375
	2000	1600909	1111706	424442	43305	59174	19576	635376	594817	39317	5730
	2001	1556601	1077616	402618	47193	66238	22924	632776	592306	39183	5653
	2002	1624714	1124770	420236	49258	69136	23927	660465	618224	40897	5900
Developed economies 1/,2/	1998	931989	699006	184370	22382	41052	11665	492699	455492	36136	3677
	1999	933600	705062	185878	18711	37678	8743	486712	451332	34289	3348
	2000	968752	713339	210903	19348	40376	10126	473493	439258	33148	3418
	2001	940243	689598	197165	21054	45212	12395	472334	437222	34032	3338
	2002	966551	708893	202682	21643	46477	12742	485550	449455	34984	3431
Developing economies 1/,2/	1998	481306	290673	181846	18940	7561	3920	105668	101604	3973	1984
	1999	493427	306825	179504	18703	6070	2991	106441	102598	3729	1990
	2000	561904	349901	203440	22835	7402	3901	119124	114048	4942	2270
	2001	544119	337810	196031	24744	8578	4733	116167	112022	4004	2278
	2002	580639	360483	209188	26405	9154	5050	123964	119540	4273	2431
OPEC	1998	49223	27013	22101	3206	93	26	13029	12835	192	68
	1999	53673	30815	22647	3103	125	36	14192	13994	193	126
	2000	57716	33147	24280	3511	177	84	14967	14761	203	129
	2001	55831	32067	23546	4154	193	104	14543	14337	202	112
	2002	55853	32080	23555	4156	193	104	14549	14343	202	112
Eastern Europe and the former USSR 1/,5/	1998	73275	48737	8982	867	12094	5954	41247	38782	2450	34
	1999	67440	45203	9120	753	10200	4697	39884	38503	1371	37
	2000	70256	48378	10117	1124	11397	5549	42670	41422	1228	42
	2001	72242	50228	9442	1396	12448	5796	44295	43082	1148	37
	2002	80179	55747	10479	1549	13816	6433	49162	47815	1274	41
Former USSR-Europe 6/	1998	31508	17359	6291	483	4722	3704	11481	9684	1789	11
	1999	27333	13606	6715	461	4139	3157	9911	9192	712	22
	2000	26479	14508	7424	755	4547	3755	10773	10228	532	17
	2001	23885	13055	6514	950	4249	3522	9346	8917	377	4
	2002	25700	14047	7009	1022	4572	3790	10056	9595	406	4
Developed economies-Europe	1998	653375	524800	83105	14850	39581	10912	444016	409585	33401	2638
	1999	636762	519416	76689	11724	36412	8223	435683	403156	31473	2370
	2000	635191	511138	82195	12399	38983	9560	419058	387769	30257	2441
	2001	632761	502407	83708	13877	43745	11763	420472	388375	31051	2448
	2002	670383	532279	88685	14702	46346	12462	445472	411467	32897	2594
European Union	1998	616381	493221	78469	14053	38804	10701	419311	385266	33039	2559
	1999	599300	487451	71940	11044	35665	8055	411441	379257	31157	2304
	2000	595969	478121	76813	11628	38161	9334	394517	363537	29979	2368
	2001	595274	471479	78107	13030	42788	11444	396504	364759	30731	2385
	2002	631534	500198	82865	13824	45394	12141	420656	386978	32603	2530
European Free Trade Association	1998	36432	31057	4601	783	771	208	24245	23872	347	79
	1999	36893	31436	4714	661	743	165	23766	23438	302	66
	2000	38696	32534	5346	757	817	223	24110	23813	265	73
	2001	36961	30441	5568	834	951	314	23528	23189	305	63
	2002	38350	31585	5777	865	987	326	24412	24061	316	65
Other developed economies	1998	278614	174206	101266	7532	1472	753	48682	45906	2735	1039
	1999	296838	185646	109189	6987	1265	520	51029	48176	2815	978
	2000	333561	202202	128708	6948	1393	567	54435	51489	2891	977
	2001	307482	187191	113457	7177	1467	632	51862	48847	2981	890
	2002	300310	182825	110811	7010	1433	617	50652	47708	2911	869

For general note and footnotes see end of table.

Exportations mondiales par classes de marchandises et par régions (suite)

En millions de dollars E.-U. f.o.b.

Economies développées 1/,2/ — Canada	U.S.A. E.-U.	Japan Japon	Australia New Zealand Australie Nouvelle-Zélande	Developing economies / Economies en voie de développement 1/,2/ — Africa Afrique	America Amerique — Total	America Amerique — LAIA ALADI	Asia Asie — Mid. East Moyen Orient	Asia Asie — Other Autres 7/	Oceania Océanie	← Exportations vers / Année	Exportations en provenance de ↓
Articles manufacturés divers (CTCI, Rev. 2 et Rev. 3, 6 et 8)											
46420	251845	67412	17846	25615	77325	59178	46797	215106	1065	1998	Monde 1/
48813	267681	72988	18423	24573	72575	54823	41717	226147	1054	1999	
53699	302206	84305	18762	24121	83716	64067	46045	260911	990	2000	
49389	281979	80019	17145	26323	78975	59936	47281	239609	1010	2001	
51550	294318	83521	17895	27475	82431	62559	49349	250094	1120	2002	
39394	119476	25253	10964	16402	50941	40027	25426	84458	911	1998	Economies dévelopées 1/,2/
41612	127719	26025	10967	15434	49181	38753	20735	94138	901	1999	
45383	141924	29283	10651	14665	56057	44616	21558	112238	837	2000	
41303	128101	26840	9621	16151	51970	40981	21754	100354	856	2001	
42459	131685	27591	9890	16603	53424	42128	22363	103162	860	2002	
6773	127283	40563	6842	8330	25668	18716	19007	126573	732	1998	Economies en voie de développement 1/,2/
7004	136423	45635	7415	8246	22845	15740	18752	127402	723	1999	
8086	156329	53740	8073	8633	26978	19099	22174	143273	697	2000	
7894	149652	51920	7481	9372	26424	18657	22808	134886	633	2001	
8424	159696	55405	7983	10001	28198	19909	24338	143940	650	2002	
292	6232	7028	364	878	1468	1130	5285	14448	20	1998	OPEP
392	7398	8086	619	898	1298	936	5872	14527	47	1999	
410	8426	8578	635	939	1669	1252	6303	15300	57	2000	
369	8088	8385	569	1086	1621	1210	6109	14674	48	2001	
369	8091	8388	569	1086	1622	1210	6111	14680	50	2002	
254	5087	1596	40	883	720	438	2366	4081	2	1998	Europe de l'Est et l'ancienne URSS 1/,5/
197	3540	1328	41	893	553	333	2231	4613	1	1999	
230	3953	1282	38	823	685	356	2315	5406	1	2000	
192	4226	1259	43	800	585	302	2721	4375	2	2001	
213	4690	1397	48	888	649	335	3020	4856	2	2002	
109	3865	1507	3	532	410	190	1713	3539	1	1998	l'ancienne URSS-Europe 6/
93	2241	1240	5	587	333	163	1611	4093	0	1999	
72	2377	1192	4	540	410	130	1543	4822	0	2000	
38	2419	1160	9	519	313	94	1859	3770	0	2001	
41	2603	1248	10	558	337	101	2000	4057	0	2002	
4495	50990	11732	4784	13584	13427	10896	19927	29654	369	1998	Economies développées-Europe
4602	53135	11974	4716	12621	11496	9126	15813	30988	374	1999	
4975	59767	13244	4567	12056	12134	9732	17131	35041	366	2000	
4536	52688	12409	3981	13532	12185	9823	17114	34503	377	2001	
4806	55821	13147	4218	14337	12909	10407	18132	36554	360	2002	
4306	46622	10161	4547	13382	12851	10491	18821	27008	361	1998	Union Européenne
4409	48339	10223	4439	12390	10968	8767	14865	28049	367	1999	
4771	54285	11358	4311	11875	11549	9342	16091	31570	355	2000	
4350	48273	10803	3732	13308	11609	9450	16005	30931	363	2001	
4615	51213	11461	3959	14119	12316	10026	16980	32815	355	2002	
188	4315	1565	237	187	575	405	1102	2633	7	1998	Association Européenne de Libre Exchange
192	4746	1749	276	212	526	359	944	2928	7	1999	
202	5435	1884	255	166	583	389	1035	3458	10	2000	
184	4376	1602	249	211	573	372	1104	3560	13	2001	
191	4540	1662	258	219	595	386	1146	3694	14	2002	
34899	68485	13521	6180	2818	37513	29131	5499	54804	543	1998	Autres economies développées
37010	74584	14052	6251	2813	37685	29627	4922	63150	527	1999	
40409	82157	16039	6084	2609	43923	34884	4427	77198	472	2000	
36768	75412	14431	5640	2619	39785	31158	4640	65851	479	2001	
35910	73653	14094	5508	2558	38857	30431	4532	64315	480	2002	

Voir la fin du tableau pour la remarque générale et les notes.

SPECIAL TABLE: D

World exports by commodity classes and by regions (continued)

In million U.S. dollars f.o.b.

Exports to → / ↓ Exports from	Year	World / Monde 1/	Developed economies / Econ. dévelop-pées 1/,2/	Developing economies / economies en voie de développement 1/,2/: Total	Developing economies: OPEC / OPEP	Eastern Europe and fmr. USSR-Europe / Europe de l'Est et l'anc. URSS-Europe: Total 1/,5/	Eastern Europe and fmr. USSR-Europe: Former USSR-Eur. 6/	Developed economies: Europe: Total	Europe: EU / UE	Europe: EFTA / AELE	Developed economies: South Africa / Afrique du Sud
		Other manufactured goods (SITC, Rev. 2 and Rev. 3, 6 and 8) (continued)									
Canada	1998	48351	46307	1914	240	130	66	2475	2301	172	25
	1999	51816	49990	1735	216	90	37	2599	2474	125	17
	2000	57743	55663	1985	201	94	43	2749	2643	103	23
	2001	54502	52543	1884	217	75	36	2716	2625	88	20
	2002	52930	51028	1830	211	73	35	2638	2549	85	19
United States	1998	130068	76369	52837	3494	860	427	27963	26424	1518	517
	1999	131774	77786	53294	2896	692	256	27702	26100	1578	452
	2000	150389	87292	62342	2721	753	270	31486	29753	1691	443
	2001	139606	82688	56014	2862	899	363	31412	29436	1958	434
	2002	132549	78508	53182	2717	854	345	29824	27948	1859	412
Japan	1998	73855	34261	39286	3274	307	184	12348	11642	691	309
	1999	79968	34848	44798	3199	320	160	12525	11944	572	300
	2000	89963	35674	53913	3425	374	180	12173	11650	516	302
	2001	76747	30705	45712	3469	327	159	10888	10383	496	255
	2002	79290	31722	47227	3584	338	164	11249	10727	512	263
Australia, New Zealand	1998	10137	5713	4006	322	8	4	1117	1067	48	111
	1999	10828	5800	4342	398	7	2	1096	1026	69	116
	2000	12382	6256	4912	406	9	2	1033	996	37	91
	2001	12046	6307	4747	370	12	5	1149	1115	34	72
	2002	12150	6362	4788	373	12	5	1159	1125	34	73
Developing economies-Africa	1998	12734	10188	2218	500	33	12	8838	8722	110	191
	1999	12394	10242	1850	375	23	10	8947	8816	126	229
	2000	17963	15371	2391	555	45	25	13548	12658	878	356
	2001	18461	15571	2308	542	39	22	13809	13627	172	532
	2002	19395	16385	2425	569	41	23	14543	14352	181	559
Developing economies-America	1998	61936	43834	17779	2009	127	49	7775	7622	150	71
	1999	63478	48023	15311	1430	67	20	7492	7299	191	71
	2000	72928	54875	17791	1967	65	25	8098	7728	368	102
	2001	71045	53120	17666	2449	70	33	7917	7597	318	94
	2002	71992	53833	17902	2482	71	33	8027	7702	322	95
Developing economies-Europe 3/	1998	8101	6064	1505	82	522	148	5611	5260	349	4
	1999	7191	5330	1442	74	413	82	4935	4741	193	3
	2000	7602	5502	1600	70	496	100	5022	4798	222	4
	2001	7882	5572	1748	77	560	133	5195	4957	236	4
	2002	8317	5885	1845	81	591	140	5487	5236	249	4
Developing economies-Middle East	1998	49276	28926	18004	3930	1737	955	18636	18299	317	67
	1999	49373	29719	18008	3420	1077	468	18906	18565	311	58
	2000	51312	31143	18385	3693	1059	504	19383	19045	303	70
	2001	54761	32517	19869	5071	1553	835	20421	20082	293	80
	2002	55757	33109	20231	5163	1581	850	20793	20447	298	81
Developing economies-Other Asia	1998	347727	200636	141918	12419	5057	2756	64586	61487	3038	1645
	1999	359384	212485	142286	13404	4488	2411	65904	62930	2898	1626
	2000	410362	241963	162538	16543	5735	3247	72831	69582	3166	1738
	2001	390262	230044	153719	16598	6354	3710	68648	65586	2980	1568
	2002	426917	251651	168157	18157	6951	4058	75096	71746	3260	1715
Former USSR-Asia 7/.	1998	2549	1421	707	71	418	403	1282	1240	42	1
	1999	2593	1372	801	97	418	405	1238	1168	70	0
	2000	3265	1696	1097	207	470	439	1517	1278	239	0
	2001	3169	1677	1024	200	466	436	1503	1262	241	0
	2002	3490	1862	1128	220	513	480	1670	1404	265	0
Developing economies-Oceania	1998	1532	1020	422	0	85	0	217	208	9	6
	1999	1606	993	607	0	2	0	225	215	10	3
	2000	1737	996	734	7	2	0	193	188	5	0
	2001	1708	980	721	7	2	0	171	167	5	0
	2002	1696	1147	898	9	9	0	294	264	66	0

For general note and footnotes see end of table.

Exportations mondiales par classes de marchandises et par régions (suite)

En millions de dollars E.-U. f.o.b.

Economies développées 1/,2/ Canada	U.S.A. E.-U.	Japan Japon	Australia New Zealand Australie Nouvelle-Zélande	Developing economies Economies en voie de développement 1/,2/ Africa Afrique	America Amerique Total	America Amerique LAIA ALADI	Asia Asie Mid. East Moyen Orient	Asia Asie Other Autres 7/	Oceania Océanie	Année	← Exportations vers / Exportations en provenance de ↓
Articles manufacturés divers (CTCI, Rev. 2 et Rev. 3, 6 et 8) (suite)											
.	42759	855	134	82	811	604	159	853	1	1998	Canada
.	46391	818	106	96	673	484	158	797	1	1999	
.	51858	860	116	74	775	592	145	986	2	2000	
.	48994	638	103	65	762	587	138	915	2	2001	
.	47581	620	100	63	740	570	134	889	2	2002	
33539	.	10564	2618	1103	34132	26245	2538	14965	52	1998	Etats-Unis
35763	.	10167	2526	1038	34686	27067	2273	15191	52	1999	
39012	.	12346	2523	926	40425	31849	1891	18998	54	2000	
35584	.	11325	2271	993	36577	28382	1878	16465	48	2001	
33785	.	10753	2156	943	34728	26947	1783	15633	46	2002	
1062	19034	.	1415	634	2135	1910	2489	33921	89	1998	Japon
952	19472	.	1442	547	1894	1708	2125	40132	84	1999	
1076	20585	.	1375	461	2187	1974	2010	49157	83	2000	
894	17355	.	1200	477	2039	1831	2236	40879	69	2001	
924	17930	.	1240	493	2107	1892	2310	42234	71	2002	
123	1043	1503	1802	30	125	92	95	3356	399	1998	Australie, Nouvelle-Zélande
69	1113	1432	1954	33	94	60	113	3716	386	1999	
76	1329	1839	1853	29	135	94	98	4318	331	2000	
76	1396	1705	1872	26	81	59	96	4201	342	2001	
77	1408	1720	1888	26	82	60	97	4237	345	2002	
30	883	219	10	1416	21	15	285	483	1	1998	Economies en voie de développement-Afrique
29	852	164	11	1329	146	110	186	174	1	1999	
43	1086	270	25	1464	87	44	432	388	2	2000	
31	920	235	17	1474	40	31	464	318	1	2001	
33	967	247	18	1549	42	33	487	334	1	2002	
793	33791	1234	142	288	14263	11209	466	2752	3	1998	Economies en voie de développement-Amérique
701	38171	1392	151	279	12007	8931	289	2726	3	1999	
740	44188	1563	153	296	13905	10587	499	3083	3	2000	
779	43103	1065	130	316	14151	10628	395	2794	4	2001	
789	43678	1079	132	320	14340	10770	400	2831	4	2002	
23	391	7	7	57	34	32	122	28	0	1998	Economies en voie de développement-Europe 3/
21	332	10	8	48	28	22	120	38	0	1999	
40	393	9	7	39	42	19	175	48	0	2000	
33	291	8	13	51	41	14	157	42	1	2001	
35	307	8	14	54	43	15	166	44	1	2002	
249	4072	5476	61	1497	182	87	6069	10123	0	1998	Economies en voie de développement-Moyen Orient
278	4460	5461	73	1243	168	79	6252	10198	0	1999	
266	5320	5505	85	986	182	95	6637	10443	0	2000	
251	5535	5543	84	1319	230	130	7433	10737	0	2001	
256	5636	5644	86	1343	234	132	7568	10932	0	2002	
5677	88007	33118	6474	5072	10895	7127	12065	113069	698	1998	Economies en voie de développement-Autres Pays d'Asie
5974	92485	38108	7029	5347	10074	6206	11905	114112	688	1999	
6971	105204	45887	7670	5845	12294	7886	14431	129074	667	2000	
6774	99666	44567	7094	6209	11480	7372	14359	120785	602	2001	
7411	109027	48753	7760	6792	12559	8064	15707	132130	659	2002	
8	68	56	0	36	44	28	185	442	0	1998	l'ancienne URSS asiatique 7/
7	90	30	0	14	51	2	207	527	0	1999	
6	152	13	0	19	60	16	375	641	0	2000	
5	148	13	0	18	57	16	335	612	0	2001	
6	163	14	0	20	63	18	369	674	0	2002	
1	139	509	148	0	273	246	0	118	30	1998	Economies en voie de développement-Océanie
1	122	500	143	0	422	392	0	154	31	1999	
26	138	506	133	3	468	468	0	237	25	2000	
26	137	502	143	3	482	482	0	210	25	2001	
26	136	498	193	4	479	479	0	295	32	2002	

Voir la fin du tableau pour la remarque générale et les notes.

SPECIAL TABLE: D

World exports by commodity classes and by regions (continued)

In million U.S. dollars f.o.b.

Exports to → / ↓ Exports from	Year	World Monde 1/	Developed economies Econ. développées 1/,2/	Developing economies / economies en voie de développement 1/,2/ Total	Developing economies OPEC OPEP	Eastern Europe and fmr. USSR-Europe / Europe de l'Est et l'anc. URSS-Europe Total 1/,5/	Eastern Europe and fmr. USSR-Europe Former USSR-Eur. 6/	Developed economies Europe Total	Developed economies Europe EU UE	Developed economies Europe EFTA AELE	Developed economies South Africa Afrique du Sud
									Textile yarn and fabrics (SITC, Rev. 2 and Rev. 3, 65)		
World 1/	1998	161024	80836	68282	6630	9749	2586	56494	54214	2136	785
	1999	155994	77338	68639	6922	8978	2225	51843	49713	1992	758
	2000	164623	76811	77304	7740	9507	2641	49265	47295	1846	769
	2001	158067	73869	72902	7898	10581	3041	48087	46162	1803	742
	2002	164984	77101	76092	8244	11044	3174	50191	48182	1882	774
Developed economies 1/,2/	1998	81256	53600	18847	1686	7218	1325	42948	41052	1784	225
	1999	76015	49185	19354	1464	6835	1184	38648	36914	1636	190
	2000	74710	46061	21110	1401	7011	1338	35128	33564	1481	193
	2001	73081	44002	21071	1441	7729	1528	33667	32114	1470	177
	2002	75126	45233	21661	1481	7945	1571	34609	33013	1511	182
Developing economies 1/,2/	1998	75427	24614	49072	4917	1264	516	11149	10844	274	558
	1999	76048	25574	49007	5444	1102	444	10791	10467	285	567
	2000	85618	27902	55921	6323	1370	632	11468	11140	287	576
	2001	80502	26842	51576	6440	1653	824	11549	11255	256	563
	2002	85905	28644	55038	6872	1764	879	12324	12010	273	601
OPEC	1998	3632	1876	1736	342	19	4	1262	1208	53	19
	1999	4401	2153	2218	469	22	5	1301	1250	51	36
	2000	4893	2199	2638	512	43	23	1242	1199	43	34
	2001	4493	2042	2411	549	38	15	1152	1124	28	34
	2002	4495	2043	2412	549	38	15	1152	1124	28	34
Eastern Europe and the former USSR 1/,5/	1998	4341	2622	363	28	1268	745	2397	2318	78	1
	1999	3931	2578	278	13	1041	598	2404	2332	72	1
	2000	4296	2849	273	16	1127	671	2669	2590	78	1
	2001	4484	3024	256	18	1199	689	2871	2793	77	1
	2002	4977	3356	284	20	1331	765	3186	3100	85	1
Former USSR-Europe 6/	1998	1418	560	194	17	628	544	453	437	16	0
	1999	1198	525	154	5	486	422	448	436	12	0
	2000	1293	585	129	4	579	512	512	501	11	0
	2001	1261	592	106	4	563	500	536	520	16	0
	2002	1357	637	114	4	606	538	577	560	17	0
Developed economies-Europe	1998	63194	44849	9661	898	7102	1266	40259	38423	1731	179
	1999	56918	40661	8878	800	6744	1149	36300	34619	1586	148
	2000	53724	37282	8997	773	6920	1298	32787	31273	1432	145
	2001	53493	36021	9556	871	7640	1489	31661	30154	1425	140
	2002	56674	38163	10124	923	8094	1578	33543	31947	1510	148
European Union	1998	61170	43144	9458	854	6986	1241	38719	36903	1713	174
	1999	55052	39126	8673	761	6619	1126	34918	33256	1570	144
	2000	51979	35872	8788	730	6794	1273	31530	30034	1417	142
	2001	51841	34725	9332	818	7508	1462	30501	29010	1412	137
	2002	54999	36840	9900	868	7965	1551	32359	30777	1498	145
European Free Trade Association	1998	2000	1683	202	44	116	25	1519	1499	18	5
	1999	1841	1512	204	39	125	24	1359	1340	16	3
	2000	1722	1388	208	43	126	25	1237	1219	15	3
	2001	1627	1272	223	52	131	27	1140	1124	13	3
	2002	1688	1320	231	54	136	28	1183	1166	13	3
Other developed economies	1998	18061	8750	9186	788	116	59	2689	2630	53	47
	1999	19097	8524	10476	665	91	35	2348	2296	50	42
	2000	20985	8779	12113	628	91	40	2341	2291	49	48
	2001	19588	7981	11514	570	89	39	2006	1960	44	38
	2002	19131	7795	11245	557	87	38	1959	1914	43	37

For general note and footnotes see end of table.

Exportations mondiales par classes de marchandises et par régions (suite)

En millions de dollars E.-U. f.o.b.

Economies développées 1/,2/				Developing economies Economies en voie de développement 1/,2/						← Exportations vers	
Canada	U.S.A. E.-U.	Japan Japon	Australia New Zealand Australie Nouvelle-Zélande	Africa Afrique	America Amerique Total	America Amerique LAIA ALADI	Asia Asie Mid. East Moyen Orient	Asia Asie Other Autres 7/	Oceania Océanie	Année	Exportations en provenance de ↓
Fils et tissus de matières textiles (CTCI, Rev. 2 et Rev. 3, 65)											
3979	13057	4038	1841	5908	9186	6568	7495	43483	563	1998	Monde 1/
3953	13986	4251	1899	5984	9377	6788	6949	44587	480	1999	
4043	15552	4771	1795	6197	11395	8243	7650	50350	467	2000	
3701	14534	4635	1605	6919	10865	7226	7652	45707	395	2001	
3863	15170	4838	1675	7222	11340	7542	7987	47707	400	2002	
3093	5098	1060	809	3532	4194	3253	2610	7094	127	1998	Economies dévelopées 1/,2/
3026	5285	902	792	3428	4749	3901	2166	7879	113	1999	
3079	5680	986	701	3229	5921	4827	2130	8720	102	2000	
2841	5448	976	634	3660	6030	4201	2086	8125	77	2001	
2920	5600	1003	652	3762	6199	4319	2144	8352	78	2002	
866	7772	2969	1026	2359	4978	3310	4772	36254	436	1998	Economies en voie de développement 1/,2/
914	8556	3342	1101	2529	4613	2878	4705	36613	367	1999	
951	9718	3781	1090	2952	5462	3412	5449	41514	365	2000	
849	8958	3654	967	3246	4819	3017	5490	37495	318	2001	
906	9559	3899	1032	3464	5142	3219	5858	40012	315	2002	
81	256	204	52	116	195	160	457	966	2	1998	OPEP
133	252	330	100	155	182	145	617	1259	4	1999	
98	392	337	96	173	255	199	671	1525	7	2000	
54	409	315	79	186	252	205	644	1319	6	2001	
54	409	315	79	186	252	205	644	1320	7	2002	
19	187	9	6	18	13	5	113	135	0	1998	Europe de l'Est et l'ancienne URSS 1/,5/
13	146	8	5	27	15	9	79	95	0	1999	
13	155	5	4	16	12	5	71	116	0	2000	
12	128	6	4	13	15	8	77	87	0	2001	
13	142	7	4	14	17	9	85	97	0	2002	
2	98	6	0	3	6	2	62	106	0	1998	l'ancienne URSS-Europe 6/
2	70	5	0	19	9	7	39	73	0	1999	
2	69	2	0	5	4	0	19	93	0	2000	
2	50	3	0	4	6	3	17	69	0	2001	
2	54	3	0	4	6	3	18	74	0	2002	
334	2624	799	356	3399	877	719	1943	2142	17	1998	Economies développées-Europe
305	2639	660	339	3282	715	578	1649	2203	18	1999	
310	2802	700	302	3092	767	627	1679	2436	20	2000	
305	2703	726	276	3500	757	622	1647	2545	22	2001	
323	2864	769	292	3708	802	659	1745	2696	23	2002	
323	2517	772	348	3375	854	699	1872	2069	17	1998	Union Européenne
295	2539	636	330	3258	694	560	1578	2124	18	1999	
299	2706	673	292	3074	746	608	1602	2353	19	2000	
296	2621	697	271	3470	736	602	1574	2455	21	2001	
314	2781	739	288	3681	781	639	1670	2605	22	2002	
11	107	27	8	23	23	20	71	73	0	1998	Association Européenne de Libre Exchange
10	99	23	10	24	20	18	71	79	0	1999	
10	95	26	10	18	21	19	76	83	0	2000	
9	82	27	5	29	21	20	73	90	0	2001	
9	85	28	5	30	22	21	76	93	0	2002	
2759	2474	261	453	133	3317	2534	667	4952	109	1998	Autres economies développées
2721	2646	242	453	146	4034	3323	516	5675	95	1999	
2769	2878	286	399	137	5154	4199	450	6284	83	2000	
2536	2745	250	359	161	5273	3579	439	5580	56	2001	
2477	2681	244	351	157	5150	3496	429	5450	55	2002	

Voir la fin du tableau pour la remarque générale et les notes.

SPECIAL TABLE: D

World exports by commodity classes and by regions (continued)

In million U.S. dollars f.o.b.

Exports to → / ↓ Exports from	Year	World / Monde 1/	Developed economies / Econ. dévelop-pées 1/,2/	Developing economies / economies en voie de développement 1/,2/		Eastern Europe and fmr. USSR-Europe / Europe de l'Est et l'anc. URSS-Europe		Developed economies			
								Europe			South Africa
				Total	OPEC / OPEP	Total 1/,5/	Former USSR-Eur. 6/	Total	EU / UE	EFTA / AELE	Afrique du Sud
											Textile yarn and fabrics (SITC, Rev. 2 and Rev. 3, 65) (continued)
Canada	1998	1919	1812	91	12	16	7	107	105	2	6
	1999	2032	1950	71	7	11	4	94	92	2	3
	2000	2205	2122	75	8	8	2	83	81	2	7
	2001	2163	2084	73	7	6	1	64	63	1	3
	2002	2101	2024	71	7	6	1	62	61	1	3
United States	1998	8984	4692	4215	284	77	37	1491	1466	24	29
	1999	9252	4321	4870	204	60	20	1191	1171	20	25
	2000	10548	4484	6013	166	51	22	1288	1268	19	29
	2001	10096	3995	6047	156	54	25	1105	1081	23	23
	2002	9586	3793	5741	148	51	24	1049	1026	22	22
Japan	1998	5971	1395	4561	465	15	11	721	695	23	8
	1999	6598	1397	5189	419	13	8	711	686	23	9
	2000	7023	1337	5665	419	21	12	645	622	23	8
	2001	6198	1104	5075	374	19	9	544	527	16	7
	2002	6403	1141	5243	386	20	9	562	544	17	7
Australia, New Zealand	1998	483	293	185	15	0	0	44	43	0	3
	1999	503	302	199	19	0	0	38	37	0	3
	2000	480	288	190	22	0	0	40	40	0	3
	2001	445	291	153	18	0	0	30	30	1	4
	2002	449	294	154	18	0	0	30	30	1	4
Developing economies-Africa	1998	1073	744	274	59	7	1	581	571	8	24
	1999	1000	670	279	74	6	2	543	531	11	24
	2000	1206	841	307	62	7	3	657	641	11	44
	2001	1036	711	262	37	6	3	562	550	8	49
	2002	1088	748	275	39	6	3	592	579	8	51
Developing economies-America	1998	4181	2415	1727	195	10	3	279	265	14	3
	1999	4187	2685	1487	148	6	1	242	231	11	3
	2000	4630	2896	1703	179	5	1	235	224	11	5
	2001	4000	2456	1516	208	5	1	257	248	9	4
	2002	4053	2489	1536	211	5	1	261	251	9	4
Developing economies-Europe 3/	1998	605	367	193	6	44	12	336	334	2	0
	1999	464	319	105	5	39	9	292	289	3	0
	2000	474	320	102	4	52	17	296	292	5	0
	2001	523	331	132	6	59	21	311	307	4	0
	2002	552	350	139	6	62	22	328	324	4	0
Developing economies-Middle East	1998	4887	3258	973	363	348	172	2645	2557	79	32
	1999	4982	3485	1002	370	277	103	2740	2641	84	24
	2000	5267	3586	1060	383	364	137	2732	2647	73	29
	2001	6061	3848	1467	640	482	180	3018	2951	55	27
	2002	6171	3918	1494	652	491	183	3073	3005	56	27
Developing economies-Other Asia	1998	64656	17816	45895	4294	854	329	7307	7117	170	498
	1999	65388	18400	46122	4847	774	329	6973	6775	175	516
	2000	74002	20243	52725	5694	941	474	7548	7337	187	498
	2001	68840	19480	48173	5549	1101	619	7400	7199	181	483
	2002	75306	21310	52698	6070	1204	677	8095	7875	198	528
Former USSR-Asia 7/.	1998	126	32	60	2	34	31	31	31	1	0
	1999	156	26	95	7	35	32	25	25	0	0
	2000	161	25	100	15	36	34	24	24	0	0
	2001	135	25	78	11	33	30	23	23	0	0
	2002	149	28	86	12	36	33	26	26	0	0
Developing economies-Oceania	1998	25	15	10	0	0	0	0	0	0	0
	1999	27	15	12	0	1	0	0	0	0	0
	2000	40	15	25	1	0	0	0	0	0	0
	2001	42	16	25	1	0	0	0	0	0	0
	2002	42	19	31	1	0	0	0	0	0	0

For general note and footnotes see end of table.

Exportations mondiales par classes de marchandises et par régions (suite)

En millions de dollars E.-U. f.o.b.

Economies développées 1/,2/				Developing economies Economies en voie de développement 1/,2/						← Exportations vers	
Canada	U.S.A. E.-U.	Japan Japon	Australia New Zealand Australie Nouvelle-Zélande	Africa Afrique	America Amerique Total	America Amerique LAIA ALADI	Asia Asie Mid. East Moyen Orient	Asia Asie Other Autres 7/	Oceania Océanie	Année	Exportations en provenance de ↓
Fils et tissus de matières textiles (CTCI, Rev. 2 et Rev. 3, 65) (suite)											
.	1677	7	13	2	43	36	16	31	0	1998	Canada
.	1833	5	12	2	34	29	8	26	0	1999	
.	2014	5	11	2	36	31	8	29	0	2000	
.	1998	6	10	2	32	27	6	32	0	2001	
.	1940	6	10	2	31	26	6	31	0	2002	
2693	.	241	179	44	3168	2404	248	745	6	1998	Etats-Unis
2660	.	223	159	41	3906	3211	183	727	5	1999	
2710	.	268	141	36	5019	4076	129	823	4	2000	
2485	.	233	110	50	5151	3470	128	713	3	2001	
2359	.	221	104	47	4891	3295	122	677	3	2002	
40	550	.	75	24	71	60	384	4051	30	1998	Japon
38	558	.	77	27	60	52	307	4765	29	1999	
40	583	.	56	23	59	52	288	5264	31	2000	
34	475	.	41	29	53	45	279	4695	19	2001	
35	491	.	42	30	55	46	288	4851	20	2002	
17	51	8	168	4	3	3	3	101	74	1998	Australie, Nouvelle-Zélande
13	52	8	187	5	2	2	3	127	62	1999	
8	52	9	176	2	4	4	4	132	48	2000	
5	58	7	185	2	4	4	4	109	34	2001	
5	59	7	187	2	4	4	4	110	34	2002	
3	131	2	2	203	3	3	42	16	0	1998	Economies en voie de développement-Afrique
4	94	3	2	219	6	6	28	17	0	1999	
6	126	3	4	217	10	10	45	21	0	2000	
4	90	4	2	192	4	4	39	21	0	2001	
4	95	4	2	202	4	4	41	22	0	2002	
110	1960	50	12	7	1644	1385	31	43	0	1998	Economies en voie de développement-Amérique
99	2277	50	13	5	1371	1133	20	90	1	1999	
104	2482	52	17	6	1524	1269	14	158	0	2000	
98	2045	39	10	7	1369	1160	14	125	1	2001	
99	2072	40	10	7	1387	1175	14	127	1	2002	
3	26	0	0	3	1	1	11	2	0	1998	Economies en voie de développement-Europe 3/
2	24	0	0	3	2	0	9	2	0	1999	
1	22	0	0	2	2	1	10	2	0	2000	
1	18	0	0	4	1	0	11	2	0	2001	
1	19	0	0	4	1	0	12	2	0	2002	
100	362	32	12	132	26	19	510	246	0	1998	Economies en voie de développement-Moyen Orient
116	450	44	19	179	33	24	500	233	0	1999	
81	586	49	21	153	43	35	538	278	0	2000	
46	602	51	17	245	50	41	807	310	0	2001	
47	613	52	17	249	51	42	822	316	0	2002	
652	5292	2884	986	2013	3300	1901	4178	35946	432	1998	Economies en voie de développement-Autres Pays d'Asie
693	5710	3245	1054	2124	3198	1714	4147	36267	363	1999	
758	6501	3677	1035	2574	3883	2097	4842	41034	361	2000	
699	6202	3560	922	2797	3396	1812	4619	37016	314	2001	
765	6785	3894	1009	3060	3715	1982	5053	40493	343	2002	
0	1	0	0	0	0	0	52	8	0	1998	l'ancienne URSS asiatique 7/
0	1	0	0	0	0	0	85	9	0	1999	
0	1	0	0	0	0	0	92	8	0	2000	
0	1	0	0	0	0	0	71	7	0	2001	
0	1	0	0	0	0	0	78	8	0	2002	
0	1	0	14	0	3	2	0	2	4	1998	Economies en voie de développement-Océanie
0	1	0	13	0	4	2	0	4	3	1999	
0	1	0	14	0	0	0	0	21	3	2000	
0	1	0	15	0	0	0	0	22	3	2001	
0	1	0	20	0	0	0	0	31	4	2002	

Voir la fin du tableau pour la remarque générale et les notes.

SPECIAL TABLE: D

World exports by commodity classes and by regions (continued)

In million U.S. dollars f.o.b.

Exports to → / ↓ Exports from	Year	World / Monde 1/	Developed economies / Econ. dévelop-pées 1/,2/	Developing economies / economies en voie de développement 1/,2/ — Total	Developing economies — OPEC / OPEP	Eastern Europe and fmr. USSR-Europe / Europe de l'Est et l'anc. URSS-Europe — Total 1/,5/	Eastern Europe — Former USSR-Eur. 6/	Developed economies — Europe — Total	Europe — EU / UE	Europe — EFTA / AELE	South Africa / Afrique du Sud
											Iron and steel (SITC, Rev. 2 and Rev. 3, 67)
World 1/	1998	142713	89210	45071	6224	5624	1570	61327	57784	3499	407
	1999	124976	76028	41623	4760	4835	1452	52454	49782	2636	297
	2000	136315	83781	47170	5808	5052	1242	56726	53933	2756	309
	2001	128011	76984	44933	6925	5831	1599	54788	52032	2676	291
	2002	133612	80353	46899	7228	6086	1669	57185	54309	2793	304
Developed economies 1/,2/	1998	93742	68689	21848	3505	2910	603	52427	49221	3171	280
	1999	82498	59147	20357	2720	2805	725	45638	43086	2521	204
	2000	89226	63216	22813	2792	3007	569	48016	45577	2410	195
	2001	85340	59348	22484	3338	3356	672	46351	43976	2340	202
	2002	87728	61009	23113	3431	3450	691	47648	45206	2405	208
Developing economies 1/,2/	1998	32742	14094	18369	2190	248	161	4765	4578	179	112
	1999	29012	12521	16196	1661	249	158	3593	3525	63	80
	2000	35525	15477	19667	2417	286	169	4822	4572	243	94
	2001	31538	12601	18358	2887	478	357	4130	3903	220	85
	2002	33655	13447	19590	3081	510	381	4407	4165	235	91
OPEC	1998	2105	730	1374	317	1	0	258	256	2	1
	1999	2084	694	1373	227	0	0	226	223	2	0
	2000	2415	844	1525	371	10	9	326	325	1	6
	2001	2109	771	1301	452	34	33	334	331	3	2
	2002	2110	771	1302	452	34	33	334	331	3	2
Eastern Europe and the former USSR 1/,5/	1998	16229	6427	4853	529	2466	806	4134	3984	148	15
	1999	13465	4360	5070	380	1781	569	3223	3170	52	13
	2000	11564	5088	4690	598	1759	505	3888	3784	103	20
	2001	11133	5035	4091	701	1997	571	4306	4153	115	4
	2002	12356	5588	4540	778	2216	634	4779	4609	128	4
Former USSR-Europe 6/	1998	10597	3244	3813	332	1084	719	1314	1250	64	10
	1999	9301	2007	4223	282	819	526	1120	1110	10	8
	2000	6612	2212	3806	476	594	435	1355	1313	43	17
	2001	6022	2167	3195	531	658	483	1681	1600	43	2
	2002	6480	2332	3438	571	708	520	1809	1722	46	2
Developed economies-Europe	1998	67315	56105	8072	1832	2846	553	50428	47545	2849	222
	1999	57584	48520	6152	1322	2723	669	43787	41450	2306	160
	2000	61582	51569	6903	1426	2922	518	45744	43510	2206	149
	2001	60549	49339	7774	1823	3285	627	44315	42126	2155	167
	2002	64149	52273	8236	1931	3480	664	46950	44631	2283	177
European Union	1998	65312	54223	7994	1814	2803	548	48711	45838	2840	219
	1999	55812	46845	6092	1317	2687	668	42283	39956	2297	158
	2000	59876	49974	6839	1419	2874	513	44333	42109	2196	147
	2001	58932	47835	7714	1815	3233	621	42946	40769	2143	165
	2002	62522	50749	8184	1926	3430	659	45562	43252	2274	175
European Free Trade Association	1998	2002	1883	77	18	43	5	1717	1707	9	3
	1999	1771	1675	60	5	36	1	1503	1494	8	2
	2000	1706	1594	64	7	48	5	1411	1400	10	2
	2001	1615	1504	60	7	52	6	1369	1356	12	2
	2002	1676	1561	62	7	54	6	1420	1407	12	2
Other developed economies	1998	26427	12584	13777	1673	64	50	1999	1676	322	58
	1999	24915	10626	14205	1397	83	56	1852	1636	215	44
	2000	27643	11647	15910	1366	85	50	2272	2067	204	46
	2001	24792	10009	14710	1515	72	45	2036	1851	185	35
	2002	24214	9776	14367	1480	70	44	1989	1808	181	34

For general note and footnotes see end of table.

Exportations mondiales par classes de marchandises et par régions (suite)

En millions de dollars E.-U. f.o.b.

Economies développées 1/,2/				Developing economies / Economies en voie de développement 1/,2/						← Exportations vers	
Canada	U.S.A. / E.-U.	Japan / Japon	Australia New Zealand / Australie Nouvelle-Zélande	Africa / Afrique	America / Amerique: Total	America / Amerique: LAIA / ALADI	Asia / Asie: Mid. East / Moyen Orient	Asia / Asie: Other / Autres 7/	Oceania / Océanie	Année	Exportations en provenance de ↓
Fer et acier (CTCI, Rev. 2 et Rev. 3, 67)											
4294	18881	2647	1088	4038	7330	6166	6561	26079	117	1998	Monde 1/
3966	14856	2933	1063	2935	5395	4374	5399	27035	100	1999	
4790	17043	3418	1045	2719	6443	5317	6134	30886	108	2000	
3987	14087	2418	987	3273	6431	5242	6789	27446	125	2001	
4161	14703	2524	1030	3416	6712	5471	7086	28647	127	2002	
3628	10971	333	758	2319	3912	3432	3189	11877	92	1998	Economies dévelopées 1/,2/
3351	8499	507	728	1670	3123	2745	2302	12762	81	1999	
3888	9604	632	665	1560	3613	3213	2580	14521	77	2000	
3335	8171	440	639	1924	3664	3270	2871	13457	84	2001	
3428	8400	452	657	1978	3767	3361	2951	13834	80	2002	
540	6007	2160	329	1228	2963	2384	1979	12058	24	1998	Economies en voie de développement 1/,2/
538	5548	2273	334	793	1963	1427	1724	11602	20	1999	
803	6477	2741	379	742	2386	1846	2322	14052	31	2000	
614	5335	1943	345	873	2371	1778	2776	12164	41	2001	
655	5693	2073	368	932	2530	1897	2962	12980	40	2002	
45	393	25	7	224	311	254	450	389	0	1998	OPEP
23	381	53	11	135	220	174	555	462	1	1999	
36	427	41	9	90	348	287	674	402	10	2000	
24	354	40	17	86	304	255	565	343	3	2001	
24	354	40	17	86	304	255	565	343	2	2002	
126	1902	155	1	492	456	349	1394	2144	1	1998	Europe de l'Est et l'ancienne URSS 1/,5/
77	809	153	1	472	309	202	1374	2672	0	1999	
99	962	46	1	416	444	257	1232	2313	0	2000	
38	580	35	3	476	396	193	1142	1824	0	2001	
42	644	39	3	528	440	214	1267	2024	0	2002	
70	1668	141	0	363	245	172	1146	2008	1	1998	l'ancienne URSS-Europe 6/
62	616	143	0	379	202	118	1103	2522	0	1999	
49	703	40	0	344	284	117	923	2186	0	2000	
12	400	24	1	376	267	77	832	1698	0	2001	
13	430	26	1	405	287	83	895	1827	0	2002	
647	4165	159	260	1598	1440	1247	2186	2373	21	1998	Economies développées-Europe
546	3508	135	218	1095	1041	878	1489	2085	26	1999	
665	4416	195	225	1120	1111	959	1867	2329	23	2000	
541	3783	182	195	1414	1179	1029	1892	2790	20	2001	
573	4008	193	207	1498	1249	1090	2004	2956	21	2002	
639	4041	138	251	1583	1434	1244	2172	2334	21	1998	Union Européenne
539	3378	116	206	1079	1035	872	1483	2057	26	1999	
660	4277	170	215	1106	1102	951	1859	2299	23	2000	
535	3687	157	190	1399	1174	1025	1885	2759	20	2001	
568	3912	167	202	1484	1246	1087	2000	2927	19	2002	
8	124	21	8	15	5	4	13	39	0	1998	Association Européenne de Libre Exchange
7	129	19	13	16	7	6	6	29	0	1999	
6	139	25	10	14	9	8	7	30	0	2000	
6	96	25	5	15	5	5	7	31	0	2001	
6	100	26	5	16	5	5	7	32	0	2002	
2981	6806	173	499	721	2472	2185	1003	9504	71	1998	Autres economies développées
2806	4991	373	509	575	2081	1867	813	10677	55	1999	
3222	5188	437	440	441	2502	2254	713	12191	55	2000	
2794	4388	258	444	510	2485	2241	979	10668	63	2001	
2729	4286	252	434	498	2427	2189	956	10419	60	2002	

Voir la fin du tableau pour la remarque générale et les notes.

SPECIAL TABLE: D

World exports by commodity classes and by regions (continued)

In million U.S. dollars f.o.b.

Exports from ↓ / Exports to →	Year	World Monde 1/	Developed economies Econ. dévelop-pées 1/,2/	Developing economies economies en voie de développement 1/,2/ Total	Developing economies OPEC OPEP	Eastern Europe and fmr. USSR-Europe Europe de l'Est et l'anc. URSS-Europe Total 1/,5/	Eastern Europe and fmr. USSR-Europe Former USSR-Eur. 6/	Developed economies Europe Total	Developed economies Europe EU UE	Developed economies Europe EFTA AELE	Developed economies South Africa Afrique du Sud
											Iron and steel (SITC, Rev. 2 and Rev. 3, 67) (continued)
Canada	1998	3134	3064	67	7	4	3	51	48	4	1
	1999	2888	2818	69	6	1	0	48	46	1	0
	2000	3216	3129	84	4	3	0	46	46	1	0
	2001	2800	2696	101	2	3	0	49	49	0	1
	2002	2719	2618	98	2	3	0	48	48	0	1
United States	1998	5706	3273	2420	366	13	9	531	503	28	11
	1999	5193	3211	1970	139	12	8	477	438	38	8
	2000	5959	3789	2142	148	28	20	668	600	68	10
	2001	5658	3358	2269	168	31	22	592	554	38	11
	2002	5372	3188	2154	160	29	21	562	526	36	10
Japan	1998	14867	4790	10029	1160	47	37	912	624	287	38
	1999	13459	2670	10721	1099	67	47	590	428	161	29
	2000	14832	2517	12264	1095	51	28	586	459	127	26
	2001	13570	2444	11090	1217	36	22	663	525	137	19
	2002	14020	2525	11457	1257	37	23	685	542	142	20
Australia, New Zealand	1998	1305	717	587	49	0	0	182	182	0	8
	1999	1014	526	487	68	0	0	87	87	0	6
	2000	811	431	379	52	0	0	84	84	0	10
	2001	526	227	298	34	0	0	24	24	0	3
	2002	531	229	301	34	0	0	24	24	0	3
Developing economies-Africa	1998	673	332	339	56	1	0	244	244	0	12
	1999	593	299	293	26	0	0	201	198	3	14
	2000	799	384	401	78	11	9	242	227	14	20
	2001	730	350	369	78	6	5	230	215	15	13
	2002	767	368	388	82	6	5	242	226	16	14
Developing economies-America	1998	8367	4766	3566	557	24	13	1156	1141	15	12
	1999	7086	4557	2517	263	11	6	1164	1152	12	11
	2000	7971	5024	2928	383	9	7	1339	1319	20	19
	2001	7185	4296	2873	535	9	6	1141	1132	9	11
	2002	7281	4354	2911	542	9	6	1157	1148	9	11
Developing economies-Europe 3/	1998	837	652	141	9	44	2	592	451	140	0
	1999	528	379	112	3	37	6	335	317	18	0
	2000	737	516	173	3	48	8	418	402	16	0
	2001	647	426	171	5	50	9	393	373	20	0
	2002	683	450	180	5	53	9	415	394	21	[illegible]
Developing economies-Middle East	1998	2599	922	1641	696	18	7	574	563	5	0
	1999	2563	969	1528	462	25	3	661	654	2	1
	2000	2827	1180	1540	615	28	2	783	771	6	6
	2001	3416	1229	1866	908	235	194	839	833	1	2
	2002	3478	1251	1900	925	239	198	854	848	1	2
Developing economies-Other Asia	1998	20047	7287	12597	872	162	139	2120	2100	19	85
	1999	18013	6177	11658	906	176	143	1151	1122	28	5[illegible]
	2000	22816	8147	14478	1338	190	142	1910	1723	186	49
	2001	19249	6110	12958	1361	178	143	1419	1242	176	5[illegible]
	2002	21057	6684	14175	1489	195	156	1552	1359	193	6[illegible]
Former USSR-Asia 7/.	1998	725	186	413	50	126	122	127	127	0	[illegible]
	1999	750	137	483	70	130	127	55	40	15	[illegible]
	2000	1136	313	687	185	135	129	269	102	167	[illegible]
	2001	1084	301	656	180	127	121	260	102	158	[illegible]
	2002	1194	334	723	198	140	133	289	113	174	[illegible]
Developing economies-Oceania	1998	220	134	85	0	0	0	79	79	0	[illegible]
	1999	229	140	89	0	0	0	82	82	0	[illegible]
	2000	375	227	147	0	0	0	130	130	0	[illegible]
	2001	311	189	122	0	0	0	108	108	0	[illegible]
	2002	309	221	152	0	0	0	186	171	0	[illegible]

For general note and footnotes see end of table.

Exportations mondiales par classes de marchandises et par régions (suite)

En millions de dollars E.-U. f.o.b.

Economies développées 1/,2/ — Canada	U.S.A. E.-U.	Japan Japon	Australia New Zealand Australie Nouvelle-Zélande	Developing economies Economies en voie de développement 1/,2/ — Africa Afrique	America Amerique — Total	America Amerique — LAIA ALADI	Asia Asie — Mid. East Moyen Orient	Asia Asie — Other Autres 7/	Oceania Océanie	Année	← Exportations vers / Exportations en provenance de ↓
Fer et acier (CTCI, Rev. 2 et Rev. 3, 67) (suite)											
.	2999	6	7	2	30	24	4	31	0	1998	Canada
.	2761	4	5	3	28	22	6	32	0	1999	
.	3071	8	3	2	39	29	4	39	0	2000	
.	2634	7	4	0	64	57	3	34	0	2001	
.	2558	7	4	0	62	55	3	33	0	2002	
2558	.	101	43	237	1622	1447	135	424	2	1998	Etats-Unis
2557	.	114	32	172	1391	1275	53	351	1	1999	
2910	.	149	33	50	1596	1474	58	430	1	2000	
2593	.	106	27	108	1691	1554	77	391	1	2001	
2462	.	101	26	103	1606	1475	73	371	1	2002	
324	3224	.	289	269	670	596	753	8332	4	1998	Japon
190	1563	.	295	188	513	454	647	9370	2	1999	
227	1416	.	259	190	650	565	562	10856	6	2000	
145	1359	.	256	193	594	512	820	9473	9	2001	
150	1404	.	264	199	614	529	847	9787	9	2002	
55	296	52	124	4	66	40	20	432	66	1998	Australie, Nouvelle-Zélande
6	247	32	148	7	45	15	24	360	52	1999	
12	179	32	114	4	53	24	19	256	47	2000	
9	58	8	125	2	22	10	6	216	52	2001	
9	59	8	126	2	22	10	6	218	52	2002	
3	40	31	0	274	0	0	59	6	0	1998	Economies en voie de développement-Afrique
0	47	37	0	231	19	19	35	8	0	1999	
8	47	64	3	197	13	10	103	87	1	2000	
5	40	59	2	204	8	6	97	60	0	2001	
5	42	62	2	214	8	6	102	63	0	2002	
270	3161	150	17	102	2460	2038	230	772	0	1998	Economies en voie de développement-Amérique
188	2934	251	10	136	1510	1178	88	782	0	1999	
260	3182	209	14	139	1833	1480	165	790	0	2000	
272	2726	132	11	141	1843	1448	172	716	0	2001	
276	2762	134	11	143	1868	1467	174	726	0	2002	
1	55	0	0	10	1	1	20	1	0	1998	Economies en voie de développement-Europe 3/
2	39	0	0	3	1	1	24	1	0	1999	
21	74	0	0	1	0	0	59	3	0	2000	
16	14	0	0	2	0	0	45	4	0	2001	
17	15	0	0	2	0	0	47	4	0	2002	
38	165	9	2	378	97	24	805	357	0	1998	Economies en voie de développement-Moyen Orient
38	133	5	1	201	81	15	848	392	0	1999	
41	237	2	1	158	79	22	939	362	0	2000	
39	232	2	1	276	106	38	1064	414	0	2001	
40	236	2	1	281	108	39	1083	422	0	2002	
228	2566	1937	309	464	401	319	865	10842	22	1998	Economies en voie de développement-Autres Pays d'Asie
310	2375	1946	322	222	350	213	730	10334	18	1999	
473	2905	2403	359	247	460	334	1056	12666	29	2000	
283	2296	1698	330	250	414	286	1398	10850	40	2001	
310	2512	1857	361	273	453	313	1529	11869	44	2002	
6	33	17	0	35	43	28	96	239	0	1998	l'ancienne URSS asiatique 7/
5	54	22	0	12	50	2	78	342	0	1999	
4	36	0	0	17	59	16	225	385	0	2000	
4	32	0	0	16	56	16	217	365	0	2001	
4	35	0	0	18	62	18	239	402	0	2002	
0	19	33	1	0	3	1	0	81	2	1998	Economies en voie de développement-Océanie
0	20	34	1	0	3	1	0	84	2	1999	
0	32	64	1	0	0	0	0	146	1	2000	
0	27	53	1	0	0	0	0	120	1	2001	
0	27	53	1	0	0	0	0	168	1	2002	

Voir la fin du tableau pour la remarque générale et les notes.

SPECIAL TABLE: D

World exports by commodity classes and by regions (continued)

In million U.S. dollars f.o.b.

Non-ferrous metals (SITC, Rev. 2 and Rev. 3, 68)

Exports from ↓ / Exports to →	Year	World Monde 1/	Developed economies Econ. dévelop-pées 1/,2/	Developing economies economies en voie de développement 1/,2/ Total	Developing economies OPEC OPEP	Eastern Europe and fmr. USSR-Europe Europe de l'Est et l'anc. URSS-Europe Total 1/,5/	Eastern Europe and fmr. USSR-Europe Former USSR-Eur. 6/	Developed economies Europe Total	Developed economies Europe EU UE	Developed economies Europe EFTA AELE	Developed economies South Africa Afrique du Sud
World 1/	1998	111433	76282	31850	2182	2432	628	46107	42460	3629	240
	1999	111040	74762	32633	2145	2421	609	43130	40400	2707	230
	2000	125507	82656	38564	2489	2879	777	47596	44950	2614	293
	2001	117948	77845	35467	2547	3007	849	46004	43353	2614	274
	2002	123109	81251	37019	2658	3139	886	48017	45250	2728	286
Developed economies 1/,2/	1998	60437	47180	11401	942	1322	253	31393	29576	1799	198
	1999	61971	47548	12165	906	1348	230	29889	28139	1735	156
	2000	69777	52359	14427	898	1662	328	32893	31141	1735	196
	2001	65730	49783	13032	963	1755	355	32699	30775	1907	112
	2002	67569	51176	13397	990	1804	365	33614	31636	1960	115
Developing economies 1/,2/	1998	39019	18756	19850	1228	279	208	7210	6918	290	41
	1999	39218	18951	19840	1231	289	220	7071	6718	350	74
	2000	44230	20983	22828	1579	350	244	7685	7197	482	97
	2001	42249	19970	21443	1574	377	269	7793	7295	492	161
	2002	45085	21310	22882	1680	402	287	8316	7785	525	172
OPEC	1998	15099	6686	8410	537	3	0	721	699	22	1
	1999	15381	6855	8521	535	1	1	672	666	6	0
	2000	15827	7039	8783	539	1	1	732	716	15	1
	2001	15819	7044	8771	575	3	3	750	732	16	4
	2002	15825	7047	8775	575	3	3	750	732	16	4
Eastern Europe and the former USSR 1/,5/	1998	11977	10346	598	12	831	167	7505	5966	1539	1
	1999	9851	8262	627	8	784	159	6170	5542	622	0
	2000	11501	9314	1309	13	866	206	7018	6612	397	0
	2001	9968	8092	992	10	876	225	5511	5283	216	1
	2002	11063	8981	1101	11	972	250	6117	5863	240	1
Former USSR-Europe 6/	1998	9297	8387	364	10	353	85	5618	4104	1514	0
	1999	7255	6319	407	4	353	97	4319	3725	589	0
	2000	8312	6913	1024	3	375	148	4736	4364	362	0
	2001	6892	5908	676	6	307	133	3408	3220	174	0
	2002	7416	6357	727	6	330	143	3667	3465	187	0
Developed economies-Europe	1998	37588	32640	3393	487	1293	243	28285	26637	1631	123
	1999	36305	31278	3242	391	1325	223	26769	25331	1423	82
	2000	42393	36150	4062	396	1628	311	29947	28398	1534	133
	2001	40703	34353	4050	490	1721	339	29314	27669	1629	87
	2002	43123	36396	4291	519	1823	359	31057	29314	1726	92
European Union	1998	31870	27338	3010	469	1259	236	24145	22641	1486	121
	1999	30085	25559	2772	380	1295	220	22532	21211	1306	80
	2000	34541	29037	3367	385	1582	292	24807	23348	1444	131
	2001	34197	28696	3250	477	1671	325	24757	23230	1512	86
	2002	36280	30444	3448	506	1773	345	26265	24645	1604	91
European Free Trade Association	1998	5711	5295	382	18	34	7	4134	3989	145	2
	1999	6214	5713	471	11	30	3	4231	4114	117	2
	2000	7849	7108	695	11	45	19	5136	5046	90	2
	2001	6504	5655	799	13	49	13	4555	4437	117	2
	2002	6748	5868	829	13	51	13	4726	4604	121	2
Other developed economies	1998	22848	14540	8009	455	30	10	3107	2939	168	75
	1999	25666	16271	8923	515	23	7	3120	2808	312	74
	2000	27383	16209	10364	502	34	17	2946	2744	201	63
	2001	25028	15430	8982	473	34	17	3385	3106	278	25
	2002	24444	15070	8772	462	33	17	3306	3034	272	24

For general note and footnotes see end of table.

Exportations mondiales par classes de marchandises et par régions (suite)

En millions de dollars E.-U. f.o.b.

Economies développées 1/,2/				Developing economies / Economies en voie de développement 1/,2/						← Exportations vers	
Canada	U.S.A. / E.-U.	Japan / Japon	Australia New Zealand / Australie Nouvelle-Zélande	Africa / Afrique	America / Amerique: Total	America / Amerique: LAIA / ALADI	Asia / Asie: Mid. East / Moyen Orient	Asia / Asie: Other / Autres 7/	Oceania / Océanie	Année	Exportations en provenance de ↓
Métaux non férreux (CTCI, Rev. 2 et Rev. 3, 68)											
2405	14260	12184	732	671	3903	3507	2368	24472	20	1998	Monde 1/
2516	15292	12536	670	603	3517	3189	2188	25926	19	1999	
2779	17645	13287	639	672	4311	3889	2652	30477	20	2000	
2410	16791	11453	541	774	3769	3435	2740	27688	17	2001	
2515	17526	11954	565	808	3934	3585	2860	28900	18	2002	
2266	9576	2960	509	467	2245	2098	1020	7401	15	1998	Economies dévelopées 1/,2/
2370	10587	3767	484	418	2084	1964	867	8548	15	1999	
2665	11975	3900	413	438	2374	2255	848	10485	16	2000	
2307	11239	2811	344	509	2002	1897	863	9353	14	2001	
2372	11553	2890	354	523	2058	1950	887	9615	15	2002	
131	3183	7913	223	189	1551	1406	1078	16943	4	1998	Economies en voie de développement 1/,2/
142	3702	7707	185	169	1390	1224	1192	17016	4	1999	
102	4518	8278	224	203	1854	1632	1519	19151	4	2000	
90	4094	7556	192	240	1746	1537	1450	17905	3	2001	
96	4369	8063	205	256	1863	1640	1547	19107	3	2002	
0	374	5573	17	49	213	185	612	7535	0	1998	OPEP
1	411	5760	12	9	151	130	647	7712	1	1999	
6	399	5895	7	7	225	196	638	7911	2	2000	
2	457	5825	7	16	230	194	623	7903	0	2001	
2	457	5827	7	16	230	194	623	7906	0	2002	
8	1501	1312	0	15	107	3	270	129	0	1998	Europe de l'Est et l'ancienne URSS 1/,5/
4	1003	1062	1	17	44	1	128	362	0	1999	
12	1153	1109	2	32	83	1	284	841	0	2000	
13	1457	1087	4	25	21	1	427	431	0	2001	
14	1617	1206	4	28	23	1	474	478	0	2002	
5	1448	1305	0	1	105	1	191	60	0	1998	l'ancienne URSS-Europe 6/
1	927	1057	0	1	40	0	77	267	0	1999	
4	1067	1097	1	7	74	1	174	759	0	2000	
3	1402	1082	4	3	2	1	321	347	0	2001	
3	1509	1164	4	3	2	1	345	373	0	2002	
150	2783	935	172	411	462	418	800	1463	5	1998	Economies développées-Europe
157	2884	1075	140	357	431	390	607	1608	6	1999	
180	4195	1383	150	380	556	510	632	2223	6	2000	
161	3820	712	126	443	548	500	655	2109	6	2001	
171	4047	754	133	469	581	530	694	2234	5	2002	
140	2109	486	154	398	442	406	753	1165	5	1998	Union Européenne
145	2016	497	124	347	409	376	559	1221	6	1999	
164	2913	730	135	374	529	491	604	1593	6	2000	
147	2957	506	114	438	533	491	614	1374	6	2001	
156	3137	537	121	465	565	521	651	1458	5	2002	
10	674	449	17	13	20	11	48	298	0	1998	Association Européenne de Libre Exchange
12	868	578	16	10	22	15	49	387	0	1999	
16	1282	654	15	7	27	19	28	630	0	2000	
14	863	205	11	5	15	8	41	735	0	2001	
15	895	213	11	5	16	8	43	763	0	2002	
2116	6793	2024	337	56	1783	1680	220	5937	11	1998	Autres economies développées
2214	7703	2692	343	61	1652	1574	260	6940	9	1999	
2485	7780	2517	263	57	1818	1745	216	8262	9	2000	
2146	7419	2099	218	66	1454	1397	207	7244	8	2001	
2096	7246	2050	213	64	1420	1364	202	7075	8	2002	

Voir la fin du tableau pour la remarque générale et les notes.

SPECIAL TABLE: D

World exports by commodity classes and by regions (continued)

In million U.S. dollars f.o.b.

Exports from ↓ / Exports to →	Year	World / Monde 1/	Developed economies / Econ. dévelop-pées 1/,2/	Developing economies / économies en voie de développement 1/,2/: Total	Developing economies / économies en voie de développement 1/,2/: OPEC / OPEP	Eastern Europe and fmr. USSR-Europe / Europe de l'Est et l'anc. URSS-Europe: Total 1/,5/	Eastern Europe and fmr. USSR-Europe / Europe de l'Est et l'anc. URSS-Europe: Former USSR-Eur. 6/	Developed economies: Europe: Total	Developed economies: Europe: EU / UE	Developed economies: Europe: EFTA / AELE	Developed economies: South Africa / Afrique du Sud
											Non-ferrous metals (SITC, Rev. 2 and Rev. 3, 68) (continued)
Canada	1998	7538	7137	398	27	4	0	817	707	110	3
	1999	7213	6922	287	14	3	0	561	494	67	1
	2000	8172	7734	437	17	1	0	596	551	45	2
	2001	7593	7220	371	15	1	0	626	590	36	4
	2002	7374	7012	360	15	1	0	608	573	35	4
United States	1998	6893	4332	2547	158	14	5	1597	1546	52	7
	1999	6303	3943	2350	142	10	5	1121	1071	50	22
	2000	7388	4619	2751	115	18	9	1455	1345	109	24
	2001	6626	4372	2233	120	21	11	1725	1528	196	5
	2002	6291	4151	2120	114	20	10	1638	1451	186	5
Japan	1998	3914	880	3029	123	5	0	244	242	2	7
	1999	4201	826	3370	148	4	0	253	248	5	12
	2000	4854	1004	3842	146	8	3	344	335	9	12
	2001	4220	944	3271	135	5	2	333	297	35	3
	2002	4360	975	3379	139	5	2	344	307	36	3
Australia, New Zealand	1998	3924	1790	1863	135	0	0	216	216	0	58
	1999	4378	1761	2168	176	0	0	295	289	6	39
	2000	5604	2174	2656	194	0	0	296	292	4	25
	2001	5403	2281	2540	169	0	0	422	416	6	13
	2002	5450	2301	2562	170	0	0	426	420	6	13
Developing economies-Africa	1998	1419	811	508	118	3	0	589	547	42	7
	1999	1180	965	119	30	0	0	789	725	64	45
	2000	1450	1178	270	48	1	0	823	750	72	63
	2001	1889	1269	235	42	1	0	925	861	64	120
	2002	1985	1335	247	44	1	0	974	907	67	126
Developing economies-America	1998	9414	6670	2728	172	1	0	3449	3410	39	8
	1999	9487	7014	2455	138	0	0	3196	3109	87	5
	2000	11156	7870	3248	260	8	2	3415	3216	200	7
	2001	10069	7306	2735	187	1	0	3422	3216	206	4
	2002	10203	7404	2772	189	1	0	3469	3261	209	4
Developing economies-Europe 3/	1998	759	598	105	3	55	7	563	431	132	1
	1999	627	502	80	3	45	3	475	378	97	1
	2000	778	600	124	3	54	3	573	455	117	1
	2001	814	619	136	3	58	3	595	469	126	1
	2002	859	654	144	3	61	3	628	495	133	1
Developing economies-Middle East	1998	14807	6406	8362	736	19	10	767	757	9	0
	1999	14970	6449	8476	750	21	8	797	773	24	1
	2000	15289	6562	8662	822	28	7	841	824	16	2
	2001	15458	6591	8784	916	37	12	879	860	17	7
	2002	15739	6711	8944	933	38	12	895	876	17	7
Developing economies-Other Asia	1998	12616	4270	8144	199	201	191	1841	1773	68	24
	1999	12951	4022	8706	310	223	209	1814	1734	78	22
	2000	15554	4772	10521	445	260	232	2032	1951	76	25
	2001	14015	4183	9551	425	280	254	1972	1889	79	29
	2002	15331	4576	10448	465	306	278	2157	2066	86	32
Former USSR-Asia 7/.	1998	1464	1119	155	16	190	184	1055	1014	41	0
	1999	1439	1071	161	14	207	201	1052	1000	52	0
	2000	1737	1284	219	5	234	216	1176	1113	64	0
	2001	1711	1257	206	6	247	229	1155	1085	70	0
	2002	1884	1396	227	7	272	252	1284	1207	77	0
Developing economies-Oceania	1998	3	0	2	0	0	0	0	0	0	0
	1999	3	1	2	0	0	0	0	0	0	0
	2000	4	1	2	1	0	0	1	1	0	0
	2001	3	1	2	1	0	0	1	1	0	0
	2002	3	1	2	1	0	0	2	2	0	0

For general note and footnotes see end of table.

Exportations mondiales par classes de marchandises et par régions (suite)

En millions de dollars E.-U. f.o.b.

Economies développées 1/,2/ Canada	U.S.A. E.-U.	Japan Japon	Australia New Zealand Australie Nouvelle-Zélande	Developing economies Economies en voie de développement 1/,2/ Africa Afrique	America Amerique Total	America Amerique LAIA ALADI	Asia Asie Mid. East Moyen Orient	Asia Asie Other Autres 7/	Oceania Océanie	Année	← Exportations vers / Exportations en provenance de ↓
Métaux non férreux (CTCI, Rev. 2 et Rev. 3, 68) (suite)											
.	5956	329	25	3	80	73	22	293	0	1998	Canada
.	6047	296	13	1	26	23	9	251	0	1999	
.	6794	321	17	1	60	57	9	368	0	2000	
.	6358	214	15	1	37	34	6	327	0	2001	
.	6175	208	15	1	36	33	6	318	0	2002	
2081	.	488	91	13	1655	1560	94	784	1	1998	Etats-Unis
2180	.	463	83	8	1564	1489	102	674	0	1999	
2440	.	554	43	9	1654	1589	79	1007	1	2000	
2094	.	426	30	15	1349	1297	79	788	0	2001	
1988	.	404	28	14	1281	1231	75	748	0	2002	
19	577	.	31	1	31	30	68	2928	0	1998	Japon
11	514	.	33	3	28	28	85	3254	0	1999	
23	590	.	31	4	31	30	72	3735	0	2000	
24	557	.	24	3	25	24	62	3180	0	2001	
25	575	.	25	3	26	25	64	3285	0	2002	
8	172	1146	183	2	4	4	18	1829	10	1998	Australie, Nouvelle-Zélande
9	157	1039	207	2	7	7	33	2119	8	1999	
12	255	1399	165	2	22	18	25	2599	8	2000	
15	374	1295	145	2	11	10	31	2489	8	2001	
15	377	1306	146	2	11	10	31	2511	8	2002	
3	36	174	0	60	1	0	78	369	0	1998	Economies en voie de développement-Afrique
3	32	96	0	57	0	0	24	38	0	1999	
4	121	164	1	71	35	3	54	110	0	2000	
3	85	133	0	78	2	2	72	83	0	2001	
3	89	140	0	82	2	2	76	87	0	2002	
71	2261	873	4	12	1493	1353	24	1198	0	1998	Economies en voie de développement-Amérique
77	2777	941	4	10	1310	1157	70	1065	0	1999	
20	3279	1135	7	17	1724	1559	199	1308	0	2000	
28	3118	720	7	26	1646	1471	92	971	0	2001	
28	3160	730	7	26	1668	1491	93	984	0	2002	
0	25	0	1	6	7	6	10	0	0	1998	Economies en voie de développement-Europe 3/
0	15	0	2	5	5	1	8	2	0	1999	
2	17	0	1	6	21	1	11	1	0	2000	
2	12	0	2	7	25	1	13	0	0	2001	
2	13	0	2	7	26	1	14	0	0	2002	
4	185	5412	10	81	1	0	828	7451	0	1998	Economies en voie de développement-Moyen Orient
2	220	5388	8	52	4	3	893	7525	0	1999	
3	244	5424	16	64	1	1	959	7633	0	2000	
2	200	5455	15	71	3	2	996	7710	0	2001	
2	204	5554	15	72	3	2	1014	7850	0	2002	
54	676	1455	207	29	48	45	137	7925	4	1998	Economies en voie de développement-Autres Pays d'Asie
59	657	1281	170	45	70	62	198	8386	4	1999	
74	856	1555	200	45	73	69	296	10098	4	2000	
55	679	1246	168	59	71	61	277	9139	3	2001	
60	743	1363	184	65	78	67	303	9997	3	2002	
0	25	39	0	0	0	0	29	126	0	1998	l'ancienne URSS asiatique 7/
0	11	8	0	0	0	0	29	132	0	1999	
0	97	11	0	1	0	0	26	191	0	2000	
0	92	10	0	1	0	0	21	184	0	2001	
0	101	11	0	1	0	0	23	203	0	2002	
0	0	0	0	0	1	1	0	1	0	1998	Economies en voie de développement-Océanie
0	0	0	0	0	2	1	0	1	0	1999	
0	0	0	0	0	0	0	0	2	0	2000	
0	0	0	0	0	0	0	0	2	0	2001	
0	0	0	0	0	0	0	0	3	0	2002	

Voir la fin du tableau pour la remarque générale et les notes.

SPECIAL TABLE: D

World exports by commodity classes and by regions (continued)

In million U.S. dollars f.o.b.

Exports to → / ↓ Exports from	Year	World Monde 1/	Developed economies Econ. dévelop-pées 1/,2/	Developing economies – economies en voie de développement 1/,2/ Total	Developing economies OPEC OPEP	Eastern Europe and fmr. USSR-Europe – Europe de l'Est et l'anc. URSS-Europe Total 1/,5/	Eastern Europe and fmr. USSR-Europe Former USSR-Eur. 6/	Developed economies – Europe Total	Europe EU UE	Europe EFTA AELE	South Africa Afrique du Sud
		Other manufactured metal products (SITC, Rev. 2 and Rev. 3, 691-695, 699 and 812)									
World 1/	1998	111984	78780	26944	3388	5766	1649	52146	48345	3716	470
	1999	113890	81478	26613	2987	5610	1383	53255	49648	3511	454
	2000	118170	83177	28538	3179	6215	1786	51161	47912	3150	461
	2001	116789	81783	27857	3635	6761	1792	51181	47873	3200	522
	2002	121899	85362	29076	3794	7057	1870	53421	49968	3340	545
Developed economies 1/,2/	1998	81464	60923	15784	2027	4396	1032	44481	40907	3492	334
	1999	81642	61795	15539	1756	4203	690	44688	41372	3228	318
	2000	82114	60800	16725	1708	4474	793	41828	38842	2899	305
	2001	80604	59361	15823	1915	5181	1036	42128	39106	2928	346
	2002	82859	61022	16266	1969	5326	1065	43307	40200	3010	356
Developing economies 1/,2/	1998	24953	14019	10613	1328	254	118	4007	3874	129	134
	1999	26095	15032	10763	1195	249	96	4175	3988	179	135
	2000	29214	17406	11461	1428	266	95	4632	4478	143	153
	2001	29367	17581	11367	1633	307	128	4502	4353	137	173
	2002	31338	18761	12130	1743	328	137	4804	4645	146	185
OPEC	1998	2600	188	2410	425	2	1	75	61	15	0
	1999	2688	200	2476	318	2	1	59	58	1	1
	2000	2799	288	2493	327	2	1	73	72	1	2
	2001	2889	282	2600	485	1	1	95	94	1	1
	2002	2890	282	2601	485	1	1	95	94	1	1
Eastern Europe and the former USSR 1/,5/	1998	5567	3838	546	33	1116	499	3659	3564	94	2
	1999	6153	4651	312	36	1157	597	4392	4287	104	1
	2000	6842	4971	353	43	1474	898	4700	4592	107	3
	2001	6818	4840	667	87	1274	628	4551	4415	135	4
	2002	7567	5372	740	97	1414	697	5051	4900	150	4
Former USSR-Europe 6/	1998	1106	360	374	7	340	308	269	262	8	0
	1999	1775	1067	166	13	513	461	926	908	18	0
	2000	2148	1141	208	23	800	732	1012	997	15	0
	2001	1524	573	495	65	430	394	431	416	15	0
	2002	1640	617	533	70	463	424	464	448	16	0
Developed economies-Europe	1998	58494	46204	7690	1409	4264	975	41130	37698	3352	254
	1999	57863	46655	7054	1230	4061	658	41354	38155	3113	239
	2000	54896	43864	6606	1107	4325	756	38525	35672	2767	223
	2001	56451	44033	7164	1292	5027	1000	38743	35850	2800	260
	2002	59807	46651	7590	1369	5326	1059	41047	37982	2966	275
European Union	1998	55226	43252	7463	1380	4176	954	38585	35187	3323	245
	1999	54710	43798	6841	1204	3979	639	38920	35749	3090	230
	2000	51723	41007	6381	1082	4235	737	36090	33265	2745	214
	2001	53434	41368	6930	1264	4909	972	36431	33562	2780	252
	2002	56689	43888	7352	1341	5208	1031	38650	35606	2949	267
European Free Trade Association	1998	3258	2944	225	28	88	20	2537	2505	28	9
	1999	3143	2850	211	26	82	19	2426	2399	23	8
	2000	3160	2848	222	24	90	19	2427	2399	22	9
	2001	3007	2658	231	26	117	28	2305	2282	20	7
	2002	3120	2758	240	27	121	29	2392	2368	21	7
Other developed economies	1998	22970	14719	8094	618	132	57	3351	3208	141	80
	1999	23780	15140	8485	526	142	32	3334	3217	116	79
	2000	27218	16936	10118	601	149	37	3303	3170	133	82
	2001	24154	15328	8659	623	154	36	3385	3256	128	86
	2002	23591	14970	8457	608	150	35	3306	3180	125	84

For general note and footnotes see end of table.

Exportations mondiales par classes de marchandises et par régions (suite)

En millions de dollars E.-U. f.o.b.

Economies développées 1/,2/				Developing economies Economies en voie de développement 1/,2/						← Exportations vers	
Canada	U.S.A. E.-U.	Japan Japon	Australia New Zealand Australie Nouvelle-Zélande	Africa Afrique	America Amerique Total	America Amerique LAIA ALADI	Asia Asie Mid. East Moyen Orient	Asia Asie Other Autres 7/	Oceania Océanie	Année	Exportations en provenance de ↓
Autres produits en metal manufacturés (CTCI, Rev. 2 et Rev. 3, 691-695, 699 et 812)											
5604	16204	2631	1267	2239	6984	5863	3929	12761	174	1998	Monde 1/
6057	17376	2605	1288	2456	6958	5886	3507	12676	174	1999	
7205	19474	3154	1285	2090	8000	6893	3572	13886	158	2000	
6009	19137	3288	1219	2225	7227	6020	3934	13396	157	2001	
6272	19974	3432	1272	2322	7543	6283	4106	13982	159	2002	
5144	8760	1018	806	1678	5405	4696	2121	5794	133	1998	Economies dévelopées 1/,2/
5581	9186	886	785	1728	5513	4856	1748	5772	134	1999	
6670	9899	1009	759	1522	6480	5822	1673	6309	124	2000	
5468	9433	944	725	1636	5655	4947	1739	5989	126	2001	
5621	9697	970	745	1682	5813	5085	1788	6157	127	2002	
452	7308	1593	457	542	1565	1157	1716	6608	41	1998	Economies en voie de développement 1/,2/
466	7969	1707	498	710	1421	1011	1702	6747	40	1999	
525	9361	2113	522	548	1503	1061	1843	7379	34	2000	
529	9476	2313	491	570	1545	1053	1892	7157	31	2001	
565	10112	2468	524	608	1649	1124	2019	7637	32	2002	
1	77	32	2	65	145	116	980	1212	6	1998	OPEP
3	94	35	8	56	99	78	1002	1310	8	1999	
2	133	60	18	46	109	80	1019	1313	6	2000	
2	113	59	12	60	119	90	1046	1370	5	2001	
2	113	59	12	60	119	90	1046	1371	5	2002	
7	136	20	3	20	14	10	92	359	0	1998	Europe de l'Est et l'ancienne URSS 1/,5/
9	220	12	4	18	24	20	57	157	0	1999	
9	215	31	4	20	17	9	56	198	0	2000	
12	228	31	2	19	28	19	304	249	0	2001	
13	253	34	2	21	31	21	337	276	0	2002	
3	69	15	1	7	2	0	34	329	0	1998	l'ancienne URSS-Europe 6/
3	123	10	3	4	2	1	20	138	0	1999	
2	97	27	1	2	10	4	25	168	0	2000	
2	111	25	1	6	5	4	263	218	0	2001	
2	119	27	1	6	5	4	283	235	0	2002	
364	3254	513	384	1417	1633	1341	1749	2198	50	1998	Economies développées-Europe
497	3413	488	391	1384	1463	1173	1468	2058	46	1999	
426	3526	564	343	1172	1374	1106	1379	2027	48	2000	
363	3588	518	314	1349	1420	1118	1443	2235	52	2001	
385	3801	549	333	1429	1504	1184	1529	2368	53	2002	
344	2954	465	369	1402	1594	1307	1703	2080	49	1998	Union Européenne
477	3098	444	377	1366	1429	1144	1433	1941	45	1999	
403	3218	514	329	1157	1336	1071	1344	1903	48	2000	
344	3327	476	302	1305	1382	1084	1411	2123	52	2001	
365	3530	505	320	1384	1466	1150	1497	2252	51	2002	
20	300	48	15	14	39	35	46	117	0	1998	Association Européenne de Libre Exchange
20	314	44	14	17	34	30	35	116	1	1999	
23	308	50	14	14	38	35	35	124	0	2000	
19	261	42	12	42	38	34	31	111	0	2001	
20	271	44	12	44	39	35	32	115	0	2002	
4780	5506	505	422	261	3772	3355	372	3596	83	1998	Autres economies développées
5084	5773	399	395	344	4050	3682	280	3714	88	1999	
6244	6372	446	416	350	5106	4716	294	4282	75	2000	
5106	5846	426	412	287	4235	3829	296	3755	73	2001	
4987	5710	416	402	280	4136	3740	289	3667	75	2002	

Voir la fin du tableau pour la remarque générale et les notes.

SPECIAL TABLE: D

World exports by commodity classes and by regions (continued)

In million U.S. dollars f.o.b.

Exports from ↓ / Exports to →	Year	World Monde 1/	Developed economies Econ. dévelop-pées 1/,2/	Developing economies economies en voie de développement 1/,2/ Total	OPEC OPEP	Eastern Europe and fmr. USSR-Europe Europe de l'Est et l'anc. URSS-Europe Total 1/,5/	Former USSR-Eur. 6/	Developed economies Europe Total	EU UE	EFTA AELE	South Africa Afrique du Sud
Other manufactured metal products (SITC, Rev. 2 and Rev. 3, 691-695, 699 and 812) (continued)											
Canada	1998	3990	3841	126	15	23	10	163	159	4	[illegible]
	1999	4221	4077	118	26	26	7	165	163	3	[illegible]
	2000	4700	4561	117	15	21	7	160	157	3	[illegible]
	2001	4389	4256	117	14	16	4	164	161	3	[illegible]
	2002	4262	4133	114	14	16	4	159	156	3	[illegible]
United States	1998	12182	7234	4895	306	52	27	1950	1861	87	[illegible]
	1999	12462	7513	4904	232	44	14	1969	1900	69	[illegible]
	2000	14735	8623	6059	255	53	19	1903	1819	84	[illegible]
	2001	12697	7520	5107	257	71	22	1961	1871	89	[illegible]
	2002	12055	7140	4849	244	67	21	1862	1776	85	[illegible]
Japan	1998	5220	2658	2542	212	20	8	812	776	36	[illegible]
	1999	5527	2584	2899	190	44	4	794	761	33	[illegible]
	2000	6114	2675	3396	270	43	6	781	746	35	[illegible]
	2001	5485	2542	2907	270	36	5	843	816	26	[illegible]
	2002	5667	2626	3003	279	37	5	871	843	27	[illegible]
Australia, New Zealand	1998	536	274	246	60	1	0	33	32	1	[illegible]
	1999	515	287	227	62	1	0	39	38	1	[illegible]
	2000	507	306	197	49	1	0	39	38	1	[illegible]
	2001	541	307	232	58	1	0	40	39	1	[illegible]
	2002	546	310	234	59	1	0	40	39	1	[illegible]
Developing economies-Africa	1998	236	111	114	33	1	0	90	89	0	[illegible]
	1999	336	187	143	29	1	1	133	127	6	[illegible]
	2000	390	248	136	42	2	1	173	146	27	[illegible]
	2001	375	257	112	34	1	0	165	139	25	[illegible]
	2002	394	270	118	36	1	0	174	146	26	[illegible]
Developing economies-America	1998	3969	2795	1135	101	4	1	170	153	16	[illegible]
	1999	4075	3110	958	75	3	0	123	119	3	[illegible]
	2000	4843	3795	1014	99	3	0	150	133	17	[illegible]
	2001	5389	4297	1064	115	2	1	149	134	15	[illegible]
	2002	5461	4355	1078	117	2	1	151	136	15	[illegible]
Developing economies-Europe 3/	1998	537	335	145	7	56	19	320	314	6	[illegible]
	1999	519	336	137	5	46	12	318	311	6	[illegible]
	2000	561	365	147	6	47	9	346	338	8	[illegible]
	2001	595	376	168	7	50	14	358	347	11	[illegible]
	2002	628	397	177	7	53	15	378	366	12	[illegible]
Developing economies-Middle East	1998	2809	382	2341	466	67	42	301	293	7	[illegible]
	1999	2849	413	2345	358	52	26	327	320	6	[illegible]
	2000	2852	420	2340	364	48	21	332	325	6	[illegible]
	2001	3036	442	2446	538	72	27	374	365	7	[illegible]
	2002	3091	450	2491	548	73	27	381	372	7	[illegible]
Developing economies-Other Asia	1998	17394	10392	6874	721	127	55	3125	3024	99	[illegible]
	1999	18305	10981	7175	728	147	57	3273	3110	157	[illegible]
	2000	20560	12573	7820	917	166	63	3630	3535	85	[illegible]
	2001	19965	12205	7574	940	182	86	3455	3366	79	[illegible]
	2002	21840	13351	8285	1028	199	94	3780	3682	86	[illegible]
Former USSR-Asia 7/.	1998	23	3	7	1	13	13	3	3	0	[illegible]
	1999	17	3	9	1	5	5	3	3	0	[illegible]
	2000	28	8	10	1	10	10	5	4	1	[illegible]
	2001	26	8	9	1	9	9	5	4	1	[illegible]
	2002	29	9	10	1	10	10	6	4	1	[illegible]
Developing economies-Oceania	1998	9	4	5	0	0	0	1	1	0	[illegible]
	1999	12	6	5	0	0	0	1	1	0	[illegible]
	2000	8	5	3	0	0	0	1	1	0	[illegible]
	2001	7	4	3	0	0	0	1	1	0	[illegible]
	2002	7	5	4	0	0	0	2	2	0	[illegible]

For general note and footnotes see end of table.

Exportations mondiales par classes de marchandises et par régions (suite)

En millions de dollars E.-U. f.o.b.

Economies développées 1/,2/ Canada	U.S.A. E.-U.	Japan Japon	Australia New Zealand Australie Nouvelle-Zélande	Developing economies Economies en voie de développement 1/,2/ Africa Afrique	America Amerique Total	LAIA ALADI	Asia Asie Mid. East Moyen Orient	Other Autres 7/	Oceania Océanie	← Exportations vers Année	Exportations en provenance de ↓
Autres produits en metal manufacturés (CTCI, Rev. 2 et Rev. 3, 691-695, 699 et 812) (suite)											
.	3628	27	14	9	71	45	7	37	0	1998	Canada
.	3879	18	9	13	68	45	10	26	0	1999	
.	4367	18	12	5	59	35	13	40	0	2000	
.	4061	14	14	4	58	35	7	46	0	2001	
.	3944	14	14	4	56	34	7	45	0	2002	
4612	.	428	155	66	3457	3086	201	1163	6	1998	Etats-Unis
4970	.	341	141	83	3680	3349	159	968	10	1999	
6104	.	366	154	95	4787	4438	179	985	8	2000	
4972	.	358	136	88	3888	3526	152	964	6	2001	
4721	.	340	129	84	3691	3348	144	915	6	2002	
121	1595	.	93	27	189	173	123	2194	8	1998	Japon
71	1612	.	67	33	249	237	73	2538	6	1999	
93	1693	.	70	24	217	205	73	3075	5	2000	
92	1483	.	80	20	249	233	98	2534	5	2001	
95	1532	.	83	21	257	241	101	2618	5	2002	
19	59	18	140	7	9	8	17	143	69	1998	Australie, Nouvelle-Zélande
16	63	13	151	8	5	5	18	124	71	1999	
15	69	23	155	2	4	4	12	117	61	2000	
9	76	20	157	7	6	5	11	147	61	2001	
9	77	20	158	7	6	5	11	148	62	2002	
0	4	1	0	95	2	1	13	3	1	1998	Economies en voie de développement-Afrique
0	7	16	0	74	53	53	11	4	0	1999	
1	9	20	2	95	9	9	24	8	0	2000	
1	6	21	1	85	11	9	10	6	0	2001	
1	6	22	1	89	12	9	11	6	0	2002	
50	2552	7	11	27	1076	768	14	17	1	1998	Economies en voie de développement-Amérique
61	2907	6	10	12	911	618	9	25	0	1999	
55	3569	7	10	19	955	629	11	28	1	2000	
66	4062	8	7	13	1014	651	5	31	0	2001	
67	4116	8	7	13	1028	660	5	31	0	2002	
2	11	0	0	7	2	2	11	3	0	1998	Economies en voie de développement-Europe 3/
1	15	0	0	5	1	1	8	5	0	1999	
0	17	0	0	4	2	1	9	4	0	2000	
1	14	0	0	4	1	1	10	6	0	2001	
1	15	0	0	4	1	1	11	6	0	2002	
1	60	2	2	86	12	11	1054	1173	0	1998	Economies en voie de développement-Moyen Orient
1	53	1	3	77	8	7	1072	1168	0	1999	
2	54	2	3	74	6	5	1091	1155	0	2000	
2	30	3	2	95	15	13	1137	1183	0	2001	
2	31	3	2	97	15	13	1158	1205	0	2002	
399	4680	1583	441	327	472	375	623	5412	37	1998	Economies en voie de développement-Autres Pays d'Asie
403	4986	1683	480	541	447	331	602	5544	36	1999	
467	5710	2084	505	356	531	417	708	6183	31	2000	
459	5362	2280	479	373	504	378	730	5931	28	2001	
502	5866	2494	524	408	551	414	799	6488	31	2002	
0	0	0	0	0	0	0	1	5	0	1998	l'ancienne URSS asiatique 7/
0	0	0	0	0	0	0	1	8	0	1999	
0	0	2	0	0	0	0	1	8	0	2000	
0	1	2	0	0	0	0	2	8	0	2001	
0	1	2	0	0	0	0	2	9	0	2002	
0	0	0	3	0	1	0	0	1	3	1998	Economies en voie de développement-Océanie
0	0	0	5	0	1	0	0	2	3	1999	
0	2	0	2	0	0	0	0	1	2	2000	
0	1	0	2	0	0	0	0	1	2	2001	
0	1	0	3	0	0	0	0	1	3	2002	

Voir la fin du tableau pour la remarque générale et les notes.

SPECIAL TABLE: D

World exports by commodity classes and by regions (continued)

In million U.S. dollars f.o.b.

Exports to → / ↓ Exports from	Year	World Monde 1/	Developed economies Econ. dévelop-pées 1/,2/	Developing economies économies en voie de développement 1/,2/ Total	Developing economies OPEC OPEP	Eastern Europe and fmr. USSR-Europe Europe de l'Est et l'anc. URSS-Europe Total 1/,5/	Eastern Europe and fmr. USSR-Europe Former USSR-Eur. 6/	Developed economies Europe Total	Developed economies Europe EU UE	Developed economies Europe EFTA AELE	Developed economies South Africa Afrique du Sud
											Clothing (SITC, Rev. 2 and Rev. 3, 84)
World 1/	1998	198150	155937	34781	3639	6963	3390	90500	85574	4752	353
	1999	197685	158439	33010	3690	5823	2567	90083	85264	4636	347
	2000	208768	166723	35287	4146	6426	3138	87376	82817	4377	486
	2001	207583	165530	34170	4567	7494	3668	87809	83232	4400	459
	2002	216666	172773	35665	4767	7822	3829	91651	86874	4593	479
Developed economies 1/,2/	1998	64216	49375	11700	919	3121	1236	40866	37402	3311	44
	1999	62286	48492	11006	796	2765	883	40193	36845	3191	39
	2000	59058	44630	11517	812	2873	1075	35915	32918	2843	35
	2001	59383	45434	10435	928	3471	1406	36708	33545	3008	34
	2002	61045	46705	10727	954	3568	1445	37735	34484	3092	35
Developing economies 1/,2/	1998	124658	98186	22982	2712	3300	1835	41657	40329	1308	309
	1999	126117	101412	21929	2890	2592	1470	41738	40406	1307	308
	2000	140853	113847	23704	3327	3052	1826	43624	42204	1392	451
	2001	138535	111215	23647	3633	3331	1960	42624	41371	1234	424
	2002	147833	118680	25234	3877	3555	2092	45485	44148	1317	452
OPEC	1998	12832	12223	585	253	24	11	8704	8641	63	23
	1999	14282	13281	966	395	34	14	9268	9180	87	33
	2000	15342	14201	1108	449	32	15	9579	9490	88	28
	2001	15193	13979	1181	491	31	16	9456	9376	79	23
	2002	15199	13985	1181	491	31	16	9460	9380	79	23
Eastern Europe and the former USSR 1/,5/	1998	9277	8376	99	8	542	319	7977	7844	133	0
	1999	9282	8534	76	4	466	213	8152	8013	138	0
	2000	8858	8246	65	7	501	237	7837	7695	141	0
	2001	9665	8880	89	6	693	302	8476	8316	159	0
	2002	10727	9856	99	7	769	335	9407	9230	176	0
Former USSR-Europe 6/	1998	1849	1332	51	0	245	212	1168	1140	28	0
	1999	1857	1450	35	0	170	137	1275	1249	26	0
	2000	1432	1240	28	1	164	145	1103	1078	24	0
	2001	1526	1293	35	1	198	174	1161	1133	28	0
	2002	1642	1391	38	1	213	187	1249	1219	30	0
Developed economies-Europe	1998	52514	44906	4502	796	3086	1209	39879	36462	3265	39
	1999	50794	43947	4082	688	2746	874	39293	35983	3152	34
	2000	47041	39890	4254	716	2860	1069	35107	32139	2816	31
	2001	49218	41034	4682	814	3460	1400	35950	32811	2984	31
	2002	52144	43474	4960	862	3666	1483	38087	34762	3161	33
European Union	1998	51566	44034	4457	786	3055	1197	39155	35749	3254	38
	1999	49871	43100	4034	678	2718	867	38597	35298	3142	34
	2000	46227	39145	4207	711	2838	1062	34514	31554	2807	31
	2001	48346	40242	4627	808	3435	1389	35328	32198	2976	30
	2002	51291	42693	4909	857	3644	1474	37480	34159	3157	32
European Free Trade Association	1998	792	718	44	9	30	12	574	563	10	1
	1999	765	695	43	6	28	7	543	534	9	0
	2000	682	614	46	4	22	7	465	456	9	1
	2001	733	655	53	6	25	12	488	480	7	1
	2002	761	680	55	6	26	12	506	498	7	1
Other developed economies	1998	11702	4470	7198	123	34	26	987	940	46	5
	1999	11492	4545	6924	108	18	9	900	861	38	4
	2000	12017	4740	7263	97	12	6	807	779	28	4
	2001	10165	4400	5753	114	11	6	759	734	24	3
	2002	9928	4297	5619	111	11	6	741	717	23	3

For general note and footnotes see end of table.

Exportations mondiales par classes de marchandises et par régions (suite)

En millions de dollars E.-U. f.o.b.

Economies développées 1/,2/				Developing economies Economies en voie de développement 1/,2/						← Exportations vers	
Canada	U.S.A. E.-U.	Japan Japon	Australia New Zealand Australie Nouvelle-Zélande	Africa Afrique	America Amerique Total	America Amerique LAIA ALADI	Asia Asie Mid. East Moyen Orient	Asia Asie Other Autres 7/	Oceania Océanie	Année	Exportations en provenance de ↓
Vetements (CTCI, Rev. 2 et Rev. 3, 84)											
3063	45585	14189	1875	2388	10683	5277	3804	17136	116	1998	Monde 1/
3039	47030	15489	2064	2341	10392	5025	3793	15713	111	1999	
3440	53839	18755	2304	2202	11524	5455	4232	16570	104	2000	
3548	52063	18843	2197	2291	10137	5210	4536	16332	105	2001	
3703	54341	19668	2293	2391	10581	5438	4734	17047	110	2002	
910	4772	2201	317	1042	7176	3288	1327	1607	55	1998	Economies dévelopées 1/,2/
822	4974	1936	319	974	6814	3073	1149	1546	49	1999	
830	5454	1908	285	986	7073	2837	1175	1789	43	2000	
810	5451	1962	280	1038	5600	2436	1268	1982	43	2001	
833	5604	2017	288	1067	5757	2504	1303	2037	44	2002	
2126	40451	11983	1558	1340	3496	1987	2458	15478	61	1998	Economies en voie de développement 1/,2/
2194	41703	13549	1744	1357	3573	1951	2634	14132	62	1999	
2595	47998	16843	2018	1215	4444	2616	3041	14757	61	2000	
2720	46235	16876	1916	1247	4527	2772	3251	14320	62	2001	
2903	49338	18009	2045	1331	4831	2958	3469	15281	60	2002	
100	3253	125	19	97	79	37	262	143	3	1998	OPEP
136	3634	169	41	169	111	50	395	281	7	1999	
148	4215	192	40	200	125	57	439	334	8	2000	
167	4118	183	33	265	125	58	451	330	9	2001	
167	4120	183	33	265	125	58	451	330	9	2002	
27	362	6	1	6	11	2	19	51	0	1998	Europe de l'Est et l'ancienne URSS 1/,5/
23	352	4	1	10	6	1	11	35	0	1999	
14	387	4	1	2	7	1	15	25	0	2000	
17	377	5	1	7	10	2	16	30	0	2001	
19	418	6	1	8	11	2	18	33	0	2002	
15	148	0	0	1	9	0	1	40	0	1998	l'ancienne URSS-Europe 6/
10	163	0	0	1	5	1	1	27	0	1999	
2	135	0	0	0	5	0	1	21	0	2000	
4	129	0	0	2	7	0	0	25	0	2001	
4	139	0	0	2	8	0	0	27	0	2002	
251	2636	1720	133	1000	508	412	1234	1242	29	1998	Economies développées-Europe
223	2589	1486	125	933	440	346	1081	1125	29	1999	
238	2757	1449	119	938	453	361	1110	1275	29	2000	
271	2895	1600	112	995	510	406	1203	1443	29	2001	
287	3067	1695	119	1054	540	430	1275	1529	30	2002	
242	2543	1681	127	998	504	409	1222	1217	29	1998	Union Européenne
215	2492	1446	118	927	436	343	1073	1099	29	1999	
230	2660	1412	111	937	448	357	1101	1247	29	2000	
263	2779	1561	106	992	504	401	1192	1412	28	2001	
279	2948	1656	112	1052	535	425	1265	1498	29	2002	
9	88	39	6	1	4	3	12	25	0	1998	Association Européenne de Libre Exchange
8	96	39	7	1	4	4	8	26	0	1999	
8	97	36	8	1	5	4	9	28	0	2000	
8	114	38	6	1	6	5	10	31	0	2001	
8	118	39	6	1	6	5	10	32	0	2002	
658	2136	480	183	42	6668	2876	93	366	26	1998	Autres economies développées
599	2385	450	194	41	6373	2726	67	420	20	1999	
592	2697	459	166	48	6620	2476	65	514	14	2000	
539	2557	362	168	43	5090	2030	66	539	14	2001	
526	2497	354	164	42	4971	1983	64	526	15	2002	

Voir la fin du tableau pour la remarque générale et les otes.

SPECIAL TABLE: D

World exports by commodity classes and by regions (continued)

In million U.S. dollars f.o.b.

Exports from ↓ / Exports to →	Year	World / Monde 1/	Developed economies / Econ. dévelop-pées 1/,2/	Developing economies / économies en voie de développement 1/,2/: Total	Developing economies: OPEC / OPEP	Eastern Europe and fmr. USSR-Europe / Europe de l'Est et l'anc. URSS-Europe: Total 1/,5/	Eastern Europe and fmr. USSR-Europe: Former USSR-Eur. 6/	Developed economies: Europe: Total	Developed economies: Europe: EU / UE	Developed economies: Europe: EFTA / AELE	Developed economies: South Africa / Afrique du Sud
											Clothing (SITC, Rev. 2 and Rev. 3, 84) (continued)
Canada	1998	1706	1677	21	4	9	7	52	48	4	0
	1999	1881	1864	14	4	3	2	48	43	5	0
	2000	2077	2057	17	4	3	2	44	41	4	0
	2001	1943	1925	17	5	2	1	45	42	2	0
	2002	1887	1869	17	5	2	1	44	41	2	0
United States	1998	8508	1637	6850	99	21	15	479	447	31	3
	1999	7960	1426	6522	78	12	5	363	338	24	3
	2000	8173	1383	6783	74	7	3	328	313	15	2
	2001	6532	1233	5292	91	7	3	332	317	14	2
	2002	6202	1171	5024	86	7	3	315	301	13	2
Japan	1998	408	203	204	8	2	1	115	108	7	1
	1999	456	205	251	6	0	0	117	112	5	0
	2000	534	222	311	5	1	0	119	114	4	1
	2001	470	179	290	5	0	0	86	83	3	0
	2002	486	185	300	5	0	0	89	86	3	0
Australia, New Zealand	1998	278	198	79	3	2	2	15	14	0	0
	1999	285	209	75	6	1	1	16	16	0	0
	2000	285	203	81	7	1	0	18	18	1	1
	2001	309	222	86	4	1	1	25	25	1	1
	2002	312	224	87	4	1	1	25	25	1	1
Developing economies-Africa	1998	6430	6269	109	43	6	4	5691	5674	13	19
	1999	6179	6042	91	25	3	1	5467	5451	14	17
	2000	6165	5998	120	50	3	1	5259	5242	13	69
	2001	6196	6029	116	48	3	2	5331	5315	13	110
	2002	6510	6344	122	50	3	2	5614	5598	14	116
Developing economies-America	1998	8823	7947	848	131	9	8	219	214	4	0
	1999	9942	9039	882	106	3	3	191	187	4	0
	2000	11150	10154	975	174	2	2	253	201	52	0
	2001	10551	9466	1064	264	2	2	185	178	8	1
	2002	10692	9593	1078	268	2	2	188	180	8	1
Developing economies-Europe 3/	1998	1727	1611	101	6	13	3	1499	1480	19	0
	1999	1461	1357	93	6	9	2	1279	1260	19	0
	2000	1355	1251	90	6	13	2	1164	1143	20	0
	2001	1386	1273	97	6	14	2	1200	1177	23	0
	2002	1463	1344	102	6	15	2	1267	1243	24	0
Developing economies-Middle East	1998	17666	15942	845	352	828	416	12870	12692	177	25
	1999	17454	16212	795	352	405	194	12836	12688	147	21
	2000	17781	16829	612	279	260	176	12961	12814	147	20
	2001	18667	17432	754	348	316	216	13224	13080	143	19
	2002	19007	17749	768	354	322	220	13465	13318	146	19
Developing economies-Other Asia	1998	89012	65725	20856	2180	2361	1404	21266	20157	1094	262
	1999	90062	68112	19696	2400	2173	1270	21854	20708	1124	269
	2000	103342	79033	21432	2818	2774	1646	23954	22771	1159	362
	2001	100633	76408	21126	2967	2995	1738	22650	21586	1047	294
	2002	110085	83585	23110	3246	3276	1901	24777	23613	1145	322
Former USSR-Asia 7/.	1998	38	14	6	1	16	16	8	8	0	0
	1999	48	22	10	0	14	14	10	10	0	0
	2000	60	18	29	0	12	11	9	9	0	0
	2001	51	18	22	0	10	9	10	10	0	0
	2002	56	20	24	0	11	10	11	11	0	0
Developing economies-Oceania	1998	999	691	224	0	83	0	112	112	0	4
	1999	1019	652	371	0	0	0	112	112	0	0
	2000	1060	583	475	0	0	0	34	34	0	0
	2001	1100	608	490	0	0	0	35	35	0	0
	2002	1092	712	610	0	0	0	60	55	0	0

For general note and footnotes see end of table.

Exportations mondiales par classes de marchandises et par régions (suite)

En millions de dollars E.-U. f.o.b.

Economies développées 1/,2/ Canada	U.S.A. E.-U.	Japan Japon	Australia New Zealand Australie Nouvelle-Zélande	Developing economies Economies en voie de développement 1/,2/ Africa Afrique	America Amerique Total	LAIA ALADI	Asia Asie Mid. East Moyen Orient	Other Autres 7/	Oceania Océanie	← Exportations vers Année	Exportations en provenance de ↓
Vetements (CTCI, Rev. 2 et Rev. 3, 84) (suite)											
.	1611	11	1	0	12	5	5	4	0	1998	Canada
.	1802	11	1	0	5	4	4	3	0	1999	
.	1996	12	1	0	6	4	5	6	0	2000	
.	1866	10	1	2	3	2	5	7	0	2001	
.	1812	10	1	2	3	2	5	7	0	2002	
647	.	460	29	16	6647	2864	70	112	3	1998	Etats-Unis
588	.	432	29	11	6352	2708	49	106	3	1999	
578	.	437	27	12	6605	2466	41	120	3	2000	
526	.	340	24	10	5080	2023	39	158	4	2001	
499	.	323	23	9	4823	1921	37	150	4	2002	
4	79	.	4	1	3	1	7	192	0	1998	Japon
3	78	.	6	2	2	2	5	242	0	1999	
5	92	.	5	1	2	2	4	304	0	2000	
4	86	.	3	1	1	1	3	285	0	2001	
4	89	.	3	1	1	1	3	294	0	2002	
1	28	6	147	0	1	1	1	54	22	1998	Australie, Nouvelle-Zélande
1	31	5	156	0	0	0	2	56	16	1999	
1	44	7	132	0	1	0	1	68	11	2000	
1	47	9	139	0	0	0	1	73	10	2001	
1	47	9	140	0	0	0	1	74	10	2002	
17	538	4	0	78	6	4	18	4	0	1998	Economies en voie de développement-Afrique
16	535	5	1	66	6	5	12	5	0	1999	
20	643	6	1	70	5	3	39	6	0	2000	
14	567	7	1	67	4	2	40	5	0	2001	
15	596	7	1	70	4	2	42	5	0	2002	
38	7677	9	3	4	822	495	19	3	0	1998	Economies en voie de développement-Amérique
51	8784	9	4	1	847	407	9	24	0	1999	
60	9827	10	3	2	950	536	12	11	0	2000	
66	9200	8	5	3	1022	597	14	25	0	2001	
67	9323	8	5	3	1036	605	14	25	0	2002	
2	110	0	0	1	0	0	7	0	0	1998	Economies en voie de développement-Europe 3/
1	76	0	0	1	0	0	7	0	0	1999	
0	86	0	0	0	0	0	9	0	0	2000	
0	71	0	0	1	0	0	9	0	0	2001	
0	75	0	0	1	0	0	9	0	0	2002	
85	2921	9	1	456	22	15	272	78	0	1998	Economies en voie de développement-Moyen Orient
92	3190	10	2	379	21	15	255	127	0	1999	
104	3630	13	3	161	21	14	261	160	0	2000	
113	3929	16	2	161	23	15	373	186	0	2001	
115	4000	16	2	164	23	15	380	189	0	2002	
1983	29113	11579	1450	801	2429	1257	2142	15389	57	1998	Economies en voie de développement-Autres Pays d'Asie
2034	29036	13163	1642	909	2339	1166	2350	13966	59	1999	
2387	33731	16464	1918	982	3002	1596	2720	14573	58	2000	
2502	32380	16485	1808	1015	2998	1677	2816	14097	58	2001	
2737	35421	18033	1978	1110	3280	1835	3080	15421	63	2002	
0	6	0	0	1	0	0	2	3	0	1998	l'ancienne URSS asiatique 7/
1	11	0	0	0	0	0	9	1	0	1999	
1	7	0	0	0	0	0	27	1	0	2000	
1	7	0	0	0	0	0	20	1	0	2001	
1	8	0	0	0	0	0	22	1	0	2002	
1	92	380	102	0	217	215	0	4	3	1998	Economies en voie de développement-Océanie
1	81	363	95	0	359	358	0	9	3	1999	
25	82	350	92	0	466	466	0	6	3	2000	
25	88	360	100	0	480	480	0	6	3	2001	
25	87	357	135	0	477	477	0	8	4	2002	

Voir la fin du tableau pour la remarque générale et les notes.

SPECIAL TABLE: D

World exports by commodity classes and by regions (continued)

General note

The purpose of this table is to provide data on the network of flows of broad groups of commodities within and between important economic and geographic areas of the world.

The regional analysis in this table is in accordance with that of Special Table A in this issue.

Export data in this table are largely comparable to that shown in Special Table A except that Special Table A contains revised data for total exports which are not incorporated into this table if the corresponding revised data at the commodity/destination level are not available. Also, the regional totals shown in Special Table A have been adjusted to exclude the re-exports of countries comprising each region. This adjustment is not made in this table since re-exports are often not available by commodity and by destination.

The commodity classification is in accordance with the United Nations' Standard International Trade Classification (SITC), Revision 3, except for countries wich report trade data only in terms of the SITC, Revision 2, or the SITC, Revised.

The data approximate total exports of all countries and areas of the world. They are based on official export figures converted, where necessary, to U.S. dollars according to conversion factors published in Table C for each country in this volume. Where official figures are not available estimates based on the imports reported by partner countries and on other subsidiary data are used. Some official national data have been adjusted

(a) to approximate the commodity groupings of the SITC and

(b) to approximate calendar years.

The data include special category (confidential) exports, ships' stores and bunkes and exports of minor importance, the destination of which cannot be determined. These data are included in the world totals for each commodity group and in total exports, but are excluded from all regions of destination.

1/ Exports for which country of destination is not available are included in the totals for the 'World', the 'Developed economies', the 'Developing economies' and 'Eastern Europe and the former USSR' but are excluded from the regional components of these groupings.

2/ This classification is intended for statistical convenience and does not, necessarily, express a judgment about the stage reached by a particular country in the development process.

3/ Data refer to Serbia and Montenegro, Croatia, Slovenia, Bosnia and Herzegovina, and the former Yugoslav republic of Macedonia.

4/ Section 9 of the SITC, which comprises commodities and transactions not classified elsewhere, is included in the total trade but is not shown separately in this table.

5/ Includes Eastern Europe and the European countries of the former USSR.

6/ Includes Belarus, Estonia, Latvia, Lithuania, Republic of Moldova, the Russian Federation, and Ukraine.

7/ Includes Armenia, Azerbaijan, Georgia, Kazakhstan, Kyrgyztan, Tajikistan, Turkmenistan, and Uzbekistan.

Exportations mondiales par classes de marchandises et par régions (suite)

Remarque générale

Le but de ce tableau est de fournir un apercu du courant des marchandises entre les régions importantes économiques et géographiques du monde et de leur commerce intérieur.

L'analyse régionale dans ce tableau est conforme à celle du Tableau Spécial A du présent numéro.

Les données des exportations dans ce tableau sont en générale comparables aux chiffres qui sont inclus dans le Tableau Spécial A, exceptées que celles du Tableau Spécial A comportent des revisions aux exportations totales qui ne sont pas inclus dans ce tableau si les revisions des données correspondantes au niveau de marchandise/destination ne sont pas disponibles. De plus, les totaux régionaux inclus dans le Tableau Spécial A ont été ajustés pour exclure les re-exportations des pays qui comprennent la région. Cet ajustement n'est pas fait dans ce tableau parce que des re-exportations ne sont pas disponibles fréquemment par marchandise et par destination.

La classification par marchandise utilisée est la Classification type pour le commerce international (CTCI), des Nations Unies, Revision 3, en dehors des pays qui rapportent exclusivement les données du commerce en accord avec la CTCI, Revision 2, ou la CTCI, Revisée.

Les données approachées des exportations totales de tous pays et régions du monde. Elles sont basées sur les chiffres de exportations officielles nationales convertis en dollars E.-U. selon les facteurs de conversion publiés dans le de conversion publiés dans le Tableau C pour chaque pays dans ce tome.

Quand les chiffres officiels ne sont pas disponibles on a recours a des estimations basées sur les importations rapportées par les pays partenaires ou sur d'autres données subsidiaries. Quelques données officielles nationales ont étée ajustées

(a) qu'elles correspondent aux groups des marchandises de la CTCI et
(b) qu'elles correspondent aux années civiles.

Les données comprises les exportations de 'special category' (confidentielles), les approvisionnments des navires et combustible de soute et autres exportations de moindre importance dont la destination n'a pu être déterminée. Ces donnés sont comprises dans le totaux de chaque groupe de marchandise et dans les exportations totales, mais elles ne sont pas comprises dans les régions de destination.

1/ Les exportations dont les pays de destination ne sont pas disponibles sont comprises dans les totaux du 'Monde', des 'Economies développées', des 'Economies en voie de développement' et de 'Europe de l'Est et l'ancienne URSS', mais ils ne sont pas comprises dans chaque partile composant ces régions.

2/ Cette classification est utilisée pour plus de commodité dans la présentation des statistiques et n'implique pas nécessairement un jugement quant au stade de développement auquel est parvenu un pays donné.

3/ Les données se rapportent à Sebie-et-Monténégro Croatie, Slovénie, Bosnie-Herzégovine et l'ancienne République yougoslave de Macédoine.

4/ Section 9 de la CTCI, qui représente les articles et transactions non classes ailleurs est comprise dans le commerce total mais n'est pas présentée séparément dans ce tableau.

5/ Y compris de l'Europe de l'est et les pays européens de l'ancienne URSS.

6/ Y compris Bélarus, Estonie, Lettonie, Lituanie, République de Moldova, Fédération de Russie, et Ukraine.

7/ Y compris Azerbaïdjan, Arménie, Géorgie, Kazakhstan, Kirghizistan, Tadjikistan, Turkménistan, et Ouzbékistan.

SPECIAL TABLE: E

Growth of world exports by commodity classes and by region

Annual average rate: in per cent

SITC	Commodity classes (Origin or destination →)	Year	World Monde 1,2	Developed economies / Economies développées 1,2	Developing economies / economies en voie de développement 1,2: Total	Developing economies 1,2: OPEC OPEP	Eastern Europe & fmr. USSR-Europe / Europe de l'Est et l'ancienne URSS-Europe: Total 1,4	Eastern Europe & fmr. USSR-Europe: Fmr USSR-Europe 5	Developed economies Europe: Total	Developed economies Europe: EU UE	Developed economies Europe: EFTA AELE
	Origin of exports of major commodity classes										
0-9	All commodities 3	1998/02	4.2	2.4	7.4	10.2	8.5	7.8	2.9	2.8	5.4
		1998/99	3.6	1.8	8.5	22.1	-1.9	-2.8	0.0	-0.4	5.4
		1999/02	4.4	2.6	7.1	6.5	12.3	11.5	3.9	3.8	5.4
		2000/02	0.5	0.4	-0.2	-7.1	6.8	1.6	4.3	4.5	2.2
		2001/02	4.6	3.7	5.5	0.2	9.5	5.4	7.4	7.6	4.6
0&1	Food, live animals, beverages and tobacco	1998/02	1.0	1.2	0.0	-2.2	4.7	11.9	1.0	1.1	0.0
		1998/99	-2.7	-0.9	-5.1	-4.2	-17.6	-18.8	-1.4	-1.5	1.3
		1999/02	2.2	1.9	1.8	-1.5	13.3	24.5	1.9	2.0	-0.4
		2000/02	4.0	4.6	1.4	1.4	19.3	34.8	6.5	6.7	2.9
		2001/02	4.7	6.2	-1.0	3.2	34.1	91.4	10.5	10.7	7.4
2&4	Crude maerials, oils and fats, (fuels excluded)	1998/02	0.9	0.6	1.5	6.1	0.4	-1.3	1.0	1.0	0.6
		1998/99	-5.3	-6.3	-2.8	-0.2	-9.1	-15.7	-8.9	-9.1	-3.5
		1999/02	3.1	3.0	3.0	8.3	3.8	4.1	4.5	4.6	2.0
		2000/02	1.0	1.2	1.0	6.5	-0.2	-0.9	6.2	6.4	-0.5
		2001/02	6.7	5.4	5.8	15.4	30.1	45.2	11.6	11.9	1.8
3	Mineral fuels, lubricants and related material	1998/02	16.1	14.2	16.7	16.9	18.5	19.0	15.8	14.3	19.8
		1998/99	26.4	14.0	37.2	44.3	8.6	9.8	17.8	13.5	29.7
		1999/02	12.8	14.2	10.6	9.0	22.0	22.3	15.2	14.6	16.7
		2000/02	-4.9	-2.9	-7.6	-9.4	4.4	3.8	-2.0	-1.5	-2.9
		2001/02	-0.4	0.4	-2.4	1.2	8.2	7.8	5.1	7.9	-0.6
5	Chemicals	1998/02	5.5	5.3	6.6	0.7	4.5	3.5	5.6	5.5	7.4
		1998/99	2.8	2.8	5.2	-2.8	-9.1	-6.7	1.4	1.1	4.6
		1999/02	6.4	6.2	7.1	2.0	9.5	7.1	7.1	7.0	8.3
		2000/02	5.6	6.5	2.0	-4.0	3.6	-0.3	9.5	9.1	15.1
		2001/02	7.7	8.4	3.7	-16.7	15.4	21.0	11.2	10.8	15.9
7	Machinery and transport equipment	1998/02	3.8	1.5	9.5	10.3	11.9	4.0	2.5	2.6	-0.2
		1998/99	5.0	2.7	12.8	4.2	1.0	-14.8	0.3	0.3	0.1
		1999/02	3.4	1.1	8.4	12.5	15.8	11.2	3.2	3.4	-0.3
		2000/02	-0.7	-1.8	0.8	-3.5	13.4	4.7	3.1	3.2	0.3
		2001/02	4.9	2.5	9.7	4.5	18.6	22.1	6.2	6.3	0.1
6&8	Other manufactured goods	1998/02	2.4	1.2	4.3	2.3	4.5	0.9	0.9	0.8	1.7
		1998/99	0.6	0.2	2.6	8.8	-8.1	-13.4	-2.5	-2.8	1.3
		1999/02	3.0	1.5	4.8	0.3	9.0	6.2	2.0	2.0	1.9
		2000/02	0.8	0.4	0.6	-3.0	6.4	-1.1	3.2	3.3	0.4
		2001/02	4.7	3.4	4.8	-3.1	21.5	38.4	6.1	6.2	5.6
	Destination of exports of major commodity classes										
0-9	All commodities 3	1998/02	4.2	3.5	4.9	3.6	4.8	2.6	2.7	2.8	0.0
		1998/99	3.6	5.5	3.6	-9.5	-12.5	-26.0	2.6	3.0	-4.4
		1999/02	4.4	2.8	5.4	8.4	11.3	14.4	2.7	2.8	1.5
		2000/02	0.5	0.1	0.1	6.9	9.1	10.4	2.0	2.1	1.3
		2001/02	4.6	3.9	5.5	2.3	10.1	8.6	5.6	5.6	5.1
0&1	Food, live animals, beverages and tobacco	1998/02	1.0	1.3	1.1	1.3	-3.1	-5.5	0.4	0.4	1.5
		1998/99	-2.7	0.7	-6.1	-6.3	-25.2	-32.1	-1.2	-1.3	2.8
		1999/02	2.2	1.5	3.6	4.0	5.6	5.5	0.9	0.9	1.0
		2000/02	4.0	4.3	2.3	3.0	9.6	9.9	5.9	5.9	5.5
		2001/02	4.7	6.7	-0.6	-6.3	6.3	5.5	8.5	8.5	8.0
2&4	Crude maerials, oils and fats, (fuels excluded)	1998/02	0.9	-0.5	3.7	1.9	2.9	4.2	-0.8	-0.9	1.8
		1998/99	-5.3	-5.3	-2.6	2.1	-12.2	-8.5	-9.5	-9.6	-7.7
		1999/02	3.1	1.2	6.0	1.8	8.5	8.8	2.3	2.1	5.2
		2000/02	1.0	-0.2	3.2	1.2	5.3	4.6	2.2	2.1	3.7
		2001/02	6.7	5.8	7.9	5.8	21.3	19.0	8.0	8.0	8.0
3	Mineral fuels, lubricants and related material	1998/02	16.1	16.3	14.9	13.0	10.5	8.1	16.5	17.0	10.0
		1998/99	26.4	37.1	68.0	14.4	-3.1	-14.7	32.8	34.3	8.5
		1999/02	12.8	10.2	1.2	12.6	15.4	17.0	11.6	11.8	10.5
		2000/02	-4.9	-4.9	-7.4	-6.1	0.0	5.5	-2.8	-2.7	1.4
		2001/02	-0.4	-2.2	0.5	-7.0	1.6	-1.8	3.7	2.7	30.9
5	Chemicals	1998/02	5.5	5.8	5.5	5.4	7.5	7.9	5.2	5.2	5.6
		1998/99	2.8	3.6	4.7	0.5	-7.7	-21.2	1.0	0.8	3.6
		1999/02	6.4	6.5	5.8	7.0	13.1	19.9	6.7	6.7	6.3
		2000/02	5.6	6.9	1.2	5.0	12.9	15.8	8.4	8.3	10.3
		2001/02	7.7	8.9	4.8	0.2	14.2	13.9	11.3	11.2	13.2
7	Machinery and transport equipment	1998/02	3.8	3.0	5.3	4.1	7.4	6.1	2.2	2.3	-1.0
		1998/99	5.0	6.8	1.5	-15.7	-12.1	-33.2	4.2	4.6	-3.0
		1999/02	3.4	1.7	6.6	11.7	14.9	23.9	1.5	1.6	-0.3
		2000/02	-0.7	-1.2	-0.3	10.7	13.4	23.6	0.9	0.9	-0.4
		2001/02	4.9	3.4	7.0	7.7	18.1	21.2	4.0	4.1	0.2
6&8	Other manufactured goods	1998/02	2.4	1.9	3.5	4.3	5.3	4.5	0.8	0.9	-0.6
		1998/99	0.6	1.8	-0.1	-8.6	-11.4	-24.4	-1.0	-0.6	-7.5
		1999/02	3.0	2.0	4.7	9.0	11.5	16.4	1.5	1.4	1.8
		2000/02	0.8	0.3	0.4	7.1	11.1	12.6	1.9	1.9	2.6
		2001/02	4.7	3.9	7.4	5.5	15.2	18.0	5.0	4.7	8.9

For general note and footnotes see end of Special Table F.

Croissance des exportations mondiales par catégories de marchandises et par régions

Taux annuel moyen: en pourcentage

conomies / véloppées 1, 2			Developing economies / Economies en voie de développement 1, 2						◄── En provenance ou vers		
anada	U.S.A / E.-U.	Japan / Japon	Australia New Zealand / Australie Nouvelle-Zélande	Africa / Afrique	America / Amerique	Asia / Asie: Mid.East / Moyen Orient	Asia / Asie: Other / Autres 6	Oceania / Océanie	Année		CTCI: Classes de marchandises ▼
Provenance des exportations de grandes catégories de marchandises											
4.1	-0.2	1.8	5.2	11.5	5.9	11.2	7.1	-4.2	1998/02	0-9	Tous produits 3
11.3	1.2	7.6	0.2	23.8	6.6	21.5	6.3	-5.9	1998/99		
1.9	-0.7	-0.1	6.9	7.7	5.6	8.0	7.4	-3.7	1999/02		
-4.6	-6.0	-6.8	2.0	-6.1	-1.0	-2.8	1.0	-10.3	2000/02		
-2.9	-5.5	3.3	3.8	7.3	1.2	-6.4	9.2	-6.3	2001/02		
4.6	-0.8	1.9	5.9	-0.8	-2.0	-1.6	2.5	-11.1	1998/02	0&1	Produits alimentaires, boissons et tabacs
2.1	-2.5	5.1	6.6	-5.9	-8.1	-5.4	-1.9	4.1	1998/99		
5.5	-0.2	0.8	5.7	1.0	0.1	-0.2	4.1	-15.6	1999/02		
3.8	-2.3	1.2	5.4	0.7	0.2	2.1	2.3	-2.3	2000/02		
-1.8	-4.5	-28.4	5.6	0.5	-4.6	-16.5	5.2	-12.7	2001/02		
-2.2	0.7	5.4	1.1	7.0	1.4	0.2	1.2	-9.8	1998/02	2&4	Matières premières huiles & graisses (combust. exclu.)
3.0	-10.3	1.8	-4.5	8.8	-6.5	0.9	-2.4	-9.8	1998/99		
-3.9	4.7	6.6	3.0	6.4	4.2	-0.1	2.4	-9.8	1999/02		
-8.4	-0.6	3.9	-1.5	7.7	1.5	3.4	-0.2	-18.4	2000/02		
-3.3	1.7	5.7	-1.9	32.5	1.8	-23.4	8.8	-13.0	2001/02		
15.9	3.7	3.2	9.1	16.4	18.1	18.5	13.0	3.4	1998/02	3	Combustibles minéraux et produits
14.6	-1.6	-0.9	-1.2	52.8	37.0	44.8	14.9	-80.2	1998/99		
16.3	5.6	4.6	12.8	6.3	12.4	10.8	12.4	79.6	1999/02		
-6.3	-6.3	-3.9	0.4	-13.8	-5.2	-6.9	-5.2	-16.6	2000/02		
-13.1	-8.1	-7.0	2.4	5.9	6.1	-8.7	-0.4	-19.6	2001/02		
5.8	3.8	5.1	8.2	2.8	4.7	0.6	8.3	0.8	1998/02	5	Produits chimiques
5.6	3.6	12.8	11.4	-2.5	-1.3	-0.9	8.9	4.7	1998/99		
5.9	3.9	2.7	7.2	4.7	6.7	1.1	8.2	-0.5	1999/02		
1.6	-0.5	-2.7	4.0	4.4	1.7	0.0	2.2	2.4	2000/02		
1.8	-1.3	8.4	1.3	15.8	1.3	-19.3	7.4	3.1	2001/02		
2.4	-1.6	1.1	9.6	8.0	7.5	10.9	10.0	-9.4	1998/02	7	Machines et matèriels de transports
16.4	2.1	6.8	10.3	16.9	13.3	10.5	13.0	14.2	1998/99		
-1.9	-2.8	-0.8	9.4	5.1	5.7	11.0	8.9	-16.1	1999/02		
-7.1	-8.2	-7.8	3.3	9.6	-1.3	12.1	0.9	-9.1	2000/02		
-3.2	-7.1	3.2	8.4	7.8	-0.4	12.6	11.9	29.3	2001/02		
3.3	0.2	1.5	4.4	11.1	4.5	3.2	4.2	2.5	1998/02	6&8	Articles manufacturés divers
7.2	1.3	8.3	6.8	-2.8	2.3	0.6	3.3	8.4	1998/99		
2.1	-0.1	-0.6	3.6	16.2	5.2	4.1	4.5	0.6	1999/02		
-2.3	-6.6	-6.6	-1.4	6.4	0.5	4.6	-0.1	-4.0	2000/02		
1.1	-6.0	2.3	3.3	2.9	3.8	2.2	5.4	2.7	2001/02		
Destination des exportations de grandes catégories de marchandises											
2.3	5.5	4.3	3.2	2.2	0.2	2.9	7.3	6.1	1998/02	0-9	Tous produits 3
6.7	11.9	8.8	5.9	-2.9	-5.3	-8.0	10.7	9.7	1998/99		
0.8	3.5	2.8	2.4	3.9	2.1	6.8	6.2	4.9	1999/02		
-3.0	-2.2	-4.2	2.5	4.6	-4.3	4.1	0.0	5.7	2000/02		
0.4	2.4	-2.6	11.7	4.7	-4.2	9.5	7.9	6.5	2001/02		
5.3	4.8	0.3	5.7	1.4	-1.6	0.4	2.7	-1.0	1998/02	0&1	Produits alimentaires, boissons et tabacs
2.4	4.8	5.0	12.2	-10.7	-14.4	-0.3	-2.2	-0.5	1998/99		
6.2	4.9	-1.2	3.5	5.8	3.1	0.6	4.4	-1.2	1999/02		
5.8	4.8	-3.7	4.0	5.0	2.3	-1.4	2.6	2.1	2000/02		
6.7	6.8	-2.1	11.8	4.1	-2.1	-6.7	0.5	4.6	2001/02		
0.8	-0.1	-0.2	-2.1	2.4	-1.8	1.5	5.6	-2.7	1998/02	2&4	Matières premières huiles & graisses (combust. exclu.)
-2.2	4.0	0.8	3.6	-3.0	-18.1	-14.4	3.6	-6.9	1998/99		
1.8	-1.4	-0.5	-3.9	4.3	4.3	7.4	6.3	-1.3	1999/02		
-3.8	-3.3	-4.5	-6.0	8.3	1.0	6.4	2.6	0.5	2000/02		
0.2	1.9	2.3	7.1	37.1	5.9	20.5	4.1	-9.6	2001/02		
11.9	19.6	7.7	16.5	14.9	16.0	17.1	13.7	14.6	1998/02	3	Combustibles minéraux et produits
28.9	51.6	25.0	39.3	79.9	36.0	52.5	88.0	20.3	1998/99		
6.7	10.5	2.5	9.7	-1.1	10.1	7.3	-3.8	12.7	1999/02		
-8.2	-7.3	-9.0	5.1	-6.9	-7.7	-6.8	-7.9	-10.8	2000/02		
-11.4	-5.9	-19.3	7.9	8.2	4.5	14.5	-5.5	-8.8	2001/02		
4.7	9.4	5.1	1.5	2.2	2.5	4.1	7.4	4.5	1998/02	5	Produits chimiques
7.0	13.6	8.0	5.8	-7.1	-3.8	-0.6	11.2	7.6	1998/99		
3.9	8.1	4.2	0.1	5.5	4.7	5.7	6.1	3.4	1999/02		
1.4	5.6	0.3	1.6	6.5	-0.4	4.1	0.4	8.1	2000/02		
0.6	6.6	1.1	-1.9	2.2	-3.8	8.6	7.6	12.6	2001/02		
0.8	4.3	6.8	4.4	1.3	-2.1	1.8	8.8	15.8	1998/02	7	Machines et matèriels de transports
7.4	11.7	10.5	7.8	-7.6	-7.6	-16.3	9.5	27.6	1998/99		
-1.3	2.0	5.6	3.3	4.5	-0.3	8.7	8.6	12.1	1999/02		
-4.9	-3.6	-3.8	3.4	4.4	-6.6	6.4	-0.1	22.8	2000/02		
1.4	2.3	2.6	17.9	3.6	-7.6	17.7	10.1	18.3	2001/02		
1.9	4.0	3.8	1.6	1.9	-0.4	3.2	4.9	-2.3	1998/02	6&8	Articles manufacturés divers
5.0	6.1	8.9	3.8	-4.2	-6.5	-10.6	5.2	-1.0	1998/99		
0.9	3.3	2.2	0.9	4.0	1.8	8.2	4.9	-2.7	1999/02		
-3.4	-1.3	-4.0	0.4	6.1	-4.5	6.7	0.0	-1.4	2000/02		
1.2	3.4	-2.9	10.8	7.9	-3.4	11.8	9.8	5.8	2001/02		

Voir la fin du Tableau Spécial F pour la remarque générale et les notes.

SPECIAL TABLE: F

Structure of world exports by commodity classes and by region

In per cent

Origin or destination → / ↓ SITC Commodity classes		Year	World Monde 1,2	Developed economies / Economies développées 1,2	Developing economies / economies en voie de développement 1,2: Total	Developing economies: OPEC OPEP	Eastern Europe & fmr USSR-Europe / Europe de l'Est et l'ancienne URSS-Europe: Total 1,4	Eastern Europe: Fmr USSR-Europe 5	Developed economies – Europe: Total	Developed economies – Europe: EU UE	Developed economies – Europe: EFTA AELE
Origin of exports of major commodity classes											
0-9	All commodities 3	1998	100.0	67.7	28.5	4.0	3.9	1.9	42.5	40.2	[illegible]
		1999	100.0	66.5	29.8	4.7	3.7	1.8	41.0	38.7	[illegible]
		2000	100.0	63.3	32.7	5.8	4.0	2.2	37.6	35.3	[illegible]
		2001	100.0	63.7	31.9	5.2	4.3	2.2	39.4	37.0	[illegible]
		2002	100.0	63.2	32.2	5.0	4.5	2.2	40.5	38.1	[illegible]
0&1	Food, live animals, beverages and tobacco	1998	100.0	65.7	31.4	2.9	2.9	1.0	46.0	44.0	[illegible]
		1999	100.0	66.9	30.6	2.9	2.5	0.8	46.6	44.5	[illegible]
		2000	100.0	65.6	31.8	2.7	2.6	0.9	44.0	42.0	[illegible]
		2001	100.0	65.4	31.9	2.6	2.6	0.8	43.6	41.8	[illegible]
		2002	100.0	66.4	30.2	2.6	3.4	1.5	46.1	44.2	[illegible]
2&4	Crude materials, oils and fats, (fuels excluded)	1998	100.0	59.4	34.7	3.9	5.9	4.2	27.3	26.4	[illegible]
		1999	100.0	58.7	35.6	4.1	5.7	3.7	26.2	25.4	[illegible]
		2000	100.0	58.5	35.6	4.3	6.0	4.0	24.7	23.9	[illegible]
		2001	100.0	59.4	35.8	4.4	4.8	2.8	26.1	25.3	[illegible]
		2002	100.0	58.7	35.5	4.8	5.8	3.8	27.3	26.5	[illegible]
3	Mineral fuels, lubricants and related material	1998	100.0	33.4	56.0	35.2	10.6	9.4	20.8	15.3	[illegible]
		1999	100.0	30.1	60.7	40.1	9.1	8.2	19.4	13.7	[illegible]
		2000	100.0	29.9	60.5	39.8	9.6	8.8	19.4	13.4	[illegible]
		2001	100.0	31.0	58.4	35.7	10.6	9.6	19.5	13.2	[illegible]
		2002	100.0	31.3	57.2	36.2	11.5	10.4	20.6	14.3	[illegible]
5	Chemicals	1998	100.0	80.9	16.3	2.2	2.8	1.3	58.4	53.7	[illegible]
		1999	100.0	80.9	16.7	2.1	2.5	1.2	57.6	52.8	[illegible]
		2000	100.0	79.0	18.2	2.2	2.8	1.4	54.5	50.3	[illegible]
		2001	100.0	79.9	17.6	2.4	2.5	1.1	56.8	52.2	[illegible]
		2002	100.0	80.4	17.0	1.8	2.7	1.2	58.7	53.7	[illegible]
7	Machinery and transport equipment	1998	100.0	74.7	23.1	0.5	2.2	0.5	42.8	41.3	[illegible]
		1999	100.0	73.1	24.8	0.5	2.1	0.4	40.9	39.5	[illegible]
		2000	100.0	69.9	27.8	0.6	2.3	0.5	37.8	36.6	[illegible]
		2001	100.0	70.0	27.3	0.6	2.6	0.4	40.2	38.9	[illegible]
		2002	100.0	68.4	28.6	0.6	3.0	0.5	40.7	39.4	[illegible]
6&8	Other manufactured goods	1998	100.0	61.1	34.1	3.2	4.8	2.1	42.8	40.4	[illegible]
		1999	100.0	60.8	34.8	3.5	4.4	1.8	41.5	39.1	[illegible]
		2000	100.0	58.6	36.7	3.5	4.7	2.0	38.4	36.1	[illegible]
		2001	100.0	58.9	36.6	3.5	4.5	1.5	39.8	37.4	[illegible]
		2002	100.0	58.2	36.6	3.2	5.2	2.0	40.3	37.9	[illegible]
Destination of exports of major commodity classes											
0-9	All commodities	1998	100.0	67.1	26.7	3.0	4.0	1.7	40.5	38.0	[illegible]
		1999	100.0	68.4	26.7	2.7	3.4	1.2	40.1	37.8	[illegible]
		2000	100.0	65.9	27.7	2.6	3.5	1.3	37.1	35.0	[illegible]
		2001	100.0	65.7	27.2	3.0	3.9	1.5	37.8	35.7	[illegible]
		2002	100.0	65.3	27.5	3.0	4.1	1.6	38.2	36.1	[illegible]
0&1	Food, live animals, beverages and tobacco	1998	100.0	67.8	25.4	5.0	5.5	3.7	45.8	44.3	[illegible]
		1999	100.0	70.1	24.5	4.8	4.3	2.6	46.5	44.9	[illegible]
		2000	100.0	68.3	26.4	5.2	4.2	2.6	43.2	41.6	[illegible]
		2001	100.0	67.4	26.9	5.7	4.6	2.8	43.2	41.6	[illegible]
		2002	100.0	68.7	25.5	5.1	4.7	2.9	44.8	43.2	[illegible]
2&4	Crude materials, oils and fats, (fuels excluded)	1998	100.0	62.1	31.7	3.0	3.7	1.5	39.4	37.5	[illegible]
		1999	100.0	62.0	32.6	3.2	3.4	1.5	37.7	35.8	[illegible]
		2000	100.0	60.1	33.9	3.1	3.6	1.6	36.0	34.1	[illegible]
		2001	100.0	59.2	35.0	3.1	3.5	1.5	36.4	34.5	[illegible]
		2002	100.0	58.7	35.4	3.1	3.9	1.7	36.8	34.9	[illegible]
3	Mineral fuels, lubricants and related material	1998	100.0	53.9	20.7	1.0	5.6	2.8	29.7	27.6	[illegible]
		1999	100.0	58.4	27.5	0.9	4.3	1.9	31.2	29.4	[illegible]
		2000	100.0	54.3	20.9	0.9	4.1	1.7	28.8	27.3	[illegible]
		2001	100.0	55.3	19.7	1.0	4.5	2.1	28.9	27.7	[illegible]
		2002	100.0	54.3	19.8	0.9	4.6	2.1	30.2	28.5	[illegible]
5	Chemicals	1998	100.0	65.4	28.2	3.0	4.3	1.6	46.1	43.2	[illegible]
		1999	100.0	65.9	28.7	3.0	3.8	1.2	45.3	42.3	[illegible]
		2000	100.0	64.4	30.7	3.0	4.0	1.4	43.3	40.5	[illegible]
		2001	100.0	65.3	29.0	3.2	4.4	1.6	44.2	41.3	[illegible]
		2002	100.0	66.0	28.2	3.0	4.6	1.7	45.6	42.7	[illegible]
7	Machinery and transport equipment	1998	100.0	68.3	27.8	3.0	3.2	1.1	38.7	36.7	[illegible]
		1999	100.0	69.5	26.9	2.4	2.7	0.7	38.4	36.5	[illegible]
		2000	100.0	66.9	29.3	2.5	2.9	0.8	35.3	33.6	[illegible]
		2001	100.0	67.2	28.9	3.0	3.3	1.1	36.7	34.9	[illegible]
		2002	100.0	66.2	29.5	3.1	3.7	1.2	36.4	34.7	[illegible]
6&8	Other manufactured goods	1998	100.0	69.6	25.7	2.9	4.1	1.5	42.4	39.6	[illegible]
		1999	100.0	70.4	25.5	2.6	3.6	1.1	41.8	39.1	[illegible]
		2000	100.0	68.9	26.9	2.7	3.8	1.3	39.0	36.5	[illegible]
		2001	100.0	68.8	26.1	3.1	4.2	1.5	39.8	37.3	[illegible]
		2002	100.0	68.3	26.8	3.1	4.6	1.6	39.9	37.3	[illegible]

For general note and footnotes see end of table.

TABLEAU SPECIAL: F

Structure des exportations mondiales par categories de marchandises et par regions

En pourcentage

conomies ėveloppées 1, 2			Developing economies Economies en voie de développement 1, 2						← En provenance ou vers		
Canada	U.S.A E.-U.	Japan Japon	Australia New Zealand Australie Nouvelle-Zélande	Africa Afrique	America Amerique	Asia Asie Mid.East Moyen Orient	Asia Asie Other Autres 6	Oceania Océanie	Année		CTCI: Classes de marchandises ↓
Provenance des exportations de grandes catégories de marchandises											
4.0	11.9	7.3	1.2	1.3	5.1	3.0	18.7	0.1	1998	0-9	Tous produits 3
4.3	11.6	7.5	1.2	1.5	5.3	3.5	19.1	0.1	1999		
4.4	11.4	7.7	1.2	1.9	5.6	4.1	20.6	0.1	2000		
4.3	11.1	6.7	1.3	1.6	5.7	4.3	19.9	0.1	2001		
4.0	10.0	6.6	1.3	1.7	5.5	3.9	20.8	0.1	2002		
3.6	11.0	0.5	3.9	2.9	12.7	2.5	12.7	0.2	1998	0&1	Produits alimentaires, boissons et tabacs
3.7	11.1	0.5	4.2	2.8	12.0	2.5	12.8	0.2	1999		
4.1	11.7	0.5	4.6	2.8	12.1	2.4	14.0	0.1	2000		
4.4	11.3	0.7	4.6	2.8	12.3	2.9	13.4	0.2	2001		
4.1	10.3	0.5	4.7	2.7	11.3	2.3	13.5	0.1	2002		
9.7	13.5	1.4	6.1	3.3	11.7	1.9	16.6	0.9	1998	2&4	Matières premières huiles & graisses (combust. exclu.)
10.6	12.8	1.5	6.1	3.7	11.5	2.0	17.1	0.9	1999		
10.5	13.8	1.6	6.4	3.6	11.8	1.7	17.1	0.9	2000		
9.5	14.0	1.7	6.6	3.3	12.5	2.5	16.4	0.7	2001		
8.6	13.4	1.7	6.1	4.1	11.9	1.8	16.7	0.6	2002		
5.5	3.1	0.4	3.0	9.5	8.9	23.7	13.5	0.2	1998	3	Combustibles minéraux et produits
5.0	2.4	0.3	2.4	11.5	9.7	27.1	12.3	0.0	1999		
5.7	2.0	0.2	2.1	11.7	9.6	26.7	12.2	0.1	2000		
6.3	2.2	0.3	2.3	9.1	9.0	28.0	12.2	0.1	2001		
5.5	2.0	0.2	2.4	9.6	9.6	25.6	12.2	0.1	2002		
2.4	13.3	5.3	0.6	0.6	2.8	1.8	10.7	0.0	1998	5	Produits chimiques
2.4	13.4	5.8	0.6	0.6	2.7	1.8	11.3	0.0	1999		
2.6	14.0	6.2	0.6	0.6	2.9	1.7	12.7	0.0	2000		
2.5	13.6	5.2	0.7	0.5	2.9	2.0	11.9	0.0	2001		
2.4	12.5	5.2	0.6	0.5	2.7	1.5	11.9	0.0	2002		
4.0	14.9	12.2	0.3	0.1	4.0	0.5	18.2	0.0	1998	7	Machines et matèriels de transports
4.4	14.5	12.4	0.3	0.1	4.4	0.5	19.6	0.0	1999		
4.3	14.1	12.7	0.3	0.1	4.7	0.5	22.3	0.0	2000		
4.1	13.6	11.1	0.3	0.1	4.9	0.6	21.6	0.0	2001		
3.8	12.1	11.0	0.3	0.1	4.7	0.6	23.0	0.0	2002		
3.2	8.5	4.8	0.7	0.8	4.1	3.2	25.3	0.1	1998	6&8	Articles manufactués divers
3.4	8.6	5.2	0.7	0.8	4.1	3.2	26.0	0.1	1999		
3.5	9.1	5.4	0.7	1.0	4.4	3.1	27.6	0.1	2000		
3.4	8.7	4.8	0.7	1.2	4.4	3.4	27.0	0.1	2001		
3.3	7.8	4.7	0.7	1.2	4.4	3.3	27.1	0.1	2002		
Destination des exportations de grandes catégories de marchandises											
3.4	16.5	4.5	1.3	1.9	5.9	3.2	15.1	0.1	1998	0-9	Tous produits 3
3.5	17.9	4.7	1.3	1.8	5.4	2.9	16.1	0.1	1999		
3.4	18.4	4.9	1.2	1.6	5.6	2.9	17.2	0.1	2000		
3.3	17.8	4.8	1.1	1.7	5.5	2.9	16.5	0.1	2001		
3.1	17.4	4.5	1.2	1.7	5.1	3.1	17.0	0.1	2002		
2.4	9.7	8.4	0.8	3.6	6.1	4.6	10.3	0.2	1998	0&1	Produits alimentaires, boissons et tabacs
2.5	10.5	9.0	0.9	3.3	5.4	4.7	10.3	0.2	1999		
2.7	11.1	9.5	0.9	3.6	5.7	5.0	11.3	0.2	2000		
2.7	11.1	8.7	0.9	3.7	5.9	5.0	11.5	0.2	2001		
2.8	11.3	8.2	0.9	3.7	5.5	4.5	11.0	0.2	2002		
2.6	10.1	8.6	0.7	2.6	5.3	3.4	20.0	0.1	1998	2&4	Matières premières huiles & graisses (combust. exclu.)
2.7	11.1	9.1	0.7	2.6	4.5	3.1	21.9	0.1	1999		
2.9	10.6	9.2	0.7	2.4	4.7	3.1	23.2	0.0	2000		
2.8	10.2	8.6	0.6	2.1	4.7	3.1	24.6	0.1	2001		
2.6	9.7	8.2	0.6	2.7	4.7	3.5	24.0	0.0	2002		
1.6	15.1	6.3	0.8	1.3	5.1	2.5	11.1	0.2	1998	3	Combustibles minéraux et produits
1.6	18.1	6.3	0.9	1.8	5.5	3.0	16.6	0.2	1999		
1.5	17.9	5.1	0.6	1.3	5.4	2.7	10.9	0.2	2000		
1.6	18.0	5.8	0.7	1.1	4.8	2.2	10.8	0.2	2001		
1.4	17.0	4.7	0.8	1.2	5.1	2.6	10.3	0.2	2002		
3.2	10.1	3.4	1.5	2.0	6.8	3.3	15.6	0.1	1998	5	Produits chimiques
3.3	11.2	3.6	1.6	1.8	6.3	3.2	16.9	0.1	1999		
3.4	11.7	3.7	1.4	1.7	6.8	3.2	18.5	0.1	2000		
3.3	11.8	3.6	1.4	1.8	6.7	3.1	16.7	0.1	2001		
3.1	11.7	3.4	1.3	1.7	6.0	3.1	16.7	0.1	2002		
4.2	19.8	3.2	1.4	1.7	6.4	3.1	16.2	0.1	1998	7	Machines et matèriels de transports
4.3	21.1	3.4	1.4	1.5	5.6	2.5	16.8	0.1	1999		
4.1	21.5	3.8	1.3	1.4	5.7	2.5	19.3	0.1	2000		
3.9	20.7	3.7	1.3	1.6	5.8	2.5	18.6	0.1	2001		
3.8	20.2	3.6	1.4	1.6	5.1	2.9	19.5	0.1	2002		
3.1	17.2	4.6	1.2	1.7	5.2	3.2	14.9	0.1	1998	6&8	Articles manufacturés divers
3.2	18.1	5.0	1.3	1.7	4.8	2.8	15.6	0.1	1999		
3.3	19.0	5.4	1.2	1.5	5.1	2.9	16.7	0.1	2000		
3.1	18.5	5.3	1.1	1.7	5.0	3.1	15.7	0.1	2001		
3.0	18.2	4.9	1.2	1.7	4.6	3.3	16.5	0.1	2002		

Voir la page suivante pour la remarque générale et les notes.

SPECIAL TABLE: F

Structure of world exports by commodity classes and by region

In per cent

SITC Commodity classes	Year	World / Monde 1,2	Developed economies / Economies développées 1,2	Developing economies / economies en voie de développement 1,2: Total	Developing economies 1,2: OPEC / OPEP	Eastern Europe & fmr USSR-Europe / Europe de l'Est et l'ancienne URSS-Europe: Total 1,4	Eastern Europe & fmr USSR-Europe: Fmr USSR-Europe 5	Developed economies – Europe: Total	Developed economies – Europe: EU / UE	Developed economies – Europe: EFTA / AELE
Commodity composition of the total exports of selected regions										
0-9 All commodities	1998	100.0	100.0	100.0	100.0	100.0	100.0	100.0	100.0	100.0
	1999	100.0	100.0	100.0	100.0	100.0	100.0	100.0	100.0	100.0
	2000	100.0	100.0	100.0	100.0	100.0	100.0	100.0	100.0	100.0
	2001	100.0	100.0	100.0	100.0	100.0	100.0	100.0	100.0	100.0
	2002	100.0	100.0	100.0	100.0	100.0	100.0	100.0	100.0	100.0
0&1 Food, live animals, beverages and tobacco	1998	7.6	7.4	8.4	5.6	5.8	3.9	8.2	8.3	6.1
	1999	7.1	7.2	7.3	4.4	4.9	3.3	8.1	8.2	5.9
	2000	6.2	6.5	6.1	2.9	4.0	2.6	7.3	7.4	4.9
	2001	6.7	6.9	6.7	3.4	4.1	2.5	7.4	7.5	4.8
	2002	6.7	7.0	6.3	3.5	5.0	4.6	7.6	7.8	5.0
2&4 Crude, materials, ooils and fats, (fuels excluded)	1998	4.0	3.5	4.8	3.9	6.1	8.6	2.5	2.6	1.4
	1999	3.6	3.2	4.3	3.2	5.7	7.5	2.3	2.4	1.3
	2000	3.5	3.2	3.8	2.6	5.1	6.4	2.3	2.3	1.3
	2001	3.4	3.2	3.8	2.9	3.8	4.4	2.3	2.3	1.2
	2002	3.5	3.2	3.9	3.4	4.5	6.1	2.4	2.4	1.2
3 Mineral fuels, lubricants and related material	1998	6.0	2.9	11.7	53.0	16.4	29.1	2.9	2.3	14.6
	1999	7.3	3.3	14.8	62.6	18.2	32.9	3.4	2.6	17.9
	2000	10.3	4.9	19.1	70.5	24.4	41.6	5.3	3.9	26.9
	2001	9.7	4.7	17.7	66.4	23.6	42.4	4.8	3.5	25.6
	2002	9.2	4.5	16.3	67.1	23.3	43.4	4.7	3.5	24.3
5 Chemicals	1998	9.6	11.5	5.5	5.3	6.9	6.7	13.2	12.8	19.6
	1999	9.5	11.6	5.3	4.2	6.4	6.4	13.3	13.0	19.5
	2000	9.1	11.4	5.1	3.5	6.3	5.9	13.2	13.0	16.7
	2001	9.8	12.3	5.4	4.5	5.7	5.0	14.1	13.8	19.1
	2002	10.1	12.8	5.3	3.7	6.0	5.7	14.6	14.2	21.1
7 Machinery and transport equipment	1998	41.2	45.4	33.4	4.9	23.6	10.7	41.4	42.3	25.7
	1999	41.7	45.8	34.7	4.2	24.3	9.4	41.6	42.6	24.4
	2000	41.5	45.9	35.3	4.6	23.7	8.7	41.8	43.1	21.4
	2001	40.4	44.4	34.6	4.7	24.6	8.0	41.2	42.5	21.5
	2002	40.6	43.9	36.0	5.0	26.7	9.3	40.8	42.0	20.6
6&8 Other manufactured goods	1998	28.5	25.8	34.2	23.3	35.7	30.9	28.8	28.7	30.1
	1999	27.7	25.3	32.3	20.8	33.5	27.5	28.0	28.0	28.9
	2000	26.5	24.6	29.8	15.9	30.9	25.0	27.1	27.1	27.0
	2001	26.6	24.6	30.5	17.9	27.6	18.1	26.8	26.9	25.8
	2002	26.7	24.5	30.3	17.3	30.7	23.8	26.5	26.6	26.1
Commodity composition of the world exports to selected regions										
0-9 All commodities	1998	100.0	100.0	100.0	100.0	100.0	100.0	100.0	100.0	100.0
	1999	100.0	100.0	100.0	100.0	100.0	100.0	100.0	100.0	100.0
	2000	100.0	100.0	100.0	100.0	100.0	100.0	100.0	100.0	100.0
	2001	100.0	100.0	100.0	100.0	100.0	100.0	100.0	100.0	100.0
	2002	100.0	100.0	100.0	100.0	100.0	100.0	100.0	100.0	100.0
0&1 Food, live animals, beverages and tobacco	1998	7.6	7.7	7.2	12.6	10.4	16.9	8.6	8.8	4.6
	1999	7.1	7.3	6.5	13.0	8.9	15.5	8.3	8.5	4.9
	2000	6.2	6.5	5.9	12.4	7.5	12.3	7.3	7.4	4.5
	2001	6.7	6.9	6.6	12.5	7.9	12.5	7.6	7.8	4.8
	2002	6.7	7.0	6.2	11.5	7.6	12.2	7.8	8.0	4.9
2&4 Crude materials, oils and fats, (fuels excluded)	1998	4.0	3.7	4.7	3.9	3.6	3.6	3.9	3.9	3.1
	1999	3.6	3.3	4.4	4.4	3.6	4.4	3.4	3.4	3.0
	2000	3.5	3.2	4.2	4.0	3.6	4.3	3.4	3.4	3.2
	2001	3.4	3.1	4.4	3.5	3.0	3.5	3.3	3.3	3.2
	2002	3.5	3.1	4.5	3.6	3.3	3.8	3.4	3.4	3.3
3 Mineral fuels, lubricants and related material	1998	6.0	4.8	4.6	2.0	8.3	9.9	4.4	4.3	4.1
	1999	7.3	6.2	7.5	2.5	9.2	11.4	5.7	5.7	4.7
	2000	10.3	8.5	7.8	3.6	12.2	13.4	8.0	8.0	6.1
	2001	9.7	8.1	7.0	3.0	11.1	13.5	7.4	7.5	4.9
	2002	9.2	7.7	6.6	2.8	10.2	12.2	7.3	7.3	6.1
5 Chemicals	1998	9.6	9.3	10.1	9.6	10.2	9.0	10.9	10.9	11.7
	1999	9.5	9.2	10.2	10.6	10.8	9.6	10.7	10.6	12.7
	2000	9.1	8.9	10.1	10.6	10.5	10.0	10.7	10.6	12.3
	2001	9.8	9.7	10.4	10.4	10.9	10.5	11.4	11.3	13.6
	2002	10.1	10.2	10.3	10.2	11.3	11.0	12.0	11.9	14.6
7 Machinery and transport equipment	1998	41.2	41.9	42.8	41.1	33.3	27.7	39.3	39.7	33.5
	1999	41.7	42.4	42.0	38.4	33.4	25.0	40.0	40.3	34.0
	2000	41.5	42.2	43.9	39.1	34.0	25.3	39.5	39.9	33.3
	2001	40.4	41.3	42.9	39.8	34.2	28.4	39.2	39.5	33.8
	2002	40.6	41.1	43.5	41.9	36.7	31.7	38.6	39.0	32.2
6&8 Other manufactured goods	1998	28.5	29.6	27.5	27.1	29.2	25.9	29.9	29.7	33.8
	1999	27.7	28.6	26.5	27.4	29.6	26.5	28.8	28.7	32.7
	2000	26.5	27.8	25.8	27.7	28.6	26.8	27.9	27.7	32.2
	2001	26.6	27.9	25.5	27.0	28.4	25.6	28.0	27.8	31.9
	2002	26.7	27.9	26.0	27.8	29.6	27.8	27.8	27.6	33.0

For general note and footnotes see end of table.

Structure des exportations mondiales par categories de marchandises et par regions

En pourcentage

Economies développées 1, 2			Developing economies / Economies en voie de développement 1, 2						← En provenance ou vers		
Canada	U.S.A / E.-U.	Japan / Japon	Australia New Zealand / Australie Nouvelle-Zélande	Africa / Afrique	America / Amerique	Asia / Asie: Mid.East / Moyen Orient	Asia / Asie: Other / Autres 6	Oceania / Océanie	Année	CTCI: Classes de marchandises ↓	
Composition par marchandises des exportations totales des régions selectionnées											
100.0	100.0	100.0	100.0	100.0	100.0	100.0	100.0	100.0	1998	0-9	Tous produits 3
100.0	100.0	100.0	100.0	100.0	100.0	100.0	100.0	100.0	1999		
100.0	100.0	100.0	100.0	100.0	100.0	100.0	100.0	100.0	2000		
100.0	100.0	100.0	100.0	100.0	100.0	100.0	100.0	100.0	2001		
100.0	100.0	100.0	100.0	100.0	100.0	100.0	100.0	100.0	2002		
6.7	7.0	0.5	24.1	17.2	18.7	6.5	5.2	15.8	1998	0&1	Produits alimentaires, boissoins et tabacs
6.2	6.8	0.5	25.7	13.1	16.2	5.0	4.8	17.5	1999		
5.8	6.4	0.4	23.2	9.4	13.5	3.6	4.2	9.9	2000		
6.8	6.8	0.7	24.4	11.5	14.6	4.4	4.5	12.6	2001		
6.8	6.9	0.5	24.8	10.8	13.8	4.0	4.3	11.8	2002		
9.6	4.5	0.8	19.9	10.3	9.1	2.5	3.5	36.0	1998	2&4	Matières premières huiles & graisses (combust. exclu.)
8.9	4.0	0.7	18.9	9.0	7.9	2.1	3.2	34.5	1999		
8.1	4.2	0.7	18.1	6.6	7.3	1.4	2.9	34.3	2000		
7.5	4.3	0.9	17.9	7.0	7.6	2.0	2.8	30.5	2001		
7.5	4.7	0.9	16.9	8.7	7.6	1.6	2.8	28.4	2002		
8.2	1.6	0.3	15.0	45.1	10.4	47.4	4.3	8.7	1998	3	Combustibles minéraux et produits
8.5	1.5	0.3	14.8	55.7	13.4	56.4	4.7	1.8	1999		
13.1	1.8	0.3	17.8	63.7	17.6	66.5	6.1	13.7	2000		
14.1	1.9	0.4	17.6	54.3	15.4	62.4	5.9	13.8	2001		
12.6	1.8	0.3	17.3	53.7	16.1	60.9	5.4	11.9	2002		
5.7	10.7	7.0	4.4	4.6	5.2	5.9	5.5	1.2	1998	5	Produits chimiques
5.4	11.0	7.4	4.9	3.6	4.8	4.8	5.6	1.3	1999		
5.3	11.2	7.3	4.7	2.7	4.7	3.8	5.6	1.1	2000		
5.8	12.0	7.6	5.0	3.1	4.9	4.6	5.8	0.3	2001		
6.0	12.6	8.0	4.9	3.3	5.0	4.0	5.7	1.4	2002		
40.7	51.8	69.2	9.4	3.2	32.4	6.3	40.3	5.2	1998	7	Machines et matériels de transports
42.6	52.3	68.7	10.4	3.0	34.4	5.8	42.8	6.3	1999		
40.2	51.4	68.8	10.8	2.1	34.7	4.7	44.9	4.1	2000		
38.2	49.8	67.3	10.6	2.8	35.1	5.2	43.7	3.0	2001		
38.1	49.0	67.2	11.1	2.8	34.5	6.3	44.7	4.2	2002		
22.5	20.5	19.0	15.6	18.9	22.6	31.0	38.7	26.9	1998	6&8	Articles manufacturés divers
21.7	20.5	19.1	16.7	14.8	21.7	25.7	37.7	31.0	1999		
20.8	21.1	18.8	16.2	14.5	20.8	19.8	35.5	30.8	2000		
21.0	21.0	19.0	15.2	19.4	20.9	21.0	36.0	32.2	2001		
21.8	20.8	18.8	15.1	18.6	21.4	23.0	34.7	35.3	2002		
omposition par marchandises des exportations mondiales vers régions selectionnée											
100.0	100.0	100.0	100.0	100.0	100.0	100.0	100.0	100.0	1998	0-9	Tous produits 3
100.0	100.0	100.0	100.0	100.0	100.0	100.0	100.0	100.0	1999		
100.0	100.0	100.0	100.0	100.0	100.0	100.0	100.0	100.0	2000		
100.0	100.0	100.0	100.0	100.0	100.0	100.0	100.0	100.0	2001		
100.0	100.0	100.0	100.0	100.0	100.0	100.0	100.0	100.0	2002		
5.3	4.5	14.3	4.7	14.4	7.8	10.7	5.2	13.6	1998	0&1	Produits alimentaires, boissons et tabacs
5.1	4.2	13.8	4.9	13.3	7.1	11.6	4.6	12.3	1999		
5.0	3.8	12.1	5.0	13.9	6.4	10.8	4.1	11.0	2000		
5.6	4.2	12.2	5.1	14.1	7.1	11.4	4.7	10.5	2001		
5.9	4.3	12.2	5.1	14.0	7.3	9.7	4.3	10.3	2002		
3.1	2.4	7.7	2.1	5.4	3.5	4.2	5.3	2.1	1998	2&4	Matières premières huiles & graisses (combust. exclu.)
2.8	2.3	7.1	2.1	5.4	3.1	3.9	4.9	1.8	1999		
2.9	2.0	6.5	2.1	5.1	2.9	3.8	4.7	1.6	2000		
2.9	2.0	6.1	1.8	4.1	2.9	3.6	5.1	1.7	2001		
2.9	1.9	6.4	1.7	5.4	3.3	4.0	4.9	1.5	2002		
2.8	5.4	8.5	3.7	4.0	5.1	4.6	4.4	10.0	1998	3	Combustibles minéraux et produits
3.4	7.4	9.7	4.8	7.4	7.4	7.6	7.5	10.9	1999		
4.5	10.0	10.7	5.7	8.1	9.9	9.6	6.6	19.0	2000		
4.6	9.8	11.7	6.1	6.2	8.5	7.3	6.3	15.8	2001		
4.1	9.0	9.7	5.9	6.4	9.2	7.7	5.6	13.5	2002		
9.1	5.9	7.4	11.5	9.9	11.0	9.7	9.9	5.7	1998	5	Produits chimiques
9.1	5.9	7.3	11.5	9.5	11.1	10.5	9.9	5.6	1999		
9.1	5.8	7.0	11.0	9.5	11.1	10.2	9.8	5.1	2000		
9.9	6.5	7.3	12.3	10.1	12.0	10.3	9.9	5.0	2001		
10.0	6.8	7.6	10.8	9.9	12.0	10.2	9.9	5.3	2002		
51.5	49.2	29.7	44.8	37.6	44.7	39.3	44.0	30.4	1998	7	Machines et matériels de transports
51.8	49.1	30.1	45.7	35.8	43.6	35.8	43.6	35.3	1999		
50.6	48.4	32.4	46.1	36.5	42.6	36.1	46.7	31.9	2000		
48.2	47.1	31.1	44.4	36.8	42.2	35.1	45.6	38.8	2001		
48.7	47.0	32.7	46.9	36.4	40.7	37.7	46.6	43.1	2002		
26.0	29.6	29.8	27.2	26.3	24.9	28.1	28.3	31.0	1998	6&8	Articles manufacturés divers
25.6	28.1	29.8	26.7	25.9	24.6	27.3	26.9	28.0	1999		
25.9	27.4	29.2	26.7	25.3	24.5	27.1	25.9	25.6	2000		
25.5	27.6	29.4	25.8	25.2	24.2	27.8	25.4	22.5	2001		
25.7	27.9	29.3	25.6	26.0	24.4	28.4	25.8	22.3	2002		

Voir la page suivante pour la remarque générale et les notes.

SPECIAL TABLE: F

Structure of world exports by commodity classes and by regions (continued)
Structure des exportations mondiales par catégories de marchandises et par régions (suite)

General note

The regional analysis in Special Tables E and F is in accordance with Special Table A of this issue.

The figures in tables E and F are derived from the data in Special Table D.

The commodity classification is in accordance with the United Nations' Standard International Trade Classification (SITC), Revision 3, except for for countries which report trade data only in terms of the SITC, Revision 2, or the SITC, Revised.

The data approximate total exports of all countries and areas of the world. They are based on official export figures converted, where necessary, to U.S. dollars according to conversion factors published in Table C for each country in this volume. Where official figures are not available estimates based on the imports reported by partner countries and on other subsidiary data are used. Some official national data have been adjusted

(a) to approximate the commodity groupings of the SITC and

(b) to approximate calendar years.

The data include special category (confidential) exports, ships' stores and bunkers and exports of minor importance, the destination of which cannot be determined. These data are included in the world totals for each commodity group and in total exports, but are excluded from all regions of destination.

1 Exports for which country of destination is not available are included in the totals for the 'World', the 'Developed economies', the 'Developing economies' and 'Eastern Europe and the former USSR' but are excluded from the regional components of these groupings.

2 This classification is intended for statistical convenience and does not, necessarily, express a judgement about the stage reached by a particular country in the development process.

3 Section 9 of the SITC, which comprises commodities and transactions not classified elsewhere, is included in the total trade but is not shown separately in this table.

4 Includes Eastern Europe and the European countries of the former USSR.

5 Includes Belarus, Estonia, Latvia, Lithuania, Republic of Moldova, the Russian Federation, and Ukraine.

6 Includes Armenia, Azerbaijan, Georgia, Kazakhstan, Kyrgyzstan, Tajikistan, Turkmenistan, and Uzbekistan.

Remarque générale

L'analyse régionale dans les Tables Spécial E et F est conforme au Tableau Spécial A de ce numéro.

Les données de les tables E et F sont derivées de celles publiées dans le Tableau Spécial D.

La classification par marchandise utilisée est la Classification type pour le commerce international (CTCI), Revision 3,) en dehors des pays qui rapportent exclusivement les données du commerce en accord avec la CTCI, Revision 2, ou la CTCI, Revisée.

Les données approchées des exportations totales de tous pays et régions du monde. Elles sont basées sur les chiffres des exportations officielles nationales convertis en dollars E.-U. selon les facteurs de conversion publiés dans le Tableau C pour chaque pays ce tome. Quand les chiffres officiels ne sont pas disponibles on a recours a des estimations basées sur les importations rapportées par les pays partenaires ou sur d'autres donées subsidiaries. Quelques données officielles nationales ont été ajustées

(a) qu'elles correspondent aux groups des marchandises de la CTCI et

(b) qu'elles correspondent aux années civiles.

Les données comprises les exportations de 'special category' (confidentielles), les approvisionnements des navires et combustible de soute et autres exportations de moindre importance dont la destination n'a pu être déterminée. Ces données sont comprises dans les totaux de chaque chaque groupe de marchandise et dans les exportations totales, mais elles ne sont pas comprises dans les régions de destination.

1 Les exportations dont les pays de destination ne sont pas disponibles sont comprises dans les totaux du 'Monde', des 'Economies développées', des 'Economies en voie de développement' et de 'Europe de l'Est et l'ancienne URSS', mais ils ne sont pas comprises dans chaque partie composant ces régions.

2 Cette classification est utilisée pour plus de commodité dans la présentation des statistiques et n'implique pas nécessairement un jugement quant au stade de développment auquel est parvenu un pays donné.

3 Section 9 de la CTCI, qui représente les articles et transactions non ailleurs est comprise dans le commerce total mais n'est pas présentée séparément dans ce tableau.

4 Y compris de l'Europe de l'est et les pays européens de l'ancienne URSS.

5 Y compris Bélarus, Estonie, Lettonie, Lituanie, République de Moldova, Fédération de Russie, et Ukraine.

6 Y compris Azerbaïdjan, Arménie, Géorgie, Kazakhstan, Kirghizistan, Tadjikistan, Turkménistan, et Ouzbékistan.

Special Table G - Tableau Special G

Total exports and imports by countries or areas

Volume, unit value/price, terms of trade and purchasing power of exports, in US dollars: (1990 = 100)

Exportations et importations totales par pays ou zones

Volume, valeur unitaire/prix, termes de l'échange et pouvoir d'achat des exportations, en dollars É.-U.: (1990 = 100)

Country or Area	1985	1994	1995	1996	1997	1998	1999	2000	2001	2002	Pays ou Zone
Argentina											**Argentine**
Imports: Volume	...	459	503	601	789	856	738	732	605	275	Importations: volume
Imports: Unit Value	...	100	98	97	95	90	85	85	82	80	Importations: valeur unitaire
Exports: Volume	...	179	152	162	186	207	206	212	221	221	Exportations: volume
Exports: Unit Value	...	115	111	119	115	103	92	101	97	93	Exportations: valeur unitaire
Terms of Trade	...	*115*	*113*	*122*	*121*	*115*	*108*	*119*	*118*	*116*	*Termes de l'échange*
Purchasing Power of exports	...	*206*	*173*	*198*	*225*	*237*	*222*	*251*	*261*	*256*	*Pouvoir d'achat des Export.*
Australia											**Australie**
Imports: Volume	77	133	148	161	180	195	215	233	223	252	Importations: volume
Imports: Unit Value[1]	77	105	109	109	103	95	95	94	88	89	Importations: valeur unitaire[1]
Exports: Volume	81	139	141	157	179	178	187	205	211	213	Exportations: volume
Exports: Unit Value[1]	71	86	94	95	91	81	77	80	79	81	Exportations: valeur unitaire[1]
Terms of Trade	*92*	*82*	*85*	*87*	*88*	*85*	*81*	*86*	*89*	*91*	*Termes de l'échange*
Purchasing Power of Exports	*74*	*114*	*120*	*136*	*158*	*152*	*151*	*176*	*188*	*194*	*Pouvoir d'achat des Export.*
Austria											**Autriche**
Imports: Volume	68	140	125	129	164	188	206	223	237	243	Importations: volume
Imports: Unit Value	72	94	108	98	80	74	69	60	58	60	Importations: valeur unitaire
Exports: Volume	69	152	140	147	192	220	269	268	292	308	Exportations: volume
Exports: Unit Value	69	84	97	89	72	67	56	54	51	54	Exportations: valeur unitaire
Terms of Trade	*96*	*90*	*90*	*91*	*90*	*91*	*81*	*89*	*88*	*90*	*Termes de l'échange*
Purchasing Power of Exports	*66*	*138*	*126*	*134*	*173*	*200*	*218*	*240*	*256*	*279*	*Pouvoir d'achat des Export.*
Belgium											**Belgique**
Imports: Volume	73	115	121	126	131	141	141	155	161	175	Importations: volume
Imports: Unit Value	64	91	106	105	96	93	90	88	87	90	Importations: valeur unitaire
Exports: Volume	76	123	131	134	144	151	156	171	175	190	Exportations: volume
Exports: Unit Value	60	94	110	107	98	96	92	87	86	90	Exportations: valeur unitaire
Terms of Trade	*93*	*103*	*103*	*102*	*102*	*104*	*102*	*99*	*99*	*101*	*Termes de l'échange*
Purchasing Power of Exports	*71*	*127*	*135*	*137*	*146*	*156*	*159*	*170*	*174*	*191*	*Pouvoir d'achat des Export.*
Bolivia											**Bolivie**
Imports: Volume	...	...	...	...	...	...	...	...	...	...	Importations: volume
Imports: Unit Value	...	...	...	...	...	...	...	...	...	...	Importations: valeur unitaire
Exports: Volume	88	95	91	93	98	93	85	97	103	124	Exportations: volume
Exports: Unit Value	89	66	73	72	55	49	48	61	58	50	Exportations: valeur unitaire
Terms of Trade	...	...	...	...	...	...	...	...	...	...	*Termes de l'échange*
Purchasing Power of Exports	...	...	...	...	...	...	...	...	...	...	*Pouvoir d'achat des Export.*
Brazil											**Brésil**
Imports: Volume	69	142	176	178	174	181	170	185	185	180	Importations: volume
Imports: Unit Value	96	113	136	141	178	150	137	143	142	124	Importations: valeur unitaire
Exports: Volume	96	116	120	119	125	138	137	146	163	177	Exportations: volume
Exports: Unit Value	87	119	124	128	136	119	112	120	114	109	Exportations: valeur unitaire
Terms of Trade	*91*	*106*	*91*	*91*	*76*	*79*	*82*	*84*	*80*	*88*	*Termes de l'échange*
Purchasing Power of Exports	*87*	*123*	*109*	*108*	*95*	*109*	*112*	*123*	*131*	*155*	*Pouvoir d'achat des Export.*
Canada											**Canada**
Imports: Volume	72	133	143	151	179	190	207	226	226	216	Importations: volume
Imports: Unit Value	86	98	102	102	101	98	97	100	96	98	Importations: valeur unitaire
Exports: Volume	80	138	152	161	175	189	210	229	229	220	Exportations: volume
Exports: Unit Value	84	94	102	103	101	94	94	102	98	98	Exportations: valeur unitaire
Terms of Trade	*97*	*96*	*100*	*101*	*100*	*96*	*97*	*103*	*103*	*100*	*Termes de l'échange*
Purchasing Power of Exports	*77*	*133*	*152*	*163*	*174*	*182*	*204*	*234*	*235*	*219*	*Pouvoir d'achat des Export.*

Special Table G - Tableau Special G

Total exports and imports by countries or areas

Volume, unit value/price, terms of trade and purchasing power of exports, in US dollars: (1990 = 100) *[cont.]*

Exportations et importations totales par pays ou zones

Volume, valeur unitaire/prix, termes de l'échange et pouvoir d'achat des exportations, en dollars É.-U.: (1990 = 100) *[suite]*

Country or Area	1985	1994	1995	1996	1997	1998	1999	2000	2001	2002	Pays ou Zone
China, Hong Kong SAR[2]											**Chine, Hong-Kong RAS[2]**
Imports: Volume	44	187	213	222	238	221	221	261	256	276	Importations: volume
Imports: Unit Value	83	105	110	109	106	101	99	99	96	92	Importations: valeur unitaire
Exports: Volume	43	176	197	207	219	210	218	255	247	267	Exportations: volume
Exports: Unit Value	85	105	109	108	107	103	100	99	97	94	Exportations: valeur unitaire
Terms of Trade	*103*	*100*	*99*	*100*	*100*	*102*	*101*	*100*	*101*	*102*	*Termes de l'échange*
Purchasing Power of exports	*45*	*177*	*195*	*206*	*220*	*213*	*220*	*255*	*248*	*273*	*Pouvoir d'achat des Export.*
Colombia											**Colombie**
Imports:Volume	...	...	...	...	...	...	...	...	...	...	Importations: volume
Imports: Unit Value	107	94	100	101	99	91	85	82	81	78	Importations: valeur unitaire
Exports:Volume	...	...	...	...	...	...	...	...	...	...	Exportations: volume
Exports: Unit Value	131	104	112	104	116	103	96	100	89	85	Exportations: valeur unitaire
Terms of Trade	*123*	*111*	*112*	*104*	*117*	*113*	*114*	*122*	*111*	*109*	*Termes de l'échange*
Purchasing Power of Exports	...	...	...	...	...	...	...	...	...	...	*Pouvoir d'achat des Export.*
Denmark											**Danemark**
Imports: Volume	93	118	126	128	139	145	148	156	158	168	Importations: volume
Imports: Unit Value	65	93	107	104	94	93	88	82	82	85	Importations: valeur unitaire
Exports: Volume	84	122	116	119	127	128	135	144	157	166	Exportations: volume
Exports: Unit Value	59	94	107	105	94	92	89	83	80	84	Exportations: valeur unitaire
Terms of Trade	*92*	*102*	*100*	*101*	*100*	*99*	*100*	*102*	*98*	*98*	*Termes de l'échange*
Purchasing Power of Exports	*77*	*124*	*116*	*120*	*126*	*127*	*136*	*146*	*154*	*163*	*Pouvoir d'achat des Export.*
Dominica											**Dominique**
Imports: Volume	57	...	...	...	...	...	...	...	...	...	Importations: volume
Imports: Unit Value	79	...	...	...	...	...	...	...	...	...	Importations: valeur unitaire
Exports: Volume	62	107	68	90	87	80	79	86	67	62	Exportations: volume
Exports: Unit Value	81	97	100	93	119	100	101	89	90	90	Exportations: valeur unitaire
Terms of Trade	*103*	...	...	...	...	...	...	...	...	...	*Termes de l'échange*
Purchasing Power of Exports	*64*	...	...	...	...	...	...	...	...	...	*Pouvoir d'achat des Export.*
Dominican Republic											**République dominicaine**
Imports: Volume	...	...	...	...	...	...	...	...	...	...	Importations: volume
Imports: Unit Value	...	...	...	...	...	...	...	...	...	...	Importations: valeur unitaire
Exports: Volume	110	92	96	101	104	99	...	...	...	...	Exportations: volume
Exports: Unit Value	71	90	101	102	106	83	...	...	...	...	Exportations: valeur unitaire
Terms of Trade	...	...	...	...	...	...	...	...	...	...	*Termes de l'échange*
Purchasing Power of Exports	...	...	...	...	...	...	...	...	...	...	*Pouvoir d'achat des Export.*
Ecuador											**Equateur**
Imports: Volume	...	103	138	133	182	228	132	137	171	216	Importations: volume
Imports: Unit Value	...	...	...	...	...	...	...	...	...	...	Importations: valeur unitaire
Exports: Volume	98	138	154	157	157	149	143	154	156	153	Exportations: volume
Exports: Unit Value	128	83	84	96	94	70	85	110	95	102	Exportations: valeur unitaire
Terms of Trade	...	...	...	...	...	...	...	...	...	...	*Termes de l'échange*
Purchasing Power of Exports	...	...	...	...	...	...	...	...	...	...	*Pouvoir d'achat des Export.*
Ethiopia											**Ethiopie**
Imports: Volume	...	...	...	...	...	...	...	...	...	...	Importations: volume
Imports: Unit Value	...	...	...	...	...	...	...	...	...	...	Importations: valeur unitaire
Exports: Volume	96	94	80	...	...	...	...	...	...	...	Exportations: volume
Exports: Unit Value	110	94	118	...	...	...	...	...	...	...	Exportations: valeur unitaire
Terms of Trade	...	...	...	...	...	...	...	...	...	...	*Termes de l'échange*
Purchasing Power of Exports	...	...	...	...	...	...	...	...	...	...	*Pouvoir d'achat des Export.*

Special Table G - Tableau Special G

Total exports and imports by countries or areas

Volume, unit value/price, terms of trade and purchasing power of exports, in US dollars: (1990 = 100) *[cont.]*

Exportations et importations totales par pays ou zones

Volume, valeur unitaire/prix, termes de l'échange et pouvoir d'achat des exportations, en dollars É.-U.: (1990 = 100) *[suite]*

Country or Area	1985	1994	1995	1996	1997	1998	1999	2000	2001	2002	Pays ou Zone
Finland											**Finlande**
Imports: Volume	75	95	102	110	119	129	129	135	132	140	Importations: volume
Imports: Unit Value	66	91	108	104	95	92	92	90	89	87	Importations: valeur unitaire
Exports: Volume	92	133	143	151	169	178	185	200	199	209	Exportations: volume
Exports: Unit Value	55	83	106	100	90	90	87	85	82	80	Exportations: valeur unitaire
Terms of Trade	*84*	*92*	*98*	*96*	*95*	*97*	*95*	*94*	*92*	*91*	*Termes de l'échange*
Purchasing Power of exports	*77*	*122*	*141*	*146*	*161*	*173*	*176*	*189*	*183*	*191*	*Pouvoir d'achat des Export.*
France											**France**
Imports:Volume	72	117	123	126	135	146	152	168	180	189	Importations: volume
Imports: Unit Value	68	92	104	103	92	90	86	70	67	66	Importations: valeur unitaire
Exports:Volume	79	120	129	134	147	157	166	185	191	242	Exportations: volume
Exports: Unit Value	60	99	111	109	98	96	91	70	68	69	Exportations: valeur unitaire
Terms of Trade	*89*	*107*	*107*	*105*	*106*	*106*	*106*	*100*	*102*	*104*	*Termes de l'échange*
Purchasing Power of Exports	*70*	*127*	*137*	*141*	*155*	*166*	*175*	*185*	*195*	*251*	*Pouvoir d'achat des Export.*
Germany											**Allemagne**
Imports: Volume	70	114	115	122	133	146	153	172	173	172	Importations: volume
Imports: Unit Value	66	94	110	102	91	88	82	79	77	77	Importations: valeur unitaire
Exports: Volume	82	112	116	125	140	152	159	182	188	190	Exportations: volume
Exports: Unit Value	56	93	107	100	87	85	80	72	72	74	Exportations: valeur unitaire
Terms of Trade	*85*	*98*	*98*	*98*	*96*	*97*	*98*	*91*	*93*	*95*	*Termes de l'échange*
Purchasing Power of Exports	*70*	*110*	*114*	*123*	*134*	*148*	*155*	*166*	*174*	*181*	*Pouvoir d'achat des Export.*
Greece											**Grèce**
Imports: Volume	62	150	163	178	180	219	231	257	...	...	Importations: volume
Imports: Unit Value	69	72	77	69	65	66	64	58	56	62	Importations: valeur unitaire
Exports: Volume	86	149	164	175	194	221	235	244	...	...	Exportations: volume
Exports: Unit Value	66	79	84	69	58	61	72	68	65	73	Exportations: valeur unitaire
Terms of Trade	*96*	*110*	*109*	*100*	*90*	*93*	*112*	*118*	*117*	*118*	*Termes de l'échange*
Purchasing Power of Exports	*83*	*164*	*179*	*175*	*174*	*205*	*263*	*289*	...	...	*Pouvoir d'achat des Export.*
Guatemala											**Guatemala**
Imports: Volume	70	148	...	...	...	...	...	...	...	...	Importations: volume
Imports: Unit Value	101	109	...	...	...	...	...	...	...	...	Importations: valeur unitaire
Exports: Volume	81	147	...	...	...	...	...	...	...	...	Exportations: volume
Exports: Unit Value	109	88	98	89	...	...	...	...	...	...	Exportations: valeur unitaire
Terms of Trade	*107*	*81*	...	...	...	...	...	...	...	...	*Termes de l'échange*
Purchasing Power of Exports	*87*	*119*	...	...	...	...	...	...	...	...	*Pouvoir d'achat des Export.*
Honduras											**Honduras**
Imports: Volume	...	...	...	...	...	...	...	...	...	...	Importations: volume
Imports: Unit Value	...	...	...	...	...	...	...	...	...	...	Importations: valeur unitaire
Exports: Volume	115	79	83	95	72	91	83	118	122	139	Exportations: volume
Exports: Unit Value	98	89	123	115	130	117	99	98	111	107	Exportations: valeur unitaire
Terms of Trade	...	...	...	...	...	...	...	...	...	...	*Termes de l'échange*
Purchasing Power of Exports	...	...	...	...	...	...	...	...	...	...	*Pouvoir d'achat des Export.*
Hungary											**Hongrie**
Imports: Volume	99	136	131	138	174	218	249	300	313	328	Importations: volume
Imports: Unit Value	92	121	134	133	123	120	114	108	109	115	Importations: valeur unitaire
Exports: Volume	96	97	106	110	143	176	204	248	267	283	Exportations: volume
Exports: Unit Value	90	113	126	123	115	114	106	98	99	105	Exportations: valeur unitaire
Terms of Trade	*97*	*93*	*94*	*93*	*93*	*95*	*93*	*91*	*90*	*91*	*Termes de l'échange*
Purchasing Power of Exports	*94*	*91*	*99*	*102*	*134*	*167*	*190*	*225*	*242*	*257*	*Pouvoir d'achat des Export.*

Special Table G - Tableau Special G

Total exports and imports by countries or areas

Volume, unit value/price, terms of trade and purchasing power of exports, in US dollars: (1990 = 100) *[cont.]*

Exportations et importations totales par pays ou zones

Volume, valeur unitaire/prix, termes de l'échange et pouvoir d'achat des exportations, en dollars É.-U.: (1990 = 100) *[suite]*

Country or Area	1985	1994	1995	1996	1997	1998	1999	2000	2001	2002	Pays ou Zone
Iceland											**Islande**
Imports: Volume	88	90	96	111	118	147	154	160	145	...	Importations: volume
Imports: Unit Value	61	99	111	111	104	103	99	98	96	...	Importations: valeur unitaire
Exports: Volume	86	108	105	115	117	113	122	122	131	...	Exportations: volume
Exports: Unit Value	59	94	108	104	100	107	104	98	97	...	Exportations: valeur unitaire
Terms of Trade	*97*	*96*	*97*	*93*	*96*	*105*	*104*	*100*	*101*	...	*Termes de l'échange*
Purchasing Power of exports	*84*	*103*	*102*	*107*	*113*	*119*	*127*	*122*	*133*	...	*Pouvoir d'achat des Export.*
India											**Inde**
Imports:Volume	65	168	261	186	199	292	309	346	370	303	Importations: volume
Imports: Unit Value	92	68	59	83	102	59	58	62	57	77	Importations: valeur unitaire
Exports:Volume	52	154	189	236	205	206	213	287	324	336	Exportations: volume
Exports: Unit Value	84	94	90	78	91	85	93	84	74	77	Exportations: valeur unitaire
Terms of Trade	*92*	*137*	*152*	*93*	*89*	*143*	*161*	*134*	*130*	*100*	*Termes de l'échange*
Purchasing Power of Exports	*48*	*211*	*286*	*220*	*182*	*294*	*343*	*384*	*421*	*336*	*Pouvoir d'achat des Export.*
Indonesia											**Indonésie**
Imports: Volume	...	...	...	...	...	...	...	...	...	...	Importations: volume
Imports: Unit Value	...	...	...	...	...	...	...	...	...	...	Importations: valeur unitaire
Exports: Volume	91	163	171	179	230	214	176	209	253	209	Exportations: volume
Exports: Unit Value	125	97	111	117	111	87	70	108	97	67	Exportations: valeur unitaire
Terms of Trade	...	...	...	...	...	...	...	...	...	...	*Termes de l'échange*
Purchasing Power of Exports	...	...	...	...	...	...	...	...	...	...	*Pouvoir d'achat des Export.*
Ireland											**Irlande**
Imports: Volume	72	128	146	161	185	218	236	275	274	268	Importations: volume
Imports: Unit Value	67	98	109	107	102	99	96	90	90	93	Importations: valeur unitaire
Exports: Volume	65	153	184	202	232	289	336	401	422	419	Exportations: volume
Exports: Unit Value	67	94	102	102	97	94	94	85	84	88	Exportations: valeur unitaire
Terms of Trade	*100*	*96*	*94*	*94*	*95*	*95*	*97*	*94*	*93*	*95*	*Termes de l'échange*
Purchasing Power of Exports	*65*	*147*	*173*	*191*	*221*	*275*	*328*	*379*	*391*	*399*	*Pouvoir d'achat des Export.*
Israel											**Israël**
Imports: Volume	74	166	182	194	197	197	226	257	238	240	Importations: volume
Imports: Unit Value	73	94	102	101	96	91	88	91	90	90	Importations: valeur unitaire
Exports: Volume	75	140	150	161	177	188	206	260	246	249	Exportations: volume
Exports: Unit Value	69	100	105	105	104	101	101	101	98	98	Exportations: valeur unitaire
Terms of Trade	*94*	*107*	*103*	*104*	*108*	*111*	*114*	*110*	*110*	*110*	*Termes de l'échange*
Purchasing Power of Exports	*71*	*150*	*155*	*167*	*191*	*208*	*236*	*287*	*269*	*273*	*Pouvoir d'achat des Export.*
Italy											**Italie**
Imports: Volume	72	108	119	113	124	135	145	158	158	161	Importations: volume
Imports: Unit Value	70	85	73	78	71	68	64	63	63	64	Importations: valeur unitaire
Exports: Volume	81	125	141	138	145	149	149	167	168	167	Exportations: volume
Exports: Unit Value	57	116	96	106	96	95	91	83	84	87	Exportations: valeur unitaire
Terms of Trade	*82*	*136*	*131*	*136*	*135*	*140*	*141*	*130*	*133*	*136*	*Termes de l'échange*
Purchasing Power of Exports	*66*	*169*	*184*	*188*	*195*	*209*	*211*	*218*	*224*	*227*	*Pouvoir d'achat des Export.*
Japan											**Japon**
Imports: Volume	63	121	136	143	145	138	151	167	165	168	Importations: volume
Imports: Unit Value	88	97	105	104	99	87	87	96	90	85	Importations: valeur unitaire
Exports: Volume	88	103	107	107	120	119	121	132	119	129	Exportations: volume
Exports: Unit Value	71	134	145	133	122	114	120	126	118	113	Exportations: valeur unitaire
Terms of Trade	*80*	*138*	*138*	*128*	*123*	*132*	*138*	*131*	*131*	*132*	*Termes de l'échange*
Purchasing Power of Exports	*71*	*143*	*147*	*138*	*148*	*156*	*167*	*173*	*156*	*170*	*Pouvoir d'achat des Export.*

Special Table G - Tableau Special G

Total exports and imports by countries or areas

Volume, unit value/price, terms of trade and purchasing power of exports, in US dollars: (1990 = 100) *[cont.]*

Exportations et importations totales par pays ou zones

Volume, valeur unitaire/prix, termes de l'échange et pouvoir d'achat des exportations, en dollars É.-U.: (1990 = 100) *[suite]*

Country or Area	1985	1994	1995	1996	1997	1998	1999	2000	2001	2002	Pays ou Zone
Jordan											**Jordanie**
Imports: Volume	101	219	152	164	160	151	149	178	186	...	Importations: volume
Imports: Unit Value	104	83	94	101	99	98	96	98	100	...	Importations: valeur unitaire
Exports: Volume	72	153	137	134	143	147	151	163	200	...	Exportations: volume
Exports: Unit Value	98	96	111	117	113	107	104	100	101	...	Exportations: valeur unitaire
Terms of Trade	*94*	*115*	*118*	*115*	*114*	*109*	*109*	*101*	*101*	...	*Termes de l'échange*
Purchasing Power of exports	*67*	*176*	*162*	*154*	*163*	*160*	*164*	*165*	*202*	...	*Pouvoir d'achat des Export.*
Kenya											**Kenya**
Imports:Volume	72	121	141	140	149	150	136	157	...	...	Importations: volume
Imports: Unit Value	91	78	96	95	100	98	92	94	...	...	Importations: valeur unitaire
Exports:Volume	81	153	183	...	...	...	...	...	...	...	Exportations: volume
Exports: Unit Value	117	111	129	123	141	138	112	110	...	...	Exportations: valeur unitaire
Terms of Trade	*130*	*143*	*134*	*130*	*142*	*141*	*122*	*118*	...	...	*Termes de l'échange*
Purchasing Power of Exports	*105*	*219*	*246*	...	...	...	...	...	...	...	*Pouvoir d'achat des Export.*
Korea, Republic of											**Corée, République de**
Imports: Volume	52	287	187	216	220	165	213	253	247	278	Importations: volume
Imports: Unit Value	87	95	104	99	95	78	77	89	81	78	Importations: valeur unitaire
Exports: Volume	60	264	181	213	244	291	326	393	396	448	Exportations: volume
Exports: Unit Value	78	117	106	92	86	67	65	66	57	55	Exportations: valeur unitaire
Terms of Trade	*91*	*123*	*102*	*93*	*90*	*86*	*84*	*74*	*71*	*70*	*Termes de l'échange*
Purchasing Power of Exports	*54*	*324*	*185*	*197*	*220*	*251*	*275*	*290*	*279*	*315*	*Pouvoir d'achat des Export.*
Malaysia											**Malaisie**
Imports: Volume	...	...	...	...	...	...	...	...	...	...	Importations: volume
Imports: Unit Value	...	...	...	...	...	...	...	...	...	...	Importations: valeur unitaire
Exports: Volume	76	84	84	...	...	...	...	...	...	...	Exportations: volume
Exports: Unit Value	112	...	...	...	...	...	...	...	...	...	Exportations: valeur unitaire
Terms of Trade	...	...	...	...	...	...	...	...	...	...	*Termes de l'échange*
Purchasing Power of Exports	...	...	...	...	...	...	...	...	...	...	*Pouvoir d'achat des Export.*
Mauritius											**Maurice**
Imports: Volume	...	...	...	...	...	...	...	...	...	...	Importations: volume
Imports: Unit Value	83	105	115	119	103	96	98	97	94	...	Importations: valeur unitaire
Exports: Volume	...	...	...	...	...	...	...	...	...	...	Exportations: volume
Exports: Unit Value	61	107	117	126	110	111	105	99	91	...	Exportations: valeur unitaire
Terms of Trade	*74*	*102*	*102*	*106*	*107*	*115*	*108*	*102*	*97*	...	*Termes de l'échange*
Purchasing Power of Exports	...	...	...	...	...	...	...	...	...	...	*Pouvoir d'achat des Export.*
Mexico											**Mexique**
Imports: Volume	...	...	...	...	...	...	...	...	...	...	Importations: volume
Imports: Unit Value	...	...	...	111	111	111	110	113	...	...	Importations: valeur unitaire
Exports: Volume	...	...	...	...	...	...	...	...	...	...	Exportations: volume
Exports: Unit Value	...	...	...	...	...	...	...	...	...	...	Exportations: valeur unitaire
Terms of Trade	...	...	...	...	...	...	...	...	...	...	*Termes de l'échange*
Purchasing Power of Exports	...	...	...	...	...	...	...	...	...	...	*Pouvoir d'achat des Export.*
Morocco											**Maroc**
Imports: Volume	66	96	110	106	111	136	141	...	...	...	Importations: volume
Imports: Unit Value	83	102	110	110	101	87	89	...	...	...	Importations: valeur unitaire
Exports: Volume	66	115	113	110	118	121	127	...	...	...	Exportations: volume
Exports: Unit Value	74	84	140	...	...	...	...	...	...	...	Exportations: valeur unitaire
Terms of Trade	*89*	*82*	*127*	...	...	...	...	...	...	...	*Termes de l'échange*
Purchasing Power of Exports	*59*	*95*	*144*	...	...	...	...	...	...	...	*Pouvoir d'achat des Export.*

Special Table G - Tableau Special G

Total exports and imports by countries or areas

Volume, unit value/price, terms of trade and purchasing power of exports, in US dollars: (1990 = 100) *[cont.]*

Exportations et importations totales par pays ou zones

Volume, valeur unitaire/prix, termes de l'échange et pouvoir d'achat des exportations, en dollars É.-U.: (1990 = 100) *[suite]*

Country or Area	1985	1994	1995	1996	1997	1998	1999	2000	2001	2002	Pays ou Zone
Myanmar											**Myanmar**
Imports: Volume	...	...	...	...	...	...	...	...	...	...	Importations: volume
Imports: Unit Value	...	...	...	...	...	...	...	...	...	...	Importations: valeur unitaire
Exports: Volume	100	145	151	104	110	...	...	...	...	...	Exportations: volume
Exports: Unit Value	98	91	150	139	133	...	...	...	...	...	Exportations: valeur unitaire
Terms of Trade	...	...	...	...	...	...	...	...	...	...	*Termes de l'échange*
Purchasing Power of exports	...	...	...	...	...	...	...	...	...	...	*Pouvoir d'achat des Export.*
Netherlands											**Pays-Bas**
Imports:Volume	77	121	136	143	152	166	179	187	188	176	Importations: volume
Imports: Unit Value	67	92	104	100	92	88	84	81	81	84	Importations: valeur unitaire
Exports:Volume	77	129	140	146	159	171	179	195	195	198	Exportations: volume
Exports: Unit Value	67	92	106	101	93	89	83	82	82	81	Exportations: valeur unitaire
Terms of Trade	*100*	*100*	*102*	*101*	*102*	*101*	*98*	*100*	*101*	*97*	*Termes de l'échange*
Purchasing Power of Exports	*77*	*129*	*143*	*148*	*162*	*173*	*176*	*195*	*197*	*191*	*Pouvoir d'achat des Export.*
New Zealand											**Nouvelle-Zélande**
Imports: Volume	76	122	129	134	139	142	161	157	160	173	Importations: volume
Imports: Unit Value	83	104	113	115	110	92	93	93	87	91	Importations: valeur unitaire
Exports: Volume	93	130	134	140	147	146	149	157	165	174	Exportations: volume
Exports: Unit Value	67	102	110	111	104	89	89	89	90	89	Exportations: valeur unitaire
Terms of Trade	*81*	*98*	*97*	*97*	*95*	*96*	*96*	*96*	*103*	*98*	*Termes de l'échange*
Purchasing Power of Exports	*75*	*127*	*130*	*135*	*140*	*141*	*142*	*152*	*170*	*169*	*Pouvoir d'achat des Export.*
Norway											**Norvège**
Imports: Volume[3]	94	122	134	147	160	181	182	194	196	201	Importations: volume[3]
Imports: Unit Value[3]	65	86	97	94	84	78	73	67	65	68	Importations: valeur unitaire[3]
Exports: Volume[3]	67	136	145	163	172	172	176	185	194	197	Exportations: volume[3]
Exports: Unit Value[3]	86	75	86	91	84	70	77	98	92	94	Exportations: valeur unitaire[3]
Terms of Trade	*133*	*87*	*89*	*97*	*100*	*89*	*105*	*147*	*140*	*137*	*Termes de l'échange*
Purchasing Power of Exports	*88*	*119*	*128*	*158*	*172*	*154*	*186*	*273*	*271*	*269*	*Pouvoir d'achat des Export.*
Pakistan											**Pakistan**
Imports: Volume	77	120	129	127	130	130	140	138	155	170	Importations: volume
Imports: Unit Value	99	98	107	103	47	41	44	48	45	46	Importations: valeur unitaire
Exports: Volume	56	139	110	130	123	119	134	150	153	164	Exportations: volume
Exports: Unit Value	85	96	117	114	114	117	108	99	93	89	Exportations: valeur unitaire
Terms of Trade	*86*	*99*	*110*	*111*	*245*	*282*	*244*	*206*	*206*	*196*	*Termes de l'échange*
Purchasing Power of Exports	*48*	*137*	*121*	*144*	*300*	*336*	*326*	*309*	*315*	*321*	*Pouvoir d'achat des Export.*
Panama											**Panama**
Imports: Volume	...	...	...	...	...	...	...	...	...	...	Importations: volume
Imports: Unit Value	...	...	...	...	...	...	...	...	...	...	Importations: valeur unitaire
Exports: Volume	...	...	...	...	...	113	84	79	...	...	Exportations: volume
Exports: Unit Value	...	...	...	...	...	...	...	...	...	...	Exportations: valeur unitaire
Terms of Trade	...	...	...	...	...	...	...	...	...	...	*Termes de l'échange*
Purchasing Power of Exports	...	...	...	...	...	...	...	...	...	...	*Pouvoir d'achat des Export.*
Papua New Guinea											**Popouasie-Nouvelle-Guinée**
Imports: Volume	...	...	...	...	...	...	...	...	...	...	Importations: volume
Imports: Unit Value	129	...	...	...	...	...	...	...	...	...	Importations: valeur unitaire
Exports: Volume	92	154	149	139	125	...	...	...	...	...	Exportations: volume
Exports: Unit Value	87	124	137	132	135	105	95	...	...	...	Exportations: valeur unitaire
Terms of Trade	*68*	...	...	...	...	...	...	...	...	...	*Termes de l'échange*
Purchasing Power of Exports	*63*	...	...	...	...	...	...	...	...	...	*Pouvoir d'achat des Export.*

Special Table G - Tableau Special G

Total exports and imports by countries or areas

Volume, unit value/price, terms of trade and purchasing power of exports, in US dollars: (1990 = 100) *[cont.]*

Exportations et importations totales par pays ou zones

Volume, valeur unitaire/prix, termes de l'échange et pouvoir d'achat des exportations, en dollars É.-U.: (1990 = 100) *[suite]*

Country or Area	1985	1994	1995	1996	1997	1998	1999	2000	2001	2002	Pays ou Zone
Peru											**Pérou**
Imports: Volume	...	...	...	...	...	...	...	...	...	...	Importations: volume
Imports: Unit Value	...	...	...	...	...	...	...	...	...	...	Importations: valeur unitaire
Exports: Volume	118	132	133	141	153	132	148	168	191	216	Exportations: volume
Exports: Unit Value	85	86	106	112	109	84	90	120	100	106	Exportations: valeur unitaire
Terms of Trade	...	...	...	...	...	...	...	...	...	...	*Termes de l'échange*
Purchasing Power of exports	...	...	...	...	...	...	...	...	...	...	*Pouvoir d'achat des Export.*
Philippines											**Philippines**
Imports:Volume	41	70	41	48	52	41	46	49	48	...	Importations: volume
Imports: Unit Value[1]	106	101	101	104	94	70	68	58	49	...	Importations: valeur unitaire[1]
Exports:Volume	60	93	60	67	79	85	93	107	95	...	Exportations: volume
Exports: Unit Value[1]	98	...	...	...	...	69	79	65	54	...	Exportations: valeur unitaire[1]
Terms of Trade	*92*	...	...	...	...	*98*	*116*	*113*	*112*	...	*Termes de l'échange*
Purchasing Power of Exports	*55*	...	...	...	...	*84*	*108*	*121*	*107*	...	*Pouvoir d'achat des Export.*
Poland											**Pologne**
Imports: Volume	113	211	254	325	397	473	492	526	543	582	Importations: volume
Imports: Unit Value[1]	125	94	100	105	98	97	90	85	85	87	Importations: valeur unitaire[1]
Exports: Volume	77	111	130	142	162	173	183	226	253	274	Exportations: volume
Exports: Unit Value[1]	110	102	116	113	105	107	100	92	94	99	Exportations: valeur unitaire[1]
Terms of Trade	*87*	*109*	*117*	*108*	*107*	*109*	*110*	*108*	*111*	*114*	*Termes de l'échange*
Purchasing Power of Exports	*67*	*121*	*152*	*154*	*174*	*189*	*202*	*245*	*281*	*312*	*Pouvoir d'achat des Export.*
Portugal											**Portugal**
Imports: Volume	43	115	117	125	138	158	174	...	...	...	Importations: volume
Imports: Unit Value	72	90	104	104	94	91	85	80	78	...	Importations: valeur unitaire
Exports: Volume	56	111	116	127	138	146	151	...	...	...	Exportations: volume
Exports: Unit Value	62	97	113	110	99	96	92	84	83	...	Exportations: valeur unitaire
Terms of Trade	*86*	*107*	*108*	*105*	*105*	*107*	*108*	*105*	*106*	...	*Termes de l'échange*
Purchasing Power of Exports	*48*	*119*	*126*	*134*	*144*	*155*	*164*	...	...	...	*Pouvoir d'achat des Export.*
Rwanda											**Rwanda**
Imports: Volume	...	...	...	...	...	...	...	...	...	...	Importations: volume
Imports: Unit Value	...	...	...	...	...	...	...	...	...	...	Importations: valeur unitaire
Exports: Volume	67	30	51	49	121	129	...	...	...	...	Exportations: volume
Exports: Unit Value	162	61	127	124	140	67	...	...	...	...	Exportations: valeur unitaire
Terms of Trade	...	...	...	...	...	...	...	...	...	...	*Termes de l'échange*
Purchasing Power of Exports	...	...	...	...	...	...	...	...	...	...	*Pouvoir d'achat des Export.*
Seychelles											**Seychelles**
Imports: Volume	60	124	135	227	200	243	310	294	...	...	Importations: volume
Imports: Unit Value	88	89	92	89	91	85	75	62	...	...	Importations: valeur unitaire
Exports: Volume	18	172	139	256	343	343	521	672	...	...	Exportations: volume
Exports: Unit Value	125	95	125	116	147	190	151	133	...	...	Exportations: valeur unitaire
Terms of Trade	*142*	*106*	*135*	*130*	*161*	*225*	*202*	*214*	...	...	*Termes de l'échange*
Purchasing Power of Exports	*25*	*183*	*187*	*333*	*552*	*771*	*1052*	*1435*	...	...	*Pouvoir d'achat des Export.*
Singapore											**Singapour**
Imports: Volume	50	157	177	188	203	184	194	220	196	198	Importations: volume
Imports: Unit Value[1]	86	108	116	115	107	94	94	100	97	96	Importations: valeur unitaire[1]
Exports: Volume	46	187	216	229	245	248	261	302	288	303	Exportations: volume
Exports: Unit Value[1]	94	98	104	103	97	84	83	86	80	78	Exportations: valeur unitaire[1]
Terms of Trade	*108*	*91*	*90*	*90*	*90*	*90*	*89*	*86*	*83*	*81*	*Termes de l'échange*
Purchasing Power of Exports	*50*	*171*	*194*	*207*	*221*	*223*	*232*	*260*	*238*	*246*	*Pouvoir d'achat des Export.*

Special Table G - Tableau Special G

Total exports and imports by countries or areas

Volume, unit value/price, terms of trade and purchasing power of exports, in US dollars: (1990 = 100) *[cont.]*

Exportations et importations totales par pays ou zones

Volume, valeur unitaire/prix, termes de l'échange et pouvoir d'achat des exportations, en dollars É.-U.: (1990 = 100) *[suite]*

Country or Area	1985	1994	1995	1996	1997	1998	1999	2000	2001	2002	Pays ou Zone
South Africa											**Afrique du Sud**
Imports: Volume	88	125	136	147	155	157	146	156	156	...	Importations: volume
Imports: Unit Value	73	100	112	103	102	95	94	96	91	...	Importations: valeur unitaire
Exports: Volume	90	115	119	130	137	140	142	156	157	...	Exportations: volume
Exports: Unit Value	67	100	114	106	105	97	93	93	89	...	Exportations: valeur unitaire
Terms of Trade	*92*	*99*	*102*	*103*	*102*	*102*	*98*	*97*	*98*	...	*Termes de l'échange*
Purchasing Power of exports	*83*	*114*	*122*	*134*	*140*	*143*	*140*	*151*	*154*	...	*Pouvoir d'achat des Export.*
Spain											**Espagne**
Imports:Volume	44	131	...	...	...	...	...	...	...	...	Importations: volume
Imports: Unit Value[1]	77	81	91	90	81	77	74	72	70	71	Importations: valeur unitaire[1]
Exports:Volume	76	160	...	...	...	...	...	...	...	...	Exportations: volume
Exports: Unit Value[1]	57	83	95	94	84	83	78	72	72	76	Exportations: valeur unitaire[1]
Terms of Trade	*74*	*102*	*104*	*105*	*105*	*107*	*106*	*100*	*103*	*106*	*Termes de l'échange*
Purchasing Power of Exports	*57*	*164*	...	...	...	...	...	...	...	...	*Pouvoir d'achat des Export.*
Sri Lanka											**Sri Lanka**
Imports: Volume	105	153	178	179	201	218	219	244	221	245	Importations: volume
Imports: Unit Value	70	98	109	112	109	...	...	...	...	...	Importations: valeur unitaire
Exports: Volume	83	118	145	151	167	165	171	205	188	190	Exportations: volume
Exports: Unit Value	81	98	132	136	140	146	135	133	129	124	Exportations: valeur unitaire
Terms of Trade	*114*	*100*	*120*	*122*	*128*	...	...	...	...	...	*Termes de l'échange*
Purchasing Power of Exports	*95*	*117*	*175*	*184*	*214*	...	...	...	...	...	*Pouvoir d'achat des Export.*
Sweden											**Suède**
Imports: Volume	80	108	109	112	124	136	140	158	149	147	Importations: volume
Imports: Unit Value[1]	66	90	103	106	95	90	89	86	80	85	Importations: valeur unitaire[1]
Exports: Volume	90	114	112	118	131	143	151	168	163	167	Exportations: volume
Exports: Unit Value[1]	60	85	97	98	87	83	79	74	67	70	Exportations: valeur unitaire[1]
Terms of Trade	*90*	*94*	*94*	*93*	*92*	*92*	*89*	*86*	*83*	*82*	*Termes de l'échange*
Purchasing Power of Exports	*81*	*108*	*105*	*110*	*120*	*132*	*135*	*144*	*136*	*136*	*Pouvoir d'achat des Export.*
Switzerland											**Suisse**
Imports: Volume	75	102	109	110	117	126	137	146	146	142	Importations: volume
Imports: Unit Value	60	97	109	104	94	90	85	80	82	85	Importations: valeur unitaire
Exports: Volume	82	109	114	115	124	130	135	144	147	148	Exportations: volume
Exports: Unit Value	54	104	117	113	100	99	97	89	91	96	Exportations: valeur unitaire
Terms of Trade	*91*	*107*	*107*	*108*	*107*	*110*	*114*	*111*	*111*	*113*	*Termes de l'échange*
Purchasing Power of Exports	*75*	*117*	*122*	*125*	*132*	*143*	*153*	*160*	*164*	*167*	*Pouvoir d'achat des Export.*
Syrian Arab Rep.											**République arab syrienne**
Imports: Volume	161	276	248	250	218	...	...	...	...	...	Importations: volume
Imports: Unit Value	198	105	118	125	107	...	...	...	...	...	Importations: valeur unitaire
Exports: Volume	45	171	167	164	183	...	...	...	...	...	Exportations: volume
Exports: Unit Value	273	72	90	95	75	...	...	...	...	...	Exportations: valeur unitaire
Terms of Trade	*138*	*69*	*76*	*76*	*70*	...	...	...	...	...	*Termes de l'échange*
Purchasing Power of Exports	*62*	*117*	*127*	*125*	*128*	...	...	...	...	...	*Pouvoir d'achat des Export.*
Thailand											**Thaïlande**
Imports: Volume	41	151	170	154	137	100	124	150	134	149	Importations: volume
Imports: Unit Value	96	111	125	139	136	122	119	125	136	128	Importations: valeur unitaire
Exports: Volume	59	177	243	219	235	254	284	346	327	371	Exportations: volume
Exports: Unit Value	76	111	121	132	126	110	106	104	102	95	Exportations: valeur unitaire
Terms of Trade	*80*	*100*	*97*	*95*	*93*	*90*	*89*	*83*	*75*	*74*	*Termes de l'échange*
Purchasing Power of Exports	*47*	*177*	*235*	*207*	*218*	*229*	*253*	*287*	*246*	*275*	*Pouvoir d'achat des Export.*

Special Table G - Tableau Special G

Total exports and imports by countries or areas

Volume, unit value/price, terms of trade and purchasing power of exports, in US dollars: (1990 = 100) *[cont.]*

Exportations et importations totales par pays ou zones

Volume, valeur unitaire/prix, termes de l'échange et pouvoir d'achat des exportations, en dollars É.-U.: (1990 = 100) *[suite]*

Country or Area	1985	1994	1995	1996	1997	1998	1999	2000	2001	2002	Pays ou Zone
Tunisia											**Tunisie**
Imports: Volume	77	120	...	...	...	...	...	...	...	...	Importations: volume
Imports: Unit Value	75	...	...	...	...	...	...	...	...	...	Importations: valeur unitaire
Exports: Volume	82	137	...	...	...	...	...	...	...	...	Exportations: volume
Exports: Unit Value	80	87	...	...	...	...	...	...	...	...	Exportations: valeur unitaire
Terms of Trade	*108*	...	...	...	...	...	...	...	...	...	*Termes de l'échange*
Purchasing Power of exports	*89*	...	...	...	...	...	...	...	...	...	*Pouvoir d'achat des Export.*
Turkey											**Turquie**
Imports:Volume	68	99	128	166	205	200	198	262	197	238	Importations: volume
Imports: Unit Value	102	95	111	105	96	92	87	91	90	89	Importations: valeur unitaire
Exports:Volume	65	134	143	157	178	195	201	224	274	317	Exportations: volume
Exports: Unit Value	84	95	107	102	97	93	87	83	81	80	Exportations: valeur unitaire
Terms of Trade	*82*	*99*	*96*	*97*	*102*	*102*	*100*	*92*	*90*	*89*	*Termes de l'échange*
Purchasing Power of Exports	*53*	*133*	*137*	*153*	*181*	*199*	*202*	*206*	*246*	*283*	*Pouvoir d'achat des Export.*
United Kingdom											**Royaume-Uni**
Imports: Volume	70	108	112	123	135	148	159	178	183	186	Importations: volume
Imports: Unit Value[1]	67	99	112	111	109	103	99	97	92	103	Importations: valeur unitaire[1]
Exports: Volume	80	116	125	136	146	148	155	173	174	172	Exportations: volume
Exports: Unit Value[1]	68	101	111	111	110	105	102	99	94	104	Exportations: valeur unitaire[1]
Terms of Trade	*101*	*102*	*99*	*100*	*101*	*102*	*102*	*102*	*102*	*101*	*Termes de l'échange*
Purchasing Power of Exports	*81*	*118*	*124*	*135*	*147*	*151*	*159*	*176*	*178*	*174*	*Pouvoir d'achat des Export.*
United States											**Etats-Unis**
Imports: Volume	79	131	140	148	166	186	206	230	224	234	Importations: volume
Imports: Unit Value[1]	87	102	106	107	105	98	99	106	102	100	Importations: valeur unitaire[1]
Exports: Volume[4]	63	126	137	145	162	166	173	190	179	171	Exportations: volume[4]
Exports: Unit Value[1,4]	88	104	109	109	108	104	103	105	104	103	Exportations: valeur unitaire[1,4]
Terms of Trade	*102*	*102*	*102*	*102*	*103*	*106*	*104*	*99*	*102*	*103*	*Termes de l'échange*
Purchasing Power of Exports	*64*	*128*	*140*	*148*	*167*	*176*	*179*	*188*	*182*	*177*	*Pouvoir d'achat des Export.*
Uruguay											**Uruguay**
Imports: Volume	...	...	...	...	...	...	...	...	...	...	Importations: volume
Imports: Unit Value	...	...	...	...	...	...	...	...	...	...	Importations: valeur unitaire
Exports: Volume	...	...	...	...	...	...	...	...	...	...	Exportations: volume
Exports: Unit Value	79	95	105	102	100	99	85	84	82	78	Exportations: valeur unitaire
Terms of Trade	...	...	...	...	...	...	...	...	...	...	*Termes de l'échange*
Purchasing Power of Exports	...	...	...	...	...	...	...	...	...	...	*Pouvoir d'achat des Export.*
Venezuela											**Venezuela**
Imports: Volume	...	...	...	...	...	...	...	...	...	...	Importations: volume
Imports: Unit Value[1]	120	108	139	122	129	134	135	131	133	130	Importations: valeur unitaire[1]
Exports: Volume	...	...	...	...	...	...	...	...	...	...	Exportations: volume
Exports: Unit Value	100	...	...	...	...	...	...	...	...	...	Exportations: valeur unitaire
Terms of Trade	*83*	...	...	...	...	...	...	...	...	...	*Termes de l'échange*
Purchasing Power of Exports	...	...	...	...	...	...	...	...	...	...	*Pouvoir d'achat des Export.*

Special Table G - Tableau Special G

Total exports and imports by countries or areas

Volume, unit value/price, terms of trade and purchasing power of exports, in US dollars: (1990 = 100) *[cont.]*

Exportations et importations totales par pays ou zones

Volume, valeur unitaire/prix, termes de l'échange et pouvoir d'achat des exportations, en dollars É.-U.: (1990 = 100) *[suite]*

General Note: The volume and unit value/price indices are as compiled by countries. They show the changes in the volume (volume index) and the average price (unit value/price index) of total imports and exports. Using these indices, the United Nations Statistics Division calculates the terms of trade indices (export unit value/price indices divided by the corresponding import unit value/price indices), and the index of the purchasing power of exports (the terms of trade multiplied by the volume index of exports). Country footnotes which appear in Special Table B of this volume also apply to the country indices published in this table.

1 Price indices.
2 See explanatory notes pertaining to Hong Kong SAR and Macao SAR on page v.
3 Index numbers exclude ships.
4 Excluding military goods.

Remarque générale: Les indices du volume et les indices de la valeur unitaire/prix sont comme compilées par les pays. Ils indiquent les variations des quantitées (indice du volume) et des prix moyens (indice de la valeur unitaire/prix) des importations ou exportations totales. Utilisant ces indices la Division de Statistique des Nations Unies calcule les indices des termes de l'échange (sont obtenus en divisant les indices de la valeur unitaire à l'exportation par ceux à l'importation), et l'indice du pouvoir d'achat des exportations (sont obtenu en multipliant l'indice des termes de l'échange du volume des exportations). Les notes se rapportant aux pays qui apparaissent dans le Tableau Spécial B de ce tome s'appliquent aussi aux indices de ce tableau.

1 Les indices des prix.
2 Voir les notes explicatives concernant Hong-Kong RAS et Macao RAS à la page vii.
3 Non compris les navires.
4 Non compris les importations des economats militaires.

Special Table H - Tableau Special H

Total exports and imports by regions

Volume and unit value indices and terms of trade in US dollars (1990 = 100)

Exportations et importations totales par régions

Indices du volume et de la valeur unitaire et termes de l'échange en dollars É.-U. (1990 = 100)

Regions - Régions	1985	1992	1993	1994	1995	1996	1997	1998	1999	2000	2001	2002
Exports - Unit value index / Exportations - Indice de la valeur unitaire[1]												
Total - Totaux	73	102	97	101	109	108	101	94	91	91	87	86
Developed economies - Economies développées[2]	67	103	97	100	109	107	99	95	92	88	86	87
Africa - Afrique[3]	67	101	96	100	114	106	105	97	93	93	89	...
North America - Amérique du Nord	87	100	99	101	107	108	106	102	101	104	102	101
Asia - Asie	71	113	123	132	143	131	121	113	119	124	116	111
Europe	61	103	93	95	105	103	93	90	86	79	77	80
EU - UE	60	103	93	96	105	103	93	91	86	78	77	79
EFTA - AELE	64	96	89	92	104	103	93	87	88	93	91	95
Oceania - Océanie	70	89	85	89	97	98	94	82	79	82	81	82
Developing econ. - Econ. en voi de développement[2]	93	99	97	102	108	111	106	91	89	96	89	83
Africa - Afrique	110	89	82	88	100	91	84	64	75	86	76	57
America - Amérique	90	93	89	91	98	118	122	112	113	121	108	101
Asia - Asie	98	101	100	105	111	111	104	89	86	93	86	82
Asia Middle East - Moyen-Orient d'Asie	127	94	87	89	97	106	100	74	101	136	126	116
Other Asia - Autres Pays d'Asie	87	104	103	110	114	112	105	93	83	85	79	76
Europe[4]	74	...	...	...	...	...	...	...	...	...	...	...
Imports - Unit value index / Importations - Indice de la valeur unitaire[1]												
Total - Totaux	77	99	94	97	105	104	99	93	91	92	88	88
Developed economies - Economies développées[2]	74	99	93	95	103	102	95	90	88	87	85	86
Africa - Afrique[3]	73	106	99	100	112	103	102	95	94	96	91	...
North America - Amérique du Nord	86	101	100	101	106	106	104	98	99	105	101	99
Asia - Asie	87	96	96	97	105	103	99	87	87	96	90	86
Europe	67	99	89	92	101	99	90	87	82	77	77	79
EU - UE	67	99	88	92	101	99	90	87	82	78	77	79
EFTA - AELE	61	100	91	94	105	101	91	86	81	76	76	80
Oceania - Océanie	78	99	99	104	110	111	105	95	95	93	88	89
Developing econ. - Econ. en voi de développement[2,5]	88	99	97	101	113	112	111	102	103	108	99	96
Africa - Afrique	76	99	95	98	108	101	96	88	...	...	...	...
America - Amérique	102	95	94	105	126	125	152	141	134	137	126	116
Asia - Asie	89	99	98	100	111	111	106	95	99	104	95	93
Asia Middle East - Moyen-Orient d'Asie	90	100	92	95	103	104	99	92	90	92	93	...
Other Asia - Autres Pays d'Asie	88	99	99	101	112	112	107	96	101	107	95	92
Europe[4]	82	116	121	...	...	...	...	...	...	...	...	...
Terms of trade / Termes de l'échange[6]												
Developed economies - Economies développées[2]	90	104	105	106	106	105	104	105	105	101	101	102
Africa - Afrique[3]	92	96	98	99	102	103	102	102	98	97	98	...
North America - Amérique du Nord	100	99	100	100	101	101	102	103	102	99	101	102
Asia - Asie	81	118	128	137	136	127	122	130	136	129	130	130
Europe	90	103	104	104	104	104	103	104	104	101	101	101
EU - UE	89	104	105	104	104	104	103	104	104	100	100	100
EFTA - AELE	105	96	97	98	99	102	103	101	109	123	120	120
Oceania - Océanie	90	90	86	85	88	88	89	87	83	87	92	92
Developing econ. - Econ. en voi de développement[2,5]	106	101	100	101	96	99	95	89	86	89	89	87
Africa - Afrique	144	90	86	90	92	90	87	73	...	...	...	...
America - Amérique	88	98	95	87	78	94	80	79	84	88	86	86
Asia - Asie	110	102	102	105	100	100	99	93	87	89	90	89
Asia Middle East - Moyen-Orient d'Asie	141	94	94	93	94	102	101	80	112	148	135	...
Other Asia - Autres Pays d'Asie	99	105	105	109	102	100	98	96	83	80	83	83
Europe[4]	90	...	...	...	...	...	...	...	...	...	...	...

Special Table H - Tableau Special H

Total exports and imports by regions

Volume and unit value indices and terms of trade in US dollars (1990 = 100) *[cont.]*

Exportations et importations totales par régions

Indices du volume et de la valeur unitaire et termes de l'échange en dollars É.-U. (1990 = 100) *[suite]*

Regions - Régions	1985	1992	1993	1994	1995	1996	1997	1998	1999	2000	2001	2002
Exports - Volume index / Exportations - Indice du volume[7]												
Total - Totaux	74	107	112	122	135	142	157	167	177	199	199	209
Developed economies - Economies développées[2]	79	105	108	118	129	136	150	157	164	182	182	184
Africa - Afrique[3]	103	97	106	107	103	116	126	115	122	138	141	...
North America - Amérique du Nord	70	112	117	127	137	145	160	166	175	189	179	172
Asia - Asie	87	103	102	104	108	109	121	120	122	136	121	130
Europe	79	102	106	117	130	138	152	162	170	191	195	200
EU - UE	80	102	106	117	131	139	154	164	172	194	198	203
EFTA - AELE	76	102	104	112	118	124	133	136	141	148	153	154
Oceania - Océanie	83	120	127	136	139	155	167	166	174	190	191	192
Developing econ. - Econ. en voi de développement[2]	60	114	123	137	153	160	179	197	219	250	254	289
Africa - Afrique	75	98	95	97	100	120	129	152	152	164	165	229
America - Amérique	67	111	124	152	159	148	158	172	181	202	217	237
Asia - Asie	56	118	128	141	161	171	194	212	241	279	281	318
Asia Middle East - Moyen-Orient d'Asie	58	108	118	115	117	123	139	160	146	151	154	169
Other Asia - Autres Pays d'Asie	56	120	130	147	172	183	208	226	269	319	320	365
Europe[4]	70	...	...	...	...	...	...	...	...	...	...	...
Imports - Volume index / Importations - Indice du volume[7]												
Total - Totaux	72	110	114	125	136	144	156	165	176	197	197	203
Developed economies - Economies développées[2]	72	106	107	118	129	136	148	160	173	191	188	191
Africa - Afrique[3]	85	100	109	127	150	160	177	169	155	171	171	...
North America - Amérique du Nord	80	106	116	129	137	144	163	180	199	220	214	221
Asia - Asie	65	103	108	123	138	145	146	138	152	167	166	166
Europe	71	106	104	113	125	131	143	157	166	186	184	185
EU - UE	70	107	104	114	126	132	145	158	168	188	186	188
EFTA - AELE	78	91	91	101	108	113	122	134	140	151	149	148
Oceania - Océanie	80	103	107	121	132	140	148	157	169	176	167	187
Developing econ. - Econ. en voi de développement[2]	68	124	136	149	159	171	181	178	183	213	221	241
Africa - Afrique	101	92	92	95	102	111	118	146	...	...	...	...
America - Amérique	64	140	154	173	152	170	164	185	187	211	225	229
Asia - Asie	63	126	140	153	171	182	194	180	188	225	232	258
Asia Middle East - Moyen-Orient d'Asie	88	125	133	112	124	138	154	160	159	196	187	...
Other Asia - Autres Pays d'Asie	57	126	140	161	180	190	202	182	192	229	239	267
Europe[4]	79	65	71	...	...	...	...	...	...	...	...	...

Special Table H - Tableau Special H

Total exports and imports by regions

Volume and unit value indices and terms of trade in US dollars (1990 = 100) *[cont.]*

Exportations et importations totales par régions

Indices du volume et de la valeur unitaire et termes de l'échange en dollars É.-U. (1990 = 100) *[suite]*

Source:
Compiled by the United Nations Statistics Division from international and national publications.

Note:
For the composition of the regions, see Special Table A of this issue.

1 Regional aggregates are current period weighted.

2 This classification is intended for statistical convenience and does not, necessarily, express a judgement about the stage reached by a particular country in the development process.

3 Beginning January 1998, data refer to South Africa only. Prior to January 1998, data refer to Southern African Common Customs Area.

4 Beginning 1 January 1992, data refer to the Federal Republic of Yugoslavia (Serbia and Montenegro). Prior to that date, data refer to the Socialist Republic of Yugoslavia.

5 Indices, except those for Europe, are based on estimates prepared by the International Monetary Fund.

6 Unit value index of exports divided by unit value index of imports.

7 Volume indices are derived from value data and unit value indices. They are base period weighted.

Source:
Compilé par la Division de statistique des Nations Unies à partir de publications internationales et nationales.

Note:
Pour la composition des régions, voir tableau special A du présent numéro.

1 Les totaux régionaux sont à coéfficients de pondération correspondant à la période en cours.

2 Cette classification est utilisée pour plus de commodité dans la présentation des statistiques et n'implique pas nécessairement un jugement quant au stade de développement auquel est parvenu un pays donné.

3 A compter de janvier 1998, les données se rapportent qu'à l'Afrique du Sud. Avant janvier 1998, les données se rapportent à l'Union Douanière de l'Afrique Mèridionale.

4 A partir de 1er janvier 1992 les données se rapportent à la République fédérative de Yougoslavie (Serbie et Monténégro). Avant cette date les données se rapportent à la République socialiste fédérative de Yougoslavie.

5 Le calcul des indices, sauf ceux pour l'Europe, sont basés sur les estimations preparées par le Fonds monétaire international.

6 Indice de la valeur unitaire des exportations divisé par l'indice de la valeur unitaire des importations.

7 Les indices du volume sont calculés à partir de chiffres de la valeur et des indices de la valeur unitaire. Ils sont à coéfficients de pondération correspondant à la période en base.

SPECIAL TABLE: I

Manufactured goods exports

1990 = 100

Region, country or area	1985	1992	1993	1994	1995	1996	1997	1998	1999	2000	2001	2002
	Unit Value Indices in U.S. dollars - Indices de valuer unitaire en dollars des E.-U.											
Total 1/	66	103	99	101	110	106	99	97	92	90	87	...
Developed economies	64	103	97	99	110	106	99	98	93	89	86	86
America	89	100	99	99	102	102	103	102	101	102	101	101
Canada	90	91	88	84	87	88	89	85	83	84	81	80
United States 2/	88	103	103	104	107	106	108	108	108	109	108	111
Europe	57	102	91	93	107	104	93	93	87	79	78	79
EU	57	102	92	93	107	103	92	92	87	79	77	78
Austria 3/	60	99	91	90	104	94	77	72	60	51	48	51
Belgium/Luxembourg 4/	58	99	90	94	109	106	97	96	91	86	85	90
Denmark	55	102	92	97	112	108	98	97	94	84	84	86
Finland	54	90	74	83	105	99	89	88	85	82	78	82
France	62	100	94	98	111	107	96	96	90	80	78	67
Germany 5/	55	103	93	94	108	101	87	89	80	72	71	74
Greece	63	95	78	83	88	84	72	66	63	59	...	...
Ireland 4/	63	97	96	89	98	97	81	75	...	...	...	...
Italy 4/	55	105	89	86	96	98	90	95	91	80	80	...
Netherlands 6/	57	102	92	92	109	102	91	89	85	77	...	...
Portugal 4/	63	106	98	94	111	105	94	92	88	81	80	...
Spain 4/	55	109	85	86	99	99	88	86	...	...	...	...
Sweden	58	102	82	85	105	106	94	90	85	80	...	...
United Kingdom	60	102	98	103	114	113	113	112	106	98	92	95
EFTA	56	101	87	96	116	114	101	99	97	90	92	96
Iceland 4/	57	86	76	80	114	106	101	89	...	...	...	...
Norway	58	92	80	82	102	96	88	85	80	75	73	75
Switzerland 4/	55	103	88	99	120	118	105	104	101	93	97	102
Other developed economies	70	113	120	129	138	128	121	115	113	116	110	104
Australia	67	86	81	88	96	94	89	78	78	80	72	73
Israel	69	101	102	101	105	105	102	105	114	137	...	...
Japan	71	115	124	134	144	133	126	121	119	121	118	111
New Zealand	66	89	89	98	112	109	102	84	80	83	81	83
South Africa	60	101	100	101	123	107	...	...	...	...	...	...
Developing economies	80	101	102	104	111	105	99	96	89	92	90	...
China, Hong Kong SAR	...	104	104	105	108	108	104	101	99	97	93	90
India	76	92	89	88	86	69	84	79	90	74	...	...
Korea, Republic of 6/	72	96	95	98	103	94	85	76	62	75	70	62
Pakistan	81	101	98	107	125	123	129	127	117	110	110	...
Singapore	...	103	99	108	112	109	102	92	90	88	86	88
Turkey 7/	93	100	95	90	106	97	89	84	80	85	84	82
	Unit value indices in 'SDR' - Indices de valuer unitaire en 'DTS'											
Total	89	99	96	95	99	99	97	97	91	92	94	...
Developed economies	86	99	95	94	99	99	97	98	93	91	92	90
Developing economies	107	97	99	99	99	98	97	96	88	95	97	...

For general note and footnotes see end of Special Table K.

Exportations des produits manufacturés (suite)

In thousand million U.S. dollars — En milliards de dollars E.-U.

1985	1992	1993	1994	1995	1996	1997	1998	1999	2000	2001	2002	Région, pays ou zones
Unit value indices in national currency - Indices de valuer unitaire en monnaie nationale												
.	.	.	.	.	.	.	.	.	.	.	.	**Totaux 1/**
.	.	.	.	.	.	.	.	.	.	.	.	**Economies dévelopeées**
.	.	.	.	.	.	.	.	.	.	.	.	Amérique
106	94	98	99	102	103	105	108	106	106	108	108	Canada
88	103	103	104	107	106	108	108	108	109	108	111	Etats-Unis 2/
.	.	.	.	.	.	.	.	.	.	.	.	Europe
.	.	.	.	.	.	.	.	.	.	.	.	UE
110	96	93	91	92	88	83	78	68	67	65	65	Autriche 3/
...	...	...	...	...	...	...	...	...	...	...	...	Belgique / Luxembourg
94	100	97	100	102	102	105	105	106	110	112	109	Danemark
88	106	112	112	120	119	121	123	124	138	135	135	Finlande
102	97	98	100	101	101	103	104	102	104	105	86	France
100	100	95	94	96	94	94	97	92	95	97	98	Allemagne 5/
55	114	112	127	128	128	123	123	122	136	...	...	Grèce
...	...	...	...	...	...	...	...	...	...	...	...	Irlande
...	...	...	...	...	...	...	...	...	...	...	...	Italie
104	98	94	92	96	95	97	97	97	102	...	...	Pays-Bas 6/
...	...	...	...	...	...	...	...	...	...	...	...	Portugal
...	...	...	...	...	...	...	...	...	...	...	...	Espagne
84	100	108	111	126	120	121	120	119	124	...	...	Suède
83	104	117	120	129	129	123	121	117	116	114	114	Royaume-Uni
.	.	.	.	.	.	.	.	.	.	.	.	AELE
...	...	...	...	...	...	...	...	...	...	...	...	Islande
79	92	92	93	104	99	100	103	100	107	106	97	Norvège
...	...	...	...	...	...	...	...	...	...	...	...	Suisse
.	.	.	.	.	.	.	.	.	.	.	.	Autres économies dévelopées
75	91	94	94	102	94	94	97	94	108	112	105	Australie
...	...	...	...	...	...	...	...	...	...	...	...	Israël
116	101	95	95	93	101	106	109	94	91	99	96	Japon
80	99	98	99	101	94	92	93	90	109	115	106	Nouvelle-Zélande
52	111	127	139	173	178	...	...	...	...	...	...	Afrique du Sud
.	.	.	.	.	.	.	.	.	.	.	.	**Economies en voie de développement**
...	103	103	105	107	107	103	100	98	97	93	91	Chine, Hong-Kong RAS
53	136	154	158	160	141	174	187	221	190	...	...	Inde
89	106	108	111	112	107	114	150	122	120	126	109	Corée, République de
59	117	127	151	182	203	245	265	270	269	314	...	Pakistan
...	...	...	...	...	...	...	...	...	...	...	...	Singapour
...	...	...	...	...	...	...	...	...	...	...	...	Turquie

Voir la fin du Tableau Special K pour la remarque générale et les notes.

SPECIAL TABLE: I

Manufactured goods exports

1990 = 100

Region, country or area	1985	1992	1993	1994	1995	1996	1997	1998	1999	2000	2001	2002
						Quantum indices - Indices de volume						
Total 1/	71	111	115	130	141	152	171	176	191	215	217	...
Developed economies	76	106	108	121	129	137	153	157	166	185	191	192
America	62	114	121	137	152	162	179	183	193	207	214	187
Canada	75	119	135	164	187	193	204	223	253	254	263	262
United States	59	113	117	130	142	153	172	172	176	194	200	166
Europe	77	104	106	119	126	135	153	158	166	188	198	205
EU	77	105	105	120	127	137	155	160	168	191	202	210
Austria	66	108	107	119	130	147	181	190	223	259	321	297
Belgium/Luxembourg	72	104	112	123	128	132	142	157	164	185	194	261
Denmark	82	114	111	118	125	128	145	152	170	180	189	205
Finland	86	97	117	132	144	153	172	188	188	211	217	207
France	72	112	104	116	122	129	143	154	163	189	225	226
Germany	81	104	100	112	117	126	145	148	158	184	193	200
Greece	85	126	139	133	153	168	195	215	199	232	...	...
Ireland	64	122	124	166	193	232	320	434	...	...	...	...
Italy	82	100	112	132	144	153	159	153	151	176	184	...
Netherlands	78	105	107	121	130	139	184	170	180	205	...	...
Portugal	52	110	100	120	132	143	157	173	183	195	202	...
Spain	73	109	132	157	169	191	220	231	...	...	...	...
Sweden	88	97	108	128	131	131	156	157	171	171	...	...
United Kingdom	75	101	95	108	116	128	139	139	140	156	151	161
EFTA	80	101	111	108	106	108	119	125	134	141	136	126
Iceland	96	94	102	131	120	130	149	168	...	...	...	...
Norway	90	106	105	96	100	106	136	147	149	155	142	152
Switzerland	77	100	112	111	107	108	114	120	130	138	134	119
Other developed economies	86	104	104	107	112	115	124	120	133	148	132	144
Australia	67	138	161	180	196	254	277	267	291	320	323	333
Israel	72	111	126	146	155	170	194	197	203	207	...	...
Japan	87	103	101	103	107	107	115	110	121	135	116	127
New Zealand	88	120	132	152	155	162	178	203	221	222	240	234
South Africa	85	107	114	126	134	159	...	...	...	...	...	...
Developing economies	51	133	146	171	196	218	250	260	300	348	335	...
China, Hong Kong SAR	...	100	95	93	95	87	90	84	78	84	74	78
India	55	132	147	181	215	278	246	253	259	375	...	...
Korea, Republic of	63	122	132	151	184	202	232	252	346	341	321	321
Pakistan	48	130	136	137	124	146	132	128	146	162	164	...
Singapore	...	125	155	195	236	255	274	267	292	354	315	318
Turkey	59	119	130	164	170	197	250	279	294	297	343	412

For general note and footnotes see end of Special Table K.

Exportations des produits manufacturés (suite)

In thousand million U.S. dollars — En milliards de dollars E.-U.

1985	1992	1993	1994	1995	1996	1997	1998	1999	2000	2001	2002	Région, pays ou zones
					Value - Valeur							
1138	2747	2730	3142	3744	3873	4069	4104	4226	4641	4564	...	**Totaux 1/**
955.5	2148	2064	2346	2775	2847	2960	2993	3032	3212	3208	3222	**Economies dévelopées**
199.2	413.8	435.1	490.1	557.0	593.7	667.7	675.6	703.7	763.6	781.4	685.2	Amérique
53.82	84.61	93.80	109.2	128.2	134.0	142.9	148.7	165.6	167.3	168.8	166.5	Canada
145.3	329.2	341.3	380.9	428.8	459.7	524.8	527.0	538.1	596.3	612.6	518.8	Etats-Unis
571	1373	1244	1432	1741	1803	1831	1894	1867	1922	1980	2077	Europe
537	1295	1171	1353	1647	1709	1739	1799	1768	1825	1884	1984	UE
15.06	40.66	36.70	40.88	51.38	52.28	53.05	51.65	50.44	49.82	58.30	57.09	Autriche
39.75	97.60	95.90	110.7	133.1	133.3	131.2	143.3	142.5	151.4	156.7	222.8	Belgique / Luxembourg
9.61	24.66	21.65	24.30	29.43	29.22	30.17	31.22	33.76	31.83	33.45	37.16	Danemark
10.80	20.05	20.05	25.11	34.68	34.77	35.12	38.00	36.70	39.71	38.85	38.87	Finlande
73.71	184.6	162.8	187.2	222.9	229.4	225.8	244.3	242.5	249.2	290.2	251.9	France
161.6	387.5	334.6	380.4	455.8	459.7	455.3	477.9	461.1	481.0	499.2	534.8	Allemagne 5/
2.37	5.31	4.83	4.88	5.99	6.29	6.21	6.34	5.58	6.06	5.99	...	Grèce
6.66	19.56	19.58	24.29	31.21	36.99	42.82	53.58	59.55	65.59	75.13	77.65	Irlande
67.77	158.4	150.1	170.6	209.0	226.9	215.0	219.7	206.7	212.6	223.2	223.3	Italie
35.54	85.31	79.18	89.86	113.9	114.0	133.5	121.7	122.2	127.5	120.9	...	Pays-Bas
4.32	15.38	12.88	14.86	19.45	19.85	19.48	21.10	21.33	20.96	21.35	...	Portugal
17.27	50.61	47.54	57.74	71.35	80.45	82.32	84.75	88.72	89.43	91.38	...	Espagne
24.80	48.49	43.13	53.35	67.44	67.70	71.39	68.70	71.11	67.16	58.69	66.86	Suède
67.92	156.6	141.6	168.7	201.3	218.4	237.7	236.4	225.6	232.5	210.2	232.6	Royaume-Uni
33.48	76.60	72.26	78.21	92.70	92.26	90.34	93.84	97.39	95.38	94.31	91.13	AELE
0.16	0.23	0.23	0.31	0.40	0.40	0.44	0.44	0.56	0.61	0.67	0.73	Islande
7.43	13.84	12.05	11.20	14.46	14.39	17.01	17.67	16.84	16.60	14.82	16.26	Norvège
25.89	62.53	59.98	66.70	77.84	77.47	72.88	75.73	79.99	78.18	78.82	74.13	Suisse
185.4	361.6	385.1	423.7	476.2	450.4	461.3	423.7	461.0	525.6	447.4	459.8	Autres économies dévelopées
3.69	9.83	10.85	13.07	15.63	19.75	20.43	17.29	18.73	21.21	19.32	20.23	Australie
5.26	11.74	13.48	15.50	17.09	18.79	20.84	21.67	24.22	29.71	27.59	27.53	Israël
170.8	328.5	348.6	381.1	425.8	393.6	402.1	369.6	397.5	454.8	378.0	391.8	Japon
1.48	2.73	2.98	3.78	4.38	4.46	4.60	4.32	4.50	4.69	4.95	4.91	Nouvelle-Zélande
4.19	8.78	9.22	10.28	13.36	13.79	13.31	10.81	16.12	15.21	17.49	15.33	Afrique du Sud
182.7	599.2	665.3	795.6	969.6	1026	1109	1111	1194	1430	1355	...	**Economies en voie de développement**
15.83	28.42	27.12	27.11	28.22	25.83	25.69	23.26	21.16	22.43	18.94	19.42	Chine, Hong-Kong RAS
5.23	15.35	16.42	20.15	23.34	24.32	25.97	25.28	29.27	35.01	33.55	...	Inde
27.77	71.38	76.79	89.86	115.5	116.0	120.0	116.3	130.6	156.9	137.3	121.4	Corée, République de
1.68	5.72	5.79	6.38	6.74	7.76	7.40	7.08	7.41	7.73	7.79	8.42	Pakistan
11.96	49.33	58.74	80.54	101.0	106.0	106.6	94.15	99.68	119.3	103.7	106.7	Singapour
4.95	10.64	11.17	13.30	16.32	17.32	20.02	21.04	21.19	22.70	25.98	30.33	Turquie

Voir la fin du Tableau Special K pour la remarque général et les notes.

SPECIAL TABLE: J

Fuel imports

Developed economies

1990 = 100

Region, country or area	1985	1992	1993	1994	1995	1996	1997	1998	1999	2000	2001	2002
	Unit Value Indices in U.S. dollars - Indices de valuer unitaire en dollars des E.-U.											
Developed economies	115	86	80	75	82	93	88	65	76	115	105	106
America	115	83	77	72	78	95	87	62	78	129	113	110
Canada	113	79	74	68	74	84	80	62	67	91	101	99
United States 2/...............	115	83	78	73	79	96	88	62	79	133	114	111
Europe	112	87	79	75	83	92	86	66	74	105	100	105
EU	112	87	79	75	83	92	86	66	74	105	100	105
Austria 3/........................	109	89	78	74	82	85	74	70	87	104	97	96
Belgium/Luxembourg 4/....	74	89	75	80	93	91	84	83	80	76	75	101
Denmark	115	89	76	76	84	96	91	72	76	110	102	109
Finland	104	88	77	78	87	87	84	74	89	126	114	114
France	121	87	79	75	81	90	84	66	73	99	97	100
Germany 5/.....................	118	87	77	74	82	91	88	65	71	111	108	111
Greece	147	98	107	90	97	111	110	84	82	130	...	...
Ireland 4/........................	64	88	81	80	85	92	86	65	...	...	...	...
Italy 4/............................	98	84	79	73	80	94	86	55	...	...	...	...
Netherlands 4/	123	87	85	72	80	92	...	...	...	...	...	...
Portugal 4/	124	81	71	68	74	85	77	53	68	109	101	...
Spain 4/..........................	149	82	78	75	83	95	91	63	...	...	...	...
Sweden	116	84	75	73	80	89	82	65	76	118	...	...
United Kingdom	121	89	78	75	84	96	90	68	82	117	106	105
EFTA	109	86	78	76	81	92	86	67	72	108	102	98
Iceland 4/.......................	117	99	89	85	92	95	109	87	...	...	...	...
Norway	104	85	76	82	86	99	85	69	75	94	94	9[illegible]
Switzerland 4/.................	110	86	79	74	78	89	85	66	70	112	104	98
Other developed economies ..	126	90	85	78	85	93	94	69	76	116	103	10[illegible]
Australia	127	77	74	73	72	82	81	59	71	109	92	9[illegible]
Israel	130	80	70	68	75	86	80	63	74	113	...	...
Japan	126	91	86	79	87	96	99	71	79	123	109	110
New Zealand	123	88	84	78	86	98	98	68	78	123	109	11[illegible]
South Africa	...	...	...	...	...	...	...	...	...	...	...	...

For general note and footnotes see end of Special Table K.

Importations de produits énergétiques (suite)

Pays à économies développées

In thousand million U.S. dollars — En milliards de dollars E.-U.

1985	1992	1993	1994	1995	1996	1997	1998	1999	2000	2001	2002	Région, pays ou zones
Unit value indices in national currency - Indices de valuer unitaire en monnaie nationale												
.	.	.	.	.	.	.	.	.	.	.	.	**Economies dévelopeées**
.	.	.	.	.	.	.	.	.	.	.	.	Amérique
133	82	81	80	87	99	95	79	85	116	135	133	Canada
115	83	78	73	79	96	88	62	79	133	114	111	Etats-Unis 2/
.	.	.	.	.	.	.	.	.	.	.	.	Europe
.	.	.	.	.	.	.	.	.	.	.	.	UE
198	86	80	74	73	79	80	76	99	137	131	123	Autriche
...	...	78	80	82	85	90	90	90	99	102	129	Belgique/ Luxembourg
195	87	80	78	76	90	98	78	86	144	136	139	Danemark
168	104	116	105	99	105	114	104	130	212	198	189	Finlande
199	85	82	76	75	85	90	71	82	130	131	128	France
216	84	80	74	73	85	95	71	81	147	146	147	Allemagne 5/
130	118	155	137	142	169	190	156	159	299	...	...	Grece
...	...	...	...	...	...	...	...	...	...	...	...	Irlande
...	...	...	...	...	...	...	...	...	...	...	...	Italie
...	...	...	...	...	...	...	...	...	...	...	...	Pays-Bas
...	...	...	...	...	...	...	...	...	...	...	...	Portugal
...	...	...	...	...	...	...	...	...	...	...	...	Espagne
168	83	99	95	97	101	106	87	107	184	...	...	Suède
168	90	92	87	95	109	98	73	90	138	131	124	Royaume-Uni
.	.	.	.	.	.	.	.	.	.	.	.	AELE
...	...	...	...	...	...	...	...	...	...	...	...	Islande
142	85	86	92	87	102	96	83	94	133	135	119	Norvège
...	87	84	72	66	79	89	68	76	137	129	111	Suisse
.	.	.	.	.	.	.	.	.	.	.	.	Autres économies dévelopées
142	82	85	78	76	82	85	73	85	147	144	134	Australie
...	...	...	...	...	...	...	...	...	...	...	...	Israël
208	80	66	56	57	73	83	65	63	92	96	95	Japon
148	98	92	78	78	85	89	76	88	162	155	145	Nouvelle-Zélande
...	...	...	...	...	...	...	...	...	...	...	...	Afrique du Sud

Voir la fin du Tableau Special K pour la remarque général et les notes.

SPECIAL TABLE: J

Fuel imports (continued)

Developed economies

1990 = 100

Region, country or area	1985	1992	1993	1994	1995	1996	1997	1998	1999	2000	2001	2002
	Quantum indices - indices de volume											
Developed economies	85	106	107	112	111	117	124	125	126	139	144	136
America	69	102	110	119	116	117	137	146	145	156	165	159
Canada	56	92	98	105	111	121	152	151	148	188	168	151
United States	71	103	111	120	116	117	136	146	145	152	164	160
Europe	97	109	106	109	105	114	117	116	116	135	138	126
EU	98	109	107	109	106	114	117	116	116	136	139	126
Austria	90	99	99	104	115	134	146	106	83	113	134	145
Belgium/Luxembourg	131	110	115	112	105	127	133	108	124	212	218	160
Denmark	123	108	91	88	78	78	82	82	84	104	82	82
Finland	98	95	94	109	94	117	112	101	95	101	106	106
France	89	105	102	105	102	113	116	113	116	139	155	125
Germany 5/	93	123	123	127	121	136	132	137	131	140	137	126
Greece	134	154	143	154	127	147	97	170	122	203	...	...
Ireland	140	99	95	93	94	107	118	130	...	...	...	...
Italy	129	101	92	99	99	98	102	117	...	...	...	...
Netherlands	90	101	99	112	114	117	...	...	...	...	...	...
Portugal	60	111	111	124	135	113	126	140	146	137	138	...
Spain	71	120	107	113	110	118	119	130	...	...	...	...
Sweden	94	104	106	106	101	107	111	95	108	103	...	...
United Kingdom	81	99	105	87	78	82	85	81	78	90	98	98
EFTA	94	99	93	95	94	109	124	115	112	110	117	111
Iceland	74	87	86	88	84	103	86	91	...	...	...	...
Norway	111	88	89	87	94	132	120	117	116	117	121	111
Switzerland	88	104	95	98	94	100	127	115	112	108	117	113
Other developed economies	77	104	104	109	117	122	126	120	126	128	131	133
Australia	58	141	163	151	184	215	212	213	249	249	255	249
Israel	77	134	160	155	165	157	211	210	...	235	...	...
Japan	77	102	100	106	107	110	110	106	110	110	112	112
New Zealand	85	94	102	117	119	130	134	151	155	170	179	...
South Africa	...	...	...	...	...	...	...	...	...	...	...	...

For general note and footnotes see end of Special Table K.

Importations de produits énergétiques (suite)

Pays à économies développées

In thousand million U.S. dollars — En milliards de dollars E.-U.

1985	1992	1993	1994	1995	1996	1997	1998	1999	2000	2001	2002	Région, pays ou zones
					Value - Valeur							
273.65	253.80	236.02	231.99	252.59	301.95	305.93	226.93	266.54	443.33	420.09	402.31	**Economies dévelopeées**
60.34	63.99	64.48	65.26	68.93	84.50	91.32	68.91	86.41	152.10	141.40	132.75	Amérique
4.59	5.33	5.24	5.16	5.94	7.43	8.78	6.76	7.14	12.48	12.38	10.82	Canada
55.75	58.66	59.24	60.10	62.98	77.06	82.55	62.15	79.27	139.62	129.01	121.93	Etats-Unis
153.64	132.27	117.38	114.03	122.22	147.44	141.30	107.25	120.97	198.98	195.04	185.37	Europe
148.97	128.32	113.98	110.68	118.72	142.78	136.40	103.70	117.18	193.40	189.43	180.21	UE
3.10	2.77	2.45	2.44	2.98	3.59	3.42	2.32	2.28	3.71	4.09	4.36	Autriche
9.32	9.49	8.33	8.59	9.43	11.16	10.78	8.54	9.51	15.39	15.77	15.58	Belgique/ Luxembourg
3.12	2.11	1.53	1.47	1.44	1.65	1.65	1.30	1.41	2.52	1.83	1.96	Danemark
3.23	2.67	2.30	2.70	2.59	3.25	2.98	2.39	2.67	4.02	3.81	3.86	Finlande
24.10	20.56	17.86	17.52	18.55	22.76	21.80	16.70	18.88	30.77	33.62	27.84	France
31.39	30.42	27.15	26.66	28.31	35.05	33.20	25.34	26.44	44.43	41.97	39.79	Allemagne 5/
3.00	2.29	2.33	2.10	1.88	2.48	1.63	2.16	1.53	4.00	4.28	...	Grèce
1.20	1.17	1.03	0.99	1.06	1.32	1.36	1.13	1.28	2.06	2.05	1.69	Irlande
23.92	15.96	13.74	13.64	14.95	17.41	16.49	12.03	14.15	23.03	22.45	21.93	Italie
14.54	11.56	11.11	10.66	12.11	14.27	14.10	10.48	12.70	20.02	18.97	...	Pays-Bas
2.03	2.46	2.14	2.31	2.73	2.64	2.66	2.05	2.69	4.10	3.82	...	Portugal
10.89	10.15	8.69	8.70	9.44	11.50	11.12	8.52	10.58	18.55	17.35	...	Espagne
5.41	4.35	3.93	3.82	4.00	4.75	4.51	3.05	4.09	6.06	4.74	5.86	Suède
13.74	12.35	11.39	9.09	9.25	10.93	10.70	7.71	8.97	14.73	14.69	14.31	Royaume-Uni
4.58	3.84	3.30	3.24	3.39	4.51	4.76	3.45	3.64	5.34	5.38	4.90	AELE
0.14	0.14	0.12	0.12	0.13	0.16	0.15	0.13	0.13	0.22	0.19	0.18	Islande
1.36	0.89	0.80	0.84	0.95	1.54	1.19	0.95	1.03	1.30	1.34	1.21	Norvège
3.07	2.81	2.38	2.28	2.32	2.81	3.42	2.38	2.48	3.82	3.85	3.51	Suisse
59.66	57.55	54.16	52.70	61.44	70.02	73.31	50.77	59.16	92.25	83.66	84.19	Autres économies dévelopées
1.59	2.37	2.61	2.39	2.88	3.84	3.72	2.71	3.81	5.90	5.11	5.05	Australie
1.35	1.46	1.51	1.43	1.67	1.83	2.27	1.80	...	3.59	3.17	3.12	Israël
55.90	53.03	49.34	48.15	53.92	60.86	62.83	43.27	49.89	77.43	70.23	70.36	Japon
0.76	0.60	0.62	0.66	0.74	0.93	0.95	0.75	0.88	1.51	1.42	...	Nouvelle-Zélande
0.06	0.09	0.07	0.07	2.22	2.56	3.53	2.23	2.44	3.83	3.74	3.27	Afrique du Sud

Voir la fin du Tableau Special K pour la remarque général et les notes.

SPECIAL TABLE: K

Some indicators on fuel imports
Developed economies

1990 = 100

Region, country or area	1985	1992	1993	1994	1995	1996	1997	1998	1999	2000	2001	2002
	Fuel Imports as percent of total imports Importation des produits énergétiques en pourcentage des importations totales											
Developed economies	19.7	9.2	9.2	8	7.3	8.5	8.4	6.1	6.8	10.1	9.9	9.3
America	13.8	9.5	8.8	7.8	7.4	8.5	8.3	6	6.8	10.2	10.1	9.3
Canada	6	4.3	4	3.5	3.6	4.3	4.5	3.4	3.3	5.2	5.6	4.9
United States	15.4	10.6	9.8	8.7	8.2	9.4	9.2	6.6	7.5	11.1	10.9	10.1
Europe	19.8	7.6	7.8	6.7	6	7.1	6.8	4.9	5.5	8.5	8.2	7.7
EU	20.5	7.8	8	7	6.2	7.3	7	5.1	5.7	8.7	8.4	7.9
Austria	14.9	5.1	5	4.4	4.5	5.3	5.3	3.5	3.7	5.8	6.2	6.4
Belgium/Luxembourg	16.6	7.6	7.5	6.8	6.1	7.1	7.1	5.1	5.9	8.8	8.9	7.8
Denmark	17.3	6.3	5	4.1	3.3	3.8	3.8	2.8	3.1	5.7	4.1	4
Finland	24.4	12.6	12.8	11.5	8.8	10.5	9.6	7.4	8.5	11.9	11.5	11.5
France	22.4	8.6	8.9	7.7	6.8	8.3	8.2	5.8	6.6	9.9	9.5	9.2
Germany	19.8	7.4	7.9	7	6.1	7.9	7.6	5.5	5.7	8.7	8.5	8.1
Greece	29.5	9.8	10.6	9.8	7.2	8.7	6.5	7.5	5.8	13.4	15.2	...
Ireland	11.9	5.2	4.8	3.8	3.3	3.7	3.5	2.5	2.8	4.1	3.9	3.2
Italy	26.3	8.5	9.3	8.1	7.3	8.4	7.9	5.6	6.5	9.8	9.3	9
Netherlands	22.3	8.6	9.6	8.2	7.7	8.9	8.7	6.7	7.6	11.5	11.6	...
Portugal	26.5	8	8.8	8.5	8.1	7.8	8.1	5.5	7.3	10.3	9.7	...
Spain	36	10.2	10.9	9.4	8.3	9.3	8.9	6.5	7.2	12.1	11.2	...
Sweden	18.9	8.7	9.2	7.4	6.5	7.4	7.2	4.8	6.4	8.9	8	8.8
United Kingdom	12.5	5.6	5.4	4	3.5	3.9	3.5	2.5	2.8	4.5	4.3	4.1
EFTA	9.7	4.1	3.8	3.3	3	3.9	4.2	2.9	3	4.4	4.5	4.1
Iceland	15.7	8.3	9.2	8.3	7.2	7.8	7.6	5.2	5.4	9.4	8.9	8.6
Norway	8.7	3.4	3.3	3.1	2.9	4.5	3.3	2.5	3	3.8	4.1	3.5
Switzerland	10	4.3	3.9	3.4	2.9	3.5	4.5	3	3	4.6	4.6	4.2
Other developed economies	33.6	17.9	16.3	13.8	13.3	14.5	15.4	12.5	13.3	17.5	17.3	17.3
Australia	6.9	5.5	5.9	4.8	5	6.2	6	4.5	5.8	8.3	8.5	7
Israel	16.3	7.7	7.4	6	5.7	6.1	7.8	6.6	...	10	9.5	8.8
Japan	43.1	22.8	20.5	17.5	16	17.4	18.5	15.4	16.1	20.4	20.1	20.8
New Zealand	12.7	6.5	6.4	5.6	5.3	6.3	6.6	6.6	6.1	10.4	8.5	...
South Africa	0.6	0.5	0.4	0.3	8.3	9.5	11.4	8.4	10.1	14.4	15.4	12.5
	Ratio of unit value indices of manufactured goods exports and fuel imports Quotient des indices de la valeur unitaire des exportations des produits manufacturés et des importations des produits énergétiques											
Developed economies	56	120	122	133	135	114	112	150	123	77	82	81
America	77	121	129	137	130	107	118	165	129	79	90	92
Canada	80	114	120	124	118	104	111	137	125	92	80	81
United States	77	124	133	143	136	111	122	175	136	82	95	100
Europe	51	118	116	125	130	113	108	142	117	76	77	75
EU	51	118	116	125	129	112	107	141	116	75	77	74
Austria	55	112	116	122	127	110	104	103	69	49	50	53
Belgium/Luxembourg	78	110	120	118	117	116	115	116	115	114	113	89
Denmark	48	115	121	128	133	113	108	135	123	76	82	79
Finland	52	102	97	106	121	113	106	118	96	65	68	71
France	51	114	120	131	136	119	114	145	124	80	80	68
Germany	46	119	120	127	132	111	98	137	113	65	66	67
Greece	42	97	73	92	91	76	65	79	76	45	...	...
Ireland	98	110	118	111	116	105	94	115	...	...	...	...
Italy	56	125	112	118	120	104	105	175	...	...	...	...
Netherlands	46	117	109	128	135	111	...	...	...	...	...	...
Portugal	51	131	139	138	150	123	122	173	131	75	79	...
Spain	37	133	108	115	119	105	97	136	...	...	...	...
Sweden	50	121	109	117	131	119	115	139	111	68	...	...
United Kingdom	50	115	127	138	135	118	125	164	130	84	86	91
EFTA	51	117	111	126	144	123	118	148	135	83	90	98
Iceland	49	87	86	94	124	111	93	103	...	...	...	...
Norway	56	108	106	101	119	97	104	123	106	80	78	81
Switzerland	50	120	112	134	153	133	123	158	145	83	93	104
Other developed economies	56	125	142	164	163	138	129	168	149	100	107	101
Australia	52	111	110	120	134	114	110	133	110	73	78	78
Israel	54	126	146	148	140	122	128	165	154	121	...	...
Japan	56	126	144	169	164	139	127	169	150	98	108	101
New Zealand	54	102	106	127	129	111	104	123	103	68	74	74
South Africa	...	...	...	...	...	...	...	...	...	...	...	...

For general note and footnotes see end of table.

Quelques indicateurs sur les importations de produits énergétiques
Pays à économies développées

1985	1992	1993	1994	1995	1996	1997	1998	1999	2000	2001	2002	Région, pays ou zones
Fuel imports as percent of total exports Importations des produits énergétiques en pourcentage des exportations totales												
21.6	9.5	9.2	9.1	7.4	8.6	8.3	6.2	7.1	10.9	10.6	10	**Economies dèvelopeées**
20.5	11.4	11	10.1	9.3	10.8	10.6	7.7	9.3	14.4	14.3	14	Amérique
5.3	4	3.6	3.1	3.1	3.7	4.1	3.2	3	4.5	4.8	4.3	Canada
27	13.8	13.5	12.5	11.5	13.2	12.8	9.1	11.4	17.8	17.6	17.6	Etats-Unis
20.4	7.9	7.6	6.5	5.7	6.7	6.2	4.7	5.3	8.4	8	7.3	Europe
21.1	8.2	7.9	6.7	5.9	6.9	6.4	4.8	5.4	8.7	8.2	7.5	UE
18	6.2	6.1	5.4	5.2	6.2	5.8	3.8	3.5	6.3	6.6	6.4	Autriche
17.4	7.7	6.9	6.3	5.6	6.6	6.5	4.8	5.4	8.1	8.1	7.3	Belgique/Luxembourg
18.9	5.3	4.1	3.5	2.9	3.4	3.5	2.7	2.8	5.1	3.6	3.5	Danemark
23.9	11.2	9.8	9.1	6.4	8	7.3	5.5	6.4	8.8	8.6	8.7	Finlande
24.7	8.9	8.7	7.5	6.5	8	7.7	5.6	6.3	10.2	9.6	9.1	France
17.1	7.1	7.1	6.2	5.4	6.8	6.5	4.7	4.9	7.9	7.4	6.5	Allemagne
66.1	23.3	26.6	22.4	17.1	20.9	15.1	20.1	15.1	36.5	41.6	...	Grèce
11.5	4.1	3.6	2.9	2.4	2.9	2.5	1.8	1.8	2.7	2.4	1.9	Irlande
30.3	9.5	8.2	7.2	6.5	6.9	6.9	5	6.1	9.7	9	8.7	Italie
21.3	8.3	8.5	7.3	6.8	8	5.9	6.2	6.3	9.6	8.7	...	Pays-Bas
35.7	13.2	13.9	12.9	11.7	11.4	11.7	8.5	11	16.8	15.6	...	Portugal
44.8	15.8	14.3	11.9	10.5	11.3	10.5	8	9.5	16.4	14.9	...	Espagne
17.8	7.8	7.9	6.2	5.2	5.7	5.6	3.7	4.8	7.8	6.2	7.2	Suède
13.6	6.5	6.6	4.5	3.9	4.2	3.8	2.9	3.4	5.3	5.7	5	Royaume-Uni
9.5	3.8	3.4	3	2.7	3.4	3.8	2.8	2.8	3.7	3.8	3.3	AELE
17.5	9.2	8.9	7.5	7	8.4	8.3	6.7	5.7	11.8	9.2	8	Islande
6.8	2.5	2.5	2.4	2.3	3.1	2.5	2.3	2.3	2.2	2.3	2	Norvège
11.2	4.3	3.8	3.2	2.8	3.5	4.5	3	3	4.7	4.7	4	Suisse
27.2	13.5	12	38.1	11.1	13.3	13.4	10.1	11	14.9	15.6	15.2	Autres économies dévelopées
7.2	5.7	6.4	5.3	5.7	6.7	6.2	5.1	6.8	8.8	8.1	7.8	Australie
21.6	11.1	10.2	8.4	8.8	8.9	10.1	7.7	...	11.4	10.9	10.6	Israël
31.8	15.6	13.7	121.7	12.2	14.8	14.9	11.1	11.9	16.2	17.4	16.9	Japon
13.7	6.4	6.1	5.6	5.6	6.6	6.9	6.2	7	10.9	9.2	...	Nouvelle-Zélande
0.6	0.4	0.3	0.3	7.9	10.9	11.8	8.8	9.3	14.7	13.4	11.8	Afrique du Sud

SPECIAL TABLES: I, J and K

General note: Manufactured goods are here defined to comprise sections 5 through 8 of the Standard International Trade Classification (SITC). These sections are: chemicals and related products, manufactured goods classified chiefly by material, machinery and transport equipment and miscellaneous manufactured articles. Fuels are here defined to comprise all the products in section 3 of the SITC. These products are: coal, coke and briquettes, petroleum, petroleum products and related materials gas and electric current. The economic and geographic groupings in this table are in accordance with those of Special Table A in this issue, although Special Table A includes more detailed geographic sub-groups which make up the groupings 'Other developed economies' and 'Developing economies' of this table. In 1990 the exports of manufactured goods by all Developed' and Developing' economies accounted for approximately 96 per cent of world exports of manufactured goods. The unit value indices are obtained from national sources, except those of a few countries which the United Nations Statistics Division compiles using their quantity and value figures. For countries that do not compile indices for manufactured goods exports and fuel imports conforming to the above definition, sub-indices are aggregated to approximate an index of SITC sections 5-8 and SITC section 3 respectively. Unit value indices obtained from national indices are rebased, where necessary, so that 1990=100. Indices in national currency are converted into U.S. dollars using conversion factors obtained by dividing the weighted average exchange rate of a given currency in the current period by the weighted average exchange rate in the base period. All aggregate unit value indices are current period weighted. The indices in SDRs are calculated by multiplying the equivalent aggregate indices in U.S. dollars by conversion factors obtained by dividing the SDR/$US exchange rate in the current period by the rate in the base period. The quantum indices are derived from the value data and the unit value indices. All aggregate quantum indices are base period weighted. The figures in Special Table K are calculated from those prepared for Special Tables I and J. Total imports and exports used in the calculations are, in general, those published in Special Table A.

1/ Excludes trade of the countries of Eastern Europe and the former USSR.

2/ Beginning 1989, derived from price indices; national unit value index is discontinued.

3/ Series linked at 1988 and 1995 by factors calculated by the United Nations Statistics Division.

4/ For the years beginning 1981, indices are calculated by the United Nations Statistics Division; for Netherlands beginning 1988, for Belgium 1988-1992, and for Switzerland 1988 to 1995.

5/ Data prior to January 1991, pertain to the territorial boundaries of the Federal Republic of Germany and the former German Democratic Republic prior to 3 October, 1990 (see explanatory notes on data pertaining to Germany on page vi).

6/ Derived from sub-indices using current weights; for Netherlands from 1989 to 1996.

7/ Industrial product.

Remarque générale: Les produits manufacturés comprennent les sections 5 à 8 de la Classification type pour le commerce international (CTCI). Ces sections sont produits chimiques et produits connexes, articles manufacturés classés principalement d'après la matière primière, machines et matérial de transport et articles manufacturés divers. Les produits énergétiques comprennent tous les produits appartenant à la section 3 de la CTCI. Ces produits sont huilles, cokes et briquettes, pétrole, produits dérives du pétrole et produits connexes, gaz et énergie électrique. Les groupes économiques et géographiques de ce tableau sont conformes aux groupes des pays ou zones qui paraissent dans le tableau special A de ce numéro, bien que le tableau special A comprend plus de détails en ce qui concerne les sous-groupes des Autres economies dévelopées et 'Economies en view de développement' de ce tableau. En 1990, les exportations des produits manufacturés par tous les Economies développées' et les 'Economies en voie de développement' representaient approximativement 96 pourcent de l'ensemble des exportations mondials des produits manufacturés. Les indices de la valeur unitaire sont obtenus de sources nationales, á l'exception de quelque pays pour lesquels la Division de Statistique des Nations Unies calcule ces indices en utilisant le chiffres de la valeur et du volume fournis par ces pays. Pour les pays ne calculant pas leurs indices des exportations des produits manufacturés et importations des produits énergétiques selon la definition décrite ci-dessus les sous-indices sont agrégés en un indice qui se rapproche les sections 5 à 8 de la CTCI et la section 3 de la CTCI respectivement. Les indices en monnaie nationale son convertis en dollars des E.-U. en les multipliant par un facteur de conversion obtenu en divisant le taux de change courant, moyenne pondérés, d'une monnaie donnée par celui de la période de base. Tous les agrégés des indices de la valeur unitaire, sont à coéfficients de pondération correspondant à la période indiquée. Les indices indices en DTS son calculés en multipliant les indices totaux equivlents en dollars E.-U. par un facteur de conversion obtenu en divisant le taux de change cournat du DTS/$E-U d'une monnaie donnée par celui de la période de base. Les indices du quantum sont calculés à partir de chiffres de la valeur et lés indices de la valeur unitaire. Tous les agrégés des indices du quantum sont à coéfficients de pondération correspondant à la période en base. Les chiffres dans tableau special K sont calculés selon des données preparées pour les tableaux spéciaux I et J. Les totales des importations et exportations utilisées dans les calculs sont, en générale, celles publiées dans le Tableau Spécial A.

1/ Non compris le commerce des pays de l'Europe de l'Est et l'ancienne URSS.

2/ A partir de 1989, calculés à partir des indices des prix; l'indice de valeur unitaire national est discontinué.

3/ Les series sont enchainées à 1988 et à 1995 par facteurs calculé par la Division de Statistique des Nations Unies.

4/ Pour les années à partir 1981, les indices sont calculés par la Division de Statisque des Nations Unies; pour les Pays-Bas à partir de 1988, pour la Belgique 1988-1992, et pour la Suisse 1988-1995.

5/ Les données relatives à la période précédent janvier 1991 correspondent aux limites territoriales de la République Fédérale d'Allemagne antérieur au 3 octobre 1990 (Aussi voir les notes explicatives sur les données concernant l'Allemagne à la page vi).

6/ Calculés à partir de sous-indices à coéfficients de pondération correspondant à la période en cours; pour les Pays-Bas de 1989 à 1996.

7/ Produit industriel.

كيفية الحصول على منشورات الأمم المتحدة

يمكن الحصول على منشورات الأمم المتحدة من المكتبات ودور التوزيع في جميع أنحاء العالم . استعلم عنها من المكتبة التي تتعامل معها أو اكتب إلى : الأمم المتحدة ، قسم البيع في نيويورك أو في جنيف .

如何购取联合国出版物

联合国出版物在全世界各地的书店和经售处均有发售。请向书店询问或写信到纽约或日内瓦的联合国销售组。

HOW TO OBTAIN UNITED NATIONS PUBLICATIONS

United Nations publications may be obtained from bookstores and distributors throughout the world. Consult your bookstore or write to: United Nations, Sales Section, New York or Geneva.

COMMENT SE PROCURER LES PUBLICATIONS DES NATIONS UNIES

Les publications des Nations Unies sont en vente dans les librairies et les agences dépositaires du monde entier. Informez-vous auprès de votre libraire ou adressez-vous à : Nations Unies, Section des ventes, New York ou Genève.

КАК ПОЛУЧИТЬ ИЗДАНИЯ ОРГАНИЗАЦИИ ОБЪЕДИНЕННЫХ НАЦИЙ

Издания Организации Объединенных Наций можно купить в книжных магазинах и агентствах во всех районах мира. Наводите справки об изданиях в вашем книжном магазине или пишите по адресу: Организация Объединенных Наций, Секция по продаже изданий, Нью-Йорк или Женева.

COMO CONSEGUIR PUBLICACIONES DE LAS NACIONES UNIDAS

Las publicaciones de las Naciones Unidas están en venta en librerías y casas distribuidoras en todas partes del mundo. Consulte a su librero o diríjase a: Naciones Unidas, Sección de Ventas, Nueva York o Ginebra.

Litho in United Nations, New York
03-62988—February 2004—3,005
ISBN 92-1-061205-1

United Nations publication
Sales No. E/F.04.XVII.3, vol. II
ST/ESA/STAT/SER.G/51

DATE DUE

GAYLORD PRINTED IN U.S.A.